- Suggested pronunciations for biblical persons and places
- Main entries with Hebrew, Greek, and transliteration fonts
- Summary introductions for long articles
- Helpful outlines for long articles
- Bibliographies
- List of abbreviations
- Index of maps, charts, photos, and illustrations
- Peer reviewed by congregational leaders
- Fully searchable CD-ROM with full text database and color illustrations included at no extra charge when the complete set is purchased by subscription

THE NEW INTERPRETER'S® DICTIONARY OF THE BIBLE

Me-R

VOLUME 4

Editorial Board

THE NEW INTERPRETER'S® DICTIONARY OF THE BIBLE

Me-R

VOLUME 4

ABINGDON PRESS
Nashville

THE NEW INTERPRETER'S® DICTIONARY OF THE BIBLE
Me-R
VOLUME 4

This book is printed on recycled, acid-free paper.

Library of Congress Cataloging-in-Publication Data

The New Interpreter's Dictionary of the Bible.
p. cm.
Includes bibliographical references.
ISBN 0-687-05427-3 (alk. paper)
1. Bible--Dictionaries. I. Abingdon Press.

BS440.N445 2006
220.3--dc22

2006025839

ISBN-13: 978-0-687-33375-2

English language fonts are from the Weidemann family. Ancient language fonts were developed in the public domain for scholars who comprise the Society of Biblical Literature, including SPTiberian for Hebrew, SPIonic for Greek, and SPAtlantis for transliteration.

PUBLICATION STAFF

Project Director: John F. Kutsko
Project Manager: Marianne Blickenstaff
Reference Editor: Heather R. McMurray
Associate Editor: Tim West
Publishing Consultant: Jack A. Keller
Contracts Manager: Lori C. Patton
Production & Design Manager: Ed Wynne
Typesetter: Kevin A. Wilson
Print Procurement: Clara Vaughan
Marketing Manager: Teresa Alspaugh

EXECUTIVE STAFF

President and Publisher: Neil M. Alexander
Editor-in-Chief, Abingdon Press: Mary Catherine Dean

1 2 3 4 5 6 7 8 9 10 – 09 10 11 12 13 14 15 16 17 18

MANUFACTURED IN THE UNITED STATES OF AMERICA

Acknowledgements

Alinari/Art Resource, NY: PERSEPOLIS Fig. 1

Bildarchiv Preussischer Kulturbesitz/Art Resource, NY: MONEY, COINS Fig. 1; PORTRAYALS OF BIBLICAL FIGURES IN ISLAMIC TRADITION Fig. 1

David Bivin/LifeintheHolyLand.com: ROME, CITY OF Fig. 2

Todd Bolen/BiblePlaces.com: MIRROR Fig. 1; MONEY, COINS Fig. 1; MORTAR AND PESTLE Fig. 1; MOUNT OF OLIVES Fig. 1; MUREX Fig. 1; NILE RIVER Fig. 1; OLIVE, OLIVE TREE Fig. 1; OSTRACA Fig. 1; ROME, CITY OF Fig. 1; ROSETTA STONE Fig. 1

British Academy: QUMRAN Fig. 1

British Museum/Art Resource, NY: MEDICINE AND HEALING, GODS OF Fig. 1; MONEY, COINS Fig. 2; OSIRIS Fig. 1

École Biblique: MUSICAL INSTRUMENTS Fig. 4

Matt Floreen/www.mattfloreen.com: MERNEPTAH Fig. 1

Werner Forman/Art Resource, NY: PYRAMID TEXTS Fig. 1

Foto Marburg/Art Resource, NY: ROMAN RELIGIONS Fig. 1

F. Nigel Hepper: MINT Fig. 1; MUSTARD Fig. 1; MYRTLE Fig. 1; PLANTS OF THE BIBLE Fig. 1, 2, 3, 4, 5; RUSHES Fig. 1

Israel Antiquities Authority: MUSICAL INSTRUMENTS Fig. 1, 2, 3

John C. H. Laughlin: POT Fig. 1; POTSHERD Fig. 1; POTTERY Fig. 1

Erich Lessing/Art Resource, NY: MENORAH Fig. 1; MOABITE STONE Fig. 1; MONEY, COINS Fig. 3; MYSTERY RELIGIONS Fig. 1; OBELISK, BLACK Fig. 1; OSSUARIES Fig. 1; PERSIA, HISTORY AND RELIGION OF Fig. 1; PHILISTINES Fig. 1; PHOENICIA Fig. 1; QURAN Fig. 1;

Jodi Magness: QUMRAN Fig. 2

The Megiddo Expedition, The Institute of Archaeology, Tel Aviv University: MEGIDDO Fig. 1, 2, 3, 4, 5, 6, 7, 8

Meiron Excavation Project: Fig. 1, 2

Studium Biblicum Franciscanum Archive, Jerusalem: MEDEBA Fig. 1; NEBO, MOUNT Fig. 1; PELLA Fig. 1

Vanni/Art Resource, NY: OBELISK Fig 1

John Mark Wade: PETRA Fig. 1

Consultants

Archaeology Consultant

John C. H. Laughlin
Averett University
Danville, VA

Consulting Readers

Eric Elnes
Scottsdale Congregational United Church of Christ
Scottsdale, AZ

Dottie Escobedo-Frank
Cross Roads United Methodist Church
Phoenix, AZ

Renae Extrum-Fernandez
Walnut Creek First United Methodist Church
Walnut Creek, CA

Tyrone Gordon
St. Luke Community United Methodist Church
Dallas, TX

Kevass J. Harding
Dellrose United Methodist Church
Wichita, KS

James A. Harnish
Hyde Park United Methodist Church
Tampa, FL

Judi K. Hoffman
Edgehill United Methodist Church
Nashville, TN

Robert Johnson
Windsor Village United Methodist Church
Houston, TX

Chan-Hie Kim
Upland, CA

Sungho Lee
Korean United Methodist Church of Santa Clara Valley
San Jose, CA

Merry Hope Meloy
Doylesburg, PA

H. Mitchell Simpson
University Baptist Church
Chapel Hill, NC

Evelene Sombrero-Navarrete
Holbrook United Methodist Church
Holbrook, AZ

Mariellen Sawada-Yoshino
San Jose United Methodist Church
San Jose, CA

Contributors

Judith Z. Abrams
MAQOM
Houston, TX

Paul J. Achtemeier
Union Theological Seminary and
Presbyterian School of Christian Education
Richmond, VA

Susan Ackerman
Dartmouth College
Hanover, NH

A. K. M. Adam
Duke Divinity School
Durham, NC

Martin C. Albl
Presentation College
Aberdeen, SD

Yairah Amit
Tel Aviv University
Tel Aviv, Israel

Garwood P. Anderson
Nashotah House Theological Seminary
Nashotah, WI

Kevin L. Anderson
Asbury College
Wilmore, KY

Bill T. Arnold
Asbury Theological Seminary
Wilmore, KY

Hector Avalos
Iowa State University
Ames, IA

Carol Bakhos
University of California Los Angeles
Los Angeles, CA

David M. Battle
Orangeburg, SC

David R. Bauer
Asbury Theological Seminary
Wilmore, KY

Michael G. W. Becker
Ludwig-Maximilian Universitaet
Munich, Germany

Alice Ogden Bellis
Howard University
Washington, DC

Dianne Bergant, C.S.A.
Catholic Theological Union in Chicago
Chicago, IL

Adele Berlin
University of Maryland College Park
College Park, MD

Johannes Beutler, S.J.
Frankfurt, Germany

Mark E. Biddle
Baptist Theological Seminary at Richmond
Richmond, VA

Julye M. Bidmead
Chapman University
Orange, CA

Gerald M. Bilkes
Puritan Reformed Theological Seminary
Grand Rapids, MI

ELLEN BIRNBAUM
Boston University
Boston, MA

J. TED BLAKLEY
University of St. Andrews
St. Andrews, United Kingdom

MARIANNE BLICKENSTAFF
Abingdon Press
Nashville, TN

L. GREGORY BLOOMQUIST
St. Paul University
Ottawa, ON, Canada

DARRELL L. BOCK
Dallas Theological Seminary
Dallas, TX

KEITH BODNER
Atlantic Baptist University
Moncton, NB, Canada

HELEN K. BOND
New College, University of Edinburgh
Edinburgh, United Kingdom

M. EUGENE BORING
Brite Divinity School
Texas Christian University
Fort Worth, TX

ODED BOROWSKI
Emory University
Atlanta, GA

ALEJANDRO F. BOTTA
Boston University
Boston, MA

MARY P. BOYD
University Temple United Methodist Church
Seattle, WA

JOHN M. BRACKE
Eden Theological Seminary
St. Louis, MO

KENT V. BRAMLETT
University of Toronto
Toronto, ON, Canada

JOACHIM BRAUN
Bar Ilan University
Ramat-Gan, Israel

ANNA BRAWLEY
Chicago, IL

TERRY L. BRENSINGER
The Grantham Church, Brethren in Christ
Grantham, PA

MARC ZVI BRETTLER
Brandeis University
Waltham, MA

THOMAS V. BRISCO
Logsdon School of Theology
Hardin-Simmons University
Abilene, TX

AARON BRODY
Pacific School of Religion
Berkeley, CA

FRANÇOIS BRON
Section des Sciences historiques et philogiques,
EPHE
Paris, France

JAMES A. BROOKS
Bethel Seminary (Emeritus)
St. Paul, MN

WILLIAM P. BROWN
Columbia Theological Seminary
Decatur, GA

THEODORE W. BURGH
University of North Carolina at Wilmington
Wilmington, NC

JOEL S. BURNETT
Baylor University
Waco, TX

RICHARD A. BURRIDGE
King's College London
London, United Kingdom

GAY L. BYRON
Colgate Rochester Crozer Divinity School
Rochester, NY

SUSAN A. CALEF
Creighton University
Omaha, NE

ALLEN DWIGHT CALLAHAN
Brown University
Providence, RI

William Sanger Campbell
The College of St. Scholastica
Duluth, MN

Timothy B. Cargal
Northwood Presbyterian Church
Silver Spring, MD

Philippa Carter
McMaster University
Hamilton, ON, Canada

Warren Carter
Brite Divinity School
Texas Christian University
Fort Worth, TX

Tony W. Cartledge
Biblical Recorder
Raleigh, NC

Joseph R. Cathey
Southwestern Baptist Theological Seminary
Fort Worth, TX

Marvin L. Chaney
San Francisco Theological Seminary
San Anselmo, CA

James H. Charlesworth
Princeton Theological Seminary
Princeton, NJ

Mark W. Chavalas
University of Wisconsin-La Crosse
La Crosse, WI

Emily R. Cheney
Athens, GA

Samuel Cheon
Hannam University
Daejeon, Republic of Korea

Bruce Chilton
Bard College
Annandale on Hudson, NY

L. Juliana Claassens
Baptist Theological Seminary at Richmond
Richmond, VA

Richard J. Clifford, S.J.
Boston College
Chestnut Hill, MA

Trevor D. Cochell
Baylor University
Waco, TX

Gary Colledge
Akron, OH

John J. Collins
Yale University
New Haven, CT

Raymond F. Collins
The Catholic University of America
Washington, DC

Edgar W. Conrad
University of Queensland
Brisbane, Australia

Michael D. Coogan
Stonehill College
Easton, MA

Edward M. Cook
Cincinnati, OH

Joan E. Cook, S.C.
Georgetown University
Washington, DC

Steve Cook
Vanderbilt University
Nashville, TN

Kathlyn Mary Cooney
University of California Los Angeles
Los Angeles, CA

Wendy Cotter, C.S.J.
Loyola University of Chicago
Chicago, IL

J. R. C. Cousland
University of British Columbia
Vancouver, BC, Canada

Sidnie White Crawford
University of Nebraska
Lincoln, NE

Jerome F. D. Creach
Pittsburgh Theological Seminary
Pittsburgh, PA

Stephanie Buckhanon Crowder
Belmont University
Nashville, TN

A. ANDREW DAS
Elmhurst College
Elmhurst, IL

JAMES R. DAVILA
St. Mary's College
University of St. Andrews
St. Andrews, United Kingdom

JOHN DAY
Oxford University
Oxford, United Kingdom

LINDA DAY
Pittsburgh, PA

L. J. DE REGT
United Bible Societies
The Hague, Netherlands

J. ANDREW DEARMAN
Austin Presbyterian Theological Seminary
Austin, TX

NANCY DECLAISSÉ-WALFORD
McAfee School of Theology
Mercer University
Atlanta, GA

MARK DELCOGLIANO
Emory University
Atlanta, GA

WILLIAM G. DEVER
Mountoursville, PA

LAMOINE F. DEVRIES
Missouri State University (Emeritus)
Springfield, MO

JAMES A. DIAMOND
University of Waterloo
Waterloo, ON, Canada

LORENZO DITOMMASO
Concordia University
Montreal, QC, Canada

FRED W. DOBBS-ALLSOPP
Princeton Theological Seminary
Princeton, NJ

MARY KAY DOBROVOLNY, R.S.M.
College of St. Mary
Omaha, NE

TERENCE L. DONALDSON
Wycliffe College
Toronto, ON, Canada

CLAUDE DOUMET-SERHAL
University College London
London, United Kingdom

F. GERALD DOWNING
University of Manchester
Manchester, United Kingdom

JOEL F. DRINKARD, JR.
Review & Expositor
Louisville, KY

JAMES D. G. DUNN
University of Durham
Durham, United Kingdom

RUBÉN R. DUPERTUIS
Trinity University
San Antonio, TX

NICOLE WILKINSON DURAN
Trinity Presbyterian Church
Bryn Mawr, PA

PATRICIA DUTCHER-WALLS
Vancouver School of Theology
Vancouver, BC, Canada

JASON C. DYKEHOUSE
Baylor University
Waco, TX

TERRY W. EDDINGER
Carolina Evangelical Divinity School
High Point, NC

CARL S. EHRLICH
York University
Toronto, ON, Canada

GÖRAN EIDEVALL
University of Uppsala
Uppsala, Sweden

YOEL ELITZUR
Herzog College
Alon Shvut, Israel

SUSAN M. ELLIOTT
Red Lodge, MT

JOHN C. ENDRES, S.J.
Jesuit School of Theology at Berkeley
Berkeley, CA

MILTON ENG
William Patterson University
Wayne, NJ

TAMARA COHN ESKENAZI
Hebrew Union College—Jewish Institute of Religion
Los Angeles, CA

JANET S. EVERHART
Simpson College
Indianola, IA

BENJAMIN FIORE
Campion College, University of Regina
Regina, SK, Canada

PAUL E. FITZPATRICK, S.M.
Blessed John XXIII National Seminary
Weston, MA

PETER W. FLINT
Trinity Western University
Langley, BC, Canada

CAROLE R. FONTAINE
Andover Newton Theological School
Newton Centre, MA

MARY F. FOSKETT
Wake Forest University
Winston-Salem, NC

TERENCE E. FRETHEIM
Luther Seminary
St. Paul, MN

RUSSELL FULLER
University of San Diego
San Diego, CA

JOHN GAY
Madisonville, TN

HEIDI S. GEIB
Vanderbilt University
Nashville, TN

FRANCES TAYLOR GENCH
Union Theological Seminary and
Presbyterian School of Christian Education
Richmond, VA

BRUCE W. GENTRY
Southeast Missouri State University
Cape Girardeau, MO

DAVID W. J. GILL
Swansea University
Swansea, United Kingdom

FLORENCE MORGAN GILLMAN
University of San Diego
San Diego, CA

MARK D. GIVEN
Missouri State University
Springfield, MO

MARK S. GOODACRE
Duke University
Durham, NC

FRANK H. GORMAN
Muncie, IN

DONALD E. GOWAN
Pittsburgh Theological Seminary (Emeritus)
Pittsburgh, PA

LESTER L. GRABBE
University of Hull
Hull, United Kingdom

DAVID F. GRAF
University of Miami
Coral Gables, FL

JOEL B. GREEN
Fuller Theological Seminary
Pasadena, CA

MARK D. GREEN
Indiana State University
Terre Haute, IN

JAMES P. GRIMSHAW
Carroll University
Waukesha, WI

CAROL STUART GRIZZARD
Pikeville College
Pikeville, KY

George H. Guthrie
Union University
Jackson, TN

Michael E. Hardwick
Pontifical Paul VI Institute and St. Louis University
St. Louis, MO

R. Justin Harkins
Vanderbilt University
Nashville, TN

J. Albert Harrill
Indiana University
Bloomington, IN

Hannah K. Harrington
Patten University
Oakland, CA

J. Gordon Harris
Sioux Falls Seminary
Sioux Falls, SD

Ralph K. Hawkins
Kentucky Christian University
Grayson, KY

Heidi E. Hawks
Pfafftown, NC

Charles W. Hedrick
Missouri State University (Emeritus)
Springfield, MO

Charlotte Hempel
University of Birmingham
Birmingham, United Kingdom

F. Nigel Hepper
Royal Botanic Gardens
Kew, United Kingdom

Theodore Hiebert
McCormick Theological Seminary
Chicago, IL

Carolyn Higginbotham
Christian Theological Seminary
Indianapolis, IN

T. R. Hobbs
McMaster University
Hamilton, ON, Canada

Michael W. Holmes
Bethel University
St. Paul, MN

Leslie J. Hoppe, O.F.M.
Catholic Theological Union
Chicago, IL

Teresa J. Hornsby
Drury University
Springfield, MO

Fred L. Horton
Wake Forest University
Winston-Salem, NC

Edwin C. Hostetter
The George Washington University
Washington, DC

Bonnie Howe
Dominican University of California
San Rafael, CA

Herbert B. Huffmon
Drew University
Madison, NJ

Susan E. Hylen
Vanderbilt University
Nashville, TN

David Instone-Brewer
Tyndale House
Cambridge, United Kingdom

Stuart Irvine
Louisiana State University and
Agricultural and Mechanical College
Baton Rouge, LA

Ada Maria Isasi-Díaz
Drew University Theological School
Madison, NJ

Daegyu J. Jang
Korea Baptist University
Daejeon, Republic of Korea

Ann Jervis
Wycliffe College
Toronto, ON, Canada

Andy Johnson
Nazarene Theological Seminary
Kansas City, MO

Marshall D. Johnson
Minneapolis, MN

Philip S. Johnston
Wycliffe Hall, Oxford University
Oxford, United Kingdom

William Johnstone
King's College, University of Aberdeen
Aberdeen, United Kingdom

A. Heath Jones, III
Nashville, TN

Judith Anne Jones
Wartburg College
Waverly, IA

Scott C. Jones
Covenant College
Lookout Mountain, GA

Martha Joukowsky
Brown University (Emerita)
Providence, RI

Ljubica Jovanovic
Cornell University
Ithaca, NY

Nyasha Junior
University of Dayton
Dayton, OH

Ted Kaizer
University of Durham
Durham, United Kingdom

Isaac Kalimi
Northwestern University
Evanston, IL

John Kaltner
Rhodes College
Memphis, TN

John I. Kampen
Methodist Theological School in Ohio
Delaware, OH

Brad E. Kelle
Point Loma Nazarene University
San Diego, CA

D. Andrew Kille
Bible Workbench
San Jose, CA

Hyun Chul Paul Kim
Methodist Theological School in Ohio
Delaware, OH

Uriah Y. Kim
Hartford Seminary
Hartford, CT

Paul J. Kissling
TCMI Institute
Heilingenkreuz, Austria

Raz Kletter
Tallinn, Estonia

Amos Kloner
Bar Ilan University
Ramat-Gan, Israel

Ernst Axel Knauf
Universität Bern
Bern, Switzerland

Craig R. Koester
Luther Seminary
St. Paul, MN

Jennifer L. Koosed
Albright College
Reading, PA

Edgar Krentz
Lutheran School of Theology at Chicago
Chicago, IL

Robert Kugler
Lewis & Clark College
Portland, OR

Jeffrey S. Lamp
Oral Roberts University
Tulsa, OK

Peter Lampe
University of Heidelberg
Heidelberg, Germany

John C. H. Laughlin
Averett University
Danville, VA

Dale F. Launderville
Saint John's University
Collegeville, MN

John I. Lawlor
Grand Rapids Theological Seminary
Grand Rapids, MI

Beatrice J. W. Lawrence
Hebrew Union College—Jewish Institute of Religion
Los Angeles, CA

Archie C. C. Lee
The Chinese University of Hong Kong
Shatin, Hong Kong

Eunny Lee
Princeton Theological Seminary
Princeton, NJ

Joel Marcus LeMon
Emory University
Atlanta, GA

Jutta Leonhardt-Balzer
School of Divinity and Religious Studies
King's College, University of Aberdeen
Aberdeen, United Kingdom

Barbara Mei Leung Lai
Tyndale Seminary
Toronto, ON, Canada

Baruch A. Levine
New York University
New York, NY

Irina Levinskaya
Cambridge, United Kingdom

Gregory L. Linton
Johnson Bible College
Knoxville, TN

Oded Lipschits
Tel Aviv University
Ramat Aviv, Israel

Kenneth D. Litwak
Azusa Pacific University
Azusa, CA

Francisco Lozada, Jr.
Brite Divinity School
Texas Christian University
Fort Worth, TX

Lamontte M. Luker
Lutheran Theological Southern Seminary
Columbia, SC

Temba L. J. Mafico
Interdenominational Theological Center
Atlanta, GA

Jodi Magness
University of North Carolina at Chapel Hill
Chapel Hill, NC

Bruce J. Malina
Creighton University
Omaha, NE

Dale W. Manor
Harding University
Searcy, AR

Claude Mariottini
Northern Baptist Theological Seminary
Lombard, IL

Steven D. Mason
LeTourneau University
Longview, TX

Susan F. Mathews
University of Scranton
Scranton, PA

Victor H. Matthews
Missouri State University
Springfield, MO

Gerald L. Mattingly
Johnson Bible College
Knoxville, TN

Kathy R. Maxwell
South Texas School of Christian Studies
Corpus Christi, TX

Nathan D. Maxwell
South Texas School of Christian Studies
Corpus Christi, TX

Amihai Mazar
The Hebrew University of Jerusalem
Jerusalem, Israel

Byron R. McCane
Wofford College
Spartanburg, SC

P. Kyle McCarter, Jr.
Johns Hopkins University
Baltimore, MD

C. Mark McCormick
Stillman College
Tuscaloosa, AL

Lee Martin McDonald
Acadia Divinity College (Emeritus)
Wolfville, NS, Canada

Bernard McGinn
Divinity School at the University of Chicago (Emeritus)
Chicago, IL

Michael C. McKeever
Judson University
Elgin, IL

John L. McLaughlin
University of St. Michael's College
Toronto, ON, Canada

Phillip McMillion
Harding University Graduate School of Religion
Memphis, TN

James K. Mead
Northwestern College
Orange City, IA

Tim Meadowcroft
Laidlaw College
Waitakere City, New Zealand

Sarianna Metso
University of Toronto
Toronto, ON, Canada

Marvin Meyer
Chapman University
Orange, CA

Carol Meyers
Duke University
Durham, NC

J. Ramsey Michaels
Missouri State University (Emeritus)
Springfield, MO

David M. Miller
Briercrest College and Seminary
Caronport, SK, Canada

Robert D. Miller, II
The Catholic University of America
Washington, DC

R. W. L. Moberly
University of Durham
Durham, United Kingdom

David P. Moessner
University of Dubuque
Dubuque, IA

Philip G. Monroe
Biblical Seminary
Hatfield, PA

Douglas Moo
Wheaton College
Wheaton, IL

Milton Moreland
Rhodes College
Memphis, TN

William S. Morrow
Queen's Theological College
Kingston, ON, Canada

James C. Moyer
Missouri State University
Springfield, MO

STEPHEN MOYISE
University of Chichester
Chichester, United Kingdom

HANS-FREDRICH MUELLER
Union College
Schenectady, NY

E. THEODORE MULLEN, JR.
Indiana University—Purdue University Indianapolis
Indianapolis, IN

FREDERICK J. MURPHY
College of the Holy Cross
Worchester, MA

JEROME MURPHY-O'CONNOR, O.P.
École Biblique
Jerusalem, Israel

JUDITH H. NEWMAN
Toronto School of Theology and
the University of Toronto
Toronto, ON, Canada

JEROME H. NEYREY, S.J.
University of Notre Dame
Notre Dame, IN

PETER OAKES
University of Manchester
Manchester, United Kingdom

JULIA M. O'BRIEN
Lancaster Theological Seminary
Lancaster, PA

JOHN J. O'KEEFE
Creighton University
Omaha, NE

DENNIS T. OLSON
Princeton Theological Seminary
Princeton, NJ

SHARON PACE
Marquette University
Milwaukee, WI

KIM PAFFENROTH
Iona College
New Rochelle, NY

EUGENE EUNG-CHUN PARK
San Francisco Theological Seminary
San Anselmo, CA

DONALD W. PARRY
Brigham Young University
Provo, UT

DALE PATRICK
Drake University
Des Moines, IA

KIMBERLY R. PEELER
Vanderbilt University
Nashville, TN

DAVID PENCHANSKY
University of St. Thomas
St. Paul, MN

KEN M. PENNER
St. Francis Xavier University
Antigonish, NS, Canada

PHEME PERKINS
Boston College
Chestnut Hill, MA

DAVID L. PETERSEN
Emory University
Atlanta, GA

BRIAN K. PETERSON
Lutheran Theological Southern Seminary
Lexington, SC

MICHELE PICCIRILLO, O.F.M.†
Studium Biblicum Franciscanum
Jerusalem, Israel

SUSAN M. PIGOTT
Logsdon School of Theology
Hardin-Simmons University
Abilene, TX

JOHN J. PILCH
Georgetown University
Washington, DC

ELIZABETH E. PLATT
University of Dubuque Theological Seminary
(Emerita)
Dubuque, IA

Adam L. Porter
Illinois College
Jacksonville, IL

Emerson B. Powery
Messiah College
Grantham, PA

James J. H. Price
Lynchburg College
Lynchburg, VA

Paul J. Ray, Jr.
Andrews University
Berrien Springs, MI

Mark Reasoner
Bethel University
St. Paul, MN

Stephen Alan Reed
Jamestown College
Jamestown, ND

Barbara Reid, O.P.
Catholic Theological Union
Chicago, IL

David M. Reis
Bridgewater College
Bridgewater, VA

Bennie H. Reynolds, III
University of North Carolina at Chapel Hill
Chapel Hill, NC

Victor Rhee
Talbot School of Theology
Biola University
La Mirada, CA

David Rhoads
Lutheran School of Theology at Chicago
Chicago, IL

Earl J. Richard
Loyola University New Orleans (Emeritus)
New Orleans, LA

Rainer Riesner
Technische Universität Dortmund
Dortmund, Germany

Ellen Robbins
Johns Hopkins University
Baltimore, MD

Gregory Allen Robbins
University of Denver
Denver, CO

J. J. M. Roberts
Princeton Theological Seminary (Emeritus)
Princeton, NJ

Calvin J. Roetzel
University of Minnesota—Twin Cities
St. Paul, MN

Gary O. Rollefson
Whitman College
Walla Walla, WA

Christopher A. Rollston
Emmanuel School of Religion
Johnson City, TN

Mark Roncace
Wingate University
Wingate, NC

Christopher Rowland
Queen's College, University of Oxford
Oxford, United Kingdom

Rodney S. Sadler, Jr.
Union Theological Seminary and
Presbyterian School of Education at Charlotte
Charlotte, NC

Stanley P. Saunders
Columbia Theological Seminary
Decatur, GA

Kenneth L. Schenck
Indiana Wesleyan University
Marion, IN

Lawrence H. Schiffman
New York University
New York, NY

Jeremy Schipper
Temple University
Philadelphia, PA

Brian B. Schmidt
The University of Michigan
Ann Arbor, MI

Philip C. Schmitz
Eastern Michigan University
Ypsilanti, MI

Eckhard J. Schnabel
Trinity Evangelical Divinity School
Deerfield, IL

Tammi J. Schneider
Claremont Graduate University
Claremont, CA

Daniel N. Schowalter
Carthage College
Kenosha, WI

Andreas Schuele
Union Theological Seminary and
Presbyterian School of Christian Education
Richmond, VA

Michael J. Schufer
Claremont Graduate University
Claremont, CA

Ian W. Scott
Tyndale Seminary
Toronto, ON, Canada

JoAnn Scurlock
Elmhurst College
Elmhurst, IL

Alan F. Segal
Barnard College
Columbia University
New York, NY

C. L. Seow
Princeton Theological Seminary
Princeton, NJ

Phillip Michael Sherman
Knoxville, TN

Stephen J. Shoemaker
University of Oregon
Eugene, OR

Matthew L. Skinner
Luther Seminary
St. Paul, MN

P. Oktor Skjaervø
Harvard University
Cambridge, MA

Thomas B. Slater
McAfee School of Theology
Mercer University
Macon, GA

Abraham Smith
Perkins School of Theology
Southern Methodist University
Dallas, TX

Daniel L. Smith-Christopher
Loyola Marymount University
Los Angeles, CA

Marion L. Soards
Louisville Presbyterian Theological Seminary
Louisville, KY

Will Soll
Webster University
St. Louis, MO

Elna K. Solvang
Concordia College
Moorhead, MN

F. Scott Spencer
Baptist Theological Seminary at Richmond
Richmond, VA

Richard A. Spencer
Appalachian State University
Boone, NC

Ephraim Stern
Hebrew University of Jerusalem
Jerusalem, Israel

D. Matthew Stith
Community Presbyterian Church
West Fargo, ND

Matthew W. Stolper
Oriental Institute, University of Chicago
Chicago, IL

Lawson G. Stone
Asbury Theological Seminary
Wilmore, KY

James Riley Strange
Samford University
Birmingham, AL

Brent A. Strawn
Candler School of Theology, Emory University
Atlanta, GA

Channa Cohen Stuart
Free University Amsterdam
Amsterdam, The Netherlands

R. S. Sugirtharajah
University of Birmingham
Birmingham, United Kingdom

William M. Swartley
Associated Mennonite Biblical Seminary
Elkhart, IN

Kim Huat Tan
Trinity Theological College
Singapore, Republic of Singapore

Robert C. Tannehill
Methodist Theological School in Ohio (Emeritus)
Delaware, OH

Jason R. Tatlock
Armstrong Atlantic State University
Savannah, GA

Nicholas H. Taylor
University of Zululand
KwaDlangezwa, South Africa

Eugene TeSelle
Vanderbilt Divinity School (Emeritus)
Nashville, TN

Anthony C. Thiselton
University of Nottingham
Nottingham, United Kingdom

David L. Thompson
Asbury Theological Seminary
Wilmore, KY

James W. Thompson
Abilene Christian University
Abilene, TX

Mark A. Thronveit
Luther Seminary
St. Paul, MN

Bonnie Bowman Thurston
Wheeling, WV

Jessica Tinklenberg de Vega
Morningside College
Sioux City, IA

Wesley I. Toews
Canadian Mennonite University
Winnipeg, MB, Canada

W. Sibley Towner
Union Theological Seminary and
Presbyterian School of Christian Education (Emeritus)
Richmond, VA

Joseph L. Trafton
Western Kentucky University
Bowling Green, KY

Phyllis Trible
Wake Forest University Divinity School
Winston-Salem, NC

Allison A. Trites
Acadia Divinity College (Emerita)
Wolfville, NS, Canada

Johannes Tromp
Leiden University
Leiden, The Netherlands

Patricia K. Tull
Louisville Presbyterian Theological Seminary
Louisville, KY

John D. Turner
University of Nebraska-Lincoln
Lincoln, NE

Mary Donovan Turner
Pacific School of Religion
Berkeley, CA

David Ussishkin
Tel Aviv University
Ramat Aviv, Israel

Eveline J. van der Steen
Liverpool University
Liverpool, United Kingdom

ROBERT E. VAN VOORST
Western Theological Seminary
Holland, MI

JAMES C. VAMDERKAM
University of Notre Dame
Notre Dame, IN

MICHAEL G. VANZANT
Mount Vernon Nazarene University
Mount Vernon, OH

ALYS VAUGHAN-WILLIAMS
Consultant archaeobotanist
Cromford, United Kingdom

T. DELAYNE VAUGHN
Baylor University
Waco, TX

RICHARD B. VINSON
Salem College
Winston-Salem, NC

BURTON L. VISOTZKY
Jewish Theological Seminary of America
New York, NY

PAULINE A. VIVIANO
Loyola University of Chicago
Chicago, IL

BARRY DOV WALFISH
University of Toronto
Toronto, ON, Canada

SZE-KAR WAN
Perkins School of Theology
Southern Methodist University
Dallas, TX

CECILIA WASSÉN
Uppsala University
Uppsala, Sweden

DUANE F. WATSON
Malone College
Canton, OH

RANDALL C. WEBBER
Louisville, KY

JAMES E. WEST
Quartz Hill School of Theology
Quartz Hill, CA

TRISHA GAMBAIANA WHEELOCK
Gustavus Adolphus College
Saint Peter, MN

PETER WIDDICOMBE
McMaster University
Hamilton, ON, Canada

DAVID S. WILLIAMS
University of Georgia
Athens, GA

TIMOTHY A. WILLIS
Pepperdine University
Malibu, CA

KEVIN A. WILSON
Merrimack College
North Andover, MA

JOHN D. WINELAND
Kentucky Christian University
Grayson, KY

DEREK E. WITTMAN
Baylor University
Waco, TX

LISA MICHELE WOLFE
Oklahoma City University
Oklahoma City, OK

ARCHIE T. WRIGHT
Regent University School of Divinity
Virginia Beach, VA

FRANK M. YAMADA
McCormick Theological Seminary
Chicago, IL

JOHN Y. H. YIEH
Virginia Theological Seminary
Alexandria, VA

SHARON ZUCKERMAN
The Hebrew University of Jerusalem
Jerusalem, Israel

General Editor's Preface

On behalf of the Editorial Board, I welcome you to the company of users of *The New Interpreter's® Dictionary of the Bible*, a five-volume set offering the best in contemporary biblical scholarship. This new dictionary stands in the continuing tradition of the Interpreter's® series, developed for church and synagogue teachers and preachers and with the goal of supporting congregations and all students of the Bible as they seek to learn and grow.

The dictionary covers all the persons and places mentioned in the Bible. It contains a full range of articles on the cultural, religious, and political contexts of the Bible in the ancient Near East and the Greco-Roman world, and it offers many articles explaining key methods of biblical interpretation. The dictionary includes numerous articles on theological and ethical themes and concepts important to understanding the biblical witness.

The original *Interpreter's Dictionary of the Bible*, published in the 1960s, remained a key reference tool for pastors and teachers for nearly half a century. Yet it was of course a product of its time. Biblical scholarship moved an enormous distance in the intervening years, in knowledge of the literature and culture of the ancient world, and in the development of new approaches that have opened fresh horizons of interpretation, for individual books of the Bible, and for many theological concepts. Study of the Dead Sea Scrolls, of ancient Gnostic documents, and of extra-biblical prophetic texts from the ancient Near East are but a few of the many areas in which scholarship focused on extra-biblical texts has developed new data of great significance for understanding the Bible. Increased attention to gender, ethnicity, and economic class offers new insights into previously neglected aspects of the culture of the biblical world, which in some cases leads to striking new perspectives on biblical texts. Archaeology teams up with a wide range of natural sciences to develop methods that give greater insight into ancient community life, in addition to military upheavals. Newly discovered inscriptions and artifacts shed new light on biblical history and on religious beliefs and practices of ancient Israel and early Christianity. Recent progress in the analysis of Hebrew poetry, in understanding of Greek rhetoric, in theories of characterization, as well as new models of social-scientific analysis and cultural studies offer new avenues of inquiry in support of theological reading of the biblical text. To account for these and many other exciting developments, we have produced an entirely new dictionary rather than a revision of the old. While there may not be new information on certain obscure biblical persons or places, the major articles, almost without exception, introduce fresh material and even entirely new topics that were not on the 1960s scholarly horizon.

Of course these many changes in biblical studies have not taken place in a vacuum. The world itself has also changed greatly. As we move through the 21st century, we face a world grown smaller by speed of communication, yet in many ways politically and economically more fragmented (or at least we are more aware of the fragmentation) than ever before. Ecologically we face a possibly precarious future; factionalism and hostility seem on the increase within and among some religious and racial/ethnic groups, even as signs of reconciliation and search for common ground blossom in unexpected places. While such issues will not be addressed directly on every page, it is the aim of this dictionary to enable wise use of the biblical tradition in theological and ethical approaches to these difficult issues.

As the knowledge of the world surrounding the Bible and also methods for studying the Bible have expanded and changed, so also has the profile of the leaders in biblical scholarship. *The New Interpreter's Dictionary* contributors number approximately 900 women and men in more than 40 different countries from Australia to Africa, from the Americas to Europe, Asia, and the Middle East. Chosen for their scholarly expertise and publication in the areas of their articles, they are identified with Catholic, Orthodox, Jewish, and many different Protestant traditions; they range in personal commitment from conservative to liberal and come from many racial/ethnic and cultural backgrounds. The wide scope of the contributors' contexts reflects the global scope of biblical scholarship of the 21st century.

The Editorial Board took joint responsibility for nominating the wide range of authors who have contributed to this dictionary. Meetings, followed by numerous conference calls and innumerable rounds of email communication enabled comment and consensus building around the hundreds of nominees. Access to such a global span of contributors was greatly eased by computer and internet technology that could not have been feasible even a decade ago, with a website through which more than 7,100 articles were moved seamlessly and without paper from author to press and then through the various editorial stages. All but the very briefest articles were reviewed for content, balance of perspective, and accessibility by at least one member of the editorial board, and web and email facilitated discussion with authors of any proposed revisions. In addition, experienced pastors were recruited for further review of select longer articles, as an additional check on the readability and theological usefulness of the material for the intended audience.

In guidelines for authors and editors, this project has emphasized openness and generosity to various points of view. In an era when the very notion of one right answer to every question is itself increasingly called into question, we have asked our authors to offer their own perspectives on their topics while still including a clear and charitable presentation of significant alternative scholarly viewpoints. The editors are grateful to the authors for their willingness to write in this style, which will provide a fuller interpretive context for readers who are seeking an introduction to a subject.

As General Editor, it is my joy to express appreciation to the entire Editorial Board for their untiring efforts. The Board itself reflects something of the ecclesial, cultural, and racial/ethnic diversity, as well as the range of scholarly expertise that we have worked to bring to fruition in our contributing authors. Thanks, then, to Samuel Balentine, Brian Blount, Joel Green, Kah-Jin Jeffrey Kuan, Pheme Perkins, and Eileen Schuller for all that each of you has brought to our common work; and thanks to the staff of Abingdon Press, who have shepherded this long process with intelligence, imagination, and love.

KATHARINE DOOB SAKENFELD, GENERAL EDITOR

Features of the New Interpreter's® Dictionary of the Bible

A. The Main Entry

1. Title. Main entries are set in a bold font and highlighted in red. In most instances, where more than one person or place in the Bible shares a name, one article covers all instances of that proper name. For example, the article on JOSHUA will include Joshua, high priest and Joshua, son of Nun. However, in some instances, where the subject material is especially important, we divide articles between experts in various fields, to obtain the best treatments. For example, instead of one article on Abraham, we have ABRAHAM, NT and ABRAHAM, OT.

The articles are listed in alphabetical order, with rare exceptions; e.g., when listing all of the entries pertaining to BAAL some minor content sequencing was required.

2. Pronunciation. If the main entry is a person or place in the Bible, it is followed by a preferred pronunciation that is endorsed by the Society of Biblical Literature and derived from the *Harper-Collins Bible Pronunciation Guide* (ed. William O. Walker, Toni Craven, and J. Andrew Dearman. Revised edition, 1994). The following pronunciation key is a useful guide to the sounds that are intended.

a	cat	ihr	ear	ou	how
ah	father	j	joke	p	pat
ahr	lard	k	king	r	run
air	care	kh	ch as in German *Buch*	s	so
aw	jaw	ks	vex	sh	sure
ay	pay	kw	quill	t	toe
b	bug	l	love	th	thin
ch	chew	m	mat	*th*	then
d	do	n	not	ts	tsetse
e, eh	pet	ng	sing	tw	twin
ee	seem	o	hot	uh	ago
er	error	oh	go	uhr	her
f	fun	oi	boy	v	vow
g	good	oo	foot	w	weather
h	hot	*oo*	boot	y	young
hw	whether	oor	poor	z	zone
i	it	or	for	zh	vision
i	sky				

Stress accents are printed after stressed syllables. ´ is a primary stress. ´ is a secondary stress.

3. Biblical Languages. The editors think it is important for a dictionary to make the original biblical languages a part of appropiate entries. To satisfy those readers who are trained in

Hebrew, Aramaic, and Greek, the key terms are rendered in the original language as part of the main-entry heading. A transliteration is provided in the heading, and also with the first occurrence of any Hebrew or Greek font that is introduced in the body of an article. The transliteration style is based on the "general purpose" guide in the *SBL Handbook of Style*. For some students of the ancient languages, the transliteration style functions as a pronunciation guide, though this dictionary makes no attempt to reconcile English pronunciations with ancient-language transliterations.

4. Outline. Entries with more than 2,000 words ordinarily have an outline to help the reader navigate the information contained in the article.

5. Cross References. In the body of the main entry a reader will encounter words presented in all CAPITALS to signal that this topic exists as a separate entry in the dictionary. It would diffuse the purpose of special emphasis to signal a cross reference through capitalization for every person or place in the Bible. The capitalized cross reference means that information in another article is available to enhance the reader's understanding of a concept or to further explain the meaning of a technical term.

One of the risks of publishing five volumes over the course of several years is the potential of including "blind" cross references that lead the reader to another cross reference rather than to an article. Great care is taken in our database to prevent this frustration for the reader; if any blind references occur (perhaps if an article failed to appear), we will correct the link upon reprint.

6. Bibliography. This dictionary is not intended as a technical reference tool; therefore, entries do not contain detailed citations within the body of the article, nor footnotes at the end. However, a limited number of technical articles contain citations of an author's name, with bibliographic reference at the end of the entry. Bibliographies for articles are necessarily short and select. Works published before the mid-20th cent. generally are avoided in favor of more current works that build on earlier publications.

B. Main Entry List

The definitions included in this dictionary are written in a style that is accessible to students, pastors, and teachers of the Bible. Style decisions are based on the needs, interests, and skills in the primary audience. A group of consulting readers (all pastors of churches) aided us in vetting these articles for comprehension and usefulness in their daily tasks.

We began with the main entries from *The Interpreter's Dictionary of the Bible* (1964, 1975). We subtracted from this list several hundred King James Version spellings of persons, places, and obsolete terms, and replaced these with spellings or terms found in the *New Revised Standard Version* of the Bible. To the list of entries we added terms from other theological handbooks and Bible dictionaries, as well as topics recommended by members of the editorial board and authors. Author input was crucial as we responded to suggestions about dated topics, emerging trends, and more recently published primary sources.

The authors have moved away from the word-study approach that dominated biblical scholarship when the *Interpreter's Dictionary* was published. Scholars have learned that literary context is more important for present day Bible readers than etymology (word origins) or later theological notions of what a word means. A Bible dictionary, like any other dictionary, indexes single words or phrases that label people, places, and subjects. The challenge for the author of a Bible dictionary article is to convey (within the limited word count) the diverse range of meaning that can be represented by major terms.

C. Sources of Style

For English style (e.g., spelling and abbreviations), we relied on a blend of three sources: the *SBL Handbook of Style* (1999), produced by the Society of Biblical Literature, the *Chicago Manual of Style,* 15th Edition, and for issues unique to our project, the *New Interpreter's®* style guide.

When appropriate, we based translation of texts on the *New Revised Standard Version* of the Bible (NRSV), to promote uniformity among articles. Some familiar terms from the King James Version have been omitted, but Volume Three of the dictionary includes an article called KING JAMES VERSION, ARCHAIC TERMS. Readers are also encouraged to read the articles on BIBLE TRANSLATION THEORY; BIBLICAL INTERPRETATION, HISTORY OF; VERSIONS, AUTHORIZED; VERSIONS, BIBLE; and VERSIONS, ENGLISH for more information.

Other *New Interpreter's®* products consistently use the label "Old Testament" (OT). We decided with this dictionary to maintain the same style. Of course, when discussing the ancient languages more directly, articles refer as necessary to the Hebrew Bible (e.g., the Masoretic Text, with the abbreviation Heb.) or the Septuagint (the Greek text, with the abbreviation LXX).

We use the terms in small caps that are preferred by most scholars for identifying dates: BCE, "Before the Common Era" (in place of B.C., "Before Christ") and CE for "Common Era" (instead of A.D. for *Anno Domini,* "Year of our Lord").

For further help in navigating the dictionary, please see the list of ABBREVIATIONS at the end of each volume.

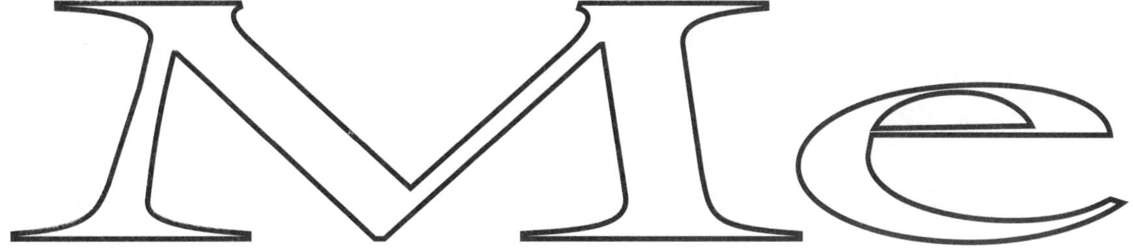
Me

MEAL [סֹלֶת soleth, קֶמַח qemakh]. Grain that was ground up, parched, and eaten in loaves of bread. Every village and town would have been familiar with the sound of millstones grinding grain into flour (Isa 47:2) or the sight of women sitting before their houses grinding meal by hand in a quern (Luke 17:35). As part of its daily provisions, every household kept a store of meal in jars (1 Kgs 17:12) that they would mix with olive oil and then fashion into unleavened cakes (Gen 18:6; Judg 6:19; NRSV, "choice flour"). The royal household was well supplied with meal (1 Kgs 4:22 [Heb. 5:2]). In times of famine, the price of this everyday commodity soared, and people longed for the day when it would be cheaply available (2 Kgs 7:1-2, 16-20). At harvest time, the finest quality, "the first of your ground meal" (ʿarisah עֲרִיסָה, author's trans.; NRSV, "dough"), was offered to God in the form of cakes or loaves as a thank offering (Num 15:20-21; Ezek 44:30; Neh 10:37 [Heb. 10:38]). *See* BARLEY; MILL, MILLSTONE; THRESHING; WHEAT.

VICTOR H. MATTHEWS

MEAL CUSTOMS. Meal customs reflected in the Bible were influenced by the larger cultural contexts of the ANE, Judaism, and the Greco-Roman world and served to shape social and theological relationships.

The number of MEALS and the amount of food consumed each day depended on socioeconomic status (1 Kgs 4:22-23; 17:8-16). For many, two meals were the norm: a simple meal in the late morning (e.g., parched grain and bread dipped in sour wine; Ruth 2:14) and the main meal in the evening after the day's work (e.g., bread and lentil stew; Gen 25:29-34).

Many meals represented in the Bible were not typical daily meals but feasts or banquets. These meals were special occasions, usually served in the evening, and were integral parts of weddings (Gen 29:21-22; Matt 22:1-13; John 2:1-11), religious festivals (e.g., Passover; Exod 12; Mark 14:12-25), ratifications of political treaties or covenants (Gen 26:26-33; Exod 24:9-11), offers of HOSPITALITY (Gen 18:1-8; Ps 23), or gatherings of organizations (1 Cor 10:17-33).

Distinctive meal customs were common in these cultural contexts. Jewish DIETARY LAWS specified the type of food fit for consumption and the manner in which food was to be prepared (e.g., blood is to be drained). The practice of these laws, outlined in Lev 11 and Deut 14, was associated with holiness (Lev 11:44-45; Deut 14:21) and influenced Jewish-Gentile relationships in the OT and NT (see Acts 15).

Ancient Near Eastern and Greco-Roman customs associated with formal evening meals called BANQUETs became prevalent by the 1st cent. BCE. The first part of this social event was dinner. Invitations were sent to the guests (Luke 14:10, 12, 16). When arriving, guests would have their feet washed (Judg 19:21; compare John 13:1-16) and might be anointed on the head with oil or perfume (Mark 14:3; Luke 7:46). Around the table, guests would be seated according to rank (Gen 43:33; Luke 14:7-11). Before eating, guests would wash their hands (Mark 7:1-8) and a thanksgiving would be offered (Matt 26:26-27; Mark 8:6). While at ordinary meals women and men ate together, at banquets typically only men reclined around the table, leaning on their left elbow so they could eat with their right hand (John 13:23-25).

The second part of the event, the symposium, included the drinking of wine, philosophical conversations, and various forms of entertainment such as singing and dancing (Mark 6:22). In the last supper, the guests drank wine after supper (Luke 22:20) and engaged in conversation (Luke 22:24-30).

Failure to follow meal customs in the ancient world might warrant a critique. Those who did not offer hospitality were condemned (Deut 23:3-4; Luke 10:10-12). Jesus admonished his dinner host for not bathing his feet, greeting him with a kiss, or anointing his head with oil (Luke 7:36-50). The wealthy who participated in luxurious dining to the exclusion or detriment of the poor were criticized (Amos 6:4-7; Luke 14:12-14; 16:19-30; 1 Cor 11:17-34). While Mark and Luke portrayed women participating in more traditional meal customs as servants or in private settings (Mark 1:29-31; Luke 10:38-42), Matthew advocated a more egalitarian, inclusive, and public role for women and children in meal settings (Matt 14:13-21; 15:32-39; 25:1-13). *See* FEASTS AND FASTS; FESTIVALS, GRECO-ROMAN; LAST SUPPER, THE; LORD'S SUPPER; MESSIANIC BANQUET; PASSOVER AND FEAST OF UNLEAVENED BREAD; TABLE FELLOWSHIP.

Bibliography: Dennis E. Smith. *From Symposium to Eucharist: The Banquet in the Early Christian World* (2003).

JAMES P. GRIMSHAW

MEAL OFFERING. *See* SACRIFICES AND OFFERINGS.

MEALS. Meals serve the practical function of providing nourishment and become an opportunity for fellowship, celebration, and commemoration of important events in the life of a community.

A. Meals in the Old Testament

1. Diet

Meals in the OT largely were determined by the socioeconomic circumstances of their partakers. A meal could be as simple as crushed barley and bread dipped in a condiment of vinegar that the laborers ate in Ruth 2:14, or as lavish as what is described as King Solomon's daily fare in 1 Kgs 4:22-23: "thirty cors of choice flour, and sixty cors of meal, ten fat oxen, and twenty pasture-fed cattle, one hundred sheep, besides deer, gazelles, roebucks, and fatted fowl."

Bread formed the basic fare for most people in the OT. The midday meal tended to be light—ordinarily bread accompanied by various vegetables (e.g., olives, leeks, gourds) and fruits (e.g., figs, raisins, dates). The main meal of the day was the evening meal. Depending on the household's economic circumstances, a one-pot stew of vegetables, grain or legumes (lentils), and sometimes meat would be served with bread and wine on the side. Meat was considered a luxury food and accordingly was associated with special occasions such as festivals or banquets in addition to temple sacrifice, in which instance people would eat of the meat brought to the Temple (compare the sacrifice of well-being in Lev 7:11-18; 22:29-30). *See* AGRICULTURE; FOOD.

2. Social and symbolic significance

Meals in the OT were occasions for food and drink, but beyond mere nourishment and daily sustenance, the meals also exhibited social and symbolic significance. So the meals in the OT denoted a sense of community—occasions where people came together to eat (*see* SABBATH). Kenneth Craig summarizes the significance of these meals' celebration of life by people united against the darkness of the night.

a. Fellowship and group identity. Meals served as a sign of joy (Eccl 9:7), fellowship (Exod 2:20), and peace (Gen 26:28-30). Sharing meals and drinking wine together contributed to the establishment of a group identity that marked boundaries of inclusion and exclusion among the participants (compare the function of food prohibitions such as those listed in Lev 11 and Deut 14). *See* CLEAN AND UNCLEAN.

b. Festivals. Special occasions were marked by festivals where the community came together ingesting meat and wine in abundance, accompanied by dancing and entertainment (e.g., the warnings in Isa 5:11-12 [compare Amos 6:4-6] of people feasting while being oblivious to social justice concerns). *See* FEASTS AND FASTS.

In particular, banquets form a central theme in the book of Esther (see Craig, 62–68). The book starts with two separate banquets held by King Ahasuerus and Queen Vashti—the king's lavish banquet with seven days of feasting (and drinking) leading to the queen's dethronement when she refuses to be paraded before the intoxicated male guests. Queen Esther later hosts a banquet (5:4-8; 7:1-9), using the meal to gain power, as the king would more likely look kindly upon her request over generous amounts of food and wine. At the end of the book, the PURIM festival serves as a poignant symbol of life in the midst of death—indicating a sense of group solidarity as well as an ongoing tradition as this day with its accompanying meal will be celebrated in coming years (9:17-19). In addition to Purim, meals are part of the celebrations of several festivals, including, e.g., Passover, Festival of Booths, Feast of Dedication, and HANUKKAH (*see* BOOTHS, FEAST OR FESTIVAL OF; FEAST OF DEDICATION; PASSOVER AND FEAST OF UNLEAVENED BREAD).

c. Fellowship with God. Meals in the OT furthermore denote fellowship of humans with God. In Exod 24:9-11, God and humans are said to dine together on the mountain (compare also God's presence at the meal during the occasions of sacrifice, e.g., Lev 9:18-24). And in Isa 25:6, the "golden age" is imaged in terms of a banquet, an ongoing meal where God is the host who presents a feast of rich food, and feast of well-aged wines (compare also Prov 9:1-5 where Wisdom is said to host a banquet as a symbol of an invitation to embrace wisdom and life). *See* MESSIANIC BANQUET.

3. Hospitality

The social obligation of hospitality (i.e., to provide for guests) forms an important aspect of meals in the OT. So the best portions were to be given to the guest (e.g., Saul receiving the best part in 1 Sam 9:23-24). Moreover, there always ought to be room at the table for guests, as in the classic narrative in Gen 18 of

Abraham and Sarah entertaining three strangers who turned out to be divine messengers on a sumptuous meal of cakes, a roasted calf, curds and milk (compare Heb 13:2).

Bibliography: Kenneth M. Craig Jr. *Reading Esther: A Case for the Literary Carnivalesque* (1995); Philip J. King and Lawrence E. Stager. *Life in Biblical Israel* (2001).

L. JULIANA M. CLAASSENS

B. Meals in the New Testament

1. Diet

What did typical peasants eat? What foods were available? Sirach itemizes the basic staples: "The basic necessities of human life are water and fire and iron and salt and wheat flour and milk and honey, the blood of the grape and oil and clothing" (Sir 39:26). But we have more detailed knowledge of Roman Palestine from a rabbinic text that instructs a husband to provide an estranged wife with bread, legumes, oil, and fruit (*m. Ketub.* 5, 8–9). Of these three commodities —grain, oil, and wine—by far the most important was grain and the products made from it. Half of the daily caloric intake was provided by breads. Wheat was valued more than barley; hence barley bread was the food of the poor and slaves. Vegetables, although common, were inferior foods. We find in the Talmud a comment on hospitality, which suggests that a host serves the better food early in a guest's stay, but later "gives him less and less until he serves him vegetables" (*Pesiq. Rab Kah.* 31). Of the vegetables, legumes were the more desirable: lentils, beans, peas, chickpeas, and lupines. The food of the poor was turnips, which gave rise to the saying "Woe to the house in which the turnip passes" (*m. Ber.* 44:2). Of the green leafy vegetables, cabbage was the most popular. In addition, the husband must provide olive oil and fruit, principally dried figs. Wine supplied another quarter of the caloric intake, especially for males and wealthy women. Fish was a typical Sabbath dish. Milk products consisted of cheese and butter; eggs were also an important food. Honey, the primary sweetener, was widely used in the Roman period. Salt gave food flavor; pepper, ginger, and other spices, because imported, were expensive.

Reports about diet in the NT focus on bread, daily and abundant (Mark 6:38-44; 8:1-10). We consider it extremely rare that subsistent peasants "ate their fill," as they did at these feedings, such that a considerable surplus remained. Dried fish was served at the first multiplication of loaves, and appears most frequently in post-resurrection appearances (Luke 24:41-43; John 21:9-14). Roasted lamb was eaten at Passover. Oil was common, and more so wine (Luke 10:34; John 2:1-10). Figs were plentiful (Mark 11:11-21), as well as honey (Mark 1:6). These foods were inherently kosher and required only the paying of a tithe to make them holy.

2. Social and symbolic significance

Meals, food, table etiquette, and commensality remained a constant problem in the story of Jesus and the early church. These items symbolize group boundaries as well as social conflict. The Israelite concern over kosher diet was abrogated first by Jesus ("Thus he declared all foods clean," Mark 7:19; "eating and drinking whatever they provide ..., eat what is set before you," Luke 10:7-8) and then by the early church (Acts 10:14-16; 1 Cor 10:23-27). Peter's vision of unclean foods descending from heaven (Acts 10:9-15) functions both in regard to foods and as a cipher for impartial membership in the church (10:28-29, 34). Thus, the shift from a restricted to an open diet symbolizes for the disciples of Jesus a change in membership (Acts 10:28; 15:23-29). Paul's longest exhortation in 1 Corinthians addresses food and eating, namely the eating of meat sacrificed to idols (8; 10); foods and etiquette at the Lord's Supper (11:17-34) have social repercussions.

a. Jesus' eating anomalies. Jesus' own eating customs provoked controversy. He ate with the wrong people, tax collectors and sinners (Matt 9:10-13), even egregious tax collectors (Luke 19:1-10). If the cultural rule of the times was "likes eat with likes," Jesus should be eating with observant Israelites, if he really is God's agent. One of Jesus' parables showed that the least likely people will sit at the rich man's table: "'Go out at once into the streets and lanes of the town and bring in the poor, the crippled, the blind, and the lame.' And the slave said, 'Sir, what you ordered has been done, and there is still room.' Then the master said to the slave, 'Go out into the roads and lanes, and compel people to come in, so that my house may be filled'" (Luke 14:21-23). In addition, Jesus instructs one of his hosts on whom to invite to a meal: "When you give a luncheon or a dinner, do not invite your friends or your brothers or your relatives or rich neighbors, in case they may invite you in return, and you would be repaid. But when you give a banquet, invite the poor, the crippled, the lame, and the blind" (Luke 14:12-13). Jesus was accused of excess in food and drink: "The Son of Man has come eating and drinking, and you say, 'Look, a glutton and a drunkard, a friend of tax collectors and sinners!'" (Luke 7:34).

b. Paul and clean/unclean foods. Paul has much to say about the eating habits of the Corinthian community, where certain foods, i.e., meat sacrificed to idols, have become a major source of disunity (1 Cor 8:7-13; 10:14–11:1; 11:17-34). In Rom 14–15, Paul speaks to a comparable problem concerning food, commensality, group identity, and unity. Moreover, Paul criticizes Peter's eating practices at Antioch, for he ate first with Gentiles, but withdrew to eat with Judeans (Gal 2:11-14). According to Acts, Paul was confronted with eating customs among the Gentiles that were not in accord with Pharisaic observance. Paul and Barnabas were commissioned to bring to their communities a letter from James detailing avoidance of meat that is strangled or from blood (Acts 15:22-29). But nothing is said about foods, probably because of Peter's vision of foods both clean and unclean descending from heaven: "What God has made clean, you must not call profane" (Acts 10:15).

c. Peter, foods, and Cornelius. Peter, who is already hungry, receives a vision of a sheet coming down from heaven in which "were all kinds of four-footed creatures and reptiles and birds of the air" (Acts 10:12). Evidently the descending sheet in Peter's vision contained CLEAN AND UNCLEAN foods, a distinction made by an observant Israelite. When commanded to "kill and eat," Peter, an observant Jew, at first refuses (10:13-14). Clearly an Israelite is confronted by food laws that prohibit the eating of unclean animals. Heaven intervenes to change Peter's classification, removing its severe ethnic focus: "What God has made clean, you must not call profane" (10:15). The complete episode occurs a second and third time, leaving no doubt that dietary restrictions are erased (10:16). All foods are clean. But this vision is about more than food laws. The agents of a centurion named Cornelius ask Peter to come with them, which tests another Israelite custom (10:19-33). Peter then makes the connection between foods and people: "You yourselves know that it is unlawful for a Jew to associate with or to visit a Gentile; but God has shown me that I should not call anyone profane or unclean" (10:28). There were no longer to be clean and unclean foods and persons. Peter concludes that with the abolition of food and ethnic customs, God is showing a new face: "I truly understand that God shows no partiality" (10:34). One may conclude that Peter and Cornelius enjoyed many a meal together, celebrating the new food and commensality of the impartial God.

This ideal scene in the eyes of others is outrageous and demands an explanation. When Peter goes up to Jerusalem, the circumcised believers (Jewish Christians) criticize him for eating with uncircumcised men (Acts 11:2-3). Peter responds by repeating in detail the vision of the sheet with clean/unclean animals, the visit to Cornelius, and the extraordinary outpouring of the Spirit on these Gentiles—on the enemy, a Roman soldier, no less. The group agrees with Peter and accepts that God has given the Gentiles a means of repentance that leads to life (Acts 11:18). Peter's story is particularly important because it thematically lays out the issues (clean/unclean foods; clean/unclean people; the separation of Israelite and Gentile). As a result, all peoples may eat any foods when these diverse disciples gather for a meal.

d. The Last Supper. The Synoptic Gospels indicate that Jesus' last meal with his disciples before his crucifixion was a Passover meal (*see* LAST SUPPER, THE); therefore, the traditions of Passover shaped the worship of the early church around the celebration of the LORD'S SUPPER.

The blessing of bread and cup at the Last Supper follow the Passover liturgy, and although the traditions do not indicate a telling of the Passover Haggadah, Jesus serves as the head of the family and has the only speaking role. Moreover, the sequence of gestures, such as the dipping of bread in the herbs (Mark 14:20) and singing the hallel psalms (Mark 14:26), further anchors the beginning and ending of the traditional meal. Finally, the formula of the Lord's Supper maintains awareness of the tradition: "I received from the Lord what I also handed on to you ..." (1 Cor 11:23).

John sees some analogy between the Passover lamb and Jesus. According to him, Jesus dies at the very time when lambs are being slaughtered in the Temple (John 19:31, 42); then the evangelist tells us: "None of his bones shall be broken" (John 19:36), a clear reference to the Passover lamb at time of the exodus (Exod 12:46; Num 9:12). *See* PASSOVER AND FEAST OF UNLEAVENED BREAD.

3. Meals and social status

Meals often involved the issue of who could eat with whom (see *Clementine Homilies* 13.4) as well as elaborate seating arrangements by status (Luke 14:7-11). Audiences found Jesus' parable of the great feast shocking because the rich man filled his banquet hall with the riffraff of the city instead of the elite members (Luke 14:21-23). Jesus' eating with tax collectors and non-observant Israelites was countercultural and thus drew attention (Matt 9:11; 11:19; Mark 2:16; Luke 5:30). Meals became especially complicated when Jews and Gentiles tried to eat together (e.g., 1 Cor 8:1-13; Gal 2:11-14).

Meals involved issues of honor and precedence (e.g., Lucian, *Symp.* 8–9). Not all invited to a meal were treated equally, for seating location and food portion were typical strategies to confirm the high status of the host and chief guests (e.g., Luke 14:10).

Ranking and precedence also apply to the foods consumed: not all receive the same food, the same drink, and the same courtesies. The host of a feast might reserve the best food and wine for himself and honored guests, a lesser grade of food and wine for the next tier of guests, and the poorest fare for freed slaves (Seneca, *Ep.* 2.6.1–5).

Competition for status seems to inform the chaos at the Corinthian meal. Paul attempts to bring them back to a form of table fellowship that comports with the teachings of Jesus: "For when the time comes to eat, each of you goes ahead with your own supper, and one goes hungry and another becomes drunk. What! Do you not have homes to eat and drink in? Or do you show contempt for the church of God and humiliate those who have nothing?" (1 Cor 11:21-22). "So then, my brothers and sisters, when you come together to eat, wait for one another. If you are hungry, eat at home, so that when you come together, it will not be for your condemnation" (11:33-34). *See* BANQUET; BREAD; FAST, FASTING; FOOD; MEAL CUSTOMS; MIRACLE; TABLE FELLOWSHIP; WINE.

Bibliography: Gordon Bahr. "The Seder of Passover and the Eucharistic Words." *NovT* 12 (1970) 181–202; Magen Broshi. "The Diet of Palestine in the Roman Period—Introductory Notes." *The Israel Museum Journal* 5 (1986) 41–56; Gildas Hamel. *Poverty and Charity in Roman Palestine: The First Three Centuries* (1990) 8–56; Joachim Jeremias. *The Eucharistic Words of Jesus.* 3rd ed. (1968); Jerome Neyrey. *The Social World of Luke–Acts: Models for Interpretation* (1991) 361–87; Dennis Smith. "The Historical Jesus at Table." *SBLSP* (1989) 466–86; Dennis Smith. "Table Fellowship as a Literary Motif in the Gospel of Luke." *JBL* 106 (1987) 613–38; E. Springs Steele. "Luke 11:37-54—A Modified Hellenistic Symposium?" *JBL* 103 (1984) 379–94; Siegfried Stein. "The Influence of Symposia Literature on the Literary Form of the Pesah Haggadah." *JJS* 8 (1957) 13–44.

JEROME H. NEYREY, SJ

MEARAH mee-air´uh [מְעָרָה me῾arah]. This cave region in LEBANON east of SIDON belonged to the Sidonians and appears in a list of territories not conquered by Joshua (Josh 13:4).

MEASURES. *See* WEIGHTS AND MEASURES.

MEAT [בָּשָׂר basar, שְׁאֵר she᾽er; κρέας kreas]. In the biblical traditions, meat was considered not a basic necessity but a luxury to the majority of the population. *Meat* does not form part of Sirach's FOOD list denoting the basic necessities of human life (Sir 39:26). Rather, the consumption of meat more often than not signaled a special occasion, such as King Solomon's inaugural festival in 1 Kgs 8:63-65 where 22,000 oxen and 120,000 sheep served as a sign of great festivity (see also the wedding meal in Matt 22:4 that consisted of oxen and fattened calves).

In discerning what type of meat was consumed during the biblical period, the field of zooarchaeology (the study of animal bones found at archaeological sites) helps to determine what type and what number of animals were kept at a certain site, as well as the age and sex of the slaughtered animals. So the zooarchaeological record can reveal much about the socioeconomic standing of the community—e.g., the presence of cattle indicates a more settled environment. References to meat in the biblical text regularly function as a sign of wealth (e.g., the reference to large cattle together with small cattle in Gen 12:16; 13:5). Likewise, King Solomon's meat consumption for one day included ten fat oxen and twenty pasture-fed cattle (1 Kgs 4:22-23). In Amos 6:4, the prophet critiques the utter opulence of the people who recline on beds of ivory, dining on the delicacies of fattened lambs and calves (see also Ezek 34:3).

Because of meat's associations with affluence, it was served as a symbol of fertility and prosperity. So Deut 32:14 lists the fat of choice lambs and rams together with Bashan bulls and goats as part of the food God has provided to Israel.

In light of meat's connotations as the best food available, it is not surprising that the benefits of Woman Wisdom's gifts are imaged in terms of Wisdom preparing meat for a lavish, expensive banquet (Prov 9:2). And when the biblical writers had to envisage the end time, they used an image of a banquet where rich dishes filled with marrow, the most succulent part of meat, are on the menu (Isa 25:6).

Meat also was considered a sure sign of hospitality. To slaughter a calf for guests, as in Gen 18:2-8, served as an exceedingly generous act, as it would deprive the host of several hundred more pounds of meat if the animal was allowed to reach maturity. In this regard, it is interesting to note how meat's connotations very much depended on its sociocultural context. So, goat's meat, which was prized in Israel's early pastoral history as a suitable way to entertain guests (Judg 6:19-20; 13:15), receded in NT times when in the parable of the prodigal son, the eldest son complains that his father did not even give him a kid, but gave to his brother the fatted calf (Luke 15:21-30).

Meat's significance in the biblical tradition is most often connected to the phenomenon of sacrifice (*see* SACRIFICES AND OFFERINGS). So we read in Num 28 (see also Lev 23) specifications for the various meat sacrifices for the regular burnt offering (two year-old male lambs without blemish), the special occasions such as the Festival of Weeks and the Passover offering (two young bulls, one ram, seven year-old male lambs), and the guilt offering that always consisted of one male goat. Oded Borowski notes that keeping an animal for one year brings it to the point of reaching maximum weight with minimum investment. Moreover, it made sense for a male animal to be sacrificed, as the female animals that served as a source of milk usually were kept around longer.

Meat's religious significance is evident in the rich symbol of the roasted lamb at Passover that served the function of reminding Israel of God's liberative action. This symbol received new significance in the Christian tradition, which regarded Jesus Christ as the Passover lamb (1 Cor 5:7; 1 Pet 1:18-19). In addition to meat's theological significance, the sacrifices had the further function of providing for the upkeep of the Levites as the priests were entitled to a part of the food offering (Deut 18:1-3). First Samuel 2:11-17 narrates how this provision is corrupted when Eli's sons take more than they were entitled to take.

The consumption of meat was strongly regulated in the biblical text. So one finds in Lev 7:26-27 and 17:10-14 a strict prohibition against eating blood, warning that the person who eats blood will be cut off from the people. Here one sees something of the function of meat as a boundary marker that played a prominent role in the creation of Israel's identity over against the Gentiles.

A similar dynamic is at work in the custom to abstain from pork (see the list of clean and unclean foods in Lev 11; Deut 14; see also Ezek 33:25; Hos 9:3, which equate idolatry with eating unclean food; *see* CLEAN AND UNCLEAN). In post-biblical literature such as 4 Macc 5–17, Jewish heroes and heroines like Eleazar, his seven brothers, and their mother are revered for abstaining from pork to the point of becoming martyrs of the faith, so maintaining their Jewish identity. The connection between meat and identity is also evident today in Jewish kosher rituals, e.g., the contemporary custom to separate dairy and meat that goes back to the prohibition of boiling a kid in its mother's milk (Exod 23:19; 34:26; Deut 14:21).

In the NT, the role of meat as boundary marker forms a central theme in the emerging church's efforts to discern its identity. So Peter's vision in Acts 10:10-16 uses the typical categories of clean and unclean meat to reveal something of the early church's decision to relax the food laws, which made it easier to socialize with Gentile pagans. And in 1 Cor 8 and 10, Paul addresses the pastoral concern of how a divided community ought to deal with the question of whether or not it is appropriate to eat meat sacrificed to idols.

Bibliography: Oded Borowski. *Every Living Thing: Daily Use of Animals in Ancient Israel* (1998); Dennis E. Smith. *From Symposium to Eucharist: The Banquet in the Early Christian World* (2003).

L. JULIANA CLAASSENS

MEAT OFFERING. *See* SACRIFICES AND OFFERINGS.

MEBUNNAI mi-buhn'*i* [מְבֻנַּי **mevunnay**]. Mebunnai the Hushathite (*see* HUSHAH) is listed as one of the Thirty, DAVID'S CHAMPIONS, in 2 Sam 23:27, but the name may be a corruption of SIBBECAI the Hushathite (2 Sam 21:18; 1 Chr 11:29; 20:4; 27:11).

MECHERATHITE mi-ker'uh-th*i*t [מְכֵרָתִי **mekherathi**]. HEPHER the Mecherathite is listed among David's warriors (1 Chr 11:36). But "Mecherathite" may be a corruption of MAACAH (2 Sam 23:34). *See* ELIPHAL.

MECONAH mi-koh'nuh [מְכֹנָה **mekhonah**]. One of the villages in southern Judah where Israelites settled after returning from the exile in Babylon (Neh 11:28).

MEDAD mee'dad [מֵידָד **medhadh**]. ELDAD and Medad, among seventy elders chosen to relieve Moses' burden of leadership, remained in camp prophesying under the influence of the spirit while the others were at the TENT OF MEETING (Num 11:24-30). When Joshua complained about the usurpers, Moses defended them. *See* ELDAD AND MEDAD.

MEDAN mee'dan [מְדָן **medhan**]. One of the sons of Abraham and KETURAH (Gen 25:2; 1 Chr 1:32). Since all of Abraham's children except Isaac were eventually sent into the desert where they became the ancestors of Arab tribes (Gen 25:6), Medan was probably the ancestor of such a group. The name is not likely connected with the Midianites since Midian and Medan are mentioned separately. Wadi Mudan, south of Midian, may have been an area associated with a tribe of Medan.

RALPH K. HAWKINS

MEDEBA med'uh-buh [מֵידְבָא **medheva'**; Μηδαβά **Mēdaba**]. Modern Madaba. The main city on the Mishor Moab, on the high plateau east of the Dead Sea. The site is located 7 km east of Mount Nebo and 30 km south of Rabbath Ammon. The city is mentioned several times in the OT as a city conquered and occupied by the Israelites (Num 21:30; Josh 13:9, 16). According to the MESHA stele lines 7–9 (9th cent. BCE), Mesha was able to take the city, and it is later listed as a city of Moab (Isa 15:2).

Medeba was under Jewish control from the time of John Hyrcanus (Josephus, *Ant.* 13.254) until Hyrcanus II gave it back to King Aretas of Petra (*Ant.* 14.17–20). It was a city of the Province of Arabia created by Emperor Trajan in 106 CE. Eusebius' *Onomastikon* (112.14–17) mentions Qurayat as a Christian village in the territory of Madaba.

Christian families coming from the region of Karak in 1880 discovered the first mosaic floors. The MADABA MAP (ca. 6th cent. CE) was discovered during the construction of the new church on the foundation of an older Byzantine sacred building. Excavations revealed mosaic floors in religious and civil buildings, but more common are mosaic floors in the numerous churches of the city. The flourishing period of the "Madaba Mosaic School" is to be dated to the 6th cent.

Bibliography: M. Piccirillo, ed. *The Madaba Map Centenary (1897–1997)* (1999).

MICHELE PICCIRILLO

MEDES, MEDIA meed, mee'dee-uh [מָדַי **madhay**, מָדִי **madhi**; Μῆδος **Mēdos**]. The Table of Nations in Genesis portrays MADAI, possibly representing the eponymous ancestor of the Medes, as a grandson of Noah and son of Japheth, as well as the brother of Gomer, Magog, Javan, Tubal, Meshech, and Tiras (Gen 10:2).

The Medes were nomadic peoples who wandered into the mountainous lands between the Zagros Mountains and the Salt Desert in northwestern Iran southwest of the Caspian Sea ca. 14th–10th cent. BCE. Assyrian inscriptions of Shalmaneser III and Adadnirari

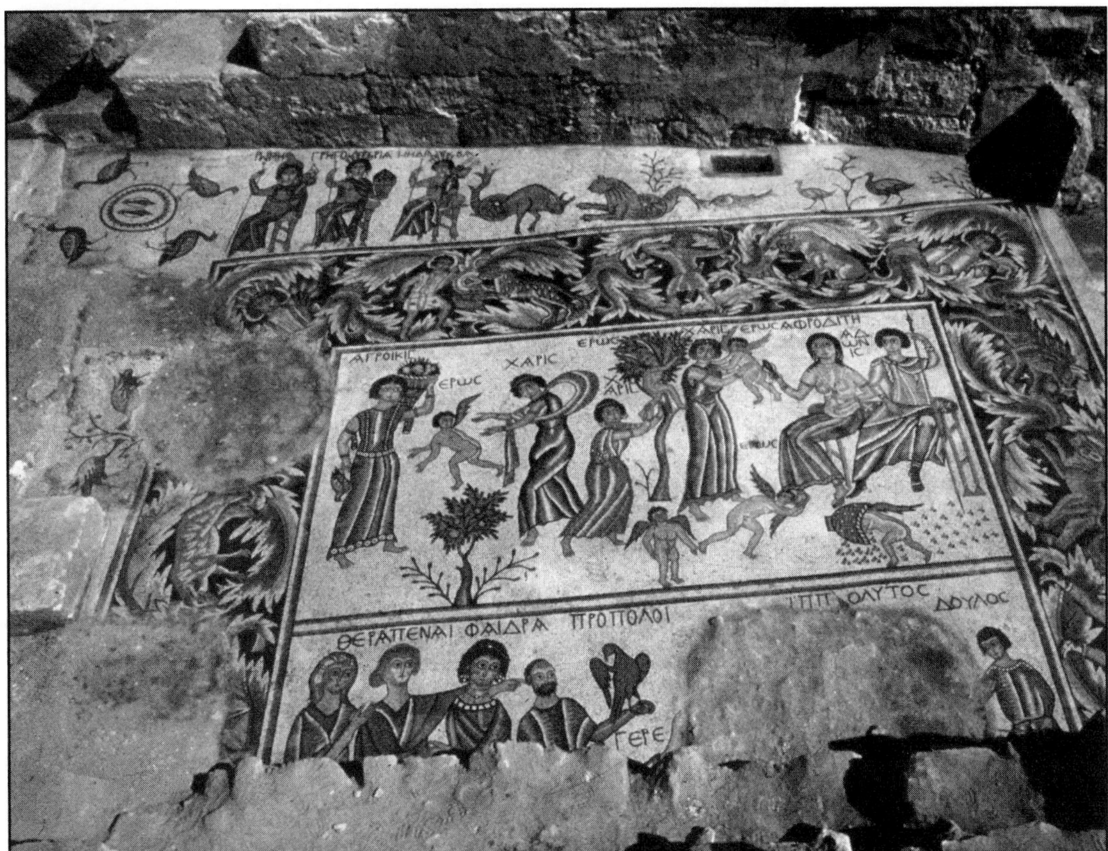

Studium Biblicum Franciscanum Archive, Jerusalem

Figure 1: The mosaic floor of the Hippolythus Hall in the Church of the Virgin Complex in the center of Madaba, Jordan (6th cent. CE).

III from the 9th cent. BCE allude to various tribal groups with no central Median state (*ARAB*, I, 581, 739). These tribal groups raided one another and neighboring states such as Urartu and Mannai, stirring Tiglath-pileser III of Assyria into action. He took control over portions of Media while exiling 65,000 people (ca. 740 BCE, *ARAB*, I, 784, 795). Sargon II deported Israelites to Media (2 Kgs 17:6; 18:11) after bringing the Medes, Urarteans, and Manneans under his control (ca. 721 BCE, *ARAB*, II, 56). Sargon notes the capture of a Median chief named Dayaukku.

In the mid-7th cent. BCE, Scythians and Cimmerians from the north invaded Media. The invasion included Mannai, which provided horses to Assyria. The invaders drove out the small force of Assyrians in the region. Three of the tribal leaders called on Assyria for help. Thus, for the sake of his horses and to exact revenge on the invaders, Esarhaddon gladly entered the region and removed the Scythian threat, but forced Media into a vassal relationship (672 BCE). Other than brief notes on Media in the writings of Ashurbanipal (ca. 660 BCE, *ARAB*, II, 854), little is known of Media until 615 BCE.

Herodotus (*Hist.* 1.96–98) describes the formation of the state of Media under Deioces (Dayaukku?) in the 8th cent. BCE. The Medes comprised clans or tribes with local leaders similar to other nomadic groups of the time in the ANE. Because of his reputation for wisdom and justice, six major tribal leaders agreed to make Deioces king and to build the capital of Ecbatana (Hamadan) if he would settle their disputes.

Following Deioces' fifty-three-year reign, his son Phraortes ruled another forty years before dying in combat against the Assyrians. During Phraortes' reign it appears that he defeated the Persians. Much of the information regarding these early leaders and their reigns is in question.

Phraortes' son, Cyaxares, is attested through a combination of Greek and Babylonian texts. He brought Media to prominence in the 7th cent. BCE by developing a standing army and forming a coalition with the Babylonians against the Assyrians. It is clear that the Medes joined with Nabopolassar of Babylon in the final destruction of Nineveh in 612 BCE, effectually ending the Neo-Assyrian Empire. Jeremiah and Isaiah envisioned the Medes as the vehicle of God's vengeance against the Babylonians (Isa 13:17; Jer 51:11, 28). The empire was divided between Babylonia and the Medes. The new territory included much of the Iranian Plateau and eastern Iran, possibly to the area of modern Tehran.

After his forty-year reign, Cyaxares' son, Astyages, ruled Media from Ecbatana for another thirty-five years until he was overthrown by CYRUS the Great of Persia in 550 BCE. The Persian Empire's capture of Media thus included great reaches of the highlands in the ANE.

Yet the Medes continued to exert influence within the Persian Empire for many years. Cyrus declared Ecbatana his capital, which became known as the capital of the province of Media (Ezra 6:2). Cyrus apparently adopted the Median system of government and placed Medes in positions of power. Daniel's version of the conquest of Babylon (539 BCE) relates the Persian victor as DARIUS the Mede (Dan 5:31). In his interpretation of the writing on the wall, Daniel tells Belshazzar that his kingdom "is divided and given to the Medes and Persians" (5:28). In fact, Daniel consistently places the Medes first in the dual designation (6:8, 12, 15). First Maccabees is set during the time just after Alexander defeated Darius and succeeded him as king (1 Macc 1:1).

Second Esdras indicates that Media was a Persian province where Jews lived in exile during the 5th cent. BCE (2 Esd 1:3). The appointment of governors of provinces was possibly predicated on Median policy. The designation for these governors as satrap (Dan 6:1) is Median in origin (*see* SATRAP, SATRAPY). The book of Esther provides the dual designation of "Persia and Media" for the empire (Esth 1:3, 14, 18). Ahasuerus (Xerxes I) maintained advisors, which included "seven officials of Persia and Media, who had access to the king, and sat first in the kingdom" (Esth 1:14). Fear that Queen Vashti's offense of refusing to appear before Ahasuerus might bring rebellion among the "noble ladies of Persia and Media" led him to proclaim a written order "among the laws of the Persians and the Medes" that banished her from the palace (1:18-19; compare Add Esth 1:14-19).

The book of Judith is a fictional story set during a war involving the Medes (Jdt 1:1-6). The storyteller praises Judith for her boldness in killing Holofernes: "the Medes were daunted at her daring" (Jdt 16:10). The book of Tobit is a story of exiles doing their best to live as righteous Jews in a Gentile land (Tob 1:1-2). Tobit's son Tobias travels to Media to reclaim his father's money (Tob 1:13-15; 4:1, 20; 5:1-8), marries a woman from Media, and ends up living there, because it is a safe haven from the Assyrians (Tob 14:4-15). Many scholars think it is unlikely that the "Media" and "Assyrians" to which these novels refer are the actual regions; rather, they are fictional settings. In the NT, Medes were present on the day of Pentecost during Peter's sermon (Acts 2:9). These Medes were probably from a state in alliance with Rome named Media Atropatene.

Little is known regarding the religion of the ancient Medes prior to the conquest of Cyrus (550 BCE). Median language is also a mystery since no texts defined as specifically Median have been found. Still, philological evidence is seen in loanwords and quotations. Script may have been cuneiform. The few excavations in Iran/ancient Persia have provided images of Median individuals. *See* PERSIA, HISTORY AND RELIGION OF.

Bibliography: Peter Jackson and Lawrence Lockhart, eds. *Cambridge History of Iran.* Vol. 2: *The Median and Achaemenian Periods* (1985).

MICHAEL G. VANZANT

MEDIATOR, MEDIATION [מֵלִיץ **melits;** μεσίτης **mesitēs**]. A mediator is a go-between. While actual words for mediators and mediation are relatively scarce in the Bible, the concept of mediation between God and humanity is fundamental both to the OT and NT.

A. Mediation in the Old Testament
   1. Sacrifice
   2. Moses and the law
   3. Seers and prophets
   4. The king
   5. Priests and the Temple
   6. The servant of the Lord
   7. Angels
   8. The wisdom and word of God
B. Mediation in the New Testament
   1. Greco-Roman background
   2. Christ as prophet and Word of God
   3. Christ as priest and servant of God
   4. Christ as king and God
   5. Mediation of the exalted Christ
C. Conclusion
Bibliography

A. Mediation in the Old Testament

1. Sacrifice

In terms of mediating value, the two most important functions of sacrifice are 1) as gifts to God and 2) as expiations for sin and uncleanness.

Since all SACRIFICES AND OFFERINGS involve the presentation of something to God, the gift aspect is perhaps their most fundamental characteristic. It is no coincidence that the most generic Hebrew words for sacrifice have the connotations of a gift: **minkhah** (מִנְחָה), **mattanah** (מַתָּנָה), and **qorban** (קָרְבָּן). As gifts, sacrifices perform the same mediating functions that gifts do between humans. Some are offered to secure God's favor, such as when Saul offers a sacrifice before going to battle (1 Sam 13:9). Votive sacrifices and offerings are either offered when making a vow or upon its successful completion. Jephthah keeps such a vow when he sacrifices his daughter after he returns from a victorious battle (Judg 11:30-31, 39). The gift of a sacrifice can propitiate God's wrath toward an individual or a people. After the Lord has sent a pestilence on Israel for David's census, God's anger is finally satisfied when David erects an altar on the threshing floor of Araunah the Jebusite and offers burnt offerings there (2 Sam 24:15-25).

In the same vein, regular sacrifices maintain God's favor and give him thanks for good things. Such gifts function somewhat like the tributes one might give to a king for his protection and blessing. The gift of the firstfruits gives God thanks for the way he has blessed the soil while at the same time looking to future blessing. Sacrificial gifts thus mediate good relationships between God and humanity in ways that humans can easily understand.

The expiatory function of sacrifices is one of the most familiar and yet most misunderstood. In general, sacrificial law was not designed to restore an individual's relationship with God for intentional sin, so-called high-handed sins (e.g., Num 15:30-31). The **khatta'th** (חַטָּאת), or "sin offering," thus mediated more in relation to impurity and uncleanness than to what we would consider "moral" sin, the distinction between the two being very loose in OT times (compare Lev 4:2). A person "impaired" by things like childbirth, leprosy, or the inadvertent violation of a taboo might be restored to wholeness by way of this "purification offering."

The idea that the sacrificial animal substituted for the person sacrificing perhaps has some element of truth, but is prone to overstatement given modern debates about penal substitution. In the Day of Atonement ritual, we should probably think more of defilement, rather than the guilt of sin, being transferred from the community of Israel to the animal. The animal then takes that pollution out of the community and into the desert. The sense of substitution is thus far more abstract than any straightforward substitution of penalty. Modern notions of guilt also seem anachronistic in relation to the Levitical system of Israel. The so-called guilt offering (**'asham** אָשָׁם) functioned almost like a fine, a penalty offered because one had inadvertently wronged God (e.g., Lev 5:15, 17). In this case, the amount of the sacrifice was not gradated in accordance with the level of the offense and thus does not figure well as a precise substitution for the offender's guilt.

In general, the mediation provided by these kinds of offerings primarily had to do with cleansing impurity and thus with restoring wholeness. The verb **kipper** (כִּפֶּר) has a range of meanings, but perhaps primarily has the sense of "wiping away." Many texts in which this verb features have a somewhat impersonal sense of atonement, such as Lev 17:11, where God has given blood for "washing" or for atonement of lives. The verse does not discuss such blood in terms of reconciliation with God, penalty for wrongdoing, or some substitution for the offender. Rather, God has placed power within blood itself to wash away impurity. In the theology of this passage in Leviticus, the mediating power of blood apparently functions in an impersonal way.

The OT is not uniform in its affirmation of sacrifice as a way to mediate God's favor. Several OT passages either qualify the benefit of sacrifice or even deny that God accepts it, particularly if the attitude of the one offering it is not appropriate (see Philo, *Moses* 2.107–108). Isaiah 1:10-20 denies the value of Israel's sacrifices because of its failure to "do good; seek justice, rescue the oppressed, defend the orphan, plead for the widow" (v. 17). We find similar statements in Amos (5:21-24), Hosea (6:6), and Micah (6:6-8), all of which reject sacrifice in preference to social justice and fidelity to God. If the two are pitted against each other, God delights more in obedience than sacrifice (1 Sam 15:22; Ps 51:16-17). Psalm 40:6 even says that God has not required burnt offerings and sin offerings but "an open ear." Hebrews 10:5-7 later takes up this passage to argue for the full sufficiency of Christ's sacrificial death and the end of the Levitical sacrificial system.

2. Moses and the law

In the OT, Moses is the single most important mediator between God and Israel, a servant whom God entrusted with his entire house (Num 12:7). In Deut 18:15, Moses describes his role in Israel as that of a prophet, although he is from the tribe of Levi and functions in some ways like a king. When God called Moses initially, he recruited him to serve as a mediator in the exodus of the Israelites from slavery in Egypt (Exod 3:10, 13). His mediation of God's authority before Pharaoh was so fearsome that the Lord could say, "I have made you like God to Pharaoh" (7:1). When Israel sinned with the golden calf, it was Moses who interceded for God not to destroy them (32:11-14). At Mount Sinai, Israel begged him to mediate between them and God, for they were afraid of the thunder and lightning coming from the mountain (20:18-21; Deut 5:5). Moses thus served both as a mediator for Israel to God as well from God to Israel.

The most important words from God that Moses mediated to Israel are of course the words of the covenant and the law. Leviticus 26:46 describes the statutes, ordinances, and laws of the covenant as ones "that the LORD established between himself and the people of Israel on Mount Sinai through Moses." Galatians 3:19 likely echoes this verse when it says that the law was "ordained through angels by a mediator," where the mediator in question is Moses. Throughout history, the significance of Moses as a mediator between God and Israel has understandably risen or fallen depending on the centrality of the law in Jewish faith.

Deuteronomy 28 sets out an extensive list of blessings and curses that follow in consequence of Israel either keeping or violating the law. Accordingly, the DtrH of Joshua, Judges, Samuel, and Kings interprets the vicissitudes of Israel's fortune in relation to its keeping of the law, in particular the law to serve no other gods but the Lord (2 Kgs 17:7-18). Much of the OT thus understands the law to continue to mediate God's relationship with Israel long after Moses. Psalm 1 declares that those who prosper are those whose "delight is in the law of the LORD, and on his law they meditate day and night" (v. 2). Psalm 119:105 says that God's "word is a lamp to my feet and a light to my path," a word that the broader psalm makes clear is the law (e.g., 119:113-114). These texts understand the law to mediate a prosperous relationship between God and his people.

3. Seers and prophets

Sacrifices served largely to mediate the approach of mortals to God. By contrast, prophets primarily, though not exclusively, mediated revelation from God to humanity (*see* PROPHET, PROPHECY). First Samuel 9:9 mentions that the earliest prophets went by the name **roʾeh** (רֹאֶה), "seer." These individuals served both priestly and prophetic functions, and a person went to them to inquire of God. The seer that Saul seeks out for guidance in 1 Sam 9 turns out to be none other than Samuel, who was coming to a certain city to offer sacrifice to Yahweh at a high place.

The "man of God" (**ʾish haʾelohim** אִישׁ הָאֱלֹהִים) in this period was not distinguished by what we would think of as moral virtue, nor did the Spirit of the Lord come only on the "righteous." In Num 22:4-7, Balak hires a practitioner of divination, Balaam, to put a curse on Israel. Balaam, a non-Israelite, is thus a kind of "seer for hire" who uses sacrifice to manipulate the divine in favor of those who solicit his services. In this instance God forbids Balaam from cursing Israel, and after Balak offers multiple sacrifices under Balaam's direction, Balaam only blesses Israel.

In early Israel, prophets formed a kind of guild. At more than one point, Saul is said to be among a band of prophets (1 Sam 10:10-13; 19:23-24) in which he is naked in a "prophetic frenzy" (19:20). Prophets also performed acts of various kinds in addition to bringing words from the Lord. Elijah and Elisha both performed miracles echoed later in the ministry of Jesus. Occasionally their prophetic acts were violent or even subversive. The 8th cent. BCE saw the rise of the "classic" prophets, who mediated God's word to Israel and Judah in numerous settings. These prophets indicted Israel for its oppression of the poor (Amos 4:1), its failure to defend the orphan and widow (Isa 1:17), and its worship of other gods and idols (Hos 11:2). At the same time, the prophets also brought hope in times of crisis and judgment (Isa 40–66; Ezek 40–48).

4. The king

Ideally, the king represented God to the people and the people to God (*see* KING, KINGSHIP). God's desire in seeking out a king was to find "a man after his own heart" (1 Sam 13:14). The ideal king was to "have a copy of this law written for him in the presence of the levitical priests" (Deut 17:18). Unlike the priests, however, the king had the power to enforce God's will on earth with regard to the law. Time and time again, credit or blame is laid at the king's feet for the status of Israel's relationship with the Lord (e.g., 1 Kgs 15:11-15; 16:26; 2 Kgs 10:29; 18:3-8; 21:2; 22:2).

As God's representative, the king was meant to protect, shepherd, and provide sound judgment for the people. The Lord called David to "be shepherd of my people Israel" (2 Sam 5:2) on his behalf. Because of his wisdom from God, the ideal king should be like "the angel of God to know all things that are on the earth" as God does (2 Sam 14:20; compare v. 17). Psalm 72 implores, "Give the king your justice, O God, and your righteousness to a king's son. May he judge your people with righteousness, and your poor with justice" (vv. 1-2). The king was thus to mediate God's justice on earth to his people, and to protect his people from their enemies. A good king also interceded for the people when they provoked God's anger, as Moses did.

Since the king of Israel represented God to his people, both those within and without were obligated to show the king the respect due God's "son." Psalm 2:2 warns those nations that might rage against the Lord's anointed. He who sits in the heavens will defend the king's honor as a reflection of his own. On more than one occasion, David refuses to harm King Saul despite the fact that Saul himself is trying to kill David. In each case, David refuses to raise his hand against "the LORD's anointed" (1 Sam 24:10; 26:9, 23). The office of the king thus represented the kingship of God in the strongest terms.

5. Priests and the Temple

If prophets primarily mediated God's word to Israel, priests mediated the approach of humanity to God by way of sacrifice. Although a substantial portion of the OT does not assume that Levitical priests must be involved in sacrifice, only Levitical priests are authorized to administer them in the ideal Israel of the Pentateuch (Num 3:5-10). In addition, they must only offer these sacrifices in the singular location where God has placed his name (Deut 12), which the books of Kings understand to be Jerusalem (1 Kgs 8:20; 11:36). If a prophetic strand in the OT denies any need for sacrifice, another strand considers the Levitical system to be essential to the worship of the Lord and the maintenance of a proper relationship with him.

In the ANE, temples served as the earthly address of a god. A deity's honor was tied to his or her temples. It is thus no surprise to find that some Israelites did not think God would allow his Temple in Jerusalem to be destroyed, regardless of their actions. The prophet Jeremiah records their defense: "This is the temple of the LORD, the temple of the LORD, the temple of the LORD" (Jer 7:4). This perspective considers the Temple a key mediating factor between God and Israel. In such an outlook, it is not merely the sacrifices or priests in the Temple that effect God's blessing. Rather, the very presence of the Temple in Jerusalem provides security from aggressors on the assumption that God will defend the house where he has placed his name.

Certainly a number of psalms see the Temple as the focal point of God's worship and his blessing of Israel.

Psalm 122 rejoices in the thought of going to the house of the Lord. Many of the so-called psalms of ascent similarly delight in Zion and, by implication, its Temple (Pss 120–137). Psalm 132 pictures the Lord enthroned in Zion's Temple and pleads for him to remember his promise to place a descendant of David on the throne forever. Psalm 84 rejoices in the courts of the Lord and the altars of the psalmist's King. In all these psalms, the Temple and Zion itself are understood to mediate the presence and blessing of the Lord.

In earlier days, God's presence was perhaps more directly associated with the ark of the covenant. Psalm 24 may picture a procession in which the ark is brought into the Temple along with a company of those who seek the God of their salvation (v. 5). In such a procession, the King of glory would enter the Temple as the ark entered the Temple. Certainly the books of Samuel and Kings closely identify God's presence with the ark of the covenant. Hophni and Phinehas, the sons of Eli, take the ark into battle thinking that it will mediate God's power on the battlefield (1 Sam 4:3). In the hands of the Philistines, the ark causes Dagon to fall on his face in his own temple, with his head and hands broken off before the ark of the Lord (5:4). Elsewhere the ark brings tumors and death in Ashdod, Gath, and Ekron (5:6, 9, 10).

In contrast with the identification of God's presence with the ark or with the Temple itself, a significant strand of OT teaching warns against any straightforward equation of the two. As Solomon is inaugurating the Temple, he warns in prayer, "But will God indeed dwell on the earth? Even heaven and the highest heaven cannot contain you, much less this house that I have built!" (1 Kgs 8:27). Already Isa 6 seems to hint that the earthly Temple is only a surrogate for a reality far more profound in scope. Isaiah 66:1 develops this insight to the fullest when it declares that "Heaven is my throne and the earth is my footstool; what is the house that you would build for me, and what is my resting place?" Stephen will take up this theme in Acts 7:49, and Hebrews will emphasize that the true sanctuary of God is in heaven itself (Heb 9:24).

6. The servant of the Lord

From a NT perspective, the four "servant songs" of Isaiah are of particular interest, especially the fourth (42:1-4; 49:1-6; 50:4-11; 52:13–53:12). The identity of the servant in the context of Isaiah has caused as many difficulties for modern interpreters as it apparently did for the Ethiopian eunuch of Acts 8:34 (*see* SERVANT OF THE LORD, THE). Is the servant a personification of corporate Israel, a king of some sort, or a prophet such as Deutero-Isaiah or Moses? Of these suggestions, the idea that the servant might be a personification of corporate Israel commands the most support, not least because the surrounding chapters explicitly identify the servant with Israel or Jacob at numerous points (e.g., 41:8; 42:19-25; 44:1, 21; 45:4; 48:20; 49:3).

Isaiah 52:1 tells Jerusalem to awake and prepare itself, presumably for the return of Israel from exile. Messengers come across the mountains to proclaim the good news of restoration to Zion (52:7). The ruins of Jerusalem are told to break forth into singing, because God has comforted and redeemed the city (52:9; compare 40:1-11). These images reiterate and presuppose the announcement of Cyrus allowing the captives of Babylon to return to Jerusalem (see Ezra 1:1-4). In this context, the fourth servant song speaks of the exaltation and prosperity from God that Israel can now expect (Isa 52:13; 53:10). God will now allot Israel a portion with the great (53:12). The appearance of Israel returning from captivity, however, is deeply marred, beyond human semblance (52:14). The Israel that was taken away to Babylon was "despised and rejected by others" (53:3). At the same time, this suffering of Israel mediates the restoration of Israel and of the returning remnant in particular (53:5).

Regardless of the original referent of this song, the idea that suffering can mediate restoration later resonated with various Jewish traditions, including Christianity. Whether this idea was truly a part of the fourth servant song originally, later interpreters certainly heard it in these terms. In the DtrH, suffering and defeat are only the consequence of someone's sin, whether of the individual who suffers or of the group to which that person belonged (e.g., Jer 31:29; Ezek 18:2). After the exile, Jewish thought increasingly concluded that the righteous could suffer even though they had not sinned. Later Jewish interpreters would find in the words of this servant song the possibility that righteous suffering might have atoning value.

7. Angels

Angels appear occasionally in the OT as messengers and mediators for God (*see* ANGEL). Angels (mal'akhim מַלְאָכִים) come to Abraham and announce what the Lord is about to do to Sodom and Gomorrah (Gen 18:2; 19:1). Jacob has a dream of angels ascending and descending a stairway to heaven at Bethel (Gen 28:12; compare 32:1-2). The angel of the Lord appears to Manoah and his wife to announce the birth of Samson (Judg 13:3-23). The identification of God with such messengers is sometimes so close that the biblical texts flow imperceptibly from one to the other. Genesis 32:24 commences with Jacob wrestling with a "man," but by the end of the story Jacob has been wrestling with God, face to face (32:30). While it is the "angel of the LORD" who appears to Moses in the burning bush (Exod 3:2), it is God who speaks to him (3:4). Judges 13 repeatedly indicates that it is the angel of the Lord who has spoken to Manoah, yet Manoah says to his wife, "We shall surely die, for we have seen God" (v. 22).

Despite these clear references to angels in the OT, it was not until the Second Temple period that angelic speculation flourished. This interest in angels did not come because of some weakened sense of God's presence among the Jews. It is more likely the demotion of the gods of the nations and an increasing sense of the scope of God's rule that facilitated developments in thinking about intermediary beings. Further, postexilic Jews observed the impressive and massive scope of imperial rule with layers of hierarchy. How could the "administration" of God's rule be any less impressive? The result was that some Jews began to name and rank angels while arranging them into hierarchies with greater and lesser authority. The group behind the Enochic writings in particular had great interest in angels.

We find angels in this period performing a number of mediatorial roles beyond the bringing of messages from God. The book of *Jubilees* understands the angel of the presence to have spoken the law to Moses (1.29; 2.1). The NT thus repeatedly implies that the law was delivered through angels (Acts 7:53; Gal 3:19; Heb 2:2). Some Dead Sea Scrolls see the presence of angels among the congregation as a guarantee of proper holiness among those who worship (e.g., CD XV, 17), a view that some see in the background of 1 Cor 11:10. In *Songs of the Sabbath Sacrifice*, earthly worship appears to mirror the worship of the angels in heaven, a view that may shed light on Col 2:18. The *Testament of Levi* goes so far as to see archangels offering bloodless sacrifices for the sins of ignorance committed by the righteous (3.5–6). Only with Philo of Alexandria do we get the sense that angels are necessary messengers because of the transcendence of God (e.g., *Giants* 16), and even here no weakened sense of God's presence accompanies his transcendence.

8. The wisdom and word of God

The wisdom and word of God largely function on a literal level in the OT (*see* WISDOM IN THE OT; WORD, THE). The exception is Prov 8, which portrays God's wisdom as a woman who is a master worker at God's side in the fashioning of the world (8:30). Nevertheless, several OT passages provide background for later Jewish traditions that seem to have impacted the NT. Genesis 1, e.g., presents the creation of the world as a sequence of "words" spoken by God. Isaiah 55:11 captures what must have been the assumption of Jews about what God says—his word always accomplishes whatever God wants it to do.

Around the time of Christ, one strand of Judaism merged this biblical imagery with certain philosophical currents of the day. Stoics understood the world to be governed by logos (λόγος), or "word," which they equated with divine reason. Some philosophers in the Egyptian city of Alexandria merged this idea with Plato's sense that the physical world was a copy of the ideal world we can only access with our mind. The result was "Middle Platonism," a mixture of Platonism with Stoicism. In the hands of certain Alexandrian Jews, these ideas became a template through which they could view the creation of the world and the way a transcendent God operated in the world.

Philo of Alexandria thus saw God's logos as the instrument through which he created the world (e.g., *Cherubim* 127), just as Gen 1 presents God creating by speaking. This logos, however, was also for Philo the collection of all the ideas in God's mind that stood behind the physical world (e.g., *Creation* 24). It was further the image of God, the ideal human of Gen 1:27 from which we embodied humans are copied (e.g., *Creation* 25). As such, Philo's logos sometimes took on a quasi-personal character and became somewhat of a hypostasis—not quite a person but not exactly a personification either. It certainly becomes for Philo the chief intermediary between God and the creation, God's chief angel (e.g., *Heir* 205–206). Meanwhile, the idea of God's word and his wisdom could flow almost imperceptibly from one to the other (e.g., *Alleg. Interp.* 1.65; compare Wis 9:1-2), with both sometimes presented literally and sometimes presented as personified attributes of God.

It is quite possible that some of these dynamics stand behind the NT's application of logos imagery to Jesus, not only in John 1 but implicitly in passages like 1 Cor 8:6; Col 1:15-17; and Heb 1:3. These passages employ a use of prepositions like the phrase "through whom" (di hou δι' οὗ) that is highly reminiscent of certain Middle Platonic philosophical circles such as that on which Philo drew. The NT also seems to equate Jesus with the wisdom of God. If Luke 7:35 and 11:49 represent the more original forms of Q sayings on which Matt 11:19 and 23:34 draw, respectively, then Matthew has apparently modified these sayings in order to equate Jesus with divine wisdom. If Matt 11:28-30 alludes to Sir 24:19 and 51:26—passages in which wisdom is personified as in Prov 8—then it is all the more likely that Matthew meant to portray Jesus as the wisdom of God.

B. Mediation in the New Testament

1. Greco-Roman background

The term mesitēs only appears six times in the NT (Gal 3:19, 20; 1 Tim 2:5; Heb 8:6; 9:15; 12:24), even though the concept of mediation is fundamental to it. The word seems to have had two basic meanings, namely, a guarantor and then an intermediary proper. As a guarantor, a mediator might guarantee the payment of a debt or assure that a contract would be followed. Hebrews' use of mesitēs may have overtones of this sense of the word, for the idea that Jesus is the mediator of a better covenant (8:6) is closely paralleled by the claim that he is the "guarantee" (engyos ἔγγυος) of a better covenant (7:22). Hebrews 9:16-17 also present the new "covenant" (diathēkē διαθήκη) for a moment in testamental and thus contractual terms.

The sense of a mesitēs as an intermediary, however, dominates its NT occurrences. Nowhere is this clearer than in 1 Tim 2:5, where the human Christ Jesus is the "one mediator between God and humankind." Such intermediaries can function in various ways as well. A mediator might simply be the middle element in the movement between two parties. Perhaps most understand Gal 3:19 in this way. Since the law involved more than one party, a mediating element, it is intrinsically inferior to the one God (see v. 20). On the other hand, a mediator might also serve as an arbitrator to reconcile or bring together divergent parties. Accordingly, Gal 3:19 might depict Moses arbitrating between God and the angels in the giving of the law.

To appreciate mediation in the NT fully, it is necessary to have some sense of how patron-client relationships worked in the ancient Mediterranean world. Informal networks of patronage pervaded life in NT times. Those who had excess resources graciously (**charis** χάρις) provided gifts (**charismata** χαρίσματα) to those in need. In return, the "clients" of such "patrons" were expected to return gratitude and honor to their donors, perhaps in addition to performing various tasks for them. When the distance between patron and client was significant enough, "brokers" came into the equation, mediators of patronage. This model of mediation likely stands in the background of some NT thinking with regard to Christ as a mediator. When viewed through this lens, Jesus becomes the appointed broker of God's grace as patron to humanity as client.

2. Christ as prophet and Word of God

The Gospel of Luke introduces the earthly ministry of Jesus by way of Isa 61:1-2, setting up a prophetic lens through which to view his mission (Luke 4:16-21). The Spirit of the Lord anointed Jesus to mediate and proclaim good news to the poor, liberty to captives, and sight to the blind. Jesus likely did refer to himself as a prophet on more than one occasion (e.g., Matt 13:57; Luke 13:33), and others also seem to have understood him in this way (Matt 21:11; Mark 6:15). The book of Acts views Jesus as the prophet like Moses predicted in Deut 18:15 (Acts 3:22; 7:37; compare John 1:21, 25; 6:14; 7:40). Therefore, among the many facets of Jesus' identity, one of the most central is that of a prophetic mediator.

We can speak of Jesus' prophetic mediation on two levels. On one level, Jesus functioned in Galilee as a prophet who brought on God's behalf both good news to the "lost sheep of Israel" and warnings of coming judgment. The miracles he performs echo those of Elijah and Elisha, and his symbolic acts find their meaning against the backdrop of the words of prophets like Jeremiah (e.g., Jer 7:11; compare Mark 11:15-17). On another level, Jesus' cosmic ministry brokers a new covenant with all humanity. In this prophetic role Jesus preaches a more abstract "word of salvation" through his incarnation (John 6:14), death, and resurrection (Heb 2:3). He is the "apostle ... of our confession" (Heb 3:1), whom God sent as a mediator to reconcile the world to himself (2 Cor 5:18).

Jesus brokers this new covenant just as Moses brokered the old: "The law indeed was given through Moses; grace and truth came through Jesus Christ" (John 1:17). The idea that Jesus brokered God's gracious patronage to both Jew and Gentile is a key concept for Paul's writings. The "law brings wrath" (Rom 4:15), "since all have sinned" (3:23). Salvation, escape from God's wrath, is a gift of God (compare Eph 2:8) that follows from God's willingness to justify the ungodly on the basis of their faith (Rom 4:5). Justification thus "depends on faith, in order that the promise may rest on grace" (4:16).

For Paul, such grace cannot come directly, as it apparently did in the case of Abraham, who "believed God, and it was reckoned to him as righteousness" (Rom 4:3; see also Gen 15:6). God has rather brokered this new covenant through Jesus Christ. Several NT writers emphasize the exclusivity of this path to God: "There is salvation in no one else, for there is no other name under heaven given among mortals by which we must be saved" (Acts 4:12); "I am the way, and the truth, and the life. No one comes to the Father except through me" (John 14:6). Salvation is possible now because of the consummate mediatorial act Paul describes as the faith of Jesus Christ (Rom 3:22; Gal 2:16), his obedience "to the point of death" (Phil 2:8). Only "by the one man's obedience the many will be made righteous" (Rom 5:19). The NT thus understands Jesus to be the only truly effective broker of God's grace.

Paul presents the cosmic scope of this mediation through the image of Jesus as the "last Adam." "Sin came into the world through one man," Adam, "and death came through sin" (Rom 5:12). By contrast, with Christ, "one man's act of righteousness leads to justification and life for all" (Rom 5:18). "The first man, Adam, became a living being" but "the last Adam became a life-giving spirit" (1 Cor 15:45). Indeed, the exalted Christ has brokered a new covenant in which the Spirit of Christ inhabits the renewed children of God (see Rom 8:9, 14; 2 Cor 3:6).

Christ is thus a prophetic mediator well beyond the bounds of any OT prophet, including Moses. "Long ago God spoke to our ancestors in many and various ways by the prophets, but in these last days he has spoken to us by a Son" (Heb 1:1-2). This prophetic **logos** is the very Word of God itself, God's highest ambassador (John 3:16). The Gospel of John draws on the Middle Platonic idea of God's **logos** and applies it to Jesus as the very will and purpose of God for the world. This conceptual framework may stand behind NT imagery elsewhere of Christ as the instrument of God in creation, the one "through whom he also created the worlds" (Heb 1:2; compare John 1:3; 1 Cor 8:6; Col 1:16).

3. Christ as priest and servant of God

Romans 8:34 states that Christ intercedes for us at the right hand of God. This may indicate that by the time of Paul, some Christians thought of Christ in priestly terms. Certainly the idea that Christ is a sacrifice appears in the earliest writings of the NT. Romans 3:25 may very well draw on an early Christian affirmation Paul himself inherited when it says that God put Jesus "forward as a sacrifice of atonement." Romans 8:3 may refer to Jesus' death as a sin offering, and 1 Cor 5:7 pictures Christ as a Passover lamb.

We can imagine that it did not take long before Jesus' death on the cross was interpreted in sacrificial and salvific terms (*see* ATONEMENT). Indeed, it is possible that Jesus anticipated his own death and drew an analogy between it and the Passover lamb. The saying in Mark 10:45 surely indicates what at the very least must have been an early understanding of Jesus' death: "For the Son of Man came not to be served but to serve, and to give his life a ransom for many." This saying may very well presuppose an identification of Jesus with the suffering servant of Isa 53, God's servant who "shall make many righteous" (v. 11; compare Acts 8:32-35).

Christ's death served to mediate atonement and reconciliation with God in the manner of a sacrifice. Several Jewish texts are regularly brought into discussion of how early Christians might have conceptualized the mediating value of Christ's death. Wisdom of Solomon 2–3 discusses the fate of a son of God who has died an unjust death at the hands of the ungodly. The souls of such individuals are said to be in the hand of God (3:1), who has accepted them "like a sacrificial burnt offering" (3:6). In 2 Macc 7:38, one of seven brothers faces his impending death in hope "through me and my brothers to bring to an end the wrath of the Almighty that has justly fallen on our whole nation." Even more explicitly, 4 Macc 6:28-29 tells of a righteous martyr asking God to "let our punishment suffice for them [Israel]. Make my blood their purification, and take my life in exchange for theirs." These passages indicate that some Jews believed a righteous individual's death might have mediating value of some sort before God.

Hebrews is the only NT book to refer to Christ explicitly as a priest, as it moves beyond sacrificial imagery in other parts of the NT. Nowhere else does the NT argue that Christ's death indicates the end of the sacrificial system (compare Acts 21:26), nor do books prior to Hebrews indicate that Christ's death atones in some way for the righteous under the old covenant. In this respect, Hebrews presents startling claims with regard to the priestly mediation of Christ. It claims that none of the sacrifices under the old covenant were actually able to take away sins (10:11). Accordingly, none of the witnesses to faith in the old covenant could be made perfect until the sacrifice of Christ (11:13, 40). By contrast, "by a single offering he has perfected for all time those who are sanctified" (10:14). The priestly mediation of Christ is thus universal in scope and time, the only effective means of atonement and reconciliation between God and humanity.

The word mesitēs occurs three times in Hebrews (8:6; 9:15; 12:24). In each instance it refers to Christ's role as the mediator of a new covenant, namely, one with better promises than the one mediated through Moses (8:6). This is the promise of true redemption (9:15), of the actual forgiveness of sins. The blood of the new covenant "speaks a better word than the blood of Abel" (12:24; compare 1 Cor 11:25). Hebrews thus conceptualizes Christ's mediation almost entirely in cultic terms.

4. Christ as king and God

As king, Jesus also plays a mediating role between God and the world. For Judaism, the Messiah was an "anointed one" who would restore the fortunes of Israel (e.g., *Pss. Sol.* 17.21–25; Acts 1:6; *see* MESSIAH, JEWISH). The NT expands the kingship of CHRIST well beyond the borders of Israel. Those who trust in Christ will certainly be a part of his coming kingdom (Rom 10:9, 13). Since God has shown his righteousness through Christ (Rom 1:17; 3:21; 10:3), submission to the lordship of Christ implies submission to the lordship of God as well. For those who do not come to know the righteousness of God, whether Jew or Gentile, Christ will eventually mediate judgment as God's representative (2 Cor 5:10). Jesus will mediate God's royal authority over all the people of the earth at his Parousia.

Christ's mediation of God's kingship extends beyond the realm of mortals to that of angels and demonic forces (e.g., 1 Cor 6:3). His exorcisms while on earth already demonstrated the rule of God over such powers (Luke 10:18; 11:20). Colossians similarly indicates that Jesus is the "firstborn of all creation" (1:15), as it addresses a Jewish "philosophy" with an exaggerated view of angels. All things were created through him—"things visible and invisible, whether thrones or dominions or rulers or powers" (1:16). He is indeed the "head of every ruler and authority" (2:10).

The Philippian hymn captures this cosmic lordship of Christ over all creation when it gives God's demand that "at the name of Jesus every knee should bend, in heaven and on earth and under the earth, and every tongue should confess that Jesus Christ is Lord" (2:10-11). Paul does not understand this lordship of Christ to be independent of God. It is rather a lordship that mediates God's lordship. The confession of Jesus as Lord is "to the glory of God the Father" (Phil 2:11). Indeed, the subordination of Christ's enemies to him occurs in preparation for the ultimate subordination of everything to God himself. "When all things are subjected to him [Christ], then the Son himself will also be subjected to the one who put all things in subjection under him, so that God may be all in all" (1 Cor 15:28).

Christ's kingship thus represents and mediates God the Father's kingship over the entire creation. Jesus Christ is Lord, but "the LORD says to my lord" to sit at his right hand (Ps 110:1; compare Mark 12:36-37).

Jesus Christ is God whose throne is forever and ever (Heb 1:8), but "God, your God, has anointed you" (1:9). In each case, the lordship and divinity of Christ is subordinate and representative of the ultimate lordship and divinity of God the Father. Christ's kingship over the cosmos thus serves to mediate the kingship of God the Father.

5. Mediation of the exalted Christ

With Christ exalted to heaven, the HOLY SPIRIT becomes the primary mediator of Christ's presence on earth. In John, Jesus promises that "I will ask the Father, and he will give you another Advocate, to be with you forever" (14:16). This Advocate is the "Spirit of truth who comes from the Father" (15:26). For Paul, the Holy Spirit defines (2 Cor 1:22), directs (Rom 8:14), and empowers (Gal 5:16) the collective body of Christ in which the Spirit dwells (1 Cor 3:16; 12:13). Perhaps most significantly, the early Christians understood the Holy Spirit to speak through the Jewish Scriptures, which made those Scriptures the most powerful mediation of God's voice to them (*see* INSPIRATION AND REVELATION).

From a Christian standpoint, the NT itself is the collection of teaching given through the Holy Spirit to Christian apostles and prophets. Already with Ephesians we have such apostles and prophets added to the foundation of the church (2:20), now supplementing Christ as the foundational mediator (1 Cor 3:11). The Pastoral Epistles emphasize the "deposit" (parathēkē παραθήκη) of teaching left by Paul to those who would follow after him (2 Tim 1:14). The later books of the NT embody tensions among differing understandings of how God's direction for the church is to be mediated. One stream looked to direct mediation from the Spirit through "charismatic" individuals such as Paul and Christian prophets. As the earlier generation began to pass, however, Christians thought more and more about deposits of teaching and established traditions, with an increasing emphasis on appropriate leadership.

C. Conclusion

Despite the diversity of the biblical texts, the theme of mediation between God and humanity is a common thread throughout both testaments. Many OT texts reflect a time when people turned to seers and sacrifices in an attempt to influence the divine. Other texts (that some scholars view as reflecting a later period) indicate that sacrifices were being made exclusively in the Temple and that the practice of Torah was regarded as a means to mediate relations between God and Israel. From the standpoint of the NT, however, Christ is the "one mediator between God and humankind" (1 Tim 2:5). The NT claims to give witness to the only effective way for humanity to approach God: Jesus Christ.

Bibliography: Walter Brueggemann. *Theology of the Old Testament: Testimony, Dispute, Advocacy* (2005); David A. deSilva. *Honor, Patronage, Kinship and Purity: Unlocking New Testament Culture* (2000); Mary Douglas. *Natural Symbols: Explorations in Cosmology* (1982); James D. G. Dunn. *Christology in the Making: An Inquiry into the Origins of the Doctrine of the Incarnation* (1989); Stephen Finlan. *The Background and Content of Paul's Cultic Atonement Metaphors* (2004); Lester L. Grabbe. *Priests, Prophets, Diviners, and Sages: A Socio-historical Study of Religious Specialists in Ancient Israel* (1995); Joel B. Green and Mark D. Baker. *Rediscovering the Scandal of the Cross: Atonement in New Testament and Contemporary Contexts* (2000); Larry W. Hurtado. *One God, One Lord: Early Christian Devotion and Ancient Jewish Monotheism* (1988); Scot McKnight. *Jesus and His Death: Historiography, the Historical Jesus, and Atonement Theory* (2005); Simon Mowinckel. *He That Cometh* (1956); Gregory E. Sterling. "Prepositional Metaphysics in Jewish Wisdom Speculation and Early Christological Hymns." *SPhilo Annual* 9 (1997) 219–38.

KENNETH SCHENCK

MEDICINE. *See* BALM; CIRCUMCISION; DISEASE; HEALING; HEALTH CARE; KING, KINGSHIP; LEPROSY; MANDRAKE; MEDICINE AND HEALING, GODS OF; PERFUME.

MEDICINE AND HEALING, GODS OF. Deities associated with healing such as Asclepius, Serapis, and Isis played a key role in the health care system of antiquity. As medicine became a form of practical knowledge in 5th cent. BCE Athens, devotion to Asclepius also emerged. A plague in 426 BCE led the Athenians to purify the island of Delos and establish the sacred festival of Apollo, observance of which delayed Socrates' execution in 399 BCE. Socrates ordered a cock sacrificed to Asclepius moments before his death (Plato, *Phaed.* 118a).

The legend in Pindar (*Pyth.* 3; ca. 476–67 BCE) had Asclepius born of Apollo and the human mother Koronis. Apollo snatched the infant from his mother's womb as she was being incinerated for betraying the god with a mortal. The centaur Chiron, a successful doctor until greed led him to bring people back from the dead, raised the child. For that act of hubris, Zeus killed Chiron. Legends persisted in attributing to Asclepius similar powers to restore life to the dead (Pausanius, *Descr.* 2.26.5; 2.27.4). Several cities claimed to be Asclepius' birthplace. The cult appears to have spread from Thessaly into the rest of Greece. By the mid-5th cent. BCE the healing sanctuary at Epidaurus had established a pattern for such sacred precincts that would spread around the Greco-Roman world from the 4th cent. BCE to the 3rd cent. CE in such cities as Cos, Pergamum, Corinth, and Rome, where the sanctuary was located on an island in the Tiber. The emperor Claudius had to intervene to prevent owners from dumping sick slaves there (ca. 50 CE).

A latecomer to most local pantheons, shrines to Asclepius are rarely part of the main religious area. In Athens his sanctuaries were on Delos and in the port Piraeus; in Cos, Pergamum, and Epidaurus the sacred temple and groves were a good walk from the city, and elsewhere as at Rome outside city walls along river banks. The basic procedure at the shrine opens with purification at a sacred spring, sacrifice to the god, donning white robes, and additional purification. Then the petitioner entered the abaton (**abaton** ἄβατον), a building in which the sick would receive the god's instruction while sleeping. Or, if a complex lacked a special facility, petitioners might sleep in the temple precincts. Dreams might be a riddle interpreted by temple priests. Though Asclepius is sometimes credited with healing the worshiper directly, often the cure involved elaborate procedures to be carried out. Those instructions might correspond to treatments prescribed by physicians.

Asclepius was assimilated to earlier, local healing deities upon being introduced to a region, especially local manifestations of Apollo. Any deity could heal his or her devotees. Asclepius is the only deity whose sole function is healing. The popularity and growth of the Asclepius cult is attested by propagandistic inscriptions detailing the miraculous cures effected by the god at Epidaurus, Pergamum, Rome, and Lebna. The god overcomes skeptics who mock his claims and heals such chronic conditions as paralysis, facial blemishes, blindness, dropsy, barrenness, and multi-year pregnancies. Excavations at Corinth and other sanctuaries have yielded terracotta models of body parts (hands, feet, legs, arms, breasts, genitalia) attesting to the god's abilities.

Among the literary elite, the philosopher and orator Aelius Aristides (117–81 CE) trumpeted the healing powers and personal concern shown him by the god in an account of his dream visions and cures, *The Sacred Discourses.* Chronically ill, Aristides not only stayed in various shrines devoted to Asclepius, he also visited those of other gods, Apollo and the Egyptian deity Serapis. In some cases he was visited by physicians while residing in a sacred precinct.

Other evidence that physicians invoked and cooperated with the healing deities can be found as early as the 4th cent. BCE. In Athens doctors participated in a biannual, state-sponsored sacrifice to Asclepius and his daughter, Hygeia. A marble plaque honoring Pheidas of Rhodes as Athens' public physician was put up in the Asclepeion (ca. 304 BCE). Decrees honoring doctors also appear in the sanctuary at Cos. Major reconstruction and expansion of the sanctuary there during the 50s and 60s CE was financed by the imperial physician. The two-day festival in honor of Asclepius held at Ephesus incorporated contests in medicine and surgery for doctors. The philosopher-physician Galen (ca. 127–200 CE), from Pergamum, also home to a famous sanctuary, was a lifelong devotee of Asclepius. He alleged that the god had appeared to him in dreams. The Hippocratic oath asked physicians to swear by Apollo, the healer, Hygeia, Panaheia, and "all the other powers of healing."

Photo Credit : © British Museum / Art Resource, NY

Figure 1: Votive relief from a healing sanctuary. Greek, 100–200 CE. The inscription on this marble relief can be translated: "Tyche [dedicated this] to Asclepius and Hygieia as a thank offering." From the island of Milos. British Museum, London, Great Britain

Galen also studied in Alexandria, the home of the most important Egyptian deity associated with healing, Serapis. Creation of the popular Hellenized version of the cult and mysteries of Isis and Serapis is attributed to Ptolemy I (366–282 BCE). As in the Asclepius sanctuaries, the afflicted would sleep in the precincts hoping for a dream prescription from the god or goddess (Diodorus Siculus, *Bib. Hist.* 1.25.3–5). The Serapeion in Alexandria underwent extensive renovations under the emperor Hadrian (117–38 CE). Aelius Aristides composed a prose hymn honoring the god. Sanctuaries to the Egyptian gods can be found throughout the Greco-Roman world. Sinope, an important center in Asia Minor, had a simple building near the north market. Tacitus repeats a legend in which terrifying dreams lead Ptolemy to demand that a statue of the god be transferred from Sinope to Alexandria (Tacitus, *Hist.* 4.83–84). An elaborate complex dedicated to the Egyptian gods existed at Ephesus. An avenue of sphinxes led up to the shrine on Delos (2nd cent. BCE). Traders from that island likely introduced the cult to Italy in the 2nd cent. BCE. Decrees prohibiting worship of foreign cults in Rome during the 1st cent. BCE indicate that devotees of the Egyptian gods provoked tensions in the city. Caligula (12–41 CE) had the Isis shrine demolished under Tiberius rebuilt on the Campus Martius. Though diffusion of the cult began in the 3rd cent. BCE, the height of devotion to the Egyptian deities based on prevalence of archaeological remains was in the 2nd and 3rd cent. CE. Caracalla (188–217 CE) dedicated a large temple to Serapis on the Quirinal hill. Images of Serapis on coins from Pergamum suggest that he was one of the gods worshiped there along with Asclepius, whose presence is well documented in Aelius Aristides.

In addition to widespread cults and sanctuaries that might draw visitors from around the Greco-Roman world, local deities were credited with healings. Graffiti testify to the presence of Roman pilgrims at Egyptian healing sanctuaries in Abydos and Deir el-Bhari. A mud-brick sanatorium was constructed in the precinct of Hathor at Dendara in the 1st cent. CE. An inscription along the road to Ostia indicates that a slave cured of blindness sacrificed a white cow to the rustic Bona Dea Felicula. Doctors had given up on his condition after ten months of treatment. *See* DISEASE; GREEK RELIGION AND PHILOSOPHY; HEALING; MIRACLE; MIRACLE WORKERS; ROMAN RELIGIONS; SUFFERING AND EVIL.

Bibliography: Wendy Cotter. *Miracles in Greco-Roman Antiquity: A Sourcebook* (1999); Ralph Jackson. *Doctors and Diseases in the Roman Empire* (1988); Vivian Nutton. *Ancient Medicine* (2004).

PHEME PERKINS

MEDITERRANEAN. *See* SEA, GREAT; WESTERN SEA.

MEDIUMS. *See* DIVINATION; ENDOR, MEDIUM OF; NECROMANCY.

MEEKNESS [עָנָו ʿanaw; πραΰς praus, πραΰτης prautēs]. Meekness reflects HUMILITY before God. The meek receive special treatment: God will hear the desire of the meek (Ps 10:17); the meek will inherit the land (Ps 37:11); the "shoot [that] shall come out from the stump of Jesse" will judge the poor and give equity to the meek (Isa 11:4), and they will "obtain fresh joy in the LORD" (Isa 29:19). Believers are to be marked by meekness (Col 3:12; Jas 1:21). In the Sermon on the Mount, Jesus says that the meek will inherit the earth, reflecting Ps 37:11 (Matt 5:5; *see* BEATITUDES).

Praus encompasses being considerate, humble, gentle, and not having an inflated sense of self. Paul refers to "the meekness (prautēs) and gentleness of Christ" as his own posture toward the Corinthians (2 Cor 10:1). Matthew 21:5 cites Zech 9:9 at Jesus' triumphal entry (praus, here rendered "humble" in NRSV) where Jesus' entrance as king, without violence, on a humble donkey, demonstrates his meekness (see also Matt 11:29).

Meekness can be understood in part by surrounding words in lists of ethical attributes and by the words it opposes. In Gal 5:22-23, meekness (NRSV, "gentleness"), love, joy, peace, patience, kindness, generosity, faithfulness, and self-control characterize the fruit of the Spirit, in contrast to works of the flesh such as jealousy, anger, rivalry, and causing dissension (Gal 5:20). Unlike those who malign believers, Christians should respond to them, providing reasons for faith with meekness (1 Pet 3:16; NRSV, "gentleness").

KENNETH D. LITWAK

MEGADIM, TEL. A site located 1 mi. north of Athlit on the Carmel coast. Excavated remains range from the Early Bronze Age to the Byzantine period, but findings came primarily from a well-preserved Persian-period town. Further excavations revealed occupation in the Chalcolithic, Early Bronze Age I and IV, Middle Bronze Age II, Late Bronze Age II, Persian, and Byzantine periods. Early Bronze remains included stone walls, buildings, and a circular tower. The Middle Bronze Age stratum, except for sixteen tombs and seven storage-jar burials, was poorly preserved. Numerous pieces of Cypriot imported pottery were among Late Bronze Age remains. In the Roman-Byzantine period, a large building on the summit of the mound probably served as a horse-changing station and caravanserai.

RALPH K. HAWKINS

MEGIDDO mi-gid'oh [מְגִדּוֹ meghiddo]. A prominent mound, called Tel Megiddo in Hebrew and Tell el-Mutesellim in Arabic ("the tell of the governor"), marks the site of biblical Megiddo. The mound rises about 30 m above the surrounding plain, and its summit covers about 13 ac. A lower terrace, settled during the Bronze Age, extends to the northeast of the mound. Two springs, Ein el-Kubbi to the northeast of the site and another spring to its west, supplied ample amounts of water, which covered all the needs of the settlement. Tel Megiddo is presently kept by The Nature and National Parks Authority, and has recently been declared by UNESCO a World Heritage Site.

Megiddo is located in the Jezreel Valley, at the very point where the narrow brook of Nahal Iron (in Arabic, Wadi Ara), which crosses the ridge of Mount Carmel, opens into the valley. The main highway from Egypt to Asia, known as the Via Maris, passed through Nahal Iron, and thus Megiddo controlled the highway. Three factors—the fertile valley, the ample supply of water, and its unique strategic position along the international

The Megiddo Expedition, The Institute of Archaeology, Tel Aviv University
Figure 1: Tel Megiddo, from north

highway—turned ancient Megiddo into one of the most important centers in the country.

The identification of Megiddo with Lejjun, located 1.5 km to the south of the mound, to where the settlement shifted in the Roman period, was first proposed by the Jewish writer Ishtori Haparchi in his book *Caphtor Waperach* in the 14th cent. CE.

A. Excavations

The German Society first initiated excavations at Tel Megiddo for the Study of Palestine. The work was directed by Gotlieb Schumacher, an architect from Haifa, between 1903 and 1905. Schumacher surveyed the site and the remains of the Roman settlement to its south, and cut a wide, deep trench across the summit of the mound from north to south. In addition, he excavated parts of the eastern and southern Israelite palaces (nos. 338 and 1723) and dug additional narrow trenches across the mound and its slopes.

In 1925, J. H. Breasted, the director of the newly founded Oriental Institute of the University of Chicago, initiated the resumption of the excavations on a very large scale. The original plan was to dig in their entirety one city level after the other. The plan, however, was too ambitious: the three upper strata (III–I) were excavated in their entirety, but eventually excavation was limited to five fields in different parts of the site (Areas AA and DD in the north, BB in the east, CC in the south, and E in the west). The lower strata were unearthed only in Area BB at the eastern slope, where bedrock was reached. In addition, a large area was dug on the eastern slope in preparation for turning it into a main dumping place for soil excavated on the summit.

The Chicago expedition was successively directed by C. Fisher (1925–27), P. L. O. Guy (1927–34; see Lamon and Shipton), and G. Loud (1934–39). In 1939 the project came to an end due to World War II.

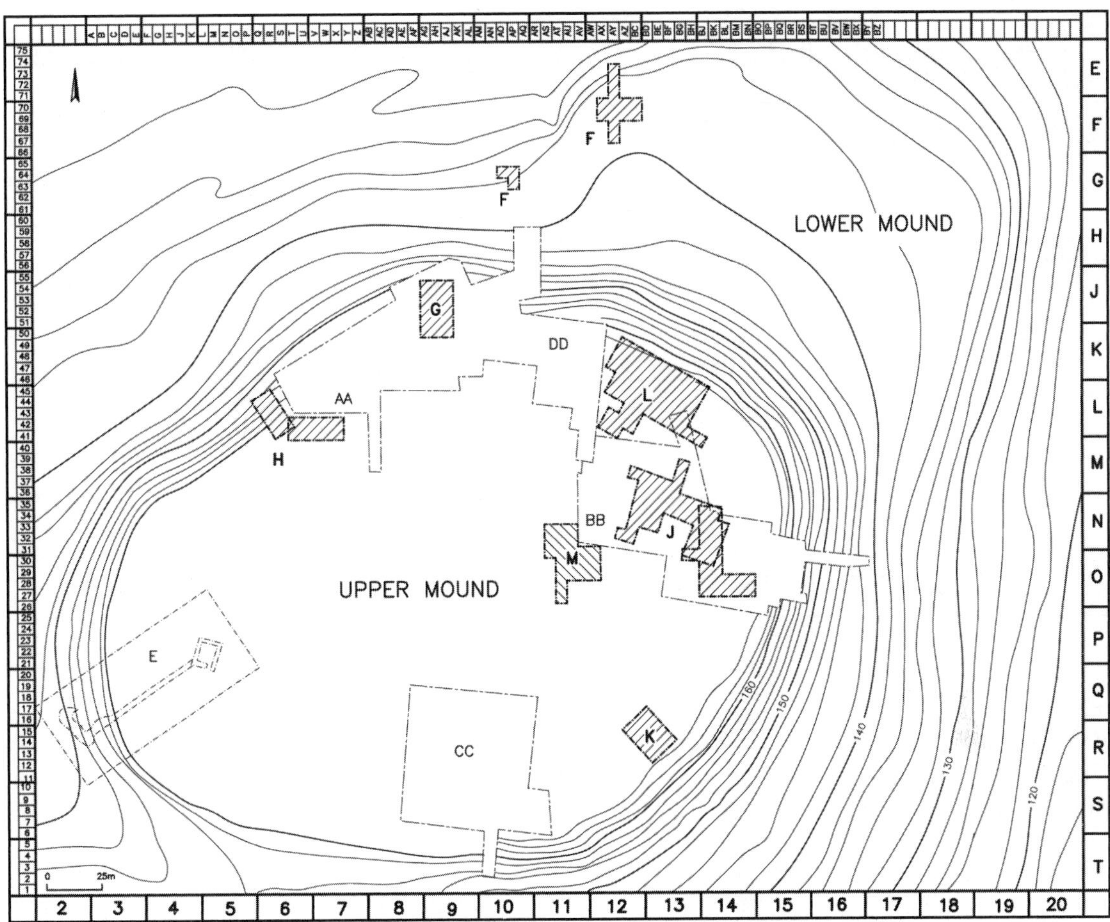

The Megiddo Expedition, The Institute of Archaeology, Tel Aviv University
Figure 2: Tel Megiddo: Plan of excavation areas

Between 1960 and 1972 Y. Yadin of the Hebrew University of Jerusalem conducted small-scale excavations aiming at elucidating the stratigraphy of the Israelite strata. The northern Israelite palace (no. 6000) was discovered in these excavations.

In 1994 large-scale excavations were resumed by Tel Aviv University in collaboration with other academic institutions around the world. The ongoing excavations are conducted by I. Finkelstein and D. Ussishkin, with E. Cline as associate director (B. Halpern was co-director until 2004). The excavations take place once in two years and aim at a systematic study of Megiddo and its history. Excavation fields were opened in various parts of the site (J in the cultic area, M in Schumacher's trench, H and L in the north, K in the southeast, and F in the lower terrace). A regional survey was conducted in the adjacent parts of the Jezreel Valley and in Nahal Iron.

B. Stratigraphy

1. Early periods

The earliest settlement remains were uncovered in a deep trench (Area BB) located on the eastern slope where excavation reached bedrock. Pre-Pottery Neolithic remains were uncovered in one cave and were labeled Str XX. The first settlement (Str XX) belongs to the Yarmukian culture of the Pottery Neolithic B period. Remains of walls and floors, as well as pottery, flint sickle blades, and a clay figurine were recovered.

By the Early Bronze I period Megiddo became a large settlement, perhaps the largest settlement in the country. As shown by surveys, an area of about 150 ac. to the east of the mound was also settled at that time. Excavations on the eastern slope indicated that this area was extensively settled as well (Stages VII–IV).

By that time the large cultic area was crystallized on the eastern side of the mound. It was excavated by the Chicago expedition (Area BB), and recently by the Tel Aviv University expedition (Area J). A small shrine (no. 4050), which had two phases, was built in Str XIX; it faced east with its courtyard extending on the slope. Later, in Str XVIII, a huge temple was built facing northeast, possibly oriented to the spring near the northeast of the site. This temple, which has only partly been uncovered, was apparently destroyed in an earthquake and later restored. A massive wall found at the bottom of the slope (no. 4045) possibly was a fortification wall surrounding the acropolis of

Period	Dates BCE	Strata	Observations
Neolithic–Chalcolithic	7000–3300	XX	
Early Bronze I	3300–3000	XIX–XVIII	Large city; cultic area
Early Bronze II	3000–2700		Gap in settlement?
Early Bronze III	2700–2200	XVII–XV	"Megaron" temples
Intermediate Bronze	2200–2000	XIV	Shaft tombs
Middle Bronze I	2000–1750	XIII–XII	Egypt's Middle Kingdom
Middle Bronze II	1750–1550	XI–X	Egypt's Second Intermediate
Late Bronze I	1550–1400	IX	
Late Bronze II–III	1400–1130	IX–VIIA	Egypt's New Kingdom
Iron I	1130–950	VI	Late Canaanite city
Iron II	950–800	VB, VA–IIB	Earlier Israelite city
	800–730	IVA	Later Israelite City
	730–600	III–II	Assyrian rule
Babylonian–Persian	600–332	I	
Roman	31 BCE–324 CE		New settlement at Lejjun

Table 1: The stratigraphy of Tel Megiddo (dates BCE are approximate; note that the dates of the periods and strata vary in different studies)

the city. It appears that by the end of Early Bronze I Megiddo was abandoned and no remains of Early Bronze II have so far been found.

By the Early Bronze III, in Str XVII–XVI, the cultic area was rebuilt, and various houses and a unique, large round altar (no. 4017) were built here. A large palatial building was built on the lower slope. Later, probably at the very end of the Early Bronze period (Str XV), the houses were replaced by three temples identical in plan and size (the "megaron" type temples), and the round altar was rebuilt.

During the Intermediate Bronze period (Early Bronze IV; Middle Bronze I), settlement on the mound, as has been discerned in the cultic area, continued but declined. Remains of small houses, pits, and pottery were found here (Str XIV; elements of Str XIIIB). Megaron Temple 4040 of Str XV and the adjacent round altar were reused. The cella of the temple was filled with rubble, and a small cell with a cultic niche was built in its center.

The Megiddo Expedition, The Institute of Archaeology, Tel Aviv University

Figure 3: Cache of Egyptianized pottery from the Early Bronze I temple

Several unusual rock-cut tombs were uncovered on the eastern slope. Their plan is based on a vertical entrance shaft leading to a rectangular chamber through a horizontal entrance; three smaller chambers were cut at the sides of the rectangular chamber. The pottery found in the tombs resembles the "caliciform" pottery of northern Syria.

2. The Middle Bronze Age

The renewal of urbanization in the cities of Canaan at the beginning of the Middle Bronze period parallels the Middle Kingdom—the period of the Twelfth Dynasty—in Egypt. At that time Egyptian presence and interests in Canaan were renewed, and continued with variations until the end of the Late Bronze Age in the 12th cent. BCE. The history of the Canaanite city-state of Megiddo parallels the developments in the rest of the country during that period. The fortified, urban settlement of Str XIII marks the advent of Middle Bronze I period (Middle Bronze IIA). Canaanite Megiddo lasted with changes until the destruction of Str VII at the end of the Late Bronze period.

It is not clear how strong Egyptian influence was in Megiddo during the Middle Bronze I period. The city is not mentioned in the Execration Texts, possibly an indication of Egyptian domination of Megiddo at that time. A broken statue of Thuthotep, an Egyptian high official of the Twelfth Dynasty, was found buried in the destroyed "tower temple" of Str VII, and it can be assumed that it stood for centuries in the temple before its plunder and final destruction in the 12th cent. BCE. Opinions vary with regard to the importance of the statue for elucidating the history of Megiddo in Middle Bronze I.

During the Middle Bronze II period, which parallels the Second Intermediate period in Egypt, the Egyptian influence in Megiddo weakened. This period is covered by Str XI–X, and according to several scholars Str XII as well. Egyptian influence is mainly expressed in a large variety of scarabs.

Middle Bronze Megiddo is characterized by a series of massive fortifications uncovered by the Chicago expedition in Areas AA, BB, and CC, by Schumacher in seven narrow trenches cut on the slopes of the mound, and by Tel Aviv University in Area F in the lower terrace.

In the north side (Area AA) the Str XIII buttressed city wall supported by a glacis and the city gate were uncovered. The gate had a stepped approach, and the outer and inner entrances of the gatehouse were oriented at a straight angle to each another—indications that the gate was mainly used by pedestrians. Further glacis supported by walls were built in this area in Str XII–XI. The rampart and retaining wall of the lower terrace (Area F) are probably contemporary with the rebuilding of the glacis on the upper mound in Str XI. The main city-gate complex to both the upper mound and the lower terrace was probably built at the northern side, in the topographical depression to the north of the Late Bronze gate. Ramparts supported by massive mud-brick walls that formed part of the substructure were uncovered in Areas BB and CC (Str XIII–XI) and in Schumacher's trenches—all indicating that Megiddo was strongly fortified in that period.

Megiddo was densely populated during the Middle Bronze period, and well-built houses were uncovered in the various excavation fields. A large building with a central courtyard was uncovered in Str X at the north side (Area AA), at the very place where the ruler's palace was built in the Late Bronze period; the Middle Bronze ruler's palace, however, was probably located in the center of the settlement. The custom of intramural burial, inside and outside the houses, was common. Many graves and stone-built tombs were found, and in many cases it is difficult to assign them to the correct city level. Two exceptionally well-constructed stone tombs were uncovered by Schumacher in a structure (the Mittelburg) in the center of the mound.

A fine group of pottery known as bichrome ware, characterized by its painted decoration in red and black colors, appears in Megiddo at the end of the Middle Bronze and at the Late Bronze I periods. Similar pottery is known from other sites in Canaan and Cyprus. Neutron activation analyses indicated that one group of this pottery originated in Cyprus, while another, distinctive group originated in Megiddo.

3. The Late Bronze Age

The beginning of the Late Bronze period is usually associated with the expulsion of the Hyksos from Egypt, the campaign of Pharaoh Ahmose to Canaan, and the renewal of Egyptian influence in the country. Correlation between the archaeological data from Canaan with the Egyptian evidence is not easy. It appears that many cities in southern Canaan and the inland areas were destroyed at the end of the Middle Bronze period, but not Megiddo and other cities in the Coastal Plain.

It appears that the Egyptian conquest of Megiddo occurred at the end of Str IX, during the first Asian campaign of Pharaoh Thutmose III in ca. 1479 BCE. The events in Megiddo are recorded in detail. Thutmose III and his army advanced along the coastal highway, and then turned to cross the Carmel Ridge through the Nahal Iron pass. The Canaanite armies led by the king of Kadesh in Syria concentrated their forces near Megiddo in order to challenge the Egyptian army at the place where the narrow pass opens into the Jezreel Valley. Thutmose III learned in advance of the Canaanite battle plan, and his commanders advised him to reach the Jezreel Valley by alternative routes to the south or north of the Nahal Iron pass. The pharaoh decided to follow the direct route, crossed Nahal Iron, and took the Canaanite armies by surprise. Thutmose III won the battle with them, and then laid a seven-month siege to Megiddo and conquered the city. The Egyptians took large amounts of booty.

The battle of Megiddo established the Egyptian hegemony of Canaan and Megiddo, which lasted with ups and downs until after the reign of Ramesses VI in ca. 1130 BCE. Megiddo is not mentioned in the descriptions of the campaigns of Amenhotep II (1427–1401 BCE), probably because it was firmly held by Egypt at that time. This is corroborated by two contemporary sources. A letter found in nearby Taanach orders the local ruler to send soldiers and provisions to the Egyptian commander at Megiddo. Papyrus Hermitage 1116A, dated to the reign of Amenhotep II, records presentations by Egyptian officials of beer and grain to envoys of Canaanite rulers, Megiddo being one of them.

Eight cuneiform letters from the el-Amarna archive, dated to the reigns of Amenhotep III and Amenhotep IV in the 14th cent. BCE, were sent from Megiddo (nos. 242–48, 365; *see* AMARNA LETTERS). Biridiya, the ruler of Megiddo, sent six letters made of local clay. They express Biridiya's loyalty to Egypt, and some of them discuss his struggle with Labaya, the ruler of Shechem, who apparently attempted to take Megiddo by force and failed. In one letter (no. 244), Biridiya appealed for Egyptian troops to prevent the fall of the city. Two letters discuss cultivation of estates in Shunem by forced labor.

By the beginning of the Late Bronze period the ruler's palace was built on the northern side along the upper periphery of the mound and near the city gate. Several superimposed palaces were uncovered here by the Chicago expedition (Area AA) in Str IX–VIIB-A. Particularly impressive is the Str VIII palace. A large courtyard lay in its center, and its walls were about

2 m thick. The Str VII palace used the same courtyard, and an annex used as the palace treasury was added. A large assemblage of ivory objects and other precious items was found here. Although Biridiya's letters found in el-Amarna must have been composed and sent from the palace, no written documents were uncovered here. A broken cuneiform tablet that possibly originated in the palace was found in the agricultural fields to the north of the site after the termination of the excavations. It included a section of the Epic of Gilgamesh hinting at the existence of a scribal school at Megiddo.

A large four-chambered city gate was built to the east of the palace. It was uncovered by the Chicago expedition and later by Tel Aviv University. The gatehouse was built of ashlars, apparently taken from an earlier structure. Beams of olive tree were incorporated in the walls. Significantly, the gatehouse does not have towers flanking the gate passage nor does it have deeply set foundations beneath floor level. The gate seems to have been incorporated in the Middle Bronze glacis surrounding the slopes of the site, which apparently continued to function in the Late Bronze period. In any case, no city wall dating to the Late Bronze period was discovered. The buildings located along the upper periphery of the mound possibly formed the defense line of the city that faced the Egyptian army of Thutmose III in about 1479 BCE.

Tower temple 2048, located in the cultic area at the eastern part of the mound above the Early Bronze round altar (Area BB), was the main temple of the city. The first stage of the temple was probably founded already in the Middle Bronze period. The building had a single hall and very thick walls, indicating that it rose to a considerable height.

A large complex—the Nordburg—was excavated in the center of the mound by Schumacher, and then by the Chicago expedition (Area BB). It was usually considered to be a Middle Bronze palatial building; the renewed excavations (Area M), however, established that it dates to Str VII.

Late Bronze Megiddo was a prosperous city expressing the rich Canaanite culture and art of the period. The finds indicate the developed commercial and cultural connections of Canaan with the surrounding countries at that time. Many valuable objects were found, such as cylinder seals, bronze figurines, gold and ivory objects, alabaster vessels, and gold jewelry. Of special importance is the assemblage of 382 carved ivories found in the treasury of the ruler's palace—the richest Bronze Age ivories assemblage found in the Near East. The assemblage forms an assortment of objects of many types and various styles—locally produced ivories in Canaanite style and imported items in Egyptian, Aegean, Assyrian, and Hittite styles.

4. The end of the Canaanite city

The prosperous Str VII city was destroyed completely, possibly by the immigrating Sea Peoples, and the settlement was abandoned for a while. Remains of heavy destruction were uncovered in the ruler's palace and in the tower temple. The city gate adjacent to the palace was blocked, and ovens found inside indicate that people settled here either shortly before the destruction of the city or immediately afterward.

The Megiddo Expedition, The Institute of Archaeology, Tel Aviv University

Figure 4: The Late Bronze city gate

Two Egyptian objects indicate the date of the destruction. An ivory pen case bearing a cartouche of Ramesses III (1182–1151 BCE, low chronology) was found sealed beneath the destruction debris in the treasury of the ruler's palace. It proves that the Str VII city was not destroyed prior to the reign of that pharaoh. A statue base of Ramesses VI (1141–1133 BCE, low chronology) was found buried in a pit. The statue may have been placed in a temple, possibly the tower temple, and buried after the latter's destruction. The statue base indicates the continuation of Egyptian hegemony in Megiddo and southern Canaan during the reign of Ramesses VI. We can assume, therefore, that Str VII was destroyed about 1130 BCE, when the Egyptian hegemony in Canaan came to an end.

The king of Megiddo is mentioned in the list of kings defeated by Joshua (Josh 12:21). We are informed in Josh 17:11-12 and Judg 1:27 that the Canaanites continued to live in Megiddo until their subjection at a later period by the tribe of Manasseh (also 1 Chr 7:29). W. F. Albright believed that the expression "at Taanach, by the waters of Megiddo" (Judg 5:19) in the Song of Deborah refers to a time when Megiddo was not settled, and he assigned the poem and the events described in it to the period immediately following the destruction of the Str VII city.

The Str VIA settlement followed a poor settlement of Str VIB. Stratum VI apparently represents the last settlement in Canaanite tradition, rather than an Israelite settlement. It was studied by the Chicago expedition, and recently by Tel Aviv University in Area K. Stratum VIA was a densely populated, unfortified settlement. The tower temple was restored, and a public building (no. 2072) was uncovered in Area AA—these being the sole public buildings uncovered in addition to domestic structures. A large assemblage of pottery—including collared-rim storage jars and Philistine pottery, as well as many bronze objects—was recovered. The settlement was destroyed by fire in an enemy attack; the theory that the destruction was caused by an earthquake is not convincing. The destruction apparently occurred in the 10th cent. BCE, and scholarly opinions differ as to its exact date.

Finally, "Chamber f"—a unique, monumental, subterranean chamber with corbelled ceiling and a shaft entrance—was uncovered by Schumacher in association with the Nordburg. The chamber was found empty. It was investigated afresh in the renewed excavations (Area M). Chamber f was constructed either in Str VII, or more likely in Str VI, and is associated with a small sanctuary(?) of Str VI. It was either a monumental burial chamber that was never used, or alternatively a subterranean cult place associated with the overlying building.

5. The earlier Israelite city

Stratum VB forms the first Israelite settlement. This level includes remains of domestic structures in various parts of the site, probably the remains of a small, unfortified settlement. In the course of time the settlement developed, and the next stratum up, Str VA–IVB, is a large administrative city, characterized by three palatial buildings.

The stratigraphy and dating of these two strata have been extensively debated in the scholarly world. The identification of the Solomonic city and the understanding of its character formed a cardinal issue in the debate. Megiddo was included, together with Taanach and Beth-shan, in the fifth administrative district of Solomon (1 Kgs 4:12) and apparently here was the residence of the district governor, Baana son of Ahilud. In 1 Kgs 9:15 Megiddo is mentioned together with Jerusalem, Hazor, and Gezer as a central city built by Solomon and financed by the levies imposed by the king. According to more traditional views (e.g., Albright, Wright, Yadin) Str VA represents the settlement dating to David's reign while Str VA–IVB represents the city built by Solomon. The attribution of Str VA–IVB to Solomon gained support when Yadin dated the four-entry city gate to this time. Based on the low chronology concept (advocated by Finkelstein), Str VA–IVB dates to the time of the Omride Dynasty (9th cent. BCE). It follows that Ahaziah king of Judah was probably killed in that city when he fled from nearby Jezreel during Jehu's revolt (2 Kgs 9:27). In that case, the underlying Str VA probably represents the settlement of Solomon's time. The Str VA–IVB city was apparently destroyed by fire, probably in an Aramean campaign during the second half of the 9th cent. BCE.

By ca. 925 BCE Pharaoh Shoshenq I (biblical SHISHAK) conducted a campaign to Canaan. The campaign is discussed in 1 Kgs 14:25-28 and 2 Chr 12:2-12, and a list of the conquered cities accompanied by a relief was carved on the walls of the temple in Karnak. Megiddo is mentioned in the Karnak inscription. A fragment of a stele ca. 3.3 m high and 1.5 m wide erected by Shoshenq I in Megiddo was uncovered at the eastern side of the summit by the Chicago expedition. The erection of the stele in Megiddo apparently indicates that Shoshenq I did not destroy the city, and intended to hold it in the future. It follows that Shoshenq I's campaign was meant to renew the Egyptian foothold in Canaan with Megiddo being a major base for the purpose. However, Shoshenq I died a year later, and the ambitious venture was abandoned.

Stratum VA–IVB includes three palatial edifices (nos. 338, 1723, 6000) built at the southern, northern, and eastern sides of the site. They were positioned at the edge of the city, their facades facing its center, and their back wall reaching the upper periphery of the site. The palaces opened into spacious courtyards. The monumental gate to the compound of the southern palace was uncovered by Schumacher, who labeled it "der Palast." The excavation of the palace and the compound was completed by the Chicago expedition. A large administrative building (no. 1482) was uncovered to the west of the southern palace compound and was apparently associated with it. The eastern palace (no. 338) was first excavated by Schumacher, who identified it as a sanctuary. The excavation was continued by the Chicago expedition, which assigned the building to Str IVA, but it appears to have belonged to Str VA–IVB. The northern palace (no. 6000) was discovered by Y. Yadin, and its excavation has been completed in the renewed excavations.

The ceremonial wings of the southern and northern palaces (nos. 1723 and 6000) were apparently based on the ground-plan of a north Syrian palace type known as bit-hilani. It was characterized by an entrance with a portico leading to an entrance hall, which in turn opened into the main hall of the edifice.

Ashlar masonry, possibly quarried on the eastern slope, was lavishly used in the construction of the palatial buildings. The monumental entrances of these buildings were apparently decorated with pilasters or free-standing pillars topped by Proto-Ionic stone capitals. Unfortunately, these edifices were largely demolished when their ashlars were taken for secondary use in Str IVA. Construction with ashlar masonry had originated in Egypt and appeared for the first time in Canaan in the Late Bronze tower temple and city gate of Megiddo. It was later introduced on a large scale in Israelite sites, in particular Megiddo and Samaria, apparently due to Phoenician influence.

Large quarters of domestic buildings were uncovered along the eastern and northern edges of the summit. A sanctuary (no. 2081) was uncovered in the northern quarter. According to Yadin's theory a casemate wall formed the fortification line of the city, but it appears that the palatial and domestic buildings extending along the upper periphery of the site formed a line of defense. A small two-chambered gatehouse uncovered beneath the so-called Solomonic gate at the northern side, approached by a wide, lime-paved ramp, formed the gate of the city. A postern built at the western edge of the summit facilitating the approach to the spring at the lower slope was assigned by the Chicago expedition and Yadin to this period, but it has recently been suggested that it formed part of the Str IVA city wall.

6. The later Israelite city

The Str IVA city radically differs from the previous Str VA–IVB city. Instead of an administrative center characterized by palatial buildings, the city was now heavily fortified and characterized by stables for horses. The change in the character and function of the rebuilt city may be associated with the destruction of the Jezreel enclosure, probably the main military base of the kings of the Omride Dynasty, which apparently occurred in parallel to the destruction of the Str VA–IVB city. The palatial buildings of Str VA–IVB have now been demolished, and their ashlars were reused in the newly erected buildings. Stratum IVA was assigned by Yadin to the 9th cent., to the time of the Omride Dynasty. However, it was probably built at the end of the 9th or the beginning of the 8th cent. and lasted until the Assyrian conquest in 732 BCE.

City Wall 325, a massive stone wall with its faces built with insets and offsets, surrounded the city. It was attached to a complex city gate—the so-called Solomonic city gate. A roadway led up to an outer, two-chambered gatehouse. This gate opened to an open court, which in turn opened to an inner, six-chambered gatehouse. The inner gatehouse rested on massive foundations, supported by a constructional fill, which were uncovered by the Chicago expedition. The structure was built with ashlars taken from the buildings of the earlier Israelite city. The ground-plan and foundations structure of the gate complex are similar to those of several other Iron Age city gates, notably those in Gezer, Hazor, Lachish, Ashdod, and probably Tel Batash (ancient Timnah).

Yadin suggested that the six-chambered inner gatehouse originated in Str VA–IVB and dates to the reign of Solomon. This dating is primarily based on the similarity in plan between this gate and the six-chambered gates in Hazor and Gezer—all three cities being mentioned together in 1 Kgs 9:15 as built by Solomon. Yadin's view is followed by many scholars. However, as the gate adjoins City Wall 325 of Str IVA it is clear that it was built in that stratum.

An impressive water system uncovered by the Chicago expedition enabled an easier approach to the spring located at the bottom of the west slope. A vertical shaft was dug from the surface of the site through the levels of accumulated debris, and then cut through the natural rock. Stairs were prepared along its sides. A horizontal tunnel led from the bottom of the vertical shaft to the spring. In a later stage the horizontal tunnel was deepened, enabling the water to flow to the bottom of the shaft. The excavator, R. S. Lamon, dated the water system to the 12th cent. BCE. Yadin argued for dating it to Str IVA, and his view is generally accepted today.

Two complexes of stables for horses were the dominant architectural features of the city. P. L. O. Guy was the first to identify them as stables and associate them with Solomon's "cities for his chariots" and "cities for his cavalry" (1 Kgs 9:19). Alternative suggested interpretations of the structures as barracks, storehouses, or marketplaces seem unlikely. It seems that Megiddo in the 8th cent. BCE served as a central base for the Israelite cavalry and chariot units, or alternatively, as a central base for training and trade of horses.

Each complex contains several stabling units. Each unit was rectangular and contained a central, lime-paved passage flanked by two stone-paved aisles where the horses stood. Each aisle was separated from the central passage by a row of stone pillars alternating with stone mangers—all being ashlars taken from the

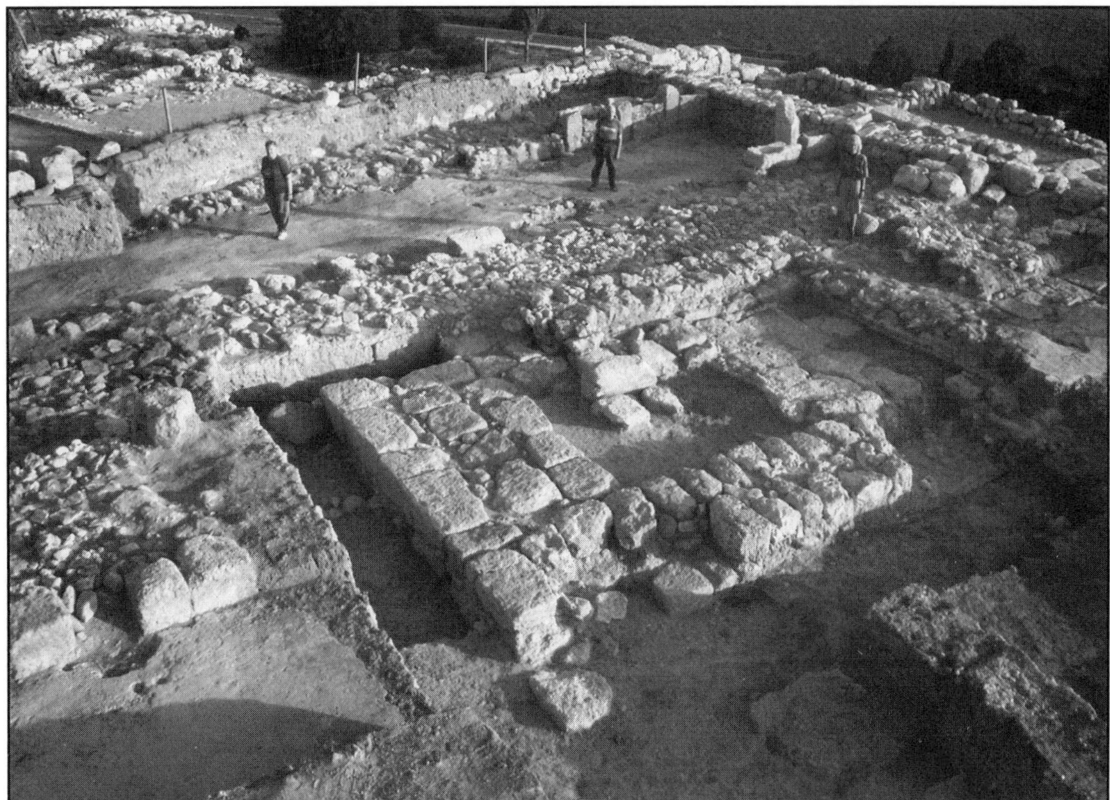

The Megiddo Expedition, The Institute of Archaeology, Tel Aviv University
Figure 5: The Israelite Northern Palace

disused palaces of Str VA–IVB. The stabling units of the southern complex opened into a large, lime-paved courtyard, possibly used for training of chariots. It has been calculated that about 450 to 480 horses were kept in the two stable complexes.

Large amounts of water and food had to be provided for these horses. Water was supplied by the water system; a square brick-built installation in the courtyard of the southern stable complex was assumed to serve as a water tank.

Two fine Hebrew seals discovered by Schumacher are usually assigned to this stratum. The seals were found in association with the monumental gate of the Str VA–IVB southern palace, and hence, based on the stratigraphical data, they could have belonged to the latter stratum. The first seal is carved of jasper, portraying a roaring lion and inscribed "(belonging) to Shema, Servant of Jeroboam"—apparently Jeroboam II, king of Israel.

The Megiddo Expedition, The Institute of Archaeology, Tel Aviv University
Figure 6: The seal of "Shema, Servant of Jeroboam"

The second seal is carved of lapis lazuli, portraying a griffin and inscribed "(belonging) to Asaph." A third fine seal was uncovered by Guy on the surface of the mound. Carved of serpentine, it depicts a griffin and a locust and is inscribed "Haman."

7. The Assyrian city

In 732 BCE Tiglath-pileser III conquered and annexed to Assyria the northern parts of the kingdom of Israel. This event marks the end of Israelite Megiddo, and Str IVA was probably destroyed at that time. Megiddo (Str III) was rebuilt as the capital of the Assyrian province Magiddu.

Large areas of the city were excavated, revealing well-planned residential quarters that apparently covered the entire top of the mound. The houses were arranged in blocks separated by parallel and evenly spaced streets.

On the northern side two large public buildings were uncovered. They portray Assyrian architectural features, notably central, rectangular courtyards, and almost certainly served as the center of the Assyrian administration and as residence of the Assyrian governor of the province.

The Megiddo Expedition, The Institute of Archaeology, Tel Aviv University
Figure 7: The seal of "Ahaz"

The massive Israelite city wall (no. 325) continued to be in use, but the city gate was rebuilt. Remains of one or two city gates built above the ruined six-chambered inner gatehouse of Str IVA were uncovered. The upper one was the two-chambered gatehouse of Str III. Remains of a four-chambered gatehouse were found beneath, and the excavators believed that it was never completed due to a change of plans. Yadin, however, believed that it was in use in Str IVA, replacing the earlier six-chambered gatehouse.

8. Later periods

The Assyrian domination in the country apparently disintegrated about the middle of the 7th cent. BCE. Stratum II represents the continuation of the settlement in the later part of the 7th cent. BCE and possibly later. New houses were now built along the same pattern of residential quarters and streets. It appears that the city wall fell into disuse in Str II or in Str I.

A large structure was uncovered by Schumacher at the eastern edge of the summit during the excavation of the Tempelburg, and Fisher later identified it as a fortress. The structure is built of thick walls and has a central courtyard. According to the Chicago excavators it was built above the disused city wall; hence it functioned as a citadel when Megiddo was no longer fortified. However, nowhere did the walls of the structure reach the city wall. The structure surrounds the buried sanctuary of the eastern palace (no. 338) and is possibly related to it.

The Megiddo Expedition, The Institute of Archaeology, Tel Aviv University
Figure 8: Israelite cult vessel from Stratum IVA

In 609 BCE Pharaoh NECO sojourned in Megiddo on his way to Carchemish to aid Assyria in its struggle with the Babylonians. Josiah, king of Judah, traveled to Megiddo and was killed there by Neco (2 Kgs 23:29-30; 2 Chr 35:20-24). It appears that Josiah was executed when he came to Megiddo to pay homage to his Egyptian overlord. The alternative interpretation that Josiah came to Megiddo to challenge militarily the Egyptian pharaoh is less likely. In any case, it is clear that following the disintegration of the Assyrian domination, the region of Megiddo was dominated for a while by the Egyptians before the Babylonians took over.

Stratum I represents the last period of settlement on the mound in the Babylonian and Persian periods. The remains of these periods are relatively poor. They include many small houses, three long storerooms near the city gate, and cist tombs. The mound was finally abandoned in the 4th cent. BCE.

The reference to "the mourning for Hadad-rimmon in the plain of Megiddo" in Zech 12:11 probably dates to the Persian or Hellenistic periods. The text possibly refers to a fertility cult associated with the storm god Hadad-rimmon. It indicates that in that period Megiddo already lay in an area regarded by the Jews as alien and pagan.

In later periods settlements in Megiddo continued to the south of the mound. A Jewish village named Kefar Otnay existed here ca. 100 CE. During the reign of Hadrian, in the 2nd cent. CE, the Legio II Traiana was stationed here, and it was later replaced by the

Legio VI Ferrata. Kefar Otnay was renamed Legio. It became the center of an administrative district, and from this name the later Arab village of Lejjun derived its name.

Extensive remains to the south of the tell, including aqueducts, a theater, and tombs, as well as a possible site of the Roman camp, were investigated by Schumacher. A thorough survey of this area, including soundings, has been recently carried out by Y. Tepper on behalf of the Israel Antiquities Authority. Salvage excavations conducted by him in the grounds of the Megiddo Prison revealed remains of the 3rd cent. CE settlement, including a Christian prayer hall with an inscribed mosaic pavement.

Bibliography: W. F. Albright. "The Song of Deborah in the Light of Archaeology." *BASOR* 62 (1936) 26–31; G. I. Davies. *Megiddo* (1986); I. Finkelstein, D. Ussishkin, and B. Halpern, eds. *Megiddo III: The 1992–1996 Seasons* (2000); I. Finkelstein, D. Ussishkin, and B. Halpern, eds. *Megiddo IV: The 1998–2002 Seasons* (2006); C. S. Fisher. *The Excavation of Armageddon* (1929); P. L. O. Guy. *New Light from Armageddon* (1931); T. P. Harrison. *Megiddo 3: Final Report on the Stratum VI Excavations* (2004); A. Kempinski. *Megiddo: A City-State and Royal Centre in North Israel* (1989); R. S. Lamon. *The Megiddo Water System* (1935); R. S. Lamon and G. M. Shipton. *Megiddo I: Seasons of 1925–34; Strata I–V* (1939); G. Loud. *The Megiddo Ivories* (1939); G. Loud. *Megiddo II: Seasons of 1935–1939* (1948); G. Schumacher. *Tell el-Mutesellim; I: Fundbericht* (1908); N. A. Silberman, I. Finkelstein, D. Ussishkin, and B. Halpern. "Digging at Armageddon." *Arch* 52 (1999) 32–39; D. Ussishkin. "King Solomon's Palace and Building 1723 in Megiddo." *IEJ* 16 (1966) 174–86; D. Ussishkin. "Was the 'Solomonic' City Gate at Megiddo Built by King Solomon?" *BASOR* 239 (1980) 1–18; D. Ussishkin. "Schumacher's Shrine in Building 338 at Megiddo." *IEJ* 39 (1989) 149–72; D. Ussishkin. "The Destruction of Megiddo at the End of the Late Bronze Age and Its Historical Significance." *TA* 22 (1995) 240–67; G. E. Wright. "The Discoveries at Megiddo, 1935–39." *BA* 13 (1950) 28–46; Y. Yadin. "Megiddo of the Kings of Israel." *BA* 33 (1970) 66–96; Y. Yadin. "Solomon's City Wall and Gate at Gezer." *IEJ* 8 (1958) 80–86.

DAVID USSISHKIN

MEGIDDO, PLAIN OF mi-gid´oh [בִּקְעַת מְגִדּוֹ **biqʿath meghiddo**]. The portion of the JEZREEL Valley near MEGIDDO where King JOSIAH was slain (2 Chr 35:22). Zechariah (12:11) alludes to the custom of mourning for the deity HADAD-RIMMON in the Plain of Megiddo.

MEGIDDO, WATERS OF mi-gid´oh [מֵי מְגִדּוֹ **mey meghiddo**]. The site of the battle in the Song of Deborah (Judg 5:19); its exact location (near MEGIDDO?) is unclear. *See* DEBORAH, SONG OF.

MEGILLOTH mi-gil´oth [מְגִילּוֹת **meghilloth**]. Meaning "scrolls," the term refers to five short books grouped together within the KETHUBIM, "writings," in the Hebrew Scriptures and probably copied together in antiquity. Each is read at certain Jewish festivals: Song of Songs at Passover, Ruth at Shavuot, Lamentations at Tisha B'Av, Ecclesiastes at Sukkot, and Esther at Purim.

BEATRICE J. W. LAWRENCE

MEHETABEL mi-het´uh-bel [מְהֵיטַבְאֵל **mehetavʾel**]. Means "favored of God." 1. The daughter of Matred, and one of the wives of HADAD, king of Edom (Gen 36:39).

2. Shemaiah, son of Delaiah, son of Mehetabel, was a prophet who was paid to tell Nehemiah, falsely, of a plot to kill him (Neh 6:10).

MEHIDA mi-h*i*´duh [מְחִידָא **mekhidhaʾ**; Μεεδδά **Meedda**]. Ancestor of a family of temple servants who were among the first group to return to Judah from the Babylonian exile (Ezra 2:52; Neh 7:54; 1 Esd 5:32).

MEHIR mee´huhr [מְחִיר **mekhir**]. The son of CHELUB and father of Eshton (1 Chr 4:11), according to the Chronicler's genealogy of Judah (1 Chr 4).

MEHOLATHITE mi-hoh´luh-th*i*t [מְחֹלָתִי **mekholathi**]. ADRIEL, husband of Saul's daughter Merab, is described as a Meholathite (1 Sam 18:19) as is Adriel's father BARZILLAI (2 Sam 21:8), likely indicating they were from a place named Meholah, possibly ABEL-MEHOLAH (1 Kgs 4:12).

MEHUJAEL mi-hy*oo*´jay-uhl [מְהוּיָאֵל **mehuyaʾel**]. Possibly means "God gives life." The son of Irad, father of Methushael, and grandfather of Lamech (Gen 4:18).

MEHUMAN mi-hy*oo*´muhn [מְהוּמָן **mehuman**]. One of the seven eunuchs who served King AHASUERUS and was charged with bringing Queen VASHTI before the king (Esth 1:10-11).

MEIRON. A settlement in the mountains of upper Galilee dating from 200 BCE to 363 CE. The area was resettled beginning in the 8th cent. CE when it became a pilgrimage site. The population of Meiron expanded considerably from the 2nd to the early 4th cent. CE, and a large synagogue was built on the acropolis. The 28 m rectangular synagogue was destroyed in 363 CE during a major earthquake. In the 3rd cent., the city played a major role in the olive oil industry of Galilee; coins from the site suggest trade relations with Tyre to the north and Hippos to the southeast. *See* SHEMA, KHIRBET; SYNAGOGUE.

MILTON MORELAND

Courtesy of Meiron Excavation Project
Figure 1: Synagogue standing facade

Courtesy of Meiron Excavation Project
Figure 2: Synagogue reconstruction

ME-JARKON mi-jahr'kon [מֵי הַיַּרְקוֹן mey hayyarqon; θάλασσα Ἱεράκων thalassa Hierakōn]. A site included within the initial tribal allotment of Dan (Josh 19:46). The Hebrew literally reads "the waters of Jarkon." The LXX translates "and west of the Jarkon the border was near to Joppa." While some scholars have inferred a site or settlement called Jarkon, the LXX seems to interpret the Hebrew as a reference to a river instead, which some identify with Wadi el-Barideh, while others associate it with Wadi ʿAuja.

Bibliography: A. Demsky. "The Boundary of the Tribe of Dan (Joshua 19:41-46)." *Sefer Moshe: The Moshe Weinfeld Jubilee Volume.* C. Cohen, A. Hurvitz, and S. M. Paul, ed. (2004) 261–84.

RALPH K. HAWKINS

MEKILTA [מְכִילְתָא mekhilta']. An early rabbinic (Tannaitic) commentary on Exodus, the Mekilta is attributed to the "school" of Rabbi Ishmael. Beginning with Exod 12:1, it is approximately one-half HALAKHAH and one-half HAGGADAH. Another Mekilta, attributed to Rabbi Shimeon ben Yohai of the school of Rabbi Akiva (*see* AKIVA, RABBI), comments on most of Exodus. The Mekilta is a Tannaitic or Halakhic MIDRASH (*see* SIFRA, SIFRE), redacted in the 3rd cent. CE.

BURTON L. VISOTZKY

MELAH, TEL tel-mee'luh [תֵּל מֶלַח tel melakh; Θερμέλεθ Thermeleth]. An unknown location listed in parallel passages (Ezra 2:59; Neh 7:61; 1 Esd 5:36) from where descendants of Delaiah, Tobiah, and Nekoda came to join the priestly ranks of the returning exiles. Scholars propose that it was an impoverished town built upon ruins in the Nippur region on the Kebar River just east of Babylon. Some associate it with Thelma, which Ptolemy locates on the salt flats near the Persian Gulf (*Geography* 5.20). The etymology of the name is uncertain; it may mean "mound of salt" or "hill of sailors."

DAVID M. BATTLE

MELATIAH mel'uh-t*i*'uh [מְלַטְיָה melatyah]. Melatiah the Gibeonite was one of the people who repaired the west wall of Jerusalem (Neh 3:7) after the exile.

MELCHI mel'k*i* [Μελχί Melchi]. The name occurs twice in Luke's genealogy of Jesus. 1. Father of Levi (Luke 3:24).

2. Father of Neri (Luke 3:28).

MELCHIEL mel'kee-uhl [Μελχιήλ Melchiēl]. The father of Charmis, one of the elders of Bethuliah (Jdt 6:15) to whom the Israelites brought ACHIOR. The Hebrew name is MALCHIEL (e.g., Gen 46:17).

MELCHIOR. *See* MELKON.

MELCHIZEDEK mel-kiz'uh-dek [מַלְכִּי־צֶדֶק malki-tsedheq; Μελχισέδεκ Melchisedek]. Melchizedek ("Zedek's king") is the first priest mentioned in Genesis (14:18) and for that reason has been the object of speculation over the centuries despite his relatively minor role in the story of the celebration of Abram's victory over CHEDORLAOMER in Gen 14:17-20. Melchizedek was king of SALEM and priest of EL ELYON. As king, he brought out bread and wine to Abram. As priest, he blessed Abram by El Elyon, "maker of heaven and earth" (14:19). These events occurred in the King's Valley, a site possibly near Jerusalem (2 Sam 18:18; *see* SHAVEH, VALLEY OF). In Ps 110:4 the king of Judah receives eternal priesthood "according to the order of Melchizedek."

Some have explained Gen 14:17-20 and Ps 110:4 on the basis of the structural similarity between the name Melchizedek and the name of the king of JERUSALEM in Josh 10:1, 3, ADONI-ZEDEK (ʾadhoni-tsedheq אֲדֹנִי־צֶדֶק). The word tsedheq in both names likely refers to a Canaanite deity, and the first elements, malki and ʾadhoni, are old forms of the Hebrew construct. Both names mean essentially the same thing:

"Zedek's king" (Melchizedek) and "Zedek's lord" (Adoni-zedek). One might speculate that if Adoni-zedek was king of Jerusalem, then the Salem over which Melchizedek ruled could also have been Jerusalem and the names Melchizedek and Adoni-zedek were throne names for pre-Davidic kings of Jerusalem. A memory of this priestly kingship remains in the oracle of Ps 110:4 that allowed the Davidic kings to boast the title "priest forever according to the order of Melchizedek." Attractive as this possibility is, there is little evidence for it beyond a similarity of names.

Given the secondary role of Melchizedek in Genesis and Psalms, readers of the Letter to the Hebrews (*see* HEBREWS, LETTER TO THE) may be surprised to find that Melchizedek and his priesthood are given great significance there (Heb 5:6, 10; 6:20; 7:1, 10, 11, 15, 17), providing Christ a priestly order and prefiguring its superiority to the Jewish priesthood. Striking is Hebrews' claim that Melchizedek was "without father, without mother, without genealogy, having neither beginning of days nor end of life" (Heb 7:3). Melchizedek has become like the Son of God, "resembling the Son of God," not vice versa. Many secondary characters in Genesis have no family or genealogy and have no account of their birth or death. Indeed, in Gen 14 alone this might be said of all the kings Abram defeated as well as the king of Sodom. Why does the author single out Melchizedek?

The Qumran texts provide evidence for a continuing interest in Melchizedek. Although the *Genesis Apocryphon* from Cave 1 merely retells Gen 14:17-20 (1Qap Gen[ar] XXII, 11–17), adding only that Salem is Jerusalem, Cave 11 has yielded another text in which Melchizedek is a heavenly redeemer who will appear at the tenth jubilee to atone for the sons of light (11Q13 II, 7–11), a role that has no biblical precedent (*see* MELCHIZEDEK TEXT).

One reason, at least, for the intense speculation about Melchizedek at Qumran and in Hebrews stems from the fact that Melchizedek was the first priest mentioned in Scripture. For Philo of Alexandria (20 BCE–40 CE), Melchizedek represented the Logos, but he also held a "self-taught and instinctive" priesthood (*Prelim. Studies* 99), a reference to his lack of predecessors. Josephus wrote that Melchizedek became the first priest of God and built the first temple in **Hierosolyma** (῾Ιεροσόλυμα), previously called **Solyma** (Σόλυμα; *J.W.* 6.438).

It is impossible to disentangle a line of Melchizedek tradition from the OT to the important roles Melchizedek played at Qumran (heavenly redeemer), in Philo (Logos), Hebrews (prototype of Christ's priesthood), and Josephus (first priest of God, first builder of the Temple in Jerusalem). This is not to say that there was no such tradition, but Melchizedek's priestly priority in Genesis could account for any or all of these interpretations, thus obscuring evidence of a coherent development of a tradition.

Bibliography: Fred L. Horton. *The Melchizedek Tradition: A Critical Examination of the Sources to the Fifth Century A.D. and in the Epistle to the Hebrews* (2005).

FRED L. HORTON

MELCHIZEDEK TEXT. The Qumran Melchizedek Document (11Q13, 11QMelchizedek) is a *pesher* (an eschatological commentary; *see* PESHARIM) on a string of texts, Lev 25:13; Ps 82:1-2; and Isa 52:7, that may derive from a DAY OF ATONEMENT liturgy. According to this text, Melchizedek and his armies will appear on the tenth Jubilee to make atonement for the Sons of Light (11Q13 II, 8–9). He will oppose BELIAL and allied spirits and rescue the redeemed from their control (11Q13 II, 12, 22, 25). An Anointed of the Spirit will come with Melchizedek in fulfillment of Daniel's prophecy (Dan 9:26) and will declare peace, comfort the congregation, and instruct them in the "ages of the w[orld]," i.e., a ten-Jubilee schema (11Q13 II, 15–21).

Of particular note is the identification of Melchizedek in 11Q13 II, 11 with the ʾ**elohim** (אֱלֹהִים, "God") of Ps 82:1. Melchizedek as ʾ**elohim** takes his place in the congregation of El (the high God) and in the midst of the ʾ**elohim** ("gods"). There can be no doubt that this passage identifies Melchizedek as a heavenly being. Indeed, the role of Melchizedek in this document is practically identical with the role of Michael in Daniel, *1 Enoch*, *Assumption of Moses*, *Testament of the Twelve Patriarchs*, and *3 Baruch*, but unhappily we never see the name Melchizedek in any other eschatological context at Qumran. Milik and Kobelski have argued that Melchireša in *Visions of Amran* (4Q543–8) and Curses (4Q280) is the cosmic opponent of Melchizedek otherwise called Belial or Satan.

Paleography dates the existing manuscript to roughly the middle of the 1st cent. BCE, but J. T. Milik believed that composition of the original document occurred around 120 BCE. The 11Q13 is part of a longer document, and Milik proposed that 11Q13, 4Q180 and 4Q181 represented three copies of the same longer work, a Book of Periods, because they share a periodization of history based on Jubilee cycles. *See* DEAD SEA SCROLLS; MELCHIZEDEK; QUMRAN.

Bibliography: F. Garcâia Martâinez, E. J. C. Tigchelaar, A. S. Woude, J. P. M. Ploeg, and E. D. Herbert. *Qumran Cave 11. DJD* 23 (1998) 221–41; P. J. Kobelski. *Melchizedek and Melchireša* (1981); J. T. Milik "Milki-sedek et Milki-rešaʿ dans les anciens écrits juifs et chrétiens." *JJS* 23 (1972) 95–144; É. Puech. "Notes sur le manuscrit de XIQMelkîsédeq." *RevQ* 12 (1987) 483–513.

FRED L. HORTON

MELEA mee´lee-uh [Μελεά **Melea**]. ELIAKIM's father and MENNA's son in Jesus' genealogy (Luke 3:31).

MELECH mee′lik [מֶ֫לֶךְ melekh]. With PITHON, TAREA, and AHAZ, one of MICAH's four sons and a descendant of Benjamin (1 Chr 8:35; 9:41).

MELITO, PSEUDO-NARRATIVE OF. A medieval Lat. account of Mary's assumption into heaven. *See* VIRGIN, ASSUMPTION OF THE.

MELKON mel′kon. According to late tradition, Melkon (or Melchior), king of Persia, was one of the three MAGI who visited Jesus' manger in Bethlehem, expanding the canonical account (Matt 2:1-12), which does not specify the names, numbers, or genders of the visitors from the east. Later tradition commonly limited the visitors to three (the number of gifts mentioned in Matthew): Melkon, GASPAR, and BALTHASAR. The Armenian Infancy Gospel records Melkon as the bearer of a letter to Adam that was written and sealed by God and saved in the archives of the kings of Persia. *See* APOCRYPHA, NT; GOSPEL OF THE INFANCY, ARMENIAN.

MARY KAY DOBROVOLNY, R.S.M.

MELONS [אֲבַטִּחִים ʾavattikhim]. The word for melon appears once in the OT when Israel yearned for the melons they had to eat in Egypt (Num 11:5). Scholars typically identify this fruit as the *citrullus vulgaris* or *lanatus*—a watermelon-type plant with sweet juicy flesh cultivated along the Nile River. *See* CUCUMBER; PLANTS OF THE BIBLE.

L. JULIANA CLAASSENS

MEM [מ ם m]. The thirteenth letter of the Hebrew alphabet, which derives from the original Semitic word *maym-, "water." *See* ALPHABET.

MEMBERS [μέλη melē]. *Members* refers to parts of a body that constitute a unit, whether literally in the sense of a physical body or figuratively regarding a group of individuals.

In both the OT and NT the word *members* can refer to parts of a group. In the OT the NRSV translates a variety of Hebrew terms as *members*: "all the souls" (kol-nafshoth [כָּל־נַפְשׁוֹת], Gen 36:6); "household of" (beth [בֵּית], Gen 39:14); "brothers of" (ʾakhe [אֲחֵי], Deut 1:16; 17:20; 18:2; 2 Chr 21:13); "all the descendants" (kol-marrebith [כָּל־מַרְבִּית] 1 Sam 2:33); "sons of" (beni [בְּנֵי], 2 Kgs 5:22); and "men" (ʾanshe [אַנְשֵׁי], Mic 7:6).

The NT also refers to members of a group of disciples or of a family/household. Terms include: "family member" (oikiakos [οἰκιακός], Matt 10:36); "from among them" (ex autōn [ἐξ αὐτῶν], Acts 15:22); and "relative" (oikeios [οἰκεῖος], 1 Tim 5:8). The NRSV sometimes uses *member* as a gender-inclusive alternative to *brother* (ʾakh [אָח], Deut 17:20; 2 Chr 21:13; adelphos [ἀδελφός] Matt 18:15-20; Gal 1:2; 1 Tim 6:2). *See* BROTHER, BROTHERHOOD; FAMILY; HOUSEHOLD, HOUSEHOLDER.

In the Bible *members* can be used to refer to body parts. Job speaks of all his body parts as his *members* (yetsurim [יְצֻרִים], Job 17:7). *Member* is sometimes a EUPHEMISM for the male genitalia: where the Hebrew has *flesh* (besar [בְּשָׂר], e.g., Lev 15:2-3; Ezek 23:20), the NRSV translates "member." In the Gospel of Matthew Jesus twice notes that "it is better for you to lose one of your members" (hen tōn melōn ἐν τῶν μελῶν), here either the eye or hand, than to find yourself in hell (Matt 5:29, 30; 18:8-9; compare Col 3:5).

In Romans Paul explains how human beings face an internal struggle with sin that pervades their very selves (Rom 7:5, 23). No matter how mindful one is of the divine law, the law of sin wages a constant battle in the flesh. "For I delight in the law of God in my inmost self," says Paul, "but I see in my members (melē) another law at war with the law of my mind, making me captive to the law of sin that dwells in my members" (Rom 7:22-23).

James uses melē in reference to the tongue (3:6). James notes that the tongue is "a world of iniquity" placed among our members that must be controlled since it "stains the whole body." *See* BODY; FLESH IN THE NT; FLESH IN THE OT.

In Romans, Paul moves from the realm of members that constitute the individual (Rom 7:22-23) to individuals as members of the community of believers and the contribution each brings to the body that is "in Christ" (Rom 12:4-5). In 1 Corinthians Paul exhorts believers to avoid sin since their bodies are members of Christ (ta sōmata hymōn melē Christou estin τὰ σώματα ὑμῶν μέλη Χριστοῦ ἐστιν, 6:15). Later, Paul extends the imagery and notes that each individual is a member and contributes in a context of mutuality to the body, which is explicitly stated to be the "body of Christ" (1 Cor 12:27). Although ostensibly different from both 1 Cor 6:15 and Rom 12:4-5, one should be cautious in attributing to Paul here the idea that the body of Christ is the church; rather, he is stating that the body constituted by believers belongs to Christ and not to any other authority.

Ephesians reflects but also transcends this figurative language in a new soteriological and ecclesiological key. Believers are "members of his [Christ's] body" (Eph 5:30) because they are beloved of him. Ephesians also reflects Paul's use of the term that insists that believers are members of each other (esmen allēlōn melē [ἐσμὲν ἀλλήλων μέλη], Eph 4:25). *See* BODY OF CHRIST; CHURCH, IDEA OF THE.

PHILIPPA A. CARTER

MEMMIUS, QUINTUS kwin′tuhs mem′ee-uhs [Κόιντος Μέμμιος Kointos Memmios]. One of two Roman ambassadors who bore a letter to the Jews after their victory over Lysias in 164 BCE (2 Macc 11:34). Attempts to identify him with other known Roman officials from the era have failed, and nothing else is known about him.

MARK DELCOGLIANO

MEMORIAL, MEMORY [אַזְכָּרָה ʾazkarah, זֵכֶר zekher, זִכָּרוֹן zikkaron; ἀνάμνησις anamnēsis]. Both the OT and NT contain several Hebrew and Greek concepts related to divine and human remembrance as well as cultic memorials.

A. Remember
B. Memory/Remembrance
C. Memorial
D. Cultic Memorial

A. Remember

Zikkaron ("memorial") is derived from the verb **zakhar** (זָכַר; "to think about, meditate on, remember"). While the verb denotes an action of calling to mind, it often implies that appropriate action is taken as a result of remembering. In several places, it is God who is mindful or who remembers. Though there are instances where God's remembering might have given rise to affliction (Neh 13:29; Pss 25:7; 79:8; Isa 64:9; Jer 14:10; Ezek 18:22, 24; Hos 7:2; 8:13; 9:9), divine remembering is usually favorable: opening the womb of barren women (Gen 30:22; 1 Sam 1:11); securing victory (Judg 16:28); rewarding fidelity (Neh 13:31).

When God is the subject of the verb, the divine activity usually benefits human beings; when human beings are the subjects of the verb, it is generally an act of divine graciousness that is remembered. Recalling God's past blessings, particularly those that comprised the experience of deliverance from Egyptian bondage, was a prominent feature of ancient Israelite religion (Deut 7:18; 16:12; 24:18). It prompted the people to be grateful for those past blessings and to hope for comparable blessings in the future. The needy cried out to God to remember their righteousness and come to their assistance (2 Kgs 20:3//Isa 38:3; Neh 1:8; 5:19; 13:14; Pss 74:2; 106:4; 119:49).

Divine remembering is usually rooted in one of the covenant relationships inaugurated by God. Such relationships can be traced as far back as the account of the covenant God made through Noah with all of creation (Gen 9:15). In this tradition, remembering the past was clearly looked upon as a guarantee of future protection. In another instance, God's graciousness to those enslaved in Egypt was prompted by God's remembrance of a promise made to the ancestors (Exod 2:24; 6:5; 32:13; Lev 26:42, 45; Ps 105:42). The nation's cry for help in times of distress was frequently dependent upon divine election, deliverance from bondage, and the covenant established with the entire nation through Moses (Ps 106:45; Ezek 16:60). Later the people sought the assurance of security in the covenant pledge attached to the monarchy (2 Chr 6:42; Ps 89:49-50). The people's own responsibility for fidelity was based on God's past graciousness (Deut 7:18; 8:2, 18; 15:15; 16:12; 24:9, 18, 22; 1 Chr 16:12, 15).

The Greek verb "to remember" (**mimnēskō** μιμνήσκω, **mnēmoneuō** μνημονεύω) functions in both the LXX and the NT in much the same way as did its Hebrew counterpart in the OT. It has the same general meaning of remembering past events (Matt 16:9; Luke 16:25; Rom 11:18; Rev 3:3). Furthermore, remembering God's promises functioned as a spur to trust and courage (Matt 28:20; Luke 24:6). Finally, as with God in the OT, Jesus' remembering was considered an assurance of forgiveness and blessing (Luke 23:42). The disciples were told to remember the words and deeds of Jesus in the same way as they remembered the gracious acts of God. Thus remembering became an act of faith for them (Matt 16:9; Mark 8:18; John 2:17; 16:4; Acts 11:16). After the resurrection, the disciples' remembering brought with it a profound realization of the meaning of these words and actions (Luke 24:6, 8; John 12:16).

In the NT, remembering took on a particular theological meaning because of the messianic expectations that were so much a part of Israelite religious thought. In their writings the NT authors pointed to the fulfillment of long-revered prophecies. There they explained that the believers' astonishment at the wonders performed by Jesus was abated when a salient ancient adage was remembered and now fully understood. It was by remembering that they gained insight into Jesus' true identity.

B. Memory/Remembrance

Though they are often used interchangeably in translations, these two words are really different. **Zekher** ("memory") refers to that which is remembered. Since the early Israelites did not have a well-developed concept of an existence after this life, they believed that it was their memory that survived, either through descendants (2 Sam 18:18) or through their own good works. If the memory of one's life perished, one's very existence might have been questioned. Thus the greatest punishment was to have the memory of one's self blotted out (Exod 17:14; Deut 25:19; 32:26; Job 18:17; Pss 9:6; 34:16 [Heb. 34:17]; 109:15; Eccl 9:5; Isa 26:14). When good works and a life of righteousness were remembered, that remembrance often took public expression, usually in acclaiming that person's good name (Ps 112:6; Prov 10:7). Thus in various translations **zekher** is rendered "name," as can be seen in passages that speak of remembrance and public acclamation of God's good works (Exod 3:15; Pss 6:5 [Heb. 6:6]; 30:4 [Heb. 30:5]; 97:12; 102:12 [Heb. 102:13]; 111:4; 135:13; 145:7; Isa 26:8; Hos 12:5).

The word **ʾazkarah** ("remembrance") is a cultic term and is only found in the P tradition of the Pentateuch. It refers to that portion of the **minkhah** (מִנְחָה; "gift offering") that was burned during certain sacrifices (Lev 2:2, 9, 16; 6:15). The **minkhah** itself consisted of flour mixed with oil, to which was added incense. When burned it became a "sweet-smelling sacrifice" (Sir 38:11; compare 45:16). The burning signified that a portion had been set aside as belonging exclusively to God. The sweet smell symbolized the hope that God would be pleased and would accept the petitioner's offering. It is not clear whether the actual memorial offering was the sweetened bread or the incense, since in one passage the priests ate the bread and merely burned the incense (Lev 24:7-9). However, there is mention of a "memorial" offering in a text describing a sin offering (Lev 5:12) and one detailing a test of a woman's marital fidelity (Num 5:15, 26). In neither case is incense included in the sacrifice. *See* SACRIFICES AND OFFERINGS.

There is a question regarding the naming of this memorial offering. It may be that since the name of God was solemnly pronounced when the ʾ**azkarah** was being offered that the term became associated with the remembrance of God.

C. Memorial

Like ʾ**azkarah** ("remembrance"), **zikkaron** ("memorial") is more than a mental image. It denotes a physical sign that functions as a reminder of an object or event of importance: stones on the priestly garment of Aaron on which are inscribed the names of the twelve sons of Jacob reminded the assembly of its intimate participation in cultic action (Exod 28:12, 29; 39:7); the tax levied to ward off divine wrath incurred because of census-taking was a reminder of the Israelites' expiation (Exod 30:16); the sound of the trumpets blown during cultic celebrations reminded the people of the observance of festivals and new moons (Num 10:10); the hammered plates made from the censors of the sinful priests reminded the people of the uniqueness of the Aaronite house (Num 16:40 [Heb. 17:5]); the royal crown placed in the Temple reminded the people that a civil leader was responsible for its rebuilding (Zech 6:14).

Zikkaron also signifies a historical record of significant deeds or maxims: scrolls of indictment (Exod 17:14); the royal annals of the Persian nation (Esth 6:1); the adages of the men who visited Job (Job 13:12); the fleeting memory of people of years gone by (Eccl 1:11; 2:16); a record of the names of the just (Isa 56:5; Mal 3:16).

Frequently, remembering is reinforced by the addition of a sign (ʾ**oth** אוֹת): at the time of the deliverance from Egypt, the blood on the house was a sign of salvation, and the commemoration of that day of deliverance became the memorial of the event of salvation (Exod 12:13-14); wearing phylacteries on the hand and forehead was an external sign of remembrance of the people's deliverance from bondage in Egypt (Exod 13:9, 16); the stones set up at Gilgal became a memorial sign of the people's miraculous crossing into the land of promise (Josh 4:6-7). The connection between **zikkaron** and ʾ**oth** is also found in the poetic vision of God reconstituting a purified people (Isa 55:13).

D. Cultic Memorial

The term **zikkaron** also denotes a cultic memorial instituted by God. Just as mental remembering brought the past to consciousness, so cultic remembrance, because of the involvement of divine power, brought the past event into present reality. God instituted these festivals as memorials of God's own saving action in the history of the people. Cultic realization of past events resembles the dynamic of performative speech that actually effects what it represents—"And God said . . . and it was" (Gen 1:1-28). When the people observed the festivals, the saving power of God that was operative in the original event was thought to be somehow again realized in the present cultic memorial celebration.

The basic cultic remembrance was the SABBATH. The directive to observe this day as a day set apart is found in the only injunction of the Decalogue that charges the people to "remember" (Exod 20:8). The people are told to refrain from work on this day, for God rested on the seventh day (Lev 23:3). The reason for this rest is not the physical refreshment of the Israelites, for that could have been achieved by engaging slaves or draft animals to do necessary work. The issue here is the work itself. The people are to abstain from any kind of work, for God rested on the seventh day after six days of creative work (Gen 2:1-4*a*). "Remembering" God's example of rest was an act of reverence toward God and an acknowledgment of human finitude. It stated publicly that no one should attempt to compete with the supremacy of God.

Besides the injunction to observe the Sabbath, the Israelites were told: "Three times in the year you shall hold a festival for me" (Exod 23:14). These cultic memorials were the great pilgrimage festivals of Unleavened Bread, Weeks or Pentecost, and Ingathering or Booths. These harvest festivals were celebrated with great ceremony (Num 10:10), and their observance eventually took on historical meaning.

The first pilgrimage festival mentioned is Unleavened Bread, not Passover. Probably independent spring celebrations, these two feasts were eventually combined and celebrated as one (*see* PASSOVER AND FEAST OF UNLEAVENED BREAD). Unleavened Bread may have originally been the more significant festival, but the stories preserved in the Bible accord that distinction to Passover. Passover, a nomadic ritual meant to ensure the safety of the flock as it moved from one pasturage to another, was celebrated as the cultic memorial of the people's deliverance from Egyptian bondage (Exod 12:14). The original Passover offering was an animal sacrifice that secured the people's deliverance (Exod 12:1-32); the commemoration of the event was a week-long remembrance festival celebrating that deliverance (Lev 23:5-8; Num 28:16-25; Deut 16:1-8).

The Feast of Weeks or Pentecost (*see* PENTECOST; WEEKS, FEAST OF), a wheat harvest festival, was celebrated seven weeks after the beginning of the barley harvest (Unleavened Bread). According to the exodus story, the Israelites arrived at Sinai seven weeks after their escape from Egypt (Exod 19:1). Because the date of their arrival and the harvest festival concurred, historical significance was now attached to the festival. Eventually it was celebrated as a cultic memorial of the Sinai covenant. As the feast took on more importance, holocausts, sin offerings, and peace offerings were added to the harvest cereal offerings (Lev 23:15-22; Num 28:26-31; Deut 16:9-12).

The Feast of Ingathering or Booths, celebrated during the autumn harvest, was the major feast of the year (*see* BOOTHS, FEAST OR FESTIVAL OF). Living in booths in order to harvest the crops reminded the people of their ancestors' sojourn in the wilderness, and so the historicized feast commemorated that deliverance. Tradition claims that Solomon dedicated the Temple during this festival (1 Kgs 8:2). This added to the importance of Jerusalem as the favored place for the celebration of the feast (Lev 23:33-43; Num 29:12-39; Deut 16:13-15).

In the NT, anamnēsis ("remembrance") refers to a cultic memorial. It is found in only three places, all of which discuss cultic commemorations (Luke 22:19; 1 Cor 11:24-25; Heb 10:3). The accounts of the institution of the eucharist clearly indicate that the saving power present in the past event is operative each time that event is "remembered" in cultic reenactment. This same idea is presumed in Hebrews, which argues that former cultic memorials were ineffective. Only the blood of Christ was a satisfactory "sin offering."

DIANNE BERGANT

MEMPHIS mem′fis [מֹף mof, נֹף nof; Μέμφις Memphis]. Memphis, 13 mi. south of modern Cairo on the west bank of the Nile River, was one of the most important cities in ancient EGYPT. Administratively part of Lower Egypt (i.e., the Delta) and capital of the first nome (province) of Lower Egypt, Memphis actually lay outside the Delta proper in a narrow stretch of the Nile Valley just south of the apex of the Delta.

The earliest recorded name of Memphis is inb-ḥḏ, White Wall or White Fortress. Later it was known by the names of its most famous structures, the temple of Ptah (ḥwt-k*3*-ptḥ; Gk. Aigyptos [Αἴγυπτος], i.e., Egypt) and the pyramid complex of King Pepy I (mnnfr). Memphis is the Greek form of the latter (Coptic Menfe; Heb. nof or mof).

Memphis appears in the Bible in prophetic oracles against Egypt (Isa 19:13; Jer 46:14, 19; Ezek 30:13, 16) and prophetic warnings against foreign entanglements (Jer 2:16; Hos 9:6). When Jeremiah (44:1) addresses the Judeans living in exile in Egypt, he names Memphis along with Migdol, Tahpanhes, and Pathros as the cities/regions where they reside. Memphis is also mentioned in Jdt 1:10 in a list of Egyptian sites to which the Assyrian king Nebuchadnezzar sends messengers.

Most Egyptian kings located their primary residence and administrative center at or near Memphis due to its strategic location at the boundary between Upper and Lower Egypt. Tradition accords the city's founding to the king who first united Upper and Lower Egypt at the end of the 4th millennium BCE. From then until the end of the Old Kingdom, Memphis was the sole capital. Following the political disintegration of the First Intermediate Period, the Twelfth Dynasty kings established their capital a short distance south of Memphis, in the vicinity of modern el-Lisht.

Whether Memphis was the royal residence or not, control of the city was imperative for any king with pretensions to rule all Egypt. Memphis was conquered by the HYKSOS at the beginning of the Second Intermediate Period and passed to Theban control at the beginning of the New Kingdom. When the Eighteenth Dynasty kings divided the administration of the country into two vizierates, they selected Memphis as the northern administrative center and primary royal residence. Memphis continued to function as a major administrative center through most of the New Kingdom, even after the royal residence was transferred to the eastern Delta under RAMESSES II. The city fell from prominence during the Third Intermediate Period and was sacked twice in less than a century, first by King Piye and later by the Assyrians. Memphis regained its status as royal residence under the Twenty-fifth Dynasty and continued to serve as Egypt's capital for much of the Late Period and into the Ptolemaic Period, when it was displaced by Alexandria as Egypt's political center.

The patron god of Memphis is Ptah, who had two primary roles in the Egyptian pantheon—as one of several creator deities and as the patron of artisans. Ptah is the central figure of the Memphite Theology, in which he calls the world into being by thought and speech. Although written in archaizing fashion, the MEMPHITE THEOLOGY is probably not much older than the Twenty-fifth Dynasty monument, the Shabaka Stone, on which it is recorded. The text elevates Ptah over all the other deities of Egypt as their creator and ruler and accords to him the establishment of the political and cultic systems. As the syncretistic deity Ptah-Sokar, later Ptah-Sokar-Osiris, Ptah appears also in funerary texts. Ptah's consort was the lion-headed plague goddess Sekhmet. The lotus god Nefertum was their son.

The temple of Ptah at Memphis and its priesthood formed a famed and powerful institution. The high priest, the *sem*-priest of Ptah and chief overseer of artisans, was one of the most important priests in Egypt. The temple that Ramesses II constructed for Ptah was one of the largest in all Egypt, rivaling in size the contemporary Amun-Re temple at Thebes. The Ptolemaic rulers favored the cults of Ptah and Apis and bestowed favors on the priesthood of the Memphite temple in exchange for its support. They traveled to Memphis to be crowned by the high priest.

Although bull-gods are known throughout Egypt, the local bull-god of Memphis, the Apis (Egyptian hp), rose to national prominence as the manifestation of Ptah. The living APIS bull resided in a temple just south of the temple of Ptah. Upon death the Apis bull was embalmed and buried with elaborate ceremony in the Memphite necropolis. The identification of the new living Apis involved a nationwide search for a black bull with the requisite markings in white on its forehead and back.

Jeremiah 46:15 uses the Apis bull as a symbol of Egypt's not-so-mighty gods. Although the MT reads "has been overthrown" (niskhaf נִסְחַף), the LXX (26:15) is almost certainly correct in dividing into two words: nas khaf (נָס חַף) translating it as ephygen ho Apis (ἔφυγεν ὁ Ἆπις), "Apis has fled." The passage thus opens with two rhetorical questions: "Why has Apis fled? Why did your bull [or "mighty one"] not stand?" The reading is further supported by the reference to Memphis in the preceding verse.

The Memphite necropolis, Saqqara, lay to the west of the city. Used almost continuously for 3,500 years, it contains historically significant tombs, including Old Kingdom pyramids, tombs of New Kingdom officials, and the Serapeum.

The step pyramid of the Third Dynasty king Djoser was the first pyramid and the direct predecessor of the true pyramid. The pyramids of Unas (last king of the Fifth Dynasty) and the kings of the Sixth Dynasty are inscribed inside with funerary texts, known as Pyramid Texts.

Numerous New Kingdom officials were buried at Saqqara. In addition to the treasurer Nehesi and the vizier Aper-El, the army commander Horemheb built a tomb complex at Saqqara. When Horemheb became king of Egypt, he discontinued plans to use the complex for his burial. Nonetheless, after his death a cult chapel was constructed for the worship of the deified king.

The funerary complex of the Apis bull, including associated chapels and small temples, formed the Serapeum. The complex comprised two large underground galleries in which the bulls were interred, one constructed in the reign of Ramesses II and the other in the Twenty-sixth Dynasty. Other embalmed animals, including the "Mother of the Apis" cows, ibises, falcons, and baboons, were interred in another section of the necropolis.

Bibliography: David Jeffreys. *The Survey of Memphis* (1985); Geoffrey T. Martin. *The Hidden Tombs of Memphis: New Discoveries from the Time of Tutankhamun and Ramesses the Great* (1991); Dorothy Thompson. *Memphis under the Ptolemies* (1988).

CAROLYN HIGGINBOTHAM

MEMPHITE THEOLOGY. An ancient Egyptian creation myth found on the Shabaka Stone, an inscription set up by Pharaoh Shabaka of the Twenty-fifth Dynasty (Nubian). According to the Memphite Theology, all of creation is the result of the work of the god Ptah. All other gods are merely aspects of Ptah and do his bidding in creation. In contrast to other Egyptian cosmologies, where creation is done through physical actions, the Memphite Theology presents Ptah as creating through his will and his spoken word. Ptah creates not only the world but also cities and the Egyptian nomes, thereby establishing the order of society. *See* CUSH, CUSHITE; EGYPT; NUBIA.

KEVIN A. WILSON

MEMPHITIC VERSION. *See* VERSIONS, COPTIC.

MEMUCAN mi-my*oo*'kuhn [מְמוּכָן memukhan]. One of seven officials of Media and Persia advising King AHASUERUS, Memucan operates as spokesperson when Ahasuerus seeks counsel concerning Queen VASHTI (Esth 1:14, 16, 21).

MEN AND MASCULINITY IN THE BIBLE. While often given less analytical attention than their female counterparts, male roles and identities are often just as fixedly prescribed and ordered within biblical texts. In general, constructions of proper maleness are reinforced by divine imagery in which God is portrayed as male and exhibiting attributes of strength, might in battle, familial and civic authority, self-control, wisdom, and justice. Men, then, are held to these divinely inscribed standards, and display them in the predominantly "male" arenas of civic life, battle, and sexuality. Throughout the Bible generally, men are overtly and covertly judged according to these constructions of maleness. To the degree that they conform, they are held as moral models or offered reward; in cases in which they resist or fail, biblical men are often punished or portrayed as effeminate, foolish, or lacking basic maleness. However, on occasion biblical authors offer competing interpretations of masculinity in which the definitions of manliness are broadened and challenged.

It would be impossible to review all examples of maleness, given the sheer number of occurrences of male figures in the biblical text. Instead, this article will emphasize a few critical and useful examples of how male stories and male authors are preoccupied with addressing male concerns, particularly "proper" forms of male behavior. Throughout, the terms "maleness" and "masculinity" will refer to these "proper" behaviors, mirroring the understanding in masculinity studies that gender is a socially created category apart from biological sex. (*See* MASCULINITY STUDIES.)

A. The Maleness of God
B. Masculinity in the Old Testament
    1. Torah
    2. History
    3. Prophets
    4. Poetry and Writings

C. Masculinity in the New Testament
1. Gospels
2. Pauline epistles
3. The Apocalypse of John
Bibliography

A. The Maleness of God

By far the most common presentation of God in the biblical text is masculine. (This is not to suggest that there are no feminine metaphors or allusions, simply that masculine metaphors are in the significant majority.) Biblical writers imagine God as warrior, king, judge, husband, father, and lord, with the masculine pronoun being employed in both the OT and NT. These images, of course, are drawn from a lived context, but they also create constructions beyond their simple meanings.

For example, for biblical writers to declare that "the LORD of hosts is mustering an army for battle" (Isa 13:4) or that God is "the King of glory ... the LORD, strong and mighty, the LORD, mighty in battle" (Ps 24:8) is to draw upon allusions already present in the mind of the author and reader. Such images suggest that God is a warrior. Since war most often took place between nations, kings, or powerful men, this construction has consequences for both the masculinization of the divine and the making of masculinity in general. The militarization of God metaphors both informs and reinforces the ideals of military might and those who engage in warfare. It makes their realm of battle the truest expression of masculinity and makes power in external affairs a mark of the male realm. Divine imagery reinforces the powerful construction of masculinity, and lends it eternal weight. Thus God the warrior and the masculinity of the human warrior are often bound up together.

We can see similar implications for masculinity built around metaphors of God's kingship and lordship. The kingship of God is well attested in the Bible, and as already noted the idea of a divine ruler is sometimes linked to military might (Ps 24:8; Rev 17:14). God's kingship in biblical texts, however, is also associated with justice and righteousness (Ps 96:10-13; Isa 33:5; Matt 25:31-46). As with battle, metaphors of God the king and judge emphasize the civic and political realm as important to maleness. Justice and righteousness in the administration of public affairs thus becomes a mark of idealized masculinity, particularly for kings (1 Sam 10:9; Isa 9:7; Jer 23:5).

Even metaphors that do not deal with the civic or military realm often reinforce an image of God as male, usually by relying on representations of the father or husband. In these instances, the relationship to humanity is more intimate than the nationalistic metaphors above. Father language for God is common, especially in the NT, and in some cases these images are quite tender (1 Chr 17:13; 1 John 3:1). Likewise, human fathering is most commonly portrayed as affectionate (Gen 37:3; Ps 103:13; Mark 9:21-25). However, both OT and NT authors on occasion place images of violence alongside fatherhood when referencing God (see Isa 64:8-9 [Heb. 64:7-8], in which God is an "exceedingly angry" father; and 1 Cor 15:24-26, in which God the Father destroys "every ruler and every authority and power").

Images of God as "husband" are less common in biblical texts. We see these images most often in prophetic literature, and they are marked by a far more obvious orientation toward power and anger or violence. Indeed, Hosea sees God as a wronged husband, with the power to "strip [Israel] naked and expose her as in the day she was born" (2:3 [Heb. 2:5]). Likewise, Ezekiel understands the Lord as both husband and father to the nation, condemning "her" as a "whore" or "prostitute," and commenting finally that leaving her naked and bare in the presence of her "lovers" (other nations) will "satisfy my fury on you" (16:1-43). The power of the divine is portrayed here as both familial and sexual in its manifestation. In contrast, however, the Apocalypse of John portrays God as Jerusalem's husband, wiping away tears and living with the city as bride (21:2-4).

These masculine images of God are critical to a more general understanding of masculinity in the Bible. While Howard Eilberg-Schwartz has (rightly) emphasized that such masculine images create a scenario in which even males must "play" feminine roles in deference to the masculinity of the divine, their presence also creates a desire for human men to copy divine manliness. Images of God as king, father, or husband create paradigms for human males. Mary Daly concludes that God-language that relies on images of dominance creates human ideals in which dominance, power, and violence are expected of men; conversely, then, images in which God is a tender father or righteous king promote compassion and justice. Indeed, as we shall see below, the men of the Bible are to a great degree judged masculine (or not) to the extent that they mirror the attributes in these divine images.

B. Masculinity in the Old Testament

1. Torah

The centrality of gender for the biblical writers becomes apparent even in the Bible's first story. Maleness and femaleness are built into the structure of creation, and gender is seen as reflecting the divine (Gen 1:27-28). Interestingly, however, the author/redactor of this first account offers no content for maleness that differs from femaleness, noting that both are created in the divine image. The second creation story (Gen 2) is markedly different in respect to gender. Here, maleness and femaleness are set apart when the second being is created, and she is called "Woman, for out of Man this one was taken" (Gen 2:23). Further, in only this account is maleness understood sexually. The humans are specifically described as naked, and the male seeks to become "one flesh" with the female in marital sex. Finally, the punishments are gender-specific: the husband will "rule over" the wife for her transgression (Gen 3:16) and the man (only) will toil against the earth in order to eat (Gen 3:17). In this second account, then, we see a more fully developed construction of masculinity, in which the male is uniquely related to the divine, seen as an intrinsically sexual being, in a position of authority over the woman, and driven by command to participate in the outside world of work.

The patriarchal narratives offer several occasions for considering biblical masculinities. Often, these tales point to ideals of masculinity as oriented on powerfulness, but opposing or recessive models of masculinity may also be found. In the story of Esau and Jacob, e.g., two contrasting masculine ideals emerge. Jacob's elder son, Esau, is "a man of the field" and hunter; the younger, Jacob, is a "quiet man, living in tents" (Gen 25:27). The "quiet" one is preferred by his mother. The hunter, Esau, who is also described as red and hairy, is preferred by the father. Allied with his mother, and not possessing the physical attributes of his hunter-brother, Jacob is forced to rely on trickery to inherit the birthright (Gen 27). Lori Hope Lefkovitz notes that the rather unlikely "performance" of Jacob dressing in animal skins to be the man his father wishes him to be is a sort of "drag show" in which maleness of one (preferred) kind is played out by another. Indeed, Esau conforms to the warrior ideal of masculinity in ways his brother does not. In this narrative that warrior-masculinity is both upheld as the ideal and overturned in the actual course of the tale.

A second example of competing masculinities is evident in the single person of Joseph (Gen 37; 39–50). In many ways, Joseph emulates the widespread models of masculinity already discussed: he is successful in civic and political affairs (Gen 39:3; 41:33) and he exhibits significant authority over others (39:6, 22; 41:45). In perhaps the most lyrical of the examples of this last attribute, Joseph is described in Jacob's final speech as having a taut bow (Gen 49:24), a metaphor for both military and sexual power. However, Joseph is also described in ways that are otherwise reserved for women. Joseph is "beautiful of form and beautiful of features" (author's trans; NRSV, "handsome and good-looking"; Gen 39:6), a phrase used elsewhere only of Rachel (Gen 29:17). Jacob gives Joseph a **kethoneth passim** (כְּתֹנֶת פַּסִּים, "a long robe with sleeves"; Gen 37:3), which (according to 2 Sam 13:18) is the garment worn by virgin daughters of the king. Twice, Joseph does not fight back when attacked and is stripped (Gen 37:23; 39:12). These unexpectedly "feminized" depictions of Joseph provide evidence that competing masculinities are present in the biblical text, occasionally in the same tale.

Men's stories in the Torah are dependent, in part, on the concept of circumcision as a mark of patrilineal descent. Among Abraham's sons, the removal of the foreskin is closely associated with the continuity of the promise among males (Gen 17:9-14). This act has been understood as related to masculinity in various ways: 1) as a form of sacrifice, which removes the power of matrilineal descent (Jay); 2) as a male counterpart to menstruation, which allows men access to fertility in a ritual sense (Silverman); or 3) as a way of delineating "insider" from "outsider" males, in determining a "bloody boundary" of true manliness in the community (Mark).

2. History

The warrior is perhaps the most prominent male image in the books of history. More than any other arena, battle is understood in these stories as the domain of males, and men are judged in part according to their military prowess and might.

In Judges, we are confronted with men who both conform to and defy the warrior paradigm, and we can see clearly the condemnation for failure to meet convention. Barak, a general summoned by Deborah, refuses to conform to the warrior role; he fears the army of Sisera, and tells Deborah, "If you will not go with me, I will not go" (Judg 4:8). In response, Deborah predicts the Lord will instead "sell Sisera into the hand of a woman" (4:9). In the subsequent victory song, the point is repeated: Jael's power and Deborah's authority are lauded, but Barak is hardly mentioned (5:12). One prevailing paradigm of manliness—might in battle, particularly—is reinforced here by laying plain the atypical scenario that follows when males do not take their "proper place" as it is understood by the Deuteronomistic compiler.

Similarly, the judge Samson (Judg 14–16) is able to bring down a thousand Philistines with a donkey's jawbone, tear apart a lion with his hands, and is powerful in his anger (14:9). However, his masculinity (called his "strength" in 16:5) is threatened by an unrelenting woman who "pestered him, [until] he was tired to death" (16:16). The tale seems intended to serve at least in part as cautionary, as does the Barak/Deborah/Jael cycle. In these stories, males who surrender power to women or do not accept military authority imperil their own masculinity.

Perhaps there is no more paradigmatic figure for the study of masculinity in the OT than King David. David, as portrayed in the books of Samuel and Kings, is the consummate warrior and civic powerhouse. When he is brought into the household of Saul, the servant providing the introduction reports, "[He] is skillful in playing, a man of valor, a warrior, prudent in speech, and a man of good presence" (1 Sam 16:18). Certainly, it is David's valorous and warring aspects that are most often lauded in the course of his narrative. David Clines notes, e.g., that David leads an army of over a million between those of Israel and Judah, and that his personal "body count" is approximately 140,000 people. While the historical reality of David's military is unknowable, these numbers function to emphasize the power of

David's kingship. David's taunting words to Abner, "Are you not a man?" (1 Sam 26:15), because Abner had not guarded Saul, sets the point clearly: part of what makes David the ideal man is his military might. However, even as David is lauded for his victories in battle, he is also commended for ruling the nation with "justice and equity" (2 Sam 8:15), indicating that the military (and masculine) authority of kings must be restrained by good judgment in service to the nation (see also Jer 13:22-27).

3. Prophets

Prophetic biographical materials, perhaps because of the social locations from which individual prophets arise, tend not to emphasize civic and military authority. Instead, male prophets tend to be presented in terms of hierarchical personal relationships. However, images of violence, strength, and power continue to appear within the masculine identity structure of prophets about whom we have biographical narratives.

Jeremiah's prophetic call underscores the more personal imagery found throughout the prophets. When Jeremiah wishes to avoid his prophetic role, he calls himself a "boy" (**naʿar** [נַעַר]; Jer 1:6). However, the Lord responds that he is not a boy; he has been transformed instead into one able to "pluck up and to pull down, to destroy and to overthrow" (1:6-10). He is changed, in essence, from a boy to a man, and commanded to "gird up his loins" to speak (Jer 1:17). The construction, while having some military allusions, is primarily on a personal level. Jeremiah is not a boy, and thus his authority as a prophet is equated with being a man. Hosea also emphasizes interpersonal masculine authority in his prophetic speech. Conflating the Lord's relationship to Israel with his own relationships, Hosea chooses and then uses a wife and children to express God's lack of mercy (Hos 1:6; 2:4 [Heb. 2:6]) upon and the consequent shaming (2:3 [Heb 2:4]) of idolatrous Israel, portrayed as a promiscuous wife. Hosea asserts his masculinity (as strength and power) in the service of prophetic metaphor. Divine forgiveness and restoration are later offered (Hos 2:14-21 [Heb. 2:16-25]), but cannot completely erase the effect of the initial imagery.

4. Poetry and Writings

While the poetry of the OT relies heavily on metaphorical language (as befits the genre), some of the Writings also offer concrete descriptions of proper manliness. In these Writings, we see similar themes of strength and familial authority, as well as an emphasis on wisdom and righteousness as fitting for a good man.

Both the Psalms and Ecclesiastes laud the man who exhibits virility in his household. The man who "fears the LORD" will have a fruitful wife and children as numerous as olive shoots (Ps 128:3-4). He will have a quiver full of sons, and will not be shamed in the presence of his enemies—a phrase that may have sexual connotations (Ps 127:3-5). In both cases, however, the sexual dominance and familial power of the father in the household is dependent upon his submission to the power of God: "Unless the LORD builds the house, those who build it labor in vain" (127:1). Similarly, in Ecclesiastes, men are seen as impressive if they "beget a hundred children, and live many years" (6:3); however, as with the psalms, this manly power must be complimented with a proper mental state. In this case, it is enjoyment (6:3) and elsewhere wisdom (9:16), but in all these instances masculinity understood as virility is coupled with a proper internal state as well.

Indeed, the sense of maleness as more than brute force is emphasized throughout the Writings. A proverb asserts, "Wise warriors are mightier than strong ones" (24:5), and Ecclesiastes contends that "Wisdom gives strength to the wise more than ten rulers that are in a city" (7:19). It is no surprise, of course, that wisdom literature would emphasize the power of wisdom. However, in regard to masculinity, the inclusion of wisdom with strength, might, and civic authority suggests a broadening of categories. The Writings do not dismiss strength (or virility, as above) as important to true manliness, but instead wish to emphasize an internal state (fear of the Lord, wisdom) that corresponds to a man's external position.

Of note for masculinity studies of Job is the repetition of the phrase "gird up your loins like a man," which God speaks twice out of the whirlwind (38:3; 40:7). The phrase "gird up your loins" and similar phrasing elsewhere in the OT indicates preparation (for the Passover in Exod 12:11; for running in 1 Kgs 18:46; for going to meet another in 2 Kgs 4:29 and 2 Kgs 9:1; and for prophetic power in Jer 1:17). In Job, it certainly conveys the need for Job to be prepared for God's response. However, in none of the above instances is the addition "like a man" included. Here, then, an association is being made between Job's manliness and his preparation for God's response to his suffering. For Job to gird his loins "like a man" is to prepare himself to confront a divine being who is about to present himself as a source of overwhelming power to create and destroy (40:8-13). In this interpretation, Job's response is particularly telling: he lays his hand on his mouth, calling himself insignificant (40:4), and when God again asks him to gird his loins, he humbles himself in the dust (42:6). In neither case does Job respond to God's power with any power of his own. Indeed, it may well be that Job is mirroring other wisdom literature, which sees deference to God and internal rightness as more "manly" than strength. In any case, these texts from Job indicate an extension of the boundaries of proper manliness; for after Job girds his loins "like a man," God declares that Job's response alone was right (42:7).

The book of Daniel, because of its significantly later date of writing, begins to betray a more Hellenistic mentality toward masculinity. While strength continues to be important for male identity (as in Dan 10:17-

20), constructions in which manliness is equated with beauty, self-control, and prudence gain in prominence. Daniel himself is described as responding to crises with "prudence and discretion" (2:14), and having "an excellent spirit, knowledge, and understanding" (5:12). He and his fellows in the court of Nebuchadnezzar have "knowledge and skill in every aspect of literature and wisdom" (1:17) and are among the "young men without physical defect and handsome" (1:4). These characteristics—beauty, self-control, wisdom, moral excellence—were commonly held as ideals for men in Greco-Roman antiquity, and their presence in Daniel indicates a movement toward Hellenization even among Jewish writers.

C. Masculinity in the New Testament

1. Gospels

Much has been written elsewhere about the Greco-Roman backgrounds for masculinity studies of the NT (see bibliography). Generally, scholars have suggested that (free) men of the Mediterranean world expressed idealized masculinity as some form of control, whether over others (less powerful men, women, children, or slaves) or the self. Self-control was exhibited in mastery of emotion, the mind, speech, and the bodily passions. In the Roman household, the idea of *patria potestas* (complete paternal power) likely never measured up to its idealized presentation, but it was nonetheless represented as an ideal. Outside the household, control often took the form of dominance in civic life, especially in oratorical skill. This emphasis on control, particularly in regard to the masculinity of Jesus, is not found equally in all Gospels, but each makes some use of the categories of maleness already established in the Hellenized world.

Among the Synoptic Gospels, Mark portrays Jesus as a man both authoritative and humiliated. The man Jesus is filled with power such that he is aware of its drain, as in the story of the hemorrhaging woman (5:30//Luke 8:46). This power is both authoritative (6:7) and apocalyptic (13:26; 14:62). And yet Mark also concedes that Jesus' authority is dependent upon the receptiveness of others (6:5). Further, Mark arranges the structure of the Gospel in terms of suffering, humiliation, and death at the hands of the enemy (8:31; 9:30-32; 10:33-34). At his passion, Jesus is mocked (15:20, 29, 31) and in need of assistance with tasks requiring strength (15:21). Jesus loses self-control at the moment of his death, crying out in a loud voice, and at that moment he is recognized as the Son of God (15:39). Graham Ward contends that this stripping of masculine ideals in Mark's passion serves to strip Jesus of his masculinity for the community, making his presence in the eucharist more available to all. At the very least, it indicates that, while Mark was familiar with standard constructions of maleness in the Hellenistic world, he also understood an alternative construction in which powerlessness had a salvific effect.

In the unique (non-Markan or Q) sections of Matthew, male figures are highlighted as significant to the life and ministry of Jesus. The genealogy emphasizes the male line of Joseph, and the birth story favors Joseph's over Mary's role (1:1–2:23). As specifically relates to Jesus, Matthew makes comparisons to idealized males of the OT, especially Moses (chaps. 2; 5) and David (chap. 1), who embody the law-oriented wisdom and king/warrior traditions of Judaism. Within the Gospel, others are able to identify Jesus by acts of authority (8:27), wisdom, and power (13:54), characteristics that were important in defining Greco-Roman maleness. Indeed, at the crucifixion, Matthew downplays the Markan emphasis on Jesus' humiliation, suggesting instead that it is in acts of power (the earthquake, resurrection of the dead) that Jesus is made known as the Son of God (27:54). Matthew even concludes with an appeal to Jesus' cosmic authority (28:18) as the foundation of the mission of the disciples.

Luke–Acts presents an interesting case for masculinity studies in that the sheer volume of material offers a broad range of male behavior and ideals. Certainly, in Luke–Acts we find evidence of some masculine ideals from the wider Greco-Roman world. In Luke, Jesus is powerful and strong (4:36; 6:19), wise (2:52), and imbued with both heavenly and earthly authority (9:1; 10:19). John the Baptist, too, embodies these characteristics: he is filled "with the spirit and power of Elijah ... to turn the hearts of fathers [NRSV, parents] to their children, and the disobedient to the wisdom of the righteous" (1:17). Paul, as presented in Acts, is an accomplished and persuasive public speaker (chaps. 13, 21, 26), and lectures Felix on justice and self-control (24:25).

However, the Lukan material also includes parables and social interactions that seem to reverse or undermine expected patterns of masculinity. For example, in the Magnificat, Luke announces the advent of a time when the powerful are brought low, and the lowly are lifted up (Luke 1:46-55). In some parables, Jesus speaks of reversed masculinities. Male officials, the standards of civic power, are seen as unwise (18:1-8), e.g., and the "father" in the parable of the prodigal son shows compassion as he runs to embrace his wayward child (15:11-32). Even in the male social hierarchy power roles are reversed (16:19-31). In other places, usually dominant male voices are pressed into the background (as with Zechariah, 1:20-23) or silenced by the acts of (unseemly) women (7:44-47, in the section of this story unique to Luke). In Acts, Peter quotes Joel's inclusive pronouncement that sons, daughters, young men, old men, and male and female slaves will receive the Spirit, a statement that seems to defy the standard masculine social hierarchy (2:17-18). Luke–Acts, then, both endorses and critiques various aspects of the dominant models of masculinity.

2. Pauline epistles

The Pauline corpus, perhaps because of the epistolary format, tends to deal with societal maleness rather than idealized portraits of individual males. Throughout, Paul comments on concrete situations in which male roles, identities, and relationships dominate.

Circumcision is a central preoccupation. Paul's position against the "Judaizers" is clearly opposed to circumcision (e.g., Gal 5:2). Paul also claims that circumcision is "nothing," in view of the "impending crisis" of the Parousia (1 Cor 7:19, 26). And yet, as we have already noted, the act of circumcision was a defining feature of the patriarchal orientation of the covenant and of the physical marking of males as a group set apart. What then, does the Pauline dismissal of circumcision accomplish for masculine identity? For one, it seems to blur maleness and femaleness, at least in terms of entry into the covenant community. Paul's famous statement that in Christ "there is no longer male and female" (Gal 3:28) occurs in the context not of social equality, but of the Abrahamic covenant and law. "If you belong to Christ [in baptism], then you are Abraham's offspring" (3:29; compare Rom 8:9). Thus, the maleness that was central to the covenant is displaced by a more generalized "offspring." However, the baptismal formula does not entirely override the prevailing roles of males (and females) within the community; in 1 Corinthians, Paul is still inclined to see male authority in families (11:3), in worship (11:4-7), and in Paul's own biblical interpretation (11:8-12), all of which show no sign of blurring gender boundaries.

Paul upholds Roman constructs of maleness in his description of those who will not enter the kingdom (1 Cor 6:9-20; compare 1 Tim 1:10). Here, Paul lists males whose bodies are ill-used: fornicators (pornoi πόρνοι), adulterers (moichoi μοιχοί), "soft people" (malakoi μαλακοί), and "men who go to bed" (arsenokoitai ἀρσενοκοῖται). The term malakoi was commonly used as a term of derision toward un-manly men, and it has been suggested that these terms refer to men who engage in male-male sexual activity, possibly in the role of the "passive" partner. The "passive" role would have been contrary to Roman constructs of proper use of the male body; males were to be the active, dominant, and penetrating participants in sexual matters.

Paul balances his rhetoric on masculine roles with maternal imagery, putting himself in a role that does not conform to cultural ideals of male authority (Gaventa). He calls the Galatians "my little children" and tells them he is in labor until Christ is born in each of them (Gal 4:19). He describes his work among the Thessalonians as that of a nurse caring for her own children (1 Thess 2:7). He tells the Corinthians that they are still "infants" in Christ whom he has fed with milk instead of solid food (1 Cor 3:1-2). Even though Paul would not count himself among the un-manly men who will not enter the kingdom (1 Cor 6:9-20), he is content to use these feminine, nurturing metaphors to express his love and concern for his communities.

The deuteropauline epistles give evidence that some communities are conforming to the societal and familial structure and propriety of Roman households. Such hierarchical family structures emphasize male dominance and authority. At the same time, these epistles exhort men in such positions of power to balance their authority with compassion. Colossians entreats men to "love your wives and never treat them harshly," to "not provoke your children," and to "treat your slaves fairly" (3:18–4:1). Similarly, Ephesians calls for mutual submission before observing that the "husband is the head of the wife" in the same way that Christ is the head of the church and must love her accordingly. Fathers are to bring up their children in the discipline of the Lord; masters are to "stop threatening" their slaves (5:21–6:9). To varying degrees, these pronouncements depend on a hierarchical view of the family that emphasizes both the authority and the duty of the *pater-familias*, while balancing this authority with compassion for those in the care of the head of household—and, in the case of Eph 5:21, mitigating hierarchy with an appeal to mutuality.

While echoing much of the household-code language of Colossians and Ephesians, Titus makes an additional appeal to men unrelated to familial obligation, but that also uses the Greco-Roman categories of self-control as central to maleness. Titus exhorts older men (presbytas πρεσβύτας; also translated "ambassadors") to be "prudent" (sōfronas σώφρονας) and "sound" (hygiaiontas ὑγιαίνοντας) and younger men (neōterous νεωτέρους) to likewise be "self-controlled" (sōfronein σωφρονεῖν) and of sound (hygiē ὑγιῆ) speech (2:2-8).

3. The Apocalypse of John

The Apocalypse of John returns to emphasizing moral models in its rhetoric of masculinity, but in this case the figures/models are cosmic in scope, as is often true of apocalypses. The warrior ideal returns, but here he has the enormous power to destroy "the flesh of kings, the flesh of captains ... flesh of all" (Rev 19:17-21) or fight dragons and cosmic monsters (12:7-8). The kingship ideal also reappears, but the sovereign Lamb vanquishes not just human but cosmic-mythic enemies (17:9-14). The Lamb has "power and wealth and wisdom and might and honor" (5:12), all elements noted throughout the Bible as important to idealized masculinity, but here broadened in scope to make him cosmically authoritative. Tina Pippin, noting the resurgence of such imagery, laments that the apocalypse reinscribes "traditional" masculinities of power in a cosmic arena. However, other scholars note that the language of the apocalypse actually overturns expected masculinities. The cosmic power and worth of the Lamb, e.g., is wrought through suffering instead of might in battle (the Lamb is "slaughtered," and his blood is a ransom for the saints; Rev 5:9). Lynn Huber notes that the emphasis on male sexual abstinence in Rev 14:4 likely contrasted with prevalent Roman models of masculine sexual power. The Apocalypse, then, confirms what is apparent throughout the Bible, namely that views of what constitutes proper maleness (while often structured in terms of authority, control, or strength) are diverse and varied, and that the communities who produced these texts sometimes spoke over and against their cultural setting to portray different norms for masculinity.

Bibliography: Janice Capel Anderson and Stephen Moore. "Matthew and Masculinity." *New Testament Masculinities.* Stephen D. Moore, ed. (2003) 67–91; Peter Brown. *The Body and Society* (1988); David Clines. "David the Man: The Construction of Masculinity in the Hebrew Bible." *Interested Parties: The Ideology of Writers and Readers of the Hebrew Bible* (1995) 212–41; Colleen Conway. *Behold the Man: Jesus and Greco-Roman Masculinity* (2008); Mary Daly. *Beyond God the Father* (1974); Howard Eilberg-Schwartz. *God's Phallus and Other Problems for Men and Monotheism* (1994); Beverly Gaventa. "Our Mother St. Paul: Toward the Recovery of a Neglected Theme." *A Feminist Companion to Paul.* Amy-Jill Levine, ed. (2004) 85–97; Erik Gunderson. *Staging Masculinity* (2000); Harry A. Hoffner. "Symbols for Masculinity and Femininity: Their Use in Ancient Near Eastern Sympathetic Magic Rituals." *JBL* 85 (1966) 326–34; Lynn Huber. "Sexually Explicit? Re-reading Revelation's 144,000 Virgins as a Response to Roman Discourses." *Journal of Men, Masculinities, and Spirituality* 2 (2008) 3–28; Nancy Jay. *Throughout Your Generations Forever: Sacrifice, Religion and Paternity* (1992); Mathew Keufler. *The Manly Eunuch* (2001); Jennifer Larson. "Paul's Masculinity." *JBL* 123 (2004) 85–97; Lori Hope Lefkovitz. "Passing as a Man: Jewish Narratives of Gender Performance." *Narrative* 10 (2002) 91–103; Elizabeth Wyner Mark. "Wounds, Vows, Emanations: A Phallic Trope in the Patriarchal Narrative." *The Covenant of Circumcision: New Perspectives on an Ancient Jewish Rite* (2003) 3–17; Stephen Moore. "'O Man, Who Art Thou?' Masculinity Studies and New Testament Studies." *New Testament Masculinities* (2003) 1–22; Stephen Moore and Janice Capel Anderson. "Taking It Like a Man: Masculinity in 4 Maccabees." *JBL* 117 (1998) 249–73; Todd Penner and Caroline Vander Stichele. "Gendering Violence: Patterns of Power and Constructs of Masculinity in the Acts of the Apostles." *A Feminist Companion to the Acts of the Apostles.* Amy-Jill Levine and Marianne Blickenstaff, eds. (2004) 193–209; Tina Pippin. *Death and Desire: The Rhetoric of Gender in the Apocalypse of John* (1992); Joseph Roisman. *The Rhetoric of Manhood: Masculinity in the Attic Orators* (2005); Michael A. Satlow. "Try to Be a Man: Rabbinic Constructions of Masculinity." *HTR* 89 (1996) 19–40; Elisabeth Schüssler Fiorenza. *The Book of Revelation: Justice and Judgment* (1989); Eric Kline Silverman. *From Abraham to America: A History of Jewish Circumcision* (2006); Diane Swancutt. "'The Disease of Effemination': The Charge of Effeminacy and the Verdict of God." *New Testament Masculinities.* Stephen D. Moore, ed. (2003) 193–234; Graham Ward. "Theology and Masculinity." *The Journal of Men's Studies* 7 (1999) 281–86; L. Michael White. "Paul and Pater Familias." *Paul in the Greco-Roman World* (2003); Craig A. Williams. *Roman Homosexuality: Ideologies of Masculinity in Classical Antiquity* (1999); David F. Wright. "Homosexuals or Prostitutes? The Meaning of *Arsenokoitai* (1 Cor 6:9; 1 Tim 1:10)." *VC* 38 (1984) 125–53.

JESSICA TINKLENBERG DEVEGA

MENAHEM men´uh-hem [מְנַחֵם menakhem]. The son of Gadi, he was the sixteenth king to rule in the Northern Kingdom (ca. 745–738 BCE). Some scholars have proposed that he was originally from Gad, but "ben Gadi" is a reference to his father and not to his place of birth (2 Kgs 15:14). According to Josephus (*Ant.* 9.228–29), Menahem was an army general who served under ZECHARIAH, the son of Jeroboam II. Zechariah had reigned six months when he was murdered by a pretender to the throne, Shallum son of Jabesh (2 Kgs 15:8-10). Zechariah was the last king of the dynasty of Jehu. His assassination most likely was motivated by the preaching of Amos and Hosea. The two prophets of the Northern Kingdom had pronounced judgment against the royal house of Jeroboam (Amos 7:10-17) and against the dynasty of Jehu (Hos 1:4-5).

It is possible that the accession of Shallum and his reign in Samaria may indicate a division in the army. Shallum did not have the support of the people, and whatever support he had among the army officers was insufficient to keep him in power. At the time Shallum became king, Menahem was stationed at TIRZAH, the old capital of the Northern Kingdom from the days of Jeroboam I until the days of Omri, who built Samaria as the new capital (1 Kgs 14:17; 16:23-24).

If Menahem was from Tirzah, he was probably from the tribe of Manasseh. He marched from Tirzah, where Israel's main army was posted. He came with some troops to Samaria, and killed Shallum in order to avenge the death of Zechariah (2 Kgs 15:14). The revolt of Shallum was suppressed after he had reigned one month as king of Israel. Shallum's short reign reflects the political instability of the Northern Kingdom at the time Menahem became king.

After Menahem became king, he took revenge against the citizens of TIPHSAH (or Tappuah). The reason for Menahem's atrocities is not very clear. Menahem's brutal action may have been an attempt to strengthen his hold on the throne after the assassination of Shallum. If the population of Tiphsah had refused to support Menahem's bid for the throne, then his vicious action against them could be seen as a punishment for their lack of support. Menahem invaded the city and punished its population; he sacked the city and "ripped open all the pregnant women in it" (2 Kgs 15:16), an atrocious practice well known among the Assyrians and used also by the Arameans (2 Kgs 8:12) and the Ammonites (Amos 1:13). Another reason for the brutality of his actions may be due to the tribal rivalry that existed between Ephraim and Manasseh. If the city was the Tappuah located in Ephraim (Josh 16:8; 17:8), and Shallum was from a place located near Tappuah, then the massacre of the population was because of their support for Shallum and his coup against Zechariah.

At the time Menahem came to the throne, the tumultuous situation in Israel produced instability and unrest in its political life. This instability was caused by the ascendancy of Assyrian hegemony and the accession of TIGLATH-PILESER III to the throne of Assyria and by the different political groups fighting for control. Tiglath-pileser came to the throne in 745 BCE and was the most aggressive Assyrian king of the new empire. His desire to enlarge the Assyrian Empire brought Israel into the sphere of his influence. Israel simply had to be conquered in order for Tiglath-pileser to fulfill his dream: complete domination of the Middle East. The political leaders of Israel were divided among those who favored cooperation with Assyria and those who favored cooperation with Syria. The anti-Assyria group favored an alliance with Syria in order to resist Assyrian ambitions. Those who were pro-Assyria promoted a position of neutrality or submission to Assyria, as the dynasty of Jehu had done in the past.

Later in his reign, Menahem was confronted with a possible Assyrian invasion and was threatened by Tiglath-pileser. Tiglath-pileser's name appears in the biblical text as Pul (2 Kgs 15:19), the name he assumed when he conquered Babylon. During the end of Menahem's reign, Assyria came up against the nations of Palestine, and Menahem voluntarily submitted himself to the king of Assyria.

In order to secure his throne and avert a possible invasion, Menahem paid Tiglath-pileser 1,000 talents of silver (3 million shekels). The tribute was high and beyond Menahem's capability of paying the assessment from the royal funds. The money for the tribute was exacted from 60,000 wealthy men who paid fifty shekels each. With this act of submission Menahem became a loyal vassal of Assyria, and Israel paid tribute until Menahem's death. By payment of the tribute and by becoming an Assyrian vassal, Menahem received the benefit of Assyrian protection. The longevity of his reign came probably because of the loyalty of the army and because of the support of Assyria after the payment of the tribute.

The act of submission to Assyria was hardly popular among those who favored an alliance with the Arameans. The internal troubles that Menahem had avoided by submission to Assyria broke out again at or shortly after his death. Menahem died in peace and rested with his ancestors (2 Kgs 15:22). The writers of 2 Kings accuse Menahem of following the religious practices of Jeroboam I (2 Kgs 15:18). This judgment is the conventional way every king of the Northern Kingdom was evaluated by the writers of Kings. After the death of Menahem, his son Pekahiah became king of Israel and continued his father's policy of cooperation with Assyria. *See* ASSYRIA AND BABYLONIA.

Bibliography: Menahem Haran. "The Rise and Decline of the Empire of Jeroboam ben Joash." *VT* 17 (1967) 266–97.

CLAUDE MARIOTTINI

MENAHOT [מְנָחוֹת **menakhoth**]. Means "offerings." The second tractate of the fifth order of the MISHNAH (*Kodashim*). Menahot discusses various aspects of the sacrificial system, with emphasis on intention.

MENANDER muh-nan´duhr. 1. The putative author of the pseudepigraphical work *The Sentences of Syriac Menander*, a collection of popular wisdom sayings similar to Jewish wisdom texts (e.g., Sirach). The text is traditionally dated from the 3rd cent. CE.

2. Josephus quotes Menander of Ephesus, who wrote a history of the kings of Phoenicia using Phoenician historical records as his sources (*Ag. Ap.* 1.116–20).

MICHAEL J. SCHUFER

MENE, MENE, TEKEL, AND PARSIN mee´nee tek´uhl pahr´sin [Aram. מְנֵא מְנֵא תְּקֵל וּפַרְסִין **meneʾ meneʾ teqel ufarsin**]. These three (the ancient versions of LXX, Theod., Vg. all omit the second **meneʾ**) or four words are the famous "handwriting on the wall" (Dan 5:25) that terrified the putative last Babylonian king, BELSHAZZAR. No wonder! They were written by a ghostly, disembodied hand even as the drunken king and his entourage were feasting from the precious vessels looted from the Jerusalem Temple by "his father," Nebuchadnezzar (2 Kgs 24:13; 2 Chr 36:18; Dan 1:1-2; 5:2).

Drawing upon Jewish legend, the artist Rembrandt offered an explanation for why the king and all his wise men failed to make sense of the four mysterious Aramaic words. In his famous painting *Belshazzar's Feast*, he depicted the pale handwriting vertically instead of horizontally, thus creating a kind of anagram. The words may indeed have been meant to be ominously obscure. In Dan 5:24-28, the Jewish sage and riddle-solver DANIEL, brought into the banquet at the insistence of the queen (vv. 10-12), uses puns in order to create an oracle of judgment against the king. He vocalizes all three words as passive participles rather than nouns. Hence **meneʾ** means "numbered" (in the sense of "delimited"), **teqel** means "weighed," and from the plural parsin (sg. peres פְּרֵס) he derives "divided."

For more than a century now, many critical interpreters have regarded the three words as nouns, names of ANE coins valued by weight, i.e., meneʾ = mina; teqel = SHEKEL; peres = half-mina (or possibly half-shekel). The sequence is peculiar, in that the middle term is the least valuable coin (at a ratio of about 50:1:25). Perhaps the riddle was intended to offer an evaluation of rulers in descending order of merit (compare Dan 2:36-45), with peres displaced to the third position to anticipate the king's imminent overthrow by the Medes and the Persians (v. 28). *See* MONEY, COINS; WEIGHTS AND MEASURES.

W. SIBLEY TOWNER

MENELAUS men´uh-lay´uhs [Μενέλαος Menelaos]. Menelaus was the high priest from 172–162 BCE, during the time of the Maccabean Revolt (167–164 BCE). Menelaus and his family, already important in Jerusalem, sought higher authority through unscrupulous means.

JASON bribed ANTIOCHUS IV Epiphanes to appoint him high priest, replacing his brother Onias III in 174 BCE (2 Macc 4:7-9). Jason introduced Hellenistic customs to Jerusalem.

Two years later, Menelaus, a non-Zadokite priest (2 Macc 3:4, corrected), offered Antiochus a larger bribe and was appointed high priest. Once in power, Menelaus appointed his brother, Lysimachus, as his deputy.

Menelaus' reign as high priest was tumultuous. A crowd lynched Lysimachus because Menelaus stole temple property to pay Antiochus (2 Macc 4:42). Jason attacked Jerusalem, leading Antiochus, who believed Judea was in revolt, to pillage Jerusalem and loot the Temple (2 Macc 5:11-21). Shortly thereafter Antiochus prohibited the observance of Jewish customs (2 Macc 6), prompting the Maccabean Revolt.

Some scholars argue that Menelaus was a hellenizer, but the sources mention no Greek customs introduced by Menelaus (rather than Jason). Rather, they suggest that Menelaus sought power and violated Jewish customs to get it. Antiochus Epiphanes probably knew little of Judaism, so the prohibition of Judaism was most likely done at the behest of Menelaus. Supporting this is the suggestion that the king continued to see Menelaus as his representative (2 Macc 11:27-33) and that, later, the Syrian Lysias blamed Menelaus for all the troubles (2 Macc 13:4). This resulted in Menelaus' execution. Menelaus' motives are opaque and scholars have offered various explanations for his actions (Grabbe). *See* CHIEF, HIGH PRIEST; MACCABEES, MACCABEAN REVOLT.

Bibliography: Lester Grabbe. *Judaism from Cyrus to Hadrian.* Vol. 1 (1992).

ADAM L. PORTER

MENESTHEUS mi-nes´thee-uhs [Μενεσθεύς Menestheus]. Menestheus is the father of APOLLONIUS (2 Macc 4:4, 21), governor of Coelesyria and Phoenicia around the time of Antiochus IV Epiphanes, who is mentioned in this context in connection with his support of Simon the Benjaminite against the high priest ONIAS III.

MENI muh-nee´ [מְנִי meni]. The name of a deity, translated "DESTINY" by the NRSV (Isa 65:11). The name is related to the verb meaning "count," "number," or "assign." A group in postexilic Judah was participating in libation rituals for the deities Gad (Fortune)and Meni (Destiny), and, in a play on the latter deity's name, Yahweh says he will "destine" this apostate group to the sword (Isa 65:12). *See* GODS, GODDESSES.

TREVOR D. COCHELL

MENNA men´uh [Μεννά Menna]. Appears only in Luke's genealogy of Jesus. Menna is the son of Mattatha and the father of Melea (Luke 3:31).

MENORAH muh-nor´uh [מְנוֹרָה menorah]. The golden LAMPSTAND (or lampstands), one of the most prominent furnishings of ancient Israel's sacral structures—the wilderness TABERNACLE and the Jerusalem Temple (*see* TEMPLE, JERUSALEM)—is often referred to as the menorah, the Hebrew word for the support, or stand, for a light source. Like all national shrines in the ANE, the tabernacle and Temple were considered dwelling places for the deity and as such required the furnishings appropriate to a palatial residence. The menorah was thus no ordinary lampstand but rather an elaborate and costly piece of equipment. The tabernacle menorah appears in the Priestly writings of the Pentateuch (mainly in Exodus but also in Leviticus and Numbers), and those of the Temple are mentioned in Kings and Chronicles (and also Jeremiah and Zechariah). *See* LAMP, OT.

The most detailed information comes from the tabernacle texts of Exod 25:31-40 and 37:17-24. The menorah was to be a stand with six branches, with two sets of three opposite each other on each side of the central stand. However, it is neither clear that these branches would all have reached the same height nor that lamps were atop each one. All seven lamps may have been placed on the central stand; and one Priestly reference (Lev 24:2-4) refers to a single lamp, perhaps a seven-spouted one like those known from archaeology, set on the menorah of the tent of meeting. No indication of size is given for the menorah, in contrast to the fact that dimensions are provided for the other interior furnishings of the tabernacle. The menorah is to be made of pure gold, hammered into the specified shape. This kind of gold work would have been impossible without an underlying wooden form, although none is mentioned. The elaborate and yet incomplete information about the tabernacle menorah may reflect the fact that the Priestly texts in which it appears were shaped at the end of the Iron Age, perhaps reflecting information about the menorah of the early Second Temple superimposed on a simpler, single lamp menorah of a premonarchic Israelite shrine.

The incomplete details may not allow for an accurate reconstruction of the tabernacle menorah, but they do suggest something of its iconic value. The instructions in Exodus are replete with botanical terms: calyxes, petals, branches, and almond blossoms; and the overall branched form is strikingly similar to stylized trees depicted in representational art of the east Mediterranean in the Late Bronze and Iron ages. Such trees-of-life signify the divine power that provides the fertility of plant or even human life. When combined with the symbolism of its lamps, perhaps connoting divine omniscience, the menorah contributes to the conceptualization of God's presence in the tabernacle and also invokes cosmic paradigms of a tree (on a sacred mountain) as the center of the world.

The account in the book of Kings of the construction of the Jerusalem Temple devotes only one verse (1 Kgs 7:49) to the menorah. It specifies that there are to be ten golden menorahs, five on each side of the main hall of the building. Because no information about branches or multiple lamps for each menorah is provided, it is possible that each of these menorahs was a cylindrical stand on which a multi-spouted lamp was placed in accordance with the menorah of Zech 4:2. The object in Zechariah's vision, which probably dates to a time very soon after the dedication of the Second Temple, apparently has seven seven-spouted lamps atop a cylindrical stand. As a visionary object, it is likely more complicated than an actual menorah; yet it may indicate the remembered form of the First Temple menorahs.

Israel Erich Lessing/Art Resource, NY

Figure 1: A menorah on a bronze coin issued under Antigonos II. Location: Israel Museum (IDAM), Jerusalem

The menorah of the Second Temple is known from Josephus and rabbinic literature and also from artistic representations from the end of the Second Temple period and in the centuries immediately following its destruction in 70 CE.

Those sources do not agree on all aspects of the menorah's appearance but are virtually unanimous in indicating that the Second Temple had a single seven-branched menorah with a single-spouted lamp atop each of the branches. The Chronicler, writing in the Second Temple period, refers to the menorah (singular), not menorahs, of the First Temple and is likely influenced by the single menorah of his day (2 Chr 13:11).

Bibliography: Carol L. Meyers. *The Tabernacle Menorah: A Synthetic Study of a Symbol from the Biblical Cult* (2003).

CAROL MEYERS

MENSTRUATION [נִדָּה niddah]. Niddah, a nominal construction from the root ndd (נדד, or possibly ndh [נדה], a near synonym), carries the sense of "distancing, separation, chasing away" and literally means "expulsion, elimination." Niddah originally referred to menstrual discharge but later came to signify the menstruant herself. Other terms used for menstruation, although rare, include dawah (דָּוָה), "menstruating, sick, faint" (e.g., Lev 15:33) and ʿiddah (עִדָּה), "menstrual period" (e.g., Isa 64:6 [Heb. 64:5]). The LXX usually uses the term aphedros (ἄφεδρος) to translate niddah. The word *menstruation* does not occur in the NT, but note the example of the hemorrhaging woman of Mark 5:25, who may have had an abnormal menstrual flow (*see* WOMAN WITH FLOW OF BLOOD).

Menstruation conjures a paradox. On the one hand, it is a blessing because it denotes a fertile woman. On the other hand, it is a curse signifying lack of conception and sometimes miscarriage. In biblical thought, the loss of life-giving fluids and its reminder of human mortality probably gave rise to labeling menstruants impure (*see* CLEAN AND UNCLEAN). A menstruant must bathe and launder after seven days, and then she is considered pure at sunset. Bathing is not explicitly required; however. a person who touches her bed/seat (Lev 15:19-22) must bathe, *a fortiori*, the menstruant (compare *m. Mikw.* 8:1, 5). *See* BATHING; MIQVAH, MIQVEH.

Like other impurity bearers in the ANE, the menstruant was expected to keep away from sacred things. Sacred festivals and sacred food were off limits. This cross-cultural phenomenon is reflected in Greco-Roman culture (Pliny the Elder, *Nat. Hist.* 7.65; 28.23.78–80).

While Jewish concern was primarily directed at maintaining the purity of sancta, many Jews, e.g., the Pharisees, also attempted to keep purity in the ordinary realm. Indeed, according to Lev 15:31, the buildup of impurity in the community defiles the sanctuary situated within it even without direct contact. Thus, in many families, menstruants were avoided (compare Gen 31:35; 4Q274 1 I, 4–6) and, in some communities, they were probably sequestered (compare the Temple Scroll [11Q19 XLVIII, 16–17]; Josephus [*Ant.* 3.261] and the Mishnah [*m. Nid.* 7:4]).

According to Israelite law, a man who has sexual intercourse with a menstruant takes on himself her impurity, and is subject to death by divine agency (Lev 15:24; 18:19, 29; Ezek 18:6). The Dead Sea Scrolls complain of priests who sin by sleeping with menstruants (4Q266 6 II 2). In order to avoid violation of the Torah, rabbinic law requires women to count their days of impurity strictly and inspect themselves for any appearance of menstrual blood (*m. Nid.* 66*a*, 67*b*).

In nonlegal texts, the term **niddah** is used for impurity in general. Several writers refer to sin metaphorically as **niddah** (e.g., 2 Chr 29:5; Ezra 9:11; Lam 1:17; Ezek 7:19-20). In the Dead Sea Scrolls **niddah** often refers to the degenerate human condition (1QH IX, 22; "sin of humanity," 1QS XI, 14–15).

Bibliography: Shaye Cohen. "Menstruants and the Sacred in Judaism and Christianity." *Women's History and Ancient History.* Sarah B. Pomeroy, ed. (1991) 273–99; Moshe Greenberg. "The Etymology of *Niddah* '(Menstrual) Impurity.'" *Solving Riddles and Untying Knots.* Z. Zevit et al., eds. (1995) 69–77; Hannah K. Harrington. *The Purity Texts* (2004); Amy-Jill Levine. "Discharging Responsibility: Matthean Jesus, Biblical Law, and Hemorrhaging Woman." *A Feminist Companion to Matthew.* Amy-Jill Levine, ed. (2001) 70–87; Jacob Milgrom. *Leviticus 1–16.* AB 3A (1991); Rahel Wasserfall, ed. *Women and Water: Menstruation in Jewish Life and Law* (1999).

HANNAH K. HARRINGTON

MENUHOTH min-*yoo*'hoth [מְנֻחוֹת **menukhoth**]. A half-tribe referred to by the proper name HAROEH (1 Chr 2:52) and descended from SHOBAL (Gen 36:20, 23-29; etc.). The Menuhoth are unknown, unless they are related to the "half of the Manahathites" (v. 54), which seem to be etymologically related (*see* MANAHATH, MANAHATHITES). An Edomite chieftain named Shobal appears with a son named Manahath (Gen 36:23, 1 Chr 1:40), highlighting the links between Judah and its southern neighbors.

RALPH K. HAWKINS

MEONOTHAI mee-on'oh-th*i* [מְעוֹנֹתַי meʿonothay]. In Judah's genealogy, one of OTHNIEL's two sons and the father of OPHRAH (1 Chr 4:13-14).

MEPHAATH mi-fay'ath [מֵפַעַת mefaʿath]. Means "splendor," "height." One of the Levitical cities (Josh 13:18; 21:37; 1 Chr 6:79) among the cities of the tribe of Reuben, east of the Dead Sea. Later a Moabite city, it was mentioned as a punished city in Jer 48:21. *See* LEVITICAL CITIES, TOWNS; MERARI, MERARITES.

MEPHIBOSHETH mi-fib'oh-sheth [מְפִיבֹשֶׁת **mefivosheth**]. Second Samuel uses the name Mephibosheth ("out of the mouth of shame") for two characters. 1. The son of Saul and Rizpah whom David delivers to the Gibeonites for execution along with six other sons of Saul (2 Sam 21:8-9).

2. Jonathan's son and Saul's grandson whom David spares due to his promise to treat Jonathan's family kindly (2 Sam 21:7; compare 1 Sam 20:14-15). It is possible that the use of the name Mephibosheth for both son of Saul and the son of Jonathan could be the result of scribal alteration. Rather than Mephibosheth, the name of Jonathan's son may be MERIB-BAAL based on the genealogies in 2 Chr 8:34 and 9:30. Although Jonathan's son continues King Saul's lineage (2 Sam 9:12), some interpreters suggest that David spares him because he does not consider him a legitimate threat to his throne due to Mephibosheth's disability (4:4; 9:3, 13; 19:26). Thus, David could afford not only to spare him, but even restore Saul's land to him and give him a permanent place at the king's table (9:7-13). David, however, explains this ostensible kindness to Mephibosheth as an expression of loyalty to Jonathan (9:7).

Other interpreters suggest that David perceives Mephibosheth as a threat. David may have given him a permanent place at his table in order to keep an eye on him. In fact, when Ziba accuses Mephibosheth of disloyalty to David during Absalom's revolt, David takes Saul's property away from him and gives it to Ziba (2 Sam 16:1-4). After Absalom's revolt, Mephibosheth tells David that Ziba slandered him (19:24-30). David responds by dividing Saul's property equally between Ziba and Mephibosheth (19:29).

Although the Bible does not report which party actually tells David the truth, the majority of interpreters sympathize with Mephibosheth over Ziba. According to some rabbinic traditions, the Davidic kingdom was divided, fell into idolatry, and went into exile because David divided the property promised to Mephibosheth (*b. Shabb.* 56b). Several other rabbinic writings even present Mephibosheth as a great Torah scholar since the Hebrew word **bosheth** (בֹּשֶׁת, "shame") appears as both an element of the name Mephibosheth and in reference to one who speaks Torah before kings in Ps 119:46 (*b. Ber.* 4a; compare *b. Eruv.* 53b; *y. Qidd.* 65c).

Nonetheless, interpretative opinions about Mephibosheth vary. The rabbis also claim that David divided Saul's property because he thought Mephibosheth showed a disrespectful attitude (*b. Shabb.* 56b). They suggest that this is why Chronicles calls him "Merib-baal," which they understand as meaning "one who strives with his lord."

Bibliography: Gordon Hamilton. "New Evidence for the Authenticity of bšt in Hebrew Personal Names and for Its Use as a Divine Epithet in Biblical Texts." *CBQ* 60 (1998) 228–50; Stuart Lasine. "Judicial Narratives and the Ethics of Reading: The Reader as Judge of the Dispute between Mephibosheth and Ziba." *HS* 30 (1989) 49–69; Jeremy Schipper. *Disability Studies and the Hebrew Bible: Figuring Mephibosheth in the David Story* (2006).

JEREMY SCHIPPER

MERAB mee′rab [מֵרַב merav]. Means "increase." Eldest daughter of King Saul (1 Sam 14:49). In accordance with the promise he made before the engagement with Goliath (1 Sam 17:25) Saul betrothed Merab to David. Before that marriage Merab's younger sister MICHAL had displayed her attachment to David, so Michal married David instead of Merab. Merab was then married to ADRIEL the Meholathite, to whom she bore five sons (2 Sam 21:8).

CHANNA COHEN STUART

MERAIAH mi-ray′yuh [מְרָיָה merayah]. According to Nehemiah's list of priests in the days of JOIAKIM, Meraiah was head of the ancestral house of Seraiah (Neh 12:12).

MERAIOTH mi-ray′yoth [מְרָיוֹת merayoth]. Priestly name in the OT. 1. A high-priestly descendant of Aaron who was an ancestor of Zadok (1 Chr 6:6-7, 52) and of Ezra (Ezra 7:3).

2. Zadok's father (1 Chr 9:11; Neh 11:11), in contradiction to references to Ahitub as the father of Zadok (e.g., 1 Chr 6:8; 18:16).

3. A postexilic priestly family according to Neh 12:15. In Neh 12:3 the family name is instead MEREMOTH.

CECILIA WASSÉN

MERARI, MERARITES mi-rah′ri, mi-rah′rit [מְרָרִי merari, בְּנֵי מְרָרִי bene merari; Μεραρί Merari]. 1. The third-born son of Levi (Gen 46:11).

2. The Levites descended from Merari (Num 26:57). They formed the third branch of the Levites and were divided into two clans named after the sons of Merari, MAHLI and MUSHI (1 Chr 6:19). According to Num 4:29-33, the Merarites were in charge of carrying the poles and bases that made up the frame of the tabernacle. They were provided with four wagons and eight oxen to assist them with this task (Num 7:8). When the tabernacle was set up, the Merarites were to camp on the north side, forming a barrier between the Israelites and the sacred precinct (Num 3:35). It is likely that the Merarites functioned as priests at some point in Israel's history, but the scheme presented in the books of Numbers and Chronicles subordinates them to the Aaronic priests.

First Chronicles 6:44-48 states that the Merarites served as musicians in the Temple of Solomon in Jerusalem. Merarites, along with the Kohathites, also functioned as gatekeepers in the Temple (1 Chr 26:12-19). During the reign of HEZEKIAH Merarites were part of the group that cleansed the Temple (2 Chr 29:12-15), a job they performed again during the reforms of Josiah (2 Chr 34:12). In the postexilic period, Merarites formed part of the group that returned from Babylon with Ezra (Ezra 8:15-20). If the SHEREBIAH in Neh 8:7 is the same as the Sherebiah in Ezra 8:18, then the Merarites were among those who interpreted when Ezra read the law to the people (Neh 8:5-8). *See* CHRONICLES, FIRST AND SECOND BOOKS OF; DOORKEEPER; EZRA AND NEHEMIAH, BOOKS OF; LEVI, LEVITES; MUSICAL INSTRUMENTS; PENTATEUCH; TABERNACLE; TEMPLE, JERUSALEM.

3. The father of Judith (Jdt 8:1; 16:6). *See* JUDITH; JUDITH, BOOK OF.

KEVIN A. WILSON

MERATHAIM mer′uh-thay′im [מְרָתַיִם merathayim]. Meaning "double rebellion." A land mentioned in Jer 50:21, referring by synecdoche to Babylon. The name plays on the Akkadian name Marratu, for the salt-marshes of southern Babylonia. PEKOD (meaning "punishment") in the par. line refers to another region of Babylonia, where the Puqudu tribe lived.

MERCENARY [שָׂכִיר sakhir; μισθωτός misthōtos, δύναμις dynamis]. A military person hired to fight for wages, explicitly occurring only once in the OT, as mercenaries of Egypt (Jer 46:21), but the practice of hiring military fighters is clearly an integral element in many biblical stories. The band of fighting men who join and follow David in 1 and 2 Samuel are clearly to be considered mercenaries, particularly in narratives where they benefit directly from the victories (1 Sam 30). To this group may also belong the warriors who follow David even after he has become king in Jerusalem. The groups identified as the Pelethites, Cherethites, and Gittites came from different groups of the Philistines, were hired by David during the time he lived in the south, and led raids against different Philistine territories and cities (2 Sam 8:18; 15:18; 20:7, 23). As a matter of continued practice, there are allusions in 2 Kgs 18:21 to Hezekiah's relying upon Egyptian assistance against Assyria. In Judith, Achior and his associates were said to be mercenaries (Jdt 6:2, 5), and various groups involved in the Maccabean Revolt hired mercenaries (1 Macc 4:35; 6:29; 15:3; 2 Macc 10:14, 24). *See* CHERETHITES AND PELETHITES; WAR, METHODS, TACTICS, WEAPONS OF (BRONZE AGE THROUGH PERSIAN PERIOD); WAR, METHODS, TACTICS, WEAPONS OF (HELLENISTIC THROUGH ROMAN PERIODS).

C. MARK MCCORMICK

MERCHANT [כְּנַעַן khena'an, סוֹחֵר sokher, רוֹכֵל rokhel; ἔμπορος emporos]. An itinerant trader or businessperson, whose traveling about is reflected by the

Hebrew roots skhr (סחר) and rkhl (רכל), which can both mean to "turn" or "go about." The itinerancy of merchants included travel to purchase homespun fabric from farmers (Prov 31:24) and to market their wares door-to-door (Neh 13:16). In a well-known parable, an emporos is traveling "in search of fine pearls" (Matt 13:45). It was not unusual for merchants to travel great distances in order to secure their merchandise, as, e.g., with incense and spices from Arabia (e.g., Ezek 27:22-23) and gold from Africa (e.g., 1 Kgs 9:26-27). A network of trade routes spanned the ANE, making it possible for caravans to travel to and from these distant locations. When they were not engaged in overland trade, merchants traveled to and from the marketplace or bazaar where they set up shop (Neh 3:31-32; 13:19-20).

Merchants were regulated by both custom and law codes in the ancient world. Many of the Mari and Nuzi tablets illustrate the customs of ancient Semitic merchants. Both the Code of Hammurabi (108) and the Torah (Lev 19:35-36; Deut 25:13-16) regulated weights and measures. Prophetic oracles include denouncements of dishonesty among merchants (e.g., Hos 12:7; Amos 8:5-6; Mic 6:10-11). As part of his call for transformation among God's people, Ezekiel demanded that practical justice be applied to the marketplace (Ezek 45:10-12). In Rev 18:3, "merchants of the earth" are highlighted among those who will mourn the fall of Babylon. *See* HAMMURABI, CODE OF; TRADE AND COMMERCE; TRADER.

RALPH K. HAWKINS

MERCY SEAT [כַּפֹּרֶת kapporeth]. From the Hebrew root kpr (כפר), meaning "to cover over," referring specifically to "covering" wrong, this was the covering for the ARK OF THE COVENANT. Two cherubim faced each other and spread their wings over the elaborate, gold mercy seat (Exod 25:16-21).

The ark was placed in the MOST HOLY PLACE in the TABERNACLE and functioned as the point where the priests sprinkled blood for the atonement of Israel (Lev 16:14-16), as well as the place above which God met with Moses (Exod 25:22; Lev 16:2). This element in the Priestly description transforms the ark from a container for the covenant into a portable throne for the DIVINE PRESENCE.

C. MARK MCCORMICK

MERCY, MERCIFUL [רָחַם rakham, רַחֲמִים rakhamim, רַחוּם rakhum; ἐλεέω eleeō, ἔλεος eleos, οἰκτιρμός oiktirmos]. Mercy is a synonym for *compassion* and means to have pity or to feel sorry for someone.

A. Old Testament

The most common words in Hebrew to express mercy or compassion are rakham ("to have compassion") and its derivatives, the noun rakhamim and adjectives rakhum and rakhamani (רַחֲמָנִי). Rakham appears forty-seven times in Hebrew, rakhamim thirty-nine times, rakhum thirteen times, and rakhamani once. While the rakham word group is used largely to describe the mercy of Yahweh, khamal (חָמַל, "to have compassion on," "to be sorry for"; forty-one times) and its derivative khemlah (חֶמְלָה; twice) and khus (חוּס, "to have compassion or pity"; twenty-four times) are used more broadly.

In only a few cases is human mercy indicated with the noun rakhamim. Joseph is overcome with rakhamim for his brothers (Gen 43:30), and the rakhamim of the mother "burns" for her child about to be divided up (1 Kgs 3:26). In both, rakhamim affects Joseph and the mother emotionally and physically. In Prov 12:10, "the mercy of the wicked" is said to be cruel, but that is tantamount to saying the wicked lack mercy. In these texts, rakhamim is an emotion triggered by afflictions in others that results in binding one to the afflicted empathically. At the same time, rakhamim also separates one from the afflicted, since mercy presupposes a differential between the granter of mercy and its recipient. For the recipient, accepting mercy means accepting the relationship and its structure, and rejecting mercy means the dissolution of that bond. Thus God has to allow Daniel to receive compassion from the palace master (Dan 1:9), for Daniel's allegiance lies first with God.

This differential is at the heart of divine mercy toward human beings, though divine mercy is less an emotion than an act. Divine mercy is initiated by Yahweh, who has absolute freedom to show or withhold compassion, and human beings are only in the position to receive mercy. Thus, even human mercy is a gift from God. In Exod 33:19, God establishes a covenant with Moses by proclaiming God's own name: "I will be gracious to whom I will be gracious, and will show mercy (rakham) on whom I will show mercy (rakham)." Grace and mercy, along with steadfast love (khesedh חֶסֶד) and faithfulness (ʾemeth אֱמֶת), are concrete expressions of God's covenantal election, through which Israel becomes a people (Isa 54:10). Accepting divine mercy means accepting this unequal relationship and the commandments stipulated therein. *See* KHESED.

Within the boundaries of the covenant, only insiders who keep the ordinances of the covenant can receive mercy. In a hymn praising God's salvation in the wilderness (Ps 103), Yahweh, as a father to his children, shows compassion only to those who fear him and keep his commandments (vv. 13, 17-18), though God's compassionate nature mitigates the anger (vv. 8-10). Jeremiah 12:14-17 seems at first sight to be an exception, for Yahweh is said to show compassion to Israel's evil neighbors. But that comes with a condition—only if they swear off their allegiance to Baal and "diligently learn the ways of my people, to swear by my name" (v. 16).

When divine mercy is so closely tied to the covenant, the exile casts doubt on the covenant's continual validity. The exile happened because Yahweh's mercy was withdrawn. Seen from this perspective, sin is a refusal of mercy and its consequence is abandonment (Isa 60:10; 63:15). Yahweh withdraws steadfast love and mercy from Judah and hastens its collapse (Jer 16:5). Yahweh delivers Judah and Israel into the hands of Babylon who, in contrast to God, will show no mercy (Isa 47:6; Jer 21:7). Yahweh, too, shows no mercy to Israel, all foreign occupiers, even orphans and widows (Isa 9:11-21 [Heb. 9:10-20]).

Postexilic appeals to the mercy of God take two forms: mitigation of punishment and hope for restoration. Jeremiah appeals to God to show mercy, so that the king of Babylon will show Israel mercy and let the people return to their homeland (Jer 42:12). Thus even the captors' mercy finds its ultimate source in Yahweh (see 1 Kgs 8:50; 2 Chr 30:9). Nothing, therefore, escapes the hand of the Lord, be it destruction of Israel (Jer 6:23) or Israel's enemies (Isa 13:18; Jer 50:42). A second form in which divine mercy manifests itself is to give hope for restoration (Isa 14:1; 27:7-11; 30:18; 54:7-8; Jer 30:18; 31:20; 33:26; Mic 7:18-19). Yahweh turns away from Israel in anger, but only for a short while, for Yahweh remembers his own mercy even in anger (Hab 3:2). This juxtaposition of anger with compassion is starkest in Hosea's warnings. Judgment against Israel (1:6) is pitted against mercy on Judah (1:7; 2:23 [Heb. 2:25]), and the frightful warning of no mercy on Israel's children (2:4 [Heb. 2:6]) is set against the promise of a new covenant in righteousness, justice, steadfast love, and mercy (2:18-20 [Heb. 2:20-22]). In less striking but no less vivid fashion, the second Servant Song (Isa 49) paints the servant as "one deeply despised, abhorred by the nations, the slave of rulers" (v. 7), before reminding him of the covenant established long ago (vv. 7*a*-8). The compassion of the Lord, even greater than a mother's love for her newborn (v. 15), will guide the restored people to springs of water (v. 10).

Within the context of postexilic yearning for restoration, the parallelism between mercy (**rakhamim**) and God's steadfast goodness (**khesedh**) is crucial for the development of both concepts. While mercy is momentary and circumstantial, intently focused on the afflicted, steadfast love is a constant attribute of Yahweh in his covenant with Israel (see Isa 54:7-8). On the other hand, while **khesedh** in secular usage never means forgiveness, its connection with **rakhamim** helps stretch its meaning to include that very quality. Thus, in a lament, the psalmist pleads that Yahweh not remember his sins out of mercy and steadfast love (Ps 25:6-7). Likewise in Pss 40 and 51, a plea for mercy points to personal and corporation salvation, while steadfast love shows God's constant commitment to the covenant (40:11-12 [Heb. 40:12-13]; 51:1 [Heb. 51:3]; compare Ps 69:16 [Heb. 69:17]; 77:9 [Heb. 77:10]; Isa 63:7; Hos 2:19 [Heb. 2:21]).

Both **khesedh** and **rakhum** feature prominently in Exod 34:6-7, where Moses hears the Lord's self-proclamation as "a God merciful and gracious, slow to anger, and abounding in steadfast love and faithfulness, keeping steadfast love for the thousandth generation." "Merciful and gracious" (Spieckermann's compassion formula) is used as a title of Yahweh ten times (2 Chr 30:9; Neh 9:17, 31; Pss 86:15; 103:8; 111:4; 145:8; Joel 2:13; Jonah 4:2), and all are connected to the covenant. Here the compassion formula, combined with **khesedh** and **ʾemeth**, is balanced by a severe note of judgment: "Keeping steadfast love for the thousandth generation, forgiving iniquity and transgression and sin, yet by no means clearing the guilty, but visiting the iniquity of the parents upon the children and the children's children, to the third and the fourth generation" (Exod 34:7). This very tension is also found in Deut 4, where the consuming God of v. 24 is met by the merciful God of v. 31 (also see Deut 5:9-10, par. Exod 20:5-6; and Deut 7:9-10). The tension with punishment remains a defining characteristic of biblical mercy.

Twice human beings are bidden to emulate divine mercy. In Zech 7:9-10, the Lord says to Zechariah, "Render true judgments, show kindness and mercy to one another; do not oppress the widow, the orphan, the alien, or the poor; and do not devise evil in your hearts against one another." This prophecy clearly addresses an authority figure who could realize justice and mercy. In Ps 112, the compassion formula is used for the only time to address a human subject. Those who fear the Lord will "rise in the darkness as a light for the upright; they are gracious, merciful, and righteous" (v. 4). Psalms 111 and 112 form the two halves of a hymn of praise: the deeds of Yahweh rhapsodized in the first half ("the LORD is gracious and merciful," 111:4) are the model for human deeds (compare 112:5-9).

Uses of **khus** ("to spare" or "to pity") are primarily negative, as in the stereotypical formula "show no mercy or pity" (lit., "your eye will not spare"). The formula is found in Deut 7:16; 13:8 [Heb. 13:9]; 19:13, 21; 25:12; Ezek 5:11; 7:4, 9; 16:5. The same full formula is used in Isa 13:18, where **khus** is paralleled by **rakham**. In Ezek 24:14, the formula appears without *eye* but has the verb in the first-person singular. This slight variation is followed in Jer 13:14 (parallel **rakham**); 21:7. Occasionally, **khus** is used positively, "my eye spared them" (Ezek 20:17; compare Neh 13:22; Joel 2:17). In all these cases, **khus** refers to limiting punishments to the culprit that are otherwise deserved. Its background might well be casuistic law and apodictic legal formulation. The parallel term **khamal** ("to have compassion or pity on," "to be sorry for") is also used largely negatively to express pitilessness (Hab 1:17; Zech 11:6). In seven of the eight occurrences of the word in Ezekiel, the negative uses of **khamal** are intensified by adding **khus** as parallel. The result is a strong expression of "pitilessness and mercilessness."

B. New Testament

Three word groups are used to express mercy or compassion in the NT. The noun **eleos** appears twenty-seven times, the verb **eleeō** (or its bi-form **eleaō** ἐλεάω) thirty-two times, and the adjective **eleēmōn** (ἐλεήμων) twice. In the LXX, **eleos** normally translates **khesedh** and occasionally translates **rakhamim** (six times), while **eleos** is used for **khanan** (חָנַן) and **rakham** and **eleēmōn** mostly for **khannun** (חַנּוּן). The noun **oiktirmos**, a synonym of **eleos**, is used in the NT five times, the adjective **oiktirmōn** (οἰκτίρμων) three times, and the verb **oiktirō** (οἰκτίρω) twice. In the LXX **oiktirmos** translates **rakhamim** twenty-five times, while **oiktirmōn** translates **rakhum** twelve times and occasionally different forms of **khanan** (three times), and **oiktirō** translates **khanan** ten times and **rakham** twelve times. The noun **splanchnon** (σπλάγχνον; lit. "entrails" but fig. "compassion" in the NT; always in plural) and the verb **splanchnizomai** (σπλαγχνίζομαι, "to have compassion") are used infrequently in the LXX. In Prov 12:10 the noun is used for **rakhamim** and in 26:22 for **beten** (בֶּטֶן, "womb" or "belly"), but is otherwise found in passages with no Hebrew equivalents. The NT references to mercy and compassion are concentrated especially in the Synoptic Gospels and in Paul.

1. Synoptic Gospels

Luke seems to favor **eleos**, using it six times, five of which are in the birth narrative. Matthew uses it three times, but two of them come from Hos 6:6. Mark does not use **eleos** but uses **eleeō** three times. Matthew uses it seven times (three from Mark), with all but one with Jesus as subject, and Luke uses it four times (two from Mark), all but one with Jesus as subject. The **oiktirmos** word group does not appear in the Synoptics at all. **Splanchnon** appears in Luke–Acts twice but only once for mercy, whereas **splanchnizomai** appears only in the Synoptics, totaling twelve times. Of these, four are found in Mark, all with Jesus as subject. It appears in Matthew five times: three from Mark, one takes a human master as subject, and another has Jesus as subject, the last probably the result of emulating Mark. Luke uses the verb three times, only once with Jesus as subject. It follows that the use of **splanchnizomai** to express Jesus' compassion is ultimately traceable to Mark.

There seems to be no appreciable distinction between the three word groups in the Synoptics, though the only evidence comes from Luke. The good Samaritan who "was moved with pity" (**splanchnizomai**) toward the victim (10:33) is said to have done an **eleos** (v. 37). That **eleos** ("mercy") is used primarily to translate **khesedh** ("steadfast love") in the LXX might contribute to our hearing echoes of covenantal language. In later Judaism **khesedh** tends to blend with **rakhamim** since together the terms express God's covenantal faithfulness. This is especially clear in Luke 1–2, where there is a preponderance of covenantal themes. The mercy of God (1:50) recalls the covenantal Ps 103, except the fear formula (103:11, 17-18) is now eschatologically appropriated. Likewise, "remembrance of his mercy" (Luke 1:54) alludes to God's covenantal steadfast love (**khesedh**) and faithfulness in Ps 98:3. The covenant of "our ancestors" is explicitly mentioned in Luke 1:72 (compare Mic 7:20), but as is true in the Lukan prologue as a whole, the covenantal language is placed in an eschatological context. Thus, God's "tender mercy" (**splanchna eleous** [σπλάγχνα ἐλέους], Luke 1:78, which is unique in the NT but found also in *T. Zeb.* 7:3; 8:2, 6) would prompt "the dawn from on high" to break.

This dawning of the eschaton is illustrated in Jesus' healing the demoniac, because it is a demonstration that the Lord has compassion on the possessed (Mark 5:19). The healing not only heralds God's reign and the promised covenantal renewal, but it is brought about here and now by Jesus the Lord. The plea by the blind man of Jericho makes the same point (Mark 10:47-48 par. Matt 9:27; 20:30-31; Luke 18:38-39). He addresses Jesus by the biblical title "Son of David" in order to stress that Jesus is the fulfillment and bringer of divine mercy (for other uses of **eleēson me** [ἐλέησόν με], see Matt 15:22; 17:15; Luke 17:13). Biblical covenantal language now gives way to and is enfleshed by Jesus' practice of mercy and compassion. In anticipating the birth of Jesus the new age is announced, but in Jesus himself biblical mercy now finds its eschatological fulfillment. Accordingly, human mercy to one another must mirror this new eschatological situation (Matt 18:33). Only the merciful will be rewarded with God's mercy in the new reign (Matt 5:7).

2. Paul

Following Jewish tradition, Paul uses mercy in greeting (Gal 6:16). But Paul also goes beyond traditional usage by taking "Father of mercies" (2 Cor 1:3) to refer to the source of mercy in God. In this regard, *mercy* is synonymous with "divine grace" or "spiritual gift" (Rom 12:8; 1 Cor 7:25; 2 Cor 4:1; perhaps Phil 2:1), even healing (Phil 2:27).

Covenantal mercy colors Paul's usage of the **eleos** and **oiktirmos** word groups (used interchangeably by Paul). Derivatives from these two groups total nineteen times, eleven of which are found in Rom 9–11, where Paul elaborates on the paradox between divine faithfulness and freedom. All uses of mercy words stem from Exod 33:19, cited in Rom 9:15, 18. God's freedom to show mercy and wrath is reiterated in 9:23, which sets the stage for the allegory of the olive tree (11:17-24) and the complex citation of Isa 59:20-21 in Rom 11:26*b*-27. From there Paul draws the conclusion in

11:30-32 that even belief is dependent on election and freedom. Just as Jewish disbelief has led to mercy shown to the Gentiles, the Jews will indeed be shown mercy again (omitting second "now"). The whole discussion of covenantal mercy is recapitulated in "the mercies of God" of 12:1, a bridge to the ethical section of 12:1–15:13, and again in 15:9.

Paul only uses the noun **splanchnon**, which for Paul stands for the whole person as related to his or her affection for another. Thus, in 2 Cor 6:12 and 7:15, the term refers to Paul's and Titus' immense capacity to love the Corinthians. When Paul asks Philemon to refresh (**anapauō** ἀναπαύω) the **splanchna** (plural of **splanchnon**) of the saints (Phlm 7, 20), Paul in effect asks that they renew the mutual affections they have for one another. It is this connection between persons that enables Paul to use "compassion (**splanchna**) of Christ Jesus" to express his yearning for his readers (Phil 1:8). His in-Christness has so transformed the new community that they could become one. This unity in Christ, first formulated in Gal 3:28, thus extends the boundaries of **splanchna** from the individual to the communal, so that the Philippians' affection and mercy could complete Paul's joy (Phil 2:1-2). This is perhaps the only way to understand why Paul could call the converted Onesimus his very own **splanchna** (Phlm 12). *See* LOVE IN THE NT; LOVE IN THE OT.

Bibliography: E. C. MacLaurin. "The Semitic Background of Use of '*en splanchnois*.'" *PEQ* 103 (1971) 42–45; Katharine D. Sakenfeld. *The Meaning of* חֶסֶד *in the Hebrew Bible: A New Inquiry* (1978); H. Spieckermann. "Barmherzig und gnädig ist der Herr." *ZAW* 102 (1990) 1–18.

SZE-KAR WAN

MERED mee'rid [מֶרֶד **meredh**]. In Judah's genealogy, one of Ezrah's four sons. He married Bithiah, Pharaoh's daughter, and an unnamed Jewish wife (1 Chr 4:17-18).

MEREMOTH mer'uh-moth [מְרֵמוֹת **meremoth**; Μαρμωθί **Marmōthi**]. 1. Uriah's son who received the silver, the gold, and the vessels that Ezra brought to the Temple (Ezra 8:33; 1 Esd 8:62). He is listed as among those making repairs on the wall near the Fish Gate (Neh 3:4). He also worked on repairs extending from the door to the end of Eliashib's house (Neh 3:21).

Initially, he was excluded from the priesthood because his name was absent in the records (Ezra 2:61).

2. A descendant of Bani who dismissed his foreign wife and their children (Ezra 10:36).

3. A participant in the community's covenant renewal whose name appeared on the sealed document (Neh 10:5). Meremoth is listed as one of the priests and Levites who returned with Zerubbabel.

EMILY R. CHENEY

MERENPTAH. *See* MERNEPTAH.

MERES mee'reez [מֶרֶס **meres**]. One of the seven officials of Media and Persia who occupied a high rank and advised King AHASUERUS (Esth 1:14).

MERIBAH mer'i-bah [מְרִיבָה **merivah**]. In REPHIDIM the people complain to Moses because there is no water (Exod 17:1-7). Moses presents their complaint to God, who commands Moses to strike the rock at Horeb. Moses does so, producing water, and the name Rephidim is changed to MASSAH, "testing," and Meribah, "quarreling." Numbers 20:1-13 contains a parallel story where the name is changed to Meribah with no mention of Massah. This tradition is somewhat different in Deut 33:8 and Ps 81:7. Aaron's rebellion at Meribah is the reason he will not enter Canaan (Num 20:24). *See* KADESH, KADESH-BARNEA; ZIN, WILDERNESS OF.

KEVIN A. WILSON

MERIB-BAAL mer'ib-bay'uhl [מְרִיב בַּעַל **meriv baʿal**, מְרִי־בַעַל **meri-vaʿal**]. The son of JONATHAN (1 Chr 8:34; 9:40). Meri-baal means "rebellion of Baal," while Merib-baal means "opponent of Baal." Some have advocated reading these names in a more positive light as "hero of Baal" and "advocate of Baal," respectively.

In 1 Samuel, the name of Jonathan's son is MEPHIBOSHETH (**mefivosheth** מְפִיבֹשֶׁת), meaning "from the mouth of shame," and is probably a constructed replacement to avoid using the name of Baal. Similar changes can be seen in the change of Ishbaal (1 Chr 9:39) to Ishbosheth (2 Sam 2:8).

C. MARK MCCORMICK

MERIBATH-KADESH mer'i-buhth-kay'dish [מְרִיבַת קָדֵשׁ **merivath qadhesh**]. At two places named MERIBAH, Moses struck a rock to produce water for the Israelites. The second, located near Kadesh (Num 20:1-13), became known as Meribath-kadesh because of its proximity to Kadesh. Because Yahweh was displeased with Moses and Aaron there, he barred them from entering Canaan (Num 27:14; Deut 32:51). Meribath-kadesh is used as a synonym for Kadesh (or KADESH-BARNEA) in descriptions of the southern border of Judah (Ezek 47:19; 48:28).

A. HEATH JONES III

MERIT. Biblical merit is found at the intersection of divine freedom and human responsibility. All rewards from God are gifts granted out of God's generosity; no one merits rewards with good work or proper ritual. Appearing to Abraham, the Lord promises a covenant with him as a REWARD, even though the context makes no mention of merit. By juxtaposing gift with reward, however, the door is open to earning a reward by merit. This understanding is especially prevalent in the wisdom literature (so, e.g., Prov 11:18). In the kingdom sayings of Jesus, gift and merit stand in eschatological tension. While heavenly reward seems to be based on human merit (Mark 10:21 and par.), ultimately God gives freely according to divine freedom. Thus, workers in the vineyard receive the same wage no matter how long they have labored because it is based not on their work but on the generosity of the owner (Matt 20:1-16). Paul maintains the same tension: justification is spoken of as a reward only as a result of GRACE (Rom 4:4). But if justification is not based on merit, merit loses its sense of desserts, and good work becomes an end in itself. *See* JUSTIFICATION, JUSTIFY.

SZE-KAR WAN

MERKAVAH MYSTICISM. The rabbinic literature regarded the **merkavah** (מֶרְכָּבָה), the heavenly "throne-chariot" of God described in Ezek 1 and 10, as a dangerous topic that could actually harm those who studied it. The Babylonian Talmud tells of four 2nd-cent. rabbis who entered "paradise" (arguably the celestial Temple, site of the **merkavah**), where one died, one went mad, one became a heretic, and only Rabbi Akiva returned unharmed.

The Hekhalot literature is a bizarre collection of Jewish mystical texts in Hebrew and Aramaic that forms the basis of "merkavah mysticism." It seems to have been composed from late antiquity to the early Middle Ages and the contents of the individual works often vary widely in the manuscripts (*see* ENOCH, THIRD BOOK OF). These works tell of mystical adventures (including the story of the four who entered paradise) and quasi-shamanic ritual practices pseudepigraphically attributed to certain 2nd-cent. rabbis. The texts purport to describe either how to "descend" (i.e., ascend) through the seven celestial "palaces" (**hekhaloth** הֵיכָלוֹת) to the **merkavah** to sing the celestial liturgy with the angels, or else how to compel angels, especially the **sar torah** (שַׂר תּוֹרָה) or Prince of Torah, to descend from heaven to earth and grant the summoner supernatural knowledge of Torah and other powers.

Bibliography: James R. Davila. "The Hodayot Hymnist and the Four Who Entered Paradise." *RevQ* 17/65–68 (1996) 457–78; James R. Davila. *Descenders to the Chariot: The People behind the Hekhalot Literature* (2001); Peter Schäfer. *The Hidden and Manifest God: Some Major Themes in Early Jewish Mysticism* (1993).

JAMES R. DAVILA

MERNEPTAH muhr´nep-tah´. Merneptah, fourth king of the Egyptian Nineteenth Dynasty, was the thirteenth and oldest surviving son of the long-lived king RAMESSES II. His name means "beloved of Ptah."

Matt Floreen/www.mattfloreen.com

Figure 1: Merneptah Stele, closeup of Israel, collection of Egyptian Museum

Merneptah defended Egypt against incursions by the Libyans and Sea Peoples. *See* EGYPT; PHARAOH.

The earliest reference to Israel appears on the so-called "Israel stela," a victory stela commemorating Merneptah's victory over the Libyans in his fifth year. The conclusion extols the king as pacifier of Syria-Palestine, specifically Canaan, Ashkelon, Gezer, Israel, and Yanoam. The text attests the existence of Israel in the late 13th cent. BCE. The orthography suggests that the scribe understood Israel to be a tribe rather than a town or territory; the writing of Israel concludes with the people determinative rather than the town or hill-country determinative. The Judean locale Nephtoah (Josh 15:9; 18:15) is named after Merneptah.

CAROLYN HIGGINBOTHAM

MERODACH mi-roh′dak [מְרֹדָךְ merodhakh]. A long form of the name of the Babylonian god MARDUK. It appears in Jer 50:2 and in the names of the Babylonian kings MERODACH-BALADAN (2 Kgs 20:12; Isa 39:1) and EVIL-MERODACH (2 Kgs 25:27; Jer 52:31). The god was also known as BEL.

MERODACH-BALADAN mi-roh′dak-bal′uh-duhn [מְרֹדַךְ בַּלְאֲדָן merodhakh bal'adhan, בְּרֹאדַךְ בַּלְאֲדָן bero'dhakh bal'adhan]. Marduk-apla-iddina II (Akkadian) was sheikh of the Chaldean Bit Yakin tribe whose territory lay in the marshes of southern Iraq and who profited from the camel caravan trade to Arabia. In 729 BCE, he paid tribute to Tiglath-pileser III as king of Assyria and Babylon and was recognized by him as king of the Sealand. Taking advantage of the confusion surrounding the overthrow of Shalmaneser V by Sargon II (722), he seized the throne in Babylon. Sargon II dethroned Marduk-apla-iddina (710) and besieged him in his capital Dur-Yakin (709–707), but he managed to escape and take refuge with his Elamite allies. Riding on the heels of a successful revolt against the new king, Sennacherib, by a Babylonian Marduk-zakir-shumi II, Marduk-apla-iddina ousted the latter and reclaimed Babylon (703). His allies included Elamites, Arabs, and Hezekiah of Judah. Isaiah strongly disapproved of the connection and warned that no good would come of it (2 Kgs 20:12-19; Isa 39). Marduk-apla-iddina was ousted after nine months by Sennacherib. In the face of a second campaign (700), he collected the gods of his land and the bones of his fathers from their graves and fled by ship to Elam, where he died (ca. 694). His descendants continued to lead the tribe of Bit Yakin after his death. Some were loyal Assyrian governors; others tried and failed to emulate their ancestor's achievements.

JOANN SCURLOCK

MEROM, WATERS OF mee′rom [מֵי מֵרוֹם me merom]. The Israelite army under Joshua and a Canaanite coalition of armies did battle by the waters of Merom (Josh 11:5, 7), whose actual location is unknown. A common identification has been with Lake Huleh in northern Galilee, above the Sea of Galilee. However, several questions have been raised: why it would be called "waters" rather than "sea" as are both the Sea of Galilee and Dead Sea, the directions of flight from the battle, and the absence of a specific site identified as Merom.

Another common identification has been MEIRON, a site near Wadi Meiron in the foothills of Mount Meiron (Jebel Jarmaq). However, excavations at that site indicated no permanent settlement there prior to the Hellenistic period, and excavators specifically say the site should not be confused with Merom.

Merom is mentioned in the reports of the campaigns of Thutmose III, Tiglath-pileser III, and Ramesses II as conquered by them, suggesting Merom was a significant Canaanite site in northern Galilee from at least the Late Bronze Age (Thutmose) until mid-8th cent. BCE (Tiglath-pileser).

Yohanan Aharoni suggested Merom be identified with Tell el-Khirbeh, approximately 8 mi. west-northwest of Hazor. More recently, Gal suggested Merom as Tel Qarney Hittin, approximately 4 mi. west of the Sea of Galilee near its north-south midpoint. Gal sees Josh 11 as recording a list of major Canaanite cities in the valleys encircling Galilee: Hazor in the Huleh Valley, Shimron in the Jezreel Valley, Achshaph in the Plain of Akko, and Tel Qarney Hittin between Hazor and Shimron in the Plain of Kinnereth/Gennesaret.

Bibliography: Yohanan Aharoni and Michael Avi-Yonah. "The Battle of the Waters of Merom." *The Macmillan Bible Atlas* (1977); Zvi Gal. "The Late Bronze Age in Galilee: A Reassessment." *BASOR* 272 (1988) 79–83.

JOEL F. DRINKARD JR.

MERONOTHITE mi-ron′oh-th*i*t [מֵרֹנֹתִי meronothi]. Jehdeiah the Meronothite was the official in charge of donkeys during David's reign (1 Chr 27:30). Jadon the Meronothite helped to repair the wall of Jerusalem after the exile (Neh 3:7). The location of Meronoth is unknown; Jadon's colleagues, however, came from cities in Benjamin.

MEROZ mee′roz [מֵרוֹז meroz]. The town of Meroz appears in the Song of Deborah's description of the battle between the forces of Barak and Sisera. Meroz (Judg 5:23) likely was located in the Jezreel Valley because the battle took place in the Jezreel Valley "at Taanach, by the waters of Megiddo" (Judg 5:19). While the exact location of Meroz is unknown, its inclusion in the song and the cursing of its people suggest that it had a choice to support Barak against Sisera, but it instead remained neutral. The town's name is remembered because of this shameful failure (compare Chorazin, which only appears in the Bible as an example of a town that rejected Jesus; Matt 11:21//Luke 10:13).

VICTOR H. MATTHEWS

MERRAN mer´uhn [Μερράν Merran]. A city along with TEMAN in Edom known for wisdom (Bar 3:23). The name may actually have been a misreading of MEDAN or Midian.

MESAD HASHAVYAHU. This archaeological site in the Judean region of Yabneh Yam yielded archaeological remains from the Iron II and Persian periods along with some "Greek" sherds. Most significantly, several Old Hebrew ostraca were also discovered and are dated in the late 7th cent. BCE. The largest of the ostraca, a letter, contains important legal material that complements pentateuchal materials (Exod 22:25-26; Deut 24:10-13). *See* INSCRIPTIONS.

Bibliography: Joseph Naveh. "A Hebrew Letter from the Seventh Century B.C." *IEJ* 10 (1963) 129–39; Joseph Naveh. "The Excavations at Mesad Hashavyahu: Preliminary Report." *IEJ* 12 (1962) 89–113; Joseph Naveh. "More Hebrew Inscriptions from Mesad Hashavyahu." *IEJ* 12 (1962) 27–32.

CHRISTOPHER A. ROLLSTON

MESALOTH mes´uh-loth [Μεσσαλώθ Messalōth, Μαισαλώθ Maisalōth]. Demetrius I dispatched Bacchides to besiege Mesaloth in the West Galilean town of Arbela after the death of Nicanor (1 Macc 9:1-2). Hebrew etymology and Josephus' account (*Ant.* 12.420–25) indicate that Mesaloth was probably an ascent (steps) to caves rather than a place-name.

MESHA mee´shuh [מֵשָׁא mesha᾽]. 1. A place marking a boundary of the territory where SHEM's descendants through ARPACHSHAD lived (Gen 10:30). It is unclear whether Mesha was a city or a territory, and suggested identifications of Mesha are highly speculative. SEPHAR, the other location in Gen 10:30, is also unknown.

2. A son of Caleb (1 Chr 2:42). The LXX reads MARESHAH instead of Mesha.

3. One of the sons of SHAHARAIM, a Benjaminite living in Moab (1 Chr 8:9), who had sent away two of his wives. Another wife, HODESH, bore him Mesha. *See* MASSA.

KEVIN A. WILSON

4. Mesha (mesha῾ מֵישַׁע), which means "salvation," was a mid-9th cent. BCE Moabite king known through two sources: 2 Kgs 3 and the MOABITE STONE (also known as the Mesha Stele). According to the Mesha Stele, Mesha was the son of Chemosh[yat], who ruled Moab for thirty years prior to Mesha; he was a devotee of the god CHEMOSH, whom Mesha believed to have intervened in his behalf. Both the OT and the Mesha Stele indicate that during a period of the Israelite Omride dynasty, Moab was under Israelite domination (Mesha Stele line 5; 2 Kgs 3:4). Israel's annual tax on Mesha consisted of large quantities of sheep and of rams' wool (2 Kgs 3:4). At some point during the reign of the Omrides (during the reign of either Ahab [Mesha Stele] or Jehoram [2 Kgs 3:1]) Mesha rebelled against this domination. In the biblical text, Mesha faces a coalition of Jehoram, Jehoshaphat (king of Judah), and the king of Edom, supported by the Israelite prophet Elisha. Mesha's defeat by the coalition ends with him offering his son as a burnt offering on the wall of Kir-hareseth (2 Kgs 3:25-27). The Mesha Stele portrays Mesha both as successful in his endeavor to rid Moab of Israelite oppression and as a successful builder of the Moabite kingdom. *See* MOAB, MOABITES.

JOHN I. LAWLOR

MESHA STELE. *See* MOABITE STONE.

MESHACH. *See* SHADRACH, MESHACH, ABEDNEGO.

MESHASH, KHIRBET EL. This archaeological site, whose modern Israeli name is Tel Masos, consists of three discrete areas of settlement in the BEER-SHEBA region: the Middle Bronze Age, the Iron Age I, and the Iron Age II. The site is situated at the intersection of the region's north-south and east-west routes. Although various proposals have been made, there is no consensus regarding the ancient name of this site.

The most important of the Middle Bronze Age architectural remains is a RAMPART that enclosed some 4 ac. of land. Near the Middle Bronze settlement was the Iron Age I settlement, unfortified, consisting of some 15 ac., established on top of Chalcolithic cave dwellings, and reportedly revealing three strata totaling five distinct phases. The first phases might reflect the presence of some sort of semi-nomadic group, but the later phases have features such as a four-roomed house that reflect some sort of sedentary population. Significantly, there is an absence of collared-rim jars that some consider to be markers of the early Israelites, but present are examples of coastal pottery (e.g., Philistine pottery, Phoenician "bichrome" ware). A scarab associated with the reign of Sethi II has also been found. Although sometimes the Iron I site is said to have been occupied by early Israelites, some debated markers traditionally associated with Israelite identity are missing thus indicating the complexity of issues surrounding questions of ethnic identity (*see* ARCHAEOLOGY).

The Iron II tell, located some 200 m from the Iron I settlement, should be considered a small fortress, but several fragmentary Iron II Old Hebrew ostraca have been found, at least two of which contain lists of personal names. Arguably, these may be the products of a small Judean administrative apparatus in the south. *See* INSCRIPTIONS.

Bibliography: Yohanan Aharoni. "Excavations at Tel Masos." *Tel Aviv* 2 (1975) 97–124; Volkmar Fritz. "The

Israelite 'Conquest' in the Light of Recent Excavations at Khirbet el-Meshash." *BASOR* 241 (1981) 61–73.

CHRISTOPHER A. ROLLSTON

MESHECH mee'shek [מֶשֶׁךְ meshekh]. 1. In the Table of Nations, Meshech is related as the seventh son of Japheth, and comes immediately after TUBAL (Gen 10:2//1 Chr 1:5).

2. In 1 Chr 1:17 Meshech appears among the sons of Shem, instead of Mashin the par. text of Gen 10:23. But since the Peshitta and Vulgate versions of Chronicles read Mash as in Genesis, it is possible that the Chronicler either reflects his *Vorlage* (LXX Gen 10:23: Mosoch Μόσοχ) or attempts to identify the unfamiliar name with a familiar one.

3. A land located in east Asia Minor (modern Turkey), known from the Greek sources as Phrygia, and populated with non-Semitic inhabitants. As a result of their geographic proximity, Meshech and Tubal are mentioned together in various biblical and extrabiblical texts. This picture is reflected in the prophetic literature, particularly the book of Ezekiel, e.g., in the oracle on Tyre: "Javan, Tubal, and Meshech traded with you; they exchanged human beings and vessels of bronze for your merchandise" (Ezek 27:13; see also 32:26; 38:2-3; 39:1).

In the MT of Isa 66:19, which lists several names of lands/people, the words moshekhe qesheth (מֹשְׁכֵי קֶשֶׁת), "which draw the bow" (i.e., archers), are out of context. Most probably, the word moshekhe is corrupted from the name meshekh, and the word qesheth is a late addition to give some meaning to the unfamiliar term moshekhe (maybe by influence of Jer 46:9). To be sure, the LXX reads here Mosoch. Nevertheless, Meshech appears here prior to Tubal.

Meshech and Tubal sometimes come together as Mushki and Tabal in the Assyrian documents. The earliest record of Mushki is in the inscriptions of King Tiglath-pileser I (1114–1076 BCE), who in his first year attacked the five kings of the land Mushki, defeated them, and killed 20,000 (another version: 12,000) of their soldiers. They are probably mentioned also in the inscriptions of Ashur-bel-kala and Tukulti-ninurta II (885 BCE). In 883 BCE, Ashurnasirpal II reports receiving tribute from Katmuhu and Mushki, which included cattle, sheep, wine, and a large number of bronze vessels (for the latter item compare Ezek 27:13; Gen 4:22: "Tubal-cain, who made all kinds of bronze and iron tools"). His son Shalmaneser III also recounts receiving taxes from Mushki and Tabal (837/6 BCE). Shamshi-ilu, the turtanu (i.e., the chief commander; compare Isa 20:1) of Shalmaneser IV (783–773 BCE), mentions Mushki together with Urartu as enemies of Assyria.

During Sargon's reign (722–705 BCE), King Mita (= Midas of the Greek sources) of Mushki/Meshech attempted to undermine Assyrian rule in Anatolia. In 717 BCE, together with Pisiris of Carchemish, he rebelled against Assyria, and subsequently Carchemish became an Assyrian province. Two years later (715 BCE), Mita conquered territories from Que (= Cilicia of the Greek sources). In 713, he persuaded other kingdoms, among them Tabal and Urartu, to join the anti-Assyrian coalition. Following the defeat of Urartu by the Assyrians, Mita lost his influence in Tabal, which became an Assyrian province. After the capture of Gurgum (711/10 BCE), Mita was confronted directly with Assyria. Nonetheless, in 709, due to the pressure of the Cimmerian warriors from southern Russia, Mita took a different political position toward Assyria. He cooperated with Sargon in order to face the new common threat. However, the efforts of Mushki and Assyria (as well as some other small kingdoms) to stop the Cimmerians were useless. In 705, Sargon, who was forced to campaign against Tabal, was defeated by the Cimmerians and killed in battle. This political constellation probably changed again in the time of Esarhaddon, king of Assyria (681–669 BCE): in 675, Mushki, Tabal, and Melid were joined to the Cimmerians and fought against the Assyrian Empire.

In Greek historiography, Herodotus recounts that the Moschoi (Μόσχοι) and Tibarēnoi (Τιβαρηνοί) were located at the south of the Black Sea and were allies of Persians (*Hist.* 3.94; 7.78). Thus, they are probably identical with the Phrygians of the Greek sources (though this identification is not accepted unanimously in the scholarship). In Ps 120:5, "Woe is me, that I am an alien in Meshech, that I must live among the tents of Kedar," Meshech probably marks the northern rim of the civilized world, while Kedar in the Syrian-Arabian desert the southeastern rim.

Bibliography: I. Kalimi. "Three Assumptions about the Kenites." *ZAW* 100 (1988) 386–93; H.-J. Kraus. *Psalms 60–150.* CC (1993); D. D. Luckenbill. *Ancient Records of Assyria and Babylonia.* Vols. 1–2 (1926–27); J. G. Macqueen. "The History of Anatolia and the Hittite Empire: An Overview." *Civilizations of the Ancient Near East.* J. M. Sasson et al., eds. (1995) 2.1085–1105; M. Mellink. "The Native Kingdoms of Anatolia." *The Cambridge Ancient History.* 2nd ed. (1991) 3/2.619–43; S. Parpola. *Neo-Assyrian Toponyms* (1970); I. L. Seeligmann. *The Septuagint Version of Isaiah and Cognate Studies* (2004).

ISAAC KALIMI

MESHELEMIAH mi-shel'uh-m*i*'uh [מְשֶׁלֶמְיָה meshelemyah]. A gatekeeper, a Levite, a descendant of Korah, and the father of seven sons, including Zechariah, who was also a gatekeeper (1 Chr 9:21; 26:1-3). Also referred to as Shelemiah (1 Chr 26:14) and may be the same as SHALLUM.

MESHEZABEL mi-shez'uh-bel [מְשֵׁיזַבְאֵל meshezav'el]. The Aramaic means "God delivers" and appears three times in Nehemiah, possibly referring to the same person. 1. Father of Berechiah, father of

Meshullam who made repairs to the Jerusalem wall (Neh 3:4; compare 3:30).

2. One of forty-four leaders of the people who signed Ezra's covenant to keep the law (Neh 10:21).

3. Descendant of Zerah and father of Pethahiah, the representative of Judean concerns to the Persian king (Neh 11:24).

KEN M. PENNER

MESHILLEMITH mi-shil´uh-mith [מְשִׁלֵּמִית meshillemith]. Ancestor of Jeroboam and priest listed in the genealogy of 1 Chr 9:10-13. Probably the same person as MESHILLEMOTH in Neh 11:13.

MESHILLEMOTH mi-shil´uh-moth [מְשִׁלֵּמוֹת meshillemoth]. 1. Father of Berechiah, an Ephraimite chief (2 Chr 28:12).

2. Son of Immer and ancestor of Amashsai, a priest in Jerusalem in Nehemiah's time (Neh 11:13). He may be identical to MESHILLEMITH, son of Immer (1 Chr 9:12).

MESHOBAB mi-shoh´bab [מְשׁוֹבָב meshovav]. Clan leader in the Simeonite tribe who prospered in the east side of the valley (1 Chr 4:34).

MESHULLAM mi-sh*oo*l-uhm [מְשֻׁלָּם meshullam]. The name of several individuals in the OT. 1. Grandfather of Shaphan, the secretary of King Josiah (2 Kgs 22:3; *see* JOSIAH).

2. One of the sons of Zadok and the father of the priest Hilkiah (1 Chr 9:11; Neh 11:11), who found "the book of the law" (2 Kgs 22:8).

3. A Kohathite who was appointed as one of the overseers of the temple repairs (2 Chr 34:12). Josiah sent Shaphan and Hilkiah to the prophetess Huldah, the wife of Shallum (an alternative form of Meshullam), to inquire about "the book of the law." Huldah told them that Josiah would die in peace (2 Kgs 22:20; the Hebrew word for "peace," shalom [שָׁלוֹם], is the same word on which the name Meshullam is based). It is ironic that although Josiah was surrounded by "peace," he died a violent death (2 Kgs 23:29; 2 Chr 35:23-24).

4. One of three children of Zerubbabel (1 Chr 3:19).

5. A Benjaminite whose son Shallu was one of the first returned exiles (1 Chr 9:7; Neh 11:7).

6. Another Benjaminite who was one of the first returned exiles; son of Shephatiah (1 Chr 9:8).

7. Another member of the priestly family of Zadok; his great-grandson was a returned exile (1 Chr 9:12).

8. One of eleven leading men whom Ezra sent to recruit Levites to join the company of exiles returning to Jerusalem (Ezra 8:16).

9. One of four leading men who opposed Ezra's policy against marriage to foreign women (Ezra 10:15).

10. A son of Bani who had married a foreign wife and was among those who sent their wives away with their children in accordance with Ezra's policy (Ezra 10:29).

11. A son of Berechiah, he was a leader of one of the groups assigned to repair the wall of Jerusalem (Neh 3:4, 30). His daughter was married to Jehohanan, son of Tobiah (Neh 6:18); Tobiah conspired against Nehemiah and his building projects.

12. A son of Besodeiah who helped repair the Old Gate (Neh 3:6).

13. One of the leaders who was given the honor of standing at the left hand of Ezra as he read from "the book of the law of Moses" (Neh 8:4).

14. One of the priests who signed the covenant drawn up by Nehemiah (Neh 10:7).

15. One of "the leaders of the people" who also signed the covenant drawn up by Nehemiah (Neh 10:20).

16. The head of the priestly family of Ezra in the time of the high priest Joiakim (Neh 12:13).

17. The head of the priestly family of Ginnethon in the time of the high priest Joiakim (Neh 12:16).

18. A gatekeeper during the time of the high priest Joiakim (Neh 12:25).

19. One of the priests who participated in the dedication ceremony of the city wall (Neh 12:33).

20. A descendant of Gad who lived in Bashan (1 Chr 5:13).

21. A descendant of Benjamin, son of Elpaal (1 Chr 8:17).

URIAH Y. KIM

MESHULLEMETH mi-sh*oo*l´uh-mith [מְשֻׁלֶּמֶת meshullemeth]. The mother of Amon, the daughter of Haruz, and the wife of Manasseh, Judah's king (2 Kgs 21:19).

MESOPOTAMIA mes´uh-puh-tay´mee-uh [אֲרַם נַהֲרַיִם ʾaram naharayim; Μεσοποταμία Mesopotamia]. The Gk. term means literally "in the midst of the river(s)" and has come secondarily to denote the vast land between the Tigris and Euphrates rivers, the region from which international powers ruled the ancient world, including ASSYRIA AND BABYLONIA in the 1st millennium BCE. More narrowly, *Mesopotamia* is used in OT passages in translating the Hebrew name ARAM-NAHARAIM, the traditional homeland of Israel's ancestors, denoting a region more specifically in the northwest bend of the Euphrates River. The term *Mesopotamia* as a translation for this region is therefore inexact, and some translations choose instead to use "Aram-naharaim" as a more precise appellation for this region in north Mesopotamia. In the NT, *Mesopotamia* appears only in the book of Acts.

A. Terminology and Geographical Features
B. History
C. Biblical Usage
Bibliography

A. Terminology and Geographical Features

Mesopotamia formed a cultural and geopolitical unit distinct from Iran to the east and the Mediterranean coastline to the west throughout ANE history (ca. 4000–330 BCE), although it also extended beyond simply the Tigris-Euphrates Valley and its tributaries (*see* EUPHRATES RIVER; TIGRIS RIVER). The region went by a variety of names in the respective languages of antiquity until the Greeks referred to a satrapy formed by Alexander the Great as "Mesopotamia," a designation strictly true only if viewing the country from the west. Mesopotamia generally extends from the mouth of the Persian Gulf northwestward along the bend in the Euphrates and reaches eastward to the Tigris at the foot of the Zagros Mountains. All of modern Iraq and Kuwait, and parts of Iran, Syria, and Lebanon make up the area known as Mesopotamia.

The various subregions of greater Mesopotamia share cultural features: the economy was based almost entirely on agriculture and animal husbandry, while trade and transportation were critically important due to a lack of natural resources beyond soil, water, fish, etc. On the other hand, there are climatic and geographical differences between north and south Mesopotamia. In particular, the Zagros Mountains in the north and east give way gradually to the undulating hills of north Mesopotamia, where the Tigris River flows rapidly, making it less useful for transportation. Here too, in the north, the rain shadow provides adequate rainfall in a pleasant climate, making it possible to settle almost anywhere without dependence on irrigation for crops. Similarly in the northwest, in the great bend of the Euphrates adequate rainfall, in addition to a slower-flowing Euphrates and its many tributaries of the Khabur and Balikh rivers, made for extensive settlements early in human history.

By contrast, south Mesopotamia is characterized by an alluvial plain formed where the Tigris and Euphrates flow closest together just south of modern Baghdad, extending southeastward to the marches of the Persian Gulf. Rainfall is limited in the alluvial plain, so that most settlements were located in proximity to the slower moving Euphrates and its usefulness for irrigation. The erratic water supply and high water table meant relatively frequent flooding, and the scarcity of metals, stone, and wood made trade imperative in the south, usually in exchange for textiles and leatherwork. Cultural influence may be the south's greatest contribution to human history, since south Mesopotamia, or simply "Babylonia," may be credited with establishing the ideological and social infrastructure for much of ANE culture, and was often held in high regard for its cultural sophistication (Arnold). The differences between north and south Mesopotamia were prevalent throughout ANE history, although the distinctions during the 1st millennium BCE between Assyria and Babylonia are of most interest for readers of the Bible.

So the term *Mesopotamia* may justifiably be used for this vast region of the ANE as first coined in Alexandrian times. However, evidence suggests that the pre-Hellenistic names for Mesopotamia, such as Aram-naharaim and variants in other ancient languages, connoted an association with one river only, the Euphrates, and not at all with two rivers as the name has been understood since the Alexandrian age (Finkelstein). Geographically, all city names associated with earlier names for the region are located in the extreme western portion, and none are east of the Khabur Valley. Lexicographically, the Aramaic and Akkadian terms that preceded the Greek form do not necessarily connote two rivers, since the Hebrew word naharayim appears to be dual in form only but not meaning. In fact, in all likelihood, the original connotations of the earliest terms referred to the great bend of the Euphrates itself, the large U-shaped curvature in the northwest, and to the territory enclosed by the Euphrates on three sides (Finkelstein). No other river was designated by naharayim or its cognates in other languages, and the region in view was the great riverine peninsula surrounded by the Euphrates in the northwest. Thus Aram-naharaim itself is more specifically this region in the northwestern bend of the Euphrates River.

B. History

When taken together with the Egyptian Nile Valley, Mesopotamia constitutes the matrix of ANE culture and the birthplace of human civilization. Because Mesopotamia is geographically open and easily accessible from nearly all its borders, the region was impacted by a steady infusion of different nationalities and people groups throughout ancient history. The distinctive cuneiform script used in the earliest written language of ancient Mesopotamia, Sumerian, was adapted by Semitic newcomers in the 3rd millennium BCE and subsequently exported to all points of the compass for varied use in many languages of western Asia.

For reasons that are obscure, southern Mesopotamia was the site of the world's first urban civilization. Artificial irrigation in the alluvial plain made crop yields higher than was possible anywhere else in the ancient world and large settlements possible over less land. The meandering and slow-moving Euphrates provided a resource for irrigation, and the oldest and most important cities of the world were located in the south along its many canals and tributaries. An urban explosion occurred in the 4th millennium BCE in southern Mesopotamia. The process of urbanization continued into the 3rd millennium, accompanied by the invention of writing, widespread prosperity, and refined irrigation systems. During the first centuries of the 3rd millennium, Sumerian influence was felt most prominently in the southern regions of the alluvial plain, organized mostly among certain powerful city-states. By contrast, the northern alluvium was occupied predominantly by Semitic Akkadians, governed by something more like a territorial state than city-states. By the mid-3rd millennium, scribes at the city of Ebla in the northwest were using cuneiform script to record their extensive economic activities.

Sometime around 2300 BCE, north and south were unified briefly under the leadership of Sargon I of Akkad. Semitic populations had participated in Mesopotamian society for many centuries, but Sargon succeeded in replacing the Sumerian city-states of the south with Akkadian governors loyal to a central administration at Akkad, and his successful military campaigns gained control of important trade routes, leading briefly to a unified Mesopotamia more like an empire than a territorial state. The Old Akkadian language came into use for royal inscriptions, archives, and administrative texts, and Semitic religion became more prominent during this period. After the collapse of this first Semitic empire, a brief Sumerian renaissance occurred in the so-called Third Dynasty of Ur (ca. 2112–2004 BCE). Under the leadership of Ur-Nammu and his son and successor, Shulgi, administrative and economic reforms transformed the city of Ur in the south into a centralized territorial state with its core in southern Mesopotamia and its periphery in provinces and cities in military buffer zones to the east and northwest. Sumerian literature enjoyed a brief revival during this period, although its contributions as a living and creative language began to wane with the turning of the new millennium.

Toward the end of the 3rd millennium BCE, the Sumero-Akkadian culture of Mesopotamia had advanced remarkably with regard to literature, economics, religion, and the arts. The arrival of the AMORITES into central and southern Mesopotamia as the 2nd millennium dawned was a turning point in ancient history. New Amorite city-states of various sizes began to supplant the Sumero-Akkadian culture of the previous millennium. Emerging from this widespread balance of power were the city-states of Asshur in the north along the Tigris under Shamshi-Adad I (1813–1781 BCE), the city of Mari on the west bank of the Euphrates under the Lim Dynasty (Yaggid-Lim, Zimri-Lim, etc.), and the first dynasty of Babylon in the south, which eventually rose to prominence under its sixth ruler, Hammurabi (1792–1759 BCE). The latter ushered in the Old Babylonian Period, creating an empire in and beyond Mesopotamia of such magnitude that it would leave an indelible mark on the rest of human history.

After the collapse of the Old Babylonian Empire and the fall of Babylon to the Hittites in 1595 BCE, a power vacuum in southern Mesopotamia was filled by the Kassites, a new ethnic group from Iran. Although this was not particularly an age of political strength or expansion for Mesopotamia, the stability provided by four centuries of Kassite Babylonian rule (down to 1155 BCE) brought renewed cultural significance to southern Mesopotamia, which came to be venerated as an ancient and prestigious cultural capital of the world. The Kassite period of Mesopotamian history brought a new political unification and centralized administration, resulting in an impressive period of prosperity and affluence for southern Mesopotamia. Across the ANE, the Late Bronze Age (1550–1200 BCE) was one of internationalism, in which nation-states along the Mediterranean coastal rim (Egypt, the Hittites of Anatolia, the rich city-states of the Levant, and the Hurrians in northern Mesopotamia) all vied for political and military advantage. Among this "Great Powers Club," the Assyrians eventually began to emerge in northern Mesopotamia toward the end of the period. But the literary florescence and cultural prestige of southern Mesopotamia were preserved by the Kassites and are brilliantly illustrated by the use of the Babylonian language as the lingua franca for diplomatic correspondence among the nations (the "Amarna Age," named for the archive of cuneiform tablets from El-Amarna in Egypt preserving the correspondence between the great powers of the day).

The demise of Bronze Age culture in the ANE coincides with the collapse of the dominant empires of the Mediterranean world, the Hittites of Asia Minor and the Mycenean civilization on the mainland of Greece, as well as most of the city-state polities in the Levant. Within a fifty-year period around 1200 BCE, nearly every city in the eastern Mediterranean world collapsed suddenly. These political events, marking the transition from Bronze to Iron ages, were also accompanied by new cultural developments. The age of internationalism was officially over, and the Babylonian dialect ceased to be used as the lingua franca. A more convenient form of writing, the alphabet, spread beyond the Levant and changed the accessibility of written communication. New political systems began to emerge, and new ethnic entities emerged in the vacuum in the form of the Aramean city-states of Syria and the Israelites and Philistines in the southern Levant. The cause of the changes is most likely the Sea Peoples, the immigration of dozens of small groups from the Aegean, flowing into the Mediterranean basin and disrupting the previous balance of power, although the specific nature of these Sea Peoples is uncertain (*see* PHILISTINES; PHOENICIA).

The destruction of urban life across the eastern Mediterranean and the collapse of Bronze Age culture in general radically changed the political realities of the ANE. With the collapse of the Hittites and Egyptians in the west, the center of power shifted to the east, especially to Assyria and Babylonia. Babylonia itself remained relatively stable and experienced little impact from the carnage in Anatolia and the Mediterranean rim. By contrast, the domino-like effect of the events in the eastern Mediterranean probably led to the arrival of the Arameans into central and southern Mesopotamia. In northern Mesopotamia, the presence of the Arameans contributed to the temporary decline of Assyria at the end of the 12th cent. BCE, and by the beginning of the 1st millennium, Arameans controlled not only southern Syria, but the western territories of Babylonia. At the beginning of the 1st millennium, Mesopotamia was clearly divided into north and south, Assyria and Babylonia, the emerging new political entities of the Iron Age, thus marking the beginning of Assyro-Babylonian conflict as a central feature of Mesopotamian politics of the 1st millennium.

Political history in Mesopotamia in the 1st millennium BCE was largely a series of imperial powers, commencing with the Assyrian Empire, followed by the brief Babylonian Empire, the Persians, and subsequently Greek rule. Dominating throughout the first half of the 1st millennium was a single political identity in northern Mesopotamia, Assyria. The empire waxed and waned for centuries, but always played an intimidating role when it was on the rise. In Syria-Palestine, city-states and small territorial states fought each other until Assyria began to grow strong again, at which time they frequently forged alliances to hold off the Assyrian threat. The northern Israelites were often caught in these political machinations, and eventually fell victim to Assyrian might near the end of the 8th cent. BCE. For a brief period of time during the 7th and 6th cent., after the fall of the Assyrian Empire, Babylon rose again to premier international status and enjoyed a spectacular period of strength and prosperity in what may be called the Neo-Babylonian Empire (also sometimes known as the Chaldean Empire). Although extremely brief in duration, the grandeur of the empire, especially under Nebuchadnezzar II, and its legacy in the biblical and classical sources left an indelible mark on subsequent history, making this one of the most interesting periods of Mesopotamian history. The Persian capture of Babylon in 539 BCE ended the last native Semitic empire of ancient Mesopotamia.

C. Biblical Usage

While some have taken the Hebrew ʾaram naharayim as a dual, and thus as "Aram of the Two Rivers," assuming the two rivers are the Euphrates and the Khabur in north Mesopotamia, it more likely connotes "Aram of the River-land," as we have seen, denoting the riverine peninsula in the upper middle Euphrates. This geographical name occurs five times in the OT. First, the Yahwist identified the ancestral home of Abraham as the city of Nahor in Aram-naharaim (Gen 24:10). The "city of Nahor" is almost certainly HARAN, which confirms the location of Aram-naharaim as a region on the middle Euphrates. The Priestly traditions appear to know the place as PADDAN-ARAM (e.g., Gen 25:20; 28:2).

Second, Aram-naharaim (or Mesopotamia) is also the homeland of Balaam, son of Beor, who is said to be from the city of Pethor (Deut 23:4 [Heb. 23:5]). In Num 22:5, Pethor is identified as "on the Euphrates, in the land of Amaw," and Balaam further identifies himself as from Aram (Num 23:7), placing Pethor generally in Aram. More specifically, an inscription of Shalmaneser III locates Pitru/Pethor on the west bank of the Euphrates in northern Mesopotamia near the point where it joins the river Sagura (*COS* 2.113A:263). Although positive identification of the site is not yet possible, Tell Ahmar, also known in antiquity as Til Barsip, near Carchemish, is a candidate.

The third occurrence of ʾaram naharayim is as the country ruled by King Cushan-rishathaim, one of the first enemies of Israel during the Judges period (Judg 3:8). This reference is of little value in determining the region denoted by the name. The fourth and fifth occurrences relate to David's wars with the Ammonites, who purchased matériel and hired infantry soldiers from Mesopotamia, or Aram-naharaim (1 Chr 19:6; Ps 60; compare 2 Sam 10:6).

Of these five occurrences of ʾaram naharayim in the OT, four of them are translated by the LXX as "Mesopotamia" or "Syrian Mesopotamia," and once as "Syria of the Rivers" (Judg 3:8). The NRSV twice translates ʾaram naharayim simply as "Mesopotamia" (Deut 23:4; 1 Chr 19:6), although elsewhere it uses "Aram-naharaim," a more precise designation for the region (compare JPS, NAB, NIB, NIV, NLT, etc.; NJB has "Upper Mesopotamia").

The context of ʾaram naharayim in these occurrences confirms that the geographical name denotes the great bend of the Euphrates itself, its large U-shaped curvature in the northwest, and, specifically, the territory enclosed by the Euphrates on three sides, a so-called riverine peninsula. The use of "Syria of the Rivers" or "Syrian Mesopotamia" by the LXX translators only confirms this conclusion. English translations using "Mesopotamia" in the OT texts may be slightly misleading, since upper or northwest Mesopotamia is in view, so "Aram-naharaim" is preferable.

In the NT, "residents of Mesopotamia" are included in the list of devout Jews from every nation living in Jerusalem who, on the day of Pentecost, hear the rushing violent wind and the speech of the disciples and marvel that they hear in their own language the disciples proclaiming God's deeds of power (Acts 2:9). The last occurrence of *Mesopotamia* in the Bible is Stephen's identification of Abraham as living there prior to living in Haran (Acts 7:2). This assumes UR of the Chaldeans was in south Mesopotamia, rather than another Ur in Upper Mesopotamia (compare Gen 11:28, 31; 15:7).

Bibliography: Bill T. Arnold. *Who Were the Babylonians?* (2004); J. J. Finkelstein. "Mesopotamia." *JNES* 21 (1962) 73–92; Edward Lipiński. *The Aramaeans: Their Ancient History, Culture, Religion* (2000); A. Leo Oppenheim. *Ancient Mesopotamia: Portrait of a Dead Civilization* (1977); J. Nicholas Postgate. *Early Mesopotamia: Society and Economy at the Dawn of History* (1992); Michael Roaf. *Cultural Atlas of Mesopotamia and the Ancient Near East* (1996); Wolfram von Soden. *The Ancient Orient: An Introduc-*

tion to the Study of the Ancient Near East (1994); Claus Westermann. *Genesis 12–36: A Commentary.* CC (1985).

BILL T. ARNOLD

MESSAGE [דָּבָר davar; λόγος logos]. *Message* does not routinely translate any particular term in the OT or NT, being a suitable translation in various contexts for at least five Hebrew and seven Greek terms (and as many as a dozen of the sixty NRSV uses have no counterpart in the original but are supplied to give idiomatic sense to the English). Thus, it would be somewhat arbitrary to limit a survey only to occurrences of the English word. Nonetheless, the two most commonly translated terms are the Hebrew davar (thirteen times) and Greek logos (seventeen times), both of which might be, and more often are, translated more literally as "word." So, for example, the common expression "word of the LORD/God" could quite appropriately be translated "message of God" or perhaps even "message from God."

In its secular usage, a message is characteristically transmitted from one political entity to another (Josh 10:3; Judg 3:19; 11:28; 1 Kgs 5:8; 20:12), or from prophet to king (2 Kgs 5:8; 9:5) or vice versa (Num 22:7, 10; 2 Chr 34:28), often by means of intermediaries (e.g., 1 Sam 11:5; but see Prov 26:6). Although no particular theological significance routinely attaches to the term on such occasions, in certain contexts it is clear that the "message" is from God (e.g., Judg 3:19-20; 2 Sam 12:25; 19:11; 2 Kgs 22:18-20; Hag 1:13), always so with the expression "word of the LORD." The actual content of the "word of the LORD" varies considerably, from private disclosures to words of public rebuke, from prophetic warning of imminent calamity to words of reassurance and promise. Characteristically, but not exclusively, the "word of the LORD" "comes to" the prophet on behalf of the people, as in the stereotyped introductions to many prophetic writings (Jer 1:2; Ezek 1:3; Hos 1:1-2; Joel 1:1; Jonah 1:1; etc.), thus characterizing the message as extrinsic to the prophet. As depicted especially in the prophetic corpus, the "word of the LORD" not only communicates abstractly, but dynamically accomplishes its objective (Ps 107:20; Isa 24:1-3; 55:9-11). This dynamic "word of LORD" sometimes even hypostatizes by means of metaphor or personification (e.g., Ps 147:15-18; Ezek 3:1-3; Wis 18:15-17).

As a way of referring in summary fashion to Christian proclamation and teaching, NT references to *message* are consistently theological in character. In a characteristic NT expression, the message (logos) is qualified by a descriptive genitive by which the message's character or goal is further specified: e.g., message of salvation (Acts 13:26), of the good news (Acts 15:7), of God's grace (Acts 20:32), of the cross (1 Cor 1:18), of reconciliation (2 Cor 5:19). Several NT passages comprise what might be regarded as summaries of the early Christian proclamation of the message (e.g., Rom 1:1-4; 1 Cor 15:2-5; Phil 2:6-11; 1 Pet 3:18-22). Likewise, the apostolic speeches of Acts suggest the contours of early Christian preaching, though surely not to the exclusion of Lukan theological interests (e.g., 2:14-40; 13:16-41; 17:22-31). On the basis of such material, an outline of the primitive Christian message (or KERYGMA) has been reconstructed: 1) Jesus as the fulfillment of the OT; 2) Jesus' ministry culminating in his death; 3) his resurrection and exaltation; 4) the giving of the Spirit; and 5) a summons to repentance and faith. Not all are persuaded, however, that the early Christian message was so homogenous, and some regard such a scheme as the imposition of an artificial conformity upon what was a more theologically diverse movement. Whatever one makes of that issue, it at least remains the case that alongside the message about Jesus the NT gives equal voice to the message of Jesus. Any account of the early Christian message will need to do justice to a gospel that proclaimed Jesus as well as the message Jesus proclaimed, in particular his announcement of the presence of the kingdom of God and the summons to follow him in radical discipleship (Matt 4:17; Mark 1:14-15; Luke 4:18-19). *See* GOSPEL, MESSAGE; WORD, THE.

Bibliography: James D. G. Dunn. *Unity and Diversity in the New Testament: An Inquiry Into the Character of Earliest Christianity.* 2nd ed. (1990); John T. Greene. *The Role of the Messenger and Message in the Ancient Near East* (1989); Joachim Jeremias. *New Testament Theology: The Proclamation of Jesus* (1971); G. N. Stanton. *Jesus of Nazareth in New Testament Preaching* (1974); David Wenham. *Paul: Follower of Jesus or Founder of Christianity?* (1995).

GARWOOD P. ANDERSON

MESSENGER [מַלְאָךְ mal'akh; ἄγγελος angelos, ἀπόστολος apostolos]. Messengers are often sent to speak or act on behalf of other human beings. Other messengers are sent from God, sometimes speaking for God legitimately and sometimes delivering false messages (sometimes sent from God). They may be human or angelic. The purpose of God's legitimate messengers is always to inform, enable, and guide the people of God and occasionally to punish.

Messengers sent by human beings ask favors (Num 21:21-22), spy in enemy territory (Josh 2:1-21), communicate between general and king or between enemies (2 Sam 12:27-29; 2 Kgs 18:17-35), and communicate with allies (2 Sam 5:11). In Jephthah's diplomatic overture to the Ammonites, his messengers say to the king, "What is there between you and me, that you have come to me to fight against my land?" (Judg 11:12). They speak as Jephthah would if he were there.

God's messengers speak similarly on God's behalf. The most prominent are prophets, often prefacing their speeches with "Thus says the LORD" (Amos 1:3,

6, 9, 11, 13; *see* PROPHET, PROPHECY). This comes out of their understanding that God has called them to give specific messages to nations and individuals; the prophet is God's AMBASSADOR. Sometimes their words offer peace and blessing (Isa 40:1-5); more often they warn of judgment (Jer 7:16-20; Ezek 16:44-58; Hos 4:1-10). Others who are not called prophets deliver God-given information less formally (Joseph in Gen 41:25-36; Jonathan in 1 Sam 23:17; Saul in 1 Sam 24:20; Abigail in 1 Sam 25:26-31). There are also those who claim to be prophets of Yahweh but are not. God apparently does not send the Rabshakeh of 2 Kgs 18 as he claims in v. 25 (compare 2 Kgs 19:35-37). Jeremiah's foe Hananiah falls into this category as well (Jer 28:1-17).

The ANGEL of the LORD frequently speaks as God does, saying to Hagar in Gen 16:10, "I will so greatly multiply your offspring that they cannot be counted for multitude" (see Gen 13:16), and telling Abraham as he prepares to kill Isaac, "Do not lay your hand on the boy ... since you have not withheld your son ... from me" (Gen 22:12). The angel informs Hagar of her son's destiny (Gen 16:11-13) and Manoah and his wife of their impending parenthood (Judg 13); Manoah, like Hagar, believes this angel is God (v. 22). The angel of the LORD also saves Hagar and Ishmael (Gen 21:17-19), acts to prevent transgression of God's will (Num 22:22-35; in v. 22 this angel is called satan [שָׂטָן, "adversary"]), calls people to God's service and sustains them in it (Judg 6:11-18; 1 Kgs 19:4-8; Zech 1:12-17), and carries out God's punishments (2 Sam 24:15-17; Ps 35:6; Isa 37:36).

God also sends an angel to guide and instruct the people on the way to Canaan (Exod 23:20-24). The seraphs of Isa 6 articulate one of Isaiah's main themes: "Holy, holy, holy is the LORD of hosts; the whole earth is full of his glory" (v. 3). Finally, a WATCHER (an angel; see *The Book of the Watchers* in *1 Enoch*) cries aloud the judgment on Nebuchadnezzar in his dream (Dan 4:13-17).

Evil spirits from God trouble Saul (1 Sam 16:14; 18:10; 19:9). Another spirit is sent by God to lie to Ahab's 400 prophets so that he will fight in the war in which he will die (1 Kgs 22:20-23). These passages predate the belief in an evil force opposing God; anything that happens must therefore come from God.

An animal is also seen acting as an agent of God, if not as a messenger. In Num 22:16-35 Balaam, who has been hired by the king of Moab to curse the Israelites, journeys to Moab. As he travels, the angel of the LORD blocks his way with a drawn sword. Balaam's donkey sees the angel and refuses to go further. The angel of the LORD tells Balaam that he would have killed him if the donkey had not seen and avoided what the famous seer could not see (v. 33). The donkey kept Balaam alive, so God's desire to bless the Israelites succeeded.

In the NT, Jesus is called the perfect messenger (Heb 1:1–2:18; 7:1–10:25). He both speaks and acts for God, completely yielding his will to God's (Mark 14:36). Humans are used as messengers as well: Joseph receives dreams that enable him to save the infant Jesus (Matt 1:18–2:23). Elizabeth is the first person to confirm Mary's pregnancy (Luke 1:39-45); the shepherds (Luke 2:8-20), Simeon (Luke 2:25-35), Anna (Luke 2:36-38), and the wise men (Matt 2:1-12) are given insights to share with Jesus' family. John the Baptist prophesies Jesus' coming and baptizes him (Mark 1:7-9 and par.). Jesus' followers who preach in his name (the Twelve, the Seventy, the apostles [including Paul], and others) are also seen as God's messengers, as are John the prophet and the two witnesses in Rev 11:1-13. *See* APOSTLE.

Like the angel of the LORD in the OT, Gabriel informs Zechariah (Luke 1:5-20) and Mary (Luke 1:26-38) that they will have children; "an angel of the Lord" comes to Joseph in a dream (Matt 1:20). The heavenly host announces Jesus' birth to the shepherds (Luke 2:8-14). Angels also appear at Jesus' tomb and speak to those who come (Matt 28:2-7; John 20:11-13), as do one or more "men in white" (Mark 16:4-7; Luke 24:1-7; Acts 1:10-11). There are many angels in Revelation who act as messengers of God through word and action (7:2-3; 8:3–9:11).

The use of supernatural beings as God's messengers therefore underscores God as "Lord of Hosts." It shows that there was a belief in beings who know more of God's nature and plans than humans do, but who are still less than God (Rev 19:10; 22:8-9); that, like humans, they can fall (Rev 12:7-17); and that there are barriers in human relationships with them (Gen 6:1-4; see also *The Book of the Watchers* in *1 Enoch*). The use of human beings as God's messengers shows that even in our fallen state we may be of use to God, his kingdom, and each other. *See* GOSPEL, MESSAGE; MESSAGE.

CAROL STUART GRIZZARD

MESSIAH, JEWISH muh-sī'uh [מָשִׁיחַ mashiakh]. *Messiah* (mashiakh) means "anointed one." Kings were anointed in Israel and Judah, as were high priests. There is also limited evidence for the anointing of prophets (*see* ANOINT). The term mashiakh refers to the legitimate king (*see* KING, KINGSHIP). It does not have a future or eschatological connotation in the OT. In the Second Temple period, when there was no longer a king on the throne, the term came to refer to the one who would restore the kingship. The same figure could also be designated by other terms such as "Branch of David." Ideal, even supernatural characteristics were often attributed to him.

A. Old Testament Evidence
  1. The royal ideology
  2. The promise to David
  3. Messianic expectation in the Prophets
B. The Septuagint

A. Old Testament Evidence

1. The royal ideology

The messianic ideal has its roots in ANE royal ideology. In Egypt, the pharaoh was thought to be son of the sun-god, Re, and some texts from the New Kingdom period describe his begetting in sexual terms. In Mesopotamia and Canaan, the king was also said to be son of a god, but there was less emphasis on his divinity. Traces of similar royal ideology survive in the psalms. According to Ps 2, the Lord has set his king (also called his "anointed") on Zion, and commanded him to rule in the midst of his enemies. He also tells him: "You are my son; today I have begotten you" (v. 7). When the nations plot against the king, the Lord laughs them to scorn. A reference to divine begetting should also be restored in Ps 110:3. The Hebrew is corrupt, but it should be restored, following the Gk., to read "I have begotten you" (perhaps: "from the womb, from dawn, you have the dew with which I have begotten you"). The Lord invites the king to sit at his right hand and make his enemies his footstool, and also tells him that he is a priest forever according to the order of Melchizedek (king of Salem/Jerusalem in the time of Abraham). Both the motif of recognition ("you are my son") and the enthronement on the right hand are Egyptian motifs. Jerusalem had been subject to Egypt in pre-Israelite times and it is likely that old formulas and traditions were taken over by the kings of Judah. The king is addressed as **ʾelohim** (אֱלֹהִים, "god") in Ps 45:6, although he is clearly subordinate to the Most High ("your God," v. 7). Other psalms ascribe extraordinary divine blessing to the king. So Ps 21:4: "He asked you for life; you gave it to him—length of days forever and ever." Whether this should be taken to imply that at least some kings were granted immortality, or should be taken as hyperbolic, is not clear.

2. The promise to David

The special status of the king was confirmed in the promise to David in 2 Sam 7. This passage is embedded in the DtrH, and so the formulation is relatively late, perhaps exilic, but it preserves an old tradition. On the one hand it declares the king to be son of God (7:14*a*: "I will be a father to him, and he shall be a son to me") and promises that the kingship will never be taken away from the house of David (7:16: "Your house and your kingdom shall be made sure forever before me; your throne shall be established forever"). On the other hand, it acknowledges the fallible humanity of the king: "When he commits iniquity, I will punish him with a rod such as mortals use" (7:14*b*). This threat of punishment is a far cry from the rhetoric of the Egyptian kings. The main importance of the promise was that it seemed to guarantee that there would always be a descendant of David on the throne in Jerusalem. After the capture of Jerusalem by the Babylonians in 586 BCE, however, this was no longer the case. The cognitive dissonance caused by the discrepancy between the divine promise and present reality is the root of messianic expectation.

3. Messianic expectation in the Prophets

The prophet who concerned himself most with the Jerusalem kingship was Isaiah. Isaiah 7:14 ("the young woman is with child and shall bear a son") was a sign of hope to King Ahaz about the future of the royal line. The child in question is often identified as Hezekiah (also in rabbinic tradition), but he is not necessarily a future king. In any case, he is not a messiah, and was not interpreted as one in Jewish tradition. The poem in Isa 9 ("For a child has been born for us, a son given to us" [v. 6]) is most probably a poem for the enthronement of a king, perhaps Hezekiah. The titles given to this "child"—"Wonderful Counselor, Mighty God, Everlasting Father, Prince of Peace"—conform to the royal ideology in ascribing divinity, in some sense, to the king. Here again the king in question belongs to the present rather than the future. In Isa 11:1-9, however, there is a genuine messianic oracle (in the sense of a future ideal king), which predicts "a shoot from the stump of Jesse" who will usher in a wonderful age when the wolf will live with the lamb. There is no consensus as to when this oracle was composed. The reference to the "stump of Jesse" implies that the "tree" has been cut down. Some scholars see this as a reference to the assassination of King Amon, father of Josiah (2 Kgs 21:23), and see the wonderful king as Josiah, who was only eight years old when he began to reign (see Isa 11:6: "a little child shall lead them"). Many scholars, however, think that the "stump" presupposes the definitive fall of the Davidic kingship to the Babylonians in 586 BCE, and see the "shoot" as a figure wished for in the utopian future.

Equally uncertain is the provenance of the oracle in Mic 5:2, which refers to a future ruler of Israel, to come from Bethlehem. This oracle implies a critique of the Jerusalem kingship, but not a rejection of the Davidic line. Rather, it calls for a new beginning, in humble circumstances. Such a critique could have been made while there was a king in Jerusalem, but it could also have originated during or after the exile, with the implication that it was the arrogance of the rulers in Jerusalem that led to the fall.

Jeremiah, who prophesied at the time of the Babylonian invasion, was famously critical of the rulers of his day. His oracle on the occasion of the deportation of King Jehoiachin in 597 BCE seems to ring the death knell for the Davidic dynasty: "Record this man as childless ... for none of his offspring shall succeed in sitting on the throne of David, and ruling again in Judah" (Jer 22:30). A king, however, could be a descendant of David without being a descendant of Jehoiachin. (His uncle Zedekiah in fact succeeded him.) According to the following chapter in Jeremiah, "The days are surely coming, says the LORD, when I will raise up for David a righteous Branch, and he shall reign as king and deal wisely, and shall execute justice and righteousness in the land.... And this is the name by which he will be called: 'The LORD is our righteousness'" (Jer 23:5-6). The latter expression (**yhwh tsidhqenu** יהוה צִדְקֵנוּ) appears to be a play on the name of Zedekiah (**tsidhqiyah** צִדְקִיָּה). Whether the oracle should be read as affirming Zedekiah as a righteous king, or rather as saying that only a future king will live up to Zedekiah's name, is uncertain, but the latter seems more likely in view of the general tenor of Jeremiah's prophecy. This oracle is further updated in Jer 33:14-16, which says that the "Branch" will be raised up "in those days and at that time." This passage is not found in the Gk. translation of Jeremiah and is almost certainly an addition to the Hebrew text from some time in the postexilic period (*see* BRANCH).

The future restoration of the Davidic line is also affirmed in Ezekiel, where the future king is usually, but not exclusively, referred to as **nasi'** (נָשִׂיא "prince") rather than as king. In Ezekiel's vision of the new Jerusalem, however, the role of the king is greatly reduced. He is primarily responsible for providing the offerings for the temple service (Ezek 45:17).

One other prophetic passage that predicts a future restoration of the kingship should be noted. Zechariah tells Jerusalem, "Lo, your king comes to you; triumphant and victorious is he, humble and riding on a donkey, on a colt, the foal of a donkey" (Zech 9:9). The donkey was the preferred means of transport of tribal leaders in the period of the judges. The reference here is a throwback to that time, and implies the rejection of the horse, the favored animal in warfare. The Heb. refers to "sons of Greece" as the adversaries of the sons of Zion in 9:13, and for that reason many scholars have dated this oracle to the time of Alexander the Great. The reading is doubtful, however, and there is no consensus on the provenance of this passage. It is noteworthy that some messianic oracles (also Mic 5) express disillusionment with the attempts of kings to engage in warfare and look instead for someone who will rely on divine help.

When Jews were allowed to return from Babylon and rebuild the Temple, there seems to have been a brief flurry of messianic expectation associated with the figure of Zerubbabel (Hag 1–2; Zech 1–6). Haggai tells Zerubbabel that the Lord is about to overthrow nations and make him like a signet ring (2:21-23). Zechariah says that the Lord is going to bring "my servant the Branch" (Zech 3:8), an apparent reference to Jeremiah's prophecy. (It is possible that the oracle in Jeremiah is a late addition and presupposes Zechariah. Zerubbabel's name means "shoot of Babylon.") Zechariah announces the arrival of the Branch: "Here is a man whose name is Branch" (Zech 6:12). These words were almost certainly addressed to Zerubbabel, but his name has been excised from the text, so that the words now seem to be addressed to the high priest Joshua. Zerubbabel disappears abruptly from history.

The Persians allowed the Jews to rebuild their Temple, but they were not prepared to accept a restored Jewish kingdom. Second Isaiah was perhaps more realistic than Haggai and Zechariah when he said that Cyrus of Persia, who was neither Davidic nor Jewish, was the **mashiakh** of the Lord (Isa 45:1).

B. The Septuagint

It is clear enough that some messianic prophecies were introduced into the biblical text in the postexilic period. These prophecies, however, are difficult to date, and so we have no clear picture of the extent of messianic expectation in the Persian or early Hellenistic periods. One possible window into the early Hellenistic period is provided by the Gk. translation of the Bible (the LXX), of which the Pentateuch was translated by the mid-3rd cent. BCE (*see* SEPTUAGINT).

Despite some claims to the contrary, the LXX Pentateuch provides little evidence of messianic expectation. The pentateuchal passage that was most often read as messianic prediction in ancient Judaism is an enigmatic passage in the blessing of Jacob: "Until **shiloh** (שִׁילֹה) comes, and the obedience of the people is his" (Gen 49:10). The majority reading of the LXX manuscripts translates **shiloh** as "the things laid away for him," and fails to associate the future glory of Judah with an individual ruler. The Gk. version of BALAAM's oracles (Num 24:7, 17) speaks of a "man" who will have a kingdom, and this is of some significance for messianism in the Hellenistic period, even though this passage refrains from calling him a king. Of course, the Pentateuch did not provide many opportunities for the translators to indulge in messianic speculation.

The situation is different in the Prophets and Psalms, which were translated later (2nd or 1st cent. BCE). Passages such as Isa 11 were translated faithfully, but there were also some cases where the translators introduced messianic references without foundation in the Hebrew text. For example, in Amos 4:13, the Lord reveals to humanity **mah-ssekho** (מַה־שֵּׂחוֹ, "what is his thought"). The Gk. reads: "announcing to humanity his anointed" (**ton christon autou** τὸν χριστὸν αὐτου). The translator may have misread the Hebrew letters, but he evidently found it plausible that the Lord should be spoken of as announcing his anointed. Moreover, texts such as Ps 2 that originally referred to a historical king were now presumably read as referring to a king who was to come, in effect, an eschatological messiah.

C. The Dead Sea Scrolls

Since the promise to David was part of received Scripture, it is unlikely that it ever lapsed entirely, but the testimonies for much of the Second Temple period are very sparse. Several major works (Chronicles, Ezra–Nehemiah, Sirach) show no interest in messianic expectation. More remarkable is the lack of clear references to the Messiah in the early apocalypses of *Enoch* and Daniel, in the early 2nd cent. BCE. The "one like a son of man" (NRSV, "one like a human being") in Dan 7:13 receives a kingdom on behalf of the people, but he is most plausibly understood as an angelic figure rather than as a Davidic messiah (of whom there is no other indication in Daniel; the word **mashiakh** is used twice in Dan 9:25-26 with reference to priestly leaders, although these references were later reinterpreted as messianic). It would seem then that messianic interpretation was largely dormant in the early Hellenistic period, down to the Maccabean Revolt.

1. The Davidic Messiah

The DEAD SEA SCROLLS, in contrast, which were mostly written in the first half of the 1st cent. BCE, provide ample though fragmentary evidence of a revival of messianic expectation under the Hasmoneans. Much of this evidence is found in exegetical contexts. The pesher on Isaiah (4Q161) cites Isa 11:1-5, and comments: "[The interpretation of the matter concerns the Branch of] David, who will arise at the end of days" (8-10 18; author's trans.). The context refers to a battle with the Kittim, a name (derived from Citium in Cyprus) that may refer either to Greeks or Romans, but refers to Romans in the Pesharim. A fragment of the *War Rule*, 4Q285 (5 2) also refers to "Isaiah the prophet" and cites Isa 11:1 ("there shall come forth a shoot from the stump of Jesse"). Another line reads "the Branch of David and they will enter into judgment with ..." (5 3). The Branch (**tsemakh** [צֶמַח], the word used in Jer 23:5) is apparently taken as the fulfillment of Isaiah's prophecy about the shoot from the stump of Jesse. Another fragmentary line reads "the Prince of the Congregation, the Br[anch of David] will kill him" (5 4; Vermes 150). (When the fragment was first published, this verse was initially read by Eisenman and Wise as "they will kill the Prince of the Congregation, the Bran[ch of David]," but in all the parallel passages, and in Isa 11 itself, the messianic figure does the killing.) While the word **mashiakh** does not occur in either the pesher or 4Q285, there is little doubt that the Branch of David is the messianic king. In 4Q252 (*Pesher Genesis*) the Branch is explicitly called **mashiakh** in the context of an interpretation of Gen 49:10:

> Whenever Israel rules, there shall [not] fail to be a descendant of David upon the throne. For the ruler's staff is the Covenant of kingship, [and the clans] of Israel are the divisions, until the Messiah of Righteousness comes, the Branch of David. For to him and his seed is granted the Covenant of kingship over his people for everlasting generations ... (V, 1–4; Vermes, 302)

The phrase "Messiah of Righteousness" echoes the "righteous Branch" of Jeremiah.

The fragment of 4Q285 also shows that the "Prince of the Congregation" was none other than the Branch of David. This should also be apparent from the *Rule of the Blessings* (1Q28b), which includes a blessing for the Prince, which draws heavily on Isa 11:

> The Master shall bless the Prince of the Congregation ... and shall renew for him the Covenant of the Community that he may establish the kingdom of His people for ever, [that he may judge the poor with righteousness and] dispense justice with [equity to the oppressed] of the land (Isa 11:4*b*) ... (V, 20–22; Vermes, 270)

The blessing continues:

> [May you smite the peoples] with the might of your hand and ravage the earth with your sceptre; may you bring death to the ungodly with the breath of your lips! (Isa 11:4*b*). [May He shed upon you the spirit of counsel] and everlasting might, the spirit of knowledge and of the fear of God; may righteousness be the girdle [of your loins] and may your reins be girdled [with faithfulness]! (Isa 11:5). (V, 24–26; Vermes, 270)

It goes on to compare the prince to a young bull with horns of iron and hooves of bronze, and probably also to a lion (see Gen 49:9). Also notable is the statement "for God has established you as the scepter," which is probably an allusion to Balaam's oracle in Num 24:17.

The Branch of David also appears in the *Florilegium* (4Q174). This fragmentary text strings together commentaries on 2 Sam 7:10-14; Ps 1:1; and Ps 2:1. Second Samuel 7:14 ("I will be a father to him, and he shall be a son to me") is said to refer to "the Branch of David who shall arise with the Interpreter of the Law [to rule] in Zion [at the end] of time" (1 11–12). Also, we are told that "the fallen tent of David" (Amos 9:11) is "he who shall arise to save Israel" (1 12–13; Vermes 354).

The Prince of the Congregation also appears with messianic overtones in CD VII, 20, in the context of a citation of Balaam's oracle from Num 24. The two manuscripts of CD (the *Damascus Document* from the Cairo Geniza) have different texts at this point. In MS A, a citation of Amos 5:26-27, which mentions "Kaiwan your star-god," and Amos 9:11 is followed by Num 24:17: "The star is the Interpreter of the Law who shall come to Damascus; as it is written, A star shall come forth out of Jacob and a sceptre shall rise out of Israel. The sceptre is the Prince of the whole congregation, and when he comes he shall smite all the children of Seth" (VII, 18–21; Vermes 103).

The messianic interpretation of Balaam's oracle is well attested. The most famous example is the story that Rabbi Akiba thought that the star was Simon bar Kosiba, who led the revolt against Rome in 132 CE and was henceforth known as Bar Kochba, "son of the star" (*j. Taan.* 68d). As we have seen, the LXX translates "scepter" as "man" and Philo of Alexandria says that this "man" is a warrior who will subdue great nations (*Rewards* 95). Philo's familiarity with this interpretation of Balaam's oracle is all the more significant because he was not generally interested in messianism. The star and scepter are also interpreted messianically in *T. Jud.* 24:1-6. In the *Damascus Document* (CD) the star and scepter are taken as two separate figures. Balaam's oracle is cited without interpretation in the *Testimonia* (4Q175) and in 1QM XI, 6–7.

The picture of the Davidic messiah that emerges from the passages we have discussed so far is one of a mighty warrior who would drive out the Gentiles. This picture is based on a small network of biblical prophecies, most prominently Gen 49, Isa 11, Jer 23 (the Branch), and Balaam's oracle in Num 24. This picture was in no way peculiar to the sect of the Scrolls. The *Psalms of Solomon*, extant in Gk. but probably composed in Hebrew around the middle of the 1st cent. BCE, are often thought to be Pharisaic in origin. *Psalms of Solomon* 17 recalls the promise to David, and complains that "those to whom you did not make the promise" have "despoiled the throne of David." These people are not Gentiles, but the Hasmonean rulers (descended from the Maccabees) who had declared themselves kings at the end of the 2nd cent. BCE. (Their kingdom lasted about forty years, until the Roman general Pompey captured Jerusalem in 63 BCE.) The *Psalms of Solomon* are bitterly critical of the HASMONEANS, and pray that God will restore a descendant of David:

> Undergird him with the strength to destroy the unrighteous rulers, to purge Jerusalem from gentiles who trample her to destruction; in wisdom and in righteousness (see Isa 11) to drive out the sinners from the inheritance; to smash the arrogance of sinners like a potter's jar (see Ps 2:9); To shatter all their substance with an iron rod (see Ps 2:9); to destroy the unlawful nations with the word of his mouth (see Isa 11:4). (*OTP* 2, 667)

This picture of a warrior messiah was shared across sectarian lines, and was even reflected in the writings of Philo of Alexandria.

The *Psalms of Solomon* also provide a clue as to why there was a revival of messianic expectation in the early 1st cent. BCE. The Hasmoneans had renewed native Jewish kingship, but they were not descendants of David. Hence the desire, by various opposition groups, that the Lord would raise up a Davidic king, rather than one of those to whom the promise had not been given.

2. Two messiahs

The messianic expectation of the Scrolls was distinctive, however, in another respect. The *Community Rule* (1QS IX, 11) says that the men of the community should depart from none of the rules "until there shall come a prophet and the messiahs of Aaron and Israel" (**mshykhy ʾhrwn wysrʾl** משיחי אהרון וישראל). The *Damascus Document* (CD XII, 23) uses a similar expression: **mshykh ʾhrwn wysrʾl** (משיח אהרון וישראל). The latter expression has sometimes been read as a singular, but it is not apparent why one messiah should be said to be from both Aaron and Israel. Moreover, several other scrolls pair the Messiah of Israel with another figure. 1Q28a, the *Rule of the Congregation*, the eschatological rule for the end of days, insists that the Messiah of Israel should not extend his hand to the bread before the priest says the blessing (II, 18–21). In the pesher on Isaiah, the statement in Isa 11:3 that the Messiah "shall not judge by what his eyes see" is taken to mean that he will defer to "priests of renown" (8-10 25). In the *Florilegium*, the Branch of David is accompanied by the Interpreter of the Law, and likewise in CD VII, 18–19 the Prince of the Congregation is linked with the Interpreter. In the *Temple Scroll*, too, the king is clearly subject to the authority of the priests.

The idea of two messiahs has a biblical precedent in the "two sons of oil," translated as "two anointed ones," most probably Zerubbabel and the high priest Joshua, in Zech 4:14. It reflects the priestly character of the sect of the Dead Sea Scrolls, which valued the priesthood even more highly than the messianic kingship. But this feature of messianic expectation in the Scrolls may also be explained by opposition to the Hasmoneans. The latter had not only appropriated the kingship, to which they had no traditional right, they had also appropriated the high priesthood and combined the offices of king and high priest. Even though Ps 110:4 had told the king that he was a priest forever after the order of Melchizedek, the sectarians whose views are reflected in the Scrolls held firmly that the two offices should be distinct. Hence their hope for two messiahs at the end of days.

3. Controversial texts

Three other texts from the Dead Sea Scrolls require comment: 4Q246, 4Q521, and 4Q541. The text 4Q246 is popularly known as "the Son of God text." The text consists of two columns, of which the first is torn down the middle so that only the second half of the lines survives. Someone is said to fall before a throne. There is mention of a vision. The fragmentary text continues with references to affliction and carnage, and mentions "the king of Assyria and [E]gypt" (I, 6).

The second column is fully preserved. It speaks of someone who will be called "Son of God" and "Son of the Most High" (II, 1). There will be a period of tumult "until the people of God arises" and all rest from the sword (II, 4). Then there will be an everlasting kingdom.

There has been a lively debate as to whether the figure called "Son of God" is a negative figure or a positive one, allied with the people of God. There is a lacuna before the phrase "until the people of God arises," and this has led some scholars to assume that the "Son of God" belongs to the time of distress, and so must be a negative, evil figure. But by far the closest parallel to the titles in question is explicitly messianic. In Luke 1:32 the angel Gabriel tells Mary that her child "will be great, and will be called the Son of the Most High, and the Lord God will give to him the throne of his ancestor David. He will reign over the house of Jacob forever, and of his kingdom there will be no end." In 1:35 he adds: "he will be called Son of God." The Gk. titles "Son of the Most High" and "Son of God" correspond exactly to the Aram. fragment from Qumran. Both texts refer to an everlasting kingdom. Luke would hardly have used the Palestinian Jewish titles with reference to the Messiah if they were primarily associated negatively with a Syrian king. The basis for referring to the Messiah as SON OF GOD is clear, not only in Ps 2 but also in 2 Sam 7 and in the *Florilegium* from Qumran. The role of the Son of God conforms to the traditional role of the Messiah, to impose peace on earth by the power of God.

The text 4Q521 speaks of a messiah whom heaven and earth will obey. It goes on to say that "the glorious things that have not taken place, the Lord will do as he said, for he will heal the wounded, give life to the dead and preach good news to the poor" (2 11–12; author's trans.). These are works of the Lord, but preaching good news is usually the work of a herald or messenger. In Matt 11:2-6 the same works are attributed to Jesus. It is likely that in 4Q521 too the messiah whom heaven and earth obey is the agent through whom the Lord acts. If so, the messiah is here depicted as an Elijah-like figure, and should be identified as a prophetic rather than a royal messiah. An eschatological herald or messenger (compare Isa 52:7) also plays a part in 11Q13.

The very fragmentary Aram. text 4Q541 speaks of a figure who "will atone for all the children of his people" (9 2). He is a teacher, and "his light will be kindled in all the corners of the earth, and it will shine on the darkness" (9 4). This figure will nonetheless encounter difficulties. "They will speak many words against him, and they will invent many ... fictions against him and speak shameful things about him" (9 5–6). It has been argued that this passage concerns a "suffering servant" modeled on Isa 53. He is not called a messiah, but the spread of his light might be taken to have eschatological significance. The motif is paralleled in a poem about an eschatological priest in *T. Levi* 18. Since the figure in 4Q541 atones for his people, he is presumably a priest, and atones by offering the prescribed sacrifices. (Priests were also teachers.) There is no indication that his suffering was thought to have atoning significance. The abuse he encounters is similar to the opposition to the TEACHER OF RIGHTEOUSNESS, as reflected in the *Hodayot* (1QH[a]).

There is very little evidence for Isa 53 as a messianic prophecy in pre-Christian Judaism, but there was a possible textual basis. In Isa 52:14, the passage "so marred (**mishkhath** מִשְׁחַת) was his appearance, beyond human semblance" is read as "so I have anointed (**mshkhty** משחתי) [his appearance beyond that of a man]" in the great Isaiah scroll from Qumran (1QIsa[a]). This may be a scribal error, but it lent itself to a messianic interpretation, especially in light of Isa 61:1, where the prophet says that God has anointed him. Whether the text was read this way at Qumran is an open question. There are many allusions to Isa 53 in the *Hodayot*, and it is arguable that the Teacher of Righteousness understood himself as the suffering servant. There is no good evidence, however, that the Teacher was ever regarded as a messiah.

D. Messiah and Son of Man

In Dan 7 "one like a son of man" appears on the clouds and is given a kingdom on behalf of "the holy ones of the Most High." He appears in contrast to four beasts, which symbolize four kingdoms. In the context of Daniel, this figure is not the Messiah, but rather the patron angel of Israel, MICHAEL (see Dan 10:21; 12:1). By the 1st cent. CE, however, the two figures were associated (*see* SON OF MAN).

The Similitudes of Enoch (*1 En.* 37–71) was most probably written in the early or mid-1st cent. CE. It has not been found in the Dead Sea Scrolls. It describes three visions of Enoch. In one of these he sees "one who had a head of days, and his head was like white wool. And with him was another, whose face was like the appearance of a man; and his face was full of graciousness like one of the holy angels" (*1 En.* 46:1; Nickelsburg and VanderKam, 59). These are evidently the same as the figures seen by Daniel. The "Son of Man" is an angelic figure, although he is distinguished from Michael in this text. We are told that "his name was named" even before the sun and the constellations were created. Later, he sits as judge on the throne of glory. In two passages, 48:10 and 52:4, he is referred to as "his Anointed One" or Messiah. At the end of the Similitudes, Enoch is taken up to heaven; and in chap. 71, in what appears to be a secondary appendix, he is greeted as "Son of Man." Whether, or in what sense, he is identified with the Son of Man of his visions is disputed. Up to that point, there is no indication that the Son of Man ever had an earthly career. While he is called Messiah, he is not associated with the line of David. We have already seen that the term *messiah* was not restricted to the Davidic king, but could also be applied to a future priest, and perhaps also to a prophet. The Similitudes illustrate another usage, with reference to a heavenly, angelic figure. A similar figure is described in 11Q13, where he is given the name of the ancient priest-king of Salem (Gen 14; compare Ps 110), but is described as an ʾ**elohim** (divine or angelic being) who executes the judgments of God. Melchizedek is not called "messiah."

Imagery associated with the Son of Man is used in connection with the Davidic messiah in *4 Ezra*, an apocalypse from the end of the 1st cent. CE, which survives in Latin and other versions. There Ezra is told that "my son the Messiah shall be revealed with those who are with him, and those who remain shall rejoice four hundred years. And after these years my son the Messiah shall die, and all who draw human breath" (*4 Ezra* 7:28-29; *OTP* 2, 537). Then the world will be returned to primeval silence for seven days, after which the resurrection will follow. The Messiah is not killed, but apparently dies of natural causes. (The roughly contemporary apocalypse of [Syriac] *2 Baruch* says that "when the time of the presence of the Messiah has run its course ... he will return in glory," presumably to heaven. Then the resurrection will follow [*2 Bar.* 30:1].) The four-hundred-year reign, like the millennium in the book of Revelation, provides for an era of earthly fulfillment, in line with traditional OT expectation, before the end of the world and new creation that is characteristic of apocalyptic literature.

In *4 Ezra* 11–12, the visionary sees an eagle come up out of the sea, which is then confronted by a lion. He is told that the eagle "is the fourth kingdom which appeared in a vision to your brother Daniel. But it was not explained to him as I now explain ... it to you" (12:11-12). The eagle obviously symbolizes Rome. The lion is identified as "the Messiah whom the Most High has kept until the end of days, who will arise from the posterity of David" (12:32; *OTP* 1, 550). In chap. 13, Ezra sees "something like the figure of a man" come up from the sea and fly with the clouds. He takes his stand on a mountain, and destroys the nations who attack him with the breath of his lips. He is identified as "my son," whom the Most High has been keeping for many ages, and the mountain is identified as Mount Zion. While the imagery of riding on the clouds recalls the "Son of Man," the stand on Mount Zion and the fiery breath are clearly messianic images (compare Ps 2; Isa 11). While the Messiah is said to be from the posterity of David, he is also said to be a preexistent figure, like the Son of Man in the Similitudes, whom the Lord has been keeping for many ages. The Messiah is also said to be preexistent in the LXX translation of Ps 110 (109 in Gk.), where he is said to have been begotten "before the Day Star." (The Hebrew has "from dawn.")

The idea of a savior figure who comes from heaven is also found in the fifth book of *Sibylline Oracles*, composed in Egypt in the early 2nd cent. CE. He is variously described as "a king sent from God" (108–9), an "exceptional man from the sky" (256), or "a blessed man ... from the expanses of heaven with a scepter in his hands which God gave him" (414; *OTP* 1, 395–403). While he is not said to be anointed, as an eschatological king sent by God he is clearly a messianic figure. His heavenly origin recalls the "Son of Man," but the language is not especially close to that of Daniel. It is apparent, in any case, that the figure of the Messiah had taken on a supernatural character by the late 1st–early 2nd cent. CE.

E. Messianic Pretenders

More traditional ideas of a human, warrior messiah also continued to flourish. Josephus reports a series of royal pretenders in the 1st cent. CE, beginning after the death of Herod, with Judas, whose father had been killed by Herod; Simon, a servant of Herod of imposing size; and Athronges, another person distinguished by size (Josephus, *Ant.* 17.271–85). We know little about these people apart from the unsympathetic account of Josephus. Josephus also claims that messianic expectation, based on some people misinterpreting Scripture, was a significant factor in the outbreak of the revolt against Rome in 66 CE (*J.W.* 6.312–13). Josephus held that the oracle really referred to Vespasian, who was proclaimed emperor while in Judea. Josephus portrays two of the rebel leaders as royal pretenders: Menahem, son of Judas the Galilean (*J.W.* 2.433–34), and Simon bar Giora (*J.W.* 4.503). The latter was ceremonially executed in Rome as the leader of the defeated Judeans. In 115–117 CE a revolt swept the Diaspora in Cyrene and Egypt, which was led by a messianic pretender whose name is variously given as Lukuas or Alexander (Eusebius, *Hist. eccl.* 4.2.1–5; Cassius Dio, *Rom.* 68.32.1–3). Simon Bar Kosiba, known as Bar Kochba, who led the last Jewish revolt against Rome in 132–35 CE, was allegedly hailed as messiah by Rabbi Akiba (*see* BAR KOCHBA, SIMON). Coins from the revolt refer to him as "prince" (nsyʾ נשיא), which we have seen as a messianic title in the Dead Sea Scrolls, and sometimes mention him with the high priest Eleazar.

F. Later Jewish Tradition

In the wake of the failed revolts, the compilers of the Mishnah turned away from messianism. The Mishnah only makes passing reference to "the days of the messiah" twice (*m. Ber.* 1:5 and *m. Sotah* 9:15). Ongoing messianic hope is attested in the Jewish daily prayer, the Eighteen Benedictions, which prays explicitly for the restoration of the throne of David and coming of the Branch of David, and also in the Aramaic biblical paraphrases, the Targums. The picture of the Messiah in these sources is in line with what we have seen in the Dead Sea Scrolls. Targum Pseudo-Jonathan on Gen 49 speaks of the King Messiah girding his loins for battle, and reddening the mountains with the blood of the slain. Expectation of the Davidic messiah is well attested in the Talmud (e.g., *b. Sanh.* 98–99a).

Later Jewish tradition also refers to an Ephraimite messiah, son of Joseph, who would be killed (*b. Sukkah* 52a and later traditions). This figure was apparently expected to precede the messianic son of David. This tradition might have arisen after the failure of the messianic revolts in the early 2nd cent. CE, but it remains obscure.

There is some evidence for a messianic interpretation of the suffering servant in later Judaism. The Targum of Isaiah, which is no earlier than the 2nd cent. CE but may contain older traditions, glosses the word *servant* with *messiah* (ʿbdy mshykhʾ עבדי משיחא). The Targum consistently changes the meaning of Isa 53 so that the servant is not suffering but triumphant. But in the Talmud tractate *Sanhedrin* 98b the Messiah is called "the sick one" (or, according to another reading, "the leper") and Isa 53:4 is cited as proof-text. The idea of a suffering messiah, however, is late and marginal in Judaism, and is not attested before the rise of Christianity. *See* CHRIST; DAVID.

Bibliography: J. H. Charlesworth, ed. *The Messiah* (1992); J. H. Charlesworth, ed. *The Old Testament Pseudepigrapha.* 2 vols. (1983–85); A. Y. Collins and J. J. Collins. *King and Messiah as Son of God* (2008); J. J. Collins. *The Scepter and the Star* (1995); J. Day, ed. *King and Messiah in Israel and the Ancient Near East* (1998); Robert Eisenman and Michael Wise. *The Dead Sea Scrolls Uncovered: The First Complete Translation and Interpretation of 50 Key Documents Withheld for over 35 Years* (1992); W. Horbury. *Jewish Messianism and the Cult of Christ* (1998); S. Mowinckel. *He That Cometh* (1956; reprint, 2005); George W. E. Nickelsburg and James C. VanderKam. *1 Enoch: A New Translation* (2004); K. E. Pomykala. *The Davidic Dynasty Tradition in Early Judaism* (1995); W. Schniedewind. *Society and the Promise to David* (1999); Geza Vermes. *The Dead Sea Scrolls in English* (1995); M. O. Wise. *The First Messiah* (1999).

JOHN J. COLLINS

MESSIAH, TITLE FOR JESUS. *See* CHRIST.

MESSIANIC BANQUET. The term "messianic banquet" is not found in the Bible, but has been used by modern scholars as a convenient designation for that cluster of imagery in which eschatological salvation is portrayed as a grand banquet, whether or not the Messiah is specifically mentioned. For most of the world's population throughout history, scarcity and hunger have been the experienced reality or constant threat. Thus it is not unexpected that metaphors of eschatological salvation would include the image of a great feast in which there was abundant food for all (*see* MESSIAH, JEWISH; SALVATION).

The motifs that developed into the image of the messianic banquet are illustrated in an oracle from Israel's earliest days. Genesis 49:10 seems to be an oracle that celebrates the good life that had come with the conquests of David, but realizes this cannot be the ultimate fulfillment of God's purpose and so looks forward to the eschatological time. The oracle combines the motifs of the coming deliverer and the good time coming when there will be plenty to eat and drink. When the ultimate savior figure comes, the time of scarcity will be replaced by the time of extravagant plenty. This will also be the time of the ultimate victory of God's ruler to whom other peoples will be subject.

Such imagery affected the ways Israel's prophets and teachers depicted their ultimate hopes, as well as their present life as an anticipation of the eschatological future. Deuteronomy 12:9-14 is a representative text in which such themes are woven together: the dialectic of already/not yet; the ultimate rest (**menukhah** מְנוּחָה) and possession (**nakhalah** נַחֲלָה) of the land as God's gift, rather than a human achievement, is already celebrated in the sacrificial feast; the final victory of God in which the enemies are destroyed; and the unity and equality of the people of God gathered in the holy city about the one shrine in which men, women, and children, slave and free, rich and poor, all join in one grand festive meal.

As prophecy modulated into apocalyptic, such imagery became more specific and vivid. Isaiah 25:6-8 compresses several scattered motifs into one stunning scene:

> On this mountain the LORD of hosts will make for all peoples a feast of rich food, a feast of well-aged wines, of rich food filled with marrow, of well-aged wines strained clear. And he will destroy on this mountain the shroud that is cast over all peoples, the sheet that is spread over all nations; he will swallow up death forever. Then the Lord GOD will wipe away the tears from all faces, and the disgrace of his people he will take away from all the earth, for the LORD has spoken.

The LORD is the host, and no messianic figure is mentioned, but the feast is now clearly universal, including all nations. Death is destroyed. Here, the blindness of the nations is healed, and they are included in the feast; in other texts, the banquet is the celebration of God's destruction of the enemy (e.g., 46:10; Isa 34:5-7; Jer 25:15-34; Ezek 39:7-10; Zeph 1:9). The menu is not given, but in some texts the ancient chaos monster is sacrificed and presumably eaten by the banqueters, though this is not specified (Ps 74:12-17; compare Ezek 29:3-5; 32:2-8; *see* ESCHATOLOGY OF THE OT).

Jewish sources from the same general period as the beginnings of Christianity refer to the messianic banquet only rarely, but their manner of reference and the way banqueting imagery is used suggest that the idea had become common and could be generally presupposed. In *2 Bar.* 29:4-8 the coming of the Messiah will bring abundance of food and drink, when the redeemed will dine not only on the Leviathan and

Behemoth, but extravagant harvests of fruit and the return of the heavenly MANNA. *First Enoch* 62:14 promises that the righteous and elect "shall eat and rest and rise with that Son of Man forever and ever."

The Qumran community looked forward to the coming of two Messiahs, a lay Messiah and a priestly Messiah, who would preside at the eschatological meal. The directions given for the future ritual also seem to apply to the present communal meals, which were thought of as in some way an anticipation of the eschatological banquet (see 1Q28a II, 17–20; 1QS VI, 4–6). *See* ESCHATOLOGY IN EARLY JUDAISM; FEASTS AND FASTS.

The apocalyptic hope of Revelation includes as a central theme the great eschatological banquet, when the redeemed will rejoice together at the "marriage supper of the Lamb" (19:9), a motif woven into the visions in various ways. That the messianic feast will be a wedding celebration in which the Messiah celebrates with his bride, the church, is also reflected in other NT texts (Matt 22:1-14 [compare Luke 14:15-24]; 25:1-13; Luke 12:35-38). Jesus' teaching sometimes portrayed the eschatological kingdom of God as a grand banquet including Jews and Gentiles (Matt 8:11-12//Luke 13:28-30), without specifically pointing to his presence as Messiah. Other texts make it explicit that Jesus plays the role of the messianic host (Luke 22:28-30; compare Rev 19:9). The ministry of Jesus, especially the stories in which he feeds the hungry multitudes, and the eucharistic and fellowship meals of the church are portrayed as anticipating the joyful inclusiveness of the messianic banquet (Mark 2:18-20//Matt 9:14-17; Mark 6:30-44//Matt 14:13-21//Luke 9:12-17//John 6:1-14; Mark 8:1-10//Matt 15:32-39; *see* AGAPE; COMMUNION; EUCHARIST; LORD'S SUPPER; MIRACLE; TABLE FELLOWSHIP). Luke–Acts' ubiquitous table scenes are redolent of the coming eschatological joy (Luke 5:29-39; 7:36-50; 11:37-54; 14:1-24; 22:14-38; 24:30-32, 36-49; Acts 2:42, 46; 20:7). At the Last Supper, Jesus points to the future kingdom in which he will eat and drink with the disciples; the church's eucharistic celebrations are already a foretaste of the eschatological banquet (Matt 26:29; Mark 14:25; Luke 22:15-18; compare 1 Cor 11:26, which gives an eschatological tone to the meal as such). *See* APOCALYPTICISM; ESCHATOLOGY OF THE NT; MEALS.

Bibliography: John J. Collins, ed. *The Encyclopedia of Apocalypticism* (1998).

M. EUGENE BORING

MESSIANIC MOVEMENTS. Messianic movements are social movements inspired by religious convictions that a better world is on its way whose coming can be inaugurated by an agent (the messiah) and the movement around that figure. The inspiration for such movements lies in the Bible and specifically in the passages relating to an anointed figure who would fulfill the divine promises for human history (e.g., Isa 11; 61). Such movements have a long history in both Judaism and Christianity; their importance for the latter in particular lies in the fact that Christianity started as a messianic movement.

The 1st-cent. CE Jewish historian Flavius Josephus describes movements led by various individuals promising deliverance and liberation. Strictly speaking these are not messianic movements, at least as described by Josephus, in that there is no evidence that the leader regarded himself as messiah. While Josephus was aware of the suffering of ordinary people (*J.W.* 7.260) and the provocation caused by Roman actions (e.g., *Ant.* 18.60, 274), he regarded it with distaste (*Ant.* 20.124). In the last days of the Temple, Jesus son of Ananias suffered for preaching a message of doom on the Temple (*J.W.* 6.309). The so-called sign prophets (*J.W.* 6.285–87; *Ant.* 20.97–99, 167–72, 188) engaged in significant actions that recalled, and perhaps recapitulated, liberative moments from the past, such as the crossing of the Jordan and regarding the wilderness as an arena of catharsis and hope. Such symbolic actions have their parallels in other acts of protest in the late Second Temple period (*J.W.* 1.648; *Ant.* 18.55–59).

The situation seems to be rather different with the so-called second Jewish revolt in 132–135 CE where Simeon ben Kosebah was, so rabbinic tradition has it (*y. Taan.* 68d), hailed as "son of a star" ("Bar Kochba," and therefore the fulfillment of Num 24:17; *see* BAR KOCHBA, SIMON). The mystical messianism of Abraham Abulafia in the Middle Ages, and Sabbatai Sevi in the 17th cent, indicate the way in which messianism, linked with mystical experience, continued to be a potent force within Jewish history, with similar contours to earliest Christianity and later Christian millenarian movements. Indeed, Christianity's origins were a form of messianism, in which there was the restoration of Jewish fortunes and the coming of a reign of peace and justice on earth, by means of a divinely appointed agent. The main difference about early Christianity, as compared with what we now know of these other movements in Second Temple Judaism led by a prophetic figure, is that this was a messianic movement that survived the trauma of the death of its leader to become part of the tapestry of religion in the last decades of Second Temple Judaism (*see* JESUS CHRIST).

The "this worldly" eschatology that is typical of such messianic movements has been described by sociologists of religion as "millenarian," in which there is an imminent reversal of political arrangements in this age, so that the downtrodden either become the leaders in the new age or have a share in a quality of life denied to them in the old age. A particularly important category of millenarians are those who see such beliefs not just as a matter of belief but of actualization, who thereby seek to enact or bring in the messianic age. The sign prophets mentioned by Josephus, as well as Jesus and Paul, fall into this category, and their careers are illuminated by parallel movements in both Judaism and Christianity. See ESCHATOLOGY IN EARLY JUDAISM; MESSIAH, JEWISH.

Bibliography: Dale C. Allison. *Jesus of Nazareth: Millenarian Prophet* (1998); A. Bradstock and Christopher Rowland. *Radical Christian Writings: A Reader* (2002); W. D. Davies. "From Schweitzer to Scholem: Reflections on Sabbatai Svi." *Jewish and Pauline Studies* (1984) 257–77; John Gager. *Kingdom and Community* (1975); R. Gray. *Prophetic Figures in Late Second Temple Jewish Palestine* (1993); M. Idel. *Messianic Mystics* (1998); K. Mannheim. *Ideology and Utopia* (1960); Christopher Rowland. *Christian Origins: An Account of the Setting and Character of the Most Important Messianic Sect of Judaism.* Rev. ed. (2002); Christopher Rowland. *Radical Christianity: A Reading of Recovery* (1988); G. Scholem. *Sabbatai Sevi: The Mystical Messiah 1626–1676* (1973); Brian R. Wilson. *Magic and the Millennium: A Sociological Study of Religious Movements of Protest among Tribal and Third-World Peoples* (1973).

CHRISTOPHER ROWLAND

MESSIANIC RULE. *See* DEAD SEA SCROLLS; RULE OF THE COMMUNITY.

MESSIANIC SECRET. *See* MARK, GOSPEL OF; SECRET, MESSIANIC.

MESSOS, APOCALYPSE OF. A lost Gnostic text, likely in the Sethian tradition, which is identified by Porphyry along with four other known "apocalypses" of Sethian inclination (*Vit. Plot.* 16). The figure "Messos" is also mentioned in the tractate Allogenes as the speaker's son, to whom the speaker entrusts revelations he has received.

JESSICA TINKLENBERG DEVEGA

METALLURGY. Metallurgy is the whole process of creating metal objects out of metal ore. It consists of a number of stages, starting from the moment the ore is mined: the roasting, smelting, cleaning, alloying, carburizing (in case of steel), and shaping into objects. The metallurgical process varies by metal, a difference that is discernible in the numerous biblical references to metallurgy and the profession of SMITH. According to biblical tradition the inventor of metallurgy was TUBAL-CAIN (Gen 4:22). He was also the eponymous ancestor of the KENITES, a tribe that accordingly was associated with metalworking. Job 28:1-2 aspires to cover the whole field of metallurgy, referring both to all the main metals in use, and to the beginning and end stages of metallurgy, from MINING to REFINING.

The most important metal in the southern Levant in quantitative terms was undoubtedly COPPER, or rather its alloy BRONZE. Evidence of copper smelting in the southern Levant is found in the Wadi Arabah, where there are two major copper ore fields: Timna and the Wadi Feinan (*see* FEINAN, WADI). In pre-Roman times copper ore was smelted in small furnaces, many of which have been found in the Wadi Arabah copper mining centers. These furnaces consisted of small shaft-like structures made of clay, rarely more than 60 cm in diameter, with a hole in the base for letting out the molten slag, and smaller holes in the sides for tuyeres (blowpipes). The bottom contained a hollow, in which the reduced metal was collected. To start the smelting process the furnace was stacked with alternate layers of charcoal, crushed ore, and flux (which was added to speed up the process and lower the firing temperature, and often consisted of iron ore). It was then kept burning, using tuyeres and bellows, for several days. Charcoal had to be added frequently during the process. After the slag was let out, and the furnace had cooled off, it was broken down in order to reach the metal that had collected at the bottom. This was then remelted in crucibles and shaped into ingots.

Alloying of copper with TIN to acquire bronze started in the 3rd millennium, and it gave its name to the period called the Bronze Age. Biblical references to copper or BRASS (**nekhosheth** נְחֹשֶׁת) usually refer to tin-bronze. The origin of the tin used in the Levant to create bronze is still a subject of discussion, but it probably originated in Anatolia. Tin was occasionally used as a metal on its own, and it has a place in various lists of metals such as Num 31:22 and Ezek 27:12, but its main use was in the production of bronze. Bronze is acquired by heating copper in a crucible with cassiterite (or another tin-ore) and charcoal. This step, the production of bronze, and the next, the melting and casting of bronze objects, were relatively simple techniques, and melting sites have been found all over the Levant in the Bronze and Iron ages, generally in towns and villages.

Archaeological evidence of bronzeworking typically includes remains of crucibles, tuyeres, slag, small drops of copper or bronze, lumps of tin ore, and the remains of hearths. Stone molds for casting small objects such as jewelry or small tools are also found occasionally. The description of the tabernacle furniture in Exodus mentions several techniques, such as casting of objects made of massive bronze, and hammering of copper plate, which was either used of itself or to overlay objects made of other materials (e.g., Exod 27; 30; compare Num 16:37-39).

Solomon ordered the furniture for the Temple in Jerusalem to be made by Hiram of Tyre, who was highly skilled in bronzework (1 Kgs 7:13-47). These were large objects, such as pillars with capitals, the "molten sea" of bronze, and the lavers. Casting of these large objects required special skills, in which Hiram was reputed to be expert. The temple furniture was cast in clay molds in the plain between Succoth and Zarethan, located in the east Jordan Valley north of the Wadi

Zerqa (the river Jabbok). On the tell of Deir ʿAlla (*see* DEIR ʿALLA, TELL), which is generally identified with Succoth, a sequence of installations has been found that has been interpreted as furnaces for bronzeworking. The installations consist of rectangular rooms of mudbrick with heavy walls, an outer diameter of 4–5 m, and an inner diameter of 2 m. They were heavily burned inside, and along the sides were small holes that may have served as airholes. Small drops of copper or bronze were found in the immediate surroundings, as well as one tuyere.

Comparison with an installation found in Qantir, in the eastern Nile Delta, and dated to the Eighteenth Dynasty (Late Bronze Age) suggests that the installation in Deir ʿAlla may well have been used for the casting of large objects, comparable to the pillars, capitals, vessels, and other objects that are mentioned in 1 Kgs 7. The workshop at Qantir consisted of four very large furnaces, and "melting batteries" (rows of fireplaces that held crucibles in which the metal was melted). The large furnaces were used to fire large clay molds, which were then left in place on the furnace and kept hot. In the melting batteries large quantities of bronze could be melted simultaneously. The molten metal was poured into the molds. For very large objects several subsequent batches of melted bronze would be necessary, and the bronze already in the molds had to be kept fluid, which is why the molds were kept hot on the furnaces.

The installation at Deir ʿAlla may have been part of a comparable workshop, somewhat smaller and probably less sophisticated. No melting batteries have been found here, but much of the tell remains unexcavated, and they may still be found. The installations at Deir ʿAlla are dated to the Early Iron Age (12th–11th cent. BCE), about two centuries before the reign of Solomon and the building of the first Temple. They therefore cannot be associated with Hiram of Tyre. No comparable installations from the 10th cent. have been found. However, the finds at Deir ʿAlla make clear that in the Early Iron Age this region was reputed for the casting of large bronze objects. The reference in 1 Kgs 7:46 proves that this reputation must still have existed in later periods and explains why Solomon had his large temple furniture cast in the plain of Succoth and Zarethan.

GOLD and SILVER were worked much in the same way as bronze: after the metal had been smelted from the ore and shaped into ingots, it could be cast into small objects (mostly jewelry or smaller elements of the tabernacle furnishings) or hammered into a gold or silver sheet. This sheet could then be used for objects of pure metal such as gold vessels or the silver trumpets used to call the congregation (Num 10:2), or to overlay objects made of other materials such as wood or bronze. Much of the metal industry involved the reuse of old metal objects, which is the main reason why relatively little precious metal is found in archaeological sites.

In order to enhance their purity and therefore their value, precious metals such as gold and silver had to be refined. This process is mentioned often in the Bible, both in a literal sense, referring to the purity of the metal itself (1 Chr 28:18; 29:4), and in a metaphorical sense, when the refining of gold and silver is compared to the removal of moral impurities—a painful process, but one that leads to purity and righteousness (Mal 3:2-3). In order to be refined, the metal was placed in a crucible, together with another, baser metal such as lead. The metals were then melted together and the impurities were bound to the baser metal, and so separated from the pure gold or silver. Refining of silver involved the addition of lead, which would absorb the impurities of the silver, and then be oxidized and evaporated, a process described in Jer 6:29. It could also be removed with the use of sodium hydroxide (lye), which would turn it into dross, a solid slag that floated on top of the liquid silver. This dross, which contained all the impurities of the silver, could then be removed, after which the pure silver could be cast (Prov 25:4; Isa 1:25).

While gold, silver, and bronze could easily be melted and cast, the production of IRON required different techniques, both for extracting it from the ore and for forging it into tools and weapons. Iron is one of the most common ores, but the extraction of metal from it is a complicated process, involving both high temperatures and complex technology. Even then, in order to make its qualities superior to those of bronze, it had to undergo complex treatment involving carburizing and annealing. It was, therefore, not until the 12th cent. BCE, the beginning of the Iron Age, that iron began to be produced on any scale. There are several references in the Bible to the production of iron. The ban on blacksmiths (1 Sam 13:17-22) and the references to the iron chariots of the Canaanites (e.g., Josh 17:18) suggest that the early Israelites did not produce iron. However, the biblical writers were well aware of the technology, as is shown by the references to the extreme heat of an iron furnace (minimum 1200° C; see Deut 4:20; 1 Kgs 8:51) and the forging of iron objects (Isa 44:12).

Until very recently little was known about iron production in the Iron Age, the earliest smelting sites in the Levant dating from the Roman period. However, an iron-smelting site has been found in the central east Jordan Valley, at Tell el-Hammeh, where iron was extracted out of iron ore. This site has been dated to the 10th cent. BCE (930 Cal BCE) and is the world's oldest known iron-smelting site. Tell el-Hammeh is located in one of the major iron ore fields in the region, near Mugharet el-Wardeh west of Amman. A number of furnaces have been found here, together with large amounts of both smelting and smithing slag and ore, as well as large numbers of tuyeres. These furnaces were generally large (1.5 to 2.5 m in diameter), and analysis of the remains has shown that highly sophisticated techniques were applied, producing a high metal yield.

Further research has also revealed information about the social organization of these Iron Age metalsmiths. A comparison of the material remains of Tell el-Hammeh with those of Beth-Shemesh (west of the Jordan, in the traditional territory of Judah) has revealed that iron produced on Tell el-Hammeh was smithed in Beth-Shemesh, and that the same smiths were likely involved. These smiths belonged to a local group or tribe and practiced their trade independently, probably on a seasonal basis. They would take their raw iron to cities such as Beth-Shemesh, where they set up shop and produced tools and weapons, which they then sold to the local population. This situation can be compared to more recent forms of social organization in the same region. Until the 19th cent. CE there were special tribes of itinerant metalsmiths who would travel among towns, villages, and nomadic tribes, or settle among them, to practice their trade. The social organization of the 10th cent. BCE and the recent discoveries at Hammeh and Beth-Shemesh suggest that the smiths of Tell el-Hammeh, from the early biblical period, may also have belonged to a separate tribe, possibly Kenites.

Bibliography: P. T. Craddock. *Early Metal Mining and Production* (1995); T. A. Wertime and J. D. Muhly, eds. *The Coming of the Age of Iron* (1980).

EVELINE J. VAN DER STEEN

METAPHOR IN THEOLOGY. From the outset, theologians have wrestled with the status and function of the figurative and imaginative in Scripture and interpretation. Metaphors shape the work of every theologian.

Early Christian theologians presupposed a powerful metaphor: the Scriptures are words of God. They tend to assume a stark literal/figurative split that parallels human/divine and material/spiritual dichotomies. In essence, God and humanity belong to separate spheres that metaphor bridges. Origen's (b. 185 CE) model distinguished between the literal level of "the letter" (gramma γράμμα) and an advanced level in which readers discern "shadows" and signs, the spiritual gospel. The idea that deeper truth is accessible only to insiders who decode the metaphorical and allegorical has persisted, notably in Augustine (b. 354 CE). Thomas Aquinas (b. 1224 CE) would later open his *Summa Theologiae* arguing that, since God uses metaphors in sacred Scripture, they must have a role in revelation and that "therefore this sacred science (theology) may use metaphors" (1.1.9).

Currently, metaphor is again a focal topic as, in the wake of the Enlightenment, theologians explore again the significance of the imaginative in hermeneutics and theological construction. Garrett Green ("hermeneutic imperative") and David Tracy ("analogical imagination") bring metaphor to center stage. J. D. Crossan echoes Derrida's assertion that biblical language is "a metaphor of a metaphor" and creates a "world." Sally McFague points to the metaphorical nature of models of God. The notion of a concept/figure split persists, however, in much of this work. Paul Ricoeur insists on metaphor's importance—"rule"—as it operates beneath the literary or linguistic level and is key to narrative coherence and interpretation. In ways yet to be explored fully among theologians, cognitive metaphor theories confirm the importance of metaphor that early theologians intuited, but deny the literal/figurative split: metaphor works at the conceptual level, not as mere embellishment. Theologians' work must therefore be characterized and constrained by metaphor. *See* ANALOGY; GOD, METAPHORS FOR; IMAGE, IMAGERY; JESUS, METAPHORS FOR; METAPHOR IN JEWISH THEOLOGY; SIMILITUDES; THEOLOGICAL HERMENEUTICS.

Bibliography: J. D. Crossan. *The Dark Interval: Towards a Theology of Story* (1988); J. Derrida. "The White Mythology: Metaphor in the Text of Philosophy." *New Literary History* 6 (1974) 5–74; Garrett Green. *Theology, Hermeneutics, and Imagination* (2000); George Lakoff and Mark Johnson. *Metaphors We Live By* (1980); Sally McFague. *Metaphorical Theology* (1982); Sally McFague. *Models of God* (1987); Paul Ricoeur. *Figuring the Sacred* (1995); Paul Ricoeur. *The Rule of Metaphor* (1993); David Tracy. *Analogical Imagination* (1998).

BONNIE HOWE

2. The centrality of metaphor in Jewish theology originates in the OT. Israel's relationship with Yahweh is often portrayed as spousal and, correspondingly, idolatry becomes an act of adultery (e.g., Hos 4:12-13). Israel's exclusive fealty to its God is also expressed through the metaphors of God as king, father, and master, which also become the metaphoric staples of prayerful address to God (*see* GOD, METAPHORS FOR).

Prophetic oration is rife with metaphor, which extends to performance as well, when, as in modern street theater, the prophet conveys his message through metaphoric act. Ezekiel portends exile by his own exit from his house (Ezek 12:1-16) and dramatically captures the doomed fate of his community by weighing, burning, and scattering his own hair and beard shavings (5:1-4). Hosea's family life acts as metaphor for Israel's infidelities: Israel's infidelities to Yahweh are like being married to a prostitute, and the children's names ("Not pitied" and "Not my people") are living metaphors of abandonment (Hos 1:2-8).

The classical rabbinic sages employ metaphor within a common trope of rhetorical PARABLE, which entices its audience to deduce a moral lesson or theological principle for themselves. Metaphor is an ideal esoteric mode of communication that delivers potentially subversive thought to audiences used to traditional conceptions of God. The rabbi replaces the prophet as the purveyor of religious tradition, and concomitantly God's word is no longer heard directly (through the prophets) but is rather mined out of the prophetic textual legacy—the TORAH. As God's speech, the text is hyper-meaningful, encouraging a multilayered reading where the literal is informed by metaphor, disclosing deeper strata of meaning. The Torah is metaphorically a marriage contract between the Jews and God, and it replaces God as spousal partner. Torah-study as the cardinal activity of the rabbis is erotically symbolized, making any distraction from this supreme rabbinic enterprise adulterous. Metaphor allows for the transference of a biblical paradigm to a new rabbinic one.

Beginning with Philo and through the Middle Ages, metaphor becomes the central instrument of reconciliation of clashes between Torah and culturally informed values and truths. Maimonides (d. 1205), the chief exponent of Jewish rationalism, "cleanses" the Torah of its philosophically difficult anthropomorphisms by reading them as metaphor. The purpose of metaphor for Maimonides was not to provide another layer of meaning but to displace the literal.

The Jewish mystical tradition is symbolically charged with representations of the Godhead, in which metaphor is not mere replacement of the signifier by the signified, but allows both to cohere in a transcendent mirroring of each other. *See* ANALOGY; BIBLICAL INTERPRETATION, HISTORY OF; IMAGE, IMAGERY; SIMILITUDES; THEOLOGICAL HERMENEUTICS.

JAMES A. DIAMOND

METAPHORS FOR GOD. *See* GOD, METAPHORS FOR.

METAPHORS FOR JESUS. *See* JESUS, METAPHORS FOR.

METEORITES [βαίτυλος **baitylos**]. A meteorite is a piece of a meteor or "falling star" that reaches the surface of the earth without being completely vaporized. The Greek word for meteorite is identified with the name of the Semitic deity Bethel, whose presence is experienced in meteorites. For the ancients of the eastern Mediterranean, the meteorite was a celestial artifact. The meteorite had all the sacred qualities and powers that the sky exerts over human beings. Without the aid of altered states of consciousness, human beings could not reach up to the sky. With a meteor, however, humans could experience the material out of which celestial structures of the deities were built—material that previously had come in contact with celestial beings and their power. The meteorite, therefore, had living power, could perform phenomena, and could give oracles.

At a shrine devoted to the deity named Bethel, Jacob experienced a vision of the opening in the sky where angels went up and down (Gen 28; 35; compare Jer 48:13; Amos 3:14; 5:5). The sacred stone of Bethel is considered by some scholars to have been a meteorite, enshrined in a Canaanite sanctuary to Bethel (Gen 28:11-19). The Judean community at Elephantine likewise venerated Baitylos/Bethel. Phoenicians associated black stones from the sky with various deities. In Islam, the possible meteorite enshrined in the Kaba in Mecca (12 in. in diameter) is said to have been given to Ishmael by the angel Gabriel. *See* ASTRONOMY, ASTROLOGY; BETHEL, DEITY; PORTRAYALS OF ISHMAEL IN ISLAMIC TRADITION.

BRUCE J. MALINA

METHEG-AMMAH mee'thig-am'uh [מֶתֶג הָאַמָּה **methegh ha'ammah**]. After defeating the Philistines, David seized Metheg-ammah (2 Sam 8:1), which translators have viewed as either a proper name (KJV, RSV, NRSV) or a descriptive phrase denoting the conquest of the most prominent Philistine town ("the bridle of the mother city," ASV).

METHUSELAH mi-th*oo*'suh-luh [מְתוּשֶׁלַח **methushelakh**; Μαθουσαλά **Mathousala**]. Methuselah, son of Enoch and father of Lamech (Luke 3:37), lived 969 years, the longest life span of anyone in the Bible, according to Gen 5:21-27. The name means "man of **shelakh** (שֶׁלַח)," with **shelakh** representing either the name of a Canaanite deity or some sort of weapon. According to the chronology of Gen 5–6 Methuselah died in the 600th year of Noah, the year of the flood. *See* METHUSHAEL.

STEVEN D. MASON

METHUSHAEL mi-th*oo*'shay-uhl [מְתוּשָׁאֵל **methusha'el**]. Descendant of Cain and son of Mehujael and father of LAMECH (Gen 4:18), this name is the J-source equivalent of the P-source METHUSELAH (Gen 5:21-26) and credited as the longest-lived human. The name is likely derived from Akkadian **mutu sha ili** ("man of god"). *See* DEITIES, UNDERWORLD.

R. JUSTIN HARKINS

MEUNIM mi-y*oo*'nim [מְעוּנִים **me'unim**]. An unknown group or groups. The Qere in 1 Chr 4:41 and Ezra 2:50 reads Meunim, while the Kethibh reads Meinim. The Hebrew of 2 Chr 26:7 (NRSV, "Meunites") and Neh 7:52 reads Meunim. One suggestion is that the names of two different peoples have been conflated, Meunim being the inhabitants of one of three cities named MAON in Moab, in Edom, and in Judah, while the Meinim come from the south Arabian city of Ma'in. The NRSV emends the text of 2 Chr 20:1 to read "Meunites," although the underlying Hebrew refers to the Ammonites.

KEVIN A. WILSON

MEUNITE. *See* MEUNIM.

MEVORAKH, TELL. A small mound in the Sharon plain, on the southern bank of Nahal Taninim. The earliest settlement uncovered (Str XV) was a rectangular fortress built of mud bricks founded on the low natural hill in the Middle Bronze Age IIA. Later in the Middle Bronze Age IIA (Str XIV), the fortress was surrounded by many unwalled residential houses that covered the entire hill.

During the Middle Bronze Age IIB (Str XIII), the inhabitants constructed a rampart that buried the previous fortress and buildings to a height of 3 m. Some residential rooms and a large kitchen had been built inside the crater for the use of the settlers—probably soldiers of a small unit stationed there—and their families. Several burial jars of infants were discovered beneath the floors of the structures.

After the destruction of this settlement, another was built on the same location in the Middle Bronze Age IIC (Str XII). The main difference between the latter two Middle Bronze Age settlements is the burial methods. The infant burial jars of Str XII had not been buried under the floors as had been done in Str XIII, but in the outer slopes of the ramparts. On some of these jars are HYKSOS stamp impressions.

Stratum XI, the first settlement of the Late Bronze Age, included the remains of a large building that occupied the entire excavation area. This 10 m × 5 m sanctuary was oriented on an east-west axis. Other structural remains include a plastered platform (ca. 0.6 m high) with five steps leading up to it from the east and a plastered bench that ran along the west (short) end of the hall. In the center of the hall stood a large round stone, which may have served as a column base.

The sanctuary of Str X consisted of the same building layout and orientation, but the platform and steps of the earlier period were enclosed and buried within two low walls that formed a new and higher platform (ca. 1 m high). Numerous small finds were recovered including Mitannian-style cylinder seals and imported Cypriot vessels. Interesting local ware include many jars, jugs, juglets, bowls, lamps, and especially decorated chalices and goblets. The only hint of the type of cult that was practiced here was the discovery of a well-preserved bronze snake, about 20 cm long, which closely resembles the bronze snakes found in contemporary sanctuaries at Timna and Hazor.

The sanctuaries of both Strata XI and X were bounded on the south and west by large stone-paved courtyards. These structures occupied almost the entire area of the Late Bronze Age site and may represent a wayside sanctuary, the first of its kind to be discovered in Israel. Stratum IX, which consists of the remains of a large building, stood over the remains of the earlier sanctuaries. The purpose and function of this Late Bronze Age building remain unclear.

The Str VIII of the Iron Age (IB) is represented by a rectangular platform surrounded on the west, south, and east by a stone wall more than 1 m thick, while on the north it was set into the Middle Bronze Age II rampart. This platform apparently served as the foundation of a building, the purpose of which is unknown.

Above the remains of the stratum VIII platform was a four-room house, also from the Iron Age IB (Str VII), dated to the 10th cent. BCE. A large building was surrounded by a broad courtyard with a floor made of a thick layer of beaten lime, and the whole complex was encircled by a wall about 1 m thick. The pottery included local red hand-burnished ware and undecorated pottery, as well as imported Cypriot vessels, among them Cypro-Phoenician, Bichrome, and White Painted ware. This complex has been identified as either an administrative center or an official storehouse.

There are also three Persian phases, but only the last two (Str V, IV) preserved remains from what may have been an administrative center or large estate.

Above the Persian levels remains of the Hellenistic (Str III) and Roman/Byzantine (Str II) periods were discovered. Stratum I consisted of the entire surface of the site, which was densely covered by numerous graves of the Arab period.

Bibliography: A. Knauf. "The Uniqueness of the LB Temple at Tell Mevorak." *BA* 41 (1978) 135; Ephraim Stern. "The Excavations at Tell Mevorakh and the Late Phoenician Elements in the Architecture of Palestine." *BASOR* 225 (1977) 17–28; Ephraim Stern. "Excavations at Tel Mevorakh Are Prelude to Tell Dor Dig." *BAR* 5 (1979) 34–39; Ephraim Stern. "A Late Bronze Age Temple from Tel Mevorakh." *BA* 40 (1977) 89–91.

EPHRAIM STERN

MEZAHAB mee´zuh-hab [מֵי זָהָב me zahav]. Mother of Matred and grandmother of Mehetabel, wife of King Hadad (II) of Edom (Gen 36:39; 1 Chr 1:50). While the gender of the name has been disputed, pre-Islamic Arabian parallels suggest it is female. Me-zahab means "waters of gold" and may also refer to a location.

RALPH K. HAWKINS

MEZOBAITE mi-zoh´bay-*i*t [מְצֹבָיָה metsovayah]. JAASIEL the Mezobaite was one of an elite group of soldiers handling special assignments for David (1 Chr 11:47). Mezobaite probably means "from ZOBAH."

MEZUZAH muh-*zoo*´zuh [מְזוּזָה mezuzah]. Hebrew word for "doorpost" or "gatepost." The meaning depends on the structure to which it is attached. The word can refer to the doorposts of the Temple (1 Kgs 7:5), of a house (Exod 12:7, 22, 23; Deut 6:9; 11:20), or of other structures (e.g., Ezek 43:8).

The doorpost is a symbolic marker for the THRESHOLD, and is therefore significant as the place where the blood of the Passover lamb was spread to protect the Israelites from the angel of death (Exod 12). It is also significant as the position for the inscription of the Shema and is paired with the PHYLACTERIES as a method for marking oneself as remembering of the commands of the covenant (Deut 6:9; 11:20). *See* SHEMA, THE.

C. MARK MCCORMICK

MIBHAR mib'hahr [מִבְחָר **mivkhar**]. Hagri's son, one of David's MIGHTY MEN called the Thirty (1 Chr 11:38), but not included in the par. text (2 Sam 23:36).

MIBSAM mib'sam [מִבְשָׂם **mivsam**]. 1. Son of Ishmael and brother of Mishma (Gen 25:13; 1 Chr 1:29).

2. A Simeonite, the son of Shallum and father of Mishma (1 Chr 4:25).

Because MISHMA is associated with each Mibsam, it is possible that the names represent two tribes regarded as Ishmaelite or Simeonite in different genealogical traditions.

A. HEATH JONES III

MIBZAR mib'zahr [מִבְצָר **mivtsar**]. The name means "fortress" and is used twice to refer to one of the tribal chiefs of Edom (Gen 36:42; 1 Chr 1:53). It is probably a place name; Eusebius' *Onom.* 124.20 associates it with Mabsara, a large village in the Gebalene dependent upon PETRA.

MICA mi'kuh [מִיכָא **mikha'**, מִיכָה **mikhah**]. 1. Mephibosheth's son and descendant of Saul. He had four sons. David provided for his father MEPHIBOSHETH as if he were his son (2 Sam 9:12). In 1 Chr 8:34-35; 9:41, Mica appears as MICAH the son of MERIB-BAAL.

2. A Levite; Asaph's grandson, Zichri's son, and Mattaniah's father (1 Chr 9:15; Neh 11:22). In Neh 11:17, Zabdi is his father; and in Neh 12:35, where his name is spelled MICAIAH, Zacar is his father.

3. A Levite who placed his name on the sealed covenant document (Neh 10:11).

EMILY R. CHENEY

MICAH mi'kuh [מִיכָה **mikhah**, מִיכָיָה **mikhayah**, Μειχά **Micha**]. Means "who is like the Lord." 1. Resident of the hill country in Ephraim, who stole from and later returned to his mother 1,100 silver shekels. Micah's mother made an idol out of silver for his shrine. Micah placed his son as priest over the shrine then later replaced him with a Levite from Bethlehem in Judah (Judg 17:1–18:4).

2. Son of Joel and a descendant of Reuben (1 Chr 5:5).

3. Son of Merib-baal (MEPHIBOSHETH in 2 Sam 9:12), descendant of Jonathan and Saul (1 Chr 8:33-35; 9:40-41). *See* MICA.

4. A Levite and the elder son of Uzziel during Solomon's reign and David's last days (1 Chr 23:20; 24:24-25).

5. Father of Abdon (2 Chr 34:20). Called MICAIAH in 2 Kgs 22:12.

6. A prophet (Mic 1:1; *see* MICAH, BOOK OF).

7. Father of Uzziah, a magistrate (Jdt 6:15).

EMILY R. CHENEY

MICAH, BOOK OF mi'kuh [מִיכָה **mikhah**; Μιχαίας **Michaias**]. Micah, a shortened form of Micaiah, means "Who is like Yah(weh)?" The question is rhetorical and expresses Yahweh's incomparability. While Micah is a common name in biblical and extrabiblical sources alike, it here designates the prophet associated with the BOOK OF THE TWELVE—the sixth in the Hebrew collection, the third in the Greek. Micah is identified in the book's superscription (Mic 1:1) as having come from the town of MORESHETH in the Judahite SHEPHELAH—probably the same as Moresheth-gath in 1:14—and having prophesied during the reigns of Judahite kings of the latter part of the 8th cent. BCE. In Jer 26:18, Micah is remembered for the prophecy of Jerusalem's destruction found in Mic 3:12. The book bearing Micah's name contains both oracles of judgment for the capital cities of Samaria and Jerusalem and their leaders, and visions of future restoration, vindication, and peace for Jerusalem and Jacob. Discerning how these two vectors are related is key to the interpretation of the book.

A. Structure of Micah

I. Superscription (1:1)
II. Making the Punishment Fit the Crime (1:2–3:12)
  A. Samaria—Jerusalem's precursor (1:2-7)
    1. Theophany of the divine judge (1:2-4)
    2. Judgment for Samaria (1:5-7)
  B. Lament—Shephelah decimated, Jerusalem threatened (1:8-16)
  C. The dispossessors will be dispossessed (2:1-5)
  D. Dispute—false words cloak evil deeds (2:6-11)
  E. Yahweh will lead a remnant (2:12-13)

F. Leaders mislead (3:1-12)
1. Rapacious rulers (3:1-4)
2. Pernicious prophets (3:5-8)
3. Jerusalem will fall—venal leaders to blame (3:9-12)

III. Visions of Hope for Jerusalem and Israel (4:1–5:15 [Heb. 5:14])
A. Future peace under Yahweh's just rule (4:1-5)
B. A remnant will return to Jerusalem (4:6-7)
C. Restoration of Jerusalem's rule (4:8)
D. Distress, exile, and restoration for Jerusalem (4:9-10)
E. Jerusalem's fortunes reversed (4:11-13)
F. (Davidic) kings—present and future (5:1-4 [Heb. 4:14–5:3])
G. Role reversal with "Assyria" (5:5-6 [Heb. 5:4-5])
H. The remnant of Jacob will be mighty among the peoples (5:7-9 [Heb. 5:6-8])
I. God's purge (5:10-15 [Heb. 5:9-14])

IV. From Indictment to Restoration (6:1–7:20)
A. Many questions—Yahweh's case against Israel (6:1-8)
1. A covenant lawsuit (6:1-5)
2. What does Yahweh require? (6:6-8)
B. The city" judged (6:9-16)
1. Poetic justice for economic crimes (6:9-15)
2. The Omrids as object lesson (6:16)
C. A prophetic complaint (7:1-20)
1. Lament over a perverse society (7:1-7)
2. From darkness into light (7:8-10)
3. A day of (Jerusalem's) restoration (7:11-13)
4. Reversal of fortunes for Israel and its enemies (7:14-17)
5. God's compassion and forgiveness for a remnant (7:18-20)

B. Detailed Analysis

1. Text

In a number of places, the received Hebrew text of Micah seems to have suffered considerable corruption in the course of transmission. While the ancient versions and fragmentary ancient manuscript finds from the Judean wilderness occasionally provide alternate readings of interest in Micah, the text they witness does not on the whole vary markedly from the Masoretic Text. The most serious textual problems in the book appear to antecede these ancient witnesses. All English translations include not a little uncertainty and conjecture—of necessity. Readers dependent upon translations may wish to compare several. Where they diverge widely or offer cautioning footnotes, the reader is at least alerted to the underlying problems.

2. Views of composition

Virtually all informed opinion points to a certain tension in the book of Micah. On one hand, it contains a number of individual literary units that are quite diverse in content, style, and apparent address. The casual modern reader, as a result, often finds it difficult to follow any "thread" in the book. Read by itself, any given unit may appear to contradict another rather directly. Repeated, careful reading of the entire book, on the other hand, reveals a more arcane unity based upon subtle structuring devices, the repetition of vocabulary and motifs at significant junctures, and strategic juxtapositions.

Beyond descriptive agreement about the book's diversity and unity, however, lies no scholarly consensus about how to understand or account for its tensive reality. Each of the logical options has distinguished proponents. Some view the vast majority of the book as deriving from the 8th-cent. prophet or his immediate followers. They see the book's unity as rooted in the prophet's person and message, and point to different social and historical situations to account for the diversity. Others start with the received book's arcane unity. Some of these prefer to proceed on literary grounds, bracketing out most historical questions as unanswerable. Other "final-form" interpreters view the book as a product of postexilic literati. For them, earlier stages of traditions incorporated into the book, including any that may derive from an 8th-cent. prophet, are simply unrecoverable.

Another stream of scholarship, represented in what follows, sees in the book of Micah the end result of a kind of traditioning process well attested elsewhere in the ANE. While this process is thought to have its fountainhead in the named prophet of the 8th cent., different periods of the ancient community of faith are seen as having "recomposed" the growing Micah tradition as they sought to honor and appropriate it in their situation. The end result is a literary "collage"—or even "a collage of collages"—in which older, independent units carry forward meanings relative to their context of origin, but are then juxtaposed to other material from other contexts. The juxtapositions, too, have their motivating situations and contextual meanings. Each subsequent stage of recomposition incorporates the former stage(s), lending new meanings without erasing the old.

Scholars who currently pursue this line of inquiry know that they cannot explicate the process in full historical or literary detail. They seek instead to define systemically distinct contexts that carried the tradition, and to discern how the needs, interests, and perspectives of each such context may have shaped it. Although the full process was undoubtedly more complex, the Micah tradition will be examined here against the background of three situations: 1) the socioeconomic changes in Judah and Israel during the latter part of the 8th cent. BCE; 2) the royal reforms of the late Judahite monarchy; and 3) a less well-defined context during the exilic and early Second Temple periods.

3. Three levels of tradition for three different contexts

a. Self-contained oracles for the 8th century. Recent studies have illuminated the dynamics of political economy in Israel and Judah during the time of Micah and his fellow 8th-cent. prophets—Isaiah, Hosea, and Amos. Both kingdoms were actively engaged in international trade. They imported luxury goods, military matériel, and certain construction materials for monumental architecture. To pay for these imports, they exported fiber and foodstuffs, especially wheat, olive oil, and wine. While the imports benefited primarily the top of the social pyramid, the exports came from peasant farmers, with whose subsistence they competed directly. A royal standardization of wine and oil amphorae to expedite this trade, regional specialization and intensification of agriculture, concentrated cropping, effacement of traditional risk-spreading measures, explosive population growth, pressure on arable land, consolidation of land ownership, growth of absentee landlordism, and landlord usurpation of decisions about agricultural priorities and techniques all ensued.

When faced with drought, blight, pestilence, or other exigencies of the erratic natural environment, peasants were now bereft of the intricate webs of support that traditional village systems had previously provided. To secure grain to seed their fields and feed their families, they were forced to take out survival loans at usurious rates of interest. As surety for these debts, they had only their fields and the indentured labor of family members to offer. The village courts that were called upon to process the inevitable foreclosures had very few procedural safeguards and were easily suborned or coerced by the few with power and wealth. These foreclosures, in turn, exacerbated all the dynamics that had led to them.

Like his prophetic contemporaries, Micah appealed these cases to God's court of last resort. Tradition regarding these appeals is found in a series of self-contained speeches in much of chap. 1, most of chaps. 2 and 3, and, perhaps, in 6:9-15 and elsewhere. These speeches all address and accuse the powerful and wealthy leaders of society, not Israel or Judah as a whole. Their basic message is the same—the powerful have oppressed the powerless and have been judged guilty of that crime in God's court. Address is direct. Irony and wordplay occur frequently, but they reinforce the basic thrust of the oracles, rather than qualifying or subverting it. These units appear to have been composed for oral delivery and employ a limited number of genres. Each is complete in itself and does not depend on juxtaposition with others for meaning. They conceive of the prophet as auditor of proceedings in Yahweh's court. The language is forensic, with single units often including both indictment and sentence. Measure-for-measure correspondence between the two is favored, thus ensuring that justice is poetic. Sentence, which has already been passed and is fulfillable, is announced as inevitable catastrophe.

b. Reformist recomposition for the late Judahite monarchy. After Samaria's fall to Assyrian might in 722 BCE and the narrow escape of Jerusalem and HEZEKIAH from SENNACHERIB's siege in 701 BCE, the Micah tradition functioned in a different context. Samaria's destruction vindicated Micah's proclamation of inevitable catastrophe (1:6). Jerusalem's near miss focused attention on its fortunes relative to Samaria's. How could it avoid Samaria's fate? The centralizing reforms of King JOSIAH (ca. 640–609 BCE) accentuated national independence and identity, focusing upon the ruling Davidid, his royal chapel (the Temple in Jerusalem), and implementation of Deuteronomic law.

In that context, the Micah tradition was taken to address the nation as a whole and undifferentiated (e.g., 6:1-5). Society-wide transgressions of Deuteronomic law, particularly those involving cultic matters, were stressed (e.g., 1:5, 7 [portions]; 5:12-14 [Heb. 5:11-13]). A tradition now carried in writing by scribes attached to the royal court and Temple could maintain open-ended ambiguity by juxtaposing indictment for transgressions with exhortation to choose reform (6:6-8). Doom that had been ineluctable now became contingent. Samaria functioned as a negative object lesson (1:5-7; 6:16*a*), as it did in the DEUTERONOMISTIC HISTORY (e.g., 2 Kgs 17:5-18*a*), a work in which Josiah's scribes also likely had a major hand. Judgment oracles, with their sentence of inevitable catastrophe, were understood as having been fulfilled already. The prophetic lawsuit (Mic 6:1-5), by contrast, both demanded reform and offered the choice of an open future (6:6-8). Since such exhortation, by its nature, was not fulfillable, its open possibilities carried the irony of almost perpetual crisis.

c. Micah's message for exile and restoration. The fall of Jerusalem to the Babylonians in 587 BCE, attended by deportations into exile, again changed the context in which the Micah tradition was carried, understood, and shaped. Exhortations to reform, lest Jerusalem suffer Samaria's fate, gave way to acknowledgment that Jerusalem, like Samaria, had been justly punished for its sins. When the edict of Cyrus (538 BCE) led to the return of some exiles from Babylon to Jerusalem, the eventual rebuilding of its Temple (520–515 BCE), and an extended struggle of the community gathered around this Second Temple for identity and survival, the Micah tradition was recomposed to reflect and reflect upon that new chapter in Jerusalem's story.

Materials of diverse genres and origins, as well as the canonical shape of the book of Micah, emphasized Yahweh's compassion and salvation for Jerusalem and Jacob, Jerusalem's restoration to its former dominion, its triumph over the nations that had destroyed and oppressed it, and Zion's future role as the seat of Yahweh's peaceful reign over all the nations. That final shaping of the book, with its numerous announcements of salvation, did not erase or obviate the earlier judgment oracles or exhortations to reform. They and their role in Jerusalem's story were remembered and retained as a warning against the sort of behavior that brought Jerusalem's fall. While literary analyses differ in detail, all agree that the structure of the book of Micah alternates judgment (1:2–2:11; 3:1-12; 6:1–7:7) with salvation (2:12-13 [in its final form and placement]; 4:1–5:15 [Heb. 5:14]; 7:8-20), both within its sections and in the book as a whole.

C. Theological and Religious Significance of Micah

1. Judgment and salvation

Judgment and salvation are often thought to vary in inverse proportion—more of one necessarily means less of the other. Taken as a whole, the book of Micah is a powerful antidote to this notion. In close human relationships, love plumbs some of its greatest depths in naming antisocial or self-destructive behaviors and pointing out their intrinsic consequences. Unconditional acceptance following disaster and/or repentance flows from that same love. Legitimate anger raises rhetorical and emotional stakes to call attention to violations unacknowledged or denied. When it has its desired effect and the violation is remedied, reconciliation and closer bonding follow in its wake. Anger is not the opposite of love; indifference is. Such realities are readily intelligible in the interpersonal relationships of human beings. Their use by analogy to explicate the divine-human relationship should be understood with equivalent suppleness, and not be held prisoner to the strictures of reductionist logic.

2. An epitome of prophecy

Micah 6:6-8, the most familiar passage from Micah in many circles, is a self-conscious epitome of prophecy that seeks the theological taproot beneath specific prophetic issues. Since God is not the problem, it observes, placating God with conspicuous or extravagant religiosity is not the solution. Rather, God seeks from human beings only what is "good" for all concerned (6:8)—"to effect justice, to love covenant loyalty, and a making humble to walk with your God" (author's trans.; NRSV, "to do justice, and to love kindness, and to walk humbly with your God"). The first quality of life delineated involves not only acting justly in personal conduct, but taking responsibility for justice in institutional processes. The second emphasizes a mutuality of concern and commitment that is tenderly sensitive to others' needs. The third, unique to this passage, expresses more a summation than an addition. It says that the qualities sought derive not from false or self-effacing humility but from an attentiveness to God's view of the "good" that is fully commensurate with God's radical otherness.

3. The realism of a utopian vision

Because Mic 4:1-4 (see Isa 2:2-4) is transparently utopian, it is sometimes dismissed as merely utopian. The following points caution against easy acceptance of that utilitarian truncation of canon. First, the text's vision is deeply rooted in human needs, hopes, and longings that are perennial and fundamental. Real people make decisions and act upon the basis of such visions. Second, utopian poetry is an act of imagination that creates a sphere of freedom. It thereby subverts the present order with its notion that its own oppressions are inevitable. Note that the book of Micah juxtaposes 4:1-4 with a culminating oracle of judgment upon such oppressions in 3:9-12, thereby contrasting human rule with divine. Third, as every hard-headed realist knows, nothing is more "real-world" than deciding the priorities of resource allocation. In its classic evocation of the "guns-or-butter" issue, Mic 4:1-4 knows that better than some self-proclaimed "realists." Fourth, nations "learn" warfare. Its perpetration requires training and indoctrination. It can be unlearned. Alternative skill sets and doctrinal perspectives can be learned in its stead. Fifth, "Truth is the first casualty of war," says an aphorism that understands the role of "spin" and dissembling in the provocation and perpetration of war. Micah 4:1-4 enunciates the reverse corollary—full, fair, and truthful adjudication born of God is prerequisite to ending the terror of war.

4. Leaders real and ideal

Micah's judgment oracles find particularly culpable human leaders who use their power to exploit and oppress those vulnerable to them. Juxtapositions in the book contrast such leaders with the peace, justice, and equity of Yahweh's future rule. Citizens of agrarian monarchies have often longed for a future, ideal king to deliver them from the rapacity of their present leaders. While the exact nature and origins of the unit in Mic 5:1-4 (Heb. 4:14–5:3) are obscure, it foresees a future Davidid whose rule will be consonant with Yahweh's. Matthew 2:6 (see John 7:42; 21:16) reports the fulfillment of this messianic expectation in the birth of Jesus.

Bibliography: Juan I. Alfaro. *Justice and Loyalty: A Commentary on the Book of Micah* (1989); Leslie C. Allen. *The Books of Joel, Obadiah, Jonah and Micah.* NICOT (1976); Francis I. Andersen and David Noel Freedman. *Micah.* AB 24E (2000); Ehud Ben Zvi. *Micah.* FOTL 21B (2000); Marvin L. Chaney. "Micah—Models Matter: Political Economy and Micah 6:9-15." *Ancient Israel: The Old Testament in Its Social Context.* Philip F. Esler, ed. (2006) 145–60; Robert B. Coote. *Amos among the Prophets: Composition and Theology* (1981); Delbert R. Hillers. *Micah.* Hermeneia (1984); James Limburg. *Hosea–Micah.* Int.(1988); William McKane. *Micah* (1998); James Luther Mays. *Micah: A Commentary.* OTL (1976); Erin Runions. *Changing Subjects: Gender, Nation and Future in Micah* (2001); Daniel J. Simundson. "The Book of Micah." *NIB* 7 (1996) 531–89; Marvin A. Sweeney. *The Twelve Prophets.* Berit Olam (2000) 2.337–416; Hans Walter Wolff. *Micah.* CC (1990).

MARVIN L. CHANEY

MICAIAH mi-kay´yuh [מִיכָה mikhah, מִיכָיָה mikhayah, מִיכָיְהוּ mikhayehu]. The name also appears in the contracted form of MICAH. 1. The son of Imlah, who prophesied about the death of Ahab in his attempt to conquer Ramoth-gilead from the Arameans (1 Kgs 22:4-28; 2 Chr 18:3-27). The prophecy of Micaiah took place at the time Ahab, king of Israel, persuaded Jehoshaphat, king of Judah, to join him in a battle to take back Ramoth-gilead, an important city in Gilead, which was under Aramean control. Jehoshaphat agreed, but he also desired to inquire about the word of the Lord concerning the war. Dissatisfied with the unanimous view of the court prophets, Jehoshaphat asked whether there was a prophet of the Lord from whom they might inquire about the will of the Lord. Ahab mentioned Micaiah, the son of Imlah, a prophet who was not associated with the court. While Jehoshaphat waited for the arrival of Micaiah, Ahab's prophets, represented by ZEDEKIAH, emphasized that the king would be victorious in battle. When Micaiah came before Ahab and Jehoshaphat and was asked by the king whether he would be victorious in the battle for Ramoth-gilead, Micaiah replied by giving the same assurance of victory that was given by Ahab's prophets.

However, Ahab perceived that Micaiah's words were not true and asked him to speak only truth in the name of the Lord. Micaiah then told Ahab of his vision: he saw Israel scattered like sheep without a shepherd. Micaiah's words meant that Ahab would die in his attempt to conquer Ramoth-gilead and that Israel's army would be scattered. Micaiah then described his second vision: he saw the Lord sitting upon his throne and the heavenly council gathered around him. In the deliberation concerning Ahab's fate, a member of the court offered to be a lying spirit in the mouth of Ahab's prophets.

Zedekiah, outraged by Micaiah's words, slapped him on the cheek. Micaiah responded by saying that Zedekiah would flee in terror when the day of disaster came upon Israel. Ahab ordered Micaiah to be sent to prison and be kept alive on bread and water until his return from the battlefield. The death of Ahab in battle was evidence that Micaiah was a true prophet of the Lord (*see* PROPHET, PROPHECY).

2. The father of Achbor, who was one of the people sent to the prophetess Huldah to inquire of the Lord concerning the book found at the occasion of the repair of the Temple (2 Kgs 22:12). In the par. passage, Achbor appears as Abdon, the son of Micah (2 Chr 34:20).

3. The daughter of Uriel of Gibeah, who was the wife of Rehoboam, king of Judah, and the mother of Abijah (2 Chr 13:2). In the par. stories of the reign of Abijah her name appears as MAACAH, the daughter of Abishalom/Absalom (1 Kgs 15:2; 2 Chr 11:20).

4. One of the royal officers sent by Jehoshaphat, king of Judah, throughout all the cities of Judah to teach the people the law of the Lord (2 Chr 17:7-9).

5. The son of Zaccur and a descendant of Asaph, the temple musician. Micaiah's great-great-grandson Zechariah was one of the priests who participated in the procession and blew the trumpet during the dedication of the wall of Jerusalem in the days of Nehemiah (Neh 12:35).

6. One of the eight Levitical musicians who blew the trumpet in the Temple and stood with Nehemiah, the leaders of Judah, and the priests during the ceremonies at the occasion of the dedication of the wall of Jerusalem (Neh 12:41).

7. The son of Gemariah and the grandson of Shaphan (Jer 36:11). Micaiah, a contemporary of the prophet Jeremiah, reported to the princes of Judah the words Baruch read from the scroll in the Temple, at the command of Jeremiah, in the fifth year of King Jehoiakim (Jer 36:9).

Bibliography: R. W. L. Moberly. "Does God Lie to His Prophets? The Story of Micaiah ben Imlah as a Test Case." *HTR* 96 (2003) 1–23.

CLAUDE MARIOTTINI

MICE. *See* MOUSE.

MICHAEL m*i*´kay-uhl [מִיכָאֵל mikhaʾel; Μιχαήλ Michaēl]. Meaning "who is like God?" 1. An Asherite, the father of Sethur, who was one of the twelve spies sent to reconnoiter in Canaan (Num 13:13).

2. A Gadite who settled in Bashan in the days of Jotham and Jeroboam II (1 Chr 5:13).

3. A Gadite, the son of Jeshishai and father of Gilead (1 Chr 5:14).

4. A Levite singer, the great-grandfather of Asaph (1 Chr 6:40).

5. An Issacharite, son of Izrahiah, who served as a military leader in the time of David (1 Chr 7:3).

6. A Benjaminite, son of Beraiah, who resided in Jerusalem (1 Chr 8:16).

7. A military leader from the tribe of Manasseh who deserted Saul at Ziklag and was made a commander of David's forces (1 Chr 12:20).

8. An Issacharite, father of Omri, who oversaw Issachar during David's reign (1 Chr 27:18).

9. A son of King Jehoshaphat of Judah, who was assassinated when his older brother Jehoram assumed the throne (2 Chr 21:2-4).

10. The father of Zebadiah, who led eighty men back from Babylon with Ezra, in the time of Artaxerxes (Ezra 8:8).

11. ARCHANGEL and heavenly prince. Michael and GABRIEL are the only two angels mentioned by name in the Bible. In the OT, Michael is distinguished as the special patron and guardian of Israel, while Gabriel acts as the interpreter of the heavenly mysteries to Daniel. Michael is identified only at Dan 10:13, 21; 12:1, where he is described as "one of the chief princes" or the "great prince" in charge of God's people. These

designations reflect the notion that each nation has its patron ANGEL in the heavenly realm (Sir 17:17).

In the NT, Michael is mentioned by name only twice, at Jude 9 and Rev 12:7. The reference in Jude evidently alludes to the lost ending of the *Testament of Moses*, a pseudepigraphal work in which Michael contests SATAN's legal claim to the body of Moses. Satan's claim apparently arises from Moses' blood guilt for murder (Exod 2:12), but rather than rebuke Satan himself, Michael says "the Lord rebuke you" (compare Zech 3:2), and, as Moses' advocate, he is able to reclaim Moses' body and vindicate his reputation. At Rev 12:7, Michael leads the unfallen angels against the dragon, Satan, and his rebellious host and casts them out of heaven. Michael's victory anticipates Christ's ultimate triumph over Satan (Rev 19:11–20:10).

These biblical references reflect a distinctive angelology that emerged in the Hellenistic period and became increasingly elaborated in extra-biblical writings over the following centuries, amplifying the features already apparent in the biblical record. For instance, in keeping with his role in Daniel, Michael figures as the patron angel of Israel, serving as legal champion, military protector, and commander (*2 En.* 22:6; compare *T. Levi* 5:6; *T. Dan* 6:2-3). He defends Israel against Satan (*T. Mos.* 10:2), and also fights against the Kittim (i.e., Rome; 1QM IX, 15–16; XVII, 6–8). Michael's mandate extends to humans in general (*1 En.* 20:5): he acts as their intercessor (*2 En.* 33:10) and as an *angelus interpres* who reveals heavenly mysteries to humans and then provides them with interpretations (*1 En.* 60:4-9; 71:3-4). Michael enjoins Satan to worship Adam and Eve (*L.A.E.* 13–15) and serves as the first couple's advisor, providing them with seeds to plant (*L.A.E.* 22:2) and offering instruction in the performance of burials (*Apoc. Mos.* 43:1-3). He further acts as psychopomp (or soul guide) to Abraham, leading him to heaven (*T. Ab.* 20:10-12), and is likely the intermediary between God and Moses at the giving of the Law on Mount Sinai (*Jub.* 1:27; 2:1; Acts 7:38; compare 4Q470).

In the heavenly realms, Michael is the chief and leader of the angels (*Ascen. Isa.* 3:16; *1 En.* 24:6), and the first angel of the divine presence, who stands before the throne of God together with the archangels Raphael, Gabriel, and Phanuel (*1 En.* 40:8-9). In his capacity as recording angel, Michael assumes an active role in the final judgment (*Ascen. Isa.* 9:22-23), overseeing the punishment of the hosts of Azazel, as well as of Semjaza and the other angels who had slept with the daughters of men (*1 En.* 54:5-6; 68:1–69:3). In the later post-biblical period, narratives about Michael continued to expand and proliferate, affording the basis for ongoing speculation in the Western religious traditions.

Bibliography: D. Hannah. *Michael and Christ: Michael Traditions and Angel Christology in Early Christianity* (1999).

J. R. C. COUSLAND

MICHAL m*i*'kuhl [מִיכַל mikhal]. Means "who is like God?" King Saul's younger daughter who loves and marries DAVID. Saul tries to use her to bring about David's death, but David uses her to become the king's son-in-law (1 Sam 18:21, 26). As a daring and loving wife she saves David from her father by urging him to flee and making it possible for him to do so (1 Sam 19:11-17). In retaliation, Saul gives her as a wife to PALTI (1 Sam 25:44), from whom she is taken later at David's bidding (2 Sam 3:12-27). Initially loving David (the only woman in biblical narratives said to love a man; 1 Sam 18:20, 27), Michal later despises David and criticizes him for unseemly behavior (2 Sam 6:17-21). *See* SAUL, SON OF KISH.

Second Samuel 6:23 reports that she had no children till her death, but some Hebrew manuscripts of 2 Sam 21:8 refer to her as Adriel's wife and the mother of five whom David turns over to the Gibeonites for execution (Adriel's wife in 1 Sam 18:19 is MERAB, Michal's older sister).

TAMARA COHN ESKENAZI

MICHAL, TEL. Occupying five adjacent hills immediately north of Tel Aviv in present-day Herzliya, Michal (or Mikhal) was once a thriving maritime town frequently inhabited from the 17th cent. BCE (Middle Bronze IIB) to the turn of the Common Era. Subsequently, the site experienced limited settlement around the 8th to 9th cent. CE (Early Arab). The ancient toponym is uncertain: "Michal" is a reconstruction based upon the Arabic designation of the area, Dhahrat Makmish, which supposedly preserves the end of Reshef-Mekal, the name of a Phoenician deity.

Bibliography: Ze'ev Herzog, George Rapp Jr., and Ora Negbi, eds. *Excavations at Tel Michal, Israel* (1989).

JASON R. TATLOCK

MICHMASH mik'mash [מִכְמָס mikhmas, מִכְמַשׂ mikhmas, מִכְמָשׂ mikhmash; Μαχμάς Machmas]. A Benjaminite town located near the border between Benjamin and Ephraim, east of the central Benjamin plateau and the north-south ridge route that extends from Bethlehem to Shechem. Michmash was situated between two precipices of the Wadi Suweinit (BOZEZ on the north and SENEH on the south [1 Sam 14:4]; meanings of both uncertain), a western tributary of the Wadi Qilt. The "Michmash Pass" (1 Sam 13:23; Isa 10:28-29) lay between Michmash and Geba a short distance to the southwest. Eusebius locates it 9 Roman mi. from Ramah (*Onom.* 132.23). Its location plays a significant role in the extended 1 Sam 13–14 narrative of the Saul/Jonathan confrontation with the Philistines.

The present-day village of Mukhmas is generally considered to mark the OT site, although this has not been confirmed by excavation; other suggestions have been offered, but with no more foundation than that site, which seems to sustain some etymological relationship to the OT site.

That the Philistines were mustered and encamped (1 Sam 13:5, 16) at Michmash is to be understood as a serious threat to the fledgling Israelite nation in light of the identification of Philistine territory as that of the five cities in the coastal plain west of the Judean hill country—Gaza, Ashdod, Ashkelon, Gath, and Ekron (Josh 13:3). Furthermore, according to 1 Sam 13:19-22, the Philistines were in control of the iron industry to the extent that the craft was not available to Israel. A Philistine encampment in Michmash suggests a gradual erosion of Israelite control of the hill country and a threatening advance of Philistine access across (east of) the main north-south ridge route, thus bisecting the hill country. This situation eventually reaches a climax when Saul is slain in battle with the Philistines at Mount Gilboa (1 Sam 31). Saul's inability to deal with the Philistines at Michmash is quite evident in 1 Sam 13–14, and is the very situation that gave rise to Jonathan's decision to take matters into his own hands.

Michmash is briefly referenced in only four other OT texts. Isaiah 10:28 speaks of an invasion of Judah/Jerusalem by an unidentified force that, while moving south along the ridge route, traverses the difficult and treacherous terrain of the Michmash Pass—leaving its baggage at Michmash, apparently while it crossed the Wadi Suweinit. The postexilic texts Ezra 2:27 and its par. Neh 7:31 agree in reporting that 122 "people of Michmas" were participants in the return to Judea from Babylon under the decree of Cyrus; Neh 11:31 records a postexilic occupation of Michmash by Benjaminites.

First Maccabees 9:73 and Josephus (*Ant.* 13.1–34) report that the Hasmonean Jonathan, son of Mattathias, replaced his brother Judas as leader/judge upon the latter's death. Subsequent to an encounter with Bacchides and hellenized Jews, Jonathan took up residence in Michmash and governed his people from that location.

JOHN I. LAWLOR

MICHMETHATH mik´muh-thath [מִכְמְתָת **mikhmethath**]. A town or a topographical feature "east of Shechem" (Josh 17:7), midpoint in the border between Manasseh and Ephraim. To the east, the boundary turned toward Taanath-shiloh (possibly Khirbet Tana el-Foqa) and then Janoah (the ridge of modern Yanun) (Josh 16:6), probably along the southern edge of the Bet Dagan Valley. Toward the west the border continued southward to the settlement near the spring of Tappuah, and then descended westward with the brook of Kanah (Josh 17:7-9). Accordingly, Michmethath should be located on the northwestern peak of the Yanun ridge, where the ruins of Khirbet Ibn Nasr are located.

YOEL ELITZUR

MICHRI mik´r*i* [מִכְרִי **mikhri**]. A family head whose descendants lived in Jerusalem. He was the grandfather of ELAH and a descendant of Benjamin (1 Chr 9:8). *See* BENJAMIN, BENJAMINITES.

MIDDIN mid´uhn [מִדִּין **middin**]. One of six towns, including EN-GEDI, with fortresses and supporting villages located in the wilderness west of the Dead Sea listed in Josh 15:21-62 as part of the land allotment given to Judah. Archaeological evidence of habitation that may have supported the Judahite wilderness towns suggests that Middin was probably located in el-Buqe'ah, the Valley of Achor, perhaps at Khirbet Abu Tabaq.

HEIDI E. HAWKS

MIDDLE EAST. A region comprising the countries in southwest Asia and northeast Africa. The boundaries of the region are not well defined. Almost all delimitations include Egypt, Israel and Palestine, Jordan, Syria, Lebanon, Turkey, Iraq, Iran, Kuwait, Saudi Arabia, Qatar, the United Arab Emirates, Oman, and Yemen. Countries along the north coast of Africa are sometimes included, as are areas to the east and northeast of Iran. The term has been criticized for its Eurocentrism, since the region is only "middle" from a Western perspective. When referring to this region in biblical times, most scholars employ the term "ancient Near East."

KEVIN A. WILSON

MIDIAN, MIDIANITES mid´ee-uhn, mid´ee-uh-n*i*t [מִדְיָן **midhyan**, מִדְיָנִים **midhyanim**]. Abraham's descendants through Keturah (Gen 25:2) included six sons, one named Midian. The name's philological origin is difficult to ascertain, yet may be related to the designation used for the Medes (**madhi** מָדַי) several centuries later. Throughout the OT the Midianites are found in various relationships with Israel. The majority of the Midianite occurrences within Scripture are within the narratives dealing with pre-monarchical Israel. These narratives present a confusing mosaic of extremes that range from friendly and familial connection with the Midianites (Exod 2:15-18) to intense battle and attempted genocide of the Midianites by Israel (Num 31:1-9).

Genesis 25:1-6 states that Abraham sent his six sons born by Keturah away from Canaan to the east. The Midianites became a tribal and ethnic entity whose territory consisted of the desert regions of the southern Transjordan, south and east of the Dead Sea. Thus, the Midianites are understood to be part of the ancestry and precursors of the Arabic-speaking tribes of the Western Arabian Desert.

Trade commerce was a staple of existence for the desert tribes with numerous routes for caravans throughout the ANE developing over time. The first mention of Midian as a people group involved participation in the CARAVAN trade. Joseph's purchase as a slave in Gen 37:25-36 portrays the Midianite CAMEL caravan traveling from Gilead in northern Transjordan toward Egypt carrying aromatic spices and incense such as gum, balm, and myrrh. Evidently, the Midianites included slaves in their market wares also. It is interesting to note that within the stories of Joseph the term *Ishmaelite* is interchanged with *Midianite.* The term *Ishmaelite* may have served as a generic term to define desert peoples at the time of the final formation of the text (see Jdg 8:22-24). The angel of the Lord's words to Hagar in Gen 16:11-12 describe the future habitation for Ishmael as "far to the east of his brothers." Ishmaelites, Midianites, and other "peoples of the east" shaped the landscape of later Arab lands and peoples (*see* ISHMAEL, ISHMAELITES; JOSEPH, JOSEPHITES).

The historicity of the Exodus–Sinai narratives cannot be proved archaeologically or historically. Yet, the purpose of the accounts is defined through the text as received. The Exodus tradition reads like a rite of passage (Propp). Israel's formation into a nation began through the intense experience in Egypt. As in a rite of passage story, Israel returns to Canaan from Egypt. Yet the hero of the story is portrayed in great detail with surprising help from a providential meeting. In the story of Moses' flight from Egypt following his murder of the Egyptian taskmaster, he finds himself in the "land of Midian." He met a Midianite priest named JETHRO (also named Ruel or Hobab), and married Jethro's daughter ZIPPORAH (Exod 2:15-21). Moses and Zipporah produced two sons, Gershom (a Midianite name) and Eliezer (a Hebrew name). All of the Midianite names in these stories are represented in pre-Islamic Arabic inscriptions.

The Midianites are protrayed as shepherds rather than the traders of the Joseph story. This juxtaposition of traders and shepherds within the desert tribes is part of Bedouin life to this day (*see* PASTORAL NOMADS). In Exod 18 Jethro became an important advisor to Moses at Sinai. His priestly status is proved through burnt offerings and sacrifice performed with the "elders of Israel" (Exod 18:12). The following communal meal of all parties in the story possibly served as a covenant peace agreement between the new Israelite people and the Midianites.

Jethro's participation in worship with the Israelites has been used to support the concept that Yahweh came from the desert. Moses' encounter with Yahweh on Horeb occurred in the grazing lands of Midian. The book of Judges notes Moses' father-in-law as a Kenite (1:16; 4:11; *see* KENITES). Some scholars propose that worship of Yahweh began with the wandering tribes of the desert. This is highly speculative; however, throughout the biblical texts traditions celebrate the formation of Israelite faith within the WILDERNESS.

Numbers 10:29-32 details the valuable assistance of Jethro in leading Israel through the wilderness, apparently in addition to the pillar of cloud and pillar of fire (see Exod 13:21-22; Num 9:15-23). Jethro's advice to Moses in naming leaders of "thousands, hundreds, fifties, and tens" (Exod 18:13-27) follows the form of military formations throughout the ANE and may be seen in the census lists in Num 1 and 26.

The people of Midian were invited by Moses to join Israel in entering the promised land (Num 10:29), but the Midianites rejected the invitation. In the exodus traditions, Moses departed Egypt with a "mixed multitude" that was shaped into the people of the covenant blessing. Jethro's participation in Yahweh worship (Exod 18:12) seemingly provides the impetus for Moses' offer.

Following the wilderness wanderings, Israel circumvented Edom in southern Transjordan and approached the border of Moab. Numbers 22 reflects some form of cooperation, possibly trade commerce between Midian and Moab in securing the services of BALAAM. The main trade route north and south through Transjordan, the King's Highway, ran through Moab. Midianite caravans moving north provided opportunity for commercial gain for Moab.

In drastic contrast to the Jethro–Moses stories, the next account of Israel and Midian was tragic. Numbers 25 describes the apostasy of Israel with Moabite women near Mount Nebo at Baal-Peor. The apostasy resulted in the brutal death of an Israelite man and Midianite woman. COZBI, the Midianite woman, was the daughter of Zur, the head of Midian (Num 25:15). Because of these events Moses finally declared war to eliminate all Midianites (Num 31:1-17). The war resulted in the defeat of five kings ("chiefs" in Josh 13:21) of Midian, including Zur.

The final mention of the Midianites as a people is the detailed story of Gideon in Judg 6–8. The Midianites are portrayed as camel-riding warriors who invade Canaan periodically for the collection of agricultural "taxes." The arid land of Midian was incapable of supplying a consistent living for the tribal population. Canaan's productive farmland became the target of marauding Midianites during harvest time, to supplement their meager food sources. Gideon's defeat of the Midianites with a small band selected by God stretched from Canaan back across the Jordan as the invaders fled for home. The victory was long remembered in Israel's faith traditions as a symbol of God's faithfulness (Isa 9:4; 10:26; Ps 83:9).

The Gideon story, together with the Num 31 events, provides a glimpse of a politically cohesive Midian led by chieftains. Further, Judg 6:3 places Midian in a coalition with the Amalekites and the "people of the east" (*see* PEOPLE OF THE EAST). The prolonged time of Midian's effective run of Israelite territory may depict the strength and domination of the combined desert dwellers over Transjordan. Midianite connection with these known nomadic and semi-nomadic peoples displays the way of life of the Midianites.

Later biblical references to Midian are geographic designations. First Kings 11:18 places Midian in southern Transjordan, south of Edom. Israel's slaughter of Edomite males resulted in Hadad fleeing from Midian to Egypt. Both Isa 60:6 and Hab 3:7 contain prophecies that depict Midian in solely geographic terms.

Yet, Midianite territory is difficult to define or articulate in the narratives. The nomadic background of the tribal people dictates this lack of specific location. While most references seem to locate Midian in the southern areas of the Transjordan, 1 Kgs 11 locates the area east of Paran and west of Edom, the Arabah of the Great Rift Valley. Greek sources provide a consistent view of Midian settling in Northwest Arabia. Archaeological evidence in the region revealed a developed civilization that consisted of walled cities, mining and smelting operations, and advanced agricultural practices in the Hejaz of the Arabian Peninsula, opposite the Sinai regions of the exodus accounts. The literary and archaeological evidence depicts the social and cultural flow seen in various regions of Transjordan. Nomadic practices of traveling hundreds of kilometers in search of grazing land resulted in Midianite presence in Sinai and in Transjordan. In the battle between the desert and the "sown" arable land, relative long-term climatic issues effected forms of subsistence for semi-nomadic peoples. When proper natural resources were available, sedentary practices with development of farming villages and even cities followed. Yet, the desert peoples in times of climatic difficulties were able to return to their roots of pastoral migration. Often a blended, semi-nomadic coexistence between agriculture and pastoralism developed.

Distinctive Midianite pottery found in the Arabian Desert has been discovered in the Jordan Valley and in Palestine. According the archaeological record, Midian was a significant political and social entity by the Late Bronze and early Iron periods. The people of Midian, as well as other nomadic groups of the ANE, were capable of a complex society that held influence commercially from Egypt north to Mesopotamia until the rise of Islam.

Bibliography: John I. Durham. *Exodus.* WBC 3 (1987); William C. Propp. *Exodus 1–18.* AB 2 (1999).

MICHAEL G. VANZANT

MIDRASH mid′rash [מִדְרָשׁ **midhrash**]. Midrash is rabbinic commentary on the Scriptures, particularly the TORAH ("law" or "teaching"). The verbal root of **midhrash** is **darash** (דָּרַשׁ), "to search out." Sometimes collections of midrash are referred to in the plural: midrashim (**midhrashim** מִדְרָשִׁים).

A. Biblical Origins

The verbal root of the term **midhrash** (**darash**) originates in the Bible, usually in reference to seeking God's will. For example, in Gen 25:22, Rebecca is having a difficult pregnancy and seeks (**lidhrosh** לִדְרֹשׁ) an oracle from God. In 1 Kgs 22:5, a subtle difference is introduced when Jehoshaphat asks the king of Israel to "inquire (**derash** דְּרָשׁ) first for the word of the LORD." This shift from a direct to indirect approach to seeking God's word is concretized in Ezra 7:10, where Ezra "set his heart (**lidhrosh**) to study or expound the Torah. There is similar use of the term in the Dead Sea Scrolls for expounding the Torah (1QS VI, 6).

In the earliest layers of RABBINIC LITERATURE, *midrash* refers to RABBINIC INTERPRETATION of the Bible. This creative EXEGESIS is accomplished through a series of hermeneutic rules, many of which were explicitly enumerated by the rabbis, who saw the origins of their midrashic exegesis in the Bible itself. For example, on Gen 5:29, "He named him Noah (**noakh** נֹחַ), saying, '. . . this one shall bring us relief (**yenakhamenu** יְנַחֲמֵנוּ),' " the rabbis comment, "the name [Noah] is not the midrash and the midrash ['he shall bring us relief'] is not the name" (*Gen. Rab.* 25:2; author's trans.). While the objection is that the root (**nkhm** נחם) of the word **yenakhamenu** ("he will bring us relief") does not replicate the root of Noah's name (**nwkh** נוח), the rabbis nevertheless accept this biblical explanation of the origin of Noah's name as "midrash."

Many scholars follow Michael Fishbane in tracing the origins of rabbinic midrash to these types of inner-biblical interpretations (a biblical text interpreting itself or another biblical text). According to this argument, Deuteronomy may be seen as a form of midrash on the exodus and wilderness traditions; certain prophets may be seen as doing midrash on the laws of Torah; and the book of Chronicles may be seen as a midrash on the histories of Samuel–Kings. *Leviticus Rabbah* 1:3 states that Chronicles was given precisely for the sake of midrash. *See* INTERTEXTUALITY.

B. Pre-rabbinic and Early Parallels

In the pre-rabbinic period, it is difficult to determine the exact content of the biblical canon: what was considered to be "Scripture," and what was commentary on Scripture? Midrashic commentary was a form of filling in the gaps, answering questions that the Scripture itself did not make clear. Accordingly, we might consider certain of the apocryphal writings under the broad rubric of proto-midrash. The midrashic Greek Esther, e.g, consciously addresses a fact that was evidently perplexing to the rabbis: the lack of explicit mention of God's name in the Hebrew text of the book of Esther (*see* ESTHER, ADDITIONS TO). The Apocrypha contains the book of Baruch, rabbinic exegesis on Jeremiah that is purported to be written by Jeremiah's scribe Baruch (compare Jer 32:12-16; 36; 43:1-7; 45). There are episodes in the life of Daniel recorded in Greek Daniel, not found in the Hebrew text, that represent rabbinic interpretation of the book of Daniel (*see* DANIEL, ADDITIONS TO). All of these might be considered instances of "gap-filling" that characterizes later rabbinic midrashim.

The Greek works of Philo and Josephus (esp. *Jewish Antiquities*) also expand the biblical text, fill in gaps, allegorize, and otherwise interpret the Bible in ways reminiscent of the rabbis. Many of the traditions that these Jews quote in their interpretations of Jewish Scripture find parallels in rabbinic midrash. Similarly, the Hebrew and Aramaic writings at Qumran, particularly the genre called pesher, show affinities for the methods found in the rabbinic midrashim (*see* PESHARIM). While none of these conclusively demonstrate direct influence from midrashic literature, much of the interpretative process is similar.

This is also true for NT interpretation of the OT, and later patristic interpretation of the OT and NT. In patristic exegesis there is evidence for parallel development with the midrashim, as well as borrowing from and polemic against one another. Particularly the Greek fathers' parallels and similarities with midrash may stem from shared reading and interpretative strategies in the common Hellenistic milieu.

C. Tannaitic Midrash (ca. 70–250 CE)

The earliest rabbinic midrashim were redacted at the end of the Tannaitic period, about the time of the publication of the MISHNAH, ca. 200 CE. These works contain traditions of earlier scholars and of rabbis (*see* ORAL LAW, ORAL TORAH) who flourished following the destruction of the Jerusalem Temple in 70 CE. Some of the earliest examples of this type of midrash are found in the Passover HAGGADAH, which expounds Deut 26. Explanations are offered for biblical texts, sometimes by merely juxtaposing one verse with another, so that both verses may be mutually illuminated. Deuteronomy 26:5 reports that the Israelites descended to Egypt "few in number"(bimethe meʿat בִּמְתֵי מְעָט). The verse is juxtaposed with Deut 10:22, "seventy persons." The midrash of the Passover haggadah thus notes that "seventy" is how "few" descended, and that the rare word mete (perhaps meaning "mortals") can be understood as "persons."

Midrash in this early period determines the meanings of texts. It also discerns from Scripture the demands of developing rabbinic HALAKHAH and its relationship to biblical authority. Many verses of Torah required exegesis, as well as harmonization with received Jewish traditions. Ultimately two "schools" of thought arose in this period, those of rabbis Akiva and Ishmael. The latter preferred reading using hermeneutic norms that could be traced to Scripture. Rabbi Akiva (*see* AKIVA, RABBI) was a more radical reader, inferring Jewish law from repetitions (such as infinitive absolutes) and apparently extraneous words in a verse. Rabbi Ishmael demurred that the Torah speaks in normal human language. The so-called schools of Akiva and Ishmael disagree primarily over matters of interpretation of Torah to derive Jewish law. Despite this focus, the two interpretative strategies find parallels among the Alexandrian and Antiochene "schools" of the church fathers (*see* PATRISTIC BIBLICAL INTERPRETATION).

While there is almost no legal material in Genesis, the schools of Akiva and Ishmael have each redacted commentaries on Exodus (*see* MEKILTA), Leviticus, Numbers, and Deuteronomy (*see* SIFRA, SIFRE). There is debate among scholars as to the existence of these schools or whether they are a 19th-cent. historiographic construct. Even for those who accept the existence of such schools, it is difficult to determine the precise strands of each school's traditions. Further, the texts attributed to the separate schools share in common the Midrash Haggadah on the narrative passages in those four books of the Pentateuch.

D. Amoraic Midrash (ca. 250–550 CE)

By the end of the Tannaitic period, a corpus of rabbinic literature existed that included apodictic legal works such as Mishnah and Tosefta (*see* TOSEPHTA, TOSEPTA, TOSEFTA), as well as the biblical commentaries of the Tannaitic midrash listed above. While the latter focused on halakhah, they shared exegetical traditions on the nonlegal materials, thus ensuring rabbinic traditions of both legal and narrative midrashim. This is reflected in the collection of traditions on the first book of the Torah, called *Genesis Rabbah* (ca. early 5th cent. CE), a work that comments on virtually every verse of Genesis, most often separating the verse (or part thereof) from its biblical context. This atomistic strategy of reading allowed the rabbis to make ideological points and read them into (and out of) the Torah text with playful freedom.

The same is true of the freedom with which the rabbis superimpose their own agenda on the book of Leviticus in the contemporary *Leviticus Rabbah.* Here, the rabbis ignore the legal intricacies of Leviticus, treating less than 20 percent of its verses, and even these only serve as rubrics for advancing the rabbinic worldview. This miscellany of rabbinic haggadic traditions, while giving lip service to the destroyed Temple and its priesthood, presents the rabbis as the new leadership of the people Israel and Torah study as the replacement for sacrifice. The work called *Pesiqta of Rab Kahana* advances a similar agenda, organized around the synagogal lectionary cycle of special Sabbath and holiday Torah readings.

Lamentations Rabbah, also redacted in the 5th cent. CE, grapples with questions of theodicy and God's relationship to Israel following the destruction of the Second Temple. While ostensibly commenting on the destruction of the First Temple in Lamentations, the midrash addresses more contemporary issues (including, perhaps, the role of Israel in light of the rise of Christianity). The contemporary *Song of Songs Rabbah* treats the biblical book of erotic love poetry as an allegory of God's love for Israel expressed either at the crossing of the Reed Sea or during the theophany at Sinai. This mode of allegorization of Song of Songs is also used by the church fathers, who read the OT scroll as an allegory on Christ's love for the church.

E. Talmudic Midrash and Sage Tales

Many of the midrashic traditions found in *Genesis Rabbah* and *Leviticus Rabbah* are also redacted in the Palestinian Talmud (*see* TALMUD, JERUSALEM). This Talmud, like the works described above, narrates stories about the rabbis themselves in addition to its biblical exegesis. These "sage tales" are akin to the church's lives of the saints, or the Hellenistic lives of the sophists, in that they are didactic literature and not reliable biography. These sage tales are often formulated as a Greco-Roman **chreia** (χρεία), or pronouncement story, in which rabbis teach about moral behavior or Jewish ideology and law. Most often, these stories quote biblical verses, or the sentiments of Scripture are embedded within the narrative, so that these tales also may be considered midrashim.

The Babylonian TALMUD repeats many of these tales about Palestinian sages, recasting them according to the ideology of the Babylonian rabbinic academies. The Babylonian Talmud also offers midrash on Scripture (including a sustained exegesis of Esther in tractate *Megillah*). By the time of the Babylonian Talmud, the rabbis have begun to make a distinction between **peshat** (פְּשַׁט), or contextual reading, and **derash**, which is rabbinic interpretation. By this era midrash represents the reenvisioning of biblical narrative through the lenses of rabbinic theology and ideology. The triumph of rabbinic interpretation may be witnessed by a late 5th-cent. rabbi explaining that while he had studied all of rabbinic tradition (**talmudha'** תַּלְמוּדָא), he did not yet know that Scripture cannot lose its contextual meaning (**peshuta'** פְּשׁוּטָא) (*b. Shabb.* 63a).

F. Gaonic Midrash (ca. 550–1000 CE)

Ecclesiastes Rabbah was compiled contemporary with or just following the redaction of the Babylonian Talmud. The work has been characterized as an encyclopedia of rabbinic traditions that uses the verses of Ecclesiastes as rubrics to organize the rabbinic curriculum.

Midrash Mishle is a 9th-cent. midrash on the book of Proverbs. Its often terse exegeses foreshadow later rabbinic Bible commentary. In the same era, we find retellings of the Bible. *Pirqe Rabbi Eliezer* imaginatively recounts the biblical narrative from creation (including allusions to mystical speculation) up to the death of Miriam, where the text abruptly comes to an end. Many of the traditions recounted in this work are paralleled in the Aramaic Targum called *Pseudo-Jonathan* (*see* TARGUMS). Another midrashic work from this period is the moralistic first-person narrative *Seder Eliyahu.* These three works retain rabbinic polemics against the Karaite sect.

During this period, named for the leader (ga'on גָּאוֹן) of the rabbinic academies of Palestine and Jewish Babylonia, midrashic literature was composed away from the Holy Land, in places as diverse as Iraq, North Africa, and Europe. Certain of these works are characterized by a format in which the midrash begins with a legal question that is answered by a quotation from the Mishnah and then a homiletic exposition of the week's annual lectionary ensues. Works in Aramaic (*Sheiltot*) and Hebrew (*Tanhuma–Yelamdenu*) follow this format for the entire Pentateuch.

G. Medieval Midrash (ca. 1000–1650 CE)

By the Middle Ages, rabbis turned their creativity to collecting and organizing midrashic literature. In North Africa, Rabbenu Nissim Gaon (d. 1062) collected rabbinic sage tales and published them in Arabic. Hebrew collections of rabbinic commentaries on the Bible, such as the *Yalqut Shimoni* (Franco-Germany, 13th cent.) and *Yalqut HaMechiri* (Spain, 14th cent.) became popular compendia. *Midrash HaGadol* (Yemen, 14th cent.), a compendium on the Torah cycle, includes introductions and poetry on the weekly lection, in addition to its sampling of midrash. Rabbi Ya'akov ibn Habib (ca. 1440–1515 CE) edited the midrashic and haggadic sections of the Babylonian Talmud in a work called *'Ayn Ya'akov.* The work was completed posthumously and printed in Saloniki just after his death.

Two 12th-cent. compendia deserve mention in this survey of medieval midrash: *Midrash Leqah Tov* (Bulgaria?) and *Midrash Sekhel Tov* (Italy). These works pay more attention to context, are less atomistic, and are less inclined to long homilies or narratives than earlier midrashim. They serve as another step in the transition from midrash to rabbinic biblical commentary. Two examples of commentary must suffice. Rabbi Solomon ben Isaac (known by the acronym RASHI, ca. 1040–1105 CE, Troyes, France) epitomized all of midrashic literature in his terse commentary on most of the Bible. Rashi's grandson, Rabbi Samuel ben Meir (Rashbam, ca. 1080–1174 CE), opposed this style of commentary in favor of **peshat**. Rashbam thought midrashim to be false to the Bible text and preferred his literalist, contextual commentary. Fortunately, this radical divide between **peshat** and **derash** did not bring an end to midrash.

H. Modern Midrash

The playful, ideological interpretations of the rabbis that so annoyed Rashbam continued to hold fascination for rabbinic Jews in the centuries that followed. Collectors such as Louis Ginzberg compiled rabbinic midrashim interlaced with Hellenistic biblical exegesis and even some Jewish material embedded in the writings of the church fathers. Zionist poet Hayim Nahman Bialik collected biblical commentary and sage tales.

In recent decades, Jewish fiction writers and especially feminists have utilized both classical midrashim, as well as the process of midrash, to give voice to female characters of the Bible. As a mode of reading the Bible, midrash continues to garner new readers and writers, as well as serve as a window into the rabbinic Jewish mindset of centuries past.

Bibliography: Hayim Nahman Bialik. *Sefer HaAggadah* (1930); Michael Fishbane. *Biblical Interpretation in Ancient Israel* (1985); Louis Ginzberg. *The Legends of the Jews* (1909–1938); Saul Lieberman. "Rabbinic Interpretation of Scripture." *Hellenism in Jewish Palestine* (1950) 47–67; Jeffrey Rubenstein. *The Culture of the Babylonian Talmud* (2003); Herman L. Strack and Günter Stemberger. *Introduction to the Talmud and Midrash* (1992); Burton Visotzky. *Golden Bells and Pomegranates: Studies in Midrash Leviticus Rabbah* (2003); Burton Visotzky. "Jots and Tittles: On Scriptural Interpretation in Rabbinic and Patristic Literatures." *Fathers of the World: Essays in Rabbinic and Patristic Literatures* (1995) 28–40.

BURTON L. VISOTZKY

MIDWIFE [מְיַלֶּדֶת **meyalledheth**]. A woman trained to assist mothers in childbirth. Three narratives in the OT feature midwives: Benjamin's birth to RACHEL (Gen 35:17), the birth of the twins Perez and Zerah to TAMAR (Gen 38:28), and the defiance of SHIPHRAH and PUAH, midwives who protect the male Hebrew infants from Pharaoh's orders of extermination (Exod 1:15-21).

These accounts show that midwives not only assisted in birth but also provided comfort to mothers in distress, and at times participated in the important task of naming newborns. The extraordinary narrative of Shiphrah and Puah, whose ethnic origins are ambiguous, portrays them as heroines. They shrewdly defy Pharaoh's commands in order to save the Hebrew boys, stating that the Hebrew women are, literally, "beasts" (**khayoth** חָיוֹת) who give birth before the midwives can arrive (Exod 1:19). In an account where even Pharaoh's identity is not mentioned, the midwives' names as well as God's reward to them are pointedly recorded. *See* BIRTH.

SHARON PACE

MIGDAL-EL mig′duhl-el′ [מִגְדַּל־אֵל **mighdal-ʾel**]. Means "tower of El." One of the fortified villages that was allotted to the tribe of Naphtali (Josh 19:38). Sometimes it has been identified with the town MAGDALA mentioned in Matt 15:39 and the home of Mary Magdalene. *See* NAPHTALI, NAPHTALITES.

MIGDAL-GAD mig′duhl-gad′ [מִגְדַּל־גָּד **mighdal-gadh**]. Means "tower of Gad." A city in the lowlands (the SHEPHELAH) in the region allotted to Judah (Josh 15:37), possibly the site of modern-day el-Mejdel.

MIGDOL mig′dol [מִגְדֹּל **mighdol**]. A site on the exodus itinerary near PI-HAHIROTH, BAAL-ZEPHON, and the Red Sea (Exod 14:2; Num 33:7). The biblical description places it somewhere east of SUCCOTH (Tell el-Maskuta). If the name comes from the Hebrew word **migdhol**, meaning "tower, fortress," Migdol may be identified with one of the Egyptian fortresses on the northeast border. According to Jer 44:1, a number of Judeans sought refuge in the cities of Egypt, including Migdol, after the first deportation by Nebuchadnezzar in 597 BCE. This Migdol has been associated with Tell el-Her, although this may represent a different place than the Migdol of the exodus. Jeremiah prophesied that those in Egypt would not escape punishment (Jer 44:7-14). Because of its location at the northeast corner of Egypt, Migdol could serve with SYENE as an inclusio for the entirety of Egypt (Ezek 29:10; 30:6).

KEVIN A. WILSON

MIGHTY MEN [גִּבֹּרִים **gibborim**]. A term applied to men who are strong, courageous, bold, or outstanding in many different ways. It is applied to non-Israelites (Josh 10:2), to heroes from the distant past (Gen 6:4; *see* NEPHILIM), or to a contemporary warrior, like David, who is recognized as particularly brave and cunning (2 Sam 17:10). The members of David's mercenary band of WARRIORS led by Joab (2 Sam 10:7) and Benaiah (1 Kgs 1:10) were called "mighty men." In Song 3:7, Solomon is being carried on a litter accompanied by "sixty mighty men of the mighty men of Israel."

C. MARK MCCORMICK

MIGHTY ONE [אָבִיר **ʾavir**; δυνάστης **dynastēs**, δυνατός **dynatos**]. Occurs in the epithets "Bull/Mighty One of Jacob" (Gen 49:24; Ps 132:2, 5; Isa 49:26; 60:16; Sir 51:12) and "Bull/Mighty One of Israel" (Isa 1:24), and "the Mighty One" of Sir 46:5, 6, 16 and Luke 1:49. *See* GOD, NAMES OF.

MIGHTY WORKS. *See* MIRACLE; MIRACLE WORKERS; SIGNS AND WONDERS.

MIGRON mig′ron [מִגְרוֹן **mighron**]. A site in the tribal area of Benjamin where Saul sat under a pomegranate tree preparing for battle with the Philistines (1 Sam 14:2). The text mentions it as on the outskirts of Gibeah. Some scholars suggest the text reads "near the threshing floor" rather than the site name Migron. The Assyrian army passed Migron on its way to Jerusalem (Isa 10:28). In this passage, Migron is located between Aiath (Ai) in the north, Geba in the south, and near Michmash. Migron has been associated with Tell Miryam but this identification is uncertain.

TERRY W. EDDINGER

MIJAMIN mij′uh-min [מִיָּמִן **miyamin**, מִיָּמִין **miyamin**; Μιαμείν **Miamein**]. 1. During David's last days, the head of the sixth division and therefore the ancestor of a priestly family in postexilic times (1 Chr 24:9).

2. Among the descendants of Parosh who dismissed their foreign wives and children in accordance with God's command through Ezra (Ezra 10:25; 1 Esd 9:26).

3. A priest who placed his name upon Ezra's sealed covenant document (Neh 10:7). Possibly the same as MINIAMIN (Neh 12:17, 41).

4. A priest who returned to Jerusalem after the exile with Zerubbabel (Neh 12:5).

EMILY R. CHENEY

MIKLOTH mik'loth [מִקְלוֹת **miqloth**]. The name of two people in the OT. Its meaning is uncertain. 1. A descendant of Benjamin, Mikloth is the son of Jeiel and father of Shimeam (also called Shimeah) (1 Chr 8:32; 9:37-38).

2. An officer under Dodai (*see* DODO) in the army of David; he led the division of the second month, which had 24,000 men (1 Chr 27:4). The text of this verse is highly problematic; when emended, the name Mikloth does not appear in some translations (as in RSV).

MARK RONCACE

MIKNEIAH mik-nee'yah [מִקְנֵיָהוּ **miqneyahu**]. One of the second rank of Levites chosen to play a musical instrument during David's second attempt at processing into Jerusalem with the ark (1 Chr 15:18, 21). Mikneiah, meaning "Yahu creates" or "Yahu acquires," is not found in a similar list in 1 Chr 16:5.

MIKTAM mik'tam [מִכְתָּם **mikhtam**; στηλογραφία **stēlographia**]. A term in the superscriptions of several psalms associated with David (Pss 16; 56–60). The LXX translates the term as "stela inscription," perhaps indicating these psalms were written on a stone. Other proposals include "golden psalm," "atonement psalm," and "secret prayer." Because of the similar form and superscription of the prayer in Isa 38:10-20 ("a writing [**mikhtav** מִכְתָּב] of King Hezekiah," Isa 38:9), it too may be a miktam. *See* MUSIC.

JOEL MARCUS LEMON

MILALAI mil'uh-l*i* [מִלֲלַי **milalay**]. One of the priests and musicians who participated in the dedication of the Jerusalem wall in the postexilic reconstruction (Neh 12:36).

MILCAH mil'kuh [מִלְכָּה **milkah**]. 1. Abraham's niece and daughter of HARAN, who married Abraham's other brother NAHOR (Gen 11:29). She was the grandmother of REBEKAH (Gen 24:15, 24, 47).

2. One of the daughters of Zelophehad, of the tribe of Manasseh, who were involved in establishing Mosaic legislation regarding a daughter's right to inheritance in the event of no male heir (Num 27:1; Josh 17:3).

STEVEN D. MASON

MILCOM mil'kuhm [מִלְכֹּם **milkom**]. The Ammonite god (1 Kgs 11:5, 33; 2 Kgs 23:13). Vocalized differently, the Hebrew consonants **mlkm** could read "their king" (2 Sam 12:30). *See* MOLECH, MOLOCH.

MILDEW [יֵרָקוֹן **yeraqon**]. English translation of **yeraqon**, a plant malady of uncertain nature. The word, which always appears in conjunction with BLIGHT (**shiddafon** שִׁדָּפוֹן) as a manifestation of divine judgment, signifies a yellowish or pale-green color and probably describes the effects of a scorching wind. *See* EAST WIND; ISRAEL, CLIMATE OF; MOLDY.

T. DELAYNE VAUGHN

MILE [μίλιον **milion**, στάδιος **stadios**]. A **milion** is a Roman measure of of about 1,480 m (an English mile is a little over 1,600 m). A **stadios**, often translated "mile" (Luke 24:13; John 6:19), is only 185 m. Roman soldiers could compel citizens of the regions they occupied to help carry their equipment (Epictetus, *Diss.* 4.1.79; see Mark 15:21, where soldiers compel Simon of Cyrene to carry Jesus' cross). Jesus told his disciples to walk two miles (**milion**) when compelled to walk one (Matt 5:41). In so doing, they would offer kindness to their enemies, a prominent theme in the SERMON ON THE MOUNT. *See* WEIGHTS AND MEASURES.

KIMBERLY R. PEELER

MILETUS m*i*-lee'tuhs [Μίλητος **Milētos**]. Miletus was a seaport located on the Aegean coast 30 mi. south of EPHESUS in southwest Asia Minor, situated on a peninsula extending from the southern shore of the Gulf of Latmos, a deepwater inlet, and near the mouth of the winding Meander (modern Büyük Menderes) River. The city had four natural harbors and relied primarily on its maritime potential for growth and prosperity. Over the centuries accumulated sediment from the Meander turned the Gulf of Latmos into an inland lake (Bafa Lake) and moved the city, which was finally abandoned in the 17th cent. CE, 5 mi. from the coast to its current location near the Turkish village of Balat 20 mi. south of Söke.

Excavations indicate that it was inhabited as early as the 4th millennium BCE, but archaeologists have been unable to determine the origins of the inhabitants in this early period. The first identifiable occupants were settlers from CRETE who colonized the area during the Minoan expansion (ca. 1900–1500 BCE) and apparently named it after a Cretan city (Strabo, *Geogr.* 14.1.6). In the 14th cent. BCE, Miletus was overtaken by Myceneans from the Greek mainland who built the first city walls and made it a fortified outpost. For the next several centuries, control of the city alternated between the Myceneans and the Hittite Empire, the major power in Asia Minor during that period.

Archaeological evidence indicates that Miletus was destroyed ca. 1200 BCE, although no literary account exists to explain why or by whom. Shortly thereafter, the city played a leading role in the Ionian migration from Greece. Resettled by the Ionians, Miletus became the most prosperous and prominent of the twelve Ionian cities established in Asia Minor. By the 7th cent. BCE it was the leading city in Asia Minor in commerce and colonization and the foremost Greek city in the east, surpassing even its neighbor Ephesus, and Athens and Sparta on the Greek mainland, in size, wealth, power, and influence. Indeed, it maintained three bustling marketplaces simultaneously and was one of the first cities to mint coins, both of which testify to its commercial success. Its prosperity was due in no small measure to its colonizing activities. Pliny put the number of colonies established by Milesians at ninety (Pliny, *Nat.* 5.112; compare Strabo, *Geogr.* 14.1.6), but the actual number is estimated to be between thirty and fifty, still more than any other Greek city. The colonies were located as far away as Egypt and the Black Sea, and each contributed to the mother city's wealth through favorable trade agreements.

Although there was continuous rivalry with Lydia (*see* LYDIA, LYDIANS), Miletus remained free until it came under Persian rule in 546 BCE. The conquest by Persia was bloodless as Miletus was spared human casualties, as well as damage to its buildings and interruption of its commerce, by agreeing to peace terms without going to war (Herodotus, *Hist.* 1.141.3; 1.143.1). In 499 BCE, however, Miletus led a revolt by the Ionian cities against the Persians. The Persian army conquered the city in 494 BCE and, in retaliation for its role in the rebellion, demolished it and killed or deported most of its inhabitants (Herodotus, *Hist.* 6.18–22). It was rebuilt following the defeat of the Persians by the Greeks in 479 BCE and, although it never regained its former stature, remained an important metropolis into the Roman period and beyond. At the end of the Peloponnesian War (ca. 401 BCE), Miletus was forced to resubmit to Persia, and thereafter was never again a free city. It surrendered to ALEXANDER THE GREAT in 334 BCE, and during the Hellenistic period it was the object of territorial competition between the Seleucids and the Attalids. The city was part of the PERGAMUM Empire bequeathed to Rome following the death of Attalus III in 133 BCE.

In addition to its commercial significance, Miletus was also an intellectual and cultural center. It was home to the natural philosophers Thales (the father of Western philosophy), Anaximander, and Anaximenes; the geographer and logographer Hecataeus; the rhetorician Aeschines; the writer Aristides; and the urban planner Hippodamus, who popularized the widely used orthogonal city layout. Indeed, when Miletus was rebuilt following liberation from Persia in 479 BCE, it became the first Greek city planned and constructed completely according to the Hippodamian grid design. Archaeological remains attest to the city's architectural achievements, and include a theater, gymnasium, nymphaeum (monument containing fountain and pool), bouleterion (council house), baths, and temples to Athena and to Apollo. The temple to Apollo, considered the most magnificent of the Ionic shrines, was built and maintained by the Milesians at Didyma 10 mi. south of Miletus. Miletus' architectural splendor lasted at least through the end of the 1st cent. CE, given that Faustina, wife of the Roman emperor Marcus Aurelius (161–180 CE), was one of the most generous contributors to the city's building program. Archaeologists have also discovered a synagogue and an inscription reserving a seating area for Jews in the theater, confirming Josephus' information that Miletus had a well-established Jewish community by the Roman period (*Ant.* 14.244–46).

Miletus is mentioned three times in the NT, each instance in reference to Paul's mission. Acts 20:15-17 tells of the apostle stopping at Miletus on his way to Jerusalem and sending for the leaders of the Jesus movement in Ephesus to meet him there so that he could deliver his farewell address to them. In its final greetings, 2 Tim 4:20 notes that Paul left Trophimus behind in Miletus because he was too ill to travel. *See* ASIA; GREECE; PAUL, THE APOSTLE; PERSIA, HISTORY AND RELIGION OF; ROMAN EMPIRE.

Bibliography: Ekrem Akurgal. *Ancient Civilizations and Ruins of Turkey: From Prehistoric Times until the End of the Roman Empire.* 6th ed. (1985); Vanessa B. Gorman. *Miletos, the Ornament of Ionia: A History of the City to 400 B.C.E.* (2001); A. John Graham. *Colony and Mother City in Ancient Greece* (1964); George M. A. Hanfmann. "Ionia, Leader or Follower." *HSCP* 61 (1953) 1–37; M. J. Mellink. "Archaeology in Anatolia." *AJA* 93 (1989) 122–25; Stephen Mitchell. "Archaeology in Asia Minor 1979–84." *Archaeological Reports* 31 (1984–85) 70–105.

WILLIAM SANGER CAMPBELL

MILH, TELL EL. *See* MALHATA, TEL.

MILK [חָלָב khalav; γάλα gala]. Primarily from goats and secondarily from sheep (Deut 32:14; Prov 27:27), milk was a versatile and nourishing drink that regularly accompanied meals in the biblical traditions (Sir 39:26). Only a small quantity was consumed fresh, and the remainder was turned into dairy products such as CURDS, butter, and cheese (Gen 18:8; 2 Sam 17:29). Milk's nutritional value and versatility are responsible for its symbolic use. Milk, in conjunction with HONEY, serves as a symbol of fruitfulness (e.g., the reference to the land flowing with milk and honey in, e.g., Exod 3:8, 17; Lev 20:24, as well as the image of restoration in Joel 3:18 in which the hills will be flowing with milk). Moreover, in some texts milk conceivably exhibits sexual overtones (Song 4:11; 5:1; Judg 4:19; 5:25).

In the NT milk is used as a symbol for learning or teaching (as with a similar connection in the invitation to drink milk in Isa 55:1). In 1 Cor 3:2, Paul writes that he has fed the young converts with milk, not solid food. Milk here functions as an image for elementary Christian teachings that are easily digested by those who are "babies" in the faith (see also Heb 5:12-13; 1 Pet 2:2). Milk furthermore has a rich history of interpretation when interpreters like Clement of Alexandria (*Paed.* 1.6.46.1) use milk as an image of making God's word one's own, denoting the believer's complete dependence on one's mother, God.

L. JULIANA CLAASSENS

MILL, MILLSTONE [פֶּלַח pelakh, רֵחַיִם rekhayim; μύλος mylos]. Throughout the villages and towns of the ANE, GRAIN (primarily wheat and barley) formed the staff of the daily diet. In order to process it into flour for loaves and cakes, the women of each household would grind it by hand between an upper and lower millstone, sometimes referred to as the saddle-quern based on its concave shape (compare Num 11:8; Matt 24:41). Numerous examples of these stones have been recovered in excavations, demonstrating that the lower stone was 1.5–2.75 ft. long and 10–15 in. wide. The hand grinder was generally 4–8 in. long and 2.75–6 in. wide. This would have been heavy and dirty work, requiring the woman to kneel over the lower stone while crushing the kernels with a back and forth motion of her handmill. The work sometimes was relegated to slaves (Exod 11:5), and it was a task no upper-class woman would wish to do since it coarsened the hands (Isa 47:2).

A handmill of this type, probably shaped with basalt, would have been a precious possession (equated with life itself), and the law forbade the giving of either the upper or lower millstone in pledge of a debt (Deut 24:6). The millstone was possibly handed down from mother to daughter as a legacy of their role within the household. Thus a woman of the besieged city of Thebez carried her hand grinder with her when she fled for her life. However, it then became an effective and lethal weapon when she cast it down upon Abimelech's head (Judg 9:53; 2 Sam 11:21). Milling grain was so closely associated with "women's work" that it became an insult for men. The Philistines made sport of the blinded and shorn Samson by putting him to work grinding at the millstone in prison (Judg 16:21), and the young men of Judah were forced to toil at millstones after the fall of Jerusalem (Lam 5:13; *see* GRIND, GRINDING).

In larger settlements, huge circular millstones (Rev 18:21) were shaped to process mass quantities of grain and seeds for local consumption, to pay taxes and tithes, and as an item of trade. The common sound of the grinding stone was associated with the prosperity of people and a time of peace. For this reason it is equated in Jer 25:10 with the mirthful voices of a bridal party and the warm glow of the oil lamp. The author of Rev 18:21-23 provides an augmented list of sounds and sights, including the millstone, in describing a time of trouble when all normalcy is lost. The physical properties of the millstone equate it with the hard heart of the savage Leviathan (Job 41:24) and as a means of committing suicide for those in despair (Matt 18:6; Mark 9:42; Luke 17:2). *See* AGRICULTURE.

VICTOR H. MATTHEWS

MILLENNIUM muh-len´ee-uhm. The term *millennium* never occurs in the Bible. It comes from the Lat. *mille anni*, meaning "a thousand years," and is a translation from the Gk. chilia etē (χίλια ἔτη, from which the English words *chiliasm* and *chiliastic* are derived). This thousand-year period is mentioned repeatedly in Rev 20:1-10. During that time, according to John, the named author of Revelation, SATAN is bound in the ABYSS (Rev 20:1-3, 7-10), and those martyred "for their testimony to Jesus and for the word of God" are raised from the dead to reign with Christ (Rev 20:4-6). At the end of it, Satan is released "for a little while" (Rev 20:3) to deceive the nations and threaten the people of God once more before being consigned finally to "the lake of fire" (Rev 20:7-10).

A stark contrast is evident between the extraordinarily long period of triumph and vindication and all other time designations within the book (half an hour, Rev 8:1; one hour, 18:10, 17, 19; one day, 18:8; three and a half days, 11:9; five months, 9:5; forty-two months, 11:2; 13:5; 1,260 days, 11:3; 12:6; "a time, and times, and half a time," 12:14). In his own way John echoes the apostle Paul in weighing present affliction against future glory (see Rom 8:18; 2 Cor 4:17). But why does John speak of a temporal kingdom, apparently on earth (see Rev 5:10), and why does it last for a millennium, "a thousand years"?

Jewish apocalyptic literature knows of an intermediate kingdom or messianic era, though not necessarily a thousand years in duration (*see* ESCHATOLOGY IN EARLY JUDAISM; MESSIAH, JEWISH). In this messianic era, the God of Israel will be victorious in this world and the world to come, both within history and beyond it. For example, according to *1 Enoch*, during the eighth and ninth "weeks" of the "Apocalypse of Weeks" in *1 En.* 91:12-17, righteousness will flourish on earth; in the tenth week, a new heaven will appear. But the length of the "weeks" is uncertain and they probably are of unequal duration. Jewish apocalyptic literature also uses the number "one thousand" in a description of God's vindication. *Second Baruch* (almost certainly later than the book of Revelation) contemplates a time when the earth will produce a miraculous bounty of grapes, when each vine will produce a thousand branches, each branch will produce a thousand clusters, and each cluster a thousand grapes (*2 Bar.* 29:5).

Irenaeus reports that PAPIAS, bishop of Hierapolis in Asia Minor, attributed these apocalyptic notions to the author of the book of Revelation (Irenaeus, *Haer.* 5.33.3–4) and believed that after the resurrection of the dead there would be a thousand years during which the kingdom of God would be physically manifested on earth (Eusebius, *Hist. eccl.* 3.39.12).

In *4 Ezra* (also later than Revelation), the period of vindication is only 400 years. God promises Ezra that God's son, the Messiah, will be revealed, and those who remain will rejoice for 400 years, after which the Messiah and all humanity will die. The world will return to a primeval state for seven days, as it was before the creation, and after seven days, the world will be awakened anew (*4 Ezra* 7:28-31).

One of the recensions of *2 Enoch* hints at a world cycle of 7,000 years, followed by an eighth day, or eighth "thousand," that occurs outside of time (*2 En.* 33:1-2). But the text is of uncertain date and uncertain (possibly Christian) provenance, and it points toward a timeless eternity rather than an actual "thousand years" on earth.

Just as inconclusive are later rabbinic reflections on the six days of creation in light of Ps 90:4 ("For a thousand years in your sight are like yesterday when it is past"). For example, the Talmud tractate *Sanhedrin* says that the world will exist for 6,000 years, and then it will be desolate for 1,000 years (during the seventh "thousand"). During the 6,000 years, the earth is desolate for 2,000 years, then the Torah flourishes for 2,000 years, then the Messianic era comes for the next 2,000 years (*b. Sanh.* 97a-b).

Paul speaks of an age during which Christ will subdue his enemies before delivering the kingdom over to God the Father (1 Cor 15:23-28), but Paul does not distinguish between a present and future millennial expression of that kingdom. Second Peter uses Ps 90:4 to explain why the coming of Christ is so long delayed, reminding readers "that with the Lord one day is like a thousand years, and a thousand years are like one day" (2 Pet 3:8). It is but a short step to assign one thousand years to the DAY OF THE LORD when it finally comes (2 Pet 3:10). That step is taken in Rev 20.

According to the *Epistle of Barnabas* in the early 2nd cent. CE, creation in six days "means that in six thousand years the Lord will complete all things" (*Barn.* 15:4). Then, "when his Son comes he will put an end to the age of the lawless one" and "rest on the seventh day" (*Barn.* 15:5). This is followed by "an eighth day" or "another world" (*Barn.* 15:8). The author says that Christians should celebrate the eighth day with gladness, because it is the day Jesus was resurrected (*Barn.* 15:8).

Justin Martyr rationalized the "thousand years" of Revelation by appealing to Ps 90:4, Isa 65:22 ("like the days of a tree shall the days of my people be"), and God's warning to Adam that on the "day" he ate of the tree of life he would die (Gen 2:17), noting that Adam in fact died within a thousand years. Finally, while acknowledging that some true Christians disagree, Justin said that those who believe in Christ will live for a thousand years in Jerusalem, after which the judgment of all people will take place (*Dial.* 80–81).

Irenaeus too argued that the day of the Lord is as a thousand years; because it took six days to create the world, the world will come to an end at the conclusion of the six-thousandth year (*Haer.* 5.38.3).

Later, in the *Apocalypse of Elijah* (*Apoc. El.* 5:36-39), the millennium came to represent a NEW HEAVEN AND NEW EARTH where there would be no evil, where Christ will rule for a thousand years.

John's concept of the millennium left its imprint on Christian theology. Because it occurs in only one passage of one rather atypical NT book, it has become a kind of test case for how much diversity within the canon one can tolerate. Some, finding it at odds with the rest of the Bible, simply chose to leave John's imagery back in the 1st cent. where it originated. Others, without necessarily taking "a thousand years" literally, still took the idea of the millennium seriously and regarded it as a finite period of time during which the kingdom of God comes to realization on earth (see Matt 6:10, "on earth as it is in heaven"). Certain millenarian groups (e.g., Montanists, "French Prophets," Shakers, Irvingites, some Anabaptists, Adventists, and others) built their very identity around such millennial expectations. Other "premillennialists" (so-called because Christ returns before the thousand years), anticipating the conversion of the Jews to Christianity (see Rom 11:26), interpreted the millennium as a way of making room for the literal fulfillment of biblical prophecies relating to Israel and the Jewish people. This group includes dispensationalists, other fundamentalists, and some present-day evangelicals. "Postmillennialists" saw the thousand years as Christianity's triumph throughout the world before (or even instead of) Christ's literal return to earth, in much the same way that secular utopians envision society's gradual transformation through education and technology. Another kind of "postmillennial" approach (going back to Augustine) domesticated John's millennium by making it one metaphor among many for Christ's lordship in the present age or for the intermediate state of Christians who had died. This view was called "amillennialism" because its practical effect was to do away with the millennium altogether, while retaining a belief in Christ's second coming.

Whatever else it may mean in the book of Revelation, the concept of the millennium stands as a reminder of the Jewish context of early Christianity. The God of Israel cares about this world no less than the heavenly one to come. Just as those martyred for their faith await the redemption of their bodies (and not just their spirits), so they await vindication not only in heaven but also in the same earthly arena where they suffered and died (so Irenaeus, *Haer.* 5.32.1). Moreover, Revelation's depiction of the thousand years of peace followed by evil's brief resurgence at the end (Rev 20:7-10) allows the author to imply that the evil forces at work in the Roman Empire in his day—such as the beast and the false prophet (Rev 13:1-18)—would not be the world's last manifestations of evil, but that "the dragon . . . who is the Devil and Satan" (Rev 20:2) would rise once more to deceive the nations. To that extent, John qualifies his initial insistence that "the time is near" (Rev 1:3), because he says that Satan is destroyed in two stages, with one still to come. Far from making John's Revelation irrelevant to the present, the concept of the millennium reminds us that the conflict between good and evil still goes on, taking many forms, but that through it all the promise "I am making all things new" (Rev 21:5) is being fulfilled in real time and real history. *See* APOCALYPTICISM; ESCHATOLOGY OF THE NT; PAROUSIA; REVELATION, BOOK OF.

Bibliography: David E. Aune. "Excursus 20A: The Temporary and the Eternal Kingdom." *Revelation 17–22.* WBC 52C (1998) 1104–1108; Robert G. Clouse, ed. *The Meaning of the Millennium: Four Views* (1977); Charles E. Hill. *Regnum Caelorum: Patterns of Millennial Thought in Early Christianity* (2001); J. Webb Mealy. *After the Thousand Years: Resurrection and Judgment in Revelation 20* (1992).

J. RAMSEY MICHAELS

MILLET [דֹּחַן dokhan, פַּנַּג pannagh]. A type of grass whose small seeds are used for food. While it is difficult to specify the variety of grain translated as "millet" in Ezek 4:9, most scholars identify dokhan as *Panicum miliaceum* (broomcorn or proso millet). This variety, which appears early in the archaeobotanical record in China, the Near East, India, and Africa, has low water requirements and can be sown in nearly any type of soil other than coarse sand. It is planted in the spring since it is intolerant to cold weather, and has a 60–65-day growing season. Ezekiel is instructed to use millet as one of several ingredients in his ration of unleavened bread in order to dramatize the scarcity of food faced by the exiles.

In Ezek 27:17, *millet* translates pannagh, a rare word derived from the Akkadian word for flour (pannigu). It appears in Ezekiel's list of the trade goods Israel regularly sent to Tyre. Pannagh, however, may in fact refer to a medicinal plant from which galbanum is derived. *See* GRAIN; PLANTS OF THE BIBLE.

VICTOR H. MATTHEWS

MILLO mil'oh [מִלּוֹא millo']. An unspecified place in the "City of David." Its possible derivation from male' (מָלֵא, "to be full" or "to fill") may indicate some kind of stone filling, perhaps a stepped stone foundation that served as a supporting terrace along the eastern ridge of the city. "The Millo" already existed at the time of David (2 Sam 5:9); Solomon enlarged and reinforced it (1 Kgs 9:15, 24; 11:27; 1 Chr 11:8); Hezekiah later repaired it (2 Chr 32:5). *See* BETH-MILLO; DAVID, CITY OF; JERUSALEM.

Bibliography: J. M. Cahill and D. Tarler. "Excavations Directed by Yigal Shiloh at the City of David, 1978–1985." *Ancient Jerusalem Revealed.* H. Geva, ed. (2000) 31–45.

RALPH K. HAWKINS

MIMESIS [μίμησις mimēsis; Lat. *imitatio*]. Imitation is a significant concept in Greco-Roman antiquity in philosophical discussions of the nature of reality, artistic representation, and education. Plato uses the concept in a number of different ways, but is most famous for banishing the poets from his ideal state for creating mimetic realities that could only approximate the true forms of things, for being derivative. Aristotle saw the origins of art in humans' natural inclination to imitate what we know and to learn by that process. Elizabeth Castelli has shown that mimēsis features in a number of different discourses, including discussions of the relation of the sensible world to the intelligible world, human imitation of the divine, and the relation between a king, that person appointed by the gods and therefore closest to them, and the divine realm. These discourses provide an important context for understanding Paul's use of the term mimētēs (μιμητής, "imitator"). Paul praises Christians in Thessalonica for becoming imitators of Paul and his co-workers, of the Lord, and of Judean Christian communities (1 Thess 1:6-7; 2:14). As an imitator of Christ, Paul considers himself an example, urging Christians to imitate him (1 Cor 11:1; compare 1 Cor 4:16; Phil 3:17).

The most widespread use of mimēsis and related terms is in the realm of Greco-Roman education, where imitation stood at the heart of the process of learning to read and write. Through all stages of Greek education students imitated a handful of select models, drawn mostly from classical poetry, interacting with them in increasingly complex ways. In the first stage, students started by copying the letters, words from lists to learn vocabulary, and short passages from poetry, often from Homer's epics. The second stage consisted of more detailed imitation of the same models, this time applying grammatical categories. The third stage, rhetorical training, marched students through complex exercises again interacting with the same classical models. The result of this educational process is a later literary and rhetorical practice that is marked by a mimetic compositional ethos. Students were encouraged to borrow from multiple models and to seek to improve on them. Recently, scholars have seen in some NT texts evidence of a mimetic relationship to models. An obvious model for Christian writers is the LXX; literary imitation has helped explain the relationship of parts of Luke and Acts to the LXX, particularly the stories of Elijah and Elisha. Less obvious, but no less important, is the NT's relationship to Greek classical models. Dennis Macdonald has argued that episodes of Mark, Luke, and Acts are modeled on such Greek writers as Homer, Plato, and Euripides, all of whom were prominent models in Greek education. Mimēsis is also applied more generally to Christian use of generally accepted literary models or themes. *See* EDUCATION, NT; INTERTEXTUALITY.

Bibliography: Jo-Ann A. Brant. "The Place of Mimēsis in Paul's Thought." *SR* 22 (1993) 285–300; Elizabeth A. Castelli. *Imitating Paul: A Discourse of Power* (1991); Dennis R. MacDonald. *Does the New Testament Imitate Homer? Four Cases from the Acts of the Apostles* (2003); Dennis R. MacDonald. *The Homeric Epics and the Gospel of Mark* (2000).

RUBÉN R. DUPERTUIS

MINA. *See* WEIGHTS AND MEASURES.

MINCING [טָפַף tafaf]. A word occurring only in Isa 3:16 to describe the affected walk of the excessively haughty daughters of Jerusalem. Related to a Hebrew word for child (taf טַף; e.g., Jer 43:6), the term probably describes a particularly dainty walk and might be translated "tripping" or "skipping."

MIND [לֵב lev, לֵבָב levav; νοῦς nous]. There is no word in biblical Hebrew for "mind." That lev and levav ("heart") are rendered in the LXX regularly by kardia (καρδία, "heart") and occasionally by nous ("mind") reflects the Hebraic understanding of the heart as the seat of compassion as well as intellection (*see* HEART). The notion of thinking (bin בִּין) appears in the wisdom literature, where it is not a natural human attribute but a gift of divine wisdom. In Judaism, most of the characteristics of Hellenistic "mind" are taken over by the Greek term for wisdom, sophia (σοφία). These examples stress right actions in relationship rather than mere right thinking (*see* WISDOM IN THE OT). In the NT, nous can mean one's inner orientation or moral attitude (e.g., Rom 1:28; 12:2; compare Eph 4:17, 23; Col 2:18; 1 Tim 6:5; 2 Tim 3:8), practical reasoning that determines will and action (Rom 7:23, 25), intellectual organ or reasoning faculty (Luke 24:45; Phil 4:7; 2 Thess 2:2; Rev 13:18; 17:9), and thought or judgment (Rom 14:5-6). "Mind" becomes a theological category as the result largely of Paul's writing. Of the twenty-six uses of nous, only three occur outside the Pauline corpus. In adapting the Hellenistic term, Paul does not prioritize mind as the ruler of the tripartite soul, as in Plato. There is no evidence that Paul subscribed to Pindar's notion that the nous was divine and immortal, imprisoned in the body until death, or to a neoplatonic idea of using the mind for spiritual intuition and ecstatic apprehension of God.

Paul's lack of precision in using the term *mind* means that nous is not a technical term. Paul could use the word to represent the whole person, as in Rom 7:23-25. He vouchsafes that while he desires to serve the law of God with his mind, he instead serves the law of sin in his flesh (Rom 7:18-23). "Mind" in this internal battle is identical to "the inner person," which according to Rudolf Bultmann is a person's real self in distinction from his or her objectivized self. Bultmann is probably correct in applying this meaning to Rom 7, the only such usage in Paul.

In critiquing glossolalia, Paul suggests that the human spirit and mind do not coexist: "For if I pray in a tongue, my spirit prays but my mind is unproductive" (1 Cor 14:14). Speaking in tongues is an ecstatic experience that renders the reasoning faculty inactive and the speaker unable to communicate with others or build them up (v. 16). Paul does not denigrate speaking in tongues, since he claims to do so himself (v. 18), but for the sake of the community, he would rather speak five words with his mind than ten thousand in tongues (v. 19). "Mind" in this context represents the exercise of rational faculty for communication.

Paul's unique contribution to nous, however, grounds it in communal ethics, thus asking a group to achieve a common mind. In 1 Cor 1:10, Paul confronts the factions by exhorting them to "be united in the same mind and the same purpose." Here nous stands in the singular and in parallel to gnōmē (γνώμη, "purpose"), so that it cannot refer to an individual's rational faculty. It stands for a set of common thoughts or assumptions that can form the basis of unity. The same idea is captured in the expression "to be of the same mind" (Phil 2:2; 4:2; compare Rom 12:16; 15:5; 2 Cor 13:11)—literally, "to think the same thing" (phronein to auto φρονεῖν τὸ αὐτό).

Paul refers to this communal nous with the enigmatic nous tou Christou (νοῦς τοῦ Χριστοῦ, "mind of Christ") in 1 Cor 2:16*b*. It has been suggested that the union between nous and pneuma (πνεῦμα, "Spirit"; 2:12) reflects Hellenistic MYSTERY RELIGIONS and GNOSTICISM in which the initiates receive saving gnōsis (γνῶσις) by achieving union with the God-Nous. The parallelism between nous and pneuma is indisputable, but the context of Paul's thought is not Hellenistic mysticism but the early community. The nous tou Christou epitomizes an elaborate discussion of the Spirit initiated in v. 6. But the parallelism is already required by the citation of LXX Isa 40:13 in v. 16*a*, "For who has known the mind of the Lord [nous kyriou νοῦς κυρίου]?" where nous translates ruakh (רוּחַ, "spirit"). Paul's answer is "No one"—with the crucial exception that "we have the mind of Christ" (v. 16*b*). The Lord-Christ comparison is intended as a pastoral reminder to the Corinthians concerning the kind of mind or Spirit they have received. While the Corinthians revel in their spiritual accomplishments, Paul ironically criticizes them by equating the wisdom of God with what is foolishness to the world. The wisdom of God is embodied in the paradox of the cross, and rulers of this age are ignorant of it (2:8; compare 1:18-25). The Corinthians have indeed received the Spirit, Paul accedes, but this Spirit is the mind of Christ, which finds its truest expression in the cross. And this common mind-set forms the bedrock of unity. Isaiah 40:13 is again cited in Rom 11:34, but here the "mind of the Lord" refers to the mystery of God's salvific plans.

In Phil 2:6-11, Paul introduces a christological basis for unity. Christ's self-emptying, which led to the cross, is paradigmatic (*see* KENOSIS). The Philippians are asked literally "to think [**phronein**] this" among themselves (v. 5), which is to say, to establish a common mind-set based on Christ's humility, so that mutual humility might become normative behavior between members and that unity of the community might be a possibility.

The communal mind is likewise the focus of Rom 12:1-2, where Paul lays a foundation for ethical behaviors. Presentation of bodies (plural) is accompanied by transformation and renewal of the mind (singular **nous**). The language here recalls 2 Cor 3:18 and 4:16, where daily encounters with the "Spirit of the Lord" (3:16-17) and "the death of Jesus" (4:10-12) effect internal changes. The thought in Rom 12 is similar, except Paul explicitly applies it to the whole community. Unity is maintained if no one thinks more highly (**hyperphronein** ὑπερφρονεῖν) than one ought to think (**phronein**) and everyone thinks (**phronein**) with sobriety (**sōphronein** σωφρονεῖν) each according to the measure of faith (12:3). Humility informs this mind-set and is instrumental to unity, for to think the same thing means not to think haughtily (**mē ta hypsēla phronein** μὴ τὰ ὑψηλὰ φρονεῖν) toward others (12:16). This last expression echoes 11:20, where Gentiles are warned not to treat Jews with arrogance, for Paul desires unity between the two ethnic groups.

For Paul, therefore, "mind" means not so much rational faculty as a theological mode of thinking founded on the paradox of the cross. As summarized by R. Jewett, the mind is a constellation of thoughts based in the gospel that provides for the unity of the church. Such a general definition of **nous** would throw light on the "debased mind" of Rom 1:28. Regarding Gentiles who do not accept God as proved in spite of God's knowability through creation (vv. 19-21), God delivers them into a state in which the mind is incapable of proving anything to be true. The "debased mind" refers to a state in which someone who rejects God is given over to a demonic reality (Jewett). *See* UNITY; WISDOM IN THE NT.

Bibliography: R. Bultmann. *New Testament Theology I.* K. Grobel, trans. (1951) 211–16; R. Jewett. *Paul's Anthropological Terms: A Study of Their Use in Conflict Settings* (1971) 358–90, 450–51; R. Reitzenstein. *Hellenistic Mystery-Religions: Their Basic Ideas and Significance.* J. E. Steely, trans. (1978); G. Theissen. *The Psychological Aspects of Pauline Theology.* J. P. Galvin, trans. (1987); A. Thiselton. *The First Epistle to the Corinthians.* NIGTC (2000) 271–76, 1108–11; W. Willis. "'The Mind of Christ' in 1 Corinthians 2,16." *Bib* 70 (1989) 110–22.

SZE-KAR WAN

MINEAN min-ee'uhn [Μιναῖος **Minaios**]. The Mineans were a Semitic people who ruled the kingdom of Ma'in, located in modern North Yemen, and founded by the kings of Hadhramaut (southern Arabia) about 400 BCE (*see* HAZARMAVETH). Its trading industry extended as far as colonies in Egypt, Gaza, Sidon, and DEDAN. In the 1st cent. BCE it was absorbed by its southern neighbor Saba (*see* SABEANS).

The name is used in the LXX in place of the MEUNIM (Qere) or Meinim (Kethibh) in 1 Chr 4:41 and Ezra 2:50 and in the LXX in place of Meunim in 2 Chr 26:7 and Neh 7:52. The LXX also uses the name where the Hebrew refers to the Ammonites (perhaps a corruption of Meunim or Meinim) in 2 Chr 20:1; 26:8. The term "Meinim" may refer to the Mineans, whereas "Meunim" may refer to inhabitants of MAON, a name that is attached to several different locations.

GREGORY L. LINTON

MINIAMIN min'yuh-min [מִנְיָמִן **minyamin**, מִנְיָמִין **minyamin**]. Meaning "from the right" or "luck, lucky person." 1. One of Kore's assistants overseeing the gathering of freewill offerings during King Hezekiah's reign (2 Chr 31:15). The LXX, Vulgate, and Peshitta record "Benjamin" here.

2. One of the priestly houses during Joiakim's term as high priest (Neh 12:17).

3. A trumpet-playing priest present for the dedication of the Jerusalem wall rebuilt under Nehemiah's supervision (Neh 12:41). *See* MIJAMIN.

HEIDI E. HAWKS

MINIM [מִינִים **minim**]. A rabbinic designation for heterodox or heretical followers of Judaism, possibly gnostic or Christian Jews. In the Mishnah and Talmud, **minim** usually focuses on heterodox beliefs (e.g., the belief in "two powers") or practice (e.g., the use of protective amulets). The synagogue prayer *Birkhat Ha-Minim* ("Blessing of the Heretics") beseeches God to let the **minim** be destroyed.

JESSICA TINKLENBERG DEVEGA

MINING. Job 28 is an extensive and detailed description of the various aspects of mining. The process of mining, digging into the earth and rock to extract ores and precious stones, is used as a metaphor, comparing probing into the depths of the earth with the search for true wisdom. The description also shows that the author of Job had a practical knowledge of several aspects of mining. Mining, particularly of COPPER and IRON, was known in ancient Israel because of the copper mines in the Wadi Arabah and the iron mines in Gilead, both of which were exploited during the biblical period. This is also reflected in Deut 8:9, which refers to "a land whose stones are iron and from whose hills you may mine copper."

The copper ore fields of TIMNA and Wadi Feinan (*see* FEINAN, WADI), in the southwest and northeast of the Wadi Arabah, respectively, were originally one geological feature, cut through by the great African rift, of which the Wadi Arabah forms a part. As a result of horizontal shifting of the two tectonic plates, the two fields are now about 100 km apart. The Timna ore fields were exploited from the Neolithic period onward. The latest extensive period of exploitation prior to the Islamic era was in the Late Bronze Age, from the 14th to the 12th cent. BCE, by the pharaohs of the Egyptian New Kingdom. After the collapse of the Egyptian Empire exploitation may have continued for a short while by Midianite tribes, but it stopped in the 12th cent. The suggestion that the Timna mines were exploited by Solomon, a suggestion that is reflected in the name "King Solomon's mines" that has been given to the site, is therefore not substantiated by archaeology. If Solomon's legendary wealth was (partly) due to his exploitation of the copper mines, a more likely candidate for this title is the Wadi Feinan.

Copper mines in the Wadi Feinan have been exploited from Chalcolithic times onward. The copper treasure from Nahal Mishmar, dated to the Chalcolithic period, was made from copper that was mined in the Wadi Feinan. There is evidence for exploitation of the ore fields of Khirbet en-Nahas, a site in the Wadi Feinan, from the 11th cent. BCE onward, probably by a local semi-nomadic population. In the 10th cent. a fortress was built in Khirbet en-Nahas, testifying to the importance of the copper mining industry at the time. Copper exploitation in the Wadi Feinan reached its zenith during Neo-Assyrian times, when some 13,000 tons of copper were produced in the Wadi Fidan. Copper mining, together with the Arabian trade, was one of the economic pillars of the kingdom of Edom.

Job 28:4 refers to the shafts that are dug to reach the ore. Shaft mining as a way to reach the copper ore was used certainly from New Kingdom times onward. Both in Timna and in the Wadi Feinan thousands of shafts have been found that give access to extensive networks of underground galleries and caves. The shafts are well dug, square or rounded, with steps cut into the walls to ease access. Because of the lack of artifacts found in connection with these shafts, they can be hard to date, but it is likely that they were reused in different periods. Some of them were as deep as 30 m. Airholes have been found that served to ventilate and light the multi-level galleries. Nevertheless, work must have been difficult and dangerous, as testified by Job 28:4. In the Roman period the mines of Wadi Feinan were exploited extensively, mostly with the use of prisoners, who never survived for long due to the excruciating circumstances in the mines.

Iron ore is the commonest ore in existence, but due to the difficulties of extracting the metal, iron ore was not exploited until the beginning of the Iron Age, ca. 1200 BCE (*see* METALLURGY). Biblical Gilead, in the Ajlun area, east of the Jordan, contains the largest iron ore field in the region. Recent research in this area has revealed the existence of a mining and smelting industry for iron, with a starting date in the 10th cent. BCE (930 BCE). The smelting site, Tell el-Hammeh, was several kilometers away from the mining site of Mugharet el-Wardeh, but technological analysis shows that the iron ore was almost certainly mined at Mugharet el-Wardeh. Earlier research revealed the existence of horizontal mining shafts in the caves of Mugharet el-Wardeh, leading into large artificial caves in the mountain itself, with roofs supported by rock pillars that were left in place by the miners. There was no evidence for smelting, or for that matter any activity near the caves during the Iron Age, which suggests that the ore was mined and immediately transported to the smelting site. The miners probably belonged to a semi-nomadic population. Evidence of their presence has also been found in Beth-Shemesh, west of the Jordan, suggesting that they may have worked the mines on a seasonal basis, working as itinerant smiths during the rest of the year. SILVER was extracted from lead ore by various processes (*see* LEAD, METAL). The nearest lead mines where silver was extracted were in Cyprus.

Bibliography: P. T. Craddock. *Early Metal Mining and Production* (1995); B. Rothenberg. *Were These King Solomon's Mines?* (1972).

EVELINE J. VAN DER STEEN

MINISTER IN THE OT [שָׁרַת sharath]. In the NRSV the word *minister*, which is used only as a verb, refers to the acts of the PRIESTS AND LEVITES who serve God in the sanctuary or Temple by offering sacrifice.

Throughout the OT, various presentations are given regarding the specific tasks of the divisions (clans) of the Levites—the tribe descended from Levi, one of the twelve sons of the patriarch Jacob. In Exodus, Numbers, and Chronicles, the descendants of Aaron alone are designated as God's priests; Ezekiel further specifies that only the Zadokites, descended from Aaron's son Eleazar, may so function. Deuteronomy, however, underscores that all Levites, because they have no portion of land as do the other tribes, "stand before the LORD to minister to him"; the God of Israel alone is their inheritance (Deut 10:8-9).

In the book of Exodus, the location of priestly ministry occurs either at the altar or at the tent of meeting (Exod 30:20). The sanctuary (and later the Temple) is the meeting ground of heaven and earth, where God had promised to dwell among the people. There the priests minister by performing the rites of sacrifice and prayer, offering praise, thanksgiving, and acts of atonement, thus continually binding the people with God. The sanctity of their actions is indicated by the distinctive garments that they wear while ministering (Ezek 42:14); by the fact that their actions are punishable by death at the hand of God if performed improperly; and by God's designation of the duration of their service for a "perpetual ordinance" (Exod 28:43). Before ministering at the altar or entering the tent of meeting, the priests wash their hands and feet, an act of purification that saves them from death (Exod 30:20-21); similarly, because they are anointed with oil, the holiness of Aaron's sons is underscored (30:30; 40:15).

In those texts that understand the Levites to be subordinate to the Aaronide priests, the Levites' various duties are presented as divine service as well. The Levites assist the priestly sacrifices by guarding the precincts of the sanctuary and Temple, by carrying all the components and sacrificial items during transport of the portable shrine, and by attending to the various items used for sacrifice. The Levites are responsible for the items "with which the priests minister," namely, the ark of the covenant (compare Deut 10:8; 1 Chr 15:2; 16:37); the table, on which the Bread of Presence is placed; the lampstand, or seven-branched menorah; the altar, used for sacrifice; the vessels of the sanctuary; and the screen, or curtain, used to separate the inner sanctuary from the holy of holies (Num 3:31).

The critical responsibility that the Levites have for the entirety of the people is indicated by the information that they serve as substitutes for the firstborn—to whom God is entitled—by offering sacrifices to God (Num 3:11-13). Moses instructs the congregation to provide portions of their sacrificial offerings to them, "For the LORD your God has chosen Levi out of all your tribes, to stand and minister in the name of the LORD, him and his sons for all time" (Deut 18:5).

The sacrificial acts, or ministry, of the priests are closely associated with other responsibilities. These include the carrying of the ark of the covenant, the recitations of the blessings in God's name, and duties within the judicial system. The ark was used not only as a container for the law, but also as a guide for the Israelites in the wilderness and as a palladium during battle. Its unparaleled importance can be seen by the dire consequences that both the Israelites and Philistines suffered when the latter captured it (1 Sam 3–6). The importance of the Levites' recitation of the priestly blessing is indicated not only by the multiple references in the Bible to their blessings of the people (Deut 21:5; Lev 9:22) but also by the very record of the blessing itself (Num 6:22-27). The discovery of two tiny silver scrolls (late 7th or early 6th cent. BCE) at Ketef Hinnom, a hillside burial site near Jerusalem, demonstrates that these words of the blessing were sometimes worn as silver amulets. Variants and echoes of the blessing are also found in the Dead Sea Scrolls (1QS II, 2–4 [= 4Q256 II, III; 4Q257 II, III; 5Q11], 1Q28b II, 2–4 [= 1QSb], and 4Q285 [4QSM] 1 3–5). This blessing is still recited in Jewish and in Christian liturgies today. In addition, the connection between the Levites' ministry and the pursuit of justice is seen in the account of the expiation of bloodguilt for an unsolved murder (Deut 21:1-9). Although the specifics of their role are not given, they pursue justice by rendering decisions in "cases of dispute and assault" (Deut 21:5; see also 17:12).

Besides the priests and Levites, who retain the distinction of ministering to the Lord in prayer and sacrifice, the people have a role in the divine service as well. The psalmist states that whoever is faithful, keeping the commandments, ministers to God (Ps 101:6). The eschatological hope for all people is that when foreigners keep the commandments, they too please God with ministry (Isa 56:6). Not only foreign individuals but also their kings and even their flocks will be accepted as sacrifice and thus "minister" to God (Isa 60:7, 10).

SHARON PACE

MINISTRY, CHRISTIAN [διακονία diakonia]. From the ancient church to contemporary communities of faith, a major unresolved issue is the nature of Christian ministry. After centuries of dialogue, Christian traditions have come to no shared understanding of such matters as the relation of the people of God to ordained ministers, the authority to administer the sacraments, and the organizational structure of offices within the church. Some define ministry in terms of offices, while others define it in terms of functions. In addition to traditional questions about the nature of ministry, the contemporary church faces other challenges in defining ministry that are rooted not in ancient doctrinal debates but in the influence of therapeutic professions or business models. This uncertainty has resulted in a new call to examine the foundations of Christian ministry in the ancient church.

A. Terms for Ministry

The uncertainty over the nature of Christian ministry may reflect the diversity of the biblical witness, for the NT offers no uniform church order or nomenclature for describing Christian ministry. Indeed, the variety in NT nomenclature contributes to this uncertainty. "Ministry" (Acts 1:17; 20:24; 21:19; Rom 11:13; 12:7; 15:31; 2 Cor 3:7-11) is a translation of diakonia, which is also rendered as "service" (Acts 6:4, "serving the word"; 1 Cor 12:5; 16:15; see also "relief" in Acts 11:29). The verb diakoneō (διακονέω) is rendered either as "to minister" (Rom 15:25) or "to serve" (Matt 8:15; 20:28; Luke 12:37; 17:8; Heb 6:10; Phlm 13; 1 Pet 1:12; 4:10; see also Matt 25:44, "take care of"; 27:55, "provide for"; Acts 6:2, "wait on"). The noun diakonos (διάκονος), used in a variety of contexts, is rendered either as "minister" (2 Cor 3:6; 11:23; Eph 6:21) or "servant" (Matt 20:26; John 2:5; 12:26; Rom 13:4; 15:8; 1 Cor 3:5; 2 Cor 6:4; Eph 3:7; Col 1:7; 4:7) and is occasionally translated as "deacon" (Rom 16:1; Phil 1:1; 1 Tim 3:8, 12). This group of words appears about 100 times in the NT, but is rarely used in the OT. The alternative translations of the word contribute to the uncertainty over the nature of ministry. Contrary to earlier views that identified the root meaning as serving tables, John Collins has shown that the word is used in secular Greek literature for a variety of activities that one does on behalf of another, including being a go-between or messenger. Paul employs diakonia and diakonos as the comprehensive terms for his vocation (2 Cor 3:3, 6; 11:23) as spokesperson for God (*see* SERVE, TO).

Other NT words have shaped Christian interpretations of ministry. The NT uses the term *pastor* (poimēn ποιμήν) only once (Eph 4:11) for leaders other than Jesus (compare *shepherd* in John 10:2, 12; Heb 13:20; 1 Pet 2:25) but employs the pastoral image in several instances, using the verb poimainō (ποιμαίνω) for the task of leaders who have responsibility for the people (John 21:16; Acts 20:28; 1 Pet 5:2). In other NT witnesses, prophets (Acts 11:27; 15:32; 1 Cor 12:28), teachers (1 Cor 12:28; Eph 4:11), elders (Acts 14:23; 20:17; 1 Tim 5:17; Titus 1:5), and bishops (Phil 1:1; 1 Tim 3:1) perform tasks on behalf of the church. In some instances, the terms appear to be titles, while in other instances they describe functions or status in life. Thus an examination of the beginnings of Christian ministry involves not only the survey of offices or terms, but the complex web of activities and terms for those who act on God's behalf for the sake of the people.

Although the word group diakon- appears only rarely in the OT (LXX), God's covenantal love toward Israel requires the work of those who speak for God to call Israel to faithfulness. God is Israel's SHEPHERD (Gen 48:15; Pss 23:1; 80:1) who does not leave Israel as "sheep without a shepherd" (Num 27:17; Isa 13:14). Consequently, God appoints prophets and kings to be shepherds on God's behalf (2 Sam 5:2; 7:7; Ezek 34:5-24). Prophets who are called (Isa 6:1-8; Jer 1:4-10; Ezek 1:1-3) and sent (Isa 6:8; Jer 1:7; Ezek 2:3) to speak to Israel anticipate the similar roles of apostles and ministers in early Christianity whom Christ calls and sends to speak to the people (Matt 10:5, 40; Rom 10:15; 1 Cor 1:17).

B. Jesus Remembered

Although Jesus is known to us only through the portraits in the Gospel traditions, these narratives contain not only the perspective of the evangelists a generation later, but also the church's memory of the beginnings of the Jesus movement. According to the united witness of the Synoptic Gospels, Jesus came into Galilee preaching the coming of the kingdom of God and summoning Israel to repent in view of the coming eschatological hour (Mark 1:14-15 par.). Jesus' public ministry consisted of PREACHING (kēryssō κηρύσσω, Matt 4:17, 23), teaching (didaskō διδάσκω; Matt 4:23; 5:2; 7:29; 9:35), and HEALING (therapeuō θεραπεύω; Matt 4:23; 8:16; sōzō σῴζω; Matt 9:21-22; Luke 8:36) in order to reclaim all Israel, including the outcasts, for the kingdom.

The roots of Christian ministry are evident in the synoptic accounts of Jesus' call to the disciples and the commission to extend his ministry in a ministry of preaching, teaching, and healing (see Matt 10:2-8). Their ministry, therefore, involved the dual aspects of being called (Matt 10:1; Mark 3:13) and sent (Matt 10:5; Mark 3:14) to act on behalf of the one who sent them. They were the representatives of Jesus with the authority to speak on his behalf (Matt 10:40; Luke 10:16) and to minister to Israel's outcasts. Those who participated in Jesus' ministry also share his precarious existence (Matt 8:18-22; 10:9-36) and take up a cross (Matt 10:38; Mark 8:34; Luke 9:23).

All three Synoptics report the disciples' struggle to define Christian ministry. When they indicate their desire for the first places in the kingdom, Jesus responds with the claim that his community has a countercultural understanding of leadership. While "the Gentiles" exercise power over others (Mark 10:42), among the disciples "whoever wishes to become great among you must be your servant" (diakonos; Mark 10:43). In all three synoptic accounts Jesus identifies himself as a diakonos (or "one who serves," e.g., Luke 22:27), making himself a model for Christian ministry and defining the mission of those who follow him in the language of being at the disposal of others.

The traditions about the apostles in Acts indicate the continuity between their role during the life of Jesus and after his departure. Under the power of the Spirit, the apostles continue the signs and wonders that they began when they were first sent out by Jesus (Acts 2:43; 4:30; see 6:8) and proclaim the name of Jesus in the presence of the authorities (4:5-12), an indication of their readiness to share the destiny of Jesus.

C. Paul and His Churches

1. Paul's ministry

Because Paul does not belong to the circle of the Twelve, his need to defend his apostleship results in considerable reflection on the nature of his apostleship and Christian ministry. Because he has both "seen the Lord" (1 Cor 9:1; see 15:1-8) and been called (Gal 1:15; see Rom 1:1), he is the equal of the other apostles (1 Cor 9:1-2; 15:4-8; Gal 2:1-10). In describing his calling and work in language that is reminiscent of the prophets, he places his role alongside theirs as a spokesman for God (*see* APOSTLE). Like Jeremiah, he was "set apart" before he was born (Jer 1:5; Gal 1:15; see Isa 49:1) and now serves under divine compulsion (Jer 20:9; 1 Cor 9:16) with the task of building and planting (Jer 24:6; 2 Cor 10:8) the people of God.

Just as Jesus commissioned the Twelve to preach (kēryssō) the kingdom to Israel, the risen Lord commissioned Paul to proclaim the gospel (euangelizō εὐαγγελίζω; 1 Cor 1:17; 9:16) where Christ had not been named (Rom 15:20). Paul's preaching, like that of Jesus and the disciples, resulted in the establishment of communities that he describes with the metaphors of planting (1 Cor 3:6), laying a foundation (1 Cor 3:10), and becoming a father (1 Cor 4:15). Paul defines his ministry not only in terms of laying a foundation and planting the community but also according to the ultimate outcome of his work. He envisions a corporate narrative for his communities that extends from the moment when God "began a good work" at their reception of the gospel (Phil 1:6; see 1 Thess 1:5) until the time when the community will be "blameless" (Phil 1:10; 1 Thess 3:13; 5:23) in holiness at the day of Christ (2 Cor 1:14; Phil 1:10; 2:16). Paul's frequent statements that his "boast" will be the presentation of a blameless community at the coming of Christ (Rom 15:15-17; 2 Cor 1:12-14; Phil 2:16-18; 1 Thess 2:19) indicates that he understands ministry as a participation with God in the transformation of the community of faith into the likeness of Christ. The failure to fulfill this goal will mean that he has "run in vain" (Gal 2:2; Phil 2:16). In 1 Thessalonians, he employs the familial metaphor to describe himself as both the nurse caring for infants (2:7) and the father (2:11-12) urging his children to ethical living. He is the priest offering a sacrifice of Gentiles who have been sanctified (Rom 15:16-17), the architect who laid the foundation of a building that will be completed only if it survives until the end (1 Cor 3:10-17), the father of the bride who hopes to present the church blameless at the end (2 Cor 11:2), and the pregnant mother (Gal 4:19) in the travail of birth pangs for her children. Because his task is to participate in the formation of communities, he experiences "anxiety for all of the churches" (2 Cor 11:28) and writes letters to confirm communities in their faith.

Paul's most detailed articulation of his view of Christian ministry comes in response to Corinthian opponents who challenge the legitimacy of his ministry. When the Corinthians evaluate their leaders on the basis of wisdom and rhetorical power (see 1 Cor 3:1-4, 18-23; 4:3), Paul describes himself and Apollos as "servants" (diakonos) through whom they had believed (1 Cor 3:5), "servants (hyperetēs ὑπερέτης) of Christ and stewards (oikonomos οἰκονόμος) of God's mysteries" (1 Cor 4:1). Using the language for those who are at the disposal of another, Paul insists that the basic requirement for ministers is that they are faithful in managing a trust. As Paul indicates in other instances (1 Cor 9:17; 1 Thess 2:4), he is at the disposal of the gospel, commissioned for the task before him. Thus he challenges the Corinthians' own evaluation of the nature of ministry.

The nature of Christian ministry is the central issue of 2 Corinthians, as Paul confronts the challenge offered by opponents who claim to be both apostles (11:13; note Paul's ironic designation "super-apostles" in 11:5; 12:11) and "ministers of Christ" (11:23). Even if the letter is a composite of more than one communication from Paul, as many scholars argue, the nature of ministry is the issue that Paul pursues from beginning to end. Paul's responses to direct attacks (10:2, 10-11; 11:7) and focus on boasting (10:13; 11:1–12:10) and self-commendation (10:12, 18) indicate that the opponents compared themselves to Paul, boasting of their achievements and criticizing Paul's weakness (10:10).

Paul responds to the opponents with the consistent claim that ministry is defined not by the secular standards represented by the opponents but by the story of the crucified and risen Lord. In the peristasis catalogs (2 Cor 6:4-10; 11:23-33; 12:10), a distinguishing feature of 2 Corinthians, Paul defines his ministry in cruciform terms, indicating that he embodies the cross and resurrection. As a weak earthen vessel (4:7), he carries "in the body the death of Jesus, so that the life of Jesus may also be made visible in our bodies" (4:10). Paul boasts in his weakness (11:29-30), declaring, "Whenever I am weak, then I am strong" (12:10), indicating that the minister participates in God's power only by sharing in the cross and embodying the message of the cross and resurrection (13:4).

2. Paul's co-workers

As Paul indicates in his description of himself as planter and builder (1 Cor 3:6-9), others participate in the work of ministry, building onto the work that he established (1 Cor 3:10). Paul mentions several itinerant CO-WORKERs who extend his ministry by serving as his spokespersons and participating in his way of life. In describing them with the terms *partner* (koinōnos κοινωνός; 2 Cor 8:23), "fellow soldier" (systratiōtēs συστρατιώτης; Phil 2:25; see Phlm 2), "fellow prisoner" (synaichmalōtos συναιχμάλωτος; Phlm 23; Rom 16:7), and "fellow worker" (synergos συνεργός; Rom 16:3; 1 Cor 3:9; Phlm 24), Paul indicates their participation in his ministry. The most prominent traveling companion is Timothy, whom Paul entrusts with the task of explaining his ways (1 Cor 4:17) because he does the same work that Paul does (1 Cor 16:10). Paul sends him to Thessalonica to continue Paul's own work of strengthening and encouraging the community in the midst of the persecutions they faced (1 Thess 3:2). In addition to speaking for Paul, Timothy embodies the self-denial that characterizes the apostle (Phil 2:20-21). Apollos is, like Paul, a servant (diakonos, 1 Cor 3:5) who joins in Paul's work and whom Paul sends to extend his ministry (1 Cor 16:12). As Paul's partner

(2 Cor 8:23), Titus also speaks for Paul and shares his anguish and joy over the condition of the churches (see 2 Cor 7:13-16). Paul describes Luke (Rom 16:21; Phlm 24) and Demas (Phlm 24) as fellow workers. In the disputed letters Ephesians and Colossians, emissaries function in the same way as in earlier letters. Epaphras is a "faithful minister" (**diakonos**, Col 1:7) who wrestles in prayer on behalf of the Colossian church (4:12). Archippus has received a ministry (**diakonia**; NRSV, "task") from the Lord (Col 4:17). Tychicus will "report everything" to the Ephesians (Eph 6:21). The co-workers, like Paul, are commissioned and sent on a mission to speak on behalf of the one who sent them, and they share Paul's goal of building up communities of faith.

3. The Pauline churches

Paul depends not only on traveling co-workers to sustain his work but also on the local communities he had founded. Although one cannot assume uniformity of ministerial practice in the Pauline churches, the letters suggest that Paul expects all of his churches to continue his work of building onto the foundation that he laid (1 Cor 3:10). Within the familial atmosphere created by the household setting, Paul addresses his communities as siblings (1 Thess 2:1, 9; 4:1), encouraging them to adopt the familial atmosphere in order to replace the families that many members had lost at their conversion (Rom 12:9-21; 1 Thess 4:9-12). He writes to the entire church, encouraging all of the members to take responsibility for building the community (Rom 15:14; 1 Cor 14:1-5; 1 Thess 5:11) and for encouraging others (1 Thess 4:18). He does not designate liturgical responsibilities to specific leaders in the church. The fact that the entire community has received SPIRITUAL GIFTS "for the common good" (1 Cor 12:7) indicates the involvement of the entire community in the ministerial task. Similarly, the image of the body and the members (Rom 12:3-8; 1 Cor 12:12-31) focuses on the interdependence of all the members in building up the local church.

This emphasis on mutual ministry led many scholars in the 20th cent., following the claims of Rudolf Sohm, to argue that the Pauline churches followed a progression from the equality of all members through the exercise of charismatic gifts in the early period to the development of church offices in the later period. However, the evidence from the Pauline churches suggests that this claim is overstated inasmuch as the mutual ministry characteristic of Paul's churches does not preclude the emergence of local leaders who undertake specific ministries within the church. For example, while Paul assumes the involvement of the whole church in ministry (1 Thess 5:15-21), he also encourages them to "respect those who labor among you, and have charge of you in the Lord and admonish you" (5:12) and to "esteem them very highly ... because of their work" (5:13). The use of one definite article in 1 Thess 5:12 suggests the presence of a single group that has taken on the three tasks Paul mentions. Thus a dialectical relationship exists between the responsibilities of everyone for the edification of the church and the responsibilities of leaders. Although the entire community is involved in instructing and admonishing others, the community recognizes those who engage in evangelism (i.e., **kopiōntas** [κοπιῶντας], "those who labor among you," from **kopiaō** [κοπιάω], "work, labor"; 5:12), leadership (**proistamenous** [προισταμένους], "those who are over you," from **proistēmi** [προΐστημι], "have authority, have charge, give aid"; 5:12), and teaching (**nouthetountas** [νουθετουντας], "those who admonish you," from **noutheteō** [νουθετέω], "instruct, teach, warn"; 5:12) roles. Paul's use of Gk. participles rather than nouns to describe their work indicates a focus on functions rather than titles. These roles may reflect the leadership roles of the householders who made their homes available for the community. The term **proistēmi** with the dual meanings of "have charge" and "give aid" (see Rom 12:8), suggests the role of the father who manages the household (1 Tim 3:4) with both authority and care.

A similar relationship between the ministry of the entire community and that of individual leaders is evident in the other letters. Although Paul writes to the entire congregation at Philippi, he refers also to the bishops and deacons (Phil 1:1). He does not specify the roles of these ministers, but his terminology may suggest roles similar to those of leaders at Thessalonica. Paul refers also to Euodia and Syntyche, who struggled with him in the work of the gospel along with Clement and other co-workers (4:2-3). In Galatians, he encourages members to "bear one another's burdens" (6:2), but also assumes that "those who are spiritual" (6:1) will assist faltering members and that those who are taught will share with their teachers (6:6). In 1 Corinthians, while Paul insists that all members are indispensable within the body of Christ (1 Cor 12:12-26) and lists a variety of ministries (12:5-10), he encourages the church to recognize the household of Stephanas, the "first converts in Achaia," because they "devoted themselves to the service (**diakonia**) of the saints." Paul urges the Corinthians to put themselves "at the service of such people, and of everyone who works and toils with them" (1 Cor 16:15-16). He also refers to Phoebe as a DEACON (**diakonos**) of the church at Cenchreae and a benefactor (**prostatis** προστάτις) of many (Rom 16:1-2). Paul's references to individuals suggest that both men and women emerged to take ministerial roles in the church. Their experience and involvement in acts of service for the community were the basis for their recognition by the church.

D. Ministry in the Pastoral Epistles

Although the dating and provenance of the Pastoral Epistles is a matter of dispute, the significance of all three letters for the development of Christian ministry subsequent to the undisputed Pauline letters is evident. Despite the attention that these letters give to offices within the church, the primary issue in all three is the author's concern to protect the deposit of faith against false teaching (1 Tim 6:20; 2 Tim 1:12, 14). The author's solution to the problem is to ensure that leaders will preserve the deposit and transmit it to others. As one who regards the gospel as a trust (2 Tim 1:11; Titus 1:3), Paul is the model for others (1 Tim 1:14-16). As Paul's envoys, Timothy and Titus speak on his behalf with two primary dimensions to their work: to model behavior that is appropriate to the gospel message (1 Tim 4:12; Titus 2:7) and to teach local communities (1 Tim 4:6, 11; 6:2; Titus 2:1).

Timothy and Titus ensure that local communities are equipped to meet the challenge of heresy and to protect the deposit of faith. According to 2 Tim 2:2, Timothy's task is to commit (lit., "deposit") what he has learned to faithful people who will teach others. In 1 Timothy and Titus, the restriction of these functions to those who meet the criteria reflects the emergence of offices in the local communities. Titus' commission to appoint elders (presbyteroi πρεσβύτεροι) in every city (Titus 1:5) presupposes an office that is not mentioned in the undisputed Pauline letters (*see* ELDER IN THE NT). First Timothy mentions the qualifications for a variety of offices, including the offices of BISHOP (1 Tim 3:1-7) and deacon (1 Tim 3:8, 12), which probably reflect continuity and development from the bishops and deacons (Phil 1:1) and "those who have charge" (1 Thess 5:12) in the undisputed Pauline letters. The elders mentioned in 1 Tim 5:17 may be the equivalent of the office of bishop in 3:1. Although the office of bishop was limited to men ("husband of one wife," 1 Tim 3:2), the office of deacon probably included both men and women, as the reference to women (i.e., women deacons) in 3:11 suggests.

Although 1 Timothy and Titus focus on the qualifications for these offices rather than the precise tasks of the officeholders, the texts offer important insights into the development of Christian ministry. In the first place, the qualifications for the respective offices indicate that Christian ministers embody ethical standards that are consistent with the Christian message and, like Paul and Timothy, serve as models of Christian practice. In the second place, Christian ministers are the community's teachers (1 Tim 3:2; 5:17), protecting it against false teachers (Titus 1:9-11). In the setting of the house church, leaders exercise authority analogous to the head of the household (1 Tim 3:4; 5:17). Although the Pastoral Epistles, in contrast to the undisputed letters of Paul, assume a church with established offices, Christian ministers maintain the original functions of building the community through the ministry of teaching and personal example.

E. Other New Testament Witnesses

1. Luke–Acts

Writing at a time after 70 CE, the author of Luke–Acts portrays the (reconstituted, see Acts 1:15-26) twelve apostles as the successors who continue the work of Jesus and provide the foundation for the continuing ministry of the church. Their task is to be the witnesses of Jesus (Acts 1:8; 4:33), proclaiming his cross and resurrection, and continuing the call to repentance (Acts 2:38; 3:19) initiated by John the Baptist (Luke 3:8) and Jesus (Luke 13:3). Luke's description of their commitment to the ministry of the word (Acts 6:4, diakonia tou logou [διακονία τοῦ λόγου]) and their appointment of seven men for the ministry (6:3) of serving tables (6:2, diakoneō trapezais [διακονέω τραπέζαις]) probably reflects the twofold ministry of his own community. At the Jerusalem conference, the elders of the Jerusalem church appear alongside the apostles (15:2, 4, 6, 22-23) to consider the issue of conditions for Gentile membership in the church. James, as the leader of the Jerusalem elders, makes the decision (15:19), which is ratified by the elders and confirmed by the entire church (15:22). From this point on in the narrative of Acts, the apostles disappear from the scene and are succeeded in Jerusalem by James and the elders (21:18). Having described the elders previously as the recipients of relief funds (Acts 11:30), the author now presents them as the decision-making body for the church in Jerusalem.

Luke portrays continuity between the forms of Christian ministry in Jerusalem and in the churches associated with the Pauline mission. Both men and women are included among the prophets. In Jerusalem, prophets predict events of the future (Acts 11:27; 21:10); in Caesarea, Philip's four daughters prophesy (Acts 21:9). In Antioch, Saul and Barnabas are included among the prophets and teachers who commission the first missionary journey (13:1-3). The task of the prophets is not only to predict the future but also to encourage and strengthen the believers (Acts 15:32).

Although Luke refers to the work of prophets, the primary focus in his portrayal of Christian ministry in the local communities is the role of the elders in the Pauline churches. Just as he envisions succession from apostles to elders in the Jerusalem churches, he envisions the churches of the Pauline mission under the guidance of elders (14:23). Paul's final speech to the Ephesian elders before his arrest and death (Acts 20:17-35) addresses the issue of succession in a manner that is reminiscent of the Pastoral Epistles. Paul recalls that his sacrificial conduct provided an example (20:17-19, 22-26) and that he has taught them the whole counsel of God (11:27). Thus he commissions the elders to act in his absence and to "keep watch" over "all the flock, of which the Holy Spirit has made [them] overseers," and to "shepherd the church of God that he obtained with the blood of his own Son" (20:28). The elders are, therefore, the guardians of the church, ensuring that the church will be nurtured by true teaching. Thus the Lukan narrative envisions Christian ministry in the post-apostolic situation under the guidance of elders, who teach and have authority over the church in the context of both internal and external threats.

2. Hebrews and 1 Peter

Hebrews and 1 Peter, two homilies written in the late 1st cent., attest to the development of ministry along similar lines. The high degree of mutual ministry (Heb 3:12; 10:24-25; 12:15; 1 Pet 4:11-13) in both homilies does not preclude the presence of authoritative leaders with special responsibilities. The author of Hebrews reminds the readers of their indebtedness to past leaders who taught the word of God (13:7) and encourages them to obey and submit to the current leaders who watch over them (13:17). In 1 Peter, elders "tend the flock of God," exercise authority, and serve as examples for others (1 Pet 5:2-3). Thus both homilies assume a dialectical relationship between the responsibility of the whole community and of leaders that is similar to the ministries in the Pauline churches.

3. The Gospel of Matthew

Faced with the problem of false prophets within the community on one side (Matt 7:21-22; 24:11, 24) and hypocritical leaders on the other (6:1-18), the author of Matthew articulates a view of Christian ministry that maintains continuity with Jesus' teaching and offers an alternative to leadership by the Pharisees. In contrast to those who insist on titles and recognition (6:1-18; 23:5-7), the author insists that the disciples reject the common titles for leadership (23:8-12) because they belong to the same family (23:9). Community conflicts will be settled by the whole church, which has the authority to bind and loose in Jesus' name (18:18). Jesus' final charge to the disciples indicates that Matthew's church is engaged in a mission to proclaim and to teach all that Jesus had commanded them (28:19-20). Thus Christian ministry consists of transmitting the teachings of Jesus to new converts.

4. The Gospel of John

John's understanding of Christian ministry is evident in the role of the disciples. The account of Jesus' washing of the disciples' feet (13:1-9) presents Jesus as the model for the conduct of his followers (13:14-15) and defines Christian ministry as the imitation of Jesus. The disciples have no hierarchy, but live as friends (15:14), sharing the fate of Jesus (15:18). Living in the period after the departure of Jesus, the disciples are empowered by the Holy Spirit (14:26; 15:26; 16:7-11) to continue the work of Jesus. Their role becomes evident in the high priestly prayer: "As you have sent me into the world, so I have sent them into the world" (17:18). As in the synoptic accounts, Jesus sends the disciples out to continue to witness on his behalf (20:21). Whereas the disciples have the authority to bind and loose in Matt 18:18, in John they forgive sins in Jesus' name (John 20:23).

F. Ministry after the New Testament

Although the evidence suggests that Jesus' call to the disciples to extend his mission and share his life of service set in motion a variety of leadership forms, the Pastoral Epistles, with their focus on specific offices, mark the transition to the Christian ministry of the 2nd cent., leading to the emergence of the monepiscopacy as represented in the letters of Ignatius. Clement of Rome described permanent leaders appointed by the apostles who have the authority to appoint others (*1 Clem.* 44:2). He describes ministers variously as "leaders" (hēgomenos [ἡγόμενος], 1:3; proēgoumenoi [προηγούμενοι], from proēgeomai [προηγέομαι], "lead the way," 21:6), "appointed elders" (kathestamenoi presbyteroi [καθεστάμενοι πρεσβύτεροι], from kathistēmi [καθίστημι], "appoint," 54:2), and "bishops" (episkopoi [ἐπίσκοποι], 42:4), and he does not distinguish among them. Ignatius confronts heretical teachings by insisting on governance by a single bishop, whose primary task is correct teaching (Ing. *Pol.* 1:2), care for the widows (Ing. *Pol.* 4:1), and presiding at the eucharist (Ing. *Smyrn.* 8:1). The DIDACHE's instruction to appoint bishops and deacons (*Did.* 15) reflects a view of Christian ministry similar to that of the Pastoral Epistles. In subsequent developments, the single bishop gained increasing authority and took on increased liturgical functions. *See* CHURCH, LIFE AND ORGANIZATION OF; LEADER, LEADERSHIP, NT.

Bibliography: Efrain Agosto. *Servant Leadership: Jesus and Paul* (2005); Robert Banks. *Paul's Idea of Community* (1980); David Bartlett. *Ministry in the New Testament* (1993); Alastair Campbell. *The Elders: Seniority within Earliest Christianity* (1994); H. Von Campenhausen. *Ecclesiastical Authority and Spiritual Power in the Church of the First Three Centuries* (1969); John Collins. *Diakonia* (1990); J. D. G. Dunn. *Unity and Diversity in the New Testament.* 2nd ed. (1990); E. E. Ellis. "Paul and his Co-workers." *NTS* 17 (1970) 440–45; B. Holmberg. *Paul and Power* (1978); Morna Hooker. "A Partner in the Gospel: Paul's Understanding of His Ministry." *Theology and Ethics in Paul and His Interpreters* (1996) 83–100; M. Y. MacDonald. *The Pauline Churches* (1988); H. O. Maier. *The Social Setting of the Ministry as Reflected in the Writings of Hermas, Clement and Ignatius* (1991); Andrew Purves. *Pastoral Theology in the Classical Tradition* (2001); Rudolf Sohm. *Kirchenrecht* (1892); James W. Thompson. *Pastoral Ministry according to Paul* (2006).

JAMES W. THOMPSON

MINNI min´*i* [מִנִּי minni]. Appears only in Jer 51:27 as one of three states, at that time controlled by the Medes, called to attack Babylon. It is located in the area south of Lake Urmia, a salt lake in the Azarbaijan region of northwestern Iran. The other two nations mentioned with Minni are Ararat and Ashkenaz, located in the northern regions of west Asia, modern Iran, and extending into southeast Turkey. Minni is typically identified with the MANNEANs, a people who frequently appear in Assyrian historical inscriptions from the time of the reign of Shalmaneser III (858–824 BCE) to the end of the Assyrian Empire. Armenia is regarded by some as har minni, that is, the mountainous region of Minni. Hence, Minni would be an abbreviated form of Armenia. *See* MANNEAN.

MARK RONCACE

MINNITH min′ith [מִנִּית minnith]. Minnith was one of twenty Ammonite cities taken by JEPHTHAH (Judg 11:33), and, additionally, the source of wheat traded to Tyre (Ezek 27:17; some modern translations, e.g., RSV, amend the Hebrew from "the wheat of Minnith" to "wheat and olives"). The location has been debated, and disagreements between the MT, LXX, and Targumim indicate the ancient translations were trying to make sense of the geography in terms of the later Israelite loss of the territory between the Arnon and Jabbok rivers. Jephthah's Ammonite rout progressed from a lesser-known AROER east of the Ammonite royal citadel at Rabbah past Minnith somewhat to the south, then northwest to Abel-Keramim, inferring the capture of a swath of Ammonite border towns, thereby circumscribing Ammonite expansionism.

KENT V. BRAMLETT

MINOR PROPHETS. *See* BOOK OF THE TWELVE; CANON OF THE OLD TESTAMENT.

MINT [ἡδύοσμον hēdyosmon]. The Mediterranean variety of horse-mint (*Mentha longifolia*) is a fragrant, edible perennial with an erect stem and narrow, lance-shaped leaves. Jesus accused some people of being more concerned with laws of tithing, including mint, than they were with following the laws concerning justice (Matt 23:23; Luke 11:42). *See* PLANTS OF THE BIBLE.

VICTOR H. MATTHEWS

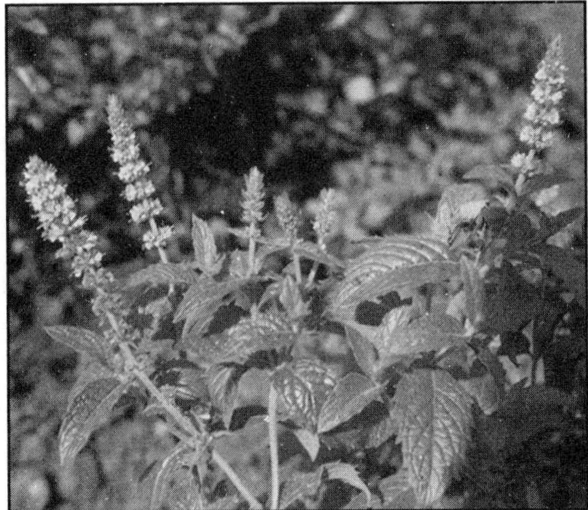

F. Nigel Hepper

Figure 1: Mint (*Mentha longifolia*)

MINUCIUS FELIX. Late 2nd- or early 3rd-cent. Christian Latin apologist who wrote the dialogue *Octavius.* Based solely on philosophical arguments, particularly Stoicism, and drawing on a large number of classical and Christian writers, the Christian interlocutor attempts to convince his pagan opponent of the truth of Christianity without resource to scriptural texts or teachings.

MARK DELCOGLIANO

MINUSCULE min′uh-sky*oo*l. Derived from the Latin *minusculus,* meaning "somewhat small," this term designates the smaller handwriting that gradually replaced the older UNCIAL, or "capital-letter," script in producing Gk. and Lat. manuscripts during the 8th and 9th cent. By extension, manuscripts written in a minuscule script are called "minuscules." *See* ALPHABET; TEXT CRITICISM, NT.

MARK DELCOGLIANO

MIQSAT MA῾ASE HA-TORAH. *See* HALAKHIC LETTER.

MIQVAH, MIQVEH [מִקְוָה miqwah, מִקְוֶה miqweh]. A large ritual bath, deep enough to allow complete immersion, dug into bedrock and waterproofed by plastering. Most miqvaoth (plural of miqvah) have steps to facilitate entry and exit. Archaeologists have found many miqvaoth in Jerusalem, Judea, and Galilee. Ritual impurity could often be removed by "bathing" (Lev 15:13), which Jews understood to mean bodily immersion in "living" water (a spring, stream, or ocean) or in a miqvah that collected "living" water. Thus John the Baptist baptized people in the "living" water of the Jordan that could restore them to ritual purity. The Christian rite of baptism derives from this Jewish custom and originally Christians, too, preferred baptism in "living" water (*Did.* 7). *See* BAPTISM; BATHING; CLEAN AND UNCLEAN.

ADAM L. PORTER

MIRACLE [אוֹת ʾoth, מוֹפֵת mofeth; δύναμις dynamis, σημεῖον sēmeion]. The English term "miracle" is derived from Latin *miraculum* (a "marvel"), but *miraculum* is never used in the Vulgate (the Latin translation of the OT and NT by Jerome in the late 4th cent. CE). In the OT, the LXX, and the NT, several Hebrew and Greek terms have been used to describe miracles. Most often in the OT and NT, a miracle functions as a sign, a communication of God's relationship with humankind and history.

A. The Old Testament
  1. Everything is a miracle
  2. Terms for miracles in the Old Testament
  3. Signs from heaven and earth
    a. Sun
    b. Clouds
    c. Fire
    d. Thunder and lightning

A. The Old Testament

1. Everything is a miracle

In the beginning, everything was a miracle. Prior to the 5th cent. CE, people believed that everything within the cosmos and every activity was an act of God's intervention. The rising of the sun every morning, the breeze that came up on the sea, the nighttime panorama of moon and stars: all this was miracle. No ideas about laws of nature existed, and there was no notion of an independent set of patterns interlinked with impersonal forces.

Genesis 1 and 2, although from separate traditions, agree that each element of creation is a beneficent intervention by the one life-giving God. The sophistication of the Priestly tradition (Gen 1) begins with nothingness, from which an ever-greater development and definition, refinement and complexity of creation springs into existence at the word of God, beginning with light and climaxing in the creation of humankind, male and female. The earlier anthropomorphic Yahwist tradition (Gen 2) makes a man the first of God's creations, and God created the rest of the cosmos to care for him and to please him, and to be under his care. Eventually God gives him a woman, a partner to save him from loneliness. All of creation is a miracle (compare Ps 8). Moreover, people believed that creation was completely dependent at every moment for the continuing intervention of God to sustain life, so that God remains vigilant, especially for the needs of humankind (compare Ps 11:4). Beside the miracle of creation, Jewish tradition recognizes those very special occasions when God intervenes in the ordinary activity of creation to communicate in a surprising and dramatic way with humankind, to reinforce the truth of God's ultimate authority and power over all other imagined deities or attractions or to perform an act of salvation, out of love.

2. Terms for miracles in the Old Testament

Hebrew uses several words when describing these special deeds but the two most common are ʾ**oth** ("sign") and **mofet** ("wonder"), ʾ**oth** being the more common of the two. Of the seventy-eight uses of ʾ**oth** in the OT, only twenty-seven occur in non-miraculous contexts. The plentiful use of ʾ**oth** emphasizes the importance of the miracle and is a reminder of God's authority and power. The LXX most often translates ʾ**oth** with the Greek word for "sign" (**sēmeion**). **Sēmeion** also translates the Hebrew word for "wonder" (**mofet**). A combination of "signs and wonders" is found in twelve instances spread across a variety of OT texts (Deut 13:1, 2; 28:46; 29:3; 34:11; Neh 9:10; Jer 32:20, 21; Dan 6:27; Wis 8:8; 10:16, 19). Six of these texts refer to the miracles Moses performed during the exodus (Deut 29:3; 34:11; Jer 32:20, 21; Neh 9:10; Wis 10:16).

3. Signs from heaven and earth

In the OT, it is clear that God is directly involved in miracles. Sometimes God speaks directly to human leaders, giving directions as well as interpretive messages to the people. More commonly, God uses creation to intervene in ways that are dramatic and extraordinary.

a. Sun. God withdraws the sunlight from the Egyptians (but not the Israelite dwellings) in the ninth plague (Exod 10:21-23) as a sign of God's punishment for Egyptian arrogance toward God. In Josh 10:12-14, God halts the progress of the sun in order to allow Joshua and his armies a longer day in which to destroy the Amorites. A more benign context is found in 2 Kgs 20:8-11, where God makes the sun move back across the sky "ten steps" as a sign to King Hezekiah that God has granted his prayer for a longer life.

b. Clouds. Clouds gather to cloak God's presence. They conceal the LORD when he takes his place at the head of the column of Israelites to guide them through the desert by day (Exod 13:21*a*). At Mount Sinai, they cover the mountain for seven full days (Exod 24:16). Clouds gather over the tent of meeting while the LORD hears the people's complaints against Moses and Aaron (Num 16:42).

c. Fire. God uses fire to instruct, to express favor, and to destroy those who oppose God's chosen leaders. God causes a bush to blaze with fire that does not consume it. From within the bush Moses hears God call to him, "Come no closer! Remove the sandals from your feet, for the place on which you are standing is holy ground" (Exod 3:5). God is concealed in the pillar of fire that travels at the head of the column of Israelites to guide them at night (Exod 13:21-22). On some occasions God sends fire to consume the sacrifices made by faithful leaders as a sign of favor (e.g., sacrifices offered by Abraham [Gen 15:17]; Aaron [Lev 9:24]; Gideon [Judg 6:21]; Solomon [2 Chr 7:1]; and Elijah [1 Kgs 18:38]). But God sends fire to consume those persons who dare offer sacrifice unworthily (e.g., Aaron's sons Nadab and Abihu [Lev 10:1-21], and the 250 men opposing Moses who offer incense to the LORD [Num 16:35]). God sends fire to burn some of the Israelite camp when the people constantly complain (Num 11:1-3). As a sign to Elisha that the LORD accepts him as the LORD's prophet, God completely destroys by fire the army of the arrogant King Ahaziah (2 Kgs 1:10-12).

d. Thunder and lightning. Thunder and lightning signal the LORD's presence on Mount Sinai as Moses goes up to meet him (Exod 19:16-20). God uses it as a sign of his displeasure in 1 Sam 12:16-18 when the people ask Samuel for a king like the other nations.

e. Rain. God sometimes sends rain to flood and sometimes withholds rain to destroy by drought as a sign of God's wrath. For example, the LORD opens up the waters of the heavens to flood the earth, and only Noah and his family survive (Gen 7:1–8:17). The LORD completely stops up the waters to create a drought to punish King Ahab of Samaria for his adoration of the fertility god Baal (1 Kgs 17:1-7). The drought stretches all the way to Sidon, Baal's home territory, to prove that all fertility is reliant on the LORD alone. Only when Elijah slays the prophets of Baal does the LORD send the clouds to bring rain (1 Kgs 18:41-45).

f. Hail. Hail destroys on a large scale. For the seventh plague, God sends hail as a sign of his displeasure to destroy the crops of the Egyptians (Exod 9:18-34). The LORD uses hail to wound the armies of the Canaanite kings who dare to war against Joshua (Josh 10:11).

g. Dew. In the miracle of dew, the LORD sends a sign to Gideon to let him know that the LORD is calling him to be a judge. Gideon leaves a fleece on the ground, and God soaks the fleece with dew, while the earth all around stays completely dry (Judg 6:37-40).

h. Plagues. The plagues that God sends to the Egyptians include blood in the Nile (Exod 7:14-25), frogs (8:1-15), gnats (8:16-19), flies (8:20-32), cattle dying (9:1-7), boils (9:8-12), locusts (10:1-20), darkness (10:21-23), and the death of the firstborn (11:4-7; 12:29-30).

i. Earth. The ground opens up to swallow Dathan and Abiram, sons of Korah, for their collusion against Moses (Num 16:28-33 [compare Deut 11:6-7]). In a second miracle, the ground shakes only under the statue of the Philistine god Dagon, which is found lying face-first on the ground. God toppled the statue as a sign of displeasure because the Philistines had the temerity to place the stolen ark of the covenant in Dagon's shrine (1 Sam 5:1-4).

j. Water. Moses parts the sea to allow his people to escape on dry land as they flee from Egypt (Exod 14:1-31). Joshua orders his men to carry the ark across the Jordan River, and the water parts before them (Josh 3:9–4:13). Elijah and Elisha both part the waters of the Jordan (2 Kgs 2:8, 14).

4. Miracles to meet human need

a. Drinking water. The wandering Israelites complain to Moses that they cannot drink the bitter waters of Marah. God orders Moses to throw a certain log into the water that renders the waters sweet (Exod 15:25). Elisha sweetens the water of Jericho by throwing some salt into its source (2 Kgs 2:19-22), possibly a reference to Moses' miracle at Marah.

God also provides water where there is none. God orders Moses to strike the rock at Meribah, and the water flows from the rock (Exod 17:5). God provides water for Samson by splitting a "hollow place" from which gushes a spring of water (Judg 15:18-19).

b. Food. The miraculous provision of food is a great testimony to God's power, but also to the degree of tender care for the people. The major miracle of the OT is God's gift of manna to the wandering Israelites. Thus, when the people complain that they will die of hunger in the wilderness, God sends Moses to announce that it will rain bread from heaven. God causes the MANNA to appear on the ground every morning to sustain the Israelites throughout their forty years of wandering (Exod 16:4-35). God also sends quail on one occasion (Exod 16:12-13).

God provides food for Elijah, who is hiding from King Ahab, by sending ravens with meat (1 Kgs 17:6). In a second miracle, God feeds Elijah when the prophet flees to the wilderness to escape the vengeful Queen Jezebel. Although Elijah wants to die, an angel brings him water and a cake baked on hot stones (1 Kgs 19:1-8). This meal sustains the prophet for forty days and forty nights (1 Kgs 19:8; compare Exod 34:28 and Deut 9:11). The miracle of food connects Moses and Elijah. Elijah also acts as God's agent when he supplies food to the starving widow of Zarephath and her son. God provides a never-ending supply of oil and flour for three years (1 Kgs 17:15).

Elisha also supplied unfailing oil to a widow. With debts mounting, the widow was going to have to sell her two sons into slavery to pay what she owed. Elisha tells her to find as many vessels as possible and to fill them from the little cruet of oil she has left. The oil keeps flowing until it fills every jar, and the widow sells it to pay her debts (2 Kgs 4:1-7). In a second miracle, Elisha feeds 100 men on just twenty loaves of barley and wheat (2 Kgs 4:42-44).

c. Healing and illness. Since God is the constant sustainer of life itself, health given or removed is a powerful expression of God's care or anger.

Elisha heals Naaman, the Syrian general, from his leprosy. Elisha tells the general to wash in the Jordan seven times (2 Kgs 5:10). No mention is made of Elisha's petition to God, but Naaman sees his role as a man of God as a clear representation of God. His response to his healing makes the narrator's point: "Now I know that there is no God in all the earth except in Israel" (2 Kgs 5:15). But God strikes Miriam with leprosy when she speaks against Moses; God later heals her (Num 12:10-15).

Isaiah prophesies to King Hezekiah that his sickness will soon end in death (2 Kgs 20:1), but the king appeals to God to remember his many acts of faithfulness, and God relents. Before Isaiah is out of the palace he receives God's new message to the king that he shall live (2 Kgs 20:8-11).

Occasionally God strikes wrongdoers with illness. For example, when the Philistines touch the ark of the covenant, which they have stolen, God gives them terrible tumors (1 Sam 5:9-12). God paralyzes the hand of Jeroboam, when Jeroboam commands that a prophet from Judah be arrested (1 Kgs 13:1-4).

d. Life and death. Occasionally God sends death as punishment. When the Israelites rise up in protest against Moses and Aaron, God sends a plague that kills 14,700 people. Only Aaron's expiating offering of incense appeases God's anger (Num 16:46-50). David's illegitimate child through his adulterous union with Bathsheba dies, despite David's prayers (2 Sam 12:12-19). God punishes David's arrogance in conducting a census by killing 70,000 of his people (1 Chr 21:14). Only David's prayers, sacrifices, and self-accusation of pride save Jerusalem. God strikes Uzzah dead for daring to touch the ark of the covenant to steady it, when it was being transported to safety on a cart that threatened to tip (2 Sam 6:1-8). These examples have the common theme of punishment for anyone who shows irreverence toward the sacred.

There are three miracle stories in the OT in which God brings the dead back to life, and all three occur in the Elijah and Elisha traditions. Elijah calls on God to have mercy on the widow of Zarephath when her son dies. The child's spirit returns, and the woman says, "Now I know that you are a man of God, and that the word of the LORD in your mouth is truth" (1 Kgs 17:24). A story of Elisha has certain parallels: the Shunammite woman has a son who has died. The story has been drawn out with delays in Elisha's return to the house to save the boy, and ineptitude on the part of Elisha's messenger. But Elisha prays for the boy in the same dramatic gesture as Elijah, stretching himself on the child and breathing into him as he prays. God answers the prayer, and the child lives (2 Kgs 4:18-37). The final miracle is less known. Some Israelites were burying a corpse when they caught sight of Moabite raiders. In their fear, they threw the body into the grave of Elisha. As soon as the body touched the bones of Elisha, life returned to the corpse (2 Kgs 13:20-21).

5. Repetition of significant miracles

The repetition of significant miracles joins traditions and affirms successors. For example, miracles performed by Moses are repeated by his successors as a sign of divine affirmation of their role.

When God tells Moses to separate the waters before the fleeing Israelites (Exod 14:1-31), the miracle proves God's supreme power and also establishes Moses as God's favored leader. In this miracle, Moses obeys God's command to raise his arms, and as he does so, God parts the sea, allowing the people to pass "on dry ground" (Exod 14:29). When Moses lowers his arms again, the walls of water close and drown the pursuing Egyptians. "So the people feared the LORD and believed in the LORD and in his servant Moses" (Exod 14:31*b*).

A similar miracle occurs when Joshua must lead the Israelites across the Jordan River. Joshua, Moses' successor, orders the priests to carry the ark of the covenant right into the Jordan. As they do so, the waters part so that the people can cross (Josh 3:9–4:13). When God commands Joshua to call the priests from the Jordan, the Jordan waters close (Josh 4:18). The intentional similarity to the Moses miracle is evident in Josh 3:7, where the Lord earlier promised Joshua, "This day I will begin to exalt you in the sight of all Israel, so that they may know that I will be with you as I was with Moses." After the crossing, the narrator affirms the fulfillment of God's promise: "On that day the LORD exalted Joshua in the sight of all Israel; and they stood in awe of him, as they had stood in awe of Moses, all the days of his life" (Josh 4:14).

Elijah is identified as a leader like Moses when he parts the Jordan River. Elijah rolls up his cloak, strikes the Jordan, and it parts, so that he and his disciple, Elisha, may cross over on dry ground (2 Kgs 2:8; Exod 14:22, 29). Elisha himself is shown to be the successor of Elijah, approved by God, and in continuity with Moses, when he picks up Elijah's mantle as it falls from the fiery chariot that takes Elijah up to heaven. Elisha strikes the Jordan with the mantle crying, "Where is the LORD, the God of Elijah?" and the waters part for him. The significance of this event is supplied by the exclamation of the waiting prophets, "The spirit of Elijah rests on Elisha," and by their reverence toward him, and "they came to meet him and bowed to the ground before him" (2 Kgs 2:15).

These examples demonstrate how repetition of miracles functions to affirm the legitimacy of successors to Moses, no matter the span of time. The repetition asserts God's choice of these leaders to be "men of God" whom the people are to trust.

B. The Greco-Roman World

1. A new cosmology

Before the 5th cent. BCE, most Mediterranean people thought of the world as a half-sphere upside down on a plate. The plate represented the earth, where mortals lived, and the spherical portion represented the heavens, where the deities lived. In the 5th cent., Greek philosophers called Pythagoreans proposed that the cosmos was a perfect sphere, at the center of which was the earth, with planets orbiting it at graduated distances. This new cosmology raised questions about where the deities lived and where chaos existed.

Philosophical responses included that of the Stoics, who viewed the patterns of a natural law as a sign that all creation was sacred, the product of divine fire and matter, where every movement was an expression of divine providence. Platonists affirmed the intervention of the divine on earth, while Skeptics wondered whether humans could comprehend the divine at all. A new element of doubt had entered the world, and the place of miracles was changing.

2. Mystery cults and the search for divine mercy

Religious trends of the 1st cent. CE offer clear evidence about social needs. An outstanding feature of this period is the shift toward the merciful and benevolent deities of the mystery cults (e.g., Demeter-Persephone, Magna Mater, Isis, and Dionysus). Myths about Demeter, Magna Mater, and Isis told how they each had suffered the death of a child, a lover, or a husband, and then mysteriously had their loved one returned to life again. Thus these chthonic deities had experienced true sorrow that no Olympian god or goddess could ever know, and therefore, they could be sympathetic to human grief. The growing popularity of their cults suggests that the general population felt hope that perhaps these compassionate deities might see fit to work a miracle for them, preserve the life of their child, give them a sign of danger, or heal them through their power, so that life might be longer and better.

3. The divinely empowered hero

The Hellenistic world introduced the concept of the divinely empowered hero, someone whose role was not to petition the gods but to whom divine power was given, so that nature could refuse him nothing (*see* DIVINE MAN). The Pythagorean philosophers and certain kings and emperors of the Mediterranean world represent some of these "divine men."

Pythagoras and his disciples were among the first to probe the laws of nature, and to do so with such reverence that they believed that the elements of nature knew them and honored their wishes. The idea that nature's elements were rational, living forces explains miracle stories surrounding the Pythagoreans. For example, Pythagoras greeted a stream of water as he crossed it, and his disciples heard its friendly response to him (Porphyry, *Vit. Pyth.* 27; Iamblichus, *Life of Pythagoras* 28.134). In another example, Pythagoras stilled water so that his friends could cross over (Porphyry, *Vit. Pyth.* 29; Iamblichus, *Life of Pythagoras* 135). Some of his friends reported that he could be in two places at the same time (Porphyry, *Vit. Pyth.* 27; Iamblichus, *Life of Pythagoras* 3.15–16; 28.134).

In the late 1st cent. CE, the itinerant holy man Apollonius of Tyana, who called himself a Pythagorean, was able to exorcise demons (Philostratus, *Vit. Apoll.* 4.20, 25), raise a young woman from the dead (4.45), and be in two places at once (8.10). *See* MEDICINE AND HEALING, GODS OF.

4. Divine rulers

Another type of divinely empowered hero was the divine ruler. Although the Egyptians had adored their pharaoh as divine for many centuries, the concept of a divine ruler did not enter Western thought until ALEXANDER THE GREAT promulgated his own divinity, claiming to be fathered by Zeus Ammon (Plutarch, *Alex.* 3.1, 3). How else could one explain Alexander's conquest of the known world as anything other than divine favor and divine empowerment? The miracle stories in which nature accommodated Alexander were so well known that Josephus appeals to them in his exposition of Moses' parting the sea at the exodus. He asked why people were so surprised and incredulous about Moses' parting the sea, when they were quite willing to believe that when Alexander needed to cross the Paphlagonian sea, it pulled back and curled over before him in a bow and allowed him to cross with ease (*Ant.* 2.347–48).

Augustus Caesar was also portrayed as divine hero. An intaglio carved after the battle of Actium (31 BCE) illustrates Augustus riding across the waves on two dolphins, the usual iconography for the Roman god of the sea, Neptune. Thus, it claims that Augustus won the battle because he was endowed with the power of Neptune, so that nothing could overpower him on the sea. Although Augustus himself never publicly allowed himself to be called a god, he did allow himself to be represented with the eagle of Zeus.

Philo expresses Augustus' contribution to the *pax Romana* ("Roman peace") by using the metaphor of a nature miracle, claiming that all of humanity was about to destroy itself until Augustus "calmed the torrential storms" (Philo, *Embassy* 10.144).

The god Serapis gave the emperor Vespasian the power to heal a lame man and a blind man (Suetonius, *Vesp.* 7.2). Tacitus reports that Vespasian restored a man's paralyzed hand and could give sight to the blind (Tacitus, *Hist.* 4.81). Vespasian's divine gift of healing was a sign of divine approval of his leadership as emperor.

In the 1st cent. CE, under the influence of these trends, Philo portrays Moses as a type of divine man cut from the same fabric as Hellenistic heroes: "He was named a god and king of whole nations" (*Moses* 1.158). He also declares that because God had given the world to Moses, all the elements obeyed him (*Moses* 1.155).

C. The New Testament

1. Terms for miracle in the New Testament

The most common reference to a miracle in the NT is **dynamis** ("a mighty work" or "deed of power"; e.g., Matt 7:22; 11:20, 21, 23; 13:54, 58; Mark 5:30; 6:2, 5, 14; 9:39; Luke 1:17; 10:13; 19:37; Acts 2:22; 8:13; 10:38). The word **sēmeion** ("sign"), apart from its use in John's Gospel, usually refers to great cosmic miracles, sometimes with an apocalyptic/eschatological sense (e.g., Matt 12:38, 39; 16:1, 3, 4; 24:3, 24, 30; Mark 8:11, 12; 13:4, 22; Luke 11:16, 29, 30; 21:7, 11, 25; 23:8; Acts 2:19, 22, 43; 4:30; 6:8; 7:36; 14:3; 15:12). **Sēmeion** combines with **teras** (τέρας, "wonder") as "signs and wonders" (**sēmeia kai terata** σημεῖα καὶ τέρατα) in Matt 24:24; Mark 13:22; John 4:48; Acts 2:19, 22, 43; 4:30; 5:12; 6:8; 7:36; 14:3; 15:12; Rom 15:19; 2 Cor 12:12; 2 Thess 2:9; and Heb 2:4). In John's Gospel, all miracles are called **sēmeia** ("signs"), as in the OT tradition discussed above (John 2:11, 18, 23; 3:2; 4:48, 54; 6:2, 14, 26, 30; 7:31; 9:16; 10:41; 11:47; 12:18, 37; 20:30). A very few times the word *work* or *deed* (**ergon** ἔργον) refers to a miracle (e.g., Matt 11:2; Luke 24:19; John 7:3, 21; 9:3, 4; 10:25, 32, 37, 38; 14:10, 11, 12; 15:24).

2. Signs from heaven and earth

a. Heavenly miracles. The heavens are torn in two (Mark 1:10) or "opened" (Matt 3:16; Luke 3:21) at the baptism of Jesus. The sun is hidden, and darkness covers the land as Jesus is dying on the cross, during what should be the brightest part of the day (Matt 27:45). Clouds cover Jesus, Elijah, and Moses in the transfiguration (Mark 9:7//Matt 17:5//Luke 9:34); and God sends tongues of fire from heaven to signal the descent of the Holy Spirit upon the waiting apostles on Pentecost (Acts 2:3-4).

b. Healings. Jesus heals Peter's mother-in-law of a fever (Mark 1:29-30//Matt 8:14-17//Luke 4:38-41). Paul cures the elderly father of his host, Publius, who has been lying sick with fever and dysentery (Acts 28:7-8). Jesus restores health to one leper (Mark 1:40-45//Matt 8:1-4//Luke 5:12-16) and then to ten (Luke 17:11-19). Jesus' healing of a paralyzed man (Mark 2:1-12//Matt 9:2-8//Luke 5:17-26) is echoed by his disciple Peter when he heals Aeneas, who was paralyzed for eight years (Acts 9:32-35). Similar miracles of restoring incapacitated people occur in Acts 3:2-11 when Peter and John cure a lame man, and in Acts 14:8-9 when Paul cures a man crippled from birth. In the Gospel of John, Jesus restores a man who had been crippled for thirty-eight years (John 5:1-18). Jesus restores a man's withered hand (Mark 3:1-6//Matt 12:9-14//Luke 6:6-11). Jesus halts the chronic hemorrhage of a woman who suffered with it for twelve years (Mark 5:24-34//Matt 9:18-26//Luke 8:40-56). Jesus restores hearing to a deaf man with a speech impediment (Mark 7:31-37//Matt 15:29-31).

Stories of restoration of sight are especially important, for to be deprived of the light was often considered divine punishment and therefore carried with it a special stigma. Jesus gives sight to a man from Bethsaida (Mark 8:22-26) and to the blind beggar Bartimaeus (Mark 10:46-52//Matt 20:29-34//Luke 18:35-43). In the Johannine tradition, Jesus gives sight to a man born blind (John 9:1-4). On occasion, God strikes someone with temporary blindness as a means of getting that person's attention. God strikes Paul with temporary blindness; a few days later, God sends Ananias to restore his sight (Acts 9:1-19). Paul himself pronounces a sentence of temporary blindness on the magician Elymas, who tries to obstruct Paul's preaching (Acts 13:11).

Jesus heals the centurion's servant without ever going to the man's house (Matt 8:5-13//Luke 7:1-10). John's Gospel has a similar story, except it is a royal official's son who needs a miraculous healing that Jesus grants (John 4:46-54). Jesus heals a man suffering from generalized edema (Luke 14:1-6). Jesus restores the ear of Malchus the high priest's servant after a sword severs it during the arrest of Jesus (Luke 22:49-51).

Jesus expels demons from a man in a synagogue (Mark 1:21-29//Luke 4:31-37), from a Gerasene demoniac (Mark 5:1-20//Matt 8:28–9:1//Luke 8:26-39), from a Syro-phoenician woman's daughter (Mark 7:24-30//Matt 15:21-28), and from a boy (Mark 9:14-29//Matt 17:14-21//Luke 9:37-43*a*). Jesus frees a woman from a spirit of infirmity (Luke 13:10-17). Paul exorcizes a girl in Jesus' name (Acts 16:16-18). Note that the formal command (v. 18) echoes the command of Jesus in Mark 9:25.

Jesus raises Jairus' daughter, who has just died (Mark 5:21-24, 35-43//Matt 9:18-19, 23-26//Luke 8:40-42, 49-56). Jesus raises the widow of Nain's son (Luke 7:11-17), echoing the Elijah and Elisha traditions covered above. Jesus raises Lazarus, who had been dead for several days (John 11:1-44). Both Peter and Paul raise the dead (Acts 9:36-42; 20:7-12).

c. Nature miracles. Jesus stills a storm (Mark 4:35-41//Matt 8:23-27//Luke 8:22-25) and walks on water (Mark 6:45-52//Matt 14:22-33//John 6:15-21). In John 2:1-11, he turns water into wine. In Matthew's tradition, Peter is empowered by Jesus to walk on water (Matt 14:28-29).

In the Matthean tradition, Jesus has Peter catch a fish with a coin in its mouth to pay their taxes (Matt 17:24-27). Jesus causes a great number of fish to enter the nets of Peter (Luke 5:1-11).

Jesus provides food for 5,000 people from a few loaves of bread and fish (Mark 6:32-44//Matt 14:13-21//Luke 9:10*b*-17; John 6:1-15); he feeds 4,000 in a similar manner (Mark 8:1-10//Matt 15:32-39).

God causes an earthquake to occur at Jesus' death, and rocks split (Matt 27:51). In Acts 16:26, an earthquake miraculously opens the doors of the prison where Paul and Silas are being held captive. In a related story, an angel causes chains to fall off Peter's wrists (Acts 12:6-11). Philip is carried away by the Spirit in Acts 8:39.

3. The interpretation of miracle stories

a. The form of the miracle story. Rudolf Bultmann examined all the Gospel miracles for any constants in their form. He concluded that miracle stories have three elements: an introduction in which the problem is identified (e.g., "Simon's mother-in-law was in bed with a fever" [Mark 1:30*a*]); the response of the miracle worker to the situation in command, deed, or both (e.g., "He came and lifted her up" [Mark 1:31*a*]); and the resolution with either a demonstration (e.g., "Then the fever left her, and she began to serve them" [Mark 1:31*b*]) or an acclamation from those watching, typical in the case of exorcisms (e.g., "He commands even the unclean spirits, and they obey him" [Mark 1:23-27]). Bultmann reasoned that the more embellishments that appeared on a miracle story, the more editing and retelling had occurred as it was passed down.

b. Miracles in Mark's Gospel. Mark's Gospel begins with Jesus' identification as Son of God (Mark 1:1). When Jesus begins his public life, he announces: "The time is fulfilled, and the kingdom of God has come near; repent, and believe the good news" (Mark 1:15). Jesus has power and authority as Son of God, and miracles are signs of this new kingdom where the ordinary is overturned. Jesus restores health and life in this dark world where spiritual blindness is the norm. Jesus' miracles show that he has authority over the forces of nature. He stills a storm, walks on water, and increases the amount of food available to feed a crowd. Even though they witness these miracles, the disciples do not "see," they do not understand. Despite the miracles they have seen, they are confused when Jesus says he must suffer and die. When Jesus dies on the cross, the curtain in the Temple rips from top to bottom, and the centurion on duty does understand who Jesus is: "Truly this man was God's Son" (Mark 15:39). In Mark, miracles are meant to give the listener confidence in Jesus' authority and ability to restore both physical and spiritual sight, so that listeners can experience the in-breaking of the kingdom of heaven.

c. Miracles in Matthew's Gospel. Matthew's placement of miracles and his redaction of them function to emphasize faith and commitment in a disciple. Immediately following the Sermon on the Mount (Matt 5–7) he situates three healing stories, the leper (Matt 8:1-4), the centurion's servant (vv. 5-13), and Peter's mother-in-law (vv. 14-17). This ordering shows that Jesus is a man not only of words but also of deeds. These miracle stories feature persons ordinarily "invisible" to regular society. Jesus shows his disciples how compassion is a hallmark of the righteousness demanded by the Torah. Matthew expounds on the theme of faith in the story of Jesus empowering Peter to walk on the water. Impetuous Peter steps out of the boat to walk on the sea, but when he sees the wind and is afraid, he begins to sink, and calls out, "Lord, save me!" Jesus raises him immediately, but not without a reproach for his doubt (Matt 14:22-33). This miracle story sets up a precedent for Peter's loss of faith and his denial of Jesus after the soldiers come to arrest him. Finally, Matthew uses miracles as reminders that God's power is at work as the end time approaches. In his version of the Gersasene demoniac (Matt 8:28–9:1) the cry of the demons is not quite the same as it is in Mark, where the demon simply asks Jesus not to torment him (Mark 5:7). In Matthew, the demons say, "Have you come here to torment us before the time?" (Matt 8:29). The "time" is the time of judgment. For Matthew, Jesus' exorcisms are to be seen as part of the larger cosmic plan of God as the time for the judgment comes closer. Thus the Matthean miracle stories show that Jesus is a man of compassionate works who demands faith of his disciples and whose miracles are part of the coming kingdom of heaven and judgment.

d. Miracles in Luke's Gospel. The key to understanding Luke's miracle stories is found in Jesus' visit to Nazareth (Luke 4:16-30) where the appeal to Isa 58:6; 61:1-2 defines Jesus' role:

> The Spirit of the Lord is upon me, because he has anointed me to bring good news to the poor. He has sent me to proclaim release to the captives and recovery of sight to the blind, to let the oppressed go free, to proclaim the year of the Lord's favor.

All miracles in the Gospel of Luke manifest the freeing of people from every kind of bondage. Jesus links himself with the traditions of Elijah and Elisha to make clear that God's Spirit offers salvation to all. He reminds the people that Elijah was sent to a Sidonian widow, even though there were many widows in Israel, and that Elisha healed the Syrian, Naaman, although there were many lepers in Israel (Luke 4:25-27). This universalism is seen throughout the Gospel, and articulated explicitly in Luke's extension of the Isaiah passage found in Mark 1:2-3 (Luke 3:4 = Isa 40:3): "Every valley shall be filled, and every mountain and hill shall be made low, and the crooked shall be made straight, and the rough ways made smooth; and all flesh shall see the salvation of God" (Luke 3:5-6).

The Lukan stories focus especially on God's mercy to the poor in order to heighten the listeners' sensitivity to the worldwide breadth in Jesus' saving message. Moreover, Luke's Gospel adds two miraculous healings not found elsewhere in the Gospels: the freeing of a woman from the spirit of infirmity (Luke 13:10-17) and the healing of the man with dropsy (Luke 14:1-6). Jesus heals these people out of his overwhelming compassion, not because anyone asked him to do so. Again in Luke 7:11-18, no one asks Jesus to attend to the widow's only son. He approaches the bier and raises the boy to life because he is moved by the widow's grief. This healing echoes the Elijah and Elisha miracle stories. The people cry out, "A great prophet has risen among us," but the audience of the Gospel knows from the infancy narrative that this is God's true Son, and that this miracle is part of the liberating power Jesus brings.

e. Miracles in John's Gospel. The first chapter of the Gospel proclaims Jesus the Logos made flesh (John 1:1-18) so that the Jesus who appears in every one of the eight miracles carries an almost otherworldly aura. All miracles are "signs" in the Gospel of John. Jesus revealed his glory in the first sign (changing water into wine), and his disciples believed in him (John 2:11). Two of the signs do not receive much comment (the healing of the official's son [John 4:46-54] and the stilling of the storm [John 6:16-21]), but the other five are treated as introductions to important discourses where Jesus may clarify his identity, the significance of his actions, and his relationship to the world and the believer. Note for each of the miracles that the proportion of text that describes the miracle account is much smaller than the amount given to the discourse that follows. For example, in the healing of the man at the pool of Bethsaida (John 5:2-47), vv. 2-9 are devoted to the miracle story, and vv. 16-47 are devoted to discourse/dialogue with religious authorities. In the multiplication of bread (John 6:1-71), vv. 1-15 are devoted to the miracle, and vv. 22-71 compose a discourse on Jesus as "bread from heaven." The story of Jesus' healing the man born blind (John 9) devotes only the first seven verses to the miracle and the rest of the chapter to a debate on Jesus' holiness. In the miracle of the raising of Lazarus (John 11:38-54), the miracle is reported briefly in vv. 38-44, while vv. 42-54 record the ensuing collusion against Jesus. In the story of the miraculous catch of fish (John 21:1-19), the miracle story and discourse are proportionate: the miracle is narrated in vv. 1-14, and the reconciliation of Peter and Jesus is reported in vv. 9-19.

f. Miracles in the Acts of the Apostles. The miracle stories in Acts function to affirm the Holy Spirit's guidance of the church. In particular, certain miracles of Peter and Paul seem to repeat the miracles of Jesus (for Peter, see Acts 9:34, 40; for Paul, see Acts 9:1-18; 14:10; 16:18; 20:9-12; 28:1-9). Thus, Acts uses miracle stories to demonstrate how the emerging church is a continuation of Jesus' ministry.

4. Conclusion

The miracles of the NT attest to the authority of Jesus as God's Son, and they impress the listener with how much God loves persons from every stratum and class, but especially the poor. The power of Jesus over sickness, demons, the nature, and even over death are small expressions of the life-giving and eternal character of the kingdom that is promised. The repetition of Jesus' miracles by his disciples, as recorded in Acts of the Apostles, assure the community of the continuity between Jesus and the church.

Bibliography: Paul J. Achtemeier. "The Origin and Function of the Pre-Marcan Miracle Catenae." *JBL* 91 (1972) 198–221; Paul J. Achtemeier. "Towards the Isolation of Pre-Markan Miracle Catenae." *JBL* 89 (1970) 265–91; Raymond E. Brown. *The Gospel of John* (1970); Rudolf Bultmann. *History of the Synoptic Tradition* (1968); Walter Burkert. *Ancient Mystery Cults* (1987); Brevard Childs. *The Book of Exodus.* OTL (1974); George W. Coats. *Exodus 1–18.* FOTL (1998); Robert L. Cohn. *2 Kings.* Berit Olam (2000); Wendy Cotter. *The Miracles of Greco-Roman Antiquity* (1999); John R. Donahue. *The Gospel of Mark.* SP (2002); Terence E. Fretheim. *First and Second Kings.* Westminster Bible Companion (1999); Daniel J. Harrington. *The Gospel of Matthew.* SP (1991); Cornelius Houtman. *Exodus* (1993); Carol Meyers. *Exodus.* New Cambridge Bible Commentary (2005); Richard Nelson. *First and Second Kings.* IBC (1987); Charles H. Talbert. *Literary Patterns, Theological Themes, and the Genre of Luke-Acts* (1964–65); Jerome T. Walsh. *1 Kings.* Berit Olam (1996); Marsha C. White. *The Elijah Legends and Jehu's Coup* (1994).

WENDY COTTER, C.S.J.

MIRACLE WORKERS. Miracles in the biblical tradition are for the most part proprietary deeds of God (Pss 72:18; 136:4) and of the prophets God sent (*see* MIRACLE). Biblical miracle working reveals the powerful closeness of God, and serves to legitimate the human performer (Exod 7:9; Acts 2:22) and authenticate a message (Exod 4; Luke 11:20; but Deut 13). The OT and NT also discuss false prophecy (1 Kgs 22; Jer 28) and non-legitimate miracle working; people such as Simon Magus are criticized as performers of magic (Acts 8:9-25; *see* MAGIC, MAGICIAN).

The most influential miracle workers of the OT are MOSES (Exod 4; 7–12; 14–17; Num 11; 20–21), ELIJAH (1 Kgs 17–19; 2 Kgs 1–2), and ELISHA (2 Kgs 2–6; 8; 13). They bring healing or illness and influence nature by speaking and using miraculous instruments (e.g., the rod of Moses). In the NT Jesus, his disciples, and the apostles perform miracles (*see* JESUS CHRIST), typically connected with the eschatological message of the nearness of God's kingdom (Matt 11:5-6; Luke 11:20). The Gospels witness a theological interpretation, especially the understanding of "signs" in John (*see* SIGNS IN THE NT). Further more, the apostles are pictured as miracle workers, especially in Acts and the apocryphal tradition. Paul's catalog of charismata includes a charisma of HEALING and miracle working (1 Cor 12:9-10, 28-30).

There is some early Jewish and pagan influence on the shape of the traditions of Jesus' miracle working. A typology of miracle workers (charismatic/ritual/magic type or "divine man") can show some analogies to Jesus' deeds, but cannot give a complete interpretation of them. Most prominent are the rabbinic traditions about HONI the Circle-Drawer (*m. Taan.* 3:8; Josephus, *Ant.* 14.22–24) and HANINAH BEN DOSA (*m. Ber.* 5:5; *Abot* 3:10–11; *Sotah* 9:15; *t. Ber.* 3:20); however, the rabbis describe this miracle working as dependent on prayer and not connected with a message.

In Greek tradition, Apollo and Asclepios are considered healing gods, and many ordinary people are referred to as miracle workers. Especially the traditions about EPIMENIDES, Empedocles, and Pythagoras had some influence on the conception and description of miracle workers in Hellenistic and Roman antiquity, as Apollonius of Tyana (Philostratus, *Vita Apollonii*), Alexander of Abonuteichos, and Apuleius prove.

MICHAEL BECKER

MIRIAM mihr'ee-uhm [מִרְיָם miryam]. 1. Miriam, one of the few women to be called a "prophet" (Exod 15:20; compare also Deborah in Judg 4:4; Huldah in 2 Kgs 22:14; Noadiah in Neh 6:14), offers a mixed portrait of female leadership in a patriarchal society (*see* PROPHET, PROPHECY). In Mic 6:4, Miriam is remembered together with Moses and Aaron as one of the leaders by whom God redeemed Israel from the house of slavery in Egypt, attesting to her significance in the collective memory of Israel.

The first reference to Miriam is found in Exod 1–2 where together with the two midwives Shiphrah and Puah, Moses' mother, and the Egyptian pharaoh's daughter, Miriam works to secure the well-being of the baby MOSES and the future leader of the Israelite people. In her first appearance, though, Miriam's name is not even mentioned. The text reports only that "[the baby's] sister stood at a distance" (Exod 2:4). Miriam emerges as a canny negotiator, whose initiative is responsible for the fact that the infant will be nursed by his own mother all the while growing up safely in Pharaoh's own home. Then, after her strategic role in rescuing Moses that serves as one of the first acts of liberation in the book of Exodus and that paves the way for God's liberation in Exod 3 and beyond, Miriam fades into the shadows. The Bible does not record any further role that Miriam might have played in the struggle for liberation led by her brothers Moses and Aaron (*see* AARON, AARONITE).

The next appearance by Miriam occurs after the victory at the sea when Miriam took a tambourine in her hand, and while leading the other women, sang the following song: "Sing to the LORD, for he has triumphed gloriously; horse and rider he has thrown into the sea" (Exod 15:20-21). The words of Miriam's song echo the Song of Moses that precedes her song in Exod 15:1-18; however, because of the narrative space Moses' song is given, Miriam's song seems a pale imitation of her brother's (*see* POETRY, HEBREW; SONG OF THE SEA).

Some scholars, though, and not just those feminist in inclination, have argued that the very fact that Miriam's song survived at all suggests that Miriam's was likely the original song, which at some point was put into the mouth of Moses. Moreover, Miriam's song offers evidence of women's role in liturgical tradition (compare Jephthah's daughter in Judg 11:34 and the women proclaiming David's victory in 1 Sam 18:6-7). Thus Carol Meyers has identified numerous Iron Age terra-cotta female figurines holding handheld frame-drum type instruments that reflect a distinct tradition of women's performance (singing, drum playing, and dancing; *see* MUSIC).

The next episode in the life of Miriam occurs in the wilderness on the way to the promised land. In the context of the Israelites murmuring and grumbling and raising the issue of shared leadership (Num 11–12), Miriam and Aaron are severely reprimanded for challenging Moses' sole authority. Moving beyond their seeming dissatisfaction with regard to Moses' marriage to the Cushite wife, perhaps hearkening back to Moses' wish in Num 11:29 that all people would be prophets, and perhaps in light of Miriam's own identification as prophet, Miriam and Aaron challenge Moses: "Has the LORD spoken only through Moses? Has he not spoken through us also?" (Num 12:2). God's response in vv. 6-8 ensures that Moses' prophetic leadership is left unchallenged when God argues that Godself has spoken to Moses "face to face—clearly, not in riddles" (*see* CUSHITE WIFE, MOSES'). God goes on to punish Miriam for her insolence. It is significant that even though both Miriam and Aaron challenged Moses, only Miriam is struck by leprosy. Scholars have pointed to the unfairness of this divine response, which yields a problematic portrait of a God who punishes a woman for speaking up and claiming her role as leader. Miriam's importance for the community is evident from the fact that Aaron and Moses intercede on her behalf (Num 12:11-13) and that the whole community is said to wait until she is healed before resuming their journey (v. 15).

A final glimpse of Miriam is found in her obituary in Num 20:1, which is followed by an account of the scarcity of water (Num 20:2-13). This juxtaposition has led to some creative rabbinic interpretations, e.g., that Miriam's well, which had accompanied the Israelites on their journey through the wilderness, disappeared after her death (e.g., Pseudo-Philo, *L.A.B.* 20:8; *S. Olam. Rab.* 10).

2. Listed in v. 17 of the Judahite genealogy in 1 Chr 4 as one of three children of Bithia, Pharaoh's daughter.

Bibliography: R. J. Burns. *Has the Lord Indeed Spoken Only through Moses? A Study of the Biblical Portrait* *of Miriam* (1987); Carol Meyers. "The Drum-Dance Song Ensemble: Women's Performance in Biblical Israel." *Rediscovering the Muses: Women's Musical Traditions.* Kimberly Marshall, ed. (1993) 49–67; Phyllis Trible. "Bringing Miriam Out of the Shadows." *A Feminist Companion to Exodus to Deuteronomy* (1994) 166–86.

L. JULIANA CLAASSENS

MIRMAH mihr′muh [מִרְמָה **mirmah**]. Means "deceit." The seventh of seven sons born to SHAHARAIM and his wife HODESH in Moab, listed in the Benjaminite genealogy (1 Chr 8:10).

MIRROR [מַרְאָה marʾah, רְאִי reʾi; ἔσοπτρον **esoptron**]. Mirrors, reflective devices first made of highly polished stone, copper, and bronze, and later of other materials, are attested archaeologically for over eight millennia. Textual references to mirrors in cultures surrounding the biblical world date to at least 2500 BCE.

Todd Bolen/BiblePlaces.com

Figure 1: Late Bronze Age mirror, collection of Rockefeller Museum

Mirrors are most often associated with females, particularly female deities and women of wealth. Ancient queens and goddesses are sometimes depicted holding a mirror; the Egyptian goddess Hathor appears on mirror handles. Notably, the Egyptian symbol "ankh," or life, shaped like a hand-held mirror, is used in contemporary culture as a symbol for "woman." Many mirrors have been found in female burial sites (*see* AMARNA, TELL EL). As mirrors became more readily available during Hellenistic times, they were less frequently associated with wealth.

There are few biblical references to mirrors. Exodus 38:8 reports "serving women" near the tabernacle with mirrors, presumably bronze, which were melted down to fashion the bronze laver for the tabernacle, resulting in a symbol associated primarily with women destroyed to fashion a basin for male priests. Scholars offer various proposals for the function of the women in Exod 38:8; some infer that the women were prostitutes, connecting the text to 1 Sam 2:22, and others, more plausibly, propose a cultic or priestly function for the women. Woman Wisdom is a mirror of God's good work (Wis 7:26). Additional biblical references to mirrors include Job 37:18, which compares the sky to a "molten mirror," and 1 Cor 13:12, "now we see in a mirror, dimly." A verbal form meaning "to show as in a mirror" appears in 2 Cor 3:18.

JANET S. EVERHART

MIRSIM, TELL BEIT. A prominent 8-ac. mound at the juncture of the Judean foothills and the northern Shephelah, some 15 mi. southwest of Hebron. It was excavated by W. F. Albright in 1926–32 and promptly published, in one of the pivotal archaeological projects of the early days of the discipline. In keeping with the then-current "biblical archaeology" (which Albright fathered), the site was identified with "Debir/Kiriath-sepher" (Josh 15:16-19; Judg 1:11-15). Although Albright's pioneering methods of stratigraphic excavation and comparative ceramic chronology have been much lauded, his historical and cultural syntheses have been revised considerably. Since DEBIR is now more persuasively identified with Khirbet Rabûd, the ancient name of Tell Beit Mirsim is unknown.

Basal Str. J belongs to the Early Bronze II–III horizon, ca. 3000–2400 BCE (not later, as Albright thought). Strata I–H, then, is characteristic of Early Bronze IV (Albright's "Middle Bronze I"), with a shaft-tomb cemetery and sparse occupation in natural caves on the bedrock. The true Middle Bronze Age is represented by Str. G–D, when the site was a major fortified Canaanite city-state, destroyed no doubt by the Egyptian campaigns in the early 15th cent. BCE at the time of the expulsion of the Asiatic "Hyksos" princes from the Egyptian Delta. Rebuilt in the Late Bronze Age after a gap (Str. C), the site was again destroyed sometime in the mid-late 13th cent. BCE, although not by the Israelites ca. 1220 BCE as Albright held.

The Iron Age is represented by Str. A–B. Stratum B, with three phases, belongs to the Iron I/early Iron II period, ca. 1200–900 BCE and represents the early Israelite occupation. (There is no Philistine presence.) At the end of the final phase, Str. B_3, the walled town was destroyed, in all probability by the Egyptian pharaoh Shishak ca. 925 BCE (1 Kgs 14:25-28; 2 Chr 12:1-12).

Albright had dated the destruction of Str. A_2 to the well-known raid of the Assyrian king Sennacherib in 701 BCE, then the end of Str. A_1 to the Babylonians in 586 BCE. Today, with the related destruction of Lachish, Level III moved up by consensus from 598 BCE to 701 BCE, Tell Beit Mirsim Str. $A_{2\text{-}1}$ must be seen as ending at the end of the 8th cent. BCE. There was then little or no occupation in the 7th cent. BCE.

Bibliography: W. F. Albright. *The Excavation of Tell Beit Mirsim*, vols. I–III (1932–43); W. B. Dever and S. Richard. "A Reevaluation of Tell Beit Mirsim J." *BASOR* 226 (1977) 1–14; W. B. Dever and S. Richard. "An EB IV Tomb Group from Tell Beit Mirsim." *EI* 27 (2003) 29–36; R. Greenberg. "New Light on the Early Iron Age at Tell Beit Mirsim." *BASOR* 265 (1987) 55–80; M. Kochavi. "Khirbet Rabûd = Debir." *TA* 1 (1974) 2–33; D. Ussishkin. "The Destruction of Lachish by Sennacherib and the Dating of the Royal Judean Storage Jars." *TA* 4 (1977) 28–60; Y. Yadin. "The Tell Beit Mirsim G-F Alleged Fortification." *BASOR* 217 (1973) 22–25.

WILLIAM G. DEVER

MIRZBÂNEH, DHAHR. A rocky ridge above the springs at ʿAin es-Sâmiyeh, in the hills northeast of Ramallah. Although frequently robbed but never systematically excavated, the large region is exceptionally rich in archaeological remains, extending from at least the late 3rd millennium BCE to the Byzantine era. The major attraction was probably the spring itself, the largest in the Ephraim hill country, as well as the strategic location of the surrounding hills, at the head of the Wâdi ed-Dâliyeh that descends to the Jordan Valley just north of Jericho. East of the springs of ʿAin es-Sâmiyeh, a cemetery of hundreds of shaft-tombs belongs to the Early Bronze IV period (ca. 2400–2000 BCE). *See* DALIYEH, WADI ED; MARJAMEH, KHIRBET EL.

Bibliography: W. G. Dever. "Middle Bronze I Cemeteries at Mirzbâneh and ʿAin-Sâmiyeh." *IEJ* 22 (1972) 95–112; I. Finkelstein. "The Central Hill Country in the Intermediate Bronze Age." *IEJ* 41 (1999) 17–45; P. W. Lapp. *The Dhahr Mirzbâneh Tombs* (1966); P. W. Lapp and N. Lapp, eds. *Discoveries in the Wâdi ed-Dâliyeh* (1972); A. Mazar. "Three Israelite Sites in the Hills of Judah and Ephraim." *BA* 45 (1982) 107–78.

WILLIAM G. DEVER

MISCARRIAGE [נֵפֶל **nefel**, שָׁכֹל **shakhol**; ἔκτρωμα **ektrōma**]. In the OT miscarriage always results in a dead fetus. A **nefel** is a fetus that has fallen or been expelled from the womb prematurely. It also refers to a stillbirth or abortion. The psalmist prays that the future of the wicked would be like that of a miscarried fetus (NRSV, "untimely birth that never sees the sun"), having no chance of life (Ps 58:8 [Heb. 58:9]; see also Eccl 6:3). In despair, Job wishes he had been aborted before birth (Job 3:16).

Fertility was a covenant blessing, and thus miscarriage was not only a personal tragedy but could also be a corporate punishment. If Israel was faithful to Yahweh, her women and crops would not miscarry (Exod 23:26; Mal 3:11). Disobedience brought the reverse: "miscarrying wombs" and "dry breasts" (Hos 9:14). Causing a miscarriage (**shakhol**), however, is punishable by law (Exod 21:22).

A woman who had a jealous husband could be given a test called a "trial by ordeal" (Num 5:11-31) that might result in miscarriage, if she were pregnant. The woman was made to drink the WATER OF BITTERNESS. Those who administered this test believed that if the woman was guilty of adultery, she would have a miscarriage (*see* TRIAL BY ORDEAL).

According to the *Temple Scroll* (11Q19 L, 10–11), a pregnant woman who miscarries is rendered impure and "like a grave" as long as the dead fetus remains within her. This is a ruling of greater severity than the rabbinic interpretation, according to which a woman who miscarries becomes impure only when the fetus emerges (e.g., *m. Nid.* 3:5-7). *See* CLEAN AND UNCLEAN.

In the NT, Paul calls himself an **ektrōma** ("stillbirth, untimely birth") to emphasize his unworthiness compared to the original twelve disciples. While the Twelve had been taught directly by Jesus during his lifetime, Paul was "born" into the faith seemingly out of season (1 Cor 15:8). Here the point is not premature death, but untimely birth. *See* ABORTION; BARREN, BARRENNESS; BIRTH; CHILD, CHILDREN.

Bibliography: Judith R. Baskin. *Midrashic Women: Formations of the Feminine in Rabbinic Literature* (2002); Hannah K. Harrington. *The Purity Texts* (2007).

HANNAH K. HARRINGTON

MISHAEL mishʹay-uhl [מִישָׁאֵל **mishaʾel**]. Means "Who is what God is?" 1. A Levite, the firstborn son of Uzziel (Exod 6:22).

2. One of the men who stood beside Ezra when he read the Torah to the people (Neh 8:4). His function during the reading is unknown.

3. One of the three men from Judah who was taken to Babylon to be educated along with Daniel (Dan 1:6). Mishael served in Nebuchadnezzar's court, and he assisted Daniel with the interpretation of the king's dream (Dan 1:19; 2:17-18). The palace master changed Mishael's name to Meshach (Dan 1:7). Mishael and his friends were thrown into a furnace when they refused to bow to the king's image, but they were delivered by God (Dan 3:1-30). *See* SHADRACH, MESHACH, ABEDNEGO.

KEVIN A. WILSON

MISHAL mīʹshuhl [מִשְׁאָל mishʾal]. One of the cities ascribed to the tribe of Asher (Josh 19:26) and belonging to the Levitical tribe of Gershom (Josh 21:30; MASHAL in 1 Chr 6:74 [Heb. 6:59]). Of unknown location, Mishal is listed in military accounts as one of the towns conquered by Thutmose III.

MISHAM mīʹshuhm [מִשְׁעָם mishʿam]. One of Elpaal's sons listed in Saul's genealogy (1 Chr 8:12). ELPAAL and his sons were noted for building ONO and LOD.

MISHMA mishʹmuh [מִשְׁמָע mishmaʿ]. Means "hearing, something heard." 1. The fifth of Ishmael's twelve sons (and brother of MIBSAM) (Gen 25:14; 1 Chr 1:30).

2. A descendant of Simeon, Mishma was son of Mibsam and father of Hammuel and others (1 Chr 4:25-26). The collocation of Mishma with Mibsam in both cases suggests these names may represent two Arab tribes inhabiting the Negeb at the time of the Chronicler.

KEN M. PENNER

MISHMANNAH mish-manʹuh [מִשְׁמַנָּה mishmannah]. The fourth of eleven Gadite commanders, expert warriors, listed in 1 Chr 12:8-13, who defected to David's side at Ziklag and became officers in his army.

MISHNAH mishʹnuh [מִשְׁנָה mishnah]. The Mishnah is the premiere work of rabbinic Oral Torah (*see* ORAL LAW, ORAL TORAH). The term *Mishnah* derives from the Hebrew (**shanah** שָׁנָה) meaning "to repeat" or "recite." Some relate the term to the Hebrew for "second" (**sheni** שֵׁנִי), implying that the Mishnah is a second TORAH, or as it was called by church fathers in Greek, **deuterōsis** (δευτέρωσις). Edited by Rabbi Judah, the patriarch of the Palestinian Jewish community in ca. 200 CE, the Mishnah is a compendium of rabbinic pronouncements primarily on matters of Jewish law (*see* HALAKHAH). The Mishnah often brings differing opinions regarding a given law, and often includes both majority and minority judgments. "Why recall the opinion of a minority against a majority, when the law follows the majority? So that a [later] court might agree with the minority and rely on that precedent" (*m. Ed.* 1:5; author's trans.). These tendencies preclude identification of the Mishnah as a legal code per se and instead identify it as a compendium of rabbinic opinions.

The Mishnah offers rabbinic tradition as its source of authority, unlike the contemporary Midrash Halakhah (*see* MIDRASH; SIFRA, SIFRE), which justifies rabbinic pronouncements by linking them to biblical verses. "Rabbi So-and-so said . . ." is the primary means of introducing and transmitting Mishnaic traditions, and biblical verses are rarely cited. Authorities who flourished before the destruction of the Temple in 70 CE are sometimes cited (e.g., Hillel and Shammai). More frequently, the Mishnah quotes rabbis from the era of the Council of Jamnia (i.e., between 70 CE and the Bar Kochba revolt, ca. 132–135 CE) or the later, Ushan era (ca. 135–200 CE). These "eras" are named for rabbinic study-circles in the towns of Yavneh, on the Judean coast, and Usha, in the Galilee (*see* JAMNIA, COUNCIL OF).

While the Midrash tends to be organized by the order of biblical books, the Mishnah has a topical scheme. Six socio-anthropological categories organize the Oral Torah into the orders: Agriculture (*Zeraim*), Calendar (*Moed*), Women (*Nashim*), Torts (*Neziqin*), Sacred Things (*Qodashim*), and Ritual Fitness (*Teharot*). Each of these orders is made up of various tractates, as the chart indicates. Tractates range in content from three to two dozen chapters.

These are the sixty-three tractates of the Mishnah. Later generations of rabbinic scholars composed dialectical commentaries on many of these tractates. In Roman Palestine of the early 5th cent., thirty-nine tractates of commentary made up the Western or Jerusalem Talmud (*see* TALMUD, JERUSALEM). In late 5th- or

Zeraim	Moed	Nashim	Neziqin	Qodashim	Teharot
Berakhot	Shabbat	Yevamot	Bava Qamma	Zevahim	Kelim
Peah	Eruvin	Ketubbot	Bava Metzia	Menahot	Ohalot
Demai	Pesahim	Nedarim	Bava Batra	Hullin	Negaim
Kilim	Sheqalim	Nazir	Sanhedrin	Bekhorot	Parah
Sheviit	Yoma	Gittin	Makkot	Arakhin	Teharot
Terumot	Sukkah	Sotah	Shevuot	Temurah	Mikwaot
Maaserot	Betzah	Qiddushin	Eduyyot	Keritot	Niddah
Maaser Sheni	Rosh HaShanah		Avodah Zarah	Meilah	Makhshirin
Hallah	Taanit		Avot	Tamid	Zabim
Orlah	Megillah		Horayot	Middot	Tevul Yom
Bikkurim	Moed Qatan			Qinnim	Yadayin
	Hagigah				Uqtzin

Table 1: Mishnah chart

early 6th-cent. Sassanian Babylonia, thirty-seven tractates of commentary made up the Babylonian Talmud (*see* TALMUD).

The Tosefta (**toseftah** תּוֹסֶפְתָּה) is a companion work to the Mishnah that predates either of the two Talmuds (*see* TOSEPHTA, TOSEPTA, TOSEFTA). It is organized into the same orders and tractates as the Mishnah. The Tosefta (lit., "addition") consists of rabbinic traditions from roughly the same era as the Mishnah. The Tosefta often quotes the Mishnah, sometimes expands the purview of its laws, sometimes brings additional early rabbinic materials, and on occasion even contradicts the Mishnah. Recently scholars have suggested that the Tosefta is a commentary on an earlier redaction of the Mishnah than the one in common usage. This hypothesis explains those few passages where the Mishnah seems to be quoting the Tosefta.

Already in the time of the Talmuds the rabbis assumed that the Mishnah underwent various redactional stages. They suggest that Rabbi Akiva first gathered early rabbinic statements and arranged them by topical categories (*see* AKIVA, RABBI). His disciple, Rabbi Meir, is said to have refined the collection of Tannaitic statements. Finally, his disciple, Rabbi Judah the Prince, is credited with editing the Mishnah (*see* JUDAH THE PRINCE, RABBI). Even Rabbi Judah is recognized as making revisions in the Mishnah's text. Modern scholars debate the method of publication of the Mishnah, whether it was literally Oral Torah and thus "published" by committing it to a memory expert, or whether it was published in a written form.

As may be seen by the array of tractates in the orders of the Mishnah, a significant proportion of its focus was on the rituals of the moribund Jerusalem Temple. This points, in some measure, to the relationship of the Mishnah to early Midrashic biblical commentary. Since Leviticus is the central book of the Five Books of Moses, it was only natural for the rabbis to retain a focus on the Temple. Some scholars also suggest that this Mishnaic preoccupation with the Jerusalem cult and its priesthood indicates a desire for the rebuilding of the Temple. Still other scholars presume this to be an idealized yearning or a form of messianic speculation. Yet others consider the Mishnah's attention to the cult to be a form of co-opting the priesthood, with the intention that the rabbis be seen as having the authority of the Temple hierarchy and ultimately replacing them.

The Mishnah also lays out a program of Jewish ritual life independent of the Temple, which allowed Judaism to endure the trauma of its destruction and ultimately flourish once more. Details of Sabbath and holiday observance, food consumption rules, family law, the rudiments of tort procedures, and economic legislation all served as the basis for a Jewish polity that grew vibrant in Late Antiquity and the Byzantine era. *See* PHARISEES; RABBINIC INTERPRETATION; RABBINIC LITERATURE.

Bibliography: David Weiss Halivni. *Midrash, Mishnah and Gemara: The Jewish Predilection for Justified Law* (1986); Judith Hauptman. *Rereading the Mishnah: A New Approach to Ancient Jewish Texts* (2005); Jacob Neusner. *Judaism: The Evidence of the Mishnah* (1983); Herman L. Strack and Günter Stemberger. *Introduction to the Talmud and Midrash* (1992).

BURTON L. VISOTZKY

MISHNEH GATE. *See* OLD GATE.

MISHRAITE mish′ray-*it* [מִשְׁרָעִי **mishraʿi**]. One of the families of KIRIATH-JEARIM, located on the northern border of Judah, from whom the Zorathites and Eshtaolites descended (1 Chr 2:53).

MISPAR mis′pahr [מִסְפָּר **mispar,** מִסְפֶּרֶת **mispereth;** Μασφάρ **Masphar**]. One of the leaders returning with Zerubbabel from Babylonian exile (Ezra 2:2). Mispereth, rather than Mispar, is noted in Neh 7:7, although the LXX reads **Masphar**. Some manuscripts of 1 Esd 5:8 read **Masphar** (as with RSV).

MISPERETH. *See* MISPAR.

MISREPHOTH-MAIM mis′ruh-foth-may′im [מִשְׂרְפוֹת מַיִם **misrefoth mayim**]. Located at the southern border of Sidon, perhaps at either Khirbet Misheirefeh or ʿAin Mesherfi, Misrephoth-maim served as natural boundary and border marker. The army fleeing from Joshua's troops did not make it beyond this boundary (Josh 11:8). Sidon, marked by Misrephoth-maim, was intended to be conquered and become part of the Israelite land allotment (Josh 13:6), although Judg 2:20–3:4 recorded Sidon as remaining independent of Israel.

HEIDI E. HAWKS

MISS THE MARK [חָטָא **khata**ʾ]. Committing a mistake; not taking the right path of duty and so acting against God or other humans. *See* MARK, GOAL, SIGN; SIN, SINNERS.

MISSIONS [ἀποστολή **apostolē**]. The term *mission* (Lat. *missio*) summarizes various nouns (e.g., apostle, disciple, evangelist, good news, herald, witness, worker) and verbs (e.g., announce good news, convince, declare, go, proclaim, profess, send, serve, teach, witness), some with a metaphorical meaning (fisherman, harvest, seed, way; build, plant), that describe the missionary activity of the early Christians. *Mission* is best understood as the activity of a community of faith that distinguishes itself from its environment both in terms of religious belief (theology) and in terms of social behavior (ethics), that is convinced of the truth claims of its faith, and that actively works to win other people for the convictions and for the way of life of whose truth the members of that community are convinced.

A. The Mission of Jesus of Nazareth

1. Jesus' missionary commission

The NT sources are unanimous in attributing the beginning of the early Christian mission to a commission that the risen Jesus Christ gave to his followers (Matt 28:18-20; Mark 13:10; 14:9; Luke 24:46-49; John 20:21; Acts 1:8). The view that the missionary activity of the early church was not a maneuver initiated by Peter or by Paul, calculated to increase the number of sympathizers of Jesus beyond the initial small band of followers, but the direct result of a commission that Jesus gave to his followers, is confirmed by three facts.

a. The Old Testament. The OT Scriptures contain no charge to the people of Israel to actively spread the truth about Yahweh to people of other faiths with a view to integrate them into the commonwealth of Israel. The salvation of the nations is not a task that Israel is commissioned to carry out but a hope promised by the prophets (Isa 60:3-14; 66:23; Zech 14:16).

b. Second Temple Judaism. There was no organized effort of any of the Jewish movements during the Second Temple period, such as the Pharisees or Sadducees, to lead non-Jews to faith in Yahweh. The conversion of individuals to the Jewish faith (*see* PROSELYTE) and the presence of sympathizers with the Jewish faith in local synagogues (*see* GODFEARER) establishes the attractiveness of Jewish monotheism and Jewish ethics for many non-Jews, but not the existence of an organized Jewish missionary outreach.

c. The Greco-Roman world. While some religious cults were disseminated to other Greek and Roman cities, notably the mystery cults, there is hardly any evidence for conscious "evangelizing" in Egyptian, Greek, or Roman religions, and no evidence at all for a god whose cult required its adherents to propagate its beliefs and practices to potential converts. This is true also for the emperor cult in the 1st cent.

Thus, as there were no functional models for the active "missionary" propagation of religious beliefs and for the intentional multiplication of communities of faith and practice, the claim of the NT sources concerning the initiatory role of Jesus as regards the missionary activity of the earliest followers of Jesus must be regarded as authentic.

2. Jesus and the Twelve

The Twelve, symbolizing the reconstitution of the people of God, redefined in terms of allegiance to Jesus rather than to the traditional symbols of national Israel, were called and prepared by Jesus for their future missionary task. According to Mark 1:17 and Matt 4:19 (compare Luke 5:10), Jesus called twelve of his followers (*see* APOSTLE; DISCIPLE, DISCIPLESHIP) to be "fishers of people," i.e., to participate in his mission of rescuing the poor in spirit, the meek, those who hunger and thirst for righteousness.

3. Jesus' mission to the Jews

Jesus was a teacher who did not expect people to come to him. Rather, he went to visit all the small farms (Mark 6:56), the villages, and the towns of Galilee and urban centers such as Jerusalem. References to Jesus' geographical movement in Mark 6:6 and Luke 4:43 suggest that Jesus planned his travels in some organized manner. Jesus proclaimed his message to the powerless Galilean peasants as well as to the influential leaders of the Jerusalem establishment, to people with bad reputations and to the pious.

4. Jesus' mission to Gentiles

The proclamation of "the good news of God" that "the time is fulfilled, and the kingdom of God has come near" (Mark 1:14-15) was bound to reach beyond Israel, as the prophets had announced that in the last days the nations would stream to the Lord's temple on Mount Zion (Isa 2:2-5; 49:1-6; Mic 4:1-5; Zech 8:20-23). Jesus challenged his followers to be the light of the world (Matt 5:13-16). He ministered to Gentiles who sought him out (Matt 8:5-13; Mark 5:1-20; 7:24-30). He announced that Gentiles will share in the blessings of the kingdom (Matt 8:11-12) and that the consummation would not occur until the gospel of the kingdom had been preached to all nations (Matt 24:14; Mark 13:10).

5. The commission of the risen Christ

According to Matthew, Luke, and Paul, Jesus commanded his followers after his death on the cross and his vindication in the resurrection to go to the "ends of the earth" (Acts 1:8) to "all nations" (Matt 28:19) with the good news of God's redemptive action in Jesus the Messiah and invite them to become his followers (see also the commission to Paul in Acts 9:15; 26:15-18; Gal 1:16).

B. The Mission of the Jerusalem Church

Our knowledge of the missionary activity of the Jerusalem church is limited to hints in Luke's narrative in the ACTS OF THE APOSTLES.

1. Learning from Jesus

Following Jesus' example and his previous injunction to preach and to heal (Matt 10:7-8), the early Christian missionaries are portrayed in Acts as preaching the gospel (Acts 3:11-26; 4:1-2; 5:21), as healing people (Acts 3:1-10; 5:12), and as forming communities characterized by selfless love (Acts 4:32-37; 6:1-7). The earliest missionaries include Peter, Stephen, Barnabas, and, when Acts 13:1 is read in the light of Acts 11:20, Simeon called Niger, Lucius of Cyrene, and Manaen, who had connections with the king Herod Antipas.

2. Mission to the Jewish people

Luke reports missionary activity in the cities and villages of Judea, Galilee, and Samaria and in the coastal areas (Acts 8:14, 25; 9:31-32, 35). The praxis of the apostle Paul demonstrates that even the most prominent missionary to the Gentiles preached whenever possible first to the Jews (Rom 1:16; Acts 9:15).

3. Mission to Gentiles

Peter plays a pioneering role in the first breakthrough to the Gentiles in Caesarea (Acts 10:1–11:18). The Jerusalem church feels responsible for the missionary outreach to Gentiles in Antioch (Acts 11:19-24). As regards geography and ethnography, a messianic mission to "all the nations" would remind the apostles of the Table of Nations (Gen 10) and its continuing significance as the "Jewish" description of the world (*Jub.* 8–10; Josephus, *J.W.* 2.345–401).

4. Geography

The geographical horizon of the early Christians was not limited to the Roman Empire: evidence in Acts demonstrates awareness of regions such as Parthia in the east and Ethiopia in the south (Acts 2:9; 8:27). As regards a feasible approach to fulfilling the commission to go to "all nations," the apostles would have thought in terms of specific nations or tribes or, from a political perspective, in terms of Roman provinces (Rom 16:4; 1 Cor 16:19; 2 Cor 8:1; Gal 1:2, 22). As regards the term "ends of the earth," an exclusively Jewish outlook might think in terms of the extent of the Jewish Diaspora (Acts 2:9-11). A wider perspective informed by readily available geographical knowledge would extend the geographical horizons to the farthest points on the edge of the inhabited world: the Indians in the east (note the traditions concerning the mission of the apostle Thomas to India in the *Acts of Thomas*; note Esth 1:1 LXX; 1 Macc 6:37), the Scythians in the north (Col 3:11), Spain in the west (Rom 15:24, 28), and the Ethiopians in the south (Acts 8:27-39).

C. The Mission of Paul

We have more information about the missionary activity of Paul due to the fact that several of his letters have survived and that Luke devotes the second half of Acts to a report of Paul's ministry.

1. Missionary identity

Paul describes his work as a missionary in 1 Cor 3:10-15 and in 1 Cor 9:19-23 as follows: 1) A missionary is a servant (**diakonos** διάκονος), i.e., a person who gets something done at the behest of a superior (*see* SERVANT; SERVE, TO). Paul uses metaphors from agriculture and house construction to describe the work of missionaries, preachers, and teachers: they plant, they water, they build—tasks and activities that cannot possibly lead to boasting. 2) God is the "Lord" (**kyrios** κύριος) of missionary and pastoral work. He is the superior at whose behest the missionaries serve. 3) The relationship to the Lord establishes the unity of the ministry of all missionaries and teachers: they are "one," they have a common purpose. 4) Paul understands his task to be that of a missionary called to "plant" and to "lay the foundation" as a "skilled master builder," i.e., to establish new congregations. 5) The foundation that Paul lays is Jesus Christ himself, specifically the message of Jesus the crucified Messiah (1 Cor 1:23; 2:2). 6) Missionary success comes from God: it is God who gives growth. 7) Missionaries and teachers are accountable to God, and it is God alone who decides what constitutes success or failure of missionary and pastoral work. 8) Authentic missionaries take their listeners seriously: Paul has made himself "a slave to all, so that I might win more of them" (1 Cor 9:19). The listeners decide the form in which the gospel is proclaimed, as it is the listeners who need to understand the gospel. 9) Paul does not exclude anyone from his preaching, as he is sent to "all": he preaches both to Jews and Gentiles. 10) The goal of missionary work is to "win" (**kerdainō** κερδαίνω) people, i.e., to rescue them from condemnation in God's judgment, to lead them to saving faith in Jesus Christ, to integrate them into the community of God's family. 11) The declaration "I do it all for the sake of the gospel" (1 Cor 9:23) indicates that the normative center of missionary accommodation is the gospel, not the pragmatic motif of effectiveness.

2. Missionary strategy

Paul seeks to proclaim the message of God's saving revelation in Jesus Christ to Jewish audiences and to Gentile audiences, particularly in areas in which it had never been proclaimed (Rom 15:14-21; Gal 2:7). The planning for the implementation of this goal was relatively straightforward: he traveled from city to city, preaching the message of Jesus the Messiah and Savior and gathering the new converts in local Christian communities. This is what he did in Arabia, in Syria, in Cilicia, on Cyprus, in the provinces of Galatia and Asia, and in the provinces of Macedonia and Achaia. When it proved impossible to reach a certain region, as was the case with the prospect of traveling to the provinces of Asia, Bithynia, and Mysia (Acts 16:7-8), Paul's strategy does not break down: there are other cities in other regions that need to hear the gospel.

3. Urban strategies

Paul preached in the capitals of several Roman provinces, centers of Roman administration, of Greek culture, and of Jewish presence: in Tarsus in Cilicia, in Antioch in Syria, in Paphos on Cyprus, in Perga in Pamphylia, in Thessalonica in Macedonia, in Corinth in Achaia, in Ephesus in the province of Asia. At the same time Acts 13:48-49 suggests that Paul's missionary work was not limited to cities but also reached towns and villages that were controlled by these cities.

4. Social and ethnic strategies

Paul had contacts with members of the ruling elites; examples include Sergius Paulus, the proconsul of Cyprus (Acts 13:6-12), prominent women in Thessalonica and in Beroea (Acts 17:4, 12), and the Asiarchs in Ephesus (Acts 19:31). The high social position of the people with whom Paul has positive encounters is a function of Luke's description of the progress of the early Christian mission. In his brief comment on his self-understanding as a missionary in Rom 1:14-16, Paul asserts that he seeks to reach both Greeks and barbarians, the wise and the foolish. Paul disregards the traditional social and cultural categories and classifications that were defined and drawn up by the elites.

5. Conversion

Paul's missionary preaching aims at facilitating the conversion of both Jews and Gentiles to faith in Jesus, the crucified and risen Messiah, Savior, and Lord. Paul understands conversion and its consequences as a "demonstration of the Spirit and of power" (1 Cor 2:4; compare 1 Thess 1:5). Conversion happens through the confession by which individuals turn to and submit to God and his Messiah (Rom 10:9). Conversion effects a transformation that results from the repentance of unrecognized sin, that involves a break with many of the traditional values of contemporary society, and that entails obedience to Scripture, to the word of Jesus Christ, and to the teaching of the apostles.

6. Establishing churches

Paul's missionary work did not end with the oral proclamation of the good news of Jesus Christ and with the conversion of individual people. Paul established churches, communities of men and women who had come to faith in the one true and living God and in Jesus the Messiah and Savior. *See* GENTILES; GOSPEL, MESSAGE; JESUS CHRIST; NATIONS; PAUL, THE APOSTLE; PETER, THE APOSTLE; STEPHEN.

Bibliography: Jostein Ådna and Hans Kvalbein, eds. *The Mission of the Early Church to Jews and Gentiles* (2000); Richard J. Bauckham. "James and the Jerusalem Church." *The Book of Acts in Its Palestinian Setting.* R. Bauckham, ed. (1995) 415–80; Lukas Bormann et al, eds. *Religious Propaganda and Missionary Competition in the New Testament World* (1994); Raymond E. Brown and John P. Meier. *Antioch and Rome: New Testament Cradles of Catholic Christianity* (1983); Stephen J. Chester. *Conversion at Corinth* (2003); James D. G. Dunn, ed. *Jews and Christians: The Parting of the Ways A.D. 70 to 135* (1992); Martin Goodman. *Mission and Conversion: Proselytizing in the Religious History of the Roman Empire* (1994); Ferdinand Hahn. *Mission in the New Testament* (1981); Colin J. Hemer. *The Book of Acts in the Setting of Hellenistic History* (1989); Martin Hengel and Anna Maria Schwemer. *Paul between Damascus and Antioch: The Unknown Years* (1997); Andreas Köstenberger and Peter T. O'Brien. *Salvation to the Ends of the Earth: A Biblical Theology of Mission* (2001); Ramsay MacMullen. *Paganism in the Roman Empire* (1981); I. Howard Marshall. *New Testament Theology: Many Witnesses, One Gospel* (2004); I. Howard Marshall and David Peterson, ed. *Witness to the Gospel: The Theology of Acts* (1998); Teresa Okure. *The Johannine Approach to Mission* (1988); Lambertus Lietaert Peerbolte. *Paul the Missionary* (2003); Rainer Riesner. *Paul's Early Period: Chronology, Mission Strategy, Theology* (1998); Eckhard J. Schnabel. *Early Christian Mission.* 2 vols. (2004); James M. Scott. *Paul and the Nations* (1995); Stephen G. Wilson. *The Gentiles and the Gentile Mission in Luke–Acts* (1973); Bruce W. Winter. *Philo and Paul among the Sophists* (1997).

ECKHARD SCHNABEL

MIST [אֵד ʾedh, נָשִׂיא nasiʾ, עָנָן ʿanan; ἀτμίς atmis, ἀχλύς achlys]. Although clearly related, mist (condensation in the air) is best distinguished from DEW (condensation of water vapor on a cooled surface). In Israel the cold night air condenses into drops of water to form a misty rain or heavy fog that is quickly dissipated by the morning sunlight. This is the "morning cloud" to which Hosea compares Israel's ephemeral love for God (6:4). Similarly, James compares the fleetingness of human existence to a mist that quickly vanishes (4:14). Mist and darkness come over a magician who has been blinded by Paul (Acts 13:11); and "mists driven by a storm" is used as an image for those who have gone astray (2 Pet 2:17).

MARK RONCACE

MITANNI mi-tan'ee. Mitanni, with its capital, Washukanni, in the upper Habur River Valley, was an important Hurrian imperial state in the last half of the 2nd millennium BCE. It emerged in the middle of the 2nd millennium following the vast migration of HURRIANS into Mesopotamia, Cilicia, and Syria. The Mitanni ruling class also included an Indo-Aryan minority that were apparently responsible for introducing new horse breeding and training techniques into the area. The Hurrians' introduction of the light, horse-drawn, two-wheel chariot as a military weapon appears to have enabled Mitanni's rapid imperial expansion to the east through Assyria and to the west through most of Syria and into Palestine, though the states in these areas were not dissolved but governed loosely as vassals. The Syrian campaigns of the Egyptian kings Thutmosis I (1512–1500 BCE), Thutmosis III (1469–1436 BCE), and Amenophis II (1438–1412 BCE) weakened Mitanni and permitted the emergence of the Hittite Empire as its rival. Mitanni remained a major imperial power through the Amarna period, and the AMARNA LETTERS include communications from Tushratta of Mitanni to Amenophis III (1402–1363 BCE) and Amenophis IV (1363–1347 BCE). Revolt within Mitanni helped the great Hittite ruler Shuppiluliuma crush Tushratta and Mitanni (ca. 1350 BCE). The collapse of Mitanni, however, permitted Assyria to become independent, so the HITTITES quickly reconstituted Mitanni in the area between the Habur and the Euphrates as a buffer against the new power of Assyria. This area, known as Hanigalbat by the Assyrians, remained a battleground between the Hittites and the Assyrians until the Assyrian ruler Shalmaneser I (1273–1244 BCE) conquered it, bringing an end to the once-great Mitanni.

J. J. M. ROBERTS

MITHKAH mith'kuh [מִתְקָה mithqah]. One of the Israelites' encampments, location unknown, in the wilderness (Num 33:28-29). Means "sweetness," which may imply a water source.

MITHNITE mith'n*i*t [מִתְנִי mithni]. Family name or place of origin ascribed to Joshaphat (1 Chr 11:43), one of DAVID'S CHAMPIONS. Because of its uniqueness the text is questioned.

MITHRAS, MITHRAISM mith'ruhs, mith'ruh-iz'uhm. Mithras, known from ancient Vedic hymns and the AVESTA, is a divine figure who came to prominence in the Roman period in the mysteries of Mithras (Mithraism). While the Greco-Roman worship of Mithras may be understood to derive from early sources, the mysteries of Mithras are best understood as a Roman form of religion flourishing in the Roman Empire from the 2nd cent. CE on. Roman men, especially military men and imperial officers, were attracted to Mithraism, and sanctuaries of the Mithraic mysteries, called Mithraea, were established all around the Roman Empire.

Mithraea were designed to resemble caves. Within Mithraea devotees conducted initiations and shared sacred meals of bread and water (or a mixture of water and wine). Justin Martyr acknowledged the similarities between the Mithraic sacred meal and the Christian eucharist, though he maintains that the similarities are due to diabolical imitation of the Christian celebration. Tertullian also mentioned lustrations, ordeals, and tests of courage in Mithraic worship. Initiation into the Mithraic mysteries involved several stages of initiation. Ordinarily, seven stages are enumerated: raven, bridegroom (or occult), soldier, lion, Persian, courier of the sun, and father. The artistic centerpiece in the Mithraic sanctuary was typically the scene of Mithras slaying the bull. Inscriptions from the Mithraeum of Santa Prisca describe the Mithraic view of salvation in terms that resemble Christian formulations.

Traditionally, Mithraism has been interpreted as an ethical religion that preserved leading themes of Avestan or Zoroastrian worship into the Roman period, but more recently, a new astronomical paradigm of Mithraism has emerged, so that Mithraism may be understood to have provided a vision of the cosmos and salvation within the cosmos (Beck; Ulansey). *See* MYSTERY RELIGIONS.

Bibliography: Roger Beck. *Planetary Gods and Planetary Orders in the Mysteries of Mithras* (1988); Marvin Meyer, ed. *The Ancient Mysteries: A Sourcebook of Sacred Texts* (1999); David Ulansey. *The Origins of the Mithraic Mysteries: Cosmology and Salvation in the Ancient World* (1989).

MARVIN MEYER

MITHREDATH mith'ruh-dath [מִתְרְדָת mithredhath; Μιθραδάτης Mithradatēs, Μιθριδάτης Mithridatēs]. 1. King CYRUS of Persia's treasurer who inventoried the Jerusalem temple vessels taken by Nebuchadnezzar and returned them to SHESHBAZZAR, who brought the vessels with him when he returned from Babylonian exile to Jerusalem (Ezra 1:8; Mithridates in 1 Esd 2:11).

2. A Persian officer who, along with others, sent correspondence to King Artaxerxes opposing the rebuilding of Jerusalem and the walls surrounding the city (Ezra 4:7; Mithridates in 1 Esd 2:16).

HEIDI E. HAWKS

MITHRIDATES. *See* MITHREDATH.

MITYLENE mit'uh-lee'nee [Μιτυλήνη Mitylēnē]. Capital city and port located on the southeastern side of the island of Lesbos in the Aegean Sea, where Paul and his companions stopped before sailing on to Chios, Samos, and Miletus in making their way to Jerusalem during Paul's third missionary journey (Acts 20:14). During the time of the Roman Empire, it was known as a commercial port and the resort for wealthy Romans. When its residents revolted against the Romans for taxation in 80 CE, its acropolis and walls were destroyed, but Pompey restored its inhabitants' freedom. In 151–52 CE, an earthquake demolished it. Later, during the Middle Ages, the city's name came to be used for the whole island.

EMILY R. CHENEY

MIZAR mí'zahr [מִצְעָר mitsʿar]. Means "littleness." Possibly the name of a mountain (NRSV, "Mount Mizar"; Ps 42:6) located in the area near Hermon and the Jordan River, since no other locales are mentioned in Ps 42. Or, the Hebrew word may be only providing a contrast to the grandeur of Mount Hermon.

MIZMOR [מִזְמוֹר mizmor]. A type of song (*see* SONG, SONGS). The Hebrew term appears only in the superscriptions or titles of fifty-seven psalms, where it is translated "psalm" (*see* PSALMS, BOOK OF). Other types of song in the book of Psalms are the MIKTAM, the MASKIL, and the shiggaion (Ps 7). The distinguishing characteristics of a mizmor are difficult to establish, but the term frequently appears with a proper name: David, Asaph, or the Korahites. Several psalms are identified as both a mizmor and a "song," e.g., Pss 65–68; 92; and 108; Ps 88 is called a mizmor, a "song," and a "maskil."

WILL SOLL

MIZPAH, MIZPEH miz'puh, miz'peh [מִצְפָּה mitspah, מִצְפֶּה mitspeh; Μασσηφά Massēpha]. Means "lookout point" or "watchtower," from the Hebrew root tsph (צפה), "to look out, keep watch, spy." Five locations in the OT are given the name Mizpah or Mizpeh, which are two variant spellings of the name. 1. A land located near Mount Hermon occupied by Hivites (Josh 11:3).

2. A town in the Shephelah region of Judah (Josh 15:38).

3. A settlement in Benjamin. This Mizpah is the only one that receives repeated and detailed references in the DtrH (Josh 18:26; Judg 20–21; 1 Sam 7; 10:17-27; 1 Kgs 15:16-22; 2 Kgs 25:23, 25), and in 2 Chr 16:6; Neh 3:7, 15-19; Jer 40–41; and 1 Macc 3:46. Scholars divide the texts dealing with Mizpah of Benjamin into two groups: those with religious/cultic overtones and those with strategic significance (McKenzie). The date and historiographic value of the religious/cultic texts in Joshua, Judges, and 1 Samuel are in question, with one group placing them early, in the premonarchic period, and others viewing them as late, exilic or postexilic retrojections based on the significance of the site during the Babylonian and early Persian periods. Regardless of date, the passages indicate that Mizpah was a prominent settlement in the region of Benjamin, a small tribal territory located immediately north of Jerusalem. They reflect biblical traditions that hold that Mizpah was a place of assembly, judgment, and sacrifice; was closely linked to the career of the prophet Samuel; and was the site of the election of Saul to kingship.

The strategic and political significance of Mizpah are detailed during the period of the divided monarchy when the region of Benjamin became a border zone between the two kingdoms. This is highlighted when the Judean king Asa fortified Mizpah and Geba in Benjamin. It is reported that Asa mustered all the corvée labor available to him to build these fortifications, in direct reaction to King Baasha's aborted attempt to wall Ramah and solidify northern Israel's hold on the region (1 Kgs 15:16-22; 2 Chr 16:6). The stones and timber used at Ramah were dismantled and transferred to the building projects at Mizpah and Geba, an architectural recycling process of building materials for monumental construction that was common in the Near East. Strategically, Asa's building projects make perfect sense: Mizpah held a prominent position along the main north-south access route between Judah and northern Israel, and Geba guarded the secondary north-south road. The Judean ruler thus bolstered the frontier of his kingdom along the two most likely routes of attack from a threat coming from the north. In a much later episode, it is detailed that Asa also built a cistern at Mizpah that was in use at least down to the 6th cent. BCE (Jer 41:9). The construction of a water source within the newly walled settlement at Mizpah shows further military strategy in that it would allow occupants to better withstand a siege behind the protection of its fortifications. Cisterns and massive water tunnels are attested archaeologically at fortified sites in the southern Levant in the Iron II period, typically equated with the time of the divided monarchy, lending further credence to this detail preserved in the prophetic report.

After the reign of Asa, Mizpah is not mentioned until the period following the destruction of Jerusalem by the Babylonians in 587/86 BCE (2 Kgs 25; Jer 40–41). It is the site of the regional capital of the Neo-Babylonian province of Judah, ruled over by a local governor, Gedaliah, appointed by the imperial power. At Mizpah, Gedaliah is joined by a group of Judean officers who commanded troops in the open country. The region of Benjamin was spared the degree of devastation wrought by the Chaldeans on Jerusalem and other areas of Judah, perhaps in part due to the pro-Babylonian leanings of its Judean leadership. Benjamin was a focal point of continued Judean settlement, and with Gedaliah's encouragement was the region to which Judean refugees, who had fled before the invading Babylonian armies, returned. After the prophet Jeremiah is freed from imprisonment by the Chaldeans, his captors give him the choice to join the exiled community in Babylonia or remain in war-ravished Judah. The prophet chooses to stay with his fellow beleaguered Judeans and joins Gedaliah at Mizpah. Jeremiah is then caught up in the intrigue of the assassination of Gedaliah at the hands of Ishmael, a Judean officer from the Davidic line, whose act was perpetrated in collusion with the kingdom of Ammon. Ishmael is pursued in his escape from Mizpah by Judean forces loyal to the slain Gedaliah; however, the assassin escapes with a small band of men to the safety of neighboring Ammon. Fearing reprisals from the Chaldeans, a group of Judeans leaves Mizpah for the relative safety of Egypt, bringing Jeremiah with them. Thus, the long-standing diasporic community of Judeans/Jews in Egypt is established.

In Nehemiah's time, Mizpah of Benjamin is known to have had its own district in the empire controlled by Persia. Two separate rulers of this district are mentioned aiding in the repair of the city wall and gates of Jerusalem, presumably with laborers sent from the town (Neh 3:15-17). The final historical reference to Mizpah is from the Hellenistic period (1 Macc 3:46), when Jewish armies gather in assembly near the site to worship before their battle with the Seleucid forces. This text indicates the settlement's continued religious significance and tradition as a place of assembly and is an example of the conservation of sacred space despite the resurgence of Jerusalem during this period both religiously and politically. In this passage in 1 Maccabees, Mizpah is said to be "opposite Jerusalem," a geographic detail not found in any of the earlier texts. It is possible that by the Hellenistic period the name Mizpah, and traditions related to this earlier settlement in Benjamin, had migrated to a settlement farther south and much closer to Jerusalem.

Mizpah of Benjamin has been identified by historical geographers with the archaeological sites of Tell en-Nasbeh or Nebi Samwil. The main research goal of early expeditions (1926–35) was proving or disproving its identification with Mizpah, a question that was not answered definitively despite uncovering two-thirds of the ancient site. The Nasbeh materials have been thoroughly reworked by Jeffrey Zorn, who has demonstrated that the site's stratigraphy is a good match with the historical references to Mizpah detailed above. Perhaps the most significant links between Nasbeh and Mizpah are the impressive Iron II–period wall that surrounds the site, a fortification without parallel in the territory of Benjamin, and the settlement phase of the Babylonian/early Persian period. Nasbeh's massive fortification, with towers and city gate, is the best fit in the region of Benjamin for the public works project of King Asa at Mizpah. The size and stature of Tell en-Nasbeh's Str 2, dated by Zorn to the 6th–5th cent. BCE, is unmatched in the region and lends further credence to its identification as Mizpah, the capital of the Babylonian province of Judah. The site begins to diminish in the Persian period, when the administrative center shifts south to Ramat Rahel, and the revival of Jerusalem is begun. The recent excavation of Nebi Samwil has revived with the theory that the site is the settlement of Mizpah in Benjamin; however, the remains are not a convincing fit, especially since the site lacks an Iron II fortification and any significant phase from the Babylonian period. This further bolsters the identification of Tell en-Nasbeh with Mizpah of Benjamin, an identification that is now widely accepted. It is possible, however, that Nebi Samwil is the Mizpah mentioned in 1 Maccabees, given its elevation, proximity to Jerusalem, and impressive late Hellenistic remains. (For a similar proposal, see John Rogerson, who, however, dates the move of Mizpah from Tell en-Nasbeh to Nebi Samwil to the Babylonian period.) The traditional connection between the prophet Samuel and Mizpah may have been transferred at this time or later, as is reflected in the Arabic name of the settlement. Thus the long-standing debate may be resolved by identifying Tell en-Nasbeh with Mizpah of the Iron Age, Babylonian, and early Persian periods, and Nebi Samwil with Mizpah of the Hellenistic period. *See* ATAROTH-ADDAR; MEROM, WATERS OF.

4. A site in Gilead (Judg 11:29).

5. A settlement in Moab to which David traveled during his flight from Saul (1 Sam 22:3).

Bibliography: Oded Lipschits. "Demographic Changes in Judah between the Seventh and the Fifth Centuries B.C.E." *Judah and the Judeans in the Neo-Babylonian Period.* Oded Lipschits and Joseph Blenkinsopp, eds. (2003) 323–76; Oded Lipschits. "The History of the Benjamin Region under Babylonian Rule." *TA* 26 (1999) 155–90; Yitzhak Magen and Michael Dadon. "Nebi Samwil." *Qad* 118 (1999) 62–77; Steven L. McKenzie. "Mizpah of Benjamin and the Date of the Deuteronomistic History." *"Lasset uns Brücken bauen . . .": Collected Communications to the XVth Congress of the International Organization for the Study of the Old Testament, Cambridge 1995.* Klaus-Dietrich Schunck and Matthias Augustin, eds. (1998) 149–55; John Rogerson. *Chronicles of the Bible Lands* (2003); Jeffrey R. Zorn. "Tell en-Nasbeh and the Problem of the Material Culture of the Sixth Century." *Judah and the Judeans in the Neo-Babylonian Period.* Oded Lipschits and Joseph Blenkinsopp, eds. (2003) 413–47.

AARON BRODY

MIZRAIM miz-ray'im [מִצְרַיִם mitsrayim]. Mizraim is the most common designation for EGYPT in the OT. In Gen 10:6, the sons of Ham are Mizraim, Cush, Put, and Canaan.

Scholars debate whether Mizraim refers not to Egypt, but to Musri, an Anatolian site known from Akkadian sources. Both 1 Kgs 10:28 (//2 Chr 1:16) and 2 Kgs 7:6 feature horses, for which Anatolia was more famed than Egypt. Furthermore, the pairing of Mizraim/Musri and KUE (1 Kgs 10:28//2 Chr 1:16) resembles the monolith inscription of the 9th cent. BCE Assyrian king Shalmaneser III, which reports the inclusion of soldiers from Que and Musri in an anti-Assyrian coalition assembled in Syria. Other scholars contend that the reference to Egyptian horses/chariots alongside the horses of Kue or the chariots of Hatti is deliberate, emphasizing the extent of Solomon's economic reach (1 Kgs 10:28//2 Chr 1:16) and the power of Israel's potential allies (2 Kgs 7:6).

CAROLYN HIGGINBOTHAM

MIZZAH miz'uh [מִזָּה mizzah]. Name of REUEL's fourth son and one of Esau's grandsons (Gen 36:13, 17). Also can be understood as the name of an Edomite tribe (1 Chr 1:37).

MMŠT. **Mmšt** is known from the **lmlk** ("belonging to the king") seal impressions found on Judean storage jar handles of the late 8th cent. BCE, as are the sites Socoh, Ziph, and Hebron. Its location is uncertain, but it has been suggested that it refers to Jerusalem, a supposition based on the reconstruction of **mmšt** as ***mamšalt** from Hebrew **memšeleth** (מֶמְשֶׁלֶת, "government"). *See* LMLK SEALS.

Bibliography: H. L. Ginsberg. "MMŠT and MṢH." *BASOR* 109 (1948) 20–22; A. F. Rainey. "Wine from the Royal Vineyards." *BASOR* 245 (1982) 57–62.

JASON R. TATLOCK

MNASON nay'suhn [Μνάσων **Mnasōn**]. An early Cypriot disciple and host of Paul and his companions on Paul's final visit to Jerusalem (Acts 21:16). Some, following the Western textual variant, locate Mnason's home in an unnamed village along the journey from Caesarea to Jerusalem. If so, Paul's reception in 21:17 implies a broad welcome by the Jerusalem Christian community. If not, those welcoming Paul in Jerusalem may merely have consisted of Mnason and his associates. As an "early disciple," Mnason would possess exemplary credentials in the Jerusalem church, and his Hellenistic background would ensure a culturally sensitive host for Paul and his Gentile companions.

MICHAEL C. MCKEEVER

MNEMONIC DEVICES. A mnemonic device is something that serves as an aid to memory. English-speaking children may learn "Every Good Boy Does Fine" to remember the notes of the musical staff, or "My Very Educated Mother Just Served Us Nine Pizza Pies" to remember the planets and their order. Such mnemonics often rely on the correspondence of the initial letter of the words in the mnemonic phrase to the subject one is trying to memorize. While these kinds of mnemonics do not occur in the Bible, they do occur in later Jewish and Christian literature. A well-known example can be found in the Passover Haggadah, where Rabbi Judah ben Ilai is credited with a mnemonic for the ten plagues of the exodus and their order.

Sometimes a rhyme or song is created with a mnemonic purpose, e.g., "Thirty Days Hath September," to remember the number of days in each month. In fact, some have wondered if rhyme itself was originally introduced into poetry as an aid to memory. But mnemonic utility hardly exhausts the aesthetic appeal and potential of rhyme in verse.

In Hebrew poetry, some have suggested that the ACROSTIC form came into being as a mnemonic device (e.g., Ps 119). While on the surface such a view may seem plausible, the parallels to Babylonian name/sentence acrostics, which were clearly not written with any mnemonic purpose in view, make it difficult to maintain. The acrostic form was employed for conceptual and aesthetic reasons rather than mnemonic ones.

One text that might have been created with ease of memory in view is the TEN COMMANDMENTS. Both their brevity and the fact that there are ten of them (corresponding to the fingers of the hand) may have been guided by mnemonic considerations.

WILL SOLL

MOAB, CITY OF moh'ab [עִיר מוֹאָב ʿir moʾav]. A city on the Arnon River where Balaam meets with Balak (Num 22:36-38). Probably the same as AR (Num 21:15, 28).

MOAB, MOABITES moh'ab, moh'uh-b*i*t [מוֹאָב moʾav, מוֹאָבִי moʾavi; Μωάβ **Mōab**, Μωαβείτης **Mōabeitēs**]. 1. The son of Lot by one of his daughters according to the etiological account in Gen 19:30-38. The Ammonites are descended from Lot by his other daughter and are related to Moab. The connection drawn between the Moabites and Abraham's nephew is an explicit recognition of links between Israel and Moab (Deut 2:9).

2. *Moab* refers to a geographic region and more particularly to the plateau areas east of the Dead Sea. *Moab* is used as a geographic designation in the Late Bronze Age in Egyptian texts dating to the reign of Ramesses II, and there were always pastoral and sedentary inhabitants arranged in tribal and clan polities, whether or not there was a recognized larger Moabite polity.

Moab also refers to the nation-state in that same region during the Iron Age, with political antecedents that may reach back into the Late Bronze Age. The designation *Moabite*, therefore, can refer either to someone living in the area of Moab or to someone attached to the political entity of Moab. Both area and nation had identity markers of culture and religion. Although *Moabite* is not a racial term, it was a recognized ethnic designation.

The development of a Moabite nation has some parallels with that of other nations in the southern Levant such as Israel, Judah, and Ammon, and there are multiple references in historical documents to Moab's interaction with these neighbors. In each case, these states emerged politically at points in the Iron Age from relative or total obscurity in Bronze Age sources. They each have a strong tribal structure, monarchy, a literary heritage, and one or more patron deities of the nation.

Extant Moabite inscriptions give added detail to the descriptions of Moab and Moabites from other sources. Scholars draw upon references in Egyptian New Kingdom (Late Bronze Age) texts, the OT, and Neo-Assyrian texts in order to reconstruct ancient Moabite history. The results of modern archaeological surveys and excavations add to the textual sources scholars have at their disposal. The flowering of the Moabite state took place in Iron Age II and III (9th–6th cent. BCE). What autonomy and cohesion Moab could maintain was largely brought to an end by the Babylonian campaigns in the region (598–580 BCE).

A. Moabite Texts
B. Geography and Settlement Patterns
C. Moabite History
D. Religion and Culture
Bibliography

A. Moabite Texts

Fortunately, fragments of several monumental Moabite inscriptions are extant, and they are the primary sources for Moabite identity. There are also a number of Moabite epigraphic seals from the 8th and 7th cent. BCE that provide some insight into Moabite culture and religion (see §D). Pride of place goes to a thirty-four-line inscription on a basalt stone (referred to as the MESHA stele or inscription or MOABITE STONE) discovered at Dibon. Unfortunately, it was broken in pieces after its discovery by a Protestant missionary in 1868. The inscription narrates the highlights of the reign of King Mesha (compare 2 Kgs 3), particularly his building projects and the ways in which he freed Moab from the control of the Omride Dynasty in Israel. It mentions Omri by name and contains one of the earliest nonbiblical references to Yahweh, the name of the God of Israel.

Two brief pieces from monumental inscriptions provide evidence of several additional incomplete lines of text. A fragment discovered in Karak contains a portion of one line that has the phrase "king of Moab" preceded by a portion of what is likely a proper name. Some interpreters see the inscription as belonging either to Mesha or his father (see §C). The other fragment preserving only a few consonants was found on the surface near the ruins of ancient Dibon. Only the word *house* (**bt** בת) followed by the consonant KAF (**k** כ) remains. Some have speculated that the line contained the phrase "house of Ke[mosh]" (author's trans.).

In 2003 the Israeli National Museum displayed a fragmentary stone inscription that appeared first on the antiquities market. Its provenance is unknown, but its script and vocabulary mark it as classical Moabite. Portions of seven lines are visible, the last two of which are unintelligible. The script is similar to that of the Mesha inscription. The inscription can be rendered as follows:

1. . . . I built . . .
2. . . . many prisoners. And I built [. . . k]ing . . .
3. [And I bui]lt Beth Harosh and with Ammonite prisoners
4. [I built] a reservoir, a strong gate, and cattle
5. .....there, and the Ammonites saw that they were weak in every
6. . . .
7. . . . (author's trans.)

Collectively, these fragments demonstrate a Moabite penchant for monumental inscriptions on stone, a cultural characteristic shared with several Phoenician and Aramean parallels. Three of the four are royal inscriptions. The first and fourth share similarities regarding the use of prisoners, along with a desire to celebrate construction projects. The fourth contained an account related to Moab's Ammonite neighbors.

B. Geography and Settlement Patterns

Moab was located in the TRANSJORDAN between the Ammonites to the north (*see* AMMON, AMMONITES) and the Edomites to the south (*see* EDOM, EDOMITES). The physical geography of greater Moab comprised essentially the plateau land east of the lower Jordan Valley and the Dead Sea. That plateau has precipitous slopes on its western side in the descent to the valley floor. The Dead Sea sits some 900 ft. below sea level, while the plateau to the east is 2,500–3,500 ft. above sea level. The eastern edge of the plateau is not easily marked, but as the rainfall pattern decreases moving toward the Syrian-Arabian desert, so does the population level. The plateau area is bisected by the massive canyon of the Wadi Mujib (the Arnon River of the OT), which flows westward into the Dead Sea. The Wadi Mujib drains a large section of the plateau during times of measurable rain, although the water flow is normally weak. Its canyon is approximately 2 mi. wide and it cuts deeply between the tableland to its north and the central plateau to its south. At the southern end of the central plateau is the Wadi Hasa (the Zered River of the OT), which presents an even broader division between the central plateau and the mountainous region of Edom to the south, although the descent and ascent is less steep than that of the Mujib.

Animal husbandry, particularly sheep and goats, abounds in this region (2 Kgs 3:4). The fields of the plateaus also produce a considerable amount of grain (wheat and barley) in good seasons. Grapes are another product, especially on the tableland around ancient MEDEBA (modern Madaba).

An important trading route runs north-south through Moab, linking Arabia and the port of Aqaba with such centers to the north as Damascus and the Phoenician ports. Numbers 20:17 and 21:22 reference a KING'S HIGHWAY or route associated with royal sponsorship. The trade route was not so much a single marked road as a recognized series of stops along a couple of parallel branches. The King's Highway, therefore, may refer to the centuries-old trading route, but that is not certain. It may simply refer to a route watched over by or under the authority of a local ruler. Later, during the period of Roman rule, a highway was constructed running north-south in Transjordan, complete with paving stones and mile markers. It bore the name Via Nova Traiana, i.e., the new road sponsored by the emperor Trajan.

Archaeological surveys show that settlement patterns in Moab generally follow broader cultural and climatic influences in the southern Levant. The 3rd millennium BCE (Early Bronze III–IV) is more frequently reflected in material cultural remains than either the Middle or Late Bronze ages, although the latter are found in the archaeological record. Toward the end of the 2nd millennium BCE, sedentary existence began to increase. A number of walled settlements were constructed, beginning in the early Iron Age (12th–11th cent. BCE), with a peak in the 8th–early 6th cent. BCE.

The largest city on the central plateau is Karak, home to a massive CASTLE from the crusader period (*see* KARAK, KHIRBET). In Iron Age II, the period of the Moabite kingdom, the predecessor to Karak was likely KIR-HARESETH (2 Kgs 3:25; Isa 16:7). AR, another Moabite settlement on the central plateau, may be identified with the modern settlement of Rabbah, north of Karak. Another possibility for Ar would be Balua, an archaeological site with strong fortifications located along a southern tributary of the Mujib. There are a string of Iron Age walled settlements along the eastern edge of the central plateau, but they did not originate at one point in time as part of a national line of defense. Some date earlier than others and their roles in a regional economy may have varied. The northern plateau preserves a number of walled Iron Age sites (i.e., their ruins). Among them are Muhayat (Nebo), Jalul, Mudaynah on the Thamad, Rumayl, ʿAraʿir (Aroer), and Dhiban (Dibon), all of which have been partially excavated. The inscription of King Mesha was discovered in Dhiban, a likely indication that ancient Dibon was his capital. Mudaynah on the Thamad has undergone systematic excavation in recent years. From the 9th cent. and later, it preserves strong Iron Age fortifications, including a chambered gate, casemate walls, and a cultic installation. An incense stand discovered at the site has a brief inscription in Moabite on it from the maker Elishama dedicating the implement. The dialect of the inscription has both Moabite and Phoenician characteristics.

The central plateau similarly has several walled Iron Age sites. Mudaybi, located southeast of Karak, has a large, four-chambered gate and several proto-Aeolic capitals.

The latter have parallels in the primary Israelite cities of Samaria, Megiddo, and Hazor, and in the Judean cities of Jerusalem and Ramat Rahel (between Jerusalem and Bethlehem). Balua, located on a southern tributary of the Mujib, had an inscribed sculpture from the 13th/12th cent. BCE showing strong Egyptian artistic influence, and from the later Iron Age, several brief Moabite ostraca. The inscription on the Balua stone is weathered and obscure, but gives indication of literacy in Moab in the 2nd millennium BCE. Another stone sculpture from Jebel Shihan, a few km west of Balua, apparently dates from the late 2nd millennium BCE and depicts a warrior wearing a fighting skirt and brandishing a spear. These two sculptures are evidence for an emerging Moabite culture that developed into a nation-state in the Iron Age. The multichambered gates, capitals, and city walls discovered show that the urban culture of Moab had points of similarity with Judah and Israel in Iron Age II. In domestic architecture, both cultures reflected a common building design for family dwellings known as the four-room house.

The fact that *Moab* is a recognized geographic term masks a number of complexities and fascinating dynamics that are reflected in historical sources. The two primary sources for Moabite geography are the OT and the Mesha inscription (ca. 835 BCE). Mesha identifies himself as a Dibonite and king of Moab (lines 1–2). Apparently, Dibon was his capital. A number of sites on the plateau between Dibon and Medeba (ca. 30 mi. north) are named, along with a couple of references to subregions and related population groups. These references come in the context of Israel's domination of Moab during the Omride Dynasty, and the building projects Mesha undertook after throwing off the Israelite yoke (compare 2 Kgs 3:4-5). From Mesha's perspective, the tableland between the Arnon River and Medeba is Moabite, with Chemosh, the chief Moabite deity, its patron. In the course of the narration, Mesha refers to Baal-meon, Bezer, Beth-diblathaim, Dibon, Horonaim, Jahaz, Medeba, Nebo, Ataroth, Aroer, and Kiriathaim (biblical nomenclature), all sites known from references in the OT, and with the probable exception of Horonaim, all located on the tableland north of the Arnon. There is also a reference to the Arnon River (Wadi Mujib) and a highway or crossing point associated with it (line 26), which Mesha also claims for Moab. And if the references to Horonaim in lines 31–32 are to a site south of the Arnon on the central plateau, then it follows naturally that the plateau south of the Arnon is considered part of Moab. The discovery of the fragmentary Moabite inscription in Karak may be related to the events narrated at the end of the Mesha inscription. It does confirm Moabite presence, at least for a time, in the region.

Mesha makes an intriguing reference to the "men of Gad who lived in Ataroth for a long time" (line 10; author's trans.), which may refer to elements of the Israelite tribe of Gad (*see* GAD, GADITES). The description does not link their presence to the expansive policies of OMRI. It is obvious from other references, however, that the Omride forces had occupied a number of places on the tableland. Mesha reports that Israel had humbled Moab because Chemosh was "angry with his land" (lines 5–6). Israel controlled the area of Medeba (lines 7–8), which also included Nebo. In the struggle against Israel, Mesha had assembled fighters and attacked Nebo (west of Medeba, lines 14–18), where apparently there was a shrine dedicated to the worship of Yahweh. Lines 17–18 make reference to "[ves]sels of Yahweh" (author's trans.). Jahaz was another settlement on the tableland that Israel had fortified and where struggles ensued (lines 18–20) and the Israelites were defeated.

As a memorial stele, the Mesha inscription is a retrospective on his reign and glorifies his achievements. Its narration provides something of a "snapshot" of Israelite relations with Moab, rooted in a longer history of interaction, including a basic outline to define the land of Moab. Readers can extrapolate from Mesha's account that the Israelites also laid claim to the tableland north of the Arnon, however tendentious that claim may be from a Moabite perspective. Evidence for this claim appears in a number of biblical references. In the description of the tribal inheritance of Reuben (Josh 13:15-21; see vv. 8-9), major sections of the tableland north of the Arnon are assigned to that tribe. A number of cities in the biblical list are also named in the inscription of King Mesha (e.g., Dibon, plain of Medeba, Beth-baal-meon, Jahaz). In the list of cities of refuge and Levitical cities comes the reference to Bezer (Josh 20:8; 21:36), a city claimed and rebuilt by Mesha (line 27). According to Num 32:33-38, the tribes of Reuben and Gad built (rebuilt?) several cities east of the Dead Sea including Dibon, Ataroth, Aroer, Nebo, and Baal-meon.

The wilderness itineraries in the Pentateuch presuppose a Moabite entity living east of the Dead Sea (Num 21:10-13; Deut 2:1-37) as the Israelite tribes approach from the south. According to Num 21:10-13 the Israelites camped east of Moab. Although not stated explicitly, the reference to the river Zered is likely understood as the southern border of Moab. The northern border, however, is defined as the Arnon River. The tableland to the north of Arnon belonged to the Amorites and King Sihon, who had taken the land from the Moabites (so Num 21:26). The narratives in Deuteronomy state that Israel would not lay claim to Moabite territory, since God had assigned them an inheritance (2:9; compare Judg 11:15). The only Moabite city mentioned, however, is Ar on the central plateau south of the Arnon. Nevertheless, the connection between Moab and the tableland north of the Arnon was strong, since the name Moab is attached to it in related biblical texts. The camping place of the tribes on the tableland across from Jericho is called the "plains of Moab" (Num 22:1). The local king who opposed the Israelites camped on the plains was Balak, king of Moab (Num 22:2-4), and Israelite apostasy with Baal-peor on the plains also involved the "daughters of Moab" (Num 25:1).

Thus the wilderness itineraries represent a complicated matter. On the one hand, Israel will lay claim to the tableland as territory formerly held by the Amorites. On the other hand, there is implicit recognition that Moab is also related to the land, and the prophetic oracles against Moab dating from the 8th and 7th cent. BCE presuppose that the tableland is Moabite (Isa 15:1-2; 16:6-12; Jer 48:1-47). There are source and redaction issues related to the wilderness itineraries that make it difficult to work out systematically the ways in which early Israel related to Moab, particularly in the possession of settlements on the tableland. The lists of Levitical cities and cities of refuge may reflect a combination of early and ideal practices, and it is difficult to know what reality lies behind the claim, e.g., that the city of Bezer served both institutions. Indeed, Bezer cannot be located with any certainty, although there are several plausible candidates on the plateau near Medeba (e.g., Khirbat at Teim, Jalul, Umm al ʿAmad). From the time of Mesha onward (mid-9th cent. BCE), the tableland is de facto Moabite in a political sense, whatever connections remain with Israelites and others who may have continued living there.

The Moabite identity of the tableland in the 8th and 7th cent., confirmed by the OT's prophetic oracles, is a state of affairs that lasted essentially until the Babylonian onslaught in the region, early in the 6th cent. BCE. Possibly there were periodic tensions with the Ammonites, as they expanded southward and encroached upon Moab, or as Moab expanded northward, but these things likely were mitigated by the greater difficulties each nation had in dealing first with Assyrian encroachment and later with the Babylonians.

C. Moabite History

Mention of Moab first appears in Egyptian documents. The Egyptians under Ramesses II campaigned in Moab during the Late Bronze Age, and mentioned the city of Dibon during one encounter. Interestingly, the excavations at Dibon did not uncover any Late Bronze remains. Perhaps Late Bronze remains are buried under a portion of the modern city or the settlement represented in the campaign account was more that of a tribal encampment. The first king named in the region is Balak, whose efforts to thwart the Israelites are narrated in Num 22–24. One should not simply assume from the narrative that Balak was the king over greater Moab. It is possible that on occasion he and other Moabite kings in historical sources are chieftains or regional rulers who covet the title "king." There may have been other Moabite tribal leaders or governors of a city with regional power bases who lived simultaneously with those whose names are preserved in ancient texts.

According to Judg 3:12-30 a Moabite named Eglon expanded his power base, gathered some Ammonites and Amalekites in an army, and took up residence in the "city of palms." The location of the latter is not certainly identified, but it is likely Jericho (Deut 34:3). Although the book of Judges describes Eglon's expansion as a defeat of Israel (3:12-14), close reading of the narrative reveals that it is the Benjaminites and the nearby hill country of Ephraim most affected by Eglon. It was a Benjaminite named Ehud who killed Eglon and who organized the rebellion against his rule. Fords for the Jordan River were nearby (Judg 3:28), and when the Moabite supporters of Eglon tried to flee to the eastern side of the Jordan, they were repulsed and killed. This expansion of Moabite control to the west side of the Jordan came, of course, at the expense of the Israelite tribes living in the southern Jordan Valley and the hills immediately to the west. It is a mirror to the later expansion of Israelite control under Omri, whereby the tableland north of the Arnon was effectively controlled by Israelites living in key cities.

The short story known as the book of Ruth links Bethlehem of Judah to Moab through the marriage of Boaz to Ruth (a Moabite; *see* RUTH, BOOK OF). Two forms of a genealogy at the book's end trace the lineage of DAVID back to Boaz and Ruth (Ruth 4:17-22). Whatever can be said historically about the story itself, Moabite ancestry would not be a mark in David's favor. Its acknowledgment, therefore, is plausibly based in fact. Moreover, the brief notice that David sent his parents to the king of Moab when he was pursued by Saul makes sense as a request for help based, at least in part, on an extended clan obligation (1 Sam 22:3-4). It is also possible that the book of Ruth is a composition of the postexilic period and serves as a counterweight to the enforced divorces enacted under the Ezra–Nehemiah reforms. Yet if that is the case (and it is a plausible interpretation), one should not necessarily conclude that David's "Moabite ancestry" is a convenient fiction.

Saul engaged in struggles against the Moabites and Ammonites (1 Sam 14:47). An account in 1 Sam 11:1-11 portrays the king as responding to Ammonite aggression and expansion. Similarly, there is a notice that David subjugated the Moabites and Ammonites (2 Sam 8:2, 12), but unfortunately a narrative explaining hostilities and their conclusion exists only for the latter (2 Sam 10:1-14). These texts are part of the expansion and contraction of the borders between Israel, Moab, and Ammon seen in the book of Judges, as well as evidence for efforts to impose vassal relations upon the Transjordanian communities as Israelite political influence developed.

David treated Moab harshly in subjugating them (2 Sam 8:2), and there is no reason cited for this. It is possible that this was a result of intrigue, where Moabite forces sided with one of David's rivals, and David understood it as a transgression of a clan obligation.

At least one of Solomon's diplomatic marriages was to a Moabite, most likely a princess (1 Kgs 11:1, 3). For this he is criticized in 1 Kgs 11:6. The king also built a shrine ("high place") for Chemosh, the patron deity of Moab, on a hill east of Jerusalem (1 Kgs 11:7). Solomon did the same for an Ammonite deity. The text does not state whether the choice of the eastern hill was made, at least in part, because Moab and Ammon lie to the east, but the fact that these two shrines are singled out by the writer indicates at least something of their importance (and perceived negative influence).

A brief comment in 2 Kgs 1:1 that Moab had rebelled against Israel after the death of AHAB is elaborated in 2 Kgs 3:1-27, with an account of fighting between Moab and a coalition led by King Jehoram of Israel (*see* JORAM). Ahab was first succeeded by his son Ahaziah, who reigned only briefly while ill. Ahaziah was then succeeded by Jehoram, another son of Ahab. According to the biblical account, the Moabite king Mesha used to provide a large tribute of sheep and wool to Israel (2 Kgs 3:4-5), but chose eventually to rebel. Jehoram assembled a coalition of forces with Judah (and King Jehoshaphat) and Edom and led a campaign against Moab, which approached Moab from the south. After initial victories, the coalition forces isolated the Moabite king in Kir-hareseth, whereupon the king offered his son as a sacrifice and Israel withdrew (on this last matter, see below). Kir-hareseth is likely the Iron Age counterpart to Karak, the largest city on the central plateau. With the discovery of the Mesha inscription, the brief account in 2 Kgs 3 is set in a broader framework. Apart from passing references at the end of the inscription (lines 31–32), which unfortunately are fragmentary, the Moabite account describes struggles for the tableland north of the Arnon (Mujib).

Mesha refers to the humbling or oppression of Moab by Omri (line 5), thus providing further context for the report in 2 Kgs 3:4 that Mesha and Moab paid an onerous tribute to Israel. Lines 6–9a in the inscription are a crucial summary of recent Moabite history. What they summarize about the struggle with Israel is elaborated upon at various points in the inscription.

The reference to "forty years" in line 8 is a valuable indicator of the length of Moabite servitude, but forty years does not compute as the length of Omri's reign and half that of his son Ahab. According to 1 Kgs 16:23-29, Omri ruled for twelve years and Ahab for twenty-two. Omri's reign and half that of Ahab does not equal forty years. Moreover, the biblical reports have Moab rebelling against Israel "after" the death of Ahab (2 Kgs 1:1) or "when" Ahab died (2 Kgs 3:5), not at the midpoint of Ahab's reign, if he is the "son" of lines 6 and 8. The report that Israel had perished forever is perhaps the easiest to deal with, since it has the ring of hyperbole in celebrating the defeat and retreat of an enemy. If the inscription is a retrospective account and thus written some years after Israel's defeat, the hyperbole may also reflect the death of the last Omride Jehoram, the subsequent replacement of the house of Omri with that of JEHU (2 Kgs 10:1-17), and the hegemony of Neo-Assyria under SHALMANESER III in making Jehu a vassal. This latter reference is not mentioned in the

OT. A black obelisk commissioned by Shalmaneser III records in text and iconography that Jehu, Jehoram's successor in Israel, became a Neo-Assyrian vassal by the year 841 BCE (*see* OBELISK, BLACK).

In lines 6 and 8, the Moabite term translated as "his son" (**bnh** בנה) raises two related questions. The first is the matter of kinship. In accord with standard Semitic usage, *son* can mean descendant and successor, so *son* in either line could refer to any Omride rulers. The second is a complicated matter of the term's morphology and vocalization. Stated simply, the transliterated term **bnh** comprises the Moabite word for "son/descendant" (**bn** בן) plus the third-person singular suffix (**h** ה), meaning "his." The inscription lacks vowels, and the use of *matres lectionis* (consonants that represent vowels) is inconsistent in Iron Age inscriptions, so it is possible that **bnh** in line 8 could also be rendered "his sons." If rendered correctly as *sons*, it thus indicates that Mesha writes retrospectively from a point in time in which the Omride Dynasty is no longer ruling Israel. Moab had freed itself from Israelite control at a mid-point in the Omride Dynasty, measured as a totality. The dynasty is given a total of forty-eight years of rule in the formulas of 1–2 Kings. Interpreters face a difficulty in either taking literally the "forty years" of the Moabite inscription, when it may mean essentially a "generation" or a "number of years," or in pressing too firmly for harmony between the biblical and the Moabite accounts, when both may present a one-sided view of a more complicated history.

After the introductory summary in lines 6–9a, the inscription rehearses the wresting of the tableland away from Israel along with celebration of Mesha's (re) building projects. Lines 31–33 report that Chemosh commanded Mesha to "go down and fight against Horonaim" (**khwrnn** [חורנן] in Moabite; compare Isa 15:5; Jer 48:3, 5, 34). Interpreters, therefore, have long wondered if the inscription concluded with Mesha's version of the hostilities narrated in 2 Kgs 3. Additional support for this hypothesis comes in A. Lemaire's suggested restoration in line 31 to read "house of David" (**b[t d]wd** ב[ת ד]וד), which had taken up residence in Horonaim. According to Lemaire, a noted epigrapher, this restored phrase is an example of the political term. If this disputed reconstruction is correct, the term refers to the state of Judah and, more particularly, the ruling dynasty, for which there are biblical parallels (Isa 7:2; Jer 21:12). Lemaire based his suggestion on a fragmentary Aramaic inscription also from the mid-9th cent. BCE, which was discovered at Tell Dan and which contained a reference to the "house of David" (*see* INSCRIPTION, TELL DAN). That inscription records the killing of a king of Judah and one of Israel (whose personal names are only partially preserved). Furthermore, the inscription from Dan can be linked to the interpretation of Mesha's inscription in that its fragmentary description of regicide probably preserves yet another reference to the end of the Omride Dynasty.

To complicate matters even more, 2 Chr 20:1-30 preserves an account of a Transjordanian coalition attacking Judah and King JEHOSHAPHAT from the southeast. The coalition comprised Moabites, Ammonites, and people from Mount Seir in Edom (20:10, 23), and perhaps some "Meunites" from Edom (so some Gk. translations of 20:1; compare 2 Chr 26:7). The compilers of 1–2 Kings do not preserve a version of this account, and it is possible that the struggles narrated reflect the postexilic time of the Chronicler (ca. 350 BCE?) rather than the mid-9th cent. However the historical background is sorted out, Jehoshaphat is linked twice with struggles against the Moabites, once in concert with Jehoram of Israel and once on his own.

Neo-Assyrian incursions in the southern Levant began earlier in the 9th cent., and they were opposed by the states in the region. Moab was included in this broad sweep of affairs, although the state is not named until the following century in Assyrian records. According to the annals of Shalmaneser III, a coalition of states in the region opposed him in battle in 853 BCE. Ahab of Israel is listed in a manner suggesting that he was a ringleader of the coalition. Neither Moab nor Judah is named in the list of coalition members, but possibly both played a supporting role to Ahab, so that the forces they contributed were considered his. Indeed, this is almost certain for Moab, if it was still a vassal to Israel at the time. It is also possible, indeed likely, that the rebellion of Mesha and Moab against Israel was set in motion by the pressure exerted by the Assyrians on Israel.

With the rise of TIGLATH-PILESER III (745–727 BCE) to power in Assyria came imposition of vassal status on several states in the region, including Moab. Since Moab had access to an important trading route and proximity to the Arab tribes living on the edge of sedentary existence, the Assyrians were particularly interested in control of their territory. This is a model later followed closely by the Romans in Transjordan as they sought to shore up their eastern front and to profit from lucrative trade in the region.

Moab appears several times in Assyrian lists of states providing tribute. Whatever role Moab may have had earlier in opposing Assyrian encroachment in the region, it eventually became a vassal, as did the Ammonites and the Edomites. The fact that these other Transjordanian states are also among the vassals is strong indication of Assyrian interest in the trading connections those states had with Arabia. Thus Moab is listed among those bearing tribute in the reigns of Tiglath-pileser III, Sargon II, Sennacherib, Esarhaddon, and Ashurbanipal, covering a period of 100 years or more. Four Moabite kings are also named: Salamanu, Kamoshnabdi, Mutsuri, and Kamoshhaltu. Two of these are theophoric names and reflect the veneration of the patron deity Chemosh. The name Salamanu is taken by some interpreters also as a theophoric name, representing veneration of a Canaanite deity, Salman. If this is correct, it would be evidence for the name of another deity in the Moabite pantheon. Others, however, are reticent to make the connection with another Canaanite deity and see the name instead related to the term **slm** (שלם, "peace" or "fulfillment").

During the reign of Ashurbanipal, the Moabite king Kamoshhaltu fought against Amuladin, the king of Qedar, defeating him and handing him over to Assyria. It is the Assyrian king who provides a brief notice of the affair, and multiple entries of it were included in the Assyrian archives. One suspects that the military action was based on a combination of local tensions between Moab and the Arabian coalition centered at Qedar, and the loyalty pledged by Moab to the Assyrian overlord. The Moabite king may have seized an opportunity to expand his influence in the region and to curry favor with the imperial power to the east in capturing a pesky rebel.

The fate of Moab during the transition to Babylonian hegemony is unknown. There were multiple Babylonian campaigns in the region, two of which were directed at Judah (598/97; 587/86). According to 2 Kgs 24:2, there were bands of Moabites and Ammonites who preyed on Judah during the reign of Jehoiakim. One can only speculate whether these bands had any connection to Babylonian policy or instead came from local warlords (or something similar) taking advantage of a neighbor's weakness. A few years later, Zedekiah attempted to organize opposition to Babylon, and Moab was invited to join the ranks (Jer 27:1-3; ca. 594 BCE).

According to the Jewish historian Josephus (*Ant.* 10.181–83), Nebuchadnezzar campaigned in the region in his twenty-third year (582 BCE). He reports that both Ammon and Moab were defeated by the Babylonians. As far as historical records go, this was the end of the political state of Moab. The extended oracle against Moab in Jer 48 likely reflects some of the destruction brought upon the country by the Babylonians (compare Ezek 25:8-11).

The postexilic book of Judith describes the Moabites as working in concert with the Ammonites to advise Nebuchadnezzar about the characteristics of the Israelites (Jdt 5:1-24). One can imagine the Ammonites and Moabites in a cooperative venture, but the book of Judith has several historical inaccuracies, and it is unlikely that it reflects any independent knowledge of Moabite history. Instead, the book illustrates the postexilic author's perception of Moabites and Ammonites as enemies.

D. Religion and Culture

The primary sources for Moabite religion originate from Moab itself. In addition to the fragmentary Moabite monumental texts, there are a number of Moabite seal and seal impressions from the Iron Age (8th–7th cent. BCE) that represent cultural traits. These seals preserve both epigraphic and iconographic materials. The OT offers supplementary materials to these primary sources.

Mesha's inscription identifies Chemosh as the patron deity of Moab. This profile of Moab is consistent with the OT, which twice addresses Moab as the "people of Chemosh" (Num 21:29; Jer 48:46), and refers to Chemosh six other times. Moab belongs to Chemosh. A corresponding term in Hebrew is used to identify Israel as the "people of Yahweh" (Judg 5:11; 2 Sam 1:12; Ezek 36:20). In Mesha's inscription the state religion of Moab appears monolatrous, although there are other deities mentioned. The term "state religion" needs elaboration, however, since it essentially stands for the religion of the royal house. How widespread or exclusive the veneration of Chemosh was among the inhabitants of Moab is unknown, but it is likely that the deity provided a primary identity marker for the region. Mesha's inscription represents Moabite identity from the perspective of his own role as king, unifier of the land, and servant of Chemosh. The king reports that he had built "this high place" in Qarhoh for Chemosh because the deity had delivered Mesha from foreign threat (lines 3–4). Apparently, the inscription, which was carved into a basalt stele, was erected in or near the sacred precincts of a Moabite shrine. Qarhoh is likely the royal quarter or fortified acropolis of Dibon. The Moabite term translated as "high place" (**bmt** במת) is cognate to the Hebrew term **bamah** (בָּמָה), used to describe religious shrines.

The Moabite king interprets the political misfortune of Moab as a result of Chemosh's anger with the people (line 5). Similarly, the turning of Moab's fortunes is due to Chemosh's favorable action (line 9). When Mesha defeated the Israelites living in the city of Ataroth, he killed its inhabitants as an offering to Chemosh (lines 12–13). Similarly, Mesha devoted the Israelite inhabitants of Nebo to ritual destruction (lines 14–17). The verb used in line 17 is **khrm** (חרם), a Moabite cognate to the Hebrew term for a similar act (*see* DESTROY, UTTERLY). The death of the enemy is understood in ritual terms as a sacrifice to the victorious deity. It is possible that the perplexing reference in 2 Kgs 3:27, where the Moabite king apparently sacrifices his son, is related to this conviction of the power of human sacrifice.

The king understood that Moab's patron deity revealed his will through recognizable means, since the inscription reports twice that Chemosh "spoke" to him. Perhaps these are references to a communication received by a priest or prophet and reported to the royal court. The content of the first communication was a command to go and take Nebo from Israel, a task that Mesha successfully completed. The second comes from line 32, where Chemosh commands the king to go and fight against Horonaim.

Two other deities are named in the inscription. Line 17 makes reference to Ashtar-Chemosh and line 18 contains reference to Yahweh, the divine name of the Israelite deity. With respect to the latter, it is the earliest secure reference to the personal name of Israel's God outside of the OT. It comes in the context of the battle over Nebo, and the reference to dragging the vessels of Yahweh suggests that some form of a shrine to Israel's God was located in Nebo. The biblical text does not preserve any reference to a temple or high place at Nebo, but the association of the immediate area with Moses and his death (Deut 34:1) offers an intriguing background for the possibility of such an institution in Nebo. Moreover, the cultic site of Baal-peor (Num 25) is near Nebo, so it is understandable that the Israelite inhabitants of Nebo would have an alternative to the Baal of Peor for cultic service. One cannot tell from the king's inscription whether the worship of Yahweh had held any interest for Moabites. The ritual humiliation of Yahweh's vessels was likely intended as a sign that Chemosh and Moab had triumphed over Israel and Yahweh. On the other hand, there are indications that the worship of Chemosh was carried out in Jerusalem by the Moabite wife of Solomon (1 Kgs 11:1, 7-8). The vehemence of the rejection of that high place by the biblical writers may indicate, however, that the Moabite spouses were not the only persons to offer sacrifice and worship to Chemosh. So, correspondingly, it is possible that some inhabitants of the Moabite tableland would have worshiped Yahweh in Nebo or elsewhere.

Interpreters have long debated the meaning of the hyphenated name Ashtar-Chemosh in line 17. On the one hand, it may be simply a variant way to refer to Chemosh, not unlike the reference to Yahweh Elohim (usually translated "the LORD God") in Gen 2:4. There are references to a male deity name Ashtar/ Athtar in Ugaritic and Arabian texts, and it may be that Chemosh, who is himself mentioned in the ANE as early as the EBLA TEXTS, is to be identified with Ashtar. Not only are combination names for deities a recognized phenomenon in the ANE, there is also the related phenomenon of eventually identifying deities from different pantheons who have similar roles or profiles. On the other hand, Ashtar could be a female deity name (similar to that of Ishtar, ASTARTE, Attar in cognate languages), so that Ashtar-Chemosh is a reference to the divine spouse of Chemosh. On the basis of current knowledge, it is not possible to determine conclusively which of these options is correct, but the balance of probability seems to fall on the former option. Nevertheless, even if this is the better reading of the text, it does not preclude the possibility that Chemosh had a divine spouse.

Moabite seals and seal impressions can provide both epigraphic and iconographic indications about Moabite culture and religion. Several epigraphic seals make explicit reference to Chemosh. Indeed, the use of the name Chemosh is a primary reason to identify the seal as Moabite. Another reason, where the name is lacking, is the script itself (paleography). Two examples of theophoric names from seals are **kmshykhy** ("Chemosh gives life") and **kmshl** ("Chemosh is God"). These theophoric names follow patterns seen in Hebrew, Aramaic, Ammonite, and Edomite seals, where the patron deity of a people or city forms a part of a personal name.

With respect to Moabite names, the inscription of Mesha has a partial gap where the king provides his patronym, but a portion of the father's name survives. It is a theophoric name with Chemosh as the first element, but the second element is missing. The fragmentary Moabite inscription recovered from modern Karak, however, preserves a portion of a line that reads **shyt mlk m**ʾ**b h** (...king of Moab...). Scholars have plausibly suggested that the missing name is **[km]shyt** ("Chemosh will grant" or "Chemosh gives/has given") and that this is the patronym to be restored in line 1 of the Mesha inscription. If the fragmentary Karak inscription is correctly restored at this point, then its "author" is likely Mesha or **[km]shyt**.

The iconography of Moabite seals contains symbols for the sun, moon, and stars. A number of scholars have concluded from this fact that Moabite culture and religion in Iron Age II was shaped by interest in astral signs and that it identified cosmic phenomena with the divine world. This is a pattern in Semitic cultures, so Moab would not be unique in these aspects. On the other hand, the identity of astral symbols with Moabite religion is speculation. Such symbols on seals may not be strong religious symbols, but something else altogether such as motifs reflecting cosmic order and seasons. Nevertheless, the balance of probability is a link between astral signs and Moabite religion(s). One wonders, e.g., whether an astral sign represents Chemosh. One option would be the sun, given its prominence and that of Chemosh to the life of Moab. Another would be a prominent star like Venus, especially since the male Canaanite deity Athtar was associated with Venus by Arab tribes (line 17). Given the multiplicity of the symbols, it is possible that these symbols represent collectively a pantheon of deities to account for the phenomenal world. It could mean that Chemosh is the head of the pantheon, or rather, he is simply a prominent member (not the creator or father of the gods), whose role in the pantheon is that of patron or champion of Moab.

The OT preserves two theophoric place names on the tableland, where the divine element in the name is BAAL—a common noun for "master" or "owner" used for a number of deities in the ANE. The two sites are Baal-meon and Baal-peor. The former occurs in both the OT (Num 32:38; 1 Chr 5:8; Ezek 25:9) and Mesha's inscription (lines 9, 30). In both Josh 13:17 and the Mesha stele (line 30) the site is also named Beth-baal-meon. The ancient site is to be located in or very near the modern village of Main, 8 mi. southwest of modern Madaba (ancient Medeba), where the tableland begins its steep descent to the shore of the Dead Sea. Inclusion of the term **beth** (בַּיִת, "house") raises the prospect of a temple or shrine at the site. The noun baʿal (בַּעַל) could refer to the god Chemosh as the baʿal revealed (and worshiped) at the site, to a local deity, or to one more widely known.

More information is preserved about the site of Baal-peor, which is located west of Medeba, perhaps at ʿUyun Musa ("springs of Moses") or nearby on one of the promontories overlooking the Jordan Valley. According to Num 25 the Israelites involved themselves with Moabite women, who enticed them to worship their gods. The people are described as "yoked to Baal-peor" (25:5), a phrase that is more easily taken as a reference to a deity than to a location. These activities are remembered elsewhere as apostasy toward the Lord (Ps 106:28-29; Hos 9:10). As with Baal-meon, there is no indication of the identity of the divine master or owner celebrated at the site. Possibly the people of Baal-peor worshiped a local deity who was bound to his revelation at that place and was thus known as the [divine] master of Peor. One might compare the reference to BAAL-ZEBUB, the god of Philistine Ekron, apparently known for healing (2 Kgs 1:1-4). Yet, a powerful deity like BAAL-SHAMEM, who rose to prominence along with the economic success of Phoenicia, could also be reflected in the name of Baal-meon or Baal-peor.

These two references from the OT raise more questions than they answer about the varieties of religious devotion in Moab. On the one hand, the available evidence indicates that Chemosh was the patron deity of Moab and venerated by the royal house. On the other hand, several deities were likely venerated among the population groups of greater Moab, some of whom would be common to the Iron Age in the southern Levant, and others perhaps had a more regional flavor.

In spite of the ancestral accounts that recognize a certain kinship between Israel and Moab, the dominant reaction in the OT to Moabite religion and culture is negative. In Deut 23:3-6 Moabites and Ammonites are forbidden entry into the assembly of Israel. Historical reasons are cited for this prohibition. This negative view of Moab continues into the postexilic period. The fictional novel Judith represents the Moabites and the Ammonites as Israel's enemies and describes how these groups advised Nebuchadnezzar about the characteristics of the Israelites (Jdt 5:1-24; *see* JUDITH, BOOK OF).

Bibliography: S. Ahituv. "A New Moabite Inscription." *Israel Museum Studies in Archaeology* 2 (2003) 3–10; P. Bienkowski, ed. *Early Edom and Moab: The Beginning of the Iron Age in Southern Jordan* (1992); P. M. Michèle Daviau. "Hirbet el-Mudēyine in Its Landscape: Iron Age Towns, Forts, and Shrines." *ZDPV* 122 (2006) 13–30; P. M. Michèle Daviau. "Moab's Northern Border: Khirbat al-Mudayna on the Wadi ath-Thamad." *BA* 60 (1997) 222–28; A. Dearman, ed. *Studies in the Mesha Inscription and Moab* (1989); P. E. Dion and P. M. Michèle Daviau. "An Inscribed Incense Altar of Iron Age II at Hirbet el Mudeyine (Jordan)." *ZDPV* 116 (2000) 1–13; J. A. Emerton. "The Value of the Moabite Stone as a Historical Resource." *VT* 52 (2002) 483–92; Chang-Ho C. Ji. "Archaeological Survey of the Dhiban Plateau." *AJA* 101 (1997) 499–500; B. Jones. *Howling over Moab: Irony and Rhetoric in Isaiah 15–16* (1996); A. Lemaire. "'House of David' Restored in Moabite Inscription." *BAR* 20 (1994) 30–37; G. L. Mattingly et al. "Al-Karak Resources Project 1997: Excavations at Khirbat al-Mudaybi'a." *ADAJ* 43 (1999) 127–44; J. M. Miller, ed. *Archaeological Survey of the Kerak Plateau* (1991); A. F. Rainey. "Mesha' and Syntax." *The Land That I Will Show You: Essays on the History and Archaeology of the Ancient Near East in Honor of J. Maxwell Miller.* J. A. Dearman and M. P. Graham, eds. (2001) 287–307; B. Routledge. *Moab in the Iron Age: Hegemony, Polity, Archaeology* (2004).

J. ANDREW DEARMAN

MOABITE STONE. The Moabite Stone, also called the Mesha Stele, is a thirty-four-line inscription on a large black basalt pillar written in a Transjordanian dialect having close affinity with classical Hebrew. It recounts the achievements of MESHA, the king of Moab, a figure also known from the OT (2 Kgs 3:4). The inscription provides a Moabite perspective on the rebellion by Moab against Israel recorded in 2 Kgs 1:1; 3:4-27. It is the longest Iron Age inscription found on either side of the Jordan River and the primary source of information about the ancient Moabite language. The inscription

Figure 1: Victory stele of Mesha, king of Moab. Black basalt. Louvre, Paris, France

itself may be dated to ca. 840 BCE, recounting events occurring sometime not long before during the mid-9th cent. BCE.

The Moabite Stone was first made known to the West through an Alsatian-born Anglican missionary named F. A. Klein, working in Moab in 1868. After viewing the inscription with the help of Bedouin near modern-day Dhiban (*see* DIBON), he attempted to acquire it with the aid of the Prussian government. While his efforts ultimately failed, new interest came from Charles Clermont-Ganneau, who was more successful. But before Clermont-Ganneau could take possession of the inscription, it was shattered by locals who resented pressures from Turkish authorities in Palestine. Fortunately, Clermont-Ganneau had arranged to have a paper impression made of the inscription prior to its destruction. This impression, called a squeeze, was inexpert, but it is the sole basis for our knowledge of the content of approximately one-third of the stone. Clermont-Ganneau eventually acquired the large majority of the pieces. After some time, all the recovered fragments made their way to the Louvre, where the reconstructed stele has been housed since 1875.

The Moabite Stone memorializes the military exploits and domestic accomplishments of Mesha during his reign over Moab. It depicts Mesha as the deliverer of his people, and this message is underscored by his very name, meaning "savior." While the rule of his father, Chemosh-yat, was characterized by weakness and foreign oppression, the Moabite Stone depicts Mesha as the legitimate successor to the throne who is favored by a Moabite god, CHEMOSH, to bring an end to this oppression and to restore order to his country.

The message of the inscription may be organized topically into four parts. It consists of an introduction (lines 1–4), followed by three larger sections in which two narratives of various military campaigns (lines 4–21; 31–34) flank a central account of Mesha's domestic accomplishments in and around Dibon (lines 21–31).

After Mesha's self-presentation, the inscription conveys the occasion for its composition: "I made this high place for Chemosh in Qarhoh [. . .] because he delivered me from all the kings and because he made me gloat over all my enemies" (lines 3–4; author's trans.). The role of Chemosh in guaranteeing Mesha victory in his military campaigns is heavily emphasized throughout the battle accounts that follow. Yet the larger purpose of the inscription is to legitimate Mesha's rule by detailing both his military victories and his success in reestablishing order, particularly in Dibon.

The first major section, spanning half the total inscription, is devoted primarily to campaigns north of Dibon. As is typical of ANE conquest accounts, these narratives paint Moab's success and the enemy's failure in black and white, and the language is hyperbolic and repetitive. Its focus is the reclamation of Moabite territory from Israel. Though OMRI had "oppressed Moab for many days" (line 5; author's trans.), Mesha reversed Moab's fortunes during the reign of Omri's "son." He boasts, "I gloated over him and over his house. And Israel utterly perished forever" (line 7; author's trans.). Through Chemosh's favor, Mesha is able to reclaim MEDEBA, formerly in Omri's possession. He displaces the Gadites from ATAROTH, claiming to have killed all the people of the city. At the behest of Chemosh, he attacks Nebo in Israelite territory, plundering cultic objects from a shrine to Yahweh. Mesha even suggests that the Moabites killed 7,000 people in Nebo in a single morning. The inscription also records success at JAHAZ, which Mesha seized "to annex it to Dibon" (line 21; author's trans.). Thus Mesha not only restores old borders, but expands Moab by adding new territory from what was once Israelite land.

The second section is dedicated to recounting how Mesha created an edenic, orderly society in and around Dibon by (re)building fortifications and cosmic foundations. While Chemosh's favor was the driving force behind Mesha's military successes, his domestic accomplishments are depicted as personal achievements. "It was I who built Qarhoh: the walls of the parks and the walls of the citadel. It was I who built its gates, and it was I who built its towers. It was I who built the palace, and it was I who made the retaining walls of the reservoir for water in the middle of the city" (lines 21–24; author's trans.). Such exploits are found in other ANE royal inscriptions and in the OT (Eccl 2:4-6), symbolizing monarchical mastery over nature by cultivating land for security, sustenance, and pleasure. Still more striking is Mesha's claim to have used Israelites for slave labor in these projects. In this way, those who had caused Moab's chaos are now instrumental in reestablishing its order. As the ideological center of the Mesha inscription, Dibon and its epicenter in the acropolis of Qarhoh are depicted as the navel of the earth, much like Jerusalem and Zion in the OT. This section also makes mention of a few other building projects in the area, but without the attention given to those in Dibon.

The final section begins yet another account of military conquest, including action against HORONAIM, south of Dibon. Unfortunately, the inscription is very fragmentary at this point. However, there remains the possibility that it originally mentioned the house of DAVID, as proposed by André Lemaire. If correct, this may indicate that Mesha undertook a campaign in the south against Judahite territory, much as he had done against Israelite territory in the north.

The conflict between Moab and Israel narrated on the Moabite Stone is also mentioned in the OT: "Now King Mesha of Moab was a sheep breeder, who used to deliver to the king of Israel one hundred thousand lambs, and the wool of one hundred thousand rams. But when Ahab died, the king of Moab rebelled against the king of Israel" (2 Kgs 3:4-5). However, it proves difficult to harmonize the campaign narrative in 2 Kgs 3:6-27 with the accounts on the Moabite Stone. While some believe that the Kings narrative records a different set of events than those recounted in the Mesha inscription, many scholars understand these narratives as providing two different perspectives on the same events, each heavily shaped by the author's selective judgment.

One challenge to reconciling the perspectives of the two texts relates to the figures of Omri and his successor, mentioned in lines 4–8 of the Moabite Stone. Mesha claims that Omri occupied Medeba "during his time and half the time of his **bn** (בן)—forty years" (line 8; author's trans.). If one understands the term **bn** used in the inscription to mean "son" in the sense of immediate offspring or successor, then AHAB is in view. However, on this interpretation, the "forty years" in the inscription becomes problematic. Further, 2 Kings recounts that Moab rebelled after the death of Ahab (1:1; 3:5). To solve this, one might interpret the number forty as a round number, simply meant to signify a long period of time. Alternately, the term **bn** used in the Mesha inscription may denote Omri's grandson rather than his son, as it also sometimes does in the OT (Gen 31:55 [Heb. 32:1]; 2 Chr 22:9). If this latter interpretation is accepted, the Moabite Stone likely refers to Omri's grandson, JEHORAM, who, in alliance with JEHOSHAPHAT of Judah, took action against the Moabite rebellion in ca. 850 BCE (2 Kgs 3:6-27). The use of the term typically denoting "son" on the Moabite Stone is likely motivated by the parallel between the fates of Israelite and Moabite kings that Mesha wishes to create. While Omri had oppressed Moab, his "son" Jehoram lost control of it; while Chemosh-yat had been oppressed by Israel, his son, Mesha, regained control of Moab and gloated over Israel. *See* ARCHAEOLOGY; MOAB, MOABITES; OBELISK; STELE.

Bibliography: Andrew Dearman, ed. *Studies in the Mesha Inscription and Moab* (1989); J. A. Emerton. "Lines 25–26 of the Moabite Stone and a Recently-Discovered Inscription." *VT* 55 (2005) 293–303. J. A. Emerton. "The Value of the Moabite Stone as an Historical Source." *VT* 52 (2002) 483–92; Siegfried Horn. "Why the Moabite Stone Was Blown to Pieces." *BAR* 12 (1986) 50–61; André Lemaire. "'House of David' Restored in Moabite Inscription." *BAR* 20 (1994) 30–37; P. Kyle McCarter Jr. *Ancient Inscriptions: Voices from the Biblical World* (1996); Simon B. Parker. *Stories in Scripture and Inscriptions: Comparative Studies on Narratives in Northwest Semitic Inscriptions and the Hebrew Bible* (1997); K. A. D. Smelik. *Converting the Past: Studies in Ancient Israelite and Moabite Historiography* (1992).

SCOTT C. JONES

MOADIAH moh'uh-dī'uh [מוֹעַדְיָה mo'adhyah]. A priestly family whose head was listed as PILTAI when JOIAKIM was high priest (Neh 12:17). Perhaps the same as MAADIAH (Neh 12:5).

MOAT [חָרוּץ kharuts]. A protective trench around a city. Gabriel's revelation of the rebuilt Jerusalem describes such a feature, signifying the complete restoration and fortification of the city (Dan 9:25).

MOCHMUR mok'muhr [Μοχμούρ Mochmour]. Mochmur is a brook southeast of Dothaim (Jdt 7:18). Scholars have asserted that it is Wadi Makhfuriyeh, Wadi Qana, or a fictitious brook.

MOCK. *See* SCOFFER; TAUNT.

MODAD. *See* ELDAD AND MEDAD; MEDAD.

MODEIN moh'deen [Μωδείν Mōdein]. The town of Modein was the traditional home of the family of the HASMONEANS or Maccabees. The location is generally thought to be at Tell al-Ras, close to the village of El-Midya, whose name seems to derive from the name of the Hellenistic-age site. The location is in the Shephelah, the foothill transition region between the high hill country and the coastal plain, with Lydda (Lod) about 10 km to the west and Beth-horon about 10 km to the southeast. It seems to have been in a strategic position vis-à-vis the pass from the coastal plain to Beth-horon. Modein itself is in an accessible and level area on the Wadi en-Natuf, and would have been easily accessible to Lydda, the regional capital. Yet it also borders the Western Slopes on the north and the Gophna Hills on the east, both rugged, mountainous regions. This made it a convenient base for operations during the Maccabean Revolt (168/7–165/4 BCE; *see* MACCABEES, MACCABEAN REVOLT) because the Maccabean fighters could easily escape into the mountains if threatened by Seleucid troops, as they did on a number of occasions (e.g., 1 Macc 2:28).

Modein does not seem to be referred to in the OT but first appears in 1 Macc 2. As the religious persecutions under Antiochus IV began, MATTATHIAS supposedly left Jerusalem (with his sons) to reside in Modein (2:1). Although it is not stated in this passage, we infer from the various other passages in 1 Maccabees that Modein was the ancestral home of the Hasmoneans (esp. 2:70; 9:19). According to 1 Macc 2, Mattathias did not escape the persecutions, for Seleucid soldiers came to the village and attempted to force the local people to participate in a pagan sacrifice. Mattathias refused and then, when the soldiers persisted, killed a Jew who was complying as well as the Seleucid officer who was enforcing the command. He and his sons then fled into the hills, to begin the resistance to Seleucid oppression (1 Macc 2:28, 42-48). Not long afterward Mattathias died, and his sons buried him in the tomb of his ancestors in Modein (1 Macc 2:70).

When JUDAS ambushed the Seleucid commander Seron's force (1 Macc 3:16), it was at the ascent to Beth-horon, which, as noted above, was near Modein. This is another indication that Judas was probably operating out of Modein at the time. First Maccabees 6:18-63 describes a confrontation between LYSIAS and Judas' army over the citadel in Jerusalem: the Syrian army besieged Beth-zur, and Judas marched from Jerusalem to do battle with Lysias. Second Maccabees 13 seems to give a parallel account, stating that Judas camped near Modein before doing battle (2 Macc 13:14). This is a very strange statement since Beth-zur is quite a distance from Modein. This suggests that the author of 2 Maccabees did not have a good knowledge of Palestinian topography (unlike the author of 1 Maccabees) but inserted Modein because of its associations with Judas in other contexts.

Later, when Judas fell on the field of battle, he was buried in the ancestral tomb in Modein, just as his father had been (1 Macc 9:19). Twenty years later SIMON buried his brother JONATHAN in Modein (1 Macc 13:25-30). This time Simon erected an impressive monument to his father and brothers (*see* TOMB). According to the text, Simon's monument consisted of a stone monument over the tomb itself, with polished stone in front and behind. Apparently, in the immediate vicinity he set up seven pyramids for his father and mother and four brothers (presumably the seventh was for himself). Among them were columns on which were mounted suits of armor (a common Greek trophy format at the time, representing victory), with ships carved beside the armor. Judah did not have a navy at this time, but supposedly these could be seen by seafarers, though the passage must be referring to the columns rather than the carvings (which could not possibly be seen at that distance). Although the monument was still there "to this day" (13:30) at the time when 1 Maccabees was written, no such monument has so far been found by archaeologists. The final mention of Modein is in 1 Macc 16:4, according to which John HYRCANUS camped there with a Jewish army before confronting and defeating Cendebeus, the commander of Antiochus VII.

LESTER L. GRABBE

MODERN VERSIONS OF THE BIBLE. *See* VERSIONS, ENGLISH; VERSIONS, MODERN (NON-ENGLISH).

MOʿED QATAN [מוֹעֵד קָטָן moʿedh qatan]. Means "Minor Festival." A tractate in the second order of the MISHNAH, Moʿed ("Appointed Times"), on the observances for minor religious holidays.

MOETH. *See* NOADIAH.

MOLADAH moh'luh-duh [מוֹלָדָה **moladhah**]. A town in the extreme south "toward the boundary of Edom" (Josh 15:21), first said to have been allotted to Judah (Josh 15:26), then to Simeon (Josh 19:2), with the clarification that "[Simeon's] inheritance lay within the inheritance of the tribe of Judah" (Josh 19:1). Moladah was also one of the villages outside Jerusalem settled by returning exiles (Neh 11:26). Its name is derived from the Hebrew verb **yaladh** (יָלַד), "to give birth." Moladah has often been associated with Khirbet el-Waten, east-northeast of Beer-sheba. Tell el-Milkh has also been proposed as identifying Moladah.

RALPH K. HAWKINS

MOLDING [זֵר **zer**]. A golden band that trimmed certain furnishings of the TABERNACLE: the ARK OF THE COVENANT (Exod 25:11; 37:2), the table for the BREAD OF PRESENCE (Exod 25:24-25; 37:11-12), and the incense ALTAR (Exod 30:3-4; 37:26-27). In addition to its obvious ornamental value, the molding may have reinforced the structure of these items, which were designed to be portable. However, the exact position, size, and function of the moldings remain uncertain.

JOEL MARCUS LEMON

MOLDY [נִקֻּדִים **niqqudhim**]. With tattered garb and "dry and moldy" provisions, Gibeonites pretended to be from a far country, convincing Joshua to spare them (Josh 9:5, 12).

MOLE [חֲפַרְפָּרָה **khafarparah**]. An animal that lives below ground. Alternately identified as "shrew," and appearing only in Isa 2:20 as an emendation of the MT (**lakhpor peroth** לַחְפֹּר פֵּרוֹת) on the basis of other Hebrew and Greek manuscripts (1QIsa[a]: **khprprym** חפרפרים; Theodotian: **pharpharōth** φαρφαρώθ). In this text, moles are paired with bats, both of which occupy the dark places where people cast their idols of silver and gold on the day of the LORD (compare Isa 2:11-12). *See* ANIMALS OF THE BIBLE.

JOEL MARCUS LEMON

MOLECH, MOLOCH moh'lek, moh'lok [מֹלֶךְ **molekh**; Μόλοχ **Moloch**]. *Molech* occurs several times in the OT as the name of a detested god associated with child sacrifice (Lev 18:21; 20:2-5; 2 Kgs 23:10; Jer 32:35; see also Isa 30:33; 57:9; Jer 7:31; 19:5; Zeph 1:5; *Molech* in 1 Kgs 11:7 is a slip for "Milcom," compare vv. 5 and 33). The alternative spelling *Moloch* is one of the renderings found in the LXX and also appears in Acts 7:43 in a quotation from the LXX's inaccurate translation of Amos 5:26.

In 1935 Otto Eissfeldt argued that the word *Molech* in the OT was not the name of a god, as universally had been held, but the name of a sacrifice. He deduced this on the basis of Punic inscriptions, where **mlk** denotes a sacrifice, including (when the word **ʾadham** [אָדָם, "human"] is added) a human sacrifice. However, although Punic **mlk** is certainly a sacrificial term, recent scholarship has reaffirmed that OT Molech is equally certainly the name of a god (Heider; Day). Thus, among other reasons, Lev 20:5 condemns those who go whoring after (NRSV, "prostitute themselves to") Molech, and, whereas the OT frequently speaks elsewhere of whoring after other gods, such language is never used with regard to a sacrifice.

There is, moreover, evidence that Molech was a Canaanite underworld god. The Ugaritic texts know of a god **mlk** who dwelled at Ashtaroth, the same place as **rpʾu**, whose name indicates an underworld connection, and in another Ugaritic text **mlk** is paired with the underworld god Resheph. Moreover, two Akkadian texts equate the Mesopotamian underworld god Nergal with a deity named Malik. Similarly, Isa 57:9 locates the dwelling of Molech (reading **molekh** for Heb. **melekh** [מֶלֶךְ]) in Sheol. Again, the OT Molech sacrifices took place at the Topheth ("incinerator") in the valley of Hinnom, just outside Jerusalem; if Molech was an underworld god, this would explain why Gehenna (deriving from the Aramaic name for the valley of Hinnom) later came to denote hell. (There is no ancient evidence for the view that Gehenna became a term for hell because of a constantly burning rubbish dump in this valley.) No other suggestion regarding Molech's identity (e.g., Baal, Mot, Adad-milki, Milcom, Athtar, Chemosh, Shahar and Shalem) can claim such a weight of evidence. Quite likely, the vowels of the name Molech have been distorted with those of the Hebrew word **bosheth** (בֹּשֶׁת), "shame" (a term sometimes used in the OT of Baal), as also happened with the name of the goddess Ashtoreth (originally Ashtart). Originally, the name of the god was probably vocalized not as **molekh** but as **melokh** (מְלֹךְ) or as **melekh**, "king."

Some scholars have questioned whether Molech worship really involved child sacrifice and argued that it was a case of a more harmless dedicatory ritual involving fire, but this is certainly incorrect. Some scholars who have taken this view have queried whether the OT itself even claims to refer to human sacrifice, but the Hebrew expression "offer up in the fire" (**haʿavir baʾesh** הֶעֱבִיר בָּאֵשׁ, sometimes translated "pass through the fire") undoubtedly implies sacrifice (compare Exod 13:12, 15, where **haʿavir** "offer up" [author's trans.; NRSV, "set apart"] explicitly refers to sacrifice, and Ezek 20:26, where **haʿavir**, used of humans, is said to be horrifying). Others, while accepting that the OT mentions human sacrifice, have seen this as unreliable polemic. However, human sacrifice is known elsewhere in the Canaanite world, most especially in the case of Punic child sacrifice, which is attested not only by Punic inscriptions and archaeological evidence but also by references in classical writers. There is therefore no need to doubt the reality of child sacrifices to Molech. These were doubtless a desperate measure for desperate times: the OT allusions suggest that the high point of Molech worship was in Judah in the 8th–6th cent. BCE, a period of considerable political distress. Bearing in mind that Molech was an underworld god, it is attractive to suppose that Judah's "covenant with death," alluded to in Isa 28:15 as a means to avert national catastrophe, is a reference to the Molech cult. Kings Ahaz and Manasseh (2 Kgs 16:3; 21:6) are said to have offered up their sons in sacrifice, and this is most naturally understood as referring to the Molech cult. The cult is said to have been abolished by Josiah in his reform of 621 BCE (2 Kgs 23:10) but seems to have briefly revived subsequently (Isa 57:5, 9).

Some scholars have supposed that, when the OT speaks of sacrifices to Molech, it is really referring to the offering of the FIRSTBORN in sacrifice to Yahweh (Exod 22:29 [Heb. 22:28]; Ezek 20:25-26). This view has been encouraged by Jer 32:35, where Yahweh denies commanding sacrifices to Molech. However, in Deut 17:3 Yahweh similarly denies having commanded the worship of sun, moon, or stars. Moreover, quite apart from the fact that the sacrifices to Molech did not take place at Yahweh's Temple in Jerusalem, but rather at a separate site in the valley of Hinnom, two further serious objections to this view need to be noted. First, when the OT refers to the offering of the firstborn, it never makes mention of Molech, and, when it speaks of the sacrifices to Molech, it never alludes to the offering of firstborn. Second, the sacrifices to Molech are said to have included both girls and boys (2 Kgs 23:10; Jer 32:35), whereas the offering of the firstborn related exclusively to boys (Exod 22:29 [Heb. 22:28]; 34:19-20).

Bibliography: John Day. *Molech: A God of Human Sacrifice in the Old Testament* (1989); Otto Eissfeldt. *Molk als Opferbegriff im Punischen und Hebräischen und das Ende des Gottes Moloch* (1935); George C. Heider. *The Cult of Molek: A Reassessment* (1985); Jon D. Levenson. *The Death and Resurrection of the Beloved Son: The Transformation of Child Sacrifice in Judaism and Christianity* (1993).

JOHN DAY

MOLID moh'lid [מוֹלִיד **molidh**]. Son of Abishur and his wife Abihail in Judah's genealogy; also a descendant of Jerahmeel (1 Chr 2:29).

MOLTEN SEA. *See* SEA, MOLTEN.

MOMENT. *See* TIME.

MONARCH, MONARCHY. *See* KING, KINGSHIP.

MONEY, COINS [כֶּסֶף **kesef**; ἀργύριον **argyrion**, κέρμα **kerma**, νόμισμα **nomisma**, χαλκός **chalkos**, χρῆμα **chrēma**, χρυσός **chrysos**]. Money measures relative worth and facilitates the transaction of commodities. It is a reflex of economic action and interaction. Coinage is the minted form of money, standardized in various units. The Bible reflects the whole history of money from bartering, to primitive forms of bullion (precious metal in bars or ingots), to intricately produced forms of officially minted coins. It also contains extensive and varied teachings on the use and misuse of money in various spheres.

A. Terminology

In the OT the term *money* is almost always the word kesef ("silver"), silver being the metal of choice to function as money. This money was not coined, but bullion. The value of money was determined by its weight. The main denomination of money in Semitic languages was the SHEKEL (sheqel שֶׁקֶל; siklos σίκλος), which derives from the root of the word "to weigh." Only during the Persian period in Israel was money stamped in order to identify its value. Though barter persisted into the NT period, the preponderance of references to money here are to coined money, and frequently specified according to their denominations. Generic terms for money derive from the terms for the previous metals, GOLD (chrysos), SILVER (argyrion), and BRONZE (chalkos) that were used to mint coins. The term kerma refers to small copper change (derived from the verb "to cut up," referring to small, cut-up currency). The term chrēma refers to money in the sense of substance or possessions. Only once does the term nomisma (νόμισμα, from which we derive our term *numismatics*) occur in conjunction with the term for tribute (kēnsos κῆνσος), meaning tribute money (Matt 22:19).

B. Early Forms of Money

The origin of money is shrouded in obscurity. The most compelling theory is that money originated from customs of gift exchange. Certainly some of the early mentions of money in the Bible are connected to the exchange of gifts. Upon taking Sarai into his harem, Pharaoh enriched Abram with cattle, servants, and precious metals (Gen 12:16; 13:2). Abraham acquired the title of the cave of Machpelah from Ephron the Hittite for 400 silver shekels. This transaction was ratified through an elaborate rite of exchange (Gen 23:3-20). This detailed account has strong overtones of a well-established routine of gift exchange. Abraham proposed to pay "the full price" or "worth" of the property in silver (Gen 23:9). Finally, the transaction was formalized at that price, "according to the weights current among the merchants" (Gen 23:16). Exchange by way of precious metals alleviated the cumbersome aspects of barter or exchange with commodities such as grain. The archaeological record in Israel, as elsewhere in the ANE, attests to hoards of precious metal, jewelry, ingots, and *Hacksilber* (silver chopped into little pieces) at numerous sites throughout the various periods. Many weights, both marked and unmarked, have also been found.

When the OT refers to money, we should not think of officially stamped coins. Rather, these references are to quantities of weighed precious metals. A common form for bullion was rings bound together in a bundle. Joseph's brothers found their bundles of bullion back in their sacks "in full weight" (Gen 43:21). The unit of the shekel derives from a Semitic root meaning "to weigh." It was a customary unit of weight in the ANE. The dominant system for weights was the Babylonian so-called sexagesimal system, which divided the talent into 60 minas, and the mina into 60 shekels. There were further divisions, as well as competing standards for the precise weight of the shekel (compare Exod 30:13 and 2 Sam 14:26). Transactions involved the transfer of silver ingots, rings, and the like in the appropriate amount. Rings are specifically referred to in Gen 24:22 and Job 42:11. The technical term kikkar (כִּכָּר), translated "talent," explicitly refers to circular shapes (*see* TALENTS; WEIGHTS AND MEASURES).

Other references to money in the ancestral narratives include the reparation paid to Abraham by Abimelech of Gerar (Gen 20:16) and the enslavement of Joseph by his brothers (Gen 37:28). Personal wealth was measured not only by quantity of livestock but also in bullion (Gen 13:2; 24:35). In fact, Joseph's taxation policies in Egypt first took in the more portable bullion (Gen 47:14-16; compare Gen 43:21), and only later less portable forms of wealth (Gen 47:17).

Transactions like these are sprinkled throughout the narratives of ancient Israel. Delilah turned Samson in to Philistine officials in exchange for the hefty commission of 1,100 shekels of silver per official (Judg 16:5). Micah defrauded his mother of a similar amount and later restored it (Judg 17:2). She in turn consecrated 200 shekels for the fabrication of an image of cast metal (Judg 17:4). Ahab offered Naboth money for his proprietary land at the fair market value (1 Kgs 21:2).

There is obscurity surrounding the term qesitah (קְשִׂיטָה), often translated "money" (Gen 33:19; Josh 24:32; Job 42:11). It may refer to bullion in the shape of a lamb. That smaller quantities were frequently melted together, especially for institutional purposes, is clear from various passages. The word used in 2 Kgs 22:9 refers to melting together offerings. Zechariah 11:13 refers to the office of a founder in connection with the Temple. Herodotus details how the Achaemenid temple processed precious metals by melting them down, pouring the liquid into earthenware jars, and breaking the jar after the liquid had cooled and hardened, so that pieces could be cut off (*Hist.* 3.96).

It is not easy to gauge how monetary value was configured. A passage describing Solomonic times specifies the value of an imported Egyptian chariot and horse (1 Kgs 10:29). To consult the prophet Samuel, Saul thought a quarter of a shekel sufficient (1 Sam 9:8). David bought the threshing floor and cattle of Araunah at the mere price of 50 shekels (2 Sam 24:24; but compare 1 Chr 21:25). Preexilic Hebrew inscriptions paint a similar portrait. A late 8th- or early 7th-cent. BCE ostracon from Tell Qasile refers to the import of gold. Later ostraca from Arad and Yavneh-yam mention quantities of silver in the shekel denomination.

Meanwhile, trading with precious metals did not supplant barter. The two systems of exchange coexisted. The ancient states frequently levied and paid tribute in raw materials and livestock (1 Kgs 5:11; 2 Chr 2:10).

C. The Development of Coinage

Among economic historians there is much debate concerning the origins and chronology of minted coinage, first electrum (an alloy of gold and silver) and then silver. The consensus had favored a date in the mid-6th cent. BCE for the beginning of silver coinage, electrum predating it by a century.

Scholars also debate the function of these minted coins. Some have emphasized that the earliest coins were produced by individuals. Others have argued that early patterns of distribution preclude their immediate use for external or internal trade. It is more likely that they were used in government expenditures for convenience's sake and perhaps for profit. Contrary to oft-repeated claims, small fractional units are attested at an early stage, eg., in the 6th-cent. hoard from western Asia Minor. The paucity of evidence for these fractional units in the archaeological record can best be explained from the difficulty to detect such minute entities in the material record. Some have linked the rise of coinage with the agora, intruding on the aristocratic sphere of gift exchange.

Others have broadened the question of the development of coinage in ancient Greece to include social settings or exchange and ideologies of exchange. It is too simplistic to imagine that the development of coinage was simply the result of the expansion of markets, trade, and money use. Modern economic activity makes such distinctions between the subjects and objects of economic activity, between property and social binding relationships, between production and exchange. These distinctions were not as intrinsic to exchange in ancient societies. Neither was there the absolute concept of utility upon which contemporary economic activity is based.

Both in the question of chronology and function, the question of origins is problematic. There were developments of transition in which a point of "origins" is somewhat arbitrary. Moreover, the origin of coinage differed from region to region. In historical study, the chronological and topographical constraints of a historical setting are primary and fundamental. A more fruitful tack is the question of when precious metals began to be minted in standardized form, and functioned as a means of exchange in certain regions. It should be kept in mind that until late into the Roman period coinage and pre-coinage money continued to exist side by side.

D. Early Coinages

The date of electrum coinage is bound up with the date of the Artemisium of Ephesus. Stamped and unstamped electrum pieces, together with unmarked silver, jewelry, and other items were found under the foundation of the temple of Artemis (Artemisium) in Ephesus, probably as a votive foundation deposit to the goddess Artemis. This is the earliest archaeological context for coinage and forms the *terminus ante quem* of electrum coinage. On the basis of the earlier excavations of the Artemisium, scholars fixed the *terminus* of the deposit within the range of 590–560 BCE. Renewed excavations have confirmed the 560 BCE date for the *terminus ante quem* for the deposit. Still, the variety of electrum coins and the supposed evolution of the reverse and obverse types suggests a few decades prior to the construction of the Artemisium. Some of the coins are unmarked, others have marks and/or striations, and some have genuine designs and punches. The various provenances of the coins in the Artemisium deposit probably include Lydia, Phocea, Miletus, and perhaps others. Samos also appears to have issued electrum coins.

Often Herodotus' claim forms the point of departure in the discussion of silver and gold coinage. He wrote that the Lydians were the first he knew of to cut gold and silver into currency (*Hist.* 1.94). Indeed, the name of King Croesus of Lydia (ca. 560–547 BCE) is tied to the transition from electrum to gold and silver. It is quite widely held that Croesus began producing gold and silver coinage, replacing a preexisting electrum coinage. Gold coins were known in antiquity as "Croeseids" (**Kroiseios statēr** [Κροίσειος στατήρ] from a standard-size coin called the statēr [στατήρ]). This famous first gold coin pictured confronting foreparts of lion and bull on the obverse and two square incuse punches on the reverse. Persia under Darius (521–486 BCE) adopted the practice of minting both gold and silver coins. Meanwhile, the Greek cities limited themselves to silver mintings.

The spread of coinage was swift, and by 500 BCE there were established coinages in mainland Greece, Italy, Sicily, and Asia Minor. The three most important Greek mints were Aegina, Corinth, and Athens. The famous owl series of Athens (obverse, Pallas Athena head; reverse, owl with abbreviation of the city) did not begin until 525 BCE. They were preceded by the *Wappenmünzen*, so-called because the diverse obverses are thought to represent the heraldic emblems (*Wappen*) of the individuals who commissioned their production. There were other important mints in Euboea, Boeotia,

Phocis, Corinth, Macedonia, Thrace, Abdera, Thasos, and the Greek colonies in southern Italy and Sicily, such as Sybaris, Rhegium, Acragas, Gela, and Syracuse. In Asia Minor, there were silver issues from Sardis, the region of Caria, the island of Chios, and elsewhere.

The prestige of Athenian coinage throughout the ANE is likely the success of Solon's monetary reforms in the early 6th cent., which ensured purity and stability, combined with the prominence of Athens in the successive centuries. The flow of Greek coins to the Persian Empire began in the second half of the 6th cent. BCE, either under Cyrus II or Cambyses, and increased in the 5th cent., diminishing only with the Peloponnesian War (431–404 BCE).

The Achaemenid rulers did not introduce an imperial coinage immediately upon their territorial conquests. When Cyrus conquered Lydia, he probably left the mint of Sardis intact. Important administrative, social, and economic reforms were enacted around the turn of the 5th cent. BCE by Darius I (522–486 BCE). An effective system of imperial taxation was inaugurated and maintained throughout the 200 years of Achaemenid control. As a corollary, international trade was cultivated and promoted, not in the least under the leadership of the Phoenician cities. Sometime around 500 BCE the central administration struck the first gold DARIC (ʾadharkon אֲדַרְכּוֹן), and Persian satraps began minting standardized silver (siglos σίγλος). It has been theorized that the gold darics served political ends, occurring significantly more in the West than in the East, while the silver sigloi served as military payments, occurring mainly in Asia Minor.

Bildarchiv Preussischer Kulturbesitz/Art Resource, NY

Figure 1: Persian gold coin. Obverse showing the Persian king. 5th–4th BCE. Muenzkabinett, Staatliche Museen zu Berlin, Berlin, Germany.

Alongside the darics and sigloi, there were the so-called satrapal coinages of the Achaemenid period. Debate surrounds the function of these coins. It was commonly assumed that satraps issued coins that circulated within their satrapies, in function akin to provincial coins and city coins. It is likely that the so-called satrapal issues were either issues for mercenary salaries (e.g., the case of Pharnabazos of Cyzicus) or local issues (e.g., Tissaphernes of Mysia). Thus, satrapal coinage did not exist as a separate type of coinage. A satrapal coinage was not necessary since the local and provincial coinages fulfilled the equivalent function.

Coinage seems to have reached Cyprus about 530–525 BCE, contemporaneous with the beginning of Achaemenid control in this region. During the 5th cent. BCE, silver coins circulated mostly in the urban centers along the coast. Some extraneous coins from Athens, Aegina, and other Greek cities have been found. The 4th cent. BCE saw the emergence of bronze coinage and an increase of mints and types. Again, comparatively few coins have been found outside of the coastal cities. Foreign currency from mainland Greece, Asia Minor, and the Near East occurs again in small quantity.

The Phoenician cities began minting their own coinage ca. 450 BCE. The main cities to mint coins were first Byblos, then Tyre and Sidon, and finally Aradus. It is a puzzle why the Phoenician cities waited more than a century after the Greek cities to mint coins. Equally unclear is the reason why the Phoenicians began minting when they did. The two most likely functions of coins at this stage were commercial and military. The fact that the Phoenician coins follow the trail of Phoenician export points to the commercial function. Further, it has been suggested that the small denominations in which the coinage appears would have suited typical day wages for laborers or soldiers.

It must be clearly stated that the presence of early coins does not demonstrate a monetary economy. A few scholars have speculated that the introduction of coinage in the 5th cent. overhauled the whole Palestinian economy. This does not appear to be the case. Weighing silver continued to be practiced for centuries after the first coins were minted. This is evidenced by the coexistence of coins and unminted silver in hoards from the 5th cent. BCE. Moreover, there is evidence of cut coins, indicating that coins continued to be weighed for their value and sectioned according to need. Textual sources from Persepolis, Elephantine, and Wadi ed-Daliyeh demonstrate the survival of weighing silver in the 5th and 4th cent. BCE. Clearly the transition to a monetary economy was not a simple and rapid one.

The various prerequisites for determining the existence of a monetary economy are the presence of local mints, the circulation of small denominations, and the apparent waning of older means of economic transaction. Archaeologically speaking, coins in various denominations should be found consistently and in significant quantity in the record, with allowance for a certain degree of arbitrary preservation. In Israel these requirements are not met until the Hellenistic period, or even later. Nevertheless, money does appear prior to this.

As in Asia Minor and Greece, so in Israel there are various phases of transition between a pre-monetary economy and a monetary one. They are later and subsequently different than the transitions in the Aegean. Yet the development of coinage in Israel is not isolated. It is part of the transition from the economic mode of exchange through bullion and barter to one in which standardized coins slowly became prominent.

E. The Persian Period

In Israel, the first coins were Greek, and have been found especially in 6th-and 5th-cent. BCE contexts. At least twenty-four Greek coins from these centuries have been found in Israel. Their presence helps explain why pseudo-Athenian coinage would be minted in Israel in the 4th cent. BCE. Obviously, Athenian coinage must have been viewed as an emerging means of exchange in the 5th cent. BCE, if it was to be imitated by local mints in the 4th cent. BCE.

The proportion of Athenian coins rises markedly for the 5th cent. BCE. This reflects the increasing prominence of Athens in trade over other Greek cities around the mid-5th cent. and beyond. Together with the consistent and conservative iconography of the Athenian coins this demonstrates the political and economic stability of Athens, and conversely explains its rising hegemony in trade. The virtual disappearance of true Athenian coinage at the end of the 5th cent. BCE is undoubtedly related to the political and economic attrition of Athens as a result of the Peloponnesian War. Still, Athenian coinage was considered desirable enough that throughout the Eastern Mediterranean pseudo-Athenian coins were minted.

British Museum, London, Great Britain © British Museum/Art Resource, NY

Figure 2: Silver tetradrachm of Athens. Greek, around 480 BCE. On the obverse is the head of the goddess Athena, and on the reverse the owl, a bird associated with the goddess.

Although some of the earliest Phoenician mint series have been found in Israel, all the hoards containing Phoenician coins in Israel date from the 4th cent. BCE on, and most from ca. 350–333 BCE. Of the main cities to mint coins, the preponderance of Tyre and Sidon is unmistakable. Once the Phoenician cities began minting coins in the mid-5th cent. BCE, other local cities and provinces throughout the Levant soon followed. From about 410 BCE on, pseudo-Athenian tetradrachmas, that is, imitations of the great Athenian standard, circulated throughout the eastern Mediterranean.

Many were struck in Egypt as well as at local mints in Israel. They appear regularly in hoards and among the finds in Israel.

These mints were all located south of Galilee. It is certain that there were mints in the regions of Samaria and Yehud and the cities from the southern coast, Ashdod, Ashkelon, and Gaza. Also various desert rulers, who were in close contact with Gaza, appear to have had their own coin issues. Northern Israel continued to suffice with Phoenician coins, though it seems that Dor might have begun minting coins in the 4th cent. Generally, however, it was the cities of southern Israel that infused the coin supply with their own issues.

The designation "Philisto-Arabian" is often used for the coinage minted under the auspices of the cities Gaza, Ashkelon, Ashdod—former Philistia—and desert rulers in the southern and eastern hinterland. Minting began in the early 4th cent. BCE with imitations of the Athenian coinage of the 5th cent. BCE, the *moneta franca* of the Levant. Quickly, however, they began alternating their own types, frequently Janus heads, images of Bes, and other grotesques. As a port city at the end of the desert spice trail, Gaza was independent from both Sidon and Tyre. The chief marker of its coinage is the epigraphic indicator "Gaza," either inscribed in full or abbreviated. Its coins follow the Attic standard rather than the Phoenician. Philisto-Arabian coinage circulated in great numbers in southern Israel, such as in Gaza, Beth-Zur, and Gezer, and also in Samaria. They are not found in Galilee and rarely along the coast north of Jaffa.

The province of Yehud began striking coins in small silver denominations around 400 BCE. The first series were copies of the Athenian style, depicting the head of Pallas Athena on the obverse, and an owl with an olive branch on the reverse. The legend "Yehud" in Aramaic or Paleo-Hebrew glosses the coins. Other designs followed, including issues with the lily, the falcon with spread wings, and the head of a local leader, as in the case of the coins with the legends "Yehezqiyah the governor," "Yadduʿa," and "Yohanan the priest." The reference to a Jewish priest on a minting of this time suggests the civil control wielded by a temple authority during at least a part of the 4th cent. BCE. An intriguing Yehud coin from this era, which has prompted considerable debate, seems to depict an enthroned deity. This means that either Jewish authorities had little scruple at this point with depicting the deity, or, as some contend, a Persian official ordered the design without sanction from religious authorities.

Besides Yehud, Samaria was the only other province in the Levant to have its own coinage. Its coinage is known largely from the Samaria and Nablus hoards, as well as the recently excavated Gerizim temple. These hoards included pseudo-Athenians like the Philisto-Arabian and Yehud coins, but they too incorporated unique types. The iconography and legends seem to be more eastward and Persian in orientation than in either the Philisto-Arabian and Yehud coins. A 4th-cent. BCE coin from Samaria bears the legend "Jeroboam," a likely case of invoking an honored dynast. This is demonstrated by the presence of cuneiform writing on a number of Samarian coins.

The fractional character of the local coinages shows that they were aimed to fill the need for small transactions. This is supported by the limited circulation of such coins. Larger commercial transactions must have been handled in Phoenician, Athenian, and pseudo-Athenian currency, or still in kind.

In the par. passages Ezra 2:69 and Neh 7:69-71 we find a term for gold money that has been debated (**darkemonim** דַּרְכְּמוֹנִים). It is in parallel with minas and shekels. The consonants of the term could be taken to refer to either darics or drachmas. The LXX translates the term DRACHMA (**drachmē** δραχμή). As noted above, the drachma is a unit of measurement associated with Greek coinage, though the term may have been used earlier as a unit of weight. As far as drachma coins are concerned, they were rarely minted of gold. If the daric is meant, the reference is anachronistic, for there is no undisputed evidence that darics were minted prior to Darius. Instituting the Daric standard was part of Darius' wide-scale monetary reforms. *Daric* even appears to be short for the fuller term, **stater Dareikos** (στατέρ Δαρεικός). In 1 Chr 29:7, the Hebrew also reads the term *darics* (**'adharkonim** אֲדַרְכֹנִים) anachronistically. On the basis of this comparison, we cannot reach any solid conclusions regarding the exact significance of this reference. The fact that both words are used in conjunction with gold seems to point to *daric*.

Since the context of Ezra 2:69 and Neh 7:69-71 is one of units of weights, while the terms *drachma* or *daric* are both coin units, these references appear incongruous. It must, however, be remembered that throughout most of the Persian Empire, silver and gold served as currency only by weight. Accordingly, money did not circulate at Elephantine in the form of minted coins, but was weighed. Yet here too there was the awareness of coinage as an alternative system of payment. Three papyri from the Elephantine corpus equate two shekels with one stater in weight (C 29:3; 35:3; K 12:5, 14). In the Elephantine Papyri, various weight measurements from different systems also coexist. The shekel appears to be the Egyptian shekel of about 8.7 grams. There are, however, also Persian weight measurements such as the karsh, which appear to be superimposed upon the local weight systems.

F. The Hellenistic Period

The basic coexistence of larger silver denominations minted in Acco, Tyre, and Alexandria, and bronze Yehud coins in the smaller denominations, continued into the Ptolemaic period. The Athenian standard continued its domination under the policy of Alexander. However, rigid Ptolemaic control fostered economic isolationism, albeit with great monetary stability. The mints turned out large quantities of silver tetradrachmas with the legend "of Ptolemy the King (or Savior)." Foreign coin was melted down and reminted. Writings from this period, including the Zenon Archive, the *Letter of Aristeas*, the Wisdom of Solomon (15:12), Sirach (7:18; 18:33; 21:8; 29:5-6; 31:5; 51:28), and Tobit (5:19), regularly refer to money, though often may simply refer to bullion again.

Yehud coins continued to be minted, with the small epigraphic change from the Aramaic **yhd** (יהד) to the Hebrew legend **yhdh** (יהדה). Their iconography is mostly a representation of the Ptolemaic ruler on the obverse and one of the flagship animal emblems on the reverse. Compared to the Persian-period coins from Yehud, we see a greater tendency toward religious aniconism. After 198 BCE, however, under the Seleucid rulers, especially Antiochus IV, this tendency was reversed. Known for his propagation of the Zeus cult, Antiochus IV issued coins honoring Zeus as well as himself with symbols of deification.

The political freedom won for Jerusalem by the Maccabean Revolt resulted in a new era of independently issued Jewish coins. It is debated under whom this began. According to 1 Macc 15:6, Antiochus VII permitted Simon to mint coins. However, he never did, probably because the Seleucid king reneged his permission. It seems that Simon's son, John Hyrcanus I (134–104 BCE), minted a bronze coin in Jerusalem. The legend reads "Yehanan the high priest and the council of the Jews." John's successor, Alexander Jannaeus (103–76 BCE) first issued coins with the inscription "Jonathan the king," and emblems of lilies and anchors. There is also frequent use of the official Hasmonean emblem, two cornucopias and a pomegranate. The reverse gives the legend in Gk., "Alexander the King." Later, however, perhaps under religious pressure, he avoided the designation "king," and chose for the legend "Jonathan the high priest and the council of the Jews." After Alexander Jannaeus, coins are attested from the time of John Hyrcanus II (67–64 BCE) and Mattathias Antigonus (40–37 BCE). The Hasmonean coinage circulated for a long time in Israel, and a statistically high frequency of it has been found in the material record.

G. The Early Roman Period

As in earlier periods, during the early Roman period coins circulating in Israel came from three main sources: the Roman coins minted according to the imperial standard; the provincial coins minted at Antioch and Tyre; and local coinages minted by local governors and procurators, and the Herodians. The different standards, as well as the restrictions on money the Temple would accept, necessitated the money-changers, of whom we read frequently in the NT (Matt 21:12; Mark 11:15). Money-changers controlled daily exchange rates, as well as discounted and recycled worn coinage.

After gaining the hegemony over Judea, Herod I began minting coins bearing his name and the title *king*. However, in deference to Jewish sensitivities, he avoided images of humans or gods. We also have coins issued by the Roman procurators, such as Coponius (6–9 CE), Ambibulus (9–12 CE), Valerius Gratus (15–26 CE), Pontius Pilate (26–36 CE), and Festus (59 CE). Herod's successors likewise also minted coins, including Herod Archelaus (4 BCE–6 CE), Antipas (4–39 CE), Philip II (4–34 CE), Agrippa I (37–44 CE), Herod of Chalcis (57–92 CE), and Agrippa II (56–95 CE).

Israel Museum (IDAM), Jerusalem, Israel. Erich Lessing/Art Resource, NY

Figure 3: Bronze coin with a tripod and Greek inscription, from the period of the Herodians.

By this time the Roman monetary system had come to dominate the others. Its unit was the as. The common denarius was the equivalent of 10 asses; larger denominations were larger multiples of the as. These silver coins coexisted with bronzes like the assarius, and a large bronze, the sestertius. The denarius (dēnarion δηνάριον) is the most frequently mentioned coin in the NT (Matt 18:28; 20:2, 9, 13; 22:19; Mark 6:37; 12:15; Luke 7:41; 10:35; 20:24; John 6:7; 12:5; Rev 6:6). The denarius was valued at about a day's labor (see Matt 20:9). It was about the same value as the drachma (Luke 15:8). The coin presented to Jesus for the Roman tax (Matt 22:19; Mark 12:15; Luke 20:24) was likely a Tyrian denarius. There the imperial image on the obverse was standard (*see* DENARII, DENARIUS).

An important coin in the life of a male Jew twenty years and up was the half-shekel required for the annual temple tax according to pentateuchal law (Exod 30:13-15). According to Josephus, the only acceptable form for this tax was the Tyrian shekel (*Ant.* 3.194–96). This coin began to be minted in 126 BCE and continued being minted likely until 66 CE, shortly before the Temple's destruction. We read of this tax in Matt 17:24, where it is referred to as a DIDRACHMA, which is equal to half a shekel. Two of these would equal a stater (Matt 17:27). Ironically, the shekel depicted the head of Melkart and on the reverse, around an eagle clutching the prow of a ship, there was the legend "Tyre the Holy and Invincible." During the First Jewish Revolt a beautiful new silver shekel was minted, with a chalice on the obverse with the legend "Shekel of Israel," as well as the date, and on the reverse a stem of three pomegranates with the inscription "Jerusalem the Holy." These epigraphic adjustments reveal the nationalistic and religious zeal that characterized the revolt.

Other small denominations mentioned in the Gospels include the **lepton** (λεπτόν, Mark 12:42), the **assarion** (ἀσσάριον, Matt 10:29; Luke 12:6), and the quadrans (**kodrantēs** κοδράντης, Matt 5:26; Mark 12:42). The term **chalkos** simply refers to bronze change (Mark 6:8; 12:41). The **lepton** is the denomination referred to as the "widow's mite" (Mark 12:42; Luke 21:2). All this would have been the small change that a purse or moneybox could transport.

Even during the 1st cent. CE, exchange in kind was not atypical, especially in lease or tithe payments (Luke 16:6-7; 20:10). Here the Babylonian denominations of the talent and mina were still used (Matt 18:24; 25:14-28; Luke 19:13-25).

During the First Jewish Revolt (66–70 CE) both silver and bronze coinages were minted in Jerusalem. The coins featured vegetative and cultic symbolism, and nationalistic or religious slogans such as "Freedom of Zion." After 70 CE, the silver tetradrachmas from Tyre and Antioch became the standard coin, supplemented by bronze coins from Neapolis and Sebaste. Special propagandistic coins commemorating the defeat of Judea were issued by the Romans, bearing the ominous "Judaea Capta" legend. These were minted both in Rome and in Caesarea. During the Second Revolt led by Simon bar Kochba (132–35 CE), silver tetradrachmas and denarii were overstruck with slogans referring to the lead, the city of Jerusalem, or simply "the freedom of Israel."

H. Ethical Concerns about Money

In the OT, there are frequent warnings against greed and hoarding of money. The prophets spoke regularly against the destructive consequences of greed on persons and the whole community (2 Kgs 5:26; Amos 2:6; 8:4-5; Mic 3:18). Deuteronomy commends a lifestyle of generosity and berates tightfistedness (Deut 15:8). In the Wisdom books money is a frequent theme. On the one hand, they depict riches as a blessing from God (Prov 3:16; 22:4); while on the other hand, they warn against frequent temptations associated with riches (Prov 11:1; 22:16). These wisdom themes persist in the literature of the Second Temple period period (see, e.g., Sir 29:1-28).

In the NT Jesus frequently warns against the destructive power of the love of money. People easily and frequently fixate on acquiring more and more money. This renders money a ready idol. The love of money is so opposed to the fear of God that Jesus sets the service of wealth or substance in radical opposition to the service of God (Matt 6:24; Luke 16:13). Consequently, the Aramaic term for wealth and substance, MAMMON, has made its way into the English language as having demonic overtones, which the term by itself originally lacked. On occasion, Jesus called for the renunciation of possessions (Mark 10:21; Luke 9:3) as a radical test of discipleship. Nevertheless, he also accepted support from wealthy followers, male and female (Luke 8:2-3), and kept company with the well-to-do (Matt 11:19) (*see* POVERTY; WEALTH).

In the early Christian communities, generosity with money and substance was regarded as a mark of true commitment to the gospel. The early Christians in the urban centers comprised persons of all social strata (e.g., 1 Cor 11:22). Paul recommends that property be regarded as relative (1 Cor 7:30-31), and invested significant energy in collections for the rural poor in and around Jerusalem (Acts 11:30; Rom 15:26; 1 Cor 16:2). He viewed this as a ministry that embodied the gospel in a very concrete and compelling way (2 Cor 9). *See* ISRAEL, SOCIAL AND ECONOMIC DEVELOPMENT OF; TAXES, TAXATION; TRADE AND COMMERCE; WEIGHTS AND MEASURES.

Bibliography: M. S. Balmuth. "The Monetary Forerunners of Coinage in Phoenicia and Palestine." *Proceedings of the International Numismatic Convention, Jerusalem 1963: The Patterns of Monetary Development in Phoenicia and Palestine in Antiquity.* A. Kindler, ed. (1967) 25–31; J. W. Betylon. *The Coinage and Mints of Phoenicia* (1980); D. Edelman. "Tracking Observance of the Aniconic Tradition Through Numismatics." *The Triumph of Elohim* (1995) 185–225; H. Gitler. *The Coinage of Philistia of the Fifth and Fourth Centuries BC: A Study of the Earliest Coins of Palestine* (2006); K. Harl. *Coinage in the Roman Economy, 300 B.C. to A.D. 700* (1996); P. Machinist. "The First Coins of Judah and Samaria: Numismatics and History in the Achaemenid and Early Hellenistic Periods." *Achaemenid History*, Vol. 8: *Continuity and Change.* H. Sancisi-Weerdenburg, et al., eds. (1994) 365–80; Y. Meshorer. *Ancient Jewish Coinage.* 2 vols. (1982); Y. Meshorer and S. Qedar. *The Coinage of Samaria in the Fourth Century BCE* (1991); Sitta von Reden. *Exchange in Ancient Greece* (1995); Joachim Schaper. "The Jerusalem Temple as an Instrument of the Achaemenid Fiscal Administration." *VT* 45 (1995) 528–39.

GERALD M. BILKES

MONEY-CHANGER [κολλυβιστής kollybistēs, κερματιστής kermatistēs]. Money-changers facilitated economic exchange by converting coins to and from the many international currencies and denominations. In the Roman Empire, the profession of money-changer (*nummularius*) was closely related to that of banker (*argentarius*). Within the Roman cities the former specialized in assaying coins and exchanging currencies; the latter handled the more lucrative fiscal tasks, such as deposits, loans, and commodity speculation. Beyond the Roman cities, such as in Palestine, these two professions often merged.

There were money-changers with modest operations in small villages, and there were powerful money-changers in urban centers. Wherever there was buying and selling at any significant level, one would find money-changers. Their services were vital for any economic exchange. Also since they were experts in exchange rates, detecting counterfeit, and could readily streamline the flow of money, authorities often contracted with them to collect taxes.

Since they took in large amounts of money, ancient temples also required the services of money-changers. Throughout Greece, Babylonia, and Asia Minor, temple treasuries often functioned in ways that resembled banks. They would administer loans, deposits, exchange, etc. They maintained a distinction between accounts for cultic and non-cultic matters. In the largest cities, private banks eclipsed temples in influence, but in smaller and moderately large locales temple treasuries were a common banking option. During the Hellenistic and Roman periods, Jerusalem was no exception. This is well attested in Second Temple sources (Sir 42:7; Tob 1:14; 9:5; 2 Macc 3:1-15), as well as in later rabbinic sources (*m. Sheq.* 4:3). The NT mentions money-changers only in connection with the Jerusalem temple cult (Matt 21:12; Mark 11:15; John 2:14-15). According to the Mishnah, money-changers, undoubtedly regulated by the temple hierarchy, began to collect the half-shekel tax throughout Israel one month prior to the Passover, and within the temple precincts the last twenty days prior to Passover (*m. Sheq.* 1:3). This annual tax on Jewish males and proselytes had been developed from a pentateuchal injunction (Exod 30:11-16). It had to be paid in the form of a Tyrian stater or tetradrachm, because of its metallurgic purity (Josephus, *Ant.* 18.312; Matt 17:24). This specification necessitated the work of money-changers, who would in turn charge a percentage of interest for their service.

Jesus' act of overturning the tables of the money-changers was one of a series of actions that brought the business of the Temple to a temporary halt. In line with Jeremiah and other prophets, Jesus thus demonstrated his protest against the temple establishment, whom he indicted as corrupt, and against the infringement of noisy commerce on religious devotion. The crime of the money-changers was, according to the Gospels, to have made "the house for prayer for all the nations" into "a den of robbers" (Matt 21:13; Mark 11:17). *See* MONEY, COINS; TREASURE, TREASURER, TREASURY.

Bibliography: Neill Q. Hamilton. "Temple Cleansing and Temple Bank." *JBL* 83 (1964) 365–72; Kenneth W. Harl. *Coinage in the Roman Economy 300 B.C. to A.D. 700* (1996).

GERALD M. BILKES

MONKEY [קוֹף qof; πίθηκος pithēkos]. According to 1 Kgs 10:22 (//2 Chr 9:21) SOLOMON regularly imported "gold, silver, ivory, APEs, and peacocks." Ancient Near Eastern monarchs valued simians as expressions of wealth and international prestige and commonly gave and received monkeys as a component of international diplomacy. The OT's representation of Solomon draws upon the estimation of apes as prized, luxury goods to enhance its portrait of him as a king with wide-ranging influence. *See* ANIMALS OF THE BIBLE.

Bibliography: Steven W. Holloway. "Use of Assyriology in Chronological Apologetics in David's Secret Demons." *SJOT* 17 (2003) 245–67.

STEVE COOK

MONOLATRY muh-nol´uh-tree. Monolatry is the worship of a single god without denying the existence of other gods. The term is usually interchangeable with *henotheism*, though the two words are sometimes nuanced differently. Monolatry is often seen as an evolutionary stage between polytheism and monotheism. In ancient Israelite religion, Yahweh was considered the chief God, while the existence of other gods was accepted. In the postexilic period, however, monolatry developed into true monotheism. *See* GOD, OT VIEW OF.

Monolatry is evidenced in numerous OT texts. The commandment to have no other gods before Yahweh (Exod 20:3; Deut 5:7) presupposes the existence of other gods who might be worshiped. Yahweh is sometimes pictured as the head of a divine council made up of multiple gods (Ps 82:1; Job 1–2), though none is as powerful as Yahweh (Ps 89:6-8). Monolatry forms the background to several preexilic prophets, particularly those influenced by the Deuteronomic movement. For instance, Elijah's battle with the prophets of Baal on Mount Carmel is designed to show whether Yahweh or Baal is more powerful (1 Kgs 18:20-40), while additional prophets accuse the Israelites of worshiping other gods instead of remaining faithful to Yahweh (Jer 2:20-28; Hos 1–2).

KEVIN A. WILSON

MONOTHEISM. *See* GOD, OT VIEW OF.

MONSTER [תַּנִּין tannin]. *Monster* metaphorically describes calamitous destruction. Jeremiah 51:34 sees King Nebuchadnezzar as a monster devouring Zion. Ezra foresees apocalyptic upheaval in which "women shall bring forth monsters" (2 Esd 5:8). *See* BEHEMOTH; DRAGON; LEVIATHAN; RAHAB.

MONTANUS, MONTANISM mon´tuh-nuhs, mon´tuh-niz´uhm. An apocalyptic leader and movement of the late 2nd and early 3rd cent. Arising in Phrygia around 170 CE, Montanus and two female prophets, Prisca and Maximilla, spoke messages that their followers considered new revelation from the Holy Spirit. Montanists taught an imminent expectation of the end, urged ecstatic prophesying and asceticism, courted martyrdom, gave a wider role to women, and opposed second repentance. Montanism's most famous convert was Tertullian, who was attracted to its moral rigor. Montanism spread widely in the Roman Empire, but largely died out around 225 CE due to Catholic opposition.

Bibliography: R. D. Butler. *The New Prophecy and "New Visions"* (2006); C. Trevett. *Montanism* (2002).

ROBERT E. VAN VOORST

MONTH. *See* CALENDAR.

MONUMENT [יָד yadh, צִיּוֹן tsiyon; μνημεῖον mnēmeion]. A pillar, stone, or structure marking a location as significant, often for funerary purposes. Some OT examples denote grave markers (tsiyon in 2 Kgs 23:17; Ezek 39:15; yadh in Isa 56:5), a victory monument (1 Sam 15:12; 2 Sam 18:18; 1 Chr 18:3), or a road sign (Jer 31:21). In the NT mnēmeion can be synonymous with "tomb" (Matt 23:29; Luke 11:47). Yad Vashem (meaning "a monument and a name"), the name of the Israeli holocaust memorial in Jerusalem, comes from Isa 56:5. *See* MASSEBAH; PILLAR; TOMB.

BYRON R. MCCANE

MOON [יָרֵחַ yareakh, כֶּסֶא kese', לְבָנָה levonah; σελήνη selēnē]. The earth's satellite, considered a deity throughout the ancient Semitic world. The primary Hebrew term is yareakh; less frequent are kese' ("full moon"; Job 26:9; Ps 81:3 [Heb. 81:4]; Prov 7:20) and levonah (fem. of the word for "white," i.e., "white lady"; Isa 24:23; 30:26; Song 6:10).

Most biblical references to the moon are to the earth's satellite, although traces of its divine nature remain. In Gen 1:16 the "lesser light" is fixed in the firmament along with the SUN and the stars to distinguish between night and day. The sun and moon also serve "for signs and for seasons and for days and years" (Gen 1:14; compare Ps 104:19; Jer 31:35).

The month was based on the moon's cycle, such that one of the Hebrew words for month (yerakh יֶרַח) comes from the word for moon (yareakh). Each month began with the sighting of the lunar crescent (hence the other Hebrew word for "month": khodhesh [חֹדֶשׁ], "month, new moon") and so lasted twenty-nine or thirty days. To keep agricultural events and religious holidays within their specified seasons a month was added every four years. *See* CALENDAR.

Some religious festivals were determined by the moon's cycle. The monthly NEW MOON was a time of sacrifice and feasting (Num 28:11-15; 1 Sam 20:5, 18, 24, 27); the new moon of the seventh month was especially holy, with a day of rest added to the celebrations (Num 29:1; Amos 8:5). Passover was linked to the full moon on the fifteenth of Nisan (usually April) while Sukkoth (Booths/Tabernacles) began at the full moon on the fifteenth of Tishri (September–October). *See* BOOTHS, FEAST OR FESTIVAL OF; PASSOVER AND FEAST OF UNLEAVENED BREAD.

Created by God to rule the night, the moon was a symbol of permanence (e.g., Pss 72:5, 7; 89:37 [Heb. 89:38]). Negating the moon's light was a sign of eschatological judgment in both the OT and NT, either through an eclipse (Isa 13:10; Ezek 32:7; Joel 3:15; Mark 13:24//Matt 24:29; compare Rev 8:12) or from being turned to blood (Joel 2:31; Acts 2:20; Rev 6:12). In contrast, when Jerusalem is restored the moon will be as bright as the sun (Isa 30:26; 2 Esd 5:4) while in Isa 60:19-20 and Rev 21:23 the sun and the moon will be replaced by the light of God's presence.

A moon god is attested throughout the ancient Semitic world. In Mesopotamia he was called Nanna, Suen (also written as Sin), and less frequently, Ashimbabbar; in some texts these names refer to phases of the moon, but not consistently so. The name Nanna dominated in southern Mesopotamia, especially Ur; references to Suen can also be found at Ebla and Ugarit, while Sin is attested at Mari. Nanna and Suen may reflect different traditions, either geographically or stemming from Sumerian and Akkadian groups, but they were combined at an early stage as Nanna-Suen or Nanna-Sin. Sin was the son of ENLIL and NINLIL, and fathered the sun god. This genealogy reflects the moon god's importance: he ruled the stars, judged the netherworld while absent during the day, and symbolized rebirth and fertility through his monthly disappearance and return as the new moon. He was considered the father of the people and was represented as a bull, with the animal's horns reflecting the crescent moon.

The moon god is also found in early traditions from Syria. As noted, Suen is mentioned at Ebla (ca. 2400 BCE) along with the West Semitic name Yarikh (cognate with the Hebrew **yareakh**). The form Erakh occurs in names from Mari (ca. 1800 BCE) while at Emar (ca. 1200 BCE) Sin played a major role in festivals and was a patron of the palace; another moon god, Shaggar, also appears at Emar. The latter occurs at Ugarit (ca. 1200 BCE) as Sheger, but Yarikh is mentioned more often. He is found in god lists (often equated with Sin) and personal names, receives offerings, and appears in various texts. Yarikh celebrates his marriage to Nikkal (= Ningal) as a source of blessing and fertility for humans (*KTU* 1.24), but he also scampers like a dog at El's banquet (*KTU* 1.114). This uncomplimentary portrait reflects the much greater role of the sun god Shapash at Ugarit, including usurpation of the moon god's underworldly role found in Mesopotamia. Finally, a Canaanite-period temple at Hazor (13th cent. BCE) contained a statue with a crescent on the deity's chest, a stele with hands reaching up to a crescent, and a cult stand with a crescent.

Various lunar iconography from the 1st millennium BCE Levant has been found, and the moon god is also reflected during this period in personal names from Aram, Ammon and Phoenicia, and the Assyrian king Sennacherib ("Sin has increased the brothers"). Assyrian kings supported the moon cult at Haran, with Shalmaneser III (858–824 BCE) rebuilding the temple of Sin. It was rebuilt again by the Babylonian king Nabonidus, son of the moon god's priestess, who installed his own daughter as high priestess of Sin at Ur and tried to make Sin head of the pantheon over Marduk.

Ancient Israel shared its neighbors' moon worship. A certain Natanyahu ("Yahweh has given") owned a 7th-cent. BCE tablet depicting a crescent, while an Iron Age temple to the moon god at Bethsaida included a stele showing him as a bull. The names Jerah (Gen 10:26; 1 Chr 1:20) and Jaroah (1 Chr 5:14), Laban (from **levanah**, Gen 24:29; for an alternate interpretation of the name *see* LABAN), and Hodesh (1 Chr 8:9) are based on Hebrew words related to the moon, while the Mesopotamian Sin occurs as the first part of the names of the Judahite prince Shenazzar (1 Chr 3:18) and Sanballat (Neh 2:10, etc.). Jericho and Beth-Jerah (mentioned in rabbinic sources) may be so named because the moon was worshiped there. The golden calf at Sinai has been linked by some to the moon god, with the horns representing the crescent moon and *Sinai* itself reflecting the god Sin. Also, the monthly new moon festival and the lunar connections for Passover and Sukkoth imply roots in moon worship as well. However, while they are suggestive, we cannot be certain on any of these points.

More certain is the prohibition against worshiping the moon found in Deut 4:19 and 17:3 and the statement in 2 Kgs 23:5 that moon worship occurred in the Jerusalem Temple itself (see also Jer 8:2). In addition, 2 Kgs 21:3, 5; Jer 19:13; and Zeph 1:5 note that people worshiped the "host of heaven," of which the moon was one (*see* HOSTS, HOST OF HEAVEN). In contrast, Job denies worshiping the sun and moon (Job 31:26-28). Thus, there were people in Israel who considered the moon to be a deity; Deut 4:19 even asserts that the host of heaven are deities given to other nations by Yahweh. Moreover, Yahweh's subjugation of the moon (and sun) in Isa 24:23 is not directed at an inanimate object (note "the host of heaven" in v. 21) and the moon's negative effects in Ps 121:6 may have originally referred to the moon god's influence (compare Ps 91:5).

With the move toward monotheism the moon's divinity was downplayed. In 1 Kgs 22:19 the host of heaven are simply Yahweh's court attendants and in Ps 148:3 the moon praises Yahweh. The narrative of the moon's creation, especially calling it "the lesser light" in Gen 1:16 rather than the name it shared with the moon god, completely transformed it into an object rather than a deity.

By the NT period the moon's divine associations were mostly forgotten, although not completely lost. Mythic echoes of its earlier status occur in eschatological texts: God's defeat of the moon (god) is conveyed through the moon being blotted out (Mark 13:24// Matt 24:29) or turned to blood (Acts 2:20; Rev 6:12). The moon was one of the celestial bodies that would show signs of the end times (Luke 21:25). Paul contrasts the different types of glory displayed by the sun, moon, and stars as a metaphor to describe the transformation of fleshly bodies to resurrection bodies (1 Cor 15:41). *See* ASTRONOMY, ASTROLOGY.

JOHN L. MCLAUGHLIN

MORALITY. *See* ETHICS IN THE NONCANONICAL JEWISH WRITINGS; ETHICS IN THE NT; ETHICS IN THE OT; IMMORALITY.

MORDECAI mor'duh-k*i* [מָרְדֳּכַי mordokhay; Μαρδοχαῖος Mardochaios]. The name likely derives from the Babylonian god Marduk. 1. A leader of the Jews who returned to Judah with ZERUBBABEL after the exile (Ezra 2:2; Neh 7:7; 1 Esd 5:8).

2. Son of Jair, a Benjaminite, and cousin of ESTHER (Esth 2:5-7). Mordecai's subplot in the book of Esther begins as he demonstrates his loyalty to the king by foiling a conspiracy against him, then refuses to bow to Haman, the king's advisor. The latter act sets off the animosity between Mordecai and Haman, and their mirror-image destinies establish the seesaw of the plot. While the motivation for Mordecai's refusal to bow is obscure in the OT, the LXX additions to Esther, which tend to fill the gaps with God, elaborate on his intentions. Mordecai here explains that he acted not out of pride but to avoid worshiping anyone but God (LXX Esth 4:20-21).

The LXX thus makes Mordecai fit more neatly into the genre of the Jew in the Court of the Foreign King, as, like Daniel, Mordecai's career as courtier is now endangered by his loyalty to God, who will ultimately vindicate and save him. Together, Mordecai and Esther make up a more complete survival strategy for the religious/ethnic minority they represent—one assimilates while the other refuses. Mordecai puts on sackcloth and ashes and fasts to get Esther's attention; Esther puts on perfume and finery and feasts to gain the attention of the king. This two-step strategy then saves the Jews. *See* ESTHER, ADDITIONS TO; ESTHER, BOOK OF.

NICOLE WILKINSON DURAN

MOREH mor'eh [מוֹרֶה moreh]. 1. The "oak of Moreh" (NRSV; ʾelon moreh אֵלוֹן מוֹרֶה) is more accurately the "plain of Moreh" (following the Targums, Samaritan Pentateuch, and Jerome, contra the LXX, PESHITTA, and most modern authors). According to Gen 12:6, Shechem was in the vicinity of ʾelon moreh (*see* SHECHEM, SHECHEMITES). Deuteronomy 11:30 deliberately uses this archaic name to connect the children of Israel's entrance into the promised land with their patriarch Abraham.

2. The hill of Moreh (Judg 7:1) is north of the Jezreel Valley, near where the Midianites encamped before they were attacked by Gideon. Many associate this Moreh with modern Givat ha-Moreh (Jabal ed-Dahi) east of Afula.

YOEL ELITZUR

MORESHETH mor'uh-sheth [מוֹרֶשֶׁת moresheth]. Hometown of the prophet Micah (1:1; Jer 26:18). Its full name, Moresheth-gath, appears only in Mic 1:14 and indicates that the town was a suburb of GATH. However, today most scholars identify Moresheth with Tell ej-Judeideh, 6 mi. (10 km) southeast of Gath and the same distance northeast of Lachish, or about 25 mi. southwest of Jerusalem. Moresheth-gath is one of a dozen cities (Mic 1:8-16) whose names are connected by puns with the nature of their impending destruction, a fate that the prophet laments. Although the textual corruptions and obscurities make this a particularly difficult section to translate and interpret, Micah's pun appears to play on the word *Moresheth*, which is similar to the word *betrothed* (meʾoreseth מְאֹרֶשֶׂת), and on the idea that towns could be given up as a dowry (compare 1 Kgs 9:16). Hence, Judah will be forced to give a parting bridal gift, a dowry, to the betrothed Moresheth, as that city is given over to the enemy.

MARK RONCACE

MORESHETH-GATH. *See* MORESHETH.

MORIAH muh-r*i*'uh [מוֹרִיָּה moriyah]. Moriah is mentioned twice in the OT. 1. Moriah is the region (the Hebrew is literally "the land of the Moriah") where Abraham is sent to sacrifice his son Isaac (Gen 22:2); specifically, he is directed to one of the mountains that God would show him in that region.

2. Mount Moriah is identified as the place where Solomon built the Temple; it is the place previously revealed to David, the THRESHING FLOOR of ORNAN the Jebusite (2 Chr 3:1; Ornan = ARAUNAH in the full account in 2 Sam 24:16-24). This is where David built an altar and offered sacrifices to stay the plague God had sent as a result of David's presumptuous census.

Since these are the only occurrences of the name Moriah, they are often assumed to refer to the same place. The distance from Beer-sheba (where Abraham and Isaac's journey began, Gen 21:31-33) to Jerusalem is about 45 mi., a distance appropriate for the three-day journey (Gen 22:4). However, it is surprising that there is no mention of Abraham, the near-sacrifice of Isaac, or the altar (Gen 22:9) in the account of the threshing floor in Samuel or Chronicles.

JOEL F. DRINKARD JR.

MORNING STAR [φωσφόρος phōsphoros, ὁ ἀστὴρ ὁ πρωϊνός ho astēr ho prōinos]. References Greek images of someone bringing light or exercising power over mortals. In Revelation (2:28; 22:16), it serves as a metaphor for Christ. *See* DAWN; DAY STAR.

MORTAL SIN [ἁμαρτία πρὸς θάνατον **hamartia pros thanaton**]. Literally, "sin leading to death," this kind of offense brings what is likely spiritual rather than physical death (1 John 5:16). Earlier, John wrote that a Christian who "does not love abides in death" (3:14-15). A mortal sin committed by a non-believer may mean rejecting Christ. John may also be referring to believers who seceded from the church (2:18-25). *See* SIN, SINNERS.

KATHY R. MAXWELL

MORTAR AND PESTLE [מַכְתֵּשׁ **makhtesh**, עֱלִי **ʿeli**]. The proverb of Prov 27:22, the only biblical text in which one encounters the two functionally related components together, both references the two implements and offers a descriptive context of their use: "Crush a fool in a mortar with a pestle along with crushed grain, but the folly will not be driven out." The mortar and pestle were used for crushing or pounding a variety of grains, herbs, pigments, resins, and some liquids.

Two specific OT terms are of significance: 1) **makhtesh** describes a natural or humanly created "hollow"; note the two natural geological structures of the Negev—"Maktesh-gadol" ("the large hollow") and "Maktesh-qaton" ("the small hollow"). The humanly crafted **makhtesh** refers to the mortar, a stationary (while in use) stone vessel—normally basalt, but occasionally limestone—with a shallow concave-shaped hollow (degree of concavity varies) in which grain or other materials were ground or pounded, using the pestle. The term appears only two other times in the OT; in each case it retains its sense of "hollow" but in reference to places: Judg 15:19, where reference is made to God splitting open the "hollow place that is at Lehi"; and Zeph 1:11, which speaks of a district in Jerusalem, perhaps because of its location in a geological or topographical depression. 2) **ʿeli** is the term translated "pestle" by the NRSV in Prov 27:22, the only place in the OT where it is used. The pestle was a hand-held stone, usually basalt, used for the pounding/grinding. The pestle was often elongated in shape, but archaeologists have discovered pestles of different shapes and sizes, probably determined by the mortar/s with which they were used.

A more general term, **rekhayim** (רֵחַיִם), normally translated "millstone," is of interest because its dual ending seems to suggest that two components make up the one implement (see Exod 11:5; Num 11:8; Deut 24:6; Isa 47:2; Jer 25:10). Perhaps the dual ending includes within its frame of reference the mortar and pestle, but it may reference primarily millstones, which were a larger genre of grinding utensils. Deuteronomy 24:6 alludes to the use of the **rekhayim**—the two-piece utensil for grinding grain, but probably refers chiefly to larger millstones—"upper" and "lower," which were used for larger quantities, and perhaps certain kinds of grains, seeds, and other items. Isaiah 47:2 speaks of "grinding" (**tkhn** טחן) meal in a **rekhayim**. The LXX term **mylos** (μύλος) is characteristically used for **rekhayim**. Describing the Israelite preparation of manna, Num 11:8 speaks of "beating" (i.e., pounding) it in a vessel referred to as a "mortar" (NRSV); here the term **medhokhah** (מְדֹכָה) is used—its only use in the OT.

Archaeological excavation has yielded numerous examples of mortars and pestles; the earliest date to the Pre-Pottery Neolithic A (PPNA) period from sites in the Jordan Valley (e.g., Jericho). Various styles have been recovered, from some that are rather elaborately decorated with tripod bases to very simple, concaved "bowls" with flat bottoms.

JOHN I. LAWLOR

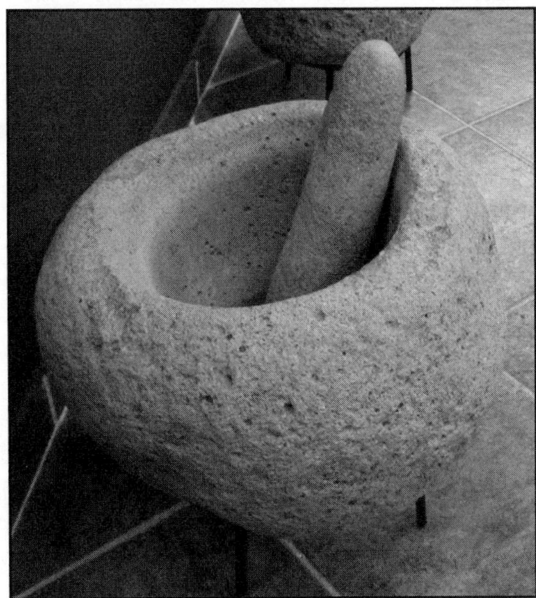

Todd Bolen/Bibleplaces.com

Figure 1: Mortar and pestle

MORTAR, THE [מַכְתֵּשׁ **makhtesh**]. This is a location in JERUSALEM, connected with the FISH GATE and the SECOND QUARTER during the reign of Josiah, where silver traders conducted their business (Zeph 1:10-11) and that will endure God's judgment and destruction on the DAY OF THE LORD. **Makhtesh** signifies a hollow place (Prov 27:22; Judg 15:19), thus a valley in Jerusalem or a place razed by the wrath of God.

STEVEN D. MASON

MOSAIC COVENANT. *See* COVENANT, OT AND NT.

MOSAIC PAVEMENT [רִצְפָּה ritsfah]. Pavement of the king's garden palace at SUSA consisting of marble, alabaster, mother-of-pearl, and colored stones (Esth 1:6), part of the opulent description of the king's palace and banquet. The Hebrew root ratsaf (רָצַף) means "to fit together," and thus the mosaic.

MOSERAH moh-see′ruh [מוֹסֵרָה moserah]. Moserah was one of the Israelites' encampments during their wilderness wanderings, next after BEEROTH-BENE-JAAKAN (Deut 10:6-7). While encamped at Moserah, Aaron died, was buried, and was succeeded as priest by his son Eleazar. Numbers 33:30-38 disagrees, naming the place Moseroth (**moseroth** מֹסֵרוֹת), placing the stop at Moseroth before Beeroth-bene-jaakan, and recording Aaron's death at Mount HOR, seven encampments after Moseroth. Moserah has no known location.

HEIDI E. HAWKS

MOSEROTH. *See* MOSERAH.

MOSES moh′zis [מֹשֶׁה mosheh; Μωυσῆς Mōysēs]. Moses is the first great leader of the people of Israel as portrayed in the OT books of Exodus, Leviticus, Numbers, and Deuteronomy. Moses is arguably the most significant human character in the OT, combining characteristics of the founding ruler, judge, law-giver, scribe, teacher, prophet, intercessor, healer, and savior for Israel. He led Israel out of slavery in Egypt in the exodus (Exod 14–15). He had a uniquely close relationship with Israel's God, speaking directly with God "face to face" (Exod 33:11; Num 12:8; Deut 34:10). He transmitted the Ten Commandments and other laws from God on Mount Sinai to the Israelites (Exod 19–20). He led the runaway Israelite slaves from Egypt through forty years of wilderness wandering until they reached the eastern boundary of the promised land of Canaan, a land he would see from a distance but not enter (Deut 34:4-5). He taught a new generation of young Israelites the essentials of their faith, leaving behind a written "book of the torah (law or teaching)" to be read and studied by each new generation (Deut 31:9-13). Moses has retained his prominence and importance in both Jewish and Christian imaginations throughout their history, extending as well to Islam and the wider culture up to modern times.

A. Moses: Historicity and Cultural Memory

The primary sources for the story of Moses are the four books of the Pentateuch in Exodus–Deuteronomy, beginning with Moses' birth story in Exod 2 and ending with the account of Moses' death in Deut 34. Elsewhere in the OT, Moses is mentioned most often in reference to the book of the law and the commandments that he transmitted (see, e.g., Josh 1:7; 23:6; 2 Kgs 14:6; 21:8; 23:25; Ezra 3:2; 7:6; Neh 1:7; 8:1; 13:1; 2 Chr 25:4; 34:14; 35:12). The figure of Moses himself is not mentioned in any of the preexilic prophets with the possible exception of Mic 6:4 (although its date is disputed). Moses is recalled in a few later exilic and postexilic prophetic texts (Isa 63:11-12; Jer 15:1; Mal 4:4). This disparity between the centrality of Moses' character in the Pentateuch and the relative absence of any mention of Moses in the earlier prophets has led to debates about the dating of the Moses traditions in Exodus–Deuteronomy. Debates about the historicity of Moses are very much entangled with scholarly disputes about the composition history of the Pentateuch.

No extant ANE text apart from the Bible mentions Moses or the dramatic event of the exodus out of Egypt that he led. Thus, evaluation of the historicity of the person of Moses relies exclusively on assessing the biblical material, particularly the traditions of the Pentateuch, as a historical source. Given the centrality of Moses in both Judaism and Christianity, the debate about the historical authenticity of the Moses traditions has been vigorous, with a wide range of opinions.

Traditional and more conservative scholars have assumed some measure of historical accuracy in the biblical narratives about Moses, locating him as a historical figure sometime in the 15th–13th cent. BCE. Following a strictly biblical chronology based on 1 Kgs 6:1, the dating of Moses' career would have been 480 years before the reign of King Solomon (around 966 BCE), suggesting a date of around 1450 BCE for the exodus. Other scholars have suggested that the history of Egypt in the 13th cent. BCE under the pharaoh Ramesses II (see Exod 1:11) provides a more plausible backdrop for dating the exodus and the life of Moses. In any case, traditionalists assume that the exodus out of Egypt was an actual historical event in which a man named Moses led a group of Israelite slaves to freedom (whether the enormous number of 600,000 men plus women and children as in Exod 12:37 or a much smaller group).

From this traditional perspective, the book of the torah of Moses (Deut 31:9-13; Josh 1:7-8) was either Moses' own eyewitness account of the events of his life, a later expanded version of some genuine Mosaic traditions, or traditions that reached back to the Mosaic period even if Moses himself did not write them. Those arguing for the historicity of Moses note at least two elements in the Moses traditions that seem unlikely to have been invented and thus ring true historically: the Egyptian form of the name "Moses," which corresponds to a frequent element in ancient Egyptian names (e.g., the pharaohs Thutmose, Ahmose, and Amenmose), and Moses' marriage to a Midianite wife, Zipporah, the daughter of a non-Israelite priest (Exod 2:16, 21).

At the other extreme, some scholars have denied any historical veracity in the stories about Moses, arguing that the Moses traditions come from a much later exilic or postexilic period (7th–5th cent. BCE). According to this position, the Moses traditions are only folktales with no genuine or authentic historical value to any period earlier than the 6th cent. BCE. Scholars of this opinion point to the curious absence of the name of Moses in any prophetic traditions clearly dating from before the 6th cent. BCE. If Moses is so deeply embedded in ancient Israel's history, why do none of the early classical prophets (8th cent. BCE) mention him? This position rests on the additional assumption that most of the major traditions of the Pentateuch come from a relatively late period in Israel's history, ranging from the later Israelite monarchy (7th cent. BCE) to the Persian period (5th cent. BCE).

Other moderating positions view the Moses stories as heroic sagas that may contain vestiges of historical material about a historical leader named Moses. These earlier sagas were taken up into larger compositions and joined with other diverse legal, poetic, and narrative traditions in a complex process of tradition-building that eventually formed the present Pentateuch. However, it remains difficult to separate out and assess the historicity of any particular detail or narrative concerning Moses. Some scholars have argued that the burial place of Moses on Mount Nebo in Deut 34:5-6 may be a genuine historical note while others point to the Song of the Sea in Exod 15, the Song of Moses in Deut 32, or the so-called Covenant Code of Exod 20:22–23:33 as particularly old historical traditions that may be associated with Moses. The earliest prophetic allusions to the exodus may be from the 8th–cent. northern Israelite prophet Hosea (assuming they are not later editorial additions). God proclaims in Hos 11:1, "Out of Egypt I called my son." Hosea 12:13 recalls a prophetic deliverer associated with the exodus without explicitly mentioning the name of Moses: "By a prophet the LORD brought Israel up from Egypt."

The Legend of Sargon, a birth story of a Mesopotamian king of Akkad from around 2300 BCE, displays a number of notable parallels to the birth story of Moses in Exod 2:1-10. The extant versions of the Sargon legend date from a much later period, the Later Assyrian and Babylonian periods (7th–6th cent. BCE), during a time when a later king of the same name, Sargon II, ruled Assyria. The legend recounts how Sargon was secretly born of a woman priest and an unknown father. Sargon was set adrift as a baby in a reed basket on the Euphrates River and then found and raised by others. Sargon eventually rose as king of Sumer and Akkad. In Exod 2, Moses' mother (of a priestly Levitical family) secretly hid her baby in a reed basket and set it afloat on the Nile River. Pharaoh's daughter discovered the baby Moses in the basket and then raised him in the Egyptian court. Eventually, Moses became not a king like Sargon but a leader of the Israelite slaves, delivering them from the oppression of the Egyptian king. Some scholars have argued that the motif of the exposure of a hero as a baby is a frequent theme in the ancient world so that the parallels between the birth accounts of Sargon and Moses do not suggest any direct dependence of one on the other. Other scholars argue that the number of parallels makes it likely that there is a relationship, whether between the Moses story and much earlier traditions of the Sargon legend that may have circulated before the 7th cent. BCE or the Moses story and the legend's 7th–6th cent. BCE versions. Thus, some scholars (presupposing a literary equivalence of the portrayal of Moses and King Josiah; Deut 34:10-12; 2 Kgs 23:25) have argued that the Moses birth story was written during the reign of Judah's 7th-cent. king Josiah as propaganda against the successors of the Assyrian king Sargon II.

Other scholars have argued that the Moses birth story is aimed more as a judgment on kingship as such and so fits better during Judah's 6th-cent. exile in Babylon when Judah's historical kingship had ended. Still other scholars argue that the birth story of the later Persian king, Cyrus, from the 5th cent. BCE, as recounted by the Greek historian Herodotus, has closer parallels and inversions of the Moses story, including a command to kill the royal baby Cyrus (compare Exod 1:22; 2:15), the transfer of the baby Cyrus from a royal family to a shepherd's family (while Moses, in contrast, is transferred from a lowly Israelite family to the royal Egyptian court, Exod 2:10), a young hot-headed Cyrus beating a playmate (as a young Moses beat an Egyptian foreman in Exod 2:12), and the major defeat and Persian conquest of the Egyptians by Cyrus' son, King Cambyses, in 525 BCE (which parallels Moses' defeat of Pharaoh).

These vigorous debates over the historicity of the figure of Moses and of the dramatic event of Israel's exodus out of the slavery of Egypt that he led testify to the centrality of Moses as a biblical character and of the exodus as a defining episode in ancient Israel's memory and theology. The capacity of the biblical character of Moses and the exodus event itself to be elastic enough to resonate across varied cultural and historical periods and conditions in ancient Israel has led some scholars to use the category of "cultural memory" rather than strict historiography to describe the ways in which the Moses and exodus traditions have long roots in ancient Israel's history that are difficult to trace to any one event or time period. Rather, the story of Moses seems capable of being called up and used in many times and conditions in Israel's various experiences of imperial, political, and social oppression (Egyptian, Assyrian, Babylonian, Persian, Greek), the loss of land and exile, the rise and fall of empires, the need for religiously shaped leadership when old structures of governance collapsed, and the survival of the people and their religious identity as the chosen people of God with whom God remained present and active. This ability to offer resource and resonance in varied times and places also accounts for the ongoing life and interpretation of the figure of Moses in post-biblical traditions reaching to the modern day.

B. Moses in Exodus–Deuteronomy

The varied portraits of Moses emerge from the richness of the biblical narratives about him in the four biblical books of Exodus, Leviticus, Numbers, and Deuteronomy. A survey of the figure of Moses in those four books reveals the multiple dimensions of his character, leadership, theological import, and narrative function as a liminal character who straddled the in-between spaces of Egypt and Israel, wilderness and promised land, past and present, humility and authority, freedom and the law, judgment and mercy, divine and human.

1. Moses as emerging leader in Exodus 1–6

The Moses story begins with a series of three brief narratives: the birth of Moses (Exod 2:1-10), Moses killing an Egyptian foreman who was beating an Israelite slave (Exod 2:11-15*a*), and Moses' rescue of seven Midianite daughters and his marriage to one of them, Zipporah (Exod 2:15*b*-22). While on the surface the three stories seem quite distinct, they contain important similarities and differences. All three stories involve an attempted rescue of an oppressed person or group. In the birth story, a foreign woman (Pharaoh's daughter) successfully rescues the endangered Hebrew baby Moses by adopting Moses into her family. In the Midianite story, Moses rescues foreign women from the harassment of shepherds and is eventually adopted into the Midianite family through marriage. In the middle story about the Egyptian foreman, Moses momentarily leaves his "home" in the Egyptian royal court and tries to help the Israelites by secretly killing an Egyptian foreman who was beating an Israelite slave. However, the next day two Israelites reject Moses' attempt to identify with them as kin as Moses intervenes to resolve their dispute (Exod 2:14). Moses is forced to flee into the wilderness as Pharaoh pronounces a death sentence on his head (Exod 2:15). At the end of the three stories, Moses names his son "Gershom" and declares the meaning of the name: "I have been an alien (ger גֵּר) residing in a foreign land" (Exod 2:22). To what land is Moses referring here? Moses is seen as a Hebrew by the Egyptians (2:6), as a non-Hebrew by the Hebrews (2:14), and as an Egyptian by the Midianites (2:19). Moses has some stake in each community (Egyptian, Israelite, Midianite), but he is not fully at home or accepted in any of them.

These three stories about the young Moses form the backdrop for the next narrative that begins with Moses shepherding sheep for his father-in-law in the wilderness (Exod 3:1-10). Moses encounters the God of his ancestors Abraham, Isaac, and Jacob in the burning bush at Horeb (or alternatively Sinai), "the mountain of God." God instructs Moses to take off his sandals, an ancient practice when entering a holy place of divine presence but also when entering someone's home (Exod 3:5-6). At last, Moses the "alien" or exile has found a place at the mountain of the God of his ancestors where he is fully at home. Fire is a common biblical symbol of God's presence (Gen 15:17; Exod 14:24; 19:18; Lev 10:2; see also Acts 2:3). The perpetually burning bush in Exod 3:2 signals the awesome, dangerous, protective, and never-failing power of the divine (*see* BUSH, BURNING). It is this divine power that will sustain Moses in his new divinely appointed rescue mission to lead the Israelites out of their Egyptian slavery and on a journey through the wilderness to the promised land of Canaan.

These initial episodes in the Moses story set forth important themes that will arise throughout the Pentateuch. As an emerging leader of the Israelites, Moses begins to experience what his fellow Israelites have experienced: Pharaoh's death threats, the loss of home, being an alien in a foreign land. Moses' identity as an alien begins to fuse with the identity of the Israelite slaves in a foreign land. In addition, Moses' actions begin to foreshadow the verbal actions that will be associated with God: "seeing" the oppression of the Israelites (Moses: Exod 2:11; God: Exod 2:25; 3:9), "striking" the Egyptians (Moses: Exod 2:12; God and the plagues: Exod 12:12, 29), "helping" and "saving" those in distress (Moses: Exod 2:17, 19; God: Exod 6:6; 14:13-14, 30). These early episodes also anticipate continuing challenges that Moses will face in the future as Israel's leader, mediating disputes and complaints within the Israelite community (Exod 2:13; 17:2; 18:13; Num 11:10-15; 12:1-2; 16:1-3). Finally, Moses' experience in crossing and straddling boundaries will define his role as a leader as he will negotiate between God and the Egyptian pharaoh, God and the Israelite people, and among different groups within Israel.

God's call to Moses to lead Israel out of slavery in Exod 3 has similarities to other call stories in the Bible in which the one who is called to be a prophet or deliverer resists and offers objections (Judg 6:14-18; Jer 1:1-10). God commands Moses to lead the Israelites out of their slavery, and Moses offers in response a series of five objections. 1) Moses claims to lack adequate qualifications ("Who am I?"), but God assures him that "I will be with you" (3:11-12). 2) The Israelites will ask Moses for God's identification or "name," and so God gives a name that is both substantive but also elusive—"I AM WHO I AM" (NRSV) or "I will be who I will be" (author's trans.; 3:13-14). 3) Moses worries that the Israelites will not believe that God has sent him, and so God gives Moses two small signs or wonders that give a glimpse of the divine power to which Moses will have access (4:1-9), a power that will be displayed in more dramatic ways through the ten plagues and the Red Sea event in Exod 7–15. 4) Moses objects that he is not eloquent, but God assures him that God will teach him what to say (4:10-12). 5) Finally, Moses exhausts his list of reasonable excuses and simply begs God to send someone else. God insists that Moses must go as God's leader, but God will also send Aaron his brother as his assistant (4:13-17). These five objections serve as a kind of theology of leadership. They underscore the frailty of human leaders, the assurance of God's presence and name as the only adequate basis for successful leadership, the need for interim "signs" and glimpses of success along the way, God's faithful provision of resources for whatever deficits faithful leaders may have, and the importance of sharing the burdens of leadership with others. This latter theme of distributing authority and leadership among others will be particularly important at three key junctures in the Moses narrative: Exod 18:13-27; Num 11:10-17, 24-30; and Deut 1:9-18.

An enigmatic text in Exod 4:24-26 recounts how God tried to kill Moses as he was returning to Egypt in obedience to God's command! Moses' wife Zipporah steps in, circumcises her son, touches the foreskin to Moses' "feet" (perhaps a euphemism for genitals), and proclaims, "A bridegroom of blood by circumcision." God relents, and Moses' life is spared. Why would God suddenly attack Moses, who has just obediently accepted the call to be God's chosen leader? Although highly enigmatic and puzzling, the motif is not unprecedented in the OT. Other specially chosen leaders or servants of God experience this mysterious threat of a divine attack as they are about to embark on their journey. Examples include Jacob (Gen 32:22-32), the prophet Balaam (Num 22:22-35), and Joshua (Josh 5:13-15). In each case, the divine threat is sudden, seemingly unprovoked, and mysterious. The sudden divine attack underscores God's sovereignty over God's chosen agents. If the chosen one strays, God the ally may quickly become an enemy. Those called by God ought not to assume uncritically that God is always and unquestionably on their side.

2. Moses as agent of God's judgment and deliverance in Exodus 7–15

As a result of Pharaoh's ongoing resistance, God sends Moses and his brother Aaron back to Pharaoh in ten encounters that result in each case with God sending a plague or ecological disaster upon the Egyptians. The plagues involve a wide range of natural disasters. The Nile River turns to blood, frogs appear everywhere in houses, gnats swarm the land, flies multiply, disease attacks animals, boils break the skin of cattle and humans, a severe hailstorm blankets the land, locusts devour the vegetation, darkness falls during the day, and finally all firstborn male offspring of Egyptian families and animals die. The plagues represent God's subtle working through the complex web of interconnection between human injustice and oppression and natural disaster. As an agent of God's judgment, Moses' repeated encounters with Pharaoh follow two alternating patterns that editors have interwoven to form the present shape of the plague cycle. One pattern (e.g., the gnats plague in 8:16-19) has the following structure:

a) God says to Moses, "Say to Aaron, 'Do *x* (a plague or "wonder")'."
b) Moses and/or Aaron do *x*.
c) The Egyptian magicians try to do *x*. Initially they succeed, later they do not.
d) Pharaoh still refuses, and his heart is hardened.

Other plague stories follow a different pattern (e.g., the flies plague in 8:20-32):

a) Moses says to Pharaoh, "If you do not let the people go, then *x* (some kind of plague) will happen."
b) Pharaoh refuses, and the plague happens.
c) Pharaoh calls Moses, and they negotiate back and forth.
d) In the end, Pharaoh's heart again is hardened, and he ends upsaying "No!"

The first pattern places emphasis on Moses' human involvement to mediate and accomplish God's will. The second pattern reduces Moses' role to one who announces what God will do, and it is God who is the primary actor.

A similar tension regarding Moses' role appears in the two traditions that have been brought together in Exod 14, which tells the story of the defeat of the Egyptians and the rescue of Israel from their slavery. In one of the two traditions now woven together in Exod 14, God comes down and is intimately present in the battle through a pillar of cloud, directly fighting against Pharaoh and the Egyptian army. God moves, drives back the sea, tosses the Egyptians, clogs their wheels, and saves the Israelites (Exod 14:19-20, 21*b*, 24-25, 27*b*). In these sections of Exod 14, Moses plays no active role. He simply announces God's coming salvation on Israel: "the LORD will fight for you, and you have only to keep still" (Exod 14:14). Alongside this version is another set of verses in Exod 14 in which God works in a more distant and mediated way through the

Exodus—Before Sinai	Numbers—After Sinai
a) Complaint about water, bitter water made sweet; The LORD heals—Exod 15:22-26	a) Unspecified complaint Angry fire of the LORD kills—Num 11:1-3
b) Manna/quail—Exod 16:1-36	b) Manna/quail—Num 11:4-15, 31-35
c) Water from the rock—Exod 17:1-7	c) Water from the rock—Num 20:1-13

Figure 1: Complaint stories

obedient words and actions of Moses and the Israelites. Moses stretches out his staff both to divide and bring back together the waters of the Red Sea, and the Israelites walk over on dry land to safety (15-18, 21*a*, 21*c*, 22-23, 26-27*a*, 28-29). The poetic Song of the Sea in Exod 15 provides yet a third version of the same deliverance event. Moses and the Israelites sing the song as an act of worship, but neither Moses nor the people appears as an actor in the poem. God alone is praised as "a warrior" who "triumphed gloriously; horse and rider he has thrown into the sea" (Exod 15:1-3).

The overall result of this interweaving of these varied patterns and traditions, one emphasizing God's direct involvement in acts of judgment and deliverance and others highlighting the mediation of God's work and power through a human agent like Moses, creates a theologically fruitful tension. As the book of Exodus recounts it, the story of Moses is not primarily a generic story of a great human liberator or heroic revolutionary with some incidental religious language attached as window dressing. God is very much the prime actor and stands behind whatever actions and words Moses may offer. The theological core of the exodus story cannot be easily disentangled from this story of liberation from slavery. On the other hand, the story of Moses is not entirely an account of a passive bystander who simply waits for God. Moses leads the people and mediates to them God's words and power as he acts and speaks. The human and the divine are intimately bound up together in this act of judgment on an imperial and oppressive national power and this act of deliverance on behalf of a less powerful and enslaved people of Israel, God's own firstborn son (Exod 4:22). Sociopolitical battles and dynamics are intimately bound up with theological realities and struggles.

3. Moses as shepherd and judge in Exodus and Numbers

Moses received his call from God in the burning bush episode as he was shepherding his father-in-law's sheep in the wilderness (Exod 3:1). The image of shepherd frequently served in the ancient world as a metaphor for a leader or king, whether human (2 Sam 5:2; 1 Kgs 22:17; Jer 23:2) or divine (Gen 49:24; Ps 23:1; Isa 40:11). A youthful David as shepherd prefigured his eventual rise to kingship as shepherd of Israel (1 Sam 16:11-13; Ps 78:70-71). Similarly, Moses' early career as a shepherd foreshadows another role that he plays in guiding the Israelites on their journey through the wilderness from Egypt to the land of Canaan.

The people complain to Moses immediately upon entry into the wilderness after the Red Sea crossing in three narratives in Exod 15:22–17:7. These three narratives are "positive" complaint stories in that the needs expressed by the people are legitimate and God responds positively to each one. If one jumps to the later wilderness wandering stories in the book of Numbers, one will find three similar murmuring stories, except that in Numbers they are all negative or illegitimate complaints. In Exodus, Moses and God respond positively to the needs of the people (providing water and manna). In Numbers, God condemns the murmuring of the people as a lack of faith or trust; each episode ends in punishment and death.

In Num 20:1-13, God condemns not only the Israelite people; God also condemns Moses and Aaron to premature deaths outside the promised land because of their failure to trust God and show God's holiness (see also Num 27:12-14). This story provides one of two alternate explanations noted in the book of Deuteronomy for why Moses will not be allowed to enter the promised land: it was because of Moses' own sin in Deut 32:48-52 and because of the people's sin in Deut 1:37; 3:23-29.

There are other parallels between the Exodus (more positive) and Numbers (more negative) wilderness stories. Moses' sister Miriam sings praises to God in Exod 15:20-21, but she rebels against Moses along with her brother Aaron in Num 12:1-2. Extra leaders are appointed to ease Moses' burdens as a friendly suggestion from his father-in-law Jethro in Exod 18. In Num 11:16-20, God similarly commands that extra leaders be appointed to help Moses, but the Numbers account involves Moses' frantic and nearly suicidal despair over the struggles of leadership. Israel attacks the oppressive enemy Amalek and is victorious in Exod 17:8-16, but in Num 14:39-45, Israel again attacks Amalek and is defeated.

Thus, Moses and God respond positively to Israel's legitimate needs and complaints early in the wilderness journey in Exodus. However, after Israel has had some long experience with Moses in the wilderness and after entering into a formal covenant with God at Mount Sinai beginning in Exod 19, the complaints of Israel in the book of Numbers are largely seen as negative failures to trust God. Thus, Moses' positive work as shepherd and provider of water and manna in Exodus is eclipsed by Moses' later frustration at being a constant object of the people's rebellion and distrust in Numbers.

One important theme in the exercise of Moses' leadership as a shepherd and judge of the people is the distribution and delegation of authority to other members of the community. Jethro's suggestion to Moses in Exod 18:13-27 to appoint judges "to bear the burden with you" underscores an important practice to be nurtured by leaders to share responsibility, for the good of the leader as well as the community (Exod 18:18). Similar accounts of Moses delegating others to share the responsibilities of judging and leading the people occur later in Num 11:10-17, 24-30 and Deut 1:9-18. The preceding account of the battle with Amalek in Exod 17:8-13 also illustrates this same theme with the image of success when Aaron and Hur help to hold up Moses' arms and thereby guarantee Israel's victory. Moreover, the concern for a regular rhythm of sabbath rest and trusting God in the manna story in Exod 16 also contributes to teaching Moses and the Israelites that God will provide. All does not depend on frenetic human achievement alone.

4. Moses as mediator of God's covenant and law

One of Moses' most central roles in the Pentateuch begins in Exod 19 as Moses prepares to transmit the commandments and laws of the covenant to the people of Israel at Mount Sinai. Scholars have long recognized that different law codes of varied age and traditions in ancient Israelite history have been gathered together in the final form of the Pentateuch and placed in the mouth of Moses as all mediated by him from God at Mount Sinai. In this way, although most scholars would agree that the legal collections of the Pentateuch had a long history of composition and collection over centuries of time and among different traditions, nearly all OT law is presented in the present form of the Pentateuch as if given by God at one time from Sinai. This centralizing of all law at Sinai invites later interpreters to seek out the one divine will within the interrelationships among these competing and sometimes conflicting law codes in the Pentateuch. Old Testament law has thereby provided a rich resource for ongoing ethical and theological reflection and debate in both Jewish and Christian traditions over the centuries.

There is one set of laws that does stand out from the rest. The Ten Commandments carry a unique authority by virtue of their prominent literary placement at the beginning of the Sinai material in Exod 20:1-17, their repetition in Deut 5:1-21 as the basis for the other laws in Deuteronomy, their portrayal as the only laws spoken directly by God to the people rather than mediated by Moses (Exod 20:1, 18-21; Deut 5:22-27), and their being on the tablets of stone written by "the finger of God" (Exod 24:12-14; 31:18; 32:15-16; 34:1; Deut 9:9-11, 15; but see Exod 34:27-28 where Moses is the writer of the stone tablets).

If the Ten Commandments are a foundational summation of Israel's central commandments in the present form of the Pentateuch, several other collections of laws in Exodus–Deuteronomy serve as extensions, adaptations, and interpretations of the Ten Commandments into the wide sphere of ancient Israel's community life as they offer guidelines for matters ranging from worship to business, from family to city and nation, from food to sex, from concern for the poor, widow, and orphan to the responsibilities of leaders, kings, prophets, judges, and elders. The disparities and varying emphases among the law codes create a fertile environment of jagged edges and unfinished legal and ethical interpretation that invites succeeding generations into dialogue with its laws. These other law codes include the so-called Covenant Code or Book of the Covenant in Exod 20:22–23:33, the cultic code in Exod 34:10-26, the Priestly laws of Lev 1–18 and Num 1–10, the Holiness Code of Lev 19–26, and the Deuteronomic law code in Deut 5–26. Moses also offers other scattered laws apart from Sinai (e.g., the Passover laws in Exod 12–13, or the later laws in Num 15; 19). These may represent later editorial additions to the Pentateuch, but their effect is to suggest the need for continued openness and interpretation in discerning the divine will even outside the boundaries of the Sinai legislation and into succeeding generations.

This need for ongoing legal and ethical reflection is also illustrated by the story of Zelophehad's daughters, who pose a legal dilemma to Moses in which two competing values or customs seem to contradict each other in Num 27 and 36. The father of the five daughters dies, and the daughters argue before Moses that they should inherit their father's land. This position would be supported by the law's concern that land remains within the family to which it was first given. Each family should retain its right to its land inheritance. On the other hand, the custom has been that only males should inherit their family's land, which would run counter to the daughters inheriting their paternal land. Moses is perplexed by the dilemma and refers the case directly to God, who sides with the daughters and directs that the concern that families retain their portion of land is more important and thus the daughters should inherit their father's land (Num 27:5-11). Not even Moses is an infallible interpreter of the law.

5. Moses as intercessor in Exodus 32–34 and Numbers 13–14

Moses is remembered outside the Pentateuch as a legendary intercessor who "stood in the breach" and turned God's wrath away from destroying a rebellious Israel (Ps 106:23; Jer 15:1).

This reputation emerges from Moses' role in the two most significant crisis points in the Pentateuch's story of God and Israel: the golden calf apostasy in Exod 32–34 and the spy story at the edge of the promised land in Num 13–14. In both cases, Israel's rebellion against God rose to such heights that God contemplated destroying the sinful Israelites in the wilderness. In a set of remarkable interchanges, it was only the arguments and intercession of Moses with God on behalf of Israel that led God to change direction and stay committed to bringing the Israelites to the promised land of Canaan.

In Exod 32, the Israelites have already committed themselves to obey all the commandments of the covenant (Exod 19:8; 24:3, 7). However, they promptly disobey the first and most important of the Ten Commandments, which prohibits the worship of other gods or the making of graven images or idols, by worshiping a golden calf while Moses is with God on top of Mount Sinai. The worship of an idol constitutes a breaking of the covenant relationship between God and Israel, and so God tells Moses that God's holy wrath will destroy Israel. God plans to abandon Israel and create a new people with Moses: "of you [Moses] I will make a great nation" (Exod 32:10). God in effect offers to start over and make of Moses a new Abraham, to whom God had given a similar promise (Gen 12:2). Moses refuses the tempting offer, however, and instead pleads with God to change God's mind and not destroy the Israelites. He offers three reasons. 1) God has a history with the Israelites, and they belong to God as God's very own people. These are "your people, whom you brought out of the land of Egypt" (Exod 32:11). 2) Abandoning the Israelites would be bad for God's international reputation. What would the Egyptians say if God allowed the Israelites to die after delivering them from Egypt (Exod 32:12)? 3) God had made a promise to Israel's ancestors (Abraham, Isaac, and Israel) that God would bring their descendants to the promised land of Canaan, and it is God's nature to keep God's promises (Exod 32:13). Remarkably, Moses' arguments are persuasive and "the LORD changed his mind about the disaster that he planned to bring on his people" (Exod 32:14). God will have the ultimate say, but God takes into account human pleas and arguments that advocate for those in need.

Although Moses had advocated for Israel before God, Moses assumes his other role as representative of God when he descends Mount Sinai and confronts the people with their sinful worship of the golden calf. He embodies the wrath of God and angrily smashes the precious stone tablets on which God had written the covenant commands, an act that signals the breaking of the covenant relationship between God and the people (Exod 32:15-19). Moses then confronts his brother Aaron, who had formed the golden calf, and Aaron (unlike his brother Moses) blames the people (Exod 32:22) and takes no responsibility himself for what he had done: "I threw [the gold] into the fire, and out came this calf!" (Exod 32:24). The contrast in leadership between Moses and Aaron is stark. Moses refuses to glorify himself and instead accepts responsibility and advocates for the people. Aaron, on the other hand, refuses to accept his own guilt and responsibility and instead places it entirely on the people.

Moses returns up Mount Sinai to meet with God a second time. God offers to send "an angel" to lead the Israelites to the promised land, since God's own holy presence cannot go "among" or "in the midst of" the sinful Israelites without destroying them (Exod 32:34; 33:2-3). However, Moses refuses to accept this compromise and insists that God's very own presence must go "with us" in their midst, for it is only God's presence that sets them apart from any other people (Exod 33:15-16). On the basis of the unique intimacy between God and Moses, God agrees to go with Israel and to dwell "in their midst" on the way to the promised land of Canaan (Exod 33:17). But how can a holy God dwell among sinful people without destroying them? The answer comes in a dramatic and unique revelation of God's inner character, glory, goodness, and name as God passes by Moses, and Moses is allowed to see the back of God but not God's face (Exod 33:19-23). As God passes by, God proclaims an expanded and altered form of the divine name and character in Exod 34:6-7 as compared to an earlier version in Exod 20:5-6. The previous description of God's character in Exod 20:5-6 had foregrounded God's jealous punishing and mentioned secondarily God's steadfast love "to those who love me and keep my commandments." In Exod 34:6-7, the description of God's love and mercy is put in first place and expanded. Forgiveness is added. The qualification of God's love only to "those who love me and keep my commandments" is deleted. God's punishment and the consequences of disobedience remain but are placed in a secondary position. It is only on the basis of this deeper insight into God's own character that Moses and Israel can proceed in confidence with their journey to Canaan, knowing that a holy and loving God can dwell even in the midst of a sinful people. Because of this definitive revelation of God's deeper merciful character, Moses oversees the construction of the tabernacle, which will be the seat of the divine presence located in the middle of the Israelite camp as they travel from Sinai to Canaan (Exod 35–40). The divine presence moves off Mount Sinai and transfers to the tabernacle in the climactic scene that concludes the book of Exodus (Exod 40:34-38).

One of the visual side effects that resulted from these intimate encounters between God and Moses on Mount Sinai is that the skin of Moses' face shone with a divine radiance or aura (Exod 34:29-35). Although Moses normally veiled his shining face, he would lift the veil whenever he communicated with God. He would also lift the veil whenever he proclaimed God's word to the people, and "the Israelites would see the face of Moses, that the skin of his face was shining" (Exod 34:35). The radiant face marked Moses as a uniquely authoritative spokesperson for God. Although no human could see the face of God and live (Exod 33:20), the people could see something of the divine in the shining face of Moses. In Exodus, the facial light of Moses mirrors in part the fiery divine light of the burning bush (Exod 3:2, 6), the divine pillar of cloud and fire veiling God's presence (Exod 13:21-22; 14:24; 33:9), and the brilliant fire and lightning associated with God's presence on Mount Sinai (Exod 19:16, 18; 24:17). As the Israelites "trembled" before God's radiant and fiery presence (Exod 19:16), so too they "were afraid" of Moses' shining face (Exod 34:30). Moses' veil, in turn, served to protect the people from their fear and the threat of overexposure to the power of divine presence that Moses embodied in their midst. The Latin Vulgate translation of the Bible mistranslated the Hebrew verb "shining/sending forth beams" as the noun "horn" (Exod 34:35; *see* MOSES, HORN OF). As a result, Moses is sometimes depicted in Christian paintings and sculpture from the medieval period onward as having horns protruding from his head. This is the case most famously with Michelangelo's statue of the horned Moses in St. Peter's Basilica in Rome.

The second major crisis in the Pentateuch that endangers God's future with Israel in the wilderness occurs in the spy story of Num 13–14. At last, Israel has arrived at the southern boundary of the promised land of Canaan after only two years of wandering in the wilderness. God's promise to Abraham and Sarah that their descendants would one day inherit the land of Canaan was seemingly about to be fulfilled (Gen 12:1, 7; 15:18-19). God instructs Moses to appoint twelve spies, one from each of the twelve tribes of Israel, to survey the land of Canaan and its inhabitants (Num 13:1-20). The spies eventually return, and the majority of the spies reports that the land is fertile, but the inhabitants, the Canaanites, are too large and powerful for the Israelites to defeat (Num 13:25-33). The people of Israel are discouraged by the news and decide not to accept God's gift of the land of Canaan. Instead, they yearn to return to Egypt or to go back and die in the wilderness (Num 14:1-4).

This failure to trust God to make good on the long-standing promise and bring them safely into the land of Canaan represents a second major breach of the covenant relationship between God and Israel in the Pentateuch. God laments to Moses, "How long will they refuse to believe in me?" God resolves to disinherit the Israelites and begin again with Moses to make a new nation, offering in effect to make Moses a new Abraham (Num 14:11-12). Once again, however, Moses refuses the offer and instead intercedes on behalf of the people of Israel. As Moses did in the golden calf incident, he reminds God that destroying Israel in the wilderness will tarnish God's international reputation, this time not only with the Egyptians but also with the Canaanites. Moses also uses the special revelation of God's deep character back in Exod 34:6-7 as "abounding in steadfast love" and "forgiving iniquity" while also "by no means clearing the guilty" as leverage for his argument that God should forgive the Israelites yet again as God has done ever since they left Egypt (Num 14:13-20).

Once again, God relents and agrees to forgive the Israelites. However, God warns Moses that the disobedience will also result in some dire consequences. The narrative seeks to keep in balance a delicate tension between the mercy of God and the judgment of God. As a stroke of poetic justice in light of the Israelites yearning to go back to the wilderness and die (Num 14:2), God resolves that the people will wander in the wilderness for thirty-eight more years for a total of forty years of wilderness wandering. In the course of that time, all the members of the old generation who had come out of Egypt will gradually die in the wilderness. At the same time, God pledges to bring the new generation of their children safely into the land of Canaan, thereby fulfilling God's Abrahamic promise of land to Israel. The parents will die for their lack of trust, but the children will live and enter Canaan (Num 14:20-35).

Moses and his brother Aaron join the older generation in being condemned to die outside the land of Canaan by virtue of their sin on another occasion later in the wilderness journey. In Num 20:2-13, the Israelites complain about the lack of water and God instructs Moses to "command the rock" to yield water for the people (20:7-8). Moses does not precisely follow the instructions to "command the rock" but instead strikes the rock twice with his staff. It is not clear whether the discrepancy is significant or not. In any case, the miracle is successful in that the rock yields water for the thirsty Israelites. However, God abruptly condemns Moses and Aaron, interpreting their actions as not trusting God or honoring God's holiness before the people. As a result, God prohibits Moses and Aaron from ever entering the land of Canaan, and thus their fate is joined to the older wilderness generation who will die in the wilderness. The exact nature of Moses' sin in Num 20 is one of the great puzzles of biblical interpretation for which a large number of solutions have been proposed from ancient times to the present. Although Moses was legendary for his ability to intercede and move God to forgive others in numerous appeals to divine mercy, he also himself experienced God's judgment and the consequences of his own disobedience (see also Num 27:12-14).

6. Moses as teacher of a new generation in Deuteronomy

Moses emerges in the book of Deuteronomy in the distinctive role of a teacher who instructs a new generation in the traditions of their ancestors just before his death narrated in the final chapter of the book (Deut 1:1-5; 4:14). Deuteronomy consists of a series of extended oral teaching sessions by Moses to the young Israelites. Moses concludes by writing all of his final teaching in "this book of the torah" (author's trans.; NRSV, "this book of the law"), which he entrusts to safekeeping with the Levitical priests so that it can be recited out loud on regular occasions to elders and all the people in succeeding generations (Deut 31:9-13, 24-29). The Hebrew word **torah** (תּוֹרָה) is often translated as "law," but in the context of Deuteronomy it is better translated as "instruction" or "teaching" (*see* TORAH). Various synonyms for the word *teach* occur at least seventeen times in Deuteronomy. Moses is repeatedly presented as a model teacher (Deut 1:5; 4:1, 5, 14; 5:31; 31:22). Moses provides the essentials of the faith through the story of the past (Deut 1:1–4:43), the laws and commandments for the present (Deut 4:44–28:68), and provisions for extending the covenant into the future (Deut 29:1–32:52). The central theme of Deuteronomy is captured in Deut 5:3: "Not with our ancestors did the LORD make this covenant, but with us, who are all of us here alive today." The word *today* or phrase "this day" occurs twenty-seven times in Deuteronomy and underscores the book's intention to catechize and educate each new generation so that the traditions and covenant with God from the past become actualized and living faith traditions for the present.

Moses embodies a Deuteronomic program of faith formation that is passed from parents or elders to children through oral education, recitation, writing, and memorization supported by written texts in ancient Israel. The Song of Moses in Deut 32:1-43 illustrates the educational intent of Moses' words. God commands Moses, "Now therefore write this song, and teach it to the Israelites; put it in their mouths, in order that this song may be a witness for me against the Israelites" (Deut 31:19). At the conclusion of the song, Moses commands the people, "Take to heart all the words that I am giving in witness against you today; give them as a command to your children, so that they may diligently observe all the words of this law (**torah**)" (Deut 32:46). "Taking to heart" involves internalizing and memorizing the words of **torah** or teaching and making them one's own through song, repetition, and hearing.

Elsewhere, Moses urges the Israelites to "love the LORD your God with all your heart" (Deut 6:5) and to "keep these words that I am commanding you today in your heart" (Deut 6:6). Moses then instructs the community on how the words of Deuteronomy can be written on the heart of the people: "Recite them to your children and talk about them" when at home or away, when rising or going to bed (Deut 6:7). This strategy of constant oral recitation combined with surrounding oneself with written emblems of Deuteronomy's teaching as constant reminders: "Bind them as a sign on your hand, fix them as an emblem on your forehead, and write them on the doorposts of your house and on your gates" (Deut 6:8-9). These strategies seek to ensure that Israel constantly remember and not "forget the LORD" (Deut 6:12). This education and faith formation begins, of course, not with children but with adults: "Remember today that it was not your children . . . but it is you who must acknowledge" God's greatness and all that God has done for God's people (Deut 11:2).

The core of Deuteronomy's curriculum of faith formation is Deut 5. All of the laws and statutes that follow in Deut 6–26 roughly follow the sequence of laws and topics as they appear in the Ten Commandments listed in Deut 5:6-21. In Deuteronomy as in Exod 20, the Ten Commandments are presented as the only words spoken directly by God to the people without Moses' mediation. The Ten Commandments are the only words that God writes on the stone tablets given to Moses (Deut 5:22). After Moses recounts how he smashed and broke the stone tablets after the golden calf apostasy, he recalls God's command to place a newly written set of stone tablets inside the ark of the covenant (Deut 10:2-5), an ornate box carried in the midst of the people that eventually ends up in Solomon's Temple in Jerusalem (1 Kgs 8:1-9). In Deuteronomy's understanding, the only function of the ark is to carry the stone tablets. At the same time, the "book of the torah" (author's trans.; NRSV, "book of the law") that Moses writes is placed beside the ark of the covenant but not in it (Deut 31:26). God's direct words are distinguished from the humanly mediated words of God through Moses in the book of the torah, which is presumably some form of the book of Deuteronomy. Later tradition will broaden the title of Torah to include all of the five books of Genesis–Deuteronomy as the books of Moses.

7. Moses as prophet

The concluding scene of the death of Moses in Deuteronomy remembers Moses as the first and greatest of Israel's prophets: "Never since has there arisen a prophet in Israel like Moses, whom the LORD knew face to face. He was unequaled for all the signs and wonders that the LORD sent him to perform" and "for all the mighty deeds and all the terrifying displays of power" (Deut 34:10-12). His uniqueness stems both from his unparalleled intimacy with God ("face to face") and his powerful "signs and wonders." Interestingly, the vocabulary of "signs and wonders . . . mighty deeds . . . terrifying displays of power" are all technical terms applied elsewhere in Deuteronomy only to God (4:34; 6:22; 7:19; 11:3; 26:8; 29:3). At the point of narrating Moses' human frailty and limits at his death, the narrative also lifts up his closeness to God in both relationship and power.

This paradoxical portrait of Moses as both a strong, heroic prophet and fragile mortal is held together in other ways at the end of Deuteronomy. In Deut 34:7, Moses is 120 years old but remains exceptionally strong and youthful: "His sight was unimpaired and his vigor had not abated." In contrast, Moses in Deut 31:2 describes himself as weak and feeble: "I am now one hundred twenty years old. I am no longer able to get about." Two conflicting explanations also coexist in Deuteronomy about why Moses had to die against his will outside the promised land of Canaan. One tradition explains the prohibition to enter Canaan as a result of Moses' own sinful act at Meribath-kadesh (Deut 32:48-52). Another tradition in Deuteronomy explains that it was because of the sin of the Israelite people that Moses had to die outside the land (Deut 1:37; 3:26; 4:21). This latter reason portrays Moses as more heroic and noble; the other portrays Moses as more flawed and sinful.

One important text concerning Moses as a prophet is embedded in the laws for leaders (judges, kings, priests, prophets) in Deut 16:18–18:22. Anticipating his own imminent death, Moses promises that in future generations God "will raise up for you a prophet like me from among your own people; you shall heed such a prophet" (Deut 18:15). The prophetic career of Jeremiah in the years leading up to the exile of Judah in 587 BCE is one of the OT's clearest examples of such a "prophet like Moses." In ways similar to Moses, Jeremiah sensed his inadequacy when called by God (Jer 1:6-8; compare Exod 3:11-12), expressed his frustration and passionate complaints to God about the challenges of being a divine spokesperson (Jer 12:1-4; 20:7-18; compare Num 11:10-15), felt a call to intercede for the people in spite of God's refusal to hear Jeremiah's prayers on their behalf (Jer 7:16; 11:14; 14:11; 15:1; Exod 32:11-14; Num 14:13-19), and offered the people hope following the judgment of God for their sinfulness (Jer 29:1–33:26; Deut 4:25-31; 30:1-10). This promise of a future prophet like Moses continued to live on beyond the OT in both Judaism and Christianity as it sometimes intersected with expectations of a future Davidic Messiah or other figure in some Jewish and early Christian traditions.

C. Moses in Post-biblical Judaism

Traditions about Moses continued to develop in post-biblical Jewish communities. The "book of the Torah" that Moses wrote came to be seen as not just some form of Deuteronomy but the whole of the Pentateuch. Hellenistic Jewish writers like Josephus and Philo (both 1st cent. CE) sought to defend the greatness of Moses by expansive traditions about his life and achievements in the face of Hellenistic attacks against Moses (Manetho and Apollonius). Moses was lifted up as a great inventor of the arts of civilization (writing, philosophy, politics, and religion), the greatest of the "prophets," an "apostle" and "man of God," as well as a model of the Hellenistic "divine man." Philo portrays Moses in the three roles of priest (compare Ps 99:6), prophet, and king, even a divine king who ascended into heaven.

Early Jewish apocalyptic texts (the *Assumption of Moses* and *Jubilees*) portray Moses as a recipient of secret knowledge about the past and future, especially the end-time. Moses continues his role as interceding on behalf of the people Israel until the Last Judgment. The Qumran community likewise honored Moses as the great prophet who provided special revelation to them through the community's unique interpretation of the Torah. The members of the Qumran desert community strongly identified with the promises and struggles of the wilderness community of Israelites that Moses led in Exodus–Deuteronomy.

The rabbinic tradition emphasized Moses' role as one who conveyed both the written law and the oral law at Mount Sinai. The written law was the Pentateuch. The oral law was the verbally transmitted set of authoritative interpretations of the Torah taught by successive generations from Moses to Joshua and forward up through the generations of the rabbis. This oral law was collected and written down to form the authoritative rabbinic tradition, eventually codified most definitively in the TALMUD (4th–6th cent. CE). The rabbis considered Moses the first of the great prophets, a true "servant of God," and most of all the great "teacher" of Torah.

D. Moses in the New Testament

The NT portraits of Moses reflect the ambivalence of the early Christian community in terms of both its continuity and discontinuity with Judaism. The Gospels highlight many parallels between Jesus and Moses while other NT writings, especially Hebrews, emphasize the superiority of Jesus to Moses. The birth story of Jesus in Matthew alludes to several parts of Moses' birth story and its embellished Jewish traditions (a royal decree to murder infants, the threat of Jesus as a rising king, the flight to Egypt by Jesus and his parents as a reversal of Moses' flight from Egypt, waiting until the king's death until his return; Matt 2; Exod 2). Jesus fasted for forty days in preparation for his temptations in the wilderness, an allusion to Moses fasting for forty days out in the wilderness at Mount Sinai (Deut 9:9; Matt 4:1-2; Luke 4:1-3). Jesus' transfiguration on the mountain with Moses and Elijah in the Gospels (Matt 17:1-8; Mark 9:2-8; Luke 9:28-36) has several parallels with Moses on Mount Sinai in Exodus: the appearance of Moses with Elijah, the shining face of Moses like the "dazzling white" appearance of Jesus (Exod 34:29-35), the cloud of divine presence and the divine voice (Exod 19:16-19), and the fear displayed by the Israelites and the disciples at the divine presence (Exod 20:18-21; Mark 9:6). The stories of Jesus feeding the 5,000 (Matt 14:13-21; Mark 6:32-44; Luke 9:10-17; John 6:1-14) recall the pentateuchal traditions of Moses as shepherd and provider of food and drink in the wilderness. In John 6:25-35, Jesus' claim to be "the bread of Life" is associated with Moses providing manna in the wilderness as "bread from heaven" (Exod 16:4). Moses lifting up the bronze serpent to heal and give life in the wilderness (Num 21:4-9) is employed as a parallel with the lifting up of Jesus on the cross in his dying, which is also his glorification (John 3:14). The ascension of Jesus in Luke 24:51 and Acts 1:9-11 draws on post-biblical Jewish traditions about Moses ascending up to heaven when he went up into the divine cloud on Mount Sinai (Exod 20:21; 24:12-18). Moses' burial place is unknown, according to Deut 34:6, resulting in an early Jewish tradition that Moses did not die but was taken up into heaven like Elijah (2 Kgs 2:1-12; see Josephus, *Ant.* 4.323–26). *See* MOSES, ASSUMPTION OF.

Implicit claims that Jesus is similar to Moses but also superior to him are made in Matthew's portrait of Jesus as giver of a new divine law in the Sermon on the Mount ("you have heard it said [by Moses], but I say to you . . . ," Matt 5:1–7:28). Luke presents Jesus as "a prophet like Moses" who led the twelve tribes (twelve disciples) on a journey through the wilderness (Luke 9:1-50), but Jesus is also more than a prophet (Luke 9:18-20). According to John 1:17, the law that "came through Moses" contrasts with the "grace and truth" that comes through Jesus. The apostle Paul wrote to the community at Corinth, urging them to interpret the story of Moses and the rebellious Israelites in the wilderness as "an example, written down to instruct us" (1 Cor 10:1-11). Yet in 2 Cor 3:1-18, the glory of the new covenant of the spirit written on tablets of human hearts and unveiled in Christ contrasts with the old covenant written on stone tablets in which the divine glory of Moses' face remained veiled and inaccessible. Hebrews draws a particularly strong divide between Jesus with his new covenant and Moses with his old covenant (Heb 7:22; 8:6-13; 9:15-22). Moses is the servant of God; Jesus is the superior "son of God" (Heb 4:14). Moses built an earthly sanctuary; Jesus built a heavenly sanctuary (Heb 8:5; 9:23-24). The Levitical priests under Moses ministered by offering sacrifices year after year. But Jesus is the great high priest who offered his life as a sacrifice once for all on the cross and now intercedes in heaven for the faithful (Heb 7:23-24; 9:25-26). The implied supersessionism or superiority of Jesus over Moses in these NT texts needs to be read within its ancient Greco-Roman context. The small fledgling Christian movement was beginning to break away from its Jewish roots and struggling for recognition in the face of the more ancient and more revered forms of traditional Judaism. Interpreting such texts in modern times requires sensitivity to the much different cultural and religious circumstances when Jews are in a minority and Christians are the majority. *See* AKHENATEN; ARK OF THE COVENANT; DATHAN; EGYPT; EXODUS, ROUTE OF; FIRSTBORN; GOD, NAMES OF; JETHRO; KADESH, KADESH-BARNEA; KORAH, KORAHITES; MIDIAN, MIDIANITES; PASSOVER AND FEAST OF UNLEAVENED BREAD; PENTATEUCH; PILLAR OF CLOUD AND FIRE; PLAGUES IN EGYPT; RED SEA, REED SEA.

Bibliography: J. Assmann. *Moses the Egyptian: The Memory of Egypt in Western Monotheism* (1997); B. Britt. *Rewriting Moses: The Narrative Eclipse of the Text* (2004); B. Childs. *Exodus.* OTL (1974); G. Coats. *The Moses Tradition* (1993); M. Dijkstra. "The Law of Moses: The Memory of Mosaic Religion in and after the Exile." *Yahwism after the Exile: Perspectives on Israelite Religion in the Persian Period.* Rainer Albertz and Bob Becking, eds. (2003) 70–98; T. Fretheim. *Exodus.* IBC (1991); R. Hendel. "The Exodus in Biblical Memory." *JBL* 120 (2001) 601–22; J. Lierman. *The New Testament Moses* (2004); D. Olson. *Deuteronomy and the Death of Moses: A Theological Reading* (1994); D. Olson. *Numbers.* IBC (1996); J. Van Seters. "Moses." *The Biblical World,* vol. 2. John Barton, ed. (2002) 194–207; H. Zlotnick-Sivan. "Moses the Persian? Exodus 2, the 'Other' and Biblical 'Mnemohistory.' " *ZAW* 116 (2004) 189–205.

DENNIS T. OLSON

MOSES, ASSUMPTION OF. A pseudepigraphical writing, also called *Testament of Moses,* that was considered lost until the mid-19th cent., when a 5th- or 6th-cent. PALIMPSEST manuscript was discovered in Milan, containing substantial fragments of a Latin version of a Greek original (*see* PSEUDEPIGRAPHA; VERSIONS, ANCIENT).

The text in its present form can confidently be dated to the first quarter of the 1st cent. CE, since it contains references to King Herod the Great (37–4 BCE) and his heirs as recent, possibly current rulers. It has been speculated that these references form part of a later editorial addition intended to update an earlier form of the text; the original document would then have to be dated to the mid-2nd cent. BCE. However, there is no real evidence to support this claim. The general consensus is that the writing originated in Jerusalem or its environs. The literary form of the *Assumption of Moses* is that of a "farewell scene" or "testament." Therefore, the writing has also been identified with another known ancient title, the *Testament of Moses.*

The contents of the writing can be summarized as follows. In the introduction (chap. 1) MOSES and JOSHUA are presented as finding themselves in the situation depicted in Deut 31. Moses is about to die and will deliver a prophecy to Joshua, in private—only at the end of time will his prophecy become known to all.

The prophecy can be divided into four parts: 2:1–3:3; 3:4–6:9; 7:1-8; 9:1–10:10. The first three of these predict how Israel, after their entrance into the promised land, will time and again become disloyal to the Lord and his commandments; therefore, foreign kings, as instruments of God, will punish them. Finally, in the dreadful circumstances brought about by the last tyrant's persecution, a small group of Jews, led by a mysterious figure designated as Taxo, will decide to remain loyal to the law of God, even if that costs them their lives. God's reaction to their steadfastness is to establish his "kingdom" throughout his creation and exalt Israel to heaven, where they will find eternal happiness.

The narrative continues with Moses giving instructions to Joshua, who, however, despairs in the face of his task as successor to Moses. The latter's accomplishments as leader of the people, and as prophet and intercessor, are mentioned in terms of the highest praise. Next, Moses is said to reassure Joshua, pointing out that he himself could accomplish his achievements only by the help of God, not because of his own merits: Joshua should accept that God's providence will take care of this people, and find in the divine promises the strength to remain faithful to the Lord and his commandments (10:11–12:13).

After this, the manuscript breaks off. It is likely that the writing's conclusion contained a description of Moses' death, his burial by the archangel Michael, and his assumption into heaven. The epistle of Jude includes a saying about Michael and Moses' body (Jude 9), a reference to this portion of the *Assumption of Moses.*

The time and place in which the *Assumption of Moses* was written was plagued by many upheavals, culminating in the Jewish war of 66–70 CE. Against this background, the author wished to convey the message that the world in which he and his audience were living was in a state of religious and moral corruption, resulting in the deplorable fact of Roman rule. Moreover, the author believed that this situation was beyond repair: human efforts were not capable of bringing improvement, and only God was able and willing to set things right. In the meantime, upright and pious Jews (such as the author and his audience), for whom the wrongs of their world were almost unbearable, are called to remain steadfast and faithful to the law and the commandments, and trust God, who has seen their affliction beforehand, but will not let them go into perdition. *See* HEROD, FAMILY; JEWISH WARS; ROMAN EMPIRE.

Bibliography: Kenneth R. Atkinson. "Herod the Great as Antiochus *redivivus*: Reading the Testament of Moses as an anti-Herodian Composition." *Of Scribes and Sages: Early Jewish Interpretation and Transmission of Scripture I.* C. A. Evans, ed. (2004) 134–49; Johannes Tromp. "Origen on the Assumption of Moses." *Jerusalem, Alexandria, Rome: Studies in Ancient Cultural Interaction in Honour of A. Hilhorst.* F. García Martínez and G. P. Luttikhuizen, eds. (2003) 323–40.

JOHANNES TROMP

MOSES, HORN OF. The artistic depiction of Moses with horns has its origin in Jerome's translation of the Hebrew verb qaran (קָרַן) as tharan (θαραν) in Exod 34:29: "And when Moses descended from Mount Sinai ... he did not know that his face was horned (*cornuta esset*) because of his conversation with God." Following the LXX (dedoxastai δεδόξασται) and the mainstream rabbinic interpretation, most modern scholars prefer a translation like "the skin of his face shone" (thus NRSV). That JEROME himself understood the meaning of the passage similarly is shown in his comment that "the face of Moses was glorified (*glorificata erat*), or as it is said in the Hebrew, horned (*cornuta*)" (*Comm. Ezech.* 50; CCSL 75.557).

Bibliography: Ruth Mellinkoff. *The Horned Moses in Medieval Art and Thought* (1970).

MARK DELCOGLIANO

MOSES, TESTAMENT OF. *See* MOSES, ASSUMPTION OF.

MOST HIGH [עֶלְיוֹן ʿelyon; Aram. עִלָּי ʿillay; ὕψιστος hypistos]. The English translation of the Hebrew ʿelyon and variants (e.g., 1 Sam 2:10; Ps 106:7), as well as its Aramaic (e.g., Dan 5:18, 21; 7:18, 22) and Greek equivalents in the LXX and in the NT (nine times, seven in Luke). It often occurs as the epithet "God Most High" (or "Most High God"). *See* EL ELYON; ELYON; GOD, NAMES OF.

C. L. SEOW

MOST HOLY PLACE [קֹדֶשׁ הַקֳּדָשִׁים qodhesh haqqodhashim, קֹדֶשׁ קָדָשִׁים qodhesh qadhashim]. This is the inner domain behind a veil (*see* VEIL OF THE TEMPLE) within the TABERNACLE (Exod 26:34) where the Israelites kept the ARK OF THE COVENANT. The high priest entered the Most Holy Place once a year (*see* DAY OF ATONEMENT) in order to make ATONEMENT for Israel.

This terminology is part of a Priestly gloss in the description of the Temple of Solomon in 1 Kings. The text describes an inner chamber (devir דְּבִיר) as the place for the ark. The phrase qodesh haqqodashim is placed in apposition so that readers identify the innermost chamber with the Most Holy Place of the tabernacle of the book of Exodus (1 Kgs 6:16; 8:6).

The Chronicler's description of the construction of the Temple replaces the innermost chamber (devir) with the Most Holy Place (qodesh haqqodashim) (2 Chr 3:8, 10). The innermost chamber returns in the description of the dedication (2 Chr 5:7), and is there again glossed with qodesh haqqadashim.

The use of this phrase as a gloss for the innermost chamber establishes continuity between the Temple in Jerusalem and the tabernacle in the wilderness, which may have served to legitimate the restored cult in the Persian Period.

C. MARK MCCORMICK

MOT. Texts from a Canaanite port city in Syria dating to about 1400–1200 BCE mention a god named Mot and describe him as a god of sterility, drought, disease, death, and the netherworld. He is contrasted with BAAL, the Canaanite weather god, who gives life and fertility through rain. These two gods battle with each other, symbolizing the struggle between death and life that takes place on earth in both agriculture and human life. The major texts describing this struggle between Mot and Baal are given in the Baal cycle of texts. Mot lives in the netherworld, and he swallows all who die. Baal himself is devoured by Mot.

For four months of the year, Baal "dies." This is during the summer months when there is no rain in countries around the Mediterranean Sea. Baal is held captive in the netherworld for these four months by Mot. The goddess Anat rescues Baal from Mot. He comes alive again for about eight months of the year to storm and rain on the land and produce fertility. The struggle between Baal and Mot continues again in a fierce battle.

The goddess Shapshu ends the struggle by telling Mot that he will not prevail. Mot eventually withdraws, and Baal prevails. All of this depicts the agricultural year in Syria with its dry season for four months followed by the wet season for eight months. It also depicts the struggle for human existence between life and death and the living and the dead.

Mot is not mentioned in the OT, but the Hebrew terms for the words *die* (**muth** מוּת) and *death* (**maweth** מָוֶת) are occasionally personified as in these representative passages: Mot's insatiable appetite is paralleled in Hab 2:5, "They open their throats wide as SHEOL; like Death (**maweth**) they never have enough." Mot's swallowing his many victims is echoed in Isa 25:7(8), "He [God] will swallow up death forever." The "covenant with death and Sheol" in Isa 28:15, 18 is also similar to the depiction of Mot. Death is personified twice in Hos 13:14, where Ephraim is redeemed from Death and Sheol. Finally, in Ps 49:14 [Heb. 49:15], Death is depicted as the shepherd for everyone who descends into Sheol. *See* DEATH, OT; DEITIES, UNDERWORLD; IMMORTALITY; UNDERWORLD, DESCENT INTO THE.

Bibliography: Victor H. Matthews and Don C. Benjamin. *Old Testament Parallels.* 3rd ed. (2007) 271; Mark S. Smith. *The Early History of God: Yahweh and Other Deities in Ancient Israel* (2002); Mark S. Smith. *The Origins of Biblical Monotheism: Israel's Polytheistic Background and the Ugaritic Texts* (2001).

JAMES C. MOYER

MOTH [סָס sas, עָשׁ ʿash; σής sēs]. A moth is an insect, order Lepidoptera. In the Bible all moths are cloth-eating (e.g., Job 13:28; Isa 50:9; Luke 12:33). Because the moth consumes cloth when it is in its larvae stage, sometimes the Hebrew words are translated "WORM" or "MAGGOT" (Hos 5:12). In some passages, the moth itself is a symbol of fragility (Job 4:19). In others passages, the moth itself symbolizes destruction (Isa 51:8). *See* INSECTS OF THE BIBLE.

Bibliography: G. S. Cansdale. *All the Animals of the Bible Lands* (1970).

JENNIFER L. KOOSED

MOTHER [אֵם ʾem, אִימָא ʾimaʾ; μήτηρ mētēr]. A well-rounded understanding of mothers in the Bible and biblical world is elusive. Reconstructions are complicated not only by the Bible's historical and sociological distance from contemporary society but also by social change over the centuries through which the Bible took shape. Relative lack of attention to women, who comprise less than 10 percent of the named figures in Scripture, paucity or absence of women's own writings, and lack of depictions of mother-daughter relationships all contribute to difficulty in reconstructing three-dimensional portrayals of motherhood. In addition, one must ask whether biblical writers described norms they saw or prescribed those they wished to promote, and whether actions in any particular story are usual or exceptional.

A. Everyday Lives of Mothers

Findings from archaeology and cultural anthropology have supplemented the biblical picture of mothers' lives and roles. Families in the villages of ancient Israel produced most of their own food, clothing, and tools. Daughters who married left their parents to join the families of their husbands, where their lives were spent not only in childbearing and childrearing but also in carrying out complex tasks to produce food and goods for the household's use. Women planted, weeded, and harvested crops, cultivated fruits and vegetables, tended domestic animals, and preserved, processed, and cooked foods. They also spun, wove, and sewed clothing, and produced pottery and baskets.

Mothers tended and educated their children at home while carrying on the other tasks of subsistence living, with which young children helped. Women were primary caregivers and instructors for sons until the boys were ready to join their fathers in the fields and continued to instruct daughters until the girls left to join their in-laws' households.

The biblical command to "be fruitful and multiply" (Gen 1:28), the early age of marriage, and the need for many workers may seem to suggest that biblical families were quite large. On the contrary, although a great percentage of women's lives was spent in childbearing and childrearing, the number of children who survived into young adulthood was limited by the high mortality rate of babies and mothers. Nearly half of all children died in infancy or youth. The many pregnancies needed to produce three or four surviving offspring increased the risk to mothers, whose life expectancy was about thirty years. Breast-feeding children for two or more years also limited the birthrate.

The centralization of government and the rise of larger cities in monarchic times and beyond drew some men away from home into armies and bureaucracies. As society became economically stratified, women's household contributions were disrupted by the availability of goods through trade. As urbanization increased, the wealth of some families both eased women's burdens and circumscribed their skilled roles and spheres of influence.

B. Motherhood in Prescriptive Passages

Pentateuchal law reflects a patricentric society, in which women's primary contribution is to produce their husbands' children. This contribution is guarded by severe strictures against women's adultery and fornication as threats to men's securing of progeny. The LEVIRATE LAW, in which a childless widow is given to her husband's brother to sire a son for the dead man, extends his right to an heir even past his lifetime, while presumably providing the mother a caregiver in her old age.

Maternity afforded women status alongside their husbands in relation to offspring who were commanded: "honor your father and your mother" (Exod 20:12; Deut 5:16; see Lev 19:3; Deut 27:16). Children who were rebellious, or who struck or cursed father or mother, were subject to death (Exod 21:15, 17; Deut 21:18-21; see Prov 20:20; 30:17). In at least two instances, mothers' participation in judicial proceedings seems designed to protect offspring from false accusations: in defense of a daughter accused by her husband of sexual impurity (Deut 22:15-19); and as a second witness against a disobedient son (Deut 21:18-21), presumably protecting him from a father's false charge.

The book of Proverbs, offering moral and religious instruction to sons, places the mother's admonition parallel to that of the FATHER (1:8; 6:20; 10:1). Rarely is the father mentioned without the mother. In the book's final chapter, praise of the strong woman who manages and provides for her household (Prov 31:10-31) follows a queen mother's exhortations to her son to reign temperately and justly (Prov 31:1-9). While Ben Sirach displays perhaps the most negative of biblical attitudes toward women in general, Sir 3:1-16 (see also 7:27-28) extrapolates from the fifth commandment a detailed exhortation to respect mother and father.

Jesus' words and actions in the synoptic Gospels are somewhat paradoxical. On the one hand, citing the fifth commandment, he criticizes contemporaries who for religious reasons deny their parents support (Matt 15:3-6; Mark 7:8-13). The crucified Jesus gives his mother into the care of the Beloved Disciple (John 19:26-27). Honoring father and mother is also mentioned in other contexts (Matt 19:19 and par.).

On the other hand, the Gospel writers seem to endorse Jesus' apparent indifference toward his mother's solicitude not only when he disappears to the Temple as a youth (Luke 2:48-49) but also when as an adult he rebuffs her visit by naming whoever does the will of God his "brother and sister and mother" (Matt 12:46-50 and par.). Similar themes emerge in his response to the woman who blesses his mother (Luke 11:27-28). His sayings that place commitment to the gospel in direct competition with familial loyalty stand in tension with the commands and customs of other parts of Scripture (Matt 10:34-38 and par.). They may reflect continuity, however, with calls in Second Temple Judaism to steadfast faith that surpasses familial protection, such as the story in 2 Macc 7 of the mother who encouraged her seven sons to suffer torture and death rather than to transgress the law. In the deuteropauline epistles, mothers' relationships with their children are overshadowed by their submissive roles as wives. The command to honor father and mother is quoted in Eph 6:1-3 following instructions to women to be subject to their husbands (5:22-24) and to men to love their wives (5:25-33). While fathers are instructed regarding their children, mothers are not, neither here nor in Col 3:18-21.

C. Mothers in Biblical Narratives

The portrayal of mothers in biblical narrative is complex to evaluate, since it refracts their experiences and deeds through the viewpoints of male authors and robs them of psychic complexity comparable to that of males in the same narratives. While women as wives and daughters show variety in personality, aims, and actions, women as mothers are portrayed with more homogeneous and uncomplicated character traits.

A dominant motif throughout Genesis, and recurring in Exodus, Judges, Ruth, Samuel, and Kings, and the Gospel narratives, is that of the childless woman who is blessed with a SON, often because of her prayer, piety, or proactive deeds. An obstacle such as the mother's age (Sarah) or barrenness (Rebekah; Rachel; Samson's mother; Hannah; Elizabeth), or the lack or loss of a husband (Lot's daughters; Tamar; Ruth; Mary) must usually be overcome (*see* BARREN, BARRENNESS). Sometimes children are given to reward faithfulness (Shiphrah and Puah in Exod 1; the Shunammite woman in 2 Kgs 4). Unlike men, women are depicted without ambivalence toward their parental roles. Biblical writers assume that women desire sons, even when they come in inopportune ways (Hagar in Gen 16) and times (Mary the mother of Jesus). The birth narratives of Jesus draw from the collection of motifs of barren and husbandless women, and angelic messengers to both fathers and mothers, to add resonance to the maternal portrayals of Mary in Matthew and of both Mary and Elizabeth in Luke.

Women in the biblical narratives not only desire sons, they also zealously protect their interests, whether as infants (the mother of Moses in Exod 2; the prostitute mother in 1 Kgs 3) or as adults (Rebekah in Gen 27; Bathsheba in 1 Kgs 1; the mother of James and John in Matt 20)—and even after their deaths (Rizpah in 2 Sam 21). When the interests of their own sons conflict with those of other mothers' offspring, ruthlessness may emerge (Sarah in Gen 21; Sisera's mother in Judg 5, as imagined by Deborah and Barak). Otherwise, maternal protection extends to other children (the midwives in Exod 1; Pharaoh's daughter in Exod 2; Jehosheba in 2 Kgs 11). While a man's neglect, endangerment, or murder of his offspring is taken in stride (Gen 19; Judg 11; 1 Sam 14; 2 Sam 13), or commanded (Gen 21), or praised (Gen 22), the only action described for women against their offspring is understood as an atrocity—cannibalism for survival (2 Kgs 6:28-29; Lam 2:20; 4:10).

The most natural of sympathetic relationships one might expect is that of a mother with her DAUGHTER. But such stories are scarce. When daughters are endangered, mothers are conspicuously absent (Lot's daughters in Gen 19; Dinah in Gen 34; Jephthah's daughter in Judg 11; the Levite's wife in Judg 19; the two Tamars in Gen 38 and 2 Sam 13). The Canaanite woman who demands that Jesus heal her daughter stands out (Matt 15; see also Mark 7), as do the dialogues between Naomi and Ruth, the only words between women that do not center on the welfare of men or boys. Their devotion must stand in for the many mother-daughter stories missing from the Bible, whose richness can only be glimpsed in Rebekah's mother's wish that her suddenly betrothed daughter tarry at home (Gen 24:55) and in the mother's delight in her flawless, darling daughter in Song 6:9.

D. Metaphorical Mothers

While masculine pronouns and images for God clearly predominate, maternal imagery emerges as well. In two consecutive verses, Isaiah portrays God as a soldier joining battle and a woman crying out in labor (Isa 42:13, 14). Other maternal images include God's giving birth to mountains, earth, and world (Ps 90:2) and to Israel itself (Deut 32:18); God's remembering Israel as a woman would her nursing child (Isa 49:15) and comforting as a woman comforts her child (Isa 66:13); and trust in God compared with the calm of a child with its mother (Ps 131). Similarly in the NT, Jesus expresses the wish to gather Jerusalem's people like a mother hen (Luke 13:34).

Images of God as mother intermingle with imagery of Israel and Jerusalem (Zion) as mother to her inhabitants. Hosea likens Israel to an unfaithful mother whose children must plead with her; because of her, they will receive no pity (Hos 2:1-4). Lamentations, by contrast, gives sympathetic voice to Zion's pleas against God for her own suffering and that of her children, the city's inhabitants (Lam 1:17; 2:13; 4:2). In Second Isaiah, Zion becomes the city to be redeemed by her children's joyful return from exile (Isa 50:1; 51:11, 16; 52:1-10; 62:11). In later parts of Isaiah, Zion's consoling breast symbolizes the restoration of prosperity (Isa 66:8-11), and in Baruch, Zion herself recounts her sufferings and hopes and instructs her children in courage and faithfulness (Bar 4:9-14). Paul turns this metaphor on its axis when he envisions "the present Jerusalem" (which he calls Hagar and Mount Sinai) and her offspring as slaves to the Mosaic law and "Jerusalem above" (Sarah) as the free mother of Christians (Gal 4:22-31). Though the depiction of women in Scripture displays variation over time, both symbolic and literal women were overall viewed most sympathetically when they were mothers. *See* BIRTH; CHILD, CHILDREN; FAMILY; HOUSEHOLD, HOUSEHOLDER; MARRIAGE, NT; MARRIAGE, OT; WOMEN IN THE ANCIENT NEAR EAST; WOMEN IN THE NT; WOMEN IN THE OT.

Bibliography: David L. Balch and Carolyn Osiek. *Families in the New Testament World: Households and House Churches* (1997); Esther Fuchs. "The Literary Characterization of Mothers and Sexual Politics in the Hebrew Bible." *Semeia* 46 (1989) 151–66; Carol L. Meyers. *Discovering Eve: Ancient Israelite Women in Context* (1988); Carol Meyers, Toni Craven, and Ross Kraemer, eds. *Women in Scripture: A Dictionary of Named and Unnamed Women in the Hebrew Bible, the Apocryphal/Deuterocanonical Books, and the New Testament* (2000); Carol Newsom and Sharon Ringe, eds. *The Women's Bible Commentary.* Rev. ed. (1998); Leo G. Perdue, Joseph Blenkinsopp, John Joseph Collins, and Carol L. Meyers. *Families in Ancient Israel* (1997).

PATRICIA K. TULL

MOTHER-IN-LAW. *See* FAMILY; NAOMI.

MOTHER-OF-PEARL [דַּר dar]. One of the materials in the MOSAIC PAVEMENT at Susa in the court of the king's palace garden (Esth 1:6).

MOUNT AZOTUS. *See* ASHDOD.

MOUNT CARMEL. *See* CARMEL, MOUNT.

MOUNT EBAL. *See* EBAL, MOUNT.

MOUNT GERIZIM. *See* GERIZIM, MOUNT.

MOUNT GILBOA. *See* GILBOA, MOUNT.

MOUNT HAURAN. *See* HAURAN.

MOUNT HEBRON. *See* HEBRON, HEBRONITES.

MOUNT HERMON. *See* HERMON, MOUNT.

MOUNT HOR. *See* HOR.

MOUNT HOREB. *See* SINAI, MOUNT.

MOUNT JEARIM. *See* JEARIM, MOUNT.

MOUNT MORIAH. *See* MORIAH.

MOUNT NEBO. *See* NEBO, MOUNT.

MOUNT OF ASSEMBLY [הַר־מוֹעֵד har moʿedh]. The mountain where the DIVINE ASSEMBLY met. Called Zaphon (which also means "north"; *see* ZAPHON, MOUNT) at Ugarit and Mount Casius in classical literature, it is identified with modern-day Jebel ʾel-Aqraʿ near the mouth of the Orontes River in northern Syria. The phrase occurs only at Isa 14:13, identifying it with "the heights of Zaphon"; the myth of a deity expelled from heaven for attempting to usurp the divine throne is used to condemn the Babylonian king's pride. Psalm 48:1-3 treats Jerusalem as the mount of assembly by calling Zion "the heights of Zaphon" (NRSV, "in the far north"). *See* DAWN; DAY STAR; MYTH IN THE OT.

JOHN L. MCLAUGHLIN

MOUNT OF DESTRUCTION [הַר הַמַּשְׁחִית har hammashkhith]. The peak at the south end of the ridge known as the Mount of Olives, which lies to the east of Jerusalem. Its name comes from the idolatry practiced there; King SOLOMON built "high places" there for the Moabite god CHEMOSH, the Ammonite god Molech, and the Sidonian goddess ASTARTE (1 Kgs 11:7; 2 Kgs 23:13). These were later destroyed by the reforming king Josiah. The original name of the mount may have been "Mount of Ointment" (har hammishkhah הַר הַמִּשְׁחָה), since the olives that are made into ointment for anointment grew there. Because of a wordplay with the very similar Hebrew word for destruction (mashkhith) and the idolatry that went on there, the name was changed to "Mount of Destruction," thus bringing it into line with prophecies found in Jer 7:32 and 51:25. It is also known as the Mount of Corruption, Mount of Offense (Vulgate), and the Mount of Scandal. *See* JOSIAH; MOLECH, MOLOCH; MOUNT OF OLIVES.

KIM PAFFENROTH

MOUNT OF OLIVES [הַר הַזֵּיתִים har hazzethim, מַעֲלֵה הַזֵּיתִים maʿaleh hazzethim; τὸ ὄρος τὸ καλουμένον ἐλαιῶν to oros to kaloumenon elaiōn, τὸ ὄρος τὸ καλουμένον ἐλαιῶνος to oros to kaloumenon elaiōnos, τὸ ὄρος τῶν ἐλαιῶν to oros tōn elaiōn]. A ridge with three crests, approximately 2 mi. long, located across the Kidron Valley from Jerusalem. With the highest point reaching approximately 2,700 ft., it stands just over 100 ft. above the Temple Mount in Jerusalem to the east, and about 4,000 ft. above the Dead Sea to the west, thus affording dramatic views of the surrounding area. In biblical times, it supported a plentiful stand of olive trees, from which it received its name (*see* OLIVE, OLIVE TREE).

Although the name Mount of Olives appears only once in the OT (Zech 14:4), we find additional references, both explicit and implicit. When escaping from Absalom, David crossed the Wadi Kidron (2 Sam 15:23) and "went up the ascent of the Mount of Olives" (lit., "the ascent of the olive trees," 15:30). With the steep drop of the Kidron Valley and the relative height of the summit, the Mount of Olives had military significance

Todd Bolen/BiblePlaces.com

Figure 1: The Mount of Olives from the Golden Gate

both for the protection of Jerusalem (see Ps 125:2) and, as David's route demonstrates, for those seeking to escape from it.

References in the OT to a mountain presumably to be identified with the Mount of Olives underscore its religious significance, including its importance as a worship site for gods other than Yahweh. The narrator of 2 Samuel refers to the summit of "the ascent of the olive trees" as the site of a sanctuary (15:32). In his recounting of the biblical story, Josephus writes that when David reached the crest of the Mount of Olives, with tears of grief he called upon God and received comfort (*Ant.* 7.202–4). Identification with the Nob mentioned in 1 Sam 21–22 (see Isa 10:32) is possible. Solomon is reported to have constructed sanctuaries for "Chemosh the abomination of Moab, and for Molech the abomination of the Ammonites, on the mountain east of Jerusalem" (1 Kgs 11:7), but these were later destroyed by Josiah (2 Kgs 23:13-14). In Ezekiel's vision of the destruction of the Jerusalem Temple, the glory of Yahweh, accompanied by the cherubim, "stopped on the mountain east of the city" (11:23)—presumably the Mount of Olives. Later, the prophet foretells the return to the Temple of "the glory of the God of Israel," entering the gate facing east; that is, the glory of God would return from the direction of the Mount of Olives (43:1-5). For Zechariah, the DAY OF THE LORD will be signaled by the return of the Lord to the Mount of Olives: "On that day his feet shall stand on the Mount of Olives, which lies before Jerusalem on the east; and the Mount of Olives shall be split in two from east to west by a very wide valley; so that one half of the Mount shall withdraw northward, and the other half southward" (14:4). In his apocalyptic vision, the strategic protection provided by the Mount of Olives will no longer be needed as the Lord will deliver his people against the armies aligned against them.

Post-biblical Jewish sources continue to speak of the Mount of Olives. Talmudic tradition associates the red heifer ritual (Num 19:2-19; compare Heb 9:13) with the Mount of Olives (*Parah* 3). Leaving the Temple by the east gate, the procession led by the high priest crossed the Kidron Valley and climbed to the summit where the heifer was sacrificed. With reference to Ezekiel's vision of the departure of God's glory (called the SHEKINAH, from **mishkhan** מִשְׁכָּן, meaning "dwelling" or "residence") from the first Temple, it is said that the Shekinah waited on the Mount of Olives for three and a half years hoping that Israel might repent, then ascended to heaven from the Mount (*Lam. Rab.* Proem 25). Eschatological associations are likely presumed when an Egyptian false prophet used the Mount of Olives as an assembly point for an army set to launch an attack on Jerusalem (Josephus, *J.W.* 2.26–63; *Ant.* 20.169–72).

References to the Mount of Olives in the NT are limited to the Jesus-tradition reported in the Gospels and Acts. Jesus' familiarity with the Mount is evident from his lodging with friends in Bethany (e.g., Mark 11:11; 14:3), located on the ridge of the Mount. For his part, Luke simply reports that, during his final week teaching in the Temple, Jesus "would go out and spend the night on the Mount of Olives, as it was called" (21:37). It is from the Mount of Olives that Jesus sends two disciples to prepare for his entry into Jerusalem, and his TRIUMPHAL ENTRY would have begun from BETHPHAGE on its summit (Matt 21:1-11; Mark 11:1-10; and Luke 19:29-40 read "Bethphage and Bethany"; see John 12:12-15). Luke adds that, on the way down the Mount of Olives, Jesus wept over the city (19:41-44). The site of ancient Bethany is probably to be identified with the modern village el-Azariyeh, but the exact location of Bethphage is contested; presumably, it was along the ridge nearer the summit. According to Matt 24 and Mark 13, Jesus warned of the eschatological destruction of the Temple while seated with his disciples on the Mount of Olives.

In the Gospels of Matthew and Mark, the garden of GETHSEMANE is the site of Jesus' struggle in prayer with God regarding his impending death, and subsequently of his betrayal by Judas and his arrest (Matt 26:36; Mark 14:32). The word **Gethsēmani** (Γεθσημανί) is a transliteration of the Hebrew/Aramaic **gath shemane** (גַּת שְׁמָנֵי, "oil press") and refers to an olive grove (specifically, to a cave housing an olive press) on the slope of the Mount of Olives (Matt 26:30; Mark 14:26). Luke, who avoids Hebrew or Aramaic place names, locates the incident on the Mount of Olives (22:39). John locates the arrest of Jesus in a garden across the KIDRON VALLEY (18:1-2). All four Gospels thus refer generally to the same place.

Luke also locates the ASCENSION of Jesus on the Mount of Olives. In Luke 24:50-51, he ascends from Bethany, whereas the report of the ascension in Acts 1:9-11 is followed by a more general reference to "the mount called Olivet, which is near Jerusalem, a sabbath day's journey away" (1:12). "A sabbath day's journey" signifies the distance one was allowed to travel on the Sabbath. Its importance derives from Exod 16:29, "Do not leave your place on the seventh day." "Your place" was apparently interpreted in light of Num 35:5, which defines the land extending 2,000 cubits (approximately 2,900–3,300 ft.) outside the city walls as belonging to the Levites (see *Tg. Yer.* Exod 16:29). The Cairo Genizah *Damascus Document* (CD X, 20) legislates that no one will walk more than 1,000 cubits (approximately 1,450–1,650 ft.) beyond the town (compare Num 35:4?), while CD XI, 5–6 speaks of 2,000 cubits as the maximum one might walk after a beast to pasture it outside the town (see *m. Eruv.* 4.11, which says 2,000 medium steps). Josephus gives the distance from the Mount of Olives as 5 stadia (approximately 3,035 ft.) in *J.W.* 20.169 and as 6 stadia (approximately 3,640 ft.) in *Ant.* 5.70.

Reflecting both the importance of the Mount of Olives in the Gospels and its panoramic views of

Jerusalem and the surrounding region, the site has been a favorite among Christian pilgrims since the 4th cent. CE. Today, shrines dot the hillside, sometimes with competing claims regarding their preservation of the actual locations of events in Jesus' final week.

Bibliography: Jerome Murphy O'Connor. *The Holy Land: An Archaeological Guide.* 4th ed. (2008).

JOEL B. GREEN

MOUNT PARAN. *See* SINAI, MOUNT.

MOUNT PERAZIM. *See* PERAZIM, MOUNT.

MOUNT PISGAH. *See* PISGAH, MOUNT.

MOUNT SAMARIA. *See* SAMARIA.

MOUNT SEIR. *See* SEIR, MOUNT.

MOUNT SINAI. *See* SINAI, MOUNT.

MOUNT TABOR. *See* TABOR, MOUNT.

MOUNT ZAPHON. *See* ZAPHON, MOUNT.

MOUNT ZEMARAIM. *See* ZEMARAIM.

MOUNT ZION. *See* ZION.

MOUNT, MOUNTAIN [הַר har; ὄρος oros]. *Mountain* is a relative term for a high elevation in a particular region; there is no consensus on what height determines the difference between a mountain and a hill. Named mountains in Israel range in height from about 1,600 ft. above sea level (Gilboa) to over 9,000 ft. (Hermon).

The mountains of the biblical world, which extend nearly 4,000 mi. from modern Turkey to Mozambique in east Africa, are the product of tectonic uplifting along the Great Rift System between the Arabian and African plates. Africa's two highest mountains (Kilimanjaro and Kenya) are a part of this system. The mountain range runs along a north-to-south line from ancient Antioch, through western Lebanon, along both sides of the Jordan River Valley, across the Sinai peninsula, and continues along the western shore of the Red Sea. Biblical references to mountainous regions include Gilboa (2 Sam 1:21), Zion (Ps 133:3), and Ragau (Jdt 1:15).

The stories of earth's opening up at Kadesh-barnea (Num 16:32) and the collapse of Jericho's walls (Josh 6:20) may reflect the experience of seismic activity caused by plate movement along this boundary. The region remains tectonically active today and continues to be the source of frequent earthquakes.

Throughout the cultures of the ANE, mountains were important both for their physical presence and their theological meaning. Several events associated with mountains were so central to the story of the people of Israel that the mere mention of their names calls to mind some of the great moments from the biblical narrative. The first occurrence of the word *mountains* occurs in the account of the great flood (Gen 7:19), which later identifies the final resting place of the ark as the mountains of ARARAT (Gen 8:4). It was on Mount Horeb (the "mountain of God") that God first called Moses to deliver his people from their captivity (Exod 3:1) and later instructed Moses to strike the rock so that water might come out for the people to drink (Exod 17:6). The top of Mount Sinai was chosen by God to communicate the commandments to the people through Moses (Exod 19–20). Scholars generally regard Horeb and Sinai as alternative names for the same mountain, so that both Moses' call and the revelation of the Decalogue occurred at the same location (*see* SINAI, MOUNT).

God chose Mount Nebo as the site where Moses would die (Deut 32:49-50; *see* NEBO, MOUNT). Mount MORIAH (also ZION), first introduced as the site where Abraham was asked to sacrifice his son Isaac (Gen 22:2), was later purchased by David and eventually became the site where Solomon built the first temple to Yahweh (2 Chr 3:1).

Jesus first taught and prayed with his disciples on the MOUNT OF OLIVES (Luke 22:39). The vision of the end time in Zech 14:4-9 pictures the LORD as king over all the earth standing on the Mount of Olives; the NT reflects this OT tradition in Rev 20–22 and in the setting of Jesus' apocalyptic discourse on the Mount of Olives in Mark 13:7-27. *See* SERMON ON THE MOUNT.

Because their higher elevation frequently brought greater amounts of precipitation and cooler temperatures than neighboring plains and valleys, mountains and associated upland regions played important roles in the lives of the people in the ancient biblical world. They were cultivated for vineyards (Jer 31:5) and provided a secure habitat for a wide variety of fauna (gazelles, 1 Chr 12:8; wild goats, Ps 104:18; young stags, Song 2:17; leopards, Song 4:8; partridges, 1 Sam 26:20; sheep, Matt 18:12).

Mountains were a place to hide and take refuge (Judg 6:2; Jdt 7:10; Luke 21:21), the place where Jephthah's daughter wandered (Judg 11:37), an ideal setting for signaling (Isa 18:3), a place for sacrifice (Hos 4:13), and the home of the Gerasene demoniac (Mark 5:5).

However, more important than their physical presence in the biblical narrative, it was their use as vivid symbols of God and God's attributes that is most striking. Both God's creation (Amos 4:13; Ps 95:4) and God's dwelling-place (Ps 74:2), mountains are often used to illustrate God's sovereignty over the natural world. Mountains are said to quake (Judg 5:5; Isa 5:25; Nah 1:5; Sir 16:19), tremble (Ps 18:7), and shatter before God (Hab 3:6). They melt like wax in God's presence (Ps 97:5; Mic 1:4), smoke at God's touch (Pss 104:32; 144:5), and can be removed at God's will (Job 9:5). Mountains symbolize God's eternal nature (Gen 49:26), righteousness (Ps 36:6), persistent love (Isa 54:10), majesty (Ps 76:4), and, if appropriate, anger (Deut 32:22). And as God's creation, mountains are said to sing (Isa 49:13) and offer praise to God (Pr Azar 1:53). *See* CARMEL, MOUNT; EBAL, MOUNT; GERIZIM, MOUNT; GILBOA, MOUNT; HERMON, MOUNT; HILL, HILL COUNTRY; ISRAEL, GEOGRAPHY OF; LEBANON MOUNTAINS; MASADA; PISGAH, MOUNT; RAGES; SEIR, MOUNT; TABOR, MOUNT; ZAPHON, MOUNT.

MARK D. GREEN

MOUNT, SERMON ON THE. *See* SERMON ON THE MOUNT.

MOUNTAIN-SHEEP [זֶמֶר zamer]. An unidentified wild animal, placed in a list of similar animals such as ox, deer, goat, and sheep that had hooves split in two, chewed the cud, and were therefore edible (Deut 14:4-5). This animal is presumed to be a species of wild sheep, which can still be found in the Mediterranean area, and was probably living in or near the Levant.

HEIDI E. HAWKS

MOURNING [מִסְפֵּד mispedh; ἀλαλάζω alalazō, δακρύω dakryō, θρηνέω thrēneō, κλαίω klaiō, κόπτομαι koptomai, ὀλολύζω ololyzō, πενθέω pentheō, πένθος penthos, ταλαιπωρέω talaipōreō]. The word *mourning* refers to a range of emotive responses such as sadness, grief, lamenting, and weeping in relation to someone's death or a sorrowful or distressing event.

A. Overview of Mourning in the Ancient Near East
B. Egypt
C. Mesopotamia
D. Israel
Bibliography
E. Mourning in the New Testament
Bibliography

A. Overview of Mourning in the Ancient Near East

Mourning includes both private expression of grief and formal, public enactment of lamentation. Contemporary custom in the West calls for decorum and for controlling grief in public at funerals, largely to protect the feelings of the other guests. Ancient Near Eastern custom valued precisely the converse: grief was to be displayed very publicly and loudly. Not to do so was considered insulting to the dead and to the grieving relations, as it implied lack of affection and respect for the dead, the family, the clan, and the nation (1 Kgs 14:13; Job 27:15; Jer 16:4, 6; 22:18; 25:33; 34:5).

The Hebrew root spd (ספד) signifies wailing, lamenting, crying. It is used in parallel construction with verbs for crying (Gen 23:2) and wailing (Jer 4:8; 49:3; Joel 1:13; Mic 1:8). The use of the verb with the preposition lifne (לִפְנֵי, "before") can suggest leading the procession of the bier. The passive form of the verb expresses "being mourned over." In the ancient world, other symbolic gestures of mourning included heaping ashes on oneself, covering one's face, and fasting (Job 1:20; 2:8, 12).

Hebrew funeral rites both reflect ANE custom and contrast with it. For people of prominence or means in ANE cultures, lamentation was deliberate and professional. The more important the person, the more prominent, long, and elaborate the funeral oration. Several examples of funeral orations survive in biblical literatures (2 Sam 1:17-27; 3:33, 34; 18:33; 2 Chr 35:25).

B. Egypt

In Egypt, a royal funeral was carried out after the long mummification process was complete (*see* EMBALM, EMBALMING), though the planning may have started many years prior, as the tombs, mortuary chapels, and other buildings in the complex had usually been under construction since the beginning of the pharaoh's reign. One wall of a tomb chapel normally depicted the funeral. Typically, it began with a funeral cortege, drawn over the sand by sledge. For royal burials and perhaps others as well, the processions included professional women mourners who wailed and covered themselves with dust. Porters bore furniture, offerings, and garlands to the tomb. In the tomb of Tutankhamun there were jars of fats and oils, baskets of grains, fruits, vegetables, fabrics, clothing, sandals, gloves, weapons, chariots, models, lamps, vases, stools, chairs, beds, statues, jewels, musical instruments, writing equipment, fans, drinking vessels, toys, games, scepters, seals, and shrines.

Transportation to the tomb was normally by the Nile and connecting canals, necessitating a grand river procession. Two boats, one under sail and the other under oar, were used for the round-trip to Abydos, the shrine of Osiris. The last and most important ritual before deposition of the body was "The Opening of the Mouth," in which the mummified body was touched with a ritual adze, signifying that the mummification and revivification process was complete (Palermo Stone). Even though Egyptians believed in a beatific AFTERLIFE, the grief and loss expressed in lamentation was real. Egyptians may have prepared for death, but their tomb paintings also show an acute appreciation for life and for the provisions that make life enjoyable.

C. Mesopotamia

In Mesopotamia, funerals and lamentation also characterized mourning, but mummification was absent. Perhaps the most famous ancient lamentation, other than the biblical book of Lamentations itself, is the lamentation of Gilgamesh for his friend Enkidu. He calls death the fate of all humanity but refuses to accept his friend's death until a worm drops out of his corpse, an important trope for mortality but one that also indicates the lack of embalming in Mesopotamia.

Besides lamentation and a week-long period of mourning for important people, Mesopotamians also took off fine clothing, tore their garments, wore sackcloth, removed headcoverings, let their beards grow unkempt and otherwise neglected their appearance, heaped ashes on themselves, and hired professional mourners, male and female, to swell the numbers of the grieving (*ANET* 87–89). Grave goods and provisions for the journey to the underworld were common—particularly beer and bread. In times of difficulty, such as a particularly inauspicious eclipse, an effigy king might be buried in a substitute funeral. Such rites helped the community ward off evil, including the evil that an unappeased ghost might perform on the body politic. Once a funeral was correctly accomplished, the mourners undertook a particular set of rituals to reintegrate into normal life, such as eating, bathing, and wearing fresh garments (*ANET* 90). The dead were then safely delivered to their afterlife and were no longer a possible threat to the community (*ANET* 91).

Lamentations for cities are not unknown outside of the Bible. The city of Ur fell to the Amorites and Elamites in about 2000 BCE. Whatever the exact events, LAMENTs are extant over the destruction of Ur. One lament describes Ninlil, wife of Ur's city god Nanna. She pleads before the council of the gods for the deliverance of the city. The second lament is spoken by Nanna himself, first pleading for his city, then abandoning it to its destruction (*ANET* 455–63). These lamentations are parallels to the biblical book of Lamentations, though the Israelite God, who accepts sole authority for good and evil, is certainly very different from the well-populated Sumerian pantheon (*see* LAMENTATIONS, BOOK OF). Thus, all misfortune for the Hebrews was due to their having disappointed or disobeyed their one God.

D. Israel

In Israel, lamentation and other funerary rites were just as imperative. Israelites were buried with grave goods (Bloch-Smith). Unlike the Egyptians, they neither embalmed nor delayed the funeral. The correct procedures for the dead were imperative. Not to accomplish them was a serious misfortune for the deceased. Family and friends attended funerals. All participated in mourning important people like kings, prophets, and priests, beginning with the family and then the friends and associates. Tears were to be shed at proper moments (Matt 11:17; Luke 7:32).

Usually, the most severe mourning lasted seven days (Gen 50:10; 1 Sam 31:13; 1 Chr 10:12; Jdt 16:24). For Moses and Aaron, mourning lasted thirty days (Num 20:29; Deut 34:8), and for Jacob, seventy days, perhaps according to the Egyptian custom (Gen 50:3). In First Temple times, the deceased might be deposited in graves, but it was more common for them to be deposited in a cave, TOMB, or an excavated cellar-like structure in these cases; the dead were laid out on a bier or ledge until the flesh decayed. The bones of the deceased might be gathered or pushed aside when a new burial arrived. In Hellenistic times, where secondary BURIAL was more common, the last date, after a year had passed, is thought to correspond to when the family gathered and deposited the bones in an ossuary (*see* OSSUARIES). No texts actually demonstrate this connection. Nor does it appear that the popularity of secondary burial in any way depends on the conception of resurrection, which gained in popularity among Jews and later also among Christians from the 2nd cent. BCE to the early centuries CE. *See* RESURRECTION, EARLY JEWISH; RESURRECTION, NT.

Bibliography: Tzvi Abush. "Mourning the Death of a Friend: Some Assyriological Notes." *Gilgamesh: A Reader.* John Maier, ed. (1997); Elizabeth Bloch-Smith. *Judahite Burial Practices and Beliefs about the Dead* (1992); Rachel Hachlili. *Jewish Funerary Customs, Practices and Rites in the Second Temple Period* (2005); Saul Olyan. *Biblical Mourning: Ritual and Social Dimensions* (2004); Alan F. Segal. *Life After Death: A History of the Afterlife in Western Religion* (2004).

ALAN F. SEGAL

E. Mourning in the New Testament

Jewish funerary customs included keening over the deceased by relatives, friends, and even professional keeners, as a way of honoring the dead through conventional displays of sorrow. Whereas grieving might be limited to a day or two ("Let your weeping be bitter and your wailing fervent; make your mourning worthy of the departed, for one day, or two, to avoid criticism; then be comforted for your grief"; Sir 38:17), rituals of mourning could go on for seven days (Sir 22:12). At the time of burial, keening women would begin the lament in the home of the deceased and continue along the route of the funeral procession, with others from the community joining along the way. Though the NT does not describe funerary rites in any detail, we do find references to mourning at someone's death that fit customary Jewish practices (e.g., Mark 5:38-39; Luke 7:12-13; 8:52-53; John 11:31, 33, 35; Acts 9:39; compare Matt 2:18). Additionally, the ritualized pattern of mourning at a BURIAL stands behind the poetic verse in Luke 7:32: "We played the flute for you, and you did not dance; we wailed, and you did not weep" (compare Matt 11:17; Herodotus, *Hist.* 1.141; Aesop, *Fab.* 27; *Acts of John* 95).

Luke's passion narrative includes among those following Jesus to the site of crucifixion some "women who were beating their breasts and wailing for him"

(Luke 23:27). "Beating one's breast" is an expression of grief, and "wailing" (thrēneō) can be used of singing a funerary hymn or dirge. Apparently, these women are depicted weeping in anticipation of Jesus' death (compare the anticipatory anointing for burial in Mark 14:3-9), but Jesus directs them to weep instead for themselves and their children in light of the impending cataclysm (Luke 23:28-31; see below). According to the Gospel of Luke, Jesus himself had wept over Jerusalem for just this reason as he approached the city (19:41-45), so in essence he is inviting these "daughters of Jerusalem" to adopt his perspective and grieve for the holy city. Elsewhere, Jesus' death is the focus of mourning in Luke's scene of Jesus' death (where the Jewish crowds are portrayed as "beating their breasts," 23:48), in the context of the discovery of the empty tomb and post-resurrection appearances in John's Gospel (20:11, 13, 15), and in the longer ending of Mark (16:10).

The emotional heaviness that the terminology of mourning draws from funerary practices underscores the importance of the reversal of mourning promised in the advent of salvation, both during the career of Jesus of Nazareth and anticipated in the eschaton (*see* RESURRECTION, NT). The Sermon on the Mount famously includes the beatitude, "Blessed are those who mourn, for they will be comforted" (Matt 5:4). The Sermon on the Plain pairs the beatitude and contrasting woe: "Blessed are you who weep now, for you will laugh. . . . Woe to you who are laughing now, for you will mourn and weep" (6:21*b*, 25*b*; compare Ps 126). Accordingly, we find reports that Jesus directed family members to cease mourning for the death of a child, whom Jesus then resuscitates (Mark 5:38-43; Luke 7:13-14; 8:51-56). Indeed, the period of Jesus' ministry is a time of rejoicing, not mourning (Matt 9:15; compare John 16:20). For the book of Revelation, the coming of the eschaton marks the dwelling of God among humanity, at which time God "will wipe every tear from their eyes. Death will be no more; mourning and crying and pain will be no more" (Rev 21:4; compare 7:17). Undoubtedly, the cessation of mourning is to be correlated with the death of evil, and the death of death itself (Isa 25:8; *2 Bar.* 21:22-23).

A more general use of the concept of mourning appears in Paul and James to connote responses that should be evoked by sin and idolatry. Mourning rather than arrogance ought to have been the Corinthians' response to sexual immorality (1 Cor 5:1-2), just as Paul anticipates that, when he arrives in Corinth, he "may have to mourn over many who previously sinned and have not repented of the impurity, sexual immorality, and licentiousness that they have practiced" (2 Cor 12:21). In an expression reminiscent of OT prophetic discourse concerning sorrow at God's judgment on idolatry, James urges his audience to repent: "Lament and mourn and weep. Let your laughter be turned into mourning and your joy into dejection" (Jas 4:9; compare 4:7-10). Similar connotations are present in Luke 18:13, where the toll collector praying in the Temple averts his eyes and beats his breast—demonstrations of shame, humility, and, perhaps, repentance (23:48; Ezra 9:6; Josephus, *Ant.* 7.252; *Jos. Asen.* 10:15)—while calling on God for mercy.

Finally, in a number of NT texts mourning is associated with endtime JUDGMENT, sometimes pictured in terms of apocalyptic cataclysm. Matthew collocates darkness with "weeping" and gnashing of teeth in a series of texts (8:12; 13:42, 50; 22:13; 24:51; 25:30) so as to portray in deathly terms the misery of separation from God that results from eschatological reversal (Matt 5:4). Luke 13:28-29 provides a related picture of the end-time banquet, with some ("evildoers") excluded from the feast. "Gnashing of teeth" likely refers in these settings to anguished despair in the face of judgment (Ps 111:10 LXX; *1 En.* 108:3-7). Deploring the fate of the wealthy, James employs the prophetic lament genre to mark the advent of disastrous misery at the judgment (5:1). Jesus' judgment oracle in Luke 23:28-31 directs those who were mourning his impending death to join him instead in mourning the coming judgment on Jerusalem. Echoing earlier prophecies of its destruction (Luke 13:34-35; 19:41-44; 21:20-24), he predicts Jerusalem's fall, anticipates the coming eschatological reversal, and, borrowing from Hos 10:8, portends destruction of the city for its departure from faithfulness to God in pursuit of idolatry. This, not Jesus' crucifixion, ought to elicit the beating of breasts and wailing. In a remarkable expression of self-idolatry, Babylon (a cipher for Rome in Rev 18) claims immortality for itself (18:7; compare Isa 47:7-8), a claim that stands in sharp contrast to the reality of its catastrophic destruction: "her plagues will come in a single day—pestilence and mourning and famine—and she will be burned with fire; for mighty is the Lord God who judges her" (18:8). Those who participate in Babylon's injustice and those so bedazzled by her opulence that they fail to see its injustice mourn her fall; after all, their own wealth and prestige has been tied to hers (18:8-19; compare Ezek 27). *See* DEATH, NT; EMOTIONS.

Bibliography: Rachel Hachlili. *Jewish Funerary Customs, Practices and Rites in the Second Temple Period* (2005).

JOEL B. GREEN

MOUSE [עַכְבָּר ʿakhbar]. Mice were known to damage agricultural crops, as when the Philistines are told to include gold images of the mice ravaging their land to be returned with the ARK OF THE COVENANT (1 Sam 6:4-5), which had earlier been captured from the Israelites. The prohibition against consuming mice (Lev 11:29) and Isaiah's admonition against those "eating the flesh of pigs, vermin, and rodents" (Isa 66:17) suggest that mice were part of the diet of certain segments of society. *See* ANIMALS OF THE BIBLE.

Bibliography: Oded Borowski. *Agriculture in Iron Age Israel* (2002).

ODED BOROWSKI

MOUTH [פֶּה peh; στόμα stoma]. *Mouth* refers to a location (literal or metaphorical), the vehicle of speech, and the symbol for God's communications. The human mouth is a powerful orifice because it marks the boundary between "inner thought" and "outer speech." Judging by speech, hearers draw conclusions about character and purpose. Words from the mouth come from the "abundance of the heart" (mind), confirming a basic identity between words and character (Matt 15:18; Luke 6:45).

As a location, the mouth is an opening that allows for the transference of items from one place to another, especially nourishment, God's word, and human praise or foolishness. In particular, the mouth indicates the outlet nearest the opening, and is often used metaphorically (as in the "mouth of the bay" in Josh 15:5; compare Gen 29:3; Josh 10:27; Jer 48:28; Dan 6:17). The earth can open its mouth to testify against human evil (Gen 4:11) or swallow the wicked as judgment (Num 16:32).

As metaphor of engagement, *mouth* refers to reliable teaching, as in "by word of mouth" (Acts 15:27), or the nearness of God's instructions, laws, decrees, and prophecies (Deut 30:14). God's mouth can heal, feed, or punish, and human mouths can be a source of joy (Song 1:2) and wisdom (Prov 10:11, 31) or ruin, evil, and cruelty. Proverbs strives to teach youngsters to guard their speech, refraining from gossip or perjury. The Messiah will smite the wicked with the "rod of his mouth" (Isa 11:4), a theme taken up in Rev 2:16; 19:15.

CAROLE R. FONTAINE

MOWING [גֵּז gez; ἀμάω amaō]. Cutting herbaceous plants. Amos 7:1 refers to the "king's mowing"—the first cut of grass or grain taken as tax (compare Ps 72:6, likening the king to rain falling on mown grass). In the NT, Jas 5:4 denounces the rich for cheating those who mow their fields.

JOEL MARCUS LEMON

MOZA moh'zuh [מוֹצָא motsa']. 1. Descendant of Judah, son of Caleb and his concubine EPHAH (1 Chr 2:46).

2. One of Saul's descendants, the son of ZIMRI (1 Chr 8:36-37; 9:42-43).

MOZAH moh'zuh [מֹצָה motsah]. One of the cities listed among those given to the tribe of Benjamin, along with Mizpeh and CHEPHIRAH, in Josh 18:26. The location of Mozah is unknown, although (along with all of the Benjaminite cities) it would have likely been located in the territory directly north of Jerusalem. *See* MIZPAH, MIZPEH.

JESSICA TINKLENBERG DEVEGA

MT, MASORETIC TEXT. "MT" is the abbreviation for "Masoretic Text," the text of the Tanakh based on the Masora, the text tradition of the Masoretes of Tiberias. "MT" has become a common term for the standard text of the Tanakh used by academics (e.g., *Biblia Hebraica Stuttgartensia*) that contains, along with the Hebrew letters, Masoretic vowel points, accent marks, and notations in the margins. *See* HEBREW BIBLE; MASORA; MASORETES; MASORETIC ACCENTS; TEXT, HEBREW, HISTORY OF.

MARIANNE BLICKENSTAFF

MU [μ M m]. The twelfth letter of the Greek alphabet, based on the Phoenician *mom [<*mawm] or *mem [<*maym]. *See* ALPHABET.

MUGHARAH, WADI EL. Wadi el-Mugharah, in Mount Carmel about 4 km east of the Mediterranean shore, is known for the four caves at its mouth that contain sediments dating from the Lower, Middle, and Upper Paleolithic and the Natufian periods (i.e., the past 400,000 years). Two Neanderthal skeletons came from Tabun Cave, and ten archaic *Homo sapiens* were excavated from the Skhul rockshelter. Modern human skeletons were found in Upper Paleolithic and Natufian layers in el-Wad cave.

GARY O. ROLLEFSON

MUJERISTA INTERPRETATION. A *mujerista* interpretation of the Bible is guided by Latinas' struggle for survival and the conviction that biblical interpretation should contribute to their liberation. A *mujerista* interpretation is rooted in Latinas' religious faith and the role it plays in their daily lived experiences, in *lo cotidiano.* Such an interpretation demands a critical cultural, sociohistorical, political, and economic analysis of their reality. A *mujerista* interpretation starts with a thorough study of a biblical pericope, using cultural criticism more than historical criticism, focusing particularly on the daily reality of the biblical characters. Their relationship with and understanding of Yahweh grew out of their daily lives just as it grows out of *lo cotidiano* of Latinas. The importance of the Bible's message lies in how its revelation about the divine is used by and helps the struggle for survival of those to whom it refers and those who embrace it now as the word of God.

Mujerista interpretation seeks to highlight biblical texts that refer to *lo cotidiano* and interpretations that focus on the centrality and importance of everyday experience. The act of resistance of two ordinary midwives, Shiphrah and Puah (Exod 1:15-21), the relevance of the faithfulness and intimacy of Ruth and Naomi for the people of Israel (Ruth 3:13-17), the need for Jesus to be touched and taken care of by the woman who washed his feet with her tears (Luke 7:36-50), Jesus' desire to share with others in order to understand himself and his mission (Luke 9:28-36), the centrality of personal, bodily needs in the kingdom of God (Matt 25:31-46)—these ordinary, daily realities of *lo cotidiano* are central to a *mujerista* reading and interpretation of the Bible.

The goal of *mujerista* theology is the liberation or fullness of life for Latinas living in the United States of America and for all poor and oppressed people. A *mujerista* interpretation listens to grassroots Latinas whose readings may not be scholarly but are valid insofar as they are life-giving to them and their communities. This recognition of the authority of Latinas to interpret the Bible is intrinsic to a *mujerista* praxis of liberation that seeks to contribute to the strengthening of these women's moral agency and self-definition. Their interpretations point to the dissonance that exists between Latinas' experiences and values and traditional interpretations of biblical texts. This dissonance gives rise to the suspicion that all reading and interpretation of the Bible are ideological, and *mujerista* interpretation privileges the worldview of the grassroots Latinas. *Mujerista* interpretation does not exclude any method of biblical interpretation but uses a wide variety of them while incorporating ideological and READER RESPONSE CRITICISM. *See* BIBLICAL CRITICISM; IDEOLOGICAL CRITICISM; POSTCOLONIAL BIBLICAL INTERPRETATION; SOCIAL SCIENTIFIC CRITICISM, NT; SOCIAL SCIENTIFIC CRITICISM, OT.

Bibliography: Nancy Cardoso Pereira. "Hermenéutica feminista: ¿caminos de enemistad o espacios sabrosos?" *RIBLA* 50 (2005) 135–39; Nancy Cardoso Pereira. "La profecía y lo cotidiano. La mujer y el niño en el ciclo del profeta Eliseo." *RIBLA* 15 (1993) 7–21; Fernando F. Segovia. *Decolonizing Biblical Studies: A View from the Margins* (2000); Fernando F. Segovia. "The Text as Other: Towards a Hispanic American Hermeneutic." *Text and Experience: Towards a Cultural Exegesis of the Bible.* Daniel Smith-Christopher, ed. (1995) 276–98.

ADA MARÍA ISASI-DÍAZ

MUJIB, WADI EL. This is the Arabic name for the river known in the OT as ARNON. It is one of four generally east-to-west flowing river systems that divide TRANSJORDAN into natural geographic regions: (north to south) the Yarmuk, the Jabbok, the Arnon, and the Zered (Wadi el-Hasa). The Wadi Mujib forms the northern boundary of the central Moabite plateau. Known as Jordan's "Grand Canyon," the Mujib canyon is as wide as 4.5 m and as deep as 750 m. The Wadi el-Mujib system drains the central Moabite plateau via its northern, eastern, and southern extensions. The wadis Nittil, Zaʾfaran, eth-Thamad, and esh-Shabik—all of which drain the region north and east of Dhiban—flow into the Wadi el-Wala; the Wadi el-Wala in turn flows into the Wadi el-Heidan, which drains the region west of Dhiban. The Wadi el-Heidan joins the Mujib system at Jebel el-Hamra, a few kilometers east of where the Mujib empties into the Dead Sea. The easternmost extension of the Mujib begins with the wadis Hallufa and et-Tuwai—both east of Jordan's desert highway, east-southeast of Siwaqa—and becomes the Wadi Suʿeida west of the desert highway; this in turn joins the Wadi Mujib southeast of Lahun. The Mujib's southern extension, comprised of the wadis el-Balu and en-Nukheita, drains the region east of the KING'S HIGHWAY and north of the Qatrana-Kerak road; these converge with the Wadi Suʿeida southeast of Lahun and become the Wadi el-Mujib. To facilitate water conservation, the Jordanian government built a dam at the point where the King's Highway crosses the basin of the Mujib, creating a reservoir to the east. In anticipation of this major project the Jordanian Department of Antiquities conducted an extensive survey and salvage excavations of antiquities sites targeted for inundation.

JOHN I. LAWLOR

MUKHAYYAT, KHIRBET EL. *See* NEBO, MOUNT.

MULBERRY, MULBERRY TREE [μόρον moron, συκάμινος sycaminos]. The black mulberry (*Morus nigra*), a short, stout tree with hairy, heart-shaped leaves, and deep red, edible fruits composed of a number of juicy globules, is mentioned in Luke 17:6 concerning believers' faith. Introduced into Palestine shortly before NT times from its native Iran (Persia), it is sometimes confused with the sycamore fig-tree, *Ficus sycomorus*, presumably owing to their superficial similarities. The fruit, moron, is mentioned as food for arousing elephants for battle (1 Macc 6:34). *See* BALSAM; PLANTS OF THE BIBLE; POPLAR; SYCAMORE.

F. NIGEL HEPPER

MULE [פֶּרֶד peredh, פִּרְדָּה pirdah; ἡμίονος hēmionos]. The mule, hybrid of a DONKEY and HORSE, is sterile and cannot reproduce, thus it was prized. It was a working animal (1 Kgs 18:5; Zech 14:15; Ps 32:9) but also a prestigious riding animal fit for a king (1 Kgs 1:33, 38, 44) and the king's sons (2 Sam 13:29). Valued more than sheep, oxen, and horses, mules appear in booty lists. Solomon received mules as annual tribute from his vassals (1 Kgs 10:25; 2 Chr 9:24). *See* ANIMALS OF THE BIBLE.

Bibliography: Oded Borowski. *Every Living Thing: Daily Use of Animals in Ancient Israel* (1998).

ODED BOROWSKI

MUPPIM muh'pim [מֻפִּים muppim]. A son of Benjamin (Gen 46:21), probably known by different names elsewhere—SHEPHUPHAM in Num 26:39 and Shephuphan in 1 Chr 8:5.

MURABBAAT, WADI. The Arabic name of the easternmost section of a wadi that begins east of Bethlehem and drains into the Dead Sea 11.5 mi. south of QUMRAN (*see* DEAD SEA SCROLLS). The modern Hebrew name is Nahal Darga. Four caves in the north wall of the wadi were occupied by Jewish refugees in the revolts against Rome in 66–74 CE and 132–35 CE.

The second occupation is dated by two letters (Mur 43, 44) from Simeon ben Kosiba, the leader of the revolt, and two legal documents dated 131 (Mur 22) and 133 (Mur 24). The badly torn biblical texts recovered all represent the standard MT. In 1955 a Hebrew text of the twelve Minor Prophets was found in a cave in the south wall some 300 m upstream from Caves 1–4.

Bibliography: P. Benoit, J. Milik, and R. de Vaux. *Les Grottes de Murabbaʿat* (1960).

JEROME MURPHY-O'CONNOR

MURASHÛ, ARCHIVES OF. A group of legal documents discovered in 1893 at NIPPUR, in central Babylonia, written in Akkadian cuneiform between 454 and 404 BCE. Approximately 885 known tablets and fragments represent some 750–800 original documents, contracts, and receipts arising from business done by descendants of a man named Murashû. Most involve either agricultural contracting, as the Murashû family and its agents leased fields and orchards from proprietors around Nippur and subleased them, along with draft animals, seed, and equipment to their own tenants; or obligations created when the Murashû family supplied short-term credit to holders of small land-grants from the Persian crown. A few deal with other matters.

Along with other non-Babylonian names in the texts, noteworthy for Bible study are approximately eighty personal names compounded with the divine name Yahweh and other names considered Jewish and thought to be descendants of Judean exiles, although nothing sets them apart from bearers of the other approximately 2,200 names in the Murashû texts.

Bibliography: Guillaume Cardascia. *Les archives des Murašû* (1951); Veysel Donbaz and Matthew W. Stolper. *Istanbul Murašû Texts* (1997); Govert van Driel. "The Murašûs in Context." *JESHO* 32 (1989) 203–29; Michael Jursa. *Neo-Babylonian Legal and Administrative Documents* (2005) 113–14; Matthew W. Stolper. *Entrepreneurs and Empire* (1985); Matthew W. Stolper. "Fifth Century Nippur: Texts of the Murašûs and from Their Surroundings." *JCS* 53 (2001) 83–132.

MATTHEW W. STOLPER

MURATORIAN CANON myoor′uh-tor′ee-uhn kan′uhn. A catalog of Christian Scriptures that constitutes an important witness in the history of the formation of the NT canon. Fragmentary, it consists of eighty-five lines preserved in a 7th- or 8th-cent. codex discovered in the Ambrosian Library in Milan. The original language of the list was almost certainly Greek, but it survives in a clumsy Latin translation. The opening lines of the document are mutilated. Other pieces of the same work were found at Monte Cassino in four manuscripts of the Pauline corpus (ca. 11th or 12th cent.). The list is notable for the twenty-four texts it deems authoritative. They include, presumably, the Gospels of Matthew, Mark, Luke, and John (if the usual reconstruction of the lacuna is accepted), the Acts of the Apostles, thirteen letters attributed to Paul, Jude, 1 and 2 John, the Wisdom of Solomon, the Apocalypse of John, and the Apocalypse of Peter (though the author admits the status of the latter is contested). Writings not mentioned are Hebrews, James, 1 and 2 Peter, and 3 John. Certain Christian works are explicitly rejected: the *Shepherd of Hermas* (although orthodox, its composition is deemed too late to be apostolic); and several gnostic, Marcionite, and Montanist writings that are characterized as forgeries and heretical. The Muratorian fragment was previously regarded as the earliest witness to the NT "canon," thought to have been promulgated in Rome at the end of the 2nd cent. That traditional provenance and the concomitant claim that the notion of a NT canon developed early still have ardent defenders. However, many scholars believe the contents of the Muratorian fragment are better accounted for by a 4th-cent. dating and an Eastern provenance—Palestine or Syria. Its closest and earliest datable parallel is the enumeration and categorization Eusebius of Caesarea gives (*Hist. eccl.* 3.25.1–7). Other Eastern lists dating to the 4th cent., e.g., those found in Cyril of Jerusalem's *Catechetical Lecture* 4.33–36, Epiphanius' *Pan.* 76, in *Codex Claromontanus*, a Syriac catalog, John Chrysostom's *Synopsis Veteris et Novi Testmenti*, and the Stichometry of Nicephorus, bear considerable and closer resemblance. *See* CANON OF THE NEW TESTAMENT.

Bibliography: Geoffrey Hahneman. *The Muratorian Fragment and the Development of the Canon* (1992); Lee Martin McDonald and James A. Sanders, eds. *The Canon Debate* (2002).

GREGORY ALLEN ROBBINS

MURATORIAN FRAGMENT. *See* MURATORIAN CANON.

MURDER. *See* CRIMES AND PUNISHMENT, OT AND NT.

MUREX. *Murex* is a genus of carnivorous marine gastropods used in the manufacture of the color PURPLE for DYE. The dyer extracted leuco-base from the hypobranchial gland and produced the dye through a lengthy process. Purple fabric was a sign of wealth and prestige. TYRE was famed for its purple dye.

MARY P. BOYD

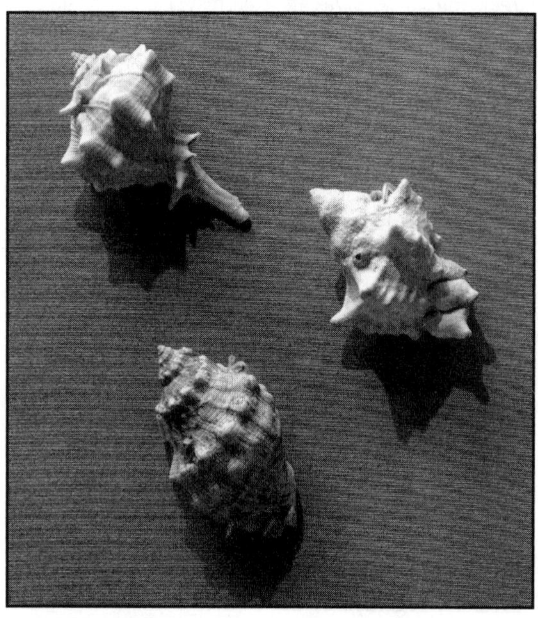

Todd Bolen/BiblePlaces.com

Murex shells for purple dye, collection of British Museum.

MURMUR [לוּן lun, תְּלֻנָּה telunnah; γογγύζω gongyzō, γογγυσμός gongysmos, διαγογγύζω diagongyzō]. In the exodus stories, the Israelites express dissatisfaction with Moses and Aaron by murmuring (NRSV, "complaining") against them. Scholars often refer to the murmuring stories in the wilderness traditions found in both Exodus and Numbers. Their dissatisfaction often stems from the hunger and thirst they experience in the wilderness (e.g., Exod 15:24; 16:2; *see* GRUMBLING; WANDER; WILDERNESS). The Israelites also murmur at the unfavorable report concerning the land of Canaan that is brought back by spies (Num 14:2). In this case, their murmuring leads to God's promise that the original generation will die in the wilderness (Num 14:27-31). Although the immediate targets for the Israelites' complaints are Moses and Aaron, murmuring is interpreted as rebellion against God (e.g., Exod 16:7-8; Deut 1:27; Ps 106:25).

In the NT, John characterizes the response to Jesus in similar terms by stating that both the Jews (John 6:41, 43) and the disciples (6:61) murmur against Jesus during his discourse on the manna (6:31-58; compare 7:12, 32). Their disbelief is thus portrayed as being like that of the Israelites in the wilderness period. Their murmuring identifies them as people who do not trust God. The word *murmur* (NRSV, "complain" or "grumble") is also used without reference to the exodus story as a general term for complaint (Phil 2:14).

SUSAN E. HYLEN

MUSA, WADI. Wadi Musa is the present name of a town immediately to the east of PETRA, deriving from a regional name anchored on ʿAyn Muisa, the "spring of Moses." Pre-Islamic and pre-Christian tradition locates MERIBAH at Wadi Musa (Num 20:1-13). The ancient name of the town was Gaia (Aram. "the valley"). Due to its strong water supply and easy accessibility, the venue makes an ideal resting place for caravans. Tawilan, where Midianite sherds (13th–10th cent. BCE) and a small Edomite settlement were found, now forms part of the town. In its center there is evidence for continuous occupation since at least the Persian period. While Nabatean religious institutions (and the upper-class living quarters) were located at Petra, civic and commercial functions logically remained at Gaia. Architectural fragments attest to at least one monumental temple at Wadi Musa, attributable to "Dusares of Gaia," the main deity of the NABATEANS. Gaia could also be intended in the 1 Chr 4:39 reference to "the valley" (haggayeʾ הַגַּיְא).

Bibliography: J. F. Healey. *The Religion of the Nabataeans* (2001); E. A. Knauf. "Mount Hor and Kadesh Barnea." *BN* 61 (1992) 22–26.

ERNST AXEL KNAUF

MUSHI my*oo*ʹsh*i* [מוּשִׁי mushi]. Mushi and his brother MAHLI were Levites, sons of Merari (Exod 6:19), and heads of the two divisions of Merarites (Num 3:33). Mushi had three sons, Mahli, EDER, and JEREMOTH (1 Chr 23:23; 24:30). Some view "Mushi" as a variant of "Moses" and posit an early group of priests descended from Moses. If so, these priests have now been demoted to Levites and separated from the figure of Moses. *See* LEVI, LEVITES; MERARI, MERARITES.

KEVIN A. WILSON

MUSIC [שִׁיר shir, שִׁירָה shirah; συμφωνία symphōnia]. We would be hard pressed to find a culture, ancient or modern, that does not incorporate music in some aspect of daily life. Various forms of music complement how people praise and worship deities, announce warfare and implement specific military strategies, initiate communal gatherings, and even provide entertainment. A plethora of instruments are utilized by trained and untrained persons to create organized sounds that are distinct for each culture. Like other features of societies and cultures (e.g., clothing, pottery), instruments and the types of sounds musicians produce with them can and do change over time. Examination of biblical and other ANE texts, in addition to archaeological remains from specific time periods and cultures, helps to explain how people in antiquity used a number of instruments to employ this artistic medium. Without question, cultures known and identified throughout the biblical world influenced one another for centuries, and this is evident in the depictions of musicians, instruments, and performances.

While the specific geographical and cultural origins of some instruments may be clearer than others, it is apparent that various forms of instruments, such as drums, lyres, harps, and pipes, were staples of most ANE cultures, particularly those mentioned in the Bible.

While archaeology and texts have produced useful insights into the ancient practices of music and the world and peoples from which they came, the precise sounds are lost to us. Instrument remains, textual descriptions regarding their construction, discussions about musical performance, specific musicians, and instruction provide some answers, as well as producing additional perplexing questions, but still leave us wondering how the music sounded. Although some of these data are readily available, we are faced with the challenge of analyzing the role of music in past cultures and, furthermore, comprehending and interpreting information provided by one of our best-known informants: the biblical witness.

All data have their unique complications, and those that speak about the musical practices of the biblical world are no exception. In addition to the lack of information about musical sound, a number of other complications must be considered. For instance, remains of instruments are scant, and instruments are seldom found whole. When they are discovered, researchers must often study comparative archaeological remains of ancient and some modern instruments. Typically, depictions of musical performance from antiquity are not accompanied with textual descriptions or detailed explanation. Additionally, some renderings of musical activity are difficult to decipher due to damage to the artifact, schematic or highly stylized artistic renderings, or the display of unknown or enigmatic practices. Consequently, those who study music and ancient cultures (archaeomusicologists or music archaeologists) must employ interdisciplinary methods from fields such as art, anthropology, ethnomusicology, computer science, cultural studies, philology, and textual studies. Researchers are able to make competent, well- researched, informed attempts to look through the eyes of the ancient writers and examine material remains from a number of perspectives.

In addition to developing special methods to research this area of ancient cultures, some essential questions must be considered, particularly when examining what we understand to be past theological and cultural practices involving music. For example, what do we want to know about culture, music, and the biblical world? Also, knowing the data that are available, what can we expect to comprehend? Last, how can or should we interpret and employ the findings? With these issues in mind, the following entry discusses some of the cultural and theological functions of music in antiquity. The focus will be on the general ANE, the OT, the Greco-Roman world, and the NT.

A. General Role of Music in the Ancient Near East

Various forms of chordophones, aerophones (e.g., pipes, flutes), membranophones (drums), and idiophones (rattles; cymbals may be considered by some a combination idiophone and membranophone) found their way into the music cultures of the ANE (*see* MUSICAL INSTRUMENTS). Through interactions such as trade, syncretism, intermarriage, and the desire to incorporate different sounds and rhythms, people fused instruments from other cultures with their own indigenous sound tools to create their specific musical cultures. Performers used these selected instruments in many everyday activities, but most of our knowledge of their music comes from depictions and descriptions of what we understand to be religious practices. In general, all known ANE cultures used combinations of instruments to pay homage to deities and to enhance specific religious practices and ceremonies.

Throughout the Near East these religious activities were at times very formal, structured, orchestrated, and exclusive, but in each culture there were also instances in which they were spontaneous, fluid, and inclusive. For the most part, ANE religious music practices were diverse, but contained a number of strong universal elements that united them. In different chronological periods, e.g., each Near Eastern culture incorporated lyres, harps, and other similar stringed instruments (e.g., lute), pipes, various forms of drums, rattles, and cymbals for performance in some aspect of society. Delineations of sacred and secular are later societal constructions; in the world of the ANE, there were no designations such as this. However, we employ these divisions for analyzing and research. While the following discussion of Near Eastern peoples is not exhaustive, it will provide a basic overview of how music functioned culturally and theologically among some of these groups.

1. Mesopotamia

In antiquity, Mesopotamia—the land between the Tigris and Euphrates rivers—included groups such as the Sumerians, Akkadians, Babylonians, Amorites, Hittites, Elamites, Kassites, and Chaldeans. Artifacts and texts from the geographical area reveal that all Mesopotamian cultures skillfully incorporated music into aspects of daily life. There were instances in which certain instruments suggest that musical performance was intricate, organized (e.g., a designated ensemble, specific songs arranged in a particular manner), and performed by trained musicians. The famous Golden or Bull Lyre of Ur from the tomb of Queen Puabi (ca. 2600–2500 BCE), for instance, is one of the most well-known archaeological finds concerning music from this region. Although the find has been replicated for the most part from the archaeological remains, its construction indicates that it was a special instrument and not just anyone played it.

The materials used in making the lyre—including precious stones such as lapis lazuli, metals like gold and silver, and rare, expensive wood—and its association with a queen suggest that the chordophone had a unique place within cultural practices. Although the Bull Lyre, along with other instruments (i.e., pipes, lyres), was found in a grave as part of the objects to accompany the deceased in the afterlife, it is possible that it may have been played in what we might interpret as secular and religious contexts and in combination with other instruments. In other words, it does not appear that the lyre was assigned exclusively to either societal realm. Yet the fact that the lyre and other instruments were a part of the cache of material remains of an elaborate royal burial should not be overlooked. The inclusion of music and musical instruments in tombs illuminates some of the ways ancients may have viewed an afterlife. This practice of burying servants, musicians, food, and other tangible items reveals that in the eyes of this group and others (e.g., Egyptians) there was life after death, and it was similar in some ways to the life from which they were departing. Moreover, the items contained in the burial would accompany them in transition to the next life. With musical instruments and musicians included in the mix, we see the importance of the art form in the lives of Mesopotamians, Egyptians, and possibly others, in this world and the next. In essence, some forms of musical performance can project a microcosm of life within a culture.

There are early Mesopotamian texts that discuss musical performances by different cultures, and some give descriptions of musical "superstars" of the time. For instance, Sumerian texts speak of Shulgi, the son of Ur-Nammu (2094–2047 BCE), who was not only a king and writer of laws but also a creator of instruments and a composer of hymns. Although Shulgi composed hymns for deities, the texts also reveal that he was not bashful in speaking about his musical talents. Shulgi's musical characteristics bear some resemblance to two prominent Israelite kings of the later biblical period, David and Solomon. The biblical writers do not say anything about either king boasting of their musical talents, but David and his son Solomon, much in the same fashion as Shulgi, composed music and were responsible for the construction of musical instruments used in what most interpret as sacred performance according to biblical traditions. Shulgi's composition of hymns for deities provides a means through which this royal figure expressed a form of theological expression and interpretation of his and his people's relationships with the pantheon of gods.

Archaeologists have discovered tablets dating to the 3rd millennium BCE that indicate possibly the earliest musical notation in the ANE (two cuneiform tablets from Ur, one from Assur, and one from Nippur; others have been found at Ras Shamra, Ugarit). One piece connected with the tablets is a mathematical text that provides insight into the levels of sophistication in Mesopotamian music in general as well as aspects of theoretical development. The mathematical text assisted in deciphering a musical hymn named *The Hurrian Cult Song.* The hymn employs musical notation from Ugarit. Assyriologist Anne Kilmer and a team of scholars translated this work, and the results of their efforts generated a recording titled *Sounds from Silence.* The skillfully crafted album uses reconstructed chordophones and also provides an interpretation of the Hurrian hymn, discussion of musical theory, and other musical selections. This discovery further demonstrates Mesopotamian, or more specifically, Hurrian theology and the use of hymns about and for deities in Mesopotamian cultures. While there are some issues in precisely translating the words of the hymn and even parts of the musical theory interpretation, we nevertheless have evidence of the use of music in this culture to pay homage to the pantheon of deities.

The Assyrians and Babylonians, dominant superpowers of Mesopotamia and at times the entire Near East, had creative music cultures, and some segments were well organized. Although both groups existed for centuries, many would consider the Assyrian and Babylonian musical golden ages to be during the 1st millennium BCE, particularly the Iron Age, also known to some as the biblical period (1200–586 BCE). Iconographic depictions (line drawings) and texts demonstrate the use and importance of music in these groups. For example, a 7th-cent. depiction from a palace wall of Assyrian king Sennacherib presents the use of elaborate harps, dulcimers, drums, handclapping, and possibly human voices (e.g., singing, chanting) in what appears to be a victorious war celebration, processional, or march. The group is organized in the following manner: tallest to shortest person, harps held by bearded and clean-shaven men, dulcimer player(s), and women and children who are possibly singing, clapping, and so on. Performing celebratory songs to a deity for deliverance or to or about specific warriors regarding their accomplishments on the battlefield was known to groups throughout the ANE. This cultural singing practice may have given adoration and praise to a deity and its actions, or the participants may have sung specifically about heroic acts of particular soldiers.

With Babylonian culture, in addition to entertaining, aiding in prophetic activity, and easing methodical labor, the biblical text indicates that music was used to signal specific times for praise and worship of specific deities. The book of Daniel describes the use of music for people to pay homage to a statue erected by King Nebuchadnezzar: "You are commanded, O peoples, nations, and languages, that when you hear the sound of the horn, pipe, lyre, trigon (possibly a small harp), harp, drum, and entire musical ensemble, you are to fall down and worship the golden statue that King Nebuchadnezzar has set up" (Dan 3:4-5). As with a number of practices, the use of music in this fashion was common throughout the ANE. The primary instruments of choice in Mesopotamian religious musical performance were harps and lyres, and they were often combined with drums, cymbals, and pipes.

Questions regarding sex and gender in Mesopotamian secular and religious musical performance remain unanswered. When attempting to interpret or comprehend enigmatic aspects of ancient cultures, we sometimes project images of the present on the past or analyze ancient peoples, societies, and cultural practices with blanket assumptions. This approach is dangerous and contributes further to the already difficult task of interpreting the past. When assessing musical practices of the ANE, particularly sex and gender, assumptions have been made regarding musical performance. A general thought when it comes to the Near East has been that males and females played specific instruments and they did not perform together in any contexts. However, it appears that in Mesopotamia men and women played each of the known instruments in religious and secular contexts and possibly performed together in some situations. Mesopotamian texts also reveal that cross-dressing was a part of musical performance, pantomime, other theatrical activity, and possibly in some religious performances. The Babylonians celebrated the Akitu Festival, also known as the New Year's Festival, which involved the Babylonian gods leaving their cities and visiting Marduk to share plans for the coming year. The event, which lasted eleven days, consisted of processions, sacrifices, and the possible reenactment of a sacred marriage ceremony, DANCING, and singing, most of which incorporated musical performance. The length of the event indicates its importance to the culture and the people. Musicians, special compositions, and specific instruments would have been a staple in this annual event. Music played a major role in the daily life of Mesopotamian cultures, and helped to facilitate and enhance a variety of cultural practices and to express their theological views of deities and how they comprehended the world around them.

2. Egypt

The land of EGYPT and its music culture are very similar to those in Mesopotamia and others throughout the Near East, but because there are more available artifacts, we are able to see even more of the unique characteristics of this highly developed and influential society. Music was a part of Egyptian culture since its inception, and the art form permeated nearly every aspect of life. Temple activities, warfare, prophecy, dance, banquets, and burials were some of the aspects of Egyptian culture in which music played a role. Some of the primary instruments in the early dynasties of Egypt (Old Kingdom) include the nay (aerophone), an end-blown pipe played at an oblique angle, oboe, harps, lyres, clappers (ca. 24–36-in.-long wood or ivory sticks, sometimes painted or carved to look like forearms with hands), cymbals, and various types of drums. The nay seems to disappear from use in the later kingdoms, but forms of the others continue. Although we have more depictions, figurines, and statues of musical scenes and musicians from Egypt than other Near Eastern cultures, the contexts of many are uncertain. Yet it appears that types of the aforementioned instruments were used in a variety of combinations for religious and secular performances and continued in some form throughout Egyptian chronology and cultural and theological development.

Egyptian gods and goddesses at times were closely associated with music and performance. For instance, the goddess Merit (also identified as the goddesses of inundation) was considered to be the personification of music. Although she is not identified with a specific instrument, Merit is connected with chironomy, the act of directing musicians and singers through hand gestures and possibly vocal commands. It is believed that this act was very similar to modern idea of conducting (Hickmann). Another deity known for his connection with music is Bes. This dwarf god with his strong connection to music and musical performance was said to appear at conception and childbirth (Manniche). There are iconographic depictions of Bes in intimate scenes between men and women (some include musical instruments, e.g., lyre); female musicians would at times display images of the god tattooed on their upper thighs (Manniche). Artists have shown Bes playing the frame drum and lyre, although it does not appear that he is associated with either of these instruments exclusively. The goddess Hathor also possessed a connection with music in Egyptian culture, as she is referred to as the "mistress of dance" and the "mistress of music." Bastet, the cat goddess, whose characteristics are similar to Hathor, is associated with music, and at times artisans depicted her, as well as Hathor, with a sistrum. The sistrum is a rattle-like instrument with strings and disks and sometimes with an ivory handle (combination idiophone–chordophone). The instrument was often used in religious practices with other deities and has been found in other Near Eastern cultures' musical corpuses. Its shape is similar to the ankh, the symbol for life, which may have some connection with sacred performance. Some scholars associate the sistrum with sex and sensuality, as its shape is similar to a part of a woman's reproductive organs.

Sex and gender identifications of musicians in Egyptian musical performance are somewhat clearer due to the types of available data. Iconographic depictions show men and women playing various shapes, types, and sizes of lyres, harps, pipes, drums, and clappers. There may be some question regarding the sistrum being played by women specifically, but it appears that both men and women played most instruments. Women's ensembles consisting of oboe, lute, harp, lyre, and vocalists performed for banquets and other public events. They also accompanied dancers (typically female) during these types of activities. There are also scenes in which men and women are depicted performing together, leading each other through chironomy. While it is debatable, it appears that musicians incorporated chironomy in both secular and sacred contexts. For the most part, however, the data suggest that women led women and men led men. In some of the earlier Egyptian periods, artistic renderings present blind male harpists/lyrists playing for singers and dancers. Whether these performers were born blind or blinded due to the performance contexts is uncertain. In other words, it is possible that just as eunuchs who worked among women were castrated in some cultures, specific musicians in Egyptian culture who performed for female dancers might have been blinded purposely. While some of the contexts shown by the artists are unknown, the majority of them are apparently elaborate and involved affairs: performers are dressed in special clothing; musical instruments, in some cases, are exquisite; and a number of additional activities take place simultaneously.

Because the dynamics of culture are so tightly intertwined, any act within nearly any aspect of culture and society affects all other aspects to some degree. Although it is not always readily apparent, this is true when it comes to music. In Egypt one instance in particular provides an excellent example. With AKHENATEN's (Amenhotep IV, 1352–1336 BCE) advent to the throne, Egypt changed dramatically. With his reign came the practice of monotheism (also possibly a version of MONOLATRY), which wiped out numerous jobs that were connected to other deities and temples. In a radical move, he established a new capital in Amarna, which essentially uprooted the previous capital city of Thebes (*see* AMARNA, TELL EL). Needless to say there were many who opposed Akhenaten's extreme decisions, but if we view these changes through the lens of music, we can see their effects upon the art form. With the "downsizing" of the Egyptian pantheon, a number of musicians lost their positions and would have had to change occupations or try to use their musical skills to work within the new religious structure. Furthermore, if there were any musical instruments associated with particular deities, they may have been banned or completely abandoned. These extreme developments were not restricted to Egypt. NABONIDUS in Babylon, who elevated the god Sin, and even those kings' reigns that brought polytheism, would have affected musical practices.

As discussed in regard to Babylonian culture, hymns were a staple in Egyptian culture. Hymns to Egyptian deities were commonplace and often expressed adoration and praise of specific gods. The words to hymns dedicated to deities such as Hathor, Amun, Aten, and others are often found in ancient texts and further express relationships between the people and gods. Also, stelae sometimes contain inscriptions as well as depictions of musicians, choirs, and so on that express theological ideas and thoughts.

These types of expressions were creative and innovative and were an integral part of Egyptian culture throughout its chronological periods. It should be understood that although Egypt was at times a dominant culture and influenced much of the Near East, the effects of surrounding peoples and cultures upon Egypt are evident in pottery, technology, theology, and musical instruments.

3. Ancient Israel and the Old Testament

The land of Israel is considerably smaller geographically than the areas mentioned up to this point. However, like those mentioned previously, ancient Israel had a distinct music culture that played a major role in the culture and theology. What we know about Israelite music culture comes primarily from the OT. While the heyday of this group's music culture was during the Iron Age or biblical period, archaeological excavations have produced evidence of music culture in this region during the prehistoric eras. Among bone pipes, rattle-like instruments, and bull-roarers dating to the Neolithic period (8300–4500 BCE), a depiction of an Early Bronze Age (3300–2200 BCE) figure with a lyre on a flagstone was unearthed in front of a palace/temple (Loud).

While it is beyond the scope of this article to explain the origins of music in general, which are extremely complex and unclear, a brief word is in order when discussing music, ancient Israel, and the OT. As mentioned, there are more questions than answers regarding the origin of music and musical instruments in ancient Israelite culture. There is, however, a somewhat cryptic etiological explanation from the biblical text regarding the origin of music and at least two types of musical instruments in the book of Genesis. The biblical writer explains that "Adah bore Jabal; he was the ancestor of those who live in tents and have livestock. His brother's name was Jubal; he was the ancestor of all those who play the lyre and pipe" (Gen 4:20-21). Although this is not meant to be a literal explanation of the origin of music, there may be some information present regarding some of the more popular instruments in ancient Israelite culture, particularly during the Early Bronze Age. Some forms of the pipe and other stringed instruments continue through subsequent chronological periods and cultural developments. We can also note that the writers describing this etiology do not discuss any religious or theological implications regarding the instruments. Moreover, there are secular and sacred scenes in the OT that involve the pipe and lyre. Again, the writers may give some indication of how ubiquitous these instruments were in Israelite culture and society.

a. Performance contexts in the Old Testament. Israelite cultural activities that involved music are much like numerous others in the ANE (warfare, funerals, homage to deities, celebrations, etc), but we have learned that like other ANE cultures, Israelite culture involving music had distinct characteristics. For example, at Israelite/Judean funerals dating to the biblical period, songs of lament accompanied wailing women. These "trained" women attended funerals and displayed their developed craft (Jer 9:20). Also, singers or musicians may have composed laments for specific events or individuals (e.g., 2 Sam 1:17-27).

The biblical text also provides insight regarding the practice of employing music with prophetic activity in ancient Israel. First Samuel 10:5 describes Saul's encounter with a band of prophets and a group of musicians just before he became the first king of Israel. Samuel advises Saul that he will be caught up in a "prophetic frenzy" with the group of prophets and musicians as they approach. Although there are different views of what exactly a "prophetic frenzy" entailed, it appears that this activity was induced or sustained by the music performed by musicians on the double pipe, cymbals, frame drum, lyre, and harp. Some forms of each of these instruments in the prophetic ensemble have continued into modern cultures of the Middle East (e.g., **mijwiz, zummara, duff**). Although there is no clear direct link, some have likened the prophetic frenzy to the practices of the Whirling Dervishes of the Middle East. These performers are known for their mesmerizing twirling in long flowing robes. This hypnotic, spiritual, ecstatic activity may go on for hours, with performers whirling and twirling faster and faster. The intensity of the music matches the performers' energies. If one has ever witnessed this event, it will be understandable how the Dervishes' actions have been paralleled to the "prophetic frenzy" described by the Samuel writer. Moreover, this activity the biblical writers describe provides additional information regarding the connection between prophecy and music. Music seems to have played a role in aiding prophets of the OT in prophesying, comprehending, and conveying the will of God.

Performance contexts may also indicate who was involved in specific musical activities in the culture of ancient Israel. For instance, while many events described in the OT include the general populace, the activity described by the writer of 1 Sam 10:5 presents a performance context that is exclusive. Note that the band of musicians is connected with the group of prophets who have been together at a high place and are coming back into town. Moreover, they are participating in a specific act—prophetic frenzy—although this action is ambiguous. People stand, watch, and comment, but none join the prophets or the musicians. Samuel tells Saul that he will soon be an involuntary participant in this restricted club, and this happens just as Samuel stated. While participation is exclusive within the ranks of the musicians and the prophets, the performance context includes onlookers or an audience. A number of the musical activities take place outside in open areas. The writer seems to imply that this combination of music and prophetic activity was a common occurrence.

Another case involving the use of music and prophecy appears in 2 Kgs 3. In this instance, Jehoshaphat, king of Judah, wanted to know how to proceed in a potential conflict with the king of Moab. In order to hear from Yahweh, he asked if there was a prophet in the land. One of his servants advised that Elisha, the protégé of Elijah, was in the area and could inquire of Yahweh on his behalf. Elisha agrees to Jehoshaphat's request. However, before the prophet begins his prophetic query for Jehoshaphat, he requests a musician. When the musician performs, "the power (lit., 'hand') of the LORD came upon him" (2 Kgs 3:15). An obvious question of course is "What instrument did the musician play?" The passage does not provide a clear answer. Although most of the instruments known to ancient Israelite culture could have served in this capacity, strong candidates may be the harp and lyre. The primary reason for this interpretation is that the Chronicler explains that these chordophones were used in prophetic activity during temple musical performances (1 Chr 25:1).

Music and prophecy appear to have gone together in ancient Israel and the Near East in general. Select instruments appear to have helped induce the prophet to connect with the deity. Furthermore, music served as an active and passive catalyst in prophecy. Saul, e.g., was passively caught up by the music and prophetic activity, while Elisha actively employed music to prophesy. This powerful art form has an indelible tie to prophecy.

b. Locations of performances. An area that is often overlooked is where music was performed. While the biblical text and archaeological record indicate that people performed music outside in open areas, the evidence suggests they also performed music in enclosed structures such as temples and other public buildings. The Chronicler presents a number of examples of temple music performance. Organized and spontaneous performances also took place outdoors as people watched. For example, when the writers of Samuel explain that the prophet Samuel reveals to Saul that he will be involved in a prophetic activity, it appears the incident takes place outside. Taking this incident into consideration, there is another aspect of musical performance that is often overlooked—the location of the audience. Although we cannot always be certain, we may reasonably speculate that performances took place in front of an audience. Size and location are questions still waiting to be researched; yet they are issues that must be considered. Also, people were aware of cultural song traditions and more than likely knew "their places" when it came time for performance. For example, people probably knew where to go and what to do when women came out of the villages to greet warriors returning from battle with song and dance (1 Sam 18:6).

c. Performers. The ancient Israelites consistently incorporated music in their lives. The importance of this art form should not be underestimated. We explored briefly an Israelite etiology of music, performance contexts, and musical instruments. But who were the performers? Ancient Near Eastern artifacts and textual descriptions provide simple-to-elaborate scenes of people involved in musical performance. While the scenes are primarily what we define as religious, the general thought is that for the most part men were the only musicians. A closer look at these data reveals that women were heavily involved as well. The etiology in Genesis does not involve women, but in Exodus the author describes Miriam and a group of women singing praises to Yahweh with their voices and frame drums after their dramatic escape (Exod 15:20). The book of Judges presents Deborah and Barak singing following their victory over Sisera (Judg 5). Some scholars argue convincingly that Barak's name was added as part of a later redaction and that the composition is actually the "Song of Deborah" (Poethig; Ackerman). Israelite culture contained a victory song tradition in which select women sang the praises of soldiers returning from battle. As mentioned previously, the biblical writers share an episode (1 Sam 18:6) in which women gather with frame drums and sing to Saul and David, singing to each other: "Saul has killed his thousands, and David his ten thousands." There is a similar scene in Judg 11:34 when the daughter of Jepthah sings to her father with frame drums and dances to celebrate his victory against the Ammonites.

The women described in these instances show at least two types of praise practiced by individuals and ensembles: 1) praise to Yahweh for deliverance; and 2) praise to individuals/men/warriors for victory in battle. The praise is rendered through voice, sometimes with frame drum accompaniment.

Men and women also worked together in religious contexts. There might have been some cultural or sex-gender restrictions, but they did collaborate in musical performance. The Chronicler discusses musical structure and hierarchy in the Temple of Jerusalem and presents an intriguing description in 1 Chr 25:1-6. ASAPH, HEMAN, JEDUTHUN (each of whom was to prophesy with lyres, harps, and cymbals) and their children had specific duties in the Temple, which primarily involved music. The daughters' names are not in the list that follows, but the list has a number of issues and their names may have been eliminated through editing. However, it would be difficult to argue that women were not involved in temple musical activity (see Ps 68:25 [Heb. 68:26]). Moreover, archaeological material indicates that women with musical instruments were depicted in clay figurines, particularly during the biblical period. Plaque figurines and figurines in the round show women with frame drums, lutes, lyres, harps, and pipes. These artifacts and the descriptions from the Bible and other ANE documents show that women, along with men, used music in the culture and theological life of Israel.

d. Styles of music performances in the Old Testament. We have discussed a number of musical performances, instruments, and performers, as well as interpretations of the use of music in the OT. Nevertheless, there are two basic types of religious musical performance presented, which are here designated "Style A" and "Style B."

Style A religious musical performances appear primarily in the Pentateuch and DtrH and have five distinct characteristics (Burgh). 1) Religious performance is inclusive. To indicate inclusiveness, the biblical writers used specific phrases such as "all of Israel," "the house of Israel," or "everyone" in their musical descriptions (e.g., 2 Sam 6:5), which implies that in some instances large groups of people who were not necessarily trained or skilled musicians participated. 2) Religious performances can consist of a mixed sex or gender ensemble. It appears that there were times when men and women performed together in religious musical contexts, as seen in the example of the vocal duet of Deborah and Barak (Judg 5:1). Although it has its complications, this passage indicates that a woman and man blend their voices in song to celebrate deliverance from an enemy with the assistance of Yahweh. 3) The religious performance is organized. The Pentateuch and Deuteronomistic writers present events in which people involved in religious musical performances lead songs through singing, with instruments, or a combination of both. These actions demonstrate that there was a dimension of order and structure initiated and led by an individual (e.g., Exod 15:20). 4) Musical instrumentation varied in religious musical performance. In many instrumental ensembles for religious activities, musicians performed on lyres, drums, cymbals, trumpets, pipes, and rattles in numerous combinations, with or without singers (e.g., 1 Sam 10:5; 2 Sam 6:5; 1 Kgs 1:40). 5). There was diversity in the religious music performance personnel. As mentioned previously, biblical writers sometimes use the term "all of Israel" or "everyone" in describing some religious musical activity. Social or hierarchical divisions within the culture do not appear to have segregated musicians when it comes to religious music performance in Style A. For instance, David the king played music with the (common) people of Israel in religious contexts without any apparent tensions (2 Sam 6:5). In contrast, there are musical groups that apparently contained only women who performed what would be defined as religious and secular music (e.g., Judg 11:1-40; 1 Sam 18:6).

Style B religious musical performances are presented primarily in Chronicles, and although the characteristics are similar to Style A, there are also some additional features and distinct differences. Five characteristics of Style B performances are very similar to Style A. 1) Style B and A are similar in that there is a dimension of structure, but Style B has much stronger and more rigid elements of organization. For example, Style B religious performances take place for the most part in specific areas (e.g., inside a tent or a temple, or in close proximity to these areas, with selected personnel playing the music; e.g., 1 Chr 6:31-48). 2) Style B is structured. Specific actions take place, sometimes at designated or assigned times, and there is often choreography of religious activity and musical performance (e.g., 1 Chr 16:4-6). 3) In Style B there are distinct musical personnel and a hierarchical musical system in place that coincides with the organization of the religious structure (e.g., 1 Chr 6:31-48). Persons participating in the services are selected and in many instances hand-picked to perform certain musical tasks. There are musical leaders, musical instructors, and other individuals who have distinct skills (e.g., apparent simultaneous prophesying and musical performance, e.g., 1 Chr 15:16-24). Also, the musical organization of ancient Israel described in Style B religious activity as a whole is kin- or family-based. 4) Style B religious musical performance also involves the use of various types of instruments. The instrumentation is very much akin to Style A (e.g., chordophones, aerophones, idiophones, human voices), but descriptions of Style B performance do not mention membranophones specifically. Interestingly, there are no taboos or derogatory connotations associated with instruments of this family, and the writer does not mention them in the same manner as in passages describing Style A religious performances. Style B performances, however, do employ the ambiguous phrases "musical instruments of David" and "instruments of praise I have made" (e.g., 1 Chr 23:5; 2 Chr 29:25-30), which may have included membranophones, idiophones, and other instruments of which we are unaware at this point. 5). There are specific names of musical personnel mentioned in Style B, which is a sharp contrast to the few names of participants found in Style A. For instance, the Chronicler names and discusses individuals who serve in designated musical capacities, and their names appear throughout Style B performances.

e. Psalms. A discussion of music in the OT is not complete without some mention of the book of Psalms (*see* PSALMS, BOOK OF). While a simple definition of the term *psalm* is a song, the psalter does not contain as much information regarding music as one may think. Typically, the headings or superscriptions (which were later additions) explain or give some musical direction, indicate specific choir guilds, or tell the type of instruments for which the psalm was supposedly composed. For instance, headings provide messages such as "for the flutes" (Ps 5) or "to the leader: with the stringed instruments" (Ps 76). Nevertheless, the psalmists provide perspectives on how they viewed and interpreted the world around them. Communal and individual laments, songs of thanksgiving, songs of ascent, royal psalms, and hymns express reflections and interpretations of situations encountered. Although it is clear that musicians employed instruments to perform the psalms, particularly in praise, the writers also use them as literary devices, e.g., symbolically and metaphorically (Pss 49; 108).

The psalms display various theological themes and emotions expressed through music. At times psalmists lament and demand the presence of God (Ps 4); in others they praise the deity for all that has and will be done (Ps 100). Although some of the superscriptions give enigmatic information, the Psalter demonstrates the importance of musical expression to Israelite culture.

B. Music in the Greco-Roman World and New Testament

The Greco-Roman world (332 BCE–6th cent. CE) from which the NT comes consists of a plethora of cultures, enigmatic rituals, theological ideas, secret societies, and unique musical instruments and practices. Chordophones, aerophones, membranophones, and idiophones continue from the OT period, and instrument types in these families are presented throughout NT writings. The number of instruments that appears in the NT is smaller than in the OT, but it nevertheless give a snapshot of the kinds used. Changes in politics, religious practices, environment, and cultural characteristics affected musical performance. The destruction of the Temple in Jerusalem in 70 CE, e.g., brought about the demise of the Levitical guilds described by the Chronicler and others. Furthermore, Greek and Roman laws, as well as rabbinic religious restrictions such as the limitation of the performance of music on the Sabbath, brought about changes during this time (Sendrey). Instrumental music was no longer a part of synagogue activities, but interestingly, singing appears to have developed further. Singing in synagogues would have taken on a new theological understanding within the emerging Christian sect. Over time, international as well as local influences and larger sociopolitical or sociocultural movements such as Hellenism would have contributed to the continued development and use of instruments.

1. Chordophones

Chordophones continue their presence. The **kithara** (κιθάρα), one of the more popular chordophones during this period, is a lyre-type instrument. The term appears in a number of instances in the NT (1 Cor 14:7; Rev 5:8; 14:2; 15:2; 18:22). Some versions such as the NRSV mistakenly translate **kithara** with the word *harp*, but iconographic depictions reveal that it is a lyre (*see* MUSICAL INSTRUMENTS §D6). While the NT writers describe the instrument in performance contexts, quite often they employ the chordophone as a symbolic instrument. For example, in one instance, the writer of Revelation describes a vision in which he hears a voice that sounds like "the sound of harpists playing on their harps (**kithara**)" (Rev 14:2). Earlier in the vision, the writer saw "twenty-four elders worshiping before the Lamb, each holding (or playing) a harp (**kithara**)" (Rev 5:8). Also, the writer observes a number of chordophones in performance: "And I saw what appeared to be a sea of glass mixed with fire, and those who had conquered the beast and its image and the number of its name, standing beside the sea of glass with harps (**kithara**) of God in their hands" (Rev 15:2). The image presented by the writer is a familiar one from the OT, as the lyrists sing and perform with their instruments. The song they sing connects the testaments through one of their most prominent figures, Moses: "And they sing the song of Moses, the servant of God, and the song of the Lamb" (Rev 15:3). The term *lyre* (NRSV, *harp*) might serve a dual role, as it may possibly refer to a single instrument or a class of instruments.

Performers on lyres and harps played with a plectrum (a small piece of material used for plucking the strings) and fingers. Like their predecessors, the material of construction for these types of instruments is wood for the body, with some type of animal gut used for the strings. Ivory, metal, or precious jewels may have been used for decoration. The precise sound of the instrument is uncertain. Performers played the instrument while standing or sitting. Some players used a shoulder strap or strap around the wrist to secure the instrument; most leaned it against the shoulder while playing. Players, both male and female, performed instrumental solos, sometimes singing while playing, or accompanied others. Musicians used the instrument in secular and sacred contexts.

2. Aerophones

The **aulos** (αὐλός; Lat. *tibia*) is one of the best-known aerophones of the NT period. It is a single or double pipe/reed instrument. The **aulos** is very similar to the **khalil** (חָלִיל) described in the OT and is sometimes compared to the recorder. In the case of the double pipe, one pipe typically serves as a drone. Bone, wood, reed, and ivory were often the materials used in construction of the **aulos**. Musicians performed on the instruments at a number of activities, including weddings, sporting events, dramas, laments for the dead, and sacrifices. It appears that both men and women played the **aulos**. Women who played the instrument were often connected with prostitution. Male performers often wore a **phorbeia** (φορβεία), which is a leather strap or cloth tied around the player's head, neck, and cheeks. An opening was left in the **phorbeia** for the mouthpiece. The purpose of the **phorbeia** was to keep the lips shut tight and the mouthpiece in place. It may have been an aid in producing a strong tone or circular breathing. Like the **kithara**, it should be noted that the term might serve a dual role, possibly referring to a single instrument or a class of instruments.

The **salpinx** (σάλπιγξ; Lat. *tuba*) is another popular instrument of the NT period. This aerophone is very similar to the **khatsotsrah** (חֲצֹצְרָה) or trumpet described in the OT, and it functioned in a similar manner. The instrument bears the title "God's trumpet" (1 Thess 4:16). In this instance, the writer describes the archangel of the Lord blowing a **salpinx** to call "the dead in Christ." There appear to be connections with the **shofar** (שֹׁפָר) from the OT (e.g., Josh 6:4), which was used to organize, move, and warn the Israelite camps. The instrument also demonstrates an affinity with the **khatsotsrah** that Yahweh commissioned Moses to build (Num 10:1-10).

The **salpinx** served a symbolic role as well. In the book of Revelation, John describes part of a vision in which he states, "I heard behind me a loud voice like a trumpet (**salpinx**)" (Rev 1:10). Later in the same text, the writer presents a climactic scene involving trumpets. Following the opening of the seventh seal, seven angels with seven trumpets are set to play. Following the blowing of the instruments by each angel, specific actions are set in motion (Rev 8:7–10:7). For example, the writer states that following the blowing of the first trumpet, "there came hail and fire, mixed with blood, and they were hurled to the earth" (Rev 8:7).

This instrument is often associated with the voice of God. While this is certainly debatable, the interpretation may not be out of the question. From the commissioning of the **khatsotsrah** (Num 10:1-10), the uses of the **shofar** (Josh 6:5) and **salpinx** (Rev 8–11), and their association with instructions, directions, and actions/judgments from God, there appears to be a connection with the **salpinx** and the others with the deity.

3. Membranophones

Drums (**symphōnia**; Lat. *tympana*) were played by men and women. Although the NT does not give specific examples of the use of drums, their presence is seen in iconographic depictions during this period and other textual descriptions. For example, during the Roman period, the cult of Cybele was active. This bloody cult involved priests and priestesses, people cutting themselves, male castration, and wild chanting and dancing to the music of drums and cymbals.

4. Idiophones

Kymbalon (κύμβαλον) is synonymous with the cymbals of the OT period. In the NT, the term appears once (1 Cor 13:1). Here, Paul speaks about love and mentions the **kymbalon** along with **chalkos ēchōn** (χαλκὸς ἠχῶν), which translates as "sounding or booming brass" (author's trans.; NRSV "noisy gong") to establish a metaphor. In addition to **kymbalon**, performers also incorporated forked cymbals (Lat. *crotala*; sing. *crotalum*). *Crotala* may demonstrate a development of cymbals from the unattached types of the Late Bronze and Iron ages. It appears that *crotala* were in use as early as the 5th cent. BCE as Herodotus mentions them in the description of a boat pilgrimage to Bubastis (*Hist.* 2.60). He explains that some of the female passengers play *crotala* and *auloi* as they make their journey. Archaeological excavations have produced examples of these idiophones. Bells also continue into the Hellenistic–Roman period, but in addition to being a part of robes they are now used more as instruments, much like rattles. They appear in a number of shapes and sizes, with three basic forms: 1) semi-spherical; 2) conical; and 3) church bell (Braun). Idiophones were also worn as jewelry and even used as forms of communication.

C. Written Music in Antiquity

To date, there are no depictions of persons in the OT period in the act of reading or writing music, but the biblical writers mention people who are knowledgeable about music and performance (e.g., Miriam, David, Heman, Jepthah, and Chenenaiah). This musical hierarchy indicates that there was a musical system in Israelite culture, whether written or oral. As discussed, iconographic depictions show that the Egyptians employed chironomy, which appears to have been a way of directing performers through a system of hand gestures and/or oral commands. It was part of Egyptian culture as early as the 4th cent. BCE (Haik-Vantoura). Also, as mentioned previously, Anne Draffkom Kilmer has revealed the presence of a written musical system in Mesopotamia. There are ongoing debates regarding her interpretations, but the work is phenomenal and does shed light on how some ANE cultures may have understood and conveyed musical ideas. In Israel in particular, there has been some work done in researching possible notation systems in the Masoretic text (*see* MASORETIC ACCENTS). Suzanne Haik-Vantoura has proposed a complex method for performing music that incorporates scales and modes with deciphering signs in the biblical text.

It is likely that many cultures in the ANE eventually developed written musical notation systems, but in the beginning, musical information was conveyed orally and through participation. Like many Middle Eastern and Western traditions, there was room for improvisation. In other words, there would have been a standard form or song, a known melody, and specific words, but parts of the performance would have been open for improvisation.

Bibliography: Susan Ackerman. "Digging Up Deborah: Recent Hebrew Bible Scholarship on Gender and the Contribution of Archaeology." *NEA* 66 (2003) 172–84; Joachim Braun. *Music in Ancient Israel/ Palestine* (2002); Theodore W. Burgh. *Listening to the Artifacts: Music Culture in Ancient Palestine* (2006); Suzanne Haik-Vantoura. *Music of the Bible Revealed* (1991); H. Hickmann. *Agypten* (1961); Anne Draffkom Kilmer. *Sounds from Silence: Recent Discoveries in Ancient Near Eastern Music.* Recording. CBS 10996 (1979); Anne Draffkom Kilmer. "World's Oldest Musical Notation Deciphered on Cuneiform Tablet." *BA* 5 (1980) 14–25; G. Loud. *The Megiddo Ivories* (1969); Lise Manniche. *Music and Musicians in Ancient Egypt* (1991); Carol Meyers. "The Drum-Dance Song Ensemble: Women's Performance in Biblical Israel." *Rediscovering the Muses: Women's Musical Traditions.* Kimberly Marshall, ed. (1993) 49–67; Eunice B. Poethig. *The Victory Song Tradition of the Women of Israel.* PhD diss. (1985); Alfred Sendrey. *Music in Ancient Israel* (1969).

THEODORE W. BURGH

MUSICAL INSTRUMENTS. Sound tools (not always "instruments" in the modern sense) accompanied everyday life from the beginnings of humanity and are part of the biblical narrative from its first books (Gen 4:21) to the last lines of the NT (Rev 18:22). Music is a pattern of human behavior defined by modern musicologists as the sound produced by tools in reflection of cultural contexts. Musical instruments are among the most perplexing phenomena of the past because of the ephemeral nature of both music itself and the indirect sources of study—written, archaeological, iconographical, and comparative—and because only a few of the instruments discovered in excavations (cymbals, rattles, conch horns) are still able to produce sound.

A. Introduction and History of the Topic
B. Sources
C. Classification of Musical Instruments
D. Musical Instruments in the Old Testament and Apocryphal/Deuteroncanonical Books
  1. Bell
  2. Castanets
  3. Cymbals
  4. Drum
  5. Flute
  6. Harp
  7. Horn
  8. Lute
  9. Lyre
  10. Pipe

A. Introduction and History of the Topic

The interpretation and understanding of musical instruments mentioned in the OT and NT reaches back to the first readings of the Scripture and first translations, the LXX, Peshitta, and Vulgate. From an early stage, the names of the instruments seem to have partly lost their correct meaning, as may be concluded from the inconsistent translations in the LXX. For example, the ʿughav (עוּגָב) is translated with three different Greek terms: **kithara** (κιθάρα; Gen 4:21), **psalmos** (ψαλμός; Job 21:12; 30:31), and **organon** (ὄργανον; Ps 150:4). **Organon** was unspecific and referred to any instrument. Just as confusing is the LXX translation of the two string instruments **nevel** (נֵבֶל) and **kinnor** (כִּנּוֹר) with a variety of Greek words (e.g., **nabla** [νάβλα], **psaltērion** [ψαλτήριον], **organon**, **kinyra** [κινύρα], **kithara**; see §D6, §D8, and §D9); the rendering of both string instruments as *psalterion* ("harp") in some verses of the Vulgate as well as the adoption of the term *psalter* for the designation of the book of Psalms led to additional misunderstandings, such as the misinterpretation of **kinnor** as a harp and the iconographic tradition of depicting King David playing the harp (an early example is the 8th-cent. CE carved book cover of a psalter at the Musée du Louvre).

The confusion increased in the next centuries when both Christian and Jewish exegetes, hardly informed on musical matters, introduced fantastic theories regarding music in biblical times. For example, in a manuscript by the prominent Jewish scholar Joshua ibn Ga'on (*Second Kennicot Bible*, Soria, 1306), the author presents a fantasy drawing of an instrument, supposedly used in the Second Temple that had ten holes that produced ten different melodies (see *b. Arak.* 11a). These bizarre ideas penetrated into secondary literature and were verbalized in modern translations. The KJV translated **nevel** with the term *viol*, an instrument that appeared in the late Middle Ages. In the 16th–17th cent. CE, the first commentaries on biblical musical instruments simultaneously appeared in Jewish and Christian circles. Rabbi Abraham ben David Portaleone's *Shiltei ha-giborim* ("Shields of the Heroes," published in Mantua, 1612) came first, followed several years later by Michael Praetorius' *Syntagma musicum* (published in Wittenberg, 1614–19). Without archaeological research available, Praetorius concluded that there were no vestiges of ancient instruments left in Palestine. This misleading judgment appears unfortunately in some scholarly publications even today.

B. Sources

The biblical text offers little information on the building material and structure of musical instruments. Materials are mentioned only three times: two silver trumpets made of "hammered work" (Num 10:2), almug wood for lyres and harps (1 Kgs 10:12), and bronze cymbals (1 Chr 15:19). Only once is the method of performance indicated: "David took the lyre and played it with his hand" (1 Sam 16:23). The sound of the instruments is described in a very general way, mostly in terms of dynamics: sounding an alarm or blowing the trumpet without alarm (Num 10:6-7); "a blast of a trumpet so loud that all the people who were in the camp trembled" (Exod 19:16); or allegorically, as in "I am a noisy gong" (1 Cor 13:1) and "a voice from heaven ... like the sound of harpists playing on their harps" (Rev 14:2).

Much richer is the biblical information on the social function of musical instruments; nearly every instrument is placed into a certain social context. The text of the Scripture is sometimes contradictory, however. The orgiastic band that accompanied David with the ark ascending to Jerusalem (2 Sam 6:5) is replaced in 1 Chr 13:1-5 by an orderly liturgical vocal-instrumental ensemble (see §D2 and §D3). Important details and new nuances of instrumental performance, especially concerning the art of trumpeting, have been discovered from the Qumran scrolls (e.g., 1QM).

Information on instruments can be derived from later Roman authors, although even such sources as Athenaeus (*Deipnosophistae*), Flavius Josephus (*Jewish Antiquities*), Philo (*On the Contemplative Life*), Strabo (*Geography*), or Plutarch (*Quaestiones Conviviales libre IX*) should be considered with caution. Post-biblical literature, in particular the Talmud treatises, often draw idealized pictures of musical instruments and musical events, particularly when describing the musical liturgy of the Second Temple.

Helpful for the recreation of the musical world of the Bible is the evidence of all kinds of comparative sources (Egyptian, Mesopotamian, Greek, and Roman) and contemporary traditional musical instruments that may have preserved characteristics of earlier centuries. But here also unjustified and misleading comparisons are frequent, as, e.g., the popular depictions of Egyptian Eighteenth Dynasty harps or even lyres from Mesopotamian Ur First Dynasty Kings that are sometimes used to illustrate musical life in ancient Israel.

In the past, musical historiography of ancient Israel/Palestine and especially organology (the study of musical instruments) was based on written sources only, mainly biblical texts. The development of archaeology in the last decades, especially the archaeology and iconography of music, presents new research possibilities and new judgments. Studies in this field show that the use of archaeological-iconographical data with a broad interdisciplinary approach involving written sources, etymology, ethnology, and other comparative material is the preferred method for the study of biblical musical instruments.

C. Classification of Musical Instruments

We can no longer determine whether any internal, cultural division of musical instruments ever existed in biblical times, though the oral tradition fixed in the written text of the OT suggests as much. Closer examination does in any case reveal a specific symbolism of musical instruments or socio-musical semantics that may or may not reflect a fixed system. Chronicles seems to group the musical instruments of the priests and of the Levite clan and musical guilds in a way that might reflect such a system (1 Chr 15–16; 2 Chr 5; 7). This manner of classifying instruments according to a socio-musical principle has been incorporated into the work of various scholars. The "observer-imposed/artificial" schema represented in Erich M. Hornbostel and Curt Sachs' classification system reflects the thinking of their time rather than an understanding intrinsic to the Bible. Accepted since the beginning of the 20th cent. by modern scholarship, their schema is used by most scholars and most reference sources. This system divides instruments according to the source of sound or the nature of the vibrating body: idiophones (self-sounders, sound produced by the vibrations of the substance of the instrument's body, e.g., cymbals, rattles); membranophones (sound produced by the vibration from a tight starched membrane, e.g., drums); aerophones (the air column within a tube is set in vibrations by breath entering the instrument in different ways: without additional mouthpiece across the edge of the tube [flutes], via a single reed [clarinets], a double reed [oboes], or the performer's lips [trumpets]); and chordophones (sound produced by the vibrations of stretched strings roused by plucking, rubbing, or bowing). The chordophones that appear in the Bible are plucked instruments, classified according to the way strings are placed on the body of the instrument (usually a resonator): 1) the strings are attached to a crossbar on the same plane as the resonator (lyre); 2) the strings are stretched between the resonator and the vertical extension of the resonance body (harp); 3) the strings are stretched along the body and the neck of the instrument, which serves as a handle as well (lute); 4) zither instruments, where the instrument consists of a string-bearer only, probably did not appear in a biblical context. For convenience, the present entry accepts the alphabetical order of English names of musical instruments.

D. Musical Instruments in the Old Testament and Apocryphal/Deuterocanonical Books

1. Bell

Bells (paʿamon פַּעֲמֹן; kōdōn κώδων), mentioned in Exod 28:33-34; 39:25-26; Sir 45:9, consisted of a hollow open-ended body, usually of metal with a clapper inside. Bells made of gold and fastened to the lower hem of Aaron's robe: "a golden bell and a pomegranate alternating all around the lower hem of the robe" (Exod 28:34). According to Josephus the sound of the golden bells symbolizes thunder, while the pomegranates symbolize lightning (*Ant.* 3.184). For Philo they symbolize the cosmic harmony (*Moses* 2.24). Sirach 45:9 recounts that the ringing of the golden bells was heard in the Temple, and Josephus describes the golden bells appended to the high priest's garment (*Ant.* 3.159–60). Archaeological finds confirm that bells were attached to cloth, and recently a depiction of bells on the robe of Aaron was discovered on a 5th-cent. mosaic from the SEPPHORIS synagogue. The bell is known in the ANE at least from the 15th cent. BCE, primarily as an apotropaic and prophylactic amulet in connection with exorcism. The oldest items (height 2–6 cm) unearthed in ancient Israel (Megiddo, Achziv, Gezer, Tel Batash) date to the 9th–8th cent. BCE. From that time on they were an integral part of the sound-world. Nearly 100 examples, mainly from the Hellenistic to Byzantine periods, have been discovered.

2. Castanets

In the context of 2 Sam 6:5, the English term *castanets* and Greek kymbalon (κύμβαλον) are hardly a correct translation for menaʿanʿim (מְנַעַנְעִים). Castanets—a popular instrument in Spain—were not part of the local ancient Israelite music culture and certainly do not fit into the chronology of the books of Samuel. The identification for menaʿanʿim preferred by modern musicology is "clay rattle."

Courtesy of the Israel Antiquities Authority

Figure 1: Clay rattle from Hazor

The archaeological clay rattle is the most verified sound tool in this region and at least 100 items are dated to the period from the Late Chalcolithic to the late Iron Age. They usually are closed clay containers of some 10–15 cm filled with small clay balls, made by hand or, later, wheel-made by local artisans. The sound was produced by rattling, which corresponds to the linguistic root **nua**ʿ (נוּעַ, "to shake, tremble"). The rattle is mainly discovered at burial sites and may be defined as a cult instrument, broadly used by the masses. It was at some point eliminated from the OT texts, perhaps to destroy the image of this pagan sound tool and erase it from folk memory.

3. Cymbals

Cymbals (**metsiltayim** מְצִלְתַּיִם, **tseltselim** צֶלְצְלִים; **kymbalon**), a form of clapper generally made of copper or brass, consist of two plates with concave centers (2 Sam 6:5; 1 Chr 13:8; 15:16, 19; 2 Chr 5:12-13; Ezra 3:10; Neh 12:27; Ps 150:5). One of a pair is held in each hand and by clashing them together a sound of indefinite pitch is produced. The term **metsiltayim**, existing in its dual form only, derives from the onomatopoeic root **tsltsl** (צלצל; "to ring, tremble"). Known from the late Sumerian (Ur III) culture (ca. 2000 BCE) and mentioned as early as the 14th cent. BCE in Ugaritic sources, they clearly were ceremonial cultic instruments in the ANE and in this capacity considered in the Bible as instruments of the Levites (*see* WORSHIP, OT). The books of Ezra and Chronicles identify the cymbal players as sons of Asaph, Heman, and Etan. Only two written sources describe the biblical cymbals: 1 Chr 15:19 speaks of "bronze cymbals," while Josephus reports that the cymbals were "broad and large instruments ... made of brass" (*Ant.* 7.306). The Hebrew biblical term **tseltselim** in 2 Sam 6:5, considered to designate a more primitive metal rattle-type idiophone, is translated in the NRSV as "cymbals" as well (see §D2). Archaeological evidence on cymbals is rich. Some thirty cymbals of two different sizes (7–12 and 3–6 cm) have been unearthed, and they belong to two distant chronological periods (14th–12th cent. BCE and the Hellenistic–Roman period). This archaeological gap of nearly 1,000 years is difficult to explain at the present. Although the two types of archaeological cymbals may correspond to the two groups mentioned in Ps 150 ("clanging cymbals" and "loud clashing cymbals"), we have to consider the fact that **metsiltayim** are mentioned exclusively in postexilic writings and that the earlier references relate only to **tseltselim**.

4. Drum

Daniel 3:5-15 is the only place where the NRSV uses the term *drum*—the name for most membranophones (see §D11)—to translate the very dubious Aramaic (**sumponeyah** סוּמְפֹּנְיָה) name of a musical instrument in the description of Nebuchadnezzar's music ensemble. A matter of intense dispute, the interpretations of the meaning of the Greek **symphōnia** (συμφωνία) range from "pipe" and "double-flute" to "hydraulis," "bagpipe," "dulcimer," and "drum." The lack of another recognizable name of a membranophone in Nebuchadnezzar's orchestra may have suggested the last interpretation. However, in antiquity the word **symphōnia** meant "consonant harmony" and referred to "making music in consort," as can be deduced from Luke 15:25. Modern musicology also prefers this interpretation (see §D14).

5. Flute

Terms for flute are found in 1 Sam 10:5; Isa 5:12; 30:29; Jer 48:36; 1 Esd 5:2; Sir 40:21; and 1 Macc 3:45. The Hebrew **khalil** (חָלִיל; from the root **khll** חלל, "to hollow out, pierce"; Akk. *khalilu*), as well as the Greek **aulos** (αὐλός), is considered to belong to the reed-instrument group (see §C) and should not be translated "flute" as in some modern translations. In the OT, it appears in connection with the joyous anointing of the king (1 Kgs 1:40; NRSV, pipes), victorious celebration (Isa 30:29), and prophetic ecstasy (1 Sam 10:5), but also symbolizes lament (Jer 48:36) and is associated with the excessive revelry of sinners (Isa 5:12). While the OT does not mention the **khalil** in the temple service, Talmudic sources refer to the **khalil** as a temple instrument made of a reed cane, point out the sweet sound of the instrument, and decry the later Hellenistic practice of covering the **khalil** with metal because it damaged the sound (*b. Arak.* 10a).

6. Harp

A variety of references to the harp (**kinnor**, **nevel**; **kithara**, **kinyra**, **nabla**, **organon**, **psaltērion**) are found in the Bible (1 Kgs 10:12; 1 Chr 13:8; 2 Chr 5:12; Neh 12:27; Pss 49:4 [Heb. 49:5]; 71:22; 92:3 [Heb. 92:4]; 108:2 [Heb. 108:3]; 137:2; 150:3; Isa 5:12; 14:11; 16:11; 23:16; Dan 3:5, 7, 10, 15; Sir 39:15; 1 Macc 3:45). The term *harp* is used in the NRSV to translate two Hebrew names of musical instruments, the **nevel** and **kinnor** ("ten-stringed harp" relates to **nevel** ʿ**asor** [נֶבֶל עָשׂוֹר]; e.g., Pss 33:2; 144:9). The etymology of **nevel** is ambiguous. The word **kinnor**, a central cultural term attested throughout the ANE that transcends geographic and linguistic boundaries, is of unknown etymology. The term **kinnaratim** ("lyre player") is first attested in 18th-cent. BCE documents of the Mari archives, and the root is also incorporated into many ANE names of deities, plants, or toponymy. The biblical **kinnor** and **nevel** usually appear together; when mentioned separately, their translation is inconsistent, the term *harp* being used alternately for both. Modern research, however, does not accept the identification of **kinnor**/**nevel** as a harp, but considers both instruments to be lyres (see §C), the **kinnor** being a solo melody lyre and the **nevel** an accompaniment tenor-bass instrument. This conclusion is based primarily on archaeological evidence: more then thirty depictions of the lyre have been discovered, but no archaeological artifact depicting the harp can be dated between the 3rd millennium BCE and the Hellenistic–Roman period (see also §D9). The **kinnor** and **nevel** were usually played together in larger groups of musical instruments (1 Sam 10:5), and both were quite versatile. They accompanied the transport of the ark (2 Sam 6:5), and prophetic ecstasy (1 Sam 10:5). The **kinnor** appears in the first mention of music (Gen 4:21), in connection with therapeutic healing (1 Sam 16:16), related to prostitution (Isa 23:16), and connected to God's anger (Isa 24:8). The **nevel**, independent of the **kinnor**, is associated with happiness (Isa 24:8, 32; Amos 5:23; 6:5).

7. Horn

The horn (**qeren** קֶרֶן, **qeren hayyovel** קֶרֶן הַיּוֹבֵל, **shofar** שֹׁפָר, **shofar hayyovel** שֹׁפַר הַיּוֹבֵל; **keratinēs** κέρατινης, **salpinx** σάλπιγξ) is found in Josh 6:4-6, 8; 1 Chr 15:28; 2 Chr 15:14; Ps 98:6; Dan 3:5, 7, 10, 15; and Hos 5:8. Standing generally for the Hebrew **qeren** ("animal's horn") or **qeren hayovel** ("ram's horn"), *horn* is used several times as a translation of **shofar** (which in most OT verses is translated by the term *trumpet*; see §D13). The word **qeren** derives from an ancient Semitic root and dates to the earliest stages of culture. It refers to an animal horn and as such is mentioned over seventy times. In the sense of a musical instrument, it is mentioned only once as **qeren hayovel** (ram's horn), at the destruction of the walls of Jericho.

8. Lute

The term *lute* (**nevel**, **ʿasor** עָשׂוֹר; **kinyra**) occurs in Pss 92:3; 150:3; and 1 Macc 4:54, although it seems to be an unsuitable translation for the underlying Hebrew words. The archaeological record definitively does not show any lute instruments present in Israel between the 11th cent. BCE and the late Hellenistic time. Moreover, when the lute appears in the 2nd cent. BCE, it is seen only in the hands of Bacchus or a naked female figure. Suggestively, a painting from the famous DURA EUROPOS synagogue (2nd–3rd cent. CE) shows the Dagon temple in Ashdod (1 Sam 5:1-5) with the Philistine god mutilated and his temple implements—including two lutes—scattered over the entire hall. Not until the 13th cent. CE did Jewish negativity toward this instrument disappear. In the mentioned verses the stringed instruments should be identified as lyres or—in the case of **ʿasor**—as "ten-stringed lyres" (see §§D6 and D9).

9. Lyre

The lyre (**kinnor**, **nevel**, **nevel ʿasor**; **kithara**, **psaltērion**) can be found in Gen 4:21; 1 Sam 10:5; 18:10; 2 Sam 6:5; 1 Chr 13:8; 2 Chr 5:12, 25; 9:11; 20:28; 29:25; Neh 12:27; Job 21:12; 30:31; Pss 33:2; 57:8; 81:2; 150:3; 151:2; Isa 5:12; Ezek 26:13; and Dan 3:5-15. The term *lyre* is used alternately to indicate the two biblical chordophones—**kinnor** and **nevel**—and, according to modern scholarship, is the most satisfactory translation (see §D6). This conclusion is based mainly on archaeological evidence, the most convincing of which is the recent discovery in Dion (Greece) of a funerary stele from Roman times with an engraved encomium to the **nabla** and a depiction of a lyre in relief. Acco and Bar Kochba coins from Hellenistic–Roman times show two types of lyres: a larger type, with a sack-like resonator-body and five to eight strings (**nevel**), and a smaller, more refined and elegant instrument with only three to five strings (**kinnor**). According to the biblical text both instruments were said to be made of "almug wood" (1 Kgs 10:11-12). The **nevel** depicted on coins had a bag-shaped resonator probably made of leather ("water-skin"; see §D6). According to the Mishnah, there should never be more than six **nevel**-instruments in worship and no fewer than nine more **kinnor** instruments should be added (*m. Arak.* 2:5). This ratio actually provides a balanced proportion of melody and bass instruments in an ensemble (*see* WORSHIP, EARLY JEWISH).

10. Pipe

The pipe (**khalil**, **mashroqi** מַשְׁרוֹקִי, **ʿughav** עוּגָב; **aulos**, **kithara**, **syrinx** σῦριγξ) occurs in Gen 4:21; 1 Kgs 1:40; Job 21:12; 30:31; Pss 150:4; 151:2; Dan 3:5, 7, 10, 15. The generic term *pipe* is used mainly for the biblical **ʿughav**, an instrument whose identification is still uncertain. Its unique status in the OT is manifested in Gen 4:21, where we read that Jubal "was the ancestor of all those who play the lyre (**kinnor**)

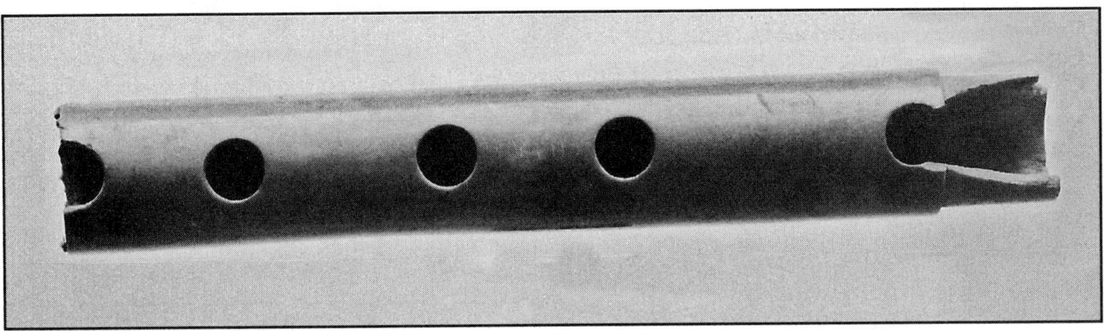

Courtesy of the Israel Antiquities Authority

Figure 2: Aulos, Samaria

and pipe (ʿughav)." Already in the LXX the meaning of this term has been lost and the various translations are confusing (see §A). The Talmud identifies the ʿughav as the temple instrument **hydraulis** (ὕδραυλις; in rabbinic sources also **maghrefah** מַגְרֵפָה; *y. Sukkah* 55c). This lack of clarity on the ʿughav resulted in a variety of interpretations. In the following centuries of the postexilic period the term ʿughav changed its meaning to an **aulos**-type reed instrument.

11. Tambourine/timbrel

The tambourine or timbrel (**tof** תֹּף; **tympanon** τύμπανον) is mentioned in Gen 31:27; 2 Sam 6:5; 1 Chr 13:8; Job 21:12; Pss 81:2 [Heb. 81:3]; 149:3; 150:4; Isa 5:12; 24:8; 30:32; Jdt 3:7; 16:1; and 1 Macc 9:39. Both terms are later 12th–14th-cent. designations for the ancient frame drum (biblical **tof**), which in different sizes (from 40–50 cm to 1–2 m) first appeared in ancient Mesopotamia (3rd millennium BCE), and via Asia and Egypt, came to Israel. It became one of the most popular musical instruments, accompanying singing and beating the rhythm for dance (*see* DANCING). The same root in Ugaritic is attested from the 14th cent. BCE and is widespread in the Middle East as extending from Sumerian to Akkadian, Arabic, Phoenician, and Egyptian. It is primarily women whom we encounter playing the **tof** (e.g., Exod 15:20: Judg 11:34; 1 Sam 10:5). Even today, Yemenite women of Jewish heritage continue this tradition. However, the **tof** was not exclusively a women's instrument, since it was played by both males and females as part of an orchestra.

The **tof** is never mentioned in connection with temple music proper, but always accompanies cultic dances and hymns, as well as religious celebrations and processions, where the female drummers are placed second after the singers, but before all other instrumentalists (Ps 68:25 [Heb. 68:26]). As in other musical cultures this type of hand drum in the OT is a sexual symbol (compare Jephthah's daughter in Judg 11:34 or the "virgin Israel" in Jer 31:4). Modern interpretations, primarily on the basis of archaeological evidence, agree that the drum was a circular frame drum, though unlike the modern tambourine, without metal jingles attached to its sides. Archaeological finds of two types of terra-cotta figures attest the female drummer as an explicit local Iron Age iconographic topos.

Bell-shaped figurines with long garments discovered in burial sites suggest a cultic function and are considered to be of multiethnic Moabite-Judean-Israelite-Phoenician origin. Terra-cotta plaque female figures are naked or half-naked with rich adornments. This last group seems to represent a belief system not represented in the biblical text because it stood in conflict with the official cult of Judah.

12. Trigon

The term *trigon* (**sabbekha**ʾ שַׂבְּכָא; **sambykē** σαμβύκη) appears only in Dan 3:5-15. It has often been identified as a lyre, though modern research suggests that it was a small vertical angular harp. This instrument fit well into the Babylonian orchestra and might have sounded strange to the Israelites, who were not familiar with it.

13. Trumpet

Hebrew and Greek words for trumpet include **khatsotsrah** חֲצֹצְרָה, **shofar**, and **salpinx**. The trumpet is featured in numerous OT passages, including Exod 19:16, 19; 20:18; Lev 25:9; Num 10:2-10; Josh 6:16, 20; Judg 3:27; 6:34; 7:8-22; 1 Sam 13:3; 2 Sam 2:28; 15:10; 1 Kgs 1:34-41; 2 Kgs 11:14; 12:14; 1 Chr 13:8; 2 Chr 5:12-13; Neh 12:35, 41; Job 39:24, 25; Pss 47:5 [Heb. 47:6]; 98:6; 150:3; Isa 18:3; Jer 4:5; 6:1; 51:27; Ezek 33:3-6; Hos 5:8; 8:1; Joel 2:1, 15; Amos 2:2; 3:6; Zeph 1:16; Zech 9:14; and 1 Esd 5:59-66. *Trumpet* is used for both the **shofar** ("ram's horn," see §D7) and **khatsotsrah**, thus carrying on the tradition of the LXX translation where both instruments are named **salpinx**—a misleading translation from a historical, theological, and acoustical point of view.

The **shofar** (etymologically uncertain, possibly from Akkadian/Sumerian **shapparu/shegbar**, "ibex, wild goat") is the most frequently mentioned instrument in the OT, and the only instrument to have survived

Courtesy of the Israel Antiquities Authority

Figure 3: Female terra-cotta bell-shaped figurine with drum from Shiqmona

Ecole Biblique

Figure 4: Female terra-cotta plaque figurine with drum

unchanged within liturgical service from biblical times to our days. Information on its structure and shape does not appeared prior to the Talmudic writings and Qumran scrolls, which tells us that two kinds of horns were to be used: the straight horn with a mouthpiece covered with gold, and a curved horn covered with silver for the day of fasting. Only the horn of a ram—a sacrificial animal—should be used (*m. Rosh. Hash.* 3:2-4). The earliest iconographical evidence for the **shofar** is from the Roman period, when it appears as part of a symbolic group: the menorah, mahta (incense pan), lulav (palm branch), and etrog (citrus fruit). At this point the **shofar** was already viewed as a symbol of national and ethnic identity, functioning as such in both sacral and secular contexts.

In nearly all OT occurrences the **shofar** appears as a solo instrument, reflecting its unique position in the biblical world of sound. The **shofar's** tonal capacity was limited to two or three strong tones described in the Bible as a "voice" (**qol** קֹל), and the instrument functioned in a variety of situations: to raise an alarm, to scare the enemy, or to evoke a magical or eschatological atmosphere. It also announced the Sabbath and the new moon. The order of the **shofar** blast, however, was not clearly expressed until the 4th cent. CE, when R. Abiyehu of Caesarea determined three terms for **shofar** blowing—a blast or long tone, a shout or quavering tremolo, and breaks or broken tones was fixed in a graphical form for the first time in the 10th-cent. prayer book by Sa'adiah Gaon.

The **khatsotsrah** (probably from an Arabic root meaning "to shout") was mainly used in the postexilic time. It is mentioned in Num 10, where exact instructions are given concerning manufacture and use of the instrument, as well as the sound of the trumpet blast (*see* BLAST OF TRUMPET OR DIVINE BREATH). The **khatsotsrah** was clearly an instrument of the priests (1 Chr 15:24; 16:6) used at many occasions, including the temple liturgy, the laying of the temple foundation (Ezra 3:10), and the king's anointing (2 Kgs 11:14). The form of the biblical trumpet cannot be firmly established by archaeological-iconographical sources; the often-cited examples of archaeological-iconographical evidence—the Arch of Titus in Rome (depicting a Roman *tuba*) and the Bar Kochba silver denarii (probably depicting the two-reed *zumra*)—are not reliable evidence of the trumpet as a temple instrument. In addition to the OT itself and Talmudic literature (*m. Rosh. Hash.* 3:3; *m. Arak.* 2:5), information on the use of the trumpet is provided by the apocalyptic *War Scroll* from Qumran (1QM). Among several details contained in the scroll are mention of engraved inscriptions on trumpets, such as "Mustered by God" and "the Princes of God" (1QM III, 3). There are trumpets of summons or alarm, trumpets of ambush, and trumpets of pursuit (1QM III, 1–3). These, as well as those mentioned in postbiblical Talmudic writings, are probably the only sources of information about the use of the trumpet and its function as a symbol of the institutionalized sacral-secular and autocratic powers during the Second Temple period.

14. Collective terms

The NRSV also employs several terms that refer to instruments as a group or to particular types of instruments. The manifold and diverse collective terms for instrumental performance almost all appear in postexilic books, thus indicating a radical change in the cultural and musical life of postexilic Judaism, manifested among other ways in the versatile use of musical instruments and new intrinsic systematization principles. The term *instrument* (**keli** כְּלִי) is often used together with an indicative term, such as "instruments of David" (**kele dawidh** כְּלֵי דָוִיד; 2 Chr 29:26-27), "musical instruments" (**kele shir** כְּלֵי שִׁיר; 1 Chr 15:16; 16:42), and "stringed instruments" (**kele nevel** כְּלֵי נֶבֶל; NRSV, "harp"; Ps 71:22). Most of the collective terms relate to stringed instruments (**nevel**, **kinnor**); their frequent appearance in the biblical text underlines the unique place of stringed instruments—the musical instruments par excellence—in the musical culture of the Bible.

15. Terminology in Psalms

The 117 psalm superscriptions, many of which have musical implications, are among the most unexplained and obscure lines in the OT. Textual analysis confronted with linguistic and musicological problems has generated a long and complicated history of interpretation. The diversity of the early Greek and Latin translations proves that the meaning of these texts had already been lost in antiquity. Modern scholars now generally agree that these superscriptions primarily represent performance guidelines. Some of them provide the name of musical instruments. In Ps 5, ʾel-hannekhiloth (אֶל־הַנְּחִילוֹת) is translated "for the flutes" (see §D10). The NRSV translates ʿal-haggittith (עַל־הַגִּתִּית) in Ps 8 as "according to The Gittith," which some interpret as "the instrument of Gath." In Pss 4 and 54, bineghinoth (בִּנְגִינוֹת; from naghan [נָגַן], "to touch the strings, play stringed instruments") may be explained as instructions that the song is to be performed on stringed instruments. Of special interest is the expression bineghinoth ʿal-hasheminith (בִּנְגִינוֹת עַל־הַשְּׁמִינִית; Ps 6). The NRSV provides the translation "with stringed instruments; according to the Sheminith." It may be more accurate to translate the phrase as "on the sheminith" (שְׁמִינִית), which can be interpreted as "playing a stringed instrument with eight strings" or "with strings arranged in an octave." The expression ʿal-hasheminith also occurs in 1 Chr 15:21, where it may be understood as a stringed instrument used by the Levites. Since the heptatonic tonal system was known in ancient Ugarit, we could expect it also for the music of the Levites (*see* MUSIC).

E. Musical Instruments in the New Testament

The NT mentions musical instruments only twenty-nine times, and even that number is deceptive, since the twelve references in Revelation are almost verbatim repetitions. The NT does not offer any variety, since only four different instruments are mentioned (aulos, kithara, salpinx, kymbalon); the value of these verses is restricted largely to metaphorical meaning and is of minor importance from an organological perspective. But there are in the NT very significant new aspects in the usage of musical instrument terms. The most important are probably the verses in 1 Cor 14:7-8: "It is the same way with lifeless instruments that produce sound, such as the flute or the harp. If they do not give distinct notes, how will anyone know what is being played? And if the bugle gives an indistinct sound, who will get ready for battle?" This is a clear demand for the exactness of performance. Repeatedly emphasizing the importance of the clarity of sound and comparing it with the comprehensibility of the spoken word, this passage reflects a new articulation of what musical performance and music itself had come to mean. Not less meaningful is the comparison of "speech without love" with the sound of a "noisy gong or a clanging cymbal" (1 Cor 13:1)—two instruments with restricted musical expressiveness—and the passage in Rev 18:22 where the destruction of the Roman Empire is equated to the image of all music instruments falling silent.

1. Bugle

Bugle is an obsolete name for an animal horn, borrowed in the 13th cent. from Old French and stemming from Latin *buculus*. Mentioned only once in the NT (salpinx; 1 Cor 14:8), it indicates here a battle signal trumpet (see §D13). The significance of this NT passage may be seen in its strong accent on distinct notes to be played.

2. Cymbal

The Greco-Roman cymbals (kymbalon) popular in the Dionysian and Cybele cult are hardly held in esteem in the NT (see 1 Cor 13:1). Mentioned but once in a passage together with the gong (see §E4), they symbolize affected proclamations.

3. Flute

The mono- or double-aulos, a popular Greek-Roman reed instrument, wrongly translated as "flute" (see §D5), is played in the NT, as in the OT, at laments for the dead (Matt 9:23) and is associated with wedding activites (Matt 11:17); sometimes, as in Rev 18:22, the instrument is used metaphorically.

4. Gong

Gong is the term used in the translation of the phrase chalkos ēchōn (χαλκὸς ἠχῶν), literally "sounding or booming brass" (1 Cor 13:1). It was previously thought to be a musical instrument, but recent research understands this term as an unequivocal reference to a resonating vase made of brass that was placed at the rear of Greek amphitheaters to resonate sympathetically to the various pitches of the actors' or singers' voices, providing a kind of acoustic amplification. This also is in accord with Paul's metaphor, which compares the "noisy gong"—the artificial amplifier of the cymbals—with loveless speech (1 Cor 13:1).

5. Harp

The references to kithara in the NT are usually of symbolic nature (see §D6). The sound of the harps of God (Rev 15:2) is compared to a "voice from heaven" (Rev 14:2). The same passage compares the sound of the kithara to the rushing of "many waters" and the rolling of "loud thunder." The Roman stringed instruments and the performance virtuosity developed to such remarkable degree during this period that listeners may have perceived the sheer power of their sound to be overwhelming and symbolizing the spiritual power of the "new song" of Christianity (compare Rev 14:2-3).

6. Trumpet

The trumpet (see §D13), usually used for signaling and communication, is in the NT mostly an instrument of supernatural power, often of apocalyptic nature (Matt 6:2; 24:31; 1 Cor 15:52; 1 Thess 4:16; Heb 12:19; Rev 1:10; 4:1; 8:2-13; 9:1, 13-14; 11:15;

18:22). The OT already alluded to the eschatological significance of the **salpinx** (Exod 20:18-19), but the NT picks up on the theophanic feature of its sound and equates it with God's voice (*see* THEOPHANY IN THE NT). Carried to the extreme, these features elevate the trumpet to the supreme instrument of divine praise and veneration and transform it into the "last trumpet," which proclaims the resurrection of the dead (1 Cor 15:52; compare 1 Thess 4:16).

Bibliography: Bathyah Bayer. *The Material Relics of Music in Ancient Palestine and Its Environs: An Archaeological Inventory* (1963); Bathyah Bayer. *The Titles of the Psalms* (1982) 28–123; Joachim Braun. *Music in Ancient Israel/Palestine: Archaeological, Written, and Comparative Sources* (2002); Joachim Braun. *On Jewish Music: Past and Present* (2006); William Harris. "'Sounding Brass' and Hellenistic Technology." *BAR* 8 (1982) 38–41; Erich M. Hornbostel and Curt Sachs. "Systematik der Musikinstrumente: Ein Versuch." *Zeitschrift für Ethnologie* 46 (1914) 553–90; Margaret J. Kartomi. *On Concepts and Classifications of Musical Instruments* (1990); Sybil Marcuse. *A Survey of Musical Instruments* (1975); James McKinnon. *Music in Early Christian Literature* (1987); James McKinnon. *The Temple, the Church Fathers, and Early Western Chant* (1998); Carol Meyers. "The Drum-Dance Song Ensemble: Women's Performance in Biblical Israel." *Rediscovering the Muses: Women's Musical Traditions.* Kimberly Marshall, ed. (1993) 49–67; T. C. Mitchell and R. Joyce. "The Musical Instruments in Nebuchadnezzar's Orchestra." *Notes on Some Problems in the Book of Daniel.* Donald J. Wiseman et al., eds. (1965) 19–27; Joan Rimmer. *Ancient Musical Instruments of Western Asia in the British Museum* (1969); Curt Sachs. *The History of Musical Instruments* (1940); Alfred Sendrey. *Music in Ancient Israel* (1969); John A. Smith. "The Ancient Synagogue, the Early Church, and Singing." *Music and Letters* 65 (1984) 1–16; William S. Smith. *Musical Aspects of the New Testament* (1962); Eric Werner. *The Sacred Bridge: The Interdependence of Liturgy and Music in Synagogue and Church during the First Millennium.* Vols. 1–2 (1959, 1984).

JOACHIM BRAUN

MUSICAL MODES. *See* MUSIC.

MUSICIANS. *See* ASAPH; DAVID; ETHAN; HEMAN; JEDUTHUN; KORAH, KORAHITES; MIRIAM; MUSIC.

MUSRI my*oos'ri.* An ancient territory mentioned in cuneiform sources (e.g., the Black Obelisk of Shalmaneser III) and possibly related to the Hebrew term MIZRAIM. *See* OBELISK, BLACK.

MUSTARD [σίναπι sinapi]. The smallness of the mustard seed is used in Jesus' teaching to depict the kingdom of God (Matt 13:31-32//Mark 4:30-32//Luke 13:18-19; compare *Gos. Thom.* 20) and faith (Matt 17:20//Luke 17:6). Although there has been debate over exactly to what plant the Gospel passages might be referring, it is almost certainly the black mustard (*Brassica nigra*). Proverbially known as the smallest of seeds in the ancient Mediterranean world (mentioned in both Hellenistic and Jewish sources), its diameter is about 0.1 in. But the plant can normally grow 6 ft. high. When conditions are favorable, a height of 15 ft. is attainable, with the main stem as thick as a human arm. This is sufficient to hold the weight of small birds that come to eat its aromatic seeds, which have been used since ancient times as a spice. Being a hardy plant, it can thrive on different types of soils and endure extremes of weather. The dramatic contrast between the proverbial smallness of the mustard seed and its eventual size serves as an apt parabolic depiction of the glorious denouement of God's kingdom that eventuates from its inconspicuous beginning. *See* PARABLE; PLANTS OF THE BIBLE.

KIM-HUAT TAN

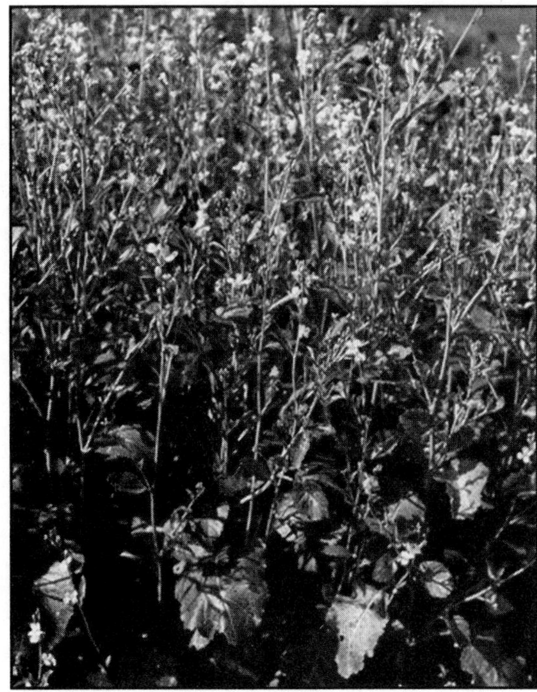

F. Nigel Hepper

Figure 1: Black mustard (*Brassica nigra*).

MUSTER GATE [שַׁעַר הַמִּפְקָד sha'ar hammifqadh]. The Muster Gate stood opposite "the house of the temple servants and of the merchants," suggesting it and the WATER GATE pierced the eastern wall of a compound enclosing the temple courts and priestly residences (Neh 3:26, 31). *See* BENJAMIN GATE; GATE; GATE OF THE FOUNDATION; GUARD, GATE OF THE; JERUSALEM; NEHEMIAH; SUR GATE.

JAMES RILEY STRANGE

MUTE [אִלֵּם ʾillem; κωφός kōphos]. The inability to speak, whether from physical impediment or other causes (Exod 4:11; Isa 36:10; Matt 12:22; Luke 1:22; 11:14). Used figuratively of false idols (Isa 35:6). *See* DEAFNESS; DISABILITY; DISEASE.

MUTH LABBEN. *See* MUSIC.

MUTILATION [גָּדַד gadhadh, קָצַץ katsats; ἀποκόπτω apokoptō, ἐκκόπτω ekkoptō]. Four primary categories of mutilation are present in the Bible: mutilation of enemies, mutilated genitalia, self-mutilation in mourning, and metaphorical self-mutilation.

Violence against enemies is a ritual that appears in many OT texts reflecting the attitudes of Israel and its neighbors (1 Sam 10:27–11:11; 2 Sam 10; Jdt 13–14). Judges 1:6-7 describes a ritual mutilation practice among Canaanites and surrounding nations that involved cutting off the thumbs and big toes of a king defeated in battle. David removes Goliath's head (1 Sam 17:51), and the Philistines cut off the head of King Saul and hang his body and the bodies of his sons on the wall at Beth-shan (1 Sam 31:9-10). Sheba, son of Bichri, loses his head for opposing King David (2 Sam 20:22). David orders his soldiers to kill those who killed Ishbosheth (whose head was severed, 2 Sam 4:7-8), cut off their hands and feet, and hang their bodies in Hebron (2 Sam 4:12).

Males with mutilated genitalia are excluded from participation in the temple rituals (Deut 23:1). Further, no mutilated animal—with crushed or missing testicles—may be offered as a sacrifice to the Lord (Lev 22:24). Several texts use the terms saris (סָרִיס); and eunouchos (εὐνοῦχος; *see* EUNUCH) to refer to officials or members of the king's court in both Israelite and foreign courts. These officials may or may not have been emasculated (2 Kgs 20:18; 23:11; Esth 1:10; 2:3, 14, 15; Jer 38:7; 41:16; Acts 8:27-39).

In addition, there is evidence of self-mutilation in connection with religious rituals among Israel's neighbors (1 Kgs 18:24-29). Mutilation during times of mourning is frequently associated with the term gadhadh (Lev 19:28; Deut 14:1; Jer 16:6; 41:5; 48:37). Self-mutilation is perhaps a characteristic of demonic oppression in Mark 5:1-20, which describes a demonized man who cuts himself with stones.

Self-mutilation is sometimes a metaphor for avoiding sin or becoming prepared for the kingdom of God. Jesus suggests (metaphorically) that it is better to mutilate oneself (ekkoptō or apokoptō) by cutting off MEMBERS of the body that offend rather than to sin (Matt 5:30; 18:8; Mark 9:43, 45; compare Rom 7:22-23). Jesus also suggests that men "become eunuchs for the kingdom of heaven" (eunouchizō εὐνουχίζω; Matt 19:12); here Jesus does not mean literal self-emasculation, but more likely refers to remaining unmarried, or celibate in expectation of the coming kingdom of heaven (compare 1 Cor 7:25-35).

When Paul writes to the Galatian church in response to his opponents (who required circumcision as a prerequisite for joining the church), he crudely and sarcastically retorts that he wishes those who urge circumcision would castrate themselves (apokoptō; "mutilate, castrate," Gal 5:12). CIRCUMCISION itself was never regarded as mutilation; here, Paul uses hyperbole to make his point more strongly. *See* ASCETICISM; CRIMES AND PUNISHMENT, OT AND NT; SACRIFICES AND OFFERINGS.

ARCHIE T. WRIGHT

MUZZLE [חָסַם khasam; φιμόω phimoō, κημόω kēmoō]. Muzzling is closing and keeping the mouth of an animal shut with a device. The law "Do not muzzle the ox" (Deut 25:4) was applied in the NT to mean "Do not neglect to pay Christian ministers" (1 Cor 9:9; 1 Tim 5:18). A possible allegorical interpretation is suggested by Paul's rhetorical question "Is God concerned with oxen?" (compare Philo, *Spec. Laws* 1.260). Or Paul may be pointing out that the literal law concerns not only oxen, because if mere oxen have these rights, all workers should surely also have them—which is how rabbinic authorities applied biblical legal principles (compare the Pharisee-Sadducee dispute in *m. Yad.* 4:7). Philo (*Virtues* 145–48) and Josephus (*Ant.* 4.233 [8.21]) both cite Deut 25:4 to show the law is humane, but for Jews it was sufficient that God had ordained it (compare *Num. Rab.* 19:8).

DAVID INSTONE-BREWER

MYNDOS min´dohs [Μύνδος Myndos]. Myndos (modern Gümüslük) is on the west end of a peninsula on the southwest coast of Asia Minor. Myndos appears in the list of cities (1 Macc 15:23) that received a letter from Lucius, the Roman consul in 142 BCE, requesting kindly treatment of Jews and the return of Judean "scoundrels" to Judea (v. 21). Few archaeological remains have been found at the site.

ADAM L. PORTER

MYRA m*i*´ruh [Μύρα Myra]. Acts 27:5-6 records that Paul and his company traveled from Caesarea on a ship of ADRAMYTTIUM to Myra, then transferred to a grain ship that had traveled from Alexandria and was bound for Rome. Myra was located about 3.5 mi. from the southwestern coast of Asia Minor in the region known as LYCIA.

Grave reliefs discovered at Myra indicate that it existed during the Persian period. During the Hellenistic period, it was one of the six largest cities of the twenty-three-member Lycian Union. Later, the Romans made Myra the capital of the province of Lycia. The partially excavated remains of the site (located north of present-day Demre-Kale) include a Roman theater, baths, and numerous tombs.

Saint Nicholas, bishop of Myra during the 4th cent. CE, was revered as the patron saint of Greece, Russia, children, sailors, merchants, scholars, and travelers. His Dutch name, Sinterklaas, transferred into English as "Santa Claus."

GREGORY L. LINTON

MYRIAD mihr´ee-uhd [רְבָבָה revavah; μυριάς myrias]. Quantitative noun used literally throughout the Bible as the specific number 10,000 (Lev 26:8; Matt 18:24). Both Testaments also use the noun as an indefinite, very large number in reference to people in a crowd, troops, angels, coins, and other things, especially units of value (Gen 24:60; Deut 33:2, 17; Rev 5:11; Jdt 16:3). *See* NUMBERS, NUMBERING.

KATHY R. MAXWELL

MYRRH [לֹט lot, מֹר mor; μύρον myron, σμύρνα smyrna]. Used as an ingredient in certain perfumes, cosmetics, and medicines, myrrh (*Commiphora myrrha*) is a reddish-colored resin obtained from a thorny bush that generally grows no more than 9 ft. in height. Since it is found in the arid regions of Yemen, Somalia, Arabia, Madagascar, and India, it stands leafless for much of the year and its bark peels off easily. When the inner bark is lacerated, a pale yellow liquid exudes and then hardens into a reddish-brown mass resembling tears. After it was harvested, myrrh was transported along the incense caravan routes throughout the ANE (see Gen 37:25; compare Rev 18:13). Its precious nature and expense are reflected in its being given as a gift by Jacob to Pharaoh (Gen 43:11) and by the magi to the baby Jesus (Matt 2:11). Myrrh's antibiotic qualities, which reduced the process of decay, were recognized by the ancient Egyptians, who used it as one of the ingredients in the embalming of mummies. An indication of its use in preserving the bodies of the dead is found in the mixture of aloes and myrrh that Nicodemus brought to anoint Jesus' body after the crucifixion (John 19:39). The medicinal uses of myrrh include its use as an astringent wash, a tonic for dyspepsia, and a stimulant for the appetite. Most important among its ancient uses, however, was as a PERFUME or fumigant. The formula for the sacred anointing oil (Exod 30:22-24) includes liquid myrrh; myrrh mixed with oil formed part of the cosmetic regimen as Esther was prepared to meet the Persian king (Esth 2:12). The sweet aroma of myrrh perfumed women's bodies (Song 1:13), robes (Ps 45:8), and bed furnishings (Prov 7:17). *See* PLANTS OF THE BIBLE.

VICTOR H. MATTHEWS

MYRTLE [הֲדַס hadhas]. An evergreen bush (*Myrtus communis*) that grows densely along hillsides and near streams and rivers (see Isa 41:19; 55:13; Zech 1:8, 10, 11). It grows to a height of 6 to 8 ft. and has glossy, fragrant leaves that were used as spices, perfumes, and in wreathes for brides and victors in the ancient Olympic games. The oil from its leaf was, and still is, used to treat digestive and urinary tract disorders. Its white flower gives way to a dark blue berry that was used to flavor food. Its wood was employed for a variety of purposes, including furniture. Myrtle was used for decoration at the Feast of Booths, that is, Sukkoth (Neh 8:15). Myrtle is a symbol of peace, joy, and blessings from the deity. The name "HADASSAH"—Esther's Jewish name—is derived from this word (Esth 2:7). *See* BOOTHS, FEAST OR FESTIVAL OF; PLANTS OF THE BIBLE.

MARK RONCACE

MYSIA mis´ee-uh [Μυσία Mysia]. A region of the Roman province of Asia Minor, north of Lydia, south of Bithynia, and bordered on the east by the Aegean. In Acts 16:7-8, Luke says that Paul and his companions wanted to enter Mysia, but being prevented from doing so, "went down to TROAS" instead. Most ancient writers located Troas (and ASSOS, Acts 20:13) in Mysia, but it would appear that to Luke, the name indicated a smaller district. PERGAMUM (Rev 1:11; 2:12-17) was the capital of Mysia from 190 BCE, when Rome awarded Mysia to Eumenes II, to 133 BCE, when his son Attalus III bequeathed Mysia to Rome. The Attalid kings decorated Pergamum with large temples to Zeus, Athena, Dionysus, and Asklepios, and claimed the title "Soter" ("savior") for their roles in Asian politics. After the death of Attalus III, a man claiming to be Eumenes' son led a brief fight for control of Mysia, but was defeated in 130–129 BCE by Rome and its other Asian allies. In 2 Macc 5:21-26 (and probably 1 Macc 1:29-40), a contingent of Mysian mercenaries attacked Jerusalem at the behest of Antiochus IV, killing many after first feigning peaceful intent.

RICHARD B. VINSON

MYSTERY [רָזָה razah; μυστήριον mystērion]. In biblical texts, *mystery* does not refer to undisclosed secrets, but rather to divine secrets now revealed by divine agency. In the Greco-Roman world, the term *mysteries* normally refers to the mystery religions.

In the OT and Jewish apocalyptic texts the term *mystery* first appears in Daniel, as a translation of **razah**, in reference to things that God reveals (Dan 2:18, 19, 27, 30, 47; and 4:9). Thereafter it occurs regularly in Jewish apocalypses (e.g., *1 En.* 41:1; 46:2; 103:2; 104:10, 12; 106:19; *2 En.* 24:3; *4 Ezra* 10:38; 12:36-38; 14:5; *Gk. Apoc. Ezra* 1:5; *2 Bar.* 48:3; 81:4) and in the Dead Sea Scrolls (e.g., 1QS III, 23; IV, 18; 1QpHab VII, 5; 1Q27). The term, indeed, is at the heart of apocalyptic thought (*see* APOCALYPTICISM): what has been revealed to the seer is precisely the mystery of how the cosmos functions, and particularly of how God's purpose will achieve its predetermined end.

The most common meaning for **mystērion** in the Greco-Roman world of the 1st cent. CE would have been in reference to the MYSTERY RELIGIONS, often called "the mysteries." The term derives from the various cults' secret teachings and rituals, known only to initiates, and kept secret so effectively that we today know little about them. That these mysteries are alluded to in Wis 14:15, 23 and 3 Macc 2:30 shows how widespread was the knowledge of the mystery cults. Philo does not hesitate to use the language of the cults when he speaks of being initiated into the mysteries of the Lord (*Embassy* 3.71, 100; *Cherubim* 42, 48, 49; *Sacrifices* 60, 62; *Giants* 54, 61; *Rewards* 121; compare Wis 8:4). Given his long association with Corinth, Paul would have been well aware of the most famous of the mysteries, those celebrated at Eleusis in Attica. The cult of Attis had been given official status in Rome under Claudius, and we know that the mysteries of Isis were celebrated both at Rome and near Corinth. At the end of the 19th cent. the history of religions school began to look at earliest Christianity as one among various religious cults and philosophies of the 1st-cent. Greco-Roman world. A parallel between baptism and the Lord's Supper on the one hand and the language and rituals of the mystery cults on the other seemed obvious to some scholars. At the heart of this new thrust was the growing conviction that Christianity itself was a syncretistic religion—that it was in appearance and effect one more mystery cult emerging from the East into the Greco-Roman world.

That early assessment had to be considerably qualified given how little we know about the mysteries themselves. From what we can discern, water rituals seem to have served as preliminary purifications and were not part of the initiation itself. Participants seem to have been motivated by the desire to be spared the terrors of the afterlife rather than a quest for redemption from sin and reconciliation with God. While the idea of a meal presided over by the god appears similar to some accounts of the eucharist (1 Cor 10:20-21), the Dionysian ritual of "eating raw meat" hardly provides a precedent for the Lord's Supper.

Nevertheless, some of Paul's Corinthian converts may have regarded baptism as forging an almost mystical bond between baptizer and baptisand (1 Cor 1:12-17). And Col 2:18 may refer to visions experienced at initiation, using a term (**embateuōn** ἐμβατεύων) attested in talk of initiation into a mystery cult. Paul himself evidently saw a dangerous parallel between the chaotic enthusiasm of the Corinthian worship (1 Cor 14:23) and the abandoned ecstasy of the Dionysian cult (12:2). And the suggestion that the bread and wine, consumed in a wrong spirit, could have destructive effect (11:29-30) has an unnerving ring. More broadly, social-anthropological appreciation of the function of rites of passage, of experiences of conversion and liminality, of eating rituals as community defining, and of the pervasiveness of magical beliefs and practices in the ancient world has reinforced the history of religions' conviction that unless the resonances between earliest Christianity and its religious environment are properly recognized the history of earliest Christianity cannot be adequately appreciated.

The term **mystērion** in the NT appears predominantly in the Pauline letters (twenty of the twenty-seven occurrences). Unlike the Alexandrian Judaism of the Wisdom of Solomon and Philo, Paul's usage shows no knowledge whatever of the vocabulary of the mysteries, with the possible exception of Col 2:18. The background that informs his usage is almost exclusively Jewish, and specifically the language of Jewish apocalypses.

Like apocalyptic Jewish texts, the Christian apocalypse of John (*see* REVELATION, BOOK OF) identifies *mystery* as the climax of the divine purpose for history being revealed to John (Rev 1:20; 10:7; 17:5, 7). The only other non-Pauline occurrence reflects the same influence: the "mystery of the kingdom of God" revealed to Jesus' intimates (Mark 4:11 and par.).

In the Pauline corpus, *mystery* is preeminently the mystery of God's intention from the first to include at the last Gentiles with Jews as God's people. The first clear reference is Rom 11:25, when Paul draws on the term to explain why his own people Israel seem to have rejected the gospel of Messiah Jesus. The mystery now revealed to him is that Israel has been hardened only in part, "until the full number of the Gentiles has come in"; then "all Israel will be saved" (11:25-26). Paul does not indicate when the mystery was so revealed, but presumably the revelation was given to him in response to his deep anguish and puzzlement over Israel's refusal of the gospel (9:2-3; 10:1). The immediately following quotation of Isa 59:20-21 (Rom 11:26-27) suggests that the revelation may have come to him through reading this Scripture.

The same significance is elaborated in what is probably a redactional addendum at the end of the letter (Rom 16:25-27): "the mystery that was kept secret for long ages but is now disclosed, and through the prophetic writings is made known to all the Gentiles ... to bring about the obedience of faith." A similar elaboration appears in Colossians, with particular emphasis on Christ himself as the resolution of the mystery: the mystery of the divine purpose that was hidden but is now revealed, "this mystery among the nations, which is Christ in you, the hope of glory" (Col 1:27; author's trans.). Colossians also speaks of the "knowledge of God's mystery, that is, Christ himself, in whom are hidden all the treasures of wisdom and knowledge" (2:2-3). Paul's commission is to "declare the mystery of Christ" (4:3). And still more fully in Ephesians: "the mystery of (God's) will ... set forth in Christ" (Eph 1:9). Ephesians says that the mystery revealed is God's acceptance of the Gentiles as fellow heirs, members of the same body, and sharers in the promise in Christ Jesus through the gospel (3:3-6). This is the mystery that Paul had been specially commissioned to unfold in his preaching to the Gentiles (3:8-10; 6:19). By extension the same language can be used of the mystery of Christ's union with the church, the coming together of Jew and Gentile to be "one new person" (2:14-16) reflected in the union of husband and wife (5:30-32).

Elsewhere Paul evinces the same conviction of being a steward of God's mystery/mysteries (1 Cor 2:1; 4:1), in this case the mystery of God's achieving his purpose through a crucified Messiah (2:7-10), alternatively described as "the wisdom of God" (1:23-24; 2:7). First Corinthians 14:2 uses the term in the more common sense: the speaker in tongues speaks mysteries that are unintelligible to his listeners; but in 1 Cor 13:2, Paul uses the term in the more apocalyptic sense of mysteries revealed. A further mystery that has been revealed to Paul is that not all will die, but all will be changed at the Parousia and resurrection (1 Cor 15:51-52).

In 2 Thess 2:7, there is a different aspect of the sequence of the end-time climax—"the mystery of lawlessness"—the mystery (now revealed) that there will be a period before the end when an antichrist figure will dominate and deceive before being finally destroyed (2:3-12). In 1 Timothy "the mystery of faith" and "the mystery of godliness" seem to have become formalized as liturgical phrases (1 Tim 3:9, 16), the latter again focusing on the Christ revealed in the flesh and vindicated in the Spirit, proclaimed among Gentiles and believed in throughout the world (3:16).

Bibliography: R. E. Brown. *The Semitic Background of the Term "Mystery" in the New Testament* (1968); H.-J. Klauck. *The Religious Context of Early Christianity: A Guide to Graeco-Roman Religions* (2000) 81–249; C. Rowland. *The Open Heaven: A Study of Apocalyptic in Judaism and Early Christianity* (1982); A. J. M. Wedderburn. *Baptism and Resurrection: Studies in Pauline Theology against Its Graeco-Roman Background* (1987).

JAMES D. G. DUNN

MYSTERY RELIGIONS [μυστήριον mystērion]. The mystery religions were secret religious organizations that flourished during the Greco-Roman period. Although varied in their places of origin and theological formulations, they represent a common form of spirituality.

The mystery religions typically originated in ancient tribal and fertility worship, and stressed the salvation of individuals initiated into what were thought to be the inner secrets of life in the world and beyond. Some of the celebrations of the mysteries occurred in public (parades, processions, purifications, sacrifices), while other ceremonies were private, and the precise nature of these secret observances remains largely unknown.

Among the mystery religions of Greek origin are the Eleusinian mysteries, the Andanian mysteries, and the mysteries of Dionysus. In addition, mysteries of the Kabeiroi (Cabiri, the great gods) were celebrated on the island of Samothrace, and lesser-known mysteries were established at Phlya. Lucian of Samosata also satirized mysteries that featured the serpent Glykon, the incarnation of Ascelpius (*see* MEDICINE AND HEALING, GODS OF).

The Eleusinian mysteries were held at Eleusis near Athens, and eventually elsewhere as well, in honor of the grain mother Demeter and her daughter Kore, the dying and rising maiden whose death and life reflected the life and death of grain. The secret ceremonies of the Eleusinian mysteries are said to have taken the form of legomena (λεγόμενα, "things recited"), deiknymena (δεικνύμενα, "things shown"), and drōmena (δρώμενα, "things performed"), and these ceremonies may have been practiced in other mystery religions as well. The Christian author Hippolytus suggests in *Refutation of All Heresies* that among the deiknymena within the Eleusinian mysteries was a single head of grain viewed in silence, apparently as a reminder of the life in grain and in human beings (*Haer.* 5.8.39). Many of the mystery religions seem to have included a sacred meal shared by those initiated into the mysteries. Moreover, the experiences of those who underwent initiation could often be described as the passage through death to life. Thus, in his *Metamorphoses* (Book 11), Apuleius discusses such a transition in the mysteries of Isis and refers to one who is *renatus* (Lat. "reborn" or "born again"). Apuleius employs language that is deliberately vague in his description of the experience of initiation, and he writes that during the evening the initiate Lucius approached the border of death, passed through all the elements, and returned. According to Apuleius, the next morning Lucius was adorned like the sun and celebrated the new day as a birthday.

The Andanian mysteries, practiced in the southwestern Peloponnesus, were dedicated to Demeter, Hermes, Apollo Karneius, Hagna ("holy one," "pure one"—Kore?), and the great gods. The Rule of the Andanian Mysteries, which still survives, outlines regulations for the organization and celebration of these mysteries.

The mysteries of DIONYSUS reflected the character of Dionysus, who was a god of fertility, animal maleness, wine, drama, and ekstasis (ἔκστασις, "ecstasy"). Frescoes in the Villa of the Mysteries at Pompeii incorporate Dionysian themes and hint at aspects of sexuality, and rumors of sexual irregularities in the Roman Bacchanalia prompted the Senate to enact legislation (*Senatus Consultum de Bacchanalibus*) to control the festivities. The Rule of the Iobacchoi describes more domesticated activities of an Athenian Bacchic club devoted to good eating, good drinking, and the enjoyment of drama. Further, Orphic texts reject the savage traditions of Dionysian lore and embrace a life of purity and spiritual bliss.

Among the mystery religions of Middle Eastern origin are the mysteries of the Great Mother and Attis, the mysteries of Isis and Osiris, and the mysteries of Mithras. Ancient sources also refer to mysteries of the Syrian goddess and ceremonies surrounding the slain youth Adonis.

The mysteries of the Great Mother and Attis present the mother goddess, often named Kybele (Cybele), along with a young lover Attis who dies in a bloody act of self-castration. Texts describe a spring passion festival in which the death of Attis was commemorated and life was anticipated. Some followers of the Great Mother and Attis, called Galli, became eunuchs dressed in transvestite garb in devotion to the Great Mother, and accounts are given of ritual baths or baptisms in the blood of a bull (*taurobolium*) or a ram (*criobolium*), so that, as one inscription puts it, a person may be *in aeternum renatus* ("reborn for eternity").

In the mysteries of ISIS and OSIRIS, the Egyptian goddess Isis is associated with Osiris, the lord of the realm of death, and Isis is claimed to have the power to save and humanize those initiated into the mysteries, as she is said to have done for Lucius in Apuleius' *Metamorphoses*. The worship of Isis also helped to shape Christian devotion to Mary the mother of Jesus and influenced portrayals of the Virgin Mary in Christian art.

The mysteries of Mithras adopted the Persian hero Mithras and incorporated him into a Roman form of worship. In the Mithraic mysteries, initiates worshiped in cave-like sanctuaries, participated in ceremonies with several stages of initiation, and shared meals reminiscent of the Christian eucharist. *See* MITHRAS, MITHRAISM.

Much of the interest of scholars in the mysteries stems from the issue of the relationship between the mystery religions and early Christianity. Like the mystery religions, early Christianity was a religion of salvation and personal choice, and Christians also included ceremonial rituals, forms of initiation, and sacred meals in their worship. Like the mysteries, early Christians could describe salvation as the experience of a dying and rising figure. In 1 Cor 15 Paul compares the MYSTERY of the death and resurrection of human beings to the planting and sprouting of seed in a manner that recalls the Eleusinian mysteries.

In *Exhortation to the Greeks* (12.120), Clement of Alexandria concludes that Christianity may be considered to be a mystery religion, but he contrasts the true Christian mysteries with what he considers to be the corrupt Greco-Roman mysteries. Today a reasonable and judicious approach to the question of the relationship between the mystery religions and Christianity avoids simplistic conclusions about dependence, and rather recognizes the parallel development of the mystery religions and early Christianity in a Mediterranean environment that was deeply interested in salvation and employed syncretistic means of articulating ways of salvation. *See* GREEK RELIGION AND PHILOSOPHY.

Bibliography: Walter Burkert. *Ancient Mystery Cults* (1987); Eldon J. Epp. "Mystery Religions of the Greco-Roman World." *Sourcebook of Texts for the Comparative Study of the Gospels*. David L. Dungan and David R. Cartlidge, eds. (1974) 355–74; Marvin Meyer, ed. *The Ancient Mysteries: A Sourcebook of Sacred Texts* (1999); Jonathan Z. Smith. *Drudgery Divine: On the Comparison of Early Christianities and the Religions of Late Antiquity* (1990).

MARVIN MEYER

MYSTICAL BIBLICAL INTERPRETATION. Discerning the mystical, or hidden, meaning of the Bible was the goal of Christian exegetes from the 2nd through the 15th cent. CE. The 12th-cent. revival of attention to the literal sense qualified, but did not challenge, the preeminence of the spiritual or mystical meaning. Even the Reformers' emphasis on the importance of the study of the letter and original languages of the Bible did not spell the end of concern for an inner appropriation of Scripture as a guide to attaining direct contact with God.

The Greek qualifier mystikos (μυστικός; Lat. *mysticus*) was a generic term for anything hidden that came to be used for the rites of the mystery cults of antiquity. The word does not occur in the Greek Bible, but by the 2nd cent. CE, especially in Clement of Alexandria (d. ca. 215), it was employed to indicate the hidden meaning of Christian beliefs and practices, especially the deep personal signification of the texts of both the OT and the NT. For Clement, as well as for his successor, Origen (d. 254), the work of the exegete (both the catechist giving general instruction to the community, as well as the "gnostic" teacher revealing the inexhaustible riches of God's word) was fundamentally an exercise in mystical interpretation. The proper reading of the Bible, as Origen once put it, would enable the soul to contemplate God with pure and spiritual love (Prologue, *Commentary on the Song of Songs*).

Mystical biblical interpretation as practiced by ORIGEN and his successors aimed at inscribing the inner meaning of the letter within the depths of the soul in order to bring the believer back to God. This mode of anagogic reading was favored by almost all exegetes of the patristic and medieval periods, though never to the exclusion of literal forms of exegesis that were the foundation of the work of the exegete. In the East classic exponents of mystical exegesis include Gregory of Nyssa, Cyril of Alexandria, and Maximus the Confessor; in the West, Augustine of Hippo, Cassian, and Gregory the Great provided models that were developed by later exegetes. Twelfth-century interpreters, especially the Cistercians (such as Bernard of Clairvaux) and the Victorines (like Hugh and Richard), were outstanding exponents of mystical interpretation. Although mystical exegesis was applied to the entire Bible, some texts, like the Song of Songs and John's Gospel, naturally lent themselves more readily to this form of interpretation.

Mystical interpretation did not die out with the changes in Western mysticism that became evident from the 13th cent. on. Much late medieval exegesis still sought to discern a living message about the soul's relation to God hidden within the letter of the text. Though largely marginalized in the modern period, the importance of the mystical dimension of biblical interpretation has been integral to the reception of the Bible in Christian history. *See* ALLEGORY; BIBLICAL INTERPRETATION, HISTORY OF; METAPHOR IN THEOLOGY.

Bibliography: Bernard McGinn. *The Presence of God.* 4 vols. (1991–); Karen Jo Torjeson. *Hermeneutical Procedure and Theological Method in Origen's Exegesis* (1986).

BERNARD MCGINN

MYTH IN THE NT [μῦθος mythos]. The word mythos ("myth"), originally meaning "word," "speech," "conversation," had by the 5th cent. BCE come to mean a fictional story or a story that was not necessarily true, in contrast to the truth established by rational inquiry. For example, Herodotus opens his history by treating the myths about Io's wanderings as the abduction of a king's daughter by Phoenician traders, followed by similar comments on Helen of Troy (*Hist.* 1.1–5). Plato bans the tales that people tell about the Homeric gods from his educational program because they depict gods as immoral, deceitful, and the source of evils (*Resp.* 379c–383c). Platonists in the imperial period (2nd–4th cent. CE) considered such tales about the gods and heroes riddling or coded speech, whose philosophical truth about the soul had to be decoded by skilled interpreters (Plutarch, *Pyth. orac.* 406b–407f; Porphyry, *On the Cave of the Nymphs*; Julian, *Oration* 7). The word *myth* refers to false stories that corrupt true Christian teaching in the NT (1 Tim 1:4; 4:7; 2 Tim 4:4; Titus 1:14; 2 Pet 1:16).

The anthropological and ethnographic recovery of myths about the origins and wars of the gods, the emergence of the cosmos and humankind, and the deeds of ancestral heroes opened up new approaches to the study of myth in the 19th and 20th cent. The "truth" to be uncovered was no longer limited to a dim memory of a historical event or natural phenomenon or to an allegorized philosophical teaching. A culture's mythic stories symbolized the social worlds of human interaction, provided the foundations of important rites of passage such as initiation into adulthood, marriage, and death, or perhaps reflected universal archetypes buried deep in the human psyche.

The recovery of myths from Anatolia and the ANE changed the landscape for both classicists, who discovered the roots of archaic Greek stories in cultural exchanges with the Near East, and biblical scholars, who discovered the roots of stories in Genesis, archaic poetry, and images of the Lord as divine warrior triumphant over Sea, the monstrous chaos. The emergence of Jewish apocalyptic visions (*see* APOCALYPTICISM) of God's triumphant victory over the powers of evil, God's joyous return to his temple mount, the festive banquet with the redeemed, and the like gave new life to these ancient mythic themes (e.g., Dan 7–12; 2 Esdras). Revelation recasts a heritage of images from the OT prophets and Jewish apocalyptic literature along with elements of Greco-Roman myth familiar to inhabitants of Asia Minor into a Christian apocalypse.

Anthropologists often see the function of myths in terms of cultural integration and stability. Students of Jewish and Christian apocalyptic take the opposite approach. They see the displacement of hopes for the renewal of society through ordinary kingship and priesthood in the visions of angelic emissaries and battles that involve the heavens against human foes that embody demonic power. Taking a cue from the persecuted seer of Rev 1:9 and the martyred saints awaiting divine vindication (Rev 6:9-11), they see apocalyptic visions as supporting resistance by a suffering minority. Jewish apocalyptic established the code by which the "world rulers"—Babylon, Persia, Greece, Rome—were cast as beasts in the mold of the archaic chaos monster. Revelation intensifies that theme in describing imperial Rome and her allies among the political and social elite of the Asia Minor city-states. As the cities vied with one another to become centers for cultic veneration of the divine emperor(s) and Rome, resistance to imperial ideology was as much a religious question of who is Lord as a socioeconomic or political one. Revelation 12 employs echoes of Greek myths of the birth of Apollo in depicting the dragon's assault on the mother of the Messiah and her children (believers). According to Suetonius (*Aug.* 94.4), Augustus was said to have been conceived by Apollo (as a snake), when his mother spent a night in his temple.

Suetonius' biography begins with a perfectly ordinary account of Augustus' birth and childhood, though certain locations had become "tourist spots" by the end of the 1st cent. CE. His readers certainly recognized the political point behind the "divine conception" as well as the postmortem apotheosis of the emperor. Luke may expect a similar smile of knowledgeable superiority from his readers when he tells a story of the people from Lystra mistaking Paul and Barnabas for Hermes and Zeus in disguise and attempting to honor them with a sacrifice (Acts 14:8-18). Do they also know the myth of local disaster when the only ones who would offer the divine pair hospitality were an elderly couple, Philemon and Baucis (Ovid, *Metam.* 8.620–724)? Royal pretensions to elicit or accept the honors due a god meet swift divine retaliation in the story of Herod Agrippa's death (Acts 12:20-23; compare Ezek 28:2, 6). Josephus expands on the crowd's acclamation by adding that the people seek favors from a powerful benefactor by flattering Agrippa with such honors (*Ant.* 19.345). The addition clarifies the social function of the exercise.

For 1st-cent. Jews living in the great urban cities like Rome, Corinth, Alexandria, Ephesus, or Antioch, the temples, statues, artistic representations, civic festivals, and celebrations of private cult associations kept the myths of gods, goddesses, and local heroes on public view. Explanations for such widespread ignorance of the one true God ranged from a Euhemeristic account (Wis 13–15) to a deserved punishment for rejecting the knowledge of God that had been available to all (Rom 1:18-32). Gentile converts to Christianity had to renounce as the work of demons the gods and rituals they had once treasured (1 Cor 8:4-13; 10:1-22; 1 Thess 1:9-10; 1 John 5:21). When familiar images, bits of mythology from non-Jewish or even Jewish sources, or acclamations of Jesus as a divine Savior triumphant over cosmic powers are employed in the NT, how is the reader to take them?

That question has troubled scholars since the 19th and early 20th cent., as the History of Religions school showed how deeply indebted the Bible is to ANE mythology for its cosmology, anthropology, and the imagery depicting how the God of Israel interacts with his people. Added to that heritage, NT authors describe Jesus as one who had a unique relationship with God, in or prior to creation (John 1:1-5; 1 Cor 8:6), became a human being (John 1:14; Phil 2:6-8), and after a triumphant conquest of the power of death has been installed even more gloriously on God's throne, superior to every power in the cosmos—demonic or angelic (Eph 1:20-23; Phil 2:9-11; Col 1:15-20; Heb 1:1-14; Rev 5:6-14). His return in judgment will mark the end of this cosmos in the final triumph of divine justice (Matt 25:31-46), the transformation of the resurrected faithful into the glorious image of Christ (1 Cor 15:50-57; Phil 3:21), and the new paradise, a heavenly Jerusalem in which God dwells with his people (Rev 20:11–21:27). Laid out in sequence, the basic story of the CHRISTOLOGY of the NT uses more of the poetry and images of myth than the logical inquiry of history, biography, or philosophy.

Some scholars suggested that Christianity had adapted a myth of the heavenly Redeemer who descends into the cosmos ruled by the demonic creator and his powers to enlighten and rescue those humans with a spark of divine light from GNOSTICISM. However, the existence of such a gnostic redeemer myth in the early 1st-cent. CE cultural context of the NT is unlikely. Others insist that all of the elements of early christology can be paralleled in Jewish sources of the period. Even so, the possibility remains that the foundational story that the NT authors tell in declaring a certain Jesus of Nazareth "both Lord and Messiah" (Acts 2:36) is itself a myth that emerged in the Gentile churches as a "Hellenized" mutation or even distortion of the Jewish Jesus movement. Classicists might compare the cult myth focused on Jesus with other popular "new religions" in the 1st and 2nd cent. CE, such as the Hellenistic version of the Egyptian goddess Isis or the popular oracle shrine created by Alexander of Abonoteichos (see Lucian, "Alexander the False Prophet"). Ethnographers who study the myths, rituals, visionary journeys, and healings of shamans in traditional societies around the globe find the modern lens that separates "facts" from myth, religion, or legend inadequate. They argue that the stories told about Jesus, including triumph over demonic figures, are comparable to those found in other cultures.

Such studies in religion challenge the theological isolation of the Bible from the rest of human culture as well as the priority given to ancient Greek mythology in scholarly treatments of myth. At the same time, the gap between the world of the biblical writers and that of contemporary Christians appears to be widening. Two strategies from the 19th and early 20th cent. continue to be pursued in 21st-cent. variations: 1) historical Jesus research; and 2) de-mythologizing. Of course, scholars may pursue the task of reconstructing a 1st-cent. Jewish context and probable history of Jesus of Nazareth simply as an intellectual task. Christians who find the mythic story of Jesus as divine redeemer implausible often look to the Jesus presented as "historical" for values of solidarity, global community, compassion, and self-sacrifice. Or they may seek a Jesus who models a path of inner transformation and spirituality—a Jesus without the church.

The program of de-mythologizing articulated by the great 20th-cent. exegete Rudolf Bultmann takes the opposite position. The historical Jesus of Nazareth is the presupposition for the existence of Christian faith but not its content. The risen Lord who has saved humanity as presented in the founding theological visions of Paul and John is the object of faith. One cannot avoid the mythological categories in which persons in premodern societies understand and describe the world when reading the NT. Believers can find a way of interpreting the biblical texts that speaks about the real dimensions of human life in our time. Bultmann adapted the existentialist description of the human subject cast into a world of temporality, anxiety, confrontation with the other, striving for authenticity, care, and the experiences of new possibility. To those critics who saw this effort to present the message of the gospel drawing on a philosophical system that did not incorporate God, Bultmann insisted that theology was not philosophy. Always the theologian and preacher as well as a scholar, Bultmann agreed that believers will continue to speak of God acting in the world and being present to their experiences of "new possibilities of being" in ways that outsiders reject as "myth."

Existentialist philosophy never captured the public imagination in North America as it did in Europe. But it is possible to find heirs to Bultmann's de-mythologizing program in contemporary liberation theologies. For these scholars, the world of demonic powers whose control must be broken for humans (and the planet) to flourish are social and political structures. Such powers privilege vast inequalities that can seem so natural or inevitable that people see no way out. "Globalization," "the market forces," a persistent state of racial, ethnic, or religious violence, crushing poverty, and degradation of the environment shape the modern experience of a world out of control and needing redemption. The apocalyptic myth of the NT can be a powerful source of hope as long as the passivity built into its ancient expressions does not get translated into disengagement from the political, social, and environmental problems of the day. *See* GREEK RELIGION AND PHILOSOPHY.

Bibliography: Rudolf Bultmann. *Jesus Christ and Mythology* (1958); Larry W. Hurtado. *Lord Jesus Christ: Devotion to Jesus in Earliest Christianity* (2003); Roger A. Johnson. *The Origins of Demythologizing* (1974); Hans-Josef Klauck. *The Religious Context of Early Christianity* (2000); Peter W. Macky. *St. Paul's Cosmic War Myth* (1998); Walter Wink. *Naming the Powers* (1986).

PHEME PERKINS

MYTH IN THE OT. The term *myth* has a decidedly mixed history in OT studies, since scholars have never found a definition for myth on which they could all agree, nor have they reached a consensus about its suitability for describing OT thought. Moreover, scholars do not always explicitly state their particular definition or justify their use of the word, so encountering the term *myth* in biblical scholarship and making sense of it can be a frustrating experience. The aim of this article is, first, to clarify the discussion of myth by laying out the major definitions of and opinions about myth among OT scholars during the past century and, second, to provide some assistance in assessing the value of the term for understanding biblical thought and literature.

A. The Critique of Myth in Old Testament Studies

For the last century, most OT scholars have rejected the word *myth* as an appropriate designation for OT thought and literature. They agree that myth is a valid label for some of the stories of Israel's neighbors about their gods, but they argue that biblical stories about Israel's God are so different that the term *myth* is not useful. Two themes are present in these discussions of myth. First, myths are other peoples' stories: they are indigenous to Israel's neighbors but not to Israel itself. Second, when Israel did take over elements of these foreign myths, it "demythologized" them and thereby advanced to a higher and more mature level of religious thought. While no two OT scholars handle this issue in exactly the same way, it is possible to divide the history of their discussions into two phases as a rough guide to the understanding of the word *myth* in 20th-cent. biblical scholarship.

1. Polytheism versus monotheism

At the beginning of the 20th cent., OT scholars accepted a definition of myth popularized by the folklorists Jacob and Wilhelm Grimm in the 19th cent.: a myth is a story about gods. This definition was essentially a literary one, by which narratives with divine characters were distinguished from narratives with human actors. For biblical scholars, however, the key element in myth was not so much the concept of divine characters per se, but that myths were stories about gods, plural, not god, singular; that is, myths included multiple divine actors. Thus, the polytheistic stories of Israel's neighbors were true myths, but the monotheistic narratives of the Bible were not, because they spoke only of a single deity.

The most influential proponent of this approach at the end of the 19th and beginning of the 20th cent. was Hermann Gunkel. He recognized the influence of the creation myths of Israel's neighbors—especially the Babylonian myth *Enuma Elish*, in which Marduk slays Tiamat, dragon of chaos, to create the world—on Israel's own creation stories, but he argued that Israel suppressed the mythological elements in its sources, in particular their polytheistic character. The Priestly story of creation in Gen 1:1–2:4*a*, e.g., reflects elements of ANE creation myths, but it is staunchly monotheistic, knowing only a sole God who creates the world unopposed. So strong was this rejection of polytheism among biblical authors, in Gunkel's opinion, that he described the Bible as possessing an abhorrence for myth. This rationale for rejecting myth is common in the first part of the 20th cent.

Most scholars today, inside and outside of biblical studies, would have problems with this approach to myth. The definition of myth as a story about the gods, while still a key ingredient in some more recent theories of myth and while still predominant in much OT scholarship, is now widely considered too narrow on its own terms to adequately describe myth. Furthermore, the simple equation of myth with polytheism was a narrow interpretation in its own day, and it was a convenient method for demonstrating the uniqueness and superiority of biblical religion. Both Gunkel and Skinner spoke of the "crude mythology" in the creation accounts of Israel's neighbors. Of course, the contrast between the monotheistic impulse in biblical religion and the polytheism of Israel's neighbors is an important one, but it is more complex than these scholars claimed, and it is now believed to be a much too limited way for deciding the merits of the concept of myth for understanding the Bible.

2. Cosmos versus history

Around the middle of the 20th cent., a distinct shift occurred in the way biblical scholars understood myth and in their reasons for rejecting it. But the results were the same: the OT does not contain myth. Old Testament scholars still accepted myth as a story about gods, but they no longer saw as its key ingredient its polytheism but rather its focus on the establishment of cosmic order. According to this definition, a myth deals primarily with the gods' establishment and maintenance of the orders and rhythms of nature, and it locates divine activity in the timeless realities established in the primordial age and in the unchanging cycles of nature. According to OT scholars, this view of divine reality described in myth contrasted sharply with Israel's strong historical consciousness. Israel understood God's activity not primarily in the eternal rhythms of the cosmos but in the contingencies and unrepeatable events of human history. Its religious literature, therefore, is not so much about timeless cosmic structures, that is, myth, but about Israel's experiences within the successive events of chronological time, that is, history. This viewpoint coincided with a powerful movement in biblical studies during this time that stressed the primacy of *Heilsgeschichte*, "sacred history," in Israel's religious thought.

Though scholars adopted this approach with different nuances, it became the dominant way to understand myth and to reject it as a biblical category in the second half of the 20th cent. and the beginning of the 21st. One of the first and most influential statements of this position was made by two professors of ANE civilizations, Henri and H. A. Frankfort, who argued that ancient Israel began "the emancipation of thought from myth." They called the "primitive" mentality behind myth "mythopoeic" thought, a way of viewing the world that was not rational, speculative, and abstract like modern thought, and that did not separate the gods and humanity from nature as subject and object, but that saw the gods and humanity directly related to cosmic phenomena and natural rhythms. According to the Frankforts, Israel broke with this mentality by dissociating God from nature and reconceiving God as pure being, and by identifying historical experience rather than nature as the realm of divine activity and ultimate meaning.

Many prominent OT scholars adopted some version of this approach to myth. G. Ernest Wright argued that Israel broke from the natural religions of its neighbors expressed in myth, and he identified biblical religion as history interpreted by faith rather than as mythology. Brevard Childs described the effort of biblical writers to destroy the foreign understanding of reality carried in myth and to replace it with a new understanding of existence rooted in the totality of Israel's concrete historical experiences. Frank Cross maintained that the events in Israel's history that it considered ultimately meaningful displaced the mythic pattern and led to a new kind of literature, epic, in which mythic and historical features are combined in a perennial tension. James Barr presented his own version of this basic approach. Major commentaries on Genesis during this period, such as those by Gerhard von Rad, Claus Westermann, Walter Brueggemann, Gordon Wenham, Nahum Sarna, and Victor Hamilton, illustrate in one form or another this approach to rejecting myth as an appropriate category for biblical literature and thought.

This approach to biblical religion and its rejection of myth has become so widespread in biblical scholarship that it is hardly questioned, yet it assumes several dubious dichotomies. The contrast between primitive and modern modes of thinking and the contrast between nature and history that are present in most forms of this rejection of myth as a biblical category are both problematic in certain respects. The idea that ancients thought differently from moderns, in particular that they possessed only a mythopoeic consciousness lacking logical and rational thought, as the Frankforts described them, is now one of the least popular understandings of myth among scholars. It represents an inaccurate and paternalistic understanding of the complexities of ancient thought. Further, the contrast between nature and history in these reconstructions of biblical thought is a stark oversimplification of biblical religion, in which both cosmic and historical orders are sacred and integrated in biblical literature (*see* CREATION). Finally, as with the rejection of myth as polytheistic in the first half of the 20th cent., this approach too seeks to promote the uniqueness and superiority of Israelite religion.

B. The Use of Myth in Old Testament Studies

While a majority of biblical scholars during the last century have rejected myth as an OT category, some have embraced myth as a useful way of talking about biblical literature and thought. Though in the minority, these scholars have kept the concept of myth alive in biblical studies and debates in several important ways.

1. Myth and ritual

The most prominent scholars who have argued that the concept of myth is an important category of biblical literature and thought are those who connect its use closely with Israel's liturgical rituals. According to their definition, myth is the spoken counterpart to that which is performed in ritual. Myth is the text of the liturgical drama, so to speak. This definition of myth arises from the recognition of the central role of ritual in ancient cultures, including that of biblical Israel, and the view that religious texts grew out of a culture's ritual practices. In their ritual reenactments and recitation of religious texts related to them, these cultures believed they could participate in the renewal of cosmic orders and powers. This definition shares the idea of myth as the expression of cosmic order, which was a prominent part of the definition accepted in the second half of the 20th cent. by most scholars who rejected myth as a biblical category, as has just been noted. By contrast, members of the myth and ritual school embraced myth as an authentic element in Israelite worship.

The Norwegian scholar Sigmund Mowinckel was a prominent practitioner of this approach to myth. Mowinckel focused his research on the relationship of the psalms to the rituals of Israel's cult, in particular to the rituals of the enthronement festival of the New Year, when God's rule of the world was reenacted and celebrated. At Israel's festivals, the myth of God's rule expressed in the psalms was not so much recited as experienced, not so much told as acted. The content of this myth as expressed in the psalms takes many forms, including the celebration of God's defeat of chaos and establishment of cosmic order and also the commemoration of God's historical acts on Israel's behalf and God's covenant-making with Israel. Like other scholars in the second half of the 20th cent., Mowinckel believed that Israel was unique in celebrating God's control of history, but unlike his contemporaries, he considered the recitation of God's deeds of salvation in history—the exodus, the covenant, the election, the immigration—as a part of Israel's festal myths. Thus Israel's historical traditions were not a threat to myth but myths themselves, along with Israel's myths of cosmic ordering. Both were recited within Israelite cultic ritual.

The primary critique of the approach to myth in the myth and ritual school is that the direct connection between a culture's traditions and its rituals, upon which this definition of myth is based, cannot always be established and in some cases seems quite unlikely. Thus, to define myth as the text of a liturgical drama can be precarious. For our purposes, it is worth noting that Israel's biblical traditions about its history could here be accepted as myth, since they accompanied the ritual reenactment of the cult, while, among other scholars described above, these same historical traditions could be interpreted as entirely antithetical to myth. The definition selected determines the suitability of the term for biblical studies.

2. Other approaches

While the appropriation of myth as a useful category for biblical studies has been most prominent in the myth and ritual school, scholars have suggested a number of other definitions for the term that they believe make it a viable concept for biblical interpretation. Scholars in the fields of classics, anthropology, and comparative religion relate a number of these definitions to developments in the study of the traditional stories of other cultures. J. W. Rogerson proposes a functional definition by which myth be viewed as literature that expresses the faith or worldview of a people. Though helpful in understanding key aspects of biblical traditions, this definition of myth is so general that it would apply, as Rogerson expresses it, to the entire Bible, and if that is so, its usefulness as an explanatory term in biblical studies is certainly debatable.

As a part of his definition of myth, Rogerson also claims that myth expresses a people's intuitions of transcendent reality. This idea is central for G. Henton Davies, who identifies myth as a way of thinking about and imagining the divine, and who identifies myth with the theme of divine presence in the OT, encompassing such motifs as the divine name, glory, cloud, ark, tent, tabernacle, and Temple. The idea here seems to be the general notion that myth is literature about God. Related to this idea, but grounded more in the concept that ancients spoke differently about God than moderns do, is the claim, put forward by J. L. McKenzie and Bernhard Anderson, that the Bible does actually contain the mythopoeic thought that most scholars denied to biblical texts. These approaches all in one sense appear to equate myth with speech about God and reflect in more sophisticated form the old definition that myths are stories about gods.

C. The Value of Myth for Old Testament Studies Today

This very mixed history of different approaches to myth by biblical scholars and of their contradictory decisions about its usefulness as a category of biblical literature and thought raises serious questions about its continuing value for biblical studies. What follows is a brief assessment of the key problems and possibilities that the term *myth* presents for us today.

1. Problems

The most obvious problem for employing the term *myth* in biblical studies today, as the survey of its usage above clearly shows, is that it has acquired so many different meanings. J. W. Rogerson concludes that given the many ways in which OT interpreters use the concept of myth, it is nearly impossible to agree on a single definition, and nothing would be gained by trying to shape all relevant material into one such definition. Then he goes on to list the different meanings of myth he has discovered under twelve different headings. Indeed, when modern English dictionaries try to define the term, their definitions vary considerably. Moreover, they customarily piece together different scholarly proposals for the term into a kind of eclectic definition that few individual scholars would subscribe to in just this way.

Still another meaning of the term *myth* that we have not even discussed complicates the situation even more. That is the popular meaning most people associate with the word *myth*: a fiction or half-truth, something that did not happen at all. The English word *myth* derives from the Greek word mythos (μῦθος), which originally meant anything spoken, but eventually came to mean also rumor, false or untrue speech, the meaning with which it is, in fact, used in the NT (e.g., 2 Pet 1:16; 1 Tim 4:7). Early Christian writers continued to use the term in this way to refer to the stories of non-Christian religions, and in common modern English usage it is probably the meaning most people think of first when they hear the word. While this, of course, is not a scholarly definition of myth, it is doubtful whether scholars can employ the term for any general audience without conjuring up this negative connotation of the term and ultimately confusing the point they wish to make.

The word *myth* is now so complicated that it tends to obscure rather than clarify discussions about biblical literature and thought. Even should scholars be consistent in telling us clearly what they choose to mean by the term—which they do not always do—it is almost impossible for them to escape the popular background noise of its negative connotations and to exclude all other aspects of its sense that their listeners may bring to the discussion. Indeed, Rogerson claims in the final sentence of his book that his entire survey of the use of myth in biblical studies will have been worthwhile if all it does is to make future scholarship more cautious about the use of the concept of myth.

2. Possibilities

While the term *myth* itself may have become irretrievably problematic for biblical studies, the problem for which it has been employed as a solution is a crucial problem that all modern Bible readers must address in one way or another, and the results of the scholarship on myth, with its many definitions, may provide some insight into ways to address it. That problem is the challenge to the simple truth of the biblical record resulting from modern scientific and historical research. Until the modern period, the biblical story was taken as a simple record of past events that happened just as narrated, and therein was seen its truth. It is now impossible to square the biblical stories of the beginnings of the world and of human culture with the findings of modern science, and it is also impossible, and often improbable, to try to establish the historical veracity of Israel's narratives of its historical beginnings in the Pentateuch. This leads students of the Bible to a very fundamental question: if its stories did not happen as told and are not true in that sense, how is one to understand the truth of the Bible?

In a basic sense, this is the question students of comparative mythology try to address: if the stories ancient and contemporary traditional societies tell about the world and about themselves are not simple accounts of what actually happened, what are they? What purpose do they serve for those who tell them? The major theories of myth have been developed to answer this question, and these theories may provide insights also into the larger purpose of biblical stories that, like the stories of many ancient and contemporary cultures, are no longer viewed as simple historical records of events. Theories of myth make the claim that the truth in traditional stories lies not so much in whether the events they narrate happened but in the larger claims and affirmations they make about the world and about human experience. Theories of myth may help us move beyond debates about the historicity of biblical literature and give us a better understanding of some of the deeper aims and concepts in biblical texts.

One of the earliest theories of myth, still influential today, is that myth attempts to explain phenomena in nature and society. This theory, which goes back to the early anthropologist E. B. Taylor, assumes that ancients possessed the same intellectual needs and skills as the modern scientists, anthropologists, and historians whose research aims to explain the origins of the world, its life, and its societies, and that their traditional tales aimed to provide such explanations. This explanatory impulse is clearly present in the abundant etiologies in Genesis, where most narratives explain common realities in the lives of its storytellers and their audiences. The Priestly creation account in Gen 1:1–2:4*a* explains both natural and social phenomena, including, e.g., the sources of both springs and rain in the reservoirs of water surrounding the earth (1:6-8) and the observance of the Sabbath on the seventh day of the week (2:1-3). Our reading of these narratives should thus take into account their explanatory purpose, their aim to provide answers, within their own intellectual and social milieu, for basic questions ancient Israelites entertained about the world and about themselves.

Another theory of myth, which has particular value in explaining the character of Israel's narratives of its origins in the Pentateuch, stresses the social function of traditional stories. According to this approach, which is connected most strongly with the work of the anthropologist Bronislaw Malinowski, traditional narratives are often designed and told to describe the identity and unity of the culture that creates them and to legitimate and support that group identity. Myths are thus social charters that establish the essential character of a people. This feature is a prominent element in all of the stories of Genesis. The genealogical narratives from Noah on show in a progressively more specific way how the people of Israel are related to but distinct from their neighbors. At the conclusion of these stories, the accounts of Jacob and his sons establish and legitimate the relations between the twelve tribes of Israel that comprise their descendants. Thus the significance of these stories is not so much their historical veracity but their interest in supporting the identity and unity of Israel at the time of the story's narrators.

Other theories of myth have been influential in the study of such traditional stories, among them the structuralist approach originating with the anthropologist Claude Lévi-Strauss, which sees in myth a logical model capable of overcoming the deep contradictions people sense about themselves and their place in the world. All of these theories provide ways of looking at a culture's traditional stories that place emphasis not on their historical accuracy but upon larger purposes they serve for their cultures. By these insights, such theories can provide biblical scholars with useful lenses for seeing the purposes of biblical narratives. Since, however, the term *myth* itself has had such a complicated and contradictory history in biblical scholarship, it is doubtful whether the insights achieved from the comparative study of mythology can be applied to the Bible under the banner of the word *myth.* More clarity will be achieved by talking about theories of myth and their insights with other terminology that describes more precisely the specific literary dynamics and modes of thought toward which scholars wish to point us. *See* COSMOGONY, COSMOLOGY; FORM CRITICISM, OT; MYTH IN THE NT.

Bibliography: Bernhard W. Anderson. *From Creation to New Creation: Old Testament Perspectives* (1994); James Barr. "The Meaning of 'Mythology' in Relation to the Old Testament." *VT* 9 (1959) 1–10; Walter Brueggemann. *Genesis.* IBC (1982); Brevard S. Childs. *Myth and Reality in the Old Testament* (1960); Frank Moore Cross. *Canaanite Myth and Hebrew Epic* (1973); G. Henton Davies. "An Approach to the Problem of Old Testament Mythology." *PEQ* 88 (1956) 83–91; Henri Frankfort, H. A. Frankfort, John A. Wilson, and Thorkild Jacobsen. *Before Philosophy: The Intellectual Adventure of Ancient Man* (1949); Hermann Gunkel. *Genesis.* Mark E. Biddle, trans. (1997); Victor Hamilton. *Genesis.* NICOT (1990); Claude Lévi-Strauss. *Myth and Meaning* (1995); Claude Lévi-Strauss. *The Raw and the Cooked* (1983); Bronislaw Malinowski. *Magic, Science, and Religion: Essays* (1948); J. L. McKenzie. "Myth and the Old Testament." *CBQ* 21 (1959) 265–82; Sigmund Mowinckel. *The Psalms in Israel's Worship.* D. R. Ap-Thomas, trans. (1967); Gerhard von Rad. *Genesis.* OTL (1972); J. W. Rogerson. *Myth in Old Testament Interpretation* (1974); Nahum Sarna. *Genesis.* JPS Torah Commentary (1989); J. Skinner. *Genesis.* ICC (1910); E. B. Taylor. *Anthropology* (1930); Gordon Wenham. *Genesis.* WBC (1987); Claus Westermann. *Genesis.* CC (1974); G. Ernest Wright. *God Who Acts: Biblical Theology as Recital* (1952).

THEODORE HIEBERT

MYTHOLOGY IN BIBLICAL INTERPRETATION. *See* ARCTURUS; BEHEMOTH; BIBLICAL CRITICISM; BIBLICAL INTERPRETATION, HISTORY OF; COSMOGONY, COSMOLOGY; DEMON; LEVIATHAN; LILITH; MYTH IN THE NT; MYTH IN THE OT; ORION; PLEIADES; RAHAB; RESHEPH.

MYTILENE. Post-New Testament spelling for MITYLENE.

Nn

NAAM nay´uhm [נַ֫עַם naʿam]. Among Judah's descendants, he was JEPHUNNEH's grandson and Caleb's third son (1 Chr 4:15).

NAAMAH nay´uh-muh [נַעֲמָה naʿamah]. 1. Daughter of LAMECH and his wife Zillah; sister of Tubal-cain (Gen 4:22).

2. A town in the lowlands of Judah, near Lachish (Josh 15:41).

3. One of Solomon's Ammonite wives (1 Kgs 11:1), and mother of REHOBOAM, Solomon's successor (1 Kgs 14:21, 31; 2 Chr 12:13). Because Solomon worshiped the gods of his non-Israelite wives, Yahweh declared that his heir would rule over Judah, but not Israel (1 Kgs 11:3-13). Like his father (and mother?), Rehoboam led Judah in the worship of foreign deities (1 Kgs 14:22-24).

SUSAN M. PIGOTT

NAAMAN nay´uh-muhn [נַעֲמָן naʿaman; Ναιμάν Naiman]. 1. A descendant of Benjamin. Naaman appears as Benjamin's son (Gen 46:21) and as his grandson (Num 26:40). He also appears as the son of Bela, Benjamin's firstborn (1 Chr 8:4). Naaman was the ancestor of the Naamites (Num 26:40).

2. The commander of the army of the king of Aram (Syria). Although the names are given in the text, the story takes place in the 9th cent. BCE, at the time when Ben-hadad II was king of Damascus and Jehoram was king of Israel. Naaman was afflicted with a skin disease (sometimes identified as LEPROSY, although most scholars do not consider this to be the correct term for his condition). He was healed of his skin disease through the intervention of ELISHA, a prophet of the Northern Kingdom (2 Kgs 5:1-27). The healing of Naaman is one of the many miracles that appear in the stories of Elisha. At the beginning of his prophetic ministry, Elisha asked Elijah for a double portion of his spirit (2 Kgs 2:9). Naaman was a successful soldier and highly regarded by the king of Aram. The nature of his illness is unknown since it did not force him to live in isolation and he was able to carry on his duties and serve the Aramean king. A young Hebrew girl who was captured in battle and who served as a servant to Naaman's wife told her mistress that a prophet in Samaria could cure the skin disease. Naaman decided to go to Samaria and secure the services of the prophet of God. He went to his king and reported what the servant girl from Israel had said. The Aramean king, eager to help his commander, sent a letter to the king of Israel requesting that Naaman be cured. Naaman took with him a gift to the prophet consisting of ten talents (750 lbs.) of silver, 6,000 shekels (150 lbs.) of gold, and ten sets of garments.

When the king of Israel read the letter, he was angry with the request and displayed his distress by tearing his garments. The reason for the king's distress was his suspicion that the king of Aram was looking for an occasion to fight against him. When the prophet Elisha heard of the king's anxiety, he sent his servant to the king with a request that the king send the Aramean commander to him. When Naaman arrived at Elisha's house, the prophet, through his messenger, told Naaman to bathe seven times in the Jordan River and he would be healed from his skin disease.

Naaman was angry at the prophet's word because he expected the prophet to welcome him personally and to heal him from his skin disease. He was also disappointed because he considered the waters of the JORDAN RIVER to be inferior to the waters of the Abana and the Pharpar, two rivers in Damascus. At the insistence of his servants, Naaman obeyed the words of Elisha, washed himself seven times in the waters of the Jordan River, and was healed from his skin disease. The symbolism associated with the number seven indicates that the healing was the work of God. Naaman returned to Elisha's house to express his gratitude to the prophet. Naaman told Elisha that now he knew that there is no other God but the God of Israel. In gratitude for his healing, Naaman offered to give Elisha a gift, but the prophet refused to accept Naaman's gift.

Naaman requested that he be allowed to take two mule-loads of earth to make an altar in Damascus to the Lord. Naaman pledged to worship only the God of Israel but since he still served the king of Aram, he would be required to participate in the official worship of Rimmon, the god of Damascus. Rimmon is an abbreviated name for Hadad-Rimmon, a god of rain and thunder.

After Naaman departed to return to Damascus, Gehazi, Elisha's servant, went after Naaman and in Elisha's name asked for a portion of the treasure the prophet had refused. Out of a sense of gratitude, Naaman gave Gehazi more than that for which he had asked. Elisha rebuked his servant and declared that Naaman's skin disease would be transferred to Gehazi and his descendants forever (2 Kgs 5:27). Naaman's healing is mentioned in the NT (Luke 4:27) where Jesus mentions "Naaman the Syrian" as an example of divine grace given to an individual who was not an Israelite.

CLAUDE MARIOTTINI

NAAMATHITE nay´uh-muh-th*ı*t [נַעֲמָתִי na`amathi]. One from Naamah, probably a South Arabian locale, not NAAMAH (Josh 15:41). This gentilic occurs only in reference to Job's friend ZOPHAR (e.g., Job 2:11).

NAARAH nay´uh-ruh [נַעֲרָה na`arah]. 1. A city mentioned in Josh 16:7 and 1 Chr 7:28 (as Naaran), on the border of Ephraim and Manasseh, commonly identified as modern Tel el-Jisr, near 'Ain Duk, about 3.5 mi. northwest of Jericho.

The site is significant for its 6th cent. CE synagogue. The three-aisled basilical synagogue was entered from the north. The nave of the synagogue was decorated with a mosaic carpet, comprised of three bands. The first (northern) band is decorated with a geometric pattern and animal roundels. The middle band depicts a solar chariot surrounded by twelve zodiac signs and the four seasons. The third band shows a torah ark, flanked by seven branched candelabra. Below this are two lions flanking a man. Most of the images have been defaced. This design is similar to those of other Byzantine-period synagogues, such as Beth-Alpha, Hammat Tiberias, and Sepphoris.

2. One of two wives of Ashhur, father of Tekoa. The four sons she bore to Ashhur are listed in 1 Chr 4:5-6.

ADAM L. PORTER

NAARAI nay´uh-r*i* [נַעֲרַי na`aray]. Son of Ezbai and one of David's "Thirty" (1 Chr 11:37). In the par. list (2 Sam 23:24-39), the name appears as "PAARAI the Arbite."

NAARAN. *See* NAARAH.

NAATHUS nay´uh-thuhs [Νάαθος Naathos]. A descendant of ADDI, he dismissed his foreign wife and children in Ezra's reform (1 Esd 9:31).

NABAL nay´buhl [נָבָל naval]. Nabal (meaning "fool," as suggested in 1 Sam 25:25), a wealthy Calebite sheep owner, is described as "surly," and later as a "wicked man" by his wife ABIGAIL (25:3, 25). When David's troops, who had protected Nabal's shepherds, asked for food during a time of feasting, Nabal declined. David, infuriated, mustered his men to kill Nabal's men. Abigail intervened with provisions while Nabal feasted and became drunk (1 Sam 25:23-36). He died ten days later and Abigail became David's wife (25:37-39). Nabal's hot-headedness is contrasted with the cleverness of his wife; she, through her wit, saves many, but he, on account of his foolishness, dies.

Bibliography: Peter J. Leithart. "Nabal and His Wine." *JBL* 120 (2001) 525–27.

JESSICA TINKLENBERG DEVEGA

NABARIAH nab´uh-r*ı*´uh [Ναβαρίας Nabarias]. One of the witnesses who stood on the platform while listening to Ezra's reading of the law (1 Esd 9:44).

NABATEANS nab´uh-tee´uhn [Ναβαταῖοι Nabataioi]. The Nabateans are identified as people from the Arab kingdom of Nabatea. They referred to themselves as Nabatu (nbtw נבטו) on Aramaic inscriptions. The Nabateans come into prominence in the late 1st cent. BCE through the lucrative trade in frankincense, myrrh, spices, gold, precious gems, silks, and medicinal products. They also became prosperous from harvesting Dead Sea bitumen. Nabatea and its capital PETRA are famous for extraordinary architecture, exquisite eggshell thin pottery painted with geometric and foliate designs, the Nabatean script (a variant of Aramaic), and ingenious hydraulic systems allowing a successful agricultural economy in the desert climate. The Nabateans were a major regional power for ca. 300 years.

In the Persian period (550–332 BCE), the Nabateans, an Arab tribe, settled in Edom and taxed those who traveled the corridor from the Red Sea to Syria (*see* EDOM, EDOMITES). Diodorus Siculus (ca. 30 BCE; *Bib. hist.* 2.48-49) states that the nomadic Nabatean merchants of exotics from Arabia, Africa, and India took refuge in Petra when attacked by King Antigonus I in 312 BCE. They are described as a people fond of freedom with camels and cattle, living under the open sky country without springs or rivers. But Strabo's later account portrays them as traders living in luxurious houses and practicing viticulture (*Geogr.* 16.4). These are a wealthy, cosmopolitan, settled people numbering 10,000 men, who are ruled by a monarch and boast a fleet in the Red Sea for merchandising spices, incense, and myrrh. By the late 2nd cent. BCE they controlled an area from the Hejaz to the HAURAN in the north and from the Nile Delta to the Syrian Desert and were actively trading with the Persian Gulf.

In 190 BCE, Antiochus IV ruled the SELEUCID EMPIRE. Having seized most of Palestine and Jordan, the Maccabees under Judas Maccabeus with John Hyrcanus I led a revolt against Antiochus IV. As Seleucid power declined, the HASMONEANS ruled an independent Judea from 142 to 63 BCE. From 135 to 104 BCE, the governor–king John Hyrcanus I conquered the Negev and land north to the Galilee. His successor Aristobulus took the Galilee. Alexander Jannaeus gained the throne in 103 and ruled from Dan to Beersheba until he died in 76 BCE. He provoked a conflict with the Nabateans, who were in control of the coveted trade routes. The Nabateans responded by allying with the Seleucid king Demetrius III and temporarily defeated the Hasmoneans, but Alexander Jannaeus regained control. He died, leaving his widow Salome Alexandra ruling (76–67 BCE). Her sons John Hyrcanus II and Aristobulus began a civil war, but with Idumean Antipater and the military support of the Nabatean king Aretas III, John Hyrcanus II took his brother captive. Fighting between the Seleucids and Ptolemies allowed the Nabateans to maintain control over the caravan routes between Arabia and Syria. Nabatean trade flourished and Petra became a metropolis with an estimated population of 20,000–30,000.

The Roman general Pompey reached Damascus in 63 BCE and forced Aretas III's troops to withdraw from Jerusalem. Pompey selected John Hyrcanus II to rule as high priest and incorporated his territory into the Roman province of Syria. Aristobulus was exiled to Rome, where he started a rebellion; this insurrection was halted by Mark Antony, and after a second rebellion in 55 BCE the Romans appointed Antipater governor. The Parthians invaded Palestine in 40 BCE and placed the Hasmonean Antigonus on the throne in Jerusalem, taking John Hyrcanus II prisoner (*see* PARTHIA, PARTHIANS). The Nabateans made a tactical blunder by siding with the Parthians; for Rome, backing the Roman vassal king Herod the Great, defeated the Parthians and captured Jerusalem. After the defeat of the Parthians, the Nabateans were forced to pay a heavy fine to Rome. Jerusalem fell to Herod in 37 BCE and Nabatea crumbled in 31 BCE; Rome now controlled a large area of Nabatean territory and ended its independent status. Although geopolitically the Nabateans lost their "national identity," their culture continued to flourish. The forces of Malichus I were overpowered at Philadelphia (modern Amman), and Antony and Cleopatra were defeated by Octavian at Actium. The Roman Empire controlled the Near East, and Octavian received the title "Augustus Caesar," becoming the first Roman emperor.

By the mid-2nd cent. BCE, the Nabateans controlled the trade routes from the Hejaz through Jordan and the Negev to the Mediterranean. Although the early rulers are unknown, coins and inscriptions permit historians to trace a single royal line from the 2nd cent. BCE to 106 CE. The eleven Nabatean kings begin with King Aretas I (ca. 168 BCE), who is referred to as the "tyrant of the Arabs" and the "King of the Nabat" in the war against the Seleucid king Antigonus of Syria. Scholars debate whether Aretas I was succeeded by Rabbel I; however, by ca. 110 BCE Aretas II ruled. He is mentioned as the victor in the siege of Gaza over the Hasmonean king Alexander Jannaeus. In ca. 96 BCE, Obodas I, the son of Aretas II, ascended to the throne and ruled until 85 BCE, inheriting the fight against Alexander Jannaeus. Ambushed, Alexander Jannaeus was driven by camels into a deep ravine and barely escaped, and Obodas I took land in Moab and Galaaditis. In a crucial battle at Cana in southern Syria in 87 BCE, Obodas I and his forces defeated the army of the Seleucid Antiochus XII. Obodas was so revered that the city of Oboda in the Negev was named for him and served as the seat of his royal cult. From 85 to 62 BCE Nabatea was ruled by Aretas III who expanded Nabatean territory to include Damascus. In 63 BCE the Roman general Pompey captured Jerusalem, and Nabatea became a client state of Rome.

Nabatean coinage was minted for 170 years to meet specific military needs. Coins were first struck ca. 62 BCE by Obodas II (62/61–59 BCE) and by his successor Malichus I (59/58–30 BCE). This was a time of political upheaval in Rome when fortunes changed. Caesar defeated Pompey, who fled to Egypt where he was murdered in 48 BCE. In 47 BCE Malichus I supplied military aid to Caesar in Alexandria, but shifted his alliance to support the Parthian invasion of Judea. In 40 BCE, the Parthians invaded Syria and captured Jerusalem, incurring the enmity of Mark Antony as well as his ally Herod the Great. With the assignation of Antipater, Herod became the governor of Judea. After the Roman victory, Malichus I was forced to pay an indemnity to Rome. Under King Obodas III (30–9/8 BCE) Nabatean relations with Rome and Judea were peaceful.

The rule of Aretas IV (9 BCE–40 CE) marks a forty-eight-year golden age for the Nabateans. To his people Aretas was known as "Haretat [Aretas] the King who Loves His People." Once again Damascus came under Nabatean control. On his coinage, his queens Huldu (until 16 CE) and Shaqilat (from 18 CE) are shown in profile, indicating that royal women enjoyed a position of power in the Nabatean court. The monuments at Petra reflect a flourishing economy and unsurpassed wealth from international trade.

Aretas IV's rule is recognized as the most creative era in Nabatean history. As Hellenistic culture was pervasive, the now wealthy but eclectic Nabateans borrowed art and architectural ideas from Egypt, Assyria, Parthia, Arabia, and Greece both for their buildings and for their artifacts. Aretas IV reigned over a cosmopolitan Nabatea with splendid temples, colonnades, palaces, fountains and ornamental pools, gardens, a theater, and 800 tombs with *triclinia* (a room with three rock-cut benches). Column capitals were adaptations of the Ionic and Corinthian styles. Whole façades were plastered and interiors were decorated with wall paintings and elaborate stucco moldings depicting animals, human faces, and figures. Nonfigurative decoration with cubic blocks, called "god blocks" because they appear to stand for the main deity Dushara, coexisted with finely carved vases, rosettes, flowers, fruits, leaves, entwined fronds, and mythological gods and animals, including Asian elephants. These decorative ideas are found not only in Petra but also at Hegra (Egra) in the Hejaz (Medain Saleh, in Saudi Arabia) and along the route to Gaza in the Israeli Negev.

Relations between Nabatea and the Herodians were generally peaceful. One of the daughters of Aretas IV was married to Herod Antipas (Herod's son), who divorced her to marry his half brother's wife, Herodias (Mark 6:17-18; Josephus, *Ant.* 18.109–10). The aftermath was a defeat by Aretas IV that cost Herod his entire army. Under Malichus II (40–70 CE), Nabatea is thought by some scholars to have witnessed a decline in its fortunes. This may not be the case, however, for it has now been confirmed that Malichus II was the king to which the *Periplus of the Erythraean Sea* referred (19.49), describing the great commercial success resulting from linking the Red Sea port city of Leuke Kome to Petra. The Nabateans were commercially and militarily successful at Hegra and occupied the north Arabian oasis in Wadi Sirhan.

In 67 CE, Josephus (*J.W.* 3.68–69) states that Malichus II commissioned 5,000 infantrymen, as well as archers and 1,000 cavalry, to suppress the First Jewish Revolt. Rabbel II (70–106 CE) ascended the throne, with his queen mother Shaqilat II serving as regent until he came of age in 75 CE. At this time, the city of Bostra in the Hawran (Syria) became a prominent city of Nabatea. Rabbel's reign ended in 106 CE and Rome absorbed Nabatea, which completely succumbed to Roman hegemony under the emperor Trajan and became the Roman province known as *Provincia Arabia.* In 130 CE, the Roman emperor Hadrian named Petra after himself, giving it an imperial imprint.

With Roman seafaring trade circumventing Arabia (directly related to the discovery of the monsoons), Nabatea began to decline as a leading trade center. The Nabatean language continued in use for administrative and legal purposes, but Greek, and to a lesser extent Latin, was used as well. The potters of Nabatean fine wares maintained their production, although the yield from this time demonstrates deterioration in the painting. By 114 CE Trajan had granted Petra the title of metropolis and it served the Romans as the principal center for their southern holdings, extending from the south shore of the Dead Sea to the Gulf of Aqaba. Nabatean kings were no more, having been replaced by Roman legates or deputies and members of the senatorial rank serving as governors.

Bibliography: Judith MacKenzie. *The Architecture of Petra* (1990); Fergus Millar. *The Roman Near East. 31 BC–AD 337* (1993); Avraham Negev. *Nabataean Archaeology Today* (1986).

MARTHA JOUKOWSKY

NABONIDUS nab´uh-n*i*´duhs. Nabonidus (Babylonian nabu-naʾid, "[the god] nabu is praiseworthy") is not mentioned in the Bible, but as the last king of Babylon (r. 555–539 BCE) he played an important role in ANE history. Moreover, some of the traditions found in Scripture, though attributed to others, especially Nebuchadnezzar, apparently concern Nabonidus, at least indirectly.

Details about Nabonidus' origins and family are unclear. He was apparently not of royal descent, but the son of Nabu-balatsu-iqbi, a scholar, and Adad-Guppi, a devotee of the moon-god Sin who may have had connections to the court of Nebuchadnezzar II and Neriglissar (see her fictional autobiography, discovered at Harran, in *COS* 1.147). Indeed, Nabonidus may have married one of Nebuchadnezzar's daughters and he was probably involved in the assassination of Neriglissar's son and successor, Labashi-Marduk, who reigned a scant three months and may have been only a child. Nabonidus subsequently assumed power, evidently to general acclaim and with the support of the army, perhaps because he was an experienced soldier himself (some identify him with the Babylonian mediator Labynetus, mentioned in Herodotus, *Hist.* 1.74). Nabonidus took the throne at an advanced age, perhaps as old as sixty (his mother died at 102 or 104 years of age in his ninth regnal year), and so his son Bel-shar-usur (Belshazzar) was probably instrumental in the coup, and likely a powerful figure, at times even coregent, throughout Nabonidus' reign.

Nabonidus undertook various campaigns to solidify or reestablish Babylonian hegemony, returning in some ways to earlier notions of Assyrian imperial ideology. He was largely successful in these military endeavors as well as in the various building projects he engaged, in which he proved to be something of an antiquarian and archaeologist, unearthing numerous early foundation deposits as part of his renovation work. However, not long into his reign, Nabonidus relocated to the oasis city of Teiman (biblical TEMA) and remained there ten years (553–543 BCE). This move proved critical, leaving an important mark on subsequent events and traditions that were picked up in Scripture in various ways.

First, while in Teiman, Nabonidus delegated power to Belshazzar. Baruch calls Belshazzar the son of Nebuchadnezzar (Bar 1:11-12) and he is mentioned several times in Daniel, where he is identified as "king" (see Dan 5:1, 9, 30; 7:1; 8:1). Belshazzar was neither of these, being the son of Nabonidus (though perhaps the grandson of Nebuchadnezzar if Nabonidus had married one of his daughters) and, at most, coregent under Nabonidus. Hence, on the one hand, the historical data about Nabonidus reveal certain details in the biblical traditions regarding Belshazzar (and Nebuchadnezzar) to be inaccurate—perhaps because they are simply too far removed from the actual events. On the other hand, these very same data help to explain the why and whence of these "inaccuracies": 1) Belshazzar, for all intents and purposes, did function as king during Nabonidus' absence (hence the royal epithet in Daniel); 2) his coregency may explain why he is mentioned together with Nebuchadnezzar (*sic*) in Baruch; and 3) Daniel is called "third" in the kingdom (Dan 5:29; compare 5:7, 16) because he comes after Nebuchadnezzar (so Daniel, erroneously; actually Nabonidus) and Belshazzar.

In this same vein, many scholars have wondered if the traditions of the madness of Nebuchadnezzar in Dan 4 are in fact better attributed to Nabonidus, who really did "wander" far from the capital. That the attribution of Nabonidus' oddities to Nebuchadnezzar may be more than simple historical error may be revealed in a text from Qumran (4Q242 = 4QPrayer of Nabonidus), which records a prayer uttered by Nabonidus when he was afflicted with illness in Teiman for seven years (frags. 1–3 1-3; compare Dan 4:16, 23, 25, 32 on "seven times") before being healed (forgiven) by a Jewish exile. Unfortunately, the text is rather fragmentary. Still, if this tradition is older than Daniel, as some scholars have suggested, it may be superior by showing that Nabonidus' illness is wrongly applied to Nebuchadnezzar in Daniel. Other scholars, however, are not convinced of the priority of 4Q242. Whatever the case, at the very least 4Q242 raises the possibility that the traditions at work in Daniel and Baruch may have as much to do with literary and theological (re)presentation and messaging as they do with historical facticity (or lack thereof). That is to say that details from other kings may have accrued to Nebuchadnezzar largely because he was infamously remembered for the destruction of Jerusalem.

A second crucial outcome of Nabonidus' relocation to Teiman was that the New Year's festival—an important celebration in Babylonian culture and religion—was not celebrated due to the king's absence. This situation certainly met with great disapproval on the part of the priests of Marduk, the high god of the Babylonian pantheon. Indeed, a stele in Harran (see *ANET*, 562), a city known for its devotion to Sin that Nabonidus rebuilt (along with Sin's temple there; see *COS* 2.123A), indicates that the king's relocation to Teiman may have been caused by priest-led uprisings against him in Babylon, Borsippa, Nippur, Uruk, Ur, and Larsa. If so, these uprisings may be the direct result of Nabonidus' favoring of the moon-god's cult and his exaltation of Sin to chief position in the pantheon (reflected in both texts and iconography from his reign).

Unfortunately, it is difficult to adjudicate our sources at this point, many of which are ambiguous and/or chronologically unclear. Certainly the Harran inscriptions mention Sin, but this is to be expected since he was the local god there. And, while it must be admitted that Marduk is noticeably absent from the Harran stelae, Marduk is quite prominent in another inscription documenting Nabonidus' rise to power (see *ANET*, 308–11). Most of the anti-Nabonidus data we have dates after 539, when Cyrus conquered Babylon and promulgated a pro-Marduk, pro-Babylon policy—in service to his own propagandistic purposes—for its citizens, especially the priests (see *ANET*, 312–14). Hence, the reasons for Nabonidus' relocation to Teiman were probably complex and multiple: family dynamics with his mother and son most certainly played a role as did political and economic interests such as Nabonidus' desire to control trade routes through Arabia. This would have been a great achievement, adding to the wealth and imperial reach of Babylon. Teiman controlled several other oases and the years away from Babylon could simply reflect the difficulties of military expeditions in that habitat. Alternatively (or additionally), Nabonidus' departure could reflect a concern over Persia's growing power to the east or the Medes' expansion across northern parts of Mesopotamia, or he may have been inspired by a dream oracle (compare *ANET*, 560–61). Regardless, while in Teiman, Nabonidus received delegations from Egypt, the Medes, and Arabs, indicating that he was an important political figure with a wide reputation. In short, the pro-Marduk religious polemic against Nabonidus may be overstated, coming as it does primarily, if not exclusively, in texts that support Cyrus. Even so, Nabonidus could not have hoped to curry much favor with the citizens of Babylon and especially its powerful priesthood by extending his absence from the capital and its religious ceremonies. So it comes as no surprise, and is a widely known fact, that only a few short years after the king returned to Babylon (543 or 542) and reinstated the New Year's festival, Cyrus advanced and took Babylon without a fight in 539 (see *Babylonian Chronicles* 7 iii 16; Herodotus, *Hist.* 1.191; Xenophon, *Cyr.* 7.26–37), perhaps because he was assisted by dissidents on the inside. Nabonidus surrendered and, according to the later historian Berossus, he was spared and lived the rest of his life in Carmania. *See* ASSYRIA AND BABYLONIA; BELSHAZZAR; CYRUS; MESOPOTAMIA; NEBUCHADNEZZAR, NEBUCHADREZZAR.

Bibliography: Bill T. Arnold. *Who Were the Babylonians?* (2004); Paul-Alain Beaulieu. "Nabonidus (2.123)." *COS* 2 (2000) 310–14; Paul-Alain Beaulieu. *The Reign of Nabonidus, King of Babylon 556–539* BC (1989); John J. Collins. *Daniel: A Commentary on the Book of Daniel* . Hermeneia (1993); A. K. Grayson. *Assyrian and Babylonian Chronicles* (1975); Amélie Kuhrt. *The Ancient Near East* (1995); Ronald H. Sack. "The Nabonidus Legend." *RA* 77 (1983) 59–67.

BRENT A. STRAWN

NABONIDUS, PRAYER OF. The Prayer of Nabonidus (4Q242) is a fragmentary Aramaic text discovered in 1952 among the DEAD SEA SCROLLS. It contains the beginning of the story of how NABONIDUS, king of Babylon, was healed by the true God from a "severe inflammation" after praying in vain for seven years to the gods of "silver, gold,...wood, stone, and clay." An anonymous Jewish "diviner" plays a role in the healing and commands the king to circulate the story in writing so that God may be glorified. Presumably, most of the missing text contained the prayer of thanksgiving.

The surviving text, dated paleographically to the 1st cent. BCE, consists of four fragments, three from the first paragraph of the scroll, preserving eight lines, and the fourth (three lines) from a later part of the scroll. Although there is general agreement on the overall meaning, scholars differ on where to place the first three fragments and on the wording of the reconstructed text between the fragments. These differences affect the translation and interpretation. For example, it is not clear whether it is God or the Jewish diviner who forgives the sin of the king (4Q242 1–3, 4). If it is the diviner (as many think), then the text provides important background for Jesus' claim to have the authority to forgive sins in, e.g., Mark 2:1-12.

Similarities between 4Q242 and the story of Nebuchadnezzar in Dan 4 (first-person narration, affliction of a Babylonian king, intervention of a Jewish sage, seven years of exile [Dan 4:32]) suggest the Nabonidus story as a precursor to the biblical one. The story of Nebuchadnezzar's madness and exile in Daniel also bears some resemblance to the experience of the historical Nabonidus, who, according to Babylonian inscriptions, retreated to Teima for ten years and was considered deranged by his opponents. It is hypothesized that in Jewish circles, the history of Nabonidus and the legend of his affliction developed into a tale of healing and conversion to monotheism; this story in turn was later assigned to the more famous Nebuchadnezzar. Still, the differences between 4Q242 and Dan 4 are significant (for instance, Nabonidus in 4Q242 suffers a physical, not mental, affliction), and the similarities may be simply common literary motifs.

Bibliography: J. Collins. "The Prayer of Nabonidus." *Qumran Cave 4 XVII: Parabiblical Texts, Part 3.* DJD 22 (1996) 83–93; F. M. Cross. "Fragments of the Prayer of Nabonidus." *IEJ* 34 (1984) 260–64; F. García Martinez. "The Prayer of Nabonidus: A New Synthesis." *Qumran and Apocalyptic* (1992) 116–36.

EDWARD M. COOK

NABOPOLASSAR nab´uh-puh-las´uhr. Chaldean tribesman who took advantage of a succession crisis in Assyria to make himself king in Babylon (626–605 BCE). The priests of Marduk acquiesced. Other cities had to be subdued by conquest or bribed with tax exemptions. Uruk's goddess Nanaya was given to the Elamites, resulting in the Uruk Prophecy, reminiscent of the Dan 2, which predicted the fall of Nabopolassar's dynasty and its replacement by an ideal king. Nabopolassar's coalition of Babylonians, Elamites, and Medes took Assur and Calah (614), Nineveh (612), and Harran (609). During his military campaigns with his son Nebuchadnezzar, the gods, temples, and physical structures of every major city of northern Iraq and Syria (the Assyrian Empire) were thoroughly destroyed, a campaign of slaughter and deportation of truly apocalyptic proportions. His ally Josiah's battle against Assyria's ally NECO at Megiddo (609) is the model for the battle of Armageddon and the battle of Carchemish (605) for the apocalyptic battle of the Qumran War Scroll. Allegedly in revenge for the destruction of Babylon by Sennacherib, this scorched earth policy was probably intended to prevent the Medes from profiting from their share of the Assyrian Empire.

Bibliography: J. A. Brinkman. "Nabopolassar." *RlA* 9 (1998) 12–16; JoAnn Scurlock. "Whose Truth and Whose Justice? The Uruk and Other Late Akkadian Prophecies Re-Revisited." *Orientalism, Assyriology and the Bible.* Steven W. Holloway, ed. (2006) 449–67.

JOANN SCURLOCK

NABOTH nay´both [נָבוֹת navoth]. Naboth lived in Jezreel during the reign of AHAB, king of Israel, and owned a vineyard adjacent to the royal palace (1 Kgs 21:1-2). Ahab desired Naboth's land for a vegetable garden, offering a better vineyard or the value of the land in money. Naboth refused to sell his property because it was the inheritance he had received from his father. The law of inheritance in Israel was designed to protect the economic viability of every family. God was the real owner of the land, thus, each family received a portion of the land in trust from God (Num 33:54). The land was kept by the family in perpetuity; it could not be sold, nor could it be confiscated (Lev 25:23). The king's wife, JEZEBEL, plotted to kill Naboth and his sons and take possession of his land.

After the reprehensible crime, when Ahab came to take possession of Naboth's land, ELIJAH met Ahab and pronounced an oracle announcing the divine punishment upon him and his house (1 Kgs 21:19-24). Only Ahab's repentance prevented the judgment from coming upon him during his lifetime (1 Kgs 21:27-29). After Ahab's death, Elijah's oracle was fulfilled when JEHU revolted against the house of Ahab and killed the royal family (2 Kgs 9:21-26). *See* INHERITANCE IN THE OT; JEZREEL, JEZREELITE.

CLAUDE MARIOTTINI

NACHMANIDES. Moses ben Nachman, Nachmanides (1194–1270), was a Jewish biblical exegete, Talmudist, kabbalist, and communal leader in Gerona, Spain, best known for his commentary on the Pentateuch, which marks a new stage in the history of exegesis as the first commentary influenced by both the Andalusian and Ashkenazic exegetical traditions. Although a product of Christian Spain, he undoubtedly felt himself to be part of the Andalusian exegetical tradition and indeed enriched the enterprise of contextual (peshat פְּשָׁט) exegesis with many insightful comments. He had absorbed the work of RASHI and the Northern French school, and held it in high regard, but did not hesitate to utilize the vast resources of rabbinic literature. Although certainly trained in grammar and philology, he found the Spanish approach, exemplified by Abraham Ibn Ezra, too grammatocentric and limiting. He was therefore sympathetic to Rashi and his selective use of midrashic material, seeking to strike a balance between the two approaches and to adopt a more holistic approach to the text. He expanded the exegetical enterprise to encompass issues of theology, ethics, history, and character analysis, thus weaving a particularly colorful and variegated tapestry operating on several levels. His commentary is famous for its psychological insights and deep understanding of human nature. Nachmanides was also a genuine kabbalist, steeped in the mystical traditions of the Provençal school of kabbalah, and included in his commentary are numerous allusions to esoteric meanings of various biblical texts. *See* HAGGADAH; HALAKHAH; IBN EZRA, RABBI ABRAHAM; MIDRASH; TALMUD.

BARRY DOV WALFISH

NACON nay'kon [נָכוֹן nakhon]. Name of the town or the owner of the THRESHING FLOOR in Judah where UZZAH died (2 Sam 6:6). The par. account in 1 Chr 13:9 associates this threshing floor with CHIDON. Both accounts agree that the site was renamed PEREZ-UZZAH (2 Sam 6:8; 1 Chr 13:11).

A. HEATH JONES III

NADAB nay'dab [נָדָב nadhav; Ναδάβ Nadab]. 1. The first of four sons whom ELISHEBA bore to Aaron (Exod 6:23; Num 3:2), appointed to priestly service together with his father and brothers (Exod 28:1). Alongside his younger brother Abihu, Nadab appears in hierarchy just below Moses and Aaron. These four, accompanied by seventy elders of Israel, ascended the mountain of God and "saw the God of Israel" (Exod 24:1, 9-11). After the ordination of Aaron and his sons, when the glory of Yahweh appeared and fire from Yahweh consumed sacrifices (Lev 8–9), there follows a brief story of Aaron's great disgrace when Nadab and Abihu "offered unholy fire before the LORD" and were consumed by Yahweh's fire (Lev 10:1-7; Num 3:4).

2. Succeeded his father Jeroboam I as second king of Israel, but after a two-year reign, he was murdered by his successor BAASHA (1 Kgs 15:25-28).

There is a correspondence between the names of Jeroboam's two sons (Nadab and Abijah) and Aaron's first two sons (Nadab and Abihu) that some scholars view as more than coincidental. Albertz posits that the priests of the Bethel sanctuary, which Jeroboam had refurbished, were Aaronides who gave homage to Jeroboam by inserting the names of his sons into their own genealogy.

3. A descendant of Judah (1 Chr 2:28, 30).

4. A descendant of Benjamin (1 Chr 8:30; compare 9:36).

5. A guest at the wedding feast Tobit held for his son Tobias and his bride Sarah (Tob 11:18). Nadab attempted to murder his uncle Ahikar but died in the trap he had set (Tob 14:10-11).

Bibliography: R. Albertz. *A History of Israelite Religion in the Old Testament Period.* OTL (1994); B. D. Bibb. "Nadab and Abihu Attempt to Fill a Gap: Law and Narrative in Leviticus 10.1-7." *JSOT* 96 (2001) 83–99; W. Houston. "Tragedy in the Courts of the Lord: A Socio-Literary Reading of the Death of Nadab and Abihu." *JSOT* 90 (2000) 31–39.

WESLEY I. TOEWS

NADABATH nad'uh-bath [Ναδαβάθ Nadabath]. A town in Transjordan near MEDEBA (modern Madaba). The Maccabees sent John and their possessions to the Nabateans for safekeeping, but the JAMBRI family from Medeba attacked the caravan, killing John and stealing the baggage (1 Macc 9:35-37). Later, Jonathan and Simon retaliated by attacking the Jambris' wedding party while it was traveling from Nadabath to Medeba. They slew many and stole its baggage (1 Macc 9:37-42).

Because the account in 1 Maccabees is vague, establishing the location of Nadabath is difficult. It has been identified with Nebo, northwest of Madaba; Khirbet et-Teim, 2 km south of Madaba; and Main, 7 km southwest of Madaba.

ADAM L. PORTER

NAG HAMMADI TEXTS nahg'huh-mah'dee. Two brothers digging for fertilizer near Nag Hammadi, a small town in Upper Egypt, found a large jar containing twelve books and several pages from a thirteenth that had been put inside the cover of one of the others. Each book (called a CODEX) contained copies of early Christian writings that are collectively referred to as the "Nag Hammadi texts" after the nearest sizable town. Discovered in December 1945, Codex III was purchased by the Coptic Museum in Cairo in October 1946. All of the surviving material from this discovery now resides there.

Study of these texts has made important contributions to the study of the NT. For example, the *Gospel of Thomas* contains a collection of Jesus' sayings and parables, many of which are comparable to sayings and parables in the Synoptic Gospels.

- A. Discovery and Publication
- B. Contents of the Collection
- C. Importance for the Study of Christianity
    1. Jesus traditions: sayings, passion, and resurrection
    2. Christology: divine beings identified with Jesus
    3. Revelations by the risen Jesus
    4. Disciples as authoritative teachers
    5. God as transcendent, not creator
    6. Revisiting the patristic view of gnostic heretics and sects
    7. Emergence of the Christian canon
- D. Importance for the Study of Antiquity
    1. Jewish traditions in myths of human origins
    2. Platonic philosophy in accounts of the divine world
    3. Hermetic writings

A. Discovery and Publication

The peasants who found the jar containing these texts in 1945 had no idea of their value. Their mother burned Codex XII as fuel. Only a few scraps survive. The rest were left with a local Coptic priest, who recognized the language but could not read it. His brother-in-law was responsible for bringing Codex III to Cairo, where it was acquired by the Coptic Museum. Its acquisition was not announced until 1948. By the end of 1946 French scholars had recognized that its *Apocryphon (Secret Book) of John* and *Gospel of the Egyptians* probably came from early Christian sects classified as "gnostics" (*see* GNOSTICISM).

How the other volumes found their way onto the antiquities market is unclear. The French scholar Jean Doresse, who had seen Codex III, was shown several others in the fall of 1948 and identified their contents as gnostic from the titles. Eventually Egyptian antiquities authorities took over most of the collection. The director of the Coptic Museum, Togo Mina, had Doresse do a detailed inventory of their contents in the spring of 1949. The first public reports did not appear until 1949 (Doresse) and 1950 (Puech). The Coptic Museum finally purchased the collection in 1952. Efforts at conservation and publication did not begin until 1956.

Translations of the *Gospel of Thomas* and other writings from Codex II began appearing in German and other modern languages in 1958/1959. However, publication of the photographic facsimile edition under UNESCO auspices (1972–84) and a critical edition of the Coptic texts by a team under the direction of James M. Robinson from the Institute for Antiquity and Christianity was not completed for several decades.

Codex I had been taken out of Egypt and purchased by the Jung Institute of Zurich in May 1952. The *Gospel of Truth* (I, 3) was published in 1956. After publication of its treatises, the "Jung Codex" was returned to Egypt. The collection contains material from thirteen codices that average 35 cm. × 15 cm. Codex I is only 29 cm. × 14 cm. Each page contains a single column of text. Detailed analysis concluded that some 1,153 pages of an original total of about 1,257 survive, though many are only partially preserved.

Fragments of letters and receipts used in the leather bindings bear dates in the 340s CE and indicate that the codices were manufactured in the region, an area that was home to Pachomian monks in the 4th cent. But the codices were not manufactured by a single workshop. Unfortunately, surveys and excavations in the area have not turned up any evidence directly related to this find. Some scholars imagine that the writings that make up the Nag Hammadi collection were copied into codices intended for a monastic library. Perhaps efforts to enforce official orthodoxy among the monks at the end of the 4th cent. led to the removal and burial of this collection.

Lacking secure evidence, one cannot say what purpose this collection served. Since the codices contain duplicates of some works that were manufactured differently, the collection may have been assembled from previous owners. That suggestion has been reinforced by differences in scribal handwriting. Handwriting analysis permits one to suggest that some of the codices were copied together.

B. Contents of the Collection

Codex I contains: 1) The *Prayer of the Apostle Paul*, a prayer of Paul on ascending to a vision of the Redeemer, with a Greek colophon. 2) The *Apocryphon of James*, a report of a post-resurrection revelation to Peter and James prior to Jesus' ascension that is embedded in a letter to an unnamed teacher. 3) The *Gospel of Truth* (also XII, 2), a meditation on the true gospel (= message of salvation) that the Father has become known in the world of forgetfulness through Jesus and that appears to be a Valentinian meditation on Christian themes. 4) The *Treatise on the Resurrection*, presented as a letter from a teacher to a student, Rheginos. The *Treatise* argues against bodily resurrection and for spiritual resurrection as taught in the transfiguration narratives about Jesus. 5) The *Tripartite Tractate*, a Valentinian theological tract in three parts, including the Father and the divine realm, the creation of humanity, the descent of the Savior, and the process of salvation. This tractate may be responding to 3rd cent. Christian critics. Codex II contains: 1) The *Apocryphon of John* (also IV, 1; shorter recension III, 1; BG 8502, 2), a post-resurrection revelation of Jesus to the apostle John, which he conveys to the other disciples. It incorporates an account of the divine world, a myth story of Wisdom's fall, the lower (Jewish) creator and the imprisonment of light in humanity linked to interpretations of Genesis. 2) The *Gospel of Thomas*, a collection of sayings and parables of Jesus that promises eternal life to those who discover their true interpretation. 3) The *Gospel of Philip* is a compendium of teachings, perhaps from different schools, that incorporates Valentinian sacramental catechesis. 4) The *Hypostasis of the Archons* is a mythologized interpretation of Gen 1–6 that claims that the descendants of Seth are the immortal, spiritual race. 5) *On the Origin of the World* (also XIII, 2) is a tractate assembled from various sources that presents a gnostic account of the origins of the lower world, Wisdom's activity, the creation of Adam in paradise, and the emergence of the spiritual race. 6) The *Exegesis on the Soul* is a tale of the soul's fall from androgynous unity into the body, passion, and mortality illustrated with passages from the prophets, NT, psalms, and Homer's *Odyssey*. 7) The *Book of Thomas the Contender* is a post-resurrection revelation dialogue advocating ascetic flight from the bodily passions and their demonic rulers.

Codex III contains: 1) The *Apocryphon of John* (see II, 1). 2) The *Gospel of the Egyptians* (also IV, 2), an account of the emanation of the divine world with the heavenly Seth's descents to save his "seed." It incorporates elements of sectarian baptismal rites. 3) *Eugnostos the Blessed* (also V, 1), a discourse on the divine world. 4) *Sophia of Jesus Christ* (also BG, 3), a dialogue between the risen Jesus and his male and female disciples incorporating a *Eugnostos* version of the divine world, the origin of humanity, and salvation of Wisdom's seed by the Savior. 5) The *Dialogue of the Savior*, a fragmentary dialogue between Jesus and disciples incorporating an apocalyptic vision of the soul's fate with wisdom sayings about creation and ascetic exhortation. Codex IV contains: 1) The *Apocryphon of John*; and 2) the *Gospel of the Egyptians.*

Codex V contains: 1) Another copy of *Eugnostos the Blessed.* 2) The *Apocalypse of Paul*, an account of Paul's ascent into the heavens. 3) The *(First) Apocalypse of James*, a revelation of the risen Jesus to his brother James that incorporates a docetic view of the crucifixion and a formula for the soul's post-mortem ascent. 4) The *(Second) Apocalypse of James*, a fragmentary discourse that includes an encounter between James and the risen Jesus and an account of James' martyrdom. 5) The *Apocalypse of Adam*, a revelation of Adam to his son Seth that interprets Genesis as the creator's attempts to prevent human enlightenment that incorporates a catalogue of false stories of the Savior's origins.

Codex VI contains: 1) *Acts of Peter and the Twelve Apostles*, an allegorical tale in which the apostles encounter Jesus in a mysterious stranger and journey to his city. 2) *Thunder: Perfect Mind*, a first-person aretalogy by Wisdom that catalogues her paradoxical attributes. 3) The *Authoritative Teaching*, a homiletic discourse on the soul's fall into the material world and its healing by the heavenly bridegroom. 4) *Concept of Our Great Power*, an apocalyptic salvation-history in three ages: flesh (ending with the flood); psychic (of Jesus, ending with war among the powers and fire); and Savior, end-time, when enlightened ones find rest. 5) A copy of Plato, *Republic* 588A–589B (a poor translation). 6) *Discourse on the Eighth and Ninth*, a hermetic tract on final unity with the universal mind (*see* HERMETIC LITERATURE). 7) The *Prayer of Thanksgiving*, a hermetic prayer of thanksgiving followed by a scribe's note on what has been copied (or not). 8) *Asclepius*, a version of chaps. 21–29 of a hermetic tract that also survives in Latin.

Codex VII contains: 1) *Paraphrase of Shem*, an apocalypse received by Shem, ancestor of the gnostic race, depicting the emergence of the watery material world of evil from three primeval powers, the polluted water baptism, Shem's heavenly ascent, and the end-time salvation. 2) *Second Treatise of the Great Seth*, containing a discourse by the exalted Christ on salvation in the heavenly church, an explanation of the Redeemer's incarnation, a docetic crucifixion account, and a litany mocking Jewish figures as "a laughingstock." 3) *Apocalypse of Peter* (no relation to the Ethiopic *Apocalypse of Peter*), in which the Savior reveals to Peter his inner spiritual reality that was not crucified and opposes orthodox claims to Petrine tradition and belief in salvation through Jesus' death. 4) The *Teachings of Silvanus*, a collection of early Christian wisdom teachings that summons the soul to master irrational passions and incorporates Alexandrian traditions. 5) The *Three Steles of Seth,* liturgical hymns addressed to each member of the divine Triad.

Codex VIII includes: 1) *Zostrianos*, an apocalypse describing the seer's ascent through and initiations in the multiple heavenly regions, known to students of Plotinus in the mid-3rd cent. (Porphyry, *Vit. Plot.* 16). 2) The *Letter of Peter to Philip* echoes the opening chapters of Acts, and the risen Jesus sends the Twelve to preach a gnostic gospel.

Codex IX contains: 1) *Melchizedek*, angelic revelations about the Savior that attack a docetic view of Jesus (5, 2–11). 2) *Thought of Norea*, a prayer or ode celebrating Norea's return to the Pleroma. 3) *Testimony of Truth*, an ascetic tract on truth that opposes Jewish traditions with a midrash on the serpent (Gen 3), martyrdom, physical resurrection, and other gnostic groups.

Codex X contains: 1) *Marsanes*, a poorly preserved heavenly journey, perhaps among the books known in Plotinus' circles.

Codex XI contains: 1) *Interpretation of Knowledge*, a tract on the gnostic interpretation of Jesus' teaching, passion, and letters of Paul that is unusual in its concern for unity in the church. 2) The *Valentinian Exposition*, a Valentinian account of creation and redemption followed by comments on the sacraments of anointing, baptism, and eucharist. 3) *Allogenes,* revelations of the seer's ascent through the divine realm to a revelation of the Unknowable One, known to Plotinus' students. 4) *Hypsiphrone*, fragmentary pages on the descent of a wisdom figure.

Codex XII contains: 1) The *Sentences of Sextus*, a Coptic version of a Greek wisdom book also known in Latin, Syriac, Armenian, and Georgian. 2) Fragments of the *Gospel of Truth.* 3) Another fragmentary tractate. Codex XIII includes: 1) The *Trimorphic Protennoia*, a tractate that gives the first-person speech of three manifestations of the divine Protennoia ("first thought") as Voice, Speech, and Word.

C. Importance for the Study of Christianity

1. Jesus traditions: sayings, passion, and resurrection

Jesus traditions found in the Nag Hammadi Library (NHL) are its best-known contribution to our understanding of early Christianity. Because the sayings and parables collected in the *Gospel of Thomas* include many that are variants of or comparable to those known from the Synoptic Gospels, new editions of the

Gospel parallels often include sayings from the *Gospel of Thomas.* Scholars have also sought to find antecedents from the unique discourses of the Johannine Jesus in such works as *Gospel of Truth*, *Dialogue of the Savior*, and *Trimorphic Protennoia* (Logos). Gnostic writings use mythological and symbolic language with little interest in historical details, so that the crucifixion accounts and resurrection stories in these works contain no new information. Rather, they exemplify a docetic separation between the heavenly redeemer and bodily reality or suffering (*see* DOCETISM). Resurrection appearances involve the teaching of a luminous, heavenly being, not Jesus' bodily transformation. For example, at the end of *Trimorphic Protennoia* the divine Revealer gathers up the crucified Jesus into the heavens.

2. Christology: divine beings identified with Jesus

Christology in the NHL presumes that redemption takes the form of one or more beings from the divine world above the creator god and his powers. These figures may represent the heavenly Human Being (Adamas) or an emanation of the "Son" of the Unknown Father and the male-female Barbelo or the ancestor of the enlightened race, Seth. The heavenly Christ is identified with one of these heavenly figures, sometimes speaking with the feminine voice of Pronoia ("providence") or Protennoia ("first thought").

3. Revelations by the risen Jesus

Revelations by the risen Jesus to one or more disciples are a popular scenario in the NHL. The resurrection stories familiar from the canonical Gospels restore the community of disciples and dispatch them to preach the gospel but contain no additional teaching. John admits that Jesus' disciples did not understand his words and deeds until after the resurrection (John 2:22). Luke infers that the risen Jesus must have conversed with his disciples about the kingdom (Acts 1:3). This gap in the record provided an opportunity for later authors to suggest that the risen Christ had given a hidden teaching to one or more disciples. Some of these revelations anticipate a secret chain of transmission and a temporal gap between the post-Easter period and the emergence of the enlightened race (*Apocryphon of James, (First) Apocalypse of James*). Others suggest that the gospel that the Twelve set out to preach was as conveyed in its teaching (*Apocryphon of John, Sophia of Jesus Christ, Letter of Peter to Philip*). Unlike the canonical resurrection stories, which underline the physical continuity between the crucified Jesus and the risen One, the NHL discourses identify the Revealer with a luminous divine being. In *Apocryphon of John* he is the "Son" of the highest divine Triad (*see* RESURRECTION, NT).

4. Disciples as authoritative teachers

Disciples as authoritative teachers have a familiar role in the NT. Paul must establish his authority as an APOSTLE like the Twelve, as well as James, the brother of the Lord (1 Cor 15:3-11). He claims that his gospel to non-Jews was accepted by the three "pillars" in Jerusalem: Peter, John, and James, the brother of the Lord (Gal 2:9). Paul points to his vision of the risen Lord and the fruitfulness of his ministry as evidence that he is an apostle. Luke restricts the designation of apostle to the Twelve, who had witnessed Jesus' ministry from John's baptism to the ascension (Acts 1:2-5, 20-26).

For many texts in the NHL a revelation from the risen Christ (so *Apocryphon of John, Apocryphon of James, Sophia of Jesus Christ*) or a vision given by the Savior prior to his return to the divine world (*(First) Apocalypse of James, Apocalypse of Peter*) is necessary to comprehend the meaning of Jesus' teaching. An author may claim the Twelve as a group (so *Sophia of Jesus Christ, Acts of Peter and the Twelve Apostles, Letter of Peter to Philip*) as one of the three "pillars" (*Apocalypse of Peter, Apocryphon of James, (First) Apocalypse of James, Apocryphon of John*) or Paul (*Apocalypse of Paul*) as the teacher of gnostic wisdom.

Other NHL texts appeal to figures named in the NT who were not as celebrated, sometimes suggesting a conflict between these figures and Peter or the Twelve. Jude Thomas and Mary Magdalene are most prominent (*Gospel of Thomas, Book of Thomas the Contender*). Another Coptic codex contains a *Gospel of Mary* that includes a scene of Peter and Andrew rejecting what Jesus had taught her (*Gos. Thom.* 114; *see* MARY, GOSPEL OF). The Coptic version concludes with all the apostles going to preach as Jesus commanded, much as *Sophia of Jesus Christ* has the twelve male and seven female disciples instructed to go out to preach. However, surviving fragments of the Greek version end with only Mary's defender, Levi, going out to preach. Therefore a move to claim that the Twelve and the women followers conveyed the same esoteric teaching may be a response by gnostic Christians to arguments against their reliance upon traditions alleged to have been transmitted by individual apostle visionaries.

5. God as transcendent, not creator

The NHL texts portray God as a transcendent, immutable, unfathomable divine being who could not have created the material world with its attendant evils. This God could not have allowed the alienation of human beings to be subject to the forces of the material world, the body, and its passions. Human beings could not be so mired in the material world and so unconscious of their inner divine nature unless some malicious lesser creator figure stepped in to drive them into ignorance and death. Several NHL texts incorporate extensive reflections on the complete disjunction between God and our conceptual categories (so *Apocryphon of John*, *Eugnostos the Blessed*, *Sophia of Jesus Christ* [based on *Eugnostos*?], *Tripartite Tractate*). Those which circulated among Plotinus' students in mid-3rd-cent. Rome incorporate the soul's ascent and transformation by vision of each level of the divine Triad/One (*Zostrianos*, *Allogenes*, *Three Steles of Seth*, *Marsanes* [?]). As a consequence of divine transcendence, the Wisdom incorporated in material creation is a fallen, disordered figure, who must herself be restored by a Savior from the heavenly aeons.

6. Revisiting the patristic view of gnostic heretics and sects

Revisiting the patristic view of gnostic heresies in light of the NHL began with attempts to match the titles of these works with those mentioned in patristic writings and to assign them to teachers or sects in the classifications found in the heresiologists. As scholars became more familiar with the range and diversity of materials in the NHL, they recognized that patristic categories did not fit the evidence. Some interpreters employ three broad categories to describe groups of related texts and broad lines of development: "Sethian" texts have closely related mythologies that reinterpret Genesis and see the heavenly Adam or Seth figure as Savior. "Valentinian" texts exhibit Christian theologoumena and "sacraments" broadly related to Valentinian theology found in patristic sources. Traditions associated with Jude Thomas may represent ascetics in Syria. Other scholars call for dismantling all of the earlier categories, even the category of gnosticism itself.

7. Emergence of the Christian canon

Studies of how the Christian canon was formed will be enriched by study of the use and implicit authority of biblical materials in the NHL. For example, the *Apocryphon of James* opens with a scene of the various disciples writing memoirs when the Savior appears and takes Peter and James, the Lord's brother, apart for a revelation that culminates in the Savior's ascension. Narrative elements in *Letter of Peter to Philip* invoke the opening chapters of Acts. Many other examples of intratextual allusions to the NT depend upon its public authority. The esoteric revelations in the NHL were not intended as an alternate Bible for the majority of Christians (*see* CANON OF THE NEW TESTAMENT).

D. Importance for the Study of Antiquity

1. Jewish traditions in myths of human origins

Jewish traditions of human origins have provoked considerable debate over whether or not the mythemes characteristic of gnostic accounts of origins (see *Apocryphon of John*, *Hypostasis of the Archons*, *On the Origin of the World*, *Apocalypse of Adam*) were dependent upon some form of 1st or early 2nd cent. Jewish esotericism. Some sections of these works that cite and then reinterpret OT texts have been described as MIDRASH (see *Hypostasis of the Archons* and *Testimony of Truth* 45, 23–48, 18). Thematic similarities can be found between gnostic mythemes and speculation in Jewish authors about such topics as the creator's angelic assistants (*Jub.* 3:4); the dual creation of Adam; the fallen angels who defiled human women (*1 En.* 6–16, "Book of the Watchers," or fail in attacking the spiritual Eve in gnostic sources); and envy as the motive for the devil (or "demiurge" or "creator" in NHL texts) introducing death into the world (Wis 2:24). Some Semitic wordplays are employed in naming the creator and his angelic offspring along with the Genesis wordplays on Adam and Eve. Therefore some scholars described gnostic interpretations of the OT as "protest exegesis" and even postulated its origins among Jews whose apocalyptic hopes had been crushed in the revolts of 70 and 132 CE. More recent scholarship has emphasized the diverse treatments of the OT among Christians in the 2nd cent. CE. Unlike Marcion's outright rejection of the OT, NHL authors employ myth and allegory to decode its true meaning (*see* MARCION, MARCIONISM). Their target is more likely to be Christians who revere the OT as Scripture.

2. Platonic philosophy in accounts of the divine world

Elements of Platonic philosophy figure in accounts of God as the One-Beyond-Being, the triadic character of the divine Father or Father-Mother dyad, and the emanation of the divine world of beings from the One to which they are bound in contemplation. However, the gap between the divine and the material world exacerbated by the number of divine emanations and the gnostic mythologizing of the Demiurge represents a major departure from Platonism, as Plotinus protested (*Enn.* 2.9). Scholars have detected philosophical motifs from other schools in the 2nd and 3rd cent. CE.: Stoic speculation concerning the rule of providence, astrological influences on parts of the human body and the passions, along with neo-Pythagorean and Aristotelian variants on the divine mind and human participation in the active intellect. For example, *On the Origin of the World* and *Eugnostos the Blessed* promise readers a revelation that will correct false philosophical views about the origins of the cosmos.

3. Hermetic writings

Hermetic writings found in Codex VI include a previously unknown tractate called *Discourse on the Eighth and Ninth* that is close to such previously known works as Corpus Hermeticum XIII and I, as well as a prayer of thanksgiving and a section from *Asclepius*, a longer work preserved in Latin. A scribal note inserted between the prayer and the *Asclepius* selection apologizes for copying a work that "you (pl.)" may already have and mentions other texts that the scribe assumes the addressees do have. To which items the scribe is referring in Codex VI is unclear. It does suggest that hermetic tracts circulated in collections in 4th-cent. Egypt.

E. Importance for the Study of Coptic

The mixture of Coptic terms and their Greek equivalents, as well as identification of Greek papyri fragments for a few of the texts in the NHL, demonstrates that the Coptic in question is a translation language (*see* COPTIC LANGUAGE). However, the variations in previously identified Coptic dialects in the NHL not only suggest that the translation of individual works occurred in different regions in Egypt, they also enable linguists to redraw the dialect maps of Egyptian in the 3rd and 4th cent. CE.

F. Relationship to Other Coptic Codices

Other Coptic codices containing gnostic texts, sometimes with other Christian apocrypha, were already known to scholars when the NHL was discovered. A codex housed in Berlin (BG 8502) included two treatises also found in the NHL (*Apocryphon of John*, in the shorter recension of Codex III rather than the longer one of Codices II and IV, and *Sophia of Jesus Christ*). The Berlin codex also includes another gnostic revelation dialogue, *Gospel of Mary*, which is closely related to the examples of the genre found in the NHL. Its final text is a selection from an apocryphal *Act of Peter* (*see* BERLIN GNOSTIC, CODEX). In 2006, the National Geographic Society announced the existence of a badly decayed codex that contained a previously unknown gnostic revelation dialogue, the *Gospel of Judas*, along with versions of two treatises known from NHL, *Acts of Peter and the Twelve Apostles* and *(First) Apocalypse of James*, as well as a fourth work that makes some reference to "Allogenes" but is not apparently a version of the NHL text by that name (*see* JUDAS, GOSPEL OF). The best-preserved of its treatises, *(First) Apocalypse of James* (which only has the title "James" in the new codex), provides restoration for some fragmentary pages in the NHL version. It appears to be a separate Coptic translation of the original Greek text. Pending detailed studies of the Coptic texts, the significance of this codex to study of the NHL cannot be determined.

Bibliography: W. Barnstone and M. Meyer. *The Gnostic Bible* (2003); A. D. DeConick. *The Original Gospel of Thomas in Translation* (2006); M. Franzmann. *Jesus in the Nag Hammadi Writings* (1996); R. Kasser, M. Meyer, and F. Gaudard. *The Gospel of Judas.* Critical Edition (2007); K. King. *The Gospel of Mary of Magdala* (2003); K. King. *The Secret Revelation of John* (2006); B. Layton. *The Gnostic Scriptures* (1987); G. P. Luttikhuizen. *Gnostic Revisions of Genesis Stories and Early Jesus Traditions* (2006); M. Meyer and J. M. Robinson, eds. *The Nag Hammadi Scriptures.* International Edition (2007); P. Perkins. *The Gnostic Dialogue* (1980); P. Perkins. *Gnosticism and the New Testament* (1993); Z. Pleše. *Poetics of the Gnostic Universe: Narrative and Cosmology in the Apocryphon of John* (2006); K. Rudolph. *Gnosis* (1983); D. M. Scholer. *Nag Hammadi Bibliography 1948–1969* (1970); D. M. Scholer. *Nag Hammadi Bibliography 1970–1994* (1997); G. A. G. Stroumsa. *Another Seed: Studies in Gnostic Mythology* (1984); E. Thomassen. *The Spiritual Seed: The Church of the 'Valentinians'* (2006); J. D. Turner. *Sethian Gnosticism and the Platonic Tradition* (2001); J. D. Turner and A. M. McGuire, eds. *The Nag Hammadi Library after Fifty Years* (1997); M. A. Williams. *Rethinking "Gnosticism"* (1996).

PHEME PERKINS

NAG HAMMADI, ARCHAEOLOGY nahg'huh-mah'dee. Since the early part of the 19th cent., explorers, archaeologists, and Egyptologists have shown interest in the area around the Upper Egyptian city of Nag Hammadi, on account of the ancient remains to be found in the region. In more recent years, since the discovery of the Nag Hammadi library, the focus of archaeological attention has been on sites near the Jabal al-Tarif and the modern village of Faw Qibli.

A. Early Surveys and Excavations

From the first half of the 19th cent., explorers and scholars have noted the tombs and ancient sites around Nag Hammadi. John G. Wilkinson viewed, Richard Lepsius inspected, and Pierre Montet (along with others) published the rock tombs in the face of the Jabal al-Tarif dating from the Sixth Dynasty of the Old Kingdom. These tombs, the largest of which is the tomb of Thauti, contain pharaonic reliefs and hieroglyphic inscriptions. W. M. Flinders Petrie excavated the Roman temple in the ancient city of Hu (Diospolis Parva) and the cemeteries nearby. Émile C. Amélineau and Louis Théophile Lefort conducted topographical surveys in the Nag Hammadi region. Lefort highlighted the evidence for monasteries founded by Pachomius (ca. 292–346 CE), who is usually considered the father of cenobitic Christian monasticism (a form of monasticism based on community living characterized by worship, discipline, and hard work), and these sites (e.g., Tabennese, Pbow, Seneset) are among the earliest of his monastic establishments. The monastery at Pbow (or Pabau, modern Faw Qibli) is particularly noteworthy in the history of Pachomian monasticism, since this monastery functioned as the administrative center of the Pachomian monastic order. In the 1950s Fernand

Debono organized a preliminary excavation of the Pachomian monastery and basilica, with limited results. It was after the discovery of the Nag Hammadi library that archaeological interest in the area in the vicinity of the Jabal al-Tarif and the Pachomian monastery at Pbow began to increase.

B. The Discovery of the Nag Hammadi Library and the Dishna Papers

Around the end of 1945 the Nag Hammadi library was discovered near the base of the Jabal al-Tarif. Different stories emerged as descriptions of how and where the discovery may have taken place (*see* NAG HAMMADI TEXTS). Within five years of the discovery, Jean Doresse attempted to find out where the texts in question had been found, and he interviewed people from the area about the discovery. He was guided to the southern portion of a cemetery—apparently a pagan cemetery—near the Jabal al-Tarif, and it was suggested that the discovery took place there, where the ground had been disturbed and where pieces of bone, fragments of cloth, and potsherds had accumulated. Claiming that those who took him there were unaware of the true purpose of his visit, Doresse has indicated he was told that peasants from Hamra Dum and Dabba, two villages in the area, had been looking for manure and happened upon a jar filled with papyrus sheets bound into books (that is, the Nag Hammadi codices). The jar was broken and lost, and the codices were taken to Cairo. There was, Doresse has reported, no consensus about exactly where the findspot was, but it was said to be somewhere in that area.

Beginning in the early 1970s, James M. Robinson began his own investigation of the circumstances surrounding the discovery of the Nag Hammadi library. He sought out a large number of people who seemed to be connected to the discovery, interviewed them at length, and judged that Doresse's account was inaccurate. According to the story Robinson has put together, the Nag Hammadi library was discovered around December 1945 by Muhammad Ali of the al-Samman clan. As Muhammad Ali, a resident of al-Qasr, has communicated his story to Robinson, several Egyptian *fellahin* (peasant farmers), including Muhammad Ali himself, were riding their camels near the Jabal al-Tarif. (He said he recalled the date of this trip because he associated it with an act of blood vengeance that occurred around then.) Muhammad Ali said that he and the others hobbled their camels at the foot of the Jabal al-Tarif and dug around a large boulder on the talus (the slope of debris) that had formed against the face of the cliff. They were gathering a natural fertilizer (**sabakh**), and to their surprise they uncovered a large storage jar with a bowl sealed on the mouth of the jar as a lid. When Muhammad Ali smashed the jar with his mattock, he said, he caught sight of the codices of the Nag Hammadi library that had been placed within the jar. The rest of the story assembled by Robinson addresses the roles of middlemen and scholars in the disposition of the Nag Hammadi collection, which now is in the possession of the Coptic Museum in Old Cairo, Egypt.

Robinson has also explored what can be recovered of the story of the discovery of the Dishna papers (usually referred to as the BODMER PAPYRI) near the modern city of Dishna, not far from Nag Hammadi and even closer to Faw Qibli. According to the story pieced together by Robinson, the Dishna papers were found in late 1952 near the Jabal Abu Mana, off the Dishna plain. This account is somewhat reminiscent of the story of the Nag Hammadi discovery: two men from the area, Hasan Muhammad al-Samman and Muhammad Khalil al-Azzuzi, were collecting fertilizer a short distance from the base of the Jabal Abu Mana when Hasan located a storage jar, broke it open, and found the texts of the Dishna papers inside. Robinson reports that apparently some of the papers were burned and some given away, but most of the texts eventually were acquired by the Chester Beatty Library, the Bibliothèque Bodmer, and other repositories. The Dishna papers contain, among other texts, biblical manuscripts and letters from officials in the Pachomian monastic order, and Robinson has proposed that the texts may represent the archives of the Pachomian monastic library at Pbow.

C. Archaeology at the Jabal al-Tarif

Following the publication of Doresse's story of the discovery of the Nag Hammadi library, archaeological work was initiated under the sponsorship of the Institute for Antiquity and Christianity of Claremont Graduate University. The excavations were organized by James M. Robinson; the field directors for the early stages of the work were Torgny Säve-Söderbergh and Bastiaan Van Elderen, and Labib Habachi functioned as a consultant. During the first season, in 1975, archaeological work was undertaken around the Jabal al-Tarif. A proton magnetometer survey, under the supervision of Philip Hammond, was accomplished, and trial trenches were laid out in order to test Doresse's claim that a cemetery near the base of the Jabal al-Tarif was the findspot for the Nag Hammadi material, but the tests and trenches did not clearly disclose any such cemetery. Six of the tombs and caves in the face of the Jabal al-Tarif were excavated, and previously unpublished reliefs and hieroglyphs in the tomb of Thauti (T 73) were uncovered. The walls of another cave, now often termed the "Psalms Cave" (T 8), were found to include the opening lines of Ps 51–93 painted in the red paint typical of monastic use. A few artifacts were unearthed, including coins and an inscribed clasp of a bronze necklace from the Egyptian Sixth Dynasty (*see* EGYPT).

D. Archaeology at Faw Qibli

In part because of the suggestion that there may have been a link between the Nag Hammadi library and the Pachomian monastery at Pbow (the cartonnage, or scrap papyrus, lining the covers of the Nag Hammadi codices contains names suggesting monks and locales around Pbow), the second and following seasons of archaeological work sponsored by the Institute for Antiquity and Christianity (1976, 1977–78, 1979–80) turned to the ruins of the Pachomian monastery and basilica at Pbow. Peter Grossmann of the German Archaeological Institute, who was a member of the staff during the first seasons, assumed oversight of the archaeological and architectural investigation of the site during the 1980s (1986, 1989). Grossmann, together with Gary Lease, concluded that the archaeological evidence pointed to three successive churches built at this Pachomian center. Each church had five aisles, with a central nave and two aisles on each side, and each church was larger than the preceding one. The outer aisles and return aisles assumed the form of an ambulatory around the church. The increase in the size of the subsequent constructions, it has been theorized, probably was due to the growth of the Christian population in the region and the success of the Pachomian monastic order. The first and earliest of the churches (about 40 m in length) was most likely built during the lifetime of Pachomius (ca. 330–46); the second church (about 56 m in length) was constructed somewhat later (no earlier than the late 4th cent.); the third and final church at the site (about 78 m in length) may have been the great Pachomian basilica, apparently brought to completion in 459). A text identified as a sermon of Timothy II of Alexandria (said to have been delivered on the occasion of the dedication of the great basilica at Pbow) mentions that date. The great basilica must have gradually lost its importance and was seemingly abandoned, and while tradition has suggested that al-Hakim may have destroyed the church in the 11th cent., Grossmann guesses that if there is any truth to this tradition, al-Hakim may have done little more than plunder a building already in disrepair.

The Pachomian archaeological site at Faw Qibli is replete with the remains of the limestone foundation blocks, granite columns, and brick rubble of churches that were brick structures supported by reused stone pieces. More granite pieces, such as an olive press, were found scattered around the site, sometimes with hieroglyphs and artistic markings (for instance, stylized stars) indicating that the stone was recycled from an older building in the area, probably an Egyptian temple.

In the course of the excavation of the monastery and basilica at Faw Qibli, heavy equipment engaged in digging a canal in the cultivated fields around the village broke through a buried stone installation and brought up, unceremoniously and unscientifically, the remains of some sort of stone structure, apparently dating from the Roman period. The area around the excavation site in general merits further archaeological examination, though the modern village of Faw Qibli increasingly covers much of the area.

E. Surveys of al-Qasr and the Wadi Shaykh Ali

In late 1980, two surveys of nearby sites with possible monastic connections were carried out by participants in the excavations. The first, an archaeological survey of al-Qasr (ancient Seneset or Chenoboskia), consisted of a close visual inspection of the place where, according to Pachomian sources, Pachomius was converted to Christianity, learned the anchoritic life with Palamon, and thereafter founded the third monastery in his cenobitic monastic movement. Ample indications of early occupation of the site were noted, including portions of millstones, oil presses, mortars, a small marble column, door sockets, and a block of marble with a Greek Hadrianic inscription (previously published). The other survey led up the Wadi Shaykh Ali, a ravine that runs off the Dishna Plain. The team had been alerted to archaeological evidence in the Wadi Shaykh Ali, and the survey disclosed an unfinished obelisk, hieroglyphs (among them a cartouche of Pharaoh Menkaure) incised on an overhanging rock, and numerous Coptic Christian graffiti, most painted onto the rock in the red paint used by the monks of the region (*see* COPTIC LANGUAGE). Bricks observed at the site may provide hints that this spot was used for some monastic purpose, perhaps burial, and potsherds noted in passing may call to mind the sort of pottery found throughout the region, including pottery associated with the Pachomian monastic center at Pbow and the bowl Robinson acquired at al-Qasr that seems to have been used as the lid of the jar within which the Nag Hammadi library was buried. At this point, however, no confirmation for a direct connection between the Nag Hammadi library and the Pachomian monastery at Pbow can be made on the basis of the pottery or the other archaeological evidence. *See* ARCHAEOLOGY.

Bibliography: Émile C. Amélineau. *La géographie de l'Égypte à l'époque copte* (1893); H. Keith Beebe and Marvin Meyer. "Literary and Archaeological Survey of al-Qasr." *American Research Center in Egypt Newsletter* 121 (1983) 25–31; *Biblical Archeologist* 42, no. 4 (1979); Fernand Debono. "La basilique et le monastère de St. Pachôme." *Bulletin de l'Institut français d'archéologie orientale* 70 (1971) 191–220; Jean Doresse. *The Discovery of the Nag Hammadi Texts* (2005); James E. Goehring. "An Early Roman Bowl from the Monastery of Pachomius at Pbow and the Milieu of the Nag Hammadi Codices." *Coptica–Gnostica–Manichaica: Mélanges offerts à Wolf-Peter Funk.* Louis Painchaud and Paul-Hubert Poirier, eds. (2006) 357–71; Peter Grossmann. *Christliche Architektur in Ägypten* (2001); Peter Grossmann and Gary Lease. "Faw Qibli–1989 Excavation Report (= Sixth Season)." *Göttinger Miszellen* 114 (1990) 9–16; Gary Lease. *Traces of Early Egyptian Monasticism: The Faw Qibli Excavations* (1991); Richard Lepsius.

Denkmäler aus Aegypten und Aethiopien (1904); Marvin Meyer. "Archaeological Survey of the Wadi Sheikh Ali: December 1980." *Göttinger Miszellen* 64 (1983) 77–82; Marvin Meyer. *The Gnostic Discoveries* (2005); Pierre Montet. "Les tombeaux dits de Kasr el-Sayad." *Kemi* 6 (1936) 81–129; W. M. Flinders Petrie. *Diospolis Parva, the Cemeteries of Abadiyeh and Hu, 1898–99* (1901); James M. Robinson. "From the Cliff to Cairo: The Story of the Discoverers and Middlemen of the Nag Hammadi Codices." *Colloque international sur les textes de Nag Hammadi (Québec, 22–25 août 1978)*. Bernard Barc, ed. (1981) 21–58; James M. Robinson. "The Jung Codex: The Rise and Fall of a Monopoly." *RelSRev* 3 (1977) 17–30; James M. Robinson. *The Pachomian Monastic Library at the Chester Beatty Library and the Bibliothèque Bodmer* (1990); Torgny Säve-Söderbergh. *The Old Kingdom Cemetery at Hamra Dom (El-Qasr wa es-Saiyad)* (1994) John G. Wilkinson. *Modern Egypt and Thebes, Being a Description of Egypt* (1843).

MARVIN MEYER

NAGGAI nag'*i* [Ναγγαί **Naggai**]. Appears only in Luke's genealogy of Jesus as the father of Esli and the son of Maath (Luke 3:25-26).

NAHALAL, NAHALOL nay'huh-lal, nay'huh-lol [נַהֲלָל **nahalal**, נַהֲלֹל **nahalol**]. Nahalal (or Nahalol, Judg 1:30) was a Levitical town within the tribal allotment of Zebulun in the northwestern portion of the Jezreel Valley (Josh 19:15; 21:35). Currently, Moshav Nahalal retains the ancient toponym, which can be traced back to biblical Nahalal through Arabic Maʿlul and rabbinic Mahalul. Adjacent Tell el-Beida, which has yielded Iron Age remains, is a strong candidate for the ancient town. Alternatively, Tell en-Nahl, also an Iron Age site, has been equated with Nahalal, but it is situated outside of Zebulun's traditional territory. *See* ZEBULUN, ZEBULUNITE.

JASON R. TATLOCK

NAHALIEL nuh-hay'lee-uhl [נַחֲלִיאֵל **nakhaliʾel**]. A town between Mattanah and Bamoth on the exodus itinerary north of the Arnon River (Num 21:18-19). It was one of the last places passed by the Israelites before they arrived at the Plains of Moab. The name means "stream of God," suggesting it should be identified with one of the wadis in the area.

KEVIN A. WILSON

NAHAM nay'ham [נַחַם **nakham**]. Naham, Means "comfort." Naham was the leader of a tribe, HODIAH's brother, and Ezrah's brother-in-law (1 Chr 4:17-19).

NAHAMANI nay'huh-may'n*i* [נַחֲמָנִי **nakhamani**]. Means "compassionate." Nahamani is listed among the prominent Jewish leaders who returned from exile in Babylon with ZERUBBABEL, according to Neh 7:7. While a similar list of returned exiles in Ezra 2 does not contain the name, 1 Esd 5:8, another par. text, substitutes the name Eneneus (**Enēnios** Ενήνιος).

JOEL MARCUS LEMON

NAHARAI nay'huh-r*i* [נַחְרַי **nakhray**]. Naharai of BEEROTH was one of the Thirty, the main body of DAVID'S CHAMPIONS. He served as Joab's armor-bearer (2 Sam 23:37; 1 Chr 11:39).

NAHARIYEH. A village on the Mediterranean coast, at the entrance of the River Gaathon, occupied since the Middle Bronze Age. A temple, open-air court, and high place have been excavated. Female figurines, including a stone mold of a nude female figure, all found in association with the cultic structures, were likely used for the worship of ASHERAH of the Sea, the principle goddess of Ugarit. Tel Nahariyeh has been identified with MAHALAB (Josh 19:29) in the territory of Asher, or with HELBAH, included in a list of cities that Asher failed to conquer (Judg 1:31). See UGARIT, HISTORY AND ARCHAEOLOGY.

RALPH K. HAWKINS

NAHASH nay'hash [נָחָשׁ **nakhash**]. 1. Nahash was an Ammonite ruler involved in a struggle with the Israelites under the fledgling leadership of Saul (1 Sam 11:1-13; 12:12), which seems to have influenced Israel's desire to have a king (1 Sam 12:1-25), although in 1 Sam 11:15 Saul is already designated king. The chronology of the struggles with the Ammonites and Saul's public coronation as king is thus difficult to untangle (*see* AMMON, AMMONITES).

Two sons of Nahash are mentioned: HANUN succeeded his father on the throne during David's reign (2 Sam 10:1-2//1 Chr 19:1-2), and SHOBI assisted David's flight from Jerusalem during Absalom's coup (2 Sam 17:27). If a single Nahash ruled in Ammon from the beginning of Saul's reign in Israel until some time in David's reign, the period of rule was likely several decades, prompting some scholars to wonder whether Nahash was the name of both father and son Ammonite rulers.

The earliest Hebrew manuscript of Samuel (4Q51), found among the DEAD SEA SCROLLS, contains several lines about Nahash's oppression in Transjordan, partially preserved in Josephus (*Ant.* 6.68–72), that are not in the MT. The NRSV includes this textual tradition at the end of 1 Sam 10:27 to set the stage for the report in 11:1 that Nahash had come to Jabesh-gilead to besiege it.

2. A Nahash is mentioned as the father of Abigail in 2 Sam 17:25. Some connect this Nahash to the king of Ammon, but the relationship, if any, is unknown. If the Ammonite king is intended by this reference, then the reference may indicate a link between David's family and the Ammonite royal line. Abigail is also the name of David's sister according to 2 Chr 2:16.

Bibliography: F. M. Cross. "The Ammonite Oppression of the Tribes of Gad and Reuben: Missing Verses from 1 Samuel 11 Found in 4QSam." *History, Historiography and Interpretation: Studies in Biblical and Cuneiform Literatures.* H. Tadmor and M. Weinfeld, eds. (1983) 148–58.

J. ANDREW DEARMAN

NAHATH nay'hath [נַחַת nakhath]. 1. One of four sons born to REUEL, the son of Esau and Basemath. Each of these brothers is identified as the leader of an Edomite clan (Gen 36:13, 17; 1 Chr 1:37).

2. The son of ELKANAH from the priestly line descending from Levi's son Kohath (1 Chr 6:26 [Heb. 6:11]).

3. One of several priestly administrators who supervised the collection and storage of the many generous offerings provided by the Israelites in the wake of the spiritual revival that characterized Judah during the days of Hezekiah (2 Chr 31:13).

JASON R. TATLOCK

NAHBI nah'b*i* [נַחְבִּי nakhbi]. Nahbi, son of Vophsi, from the tribe of Naphtali, was one of the twelve SPIES sent by Joshua from the wilderness of PARAN into Canaan (Num 13:14).

NAHOR nay'hor [נָחוֹר nahor; Ναχώρ Nachōr]. 1. Genesis 11:22-25 places Nahor in the line of Shem as the seventh generation from Noah and identifies Nahor as the grandfather of Abram/Abraham. This Nahor, said to have died in Ur, is the Nahor in the genealogy of Jesus according to Luke (3:34). Nahor is identified as the son of SERUG and the father of TERAH, in turn the father of Abram and his younger brothers, Nahor and Haran.

2. The younger brother of Abram according to Gen 11:26. Nahor, who like Jacob had twelve sons (Gen 22:20-24), is identified in Gen 24 as the grandfather of LABAN and REBEKAH, who are subsequently in the area of HARAN (Gen 28).

3. The name Nahor reflects the city of Nah(h)ur, well documented in the Mari and later 2nd millennium BCE texts, located in the upper reaches of the Habur River. Til-Nahiri, a less compelling parallel, is attested in the time of Assurbanipal. It may well be in the west but cannot be securely located. Along with several other ancestors in the Genesis genealogies, the name Nahor is tied to places and individuals.

The biblical tradition describes a family group led by Terah, including Abram and his wife Sarai as well as Haran's son Lot who departed from Ur of the Chaldeans in southern Mesopotamia and journeyed to the city of Haran (Harran). The two cities were linked through trade and the shared cult of the moon god Sin. Joshua 24:2 describes Terah and his sons Abraham and Nahor as having worshiped other gods (compare Gen 31:53, "May the gods of Abraham and the gods of Nahor judge between us" [author's trans.; NRSV "the God of Abraham and the God of Nahor"]). Other personal names Haran, Serug, and Terah also reflect place names of the region. These various ancestors are linked with city names that do not neatly fit with their traditional places of birth or residence. Instead, these names are linked with places that represent a 2nd-millennium domain (Nahor and Haran) or, in the case of Serug and Terah, with city names from an Aramean region in north Syria attested at least by the 10th–9th cent. BCE. Haran is known from both periods.

All of these locations are consistent with the tradition in Deut 26:5 identifying the ancestors—"my father" (author's trans.; NRSV, "my ancestor")—as "a wandering/fugitive Aramean (ʾarammi ʾovedh ʾavi אֲרַמִּי אֹבֵד אָבִי)," i.e., Nahor and several other of the names of the ancestors of Israel reflect identification with the area in north Syria and south-central Turkey that was an Amorite area in the early 2nd millennium and an Aramean area by the early 1st millennium. It is this same area that is cited in the Genesis narratives as ARAM-NAHARAIM, to which Abraham dispatched his servant to find a wife for his son Isaac (Gen 24), and as PADDAN-ARAM (Gen 28; associated with Harran), the area where Jacob took refuge with the family of Laban, grandson of the younger Nahor, whose namesake city was some 200 km distant. The traditions are not seeking to present a complete or consistent history. They indicate the mobility of those involved in Israel's prehistory and their readiness to leave behind great urban centers in search of something else, and they affirm connections with the Amorite–Aramean areas of north Syria and south-central Turkey.

Bibliography: A. Kirk Grayson. *Assyrian Rulers of the Early First Millennium BC, II (858–745 BC)* (1996); Theodore Kwasman and Simo Parpola. *Legal Transactions of the Royal Court of Nineveh, Part I: Tiglath-Pileser III through Esarhaddon* (1991); Edward Lipinski. *The Aramaeans: Their Ancient History, Culture, Religion* (2000); Simo Parpola and Michael Porter, eds. *The Helsinki Atlas of the Near East in the Neo-Assyrian Period* (2001).

HERBERT B. HUFFMON

NAHSHON nah'shon [נַחְשׁוֹן nakhshon; Ναασσών Naassōn]. The brother of Aaron's wife, Elisheba (Exod 6:23), and chief of the tribe of Judah when the Israelites where wandering in the wilderness. Nahshon participated in taking the census (Num 1:7) and presenting offerings at the altar dedication (Num 7:12, 17). Nahshon appears in the genealogies of Moses and Aaron (Exod 6:14-25), David (Ruth 4:18-22; 1 Chr 2:3-17), and Jesus (Matt 1:4; Luke 3:32). *See* JUDAH, JUDAHITES.

RALPH K. HAWKINS

NAHUM nay'huhm [נַחוּם nakhum; Ναούμ Naoum]. 1. Prophesied NINEVEH's destruction (Nah 1:1; Tob 14:4; 2 Esd 1:40).

2. Ancestor of Jesus (Luke 3:25). *See* NAHUM, BOOK OF.

NAHUM PESHER nay'huhm pesh'uhr. This 1st cent. BCE scroll (4Q169) employs "continuous pesher" exegesis, a method employed in other Qumran texts. The book of Nahum is interpreted as a prophecy of judgment against the community's enemies. References to several known historical figures contribute information about the sect's history. *See* DEAD SEA SCROLLS; NAHUM, BOOK OF; PESHARIM.

DAVID M. MILLER

NAHUM, BOOK OF nay'huhm [נַחוּם nakhum; Ναούμ Naoum]. Nahum is the seventh book of the Twelve Minor Prophets (*see* BOOK OF THE TWELVE). It is solely devoted to a series of oracles against NINEVEH, the capital of the Assyrian Empire.

A. Organization of the Book
B. History of Composition
C. Genre and Literary Style
D. Theological and Religious Significance
Bibliography

A. Organization of the Book

1:1 Superscription
1:2-14 The Cosmic Divine Warrior Marches against Evil
1:15–2:13 [Heb. 2:1-14] The Divine Warrior's March on Nineveh
3:1-19 The Divine Warrior's Humiliation of Nineveh

The body of the book comprises three Divine Warrior images, each culminating in the taunt of the Assyrian king. The first begins with a theophany, in which Yahweh shakes mountains, rivers, and the sea before turning against "you" in 1:14, a male figure whose grave is made worthless. In 2:1, Yahweh is described as a "scatterer" (so MT; NRSV, "shatterer"; compare 2 Sam 22:15) who leads the divine armies against Nineveh. He also clashes with another masculine figure (2:5), who may be the king of Assyria, taunted as the impotent lion and as "you" at the close of the chapter. In chap. 3, Yahweh is disturbingly like other warriors in establishing power over the king by assaulting a female under his charge: Nineveh, personified as a woman (3:4-7). Nahum 3:18 explicitly names the male antagonist of the book as Assyria's king. Like the book of Jonah (*see* JONAH, BOOK OF), Nahum ends with a rhetorical question, even though the end of Jonah provokes pity on Assyrians while Nahum ends with taunt and humiliation.

B. History of Composition

The book is usually dated to a period between the fall of Thebes to the Assyrians in 663 BCE (3:8) and the actual fall of Nineveh to a coalition of the Babylonians and Medes in 612 BCE. While some have attempted to identify parallels between the book and other ancient accounts of Nineveh's destruction, dating is more usually based on claims that the sentiments of the book best fit a period in which hatred of the Assyrians was at its peak. If the book is seen as prophecy in a predictive sense, then it must predate 612.

Given the absence of solid historical anchors, however, Nahum, along with rest of the prophetic books, may have been written or substantially edited during the Babylonian exile to serve as an explanation of Yahweh's activity in history. From an exilic vantage point, one in which the fall of Nineveh was known to have occurred in the past, this book would have underscored that the fall of the Assyrians was Yahweh's doing, a just punishment for their brutality. Some have posited an even later, Persian period date for the final form of the book.

Since the late 19th cent., most commentators have discerned within 1:2-9 an incomplete alphabetic acrostic, believed to have been redacted into the book to widen its scope. In such an interpretation, the acrostic is an earlier independent composition, perhaps originating in a liturgical setting. Recent scholarship has challenged the presence of the acrostic, pointing to the number of emendations required to make the poem follow even the first half of the Hebrew alphabet. Proponents of the independent origin of the Divine Warrior hymn also fail to appreciate adequately the continuity between its Divine Warrior imagery and the rest of the book.

Neither the book itself nor other literature (biblical or extrabiblical) offers historical information about the prophet Nahum. Speculation about the location of ELKOSH (1:1) derives solely from inferences in the book. In light of the dearth of historical information and given the book's highly crafted style, it is usually considered an anonymous literary composition rather than the report of a particular prophet's words.

C. Genre and Literary Style

The superscription designates Nahum as an "oracle," a "vision," and a "book." The Hebrew for "oracle" is massa' (מַשָּׂא), also translated as "burden" in Jer 23:33-40. The label may be a genre marker, since it also heads prophetic collections that begin at Hab 1:1; Zech 9:1; 12:1; Mal 1:1; and oracles against foreign nations in Isa 13–23.

Each of these collections draws a clear distinction between the righteous and the wicked, and all pit the nations against Yahweh's people (although Malachi is also interested in dichotomies within the community itself). In Hab 3 and Zech 9, as in Nahum, a theophany inaugurates the people's salvation.

Based on its content, Nahum also is often designated as one of the "ORACLEs against the NATIONS," along with Obadiah, Isa 13–23, Jer 46–51, Ezek 25–32, and

Amos 1:3–2:3. Some have posited that the oracles against the nations were used in rituals related to warfare, perhaps accompanied by symbolic acts intended to actualize the predictions, but the texts offer no criteria by which to distinguish between pieces actually used as liturgies and literary imitations of earlier forms.

Nahum's vocabulary and theme link it to other biblical and extrabiblical materials that recount the acts of the Divine Warrior (e.g., Ps 68; Isa 63; Hab 3; Jdt 5). Study of this extensive literature underscores that Divine Warrior language can serve different rhetorical and political functions; it can establish creation myths, support monarchy, and/or challenge existing political structures (*see* WARRIOR, DIVINE). In Nahum, Divine Warrior language establishes Yahweh's superiority over a seemingly invincible human power, and perhaps over all human powers. When read in retrospect after the fall of Nineveh, Nahum also functions as a THEODICY. It explains the question implied by Hosea, Amos, and Micah: how could a righteous deity use unrighteous Assyrians to punish Israel?

The highly crafted literary style of the book has attracted much attention. The author employs a vast array of techniques, such as assonance, alliteration, repetition, simile, metaphor, and irony. The echoed shouts of soldiers in 2:9, the imagery of bodily responses to terror in 2:10, the rapid-fire snapshots of rearing horses and mass carnage in 3:3—all serve, like modern combat films, to recreate in the reader the confusion and terror of warfare. The personification of Nineveh in 3:4-7 as a whore draws from the common prophetic description of cities as women, wrongdoing as whoredom, and sexual assault as justifiable punishment, but in Nahum the imagery is especially brutal and is intensified by the taunts that follow.

D. Theological and Religious Significance

For its celebration of the bloody success of the Divine Warrior over the king of Assyria, piles of anonymous dead, and Woman Nineveh, Nahum has been accused of misogyny, nationalism, vengeance, and the promotion of violence. Indeed, few books have been castigated more for their violence. The literary craft that makes the book so vivid and striking also makes it graphic, disturbing, and problematic.

Those who find positive value in the book highlight what Nineveh/Assyria signified in the ancient world. The Neo-Assyrians were the dominant superpower and infamous for their cruelty, self-advertised in their palace reliefs and official documents. Read against such a background, Nahum's insistence that Yahweh is stronger than even this superpower would underscore Yahweh's justice and care for the oppressed. Rather than calling people to arms, Nahum would liberate the enslaved imagination, making it possible to believe in God's sovereignty despite all evidence to the contrary. If indeed the book was written after the fall of Nineveh, it serves like other prophetic books to underscore that God is ultimately in charge of history: the fall of Assyria does not illustrate the power of the Babylonians and Medes, who receive credit for its destruction, but rather the might of the Divine Warrior who fights alone. In this way, Nahum would serve to bolster Zechariah's attempts to assure the postexilic community that Yahweh will punish the nations and restore Jerusalem (Zech 1; 2; 8), based on how Yahweh worked in the past.

Feminist interpreters point out the danger in the description of Woman Nineveh's assault in Nah 3. Like the comparison of God's punishment of Israel with a man's punishment of his wife in Hos 2, Nahum's metaphor not only reflects the reality of women's vulnerability in war but also, by showing sexual assault as justifiable punishment carried out by the deity himself, reinforces these human ideologies and the behaviors that follow from them. Can Nahum be a partner in the call for justice if its imagery is permeated with sexism and glee over the enemy's death and humiliation? *See* PROPHET, PROPHECY.

Bibliography: Julia Myers O'Brien. *Nahum.* Readings (2002); Judith Sanderson. "Nahum." *Women's Bible Commentary.* Carol A. Newsom and Sharon H. Ringe, eds. (1992) 217–21; W. Wessels. "Nahum, an Uneasy Expression of Yahweh's Power." *OTE* 11 (1998) 615–28.

JULIA M. O'BRIEN

NAIDUS nīʹduhs [Ναϊδος Naidos]. One of those who gave up foreign wives in Ezra's reform (1 Esd 9:31).

NAIL [מַסְמֵר masmer; ἧλος hēlos]. The absence of any mention in the biblical narrative of the use of nails in the construction of private houses, furniture, and other wood items suggests that this was rare in antiquity. Based on Egyptian evidence as well as accounts related to ship building, it is more likely that holes were drilled into the wood with a bow drill and then filled with wooden pegs pounded into place with a MALLET. The Roman invention of the augur would have made this task more efficient.

In those few instances in which iron nails are mentioned in the construction process, the context is the decoration of the Jerusalem Temple (1 Chr 22:3; 2 Chr 3:9), often relating to the extravagance of affixing gold foil or plates to the inner walls of the Temple. Fifty shekels of gold were then used to overlay the heads of these small iron nails (perhaps the size of tacks). Both Jeremiah and Second Isaiah refer to the fashioning of idols using iron nails or clasps to fasten them together (Isa 41:7; Jer 10:4). To deal with the demands of heavier tasks the Romans invented forged iron nails and the claw HAMMER to remove them. Long iron nails (7.5 in. in one recovered example) would have been used and probably reused when possible for CRUCIFIXION (John 20:25; compare Col 2:14). Arms were nailed above the wrist, the legs bent, and a nail driven through the heel bones to pin the lower torso to the cross. *See* TOOLS.

VICTOR H. MATTHEWS

NAIN nayn [Ναΐν Nain]. The site of Nain is mentioned only in Luke 7:11 as the place where Jesus raised a young man, a son of a widow, from the dead. In Luke's narrative, the travel itinerary has Jesus and his followers approaching Nain from Capernaum (7:1), approximately 20 mi. by road to the northeast. The story of the raising of the widow's son is part of a series of miracle stories in Luke that foreshadow the statement to John the Baptist's disciples that Jesus is the one who was expected because he had performed many signs, including raising the dead (7:22). Most commentators understand the story to have been part of Luke's special material due to several non-Lukan elements in the story, including the reference to Nain. The story is also considered part of a pre-Lukan or Lukan interest in comparing Jesus to Elijah and Elisha, thus many commentators have seen parallels with the resurrection stories in 1 Kgs 17 and 2 Kgs 4.

A reference in the story to a gate (7:12) implies that this was a walled city. The ancient site of Nain is thought to be located at the modern town of Nein in southern Galilee. Nein sits on the northern side of the Jebel Dahi ("Hill of Moreh") facing the Jezreel Plain, northeast of the modern city of Afula and south of Mount Tabor. Recent archaeology around the modern town of Nein has revealed that the site had been continuously occupied since the Iron Age. Survey evidence suggested there had once been an ancient wall around the site. Ancient rock-cut tombs and remains of Roman-period sarcophagi have been found on the hillside and in the village.

Excavations in and around Nein have revealed material dating to the Roman through the Islamic periods, with significant evidence from the Mamluk period (14th cent.).

MILTON MORELAND

NAIOTH nay'yoth [נָוִית nawith, נָוְיַת noweyath]. After David flees from Saul to Samuel in RAMAH, both David and Samuel settle at Naioth (nayoth נָיוֹת) in Ramah (1 Sam 19:18). After sending three sets of messengers after David, Saul goes himself (1 Sam 19:20-21). A prophetic frenzy falls on Saul all the way from Ramah to Naioth. At Naioth Saul falls before Samuel, where he continues in a frenzied state all day and night (1 Sam 19:22-24). At Naioth the spirit of God is responsible for Saul's condition, as in 1 Sam 10:9-13. In both instances the question "Is Saul also among the prophets?" appears. The first instance, in 1 Sam 10:12, occurs shortly after Saul is anointed king and is positive, but the second instance, in 1 Sam 19:24, carries a negative connotation as Saul begins to actively pursue the fugitive David.

The meaning of *Naioth* is unknown, so some commentators take the word not as a place name but instead as a plural construct related to naweh (נָוֶה, "shepherd's camp"). According to this reading, David and Samuel were at a camp, possibly of prophets, at Ramah. *Targum Jonathan* renders the word as the phrase "house of learning" (beth ʾulfanaʾ בֵּית אֻלְפָנָא). The LXX, however, renders the Hebrew as a place name, Nauiōth en Rhama (Ναυιώθ ἐν Ῥαμά).

Bibliography: Hans Wilhelm Hertzberg. *1 and 2 Samuel.* OTL (1964); P. Kyle McCarter Jr. *1 Samuel.* AB 8 (1980).

HEATHER R. MCMURRAY

NAKEDNESS [מָעוֹר maʿor, עֶרְוָה ʿerwah; γυμνότης gymnotēs]. The basic idea of the term *nakedness* is "to lay bare," "to expose," "to reveal," or "to uncover." The terms are often euphemisms for genitalia (e.g., Gen 9:22; Lev 18:9). The term *nakedness* has several meanings in the Bible.

Humans are born naked and die naked (Job 1:21; Eccl 5:15 [Heb. 5:14]). Related is the statement that humans were originally naked and without shame (Gen 2:25). Nakedness is also a sign of dire poverty. As part of the call to help the poor, the Israelites are encouraged to clothe the naked (Isa 58:6-7; Job 22:6; 24:7, 10), a call Jesus continues (Matt 25:36, 43).

Nakedness before God is prohibited. Israelites are not to ascend the steps of an altar and expose their nakedness (Exod 20:26 [Heb. 20:23]; compare Rev 3:18). More pointedly, the priests are to wear linen breeches when they serve in the tent or at the altar to cover their nakedness (Exod 28:42).

Nakedness, as an exposure of the most shameful kind, is a sign of or a call for divine judgment (Isa 3:17; 20:2-4; 47:3; Hab 2:15; Mic 1:11; Nah 3:5). This usage often depicts a city or nation as a "female" who has been sexually unfaithful to her husband or sexually promiscuous (see Hos 2:2-13 [Heb. 2:4-15]). The prophets often announce Yahweh's judgments on Israel and Judah in this way (Ezek 16; 23).

To uncover the nakedness of another is a euphemism for sexual intercourse or an uncovering or shaming of a male family member through intercourse with his wife (repeatedly in Lev 18 and 20, both part of the Holiness Code material; see the story of Noah's nakedness in Gen 9:20-29). The Holiness texts identify family relations by prohibiting males from having intercourse with specific females related by blood or marriage. *See* H, HOLINESS CODE; LEVITICUS, BOOK OF; SEX, SEXUALITY.

FRANK H. GORMAN

NAME OF GOD. *See* GOD, NAMES OF.

NAME, NAMING [שֵׁם shem; ὄνομα onoma]. The simplest denotation of *name* in the Bible is a label for distinguishing persons, living things, or places from one another. This simplistic definition masks a complex concept. Most personal names and place names are hypocoristic, constituting all or part of a sentence (e.g., Gen 32:28 [Heb. 32:29], 31; 1 Kgs 9:10-13). Such a sentence might reflect something distinctive about a person's birth or character (e.g., Daniel [daniyeʾl דָּנִיֵּאל], "God is my judge" or "God judges") or it might refer to an important event associated with a place (e.g., PENUEL [penuʾel פְּנוּאֵל], "face of God," the place where Jacob claimed to have seen God face to face). These names are almost always theological in character and often include a divine name as part of the name.

There are several examples in which *name* stands in parallel with *remember* or *memory* (zakhar זָכַר, zekher זֵכֶר; Job 18:17; Prov 10:7; Isa 26:8; *see* REMEMBER, TO). Some texts use the causative form of *remember* with *name* as its object. This might reflect influence from Mesopotamia, where the verb zakaru means "to utter, name." However, there are instances from throughout the ANE in which *name* and *memory* are interchangeable, as they are in the Bible. This justifies a more literal interpretation of statements by individuals when they express a desire for their names to be "remembered" (Exod 20:24; Josh 23:7; Ps 83:4 [Heb. 83:5]), especially by their descendants (2 Sam 18:18; Jer 11:19). A name implies not only a distinguishing label, but the reputation or essence of a person or thing, so it is something by which—but also for which—someone or something is remembered (Exod 23:13; 28:12, 29; Isa 26:13; compare Isa 48:1).

The acts of giving or changing a name can be descriptive or prescriptive (that is, demonstrating the authority of the one giving the name). The former entails naming for the purpose of acknowledging how someone or something is distinctive and thus how one is remembered. This is obvious in passages that use *name* in reference to a person's existing character or reputation. One can have a good name (Prov 22:1; Eccl 7:1) or a bad name (Deut 22:19; NRSV "slandered"; Neh 6:13).

Having a good name means having a good reputation. To "make a name" means to earn and maintain a good reputation (Gen 12:2; 2 Sam 7:9, 23). Names ascribed to the child in Isa 9:6 [Heb. 9:5]—"Wonderful Counselor, Mighty God, Everlasting Father, Prince of Peace"—recount the ideal reputation (the "good name") to which royal offspring should aspire (compare Jer 23:6). Jesus nicknamed James and John "Sons of Thunder" (Boanērges βοανηργές; Mark 3:17), and he renamed Simon "Rock" or "Peter" (Petros Πέτρος) in recognition of his solid character (Matt 16:18).

A bad name indicates loss of reputation and status. An example of someone who has a "bad name" is Nabal (naval [נָבָל], "fool"), who acts toward David in a foolish manner ("as his name is, so is he," 1 Sam 25:25). The substitution of ISHBOSHETH (ʾish-bosheth [אִישׁ־בֹּשֶׁת], "man of shame") for ISHBAAL (ʾish-baʿal [אִישׁ־בַּעַל], "man of Baal") serves a similar function in indicating bad character (2 Sam 2:8-10).

Naming has a descriptive nature rather than authoritative force in several other instances. Hagar declares a special name for God—El-Roi (ʾel roʾi [אֵל רֳאִי], "God sees")—as a perpetual reminder of her unique encounter with God (Gen 16:13; *see* GOD, NAMES OF). The women of Bethlehem give OBED (ʿovedh עוֹבֵד) his name to indicate his place within the Israelite lineage as opposed to a Moabite lineage (Ruth 4:17). The prophecy concerning the naming of IMMANUEL (ʿimmanu ʾel [עִמָּנוּ אֵל], "God is with us") is a prediction of the special role that the child will play (Isa 7:14; compare Matt 1:21-23). Hosea names his children LO-RUHAMAH (loʾ rukhamah [לֹא רֻחָמָה], "no pity") and LO-AMMI (loʾ ʿammi [לֹא עַמִּי], "not my people") as prophecies for the house of Israel (Hos 1:6-8).

God's naming of created things reflects the distinctive function or status of each within CREATION. God names the light "Day," the darkness "Night," the dome "Sky," the dry land "Earth," and the waters "Seas" (Gen 1:5, 8, 10). God orders things into existence, and the naming of created things is part of God's authority over them. For the first man, however, the act of naming the animals and the woman merely identifies the nature of his relationship with the various animals and with the woman; he is not their creator, and he does not determine their destinies by naming them (Gen 2:19-20, 23).

It is clearer in other texts that the giving of a name includes God's claim to authority. God named created things (Gen 1). God "called by name" BEZALEL, thereby authorizing him to construct the tabernacle (Exod 31:2; 35:30). Yahweh "calls by name" the people of Israel and the Persian king CYRUS, commissioning them to perform divinely chosen tasks (Isa 43:1; 44:5; 45:3-4; 63:19). God functions as the superior partner in a covenant by changing the names of Abram to Abraham and Sarai to Sarah. This demonstrates God's unilateral authority to initiate a new phase in this covenant relationship (Gen 17:5, 15; compare Gen 32:27-30 [Heb. 32:28-31]; 2 Sam 12:24-25). God declares to Moses, "I know you by name," indicating that God knows Moses intimately enough to perceive his thoughts and character (Exod 33:12, 17).

Human beings also claim authority over others by naming them. The pharaoh of Egypt gives Joseph a new name as part of commissioning Joseph to be a royal administrator (Gen 41:45). Foreign conquerors replace the kings of Judah and give them new names as a demonstration of the conquerors' authority over the vanquished (2 Kgs 23:34; 24:17). An implied demonstration of authority lies behind the statement that God gives Jesus "the name that is above all names" (Phil 2:9; compare Eph 1:20-21). The renaming of cities constitutes a comparable claim to authority over those cities (Num 32:38, 41-42; Josh 14:15; 21:11; Judg 18:27-29). Joshua designates certain conquered towns "by name" to serve as Levitical cities, an act that implies a level of authority over them (Josh 21:9; compare 1 Chr 6:65 [Heb. 6:50]).

Using someone's name is an appeal to that person's authority. Messengers speak "in the name of" a king or important person who sends them (1 Sam 25:4-11; Esth 2:22; Ps 89:24 [Heb. 89:25]; Jer 29:25; *see* MESSENGER). They speak in the first person on behalf of the sender, and they carry the sender's authority in this act. Peter and John appeal to Jesus' authority when they heal "by the name of Jesus" (Acts 4:5-10). Paul denies for himself any claim to authority that would come from baptizing in his own name (1 Cor 1:12-17). Speaking or acting in someone's name implies intimate knowledge of that authority figure's thoughts. Jesus shows his personal familiarity with his followers by speaking of himself as a shepherd who knows his sheep "by name" (John 10:3). Similarly, John calls on his readers to greet others "by name" (3 John 15; compare Esth 2:14).

In antiquity, writers sometimes used a well-known and respected person's name to support their own text's authority. For example, people wrote in the name of the patriarchs, prophets, apostles, and other authoritative figures to give credence to their work or to honor the great person's teaching and memory (*see* APOCRYPHA, NT; PSEUDEPIGRAPHA; PSEUDONYMOUS WRITING).

A corollary connotation is seen in the use of *name* in relation to inheritance, entailing both descendants and property (2 Sam 14:7; Isa 14:22). Several passages mention a desire to "establish" or "perpetuate" a name. This is not simply an ontological issue because these expressions often reflect practical concerns about maintaining a familial claim to property (*see* INHERITANCE IN THE OT). A primary motivation for the marriage of Boaz and Ruth is the desire to "maintain the name" of Ruth's first husband, which involves his inheritance rights (Ruth 4:5, 9-14; compare Deut 25:6-7; *see* FAMILY; LEVIRATE LAW). Jacob declares that Ephraim and Manasseh will have a name alongside Joseph's brothers, thus establishing their descendants' inheritance rights (Gen 48:6). Conversely, there are occasional concerns or threats that someone's name will be "destroyed" or "cut off" as a result of wicked behavior. The most obvious result of this is that these individuals cannot lay claim to traditional inheritance rights (Num 27:4; 1 Sam 24:21) or they have no descendants to claim that inheritance (Deut 25:6; Ps 109:13). References to having one's name included in the Lord's book imply concerns about spiritual inheritance (Exod 32:32-33; Deut 29:20; Ps 69:28 [Heb. 69:29]).

The name of God is unlike any other name in the Bible and was considered too sacred to be uttered aloud. When Moses asked God to reveal God's name to him, God replied with the mysterious phrase, "I am who I am" (Exod 3:14; *see* GOD, NAMES OF; TETRAGRAMMATON; YAHWEH). Rather than pronounce this holy name, Jewish readers substitute the word ʾadhonay (אֲדֹנָי, "Lord"; *see* ADONAI, ADONAY) or refer to God as hashem (הַשֵּׁם, "the Name") as found in Lev 24:11. The third of the TEN COMMANDMENTS prohibits taking the name of God in VAIN.

Bibliography: Brevard S. Childs. *Memory and Tradition in Israel* (1962); George W. Ramsey. "Is Name-Giving an Act of Domination in Genesis 2:23 and Elsewhere?" *CBQ* 50 (1988) 24–35.

TIMOTHY M. WILLIS

NANEA nuh-nee´uh [Ναναία Nanaia]. Originally a Mesopotamian goddess, during the Hellenistic and Roman periods, Nanea was syncretized with local deities and worshiped from Egypt to Iran as a goddess of love and war.

According to various ancient sources, ANTIOCHUS IV Epiphanes tried to pillage a temple of Nanea in Persia, but failed (2 Macc 1:14; 1 Macc 6:1-2; Polybius, *Hist.* 31.9; Josephus, *Ant.* 12.354).

ADAM L. PORTER

NANNA. Also known as Nanna-Suen, Suen, and Ashimbabbar, Nanna is the Sumerian moon god and principal deity of UR. Sumerian tradition considers him the eldest son of ENLIL and associates him with the flourishing of herds. Nanna's family includes a wife, Ningal, and two children, the goddess Inanna and the sun god Utu.

STEVE COOK

NAOMI nay-oh´mee [נָעֳמִי naʿomi]. Meaning "my pleasantness." An Ephrathite (Bethlehemite) woman whose story is central to the book of Ruth (*see* RUTH, BOOK OF). Naomi was widowed after moving her family to Moab during a time of famine (Ruth 1:1). Her sons took Moabite wives, ORPAH and RUTH, but after they had lived there for ten years, her sons died as well (Ruth 1:5). Naomi, unable to give her daughters-in-law husbands for levirate marriage at her age, begs the women to return to their own land and gods; Orpah complies, but Ruth refuses and accompanies Naomi to Bethlehem (Ruth 1:19, 22). Upon their return, Naomi informs the women of Bethlehem that she is no longer Naomi but MARA (maraʾ מָרָא, "bitter"), "for the Almighty has dealt bitterly with me" (Ruth 1:20).

In spite of her sadness, Naomi engineers the marriage of Ruth to a kinsman named BOAZ. Naomi convinces Ruth to visit Boaz's threshing floor after meeting him while gleaning. There, she tells Ruth, "Observe the place where he lies; then, go and uncover his feet and lie down" (Ruth 3:4). Boaz pledges to take Ruth as his wife, acting as next-of-kin (Ruth 3:13; 4:5-6). Ruth bears Boaz a son, named OBED, whom Naomi herself nurses (Ruth 4:16-17). Naomi's new "son" (as the women of the neighborhood call Obed) is then revealed as the grandfather of King David (Ruth 4:17). Naomi's actions to save herself and her daughters-in-law ultimately preserve the nation as well.

Bibliography: Athalya Brenner, ed. *Ruth and Esther: A Feminist Companion to the Bible* (1999).

JESSICA TINKLENBERG DEVEGA

NAPHATH-DOR nay'fath-dor' [נָפַת דּוֹר nafath dor, נָפוֹת דּוֹר nafoth dor]. Located between Carmel and Caesarea. Archaeological evidence indicates Naphath-dor's existence from the Late Bronze Age through the 7th cent. CE. Naphath, meaning "sand dune" or "district," refers to its coastal location or its status as district seat during Solomon's reign (1 Kgs 4:11). Naphath-dor was conquered by Joshua (Josh 11:2; 12:23) and assigned to Manasseh as part of the tribe's land allotment. A variant is Naphoth-dor. *See* DOR.

HEIDI E. HAWKS

NAPHISH nay'fish [נָפִישׁ nafish]. Eleventh of the twelve sons of Ishmael (Gen 25:15; 1 Chr 1:31); founder of an Arab tribe that was besieged and conquered by the Gadites, Reubenites, and the half-tribe of Manasseh living on the east side of the Jordan (1 Chr 5:18-19). *See* ISHMAEL, ISHMAELITES.

R. JUSTIN HARKINS

NAPHOTH-DOR. *See* NAPHATH-DOR.

NAPHTALI GATE naf'tuh-l*i* [שַׁעַר נַפְתָּלִי shaʿar naftali]. In Ezekiel's vision of the new Temple and Jerusalem (Ezek 40–48), the city walls have three gates to a side, all named for Israelite tribes. The gates of Gad, Asher, and Naphtali lie on the east side (Ezek 48:34). *See* EZEKIEL, BOOK OF.

JAMES RILEY STRANGE

NAPHTALI, NAPHTALITES naf'tuh-l*i*, naf'tuh-l*it* [נַפְתָּלִי naftali, בְּנֵי נַפְתָּלִי bene naftali; Νεφθαλὶμ Nephthalim, φυλὴ Νεφθαλὶμ phyle Nephthalim]. 1. The sixth son of JACOB who became the eponymous ancestor of the tribe of Naphtali. Naphtali's birth resulted from RACHEL's desperation to stake her claim as the preferred wife over her sister and rival, LEAH. Since Rachel had no children, she offered Jacob her handmaid, BILHAH, as a surrogate mother, a practice consistent with customs of the ancient world. Bilhah had already given birth to Dan (Gen 30:1-6; *see* DAN, DANITES), but the contest with Leah had continued, and Rachel hoped to establish her primacy with the birth of a second son through Bilhah, whom she named Naphtali. His name reflects the rivalry with Leah and linguistically springs from the Hebrew root ptl (פתל) meaning "twist" or "wrestle"; hence, she affirms: "With mighty wrestlings I have wrestled with my sister, and have prevailed" (Gen 30:8).

In the course of time, Naphtali and his children descend into Egypt with Jacob's family to survive the famine (Gen 46:24). His sons included Jahzeel (Jahziel in 1 Chr 7:13), Guni, Jezer, and Shillem (Shallum in 1 Chr 7:13).

2. The Naphtalites, descended from the eponymous ancestor Naphtali, received territory in the northern extremity of Israel. When the tribes of Israel left Egypt, the tribe of Naphtali provided 53,400 men of war (Num 1:42-43). By the end of the wanderings their number had reduced to 45,400 (Num 26:48-50). Leading individuals during the wanderings were Ahira son of Enan, who facilitated the census and then served as the tribe's main leader (see Num 1:15; 2:29; 10:27), and Nahbi son of Vophsi, who represented them in the reconnaissance mission to Canaan (Num 13:14).

When Israel eventually returned to Canaan and performed the covenant renewal ceremony near Shechem, Naphtali was among the tribes to gather on the slopes of Mount Ebal, the mount of cursings (Deut 27:13). Naphtali's land allotment was in the far north in the Galilean highlands (Josh 19:32-39) with Asher on its west. The eastern boundary was the Jordan from Mount Hermon to the Sea of Galilee. Zebulun (Josh 19:10-16) and Issachar (Josh 19:17-23) were the southern neighbors. The northern border remains undefined, but would have abutted Phoenicia. How to understand the Mosaic blessing in Deut 33:23 that mentions Naphtali's possession of the territory in "the west and the south" is problematic. The word for "west" can also be rendered "sea" and may therefore refer to the Sea of Chinnereth rather than the more traditional use to refer to the Mediterranean. The reference to the "south" does not refer to the southern part of Canaan, but may refer to the area slightly south of Galilee. That general area, however, was allotted to Issachar (Josh 19:17-23) although tracing the exact boundary is challenging.

The tribal area had some notable towns within its borders; it was privileged with the presence of a city of refuge at Kedesh (Josh 20:7). In addition to Kedesh, two other towns were reserved for the Gershonite family of the Levites (Josh 21:32; minor spelling variations appear in 1 Chr 6:76). One major town in the list of cities of Naphtali is Hazor, which held significant political sway in the area when Israel entered Canaan (Josh 11:10-11). While Joshua is said to have destroyed Hazor, it appears again with Jabin as its king when the Bible notes its subjugation at the hands of Deborah and Barak (Judg 4:1-10).

During the period of the judges, Naphtali plays significantly in Israel's history. At the behest of Deborah, Barak, who hails from Kedesh in Naphtali, serves as the field commander against the Canaanite oppression under Jabin (Judg 4:6-10). The Naphtalites later join Gideon's rout of the Midianites (Judg 6:35; 7:23).

During the monarchical period, the Chronicler notes that Naphtali contributed to David's army while David was still ruling from Hebron (1 Chr 12:34-40). Solomon's reign tapped the talent of Naphtali in the person of HIRAM, a bronze worker of mixed parentage—his Naphtalite mother had married a Tyrian—who engineered the major bronze castings for the Temple of

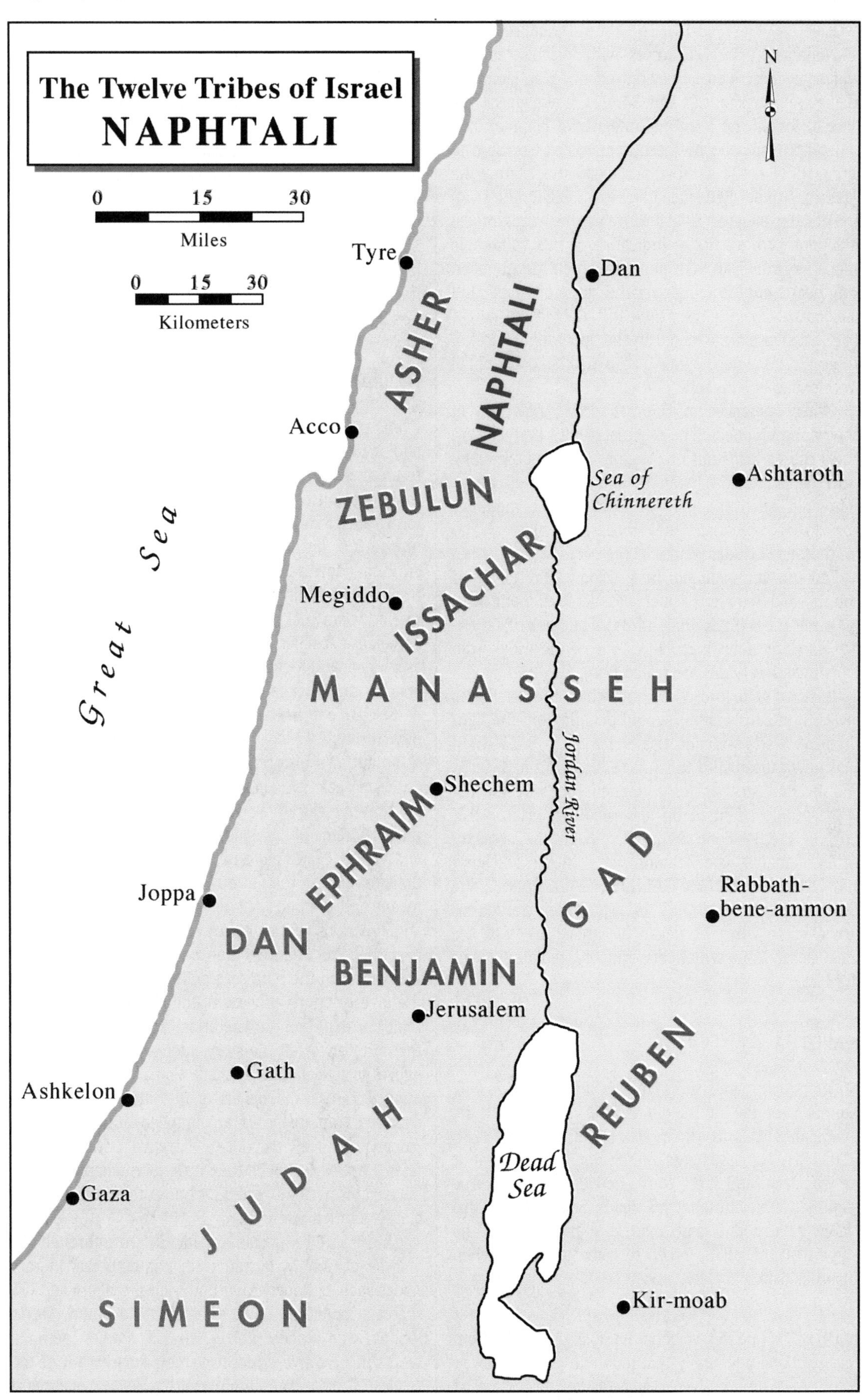
The Twelve Tribes of Israel
NAPHTALI
0 15 30
Miles
0 15 30
Kilometers
N
Tyre
Dan
ASHER
NAPHTALI
Acco
Sea of Chinnereth
Ashtaroth
ZEBULUN
Great Sea
ISSACHAR
Megiddo
MANASSEH
Jordan River
Shechem
EPHRAIM
GAD
Joppa
Rabbath-bene-ammon
DAN
BENJAMIN
Jerusalem
REUBEN
Gath
Ashkelon
JUDAH
Dead Sea
Gaza
Kir-moab
SIMEON

Jerusalem (1 Kgs 7:13-14). The last historical reference to Naphtali in the OT occurs with Josiah's reforms, which are described as having extended as far north as the tribal territory (2 Chr 34:6-7); however, by the time of Josiah, the territorial integrity of Naphtali had collapsed. Naphtali's northern and eastern exposure to foreign powers had left it vulnerable to attacks from the Arameans under Ben-Hadad (1 Kgs 15:20; 2 Chr 16:4) and it later suffered a fatal blow at the hands of the Assyrians (2 Kgs 15:29). Indicative of this vulnerable exposure is the Dan inscription, in which the Aramean king boasts of his victory over the "king of Israel" and the "house of David" (*see* INSCRIPTION, TELL DAN). The Assyrian exile is noted in the apocryphal book of Tobit (7:1-5) where some of the people of Naphtali were exiled to Nineveh.

Other references to Naphtali occur, however, in poetry and prophecy. The psalmist (68:27 [MT 68:28]) notes the participation of Zebulun and Naphtali along with Benjamin and Judah in a procession to honor Yahweh. The listing may be a geographic modification to accommodate the smallest (Benjamin) and southernmost (Judah) tribes to the northernmost tribes of Zebulun and Naphtali. In a vision of the idealized country and Temple, Ezekiel sees Naphtali along with the other tribes (Ezek 48:4, 34-35). The book of Revelation similarly notes Naphtali as one of the tribes from which God's servants are sealed (7:6).

Isaiah would foresee a time when the territories of Zebulun and Naphtali would benefit from the light shed by God's servant (Isa 9:1-2 [MT 8:23–9:1]). Matthew tapped into this image, applying it to Jesus and his ministry, as Jesus opened the way for the oppressed to be lifted up and renewed (Matt 4:13-16). In the 1st cent., what had been the areas of Asher, Naphtali, and Zebulun were known as Upper and Lower Galilee (*see* GALILEE, GALILEANS). The Galilean town of CAPERNAUM, which served as Jesus' home when he began his preaching, was the focal point from which his ministry radiated (Matt 4:23-25).

DALE W. MANOR

NAPHTHA. *See* NEPHTHAR.

NARCISSUS nahr-sis´uhs [Νάρκισσος Narkissos]. Members of the household [NRSV, "family"] of the freedman Narcissus (Rom 16:11) formed a HOUSE CHURCH. Narcissus was either not a Christian, or he was dead, and those of his house continued to be identified with him after his death. Some believe this Narcissus was the same man as a freedman of the emperor CLAUDIUS, forced to commit suicide when Claudius died in 54 CE.

MARK REASONER

NARD [נֵרְדְּ nerde; νάρδος nardos]. An herb, from the *Valerianaceae* family that grows in the Himalayan countries of Bhutan, Nepal, and Kashmir in India. The fragrant root and lower stems were dried and used to concoct a perfumed OINTMENT. It was transported in the form of a dry rhizome or oil phase extract and was considered a very expensive luxury item. By including the detail that nard was contained in an alabaster flask, Mark (14:3) demonstrated the precious nature of the nard used by the woman to anoint Jesus' head (compare John 12:3). Nard has an intense, warm, musky odor that is described as an erotic PERFUME in Song 1:12-13 suitable to entice one's lover in a similar fashion to a bag of myrrh worn around the neck. Its fragrance is matched to other aromatics (Song 4:13-14). *See* PLANTS OF THE BIBLE.

VICTOR H. MATTHEWS

NARRATIVE CRITICISM. As its name implies, narrative criticism is a methodology that analyzes the narrative (story-like) features of biblical writings. This methodology emerged in the 1970s and 1980s in reaction to the fragmentation of biblical texts that resulted from traditional historical-critical methods (such as textual, form, and redaction criticisms). Instead of breaking up the text into sources and editorial parts, narrative criticism addresses the unity and coherence of the text. In place of isolating short, form-critical episodes, narrative criticism seeks meaning in the dynamic interplay between a specific passage and the larger literary unit as a whole and focuses on the holistic, temporal experience of an audience.

Narrative criticism does not treat the text as a window through which to view, e.g., the historical Jesus or an author's historical community. Instead, narrative criticism seeks to comprehend the "story world" created by the narrative—its characters, events, and settings, its frame of time and space, and its cultural beliefs and values. Narrative critics use a set of literary questions to analyze the various configurations of plot, the means and methods of characterization, and the types and functions of the narrative's settings. In addition, narrative critics address the role of the narrator and the way in which the narrator's point of view encompasses the diverse points of view of the characters. Narrative criticism explores the rhetorical devices employed by the narrator to tell the story, such as repetition, irony, figures of speech, and imagery. From an analysis of the implicit values and beliefs of the narrative, the critic constructs an image of an "implied author" and an "ideal audience" response. Narrative critics seek to infer the ways in which the impact of the narrative may have confirmed, subverted, or transformed the world of ancient audiences.

In OT studies, narrative criticism arose through the analysis of Hebrew narratives by contemporary literary critics such as Robert Alter and Meir Sternberg and OT scholars including David Clines, David Gunn, David Jobling, and Robert Polzin. In NT studies, seminal works in narrative criticism came primarily out of the work of the Markan Seminar of the Society of Biblical

Literature (e.g., Thomas Boomershine, Joanna Dewey, Werner Kelber, Norman Petersen, David Rhoads, Robert Tannehill, and Mary Ann Tolbert).

In its methodology, narrative criticism makes use of ancient literary theories and narratives from NT times, along with contemporary methods for studying modern novels and short stories through the discipline of narratology (e.g., the work of Mieke Bal, Wayne Booth, Seymour Chatman, Gerard Genette, and Shlomith Rimmon-Kenan). Scholars have begun applying narrative criticism to works in genres other than narrative, such as the letters of Paul and the book of Revelation. *See* BIBLICAL CRITICISM.

Bibliography: Robert Alter. *The Art of Biblical Narrative* (1981); Yairah Amit. *Reading Biblical Narratives: Literary Criticism and the Hebrew Bible.* Yael Yotan, trans. (2001); Mieke Bal. *Narrative Theory: Critical Concepts in Literary and Cultural Studies* (2004); Mieke Bal. *Narratology: Introduction to the Theory of Narrative* (1997); Mieke Bal and David Jobling. *On Story-Telling: Essays in Narratology* (1991); Thomas Boomershine. *Story Journey* (1988); Wayne Booth. *The Company We Keep: An Ethics of Fiction* (1989); Wayne Booth. *The Rhetoric of Fiction* (1983); Seymour Chatman. *Coming to Terms: The Rhetoric of Narrative in Fiction and Film* (1990); Seymour Chatman. *Story and Discourse: Narrative Structure in Fiction and Film* (1980); David J. A. Clines. *Interested Parties: The Ideology of Writers and Readers of the Hebrew Bible* (1995); David J. A. Clines. *The Theme of the Pentateuch* (1999); Alan Culpepper. *The Anatomy of the Fourth Gospel: A Study in Literary Design* (1983); J. Cheryl Exum and David J. A. Clines. *The New Literary Criticism and the Hebrew Bible* (1993); Gerard Genette and Jane E. Lewin. *Narrative Discourse: An Essay in Method* (1983); David M. Gunn and Danna Nolan Fewell. *Narrative in the Hebrew Bible* (1993); David M. Gunn and David E. Orton. *Narrative and Novella in Samuel* (1991); David Jobling. *The Sense of Biblical Narrative* (1987); Stephen Moore. *Literary Criticism and the Gospels: The Theoretical Challenge* (1989); Robert Polzin. *David and the Deuteronomist: 2 Samuel* (1993); Robert Polzin. *Samuel and the Deuteronomist: 1 Samuel* (1993); Mark Powell. *What Is Narrative Criticism?* (1990); James Resseguie. *Narrative Criticism and the New Testament: An Introduction* (2005); David Rhoads. *Reading Mark, Engaging the Gospel* (2004); David Rhoads, Joanna Dewey, Don Michie. *Mark as Story: An Introduction to the Narrative of a Gospel* (1999); Shlomith Rimmon-Kenan. *A Glance beyond Doubt: Narration, Representation, Subjectivity* (1996); Shlomith Rimmon-Kenan. *Narrative Fiction: Contemporary Poetics* (2002); Meir Sternberg. *The Poetics of Biblical Narrative: Ideological Literature and the Drama of Reading* (1985); Robert Tannehill. *The Literary Unity of Luke–Acts.* 2 vols. (1986); Mary Ann Tolbert. *Sowing the Gospel: Mark's Work in Literary-Historical Perspective* (1996).

DAVID RHOADS

NARRATIVE LITERATURE. Narrative literature is one of the main GENREs in the Bible. More than one-third of OT biblical literature is in the form of narrative, and narratives are also found within the other genres, such as prophetic and wisdom literature. Approximately half of the NT is narrative. But the significance of narrative in the NT surpasses the amount of narrative material because the canonical order of books in the NT provides a narrative framework to the NT as a whole.

A. Identification and Significance of Old Testament Narrative

In addition to the volume of narrative within the OT, the importance of narrative is shown in its use as framework for other genres and in its content—for example, as the framework for the Torah laws—and as a way of delivering biblical messages and ideology via the history of the relationship between the Israelites and their God.

Most OT stories are intended to describe a real past, which is why they are accepted by many as historiography (*see* HISTORY AND HISTORIOGRAPHY, OT). Stories like Nathan's parable about the poor man's ewe (2 Sam 12:1*b*-4), or the story of the wise woman from Tekoa (2 Sam 14:5*b*-7), which are presented as fiction, are rare. On the other hand, the use of such parables shows that the authors chose the narrative as a rhetorical means of persuading their addressees.

Many of the stories are organized in a continued sequence. The description that begins with the book of Genesis and the creation of humans and ends with the book of Kings and the downfall of Jerusalem and its Temple reflects a systematic-chronological sequence, which includes the Pentateuch and the early prophets. In addition, there are narratives in some of the later prophets (e.g., Jer 32, 34, 36 and more) and in the Writings (Ruth, Chronicles, Daniel, Esther, Ezra and

Nehemiah). Independent stories, unconnected with the sequence of ancient Israelite history, such as the story of Job (Job 1–2; 42:7-17), are rare.

This literary picture raises some questions. Why were biblical authors interested mainly in the genre of narrative, specifically historical narrative? Historical narrative gave them two effective ways of communicating messages to their readers: the persuasive power of stories and the reliability of materials regarded as history, not fiction. Moreover, historical narrative was a substitute for mythology in the new monotheistic faith. This new religion tried to distance itself from the cyclical mythological background of surrounding societies, and to find a different way to learn about the single, remote God, his precepts and demands. It meant following the relationship between God and his people in the linear past. Thus, biblical authors used the past as a vehicle for learning about God's ways and his people's expected behavior.

The authors of biblical narratives, who were scribes and members of the intellectual circle of their time, knew that to spread their message beyond the elite and educated class, namely, to the whole society, the stories had to appeal to everyone, from someone who was illiterate but could listen, to the scholarly reader. Addressing the text to wider classes of people required the messages to be conveyed in an interesting, clear, and easily comprehended form. The story must therefore be understood as an imitation of reality and perceived as a simple dramatic narrative. On the higher levels of reading, it may be interpreted far beyond the imitation of reality. The episodes may be seen as motifs, the figures as archetypes, and the language as a highly stylized tool, filled with allusions and wordplay. The reader may perceive analogies, structural patterns, changes in repetitions, and the like. All these are techniques of composition that enrich the reading experience and deepen the message. Ultimately, all readers and listeners can enjoy biblical stories.

Biblical stories are short—some twenty-five verses on average. A story of more than sixty verses, like that of the marriage of Isaac and Rebekah (Gen 24:1-67), is quite rare, and the longer ones, such as the story of Joseph (Gen 37–50), or the book of Ruth, are made up of short stories. In these cases, too, each substory revolves around a conflict and leads to a change. However, there are two different combination models of short stories. Typically in the Joseph story the connection between the substories is based on cause and effect, so that almost every one of them serves the sequel like a link in the chain of the long narrative. Abraham stories, however, are not linked causally but connected by editorial comments on the time and place of the events (Gen 22:1, 20—"After these things," etc.). Every story contributes to the understanding of Abraham's personality and the values that he, the father of the nation, represents.

The study of biblical narrative in the last fifty years has discovered its advanced poetics and the different techniques employed by its authors in creating texts that are not merely didactic or homiletic, but also possess aesthetic quality and can appeal to all levels of society. The clarity of biblical narrative, the combination of its components, matching content and form, make it special and unique not only for the time of its composition, but even in our modern time.

B. Components of Old Testament Narrative

A brief examination of the story's components, such as plot, characters, narrator, time, place, and style, reveals some of its sophisticated poetics.

1. Plot

The plot is the central element in biblical narrative, not only because it attracts the interest of all readers, but also because people's actions reflect their character, and the examination of the plot is the main means of discovering it. Moreover, the development of the plot directs the reader to the meaning of the story. The chosen elements of the plot are of great importance. For example, the account of David's life consists of selected events that emphasize his failings as a human being, as a father, and as a king. The stories chosen to depict his reign do little to glorify his achievements, such as his victories and his consolidation of the kingdom (2 Sam 5–9 only!). On the other hand, much is made of his war against the Ammonites (2 Sam 10–12), in which his failings and sins are exposed, leading to his punishment and the uprisings against him in his kingdom (2 Sam 13–1 Kgs 2). The chosen elements of the plot and the associated conflicts illustrate and highlight the issues that concerned the monotheistic faith, such as the role of the king, the exposure of a mortal king's weaknesses and limitations, the role of morality as a judicial divine criterion, and the hierarchy that sets the prophet above the king.

2. Characters

The plot is moved by two kinds of characters: the divine, namely, God and his superhuman messengers, and people who are sometimes individuals—mainly leading figures such as kings, prophets, and priests—or collective entities, such the Israelites, or particular tribes. God appears as the source of all the power, while the human heroes are limited and dependent on him, who sent or chose them (Samson, Gideon, David, and others). It is interesting to examine the tension between the roles of God and humanity in the stories. The further God is from sight and the less is known about him, the more his human emissaries and people are revealed. This focus on the human is another reason why there are no perfect characters in biblical narratives. All the protagonists, including kings and prophets, are sometimes depicted as weak. Even Moses had to strike the rock twice (Num 20:7-12). In this way, biblical narrative, despite being religious-didactic texts, avoids depicting flat figures or types, and develops such rounded, complex characters as Saul and David.

3. Narrator

Biblical narrative is often told by an omniscient narrator who knows not only the human characters, but even the mind of God. He does not share his all-encompassing observations with the readers, but only as suit his intentions. For example, he tells that God repented having created human beings (Gen 6:5-8). Unlike dry factual histories, the biblical narrative allows for scenes and dialogues reproducing the "original" voices of the characters in the story world. The reader has to examine when and why the narrator appears, and when and why the stage is given to scenes and characters. It is accepted that the narrator's reports are always trustworthy, so they can serve as the yardstick for the trustworthiness of characters in the narrative. The narrator's comments tell the reader about the gap between the time of the telling and that of the described events—as, for example, "At that time the Canaanites were in the land" (Gen 12:6). Of special importance are the narrator's judgmental comments, such as the concluding statement of the story about David and Bathsheba: "But the thing that David had done displeased the LORD" (2 Sam 11:27*b*). Such comments tell the reader about the world of the authors and their aims.

4. Time and space

These short stories make up a historical sequence covering hundreds or even thousands of years. To do this, the authors had to decide which parts to skip and which to develop, while maintaining the continuity. The result was various techniques of abbreviation, such as lists (Gen 5), and the use of formulas or phrases that suggest that a long, if undefined, length of time has elapsed, such as "And the land had rest eighty years" (Judg 3:30). Yet when the subject is especially important, the author extends the time of telling. This can be achieved by repetition, as in the description of the tabernacle (Exod 25–31, 35–40), or by incorporating dialogues, as in the story of the purchase of the Cave of Machpelah (Gen 23).

Of special importance are the deviations from the diachronic time sequence that characterizes the historical descriptions. Biblical narrative allows for various kinds of prolepsis (i.e., anticipation), mainly in denoting the manifestations of God, his angels, or, primarily, his prophets. It does so also by means of dreams and various magical techniques—e.g., the consultation with the woman of Endor, who had a familiar spirit (1 Sam 28).

The narrator's anticipatory comments tell the reader that events are not haphazard, that God is orchestrating them and directing history.

As for space, the historical background is typically emphasized, mainly by mentioning the names of places. On the other hand, the authors seldom paid attention to details of the particular space.

5. Functionality

The biblical story is markedly functional, and the various details it includes are designed to serve the story. The functional quality helps keep the story short, so the appearance of a descriptive detail about a figure or a place must be intentional and meant to contribute to the story or its message.

Bibliography: R. Alter. *The Art of Biblical Narrative* (1981); Y. Amit. *Reading Biblical Narratives: Literary Criticism and the Hebrew Bible.* Y. Lotan, trans. (2001); S. Bar-Efrat. *Narrative Art in the Bible.* D. Shefer-vanson, trans. (1989); M. Buber. "Leitwort Style in Pentateuch Narrative." *Scripture and Translation: Martin Buber and Franz Rosenzweig.* L. Rosenwald with E. Fox, trans. (1994) 114–28; J. Fokkelman. *Reading Biblical Narrative: A Practical Guide* (1999); H. Gunkel. *Genesis.* M. E. Biddle, trans. (1997); M. Sternberg. *The Poetics of Biblical Narrative: Ideological Literature and the Drama of Reading* (1985).

YAIRAH AMIT

C. Identification and Significance of New Testament Narrative

The four Gospels and Acts establish the narrative foundation for reading and understanding the letters and the Apocalypse that follow. Accordingly, the four Gospels present the person and work of Jesus Christ, which the remainder of the NT explicates. Acts forms a narrative bridge between the Gospels and the letters by connecting the story of Jesus with that of the ongoing life of the church, and describing the ecclesial context in which the letters were written and received. Moreover, however one evaluates the historical accuracy of Acts' depiction of the life and ministry of Paul, the presentation of Paul there is the narrative presupposition for the letters of Paul within the NT canon. The importance of this narrative preparation for the letters is indicated by the fact that it necessitated separating the Gospel of Luke from the Acts of the Apostles, which refers readers back to the Gospel (Acts 1:1).

But the significance of narrative within the NT also emerges from the twofold narrative substructure within NT letters. On the one hand, all the letters assume the salvation-historical mega-narrative that is presented within the entire Bible, namely, the story of God's redemption of fallen humanity through the covenant God made with Israel, culminating in the Christ-event and leading ultimately to the new heaven and new earth that God will establish at the PAROUSIA of Christ. On the other hand, the letters assume also an implicit, and sometimes explicit, narrative of the history between epistolary author and audience. In some letters, such as Romans, the salvation-historical mega-narrative is dominant; while in others, such as 1 Thessalonians, the author-audience narrative predominates. But both narratives are always present. The book of Revelation, which includes the second perspective in its letters to the churches (Rev 2:1–3:22), assumes especially the broad salvation-historical mega-narrative.

Therefore, although the distinction between the genre of narrative and that of discourse (the form of logical argument found in the letters) is necessary, it is sometimes difficult to distinguish sharply between them. Thus, narrative books such as the Gospels and Acts contain speeches, or discourses, which are embedded within the narrative and derive their meaning from the narrative while contributing to narrative development (e.g., the "Sermon on the Mount," Matt 5–7; Peter's "Pentecost Sermon," Acts 2:14-36). Alternately, we frequently find narrative accounts presented within letters, such as Paul's account of his dealings with the apostles in Gal 1–2 and the account of the transfiguration in 2 Pet 1:16-18. Nevertheless, there are certain components that belong specifically to narrative and distinguish certain NT material as belonging specifically to the genre of narrative.

D. Components of New Testament Narrative

A brief discussion of the components of narrative as employed within the NT will explicate some of the distinctions between NT narratives and those found in the OT and will disclose certain chief characteristics of NT narrative.

1. Plot

Plot has to do with the ordering of events within the story of a narrative. Plot often (but not always) involves a movement toward a culmination, which is called "climax." When climax is present it indicates the essential meaning of the narrative progression. This climactic movement characterizes the plot of each of the narrative books of the NT. The plot of the Gospels moves toward the death and resurrection of Jesus; and the particular way in which each Gospel reaches its climax expresses the unique perspective of that Gospel. Thus, the Gospel of Matthew comes to a final climax in the resurrection appearance of the missionary commissioning (Matt 28:16-20); the Gospel of Mark has its essential climax in the confession of Jesus' divine Sonship by the centurion as he faces the cross (Mark 15:39); the ascension forms the climax to the Gospel of Luke (Luke 24:50-52); and John's Gospel reaches its essential climax in the statement of purpose for the entire Gospel ("that you may come to believe that Jesus is the Messiah, the Son of God," John 20:30-31), which is associated especially with the resurrection appearances. The plot of Acts finds its climax with Paul preaching the gospel at Rome, about to make his appeal to Caesar (Acts 28:11-31), suggesting that Acts is not ultimately concerned with Paul or his fate but rather with the geographical spread of the gospel from Jerusalem to Rome, the chief city of the Roman Empire and the farthest distance from Jerusalem in the world narrated in Acts.

The plot of each narrative book is also characterized by conflict. The plot presents this conflict on two levels. On the one hand, there is conflict on the human-historical level between Jesus and his followers over against their opponents, namely the religious and political authorities and eventually significant portions of the Jewish population, as well as certain Gentile adversaries. On the other hand, this human-historical conflict is an expression of the cosmic struggle between God (and God's angels) and the devil (and demons). The immediate outcome of this conflict seems to be the triumph of Jesus' adversaries; but the resurrection of Jesus in the Gospels and the overcoming victory of the church's mission in Acts support the claim that Christ and his faithful church will ultimately prevail.

Consistently the plot of NT narrative books emphasizes that the story being told is the end-time (or eschatological) fulfillment of God's salvation-historical dealings with Israel as recounted in the OT; it is the culmination of God's redemptive actions that he initiated with Abraham. Luke's Gospel is representative of this general NT perspective when it claims to describe those things which have been "fulfilled among us" (Luke 1:1). Thus, the events narrated in the NT are of critical importance; and consequently there is an emphasis upon the historical trustworthiness of the accounts, which often involves appeal to eyewitness testimony (e.g., Luke 1:1-4; John 19:35; 21:24; and the "we-sections" of Acts 16–28).

2. Characters

The primary character of each of the narrative books of the NT is Jesus Christ. This claim is manifestly true of the Gospels, but it is equally valid for Acts. Although the book of Acts is traditionally titled "the Acts of the Apostles," and in spite of the prominence of the Holy Spirit within the narrative, the chief actor in the book of Acts is the exalted Christ. When Luke declares in Acts 1:1 that in his first book (the Gospel of Luke) he dealt with all Jesus began to do and to teach, he implies that in this second volume he will narrate that which Jesus continues to do and to teach; and a close examination of Acts reveals that the exalted Christ is repeatedly the subject of critical actions throughout the narrative (e.g., Acts 1:24; 2:33; 4:10-11; 9:1-17, 34; 22:17-21).

3. Narrative world

Whenever writers create narratives they construct a "narrative world," which is the more or less self-contained system of relationships and realities that exist within the story. The primary reality in the narrative world of each of the narrative books of the NT is God. God is the sovereign power and therefore God's perspective (or "point of view") is the ultimately reliable one for the narrative worlds of the NT. The voice of the narrative ("the narrator") in the world of the NT stories is always reliable in that it always agrees with the perspective of God. And Jesus is always the perfectly reliable character, whose speech and actions are consistently true and right, because his point of view is completely aligned to that of God.

Bibliography: Richard A. Burridge. *What Are the Gospels? A Comparison with Graeco-Roman Biography* (1992); Martin Hengel. *Acts and the History of Earliest Christianity* (1979); Jack D. Kingsbury. *The Christology of Mark's Gospel* (1983); Jack D. Kingsbury. *Conflict in Luke: Jesus, Authorities, Disciples* (1991); Jack D. Kingsbury. *Matthew as Story* (1988); Norman Petersen. *Rediscovering Paul: Philemon and the Sociology of Paul's Narrative World* (1985); Bruce W. Winter and Andrew D. Clarke, eds. *The Book of Acts in Its Ancient Literary Setting* (1993); Ben Witherington III. *Paul's Narrative Thought World: The Tapestry and Tragedy of Triumph* (1994).

DAVID R. BAUER

NASBEH, TELL EN. *See* MIZPAH, MIZPEH.

NASH PAPYRUS. The Nash Papyrus consists of four pieces of inscribed papyrus that preserve a form of the Decalogue (i.e., TEN COMMANDMENTS, Exod 20; Deut 5) and the beginning of the Shema (Deut 6:4; *see* SHEMA, THE). The papyrus was acquired by W. L. Nash in Egypt at the beginning of the 20th cent. and was first published in 1902 by Stanley Cook. Subsequent studies conclusively dated the papyrus to the 2nd cent. BCE. The Nash Papyrus is either a liturgical text or a copy for private use, not a biblical manuscript. The combination of the Decalogue and the Shema in that order reflects the practice, known from the Talmud (*b. Ber.* 12a), of reciting both in sequence. In addition to its age, the Nash Papyrus is also important for the light it sheds on the text of the Decalogue and the relationship between the copies of that text in Exodus and Deuteronomy and in the LXX. It is closest to the LXX of Exodus and clearly demonstrated for the first time that the LXX is frequently a faithful translation of its Hebrew *Vorlage*, an understanding reinforced by the study of the Hebrew biblical manuscripts from the Judean Desert. *See* TEXT, HEBREW, HISTORY OF.

RUSSELL E. FULLER

NATHAN nay´thuhn [נָתָן nathan; Ναθάμ Natham]. 1. Nathan, son of David (2 Sam 5:14; 1 Chr 14:4) and elder brother of Solomon (1 Chr 3:5), whose name appears in the "day of the Lord" pronouncement in Zech 12:12 and who is included in Jesus' genealogy in Luke 3:31.

2. In Samuel–Kings, Nathan the prophet has three major appearances. He is first introduced in 2 Sam 7:2, without any background information or genealogy. He is simply referred to as "Nathan the prophet," and is in conversation with David. Settled in his court, the king indirectly suggests building a temple, perhaps seeking legitimization from the prophet. Although Nathan is encouraging ("do all that you have in mind"), God comes to the prophet later that night with a stunning oracle. God's long speech to Nathan begins with a lecture in historical theology, then moves to a stunning reversal: God will build David a house, and a son will succeed him on the throne of Israel. This announcement of a long-lasting Davidic dynasty is often cited as a key moment in the larger storyline.

Nathan's next appearance is 2 Sam 12, where he delivers a severe rebuke after the Bathsheba affair and the murder of Uriah. Nathan begins with a tale designed to evoke a response from the king. David utters severe words against "the man" of Nathan's tale, to which the prophet replies, "You are the man!" In chap. 7 Nathan announced a long-lasting house for David, but in chap. 12 it now becomes a house from which the sword will never depart (v. 10). In a short cameo near the end of the chapter, Nathan reemerges after the birth of David and Bathsheba's (second) child. The LORD sends a message through Nathan that Solomon is to be called Jedidiah ("beloved of the LORD"). Based on the Genesis model, a change of name indicates a change of destiny, and it would seem as though the young Solomon is endowed with great expectations.

Nathan's final appearance is in 1 Kgs 1. With an aged David apparently unaware of Adonijah's pretensions to kingship, Nathan approaches Bathsheba with a plan: Bathsheba is to enter the king's chambers and question him about an (alleged) "oath" that Solomon is to reign in his place. There is no record of such an oath sworn by David in 2 Samuel. There is, however, the name-change and the announcement of God's love for Solomon, so these factors may motivate the prophet's actions in 1 Kgs 1. Whether or not David swore the oath before, he eventually claims that he did, and within an hour Solomon is anointed as the king of Israel. With that, Nathan exits the stage, referred to again only in passing, in royal lists. Nathan also features in Chronicles, where he is mentioned as the author of a monarchic history.

3. Nathan of Zobah, one of David's mighty men (2 Sam 23:36) and one of the heroes in 1 Chr 11:38. He was father of Igal and brother of Joel.

4. Father of Azariah and Zabud (1 Kgs 4:5). Possibly the same Nathan as #1 or 2 above.

5. Son of Attai, a descendant of Judah from the clan of Jerahmeel. He was father of Zabad (1 Chr 2:36).

6. One of the delegates sent by Ezra to Iddo in Casiphia to recruit servants for the house of God (Ezra 8:16). He is probably the same Nathan who agreed to divorce his foreign wife (Ezra 10:39).

Bibliography: R. Alter. *The David Story* (1999); K. Bodner. "Nathan: Prophet, Politician, and Novelist?" *JSOT* 26 (2001) 43–54; G. H. Jones. *The Nathan Narratives* (1990); R. Polzin. *David and the Deuteronomist* (1993); H. S. Pyper. *David as Reader* (1996).

KEITH BODNER

NATHAN THE PROPHET, WORDS OF. *See* BOOKS REFERRED TO IN THE BIBLE.

NATHANAEL nuh-than´ay-uhl [Ναθαναήλ Nathanaēl]. Means "God has given." 1. A priest from the line of Pashhur whom Ezra required to divorce his foreign wife (1 Esd 9:22).

2. An ancestor of Judith (Jdt 8:1), the heroine of the 2nd cent. BCE Jewish apocryphal novel.

3. An Israelite whom Jesus described as having "no deceit" and whom he called to become his disciple and a witness of his future glory (John 1:45-51). The implication here is not that Nathanael was without sin, but that he was honest and sincere in his dedication to the God of Israel. Somehow, Jesus' observation of him under the fig tree reinforced this perception. John's purpose in including Jesus' encounter with Nathanael is not to show Nathanael's righteousness, but to demonstrate Jesus' supernatural knowledge (compare, e.g., John 4:17-18; 6:70; 9:3). Recognizing that Jesus had unique and special insight, Nathanael made a confession of faith in Jesus as the "Son of God" and as the "King of Israel," the rightful leader of the people of Israel. Jesus responded by promising to him a vision, reminiscent of Jacob's vision at Bethel (Gen 28:10-17), in which he would reveal himself to Nathanael as the Son of Man (John 1:51).

Nathanael is not specifically named in the Synoptics, although his association in the Fourth Gospel with others of the apostles (John 1:45-51) and his presence with the Twelve at the Sea of Galilee after the resurrection (John 21:2) have led some to identify him with persons who do appear in the Synoptics (e.g., Matthew, Simon the Canaanite, Bartholomew).

RALPH K. HAWKINS

NATHAN-MELECH nay´thuhn-mee´lik [נְתַן־מֶלֶךְ nethan-melekh]. Means "the king has given." A court official or eunuch (NRSV; saris סָרִיס) under King Josiah (2 Kgs 23:11; *see* RAB-SARIS). *King* (melekh מֶלֶךְ) may refer to Yahweh or to another deity, specifically Molech (compare v. 10) or Milcom (compare v. 13). Nathan-melech's quarters were near the entrance of the Temple, where the horses dedicated to the sun were kept.

PAULINE A. VIVIANO

NATIONALISM. The study of nationalism as a social phenomenon in biblical analysis has become a topic of serious interest at the beginning of the 21st cent. It appeared to many social and political commentators, scholars, and observers that the end of the cold war in the late 1980s would bring opportunities for internationalism, but instead resulted in the violent resurgence of older, localized loyalties in many parts of the world. Therefore, one major approach to the study of contemporary conflicts has been to revisit the 20th-cent. theories of nationalism, with particular interest in the possibility of understanding nationalist sentiment as a long-standing human preoccupation, and thus worthy of historical as well as contemporary analysis. Among the historical sources that scholars have considered as examples of ancient "nationalism" include biblical texts.

The discussion of nationalism in the Bible, however, faces serious difficulties. Any analysis of nationalism in the Bible faces the daunting task of defining the concept itself before one locates occasions of its expression in ancient texts. Furthermore, it is of the very nature of post-19th-cent. nationalism itself that ancient religious traditions unavoidably become caught up in the very same contemporary nationalist debates that often motivate aspects of the study of ancient sources. In short, it can be part of a modern "nationalist" agenda to locate "nationalism" in ancient texts.

A. Nationalism: An Ancient Reality?

In a historical survey of approaches to nationalism in contemporary analysis, Paul Lawrence emphasizes how elusive has been a widely accepted definition of nationalism. Noting that Plato certainly differentiated Greeks from barbarians (*Resp.* 5.470), and that Bede, in the 8th cent. CE, referred to the English as a single nation (Bede, *Eccl. Hist.* 1.1, 15; 2.1), there is certainly a strong basis for suggesting that some kind of recognition of large-scale membership in a geographically significant population is not a recent social phenomenon in human history. Determining the factors that construct such ancient nationalisms, however, proves difficult. In debates about ancient and modern nationalism, e.g., common language, race, geographical location, and/or shared religious or mythological traditions have all been suggested, but none of them has proved to sustain systematic arguments for national identification or affiliation in general cases—while each have arguably played important roles in specific cases. For example, European historical scholarship locates the modern discussions of nationalism to the 18th and 19th cent., often citing the different paths of German and French nationalism as a key contrast between strong centralizing nationalism seen in 19th-cent. German unification or defined more collectively as a sentiment of the citizenry, defined preeminently in the French revolution.

Modern debates on nationalism tend to focus precisely around the key issue for the study of nationalism in the Bible—namely whether nationalism is in any sense an ancient phenomenon that is ubiquitous in human experience. This view, often referred to as "perennialist" or "primordialist" in the modern literature on nationalism, reaches perhaps its farthest limits with the theories that insist that nationalist sentiment is an evolutionary extension of *Homo sapiens* kinship. Allied against such perennialist views are those who argue that nationalism is among the products of the modern, industrialized world that was uniquely able, beginning in the 19th cent. especially, to marshal large-scale attachments to an otherwise unprecedented social ideal through media (beginning with print) and the manipulation of socioreligious attitudes of allegiance and devotion. Furthermore, as sociologists frequently observed, modern nationalism in the West was able to marshal nearly (and at times explicitly) religious iconography, traditions, and ritual devotion that were considered only possible with the increased "secularization" of European Christianity since the Enlightenment. Such debates about the recent, or primordial, roots of nationalist sentiment clearly are necessary collateral arguments to the study of nationalism in ancient texts.

B. Biblical Israel

1. **The Merneptah Inscription and early conceptions of "peoplehood" in ancient Israel**

The root of "nationalism" in ancient Israel is usually considered to be the famous MERNEPTAH Inscription (normally dated to 1207 BCE, but see Kitchen). The reading of the name *Israel* in this inscription is the oldest reference in extant texts, but the precise implication of this reading is disputed. Egyptologists dispute whether the hieroglyphics indicate a "people" rather than a "state" or "nation" (Hjelm and Thompson; contra Kitchen). The term suggests an ethnic settlement, a social grouping, but not a formalized entity with centralized leadership or urban centers, much less a capital. The consensus among historians continues to be that this provides indication of the early settlements that will eventually consolidate into the united monarchy under Saul and David after 1020 BCE, also based in the highlands of Palestine, and also attests to the significance of the term *Israel* as an identification of this people, as differentiated from other names given to peoples and/or city-states in the surrounding area (e.g., Ashkelon, the coastlands, Gezer, inlands, and Yenoam for areas of Galilee). *See* ISRAEL, NAMES AND ASSOCIATIONS OF; ISRAEL, ORIGINS OF.

2. **Terms for "Israel": Ambiguous contexts**

There is a variety of terms used in the Bible for collective references to Israelites. Perhaps most common is the term **bene yisraʾel** (בְּנֵי יִשְׂרָאֵל, lit. "sons of Israel"), which suggests the use of a term of fictive KINSHIP. The collective use of an otherwise familial term is not at all unusual (e.g., **bene haggolah** [בְּנֵי הַגּוֹלָה], lit., "sons of the exile," Ezra 4:1; 6:19; NRSV, "exiles"); terms of fictive kinship are predominant mainly in the Pentateuch, but is far less common in the prophetic literature. This creates a historical difficulty depending on whether one dates some of the prophetic literature prior to the final form of the Pentateuch, or whether one can be confident about identifying older sources in pentateuchal literature. Another term, **kol-yisraʾel** (כָּל־יִשְׂרָאֵל; lit. "the whole of Israel"), is used far less prominently. It is hard to attach much significance to these terms, however, as the context only rarely speaks of a critical relationship between territory and peoples, although this is not entirely absent.

The problem of terminology is particularly acute when discussing terms normally rendered in English as "nation," particularly in the use of **goyim** (גּוֹיִם, meaning the NATIONS), which is not, however, quite the same as modern conceptions of nationality. For example, the following passage may suggest "future predictions" of a nation with a territory: "I am God, the God of your father; do not be afraid to go down to Egypt, for I will make of you a great nation there" (Gen 46:3). But it may also express awareness of the people of Israel being ethnically different from surrounding Egyptians, as is clearly stated in passages such as the following: "But the LORD will make a distinction between the livestock of Israel and the livestock of Egypt, so that nothing shall die of all that belongs to the Israelites" (Exod 9:4). Is this, however, a form of emergent national identity? At the same time, the term **goyim** can certainly speak of other nations: "I am going to bring upon you a nation from far away, O house of Israel, says the LORD. It is an enduring nation, it is an ancient nation, a nation whose language you do not know, nor can you understand what they say" (Jer 5:15).

Despite these cautions, however, it seems beyond doubt that the biblical texts most certainly represent a time when Israelite existence was to be expressed in what can be called "national" terms in the same way that other "nations" can be spoken of at that time, and quite different from transnational imperial empires such as the Assyrian, Babylonian, Persian, and Hellenistic periods. As Steven Grosby has argued, the Israelite people expressed many aspects necessary for "national" existence, including fictive kinship terminology beyond family and tribe, a religious tie to an explicitly demarcated land as "belonging to Yahweh," and thus an association of the "people of Yahweh" as a community with territorial boundaries.

3. **Borders of Israel**

Crucial to any discussion of nationalism in ancient textual traditions is a sense of place—a people that is traditionally attached to a LAND. Here again, however, the data are no more precise than they are with terms of "nation." Many scholars place considerable emphasis on the significance of Num 34:1-12 as the establishment of a "bounded territory": "The LORD spoke to Moses, saying: 'Command the Israelites, and say to them: When you enter the land of Canaan (this is the land that shall fall to you for an inheritance, the land of Canaan, defined by its boundaries) ....'" The LORD then gives boundaries, from the wilderness of Zin to Kadesh-barnea, to the Wadi of Egypt, to the Great Sea; from the Great Sea to Mount Hor to Zedad; from Ziphron to Hazar-enan; to Shepham; from Shepham to Riblah to the eastern slope of the sea of Chinnereth, then to the Jordan and the Dead Sea.

The complication in this for biblical history is, of course, the fact that the tradition represents the Israelites as a people not indigenous to any particular land, but rather given land from God, with the strong awareness that someone else was previously there: "but the hill country shall be yours, for though it is a forest, you shall clear it and possess it to its farthest borders; for you shall drive out the Canaanites, though they have chariots of iron, and though they are strong" (Josh 17:18; *see* CANAAN, CANAANITES).

Nevertheless, borders of Israelite peoples are spoken of in general terms, but it is difficult to assign to any single passage a priority. In addition to the more precise definitions provided in Num 34, e.g., there can be wider, generalized borders; note Exod 23:31, which is the first reference to borders in the Pentateuch. Furthermore, note that successful military campaigns result in "expanding borders," while peace means lack of conflict within borders (Ps 147:14; Isa 26:15; Sir 47:13).

4. Changing patterns of settlement: Yehud

Finally, the question of nationalism in ancient Israel is complicated by the fact that borders change depending on the time period. The territories under David and Solomon seem the most expansive, allowing for grandiose claims of God's blessings through conquests of foreign lands, preeminently in the time of Solomon: "For he had dominion over all the region west of the Euphrates from Tiphsah to Gaza, over all the kings west of the Euphrates; and he had peace on all sides. During Solomon's lifetime Judah and Israel lived in safety, from Dan even to Beer-sheba, all of them under their vines and fig trees" (1 Kgs 4:24-25; compare Isa 26:15).

After the devastation of 587 BCE, however, the attention of the biblical texts shifts to the postexilic communities, which are territories under Persian, then Hellenistic administration with local leadership. Scholars of the postexilic, or Persian period, typically turn to genealogical lists, or the "Golah List" (Ezra 2 // Neh 7) and try to chart the expanse of territories mentioned there. John Wright draws evidence from the study of genealogical and tribal-structure lists in the Persian period (e.g., 1 Chr 2:3–4:23 and 8:1-40) to reveal concentrations of population in Jerusalem, the Judean hill country, and the western area of Benjamin just north of Jerusalem, but it is a territory connected with a people that "expands and contracts" according to military fortunes and imperial interests; but he strongly suggests Yehud to be a polity that is closer to an ethnos rather than a bordered territory.

5. From nation to ethnos?

Finally, theories of biblical nationalism must contend with the fact that the biblical texts are not of one mind on late ideologies of communal identity (Smith-Christopher). The notion that JUDAISM became quite diverse, and developed away from strict notions of a single national existence, has been developed from recent work on the diversity of Hellenistic Judaism (see Gruen), which represents a period of rich variety of perspectives.

Finally, the devastation of 587 was interpreted by many late biblical texts as an end to older forms of nationalism, as threatened by Deut 28:63-65, where Israel is scattered among all peoples of the earth.

Many aspects of Babylonian and Persian period prophetic literature can be read not merely to develop a theology of temporary diasporic existence, but rather the beginnings of a theology of nonnational existence (e.g., Jer 29:7; *see* EXILE). While traditions of nationalism prefer to read those texts that suggest attachment to land as a primordial indication of national existence, it is clear that DIASPORA existence is not rejected as a viable lifestyle in latter biblical texts such as Daniel, Tobit, and Esther.

It is precisely the nature of communal existence that is debated in diaspora biblical literature, where, e.g., Maccabean resurgent nationalism (*see* MACCABEES, MACCABEAN REVOLT) is criticized in Dan 11 and in the widely acknowledged quietism of the wisdom tradition, as well as expressed in early rabbinic examples such as R. Yochanon Ben Zakkai's opposition to the Jewish Revolt against Rome in 67–70 CE, and in the trans-ethnic polemics of early Christianity, e.g., when the Gospel of Matthew says to make disciples of all NATIONS (Matt 28:19), and Paul breaks down national and ethnic boundaries: "there is no longer Jew or Greek .... And if you belong to Christ, then you are Abraham's offspring" (Gal 3:28-29; compare Col 3:11). The book of Acts depicts the beginnings of the early church as a gathering of people from many nations (Acts 2:5-11). The communal nature of the TABLE FELLOWSHIP in the early church promotes the ideal expressed in Isa 25:6-8 (see Matt 8:11) that the Lord of Hosts will make for all peoples a feast, and that the kingdom of God is like a great banquet to which many are invited (Luke 14:15-24).

In short, discussions of biblical nationalism must contend with the very real presence of an internal late biblical critique of the Israelite experiment with the monarchy suggesting at the very least a changed form of communal existence. This critique extends to the very request for a monarch implicit in 1 Sam 8, e.g., which is a post-587 criticism of the actual policies and experience of monarchical Israel, rather than "before the fact" prophecy (*see* KING, KINGSHIP). The long list of political and economic difficulties of the monarchy conclude with what is reported as a stubborn refusal: "But the people refused to listen to the voice of Samuel; they said, 'No! but we are determined to have a king over us, so that we also may be like other nations, and that our king may govern us and go out before us and fight our battles'" (1 Sam 8:19-20).

The biblical texts, therefore, include notable debates about the very necessity of national existence "like the other nations." Thus, any analyses of "biblical nationalism" must note that the biblical texts present both diversity and development, and thus raise questions about using biblical texts to defend a primordial theory of nationalism. *See* ETHNICITY; FOREIGN, FOREIGNER; GENTILES; ISRAEL, HISTORY OF.

Bibliography: Bede. *A History of the English Church and People.* Leo Sherley-Price, trans. (1955); C. E. Carter. *The Emergence of Yehud in the Persian Period: A Social and Demographic Study* (1999); S. Grosby. *Biblical Ideas of Nationality: Ancient and Modern* (2002); E. Gruen. *Heritage and Hellenism: The Reinvention of Jewish Tradition* (2002); I. Hjelm and T. L. Thompson. "The Victory Song of Merneptah, Israel and the People of Palestine." *JSOT* 27 (2002) 3–18; Kenneth Kitchen. "The Victories of Merenptah, and the Nature of Their Record." *JSOT* 28 (2004) 259–72; P. Lawrence. *Nationalism: History and Theory* (2005); Oded Lipshits. *The Fall and Rise of Jerusalem: The History of Judah under Babylonian Rule* (2005); Daniel Smith-Christopher. *A Biblical Theology of Exile* (2002); J. Wright. "Remapping Yehud: The Borders of Yehud and the Genealogies of Chronicles." *Judah and the Judeans in the Persian Period.* O. Lipshits and M. Oeming, eds. (2006) 67–89; John Howard Yoder. *The Jewish-Christian Schism Revisited.* M. Cartwright and P. Ochs, eds. (2003).

DANIEL L. SMITH-CHRISTOPHER

NATIONS [גּוֹיִם goyim, לְאֻמִּים leʾummim, עַמִּים ʿammim; Aram. אֻמַּיָּא ʾummayyaʾ; τὰ ἔθνη ta ethnē]. In the OT, although Israel is occasionally referred to as a *nation* (goy גּוֹי) rather than a *people* (ʿam עַם), the plural goyim, especially with the article (haggoyim הַגּוֹיִם; "the nations"), almost invariably refers to the nations other than Israel. This usage continues in the Apocrypha and the NT, though these later writings also reflect a subsequent development in which the sense of *nation* gives way to that of "non-Jewish," so that goyim and (under the influence of the LXX), ethnē (singular: ethnos ἔθνος) also come to be used with reference to groups of non-Jewish individuals. The NRSV addresses this dual sense of ethnē in the Apocrypha and the NT by using both "nations" and "GENTILES" (from the Lat. *gentilis,* "belonging to a *gens* [clan, nation]"), though it is not always easy to discern in specific instances whether the sense of *nation* has indeed been eclipsed. In the NT, where corporate identity is no longer defined unequivocally with reference to the nation of Israel, there are some instances where "(all) the nations" includes Israel.

From beginning to end the biblical narrative deals focally with a particular people, but always within a larger setting that embraces all nations. In Genesis, the story of Abraham and his descendants is prefaced by a narrative (Gen 1–11) that begins with the creation of the world and culminates in the list of Noah's descendants, from whom "the nations spread abroad on the earth after the flood" (Gen 10:32). After the tumultuous story of Israel has unfolded from the initial high point of the exodus ("I brought [them] out of the land of Egypt in the sight of the nations"; Lev 26:45) to its ignominious low point in the exile ("I swore to them in the wilderness that I would scatter them among the nations"; Ezek 20:23), the Jewish canon concludes with the edict of Cyrus, to whom "the LORD, the God of heaven, has given . . . all the kingdoms of the earth," an edict that authorized the Jewish exiles to return to Jerusalem and to rebuild the Temple (2 Chr 36:23). After recounting the story of Jesus, the servant in whose "name the Gentiles will hope" (Matt 12:21), and the work of the apostolic witnesses in proclaiming the message of Christ "to all nations, beginning from Jerusalem" (Luke 24:47), the Christian canon ends with John's vision of the new Jerusalem, at the center of which stands the tree of life, whose "leaves . . . are for the healing of the nations" (Rev 22:2). The particular stories of Israel and of Christ, then, cannot be told without reference to "the nations," who play an indispensable role in each.

In Christian reflection on these stories, an inaccurate contrast has often been drawn between the "particularism" of Israel and its scriptures and the "universalism" of Christianity and the NT. Such a contrast is one-sided and misleading. Despite Israel's sense of election and distinct identity, both the OT and subsequent Jewish literature contain their own forms of UNIVERSALISM, reflecting various ways of ascribing to Gentiles a positive place in the divine purposes. Conversely, despite the early Christian conviction that the gospel is to be proclaimed to all nations, this gospel is good news for Gentiles only insofar as they are prepared to become part of a very particular social entity. While the question of Israel and the nations is an important aspect of self-identification in both testaments, universalism and particularism are inadequate categories for dealing with the question.

- A. Terminology
  - 1. Hebrew and Aramaic
    - a. goyim
    - b. leʾummim
    - c. ʿammim
    - d. ʾummayya

   2. Greek
      a. Septuagint
      b. Apocrypha
      c. New Testament
B. Ethnological Considerations
C. The Place of the Nations/Gentiles in Biblical Discourse
   1. Old Testament
   2. Apocrypha
   3. New Testament
Bibliography

A. Terminology

Biblical material pertinent to the topic of "the nations" is by no means restricted to those words rendered as *nations* or *Gentiles* in the NRSV. References to specific nations, for example, can be just as significant; Isa 19:18-25 (mentioned below) is a striking case in point. Still, any discussion of the topic needs to begin with vocabulary.

1. Hebrew and Aramaic

a. goyim. Goy and goyim are uniformly rendered by *nation(s)* in the NRSV. As a collective entity a nation can be thought of as coming into existence at a particular time (Exod 9:24; Dan 12:1) and also as being able to diminish to the point that it no longer qualifies as such (Jer 33:24). The defining characteristics of a nation, however, tend to be assumed rather than explicitly described. Several characteristics appear frequently. 1) National existence is closely bound up with possession of a LAND. God "apportioned the nations" by "fix[ing] the boundaries of the peoples" (Deut 32:8). The increase of a nation is equivalent to the enlargement of "the borders of the land" (Isa 26:15). Israel will be tempted to think of itself as a nation like the others once it has "taken possession of [the land] and settled in it" (Deut 17:14). 2) National existence is also characterized by kingship. Israel believes that in order to become a nation "like all the nations that are around me" it is necessary to have a king (Deut 17:14; compare 1 Sam 8:5, 20). Nehemiah simply assumes that each nation has its own king (Neh 13:26). Ezekiel looks forward to a time when Israel and Judah will be "one nation in the land" with "one king . . . over them all" (Ezek 37:22). 3) One role of the king is to lead a nation in battle (1 Sam 8:20), which leads to another aspect of national identity: military engagement is so integral to nationhood that only with respect to an ideal future can the prophet imagine a nation not manufacturing sword and spear and not learning war (Isa 2:4). Consequently nationhood carries with it the possibility either of ruling over other nations (e.g., Deut 15:6) or of being subject to another nation (e.g., Isa 36:18). 4) Another defining characteristic has to do with religion and cult. It is simply assumed that each nation has its own god (e.g., Deut 12:30; Josh 23:7; 1 Kgs 11:2). In the most probable reading of Deut 32:8, the nations were apportioned by the Most High "according to the number of the gods." To "be like the nations" is to "worship wood and stone" (Ezek 20:32), that is, to follow their pattern of worship.

In addition to these major characteristics, several other things are associated with a goy: a distinctive language (e.g., Gen 10:5; Jer 5:15; Zech 8:23); descent from a common ancestor (e.g., Gen 10:5; 17:4-6; Jer 16:19); characteristic "statutes and ordinances" (Deut 4:8; also Ezek 5:7); distinctive customs (Jer 9:26), though for the most part "the way of the nations" (Jer 10:2) has to do with religious practice.

That these various characteristics were considered to be interconnected can be seen from instances in which they appear together: "the descendants of Japheth in their lands, with their own language, by their families, in their nations" (Gen 10:5); "the nations [who have been resettled in Samaria] do not know the law of the god of the land" (2 Kgs 17:26); "the gods of the nations of those lands" (2 Chr 32:13). Likewise, the characteristics of nationhood can also be discerned from the words that are used in parallel with *nations*: peoples (e.g., Gen 25:23; Ps 18:43 [Heb. 18:44]; Isa 11:10); kings (e.g., Ps 72:11; 135:10; Isa 62:2); kingdoms (e.g., Isa 13:4; Hag 2:22); countries (= lands; e.g., Ezek 6:8; Zech 10:9); provinces (medhinoth [מְדִינוֹת]; Lam 1:1).

Although Israel is to remain distinct from the nations, not following their ways or worshiping their gods (e.g., Lev 18:24; 2 Kgs 17:15), the biblical writers show no hesitation in describing Israel as a nation. God's promise to Abraham was to make of him "a great nation" (Gen 12:2); God tells Moses that Israel is to be "a priestly kingdom and a holy nation" (Exod 19:6); Moses in turn reminds God that "this nation is your people" (Exod 33:13); God speaks through Isaiah: "Listen to me, my people, and give heed to me, my nation" (Isa 51:4).

At the same time, however, when it appears in the plural (goyim), *nations* almost always refers to the nations other than Israel. The only clear exception is Ezek 37:22, which refers to the two "nations" of Judah and Israel. (In Ezek 2:3, the singular, found in the Syriac, is probably original.) The NRSV rendering of Ezek 25:8 seems to imply that Judah is one of the nations ("The house of Judah is like all the other nations"), but otherwise has no counterpart in the Hebrew.

b. leʾummim. This term is found primarily in poetic material, usually in the plural and usually in parallel with some other term (most often goyim or ʿammim). The NRSV renders leʾummim *peoples* unless it stands in parallel with ʿammim, in which case it is rendered *nations*. In four instances where the MT has ʾummim (אֻמִּים, tribes, peoples; Ps 44:14 [Heb. 44:15]; 57:9 [Heb. 57:10]; 67:4 [Heb. 67:5]; 108:3 [Heb. 108:4]), leʾummim is also the preferred reading (*see* MT, MASORETIC TEXT). The plural form always refers to peoples other than Israel. In the singular it is used once of Israel ("my nation," in par. with "my people" [ʿammi עַמִּי]; Isa 51:4) and three times in a generic sense (Prov 11:26; 14:28, 34).

c. ʿammim. While the singular ʿam is distinctively used of Israel as a people, the plural ʿammim is often used of peoples other than Israel. In a handful of instances (1 Kgs 4:34 [Heb. 5:14]; Isa 12:4; 14:2; 24:13; Ezek 38:8; Hos 9:1; 10:10) the NRSV renders ʿammim as *nations* rather than *peoples*, though no semantic distinction is apparent.

d. ʾummayyaʾ. In the Aram. portions of the OT, the NRSV consistently uses *nations* to render ʾummayyaʾ—once in Ezra (4:10) and six times in Daniel (3:4, 7; 4:1 [Aram. 3:31]; 5:19; 7:14). All but one of the occurrences in Daniel involve the set phrase "peoples (ʿammayyaʾ עַמְמַיָּא), nations and languages"; the other occurrence is a slight variation: "peoples and nations of every language" (6:25 [Aram. 6:26]). The singular form of the phrase also appears in Dan 3:29. For the most part the phrase is used directly or indirectly by the king of Babylon, and thus implicitly includes Israel. In the final occurrence, however, it refers to the dominion given to the "one like a son of man" (7:14), and thus refers to the nations other than Israel.

2. Greek

a. Septuagint. While the LXX tends to use ethnos for goy and laos (λαός) for ʿam, each Gk. word also renders a range of other Hebrew words, resulting in a certain consolidation of vocabulary. In addition, the LXX bears witness to an intensification of a tendency already present in the Heb.—namely, to use ʿam (singular) with reference to Israel and goyim (plural) with reference to the other nations. In instances where Israel is referred to as a goy, for example, the LXX often eschews ethnos, either rendering it as laos (Josh 3:17; 4:1; Isa 58:2) or formulating the clause in some other way (Josh 5:6, 8; 10:13; Ps 83:4 [Heb. 83:5]; Isa 51:4; Ezek 2:3; though for exceptions see Gen 12:2; Exod 19:6; 2 Sam 7:23). Conversely, ethnos is routinely used in instances where ʿam (singular) is used of a nation other than Israel (e.g., Exod 1:9; 15:14; Lev 20:2; Deut 1:28; 2:10). Likewise, the LXX translators routinely used ethnē for ʿammim where the Hebrew term referred to "peoples" other than Israel (e.g., Exod 19:5; 23:27; Lev 20:24, 26; Deut 2:25; 6:14). In short, the LXX reflects a development in which laos and ethnē have become almost technical terms for Israel (in its distinctive status as God's special people) and the other nations respectively. There is a parallel development in non-Jewish Greek usage, in which ethnē denotes the non-Greek nations (barbarians), though the extent to which this influenced the Jewish development is unclear.

b. Apocrypha. Several aspects of the use of ethnos/ethnē in the Apocrypha deserve mention, especially when viewed in comparison with the Septuagint. First, while the plural continues to be used as a designation for non-Jews, it frequently refers to groups of non-Jewish individuals rather than to nations per se. This is clearly the case when numbers are specified: the 3000 ethnē of 1 Macc 5:22 or the 20000 of 2 Macc 8:9 are clearly individuals, not nations. Likewise we are to think of individuals in the references to the ethnē "who dallied with prostitutes" (2 Macc 6:4) or who lived in "a certain town" (2 Macc 12:13). Although it is not always clear why the NRSV has chosen one term (*nations* or *Gentiles*) over the other, in most occurrences of *Gentiles* an individual sense is at least possible. Second, the authors or translators of the apocryphal books do not shy away from using ethnos with reference to Israel. Tobit speaks of "my kindred and my nation [NRSV "people"] who had gone with me in exile to Nineveh" (Tob 1:3); Judas refers to "the misfortunes of our nation and of the sanctuary" (1 Macc 3:59). Similarly, 2 Maccabees speaks of "the other nations" (4:35; 6:14), implying that Israel is to be considered a nation as well. In these writings laos (people) also appears frequently with reference to Israel, but the preference for laos over ethnos as a designation for Israel is not as pronounced here as in the LXX.

c. New Testament. The use of ethnos/ethnē in the NT is consistent with patterns already present in the LXX and the Apocrypha, though with some distinctively Christian developments as well. The basic sense of the term continues to be apparent, especially with the singular form, which in almost every case refers to a national entity. In Acts 7:7 and 8:9, for example, ethnos is used of specific identifiable nations (Egypt and Samaria respectively). In his apocalyptic discourse Jesus speaks of a time when "nation will rise against nation and kingdom against kingdom" (Matt 24:7 and par.). Acts 2:5 speaks of "every nation under heaven" (compare Acts 10:35; 17:26) and goes on to list some fifteen of them. This basic sense of the term is especially apparent in Revelation, where the NRSV quite appropriately chooses *nation(s)* to render all twenty-three occurrences of ethnos/ethnē. Characteristic of Revelation is the phrase "peoples and tribes and languages and nations" (11:9), which appears in several variations.

Outside Revelation, however, there are few instances where the plural form ethnē refers to nations per se (Luke 21:24-25). Most commonly the term is used with reference to a collectivity of individuals, as when Paul speaks of eating with Gentiles (Gal 2:12) or the author of Acts describes scenes in which Gentiles receive the Holy Spirit (10:45) or hear something that was said (13:48). This sense of ethnē is also apparent when it stands in parallel with *Greeks* (Acts 14:1-2; 1 Cor 1:23) or Judeans (Acts 14:5; Rom 3:29; 9:24). Although the NRSV uses *Gentile* in the singular on six occasions, nowhere is this a rendering of ethnos, which never refers to an individual in its singular form. In each case *Gentile* renders some other form, two of which deserve specific mention (the others are Mark

7:26; Acts 10:28; 15:23; Gal 2:15). One of these is Gal 2:14, where Paul uses the related adverb ethnikōs (ἐθνικῶς) to describe Peter as one who "live[s] like a Gentile and not like a Jew." The other is Matt 18:17, which contains the closest Gk. equivalent to *Gentile*—the adjective ethnikos (ἐθνικός), pertaining to a foreign nation or, in its singular form, as a substantive ("let such a one be to you as a Gentile and a tax collector"). The plural form, ethnikoi (ἐθνικοί), also as a substantive, is found in Matt 5:47; 6:7; and 3 John 7.

Israel is referred to as an ethnos on a number of occasions, but most often when the speaker is a Gentile (John 18:35; Acts 10:22) or when a Jew is addressing a Gentile (Acts 24:2; 24:17; 26:4). Only in Luke 7:5 and John 11:48-52 do we find in-house Jewish dialogue in which ethnos is used of the Jewish people, and even here the relationship of the Jews with an outside nation (specifically, Rome) is central to the context. Presumably Israel is included in the statement that God made "every nation" from one ancestor (Acts 17:26; compare Acts 10:35), though this is not explicit. The plural phrase "all the nations" (panta ta ethnē πάντα τὰ ἔθνη) clearly includes Israel in Luke 24:47 ("to all nations, beginning from Jerusalem"). Matthew's use of the phrase has occasioned significant debate, since the ending of his Gospel could be read in an anti-Judaic way if the final command of Jesus to the Eleven is to "make disciples of all the Gentiles" (28:19). Of the other three appearances of the phrase in Matthew, two are indeterminate (24:9, 14). The third concerns the gathering of panta ta ethnē for the final judgment (25:32). While it is hard to imagine the Jewish nation not being included here (or in 28:19), both passages seem to be concerned with individuals rather than nations, which would be more consistent with the reading "Gentiles."

Finally, two specifically Christian usages are to be noted. First, on a number of occasions a distinction is made between non-Jewish believers and Gentiles (1 Cor 5:1; 12:2; Eph 4:17; 1 Thess 4:5; 1 Pet 2:12; 4:3). What is implicit in most of these references is made explicit by Paul in 1 Cor 12:2 ("when you were ethnē"): by virtue of their identification with Christ, these believers are Gentiles no longer but have taken on a new identity. Second, one aspect of this new identity is that Christians themselves constitute a new ethnos. In 1 Pet 2:9 the church is described as "a chosen race [genos], a royal priesthood, a holy nation [ethnos], a people [laos] for [God's own] possession." In Matt 21:43, the kingdom is to be taken from the chief priests and Pharisees "and given to a people [ethnos] that produces the fruits of the kingdom."

B. Ethnological Considerations

In our discussion of specific vocabulary items in the preceding section, we have made use of their "equivalents" in a contemporary English translation. Since meaning is embedded in cultural context, however, both sets of culture-based meaning require critical reflection if understanding is not to be distorted or short-circuited by unexamined assumptions. We cannot simply assume that goy or ethnos meant for ancient speakers of Hebrew or Greek what "nation" means for contemporary speakers of English. Nor should we assume that any meaning attached to "nation" is the objective reality against which the meaning of other terms is to be measured. To help with the task of critical reflection, we can turn with profit to social-scientific studies of ETHNICITY.

Sociologists and cultural anthropologists generally agree that ethnic identity involves a variety of elements or indicators that persist over time—genealogical descent, territory, language, way of life, religious practice, political organization, shared experience, and the like. There is disagreement, however, as to the nature of ethnic identity itself. At one pole are the essentialist or primordialist approaches, which see ethnicity as an objective reality that is inherent in a constellation of such elements and is simply determined by them. The other pole—the constructivist or instrumentalist—conceives of ethnic identity as something that is socially constructed and maintained.

Some elements, of course, seem to lend themselves more to one pole or the other. Descent might seem more of an immutable or ascribed reality, and thus suggestive of an essentialist approach; social or religious customs might appear more a matter of convention or acquisition, and thus more in keeping with a constructivist approach. Yet such distinctions are not clear-cut. What counts for descent is subject to a measure of social construction (e.g., intermarriage and the status of resultant children). Conversely, religious observances can be perceived as forming part of an immutable reality. The most fruitful approaches, then, will be found somewhere in between the two poles, recognizing the existence of some basic raw materials, but also understanding ethnic identity as a value-added product constructed out of these materials.

To be sure, the diverse nature of the raw materials means that ethnic identity can be constructed in a variety of ways. Some groups place more emphasis on elements that come with birth, with the result that ethnic identity is something that is ascribed. OT Israel is a case in point. Others—e.g., Hellenistic Greeks and Romans—place the emphasis on elements that can be learned or acquired. To use categories suggested by Denise Kimber Buell, we can think of a spectrum stretched out between the poles of fixity (ascribed elements) and fluidity (acquired elements).

The groups just mentioned (i.e., OT Israel, Hellenistic Greeks, Romans) are not just examples, of course. Their location at different ends of the spectrum draws attention to a significant change in environment that affects the biblical material under discussion. In the OT, Israel's identity is constructed as ascribed, fixed and immutable: there is a fundamental distinction between

Israel and "the nations"; sojourners might be able to share in almost every aspect of Israel's life (e.g., Lev 24:22; also Exod 12:49; Num 9:14; 15:16, 29-30), but the only means of entry into the people of Israel is birth; while marriage into Israel is possible (e.g., Ruth), only over the course of several generations would the offspring of such a union be fully integrated into the people (compare Deut 23:8). Alexander and his successors, however, brought with them the idea that "Greek-ness" was not limited to those born of Greek parents but instead was an identity that one could take on through the acquisition of Gk. language and culture. This Hellenistic ethos was taken up by the Romans and adapted in the service of the empire.

This development had a significant impact on identity construction within Judaism and, subsequently, Christianity. First, the arrival of Hellenism both raised new questions for Jews about how to identify themselves vis-à-vis the "nations" and provided a model for a new conception of Jewishness as an identity that a Gentile could assume by becoming a proselyte (North; Cohen; *see* PROSELYTE). Second, the influx of Gentiles and the separation from Judaism were primary catalysts in the developing self-identification of early Christianity, one aspect of which was the idea that Christians themselves constituted an **ethnos** or **genos** (γένος; 1 Pet 2:9), distinguishable from "Jews or Greeks" (1 Cor 10:32; compare Aristides, *Apol.* 2.2) as a new nation (Justin, *Dial.* 119.4, 6) or race (*Diogn.* 1.1).

C. The Place of the Nations/Gentiles in Biblical Discourse

1. Old Testament

A survey of the various roles played by the nations in OT material demonstrates both the importance of the nations for Israel's self-understanding and the complexity of OT thought about the nations.

In one of their more negative characterizations, the nations function as bad examples—enticing models of wickedness from whom Israel is to remain separate but whom Israel is constantly tempted to emulate. It was because of the wickedness of the nations that God drove them out before the Israelites (Lev 18:24; Deut 9:4; 1 Kgs 14:24). Thus when Israel took possession of the land, they were commanded not to "imitate the abhorrent practices of those nations" (Deut 18:9; compare Deut 12:30; Jer 10:2). Nevertheless, Israel continued to be "snared into imitating them" (Deut 12:30), "learn[ing] to do as they did" (Ps 106:35) in their worship (2 Chr 36:14), their ordinances (Ezek 5:7) and their over-reliance on kings (Deut 17:14; 1 Sam 8:5).

The nations also play the role of Israel's enemies. In the ideal state of affairs, they are subjugated enemies (Deut 28:1), subservient to Israel (Deut 15:6; Ps 47:3 [Heb. 47:4]) or its king (2 Sam 22:44; Ps 2:8) and contributing to Israel's wealth and well-being (2 Sam 8:11). More often, of course, they are actual enemies (Neh 5:9), who "treacherously plot evil" against Israel (Ps 59:5 [Heb. 59:6]) and function as agents of desecration (Ps 79:1) and oppression (Isa 14:2). Still, the hope remains that in the future God will finally act in judgment against the nations (Isa 30:28; Ezek 30:3; Zeph 3:8), who will then submit to Israel's rule (Isa 14:2) and bring tribute to Jerusalem (Isa 60:5; Hag 2:7).

Yet even in their role as enemies the nations are not operating outside the divine purposes. The promise to Israel that "the LORD your God will set you high above all the nations of the earth" was conditional: "If you will only obey the LORD your God" (Deut 28:1). The other side of the condition was that, if Israel were disobedient, God would bring "a grim-faced nation" (Deut 28:50) from far away as an agent of punishment. Thus when Israel proved to be disobedient, God "gave them into the hand of the nations" (Ps 106:41) and "scattered [them] among the nations" (Ps 44:11; also Jer 9:16; Ezek 4:13).

Moving in a more positive direction, the nations appear in the role of witnesses to God's dealings with Israel. This role began with the exodus, as God brought them "out of the land of Egypt in the sight of the nations" (Lev 26:45; also Ezek 20:14, 22). It continued whenever God acted to bless or vindicate Israel: "then it was said among the nations, 'The LORD has done great things for them'" (Ps 126:2). This role has a negative side to it as well, in that the nations also stand as witnesses to God's judgment of Israel, recognizing that God's anger was provoked "because they abandoned the covenant of the LORD" (Deut 29:25; also Jer 22:8-9). Related to this, but representing less perception on the part of the nations, are instances where they are presented as taunting the Israelites for their misfortunes (Jer 44:8) and concluding that their God had abandoned them (Ps 79:10; Joel 2:17), a prospect that is used by Moses in beseeching God to be lenient (Num 14:15-16) and by Nehemiah in exhorting the people to repent (Neh 5:9). This role is one that will be played in the eschatological future as well, as the nations witness Israel's salvation and vindication (Isa 52:10; 62:2; Jer 33:9; Ezek 37:28).

Further, the nations appear as worshipers of God and recipients of blessing. Sometimes this role is more potential than actual, as when God declares that the nations will be blessed in Abraham and his offspring (Gen 18:18; 22:18; 26:4); Solomon calls on God to hear the prayer of the "foreigner" who comes from a distant land to pray in the Temple (1 Kgs 8:41-43); or the psalmist calls on the nations to "worship the LORD in holy splendor" (Ps 96:9; also 117:1). But instances of actual worship and blessing are recounted as well: Naaman's vow to make sacrifices only to "the LORD" (except for command performances in the house of Rimmon; 2 Kgs 5:18); gifts brought by "many" from "the nations" "to the LORD in Jerusalem" (2 Chr 32:23); and the repentance of the Ninevites, who "cr[ied] mightily to God" (Jonah 3:8; also Mal 1:11). In addition, there is the degree to which the SOJOURNER was included within the covenant life of Israel.

Participation by the nations in worship and blessing is especially pronounced in passages dealing with the eschatological future. The nations not only witness God's saving activity on Israel's behalf, but decide to make pilgrimage to Jerusalem in order to learn God's ways (Isa 2:2-4//Mic 4:1-4), to entreat God's favor (Zech 8:22-23), to share in the end-time banquet on the holy mountain (Isa 25:6-10), to celebrate the festival of booths (Zech 14:16-19), and so on. In the latter parts of Isaiah the action might seem to move in the opposite direction, as the Servant is commissioned "as a light to the nations, that my salvation may reach the end of the earth" (Isa 49:6; also 42:1, 6) and "survivors" are sent out "to declare my glory among the nations" (Isa 66:19). Even so, the outcome of this centrifugal action is that the nations will journey to "the holy mountain Jerusalem," bringing with them the exiled Israelites "as an offering to the LORD" (Isa 66:20). The expectation in Isa 19:19 that "on that day there will be an altar to the LORD in the center of the land of Egypt" is a rare exception to this Jerusalem-centered pattern.

Finally, as has become apparent already, the nations play out their various roles under the sovereignty of Israel's God, who "rules over the nations" (Ps 22:28 [Heb. 22:9]; also 2 Chr 20:6) and will "judge the peoples with equity" (Ps 96:10). It was God who "apportioned the nations" and fixed their boundaries (Deut 32:8) and who caused nations to rise and fall (Job 12:23).

2. Apocrypha

Most of the roles assigned to the nations in OT material reappear in the Apocrypha. The nations or Gentiles appear as negative models, whose ways some Israelites avoid (Tob 1:11) while others find desirable (1 Macc 1:11-15). Whole narratives are given over to their activity as enemies of Israel (Judith, 1 and 2 Maccabees) and they also play a role as agents of divine punishment (Tob 13:5; Bar 4:6) and as witnesses to God's dealings with Israel (Sir 39:10; 46:6; 2 Macc 1:27). Gentiles are also presented as recipients of divine blessing (Sir 44:21) and as worshipers of God, both in the present (see below) and in the eschatological future (Tob 13:11; 14:6).

In addition, Jewish thinking about the nations underwent certain developments in the Hellenistic period, most of which are reflected in the Apocrypha. One is the emergence of apocalyptic literature, in which Israel's troubled experience at the hand of the nations is often seen as just the earthly dimension of more cosmic struggles between God and corrupted spiritual powers (e.g., *1 En.* 6–11; 85–90). While the Apocrypha does not contain any apocalyptic work, the apocalyptic sections of Daniel (i.e., chaps. 7–12) might be mentioned in this connection. Another development has to do with proselytism (*see* PROSELYTE), as Jews came to understand their national identity as something that a Gentile could acquire through conversion (Tob 1:8; Jdt 14:10). Proselytes in turn were part of a larger phenomenon of Gentile attraction to Judaism (e.g., Philo, *Mos.* 2.17-24; Josephus, *Ag. Ap.* 2.279–84). Some Jews saw such sympathization with Judaism as simply a way station on the road to proselytism (e.g., Josephus, *Ant.* 20.43–45), while others were of the opinion that Gentile sympathizers could be acceptable to God without full conversion (e.g., *Ant.* 20.41). Although the Apocrypha contains no explicit statement of the latter view, Gentile attraction to Judaism or worship of Israel's God tends to be viewed positively (2 Macc 3:1-3, 35-36; Bel 1:41; Add Esth 16:15-16; 3 Macc 1:9; 6:33; 4 Macc 4:11-12). Finally, various Hellenistic Jews made a concerted attempt to present the Torah as a written formulation of a natural law that is accessible to all on the basis of sanctified reason. While no apocryphal writing is as generous in this regard as Philo or the *Letter of Aristeas*, the Wisdom of Solomon nevertheless presents life-giving wisdom as something that can be found by Gentiles and Jews alike (e.g., Wis 6:12).

A recurring feature of these developments in Second-Temple Judaism is what can be called their universalism, that is, an interest in the possibility that Gentiles might be included in positive ways in God's dealings and purposes. While there is considerable fluidity and ambiguity, it is nevertheless possible to identify several distinct forms in which Gentiles might be included: proselytes (full members of the covenant people); righteous Gentiles (acceptable to God on the basis of observances required for Gentiles); ethical monotheists (adherents of a natural law); participants in end-time salvation. Of course, exclusionary strains are present as well, most notably in *Jubilees* (15:26) and the Qumran material.

3. New Testament

In its first century or so, the Christian movement was transformed from a Jewish renewal group still within the structures of Judaism into a Gentile religion attempting to establish itself in the Greco-Roman world. Thus the most pertinent questions to ask about the NT are on what terms the Gentiles came to be included in the movement and how this inclusion was perceived. Although the emergent orthodox church was marked by anti-Judaic apologetic and supersessionist theology (the idea that the [Gentile] church had superseded Israel in God's purposes, taking over all that was positive in Israel's identity and heritage in the process), the initial steps toward Gentile inclusion did not in themselves represent a turning away from the Jewish frame of reference. Indeed, not only did the gospel begin to flow into the non-Jewish world along channels that were already present within Judaism, but also all of the patterns of universalism within wider Judaism manifested themselves in early Christianity.

The point can be illustrated briefly by Luke's account of the Jerusalem Council (Acts 15). What is at issue in this meeting of early Christian leaders, as Luke presents it, is precisely the terms on which Gentiles are to be included. Some argue what is essentially a form of proselytism: Gentiles need to accept circumcision and the Mosaic law in order to be admissible to the community of the "saved" (Acts 15:1). The decision taken by the council, however, is that Gentiles who have believed in Jesus need not follow the whole law of Moses but are acceptable as Gentiles as long as they adhere to a smaller set of observances (15:19-21). In the course of arguing for this position, James states that this Gentile influx should be seen as a fulfillment of the prophetic expectation that in the last days God would "look favorably on the Gentiles, to take from among them a people for his name" (Acts 15:14, citing LXX Amos 9:11-12). In other words, positions staked out here correspond in significant measure to patterns already present within Judaism.

At the same time, however, the particular character of early Christian belief meant that these patterns developed in distinctive ways. These NT patterns can be described economically by arranging them along an axis of Christian self-understanding, which, at one end, continues to use *Jews* and *Gentiles* in their traditional Jewish form and, at the other, subjects these terms to significant redefinition.

A number of NT passages might be understood as assertions of a straightforward rejection-replacement schema: Jews are rejected and Gentiles are brought in to take their place (e.g., Matt 8:11-12; Acts 13:44-48). In their broader contexts, however, such passages are generally part of larger, more nuanced constructions.

The NT writing for which the traditional categories of "Jews" and "Gentiles" are most significant is Luke–Acts. In Luke's schema, it is necessary that the gospel first be preached to Jews. Only when the Jewish community has had a chance to respond—with some "convinced" by the message and others "refus[ing] to believe" (Acts 28:24)—do the Gentiles get their opportunity. For Luke, then, the church consists of a large body of law-observant Jewish believers at the core (e.g., Acts 21:20), to which a body of Gentile believers is added. A similar pattern seems to be present in Revelation, where a redeemed Israel ("one hundred forty-four thousand, sealed out of every tribe") is then joined by "a great multitude that no one could count, from every nation" (Rev 7:4-10).

Paul also understands the church as consisting of a Jewish remnant (Rom 11:5) together with the Gentile believers who have come to join them (Rom 11:17, reading **en autois** [ἐν αὐτοῖς] as "among them"). In addition, when "the full number of the Gentiles has come in," "all Israel will be saved" (Rom 11:25-26). What sets Paul apart from Luke, however, is his argument that by virtue of being "in Christ," believing but uncircumcised Gentiles are members of Abraham's "seed" (Rom 4:16; Gal 3:29). Since such membership traditionally required circumcision (see "seed" in Gen 17:7-15), Paul's formulation represents a substantial redefinition of Abraham's family, and thus of Israel.

While John's Gospel makes no explicit reference to the "Gentiles" at all (**ethnos** appears only in the singular, with reference to the Jewish nation), the idea that Gentile believers are added to a Jewish core seems to be in view in Jesus' statement about the "other sheep that do not belong to this fold," who eventually will be brought in so that "there will be one flock, one shepherd" (John 10:16). A similar conception can be discerned in the editorial comment that Jesus was to die "not for the [Jewish] nation only, but to gather into one the dispersed children of God" (John 11:51-52). The emphasis on unity, however, together with the thoroughgoing transformation of Jewish symbols and identity in the Fourth Gospel, mean that traditional Jewish and Gentile identities are substantially transformed or even transcended.

Matthew's gospel sets up a considerable narrative tension with respect to the place of Gentiles in the ministry of Jesus. On one hand, Gentiles are drawn to Jesus from the beginning (Matt 2:1-12; 8:5-11; 15:21-28) and are commended for their faith (8:10; 15:28). On the other, Jesus restricts his own ministry (15:24) and that of his disciples (10:5-6) to "the lost sheep of the house of Israel" and explicitly forbids his disciples to go to "the Gentiles" (10:5). The tension is resolved in the conclusion of the narrative, however, where Jesus' elevation to a position of "all authority" makes it possible ("therefore") for **panta ta ethnē** to become disciples (28:18-19). If **ethnē** is to be translated as "nations" here, so that Jesus is sending out his disciples to "all the nations" including Israel, the conclusion of Matthew's gospel might represent a significant qualification of the distinction between Jews and Gentiles. Israel becomes just one of the nations from whom disciples are to be drawn, and the identity of the new community of disciples is determined not by ethnic identity markers but by baptism and Jesus' authoritative reinterpretation of the law of Moses.

A further step in the process of redefinition is apparent in 1 Peter. This epistle is directed at readers who originally were Gentiles (1:18). Now that they have come to believe in Christ, however, they are no longer Gentiles (2:12; 4:3) but are identified by terms originally ascribed to Israel: "a chosen race, a royal priesthood, a holy nation" (2:9). It is just a short step from here to Justin's straightforward assertion that Christians "are the true spiritual Israel" (*Dial.* 11.5). *See* CANAAN, CANAANITES; EXILE; FOREIGN, FOREIGNER; HABIRU, HAPIRU; MIXED MULTITUDE; NAZIR, NAZIRITE; RECHAB, RECHABITES.

Bibliography: Mark G. Brett. *Ethnicity and the Bible* (1996); Denise Kimber Buell. *Why This New Race: Ethnic Reasoning in Early Christianity* (2005); Shaye J. D. Cohen. *The Beginnings of Jewishness:*

Boundaries, Varieties, Uncertainties (1999); Terence L. Donaldson. *Judaism and the Gentiles: Patterns of Universalism (to 135 CE)* (2007); Robert Goldenberg. *The Nations That Know Thee Not: Ancient Jewish Attitudes Towards Other Religions* (1997); Jonathan M. Hall. *Hellenicity: Between Ethnicity and Culture* (2002); John North. "The Development of Religious Pluralism." *The Jews Among Pagans and Christians in the Roman Empire.* Judith Lieu et al., eds. (1992); Kenton L. Sparks. *Ethnicity and Identity in Ancient Israel* (1998).

TERENCE L. DONALDSON

NATURAL HISTORY. *See* ANIMALS OF THE BIBLE; BIRDS OF THE BIBLE; INSECTS OF THE BIBLE; NATURE, NATURAL PHENOMENA; PLANTS OF THE BIBLE.

NATURE, NATURAL PHENOMENA [φύσις physis]. *Nature* refers to the entire realm of entities that human beings experience, and which includes animals, plants, and the greater cosmos. There is no word in the OT that corresponds to our English *nature* (from Lat. *natura*), which is often used to translate the Gk. word physis. The term physis does not necessarily mean the opposite of supernatural. Aside from some weak exceptions (Luke 24:39; 1 Cor 15:40-44), any juxtaposition of *natural* with *supernatural* is not well maintained in the Bible. Physis generally refers to essential or inborn features (a common meaning in Greco-Roman literature) and may be found in some NT texts such as Rom 1:26; 1 Cor 11:14; Gal 2:15; and Jas 3:6.

There is no systematic biblical description of the structure of the cosmos. However, many scholars have reconstructed a triad consisting of Heaven(s), Earth, and Underworld. Genesis 1 assumes a triad of Heaven(s), Earth, and Sea. In addition, the OT often uses "heavens and the earth" to designate the entire cosmos (e.g., Gen 1:1). *See* COSMOGONY, COSMOLOGY.

The exact shape of the cosmos is unclear. The "circle of the earth" in Isa 40:22 is probably a reference to the circle formed by the horizon rather than a reference to any spherical shape of the earth. Many scholars think that the ancient Hebrews conceived of the cosmos as a flat disk (earth) surrounded by water, and with a metallic dome for a sky (raqiʿa in Gen 1:7). The sky was supported by pillars (Job 9:6). Cardinal directions were related to the direction from which the sun rose.

Genesis 1 provides the most familiar biblical story of how "nature" emerged (*see* CREATION). The cosmos began as a chaotic mass of water stirred by a divine wind. God shaped that mass by division and differentiation, and added, through the divine spoken word, many of the entities that populate it. A watery beginning is posited by some Greek cosmologists (Thales, 6th cent. BCE) and by the Babylonian creation epic *Enuma Elish* (early 1st millennium BCE). Fragments of other creation stories involve battling a sea monster (see Job 26:12-13), something also seen in the *Enuma Elish.*

Genesis 2 depicts God as more of a craftsman, especially in forming Adam from clay, and Eve from Adam's rib. Breathing is recognized as a crucial component of human and animal life (Eccl 3:19). A process of growth and decline of the body within a set lifespan is part of the normal course of nature (compare Ps 90:10). The menstrual cycle and its relation to impregnation is recognized (2 Sam 11:4-5). However, death and other bodily functions could be viewed as conferring impurity (Lev 12, 15).

The etymology of the word shamayim (שָׁמַיִם), translated as "heaven(s)" in the OT, has generated much debate, but one postulated meaning is "place of waters." The idea of many heavens is even more developed in deuterocanonical literature and in the NT (compare 2 Cor 12:2). In any case, heaven was thought to be the residence of Yahweh and his entourage (see Gen 11:5; Job 1:6-7). The earthly Temple mirrored important aspects of the cosmos (1 Kgs 8:12-13).

HEAVEN contained the objects we identify as sun, moon, and stars, which were sent into the dome (Gen 1:17). The sun and moon illuminated the earth and marked time, which is a necessary tool of agricultural and ritual cycles. It is uncertain whether the OT recognized planets as a specific category of heavenly objects.

The earth (ʾerets [אֶרֶץ] or ʾadhamah [אֲדָמָה]) is the place where human beings normally lived. The major features of the EARTH included mountains, plains, valleys, rivers, and wilderness (versus settled areas). Mountains were the abodes of the gods, and the meeting place between heaven and earth. The higher mountains, such as the snow-capped Lebanon Mountains, were associated with God's majesty (Ps 29:6). The earth was a source of raw materials used in construction tools, and weapons (e.g., 1 Kgs 6:7).

There was also a subterranean world. Water is stored there (Gen 7:11). Because of the widespread custom of burying the dead, the underworld, especially as designated by the term SHEOL (sheʾol [שְׁאֹל, שְׁאוֹל]), also became associated with death (1 Sam 28:13). The underworld was also where rebellious angels could be imprisoned (2 Pet 2:4). *See* DEAD, ABODE OF THE; UNDERWORLD, DESCENT INTO THE.

The seas were the home of marine creatures, many of which served as food. Sea monsters, such as Leviathan (Job 41:31) and Rahab (Job 26:12; Isa 51:9-10), inhabited the seas. The slaying or domination of the SEA, personified as a monster, has parallels in Babylonian stories of creation such as the *Enuma Elish.* The sea was a means of transportation for human beings (Ps 104:25-26).

Acquiring fresh WATER is a primary challenge in arid lands. Rivers provided water supplies and transportation. Springs, with origins deep in the ground, were often seen as miraculous (see Exod 17:1-7). Some springs became vital to fortified cities, which were vulnerable to sieges, and great effort was spent to build tunnels for access (e.g., at Megiddo). Otherwise, rain could be stored in cisterns.

Many biblical authors distinguished sharply between human beings and animals. In the story of Nebuchadnezzar's madness, for instance, part of his animalistic behavior included eating directly from the ground and being exposed to the elements (Dan 5:21). For Gen 1, however, humans are like other living things in their being created by God and thus in their relation to him. Vegetation is for both humans and animals (1:30). Animals share with humans the command to reproduce, increase, and fill the seas and the earth (1:22); and animals like humans have "life" (**nefesh** נֶפֶשׁ). The additional vocation given humanity, "to subdue" and "to have dominion" over the earth (Gen 1:26, 28), calls for human care and cultivation of nature. Ecclesiastes (3:19-21) suggests human beings bear no advantage over beasts.

Otherwise, animals were used for food and transportation. The classification of animals could be based on their utility for ritual or food (clean vs. unclean/pure vs. impure in Lev 11). Animals may also be classified into the main theater of the cosmos that they inhabit (earth, sky, sea as in Gen 1). Composite creatures, common in Near Eastern iconography, were used in biblical imagery (Dan 7:4-7; Rev 13:1-2). *See* ANIMALS OF THE BIBLE.

Plants are conceived as entities that grow while anchored to the earth (Gen 1:11-12; Matt 13:3-8). Plants served primarily as a source of food (Gen 1:29; Ps 104:14-15). Trees served in construction of homes and monumental buildings (1 Kgs 5:10; 6:15). Medical use is seen in, among other plants, figs (2 Kgs 20:7) and balsam from Gilead (Jer 8:22). Biblical imagery and poetry often appealed to various dimensions of plants, including their aesthetic value, to illustrate moral and theological themes (e.g., Ps 1; Isa 5; John 15:1). *See* PLANTS OF THE BIBLE.

Within biblical scholarship, at least two approaches can be observed on the question of the relationship between God and nature. Some scholars see the Bible as exhibiting a stark contrast between God and the natural order he created. The personal Hebrew God is then contrasted with the deities of the ANE who were identified with natural phenomena.

More recent scholarship questions such a stark distinction. Yahweh creates wind by blowing through his nostrils (Exod 15:8-10), has thunder for a voice (Job 37:5), and rides upon the clouds (Ps 68:4). Thus, Yahweh often resembles the storm gods in neighboring cultures (Baal at Ugarit; Zeus on Mount Olympus) so much that even Israelites could confuse them (Hos 2:8-9). Other biblical writers, however, strove to differentiate Yahweh from other storm gods (see 1 Kgs 19:11-12).

The study of attitudes toward nature in the Bible has become prominent in the last four decades. This prominence is often attributed to responses by biblical scholars to the widely influential critique by Lynn White, the medievalist who argued that the biblical idea of nature as an object to be used and mastered by human beings was a principal cause of our current ecological crisis (*see* ECOLOGY). Some biblical scholars (especially Simkins) believe, however, that at least three attitudes may be discerned in the biblical materials: 1) subjugation of human beings by nature (Job 38–41); 2) harmony between humanity and nature (Deut 11:13-17; Hag 1:9-10), which Simkins views as the predominant model; and 3) subjugation of nature by human beings (Gen 1:26-28).

Nature could be a teacher, and some theological concepts could be derived from the observation of nature (Rom 1:20-24; 1 Cor 11:14). Some biblical authors saw the destruction of nature by God as a means of punishment and renovation (e.g., Noah's flood). The destruction or renewal of "nature" will occur in the end of time (2 Pet 3:7; Rev 21:23-25). Otherwise, some authors recognized that human beings could damage or overtax the environment (Gen 13:6; compare 2 Kgs 2:19-20).

Bibliography: Gerard Naddaf. *The Greek Concept of Nature* (2006); Ronald A. Simkins. *Creator and Creation: Nature in the Worldview of Ancient Israel* (1994); Lynn White. "The Historical Roots of our Ecological Crisis." *Science* 155 (1967) 1203–07.

HECTOR AVALOS

NAVE nayv [בַּיִת **bayith**, הֵיכָל **hekhal**]. The largest room in the tripartite interior of the Solomonic Temple, between the holy of holies and the PORCH. Forty cubits long, twenty wide, and thirty high, with gilded wall-carvings, it contained a golden altar, ten lampstands, a table for displaying bread, and numerous small golden implements (1 Kgs 6–7; 2 Chr 3–4; Ezek 41). Scholars use archaeological evidence from ANE temples to reconstruct what the sections of the Temple might have looked like. *See* TEMPLE, JERUSALEM; TEMPLES, SEMITIC.

LJUBICA JOVANOVIC

NAVEL CORD [שֹׁר **shor**]. Shor refers to the navel or navel cord (Ezek 16:4), and can be translated more generally as "flesh" (Prov 3:8). In its description of Jerusalem as an abandoned infant whose navel cord has been left intact, Ezek 16:3-7 presupposes the customary procedures that followed the delivery of a newborn: cutting the umbilical cord with a sharp reed, washing the infant, then rubbing it down with salt and swaddling it. In ANE cultures, cutting the umbilical cord was especially meaningful because the physical separation from the mother signaled the moment when the newborn gained status as an independent human being. *See* BIRTH.

Bibliography: M. Stol. *Birth in Babylonia and the Bible: Its Mediterranean Setting* (2000).

MARY F. FOSKETT

NAZARENE, NAZARENES naz´uh-reen [Ναζαρηνός Nazarēnos, Ναζωραῖος Nazōraios]. An adjective denoting origin in the village of NAZARETH that is used in the singular only of Jesus; the plural is used as a designation for Jesus' followers.

The name *Jesus* was common in biblical times, so one way the Jesus of the NT is distinguished from others is by the attribution *Nazarene*, indicating his hometown of Nazareth. The term only occurs in the Gospels and Acts, and in two different forms. Mark uses the form Nazarēnos (1:24; 10:47; 14:67; 16:6). Matthew (2:23; 26:71) and John (18:5, 7; 19:19) use the form Nazōraios. Luke uses both forms (Nazarēnos: Luke 4:34; 24:19; Nazōraios: 18:37), but uses Nazōraios exclusively in Acts (2:22; 3:6; 4:10; 6:14; 22:8; 24:5; 26:9). The NT authors use both forms to refer to Jesus' coming from Nazareth, equivalent to the expression "the one from Nazareth" (ho apo Nazareth ὁ ἀπὸ Ναζαρέθ, Matt 21:11; John 1:45; Acts 10:38).

But there are linguistic hurdles to viewing a progression from the Semitic terms for Nazareth (notsrat נֹצְרַת, natsereth נַצֶּרֶת) and the Aram. forms of the adjective (natseraya נָצְרָיָ, natsera'a נָצְרָאָ) to the Gk. forms Nazarēnos and Nazōraios. In particular, it is difficult to account for the changes from the tsade (ts צ) in Aram. to the zeta (z ζ) in both Gk. forms and from the semi-vowel shewa (e ְ) to the long ō (ω) in Nazōraios. In addition, *Nazareth* is not mentioned in the OT, the Apocrypha, Josephus, or rabbinic literature. Thus, other derivations were suggested, such as in the Hebrew root nzr (נזר, "to vow," "to abstain") or in the Aram. natsoraya (נָצְרָיָ, "watchers," "observers") from the root ntsr (נצר). Most scholars conclude that our Gk. forms derived from the Aram. for Nazareth (natseraya or natsera'a).

Matthew 2:23 links Jesus' residence in Nazareth with the epithet *Nazarene.* Though some suggest Matthew is referring to a specific prophecy about the BRANCH (netser נֵצֶר, Isa 11:1) or to a Nazirite (nazir נָזִיר, Judg 13:7; *see* NAZIR, NAZIRITE), Matthew probably refers to the "holy one of God" (Isa 4:3; Judg 16:17 LXX) as a messiah who would be despised (*see* MESSIAH, JEWISH).

In the NT, the plural Nazōraioi (Ναζωραίοι) is used once as a title for Jesus' followers (Acts 24:5). The term may have originated as a term of derision and was indeed used so later in the execration of the notsrim (נֹצְרִים, Nazarenes) in the twelfth of the Eighteen Benedictions. This TWELFTH BENEDICTION, called the Birkat ha-Minim, "benediction of the heretics" (ca. 100 CE), asks God to doom groups, Jewish and Gentile, who were thought harmful to the Jewish people (see *b. Ber.* 28b). This benediction is evidence of the schism forming between Jews who believed Jesus was the promised Messiah, and those who did not, because if a "sectarian" or "Nazarene" were to recite it, he condemned himself to be erased from the book of life where the names of the righteous are inscribed.

Though the term *Nazarene* was replaced by *Christian* (Christianos Χριστιανός; Acts 11:26), it was retained in the Syrian, Armenian, and Arab churches, and the Hebrew notsrim endures to this day as a designation for Christians. The modern Protestant denomination, the Church of the Nazarene, purposely named itself in awareness of the lowly and derisive connotations of the word. *See* CHRISTIAN-JEWISH RELATIONS.

Bibliography: Raymond E. Brown. *The Birth of the Messiah* (1993).

KEVIN L. ANDERSON

NAZARETH naz´uh-rith [נָצְרַת natsrath; Ναζαρά Nazara, Ναζαρέθ Nazareth, Ναζαρέτ Nazaret]. A village in the Roman district of Galilee identified in the NT as the home of Joseph, Mary, and Jesus (Matt 2:23; Luke 2:4, 39, 51; *see* GALILEE, GALILEANS).

Located in Lower Galilee, Nazareth is approximately midway between the Mediterranean Sea to the west and the southern tip of the Sea of Galilee to the east. Situated on a ridge overlooking the Jezreel Valley, Nazareth had a commanding view of the large basin to the south and was in close proximity to SEPPHORIS, the capital of Galilee, and to a major highway 3 mi. to the north.

The unimportance of Nazareth is reflected in the absence of references to the name in any ancient inscriptions or texts. Nazareth is not mentioned in the OT, the writings of Josephus, or in early Jewish literature. The first references appear in the Gospels and the book of Acts. Outside the NT, the name does not appear until the 3rd cent. CE in an inscription from Caesarea Maritima that speaks of a priestly family that settled at Nazareth. A reference to the site's location appears in the writings of Eusebius in the 4th cent. CE (*Hist. eccl.* 1.7.14).

The four Gospels introduce Jesus from different perspectives that shed new light on the different identities of Nazareth. Matthew mentions Jesus' association with Nazareth as a fulfillment of prophecy: "He made his home in a town called Nazareth, so that what had been spoken through the prophets might be fulfilled, 'He will be called a Nazorean'" (Matt 2:23). This statement is inspired by Isa 11:1—"A shoot shall come out from the stump of Jesse, and a branch shall grow out of his roots"—as a play on the Hebrew word netser (נֵצֶר, "branch, root") from which the name *Nazareth* was derived.

The Gospel of Luke's concern is to depict Nazareth as a part of the larger (Gentile) world. Even though it was a small village in Galilee, according to Luke the citizenry of Nazareth had to register and recognize their responsibilities in the larger world. Therefore, "Joseph also went from the town of Nazareth in Galilee to Judea, to the city of David called Bethlehem" (Luke 2:4; *see* INFANCY NARRATIVES).

The Gospel of Mark first mentions Nazareth in the context of Jesus' baptism: "Jesus came from Nazareth of Galilee and was baptized by John in the Jordan" (Mark 1:9). When Jesus heals a man with an unclean spirit, the unclean spirit knows his identity (while others do not) and proclaims, "What have you to do with us, Jesus of Nazareth?" (Mark 1:26).

In the Gospel of John, Philip identifies Jesus not only by his fulfillment of messianic expectations but also by his origins in Nazareth: "We have found him about whom Moses in the law and also the prophets wrote, Jesus son of Joseph from Nazareth" (John 1:45). However, Nathanael reflected the popular opinion of the day: "Can any good thing come out of Nazareth?" (John 1:46). Jesus went from Nazareth to Capernaum to start his Galilean ministry (Matt 4:13). While there, he spoke in the synagogue on the Sabbath, read from Isaiah (58:6; 61:1-2), and proclaimed that he was the fulfillment of that Scripture (Luke 4:16-30). Jesus' identification with Nazareth appears in several accounts in the Gospels and Acts (Matt 2:23; Mark 1:24; Luke 18:37; John 18:5, 7; Acts 2:22; 3:6).

Evidence of habitation in the area goes back to the Neolithic period. In the time of Jesus, Nazareth was a small agricultural village with a spring and a population of approximately 400 to 500 people. Excavations were conducted under the Church of the Annunciation beginning in 1954. The project revealed evidence from the Roman period, caves used for dwellings, grain storage and cisterns, wine presses, olive oil presses, and millstones. Caves from the 3rd and 4th cent. CE provide evidence for the early veneration of the site by Christians in the form of a plaster painted surface with the design of a cross and Christian prayers on the wall. The caves were attached to a building with a floor mosaic, perhaps a Jewish Christian synagogue.

A new excavation began during the spring of 1997. Located on the southern and eastern slopes of the Nazareth Hospital, the excavation recovered evidence of terrace farming practices dated to the Roman period (*see* AGRICULTURE). Nazareth gained recognition as an important Christian site with the veneration of Mary during the 6th cent. with the building of the Church of the Annunciation and the Church of St. Joseph. Today, the predominately Arab population of the modern city of Nazareth comprises 70,000–80,000 people, both Christians and Muslims.

LAMOINE F. DEVRIES

NAZIR, NAZIRITE naz'uh-r*i*t [נָזִיר nazir]. Nazirites appear early in the OT record and are found in both the NT period and rabbinic Judaism. The Hebrew name nazir is derived from the verb nazar (נָזַר), which means "to CONSECRATE" or "to set apart." Nazirites demonstrated their devotion to God through distinctive behaviors, commonly observing prohibitions against cutting the hair, drinking wine, or touching the dead. The earliest Nazirites appear to have adopted the role as a life calling. In later periods, a practice developed in which one could become a Nazirite for a temporary period as payment of a vow. Early Nazirites were either called by God or dedicated by their parents to a lifelong state of consecration to God, outwardly identified by their unshorn hair. The oldest biblical account of a Nazirite is that of SAMSON, in the period of the Judges (11th–12th cent. BCE). Before his conception, an angel instructed Samson's mother to rear her child as a Nazirite: "No razor is to come on his head, for the boy shall be a nazirite to God from birth" (Judg 13:5). Samson's mother was instructed to avoid wine, strong drink, and unclean foods (Judg 13:4), but the only restriction spelled out for the child was that his hair not be cut. Samson partook in his wedding feast (which typically involved fermented drinks) "as the young men were accustomed to do" (Judg 14:10) and had no compunction against touching dead bodies (Judg 14:19). When Delilah relieved Samson of his hair, however, he lost the supernatural strength emblematic of his special relationship with God (Judg 16:19-20).

SAMUEL (11th cent. BCE) may also have been considered a Nazirite. When his mother, Hannah, prayed for a son, she vowed to return him to Yahweh: "I will give him to the Lord all the days of his life, and a razor shall never come on his head" (1 Sam 1:11 NASB). The NRSV follows an alternate reading found in the LXX and in the Dead Sea Scrolls (4Q51) that specifies: "then I will set him before you as a nazirite until the day of his death. He shall drink neither wine nor intoxicants, and no razor shall touch his head."

The prophet Amos (8th cent. BCE) spoke of Nazirites "raised up" by divine appointment, but who were forced to drink wine by rebellious Israelites who also commanded divinely commissioned prophets not to prophesy (Amos 2:11-12). Like prophets, then, lifelong Nazirites believed they were called to a permanent and special relationship with Yahweh. The primary symbol of their consecrated status was unshorn hair, though a prohibition against wine and strong drink also became standard.

There is no clear evidence of lifelong Nazirites after the time of Amos. Some writers think of John the Baptist as a Nazirite because the angel who announced his birth declared that he should never take any fermented drink (Luke 1:15) and because he lived an ascetic life of pious devotion. The NT describes John's eccentric choices in food and clothing in some detail, but does not mention his hair. John appears to be more desert prophet than Nazirite.

The Priestly traditions described in the book of Numbers, generally dated to the postexilic period, reflect a custom that developed in which persons adopted the strict requirements of living as a Nazirite for a temporary period. In the OT and ANE context, vows were always conditional promises. In the context of prayer, a distressed worshiper would seek a specific boon from God and promise something in return. Explicit vows occur in both narrative and poetic literature (Gen 28:20-22; Num 21:2; Judg 11:30-31; 1 Sam 1:11; 2 Sam 15:7-8; Ps 61:8 [Heb. 61:9]). While these vows seem to have been freely expressed and freely paid, the making of temporary Nazirite vows became institutionalized and was strictly regulated (Num 6:1-21).

Both men and women could vow to become temporary Nazirites for a designated period. Such Nazirites were required to observe three types of abstinence: they could not imbibe any intoxicating drink, cut their hair, or defile themselves through touching a dead body, even of a parent (Num 6:2-8). The stringent requirements for purity were similar to those of the high priest (Lev 10:9-10; 21:1-3).

The high level of sanctity accorded Nazirites is reflected in the tight requirements for completing their vows. For example, if a temporary Nazirite was accidentally defiled by touching a corpse or being anywhere near a corpse, the Nazirite was required to shave his or her hair on the seventh day following and undergo purification rituals involving the sacrifices of two pigeons and a yearling lamb. The previous period served was then declared void, and the Nazirite had to start anew the promised period of sanctification (Num 6:9-12).

The completion of a temporary Nazirite's service was marked by offerings and ceremonies (Num 6:13-21), an expensive undertaking that underscored the seriousness accorded the Nazirite vow. Sacrifices to be offered included a male lamb for a whole burnt offering, a female lamb for a sin offering, and a ram for an offering of well-being. These were accompanied by gifts of grain, oil, and wine. To complete the ritual, the Nazirite's head was shaved and the hair was burned on the altar with the sacrifices. To be released from sacred Nazirite status, the person also had to fulfill any other material vows that were made in conjunction with the Nazirite vow.

In Second Temple Judaism and the NT, poor persons sometimes made Nazirite vows but could not afford the sacrifices and offerings required to complete their obligations. It was considered a pious act for wealthier persons to accompany such Nazirites to the Temple and pay for their sacrifices, as happened with Paul in Acts 21:23-26. Mishnaic regulations suggest a normative period of thirty days for Nazirite vows (*m. Naz.* 1:3) and underscore the conditional nature of Nazirite vows in the rabbinic period (*m. Naz.* 2:7-10; 3:6).

TONY W. CARTLEDGE

NAZOREANS, GOSPEL OF THE naz´uh-ree´uhn. The gospel text used by the Nazoreans (also referred to as the Nazareans, Nazarenes) exists only in brief quotations and citations by early church writers from the late 2nd through the late 4th cent. (HEGESIPPUS, ORIGEN, EUSEBIUS, EPIPHANIUS, and JEROME). Later citations from medieval writers also exist; in the later period the gospel was known by title as "the Gospel of the Nazoreans." The earlier patristic writers, however, do not describe the gospel by title but only as the gospel in use among the Nazoreans. Sometimes they described it as a Jewish gospel, or in other citations they confused it with the Gospel of the Hebrews.

Sorting out which fragmentary patristic quotations belong to the gospel used by the Nazoreans from two other Jewish-Christian gospels (the gospels of the Hebrews and the Ebionites) known by early patristic writers is difficult because of the confusing and imprecise attribution (or generally non-attribution) of these three texts by the patristic writers. Epiphanius describes the Nazoreans as a very early Jewish-Christian group that fled from Jerusalem to Pella when Jerusalem was destroyed in 70 CE. They lived by the Jewish law but held orthodox views about Jesus. At the end of the 4th cent., Jerome claimed to have copied and translated a gospel used by the Nazoreans in the Syrian city of Beroia.

The Gospel of the Nazoreans, according to Eusebius and Jerome, was "written in Hebrew characters," which modern scholars take to have been Aramaic, sometime before 180, when the Nazorean gospel was first cited by Hegesippus. Because of its close similarity to canonical Matthew, scholars take its earliest possible date of composition to have been the latter half of the 1st cent., when Matthew was composed. The Gospel of the Nazoreans does not simply repeat Matthew's text, however, but revises it by interpolating into it new material or otherwise expanding it.

Some scholars argue that the Nazoreans had access to a version of Matthew that was written in Aramaic, and in that way they account for the Nazorean gospel being written in Aramaic. Others argue that the Nazorean gospel was a later translation into Aramaic of the Greek text of Matthew. Some scholars have questioned the existence of the Gospel of the Nazoreans, and assign its patristic fragments to the Gospel of the Hebrews. *See* EBIONITES, GOSPEL OF THE; HEBREWS, GOSPEL OF THE; NAZARENE, NAZARENES.

Bibliography: F. J. Klijn and G. J. Reinink. *Patristic Evidence for Jewish-Christian Sects* (1973); Philipp Vielhauer and Georg Strecker. "The Gospel of the Nazareans." *New Testament Apocrypha: Gospels and Related Writings.* Vol. 1 (1991) 154–65; Stephen G. Wilson. *Related Strangers: Jews and Christians 70–170 C.E.* (1995).

CHARLES W. HEDRICK

NEAH nee´uh [נֵעָה ne'ah]. A town or region in Zebulun (Josh 19:13).

NEAPOLIS nee-ap´uh-lis [Νεάπολις Neapolis]. Neapolis (lit., "New City") is the name of several municipalities in the Greco-Roman world that were founded near earlier sites. The NT mentions a Neapolis, which served as the seaport for PHILIPPI.

Ancient Neapolis is identified with the modern town of Kavala, whose name comes from the Latin for "horse" because of its connection with horse trading. Neapolis is located about ten miles from Philippi on the other side of a mountain ridge. This town became Paul's entry port into Europe on his second missionary journey. Paul sailed from Troas to the island of Samothrace and then on to Neapolis (Acts 16:11). Paul probably passed through this town again on his second visit to Macedonia (Acts 20:1), and likely left from this port on his way to Troas (Acts 20:6). In addition to its proximity to Philippi, Neapolis' importance was tied to its access to the sea and its location on the Egnatian Way.

The original founding of the town is unsure, but it was probably a colony of the island of Thasos. It was in the territory of Thrace and later became a part of the Roman province of Macedonia. This harbor town served as the mooring point for the fleet of Cassius and Brutus at the time of the battle of Philippi (42 BCE). This battle served as the decisive turning point in the victory of the Caesarians over the Republicans. Today the modern settlement covers most of the ancient remains.

JOHN D. WINELAND

NEARIAH nee´uh-rī´uh [נְעַרְיָה ne῾aryah]. Means "servant of Yahweh." 1. A descendant of Solomon, one of the six sons of Shemaiah and a father of three sons (1 Chr 3:22-23).

2. A Simeonite military leader during Hezekiah's reign. After the Simeonites conquered the pastureland near Gedor (or, following LXX, Gerar, a town in the Negeb), Neariah helped lead an expedition to destroy the Amalekites who had escaped (1 Chr 4:42). *See* AMALEK, AMALEKITES; SIMEON, SIMEONITES.

JOEL MARCUS LEMON

NEBAI nee´bī [נוֹבָי novay, נֵיבָי nevay]. A leader whose name appears on the sealed covenant document (Neh 10:19). *See* EZRA AND NEHEMIAH, BOOKS OF.

NEBAIOTH ni-bay´yoth [נְבָיוֹת nevayoth]. Means "fruitfulness." Firstborn son of Ishmael (Gen 25:13; 1 Chr 1:29) who had an Egyptian mother according to *Jub.* 17:13-14. He was the ancestor of an Arabian tribe by the same name (Isa 60:7). Genesis 28:9 and 36:3 mention Nebaioth's sister but the text gives no more information about Nebaioth. *See* ISHMAEL, ISHMAELITES.

Isaiah 60:7 mentions a pastoral northern Arabian tribe, associated with KEDAR, who would bring rams to be sacrificed to the Lord in the ideal Zion. Assyrian documents list Nebaioth and Kedar among Arab tribes Tiglath-pileser III defeated. Nebaioth has been associated with the NABATEANS, a view long and widely held; however, recent scholars discount the connection based upon linguistic and historical considerations.

TERRY W. EDDINGER

NEBALLAT ni-bal´uht [נְבַלָּט nevallat]. This placename only appears in the list of Benjaminite settlements following the return from Babylonian exile (Neh 11:34). It has been identified with Beit Nabala (Horvat Nevallat), at the western extreme of the tribal territory and approximately 4 mi. northeast of LOD in the northern Shephelah. The list of resettled cities (compare Josh 18:11-28) may represent an attempt to restore traditions associated with Israel's earlier history. *See* BENJAMIN, BENJAMINITES.

VICTOR H. MATTHEWS

NEBAT nee´bat [נְבָט nevat]. Father of JEROBOAM I (e.g., 1 Kgs 11:26). Not the same as NABOTH.

NEBO nee´boh [נְבוֹ nevo]. The parallelism between BEL, Nebo, and "their images" (author's trans.; NRSV, "their idols") in Isa 46:1 indicates that Bel and Nebo are to be taken as names of Babylonian deities. Akkadian Bel, like its Hebrew equivalent Baal, began as an epithet meaning "lord," but just as Baal became the more common name for the Canaanite storm god Hadad, so in the Neo-Babylonian period Bel became the more common name for MARDUK, the city god of Babylon and supreme deity in the Babylonian pantheon. Nebo is Nabu, the city god of Borsippa, the patron deity of scribes, and the son of Marduk in Babylonian theology. The divine name probably also lies behind the garbled form of Azariah's Babylonian name Abednego (Dan 1:7; 2:49; 3:12-30). The original form, Abed-nebo, would mean "servant of Nabu," a common name type in Babylonia. This presumably intentional garbling of the divine name may also help explain an oddity in the Greek textual tradition of Isa 46:1. In that passage a number of LXX manuscripts have replaced Nebo with DAGON, a god of the Philistines and, as Dagan, a god of the middle Euphrates region, but a god who is never closely associated with Marduk. Dagon's introduction into this passage is best explained if the original Nebo had been intentionally corrupted to Nego, which corresponds to no known pagan deity, leading the translators to replace an obvious corruption with Dagon, who was known from other biblical passages. If Dagon was better known to the latter translators, however, Nebo is clearly the original reading. In the Neo-Babylonian period of Second Isaiah, the god Nabu was closely associated with Bel and actually rivaled Marduk in importance, so he would have been well known to the prophet's audience, the Judean exiles in Babylon.

The point of Isa 46:1 is that even the greatest of the Babylonian gods cannot save Babylon. In fact, they are just an added burden that the Babylonians must labor to save. It is possible that the text alludes to the specific actions of Nabonidus in gathering the images of the major Babylonian gods from the outlying cities and bringing them into the city of Babylon for safekeeping. *See* GODS, GODDESSES.

J. J. M. ROBERTS

NEBO, MOUNT nee'boh [הַר־נְבוֹ har-nevo]. Mount Nebo (800 m above sea level, in the territory of Madaba in Jordan) is bounded on the east by the Wadi ʿAfrit, on the north by the Wadi ʿUyun Musa, and on the south by the Wadi al-Judaydah, which extends into the Wadi al-Kanaysah.

The two most historically important peaks are the western peak of Siyagha with the Memorial Church of Moses, and the southeastern peak of al-Mukhayyat, identified with the town of Nebo (Num 32:3-4, 38; Isa 15:2; Jer 48:1, 22; *see* MOABITE STONE). Eusebius identified this mountain with the Mount Nebo in front of Jericho and Jerusalem in the Moabite region (*Onom.* 16.24), which the prophet Moses climbed at the end of his life (Deut 34:1). Christians built a large basilica surrounded by a monastery to commemorate the event.

The Bible relates several episodes associated with Mount Nebo, which is identified with the peak of Pisgah (Deut 34:1): the Israelite tribes encamped "in the mountains of Abarim, before Nebo" (Num 33:47; Pisgah in Num 21:20); Balak took Balaam toward the summit of Pisgah to curse the tribes of Israel (Num 23:13-26); and Moses "went up from the plains of Moab to Mount Nebo, to the top of Pisgah" where he was shown the promised land (Deut 34:1). The town of Nebo appears in prophetic oracles against Moab (Isa 15–16; Jer 48) as part of the territory of Reuben (1 Chr 5:8). The Moabite Stone (9th cent. BCE) includes Nebo

Studium Biblicum Franciscanum Archive, Jerusalem.

Figure 1: The mosaic floor of the diaconicon-baptistery in the Memorial of Moses on Mount Nebo, Jordan (530 CE).

as a city conquered by King Mesha in his northern campaign against Israel (lines 14–18).

At Nebo are traces of human presence ranging from the Epipaleolithic period (18000–8300) to Arab times (7th–9th cent. CE), with main settlements dating to the 4th–3rd millennium BCE and the Iron Age. Excavations near the spring of ʿAyn al-Jadidah uncovered an urban settlement (3500–3000 BCE). A second urban settlement of the 3rd millennium BCE has been partially excavated at Qarn al-Kabesh. Iron Age II buildings were excavated at Khirbet al-Mashhad near the ʿUyun Musa Springs. Tombs of the same period (8th–7th cent. BCE) were uncovered east of Khirbet al-Mukhayyat. A village at Khirbet al-Mukhayyat dates to the Roman-Byzantine period with significant Christian and monastic presence extending into the Abbasid period. On the top of Siyagha, pilgrims visited the Memorial of Moses beginning in the 4th cent. CE (Egeria and Peter the Iberian). The first sanctuary, composed of a trichora (triconched) church and a baptistery chapel lavishly decorated with a mosaic floor made by the mosaicists Soel, Kayoum, and Elias (August 530 CE), was developed into a three-nave basilica with an elongated diakonikon chapel to the north, a baptistery chapel to the south, and the Theotokos chapel farther south (ca. 6th cent.). The renovation work was finished in the first decade of the 7th cent. according to the Greek inscriptions that accompany the mosaic floors of the three main phases of the sanctuary. The large monastery reached its largest extent in the 6th cent. It was inhabited until the 10th cent. CE.

On the top of Khirbet al-Mukhayyat three main churches and a monastery have been excavated: the church of Amos and Casiseos with the northern chapel of Priest John decorated with two superimposed mosaic floors at the time of Bishop Fidus (5th cent.) and Bishop John (middle of the 6th cent.); the church of the Holy Martyrs Lot and Procopius paved with a mosaic floor at the time of Bishop John; the church of Saint George on the highest point of the acropolis paved with a mosaic floor at the time of Bishop Elias, 536 CE; and a small agricultural monastery on the eastern slope of Wadi ʿAfrit. In the Wadi ʿUyun Musa, two small ecclesiastical edifices have been excavated: the church of Kayanos with two superimposed mosaic floors (5th and 6th cent.) with inscriptions in Greek as well as the Palestinian Aramaic spoken and used by Christians in the region from the Byzantine to the Early Islamic period; and the church of the deacon Thomas paved in the middle of the 6th cent.

In the southern wadi of ʿAyn al-Kanisah, on a spur to the east of the spring, excavations have revealed a small monastery dedicated to the Theotokos (a title for Mary meaning "Mother of God"). In the mosaic floor of the chapel built on the highest spot, two inscriptions witness the monastic presence in the 6th cent. and in the 8th cent., when the mosaic had been restored in the year 762 CE.

Bibliography: M. Piccirillo and E. Alliata, eds. *Mount Nebo: New Archaeological Excavations (1967–1997)* (1998); S. Saller. *The Memorial of Moses on Mount Nebo* (1949).

MICHELE PICCIRILLO

NEBO, TOWN OF nee'boh [נְבוֹ nevo]. One of the Moabite towns conquered by Israelites (Num 32:3-4). The Reubenites and Gadites asked Moses for the land, which the Reubenites settled (Num 32:38). The 9th-cent. BCE MOABITE STONE of King MESHA reports, "CHEMOSH said to me 'Go, take Nebo from Israel.'" Nebo apparently remained a Moabite town because it is mentioned in oracles against Moab (Isa 15:2; Jer 48:1, 22). *See* MOAB, MOABITES; REUBEN, REUBENITES.

R. JUSTIN HARKINS

NEBUCHADNEZZAR, NEBUCHADREZZAR neb´uh-kuhd-nez´uhr, neb´uh-kuh-drez´uhr [נְבוּכַדְנֶאצַּר **nevukhadhneʾtsar**, נְבוּכַדְרֶאצַּר **nevukhadhreʾtsar**; Ναβουχοδονοσόρ **Nabouchodonosor**]. There were two important kings of Babylon named Nebuchadnezzar (Akkad. **Nabu-kudurri-utsur**, "O Nabu protect my heir"), though only Nebuchadnezzar II is mentioned in the Bible. 1. Nebuchadnezzar I of the Second Dynasty of Isin ruled Babylon from 1125 to 1104 BCE. He kept Assyria at bay, but it was his successful campaign against Elam, in which he recovered the statue of Marduk, that made him great in the eyes of the Babylonians (*see* ELAM, ELAMITES).

2. Nebuchadnezzar II, who ruled Babylon for forty-three years (605–562 BCE), was the second ruler of the Neo-Babylonian dynasty founded by his father NABOPOLASSAR (626–605 BCE). Nabopolassar had rebelled against Assyria, seized the Babylonian throne, and begun a long see-saw struggle to drive Assyria from Babylonian territory (*see* ASSYRIA AND BABYLONIA).

It was only in the later stages of this struggle, following the destruction of Assyria and its replacement by EGYPT as Babylon's main enemy, that Nebuchadnezzar appears in the texts. He is first mentioned in a summer campaign of Nabopolassar's nineteenth year (607 BCE), when Nabopolassar left Nebuchadnezzar, his oldest son and crown prince, in charge of what had begun as a joint campaign and returned home to Babylon. For a couple of months Nebuchadnezzar campaigned on his own against mountain fortresses up to the border of URARTU. Then in 605 BCE, while the king remained home, Nebuchadnezzar led the Babylonian army in an attack on Carchemish. The crown prince inflicted on the Egyptian army a horrendous defeat celebrated by the prophet Jeremiah in an oracle against Pharaoh Neco of Egypt (Jer 46:1-12). Nebuchadnezzar followed this initial victory by a swift pursuit (compare Hab 1:8) of the fleeing remnants of the Egyptian army, overtaking and annihilating them in the region of Hamath.

Nebuchadnezzar proceeded to conquer all of Hamath, but when word came of his father's death in Babylon Nebuchadnezzar raced back to Babylon to assume the throne. He then returned to the west and continued to march about Syria collecting booty until the winter of 604 BCE. He briefly returned to Babylon in the spring of 604, and then marched west again to take tribute from the kings of Syria and Palestine. In late 604 he captured and destroyed the Philistine city of Ashkelon before returning to Babylon early in 603. Around this time the pro-Egyptian JEHOIAKIM of Judah submitted to Nebuchadnezzar and became his vassal for three years. In 603, 602, and 601 Nebuchadnezzar continued his annual booty-collecting marches through Syria-Palestine, but in the winter of 601 he suffered severe losses in a bloody battle with Egypt on the Egyptian border. This forced Nebuchadnezzar to spend the following year refitting his army in Babylon.

The apparent defeat and subsequent failure of the Babylonian army to march west in 600 BCE provoked Jehoiakim to rebel. In late 599, however, Nebuchadnezzar again marched west. While he secured his supply lines against the desert Arabs, Nebuchadnezzar also harassed Judah with raiding parties (2 Kgs 24:2). Then in late 598, Nebuchadnezzar marched against Jerusalem. Jehoiakim died, leaving his son JEHOIACHIN to face the Babylonian siege. Jehoiachin's rule lasted only three months. He surrendered the city to the Babylonians on March 15 or 16, 597 BCE, and Jehoiachin, his mother, and the Judean elite were taken away into Babylonian captivity, while the vessels and treasures of the Temple were taken away as booty (2 Kgs 24:13-17). Nebuchadnezzar installed Jehoiachin's uncle MATTANIAH as king of Judah in his place, giving him the throne-name ZEDEKIAH (2 Kgs 24:17).

In 596 BCE Nebuchadnezzar moved east to block an Elamite threat, and there was a rebellion in Babylonia in the winter of 595–594 that may have encouraged Judean dreams of revolt, but Nebuchadnezzar quickly suppressed the rebellion and resumed his booty-collecting marches through Syria in 594 and 593. Unfortunately, at this point the Babylonian Chronicle breaks off, and our details for the last thirty-two years of Nebuchadnezzar II's reign are very sketchy. At some point Zedekiah rebelled against Nebuchadnezzar, apparently expecting Egyptian support. In late 588 Nebuchadnezzar besieged Zedekiah in Jerusalem. The siege lasted about a year and a half, being relieved only briefly by an Egyptian sortie (Jer 37:5, 11-16) before the city wall was breached in the summer of 586. Zedekiah tried to escape, but he was captured and brought before Nebuchadnezzar at his headquarters in Riblah. Nebuchadnezzar executed Zedekiah's sons before Zedekiah's eyes, then blinded him, fettered him, and sent him to Babylon. Nebuchadnezzar also plundered and burned Jerusalem, destroyed its walls, and deported most of its remaining population into EXILE (2 Kgs 25:8-21).

From Josephus (*Ag. Ap.* 1.156) we know that Nebuchadnezzar besieged Tyre for thirteen years (ca. 585–573/72 BCE), though the outcome seems to have been a disappointment to the Babylonians. Tyre accepted Babylonian vassalage, but on reasonably favorable terms and without the plundering of their city, which the Babylonians were unable to capture. Ezekiel, who had repeatedly prophesied Nebuchadnezzar's conquest and plundering of Tyre, ultimately admits the failure of those prophecies to be realized and has God offer Nebuchadnezzar and his army Egypt as a consolation prize (compare Ezek 26:1–28:24; 29:17-20). Nebuchadnezzar may have attempted such an invasion of Egypt, because there is a broken inscription from his thirty-seventh year (ca. 568 BCE) that appears to mention an attack on Egypt, but we are lacking any further details. Nebuchadnezzar left numerous inscriptions related to his extensive building activities in Babylon, but few of them provide information on his military campaigns. Unlike the Assyrians, the Neo-Babylonian kings in their inscriptions downplayed the militaristic images and highlighted their service to the gods and their creation of well-being for the citizens of Babylon. Nebuchadnezzar clearly wanted to portray himself as the king of justice, a new HAMMURABI as it were, who brought peace and prosperity first to the Babylonians, and then eventually to all peoples under his rule. Nebuchadnezzar did bring prosperity to central Babylonia, but he did it at the expense of the periphery of his realm. Unlike the Assyrians, who tried to maintain the economic feasibility of their distant provinces, Babylon seemed satisfied to drain them of their resources. Assyria repopulated the regions it decimated with exiles from other parts of its realm, but Babylon left large regions of Palestine depopulated and in ruins to discourage Egyptian designs on the area. Habakkuk's negative oracle against Babylon (Hab 2:6-17) probably voiced the real feelings of most of Nebuchadnezzar's western subjects.

As conqueror of Jerusalem and destroyer of the Temple, Nebuchadnezzar II was the Neo-Babylonian ruler whose memory was most deeply seared into Jewish memory. The Bible clearly mentions only one other ruler of this dynasty, EVIL-MERODACH (Amel-Marduk), Nebuchadnezzar's son, who released Jehoiachin from prison (2 Kgs 25:27; Jer 52:31). The identification of the Babylonian official NERGAL-SHAREZER (Jer 39:3, 13) with Neriglissar, Evil-Merodach's successor, is less certain. Nonetheless, the Nebuchadnezzar portrayed in Daniel and Judith appears to be a composite of several different rulers. Judith confuses Nebuchadnezzar with an Assyrian king in Nineveh, while Daniel conflates Nebuchadnezzar with NABONIDUS, the last king of the Neo-Babylonian Dynasty. The traditions of Nebuchadnezzar's strange idol (Dan 3) and of his mad sojourn in the wilderness (Dan 4) appear to reflect negative Babylonian traditions about Nabonidus' cultic innovations and his long sojourn in Tema. The Prayer of Nabonidus from Qumran (4Q242) reinforces this suspicion, and BELSHAZZAR, called the son of Nebuchadnezzar in Daniel (Dan 5:2, 22) and Baruch (Bar 1:11-12), was actually the son of Nabonidus.

Bibliography: Albert K. Grayson. *Assyrian and Babylonian Chronicles* (1975); David Stephen Vanderhooft. *The Neo-Babylonian Empire and Babylon in the Latter Prophets* (1999); Donald J. Wiseman. *Nebuchadrezzar and Babylon* (1985).

J. J. M. ROBERTS

NEBUSHAZBAN neb´uh-shaz´ban [נְבוּשַׁזְבָּן nevushazban]. Nubushazban, a Babylonian official (Jer 39:13-14), helped transfer Jeremiah to Gedeliah's custody. Nebushazban is listed as a RAB-SARIS. *See* OFFICER, OFFICIAL.

NEBUZARADAN neb´uh-zuh-ray´duhn [נְבוּזַרְאֲדָן nevuzarʾadhan]. One of the Babylonian officials connected with the fall of Jerusalem, Nebuzaradan was a "captain of the guard," a high-ranking military officer (*see* OFFICER, OFFICIAL). He is described as responsible for burning Jerusalem and deporting exiles (2 Kgs 25:8-11, 18-21). After the fall of Jerusalem, Nebuzaradan oversaw the transfer of Jeremiah to Gedeliah's custody (Jer 39:13-14) and was also associated with a later Babylonian deportation of Judeans in 582/1 BCE (Jer 52:30).

JOHN M. BRACKE

NECK, STIFF. *See* STIFF-NECKED.

NECKLACE. *See* JEWELRY.

NECO nee´koh [נְכוֹ nekho, נְכֹה nekhoh]. Neco, the second PHARAOH of the Twenty-sixth Dynasty of Egypt, appears in biblical accounts of the death of King JOSIAH and in contemporary oracles of Jeremiah. He is usually designated Neco II, although he was the first king of that name to rule both Upper and Lower EGYPT. His grandfather Neco I was a regional ruler based in the delta city of Sais at the end of the Third Intermediate Period. Neco (alternate: Necho or Nekau) II, son of Psamtik I, ruled Egypt from 610 to 595 BCE. The primary sources for his reign are the Neo-Babylonian Chronicles, the Bible, and Herodotus.

The Twenty-sixth Dynasty arose in the context of competing Cushite and Assyrian expansion. In the late 8th and early 7th cent. BCE, Egypt was ruled by Cushite kings. As the Cushites extended their influence north and east, they clashed with Assyrian interests. In a series of invasions, the Assyrians drove the Cushites from power and claimed authority over the Nile Valley. The local rulers, including Psamtik I of Sais, became Assyrian vassals.

The emergence of Babylonia and Media as threats to Assyrian dominance in Mesopotamia shifted the balance of power. Assyria could not maintain its hold over its imperial periphery. Psamtik I filled the power vacuum in the Nile Valley, uniting Upper and Lower Egypt under his rule and throwing off Assyrian sovereignty. In 616 BCE the Egyptian army marched to Syria to prop up a weakened Assyria as a counter against Babylon.

Neco II continued his father's policy, mounting a series of expeditions to Syria beginning in his first year. According to biblical accounts (2 Kgs 23:29-35; 2 Chr 35:20–36:4), King Josiah of Judah intervened in the power struggle, interposing his army in the path of the Egyptians as they marched up the *Via Maris* in 609 BCE. The armies met at MEGIDDO, where Josiah was killed. Neco II deposed Josiah's successor JEHOAHAZ, replaced him with Jehoahaz's half-brother ELIAKIM, whom he renamed JEHOIAKIM, and imposed tribute on Judah. Second Kings 23:33 states that Jehoahaz was first confined at Riblah in the region of Hamath before being taken to Egypt as a prisoner of war.

The Neo-Babylonian Chronicles document Egypt's initial successes and ultimate failure combating Babylon. Egypt was able to gain control of northern Syria for several years, pushing as far as Harran on the Euphrates River before being driven back. In 605 BCE, the Babylonian army, under the command of crown prince Nebuchadnezzar, attacked the Egyptians at their Syrian base at Carchemish (*see* NEBUCHADNEZZAR, NEBUCHADREZZAR). The defeated Egyptians fell back to Hamath, where they were beaten again and forced to withdraw from Syria. In powerful poetry Jeremiah notes Egypt's defeat at Carchemish (Jer 46:2), which he calls "a sacrifice in the land of the north by the river Euphrates" (Jer 46:10).

Jeremiah warns of Nebuchadnezzar's impending attack on Egypt itself (Jer 46:13), which he expects to be successful: "Daughter Egypt shall be put to shame; she shall be handed over to a people from the north. The LORD of hosts, the God of Israel, said: See, I am bringing punishment upon Amon of Thebes, and Pharaoh, and Egypt and her gods and her kings, upon Pharaoh and those who trust in him. I will hand them over to those who seek their life, to King Nebuchad-rezzar of Babylon and his officers" (Jer 46:24-26*a*). In fact, Neco II stopped the Babylonian advance at Migdol and, according to Herodotus (*Hist.* 2.159), recaptured Gaza. Nonetheless, Egyptian domination of even southernmost Palestine was short lived. Nebuchadnezzar returned in 597 BCE and reimposed Babylonian sovereignty.

Neco II invested heavily in maritime operations in the Mediterranean and Red seas. He began construction of a canal linking the two via the Nile and the Wadi Tumilat. He maintained good relations with eastern Greece, making donations to Ionian shrines and employing Ionian and Carian mercenaries. Herodotus claims (*Hist.* 4.42) that Neco II even sponsored a three-year Phoenician expedition that successfully circumnavigated Africa.

CAROLYN HIGGINBOTHAM

NECROMANCY nek′ruh-man′see. Form of divination using spirits of the dead to foretell the future. In principle, this practice was forbidden in Israel, but there were experts who could inquire of spirits or consult with the dead (Lev 19:31; 20:27; Deut 18:11). For example, the medium of Endor is supposed to have brought back the ghost of Samuel to speak with Saul (1 Sam 28:3-25; *see* ENDOR, MEDIUM OF). The spirit or ghost was only visible and fully audible to the professional necromancer; all the consulter heard was chirping and muttering (Isa 8:19-20*a*; 29:4). The closest equivalent in ancient Mesopotamia was consulting a dream interpreter with offerings for a ghost in the hopes of receiving an answer by chance utterance. There were also professionals who used a simple form of psalter or hammered dulcimer to raise the dead for purposes of a séance. This instrument, called Ishtar's bow, was supposed to have been created from the roots and branches of a primordial tree that grew up in Sumer at the beginning of time. Ancient Mesopotamians also knew a method of direct consultation, which was to rub a magic salve on the face to make a ghost or death demon visible or onto a figurine or a skull to make the spirit speak. If things did not go as planned—e.g., the ghost came but would not speak—then a namburbi ritual was performed to dispel it. For either formal séances or private practice, it was helpful to choose an appropriate date such as the end of the fifth month Abu (the Mesopotamian Halloween), the fourth month Du'uzu (festival of Dumuzi), the ninth month Kislimu (festival of Nergal), or the tenth month Tebetu (festival of Anu), when ghosts would be already in the area to visit their relations or to beg for a handout. Offerings to the ghost were appropriate to private necromantic rituals, as also to the Anunnaki (netherworld gods) and Pabilsag, governor of the netherworld. In the classical world, the dead were consulted by means of incubated dreams or by digging blood-filled ditches as, for example, in the *Odyssey*. Evil witches were allegedly able to temporarily revive corpses for a suitable fee. In Egypt, communicating with the dead for whatever purpose was a simple matter of inserting a letter into a tomb.

JOANN SCURLOCK

NECTAR [נֹפֶת nofeth]. The sweet fluid secreted by flowers that bees collect to produce HONEY. Indeed, in most contexts **nofeth** is simply translated "honey" (e.g., Prov 5:3; 27:7). In Song 4:11, a lover describes his bride's lips as distilling (i.e., dripping) nectar, referring to the sweetness of her words—and her kisses.

JOEL MARCUS LEMON

NEDABIAH ned′uh-bī′uh [נְדַבְיָה nedhavyah]. The seventh son of King Jeconiah (*see* JEHOIACHIN) of Judah (1Chr 3:18).

NEEDLE [βελόνη **belonē**, ῥαφίς **rhaphis**]. A small tool used for SEWING or for making woven items. One end is blunt or sharpened to a fine point, and the other end has a small hole through which thread or a leather cord can be drawn. The earliest examples of needles (6th–4th millennia BCE) are made of carved bone. Bronze needles were more common during the OT and NT periods.

Needles ranged in size (from 1.5–5.5 in.) according to their function. Larger, thicker needles were used for stitching together LEATHER goods (such as tents, wineskins, and sandals), weaving on a loom, or repairing fishing nets, while smaller, finer needles were employed for sewing cloth and for decorative embroidery (*see* CLOTH, CLOTHES; EMBROIDERY AND NEEDLEWORK; TENTMAKER).

Jesus said it is more difficult for the rich to enter heaven than for a camel to fit through the eye of a needle (Matt 19:24; Mark 10:25; Luke 18:25). This absurd illustration may have been intended to jolt the wealthy out of complacency. Some later manuscripts softened the saying by substituting **kamilos** (καμίλος, "rope") for **kamēlos** (κάμηλος, "camel"). A speculative suggestion is that ancient walled cities had small gates, called the "needle's eye," through which a camel could pass, but not with a load on its back.

MARIANNE BLICKENSTAFF

NEEDLEWORK. *See* EMBROIDERY AND NEEDLEWORK.

NEGEB, NEGEV neg′eb, neg′ev [נֶגֶב neghev]. The word *Negeb*, which derives from a Hebrew root **ngb** (נגב) meaning "dry," generally designates the large area south of the hill country of Judah and northeast of the Sinai Peninsula. In its modern usage, the word *Negev* refers to a triangular-shaped region that constitutes more than half of the state of Israel, with a northern base spanning from Gaza through Beer-sheba to the Dead Sea, an eastern side running south from the Dead Sea to Elath, and a western side running north from Elath to Gaza. In its OT usage the Negeb designated the area about 15 mi. north and south of BEER-SHEBA and eastward to the Dead Sea, perhaps extending southward as far as Kadesh-barnea (*see* KADESH, KADESH-BARNEA). The boundaries of the area considered the Negeb changed over time, and its relationships to surrounding kingdoms like Judah and Edom are difficult to reconstruct.

For the OT writers, the Negeb is largely peripheral, lying outside the important areas for the story of Israel and Judah. However, for the modern study of ancient Israelite history, society, and religion, the Negeb has proved most significant. This area occupies an important location as the crossroads between Egypt and Mesopotamia, the gateway to southern Syria–Palestine, and the center of several trade routes that brought its valuable natural resources, such as copper and salt, to urban centers throughout the area. More significantly, the Negeb's dry climate has permitted the discovery of some of the best-preserved archaeological and textual finds in all of Syria–Palestine. These discoveries—such as military fortresses, texts of Judean military correspondence, and remains of apparently Yahwistic but perhaps "non-orthodox" sanctuaries and altars—have shed new light on the military, domestic, and religious life of Israel and Judah.

The Negeb's climate is generally semi-desert. The most desert-like conditions exist in the highlands south of Beer-sheba. Mountain ranges run diagonally across the region, cut by numerous wadis running east–west. The area's climate restricts the ability for agriculture, which must depend upon occasional flooding in the wadis or the ability to channel rain runoff, and supports primarily sheep and goat raising. The northern valley around Beer-sheba, however, has annual rainfall that supports more robust agriculture and grazing.

Settlement of the Negeb occurred in a series of waves that were likely the result of war, imperialism, and economic pressures rather than dramatic climate changes. Evidence of major occupation stretches back to the Chalcolithic period (ca. 4000 BCE), with significant settlement activity in the northern Negeb during the Early Bronze Age (ca. 3200 BCE). This period was followed by a 1,000-year span of little to no occupation, especially in the northern Negeb. During the first part of the Middle Bronze Age (ca. 2000 BCE) a new wave of settlement occurred primarily in the central highlands and southern area. For the rest of the Middle and Late Bronze ages (ca. 2000–1200 BCE), the majority of the Negeb was largely uninhabited, except perhaps by nomadic peoples and a few towns. This lack of significant settlement continued into the beginning of the Iron Age (ca. 1200 BCE).

Many of the OT stories of the patriarchs/matriarchs portray Abraham, Isaac, and their families as journeying throughout the Negeb, encountering various built-up towns, and dwelling in northern locations such as Beer-sheba and GERAR (see Gen 20:1; 21:31-34; 24:62; 26:6). Many of the exodus and wilderness stories are also set in the Negeb, where the Israelites are said to have encountered nomadic groups like the Amalekites (Exod 17:8-16; Num 13:29; *see* AMALEK, AMALEKITES), dwelled for an extended period at Kadesh-barnea (Num 13:25-26; Deut 1:19), and engaged in military conflict with the city of HORMAH and the king of ARAD (Num 21:1-3; Deut 1:44). The book of Joshua also tells of the conquering of the king of Arad (Josh 12:1, 14) and assigns conquered Negeb territories to the tribes of Judah and Simeon (Josh 15:21-32; 19:1-9).

The archaeological record described above raises questions about these biblical narratives. The lack of evidence for significant settlement in the Beer-sheba area during periods traditionally associated with the patriarchs and matriarchs (Middle and Late Bronze ages) has led some to question the date, nature, and/or historicity of the patriarchal narratives. During the time the Israelites are said to encounter kings and cities (Late Bronze and Early Iron ages), the northern Negeb reflects occupation patterns more consistent with pastoral nomads or villagers, leading some scholars to reenvision the kings as tribal chieftains and to propose alternative sites for settlements. As a result, some scholars suggest that these biblical traditions reflect realities of a later period.

Areas in the Negeb experienced various moments of renewed flourishing during the period of the kingdoms of Israel and Judah (10th–6th cent. BCE). The OT depicts both Saul and David as battling the Amalekites in the northern Negeb (1 Sam 15:1-9; 27:8; 30:1) and alludes to the presence of several districts throughout the region that David is said to have incorporated into Judah (see 1 Sam 27:8-10; 30:11-20; e.g., "Negeb of Judah," "Negeb of the Jerahmeelites," "Negeb of the Kenites," etc.). Mostly unfortified settlements multiplied in the northern Negeb in the first two centuries of the Iron Age and show evidence of destruction by about 1000 BCE.

The narratives about Solomon portray him as incorporating the Negeb into a vast empire ruled from Jerusalem (1 Kgs 4:21 [Heb. 5:1]), but the historicity of these traditions remains debated. Of special interest is the archaeological evidence for a number of apparently military forts throughout the Negeb that appear to have emerged in the late 11th or early 10th cent. BCE and been destroyed around the time of Pharaoh SHISHAK's invasion of Syria–Palestine (ca. 922 BCE; 1 Kgs 14:25-26). These fortified settlements are generally in the Negeb hills along the way from Arad to Kadesh-barnea. Scholars have traditionally linked these forts to a centralized state building program by Solomon undertaken to protect trade routes in the Negeb. Others note, however, that the locations and arrangement of these settlements do not indicate a system of military installments, but more likely reflect civilian settlements established by desert inhabitants expanding northward.

Throughout the remainder of the monarchic period, the Negeb was primarily a contested border region, making the area of interest to the Assyrians and Babylonians and the primary location of struggles between Judah and Edom (*see* EDOM, EDOMITES). There is evidence of various fortified Judean settlements in the northeastern Negeb throughout the 9th and 8th cent. BCE. In this period, the Judean king Jehoshaphat is said to have controlled the northern Negeb, attempted a failed maritime venture at Ezion-geber, and ruled Edom by a deputy, an arrangement against which Edom would later rebel (1 Kgs 22:47-50 [Heb. 22:48-51]). Similarly, Uzziah is said to have established forts throughout the Negeb and rebuilt the port at Elath (2 Kgs 14:22; 2 Chr 26:10). Judah's time of greatest dominance in the Negeb, however, likely began under Hezekiah in the last part of the 8th cent. Probably under Assyrian sponsorship, Judah strengthened its control over most of the areas to the southwest (2 Kgs 18:8). The city of Beer-sheba was apparently an important cultic center during this time (Amos 5:5; 8:14).

Beer-sheba and other major cities of the northern Negeb were destroyed by the Assyrians in 701 BCE. After some subsequent rebuilding, the final period of importance for the Negeb during monarchic times centered on the eastern area around Arad and spanned the last decade of the kingdom of Judah (ca. 597–586 BCE). During this period, Judah's struggles with Edom in the Negeb became pronounced. The Edomites were apparently involved in attacking Judean cities before the Babylonian invasion in 597 BCE (Jer 13:19) and are remembered as participating in the destruction of Jerusalem in 586 BCE (Ps 137:7; Obad 8-14).

The city of Arad, a key Judean fortress on the road to Edom, was the most significant site in the Negeb during this time. Excavations have revealed the presence of a Yahwistic temple, whose layout and altar were very similar to the biblical descriptions of the Jerusalem Temple. This sanctuary was destroyed in the latter 7th cent. BCE., perhaps as a part of Josiah's reform that closed sanctuaries outside of Jerusalem. The Arad sanctuary provides new insight into Judean religious practices outside the Jerusalem establishment. The Babylonian campaigns of the 6th cent. fundamentally altered the society and economy of the Negeb, and there is limited evidence of settlement between the 6th and 3rd cent. BCE. Perhaps by the late Persian period, however, the NABATEANS, nomadic traders from Arabia, were present in the Negeb, and they flourished between the 1st cent. BCE and the 1st cent. CE (*see* IDUMEA). The Romans gained control of the Negeb in the early 2nd cent. CE. During the Byzantine period, the area came under Christian influence and saw the establishment of numerous churches. The Arabs conquered the Negeb in the 630s CE, after which the region experienced little development until the modern period. *See* ISRAEL, GEOGRAPHY OF.

Bibliography: Yohanan Aharoni. "The Negeb." *Archaeology and Old Testament Study.* D. Winton Thomas, ed. (1967) 385–403; Itzhaq Beit-Arieh. *Horvat Qitmit: An Edomite Shrine in the Biblical Negev* (1995); Michael Evenari, Leslie Shanan, and Naphtali Tadmor. *The Negev: The Challenge of a Desert.* 2nd ed. (1982); Israel Finkelstein. *Living on the Fringe: The Archaeology and History of the Negev, Sinai, and Neighboring Regions in the Bronze and Iron Ages* (1995); Nelson Glueck. *Rivers in the Desert: A History of the Negev* (1959); Thomas L. Thompson. *The Settlement of Sinai and the Negev in the Bronze Age* (1975).

BRAD E. KELLE

NEGINAH, NEGINOTH. *See* MUSIC.

NEHELAM ni-hel'uhm [נֶחֱלָם nekhelam]. The family name or hometown (literally, "the Nehelamite") of SHEMAIAH, a "false" prophet condemned by Jeremiah (Jer 29:24, 31, 32). The name is otherwise unknown, as is the locality. A third, less likely, possibility is to translate it as "dreamer" (from the Hebrew root **khalam** [חָלַם]), in which case it would be a term coined by Jeremiah to mock Shemaiah. Shemaiah had sent a letter from exile in Babylon to the priesthood in Jerusalem with instructions to imprison Jeremiah for being a "madman" and prophesying a lengthy stay in Babylon—that is, for being a "false" prophet.

MARK RONCACE

NEHEMIAH nee'huh-mi'uh [נְחֶמְיָה **nekhemyah**; Νεεμίας **Neemias**]. Means "Yahweh comforts." 1. One of the leaders of the exiles who returned from Babylon with ZERUBBABEL after 538 BCE (Ezra 2:2; Neh 7:7; 1 Esd 5:8).

2. Son of HACALIAH (Neh 1:1); governor of the Persian province of Yehud (Judah) during the restoration (445–433 BCE, with a second term sometime later). Nehemiah's own first-person account, the so-called Nehemiah Memoir (Neh 1:1–7:73*a*, parts of 12:27-43, and 13:4-31), provides most of our information about this faithful, capable administrator.

Prior to his governorship, Nehemiah was "CUPBEARER to the king" (Neh 1:11), a trusted official of ARTAXERXES I Longimanus, king of Persia (465–424 BCE). The view that he was a EUNUCH stems from a LXX misreading of **eunouchos** (εὐνοῦχος, "eunuch") for **oinochoos** (οἰνοχόος, "cupbearer"). Hearing of the deplorable conditions of the Jews and the ruinous state of JERUSALEM's defenses moved Nehemiah to ask Artaxerxes for help, but only after first bringing the matter to God. The king responded with letters of safe passage and timber for the rebuilding projects (Neh 1:1–2:8).

Nehemiah's major achievement is the refortification of Jerusalem. While Josephus reports that the reconstruction took almost two years and four months (*Ant.* 11.179), the text of Nehemiah claims the project was completed in a remarkable fifty-two days (Neh 6:15). The vigorous opposition of the surrounding leaders—SANBALLAT the Horonite, governor of Samaria; TOBIAH the Ammonite; and GESHEM the Arab—manifested in various threats, intrigues, and plots culminating in accusations of sedition (Neh 2; 4; 6) add to the near-miraculous nature of the accomplishment. Some scholars suggest caution here since the memoir presents Nehemiah's version of the story, and these three leaders may have considered themselves loyal subjects of Artaxerxes honestly concerned about the reestablishment of a king in Jerusalem (Neh 6:6-7). In favor of Nehemiah's position is Artaxerxes' explicit permission and funding (Neh 2:8-9). Similar vocabulary in other Persian documents suggests that fortresses housing garrisons of soldiers for protection and tax collection were also a part of Nehemiah's mission.

Reforms initiated by Nehemiah during his first term as governor testify to his social consciousness, administrative ingenuity, and concern for morale. They include efficient dealing with the social injustice of wealthy members of the community who had taken advantage of a drought (Neh 5:1-13), the resettlement of a representative tenth of the outlying population to solve the defensive problem of an underpopulated Jerusalem (Neh 7:4-5; 11:1-2), and the joyous dedication of the walls (Neh 12:27-43).

During a second term as governor following a brief absence, Nehemiah carried out a second series of reforms regarding the misuse of the Temple (Neh 13:4-9), enforced financial support of the Levites (Neh 13:10-14), compelled observance of the Sabbath regulations (Neh 13:15-22), and required the dissolution of mixed marriages (Neh 13:23-27).

Above all, Nehemiah's capable and courageous administration grew out of his strong sense of vocation and trust in God's grace (Neh 2:8, 18, 20; 6:16). *See* EZRA AND NEHEMIAH, BOOKS OF.

3. Son of AZBUK who ruled half the district of BETH-ZUR and helped repair the walls of Jerusalem (Neh 3:16).

MARK THRONTVEIT

NEHEMIAH, BOOK OF. *See* EZRA AND NEHEMIAH, BOOKS OF.

NEHILOTH. *See* MUSIC.

NEHUM nee'huhm [נְחוּם **nekhum**]. A prominent Jew returning from Babylonian exile with ZERUBBABEL (Neh 7:7). The name, appearing only once in the OT, is virtually identical to that of the visionary NAHUM of Elkosh (Nah 1:1); indeed, the LXX renders both **Naoum** (Ναούμ). In Ezra 2:2, a parallel text, the common name REHUM replaces Nehum, suggesting scribal error in Neh 7:7.

JOEL MARCUS LEMON

NEHUSHTA ni-hoosh'tuh [נְחֻשְׁתָּא **nekhushta**ʾ]. The mother of King JEHOIACHIN of Judah (2 Kgs 24:8). The name of the king's mother often appears in Deuteronomistic king lists (see 2 Kgs 14:1-3; 15:1-3; 21:1-2; 23:31-32; 24:18), suggesting that the mother's lineage was a significant piece of the king's biography, and perhaps that she held an official role. *See* QUEEN.

Bibliography: Elna K. Solvang. *A Woman's Place is in the House: Royal Women of Judah and Their Involvement in the House of David* (2003).

JESSICA TINKLENBERG DEVEGA

NEHUSHTAN ni-hoosh'tuhn [נְחֻשְׁתָּן **nekhushtan**]. The name of the bronze serpent that King HEZEKIAH had broken into pieces in his religious reform, attempting to destroy Canaanite forms of worship (2 Kgs 18:4, the only OT reference to the name) and centralize worship in the Jerusalem Temple. The English name is a transliteration from the Hebrew, and the meaning is derived from the nouns BRONZE (**nakhush** נָחוּשׁ) and SERPENT (**nakhash** נָחָשׁ), which could have provided a double meaning. The biblical author noted that the bronze serpent, which was believed to have been the one erected by Moses in Num 21:8-9 for the purpose of healing, was destroyed because the people were making offerings to it. The influence of a possible Nehushtan cult in Jerusalem is exhibited by the name NEHUSHTA, the queen mother of King Jehoiachin (2 Kgs 24:8). Serpent iconography was a common feature among the cultures of the ANE. *See* ASHERAH; SERPENT, BRONZE.

BRUCE W. GENTRY

NEIEL ni-ī'uhl [נְעִיאֵל **ne**ʿ**i**ʾ**el**]. A town listed along with BETH-EMEK as a northern boundary marker in the allotment to the tribe of Asher (Josh 19:27). It is likely Khirbet Yaʿnin. *See* ASHER, ASHERITES.

NEIGHBOR [עָמִית ʿ**amith**, רֵעַ **rea**ʿ, שָׁכֵן **shakhen**; πλησίον **plēsion**]. A neighbor is a person who lives near another; each of a number of persons who lives in the vicinity of others. The word describes the proximate spatial relation of two or more persons. By itself this spatial designation says nothing of the social significance of being or having a neighbor. A first step in understanding what *neighbor* might mean is to understand the social system from which the word has its meanings. All the peoples described in the Bible lived in collectivistic societies, where group integrity and group support were a primary orientation (*see* COLLECTIVIST PERSONALITY). The term *neighbor* is also used in the NT as an inclusive language translation of **adelphos** (ἀδελφός, "brother"; e.g., Matt 7:3-5).

A neighbor in Israelite society is well described in Lev 19:16-18 (part of which is cited in the Synoptics; Matt 22:39; Mark 12:31; Luke 10:27): "You shall not go around as a slanderer among your people, and you shall not profit by the blood of your neighbor. . . . You shall not hate in your heart anyone of your kin; you shall reprove your neighbor, or you will incur guilt yourself. You shall not take vengeance or bear a grudge against any of your people, but you shall love your neighbor as yourself." Here *neighbor* includes "your people" and "your kin." For an Israelite, all Israelites are neighbor.

Thus, a neighbor is a member of the Israelite ingroup or we-group. *Ingroup* refers to an exclusive circle of people with a common purpose, interests, or attitudes, especially one that produces feelings of camaraderie, exclusivity, COMMUNITY, and solidarity. In Israel this ingroup consisted of those covenanted to the God of Israel, the people of the God of Israel, characterized by common blood, common land, common language, common way of life, and common worship. This is the widest circle of all Israel.

However, in daily living this wide ingroup was more constricted and focused on people in narrower circles consisting of extended family, village mates, city section mates, city mates, and the like. The boundaries of one's ingroup expanded and contracted largely in terms of who constituted the outgroup. For all Israel, foreigners were outgroup; for Galileans, the people of Judea and Perea as well as Samaria were outgroup; for the people of Nazareth, other villages and towns were outgroup (*see* FOREIGN, FOREIGNER). As a rule, then, *neighbor* describes persons who live in proximity and interact in terms of their mutual attachments and entitlements.

The fact of physical proximity is interpreted as involving some sense of self and extended self, some sense of being part of a neighborhood that involves a sort of network of people who provide one another with a sense of mutual belonging and mutual assistance. What binds neighbors in this sense are bonds of generalized reciprocity, that is, doing favors for one another in open-ended interactions. Neighbors acted like fictive kin (*see* KINSHIP). This is quite different from the neighborhood market where vendors and residents are bound by balanced reciprocity: take and pay here and now. But should the vendor provide open credit, the relationship develops into one of closer attachment, realized by generalized reciprocity. The network of interacting neighbors reaches a social boundary at which people on the other side might be general neighbors (e.g., the house of Israel), but because they do not regularly interact, they are regional non-neighbors, an outgroup. As a rule, local neighbors have no sense of obligation to these fellow ethnic people on the other side. Hence, while they are not enemies, they are like traveling vendors, treated by the norms of balanced reciprocity. And at a third social level is the realm of enemies, people who must be fended off and who have no entitlements of either balanced or generalized reciprocity. These are rightfully treated with negative reciprocity: take and give nothing in return.

The rule to love one's neighbor has the same quality as the "thou shalt nots" of the TEN COMMANDMENTS. The purpose is to maintain societal harmony and prevent conflict among the ingroup. Neighbors and conflict are a sort of contradiction (see Matt 5:43-44). Reconciliation is required for neighborhood stability and peace and confidence in interaction (emphasized in Matt 5:23-26; 18:15-22; see Luke 17:3-4). Hence the great value of village peacemakers, veritable sons of God (as in Matt 5:9).

The difficulty in antiquity was to consider people beyond the outermost rim of the ingroup as anything other than enemy, as a different species, as not belonging to the ethnocentric human race constituted of self and one's neighbors. The question of "who is my neighbor" was therefore one of significance, especially for the scribal class. Villagers knew who their neighbors were. The scribal class asked the theoretical question of how far the boundaries of neighborhood extended (as in Luke 10:29).

The parable of the Good Samaritan in Luke 10:30-37 extends the neighborhood boundary to those original Israelites, the SAMARITANS, regardless of their subsequent genealogical confusion (*see* SAMARITAN, THE GOOD). While Pharisees and their program of "no mixture" tended to exclude many in Israel, Jesus' vision of a forthcoming Israelite theocracy included as many as possible. Old Israel (Samaria) and newer Israel (Judea) are bound by the mutual obligations and entitlements of neighborly obligations.

In sum, to understand *neighbor* one might imagine three concentric social rings: the center ring includes people obliged by mutual generalized reciprocity, one's local, everyday neighbors. The next ring includes people obliged by balanced obligations, tit for tat, here referring to the house of Israel. A third ring, left unbounded on the outside, consisted of people to whom one is not bound at all.

The feat of subsequent human development during the Enlightenment was to imagine that all human beings might be neighbors, hence to include all humans within this innermost ring of generalized reciprocity. But as the period of globalization and continual aggression begun in the 20th cent. has demonstrated, this vision has not succeeded. Instead there is a new arrangement of an innermost ring consisting of persons of extreme wealth, with the rest of humankind in the balanced and negative reciprocity rings. *See* LOVE IN THE NT; LOVE IN THE OT; NATIONS; SOJOURNER; STRANGER.

Bibliography: Benedict R. Anderson. *Imagined Communities: Reflections on the Origin and Spread of Nationalism* (1983); Bruce J. Malina. *Christian Origins and Cultural Anthropology* (1986).

BRUCE J. MALINA

NEKODA ni-koh'duh [נְקוֹדָא neqodha᾽; Νεκωδά Nekōda]. 1. A temple servant whose descendants returned from Babylonia to Jerusalem after King Cyrus of Persia had ended the exile (Ezra 2:48; Neh 7:50). In 1 Esd 5:31, the name is Noeba.

2. An ancestral head of a family whose descendants had returned to Jerusalem after the exile but could not verify their descent and Israelite kinship (Ezra 2:59-60; Neh 7:62; 1 Esd 5:37). *See* EZRA AND NEHEMIAH, BOOKS OF.

EMILY R. CHENEY

NEMUEL nem'y*oo*-uhl [נְמוּאֵל nemu᾽el]. 1. Listed among the descendants of ELIAB in the Reubenite tribe (Num 26:9).

2. One of Simeon's sons and the head of one of five clans together numbering 22,200 descendants (Num 26:12; 1 Chr 4:24). He is called JEMUEL in Gen 46:10 and Exod 6:15.

NEO-ASSYRIANS. *See* ASSYRIA AND BABYLONIA.

NEOFITI, TARGUM. *See* TARGUMS.

NEOLITHIC AGE. *See* PRE-HISTORY IN THE ANCIENT NEAR EAST.

NEPHEG nee'fig [נֶפֶג nefegh]. 1. The second of three sons of Izhar and a descendant of Kohath in the genealogy of Levi (Exod 6:21).

2. A son of David, born in Jerusalem to an unnamed wife or concubine (2 Sam 5:15; 1 Chr 3:7; 14:6).

NEPHILIM nef'uh-lim [נְפִלִים nefilim; γίγαντες gigantes]. The Nephilim are mentioned in two enigmatic passages in the Pentateuch, the ambiguity of which led to differing interpretations of the Nephilim in later Judaism. The word itself is related to nafal (נָפַל, "to fall"); hence, it has the connotation of "the fallen ones." The origins of the name (e.g., who fell, who caused them to fall) are obscure.

In a rather awkward comment, the author of Gen 6:4 observes that the Nephilim were on the earth when the sons of God came in to the daughters of men and bore children by them (*see* GOD, SONS OF). The author notes that the Nephilim also lived after this time. He concludes by saying that "these were the heroes (gibborim גִּבֹּרִים) that were of old, warriors of renown." What is clear is that the Nephilim lived before the FLOOD. What is not clear is the relationship, if any, between the Nephilim and the offspring of the unions of the sons of God and the daughters of men, on the one hand, or between the Nephilim and the gibborim, on the other.

The second passage, Num 13:33, says nothing about either the sons of God and the daughters of men or the gibborim. Rather, the author recounts how the spies sent by Moses into Canaan reported that the Nephilim (further characterized as the sons of ANAK, who came from the Nephilim) were so large that the spies themselves seemed to be the size of grasshoppers. (In Deut 2:10-11 the ANAKIM, again noted for their height, are called REPHAIM, rather than Nephilim.)

From these two passages, four elements about the Nephilim were combined and developed in one way or another by later writers: 1) their antediluvian existence; 2) their possible relationship to the children of the sons of God and the daughters of men; 3) their possible relationship to the gibborim; and 4) their great size.

Some later Jewish writers seem to have ignored the relationship between the Nephilim and the children of the sons of God and the daughters of men. Picking up only the third element noted above, Ezek 32:27 speaks of the "fallen warriors" (gibborim noflim גִּבּוֹרִים נֹפְלִים) who have gone down to Sheol with their weapons of war. In the same vein, the LXX, adding the first and fourth elements, identifies the Nephilim, which it translates as "giants" (gigantes, from sing. gigas [γίγας]; *see* GIANTS), explicitly with the "heroes" in Gen 6:4. It also translates gibborim noflim in Ezek 32:27 simply as "giants" (gigantes). Similarly, Bar 3:26-28 speaks of the giants' expertise in war and their ultimate demise. Other texts like Wis 14:6 and 3 Macc 2:4 comment on the giants' destruction in the waters of the flood.

In other writers, such as *Jubilees*, the identification of the Nephilim with the offspring of the sons of God and the daughters of men was made explicit (*Jub.* 5:1; 7:22). The same idea is found in an extended, though very fragmentary expansion of the Gen 6:1-4 story in the opening columns of the *Genesis Apocryphon.* In 1QapGen[ar] II, 1, LAMECH, the father-to-be of Noah, expresses his concern that his wife has become pregnant by one of the WATCHERs and therefore belongs to the Nephilim, who are later said to have spilled some blood (1QapGen[ar] VI, 19). A much more elaborate story is contained in the *Book of Giants*, which has survived in only a few fragments from Qumran (4Q530–33), but which may be related to a later Manichean document of the same name. In an antediluvian-based narrative that mentions such luminaries as Enoch (4Q530 II, 21) and Gilgamesh (4Q530 II, 2; 4Q531 17 12), the *Book of Giants* speaks of both the Nephilim (4Q530 II, 6; III, 8; 4Q531 5 2, 8; 4Q532 2 3) and the gibborim (4Q530 II, 13, 15, 20–21; III, 3; 6 I, 8; 4Q531 4 4; 5 2, 5), though apparently distinguishing them from each other (4Q531 5 2). All of this seems to be related to the story of the fall of the Watchers found in the *Book of the Watchers* (*1 En.* 1–16), where the sons of God ("the Watchers") and the daughters of men produce "giants" that wreak havoc on the earth before being destroyed by the flood, a story that was probably assumed in the passages from the Wisdom of Solomon and 3 Maccabees noted above (*see* ENOCH, FIRST BOOK OF). Finally, it is worth noting that *An Admonition Associated with the Flood* (4Q370 I, 6) identifies those who did not escape the flood as the gibborim but does not mention the Nephilim.

JOSEPH L. TRAFTON

NEPHISIM ni-fī'sim [נְפִיסִים nefisim (Kethibh), נְפוּסִים nefusim (Qere); Ναφισί Naphisi]. Family head whose descendants belonged to the NETHINIM or temple servants, and returned to Jerusalem after Cyrus had ended the exile (Ezra 2:50; 1 Esd 5:31). The reading for this family head as Nephushesim (nefishesim נְפוּשְׁסִים) in Neh 7:52 had probably resulted from the combining of two variant spellings of the name, one with shin (sh שׁ) and the other one with samech (s ס). These temple servants were possibly related to the Naphesh Ishmaelites. *See* EZRA AND NEHEMIAH, BOOKS OF.

EMILY R. CHENEY

NEPHTHAR nef'thahr [νέφθαρ nephthar]. The combustible liquid found at the time of Nehemiah where the fire of the altar had been hidden (2 Macc 1:18-36). The account implies that the word *naphtha* (**nephthai** νέφθαι) derives from **nephthar**, and claims that it means "purification." These claims cannot be supported; the etymology is Akkadian (**naptu**). *See* MACCABEES, SECOND BOOK OF.

KEN M. PENNER

NEPHTOAH, WATERS OF nef-toh´uh [מֵי נֶפְתּוֹחַ **me neftoakh**]. Means "opening." A boundary marker of Judah and Benjamin, between Mount EPHRON and the Valley of Hinnom (Josh 15:9; 18:15), usually identified with modern Lifta/Me Neftoah, just northwest of Jerusalem. This may be the "wells of MERNEPTAH" of the Egyptian Papyrus Anastasi III. The "westward" direction of the boundary in Josh 18:15 conflicts with 15:9; the NRSV omits the direction, harmonizing the two verses. *See* HINNOM, VALLEY OF.

KEN M. PENNER

NEPHUSHESIM. *See* NEPHISIM.

NER nuhr [נֵר **ner**]. Means "lamp." Ner is sometimes listed as the father of Abner, Saul's uncle. In other instances, Ner is listed as the father of Kish and Abner. The question is complicated by the fact that verses in Samuel and Chronicles can be read to support either case.

First Samuel 14:51 records that Abiel was the father of Ner, and Ner the father of Abner. This notice fits 1 Sam 9:1, where Saul's grandfather is listed as Abiel. However, in 1 Sam 14:50, "Saul's uncle" could refer either to Abner or Ner in Hebrew. That Ner is Saul's grandfather, and Abner Saul's uncle, finds support in 1 Chr 8:33 and 9:39. Both verses list Ner as the father of Kish and Abner. First Chronicles 9:35-36, on the other hand, supports the reading that Kish and Ner were brothers (here their father is Jeiel not Abiel), which agrees with both 1 Sam 9:1 and 14:51. According to Josephus' *Ant.* 6.129–30, Ner was Saul's uncle, and this reading supports reading Ner as Saul's uncle, not Abner, agreeing with both 1 Sam 9:1 and 14:51.

In 1 Sam 10:14-16 an unnamed uncle of Saul is mentioned. Some have raised the possibility that this uncle is Ner, although nothing in the text indicates that connection.

Bibliography: Hans Wilhelm Hertzberg. *1 and 2 Samuel.* OTL (1964); Sara Japhet. *1 and 2 Chronicles.* OTL (1993); Ralph W. Klein. *1 Samuel.* WBC 10 (1983); P. Kyle McCarter. *1 Samuel.* AB 8 (1980).

HEATHER R. MCMURRAY

NEREUS nee´ri-y*oos* [Νηρεύς **Nēreus**]. Nereus is a Roman Christian greeted by Paul in Rom 16:15. Although Nereus is a Greek name, it was not uncommon in Rome, especially among slaves. Of the twenty-eight people called Nereus in 1st-cent. Roman inscriptions, at least fifteen are identified as slaves or freedmen. Nevertheless, Nereus may have been a leader in a Roman HOUSE CHURCH. He and his sister are singled out for greeting alongside PHILOLOGUS, JULIA, and OLYMPAS, while the rest of their community is mentioned generically as "all the saints who are with them." Nereus was probably a Gentile, since Paul usually highlights the ethnic background of Jews explicitly in Rom 16. In Greek mythology Nereus was a god of the sea, father of the Nereids. *See* ROMANS, LETTER TO THE.

Bibliography: Peter Lampe. *From Paul to Valentinus: Christians at Rome in the First Two Centuries* (2003).

IAN W. SCOTT

NERGAL nuhr´gal. Sumerian god of plague and of the netherworld whose seat was at Kutha. Nergal was associated with the planet Mars. He acquired the netherworld by marriage to the goddess Ereshkigal. Nergal was identified with Erra, the anti-hero of the Erra epic and destroyer of Babylon. Nergal's month was Kislimu, during which a festival was held that included a ritual scattering of palm branches reminiscent of Palm Sunday. Nergal seems to have been honored by heterodox Jews in Babylonia. The people of Cuth brought Nergal to Samaria when they were resettled there by Assyria, and he was worshiped with Yahweh (2 Kgs 17:30). As Hercules-Nergal, he appears in Parthian Hatra.

JOANN SCURLOCK

NERGAL-SHAREZER nuhr´gal-shuh-ree´zuhr [נֵרְגַל שַׂר־אֶצֶר **nerghal sar-ʾetser**]. One of the Babylonian officials who was present during and after the fall of Jerusalem (Jer 39:3, 13). The name means "Nergal, protect the king." Textual problems in Jer 39:3 make his identification tenuous. The first occurrence of the name in Jer 39:3 is followed by the word *Samgar-nebo*, which could be the name of another official, a textual corruption of the title Simmagir, or could mean "prince of Sin-magir." Nergal-sharezer is twice given the title RABMAG. It is thus unclear if 39:3 refers to two different persons with the same name, or one person with two titles. Many think that Nergal-sharezer is Neriglissar, who succeeded Amel-marduk, Nebuchadnezzar's son, as king of Babylon (559–556 BCE).

MARK RONCACE

NERI nee´r*i* [Νηρί **Nēri**]. Found only in Luke's genealogy as the father of Shealtiel (Luke 3:27). Elsewhere Jeconiah is Shealtiel's father (1 Chr 3:17; Salathiel in Matt 1:12).

NERIAH ni-r*i*´uh [נֵרִיָּה **neriyah**; Νηρίας **Nērias**]. The son of Mahseiah and the father of BARUCH, the scribe and loyal friend of JEREMIAH (Jer 32:12; Bar 1:1), and SERAIAH, the quartermaster of the exiled king Zedekiah (Jer 51:59-64). Epigraphic evidence seems to corroborate biblical descriptions of Neriah. The name nryhw (נריהו) appears as a patronym on two Hebrew seals, one belonging to a certain Berechiah (a long form of Baruch) and another belonging to Seraiah.

JOEL MARCUS LEMON

NERO nihr'oh. Nero Claudius Caesar Augustus Germanicus was Roman emperor from 54 to 68 CE, successor of CLAUDIUS, and the last emperor of the Julio-Claudian dynasty (*see* ROMAN EMPIRE).

A. Sources

How to evaluate Nero's career as emperor has been a disputed issue from earliest times. Within a generation of Nero's death, Josephus reports that many people attempted to compose a history of Nero, but those authors who had received benefits from Nero tended to present him more favorably than was truthful, and those who hated him lied about him and made him out to be worse than he was (*Ant.* 20.154–57). Except for Nero's propaganda speeches preserved in inscriptions, there are no extant autobiographical texts. The only contemporary materials dealing directly with Nero's reign are from his advisor and sponsor SENECA, written in the early period of Nero's reign while Seneca still enjoyed the emperor's favor (*De Clementia; Apocolocyntosis divi Claudii*). Josephus' fifty-six references to Nero are mostly matter-of-fact. His occasional evaluative comments are mixed, their ambivalent tendencies reflecting both the war that devastated his homeland and his debt to his (Flavian) Roman patrons.

The three later Roman historians (Tacitus, *Hist.* 1–4; *Ann.* 14–16; Cassius Dio, *Rom.* 61–63, Suetonius, *The Life of Nero*) who narrated his exploits with varying degrees of objectivity all had access to reliable information. However, like ancient historians in general, they tended to regard their craft as a combination of rhetoric and philosophy, setting forth in historical form the virtues that had made Rome great and the vices that contradicted the core values of the Roman people. In their writings, Nero tended to become the foil for their view of the ideal Roman emperor. All belonged to the Flavian period that tended to deprecate the Julio-Claudian period, particularly Nero as its last representative. Legends about Nero grew with time. Despite the tendentious nature of our only sources, the substantial accuracy of the following characterization seems to be securely grounded.

B. Life and Times

1. Birth and early life

Nero was born on December 15, 37 CE as Lucius Domitius Ahenobarbus into a family that had belonged to the Roman nobility for more than 500 years. His father, who was not related to the imperial family by blood, had married a niece of Octavian (AUGUSTUS). His mother Agrippina was the great-granddaughter of Augustus and sister of the reigning Gaius Caesar (CALIGULA). Nero's father died when he was a small child, and his mother was exiled as politically dangerous. According to Suetonius, the child was brought up in the home of his aunt Lepida in modest circumstances, with a dancer and a barber as his principal tutors (*Nero* 1). After the murder of Caligula, Claudius succeeded to the throne, recalled Agrippina from her island exile, fell under her spell, and married her. She persuaded him to adopt her only child as his son, who at age twelve became Nero Claudius Caesar Germanicus.

It was assumed that Claudius' own son Britannicus would succeed his father as emperor, but the empire was not technically a monarchy and succession was not hereditary. Agrippina, however, was diligently grooming her son to be the next emperor. She prevailed upon Claudius to recall from exile the respected teacher and writer Lucius Annaeus Seneca and to appoint him as Nero's private tutor. The boy developed skill in rhetoric, could speak persuasively in both Latin and Greek, and acquired a taste for Greek literature, art, and music. Agrippina's public relations campaign emphasized that Nero was a descendant of the Divine Augustus, and her intrigues facilitated the marriage of Nero to Claudius' daughter Octavia, a further claim to the imperial throne when Claudius died. When it appeared that Claudius might nonetheless nominate Britannicus as the next emperor, Agrippina fed him poisoned mushrooms, and Claudius died without being able to implement his plan.

The young Nero was presented to the Praetorian Guard by its prefect, Sextus Afranius Burrus, who owed his position to Agrippina. After the support of the Praetorian Guard had been secured, Burrus and Seneca then became advisors to the young emperor. Seneca wrote and Nero delivered his initial speech to the Senate setting forth his "policy statement," whereupon the Senate, in feigned ignorance of the circumstances of Claudius' death and his will affirming Britannicus as his successor, approved Nero as Claudius' legitimate successor and the fifth Princeps. The new emperor was seventeen.

There were reports that early in his reign Nero often disguised himself and went with his bodyguards through the streets of Rome, robbing and beating the common people. These stories have sometimes been considered intentional distortions by his later detractors, who twisted the legendary image often associated with the good ruler—the benevolent monarch who circulates incognito among his subjects to learn what their life is really like and what they really think of him rather than depending on the flattering reports from his courtiers. Likewise, the myth of *Nero redivivus* has sometimes been understood as a reflection of Nero's popularity among the populace, who hopefully awaited his return to restore the good times they had experienced during his rule.

2. Two periods?

Roman historians agree that Nero's reign was a mixture of good features combined with horrendous evil, but the nature of the sources has generated interpretative difficulties that have inhibited a homogeneous picture. Some historians have followed Tacitus' depiction of an early period of good government (54–59 CE) followed by the irresponsibility, cruelty, and growing megalomania in the latter part of his reign (*Ann.* 13). In this view, during the "five Golden Years" his advisors Burrus and Seneca, along with his mother Agrippina, were the real governing powers, leaving the boy to exhaust himself in youthful pleasures. It was thought that when the young emperor matured, he would assume his rightful responsibilities.

Meanwhile, the empire itself was wisely governed by the powers behind the throne, and both the economy and justice flourished. The second phase only began after Nero became suspicious of his mother and had her murdered (59 CE) and Burrus died (62 CE) amid rumors that Nero had poisoned him. The same year Seneca received permission to retire and withdrew from politics. In this view, when the young Nero emerged as the *de facto* ruler, he had become so self-centered and irresponsible that he wasted the empire's resources on his own vanities and became a monstrous tyrant.

While historical reality is rarely so chronologically neat, it is true that Nero's administration had some positive features, especially in its early period. Seneca's *De Clementia,* published in 55 or 56 CE, portrays Nero as pursuing a liberal and generous policy that minimized obtaining favors and citizenship through bribery (see Acts 22:28) and promised to end imperial trials behind closed doors. In previous administrations, the charge of *maiestas* ("treason") had been loosely defined, and emperors had decided the cases personally in their own chambers, a combination that encouraged injustice and personal vendettas. Nero seems to have kept his initial promise to end this practice, showed more respect for the power of the Senate, and won widespread support for his policies, especially among the upper classes. He was popular among the masses for the peace and prosperity that generally prevailed, for his interest in associating with them personally, and for his generous provision of food and games. His propagandists and later biographers reminded the populace that in contrast to warriors like Julius Caesar and Augustus, Nero came to power without force.

General popularity on the home front was matched by troubles on the boundaries of the empire. The most serious provincial rebellion against Roman rule in the 1st cent. was not the Jewish revolt of 66–70 CE (of most interest to biblical and Christian historians), but the 60–61 revolt in Britain. Thousands of Roman soldiers were slaughtered, and though Roman rule was maintained over the province, the cost in lives and money was deeply resented, and Nero was rightly blamed. He did not, in fact, attend as closely to the military affairs as his predecessors and followers. The Roman citizenry owed its prosperity to good management of the legions and good relations with their commanders, who during Nero's reign realized their own power in making and unmaking the emperors.

On the eastern frontier, Parthia was the constant thorn in Rome's side. The Romans needed solid pro-Roman support from the buffer state Armenia, which had to be secured by stationing strong legionary forces in neighboring Syria. Nero did not manage the political and military strategy well, though he did finally force the Armenian king to come to Rome and, in an extravagant display, to receive his crown from Nero himself. Nero's fear of placing potential rivals in key positions tended to cause him to appoint men of lesser status to provincial governorships, weakening the empire's hold on its constituency and further alienating him from the powerful Senate.

3. The great fire and the Christians

The great fire of 64 CE became a turning point in Nero's career. On July 19, a fire broke out in the *Circus Maximus* and spread rapidly within the inner city, where buildings constructed mainly of wood were crowded close together. The conflagration burned for six days and seven nights, destroying almost a quarter of the city. The popular image of a Nero who watched the fire and "fiddled while Rome burned" is legend: the violin had not yet been invented, and Nero was absent from the city when the fire began. But Suetonius reports that Nero watched the conflagration from the tower of Maecenas dressed in his stage costume and sang the whole of *The Sack of Troy* (Suetonius, *Nero* 38). Tacitus also reports this, but as a story that he neither affirms nor denies (Tacitus, *Ann.* 15.39). Nero was already under heavy criticism for his extravagant building operations, and the rumor persisted that his own agents had ignited the blaze and hindered those who attempted to extinguish it, intending after the destruction to construct an elaborate new inner city named after himself. To divert these suspicions from himself, Nero looked for scapegoats, and he found them in the new Christian group, already suspect by the Roman population for their disdained eastern religion and their unwillingness to participate in the public activities of Roman culture.

Tacitus describes how Nero made the Christians wear animal skins and be torn to pieces by dogs or caused them to be nailed to crosses and burned as illumination in the night. He created a circus of torture in his own gardens, while he circulated as host in a charioteer's costume. According to Tacitus, Nero's cruelty resulted in sympathy for the Christians, because they were being killed not for the public good but at the whim of a tyrant (Suetonius, *Ann.* 15.44). Suetonius reports both the fire and Nero's suppression of Christians, but he makes no connection between them, treating them in widely separated chapters (*Nero* 6.2 [Christians], 6.38 [fire]). Cassius Dio deals fully with the fire but does not refer to Christians at all (*Rom.* 62.16–18). Christian writers who report Nero's violence against Christians also make no reference to the fire.

Later Christians understood Nero's actions as the persecution of Christians *per se*, the first imperial persecution. Although Nero did take advantage of the widespread antagonism toward Christians and was excessively cruel in his punishment, professing the Christian faith was not criminal itself. The event stamped itself indelibly on the Christian consciousness, and the image of Nero was later to assume monstrous proportions in some Christian circles (*see* CHRISTIANS, PERSECUTION OF).

4. The divine Nero

The cult of the divine ruler was a phenomenon of Eastern culture and religion not promoted by the earlier emperors, who accepted divine honors only reluctantly. Tiberius denied the requests from cities in Greece and Asia that wished to grant him divine honors; when a similar overture came from Spain, Tiberius rejected it with an address to the Senate that explicitly declared that he understood himself as a human being performing human tasks. Yet the line between honor and worship was not crisp. The posthumous deification of Julius Caesar meant that Augustus was "son of god" (*divi filius*). Tiberius' successors were not hesitant to accept divine honors during their lifetimes, so that when Nero became emperor there was already something of a tradition of EMPEROR WORSHIP, even in Rome. This was enhanced by Nero's own growing megalomania and by his apparent desire to stamp the Roman emperor's image with the features of the (divine) Hellenistic monarch. He thus appears to have taken his own divinity more seriously than his predecessors, but the evidence that he pursued an intentional policy of self-apotheosis is slight.

5. The final phase

Nero had shown early on his interest in Greek language and culture. Even before becoming emperor, he had addressed the Senate three times in Greek. He wrote and performed Greek music and promoted it in Italy, where he also attempted to establish Roman counterparts to the Greek games. In 67–68 CE, he and his entourage toured Greece, where he performed in various artistic and athletic contests as singer, harpist, actor, athlete, or chariot driver. He was awarded the victor's crown in every contest—including a chariot race he did not complete. He announced the "Liberation of Hellas," i.e., that Greece was henceforth exempt from Roman taxation, and he set his soldiers and thousands of slaves and prisoners of war to work excavating a canal at Corinth to connect the Adriatic and the Aegean—a visionary project not completed until 1883.

His neglect of matters of state opened the door for powerful military leaders to seize the reigns of government. In the spring of 68 CE, while Vespasian's troops were suppressing the insurgency in Judea, fresh revolts broke out in Spain, Gaul, and Africa, and the empire was in civil war. Nero returned to Rome, but too late. The Senate turned against him, declaring him to be an enemy of the state. He fled to a suburban villa where he committed suicide by stabbing himself in the throat with the help of his freedman Epaphroditus. He reportedly died lamenting, "What an artist dies with me" (Suetonius, *Nero* 48–49). After eighteen months of civil war in which Galba, Otho, and Vitellius each reigned briefly in the struggle for leadership, Vespasian left the siege of Jerusalem in the hands of his son Titus, returned to Rome as emperor, and the Flavian dynasty replaced the Julio-Claudian.

C. Reflection in the New Testament

Several NT documents were written while Nero was emperor: 1 Corinthians, 2 Corinthians, Philippians, Philemon, Galatians, and Romans. The Gospel of Mark was written either in the last days of Nero or shortly after his death; it probably reflects the 66–70 CE war in Judea that erupted in Nero's time. Nero is not directly mentioned in any NT document. Neither the positive nor the negative images of Nero found in Roman historians ancient and modern are directly reflected in the NT, and the problem of interpreting the ambiguous data of his reign is not found there. Nero is, however, indirectly reflected in the NT.

1. Appointment of governors of Judea

According to Tacitus' "two-period" scheme, in Nero's early years he generally made good gubernatorial appointments but in his later period was reluctant to install potential rivals as governors. This had tragic consequences for the province of Judea. After the death of Herod Agrippa I, Claudius had reimposed the Augustan policy of direct Roman rule and had appointed Antonius Felix as governor of Judea. Nero inherited this situation, continued Felix's appointment, and followed him with Porcius Festus, Lucceius Albinus, and Gessius Florus. Nero did not consider Judea to be a major problem and did not recognize the need for sensitive and capable governors to deal with the volatile situation there. Therefore, he made poor appointments.

2. Paul's appeal and trial

Nero was the emperor to whom Paul appealed after his hearings and imprisonment in Jerusalem and Caesarea were bogged down in local political and religious concerns (Acts 25:6-12). The author of Luke–Acts portrays the Romans in generally positive terms, with the assumption that the Christian Paul, a Roman citizen, will receive justice from the emperor, who is never portrayed in a negative light. *See* APPEALS TO CAESAR BY PAUL.

3. Romans 13:1-7

Paul's letters never refer directly to any emperor, past or present, nor is he ever critical of the empire as such. In Rom 13, Paul explicitly directs Roman Christians to pay taxes to the Roman government, whose officers are appointed by God to punish evil and maintain order. Nero was emperor when Paul wrote this. The "two-period" view of Nero's reign has sometimes been invoked to explain Paul's positive view of emperor and empire. Paul wrote during the early "good" period, while Seneca was directing Roman policy. This is a questionable attempt to save Paul from apparently affirming the evils inherent in Roman rule.

4. Death of Peter, Paul, and other Christians

The fire in Rome in 64 CE and subsequent persecution of Christians was a major tragedy and crisis for the participants, contemporary Christians throughout the empire, and the later church. In the context of Nero's other outrages and atrocities, Nero's abuse of Christians was barely noticed by Roman historians of the time, especially since the Christians were a suspect and despised Eastern sect. It is likely, but not demonstrable, that both Peter and Paul died in this persecution or its associated events. If so, Nero was the emperor who not only murdered numerous Christians but also killed the two most important leaders of the first Christian generation. These events may be reflected in the retrospective allusions of Mark 10:35-40; John 21:18-19; Acts 20:38; and 1 Pet 4:12-16 (which nonetheless urges Christians to "honor the emperor," 1 Pet 2:13). *See* ROME, EARLY CHRISTIAN ATTITUDES TOWARD.

5. Revelation and *Nero redivivus*

After Nero's suicide as an enemy of the state, several versions of a myth arose that he really was not dead but would return as a conqueror from the east. Some figures actually appeared claiming to be Nero and were taken seriously by elements of the population—until apprehended and executed by the authorities. Some versions of this myth regarded Nero as a savior figure who would restore the good times of his own reign. Others saw the death of the tyrant as too good to be true, supposing that he would return in wrath to inflict punishment on his enemies—as in the post-mortem legends about Hitler and Stalin. Since Nero had persecuted Christians and had made claims to divinity, some streams of early Christianity incorporated the image of the return of Nero into their apocalyptic scenario. The returning Nero became the ANTICHRIST whose appearance would signal the end of days. The book of Revelation was probably written during the reign of DOMITIAN, who also made claims to divinity and in whose administration Christians were persecuted (*see* REVELATION, BOOK OF). The author of Revelation understood these sporadic persecutions as the leading edge of the events that would bring history to a close with the return of Christ. In Revelation, Domitian was *Nero redivivus*, the BEAST from the sea who received his power, throne, and authority from Satan (Rev 13:1), a reincarnation of Nero, a phony counterpart to Christ who had received a death-blow but still lived (Rev 13:3). Nero is most likely signified by the "mark of the beast" (Rev 13:18), since the numerical value of his name totals 666 (*see* NUMBERS, NUMBERING; SIX HUNDRED AND SIXTY-SIX).

Bibliography: Jaś Elsner and Jamie Masters, eds. *Reflections of Nero: Culture, History, and Representation* (1994); Miriam T. Griffin. *Nero: The End of a Dynasty* (1985); David Shotter. *Nero*. 2nd ed. (2005); Suetonius. *The Lives of the Caesars, II*. J. C. Rolfe, ed. and trans. (1997).

M. EUGENE BORING

NERVA. Already an old man at the time of DOMITIAN's assassination, Marcus Cocceius Nerva became emperor of Rome on September 18, 96 CE, styling himself *Imperator Nerva Caesar Augustus*. He would additionally acquire the titles *Germanicus* after a military victory in 97 by TRAJAN, his adoptive son, co-regent, and successor, and *Divus* ("god") at Trajan's request and by decree of the senate after his death on January 25, 98. Unlike his predecessor, posterity reckoned Nerva among the "good emperors." Passing over relatives, Nerva introduced the principle of succession by adoption without regard to blood relation, thereby paving the way for political stability. His reign offered an atmosphere of liberty and relief not just to Rome's senatorial class (Tacitus, *Agr.* 3), but also to Jews and Jewish converts (a category that included Christians) who had suffered abuse at the hands of informers (Cassius Dio, *Rom.* 68.1; Eusebius, *Hist. eccl.* 3.18–20). Nerva also worked to relieve tax burdens while simultaneously instituting the alimenta system (state support for poor children), redistributing land to poor citizens, and finishing Domitian's building program in Rome, the Forum Nervae. Despite his long and distinguished record of public service (including state priesthoods, regular offices, and senatorial career), descent from a distinguished family with connections even to the

Julio-Claudians, and popular measures as emperor, Nerva proved too weak to withstand the demands of mutinous praetorians who remained unhappy after the assassination of Domitian, which mutiny occasioned his felicitous adoption of Trajan in October 97 in the temple of Jupiter Optimus Maximus (Pliny the Younger, *Pan.* 8). Nerva died suddenly some three months later. *See* EMPEROR; EMPEROR WORSHIP.

Bibliography: John D. Grainger. *Nerva and the Roman Succession Crisis of AD 96-99* (2003).

HANS-FRIEDRICH MUELLER

NESSANA. A town on a major caravan route in the western Negeb (*see* NEGEB, NEGEV), close to the border of Israel and Egypt, founded by the NABATEANS in the 3rd cent. BCE. The site declined in importance after the 1st cent. CE but saw the construction of a fortress and a church complex in the early 4th cent. CE; settlement continued for another three centuries, into the Early Islamic Period. Excavators recovered a large number of papyri dating from the 5th to the 7th cent., including fragments of classical texts and early Christian literature as well as numerous contracts, receipts, and ecclesiastical and military administrative texts.

A. HEATH JONES III

NEST [קֵן qen; κατασκήνωσις kataskēnōsis]. In the OT, the bird's nest is a common metaphor for a place of refuge. Some passages allude to the inaccessibility of certain nests (Jer 49:16; Job 39:27). Other passages describe nests being plundered (Deut 22:6; Isa 10:14). Although the basic sense of kataskēnōsis is "encampment," the translation "nest" illustrates that Jesus has no place of refuge (e.g., Matt 8:20; Luke 9:58; see also Matt 13:32//Luke 13:39). *See* BIRDS OF THE BIBLE.

GÖRAN EIDEVALL

NET [חֵרֶם kherem, מִכְמָר mikhmar, מְצוֹדָה metsodhah, רֶשֶׁת resheth; ἀμφίβληστρον amphiblēstron, δίκτυον diktyon, σαγήνη sagēnē]. Like other types of snares, the net is designed to hinder the movement or escape of the prey, whether it is animals, fish, or humans. These handmade devices were usually constructed of twisted fiber or vines, woven together into a mesh that was light enough to throw or transport, but strong enough to hold the trapped creature until the hunter or fisher could secure the catch.

On land a variety of stratagems were used to net the chosen prey. For instance, an Eighteenth Dynasty papyrus (possibly a copy of a Middle Kingdom text) on "The Pleasures of Fishing and Fowling" describes how hunters weave the knots into their nets and then draw tight the ropes that enfold birds within a clap net (see Hos 7:12). Even fairly modest tombs within the Theban necropolis, such as the Tomb of Nakhte, contain painted wall scenes of hunters snaring birds. Hunting in ancient Israel was often on a smaller scale, with individual hunters using nets that were attached to wooden frames held up by a supporting stick or set to snap shut. These spring traps would then capture the bird or small animal at the slightest jarring of the trigger (Amos 3:5). Sometimes caged decoys were placed within the spring trap to lure other birds (Jer 5:26-27). The skill and patience this required is noted in Prov 1:17, which warns that it is useless to spread a baited net while the birds are in sight of your preparations. To catch larger animals, the net could be spread along trails (Lam 1:13) or over a pit to hide its entrance (Pss 57:6 [Heb. 57:7]; 140:5 [Heb. 140:6]), to trip them into falling into the pit (Job 18:8), and also to provide an entangling restraint once the creature is trapped (Ps 35:7; Jer 18:22). Occasionally, nets were strung in such a way as to close off the escape of animals driven into a cul-de-sac by beaters or to ensnare their hoofs within their cords (see the trapped antelope in Isa 51:20).

Ancient rulers clearly took advantage of this hunting image in their military and political rhetoric. For instance, the Sumerian Stele of Vultures commemorates the victory of Eannatum of Lagash over Enakalle of Umma (ca. 2550 BCE) with an image of his patron god Ninurta holding captives in the air within a massive net. Similar poetic imagery is found in the psalmist's lament that the wicked have seized the poor and drug them off "in their net" (Ps 10:9) and in Hosea's condemnation of the priests and kings of Israel, who have spread their net of oppression and corruption over Tabor (Hos 5:1). Micah likewise finds this a useful metaphor in describing an anarchic society so violent and without restraint that even brother hunts brother with a net (Mic 7:2). Wisdom literature's focus on proper social behavior cautions against flattering one's neighbor lest you set a trap for his feet by creating a false sense of pride (Prov 29:5).

Since their livelihood and the survival of their households were dependent upon the quality and durability of their tools, those who fished on the Sea of Galilee spent a great deal of time mending (Matt 4:21), washing (Luke 5:2), and drying their nets. They regularly cast these nets either from the shoreline (Matt 17:27) or the shallows, or let them down into the water from their boats (Luke 5:4; John 21:6). Fishing cooperatives that operated the larger boats employed huge drag or seine nets (75–100 ft. long and 25 ft. high; Hab 1:15; Matt 13:47) that could create a virtual walled off section in a portion of the lake, trapping large quantities of fish. Then the catch could be either hauled into the boat or dragged back to the shallows and pulled onto the shore (John 21:11). Such an image of abundance and opportunity served as a natural metaphor in the Gospels for the kingdom of heaven, which was like a net let down into the lake catching all manner of fish but leaving it up to the fishers to discern which will be placed into baskets and which will be cast into the rubbish heap (Matt 13:47-48). Similarly, the musing of Qoheleth over the uncertainties of our existence notes how humans can be ensnared like fish in a net or birds in a snare by life's calamities (Eccl 9:12). The net thus serves as a useful tool, providing for the needs of the people, and as a potential danger for the unwary and unprepared. *See* FISHING; HUNTING; TOOLS; TRAPS AND SNARES.

VICTOR H. MATTHEWS

NETAIM ni-tay'im [נְטָעִים neta'im]. A town in Judah where potters and other inhabitants in the king's service lived (1 Chr 4:23). *See* GEDERAH.

NETHANEL ni-than'uhl [נְתַנְאֵל nethan'el]. The name of eight to ten men meaning "God has given." 1. A leader of the tribe of Issachar in the wilderness period who assisted Moses with the census (Num 1:8; 2:5; 7:18; 10:15).

2. The fourth son of Jesse (1 Chr 2:13-14).

3. A priest or Levite in the time of David and one of the men appointed to blow the trumpet before the ark (1 Chr 15:24).

4. The father of the scribe Shemaiah, a Levite in the time of David (1 Chr 24:6). Possibly the same as #3 above.

5. A Korahite who was gatekeeper in the Temple during the time of David (1 Chr 26:4).

6. An official in the reign of Jehoshaphat who was sent to teach the law in Judah (2 Chr 17:7).

7. A chief of the tribe of Levi in the time of Josiah (2 Chr 35:9).

8. A priest in the postexilic period who had married a foreign woman (Ezra 10:22).

9. A priest in the time of Jehoiakim (Neh 12:21).

10. A priest or Levite in the time of Nehemiah who celebrated the rebuilding of the walls of Jerusalem (Neh 12:36). Possibly the same as #9 above. *See* LEVI, LEVITES.

KEVIN A. WILSON

NETHANIAH neth'uh-n*i*'uh [נְתַנְיָה nethanyah, נְתַנְיָהוּ nethanyahu; Ναθανίας Nathanias]. 1. Elishama's son and the father of Ishmael who murdered Gedaliah, governor of Judah, at Mizpah (2 Kgs 25:23, 25; Jer 40:8, 15; 41:1-18).

2. A Levite; second of Asaph's four sons, who with his three brothers received the fifth lot and prophesied with musical instruments under King David's direction (1 Chr 25:2, 12).

3. One of the Levites whom King Jehoshaphat sent to instruct the people throughout Judah about God's law (2 Chr 17:8).

4. One of the descendants of BANI who gave up his foreign wife (1 Esd 9:34; "Nathan" in the par. list of Ezra 10:39).

5. Jehudi's father and Shelmiah's son (Jer 36:14).

EMILY R. CHENEY

NETHINIM neth'in-im [נְתִינִים nethinim; Aram. נְתִינַיָּא nethinayya'; Ναθανείμ Nathaneim, δεδομένοι dedomenoi]. Means "appointed, given, dedicated" i.e., to the Temple. It refers to a guild of menial temple servants of diverse (including foreign) origins, but accepted in the community of Israel (*see* SERVANT; TEMPLE, JERUSALEM). They were ascribed (devoted or given) to the Temple (Ezra 7:24) to serve under the supervision of the Levites (Ezra 8:20). The noun always appears in the plural in the Bible. The NRSV translates the term as "temple servants."

The book of Ezra ascribes their institution to David, who appointed them to serve the Levites (Ezra 8:20). First Chronicles 9:2 suggests a preexilic presence of the Nethinim when it states that together with the Israelites, priests, and Levites, the Nethinim returned to their landed state (ba'akhuzzatham בַּאֲחֻזָּתָם; compare Gen 23:20; 49:30). Arad ostracon 18 (late 7th or early 6th cent. BCE) mentions "a Querosite" (line 5, qrsy = bn qrs) dwelling in the Temple of Yahweh (compare the mention of the bene-qeros [בְנֵי־קֵרֹס], "sons of Keros," in Ezra 2:44 and Neh 7:47), who might be regarded as a member of the Nethinim. According to some rabbinic traditions, their origin is associated with the Gibeonites whom Joshua (Josh 9:23, 27) made "hewers of wood and drawers of water for the congregation and for the altar of the LORD" (see *b. Yev.* 71a; 78a–79b; *b. Hor.* 4b; *b. Mak.* 13a). This tradition has additional support in the repetition of the genealogy of Gibeon after the rest of the temple personnel in Chronicles' list of returnees (compare 1 Chr 9:2, 35), where the temple personnel are the climax of 1 Chr 1–9.

Nethinim are listed along with priests, Levites, singers, and porters in Ezra–Nehemiah as part of the temple personnel (*see* PRIESTS AND LEVITES). A first contingent came under the leadership of ZERUBBABEL (Ezra 2:43-54//Neh 7:46-56//1 Esd 5:29-32). Together with the "descendants of Solomon's servants" they amount to 392 people (Ezra 2:58//Neh 7:60; 372 in 1 Esd 5:35). They are also part of the returning group assembled by EZRA in Babylon; 220 Nethinim were brought by Ezra in 458/7 BCE (Ezra 8:17, 20; compare 7:7) from the sanctuary of Casiphia. First Esdras uses the word hierodouloi (ἱεροδούλοι, "sacred servants") regularly to refer to the Nethinim, while the Levites in 1 Esd 1:3 are described as hierodouloi tou Israēl (ἱεροδούλοι τοῦ Ἰσραήλ, "sacred servants of Israel"), clearly contrasting them with the Nethinim and suggesting again the perceived foreign origins of the Nethinim. Ezekiel's diatribe (Ezek 44:6*b*-9) against the use of foreigners (bene-nekhar בְּנֵי־נֵכָר) in the sanctuary was possibly directed against the Nethinim. The Peshitta renders the Nethinim in 1 Chr 9:2 as geyora (Syr. "foreign, alien, spurious"; a cognate of Hebrew gerim [גֵּרִים]; *see* SOJOURNER; STRANGER).

The Nethinim appear together with "all who have separated themselves from the peoples of the lands to adhere to the law of God" in Neh 10:28 and were exempt from taxation, tribute, or toll as were other temple functionaries (Ezra 7:24). Isaiah is probably referring to those Nethinim when it mentions the foreigners (**ben-hannekhar** בֶּן־הַנֵּכָר) "who join themselves to the LORD to minister to him" (Isa 56:3-7). They were organized under detachment heads. Nehemiah 11:21 mentions two chiefs, ZIHA and GISHPA, in charge of the whole guild. Some of them lived in the OPHEL in Jerusalem (Neh 3:26), others lived opposite to the MUSTER GATE (Neh 3:31), and still others lived in various cities (Ezra 2:70; Neh 7:73).

A list of Nethinim is attested in one of the Dead Sea Scrolls (4Q340) that seems to be a list of people interdicted from marriage within the community. Their status in 4Q174 (assuming that **bn nkhr** is the same as **nathin** [נָתִין]) is the same as that of the proselytes; they are part of the community but proscribed from the messianic sanctuary (*see* PROSELYTE). Josephus designates them **hierodouloi** ("sacred servants"; *Ant.* 11.128). The Talmud (*b. Qidd.* 4:1) puts the Nethinim at a similar level with other groups of impaired genealogy (freed slaves, illegitimate children, "silenced ones," and foundlings). They were forbidden to marry Jews, but according to R. Yosé they will be genealogically purified in the world to come.

The Babylonian institution of the **shirkutu** displays strong similarities with the biblical Nethinim. Neo-Babylonian documents attest to the presence of **shirku**, a religious guild dedicated to the service of different deities recruited from among underprivileged social classes and foreigners. They were donated to the sanctuary and didn't have individual owners but belonged to the temple's god. The verb to describe this donation to the temple is **nadanu**, the Akkadian cognate of the Hebrew **nathan** (נָתַן, "to give"). There is evidence of some **shirkus** achieving a privileged social and economic status.

The Nethinim should not be confused with the **nethunim** (נְתֻנִים, the passive participle of **nathan**, "assigned, dedicated"), a term usually applied to the Levites in P (Num 3:9; 8:15-16, 19; 18:6). Although the Nethinim and **nethunim** share a common background of service in the Temple and both words share the same verbal stem, they point to different groups within the Bible: one generally denoting a group of servants specifically ascribed to the Temple and the other persons consecrated to serve God.

Bibliography: Joseph M. Baumgarten. "The Exclusion of Netinim and Proselytes in 4QFlorilegium." *RQ* 8 (1972) 87–96; Joseph Blenkinsopp. *Ezra-Nehemiah.* OTL (1988); Magen Broshi and Ada Yardeni. "List of Netinim." *Qumran Cave 4: XIV. Parabiblical Texts, Part 2* (1995) 81–84; Menahem Haran. "The Gibeonites, the Nethinim, and the Sons of Solomon's Servants." *VT* 11 (1961) 59–69; Baruch Levine. "The Nĕtînîm." *JBL* 82 (1963) 207–12; Baruch Levine. "Later Sources on the Netinim." *Orient and Occident.* Harry A. Hoffner, ed. (1973) 101–7; Emile Puech. "The Tell el-Fûl jar Inscription and the Nĕtînîm." *BASOR* 261 (1986) 69–72; E. A. Speiser. "Unrecognized Dedication." *IEJ* 13 (1963) 69–73; Joel Weinberg. *The Citizen-Temple Community* (1992); S. Zawadzki. "A Contribution to the Understanding of širkûtu in the Light of a Text from the Ebabbar Archive." AoF 24 (1997) 226–30.

ALEJANDRO F. BOTTA

NETOPHAH, NETOPHATHITE ni-toh'fuh, ni-tof'uh-th*it* [נְטֹפָה **netofah**, נְטֹפָתִי **netofathi**; Νετέβας **Netebas**]. 1. Town in Judah mentioned along with BETHLEHEM (1 Chr 2:54), and listed as one to which some of its residents returned after the exile (Ezra 2:22; Neh 7:26; 1 Esd 5:18). Companies of singers lived in its villages (Neh 12:28), as did Levites after the exile (1 Chr 9:16). The ruin, Khirbet Bedd Faluh, located about 3.5 mi. southeast of Bethlehem, with the nearby spring called ʿAin en-Natuf, has been identified as the site where the town of Netophah once stood.

2. Resident of Netophah: Maharai and Heleb, two of David's warriors who commanded military divisions, were Netophathites (2 Sam 23:28-29; 1 Chr 11:30; 27:13), as was Seraiah, Tanhumeth's son, who fought on behalf of GEDALIAH before Jerusalem fell to the Babylonians in 587 BCE (2 Kgs 25:23; Jer 40:8).

EMILY R. CHENEY

NETTLE [חָרוּל **kharul**, קִמּוֹשׂ **qimmos**]. Certain herbaceous plants having the ability to sting by inserting irritating liquid under the skin, in contrast to thistles and thorns that simply prick. All are common in the cultivated fields, rough places, and waysides of Israel. Nettles include the small nettle (*Urtica urens*), the Roman nettle (*U. pilulifera*), and an uncommon annual nettle (*U. membranacea*). Nettles represented the untended or abandoned and overrun in several biblical texts (Prov 24:30-34; Isa 34:14; Zeph 2:9). *See* PLANTS OF THE BIBLE; THISTLE, THORN.

F. NIGEL HEPPER

NETWORK. *See* LATTICEWORK.

NEVIʾIM, TARGUM. *See* TARGUMS.

NEW [חָדָשׁ **hadhash**; καίνος **kainos**, καινότης **kainotēs**, νέος **neos**, πρόσφατος **prosphatos**]. The Bible uses *new* with three meanings: 1) a relative sense, referring to a state or stage distinctive from what was or is, that is, from what is "old"; 2) a reference to something that has not yet been; and 3) a qualitative sense, using *new* to refer to a better version of an existing state or thing.

In the OT *new* in the sense of recent origin is used to describe material phenomena—which includes among other things garments (1 Kgs 11:29-30), grain (Lev 2:14; Num 28:26), houses (Deut 20:5; 22:8), wine (Hag

1:11), or social constructs like marriage (Deut 24:5). The word *new* can be used in order to distinguish from what is old. While some instances of newness are prohibited, for instance new gods (Deut 32:17), usually what is new is regarded positively and as being of special interest to God. In the NT *new* is used in the reference to the "new tomb" in which Jesus was buried (Matt 27:60; John 19:41) or the "new teaching" that philosophers want to hear about from Paul (Acts 17:19). Typically there is a positive value attached to what is "new" (1 Cor 5:7), although the old is also honored (Matt 13:52).

New also refers to renewal in the OT. *Moon* is by far the most common word in the OT to be qualified with *new* (*see* NEW MOON). The restored appearance of the moon is used to mark time (e.g., Exod 19:1; 1 Sam 20:18, 24, 27), especially communal liturgical time (2 Chr 8:13, 31:3; *see* NEW YEAR). The renewal of youth (Ps 103:5), strength (Isa 40:31; 41:1), and kingship (1 Sam 11:14) are other examples of *new* as the resumption of what was. Hope for renewal is connected to confidence in God's faithfulness, especially as regards Israel's eschatological hopes (Zeph 3:17). In the NT, Revelation writes of God making all things new (Rev 21:5), likely a concept similar to the one Jesus expresses in Matthew regarding the "renewal" (NRSV; lit., "rebirth") of all things (Matt 19:28).

New can refer to something that has not existed previously. Jeremiah speaks of the Lord creating a "new thing on the earth," which is that "the female protects the man" (Jer 31:22; author's trans.; NRSV, "a woman encompasses a man"). There is general agreement that this saying points to a reversal of the natural order of things and so to the creation of something that has not yet existed. God's capacity to create what is truly new is seen also in Num 16:30. Second Isaiah records God saying, "See, the former things have come to pass, and new things I now declare; before they spring forth, I tell you of them" (Isa 42:9). See also Isa 43:19 and 48:6-7, where the new is something that is created now. This is not renewal but a new thing that has never been. Typically this understanding of *new* is connected to the hope for God's creation to finally be set right. However, this positive idea of newness had a famous detractor in the poet Qoheleth (Eccl 1:9-10).

In Gal 6:15 and Col 3:10 *new* appears to refer to something that has not yet been. Since in the "NEW CREATION" the old categories of circumcision and uncircumcision are no longer valid (Gal 6:15) and by donning the "new self" (NRSV; lit., "the new") there is no longer Greek and Jew, etc. (Col 3:10-11), *new* describes a reality brought into existence for the first time. Also, Heb 10:20 speaks of a "new and living way," suggesting something new in kind.

New can refer to something that is qualitatively a better version of an existent state or thing. Isaiah speaks of Zion's being called by a "new name that the mouth of the LORD will give" (Isa 62:2). The prophets also speak of God's promise to give Israel a new spirit and heart (Ezek 36:26; also 11:19) and the requirement that Israel appropriate "a new heart and a new spirit" (Ezek 18:31). That this kind of newness carries with it the value of being better than the old is seen particularly in Jeremiah's conviction that God will make a new covenant with God's people (Jer 31:31) that will be written on their hearts (Jer 31:33) and in Isaiah's vision of new heavens and a new earth (Isa 65:17; 66:22; compare Rev 21:1) where "all flesh shall come to worship" Yahweh (Isa 66:23; *see* NEW HEAVEN, NEW EARTH). Consequently, the "new song" to which the psalmist and Isaiah refer (Pss 33:3; 40:3 [Heb. 40:4]; 96:1; 98:1; 144:9; 149:1; Isa 42:10) is a hymn that praises God for this anticipated change for the better.

Ephesians writes of a "new humanity" (Eph 2:15) and "the new self" (Eph 4:24), both of which are better versions of what people have been. Likewise, various texts speak of a "new covenant" (Luke 22:20; 1 Cor 11:25; 2 Cor 3:6; Heb 8:8, 13; 9:15; 12:24) and a "NEW COMMANDMENT" (John 13:34; 1 John 2:8). With Jesus there is a new teaching "with authority" (Mark 1:27). And 2 Peter and Revelation speak of new heavens and a new earth (2 Pet 3:13; Rev 21:1; compare Isa 65:17; 66:22). Revelation records a vision of a NEW JERUSALEM (Rev 3:12; 21:2) and the promise of a "new name" (Rev 2:17; 3:12).

In some cases the meaning of *new* can be ambiguous. Plainly, it is a matter of interpretation whether in some texts *new* should be understood to refer to renewal, to something that has not yet existed, or to a qualitatively better version of a known category. This could be said for several of the above citations in both the OT and the NT. Likewise, when 1 Peter speaks of being born anew (1 Pet 1:3, 23; *see* NEW BIRTH) and Paul refers to a "NEW CREATION" (2 Cor 5:17), this could mean the renewal of the old creation, the creation of what has not yet been, or a better version of what was. Again, depending on one's overall understanding of Paul, the NEW LIFE based on Christ's resurrection (Rom 6:4; 7:6) could mean either a better version of life as we know it or a kind of life that has never before existed.

All three uses of newness have eschatological associations. In the NT, newness is associated with the kingdom (Matt 9:17; Mark 2:21-22; Luke 5:36-39). Consequently, the newness referred to is, in a sense, the end of newness, for it is the final stage of God's saving work for God's creation. Nevertheless, this newness remains new. Colossians speaks of renewal in the context of "the new" (Col 3:10); the state of the new life includes singing a new song (Rev 5:9; 14:3) and speaking in new tongues (Mark 16:17). *See* REBIRTH, RENEWAL.

Bibliography: Roy A. Harrisville. *The Concept of Newness in the New Testament* (1960); Jack R. Lundbom. *Jeremiah 21–36*. AB 21B (2004); Choon-Leong Seow. *Ecclesiastes*. AB 18C (1997).

ANN JERVIS

NEW BIRTH. The hope of new birth or a new beginning, when all creation is in right relation, is expressed in various ways. God has given birth to Israel (Exod 4:22; Deut 32:18) and God will bring about a rebirth of the people through an outpouring of the Spirit. Isaiah speaks of a new heaven and a new earth (65:17-25); Jeremiah of a new covenant and a new heart (Jer 31:31-34); Ezekiel of hearts of stone exchanged for hearts of flesh (36:25-28), and of dry bones coming to life again (37:1-14); Joel of a time of prophesying by all God's faithful (2:26-32).

Christians experience new birth by dying and rising with Christ through baptism (Rom 6:3-14; Col 2:12; 3:1-2), the "water of rebirth" (**loutron palingenesia** [λουτρὸν παλιγγενεσία]; Titus 3:5). Being "born from above" or "born again" (**gennaō anōthen** [γεννάω ἄνωθεν]; John 3:3) is a gift from God, by water and the spirit (John 3:5), and by the word of truth (Jas 1:18). New birth into "a living hope" and into "an inheritance that is imperishable" (1 Pet 1:3-4) results in obedience to the truth, deep love of one another from the heart (1 Pet 1:22-23), sinlessness (Rom 6:3-14; 1 John 3:9), a renewal of the inner nature day by day (2 Cor 4:16), dissolution of ethnic and status divisions (Col 3:10-11), and the ability to discern the will of God (Rom 12:2)—in short, a new humanity (Eph 2:15; 4:24) and a new creation (2 Cor 5:17; Gal 6:15) that will be brought to completion at the end time (Matt 19:28).

BARBARA REID, O.P.

NEW COMMANDMENT [ἐντολή καινή **entolē kainē**]. Jesus' command to love is found in all four Gospels. The synoptic versions have a great deal in common (Matt 22:34-40; Mark 12:28-34; Luke 10:25-28): in response to a question, Jesus lifts up the OT commandments to love God and neighbor (Deut 6:5; Lev 19:18). John's version of the love commandment is notably different. One difference is the framing of the commandment as "new": "I give you a new commandment, that you love one another. Just as I have loved you, you also should love one another" (John 13:34). In claiming "newness," John is not saying the command originates with Jesus. What is "new" is the identification of Jesus as the primary example of love for his followers (*see* LOVE IN THE NT; NEW).

Second, many commentators read John's version of the love command as exclusive: the disciples are to love "one another," rather than the more inclusive "neighbor." The contrast is greatest with Luke's Gospel. There, the primary example of a neighbor is one who is an outsider, the Samaritan (Luke 10:29-37). John's version may present a rather insular picture of the Christian community, called only to love "one another." Interpreters point to language in John suggesting the community was under fire from its Jewish opponents: they will be hated by the world (15:18) and expelled from the synagogue (16:2). In this context, the call to love one another is an instruction aimed to help the community survive difficult circumstances. The instruction sets the disciples of Jesus apart from the world; they are to be identified by love (13:35).

For other interpreters, the commandment does not prescribe exclusivity but Jesus' intentions for those who follow him: they are to be a community characterized by love. Understood this way, love for "one another" must be read in connection with the instruction to love as Jesus loved. The commandment is set against the backdrop of the Last Supper in John, where Jesus' love has included washing the feet of all of his disciples, including Peter, who later denies him, and Judas, who betrays him (John 13:3-15). Jesus' example is not one of exclusion, but inclusion. The context of the passage also supports this reading. Many interpreters identify 13:31-38 as the introduction to the "Farewell Discourse," in which Jesus instructs and encourages his disciples for the time when he will not be with them. The point of the command is not to exclude love of those outside the community of believers. The command to love is part of Jesus' instructions for how the disciples will carry on without him. They are to enter into the love shared by Jesus and the Father (see 14:21).

SUSAN E. HYLEN

NEW COVENANT, THE. *See* COVENANT, OT AND NT.

NEW CREATION [καινὴ κτίσις **kainē ktisis**]. For Paul, the coming of Christ means the world of "flesh" has passed away and there is a "new creation" (2 Cor 5:17) that is superior to fleshly distinctions like circumcision and uncircumcision (Gal 6:15). Redemption is expressed as a renewal of CREATION in the promise of a new heaven and a new earth (Isa 65:17; 66:22; Rev 21:1) and in Paul's image of all creation yearning to be set free (Rom 8:20-23). *See* FLESH IN THE NT; NEW HEAVEN, NEW EARTH; NEW LIFE.

MARIANNE BLICKENSTAFF

NEW GATE [בֵּית־יְהוָה הֶחָדָשׁ **beth-yhwh hekhadhash**, שַׁעַר־יְהוָה **shaʿar-yhwh**]. Perhaps also the UPPER GATE of 2 Kgs 15:35//2 Chr 27:3, this gate was in the temple precincts (Jer 26:10; 36:10). A court convened at the gate's entrance in order to hear accusations against JEREMIAH. The route taken by the court officials suggests that the gate stood south of the JERUSALEM Temple.

JAMES RILEY STRANGE

NEW HEAVEN, NEW EARTH [οὐρανὸς καινὸς καὶ γῆ καινή **ouranos kainos kai gē kainē**]. Revelation depicts John's vision of "a new heaven and a new earth" (21:1). The old heaven and earth have departed (compare 20:11), along with the sea and its associations with CHAOS. The imagery is part of the cosmic upheaval associated with God's appearance at the end time (i.e., Rev 6:12-14). The destruction or transformation of creation is common in Jewish prophetic and apocalyptic traditions (e.g., Isa 65:17; 66:22; *1 En.* 45:4-5; *Jub.* 1:29) and the NT (Matt 5:18; Mark 13:30; Rom 8:21; 2 Pet 3:12-13). *See* REVELATION, BOOK OF.

SUSAN E. HYLEN

NEW HUMANITY [καινὸς ἄνθρωπος **kainos anthrōpos**]. The NT's anthropological concept of a "new humanity" is rooted in Paul's christological understanding of Christ as a SECOND ADAM, i.e., as a new human. In 1 Cor 15:42-49, Paul juxtaposes Adam as the first human and Christ as the second or last human, distinguishing Adam, a "living being" (psychēn zōsan ψυχὴν ζῶσαν) who has a "physical" (psychikos ψυχικός) body, from Christ, who is a "life-giving spirit" (pneuma zōopoioun πνεῦμα ζῳοποιοῦν). Paul then articulates his hope that believers will participate in Christ, the second/last human from heaven, by being resurrected as a "spiritual body" (1 Cor 15:44, sōma pneumatikon [σῶμα πνευματικόν]).

The deuteropauline letters derive the anthropological concept of a "new humanity" from Paul's christology. Colossians 3:9-10 and Eph 4:22-24 contrast "the old humanity" (ton palaiov anthrōpov [τὸν παλαιὸν ἄνθρωπον], author's trans.; NRSV, "the old self") and "the new humanity" (ton neon/kainon anthrōpon τὸν νέον/καινὸν ἄνθρωπον, author's trans.; NRSV, "the new self") respectively as what believers should put away and what they should put on (i.e., "clothe yourselves with"). The similarity between the language of these verses and the baptismal formula in Gal 3:27 ("[you] have clothed yourselves with Christ") implies that "new humanity" refers to the mystical union of believers with Christ, connecting the christological meaning of "new humanity" with the anthropological one.

The anthropological meaning of "new humanity" is further developed in Eph 2:15, in which Christ is said to have made peace by creating in himself "one new humanity" (hena kainon anthrōpon ἕνα καινὸν ἄνθρωπον) out of two groups, i.e., Jews and Gentiles. This ecclesiological statement describes the church as the body of Christ consisting of both Jews and Gentiles, but it also points to a greater vision of all humanity as one in the cosmically exalted Christ. Thus, the deuteropauline epistles proceed from the original Pauline notion of Christ as the new human to the hope that all humanity will be newly reconciled as one in Christ. *See* NEW; SON OF MAN.

EUGENE EUNG-CHUN PARK

NEW JERUSALEM [Ἰερουσαλὴμ καινή **Ierousalēm kainē**]. The culminating image of Revelation is John's vision of "the holy city, the new Jerusalem" (Rev 21:2; compare 21:10; 3:12), a vision of God's ultimate establishment of abundance and peace. The city metaphor has multiple, overlapping meanings. Many details of the city in Rev 21:1–22:5 are familiar from the restoration of Jerusalem promised by the prophets (e.g., Isa 2:1-4; 49:18; 60–62; 65:17-25; Jer 31:38; Zech 14:6-11). The measuring of the city (Rev 21:15-21) alludes to Ezekiel's vision of the restored temple (Ezek 40–47), although in Revelation God dwells directly in the city. The city as bride evokes the notion of the marriage of the church to Christ (e.g., Eph 5:25-33). *See* REVELATION, BOOK OF.

SUSAN E. HYLEN

NEW JERUSALEM BIBLE. The 1985 revision of the *Jerusalem Bible* (1966), based on the landmark Catholic biblical scholarship of the French Dominicans of Jerusalem. *See* VERSIONS, ENGLISH.

NEW LIFE [מִחְיָה mikhyah; καινότης ζωῆς **kainotēs zōēs**]. God creates new life (Gen 1–2), gives life through the birth of children (Gen 21:1-2; 1 Sam 1:19-20; Ps 113:9), and makes life-giving rivers flow in the desert (Isa 43:19). Through God's power, dead bones live again (Ezek 37:1-7; see Sir 46:12; 49:10). God also renews spiritual life through a "new heart" (Ezek 36:26) and a "new and right spirit" (Ps 51:10 [Heb. 51:12]). Jesus speaks of being born anew or born from above (John 3:3). Just as Ezra reminds his community that while they were slaves, God gave them "new life" (Ezra 9:9), Paul claims that Christ frees those in bondage to the law to receive "new life" in the Spirit (Rom 6:4; 7:4-6). *See* NEW BIRTH; NEW CREATION; REBIRTH, RENEWAL; RESURRECTION, OT; RESURRECTION, EARLY JEWISH; RESURRECTION, NT.

MARIANNE BLICKENSTAFF

NEW MOON [חֹדֶשׁ **khodhesh**; νεομηνία **neomēnia**]. The term for the time when the lunar crescent first becomes visible and then for the day that begins with the night of the crescent. The new moon figures in ancient Jewish and Christian literature in several kinds of contexts, as it does in other ancient literatures.

The new moon functions as a calendrical date. Genesis 1:14-19 assigns the sun and the moon functions in measuring time, and a series of references in the OT show that it did operate in this fashion. In a number of passages the new moon serves as a date with perhaps no other significance. Exodus 19:1 says that the third new moon after the exodus was the date on which the Israelites entered the wilderness of Sinai. The first of the first month—which may be, although is not necessarily, the day of the new moon (see the calendar of *Jubilees* and the Qumran literature)—was the time at which Ezra's group began its journey from Babylon, and they reached Jerusalem on the first of the fifth month (Ezra 7:9; see 10:16-17; Neh 8:2; 1 Esd 5:52-53, 57 [Gr. 5:51-52, 55]; 8:6; 9:16-17, 37, 40; Philo, *Spec. Laws* 2.140–44; *see* CALENDAR).

The new moon is associated with the SABBATH and/or festivals (*see* FEASTS AND FASTS). For example, Isa 1:13 mentions "[n]ew moon and sabbath and calling of convocation," and 1:14 refers to "new moons and your appointed festivals" as occasions that the Lord hates (see also Isa 66:23). Hosea 2:11 offers a fuller listing: "I will put an end to all her mirth, her festivals, her new moons, her sabbaths, and all her appointed festivals." Such passages include the new moons with other times that had cultic associations and apparently involved celebration. In Jdt 8:6 the new moon and the day before it are among the rare times when Judith did not fast (see also 1 Chr 23:31; 2 Chr 2:4; 8:13; 31:3; Ezra 3:5; Neh 10:33; Ezek 45:17; 46:1, 3; 1 Macc 10:34; 2 Esd 1:31; Col 2:16; and possibly Gal 4:10).

The new moon is associated with offerings and other cultic activities. Various texts show that the new moon or first of the month was a special occasion accompanied by rites and rituals. In the Deuteronomistic History, two passages are relevant. According to 1 Sam 20, King Saul expected David to be present for the meal on the new moon (1 Sam 20:5, 18), while the following day was also marked by a feast (1 Sam 20:27). Saul suspected David's absence was caused by his being in a state of impurity (1 Sam 20:26). In 2 Kgs 4:23, when the Shunammite woman wished to visit the prophet Elisha immediately, her husband objected: "Why go to him today? It is neither new moon nor sabbath." The text implies that such times were thought suitable for consulting a religious figure. Amos 8:5 indicates that a prohibition of trade, familiar for the Sabbath, also applied on the day of the new moon. There the people are quoted as asking: "When will the new moon be over so that we may sell grain; and the sabbath, so that we may offer wheat for sale?" (See also Arad Ostracon 7.6–8.)

The Priestly literature specifies the sacrifices and other observances that took place on the first of each month. The first of the month is included among the times when trumpets were to be blown with the offerings as a reminder to God about Israel (Num 10:10; see also Num 29:1-6 where the trumpets are to be sounded on the first of the seventh month, the day of trumpets; Ps 81:3 [Heb. 81:4]; Philo, *Spec. Laws* 2.188–92). A passage devoted strictly to the first of the month is Num 28:11-15, which prescribes the sacrifices to be offered specially on those dates in addition to the daily offerings (see also Josephus, *Ant.* 3.238). The burnt offering was to consist of two young bulls, one ram, and seven blemish-free male lambs of one year. For each of these a grain and drink offering was also stipulated, and finally one male goat was sacrificed as a sin offering. Ezekiel gives a different listing: the prince offers one bull, six lambs, and a ram, along with a grain and liquid offering for each (Ezek 46:6-7). On the first of the seventh month, besides these offerings, the legislator adds a burnt offering of one bull, one ram, and seven male lambs a year old and without blemish; each of these was accompanied by a specific grain offering, and one male goat was sacrificed as a sin offering to effect atonement (Num 29:1-6; Josephus, *Ant.* 3.239).

The Mishnah (*m. Rosh. Hash.* 1:3–3:1) reveals the importance of establishing correctly the time of the new moon through its fairly detailed description of the process by which the rabbinic court ascertained the date of the first sighting of the new moon from reliable witnesses. The proper timing of the festivals, which fall on scripturally mandated dates in the months, depended on which date was defined as the first of the month (see *m. Meg.* 3:6; *b. Meg.* 21b-22a for Num 28:11-15 as the Torah reading for the new moon).

In the NT, the specific word for "new moon" (neomēnia) occurs only in Col 2:16, where it is one in a series of items—food, drink, festivals, Sabbaths—that are not to be sources of condemnation for the Colossian Christians once Christ had defeated the powers. Rather, they are "only a shadow of what is to come, but the substance belongs to Christ" (Col 2:17). Similarly, Paul writes in Gal 4:10 that the believers were continuing in the former ways of enslavement by "observing special days, and months (mēnos μηνός), and seasons, and years." Although the matter receives no mention in the NT, the new moon was a factor in the dating of EASTER, especially for those Christians who celebrated it at the time of the Passover on the fourteenth day of the first lunar month. *See* PASSOVER AND FEAST OF UNLEAVENED BREAD.

Bibliography: William Hallo. "New Moon and Sabbaths: A Case-study in the Contrastive Approach." *HUCA* 48 (1977) 1–18; Timothy C. G. Thornton. "Jewish New Moon Festivals, Galatians 4:3-11 and Colossians 2:16." *JTS* 40 (1989) 97–100.

JAMES C. VANDERKAM

NEW TESTAMENT [ἡ καινὴ διαθήκη hē kainē diathēkē]. Commonly refers to the twenty-seven books comprising the second portion of the Christian scriptures (*see* CANON OF THE NEW TESTAMENT), the first portion being the OT. The Gk. phrase (1 Cor 11:25; 2 Cor 3:6; Heb 8:8, 13; 9:15) has a variant translation of "new covenant" in distinction to the covenant of Jer 31:31-34 (*see* COVENANT, OT AND NT). The transfer of the language from "covenant" to a body of writings reflects Paul's use of "old covenant" to refer to the writings of the Mosaic covenant (e.g., 2 Cor 3:14; *see* TESTAMENT).

MARY KAY DOBROVOLNY, R.S.M.

NEW TESTAMENT CANON. *See* CANON OF THE NEW TESTAMENT.

NEW TESTAMENT CHRONOLOGY. *See* CHRONOLOGY OF THE NT.

NEW TESTAMENT LANGUAGE. *See* GREEK LANGUAGE.

NEW TESTAMENT TEXT. *See* TEXT, NT.

NEW TESTAMENT, OT QUOTATIONS IN THE. The use of the OT in the NT invites consideration of four complex issues: 1) the authority of biblical texts (issues of canon); 2) what texts were being used (text-critical issues); 3) how they were being read (hermeneutics); and 4) how they were being appealed to (various types of uses).

It is actually anachronistic to speak of the use of the OT in the NT in the context of 1st-cent. authors and Hebrew Scriptures. There was neither an OT nor NT in place as yet; those who believed Jesus was the promised Messiah were simply appealing to respected Jewish texts they shared with other Jews and Gentiles. By the 1st cent., virtually all Jews recognized the TORAH as sacred text, and many of the Writings, Prophets, and Psalms were also held in high regard, but Judaism had not yet finalized a complete canon (*see* CANON OF THE OLD TESTAMENT). Thus the appeal to the "Old Testament" is an appeal to highly regarded texts, usually to make either a theological or christological argument (Heb 1:5-13) or to make an appeal for moral behavior (1 Pet 1:13-18). When such an appeal was being made, there did not yet exist a functioning NT canon either (*see* CANON OF THE NEW TESTAMENT). The writings that cited the Hebrew Scriptures were being composed to encourage others who had come to believe in Jesus as the center of God's plan for humanity.

There were a series of texts to which one could make an appeal. The writings that came to be a part of the NT are written in Gk., while the oldest form of the Hebrew Scriptures is in either Hebrew or Aram. There also existed various versions of the sacred texts in both Gk. and Aram. This means writers had the choice, depending on their own abilities and what was available to them, to cite the text in its original language (and various versions in which it might appear) or in translation. Several Gk. translations of the Hebrew Scriptures were available, including those of Aquila, Theodotian, Symmachus, and the version we now call the SEPTUAGINT (LXX). The situation is not unlike the plethora of English translations one can choose from today. In fact, when we look at English translations of these texts, many of them follow the Gk. text where the Gk. translation differs from the Hebrew.

It was not unusual in a Jewish context to read the text with some freedom in citation. Because much of the NT was written in a Jewish context or for a mixed group of Jewish and Gentile listeners, examples of this sort of free interpretation are evident (*see* JEWISH BIBLICAL INTERPRETATION). By reading the quotation from the OT side by side with its counterpart in the NT, one can see how the NT author has sometimes changed the citation in some small way to make a particular point. Sometimes a NT author will combine concepts from several OT texts. For example, Paul quotes 2 Sam 7:14 in 2 Cor 6:18, but he also alludes to Isa 43:6 and 55:3.

Understanding how Jewish interpretation of Scripture worked is helpful in understanding how these Scriptures are used in the NT. Among the key rules for interpretation (often called Hillel's rules; see *t. Sanh.* 7) are: 1) one can make an argument from the lesser to the greater, where what is true in a small instance is also true in a larger one (Heb 9:13-14); 2) the linking of two passages with the same term or concept allows them both to be applied to the topic (e.g., Acts 2:16-36, with numerous links between the texts and exposition); and 3) the prophetic use of pattern or typology where a near event mirrors what a later event also will look like because God has designed history in repeatable patterns (e.g., themes like new exodus, day of the Lord, and many messianic texts). Usually with this kind of interpretation, one can see the pattern escalate so that Jesus becomes a unique fulfillment of the Jewish Scriptures (e.g., Isa 7:14 in Matt 1:21-23, from birth by a virgin or "young woman" to a virgin birth). A final kind of citation reflects an eschatological reading, known as pesher (*see* PESHARIM), where "this is that" identification takes place, and the text is interpreted to explain the writer's current situation (e.g., Joel 2:28-32 in Acts 2:17-18). *See* FULFILL, FULFILLMENT; RABBINIC INTERPRETATION.

Christians and Jews shared certain suppositions about these texts. They shared the belief that these sacred texts were God's word and that they were true; that one person could represent many people (e.g., the king or messiah could represent the nation or Adam could represent humanity); and that God worked in patterns in history. But they also differed on some points. Christians argued that the days of fulfillment had come (or at least had begun), that the process of salvation was taking place in stages, not all at once, and that Jesus was the Messiah at the center of this realization (*see* MESSIAH, JEWISH).

Finally, one must pay attention to the wide variety of ways these texts are applied. The NT frequently appeals to prophetic fulfillment, which can involve simple prediction of a specific event (e.g., Mic 5:2 in Matt 2:5-6) or prophetic appeal to pattern (e.g., Hos 11:1 in Matt 2:15). The NT uses OT texts as illustrations (1 Cor 10:1-12). The NT alludes to OT persons and concepts to summarize a situation, as when Jesus says to his disciples that he is the fulfillment of the law and the prophets (e.g., Luke 24:26-27, 44). Finally, the NT appeals to OT language and imagery to make metaphorical statements, as when 1 Peter refers to a spiritual priesthood and spiritual sacrifices (e.g., 1 Pet 2:5-11). Such texts can seek to prove an idea, explain a concept, or exhort the reader.

In sum, the citation of the OT in the NT involves a variety of textual and hermeneutical ways for reading and understanding the promises of God. *See* TEXT CRITICISM, NT; TEXT CRITICISM, OT; TEXT, HEBREW, HISTORY OF; TEXT, NT.

Bibliography: G. K. Beale, ed. *The Right Doctrine from the Wrong Texts? Essays on the Use of the Old Testament in the New* (1994); Darrell L. Bock. "Scripture Citing Scripture: The Use of the Old Testament in the New." *Interpreting the New Testament Text: Introduction to the Art and Science of Exegesis.* Darrell L. Bock and Buist M. Fanning, eds. (2006) 255–76; Robert G. Bratcher. *Old Testament Quotations in the New Testament* (1984); C. H. Dodd. *According to the Scriptures: The Sub-Structure of New Testament Theology* (1952); Craig A. Evans. "The Old Testament in the New." *The Face of New Testament Studies: A Survey of Recent Research.* Scot McKnight and Grant R. Osborne, eds. (2004) 130–45; Richard N. Longenecker. *Biblical Exegesis in the Apostolic Period* (1999); Klyne Snodgrass. "The Use of the Old Testament in the New." *Interpreting the New Testament: Essays on Methods and Issues.* David Alan Black and David S. Dockery, eds. (2001) 209–29.

DARRELL BOCK

NEW YEAR [רֹאשׁ הַשָּׁנָה ro'sh hashanah]. The first day or days of an annual CALENDAR. No date or dates are labeled "the new year" in the OT. The only time the term later used for the new year—"the head/beginning of the year" (ro'sh hashanah)—appears is in Ezek 40:1, where the prophet's vision is dated to "the twenty-fifth year of our exile, at the beginning of the year [LXX: month], on the tenth day of the month." Here the words "the beginning of the year" have a general meaning, since the writer must still specify the date in the next phrase. The earliest use of ro'sh hashanah for the new year day is in the Mishnaic tractate *Rosh HaShanah. See* MISHNAH.

Though the expression ro'sh hashanah (or something closely analogous) for a new year day does not appear in the OT, several texts speak in other terms about the beginning of the year. There are two calendrical systems, one of which assumes an autumnal new year and the other a vernal inception for the calendar. The system that presupposes a fall new year is associated closely with the agricultural cycle, especially the harvest seasons. Exodus 23:16, which is part of the festal calendar section of the Covenant Code (Exod 21–23; *see* COVENANT, BOOK OF THE), refers to the third of the three pilgrimage holidays listed as "the festival of ingathering at the end of the year, when you gather in from the field the fruit of your labor." The harvest season naturally ends in the autumn, a time described literally as "the going out of the year." Whether the expression refers to the end or the beginning of the year, the time intended is the same. In Exod 34:22 the same holiday is called "the festival of ingathering at the turn of the year." The agricultural cycle is under consideration here, but the time in question is called the end/turn of the year, not of the harvest, and thus appears to have calendrical significance. The so-called GEZER CALENDAR begins its enumerations of the agricultural seasons in the autumn. *See* FEASTS AND FASTS; SEASONS.

The system that places the beginning of the year in the spring comes to expression in a series of texts that designate months by ordinal numbers. Exodus 12:1-2 reports that a particular month, the time of the exodus from Egypt, was selected as the first one in the year: "The LORD said to Moses and Aaron in the land of Egypt: This month shall mark for you the beginning of months; it shall be the first month of the year for you" (in Exod 13:4 and Deut 16:1 this is called the month of ABIB). The cultic calendar begins with the month in which Passover occurs, as is clear from the detailed lists of festivals in Lev 23 (H) and Num 28–29 (P) (*see* PASSOVER AND FEAST OF UNLEAVENED BREAD). Although both of these texts designate months by ordinals and consider the month of Passover to be the one from which the count starts, the first of the first month is never highlighted or even mentioned other than as one day that is included in the general category of all twelve firsts of the month (in Exod 40:2 the tabernacle is erected on the first of the first month; in Ezek 45:18-20 the sanctuary is purged on it, though the same happens on the seventh day of the month). Unlike the first day of the first month, the date that in rabbinic times was called the new year (the first of the seventh month [named TISHRI]) is given special treatment in the two lists (Lev 23:23-25; Num 29:1-6). Leviticus 23:24-25 orders that the day be observed as "a day of complete rest, a holy convocation commemorated with trumpet blasts. You shall not work at your occupations; and you shall present the LORD's offering by fire." Numbers 28–29 is similar, although it requires special sacrifices on the first day of each month (Num 28:11-15). Nevertheless, the first of the seventh month is still singled out as a day of holy convocation, rest, and blowing of trumpets and as having additional offerings beyond the requirements for the first days of the other months (Num 29:1-6, esp. v. 6). Some important events in the OT are also dated to the first day of the seventh month, such as Ezra's reading of the law (Neh 8:2).

Among the works found in the Qumran caves, the *Temple Scroll*, which bases its presentation on pentateuchal legislation, calls the first of the seventh month a Sabbath and a memorial with trumpet blasts (11Q19 XXV, 3; see lines 2–10 and 4Q409 1 I, 5). It also mentions the extra offerings and says it is a time for rejoicing (4Q409 1 I, 9). Unlike Num 29, the *Temple Scroll* prescribes these extra sacrifices for the first of the first month as well as the first of the seventh month (11Q19 XIV, 9–18; see *Jub.* 7:2-3 for Noah's sacrifice on the first day of the first month). *Jubilees* designates the first days of the first, fourth, seventh, and tenth months as "memorial days and days of seasons" (*Jub.* 6:23). They are memorial days in the sense that they recall dates of events that occurred during the flood; they also divide the year into four seasons of thirteen weeks each (*Jub.* 6:24-31). *Jubilees* calls none of these dates the new year, although it too uses ordinals to designate months, and the first month of its 364-day calendar is in the spring. Yet it is interesting that in *Jub.* 12:6 Abram studies the stars at the beginning of the seventh month to determine the character of the coming year—as if the agricultural year began then.

Josephus, like the author of *Jubilees*, offers a calendrical discussion directly after recounting the story of the flood. He says that Moses designated NISAN as "the first month for the festivals" (*Ant.* 1.81). He then adds, "he also reckoned this month as the commencement of the year for everything relating to divine worship, but for selling and buying and other ordinary affairs he preserved the ancient order" (*Ant.* 1.81), that is, the order in which the year starts in the fall. Philo stresses the importance of blowing trumpets in his treatment of the first days of the seventh month (*Spec. Laws* 2.188–92).

The Mishnah devotes a tractate to the new year day and calls that day **roʾsh hashanah**. In view of the multiple new years implied in the OT and Josephus' explicit statement to that effect, it is noteworthy that the tractate begins in this way: "There are four 'New Year' days: on the first of Nisan is the New Year for kings and feasts; on the first of Elul is the New Year for the Tithe of Cattle (R. Eleazar and R. Simeon say: The first of Tishri); on the first of Tishri is the New Year for [the reckoning of] the years [of foreign kings], of the Years of Release and Jubilee years, for the planting [of trees] and for vegetables; and the first of Shebat is the New Year for [fruit-]trees" (*m. Rosh Hash.* 1:1). By mentioning "heads of the year" on four occasions (1/1 [Nisan], 1/6 [Ellul], 1/7 [Tishri], and 1/11 [Shebat]), the sages documented a more developed stage in understanding the different kinds of seasons in the Scriptures. In the remainder of the tractate, however, only the first of Tishri is treated as the new year day.

While there is no explicit reference to a new year day in the OT, some scholars have speculated that there was such a holiday and that it was the occasion for a special festival—the festival of the enthronement of Yahweh. The name most commonly associated with this theory is that of Sigmund Mowinckel, although others came to similar conclusions. The theory of a festival of the enthronement of Yahweh was at least in part influenced by the information that was becoming available in the early 20th cent. about the AKITU festival in Babylon (and, to some extent, by material in the Ugaritic texts). At the Babylonian new year festival, the high god Marduk was enthroned as king in an elaborate ritual ceremony. Mowinckel and others believed there was evidence for a similar event in Israel (but in the autumn, not in the spring as in Babylon), as indicated by the psalms of the enthronement of the Lord and related scriptural material. In those psalms one meets the expression **yhwh malakh** (יְהוָה מָלָךְ), which Mowinckel understood to mean "the LORD has become king" (see Pss 93:1; 96:10; 97:1; 99:1; compare **malakh ʾelohim** [מָלַךְ אֱלֹהִים] in Ps 47:8 [Heb. 47:9]). He was also able to find in these texts a number of features tied to **roʾsh hashanah** in rabbinic texts (e.g., the blast of trumpets, memorial, judging, kingdom) and concluded that in Israel, as was the case in Babylon, there was a new year festival in which the drama of the Lord becoming king of the world was reenacted—a drama that possessed a sacramental power. Once Mowinckel had established this position to his satisfaction, he drew many other passages into connection with the festival. For example, the stories about bringing the ark of the covenant to the sanctuary (2 Sam 6:1-19; 1 Kgs 8; see also Pss 24:7-10; 132:7-9) describe the procession in which the invisible deity, thought to be enthroned on the ark, was carried to the Temple. Among the many themes and traditions he tied to this festival were creation, exodus and deliverance, and Sinai. So significant were the thoughts of past and future deliverances to it that Mowinckel believed the festival and its themes revealed the origins of Israel's eschatology.

The theory about a new year festival of the Lord's enthronement has not gained wide endorsement because it suffers from a number of debilitating defects, most prominently the lack of unequivocal evidence in the OT for such a festival and for its connection with a celebration of the new year (a date that was, on Mowinckel's view, in later times separated from the Festival of Tabernacles, the original autumnal new year holiday). Among the more particular objections that have been raised, one should mention that the phrase **yhwh malakh** may actually mean "Yahweh is king" rather than "Yahweh becomes king" and the passages about the ark's progression to the sanctuary do not relate the event to the Lord's kingship over the world.

Bibliography: Herbert Danby, trans. *The Mishnah* (1933); Josephus. *Jewish Antiquities*, vol. 5. H. St. J. Thackeray, trans. (1930); Hans-Joachim Kraus. *Worship in Israel: A Cultic History of the Old Testament* (1965); Jacob Milgrom. *Leviticus 23–27*. AB 3B (2001); Sigmund Mowinckel. *The Psalms in Israel's Worship* (1962).

JAMES C. VANDERKAM

NEZIB nee'zib [נְצִיב **netsiv**]. One of the towns listed in the inheritance of the tribe of Judah, in the fourth district of the SHEPHELAH (Josh 15:43). It is mentioned in Eusebius (*Onom.* 136:21) and identified with modern Khirbet Bet Netsiv ash-Sharqiyah. The word means "post" in the sense of pillar, garrison, or officer.

KEN M. PENNER

NIBHAZ nib'haz [נִבְחַז **nivhaz**]. Nibhaz and TARTAK were deities worshiped by the people of Avva, one of several foreign groups that the Assyrians resettled in the northern kingdom of Israel after conquering Samaria in 720 BCE and deporting the population (2 Kgs 17:24,

29-31). Neither the people nor their deity can be identified with certainty. Some scholars have associated Nibhaz with the Elamite god Ibnahaza. Others, citing the Gk. form of the name, Eblazer (Eblazer Ἐβλαζέρ), suggest that the deity had the Aram. name "Nebo-hazer," or "Nebo-who-returns" (*see* ASHIMA, ASHIMAH; NEBO). The Avvites combined the worship of Nibhaz and Tartak with the worship of Yahweh, much to the chagrin of the Deuteronomist (2 Kgs 17:33).

BRUCE W. GENTRY

NIBSHAN nib´shan [נִבְשָׁן nivshan]. Meaning "level, soft (soil)." Nibshan is one of the towns in the steppe of Judah (Josh 15:62). The initial identification with Khirbet el-Maqari, about 9 km southwest of Qumran, has been reconsidered in favor of Ein el-Ghuweir on the Dead Sea.

Bibliography: Z. Greenhut. "The City of Salt." *BAR* 19 (1993) 33–43.

KEN M. PENNER

NICANOR nī-kay´nuhr [Νικάνωρ Nikanōr]. The name Nicanor occurs frequently in the Maccabean literature. Because it was a common name in the Hellenistic period, it is difficult to establish whether all its occurrences refer to the same person.

1. The leader of the Cyprian mercenaries (2 Macc 12:2).

2. The "royal agent" who is referred to in Samaritan correspondence (Josephus, *Ant.* 12.261–64).

3. The son of Patroclus and a "chief friend" of Antiochus IV Epiphanes (1 Macc 3:38; 2 Macc 8:9).

4. The overseer of all the war elephants in the kingdom (elephantarchēs ἐλεφαντάρχης) who was made governor of Judah (2 Macc 14:12).

5. The companion of Demetrius I Soter, son of Seleucus IV, who resided with Demetrius in Rome and accompanied him to Syria in 162 BCE when Demetrius supplanted Antiochus V Eupator as king (Polybius, *Hist.* 31.14.4; see 1 Macc 7:1-4; compare Josephus, *Ant.* 12.402).

Given the relatively low status of a mercenary leader in comparison to the other Nicanors, this Nicanor is most likely not the same as Nicanor #1. The same may hold true for Nicanor #2. If, however, Nicanor #3, 4, and 5 are the same individual, then Nicanor #3 left Palestine and joined Demetrius in Rome after the death of Antiochus IV. In the episodes mentioned below, the chief actors are Nicanor #3–5.

In the spring of 166 or 165 BCE, Lysias, the regent of Antiochus IV Epiphanes, urged Ptolemy, the governor of Coele-Syria and Phoenicia, to equip Nicanor and the general Gorgias with a sizable army to subdue JUDAS Maccabeus. Both 1 and 2 Maccabees describe the ensuing battle, though they differ in essentials with 2 Maccabees highlighting the role of Nicanor, and 1 Maccabees that of Gorgias (compare 1 Macc 3:38–4:25; 2 Macc 8:8-29). The Syrians based at Ammaus (Emmaus) hoped to ambush Judas by night. Judas learned of the plan and attacked Ammaus first. Nicanor's forces were defeated, and he was (reputedly) compelled to disguise himself and flee to Antioch alone like a runaway slave (2 Macc 8:35).

Thereafter, Nicanor, having been appointed the GOVERNOR of Judea (2 Macc 14:12), adopted differing strategies in dealing with Judas. He began with appeasement and encouraged Judas to marry, settle down, and have children (2 Macc 14:18-25). Eventually, at the urging of Demetrius and of Alcimus, the newly appointed high priest, Nicanor sought to seize Judas by treachery (compare 1 Macc 7:26-30; 2 Macc 14:26-30). Judas became aware of the plot, and the conflict culminated in two battles. The location of the first battle—Capharsalama—and its outcome are uncertain. Although 1 Macc 7:31-32 affirms that Nicanor lost 500 men, Josephus' (possibly corrupt) text relates that Judas was defeated (*Ant.* 12.405). Nicanor then returned to Jerusalem, threatened to destroy the Temple, and embarked on a second battle at Beth-Horon, rashly promising that he would be able to provide the coastal cities with Jewish slaves at bargain prices (2 Macc 8:9-11). Nicanor's hubris was rewarded by the complete rout of his army and his own death. His head and right arm, both of which had threatened the Temple (2 Macc 14:33), were displayed by Judas on the battlements of Jerusalem (1 Macc 7:33-49; 2 Macc 15:25-35). Judas further established the thirteenth of ADAR (161 or 160 BCE) as an annual holiday—Nicanor's Day—to commemorate the victory (2 Macc 15:36). This was the last battle won by Judas, and 2 Maccabees concludes its narrative on this triumphant note. *See* MACCABEES, MACCABEAN REVOLT.

6. In the NT, one of the seven deacons appointed by the Jerusalem church to oversee the daily distribution of food, thereby leaving the apostles free to focus on more pressing responsibilities (Acts 6:5).

Bibliography: Bezalel Bar-Kochva. *Judas Maccabaeus: The Jewish Struggle against the Seleucids* (1989).

J. R. C. COUSLAND

NICANOR GATE nī-kay´nuhr. The Mishnah's Nicanor Gate (*m. Mid.* 1:4; 2:3) of the Jerusalem temple courts may correspond to one of two splendid gates mentioned by Josephus (*J.W.* 5.201, 204–5), and to the BEAUTIFUL GATE of Acts 3:1-10. An ossuary inscription discovered near Jerusalem in 1902 reads, "Bones of the sons of Neikanor the Alexandrian who made the doors."

JAMES RILEY STRANGE

NICODEMUS nik´uh-dee´muhs [Νικόδημος Nikodēmos]. Nicodemus appears only in the Gospel of John (John 3:1-10; 7:45-52; 19:38-42; *see* JOHN,

GOSPEL OF). Some interpreters understand Nicodemus as a historical figure who lived either during the lifetime of Jesus or in the author's community. Most scholars reject this approach, seeing Nicodemus as a representative figure who exhibits characteristics of certain people who come into contact with Jesus. Exactly which characteristics Nicodemus represents is disputed.

In Nicodemus' first appearance, he engages Jesus in debate. Jesus speaks to Nicodemus metaphorically about **gennēsis anōthen** (γέννησις ἄνωθεν). The Gk. word **gennēsis** means "birth," and **anōthen** means both "from above" and "again" (*see* NEW BIRTH). Jesus' words indicate that Nicodemus has not understood the metaphor (John 3:9).

Many interpreters understand Nicodemus as hostile to Jesus from the outset. As a Pharisee and leader of the Jews (John 3:1, *see* PHARISEES; SANHEDRIN), he represents a group who elsewhere are Jesus' enemies (e.g., John 5:18; 11:57). Yet Nicodemus' initial approach to Jesus shows understanding. He calls Jesus "rabbi" and "a teacher who has come from God" (John 3:2). Both the appellation of *rabbi* and the notion that Jesus is sent from God are important to John's presentation of Jesus (e.g., John 1:38, 49; 4:31; 6:41-42, 8:4; *see* RABBI, RABBONI).

An ambiguous detail is that Nicodemus comes to Jesus "by night" (John 3:2). This leads many readers to include Nicodemus with those who "walk at night . . . because the light is not in them" (John 11:10). On the other hand, the same words could make Nicodemus one of those who do what is true and "come to the light" (John 3:21). Readers must make judgments about such details in assessing Nicodemus' character (*see* LIGHT AND DARKNESS).

Nicodemus' later appearances may suggest a growing understanding of Jesus. In Nicodemus' second appearance (John 7:45-52), he defends Jesus, saying that the law requires that the Pharisees give Jesus a fair hearing. This is no outright confession of faith, and many see it as a lukewarm approval of Jesus. Yet others argue that Nicodemus' statement functions ironically to refute the claim by the Pharisees that none of them believes in Jesus and only those ignorant of the law follow him (John 7:48-49).

Finally, Nicodemus brings a great quantity of spices and helps JOSEPH of Arimathea bury Jesus (John 19:38-42). Some view Nicodemus' actions here as misguided—he is too focused on Jesus' death and does not understand that Jesus will rise from the dead. Others argue that the elaborate burial indicates Jesus' royal status. Jesus' kingship is an important theme in John, especially in the trial narrative, so Nicodemus's burial of Jesus could imply true understanding.

In the end, Nicodemus may simply be an ambiguous character used by John to draw the reader into the Gospel's perspective. In judging the character of Nicodemus, the reader reasons according to the terms the Gospel sets forth. For example, John states clearly that Jesus is light (John 8:12); the question is to what extent Nicodemus has "come to the light." Regardless of the answer, the reader bases his or her decision on the metaphor of Jesus as light and thus may be brought to deeper understanding of Jesus.

SUSAN E. HYLEN

NICODEMUS, GOSPEL OF. According to the Latin tradition after the 14th cent., the name for the *Acts of Pilate*. *See* PILATE, ACTS OF.

NICOLAITANS nik′uh-lay′uh-tuhn [Νικολαΐτης **Nikolaitēs**]. An early Christian sect mentioned only in Rev 2:6, 15. John the seer reports that the exalted Christ commended the Ephesians because they "hate the works of the Nicolaitans, which I also hate" (v. 6), and called on those in Pergamum to "repent" because some in that church "hold to [their] teaching" (v. 15). *See* SECTS, SECTARIANS.

The name itself suggests that the sect were partisans of NICOLAUS, but who Nicolaus might be is not indicated in Revelation. According to Irenaeus (*Haer.* 1.26.3), Nicolaus is the "proselyte of Antioch" who was among the seven men named by the Jerusalem church to attend to "the daily distribution" (Acts 6:1-5). Other apologists adopt this identification, but disagree as to whether the partisans had maintained (Hippolytus, *Haer.* 7.24) or departed from Nicolaus' own positions (Clement of Alexandria, *Strom.* 2.20). Most modern scholars view this identification as tenuous.

An alternative explanation for the name is provided by wordplays on the names Nicolaus and Balaam. BALAAM is associated with the false teachings of the sect in the Pergamum church (Rev 2:14). The name Balaam can be construed as a compound of the Hebrew **bala**ʿ (בָּלַע, "he destroyed") and ʿ**am** (עַם, "people"). In a similar manner, Nicolaus is a compound of the Gk. **nika** (νικᾷ, "he destroys") and **laon** (λαόν, "people"). There are two problems with this etymological interpretation: 1) it does not appear to have been suggested by interpreters in antiquity, and 2) whereas Balaam had a negative connotation, the Gk. name Nicolaus was culturally associated with honor. While it is doubtful that the etymological link could have led to coining the designation as a code name either by the sect itself or by its opponents, neither of the difficulties rules out the possibility of the pun.

One other etymological possibility has been suggested for naming the sect Nicolaitans by considering it a rough transliteration into Gk. of the Aram. **nikholah** (נֵיכוֹלָה), "let us eat." While this explanation has found little support among scholars, it does have the benefit of relating to one of the two things alleged against the Nicolaitans in Revelation, namely that the adherents "eat food sacrificed to IDOLs" (2:14). Together with FORNICATION, these practices of the Nicolaitans are characterized as consistent with the counsel of Balaam to Balak in leading astray the

Israelites as they wandered through Moab on their way from Egypt into Canaan (Num 22–24). While the OT story focuses on Balaam's fourfold blessing of the Israelites rather than cursing them (as Balak had sought), both ancient and modern interpreters have concluded on the basis of Num 25:1-2 and 31:16 that Balaam also advised the king how to lure the people away from God, perhaps so they would lose God's favor (Philo, *Moses* 1.295–99; Josephus, *Ant.* 4.126–30).

While Rev 2:15 refers to the "teaching" of the Nicolaitans, then, it specifically mentions only these two matters of praxis. Yet even these may refer to only a single area of concern. The allegation that they "practice fornication" may be a metaphorical way of referring to IDOLATRY rather than an indictment of sexual license. Indeed, given the identification of Pergamum as the location where the Nicolaitans had found some measure of acceptance, it may be that the imperial cult that figures so prominently in Revelation is particularly in view. If idolatry was the Nicolaitans' central teaching (perhaps they advocated joining with broader cultural observances as a means of avoiding either formal persecution or at least being socially ostracized), then the Ephesian Christians' rejection of the sect is especially noteworthy, given the importance of the Artemis cult in that city.

The practices of which the Nicolaitans are accused were both proscribed by the so-called Jerusalem Council (Acts 15:20, 29) and had been among Paul's particular concerns of libertine excess (1 Cor 5; 8). The suggestion that the Nicolaitans may have been overzealous Paulinists who realized one of Paul's great concerns (compare Rom 6:1-2, 15; Gal 5:13-26), however, goes beyond the evidence.

The Nicolaitans have been variously associated with other groups mentioned either in the NT or other early Christian literature. Since "practicing fornication" and "eat[ing] food sacrificed to idols" were promoted by a prophetess identified as Jezebel in Revelation's letter to Thyatira (2:20), some have suggested that the Nicolaitans may have been active in that city as well. Yet having explicitly named the sect in the letters to Ephesus and Pergamum, it is difficult to conceive why John would have avoided the name in the Thyatiran letter. The explicit link to Balaam in 2:14-15 has opened the possibility of a connection with the antinomian groups denounced in 2 Pet 2:12-16 and Jude 11. Yet those letters emphasize Balaam's desire for monetary gain rather than either idolatry or sexual license. Among the writers of the patristic era, the Nicolaitans were commonly associated with gnostics (Irenaeus, *Haer.* 3.11.7; Tertullian, *Praescr.* 33; Hippolytus, *Haer.* 7.36), but references to the sect are notably absent from the surviving gnostic treatises. In the final analysis, then, the association of the Nicolaitans mentioned in Rev 2:6, 15 with any of these other groups must be considered speculative. *See* REVELATION, BOOK OF.

Bibliography: Colin J. Hemer. *The Letters to the Seven Churches of Asia in Their Local Settings* (1986).

TIMOTHY B. CARGAL

NICOLAUS [Νικόλαος Nikolaos]. One of seven men chosen to care for the neglected Hellenist widows (Acts 6:5; *see* SEVEN, THE). The last listed, he is identified as a "proselyte from Antioch" (NRSV, "proselyte of Antioch"). Some have suggested that the label "proselyte" applies to all seven men, but it is more likely that Nicolaus is being singled out. That is, unlike the other six men, who were Jews from birth, Nicolaus was a pagan convert to Judaism. Nicolaus' status as a proselyte may have a theological significance in Acts, indicating how the scope of the church's mission widened to include Gentiles as well as Jews.

Nicolaus is not mentioned again in Acts or the NT. Later Christian writers, notably Irenaeus (*Haer.* 1.26.3) and Eusebius (*Hist. eccl.* 3.29.1–3), identified him as a heretic and the founder of the NICOLAITANS, who are mentioned pejoratively in Rev 2:6, 15. Aside from the coincidence of the names, however, there is no reason to associate Nicolaus and the Nicolaitans.

Bibliography: Jack T. Sanders. *The Jews in Luke-Acts* (1987).

RUBÉN R. DUPERTUIS

NICOPOLIS ni-kop'uh-lis [Νικόπολις Nikopolis]. The city of Nicopolis is located in the region of Epirus in northwest Greece, within the Roman province of Macedonia. The name, "Victory City," celebrated the victory of Octavian (later the emperor Augustus) over the forces of Marcus Antonius and Cleopatra at the naval battle of Actium in 31 BCE. The Actium Peninsula formed part of Acarnania and lay at the entrance to the Ambracian Gulf; Nicopolis was located on the opposite side of the gulf. Augustus' new "holy" city was celebrated by a poem (*Palatine Anthology* 9.553) that noted it replaced the older communities on the island of Leucas, the Corinthian colony of Ambracia, Thyrreium, and Anactorium and Argos Amphilochicum (both on the Ambracian Gulf). The forceful movement of populations is reflected by the archaeological evidence for the physical transfer of the classical temple from Kassope (north of Nicopolis) to the new city. The dual identity of Roman colony and free Greek community is reflected by Pliny the Elder (*Nat.* 4.5). The deliberate abandonment of the communities in its territory meant that the nearest civic neighbor to Nicopolis was Patras in the northern Peloponnese. Among the benefactors of the city was Herod the Great (Josephus, *Ant.* 16.147).

The city was probably formally founded in 29 BCE, coinciding with the establishment of the Actian Games that were transferred there. These games were held every four years, the cycle of the traditional Olympic festival, and coincided with the anniversary of the victory. Sparta, a city that had sided with Octavian in the civil war, was given the honor of administering the games. This festival was used to initiate a new Actian age, a chronological scheme found on several inscriptions in Greece dating to the Augustan period. The site of Actium itself was developed by the emperor Augustus. He refurbished the historic sanctuary of Apollo Aktios and in 29 BCE dedicated a monument for his naval victory. The trophy's inscription appears to have been dedicated to Poseidon (god of the sea) and Ares (god of war); such a dedication is noted by Suetonius (*Aug.* 18).

Paul intended to spend the winter at Nicopolis (Titus 3:12). This perhaps hints at a journey either along the *Via Egnatia* from Macedonia or by sea from the Gulf of Corinth. *See* TITUS, LETTER TO.

Bibliography: Euangelos Chrysos, ed. *Nicopolis I: Proceedings of the First International Symposium on Nicopolis (23–29 September 1984)* (1987); Jacob Isager. *Foundation and Destruction: Nikopolis and Northwestern Greece* (2001).

DAVID W. J. GILL

NIGER nī́guhr [Νίγερ Niger]. A Gk. loanword from the Latin *niger*, meaning "black" or "dark." It is found only in Acts 13:1, as a surname for Simeon. He is listed among the teachers and prophets in the church at Antioch (*see* ANTIOCH, SYRIAN), although it is unclear as to which group he belongs. Some interpret **Niger** as an ethnographic designation suggesting Simeon was of African origin; however, this remains conjecture. *See* ACTS OF THE APOSTLES.

MICHAEL J. SCHUFER

NIGHT [לַיְלָה laylah, לַיִל layil; νύξ nyx]. *Night* occurs over 250 times in the Bible, mostly in the OT (63 times in the NT), with the greatest number of occurrences in Psalms. *Night* is used in both a literal (between sunset and sunrise) and a metaphorical sense. In both cases, it is related to *darkness*, as in the creation when God divides light from darkness (*see* LIGHT AND DARKNESS).

Frequently darkness is connected with evil or danger (e.g., Judg 20:5; Job 4:12-14; 24:13-17; Ps 91:5; Jer 49:9; Mic 3:6). In OT apocalyptic writings, night is often a symbol for evil (that will be ended by God's coming, e.g., Zech 14:7).

However, night is not always associated with evil in the OT. Night is the time for DREAMs, which are valued as divine communication (Gen 40:5; 41:11; Dan 7:2; compare Matt 2:12). In addition, the central religious festival, Passover, celebrates the night of Israel's deliverance from Egypt (Exod 12:1-27).

Old Testament references to night frequently occur in combination with *day* to describe periods of TIME (over 200 occurrences, of which fifty are combined with *day*; *see* DAY, OT); e.g., "forty days and nights" (Gen 7:4, 12; Exod 24:18; 34:28; Deut 9:9, 11, 18, 25; 10:10). Since night is the time for rest (Ruth 3:13; 1 Kgs 3:19; Tob 2:9; 6:2), a sleepless night is lamented (Ps 6:6, 7; Eccl 2:23). In its literal usage, *night* is often divided into watches (Pss 63:6; 119:148; compare Matt 14:25; Luke 12:38).

The NT increasingly employs *night* in metaphorical ways. As in the OT, there is the literal sense of night as a period of time (Matt 12:40) and in combination with *day* to mean the complete day (Mark 4:27; Acts 26:7; *see* DAY, NT). And, as in the OT, the NT describes a significant period of time as "forty days and forty nights" (Matt 4:2) and refers to night as the time of dreaming (Acts 18:9; Matt 1:20-24). In parables of the end times, nighttime is when the faithful must be prepared for the sudden return of Jesus (as the master in Luke 12:38, as a thief in Matt 24:43; Luke 12:39, or as the bridegroom in Matt 25:6). In the Gospel of John, *night* describes both the time of day and the metaphorical darkness in which Nicodemus came searching but not yet seeing who Jesus was (3:1-10; compare 19:39). John also uses *night* metaphorically as the time of darkness when no one can do God's work (9:4; 11:10). When Judas leaves to betray Jesus, it is "night" (13:30; as with the story of Nicodemus, *night* should be understood both literally and metaphorically).

In Paul, *night* is also a metaphor for the passing age of evil because the light of salvation brings the rule of God (Rom 13:12). Paul uses *night* to describe the faithless life from which believers are redeemed (1 Thess 5:5-7). This contrast is found in the plea of Eph 5:8-11 for Christians to live as "children of light."

In Revelation, night is absent in the New Jerusalem, because God has defeated that which opposes him (21:25; 22:5).

WENDELL WILLIS

NIGHTHAWK [תַּחְמָס takhmas]. It is obvious that the Hebrew word **takhmas** in the duplicate lists of Lev 11:16 and Deut 14:15 denotes a bird that was considered unclean. Unfortunately, the literary context contains no further clues. The uncertain etymological connection to **khamas** (חָמָס), "violence," offers little help. The NRSV translates "nighthawk," despite the fact that nighthawks (family Caprimulgidae, subfamily Chordeilinae) do not seem to belong to the fauna of Palestine. From that point of view, one of the nighthawk's relatives, the nightjar (*Caprimulgus europaeus* or *Caprimulgus tamaricis*) would be a more likely alternative. However, several scholars have suggested that **takhmas** refers to some kind of owl, possibly the barn owl (Tristram) or the short-eared owl (Driver).

Bibliography: I. Aharoni. "Animals mentioned in the Bible." *Osiris* 5 (1938) 461–78; G. R. Driver. "Birds in the Old Testament: I. Birds in Law." *PEQ* 87 (1955) 5–20; Henry B. Tristram. *The Fauna and Flora of Palestine.* (1884).

GÖRAN EIDEVALL

Todd Bolen/BiblePlaces.com

Figure 1: Nile River near the Beni Hasan tombs from the east.

NILE RIVER nīl [יְאֹר yeʾor]. At over 4,200 mi. in length, the Nile is the longest river in the world, arising south of the equator in eastern Africa and flowing north through the Sudan and EGYPT to the Mediterranean Sea. The waters of the Nile gave life to the desert climate of northern Sudan and Egypt and nourished the civilizations that emerged on its shores over 5,000 years ago.

The most common Hebrew term in the Bible for the Nile and its channels is yeʾor (pl. yeʾorim יְאֹרִים). The word probably derives from Egyptian itrw, "river." Twice yeʾor is used to refer to other things: once for the Tigris (Dan 12:5-7) and once for channels cut by miners (Job 28:10).

The Nile is intimately connected with life and death in both Egyptian and biblical traditions. Although the Nile appears frequently in narratives and oracles dealing with Egypt, references to the Nile in the Bible are rarely mere geographic details. Most reflect its real and symbolic importance in Egyptian life.

The waters of the Nile derive from two primary sources: the equatorial lake plateau in east Africa, especially Lake Victoria, and the Ethiopian highlands. Its headwaters are mountain springs at elevations exceeding 9,000 ft., which tumble down dramatic waterfalls, cut deep gorges, and feed a series of lakes.

The White Nile, sections of which are called the Victoria Nile, the Albert Nile, and the Mountain Nile, flows north out of Lake Victoria through Uganda and the Sudan. In southern Sudan, the White Nile passes through an extensive swampy region known as the Sudd, which absorbs the floodwaters of the rainy season, most of which are lost to evaporation. The level of the White Nile north of the Sudd is relatively constant throughout the year.

The Blue Nile and the Atbara are fed by monsoonal rains on the Ethiopian highlands. The Blue Nile flows south out of Lake Tana and then west across Ethiopia before bending north to join the White Nile at Khartoum. The Atbara River arises north of Lake Tana and runs northward to meet the Nile.

The volume of both the Blue Nile and the Atbara varies greatly during the year, and even from year to year, depending on the rainfall in Ethiopia. The resulting flood, or inundation, accounted for the fertility of the Nile Valley in ancient times. The floodwaters replenished the fields by washing the salts out of the soil and depositing a thin layer of nutrient-rich silt on the valley floor. In Egypt the Nile began to rise in July, peaking in August/September. When the waters receded in October/November, the fields were surveyed and planted. In an average year, the river rose 20–25 ft., flooding the fields to a depth of 5–6 ft.

For the ancient Egyptians, the sufficiency of the annual inundation was literally a matter of life and death. A low flood provided inadequate water and nutrients for the crops. Too high a flood washed away villages and irrigation systems and delayed planting. The Egyptian rulers measured and recorded the maximum height of the inundation, especially in the Memphis-Cairo region. Only sporadic records survive from pre-Hellenistic Egypt, but the data from ancient, medieval, and modern Egypt indicate that low (or high) floods tended to cluster together, resulting in periods of crop failure lasting several years, alternating with periods of great productivity (compare Gen 41:17-36, 53-56).

The Egyptians gave voice to their hopes and fears in hymns dedicated to Hapy, the deified flood. One hymn praises Hapy for saving Egypt by watering the countryside to give life, creating barley and emmer, bringing abundant provisions, and providing pastures for the cattle and provisions for sacrifices. When Hapy is sluggish or stops, everyone is stricken with poverty. The food supply is destroyed, and no one has peace (Foster). Images of Hapy depict an androgynous figure with beard and large, sagging breasts and stomach, often wearing a headdress of papyrus plants. Hapy was associated with Nun, the primeval waters, and as bringer of the flood, was the source of the land's fertility and hence a creator god. Royal decrees from the late 2nd millennium endowed semi-annual festivals that included offerings to Hapy.

The Nile proper begins at Khartoum, where the Blue and White Niles join. The last Nile tributary is the Atbara, 200 mi. north of Khartoum. From there the river flows through a narrow desert valley up to 13 mi. wide, at times framed by high cliffs, creating a slender ribbon of cultivable land where the Egyptians grew emmer wheat and barley. From Khartoum to Aswan, the river's broad S-curve was punctuated by six stretches of cataracts (steep rapids). Below Aswan, the Nile was consistently navigable, and in ancient times goods traveled mostly by boat.

The FLOODS deposited their heaviest sediments along the riverbanks, forming natural levees between the river and the fields. Villages were built on the levees. Basin irrigation replaced natural irrigation. The floodplain was terraced into large basins surrounded by dikes. Canals and sluice-gates controlled the flooding of the basins, with a channel to the Faiyum depression serving as a spillway in years of extremely high flood volume. The introduction of the shaduf, a levered irrigation device consisting of a bucket with counterweight, supported the cultivation of gardens beyond the floodplain.

As the river nears the Mediterranean, the valley fans out into a broad, fertile delta of thick silt deposits dotted with swamps and brackish lagoons. Bifurcating branches of the Nile wind through the delta to the sea.

The river has shifted course over the centuries, straightening its path, forming islands, and alternately forming and filling swampy hollows. In the delta, both the number and course of the distributaries varied even as accumulating sediments built up and extended the landmass.

The Nile appears in narrative texts set in Egypt and in prophetic oracles referring to Egypt. References to the inundation are common, as are assertions of divine control over the Nile and its fertility.

In the Joseph narrative the Nile is the source of both plenty and famine. Both the seven fat cows and the seven lean cows of Pharaoh's dream come up out of the Nile (Gen 41:2-3), alluding to the consequences of normal and low inundations. The vision predicts optimal inundations for seven years followed by seven years of low inundations, resulting in famine.

Prophetic texts allude to the drying up of the Nile (Isa 37:25; Zech 10:11). The most elaborate description appears in the oracle against Egypt in Isa 19, which reflects Egyptian fears of catastrophically low inundations: "The waters of the Nile will be dried up, and the river will be parched and dry" (19:5). The result is complete agricultural collapse, affecting farmers, fishermen, weavers, and "all who work for wages" (19:10).

In accounts of the exodus, the Nile takes center stage in the contest between God and the pharaoh. Ironically, whereas in Egyptian ideology the Nile is the source of life, it is transformed into a means of death for the Israelites when the pharaoh commands the drowning of every newborn Hebrew male (Exod 1:22). Appropriately then, the first plague transforms the Nile to blood, killing all the fish and depriving the Egyptians of water to drink (Exod 7:20-21). Although the Egyptian magicians replicate this feat, it inaugurates the contest between God, represented by Moses and Aaron, and the gods of Egypt, represented by the divine pharaoh and his magicians (*see* PLAGUES IN EGYPT).

Oracles against foreign kings sometimes include condemnation for claiming ownership or control of the Nile and its life-giving power. The king of Egypt is rebuked for asserting: "My Nile is my own; I made it for myself" (Ezek 29:3). Similarly, the Assyrian king Sennacherib is chastised for his hubris, which includes the claim: "I dried up with the sole of my foot all the streams of Egypt" (2 Kgs 19:24; Isa 37:25). The rise and fall of nations is determined by God alone.

In Amos and Jeremiah the Nile's inundation appears in distinctly non-Egyptian metaphors of destruction. Amos uses the inundation in parallel with standard theophanic descriptions of the earth shaking and melting. When God comes in judgment the land will "rise like the Nile, and be tossed about and sink again" (Amos 8:8). Jeremiah envisions the flood as a surge of water, destroying cities in its path (Jer 46:8). *See* RIVER.

Bibliography: John Collins. *The Nile* (2002); John L. Foster. "Khety's Hymn to the Nile." *Hymns, Prayers, Songs: An Anthology of Ancient Egyptian Lyric Poetry* (1995) 114–16; Rushdi Said. *The River Nile: Geology, Hydrology and Utilization* (1993); Terje Tvedt. *The Nile: An Annotated Bibliography.* 2nd ed. (2004).

CAROLYN HIGGINBOTHAM

NIMRAH. *See* BETH-NIMRAH; LEOPARD.

NIMRIM, THE WATERS OF nim'rim [מֵי נִמְרִים me nimrim]. Referenced in only two OT texts (Isa 15:6; Jer 48:34). Both are embedded in sections of the respective prophetic compositions devoted to oracles against nations—more specifically, against Moab.

The specific identification of the waters' location is uncertain. Two possible geographical settings are at the center of the discussion. One view points to the region approximately 15 km northeast of the northern end of the Dead Sea, in the vicinity of Tell Nimrin and Tell Bleibil in the Plains of Moab. Wadi Nimrin is part of the system that drains the region and eventually empties into the Jordan River about 10 km north of the Dead Sea's northern tip.

The alternative view draws attention to the region approximately 10 km north of the Dead Sea's southern tip and just east of its eastern shore, in the vicinity of Tell Numeireh. A variation of this view locates the waters a little farther east, at the extreme western edge of the Moabite plateau's southern end. These virtually parallel oracles against Moab suggest that in antiquity, the Waters of Nimrim were, or provided the resources for, a very rich, fertile area of cultivation, which would be dried up and become desolate. *See* MOAB, MOABITES.

JOHN I. LAWLOR

NIMROD nim′rod [נִמְרוֹד nimrodh]. 1. Nimrod, son of Cush, and a direct descendant of Noah, was a mighty warrior and hunter who founded Nineveh and Babylon, as well as a number of other cities including Calah (Gen 10:8-12; 1 Chr 1:10; *see* CUSH, CUSHITE). The name Nimrod is derived from Akkadian **namru** or **nimru** ("shining"), an epithet of a number of Mesopotamian gods, including Marduk and Ninurta. Ninurta was the chief god of Calah and a patron of hunting as the sport of Assyrian kings. **Nimru** also means "panther," an animal that was included in the hunting park founded by Ashurnasirpal II at Calah.

The 10th-cent. Arab historian ʿAli ibn al-Husayn al-Masʿudi (896–956 CE) identifies this Nimrod (Arabic **nimrud**), son of Cush (Arabic **kush**), as the father of SENNACHERIB (*Meadows of Gold* 1103). This would make him SARGON II of Assyria, who was indeed a mighty hunter as well as a rebuilder and founder of cities, including a new capital at Dur-Sharruken (modern Khorsabad), and a new Samaria as capital of an Assyrian province. For the prophet Micah, Assyria is the land of Nimrod (Mic 5:6). *See* ASSYRIA AND BABYLONIA.

2. There was a second Babylonian Nimrod who is not mentioned in the Bible but appears in rabbinic literature (*b. Hag.* 13a; *b. Pesah.* 94b). This Nimrod (Arabic **nimrud**), son of Kanaan, is identified by al-Masʿudi as the grandson of Sennacherib (*Meadows of Gold* 1103). This would make him Shamash-shum-ukin, who led Babylon in an unsuccessful revolt against his brother Ashurbanipal and died in the flames of his palace, inspiring the legend of Sardanapalus (*see* ASHURBANIPAL, ASSURBANIPAL). This Nimrod was an archetypical rebel, as Hebrew folk etymologies of Nimrod's name (**maradh** [מָרַד], "to rebel") would imply. In Jewish and Arabic folklore, Nimrod is an evil tyrant who built the tower of BABEL to protect himself against the flood (Josephus, *Ant.* 1.113–19), presumably a reference to Nebuchadnezzar II's rebuilding of the walls of Babylon to prevent water being diverted against them (Berossus, *Hist.* 3.3.2a). Nimrod also quarreled with Abraham, whom he sought to burn in the style of Nebuchadnezzar throwing Daniel into the fiery furnace, catapulting him into a giant pyre using the world's first ballista (al-Kisaʾi, *Qisas Al-Anbiya* 1.145–49, in Janssen). According to the 10th-cent. author Ahmad Ibn-Rusta, Nimrod, like Nebuchadnezzar and Titus, is supposed to have been tormented by gnats (Kitab al-Aʿlaq an Nafisa 199, in Janssen). Another 10th-cent. Arab historian, Muhammad ibn Jarir al-Tabari (838–923 CE), portrays Nimrod as a rebel against God who shoots arrows into the sky with murderous intent while attempting to scale the heavens (al-Tabari, *The History of al-Tabari* 320). This image of Nimrod is a reference to Isa 14:12 where a "king" rises to the heavens as the DAY STAR, son of the dawn. "Lucifer" (Lat. "light-bearing") or **Heōsphoros** (Gk. Ἑωσφόρος, "bringer of the morning") is a translation of Akkadian **namru**, which means "shining." **Namru** was an epithet of the day star (the planet Mercury), so called because, like Venus, it is visible in the sky at dawn. The heliacal rising of the planet Mercury on the fifth of Nisannu during the Babylonian New Year's Festival was the occasion for a bonfire sacrifice in which a bull representing Anu, king of the heavens, was burned in a pit (as in Isa 30:33) to symbolize the rising of Marduk into the heavens as Mercury and his defeat of Anu.

Bibliography: R. D. Barnett. *A Catalogue of the Nimrud Ivories.* 2nd ed. (1975); Berossus. *The Babyloniaca of Berossus.* Stanley M. Burstein, trans. (1978); Caroline Janssen. *Babil, the City of Witchcraft and Wine* (1995); Muhammad Ibn Abd Al-Kisai. *Qisas Al-Anbiya.* Isaac Eisenberg, trans. (1922–23); Ali ibn al-Husayn al-Musadi. *Meadows of Gold.* Aloys Sprenger, trans. (1841); Muhammad ibn Jarir al-Tabari. *The History of al-Tabari.* William Brinner, trans. (1987).

JOANN SCURLOCK

NIMSHI nim′sh*i* [נִמְשִׁי nimshi]. JEHU is called "son of Nimshi" (1 Kgs 19:16; 2 Kgs 9:20; 2 Chr 22:7), but also "son of JEHOSHAPHAT son of Nimshi" (2 Kgs 9:2, 14; "son" is used to indicate direct or indirect descent). Nimshi might mean "drawn out."

KEN M. PENNER

NINE. *See* NUMBERS, NUMBERING.

NINETEEN. *See* NUMBERS, NUMBERING.

NINETY. *See* NUMBERS, NUMBERING.

NINEVEH nin′uh-vuh [נִינְוֵה nineweh; Νινευή Nineuē]. A major city in northern Mesopotamia during the Bronze and Iron Ages, and the capital of Assyria at the height of the Neo-Assyrian Empire. In the wake of its destruction in 612 BCE, the city experienced sudden reversal of political fortune, from extreme wealth and power to abject ruin.

Nineveh lay on the east bank of the Tigris River, near the confluence of the Tigris and Khosr rivers, directly across from modern Mosul on the west bank of the Tigris. The ancient city was surrounded by a roughly rectangular, double wall, approximately 2 km wide and 5 km long. With an enclosed area of 750 ha., Nineveh was truly a "great city" (Jonah 1:2). Two prominent mounds are located on the western side of the site: Kuyunjik and Nebi Yunas (meaning "Prophet Jonah"). The Khosr River entered ancient Nineveh midway along the eastern wall and traversed the width of the city, passing along the base of Kuyunjik before exiting through the western wall.

While the origins of Nineveh go back approximately to 6000 BCE, the city reached the pinnacle of its power after SENNACHERIB (704–681 BCE) made it the capital of Assyria. The king's extensive construction in the city included, most notably, his "palace without rival" (as the Assyrian inscriptions call it), the fortification of the city's perimeter wall, an elaborate water system of canals, levees, and dams, and the provision of park areas within the city. The "hanging gardens of Babylon," made famous by classical writers, may actually have been constructed by Sennacherib in Nineveh. The city continued as the capital throughout the reigns of the powerful kings ESARHADDON (680–669 BCE) and Ashurbanipal (668–627 BCE), and even beyond, during the final years of Assyria (*see* ASHURBANIPAL, ASSURBANIPAL). According to the Babylonian Chronicle, Nineveh fell to the joint forces of the Babylonians and Medes in the summer of 612 BCE. A 1st cent. BCE account of Nineveh's fall suggests that a natural overflow of the Tigris River weakened the perimeter wall and thereby helped the Babylonians and Medes to topple the city (Diodorus Siculus, *Bib. Hist.* 2.27.1–2). More likely, the attacking forces manipulated Nineveh's water system to bring about the inundation of the city (see Nah 2:6). Excavations at the site in 1987–90 yielded new evidence of the violent siege by the Babylonians and Medes. While artifactual remains at Nineveh can be interpreted to fit the idea of the city's flooding in 612, no direct evidence has yet been found to prove such flooding.

According to Gen 10:10-12, which is part of the Yahwist's contribution to the Table of Nations, the legendary hero NIMROD founded Nineveh. Nimrod, the text claims, first established his kingdom "in the land of Shinar" (Babylonia) and "from that land he went into Assyria, and built Nineveh, Rehoboth-ir, Calah, and Resen between Nineveh and Calah; that is the great city." The final clause—"that is the great city"—may have applied originally to Nineveh (see Jonah 1:2).

Second Kings 19:36-37 (compare Isa 37:37-38) presents Nineveh as the capital city of Assyria. The verses include a composite account of Sennacherib's invasion of Judah in 701 BCE. According to v. 35, the angel of Yahweh visited the Assyrian camp at night and killed 185,000 troops, and subsequently Sennacherib "left, went home, and lived at Nineveh" (v. 36). There, while the king was worshiping in the temple of NISROCH, his sons murdered him "with the sword" (v. 37). The biblical writers understand Sennacherib's death as fulfillment of Yahweh's pledge in 19:7*b*: "I will cause him to fall by the sword in his own land." The reach of Yahweh's judgment extends to the capital city of the enemy king, even to the temple of his god in Nineveh.

The 7th-cent. prophets Nahum and Zephaniah proclaim the fall of Nineveh. According to Zeph 2:13-14, Yahweh will make the city a "desolation," inhabited only by wild animals. A taunt in v. 15 contrasts this fate with Nineveh's previous glory and pride: "Is this the exultant city that lived secure, that said to itself, 'I am, and there is no one else'?"

The entire book of Nahum is "an oracle concerning Nineveh" (Nah 1:1; *see* NAHUM, BOOK OF). The sack of the city is depicted graphically in 2:1-13. Yahweh is the "scatterer" (NRSV, "shatterer") who attacks Nineveh, but he employs a well-equipped human army to conquer it (v. 3). The scene includes an assault against the city wall, the opening of the "river gates," the destruction of the royal palace, the deportation of captives, the flight of the city's defenders, the confiscation of spoil, and the panic of Nineveh's citizens (vv. 4-10). A taunt in vv. 11-12 uses lion imagery to convey the theme of reversal: the plunderer of the nations is now plundered. Nahum 3 speaks of Nineveh as a "city of bloodshed, utterly deceitful, full of booty" (v. 1) and then addresses the city as a harlot whom Yahweh will humiliate by undressing her before the nations. Nineveh is no more invincible than Thebes (v. 8), which fell to Ashurbanipal in 663 BCE. Scholars debate whether Nahum's speeches predate 612 and look forward to the city's fall, or postdate the event and reflect back on it.

The postexilic book of Jonah tells the story of Jonah son of Amittai, commissioned by Yahweh to prophesy against Nineveh (*see* JONAH, BOOK OF). Second Kings 14:25 dates the prophet to the reign of Jeroboam II (788–748 BCE). Jonah 3:3 describes the city as "an exceedingly large city, a three days' walk across" (surely an exaggeration), and 4:11 claims that Nineveh's population exceeded 120,000 people. The book narrates Jonah's proclamation of the city's imminent overthrow, the subsequent repentance of its king and citizens, and God's decision to spare Nineveh. The tale thus emphasizes divine mercy for sinners who "cry mightily to God" and "turn from their evil ways" (3:7-10).

The OT thus presents two images of Nineveh: the arrogant city that deservedly suffers divine punishment and the repentant city that God spares. The former image is picked up in the apocryphal book of Tobit, which is the story of a pious Jew exiled to Nineveh (*see* TOBIT, BOOK OF). According to 14:3-4, Tobit is old and soon to die when he urges his children to flee Nineveh, because he believes Nahum's word of judgment against the city. A similarly negative picture of the city probably is assumed in the apocryphal book of Judith (*see* JUDITH, BOOK OF). The tale begins by introducing Nebuchadnezzar as a king who "ruled over the Assyrians in the great city of Nineveh" (1:1). Historically, Nebuchadnezzar was king over the Neo-Babylonian Empire, and Nineveh lay in ruins when he rose to the throne in 605 BCE. The fictitious association of the king with infamous Nineveh and the Assyrians serves to enhance the depiction of an arrogant world power that, according to the tale, suffers defeat at the hand of the pious Israelite widow, Judith.

The image of Nineveh as a repentant city surfaces in the Jesus saying in Luke 11:32 (compare Matt 12:40-41). The saying reasons that, since the Ninevites (**Nineuitai** Νινευῖται) repented at the proclamation of Jonah, they are qualified to condemn the recalcitrant generation of Jesus on the day of judgment. *See* ASSYRIA AND BABYLONIA.

Bibliography: P. Machinist. "The Fall of Assyria in Comparative Ancient Perspective." *Assyria 1995* (1997) 179–95; J. J. M. Roberts. *Nahum, Habakkuk, and Zephaniah.* OTL (1991); D. Stronach and S. Lumsden. "UC Berkeley's Excavations at Nineveh." *BA* 55 (1992) 227–33.

STUART IRVINE

NINLIL. A deity who in Sumerian mythology is the consort of ENLIL, the patron god of Sumer. In one text, her name is Sud until she marries Enlil, at which point her name is changed to Ninlil. Her temple was located in Nippur. *See* AKKADIAN; SUMER, SUMERIANS.

NINURTA. A deity in the Sumerian and AKKADIAN pantheons; the son of ENLIL and god of agriculture, warfare, and wisdom. The name NIMROD may derive from the name Ninurta. *See* GILGAMESH, EPIC OF; SUMER, SUMERIANS.

NIPHISH [Νειφεῖς **Neipheis**]. Called MAGBISH in Ezra 2:30, his descendants returned after the exile (1 Esd 5:21).

NIPPUR ni-poor´. A city in Mesopotamia located about 60 mi. (95 km) southeast of ancient Babylon and occupied almost continually from the early 6th millennium BCE to the 9th cent. CE.

In the late 3rd and early 2nd millennia BCE, Nippur was one of the principal sites in ancient Sumer because of its central location in the great southern plain between the Euphrates and Tigris rivers. Its patron god was ENLIL, the head of the Sumerian pantheon, an indication of the city's importance. At its greatest extent Nippur covered over 370 ac. (150 ha.). Its ZIGGURAT, a stepped pyramid that served as a platform for the temple of Enlil called Ekur, is one of the best preserved in Mesopotamia, and to this temple the rulers of other Sumerian city-states and later rulers as well regularly sent offerings.

Excavations in the late 19th and early 20th cent. uncovered tens of thousands of tablets in Sumerian and Akkadian in a variety of genres and from many periods. These comprise one of the most extensive discoveries of texts from ancient Mesopotamia. Since the mid-20th cent., when political conditions have allowed, the principal expedition has been that of the Oriental Institute of the University of Chicago; its excavations have considerably clarified the site's stratigraphy and the chronology of the larger region.

Nippur is not mentioned in the Bible. According to Ezek 1:1, the prophet's inaugural vision took place "among the exiles by the river CHEBAR." Among the many texts found at Nippur are the Murashu tablets, the records of a business firm that date to the second half of the 5th cent. BCE (*see* MURASHÛ, ARCHIVES OF). These tablets twice mention a large irrigation canal in Nippur called the Kabaru, almost certainly the same watercourse referred to in the book of Ezekiel. The Murashu tablets also mention a large number of individuals with Jewish names, showing that a century and a half after Ezekiel the community of exiles from Judah had been integrated into the commercial life of Nippur.

The Jewish community at Nippur continued to thrive in subsequent centuries. Other important texts from Nippur are several hundred inscribed bowls, with incantations written in various dialects of Aramaic and dating to the 6th cent. CE. These were used by Jews to protect themselves against various evil powers, especially LILITH. *See* ASSYRIA AND BABYLONIA; SUMER, SUMERIANS.

MICHAEL D. COOGAN

NISAN nī´san [נִיסָן **nisan**]. Postexilic name for the first month in the Hebrew calendar, comparable to March–April (Neh 2:1; Esth 3:7). *See* CALENDAR.

NISROCH nis´rok [נִסְרֹךְ **nisrokh**]. Sennacherib was killed in the shrine of this god by his sons (2 Kgs 19:37; Isa 37:38). Nisroch is a punning reference to Akkadian **matsrakhu**, in Assyrian **matsrukhu**, a divine standard or "weapon." These "weapons" of Assyrian gods preceded the army on campaign and received regular sacrifices in the field. When peace was made, it was in the presence of the "weapon" of Ashur that tributaries like Hezekiah were made to swear oaths of loyalty to Assyrian kings such as Sennacherib. Since the word does not exist in Hebrew, Akkadian TSADE RESH KHET (**tsrkh**) should have been rendered phonetically. Instead, the initial letter was changed to SAMEK (**s** ס) and the last to KAF (**k** כ), producing a nonsense word. This was probably to invoke Hebrew samek resh khet (**srkh** סרח): "to run free and unrestrained; to overrun or exceed" and simultaneously tsade resh kaf (**tsrk** צרך): "to be in need," thus summarizing in a single word Isaiah's judgment on Sennacherib as a boastful and ultimately humbled "weapon" in the hand of God (Isa 10:12-16).

Bibliography: Steven W. Holloway. *Aššur Is King! Aššur Is King! Religion in the Exercise of Power in the Neo-Assyrian Empire* (2002).

JOANN SCURLOCK

NOADIAH noh´uh-d*i*´uh [נוֹעַדְיָה no'adhyah]. Means "Yahweh met." 1. Son of BINNUI, who, along with Eleazar and fellow Levite Jozabad, was present when Ezra weighed the treasure for the Temple into the hands of Meremoth the priest (Ezra 8:33). Moeth appears in the par. list instead of Noadiah (1 Esd 8:63).

2. The (false) prophetess, who along with "the rest of the prophets," intimidated Nehemiah (Neh 6:14). Her connection with SHEMAIAH, who was hired to prophesy against Nehemiah by SANBALLAT and TOBIAH (Neh 6:10-13), is not specified.

KEN M. PENNER

NOAH noh´uh [נֹחַ **noakh**, נֹעָה no'ah; Νῶε Nōe]. 1. Noah is the protagonist of the FLOOD story in Gen 6:5–9:28 and thus arguably is the center character of the primeval history. Isaiah 54:9 mentions the covenant with Noah as an example of God's steadfast love, and Ezek 14:14, 20 depicts Noah (together with Daniel and Job) as an exceptionally righteous person whose prayer can change the fortune of an entire nation. Since Isaiah and Ezekiel seem to presuppose that their readers were familiar with Noah as a literary character, it is safe to assume that the Noah tradition was known widely in the exilic and early post-exilic periods. So far, however, there are no extra-biblical references to Noah, and the name does not occur in the Mesopotamian flood traditions.

A. Noah's Place in Primeval History
B. Textual Layers of the Noah Tradition
   1. Priestly tradition
   2. Non-priestly tradition
   3. Sons of Noah
C. Apocryphal Stories of Noah
D. Noah in the New Testament
Bibliography

A. Noah's Place in Primeval History

In the primeval history, Noah is mentioned for the first time not in the flood narrative itself but in the preceding genealogy of Adam (Gen 5). A few things are remarkable about how he is introduced in Gen 5:28-32. His name is explained by way of an etymology: the authors derive **noakh** from the root **nuakh** (נוּחַ) "to rest," meaning that Noah is the one to relieve humankind from the work on the ground that God had cursed (see Gen 3:17-19), but it is not clear how human fate changes with the appearance of Noah. Exegetes have argued that the blessing that Noah and his descendants receive in Gen 9:1 has the purpose of easing or even reversing the burdens put on humankind in Gen 3:14-19. However, there is no reason to assume that farming and childbearing would be any less toilsome and painful after the flood than it had been before (see Gen 3:16-19), or that snakes would no longer pose a threat (see Gen 3:14-15). Thus it seems likely that the kind of relief that Noah brings to humankind is of a quite different nature. According to Gen 9:20, after the flood Noah becomes a tiller of the ground, just like his forefather Adam. However, Noah elicits something more enjoyable from the cursed ground than thorns and thistles: the wine that according to Judg 9:13 and Ps 104:15 gladdens the hearts of gods and humans. From a literary point of view, the etymology of Noah's name in Gen 5:28 serves as a bridge between the narrative about Adam and Eve (the post-Eden stage of humanity) and the narrative about the generation of Noah and his descendants (the post-diluvian stage of humanity).

One other interesting detail about Noah as a literary character relates to how he, as the last of the descendants of Adam, figures into the chronology of Gen 5. If one does the math with the ages of the patriarchs listed and the respective dates when they fathered their oldest sons, it turns out that Noah represents the first generation of humans who were born after the death of Adam. Regarding the structure of the primeval history, this clearly indicates that with Noah the story line moves on to a new chapter about humanity. The fact that Gen 5 separates Noah from Adam might also prepare the reader for the main message of Gen 6, namely that wickedness and violence had spread among the old "Adamite" humanity so that their demise was unavoidable. The only exception is Noah, who stands for a fresh start in the relationship between God and humankind. *See* GENESIS, BOOK OF.

B. Textual Layers of the Noah Tradition

The flood narrative in its present form is the result of a long transmission process and as such comprises a number of different textual layers. Consequently, the depiction of Noah has many facets, not all of which are compatible.

1. Priestly tradition

In what has been considered the "priestly" report of the flood, Noah is introduced as a "righteous" and "blameless" man who "walked with God" (Gen 6:9). One gets the impression that this is how the priestly authors (who also composed the creation report in Gen 1:1–2:3) envisioned a human being as the "image of God" (1:26). As such, Noah is depicted in contrast not only to the rest of humankind but to all "flesh" that had turned corrupt and violent. The priestly narrators make it clear that it was his exceptional righteousness that saved Noah and his family from the flood.

Some of the same characterizations belong to Job, who is a blameless and God-fearing person (Job 1:1.8; 2:3). An interesting tension between the two traditions exists. Whereas the flood narrative demonstrates that righteousness and piety save Noah even when the world around him falls apart, the prologue of Job problematizes such a position: even Job, the most perfect person imaginable, is not spared many hardships.

In the priestly flood narrative Noah remains in the background, and God is the main character of the story. Noah does what he has been told to do: he builds the ark by exactly following God's instructions and then herds the animals into the ark (*see* ARK OF NOAH). Eventually he sends out a bird to see if the waters have gone down enough for the inhabitants of the ark to disembark. Noah remains in a purely passive role when God announces the covenant. Noah receives a blessing and an eternal covenant that includes not only humankind but all of creation (9:1-17). *See* NOAHIC COVENANT.

2. Non-priestly tradition

The portrait of Noah becomes ambivalent in the non-priestly tradition. In Gen 6:5-8, God judges that all the devices of the human heart are evil and that it was therefore a mistake to create humankind in the first place. Noah alone had found favor (**khen** חֵן) in God's eyes (Gen 6:8). The text does not say that Noah was an outstandingly righteous person whose virtue saved his life. Rather, the text suggests that Noah might have been relatively more righteous than the rest of humankind but that he, too, had an evil heart. This view is confirmed by the end of the non-priestly flood narrative when God repeats his assessment of human nature, now with regard to Noah and his family as the only survivors: "The inclination of the human heart is evil from youth" (Gen 8:21). This tradition does not explain why Noah was saved from the flood and why he was made the primal ancestor of a new humanity that, after all, would be not so different from the old. Important in this regard is the sacrifice that Noah offers after the flood (Gen 8:20). This is the only time that Noah does something that God had not told him to do. This sacrifice seems to have no particular purpose. The way Noah's sacrifice is woven into the overall plot suggests, however, that this is his response to having been saved or, to having found favor (**khen**) in God's eyes. This, in turn, prompts God to make the unconditioned promise to never destroy the world again (Gen 8:22). Note that in this tradition, God's promise is not called a covenant, as it is in the priestly text. Rather, it can be best described as a relationship based on divine grace and human graciousness in a world marked by the reality of human sin and suffering.

3. Sons of Noah

Looking at the literary portraits of Noah in Gen 6–9, one can summarize that Noah exemplifies two different understandings of what humankind is or what it ought to be. Beyond that, there are hardly any personal characteristics included in Gen 6:5–9:19 that make Noah appear as a *dramatis persona* as one finds it with the protagonists of the Mesopotamian flood traditions (e.g., Atrahasis, Utnapishtim; *see* GILGAMESH, EPIC OF). As a matter of fact, the only "biographic" pieces of information about Noah are included in the genealogies of Gen 5 and 9:18-19, where we get to know the names of his three sons, SHEM, Ham, and JAPHETH (*see* HAM, HAMITES). The names of Noah's wife and the wives of his sons are not recorded in the canonical text.

There is consensus among scholars that the anecdote about Noah as a vinedresser (Gen 9:20-27) was not originally connected with the flood narrative but was added at a later stage, possibly as late as in the Hellenistic period. Although the plot revolves around Noah being so drunk that he uncovers himself, so that he is seen naked by his son Ham (Canaan), this is a story about the three sons. In its present literary context, the purpose of Noah's curse on Canaan (Gen 9:25-27) is to legitimize the taking over of the land of Canaan by the patriarchs of Israel and their descendants (*see* CANAAN, CANAANITES).

C. Apocryphal Stories of Noah

The *Genesis Apocryphon* mentions a "book of the words of Noah" (1 QapGen ar V, 29), which indicates that Noah, very much like Enoch, assumed the role of a prophetic figure whose words and visions were recorded apart from the canonical books (*see* GENESIS APOCRYPHON). Although now badly damaged, the *Genesis Apocryphon* contained some of these "words of Noah," as perhaps did the *Apocalypse of Noah* (*see* NOAH, APOCALYPSE OF). The *Genesis Apocryphon* retells the flood narrative as a report, first of Lamech and then of his son Noah (1 QapGen ar II,1–XV,14). The birth of Noah seems to have been the object of a debate. The *Genesis Apocryphon* reveals that there was speculation about whether he really was a human being or rather an offspring of the "Sons of God" who, according to Gen 6:2, took human wives for themselves (*see* GODS, SONS OF). In the text, Lamech's wife Bitenosh confirms that Noah was indeed Lamech's biological son. Noah introduces himself as someone who, from the moment of his birth, has walked in truth (VI, 1-3). His exceptional righteousness is what privileges Noah to receive prophetic visions. The *Genesis Apocryphon* presents the biblical episode about the "angel marriages" (Gen 6:1-4) as Noah's first vision, in which he sees the violence that the NEPHILIM (Gen 6:4) bring upon humankind.

The Noah of the primeval history is also referenced in several other sapiential and eschatological traditions, where he is characterized mostly as an exceptionally righteous and faithful human being, in contrast to the wicked ways of the world (2 Esd 3:11; 4 Macc 15:31). The priestly account of the flood narrative primarily shaped the later portrayals of Noah. He appears as the second in Sirach's eulogy of Israel's great ancestors (Sir 44:17). In the same line of tradition, Noah marries a woman of his own kin (Tob 4:12), a detail that is found nowhere in the primeval history itself. However, already in the *Genesis Apocryphon* one finds a tradition that focuses on the identity of Noah's wife: her father's name seems to have been included (VI, 7, a damaged text) and her own name is recorded as Amzara.

D. Noah in the New Testament

The NT refers to Noah as a shining example of righteousness (2 Pet 2:5) and faith (Heb 11:7). He is also mentioned in the list of Jesus' ancestors (Luke 3:36). A different adaptation of the OT flood narrative is found in one of Jesus' teachings (Matt 24:37-39// Luke 17:26-27). Here the coming of the Son of Man is compared with the flood "in the days of Noah" as an event that will occur unexpectedly and without warning.

2. One of the daughters of Zelophehad (Num 26:33; 27:1; 36:11) who, upon the death of their father, petitioned Moses for a share of the inheritance (Num 27:1). The LORD decided in their favor, and this judgment became a precedent that allowed daughters to inherit their father's property, if there were no sons (Num 27:7-9). *See* ZELOPHEHAD, DAUGHTERS OF.

Bibliography: Walter Brueggemann. *Genesis.* Interpretation (1982); Norman Cohn. *Noah's Flood: The Genesis Story in Western Thought* (1999).

ANDREAS SCHUELE

NOAH, APOCALYPSE OF. Several references in the Pseudepigrapha refer to a written document described as the Book of Noah (e.g., *Jub.* 10:13; 21:10; *T. Levi* 2:3 [Greek]). Scholars therefore speak of an Apocalypse or Book of Noah and suggest that such a "book" was connected with other texts concerning Noah. Noah's struggle against the power of evil spirits who bring sin into the world is an important aspect of these traditions. These materials usually include portions of *1 Enoch*, especially chaps. 106–107 (birth of Noah), and chaps. 6; 8–10 (sin of the Watchers in the time of Noah). *Jubilees* 10 contains a prayer of Noah to control the power of the spirits of evil, a theme connected with the story of the fall of the Watchers in *1 Enoch. Jubilees* 21 contains regulations prohibiting the shedding and consumption of blood, referring to the words of Enoch and Noah as a source. The discovery of the Dead Sea Scrolls has yielded more texts that may be related to a lost Book of Noah, especially 1Q19 and 4Q534. Traditions concerning the birth of Noah are also found in the GENESIS APOCRYPHON. These scattered references correspond only partially to the genre apocalypse (*see* APOCALYPTICISM), so it is preferable to speak of a Book of Noah. However, the actual existence of such a document remains disputed. *See* ENOCH, FIRST BOOK OF; JUBILEES, BOOK OF.

JOHN C. ENDRES, S.J.

NOAH, BOOK OF. *See* NOAH, APOCALYPSE OF.

NOAHIC COVENANT. A covenant established between God and Noah, as well as with Noah's descendants and all animals, following the flood (Gen 9:8-17). God promised never again to destroy the world by means of a flood and placed the rainbow in the clouds as a reminder of the covenant. Unlike most other covenants between God and humanity, the Noahic covenant did not impose any requirements on humans. *See* COVENANT, OT AND NT.

KEVIN A. WILSON

NOAHIDE LAWS [שֶׁבַע מִצְוֹות בְּנֵי נֹחַ **sheva' mitswoth bene noakh**]. The "Seven Commandments (of) the Children of Noah," also known as the "Seven Laws of Noah," are basic moral laws that the rabbis believed were binding on all humankind (*b. Sanh.* 58b). Maimonides, a 12th-cent. rabbi and philosopher, wrote in his commentary, the *Mishneh Torah*, that a non-Jew who keeps these laws is a "righteous Gentile" and will have a place in heaven (*Hilkhot Melakhim* 8.14). The seven laws include prohibitions on idolatry, blasphemy, murder, theft, sexual immorality, and eating living flesh, as well as exhortations for the establishment of courts of justice (compare Gen 9:4-6). *See* GENTILES; GODFEARER; NATIONS; ORAL LAW, ORAL TORAH.

MARIANNE BLICKENSTAFF

NO-AMON noh-am´uhn [נֹא אָמוֹן **no' 'amon**]. Hebrew name for the Egyptian city THEBES (NRSV). It means "city of (the god) AMON" (Nah 3:8).

NOB nob [נֹב **nov**]. DAVID flees from Saul to Nob, the city of priests, where he asks for and receives the bread of the Presence and Goliath's sword from Saul's priest AHIMELECH (1 Sam 21:1-9). These are important symbols of authority: holy bread and the sword of Israel's great enemy. When Saul discovers this from DOEG (1 Sam 21:7; 22:9), Saul orders the death of the priests. Saul's men refuse his order, but Doeg obeys. Saul, the king who refused to have his men kill all the Amalekites and their livestock, becomes responsible for the eradication of an entire priestly city with the exception of one single inhabitant: Abiathar. The result of Saul's rash behavior is that in addition to the holy bread and Goliath's sword, the priest Abiathar and the ephod reside with David, illustrating God's abandonment of Saul in favor of David. *See* SAUL, SON OF KISH.

Second Temple texts elaborate on why the priests at Nob died and who was to blame. Pseudo-Philo explains the slaughter by ascribing unrighteous behavior to the priests, who are like Eli's sons (*L.A.B.* 63:1; see 1 Sam 2:11-17). According to Josephus (*Ant.* 6.261) the death of the priests resulted from the sins of Eli's sons; Josephus, however, does not accuse the priests of questionable behavior (see 1 Sam 2:27-33). Pseudo-Philo makes Saul directly responsible for the execution of the priests. All of Israel is guilty because they did not object to Saul's rampage against hundreds, which stands in contradistinction with the people's objection to Saul ordering the death of one man, Jonathan (*L.A.B.* 63:2-3; see 1 Sam 14:45). The guilt of Saul and the Israelites is one reason why Saul and his forces fall to the Philistines. Josephus uses Saul and the story of the slaughter at Nob to show how power corrupts formerly righteous individuals (*Ant.* 6.262–68). In the NT the story functions as an example of interpreting Scripture. Jesus uses David eating the holy bread as precedent for breaking a law (Matt 12:3-4; Mark 2:25-26; Luke 6:3-4).

Nob is mentioned two other times in the OT. God will halt forces invading Judah at Nob outside Jerusalem (Isa 10:32). This may be Mount SCOPUS, approximately 1 mi. from Jerusalem. Also, Nob is a Benjaminite village outside Jerusalem reinhabited after the exile (Neh 11:31-35; *see* BENJAMIN, BENJAMINITES). Most scholars believe these Nobs are the same.

HEATHER R. MCMURRAY

NOBAH noh´buh [נֹבַח novakh]. Nobah is the leader of a group from the tribe of Manasseh who enters the region of Gilead, captures KENATH and its surrounding villages, and renames it for himself. This occurs in the narrative of the Manassite clans taking control of the region of Gilead from the Amorites (Num 32:39-42). In the period of the judges, the town is listed as being near Jogbehah, and these two towns mark the route that Gideon takes in order to catch the armies of Zebah and Zalmunna unaware at Karkor during the second battle between Gideon and the Midianites (Judg 8:11). *See* MANASSEH, MANASSITES.

C. MARK MCCORMICK

NOBLES, NOBILITY [אַדִּיר ʾaddir, חֹר khor, חֹרִים khorim, נָדִיב nadhiv, פַּרְתְּמִים partemim; δυνατός dynatos, μεγιστάν megistan]. The legal traditions of the Israelites, intended to govern the covenant community, make no provision for a nobility; rather, they tend toward egalitarianism (Exod 21:2-11; Deut 15:7-18; Lev 25). Nevertheless, that the prophets of the divided monarchy inveigh against the inappropriate and burdensome by-products of a class system is indicative of the emergence of nobles. While the OT text does not intend to chronicle that emergence, it does seem to offer some indicators of its existence. Creating and sustaining an army, as David did, even if only for periods of necessity (2 Sam 6:1; 8:1-14; 10:1-19), would seem to have had long-range economic implications for the nation, laying the groundwork for class distinction.

At least as early as the Davidic era development of a nobility to administer the monarchy is evident (1 Sam 8:15-18); growth of that ruling class multiplied in the Solomonic reign (1 Kgs 4:1-19, 27-28). The institution of the Solomonic chariotry on the one hand (1 Kgs 4:26), and a corvée to achieve his ambitious building program (1 Kgs 5:13-18) on the other, are further signals of a distinction between elitist and commoner. Two later narratives seem to point toward a continuance, if not an intensification, of such a system and its consequences. The narrative of the monarchical transition following Solomon's death and the posturing of Rehoboam and his entourage (1 Kgs 12) evidence the brashness of a younger nobility, insensitive to both the elder generation and the populace. Jezebel's arrangement for Ahab's seizure of Naboth's vineyard (1 Kgs 21) illustrates the exertion of force over a landowner by the elite—the kind of conduct that Amos so eloquently, but sharply, decries (Amos 5:10-13; 6:1-7; 8:4-8).

The demise of the monarchy, beginning with its division at the end of the Solomonic era, the fall of the Northern Kingdom, and the devastating collapse of the Southern Kingdom opened the way for the imposition of a series of administrative systems—Assyrian through Roman—on the region and people, which also brought a stratification of society. *See* KING, KINGSHIP; PROPHET, PROPHECY.

JOHN I. LAWLOR

NOD nod [נוֹד nodh]. After God marked him for the murder of ABEL, his brother, CAIN left the presence of Yahweh and lived in "the land of Nod, east of EDEN" (Gen 4:16). From a root meaning "to wander," the name Nod apparently symbolizes Cain's fate as a fugitive (Gen 4:12, 14).

JAMES R. DAVILA

NODAB noh´dab [נוֹדָב nodhav]. Together with JETUR and NAPHISH, this Hagrite tribe (*see* HAGAR; HAGRITE, HAGRITES) was fought by the Transjordanian Israelites in the Golan region (1 Chr 5:19). "Hagrites" was a designation of northern Arabia and its inhabitants current in the Persian period.

Bibliography: I. Eph'al. *The Ancient Arabs* (1982); E. A. Knauf. *Ismael* (1989).

ERNST AXEL KNAUF

NOGAH noh´guh [נֹגַהּ noghah]. One of David's sons (1 Chr 3:7; 14:6). Perhaps a dittographic mistake of NEPHEG since Nogah is missing from the list of David's sons in 2 Sam 5:15.

NOHAH noh´hah [נוֹחָה nokhah]. 1. A location in Benjamin, mentioned in the intertribal war (Judg 20:43). *See* BENJAMIN, BENJAMINITES.

2. The fourth of Benjamin's five sons according to 1 Chr 8:2; absent, however, from similar lists in Gen 46:21; Num 26:38-41; and 1 Chr 7:6.

NOMADS. *Nomads*, referred to as "Bedouin" (derived from Arabic badawiyin; "desert dwellers"), have a lifestyle and economy dependent on camels. By the end of the 2nd millennium BCE, nomads used domesticated dromedaries to travel deep into Near Eastern deserts in search of water and pasture for their livestock. Bedouin also used camels for long-distance trade and, as depicted on Assyrian reliefs, proved useful in warfare.

From antiquity until modern times, Bedouin have represented one adaptation to the arid environment; sedentary populations of villages and cities stood at the opposite end of the cultural spectrum. Certain traits characterize bedouin culture—e.g., pastoral activities, tents and temporary camps, seasonal migration, tribal organization. Their specialized economy enabled Bedouin to occupy the less hospitable regions of North Africa, the Levant (including the Sinai and the Negev), the Arabian Peninsula, and Mesopotamia. This ancient and distinctive lifestyle is disappearing.

Numerous OT passages reflect awareness of nomadic and bedouin groups, like the Amalekites. These texts refer to the bedouin occupation of desert regions, their pastoral economy and use of camels, and their hostile interaction with sedentary populations (e.g., Num 13:29; Judg 6:3, 5; 7:12; 1 Sam 30:1-2, 17; Isa 13:20; Jer 25:24; 49:28-29; Ezek 25:4-5). *See* CAMEL; PASTORAL NOMADS.

Bibliography: Ofer Bar-Yosef and Anatoly Khazanov, eds. *Pastoralism in the Levant: Archaeological Materials in Anthropological Perspective* (1992); Roger Cribb. *Nomads in Archaeology* (1991); Morris S. Seale. *The Desert Bible: Tribal Culture and Old Testament Interpretation* (1974).

GERALD L. MATTINGLY

NORTH. *See* ORIENTATION.

NORTH COUNTRY, THE [אֶרֶץ צָפוֹן ʾerets tsafon]. Ominous title used for regions north of ancient Israel, specifically SYRIA, northern Mesopotamia, and, by extension, Babylonia. Jeremiah also includes the variants "tribes of the north" (25:9) and "a people of the north" (46:24). The north country was broad enough to denote the land of the exile, from which Yahweh would redeem his people (Jer 3:12, 18; 16:15; 23:8; 31:8), even when returning from the north meant returning from all four directions (Zech 2:6 [Heb. 2:10]). Thus the north country may have a literal geographic denotation, referring to the regions north of ancient Israel, but also a literary symbolism, denoting faraway Babylonia (Petersen).

Topographical features of ancient Israel resulted in international highways running north and south because of the Mediterranean Sea to the west and the desert to the east and southeast. Hostile armies from western Asia of necessity descended into southern Syria-Palestine from the north as did enemies east and northeast of Israel (Babylonians and Assyrians, respectively). A few enemies during Israel's history came through the southwestern frontier (Egyptians or Philistines).

For Jeremiah, evil itself was imminent, about to break forth from the north against Judah (1:13-16). Jeremiah tells of Yahweh's plan to bring great destruction from the north against Judah (4–6). This destruction will be the result of a nation skilled with "the bow and the javelin" (6:22-23; 10:22; 25:9). Yet at the conclusion of the book of Jeremiah, another great and mighty nation will arise from the north country to bring destruction and vengeance—this time against Babylon itself (50:9, 41-42).

The specific identity of Jeremiah's foe from the north country is uncertain. A "Scythian hypothesis" was once popular, asserting that the SCYTHIANS, whom Herodotus reported invaded Syria-Palestine around 625 BCE, best fit the description (*Hist.* 1.104–6; McKane). This theory, however, has not stood the test of time (Holladay). Others have asserted that Jeremiah's "foe" bears a mythological flavor (Childs). No specific historical group can be positively identified with the northern foe, as is the nature of Israelite prophecy, although the Babylonians came to be so identified after 586 BCE. It is reasonable to assume that earlier, the foe from the north could be any Mesopotamian imperial power looming on the horizon, especially Assyria or Babylonia (Vanderhooft). *See* ASSYRIA AND BABYLONIA; PERSIA, HISTORY AND RELIGION OF.

Bibliography: Brevard S. Childs. "The Enemy from the North and the Chaos Tradition." *JBL* 78 (1959) 187–98; William L. Holladay. *Jeremiah 1: A Commentary on the Book of the Prophet Jeremiah, Chapters 1–25.* Hermeneia (1986); William McKane. *A Critical and Exegetical Commentary on Jeremiah, vol. 1.* ICC (1986); David L. Petersen. *Haggai and Zechariah 1–8: A Commentary.* OTL (1984); David S. Vanderhooft. *The Neo-Babylonian Empire and Babylon in the Latter Prophets* (1999).

BILL T. ARNOLD

NORTH GATE [שַׁעַר הַצָּפוֹן shaʿar hatsafon]. In Ezekiel's vision of abominations in the Temple, the Spirit lifts the prophet by a lock of hair and deposits him at a gate that faces north from the inner temple courts (Ezek 8:3), a gate referenced numerous other times (Ezek 8:14; 40:35; 44:4; 46:9; 47:2).

JAMES RILEY STRANGE

NORTH, ENEMY FROM THE. Oracles of judgment in Jer 4–10 announce the coming attack of a foe from the north who will wreak havoc on Israel and Judah. Earlier commentators identified the enemy as the Scythians. Recently, however, commentators have moved away from this theory and no consensus has emerged. In other prophetic texts the identity of the northern enemy seems clearer: Assyria (Jer 46:10, an oracle of judgment against Egypt); Babylon (Jer 25:8-14); or Persia (Isa 41:25; Jer 50:3, 9, 41-42, oracles against Babylon). *See* NORTH COUNTRY, THE.

MARK RONCACE

NORTHEASTER, THE [Εὐρακύλων Eurakylōn]. The stormy wind that struck Paul's ship on its way from Fair Havens to Phoenix and threatened to blow the ship to the African Syrtis (Acts 27:14). A twelve-point wind that rose from Thugga in Africa indicates that *euroaquilo* blew from roughly 30 degrees north of east. (The variant reading Euraklydōn [Εὐρακλύδων] would indicate an east-southeast wind.)

Bibliography: C. J. Hemer. "Euraquilo and Melita." *JTS* 26 (1975) 100–11.

KEN M. PENNER

NORTHERN ARMY [צְפוֹנִי tsefoni]. This term, occurring only in Joel 2:20, refers to a destructive swarm of locusts (Joel 2:25), a judgment that Yahweh promises to thrust into the remote desert and seas. It may also allude to an "enemy from the north" (e.g., Arameans, Assyrians, and Babylonians) as Yahweh's instrument of judgment, a theme common in other prophetic texts (e.g., Isa 14:31; Jer 1:13-15; 4:6; 6:1, 22; Ezek 38:6, 15; Zech 2:6 [Heb. 2:10]; compare Joel 2:11). Its etymology is linked to Zaphon, a sacred mountain in Ugaritic mythology (compare Isa 14:13; Ps 48:2 [Heb. 48:3]). *See* LOCUST; NORTH COUNTRY, THE; NORTH, ENEMY FROM THE; ZAPHON, MOUNT.

HYUN CHUL PAUL KIM

NORTHERN KINGDOM. *See* ISRAEL, HISTORY OF.

NOSE RING. *See* JEWELRY.

NOTHING, NOTHINGNESS [אַיִן ʾayin, הֶבֶל hevel, חִנָּם khinnam; οὐδείς oudeis]. *Nothingness* in English usage is an abstract noun denoting a state of absolute absence. In Hebrew, no one word corresponds exactly to the English *nothingness*; rather, the language uses several words of negation. The most common way to indicate nothing in Hebrew is ʾayin. For example, Isaiah describes God as the one who brings nations and princes to nothing (Isa 40:17, 23). Sometimes the enigmatic word hevel is taken to mean nothingness or something akin to nothingness. In Ecclesiastes, the writer proclaims that all is nothingness or VANITY (NRSV) (Eccl 1:2, 14; 2:17; 12:8) and that life itself is nothingness (Eccl 6:12; 9:9). The same word occurs in Ps 39:5-6, again with the meaning of "nothing," in verses synonymously paralleled with "breath" and "shadow." A word (khinnam) derived from the root meaning "grace" or "favor" can be employed to indicate nothing. It literally means "out of favor" but is translated as "for nothing" (2 Sam 24:24) or "without cause" (1 Sam 25:31). The Greek "nothing" or "nothingness" corresponds more closely to the English. In the NT, the word is used in a variety of contexts to indicate negation or absence. For example, Paul uses the word several times in 1 Corinthians. In chap. 7 he argues that both circumcision and uncircumcision are nothing (1 Cor 7:19), and in chap. 13 he argues that if he did not have love, he would be nothing (1 Cor 13:2). *See* ECCLESIASTES, BOOK OF.

JENNIFER L. KOOSED

NU [ν n, Ν N]. The twelfth letter of the Greek alphabet, based on the Phoenician *nun. *See* ALPHABET.

NUBIA. Nubia designates the territory along the Nile Valley in northern Sudan but does not include the territory of modern Ethiopia. Nubia, probably from the Middle Egyptian word for "gold" (nub), was the principal source of gold in the ancient world. The NRSV renders the region as either ETHIOPIA or Cush (e.g., Job 28:19).

RODNEY S. SADLER, JR.

NUMBERS, BOOK OF nuhmʹbuhrz [בְּמִדְבַּר bemidhbar; Ἀριθμοί Arithmoi]. The name "Numbers" translates Lat. *Numeri* and Gk. arithmoi, both of which correlate with the book's Talmudic name, khomesh happequdhim (חוּמֶשׁ הַפְּקֻדִים) "the 'fifth' of the census totals" (*m. Yoma* 7:1; *b. Menah.* 4:3; *b. Sotah* 36b). These names derive from the wilderness census records (Num 1–4; 26), which highlight the collective identity of the Israelites on their way to the promised land.

A. Structure of Numbers

Numbers 1:1–10:28 Establishing a Holy Community

1:1–2:25	Census and encampment
3:1–4:49	Levite and Kohathite priesthood established
5:1-31	Purity laws
6:1-21	Nazirites
7:1–8:26	Dedication of Levites and tabernacle
9:1-14	Passover at Sinai

9:15–10:28	Wilderness journey preparations

Numbers 11:1–20:28 In the Wilderness

11:1-35	Complaints and challenges to Moses' leadership
12:1-15	Aaron and Miriam jealous of Moses
13:1–14:45	Reconnaissance and conflict over land
15:1-41	Ritual requirements
16:1-50	Rebellion of Korah, Dothan, and Abiram
17:1-12	Aaron's staff blooms
18:1-32	Qualifications for priests and Levites
19:1-22	Red heifer and water for impurity
20:1-13	Waters of Meribah and Miriam's death
20:14-21	Passage through Edom denied
20:22-28	Aaron's death

Numbers 21:1–36:13 Conquest and Settlement of the Land

21:1-9	The bronze serpent
21:10-35	Conquest of Transjordan begins
22:1-21	Balaam encounters Balak
22:22-39	Balaam's oracles
25:1-17	Punishment for worship of Baal at Peor
26:1-65	Tribal census
27:1-11	Daughters of Zelophehad and inheritance legislation
27:12-23	Joshua appointed Moses' successor
28:1–29:40	Calendar of festivals and cultic activities
30:1-16	Regulation of vows
31:1-54	Attack on the Midianites
32:1-42	Israelite settlement in Gilead of Transjordan
33:1-49	Route from Egypt to Moab
33:50-56	Directions for conquest of Canaan
34:1-15	Borders of Canaan
34:16-29	Tribal leaders
35:1-8	Cities for the Levites
35:9-34	Cities of refuge and laws concerning murder
36:1-13	Revision to inheritance laws

B. The Contents of Numbers: Documentary Sources Interacting

Scholars remain divided regarding the order, date, existence, and importance of the sources imbedded in the Torah (*see* DOCUMENTARY HYPOTHESIS; SOURCE CRITICISM). The view to be presented here is that the formation of Numbers is significant, and that a source critical approach to reviewing its content is more helpful than outlining the book's final form.

In additions to sources J, E, and P, a possible third archive source from the Transjordan (T) may be identified in Num 21, in 22–24 (the Balaam pericope; *see* DEIR ʿALLA, TEXTS), and possibly in Num 32. JE authors incorporated selections of early poetry and transmitted the Balaam pericope (Num 22–24), composed of both poetry and prose narrative. Working with these earlier sources beginning in the 6th cent. BCE, the Priestly writers (henceforth "P," *see* P, PRIESTLY WRITERS) proceeded to expand the depiction of the WILDERNESS period, introduced legal and ritual materials, and presented their particular interpretation of the wilderness experience. Disagreement regarding the date of P continues, with certain scholars arguing for an earlier, preexilic date for P.

1. The non-Priestly materials in Numbers

It is possible to retrieve Numbers' non-Priestly record using source criticism. The JE material begins in Num 10:29–12:15. In Num 10:29-36, the Israelites encamped in southern Sinai, specifically in Hazeroth, near the Mountain of God (Num 11:35; *see* SINAI, MOUNT). This was after the momentous Sinai theophany (Exod 19–24; 32–34). MOSES then conferred with his Midianite father-in-law HOBAB, who joined the Israelites and guided them on their journey to the promised LAND. The people marched for three days, with the ARK OF THE COVENANT in the lead and the cloud of Yahweh hovering over them by day. The Song of the Ark, a poetic excerpt from an early epic source that calls upon Yahweh to disperse Israel's enemies and to bring back their forces safely, concludes chap. 10.

Numbers 11 (compare Exod 16–18) recounts challenges to Moses' leadership role. Facing grave discontent and active resistance—fueled by the hardships of the wilderness trek and the tasteless manna—Yahweh instructed Moses to alter the governance of the people. Yahweh then provided better food for the people. Yahweh alleviated Moses' leadership burden by conferring the Lord's spirit on seventy elders who were to assist Moses. In response to Joshua's concerns, Moses expressed confidence in his exclusive relationship to Yahweh, saying, in effect, that the conferring of Yahweh's spirit on others was a blessing and not a threat to him. Numbers 11 closes with the burial of those who were punished by Yahweh for their rebellion.

Numbers 12:1-15 further confirms Moses' exclusive intimacy with Yahweh by recounting how Moses' siblings, Aaron and Miriam, criticized Moses for marrying a Cushite woman (compare Exod 18:2, 6, 27). Yahweh summoned them to the tent of meeting, where he clearly defined Moses' unique charismatic status as a member of Yahweh's household, a human who beholds him face to face. As punishment, Miriam was afflicted by a pernicious skin ailment that is remitted because of Moses' entreaty (*see* CUSHITE WIFE, MOSES').

Whereas Num 10:29–12:15 presents uninterrupted JE material, P adapted the next JE section (the dispatch of spies into Canaan) in order to accommodate a divergent Priestly chronology of Israel's movements during the forty-year wilderness march. From JE in Num 32:8 we learn that the Israelites were in Kadesh when the spies were dispatched. In contrast, Num 13:3 states that they were dispatched from the Wilderness of PARAN, a P term for northern Sinai (Num 10:12). Numbers 13:26 states that the spies returned to "the wilderness of Paran, at Kadesh." However, Kadesh (Barnea) is not in Sinai or Paran, but in the Wilderness of Zin in the southern Negev (*see* ZIN, WILDERNESS OF).

Such fudging of boundaries highlights the differing traditions of JE and P. According to all sources, including the Deuteronomist (*see* D, DEUTERONOMIC, DEUTERONOMISTIC) the decree of forty years of wandering was punishment for the discouraging report of the spies, which had demoralized the people (Deut 1–3). Clearly, the spies were dispatched near the beginning of the wilderness period. If they were dispatched from Kadesh, in the Wilderness of Zin in the southern Negev, this means that the Israelites had already traversed Sinai within a year or so after the exodus (*see* NEGEV, NEGEV). The wilderness of their prolonged wanderings would not be the Wilderness of Sinai at all, but rather the desert east of Edom and southern Moab, reached by a circuitous route that took them first to the Gulf of Elath. This accords with the interpretation of the Deuteronomist (Deut 2:14; *see* KADESH, KADESH-BARNEA).

According to P, however, the Israelites spent most of the forty years in northern Sinai, and arrived in Kadesh only near the conclusion of this period. To superimpose their view of the wilderness period, P rewrote Num 13:1-3 (especially v. 3), to place the Israelites in Sinai when the spies were dispatched, not in Kadesh. In the same mode, P rewrote Num 13:26, so that the spies reported back to Moses in the Wilderness of Paran, P's reasons for retaining the Israelites in Sinai are not entirely clear. Perhaps the Priestly school sought to align its extensive ritual and cultic legislation with the Sinai theophany.

In Num 13:17*b*–21*a*, 22–24, 25–33 we have JE's version of the reconnaissance mission (v. 21*b*, P; v. 26, JE rewritten by P). The spies proceeded through the Negev to the Judean hill country, up to Hebron. (P inserted Num 13:21*b*, which correlates P's borders of the "promised land" to Num 34). JE resumes in Num 14:11-25, where v. 25 explains the necessity of proceeding from Kadesh to the Gulf of Elath. The Hebrew text of v. 25 says that the Amalekites and Canaanites inhabited the valley (**baʿemeq** בָּעֵמֶק), but v. 45 locates them in the mountains (**bahar** בָּהָר). Moreover, vv. 40-44 describe the difficulty of going into Judah through the hill country. Therefore, it might make more sense to read 14:25: "The Amalekites and the Canaanites inhabit the mountains (read: **bahar**); redirect your march into the wilderness tomorrow, on the way to the Sea of Reeds" (author's trans.). In the JE version, Caleb alone of the spies kept the faith in the face of the strength the Canaanites and their fortified towns (Num 13:17*b*-21*a*, 22-24, 31-33; 14:11-15). Admitting that the land was fruitful, the spies nevertheless doubted that the Israelites were capable of victory. Yahweh angrily struck out at the people, and Moses interceded to save them, but he could not reverse the decree. Entry into the promised land would be delayed until the faithless generation had perished in the wilderness. A valiant attempt was made to attack the Canaanites in the Negev hill country, but the Israelites were repulsed because Yahweh was not with them (Num 14:39-45).

JE braided with P begins again in Num 16, a report of a rebellion against Moses. Priestly authors rewrote Num 16:1-2, recasting what was a challenge to the authority of Moses on the part of several leading Reubenites. It may have been that these Reubenites balked at Moses' demand that they fight alongside the tribes settling west of the Jordan before settling east of the Jordan (compare Num 32). Priestly writers reframed the incident as a dispute within the Kohathite clan of Levi over the rights to the chief priesthood. The JE account continues in Num 16:12-15, 25-34. Moses appealed to the rebellious leaders Dathan and Abiram and their cohorts to desist. They persisted, at which point Moses beseeched Yahweh to destroy them. The earth opened its mouth and devoured the entire entourage. Brief mention of this rebellion along similar lines is provided by the Deuteronomist (Deut 11:6).

Although there are some tell-tale traces of JE in Num 20:1-13, the next substantial JE passage is a request for passage through Edomite territory addressed to the king of Edom (Num 20:14-21). At the time, the Israelites were in Kadesh (Num 20:16). Even after the Israelites promised to keep to the King's Highway and to pay for their food and water, their request was denied. This compelled them to proceed through the desert east of Edom and then to pursue a northward route. JE resumes in Num 21:4; the Israelites were proceeding along the Reed Sea route to circumvent Edom. Numbers 21:4–22:1 is a critical section in the JE historiography. The route of the Israelites, encircling Edom, is traced all the way to Nahal Zered at the ARNON on the Amorite border (Num 21:4, 12). The record of the march is interrupted to relate the episode of the copper serpent (Num 21:5-9).

There are compelling reasons to conclude that in the textual progression from v. 12 to v. 13 of Num 21, the wilderness generation passed away, although this milestone goes entirely unnoticed. The indications are inescapable, nonetheless: Num 21:12 places the Israelites at Nahal Zered, where they arrived in the thirty-ninth year (compare Deut 2:14). This was the last journey undertaken by the older generation. That Num 21:13 has the new generation, not the old one, proceeding to Arnon Gorge on the Moabite border with the Amorites (actually the border between southern and northern Moab) is evident from the fact that the successful military engagements with SIHON are certainly to be attributed to the new generation. The exodus generation was incapable and unworthy of such victories, hence the delay until that generation passed away. One would expect to find some reference to the change of generations in Num 21. Since the Priestly writers, for their own reasons, positioned the transition of generations just before the second census that is recorded in Num 26, it is possible that Priestly editors suppressed a JE record of this significant transition, one that had originally appeared in Num 21.

Numbers 21:14-20 contain two poetic passages, both cited as proof-texts that the Israelites had indeed arrived at the Arnon. The former is cited from an epic source "The Chronicle of the Wars of Yahweh" (see 1 Sam 18:17; 25:28), whereas the latter has become known as "The Song of the Well." When the narrative resumes, the Israelites requested right of passage, which was refused by Sihon. With no alternative access to the Jordan, the Israelites battled the Amorites and captured their entire territory from the Arnon to the Ammonite border at the JABBOK (Zerqa) River (Num 21:21-26). JE explains that at an earlier time, Heshbon had been conquered by Sihon from the Moabites, so the reader understands how it was that this northern Moabite town was Amorite territory. As if to verify this, the pattern of introducing early poetry as proof-texts continues in Num 21:27-30 with the so-called "Heshbon ballad." This ballad had originally celebrated the Israelite capture of northern Moab, but was reinterpreted to commemorate Sihon's victory over Moab (see §D). In Num 21:31-35 we read that the Israelites also invaded Bashan. Numbers 22:1 is a caption introducing the BALAAM pericope, which concludes at the end of Num 24. It informs us that the Israelites were encamped in the steppes of Moab. Narrative continuity in Numbers would not be interrupted if the Balaam pericope were to be removed (see §B2).

The remainder of JE in the book of Numbers is to be found in Num 25 and 32. Numbers 25:1-5 preserves the primary account of the BAAL-PEOR incident. That episode took place in Shittim (short for Abel-Ha-Shittim, compare Num 33:49). According to the JE chronology, the new generation went astray after Moabite women by joining them in pagan worship (compare Deut 4:3; Ps 106:28; Hos 9:10). P elaborated on the story (Num 25:6–26:18). Finally, Num 32 is a critical chapter in the presentation of JE's view of the period prior to crossing the JORDAN RIVER. The overall issue addressed by Num 32 is the legitimacy of the Israelite settlement in Gilead (*see* GILEAD, GILEADITES; TRANSJORDAN). So much interweaving has been performed by P, at times evoking Deuteronomistic language, that it is not possible to disentangle the sources as clearly as was possible in Num 13–14 and Num 16. This much can be said: Num 32:39-42 preserves an early record of Transjordanian settlement by the Machirite clan of the tribe of Manasseh, the only Israelite tribe to settle on both sides of the Jordan. Similarly, in Num 32:1 we read that the tribes of Reuben and Gad preferred to settle in the districts of Jazer and Gilead in Transjordan because of their suitability as pasture lands. Further JE material is imbedded in Num 32:6-9, 16-19. The two tribes agreed to fight alongside their brethren until the land west of the Jordan was conquered. To the extent that we are able to identify its primary stratum, Num 32 takes up where JE in Num 21:24-25 left off. There we were told that the Israelites occupied the towns of the Amorites and settled in them. Numbers 32:1, 39-42 provided more details on this settlement east of the Jordan, which became the important Israelite community of Gilead (*see* TRIBES, TERRITORIES OF).

Numbers as presented by JE adds nothing to the institutional component of Israelite religion as set forth in Exodus (e.g., the revelation of the Ten Commandments, and the Book of the Covenant in Exod 21–23). All laws, commandments, religious rites, or festival celebrations in Numbers are P. The constitutive themes of JE focused on the leadership of the prophet, Moses, who faced the daunting task of bringing the virtually unmanageable and often rebellious Israelites to the land. Thus, JE carries forward the agenda of Exod 32–34. Similarly, Num 11–12 echoes Exod 18 by recording a change in governance where Moses was to be assisted by a group of elders, although his relationship to Yahweh is unique. Both JE and the subsource T (= Transjordanist) attach special importance to victory over the Amorites by the new generation, and to encounters with the interior peoples (e.g., Edomites and Moabites). In this way, JE presages the wars of conquest found in Judges and Samuel.

2. The Balaam pericope (Num 22:2–24:25)

Numbers 22:1 registers the arrival of the Israelites at the Plains of Moab. Numbers 25:1 has the Israelites encamped in the same area, at Shittim. The prose narrative of the Balaam PERICOPE would be difficult to fit into the pattern of JE or P. The sub-source T (= Transjordan) would be the logical derivation of the poetic orations of Balaam. Study of the Balaam pericope has been advanced in recent decades by the discovery of plaster inscriptions from Tell Deir ʿAlla, which mention a seer named blʿm brbʿr (*see* DEIR ʿALLA, TEXTS).

Four principal orations are preserved in Numbers, all of which exhibit distinctive vocabulary and composition, making it difficult to fathom their precise meaning. The first oration relates how King BALAK summoned Balaam from Aram to pronounce execrations over the Israelites in the hope of defeating them. Overawed by the extent of the Israelite encampment, Balaam protests his incapacity to curse this divinely blessed people (Num 23:7-10).

In the second poem (Num 23:18-24), Balaam addresses Balak, explaining to him that El will not rescind Balaam's mission to bless Israel whose God, Yahweh, fights at their side. Both the third and fourth poetic orations register Balaam as one privy to knowledge revealed by El, Shadday, and Elyon, who appear to him in visions. Balaam predicts Israelite victories over the Amalekite king Agag (1 Sam 15). Finally, in the fourth poem (Num 24:15-19), Balaam predicts that David will conquer Moab and Edom. Appended to the four, principal orations are three brief orations referring to other nations (Num 24:20-24). Balaam predicts the demise of Amalek and foresees the Assyrian conquest of the Kenites, most likely a misnomer for the Edomites, who dwell in "the rock," an allusion to Petra (compare Jer 49:16-19). The third oration is highly cryptic, apparently predicting an invasion of Cis-Euphrates by a fleet from Cyprus.

The appellations given to divine powers in the Balaam orations raise a major interpretive issue from the outset. In the above review of the Balaam orations, El, Shadday, and Elyon have been taken as proper names of deities of the West Semitic pantheon, not as epithets of Yahweh, who is also mentioned by name as Israel's national God. Thus, Num 23:8 is taken to refer to both Yahweh and El. Viewed in this way, the Balaam orations speak for an early stage in Israelite religion when, as we read of the patriachs, El was worshiped alongside Yahweh, before the two were synthesized (*see* GOD, NAMES OF).

Intervening between the ongoing negotiations is the tale of the jinni (Num 22:22-35), a satirical poke at the clairvoyance attributed to diviners. We picture a beast of burden seeing the angel of Yahweh blocking the path at the same time that a famous seer cannot see it. This tale may mark the beginning of Balaam's denigration in biblical literature. From this point on, Balaam constructs altars, offers sacrifices, and employs an entire repertoire of cultic and magical techniques in attempts to attract a communication from Yahweh/Elohim that would enable him to curse Israel. In every case, he receives another dramatic blessing instead.

3. The Priestly content of Numbers

Numbers 1:1–10:28 is composed entirely of Priestly writings, and introduces the principal agenda of P—the constitution of Israelite society during the long march through the wilderness, and the operation of the cult of Yahweh centered around the portable TABERNACLE sanctuary. First the Israelites are organized according to tribes, mustered, and counted in a CENSUS (Num 1). Then they are organized into encampments according to units called **deghel** (דֶּגֶל; Num 2:3, 10, 18, 25; 10:14, 18, 22, 25), with the tabernacle and its cultic personnel stationed at the center. This entire arrangement complements the Priestly content of Exod 24:12–31:18; 35–40, and the book of Leviticus regarding the inauguration of the sacrificial cult and the installation of the priesthood subsequent to the exodus. Numbers 3–4 complete this process by mustering the Levites as cultic servitors, thereby highlighting their special status, one not previously institutionalized in the Priestly sections of Exodus or Leviticus. They set forth the specific assignments of the several Levitical clans. The Kohathite clan, including Aaron and his descendants, was granted a superior position among the other Levites (*see* KOHATH, KOHATHITE). This is indicated by their assigned task, which was to care for the inner sanctum of the tabernacle, the Holy of Holies, and its vessels; to bear them during transport; and to set them up and dismantle them when required.

In Numbers 5–6 a pattern is initiated by which two agendas are regularly interspersed. The chronicling of the wilderness experience is repeatedly interrupted by the introduction of ritual and legal materials that digress from the chain of events. Such shifts in content continue throughout the book. In Num 5–6 we read of procedures intended to preserve the purity of the people and the encampment during the march. Numbers 5:1-4 requires that impure persons of various types be removed from the encampment (see Lev 13–14). Numbers 5:5-10 is an addendum to the legislation of Lev 5 on the matter of sacrilege. Numbers 5:11-31 prescribes the TRIAL BY ORDEAL administered to a married woman suspected of adultery (see Lev 18; 20). The WATER OF BITTERNESS is administered to the wife in question. If found guilty, a miscarriage would result, and the woman would be a curse in the midst of her people. However, if the ordeal exonerated her, the pregnancy would continue normally.

Most of Num 6 is taken up by the law of the Nazirite. A person would characteristically vow to sanctify himself (or herself) through self-denial for a specified period of time. During the prescribed period, contact with the body of a dead person must be avoided, no wine or intoxicating product of the vine may be imbibed, and the Nazirite may not cut his hair with a razor. In effect, Num 6:1-21 brings together practices of private religion in ancient Israel (see Judg 13–16; 1 Sam 1–2; Amos 2:11-12; compare Deut 33:16; *see* NAZIR, NAZIRITE).

Numbers 6:22-27 preserves the text of the poetic Priestly benediction pronounced by Aaron, the chief priest, and precedes the consecration of the tabernacle altar (Num 7). The chieftains of the twelve tribes contributed the wagons required for the transport of the tabernacle and its accoutrements (Num 7:1-11). Then, over a period of twelve days, the chieftains of each of the twelve tribes presented identical offerings, consisting of gold and silver vessels filled with incense or semolina flour mixed with oil, and each chieftain contributed sacrificial animals (see §C).

Numbers 8 records the initial kindling of the tabernacle menorah (compare Exod 25:31-40) and then proceeds to describe the dedication of the Levites to tabernacle service, a subject first introduced in

Num 3–4. This record is clearly modeled after the consecration of the priests preserved in Lev 8–9. Like the priests, the Levites underwent purification, and sacrifices were offered on this occasion. The service of the Levites, who were dedicated but unconsecrated, constituted a redemption payment owed to Yahweh for having spared the firstborn of the Israelites in Egypt (*see* PRIESTS AND LEVITES). Numbers 9:1-14 digresses by instructing the Israelites to perform the paschal sacrifice at its prescribed time, on the fourteenth day of the first month (Exod 12–13; Lev 23). It adds a new provision to apply in cases where Israelites were distant from the sanctuary or ritually impure on the day the paschal sacrifice was to be performed. In response to a complaint by Israelites so affected, Yahweh instructed Moses that in such circumstances the paschal sacrifice must be offered in the second month on the fourteenth of the month. P returns to the record of the wilderness journey (Num 9:15–10:28) and how the portable tabernacle qualified as sacred space, a status that usually accrued to stationary sites. The cloud of Yahweh, which hovered over the tabernacle and enveloped it when the tabernacle was encamped (compare in JE; Num 10:34), would rise above it when the word came from Yahweh for the camp to resume the march. Effectively, the cloud not only guided the tabernacle and the Israelites on the march, but also sanctified the space beneath it.

Numbers 10:11-28 records the resumption of the march, and the Israelites journeyed from southern Sinai to the Wilderness of Paran (P's term for northern Sinai), where the cloud came to rest (compare JE's Num 10:33) and the spies were dispatched from the Wilderness of Paran. P then resumes in Num 13–14. Here JOSHUA joins Caleb in maintaining loyalty to the conquest plan (*see* CALEB, CALEBITES). In P, Caleb is the chieftain of Judah, as we would expect, and Joshua is chief of the tribe of Ephraim, the principal northern tribe (Num 13:6, 8, respectively). In fact, P identifies all of the spies as chieftains of the twelve tribes of Israel. In Num 14 (1-7*a*, 10, 26-38), P adds yet another episode of rebellion that serves to amplify the JE version. The entire community expressed the desire to return to Egypt, whereupon Joshua and Caleb went into public mourning, insisting that the protective deity of the Canaanites had abandoned them and that an Israelite conquest of the land was possible with the help of Yahweh. In a Priestly version of the divine decree delaying entry into the land, P elaborates on the consequences of divine wrath, whereby the chieftains acting as spies—with the exception of Joshua and Caleb—were annihilated in a plague (Num 14:26-39).

Numbers 15 again interrupts the sequence of events to prescribe ritual requirements, most of which appear to be supplemental to the legislation of Leviticus. Its contents may be outlined as follows: burnt offerings and those of the **zevakh** type (זֶבַח, "slaughter for sacrifice") must be regularly accompanied by grain offerings and libations (compare Lev 1; 6–7). This is followed by two cultic enactments: Israelites must remit a levied donation in order to desacralize all baked goods, and adds to the provisions of Lev 4 regarding inadvertent sins of the community by requiring that sin offerings be accompanied by grain offerings and libations, a ritual pattern that became standard in the public cult (*see* SACRIFICES AND OFFERINGS).

Numbers 16–17, in their composite, recount the rebellion of Korah, Dathan, and Abiram. Numbers 16 has been recast by P, whereas Num 17 consists entirely of a Priestly elaboration of the episode. It was P that introduced Korah, the Kohathite-Levite, and Moses' first cousin, into the act, thereby changing the entire character of the insurrection (*see* KORAH, KORAHITES). The Reubenites and their grievance, whatever it was, are lost in the shuffle, as the issue becomes the legitimacy of the Aaronide priesthood, with Korah and his faction challenging the exclusion of their claim. The fate of the insurgents also changes: according to JE they descended into Sheol alive, but according to P they perished in a conflagration (Num 16:35). Numbers 17:1-5 describes the aftermath of the rebellion and the annihilation of Korah's faction. In the continuation of P (Num 17:6-15) the people blamed Moses and Aaron for the death of Korah and his faction, which enraged Yahweh, who threatened to annihilate the entire people by means of a plague. Finally, Num 17:16-28 records yet another test of Aaron's legitimacy.

Numbers 18–19 once again address matters of cult and purity. Numbers 18 is a summary code specifying the perquisites of the priests and Levites pursuant to their respective assigned tasks in connection with the Tent of Meeting (compare Num 3–4, and 8). Briefly stated, the Levites were to receive a tithe in place of a territory of their own. For their part, the priests were to receive a levied donation from all sacred offerings, all offerings of first fruits, all condemned property, all firstborn of flock and herd, and the redemption payments of the firstborn Israelite males. The Levites were obligated to pay a tithe of their own to the priests, a tenth of what they had received. Numbers 19 prescribes procedures for purification from corpse contamination (*see* CLEAN AND UNCLEAN; WATER FOR IMPURITY).

Numbers 20 returns to the events of the march. It begins by recording the death of Moses' sister, Miriam, in Kadesh. There are further complaints about the lack of water. Yahweh reiterated his decree that none of the faithless generation would live to see the promised land (Num 20:12-13). When P resumes in Num 20:22-28, we read of Aaron's death at Hor.

The status of Num 21:1-3 remains unclear. This brief passage reports an ultimately successful Israelite penetration into the Negev involving a battle with the Canaanite king of Arad at Hormah. It appears to be an alternative to Num 14:44-45, which had reported an Israelite defeat under the same circumstances. In Num 21:1-3 the people recover from an initial defeat, after they vowed to devote the conquered Canaanite towns to Yahweh. Perhaps Priestly writers, intending to downplay the drama of Israelite victories in Transjordan, adapted a Deuteronomistic record of a successful Israelite penetration into southern Canaan. This same outcome is intimated in Num 33:40. P's negative attitude toward the Transjordanian Israelites may have led to the suppression of the passing of the wilderness generation, which we would have expected in Num 21:12-13. P resumes in Num 25:6-15, introducing the Midianites into the JE account of Israel following Moabite practices (Num 25:1-5). This incident triggers the war against the Midianites that is reported in Num 31.

Numbers 26–31 consists entirely of Priestly materials: legislation pertaining to P's cultic and legal agenda and reports of further events along the wilderness march. Numbers 27:1-11 presents an exceptional piece of legislation affecting inheritance, whereby the land of an Israelite who died without leaving a male heir would go to his daughter(s), not to his brothers (*see* ZELOPHEHAD, DAUGHTERS OF). The legislation of Num 27:1-11 is amended, however, in Num 36, where conditions are placed on the daughter's rights as an heir, which effectively undid the earlier provisions. A daughter qualifying as an heir must marry within the same tribe to prevent the land in question from being lost to the ancestral tribe. The hidden agenda in this sequence of laws is the claim of the tribe of Manasseh to territory west of the Jordan, it being the only tribe to inhabit both sides of the river. In this light, Num 27:1-11 and Num 36 bear the earmarks of emergency legislation occasioned by disputes over the allocation of tribal territories in the promised land. For the rest, Num 27:12-23 records the announcement of Moses' imminent death (with reports of his actual death being preserved in Deut 32:43-51; 34). Leadership of the people was transferred from Moses to Joshua. Numbers 28–29 present the calendar of the public cult, and as such represent a supplement to Lev 23, reflecting later Priestly enactments and including rites not prescribed in the earlier calendar (compare also Exod 29:38-46). It continues with additional, composite sacrifices on the SABBATH, and proceeds to ordain sacrifices for the NEW MOON, when a sin offering was to be added (Num 28:1-15). The CALENDAR year begins in the spring. The succession of annual festivals and sacred occasions proceeds with the prescribed offerings for the pilgrimage festival of unleavened bread (*see* FEASTS AND FASTS; PASSOVER AND FEAST OF UNLEAVENED BREAD).

Numbers 29 is devoted entirely to celebrations during the seventh month. The cultic calendar is followed in Num 30 by regulations regarding the votive system of ancient Israel, an aspect of private religion already encountered in Num 6, the Nazirite law. The most salient feature of the present legislation is a restriction placed on girls and women who pronounced vows. The VOW of an unmarried daughter or a married woman is binding only if her father or husband does not disavow her pronouncement. If a father or husband objected, the vow lost its legal force. A husband could annul a vow regardless of whether or not it was made before or after marriage.

Numbers 31 returns to events in the wilderness and builds on Num 25:17. Moses was ordered to avenge the Israelites by attacking the Midianites, who, according to P, were party to the unfortunate episode. Numbers 31 orders the recruitment of a fighting force, who, with the blessing of Eleazar, the chief priest, killed the kings of Midian and Balaam, Midianite males, and subsequently all females who had carnal knowledge of a man, thereby punishing the Midianites for the role of their women in having lured Israelites to pagan worship.

Numbers 32, the last text in Numbers to contain JE material, includes P's elaboration of the terms of the agreement between Moses and the two-and-one-half tribes, Reuben, Gad, and half of Manasseh. P spells out in legalistic fashion the consequences of compliance, on the one hand, and breach, on the other. In this transaction, the authority of Moses to modify the settlement process comes to the fore.

From Num 33 to the end of the book, P presents a variety of records and directives. Numbers 33:1-49 traces the route taken by the Israelites from Egypt to the Steppes of Moab. The route is problematic in two respects. Some of the many toponyms remain unidentified, and what is more significant, Num 33:1-49 projects a route that is different from that of both JE and P, and different even from the route indicated by the Deuteronomist. The overall route can be divided into two parts: 1) from Goshen in northeastern Egypt to Kadesh; and 2) from Kadesh to the Steppes of Moab. As regards the former part, the Israelites arrived at Kadesh only after first reaching Ezion-geber-eilat from southern Sinai via Jotbath. It is with respect to the second part of the route that more consequential divergences emerge. According to both JE and P the Israelites, after leaving Kadesh, circumvented Edom and Moab to the east and make their way northward to Amorite territory (north Moab). According to Num 33:1-49, they proceeded eastward into Transjordan via Punon in Edom, and then northward via Dibon-Gad, north of the Arnon, to the Steppes of Moab. The Deuteronomist's perception of the route is not entirely clear. On the one hand, Deut 2:1 speaks of an encirclement of Seir that took a long time, but on the other hand, Deut 2:4 reports that the Israelites passed through Edomite territory. It is possible that the route projected in Num 33 resulted from a Priestly effort to modify the JE route to accommodate the peaceful policy of the Deuteronomist toward Edom/Seir. Numbers 33:55-56 concludes with an admonition to Moses to destroy all pagan cult sites when they dispossess the Canaanites (*see* EXODUS, ROUTE OF).

After charting the itinerary of the forty-year march, Num 34 provides a delimitation of the borders of Canaan (Num 34:1-15) and mandates the procedure for the ALLOTMENT OF LAND to the tribes of Israel (Num 34:16-29). In effect, Canaan would have included most if not all of Phoenicia and Syria, the area known as Aram-Damascus (2 Sam 8:5-6; see §D3). Numbers 34:13-15 specifies that the land was to be apportioned to nine-and-one-half tribes, thereby excluding the tribes of Reuben, Gad, and half of the tribe of Manasseh, who had received their territories east of the Jordan. This formulation demonstrates cognizance of the contents of Num 32.

It was important for the Priestly writers to establish canons of criminal law affecting homicide to take effect once the Israelites had settled in the promised land. This was in line with their overall program, by which the Israelites were to bring their revealed way of life with them. Numbers 35 goes beyond other Torah codes of law, such as the Book of the Covenant (Exod 21–23), or Deuteronomy (19:1-13; compare 4:41-43), in defining more specifically the distinctions between intentional homicide—which is to say, murder—and unintentional homicide, something akin to manslaughter. A network of towns of asylum, essentially legislated in Deut 19, was placed under the management of the Levites and located in six of the forty-eight Levitical towns (Num 35:21; *see* AVENGER OF BLOOD; CITY OF REFUGE). The chapter ends with rules of testimony to apply in capital cases (Num 35:30-34).

C. The Literary Character of Numbers

Taken as a whole, Numbers comprises Hebrew poetry; narrative prose, mostly in the form of historiography; and Priestly ritual-legal texts and records that are formulaic or formalistic in structure.

1. Poetry

Except for the Priestly benediction (Num 6:22-27), which is properly to be regarded as poetic, all other poetic texts are found in non-Priestly sections of Numbers. A version of this Priestly benediction inscribed on silver amulets was found during archaeological excavations in the environs of Jerusalem at Ketef Hinnom (ca. 7th–6th cent. BCE). Its discovery has advanced our understanding of the biblical blessing.

Turning to the non-Priestly materials in Numbers, we find in Num 10:35-36 "The Song of The Ark" (compare Ps 68:2), derived from the epic tradition in which the ark was carried into battle. Some regard Num 12:6-8 as a statement on the unique relationship of Moses to Yahweh either in poetic form or as an example of heightened prose. In Num 21, poetic passages are intermittently cited from then-known epic collections. These include "The Record of the Wars of Yahweh" (Num 21:14-15) and a citation from an unnamed source, "The Song of the Well" (Num 21:17-18). Bards (composers of balanced verse) contributed the Heshbon ballad (Num 21:27-30), ostensibly celebrating an Amorite victory over the Moabites, but which may have originally commemorated an Israelite conquest of North Moab. Such citations from epic poetry functioned as proof-texts; they authenticated the narrative record. Like the more expansive Balaam orations, they represent beautiful examples of early Hebrew poetry, employing distinctive diction and syntax (*see* POETRY, HEBREW). The Balaam pericope (Num 22:2–24:25) preserves four poetic orations (see §B2).

2. Narrative historiography

The narrative styles of JE and the Balaam pericope differ in certain respects from that of the Priestly historiographers. Priestly writers, even when they are telling a story or recording an event, employ distinctly Priestly locutions and formulas, which lend to such accounts a distinctly cultic tone. At times, they introduce ritual legislation in a narrative manner. As an example, Num 15:32-36 tells about an Israelite who was apprehended gathering wood on the Sabbath. There was no instruction as to his punishment, but Moses received an ad hoc communication from Yahweh mandating the death penalty for such offenders. Thereupon, a statement of law ensued. Similarly, Num 9:1-14 relates that some Israelites complained about being unable to perform the paschal sacrifice at its ordained time because they were impure. Thereupon a new law was prescribed whereby Israelites in such circumstances or too distant from the sanctuary could offer the sacrifice in the second month on the same day. In this way, narrative reinforced law and ritual by providing background and rationale. A salient example of this pattern is found in Num 27, the incident of the daughters of Zelophehad, where a narrative introduces a change in the laws of inheritance.

There are distinctive stylistic features in the non-Priestly narratives. The inverted tenses are employed regularly, but are interspersed with circumstantial clauses and other syntactic variations that add interest. Dialogue is a frequent literary device for introducing speech into narrative, as is direct address. There are also tales, like that of the donkey (Num 22), the episode of the bronze serpent (Num 21), and the incident of Eldad and Medad (Num 11). Whereas Priestly writers attached great importance to specific dates and statistics, emphasizing obedience to divine command as mediated through Moses, JE and other historiographers tend to be more rhetorically descriptive in characterizing events and in rationalizing the ups and downs of the wilderness experience.

Thus, in recounting the episode of the spies (Num 13–14), JE details Moses' charge to the spies realistically. There is extensive dialogue among Moses, the spies, and the people, as well as between Yahweh and Moses. For their part, the Priestly writers are data centered; they name the spies, who were all tribal chieftains, and tell us how many days the trip lasted. They emphasize the theme of divine wrath and add even more poignancy to the reaction of the spies. Both JE and P indulge in prayerful language, as for example in Num 12:11-13 (JE), where Aaron first beseeches Moses, and then Moses intercedes with God. P preserves any number of similar entreaties by Moses to Yahweh, as in Num 16:22, where he entreats the deity to spare the community at the time of Korah's rebellion, or in Num 27:15, where he expresses concern over the selection of his successor. Priestly writers also employed prosaic chiasm, as, for instance, in Num 14:2: "If only we had died in the Land of Egypt; in this wilderness—if only we had died!" (compare Num 30:15). Priestly writers were tuned in to prophecy and wisdom (Num 17:23; compare Job 14:9; Ps 103:15; Isa 18:5; 40:6-8).

3. Formulaic and formalistic texts (Priestly)

All ritual and legal materials in Numbers are of Priestly provenance, unless one regards the new administrative setup ordained in Num 11:16-29, namely, the selection of seventy elders to assist Moses, as legal in character. In the area of both law and ritual, Numbers preserves important examples of casuistic formulation, a syntax that sets forth a condition or circumstance. In Priestly law, the subject usually precedes the verb. Thus: "A man, if/when he dies" (Num 27:8*b*).

The book of Numbers also preserves rare examples of temple records, variously adapted to narrative style. Numbers 7 shows the least adaptation and, for the most part, simply lists the cultic offerings of the tribal chieftains at the dedication of the wilderness tabernacle. It reflects an originally two-dimensional record, wherein standard items and quantities are tabulated in columns. In this class one would also include the census lists (Num 1–4; 26), the calendar of public festivals (Num 28–29), the rules for disposing of the spoils of war (Num 31), the route of the wilderness march (Num 33), and the map of Canaan (Num 34).

D. The Contexts of Numbers

Perhaps the greatest challenges facing biblical scholarship are to identify the context of specific biblical texts and of biblical books as a whole; to be able to date them at least approximately; and to reveal for whom they speak, and the contexts of their authors and compilers (*see* FORM CRITICISM, OT). The search for context directs us to a realistic interpretation of Numbers by talking about it in historical, social, and political terms. Inevitably, the investigation of context will yield conclusions that are less than specific. The first step has been taken by differentiating, in the survey of the contents of Numbers, between non-Priestly and Priestly sources.

1. Non-Priestly materials in context

As a whole, the authors of JE in Numbers pursued a retrojective agenda; they "refracted" actual events of the settlement period and the early monarchy—mainly wars—into the wilderness period, so as to produce a pre-history of Israel. The message of the JE historiography is that the historic enemies of Israel in Canaan and in neighboring countries had acted aggressively toward the Israelites even before they entered the land, while they were still in the wilderness. Their hostility was not, therefore, engendered by the Israelite conquest; they had always been hostile. This notion works to justify the Israelite conquest and settlement of Canaan and its domination of the interior regions, which is the hidden agenda of the JE historiographers. The conquest of Transjordan was easily justified: the Israelites seized it from other conquerors, the Amorites (Num 21; *see* ISRAEL, HISTORY OF).

Numbers provides historical indicators that direct us to certain periods and to specific historical situations. JE in Numbers carries the record forward from Exodus, where we read of a battle with the Amalekites (Exod 17; compare Deut 24–25). This correlates with the accounts of battles led by Saul and David with the Amalekites of the Negev (e.g., 1 Sam 15; 2 Sam 1). There we read that Amalekite settlements reached all the way to Shur at the approaches of Egypt (1 Sam 15:7), which explains why the first battle was with them (*see* AMALEK, AMALEKITES).

The Kadesh traditions of Num 13–14 recast the role of that southern district so as to make of Kadesh an advanced Israelite base from which to launch penetrations into southern Canaan. In reality, excavations at Kadesh have uncovered a network of fortifications aimed at preventing attacks from Sinai to the south. These fortifications were designed to keep hostile forces out, not facilitate the entry of foreign invaders. Such fortifications were first constructed in the 10th cent. BCE, perhaps during the reign of Solomon, and later activity can be dated to the period of Josiah in the late 7th cent.

No other example of refraction is provided by the brief gloss referring to Hebron (Num 13:22), where the founding of that Judean town is dated seven years before the founding of Tanis in Egypt, a town actually founded in the later Saitic period, which suggests that the author must have known of its existence at a later time, not in the Late Bronze Age. In fact, recent excavations in Hebron indicate that no walled town existed there during the period prior to the 10th cent. BCE (*see* HEBRON, HEBRONITES). The biblical author observed above-ground remains and reasoned that the town had stood on the site for many centuries, so much for the Canaanite inhabitants of the land.

In a similar fashion, JE reports on the interior neighbors of the Israelites. The mission to Edom (Num 20:14-21) reveals a telling indicator as to when it was composed. Historically, Edomite expansion westward began in the 8th cent. BCE, following the death of the Judean king Jotham (2 Kgs 16:5-6). An inscription from Arad, Level VIII, dated to the 8th cent. BCE, speaks of hostile Edomites (Aharoni). This period is resonated in Amos 1:11-12, where Edom is characterized as a treacherous kinsman. Both Num 20 and Amos 1 say of the Edomite king that he threatened Israel with a sword (or "with war"). The excavations at Qitmit indicate that Edomite expansion continued to the mid- to late 7th cent., but the Edomites would not have constituted a threat to Judah after the Assyrian invasions of the late 8th cent. (Beit-Arieh). It is also possible that an account depicting hostile Edomites may have been composed at the time of the Babylonian invasions (late 7th–6th cent. BCE).

JE in Numbers presents an ethnography of historical enemies; therefore, it is curious to find friendly Midianites (Num 10:29-32). Taking a cue from Exod 18, where Moses' "Midianite" father-in-law JETHRO offered him friendly counsel, JE in Numbers proceeds to tell of that same father-in-law (Hobab) who accompanied the Israelites on their route to Canaan. However, we never encounter friendly Midianites in the historical books of the OT, but read only of major battles with them during the settlement and pre-monarchic periods (Judg 6–8). Given noticeable fluctuations in ethnographic nomenclature, it has been suggested that Moses' in-laws were disguised Kenites, not actual Midianites (see Judg 4–5). In fact, it is entirely possible that in Num 31 the Priestly writers invented a war with the Midianites because they had no ready tradition to serve as background for the historical battles with the Midianites (*see* MIDIAN, MIDIANITES).

As for the Ammonites, we have only the statement that the Israelites avoided the Ammonites because their border was well fortified (Num 21:24), and in Deut 2:19, 37 we even read that Yahweh prohibited attacking the Ammonites. But then again, the Deuteronomist also prohibits war with Seir/Edom and Moab, whereas JE in Numbers has the Israelites avoiding such wars by circumventing Edom and engaging the Moabites in a hostile, but nonmilitary encounter. The JE account of the sin of Baal-peor (Num 25:1-5) is also part of the picture, since Moabite women were the ones who lured the Israelites to pagan worship. The Israelite conquest and settlement of Transjordan come to the fore in Num 21:4-35. Leaving aside the Ammonites, this adventure involved AMORITES and Moabites (*see* MOAB, MOABITES). There is considerable uncertainty about the identity of the Amorites in historic terms. It has been suggested that immigrant rulers from North Syria established ephemeral kingdoms in Transjordan after the fall of of Amurru, and that they were called Amorites by virtue of their places of origin—not because they were ethnic Amorites. These were the Amorites of whom Amos spoke (Amos 2:9-10). It is unclear, however, why the historiographers of Numbers introduced Amorites as the enemy. Perhaps this choice reflects an effort to justify the Israelite conquest and settlement of Gilead by insisting that this area no longer belonged to the indigenous Moabites at the time of the Israelite advance (compare Judg 11).

JE traces a northward route from the area of the Gulf of Eilat through eastern Transjordan, skirting Edom and Moab, by which is meant Moab south of the Arnon. The Balaam pericope establishes the fact of Moabite hostility, but actual war was avoided. There is no indication that claims to Moab south of the Arnon were in dispute according to Num 21. However, if the Israelites were to reach the Jordan they could not avoid war with the forces of North Moab, identified by Num 21 and some other biblical traditions as Amorites, whose king was Sihon. The Israelites did battle with them, conquering central Transjordan and the Bashan to the north. This brought them to the Steppes of Moab, just east of the Jordan.

It is significant that in contrast to JE, the Heshbon ballad (Num 21:27-30) projects a north–south route in Transjordan, from Heshbon, the northernmost point, down to Dibon and Medebah. In historical perspective, this is the more likely route of an invading army. The unusual south–north direction espoused by JE fits in with the ongoing saga of the forty-year trek from Egypt to Canaan. The Heshbon ballad was recycled, so to speak, to endorse the Israelite claim to North Moab, which includes Gilead, by making it sound like the celebration of an Amorite victory over Moab. In fact, there is only one explicit reference to the conquest of Moab by the Amorites in the Heshbon ballad, in Num 21:29: "He has made his sons fugitives, and his daughters captives, to an Amorite king, Sihon." Most likely, the last words are a gloss. Heshbon may have been known at one time as Sihon's capital, but the invaders of Moab who took sons and daughters captive were the Israelites, Omri himself and/or one of his heirs. In historical terms, the Heshbon ballad reflects the realities of the period prior to the military ventures of Mesah, king of Moab (*see* MOABITE STONE).

The HESHBON ballad and the historiography of Num 21 in general have stimulated extensive archaeological activity in the historical lands of the Ammonites and Moabites in search of biblical Heshbon. The archaeological study conceded that a fortified town had not stood there in the early Iron Age, although impressive remains from that early period have been discovered at nearly Tall al-ʿUmayri (*see* ʿUMAYRI, TALL AL). What probably happened was that biblical writers of a later age assumed that Heshbon had been the capital of an Amorite kingdom, whereas in reality another town like ʿUmayri might have had that status. The JE historiography of Num 21 utilized older materials to record the beginnings of Israelite settlement in Transjordan, which may have been concurrent with the earliest Israelite settlement of Canaan, west of the Jordan.

It remains to engage Num 32, whose theme is the legitimacy of the Israelite settlement in Gilead. Whereas Num 21:4-35 recounts the Israelite conquest and settlement of the Amorite towns of Transjordan as epochal events (Num 21:31, 35), Num 32 endorses the principle that Canaan lay west of the Jordan and that the divine command was "to cross over" the Jordan into the promised land. How is it, then, that the

Gileadite community, so closely tied to northern Israel especially, was accepted as part of the Israelite people? This issue, namely the inclusion of the Transjordanian Israelites, keeps cropping up in biblical literature. It produced a tradition according to which the tribes of Reuben, Gad, and certain clans of Manasseh, like the clan of Yair, had agreed in the days of Moses to take part in the conquest of Canaan. That is their justification for living where they did. Thus, the Israelite community of Transjordan was credited with a major role in the conquest of Canaan, because the Israelites could not have penetrated Canaan from the east and northeast unless Transjordan had been pacified.

Finally, the Caleb narrative of Num 13–14 illustrates the utilization of tribal and local traditions in the retelling of Israelite history. As a leader of the tribe of Judah, whose participation in the conquest is related in Judg 1 (compare 1 Sam 30:14), Caleb is configured as the living link between the generation of the exodus and the Israelites of the pre-monarchic period.

2. The contexts of the Balaam pericope

The poetic portions of the Balaam story exhibit a religious orientation different from that of the narrative sections the pericope. It appears that the OT preserves an El archive consisting of early poetry. Here Israel is blessed by the regional pantheon, who are all on their side, leaving little hope for their defeat by other peoples like the Moabites, who had been presumably abandoned by El. In historical terms, both the principal Balaam orations and the Heshbon ballad of Num 21 may well reflect the period of Israelite expansion in the early to mid-9th cent. BCE before MESHA initiated his military campaigns into northern Moab. As we shall have occasion to observe, the Balaam texts from Deir ʿAlla reflect a slightly later period. The calamity envisioned in them may refer to the Moabite threat to the population of Gilead. In literary terms, the discovery of the Deir ʿAlla inscriptions suggests that the biblical Balaam poems were also composed in Gilead and, as a corollary, that they were composed by one or more Transjordanian Israelites who worshiped El instead of Yahweh or alongside Yahweh. In fact, a broken line in the Mesha Stele probably attests to a contemporary temple of Yahweh in Nebo of Transjordan.

3. The Priestly material in context

The search for the context of the Priestly material in Numbers runs into the problem of establishing the relative chronology of the Torah sources. The approach taken here is that P provides clear responses to the singular cultic legislation of Deut 12–16, (D), endorsing the restriction of sacrifice to one, central altar. In this context, Lev 17 is a response to Deuteronomy in its opposition to multiple altars. Similarly, H. L. Ginsberg was correct in seeing an endorsement of the Deuteronomic deferral of the spring harvest festival in Lev 23, more precisely, a restructuring of the customary local or regional pilgrimages into national pilgrimages. Although Ginsberg traced the Deuteronomic restructuring of the cult to northern Israel of the mid- to late 8th cent. BCE, the Deuteronomic doctrine was not institutionalized in Judah until the latter part of the 7th cent. BCE during the reign of Josiah. This brings us down to the eve of the Babylonian exile, and suggests that much of what is preserved in the Priestly writings of the Torah is consequently postexilic.

There are further sequences, and internal indications of this historical progression. We will limit ourselves to those evident in Numbers. Thus, the unprecedented stratification of the priesthood, which clearly differentiates between priests and Levites, is first introduced in Num 3–4 and 8. This classification reflects Ezek 44:9-14, which is exilic, at the earliest. There we are told that the Levites were demoted because of their illicit service at the **bamoth** (בָּמוֹת, sing. **bamah** בָּמָה; "cult platforms"), outlawed by Josiah in 622 BCE (2 Kgs 22–23; *see* BAMAH; HIGH PLACE). The internecine rivalries within the Levitical "tribe," like those between Korah and his clan relative, Aaron (Num 16–17), presuppose a separate Levitical establishment with its own hierarchy.

Furthermore, the purity legislation of Num 19, which regards the corpse as the most extreme source of contamination, also directs us to Josiah, who defiled the altar at Bethel by piling upon it bones of the dead, taken from the nearby necropolis (2 Kgs 23:14-20). In turn, corpse contamination resulted in the prohibition of royal burial within the temple complex, a rule first encountered in Ezek 43:7-9.

Source-critical research has customarily attached primary importance to language and diction, which, in turn, directs us to comparative considerations. Thus, Num 2 and 10 employ the term **deghel** to designate a military unit, encamped with the families of the soldiers, as the basis for organizing the Israelite forces in the wilderness. The unit called **deghel** was a feature of Persian military organization, as we know not only from documents relating to the life of the Persian colony at Elephantine but also from Arad of the Achaemenid period, where there was a Persian garrison. Most of all, the recent surge of research into the imperial policies of the Achaemenid Empire respecting outlying regions like Palestine has strengthened the conclusion that the Priestly stratum in Torah literature, like Ezra–Nehemiah and Chronicles, reflects the realities of the temple-centered Judean community of the postexilic period.

Moving from law and ritual to historiography, Num 31 provides a remarkable giveaway as to the social context of its author. The list of Midianite kings slain by the Israelites during the war in Num 31:8 (compare Josh 13:21-22) can be read as a list of towns on the Nabatean trade route through North Arabia and Jordan. Thus, e.g., in Num 31:8, the Hebrew **reqem** (רֶקֶם) and Nabatean **raqmu** are Semitic names of

PETRA. This suggests that the people called Midianites were a mirror-image of the Kedarite Arabs of the Achaemenid period, those ruled by GESHEM, the Arab, about whom we read in Neh 2:19; 6:1-2. This Geshem is also known from an Aramaic inscription from Tell el-Maskhuta in northeastern Egypt and from a second inscription of the same period from Dedan. Such information correlates with the frequent references to Arabs in Ezra–Nehemiah and Chronicles (e.g., 2 Chr 21:16). Thus it was that a biblical writer of the Achaemenid period retrojected the hostility of contemporary Arabs, who were in league with Nehemiah's enemies in Transjordan, back into the wilderness period.

A subject worthy of further investigation is the issue of the legitimacy of the Transjordanian Israelite community of Gilead, a subject highlighted in Num 32, but whose traces may also be found elsewhere. JE attached great importance to the Transjordanian conquests, whereas it appears that P had problems with the records of the same events, and with the resulting legitimacy of the Israelite communities of Transjordan. Such an attitude informs Josh 24, for instance, where strong objection to the worship of Yahweh east of the Jordan is expressed. *See* LAW IN THE OT; PENTATEUCH; TORAH.

Bibliography: Yohanan Aharoni. *Arad Inscriptions.* Anson F. Rainey, trans. (1981); S. Ahituv. *Canaanite Toponyms in Ancient Egyptian Documents* (1984); William F. Albright. *Archaeology and the Religion of Israel.* 5th ed. (1968); William F. Albright. "The Oracles of Balaam." *JBL* 63 (1944) 207–33; John R. Bartlett. *Edom and the Edomites* (1989); I. Beit-Arieh et al. *Horvat Qitmit* (1995); K. H. Bernhardt. "The Political Situation in the East of Jordan during the Time of King Mesha." *Studies in the History and Archaeology of Jordan I.* A. Hadidi, ed. (1982) 163–67; I. Diakonoff. "The Naval Power and Trade of Tyre." *IEJ* 42 (1991) 168–93; Mary Douglas. *In the Wilderness: The Doctrine of Defilement in the Book of Numbers* (1993); I. Ephʿal. *The Ancient Arabs: Nomads on the Borders of the Fertile Crescent* (1982); P. Flint. "The Preliminary Edition of the First Numbers Scroll from Nahal Hever." *BBR* 9 (1999) 137–43; H. Louis Ginsberg. *The Israelian Heritage of Judaism* (1982); Baruch A. Levine. *Numbers 1–20.* AB 4A (1993); Baruch A. Levine. *Numbers 21–36.* AB 4B (2000); Jacob Milgrom. *Numbers.* JPS Torah Commentary (1990); Nadav Na'aman. *Borders and Districts in Biblical Historiography* (1986); D. Peake. "The Book of Numbers at Qumran: Texts and Context." *Current Research and Technological Development on the Dead Sea Scrolls.* D. W. Farny and S. Ricks, eds. (1993) 166–93; M. Weippert. "The Israelite 'Conquest' and Evidence from Transjordan." *Symposia Celebrating the 75th Anniversary of the ASOR (1900–1975).* David Noel Freedman, ed. (1979) 15–34; Julius Wellhausen. *Prolegomena to the History of Ancient Israel* (1965).

BARUCH A. LEVINE

NUMBERS, NUMBERING. In the ANE and Hellenistic world, numbering and calculation were highly developed. Enumeration and numbers often had magical, mystical, or symbolical significance, but biblical authors adopted only a minimum of such interpretation. When they did use numbers symbolically, traditional understandings were adapted to the faith of Israel and the church.

A. Numbers and Symbolism in the Biblical World

When the biblical authors came on the scene, significant developments in the history of calculation and writing of numbers had long since taken place. Human beings learned to count before they learned to write. Number systems were in use by 7000 BCE; language was first committed to writing ca. 3000 BCE in Sumer. Counting and calculation had been developed for millennia before written numerals were developed. Not only scratches in bone or wood, knotted strings, and pebbles (the Lat. for "pebble" is *calculus*) but also prototypes of the abacus enabled sophisticated calculation procedures prior to and apart from the use of written symbols. The oldest numerals were ideographic symbols on the outside of clay cases enclosing the actual clay symbols for numerical values.

After alphabetic writing was invented by the Phoenicians (or some northwestern Semitic people) ca. 3200 BCE, letters served as numbers. This meant that from the very beginning of written numbers, every word also had a numerical value. This inherent interplay between words and numbers facilitated the symbolic interpretation of numbers, a potential often exploited in a variety of ways. "Arabic" numbers (in reality derived from India), by which numbers are represented by their own symbols instead of letters of the alphabet, had not been devised in the biblical period. Likewise, the positioning system that allowed the same number to have different values depending on its position, and the use of zero, had not been devised. Thus the Jews, Greeks, and Romans of biblical times did not use numbers to make the kinds of calculations we make today but used an abacus or other computing device. Nonetheless, sophisticated measuring and accounting procedures were developed, including, e.g., the calculation of square roots, measuring the area of irregular objects, and precise prediction of eclipses and other astronomical phenomena.

In the biblical period represented by Israel and early Judaism, the names of the numbers were spelled out, and there were no separate symbols for numbers. In some cases, as illustrated by the ostraca unearthed from Omri's palace in Samaria (9th cent.) and the Lachish ostraca (6th cent.), and by grave inscriptions, numerical symbols from other cultures had been adopted for accounting procedures, but there were no Hebrew numbers. In some grave inscriptions from the 1st cent. BCE to the 7th cent. CE, Greek alphabetic numerals were inserted into the Hebrew text. In the NT period, letters of the Hebrew ALPHABET were just beginning to be used as numerals, as illustrated by the coins from the Second Jewish Revolt, sh b lkhr ysrʾl (ש ב לחר ישראל, "year two of the liberation of Israel"), in which *two* is represented by the second letter of the alphabet, BET (b ב). See also the Pompeii graffiti discussed in §B below.

Most numbering systems, including those in the biblical world, have used base ten (because we have ten fingers), and a few have used base twenty (fingers and toes), but some have used twelve, which is divisible by two, three, four, and six. For reasons still unknown to us, the Sumerians and Babylonians chose sixty as their base (still preserved in sixty minutes of sixty seconds and 360 degrees of a circle). In the earliest Sumerian documents, symbolic religious meanings were already attributed to numbers and number systems. The highest heavenly God received the base number sixty and is father of the earth-god (fifty), the moon-god (thirty, perhaps the number of days in a month?), and the sun-god (twenty), also the number of the king. The celestial and earthly worlds were both thought of as fitting together in a mystical numerological harmony, which made the numerical value of the name of a deity, place, person, or thing an essential attribute of its reality.

Not only numbers but also the act of counting itself often is understood as a sacral act, filled with divine potency. To count can imply having something or someone in one's power, at one's disposal. A foreign ruler demonstrates his power over a subject people by counting them.

The Hellenistic context of early Judaism and early Christianity was also replete with numerical symbolism and religious interest in numbers and numerology. For Plato, numbers represent the highest degree of knowledge, since they are perfectly consistent abstractions belonging to the ideal world, uncontaminated by material reality (Plato, *Resp.* 510D; *Phaed.* 79A). In this tradition, the Pythagoreans held that numbers provide an understanding of the true nature of the universe (Aristotle, *Metaph.* 13.1080). Pythagorean religious thought cultivated a kind of number mysticism. The base number ten was considered to be the holiest of numbers that gave the key to all things (Aristotle, *Metaph.* 13.1082). The *Arithmetical Introduction*, composed by the 2nd-cent. CE mathematician Nicomachus of Gerasa, a neo-Pythagorean from Judea, influenced mathematical thought for generations. It was not only a manual of mathematics but also was typical of his age in regarding numbers as having mystical qualities. Later gnostics had profound numerical interpretations of the name of God and various biblical phrases, but there is no clear evidence that this sort of gnostic numerology was already present in NT times, though the beginnings may be there.

B. An Illuminating Example: Gematria

The enormous variety of ways in which the ancient world understood the magical and religious potency of numbers and numbering can be illustrated by the method of gematria, a common approach used across the spectrum from conventional and trivial instances in everyday life to the sophisticated religious numerological speculations of scribes and teachers. The approach, which was to have repercussions in the biblical writings and interpretations of both Judaism and Christianity, may be illustrated by a famous bit of graffiti found on the wall of a house in Pompeii destroyed by the eruption of Vesuvius in 79 CE: philō hēs arithmos phme (φιλῶ ἧς ἀριθμός φμε, "I love the one whose number is 545" [φ = 500 + μ = 40 + ε = 5 = 545]). The letters of her name total 545. The one for whom the ancient "valentine" was intended would recognize it was written for her, for she knew the correct answer to the puzzle. The casual passerby, however, would have no clue, since every name can total only one number, but every number could point to a large number of different names. The curious observer would not know how many letters were in the name, and had no way of calculating which combination of how many letters was the correct name. One must know the name in advance and work backward; beginning with the number and working to the name produces an almost infinite number of possibilities.

In the religious world, gematria works only for insiders who have the answer given in advance. Thus in *Sib. Or.* 1:326–30, the name *Jesus* (IĒSOUS ΙΗΣΟΥΣ) is encoded as 888 (Ι = 10 + Η = 8 + Σ = 200 + Ο = 70 + Υ = 400 + Σ = 200 = 888), but here too, the reader must have the answer in advance. The name *Jesus* equals 888, but 888 can be the total numerical value of many other names.

Gematria and other symbolic understandings of numerals became popular and common in rabbinic literature, the time of the Mishnah, Talmud, and Kabbalah. Some rabbis found significance in the fact that the enigmatic yavo' shiloh (יָבֹא שִׁילֹה, "Shiloh comes" and other possible translations) of Gen 49:10 has the same numerical value as "Messiah." So also the numerical values of 'ekhadh (אֶחָד, "one") and 'ahavah (אַהֲבָה, "love") combined total twenty-six, the same total as yhwh (יהוה, Yahweh), so that *Yahweh* means "God is love." Even more complex and subtle calculations argued that maqom (מָקוֹם, "place"), used as a surrogate name to avoid pronouncing the sacred name of God, has the same numerical value of yhwh if the value of each letter is squared. It was thought that this mathematical fact could not be a coincidence but must be a matter of divine inspiration. To unravel this puzzle is to discover secrets God has hidden in Scripture and tradition for human edification. Some patristic and medieval exegesis followed the same imaginative path. For example, the 318 men of Gen 14:14 were understood in *Barn.* 9:8-9 as ciphers for Jesus and the cross: the 18 is the first two letters of Jesus (IĒSOUS ΙΗΣΟΥΣ), Ι (10) + Η (18), and the 300 is represented by a capital Τ in Greek (300) that resembles the cross.

Gematria was common in the biblical world and in later Judaism and Christianity, but the Bible itself contains only one clear example (see §C7 below on the number 666 in Rev 13:18). Gematria thus serves as both a contrast and a point of contact between the Bible and its historical and cultural context.

C. Numbers and Symbolism in the Jewish and Christian Scriptures

Generally speaking, the numerological speculations prevalent in the ANE and the Hellenistic world before and alongside Israel, Judaism, and the church played a minimal or nonexistent role in Israelite, Jewish, and Christian thinking. Standard treatments of biblical language and symbolism typically omit the subject entirely, as do the standard treatments of biblical theology, both OT and NT. This is the virtually unanimous conclusion of responsible and informed studies from across the theological spectrum, although popular and superstitious treatments of the Bible have often appealed to imaginative numerological schemes to prove the inspiration of the Bible or interpret its meaning. Biblical authors did sometimes adopt and adapt the symbolic and theological overtones attributed to particular numbers. These will be discussed below, in the context of the following general observations on the significance of numbers and numbering in biblical thought.

1. The act of numbering

Biblical writers sometimes shared the ANE view that numbering itself was a sacral act charged with divine power and prerogatives. The CENSUS of Luke 2 is not merely a practical administrative matter, but an extension of the divine power of Rome (compare Isa 33:18). A people described as "innumerable" means that it is unconquerable (e.g., Gen 15:5). God numbers Job's steps (Job 14:16), i.e., is in charge of them, numbers the hairs of people's heads (Matt 10:30), i.e., brings them under divine authority and protection, and counts the number of months of the pregnancy of wild animals (Job 39:1-2), i.e., is entirely in charge of nature beyond the realm of human control. Yahweh counts the stars, utterly beyond human ability, as a demonstration of God's sovereign power (Ps 147:4). Thus David's numbering of Israel, a census undertaken for military purposes, was an incursion into God's own sovereign claim to have Israel at his own disposal (2 Sam 24:10; 1 Chr 21:2). In the view of Israel's neighbors, to number in the sense of "allot" (one's destiny), to "mete out" (one's fate) was the divine prerogative (compare Isa 65:11).

2. Vast and exaggerated numbers

Ancient Near Eastern religious texts characteristically dealt in extravagant numbers as an expression of the majesty of the gods and ancient heroes. Primeval Babylonian kings lived 3,600 years; the army of King Keret numbered 3,000,000 men. The Bible, especially the narratives of the world's and Israel's earliest history, likewise deals in vast numbers. The antediluvian heroes lived hundreds of years (Gen 5, with the top figure attributed to Methuselah, 969 years). In Num 1 the Israelite multitude that left Egypt is numbered precisely by tribes and tallies 603,550 fighting men aged twenty and above, not counting the Levites, women, children, those unable to go to war, and the mixed multitude (Exod 12:37-38; 38:26; Num 1:46; 11:21). The warriors alone would make a column of fifty abreast 22 mi. long, with one yard between the ranks. Since ancient times, both Jewish and Christian interpreters have seen difficulties with these numbers. All Israel would have numbered 2 to 3 million or more. There would have been more than 150 births per day in such a population; yet the Israelites had only two midwives (Exod 1:15). There were precisely 22,273 firstborn males (Num 3:43); given 600,000+ males, this would mean an average of at least 27.1 sons per mother. Moses is typically pictured as assembling and talking with the whole people at once (Exod 13:3). Various apologetic devices have attempted to explain these numbers as historical or reduce them to manageable size. It is best to see the exaggerated numbers as an example of the Bible reflecting the practice of its environment. Even here, when compared with other ANE religious literature, there is a somewhat restrained appropriation of this cultural practice.

3. The book of Numbers

The fourth book of the OT is called bemidhbar (בְּמִדְבַּר, "in the wilderness"). As is the case with the other books of the Torah, the name is derived from a significant word in the opening line. The LXX designated the book arithmoi (ἀριθμοί, "numbers") because of the census data found in the opening chapters. The book contains no reflection on the meaning of particular numbers or the act of enumeration as such.

4. Conventional use of numbers

The Bible's use of numbers can be classified into three categories: "conventional," "rhetorical," and "symbolic." The classification is not precise, and the boundaries between the three groups are not sharply defined. The overwhelming majority of the occurrences of numbers throughout the Bible are simply conventional: the counting of herds and flocks and other items for practical purposes, the counting of money and people for tax and administrative purposes. Though sometimes precise numbers are given, round numbers are frequently used. For example, the census lists in the early section of Numbers are rounded off to the nearest hundred, and large numbers are sometimes expressed as "myriads," i.e., "tens of thousands."

Popular and novelistic efforts to derive some supposed deep symbolism or mystical meaning from every number in the Bible, or to find a complex system of hidden numbers embedded in the Bible, are misguided and unsupported by historical study. The meaning of the vast majority of biblical numbers is conventional and lies on the surface. The Bible has no hidden numerical codes or secret number mysticism.

5. Rhetorical use of numbers

A step beyond conventional usage is seen when biblical authors, especially in the OT, use numbers rhetorically or as a means of structuring literary units or their composition as a whole. Such usage goes back to earliest times and illustrates the biblical authors' adoption of rhetorical features from their cultural heritage. There are numerous instances of graduated or scaled numbering in the pattern x/x+1; e.g., Prov 30:15*b*-16 as one of several in this context:

> Three things are never satisfied;
> four never say, "Enough":
> Sheol, the barren womb,
> the earth ever thirsty for water,
> and the fire that never says, "Enough."

Amos 1–2 contains eight oracles introduced with the same formula:

> Thus says the LORD:
> For three transgressions . . .
> and for four, I will not revoke the punishment . . .

That the first oracle lists only one transgression shows the usage is rhetorical, in that the enumeration intensifies the charge rather than listing the actual transgressions.

Numbering can be used to structure a whole composition, such as the ACROSTIC psalms. A familiar example is Ps 119, composed of twenty-two stanzas of eight lines each. The Hebrew alphabet has twenty-two letters, also used as numbers. Each line of each stanza begins with the same letter, from ALEF (ʾ א) to TAV (t [ת]; "A to Z"), providing a sense of order and numerical completeness. The editors of the psalter divided it somewhat artificially into five books, so that it corresponded to the Pentateuch. The prophetic materials in the Minor Prophets (*see* BOOK OF THE TWELVE) were editorially arranged into twelve books (see §C6 below on the significance of the numbers five and twelve). Other biblical authors structure their compositions by numerical principles, but since they rarely make this explicit (e.g., the book of Revelation), the intended numerical structure is sometimes debated. The genealogy of Jesus in Matt 1:2-17 is an exception, because the numerical pattern of three groups of fourteen generations is identified and explained in v. 17 (*see* GENEALOGY, CHRIST).

6. Symbolic interpretation of numbers

The Bible has far less symbolic interpretation of numbers than was common in its ANE and Hellenistic contexts. This is probably due to the historical orientation of biblical faith in general. Number mysticism deals with abstractions and the static reality of things and perceives numbers to be constant, reliable, and uncontaminated by historical contingency. Biblical faith in the Creator who acts in history is related to the dynamism of history itself that cannot be captured in static mathematical formulae or speculation. In biblical theology, there is no transcendent aura associated with numbers as such or with any particular number. No number has any inherent allegorical or mystical meaning that remains constant. Thus, e.g., the numerical calculations of Dan 8–12 (e.g., 3.5, 7, 70, 2300, 1290, 1335 day-for-year principle) have to do with the intricacies of the apocalyptic calendric calculations, not with presumed deeper meanings of the numbers themselves. This approach, followed universally by historical interpreters of the Bible, is in contrast to allegorizing interpretations that claim that throughout the Bible numbers have consistent symbolic meanings (e.g., one is "God's number"; four is the "number of the earth"; six is the "number of evil," one short of seven, the "number of perfection"; nine is the number of the Spirit; twelve is the "number of the kingdom of God"; *see* ALLEGORY). This uncritical approach has numerous variations and no historical basis. Nonetheless, in some contexts, certain numbers that had played a key role in Israel's and the church's historical pilgrimage took on overtones of deeper symbolic meaning. Interpreters often disagree as to whether a particular instance represents a symbolic meaning—and if so, what this is—or whether the usage is merely conventional. This will be illustrated by brief discussions of some key numbers and relevant texts.

a. One. The number one occurs 1,322 times in the Jewish and Christian Scriptures (ʾekhadh, 977 times; heis [εἷς], 345 times), almost always in the conventional sense of identifying a single thing. Since neither Hebrew nor Greek has an indefinite article, in both Testaments the number one plays this descriptive role. During the time period represented by the OT, the number one had not yet attained explicit symbolic significance in representing Jewish monotheism. The Shema (Deut 6:4) was the fundamental confession of faith of Israel, but the final ʾekhadh was originally understood to mean "alone" or "unique," not "one" in the sense of theoretical exclusive monotheism (*see* SHEMA, THE). By NT times, however, the Shema had become an affirmation that Yahweh is the only God; the words *God* and *one* were absolutely correlated. During his martyrdom by burning, the legendary Rabbi Akiba is purported to have recited the Shema with his last breath, sustaining the last word, one, until he died. Early Christianity inherited this significance of *one* with reference to God (e.g., Mark 12:32; 1 Cor 8:6), and elaborated it anthropologically, christologically, and ecclesiologically (e.g., John 11:52; Acts 17:26; Rom 5:15; 12:5; Eph 4:4-6). Later gnosticism and Neo-Platonism developed speculative doctrines expounding God as "the One," but such philosophical and mystical associations with the number itself had not yet appeared in biblical times (*see* GOD, NT VIEW OF; GOD, OT VIEW OF).

b. Three. After the number seven (see §6d below), in the Bible the number three is used most frequently in a symbolic or sacral sense. While used most often in the conventional sense, in the ancient world three became a special number since it naturally suggests the idea of completeness (beginning/middle/end). From the observer's perspective, all reality is naturally divided into three realms (temporal: past/present/future; spatial: above/here/below or ahead/here/behind). The folk narratives of all cultures follow the "law of three"—one need only think of how many stories there are of three pigs, bears, billy goats gruff, blind mice, and the like, and how jokes and storytelling frequently follow this pattern. In the ancient world, gods were often grouped in triads of father/mother/child. It is thus not unexpected that numerous cultic features of Israelite law and calendar exhibit this sacral focus on threeness adopted from the prevalent culture, e.g., three annual festivals (Exod 23), periods of three days (Gen 30:36), three months (Exod 2:2), three years (1 Chr 21:12); sacrificial animals are to be three years old (Gen 15:9). In reference to Jesus' resurrection "after three days" (Mark 8:31; 14:58; 15:29), both Matthew and Luke replace with "on the third day" (Matt 16:21; Luke 9:22; compare also 1 Cor 15:4). There is abundant evidence in the LXX, Josephus, and rabbinic writings that these phrases have exactly the same meaning that represents the Jewish practice of counting part of a day as the whole (compare e.g., Gen 42:17-18; Exod 19:11-16; Josephus, *Life* 268–69; *Ant.* 2.72–73; *Esth. Rab.* 9:2). Thus without finding any mystical meaning in the number three itself, "three days" and "THIRD DAY" became significant phrases in Christian tradition, so that texts such as Luke 2:46 and John 2:1 could hardly be read by Christians without evoking the Easter imagery, which may well have contributed to shaping the story in the first place. Though the rudiments of later trinitarian doctrine are found in the NT (e.g., Matt 28:19; 2 Cor 13:13; the "these three are one" of 1 John 5:7 is spurious), there is no explicit theological development of the idea of threeness in the NT (*see* TRINITY).

c. Four (and multiples). From ancient Egypt to the present, the number four has sacral overtones in many cultures, no doubt due to its natural connection with the four points of the compass. Thus in the Bible too, the world is thought of as having four directions (e.g., Gen 2:10) and four corners (Isa 11:12; Rev 7:1). Given natural significance as the approximate length of a generation and historical significance as the time of Israel's wilderness wanderings, forty and its multiples appear numerous times to designate significant periods of TIME (e.g., forty days of rain before the flood, which lasts forty days, and forty days after the ark came to rest Noah opened the window of the ark [Gen 7:12, 17; 8:6]; Moses on Sinai for forty days and forty nights [Exod 34:28]; Elijah spends forty days en route to Sinai [1 Kgs 19:8]; Jesus' temptation for forty days [Matt 4:2]; after Easter Jesus teaches the apostles for forty days [Acts 1:3]). Later, the number four became so established as a sacred number that Irenaeus (*Haer.* 3.11.8–9) could argue creatively that the church must accept no more nor less than four Gospels on the basis of four winds and the four faces of the cherubim of Rev 4:7-8.

d. Seven (and multiples). Throughout the ANE and Hellenistic world, seven, along with its combinations and multiples, was a significant and sacred number, almost certainly based on observation of the four phases of the moon that divided the month into seven-day periods. Since the seven-day cycle fulfills and completes a period, seven had the connotation of fullness or completeness. Authors of both Testaments make frequent use of seven as a special number, often with the implication of wholeness, so that, e.g., the SEVEN CHURCHES of Rev 1–3 represent not merely seven particular congregations, but the church in its totality; the seven Catholic Letters are directed not to individuals or individual congregations but to the church as a whole. Seven is built into the structure of the Israelite cult, influencing the CALENDAR, sacred space, and ritual acts (Gen 2:2; Exod 20:13; 25:31-37). The differing genealogies of Jesus in Matt 1:2-17 and Luke 3:23-38 are both structured in hebdomads, but only Matt 1:17 makes this explicit. Revelation uses the number seven, its multiples and cognates, more frequently than any other NT book, with numerous sevens not always explicitly listed, and it is structured as a series of visions designated as seven seals, seven trumpets, and seven bowls. *See* SEVEN, SEVENTH, SEVENTY.

e. Ten (and multiples). Though other numerical systems existed in antiquity (especially the sexagesimal system discussed above), the decimal system was used by the Israelites throughout their history, as well as by the Greeks and Romans, so that the whole context of biblical history and literature assumes base ten. In this light, along with the convenience of counting on the fingers, the numerous tens of Scripture are not surprising. Not only such familiar items as the TEN COMMANDMENTS (Exod 20:2-17), ten PLAGUES IN EGYPT (Exod 7–12), and the TITHE (e.g., Gen 14:20; 28:22; Lev 27:30) but numerous other tens, made explicit or not, occur in the Bible, such as the ten bridesmaids of Jesus' parable (Matt 25:1-13), the ten pounds given to ten slaves, the best one rewarded with authority over ten cities (Luke 19:11-27), and the ten patriarchs prior to the flood (Gen 5). Ten is used as a small round number (e.g., Rev 2:10), as its multiples 100 or 1,000 were used as large round numbers (e.g., Rev 20:2-3). In contrast to their pagan surroundings, in Israel and early Christianity ten seems to have had no particular sacral or mystical significance. The tithe was holy, but not because of any sacredness associated with the number ten as such.

f. Twelve (and multiples). In the ANE, TWELVE was originally and commonly associated with the twelve months and the twelve signs of the ZODIAC, and some later Israelites and Jews (including both Josephus and Philo) saw cosmic symbolism in the number twelve. By far the predominant factor, however, in the numerous biblical instances where twelve plays a special symbolic or sacral role is the traditional belief that Israel was constituted by God as a people of twelve TRIBEs descended from the twelve sons of Jacob. "Twelve" thus often had the connotation "people of God," carried over into the church with the designation of Jesus' apostles as "the Twelve" (*see* TWELVE, THE). Thus Rev 21:9-14 combines the two images.

g. Other significant numbers. As the half of ten and the number of fingers on one hand, five became a convenient number for the literary division of a composition (e.g., the PENTATEUCH, the five books of the psalter, the five scrolls of the Writings called the Megilloth). An individual book could be divided into five sections (e.g., Matthew, *Ethiopic Enoch*). Three hundred and sixty(-five) could have an astrological significance corresponding to the number of days in a year. That Enoch lived 365 years before being translated to heaven is thus probably not an incidental comment (Gen 5:21-23), but its significance in pre-biblical tradition is now lost and not developed by the author of Genesis. Biblical authors generally have little interest in numerological speculation.

7. Key and illustrative texts

The differing ways in which attention to the special significance of particular numbers plays a role may be illustrated with reference to a few texts. The author of Matthew explicitly points out that his genealogy of Jesus is arranged according to a numerical pattern (Matt 1:2-17). He adopts the tradition behind 1 Chr 1–2 that counted fourteen (2 x 7) generations from Abraham to David, reflected in other Jewish sources. This may be reinforced by the fact that the numerical value of David's name in Hebrew (dwd דוד) is fourteen (d = 4, w = 6, d = 4), who was thus the fourteenth in both senses, or this observation may only reflect scholarly imagination.

The 153 fish of John 21:11 has attracted attention since ancient times, since it is a triangular number, i.e., the sum of all the numbers in the series 1–17. But since seventeen seems to have no particular significance for John, other interpreters have attempted various solutions in terms of gematria. For example, Theophanus Kerameus, *Homily 36* on John 21, saw the number as pointing to Rebecca (wife of Isaac and mother of Jacob and Esau) as a symbol of the universal church, since the name REBEKKA (PEBEKKA) = 153. If the author intended the reader to recognize symbolic meaning in the number, he does not make this explicit, and the key has been lost for later readers.

The only NT text in which numbering has explicit theological significance is Rev 13:18, the one clear biblical example of gematria (see §B above). The nature of gematria means the possibilities of interpretation are almost infinite unless one knows the meaning in advance—which, of course, John's original readers did. Of the numerous explanations, the most cogent is that the author is interpreting the current or soon-to-come Roman emperor in terms of the Nero redivivus myth, and that 666 is a gematriac cryptogram for NERO using the numeric values of nrwn qsr (נרון קסר; = Nero Caesar in Hebrew: נ = 50; ר = 200; ו = 6; ן = 50; ק =100; ס = 60; ר =200, which total 666). This understanding is supported by the fact that some manuscripts read 616, which would be the total if Nero is spelled in Hebrew without the optional final NUN (n ן). Since John elsewhere uses names in Hebrew letters symbolically (9:11; 16:16), this explanation would have been understood by contemporary readers. Suetonius (*Nero* 39) had already used gematria in explaining Nero's name; its number in the Greek system is 1005, the total of the numerical value of the letters in Nerōn idian mētera apekteine (Νέρων, ἰδίαν μητέρα ἀπέκτεινε, meaning "Nero killed his own mother"). Later explanations referring the "number of the beast" to figures present or expected in the interpreter's time have no basis in the biblical text.

Bibliography: Georges Ifrah. *The Universal History of Numbers: From Prehistory to the Invention of the Computer.* David Bellos et al., trans. (2000).

M. EUGENE BORING

NUMENIUS n*oo*-mee'nee-uhs [Νουμήνοις Noumēnois]. Numenius, son of ANTIOCHUS, was an envoy from the Hasmonean court who traveled to Rome and

Sparta at least twice. Around 143 BCE, Jonathan sent Numenius and Antipater, son of Jason, to Rome to confirm Jerusalem's "friendship" with Rome. They stopped in Sparta on their return trip (1 Macc 12:16). Around 142, Simon sent Numenius to Rome with a gold shield to confirm their alliance (1 Macc 14:24). This diplomatic strategy succeeded when Lucius, the Roman consul, wrote a letter to a number of cities and kingdoms in the eastern Mediterranean requesting kindly treatment of Jews (1 Macc 15:16-24).

ADAM L. PORTER

NUN nuhn [נ ן n]. The fourteenth letter of the Hebrew alphabet, which derives from the original Semitic word *nūn-, "serpent"[?], though the shape may derive from a by-form, *nakhsh-, "snake." *See* ALPHABET.

NUN, NUNITES nuhn [נוּן nun, נוֹן non, בִּן־נוּן bin-nun; Ναυή Nauē]. 1. With the exception of 1 Chr 7:27, the name Nun appears in the OT only as part of the designation "Joshua son of Nun" (see, e.g., Exod 33:11; Num 11:28; Deut 1:38; Josh 1:1) or in synonymous designations using variant forms of "Joshua" ("Hoshea son of Nun," Num 13:8, 16; Deut 32:44; "Jeshua son of Nun," Neh 8:17). The genealogical notice in 1 Chr 7:27, which contains the variant spelling non rather than the otherwise uniform nun, further identifies Nun as the son of Elishama and a member of the tribe of Ephraim. Since, however, this same Elishama appears elsewhere as an Ephraimite leader who was contemporary with Joshua (Num 1:10; 2:18; 7:48, 53; 10:22), his identification as Nun's father is likely a retrojection designed to enhance Joshua's lineage (Klein). Thus, the most that is known about Nun as a person is his relationship with Joshua and general connection to the Ephraimite line.

The personal name perhaps derives from an animal name. The etymology of the name may be related to that of the fourteenth letter of the Hebrew alphabet, which has the same spelling (nun). The name of this letter likely derives from the pictograph for nakhash (נָחָשׁ), meaning "snake," which the character nun may attempt to represent pictorially. Others, however, take the word as originally indicating a fish, the meaning of the cognate terms in Aramaic and Assyrian (Noth). Hence *Gen. Rab.* 97:3 refers to Joshua's father, Nun, as he whose name is like the name of the fish.

2. The word *Nun* could function as a group designation rather than a personal name and thus identify Joshua as a member of (lit., "son of") a particular tribe or clan (i.e., "Joshua, the Nunite"). The primary evidence for this understanding is morphological. The LXX renders the name with the Gk. Nauē (e.g., Josh 1:1), which may indicate that the name "Nun" is a development from the older Hebrew term naweh (נָוֶה). This term appears in both OT and Mari texts as a designation for the dwelling place, destination, or settlement of a flock or group (see Job 5:24; Isa 27:10; 65:10; Jer 10:25; 49:20; Lam 2:2). It may function to designate Joshua as a member of a group that dwelled in a certain location and may preserve an old clan name of some kind (Soggin; Boling). Against this conclusion, however, note that the LXX does not always translate nun with Nauē. Hence, the occurrences of this translation may only be the result of textual error through the confusion of letters and not the preservation of an older term. Additionally, the genealogical notice in 1 Chr 7:27 clearly preserves a tradition that understood Nun as a personal name that could take its place within a lineage of fathers and sons rather than as a tribal designation.

Bibliography: Robert G. Boling and G. Ernest Wright. *Joshua.* AB 6 (1982); Ralph W. Klein. *1 Chronicles.* Hermeneia (2006); Martin Noth. *Die israelitischen Personennamen im Rahmen der Gemeinsemitischen Namengebung* (1928); J. Alberto Soggin. *Joshua.* OTL (1972).

BRAD E. KELLE

NUNC DIMITTIS noonk´di-mit´is. In the Temple Simeon recognizes the infant Jesus as God's promised savior, and in Luke 2:29-32 he responds with a joyful hymn. *Nunc Dimittis* ("now dismiss") is the traditional Latin title for this hymn, taken from the beginning of the first line in which Simeon says, "Master, now you are dismissing your servant in peace."

Simeon represents faithful Jews who have waited long for the fulfillment of God's promises and are still expectantly waiting. He is also a Spirit-inspired prophet who received a special promise that he would not die before seeing the Messiah. The first verse of Simeon's hymn is thankful recognition that this promise has been fulfilled.

The temple scene that includes Simeon's hymn is an integral and important part of Luke's infancy narrative. Simeon's hymn should be compared to Mary's MAGNIFICAT (Luke 1:47-55) and Zechariah's BENEDICTUS (Luke 1:68-79). Together the three hymns, along with the angels' announcements, provide a progressive disclosure of the significance of Jesus' birth. In one sense Simeon's hymn is the climax, for it discloses the full scope of God's saving work, which will encompass Gentiles as well as Israel. It does so by using language from Isa 40–55, a section of Scripture affirming that God's salvation will include Gentiles.

Simeon's joyful hymn is followed by somber words to Mary that anticipate upheaval and opposition. The two statements together provide a guide to the rest of Luke-Acts, which narrates steps in fulfilling God's comprehensive saving purpose as it encounters human resistance.

Bibliography: Raymond E. Brown. *The Birth of the Messiah* (1993).

ROBERT C. TANNEHILL

NURSE [אֹמֶנֶת ʾomeneth, יָנַק yanaq, מֵינֶקֶת meneqeth; τροφός trophos]. A nurse may be a woman who is nursing or breastfeeding her own or another's child (meneqeth, Exod 2:7; 2 Kgs 11:2) or a caregiver for children (ʾomeneth, Ruth 4:16). In Isa 49:23, both meneqeth and ʾomeneth symbolize the comfort the returning captives will receive: "Kings shall be your foster fathers (lit., "nurses" or "nursing-fathers") and their queens your nursing mothers." Moses, despairing of his people's protesting the manna, asks rhetorically whether he must be Israel's nurse (Num 11:12). Paul speaks of tending to the Thessalonians "like a nurse (trophos) tenderly caring for her own children" (1 Thess 2:7). When a given nurse is identified, the one in her care is often particularly significant. After Pharaoh's attempted slaughter of all male Hebrew babies, for example, Moses' mother is hired as her son's nurse (Exod 2:7-9), allowing her to shape the identity of Israel's future leader. Deborah, Rebekah's nurse, accompanies her from Abraham's homeland to Canaan (Gen 24:59), indicating that nurses could continue in their service long after weaning. That Deborah's death and burial place are mentioned points to her own significance (Gen 35:8). Mephibosheth's nurse flees with her charge upon hearing of the loss of Jonathan and Saul, the child's father and grandfather (2 Sam 4:4). King J(eh)oram's daughter, Jehosheba, hides her nephew Joash and his nurse from Athaliah, who slays all the other rightful heirs of her own murdered son so that she can be queen (2 Kgs 11:2). *See* BREAST; FAMILY; MOTHER.

SHARON PACE

NUTS [אֱגוֹז ʾeghoz]. In Song 6:11 the writer tells of a "nut orchard," likely planted walnut trees (*Juglans regia*), long cultivated in Bible lands, having been brought from the Persian area. Walnut trees have a large crown of pinnate leaves on a tall trunk that yields splendid mottled timber. Its round fruits are ca. 4 cm (1.5 in) across with one delicious seed (nut) inside. Apart from the ALMOND, other nuts of the Bible grew wild, including the "terebinth" or "pistachio nuts" (botnim בָּטְנִים; Gen 43:11). These are likely to have been the little round seeds of the Atlantic TEREBINTH or pistachio (*Pistacia atlantica*, *P. palaestina*), still sold in local markets, rather than the true pistachio (*P. vera*) cultivated later. The seeds of the umbrella- or stone-pine (*Pinus pinea*) are popular nuts in some places and are meant in Hos 14:8 as the edible fruit of a coniferous tree (berosh בְּרוֹשׁ). *See* PLANTS OF THE BIBLE.

F. NIGEL HEPPER

NUZI n*oo*ʹzee. The more than 6500 cuneiform texts and fragments discovered at the excavations at Yorghan Tepe (ancient Nuzi, ca. 1600–1350 BCE) in northeastern Iraq and in surrounding areas (notably ancient Arrapha [modern Kirkuk] and Tell al-Fakhar [ancient Kurruhanni]) have often been utilized for comparative purposes with particular cultural practices in the OT. In fact, soon after the discovery of the Nuzi documents by Edward Chiera, there were numerous scholars who argued for parallels, primarily in legal and socioeconomic contexts. However, with the publication of literally hundreds of Nuzi texts over the past thirty years, there has been a re-evaluation of the relative importance of the Nuzi material for biblical studies. Many of the so-called "parallels" have been discounted, especially since there are significant chronological problems with the Late Bronze Age material from Nuzi and difficulties in tying the patriarchal narratives to a precise time period. Moreover, cuneiform finds from Syria in the Late Bronze Age, notably from Alalakh and Emar, provide a wider context for understanding not only the Nuzi collections but the biblical customs as well.

A. The City of Nuzi

Nuzi was occupied during the prehistoric, Akkadian (ca. 2300–2150 BCE), Mitanni (ca. 1600–1350 BCE), and Partho-Sassanian periods (ca. 200 BCE–600 CE). During the Akkadian period the site was named "Gasur," and various Sumerian, Sargonic and Old Assyrian texts have been found there. The site was called "Nuzi" during the Mitanni period, the best-attested period at the site and the one most relevant for OT comparisons.

The Mitanni period town of Nuzi appears to have been modest, as attested by the various types of settlements excavated, including the main urban, administrative, and religious centers. Portions of suburbs that were over 300 m north of the walled town were also excavated, revealing a number of socially and economically diverse houses that were part of larger neighborhoods. Much of the material remains show evidence of Nuzi's interconnections with MITANNI (evidenced by the seal of a Mitanni king, Saustatar, on a document). Artistic styles from Egypt, Syro-Palestine, and the Aegean have also been uncovered. Cuneiform tablets (both public and private documents) came from all of these areas, providing a rich context for understanding a typical ANE town in the 2nd millennium BCE. The population of the walled and unwalled town has been estimated to be about 1500–2000 people, a small size for a city, even for ancient standards. Dating the documents with precision has been particularly difficult, however. Not only are scholars divided about their date (ranging from 1600 to 1350 BCE); they are also not in agreement about the length of time the people flourished (between 150 and 200 years).

B. The Cuneiform Corpus at Nuzi

As stated, the Nuzi tablets were located in a wide variety of contexts and included the socio-economic activities of people from various social strata over a relatively short period of a few centuries. Since the private archives only contained texts that still had immediate relevance to their owners, the existing tablets were heavily concerned with real estate, a topic that continued to be of importance over a period of generations. A number of types of real estate documents have been found. Though land was inalienable, a landowner could bypass this problem by fictively "adopting" a buyer who was not a relative ("tablet of sonship"). One could also transfer real estate by a "tablet lease" in which land was leased for a period of time until the original owner redeemed the land by returning the land fee. There was also the "tablet of brothership" in which the owner passed an inheritance to a non-relative for services rendered. The "tablet of daughtership" stipulated that a person who adopted a daughter was responsible for arranging her marriage. Other types of documents concerning personnel, marriage contracts, livestock, and perishable items were found in fewer numbers. Administrative archives comprise ration lists, receipts, wills, and items related to the daily affairs of the central government, including loans and court records.

Of special interest are the large family archives discovered among the suburban households. These suburban landowners were active in terms of buying and purchasing movable and immovable property. For example, over 600 documents have been found concerning the family of Shilwa-Teshub, described as a "son of the king" and a slave owner who had multiple wives, children, and other dependents. Over 2,000 documents were found from the household of Tehip-Tilla, whose widowed mother made a number of real estate transactions. Tehip-Tilla himself purchased various plots of land in and around the vicinity of Nuzi. His sons, however, bickered amongst themselves, causing a strain on the extended family.

The language of the documents was a unique dialect of AKKADIAN, as attested by a large number of Hurrian words and expressions in the lexical corpus, as well as many personal names that expose a significant Hurrian element in the population (*see* HURRIANS). The Akkadian written dialect at Nuzi thus reflects a Hurrian background for scribes; many scholars have labeled the language used by the Nuzi scribes as "peripheral Akkadian" influenced by Hurrian.

C. Nuzi and the Hurrians

The ethnic background of many of the peoples at Nuzi was Hurrian, a people group whose origins are shrouded in obscurity. They are first described in late 3rd millennium BCE sources of the Sargonic king Naram-Sin (ca. 2200 BCE) as inhabiting the land of Subartu (Upper Mesopotamia). Soon thereafter, there were a number of well-established Hurrian states, which continued until the rise of a powerful Hurrian based kingdom of Mitanni (ca. 1600 BCE).

The kingdom of Mitanni was a confederation of Hurrian states in Upper Mesopotamia in the late 2nd millennium BCE. By 1450 BCE, Mitanni was the most powerful state in the Tigris-Euphrates region. Unfortunately, none of the state archives of Mitanni have been uncovered; thus, one has to rely upon information coming from correspondence with neighboring polities including Egypt, the Hittites, and Mesopotamia, as well as records from Mitanni vassal states such as Terqa (on the Syrian Euphrates), Alalakh and Ugarit (both in coastal Syria), and Arrapha, a small state in northern Iraq whose capital is most likely sealed under the modern town of Kirkuk. Nuzi was a city in the vassal kingdom of Arrapha. From these varied and fragmented sources it is somewhat apparent that Mitanni was a political term that was most often used to describe the confederation of Hurrian states and vassals. Each of these vassals had its own king, who was bound to Mitanni by a treaty sworn by oath. The ethnicity of the Mitanni state (and thus the town of Nuzi) was diverse. Although the state of Mitanni was dominated by Hurrians, there was a significant percentage of individuals with Indo-European personal names, as well as West Semitic speaking peoples (Hittites, Kassites, Babylonians, and Assyrians).

D. Nuzi Government and Social Structure

It is in this political context that we can view Nuzi as politically subordinate to the Mitanni state. This is evidenced by the fact that two Mitanni kings, Parrattarna and Sausatar, are described in a way that implies Mitanni rule over Nuzi, the nature of which is not entirely certain (except that Nuzi was placed in the Mitanni province of Arrapha). Although the city of Nuzi did not have a king, a mayor is mentioned who answered to the king of Arrapha. Documents describe the fact the Nuzi had relations (both economic and military) with other kingdoms, such as Kassite Babylonia and Assyria. Nuzi was probably destroyed by the Assyrians (ca. 1350 BCE), a fact implied textually and attested archaeologically by massive destruction levels.

The great variety of documents at Nuzi attests to a complex social structure. The king of Arrapha, though a vassal of Mitanni, was the head of the local government. The "sons of the king" were not necessarily literal descendants of the king but landowners who served in the military. There were also "charioteers," who were not necessarily connected with the military but were judges, mayors, and other government officials. They were heavily represented in banking, trade, real estate, and manufacture. Middle class owners were also property owners and professional workers. Similar to the rest of Mesopotamia, slaves at Nuzi were either prisoners of war or those who were forced into debt, which often meant working for someone to pay off the debt. However, a number of slaves at Nuzi often retained their property rights during this period. They were able to adopt children and buy and sell property, and some even had estates larger than the average citizen. One special group mentioned at Nuzi was the Habiru, who appeared to come from a variety of ethnic groups (*see* HABIRU, HAPIRU). They often appeared as workers for hire or domestic servants and were often described as homeless refugees. The etymological connection of the word *Habiru* and the biblical term *Hebrew*, which has been discussed at length, is unclear. Elite women at Nuzi were capable of owning property, making their own contracts, and engaging in various economic and social activities.

E. Nuzi and the Bible

In the early stages of the discovery of the Nuzi texts, many reputed parallels to the OT were claimed by scholars. Although over time many of these claims have been shown to be exaggerated, Nuzi and the OT appear to share a common ANE cultural heritage. As with other great archival discoveries (e.g., Ugarit, Mari, Ebla, and Emar), the tendency at the outset has often been to overemphasize the importance of new discoveries to the OT. But the scholar must be sober in asking certain questions about the differences in contexts, literary genre, and etymological kinship. Because of the wide geographic range of the Hurrians, particular customs at Nuzi carried by the Hurrians were likely spread throughout the ANE providing a convenient socio-economic, legal, and administrative context for both the Nuzi and OT materials. Moreover, discoveries of archives at EMAR, a Late Bronze Age period Hittite vassal town from the Middle Euphrates region of Syria, show that many of Nuzi customs were somewhat common throughout the Near East. Specific comparisons, however, are difficult to ascertain because of the unsolvable problem of dating the patriarchal narratives and the fact that the biblical cultural information is extracted from literary narratives and laws, while the Nuzi material is gleaned from contracts and court records. In light of this, our goal is not so much to evaluate the supposed cultural similarities (e.g., marriage contracts, pseudo-adoptions, and animal husbandry agreements), but to perhaps illuminate the ANE background of some biblical customs and thus provide important contextual material for understanding some of the patriarchal narratives and their historical plausibility (at least in terms of cultural practices).

In spite of this, there are some cultural bits of information in Genesis that appear to reflect a similar tradition to that in the Nuzi material. Because he was childless, Abraham made provisions to adopt Eliezar of Damascus as his heir in Gen 15:2-3, which is similar to Nuzi "pseudo-adoptions" where a childless couple "adopted" a servant as their heir. This is also known from the texts at Emar. However, the adopted son in the Nuzi contracts was provided with a wife and had to serve in the household of the adoptive father, seemingly similar to Jacob's tenure with his uncle Laban (Gen 29–31). But Jacob is nowhere described as an adopted son, although it is apparent that both parties misunderstood their relationship with each other.

Moreover, the Nuzi texts contain inheritance clauses for children born to the primary wife, similar to the story of Isaac in Gen 16. Many scholars have argued that the adoption of daughters whose fathers had no male offspring (compare Exod 21:7-11, in which a father sells his daughter to a buyer who was obliged to arrange her marriage) has parallels in the so-called Nuzi sistership contracts. However, a recent evaluation of the Nuzi contracts shows a transfer of the right to negotiate the sister's marriage from the father (or biological brother) to an adoptive brother. The daughter then had the status of sister to the adoptive brother, who had the right to share in the future marriage price. At any rate, the sisters in the Nuzi contracts did not automatically become wives. However, both the biblical and Nuzi customs betray a similar cultural milieu.

Like the teraphim in Gen 29, the Nuzi documents provide evidence that household gods were of great importance and were passed down from generation to generation. However, there is no concrete evidence that the household gods at Nuzi were used to verify the legitimacy of one's right to inherit property. In fact, household gods at Nuzi were even bequeathed to individuals who were not the chief heir. They have thus been considered as cultic symbols of family unity. Deathbed blessings, similar to those by Isaac (Gen 27) and Jacob (Deut 33), were of value at Nuzi, at least in the legal sphere (*see* INHERITANCE IN THE OT).

In sum, the sheer weight of the information argues at the very least for a common cultural milieu, rather than for specific borrowings or interconnections between Nuzi and the patriarchs. But the Nuzi material does not resolve any chronological issues, nor does it provide any concrete parallels with the biblical narratives.

Bibliography: Millar Burrows. "The Ancient Oriental Background of Hebrew Levirate Marriage." *BASOR* 77 (1940) 1–15; Edward Chiera. *They Wrote on Clay: The Babylonian Tablets Speak Today* (1956); David D. Deuel. "Apprehending Kidnappers by Correspondence at Provincial Arrapha." *Mesopotamia and the Bible: Comparative Explorations.* Mark W. Chavalas and K. Lawson Younger Jr., eds. (2002) 191–208; Barry L. Eichler. "Nuzi and the Bible: A Retrospective." *DUMU-E2-DUB-BA-A: Studies in Honor of Ake W. Sjöberg.* Hermann Behrens, Darlene Loding, and Martha T. Roth, eds. (1989) 107–19; Barry L. Eichler. *Indenture at Nuzi* (1973); Martha Morrison. "The Jacob and Laban Narrative in Light of Ancient Near Eastern Sources." *BA* 46 (1983) 155–64; David I. Owen and Gernot Wilhelm, eds. *Nuzi at Seventy-Five* (1999); David I. Owen et al.,

Studies on the Civilization and Culture of Nuzi and the Hurrians (1981–); Martin J. Selman. "Comparative Customs and the Patriarchal Age." *Essays on the Patriarchal Narratives.* Alan R. Millard and Donald J. Wiseman, eds. (1983) 91–139; E. A. Speiser. "The Hurrian Participation in the Civilization of Mesopotamia, Syria, and Palestine." *Oriental and Biblical Studies.* J. J. Finkelstein and Moshe Greenberg, eds. (1967) 244–69; Richard F. S. Starr. *Nuzi: Report on the Excavations at Yorghan Tepe Near Kirkuk, Iraq.* 2 vols. (1937–39); Gernot Wilhelm. *The Hurrians* (1989); Carlo Zaccagnini. *The Rural Landscape of the Land of Arraphe* (1979).

MARK W. CHAVALAS

NYMPHA nim´fuh [Νύμφα Nympha]. Owner of a house in Colossae in which Christians gathered for meetings and worship, and to whom Paul (or a Christian writing in Paul's name) sent greetings (Col 4:15). The accusative case of the name, the same for both masculine and feminine forms, has made ascertaining this Christian's gender difficult. Manuscripts render the pronoun accompanying the word "house" as "his" (e.g., Claromontanus) and "their" (e.g., Sinaiticus, Alexandrinus). But the NRSV renders "her" (as do RSV, NIV) with support from Codex Vaticanus, 1739, the Haraclean Syriac and the Sahidic, and some Greek minuscules. *See* COLOSSIANS, LETTER TO THE.

EMILY R. CHENEY

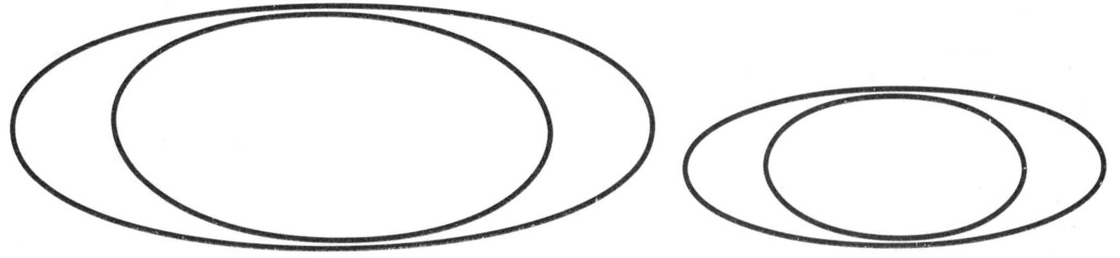

OAK [אֵלָה ʾelah, אַלָּה ʾallah, אַלּוֹן ʾallon, אֵלוֹן ʾelon]. The botanical classification of oaks (*Quercus* species) is difficult, hence no two authors seem to use quite the same names. Present-day remnants of oak woodland in the moister areas of Israel indicate a much wider occurrence in biblical times. These are bushes or large trees with evergreen and deciduous leaves in the eastern Mediterranean area, but all have the distinctive acorn-and-cup fruits of oaks. The kermes or calliprinos oak (*Quercus coccifera* or *Quercus calliprinos*) is usually seen as a nibbled bush or medium-sized tree of the mountains with evergreen, prickly leaves. One such tree is the traditional oak of MAMRE where Abraham camped (Gen 13:18). An alternative rendering of the Hebrew terms is "TEREBINTH," a large oak-like tree (*Pistacia atlantica*) of that region with a similar Hebrew name (Isa 6:13; Hos 4:13) but that is botanically very distinct. The larger, deciduous Tabor oak (*Quercus ithaborensis, Quercus aegilops*, or *Quercus macrolepis*) with lobed leaves appears on the lowland Plain of Sharon, as well as on Carmel and in the lower hill country.

The oasis-like respite provided by clumps of oak trees meant that such places were frequent camping places or villages as evidenced in such references as "oak of Moreh" (Gen 12:6; Deut 11:30), "oak at Ophrah" (Judg 6:11), "oak of Tabor" (1 Sam 10:3), and "oaks of Mamre" (Gen 13:18). Solitary oak trees were often used as landmarks (e.g., Gen 12:6; 35:4; Josh 19:33; 24:26) or markers of graves (1 Chr 10:12): Deborah, Rebekah's nurse, was buried under a particular oak (Gen 35:8), which gave rise to the place-name ALLON-BACUTH, the "oak of weeping." Offering protection from the sun, oaks were often gathering places—locations for meetings, either official or social, or even encounters with angels (Judg 6:11, 19; 9:6; 1 Sam 10:3). However, in some shady clumps immoral practices took place (Isa 57:5; Ezek 6:13; Hos 4:13). Absalom, David's son, was killed when he was caught in the branches of an oak tree while riding his mule (2 Sam 18:9-14). Reputedly sturdy trees, oaks are also often used metaphorically as symbols of strength (Isa 61:3; Amos 2:9). *See* PLANTS OF THE BIBLE.

F. NIGEL HEPPER

OAK OF TABOR. *See* TABOR, OAK OF.

OAK OF THE PILLAR [אֵלוֹן מֻצָּב ʾelon mutsav]. Abimelech was made king "by the OAK of the pillar at Shechem" (Judg 9:6). Jacob hid the foreign gods of his household beneath the oak tree near Shechem (Gen 35:4). After making a covenant with the people, Joshua set up a large stone beneath the oak at Shechem (Josh 24:22-26). All of these likely refer to the same oak, perhaps related to a shrine. *See* SHECHEM, SHECHEMITES.

TREVOR D. COCHELL

OAK, DIVINER'S. *See* DIVINER'S OAK.

OAR [מָשׁוֹט mashot, מִשׁוֹט mishot]. An oar is a long wooden pole with a flat blade at the end that is placed in the water and used to propel and steer a boat in the desired direction by applying pressure against the water. According to Ezek 27:6, oars made in Tyre consisted of oak. Large boats or galleys before the Common Era were propelled by a single tier of oarsmen synchronizing their rowing with the oars (Isa 33:21; Ezek 27:6, 26, 29). A small boat could be moved by a single rower with two oars, one on each side of the vessel. Oars existed as early as 2500 BCE, as evidenced by a limestone relief in the mortuary temple of Sahu-Re in Egypt that portrays a crew of twenty-two men seated on stools as they row. *See* SHIPS AND SAILING IN THE NT; SHIPS AND SAILING IN THE OT.

EMILY R. CHENEY

OATH [שְׁבוּעָה shevuʿah; ὅρκος horkos]. At its simplest, "swearing an oath" appears to strengthen or confirm the truth of a statement or the reliability of a promise (or threat), by invoking a divine sanction in the event that the statement proves to be false or the promise or threat proves to be empty. This may explain in part why the less frequent Hebrew form ʾalah (אָלָה) also denotes an oath or curse in certain contexts (e.g., Gen 24:41). One who swears an oath, especially in early biblical traditions, invokes a conditional curse or malediction upon himself or herself in the event that the oath turns out to be willfully false or invalid (*see* BLESSINGS AND CURSINGS). In effect, to break or to nullify an oath constitutes an act of perjury that invites penalties. Although Jesus (Matt 5:37) and James (Jas 5:12) insist that in everyday life "yes" or "no" should require no qualification and carry no less weight or reliability than an oath, situations of crisis, absence of confidence, or public need may invite the use of oaths to provide assurance that the speaker's statement, act of witness, or promise is sincere, reliable, truthful, and made in good faith. Such an emphasis upon commitment and assurance characterizes the binding nature of covenantal declarations of pledge or promise. Arguably this also characterizes the pledges enacted in dominical sacraments of baptism and the Lord's Supper or the Eucharist.

A. Biblical Hebrew and Ancient Near East Background
B. Functions and Distinctive Logic of Oaths, Including Oaths Sworn by God
   1. Sanctions
   2. Nature of God
   3. Performative force
C. Oaths in the New Testament and in Rabbinic Literature
Bibliography

A. Biblical Hebrew and Ancient Near East Background

The root for oath, **shbʿ** (שׁבע), also denotes the numeral seven (**shevaʿ** שֶׁבַע) in Hebrew and in several other ANE languages. Some scholars call attention in this context to Gen 21:22-34, where Abraham seals an oath concerning the use of a well by giving seven ewe lambs to ABIMELECH as a witness to their sworn agreement concerning the well (Gen 21:30). The narrator observes, "Therefore that place was called Beer-sheba; because there both of them swore an oath" (Gen 21:31). BEER-SHEBA (**beʾer shevaʿ** בְּאֵר שֶׁבַע) means "well of seven" but also "well of the oath." The binding oath secures Beer-sheba for Abraham and becomes the southernmost settlement of biblical Israel and a sanctuary of divine presence. Since seven in biblical traditions often signifies completeness or fulfillment and in Mesopotamian texts is also associated with deity, some argue that this suggests the notion of strengthening declarations or promises by invoking the deity as a witness to such declarations or promises. Such a connection is possible but cannot be established. The less frequent term for an oath, **ʾalah**, offers a more securely based context of thought, as indicated above. Since the word sometimes denotes a curse, many scholars argue that in early biblical thought an oath functioned as a conditional invocation of a divine sanction or curse should an oath be willfully invalidated, broken, or falsified. If an oath is taken with goodwill and sincerity, the implied protasis remains a counterfactual conditional or an unfulfilled apodosis. In the case of willful deceit, it invites retribution for what amounts to perjury. For example, in 1 Sam 3:17 Eli adjures Samuel to report truthfully his night vision with the words "May God do so to you and more also, if you hide anything from me of all that he told you." In 2 Kgs 6:31 the formula embraces both oath and vow: "So may God do to me, and more, if the head of Elisha son of Shaphat stays on his shoulders today." This understanding became so deeply embedded in the linguistic forms of oath-taking that in the course of time the full formula became truncated into an implicit indicator of an unfulfilled apodosis or counterfactual conditional by means of the use of the Hebrew **ʾim** (אִם, "if") to introduce the oath. The conjunction **ʾim** thus becomes an emphatic negative, and **ʾim-loʾ** (אִם־לֹא, "if not") an emphatic affirmative. In 2 Sam 11:11 Uriah swears to David: "As you live, and as your soul lives, I will not do such a thing" (**ʾim-ʾeʿeseh ʾeth-haddavar hazzeh** אִם־אֶעֱשֶׂה אֶת־הַדָּבָר הַזֶּה), strictly, "if I do this thing," but understood to mean "I will not do this thing."

A form such as that just cited overlaps with the logical functions of a VOW. Both forms exercise a binding force upon a declaration of intent for the future, but oaths also operate with a broader currency, referring to statements about present or past events or states of affairs as well as to promises or threats relating to the future. The binding force of an oath finds expression in the categorization of "swearing falsely" as a serious sin (Jer 7:9) and of "not swearing deceitfully" as a required virtue (Ps 24:4). An oath even has binding force on subsequent generations (Gen 50:25). Qoheleth warns his readers: "It is better that you should not vow than that you should vow and not fulfill it" (Eccl 5:5).

B. Functions and Distinctive Logic of Oaths, Including Oaths Sworn by God

In the OT, God is said to have "sworn to my servant David: 'I will establish your descendants forever, and build your throne for all generations'" (Ps 89:3*b*-4 [Heb. 89:4*b*-5]). Often this occurs within the framework of a covenant promise (Ps 89:3 [Heb. 89:4]; *see* COVENANT, NT AND OT). This theme emerges frequently: "The LORD swore to David a sure oath from which he will not turn back" (Ps 132:11). But this raises three logical problems.

1. Sanctions

Does God taking an oath still presuppose the notion of oaths as invoking hypothetical or conditional sanctions? Some argue that this principle remains implicit in such examples as Isa 45:22-23: "By myself I have sworn, from my mouth has gone forth in righteousness a word that shall not return." In the NT this becomes an issue for explicit reflection: "Because he had no one greater by whom to swear, he swore by himself, saying, 'I will surely bless you'" (Heb 6:13-14). In Hebrews the "certainty" of God's promise becomes a major theme: "The Lord has sworn and will not change his mind" (Heb 7:21).

2. Nature of God

All the same, if properties of God's character are truth and faithfulness, how can it make sense to conceive of an oath as adding to God's truthfulness or reliability? Since it is logically inconceivable that God should lie without being false to God's nature, a divine oath appears to be otiose. Hebrews asserts that it is "impossible that God would prove false" through "two unchangeable things" (Heb 6:18). These "two things" may refer to the promise itself and its confirmation by oath (Heb 6:17), but David R. Worley argues that more probably these refer to God's dual role as oath-taker and oath-witness. These provide a "hope" and a "steadfast anchor" (Heb 6:19). In 1st-cent. Judaism, Philo puzzled over how it could make logical sense for God to swear an oath on such grounds (Philo, *Sacrifices* 91–94; and *Spec. Laws* 3.203–07).

A solution depends on our avoiding the notion that an oath adds to the veracity of a speaker. The purpose of an oath is more often (as in Hebrews) to provide assurance and confidence on the part of those for whose benefit the oath is made. Thus, while there may be no legitimate reason for the Christians for whom Hebrews was written to doubt the promises of God, the writer, as a matter of grace and concession, provides further assurances that will enhance and promote "boldness" (Heb 4:16) and "full assurance" (Heb 6:11) or "full assurance of faith" (Heb 10:22) among the addressees.

3. Performative force

The logical function of oaths raises a third point. An oath does not take the form of a descriptive proposition, which is simply placed alongside the proposition to which it relates. Alfred J. Ayer and P. F. Strawson insist that there is no difference between the truth-value of "it is raining" and the truth-value of "it is true that it is raining." Strawson argues that for someone to say "it is true that" is an expression of personal endorsement or appropriation for the truth-claim in question. In this respect, the statement is like an oath. Hence, like curses and vows, oaths operate with performative or illocutionary force, not as propositions. The speaker, as it were, nails his or her colors to the mast in uttering an oath. Oaths may achieve more than this, but not less than this. Hence oaths do not fall prey to any circular argument about their use.

C. Oaths in the New Testament and in Rabbinic Literature

Both Jesus and James prohibit the use of oaths in everyday speech on the grounds that oaths distort truthful integrity by appearing to make some speech "more" truthful and reliable than straightforward statements or promises: "Do not swear at all, either by heaven . . . or by the earth. . . . Let your word be 'Yes, Yes' or 'No, No'; anything more than this comes from the evil one" (Matt 5:34-35, 37). The wording in James is almost identical with this: "Do not swear, either by heaven or by earth or by any other oath, but let your 'Yes' be yes and your 'No' be no" (Jas 5:12). The reliability of a truthful person's word renders an oath unnecessary. If transparent and habitual truthfulness characterizes someone's life, such a person should not need to resort to the use of oath. The exegesis of James yields an interpretation very close to that of Matthew. Neither passage envisages such particular contexts, e.g., as that of legal oath-taking; both concern everyday Christian discipleship.

Even so, do Jesus and the early church as represented by James reflect an attitude to oaths that is at variance with their acceptance in the OT (e.g., Num 5:19-22)? Matthean specialists do not regard the series of antitheses in the SERMON ON THE MOUNT as indicating a rejection of the OT by Jesus, even if it suggests an interpretation of the OT that accords with radical Christian discipleship. Matthew 5 and James 5 address truthful speech and personal integrity in everyday life. On the other hand, the OT witnesses to solemn occasions such as the making of a national or religious covenant in which an absence of personal knowledge of all participants requires not added truthfulness but a firm assurance of the reliability and good will of all parties concerned to make promises and pledges with good will and to perform them reliably. In addition, other passages in the NT affirm the OT traditions about divine oath-taking (Luke 1:73; Acts 2:30; Heb 6:13-17).

Hence, in Christian traditions of ecclesiology, most "mainline" churches—including Catholic, Lutheran, Calvinist, and Anglican—accept that oath-taking in law courts, e.g., comes within this public context. Dissenting interpretations are probably or normally found historically only among Anabaptists and Quakers. Melanchthon insisted that to refuse to take legal oaths or those required by the state would lead to the destruction of secular government and justice (*Augsburg Confession*, Article XVI, section 2).

Jesus engages in a particular controversy with the scribes and Pharisees about the taking of oaths in Matt 23:16-22. It is widely agreed that behind this critique lies the practice of using oaths of supposedly varying degrees of importance in order to withdraw from certain commitments, statements, or obligations by the use of a "greater" oath to countermand them. As in Matt 5:34-37, Jesus requires a transparent and non-manipulative commitment to utter truthfulness. Matthew 23:16-22 reaffirms the OT tradition that if an oath is taken, this has full binding force, whatever device of casuistry may be used to try to escape it. The notion that all the sanctions listed in Matt 23:16-22 (the sanctuary, the altar, heaven, God) are ultimately related to the holy God may perhaps recall our starting point, namely that an oath implicitly calls down a solemn and serious sanction if the oath is broken or invalidated. *See* PROMISE.

Bibliography: Alfred J. Ayer. *Language, Truth and Logic* (1990); Herbert Brichto. *The Problem of "Curse" in the Hebrew Bible* (1963); Tony W. Cartledge. *Vows in the Hebrew Bible and Ancient Near East* (1992); Meredith G. Kline. *By Oath Consigned* (1968); P. F. Strawson. "Intention and Convention in Speech Acts." *Philosophical Review* 73 (1964) 439–60; Hugh C. White.

"The Divine Oath in Genesis." *JBL* 92 (1973) 165–79; David R. Worley. "Fleeing to Two Immutable Things, God's Oath-Taking and Oath-Witnessing: The Use of Litigant Oath in Hebrews 6:12-20." *ResQ* 36 (1994) 223–36.

ANTHONY C. THISELTON

OBADIAH oh′buh-d*i*′uh [עֹבַדְיָה ʿovadhyah, עֹבַדְיָהוּ ʿovadhyahu; Ἀβδίας Abdias]. 1. Ahab's palace manager who was so devoted to Yahweh that he fed and protected a hundred prophets. As Elijah requested, he told Ahab that Elijah would meet Ahab (1 Kgs 18:3-16).

2. Arnan's son; a descendant of David through Solomon (1 Chr 3:21).

3. Izrahiah's son; a descendant of Issachar who headed a northern clan (1 Chr 7:3).

4. Azel's son; a Benjaminite and descendant of Saul (1 Chr 8:38; 9:44).

5. A Levite and descendant of Elkanah (1 Chr 9:16).

6. A Gadite warrior and an officer in David's army (1 Chr 12:9).

7. Father of Ishmaiah and Zebulunite tribal leader during David's reign (1 Chr 27:19).

8. Official of King Jehoshaphat. He taught the law to the people in the cities of Judah (2 Chr 17:7-9).

9. A Levite, Merari's son who directed temple repair during Josiah's reform (2 Chr 34:12).

10. Jehiel's son who returned with Ezra to Jerusalem (Ezra 8:9; 1 Esd 8:35), and perhaps the same Obadiah who signed the covenant (Neh 10:5).

11. A gatekeeper at the storehouses in Jerusalem after the exile (Neh 12:25).

12. Prophet whose vision is recorded in the book of Obadiah (Obad 1; *see* OBADIAH, BOOK OF). *See* PRIESTS AND LEVITES.

EMILY R. CHENEY

OBADIAH, BOOK OF oh′buh-d*i*′uh [עֹבַדְיָה ʿovadhyah; Ἀβδιού Abdiou]. The book of Obadiah is the shortest book in the OT, with a single chapter of twenty-one verses. The book contains no information regarding the prophet's lineage and origin or about contemporary rulers. Despite such brevity, the book displays aspects that are both unique and consistent with other prophetic traditions.

- A. Book
  - 1. Structure
  - 2. Textual issues
- B. Sociohistorical Settings
- C. Intertextuality
- D. Key Themes
  - 1. Divine retribution
  - 2. Kinship solidarity
  - 3. Yahweh's kingship
- Bibliography

A. Book

1. Structure

Though a single chapter, the book's structural subdivisions have been identified in various ways. In particular, scholars have considered either different elements of genres (oracles of judgment, indictment, and restoration) or distinctive redactional sources (preexilic, exilic, and postexilic compositions) to delineate various subunits and their correlations. One consistent aspect is that this book follows the patterns of oracles against the nations in the prophetic literature (*see* ORACLE).

The text exhibits a conceptual flow of argument, regardless of the issue of unity. The opening call (Obad 1-4) exhorts an envoy to announce Yahweh's decision to humiliate Edom (*see* EDOM, EDOMITES). The plan to destroy proud Edom (Obad 5-7) is compared to thieves who take what they want, and gleaners who take what they need. Unlike those scenarios, Edom will be thoroughly pillaged and will be betrayed by its former allies. The subsequent oracle (Obad 8-11) heightens the doom by depicting the violence against Edom's wise and valiant alike, based on the rationale of Edom's own violence committed against Judah. The next subunit (Obad 12-15) further delineates the preceding rationale by presenting vivid pictures of Edom's deception and violence against Israel culminating in the declaration of the day of Yahweh (*see* DAY OF THE LORD). The oracle against the nations (Obad 16-18) expands the motif of Yahweh's divine rule over the whole world and encompasses the notion of Israel's violence against Edom. The closing subunit (Obad 19-21) recapitulates the reversal motif in the eschatological vindication through which Mount Zion and its returnees will subdue Mount Esau in the kingdom ruled by Yahweh.

2. Textual issues

Amid coherent correlations of the subunits, this short text does contain both textual ambiguity and multivalence. One historically debated case concerns the relation between v. 15*a* and v. 15*b*. In light of the thematic flow, many scholars propose reversing the sentences in that verse, reading v. 15*b* as a conclusion to vv. 1-14 and v. 15*a* as an opening for vv. 16-21. Others propose taking v. 15*a-b* in its given sequence with v. 15 serving as a literary bridge between vv. 1-14 (motif of punishment) and vv. 16-21 as a separate unit (motif of salvation tied with Zion).

Another debate concerns a discrepancy of tenses in vv. 12-14. The Hebrew text reads "Do not gloat." However, both the Targum and the LXX render these phrases "You should not have gloated." Even modern Bible translations are disagreeing over which reading is preferred. The NRSV follows the LXX.

B. Sociohistorical Settings

Lack of information about the historical Obadiah makes any reconstruction of the historical settings virtually inconclusive. Although Obadiah is a name attested in the OT, the fact that it means "servant of the Lord" means it is possible that it is intended as a title instead of a personal name, thereby making it difficult to posit a historical figure. Thus, proposals concerning the social settings cover a range from as far back as the 9th cent. BCE to the other extreme of the 3rd cent. BCE.

In support of the preexilic setting, rabbinic tradition connected the prophet Obadiah with the palace official of the same name from the time of King Ahab (1 Kgs 18:1-16) and identified him as an Edomite proselyte (*b. Sanh.* 39b). This 9th-cent. setting would include the Aramean attacks against Israel (2 Kgs 6:8–7:20; 12:17-18), with Edom's possible participation.

If the book has an exilic setting, the action of Edom's looting coincides with the event of Babylon's siege and pillaging of Jerusalem in 587 BCE (Obad 10-15). Israel's bitterness and hatred toward Edom (Ps 137:7; Lam 4:21-22; Ezek 35:1–36:15; 1 Esd 4:45) further link the setting with the Babylonian conquest. The ARAD OSTRACA and other inscriptions from the eastern Negev similarly point to the Edomite violence during this period.

Supporting the postexilic setting, some scholars position the final redaction during the Persian period with the infiltration of the NABATEANS into Edom. Verses 16-21 portray the expanded eschatological motif that is representative of the Persian and Hellenistic periods (compare Mal 1:2-5). The unique term SEPHARAD (**sefaradh** [סְפָרַד]; Obad 20) may allude to either Sardis in Asia Minor or Spain, possibly signifying the expanded Diaspora.

C. Intertextuality

The book of Obadiah echoes many other prophetic texts in terms of words, phrases, and motifs. These similarities may offer helpful insights to the place and function of Obadiah in the twelve prophetic books (*see* BOOK OF THE TWELVE).

The most explicit connection is with Jer 49:7-22. Though the interconnections are apparent (Jer 49:9-10//Obad 5-7; Jer 49:14-16//Obad 1-4), their relationship has been interpreted in three possible ways: Obadiah quoting Jeremiah, Jeremiah quoting Obadiah, or both texts independently quoting another common source.

Within the Twelve Prophets, Obad 4 echoes Amos 9:2, and Obad 19 alludes to Amos 9:12. Obadiah shares comparable catchwords with Joel (Joel 2:32 [Heb. 3:5]; 3:17 [Heb. 4:17]//Obad 17; Joel 3:4, 7, 14 [Heb. 4:4, 7, 14]//Obad 15; Joel 3:19 [Heb. 4:19]//Obad 10; Joel 3:3 [Heb. 4:3]//Obad 11). Obadiah's current placement as part of the Minor Prophets was intentional because it forms a bridge between the previous books of Joel and Amos, and the following books of Jonah and Nahum. In this position, Obadiah functions as inner biblical exegesis for the books that proceed it; together with the books that follow Obadiah, it functions as an Oracle Against the Nations. Thus, the reader is pulled along through the texts based on those connections.

D. Key Themes

1. Divine retribution

That God is actively involved with human events is a fundamental premise of Obadiah's theology. Thus, the oracle starts with Yahweh's summons for nations to rise up against Edom (Obad 1). God expresses the divine plan to use other NATIONS as God's instruments to judge Edom (compare Isa 10:5-6). Furthermore, despite Edom's haughtiness, it will be humbled (Obad 3-4, 18; compare Isa 10:12-19), and the violence done against Judah will be reciprocated to Edom by divine retribution (Obad 10, 15).

2. Kinship solidarity

Edom's failure to keep kinship solidarity with Israel, especially during the time of calamity, is forcefully portrayed in Edom's cruel cowardice and atrocities. The terms *Esau* and *Jacob* emphatically echo the Genesis account for the close bond that the twin brothers should maintain. Ironically, it was Jacob who tricked his brother Esau in Genesis (25:29-34; 27:1-40; *see* ESAU, ESAUITES). Hence, if read against the context of the postexilic Persian period, the reversal of status may have multiple interpretations, intensified by the temporal ambiguity of Obad 12-14, so that the concept of solidarity can symbolize not only a Jacob–Esau relationship but also an in-group and out-group dynamic among the restored communities (compare the books of Jonah and Ruth).

3. Yahweh's kingship

The culminating announcements (Obad 19-21) broaden the horizon from Edom to other nations: Mount Zion will rule over Mount Esau, and the exiles from the farthest corners will gloriously return to regain the new kingdom. This kingdom belongs to Yahweh, who will reign with justice and peace.

Bibliography: John Barton. *Joel and Obadiah.* OTL (2001); Ehud Ben Zvi. *A Historical-Critical Study of the Book of Obadiah* (1996); Paul R. Raabe. *Obadiah.* AB 24D (1996); Daniel J. Simundson. *Hosea, Joel, Amos, Obadiah, Jonah, Micah.* AOTC (2005); Marvin A. Sweeney. *The Twelve Prophets.* Vol. 1. Berit Olam (2000); Hans Walter Wolff. *Obadiah and Jonah.* CC (1986).

HYUN CHUL PAUL KIM

OBAL oh'buhl [עוֹבָל ʿoval]. Eighth of the thirteen sons of JOKTAN (Gen 10:28), and thus a descendant of Shem, the son of Noah. The name is spelled EBAL (ʾeval אֵיבָל) in the par. list of Joktan's sons in 1 Chr 1:22. The sons of Joktan resided in the eastern hill country from Mesha to Sephar (Gen 10:30), which many scholars locate somewhere in the Arabian

Peninsula. The exact location of Obal's territory, however, is unknown.

BRUCE W. GENTRY

OBED oh'bid [עוֹבֵד ʿovedh, עֹבֵד ʿovedh; ʾΩβήθ **Ōbēth**, ʾΙωβήδ **Iōbēd**]. 1. The son of Ruth and Boaz; the father of Jesse and grandfather of King David (Ruth 4:17, 22; 1 Chr 2:12). According to some, he was the "GOEL" or "next-of-kin" for Naomi and functioned as her son (Ruth 4:14-17). In the Levirate marriage (*see* LEVIRATE LAW), he was the son (or grandson) of Naomi's husband, Elimelech (Ruth 4:3-9). In both genealogies of Jesus in Matt 1:5 and Luke 3:32, he was the son of Boaz. Because Obed is named a son of Naomi he becomes both the son of Elimelech and of Boaz; both men were of Bethlehem, Judah. Through Obed, Moab entered into the lineage of Jesus (Ruth 1:4; 4:6). *See* DAVID.

2. A descendant of Judah (1 Chr 2:37-38).

3. One of David's mighty men named in the longer list in 1 Chr 11:47, but not in 2 Sam 23 (*see* DAVID'S CHAMPIONS).

4. A gatekeeper in Solomon's Temple (1 Chr 26:7).

5. The father of Azariah, a commander (2 Chr 23:1).

6. A descendant of Adin who returned from exile (1 Esd 8:32).

BARBARA MEI LEUNG LAI

OBED-EDOM oh'bid-ee'duhm [עֹבֵד־אֱדוֹם ʿovedh-ʾedhom]. The name means "servant of (the god) Edom," apparently referring to **ʾatum** or **ʾadum**, the consort of Resheph, an underworld deity known from Egypt and Canaan. 1. The "Gittite" (i.e., from GATH) at whose house David lodged the ark of God when the procession to bring it to the City of David (2 Sam 6:1-11//1 Chr 13:1-14) was stopped by Uzzah's death. Obed-edom's name and origin could place him among Philistines loyal to David (2 Sam 15:18, 22).

2. Son of JEDUTHUN (1 Chr 15:18, 24; 16:38) who was gatekeeper for the ark of God and also performed special service as one of the lyre players accompanying the ark into the city of David (15:21; 16:5, 38).

3. Son of Korah through Kore (1 Chr 26:1, 19). Obed-edom and his sixty-two descendants were gatekeepers of the temple precinct and its related storehouses in preparation for the building of the Temple under Solomon (1 Chr 23:2; 26:4-8, 15).

4. Levitical custodian of temple treasures when JOASH, king of Israel, defeated AMAZIAH, king of Judah, and sacked Jerusalem (2 Chr 25:24). He presumably served in the gatekeeper tradition of his clan (compare 1 Chr 26:4-8, 15; and #3 above). The parallel account in 2 Kgs 14:14 omits mention of Obed-edom.

The precise relationship between these individuals remains unclear due to the nature of the work of the Chronicler, who presents one or more families of temple servants claiming ties to the caretaker of the ark under David and gives them Levitical ancestry. The son of Jeduthun and the gatekeeper under #2 above are perhaps to be understood as separate individuals (1 Chr 16:38). *See* KORAH, KORAHITES; PHILISTINES; PRIESTS AND LEVITES.

DAVID L. THOMPSON

OBEDIENCE [יִקְּהָה yiqhah, שָׁמַע shamaʿ; ὑπακοή **hypakoē**]. Many readers of the Bible may well be suspicious of the whole concept and vocabulary of obedience, in part due to the atrocities committed by people who were only "following orders," from Herod to Hitler, along with the general rejection of hierarchical authority and the affirmation of the autonomous self. Yet human society has never existed and cannot exist without some form of obedience to law and order. It is not social necessity, however, that generated the biblical authors' pervasive theology of obedience, but their understanding of God and human life.

The text of the Bible is permeated with words that express or imply obedience. In the NRSV, forms of the word group *obey/disobey* occur 283 times. When combined with related words that imply obedience (*law, command, commandment, king, ruler*), the number increases to 6,302. In addition, many biblical passages deal with the subject in profound ways without utilizing the specific vocabulary. The Bible begins with the stories of creation and fall, the obedience of the universe and the disobedience of humanity, without ever using the *obey/disobey* word group (Gen 1–3). As Dietrich Bonhoeffer recognized, the SERMON ON THE MOUNT is about obedience, concluding with a powerful contrast between those who obey Jesus as Lord and those who do not—but without any use of the specific terminology of *obey/disobey* (Matt 5–7).

English translations render several Hebrew and Greek words by the English *obey* word group. In the OT, by far the most common word for obedience is shamaʿ, the basic word for "to hear," often with the meaning "to hearken, hear-and-obey," being persuaded by and acting on what one hears. Thus the Shema (*see* SHEMA, THE) begins with "Hear, O Israel," which means much more than "listen," and proceeds immediately with the command to love and obey God (Deut 6:4-6). The Greek NT has a total of twenty-four different words that are translated by some form of the *obey/disobey* word group, but—in accord with the OT background of the NT concept of obedience—here, too, the primary words are *hear* and its derivatives, including especially **akouō** (ἀκούω), **hypakouō** (ὑπακούω), **eisakouō** (εἰσακούω), **hypakoē**, **parakouō** (παρακούω), **parakoē** (παρακοή).

It is the essential being and character of God as God the Creator and Redeemer that defines the biblical concept of obedience. The first words of God in the Bible are a command addressed to non-being, "Let there be light!" (Gen 1:3), and light obediently appears. The universe has no independent existence, nor is God one power among others who negotiates the universe into existence. God commands and the universe obeys, from the stars in their courses to the smallest animal (Gen 1–2). All creatures, great and small, are what they are in obedience to their Creator; their obedience is not a burden, but grateful praise (Pss 104; 148).

The only exception to this universal obedience is the creature called Adam (ʾadham [אָדָם]; both a personal name and the collective, "humanity"). God had given commands to Adam and Eve (Gen 2:16-17; 3:11, 17). Their disobedience represented the character of human life as such: the desire to be autonomous, to be one's own god, to be "free" in the sense of obeying no other authority except one's own.

Within disobedient humanity, God continued to call. While most were disobedient, a few responded in faith and obedience. The paradigm for this relation to God is the gracious act of God in calling into being a covenant people. Abraham and Sarah obey (Gen 12:1-4), their descendants become the covenant people by obeying the call through Moses, and they are delivered from bondage to enter into the covenant (Exod 1–19). The covenant is God's gift, but it requires obedient response (Deut 26:17; 30:16). The TEN COMMANDMENTS (Exod 20:1-17) represent God's uncompromising command, as do the host of other laws (e.g., Exod 20:22–23:33). Within the covenant, obedience to God was a virtue but not a burden, not a matter of "legalism" but of joyful celebration (Pss 19:7-14; 119). But obedience was never complete. Individual Israelites and Israel as a whole sometimes did the will of God, obeying from the heart, but for the most part the story of Israel is the story of Adamic humanity as such, and the history of the covenant people is the history of disobedience. This is the report of Israel's historians (e.g., Num 14:22; 2 Kgs 22:13; Neh 9:16), the confession and lament of Israel's psalms and prayers (e.g., Ps 106:25; Dan 9:10-11), and the accusation of Israel's prophets (e.g., Jer 3:13; 7:24; Isa 65:2 = Rom 10:21). The prophetic accusation that Israel was disobedient sometimes made clear that the obedience called for was not purely formal and authoritarian, but was inseparable from the content of the command: "to do justice, and to love kindness, and to walk humbly with your God" (Mic 6:8).

Only one human was truly obedient. The Gospels portray Jesus as wholly obedient to the will of God (e.g., Matt 4:1-11; Mark 14:36; John 4:34; 6:38). Paul twice sums up the life and death of Jesus as obedience (Rom 5:19, in contrast to humanity represented by the first Adam; Phil 2:8, of Jesus' divesting himself of divine glory and becoming a servant obedient to the point of death). The **pistis Iēsou Christou** (πίστις Ἰησοῦ Χριστοῦ, "faith of/in Jesus Christ"; Rom 3:22, 26; Gal 2:16, 20; 3:22; Phil 3:9) probably refers, in some instances, to Jesus' faithfulness, i.e., his faithful obedience to God. For Christian faith, Jesus' own obedience to God became both the basis of salvation for a disobedient humanity (e.g., Rom 5:19) and a model for the Christian life, understood as obedience to God the Creator and Jesus as Lord (e.g., Rom 6:17; 1 Pet 1:2, 22). Such obedience need not be servile, blind, or authoritarian, but can be a matter of love, trust, and insight (e.g., John 15:15—obey not as servants but as friends). Just as the person's whole response to God can be called *faith*, so it can be called *obedience*. Faith and obedience are not separate stages in a process; each embraces one's relation to God as a whole (e.g., John 3:36; Rom 1:5; 16:26). Nor is obedience an alternative or supplement to grace, which always precedes the call to obey and is its basis.

Obedience to God is sometimes expressed in the Bible as obedience to God's representatives within the community of faith. In Israel, this meant obedience to God's lawgivers, priests, and prophets (e.g., Num 27:20; Deut 17:12; Josh 1:17; 2 Kgs 18:12; Isa 50:10; Jer 35:15). In the Christian community, apostles and other church leaders called for obedience (2 Cor 10:6; Phil 2:12; 1 Thess 5:12; 2 Thess 3:14; Phlm 21). This is sometimes represented hierarchically: those who hear (obey) those commissioned by Jesus hear (obey) Jesus himself, which means they hear and obey God (Luke 10:16).

Biblical authors sometimes call for obedience to secular rulers as an aspect of one's obedience to God. Israel's prophets could declare that obedience to pagan rulers is the will of God. For Christians, the classic passage became Rom 13:1-7, in which obedience to the secular authority of the state is virtually identified with obedience to God. The ancient household was structured hierarchically, ruled by the patriarch or *pater familias*. A good household was characterized by obedience: wives to husbands, children to parents, slaves to masters. Especially in the later Pauline tradition, such obedience was encouraged as an aspect of Christian discipleship (*see* HOUSEHOLD CODES).

There are also numerous biblical examples in which disobedience to established authority, whether governmental or domestic, is considered to be obedience to God. The classical example is provided by the Maccabean martyrs who died rather than obey the edicts of Antiochus Epiphanes (e.g., 2 Macc 6:18–7:42), reflected paradigmatically in the stories of Daniel (Dan 1–6). When the choice is between obeying God or obeying human authority, even if represented by established government or religion, one must always obey God (Acts 5:29).

A major problem posed for later generations, of course, is when obedience to this-worldly authority is obedience to God and when obedience to God calls for disobedience to secular authorities, to conventional cultural norms, or even to those who claim to represent God. This issue cannot be resolved globally, as though obedience or resistance is right in every case, nor by citing texts from the Bible itself on one side or the other. Rather, it is a matter of discernment and hermeneutics. Moreover, some biblical texts raise the issue of whether the paradigm of obedience is itself so entangled with oppressive power structures that it must be abandoned: Abraham is praised for obeying God to the point of being willing to sacrifice his son (Gen 22); Saul is condemned with the words "to obey is better than sacrifice" because he saved King Agag and some animals for sacrifice, instead of destroying all the Amalekites and their property as he had been commanded (1 Sam 15:1-23). Each of these texts (and numerous similar ones) may well have a profound theological "point" not apparent to superficial reading or ideological exegesis, but the disturbing issue remains when obedience to the divine command violates the most fundamental ethical precepts—also given by God. Thus some interpreters oriented to liberation theology argue that not only the culturally conditioned forms of obedience contained in the Bible must be reinterpreted to address the (post-)modern situation (e.g., monarchy, slavery, the patriarchal family), but that the whole concept of obedience as a model for one's relation to God was part of the ancient worldview that must be abandoned in favor of equality and the autonomous self. Then the issue becomes whether the biblical message is being interpreted in terms of contemporary perspectives or replaced by them.

Bibliography: Dietrich Bonhoeffer. *The Cost of Discipleship* (1959); Ernst Käsemann. "Principles of Interpretation of Romans 13." *The Writings of St. Paul.* 2nd ed. Wayne A. Meeks and John T. Fitzgerald, eds. (2007) 573–86; Cynthia Briggs Kittredge. *Community and Authority: The Rhetoric of Obedience in the Pauline Tradition* (1998); Dorothea Soelle. *Beyond Mere Obedience* (1982).

M. EUGENE BORING

OBEISANCE [הִשְׁתַּחֲוָה hishtakhawah; προσκυνέω proskyneō]. A gesture of reverence and submission made by kneeling with nose and forehead touching the ground, including prostrating oneself before humans and worshiping gods. English Bibles render hishtakhawah as "obeisance" when it has a human object (e.g., Gen 43:28; 1 Sam 24:8) but as "worship," "bow down," and so forth when it has a divine object (e.g., Exod 20:5), thus creating a distinction absent in the original languages. The LXX translates nearly every occurrence of hishtakhawah as proskyneō, but the NRSV never renders NT occurrences of proskyneō as "obeisance" despite instances that clearly indicate prostration (Mark 15:19; Acts 10:25; Rev 22:8-9). *See* WORSHIP, EARLY JEWISH; WORSHIP, NT CHRISTIAN; WORSHIP, OT.

JUDITH ANNE JONES

OBELISK ob´uh-lisk [מַצֵּבָה matsevah; στῦλος stylos]. Derived from Gk. obeliskos (ὀβελίσκος), meaning "little needle" (see Job 41:30 [LXX 41:22]). Jeremiah warned that Yahweh was about to send Nebuchadnezzar to wreak havoc on Egypt, including breaking "the obelisks of HELIOPOLIS" (Jer 43:13). An obelisk is an upright, tall, long, thin, four-sided monument tapering at the top to a pyramidion. The first known obelisks were squat masonry monuments placed in the courtyards of Fifth Dynasty Egyptian solar temples, associating this shape with sun worship. The Egyptian word tekhen ("obelisk") is often found in connection with the word weben ("to shine"), suggesting that the obelisk is a representation of solar rays. The obelisk shape probably originates during Egyptian prehistory with the sacred benben stone, said to be the rock that caught the first light of the sun at the world's formation in Heliopolis, home of the creator god Atum-Ra. By the Twelfth Dynasty and 2nd millennium BCE, obelisks were constructed as monoliths, usually from red granite, a construction material with clear solar associations. By the New Kingdom, obelisks were placed in pairs at the pylon entrances of state temples like Karnak in Thebes.

Figure 1: Temple of Luxor, Forecourt, Obelisk of Ramesses II. Location: Temple of Amun, Luxor, Thebes, Egypt.

No obelisk pairs remain in modern Egypt because it became popular for imperial and colonial powers to ship obelisks home. Most obelisks are now found in Rome (the tallest surviving obelisk), Istanbul, London,

Paris, and New York. The largest-known obelisk lies unfinished in an Aswan granite quarry. Had it been completed, it would have been the tallest obelisk known at almost 42 m. Other cultures later copied the obelisk shape. Herod set up an obelisk at the hippodrome in Caesarea in Judea. The Black Obelisk was made by SHALMANESER III in the 9th cent. BCE to document the tribute by JEHU of Israel to Assyria. Some have made the connection between the obelisk and the standing stone MASSEBAH, used as a symbol of a god for idol worship. *See* STELE.

Bibliography: Labib Habachi. *The Obelisks of Egypt* (1978); Erik Iversen. *Obelisks in Exile* (1972); Nadav Na'aman. "Jehu Son of Omri: Legitimizing a Loyal Vassal by His Overlord." *IEJ* 48 (1998) 236–38.

KATHLYN MARY COONEY

OBELISK, BLACK. A black limestone OBELISK discovered at the ancient Assyrian capital CALAH (modern Nimrud). The Assyrian king SHALMANESER III (858–824 BCE) erected it there near the end of his reign (ca. 827 BCE) during a period of civil unrest in order to celebrate his achievements. The obelisk is four-sided and about 2 m high. At the top and bottom is a text beginning with an invocation of the gods and the epithets of Shalmaneser and then continuing with accounts of his military campaigns for every regnal year through his thirty-first year (828 BCE). The scribe then ran out of space, so there is no building account and no concluding formulae (*ANEP*, figs. 351–55).

Erich Lessing/Art Resource, NY

Figure 1: Black obelisk of Shalmaneser III, British Museum, London, Great Britain.

In the middle of this text are five panels of reliefs that run sequentially around the four sides, each portraying the tribute of a different ruler. Above each panel sequence is an epigraph identifying the tributary and listing the tribute. The five are, from top to bottom: 1) Sua the king of Gilzanu (northwest Iran); 2) JEHU the king of Israel; 3) an unnamed king of Egypt; 4) Marduk-apal-usur the Suhean (middle Euphrates); 5) Qarparunda the Patinean (region of Antakya, Turkey). The second panel portrays the Israelite king Jehu (842–814 BCE) bowing down before Shalmaneser when he paid tribute to him (841 BCE). This is the only contemporary portrayal of any Judean or Israelite king known from antiquity. *See* ASSYRIA AND BABYLONIA.

Bibliography: A. Kirk Grayson. *Assyrian Rulers of the Early First Millennium BC: II (858–745 BC)* (1991).

J. J. M. ROBERTS

OBIL oh'bil [אוֹבִיל ʾovil]. Obil was an Ishmaelite placed in charge of King David's camels, one of several civic officials to steward royal property (1 Chr 27:30).

OBLATION [מִנְחָה minkhah; προσφορά prosphora]. A type of offering (1 Kgs 18:29, 36; Pr Azar 1:15; *4 Ezra* 1:31; 3:24). The OT verses refer to the time of the "meal offering," likely indicating the daily morning and evening offerings (a burnt offering, meal offering, and libation, as in Exod 29:38-46; Num 28:1-8). *See* SACRIFICES AND OFFERINGS.

FRANK H. GORMAN

OBLIGATION [ἀνάγκη anankē]. In the Bible, the word *obligation* generally refers to religious duty and responsibility, as well as to discipleship. There is no specific Hebrew term for *obligation.* The NRSV supplies the word *obligation* to some Hebrew translations, e.g., wiheyithem neqiyiyim (וִהְיִיתֶם נְקִיִּים, "you may be exempt") becomes "you may be free of obligation" (Num 32:22). In Neh 10:32 [Heb. 10:33] the NRSV translates mitsoth (מִצְוֹת; "commandments") as "obligation" (Neh 10:32 [10:33]), and for Hebrew weʿal-hannasiʾ yiheyeh (וְעַל־הַנָּשִׂיא יִהְיֶה), "Upon the prince will be … ," it translates "This shall be the obligation of the prince …" (Ezek 45:17). The NRSV sometimes compares obligation to OATH (Gen 26:3, 28; Isa 33:8) and VOW (Num 30:6, 8, 14) to express the stipulations of a binding contract or promise.

The OT covenant tradition reflects obligation as understood in the Hittite treaties where the suzerain protected the vassal state in return for its allegiance (*see* ALLIANCE). Blessings and curses in the covenant specify the fortunes and calamities that will befall the vassal for its obedience and disobedience, respectively (see Deut 27–28). In the Bible, a covenant is not a privilege, but an obligation that characterizes the election of God's people (*see* COVENANT, OT AND NT).

In the NT, Paul considers himself obligated to proclaim the gospel, saying "for an obligation is laid on me" (anankē gar moi epikeitai [ἀνάγκη γάρ μοι ἐπίκειται], 1 Cor 9:16).

ARCHIE C. C. LEE

OBODA. A town renamed for the Nabatean ruler Obodas I. When Hasmonean John HYRCANUS and his son Alexander Jannaeus annexed parts of Moab, the move threatened the NABATEANS, for it usurped their trade routes to the Mediterranean and Damascus. The 1st-cent. BCE Nabatean ruler, Obodas I, along with the Seleucids, deployed camels as tank corps to ambush Alexander Jannaeus, who ceded Moab and Galaaditis to the Nabateans. When Obodas died, he was buried in Oboda, which was renamed in his honor. Inscriptions refer to him as "Obodas the god," indicating his deification.

Oboda was a staging post along the trade routes through the southern Negev (*see* NEGEB, NEGEV). Basically nonresidential, it became a military base serving as the protection of Nabatean caravans and a center of worship for surrounding tribes. During the Roman period, it was bypassed by a Roman road and went into decline. There are scanty remains of a temple at Oboda, perhaps dedicated to Obodas.

In the Byzantine period a large communal wine production center was constructed with separate sections for the tramping-pressing—each wine producer unloaded his grapes into his section. In modern times, Nabatean terraces and water channels have been restored as part of an experimental irrigation project. *See* ALEXANDER JANNAEUS, JANNEUS; HASMONEANS; SELEUCID EMPIRE.

MARTHA JOUKOWSKY

OBOTH oh'both [אֹבֹת ʾovoth]. The place the Israelites camped after the bronze serpent incident, between PUNON (modern Feinan) and IYE-ABARIM (Num 21:10-11; 33:43-44). The common identification as ʿAin el-Weibeh to the west of Feinan is based on the similarity of the names but requires a diversion from their northeast route. The name could mean "wineskins" (Job 32:19) or "necromancers" (NRSV, "wizards"; Lev 19:31). *See* SERPENT, BRONZE.

KEN M. PENNER

OBSCENE LANGUAGE. *See* EUPHEMISM.

OCCUPATIONS [מְלָאכָה melaʾkhah, מַעֲשֶׂה maʿaseh; ἀσχολία ascholia]. *Occupations* refers to the particular activities, professions, or tasks in which persons are habitually engaged. In Mediterranean antiquity, what one did revealed who a person was and provided a gauge of the social esteem to which a person was entitled. Such social esteem was of central concern (*see* HONOR).

As a rule, work ceased around noon, with the main meal taken at mid-afternoon. People then spent a goodly portion of the rest of the day visiting with friends and neighbors in courtyards and squares, in the work of maintaining interpersonal relations, the social security net for most ordinary people. In that world of takers (2 percent or the elite) and givers (non-elites), the kind of work in which people engaged depended exclusively on their gender and the social rank of their kin group.

In the Bible, male and female occupational roles typically were well defined and quite different. In general, women cared for the household and the inside of the kin group (e.g., Prov 31:10-27), while males took care of flocks and lands and the outside of the kin group (*see* KINSHIP). Women's occupations included midwives, maids, mourners, and prostitutes. Domestic tasks that could be performed by either men or women included weaving, pottery-making, harvesting, domestic marketing, and carrying water.

The FAMILY structures noted in the Bible changed over time. The patriarchs were tribal groups with their extended families of semi-nomadic tent-dwelling cattle keepers (Gen 46:34; 47:3-4) and raiders (Gen 14). Then sedentary groups formed on the land, and in time divided into a minority of wealthy families and a majority of poorer families (see 1 Sam 8:11-17). Elite, wealthy families included slaves and client families living on the kin group's land holdings (*see* HOUSEHOLD, HOUSEHOLDER). Non-elite families became increasingly nucleated, because the elites took their land holdings (in spite of Lev 25).

With the rise of administrative cities, owners were able to build extensive estates with secondary townhouses and temples, while the rest of the city consisted of less wealthy retainers: small merchants, tradesmen and craftsmen, priests, and various attendants (*see* CRAFTS; TRADE AND COMMERCE). Military units provided force in the service of the elites while forming fictive kin groups among themselves. People without families—childless widows, orphans—lived at the mercy of others. Finally, there were slaves owned by political units and unattached to families (*see* SLAVERY).

Along with gender and kin group, generic markers of social rank were 1) the acceptance of payment and 2) the use of one's hands ("body"). Elite occupations did not require payment. All activities requiring payment for services were considered non-elite and indicated a person's lower status. Taxes, a form of extortion destined solely for elites, were not considered payment but an entitlement of the elites (*see* TAXES, TAXATION). Further, all activities involving the use of the "hands" (manual labor) were considered to be non-elite, hence of lesser significance. As a folk healer, Jesus accepted no payment, and so could have been numbered among the elite, but he did use his own hands, a sign of the non-elite (e.g., Matt 8:3, 15; 9:29; 17:7; 20:34 and par.; compare Elisha in 2 Kgs 4:34). Elite activities did not involve manual labor. Israel's Sabbath work prohibition (Exod 20:10) forbids the use of "hands" (and feet). Therefore, on the Sabbath, all of God's people could behave like elites.

This typology based on gender, family ranking, and mode of interaction (hands, payment) can be readily applied to the occupations mentioned in the Bible and its contemporary world. Consider the occupational ranking criteria set out as common knowledge by Cicero (*Off.* 1.42). According to Cicero, proper elite activities were characterized by no payment and no use of hands. Most respected among these activities was land ownership and AGRICULTURE. Slaves did the manual labor on the large tracts of land owned by elites; these land owners then had leisure time for activities for which one received no remuneration at all. Such was the agriculture engaged in by Roman senatorial and equestrian ranks, patrician families, as well as local elites around the Mediterranean, including Judea, Galilee, and Perea. Wealth gained from agriculture was considered honest and noble under all circumstances.

Next in the hierarchy of honor came wholesale traders, long-distance importers who did not defraud others. (Hired men and slaves provided any required physical labor.) As a rule, this was the activity of the Roman equestrians, families noble by birth and activity, who also engaged in agriculture. Equestrians were remunerated by the emperor. Noble elites likewise engaged in the practice of law, senatorial office, and the direction of warfare without remuneration. There were also unpaid non-elite professions that required intelligence and benefited society: medicine, architecture, and teaching. In Israel, scribes (experts in Torah) were to be unpaid, as befits the elite occupations.

Among the vast body of non-elites, first came craftsmen. When manual labor was required, slaves were used. Soldiers, the hands and feet of the elites, ranked in this category. Next came shopkeepers, who repaired and built artifacts, and retailers (who were expected to lie and misrepresent for profit). After these were those who cater to sensual pleasures (e.g., fishmongers, butchers, cooks, poulterers, and fishermen); entertainers (perfumers, dancers, actors, musicians, and the whole corps of public entertainers); hired workmen (paid for manual labor, but only a step away from slavery). At the bottom were the reprehensible occupations that incurred people's ill will: tax collectors, usurers, pimps, and prostitutes. *See* LABOR; POVERTY; WEALTH.

Bibliography: M. M. Austin and P. Vidal-Naquet. *Economic and Social History of Ancient Greece: An Introduction* (1977); Ferdinand E. Deist. *The Material Culture of the Bible: An Introduction* (2000); Joachim Jeremias. *Jerusalem in the Time of Jesus: An Investigation into Economic and Social Conditions during the New Testament Period* (1969); Sandra R. Joshel. *Work, Identity, and Legal Status at Rome: A Study of the Occupational Inscriptions* (1992).

BRUCE J. MALINA

OCHIEL. *See* JEIEL.

OCHRAN ok'ruhn [עָכְרָן ʿokhran]. Ochran was the father of PAGIEL, a leader (*see* LEADER, LEADERSHIP, OT) of the tribe of Asher. His name occurs five times in lists of tribal leaders in the book of Numbers (1:13; 2:27; 7:72, 77; 10:26). His name seems to mean "sorrowful, distressed one." *See* ASHER, ASHERITES.

OCINA oh-si'nuh [᾿Οκεινά Okeina]. Ocina appears only in a list of towns in Jdt 2:28, described as located on the seacoast and placed to the south of Sidon and Tyre, but north of Jamnia. *Ocina* may be a corruption of Acco, an ancient harbor city, since Acco's location coincides with Ocina's position in the list in Judith. It is also possible that the name is fictitious. *See* ACCO, AKKO; JUDITH, BOOK OF; PTOLEMAIS.

Bibliography: Lawrence M. Wills. "The Book of Judith." *NIB* 3 (1999) 1073–1183.

SIDNIE WHITE CRAWFORD

OCTOPUS. A cephalopod mollusk with eight tentacled, muscular arms reaching as much as 10 ft. in length. References to the seven-headed LEVIATHAN in Ugaritic texts and Sumerian poetry and the many-headed hydra that Hercules killed suggest that the "heads" were actually the tentacles of a squid or octopus. *See* ANIMALS OF THE BIBLE.

EMILY R. CHENEY

ODED oh'did [עֹדֵד ʿodhedh, עוֹדֵד ʿodhedh]. 1. The father of AZARIAH the prophet during the reign of Asa (2 Chr 15:1). The Hebrew of 15:8 has "Oded the prophet," which the NRSV corrects.

2. A prophet who helped persuade Israel to free the Judeans taken captive during the reign of Ahaz (2 Chr 28:8-15). *See* JUDAH, JUDAHITES; PROPHET, PROPHECY.

STEVEN D. MASON

ODES OF SOLOMON. *See* SOLOMON, ODES OF.

ODOMERA od'uh-mer'uh [᾿Οδομηρά Odomēra]. Bedouin chief whom Jonathan killed along with his kindred and other townspeople in Phasiron (1 Macc 9:65-66). *See* MACCABEES, FIRST BOOK OF; PASTORAL NOMADS.

ODOR [רֵיחַ reakh; ὀσμή osmē]. In the OT the noun reakh refers to a fragrance, an odor, a scent, or a smell. The verb riakh (רִיחַ) refers to the sense of smell, the olfactory perception of a fragrance or odor. In non-cultic contexts, the "odor" may be perceived as a pleasant fragrance (see Gen 27:27; Song 1:3, 12; 2:13; 4:10, 11) or, metaphorically, as an unpleasant odor (Exod 5:21).

The most frequent usage is in the context of the Priestly sacrificial and ritual texts. A food offering (ʾisheh אִשֶּׁה; traditionally, a fire offering) presented to Yahweh and burned on the altar produces smoke that ascends heavenward and generates a pleasing, soothing, or pacifying aroma (reakh-nikhoakh רֵיחַ־נִיחוֹחַ). The anthropomorphic image of God being pleased by the aroma is generally understood to reflect Israel's ancient sacrificial practices when the sacrifices were understood to be food for the gods. The question remains, however, whether P limits the image to a purely "pleasurable experience" by Yahweh, or whether the smoke and its effect on Yahweh are a necessary element in the accomplishment of a ritual process, i.e., "Yahweh is placated by the smoke" and, because of that, looks favorably on the one who presents the sacrifice (see Gen 8:21; Lev 26:31; Sir 35:8 [LXX 35:5]; Amos 5:21 may be read as a refusal to be "appeased" or "placated" [weloʾ ʾariakh וְלֹא אָרִיחַ] by Israel's gatherings).

Leviticus uses the description of a "pleasing odor" in relation to the burnt offering (Lev 1:9, 13, 17), the grain offering (Lev 2:2, 9; 6:15 [Heb. 6:8], 21 [Heb. 6:14]; compare Sir 38:11), the well-being offering (3:5, 16), and the fat of the purification sacrifice (Lev 4:31). The "aroma" is associated with the burnt offering and the burning of the ram of ordination in the priestly ordination ritual (Lev 8:21, 28; compare Exod 29:18, 25, 41). The burned sacrifices that provide an "aroma" for Yahweh play a critical role in Israel's prescribed sacral observances (Num 28:2, 6, 8, 24; 29:2, 6, 8; compare Lev 23). Numbers 15 specifies the meal (flour and oil) and libation (wine) offerings presented in conjunction with burned sacrifices (vv. 3, 7, 10, 13), as does Sir 50:15. The sacrificing of the Passover lamb is also described as a pleasing odor (1 Esd 1:12 [LXX 1:13]).

Ezekiel declares judgment on Israel for providing a pleasing aroma for "all their idols" (6:13; 16:19; 20:28). Deuteronomy 4:28 solemnly declares to the Israelites that when they go into exile they will worship idols made by human hands that are unable to see, hear, eat, or smell (compare Ps 115:5-6). Ezekiel 20:41, however, offers hope to the Israelites with the promise that they will be a "pleasing aroma" to Yahweh when they return from exile.

The NT draws on this metaphorical imagery. Second Corinthians 2:14-15 describes the knowledge of God as a (pleasing) fragrance (osme) and Christians as the (pleasing) aroma (euōdia εὐωδία) of Christ to God. Those experiencing salvation are the fragrance of life; those perishing produce the odor of death. Ephesians interprets Christ's death as a fragrant offering and sacrifice to God (5:2). Philippians understands the monetary giving of the church as a fragrant offering, a sacrifice that is acceptable and pleasing to God (4:18). *See* INCENSE; PERFUME; SACRIFICES AND OFFERINGS; SPICE.

FRANK H. GORMAN

OFFERING. *See* ATONEMENT; CLEAN AND UNCLEAN; INCENSE; JEALOUSY; SACRIFICES AND OFFERINGS.

OFFERING FOR THE SAINTS. *See* COLLECTION, THE.

OFFERING OF WELL-BEING [זֶבַח שְׁלָמִים zevakh shelamim; θυσία σωτηρίου thysia sōteriou]. A voluntary sacrifice in which the fat of the entrails, the kidneys, and the appendage of the liver are burned as an offering to God (Lev 3:1-17). The remainder of the animal is eaten by the offerand and/or the priests (Lev 7:11-18). *See* SACRIFICES AND OFFERINGS.

KEVIN A. WILSON

OFFICER, OFFICIAL [נִצָּב nitsav, שַׂר sar; πράκτωρ praktōr, χιλίαρχος chiliarchos]. An individual endowed with civil, military, legal, or clerical authority. The Hebrew word sar is commonly used (Gen 12:15; Exod 18:21) but can also refer to an official of higher rank or nobility, such as a prince (Jer 1:18). In some instances, the NRSV translates saris (סָרִיס, "EUNUCH") as "official" (Gen 37:36).

Solomon divided the administration of Israel into twelve districts, each headed by an official (nitsav; 1 Kgs 4:27 [Heb. 5:7]). Some terms of authority are nontechnical, such as the reference to David's general, Abner, who was "over the army" (2 Sam 8:16). David and Solomon's royal bureaucracy (2 Sam 8:16-18; 20:23-26; 1 Kgs 4:2-6) is described as the "high officials," including priest (as a royal office), secretary, recorder, general, overseer of forced labor, etc. Titles such as the "king's friend" (1 Kgs 4:5) were also known in Egyptian administration.

The responsibilities of officials overlapped considerably in the biblical world. Offices that cover a variety of administrative contexts include CHIEF (nasiʾ נָשִׂיא, lit., "one lifted up," Josh 22:14), *head* (roʾsh רֹאשׁ; of one's house, Num 1:4; or of the lords of Shechem, Judg 9:39), and the officer called the *third* (the third man in the chariot, shalish [שָׁלִישׁ]; Exod 14:7). A JUDGE (shofet שֹׁפֵט) was responsible for a cross-section of legal, administrative, and military authority (i.e., Deborah; Judg 4:4-6).

The majority of references in the NT refer to Jewish Temple personnel or Roman officers. Jesus instructed making peace before being handed over to civil authority (praktōr, Luke 12:58). A Roman tribune (chiliarchos), in charge of 600–1,000 soldiers, was present at Herod Antipas' birthday banquet (Mark 6:21) and at the arrests of Jesus (John 18:12) and Paul (Acts 21:31). *See* PALESTINE, ADMINISTRATION OF.

BRUCE W. GENTRY

OFFICIAL OF THE SYNAGOGUE. *See* RULER OF SYNAGOGUE.

OFFSET [מִגְרָעָה mighraʿah, פַּעַם paʿam]. The Jerusalem Temple was surrounded on three sides by three-storied chambers. Through the use of "offsets" or recesses for beams (1 Kgs 6:6; Ezek 41:6-7), the construction of the chambers did not require that they be structurally keyed into the walls of the Temple itself. As storage areas, the side-rooms were essential, but the use of offsets allowed the Temple to remain architecturally and conceptually independent of the side-rooms. *See* ARCHITECTURE, OT; TEMPLE, JERUSALEM.

CAROL MEYERS

OFFSPRING. *See* CHILD, CHILDREN; FIRSTBORN; ISSUE.

OG og [עוֹג ʿogh]. Og was the king of BASHAN who confronted Israel on their journey through TRANSJORDAN as they moved toward the land of Canaan (Num 21:31-35). Bashan was the northern region east of the Jordan River and north of the Wadi Yarmuk. Og is reported to have reigned in the cities of ASHTAROTH and EDREI (Deut 1:4). According to Deut 3:1-4, Og and his army were destroyed in a battle at Edrei, and that defeat, along with the defeat of King SIHON, was often cited in Israel's history as evidence of Yahweh's power and protection of the people of Israel (e.g., Deut 29:7; 31:4; Josh 2:10; 9:10; Ps 135:11). Deuteronomy 3:11 lists Og as the last of the remnant of the REPHAIM, a race of giants counted among the early inhabitants of this region (Deut 2:11). His great size is supported by the reference to his iron bed as being 4 cubits wide and 9 cubits long (6 ft. × 13 ft.). Some scholars suggest that *bed* refers to a stone sarcophagus or coffin, although "iron bed" is the literal translation. When this territory is allotted in Josh 13, Bashan is given to the half-tribe of Manasseh that remains on the east side of the Jordan. The historical summary in Neh 9:22 lists Og as the ruler of Bashan. The historical psalms also refer to Og as king of Bashan (Ps 135:11; 136:20). These later references are simply a reflection of earlier tradition and do not contribute additional information about Og.

PHILLIP MCMILLION

OHAD oh'had [אֹהַד ʾohadh]. The third of six sons of Simeon and grandson of Jacob and LEAH (Gen 46:10; Exod 6:15). Ohad does not appear in the lists in Num 26:12-14 and 1 Chr 4:24-25, perhaps indicating that he died at an early age and did not become one of the Simeonite clans. *See* JACOB; SIMEON, SIMEONITES.

CLAUDE MARIOTTINI

OHEL oh'hel [אֹהֶל ʾohel]. Ohel is mentioned only at 1 Chr 3:20 where he is listed as the fifth child of ZERUBBABEL. He is mentioned as part of a second list of Zerubbabel's children. These names may have been grouped together to indicate they were born after the return to Palestine.

RUSSELL E. FULLER

OHOLAH AND OHOLIBAH oh-hoh'luh, oh-hoh'li-buh [אָהֳלָה ʾoholah, אָהֳלִיבָה ʾoholivah]. Symbolic names of SAMARIA and JERUSALEM, cities represented as unfaithful wives of Yahweh, in Ezek 23. Although both names clearly derive from *tent* (ʾohel אֹהֶל), the origin and precise meaning of these names are otherwise uncertain. Walther Eichrodt suggests "(she who has) her own tent" and "my tent (is) in her," understanding the tents as sanctuaries. Walther Zimmerli hears in the two similar names an echo of bedouin names.

The metaphor of cities as women wedded to patron gods was already in use in ANE literature prior to its adoption by earlier prophets Hosea and Jeremiah to describe "wives" of Yahweh who are punished for their unfaithfulness. Ezekiel, however, pushes this metaphor much further. In chap. 16, without resorting to a symbolic name, the prophet is told to announce Jerusalem's status as an abandoned infant whom Yahweh first rescued and then, in her adulthood, wedded, bathed, and dressed. But trusting in her own beauty, she has consorted with idols and foreign countries, engaging in worse abominations than her "sisters," Samaria and Sodom. Therefore an enraged Yahweh will punish her violently in the hope of eliciting her repentance.

When the metaphor recurs in Ezek 23, the lack of emotional engagement is striking. Here Yahweh allegorically retells the story of both Samaria and Jerusalem, who begin as young women in Egypt. Samaria (Oholah) is graphically described as lusting after the Assyrian warriors and being given into their hands, where she is killed. Though Jerusalem (Oholibah) sees this, she extends her favors to the Babylonians. Yahweh's violent punishment is described in gruesome detail. Following this, accusations and judgments against both cities are reviewed. Both are stoned, their children killed, and their houses burned, in order that women in the land will take warning. Unlike chap. 16, this chapter offers no hope of reconciliation but relates the death of both sister cities. The metaphor dies with the wives, and Ezek 40–48 envisions Jerusalem as a demythologized, inanimate city belonging to God.

The disturbing assumptions about marital ownership and violence underlying Ezekiel's metaphor merit careful examination. To justify the destruction of Yahweh's two nations, horrific crimes of apostasy are ascribed to them, thus defending divine vengeance and asserting divine control over the nations. The metaphor presents women's sexuality as subject to male control and deserving of abusive violence. Thus it seems to offer scriptural authorization of the violence of jealous men against their wives. When attributed to the holy God and his prophet, voyeurism, sadism, objectification of women, and pornographic obscenity are tragically normalized. *See* EZEKIEL, BOOK OF; IDOLATRY; MARRIAGE, OT; SEXUAL ABUSE.

Bibliography: Katheryn Pfisterer Darr. "The Book of Ezekiel." *NIB* 6 (2001) 1073–1607; Walther Eichrodt. *Ezekiel: A Commentary.* OTL (1970); Julie Galambush. *Jerusalem in the Book of Ezekiel: The City as Yahweh's Wife* (1992); Walther Zimmerli. *Ezekiel 1–24.* Hermeneia 23.1 (1979).

PATRICIA K. TULL

OHOLIAB oh-hoh´lee-ab [אָהֳלִיאָב ʾoholiʾav]. A Danite (*see* DAN, DANITES) appointed by Yahweh to assist BEZALEL in fashioning the accoutrements for the early Israelite cult, including the TABERNACLE and its accessories (Exod 31:6; 35:34; 36:1-2). Oholiab's name, meaning "father's tent," may reflect his role in the construction of the tabernacle. Whereas Bezalel seems to have specialized in metalworking and woodworking, Oholiab's province was engraving and embroidery (Exod 38:23). The two craftsmen trained others to assist them in their work; Moses alone, however, was responsible for assembling the components (Exod 40).

RODNEY S. SADLER JR.

OHOLIBAH. *See* OHOLAH AND OHOLIBAH.

OHOLIBAMAH oh-hoh´li-bah´muh [אָהֳלִיבָמָה ʾoholivamah]. A Canaanite wife of Esau and daughter of ANAH, son of Zibeon the Hivite (Gen 36:2; contrast 36:20, 25). Oholibamah is the most frequently mentioned matriarch in the genealogy of Esau/Edom (Gen 36), yet she does not appear among Esau's Canaanite wives in Gen 26:34. Three Esauite clans descend from her and an Edomite clan bears her name (Gen 36:14, 18, 41; 1 Chr 1:52). The traditions appear muddled, perhaps due to the late identification of Esau with Edom. *See* EDOM, EDOMITES; ESAU, ESAUITES.

JASON C. DYKEHOUSE

OHRMAZD. THE GOOD CREATOR GOD IN ZOROASTRIANISM. ALSO CALLED AHURA MAZDA. SEE ZOROASTER, ZOROASTRIANISM.

OIL [יִצְהָר yitshar, שֶׁמֶן shemen; ἔλαιον elaion]. While Deut 8:7-8 lists seven products of Canaan that make it a desirable, fertile, and well-watered land (wheat, barley, grape vines, figs, pomegranates, olives, and honey) the most versatile and economically important is the olive (*Olea europaea*) from which oil is extracted (*see* OLIVE, OLIVE TREE). The economic triad of olive, grape, and wheat made life possible in ancient Canaan.

Olive pits and olive wood found in archaeological excavations are evidence that the cultivation of the olive tree goes back to Neolithic times. Olives became an important factor in the economy starting with the growing urbanization in the Early Bronze Age. Even the politically motivated Jotham's Fable (Judg 9:8-9) points to the essential nature of olive oil production to the economic success (e.g., the quantities exported or sent as tribute to Egypt in Hos 12:1 [Heb. 12:2]) and the personal well-being of the people (e.g., the private sale of oil in 2 Kgs 4:7).

The process by which oil is extracted from the ripe olive has three major components: crushing, pressing, and separation of the oil from the watery lees. In earliest times the crushing of the olives was done by hand in a mortar and pestle or in a shallow hole cut into the limestone bedrock near a personal dwelling (Mic 6:15). Eventually, more efficient methods were developed, such as stone rollers pushed by hand or harnessed to an animal circling a large basin. The resulting olive mash was sometimes boiled or heated and then placed into woven baskets to be crushed by stones. The stones pressed out a fraction of the available oil. By the Iron Age period, the process was improved and the baskets were more thoroughly flattened using a lever-and-weights press such as those found at Gezer and in the huge manufacturing district at Tel Miqne-Ekron. In the Assyrian period, these presses could process hundreds of thousands of gallons of oil. From a wooden beam anchored in a stone niche in the wall, stone weights were hung to add greater pressure on the baskets so that the fluid could be collected below in a basin. The liquid oil floated to the top and was either skimmed off by hand or with a cup, or the oil was allowed to flow into a separate vessel through a small channel. The whole process was repeated three or four times in order to extract as much oil as possible. The first pressing produced the finest quality (Num 18:12), which would be used for cultic purposes such as anointing priests (Exod 29:21) or for lamp oil in the Temple (Exod 27:20). The residue from the process was formed into bricks for fuel or used as animal feed.

The ubiquitous nature of olive oil in ANE society is attested by the many uses to which it was put. Lighting people's paths at night, their homes, and their temples were oil lamps that were carried in the hand (Matt 25:3-8), placed on a table or in a niche (2 Kgs 4:10), or placed in a LAMPSTAND before the altar (Lev 24:2; *see* LAMP, NT; LAMP, OT). Sacred objects and persons were set apart by anointing them with oil (Jacob's pillar at Bethel in Gen 28:18; Samuel's anointing of kings in 1 Sam 10:1 and 16:13; *see* ANOINT). Oil was one of the items regularly offered on God's altar (Lev 2:2-7). Wheat or barley flour were mixed with oil to produce cakes, both for sacred purposes (Exod 29:2) and for one's daily bread (1 Kgs 17:12; *see* SACRIFICES AND OFFERINGS).

Oil was used to anoint the sick (Mark 6:13), as medicine on sores (Isa 1:6), in the bindings of wrapped wounds (Luke 10:34), and possibly as a liniment for sore joints (Ps 109:18). Customarily, olive oil was used after bathing to maintain skin tone (Sus 1:17), to soothe the spirit (Ps 133:2), and to cause the face "to shine" (Ps 104:15). Cosmetics to color the eyes, lips, and hair, and perfumes used by both genders depended upon oil as a base mixed with a variety of spices, roots, and dyes. The fragrant ointments, spices, and unguents used to honor the dead and mask the smell associated with their bodies were also oil based (Mark 16:1; *see* OINTMENTS).

In addition to the practical uses for olive oil, the product also provided the substance for metaphorical application. For example, the blessing of the tribe of Asher in Deut 33:24 plays on the tribal name (meaning "happy") by noting that their land, rich with olive groves, would allow them to bathe their feet in the riches provided by their oil. A person who was able to enjoy life was well fed, wore white garments, and kept the sheen of oil on his head (Eccl 9:7-9). Thus Job, in the midst of his suffering, speaks of better days when his steps were washed with milk, presumably from his many goats, and "the rock poured out for me streams of oil" (Job 29:6), a reference to the extraction process and to his abundant groves of olive trees. In a similar vein, King Hezekiah displays his riches by opening up his treasury to a Babylonian envoy, and among his vast wealth is "precious oil" (2 Kgs 20:13).

Excavations at EN-GEDI demonstrate that other precious oils contributed to the economy of ancient Israel. BALSAM oil was produced from a shrub-like tree (genus *Commiphora*) and used as a perfume (see "oil of myrrh" in Esth 2:12) and for healing purposes (possibly to be equated with the BALM of Gilead in Jer 8:22; *see* GILEAD, BALM IN). The recipe was a guarded secret of the community.

Bibliography: Rafael Frankel, Shmuel Avitsur, and Etan Ayalon. *History and Technology of Olive Oil in the Holy Land* (1994); Frank S. Frick. "'Oil from Flinty Rock' (Deuteronomy 32:13): Olive Cultivation and Olive Oil Processing in the Hebrew Bible—A Socio-materialist Perspective." *Semeia* 86 (1999) 1–17.

VICTOR H. MATTHEWS

OINTMENT [מֶרְקָחָה merqakhah, שֶׁמֶן shemen; μύρον myron]. The preparation of ointments depended upon olive OIL or oils extracted from BALSAM, MYRRH, or other spices as their base. Depending on their ingredients, ointments varied in texture, aroma, and the specific purpose for which they were produced. Flowers, fragrant resins, granulated roots, and various perfumed oils were among the organic substances commonly used in antiquity to create ointments (*see* PERFUME). Some of these products, such as the anointing oil and incense, were restricted to the exclusive use of the temple personnel and presumably were concocted by members of the priestly community (Exod 30:22-33). According to the recipes included in the text, the extensive list of ingredients required to create sacred oils and ointments included liquid myrrh, cinnamon, aromatic cane, and cassia blended in olive oil. Some of these items were employed in anointing sacred persons or objects (the ark of the covenant, basins, altars, lampstands, and utensils), and their fragrance must have contributed to the heady aromas that permeated the tent of meeting and the Temple in Jerusalem (*see* ANOINT).

A guild of professional perfumers existed in ancient Israel whose tasks included the blending of precious substances into ointments in much the same way that apothecaries did in later periods (1 Chr 9:30). Perfumers' guilds are included among the groups assigned to provide workmen to rebuild Jerusalem's walls during Nehemiah's tenure as Persian governor (Neh 3:8). The actual process of preparation by perfume makers, who could be either men or women (**raqqakhoth** [רַקָּחוֹת], 1 Sam 8:13), included crushing items into fine powders and concocting tinctures with a measured amount of oil, perhaps determined by experimentation and then kept as trade secrets by the guild members. Sometimes it was necessary for the mixtures to be steeped or boiled in a pot or cauldron (Job 41:31). While the mixtures simmered, the aromas must have served as a penetrating advertisement to passersby.

Those ointments designed for personal enhancements or cleansing agents filled a niche in the secular marketplace and in the luxury trade. Apparently, some of these products were quite costly (see the comparison between the value of a "good name" and "precious ointment" in Eccl 7:1). To enhance their sense of value, they were also packaged for the luxury market in specially designed jars and bottles. This is illustrated in the account of the woman anointing Jesus' head (Matt 26:7; Mark 14:3) in which she breaks off the neck of an alabaster flask that contains NARD, a very expensive luxury import from India whose fragrant root and lower stems were dried and used to concoct a perfumed ointment. The woman pours the cooling substance over Jesus' forehead, a practice that served as part of the hospitality ritual in wealthy households as a way of providing a luxuriant comfort and a tribute to important guests. In the parallel story that appears in Luke 7:37 a "sinful woman," as an act of supplication and respect, brings an alabaster jar of perfume with which to anoint Jesus' feet. In each of these cases, the precious character of the perfume is accented by its costly alabaster container that was designed to be used only once.

Ointments, when topically applied to the skin, formed an effective barrier against moisture loss. It is possible that wealthy women's regimens of cosmetic and cleansing treatments included various perfumed oils and ointments. For example, the wealthy widow JUDITH transforms her mournful appearance in preparation for her meeting with the general Holofernes by bathing in water and perfuming her body with precious ointment (Jdt 10:3-4). This transformation was designed to entice the general and put him off his guard. Judith's clothing and personal enhancements are reminiscent of the finery described in Isa 3:18-23, which also includes perfume. Suggestive of the incorporation of Hellenistic practices, the descriptions of preparations for Esther's beautification (Esth 2:3, 9, 12) and Susanna's bath (Sus 1:17) include a Gk. term for soap or unguent not found in the NT (smēgma σμῆγμα). In combination with the oil, this body lotion would have served as an exfoliating agent, removing the surface layer of dead skin while restoring skin tone and providing a blush to the areas where the ointment was applied. Given the damage caused by sun and wind in the Middle East, such a beauty treatment must have been very desirable and very likely was employed by both sexes when they could afford it.

Jesus' reference to the use of perfumed ointments as preparation for BURIAL (Matt 26:12) points to yet another practical purpose for these products. The substances could be used as part of the embalming process, being intermingled with the burial shroud wrappings or poured directly on the body once it had been cleansed. Among the more costly of these items was myrrh. Myrrh's antibiotic qualities would have reduced the process of decay and was therefore one of the ingredients employed by the ancient Egyptians in the embalming of mummies (*see* EMBALM, EMBALMING). Nicodemus brought a mixture of aloes and myrrh to anoint Jesus' body in preparation for his entombment (John 19:39-40).

VICTOR H. MATTHEWS

OLD AGE [זָקֵן zoqen, זִקְנָה ziqnah; γέρων gerōn, πρεσβῦτικός presbytikos]. Old age is the final adult stage of life that few reached and, therefore, was regarded as a blessing from God and a sign for respect (Lev 19:32). It brought a mixture of blessings, honor, and hardship. Related terms are zaqen (זָקֵן, "elder," "older man"), zeqenoth (זְקֵנוֹת; Zech 8:4, "older women"), yashesh (יָשֵׁשׁ; 2 Chr 36:17, "aged," "decrepit," "venerable"), sevah (שֵׂיבָה, "gray head"), presbyteros (πρεσβύτερος, "elder"), presbytēs (πρεσβύτης, "older man"), presbytis (πρεσβῦτις, "older woman"), gerōn ("elder," "older man"), and geraios (γεραιός, "old").

Literature from the ANE refers to the old person as one with white hair ("wool"). The OT describes the older person as a "gray head" (sevah, Gen 15:15; 25:8; Judg 8:32; 1 Chr 29:28; NRSV, "good old age"). Leviticus 19:32 refers to the "gray head" and face of an elder with an exhortation to rise in respect before the older person. Hebrew derives the word for "elder" (zaqen) from zaqan (זָקָן, "beard"), someone old enough to grow a beard. The book of Daniel presents the image of God as the "ANCIENT OF DAYS" who sits enthroned with hair like "pure wool" (Dan 7:9). The book of Revelation reflects this image of the "ancient of days" by referring to the royal messiah as having white hair (Rev 1:7-17). In Revelation, twenty-four elders surround the throne of God and worship the honored one (Rev 4:4; 5:5-14). Adoration from honored elders adds to the impression of power and might of the eternal ruler.

Few persons in ancient times lived to advanced years. Old age represented an exceptional achievement and divine favor (Gen 5:1-32). The Bible praises Abraham (Gen 25:8), Gideon (Judg 8:32), and David (1 Chr 29:28) for living to a "good (ripe) old age" (sevah tovah שֵׂיבָה טוֹבָה). Methuselah lived the longest of anyone in the Bible, at 969, which showed him great honor. Enoch was an exception (Gen 5:22-24), because he walked with God but lived a relatively short life span. The Bible also glorifies its heroes such as Moses (Deut 34:7) and Caleb (Josh 14:10-11) by praising their good health in their old age. In dealing with intergenerational issues, the Pastoral Epistles exhort younger people to speak to older men as "fathers" and older women as "mothers" (1 Tim 5:1-2). Older men or "elders" led Israel's tribes prior to kingship (*see* ELDER IN THE OT). The rise of monarchy eliminated the power and prestige of traditional leaders. Eldership regained power and prestige in local affairs during the exile after the dissolution of the monarchy (Jer 29:1-2; Ezek 8:1; 14:1; 20:1). After the exile, elders helped rebuild the Temple (Ezra 5:5; 6:6-7). In the Second Temple period, powerful Jewish leaders, such as the Pharisees, scribes, and Sadducees in the Sanhedrin, were known as "elders" (Matt 16:21; 26:3; Mark 8:31; Acts 4:5; 6:12; 23:14; 24:1; 25:15). Early church leaders who became overseers of the church were called "elders" as a sign of respect. Such elders "rule well," are worthy of "double honor," and are "worth their hire" (1 Tim 5:17-18). *See* ELDER IN THE NT.

Long life was a mixed blessing for people in the Bible. Older persons ultimately confronted the debilitation of aging and death. Qoheleth describes the degeneration of an aging body (Eccl 12:3-8). Failing health (loss of sight, hearing, or normal vigor) shows that old age was often filled with challenges (Gen 27:1-2; 1 Kgs 1:1-4). Older persons had to learn to live within the shadow of their own demise.

A key transition for women was menopause. It was a time of sorrow when the childless woman could no longer have children (Gen 18:11; Ruth 1:12; Luke 1:18, 36). When a man was unable to give a child to his wife, it was also a sign of advancing age (Gen 18:12).

Old age sometimes caused a loss of income and status. Jesus chastised those who used the vow of CORBAN (possessions given to God became unavailable to family) as an excuse for neglecting needs of their aging parents (Mark 7:5-13; *see* FATHER; MOTHER). Although widowhood is not exclusive to the aged, widows who had no wealth and no sons often were primary victims of poverty and had to rely on support from the community (1 Kgs 17:9-24; 2 Kgs 4:1-7; *see* WIDOW). Prophets and other writers condemned mistreatment of widows (Job 22:9; 24:3; 31:16; Ps 94:6;

Isa 1:23; 10:2), and the NT also singles out widows (old and young) as worthy of help and compassion (1 Tim 5:3-8; see Acts 6:1-7; 9:39). *See* AGING.

J. GORDON HARRIS

OLD GATE [שַׁעַר הַיְשָׁנָה shaʿar hayshanah]. Rebuilt under NEHEMIAH (Neh 3:6), part of Nehemiah's dedicatory processional (12:39), and probably located in the western city wall above the TYROPOEON VALLEY north of the EPHRAIM GATE and south of the FISH GATE.

OLD GREEK VERSIONS. *See* VERSIONS, ANCIENT.

OLD LATIN VERSIONS. *See* VERSIONS, LATIN.

OLD TESTAMENT. The Christian name for the TANAKH in contrast to the NT. Both terms are based on the "new covenant" and a perceived "old covenant" (Jer 31:31; Luke 22:20; 1 Cor 11:25, etc.). The OT is not a single canon, but has different formulations according to different branches of Christianity. The OT for Catholic and Eastern Orthodox churches was based on the SEPTUAGINT, the Greek translation of the Jewish Scriptures, and thus it contains books such as Judith. The Protestant OT is based on the Hebrew Jewish Scriptures and does not contain such Greek books. *See* CANON OF THE OT; COVENANT, OT AND NT.

JENNIFER L. KOOSED

OLD TESTAMENT CANON. *See* CANON OF THE OLD TESTAMENT.

OLD TESTAMENT CHRONOLOGY. *See* CHRONOLOGY OF THE OT.

OLD TESTAMENT LANGUAGE. *See* ARAMAIC, ARAMAISM; HEBREW LANGUAGE.

OLD TESTAMENT QUOTATIONS IN THE NT. *See* NEW TESTAMENT, OT QUOTATIONS IN THE.

OLD TESTAMENT TEXT. *See* TEXT, HEBREW, HISTORY OF.

OLIVE, OLIVE TREE [זַיִת zayith; ἐλαία elaia]. The olive is perhaps the most important plant mentioned in the Bible. Olive trees (*Olea europaea*) typify the Holy Land and adjacent territories (compare the description of the promised land in Deut 8:8).

The olive tree is a medium-sized orchard tree with a life span of hundreds of years. Its knobbly trunk may become massive and hollow with age while it still has leafy branches. When olive trees are felled, they sprout again (see Job 14:7-9), and the shoots may be seen around the base like children around a table (compare Ps 128:3). Some of the ancient trees found today in the Garden of Gethsemane could be shoots descended from trees known to Jesus.

The narrow evergreen leaves are gray-green on their upper surface and silvery beneath. There are many varieties of olive, and the skillful cultivator seeks to improve the quality by grafting better varieties onto existing trees. Paul uses the imagery of grafting to explain how the Gentiles (as wild stock) were

Todd Bolen/BiblePlaces.com

Figure 1: Olive grove near Bethlehem

being grafted into Israel, the cultivated tree (Rom 11:17-24).

In the warmth of May, the trees produce small flowers, each having four white petals and only two stamens. The rounded, elliptic fruits (about 2 cm long) ripen late in the year, staying green or turning black; the hard kernel (seed) is surrounded by oil-yielding flesh. Traditionally, olive harvest was a busy time with farmers shaking and beating each tree to make the fruits fall onto sheets spread beneath them (see Isa 17:6; 24:13). Provision could be made for sojourners, widows, and orphans if farmers left some of the fruit on the trees as Moses commanded (Deut 24:20). Excessive dropping of immature fruits was a disaster for the farmer, as there would be insufficient oil for food and ointment, and this dire situation was sometimes interpreted as a punishment for disobedience or unfaithfulness (Deut 28:40).

Once gathered, the olives were taken to the press. Heavy millstones crushed the fruit, and the pulp was placed inside shallow baskets, which were piled up for pressing or treading (Mic 6:15). The OIL squeezed out of the heap had to be purified in settling vats. Only pure oil was permitted for the lamps in the tent of meeting (Lev 24:2-4), but ordinary olive oil was used for normal lighting (*see* LAMPS, NT; LAMPS, OT).

In a dry climate, OINTMENT for the skin was much favored to make the face shine (Ps 104:15) and was poured on the head (Pss 23:5; 133:2). Olive oil could be used for healing and soothing (Luke 10:34). Oil mixed with spices was used to ANOINT sacred objects and priests in the tabernacle and later in the Temple (Exod 30:22-33; 40:9-10; see also Gen 28:18), and to anoint kings (1 Sam 10:1; 16:13).

The olive fruit was one of the three crops (cereals, grapevines, olive trees, Deut 7:13) in the Mediterranean region vital for survival in the communities of biblical times. It is probable that the acrid fruits were pickled in salt before they were eaten, although this process is not actually mentioned in the Bible. Olive oil was used for cooking, mixed with flour, and eaten with bread. *See* AGRICULTURE; FOOD; MOUNT OF OLIVES; PLANTS OF THE BIBLE.

F. NIGEL HEPPER

OLIVES, MOUNT OF. *See* MOUNT OF OLIVES.

OLYMPAS oh-lim´puhs [Ὀλυμπᾶς Olympas]. A Christian man in Rome who receives greetings from Paul in Rom 16:15, grouped with PHILOLOGUS, JULIA, and NEREUS and his sister. Family relationships among the five are possible but not specified. Due to his Gk. name, Olympas was probably a Gentile. *See* ROMANS, LETTER TO THE.

KATHY R. MAXWELL

OLYMPIAN ZEUS, TEMPLE OF [νεὼς Διὸς Ὀλυμπίου neōs Dios Olympiou]. The name given to the Temple in Jerusalem by Antiochus IV Epiphanes (2 Macc 6:2). Placing a statue of Zeus Olympios in the Temple may have accompanied attempts to compel the Jews to abandon the "laws of God" and the "laws of their ancestors" (2 Macc 6:1). The laws of sacrifice in the Temple are an integral part of the legal stipulations of the OT. This account of the defilement of the Temple in 2 Macc 6:1-11 finds a par. in 1 Macc 1:41-64, in which the inspectors appointed by Antiochus IV, along with many people who forsook the law, "erected a DESOLATING SACRILEGE on the altar of burnt offering" (v. 54). It is most likely that Antiochus IV wished to establish in Jerusalem a symbol of the origins of his dynasty and its first patron. His devotion to the Olympian Zeus is amply attested. *See* GRECO-ROMAN RELIGIONS.

JOHN I. KAMPEN

OMAR oh´mahr [אוֹמָר ʾomar]. Second-listed son of ELIPHAZ and grandson of Esau and Adah, Omar is a clan chief of Esau (Gen 36:11, 15; 1 Chr 1:36). The name could mean "lamb," "prince," or "eloquent," perhaps one of the latter due to the status and rhetorical significance of the Eliphaz of the book of Job.

JASON C. DYKEHOUSE

OMEGA oh-meg´uh [ω ō, Ω Ō]. The last letter of the Gk. alphabet. *See* ALPHA AND OMEGA; ALPHABET.

OMEN [אוֹת ʾoth; τέρας teras]. In antiquity, people believed that the divine world revealed future events to humanity through inspiration (or prophecy), and through the divining arts that involved either the observation of signs or omens, or the use of ritual techniques designed to elicit a divine response. In the ancient Mediterranean world of divining arts, omens or signs were characteristically interpreted as favorable or unfavorable and as foreshadowing evil or good consequences (*see* SIGNS AND WONDERS).

A. Identification and Interpretation of Omens
B. Ancient Near East and Old Testament
    1. Ancient Near East
    2. Egypt
    3. Syro-Canaan
    4. Old Testament
C. Greek, Roman, Jewish, and Early Christian Omen Traditions
    1. Greek traditions
    2. Roman traditions
    3. Judaism
    4. New Testament
Bibliography

A. Identification and Interpretation of Omens

Omens could be found in any deviation from the ordinary or the mundane, whether in nature or in culture, and the ritual specialist's knowledge about omens was grounded in experience and tradition. Once it was observed that a specific sign was followed by a particular event, whenever that sign recurred it was predicted that it would be followed by the same or similar event.

It would be a mistake, however, to conclude that the ancient scribes were working with some (erroneous?) notion of causation. Instead, the association of sign and event took on what has been called an "invariant" association, one of sequence or coincidence, and it was a strategy of analogy, paronomasia, or manipulation that informed the associations that made up the conventional omen statements, both the protasis (the "if"-clause) and the apodosis ("then"-clause). Either element could include observable and conceivable phenomena. When interpreted by the properly trained ritual specialist, such deviant phenomena could assist in the aversion of looming disasters or in modifying behavior that might otherwise lead to calamity. The ominous and its attendant interpretation in no way presupposed a strictly deterministic view of human fate. Rather, omens constituted a warning, a possible future that could in some instances be averted by initiating the appropriate apotropaic magical rites.

Ominous signs might be identified in unusual markings on entrails of animals, in the shapes that oil took on as it spread across water, in phenomena observed in the heavens, such as an eclipse, or in strange and wondrous happenings that took place in daily life such as anomalous animal and human births. In their written versions, and most likely in their oral antecedents as well, omens could be classified into two categories: those that could be produced when desired and those that occurred without human initiation. In other words, ritual specialists were not limited to interpreting naturally or culturally occurring portents but could obtain a particular response from the divine by initiating a series of rites designed specifically for that purpose (*see* DIVINATION).

Over the centuries, significant selections of such omens as well as their interpretations were collected and written down in various omen series in Mesopotamia. The earliest of these come from the 3rd millennium BCE (e.g., a cylinder seal of GUDEA of Lagash that shows familiarity with celestial, dream, and liver omens), though the earliest written scholarly collections of omens date to the 2nd millennium BCE (e.g., the *Summa izbu*, a Mesopotamian omen collection on monstrous births; *see* SCIENCE, MESOPOTAMIA).

B. Ancient Near East and Old Testament

1. Ancient Near East

The language employed in the written omens from the ANE has long received the attention of scholars interested in the history of religions and the philosophy of science. A conventional phrase such as "(if) the moon god mourns ..." (*CT* 16.22.238) preserved in an omen protasis has suggested to some modern interpreters that the ancients merged notions of the divine (the moon god) and natural phenomena (the moon) with the result that the ancients were thought to have embraced some type of animism owing to their mythopoeic mentality. Recent investigations have demonstrated that this is an inadequate accounting for the manner in which the omen language was understood in ancient times. Such phraseology was more likely employed as metaphoric tropes in which the natural world was described in the language used of gods (in the case at hand, the moon's eclipse was metaphorically described as the moon god's mourning). There was no implied or intended fusion of the supernatural and natural worlds on the part of the ancient Mesopotamians. In the use of such language in omens, the natural phenomena were simply described in terms of the gods. Such metaphorical statements not only facilitated analogies and comparisons that transcended the usual categories and concepts but they also upheld the conceptual distinction between a perceived phenomenon and any real or imagined phenomenon with which it might be compared.

2. Egypt

Egyptian divination involved the consultation of ORACLEs for the purpose of resolving an existing issue by means of the pronouncement of a priest or a response from the divine statue. In Egypt, DREAM interpretation was highly regarded (e.g., the Chester Beatty Papyrus III). Other divinatory practices included astrological prognostication such as the interpretation of a star's luminescence and the observance of certain types of necromancy. Forms of divination like libanomancy (vessel inquiry) and lychnomancy (lamp divination) might have been learned from other cultures. Prophecy predicting future events was widely attested in ancient EGYPT. *See* ASTRONOMY, ASTROLOGY; BOOK OF THE DEAD.

3. Syro-Canaan

In Syro-Canaan, evidence for divination is attested in artifact and text. Ornithomancy and extispicy are both mentioned on Idrimi's statue from 2nd-millennium Alalakh and attested in liver models at Megiddo and Hazor. Texts from Ugarit preserve examples of teratology, extispicy (inscribed liver and lung models), oneiromancy, an astrological report, and a lunar omen. Evidence for other forms of divination like necromancy is lacking, or at best problematic, in early Syro-Canaanite divination traditions. *See* CANAAN, CANAANITES; SYRIA.

4. Old Testament

Various practices associated with omens are similarly attested for pre-Hellenistic Israel, as preserved in the OT. Biblical writers viewed some of these practices as legitimate, such as casting LOTS, the URIM AND THUMMIM (Exod 28:30; Lev 8:8; Num 27:21; Deut 33:8; 1 Sam 14:41), consultation of the EPHOD image (Judg 8:27; 17:5; 18:14-20), belomancy (arrow divination; 1 Sam 20:20-38), hydromancy (divination with water) or lecanomancy (dropping stones in a basin of water; Gen 44:5, 15), and dream interpretation (Gen 37:5-10; 40:5-22; Dan 2:3-9, 26-36; 4:5-27). VISIONS (Gen 46:2; Ezek 1:1; Dan 1:17; Joel 2:28) and prophecy are also well attested (e.g., Isa 6:1-13; Jer 1:11-19; Ezek 1:1–3:15; 8:1–11:25; 37:1-14; 40:1–48:35; Amos 7:1-9; 8:1-3; 9:1-4; Zech 1–6). *See* PROPHET, PROPHECY; SIGNS IN THE OT.

Some, but not all, biblical writers accepted other forms of divination, including the consultation of anthropomorphic images or the TERAPHIM (Zech 10:2). These images were apparently thought to speak the divine will (Hos 3:4). NECROMANCY (1 Sam 28), sorcery, and AUGURY (Deut 18:9-14) were deemed unacceptable (*see* MAGIC, MAGICIAN). Other forms were depicted as foreign in origin, yet efficacious. In addition to the frequent mention of Babylonian astrologers (Isa 47:13; Dan 1:20; 2:2, 10, 27), the OT notes that the Babylonian king Nebuchadnezzar successfully employed liver omens, along with arrow shaking, teraphim consultation, and the casting of lots (Ezek 21:18-23). It is not entirely clear what the distinguishing factor or factors were that resulted in the acceptance or rejection of certain practices by biblical writers. Yet, one likely factor was the perceived association of such practices with religious traditions competing with or posing a direct threat to those of the biblical writers.

The OT prohibitions against selected forms of divination have been viewed as very early proscriptions directed against the Late Bronze to Early Iron Age practices of Canaanites inhabiting the southern Levant. Yet others have made the case for reading such prohibitions "against the grain" as the rhetoric of writers who directed their tirades toward the practices observed by their contemporaries at the time of writing. In such cases, the rites of the "Canaanites" might rhetorically allude to the rituals observed by the writers' overlords, whether Assyrians, Egyptians, Babylonians, Persians, or Greeks, or the neighboring Phoenicians and Arameans, or even to the rites of the "people of the land," that is, those who had settled in the southern Levant following the Assyrian and Babylonian imperial upheavals throughout the region spanning the 8th–6th cent. BCE (including, among others, Samarians from the northern regions). Finally, they may be directed at the practices of fellow, but nonsympathetic, Judeans.

C. Greek, Roman, Jewish, and Early Christian Omen Traditions

1. Greek traditions

Turning to ancient Greek divination, those who sought the divine will preferably consulted the Delphic oracle, which involved the conveyance of Apollo's divine will communicated through his temple personnel at Delphi (or at Didyma or at Claros) to a celibate female recipient who took on the name Pythia and sat on a tripod throne wearing a crown. Otherwise, a wide variety of divinatory practices were observed in institutional settings as well as in the more general public sector of society including ornithomancy (bird behavior), oneiromancy (dreams), teratoskopy (portent interpretation), belly-talkers who prophesied by means of voices speaking from their stomachs, hydromancy (water), lecanomancy (oil), lychnomancy (lamp), interpreting the sound of wind, and visions. Spontaneous events could likewise provide revelation of the divine will, such as thunder and sneezing. Dream incubation, the use of dice, and perhaps clairvoyance are also attested (Luck; Ogden). *See* GREEK RELIGION AND PHILOSOPHY.

2. Roman traditions

Roman divination similarly exemplifies a wide range of practices observed by professional ritualists and private citizens alike. These involved the interpretation of solicited signs or omens, or extispicy (perhaps of Etruscan origins), or the reading of unusual or extraordinary events or prodigies. The last could include lightning, thunder, eclipses, comets, meteors, unusual births of animals and humans, wild animals roaming Rome, unchaste Vestals, and the flight of birds (Luck; Ogden). Cicero's work titled *On Divination* (44 BCE) is set in the form of an extended debate between Cicero and his brother Quintus on the relative legitimacy of divination that in the end conveys an unresolved ambivalence about the whole enterprise. By the 2nd cent. BCE, astrology was introduced but shortly thereafter rejected by the Senate when astrologers were expelled from Rome. *See* ROMAN RELIGIONS.

3. Judaism

The important role of signs and divination in Second Temple Judaism is hinted at by a handful of fragments from among the DEAD SEA SCROLLS. Exemplars found among the scroll fragments include elements of horoscopy (astrological interpretation), physiognomy (interpretation of human physical features), zodiology, and brontology (thunder interpretation). Physiognomy predicts the future of an individual based on physical characteristics at the time of birth and in alignment with a zodiacal sign. Horoscopy predicts an individual's future based on the positions of the planets, the sun, and the moon in the ZODIAC at the moment of the individual's birth. Brontology-based oracles focus on events of a national or communal dimension and predict future mundane events on the basis of the occurrence of thunder in a particular zodiacal sign. A lunar-omen text composed in Jewish Palestinian Aramaic from the late antique period confirms the continuing influence of ancient Mesopotamian divination on the world of late Second Temple Judaism and beyond.

4. New Testament

The NT also contains accounts of the interpretation of omens, such as those that portend the birth of Jesus. The Gospel of Matthew reports that astrologers from the east followed a star and that they interpreted dreams (Matt 2:1-12; *see* MAGI). Joseph also received ominous dreams about future events (Matt 2:13-15). The Lukan infancy narrative mentions heavenly messengers who help the shepherds identify the newborn king (Luke 2:13-18). Apocalyptic texts warn against false messiahs who will produce signs and omens to lead people astray (Matt 24:24; Mark 13:22). People require a "sign" from Jesus to prove he is the Messiah (Matt 12:38; 16:1; Mark 8:11; 13:4; Luke 11:16; 21:7), and in the Gospel of John, Jesus performs several signs to indicate to his disciples who he is (e.g., John 4:54; 6:14; 12:18). In Acts 1:26, lots were cast to determine the successor to Judas Iscariot while dreams and visions are taken up as significant themes throughout the book of Acts (16:9-10; 18:9-11; etc.). In Acts, Paul encounters what is apparently a Delphic-like mantic in Philippi. Although the woman repeatedly proclaims a favorable pronouncement concerning Paul and his mission, he nonetheless expels a spirit from the woman and in so doing incurs the wrath of the locals who had profited from her special gift. They accuse him of civil disturbance and take Paul to court to sue him to recover their losses (Acts 16:16-21). The phenomenon of glossolalia (speaking in an incomprehensible or foreign language) served as a sign of divine presence, possession, and communication (*see* TONGUES, GIFT OF). *See* SIGNS IN THE NT.

Bibliography: R. M. Berchman, ed. *Mediators of the Divine: Horizons of Prophecy, Divination, Dreams and Theurgy in Mediterranean Antiquity* (1998); W. Burkert. *Greek Religion* (1985); R. David. *Religion and Magic in Ancient Egypt* (2002); G. Luck. *Arcana Mundi* (1985); J. A. North. *Roman Religion* (2006); D. Ogden. *Magic, Witchcraft, and Ghosts in the Greco-Roman Worlds: A Sourcebook* (2002); D. Pardee. "Ugaritic Science." *The World of the Aramaeans*, vol. 3 (2001) 223–54; F. Rochberg. *The Heavenly Writing* (2006).

BRIAN B. SCHMIDT

OMER oh´muhr [עֹמֶר ʿomer]. A dry measure of capacity, mentioned relative to grain in Exod 16:16-36 (NRSV, "sheaf;" Lev 23:10, 15; Deut 24:19; Job 24:10). The exact size is unknown but is probably 1 to 2 liters. *See* WEIGHTS AND MEASURES.

OMICRON [ο ο, Ο Ο]. The fifteenth letter of the Gk. alphabet, based on the Phoenician *ʿen [<*ʿayn], a voiced pharyngeal, which was not needed in Gk., and the sound was used as a voice letter, representing o; the Ionians used it as short o (o mikron [ὂ μικρόν], "little o") as distinct from OMEGA, which represented long o (o mega [ὂ μέγα], "big o"). *See* ALPHABET.

P. KYLE MCCARTER

OMISSIONS OF THE SCRIBES. *See* QERE-KETHIBH; TEXT CRITICISM, OT.

OMRI om´ri [עָמְרִי ʿomri]. 1. Omri was a king of the northern kingdom of Israel in the 9th cent. BCE (ca. 882–871). Omri is hailed king after the usurper ZIMRI set fire to his own palace and perished in the flames (1 Kgs 16:18). Despite the mere thirteen verses dedicated to Omri's story in 1 Kings with its negative evaluation, extra-biblical texts and archaeological material reveal a ruler with an international reputation who expanded the borders of the kingdom and began an impressive building campaign.

Dating Omri's reign is complicated by the apparent inconsistency of the data provided by 1 Kgs 16. The biblical text says that Zimri reigned in TIRZAH for a mere seven days, which according to 1 Kgs 16:15 correlates his reign to the twenty-seventh year of King ASA of Judah. Eight verses later the text connects the beginning of Omri's reign to the thirty-first year of Asa, which would be four years later. Omri ruled Israel for twelve years (1 Kgs 16:23), but according to 1 Kgs 16:29, Omri's son AHAB came to the throne in the thirty-eighth year of Asa, giving Omri only a seven-year reign. At issue, apparently, is what factors constitute the beginning of Omri's reign.

The text is unclear on whether ATHALIAH, who ruled Judah for a period of time (2 Kgs 11:1-16), was Omri's daughter or granddaughter. She is listed as the daughter of Ahab in 2 Kgs 8:18 and 2 Chr 21:6, but in 2 Kgs 8:26 and 2 Chr 22:2 she is labeled the daughter of Omri (NRSV, "granddaughter"). Much scholarly speculation has yielded no definitive resolution.

When Zimri killed King Elah son of Baasha (1 Kgs 16:8-10), Omri was the commander of troops encamped at Gibbethon of the Philistines (1 Kgs 16:15). According to 1 Kgs 16:16, "all Israel" made Omri king (1 Kgs 16:16). At this point, Omri withdrew from Gibbethon and lay siege to Tirzah (1 Kgs 16:17). Despite their having named Omri king, after Zimri's death the people of Israel split into factions, with some following TIBNI son of Ginath and some following Omri (1 Kgs 16:21). For reasons not explained in the text, Omri is stronger, and upon Tibni's death Omri becomes the undisputed king (1 Kgs 16:22).

The rest of the events attributed to Omri in the biblical text reveal that he reigned in Tirzah for six years, bought the hill of Samaria, and built a town there. The text associates Omri with JEROBOAM son of Nebat and his sins (1 Kgs 16:26). Omri was buried in Samaria, and his son Ahab succeeded him as king (1 Kgs 16:28).

The extra-biblical material reveals a more impressive figure than that found in Kings and Chronicles. Omri is identified by name in the mid-9th-cent. BCE MOABITE STONE. MESHA, the ruler of Moab, was not a contemporary of Omri's but refers back to him in the stela describing the history of Israel's conflict with Moab. Mesha notes that Omri occupied the whole land of MEDEBA. The area of land referenced is northern Moab, an area associated with the tribe of Gad. Thus, though there is no reference to it in the biblical text, Omri apparently used his military prowess to expand the boundaries of Israel.

The Assyrian king SHALMANESER III (858–824 BCE) also references Omri. In Shalmaneser III's Black Obelisk inscription, JEHU son of Omri (so named in a caption) is depicted bringing tribute to the Assyrian king (*see* OBELISK, BLACK). This text treats Omri as the ancestor of a kingdom, similar to how the Assyrians reference many other Aramean kingdoms they conquered in the area of Syria. The reference also dissociates Omri from Ahab (who is from Israel or Jezreel in Shalmaneser III's earlier Monolith Inscription) and associates him instead with Jehu. Later Assyrian inscriptions continue to refer to the northern kingdom of Israel as the "house of Omri" until the kingdom's destruction.

Both the biblical text and archaeology suggest significant building projects during Omri's reign. At Tirzah (Tell el-Farah [North]) the rebuilding of a palace destroyed by fire was never completed, supporting the biblical text (1 Kgs 16:18). Excavations at the site of Samaria reveal that in this period the small village on the hillock was transformed by the building of a palace (with two building stages identified) there. Palace construction also occurs at the sites of Jezreel and Tirzah. More contentious in recent years is the identification of material traditionally dated to Solomon that some now argue is Omride. Other sites possibly developed by Omri include fortifications located in strategically important locations such as Hazor, Dan, and Megiddo.

The role of Jezreel is critical because it was occupied for a brief time in the 9th cent. BCE, thereby providing archaeologists with distinctive pottery styles as possible dating indicators for the period of the Omrides at other sites (*see* JEZREEL, JEZREELITE). The pottery correlates with that found at Megiddo in levels for palaces traditionally dated to Solomon, opening up the possibility that the material belongs to Omri or his descendants rather than Solomon.

While the data address archaeological concerns, they raise the larger issue of how to correlate archaeology with the Bible and are particularly relevant for Omri since the extra-biblical material reveals that he was a ruler far more important and dynamic than the Bible suggests.

2. The fifth son of BECHER, Benjamin's firstborn (1 Chr 7:8).

3. Grandfather of UTHAI, a Judahite who settled in Jerusalem following the Babylonian exile (1 Chr 9:4).

4. An officer watching over the tribe of Issachar for King David (1 Chr 27:18). *See* ISSACHAR, ISSACHARITES.

TAMMI J. SCHNEIDER

ON on [אוֹן ʾon]. 1. A Reubenite who participates in Korah's rebellion against Moses and Aaron (Num 16:1). *See* REUBEN, REUBENITES.

2. In the phrase "POTIPHERA, priest of On," the Hebrew rendering of the name of the Egyptian city known by the Greeks as HELIOPOLIS (Gen 41:45, 50; 46:20). Ezekiel 30:17 also mentions On, although MT vocalizes the name as "AVEN" (ʾawen אָוֶן).

STEVE COOK

ONAM oh´nuhm [אוֹנָם ʾonam]. 1. Within the genealogy of Esau and the Horite clans of Edom, Onam is the son of SHOBAL (Gen 36:23). *See* EDOM, EDOMITES; ESAU, ESAUITES.

2. In the Chronicler's genealogy of the clans of Judah, Onam is the son of Jerahmeel and ATARAH (1 Chr 2:26), and he had two sons (1 Chr 2:28). *See* JERAHMEEL, JERAHMEELITES; JUDAH, JUDAHITES.

VICTOR H. MATTHEWS

ONAN oh´nuhn [אוֹנָן ʾonan]. Son of the Canaanite "BATH-SHUA" (1 Chr 2:3) and Judah; younger brother to ER, whose wife was the Canaanite TAMAR (Gen 38:2-4). The Lord deemed Er "wicked" and killed him for it (38:7). Judah in turn told Onan, whose name may mean "vigor," to impregnate Tamar, following the code of levirate marriage (*see* LEVIRATE LAW), providing lineage for the deceased and family to support the widow (Deut 25:5-10). However, Onan "wasted [his semen] toward the earth . . . , so as not to give seed [offspring] to his brother" (Gen 38:9, author's trans.). Thus all such acts of "wasting" one's semen, including masturbation, became known outside the Bible as "onanism," a misunderstanding of Onan's act in the text itself. The Lord viewed Onan's behavior as "wicked," and consigned him to the same demise as Er. The narrative's conclusion (Gen 38:26) suggests that the men's egregious act was neglect of responsibility to Tamar rather than *coitus interruptus*, masturbation, or even solicitation of a prostitute. *See* MARRIAGE; SHELAH.

LISA MICHELE WOLFE

ONE [אֶחָד ʾekhadh; εἷς eis]. A number, indicating a single object or person. *See* NUMBERS, NUMBERING.

ONESIMUS oh-nes´uh-muhs [Ὀνήσιμος Onēsimos]. 1. In the letter to Philemon, Paul refers to himself as having become father to one of his colleagues in the gospel, Onesimus, while Paul was in prison (Phlm 10). In the letter, Paul insists that Philemon receive him (i.e., Onesimus) "no longer as a slave but more than a slave, a beloved brother—especially to me but how much more to you, both in the flesh and in the Lord" (Phlm 16; *see* BROTHER, BROTHERHOOD). Traditionally, this verse has been interpreted to mean that Onesimus was the slave of Philemon, though Paul never refers to Philemon as Onesimus' master. The traditional interpretation, that Onesimus is a fugitive slave, though challenged in recent scholarship, remains dominant in scholarly and popular treatments. *See* PHILEMON, LETTER TO.

2. Colossians mentions a "faithful and beloved brother" called Onesimus (Col 4:9) whom Paul had sent to COLOSSAE and who was apparently himself a Colossian. This may be the same Onesimus from the letter to Philemon.

3. Ignatius of Antioch writes of an Onesimus, bishop of EPHESUS, "a man of indescribable charity and your bishop here on earth" (Ign. *Eph.* 1.3).

4. The 4th-cent. *Apostolic Constitutions* mentions a Bishop Onesimus of Borea in Macedonia (*Apos. Con.* 7.46).

5. The medieval Byzantine *Martyrdom of Saint Onesimus* anachronistically conflates the figure of Onesimus in the Pauline corpus with traditions about Onesimus Leontinis of Sicily, a Christian teacher martyred during the Valerian persecution in the 3rd cent. CE. According to the *Martyrdom of Saint Onesimus*, Onesimus, a "house servant" and associate of Paul, was martyred in Rome under a provincial administrator named Tertullus (390).

6. In 18th-cent. colonial America the Puritan Cotton Mather named his slave Onesimus, because Mather believed Paul's letter to Philemon was an exhortation for the master class to make their "Negroes" into willing servants of God. When a smallpox epidemic broke out in Boston in 1721, Onesimus told his master that as a child in Africa he had been inoculated against the disease with pus taken from the sore of a victim and rubbed into a cut on Onesimus's arm, a common West African practice. Mather convinced Dr. Zabdiel Boylston to experiment with the procedure. Public reaction to the experiment was violently hostile, but the inoculation drastically reduced the mortality rate among those exposed. Credit for the procedure, however, would go to Dr. Edward Jenner, a British physician who performed his first inoculation seventy-five years later. And Onesimus, like his biblical namesake, would be remembered, if at all, only as a slave. *See* SLAVERY.

Bibliography: Allen Dwight Callahan. "Paul's Epistle to Philemon: Toward an Alternative *Argumentum.*" *HTR* 86 (1993) 357–76; Allen Dwight Callahan. *The Embassy of Onesimus* (1997); Cotton Mather. *The Negro Christianized* (1706) 42–43.

ALLEN DWIGHT CALLAHAN

ONESIPHORUS on´uh-sif´uh-ruhs ['Ονησίφορος Onēsiphoros]. A supporter of Paul mentioned in 2 Timothy. In 1:16-17, Paul, or someone writing in his name, requests that the Lord grant mercy to the household of Onesiphorus, who often refreshed Paul and was not ashamed of his imprisonment in Rome. Rather, he eagerly searched there for Paul and found him. This honorable conduct contrasts with the shameful behavior of Phygelus and Hermogenes, who turned away from Paul (v. 15). Furthermore, Onesiphorus earlier rendered much service in Ephesus (v. 18). The author's request that "the Lord grant that he will find mercy from the Lord on that day" (v. 18) has provoked debate about whether "Lord" means God or Christ in each case. Because Paul greets "the household of Onesiphorus" (4:19) rather that Onesiphorus himself, some suggest that Onesiphorus has died and argue that 1:18 is the earliest Christian reference to prayer for the dead.

The suggestion that Onesiphorus is another name for ONESIMUS is not widely accepted. The apocryphal *Acts of Paul* locates Onesiphorus and his household in Iconium. Hermogenes, Titus, and Demas are also names common to both sources.

***Bibliography*:** D. R. MacDonald. *The Legend of the Apostle* (1983).

MARK D. GIVEN

ONIAS oh-n*i*´uhs ['Ονίας Onias]. Onias is the name of four individuals from a priestly family that served in Jerusalem from the late 4th to mid-2nd cent. BCE. All but the last Onias held the office of high priest. According to Josephus (*Ant.* 11.347), the line is descended from Jaddua, who is mentioned in Neh 12:11, 22. Jaddua was the son of Johanan (a scribal error has changed the text to read Jonathan). This Johanan is the son or grandson of Eliashib, who was high priest during the time of Nehemiah (Neh 3:1, 20). Eliashib's grandfather was Jeshua (Neh 12:10), who returned to Jerusalem from the Babylonian exile. Jeshua, whose ancestry can be traced to Zadok during the time of David, was the first high priest of the postexilic period. Jeshua's descendants—including Onias I, Onias II, and Onias III—served as high priests during the postexilic period until they were replaced by non-Zadokite priests around 170 BCE. 1. Onias I was the son of Jaddua (Josephus, *Ant.* 11.347), whom he succeeded as high priest upon the latter's death toward the end of the 4th cent. BCE. Onias I may be the Onias whose correspondence with King Arius of Sparta is mentioned in 1 Macc 12:5-23. His son, Simon I, became high priest after his death. Onias I and Simon I may be the Onias and Simon mentioned in Sir 50:1, although Onias II also had a son named Simon.

2. Onias II was the son of Simon I. According to Josephus, Onias II was very young when his father died, so the high priesthood was first held by Eleazar, the brother of Simon I (*Ant.* 12.42–43), and then later by Manasseh, the brother of Onias I (*Ant.* 12.157). Onias II assumed the high priesthood around the middle of the 2nd cent. BCE. Josephus negatively portrays Onias II's motivations for withholding because of his refusing to pay twenty shekels of silver as a tribute to Ptolemy III (*Ant.* 12.158). The historical background to Onias' withholding of tribute is the Third Syrian War. Onias sided with the Syrians against Ptolemy III, a move that weakened Onias' position after Ptolemy

defeated the Syrians. Joseph, Onias' nephew and the leader of the house of Tobias, used the occasion to court favor with Ptolemy. This rivalry between the Oniads and Tobiads would continue until both houses lost power during the events leading up to the Maccabean Revolt.

3. Onias III was the grandson of Onias II through his son Simon II. Onias became high priest around 190 BCE and held the office until 175 BCE. Second Maccabees preserves a very positive view of Onias III. According to 2 Macc 3:1, "the holy city [Jerusalem] was inhabited in unbroken peace and the laws were strictly observed because of the piety of the high priest Onias and his hatred of wickedness."

Second Maccabees 3–4 records the rivalry between Onias III and Simon, the leader of a hellenizing faction in league with the Tobiads. Simon and Onias had a disagreement over a question of who had jurisdiction over the city's market. Having lost the dispute, Simon went to Apollonius, the governor of Coele-Syria and Phoenicia, and made known to him the large sums of money in the Jerusalem Temple. Apollonius relayed the account to Seleucus IV, who sent Heliodorus to confiscate the money. Upon Heliodorus' arrival in Jerusalem to seize the money, the people of the city rushed from their homes to pray for the Temple. When Heliodorus attempted to enter the Temple, God sent a mighty armored horse and rider along with two bodyguards. Heliodorus was prevented from entering the Temple and was greatly wounded during the confrontation. Onias III offered sacrifices to atone for Heliodorus, who recovered from his wounds. Simon later accused Onias of having been the one who reported the funds to Apollonius. Second Maccabees 4:3-6 records that Onias recognized that the rivalry had reached crisis level. For the good of the people, Onias traveled to Antioch.

According to 2 Macc 4:7-10, Onias lost the high priesthood to his brother Jason, who offered the newly enthroned Antiochus IV 440 talents of silver for the office. Second Maccabees presents Jason as a hellenizer who introduced a number of Greek innovations to Jerusalem, including the establishment of a gymnasium in the city. Three years later, however, Jason was replaced by a higher bidder, Menelaus. When Onias, who had been in exile near Antioch, accused Menelaus of stealing from the Temple, Menelaus sent Andronicus to kill Onias (2 Macc 4:30-38). The death of Onias III is also mentioned by Josephus (*Ant.* 12.5.1) but he does not record that Onias was murdered.

4. Onias IV was the only Onias not to serve as high priest in Jerusalem. Josephus records that a son of Onias III who was also named Onias became high priest and changed his name to Menelaus (*Ant.* 12.239), but this does not comport with other sources. It seems likely, therefore, that Josephus has mistakenly confused Menelaus and Onias IV.

When Onias III died, his son Onias IV was still an infant (*Ant.* 12.237). According to Josephus, Onias IV fled to Egypt as an adult due to the political situation in Judea and his family's loss of the high priesthood (*Ant.* 12.387; 13.62–65). The date of his arrival in Egypt is debated. Josephus states that he fled from Judea after the murder of Menelaus in 162 BCE (*Ant.* 12.387). But scholars point to an Aramaic papyrus from Egypt (*CPJ* 1.132) addressed to an individual whose name is restored as Onias. It is likely that the recipient was Onias IV. The papyrus is dated to 164 BCE, which would place Onias in Egypt earlier than Josephus suggests in *Ant.* 12.387. This chronology fits well with *Ant.* 13.62–65, however, which states that Onias had already served Ptolemy Philopater for several years before requesting to build a temple in 160 BCE. Most scholars accept the evidence of the papyrus and argue that Onias came to Egypt sometime prior to 164 BCE, with some proposing that he arrived as early as 170 BCE.

In Egypt, Onias first served Ptolemy Philopater as a general in the army. Around 160 BCE, Onias led a group of Jews to Leontopolis in the Nile Delta, perhaps as part of a military force. Once in Leontopolis, he proposed to build a Jewish temple on the site of a ruined temple to the goddess Bubastis. Josephus states that Onias thought he was fulfilling a prophecy in Isa 19:19 predicting a shrine to Yahweh in the midst of Egypt. Onias petitioned Ptolemy and Cleopatra, who granted his request (*Ant.* 13.62–71). Josephus describes the temple as being similar to the Temple in Jerusalem, but of a smaller scale. (In *Ant.* 8.62–70, Josephus mistakenly credits Onias III with building the temple at Leontopolis.) Although some see the temple serving as the center of worship for Jews in Egypt, others think it served merely a local function as a shrine for a Jewish military force stationed at Leontopolis under the leadership of Onias. Regardless of its status, the temple at Leontopolis stands alongside the Jewish temple in Elephantine as the only locations other than Jerusalem that functioned as acceptable places to offer Jewish sacrifices. *See* HASMONEANS; PRIESTS AND LEVITES.

Bibliography: James C. VanderKam. *From Joshua to Caiaphas: High Priests after the Exile* (2004).

KEVIN A. WILSON

ONION [בָּצָל batsal]. Onions (*Allium cepa*) are mentioned only in the rather wistful litany of foods the Israelites could consume while they were in bondage in Egypt (Num 5:11). The spicy taste of onions and garlic would have stood in stark contrast to the steady diet of manna in the wilderness. The Egyptian variety of onion (*Allium cepa proliferum*) differs from the common onion, which forms a globular bulb underground, since its cluster of bulbs forms at the top of two- or three-foot stems. *See* AGRICULTURE; FOOD; PLANTS OF THE BIBLE.

VICTOR H. MATTHEWS

ONKELOS, TARGUM. *See* TARGUMS.

ONLY BEGOTTEN. *See* GOD'S ONLY SON; VERSIONS, ENGLISH.

ONO oh´noh [אוֹנוֹ ʾono]. A city in the plain, near Lod, mentioned in the 15th-cent. BCE list of Thutmose III. According to 1 Chr 8:12 it was occupied by the Benjaminites (*see* BENJAMIN, BENJAMINITES). Ono occurs with Lod and Hadid in the list of the towns settled by returnees after the exile (Ezra 2:33; Neh 7:37), and again among Benjaminite settlements in the days of Nehemiah (Neh 11:35; compare Neh 6:2). Rabbinical tradition counts Ono with "the walled cities from the time of Joshua" (*m. Arak.* 9:6; *b. Meg.* 4a) and locates it 3 mi. from Lod. Commonly identified with the ruined Kafr ʿAna (today southeast Or Yehudah), perhaps this site was in fact "kefar Ono" while Ono itself was 2 to 3 km southward.

YOEL ELITZUR

ONOMASTICA on´uh-mas´tuh-kuh. Lists of names of things, revolving around some heuristic component, often associated with scribal schools of the ANE. Onomastica can take different forms, such as lists of flora or fauna, gods, medical terms, or lexical data. The Onomasticon of Amenemope is representative of Egyptian lists, and there is a plethora of Mesopotamian material. It has sometimes been suggested that Solomon's "speaking of animals, and birds and reptiles" (1 Kgs 4:32) is evidence that Solomon produced onomastica.

Bibliography: David P. Silverman. *Ancient Egypt* (1997); Steve Tinney. "Texts, Tablets, and Teaching: Scribal Education in Nippur and Ur." *Expedition* 40 (1998) 40–50.

CHRISTOPHER A. ROLLSTON

ONQELOS, TARGUM. *See* TARGUMS.

ONYCHA on´i-kuh [שְׁחֵלֶת shekheleth; ὄνυξ onyx]. An ingredient in the INCENSE used in the Tabernacle (Exod 30:34; Sir 24:15). The word is a HAPAX LEGOMENON. Onycha is the closing flap of certain snails. The use of the Murex snail to make the blue dye for priests' garments has recently been verified. Thus, perhaps other mollusk by-products were used in the priestly service, burned as part of the incense. *See* PERFUME.

JUDITH ABRAMS

ONYX [שֹׁהַם shoham; σαρδόνυξ sardonyx]. A form of quartz having alternating black and white bands, similar to agate and sardonyx. Most modern versions of the Bible translate the Hebrew **shoham** as onyx, but this identification is doubtful. The cognate word in Akkadian means "red," which suggests a red stone such as CARNELIAN rather than the black and white onyx. The identification of many of the gems and semiprecious stones in the Bible is uncertain.

The "onyx" of the NRSV is a stone that is found in a number of OT passages. It is used in several parts of the vestments of the Israelite priests. Onyx is to be set into the middle of the fourth row of stones on the priest's breastplate (Exod 28:15-20). Two other onyx stones are to be engraved with the names of the twelve tribes and placed on the shoulders of the ephod (Exod 28:9). Onyx is also said to have been in the Garden of Eden (Ezek 28:13) and in the land of Havilah to the east of Eden (Gen 2:12). Onyx occurs once in the NT, where it is one of the stones decorating the city walls of the New Jerusalem (Rev 21:20). *See* AGATE; JEWELS AND PRECIOUS STONES.

KEVIN A. WILSON

OPENING [חֹר khor]. The word *opening* has a wide variety of meanings, but in the context of Song 5:4, "from the opening" or "from the latch" is probably a poetic euphemism for sexual activity.

OPHEL oh´fel [עֹפֶל ʿofel]. The Hebrew word means "hill" or "mound" but is used in the OT as a proper noun to designate a particular area of JERUSALEM: a hill (part of a ridge) south of the Temple Mount. Today, the area around the Ophel is commonly designated the "city of David" and considered the oldest area of settlement in Jerusalem. On the east, the KIDRON VALLEY separates the Ophel from the MOUNT OF OLIVES and the Silwan settlement; the Hinnom Valley is to the south and the Tyropoeon (Central) Valley is to the west (*see* HINNOM, VALLEY OF; TYROPOEON VALLEY).

As an easily defensible hill with nearby springs, the area was settled already in the Chalcolithic and Early Bronze I periods. A Canaanite settlement at the site including walls, towers, and water channels dates to the Middle Bronze II through the Late Bronze periods. Retaining walls on the Ophel likely date to the Iron Age and the first period of Judean activity in the area. Jotham built onto the "wall of Ophel" (2 Chr 27:3). Later, Manasseh built a wall around the city of David, including the Ophel (2 Chr 33:14). Hezekiah's tunnel, where the SILOAM inscription was found, cuts through the Ophel carrying water from the Gihon spring in the Kidron Valley to the pools south of the Ophel (*see* GIHON, SPRING). This tunnel supplied water to the Iron II settlement of Jerusalem during the siege by the Assyrian king Sennacherib (701 BCE). During the building of the Second Temple, temple servants lived on the Ophel (Neh 3:26; 11:21).

MILTON MORELAND

OPHIR oh´fuhr [אוֹפִיר ʾofir; Οὐφείρ Oupheir, Σωφηρά Sōphēra, Ὠφειρ Ōpheir]. A Philistine ostracon from Tell Qasile near Jaffa (8th cent. BCE) mentions 30 shekels of **zhb ʾpr** (זהב אפר)—"gold of Ophir" (Maisler). In the OT, Ophir also appears in conjunction with **zahav** (זָהָב, "gold"; 1 Chr 29:4; Sir 7:18) but more often with **kethem** (כֶּתֶם, "gold," Akkad. **kutmmu**; Job 28:16; Ps 45:9 [Heb. 45:10]; Isa 13:12).

This has led to the suggestion that *Ophir* is an epithet for *gold*, designating its high quality and not a geographical location. Nevertheless, it is clear that Ophir in other contexts refers to a geographical place where GOLD was obtained, from which the epithet is probably derived.

In the Table of Nations (the descendants of Noah in Gen 10:1-32), Ophir appears in the genealogy of Joktan and is associated with Hazarmaveth (Hadramawt), Havilah (southwestern Arabia), and Sheba (Saba) among his thirteen sons (Gen 10:29; compare 1 Chr 1:23), which suggests Ophir should be located in South Arabia.

That Ophir should be regarded as a geographical place in Arabia is also implied in the description of Solomon's maritime enterprises with Hiram of Tyre. In 1 Kgs 9:26-28, Solomon constructed a fleet of ships at Ezion-geber, which Hiram equipped with Tyrian sailors; the fleet obtained 420 talents of gold from Ophir (compare 450 talents in 2 Chr 8:17-18; 120 talents in the LXX). This cooperative maritime venture is followed by the visit of the Queen of Sheba and her camel caravan laden with spices, gold, and precious stones to Solomon (1 Kgs 10:1-10). Sheba elsewhere is associated with gold (Ps 72:10, 15; Isa 60:6; Ezek 27:22). Hiram's fleet also returned from Ophir with "gold ... almug wood and precious stones" (1 Kgs 10:11). In addition, Solomon and Hiram sent an allied fleet of Tarshish ships that came back with "gold, silver, ivory, apes, and peacocks" (1 Kgs 10:22). Elsewhere, "the kings of Tarshish and of the isles" are placed in conjunction with Sheba (Ps 72:10), and King Jehoshaphat's "Tarshish ships" were prepared to sail for Ophir before they were wrecked at Ezion-geber (1 Kgs 22:48), suggesting a Red Sea base for this expedition.

An African location has long been maintained for Ophir, and the name is linked by some with Latin *afer*, derived from a Berber context (compare Homer's *Od.* 7.8–9), but this seems highly conjectural. The ships' cargo of precious metals, monkeys, and peacocks possibly points to an African location. Other locations in western Africa also have been suggested, ranging from Zimbabwe to Nubia. Adulis, on the Eritrean coast of Somaliland, is a possible location for the cargo of the Tarshish ships that offers suitable comparisons with the Egyptian New Kingdom expeditions for exotic animals to Punt (Somalia).

An Indian location for Ophir has also been proposed based on Josephus' discussion of Hiram's sailors joining Solomon's three-year expedition to Sopheir (**Sōupheir** Σουφείρ), the Land of Gold, in India (*Ant.* 8.164), and Jerome's Vulgate also renders Ophir in Job 28:16 as "India," and this has led to its association with the Supara (Ptolemy, *Geog.* 7.1.5) and its identification with Kalyan, 40 mi. north of Mumbai. Others have suggested a location in Oman in the southeast Arabian Peninsula and associated it with the Asaba ore of Ptolemy (*Geog.* 6.7.29). Despite these suggestions, the gold-producing areas of southwestern Arabia remain the most popular proposal for the location of Ophir. In the 2nd cent. BCE, Agatharchides of Cnidus (*On the Erythraean Sea* 97) locates the gold-producing country of the Debae on the western coasts of Arabia (compare Ptolemy, *Geog.* 6.7.5), which has been identified with Dhahaban in the 'Asir province of Saudi Arabia.

A clue that Saudi Arabia was linked to Africa by trade is perhaps provided by the Greek fragments of the 2nd-cent. BCE work *Concerning the Kings in Judaea*, by the Jewish historian Eupolemus, who locates Ophir on an island in the Red Sea (Eup., frag. 2). On the major island of the Farasan Islands, off the western coast of the Arabian Peninsula, there is evidence of activity as an ancient trading center for Abbysinia in Africa and the 'Asir Mountains of Arabia. It is possible that it was a transit center for transporting the exotic animals and goods of Africa and Arabian incense and gold to ships for ports farther north in the Red Sea like Ezion-geber. Recent geological exploration has demonstrated that gold mining was widely dispersed along the Arabian Shield of the western coasts from Midian in the northwest to Yemen in the southwest, with the largest concentration in the southwestern region. Precious stones from the western coasts of Arabia are legendary, and the "ALMUG wood" is probably *juniperus*, which appears throughout 'Asir. This area of Arabia seems the most likely location for the Solomonic Ophir.

Bibliography: Mordechai Cogan. *I Kings.* AB 10 (2000); Carl R. Holladay. *Fragments from Hellenistic Jewish Authors, Vol. I: Historians* (1983); Kenneth A. Kitchen. "Sheba and Arabia." *The Age of Solomon: Scholarship at the Turn of the Millennium.* Lowell K. Handy, ed. (1997) 127–53; B. Maisler. "Two Hebrew Ostraca from Tell Qasile." *JNES* 10 (1951) 265–67; J. Naveh. "Writing and Scripts in Seventh-Century B.C.E. Philistia: The New Evidence from Tell Jemmeh." *IEJ* 35 (1985) 8–21.

DAVID F. GRAF

OPHNI of'n*i* [עָפְנִי ʿofni]. Located 2.5 mi. northwest of Bethel at modern Jifneh, Ophni is only mentioned in the Benjaminite city list in Josh 18:24. This location would actually place the city beyond the boundaries of Benjamin. However, since several other cities in the list also lie outside Judah's tribal lands, this may indicate later editorial additions based on either a fluctuation in political zones (perhaps a one-time extension of Judah during Josiah's reign) or a variation in the established district system allowing for a thirteenth district. The site of Jifneh has also been identified with Gophna, mentioned by Josephus (*J.W.* 3.51–58) as one of seven Judean toparchies. *See* BENJAMIN, BENJAMINITES.

VICTOR H. MATTHEWS

OPHRAH of'ruh [עָפְרָה ʿofrah]. 1. A city in the territory of Benjamin (Josh 18:23) identified with modern et-Taiyibeh 4 mi. northeast of Bethel. The site is named as the destination of a Philistine raiding party (1 Sam 13:17). *See* BENJAMIN, BENJAMINITES.

2. The home of GIDEON, who is also known as JERUBBAAL. At Ophrah, Gideon spoke with an angel (Judg 6:11), built an altar (Judg 6:24), installed an ephod (Judg 8:27), and was buried (Judg 8:32); also, his son ABIMELECH killed the other sons of Gideon/ Jerubbaal at Ophrah (Judg 9:5).

The location of Gideon's Ophrah is unknown. Gideon remarked that his clan, ABIEZER, was "the weakest in Manasseh" (Judg 6:15; compare Josh 17:2; *see* MANASSEH, MANASSITES). Also, Gideon engaged the Midianites in battle in the Valley of Jezreel on the north edge of the territory of Manasseh (Judg 6:33). Thus, scholars have usually assumed that Ophrah lies somewhere in Manasseh. Yet no identified site in the territory of ancient Manasseh has a name resembling *Ophrah.* The nearest candidate with a similar name is ancient ʿAffula, located north of Manasseh in the middle of the Jezreel Valley (*see* ʿAFFULA, EL).

One scholar has recently compared the name *Ophrah* to the name of the Judahite town of Ephrathah (*see* EPHRATHAH, EPHRATHITES) and suggested that Gideon was actually based in Ephrathah of Judah, which the scholar identifies as the fortress city of Ramat Rahel (*see* RAHEL, RAMAT). According to this hypothesis, an editor who sought to increase the status of King David by portraying him as the greatest hero of early Judah invented the town of Ophrah in Manasseh as a home for Gideon, thus relocating him outside of Judah and away from David.

3. The son of MEONOTHAI in the genealogy of Judah (1 Chr 4:14).

Bibliography: Lukasz Niesiolowski-Spanò. "Where Should One Look for Gideon's Ophra?" *Bib* 86 (2005) 478–93.

VICTOR H. MATTHEWS

OPPRESSION. *See* LIBERATION; LIBERATION THEOLOGY; MARGINAL, MARGINALIZATION.

ORACLE or´uh-kuhl [מַשָּׂא massaʾ, מָשָׁל mashal, נְאֻם neʾum; λόγιον logion]. A direct message from God delivered through a prophet. Although the word *oracle* often carries with it the idea of a divine answer given in response to an inquiry (e.g., the Oracle of Delphi), the terms translated as "oracle" in the Bible do not necessarily carry this connotation. Some biblical oracles are given in response to a question or petition presented to the deity (1 Kgs 22:15; 2 Chr 20:5-19), a practice that is also known from Mesopotamia, and in such cases the prophetic activity often takes place within a cultic setting (1 Chr 25:1). But the means by which the majority of oracles in the OT was received is unknown, as most are presented in their canonical form without reference to the process of intermediation that produced them.

The NRSV translates three different Hebrew words with the English term *oracle.* By far the most common is massaʾ. The meaning of the term in reference to prophecy is debated. Massaʾ means "burden" in some contexts (Num 4:24; Deut 1:12), and it has often been argued that an oracle is the burden carried by the prophet and the burden placed on the people by the divine message. Jeremiah plays off this meaning in Jer 23:33-40. When the people come to him to ask what the massaʾ ("oracle") of the Lord is, he responds by telling them that they are the massaʾ ("burden") of the Lord. Other scholars have pointed to the etymological connection of massaʾ with the verb nasaʾ (נָשָׂא, "to lift, carry"), which is used in the expression "to lift up the voice" (Gen 21:16; Judg 2:4; 2 Sam 3:32). According to this theory, an oracle is that which is spoken by the prophets when they "lift their voice." Neither of these two explanations is entirely persuasive.

Given the tentative nature of etymological explanations of the meaning of massaʾ, some scholars have attempted to arrive at a definition of the term by other means. Richard Weis, e.g., has put forth a rhetorical definition of massaʾ. Weis isolates a three-part rhetorical pattern in oracles that bear the title massaʾ: 1) an assertion is made about God's involvement in a particular set of events; 2) the massaʾ clarifies a previously given prophecy and applies it to the current situation; and 3) the massaʾ informs the hearers of appropriate responses to the current situation. Weis proposes that a massaʾ be understood as a prophetic reinterpretation of a prior divine message. Its function is to clarify a prophecy that has been previously given or to apply an older message to a new situation.

Massaʾ is frequently used as a title for prophetic speeches and collections of prophetic sayings. It does not seem to refer to a particular form-critical genre of prophetic speech, as oracles designated by this term take a variety of forms. The term seems to have arisen in the southern kingdom of Judah, and its usage is limited to prophets active in that area. It is used frequently in the oracles against the nations in Isa 13–23, although it does not appear as a title to similar oracles in Jeremiah or Ezekiel. The term massaʾ is used in the superscription of three prophetic books as a designation for the entire collection of that prophet's oracles (Nah 1:1; Hab 1:1; Mal 1:1). It is also used as a heading for two appendixes in Zechariah (Zech 9:1; 12:1). The occurrence of this word in Prov 30:1 and 31:1 is problematic. Although the NRSV translates it as "oracle" here, some have suggested it should be read as a personal or place name, e.g., "Lemuel, king of Massa" (Prov 31:1).

A second term translated "oracle" by the NRSV is neʾum (Num 24:4, 16; 2 Sam 23:1). The word, which means "utterance," is frequently used in direct quotations to indicate who is speaking (Num 14:28; Isa 14:22). In prophetic speech, its usage is parallel to the expression "thus says the LORD." It is not intended as a designation for a type of oracle, as it is also used in nonprophetic contexts (2 Sam 23:1; Prov 30:1).

The NRSV also translates the Hebrew term mashal as "oracle" in the BALAAM pericope of Num 22–24. The word is used to refer to the prophetic speeches of Balaam (Num 23:7, 18; 24:3, 15, 20-21, 23). Mashal is most commonly found in wisdom literature (Prov 1:1 etc.; Eccl 12:9). Its meaning is usually understood to derive from the comparison a mashal makes between two items (from the verb mashal [מָשַׁל], "to resemble"). Its use here to refer to prophetic speech is unique in the OT. Baruch Levine has argued that the term derives not from the content or function of the speech but from its form. In his view, a mashal is a balanced verse comprising two hemistichs. The utterances of Balaam in Num 22–24 are indeed balanced, poetic utterances. The Deir ʿAlla inscription about Balaam uses the word massaʾ to describe the message he received from El, while the Hebrew text of the OT also uses neʾum sometimes to refer to the speech of Balaam (Num 24:3-4, 15-16; *see* DEIR ʿALLA, TEXTS).

The term logion appears three times in the NT. Twice it refer to messages of God delivered in the past (Acts 7:38; Rom 3:2), while once it seems to refer to things taught by the early church (Heb 5:12). The same word also occurs in 1 Pet 4:11 where it is translated as "the very words" of God. This term as used in the NT does not necessarily refer to prophetic activity. It is used in later Christian literature to refer to the sayings of Christ and the teachings of the early church.

Bibliography: Michael H. Floyd. "The מַשָּׂא (maśśāʾ) as a Type of Prophetic Book." *JBL* 121 (2002) 401–22; Baruch A. Levine. *Numbers 21–36.* AB 4A (2000); Richard Weis. *A Definition of the Genre* Maśśāʾ *in the Hebrew Bible.* Ph.D. diss., Claremont Graduate University (1986); Robert R. Wilson. *Prophecy and Society in Ancient Israel* (1980).

KEVIN A. WILSON

ORAL LAW, ORAL TORAH. According to rabbinic tradition, oral Law or oral Torah is the authoritative interpretation of the written TORAH that was transmitted orally until it was set down in writing in order to preserve it for future generations. One of the basic premises of the tannaʾim (תַּנָּאִים; those who transmitted rabbinic teachings) is the concept of the two complementary Torahs—oral and written—that the rabbis believed were given by God to Moses on Sinai (*Sifre Deut.* 351; *see* RABBI, RABBONI; TANNA, TANNAIM). The oral Torah provided the interpretations and explanations that made possible the application of the written Torah as a way of life. Therefore, the two Torahs were of equal status and authority with each another. Further, the accuracy of the transmission of a teaching depended not only on the correctness of the contents, but also upon the mode of transmission; it had to be transmitted in the way it was believed to have been given at Sinai. Therefore, it was required that the written Torah be taught from a scroll while the oral law had to be recited orally by the tannaʾ (תַּנָּא; *y. Meg.* 74d; *b. Tem.* 14b).

According to Josephus, the PHARISEES claimed to possess ancient traditions that they inherited from past generations (*Ant.* 13.297; compare Philo, *Spec. Laws* 28.149–50). The oral law was based on these traditions with the addition of ancient customary law and midrashic exegesis of the Second Temple period. At some point between the later 1st cent. BCE and the 1st cent. CE, the notion began to be expressed that the oral law, along with the written, had been given at Sinai. Some scholars have seen this development as the result of the desire of the Yavnean rabbis to solidify their authority by claiming divine origin for their own traditions (*see* JAMNIA, COUNCIL OF). On the other hand, such ideas could have been developing within the various approaches to JUDAISM in the Second Temple period, which were all trying to provide a supplementary code to the written law to enable the Torah to be interpreted and observed. In Pharisaic Judaism (that would develop into rabbinic Judaism), this goal was accomplished by the concept of the oral law.

Rabbinic tradition has always assumed that the notion of two Torahs originating on Sinai went all the way back in time. Modern scholars can document this concept as fully developed by the aftermath of the Great Revolt (66–73 CE). By that time, the Sinaitic origin of laws was articulated, although the notion of a dual Torah and dual revelation was not yet so prominent (*see* SINAI, MOUNT). This idea was developing in Pharisaic times in the period leading up to the destruction of the Temple (70 CE), and the unwritten laws of the fathers represented an earlier stage in its conceptualization.

After the revolt, the rabbis were in the process of standardizing their teachings and authority and sought the support of the people at large (the ʿAM HAʾARETS). They appealed to the divine origin of the oral law on a few occasions (e.g., *b. Shabb.* 31a; *b. Qidd.* 66a), although only in the amoraic period (ca. 200–500 CE) was the full midrashic basis for these ideas worked out (e.g., see *Meg. Taan.* to 14 Tammuz). Then the rabbis asserted that the oral Torah and its authority were actually mentioned in the written law (*b. Ber.* 4b; interpreting Exod 24:12 as consisting of both written and oral laws).

The oral law allowed Pharisaic Judaism and later the rabbinic tradition to develop organically. It provided the basis for the assertion of continuity in Talmudic Judaism in the face of numerous adaptations and adjustments, for in the view of the rabbis it was as if there were no changes (*see* TALMUD). All later developments had already been commanded as part of the Sinaitic revelation. *See* JEWISH BIBLICAL INTERPRETATION; LAW IN EARLY JUDAISM; MISHNAH; RABBINIC LITERATURE.

LAWRENCE H. SCHIFFMAN

ORAL TRADITION. *See* TRADITION, ORAL.

ORALITY. Communication in the ancient world was primarily oral. Few people (ca. 10–20 percent) were even minimally literate. Authors composed aloud, usually in company, and recorded their initial oral compositions or their delivered speeches in writing for further oral performance(s) (e.g., Jer 36:6; Col 4:10-18). Students learned to paraphrase, summarize, and expand aloud familiar literary texts, so that learning to read and write began as oral performance.

Skilled oral communicators responded to their audiences. They used patterns of sounds and words and ideas, anticipations, repetitions, and commonplaces to help their listeners follow the story or the argument and perhaps memorize it (Plato, *Phaedr.* 227d–228c). This is the art of rhetoric (*see* RHETORIC AND ORATORY). When Paul disclaims using rhetorical sophistry (1 Thess 2:3-6), he himself deploys rhetoricians' phrases. Nonetheless, his own oral performance apparently was found to be unimpressive by some audiences (2 Cor 10:10).

Memory in an oral culture may be remarkably accurate, yet each new oral performance is a fresh interpretation, which may in turn generate new texts and performances. For example, though Jesus never wrote down his own teachings, his followers remembered and repeated his sayings. Jesus' words were compiled in written form only years later. Because of the fluidity of oral tradition, the Gospels have different versions of the same stories or teachings (*see* PARABLE; SYNOPTIC GOSPELS; SYNOPTIC PROBLEM). The words of God create the world and achieve results (Gen 1; Isa 55:11). Human beings also create acts through words: they make promises or requests or commitments (Rom 10:10). Public speakers move crowds to action. Some scholars distinguish sharply between Jesus' deeds and his sayings, yet his utterances are narrated as significant events. For example, Jesus' BLESSINGS AND CURSINGS had objective power. His verbal exorcisms and healings achieved dramatic results (see, e.g., Matt 8:8-13; 17:18; Matt 9:6-7 // Mark 2:11-12 // Luke 5:24-25; Matt 12:13 // Mark 3:5 // Luke 6:10; Mark 5:8-13; Luke 4:33-35, 38-39). Even though inscribed blessings and curses are found on tablets and amulets from the ancient world, the spoken word is more powerful than the written word. In the Scriptures, utterance takes precedence over inscription.

Biblical authors normally (and quite naturally) assumed their sequences of words would communicate. Sometimes we are told how a word is taken to work (Rom 4:3-8), and sometimes we find efforts to make words more effective (Isa 58; Heb 7:1–8:1). For explanations of how words are taken to have force (dynamis δύναμις; 1 Cor 14:11), we have to look outside the Scriptures for what people in their own cultural context took for granted. In the ancient Greco-Roman world, words were treated as names for people, things, and ideas (Eph 3:15). Dio Chrysostom (ca. 40–120 CE) explains that human beings naturally name everything that they perceive with their senses, so that when the name of something is spoken aloud, it conveys a meaning as distinct as the thing itself (*Dei cogn.* 12.65).

However, just as one person could have several names, the same name could apply to many things or ideas. That is why the methods of condensing, expanding, and paraphrasing were taught so confidently, because the ancients assumed that one could tell the same story or explain the same idea in different words. Meaning, therefore, was not contained in the words themselves, but rather words pointed to, indicated, and evoked meaning. It is this conviction, further, that underlies the practice of ALLEGORY. A written text can have plural meanings. This explains the seeming verbal freedom that the Synoptic Gospel authors display when it seems they are paraphrasing, expanding, or contracting their sources for fresh oral performances.

Important corollaries follow for exegesis. An author may have intended to say the same thing two, three, or more times in different ways in one sequence. These different sets of words may indicate fresh, complementary thoughts, or they may be editorial intrusions. Their editing is thus harder to demonstrate than many suppose. For example, variations among the Synoptic Gospels may betoken new ideas, or they may rather have been intended to say the same thing in a better way or to a different audience (*see* REDACTION CRITICISM, NT; REDACTION CRITICISM, OT).

This account of words and meanings in the ancient world might at first sight seem postmodernist and relativist. It is, however, distinctive. Certainly, words as names could be interchanged readily. But what they were intended to designate was still taken to be objective. In practice, contemporaries could check on their hearers' reactions. We today, reading written records of oral performance, are left with plural possibilities and differing judgments of plausibility. *See* ORAL LAW, ORAL TORAH; SAY, SPEAK; TRADITION, ORAL; WORD.

Bibliography: F. Gerald Downing. *Doing Things with Words in the First Christian Century* (2000); Jonathan A. Draper, ed. *Orality, Literacy, and Colonialism in Antiquity* (2004); Susan Niditch. *Oral World and Written Word: Ancient Israelite Literature* (1996); Jan Pinborg. "Classical Antiquity: Greece." *Current Trends in Linguistics. Vol. 13: Historiography of Linguistics.* Thomas A. Sekeok, ed. (1975) 69–126.

F. GERALD DOWNING

ORATORY. *See* DEMOSTHENES; RHETORIC AND ORATORY.

ORCHARD [גַּנָּה gannah, זַיִת zayith, פַּרְדֵּס pardes]. A planting of fruit trees (Song 4:13), olive trees (e.g., Exod 23:11; 1 Sam 8:14; Neh 5:11; 2 Esd 16:29), or nut trees (Song 6:11). The labor required to maintain an orchard—watering, cultivating, pruning, and harvesting—made it a luxury (see Eccl 2:5). The pleasures of its beauty and its bounty provide an apt metaphor for the lover in Song 4:13. *See* FRUIT; GARDEN; PLANTS OF THE BIBLE.

VICTOR H. MATTHEWS

ORDEAL, JUDICIAL. The extent to which judicial ordeals can be found in the Bible depends on how the concept is defined. One definition of judicial ordeal restricts it to physical tests used to determine the guilt or innocence of persons suspected of criminal activity in the absence of witnesses or material evidence. Usually, in these tests supernatural intervention was expected to protect an innocent person from a potentially harmful action. The process was reserved for extreme cases, including murder or manslaughter, sorcery, adultery, and theft. Punishment followed when the ordeal succeeded in identifying the guilty party; the ordeal itself was not the penalty. In the ANE, the best-attested ordeal of this kind is the river ordeal found in cuneiform sources (e.g., *ANET*, 166). There is no biblical parallel to such a judicial test.

However, scholars often extend the concept of ordeal to apply to various procedures that depend on supernatural means to solve difficult legal dilemmas. Therefore, discussion of judicial ordeal in the Bible has included some forms of divination and the use of oaths of innocence guaranteed by divine sanction. Of these, the most commonly attested are oaths and self-curses. The preference for an exculpatory oath reflects a belief in the efficacy of divine punishment and the necessity of leaving justice to God in cases that could not be resolved by human means (*see* OATH).

The rules for the suspected adulteress in Num 5:11-31 are often identified as a form of judicial ordeal. However, in this case, identification of the suspected adulteress and her punishment combine. The woman is brought to the sanctuary and made to drink a concoction of water and dust in which have been immersed the words of a curse. It is unclear on what grounds the woman has become suspect (pregnancy?) and what is supposed to happen if she is found guilty (spontaneous abortion of the fetus? prolapsed uterus?). But there is no indication of an additional judicial process if the woman is found guilty. The drinking of the water actuates the woman's oath, which is a form of self-curse not dependent on human agency, but on the deity. This legal procedure generated significant rabbinic commentary (*m. Sotah* 1–6).

Rabbinic tradition (*b. Abod. Zar.* 44a) saw in the command that the Israelites drink the water on which the ashes of the Golden Calf had been spread an ordeal for identifying those guilty of idolatry (Num 5:11-31). But the action of the people's drinking can also be interpreted as a reification of the condemnation brought about by violating their relationship with the Holy One. Realization of the cost of violating divine norms probably also lies behind metaphorical references to drinking divine judgment. This motif is attested both for the indictment of Israel (Ps 60:3; Isa 51:17-20; Jer 8:14; 9:13-16; 23:15; Ezek 23:31-34) and in judgments against the nations (Ps 75:8; Isa 51:21-23; Jer 25:15-29; 49:12; 51:7, 39; Lam 4:21; Obad 15-16; Hab 2:15-16; Zech 12:2).

Lament psalms in which the declaration of innocence is prominent (e.g., Pss 5; 7; 17) have also been connected with a judicial ordeal. Motifs of incubation suggest to some scholars that the wrongly accused would take an oath of innocence and spend the night at the sanctuary. This model has also been associated with a drinking ordeal, because some psalms connected to the lament genre mention a "cup" (e.g., Pss 11:6; 23:5). But it is important to note that the focus remains on a declaration of innocence. It is not clear that the procedures for unjustly accused persons alluded to in lament psalms depended on more than an exculpatory oath. Oath-taking as a form of ordeal appears in the laws of Exod 22:7-8, 9, 10-13, in which one or both parties to a suit about lost property must take an oath in the divine presence. As in Mesopotamian practice, it is likely Israelite jurists expected a guilty party to refuse the oath out of fear of divine punishment.

Some uses of DIVINATION have been described as ordeals because they rely on supernatural means for obtaining legally important information. For example, in the stories about the sin of Achan (Josh 7:13-21) and Jonathan's violation of Saul's oath (1 Sam 14:24-46) divination identifies the guilty party. Certain scholars would also consider the flowering of Aaron's rod as an instance of a divine decision obtained by an ordeal through divinatory means (Num 17). *See* CRIMES AND PUNISHMENT, OT AND NT.

WILLIAM S. MORROW

ORDER OF WIDOWS. Widows are a special concern in both the OT and NT, because they are frequently among the poor, oppressed, or abused (*see* WIDOW). The OT states that widows, along with orphans and sojourners, must be given justice and means of sustenance (e.g., Deut 24:19-21; Isa 1:17; Zech 7:10). The early church also made provision for widows (Acts 6:1). However, some of these widows were not only recipients of charity, but were members of an established ministerial group in the early church. Acts 9:36-42 describes a community of Christian widows in Joppa led by a disciple, Tabitha (also known as DORCAS), who looked after the others.

That a community of widows existed is not disputed, but whether or not it can be described as an "order" or "office" within the church depends upon the interpretation of 1 Tim 5:3-16 and the requirements for church leadership and "offices" in the PASTORAL LETTERS. In 1 Timothy "widows" are mentioned along with the offices of bishop, DEACON (1 Tim 3:1-13), and elder (1 Tim 5:17-22). Some scholars suggest that

1 Tim 5:3-16 both treats the care of needy widows (1 Tim 5:3-8) and describes the requirements for a specific office (1 Tim 5:9-16). Others argue that vv. 3-16 simply define "real" widows (that is, those who are not likely to remarry and are in need of support) against the "younger" widows (for whom the author advises remarriage).

Clues to the existence of an actual order are the terms **timaō** (τιμάω, "honor"; 1 Tim 5:3) and **katalegō** (καταλέγω, "put on the list"; 1 Tim 5:9). Because of these terms, some scholars suggest that the widows were not only recipients of benevolence, but constituted an official group with assigned duties in the Christian community. Evidently the author of 1 Timothy is instructing the church about an existing order of widows when he says that to be enrolled, a woman should have no other means of support, be sixty years old, and have been the wife of only one husband. There must also be witnesses to her good works, such as bringing up children, showing hospitality, washing the saints' feet, helping the afflicted, and doing good in every way. Once enrolled, she must remain unmarried, avoid unseemly behavior, and constantly engage in prayer (1 Tim 5:3-16).

Church historians note that the "enrolled widows" are the most celebrated group of Christian women in the first three centuries. The period is replete with literary and inscriptional evidence for their existence. During the 2nd cent. CE widows were the special concern of the bishop, both as recipients of assistance and as those specially charged with prayer (Pol. *Phil* 4:3). In the 3rd cent. instructions to widows are found in the *Didascalia Apostolorum*, where they are numbered with church officials (bishops, presbyters, deacons, acolytes, exorcists, readers, and door keepers). By the 4th cent. the image of widow at the altar of God is frequent in the literature, reflecting her sacrificial life and work of intercession. *See* LEADER, LEADERSHIP, NT.

Bibliography: Jouette Bassler. "The Widow's Tale: A Fresh Look at 1 Tim 5:3-16." *JBL* 103 (1984) 23–41; Stevan Davies. *The Revolt of the Widows* (1980); Bonnie Thurston. "1 Timothy 5:3-16 and the Leadership of Women in the Early Church." *A Feminist Companion to the Deutero-Pauline Epistles.* Amy-Jill Levine and Marianne Blickenstaff, eds. (2003) 159–74; Bonnie Thurston. *The Widows: A Women's Ministry in the Early Church* (1989).

BONNIE THURSTON

ORDINANCE [חֹק **hoq**, חֻקָּה **huqqah**, מִשְׁפָּט **mishpat**; δικαίωμα **dikaiōma**]. An *ordinance* is a statement of law, a rule established by an authority. **Mishpat** is more literally translated "judgment." The NRSV regularly translates **hoq** as "statute." Synonyms include *decree* (e.g., Deut 4:45; 6:20), *regulation* (Lev 9:16), and *law* (e.g., Deut 4:8, 44). *See* TORAH.

Exodus 21:1-17 sets forth a series of legal sentences that serve as paradigms for verdicts in the cases presented. Most of these ordinances fit the form of CASUISTIC LAW, in which a situation is described and a penalty or action prescribed. The series is well organized and makes a fine digest of law for both content and reasoning. The reference to "all the words of the LORD and all the ordinances" (Exod 24:3) looks back to the corpus of verdicts and commandments in Exod 20:23-26 and 22:21-23 (*see* COVENANT, BOOK OF THE); perhaps "words" also includes the TEN COMMANDMENTS (Exod 20:1-17). Tobit follows these ordinances (1:8).

Other examples of ordinances include the rules governing the celebration of Passover (Exod 12:14, 24, 43; 13:10), laws regarding inheritance (Num 27:11) and murder (Num 35:29), a covenant for obedience to God (Josh 24:25), rules for making burnt offerings (Ezek 43:18), and strict guidelines for who may be admitted into the Temple (Ezek 44:5). The combination of "statutes and ordinances" (**khuqqim wumishpatim** חֻקִּים וּמִשְׁפָּטִים) is used so often in legal and hortatory contexts that it becomes a general expression for all divine law (e.g., Deut 4:1, 5, 14; 5:1; 11:32).

A similar pairing of "statutes and ordinances" can be found in the Holiness Code (Lev 18:4, 5, 26; 19:37; 26:46; *see* H, HOLINESS CODE). Finding the pairing outside legal corpora (e.g., 2 Kgs 17:37; 2 Chr 33:8; Neh 9:13 and elsewhere) also suggests a standard formulation.

The term *ordinance* belongs to a piety corresponding to exhortations, e.g., in the prophets (e.g., Isa 24:5; 58:2; Jer 8:7) and writings (e.g., Pss 18:21-23; 19:9; 89:30-32; 119:5-8; 147:19-20).

In 1 Maccabees Gentile ordinances stand in contradistinction to the ordinances of the Jews. While some Jews began to follow the ordinances of the Gentiles, other Jews continued to follow the law and the ordinances of their ancestors (1 Macc 1:11-15, 57-63; 2:19-22).

Bibliography: A. Alt. "The Origins of Israelite Law." *Essays on Old Testament History and Religion.* R. A. Wilson, trans. (1967) 101–71.

DALE PATRICK

ORDINATION, ORDAIN [מָלֵא **male'**, מִלֻּאִים **millu'im**; ἐπιτίθημι χεῖρας **epitithēmi cheiras**]. Typically the terms *ordain* and *ordination* pertain to a ritual by which a person is formally appointed to and invested with a ministerial function in a religious community. Although there is no one-to-one correspondence between any biblical Hebrew or Greek term and contemporary use of "ordination," the NRSV translates **male'** as "ordain" and **millu'im** as "ordination" in Exod 28–29, Lev 8, and Num 3:3, and **epitithēmi cheiras** as "ordain" (lit., "to lay hands on") in 1 Tim 5:22. Analogs are found within the biblical tradition. In the OT, e.g., a ritual of clothing with priestly robes and anointing with oil was used in the consecration of Aaron (Lev 8) and subsequent high priests (Lev 21:10). The people of Israel laid their hands on Levites appointed to the service of the Lord, and afterward Aaron presented them to the Lord (Num 8:5-13). Moses imposed hands on Joshua, investing him with power and authority and appointing him to leadership (Num 27:15-23; Deut 34:9). *See* LAYING ON OF HANDS; PRIESTS AND LEVITES.

Josephus' description of the Roman occupation of Palestine suggests that control of the high priestly vestments was crucial to the exercise of the office (*Ant.* 18.93; 20.6–13). Hebrews speaks about the appointment of the high priest using the verb **kathistēmi** (καθίστημι, "appoint"; Heb 5:1; 7:28; 8:3; compare Acts 6:3; 7:10, 27, 35). In Greco-Roman society, candidates for priesthood were elected by a show of hands (**cheirotonia** χειροτονία) or chosen by lot. Having been scrutinized and having sworn an appropriate oath, they entered into office by offering sacrifice.

Jesus appointed the Twelve (Mark 3:14), whom he named apostles (Mark 3:14; Luke 6:13-16). These were given power and authority and sent out to preach (Luke 9:1-2; compare Matt 10:1-5; Mark 3:14-15). None of the Gospel writers describes an accompanying ritual. Luke also narrates that Jesus appointed seventy others whom he sent out (Luke 10:1), using a verb that he uses for the selection of Matthias, for whom lots were cast before he was enrolled with the eleven apostles (**anadeiknymi** [ἀναδείκνυμι]; Acts 1:24).

Luke's accounts of the choice of seven from among Hellenists and of the divine selection of the prophets Barnabas and Saul to be sent on a mission of evangelization include a ritual of imposition of hands accompanied by prayer (Acts 6:6; 13:3). Respectively alluding to Num 27 and Num 8, the Lukan accounts depict a commissioning rather than a transfer of power. Acts 6:1-6 is the fullest account of the commissioning of believers for a particular ministry in the church in the NT. Describing the appointment (**kathistēmi**; Acts 6:3) of the seven, the narrative is sometimes taken as an etiological account of the institution of the diaconate in the early church (Acts 6:1; compare 6:4). The church selected the seven; the Twelve commissioned them. Well attested in Acts (6:6; 8:17, 19; 9:12, 17; 13:3; 19:6; 28:8), the laying on of hands was a polyvalent ritual and a topic for early Christian catechesis (Heb 6:2). Prayer, rather than any specific ritual, is central to the appointment of elders in Acts 14:23. *See* ELDER IN THE NT.

Concerned with ministry in the church and with the succession of Paul, the Pastoral Epistles mention an imposition of hands on Timothy. In 1 Tim 4:14, Timothy is exhorted not to neglect the spiritual gift given to him through prophecy with a laying on of hands by the presbyterate, a council of elders. Second Timothy 1:6 mentions a spiritual gift that Timothy has through the laying on "of my [Paul's] hands." Some commentators find a reference to a commissioning ritual in 1 Tim 5:22 (see NRSV), but in this case the laying on of hands may be a gesture of forgiveness and reconciliation rather than a reference to a commissioning. Taken together, 1 Tim 4:14 and 2 Tim 1:6 represent the ritual conferral and institutionalization of a charism, a spiritual and ministerial gift. Neither text specifies any particular spiritual gift (1 Cor 12–14); they are concerned with an orderly succession in ministry. *See* LAYING ON OF HANDS.

Bibliography: Raymond F. Collins. *I Timothy and Titus.* NTL (2002); D. A. Mappes. "The 'Laying on of Hands' of Elders." *BSac* 154 (1997) 493–97.

RAYMOND F. COLLINS

ORE [אֶבֶן ʾeven]. In Job 28:2-3, the common Hebrew word for "stone" (ʾeven) indicates the raw material—the ore—from which COPPER is smelted. *See* METALLURGY.

OREB AND ZEEB or'eb, zee'uhb [עֹרֵב ʿorev, זְאֵב zeʾev]. Meaning "raven" (ʿorev) and "wolf" (zeʾev), these two Midianite captains are mentioned at the conclusion of the story of GIDEON's leading the coalition of Manasseh, Naphtali, Zebulun, and Asher against their Midianite and Amalekite oppressors during the period of the judges (Judg 7:25; *see* MIDIAN, MIDIANITES).

The Israelite coalition was much smaller than the Midianite and Amalekite armies after Gideon had pared his forces down to 300 fighting men upon the instructions of Yahweh (Judg 7:4-7). Gideon, overhearing the dream of an enemy fighter that the camp will be overthrown, knows then that Yahweh is handing him the victory and calls out his meager troops who attack and rout the enemy with little difficulty. At this point Gideon calls all the people in the hill country of Ephraim to join the battle against Midian, which they promptly do. Oreb and Zeeb are captured and killed, each at a place identified with his name: the rock of Oreb and the wine press of Zeeb. The Israelites cut off their heads and deliver them to Gideon. Contrary to the story's naming of the places, it may be that the place names gave rise to the names of the captains, but it is impossible to determine with any degree of certainty at this point which came first.

From this point on the victory over and execution of Oreb and Zeeb serve as reminders of God's power and faithfulness (Judg 8:3; Ps 83:11 [Heb. 83:12]; Isa 10:26). *See* JUDGES, BOOK OF.

C. MARK MCCORMICK

OREN or'en [אֹרֶן ʾoren]. Jerahmeel's son (1 Chr 2:25) in Judah's genealogy. *See* JERAHMEEL, JERAHMEELITES; JUDAH, JUDAHITES.

OREN, NAHAL. A cave site located on the slopes of Wadi Fallal, 10 km south of Haifa, Israel. This is to the west side of Mount Carmel. The construction of buildings on the hillside extends the site to the wadi floor. The site was first excavated in 1941, during which time the Neolithic Kebaran and Natufian traditions were found. The flint technologies since excavated indicate that the site was occupied from the Epipaleolithic (18000–12000 BCE) through to Pre-Pottery Neolithic B (PPNB) (7250–6000 BCE). Occupation debris was present throughout these periods; however, the quantity suggests that occupation was ephemeral. Typological similarities from the PPNA and B layers at Nahal Oren and Jericho indicate they were contemporary. *See* CARMEL, MOUNT; JERICHO; PRE-HISTORY IN THE ANCIENT NEAR EAST.

ALYS VAUGHAN-WILLIAMS

ORGAN. *See* TONGUE.

ORGIES [הָמוֹן **hamon**, זָנָה **zanah**]. Occasions of revelry, the exact content of which remains uncertain. In Jer 3:23 **hamon** (NRSV, "orgies") simply means "sound/excess on the mountains," which the context may suggest as a sexual euphemism.

Hosea 4:18 reads **hazneh hiznu** (הַזְנֵה הִזְנוּ), "they fornicate exceedingly" (NRSV, "they indulge in sexual orgies"), as part of a larger metaphor accusing Israel of being an adulterous "wife" to Yahweh. This passage condemns both illicit sex and worship; whether and how the two were connected is unknown. *See* ASHERAH; BAAL; DRUNKENNESS; ECSTASY; FERTILITY CULT; IDOLATRY; LICENTIOUSNESS; PROSTITUTION; WORSHIP, OT.

Bibliography: Phyllis Bird. "To Play the Harlot." *Missing Persons and Mistaken Identities: Women and Gender in Ancient Israel* (1997) 219–36.

LISA MICHELE WOLFE

ORIENTATION. Orientation refers to the means by which one gains a point of reference or gets one's bearings, often used in a geographical sense. Modern reference points are based on the compass. Both the north star, Polaris, which remains in a nearly stationary position in the northern sky, and the magnetic north pole for compasses create north as the primary orientation point.

For the ANE, with the exception of Egypt, east was the primary point of reference because it is the direction of the rising sun (*see* DAWN). The primacy of east is indicated by the vocabulary used for directions. East as the direction could be indicated by the phrase "the rising sun," but also frequently by **qedhem** (קֶדֶם and its derivatives), the direction in front of or before one: as one faced the rising sun, east was in front. Likewise, west was indicated by the phrase "the setting sun" and **ʾakhor** (אָחוֹר and its derivatives), the direction behind one. One biblical text that indicates both these directions in a context that demonstrates its meaning clearly is Isa 9:11-12: "So the LORD raised adversaries against them, and stirred up their enemies, the Arameans in the east (**miqqedhem** מִקֶּדֶם) and the Philistines in the west (**meʾakhor** מֵאָחוֹר)."

The direction south can be indicated by **yamin** (יָמִין), meaning "right hand" or "south," and related derivative terms such as **teman** (תֵּימָן). In the same manner north could be indicated by **semoʾl** (שְׂמֹאל) and its derivatives, meaning "left hand" or "north." Ezekiel 16:46 uses these two words together in an oracle against Jerusalem in a manner to show clearly the geographical meaning: "Your elder sister is Samaria, who lived with her daughters to the north of you; and your younger sister, who lived to the south of you, is Sodom with her daughters." The Egyptians used south, the source of the Nile as their primary reference for orientation. They also used the body to determine other compass points: north was behind them, west was to the right, and east was to the left.

The promise of land concerns orientation: Abraham receives all the land he can see in every direction from where he stands, northward, southward, eastward, and westward (Gen 13:14). The boundaries of the twelve tribes are also identified by the four directions (Josh 13–19; Ezek 48; *see* TRIBES, TERRITORIES OF). The configurations of the tabernacle and Temple are oriented to specific directions (Exod 26:18-20; 27:9-13; 36:23-25; 38:9-15; 2 Chr 4:4-9). The threat of enemy attack is often associated with the north (*see* NORTH COUNTRY, THE).

From certain orientations come weather systems. The north wind produces rain (Prov 25:23) and bitter cold (Sir 43:17, 20). The EAST WIND (**qadhim** קָדִים) is a destructive seasonal phenomenon in desert areas surrounding the Mediterranean (Exod 10:13; 14:21; Ps 78:26; Hos 13:15; Jonah 4:8). From the south comes heat (Job 37:17).

In the NT, east (**anatolē** [ἀνατολή], "rising," "day," dawn") is synonymous with *dawn* and is associated also with wisdom. The MAGI come from the east (Matt 2:1), and Solomon's wisdom is said to be greater than that of the sages of the east (1 Kgs 4:30). Because Jesus' empty tomb is discovered at the rising of the sun (**anatellō** ἀνατέλλω, Mark 16:2; see also Matt 28:1; Luke 24:1), the east is sometimes associated with resurrection. Messianic interpretations of passages in the LXX rely on the verbal form of **anatolē** to describe dawning light and coming redemption: a star will rise (**anatellō**) from Jacob (Num 24:17); light dawns (**anatellō**) for the righteous (Ps 97:11 [LXX 96:11]); "the glory of the Lord has risen (**anatellō**) upon you" (Isa 60:1); "I will raise up (**anatellō**) for David a righteous branch" (Jer 23:5).

As in the OT, weather patterns are identified by direction. Rain comes from the west (**dysmē** δυσμή), and scorching heat comes from the south (**notos** [νότος]; Luke 12:54). A south wind is good for sailing, but a violent wind called the "northeaster" (**typhōnikos** τυφωνικός) is responsible for storms at sea that threaten sailing ships (Acts 27:14; *see* NORTHEASTER, THE).

The orientation of the kingdom of God includes all four directions, symbolic of the whole world: "Then people will come from east (anatolē) and west (dysmē), from north (borras βορρᾶς) and south (notos), and will eat in the kingdom of God" (Luke 13:29; see Ps 107:3). The New Jerusalem is envisioned as having a wall with twelve gates, three east gates, three north gates, three south gates, and three west gates, so that all the nations can enter (Rev 21:12, 25-27; compare 1 Chr 9:24; 26:12-19).

Bibliography: Menashe Har-El. "Orientation in Biblical Lands." *BA* 44 (1981) 19–20.

JOEL F. DRINKARD JR.

ORIGEN or´uh-juhn. Born in Alexandria around 185 CE, Origen stands out as one of ancient Christianity's greatest intellects, yet he is not well known outside of academic circles. The reasons for this are multiple. According to the church historian Eusebius (*Hist. eccl.* 6.8), in his younger years Origen may have been overly zealous in his interpretation of Matt 19:12, where Jesus invites those who can bear it to become "eunuchs for the sake of the kingdom." Misunderstanding the metaphorical nature of Jesus' invitation, Origen and other young men of his generation may have castrated themselves for a higher religious purpose. Whether Origen did this or not remains a subject of scholarly debate, yet the very possibility that it is true has negatively impacted his legacy. Additionally, Origen's condemnation at the Second Council of Constantinople in 553 CE witnesses tragically to his impact: so powerful were his ideas that he could ignite controversy even 300 years after his death.

Modern readers of Origen often incorrectly locate the controversial aspects of Origen's intellectual project in his method of biblical interpretation. Origen commented prolifically on the Bible. In all of his writings he applied the ancient techniques of typological and allegorical reading. Both of these methods seek to uncover hidden, nonliteral meanings in the biblical text. For example, the story of the crossing of the Red Sea is a type of the crossing of the Christian from death to new life in baptism, and the Song of Songs is an allegory of the soul's relationship to God rather than a series of erotic love poems. Origen was a masterful interpreter and he applied these methods consistently. He differed from his contemporaries not in his application of these methods but in the depth of his theological insight (*see* ALLEGORY; METAPHOR IN THEOLOGY).

The reasons for Origen's eventual condemnation were theological rather than methodological. Just as many contemporary theologians seek to reconcile Christian faith with modern science, Origen pioneered the reconciliation of Christianity with platonic cosmology, the intellectual lingua franca of his time. His thought ranged widely: he laid the foundation for what would become the theology of the Trinity, he struggled to articulate the relationship of the divine and the human in Jesus, and he speculated on the fate and purpose of our bodily nature. By the standards of later orthodoxy and in the wake of a controversy that bears his name (the Origenist controversy), some of Origen's solutions seemed heretical. This explains his condemnation.

In retrospect, it would be fairer to call Origen a MARTYR rather than a heretic. In the year 250 CE the emperor DECIUS launched the first wide-scale persecution of the church. Origen was one of the victims. Imprisoned and tortured but not killed, Origen died a few years later as a result of his injuries. While not technically a martyr, Origen deserves to be remembered as one of the greatest of all ancient witnesses to Christ. *See* BIBLICAL INTERPRETATION, HISTORY OF.

Bibliography: David Dawson. *Christian Figural Reading and the Fashioning of Identity* (2002); John A. McGuckin. *The Westminster Handbook to Origen* (2004); Joseph W. Trigg. *Origen* (1998).

JOHN J. O'KEEFE

ORIGINAL SIN. *See* SIN, SINNERS.

ORIGINAL TEXT. *See* TEXT CRITICISM, NT; TEXT CRITICISM, OT.

ORION oh-r*i*´uhn [כְּסִיל kesil]. A translation for a constellation called kesil. In two out of three occurrences, it is mentioned alongside the constellation kimah (כִּימָה, translated PLEIADES). The constellation is cited as evidence of God's creative power (Job 9:9; 38:31; Amos 5:8). The relation of the name Orion (as translated in the NRSV) to the Hebrew word kesil is unclear since kesil can also mean "fool" (e.g., Prov 10:18). Only in the LXX of Job 38:31 is the singular form kesil translated *Orion* (Ōriōn Ὠρίων). The constellation Orion is named after a mythological Greek hunter and ironworker. Upon his death, he was conveyed to the heavens and constrained to the sky, where he became this constellation.

The Targum and Syriac render kesil as *giant*, which could correspond with "the strong one," the contemporary Arabic name for the constellation Orion. G. R. Driver postulated that kesil ("fool") pointed to a Hebrew version of a myth about a giant in which the giant, confiding foolishly in his own strength, was bound in the sky as punishment for his arrogance.

If kesil alludes to being a fool or foolishness, it may be that the Hebrew name for the constellation was intended to show the stars' inferiority to Yahweh, which stands in contradistinction to other traditions that acknowledge that the ancient Israelites often shared the ANE tendency to worship the stars and other heavenly bodies as powerful deities (e.g., Exod 20:4; Deut 4:19;

ENUMA ELISH 5.1-8; 7.125-31). Overall, biblical cosmology stresses that the heavenly bodies were not gods at all, but were merely objects created by and subject to Yahweh (e.g., Gen 1:1; 2:4; Josh 10:12-13; Isa 38:8). In each of the biblical passages where **kesil** is translated as *Orion*, the constellation is cited as evidence of God's control over the heavens. *See* ASTRONOMY, ASTROLOGY; COSMOGONY, COSMOLOGY.

Bibliography: G. R. Driver. "Two Astronomical Passages in the Old Testament." *JTS* ns 7 (1956) 1–11.

RALPH K. HAWKINS

ORMUZD. Along with OHRMAZD, a variant form of the name of the Persian high god AHURA MAZDA.

ORNAMENT. *See* JEWELRY; JEWELS AND PRECIOUS STONES.

ORNAN or'nuhn [אָרְנָן **'ornan**]. The Chronicler's spelling of the name ARAUNAH. Ornan is mentioned (1 Chr 21:15-28; 2 Chr 3:1) as the Jebusite owner of a certain threshing floor (the future site of the Jerusalem Temple) that David purchased to use as a place to offer sacrifices to avert God's destruction of Jerusalem.

DEREK E. WITTMAN

ORPAH or'puh [עָרְפָּה **'orpah**]. Orpah and Ruth were Naomi's two Moabite daughters-in-law, widowed during a famine (Ruth 1:1-14). In the narrative structure, Orpah's choice to return to her mother's house (1:8) is set in opposition to Ruth's remaining with Naomi. While the biblical story in no way condemns Orpah, the narrative oppositional arrangement gave rise to later traditions in which Orpah's descendants opposed Ruth's. Pseudo-Philo, e.g., claimed that Goliath was a descendant of Orpah's remarriage to a Philistine (*L.A.B.* 61:6), and rabbinic interpretation suggested that David is allowed to kill all four of Orpah's giant children because Ruth (David's forbear) faithfully clung to Naomi (*b. Sotah* 42b). *See* MOAB, MOABITES; RUTH, BOOK OF.

JESSICA TINKLENBERG DEVEGA

ORPHAN [יָתוֹם **yathom**; ὀρφανός **orphanos**]. The OT use of the term *orphan* does not distinguish between the loss of both parents (orphan) and the loss of the father (*see* FATHERLESS). Orphaned children were given special consideration. Torah required remnants of the harvest be left in the fields for the orphans to GLEAN, and a special collection of tithes was given every third year for their care (Deut 14:28-29; 24:19-21; 26:12; 27:19; *see* TITHES). Orphans found protection within the community and participated in celebrations (Exod 22:22-24 [Heb. 22:23-25]; Deut 24:17; 27:19; and see Ps 82:3; Prov 23:10).

God is the father of the orphan and protector of widows (Pss 10:14; 68:5 [Heb. 68:6]). God oversees justice and fairness for them (Deut 10:18; Ps 10:18). Oppressing orphans became a key example of failure to keep the covenant. These oppressors are declared sinners (Job 6:27; 22:9; 24:3, 9), while protectors of the orphaned are called righteous (Job 29:12; 31:17, 21). Orphaned daughters were especially vulnerable due to lack of inheritance rights (see Num 27:7-11). According to Lamentations, the people were like orphans after the fall of Judah (Lam 5:3). These concepts remain important for righteousness and ethical behavior in early Judaism (see, e.g., Sir 4:10; Tob 1:8); thus they become an important part of early Christian tradition as well. In keeping with Jewish tradition, the NT pairs the care of orphans with widows and mandates their care as a hallmark of religious faith and practice (Jas 1:27). Paul likens his separation from the Thessalonians to being orphaned (1 Thess 2:17). *See* ETHICS IN THE NONCANONICAL JEWISH WRITINGS; ETHICS IN THE NT; ETHICS IN THE OT; RIGHTEOUSNESS IN EARLY JEWISH LITERATURE; RIGHTEOUSNESS IN THE NT; RIGHTEOUSNESS IN THE OT.

MICHAEL G. VANZANT

ORPHISM. A Greek religion founded by Orpheus, who is best known from the myth of his descent into the underworld (*see* UNDERWORLD, DESCENT INTO THE). Orphism taught that human beings have both an evil and divine nature. The body corresponds to evil, and the soul to the divine. People who do not undergo purification in this life will be punished in the AFTERLIFE; the righteous who embrace purity will live in happiness. An important Orphic god is DIONYSUS.

MARIANNE BLICKENSTAFF

ORTHOSIA or-thoh'see-uh [Ὀρθωσία **Orthōsia**]. Orthosia (modern Artusi) was a Hellenistic city at the mouth of the river Eleutheros (al-Barid) to the north of Tripoli in northern Lebanon. It appears to be on the site of Ullaza, an Egyptian garrison during the expeditions of THUTMOSE III (1479–1425 BCE) against Syria. The city minted coins in the Ptolemaic period. In 1 Macc 15:37, TRYPHO escaped to Orthosia by ship when he fled the besieged city of Dor.

DAVID W. J. GILL

OSIRIS oh-*si*'ruhs. The Egyptian god of the underworld and the brother and husband of Isis. References to the myth of Osiris' death are found as early as the PYRAMID TEXTS. Though no one document provides a complete narrative account of how he died, his death is usually attributed to his brother, Seth. Osiris is closely connected with the afterlife and presides over the judgment of the deceased in the BOOK OF THE DEAD. He is usually depicted wrapped in mummy cloth and wearing the crown of Upper EGYPT. Originally there was a close connection between Osiris and recently deceased kings, a connection made stronger by the association of the new king with Horus, the son of Osiris. By the Middle Kingdom, however, the exclusive royal connection had been loosened and Osiris began to appear in nonroyal tombs. The primary cult sites of Osiris are Abydos in Upper Egypt and Heliopolis and Busiris in Lower Egypt. *See* SERAPIS.

KEVIN A. WILSON

OSNAPPAR os-nap´uhr [אָסְנַפַּר ʾ**osnappar**]. Osnappar was probably the same as Ashurbanipal (668–630 BCE), who succeeded ESARHADDON, the last significant king of Assyria, resettling peoples he conquered into Samaria and Transjordan (Ezra 4:10). Also known for his library at NINEVEH whose 10,000 tablets convey Assyrian history and culture. *See* ASHURBANIPAL, ASSURBANIPAL; EZRA; SARGON.

EMILY R. CHENEY

OSPREY [עָזְנִיָּה ʿ**ozniyah**; ἁλιάετος **haliaetos**]. Judging from its position within the list of unclean birds (Lev 11:13; Deut 14:12), ʿ**ozniyah** most likely denotes some bird of prey. The identification with the fish-eating osprey (*Pandion haliaetus*), made by the NRSV and other modern translations, gains support from the LXX, which has "sea-eagle." Alternative identifications suggested by scholars include the black vulture (NIV) and the bearded vulture. None of these is a conclusive identification and simply illustrates the difficulty of identifying ancient terms with specific creatures. *See* BIRDS OF THE BIBLE.

GÖRAN EIDEVALL

OSSUARIES os´y*oo*-er´ee. This term does not appear in the Bible. An ossuary is a chest or box, usually made of stone, used for secondary burial, i.e., the reburial of human bones after the flesh of a corpse has decayed. Ossuaries are typically found in Jewish tombs of the Early Roman period near Jerusalem.

Hollowed out from a single block of limestone, an ossuary is proportionate in size to the large and long bones of the body (i.e., skull and femur). Thus an average ossuary for an adult measures about 60 × 35 × 30 cm, with smaller measurements for children. Most are plain, but many are decorated with motifs from Jewish art in this period: geometric designs (the six-petaled rosette), or representations of Jewish religious themes (e.g., palm branches, **menoroth** [מְנֹרוֹת]). Most ornamentations are executed by "chip-carving," i.e., the decoration is cut into the face of the stone. Decorations often appear only on one long side of an ossuary.

Many ossuaries are inscribed, either in Hebrew, Aramaic, or Greek. Inscriptions are scrawled with charcoal or scratched with a sharp object, presumably by family members at the time of secondary burial. As a result, reading ossuary inscriptions is often difficult. Inscriptions may appear anywhere on an ossuary—the sides,

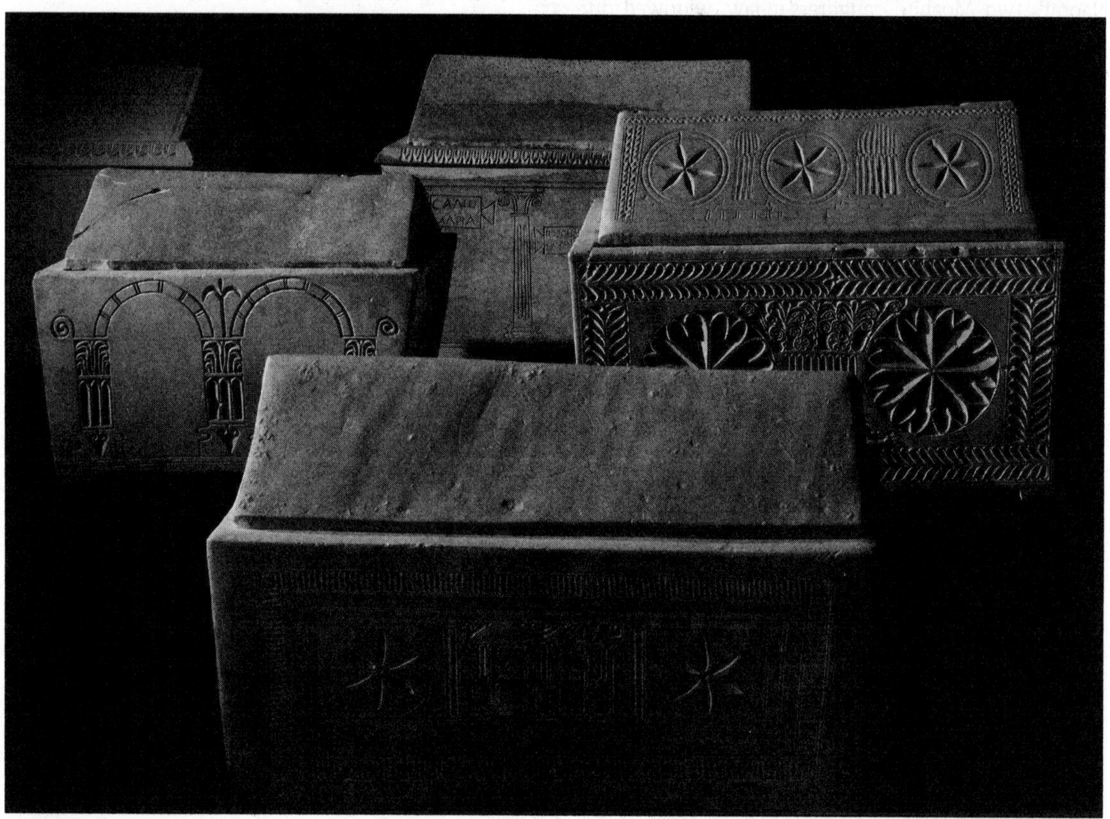

Erich Lessing / Art Resource, NY

Figure 1: Ossuaries with different decorations, from Jerusalem limestone (1st cent. BCE–1st cent. CE). Israel Museum (IDAM), Jerusalem, Israel

ends, lid, or even the inside edge. Typically recording only the name of the deceased, inscriptions may occasionally also add a nickname, patronymic, place of origin, or distinguishing fact about the deceased.

Skeletal analysis shows that many ossuaries contain the bones of more than one individual, usually members of a nuclear family. Adult females are more likely to be found in an ossuary with an adult male than by themselves. Ossuaries containing the bones of both a male and a female are more likely to be inscribed with the name of the male than the female. These trends reflect the patrilineal kinship structure of Jewish society in the Early Roman period.

Secondary burial in ossuaries was performed when decomposition of the flesh of the corpse was complete, or nearly so. Family members gathered the bones of the deceased from where they lay on a shelf or in a niche and placed them in an ossuary. The ossuary, which might be inscribed, was then positioned somewhere inside the tomb, either on the shelf, on the floor, or in a niche.

Although clay ossuaries appeared briefly during the Chalcolithic period, limestone Jewish ossuaries were unknown before the Early Roman period. Their emergence is a matter of scholarly uncertainty. They might be associated with Jewish beliefs about bodily resurrection, but no Early Roman sources connect ossuaries with resurrection, and rabbinic sources are too late to provide uncorroborated evidence for Early Roman customs. Ossuaries might reflect an effort to conserve limited space inside a tomb, but ossuaries are often found stacked up on shelves or in niches, where they consume rather than conserve space. Ossuaries might reflect the rising status of the individual in Early Roman Jewish society. Unlike earlier forms of Jewish secondary burial, ossuaries preserved individual identity after death. Thus they may have risen from the encounter between traditional Jewish customs of secondary burial and newer Hellenistic conceptions of the human individual.

BYRON R. MCCANE

OSTRACA os´truh-kuh. An ostracon (sg.; pl. ostraca) is a broken piece of pottery containing an inscription. The word *ostracon* is a Greek word, and is closely related to the word *ostracize*, meaning to banish one by means of a vote on ostraca. Specifically in reference to Israel during the period of the monarchy (ca. 1000–586 BCE, Iron Age II), most of the preserved inscriptional materials were written on ostraca. Ostraca were also used in Greece, Egypt, and other areas of the ANE. The material, broken potsherds, was readily available and involved no cost. In addition, fired pottery is exceedingly durable, much more so than papyrus, parchment, or leather, which were other common writing materials of that region. Of the large caches

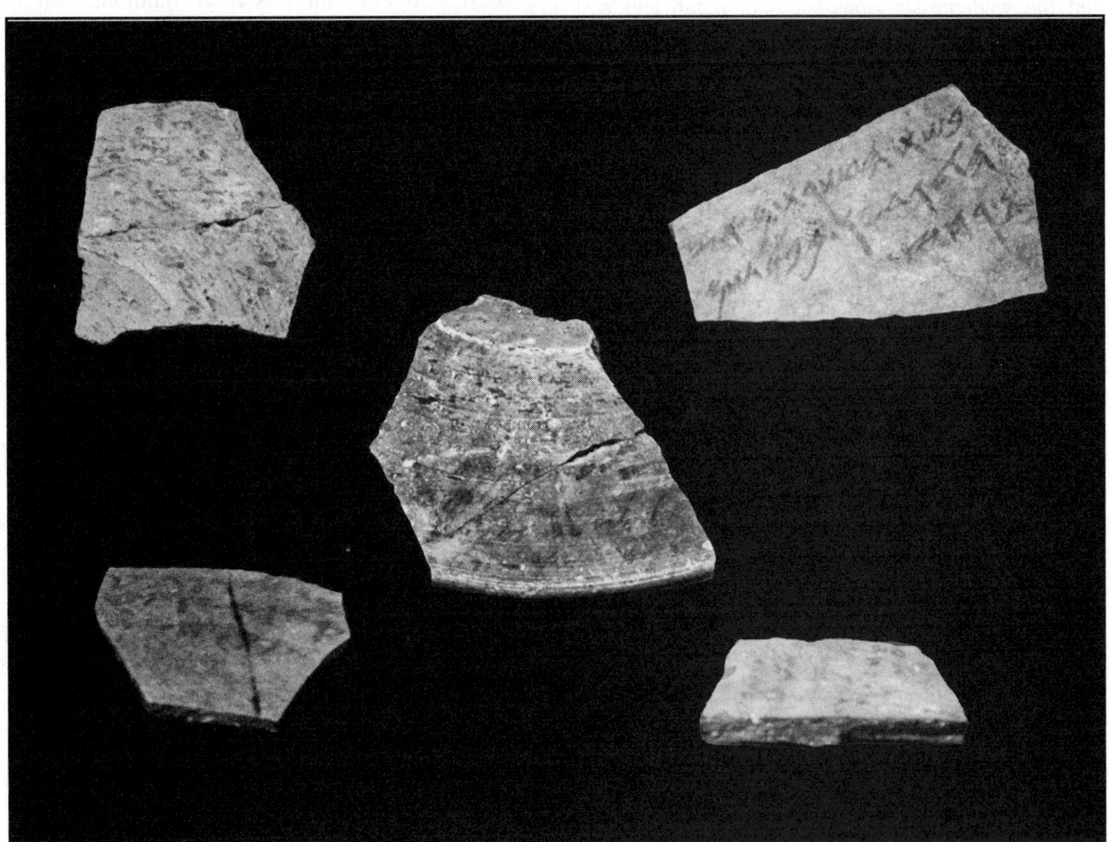

Todd Bolen/BiblePlaces.com

Figure 1: Samaria Ostraca, collection of Istanbul Archaeological Museum

of inscriptional materials from the Iron Age II period, the ARAD letters, LACHISH letters, and SAMARIA OSTRACA are all ostraca.

Israelite ostraca are typically written with ink on the potsherds. Incised potsherds may also be classified as ostraca. Some have argued that the Hebrew ostraca were just notes or drafts of official letters or receipts, and that the official documents were written on papyrus, parchment, or leather. However, the contents of many of the ostraca that have been recovered, such as the Arad letters and Lachish letters, indicate that they are the actual documents themselves. The sparsity of monumental inscriptions from the period of the monarchy coupled with the climate and circumstances of preservation make the Hebrew ostraca most important for written evidence of that period. *See* POTTERY; WRITING AND WRITING MATERIALS.

Bibliography: Alan Millard. "The Practice of Writing in Ancient Israel." *BA* 35 (1972) 98–111.

JOEL F. DRINKARD JR.

OSTRACA, SAMARIA. *See* SAMARIA OSTRACA.

OSTRICH [בַּת הַיַּעֲנָה bath hayya῾anah, יָעֵן ya῾en, רְנָנָה renanah]. The ostrich (*Struthio camelus*) is no longer found in the Middle East. In biblical times, this anomalous bird, which cannot fly, probably inhabited the wilderness regions south of Judah and east of the Jordan River. A rather detailed description of the ostrich's behavior is found in Job 39:13-18 in the midst of God's response to Job's relentless questions. In the context of God's infinite wisdom compared to Job's ability to comprehend, the ostrich is seen as a curiosity, a creature to which God has not given wisdom or understanding, and whose behavior exhibits that deficiency. This passage mentions the ostrich's habit of laying its eggs in the hot sand, where they are occasionally abandoned and exposed to dangers (39:14-15). It makes allusions to this bird's speed, which exceeds that of a horse and rider (39:18). However, the allegation that it "deals cruelly with its young" (39:16) is hardly reconcilable with facts. This notion may have arisen from the hen's habit of laying extra eggs, which serve as food for the chicks. Bath hayya῾anah can be interpreted either as "daughter of greed" or as "daughter of the desert." The bird thus designated is mentioned together with the JACKAL (Job 30:29; Mic 1:8). It is associated with the wilderness (Isa 34:13; 43:20), but also with ruined cities (Isa 13:21; Jer 50:39). Since the ostrich is omnivorous, it is not surprising that it is counted among the ritually unclean birds (Lev 11:16; Deut 14:15). *See* BIRDS OF THE BIBLE.

GÖRAN EIDEVALL

OTHER. A concept in the social sciences and philosophy used to describe a variety of social relationships in which a distinction is made between one's self or group and different selves or groups. In philosophical and psychological theory, the "other" is the outside being over against which an individual's "I" or self-awareness develops. In social and political theory, "others" are the close or distant groups, societies, or states over against which a group, society, or state defines its own identity and social meanings. How strongly or loosely a social group defines its boundaries is related to the degree of threat or friendliness it perceives in the "others" with which it shares space. In all uses of the concept, it is recognized that how one defines the "other" inherently affects one's self-identity. In biblical interpretation, the concept has been used to understand ethnicity, e.g., how ancient Israel and the early church expressed a developing ethnic identity in relation to their close cultural neighbors. The concept has also been used to analyze the social boundaries and separateness of groups in situations of stress or vulnerability, e.g., the exiles in Babylon or the house churches of the Pauline missions. *See* FOREIGN, FOREIGNER; SOJOURNER; STRANGER.

PATRICIA DUTCHER-WALLS

OTHNI oth´ni [עָתְנִי ῾othni]. A Levite son of Shemaiah and grandson of OBED-EDOM listed among the gatekeepers assigned to temple service under David (1 Chr 26:7). *See* LEVI, LEVITES.

OTHNIEL oth´nee-uhl [עָתְנִיאֵל ῾othni᾿el]. Son of Kenaz (the younger brother of Caleb) (Josh 15:17; Judg 1:13) and brother of Seraiah (1 Chr 4:13) of the tribe of Judah (Josh 15). The meaning of the name is uncertain; it appears to be a combination of ῾othni (עָתְנִי) and ᾿el (אֵל, "God"). An "Othni," son of Shemaiah, is referenced in 1 Chr 26:7. Among the most plausible of various proposals of meaning is "God is my protection." Othniel's is the first of the narratives of the delivering judges (Judg 3:7-11) raised up by Yahweh in the sequence of oppressions brought on Israel because of their doing "what was evil in the sight of the LORD," defined specifically in the Othniel narrative as "worshiping the Baals and the Asherahs" (Judg 3:7).

Apart from the so-called "minor judge" accounts (*see* JUDGES, BOOK OF), Othniel's is the shortest of the narratives, yet it is shaped by the same formulaic expressions first seen in the introductory material of Judg 2:11-19, and subsequently framing the stories of Ehud, Deborah/Barak, and Gideon (although not the "minor judge" narratives; see also the Jephthah and Samson narratives). In contrast to narratives of deliverance that follow, no details are given with respect to how he subdued the oppression of CUSHAN-RISHATHAIM of Aram. Emphasis is rather on the source of enablement: "The spirit of the LORD came upon him, ... the LORD gave King Cushan-rishathaim of Aram into his hand; and his hand prevailed over Cushan-rishathaim" (Judg 3:10). The coming of the spirit of Yahweh upon Othniel seems to anticipate other judge narratives such as Jephthah (11:29) and Samson (13:25; 14:6, 19; 15:14), and brings to mind other, later narratives: David (1 Sam 16:13) and Jahaziel (2 Chr 20:14).

Regarding Othniel's "function" among the Israelites, it is notable that, while both **moshiʿa** (מוֹשִׁיעַ, "deliverer") and **wayyoshiʿem** (וַיּוֹשִׁיעֵם, "delivered") are used in reference to Othniel (Judg 3:9), the verb **wayyishpot** (וַיִּשְׁפֹּט, "judged") is also applied to him (Judg 3:10; compare Tola, Jair, Ibzan, Elon, Abdon). *See* JUDGE.

JOHN I. LAWLOR

OTHONIAH oth′uh-n*i*′uh [Ὀθονίας **Othonias**]. A descendant of Zamoth, and one of the returning exiles whom Ezra commanded to divorce their foreign wives (1 Esd 9:28). Ezra 10:27 seems to identify him as MATTANIAH, a descendant of Zattu.

OUTCAST [נִדָּח **niddakh**]. *Outcast* can describe individuals who are deemed unequal to other members of a society because of illness or disability. God promises, "I will save the lame and gather the outcast, and I will change their shame into praise and renown" (Zeph 3:19*b-c*; compare Jer 30:17, where *outcast* is used in a metaphor of Jerusalem as a wounded person). More frequently, the term refers to those who are literally "cast out" by banishment (2 Sam 14:14) or exile. The OT repeatedly declares that God will gather the outcast exiles of Israel and Judah (Neh 1:9; Ps 147:2; Isa 11:12; 56:8). In a striking passage, Isaiah (16:3-4) calls for Judah to shelter exiles from neighboring Moab, a traditional enemy. *See* EXILE.

JASON R. TATLOCK

OVEN [תַּנּוּר **tannur**; κλίβανος **klibanos**]. The dome-shaped oven used by the Israelites for baking bread was constructed of clay and straw (Exod 8:3; compare Lev 11:35), with broken pottery used as further insulating material, and was sometimes sunk into the earth. Sticks and straw were used to kindle a fire inside the oven at the bottom of the dome (Matt 6:30), and when the fire had been reduced to hot coals the loaves were affixed to the interior walls of the oven for baking. Each household had its own oven, as the description of famine in Lev 26:26 illustrates: when grain is scarce, a single oven will suffice to bake bread for ten households. Bread baked in ovens could be leavened (Hos 7:4-7) or unleavened (Lev 2:4; 7:9). Another type of bell- or hive-shaped oven, the **tabbun** (an Arabic word not mentioned in the Bible), was heated by an exterior fire consisting of cakes of animal dung and straw. Ezekiel (4:12) may have used such an oven.

The heat of an oven was proverbial, and could serve as an image of coming catastrophe (Mal 4:1 [Heb. 3:19]). Hosea uses a heated oven as a metaphor for the hot-headed wicked (7:4-7). In Lam 5:10, the effect of famine on the exiles is compared to the effect of the heat that blackened the interior of an oven's dome: "Our skin is black as an oven from the scorching heat of famine." *See* BAKE; BREAD; FOOD; FURNACE; OVENS, TOWER OF THE; POTTERY.

VICTOR H. MATTHEWS

OVENS, TOWER OF THE [מִגְדַּל הַתַּנּוּרִים **mighdal hattannurim**]. A tower on the wall of JERUSALEM repaired under the direction of Nehemiah (Neh 3:11; 12:38). It was probably adjacent to the BAKERS' STREET, northwest of the City of David. *See* EZRA AND NEHEMIAH, BOOKS OF.

OVERLAY [צָפָה **tsafah**, רָקַע **raqaʿ**]. The verb **tsafah** ("to overlay, cover") is a technological term used mainly in reference to the process of molding a layer of precious metal (or wood) over architectural elements and furnishings of the TABERNACLE and the Jerusalem Temple (*see* TEMPLE, JERUSALEM). It occurs some twenty-five times in Exodus (25–27; 36–38) and once in Numbers (16:38) in reference to the tabernacle, and another seventeen times in Kings (1 Kgs 6 and 2 Kgs 18:26) and 2 Chronicles (3–4; 29) with respect to the Jerusalem Temple.

Some of the tabernacle's structural elements (pillars, frames, bars) are overlaid with gold, as are all the internal furnishings with their carrying poles (ark, table, incense altar), except the lampstand. Silver overlays the capitals of the courtyard pillars, and bronze covers the horns and poles of the courtyard altar. In this scheme, the most costly metal, gold, is used for the structural elements and appurtenances of the holiest space.

The construction of the Jerusalem Temple also involves overlaying the stone walls and floors with wood, which in turn is covered completely with gold, as are the wooden doors separating the internal spaces. Of the temple furnishings, the cherubim and incense altar are overlaid with gold (1 Kgs 6:14-32 // 2 Chr 3–4).

Outside the realm of sacred space, the royal throne was overlaid with gold (1 Kgs 10:18 // 2 Chr 9:17). Another Hebrew word for overlay (**raqaʿ**) is found in reference to an idol covered with gold (Isa 40:19). *See* ALTAR; ARCHITECTURE, OT; ARK OF THE COVENANT; BRONZE; CHERUB, CHERUBIM; GOLD; SILVER.

CAROL MEYERS

OVERSEER [פָּקִיד **paqidh**; ἐπίσκοπος **episkopos**]. *Overseer* refers to various officeholders who are specifically appointed to supervisory roles over others. Joseph is appointed as an overseer for the household of POTIPHAR (Gen 39:4-5), in which role he has responsibility for all of Potiphar's property. Joseph later suggests that Pharaoh appoint overseers to supervise the gathering of grain into the storehouses during the years of good harvest so that there would be plenty of food in the lean years that were coming (Gen 41:34). In Judg 9:28, **paqidh** (here translated "officer" in the NRSV) indicates a military leader or commander of troops. In 2 Chr 24:11 it refers to those "officers" appointed by the king to receive money from the priests in the Temple.

In Judg 9:28, **paqidh** is translated in the LXX with **episkopos**, a term used regularly in NT literature for individuals with supervisory responsibility for particular congregations. In Acts 20:28, the elders of the church at Ephesus are referred to as the "overseers" for that congregation. In 1 Tim 3:1-2, **episkopos** refers to an officer of the church with specific requirements and is typically translated "BISHOP." *See* JOSEPH, JOSEPHITES; LABOR; OFFICER, OFFICIAL; SLAVERY.

C. MARK MCCORMICK

OVID. The Roman poet Pubilius Ovidius Naso (ca. 43 BCE–ca. 18 CE) is best remembered for the *Metamorphoses*, a collection of retold Roman myths. Two of his works on love mention Jewish Sabbath traditions (*Am.* 3; *Ars* 1.3), indicating that Sabbath rest or synagogue attendance may have been practiced even among non-Jews of the ROMAN EMPIRE.

JESSICA TINKLENBERG DEVEGA

OWL [יַנְשׁוּף **yanshuf**, כּוֹס **kos**, קָאַת **qa'ath**, קִפּוֹד **qippodh**, קִפּוֹז **qippoz**]. Several kinds of owls (birds of the family *Strigidae*) belong to the fauna of Israel and are likely listed among the unclean birds of prey in Lev 11 and Deut 14. One may further expect that owls should be mentioned among creatures haunting deserted places, such as in Isa 34:11-15. However, it is difficult to link Hebrew terms to certain owl species. While scholarly suggestions abound, consensus is rare. It is generally acknowledged that **kos** (Lev 11:17; Deut 14:16) designates an owl, perhaps the Southern little owl (*Athene noctua glaux*). Since this bird can be heard at "waste places," it is possible that Ps 102:5-6 [Heb. 102:6-7] refers to its howling sound. It is further likely that **yanshuf** (Lev 11:17; Isa 34:11) refers to some kind of owl. In Isa 34:15, the NRSV translates **qippoz** with "owl."

The NRSV usually understands **qa'ath** to be the "desert owl" (Lev 11:18; Deut 14:17; Zeph 2:14, although not in Isa 13:11). The NRSV's rendering of **qippodh** as "screech owl" in Zeph 2:14 is contextual because the same term in Isa 14:23 is translated "hedgehog," demonstrating the difficulty of understanding ancient terms for birds and animals. *See* BIRDS OF THE BIBLE; NIGHTHAWK; OWL, GREAT.

GÖRAN EIDEVALL

OWL, GREAT [יַנְשׁוּף **yanshuf**]. It is generally agreed that **yanshuf** refers to an owl, an animal mentioned among the future inhabitants of devastated Edom (Isa 34:11) and regarded as unclean (Lev 11:17; Deut 14:16). The traditional translation is "great owl," an attempt to distinguish it from another owl (**kos** כּוֹס, "little owl"). Some have suggested that **yanshuf** means "screech owl." *See* OWL.

GÖRAN EIDEVALL

OWNER [בַּעַל **ba'al**; δεσπότης **despotēs**, κύριος **kyrios**]. Someone with legal right to the possession of land or a thing. Abraham recognized land as individual PROPERTY that could be purchased (Gen 23:1-20). The Torah recognized and protected ownership, and Israelites were expected to help one another in watching over and protecting one another's herds and material possessions (e.g., Deut 22:1-4).

Several laws in the Book of the Covenant (*see* COVENANT, BOOK OF THE) deal with ownership: of domestic animals (Exod 21:28, 29, 34, 36; 22:10-15 [Heb. 22:9-14]), houses (22:8 [Heb. 22:7]), and cisterns (21:33-34). Interestingly, the list begins with laws regulating slavery, the ownership of one human by another (Exod 21:2-11, 20-21, 26-27; compare Deut 23:15-16). While other law collections in the ANE include laws dealing with slavery, only the Torah gives it priority, probably because the ancient Israelites had experienced bondage; in the Code of Hammurabi, e.g., laws related to slaves are listed at the end and defend the rights of the owner.

The Torah regarded ownership as entailing social responsibility. Owners were to leave the edges of their fields unharvested so that the poor and the resident alien might glean them (Lev 19:9-10; 23:22). Also, it was expected that owners would look with kindness upon their employees and treat them fairly. When Tobit's nephew, Ahikar, ceased supporting him and his wife was reduced to doing so, she worked for "owners" who were benevolent to her and gave her gifts in addition to her wages (Tob 2:11-14). Jesus told a number of parables that likened God to the owners of a vineyard (e.g., Matt 20:1-16) or of a house (e.g., Luke 14:15-24). Paul writes that those who cleanse themselves from false teaching will be like utensils useful to the owner of a house (2 Tim 2:21). *See* LAND LAWS; NOBLES, NOBILITY; OFFICER, OFFICIAL.

RALPH K. HAWKINS

OX, OXEN ohks [בָּקָר **baqar**, שׁוֹר **shor**; βοῦς **bous**, μόσχος **moschos**]. A working animal often referenced in association with the DONKEY (e.g., Exod 20:17; 22:4, 9 [Heb. 22:3, 8]; 23:4). Rest is mandated for both animals in Exod 23:12: "You shall rest, so that your ox and your donkey may have relief" (also Deut 5:14). As a sacrificial animal it was on the list of such animals that could be eaten (Deut 14:4).

ODED BOROWSKI

Oxen were the principal draft animals of ancient Mediterranean agriculture. Although less productive than horses, oxen were cheaper and could be eaten as well as worked. Farmers frequently castrated male animals slated for work to make them docile, but castration probably disqualified the animal for sacrifice.

Although cattle were a major source of meat, goats were the major source of milk and cheese (*see* GOAT, GOATHERD). Oxen were the most prestigious sacrificial animals (Acts 14:13). Many of the references to oxen are in lists: sacrificial animals (e.g., Exod 20:24; 22:30; Num 22:40; Deut 14:26); possessions of a patriarch (Gen 12:16; 32:5); gifts (Gen 20:14; 21:27; Tob 10:10); captured livestock (Josh 6:21; 1 Sam 27:9); stray animals (Deut 22:1); and supplies for war (Jdt 2:17).

Potentially dangerous horns made oxen the subject of an extensive set of laws (Exod 21:28-36; *see* LAW IN THE OT). Oxen lowed (Job 6:5), had a characteristic way of eating grass (Num 22:4; Dan 4:25, 32-33; 5:21), and were attached to their owners (Isa 1:3). Most predominant was their labor: drawing carts (Num 7:3; 2 Sam 6:6), plowing (1 Sam 11:5-7; 1 Kgs 19:19-21; Prov 14:4; Amos 6:12), and even threshing (Deut 25:4). Paul uses the law against muzzling an ox while it is milling the grain as an illustration (1 Cor 9:9; 1 Tim 5:18).

The "molten sea" in the Temple rested on twelve oxen (1 Kgs 7:25, 44; *see* SEA, MOLTEN), and creatures in visions in Ezekiel and Revelation had ox-like faces (Ezek 1:10; Rev 4:7). *See* ANIMALS OF THE BIBLE; CATTLE; WILD OX.

DALE PATRICK

OXGOAD. *See* GOAD.

OXYRHYNCHUS PAPYRI ok´si-ring´kuhs puh-p*i´*r*i*. Oxyrhynchus is the name of an ancient Egyptian city about 160 km south-southwest of Cairo. It lies west of the main course of the Nile on a now dried-up canal (Bahr Yusuf). The town of el-Bahnasa, lying about 22 km west of Bani Mazar, occupies part of the ancient site. The ancient city was named after a Nile fish, which in mythology ate part of the penis of the Egyptian deity Osiris (Plutarch, *Mor.* 358: Isis and Osiris, 18). The fish was revered by the inhabitants of Oxyrhynchus (*Mor.* 353: Isis and Osiris, 7), who even went to war with another village where the fish was being eaten (*Mor.* 380: Isis and Osiris, 72). The town became a Greek city named *Oxyrhynchon polis* after the arrival of Alexander the Great (332 BCE). In Hellenistic times it served as a regional capital and was abandoned after the Arab conquest in 641 CE. For over a thousand years the inhabitants of the city dumped refuse in the desert northwest and southeast of the city.

From 1896 until 1906 excavators at the site discovered dumps that contained massive amounts of papyri, which survived through the years due to the arid conditions (*see* PAPYRUS, PAPYRI). The discoveries were published beginning with the first volume of *The Oxyrhynchus Papyri*, published by the Egyptian Exploration Society (1898); from 1898 to 2006 seventy volumes of the Gk. and Lat. papyri, and occasionally papyri in other languages, have been published. Publication proceeds at the pace of about one volume a year. In 1966 the Oxyrhynchus Papyri Project became a major research project of the British Academy and is managed jointly by Oxford University and University College London. In 1910 an Italian team began excavating at Oxyrhynchus. Some of the Italian excavation's discoveries have been published in *Papiri della Societa* (1912), but many papyri remain unpublished in Florence.

Since 2005 the Oxyrhynchus Papyri Project has been housed in Oxford at the Sackler Library. It is estimated that approximately 100,000 unpublished papyri are stored there. The unpublished papyri are kept between sheets of newspaper, each having a photograph, a preliminary catalog number, and a brief description. It took more than thirty years to put this part of the collection into such a state of preservation. There are also 500–600 boxes containing fragmentary papyri in a storage repository in the Bodleian Library. These fragments have not been photographed and are largely uncataloged. By 2003, 4,700 items had been translated, edited, and published; only about 2,000 of these have been stored between glass plates.

The Oxyrhynchus Papyri Project represents the largest collection of ancient papyri in the world and the primary reference source for EGYPT between the 4th cent. BCE and the 7th cent. CE. Project leaders estimate that while 70 percent of all known literary Gk. and Lat. papyri have come from the Oxyrhynchus collection, only about 10 percent of the collection is literary. The rest are documentary papyri, representing such things as contracts, receipts, correspondence, etc., material artifacts relating to public and private life in Egypt for a thousand years. Many biblical manuscripts and other religious texts (including the *Gospel of Thomas*) were published in the early volumes of *The Oxyrhynchus Papyri*. Between 2000 and 2006 approximately twenty new fragments of NT texts were published. The Oxyrhynchus collection remains the principal source of NT texts in the world.

It is estimated that about 50,000 of the remaining unpublished papyri are publishable, meaning that the papyri can be read and identified. Under the current editorial policy only Gk. and Lat. texts are included in the published volumes. Other languages such as Coptic, Demotic, and hieroglyphs must be published elsewhere.

Bibliography: Nikolaus Gonis, Peter Parsons, and Dirk Obbink, eds. *Oxyrhynchus: A City and Its Texts* (2006); Peter M. Head. "Some Recently Published NT Papyri from Oxyrhynchus: An Overview and Preliminary Assessment." *TynBul* 51 (2000) 1–16; *The Oxyrhynchus Papyri.* Graeco-Roman Memoirs 1–90 [vols. 1–70] (1898–).

CHARLES W. HEDRICK

OZEM oh´zuhm [אֹצֶם ʾotsem]. 1. A brother of David and Jesse's sixth son listed among Judah's descendants (1 Chr 2:15).

2. The fourth of Hezron's grandsons by his eldest son Jerahmeel listed in the aforementioned genealogy (1 Chr 2:25). *See* JERAHMEEL, JERAHMEELITES; JESSE; JUDAH, JUDAHITES.

OZIEL oh´zee-uhl [Ὀζιήλ Oziēl]. An ancestor of Judith (Jdt 8:1). Correspondingly, UZZIEL, the Hebrew form, is listed as a descendant of Simeon in 1 Chr 4:42, as is Judith in Jdt 9:2.

OZNI oz´n*i* [אָזְנִי ʾozni]. The fourth of seven sons of Gad (the name is EZBON in Gen 46:16) and eponymous ancestor of the Oznites (Num 26:16). Ozni and the clan name Oznites are the same in Hebrew (ʾozni). *See* GAD, GADITES.

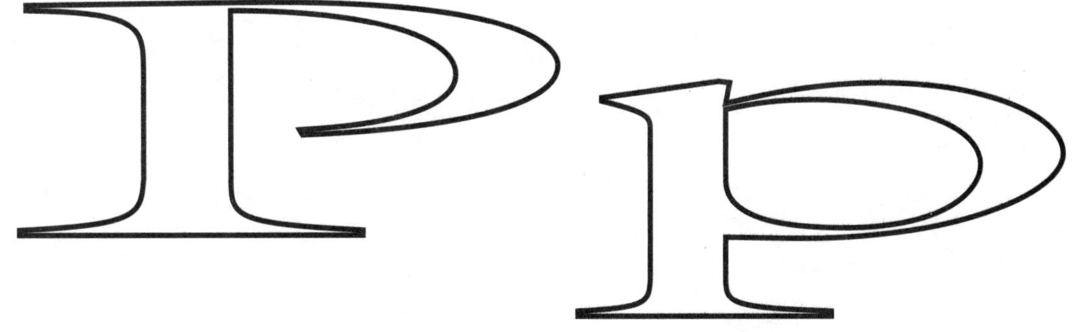

Pp

P, PRIESTLY WRITERS. One of four sources responsible for the composition of the PENTATEUCH according to traditional SOURCE CRITICISM. The Priestly source (P) is often credited with being the Torah's final redactor (editor) of the Torah; although a number of scholars have recently argued that the Holiness School—a later manifestation of Priestly thought—may have been the final editor of the Torah. Traditional source-critical scholarship held that the material contained in P was late (postexilic) and represented a devolution in ancient Israelite religion. (Such an opinion was often the result of a negative view of Judaism and/or ritual-based religion and a high appreciation for the prophetic literature.) This position is less widely held in current research. The writings of P, mainly in the later portion of Exodus, Lev 1–16, and Numbers, and sporadically in the book of Genesis, largely concern the cult. *See* DOCUMENTARY HYPOTHESIS.

PHILLIP MICHAEL SHERMAN

PAARAI pay'uh-r*i* [פַּעֲרַי pa'aray]. Paarai the Arbite (2 Sam 23:35) was one of the Thirty, the larger subset of DAVID'S CHAMPIONS. First Chronicles 11:37 lists NAARAI in place of Paarai; the difference may be the result of a spelling error.

PACHON pay'kuhn [Παχών **Pachōn**]. The apocryphal work 3 Macc 6:38 names two Egyptian months: Pachon as the ninth Egyptian solar month and EPEIPH as the eleventh. *See* CALENDAR.

PADDAN-ARAM pad'uhn-air'uhm [פַּדַּן אֲרָם **paddan 'aram**]. An area in northwest Mesopotamia along the great bend of the Euphrates. It is the home of BETHUEL and LABAN (Gen 25:20). The name occurs only in Genesis and is usually associated with JACOB (e.g., Gen 28:1-7; 35:26). Paddan-aram, HARAN (Gen 12:4-5; 27:43), and ARAM-NAHARAIM (Gen 24:10) refer to the same general area, but their exact locations are unclear.

Genesis calls the region of Paddan-aram Abraham's homeland (Haran, Gen 11:31–12:1; Aram-naharaim, Gen 24:4, 10). Abraham's brother NAHOR, ancestor of the Arameans Bethuel and Laban, settled there. Thus, Genesis indicates a close kinship between Abraham and his Israelite descendants and the Aramean peoples to the north (*see* ARAM, ARAMEANS). The Israelites perceived themselves as related to the Arameans rather than to the indigenous Canaanite population. Consequently, Abraham secures Bethuel's daughter REBEKAH as a wife for Isaac (Gen 24), and Isaac sends Jacob to Paddan-aram to marry one of Laban's daughters (Gen 28:1-7).

RALPH K. HAWKINS

PADON pay'duhn [פָּדוֹן **padhon**; Φαδών **Phadōn**]. Head of a family of temple servants (*see* NETHINIM) who returned to Judah after the exile (Ezra 2:44; Neh 7:47; 1 Esd 5:29). The name occurs only in a list of returnees preserved in three different books.

PAGANS [ἔθνος **ethnos**]. Prior polytheistic status of the Corinthian church members (1 Cor 5:1; 10:20; 12:2).

PAGIEL pay'gee-uhl [פַּגְעִיאֵל **pagh'i'el**]. Son of OCHRAN and leader of the tribe of Asher (Num 2:27; 10:26; *see* ASHER, ASHERITES). His name may mean "God has met," or "one who intercedes with God." Pagiel assisted Moses in the first wilderness census (Num 1:13) and presented the offering of the Asherites at the dedication of the tabernacle (Num 7:72-77).

KEN M. PENNER

PAHATH-MOAB pay'hath-moh'ab [פַּחַת מוֹאָב **pakhath mo'av**]. Meaning "governor of Moab" (*see* MOAB, MOABITES). It is probably a title that has been adopted as a personal name. 1. A leader in the early postexilic community who signed Nehemiah's covenant to keep the law (Neh 10:14 [Heb. 10:15]; compare Neh 3:11).

2. A postexilic clan. Ezra 2:6 notes that 2,812 people from this group were among the first to return to Jerusalem from the Babylonian exile, while Ezra 8:4 states that 200 descendants of Pahath-moab came to Yehud with Ezra. Members of this group were among those who had taken foreign wives (Ezra 10:30). Pahath-moab is identified with the descendants of Jeshua and Joab (Ezra 2:6; Neh 7:11).

KEVIN A. WILSON

PAHLAVI. The Middle Persian language of the Sasanian empire (earliest texts are 3rd-cent. CE royal and private rock inscriptions) and of the Zoroastrian "Pahlavi books" (*see* ZOROASTER, ZOROASTRIANISM). The inscription of Shâpûr I on the "Kaaba of ZARATHUSTRA" near PERSEPOLIS (ca. 260 CE) lists fires founded in the names of the royal family and provisions for sacrifices for their souls (lambs, wine, bread), while his high priest Kerdîr details in his inscriptions (ca. 270 CE) how he redressed the Mazdayasnian religious traditions and recounts a staged journey into the beyond to verify the existence of heaven and hell and the correctness of the rituals.

Like the AVESTA, the Zoroastrian Pahlavi literature was transmitted orally and only written down from the 9th cent. CE on. The texts therefore contain much material from the early Sasanian period (3rd–5th cent. CE), when Sasanian scholars worked in close proximity to their Jewish colleagues in Babylon, and reveal common concerns regarding pollution and purification.

The *Bun-dahishn*, "how things were established in the beginning," is an encyclopedia of traditional knowledge and our principal source for cosmology, anthropology, and eschatology. A similar text is the *Selections* of Zâdspram, brother of Manushchihr, from whom we have a collection of letters written to the Indian Zoroastrian (Parsee) communities ("Pahlavi *rivâyats*"), as well as a book on doctrinal issues, *Judgments of the Religion* (*Dâdestân î dênîg*). The *Dênkard*, "done according to the *dên*," is a compendium in nine books (books one and two are lost), of which books three to six discuss theological and ethical issues, book seven contains the traditional life of Zarathustra, book eight is a survey of the *Avesta*, and book nine comprises three commentaries on the *Old Avesta*, all based on Pahlavi versions of now lost Avestan texts.

Wisdom texts include *Dênkard* book six; the *Judgments of the Spirit of Wisdom* (*Dâdestân î Mênôy î khrad*); various sayings ascribed to ancient authorities, such as the famous (and legendary) 3rd-cent. Âdurbâd son of Mahrspand; and collections of "books of advice (*andarz*)" and "letters (*rivâyats*)" by various authors.

The *Book of Ardâ Wirâz* (traditionally also Wirâf) is the tale of the Righteous Wirâz, who was chosen to travel into the beyond to verify the truths of the religious tradition and returned from his journey to tell about the rewards in heaven and the punishments in hell. The battle over the new beliefs (*dên*) brought to King Wishtâsp by Zarathustra is described in the *Memorial of Zarêr* (*Ayâdgâr î Zarêrân*, an epic narrative in the style of the *Song of Roland*).

Legal texts include the *Book of a Thousand Judgments* (*Mâdayân î hazâr dâdestân*), which treats civil law, and *What One Should and What One Should Not Do* (*Shâyest nê shâyest*), on religious law. Legal and ritual commentaries are also found in the Pahlavi versions of the Avestan *Hêrbedestân* (issues in connection with priestly studies) and the *Nîrangestân* (issues of correct performance of rituals).

Other beliefs are discussed in the *Exposition to Break All Doubts* (*Shkand-gumânîg wizâr*) and in *Dênkard* book five, which contains the questions of a Christian and the answers of a Zoroastrian priest. *See* PERSIA, HISTORY AND RELIGION OF.

Bibliography: Shaul Shaked, trans. *The Wisdom of the Sasanian Sages* (*Dênkard* VI) (1979); Alan V. Williams. *The Pahlavi Rivāyat Accompanying the Dâdestân î dênîg* (1990).

P. OKTOR SKJAERVØ

PAI. *See* EDOM, EDOMITES; PAU.

PAINT [כָּחַל kakhal, פּוּךְ pukh, מָשַׁח mashakh; ζωγραφία zōgraphia, καταχρίω katachriō, σκιαγράφος skiagraphos]. Paint has been used as a medium of art at least from the Upper PALEOLITHIC and Mesolithic periods. The famous cave paintings of Lascaux in France show paint used in rich colors and realistic depictions. In the ANE, rock drawings and cave paintings are known from the Natufian period (ca. 10,000 BCE). Plastered skulls dating to Pre-pottery Neolithic from JERICHO and other Jordan Valley sites show the use of red, white, and black paint to depict facial features. In Egypt, widespread use of painting is attested in tombs.

Painting is also known in houses, especially palaces. PLASTER was applied to interior walls that were then painted. From the Herodian Northern Palace at MASADA, remains of painted walls, columns, and pillars show the use of paint to imitate more costly stone such as marble. The OT mentions painting of a building in Jer 22:14, and that for a royal palace, but certainly painting in houses was well known throughout the ANE (2 Macc 2:29). Another image the OT uses is that of whitewashing a wall, applying a thin coat of plaster or paint to cover inferior construction and make it appear as fine or strong material (Ezek 13:10-15). At Tell Deir ʿAlla, a lengthy Aramaic or Ammonite inscription dated between 700 and 600 BCE was painted on a plaster wall of a building, probably a sanctuary, using black and red paint (*see* DEIR ʿALLA, TEXTS). Pottery was also decorated with painted designs and figures, as were idols and other figures (Sir 38:27; Wis 13:14; 15:4).

Painting is also used to refer to women "painting their eyes" as a means of beautifying themselves (Jer 4:30). Jezebel paints her eyes and fixes her hair as she goes to meet her fate at the hands of Jehu (2 Kgs 9:30). These two instances of painting the eyes use the word **pukh**, which in other places is translated "ANTIMONY." *See* ARCHITECTURE, OT; COSMETICS; HOUSE.

JOEL F. DRINKARD JR.

PALACE [בֵּית הַמֶּלֶךְ beth hammelekh, בַּיִת לְמַלְכוּתוֹ bayith lemalkhutho, הֵיכָל hekhal; αὐλή aulē, βασίλειος basileios, οἰκός τῷ κυρίῳ oikos tō kyriō, οἰκός τῶν βασιλέῶν oikos tōn basileōn, πόλις polis]. *Palace* is used to designate a royal residence. A number of Hebrew words or phrases are used to designate *palace*, the most explicit being **beth hammelekh**, lit. "the king's house" (Esth 2:8), and the closely related **bayith lemalkhutho**, lit. "house for his royalty/royal dominion," i.e., "his royal house" (2 Chr 2:1, 12 [Heb. 1:18; 2:11]; LXX: **oikos tō kyriō**, "house for the lord"). In these latter instances the palace is mentioned in conjunction with the Temple (*see* TEMPLE, JERUSALEM). Solomon proposes to build a house (temple) for Yahweh and a house (palace) for himself. The parallel shows the understanding of the Temple as Yahweh's dwelling place in Jerusalem, just as the palace is the king's dwelling place. Likewise, the Hebrew word **hekhal** is used for *palace* (1 Kgs 21:1) and also for the holy place or nave of the Temple. The other words translated as *palace* (**armon** אַרְמוֹן, **birah** בִּירָה) more frequently refer to CITADELs or FORTRESSes, and indicate the strong defenses associated with a palace. In Greek, **beth hammelekh** (LXX Esth 2:8) and **hekhal** (LXX 1 Kgs 21:1) are translated with **polis**, meaning "city" or "citadel." In the NT, the high priest's dwelling is called an **aule** ("palace," Matt 26:3; Mark 15:16), a building that in Mark is associated with the PRAETORIUM or governor's headquarters.

The OT makes specific reference to the palaces of Solomon, Ahab, Ahasuerus, Nebuchadnezzar, and Pharaoh, as well as more general references to palaces. Despite the details of the size of parts of Solomon's palace in 1 Kgs 7, no specific archaeological remains have been found, although some remains of a large structure, possibly David's palace, have been excavated. However, remains of an Omride palace in Samaria have been found. Also excavations at Ramat Rahel and Lachish have revealed palaces and citadels that belonged to the later Judean monarchy, the complex at Lachish being the largest yet excavated belonging to the period of the monarchy.

In addition, significant palace remains have been found at Middle Bronze and Late Bronze Canaanite sites such as HAZOR, MEGIDDO, Shechem (*see* SHECHEM, TOWER OF), APHEK, and Tell el-ʿAjjul (*see* ʿAJJUL, TELL EL). The typical palace was of the courtyard plan—a large courtyard either flanked by or surrounded by rooms. Such palaces were often located in a complex with the primary temple of the city, or near the gate complex.

None of these palaces approaches the size and grandeur of the palaces from northern Syria and Mesopotamia. The palace of Zimri-Lim at Mari from the 18th cent. BCE had approximately 300 rooms and covered about 6 ac. Many of the walls were plastered and decorated with frescoes. Even more impressive in their size and contents were the palaces of the Assyrians, Babylonians, and Persians. The southwest Palace of Sennacherib at Nineveh, which he called "the palace without rival," had nearly 2 mi. of stone-carved reliefs covering the walls of its rooms. Each room recorded a military campaign of Sennacherib. Colossal winged bulls up to 20 ft. in height stood at the entranceways of the palace complex. The palace complex had an estimated size of 500 m by 240 m, or approximately 30 ac. These palaces demonstrated to any visitor the power of the king, both in the military victories depicted and in the sheer size of the palace and its contents. Their purpose was surely to intimidate as well as impress.

The Hasmonean rulers of Judea (134–63 BCE) built palaces near Jericho. But the premier palace builder in Judea was clearly Herod the Great (37–4 BCE) who built magnificent freestanding palaces as well as palaces incorporated within fortresses (*see* HEROD, FAMILY). Among his palaces were those in Jerusalem, JERICHO, MASADA, HERODIUM, Alexandrium, Cypros, Machaerus, Hyrcania, Doq, and Caesarea (*see* HERODIAN FORTRESSES). Josephus describes several of these, and excavations have revealed their splendor (*J.W.* 7.280–303). The Northern Palace, constructed on three terrace levels into the upper slope of Masada, was (and still remains) an engineering marvel. Unfortunately, only foundations remain of Herod's palace in Jerusalem, which was located south of the Citadel near the Joppa Gate. Remains of a significant palace, probably built by AGRIPPA II in the late 1st cent. CE, have been excavated at Banias, ancient CAESAREA PHILIPPI.

Precisely because a palace was an intimidating and impressive sign of royalty, Jesus contrasted earthly palaces to the coming kingdom of God when he asked the people crowded around John the Baptist a rhetorical question: "What then did you go out to see?" If the crowds expected someone dressed in soft robes, they should have looked in a royal palace, here **oikos tōn basileōn**, "house of kings" (Matt 11:8; in the Lukan version of this story, *palace* is **basileios** [Luke 7:25]). The crowds found quite the opposite: a homeless prophet in the wilderness (Matt 11:9-14; Luke 7:26-28). *See* ARCHITECTURE, NT; ARCHITECTURE, OT; CASTLE; STRONGHOLD; TOWER.

Bibliography: Aharon Kempinski and Ronny Reich. *The Architecture of Ancient Israel* (1992); Ehud Netzer. *The Architecture of Herod, the Great Builder* (2006); John Malcolm Russell. *Sennacherib's Palace without Rival at Nineveh* (1991).

JOEL F. DRINKARD JR.

PALAL pay'lal [פָּלָל **palal**]. Son of Uzai, and one of the builders who helped to repair the wall of Jerusalem under the direction of NEHEMIAH (Neh 3:25).

PALANQUIN [אַפִּרְיוֹן **ʾappiryon**]. An eastern means of transportation. It is a box-like LITTER in which someone rides, supported by poles carried across several people's shoulders. In Song 3:9-10, the poet describes a beautiful palanquin made of wood from Lebanon with silver posts, a golden back, a seat of purple, and an interior "inlaid with love." *See* BED; COUCH.

KATHY R. MAXWELL

PALEOLITHIC pay'lee-uh-lith'ik. A prehistoric period of time characterized by the stone tools that were made (knapped), in particular the hand ax. It is divided into three sections: Lower Paleolithic (1,400,000–250,000 BCE), Middle Paleolithic (250,000–45,000 BCE), and Upper Paleolithic (45,000–18,000 BCE). *See* PREHISTORY IN THE ANCIENT NEAR EAST.

PALESTINE AND ISRAEL, TERMINOLOGY FOR pal´uh-st*i*n, iz´ray-uhl. *Palestine* is a term of convenience used by some biblical scholars and archaeologists to designate the geographic area bounded by the Jordan River to the east, the Mediterranean Sea to the west, Lebanon to the north, and the Sinai desert to the south. Other terms used by scholars to refer to the region include the *Levant* and *Syro-Palestine.* This contemporary use of *Palestine* does not generally conform to ancient usage, a fact that does not usually come in for discussion in modern biblical studies, partly because there is no universal agreement on which term to use. In biblical studies, the word *Palestine* is normally used as a geographical designation only. The political usage of this term, especially in the context of the contemporary Israeli-Palestinian conflict, is a different issue. Today, the word refers to the state of Palestine as proposed by the Palestinian National Authority. From the earliest periods of recorded history, the terms associated with this region have shifted as empires have risen and fallen.

Incidentally, the name Palestine derives from the PHILISTINES, Israel's traditional enemies who occupied the cities of Ashdod, Ashkelon, Gaza, Ekron, and Gath on the southern coastal strip of the eastern Mediterranean. The Philistines arrived in the region at about the same time that the Israelite tribes were penetrating from the east. The name Palestine never appears in the OT or the LXX. Philistia is called **pelesheth** (פְּלֶשֶׁת) in the Hebrew. The LXX version of the Pentateuch and Joshua called the area the land of the **Phylistieim** (Φυλιστιείμ). Elsewhere, the LXX simply refers to the inhabitants of Philistia as **allophyloi** (ἀλλόφυλοι), i.e., those of a different tribe, foreigners.

Before the 2nd cent. CE, no single name was used consistently to indicate the entire area in question. Egyptian texts from the Middle Empire to the early New Empire call the area Retenu. In the New Empire, beginning particularly in the 14th to 13th cent. BCE, it is called Hurru, after the Horites who lived there. It is called Canaan in a booty list from the late 15th cent. BCE and in the AMARNA LETTERS from the following century (*see* CANAAN, CANAANITES). The name Canaan is also predominant in Genesis, Numbers, Joshua, and Judges, but less so elsewhere in the Bible. The specific boundaries of Canaan shift from source to source, sometimes encompassing Syria and sometimes being restricted to the area south of Syria. The northern coastal strip was called Phoenicia. Once the Israelite tribes occupied the hill country, that area referred to as Canaan was called **ʾerets yisraʾel** (אֶרֶץ יִשְׂרָאֵל, 1 Sam 13:19) or simply **haʾarets** (הָאָרֶץ, "the land"). It was also called the holy land, the promised land, and **ʾerets haʿivrim** (אֶרֶץ הָעִבְרִים, "land of the Hebrews"; Gen 40:15; used as late as Josephus [*Ant.* 7.53] in the 1st cent. CE and Pausanius [*Descr.* 24.8] in the 2nd cent. CE).

According to biblical tradition the entire area inhabited by Israel's tribes was united under David and Solomon in the 10th cent. BCE, but toward the end of that century the kingdom was split into the northern kingdom of Israel and the southern kingdom of Judah. In the 8th cent., the kingdom of Israel was absorbed into the expanding Assyrian Empire. In the 6th cent., the kingdom of Judah was destroyed by the Babylonians and its prominent citizens exiled to Babylonia. Cyrus the Great of Persia conquered Babylonia in 539 and in the following year he allowed the Judahite exiles to return to Jerusalem and its surrounding territory, which was part of the Persian province "Beyond the River." The official term for the former kingdom of Judah during the Persian period was **yehudh** (יְהוּד, "Judah").

During the Persian and Ptolemaic periods, COELESYRIA could be used to indicate the entire area between the Euphrates River and the Mediterranean Sea, from Cilicia to Egypt. At times, however, it could mean only the area south of Lebanon and Syria. Philo (*Embassy* 36.281), Josephus (*Ant.* 13.355–56, 392; 14.79; 16.275), and Ptolemy (*Geogr.* 5.12.22–23) use it to refer to the DECAPOLIS.

It is often claimed that Herodotus (*Hist.* 3.91) in the 5th cent. BCE was the first to extend the meaning of Palestine (**Palaistinē** Παλαιστίνη) to include more than just the coastal strip of the Philistines. Louis Feldman argues that Herodotus speaks loosely here, since the Greek historian was familiar only with the coastal area. Similarly, when Aristotle (*Mete.* 2.359a) includes the Dead Sea as part of Palestine, Feldman believes that he does so mistakenly. *Palestinian* as a noun does not occur during the ancient period at all. Nonetheless, David Jacobson insists that Herodotus was widely traveled in the area and clearly uses Palestine in the wider sense.

In the Hellenistic and Roman periods up until the time of Hadrian, the area occupied primarily by Jews was called Judea (*see* JUDEA, JUDEANS). It is attested as early as 300 BCE, used by Hecataeus of Abdera (according to Diodorus, *Bib. Hist.* 40.3) and Clearchus of Soli (according to Josephus, *Ag. Ap.* 1.179) and by Manetho (according to Josephus, *Ag. Ap.* 1.90) a bit later. That this was its official name under the Romans is attested by coins, inscriptions, and military diplomas. Authors who wrote on geography, including Pomponius Mela (*De Chorog.* 1.11.62–63) and Pliny the Elder (*Nat.* 566–72), distinguish between Palestine and Judea, and anti-Jewish writers from the 1st cent., notably Apion (according to Josephus, *Ag. Ap.* 2.33), Chaeremon (according to Josephus, *Ag. Ap.* 1.292), and Seneca (according to Augustine, *Civ.* 6.11), do not usually use the word *Palestine.* On the whole, Philo (e.g., *Moses* 1.163; *Hypothetica* 11.1; *Embassy* passim) and Josephus (*Jewish Antiquities*; *Jewish War*) refer to Judea and generally restrict the use of *Palestine* to mean the land of the Philistines. Jacobson, however, points to several passages in each author in which he seems to use *Palestine* for a wider area that includes Judea. In his letter to the Alexandrians, the emperor Claudius uses the term *Judea* (*CPJ* 153.96), as do Plutarch (*Pomp.* 45.5), Tacitus (*Hist.* 5.1; *Ann.* 2.42.5), and Suetonius (*Claud.* 28; *Galb.* 23; *Vit.* 15.1; *Vesp.* 4.5–6; 6.3; *Tit.* 4.3) at the beginning of the 2nd cent. CE. They do not mention Palestine. The last three writers also distinguish Judea from Syria, recognizing them as different provinces. When Palestine and Judea are mentioned together, they are treated as separate areas. Rabbinic texts do not use the term *Palestine* until perhaps the 5th cent. CE. Rather, they use the term **ʾerets yisraʾel**, or speak of Judea, Galilee, and the Transjordan.

After the Bar Kochba revolt (132–35 CE), the name of the region was changed from *Provincia Judea* to *Provincia Syria Palaestina*, probably as a measure to suppress Jewish identity in the area. Although there is no direct evidence that Hadrian did this, circumstantial evidence suggests it strongly. Sources from before the Bar Kochba revolt refer to the area as Judea, and that changes after the revolt. Such a change would fit with Hadrian's refounding Jerusalem as the Greco-Roman city *Aelia Capitolina*, complete with a temple to Zeus, as well as with his ban on circumcision (whether that happened before or after the revolt) and other anti-Jewish measures. *Provincia Syria Palaestina* included lands east of the Jordan. In 425 CE the area was divided into *Palaestina Prima* and *Secunda*, west of the Jordan, and *Palaestina Tertia*, east of the Jordan. *Palaestina Prima* included what had been Judea, and *Palaestina Secunda* included Galilee.

Coins and military diplomas make clear that the revolt marks the end of the use of *Judea* for the area and the beginning of the use of *Palestine* for the entire region. Even after the change of name, many authors continued to refer to the region as Judea, or to acknowledge that the area was previously called Judea. Those authors include Galen (*Simp. Med.* 9.2.5) and Celsus (according to Origen, *Cels.* 7.3) in the 2nd cent. CE, Dio Cassius (*Rom.* 69.11.1) and Origen (*Hom. Num.* 7.5) in the 3rd, and Eusebius (*Hist. eccl.* 4.2.5; 4.6; *Praep. ev.* 10.5.474a) and Jerome (*Comm. Ezech.* 25.256) in the 4th. Some inscriptions follow the same usage.

By Byzantine times, Palestine was generally accepted as the name of the region. For a short period after the Muslim conquest, the name Filistin was applied to part of the region but subsequently fell out of usage. In the Renaissance, with its renewed attention to the classical period, Palestine became the name by which European Christians knew the area. In the 20th cent. under the British mandate (1918–48), the British revived the term *Palestine*, this time with Hebrew letters appended standing for **ʾerets yisraʾel**. In 1948, part of the land became the state of Israel and part became Palestine.

Bibliography: Gideon Biger. "The Names and Boundaries of Eretz-Israel (Palestine) as Reflections of Stages in Its History." *The Land That Became Israel: Studies in Historical Geography.* Ruth Kark, ed. (1990) 1–22; Louis H. Feldman. "Some Observations on the Name of Palestine." *HUCA* 61 (1990) 1–23; David M. Jacobson. "Palestine and Israel." *BASOR* 313 (1999) 65–74; Martin Noth. "Zur Geschichte des Namens Palästina." *ZDPV* 62 (1939) 125–44.

FREDERICK J. MURPHY

PALESTINE, ADMINISTRATION OF. When, in the 8th cent. BCE, Assyrian authority expanded to include Israel, Israel was allowed to continue as a vassal state. When the Israelite kings became problematical, inefficient, or rebelled, the Assyrian emperor replaced the puppet kingdom with an Assyrian province ruled by a governor appointed in Assyria or sent directly from the capital of the empire. This pattern, with variations, was repeated during the march of empire across the territories of Israel and Judah. This article will treat the extension of Roman power into the territories of Judea, Samaria, Galilee, and the surrounding areas that became the southern part of the Roman province of Syria Palaestina (*see* ROMAN EMPIRE). (On the administration of what came to be called Palestine under the Assyrians, Babylonians, Persians, Greeks, Seleucids, and Ptolemies, *see* ASSYRIA AND BABYLONIA; HELLENISM; PERSIA, HISTORY AND RELIGION OF; PTOLEMY; SELEUCID EMPIRE.)

A. Beginnings of Roman Power in Palestine

Some biblical interpreters at Qumran understood references to the KITTIM (**kittim** כִּתִּים; from **kitti** [כִּתִּי], Cyprus; Gen 10:4; Num 24:24; 1 Chr 1:7) as referring to the Romans (1QpHab I, 6; II, 12; III, 4, 9–11), but Rome only became an influence in the political affairs of Palestine in Maccabean times (*see* KITTIM). Seleucid ambitions toward Egypt were checked when in 168 BCE the Roman legate C. Popillius Laenus confronted Antiochus IV Epiphanes on his march into Egypt and, in the name of the Roman Senate, ordered him to withdraw. When Antiochus requested time for consideration, the Roman officer drew a circle on the ground around him with the words **entautha bouleuou** (ἐνταῦθα βουλεύου "decide before leaving this circle"). This scene is reflected, in the form of a prophecy, in Dan 11:29-30, in which the Romans are represented (as at Qumran) as the Kittim. Antiochus yielded and, smarting from his humiliation, vented his rage on the inhabitants of Jerusalem who held to their ancestral faith and refused to accept the Greek culture he attempted to force on the Jewish community. This religious persecution triggered the Maccabean revolt (*see* MACCABEES, MACCABEAN REVOLT). The leader of the revolt, Judas Maccabeus, sent an embassy to Rome, which negotiated a treaty that secured the support of Rome against the Seleucids (1 Macc 8:1-32).

The revolt succeeded, and Palestine experienced almost eighty years of relative independence. Jewish leaders in Palestine administered their own affairs, in accordance with Jewish law. But from the very first, the Jewish state was beholden to Roman power, which increasingly considered Armenia, Syria, and Palestine a strategic buffer zone against the Parthians to the east, and thus under Roman control. In Maccabean times, transfer of the high priesthood to the Hasmonean family was an important political turning point (*see* HASMONEANS). The Maccabees did not belong to the priestly line; so appointment of Jason in place of the legitimate high priest was seen by the pious as a high-handed encroachment on the authority of the traditional temple state.

In 66–62 BCE the Roman general POMPEY conquered Mithridates VI of Pontus, incorporated Syria as a Roman province, and established a Roman military presence in eastern Asia Minor. Toward the end of this campaign, civil war in Judea involved Rome. At the death of Salome Alexandra, her two sons, Hyrcanus II and Aristobulus II, fought over the succession. The Nabatean king Aretas III invaded Judea in support of Hyrcanus, and defeated Aristobulus, but the country remained in turmoil. The Romans exploited the internal struggle in Judea and were happy to receive delegations not only from both the Jewish contenders who appealed to them for help, but from the Jewish people. In 63 BCE, representatives of each group appeared before Pompey in Damascus. The people's delegation wanted the Hasmonean monarchy abolished and a restoration of the old theocracy administered by the legitimate high priest. The Romans favored the people's appeal, for they too wanted to limit the powers of independent monarchs in the eastern part of the empire—thus they had previously ratified their treaties with the high priests as representing the people rather than with the Jewish kings. Pompey confirmed Hyrcanus as ruler, but denied him the title of king. Aristobulus and his followers refused to accept the decision and barricaded themselves in the Temple. After a siege of three months, Roman troops crushed the opposition. Pompey himself strode into the Temple's inner sanctum and was astounded to find it empty. Pompey reduced the territory over which HYRCANUS had authority, placing the Greek cities on the coast and those in Perea (plus Scythopolis on the west bank) into a league under Roman control, the DECAPOLIS. The proconsul of Syria, already a Roman province, was given responsibility for them and authority to exercise a general supervisory control over Judea.

Roman pacification ended the relative independence of the Hasmonean era. A tax-gathering system under publicans was instituted. Yet all did not remain quiet for long. In 57 BCE, Alexander, the son of Aristobulus II, escaped from his Roman captors, raised a small army, and fomented unrest in Judea. The proconsul of Syria, Aulus Gabinius, defeated the rebels and reorganized the province of Judea into five administrative districts, each governed by a council of local aristocrats responsible to Rome (synod [**synodos** σύνοδος] or SANHEDRIN [**synedrion** συνέδριον]). The high priest was the nominal head of the Jewish people, but the reorganization placed the authority for concrete decisions in the hands of the local councils. The high priest's remaining authority depended upon the good pleasure of Rome. A weak central authority made it easier for the Romans to pursue their own program for Palestine, and pleased the Jewish population, who could administer their own religious laws—but the line between religion and politics remained thin.

In the civil war that broke out in 49 BCE between Pompey and Julius Caesar, Pompey Hyrcanus' patron was killed. ANTIPATER, an Idumean who had been consolidating his power in Judea, advised Hyrcanus to declare his support for Caesar. Two years later, while fighting in Egypt, Caesar found himself outnumbered, and Hyrcanus supplied crucial support at the urging of Antipater. After his victory, Julius Caesar rewarded Hyrcanus by promoting him to "ethnarch of the Jews" and thus eliminated the system of five administrative districts. Once the previous reorganization into administrative districts was annulled, Antipater was made a Roman citizen and PROCURATOR (**epitropos** ἐπίτροπος) of Judea, with both military and political power. Antipater then made his two sons, Phasael and Herod, military prefects of Judea and Galilee, respectively. Herod's office was further amplified by the governor of Syria, who appointed him military prefect of Coele-Syria.

Since Julius Caesar had brought stability to Judea, his assassination on March 15, 44 BCE was a distressing blow to Jews in Palestine. Cassius, one of the assassins, became governor of Syria, which could have had negative repercussions for Palestinian Jews, but Hyrcanus and Antipater skillfully shifted their support once again. When Antipater was killed in a personal vendetta in 43 BCE, his two sons inherited the Palestinian leadership. They had to extract the required Roman tribute. Of eleven toparchies (districts organized for tax purposes) in Judea, four were unable to pay the demanded amount, and the population was sold into slavery. In the power struggles after Caesar's assassination, they nimbly shifted allegiance to whoever seemed to be winning. When Mark Antony and Octavian emerged victorious, Mark Antony became ruler of the eastern part of the empire, and nominated them to be tetrarchs of Judea. Before this arrangement could be fully implemented, in 40 BCE the Parthians took control of much of the east, including Palestine. They installed the last surviving son of Aristobulus as king and high priest. Phasael died in the struggle, but Herod escaped to Rome. The issue was whether west (Rome) or east (Parthia) would be the power behind the throne in Palestine. The Parthians had taken over Palestine and placed their puppet king on the throne. The Roman Senate, at the behest of Antony and Octavian, appointed Herod "King of the Jews." He had the title and the support of Rome, and was himself a Roman citizen by birth, but he had no kingdom (*see* HEROD, FAMILY).

B. Herod the Great

While the Romans fought the Parthians, Herod set about reconquering Judea. The more orthodox Jewish population preferred Antigonus, who, as a member of the Hasmonean family, claimed to be the sole legitimate heir to the Judean kingdom. Herod was considered an outsider, an Idumean "half Jew" who wanted to reign as a Hellenistic monarch under Roman control. Herod's supporters were mainly the Gentile and non-indigenous settlers in Samaria and Idumea, and Hellenizing Jews who saw the future of Palestine as a Hellenistic Roman state. Herod found himself fighting the Jewish population in order to establish his kingship, and actually besieging Jerusalem to establish his power. During the siege, he attempted to neutralize the objection that he had no legitimate claim to the Jewish throne by marrying a granddaughter of Hyrcanus, Mariamme. The ploy was never effective. Herod won the war and sent Antigonus to Antioch to be executed—the first time the Romans had imposed the death penalty on a king in the region. But the Jewish population continued to regard Herod as a usurper, who had destroyed the legitimate Hasmonean dynasty only with Roman support. They knew that he had been named "king" only as a countermove to Antigonus' appointment as such by the Parthians.

This popular assessment was correct. Herod was a brilliant and energetic leader, who in fact did much for the economy of Palestine by his extravagant building projects, including the reconstruction of the Temple in Jerusalem that made it one of the most magnificent sanctuary complexes in the empire. His kingdom was in all respects like the other client kingdoms under Roman sovereignty. He had the same titles, responsibilities, and privileges as the other client kings, all at the pleasure of the Roman rulers. They gave him a free hand in domestic affairs. He could rule like an independent king within his own territory, so long as his actions did not impinge on Roman interests. Thus he could not have an independent foreign policy; he could not make treaties with other rulers, nor conduct military operations without the consent of Rome. This represented a change in the earlier Roman policy during which the Romans had an alliance with the Jewish people, conducted through the Roman Senate and the Jewish people as represented by their high priest. Now, neither Rome nor Herod regarded the Jewish people as a political entity. Rome dealt directly with Herod, and Herod with Rome.

Under Rome, Herod was himself the final authority, but he did not administer the whole of Palestine personally. A complex bureaucracy maintained order and collected tribute. We know from Josephus (*J.W.* 3.54–58) that Judea was divided into eleven toparchies, Jewish Transjordan into three, and Galilee into five. We have no exact information about their internal organization, but, on the pattern in other Hellenistic kingdoms, we assume that individual villages in each district were headed by a *comarch* (kōmarchēs κωμάρχης) assisted by village clerks, with each district administered by a *toparch* (toparchos τόπαρχος) and his clerks. The toparchs were supervised by a royal official, the *strategos* (stratēgos στρατηγός) directly responsible to the king. The non-Jewish areas presumably had an analogous structure corresponding to the Hellenistic *polis* (polis πολίς), with officials, titles, and functions matching their counterparts elsewhere in the empire. Both administrative hierarchies converged at the top, where Herod himself reigned over the whole apparatus.

Herod's main obligation to Rome, aside from keeping the peace and providing a stable buffer state against the Parthians, was the annual collection of a considerable TRIBUTE. Rome thought of the land as belonging to the emperor, who leased to the client king on condition of payment of tribute. This required the extraction of taxes of numerous varieties from the population, rich and poor alike, estimated at 30–40 percent, not counting tithes and religious taxes (*see* TAXES, TAXATION). Producing such revenue required a stable and functioning economy; it was to Herod's advantage to promote peace and prosperity in his own realm. He resettled peasants who had lost their land and helped them become productive farmers again—who could pay taxes. He helped cities rebuild and become prosperous, and founded new cities. His building projects maintained employment and promoted the development of skilled workers. At the end of his reign the economic situation of the people as a whole was better than at the beginning.

Though Herod portrayed himself as an advocate of the traditional faith, he treated the office of high priest as an instrument of his political policy, a subordination made painfully clear by the fact that Herod took the sacred vestments into custody, making them available at his discretion. The Romans continued this practice after Herod's death.

Herod had maintained good relations with his Roman overlords, especially Octavian/Augustus, and had sent his sons Alexander and Aristobulus to Rome to be groomed for future leadership. In Palestine, however, Herod had ruled with intrigue and terror, eliminating several of his ten wives and numerous sons whom he considered potential threats. Reflecting Herod's lip service to Judaism that included abstinence from pork, Augustus allegedly remarked in a caustic wordplay in Greek, "It is better to be Herod's pig [hys ὗς] than his son [hyios υἱός]" (Macrobius, *Saturnalia* 2.4).

C. Herod's Heirs as Rulers

Herod's will had decreed that ARCHELAUS, the eldest son of his fourth wife Malthace, was to inherit his kingdom with the title of king. His younger brother ANTIPAS was to be subordinate to him, ruler of Galilee and Perea (except for the Decapolis) with the title of *tetrarch.* PHILIP, the son of Cleopatra of Jerusalem, was likewise to be tetrarch of the areas north and east of Galilee, variously described in Josephus and the NT (including Auranitis, Gaulanitis, Ituraea, Trachonitis, Batanaea, and Paneas; see Luke 3:1; Josephus, *Ant.* 17.189, 319). The transition was not peaceful. The brothers quarreled and went to Rome to plead their respective cases; disturbances broke out among the exploited population of Palestine. A delegation from the people had also gone to Rome to plead that the country be placed under direct control of Rome. Meanwhile, Varus, governor of Syria, pacified the Palestinian countryside with brutal force, crucifying 2,000 rebels. Augustus essentially confirmed Herod's will, except that Archelaus was denied the title *king* and was designated *ethnarch* (ethnarchēs ἐθνάρχης), thus making him ruler of Judea, Samaria, and Idumea alongside Antipas and Phillip rather than over them—perhaps with some oversight (*see* ETHNARCH).

Philip's territory was largely Gentile. He ruled it without major problems from 4 BCE until 33 CE, conducting himself as a typical Hellenistic client ruler. Banias was in his realm. Philip built a temple to Augustus at the ancient shrine city of Banias and renamed the city Caesarea Philippi. At his death his territory was added to adjoining Syria.

Herod Antipas, the King Herod of the Gospels, ruled Galilee and Perea 4 BCE–39 CE, with each area divided into five administrative districts. His official title was *tetrarch* (tetraarchēs τετραάρχης), lit. "ruler of a fourth part," but the word simply meant "prince" (*see* TETRARCH, TETRARCHY). He comported himself royally and was popularly known as "the king." He founded new cities and rebuilt others in the Hellenistic style. Ancient Sepphoris, less than 4 mi. northwest of Nazareth, was rebuilt as a shining example of the new culture, complete with a palace and a theater that seated 3,000 (see Josephus, *J.W.* 2.511; *Ant.* 18.27). SEPPHORIS was probably designated as Herod's capital, but the capital was moved to the new city of Tiberius, which Herod built on the southwest shore of the Sea of Galilee. Here too, the city was built in the Hellenistic style, with Herod's palace, splendidly decorated with animal images, and a Greek stadium. Herod chose the spot for its beauty and personal convenience (it was near the warm springs of Hammath), but without regard to traditional Jewish sensitivities. The new city was located on an ancient cemetery, thus not only showing disrespect for Jewish tradition, but also making everyone who entered it ritually unclean, ensuring that no orthodox Jew could voluntarily live and work there. Herod colonized the city by force, resulting in a mixed population of Gentiles and lapsed or compromised Jews.

We cannot be certain about the manner of government in Sepphoris and the other cities rebuilt by Herod, but Tiberius was clearly organized on the Greek pattern of free cities governed by a boulē (βουλή, "city council"). Tiberius was not in fact a free city like those of the Decapolis ("free" in this context means they were in charge of their own affairs, subject directly to Rome, not to any local ruler). Herod himself was the final authority, so the citizens could not appeal from him to the boulē. Though without the title, Herod ruled as king, careful not to displease his Roman patrons. He had his own military force; Roman troops were not stationed in his domain. He could enact the death penalty without consulting the Romans, as illustrated by his execution of John the Baptist (Mark 6:14-29; Josephus, *Ant.* 18.116–19). He could even wage minor wars, so long as his actions did not violate Rome's larger goals. Herod fought an unsuccessful war against Aretas, the Nabatean king whose capital was southeast of the Dead Sea at Petra; the defeat was avenged by Roman troops from Syria dispatched by Tiberius, but led to Herod's downfall. Antipas had divorced his Nabatean wife, the daughter of king Aretas, in order to marry Herodias; this affront to the Nabatean royal house was a factor in the war. Herodias' ambition in behalf of her husband was also a factor in ending his career. When Caligula came to power in 37 CE, Herodias persuaded Herod to petition the new emperor for the title of king. Caligula promptly deposed him and exiled him to Gaul, with his tetrarchy awarded to Agrippa (Josephus, *Ant.* 18.252; *J.W.* 2.183).

Archelaus had been awarded the core of his father's kingdom, which included the cities of Jerusalem, Samaria, Caesarea, and Joppa. He was the least competent of Herod's sons. His oppressive measures were so unbearable that a Jewish delegation sent to Rome persuaded Augustus to replace him. His rule came to an end after ten years (4 BCE–6 CE), and his territories were placed under direct Roman administration as a province of the empire.

D. Judea as a Province, 6–41 CE

Judea was considered a strategic territory and potential trouble spot and thus became a PROVINCE of the third type, with a governor of equestrian rank and the title of *praefectus.* We know from the inscription on the pedestal of a statue of Pontius Pilate at Caesarea, which was the capital, that the governors prior to Agrippa bore the title of prefect. After Agrippa's interregnum (41–44 CE) the governors were called procurators (*see* PROCURATOR). Later Roman historians anachronistically applied the title to all the governors of Judea, and this nomenclature has become traditional. The procurators of Judea were: 1) Coponius (6–9 CE); 2) Marcus Ambibulus (9–12 CE); 3) Annius Rufus (12–15 CE); 4) Valerius Gratus (15–26 CE); 5) Pontius Pilate (26–36 CE); 6) Marcellus (36–37 CE); 7) Marullus (37–41 CE). The governor's most important responsibility was procuring taxes (hence the title *procurator*). This included, however, a strong emphasis on maintaining a stable political and economic situation. The early procurators generally accommodated their administrative style to local customs and sensitivities. Not until Pontius Pilate was there any protest against specific violations of Jewish religious feelings, when images of Caesar on the Roman standards were brought into Jerusalem (Josephus, *J.W.* 2.169; *Ant.* 18.55). The peace and prosperity of the land were important for Rome's own goals.

As the basis for tax assessment, a provincial CENSUS was necessary. Such a census was conducted in 6 CE, immediately following the appointment of the first prefect, Coponius, apparently in conjunction with the census in Syria under the Syrian governor QUIRINIUS. This is the census mentioned in Luke 2:1-2, though incorrectly dated in the reign of Herod the Great. This census that tangibly brought every resident of Judea under the direct fiscal and legal authority of Rome was resisted by the revolt of Judas of Galilee (*see* JUDAS §D3). Judas was the son of Ezekias/Hiskia who had opposed Herod the Great. Judas and his followers claimed that acceptance of the Roman yoke violated the fundamental convictions of Jewish faith, for Jews could worship only the one God and must resist both the introduction of Roman images, which they considered idolatrous, and the claims by and about the emperors to divinity. They also saw, correctly, that acceptance of direct taxation from the Romans would lead to enslavement of the population when the taxes could not be paid. Judas and his followers attacked the Roman fort in Sepphoris, but they were defeated, Judas was killed, and his followers were dispersed (see Acts 5:37; Josephus, *J.W.* 2.117–18; *Ant.* 18.1–10, 23–25). The movement he had begun smoldered underground, broke out afresh from time to time, and eventually became the Zealot movement that led to the disastrous war of 66–73 CE.

Just how the tax system was administered by the procurators is unclear, and probably varied in different administrations and localities. Collection of taxes and customs duties was farmed out to publicans (**telōnai** τελῶναι; see Mark 2:14; Luke 19:2), but in some situations the municipal authorities collected the taxes. The situation in Galilee and Perea, not under direct Roman administration, remained different.

The procurator was in principle responsible for every aspect of administration. In practice, however, the administration of civil, criminal, and religious law remained in the hands of local Jewish authorities, with the priestly leaders and their associates in Jerusalem exercising great influence. Josephus claims the aristocracy and high priests actually ruled the nation under Roman supervision (*Ant.* 20.251). The legate of Syria continued to be a kind of supervisor of Judean affairs, as illustrated in the 40 CE incident in which the emperor Gaius Caligula ordered Petronius, the Syrian governor, and not Marullus, the Judean procurator, to install Gaius' image in the Jerusalem Temple. Procurators maintained the right to depose and appoint the high priest, and to keep his vestments in their own custody. Likewise, procurators retained the right to impose the death penalty for political crimes, and did not hesitate to use this authority. The Romans allowed some flexibility in the administration of the province, and expected to negotiate with Jewish leaders, who understood themselves as subsidiary partners in the government of their country. However, the picture given by the Mishnah of a permanent, central Jerusalem Sanhedrin with authority over all Jews is a later idealization. The constitution, role, and competence of the Sanhedrin, and whether it was an established continuing body or an ad hoc council with flexible membership, are all disputed points. Whether Jewish authorities retained the power to execute those deemed guilty of capital offenses in religious matters remains disputed. As throughout the empire from the time of Julius Caesar on, Judaism was a protected *religio licita* (authorized religion). Jews were exempt from Roman military service and participation in the imperial cult, and they could not be forced to violate their dietary and Sabbath laws.

E. Herod Agrippa I, 41–44 CE

When Herod Philip died in 33 or 34 CE, the Romans added his tetrarchy to the province of Syria. In 37 CE, the new emperor Gaius ("Caligula") gave these territories to Herod AGRIPPA, grandson of Herod the Great, and gave him the title of king and the Roman rank of praetor (Josephus, *Ant.* 18.228–37). Agrippa had grown up in the emperor's household in Rome. He was well known to Tiberius and Caligula and friends with Claudius. During the 40 CE crisis caused by Caligula's attempt to place his statue in the Temple in Jerusalem, Agrippa's good standing with the emperor and his diplomatic skills helped foil the plan. According to Josephus, when Caligula was assassinated, Agrippa played a major role in the negotiations that made his childhood friend Claudius emperor. In gratitude, Claudius removed the Roman governor and restored to Agrippa the remaining territories of the kingdom of his grandfather Herod the Great. From 41–44 Agrippa ruled all Palestine, though Rome remained the power behind the throne—made clear by the Roman command that Agrippa desist from refortifying Jerusalem. Agrippa was sensitive to Jewish religious traditions, observed them himself, and was popular with Jewish religious leaders. As a defender of Judaism, he had Christian leaders arrested, and executed James son of Zebedee (Acts 12:1-3). In Roman contexts, however, he behaved like any other Hellenistic client king, providing lavish support for Greek cultural institutions, erecting splendid buildings complete with pagan statuary, and sponsoring the games in Caesarea in honor of the emperor. The NT (Acts 12:20-23) and Josephus (*Ant.* 19.343–52) both report that after a splendid speech, while dressed in royal finery, he was hailed by the crowds as divine, like the Roman rulers. He accepted the acclamation and died a horrible death shortly thereafter. Acts 12:23 attributes his death to the angel of the Lord; Josephus says it was from agonizing stomach pains. He may have been poisoned by Roman officials, who did not countenance any client king becoming too popular or independent.

F. Judea as a Province, 44–66 CE

After Agrippa's death, his entire kingdom was placed under direct Roman rule. The new procurator, Cuspius Fadus, was responsible not only for Judea and Samaria, but for all of Palestine to the Syrian border, now considered the province of Judea. Tacitus (*Ann.* 12.54) claims that Galilee had a separate procurator, but this is not confirmed by other sources. This arrangement continued until 53 CE when Claudius gave the old tetrarchy of Philip and other territories around the Sea of Galilee and to its northeast to Herod Agrippa II. Sometime after he came to power in 54 CE Nero added other cities and territory. When the Jewish revolt broke out in 66 CE Agrippa II sided with the Romans, and after the war his territory was extended further.

When Fadus ordered that the Jews return the high priest's vestments to Roman control, the Jewish leaders appealed to Fadus and Longinus, the Syrian governor, to petition the emperor Claudius, who ruled in their favor (Josephus, *Ant.* 20.6–14). Fadus' successors struggled to maintain order in the increasingly troublesome province. Ventidius Cumanus (48–52 CE) was unable to maintain internal peace between Jews and Samaritans, and was deposed. Felix, his successor (52–59 CE), tried to deal with the increasing outbreaks of insurgency with brute force, which only worsened the situation, and he too was recalled. Porcius Festus (59–62 CE) seems to have been doing a creditable job, but died suddenly after three years in office. During the three months before his successor, Albinus, arrived, the high priest Ananus, with the collaboration of Jewish leaders in Jerusalem, put to death several individuals represented as opponents of the high priesthood, including James the brother of Jesus. His action was disowned by the Jewish leaders and he was deposed from the high priesthood to save the province from Roman reprisals. This incident illustrates how strictly Roman authority was maintained even in the absence of a procurator.

When Albinus arrived, his oppressive administration (62–64 CE) only further inflamed those elements of the Jewish population leaning toward revolt. Gessius Florus (64–66 CE) caused the explosive situation to ignite in open revolt. During the war that followed (66–73 CE) much of Palestine was in political chaos, with the provisional revolutionary government presumably led by the high priests and Jerusalem aristocracy. The rebels themselves were divided into several factions until the final phase of the war. From the Roman perspective, supreme authority was vested in Vespasian, sent by Nero to put down the revolt.

G. From Judea to Syria Palaestina

Following the defeat of the last Jewish rebels at Masada in 73 CE, all Palestine was incorporated into Judea and administered by Roman military governors. A rabbinic academy established at Jamnia after the war exercised great influence in religious matters and the reconstitution of Judaism after the destruction of the Temple made continuance of the sacrificial cult impossible. The priestly and lay aristocracy, predominantly Sadducean, had perished in the war; the surviving Pharisaic leadership cooperated with the Romans and did not attempt political adventures. Jewish leadership was focused on the reconstitution of JUDAISM as a religious community, and the political administration of Palestine continued in the hands of the Romans. Calm prevailed for several decades, even during the tumultuous "revolt under Trajan" (115–117 CE), which saw great unrest in the Jewish communities elsewhere (Mesopotamia, Cyprus, Cyrene, and Egypt).

A new, and final, revolt began in 132 CE under the leadership of Simeon ben Kosiba (*see* BAR KOCHBA, SIMON). Both the causes and the course of the war remain largely unknown, due to the lack of sources—there was no Josephus to record events and interpret causes, which had little interest for Roman historians (*see* JEWISH WARS). The war was apparently precipitated when the emperor Hadrian promulgated a decree banning circumcision indiscriminately in all parts of the empire, and announced plans to build a new Gentile city, Aelia Capitolina, complete with pagan temple, on the ruins of Jerusalem. The Jews fought courageously, but Roman power triumphed in 135 after desolating the whole of Judea in a bloody and costly campaign. Many of the surviving Jews were sold into slavery, and Judea became the Roman province Syria Palaestina.

Bibliography: James S. McLaren. *Power and Politics in Palestine: The Jews and the Governing of Their Land 100 BC–AD 70* (1991); Peter Schäfer. *The History of the Jews in the Greco-Roman World* (2003); E. Mary Smallwood. *The Jews under Roman Rule from Pompey to Diocletian* (1976).

M. EUGENE BORING

PALESTINE, GEOGRAPHY OF. *See* ISRAEL, GEOGRAPHY OF.

PALESTINE, GEOLOGY OF. *See* ISRAEL, GEOLOGY OF.

PALESTINIAN TARGUMS. *See* TARGUMS.

PALIMPSEST pal´imp-sest. From **palin** (πάλιν, "again") and ψάω (psaō, "rub" or "disappear"), a parchment manuscript that has been erased and reused: the original text is scraped off and new text applied on the recycled surface. *See* EPHRAEMI SYRI RESCRIPTUS, CODEX.

PALLU, PALLUITES pal´y*oo*, pal´y*oo*-*i*t [פַּלּוּא pallu ʾ]. The second of Reuben's four sons. He appears in genealogical lists in Gen 46:9 (among those Israelites who went to Egypt along with Jacob); Exod 6:14 (as the head of a Reubenite clan); and 1 Chr 5:3. Pallu is also listed in Num 26:5 as the head of the Palluite clan. In Num 26:8-9 he is mentioned as the father of ELIAB, whose sons DATHAN and ABIRAM participated in Korah's rebellion against Moses and Aaron. *See* REUBEN, REUBENITE.

DEREK E. WITTMAN

PALM TREE [תָּמָר **tamar,** תֹּמֶר **tomer,** תִּמֹרָה **timorah;** φοῖνιξ **phoinix**]. The biblical palm tree is the date palm (*Phoenix dactylifera*), which flourished in Jericho, "the CITY OF PALM TREES" (2 Chr 28:15), where the high temperatures suit it. Although palms will grow elsewhere—on "Palm Sunday" their leaves were strewn in the way when Jesus entered Jerusalem (John 12:13); and Deborah sat under a lone tree "between Ramah and Bethel in the hill country of Ephraim" (Judg 4:5)—their fruit is poor and was forbidden as a firstfruit offering, according to the Talmud. Palm leaves were used by the Greeks and Romans as symbols of victory in warfare or athletics. Judas Maccabee used them during processions at the restoration of the Temple in 164 BCE (1 Macc 13:51; 2 Macc 10:7; 14:4), and Jesus' entry may be seen as a symbol of victory over death (Rom 6:9-10).

The date palm grows 15 to 25 m high with its unbranched 30 cm-diameter trunk covered by woody leaf-bases. Its leaves create an immense head at the top of the stem as each leaf may reach 20 m in length; the stout woody midrib (which makes it appear as a "branch" in John 12:13) bears numerous linear leaflets in the manner of a huge feather. Such leaves were used at the Passover and during the Feast of Tabernacles for the construction of booths (Lev 23:40-43). There are separate male and female trees, the latter bearing large clusters of flowers that require manual pollination. The fruit is the well-known date with sugary flesh and a long, inedible seed. As well as being eaten fresh, the fruits were and still are made into a sweet drink, which some consider to be the "honey" Moses promised the Israelites (Exod 3:8). Propagation of date palms may be by seeds or, more usually, from suckers that cluster at the base of each tree. They will put down deep roots that tap into subterranean water in semi-desert areas, and they can even tolerate the brackish water often occurring in such territory.

The date palm appears to have spread eastward from Mesopotamia and gradually became established in cultivation to the west. Lebanon, formerly known as Phoenicia, may have taken the name of this palm. Other place-names such as PALMYRA in Syria and HAZAZON-TAMAR (Gen 14:7) incorporate its name. Even the feminine name TAMAR (2 Sam 13:1; Song 7:7) reflects the stately elegance of the tree. *See* BOOTH; DATES; PLANTS OF THE BIBLE.

F. NIGEL HEPPER

PALMYRA. Palmyra, also known by its indigenous name TADMOR, was situated at an oasis in the Syrian steppe. Under the aegis of Rome from Tiberius' reign onward, Palmyra reigned supreme in the caravan trade between the Parthian realm in the East and the Roman Empire in the West, prosperity reaching its climax in the 2nd and 3rd cent. CE. The 260s saw the local dynasty of Queen Zenobia staking its claim to the imperial throne, before the legitimate emperor Aurelian conquered the city in 272 CE. As regards Palmyra's origins, the name "Tadmor" is first mentioned in Assyrian cuneiform tablets from Middle Bronze Age I, and the stratification of the hill below the temple of Bel, built in the early 1st cent. CE, goes back to Early Bronze Age III. Literary sources are unhelpful to link this pre-historical phase with the fact that the city's monumental ruins all date from the Early and Late Roman periods. Josephus (*Ant.* 8.153–54) correctly draws attention to Palmyra's function as an oasis "far from the inhabited parts of Syria" (*see* SYRIA), but his account that Solomon founded the city and "surrounded it with very strong walls" follows 2 Chr 8:4, which had misinterpreted the original "Tamar in the desert" (as used in 1 Kgs 9:18) as "Tadmor in the desert." Pliny the Elder (*Nat.* 5.88) provides a realistic image of a typical oasis rather than a factual description of Palmyra, and the story of Mark Antony's abortive raid on the city in 41 BCE, as given by Appian (*Bell. civ.* 5.9), has too many inconsistencies to be of historical value. Although Palmyra's religious life was dominated by polytheistic cults, there was also a small Jewish community, shown by Hebrew inscriptions from the site itself and by Palmyrene epitaphs from the Jewish necropolis at Beth-Shearim (Galilee). The presence of the heretic bishop Paul of Samosata at

Zenobia's court (e.g., Athanasius, *H. Ar.* 71.1) implies that by the 260s Christians had settled at the oasis too, and some Manichean texts hint at the activity of Mani's followers there at the same time.

TED KAIZER

PALTI pal′t*i* [פַּלְטִי palti]. Means "My deliverance." 1. Moses sent Palti the Benjaminite, son of Raphu, into Canaan as one of the spies ordered to investigate the land in advance of an Israelite invasion (Num 13:1-16, esp. v. 9).

2. Saul gave his daughter MICHAL to Palti, the son of Laish, from Gallim, although she was already married to David (1 Sam 25:44). This notice of Saul's action, for which no justification is provided, is found in a summary of David's wives (1 Sam 25:43-44). Soon after Saul's death David negotiated with Abner, general of Ish-bosheth's army (2 Sam 3:12-21). One of David's requirements for Abner's visit was the return of Michal (2 Sam 3:13-14). She was taken from Palti, who followed weeping "all the way to Bahurim" (2 Sam 3:16, here PALTIEL) but returned to his home when so ordered by Abner (3:16). *See* BENJAMIN, BENJAMINITES.

MICHAEL G. VANZANT

PALTIEL pal′tee-uhl [פַּלְטִיאֵל palti᾽el]. Means "God is my deliverance." 1. Paltiel son of Azzan was a leader in the tribe of Issachar (Num 34:26) and one of twelve tribal leaders selected by Moses for the distribution of land to the ten tribes of Israel west of the Jordan. *See* ISSACHAR, ISSACHARITES.

2. A variant form of PALTI in the story of David's recovery of his wife MICHAL (2 Sam 3:15-16).

MICHAEL G. VANZANT

PALTITE pal′t*i*t [פַּלְטִי palti]. HELEZ, one of DAVID'S CHAMPIONS, is called "the Paltite" in 2 Sam 23:26, indicating that he came from BETH-PELET. In par. lists he is identified as "Helez the PELONITE" (1 Chr 11:27; 27:10).

PAMPHYLIA pam-fil′ee-uh [Παμφυλία Pamphylia]. A region in Asia Minor (present-day Turkey), approximately 80 mi. long and 20 mi. wide, with its southern border on the Mediterranean Sea. Pisidia borders the region on the north, Lycia on the west, and Cilicia on the east (see Acts 27:5).

Pamphylia was settled by a multitude of peoples; the Greeks named it "land of all tribes" (**Pamphylia**). In 546 BCE, the Persians gained control of the region, and by 333 BCE it had been conquered by Alexander the Great. After struggling with the Ptolemies of Egypt over the region, Antiochus III eventually made Pamphylia part of the Seleucid Empire (200 BCE), but Antiochus surrendered it to Rome in 189 BCE. From 102 to 44 BCE, Pamphylia was part of the province of Cilicia and then of Asia. It was part of Galatia from 25 to 43 CE, until the emperor Claudius created a new region called Lycia-Pamphylia. The emperor Galba reapportioned Pamphylia to Galatia, and it was reunited with Lycia under Vespasian's rule.

Because of its established Jewish population, Pamphylia was a likely destination for Paul on his missionary journeys; according to the book of Acts, it was his habit to preach in synagogues in each new region he visited (Acts 13:14; 14:1; 17:1-2, 10, 17; 18:4, 26; 19:8). Evidence for a Jewish population begins with an account of Pamphylian Jews taking part in an alliance with the Hasmoneans (1 Macc 15:23). The 1st-cent. BCE Jewish historian Philo mentions Pamphylia among cities colonized by Jews (Philo, *Embassy* 281–82). In the 1st cent. CE, Jews from Pamphylia were among the crowds at Jerusalem during Pentecost (Acts 2:10).

Indeed, the book of Acts reports that Paul, Barnabas, and John Mark sailed from Paphos on the island of Cyprus to PERGA in Pamphylia on Paul's first missionary journey, although Luke does not indicate that they preached in a synagogue there (Acts 13:13). Instead, the narrative recounts that John Mark departed for Jerusalem, while Paul and Barnabas traveled on to Pisidian Antioch (Acts 13:13-14). Luke does not indicate why the three missionaries parted ways in Pamphylia, but there seems to have been a strong disagreement, because Luke later reports that Paul considered John Mark to be a deserter (Acts 15:36-39). When Paul and Barnabas returned through Pamphylia, they preached at the capital city of Perga (Acts 14:24-25), but there is no conclusive evidence they founded a church there. *See* ACTS OF THE APOSTLES.

MARIANNE BLICKENSTAFF

PAN. *See* FIREPAN; FRYING PAN; POTTERY; VESSELS.

PANEL [בְּקָרִים beqarim, סִפּוּן sippun, פְּקָעִים peqa῾im]. Two different Hebrew terms, **peqa῾im** ("gourds") in 1 Kgs 7:24 and **beqarim** ("cattle") in 2 Chr 4:3, clearly refer to the same part of the fitting around the "molten sea" (*see* SEA, MOLTEN) and are understood in the NRSV to mean panels, although that meaning is far from certain. *See* TEMPLE, JERUSALEM.

Another term, **sippun**, from the root safan (סָפַן), which means "to cover," is often translated "ceiling" (1 Kgs 6:15). In other places where related words are used, they seem to refer to certain decorative structures covered with wood throughout, and not merely to a ceiling. These usages may correspond better to the English idea of "panel" as a wall covering (e.g., Jer 22:14; Ezek 41:16; Hag 1:4).

C. MARK MCCORMICK

PANIAS. *See* CAESAREA PHILIPPI.

PAPER [χάρτης chartēs]. Translation of Gk. word referring to a sheet or a roll of papyrus (2 John 12).

See PAPYRUS, PAPYRI; WRITING AND WRITING MATERIALS.

PAPHOS pay´fos [Πάφος **Paphos**]. The city of Paphos is located in the southwest corner of CYPRUS. It is famous for the sanctuary of Aphrodite located at Palaipaphos ("Old Paphos," also known as Kouklia). The goddess sometimes took the epithet Paphia, and her association with the city can be traced back to the Homeric epics (*Od.* 8.360–66). Coin representations show the deity, not in anthropomorphic form, but as a conical rock or *baetyl.* The sanctuary itself appears to have been in use from the 12th cent. BCE. Many of the buildings were destroyed in a great earthquake that struck Cyprus in 76–77 CE. Excavations have uncovered remains of the temple, which was in an open courtyard. The main settlement and harbor of Paphos (Nea Paphos, or "New Paphos") was located some 10 mi. away from the sanctuary. This community was founded in the late 4th cent. BCE. One of the main sanctuaries was to Artemis Agrotera. During the Ptolemaic occupation of the island, Paphos became the leading city. It also possessed its own mint issuing coins.

Paul and Barnabas traveled on the Roman road on the south coast of Cyprus from Salamis to Paphos (Acts 13:6). It was here that they encountered the Roman governor of the island, Sergius Paulus. He apparently suggested that Paul and Barnabas visit his home city of Pisidian Antioch (Acts 13:14), and they left Paphos by sea, indicating that this was the new harbor city.

Bibliography: D. W. J. Gill. "Paul's Travels through Cyprus (Acts 13:4-12)." *TynBul* 46 (1995) 219–28; F. G. Maier and V. Karageorghis. *Paphos: History and Archaeology* (1984); T. B. Mitford. "Roman Cyprus." *ANRW* II.7.2 (1980) 1285–1384.

DAVID W. J. GILL

PAPIAS pay´pee-uhs. Papias was bishop of Hierapolis in Asia Minor whom IRENAEUS describes as a "man of the early period" who was a "hearer" of John (the apostle or the "elder"?) and "a companion of Polycarp" (ca. 70 to 155–160 CE). Nothing else (including when he lived) is known about a man who appears to have been one of the leading figures of the post-apostolic era. Because he held a literal and material view of the millennium, EUSEBIUS considered him "a man of very little intelligence." His five-volume "Expositions of the Sayings of the Lord" appears to have included many traditions and legends about Jesus and the disciples (Papias was a devoted collector of anything remembered by those who followed the "disciples" or "elders"). It survives only as scattered quotations in Irenaeus and Eusebius. Of these the best known is his (puzzling) report about the authorship of the gospels of Matthew written in Hebrew and about Mark as an interpreter of Peter (Eusebius, *Hist. eccl.* 3.39). *See* APOSTOLIC FATHERS, CHURCH FATHERS; CANON OF THE NEW TESTAMENT; GOSPELS.

Bibliography: Michael Holmes. *The Apostolic Fathers: Greek Texts and English Translations.* 3rd ed. (2007).

MICHAEL W. HOLMES

PAPYRUS INSINGER. *See* INSINGER, PAPYRUS.

PAPYRUS, PAPYRI puh-p*i* ´ruhs, puh-p*i*´r*i* [πάπυρος **papyros**]. The papyrus plant flourished in antiquity in marshy regions (see Job 3:8) such as the Egyptian Delta, and the plant often reached a height of 4 or 5 m (*see* BULRUSH; REED; RUSHES). To make papyrus paper, the stem of the papyrus plant was cut into short sections, split open lengthwise, and formed into thin strips. These strips were placed on a flat surface with the fibers running in the same direction. A second layer was then placed on top of the lower layer, but at right angles; the product was a sheet of papyrus paper. The papyrus roll (or scroll) was made by gluing together the completed sheets side by side. Some papyrus scrolls could be rather long (e.g., the Harris Papyrus), but most were rarely longer than ca. 11 or 12 m.

For the field of OT studies, the Wadi Murabbaʿat Papyrus is of some significance. This papyrus is a late First Temple Hebrew PALIMPSEST: Murabbaʿat 17A (the first text written on the surface of this small papyrus) is a letter, very poorly preserved; Murabbaʿat 17B (the text written on top of the letter) is a crudely written list of names. The ELEPHANTINE PAPYRI are of enormous significance for the early Second Temple period. These Aramaic papyri of the 5th cent. BCE come from a Jewish colony on the island of Elephantine (just below the first cataract of the Nile). In part, these papyri constitute the family archives of two Jewish families. A number of these are of religious significance. For example, one of the papyri is a letter from a Jewish commander named Yedaniah to Bagoas (the governor of Judea). Within the letter, Yedaniah requests assistance in rebuilding the Temple after it was destroyed in an uprising in 410 BCE. A separate letter from Hananiah is addressed to Yedaniah and contains an exhortation for the Jews of Elephantine to observe the Passover and the Feast of Unleavened Bread.

Many of the papyri suggest religious syncretism at Elephantine. Of course, the SAMARIA PAPYRI (i.e., Wadi ed-Daliyeh Papyri), dated from the 4th cent. BCE, are also written in Aramaic, and constitute an important collection of family legal documents. The NASH PAPYRUS (a version of the Ten Commandments) is among the most famous late Second Temple papyri. W. F. Albright dated this papyrus to the 2nd cent. BCE, based on its script, and the script of this papyrus was subsequently of pivotal importance in establishing paleographic dates for the DEAD SEA SCROLLS. Some of the Dead Sea Scrolls were written on papyrus, but most were written on parchment.

Among the oldest and most important of the UNCIAL manuscripts of the NT are the CHESTER BEATTY PAPYRI and the BODMER PAPYRI. Chester Beatty Papyrus 45 is dated to the early 3rd cent. CE and preserves portions of Matthew, Mark, Luke, John, and Acts. The Chester Beatty Papyrus 46 originally contained ten epistles of Paul and is dated to ca. 200 CE. Note that the Pastoral Epistles were probably not part of this papyrus codex. Chester Beatty Papyrus 47 dates to the mid to late 3rd cent. CE and preserves portions of the book of Revelation. Bodmer Papyrus 66 preserves portions of the Gospel of John and dates to ca. 200 CE. Bodmer Papyrus 72 is the oldest copy of Jude and the two Epistles of Peter. In addition, however, it also contains the *Nativity of Mary*, Melito's *Homily on the Passover*, and the Apocryphal Correspondence of Paul to the Corinthians. This papyrus dates to the 3rd cent. CE.

The OXYRHYNCHUS PAPYRI have also proved to be of enormous importance for the fields of NT studies, because they contain some fragments of NT books (e.g., the Gospels and Revelation), early witnesses to the texts of Apollonius Rhodius, Aristophanes, Demosthenes, and Euripides, unknown texts of Menander, and various additional texts providing evidence for legal practices, economy, and society in general of Hellenes and Egyptians during the Roman and Byzantine empires. Of course, the NAG HAMMADI TEXTS constitute one of the most important collections of gnostic texts, including works such as the *Hypostasis of the Archons*, *The Gospel of Truth*, and the *Gospel of Thomas*. The Greek Magical Papyri also factor prominently in many discussions of the NT world. *See* EGERTON PAPYRUS; GNOSTICISM; INSCRIPTIONS; INSINGER, PAPYRUS; TEXT, NT; WRITING AND WRITING MATERIALS.

Bibliography: Hans Dieter Betz. *The Greek Magical Papyri in Translation*, 2nd ed. (1996); Frank Moore Cross. *Leaves from an Epigrapher's Notebook* (2003); Douglas Gropp. *Wadi Daliyeh* II. DJD 28 (2001); Larry W. Hurtado. *The Earliest Christian Artifacts: Manuscripts and Christian Origins* (2006); Bruce M. Metzger and Bart D. Ehrman. *The Text of the New Testament: Its Transmission, Corruption, and Restoration*, 4th ed. (2005); Bezalel Porten. *Archives from Elephantine* (1968); James M. Robinson, ed. *The Nag Hammadi Library* (1988).

CHRISTOPHER A. ROLLSTON

PARABLE pair'uh-buhl [מָשָׁל mashal; παραβολή parabolē]. The term *parable* is a transliteration of the Gk. parabolē, which signifies a comparison; literally it is something cast (ballō βάλλω) alongside (para παρά). Aristotle (4th cent. BCE) describes parabolē as "comparison," one of two types of examples used in argumentation (*Rhet.* 2.20.1–3; 3.19.5). In a 1st-cent. BCE Latin handbook of rhetoric, the *similitudo* (the equivalent of parabolē) is described as a type of speech that carries over a similarity or likeness from one thing to another and is used in argumentation to embellish, clarify, prove, or vivify (*Rhetorica ad Herennium* 4.45.58). In the literature of the Middle Ages the term *exemplum*, "example," designated a short story having a moral; thus the story was conceived as an example of proper or improper behavior.

A. Parable in the Ancient World

1. Old Testament

The OT uses the term mashal for literary units whose meaning is not immediately clear or easily understood (e.g., Pss 49:4 [Heb. 49:5]; 78:2; Prov 1:6). The LXX regularly translates mashal as "parable" (parabolē). In general, mashal is used to designate narratives (Ezek 17:2-10), brief figures (Ezek 24:3-5), traditional proverbs (1 Sam 24:13; Ezek 18:2), laments cast as brief narratives (Ezek 19:1-9), and sayings (Mic 2:4; Hab 2:5-6). Mashal is also used as a parallel to the RIDDLE (khidhah חִידָה; compare Ezek 17:1-2; Pss 49:4; 78:2; Hab 2:6), which is also a type of obscure or enigmatic speech. In Num 12:8 khidhah is contrasted with clear discourse. In Judg 14:12-18 and 1 Kgs 10:1 khidhah describes language that is purposely obscure and deliberately enigmatic.

A few narratives in the OT are similar to the stories Jesus told. Ezekiel 17:2-10 ("The Eagles and the Vine") is an allegory (mashal) spoken to the house of Israel (17:2), followed by an explanation (17:11-21).

Ezekiel 17:22-24 ("The Allegory of the Cedar") has no literary designation and is not followed by an explanation. Ezekiel 19:1-9 ("The Lions") and 19:10-14 ("The Vine") are narratives described as laments (**qinah** קִינָה) rather than **mashal**, but are clearly allegorical. Judges 9:8-15 is a fable, i.e., an unrealistic narrative ("The Olive Tree and the Bramble"). In the immediate context the narrative is explained allegorically (9:16-21), but no literary designation is given.

In their realism the following three narratives are the closest parallels to the stories in the NT. These narratives do not use cryptic language but reflect a mimetic fictional realism. In its literary context, 2 Sam 12:1-4 ("The Ewe Lamb") functions as an allegory (12:5-9) to expose David's mistreatment of Bathsheba and Uriah (2 Sam 11:1-27). In itself, however, the narrative is a realistic but tragic story about the abuse of the poor by the wealthy elite. David is portrayed as thinking it actually happened (12:5-6). Hence the story gives no hint of the use that Nathan will later make of it (12:7-12). Second Samuel 14:5-7 features a fictional narrative ("The Wise Woman of Tekoa") portrayed as having been invented by Joab (14:1-3, 19); the story functions in the context as an allegory of David's own behavior (14:12-13). David does not regard it as an allegory, however, but as the actual social situation of the widow (14:8-11). Hence, the story gives no hint of the use that Joab will later make of it. In itself the story appears to be an actual threat to the survival of a family. Ecclesiastes 9:14-15 is a brief narrative about a tiny city besieged by a powerful king. Lacking the forces to withstand the might of the great king, the city's destruction appeared certain, until a poor wise man by wisdom delivered the city. This portrayal of a rather typical situation in the ancient world is followed by the brief moral: "Wisdom is better than might" (Eccl 9:16).

2. Rabbinic parables

Rabbinic parables are considerably more numerous than the number of OT parables. Around 2,000 have been estimated to exist in rabbinic literature. Although the narratives in the OT antedated the time of Jesus, the texts in which rabbinic parables appear date from a much later period—anywhere from 200 to 500 years later. None of the parables in rabbinic literature have been dated in the first half of the 1st cent., although some few have been dated near the end of the 1st cent. Many rabbinic parables feature a king who generally symbolizes God and as a consequence lack the rustic village-life realism that is the hallmark of most of the stories attributed to Jesus. It is difficult to classify the rabbinic parables because of their diverse content, but some few of the stories feature animals, as is also the case with most of Aesop's fables. They are introduced similar to the ways parables in the NT are introduced. For example, "to what may the parable be likened, to ..." or "I will set forth a parable; to what may the parable be likened, to ...." A very few use simply "as" or "like." In some cases the introduction is simply "a parable" and then follows the story. The majority of the parables were followed by an application making the rabbi's point clear. Rabbinic parables were used in relation to the religious tradition that brought them into existence and concerned some aspect of God's behavior in relation to his people whether in the past or the present. Some few, however, may be described as secular stories. The parable itself was intended to serve as an explanation of the subject being addressed. *See* RABBINIC LITERATURE.

3. Aesop's fables

Aside from the narratives in the OT, a promising venue for contextualizing the stories of Jesus is the fable collections attributed to Aesop (and others). The FABLE, from the Latin *fabula* (story), is an ancient narrative form that typically, but not always, features a brief moral. Fables circulated widely in the ancient world. Usually, the fable personified inanimate objects or animals, or perhaps better, they portrayed human beings as animals and inanimate objects. The plot and dramatic action of the fable, in spite of this unrealistic characterization (viz. animals treated as human beings), were nevertheless quite realistic in the way the personified animals in the narrative interacted.

B. Parable in Early Christian Literature

1. Synoptic Gospels

In the Synoptic Gospels, narratives, proverbs, simple straightforward discourse, and other sayings with a proverbial character are designated "parable," which generally means for the evangelists that they have a deeper religious significance. Thus early Christian literature appears to designate as "parable" any saying of Jesus whose meaning is not immediately clear in terms of Christian faith and theology. Jesus, being who he was in the faith of the church, simply would not traffic in superficial discourse; therefore what appears to be banal language is judged to be figurative or comparative discourse and is given a deeper significance.

Matthew, Mark, and Luke describe a variety of Jesus' sayings as parables and sometimes differ among themselves as to what constitutes a parable. For example, a narrative (a story) describing the hazards of farming in 1st-cent. Palestine (Matt 13:3-8//Mark 4:3-8//Luke 8:5-8*a*) is described as parable and explained as figurative language describing the difficulties of evangelism in the 1st cent. (Matt 13:18-23//Mark 4:14-20//Luke 8:11-15). A saying by Jesus about how to identify a change between two seasons of the year (Matt 24:32//Mark 13:28//Luke 21:29-30) is designated as parable and followed by slightly different explanations (Matt 24:33//Mark 13:29//Luke 21:31), treating what on the surface appears to be common wisdom as a figure with religious meaning. Luke 6:39, which appears to be common sense about one blind man leading another, is identified as a parable, but Luke gives it no appended explanation. Matthew has the same saying (15:14*b*), but apparently does not regard it as a parable. Matthew bypasses "the blind leading the blind" and describes a saying about "what comes out of the mouth defiles and not what goes in" as parable (v. 15), as Mark 7:14-15 also does (v. 17). Both Mark and Matthew provide the saying (Mark 7:15//Matt 15:11) with a religious explanation (Mark 7:18-23//Matt 15:17-20). Apparently Matthew neither regards the "blind leading the blind" nor the obscure saying at Matt 15:13 ("Every plant that my heavenly Father has not planted will be uprooted") as parables having deeper significance. Luke (4:23) again describes without explanation an ancient proverb ("Doctor, cure yourself") as parable. Luke even describes a longer saying giving sensible advice (compare Prov 25:6-7) about proper etiquette at a banquet (Luke 14:7-10) as a parable, and follows it with an early Christian explanation (14:11; compare the reversal sayings; Matt 23:12; Luke 18:14; Jas 4:10). Luke designates the apparently commonsense advice about a new patch on an old garment and new wine in old wineskins (Luke 5:36-39) as a "single" parable, but provides no explanations for the two sayings. Matthew (9:16-17) and Mark (2:21-22) have the same two sayings but designate neither one as parable and do not offer an appended explanation.

Each evangelist draws theological and moral lessons from the parable for the community of faith. The evangelists' understanding of each parable is clarified by the literary contexts in which the parable is embedded, by the evangelists' revision of the story to suit the context, and particularly by the evangelists' appended conclusions and introductions. Scholars describe this comparative way of reading the text as redaction and narrative criticism (*see* NARRATIVE CRITICISM; REDACTION CRITICISM, NT). For example, the Lost Sheep story appears in Matt 18:10-14 = Luke 15:3-7 = *Gos. Thom.* 107. Each evangelist has embedded the story in a different literary context. Matthew uses the story in the context of a speech of Jesus (18:1–19:1) on matters relating to discipleship (the "little ones" are disciples, compare Matt 18:6). Matthew's conclusion informs the reader that the story is about God's ability to keep Jesus' "little ones" safe (18:14). Hence the reader is encouraged to read the "straying sheep" in the story as one of Jesus' disciples (one who "believes in him"). Luke, on the other hand, uses the story as Jesus' response to the snide criticism of the Pharisees that Jesus associated with "tax collectors and sinners." In Luke's story the sheep does not go astray but is "lost." Luke's conclusion (15:7) informs the reader that the story is about God's ability to save lost sinners. In Luke's story the shepherd returns home to celebrate with friends and neighbors the finding of the lost sheep (15:6), an allegorical flourish to emphasize the rejoicing in heaven over the redemption of even one lost sinner, an element lacking in Matthew's story. The *Gospel of Thomas* is not a narrative but simply a collection of sayings and stories arranged for the most part in no easily discernible order. The parable in *Gos. Thom.* 107, hence, has neither literary narrative context nor appended conclusion to suggest how the parable is understood by the compiler of the collection. The concluding line to the story, however, provides a reason why the shepherd left the ninety-nine sheep in the wilderness to search for one strayed (or lost) sheep ("I love you more than the ninety-nine"), an element not provided in the stories of Matthew and Luke.

2. Gospel of John

The Gospel of John neither uses the word *parable*, nor does it include any of the stories of Jesus found in the Synoptic Gospels. John does designate some of Jesus' discourse as paroimia (παροιμία), a word usually meaning "PROVERB" or "maxim" (compare 2 Pet 2:22). In the Gospel of John, however, paroimia has the character of obscure language, such as a riddle or figure, containing another more significant meaning (compare Sir 39:3). For example, Jesus' statement about the sheep and the shepherd (John 10:1-5) is described by John as paroimia (John 10:6). Such language is enigmatic discourse as opposed to clear or plain language (John 16:25-29).

3. *Gospel of Thomas*

The *Gospel of Thomas* shares with the Synoptic Gospels a number of the narratives of Jesus and also has narratives not contained in the Synoptic Gospels. But *Thomas* does not designate any of them as parables. *Thomas* also shares other sayings the Synoptic Gospels described as parables, also without describing them as parables; e.g., Luke 6:39//*Gos. Thom.* 34; Mark 7:14-15//*Gos. Thom.* 14; Mark 6:4//*Gos. Thom.* 31; Luke 5:36-39//*Gos. Thom.* 47. Although the *Gospel of Thomas* does not use the word *parable*, the initial saying in the gospel (logion 1) implies that each saying has hidden meanings: "Whoever finds the explanation of these sayings will never die." Whereas the Synoptic Gospels and John find only some sayings of Jesus to be parables or riddles, the *Gospel of Thomas* regards the entire discourse of Jesus to have specific hidden meanings.

4. *Apocryphon of James*

The *Apocryphon of James* is the only early Christian text to preserve ancient titles of parables, but the stories to which these titles relate are not identified. The titles are: "the Shepherds," "the Seed," "the Building," "the Lamps of the Virgins," "the Wage of the Workman," "the Didrachmae," and "the Woman" (*Ap. Jas.* 8:1-10). It is not certain that any of these titles can be related to the stories known in early Christian literature, even though some of the titles seem well suited to stories narrated elsewhere: e.g, "the Wage of the Workman" (compare Matt 20:1-15), the "Lamps of the Virgins" (compare Matt 25:1-12),

Parables in Order of Multiple Versions

Parables	Four Versions
The Sower	Mark 4:3-8//Matt 13:3-8//Luke 8:5-8//*Gos. Thom.* 9
The Mustard Seed	Mark 4:31-32//Matt 13:31-32//Luke 13:19//*Gos. Thom.* 20
The Vineyard	Mark 12:1-8//Matt 21:33-39//Luke 20:9-15//*Gos. Thom.* 65

Parables	Three Versions
The Leaven	Matt 13:33//Luke 13:21//*Gos. Thom.* 96
The Lost Sheep	Matt 18:12-13//Luke 15:4-6//*Gos. Thom.* 107
The Feast	Matt 22:2-13//Luke 14:16-24//*Gos. Thom.* 64

Parables	Two Versions
The Unclean Spirit	Matt 12:43-45//Luke 11:24-26
Settling out of Court	Matt 5:25-26//Luke 12:58-59
The Two Houses	Matt 7:24-27//Luke 6:48-49
The Entrusted Money	Matt 25:14-28//Luke19:12-27
Good Seed and Weeds	Matt 13:24-30//*Gos. Thom.* 57
A Merchant and a Pearl	Matt 13:45-46//*Gos. Thom.* 76
A Net Thrown into the Sea	Matt 13:47-48//*Gos. Thom.* 8
A Rich Man	Luke 12:16-20//*Gos. Thom.* 63

Parables	Single Versions
A Sprouting Seed	Mark 4:26-29
A Man Going on a Journey	Mark 13:34
The Ten Maidens	Matt 25:1-12
Settling Accounts with Servants	Matt 18:23-34
Laborers in a Vineyard	Matt 20:1-15
A Man Had Two Sons	Matt 21:28-31
Hidden Treasure	Matt 13:44
A Man and Two Debtors	Luke 7:41-42
An Injured Man on the Jericho Road	Luke 10:30-35
The Persistent Friend	Luke 11:5-7
Two Farmers and a Fig Tree	Luke 13:6-9
A Tower Builder	Luke 14:28-30
A Warring King	Luke 14:31-32
A Woman Searching for a Coin	Luke 15:8-9
The Fired Steward	Luke 16:1-7
A Father and Two Sons	Luke 15:11-32
A Rich Man and Lazarus the Beggar	Luke 16:19-31
Management of Slaves	Luke 17:7-9
The Judge and the Widow	Luke 18:2-5
A Pharisee and a Toll Collector	Luke 18:10-13
A Woman Carrying a Jar	*Gos. Thom.* 97
The Killer	*Gos. Thom.* 98
Children in a Field	*Gos. Thom.* 21
Hidden Treasure	*Gos. Thom.* 109
The Date Palm Shoot	*Ap. Jas.* 7:24-28
The Spike of Wheat	*Ap. Jas.* 12:23-27
A Grain of Wheat	*Ap. Jas.* 8:16-23

Figure 1: Parables in order of multiple versions

"the Didrachmae" (compare Luke 15:8-9), and "the Woman" (compare Matt 13:33//Luke 13:21//*Gos. Thom.* 96, 97). In the *Apocryphon of James*, two narratives (not specifically called parable in the introductory comparative frame) are treated as figures: the "Date Palm Shoot" (7:24-28) is given an allegorical explanation that is both cryptic and obscure (7:29-35). The "Spike of Wheat" (12:23-27) is cryptically explained (12:27-30) as an admonishment to "reap an ear of life and be filled with the kingdom." "A Grain of Wheat" (8:16-23) is so heavily allegorized that it is difficult to see a realistic narrative at the base of it. Its interpretation (8:24-27) suggests that people receive the kingdom through knowledge.

C. An Inventory of Narrative Parables Attributed to Jesus

There are no standardized titles to the narrative parables, but they have traditionally been titled on the basis of readers' responses to the parable. The following inventory will retain enough of the traditional title to identify the parable and will list parables in the order of their multiple versions in early Christian literature.

In those cases where multiple versions of a story exist, variations exist in the way the story is told. They are never identical, although in some cases the differences may be slight. For a story that is nearly identical in all versions, compare the story of "The Leaven" (Matt 13:33//Luke 13:21). Compare also the multiple versions of "The Sower." In Mark 4:3-8 and Matt 13:3-8 the versions are quite close but Luke's version is much shorter (Luke 8:5-8). In other cases, such marked and stylized differences change the story remarkably. For example, by comparing versions of the "Lost Sheep," we see that Luke ends the story with the shepherd bringing the previously lost sheep home to celebrate its finding with friends but leaving the ninety-nine in the wilderness to fend for themselves (15:4-6), a feature lacking in the versions in Matthew (18:12-13) and the *Gospel of Thomas* (107). In some cases the differences are so great that the versions appear to be different stories. Compare the story of "A Rich Man" in Luke 12:16-20 and the *Gospel of Thomas* (*Gos. Thom.* 63). In Luke the protagonist is already a farmer who has a bumper crop he must care for, but in the *Gospel of Thomas* he is a man who intends on becoming a farmer as a good investment. Compare also the remarkably different versions of "The Entrusted Money" in Matt 25:14-28 and Luke 19:12-27. The version in Mark 13:34 is a different story in its present form.

Scholars account for these differences with reference either to performance or interpretive variations made to the stories during their transmission through the oral period of the Jesus traditions, roughly from 30 CE (the public career of Jesus) to around 70 CE (the approximate date for the composition of the earliest extant Gospel), or to variations that occurred when the Jesus tradition reached written form. Many scholars think that Matthew and Luke used Mark as a source for their Gospels, as well as another text called Q (*see* Q, QUELLE), meaning "source," that no longer exists in manuscript form. Hence narrative parables that Matthew and Luke share with Mark are later than Mark, and the differences between them are likely due to the editing of Mark's version by Matthew and Luke. Where Matthew and Luke share a story not in Mark, the differences are due to dependence on the earlier hypothetical source Q. Scholars disagree on how the *Gospel of Thomas* and the synoptic tradition are related (*see* SYNOPTIC PROBLEM; THOMAS, GOSPEL OF).

D. Why Did Jesus Speak in Parables?

Why would Jesus have spoken in such indirect language? Early Christian literature offers three different explanations. Mark, around 70 CE, provides the earliest explanation. Jesus spoke in parables in order to ensure that the secret of the kingdom of God would only be understood by his disciples (4:10-11); for those outside the circle of his followers everything is presented in parables so that "they may indeed look, but not perceive, and may indeed listen, but not understand; so that they may not turn again and be forgiven" (4:12, taken from Isa 6:8-10 LXX). Mark says that Jesus always addressed the crowds with parables (4:34) to keep them from understanding, but 4:33 seems to leave open the possibility of limited understanding on the part of the crowds (i.e., "as they were able to hear"). And Mark does portray the religious authorities understanding that the parable of the Vineyard was directed at them (12:1-12). This breakdown of the theory of parables in Mark suggests to some that Mark may have inherited the idea from earlier tradition (Carlston).

In a parallel passage in Luke the disciples ask Jesus "what this parable [i.e., the story of the Sower] meant" (8:9). Jesus replies that the disciples have been given the ability to know the secrets of the kingdom of God but these secrets are presented to the crowds in parables, "so that 'looking they may not perceive, and listening they may not understand'" (8:10*b*); Mark's offensive last phrase ("so that they may not turn again and be forgiven") is omitted. Presumably in Luke parables about things other than the kingdom of God might be understood by the crowds.

Matthew explains that only the disciples have been given the ability to know the secrets of the kingdom (13:11), and if the crowds even have an inkling of understanding, they will lose it (13:12). Jesus speaks to the crowds in parables, because "seeing they do not perceive, and hearing they do not listen, nor do they understand" (13:13; again Mark's offensive last phrase is omitted). The crowds do not understand Jesus' parables because Isaiah's prophecy (Isa 6:8-10) is fulfilled in them: they have deliberately hardened their hearts and closed their eyes (Matt 13:14-15; but compare Matt 13:11, where the crowds were not given the ability to understand). Scholars disagree on whether any of these explanations describe the actual circumstances of Jesus' public career.

E. Narrative Parables and Literary Types

In modern study the term *parable* is frequently used as an inclusive term to describe the entire corpus of Jesus' "parabolic discourse," i.e., to include under the designation all the different literary units referred to as "parable" in early Christian literature. In a narrow sense, however, the term only designates the stories Jesus told, which are more specifically described as "narrative parables" in order to distinguish them from other literary units called "parable." The story, a narrative having a beginning, middle, and end (i.e., having a plot; see Aristotle, *Poet.* 7.1–7), is the classic form of the parable in early Christian literature (*see* NARRATIVE LITERATURE).

In early Christian literature Jesus is portrayed as regularly using figurative language—a type of discourse saying more than what was meant, or not meaning what was said, but rather something else entirely. Modern scholars have aimed at defining his discourse more precisely and have described it in the following ways.

1. Simile and similitude

A simile is a brief comparison using "like" or "as" (Matt 23:27; Luke 11:44), although this form appears very few times in the Gospel literature. More typical is the similitude, a comparative form using "like" or "as" in which the comparison is extended with more detail (see Matt 13:33, 44-46). Many scholars also identify SIMILITUDES as brief narratives used in a direct comparison with "like" or "as" (e.g., "the kingdom of heaven is like . . .") because what is being compared to the kingdom is not a simple brief statement but a minimal narrative having the basic elements of plot. In the case of Matt 13:33, 44-46 the narratives are quite brief but in other cases the narrative is rather lengthy (e.g., Matt 20:1-15). Certain other narratives are not introduced by a comparative frame but are nevertheless treated comparatively by the evangelists (e.g., Luke 18:1-8). Another form is the aphorism, a terse, somewhat puzzling statement of a principle or precept (e.g., Matt 10:16*b*; Luke 6:39; 9:60). In some cases scholars describe as aphorisms (Mark 2:21-22) sayings that seem better identified as proverbs (a short pithy statement summarizing some aspect of traditional community wisdom).

2. Allegory

Early Christians explained these stories in a variety of ways. In some cases they regarded them as elaborate allegories. An ALLEGORY deliberately composed as an allegory is a narrative whose various elements are created by the author to signify something different from what they are. But allegory has also become a hermeneutical strategy for reading non-allegorical narratives as if they were allegories. For example, the Sower (Mark 4:3-8) on its surface is a narrative about farming, but Mark explains it (4:14-20) as if it were describing Christian evangelism. In other words, the elements of the narrative are not what they appear to be on the surface, but rather they are ciphers representing something else. A sower is not a farmer but a preacher, the birds are not birds but Satan, the seed is not seed but God's word, the soils are not dirt but kinds of hearers, the hazards faced by the seed are in the allegorical reading difficulties facing 1st-cent. Christians. Besides the Sower, only two other narrative parables in the Gospels are given extensive allegorical interpretations, both in Matthew: "Good Seed and Weeds" (Matt 13:24-30, 37-43) and "A Net Thrown into the Sea" (Matt 13:47-50).

3. Example stories

One of the narrative parables ("An Injured Man on the Jericho Road," Luke 10:30-35) is explained as an example story (compare the context in which Luke embeds it: 10:25-29, 36-37) in which the Samaritan's behavior demonstrates what it means to love the neighbor. Some modern scholars have argued there are also other example stories in the corpus (e.g., Luke 12:16-21; 14:7-14; 16:19-31; 18:9-14).

4. Exhortation

Other narrative parables are explained in the Gospels as teaching Christian morality and practice, or are used for purposes of exhortation. An example of a parable understood to exhort Christians to watch for the absent Lord's return is Matt 25:1-13. Luke used a story about a farmer with an unexpected abundant harvest (12:5-21) to make the moral point that materialistic Christians are fools, for true "wealth" is spiritual (12:21).

5. Parables and the kingdom of God

Many of the narrative parables are compared to the kingdom of God/Heaven/Father. The introductory comparative frame to the story is usually translated "the kingdom of God is like . . . ." The word *kingdom*, **basileia** (βασιλεία), was used in antiquity to describe the reign, or rule, of a king, i.e., the sphere of his influence, rather than the geographical boundaries of the king's realm. Applied to God the term designates God's sphere of influence rather than a specific location, like heaven, e.g. Hence the comparison should be understood as follows: "as things go in this parable, so they go under the reign or authority of God." Out of a database of forty stories only fifteen are compared to God's reign in all extant versions. Four are compared to other things: the "Man" (*Gos. Thom.* 8), one who hears and does the words of Jesus (Matt 7:24//Luke 6:47), the return of the Son of Man (Matt 25:13-14, 31), the disciples (Luke 19:11-12), the Word (*Ap. Jas.* 8:16). Nineteen stories lack an introductory comparative frame and fifteen of the stories do not have an appended explanation. Seven of the stories have neither introductory comparative frames nor appended explanations (Hedrick).

F. Realism and the Parables

In general the parables realistically portray 1st-cent. village life in Palestine. If the stories are read for themselves rather than for underlying religious or moral significance, they are found to present such ordinary matters as, e.g., the hiring and paying of day laborers (Matt 20:1-15), dishonest employees (Luke 16:1-7), a dysfunctional family (Luke 15:11-32), two men praying in the Temple (Luke 18:10-13), a lost coin (Luke 15:8-9), how invited guests treat their invitations to a dinner party (*Gos. Thom.* 64), the risks involved in farming (Mark 4:3-8), a hidden treasure found in a field (Matt 13:44), and two farmers debating what to do about a fig tree in a vineyard (Luke 13:6-9). Since the latter half of the 1st cent., the realism of the stories has been generally ignored in favor of pursuing religious meanings in essentially secular stories.

Unlike the rabbinic parables, only a few stories treat the actions of kings and the elite class: a marriage feast is given by a king (Matt 22:2-13), a nobleman departs to receive a kingdom (Luke 19:12-27), a king goes to war against another king (Luke 14:31-32), a rich man in Hades dialogues with Father Abraham (Luke 16:19-31). When compared to the realistic stories about Palestinian village life, these stories lack realism. More likely they have been enhanced or changed in order to make them more suitable to allegorical interpretation. For example, the story of "The Vineyard" (Mark 12:1-11) is a thinly disguised allegory about God (//the vineyard owner) and Israel (//the vineyard, compare Isa 5:1-7). God sent the prophets (//the servants) to the people of Israel. They were mistreated and killed. But last of all the owner sent his beloved son (//Jesus). The tenants (//Israel's leaders) killed him, as well, and cast him out of the vineyard. The owner of the vineyard (//God) will take his judgment on the tenants (//Israel's leaders). Interestingly, these allegorical features are not found in the version of the story in the *Gospel of Thomas* (65), where the story appears as an everyday matter of leasing property and collecting rent previously agreed to.

Even in the realistic stories describing Palestinian village life one meets with unusual features, or figurative language. For example, in the story of "A Father and Two Sons" (Luke 15:11-32), the narrative unambiguously uses figurative language when it describes the prodigal son as wasting his livelihood in loose living (15:13) and characterizes him as dead/alive (15:24) and lost/found (15:32). Such figurative language is rare in the stories. In the story of "The Mustard Seed," at the end of the growth process the mustard seed is said to have become a tree in Matthew (13:32) and Luke (13:19), rather than the more realistic large shrub (Mark 4:32). The exaggeration may be due to the story's adjustment to fit Ezek 31:2-6 and Dan 4:10-12. Even Mark (followed by Matt 13:32) turns the mustard plant into the greatest of all shrubs (Mark 4:32). In the story of "The Leaven" (Matt 13:33//Luke 13:21) a woman hides a little yeast in what is equivalent to three bushels of flour. The excessive amount of flour seems almost a caricature when one thinks of a Palestinian woman baking daily bread for her family. The intrusion of the voice of God (Luke 12:20) into a story about a wealthy farmer with a bumper crop (Luke 12:16-20) is completely unexpected in such secular stories, since unambiguous religious features play a role in only four stories out of forty (Luke 10:30-35; 12:16-20; 16:19-31; 18:10-13).

G. Contemporary Hermeneutical Strategies for New Testament Narrative Parables

Extant texts from the middle 1st cent. (Paul and Josephus) provide only scanty historical information about Jesus, and neither author describes Jesus speaking in parables. The earliest extant Gospels (the last half of the 1st cent.), however, describe his language as figurative, and most describe him as one who used narrative parables in his discourse (the Gospel of John does not). Although there is no extant evidence before 70 CE that Jesus spoke in parables, the judgment of modern scholarship is that Jesus did compose and use narrative parables in his public discourse. Nevertheless, there is no way of knowing for certain what hermeneutical use he made of his parables. The first auditors of the parables made sense of them, or not, as 1st-cent. Palestinian Jews, but certainly not as post-70 CE Christians.

How the parables were treated during the period from Jesus' death (ca. 30 CE) to the earliest Gospels, shortly after the mid-1st-cent. (ca. 70 CE), is likewise unknown, again because of the lack of sources. But scholars postulate the existence of an oral period between the public career of Jesus and the writing of the earliest extant Gospels in which the Jesus traditions survived in the memories of his earliest followers and were passed on to others by word of mouth (*see* TRADITION, ORAL). During the period of their oral transmission the narratives were modified by both deliberate changes and the inevitable but unintentional changes that are a part of any repeated oral performance. The stories were expanded, condensed, and enhanced; in some cases they gained introductions and conclusions. The process of translating them from the indigenous language of the Palestinian peasant, Aramaic, into Greek, the language of the broader Greco-Roman world, also involved adjustments to the parables to accommodate the shift from one ancient culture to another (Jeremias). During the forty years or so of oral migration of the parables from one language to another, from one culture to another, the essentially secular stories of Jesus did not suit the changed circumstances of his followers; explanations were necessary to accommodate the stories for a post-resurrection community of faith. That accommodation has been going on since the latter half of the 1st cent. All of the strategies described below are currently being practiced simultaneously both in the scholarly guild and ecclesiastical circles.

1. Allegorical interpretation

Allegory is an ancient way of reading a text by ignoring its literal surface meaning and finding new meanings that are not stated as such in the text. The ancient Greeks, e.g., allegorized the Homeric epics in an attempt to protect the poet and the ancient classics from the charge of impiety. The attempts to explain away the myths were condemned by Plato as trivial (*Phaedr.* 229e–230a) and injurious to the youth, for they deceived the youth as to the true nature of the poets' compositions (*Resp.* 376e–378e). Nevertheless, allegorical interpretation persisted into the NT period and beyond. As a method, it enabled the allegorist to ignore the problems of the simple surface meaning of the text and give it a reading sympathetic to the views of the allegorist. Philo, a 1st-cent. Jew writing in Greek, explained Torah by means of allegory to make it more acceptable to the Greek mind. Paul used the method in argumentation (Gal 4:21-31) as did Matthew (1:18-23; compare Isa 7:14) and Mark (compare 4:3-9, 14-20). Reading the stories of Jesus as allegories (i.e., as narratives whose various elements are cryptic ciphers for concealed Christian truths) has remained in Christian exegesis the popular way of explaining the stories since the second half of the 1st cent.

An allegorical reading essentially works in the following way. A reader brings a different (usually Christian) story to the parable and in the reading finds points of similarity between the story brought to the reading and the parable itself. Mark's interpretation of the parable of "The Sower" (4:14-20) is a good example of the method. Craig L. Blomberg has sought a theoretical basis rehabilitating allegory as a plausible way of reading the parables. He argues for a restrained and limited allegorizing by citing certain standardized metaphors in OT and rabbinic literature, which he finds in Jesus' parables, and uses them as controls to limit excessive allegorizing. Jesus' story about "Two Farmers and a Fig Tree" (Luke 13:6-9) is therefore an allegory. The vineyard symbolizes Israel, the owner of the vineyard is an image for God, and the fig tree represents the leaders of Israel. Read against Luke's literary context (13:1-5), the parable makes two points: imminent judgment hangs over the heads of Israel's leaders, and God's mercy is extended for only a short time. "The announcement of judgment [on the tree] becomes a call to turn to God." People hearing the parable must individually make their own personal response.

2. Single moral point

No alternatives to allegory as the way of understanding the parables emerged until the late 19th cent. Adolf Jülicher argued that the essential idea of parable was comparison rather than allegory or metaphor, both of which he regarded as essentially enigmatic and indirect speech. As comparison was basic to the parable, so metaphor was basic to allegory, he argued. He sorted the parables into three types: similitude, which was a briefly expanded simile; fable (i.e., the narrative parable), which was a similitude extended into narrative; and example story, a freely invented story illustrating the truth the parable addressed. Parables comprised two parts: a picture part (the parable) and a "matter" part (the unspoken "issue," which was the real subject of the picture part). Something learned in the picture part could be applied to the unspoken "matter" part. Hence the parables were essentially instructional in nature. The stories worked by a single point of comparison between the picture part and the matter part. The single point of comparison is where the two parts came together, and it should be expressed in a universal moral of the widest and broadest generality. For example, Jülicher's "moral" for the parable of "Two Farmers and a Fig Tree" (Luke 13:6-9) is that all who do not repent will perish.

3. Metaphor

In 1935 C. H. Dodd argued that parables were metaphors. A metaphor is a way of describing one known thing in language appropriate to another known thing so as to suggest an essential similarity between them, or put another way, one thing is described as if it were the other. For example, Robert Frost, in his poem "Bereft," describes swirling leaves as a coil that hisses and strikes. In this metaphor a snake is described in language appropriate to swirling leaves on a windy day. Or put another way, the subject of the metaphor was the snake; the vehicle carrying the image of the snake was language about leaves and wind. Parables introduced by the comparative frame "the kingdom of God is like . . . ," as well as many others not so introduced, were thought to cast light upon the meaning of the concept "kingdom of God." In other words, the subject of the metaphorical story was the kingdom of God and the vehicle was language about life in Palestinian villages; or put another way, the kingdom is described in language appropriate to Palestinian village life. Hence, as things go in the story so go things under the reign of God. Exactly how the parable relates to the kingdom is never stated, however. The specifics of the comparison are left for auditors/readers to fill in. Dodd explains that the parable of the Sower, a story not introduced by a comparative frame relating the story to the kingdom, illustrates the arrival of the kingdom of God in Jesus' ministry in the vehicle of harvest. John Dominic Crossan describes the difference between allegory and metaphor in this way: allegory instructs by referencing correct information, but metaphor reveals by bringing the inexpressible into language. Robert Funk argues that the parable "An Injured Man on the Jericho Road" (Luke 10:30-35) invites readers to take up a position by the victim in the ditch, and the "meaning" depends on how readers put themselves in the story.

4. Existential narrative

In 1967 Dan O. Via Jr. argued that the narrative parables do not function as allegory, metaphor, or image. They are instead freely invented fictions and they work as any narrative does. As literary art they can be appreciated for what they are in themselves, just like any other art form. He described the parables as "literary objects," which do not reference but instead bring attention to focus on themselves. Hence they are autonomous from their creator. This meant that whatever Jesus had intended with the parables is of no consequence, since what he intended is no longer available to us today. All we have are the parables, the products of his creative activity. These brief stories dramatize how Jesus understood human existence and essentially describe different ways of being human. The different ways of being human are both positive and negative, which Via calls authentic existence (i.e., existence in faith) and inauthentic existence (i.e., existence in unfaith). In the "Laborers in the Vineyard" (Matt 20:1-15) the grumbling workers understand life only in terms of merit. They want to be responsible for their own security, and are not willing to accept the risk of relying on God's grace.

5. Stories for social reform

In 1994 William R. Herzog II argued that the parables were not figurative. Rather they were stories typifying the oppressed situation of Palestinian peasants at the hands of the wealthy elite. The stories mirrored the oppressed conditions under which the peasants lived and were intended to teach. Herzog argues that this understanding of parables posits a historical reason for the crucifixion of Jesus. He asks, why would anyone want to crucify a teacher who told charming stories encouraging morality? Herzog's answer is that Jesus was a threat to the state precisely because he sought to inform the peasants about their oppression and lead them to transform society. Thus informed, peasants are empowered to remake and humanize society. His strategy is to read the parables in the context of the social and economic world of agrarian peasants and wealthy elite. His reading of the "Laborers in a Vineyard" (Matt 20:1-15) reflects his understanding of the clash between wealthy elite and disenfranchised peasant. The owner of the vineyard is far from being a generous man; rather he takes advantage of the unemployed workers standing in the marketplace late in the day by offering them work without a wage agreement. At day's end he pays them all the same wage in the reverse order of their hiring to show the first hired how little value he placed on their full day's work. The denarius he paid to all was not a living wage, for day laborers do not work every day. When the owner is challenged by one worker about the basic unfairness of the pay, the owner banishes him, thus depriving him of future employment. The dismissal is intended to intimidate the other workers, whom he blames for the situation (Matt 20:13).

6. Parables as poetic fictions

In 1994 Charles W. Hedrick argued that the parables were invented narrative fictions, the products of Jesus' creative imagination and observation of the world about him. They realistically portray aspects of Palestinian antiquity. Successful narrative fiction works by calling attention to itself and not by being deliberately referential. Realistic fictions are designed to pull the auditor/reader into their fictional worlds, in which discoveries about self and world may be made. Readers work out discoveries for themselves (or not) in the nexus between the narrative and what they bring to it. The narrative voice of the parables does not guide readers to a specific resolution of the narrative's complications. In fact, the stories do not conclude; they simply stop with complications left unresolved. Hence parables are open-ended, leaving resolutions up to readers. Because of their polysemy (that is, the story is capable of a diversity of meanings) and what different readers bring to the parable, they are capable of a wide range of plausible readings, as the history of parables interpretation attests. In the story of "A Pharisee and Toll Collector" (Luke 18:10-13) the auditor/reader is presented with two flawed characters praying in the Temple. The Pharisee is genuinely grateful to God that he has followed Torah and been saved from a life of sin. He believes his obedience to Torah has brought him God's approval and absolution. Thus for the Pharisee God is totally predictable and must accept him as righteous. The toll collector is cast as a penitent sinner seeking God's mercy because of his sins. But oddly, he confesses no sins, makes no offer of restitution to those he has offended, and does not resolve to follow Torah in the future. He expects God to act graciously toward him on the basis of his contrite attitude alone. The complication facing the reader is this: which flawed hero will be acceptable to God? Whom might the narrator of this story pick to be the one God accepts? Hedrick says neither one; rather the design of the story suggests that God would likely pick those who can recognize the absurdity in their own cherished religious convictions that presume on the divine prerogative—something neither man in the story was able to do. *See* BIBLICAL INTERPRETATION, HISTORY OF; LITERARY INTERPRETATION, NT; METAPHOR IN THEOLOGY; READER RESPONSE CRITICISM.

Bibliography: Erich Auerbach. *Mimesis: The Representation of Reality in Western Literature* (1953); Kenneth E. Bailey. *Poet and Peasant* and *Through Peasant Eyes* (1980); M. A. Beavis. "Parables and Fable." *CBQ* 52 (1990) 473–98; Craig L. Blomberg. *Interpreting the Parables* (1990); James Breech. *The Silence of*

Jesus (1983); C. E. Carlston. *The Parables of the Triple Tradition* (1975); John Dominic Crossan. *In Parables* (1973); C. H. Dodd. *The Parables of the Kingdom* (1961); John R. Donahue. *The Gospel in Parable: Metaphor, Narrative, and Theology in the Synoptic Gospels* (1988); Robert W. Funk. *Funk on Parables* (2006); Robert Funk. *Parables and Presence* (1982); Charles W. Hedrick. *Many Things in Parables: Jesus and His Modern Critics* (2004); William R. Herzog II. *Parables as Subversive Speech* (1994); Arland J. Hultgren. *The Parables of Jesus* (2000); Joachim Jeremias. *The Parables of Jesus* (1963); Adolf Jülicher. *Die Gleichnisreden Jesu* (1899); Warren Kissinger. *The Parables of Jesus: A History of Interpretation and Bibliography* (1979); John S. Kloppenborg. *The Tenants in the Vineyard* (2006); Harvey K. McArthur and Robert M. Johnston. *They Also Taught in Parables: Rabbinic Parables from the First Centuries of the Christian Era* (1990); Marsh H. McCall Jr. *Ancient Rhetorical Theories of Simile and Comparison* (1969); Norman Perrin. *Jesus and the Language of the Kingdom* (1976); Bernard Brandon Scott. *Hear Then the Parable* (1989); Dan Otto Via Jr. *The Parables: Their Literary and Existential Dimension* (1967); Brad H. Young. *Jesus and His Rabbinic Parables* (1989).

CHARLES W. HEDRICK

PARACLETE pair´uh-kleet [παράκλητος paraklētos]. The word *paraclete* comes from the Gk. verbal adjective paraklētos, and means "someone called in assistance" or "advocate," from the verb parakaleō (παρακαλέω), meaning "give comfort or counsel." The word does not occur in the OT and is found in the NT only in John 14:16, 26; 15:26; 16:7; 1 John 2:1, translated as "advocate." Biblical scholars and theologians use *paraclete* as a technical term for the spiritual form that Jesus's presence will take in and among the Johannine community after his death and resurrection, to comfort and counsel them (John 14:16). *See* COMFORT.

Attempts to trace back the concept of "paraclete" or "advocate" to Gnostic or Jewish antecedents have largely remained inconclusive. The *Yawar* of the Mandean texts is a helper, and so are angels like Michael in the Qumran texts. This is not the primary function of the Paraclete in the Gospel of John.

An ancient tradition sees in Jesus the "advocate" of his faithful with the Father (attested in 1 John 2:1). If the faithful have sinned, Jesus Christ will be an advocate for them with the Father. Similar texts are found in Rom 8:34 and Heb 7:25; 9:24. There are reasons to assume that the author of 1 John avoided explicitly the idea of the Spirit being the advocate of the faithful due to his reserve toward charismatic tendencies of his adversaries.

In John 14:16, the "Spirit of Truth" is introduced as "another Advocate." The wording seems to imply that the HOLY SPIRIT will be sent in assistance of the faithful besides or after Christ as the advocate of his believers (see above for 1 John 2:1). In fact, the Spirit will be sent as a new form of the presence of Christ after his departure, together with a new eschatological coming of Christ himself (v. 18; 20:19, 26), alone or with the Father (v. 23). That the Spirit-Paraclete will be given (v. 16) may be inspired by the prophecy of Ezek 36:26 in reference to the new covenant.

In John 14:26 the function of the Paraclete is clarified with regards to his role for the community: he will remind the disciples of the words of Jesus and introduce them into their meaning. In this way, he assures the continued presence of Christ in his community also in the period after the hour of Jesus. The same function of the Paraclete is described in John 16:13-15. In John 15:26; 16:7-11, the Paraclete assists the disciples in their lawsuit with the world and inspires their witness. (John 15:26 seems to be influenced by Mark 13:11 and Matt 10:20). In John 16:7-11, the Paraclete is presented as an accuser of the world. He will convict the world of sin, justice, and judgment. *See* JOHN, GOSPEL OF.

Bibliography: Raymond E. Brown. "The Paraclete in the Fourth Gospel." *NTS* 13 (1966–67) 113–32; George Johnston. *The Spirit-Paraclete in the Gospel of John* (1970).

JOHANNES BEUTLER, SJ

PARADISE pair´uh-d*i*s [פַּרְדֵּס pardes; παράδεισος paradeisos]. *Paradise* is a Persian loanword (pairidaeza) in Hebrew, Aramaic, Syriac, Greek, and other languages. In Old Persian, the noun denoted an enclosure; it developed to signify a beautiful garden, like a king's garden. The concept of paradise evolved so that it symbolized streams flowing with crystal-clear and healthful water, and trees blooming constantly beside multicolored flowers. There is no sickness in this blessed place, and the temperature is always ideal for humans.

The concept "paradise" does not appear in the OT (but in the LXX of Gen 13:10, Lot sees "the paradise [paradeisos]" of God). In the LXX, the noun does appear with the meaning of forest (Neh 2:8), park (Eccl 2:5), and orchard (Song 4:13).

In the biblical world, the concept "paradise" probably first appeared in early Jewish literature sometime in the 3rd cent. BCE (see *1 En.* 32:3; 77:4). Paradise became associated with the older, well-known concept of a primordial garden, the Garden of Eden (*see* EDEN, GARDEN OF). This garden was defined by a river with four branches, the tree of life, trees abounding in fruit, and peaceful relations between humans, the creator, and all creation. This garden was eventually closed to humans because of their disobedience to God.

A barrier also separates humans from paradise, either in time (the present from the future age) or space, the distance on earth from the person to the far-distant garden, and from earth to one of the heavens.

The seer in the *History of the Rechabites* enlists two trees that bend down to lift him over an uncrossable body of water (*Hist. Rech.* 3:1-4).

Other biblical images found in the OT enriched the two concepts—the Garden of Eden and paradise—as they developed and became more similar. Among these the most important are the following: 1) Isaiah's imagery that Zion will become like Eden and the Lord's garden (Isa 51:3), and that God's people will become like a well-watered garden (Isa 58:11, compare 60:13); 2) Jeremiah's hope that God will plant the righteous in the promised land (Jer 32:41); 3) Ezekiel's imagery of God's garden, the trees of Eden, and the beatific trees by the water (Ezek 31:8-9); and 4) the psalmist's perception that the righteous are "like trees planted by streams of water" (Ps 1:1-3).

In Second Temple Judaism, the images from Genesis, Isaiah, Jeremiah, Ezekiel, and Psalm 1 coalesce to produce elegant poetic imagery for God's final planting (esp. in 1QH 16, 1QS 8, and CD 1). In early Jewish literature, paradise often has become synonymous with the Garden of Eden. In *1 Enoch*, the "Garden of Eden" in Ethiopic becomes *paradise* in the Greek translation (see esp. *1 En.* 20:7; compare 32:3). By the end of the 1st cent. CE, paradise is perceived to be the location of "the tree of life" (Rev 2:7; *4 Ezra* 8:52). (*See* TREE OF KNOWLEDGE, TREE OF LIFE.)

Descriptions of paradise are frequent in Jewish documents that were composed between ca. 300 BCE and 200 CE. The author of *4 Ezra* carries forth the traditions that the entrances to paradise are unknown (*4 Ezra* 4:7) and thus not able to be entered (*4 Ezra* 7:53). Paradise apparently existed primordially (*4 Ezra* 6:2). The paradise of delight is synonymous with the resting place (*4 Ezra* 7:36). Fruits in paradise remain unspoiled, and there is an abundance of healing (*4 Ezra* 7:123). In the age to come, paradise will be open for those few who remain faithful to God (*4 Ezra* 8:52; compare *T. Levi* 18:10-11). In Second Temple literature, the pervasive emphasis is that paradise (the Lost Eden) is reserved for God's righteous ones (examples can be found in *Life of Adam and Eve*, *4 Ezra*, *2 Baruch*, *2 Enoch*, *Testament of Abraham*, and Coptic *Apocalypse of Elijah*). In early Judaism (300 BCE to 200 CE), only rarely is *paradise* used to describe a royal garden (as in Josephus, *J.W.* 7.347).

Since no one knew the precise location of paradise, it was situated in mutually exclusive places. Some authors placed it on the earth in the north (*1 En.* 77), in the east (*1 En.* 32; *2 En.* 42), in the northeast (*1 En.* 61), between the northeast and the west (*1 En.* 70), to the far west (Josephus, *J.W.* 2.155–56), and some place (perhaps in the ocean) hidden on earth (compare the abode of the blessed ones in *Hist. Rech.* 7:2-3; 11–12). Other early Jews situated paradise in one of the heavens, especially in the third heaven (*Apoc. Mos.* 37:5; 40:1; 2 Cor 12; *2 En.* 8a), and in the seventh heaven (*Jos. Asen.* 22:13). The compiler of the *Life of Adam and Eve* (which is also the *Apocalypse of Moses*) reported that there is a heavenly and an earthly paradise (= Eden); the heavenly paradise is in the third heaven (*L.A.E.* 37:5). The Samaritans believed in an earthly and heavenly paradise, describing each as the Garden of Eden.

Since no one alive had been to paradise, it was described in conflicting ways. Some imagined it was populated (*Pss. Sol.* 14; *2 En.* 42:3b; *Apoc. Ab.* 21; *Odes Sol.* 11), others thought no one was there (*1 En.* 32; *2 En.* 8–9; *4 Ezra* 8:52). Building on the original concept of a beatific garden for the chosen ones, paradise is typically described as full of fruitful trees (*2 En.* 8a; *Odes Sol.* 11) and defined by a sweet-smelling fragrance (*1 En.* 32; *2 En.* 8a; 23; *Odes Sol.* 11). Paradise is full of trees bearing fruit. Some authors imagined that the fruit was to be eaten by the elect (Rev 2:7; *T. Levi* 18). Others believed that the trees are the elect who are planted in paradise (*Pss. Sol.* 14; *Odes Sol.* 11).

The word *paradise* appears in three NT passages: Luke 23:43; 2 Cor 12:4; and Rev 2:7. Luke emphasizes that Christ will be in paradise with the penitent thief. Paul preserves the thought that paradise is in the third heaven. The author of Revelation promises fruit from the tree of life, which is in paradise to those "who conquer."

Originally a Persian concept (as is the belief in a resurrection) that was uniquely developed within Second Temple Judaism, the concept of paradise has continued to shape the dreams of many in Western and Eastern cultures. Frequently, as in the famous work *Paradise Lost* by John Milton, paradise is described as lost (but in Christian circles opened again by Jesus Christ). In his log of 1498, Christopher Columbus expressed his belief that he had found the earthly paradise, the fringes of the long-lost Garden of Eden. *See* AFTERLIFE; HEAVEN.

JAMES H. CHARLESWORTH

PARADOX. Paradoxes put contradictory or complementary truths side by side: the gospel is both foolishness and wisdom (1 Cor 1:18-19); the first will be last (Mark 9:35; Luke 22:26); those who strive to save their souls will lose them (Matt 10:39; Mark 8:35); life is found in taking up one's cross and following the crucified one into suffering (Matt 10:38; Mark 8:34; Luke 14:27; John 12:25).

Sometimes paradoxical truths occur together in a saying ("my yoke is easy, and my burden is light," Matt 11:30), a parable, or a proverb. But paradoxical concepts are also found across the canon. For example, God is changeless and immutable (Num 23:19; 1 Sam 15:29; Ps 33:11; Mal 3:6; Jas 1:17) yet changes his mind (Exod 32:14; 1 Sam 15:35*b*; Jonah 3:10).

Paradoxical concepts clash and may push readers to stop and think more deeply, to attempt to resolve or lessen the tension between contradictory truths (paradoxos παράδοξος; 4 Macc 2:14). Sometimes the context offers ways to ease or understand the tension. To elucidate the paradoxical truth that "whoever wants to be first must be last of all," Jesus holds a child in his lap and gives a brief explanation (Mark 9:35-37).

By highlighting inconsistency in a thought process or inadequacies of a conventional understanding, a paradox can point to behavioral inconsistency. Jesus affirms the truth of the commandment "Do not murder," then asserts that certain behaviors reveal it has not truly been obeyed when the conventional interpretation has been too narrow. In this case, Jesus suggests that fully embracing the truth of the commandment entails actively seeking reconciliation with anyone one has offended, then worshiping the living God (Matt 5:21-24). But often the reader must let the paradox stand, accepting that complementary truths exist. *See* METAPHOR IN THEOLOGY; PARABLE; PROVERB; TEACHING OF JESUS.

BONNIE HOWE

PARAH pay´ruh [פָּרָה **parah**]. Parah is one of the towns inherited by the tribe of Benjamin (Josh 18:23). While the precise location of the settlement is unknown, most scholars identify it with Tell Fara, which is approximately 6 mi. northeast of Jerusalem located near a spring that still provides water to Old Jerusalem. The location is also known as "Parath" and thus could be the place (EUPHRATES RIVER) where God commanded JEREMIAH to dip his loincloth (Jer 13:4-7).

STEVEN D. MASON

PARALEIPOMENA OF JEREMIAH. *See* BARUCH, FOURTH BOOK OF.

PARALLELISM pair´uh-lel-iz´uhm. Parallelism has come to be viewed as one of the predominant characteristics of poetry, along with terseness and imagery; it is also found, to a lesser extent, in non-poetic discourse. Parallelism may be defined as the repetition of similar or related thought and/or grammatical structure in adjacent lines or verses. The repetition is rarely identical, and, indeed, the seemingly infinite ways that one line may be paralleled with another is what makes parallelism so interesting.

A. The Semantic Relationship Between Lines
B. Parallel Word Pairs
C. Grammatical Analysis
Bibliography

A. The Semantic Relationship Between Lines

There have been two schools of thought on how to describe the semantic relationship between parallel lines. The first emphasizes the sameness of the relationship and the types and degree of correspondence between the lines. There are three types or categories of parallelisms, depending on the nature of the correspondence of the lines: synonymous (the lines contain the same thought), antithetic (the lines have opposite thoughts), and synthetic (the relationship is not exactly synonymous or antithetic). In synonymous parallelism, the same thought is expressed in different words, as in Ps 117:1:

> Praise the LORD, all you nations! // Extol him, all you peoples!

In antithetic parallelism, the second line is opposed to the first line, as in Prov 11:5:

> The righteousness of the blameless keeps their ways straight,
> but the wicked fall by their own wickedness.

Synthetic parallelism, a much looser designation, accounts for parallelisms that lack exact correspondence between their parts but that show a more diffuse correspondence between the lines as a whole. An example is Song 2:4:

> He brought me to the banqueting house, // and his intention toward me was love.

A second way of looking at parallelism rejects the notion of the synonymity of parallel lines and substitutes the notion of continuity, phrasing his definition of parallelism as: "A, what's more, B." The second line of a parallelism manifests a progression or intensification of the first line. No parallelism is truly synonymous; all parallel lines embody both similarity and difference, in that the second line of a parallelism proceeds from the first line by expanding or modifying it. Indeed, this dynamic tension between sameness and difference is a hallmark of biblical parallelism.

For example, Isa 40:11:

> Like a shepherd he will pasture his flock;
> In his arms he will gather the lambs,
> and in his bosom carry them.
> He will guide the mother sheep.
> (author's trans.)

From the stock motif of God as a shepherd, Isaiah constructs a picture of intensifying protection and guidance that God will afford his people as he leads them out of captivity. Each line captures a similar thought and then develops it more. What begins as a picture of God providing for his people turns into a picture of God leading those who can walk and carrying those too weak to walk on the straight and smooth path home. The progression and intensification is especially moving in the line, "In his arms he will gather the lambs, and in his bosom carry them."

B. Parallel Word Pairs

As with the lines as a whole, the relationship between parallel word pairs became the object of study. It was noticed that certain sets of terms regularly recurred in parallel lines, such as day // night (e.g., Ps 121:6: "The sun shall not strike you by day // nor the moon by night") and heaven // earth (e.g., Isa 1:2: "Hear, O heavens // and listen, O earth"). Examples of recurring word pairs abound: Jerusalem // Judah (Isa 3:8; Jer 9:11 and passim); father // mother (Prov 1:8 and passim; Ezek 16:3;); right // left (Gen 13:9; Song 2:6).

The pairs were thought to have been fixed, i.e., they were stock pairs of words learned by poets who would then use them as the building blocks around which a parallelism could be constructed. Subsequent scholarship, however, saw these word pairs not as fixed, not as the special property of poets, but simply as commonly associated terms (like those elicited in psycholinguistic word association games) that are called forth in the process of composing parallel lines. In fact, many of the same pairs occur together in non-parallelistic discourse (e.g., right-left, Num 20:17; 22:26). Modern linguists analyze them as having either a paradigmatic relationship (coming from the same class, like Judah and Jerusalem) or a syntagmatic relationship (two words taken from a sequence). One type of syntagmatic pairing is the splitting of the components of personal or geographic names, such as Balak // king of Moab (Num 23:7) and Ephrathah // Bethlehem (Ruth 4:11).

C. Grammatical Analysis

In the 1970s and 1980s parallelism came to be viewed as a linguistic phenomenon involving linguistic equivalences and/or contrasts that may occur on the level of the word, the line, or across larger expanses of text. Linguistic equivalence means not only identity but also refers to a term or construction that, linguistically speaking, belongs to the same category or paradigm, or to the same sequence or syntagm. This kind of equivalence can easily be seen in the case of word pairs. Pairs like day and night or father and mother belong to the same grammatical paradigm ("nouns"), and might be said to belong to the same semantic paradigm ("time" and "family members").

Similarly, entire lines can be grammatically equivalent—that is, contain the same grammatical structure. Modern transformational linguistics introduced the idea of deep structure and surface structure. Parallel lines often contain the same deep structure but may vary their surface structure, yielding another dimension of the dynamic tension between sameness and difference that parallelism favors. For example, Isa 40:15:

> Even the nations are like a drop from a bucket,
> and are accounted as dust on the scales;
> see, he takes up the isles like fine dust.

Here the subject in one line ("the nations") becomes the object in a parallel line ("the isles"). (And note the intensification from "dust" to "fine dust.") Parallelism may also pair lines of different grammatical mood, as in Ps 6:5 [Heb. 6:6] where a negative indicative parallels an interrogative:

> For in death there is no remembrance of you;
> in Sheol who can give you praise?

Because there are so many ways to form parallelisms with word pairs from the same or different classes and with lines having the same or different surface structure (or even different deep structures), the variety of parallelisms is enormous and the relationships of their components is complex. An example of this complexity can be seen in Ps 111:6:

> The power of his deeds he told to his people,
> In giving to them the inheritance of nations.
> (author's trans.)

The deep structure of the syntax of the lines is not the same. The second line goes beyond the first, explaining how God's power has been manifest. Moreover, people and nations, a common word pair, do not refer to the same entity in this verse (people refers to Israel and nations refers to Canaanites). The manner in which this word pair is used is novel, but at the same time, the use of a common pair helps to draw the two grammatically different lines together. The parallel construction gives a strong sense of cohesion to the idea in this verse, that God showed his power to Israel by giving them the land of Canaan.

An example in Job 5:14 contains a double word pair:

> By day they encounter darkness,
> And as at night they grope at noon.
> (author's trans.)

Both lines express a similar thought: during the daytime it will seem like nighttime. This suggests that we should analyze the pairs as day // noon and night // darkness—these are the semantic pairs. But the structure of the lines, their word order, suggests the analysis of day // night and darkness // noon. Indeed, these are the more common word associations, the lexical pairs. In this case the lexical pairing is at odds with the semantic pairing, creating a tension between the two that in turn sets up a competing relationship between the lines, thereby binding them even more closely together.

This illustration reminds us that the sense of the entire verse comes into play in the selection of word pairs, for words are chosen to express or emphasize a particular message. The point to be made, however, is that, just as the selection of parallel words is not totally random, so is it not totally fixed. Another illustration will demonstrate the subtle difference that the choice of a word pair can make. Compare these almost-identical two verses:

> But you, O LORD, are enthroned forever;
> your name endures to all generations.
> (Ps 102:12 [Heb. 102:13])

But you, O LORD reign forever;
your throne endures to all generations.
(Lam 5:19)

The difference in the choice of one word underscores the difference in the messages of these two passages. Psalm 102 is contrasting the fleetingness of a human with the permanence of God. God's name, that is, his existence, is eternal. Lamentations, on the other hand, is lamenting the destruction of the Temple, the locus of God's throne. Despite its physical destruction, the verse maintains that God's throne—i.e., the metaphoric seat of his rulership—will remain intact.

Another aspect that may come into play in parallelism is sound. Equivalences in sound may be activated just as equivalences in grammar are. This often takes the form of pairing words with similar consonants, and is related to the broader biblical penchant for soundplay. Sound pairs may also be semantic or lexical pairs, such as **shalom** (שָׁלוֹם, "peace") // **shalwah** (שַׁלְוָה, "tranquility," author's trans.) in Ps 122:7; or they may be unrelated, as in Ps 104:19:

He made the moon for time-markers
(**mo'adhim** מוֹעֲדִים),
The sun knows its setting
(**yadha' mevo'o** יָדַע מְבוֹאוֹ).
(author's trans.)

Sound pairs reinforce the bond between lines created by grammatical and lexical pairings, yet, as in this example, need not correspond with them. Sound pairs provide yet another way to bind together two lines.

The use of seemingly infinite varieties of parallelism throughout a poem achieves a large part of the poetic effect in biblical poetry. Parallelism advances the thought of each verse while at the same time creating a close relationship between its parts. This allows for movement within the poem while promoting the sense of unity throughout the poem. An appreciation of parallelism enhances our understanding of a passage and our appreciation for the skill of the biblical poets.

Bibliography: Robert Alter. *The Art of Biblical Poetry* (1985); Adele Berlin. *The Dynamics of Biblical Parallelism* (1985); James Kugel. *The Idea of Biblical Parallelism: Parallelism and Its History* (1981).

ADELE BERLIN

PARALYSIS, PARALYTIC [παραλυτικός **paralytikos**, παραλύομαι **paralyomai**, παραλύω **paralyō**]. **Paralytikos** occurs only in a few passages: Matt 4:24; 8:5-10; 9:1-8; Mark 2:1-12. This rarity seems to underscore the severity of the condition in the ancient world. In Mark, the story's drama emerges directly from the man's paralysis: he must be carried to Jesus through the efforts of four people digging through the roof and lowering him because the crowd blocks the door. The paralysis highlights not only the healing miracle but also the density of the crowd and the desperation of those needing healing. That Jesus, moved by the carriers' faith, forgives the man's sins before healing his paralysis may point to an ancient understanding that spiritual affliction was related to physical. **Paralyō** and **paralyomai** are both more general terms for falling ill but are taken to indicate paralysis in a number of cases (e.g., Luke 5:18, 24; Acts 8:7; 9:33; Wis 17:15, 19). *See* DISEASE; HEALING.

NICOLE WILKINSON DURAN

PARAN pay'ruhn [פָּארָן **pa'ran**]. A region in the Sinai Peninsula that is usually referred to as part of the wilderness in which the Israelites wandered after they escaped Egyptian bondage. Most of the references to the region occur in the Pentateuch with a few citations in other OT books. The first possible reference to the region is in connection with CHEDORLAOMER's campaign to the Dead Sea and the Arabah during the time of Abraham. The Mesopotamian kings conquered the area as far as EL-PARAN "on the edge of the wilderness" (Gen 14:6). The compound *El-paran* includes the masculine form **'el** (אֵיל) and likely refers to Elath (**'elath** אֵילַת) on the Gulf of Aqabah (*see* ELATH, ELOTH). This site was on the edge of the Wilderness of Paran, which then extended westward into the interior of the Sinai Peninsula. It later is the region where Hagar and Ishmael found refuge after their expulsion from the family of Abraham (Gen 21:20-21). It apparently lay between Beer-sheba and the land of Shur (assuming Hagar retreated the same direction she had earlier; Gen 16:7).

When the Israelites left Mount Sinai and began their journey to Canaan, they traveled to the Wilderness of Paran (Num 10:11-12). Kadesh was in Paran and was the location from which the spies were dispatched to reconnoiter the promised land (Num 13:1-3, 25-26; *see* KADESH, KADESH-BARNEA). One poetic passage possibly alludes to Mount Sinai as Mount Paran (Deut 33:1-2; and possibly Hab 3:3; *see* SINAI, MOUNT). Perhaps corroborating this identification, the major oasis in the southern Sinai Peninsula preserves the name Paran in the name Feiran and was known in Byzantine times as Pharan.

Paran is noted in 1 Sam 25:1 as one of the places where David sought refuge in his flight from Saul. The LXX, however, reads instead that he went to the Wilderness of MAON, which would have been significantly north of the region normally considered Paran. Later, HADAD passed through the Wilderness of Paran in his flight from Midian and Edom to Egypt (1 Kgs 11:17-18).

Some confusion exists because the site of Kadesh, which is more explicitly identified as Kadesh-barnea in other passages (Num 32:8; Deut 1:2, 19; 2:14; 9:23), is mentioned as in the Wilderness of Paran (Num 13:26) but also in the Wilderness of Zin (Num 20:1;

33:36; Deut 32:51; *see* ZIN, WILDERNESS OF). Two viable explanations exist. One postulates that the site of Kadesh/Kadesh-barnea was on the border of the two wilderness regions, with Paran occupying the southern and western flank of Kadesh, and Zin being to the north and east. Another suggests that the Wilderness of Zin was a smaller part of the Wilderness of Paran, with Paran apparently stretching from the vicinity of Beersheba (Gen 21) to Kadesh-barnea (Num 13) to the Gulf of Aqabah (Gen 14) and westward to accommodate Mount Paran, which was apparently another synonym for Mount Sinai (Deut 33:1; Hab 3:3).

Bibliography: Yohanan Aharoni. *The Land of the Bible: A Historical Geography.* A. Rainey, trans. (1979).

DALE W. MANOR

PARAPET [מַעֲקֶה ma'aqeh; ἔπαλξις epalxis]. A parapet architecturally referred originally to a wall or RAMPART to protect soldiers (Jdt 14:1). It is used more commonly to describe a low wall or railing to protect the edges of a roof, balcony, bridge, or elevated platform. The one OT use is in a law requiring every house to have a parapet for the roof to protect against bloodguilt from someone falling off the roof (Deut 22:8). *See* ARCHITECTURE, OT; BATTLEMENTS; HOUSE.

JOEL F. DRINKARD JR.

PARCHED GRAIN. *See* GRAIN; PLANTS OF THE BIBLE.

PARCHMENT pahrch'muhnt [μεμβράνα membrana]. Direct biblical evidence for parchment, animal skin used as a writing surface, is scant, although passages reveal the use of a pliable or soft writing material, perhaps animal skins or papyrus, the latter made from plants (*see* PAPYRUS, PAPYRI). References to scrolls with multiple columns (Jer 36:2, 4, 23) indicate either leather or papyrus media. Ezekiel 2:9-10 refers to a scroll that was spread out before Ezekiel (see also Isa 37:14). The precise meaning of *parchments* in 2 Tim 4:13 remains elusive.

Beyond the biblical evidence, literary sources and archaeological evidence reveal that prepared animal skins served as writing surfaces for both literary and documentary texts throughout the ANE. The QUMRAN compositions (ca. 250 BCE–70 CE) provide the most complete picture of skin scrolls in antiquity. Of the 930 texts discovered at Qumran, about 800 (86 percent) were inscribed on leather. DNA evidence together with other studies reveal that the skins originated from sheep, domestic or wild goats, calves, ibexes, and gazelles. The Qumran scrolls reveal numerous aspects of leather as writing surfaces—their height and length, columnar and marginal dimensions, sheet measurements, guide dots, opisthographs, palimpsests, rulings, scribal procedures, stitching repairs, and other conventions. *See* WRITING AND WRITING MATERIALS.

DONALD W. PARRY

PARDON [כָּסָה kasah, כָּפַר kafar, נָשָׂא nasa', סָלַח salakh; ἀφίημι aphiēmi, παραιτέομαι paraiteomai]. The OT expresses a deep conviction that life as God's people depends on God pardoning sins. Though God has created a covenant with Israel and remains faithful, the people repeatedly prove themselves unfaithful. If life with God is to continue, God must pardon Israel (Exod 34:9; Num 14:19; Pss 25:11; 85:2 [Heb. 85:3]; 2 Esd 7:139).

Those who sin deliberately, however, cannot presume God's pardon. Deuteronomy 29:20 [Heb. 29:19] declares that God will not pardon the people of Israel if they think that they can sin with impunity (see also Exod 23:21; 1 Sam 15:25; 2 Kgs 24:4; Jer 5:7). Thus, God's pardon is never automatic but is always encountered as God's graciously merciful act (Wis 6:6).

God's faithfulness is seen in how deeply God desires and seeks to pardon. The unrighteous are able to repent, because the Lord "will abundantly pardon" (Isa 55:7; see Mic 7:18). God does not simply wait for the unrighteous to do so, however. God pleads with the people to allow God to pardon them (Jer 5:1). In the face of the exile, Jeremiah looks ahead to the day when God will pardon the people by removing sin itself from Israel (Jer 50:20). In Sirach, God's pardon is explicitly tied to one's own practice of forgiveness (Sir 28:2-4) and devotion to God's law (Sir 38:34*b*–39:5).

The concept of God's pardon, expressed in other language, plays a significant role in the NT. *See* ATONEMENT; FORGIVENESS.

BRIAN K. PETERSON

PARENESIS pair'uh-nee'sis [παραίνεσις parainesis]. Parenesis, or moral exhortation, reminds an audience of desirable moral practices and assumes the hearers agree. This hortatory technique differs from protreptic (protreptikos προτρεπτικός, "persuasion, a call to a new way of life") in that it is a call to continue in a life path already chosen. It is also narrower than paraklesis (paraklēsis [παράκλησις]), which focuses on the audience and encompasses exhorting, comforting, and preaching. Paul uses the term *paraklesis*, even when he engages in parenesis.

Parenesis treats conduct, behavior, and acts to be done or avoided in a friendly or philophronetic context. Thus its instruction is weaker than an order or command, which expect obedience. Parenetic injunctions expect the recipient to see their point and to fit them into a general understanding they already possess. The audience of parenetic EXHORTATION are not neophytes but members of converted communities, who are being reminded of what is expected of them.

Parenesis is a style or practice, not a specific rhetorical genre. It is akin to epideictic speech, which confirms a chosen way of life, rather than to forensic or deliberative speech, which recommends specific actions. It was used by Greco-Roman moral philosophers (e.g., Isocrates, Dio Chrysostom, Stoics such as Seneca, and Plutarch), by early Jewish writers (e.g., *Testaments of the Twelve Patriarchs*, 4 Maccabees), by NT authors (e.g., Paul, deutero-Paul, 1 Peter), and by patristic authors (e.g., Clement of Alexandria). Letters with parenetic features, written in a conversational tone, evoke the presence of the absent teacher who gives heart-to-heart advice in direct terms, without philosophical subtleties. The outlook of parenesis is over a lifetime, during which the moral instruction is to be digested and practiced.

The injunctions are drawn from traditional ethical materials and express commonly held convictions. While the advice is largely conventional, parenesis might include material appropriate to the particular audience or situation. New Testament parenesis uses theological or christological motivation or justification to support compliance, which is presumed. Examples stimulate the audience's emulation and also demonstrate that the injunctions can be acted upon with success. Negative examples steer the audience away from undesirable actions and results.

Paul, in his letter to Philemon, appeals to the common expectations of the sibling relationship in classical antiquity as he brokers improved treatment for the slave Onesimus (Aasgaard). Abraham Malherbe discovers the Greco-Roman moralists' view of education as a constant and necessary companion to ethical behavior to be the framework of the parenesis in the Pastoral Epistles. The HOUSEHOLD CODES of conduct (*Haustafeln*) and the vice and virtue lists in 1 Peter, the Pastoral Epistles, Ephesians, and Colossians are another example of traditional material adopted in service of the letters' parenetic aims (*see* LISTS, ETHICAL). A parenetic pattern of exhortation can also be found at 1 Thess 4:1-12, where the moral injunctions are affirmed by the will of God for the Thessalonians' holiness. Similarly, in Gal 5:13–6:10 the stock vice and virtue lists are linked to the Galatians' call to serve one another in Christian love as Spirit-filled followers of the crucified Christ. Christian motivation is more extensively interwoven with the multifaceted parenetic exhortation of Rom 12:1–15:13. *See* RHETORICAL CRITICISM, NT.

Bibliography: Reidar Aasgaard. "Brotherly Advice." *Early Christian Paraenesis in Context*. Troels Engberg-Pederson and James Starr, eds. (2004) 237–65; Abraham Malherbe. "Paraenesis in the Epistle to Titus." *Early Christian Paraenesis in Context*. Troels Engberg-Pederson and James Starr, eds. (2004) 297–317.

BENJAMIN FIORE, S. J.

PARENTS [אָבוֹת ʾavoth; γονεῖς goneis, πατέρες pateres]. Parents include the MOTHER and FATHER of a child. The OT does not have a generic word for parents. Instead, the plural of the term *father* (ʾavoth) indicates both male and female parents. Children are to honor their parents (Exod 20:12; Deut 5:16), and the actions of the children reflect on the parents (Prov 17:6; 28:7; 29:3), while the sins of the parents are sometimes visited upon the children (Exod 34:7; Num 14:18; Deut 5:9; compare Jer 31:27-30; Ezek 18:1-4).

The NT continues the practice of referring to parents with the plural form of *father* (pateres; Luke 1:17; Heb 11:23; NRSV, "parents"), including both fathers and mothers (but compare Eph 6:1-2, which distinguishes them). More common, however, is the term goneis, which closely parallels the English usage of the word *parent* (Matt 10:21; Mark 13:12; Luke 2:41-43; John 9:2-3; Rom 1:30; 2 Cor 12:14; Col 3:20). *See* CHILD, CHILDREN; FAMILY.

KEVIN A. WILSON

PARK [פַּרְדֵּס pardes]. A tract of land cultivated for aesthetic purposes rather than as a practical economic or agricultural asset. In Eccl 2:5, the owner brags of his parks and orchards of trees as signs of his wealth. *See* ORCHARD.

PARMASHTA pahr-mash´tuh [פַּרְמַשְׁתָּא parmashtaʾ]. One of Haman's ten sons killed by the Jews in Susa after Haman's downfall (Esth 9:9). The name reads Marmasima (Μαρμασιμά) in the LXX. *See* ADALIA; ESTHER; HAMAN.

PARMENAS pahr´muh-nuhs [Παρμενᾶς Parmenas]. One of seven men chosen to address concerns raised by the HELLENISTS regarding the distribution of the community's resources (Acts 6:5). Later tradition places him as a bishop of Soli and tells of his martyrdom in Philippi during the reign of the Roman emperor TRAJAN. *See* ACTS OF THE APOSTLES; SEVEN, THE.

RUBÉN R. DUPERTUIS

PARNACH pahr´nak [פַּרְנָךְ parnakh]. Means "delicate" or "gifted." Mentioned in the Bible as the father of ELIZAPHAN, leader of the tribe of Zebulun. Elizaphan was chosen to help with the division of the promised land among the tribes (Num 34:25). *See* ZEBULUN, ZEBULUNITE.

PARONOMASIA. *See* WORDPLAY IN THE OT.

PAROSH pay´rosh [פַּרְעֹשׁ parʿosh; Φόρος Phoros]. The ancestor of one of the families who returned to Jerusalem after Babylonian captivity. The descendants of Parosh numbered 2,172, according to Ezra and Nehemiah (Ezra 2:3; 8:3; 10:25; Neh 7:8; 10:14; 1 Esd 5:9; 8:30; 9:26). The members of the Parosh family were among those summoned to dispose of their foreign wives, as part of the campaign led by Ezra.

CHANNA COHEN STUART

PAROUSIA puh-*roo'*zhee-uh [παρουσία parousia]. Literally means "coming, arrival, presence." *Parousia* is used widely in the NT (e.g., Matt 24:3; 1 Cor 15:23; 1 Thess 5:23; 2 Thess 2:1; 2 Pet 1:16; 1 John 2:28; compare Jas 5:7). In these passages it refers to the presence of Christ eschatologically coming on the clouds of heaven (Mark 13:26) and is sometimes called the "second coming" of Christ. Nevertheless the ambiguity of the word should be noted, as when expectation of a public coming when "every eye will see him" (Rev 1:7) allowed for the possibility of the presence of Christ in other modes of experience, whether in worship or the lives of the apostles and minsters (Gal 2:20).

In Jewish texts contemporary with the NT in which the future hope is expounded, only very occasionally do we find a reference to a heavenly being coming from heaven to establish God's eschatological kingdom. Occasional reference is made to a messianic agent (e.g., *Pss. Sol.* 17:24-25; *1 En.* 46:5; 90:37; *4 Ezra* 7:29; 12:32; *2 Bar.* 29:3; 39:7; 72:2; *Sib. Or.* 3: 652-53; *T. Levi* 2:11; 4Q174; 1QS IX, 11), but the coming of a heavenly deliverer (Mark 14:62) who might also be a judge (Matt 25:31-45) is relatively rare (*see* ESCHATOLOGY IN EARLY JUDAISM). The idea of the parousia linked with the eschatological coming of the Messiah seems to be a Christian concern and may be largely a result of the development of Christian convictions.

In the Pauline Letters *parousia* is used not only of Christ's coming (e.g., 1 Thess 3:13; 2 Thess 2:8) but also of that of the apostle (2 Cor 10:10; Phil 1:26; 2:12) or his agent (1 Cor 16:17; 2 Cor 7:6-7). There is a close relationship between the parousia of Christ and the apostolic parousia (Rom 15:22, 29; 1 Cor 4:17-19; 5:3-5). Paul's presence brings with it the exercise of eschatological power despite his weakness and humility (1 Cor 4:9, 19) and will bring blessing (Rom 15:29).

The most extended parousia passages in the Pauline corpus are found in 1 Cor 15; 1 Thess 4; and 2 Thess 2. Paul uses the word *parousia* to describe Christ's appearing (1 Cor 15:23; 1 Thess 4:15). In 2 Thess 2:8 the language used is "the manifestation of his coming" (compare the reference to his revealing at 1 Cor 1:7). In 1 Thessalonians, widely assumed to be Paul's earliest letter, written as early as twenty years after Jesus' crucifixion, Paul alludes to a "word from the Lord" and refers to the coming of Christ to gather the elect, to encourage the Thessalonians not to be downcast about those who have died, because they will not be at any disadvantage at Christ's appearance. In this pasage a millennial hope (i.e., the hope that those alive when the messianic kingdom comes will get the benefits denied to those who have died) is reinterpreted by reference to Christ's coming to gather the elect whether dead or alive.

In a discussion on the belief in the resurrection and the character of the resurrection body Paul alludes to the future consummation in two passages (*see* RESURRECTION, NT). In the first Paul outlines the order in which the resurrection from the dead will take place: Christ the first fruits (which has already taken place), then those who belong to Christ at his coming (1 Cor 15:23-28; compare 1 Thess 4:15). Then comes the end when Christ hands over the kingship to God, with every rule, principality, and power destroyed. It is only when all things are subjected to the Messiah that the son will himself be subject to the father and God will be all in all (1 Cor 15:28).

A disturbance in the Thessalonian community because of eschatological enthusiasm prompted by the belief that the DAY OF THE LORD has already arrived is resolved when readers are told that a rebellion and revelation of the "lawless one" must take place first (2 Thess 2:3). The coming of the lawless one will be accompanied by signs and wonders that will deceive those who are on the way to destruction, just as the activity of the beast and the false prophet deceive the nations of the earth in Rev 13:7, 12. Finally, however, the Lord Jesus will slay the lawless one with the breath of his mouth. Isaiah 11:4 has contributed to this passage, particularly in the description of the destruction of the lawless one (compare *Pss. Sol.* 17:24; *4 Ezra* 13:8).

The eschatological discourses in the Synoptic Gospels (Matt 24–25; Mark 13; Luke 21) describe the coming of the SON OF MAN, which is linked primarily with the vindication of the elect. The element of judgment at the parousia of the Son of Man is found in the Matthean version of the eschatological discourse, in which at the final assize the Son of Man sits on God's throne (Matt 25:31-45; compare Rev 20:11-15). The criterion of judgment is ministry to the heavenly Son of Man in the form of ministry to those who are hungry, thirsty, strangers, naked, weak, and imprisoned in the present age. There is a possible link here with the much disputed *1 En.* 37–71, where the Son of Man sits on the throne of the lord of the spirits and exercises judgment (e.g., *1 En.* 69:27).

The concerns manifest in the various versions of the synoptic eschatological discourse typify the emerging Christian concern with eschatology. The future hope is focused on the coming of the Son of Man and the tribulations affecting the world, especially Christians, in the time preceding it. Little is said about the coming of the new age, familiar to us from contemporary Jewish eschatological texts and from Rev 20–21. Thus, there is none of the evocation of a this-worldly kingdom of God such as we find in a saying attributed to Jesus in the writings of Papias. Here the whole of creation is restored to a more glorious situation than it had been at the beginning of creation (Irenaeus, *Haer.* 33.3-4), themes touched on in the Beatitudes (Matt 5:3-12; Luke 6:20-23).

The coming of Jesus in the Fourth Gospel moves away from the public cosmic scenes we find in the other NT Gospels. The disciples are those to whom

Jesus comes (14:21, 23). The dwellings that Jesus goes to to prepare for the disciples can be enjoyed by the one who loves Jesus and is devoted to his words (14:2; compare 14:23). Likewise, the manifestation of the divine glory is reserved not for the world but for the disciple (14:19). Just as Jesus comes again to the disciples, so too does the PARACLETE. The world cannot receive him; and it is the Paraclete who enables the disciples to maintain their connection with the basic revelation of God, the Logos who makes the Father known (14:17; 15:26). The Paraclete thus points back to Jesus, the Word made flesh, and is in some sense at least a successor to Jesus, a compensation by his presence for Jesus' absence with the Father.

In Rev 19:11-21 there are explicit links with the vision of the Son of Man in 1:14 that inaugurate John's vision. His appearance leads to a holy war. Like the descendant of David described in Isa 11 it is with the sword proceeding from his mouth that he will rule the nations. He comes as King of kings and Lord of lords (19:16); his victory, therefore, in the struggle that is to take place is already assured (exactly what we would expect in light of 11:17). There gather together the beast and the kings of the earth to make war against him (19:19). The beast is thrown into the lake of fire and its allies slain with a sword that proceeds from the mouth of the rider on the white horse. This triumph immediately precedes the establishment of the messianic kingdom on earth (20:4). But this is not the end of the struggle against the forces opposed to the divine righteousness, as the messianic reign is a temporary phenomenon and is then followed by a final judgment that paves the way for the new heaven and earth and the establishment of God's dwelling with humankind.

How did the early church respond to the delay in Jesus' anticipated return, or parousia? In 2 Peter we have the clearest indication that the community addressed was having to wrestle with the issue of the disappointment of eschatological hope (2 Pet 3:3-7). The bulk of the evidence for the problem of the parousia's delay is implicit evidence, however. Revelation challenges Christians who "have abandoned the love you had at first" (Rev 2:4) by reminding them of the imminent expectation of Christ's coming. Similarly, in Matthew's Gospel, parables stress the fact that there has been a delay and urge readiness for the coming of Christ at a time that disciples may not expect (24:45-46; 25:1-13, 14-30). The theme of uncertainty pervades the Gospel (Matt 13:24-30, 36-43; 25:31-45). Luke–Acts emphasizes the importance of the era of the Spirit as a crucial time in the divine economy. The ascension of Christ marks the boundary between the foretaste of the messianic age in the life of Jesus and the age of the spirit.

John 21:23 indicates the shock that a community suffered with the death of a disciple who had contact with Jesus. With the death of the apostles we find a different ethos emerging, in which the present becomes less infused with eschatological significance, and where the eschatological came to be linked with the far distant future and not with the day of salvation that had dawned in the present. Inaugurated eschatology gradually diminishes to be replaced by that longing for the kingdom whose coming was detached from the life of the Christian communities in the present. Writers like Paul believed that what had happened in the Christ event was intimately linked with his own mission within the overall scheme of salvation history. The apostles themselves belong to the signs of the eschatological time, so with their death the present becomes less a day of salvation and more an anticipation of the eschatological salvation when the Twelve would soon sit on twelve thrones judging the twelve tribes of Israel (Matt 19:28).

Aspects of APOCALYPTICISM, with its orientation to the world above, offered resources for dealing with the nonfulfillment of God's reign on earth. This is anticipated in passages from the Dead Sea Scrolls (esp. in the *Thanksgiving Hymns*, 1QH[a]) where the holy community shared the lot of the angels and eschatalogical bliss in its common life. When the Letter to the Ephesians speaks of the church's being "in the heavenly places in Christ" (Eph 1:20; 2:6; 3:10; 6:12), we find reflected a similar experience of the eschatological salvation that already exists with God in heaven. The present life of the church becomes a glimpse, a foretaste of the kingdom of God, as had been the case for the holy life of the Qumran sectarians. Christ's presence in the world came to be linked more with church and sacraments, which were the vital tokens of the religion of emerging Christianity, with the ultimate appearance of Christ relegated to an item of faith, or a threat to a backsliding church rather than an all-encompssing, imminent hope for the redemption of God's world by Christ's presence in it. *See* ESCHATOLOGY OF THE NT.

Bibliography: C. Rowland. *Christian Origins: An Account of the Setting and Character of the Most Important Messianic Sect of Judaism* (2002).

CHRISTOPHER ROWLAND

PARSHANDATHA pahr-shan´duh-thuh [פַּרְשַׁנְדָּתָא parshandatha᾿]. One of the ten sons of HAMAN killed by the Jews in Susa (Esth 9:7). This name may appear on a Mesopotamian seal (LXX Pharsannestain Φαρσαννεσταίν). *See* ESTHER, BOOK OF.

PARSIN. *See* MENE, MENE, TEKEL, AND PARSIN.

PARTHIA, PARTHIANS. pahr´thee-uh, pahr´thee-uhn [Παρθία Parthia, Πάρθοι Parthoi]. Region and empire located in the southwest part of Asia, extending from the Euphrates to the Indus rivers. The Parthian people originated as a nomadic confederacy of Iranian tribes, which occupied the Satrapy of Parthia under the Persian (Achaemenid) Empire and, subsequently, under the Seleucid Empire. In 247 BCE, with the emergence of Arsaces, the founder of the Arsacid Dynasty, they secured their independence from the Seleucids, and founded an empire that was to endure for almost 500 years. The Parthian Empire reached its zenith under Mithradates I (ca. 172–138 BCE) and II (ca. 124–87 BCE), when it became second in power only to Rome. Perhaps, inevitably, conflicts erupted between the two empires, and notable battles took place in 54 BCE when the Parthians famously routed Crassus at Carrhae (OT Haran), and in 36 BCE when they repulsed Mark Antony. While the Parthians were subdued briefly by the emperor Trajan in 114–16 CE, their subjugation did not outlast his death in 116, and their empire lasted for another century until it was finally toppled by the Sasanians in 224 CE.

The only biblical mention of Parthians is at Acts 2:9, where they are the first mentioned of the fourteen peoples said to reside in Jerusalem at the time of Pentecost, and who heard the disciples speaking their own native languages. The Parthians represent the easternmost inhabitants of this catalog of nations, which, collectively, symbolizes the presence of the Jews throughout the inhabited world—among "every nation under heaven" (Acts 2:5). It has further been suggested that Luke's catalog of nations is meant to be an instance of "astrological geography," where signs of the zodiac were identified with specific countries (in this instance, Aries with Parthia), but this view has failed to command general support.

While they are not named explicitly, it is likely that allusions to the Parthians underlie some of the imagery in the book of Revelation. The descriptions of the horsemen mentioned in Revelation call to mind traits of the Parthians, who were celebrated for their cavalry and particularly their skill in shooting arrows from horseback (6:2; 9:17-19; 16:12). The famous "Parthian shot" refers to the ability of Parthian riders to turn in the saddle and shoot at their pursuers even while retreating—something that may help to explain the imagery of Rev 9:19, where the tails of horses are said to wound people.

Bibliography: Yarshater Ehsan. *The Cambridge History of Iran*. Vol 3.1-2 (1983).

J. R. C. COUSLAND

PARTRIDGE [קֹרֵא qore᾿; πέρδιξ perdix]. According to a firm tradition, qore᾿ ("caller") designates the partridge. The Chukor partridge (*Caccabis chukar*), found in mountainous regions, was probably a highly appreciated game bird already in biblical times, as indicated by the simile in 1 Sam 26:20. (See another simile in Sir 11:30.) A curious belief that the partridge has the habit of "hatching what it did not lay" is reflected in Jer 17:11, a misconception that may have arisen from the observation that the Chukor hen lays one additional clutch of eggs, to be hatched by the cock. *See* BIRDS OF THE BIBLE.

GÖRAN EIDEVALL

PARTY [גּוֹי goy, גְּרוּר gerur; ὁμιλία homilia, συμπόσιον symposion]. The NRSV uses the words *party* or *parties* to translate several Greek and Hebrew terms. The NRSV translators added it to legal discussions, to clarify what may be implied by the Hebrew or Greek (Exod 21:18; 22:9; Num 5:8; Ezek 18:8; Gal 3:20; 1 Macc 8:30). In one place *party* is used to provide a gender-neutral translation of the Hebrew (Deut 19:17).

Party is used to translate terms referring to groups of individuals, such as a group of soldiers or raiders (gerur, 1 Sam 30:15, 23), a nation or people (goy, Dan 11:23), an association or company (homilia, 3 Macc 5:18), or a group sharing a meal (symposion, 3 Macc 5:36).

In short, when the NRSV uses the word *party* in legal discussions, it is a singular noun. In other contexts, it is usually a collective noun, referring to a group or band of individuals.

ADAM L. PORTER

PARUAH puh-r*oo*´uh [פָּרוּחַ paruakh]. A member of the tribe of Issachar (1 Kgs 4:17) whose son, JEHOSHAPHAT, was one of twelve officials responsible for providing food for King Solomon and his household, each offering provisions for one month a year (1 Kgs 4:7).

PARVAIM pahr-vay´im [פַּרְוָיִם parwayim]. A place from which Solomon secured the GOLD used in the construction of the Temple in Jerusalem (2 Chr 3:6). There is some rabbinic speculation that the metal itself may have been reddish in color. It is difficult to determine with certainty the geographical location of Parvaim, although a location on the Arabian Peninsula (a known ancient source of gold) is likely. One possibility is Farwa in Yemen. *See* TEMPLE, JERUSALEM.

DEREK E. WITTMAN

PASACH pay´sak [פָּסַךְ pasakh]. Oldest of the three sons of Japhlet and great-great-grandson of the tribal ancestor Asher (1 Chr 7:33). *See* ASHER, ASHERITES; JAPHLET, JAPHLETITES.

PASCHAL LAMB pas´kuhl [פֶּסַח pesakh; πάσχα pascha]. The sacrificial offering of Passover (e.g., Exod 12:21). Jesus is portrayed as the paschal lamb (John 19:36; 1 Cor 5:7), connecting him with the lamb's role in the Passover meal and exodus. *See* PASSOVER AND FEAST OF UNLEAVENED BREAD.

PAS-DAMMIM pas-dam´im [פַּס־דַּמִּים pas-dammim]. The location where DAVID and ELEAZAR fought a heroic battle (1 Chr 11:12-14) against the Philistines, likely the same as EPHES-DAMMIM, where Goliath and the Philistines gathered (1 Sam 17:1).

PASEAH puh-see´uh [פָּסֵחַ paseakh]. 1. One of three children born to Eshton of the men of Recah according to the Heb. or Rechab in the LXX (1 Chr 4:12).

2. One of several fathers whose descendants returned from exile in the early Persian era to participate in the service of the Temple (Ezra 2:49; Neh 7:51).

3. The father of JOIADA, who rebuilt the OLD GATE of Jerusalem together with Meshullam in the days of Nehemiah (Neh 3:6). *See* EZRA AND NEHEMIAH, BOOKS OF.

JASON R. TATLOCK

PASHHUR pash´huhr [פַּשְׁחוּר pashkhur; Φάσσορος Phassoros, Φαισούρ Phaisour]. Recent scholarship suggests that the name is Egyptian and means "the son of Horus." Several individuals, often difficult to differentiate, bear this name in the Bible. 1. Son of Malchiah (*see* MALCHIJAH), the prince who owned the cistern into which JEREMIAH was thrown (Jer 38:6); one of the emissaries sent by Zedekiah in 588 BCE to seek Jeremiah's intercession with God concerning Nebuchadnezzar's impending attack. Jeremiah responded by announcing that God would fight with Babylon against Jerusalem (Jer 21:1, 3). This royal prince should not be confused with the priest of the same name (§2).

2. Son of Immer; a priest in Jerusalem in the time of Jeremiah (Jer 20:1-6). As chief officer in charge of temple security, this Pashhur ordered Jeremiah beaten and placed in the stocks following the prophet's seditious attack upon the nation and its institutions. Upon his release the next day, Jeremiah pronounced judgment on Pashhur, renaming him "Terror-all-around" and announcing that he would look on as Babylon carried the nation into exile.

3. Father of GEDALIAH, one of the temple officials who left Jeremiah to die in a muddy cistern (Jer 38:1). This Pashhur may be the one mentioned in 1 Chr 9:12; Neh 11:12.

4. Ancestor of the "sons of Pashhur" a postexilic priestly family (Ezra 2:38; Neh 7:41; 1 Esd 5:25) that returned from Babylon with Zerubbabel. The six men from this family who divorced their foreign wives are the largest priestly group to do so (Ezra 10:22; 1 Esd 9:22).

5. Either a priest who set his seal upon the firm agreement to "walk in God's law" (Neh 10:29 [Heb. 10:30]), or, more likely, the family name (#4) of one of the priestly courses presented as the personal name of such a signatory (Neh 10:3 [Heb. 10:4]).

MARK THRONTVEIT

PASS [מַעֲבָר maʿavar]. A break in a chain of mountains or hills that allowed easier passage to the other side. A number of roads in ancient Israel made use of passes as ways of travel into the Judean and Ephraimite hill country. Roads through these passes are usually termed *ascents* and *descents* (depending on the direction of travel) or *ways* in the OT and are often named after an important city on the route. The "ascent of Adummim" was the main route from Jericho to Jerusalem (Josh 15:7), while the "ascent of Ziz" ran from En-gedi to Hebron (2 Chr 20:16). The best-known pass in the OT is the pass between Michmash and Geba, where Jonathan and the forces of Saul defeated the Philistines (1 Sam 13:23–14:23). Isaiah also pictures the Assyrians using this pass as they make their way to Jerusalem (Isa 10:28-29). The Hebrew word for pass is also used to refer to the ford of a river. *See* ISRAEL, GEOGRAPHY OF.

KEVIN A. WILSON

PASSION NARRATIVES. The Passion Narratives are the portions of the Gospels that tell of the suffering and death of Jesus (usually including the accounts of his burial). Scholars debate the exact points of the beginning of each of the Passion Narratives, but all interpreters include the stories of Jesus' arrest, trial, suffering, and execution.

From the advent of form criticism interpreters contended that prior to the composition of the first written Gospel there existed a fairly well-formed, perhaps even definitely set, version of the Passion Narrative (*see* FORM CRITICISM, NT). The expanse of time between the death of Jesus in 30/33 CE and the writing of the first Gospel in the mid-60s to 70 required a process of oral transmission of tradition (*see* ORAL TRADITION). Comparison of the Passion Narratives to the other stories and sections of the Gospels found the Passion Narratives to be an extended, logically progressive sequence of scenes that were interconnected and even dependent upon one another in forming a larger coherent account. By contrast, the portions of the Gospels prior to the Passion Narratives were short, seemingly independent units that could be, and perhaps were, arranged in whatever order the evangelists desired. Moreover, whereas the pericopae composing the account of Jesus' ministry prior to the passion could stand alone and communicate a purposeful message, certain elements of the Passion Narratives had no discernible function outside of the larger account and seemed unlikely ever to have existed independently (*see* PERICOPE).

The contentions of the early form critics have undergone serious criticism by scholars attempting to disprove the existence of a pre-Gospel Passion Narrative. Yet, there are many scholars who, although dubious about the numerous and different, but precise, reconstructions of the pre-Gospel Passion Narratives, still find the basic logic of the argument for a pre-Gospel Passion Narrative persuasive. While this important interpretive issue may never be settled finally, one should not miss the central agreement by all parties in this controversy, i.e., all agree there were Passion Narrative traditions in early Christianity prior to the composition of the Gospels.

Without attempting to settle the issues of the existence and shape of a pre-Gospels Passion Narrative or Passion Narratives, one may ask whether there is evidence in the Passion Narratives of the Gospels of the oral tradition(s) from the period prior to the writing of the Gospels. Analysis of the canonical Gospels reveals a plethora of special materials in each of the works that comprehensively suggests an active interest in the passion of Jesus and implies steady elaboration of the most basic story.

In Matthew's account one finds 1) Jesus' questioning of Judas after he is kissed, 2) the story of the death of Judas, 3) the story of Pilate's wife, 4) Pilate's washing his hands and the accompanying cry of the people, 5) the offer of wine mixed with gall, 6) the signs after Jesus' death, and 7) the posting of a guard at the tomb. In Mark's Passion Narrative alone one reads of 1) the young man who fled nude from Jesus' arrest, 2) the offer of wine mixed with myrrh (similar to Matthew, but not exactly the same), and 3) Pilate's confirmation of Jesus' death. Luke offers still other items, including 1) Jesus' confronting Judas and apparently preventing the kiss, 2) the presence of the Jewish leaders at Jesus' arrest, 3) Jesus' healing of the man whose ear was cut off, 4) Jesus' being mocked as he waits at the home of the high priest, 5) the morning assembly of the Jewish leaders to consider Jesus' fate, 6) Jesus before Herod Antipas, 7) Jesus and the daughters of Jerusalem, 8) two or three words of Jesus from the cross, 9) the report of the exchange between Jesus and those with whom he was crucified, 10) the reaction of the assembled crowds who watch and see Jesus' death, and 11) the mention of the acquaintances' being present with the women and seeing the crucifixion.

John's narrative is even more distinguished by its special materials: 1) the exchange between Jesus and the crowd that came to arrest him, including his saying, "I am," and their falling to the ground, 2) the details that Simon Peter wielded the sword and that Malchus lost his ear, 3) the soldiers' seizing Jesus, 4) another disciple's accompanying Peter to the house of the high priest, 5) Jesus' being interrogated by the high priest, Annas, 6) the officer striking Jesus for his answer to the high priest and Jesus' words to the officer, 7) Annas sending Jesus bound to Caiaphas, 8) conversations between Jesus and Pilate, 9) Pilate and "the Jews" in dialogue, 10) the declaration by "the Jews," "We have no King but Caesar," 11) Jesus' bearing his own cross, 12) three words of Jesus from the cross, 13) "the Jews" requesting that Jesus' legs be broken, although he was already dead, so that his side was pierced, and 14) Nicodemus' bringing 100 pounds of spices to use in burying Jesus.

No hard and fast conclusion comes from observing these items in the Gospel Passion Narratives. But, whatever theory of synoptic interrelatedness one holds, clearly there is additional material incorporated into the Passion Narratives by the subsequent evangelists; and, in turn, whatever, if any, the relationship of the Fourth Gospel to the Synoptics, the author of that Gospel also offers a wealth of additional Passion Narrative material. While each of these unique items in the earliest Passion Narratives would require individual analysis to determine whether the material is more likely to result from the influence of oral tradition, written accounts, or from the author's own meditation and composition, it seems highly unlikely that all of these added traditions were simply the results of the authors' meditations.

Given the tendencies observed in these writings and given the natural restrictions related to ancient written materials throughout the early centuries of the life of the church, one can safely conclude that the Passion Narrative was more often told than written, more often heard than read, more often known than physically held. The process of elaboration was normal. The difficulty for the interpreter confronting the evidences of this process is twofold and sets the agenda for future studies: scholars must determine whether the additions are creations of the authors or reflections of oral and/ or written traditions, and they must assess the antiquity of the traditions when these are present in Passion Narratives accounts. *See* REDACTION CRITICISM, NT; SYNOPTIC PROBLEM.

Bibliography: R. E. Brown. *The Death of the Messiah: From Gethsemane to the Grave: A Commentary on the Passion Narratives in the Four Gospels.* 2 vols. (1994); R. Bultmann. *The History of the Synoptic Tradition* (1963); J. T. Carroll and Joel B. Green. *The Death of Jesus in Early Christianity* (1995); H. Wansbrough, ed. *Jesus and the Oral Tradition* (1991).

MARION L. SOARDS

PASSION OF PETER AND PAUL. *See* PETER AND PAUL, MARTYRDOM OF.

PASSOVER AND FEAST OF UNLEAVENED BREAD pas´oh-vuhr, uhn-lev´uhnd-bred´ [**פֶּסַח** **pesakh, חַג הַמַּצּוֹת khagh hammatsoth; πάσχα pascha, ἡ ἑορτὴ τῶν ἀζύμων hē heortē tōn azymōn]**. The Passover and Feast of Unleavened Bread are two consecutive festivals that are treated as one holiday in some biblical passages. The traditional celebration of Passover is called the SEDER.

A. The Old Testament

The two festivals figure in several kinds of passages in the OT.

1. Festival lists in the law codes

In the lists of pilgrimage festivals (Exod 23:14-17; 34:18, 22-24) only the Festival of Unleavened Bread, not Passover, is mentioned; it is said to last seven days during which only unleavened bread is to be eaten. Both lists add that it was to be observed during the month ABIB, the first month of the Hebrew CALENDAR (changed to NISAN after the exile), corresponding to the time when Israel left Egypt (Exod 23:15; 34:18). No specific time for the seven days of unleavened bread is defined. Deuteronomy 16 speaks of both Passover and the eating of UNLEAVENED BREAD and leaves the impression that this occasion lasts seven days. It stipulates that Israel was to keep the Passover in Abib. The Passover sacrifice (from the flock or herd) was not to be eaten with anything leavened. "For seven days you shall eat unleavened bread with it—the bread of affliction—because you came out of the land of Egypt in great haste" (Deut 16:3).

The festival lists in Lev 23 and Num 28–29 present a different picture: in them there are two separate but contiguous holidays. Leviticus 23:5 stipulates that Israel is to celebrate Passover in the first month, the fourteenth day, at a time defined as "between the two evenings" ("twilight" in the NRSV), when "there shall be a passover offering to the LORD." The offering is the center of attention. Leviticus 23:6-8 then deals with the Festival of Unleavened Bread that begins on 1/15, declaring that for seven days Israel is to eat unleavened bread. The first and seventh of those days were to be marked by a holy convocation and no labor, but there were to be sacrifices offered all seven days. Here the two are separate festivals. The same situation prevails in Num 28. According to v. 16 the Passover sacrifice is offered on 1/14, and vv. 17-25 provide laws for the Festival of Unleavened Bread. They include the same ones as Lev 23:6-8 but add details regarding the sacrifices that are to be presented each day, in addition to the normal daily offerings. In his list of holidays Ezekiel names and dates both holidays and identifies sacrifices connected with them (45:21-24).

Numbers 9:1-14 provides for a second Passover in response to people who were not able to celebrate it on 1/14—due to corpse defilement—but still wanted to offer the sacrifice. The divine instructions to Moses were that anyone so defiled or on a journey on 1/14 could offer the Passover on 2/14 under the same regulations as the celebration on 1/14.

2. Exodus 12:1–13:10

The two festivals—Passover and Unleavened Bread—are distinguished in other scriptural sources but are regularly mentioned side by side. In the narratives that introduce them in Exod 12–13, they appear in the general context of the tenth plague on Egypt, the death of all the FIRSTBORN. The destructive event happened around midnight (Exod 11:4) in the very night when the Israelites were celebrating the first Passover. The legislation in Exod 12 highlights these divine instructions to Moses regarding the Passover: on 1/10 the entire community was to select a LAMB, a one-year-old male without defects, one for each family group (12:3-4); none of its bones was to be broken (12:46). On 1/14 the "whole assembled congregation of Israel" was to slaughter the lamb "between the evenings" (12:6), with some blood spattered on the doorposts and lintels of the house where the meal was to be eaten. It was to be eaten that night roasted, with unleavened bread and bitter herbs, and none of it was to remain until the morning (12:8, 10). The text, which refers to the sacrifice as "the passover of the LORD" (v. 11), several times relates the term *Passover* to his passing over the Israelite houses (vv. 13, 23, 27).

Beginning at Exod 12:15, the author turns to the Festival of Unleavened Bread. There is no reference to its actually being celebrated at the time of the exodus (see Exod 13:5-7 where the Israelites are told they will celebrate it when they enter the land), but the legislation follows that for the Passover, just as the festival itself does. The holiday, during which no leaven was to be present or eaten, lasts seven days, with the first and last days being times for assemblies and no work. This festival too was tied to the exodus (12:17); the text explains that the Israelites ate their bread unleavened because of their hasty departure from Egypt (12:39). The obvious connection between Passover and the Festival of Unleavened Bread is that no yeast was to be eaten from the evening of 1/14 to the evening of 1/21, which is defined as a seven-day period (12:18). *See* EXODUS, BOOK OF.

3. Other narrative accounts

The remaining scriptural references to the holidays are few. Joshua 5:10-11 records the first Passover in the land (celebrated in the evening) and adds that on the next day "unleavened cakes (**matsoth** מַצּוֹת)" were eaten, though the Festival of Unleavened Bread is not mentioned. Centuries later, during his reform of worship on the basis of the law book found in the Temple, King Josiah ordered that the people keep Passover in Jerusalem (2 Kgs 23:21-23); apparently the provision "in Jerusalem" (v. 23, in agreement with law of the sanctuary in Deut 16) is what is meant by saying no such Passover had been held since the time of the judges. The Chronicler describes a Passover in the days of King Hezekiah (2 Chr 30) and, of course, retells Josiah's celebration of it (2 Chr 35). King Hezekiah proclaimed a Passover at the Temple in the second month of the year because, in the first month, the priests had not sanctified themselves and the people had not assembled (2 Chr 30:1-5; see v. 15: 2/14). The Levites are said to have slaughtered the Passover lambs for those who were not clean (2 Chr 30:17-20). However, 2 Chr 30:13 says it was the Festival of Unleavened Bread that the people came to celebrate in the second month; vv. 21-22 add that they kept this holiday for seven days in Jerusalem and mention the joy of the occasion and the participation of the Levites. In fact, everyone decided to celebrate the next week as well (2 Chr 30:23). According to 2 Chr 35, the priests and Levites were involved in the offering (vv. 10-11), while v. 17 says that they also observed the Festival of Unleavened Bread for seven days. Ezra 6:19-22 describes the first Passover of those who returned from exile. At that time the priests and Levites had purified themselves, and they were the ones to kill the Passover lambs (v. 20). Like 2 Chr 30:21, Ezra 6:22 notes the joy with which the seven-day Festival of Unleavened Bread was celebrated.

There has been much speculation about the origins of the two spring holidays. They differ in that the one-day Passover focuses on the sacrifice of the lamb, while the seven-day Festival of Unleavened Bread centers on the absence of yeast. Yet, whatever their origins may have been, no information has survived beyond what is found in the OT.

B. References Outside the Old Testament

Sources outside the OT document that Jewish people observed both festivals during the Persian, Hellenistic, and Roman periods.

1. Elephantine Papyri

The earliest extra-biblical reference occurs in one of the ELEPHANTINE PAPYRI. The text (TAD A4.1), which bears a date of 419 or 418 BCE, appears to relate instructions from Darius II (423–404 BCE) to Arsames, the satrap of Egypt. Though the text is broken and key words must be supplied, lines 3–4 may refer to Passover, and line 4 does mention the period from day 15 to day 21, that is, the dates of the Festival of Unleavened Bread (line 6 prohibits eating leavened bread; part of the name Nisan [the first month] can be read on line 7). The papyrus very likely indicates, therefore, that Jews in Elephantine celebrated these holidays far from the Jerusalem Temple.

2. Jubilees and Egyptian Greek texts

Jubilees (ca. 160–150 BCE) provides extended statements about the two festivals. The author briefly summarizes the exodus itself in chap. 48 and notes that 1/14 was one of the dates on which the demon Mastema was bound so that he could not accuse the Israelites (*Jub.* 48:15). The Passover legislation appears in chap. 49. One issue with which the writer deals is the time when the meal is to be eaten: the lamb had to be sacrificed before evening and the Israelites were to eat it during the evening of the fifteenth after sunset (49:1). In 49:10-12 he further specifies that the time "between the evenings" is from the third part of the day to the third part of the night. He also notes the joy of the occasion (v. 2) and the presence of wine at it (v. 6). *Jubilees* is insistent in a number of verses both that the festival should fall on the correct day and that none of the bones of the slaughtered animal be broken. It also teaches that the Passover wards off plagues for the coming year (v. 15). The Temple was the place for celebrating the Passover, and every male twenty years of age and above (a rule not mentioned in the OT) was obligated to participate (vv. 16-21). At the end of the chapter about Passover, the book makes brief reference to the Festival of Unleavened Bread and notes the joy associated with it. According to *Jubilees*, Israel actually did celebrate the seven-day holiday in the time between the exodus itself and the crossing of the sea (vv. 22-23).

Without naming it, *Jubilees* had dealt with the Festival of Unleavened Bread at an earlier point in its retelling of Genesis through Exodus. The author found the historical basis for it in the three-day journey of Abraham to sacrifice Isaac at Mount Moriah, the day there, and the three-day trip back home (17:15–18:19). Abraham celebrated this festival of the Lord with joy in the first month, just as his descendants were commanded to do (see 17:15 and 18:17-19).

Ezekiel the Tragedian, another 2nd-cent. BCE Jewish writer, briefly mentions the Passover as being offered on the eve of the full moon when the firstborn of Egypt died and the Israelites feasted (Ezek. Trag. 156–60). He also recognizes that the seven-day Festival of Unleavened Bread would be celebrated when Israel entered the land, remembering the seven days after the exodus from Egypt (Ezek. Trag. 167–71). Aristobulus (also 2nd cent.) wrote about the astronomical timing of Passover: it was to take place at the full moon, around the vernal equinox, at which time the sun and moon were in positions opposite to each other (Aristob. 1).

3. The Dead Sea Scrolls

The scribes who wrote and copied the scrolls found at Qumran referred to the two holidays several times (*see* DEAD SEA SCROLLS). The *Temple Scroll*, for one, devotes paragraphs to Passover (11Q19 XVII,6–9) and Unleavened Bread (11Q19 XVII,10–16). The Passover section names the scriptural date and stipulates that it is to be offered before the evening sacrifice (line 7); men from twenty years of age and up are to eat it in the Temple courts. The next morning they are to go home (as in Deut 16:7). Scroll 11Q19 XVII,10–16 deals with the seven-day festival that begins on 1/15 (see also 11Q19 XI, 10); there are to be solemn assemblies and no work on days one and seven, while on each of the seven days the appropriate sacrifices are to be offered (they are listed).

The calendar documents from Qumran also take note of the two festivals. Where one can calculate the dates assigned in them to the holidays, they are, of course, the ones legislated in the OT. Relatively well-preserved references are:

1. Passover: 4Q265 4 3; 4Q320 4 III, 2–12; 4Q320 4 IV, 7; 4Q320 4 V, 1, 10; 4Q320

4 VI, 6; 4Q321 2 I, 8–9 (see 4Q321 2 III, 3–4, 7); 4Q321 2 IV, 2 (see 4Q329a 4–5).
2. Unleavened Bread: 4Q326 3; 4Q365a 1 2.
3. Second Passover: 4Q319 13 4; 4Q320 4 III, 4; 4Q320 4 IV, 9; 4Q320 4 V, 3, 12; 4Q320 4 VI, 7; 4Q321 2 IV, 2; 4Q321 2 III, 8.

The *Wisdom of Solomon*, chaps. 10–19 of which focus on the events in Egypt, the exodus from it, and the wilderness period, deals with the Passover in 18:5-19. In line with the theme of this part of the book, the poetic retelling of the tenth plague and the Passover meal exemplifies how the Israelites were blessed through the means by which the Egyptians were punished.

4. Philo and Josephus

Philo of Alexandria, among other references, devoted sections to the two festivals in his survey of the scriptural holidays. In the paragraphs regarding the Passover (*Spec. Laws* 2.27, 145–49), he calls it the crossing festival and notes that for the day all Israelites became priests who slaughter the sacrificial animal. Allegorically, the occasion expresses the purification of the soul, and for that day each home becomes a temple. Philo also mentions that wine was used and hymns were sung. When he writes about the Festival of Unleavened Bread (*Spec. Laws* 2.28, 150–61), he compares conditions in the first month of the year with those at creation and dates the beginning of the holiday to the day of the full moon when there is no darkness because the sun shines all day and the moon all night. He also draws attention to the joy of the festival and finds that the lack of leaven in the bread expresses not only the incomplete state of crops at that early point in the year but also a proximity to nature, whereas leaven is a product of human art. Josephus surveys the scriptural stories about the exodus and mentions Passover and Unleavened Bread as he does so (*Ant.* 2.311–17); he also includes the other references in the biblical histories (*Ant.* 5.20–21 [Joshua]; 9.263–72 [Hezekiah]; 10.70–72 [Josiah]; 11.110 [Ezra 6]) and celebrations at later times during some of which disturbances broke out and became especially serious because of the large crowds present (*Ant.* 17.213–18 [in Archelaus' time] and 20.106–12 [in the procuratorship of Cumanus]). In his paraphrase of the law he deals with the two festivals (*Ant.* 3.248–51).

5. The New Testament

The Passover plays a central role in the NT, and the Festival of Unleavened Bread is mentioned a few times. The most famous instance is in the accounts of the Last Supper (*see* LAST SUPPER, THE), which is presented as a Passover meal (Seder) in the Synoptic Gospels. The intertwining of the two festivals is articulated in the verse that introduces the account in Mark: "On the first day of Unleavened Bread, when the Passover lamb is sacrificed, his disciples said to him, 'Where do you want us to go and make the preparations for you to eat the Passover?' " (Mark 14:12; par. Matt 26:17 and Luke 22:7). That evening Jesus and his band ate the meal at a house in Jerusalem. As they were eating, he took the bread and blessed it and gave thanks for the cup; he identified the bread with his body and the wine with his blood of the covenant that was being shed for many people (*see* EUCHARIST; LORD'S SUPPER). He would not drink that wine again until he would do so in the kingdom of God (Matt 26:26-29; Mark 14:22-25; Luke 22:14-20 [where there is a cup during and after the meal]; see also 1 Cor 11:23-26). Matthew and Mark also record that they sang a hymn before they left for the Mount of Olives (Matt 26:30; Mark 14:26).

In the Gospel of John, Jesus has a last meal with his disciples "before the festival of the Passover" (13:1); at it he washed the disciples' feet (13:3-12) and gave them a new commandment to love one another (13:34-35). Later, when he was brought to Pilate, his Jewish captors "did not enter the headquarters, so as to avoid ritual defilement and to be able to eat the Passover" (18:28). In the next chapter John again notes that it was "the day of Preparation for the Passover" and that it was about noon (19:14), the time from when the Passover lambs could be slaughtered at the Temple. As a result, Jesus, the "Lamb of God" (1:29), was killed at the time the Passover victims were sacrificed.

The festivals are named a few other times in the NT. Passover was the occasion that brought Jesus and his parents to the Temple when he was twelve years of age (Luke 2:41-42). John also mentions it as the time when Jesus cleared the Temple area of the people engaged in commerce (2:13-25; see 5:1). The Festival of Unleavened Bread figures in Acts 12:3-4 as the time at which Herod Agrippa I arrested Peter, "intending to bring him out to the people after the Passover." Paul, when commenting figuratively on clearing out the old leaven so that the community would become a new batch of unleavened dough, wrote: "For our pascal lamb, Christ, has been sacrificed. Therefore, let us celebrate the festival, not with the old yeast, the yeast of malice and evil, but with the unleavened bread of sincerity and truth" (1 Cor 5:7-8).

6. The Mishnah

The MISHNAH (ca. 200 CE) devotes a tractate to Passover and Unleavened Bread. *Pesahim* reflects the time after the destruction of the Temple and, although it deals with matters relating to the temple service (e.g., the time for the evening offering after which the Passover lambs could be sacrificed, the three groups into which the large crowd was divided and the singing of the HALLEL psalms by the Levites while each group offered the sacrifice [*m. Pesah.* 5:1, 5-7]), it focuses on other aspects of the festival. Among its concerns are rules governing the search for leaven, who may eat the meal, when work ceases, acts connected with the Passover offering that override the Sabbath, how the animal is to be roasted, issues of purity, how the first Passover differed from all subsequent ones, the four cups of wine, and the four questions (10:1-7). The tractate also examines questions related to the Second Passover (9:1-4).

Bibliography: B. Bokser. *The Origins of the Seder* (1984); J. Jeremias. *The Eucharistic Words of Jesus* (1977); J. Milgrom. *Leviticus 23–27.* AB 3B (2001).

JAMES C. VANDERKAM

PASTOR [ποιμήν **poimēn**]. A leader or overseer. The gift of pastoring is among those given by Christ to the church to equip saints for the work of ministry (Eph 4:11).

PASTORAL LETTERS pas'tuhr-uhl. The "Pastoral Letters" is a composite name for the collection of epistles that includes 1 and 2 Timothy and Titus. TIMOTHY and TITUS serve as exemplary figures with whom the reader identifies, because the letters are from an older pastor (Paul) to younger pastors (Timothy and Titus). The letters' preoccupations include church order ("how one ought to behave in the household of God, which is the church"; 1 Tim 3:15 and see 5:3-22), preservation of apostolic teaching (1 Tim 1:3-10; 3:14–4:10; 6:3-5, 20; 2 Tim 1:11-12; Titus 1:10-16), and the church's reputation (1 Tim 2:1-2; 5:14; 6:1-12; Titus 2:1-10).

Debate about authorship is lively. Those who hold Pauline authorship think the letters were written after the apostle's first Roman imprisonment, arguing he traveled east (to Gaul and Spain, Rom 15:24) and was imprisoned in Rome a second time when the letters were written. This theory relies on internal evidence from the Pastoral Epistles. Most modern scholars accept the position that these letters are pseudonymous, written in Asia Minor in the early 2nd cent. by those who applied Paul's thought to matters that arose after his death. The question of pseudonymity is important; the letters present themselves as preserving correct doctrine and practice. Using Paul's name honors the apostle and legitimates their position (*see* PSEUDONYMOUS WRITING).

The language and style of the letters differ considerably from Paul's earlier epistles. For example, while Paul uses the word *faith* as a verb (**pisteuō** πιστεύω), in the Pastoral Letters it is a noun (**pistis** πίστις), a body of knowledge to be guarded or preserved. About 20 percent of the vocabulary of the Pastorals does not occur elsewhere in the NT. Of the 306 or so words not in Paul's uncontested letters, two-thirds are used by 2nd-cent. Christian writers like Ignatius of Antioch and Polycarp. Like other deutropauline letters, the Pastorals incorporate traditional literary forms including hymn fragments (1 Tim 2:5-6*a*; 2 Tim 2:11-13), HOUSEHOLD CODES (Titus 1:5-9; 2:1-10), vice and virtues lists (1 Tim 1:9-10; 3:2-3; 6:11; 2 Tim 3:2-4; Titus 1:7-10; *see* LISTS, ETHICAL), polemical remarks, and a "trustworthy" saying formula (1 Tim 1:15; 4:9; 2 Tim 2:11).

Theologically, the Pastorals' ethical instructions suggest the gospel, properly understood, is reflected in believers' lives. The Pastoral Epistles reflect early church development and challenges. From outside there was conflict with the state. Christians were a minority vulnerable to social ostracism and political persecution, so public opinion mattered. From inside there was danger from false teaching with no structures to maintain orthodoxy, thus the concern with correct teaching (2 Tim 2:14-19) and appropriate leadership (1 Tim 3:1-12; 5:3-22; Titus 1:5-16). The letters reflect the church's movement from enthusiastic and primitive simplicity to more defined governance and doctrine, thus providing the transition to the period of the Apostolic Fathers. In the Pastoral Letters the church was settling down to live "in the world." *See* CHURCH, LIFE AND ORGANIZATION OF; TIMOTHY, FIRST AND SECOND LETTERS TO; TITUS, LETTER TO.

Bibliography: Mark Harding. *What Are They Saying about the Pastoral Epistles?* (2001); Linda Maloney. "The Pastoral Epistles." *Searching the Scriptures*, vol. 2. Elisabeth Schüssler Fiorenza, ed. (1994) 361–80; David C. Verner. *The Household of God: The Social World of the Pastoral Epistles* (1983); Frances Young. *The Theology of the Pastoral Epistles* (1994).

BONNIE THURSTON

PASTORAL NOMADS. Earlier discussions of nomadism by historical critics focused on the relation of these migrant people to the ancestral narratives in Genesis and viewed nomads as a distinct population group whose settling down to an agricultural economy contributed to the formation of the Israelite tribes in the highlands of Canaan. More recent studies have taken into account ethnographic studies and methods and have explored semi-nomadic pastoralism, a more precise term for this form of economic activity, as a social and economic adaptation. Given the scarcity of natural resources in peripheral environmental zones such as the Negeb or portions of the Jordanian Plateau, it becomes necessary to engage in periodic movement of herds and to supplement their diet and basic economy with seasonal agriculture. A subsistence group may be defined within a continuum of occupational choices and strategies from purely pastoral nomadic to purely agricultural/sedentary, but many villages contain both farmers and herdsmen and there are many regions in the Middle East where pastoral nomadic groups and agriculturalists are separate population groups living in an "enclosed" economic sphere, exploiting natural resources and living in a symbiotic relationship. The choice to engage in pastoral nomadic activity as the predominant mode of subsistence may be a long-term, conscious adaptation to the environmental realities of an area, a response to shifting political conditions, or a desire to diversify a household's economy through a mixture of farming and herding and thus ensure better chances of survival. It may also be a temporary course of action designed to meet a specific need such as that which is portrayed in the retribalization of Abram's household during its migration from Haran to Canaan and during the unsettled period of their "sojourning" prior to their return to a more sedentary lifestyle (Gen 12–20).

A. The Lifestyle of the Pastoral Nomad

The movement from a sedentary life to various levels of nomadic existence and back to a settled condition is not unusual and often is determined by wealth, political connections, and land tenure. A catastrophic climate change, the invasion of new peoples, or the desire to avoid contact with disease may trigger pastoral nomadic activity. Conversely, the acquisition of larger herds or the loss of their animals, the movement of household leaders into the political bureaucracy, or a shift in the economy may lead members of the nomadic group to make a voluntary or inescapable decision to settle down. While governments may wish to gain greater control over the pastoral nomadic groups within their political domain or even force them to become sedentarized, both ancient (Mari texts) and more recent efforts have had mixed results.

In the Middle East, pastoral nomadism involves the purposeful, regular (generally seasonal) migration of a household or a group of households from one familiar locale to another within a defined tribal territory as a means of making a living and to provide their herds of sheep and goats sufficient water and grazing. In many areas this involves what is known as transhumance, a substantial percentage of the population consciously moving the herds to and from seasonal pasturage (often from highlands to lowlands) in response to temperature and climate change. The actual migration patterns can be somewhat erratic depending upon the availability of resources given the unpredictable nature of the climate (esp. rainfall amounts) and of the political situation, but it is never aimless. It should also be noted that most pastoral nomadic groups tend to remain within easy traveling distance of their areas of cultivation and arboriculture that may require periodic attention. In this way they avoid the dangers of a single-faceted economy. Their labor-intensive social adaptation involves a juggling act by the members of the household. They must balance the need for water, pasturage, access to agricultural resources, and sociopolitical conditions with the social profile of the household (its size, relative wealth, and covenants with local villages and regional leaders). As a result, the leaders of each household are constantly assessing and reassessing conditions and making decisions to take advantage of opportunities or to counteract dangerous or threatening situations. While their movements are not dictated by external political relations, they do come into contact on a regular basis with local villagers as well as the representatives of national or regional governments. This requires them to maintain a recognized system of rights of passage, use of water resources, and periodic labor service. Both the nomadic pastoralists and the sedentary population may derive mutual benefit from these contacts with the exchange of manufactured goods, provision of items or resources not available otherwise, conveyance of news, and a temporary labor pool during harvests or shearing. For example, during the period when Abraham's household dwells in Gerar, the patriarch negotiates with King Abimelech for water rights and the digging of wells in the latter's territory (Gen 21).

B. Archaeological Evidence of Pastoral Nomadism

There has been some disagreement about whether it is possible to obtain archaeological evidence for nomadic pastoralists because of the paucity and ephemeral nature of these remains. Corrals made of brush rather than stone, wind and soil erosion, and the inundation of camping areas by seasonal marshes have contributed to this argument despite the fact that prehistorians have been able to obtain a remarkable amount of data on earlier eras and that there are documented records of pastoral nomadic groups in these regions from historical periods. For example, Egyptian administrative and monumental texts, including the Merneptah reliefs at Karnak, contain numerous references to the SHASU, who are said to range over large areas of the Levant, and state-less persons known as ʿApiru who are referred to as raiders of caravans and villages in the AMARNA LETTERS. One way to combine these documents with the archaeological record is the development of more exacting field surveys and analytic methods that will make it possible to more conclusively demonstrate that pastoral nomads can be traced throughout the Negev and Sinai ecologic zones. For instance, the evidence from Early Bronze Age occupation materials at the Camel site in the south-central Negev is an indication that even in areas where intensive agriculture is not possible there were sufficient materials for bead manufacture, small-scale metallurgy, and millstone manufacture to justify short-term occupation as long as there were nearby urban centers (in this case Arad) with which to maintain economic trade links. This and other archaeological and ethnographic data (campsites, cultic sites, cemeteries, and remains of manufacturing activity) demonstrate that from its earliest appearance, pastoral nomadism was an economic strategy employed to take fuller advantage of marginal environments like those found in portions of ancient Syro-Palestine and the Transjordanian Plateau. Generally, nomadic pastoralists functioned in symbiotic relationship to villages and towns within their sphere of activity. Semi-nomadic pastoral groups could not exist for long without a nearby settled population with which to trade and from which they could obtain grain. Without a ready source of extra food, the nomadic pastoralists were either forced into a more settled lifestyle tied to agriculture or forced to migrate to other regions where the food supply and opportunities to work as day laborers were sufficient (see Abram's move to Egypt in Gen 12:10). In addition, when there is evidence of a drastic decline in the population, such as the lack of public works and fortification projects in the Late Bronze Age in Canaan, it may be assumed that the nomadic population, which had provided part of the labor pool, had also declined.

It should also be noted that the total number of persons engaged in nonsedentary lifestyles is sometimes the result of periods of political disruption, such as the large-scale nomadization of population groups following the destruction of the Middle Bronze Age urban culture and the 12th-cent. BCE destruction of the urban centers throughout the Aegean-Anatolian, Syro-Palestinian region by the Sea Peoples. These catastrophic events, as well as periodic famines, resulted in social dislocation and in many cases widespread immigration of population groups on a scale similar to that described for Abram's household in Gen 12. For instance, the new ethnic groups entering Canaan from the former Hittite and Hurrian domains in Anatolia and north-central Mesopotamia in the 15th and 13th cent., following the collapse of their cultures, are mentioned in relation to Hebron and Jebus (Jerusalem) in the biblical narrative (Num 13:22; Ezek 16:3). The widespread redistribution of peoples resulted not only in the creation of new population mixes but also their nomadization over fairly long periods of time as they occupied new zones within which to graze their animals. Whether these forced immigrants were intent on a quick return to sedentary life is uncertain. To be sure, semi-nomadic peoples do at times make the decision to blend into a new community or claim territories for themselves, but this is not an inevitable process.

There is less evidence of long-term, pure nomadism, most often associated with the camel nomads of the Arabian Peninsula or the Sahara of northwestern Africa, during the Bronze and Iron ages. For the most part the general absence of evidence from the Iron Age sites (lack of camel bones except the intrusive deposit at ʿIzbet Sartah) indicates that pastoral nomadism in that era focused on sheep, cattle, and goat herding with a portion of the male population driving the animals to new pasturage as the seasons changed while the remainder of the village community engaged in agricultural and small cottage industries to complement their economic endeavors and better ensure the survival of the people. Large numbers of domesticated camels and the appearance of "proto-Bedouin" nomadic groups from Arabia are not documented until the 9th cent. BCE (Shalmaneser III's Qarqar inscription from 853 BCE). Thus the references to camels in Genesis, Judges, and 1 Samuel are anachronisms. The mention of nomadic pastoralists living in tents in Isaiah's vision of a desolate Babylon (Isa 13:20) and Jeremiah's reference to "nomads in the wilderness" (Jer 3:2) come from an era when political displacement and economic opportunities may have resulted in somewhat larger and more evident groups of nonsedentary peoples.

One final piece of archaeological evidence has sparked further speculation on the process or pattern of sedentarization by semi-nomadic peoples. This is based on the examination of elliptical village sites such as that found in Stratum III (12th cent.) ʿIzbet Sartah. Some scholars point to this phenomenon as evidence of the transition of semi-nomadic pastoralists into a more sedentary existence, with its reliance of construction and arrangement of the village along the lines of a pastoral encampment. Whether this reflects social transition, the elliptical arrangement of either the nomadic camp or a small village is an architectural adaptation to local climatic and geographical conditions and provides a measure of protection for the inhabitants and their stock. What seems most likely is that the increased settlement in the hill country of Canaan following the disruption of the region by the Sea Peoples included a mixed economy that took advantage of all available means of exploitation of its resources, including agriculture and pastoralism. That also means a close, symbiotic relationship between pastoral nomadic groups and the agriculturalists fleeing from the destroyed Canaanite urban centers that may eventually have coalesced into a new ethnic group.

C. Pastoral Nomadism in the Biblical Narratives

It now is generally accepted as a consensus among mainstream scholars that the ancestral narratives in Genesis and the accounts of migratory activity following the exodus from Egypt are not a historical account of events prior to the establishment of the Israelite monarchy. More likely they are a theologized saga containing a combination of cultural memories and a synthesis of a much larger chronicle based on strands of oral tradition of the mass migration and demographic instability during the period of Late Bronze and Early Iron ages (13th–11th cent. BCE). Composed and shaped in the late monarchic or postexilic period by the Deuteronomistic and Priestly editors, they function as idealized portrayals of the eponymous heroes of the Israelite nation, containing a series of social and legal precedents and providing a basis upon which to claim the right to the "promised land" under the terms of the covenant with God. As such, their usefulness is reduced to an analysis of social and economic activity.

The "nomadic ideal" expounded by Martin Noth and Albrecht Alt and used to justify a "peaceful infiltration" by pastoral nomadic biblical patriarchs into Canaan is therefore an inadequate explanation for events (*see* NOMADS). It does not take into account the ethnographic and archaeological evidence that has come to light in the past fifty years and clouds the value that may be derived from the biblical narrative about pastoral nomadic activity during the Late Bronze and Early Iron ages. In particular, it should be noted that depictions of the ancestors in Genesis are for the most part typical of semi-nomadic groups, who engage in classic strategies to make efficient use of their resources (Lot and Abram divide their herds to prevent overgrazing, Gen 13:5-9). Their economic pursuits were often centered on a central base (Hebron or Shechem) while the patriarch sent a portion of his males away to graze in either harvested fields or more distant pastures (Gen 37:12-17). When they do enter new regions, they negotiate with the local authorities for grazing rights and the use of water resources (Gen 21:22-32; 26:12-22). In addition, their movements are dictated at times by changes in the climate, forcing them to flee from famine conditions (Gen 12:10) or seek to purchase grain from Egypt (Gen 42:1-2). Similarly, the negative reaction of the tribes of Reuben and Gad to Deborah's call to war may be an indication of the desire of pastoral nomads to remain below the radar of political forces in their region. Being dependent upon both their herds and the goodwill of their neighbors to survive, these tribes would have been reluctant to respond to a conflict that may have destroyed both (Judg 5:15*b*-17). All this is an indication that the strategies employed by pastoral nomadic groups were well known and could easily be embedded into the ancestral and settlement traditions without distorting familiar economic pursuits. However, the appearance of pastoral nomadic activity in these narratives or those concerning the conquest and settlement of Canaan is not conclusive proof of the ethnic origins or emergence of the Israelites in that region. *See* HABIRU, HAPIRU; ISRAEL, SOCIOLOGY OF; MARI TEXTS, LETTERS; SOJOURNER.

Bibliography: A. Alt. *Essays on Old Testament History and Religion* (1968); Roger Cribb. *Nomads in Archaeology* (1991); William G. Dever. "Israelite Origins and the 'Nomadic Ideal': Can Archaeology Separate Fact from Fiction?" *Mediterranean Peoples in Transition, Thirteenth to Early Tenth Centuries BCE.* S. Gitin et al., eds. (1998) 220–37; I. Finkelstein. "Pastoralism in the Highlands of Canaan in the Third and Second Millennia B.C.E." *Pastoralism in the Levant.* O. Bar-Yosef and A. Khazanov, eds. (1992) 133–42; A. M. Khazanov. *Nomads and the Outside World* (1984); Thomas E. Levy and Augustin F. C. Holl. "Migrations, Ethnogenesis, and Settlement Dynamics: Israelites in Iron Age Canaan and Shuwa-Arabs in the Chad Basin." *Journal of Anthropological Archaeology* 21 (2002) 83–118; Nadav Na'aman. "The 'Conquest of Canaan' in the Book of Joshua and in History." *From Nomadism to Monarchy.* I. Finkelstein and N. Na'aman, eds. (1994) 218–81; Martin Noth. *The History of Israel.* 2nd ed. (1960); Steven A. Rosen. "Nomads in Archaeology: A Response to Finkelstein and Perevolotsky." *BASOR* 287 (1992) 75–85; Philip C. Salzman. "Pastoral Nomads: Some General Observations Based on Research in Iran." *Journal of Anthropological Research* 58 (2002) 245–64.

VICTOR H. MATTHEWS

PASTURE LANDS [מִגְרָשׁ **migrash**]. A common translation of a Hebrew noun derived from the verbal root **garash** (גָּרַשׁ, "drive out, cast out"). The term generally refers to demarcated land outside of city walls but can also refer to land used for herding livestock. While the Levites did not receive the same territorial inheritance as the other tribes of Israel, they did receive "pasture lands" (Josh 21; 1 Chr 6:54-81 [Heb. 1 Chr 6:39-66]). *See* ISRAEL, SOCIOLOGY OF.

STEVE COOK

PATARA pat'uh-ruh [Πάταρα **Patara**]. An important city of LYCIA (now in Turkey), situated about 7 mi. east of the mouth of the Xanthus River. It served as a seaport for the city of Xanthus.

Patara was known for its temple and oracle of APOLLO, delivered by a prophetess during a certain period of the year. (Herodotus, *Hist.* 1.182). Patara was conquered by Alexander the Great in the winter of 334–333 BCE. In 275 BCE Ptolemy II Philadelphius repaired the city and named it Arsinoe after his wife. In 197 BCE the city was seized by Antiochus III. Then it came under the administration of Rhodes until 167 BCE. Except for a brief capture by Brutus, the Lycians enjoyed independence until 43 CE when Claudius formally annexed Lycia and joined it to Pamphylia to form a new Roman province. The ruins of the city are located near the modern village of Gelemish.

Patara appears only once in the NT (Acts 21:1). After Paul had given a farewell address to the elders of Ephesus in Miletus (Acts 20:17-38) on his return from the third missionary journey, he set sail to COS, RHODES, and then to Patara where he found a vessel to sail to the coast of Phoenicia. *See* ACTS OF THE APOSTLES.

Bibliography: Bruce M. Metzger. *A Textual Commentary on the Greek New Testament* (1994).

VICTOR RHEE

PATH [אֹרַח **ʾorakh**, דֶּרֶךְ **derekh**, מַעְגָּל **maʿgal**, מִשְׁעוֹל **mishʿol**, נָתִיב **nathiv**; ὁδός **hodos**, τροχιά **troxia**]. The word *path* may refer literally to tracks left by wheels (e.g., Ps 23:3; Prov 2:9) or human and animal use (Gen 49:17; Ps 27:11; Mark 1:3; 4:15; Luke 8:5, 12; Acts 13:10; Rom 3:16). The image of the path is often used metaphorically to speak of the habitual "way," manner, or character of something, e.g., the "way of women" (i.e., menstruation, Gen 31:35), the sea (Ps 77:19 [Heb. 20]), wisdom (Prov 3:17), or an adulterous woman (Prov 2:18). Blessings will follow those who take the path of the righteous, but disaster overtakes those who walk in the "path that sinners tread" (e.g., Pss 1:1; 27:11; 85:13 [Heb. 85:14]; 110:7; 119:35, 105). In Deut 5:32-33, people are warned not to turn to the right or left, but to follow the exact path commanded by God. This produces long life in the land. Popular in wisdom teachings, the righteous path indicates an orientation toward life that honors the laws of God and applies them faithfully to human dealings (e.g., Job 8:13; 13:27; 33:11; Prov 1:15; 2:20; 3:6, 17; 5:21). The Hebrew prophets repeatedly call the people to reconsider their "ways" and to return to the path that God has set (Isa 3:12; 26:7; Jer 18:15; 23:12; Hos 2:6 [Heb. 2:8]; Joel 2:7; Mic 4:2). Good paths lead to life in abundance; wicked paths lead their followers down to the underworld of Sheol. *See* LIGHT AND DARKNESS; RIGHTEOUSNESS IN THE OT; SHEOL; WAY; WISDOM IN THE ANCIENT NEAR EAST; WISDOM IN THE OT.

CAROLE R. FONTAINE

PATHROS, PATHRUSIM path´ros, puh-thr*oo*´sim [פַּתְרוֹס **pathros**, פַּתְרֻסִים **pathrusim**]. Pathros signifies Upper EGYPT, the region of the Nile Valley south of Memphis to the first cataract at Aswan and the island of Elephantine. The gentilic form, **pathrusim**, occurs in the Table of Nations (Gen 10:14; 1 Chr 1:12) as one of the sons of MIZRAIM (Egypt).

Egypt was historically divided into two major administrative units: Lower Egypt, from Memphis north to the Mediterranean, and Upper Egypt. The region south of the first cataract known as Nubia or Kush was intermittently under Egyptian sovereignty, but not part of the core of Egypt. Pathros derives from the Egyptian t*3*-p*3*-rsy, "the land of the south."

Ezekiel (29:14; 30:14) includes Pathros in his oracles against Egypt. In Isa 11:11 Pathros is listed between Egypt and ETHIOPIA in the catalog of the regions from which God will restore the remnant of Israel and Judah. The same north-south sequence occurs in an inscription of the 7th-cent. BCE Assyrian king ESARHADDON, which identifies Taharqa as king of Musru, Paturisi, and Kusu.

Communities of Judeans were among the immigrant groups that settled in Upper and Lower Egypt in the Late Period (664–332 BCE). Jeremiah 44 addresses these Judean communities in exile, calling upon them to renounce the worship of the QUEEN OF HEAVEN, but they refuse. Detailed documentation exists for only one such community, the 5th-cent. BCE community at Elephantine in Upper Egypt, which worshiped at a temple of Yahweh and celebrated the Passover. *See* ELEPHANTINE PAPYRI.

CAROLYN HIGGINBOTHAM

PATIENCE [אֶרֶךְ אַפַּיִם **ʾorekh ʾappayim**, אֶרֶךְ רוּחַ **ʾerekh ruakh**; μακροθυμία **makrothymia**, ὑπομονή **hypomonē**]. Patience or ENDURANCE denotes the capacity to endure hardship, difficulty, or inconvenience without complaint, emphasizing calmness, self-control, and the willingness or ability to tolerate delay. The concept of patience in the Bible is extremely important; **ʾorekh ʾappayim** literally means "length of nose" and comes to mean, because of its picturesque imagery, someone who is not so angry as to be in confrontational proximity, nose to nose (Prov 25:15). The phrase **ʾerekh ruakh** is also used, meaning "long of spirit" with the same connotation of patience and calmness in the face of disorder or calamity (Eccl 7:8). When used of God, it describes God's willingness to wait calmly for the people to return in repentance so they can claim God's offer of forgiveness (see "slow to anger" in Exod 34:6; Num 14:18; Neh 9:17; Pss 86:15; 103:8; 145:8; Prov 14:29; 16:32; Joel 2:13; Jonah 4:2; Nah 1:3).

The idea of patience is important, too, in the NT. **Makrothymia**, the word normally rendered "patience," is variously translated "forbearance," "steadfastness," and "endurance." Also used is the more common **hypomonē**, literally meaning "to remain in place" or "to stand one's ground." Especially in ethical texts the word group (or semantic domain) calls believers to steadfastness in moral behavior in the face of the profound influences of Greco-Roman culture. For instance, Jas 1:3-4 is espcially exemplary in this regard, declaring, "You know that the testing of your faith produces endurance [**hypomonē**]; and let endurance have its full effect, so that you may be mature and complete, lacking in nothing." That is, patience, when allowed to accomplish its goal, brings about maturity and wholeness. For the author of James, patience is nothing less than the foundation upon which all Christian character is built and maintained. (See, most often, "endurance" in Rom 2:4; 2 Cor 6:4; Gal 5:22; 1 Thess 1:3; 2 Thess 1:4; 1 Tim 6:11; 2 Tim 3:10; Titus 2:2; Heb 6:12; 10:36; Jas 5:10; 1 Pet 3:20; 2 Pet 1:6.) *See* LISTS, ETHICAL.

JAMES E. WEST

PATMOS pat´muhs [Πάτμος **Patmos**]. Patmos is the AEGEAN island where the visionary called John received and recorded his vision, the book of Revelation (Rev 1:9). Patmos was probably not the backwater that is often assumed, with local cults to Apollo and Artemis. The text does not allow us to know whether John was on the island voluntarily, impelled there by a divine impulse, or banished for his prophetic activity. In later legend he was banished there by the Roman emperor himself. John writes that he is on Patmos "because of the word." This preposition construction is used elsewhere to indicate the outcome rather than the purpose of an action (e.g., Rev 2:3; 4:11), suggesting that John may have come here to hear the word rather than as the consequence of having preached the word. If, however, it is a consequence of his activity, it is most likely because some local official sent him as a result of his activities on the mainland. Patmos is the context for his trance experience (Rev 1:10), where, like Ezekiel in exile in Babylon (Ezek 1), John is enabled to understand divine mysteries about the future of the world and its political powers. *See* REVELATION, BOOK OF.

Bibliography: Ian Boxall. *The Revelation of St John.* BNTC (2006).

CHRISTOPHER ROWLAND

PATRIARCHAL LANGUAGE. Notwithstanding varied meanings of *patriarchy,* the adjective used here designates speech (oral and written) that is male-centered and male-dominated. Such speech characterizes the Bible, in the Hebrew and Aramaic of the OT and the Greek of the NT.

Crucial for understanding patriarchal language is the concept of GENDER, a word that holds three distinct yet overlapping uses, pertaining to grammar, sexual identity, and social construction. First, gender designates grammar, the formal system by which a language distinguishes words and combines them in sentences. Grammatical gender is a matter of syntax. Not all languages (e.g., Turkish) use gender, and those that do vary. Hebrew and Aramaic distinguish two genders, masculine and feminine, which apply to nouns, adjectives, pronouns, and verbs. To these two, Greek adds the category of neuter. Second, gender designates biological identification, the sexes male and female (and variations thereof). Correspondences between gender as grammar and gender as sex are partial and sometimes arbitrary. Syntax and sex should not be collapsed or confused. Third, gender designates social constructions of masculine and feminine: a continuum of human behaviors and attitudes as viewed in a particular culture at a particular time. These malleable features may or may not correspond to biological identity or grammatical formulations.

Confusion and convergence of grammatical gender with biological, social, and theological identities plague the Bible, its interpretations, and its translations. For millennia, interpreters have used its patriarchal language in deciding its meanings. Among the results have been the promotion of God as male and the legitimating of biological and social systems of sexism (i.e., male dominance and female subordination). By the 1970s, however, feminist analyses began to probe the male biases of language. These analyses showed that translators of the Bible into English have made its language even more patriarchal than required. The word ʾ**adham** (אָדָם), for instance, often carries (or allows) the generic meaning of "human" or "humankind," as do its Greek and Latin equivalents, **anthrōpos** (ἄνθρωπος) and *homo.* Yet ancient through modern translators have repeatedly rendered ʾ**adham** as "man," as if ʾ**adham** were the equivalent of ʾ**ish** (אִישׁ) in Hebrew, **anēr** (ἀνήρ) in Greek, and *vir* in Latin (compare the KJV, RSV, and NAB for Gen 1:26-27*a*). Conversely, translators have sometimes chosen a generic meaning for a word that is gender specific. In Hos 11:9, God, speaking in the first person, says, "for I am ʾ**el** (אֵל, 'God') and not ʾ**ish** ('a man')." Unlike the flexible term ʾ**adham**, the word ʾ**ish** denotes man as male or as husband (see Hos 2:16). Yet translators ancient and modern have obscured this refutation of male identity for God. They have resorted to the generic language of **anthrōpos** (the LXX), *homo* (the Vulgate), and "man," in the generic sense of all humankind (RSV), or "a mortal" (NRSV, a translation that fits the word ʾ**adham**, not ʾ**ish**).

Patriarchal language posed problems for the committee that prepared the New Revised Standard Version (NRSV; 1991). Mandated to alter the Revised Standard Version (RSV) only when necessary, the committee juggled competing values. It decided to eliminate in translation all grammatically masculine language that referred to human beings rather than to males only. (Left untouched was God-language, particularly male pronouns for deity.) That consensus reversed traditional translations making biblical language less patriarchal than it is, with gains and losses for interpretation. Changing singular nouns and pronouns to plurals became the chief solution to the problem. Psalm 8:4, traditionally rendered, "What is man that thou art mindful of him and the son of man that thou doest care for him?" (RSV), became, "What are human beings that you are mindful of them, mortals that you care for them?"

In some instances, however, the switch from singular to plural nouns and pronouns (unintentionally) distorted meaning. Proverbs 1:20-33 presents Wisdom crying out to many people. Plural nouns like "simple ones," "scoffers," and "fools" identify them, with matching pronouns and verbs forms. But at the close of the poem in Hebrew, the pronoun reference switches to the singular form as it reports the response to Wisdom. Though Wisdom addresses many, in the end only "one" hears. By changing the singular pronoun to "those who hear," the NRSV loses the contrast between the many and the one. Yet another approach changed third-person masculine pronouns to first person. Psalm 41:5, traditionally rendered the Hebrew as "My enemies say in malice: 'When will he [the psalmist] die, and his name perish?'" became "My enemies wonder in malice when I will die, and my name perish." Other approaches inserted in translation words not in the original or turned gender-specific language into generic language. "Brothers" became "brothers and sisters" (e.g., 1 Cor 1:10); in other instances "brothers" became "believers" (e.g., 1 Cor 6:8) and "my brothers" became "my friends" (1 Cor 14:26). Even in the explicitly androcentric book of Proverbs, "my son" became "my child" (e.g., 1:8; 2:1–6:1).

Where context allows, translators may simply omit masculine pronouns or substitute relevant nouns. For example, in the NRSV, Ps 62:5-6*a* begins "For God alone my soul waits in silence." It continues "for my hope is from him. He alone is my rock. . . ." By changing the words *him* and *he* to *God*, a translator can eliminate patriarchal grammar while reinforcing theological affirmation.

Further, interpreters may moderate patriarchal images for God by appeals to alternate texts that feature God in female roles or contexts. They highlight the repeated metaphor of God as a mother to signal the compassion of God (e.g., Deut 32:18; Jer 31:20) and images of the deity as provider and nurse (Exod 16:12; Num 11:11-13). Such passages can serve to override masculine grammar, temper male identity, and mitigate androcentric social constructs of the deity. By pointing to passages where God is imagined as having feminine roles alongside the better-known masculine roles, they may counter the constraints of gender. Nonetheless, despite the progress made by translators and interpreters, patriarchal language remains a formidable problem for biblical theology. In excluding women, rendering them invisible, or subordinating them to men, this language continues to promote male idolatry. *See* BIBLE TRANSLATION THEORY; FEMINIST INTERPRETATION.

Bibliography: Walter Harrelson. "Inclusive Language in the New Revised Standard Version." *PSB* 11 (1990) 224–31; Bruce M. Metzger, ed. *The Making of the New Revised Standard Version of the Bible* (1991); Carol Meyers. *Discovering Eve: Ancient Israelite Women in Context* (1988); Peter J. Thuesen. *In Discordance with the Scriptures* (1999) 152–54; Bruce K. Waltke and M. O'Connor. *An Introduction to Biblical Hebrew Syntax* (1990).

PHYLLIS TRIBLE

PATRIARCHS pay'tree-ahrk. The patriarchs are the "founding fathers" of Israel: Abraham, Isaac, and Jacob (Israel). Jacob's children were the eponymous ancestors of the twelve tribes of Israel. From this lineage the Israelites claimed their identity as a people.

A. The Patriarchal Period

Establishing the era of the patriarchs is complicated by the lack of conclusive evidence regarding their provenance and arrival in the land of Canaan. Previous scholarship located the patriarchs in the 2nd millennium BCE based on the study of names, on archaeological excavations, and by comparing the customs of the Hurrians with those of the patriarchs. The names of Israel's progenitors—Peleg, Serug, Nahor, and Terah—correspond to place names in northern Mesopotamia, suggesting that Abraham's home was Haran and not Ur of the Chaldeans (Gen 11:31). Moreover, the names Abram and Jacob attest a West Semitic connection. But because names normally remain frozen diachronically, patriarchal names may antedate the period they are purported to relate. Additionally, archaeological excavations at Shechem and Beersheba—sites that relate to the patriarchs—have so far yielded evidence that relates to the Middle Bronze II period and the Iron Age. In sum, the Genesis narratives, archaeological excavations, and extrabiblical literature do not provide conclusive data regarding the historicity of the patriarchs.

Hermann Gunkel argued that the stories of Genesis were etiological legends (stories that explain how things came to be as they are) that were transmitted by oral tradition. Albrecht Alt and Martin Noth advanced this method of interpretation to explain Israel's religion and land claim. The etiological interpretation, although questionable, elucidates the role of the patriarchal cycles (*see* ETIOLOGY). The Abraham and SARAH cycle (Gen 12–25) introduces Yahweh's promises of land and progeny (*see* ABRAHAM, OT). The military campaign against five kings in Gen 14 helps the reader to realize that Abraham, like all the patriarchs, was not a lone figure sojourning in a foreign land with his wife. Rather, he was like a tribal sheikh leading a host of people. The ISAAC and JACOB cycle (Gen 25–36) demonstrates how the Israelites occupied the promised land by supplanting Esau (Edom), the epitome of the inhabitants of the land, who lost the birthright to their land (*see* ESAU, ESAUITES). The highlight of the divine promise of the land was fulfilled after the exodus. Thus, the Joseph cycle (Gen 37–48) serves as a transition between the patriarchs in Canaan and the Israelite exodus from Egypt to the promised land (*see* JOSEPH, JOSEPHITES; JOSEPH STORY, HISTORY OF INTERPRETATION).

B. The Function of the Patriarchal Stories

The patriarchs are the cornerstone of the PENTATEUCH. Their stories were probably collected and edited during the period of the monarchy, many centuries after the events took place. To stabilize the monarchy and defend the nation, individual tribal epic stories were collected into a common historical heritage that all the twelve disparate tribes affirmed (*see* TRIBE; TRIBES, TERRITORIES OF). The story of the unity of the twelve tribes helped justify the union of the tribes under one king. The patriarchal narratives are, therefore, not to be read as objective historical accounts of Israel's humble beginnings (Deut 26:5*b*-9). Rather, they are a retrospection of Israel's early life gleaned from oral tradition, ancient songs, and poetry (*see* TRADITION, ORAL). This epic history explained how the Israelites became a great and united nation in spite of their tribal diversity. Moreover, this history provided a theocentric explanation for how a people with a precarious beginning was able to defeat strong nations that lived in fortified cities (Josh 14:12).

The redactor arranged the legends of Genesis in a chronological order that portrays Yahweh as being intrinsic in the lives of the patriarchs. Yahweh vowed to Abraham that he would have an heir whose progeny would inherit the promised land (12:1-3, 7). The promise of the LAND was subsequently made to Isaac (26:1-3) and Jacob (28:13-15). Abraham trusted Yahweh and believed that Yahweh would fulfill these promises even when it seemed hopeless (18:11-14). His faith was such that even when Yahweh commanded him to sacrifice his son Isaac, Abraham did not hesitate to obey God (22:1-3). Common ancestry, therefore, enabled the twelve tribes to live harmoniously in one land, under one king and worshiping Yahweh in one central place, Jerusalem.

C. The Religion of the Patriarchs

The constant appeal to the Israelites to reject other gods and revere only Yahweh implies that the religion of Israel was originally polytheistic (see, e.g., Exod 20:3; 1 Kgs 18:20-21; Hos 4:12-13; Mal 2:10-11). This conclusion is reached by a form-critical study of the Genesis narratives that reveals that the patriarchs worshiped several ancestral gods. Their individual names are: the Shield of Abraham (Gen 15:1); the Fear of Isaac (Gen 31:42); and the Bull of Jacob (Gen 49:24; NRSV, "Mighty One of Jacob"). The Israelites also venerated other gods, namely, El Elyon (Gen 14:18), El-roi (Gen 16:13), El Olam (Gen 21:33), and El Shaddai (Gen 17:1; 28:3). The *-el* particle in the names of gods and humans suggests that the patriarchs, like the Canaanites, revered El as their supreme god (*see* GOD, NAMES OF). There even appears to be some compatibility between Yahweh and El. For example, in Gen 35:1, Yahweh advises Jacob to build an altar to El, who had appeared to him in a theophany at Bethel. The campaign to worship Yahweh exclusively appears to have initially encountered some resistance. Thus, the adoption of Yahweh was achieved by equating the gods of the ancestors with Yahweh, who thereby bore the compound name, Yahweh Elohim. Yahweh became the supreme deity among the gods as implied in several texts, such as Exod 15:11: "Who is like you, O [Yahweh], among the gods?" The explicit articulation of monotheism appears in the period after the exile. It is in Deutero-Isaiah that we repeatedly read that Yahweh has no rival or comparison (Isa 44:6*b*-7*a*).

D. The Theology of the Patriarchal Narratives

The Genesis epic stories demonstrate how the patriarchs trusted Yahweh and believed in his promises. Even when the future of the promises looked bleak, Abraham never rebelled against Yahweh. Instead, he kept consulting with him regarding the heir (e.g., Gen 15:1-3; 17:19-21). The patriarchal unwavering faith was in stark contrast to the behavior of the later generations of the Israelites who were repeatedly accused of apostasy and rebellion against Yahweh. The patriarchs demonstrate that Yahweh will fulfill his promises in his own time (Gen 18:14). It is never too late for Yahweh to successfully intervene in a crisis (Gen 18:11*a*; see Exod 14:13). The patriarchal stories also demonstrate that God's promises are not always meant for immediate and individual fulfillment. Abraham's joy was to know that ultimately his progeny would inherit the good land of Canaan that Yahweh had promised him (Gen 12:7). The patriarchs' faith was intended to teach the Israelites of later generations to live as a people with a destiny that exceeds ethnic idiosyncrasies.

By means of covenants and signs, Yahweh required the Israelites to separate themselves from the Canaanites and their polytheistic religion (*see* CANAAN, CANAANITES). The ritual of CIRCUMCISION distinguished the Israelites from the surrounding nations (Gen 17:1-22) and initiated them into the cult of Yahweh. The lives of the patriarchs demonstrate that although God's promises are unequivocal, the process for attaining them is not. Moreover, the lives of the patriarchs show that Yahweh does not regard a promise as a divine handout; the recipient of a promise must inexorably pursue the promise in consultation with him. Thus, when the Israelites faced enemies, they prayed for victory while simultaneously training and strategizing for war (Josh 8:1-23). Yahweh condoned mistakes that patriarchs made in pursuit of their promises. For example, Yahweh blessed Jacob in spite of his life of trickery to achieve divine promises (Gen 25:29-34; 27:18-36). *See* ISRAEL, HISTORY OF.

Bibliography: Albrecht Alt. *Essays on Old Testament History and Religion.* R. A. Wilson, trans. (1967); Antony F. Campbell and Mark A. O'Brien. *Rethinking the Pentateuch: Prolegomena to the Theology of Ancient Israel* (2005); David Cotter. *Genesis.* Berit Olam (2003); Hermann Gunkel. *Genesis.* Mercer Library of Biblical Studies. Mark Biddle, trans. (1997); Martin Noth. *The History of Israel* (1960); Mark S. Smith. *The Origins of Biblical Monotheism: Israel's Polytheism and the Ugaritic Texts* (1995); Sibley Towner. *Genesis.* Westminster Bible Companion (2007).

TEMBA L. J. MAFICO

E. The Patriarchs in the New Testament

Many texts of the NT portray Jesus as the fulfillment of God's covenant with Israel (e.g., Matt 5:17-20; Luke 1:33, 45-55; Acts 3:12-13; 7:2-53; Heb 2:16-18). These texts also insinuate (and sometimes directly state) that Israel has been disenfranchised from God's promise to the patriarchs, an unfortunate theological conclusion that has resulted in anti-semitism to this day.

The Gospels of Matthew and Luke recite Jesus' genealogy to demonstrate his claim to Abraham's ancestry (Matt 1:1-2, 17; Luke 3:34), but the Gospels also redefine what being children of Abraham means (e.g., Matt 3:7-10; Luke 3:7-9), thus claiming the patriarchal promise for the followers of Jesus alone.

The book of Hebrews claims that because Abraham once paid tribute to the priest-king Melchizedek, so the children of Abraham should honor Jesus as the new high priest in the order of Melchizedek (Heb 7:1-22; see also Gen 14:17-20; *see* HEBREWS, LETTER TO THE). The most explicit is the Gospel of John, which makes the remarkable statement that Jesus preceded Abraham (John 8:58), and that only those who accept Jesus' words are the true descendants of Abraham (8:31-59).

Paul uses Abraham's faith as an example for why the Gentiles should be allowed to share in the covenant with Israel, even though they are not part of Abraham's lineage "according to the flesh" (Rom 4:1-3). Paul reasons that since Abraham's faith preceded his circumcision, he is the ancestor of all who have faith (Rom 4:9-16; Gal 3:6-18; *see* PAUL, THE APOSTLE). Paul, however, states clearly that God has not rejected the Jews (Rom 11:26-32). James 2:21-24 claims that Abraham was justified, not by faith alone, but also by works, because he offered his son Isaac (*see* Gen 22:1-19). *See* ABRAHAM, NT AND EARLY JUDAISM; ANTI-SEMITISM; CHRISTIAN-JEWISH RELATIONS; COVENANT, OT AND NT; ROMANS, LETTER TO THE.

Bibliography: Chris Boesel. *Risking Proclamation, Respecting Difference: Christian Faith, Imperialistic Discourse, and Abraham* (2008); Brendan Byrne. *Romans.* SP 6 (2007); Alan C. Mitchell. *Hebrews.* SP 13 (2007); Steve Moyise. *Evoking Scripture: Seeing the Old Testament in the New Testament* (2008).

MARIANNE BLICKENSTAFF

PATRIARCHS, TESTAMENTS OF THE TWELVE. The *Testaments of the Twelve Patriarchs* present the fictional valedictory speeches of the sons of Jacob. Satisfying the elements of the testamentary genre, they each include an introduction in which the patriarch summons his children to his pre-mortem speech; he offers autobiographical reflections, exhorts his children to avoid his vices and/or pursue his virtues, and predicts their descendants' future; then he dies and is buried by his survivors.

Seven PATRIARCHS' autobiographical accounts are rooted in Genesis (Reuben [Gen 35:22]; Levi [Gen 34]; Judah [Gen 38]; Issachar [Gen 49:14-15 LXX]; Zebulun [Gen 49:13]; Gad [Gen 37:2]; Joseph [Gen 39:6*b*-18]), and five depend on other sources and interpretive readings of Genesis (Simeon, Dan, Naphtali, Asher, and Benjamin). *See* GENESIS, BOOK OF.

The patriarchs' biographical accounts trigger their moral exhortation: right action equals pleasing God and opposing Beliar (e.g., *T. Levi* 18:12; *T. Zeb.* 9:8; *T. Naph.* 2:6; *T. Benj.* 6:1); keeping the twofold commandment to love God and one's neighbor (*T. Benj.* 5:3); and heeding traditional Greco-Roman vices (e.g., porneia [πορνεία], "unchastity," and philargyria [φιλαργυρία], "avarice"; *T. Jud.* 18:2) and virtues (e.g., haplotēs [ἁπλότης], "simplicity, uprightness"; *T. Iss.* 4:1). *See* LISTS, ETHICAL.

The eschatological sections call upon various sources to predict the patriarchs' descendants' future (Enoch: *T. Levi* 10:5; 14:1; 16:1; *T. Jud.* 18:1; the fathers: *T. Levi* 10:1; the fathers' writings: *T. Zeb.* 9:5; and heavenly tablets: *T. Ash.* 7:5). There are several types of future-oriented passages. Sin-Exile-Return (S.E.R.) sections foretell the sins of the patriarchs' descendants, the tribes' exile among the Gentiles as punishment, and God's restoration of the tribes (e.g., *T. Levi* 10; 14–15; 16; *T. Jud.* 23). Levi-Judah passages bemoan the rebellion of the patriarchs' descendants against Levi's and Judah's descendants and their defeat, but they also look forward to the descendants' loyalty to the tribes of Levi and Judah out of respect for their provision of priests, kings, and the messiah of Israel (e.g., *T. Reu.* 6:5-12; *T. Levi* 2:11; *T. Jud.* 21:1-6*a*; *T. Jos.* 19:6). Ideal savior passages are related to the Levi-Judah passages, and refer to Jesus (*T. Levi* 18; T. *Jud.* 24; *T. Zeb.* 9:8; *T. Dan* 5:10-13). A final group of future-oriented passages announce that the patriarch will be resurrected to rule over his tribe at the second coming of the messiah (*T. Sim.* 6:7; *T. Levi* 18:14; *T. Jud.* 25; *T. Zeb.* 10:1-4; *T. Benj.* 10:6-10).

Many have tried to ascertain a Jewish form of the *Testaments of the Twelve Patriarchs* behind the Christian text that survives. They have relied in particular on Hebrew, Aramaic, and Greek texts related to the testaments of Levi, Judah, and Naphtali. Such evidence, however, only certifies that Christian authors relied on Jewish sources, but not that a complete Jewish *Testaments of the Twelve Patriarchs* ever existed. As a consequence the *Testaments of the Twelve Patriarchs* are best described as a Christian argument for keeping God's universal law articulated in the speeches of the patriarchs and reaffirmed by Jesus as a path to salvation. This composition should be understood not only as a Christian composition, but also as a Christian missionary treatise for the Jews.

Bibliography: Robert Kugler. *The Testaments of the Twelve Patriarchs* (2001).

ROBERT KUGLER

PATRISTIC BIBLICAL INTERPRETATION. Patristic biblical interpretation generally refers to the writings of church fathers who lived during the late 1st cent. CE through the 8th cent. CE. Their work contains defenses against heresies, commentaries on Scripture, sermons, and discussions of doctrine (*see* APOSTOLIC FATHERS, CHURCH FATHERS).

The Patristic interpretation of Scripture was premised on the belief that the Bible was divinely inspired. As IRENAEUS commented, "The Scriptures are indeed perfect, since they were spoken by the word of God and his Spirit" (*Haer.* 2.28.2; *ANF* 1). The Fathers' main concerns were two: to demonstrate that when read aright the OT pointed to Christ and to develop a hermeneutic that would allow the nature of God and the divine will to be discerned through the texts. In the *Dialogue with Trypho*, JUSTIN MARTYR argued that when read typologically, the Jewish Scriptures attested to the existence of a second God, one who would be born from a virgin, die, and be raised. In opposition to Marcion and others who distinguished between the creator god of the OT and the Father of the NT, the Patristic authors argued for continuity between the two Testaments. Both spoke with one voice about one God and one Son: both were the work of one Spirit. The narrative of Christ's incarnation, life, death, and resurrection functioned as the hypothesis, or pattern of meaning, that ran throughout the whole of Scripture, giving it unity in all its literary variety. As AUGUSTINE explained, he and other interpreters believed they were tracking down hidden meanings in Scripture in order that they could interpret historical narratives with reference to Christ and his church (*Civ.* 16.2). The Fathers sought to read the Scriptures in order to come to the "spiritual sense" of the text. ORIGEN famously argued that the text of the Bible had three levels of meaning: the literal, the moral, and spiritual (*Princ.* 4.2.4). In practice, however, he and most of the Fathers worked only with the literal and spiritual (see Augustine, *Doctr. chr.*, 3.8–56 on rules for interpreting the Bible). All the writings of the Bible, including those of a patently historical nature, contained saving doctrines about Christ. The seemingly unedifying passages and those that contained errors, what Origen called "stumbling blocks," had been put into the text to prompt the reader to look beyond the literal level to seek the spiritual teaching to which it pointed. Two principles underlay the Patristic practice of reading. Scripture was to be used to interpret Scripture, and the methods employed were to be those warranted by the Bible itself. For many of the Fathers, the principal means for coming to the spiritual sense was allegorical interpretation. It was authorized by the Bible, most notably by Paul, who in Gal 4:24 had described the story of Hagar and Sarah as an allegory. However, not all favored this approach. Until the late 20th cent., scholarly opinion held that there were two schools of interpretation in early Christianity: the Alexandrian and the Antiochene—the former oriented to the allegorical approach, and the latter to the literal-historical approach. It is now recognized, however, that the gulf between the two was not as great as had been thought. The structure and content of a passage acted as controls for the Alexandrians; and, while the Antiochenes charged that the allegorical approach led to arbitrary readings, they themselves did not adhere strictly to the historical idiom of a passage. They too shifted to moral teaching and theological speculation, favoring the term *theoria*, discernment or spiritual insight, over that of ALLEGORY.

Augustine concluded that the Bible's use of anthropomorphisms and other seemingly unsophisticated language for God was intended to alert the reader to the incapacity of human language to encompass the divine and to the need for reading with humility in the context of the whole body of readers, the church. Any given passage was patient of a multiplicity of interpretations and no one interpreter's explanation was to be deemed definitive. All interpretations that were in accordance with the hypothesis, the Rule of Faith, were to be entertained. Interpretive skill was not something possessed by the reader, but was, like the text itself, a gift of grace, and required prayer, fasting, and sanctity. Ultimately, for all the Patristic authors, the purpose of reading the Bible correctly was the transformation of its readers through an encounter with the Word in the words. *See* BIBLICAL INTERPRETATION, HISTORY OF; TYPOLOGY.

Bibliography: John J. O'Keefe and R. R. Reno. *Sanctified Vision: An Introduction to Early Christian Interpretation of the Bible* (2005); Alexander Roberts, James Donaldson, Philip Schaff, and Henry Wace, eds. *Ante-Nicene Fathers.* 10 vols. repr. (1994); Alexander Roberts, James Donaldson, Philip Schaff, and Henry Wace, eds. *Nicene and Post-Nicene Fathers.* 14 vols. repr. (1994); Frances Young. *Biblical Exegesis and the Transformation of Christian Culture* (1997).

PETER WIDDICOMBE

PATROBAS pat´ruh-buhs [Πατροβᾶς Patrobas]. Patrobas is one of the Roman Christians greeted by Paul (Rom 16:14), included with Asyncritus, Phlegon, Hermes, Hermas, and "the brothers and sisters who are with them," which suggests that they were part of a HOUSE CHURCH in Rome. Patrobas is a shortened form of Patrobios (Πατρόβιος). *See* ROMANS, LETTER TO THE.

MARIANNE BLICKENSTAFF

PATROCLUS puh-troh´kluhs [Πάτροκλος Patroklos]. Father of NICANOR whom PTOLEMY sent to defeat the Jews and their leader JUDAS Maccabeus (2 Macc 8:9). *See* MACCABEES, SECOND BOOK OF.

PATROL [הִתְהַלֵּךְ hithhallekh; προφυλακή prophylakē]. Zechariah has visions of horsemen (Zech 1:8-11) and chariots (6:1-7) that "patrol the earth" and report to an angel. These heavenly figures are modeled on the agents who gathered intelligence for the Persian Empire. Zechariah's imagery illustrates Yahweh's omniscience (*see* ZECHARIAH, BOOK OF). An Assyrian military patrol is mentioned in Jdt 10:11.

MILTON ENG

PAU pou [פָּעוּ paʿu]. The city of HADAR (Gen 36:39; elsewhere Hadad), the last of the non-dynastic Edomite "kings," but called Pai (paʿi פָּעִי) in 1 Chr 1:50. The LXX reads Phogōr (Φόγωρ) both for Pau/Pai (otherwise unknown) and for Peor in Moab (e.g., Num 23:28). Other obscure toponyms in the list might also pertain to Moab, hinting that Pau might reflect a misrepresentation of Peor. *See* EDOM, EDOMITES.

JASON C. DYKEHOUSE

PAUL AND SENECA, LETTERS OF pawl, sen´uh-kuh. The letters of Paul and SENECA profess to be the personal correspondence between the apostle and the famous Stoic philosopher. Of the fourteen letters in the corpus, six are attributed to Paul and eight to Seneca. The letters, which place Paul within the orbit of the highest levels of Greco-Roman philosophical and political circles, seek to assert the legitimacy of Christian teachings and, ultimately, the superiority of Christianity over pagan intellectualism. Although he finds Paul's writing style unrefined (*Ep. Paul Sen.* 7; 13), Seneca nevertheless congratulates the apostle for his noble thoughts, which Seneca passed on to Nero (7), and expresses delight that Paul, the "beloved of God," is connected with his name (12). Moreover, Seneca relates his regret that innocent Christians have become the source of blame for the fires that had engulfed Rome and counsels endurance through this adversity (11). Paul, in turn, praises Seneca's reputation as a teacher (2), while simultaneously congratulating the philosopher for converting to Christianity and urging him to become a new herald of Jesus Christ (14). Although the letters purport to date from the late 50s to early 60s CE, their language and style are more representative of the 4th cent., and it is not until Jerome (*Vir. ill.* 12) and Augustine (*Ep.* 153.14) that Christian writers reference them. Jerome, however, mentions the letters' popularity, and their authenticity remained unquestioned until the Renaissance. *See* APOCRYPHA, NT.

DAVID M. REIS

PAUL AND THECLA, ACTS OF. *See* THECLA, ACTS OF PAUL AND.

PAUL, ACTS OF. An early Christian apocryphal work that recounts the missionary activity and death of the apostle Paul. It is classified among the apocryphal acts of apostles, a genre not precisely delimited but marked by stock elements: focus on an apostle's itinerant mission, an emphasis on sexual abstinence and other ascetic practices; conversion of Gentiles, especially women; persecution; and miraculous deeds. A reference to the *Acts of Paul* in Tertullian's *Baptism* (dated ca. 200 CE) indicates the latest date of composition is mid- to late 2nd cent., as well as provides what little is known about author and provenance: an unnamed presbyter in the province of Asia who wrote "out of love for Paul" (Tertullian, *Bapt.* 17).

Originally composed in Greek, the *Acts of Paul* is amply attested but not extant in its entirety. That at some point it consisted of 3,600 lines, making it longer than the 2,800 of the canonical Acts of the Apostles, is indicated by the *Stichometry of Nicephorus.* Whether the version Nicephorus saw accurately reflected the original is not known; therefore, how much of the ancient *Acts of Paul* has been lost cannot be precisely determined. The medieval manuscript tradition attests that three sections (*Acts of Paul and Thecla*, *Martyrdom of Paul*, and the correspondence between Paul and the Corinthians, also known as *3 Corinthians*) circulated independently. Recent discovery and reconstruction of a substantial papyrus (the Coptic Papyrus Heidelburg) confirms that the stories about Paul and Thecla and about his martyrdom belonged to the larger work before their eventual separation and independent circulation (*see* APOCRYPHA, NT).

Because the size and number of lacunae in the surviving manuscripts are uncertain, the original sequence of events is difficult to determine. Whether *Acts of Paul* presents a single missionary journey from Damascus to Rome, or multiple journeys, with return trips to some cities, as in canonical Acts of the Apostles, is debated. Despite the gaps in the manuscript tradition, the overall schema is clear: Paul travels to cities of the Roman east, many familiar from the Lukan Acts (e.g., Damascus, Iconium, Antioch, Myra, Ephesus, Philippi, Corinth), encounters believers, preaches a gospel of continence (**enkrateia** ἐγκράτεια) to gentiles, converting some but provoking opposition by others, and eventually arrives in Rome where he is executed by Nero. As in other apocryphal acts, it is his success in converting gentiles, especially elite women, to a virginal life that provokes the ire of government officials (*see* THECLA, ACTS OF PAUL AND).

The relationship of *Acts of Paul* to the canonical ACTS OF THE APOSTLES remains a subject of debate. There are unmistakable resemblances between the two, most notably, the narrative pattern (journey, preaching, persecution, miracles, departure) as well as similar names and places. The Jewish hostility to Paul's preaching, a prominent feature of the canonical Acts, is, however, entirely missing in *Acts of Paul*, and events at the cities to which Paul travels do not duplicate those in the Lukan account. Therefore, familiarity with the traditions in the Lukan account seems more likely than literary dependence. Numerous passages recall the language of the NT, but direct quotations are few (Matt 5:8 and 5:9 in the beatitudes of *Acts Paul* 3.5). Therefore, literary dependence on the Pauline epistles also has not been established. The influence of Pauline thought, however, is readily apparent. Most notably, the portrayal of Thecla as an apostolic witness is consistent with the glimpses of women co-workers that his letters afford (Rom 16), and the ideal of sexual abstinence reflects the influence of Pauline apocalyptic theology, particularly 1 Cor 7. *See* PAUL, MARTYRDOM OF; PAUL, THE APOSTLE.

Bibliography: Virginia Burrus. *Chastity as Autonomy: Women in the Stories of the Apocryphal Acts* (1987);

Andrew S. Jacobs. "'Her Own Proper Kinship': Marriage, Class and Women in the Apocryphal Acts of the Apostles." *A Feminist Companion to the New Testament Apocrypha.* A.-J. Levine, ed. (2006) 18–46; D. R. MacDonald. *The Legend and the Apostle: The Battle for Paul in Story and Canon* (1983); R. I. Pervo. *Profit with Delight: The Literary Genre of the Acts of the Apostles* (1987); W. Schneemelcher. "Acts of Paul." *New Testament Apocrypha,* vol. 2. W. Schneemelcher, ed. (1992) 213–70.

SUSAN A. CALEF

PAUL, ACTS OF ANDREW AND. *See* ANDREW AND PAUL, ACTS OF.

PAUL, ACTS OF PETER AND. *See* PETER AND PAUL, ACTS OF.

PAUL, APOCALYPSE OF. Paul's reference to his visionary ascent through the heavens (2 Cor 12:1-5) was the basis for two independent "Apocalypse of Paul" traditions. One apocryphal apocalypse is alleged to have been discovered in the foundations of Paul's house at Tarsus ca. 388 CE when an angel commanded a young man staying there to dig for it. Augustine notes that this apocalypse is not accepted by the church (*Tract. Ev. Jo.* 98.8). However, it was translated into many languages, with abbreviated versions focused on punishments awaiting the damned. The best manuscript evidence is a Latin version of the 6th cent. CE. This *Visio Pauli* conforms to the seven heavens structure of most Jewish and Christian apocalypses. In the third heaven, Paul is commissioned to preach against the sinfulness of humanity. Angelic guides show him both the heavenly paradise in which he encounters the Virgin Mary and great figures of the OT, and the torments that await sinners. The latter influenced representations of hell in medieval art and literature. A gnostic apocalypse among the NAG HAMMADI TEXTS recounting the apostle's ascent above the heavens of the hostile creator (an old man) adds three additional regions. Its judgment scene may have been taken from an earlier Jewish apocalypse.

PHEME PERKINS

PAUL, AUTHORSHIP. The NT contains thirteen letters that are attributed to the apostle Paul. In addition to these writings, there are still other extra-biblical correspondences that claim Paul as their author, e.g., the *Epistle to the Laodiceans,* the *Correspondence between Seneca and Paul,* and *Third Corinthians.* From at least the time of the Renaissance the extra-biblical (or noncanonical) writings have not been accepted as authentic correspondences of Paul—indeed, some were regarded as forgeries as early as the 2nd to 4th cent. CE. Thus, today, through further investigation, these documents are regarded as later, legendary writings that were produced to honor Paul, to fill gaps in the Pauline corpus (i.e., to supply letters that are mentioned in Paul's writings but that are not otherwise known), and to gratify pious curiosity concerning Paul's thought and life.

Clearly the early Christians produced pseudepigraphical writings in Paul's name (PSEUDONYMOUS WRITING). From this observation, the question arises: which from among the letters attributed to Paul are authentic correspondences between the apostle and church(s) or individual to which/whom he wrote? Critical biblical scholarship has examined the many letters attributed to Paul historically (how was the writing regarded in antiquity?), linguistically (matters of format, vocabulary, grammar, and style), and theologically (e.g., worldview, themes, and philosophical perspectives) in order to make a case for or against Pauline authorship of each of the pertinent writings. The outcomes of this analysis are 1) that none of the noncanonical writings are regarded as authentic and 2) that seven of the thirteen canonical writings attributed to Paul are thought to be indisputably authentic (Romans, First Corinthians, Second Corinthians, Galatians, Philippians, First Thessalonians, and Philemon), while the other six letters (Ephesians, Colossians, Second Thessalonians, First Timothy, Second Timothy, and Titus) are disputed—to various degrees—as to their authenticity. The conclusions one draws concerning the authenticity or inauthenticity of the canonical Pauline epistles have important implications for how one will work with the letters, especially in constructing a historical and theological understanding of Paul and, in turn, a Pauline theology. *See* PAUL, THE APOSTLE.

Bibliography: Raymond E. Brown. *An Introduction to the New Testament* (1997); Edgar Hennecke, Wilhelm Schneemelcher, and R. McL. Wilson. *New Testament Apocrypha.* Vol. 2: *Writings Relating to the Apostles; Apocalypses and Related Subjects* (1992); Luke Timothy Johnson. *The Writings of the New Testament* (1986); David G. Meade. *Pseudonymity and Canon: An Investigation into the Relationship of Authorship and Authority in Jewish and Earliest Christian Tradition* (1986).

MARION L. SOARDS

PAUL, CHRONOLOGY OF. *See* PAUL, THE APOSTLE.

PAUL, LETTERS OF. *See* PAUL, AUTHORSHIP.

PAUL, MARTYRDOM OF. Although NT authors allude to Paul's death in Rome (Acts 19:21; 23:11; 2 Tim 1:16-17), they do not explicitly speak of his martyrdom. The Apostolic Fathers (1 *Clem.* 5:5-7; Ign. *Eph.* 12:2; Ign. *Rom.* 4:1-3) add little more information, and Clement and the MURATORIAN CANON even imply that Paul died in Spain after he left Rome. Unequivocal evidence for Paul's martyrdom during the Neronian persecution in 64 CE (Tacitus, *Ann.* 15.44) does not appear until at least the latter half of the 2nd cent. in the *Martyrdom of Paul*, originally a part of the apocryphal text *Acts of Paul*, where Paul's conversion of NERO's soldiers leads to his arrest and beheading (*see* PAUL, ACTS OF). Additional conversions follow his heroic death, and Paul then reappears to condemn Nero for his injustice. Paul's martyrdom in Rome then becomes church tradition (Tertullian, *Praescr.* 36; Eusebius, *Hist. eccl.* II.25.8; III.1.3). *See* PAUL, THE APOSTLE.

DAVID M. REIS

PAUL, MARTYRDOM OF PETER AND. *See* PETER AND PAUL, MARTYRDOM OF.

PAUL, PASSION OF PETER AND. *See* PETER AND PAUL, MARTYRDOM OF.

PAUL, PRAYER OF THE APOSTLE. The *Prayer of the Apostle Paul* appears on the front flyleaf of Nag Hammadi Codex I. A Coptic translation of the Greek original, the *Prayer of the Apostle Paul* consists of an invocation to receive enlightenment from God through Jesus Christ. The prayer's appeal for divine mercy and redemption echoes the Psalms (A.3-4; see Pss 25:11; 29:11; 30:10), and Pauline allusions appear in the call to "the name [which is] exalted above every name" (A.13-14; see Eph 1:21; Phil 2:9-11) and (possibly) the plea to receive a noetic revelation (A.26-29; see 1 Cor 2:9).

The *Prayer of the Apostle Paul* also invites comparison with Hermetic and magical texts, and its vocabulary is typically gnostic. For instance, the author claims the Redeemer is his "mind" (nous νοῦς) "fullness" (plērōma πλήρωμα), and "rest" (anapausis ἀνάπαυσις) (A.6, 8-9), and asks for a revelation of "the First-born of the Pleroma of grace" for the salvation of his "eternal light soul" and "spirit" (A.22-25). These statements, along with references to the "psychic God" (A.31) who is the "beloved, elect, and blessed greatness" (A.35-37), suggest that the prayer originated in a Valentinian context, perhaps between the end of the 2nd and the end of the 3rd cent. *See* GNOSTICISM.

DAVID M. REIS

PAUL, THE APOSTLE pawl [Παῦλος Paulos]. Aside from Jesus, no one has shaped the development of early Christianity more than Paul. Even though he was the foremost advocate of the Gentile mission, an eloquent interpreter of a Jewish Messiah for a Hellenistic world, and a visionary whose journeys carried him through Asia Minor and beyond, he undoubtedly would have been surprised that his occasional letters would one day become Scripture alongside the Torah and the Prophets.

The themes at the core of Paul's gospel were Israel's traditions, Scriptures, morality, God, and a crucified Jewish Messiah whose life, death, and resurrection expanded the people of God to include believing "pagans," inaugurating a new age that would soon be brought to a grand and even revolutionary conclusion with Jesus' return. This vision suffused Paul's mission with urgency and his letters with the intensity characteristic of a time of crisis. In a great apocalyptic drama, converts lived out their faith within a community of care and hope as well as sectarian rivalry. In Paul's letters we are witness to that conflict and to a theology in the making.

Paul's teachings were controversial from the start. The fourteen writings of the NT written by or attributed to him and others' canonical and non-canonical accounts about him testify to his impact on the emergent church. His later influence on such theological giants as Augustine, Martin Luther, John Calvin, John Wesley, and John Knox continued to shape Western culture and history. But that influence has not always been benign. For example, concern that pitting Paul's Jesus-based faith against Judaism may have inspired Christian acquiescence in the Holocaust has led scholars to take a new look at Paul's writings. Noting that Christianity's development as a separate religion came after Paul's lifetime, postwar scholars have reinterpreted Paul's seeming rejection of Judaism in favor of Christianity as a reevaluation of his native religion in light of his experience of Christ (*see* ANTI-JUDAISM; ANTI-SEMITISM; CHRISTIAN-JEWISH RELATIONS). More recently, feminist scholarship has reexamined the purported misogyny of Paul's teachings to resurrect the voices and roles of women in Pauline churches. New manuscript discoveries (such as the Dead Sea Scrolls) and the steady increase of archaeological information and textual studies also help situate Paul in the 1st-cent. CE context.

A. Sources

The primary source materials for Paul's life, thought, and theologizing are his seven undisputed letters (Romans, 1 Corinthians, 2 Corinthians, Galatians, Philippians, 1 Thessalonians, Philemon). Attempts to arrive at a definitive corpus or chronology of the letters, however, are complicated by allusions to missing letters in 1 Cor 5:9 ("I wrote to you ...") and possibly 2 Cor 2:4 ("For I wrote you out of much distress and anguish of heart and with many tears ...") and doubts about the literary unity of others (2 Corinthians and Philippians).

The arguably deuteropauline letters—2 Thessalonians, Colossians, and Ephesians—provide valuable secondary sources for constructing a history of early Pauline interpretation. The even later canonical pseudepigraphic letters—1 and 2 Timothy and Titus (the Pastorals) and Hebrews—can similarly serve to decipher the legacy of Paul in the 2nd cent. and beyond (*see* PAUL, AUTHORSHIP).

The Acts of the Apostles, though also a secondary source, can be used judiciously to study Paul's life and thought. Luke clearly had access to written or oral sources about Paul and perhaps to a collection of Pauline letters. Acts' depiction of Paul's role in the expansion of the early Jesus movement and portrait of him as a figure of legendary proportions has secured Paul's place as the central figure of the early Gentile mission. It is important to recognize, however, that Luke was more author than historian and that the nine speeches Acts attributes to Paul reveal little of his pastoral theology and none of his literary style or the rhetorical character of his argumentation. Still, Paul's own autobiographical accounts have points of agreement with the fuller version given in Acts. For instance, Paul's painful memory of his earlier role as a persecutor of the church (1 Cor 15:9; Gal 1:13) is elaborated in Acts (7:58; 8:1, 3; 9:1-8; 22:4, 7, 8, 11, 14, 15), and Paul's Pharisaic lineage appears in both his letters and Acts (Phil 3:5; Acts 23:6; 26:5). Both sources agree that he was an itinerant missionary, though the emphasis on Paul's apostolic commission is muted in Acts. The mission strategy described in Acts, in which Paul turns to the Gentiles after his preaching of Christ was rejected by Jews, is at odds with that implied in Paul's letters. Both sources also refer to Paul's defense of his gospel to the Gentiles before the "apostolic council" in Jerusalem, though they disagree about the nature of that endorsement (Acts 15:1-28; Gal 2:1-10; *see* JERUSALEM, COUNCIL OF).

Some information unique to Acts has been the subject of intensive study and sometimes skepticism. For example, only Acts notes that Paul was a Roman citizen, that he was from Tarsus (9:11), that he studied under the great Gamaliel in Jerusalem (22:3), that he spoke Hebrew (21:40), that he was arrested in Jerusalem (21:33), and that he appealed to his status as a Roman citizen and was taken to Rome for trial (22:25-29). Only Acts emphasizes Paul's innocence of any crime against the Roman state or the religion of Israel (23:9). And only Acts refers to Paul's appearance before GALLIO, the proconsul in Corinth in 52 CE, a chronological peg useful for dating Paul's ministry and correspondence (Acts 18:12-17).

In a quest for the historical Paul, reliable studies lean more heavily on evidence from the undisputed letters than from Acts or other secondary sources. Where the letters and Acts disagree, the nod must go to the letters, and the historicity of materials unique to Acts should be decided on a case-by-case basis. Where material unique to Acts has a strong ideological emphasis, it must be assessed very carefully. For example, the report in Acts that Paul was born in Tarsus (Acts 22:3) appears to serve no ideological purpose and is therefore historically credible (*see* ACTS OF THE APOSTLES).

B. The Early Paul

1. Paul the Jew

Paul was born, lived, and died as a Jew. His name, **Paulos**, was linked to Saul, the first king of Israel, who also was from the tribe of Benjamin (Rom 11:1); he claimed circumcision on the eighth day, a blamelessness before the law, a preference for the Pharisaic interpretation of the law (Phil 3:5-6), and an uncommon zeal for the "traditions of my ancestors" (Gal 1:14). In one of his last letters, he railed against those who challenged his Jewishness: "Are they Hebrews? So am I. Are they Israelites? So am I. Are they descendants of Abraham? So am I" (2 Cor 11:22). Elsewhere, Paul appeals three times to his lineage as a Jew (**Ioudaios** Ἰουδαῖος; 1 Cor 9:20-23 Gal 1:13, 14), and while he radically redefines the term to include Gentile sinners (Gal 2:16), he nowhere disavows it. Referring to his native religious tradition, he notes his "earlier life in Judaism" (**Ioudaismō** Ἰουδαϊσμῷ; Gal 1:13-14) without renouncing it. He instead uses the phrase to refer to a religious enthusiasm that had earlier inspired his zeal for its traditions and his persecution of the church (*see* JEW, JEWS; JUDAISM).

Although revised in light of his experience of Messiah Jesus, Paul's Jewishness is also attested to by his apocalypticism (1 Thess 4:15–5:11), spiritualization of the sacrificial cult (Rom 12:1), monotheism (Rom 11:25-36), moral compass (1 Cor 5:1-5), and identification with its Scriptures. Even his understanding of Jesus' lineage and mission as Messiah was Jewish (Rom 1:3; 9:1-4). Thus it is inaccurate to refer to Paul as a former Jew. Along with Paul's deep roots in a Jewish tradition, however, we also know that Paul was born and grew up in a Jewish diaspora community that was influenced by and actively engaged in a lively conversation with the dominant Hellenistic culture.

2. Paul of Tarsus

The city of Paul's birth and youth was probably TARSUS (Acts 22:3), a thriving cosmopolitan crossroad between the East and the West and a vibrant intellectual center of Stoic and Cynic philosophy. Its rich political and mythic legacy is attested to by inscriptions on coins minted there, its archaeological record, and its rich literary tradition. A young Jew growing up in Tarsus would have been the beneficiary of this cosmopolitan Hellenistic environment. His first language would have been Greek; the Scriptures he read would have been in Greek translation (LXX); the literary models for his letters would have been Hellenistic; his vocabulary, rhetorical style, and philosophical outlook would have been Hellenistic; and all of these would have colored his thinking, identity, and self-understanding (*see* HELLENISM).

This foreground and Gal 1:22 (that he was "unknown by sight to the churches of Judea") contradict the claim of Acts 22:3 that Paul came to Jerusalem at a very young age to study with GAMALIEL (Acts 26:4). The symbolic focus on Jerusalem and its role as the epicenter of the early Christian mission has long been recognized as a Lukan theological construct. That Paul's letters fail to refer to his tutelage under Gamaliel when it would have been advantageous to do so (Phil 3:4-7), state that he was "unknown by sight to the churches of Judea" (Gal 1:22-23), give no hint that he knew Aramaic, and reveal his preference for the LXX make this aspect of Acts' account quite unlikely.

Although Paul clearly was an educated person, we know little about his schooling. His broad knowledge of the Greek Scriptures, his familiarity with Jewish law, traditions, myths, and legends, and his skillful use of such exegetical methods as reasoning from the lesser to the greater (e.g., Rom 5:15-21) suggest that he received a formal Jewish education of some sort. The informal educational opportunities provided by Tarsus reveal themselves in Paul's appropriation of diaspora Hellenistic Jewish culture. For example, the Stoic-Cynic DIATRIBE (Rom 6:1, 15; 7:7; 9:14; 11:1), a form of argumentation that places a question on the lips of a hypothetical objector and then crafts a response, appears regularly in Paul's defense of his apostolic authority and gospel. Paul's references to the law of nature (**physis** φύσις; Rom 2:14-15), to ascetic self-control (**enkrateia** ἐγκράτεια; 1 Cor 7:9; 9:24-27; Gal 5:23), and to lists of virtues and vices (Gal 5:19-23; Phil 4:8) reflect a blend of Hellenistic and Jewish elements. His use of words such as *conscience* (**syneidēsis** συνείδησις; Rom 2:15; 2 Cor 4:2; 5:11), *virtue, valor, honor, success,* and *fame* (from **aretē** ἀρετή; Phil 4:8) that have little or no place in the Hebrew Scriptures demonstrates how fully Paul inhabited the Hellenistic world (*see* LISTS, ETHICAL).

Although Paul's apocalypticism, monotheism, spiritualization of the sacrificial cult, core ethical convictions, and Scriptures were unmistakably Jewish, his letters reflect a dynamic synthesis of Jewish and Hellenistic features that he used to shape his teaching for predominantly Gentile churches. Of his Hellenistic influences, the SEPTUAGINT (LXX) undoubtedly had the most formative impact on his thought. More than a text calling for interpretation, the LXX was itself an interpretation. It went well beyond expressing the religion and traditions of ancient Israel to shape the religion, traditions, and identity of the Jewish community of Paul's youth. Paul's broad and nuanced Septuagintal views of law (**nomos** νόμος), the stories of Israel, and his reading of the Prophets (esp. Isaiah and Jeremiah) provided him not only with language for his theologizing and view of the world but also with a protocol for a fruitful interaction with the dominant Hellenistic culture.

Paul's most favored portions of the LXX (esp. Isaiah, in which thirty-three of the forty-four scriptural references to "world" [**oikoumenē** οἰκουμένη] appear) were those he used to support his Gentile mission. An example is the LXX of Isa 23:14-18, which instead of condemning pagan Tyre to a life of shameful prostitution with all the "nations," as did the MT (Hebrew Masoretic Text), viewed its conversion as a holy offering to God. Thus the LXX provided Paul with a sense of continuity with the ancestral traditions of Israel while allowing influences from the Hellenistic world. Trying to maintain that delicate balance may partly explain the complex and sometimes tortured reasoning he used to argue for the inclusion of GENTILES in the people of God while insisting that inclusion in no way implied God's rejection of Israel (*see* NATIONS).

Paul's thought indeed reflects a complex mix of Hellenistic and Jewish tendencies. His statement in Phil 3:4-6 that he was "as to the law, a Pharisee" (also Gal 1:14) reveals a Pharisaic inclination that Acts confirms (23:6; 26:5). Even after he became an apostle of Christ, certain features of that religious preference remained: a broad understanding of what was scriptural, belief in the immortality of the soul, an emphasis on the resurrection and judgment, a paradoxical endorsement of predestination while holding to an emphasis on human responsibility, an understanding of law (**nomos**, Hebrew TORAH), and possibly an apocalyptic tendency. Paul's spiritualizing of text and tradition in his admonition of Roman believers to present their bodies as "a living sacrifice" (12:1-2; also 15:16-19) and his references to the church as "God's temple" (1 Cor 3:16-17) and believers as "holy ones" (saints) bear marked traces of Pharisaic tendencies. Although Paul's life in Christ and commission as an apostle and free social intercourse with Gentiles would have required modification of his Pharisaic outlook, traces of it remained (*see* PHARISEES).

Although Paul's intellectual gifts and learning suggest a privileged background, they hardly prove that he was of aristocratic status or a Roman citizen. Given Paul's total silence about being a Roman in the letters, even when he feared execution was imminent (2 Cor 1:8-9) or was beaten with rods, a Roman form of punishment (2 Cor 11:25), or when it would have been advantageous to mention his citizenship (Phil 3:2-6), and his radical monotheism, which would have made it impossible for him to participate in the civic cults, pay homage to the Roman gods, or share in the imperial cult, Acts' claim does not appear credible (22:22-29). The ascription of Roman citizenship to Paul serves the theological agenda of Acts by insisting that Paul was a faithful Jew and Roman citizen to underscore his innocence and respectability at a time when the Jesus movement had come under suspicion for its unwillingness to participate in the imperial cult, its refusal of military service, and its secret meetings (*see* ROMAN EMPIRE; ROME, EARLY CHRISTIAN ATTITUDES TOWARD).

Nonetheless, there may be a grain of truth in Acts' claim. Instead of belonging to one of the few Jewish families in the East enjoying the privileges of Roman citizenship, Paul was probably a member of a **politeuma** (πολίτευμα), a Jewish community given the right to govern itself by Jewish law, tradition, and institutions. Roman emperors commonly, though not universally, accorded such autonomy to Jewish communities, exempting them from military service and participation in the imperial cult. Paul probably had humble beginnings. He was taught to work with leather and to make tents, probably by his artisan father, a skill he would later proudly employ to support his apostolic mission (1 Cor 9:6-18; 2 Cor 11:7-15; 1 Thess 2:9).

A sad chapter of Paul's pre-apostolic life was his persecution of the church, a painful memory from which he suffered to the end of his ministry. Yet letters nowhere tell us where he waged the persecution, who its victims were, or why he did it. Had Jesus' proclamation of the imminent arrival of the rule of God worried Jews that his movement would invite a brutal, indiscriminate Roman retaliation on all Jews? Did Paul haul "dangerous" Jewish followers of Jesus before SYNAGOGUE courts to discipline them? (Note Paul's reference to having himself suffered five synagogue lashings for some imagined offense [2 Cor 11:24].) Or did he invade the small HOUSE CHURCHes to ridicule the faith of the Jesus followers and attack them for their incendiary gospel? Although information is too scanty to offer any definitive answer, Paul's painful recollection of once trying to destroy "the faith" (Gal 1:23) was undoubtedly inspired by a complex mix of social, political, and theological concerns internal to the Jewish community. Roman governors would not have tolerated Jewish persecution of Gentiles or the execution of any person, Jewish or Gentile (as noted in John 18:31). What we do know is that Paul's vision of the risen Christ (Gal 1:16-17) turned him from being an adversary of Christ's followers to being an apostle of Christ.

C. Paul as Apostle of Christ

1. Paul's apostleship

In Paul's own words, his dramatic move from persecutor to apostle was not a change from one religion to another but God's "call" (Rom 1:1; 1 Cor 1:1) to be an apostle to the Gentiles (1 Cor 9:1-5; 15:1-10; Gal 1:16). Drawing on Isa 49:1-6, which speaks of being "called from the womb" and sent "as a light to the Gentiles" (LXX), Paul recalls his own commission: "But when God, who had set me apart before I was born and called me through his grace, was pleased to reveal his Son to me [or "in me"], so that I might proclaim him among the Gentiles..." (Gal 1:15-16; compare Jer 1:4-5). Neither he nor Acts (9:1-19; 22:4-16; 26:9-19) refers to this radical turning in Paul's behavior as a repudiation of one religion for another, which for a 1st-cent. Jew like Paul would imply turning away from the true God to idolatry (the reverse of what he called Gentiles to do; see 1 Thess 1:9-10).

The origin and meaning of the term *apostle* (apostolos ἀπόστολος) is uncertain. After his call, Paul recognized that others would see his claim to be an apostle of Christ as a weak one (1 Cor 15:1-11). He had never known the earthly Jesus; he had not been a disciple; and his activities as a persecutor of the church made him suspect. He had disagreements with the inner circle (Gal 2:11-21), and other itinerant apostles contested his claim to apostolic legitimacy (2 Cor 10:1–13:10). As late as the 2nd cent., an apocryphal work attributed to Peter challenged Paul's claim to apostolic legitimacy based on a vision of the resurrected Christ (*Gos. Pet.* 17.19.1–7). Although Paul was convinced of the integrity of his mission (1 Thess 2:7), he developed a fuller understanding of his call through his struggles to defend his claim to be an apostle on a par with the "so-called pillars" (author's trans.; NRSV, "acknowledged pillars") and to refute charges hurled at him by itinerant "super-apostles" (2 Cor 11:1-15; Gal 2:9). Fierce resistance to his call would eventually force Paul to challenge the special authority afforded the twelve disciples and JAMES, the brother of Jesus. That vigorous challenge achieved such a level of nuance, insight, and persuasion that a generation later others would stand in its shadow, writing letters in Paul's name.

2. Apostle to the Gentiles

As an apostle of Christ, Paul claimed a special mission as an apostle to the Gentiles (Rom 1:13; Gal 1:15-16). A grand apocalyptic scenario that would soon reach its denouement with the PAROUSIA (**parousia** [παρουσία], "coming, arrival") of Christ gave that mission a cosmic significance so that it would stretch from Jerusalem across Asia Minor into Thrace, Macedonia, and Achaia and thence to Rome and finally Spain (Rom 15:19-24). Paul's identification with the Christ who authorized his mission was so absolute that he sometimes blurred the line between their pronouncements (1 Cor 5:1-5; 16:22) and believed that even his beatings mystically participated in those of Christ. To his converts and adversaries, he presented the cuts inscribed on his back as re-presenting Jesus: "Let no one make trouble for me; for I carry the marks of Jesus branded on my body" (**stigmata tou Iēsou** [στίγματα τοῦ Ἰησοῦ]; Gal 6:17). Claiming special insight into God's salvation unfolding in his ministry, Paul conjured the grand assize at which, as a priest, he would present his Gentile converts holy and pure to Christ (Rom 15:16; 1 Cor 1:8; 2 Cor 1:14; 11:2; Phil 2:15; 1 Thess 2:10-12). He recognized, however, that his apostolic claim was weak. He had never seen Jesus in the flesh, had not been a disciple, had serious disagreements with Peter, and lacked the rhetorical gifts and physical presence claimed by other apostles (2 Cor 10:1-10). Moreover, his welcoming of Gentiles into God's elect through grace rather than observance of Jewish law met continuing resistance. Nevertheless, Paul's letters offer the most nuanced and complicated thinking anywhere in the NT about his apostolic mission to the Gentiles.

3. Paul's mission strategy

a. Travel. Driven by an overpowering sense of the imminent end of the world, Paul set out on perilous journeys crisscrossing vast expanses of Asia and Europe. On foot he faced "danger from rivers, danger from bandits, danger from [his] own people, danger from Gentiles, danger in the city, [and] danger in the wilderness" (2 Cor 11:26). At sea he survived three shipwrecks, including a day and a night adrift (2 Cor 11:25). His travels to spread the good news of God's salvation in Christ were punctuated by hunger, thirst, cold, nakedness, bone-chilling fatigue, beatings, and imprisonments (2 Cor 11:27). Even as he was founding cell groups of converts, he could be worried sick about the direction that these little house churches were taking (2 Cor 2:13; 7:5; 11:28). While traveling he would often dispatch letters or co-workers to encourage, correct, admonish, or promote reconciliation with estranged converts (*see* TRAVEL AND COMMUNICATION IN THE NT).

b. Preaching. We know little about Paul's strategy for winning and binding converts in familial assemblies, whether he won converts primarily in the workshop, on the way, in prison, in the marketplace, or in the synagogue, or if they came to Christ through casual conversation, preaching, or public disputation. While Acts portrays Paul as a great orator, highly skilled in public discourse (17:22-34), his letters indicate that his rhetorical skills left some unimpressed (1 Cor 2:1-4; 2 Cor 10:10; 11:6). His letters themselves were obviously effective, and they suggest that the good news Paul proclaimed was markedly different from that of the speech on the Areopagus in Athens that Acts ascribes to him (17:22-34).

Although the letters are hardly systematic theological treatises, they do contain the core elements of a preached theology shaped by Paul's awareness of the estrangement, alienation, and helplessness many of his listeners felt from being in the grip of capricious, careless, blind, amoral powers they could only pretend to

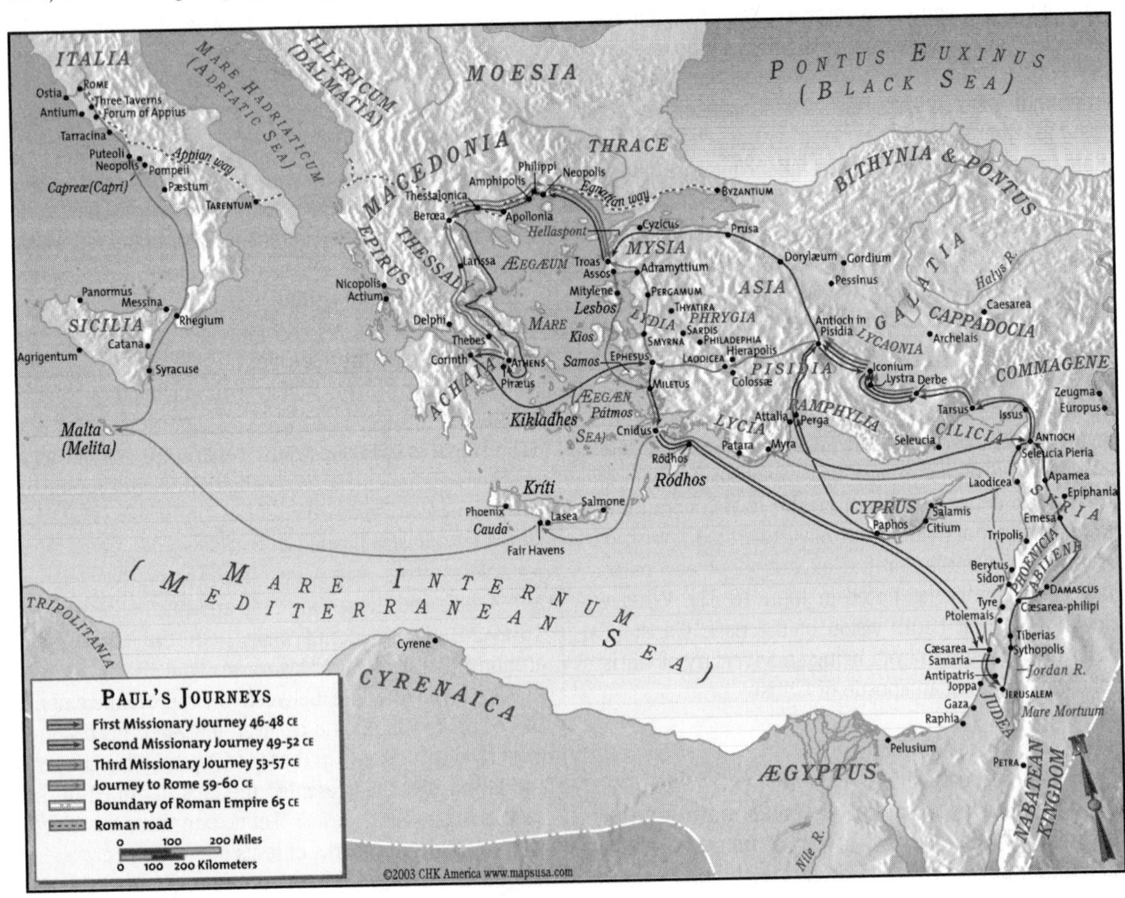

Figure 1: Paul's journeys

understand (Rom 6:12-20; 1 Cor 15:26; 2 Cor 5:19). Paul's fervent belief that through Christ God was inaugurating a new age served as his warrant for announcing deliverance from this plight.

Redemption in and through Christ's faithfulness was promised by the prophets (Rom 1:1-2) and rooted in Israel's story. Many characters and legends from that grand narrative (e.g., Adam and the myths of the garden, Abraham, Sarah, Hagar, Moses, and the prophets) find their way into Paul's letters. In Paul's telling, from that metanarrative came the Scriptures and their record of God's covenant with and promises to Israel. From Israel came the ancestors and the Messiah (Rom 9:4-5). And now, in history's final scenario, the "pagan" outsiders or "wild olive shoots" shall take life after being grafted into Israel's tame stock (Rom 11:17-24).

Thus while Paul's sermons included warnings and admonishments, they also held out promise of participation in the new creation confirmed by the outpouring of the Spirit. Scholars have suggested that these proclamations might have taken the following form: 1) Recognition of the desperate human plight (Rom 8:38; 6:20-23; Gal 1:4; 1 Thess 1:9); 2) The preexistent Messiah Jesus took slave form (Phil 2:6-7); 3) Jesus was born of the "seed of David" (Rom 1:3); 4) Jesus died "for our sins in accordance with the scriptures" (1 Cor 15:3) "to set us free from the present evil age" (Gal 1:4); 5) Jesus was crucified (1 Cor 2:2), dead, and buried (1 Cor 15:4); 6) Jesus was raised according to the Scriptures as the firstfruit of the final resurrection (Rom 1:4; 8:34; 1 Cor 15:4; 1 Thess 1:10); 7) Jesus was exalted to God's right hand (Rom 8:34; Phil 2:9); and 8) Jesus will soon return to gather God's elect and judge the world (Rom 2:16; 14:10; 1 Thess 1:10); 9) To share in this act of salvation, one must turn from sin (Rom 2:9), renounce idols (1 Thess 1:9), and accept Jesus as God's Messiah whom God raised from the dead (Rom 10:9). BAPTISM ritually marks passage from one realm to another (Rom 6:3-4; 1 Cor 12:13; Gal 3:27). The SALVATION now inaugurated will be completed in the imminent future (Rom 10:8-9).

While this mosaic has been pieced together from assorted creedal and confessional statements, traditional summaries, and ritualistic formulas, it offers a credible outline of Paul's proclamation. The letters, therefore, simply assume knowledge of this fundamental message, and with minimal reminders interpret Paul's gospel for highly situational contexts.

D. Paul as Letter Writer

In the wake of his journeys far and wide, Paul left behind cells of converts struggling to survive, to understand the gospel, to carry on the Christ experience, to meet life's challenges, to support Paul's ministry, and to face their own recurring doubts about Paul's integrity and the sufficiency of his teaching. Paul's memory of these converts set them in his presence (Gal 4:13-14; 1 Thess 2:1-11; 3:3-4), and his letters recall their shared experience and place Paul in their midst (Rom 1:8-9; 1 Cor 1:4-6; 5:1-5; Phil 1:3-8; 1 Thess 1:2). Thus the letters serve multiple functions: they bridge the distance between Paul and his churches; serve as a vehicle to exhort, advise (1 Cor 1:8; Phil 2:15; 1 Thess 5:23), and console (2 Cor 1:3-7) the assemblies; and remind these new converts of matters they might forget (e.g., 1 Thess 2:1-2, 9; 4:1-2, 13; 5:1-2). *See* LETTER.

In his absence, challenges from critics from without and within often forced Paul to respond through either emissaries or letters. In Romans, 1 and 2 Corinthians, Galatians, and Philippians, we overhear criticisms so damning that they could have fatally damaged Paul's apostolic claim. Although the argumentative style of Paul's letters is eclectic and situational, rhetorical and literary approaches and methods have been useful in analyzing Paul's vigorous defense of his Gentile gospel and the authenticity of his apostolic claim. While the basic form of Paul's undisputed letters resembles that of the Hellenistic letter, Paul was a master of the form, bending it to his ends and merging features from different epistolary traditions. Paul's letters typically though not uniformly can be outlined as follows:

1. Salutation (e.g., 1 Thessalonians)
   a. Sender (1:1*a*)
   b. Recipient (1:1*b*)
   c. Greeting (1:1*c*)
2. Thanksgiving (1:2-10; 2:13; 3:9-10)
3. Body (2:1–3:8; 3:11-13)
4. Ethical exhortation and instructions (4:1–5:22)
5. Closing
   a. Peace wish (5:23-24)
   b. Greetings (e.g., Rom 16:1-15; 1 Cor 16:19-20*a*; 2 Cor 13:13; Phil 4:21-22)
   c. Kiss (5:26)
   d. Apostolic command (5:27)
   e. Benediction (5:28)

Despite this fairly stable structure, Paul's letters reveal a high level of creativity and a theologically innovative use of the epistolary conventions of his day. A close analysis of those elements often points to distinctive Pauline emphases. In Romans, e.g., addressing a church he had neither founded nor visited and an assembly that may question his apostolic claim, the salutation calls attention to his "call to be an apostle" (1:1), then appends a number of references to support this claim: "set apart for the gospel of God ... promised beforehand through his prophets in holy scriptures, the gospel concerning his Son, who was descended from David according to the flesh and was declared to be Son of God with power according to the spirit of holiness by resurrection from the dead, Jesus Christ our Lord..." (1:2-4). By inserting this traditional material into the salutation, Paul aimed to refute slanderous rumors that he was a dangerous innovator and an agent of discord in the East. The omission of a traditional letter part can also serve Paul's rhetorical purposes. In Gal 1:6, e.g., where one expects a thanksgiving, Paul instead substitutes an expression of astonishment in which he communicates his outrage over a Galatian supplement to his gospel that required circumcision and observance of Jewish law for Gentiles to be included in the people of God.

While the form and content of the body of the letters vary, the conventional conclusion often offers valuable clues to a letter's main emphasis. First Thessalonians well illustrates how Paul uses this ritual of epistolary parting (5:12-28) to encourage and exhort his audience. Beginning with concluding exhortations directly linked to the epistolary situation (5:12-22), Paul continues with a transitional peace wish (5:23) and appends a prayer request (5:25). After the final greeting (5:26) and command to greet one another with a holy kiss (5:26; compare Rom 16:16; 1 Cor 16:20; 2 Cor 13:12), he closes with a final grace and benediction (5:28). While the peace wish definitively marks the transition to the end of the letter, it also betrays a strong Semitic trait of greeting and parting: "May the God of peace himself sanctify you entirely; and may your spirit and soul and body be kept sound and blameless at the coming (**parousia**) of our Lord Jesus Christ. The one who calls you is faithful, and he will do this" (1 Thess 5:23-24). Here Paul so defines the "peace" to involve the readers/hearers in the act of "sanctification," to exhort the disheartened to readiness, and to assure them of God's power to secure a future they had come to doubt. It alludes one last time to the promised salvation at the coming of Christ (see 1:9-10; 2:12, 19-20; 3:13; 4:6; 4:13–5:11) and finally reiterates the primary pastoral emphasis of the letter.

Thus we see Paul bending epistolary conventions to his use. His expansion of the conventional letter ending transforms that medium and makes it startlingly different from the usual Hellenistic papyrus letter ending with its simple "goodbye," "farewell," or "be strong." Paul's readers, sensitive to these subtle shifts of form and meaning, would have responded to the conclusion's emphasis on perseverance, communal solidarity, nonretaliation, moral purity, and encouragement (5:14-24).

E. Chronology of Paul's Life and Letters

1. Challenges

The paucity of historical and internal evidence makes constructing a chronology of Paul's life and letters difficult. Not one of Paul's letters is dated, and the dates of his birth and death are unknown. The exact sequence of the letters is uncertain, and some letters (2 Corinthians and Philippians) may actually be composed of fragments of multiple letters. Although Acts often disagrees with Paul's accounts in the letters (e.g., in Acts Paul makes five visits to Jerusalem, in the letters only three), some evidence from Acts can be used to confirm data from Paul or to provide chronological pegs for the construction of a tentative chronology of Paul's life.

2. Key historical data

Second Corinthians 11:32-33 refers to the ethnarch of Damascus, presumably King Aretas IV of Nabatea who ruled Damascus from 37–39 CE and from whose attempted capture Paul escaped through the wall at night (compare Gal 1:17-18). Before this nocturnal escape, which could have been in 37 CE at the earliest, he had been in Arabia (Nabatea) after his call for three years, 34–37. Thus we may hypothesize that his call came ca. 34 CE (Gal 1:17-18). If the reference "after three years" is tied to his call in 34, Paul's first trip to Jerusalem to consult with Peter and Jesus' brother James (Gal 1:18) would have come in 37/38 after his expulsion or escape from Damascus. His ministry in Syria and Cilicia would have followed in 38–47 (Gal 1:21). His second visit to Jerusalem came "after fourteen years" (Gal 2:1), and given the practice of counting any part of a year as a year, could have been as early as 46 or as late as 48 if measured from the call in 34. A seventeen-year gap between Paul's call and his second visit to Jerusalem (three plus fourteen years) has led some to suggest an earlier date for the call ("conversion"), while the hypothesis suggested here seems plausible but unprovable.

The Edict of Claudius mentioned by the Roman historian Suetonius (ca. 120 CE) refers to the expulsion of Jews from Rome to quell the turbulence caused by Chrestus (*Claud.* 5.25.4). This is probably a reference to unrest in the synagogues in which followers of Christ and non-believers were still meeting together. A date of 49 for the Edict fixed by the Christian historian and theologian Orosius (d. 420 CE) accords well with Paul's collaboration with AQUILA AND PRISCILLA (Prisca) in Corinth, whom Acts 18:2 identifies as Jews expelled under Claudius' order. Most scholars prefer the 49 date for the expulsion, but an increasing number of scholars date the expulsion to 41 CE and shift the chronology backward accordingly.

The Gallio inscription dates Gallio's tenure as proconsul in CORINTH as 52/53 CE, but illness forced him to leave his post after only a few months and before the winter weather would end the sailing season in late fall of 52. This is an important chronological peg, for Acts 18:12-17 tells of Paul's arraignment before Gallio in Corinth, and many use this date to locate Paul's time in Corinth and to chart his previous and future activities accordingly. If Acts is correct that Paul was in Corinth for eighteen months (18:11), then his ministry there began in 50. Previously he had been in Antioch and had founded churches in GALATIA, PHILIPPI, and THESSALONICA (Gal 2:11-14). A further difficulty with the Gallio reference is that we know from Paul's letters that he was in Corinth three times, and there is no way to be sure on which visit he was arraigned before Gallio.

Chronological Outline of Paul's Ministry and Writing		
Event	**Approximate dates**	**Related passages**
Jesus' crucifixion	ca. 30	
Paul's call	ca. 34	Gal 1:15, 16
Paul's ministry in Arabia/Nabatea	34–37	Gal 1:17
Paul's escape from Damascus ruled by an ethnarch, presumably Aretas IV of Nabatea	37/38	2 Cor 11:32-33
First trip to Jerusalem (two-week stay)	37/38	Gal 1:18
Mission in Syria and Cilicia (Paul's home province)	38–47	Gal 1:21
Second trip to Jerusalem; council endorses Paul's Gentile mission	ca. 47 (between 46 and 48)	Gal 2:1-10
Edict of Claudius expelling Jews from Jerusalem	49	Acts 18:2 and Suetonius, *Claud.* 5.25.4
First mission in Europe (Philippi, Thessalonica, and Achaia)	48–52	Acts 15:36–18:17
Ministry in Achaia, including Corinth	fall 50–summer 52	Acts 18:1-3
Arraignment before proconsul Gallio	summer/fall 52	Acts 18:12-17
Paul wrote 1 Thessalonians	summer/fall 52	
Paul in Ephesus	fall 52–56	
Lost letter written to Corinth	52	1 Cor 5:9
Paul wrote 1 Corinthians	53	
Letters from Ephesus and Macedonia collected in fragmentary form in 2 Corinthians	54–57	
Paul wrote Galatians	ca. 55	
Imprisonment	late 55 into early 56	2 Cor 1:8-11
Philippian correspondence from prison, probably in Ephesus	ca. 56	
Philemon possibly written during imprisonment	ca. 56	
The "painful letter" to Corinth	ca. 56	2 Cor 10:1–13:10
Reconciling letter to Corinthians from Macedonia	fall 56	2 Cor 1:1–2:13; 7:5-16
Circular letter to churches in Achaia urging completion of offering	fall 56	2 Cor 9
Paul winters in Corinth preparing the offering and delegation for delivery to Jerusalem	56–57	
Paul departs with delegation for Jerusalem with offering for the "poor among the saints" and final visit to Jerusalem	spring 57	Rom 15:25-33
Arrest, imprisonment, and transfer to Rome	57–59	Acts 25:4–28:16
Execution	60–64	*Acts of Paul and Thecla* 11.1-7

Figure 2: Chronological outline of Paul's ministry and writing

As shaky as it is, the 4th-cent. testimony of Orosius tilts the balance in favor of 52 CE. For if the Edict of Claudius was in 49 CE and Jewish-Christian refugees joined Paul in Corinth and EPHESUS, then tying Paul's arraignment to 52 CE seems more likely. Once Paul leaves Corinth for Jerusalem to deliver the offering, the record from his own hand falls silent (*see* COLLECTION, THE). Acts 23 and 24 recount Paul's arrest and imprisonment in Jerusalem under two proconsuls (Felix and Festus, 52–60 CE and 60–62 CE, respectively) and his being sent to Rome for trial. A late 2nd-cent. text, the *Acts of Paul and Thecla*, offers a legendary account of his beheading under Nero, an event, if historical, that is notoriously difficult to locate chronologically (*see* PAUL, ACTS OF). The best guess is that he was executed in Rome under Nero between 60 and 64 CE, the date of Nero's persecution of the Jesus people. Within those broad parameters, 34 as the beginning of Paul's apostolic activity and 60–64 as the end, we can attempt to place the letters chronologically.

3. The order and approximate dates of the epistles

The task of constructing a credible chronology of Paul's life and letters is complicated by evidence of later redaction (in Romans); two letters (Philippians and 2 Corinthians) were probably later compilations of multiple letter fragments. By scholarly consensus, 1 Thessalonians is Paul's earliest surviving letter, which was written after stops in Philippi and Thessalonica, where he met resistance to his message (though probably not from Jews as Acts 17:1-9 claims), left Thessalonica under pressure, and headed south. From Achaia, he dispatched TIMOTHY to Thessalonica and, in response to news Timothy brought on his return (1 Thess 1:1), Paul wrote 1 Thessalonians (ca. 50/51 CE).

After Paul's eighteen-month ministry in Corinth and arraignment before Gallio, he left in the fall of 52 CE. Thereafter ensues a long period of exchanges between Paul and the Corinthians by letter and oral communication that stretched from 53–57 CE, interrupted by a short and "painful" visit (2 Cor 2:1). Paul wrote one letter, now lost, soon after leaving Corinth (1 Cor 5:9), then oral communication was followed by 1 Corinthians, dispatched with Timothy from Ephesus (ca. 53).

The collection of letters in 2 Corinthians contains portions of as many as five letters written after Paul's founding mission to Corinth and before his final visit to prepare for the journey to deliver the offering to Jerusalem (53–57 CE). All of the fragments were probably written from Ephesus and Macedonia.

With only Paul's words about the founding of the assembly in Galatia (Gal 4:12-20) and the absence of chronological allusions, the place Galatians occupied in the sequence is uncertain. After Paul left Corinth, a visit to Galatia from Ephesus to face hostile Judaizing critics is plausible and would account for the angry missive (Galatians) that Paul dispatched later (ca. 55). Although neither Acts nor any of Paul's letters explicitly refer to an Ephesian imprisonment, a detention during his twenty-seven-month stay there (53–56 CE) after his long mission in Corinth is probable (Acts 18:19–20:35). He does speak of fighting with beasts there (1 Cor 15:32) and of being so "utterly, unbearably crushed" and in such despair that he felt he was under a death sentence (2 Cor 1:8-9). His reference to being in prison many times (2 Cor 11:23) leaves room for the Ephesian imprisonment suggested much later by the apocryphal *Acts of Paul*.

From that imprisonment, it is likely that Paul dispatched the Philippian letter(s), provoked by Jewish-"Christian" opposition to his gospel and apostolic claim, in 56 CE. Judicial hearings had taken place and execution loomed (2 Cor 1:8-11) but release remained possible (2 Cor 1:8-11; Phil 1:20, 25; 2:17, 24). Philemon also may have been written during this imprisonment, though that cannot be proved (Phlm 9). Paul wrote Romans on his third and last visit to Corinth after having passed through Macedonia, from whence he wrote a circular letter to the churches of Achaia (2 Cor 9) urging the completion of the offering and a reconciling letter to the Corinthians (1:1–2:13; 7:5-16).

When we next catch sight of Paul, the collection project is complete and delegates have gathered for the journey to Jerusalem to present the gifts to the "poor among the saints" (Rom 15:26). On the brink of departure, perhaps in early April when the shipping season opened, Paul writes Romans, the last letter we have from his hand (57 CE). About to complete a project so long in the making, Paul worries that the delivery of the offering will be seen as a provocative act. In fear of the "unbelievers" in Jerusalem (Rom 15:31), he solicits prayers for the successful reception of this gift from the Gentile churches. There Paul's own account ends, but Acts fills out the story, suggesting that Paul's worst fears were realized. After his arraignment, he first faced the proconsuls Felix and then Festus (Acts 23:33–24:26 and 25:6–26:32), possibly in 59 and/or 60 CE. He was brought to Rome for trial and, according to the apocryphal *Acts of Paul*, was executed under Nero ca. 60–64 CE.

While this construction is hypothetical, most scholars agree that Paul's apostolic activity began in the 30s and ended in the early 60s. And almost all agree that the evidence of the letters is to be preferred over that of Acts. While some scholars would arrange the letters in a different order, most agree that the majority of Paul's letters were written in the 50s, though a few place all of the letters in the 40s. Given the complexity of the available evidence, one could hardly expect a larger degree of agreement.

F. Paul as Theologian

In the 2nd cent., the venerable Polycarp complained that neither he nor anyone else could grasp Paul's wisdom (*Phil.* 3.2). Even earlier, the author of 2 Peter had admitted that many of Paul's letters are "hard to understand" (3:16). Paul's genius in bringing together elements of a Jewish gospel about Jesus, his Hellenistic habitat, and a rich store of Jewish traditions and Scriptures to deal with thorny issues in a variety of individual and communal issues in largely Gentile congregations does make them difficult to understand. One finds contradictions, highly complex arguments, and creative responses to a variety of contexts that show Paul's theologizing as a work in progress—open-ended, dynamic, and profoundly hopeful—and also how maddeningly difficult it can be to interpret the letters.

1. The nature of Paul's theologizing

Paul did not begin his mission as an apostle of Christ with a theological system that he imposed on every context. Although he claimed that his gospel was not of human origin but came from a revelation of Christ (Gal 1:11-12), that assertion hardly means it came to him whole and at once and devoid of any context. Clearly, his theologizing was informed by church traditions including the recitation of the primitive Christian kerygma, liturgical formulas, hymns, prayers, confessions, and even ethical instructions. He appealed often to the centuries-old traditions of Israel as well as their new formulations in the church's life and confession. To Paul, these were not inert, lifeless borrowings, but the essence of a living past that suffused his thinking.

Read in approximate chronological order, the undisputed letters reveal how Paul's thinking emerged through his theological and human engagement with audiences and religious traditions. Certainly, Paul's encounter with the risen Christ as God's Messiah was a dramatic, life-altering event that led him to see his role as the apostle to the Gentiles as taking place on a great cosmic stage on which the final eschatological scene was being acted out. Certainly he came to that task with a rich and venerable tradition, yet his theologizing had an ad hoc and dynamic character in response to new situations that required fresh theological reflection. His encounters with rival missionary apostles, charismatic factions in the church, hostile Jewish and Judaizing critics, disillusioned converts, faltering followers, and popular religionists provided the context for Paul's theologizing.

This Paul was hardly a theological colossus standing astride the human quest for religious insight whose very being transcended ordinary human understanding or pain. In the letters we witness his anguish when his own converts reject him, his vigorous reaction when he is vilified, his suffering from a debilitating affliction, his pain at the memory of his persecution of the church, and his doubts and anxiety about his ministry. In these struggles, Paul forged new interpretative schemes, combinations, innovations, and improvisations as he struggled heroically with issues of enormous import for the emergent church.

He wrestled with a host of questions. On what terms can pagan Gentiles be included in God's elect? By choosing Gentiles, has God rejected Israel? What are the marks of a true apostle? What does it mean to live by the "law of Christ" or the "law of the spirit"? Which of the competing versions of the early gospel is most faithful to the life of Christ? Paul obviously did not have his mind made up on all of these challenges before he faced them. Moreover, as he faced new situations, harsh critics, and vicious rivals, Paul sometimes altered his emphasis or even changed his mind (e.g., see the more positive view of law in Romans than in Galatians). Thus we see that Paul's theology was an emerging perspective rather than a fixed and consistent one.

2. Paul's Jewish roots and Gentile mission

As situational as Paul's theologizing was, it nevertheless drew strength and inspiration from deep, underlying convictions grounded in the story of Israel. From that master narrative came beliefs that he simply assumed and felt no need to justify. Foremost in that legacy was Paul's monotheism and conviction of the supremacy of the God of Israel, the creator and redeemer, the one who makes and fulfills promises, the righteous judge and merciful savior, and the sovereign and free Lord of history. His Gentile gospel was directly tied to his belief that the one God was the God of all people, his messianism to God's promises to Israel, his eschatology to the righteousness of God. So although Paul offers daring and innovative interpretations of that monotheistic tradition, he nowhere rejects it.

Paul's Pharisaic leanings are highlighted in his recounting of his place in the story of Israel. He laid claim to being a descendant of the "tribe of Benjamin," a "Hebrew born of Hebrews," to having been "circumcised on the eighth day" after his birth and blamelessness before the law, and having a surpassing zeal for the traditions of his Jewish ancestors (Acts 23:6; 26:5; 2 Cor 11:21-33; Gal 1:13-14; Phil 3:5-6). Yet a paucity of sources makes it difficult to reconstruct Paul's 1st-cent. Pharisaism. Later rabbinic texts and Gospel sources antagonistic to the Pharisees must be used with great caution. Our only writings from 1st-cent. Pharisees may come from Paul and Josephus, a Jewish historian with a questionable claim to Pharisaism who offers a mixed review of the Pharisees of the 1st cent. (*Ant.* 12–17). Paul himself tells us little about what being a Pharisee entailed or how he came to lean toward Pharisaism, and nowhere refers to interacting with Pharisees.

More useful than this consideration of Pharisaism, however, may be an understanding of Paul's use of the term **Ioudaios** (*Jew*), its foreground, and his self-understanding in relationship to it. The roots of that understanding must be located in the exile and its influence in reshaping the identity of the captive people of Judah. While in exile in the 6th cent. BCE, the Judean deportees became a confessional community with an in-group/out-group mentality that was essential for the preservation of their identity in the ghetto of Tel-abib in Babylon (Ezra 1:3; 3:1-5). Once released in 537 BCE, the returning exiles assumed control of the religious and civic administration of Judah and imposed their "ways and manners" on all within their sphere of power. This Jewish sectarianism reinscribed on Judah laid the groundwork for a geopolitical temple state that assigned second-class status to indigent Israelites, Samaritans, the people of the land, and other peoples of Israelite descent. Perpetuated and expanded under Hasmonean rule, this template was imposed on parts of Galilee and probably survived well into the 1st cent.

This sectarianism seems to have been at the center of Paul's conflict with Peter, James, John, and other leaders of the Jerusalem church. While Paul sometimes uses the word *Jew* self-referentially and nonpolemically to set one pole of difference that he hopes to reconcile (1 Cor 9:20-23), in Galatians such references occur in a harshly polemical context (Gal 1:13; 2:5). There Paul recalls an ugly incident in Antioch (2:11-18) where he angrily confronted Peter for eating with Gentiles but withdrawing when Jewish critics from Jerusalem arrived (2:12). In response, Paul begins, "We ourselves are Jews by birth and not Gentile sinners," and then subverts the exclusive and privileged claims of these **Ioudaioi** (Jews): "We know that a person is justified not by the works of the law but through the faithfulness of Jesus Christ" (2:16; author's trans.; NRSV, "faith in Jesus Christ"). While Paul can legitimately claim to be a **Ioudaios** (Gal 1:13) and to share in the genealogy of his adversaries, he vigorously resists their attempt to impose the "rules and manners" of their version of Jewish law on Gentile converts as a condition of their inclusion in the people of God (Gal 2:5). He also warns his Gentile converts in Galatia that if they follow the gospel proposed by these Jewish apostle rivals and accept circumcision as a signifier of their location in the people of God, then they would be obligated to keep the "whole law" (Gal 3:10) or be cursed. For Paul, the apocalyptic moment inaugurated by Jesus' death and resurrection redefined the terms of inclusion, and opened the way for the inclusion of Gentiles on the basis of faith (*see* FAITH, FAITHFULNESS; JUSTIFICATION, JUSTIFY).

Writing decades later about his earlier life, Paul prefers the broader, more general term *Israelite* to locate himself religiously. Note, e.g., Paul's emphatic use of the term in Rom 11:1: "I ask, then, has God rejected his people? By no means! I myself am an Israelite, a descendant of Abraham, a member of the tribe of Benjamin." Hardly a synonym for *Jew*, the more general and inclusive term *Israelite* signals his intention to define SALVATION in broad terms. Likewise, in 2 Cor 11:22, he chooses signifiers to describe himself and his rival "super-apostles" that are broader and less circumscribed than the term *Jew*: i.e., *Hebrews*, *Israelites*, and "descendants of Abraham" (compare Phil 3:5-7; *see* ABRAHAM, NT AND EARLY JUDAISM).

Paul's self-designation as an Israelite places him in a motley and mixed company of people assigned second-class citizen status. The broader term *Israelite* embraced a highly diverse multitude of people involuntarily annexed to the Hasmonean kingdom from the central hill country, Galilee, and the Transjordanian region and even traditional enemies from Edom (or Idumea), Samaritans, Galilean Arabs, Greeks, and Syrians with some claim to Israelite descent. A fundamental premise of Paul's Gentile mission was his refusal to impose the Jewish rules of identity construction and maintenance on Gentile converts as a condition of inclusion in God's elect. To secure this right, Paul had to resist pressure by the pillars of the early church to impose the rules and manners of Jews or Jewish Christians on all converts.

3. Paul's apocalyptic vision

Although Paul's thought was shaped by both Jewish and Hellenistic elements, his apocalyptic outlook was distinctly Jewish (*see* APOCALYPTICISM). His views on God's judgment and righteousness, the human plight, and the world's decline draw their energy, metaphors, language, and vision from the Jewish apocalyptic literature of his day (*see* ESCHATOLOGY IN EARLY JUDAISM), but with the difference that Paul believed the imminent return of Jesus as Lord to gather his own and proclaim God's righteous judgment would move the great cosmic drama to its final climactic, revolutionary conclusion (*see* ESCHATOLOGY OF THE NT). God's raising of Jesus from the dead confirmed his status as Lord and promised his followers a triumph over principalities and powers, sin, and death. In one short letter (1 Thessalonians), Paul refers to Jesus as **kyrios** (κύριος, "lord") twenty-three times and anticipates his imminent arrival when he would raise up believers (4:15-17). In the Hellenistic world, this highly nuanced idiomatic word, *lord*, could designate a god (e.g., Isis, Asclepius, Chronos, Artemis, Apollo, or Yahweh), powerful rulers, or any superior. Paul's use of the term, however, takes on a distinctive and apocalyptic nuance to signify Jesus who suffered, died, was raised, and would soon return (e.g., 1 Thess 1:6; 4:14-18; compare Rom 1:4; 4:24; 1 Cor 1:7, 8, 9; 5:4; 2 Cor 4:14). Yet Paul's favorite term for his lord was **Christos** (Χριστός). While the NRSV translates **Christos** as "Messiah" only once (Rom 9:5), Paul uses the title **Christos** numerous times to refer to Jesus as the Messiah, denoting function as well as mystical import (Rom 1:1, 6, 7, 8; 1 Cor 1:1-10; and so forth; *see* MESSIAH, JEWISH). For it is through the "faithfulness of Jesus Christ" (**dia pisteōs Iēsou Christou** διὰ πίστεως Ἰησοῦ Χριστοῦ; Rom 3:22), Paul claimed, that humans are released from the clutches of cosmic ruling powers such as sin, death, and demonic rule (Rom 6:1-23).

Linked to this view of cosmic deliverance by the faithfulness of Christ was Paul's conviction that believers mystically or mythically participate in Christ or in the "body of Christ." He himself speaks of being "in Christ" and of Christ being in him. He views the welts and scars left on his body from beatings as somehow participating in the "marks (**stigmata**) of Jesus" (Gal 6:17). This mystical identification carried a strong ethical imperative as well; males in Christ must not join their bodies with prostitutes, a common practice in the Hellenistic world, lest they pollute the body of Christ (1 Cor 6:12-20).

While Paul came to know Jesus only as the risen Lord, and it was this Jesus who informed Paul's gospel, he also referred to the earthly Jesus. He adopted and confirmed the creedal statement that Jesus came from the seed of David (Rom 1:3). He recognized that Jesus was born under the law (Gal 4:4). He knew of Jesus' brothers (1 Cor 9:5) and had dealings, not all pleasant, with Jesus' brother James (1 Cor 15:7; Gal 1:19; 2:9, 12). He recited with appreciation an early hymn of the church that referred to Jesus, obedient and faithful, who sacrificed himself for others (Phil 2:5-8; compare Rom 3:22-23; 1 Cor 1:17; Gal 1:4). Yet he recalled Jesus' teachings fewer than ten times in the letters (1 Cor 7:10-11; 4:12; 13:2; 9:14; Rom 13:8-10; 14:14; echoes in Rom 13:7; 14:13; 1 Thess 5:2). The death of Jesus was an important focal point for Paul's theology, for the crucifixion and resurrection represented for him God's vindication of the righteous one and the sign of the arriving new age (*see* CHRISTOLOGY).

4. Paul and the law

The Gk. term for law, **nomos**, is pluri-significant. It can refer to a "law of nature," to the Torah as a narrative of Israel's election, to commandments given by God to Moses, to the "law of the spirit," or even to the "law of Christ." Yet except for two references in Philippians (3:5, 6), an extended polemic in Galatians, and something of a corrective in Romans, Paul's letters contain few extended discussions about the law. Before the discovery of the Qumran scrolls and the link forged there between law and grace, an older view of Paul divided his life into two parts: before his "conversion," when he was frustrated by his inability to keep the law and oppressed by an unbearable burden of guilt, and after the "conversion," when he was freed from his bondage to sin and the law. The first phase was joyless; the second joyful. In the first he lived under a stern and judging God, and in the second he served under a gracious and merciful God. In this view, the Christian Paul broke with his Judaism and formed a new religion. For support, scholars pointed to Phil 3:8, where Paul discounts all of his considerable achievements under the law as "dung"; to Rom 3:21, where Paul refers to righteousness apart from the law; and to Rom 7:9, where Paul recalls two phases of his life: "I was once alive apart from the law, but when the commandment came, sin revived and I died."

But increasingly scholars have noted that Paul nowhere claims he could not keep the law and suffered under a heavy burden of guilt; to the contrary, in Phil 3:6 Paul says that he was "under the law, blameless." They have argued that his description of his achievements under the law as "dung" was less a repudiation of law than a reevaluation of those achievements in light of Christ and a sharp polemic aimed at Jewish Christian missionaries out to discredit Paul and his gospel. They have also noted that Paul hardly commended a law-free life in Christ, but presented instead a new understanding of law required by the new age dawning (see esp. Rom 8:1-8). Moreover, they claim that, read in context, Galatians was intended as a defense of Paul's gospel for Gentiles whom he included in the people of God without requiring law observance as a prerequisite. They also note the corrective that Romans appears to make to Paul's overly dismissive view of Torah in Galatians. Set in the context of Paul's apocalyptic vision, Paul speaks of the "law of Christ" (Gal 6:2) and "the law of the spirit" (Rom 8:2) in quite positive ways. In Rom 10:4 he refers to Christ as the **telos** (τέλος, "end, fulfillment"), which can be understood to mean the purpose of the law. While Paul's understanding of law is complex and enormously complicated, to say that he repudiated law altogether is inaccurate; in Rom 7:12 he says unambiguously, "The law is holy, and the commandment is holy and just and good." *See* LAW IN THE NT.

5. An emergent theology

Paul's theology emerged in and through conflict and interaction with rivals and Gentile congregations and was refined in a crucible of controversy and the needs of local churches. Examining Paul's letters in a rough chronological order reveals how his theology emerged. First Thessalonians (*see* THESSALONIANS, FIRST LETTER TO THE), Paul's earliest-known letter, addresses a predominantly if not exclusively Gentile community in distress and bears no trace of the rancorous debates later provoked by itinerant Jewish Christian missionaries contesting the legitimacy of Paul's apostleship and gospel. The letter recalls how the Thessalonians turned from idols to welcome Paul and his gospel (1:5-6, 9-10; 2:2-9; 3:2). At the center of that gospel stood Paul's emphasis on the death and resurrection of Christ (1:10; 4:14) and the exhortation to keep themselves pure and spotless as they await the return of the Lord Jesus (2:19; 3:13; 4:15; 5:23).

The context and challenges Paul faced profoundly influenced the shape his theology assumed. After the positive response to his preaching in Thessalonica and the formation of a small cell of believers who rejected their native religion for the worship of the one God of Israel, they soon experienced brutal coercion. That persecution and intimidation for their association with Christ and inclusion in God's elect (1 Thess 1:4-6; 2:1-2; 3:3-4), when coupled with the premature death of some of the believers, set off a religious or existential crisis in the community. Some worried that Paul's promise of the imminent return of Christ might be false (4:17); others risked losing all hope. Some believers despaired of ever again seeing their loved ones now departed (1:3; 2:19; 4:13; 5:8). The importance of Paul's challenge to be morally ready for the grand assize (4:3) might have escaped those who were ignorant of Jewish laws and customs and who were socialized to frequent prostitutes without shame. Still others caught up in the spirit and expecting an imminent end of the age quit work and imposed on others for support. These freeloaders (**ataktos** [ἄτακτος], "lazy, idle"; 5:14) were undermining community solidarity and trust.

Set in motion by this challenge, Paul's theologizing offers differing approaches to problems faced by his converts. Without a single citation from Scripture or explicit appeal to the Jewish tradition, Paul reinforces an identity that, nevertheless, was rooted in the Jewish apocalyptic vision of the resurrection and final judgment (*see* DAY OF JUDGMENT; RESURRECTION, NT). Reflecting his sensitivity to the pagan past of his addressees and to their persecution and discouragement, Paul appropriated inclusive election and familial language. The thanksgiving assured the persecuted that they were "beloved of God" who had chosen them (1:4). Later he made persecution and election correlates to the tradition of Christ (1:6; 2:12-16; 3:3). For those rejected by families and friends, he created a surrogate family of God (*see* GOD, HOUSEHOLD OF). While his warm and inclusive speech could hardly erase the loneliness, the confusion, and even the desperation of being an outcast, it could construct a new household to nurture, encourage, exhort, remind, and console (5:14). Headed by the patriarch, GOD THE FATHER (1:1), his "beloved" (1:3-4) could share the company of "brothers and sisters" huddled against the cold (**adelphoi** ἀδελφοί, "brothers"; used eight times for emphasis). Paul underscored his love and care for his Thessalonian converts. He recalled being "gentle" among them like a wet nurse caring for her children (2:7) and like a father encouraging and instructing his little ones (2:11-12). This special relationship to God through Christ (1:1), he reminded them, set them apart from those behaving with "lustful passion, like the Gentiles who do not know God" (4:5). And he reassured them that they could look forward to the imminent return of Christ when they would be vindicated and reunited with those momentarily torn from their embrace (4:13-18).

Later, withering criticism from the Jerusalem church and Jewish Christian apostles would force Paul to think more carefully about the inclusion of Gentiles without the imposition of law observance as a precondition. At this early stage, under the influence of his Greek Scriptures, Paul may have simply assumed that the messianic age would herald the inclusion of Gentiles and had not yet reflected on the implications of this inclusion outside the law (e.g., Amos 9:11-12 LXX; Zech 8:18-23 LXX).

The sharpest challenge to the argument that converts must observe Jewish law came later in Galatians (*see* GALATIANS, LETTER TO THE), a scathingly polemical letter addressed to churches Paul had founded in central Asia Minor (Gal 1:2; 4:13-14). There he had won converts from a sickbed and had left a Gentile congregation devoted to his gospel based on the death, resurrection, and imminent return of Christ (1:1, 4; 2:19-20; 3:1, 13; 4:4-6; 5:5, 10, 21), experience of the Spirit (3:2-5; 5:5-25), baptism into an egalitarian community (3:26-28), and salvation by grace made known through the "faithfulness of Christ" (2:16). (In Gal 2:16, the phrase **pisteōs Christou** [πίστεως Χριστοῦ, "faith or faithfulness of Christ"] refers to Christ's obedience even unto death as a saving act; the translation "faith in Christ" appears to make belief in Christ a saving work.) In his absence, however, unnamed Judaizing agitators (5:12) had declared Paul's message erroneous and dangerous and urged circumcision (1:6-7; 5:2-12; 6:12-13) and the observance of the Sabbath, festival rules (4:10), and food laws (2:12; 4:17) as a condition of salvation (4:8-9). Paul recognizes that they preach a "different gospel" (1:6-7), and in response to the arguments of these Jewish messianist critics that Gen 17:10-14 declared male circumcision a seal of the promise and a ratification of one's place among the elect, he mixes vitriol and tenderness with reason and persuasion (*see* JUDAIZING).

With utter contempt for his rivals, he curses them twice (1:8-9), expresses bitter disappointment in his converts (1:6), and fiercely defends his apostolic claim (1:1, 11-17). He attacks the scriptural appeal of his critics to Gen 17 by cleverly noting that Abraham's faith and God's promise in Gen 15:6 came without reference to the law observance that came later (Gen 17:10-14). He outlined the process by which the Galatians, like the believing Abraham, were received as adopted children into the people of God (3:15-18; 4:1-6); it was not through law observance that the Galatians were freed from sin and set in a right relationship with God, but through the "faithfulness of Jesus Christ" (2:16, 21; 3:18, 29). Recalling the liturgy of baptism (3:27-28), Paul reminds the Galatians that in Christ, "there is no longer Jew or Greek, there is no longer slave or free, there is no longer male and female." This formula appealed to a shared experience to erase the distinction between Jew and Gentile that his rivals would secure. With an ugly pun Paul threatens those seeking justification by CIRCUMCISION and law observance that they will be "cut off" from Christ (5:4); Paul the knowing Jew contemptuously scolds that "every man [i.e., Gentile believer] who lets himself be circumcised ... is obliged to obey the entire law" (5:3). Although the church would later accept Paul's argument for including Gentiles, at the time such an outcome was hardly a foregone conclusion.

News of Paul's negative view of Torah expressed in Galatians appears to have spread like a salacious rumor and later led to greater charges against him. These accusations show he was suspected of undermining the core of the religion of Israel. Apparently, in the heat of his argument with the Galatians about the gospel of the Judaizers Paul overreached himself with a view of law that was so negative that others would accuse him of repudiating God's good gift, i.e., the law, and of denying God's promises to Israel (*see* LAW IN THE OT). Such charges later provoked Paul's vigorous denial that he believed the "word of God has failed" (Rom 9:6).

When Paul composed his letter(s) to the Philippians (*see* PHILIPPIANS, LETTER TO THE) from prison (probably in Ephesus), he had already written to the Corinthians as many as four times, and possibly to the Galatians as well. He had faced a judicial hearing and awaited condemnation, execution (Phil 1:20; 2:17), or release (1:25; 2:24). When he wrote he was staring death in the face (1:7, 12-26; Acts 19:32-40; 1 Cor 15:32), and even despaired of "life itself" (2 Cor 1:8-9). Nevertheless, he found in the experience an occasion for reflecting on the death of Christ. He called on the Philippians to have in them the same mind that he found in Christ Jesus, whose preexistent celestial status, descent, life, obedience unto death, and ascent as Lord of all (Phil 2:2-11) provided an example of what life in Christ should be (compare 1 Cor 15:31; 2 Cor 5:14; 6:9). Thus his own imprisonment became an occasion for urging the Philippians to suffer for Christ's sake and to share "the same struggle (**agōn** ἀγών) that you saw I had and now hear that I still have" (1:30).

Once Paul was released, he reflected on the dangers he had faced and attributed his deliverance to God; he recalled God's consolation while in prison and held it up as a paradigm of encouragement that he offered to the Philippians (compare 2 Cor 1:9-10). Through these encounters with life's extremities he felt a bond was secured not only between him and the beaten and crucified Christ but also with his converts who at times also suffered for their faith but also came to Paul's aid when they heard he was in prison.

The letter tells of a visit from Epaphroditus, who brought money from the church in Philippi for Paul's aid, and who ministered to him. In addition to the gift from Philippi Epaphroditus also brought disquieting news. Itinerant Jewish-Christian evangelists had arrived who were quite different from those in Galatia. They urged Gentile believers to accept circumcision probably as a sign of the covenant relationship (Phil 3:2) and they emphasized participation in the glory of the resurrected life over the centrality of the cross (3:18). They seemed obsessed with a swollen self-indulgence ("their god is the belly" [3:19]), and Paul's angry response to the Judaizers who advocated circumcision as a condition of inclusion in the elect also calls on his own experience in a letter fragment (Phil 3:2–4:3). He discounts as "dung" his own considerable achievement as an Israelite, Benjaminite, super-Hebrew, and zealous Pharisee who was blameless before the law (3:5-9) in order to be found "in Christ." No repudiation was this of Paul's native religion but rather a radical revaluation of his achievements under the law in favor of Christ. Aside from its polemical context it is often misunderstood. To subvert the force of their argument Paul spiritualizes circumcision, making it apply to the uncircumcised. All believers, Jewish and Gentile, Paul names as "the circumcision" (Phil 3:2-3).

Even though Paul hurls one ugly epithet at these rivals (namely, "dogs" [3:2], the ones who pose competing claims, internal strife, and external threats), this rivalry fails to eclipse the genuine warmth and human tenderness of this letter. The conflict only seems to underscore the "partnership in the gospel" (1:5; 3:1, 9, 14; 4:21) between Paul and his Philippian converts, their common life as resident aliens with a "citizenship" (**politeuma**) in heaven (3:20), and their shared mystical life "in Christ" completely at odds with the "enemies of the cross of Christ" (3:17-18). Whether from Paul's pen or appropriated by him from a preexisting source, the great soaring Christ hymn of Phil 2:6-11 offers a stunning christological statement—a synthesis of Jewish and Hellenistic elements—that Paul lifts up for imitation (*see* KENOSIS). Philemon (*see* PHILEMON, LETTER TO) was also probably written from the same imprisonment in Ephesus (1, 9, 10, 13, 23). ONESIMUS, Philemon's slave, was with Paul when he wrote, and Paul's willingness to make good on any debt Onesimus owed suggests to some that Onesimus had stolen money from his master and fled. He had served Paul and was converted by him, and Paul wrote to Philemon and the "church in your house" urging that the returning Onesimus be treated as "more than a slave" (16). Whether Paul's diplomatic approach was masterful or allowed for continued oppression is debated, but this short letter does suggest that a partnership of early converts at opposite ends of the social scale existed in the early church.

First and Second Corinthians (*see* CORINTHIANS, FIRST LETTER TO THE; CORINTHIANS, SECOND LETTER TO THE) offer an extended record of a protracted and sometimes bitter struggle spanning several years. Although persecution was a brutal reality in Thessalonica, Philippi, and Ephesus, no such grisly prospect troubled the church in Corinth. No disillusionment darkened the mood of those converts, as in Thessalonica, and no rival Judaizing teachers as yet challenged the legitimacy of Paul's apostolic claim or sought to discredit his Gentile gospel, as in Philippi and Galatia.

The thanksgiving (1 Cor 1:4-9) praises the Corinthians for their spiritual gifts manifest "in speech and knowledge of every kind ... so that you are not lacking in any spiritual gift as you wait for the revealing of our Lord Jesus Christ" (1:5-7). But these abundant spiritual gifts had become a source of conflict, as members' identification with various mystagogues—Paul, Apollos, Cephas, and even the glorified Christ—had led to quarrels, prompting Paul's sarcastic question, "Has Christ been divided?" (1 Cor 1:11-13). He berated the pretensions of the religiously elite, which included boasting of a superior wisdom (1:20–2:16), a spiritual puffery begat by glossolalia (12:27–13:3; *see* TONGUES, GIFT OF), libertine adventurism (6:12-20), and claims of angelic status accessed through celibacy (7:1-16) and of religious wisdom, status, knowledge, and fullness above that of the apostles (4:1-13). What they claimed as an exciting spirit possession and present salvation, Paul saw as a divisive and pretentious claim giving rise to a superior and waspish behavior that threatened the very existence of the church (1:10-17; 3:3-4; 11:18-19; 12:25).

Some of Paul's most creative theologizing occurs in response to the Corinthians' religious puffery and divisive pretensions. Since the problems in Corinth at root represented exaggerations of Paul's own positions, his response required a level of diplomacy, teaching, and exhortation unequaled elsewhere in his letters. Against an arrogant claim to a superior wisdom, Paul juxtaposed a theology of the cross: "I decided to know nothing among you except Jesus Christ, and him crucified" (2:2; compare 1:17-25). Countering a spiritual elitism that made speaking in tongues the supreme charismatic gift, he made love the supreme charism (1 Cor 1:7-13; 3:1-2; 8:1; 13:1-13). Against a rampant and divisive individualistic experience of salvation in the Spirit, he emphasized the welfare of the body (1 Cor 12:12-31) and urged the completion of the Jerusalem offering (16:1-4) for the "poor among the saints" (Rom 15:26). To his converts' totalistic claims to salvation, he reminded them of the partiality of human knowledge, understanding, and vision of the future (1 Cor 13:9-13) and that believers are those in the process of "being saved" (1:18). Against pretentious claims to angelic status through celibacy and to authority based on his own example, Paul urges caution, honesty about one's own limits, and the mutual responsibility and interdependence of women and men (1 Cor 7:1-16; 11:7-16).

Second Corinthians, a collection of several letter fragments, responds to suspicions and distrust aroused by Paul's offering project. The situation worsened when itinerant Jewish apostles of Christ arrived with letters of recommendation commending them at Paul's expense (2 Cor 3:1-2). These rival apostles, skilled exegetes of Scripture (3:3-18) and radiant advocates of a gospel different from Paul's (3:12-18), sowed suspicion about Paul's ministry and honesty and the legitimacy of his apostolic claim (2 Cor 2:5–7:4 minus 6:14–7:1, and 10:1–13:10). They gained a following, with the result that some of Paul's converts abandoned him; others refused to come to his defense, and after a short catastrophic and painful visit to Corinth to settle differences, Paul had retreated in humiliation and shame (2:1-2). In the shadow of that disgraceful moment, Paul crafts a defense and makes a valiant effort to refute his critics, win back the loyalty of his alienated "children" (12:13-18), vigorously defend his apostolic credentials, and effect a reconciliation.

In the face of this challenge, Paul strikes a sometimes belligerent and angry pose (10:1-6) that segues into a brilliant theological statement about the true marks of an apostle (11:21*b*-29). To those who ridicule him as physically weak and rhetorically unskilled (10:1, 10), he redefines the nature of divine power by calling attention to the marks of shame—scars, welts, and calluses—etched on his back's flesh by whip, rod, and stones. In an epiphanic moment, the scars gain a mystical meaning from participating in the marks on Jesus' body left by the beatings he suffered and his crucifixion (11:29-30; 12:8-10; compare Gal 6:17). His recollection of the Lord's words, "for power is made perfect in weakness" (12:9), completely revises the understanding of power advanced by his rivals. His ironic use of this WEAKNESS as a signifier of apostolic authority would prove to be revolutionary.

This theological move in the letter, delivered and defended by TITUS, effects a reconciliation (1:1–2:4; 7:5-16) and the successful completion of the offering effort. In the spring of 57 CE, Paul is in Corinth; the offering project is complete; the delegation to deliver it has gathered; Paul has enjoyed the hospitality of Gaius, a leader of the congregation; and he writes Romans, possibly his last letter. And his eyes turn somewhat anxiously toward Jerusalem as he reflects on the impending delivery of the offering (2 Cor 9).

Often treated as a theological treatise, Romans (*see* ROMANS, LETTER TO THE) is a real letter, dealing with an actual situation, breathing the warmth of a letter, following the structure of a letter, and serving the function of a letter. Introducing himself to a church he had neither founded nor visited, Paul feared that the slanderous rumors and attacks on his gospel and apostolic legitimacy had preceded him (3:5-8; 6:1; 7:7). He answered charges that salvation by GRACE promoted licentiousness and that his Gentile gospel questioned the reliability of God's promises to Israel (9:1-4; 11:29). While Romans is indeed a profound, complex, and careful statement of Paul's gospel for the Gentiles, it is hardly a calm, cool, collected summary of his theology. While echoes of other letters do appear—references to Adam and Christ, charismatic gifts, law, Abraham, the love commandment, the faithfulness of Christ, salvation by grace for non-Jews, the righteousness of God, the offering, election, and a provisional eschatology—references to the cross, the eucharist, and (save 16:1-24) the church are absent altogether. Consequently, it is best to read Romans in its own right as a true letter dealing with issues vital to the defense of Paul's Gentile gospel, his anticipated missions, and conflicts between believers in Rome.

Although Romans contains no excoriation of Jewish apostles of discord (as do 2 Corinthians and Philippians), anathematization of rival Judaizing teachers (as does Galatians), sarcastic correction of enthusiastic sectarians (found in 1 Corinthians), or gentle encouragement of the persecuted and doubting who mourned unexpected loss (1 Thessalonians), it brims with theological language articulating a gospel and Gentile mission that had come under increasing criticism.

Serving as the summary of his thanksgiving (1:8-15) and theme of the epistle, 1:16-17 speaks of God's power for "everyone," Jew and Greek. In spite of the vituperation heaped on him and his gospel by critics in the East, Paul offers no apology: "I am not ashamed of the gospel; for it is the power of God for all those believing, Jew and Greek; for in it the righteousness of God is being revealed out of faithfulness unto faith and he who is righteous out of faith shall live" (author's trans.; NRSV, "For I am not ashamed of the gospel; it is the power of God for salvation to everyone who has faith, to the Jew first and also to the Greek. For in it the righteousness of God is revealed through faith for faith; as it is written, 'The one who is righteous will live by faith'"). Paul must gain some acceptance of this fundamental premise of his gospel if he is to be welcomed in Rome and his mission to Spain supported (15:22-24). For Paul, the "righteousness of God" was not a quality of being but rather God's intervention through Jesus to reclaim a crooked world, to raise up the fallen, and to offer liberation by faith through the faithfulness of Christ (3:21-22) to all in the clutches of the power of sin (3:23-26)—pagans (1:18-32) and Jews (2:1–3:8) alike. Jewish boasting and Gentile arrogance are both excluded. Since "all have sinned and fall short" (3:23), all stand in equal need of grace (3:24). Thus Paul's gospel includes but transcends individual salvation to assume cosmic proportions, declares God's redemption from the tyranny of sin and death, and provides a remedy for human brokenness and alienation (*see* SIN, SINNERS). In 4:1-22 Paul calls on Abraham's example to support his gospel for all. In Galatia, opponents had invoked Abraham (Gen 17:9-14) to counter Paul's welcome of Gentile males into God's elect without requiring circumcision. But here he finds in the Abraham story support for his inclusive gospel (Gen 15:1-6). As Israel's legendary patriarch, Abraham kept all of the laws before they were written, and as a Gentile he became, by faith, the "father of many Gentiles [not nations]" (Rom 4:17, author's trans.; NRSV, "father of many nations"). In 4:23-25, Paul comes to his point: to say that Abraham's faith "was reckoned to him" as righteousness while he was a Gentile legitimates Paul's gospel and makes it clear that Paul's gospel does not "overthrow the law" (3:31) but establishes its deeper meaning. (In proclaiming "righteousness by faith" Paul is hardly substituting one work, "faith," for another. Abraham's trust did not make him righteous; his faith was the acceptance of God's gracious work.)

Later in 5:12-21, comparing and contrasting Adam and Christ, Paul responds to the query as to how one man's act of faithfulness and righteousness could redound to others. According to Paul, just as through human sin the many share in the fate of the disobedient Adam (Gen 2:15–3:24), so even more "one man's act of righteousness" leads to "justification and life for all" (5:18). Paul's summary—"where sin increased, grace abounded all the more" (5:20)—would seem to support the charge that Paul's gospel of justification apart from works of the law encouraged licentious behavior. But in response to the slanderous jibe, "Should we continue in sin in order that grace may abound?" (6:1; compare 3:8), Paul offers three metaphors (baptism, slavery, and marriage and widowhood) and a climactic imperative of life in the Spirit. Baptism symbolizes not just the entry into the new creation and liberation from the bondage of sin but also carries the requirement to "walk in newness of life" (6:4). Freed from slavery to master sin through submission to the good master, the righteousness of God, one is free to struggle against sin's ongoing tyranny (6:12-23). Paul also notes how the death of a husband frees a wife to have children or "bear fruit" in another relationship; in like manner, those who have died to the law are freed to belong to and to bear fruit for Christ (7:1-6). Paul immediately adds, however, that it is not Torah that brings death (7:12, 16, 21-23; 8:2), but rather the crooked heart of humanity. The "law of the Spirit," Paul believed, offered a remedy for sin's infection and freed one from the "law [or principle] of sin and death" (8:2) in order to walk in newness of life (8:1-8). Paul's theology is one of hope, enabling him to see God working in all things on behalf of the called (8:28). While acknowledging human vulnerability and weakness, trauma and distress, he writes one of his most powerful statements, that believers are "more than conquerors through him who loved us" (8:37).

In Rom 9–11, a tightly reasoned climax to the first part of the letter, Paul responds to the hostile rejoinder that his earlier repudiation of Torah (in Galatians) in favor of a Gentile gospel means that God reneged on promises made to Israel. Only here does Paul carefully respond to questions about God's fairness. With deep pathos, Paul begins, "I have great sorrow and unceasing anguish in my heart" (Rom 9:2). Recalling Moses' prayer that God would take his life to substitute for that of a wayward people (Exod 32:30-32), Paul cries out, "I could wish that I myself were accursed and cut off from Christ for the sake of my own people" (Rom 9:2-3). Beginning by affirming Israel's historic privileges (9:5) and God's freedom to choose some and reject others, Paul both argues for the validity of the Gentile mission and insists that God has not rejected Israel. Paul insists on the salvation of Israel as well as Gentiles, with no preconditions whatsoever (11:26-32). He emphatically states, "As regards the gospel they are enemies of God for your [i.e., the Gentiles'] sake; but as regards ELECTION they are beloved, for the sake of their ancestors; for the gifts and the calling of God are irrevocable" (11:28-29). In wonderment as to how this could be, Paul found the answer hidden in the mystery of the Godhead itself (11:25). Moved by this conjured scenario, Paul launches into a final, climactic benediction (11:33-36):

> O the depth of the riches and wisdom and knowledge of God! How unsearchable are his judgments and how inscrutable his ways!
>
> "For who has known the mind of the Lord?
> Or who has been his counselor?"
> "Or who has given a gift to him,
> to receive a gift in return?"

For from him and through him and to him are all things. To him be the glory forever. Amen.

Despite its profundity, Paul's theologizing in the face of criticisms that his Gentile gospel fatally compromised God's word to Israel (9:6) did not long go unchallenged. In the 2nd cent., Justin Martyr thought Jewish Christians would be denied salvation (*Dial.* 47), and Jerome later ridiculed Jewish Christians whom he considered to be neither Jewish nor Christian (*Epist.* 112.13). While Paul's construction in Rom 9–11 that sought to admit difference without eschewing otherness was theologically brilliant, it was more difficult to sustain than to create.

Paul was also sensitive to the charge that his gospel of salvation apart from law encouraged immorality. While he had earlier argued by means of analogy that the freedom secured in the gospel is no license to misconduct (Rom 6–8), in Rom 12–15 he offered a more extended articulation of the imperative that went with the gospel. Opening with the admonition to all to present their bodies as "a living sacrifice" (12:1) as their daily worship, he instructs all with special gifts to use them to build the church (12:3-8; compare 1 Cor 12); he admonishes all to genuine love, perseverance in suffering, generosity to outsiders, nonretaliation in the sure confidence of vindication before the divine judgment (12:9-21), respect for governing authorities (13:1-10), and reconciliation of the weak and the strong (14:1–15:21).

In the conclusion, the Spanish mission breaks into view: "I will set out by way of you to Spain" (15:28). With the mission in the East complete from Jerusalem to Illyricum (15:19), with the offering for the "poor among the saints" in Jerusalem collected, and with the delegation gathered to deliver it (15:25-27), an anxious Paul petitions the Romans for prayers for its success and hopes a united church will support his Spanish mission as he bends back from Jerusalem to Rome. But even as he sets out on that journey to Jerusalem, his hope was mingled with fears that tradition suggests did come to pass. Finally, he closes and greets some twenty-six people, among them ten female leaders in the church with important positions (Rom 16:1-23), including PHOEBE, a deacon, who may have been the letter carrier, and Junia, the only woman in the NT who is called an apostle (16:7; *see* JUNIA, JUNIAS).

G. Conclusion

When Paul's ship moored for the last time, he left behind a rich and influential legacy. Although his letters that focus so sharply on contextual issues have an ad hoc character, they nevertheless testify to the struggle to secure the legitimacy of a Gentile mission and Paul's pastoral theology. Their multiple occasions not only taught Paul new duties, they also elicited fresh theological thinking. In Galatians and Romans, we see Paul being pushed to the limit of his ability to deal with new situations and to hold the church together. And in the letter fragments in 2 Corinthians, we see a dynamic thinker striving mightily to maintain the ties between the Gentile churches and the Jewish-Christian center in Jerusalem. And nowhere more than in 1 Corinthians do we see a form of Spirit excess that almost shattered the communal ties holding this cell of converts together. While Paul found much in the churches repugnant—immorality, religious puffery, arrogance, greedy, and self-absorbed behavior—he preached a gospel in which God through grace and the faithfulness of Christ embraced this lumpish lot among the saved.

These multiple emphases do more than offer simple variations on a common theme; they reveal at times an often ingenious and interactive theologizing process. Through bitter struggles with rival apostles and errant churches, Paul's understanding of life in Christ, the work of the Spirit, and the mission and authenticating signs of an apostle all received new and sometimes brilliant interpretations. The grand and sacred story he saw unfurling would, he believed, soon bring together Jews as God's chosen people and Gentiles as honorary Jews to blend their voices in praise to God.

Bibliography: Jouette M. Bassler. *Divine Impartiality: Paul and a Theological Axiom* (1982); J. Christiaan Beker. *Paul the Apostle: The Triumph of God in Life and Thought* (1980); Hans Dieter Betz. *2 Corinthians 8 and 9.* Hermeneia (1985); Hendrikus Boers. *The Justification of the Gentiles: Paul's Letters to the Galatians and Romans* (1994); Daniel Boyarin. *A Radical Jew: Paul and the Politics of Identity* (1994); Daniel Boyarin. "The IOUDAIOI in John and the Prehistory of 'Judaism.'" *Pauline Conversations in Context.* Janice Capel Anderson, Philip Sellew, and Claudia Setzer, eds. (2002) 216–39; Charles H. Dodd. *Apostolic Preaching and Its Development* (1960); Paula Fredriksen. "Judaism, the Circumcision of Gentiles, and Apocalyptic Hope: Another Look at Galatians 1 & 2." *JTS* 42 (1991) 532–64; Victor Paul Furnish. *1 Thessalonians, 2 Thessalonians.* ANTC (2007); Victor Paul Furnish. *II Corinthians.* AB 32A (1984); Richard B. Hays. *The Faith of Jesus Christ: The Narrative Substructure of Galatians 3:1–4:11.* 2nd ed. (2002); Richard A. Horsley. *1 Corinthians.* ANTC (1998); Leander E. Keck. *Romans.* ANTC (2005); John Knox. *Chapters in a Life of Paul* (1950); Amy-Jill Levine, ed. *A Feminist Companion to Paul* (2004); Gerd Lüdemann. *Paul, Apostle to the Gentiles: Studies in Chronology.* F. S. Jones, trans. (1984); Margaret M. Mitchell. "Paul's Letters to Corinth: The Interpretive Intertwining of Literary and Historical Reconstruction." *Urban Religion in Roman Corinth, Interdisciplinary Approaches.* Daniel N. Schowalter and Steven Friesen, eds. (2005) 307–38; Richard I. Pervo. *Dating Acts: Between the Evangelists and the Apologists* (2006); Calvin J. Roetzel. *Paul: The Man and the Myth* (1999); Calvin J. Roetzel. *2 Corinthians.* ANTC (2007); Anthony J. Saldarini. *Pharisees,*

Scribes and Sadducees (1988); E. P. Sanders. *Paul, the Law and the Jewish People* (1983); Seth Schwartz. *Imperialism and Jewish Society from 200 BCE to 640 CE* (2001); Philip Sellew. "Laodiceans and the Philippians Fragments Hypothesis." *HTR* 87 (1994) 17–28; E. Mary Smallwood. *The Jews under Roman Rule: From Pompey to Diocletian* (1976); Krister Stendahl. *Paul among Jews and Gentiles and Other Essays* (1976); Shemayarhu Talmon. "The Emergence of Jewish Sectarianism in the Early Second Temple Period." *Ancient Israelite Religion: Essays in Honor of Frank Moore Cross.* P. D. Miller, P. D. Hanson, and S. D. McBride, eds. (1987) 587–616; Sam K. Williams. *Galatians.* ANTC (1997).

CALVIN J. ROETZEL

PAULLUS, AEMILIUS. A statesman and military tactician (ca. 230–160 BCE) who was elected *curule aedile* in 192, proconsul in 191 and 167, consul in 182 and 168, and was praetor of Spain from 191 to 189. Aemilius defeated PERSEUS and ended the Third Macedonian War.

PAULUS, SERGIUS surh´jee-uhs-paw´luhs [Σεργίος Παῦλος Sergios Paulos]. In Acts 13:4-12 he is the PROCONSUL of CYPRUS who seeks out Paul and Barnabas in order to learn more about their teaching. This leads to a confrontation between the two Christian missionaries and ELYMAS, a magician who is probably being presented as an advisor to the proconsul. Paul rebukes and miraculously blinds Elymas, leading to Sergius Paulus' profession of faith. While several inscriptions have been put forward as supporting the historicity of this figure, each presents problems, leaving the results of these attempts inconclusive. This episode, at the beginning of Paul's missionary journey, is sometimes seen as part of the author's attempt to attract Roman officials by portraying them in a positive light. It is certainly part of a pattern in Acts that highlights the high social status of some of the converts to the movement, probably for apologetic reasons. Since this episode also marks the point in the narrative from which Saul is called Paul, some have suggested that Paul changed his name in honor of the proconsul, something that is highly speculative and for which there is no support. *See* ACTS OF THE APOSTLES.

RUBÉN R. DUPERTUIS

PAUSANIAS [Παυσανίας Pausanias]. A travel writer active in the mid-2nd cent. CE who was originally from Lydia but spent much of his adult life in Rome. His major work, *Description of Greece*, likely completed by 180 CE, takes readers on a tour of mainland GREECE highlighting cities, public monuments, temples, sacred groves, and various artworks, while often recounting associated myths, legends, and traditions. Written on the basis of observation and conversations with locals during his extensive travels, the work survives as the only complete example of what was a popular genre in its time. Once read as a fairly straightforward account of the region, some recent scholars understand Pausanias' interest in the Archaic and Classical periods and his choices of what sites to include in his guide as part of the literary construction of Greek identity under the Roman Empire. Some inaccuracies notwithstanding, Pausanias' *Description* is an important resource for students of Greek and Roman religion and culture in the period. *See* ASIA.

RUBÉN R. DUPERTUIS

PAVEMENT [רִצְפָּה ritsefah; λιθόστρωτον lithostrōton]. A surface that has been overlaid with stones, often flat flagstones, although sometimes rounded stones were used. Solomon's Temple is depicted as having a paved area (2 Chr 7:3), and pavement is also a feature of the restored Temple in Ezekiel's vision (Ezek 40:17-18; 42:3; *see* TEMPLE, JERUSALEM). Pilate presented Jesus to the crowd on a pavement known in Aramaic as GABBATHA (John 19:13). Both the Hebrew and Greek words can also refer to mosaic floors inlaid with precious stones (Esth 1:6; *see* MOSAIC PAVEMENT). The fact that such floors are often found in palaces (e.g., Jer 43:9) probably explains why God is depicted standing on an area tiled with sapphires in the theophany before the seventy elders on Mount Sinai (Exod 24:9-11). Although some roads were paved with stones, particularly in the Roman period, the Bible does not refer to such roads as "paved."

KEVIN A. WILSON

PAVILION. *See* SHELTER.

PAX ROMANA. The *Pax Romana*, or "Peace of Rome," refers to a period in Roman history beginning with the reign of AUGUSTUS (27 BCE) and ending with the death of Marcus Aurelius (180 CE). This was an era of relative calm and stability within the empire after long years of civil war and threat of invasion (*see* ROMAN EMPIRE). During this period, attention was given to peacetime activities such as improving roads, increasing the food supply, and building aqueducts, temples, public baths, and theaters.

To keep the peace, the Romans tolerated various religious practices, as long as proper honor also was accorded to the emperor and to public rituals of ROMAN RELIGIONS, resulting in ongoing conflict for monotheistic Jews. With improvement of the roads, travel and communication became easier, which had an impact on the nascent church: early Christian missionaries like Paul could travel all over the empire, and letters could circulate with relative ease among the churches (*see* TRAVEL AND COMMUNICATION IN THE NT). Therefore, the rapid spread of the gospel throughout the empire was largely due to the *Pax Romana.*

The term *peace* must be qualified, however, because peace often was maintained by violence. During this period, the Romans continued to expand their empire by military force, and they quickly and violently ended social uprisings. Those who threatened the social order were summarily executed as insurrectionists. Jesus was crucified as a threat to Roman peace during the volatile time surrounding the annual Passover pilgrimage to Jerusalem, when Rome kept an especially strict watch over possible Jewish unrest. Less than forty years later, Jerusalem was destroyed when the Romans put down a rebellion (70 CE), and the JEWISH WARS continued until the Romans quelled the Bar Kochba uprising in 135 CE. *See* PEACE IN THE NT.

MARIANNE BLICKENSTAFF

PE pay [פ ף p]. The seventeenth letter of the Hebrew alphabet. *See* ALPHABET.

PEACE IN THE NT [εἰρηνεύω eirēneuō, εἰρήνη eirēnē, εἰρηνικός eirēnikos]. *Peace* occurs 100 times in the NT, in every book except 1 John, with the majority (sixty-five) in Paul and Luke–Acts. The noun form **eirēnē** occurs ninety-two times. The verb **eirēneuō** occurs four times (Mark 9:50; Rom 12:18; 2 Cor 13:11; 1 Thess 5:13); the adjective **eirēnikos** twice (Heb 12:11; Jas 3:17). Noun or verb compounds occur twice (Matt 5:9; Col 1:20).

The meaning of NT **eirēnē** draws upon the OT Hebrew **shalom** (שָׁלוֹם), through the LXX. **Eirēnē** occurs 199 times in the LXX; only fourteen times does it translate words other than **shalom** and its cognates. **Eirēnē** connotes wholeness and well-being, especially through restoring relationships (between God and humans and among humans, individually and corporately). As a salutation **eirēnē** joins with GRACE (**charis** χάρις) in the epistles (e.g., 1 Cor 1:3; Gal 1:3; Phil 1:2). Toned by its theological use, the **eirēnē** greeting evokes gratitude for God's salvation and the faith community.

Eirēnē had wide use in the Greco-Roman world also. Its meaning differs from NT usage on two counts. In the context of the PAX ROMANA ("peace of Rome"), **eirēne** described the material state of prosperity following victory in war. Peace came at the cost of killing, maiming, oppressing, and subjugating. The *Ara Pacis Augustae* (Altar of Peace to Augustus) on the field of Mars erected in Rome in 9 BCE depicts this ugly, brutal side of peace. Similarly, Vespasian's Peace Temple (*Templum Pacis* Vespasian), built in 75 CE, celebrated Rome's defeat of the Jews. The famous arch of Titus testifies similarly.

Second, **Eirēnē** was the name of a Greek goddess. Gaining popularity with the peace treaty between Sparta and Athens in 375/4 BCE, devotees inaugurated

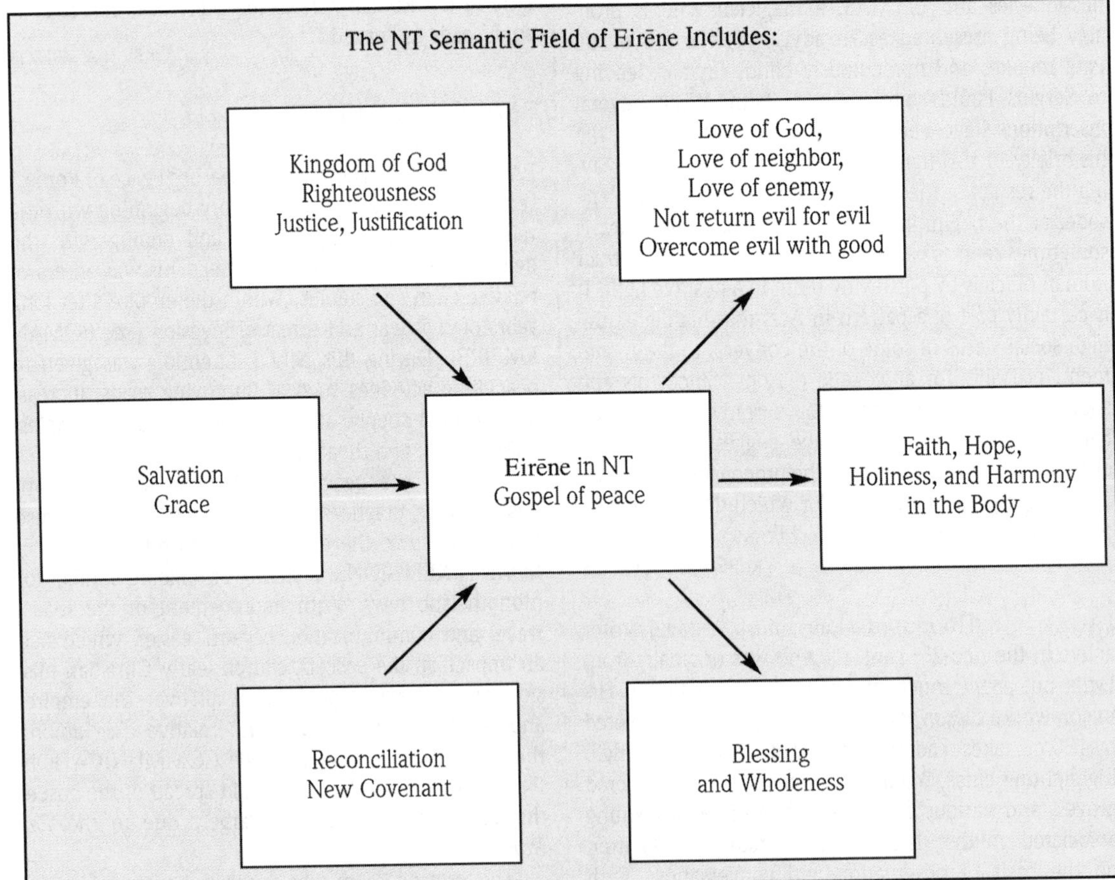

Figure 1: Peace in the New Testament semantic field chart

an annual offering to Eirēnē. In 375 BCE an Eirēnē statue was erected on Athens' Agora to celebrate cessation of war. In contrast to Eirēnē-worship celebrating destruction of enemies, NT eirēnē is God's gift reconciling former enemies through Christ by killing enmity (Eph 2:16).

On the left of eirēnē are God's gifts through Jesus Christ, the fruit of the peace-gospel restoring relationship with God and among fellow humans. On the right are the fruits of peace expressed in salvation's new creation.

In Matthew, Jesus' beatitude "Blessed are the peacemakers" (5:9) occurs in the context of his proclaiming the kingdom of heaven/God (4:17, 23), calling people to righteousness/justice (**dikaiosynē** δικαιοσύνη, occurring also in 5:6, 10), and exhorting them to "love your enemies" (5:44-45). *See* JUSTIFICATION, JUSTIFY. Both peacemaking and love of enemy mark identity as children of God (*see* LOVE IN THE NT). In Mark, Jesus' call to be at peace with one another (9:50*d*) defines the kingdom ethic in contrast to the disciples' rivalry and aspirations to greatness (9:33-34; 10:35-37). The call to humble service, contrasting with the Gentile rulers' domination (10:41-45), complements peacemaking.

Luke's fourteen uses of eirēnē are structurally strategic. Three occur in the birth narratives and set the tone of the book: Zechariah's final word, "to guide our feet into the way of peace" (1:79); Gabriel's annunciation of the Savior-Messiah, "On earth peace" (2:14); and Simeon's praise, "... now you are dismissing your servant in peace" (2:29). Three more uses of eirēnē occur near the beginning inclusio of the travel narrative (10:5-6) and two more in the ending inclusio (19:38-42). The first set, in the mission of the seventy, announces that the kingdom-gospel has come near. The last set praises heaven (19:38), antiphonal to 2:14, and concludes with Jesus' plea and judgment, "If you, even you, had only recognized on this day the things that make for peace! But now they are hidden from your eyes" (19:42). Nonetheless, the risen Jesus greets his disciples, saying, "Peace be with you" (24:36). Of Luke's seven uses of eirēnē in Acts four pertain to ecclesial dimensions (7:26; 9:31; 10:36; 15:33) and three to *Pax Romana* contexts (12:20; 16:36; 24:2). Most significant, Peter summarizes Jesus' ministry with "preaching [proclaiming] peace by Jesus Christ—he is Lord of all" (10:36). Peter quotes Isa 52:7 (LXX), **euangelizomenou eirēnēs** (εὐαγγελιζομένου εἰρήνης), which translates the Hebrew **shalom mevaser** (שָׁלוֹם מְבַשֵּׂר). Luke's use of eirēnē is not an apologetic for Rome's *Pax Romana*: it neither courts nor condemns Rome, but establishes an alternative politics of peace and justice, not the empire's "peace and security" (concurring with Paul, 1 Thess 5:3).

Of the forty-four Pauline uses, ten occur in Romans and eight in Ephesians. Most significant is Paul's virtually unique appellation "God of peace" (Rom 15:33; 16:20; 1 Cor 14:33; 2 Cor 13:11; Phil 4:9; 1 Thess 5:23; 2 Thess 3:16). "God of peace" occurs also in Hebrews' benediction (13:20). "The God of peace will shortly crush Satan under your feet" (Rom 16:20) startlingly blends peace and battle, matched in Eph 6:15, where believers wear "shoes ... to proclaim the gospel of peace" (also quoting Isa 52:7) as part of God's armor to withstand the principalities and powers, the cosmic powers of this present darkness, etc., to overcome the evil one. Believers practice peaceable living in response to God's peace uniting alienated parties through the cross of Jesus Christ (Rom 5:1-10; Eph 2:14-18 [4x]; Col 1:20). In Paul, reconciliation complements peacemaking (Rom 5:1-10; 2 Cor 5:17-20). Peace is the fruit of the Spirit (Gal 5:22), manifesting God's reign (Rom 14:17), the new Spirit-order of "life and peace" (Rom 8:6). Further, the "peace of God ... will guard your hearts and your minds in Christ Jesus" (Phil 4:7).

James specifies righteousness/justice as the harvest of peaceable peacemaking (3:18). In Hebrews Jesus is King of peace, King of righteousness, according to the order of Melchizedek (Heb 7:1-28). Believers pursue peace with holiness to ensure seeing God (12:14). First Peter calls believers to "seek peace and pursue it" (3:11) by walking in Jesus' footsteps (2:21-24).

Bibliography: Ulrich Mauser. *The Gospel of Peace: A Scriptural Message for Today's World* (1992); Willard M. Swartley. *Covenant of Peace: The Missing Peace in New Testament Theology and Ethics* (2006); Klaus Wengst. *Pax Romana and the Peace of Jesus Christ* (1987); Perry B. Yoder and Willard M. Swartley, eds. *The Meaning of Peace: Biblical Studies.* Rev. ed. (2001).

WILLARD M. SWARTLEY

PEACE IN THE OT [שָׁלוֹם **shalom**, שֶׁקֶט **sheqet**]. Peace in the OT reflects the ideal of God's good creation and describes a state of well-being. Peace is the opposite of warfare, violence, and conflict (*see* WAR, IDEAS OF). The texts of the Pentateuch, the Historical Books, the Prophets, apocalyptic literature, and Wisdom literature all represent concepts of peace in ancient Israel and Judah.

The root **shlm** (שׁלם) means "well-being" or "prosperity" (Pss 37:11; 38:3 [Heb. 38:4]; Prov 3:2)—a state of being (*see* SHALOM). However, the term is not entirely divorced from the idea of cessation of conflict. Peace negotiations to prevent or end war are **divre shalom** (דִּבְרֵי שָׁלוֹם, "words/terms of peace"; Deut 2:26; 20:10; compare Ps 35:20). In times of war, there are envoys of peace (Isa 33:7), but sometimes one does not seek peace with enemies (Deut 23:6; compare Lev 26:6).

However, the term *rest* (**sheqet**) is more closely associated with cessation of conflict, disarmament, and negotiations, as well as expressing freedom from international conflict. The late (4th–3rd cent. BCE?) historical narratives of 1 and 2 Chronicles suggest that David was denied the privilege of building the Temple because he was a man of war (1 Chr 22:8). In contrast, these texts praise Solomon as a man of peace (1 Chr 22:9). The verbal form of REST (**shaqat** שָׁקַט) implies that one can be a person who "calms" or "pacifies" conflict (Prov 15:18). Jeremiah uses the image of God putting away God's sword "at rest" (NRSV, "quiet"; Jer 47:6; compare Ezek 16:42). However, a full appreciation of biblical attitudes toward peace must move beyond studies of particular terms.

Given the widely held view that the first creation story features strong allusions to the Near Eastern creation-related motifs of the "storm god" versus the "sea god" (Baal and Yam; Marduk and Tiamat, etc.), it is seldom noted that the creation stories in Genesis actually are peaceful episodes. The Genesis creation narratives (Gen 1–2) are not about the violent conflict of the gods, but relate how the sinful violence of humanity disturbs God's originally created peacefulness. Ruptures between family members (e.g., Cain and Abel in Gen 4) and nations (Gen 14) are portrayed as violations of God's intended peace. Other stories illustrate restored peace. Isaac makes peace with Abimelech over disputed land and water (Gen 26:26-33). Jacob prays that he can return to his father's house in peace after his betrayal of Esau (Gen 28:18-21). However, Jacob "holds his peace" until the opportune time to exact vengeance against Shechem for violating his daughter (Gen 34:5).

Some of the sources offer subtle criticisms of violent foreign policies, including the portrayal of Jacob and Esau's conflict as having implications for the frequent Judean conflicts with Edom (Gen 36:8, "Esau is Edom") and the portrayal of Judean-Moabite relations in the book of Ruth.

Studies of warfare in the OT have tended to focus on the period of the monarchy (e.g., 950–587 BCE), under the assumption that historical texts (such as Samuel and Kings) reflect reliable historical assessments of the political events of that time period. These texts focus on the miraculous intervention by God as opposed to extolling the military strategy and prowess of the Israelites themselves (e.g., the miracles at the Red Sea contrasted with fighting, Exod 14:13-14; compare the miracle at Jericho, Josh 6). This is made most explicit in Judg 7, where God appears concerned that the Israelites should not believe that their own military power delivered them from danger. However, some recent scholarship posits that these "historical" narratives were likely the product of the postexilic period (e.g., post-586 BCE). The reasoning is straightforward: these scholars believe that an occupied or diaspora Jewish community, with a need to write down its history, would portray military success as the result of God's intervention, not the military prowess of the Israelites (compare 2 Chr 20). Such views are echoed in the Hellenistic period, in which Baruch teaches: "If you had walked in the way of God, you would be living in peace forever" (Bar 3:13).

Somewhat ironically, decidedly violent narratives like 1 Maccabees or Judith contain some of the most explicit references to peace negotiations. First Maccabees refers to "making peace" and "words of peace" in negotiations (**eirēnē** εἰρήνη; 1 Macc 6:49, 58, 60, 61; 7:13, 15; 11:51; 13:37; compare **eirēnikos** εἰρηνικός; Jdt 3:1; 7:24). There are also references to treaties (2 Macc 13:25).

The well-known phrase "beating swords into plowshares" (Isa 2:4//Mic 4:4) has been interpreted as a prophetic ethic of peace. However, T. Hobbs points out the opposite view (e.g., plowshares into swords, Joel 3:10) that tends to overrule the notion that the prophets spoke only of peacemaking. An excellent example of the debate is the "procession of nations" theme, of which Isa 2 and Mic 4 are examples. In some of the examples of nations streaming to Zion, the context appears to be a forced procession of conquered enemies (they will "lick the dust of your feet"; Isa 49:23). However, other texts suggest voluntary processions of former enemies, who demonstrate a strong desire to be at peace with Israel (Zech 8:20-23). In addition are the book of Jonah's universalist notions of transforming enemies (compare Isa 19).

The prophets frequently equate peace with God's blessing on the righteous (e.g., Isa 9:7; 26:3, 12; 32:17; 39:8; 55:12; 57:2; Ezek 37:26), while the unrighteous shall have no peace (e.g., Isa 48:22; 57:21; Jer 6:14; 8:11, 15; Ezek 13:10, 16). Zechariah envisions a day when there will be a "sowing of peace," in which Israel will once again be a blessing among the nations (Zech 8:12-13), and describes the coming of a humble king who will bring peace to the nations (Zech 9:9-10).

The issue of whether apocalyptic literature is in any way "peaceful" continues to be debated. K. Stendahl argued that Paul (Rom 12:20) suggests that one can treat the enemy graciously only because God will eventually punish them, and thus Paul's argument is an example of apocalyptic vengeance. The argument illustrates the perception that apocalyptic literature is an inherently violent and vengeful literature because of its imagery of war and bloodshed (e.g., Ezek 4–5; Rev 19:11-15).

John Collins has argued that the book of Daniel represents a pacifist manifesto, suggesting that the critique of "a little help" in Dan 11:34 and the rejection of the "violent ones" (NRSV, "lawless") in Dan 11:14 both describe a negative assessment of the Maccabean revolution against Greek occupation of Palestine. Jacob Licht similarly suggests that the story of Taxo in the *Testament of Moses* represents an intentionally nonmilitary form of resistance, similar to Walter Harrelson's argument about an ethic of "patient love" in the *Testament of Joseph.*

The wisdom tradition presents yet another form of biblical peacefulness (*see* WISDOM IN THE OT). The ideal "wise one" is calm and self-restrained (Prov 17:27). The wise one seeks to end conflict before it begins (Prov 17:9, 14) and will not return evil for evil, but seeks the welfare even of his enemies (Prov 17:13; compare Matt 5:43-44). "When the ways of the people please the LORD, he causes even their enemies to be at peace with them" (Prov 16:7). Wisdom contrasts with power and fortifications (Prov 16:32; 21:22). Ecclesiastes suggests that wisdom is better than might and the weapons of war (Eccl 9:16, 18; compare Prov 24:5-6). This form of wisdom is reflected in the antiwar ethos of the NT Letter of James (Jas 1:19-20; 3:17-18). *See* PEACE IN THE NT.

Bibliography: J. Collins. *Daniel: A Commentary on the Book of Daniel.* Hermeneia (1994); W. Harrelson. "Patient Love in the Testament of Joseph." *PRSt* 4 (1977) 4–13; T. Hobbs. *A Time for War: A Study of Warfare in the Old Testament* (1989); J. Licht. "Taxo, or the Apocalyptic Doctrine of Vengeance." *JJS* 12 (1961) 95–103; M. Lind. *Yahweh Is a Warrior* (1980); M. Polnar and N. Goodman. *The Challenge of Shalom: The Jewish Tradition of Peace and Justice* (1994); S. Schwarzschild. "Shalom." *Confrontation* (1981) 166–76; D. Smith-Christopher. *Jonah, Jesus and Other Good Coyotes: Speaking Peace to Power in the Bible* (2007); K. Stendahl. "Hate, Non-Retaliation, and Love: 1QS x, 17-20 and Rom. 12:19-21." *HTR* 55 (1962) 343–55; P. Yoder. *Shalom: The Bible's Word for Salvation, Justice, and Peace* (1997); G. Zampaglione. *The Idea of Peace in Antiquity* (1973); G. Zerbe. "'Pacifism' and 'Passive Resistance' in Apocalyptic Writings: A Critical Evaluation." *The Pseudepigrapha and Early Biblical Intepretation.* J. H. Charlesworth and C. A. Evans, eds. (1993) 65–95.

DANIEL L. SMITH-CHRISTOPHER

PEACEMAKER [εἰρηνοποιός eirēnopoios, εἰρηνοποιέω eirēnopoieō]. The noun (eirēnopoios) and verb (eirēnopoieō) are rare in the Bible. In Prov 10:10 (LXX) the person who reprehends a fellow openly is qualified as "making peace." In Matt 5:9, Jesus praises the peacemakers and promises them they will become "children of God." This beatitude has rabbinic parallels (*m. Abot* 1:12, 18; *m. Peah* 1:1). According to the hymn used in Col 1:20, God, or the "fullness," will "make peace" through Christ in the order of creation; peace will be worked by virtue of Christ's atoning blood on the cross. *See* BEATITUDES; PEACE IN THE NT; PEACE IN THE OT; SHALOM.

JOHANNES BEUTLER, SJ

PEACOCK. *See* BIRDS OF THE BIBLE.

PEARL [פְּנִינִים peninim; μαργαρίτης margaritēs]. In the NRSV, the only OT occurrence of *pearl* is in Job 28:18 where wisdom is said to be of more value than highly prized pearls. There are nine NT occurrences of *pearl* in the NRSV. Two are metaphors: throwing pearls before swine (Matt 7:6) and a merchant who finds one of great value (Matt 13:45, 46). Other occurrences include an ostentatious element in women's apparel (1 Tim 2:9); an emblem of the extravagance of evil Babylon (Rev 17:4; 18:12, 16); and New Jerusalem's twelve gates, each formed by a single pearl (Rev 21:21 [2x]). Today's usage of the term *pearl* refers to a gem produced as a secretion by oysters that hardens.

ELIZABETH E. PLATT

PEASANT [פְּרָזוֹן perazon]. The NRSV renders the obscure Hebrew word perazon, which only occurs in the Song of Deborah, as "peasantry" (Judg 5:7, 11). In classic anthropological usage, *peasant* is defined in terms of the peasant-proletarian class struggle. Peasants are village subsistence farmers who must pay taxes and are often exploited politically and economically by a central state government. This definition is based on the etic, or "outside observer" perspective of a post-colonial 20th-cent. anthropology. A more emic, or "native," definition would understand perazon in the Song of Deborah from the regional perspective of the Iron Age I central hill country as a collective term for the rural population, which usually lived in unwalled villages in contrast to the fortified Canaanite "towns" (ʿarim עָרִים) of the lowlands. *See* CITY; DEBORAH, SONG OF; ISRAEL, SOCIOLOGY OF; VILLAGE.

Bibliography: John Kautsky. *The Politics of Aristocratic Empires* (1982); Michael Kearney. *Reconceptualizing the Peasantry: Anthropology in Global Perspective* (1996); Gerhard Lenski. *Power and Privilege: A Theory of Social Stratification* (1966).

RALPH K. HAWKINS

PEASANT, PROTESTS OF THE ELOQUENT. This Middle Kingdom Egyptian text tells of a Job-like farmer who, robbed of his goods, loudly and repeatedly proclaims his misfortune is undeserved. Hearing of his poetic eloquence and eager to be entertained by it, Pharaoh sets up a situation similar to the debates in Job: the peasant is summoned to court where he astonishes everyone with his verbal wit, theological acumen, and disturbing social analyses. *See* JOB, BOOK OF; LAMENT; THEODICY.

CAROLE R. FONTAINE

PEDAHEL ped'uh-hel [פְּדַהְאֵל pedhahʾel]. Means "God has redeemed," "God has ransomed," or "God has delivered." Pedahel was the son of AMMIHUD and a chieftain from the tribe of Naphtali (Num 34:28). He is listed among those selected to allot portions of land in Canaan to the Israelite tribes according to the command given by Moses that land was to be apportioned under the direction of Joshua and Eleazar the priest through tribal chieftains (Num 34:16-28). *See* NAPHTALI, NAPHTALITES.

DEREK E. WITTMAN

PEDAHZUR pi-dah´zuhr [פְּדָהצוּר pedahtsur]. Means "the rock has ransomed." Known only as the father of Gamaliel, who was a leader of the people of Manasseh and aide to Moses during the Israelites' time in the wilderness (Num 1:10; 2:20; 7:54, 59; 10:23). *See* MANASSEH, MANASSITES.

PEDAIAH pi-day´yuh [פְּדָיָה pedayah, פְּדָיָהוּ pedayahu; Φαδαιά Phadaia, Φαδαίας Phadaias]. Means "Yahweh has ransomed." 1. Maternal grandfather of King Jehoiakim of Judah (2 Kgs 23:36). Pedaiah came from RUMAH, a Galilean town, showing the extent of Josiah's northern influence.

2. Third son of King Jehoiakin/Jeconiah (1 Chr 3:17-18), Pedaiah had two sons, Zerubbabel and Shimei (1 Chr 3:19). However, Zerubbabel is otherwise presented as the son of Shealtiel, Pedaiah's brother (Ezra 3:2, 8; 5:2; Neh 12:1; Hag 1:1, 12, 14; 2:2, 23; Luke 3:27).

3. Father of Joel from the half-tribe of Manasseh in the west of Jordan when David took a census (1 Chr 27:20).

4. Son of Parosh who helped to rebuild the Jerusalem wall during the time of Nehemiah (Neh 3:25).

5. One of those who stood on the left hand of Ezra when he read "the book of the law of Moses" before the people (Neh 8:4; 1 Esd 9:44).

6. Father of Joed and the son of Kolaiah, Benjaminites dwelling in Jerusalem under Nehemiah (Neh 11:7).

7. A Levite and one of three treasurers of the temple storehouses appointed by Nehemiah (Neh 13:13).

SAMUEL CHEON

PEDDLER [καπηλεύω kapēleuō]. One who sells something for profit by means of deceiving and cheating, sometimes translated as one who corrupts. The LXX uses a related word kapēlos (κάπηλος) to describe wine merchants who cheat customers with watered-down wine (Isa 1:22) and a tradesman who cannot help sinning (Sir 26:29). In the NT, Paul implies that there are some in Corinth, "peddlers," who are using God's word for personal profit. Paul writes to the Corinthians assuring them that he and his followers are not like those people; instead, Paul is sincere, speaking as one truly sent from God (2 Cor 2:17). *See* GOSPEL, MESSAGE.

KATHY R. MAXWELL

PEDESTAL [כֵּן ken]. Translated "pedestal" in 1 Kgs 7:31, ken describes the base of each of the stands for the ten bronze lavers in the court of the Solomonic Temple. Ken is also translated "base" or "stand" in reference to similar lavers of the tabernacle (Exod 30:18, 28; 31:9; 35:16; 38:8; 39:39; 40:11; Lev 8:11). *See* ARCHITECTURE, OT; LAVER; PILLAR.

JOEL F. DRINKARD JR.

PEDIMENT [מַרְצֶפֶת martsefeth]. A stone pavement upon which rested the "molten sea" in the courtyard of the Temple after King AHAZ of Judah had removed the bronze oxen upon which it had previously rested (2 Kgs 16:17), perhaps for the purpose of sending them as tribute to King TIGLATH-PILESER III of Assyria. *See* SEA, MOLTEN.

DEREK E. WITTMAN

PEG, TENT PEG [יָתֵד yathedh; πάσσαλος passalos]. A piece of wood or metal used for holding down the edge of a TENT, as in the TABERNACLE (Exod 35:18; 38:31) and in the story of JAEL and SISERA (Judg 4:21-22; 5:26). Yathedh can also be a peg for hanging or holding objects, such as the utensils of the tabernacle (Exod 27:19). Reflecting strength and security, metaphorically yathedh can indicate those upon whom community authority rests (Isa 22:23-25; Zech 10:4). Perhaps this image of the peg as symbolic of masculine power contributed to its use in Sirach, where the reader is warned that a daughter with too much freedom will "sit in front of every tent peg," a euphemism for promiscuity (26:12).

JESSICA TINKLENBERG DEVEGA

PEKAH pee´kuh [פֶּקַח peqakh]. Pekah was the son of Remaliah and the eighteenth king of Israel. Pekah's name appears on a jar handle discovered at Hazor. Pekah succeeded PEKAHIAH (738–737 BCE), the son of Menahem, after Pekahiah had reigned two years in Samaria. When Pekahiah assumed the throne of the Northern Kingdom, he continued his father's policy of cooperation with Assyria. However, the burden of the tribute paid to Assyria convinced many Israelites that the time was ready for a change.

With the help of fifty men from Gilead, Pekah, who was the third man in Pekahiah's war chariot, assassinated Pekahiah and assumed the throne of Israel. Since the two names are almost identical, it is possible that Pekah usurped the throne and assumed the name of his predecessor. The book of Isaiah may give an indication that Pekah was considered a usurper and that his reign was considered illegitimate. Isaiah generally does not use Pekah's name but simply calls him "the son of Remaliah" (Isa 7:4, 5, 9; 8:6). According to 2 Kgs 15:27, Pekah became king over Israel in the fifty-second year of Uzziah, king of Judah, and reigned in Samaria twenty years. However, the duration of Pekah's reign does not agree with the chronology found in Assyrian records. Since Assyrian records indicate that Menahem paid tribute to Assyria in 738 BCE and that Tiglath-pileser placed Hoshea on the throne in 732 BCE, it is possible that Pekah ruled over Israel for no more than five years, from 737–732 BCE. Thus, the twenty years mentioned in the biblical record may include a time when Pekah ruled as a rival king in Gilead and the years he reigned in Samaria. Another possible explanation is that Pekah considered the reigns of Menahem and Pekahiah illegitimate, since both kings had ruled as Assyrian vassals, and included the years of their reign as his own.

When Pekah became king of Israel, he might have had the support of an anti-Assyrian faction based in Gilead that supported independence from Assyria, as well as the support of those who advocated cooperation with the Arameans against Assyrian hegemony. The strategy of the anti-Assyrian coalition was to form a united front against Assyria and neutralize Assyrian control of the region. The coalition, led by Rezin, king of Damascus, turned its efforts to the south hoping to recruit the Judean king in its effort against Assyria and increase the strength, proximity, and size of its coalition. When Ahaz, king of Judah (735–715 BCE), refused to join the coalition, Pekah and Rezin marched against Jerusalem to besiege the city, to depose Ahaz, and to place on the throne of Judah a man identified as "the son of Tabeel" (Isa 7:6), someone who would favor an alliance against Assyria. This war is often referred to as the Syro-Ephraimite War.

Afraid of an invasion by the coalition and desiring to remain unconnected to the coalition, Ahaz sent messengers to Tiglath-pileser III asking for military help (2 Kgs 16:7), perhaps against the advice of Isaiah. The prophet assured Ahaz that if he trusted God, he would not be defeated by Pekah and Rezin, and would not be replaced by the son of Tabeel (Isa 7:4-6). Ahaz submitted to Tiglath-pileser, and paid a heavy tribute to Assyria by taking gold and silver from the Temple and from the royal treasury (1 Kgs 16:7-8). In response to Ahaz's invitation, Tiglath-pileser went to Palestine to help Judah. He conquered Philistia in 734 BCE, invaded Aram, killing Rezin and deporting an Aramean population to Kir (2 Kgs 16:8-9). Tiglath-pileser also conquered several cities in Galilee, Naphtali, and the land of Gilead in Transjordan and deported some of the people of the Northern Kingdom to several cities in the Assyrian Empire (2 Kgs 15:29; Isa 9:1-2 [Heb. 8:23–9:1]). As a result of the invasion, the conquered land was reorganized into three Assyrian provinces, Damascus was incorporated into the Assyrian Empire, and Judah became a vassal of Assyria.

Tiglath-pileser did not destroy Samaria, and Pekah was left with a diminished territory. With the support of Tiglath-pileser, Hoshea, the son of Elah, conspired against Pekah, killed him, and became king of Israel (2 Kgs 15:30). Hoshea ruled the Northern Kingdom, now limited mostly to Ephraim and Manasseh, as an Assyrian vassal. *See* ISRAEL, HISTORY OF; KING, KINGSHIP.

Bibliography: H. J. Cook. "Pekah." *VT* 14 (1964) 121–35.

CLAUDE MARIOTTINI

PEKAHIAH pek'uh-hi'uh [פְּקַחְיָה peqakhyah]. Son of MENAHEM and seventeenth king of the northern kingdom of Israel (2 Kgs 15:23-26), Pekahiah reigned in Samaria two years (737–736 BCE). When Pekahiah assumed the throne after the death of Menahem, Israel was paying heavy tribute to Assyria, which was resented by the population and promoted anti-Assyrian sentiments among the people. Nevertheless, Pekahiah decided to continue the pro-Assyrian policies of his father.

PEKAH, the son of Remaliah and one of the officers in Pekahiah's army, represented popular anti-Assyrian sentiments. With the help of fifty men from Gilead, Pekah conspired against Pekahiah and killed him in the citadel of the king's palace, along with Argob and Arieh, probably two of the king's advisors (2 Kgs 15:25). The political crisis created by the assassination of Pekahiah initiated a series of events that culminated with the fall of the Northern Kingdom in 722 BCE.

That there were Gileadite coconspirators may indicate that Pekah himself was from Gilead, east of the Jordan River, and that he had the support of REZIN, king of Damascus (2 Kgs 15:37). Pekah and Rezin later formed a coalition to confront Assyria and fight for independence (2 Kgs 16:9). *See* ISRAEL, HISTORY OF; KING, KINGSHIP.

CLAUDE MARIOTTINI

PEKOD pee'kod [פְּקוֹד peqodh]. The resident location of an Aramean tribe on the eastern bank of the lower Tigris River. The Puqudu were militarily and economically prosperous, though they ultimately were under the control of the Assyrians—as the records of Tiglath-pileser III, Sargon II, and Sennacherib (746–681 BCE) indicate—and subsequently the Babylonians. Pekod appears twice in the OT. In Jer 50:21, an exilic text, the poet calls for destruction of Pekod as part of the desired revenge against Babylon. Here Pekod is a wordplay on the Hebrew paqadh (פָּקַד), which can mean "punishment"; the defeat of Pekod signals the punishment of the Babylonians. In Ezek 23:23, a text that can be dated just prior to the fall of Jerusalem, the Pekod are listed as one of the illicit lovers of Oholibah (Jerusalem) whom Yahweh will use to punish the people for their religious and moral infidelity. *See* ARAM, ARAMEANS; OHOLAH AND OHOLIBAH.

MARK RONCACE

PELAIAH pi-lay'yuh [פְּלָיָה pelayah, פְּלָאיָה pela'yah; Φαλίας Phalias]. 1. The third of ELIOENAI's seven sons among David's descendants (1 Chr 3:24).

2. One of the Levites who interpreted the Mosaic law that Ezra read to the people (Neh 8:7; 1 Esd 9:48). He also signed Ezra's covenant (Neh 10:10 [Heb. 10:11]). *See* LEVI, LEVITES; NEHEMIAH.

DEREK E. WITTMAN

PELALIAH pel'uh-li'uh [פְּלַלְיָה pelalyah]. Grandfather of ADAIAH, a priest who lived in Jerusalem after the exile (Neh 11:12). The parallel genealogy of Adaiah in 1 Chr 9:12 omits several generations, including Pelaliah.

PELATIAH pel´uh-*tī*´uh [פְּלַטְיָה pelatyah, פְּלַטְיָהוּ pelatyahu]. Means "Yahweh has saved." The name is also known from the ELEPHANTINE PAPYRI. 1. The first son of HANANIAH in a list of David's descendants (1 Chr 3:21). Son or grandson of Zerubbabel.

2. One of three sons of Ishi and one of the leaders of a group of 500 Simeonites who led a raid on an Amalekite settlement on Mount Seir during the reign of King Hezekiah of Judah (1 Chr 4:42).

3. One of those whose names appear on the covenant the postexilic community made under Nehemiah (Neh 10:22).

4. An "official of the people" and son of BENAIAH, mentioned by Ezekiel in an oracle against the leaders of Jerusalem, at the end of which Pelatiah falls dead (Ezek 11:1, 13).

RUSSELL E. FULLER

PELEG pee´lig [פֶּלֶג pelegh; Φάλεκ Phalek]. Son of EBER, brother of JOKTAN, and at the age of thirty the father of REU, in the genealogy from Noah to Abraham (Gen 10:25; 11:16-19; Luke 3:35). According to the genealogy Peleg lived 239 years. The meaning of his name and an expression about him in Gen 10:25 remain disputed. According to the passage, Peleg lived during the time when "the earth was divided" (see also 1 Chr 1:19). That expression may refer to a West Semitic meaning for Peleg as "divide" (from the Hebrew root palagh (פָּלַג), meaning "split," "divide") or an Akkadian word for canals that divide civilization from nomadic life.

J. GORDON HARRIS

PELET pee´lit [פֶּלֶט pelet]. 1. One of the sons of Jahdai in the lineage of Caleb (1 Chr 2:47). *See* CALEB, CALEBITES.

2. A son of Azmaveth and brother of Jeziel. Pelet and Jeziel were Benjaminite warriors, ambidextrous archers and slingers who joined David's growing army at Ziklag (1 Chr 12:3). *See* BENJAMIN, BENJAMINITES.

A. HEATH JONES III

PELETH pee´lith [פֶּלֶת peleth]. Means "swiftness." 1. A member of the tribe of Reuben and the father of ON, who participated in Korah's rebellion against Moses at Kadesh during the exodus wanderings (Num 16:1). Because On is not mentioned again in the narrative the name seems out of place here, and "Peleth" could be a textual corruption of "Pallu," attested elsewhere as a son of Reuben (Gen 46:9; Num 26:5, 8). *See* KADESH, KADESH-BARNEA; KORAH, KORAHITES; PALLU, PALLUITES; REUBEN, REUBENITES.

2. A son of JONATHAN, descendant of Jerahmeel, assigned to the tribe of Judah (1 Chr 2:33). The Jerahmeelites lived in the Negeb, in the south of Judah, and might have been ethnic Edomites (1 Sam 27:10; 30:29). *See* CHERETHITES AND PELETHITES; JERAHMEEL, JERAHMEELITES; JUDAH, JUDAHITES; NEGEB, NEGEV.

MARSHALL D. JOHNSON

PELETHITES. *See* CHERETHITES AND PELETHITES.

PELLA pel´uh. The city of Pella of the DECAPOLIS in the Jordan Valley received its name in honor of Pella in Macedonia, birthplace of Alexander the Great. In Arabic it is called Tabaqat al-Fahl.

The city developed in a valley watered by a spring (Wadi Jirm al-Moz) that connected the eastern Transjordanian high plateau to the Palestinian coast, passing through the Beth-shan and Jezreel plains. Excavations started on the main ruins of the site in the year 1967 and extended to the top and on the slopes of the natural hill of Tell al-Husn, to the cemetery on Jabal Abu al-Khas, and on the top of Jabal Sartaba. The first evidence of human settlement dating to the Neolithic period was found in the Wadi al-Hammeh, 2 km to the northwest of the tell.

The urban center reached a period of prosperity and international renown during the Middle Bronze period, as witnessed by the Egyptian texts and the rich deposits found in the tombs. The ancient name Pahil is mentioned in Egyptian sources, starting from the Execration Texts of the 19th–18th cent. BCE. In the Roman period it was part of the Decapolis region created by Pompey the Great in 64/63 BCE. On the coins of the Roman epoch struck in the city, Pella is called in Greek "(The city) of the Philippeion and of the (inhabitants of) Pella near the Ninphaeum."

In the *Ecclesiastical History*, Eusebius relates that the valley of Pella gave refuge to the community of Jerusalem during the First Jewish Revolt (*Hist. eccl.* 3.5). In the 2nd cent. CE, a member of the Christian community of Pella was Ariston, author of the *Dispute between Jason and Papiscus about Christus*.

In the 6th cent. Zacharia, bishop of Pella, was chosen by Emperor Justinian to evaluate the damages made to the churches and monasteries of the Palaestina Secunda during the Samaritan Revolt in 529 CE.

During the 5th–6th cent. the three excavated ecclesiastical complexes—called respectively the East and West Churches and the Central Church—behind the Roman baths and theater were built. In the presbyterium of this Central Church built in the first half of the 5th cent. the original mosaic floor was changed into an upper marble opus sectile floor in the 7th cent. The three basilicas with their Western colonnaded atrium were destroyed by the 747 CE earthquake.

In the Arabic sources Pella is known for the battle of Fihl (635 CE) in which the army of the Byzantine Empire was defeated by the Muslim conquerors coming from the Arabian Peninsula. After the following and final victory on the banks of the Yarmuk River (636 CE), Pella became the capital of Jund al-Urdunn, in the new administrative division of the Palestinian territory in the Islamic Empire.

Studium Biblicum Franciscanum Archive, Jerusalem

Figure 1: The central ecclesiastical complex on the tell of Pella (Tabaqat al-Fahl).

After the 747 CE earthquake, a commercial center was built in the Abassid period on the north side of the main tell in the Wadi Khandak. During the Mamluk period (13th–15th cent.) a mosque was built on the main ruins among the poor houses of the small village of Tabaqat al-Fahl.

MICHELE PICCIRILLO

PELONITE pel´uh-n*i*t [פְּלוֹנִי **peloni**, פְּלֹנִי **peloni**]. A gentilic used of HELEZ and AHIJAH (1 Chr 11:27, 36; 27:10), two of David's "Thirty" (*see* DAVID'S CHAMPIONS). The parallel list calls Helez "the PALTITE" (2 Sam 23:26), suggesting "Pelonite" may have been a corruption of the original "Paltite." Ahijah the Pelonite appears in the parallel list as "ELIAM, son of Ahithophel the Gilonite" (2 Sam 23:34). Haplographies and scribal corrections have been proposed as an explanation for the change from the latter to the former. These textual discrepancies, along with the fact that no people known as Pelonites or place named Pelon have been identified, suggest that the 2 Samuel forms are correct.

RALPH K. HAWKINS

PELUSIUM pi-l*oo*´see-uhm [סִין **sin**]. Pelusium, modern Tell el-Farama, was a major port city at the northeastern edge of the Nile delta known for its military, industrial, and religious complexes. Its predominant cults were Amun (its patron deity), Isis and Harpokrates, and later, under Hadrian, Zeus Kasios. The city gave its name to the easternmost distributary of the Nile, the Pelusiac. It was the site of several important battles, including the Persian king Cambyses' defeat of Psamtik III in 525 BCE and Cleopatra VII's attack on her brother/husband Ptolemy XIII in 28 BCE.

In Ezek 30, the litany of Egyptian sites marked for destruction includes Pelusium (vv. 15-16). The Hebrew text uses the name **sin**, which the Vulgate and most modern translators identify with Pelusium. Two competing etymologies explain the correspondence of Hebrew **sin** with Greek **Pēlousion** (Πηλούσιον). The Greek historian and geographer Strabo derived **Pēlousion** from **pēlos** (πηλός), "clay, mud"; Hebrew **sin** could be a reflex of Egyptian **sin**, "clay." But if Pelusium derives instead from Egyptian **pr-ir-imn**, "house/temple of Amun," then Hebrew **sin** might reflect Egyptian **swn**, "tower, fortress," as Pelusium is called "the stronghold of Egypt" (Ezek 30:15). *See* EGYPT; FORTRESS.

CAROLYN HIGGINBOTHAM

PEN [חֶרֶט **kheret**, עֵט **ʿet**; κάλαμος **kalamos**]. The Hebrew **ʿet** refers to a writing instrument, such as a stylus, pen, or engraver. **ʿEt sofer** (עֵט סֹפֵר, Ps 45:1 [Heb. 45:2]; Jer 8:8) was a pen of scribes, probably a stylus or reed-pen used with ink to inscribe parchment, papyrus, wood, or ostraca. A reed-pen was created from a rush that was honed or cut obliquely and its fibers split to resemble a brush. **ʿEt-barzel** (עֵט־בַּרְזֶל, Job 19:24; compare Jer 17:1) was an iron stylus or chisel-like utensil used to engrave hard writing surfaces, a tablet, stone, or hardwood. The instrument of 3 John 1:13 (**kalamos**) was a reed-pen. **Kheret** was a graving-tool or stylus for inscribing stone or metal. Aaron employed this tool when fashioning the calf (Exod 32:4), as did Isaiah when he inscribed a tablet (Isa 8:1). *See* WRITING AND WRITING MATERIALS.

DONALD W. PARRY

PENDANT. *See* JEWELRY.

PENIEL. *See* PENUEL.

PENINNAH pi-nin´uh [פְּנִנָּה **peninnah**]. According to 1 Sam 1:2, 4, Peninnah was one of two wives of ELKANAH the Ephraimite. She had children, and consequently taunted HANNAH, the favored wife who did not have children. In that regard she was similar to HAGAR, who bore Ishmael and then tormented Sarah.

PENITENCE. *See* REPENTANCE IN THE NT; REPENTANCE IN THE OT.

PENKNIFE [תַּעַר taʿar]. A blade used for cutting a scroll (Jer 36:23). *See* WRITING AND WRITING MATERIALS.

PENNY. *See* MONEY, COINS.

PENTATEUCH pen´tuh-ty*oo*k. The Pentateuch, the first five books of Israel's Scriptures (Genesis, Exodus, Leviticus, Numbers, and Deuteronomy), constitutes the foundation of Israel's canonical collection of sacred texts. It is also known as the TORAH, the law. The name *Pentateuch,* derived from the Greek **pentateuchos** (πεντάτευχος), denotes a five-book collection. A traditional Jewish name is *Chumash,* which is a form of the Hebrew word for the number five (**khamesh** חָמֵשׁ). The construal of these five books as a unit is associated with their ascription to Moses.

This material has captured the imagination—and challenged the understanding—of both Jews and Christians down the ages. Readers are captivated by the stories of humanity created in the image of God in a world in which God delights (Gen 1); Eve and Adam are persuaded by the serpent to eat the forbidden fruit (Gen 3); Abraham is called to sacrifice his beloved Isaac (Gen 22); Moses encounters God as "I AM" at the burning bush (Exod 3); Moses receives the stone tablets with the TEN COMMANDMENTS (Exod 20; Deut 5); and many others. There is depth and enduring resonance here.

Yet for all their importance, the question of how to read these texts well is not straightforward. Long histories of debates as to how best to understand them, debates that go back to antiquity, have become particularly complicated in modernity. Indeed, many articles and books on the Pentateuch give the impression of being essentially accounts of a sophisticated scholarly puzzle-solving enterprise. The focus in this article will be on selected aspects of what is involved in reading the Pentateuch well, with a view to understanding and being able to appropriate its enduring religious significance.

A. Overview of Modern Pentateuchal Criticism

1. Development of scholarly consensus

The history of modern pentateuchal criticism has often been told (e.g., Thompson, Nicholson) and so will only be noted here in summary outline.

The traditional ascription of the Pentateuch to MOSES is related to Moses' being the prime human character within the text, the chosen leader of Israel, the privileged recipient of the law and God's self-disclosure at Sinai/Horeb, and the speaking voice in Deuteronomy. Within the texts the prime depiction of Moses as writer comes with reference to Deuteronomy's content (Deut 31:24), though there are other occasional references to Moses' writing (Exod 17:14; 24:4). The ascription of the whole Pentateuch to Moses is not part of the text's own self-presentation but early became part of its reception. Prior to modernity there was little interest in the specifics of composition as such, other than with reference to particular puzzles such as whether Moses could have written of his own death (Deut 34) or whether particular passages appeared to presuppose a post-Moses context (e.g., Gen 13:7*b*). The prime emphasis in the traditional ascription of the whole to Moses was on the religiously authoritative nature of the material.

From the 17th cent. onward scholarly interpretation became increasingly controlled by the assumption that to understand texts one had to know who the author was, as well as the author's date, context, audience, and purpose in writing. Benedict de Spinoza was the first to articulate this programmatically. In his case, the point of such an agenda was not to enhance but to diminish the religious authority of the biblical text (by emphasizing its obscurity and relegating it to the past), though scholars generally have argued that such historical knowledge could not but enhance one's understanding and appreciation. The post-Spinoza approach is sometimes conveniently designated by the epithet "historical-critical" (*see* HISTORICAL CRITICISM).

On the assumption that Moses was the author, the initial form of pentateuchal criticism was directed to the question of how Moses could have written Genesis and whether one could still discern the sources to which he must have had access, given Moses' context some 400 years after the time of the patriarchs (Gen 15:13). Yet it was not long before scholars' sense of the general diversity of terminology and perspective within the Pentateuch, together with apparent duplications of narratives and divergences between laws apparently treating the same subject, led to an altogether more complex model of the Pentateuch in which Moses steadily faded out of the picture, to be replaced by differing religious movements within Israel's history. Intensive debate in the 19th cent. led eventually to Julius Wellhausen's potent proposals (famously summarized as JEDP; *see* DOCUMENTARY HYPOTHESIS) that commanded a new consensus, a consensus that remained in place, although variously modified not least by Hermann Gunkel and Gerhard von Rad, until ca. 1970. Here the Pentateuch was seen as containing Israel's religious history as a whole, from early beginnings that were collated and reduced to writing by the Yahwist under Solomon in the 10th cent. (*see* J, YAHWIST) to the reformulation of Israel's faith during and after the exile in the Priestly texts of the 6th cent (*see* P, PRIESTLY WRITERS). The interpreter only needed to know how to rearrange the texts, as it were, so that they could be read in relation to their originating contexts, and so be properly understood (Campbell and O'Brien 1993).

2. Diversification of scholarly approaches

a. Continuing historical-critical approaches. Over the last forty years or so, this consensus has disappeared for complex reasons. Many scholars have retained the historical-critical interpretative assumptions but have shown greater divergence in interpreting the evidence of the text. The most striking change is, in essence, one of scholarly "mood." This is shown in a tendency to lower the dates of the material, especially the primary narrative strands of Genesis, Exodus, and Numbers (predominantly ascribed to the Yahwist), to the 6th cent. BCE or even later. Alongside this, however, some still hold to a 10th-cent. Yahwist, while others doubt whether we should think of a Yahwist in the first place. Though there is still some consensus about a 6th-cent. Priestly movement (despite some scholars argument for greater antiquity for priestly legislation), most else is unsettled, and previous confidence about relative internal chronology and context has disappeared.

Although some scholarly specialists continue to pursue these debates with vigor (e.g., Campbell and O'Brien 2005; Dozeman and Schmid), to the interested nonspecialist the whole scenario can be rather dismaying. We now have no more evidence than Wellhausen, Gunkel, or von Rad had, aside from some archaeological and epigraphic discoveries that have only an indirect bearing on the dating of pentateuchal narratives (*see* DEIR ʿALLA, TEXTS). The dismay is caused by the fact that mainstream scholars appeal to the same evidence and yet reach very different conclusions regarding the dating and contextualizing of some of the most famous narratives within Israel's Scriptures, sometimes differing in date by 500 years. Is dating texts as much a matter of preference or fashion or ideology as of the rigorous weighing of evidence? May there perhaps be something wrong with the way the debates are set up?

On historical-critical hermeneutical assumptions, it must surely follow from such uncertainty over date and originating context that these pentateuchal texts should be considered to be in certain respects unintelligible. For we simply do not—and apparently cannot—know what we need to know about them. Yet many interpreters would resist such a position, not least out of a sense that there is a long history of interpretation that, whatever its defects, has regularly succeeded in making the texts intelligible.

b. Literary approaches. Aside from the modification or abandonment of historical-critical hermeneutical assumptions, literary approaches have contributed to the collapse of the post-Wellhausen consensus. This movement toward literary approaches has taken many forms, often related to late 20th-cent. literary and ideological turns away from the 18th- and 19th-cent. "historical" turns. One can alternatively depict this shift in terms of movement from "author-hermeneutics" toward "text-hermeneutics" (Alonso Schökel). There has been a renewed sense of the internal literary craft and dynamics (the "poetics") of the narrative texts; narratives, which had been routinely divided between sources and redactors, have been seen afresh as skillfully fashioned and meaningful in themselves. Even if a text is recognized as being composite, the concern is to understand the point of the whole, which may be more than the sum of its parts (e.g., Alter on Korah, Dathan, and Abiram; Anderson on the flood). This approach has been undertaken especially, though by no means solely, on the part of Jewish scholars who have deep roots in the serious imaginative engagement with narratives that is historically represented by MIDRASH. More generally, this approach resonates with ways in which other classic texts are read. In order to understand and be enriched by Homer or Shakespeare one does not have to be an expert on ancient Greece or Tudor England—which is not to say that historical knowledge does not help, but only that it is not the avenue to understanding.

c. Canonical approaches. Canonical approaches, especially that pioneered by Brevard Childs, grant that there is a complex history underlying the Pentateuch but want to find significance in the ways in which the material has been shaped and preserved for future generations. The fact of canonical preservation presupposes that the material in question is capable of being meaningful in contexts other than that in which it originated (analogous to the ways in which literary classics have an ability to outlive and transcend their originating context). It may indeed be that the present shape of the Pentateuch obscures rather than represents the actual course of Israel's religious history. But its shape may be significant in its own right as a means of making the fruits of Israel's religious history accessible to subsequent generations; it can be seen as a deliberate recasting to bring out understandings and priorities that might not have been evident initially.

Moreover, the canon provides its own context of interpretation. For example, many scholars interpret Gen 1 against the background of the 6th-cent. BCE exile in Babylon and invite one to think of the reformulation of Israel's faith within the trauma of exile, which can be a valid exercise of historical imagination. Yet Gen 1 itself says nothing about Israel or the exile, and its present literary context invites reflection on the nature of God's creation at no particular time as the overture to the canonical narrative that follows. It becomes clear that the pentateuchal text has more than one context and that there is more than one set of questions that may fruitfully be asked.

d. Ideological and theological approaches. Ideologically aware interpreters, including feminists (*see* FEMINIST INTERPRETATION; IDEOLOGICAL CRITICISM), have argued that although knowledge of originating historical context remains desirable, it is also important to be able to discern the assumptions, often unconscious, that are embedded within the biblical texts, such as the priority given to males or the cultural acceptance of slavery. It is also important to discern assumptions about social status and power that readers themselves bring to the text. Ideological approaches reflect critically on the way in which the material is appropriated within a contemporary context, with concern for how certain interpretations deny power to certain persons in the changing political and socioeconomic contexts in which people today live.

Theologically, a text may have a subject matter that, although indeed molded by the assumptions of its writers, has an intrinsic significance that exceeds the author's mindset. It is very unlikely that the writer of Gen 1 had in mind or anticipated the understandings of humanity as "in the image of God" that have subsequently developed among Jews and Christians (Middleton), and other voices within Genesis seem either not to share the Gen 1 perspective or to restrict its applicability—such as Noah in Gen 9:25-27, where the corollary of YHWH's blessing on Shem (i.e., Israel) is a curse on Canaan (i.e., Canaanites) as the most abject of slaves. But this does not deny the validity of post-biblical development of the significance of "image of God." One must recognize that, in one way or other, the enduring religious authority of the Pentateuch must involve the continuing attempt to probe the possible significance and function of the text for those whose life and thought is located within communities—both Jewish and Christian—whose identity is in some way constituted by the biblical text.

B. Some Difficulties in Reading the Pentateuch

It may be helpful to consider some specific examples of difficulties that confront the careful reader of the Pentateuch—difficulties that may not admit of an entirely satisfactory explanation.

1. Narrative tensions within Genesis, Exodus, and Numbers

First, there are tensions between the implications of certain narratives on their own terms and the framework within which they are set. In Genesis this relates to issues of chronology. The famous account of Jacob deceiving Isaac and securing the blessing intended for Esau is premised on Isaac's being on his deathbed (Gen 27:2, 4, 7, 10, 41). One would naturally assume that Isaac dies soon after Jacob leaves home to avoid the murderous anger of Esau. Yet we are only told of Isaac's death after Jacob returns from his long stay with Laban, during which he has acquired wives (over a period of fourteen years; Gen 29:15-30), concubines, and numerous offspring. The joint burial of Isaac by Esau and Jacob seems to imply the reconciliation between the two after Jacob's return from Laban (Gen 35:27-29).

Alternatively, when Hagar is driven out with her son Ishmael, the story implies that Ishmael is a small child who can be carried and placed under a bush until Hagar is enabled by God to find water to give him (Gen 21:14-19). Yet Abram is eighty-six years old when Ishmael is born (Gen 16:16) and a hundred years old when Isaac is born (Gen 21:5), and Hagar's expulsion takes place only after Isaac has grown sufficiently to be weaned (which might not happen in an ancient context until a child was three), which gives rise to the tension with Ishmael (Gen 21:8-10). Thus, according to the chronological framework Ishmael is at least fifteen and possibly older when he and Hagar are expelled, hardly a portable and helpless small child.

There is some real tension between the report that Sarah is ninety years old (Gen 17:17) and Abimelech's taking her into his harem and Abraham's considering her to be a possible danger to himself because men would desire her (Gen 20:2, 11). To be sure, interpreters have regularly offered suggestions that can "make sense" of the scenario—John Calvin, e.g., first suggests Sarah had an unusual beauty that had not suffered from age, before wondering whether Abimelech was attracted more to her virtues than to her physical appearance. Yet the remarkable thing is that the narrative in itself seems unaware of any difficulty here, and the difficulty is caused by the chronological frame within which the narrative is now set.

Within Exodus and Numbers, the most famous tensions have to do with enumeration. Most of the individual narratives of Israel in the wilderness seem to presuppose a group of significant size but not huge. They can apparently be provided for by "twelve springs of water and seventy palm trees" (Exod 15:27), can all receive enough to drink from water coming out of one rock (Exod 17:6), can initially have their disputes heard by Moses alone, which is feasible even if unwise in the long term (Exod 18:13-27), and can consistently be addressed as a whole people by Moses and Aaron. This suggests perhaps several thousand people at most, maybe fewer. Yet the framework specifies "six hundred thousand men on foot, besides children" and a "mixed crowd" also (Exod 12:37-38; compare Num 1:44-46; 26:51). If women are included, then one gets a total number in the region of two million. Many interpreters have spelled out the practicalities that would be entailed by some two million Israelites in the Sinai desert, usually to show the absurdity of these numbers. The narratives themselves imply few people, while the framework specifies many.

The conventional modern approach to these internal tensions has been to explain them in terms of different literary strands: the Genesis and Exodus narratives are ancient traditions (Yahwistic), while the computations of years and numbers represent a distinct later formalizing or idealizing tendency (Priestly). But even if this were so, it is not clear that it really explains the problems in the text so much as recasts them into what may feel like a more manageable frame of reference.

2. Differences within pentateuchal laws

A second kind of difficulty concerns differences of perspective and prescription within pentateuchal laws. An interesting example of the former is afforded by the last of the Ten Commandments. In Exod 20:17 we read, "You shall not covet your neighbour's house; you shall not covet your neighbour's wife, or male or female slave, or ox, or donkey, or anything that belongs to your neighbor." Here the prime object, "house," appears to envisage not the structure within which one lives but rather "household," that is the total social resources of a well-off Israelite man. The text then goes on to specify what constitutes the household, probably in order of importance: first, his wife; second, his slaves; third, his work animals; fourth, a generalizing "anything else." In contrast, Deut 5:21 states, "Neither shall you covet your neighbor's wife. Neither shall you desire your neighbour's house, or field, or male or female slave, or ox, or donkey, or anything that belongs to your neighbor." Apart from small differences—the initial "neither" and the addition of "field"—the major difference concerns the position of "wife"; she is put in a category of her own and separated from the list of household items, which are introduced by a different verb. The significance of these differences has long been debated.

Here historical conjecture may indeed be illuminating (Daube). Elsewhere in the laws of Deuteronomy a woman can be held legally responsible for her actions, such as adultery (Deut 22:22). This responsibility contrasts with the earlier context of Genesis where, when Sarah is taken to the Pharaoh's and Abimelech's harem under false pretenses, it is Abraham and not Sarah who is reproved when the truth comes to light (Gen 12:18-19; 20:10); apparently Sarah is not accountable. Exodus 20:17 seems to belong to the more "patriarchal" frame of reference that characterizes Genesis, while Deut 5:21 seems to envisage a social context in which the wife has acquired a new legal status. What might be the precise difference of time or place between the two formulations we cannot establish; the point is the apparent development between the two versions of the Ten Commandments.

The Ten Commandments, the most famous and enduring of all pentateuchal laws, also illustrate a problem akin to our first point about tensions within the text, here between the content of the text and its self-presentation. The consistent self-presentation of the text is that the Ten Commandments are directly spoken by God to Israel, unlike all other laws, which are mediated by Moses; indeed, it is the awesome and overwhelming nature of YHWH's direct address that leads to the arrangement of Moses' speaking for God subsequently (Exod 20:18-21; Deut 5:4, 22-31). Further, God not only speaks the Commandments but writes them on stone tablets (Exod 31:18; Deut 5:22). This would lead one to expect that the wording of the Commandments would be fixed and unalterable, as in the English idiom "set in stone." Yet the versions of the Commandments in Exod 20 and Deut 5 differ. Many of the differences are minor (the most frequent difference being the connective waw [w ו], "and/or," a single stroke in Hebrew), though particular words and phrases also vary. Yet apart from differences within the tenth commandment, there is a major difference in the fourth commandment: Exodus prescribes Sabbath rest because of God's rest at creation (Exod 20:11), while Deuteronomy prescribes Sabbath rest because of YHWH's deliverance of Israel from Egypt (Deut 5:15).

Moreover, although the first two commandments are spoken by YHWH in the first person, as is appropriate in direct address, the remainder refer to YHWH in the third person (to be precise, the third, fourth, and fifth commandments, for six through ten do not mention the deity); thus the third commandment does not prohibit misuse of "my name" but of "the name of the LORD your God." Why this difference, when one would have expected YHWH to speak in the first person throughout?

Both these issues suggest a certain process of formation and interpretation that has been embodied in the biblical text. Indeed, it may well be the compiler's sense of the need to have Moses contributing something to God's words and not just repeating them that accounts for the awkward presence of Deut 5:5, which portrays Moses as "standing between the LORD and [Israel] to declare . . . the words of the LORD," despite the obvious tension between this and the immediately preceding statement that YHWH spoke with Israel "face to face," and Moses' subsequent appointment as mediator precisely because YHWH's face to face address was so overwhelming (Deut 5:4, 23-31). If the wording in the two versions of the Ten Commandments differs, it must be because Moses has modified it, though this eases one problem at the cost of creating another. A traditional Jewish approach neatly tries to make progress by proposing that Israel heard the first two commandments directly from God in the first person, and the remainder from Moses speaking about God (*b. Mak.* 24a; *b. Hor.* 8a). Yet the point remains that the text's own self-presentation in Deut 5:22 does not portray Moses fulfilling this role and at face value excludes him from it.

These examples illustrate that the text intrinsically challenges the interpreter to attempt as best as possible to understand what is going on. The question then becomes what sort of interpretive approach is most helpful and why. However, it is unlikely, judging by the history of interpretation, that any one approach will ever satisfy all.

C. The Relationship of Genesis to the Rest of the Pentateuch

Within the Pentateuch the major division is between Genesis and the other books. Genesis functions as an account of beginnings of the world as a whole (Gen 1–11) and of Israel's ancestors (Gen 12–50). In Exodus, Moses comes to center stage, Israel becomes a nation, and after the exodus the foundational covenant at Sinai/Horeb is made. How the books relate (other than simply sequentially) presents a different, but substantively weightier, kind of challenge for reading the Pentateuch.

1. The recognition and reconceptualization of a classic problem

A major issue concerns the varying ways in which religious norms should be recognized and observed. If the law (torah) as given at Sinai is normative for Israel, then how should Israel understand the PATRIARCHS who lived prior to Sinai? The patriarchs are clearly called by YHWH and are recipients of his promises, in such a way as to be "authoritative" ancestors for Israel. Yet if they did not observe torah, does this relativize the importance of torah? Or must they have in fact known torah and observed it (which is how *Jubilees* retold the material within the Hellenistic world)? Or did they somehow intuitively know what torah required as a kind of natural law and observe it? These issues are extensively canvassed in traditional Jewish interpretation (e.g., Green). (The problem is analogous to that posed by the OT for Christian faith: if Christ is normative, what is the status of those who lived before Christ?)

Remarkably, this classic problem almost entirely receded from focus in 19th- and 20th-cent. pentateuchal criticism as scholars reconceptualized the theological issue as a problem of religious history to be tackled by historical-critical methods. Scholars argued that Genesis was written during the monarchy and exile (1st millennium) and that its content, either in whole or in part, reflects the context of its composition rather than of its narrative setting (2nd millennium). The issue then ceased to be one of understanding successive "dispensations" and became instead one of discovering diverse movements and developments within Israel's overall history (*see* ISRAEL, HISTORY OF). Scholars ceased to ask about the status of pre-Mosaic religion in relation to Mosaic norms. Instead, they asked how the norms of Josiah's reform (as represented by Deuteronomy) relate to other patterns of Israelite religion, either prior to the reform (if one holds to a relatively early date for the Genesis narratives) or unaffected by the reform (if one thinks that the patriarchal narratives depict familial religion beyond its sphere of influence) or subsequent to the reform (if the Priestly legislation is subsequent to the Deuteronomic).

This change in focus illustrates the implications of differences of approach to interpreting the Pentateuch. The questions one asks and the answers that appear plausible are inseparable from the wider frame of reference and assumptions within which one works.

2. Genesis as "the Old Testament of the Old Testament"

Another way of coming at this whole issue is to ask how Moses' coming to know God as YHWH relates to the knowledge of God in Genesis. The narrative in Exod 3:13-15 implies that the name YHWH that God reveals to Moses is a new and definitive name (*see* TETRAGRAMMATON), while Exod 6:2-3 explicitly states that the patriarchs knew God as "God Almighty" (EL SHADDAI) and not as YHWH. The knowledge of God as YHWH now given to Moses was not given to the patriarchs. Yet the narrator in Genesis frequently uses the name YHWH, and the name twice appears on God's own lips (Gen 15:7; 28:13). The differing ways in which interpreters handle this puzzle can be instructive.

A more traditional or "conservative" approach argues for essential continuity between the texts. God must have been known to the patriarchs as YHWH, and what is new in Exodus is not the name as such but rather its meaning; Israel is given a new content for an already familiar name, in such a way as to convey a sense of fulfillment of the promises made to the patriarchs.

The predominant modern approach has been to argue that the Pentateuch contains more than one account of how Israel came to know the name YHWH. The Yahwist is so called because of the contention that a source/author in Genesis supposed the divine name was known from earliest times (Gen 4:26). The Elohist (Exod 3) and Priestly writers (Exod 6), in contrast, supposed that the divine name only became known in the time of Moses. Israel was apparently happy to preserve divergent accounts and simply to live with the difficulties posed thereby. For the scholar, the difficulties become a window into the complexity of Israel's religious history (*see* SOURCE CRITICISM).

A third approach is to treat the use of the divine name in Genesis as an example of using a familiar name in an unfamiliar context: God is called YHWH in Genesis because that is how Israel knows God. In other words, the usage is technically anachronistic, but it is in keeping with the common practice of storytellers (*see* NARRATIVE CRITICISM). For example, in Gen 13 the narrator uses the familiar place name Bethel (Gen 13:3), even though a later episode makes clear that in Abraham's time the place's name was Luz, and it was only subsequently renamed Bethel by Jacob (Gen 28:19). One possible advantage to the third approach is that it can be developed into a canonical approach that is both theologically rich and also plausible in regard to historical problems in the text (see Moberly 2001; Levenson 2004).

The newness of the name YHWH in the context of Moses can be linked with a larger difference between the patriarchs and Moses in the overall pattern of religious assumption and practice as the texts now stand. Patriarchal religion lacks the concept of holiness and is correspondingly open, nonmediated, not tied to one particular sanctuary, nonaggressive toward the inhabitants of Canaan, and characterized by a certain "ecumenical" outlook; e.g., both the Egyptian Pharaoh and the Hebrew Joseph are given dreams by one and the same God (the generic term for deity, ʾ**elohim** [אֱלֹהִים], is consistently used in this context) and differ only in quality of insight into the dreams. When God appears to Moses at the burning bush as YHWH, the concept of holiness is present at the outset (Exod 3:5), and thereafter the relationship between YHWH and Israel is mediated (by Moses) and characterized by demands (in covenantal torah), by exclusivity ("You shall have no other gods before me"), and by having a sanctuary (Sinai/Horeb and the tabernacle). YHWH is now God of Israel and not of Egypt or the Pharaoh, who neither knows nor acknowledges YHWH, and the Egyptians worship "gods" over whom YHWH shows power (Exod 12:12).

Yet despite these differences, the Pentateuch is emphatic that YHWH is the God of Abraham, Isaac, and Jacob. The one God can apparently be known in markedly different ways. This poses the ancient problem: how should one recognize as religiously authoritative material that is full of religious practices different from or even forbidden by Mosaic torah (compare, e.g., Jacob's setting up a pillar in Gen 28:18 with the strong prohibition of such in Deut 16:22)? What seems to have happened is that the writers/editors of the Pentateuch were willing to let much of Genesis stand in its strangeness in relation to torah (unlike the book of *Jubilees*, which consistently introduces Israel's torah and its observance into the patriarchal context), while also molding the material in certain ways so as to make it more accessible for Israel to appropriate. So, e.g., the patriarchs become types and/or figures of Israel; Abraham's descent to Egypt in time of famine and exit with wealth after plagues (Gen 12:10-20) anticipates the subsequent story of Israel's sojourn in Egypt in Exodus. God's words to Abraham—"I am the LORD who brought you from Ur of the Chaldeans"—are so resonant with the opening of the Decalogue—"I am the LORD your God, who brought you out of the land of Egypt"—that one naturally reads YHWH's dealings with Abraham as patterning YHWH's dealings with Israel (Gen 15:7; Exod 20:2). Moreover, the Abraham who lives before the giving of torah is nonetheless obedient to what torah prescribes (Gen 26:5).

In all this one sees a blurring of historical differences in the interests of appropriating the figure of Abraham within the wider context of Israel. Historical differences are not eradicated, nor are they preserved for their own sake; what appears to be at stake is a recontextualizing of the Abraham material so that it can function as religiously authoritative for Israel.

This process of recontextualization has similarities to how Christians have traditionally interpreted the OT. There is the same conviction of one God, but that God is known and served differently after a new beginning—where the coming of Jesus is, in some ways, analogous to the self-revelation of God to Moses at the burning bush and in the Sinai covenant. Reading the OT typologically or figurally is one of the ways in which Christians have sought to appropriate its distinctive content within a Christian frame of reference. Thus the relationship between Genesis and the rest of the Pentateuch sheds light on the classic Christian problem of how best to read the OT as a whole.

D. Some Hermeneutical Principles and Priorities in Pentateuchal Interpretation

In light of the fact that there are differing frames of reference and differing questions to put to the Pentateuch, a general consensus among scholars about hermeneutical principles and priorities is unlikely to occur. Nonetheless, the issue is worth raising, at least in some general outlines.

1. Characteristic differences in approach

Initially one might point out, in very broad brush stroke, characteristic differences of interpretative interest. For example, Christians tend to be more interested in pentateuchal narrative than pentateuchal law, and Jews vice versa; historically, Jewish children in synagogue would start their learning with Leviticus, while their Christian counterparts would most likely be focusing on stories of Noah, Abraham, or Moses. Alternatively, while Protestants have usually had little of interest to say about the ritual prescriptions of the Pentateuch (though some dismiss while others are piously imaginative), scholars whose own religious formation inclines them to take ritual more seriously (traditionally inclined Roman Catholics and Jews) have made sense of this material in ways that have eluded others. For example, the discussions of ritual written by Mary Douglas and Jacob Milgrom are illuminating and engaging, whereas Wellhausen had little that was constructive to offer.

2. Christian approaches to pentateuchal law

With regard to all legal material there tends to be a fundamental difference between Christians and Jews; for Jews, at least observant Jews (whose own religious formation inclines them to take ritual more seriously than nonobservant Jews), feel a certain pressure to do what the text says (via, of course, its rabbinic halakhic mediation) that tends not to characterize Christians. Because Jesus in his life, death, and resurrection is the ultimate hermeneutical key for Christians, questions of which pentateuchal laws might still need to be heeded and obeyed are always tricky. Of course, certain basic moves are already made within the NT. Genesis 17 prescribes CIRCUMCISION as a sign of the covenant in perpetuity, with no revocation envisaged. Yet Paul insists that in the light of Christ, circumcision forfeits the significance that it once had and must be reconceived (1 Cor 7:19; Gal 5:6; 6:15); although the transformation is complex, part of its deep logic appears to be that identity for Christians cannot be constituted in the biological and kinship categories of identity that Genesis undoubtedly envisages.

Alternatively, part of the significance of Israel's dietary laws is that they symbolize Israel's election to be a holy nation, in effect, as it were, a clean people among unclean peoples (Lev 20:22-26). When Peter has a vision of unclean animals and is told to kill and eat them, he initially recoils; yet God overrules him: "What God has made clean, you must not call profane" (Acts 10:10-16). The meaning of this becomes clear in what follows: Peter is summoned to take the message of Christ to a Gentile, Cornelius, and he immediately gets the point (Acts 10:28)—the abrogation of the distinction between clean and unclean animals represents the abrogation of the distinction between clean and unclean peoples, Jew and Gentile, respectively. The narrative does not say when, how, or why God has "cleansed" unclean animals; but the natural inference in the wider context is that this is what has happened in the death and resurrection of Jesus.

The commands concerning circumcision and food laws still stand within Christianity's authoritative Scriptures, and yet are seen no longer to apply; their significance is historical rather than existential or practical. But the question then becomes how much more of pentateuchal law should be seen thus. Although traditionally Christians have tended to say that moral laws still apply while civil and ritual laws do not (a principle hardly derived from the Pentateuch itself), the laws themselves often resist neat classification in such categories. Moreover, although the law that the persistently rebellious son should be put to death (Deut 21:18-21) might well be classified as moral rather than civil or ritual, most Christians would not be willing to implement it—for which they have the precedent of God himself (Hos 11:1-9).

3. Differences between Jews and Christians in interpreting the Shema

A good example of hermeneutical issues is provided by a text of prime importance, the Shema (Deut 6:4-9; *see* SHEMA, THE). What should one make of the instructions in vv. 6-9 to recite, teach, and display the foundational words that YHWH is one and is to be loved unreservedly? The first tractate of the MISHNAH begins with a discussion of the scope and implications of these instructions, for the premise is that what the text says, Israel must continue to do; the question then is what counts as due observance. Jewish commentaries on Deuteronomy also tend to give considerable space to the question of what kind of practice is envisaged in these verses (on which Jews have often differed). There is, e.g., debate as to how the "literal" practice of Orthodox Jews who, following halakhic exegesis of v. 8, bind on PHYLACTERIES at times of prayer relates to the text's own intention—which does not specify wearing only at times of prayer, and may envisage a headband and wristband to be worn at all times (Tigay).

Christian commentaries look different. Following the explicit lead of Jesus, Christians give weight to Deut 6:4-5; the words receive regular liturgical use almost always, also following Jesus' lead, in conjunction with Lev 19:18. This has the effect that the instructions of Deut 6:6-9 recede from view. A recent compilation of ancient Christian commentators on Deuteronomy (commentators not far removed in time from the Mishnah) has several pages of detailed discussion of vv. 4-5 but nothing whatsoever on vv. 6-9 (see, e.g., Lienhard, who is representative of Christian disinterest in Deut 6:6-9). A good number of modern Christian commentaries deal substantively with vv. 4-5 and only briefly with vv. 6-9, often saying little more than that the verses are to be taken figuratively or metaphorically even though many Jews (implicitly mistakenly) have taken them literally (von Rad). However, the strong historical likelihood is that the instructions are not metaphorical but envisage actual wearing and inscribing of the all-important words as a means of inculcating their content. It may be that the relative disinterest in vv. 6-9 is related to the fact that many Christians do not feel under obligation to do what the text appears to say. But contrast extensive Christian discussion of Jesus' words of institution in the Gospels and 1 Cor 11:23-26, where the "do this" is heard as obliging one to do what the text says (*see* LORD'S SUPPER).

Of course, some Christians traditionally have practices equivalent to those of Deut 6:6-9, most obviously in the regular recital of the LORD'S PRAYER and in the display of the prime Christian symbol of the cross—often on a necklace but also over the gates of cities in the historic Christian empire of Byzantium, where they symbolically depicted the identity and allegiance of the place one was entering, just as Deut 6:9 envisages the wording of the Shema doing for Israel's homes (private space) and cities (public space). Deuteronomy does not envisage the recital and display of an equivalent to the Shema, but of the Shema itself. Yet Christians only receive Deuteronomy as part of the larger canon of Scripture, which includes the NT also, and that makes the difference.

This surely well illustrates the intrinsic hermeneutical complexity of the contemporary appropriation of any law within the Pentateuch. Appropriation only becomes an issue within the context of Jewish and Christian communities whose long histories of thought and practice necessarily color the handling of Scripture and recontextualize its content. What counts as good interpretation and appropriation may not only vary over time but also be other than what the text itself might have envisaged. So, in terms of the Shema just considered, in the early 21st cent., where bodies and clothes and public buildings are increasingly "marked" with symbols and words promoting sports, sex, and capitalist consumerism, it may well be that interpreters of Deuteronomy will reconsider the possible significance of Deut 6:6-9. Perhaps those who have regarded a literal interpretation as mistaken or "legalistic" may rather see Deut 6:6-9 in terms of the importance of believers having appropriate symbols of their identity and allegiance in increasingly disparate, contested, and sometimes threatening social contexts.

E. History and Truth

Finally, a few remarks on the question of history and its relationship to the enduring value and truth of the Pentateuch are appropriate. Two things at least should be clear. First, the content of the Pentateuch has a considerable internal history. Second, the Pentateuch's enduring significance and truth should not be separable from its reception and appropriation within Jewish and Christian contexts. Perhaps the main challenge is to know how best to handle these two factors.

In terms of modern historical awareness and methods, there can be little doubt that the pentateuchal narratives stand at some distance from the contexts they depict, and they are often opaque to the priorities of the modern historian. Because of this, the question of how the literature relates to the history that underlies and has generated it is complex.

For much of the 20th cent. the scholarly consensus was that the narratives have genuinely preserved very ancient material; this was argued by German scholars primarily in terms of an underlying oral tradition (Gunkel, Alt, and Noth, in various ways) and by American scholars in terms of archaeological confirmation of various aspects of the texts (Albright, Bright, Wright). But since it became apparent that the archaeological case had been overstated (Thompson) and there was renewed doubt about our ability to discern underlying oral traditions (Van Seters), the scholarly mood has swung away from affirmations of historicity. Yet it remains an open question whether the debate might not be more fruitfully reconceived in other terms. For example, the overall internal consistency and distinctiveness of patriarchal religion has received less attention than it might, and the contemporary tendency to date much material within a relatively narrow time band—in and around the 6th cent. BCE—has not yet displayed the fruitfulness in accounting for the marked differences of content that characterized earlier 20th-cent. scholarship.

Perhaps what interpreters need is not only a sense of the underlying history as a prolonged process over time, but a corresponding understanding of how to interpret the texts as displaying a certain kind of historical and theological density that does not readily fit within modern literary categories. Von Rad (1972) offered a suggestive account of how to interpret the patriarchal stories: a prolonged history of Israel's learning to live under God is telescoped into particular moments and specific episodes. More recently, Levenson (1993) strikingly illuminates Genesis and pentateuchal law from the angle of divine election and Israel's growth in theological understanding, while Moberly (2000) offers a reading of Gen 22 that takes seriously its rendering of Abraham and Isaac while recognizing the story as a construal of the meaning of sacrifice in the Temple at Jerusalem.

In short, questions of truth and history in the Pentateuch resist easy answers. But the Pentateuch's generative fruitfulness down the centuries suggests that perhaps the best entrée to the real significance and value of Israel's foundational history is via its continuing appropriation by Jews and Christians. In these contexts, respect for the text means that it is recontextualized and transformed. The Pentateuch's truth is living; thus it changes, so that it can remain the same. *See* BIBLICAL INTERPRETATION, HISTORY OF; DEUTERONOMY,

BOOK OF; EXODUS, BOOK OF; GENESIS, BOOK OF; LEVITICUS, BOOK OF; NUMBERS, BOOK OF; SAMARITAN PENTATEUCH.

Bibliography: William Foxwell Albright. *Archaeology and the Religion of Israel* (1942); Albrecht Alt. *Essays on Old Testament History and Religion* (1968); Robert Alter. *The Art of Biblical Narrative* (1981); B. W. Anderson. "From Analysis to Synthesis: The Interpretation of Genesis 1–11." *JBL* 97 (1978) 23–29; John Bright. *A History of Israel* (1972); John Calvin. *Calvin's Commentaries, Volume 1: Genesis* (2005); Antony Campbell and Mark O'Brien. *Sources of the Pentateuch: Texts, Introductions, Annotations* (1993); Antony Campbell and Mark O'Brien. *Rethinking the Pentateuch: Prolegomena to the Theology of Ancient Israel* (2005); Brevard Childs. *Old Testament Theology in a Canonical Context* (1989); David Daube. "Biblical Landmarks in the Struggle for Women's Rights." *Juridical Review* 23 (1978) 177–80; Mary Douglas. *Leviticus as Literature* (2001); Thomas Dozeman and Konrad Schmid. *A Farewell to the Yahwist? The Composition of the Pentateuch in Recent European Interpretation* (2006); Arthur Green. *Devotion and Commandment: The Faith of Abraham in the Hasidic Imagination* (1989); Hermann Gunkel. *Genesis* (1910); Jon D. Levenson. *The Death and Resurrection of the Beloved Son: The Transformation of Child Sacrifice in Judaism and Christianity* (1993); Jon D. Levenson. "The Conversion of Abraham to Judaism, Christianity, and Islam." *The Idea of Biblical Interpretation: Essays in Honor of James L. Kugel.* Hindy Najman and Judith Newman, eds. (2004) 3–39; Joseph Lienhard, ed. *Ancient Christian Commentary on Scripture: Old Testament III: Exodus, Leviticus, Numbers, Deuteronomy* (2001); J. Richard Middleton. *The Liberating Image: The* Imago Dei *in Genesis 1* (2005) 15–42; Jacob Milgrom. *Leviticus.* CC (2004); R. W. L. Moberly. *The Bible, Theology, and Faith: A Study of Abraham and Jesus* (2000); R. W. L. Moberly. *The Old Testament of the Old Testament* (2001); Ernest Nicholson. *The Pentateuch in the Twentieth Century: The Legacy of Julius Wellhausen* (1998); Martin Noth. *Exodus.* OTL (1962); Martin Noth. *The Old Testament World* (1966); Gerhard von Rad. *Deuteronomy.* OTL (1966); Gerhard von Rad. "The Form-Critical Problem of the Hexateuch." *From Genesis to Chronicles: Explorations in Old Testament Theology.* K. C. Hanson, ed. (2005) 1–58; Gerhard von Rad. *Genesis.* OTL (1972); Luis Alonso Schökel. *A Manual of Hermeneutics* (1998); Benedict de Spinoza. *A Theologico-Political Treatise* (1951); R. J. Thompson. *Moses and the Law in a Century of Criticism Since Graf* (1970); Thomas L. Thompson. *The Historicity of the Patriarchal Narratives* (1974); Jeffrey Tigay. *The JPS Torah Commentary: Deuteronomy* (1996); John Van Seters. *Abraham in History and Tradition* (1975); Julius Wellhausen. *Prolegomena to the History of Israel* (1883); G. Ernest Wright. *Biblical Archaeology* (1957).

R. W. L. MOBERLY

PENTATEUCH, SAMARITAN. *See* SAMARITAN PENTATEUCH.

PENTECOST pen´ti-kost [πεντηκοστή pentēcostē]. Meaning *fiftieth* (day), a Greek name for the Festival of Weeks described in the holiday lists in Exod 23:14-17; 34:18, 22-24; Lev 23; Num 28–29; and Deut 16 (*see* WEEKS, FEAST OF). The LXX does not actually call the festival by the name *Pentecost*, although it does translate the phrase *fifty days* in Lev 23:16 as pentēkonta hēmeras (πεντήκοντα ἡμέρας). There is no evidence the holiday was designated *fiftieth* in Hebrew/Aramaic sources, where it is rather termed shavuʿoth (שָׁבֻעֹת, "weeks") or ʿasereth (עֲצֶרֶת, "gathering").

The name *Pentecost* was used by Greek writers for the second of the three pilgrimage festivals stipulated in the OT (Exod 23:14-17; 34:18, 22-24; Deut 16:16-17) because of the procedure arranged for determining its date. Both Lev 23:15-16 (Holiness Code) and Deut 16:9-10 say that one should count seven complete weeks from an event occurring in the first month around the time of Passover and Unleavened Bread (the waving of the sheaf in Lev 23:15; putting the sickle to the standing grain in Deut 16:9), with the next or fiftieth day being the date of the festival. Because neither of these events is assigned to a specific date, the Pentateuch prescribes no exact time for the Festival of Weeks/Pentecost; as a result, there was, at least in the Second Temple period, disagreement about when it was to be celebrated. Nevertheless, all agreed that it would fall in the third month of the Jewish calendar. The festival marked the beginning of the wheat harvest (Exod 34:22) and was to be the occasion for a number of offerings (Lev 23:17-19; Num 28:26-31), including two loaves made from wheat flour and "baked with leaven" (Lev 23:17). It was a day for a holy convocation and labor was prohibited (Lev 23:21; Num 28:26).

The Greek name *Pentecost* (pentēcostē) is attested in several Jewish texts that date from the Second Temple period or immediately after it. The earliest instance may be in the Greek translation of Tobit. At his home in Nineveh, the faithful exile Tobit and his family continued to practice the forms of piety that he had learned before the fall of Israel to the Assyrians, including travel to Jerusalem for the holidays. He reports: "At our festival of Pentecost, which is the sacred festival of weeks, a good dinner was prepared for me, and I reclined to eat" (Tob 2:1). When he noticed the large amount of food on his table, he sent his son Tobias to invite other Jews to enjoy the bounty (Tob 2:2). Enjoying the joyful meal and sharing it

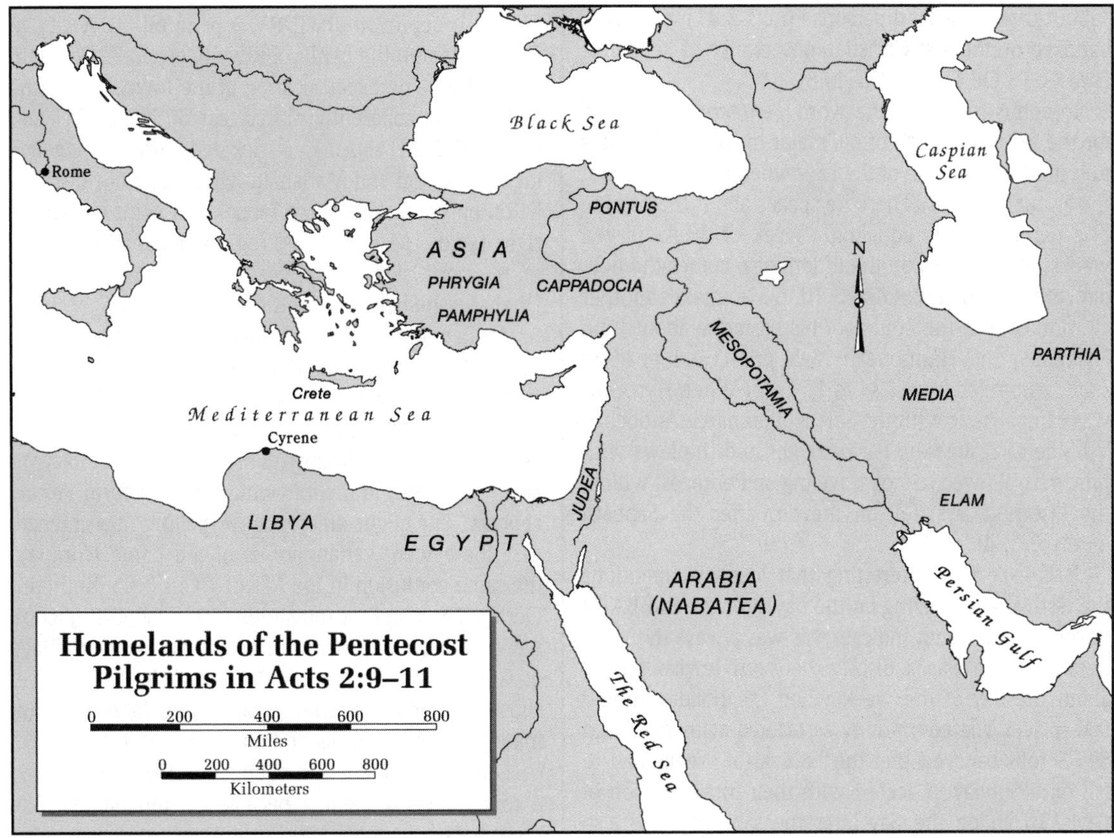

Figure 1: Homelands of the Pentecost pilgrims in Acts 2:9-11

with others appear to be how the writer of the book understood the scriptural command to rejoice at this festival (Deut 16:11). Naturally, the version of Tob 2:1 preserved at Qumran reads, "On the day of the festival of Weeks ..." (4Q196 II, 10); in a Semitic text one would not expect the Greek name for the festival. Second Maccabees, composed in Greek, also designates the holiday as *Pentecost.* In 12:31-32, it is clear that the two names for the occasion are interchangeable: v. 31 says that Judas the Maccabee and his men went to Jerusalem because the Festival of Weeks was soon to take place; v. 32 reads: "After the festival called Pentecost ...."

Philo of Alexandria several times refers to the festival by the name *Pentecost,* while he knows other designations for it. In *Rewards* 30.160 he mentions the practice of counting seven times seven weeks until Pentecost and draws attention to its character as a festival of firstfruits when loaves from the FIRST FRUITS of the wheat harvest are offered (see also *Spec. Laws* 1.183–85, where he deals with the same points). In *Spec. Laws* 2.11, 41 he enumerates the ten festivals; Pentecost is appropriately the seventh, whose date is determined by numbering seven units of seven. He also explains in *Spec. Laws* 2.30, 176–87 why it is named Pentecost and offers some numerical calculations exhibiting the virtue of the number fifty and a discussion of the fact, exceptional for an offering, that the loaves presented are to be made with leaven.

The NT contains two passing references to the holiday and one more substantial treatment of it. As Paul discusses his travel plans in 1 Cor 16, he notes that he will remain in Ephesus until Pentecost (v. 8). Acts 20 mentions the Festival of Unleavened Bread in v. 5, and in v. 16 records that Paul was eager to be in Jerusalem on the day of Pentecost. This passage reflects the apostle's desire to carry out the pilgrimage mandate. The most famous NT reference to the holiday is in Acts 2, where the HOLY SPIRIT was poured out on Jesus' first followers on the day of Pentecost (see v. 1). On that day, in obedience to the law, large numbers of Jews from many parts of the world had gathered in Jerusalem for the PILGRIMAGE holiday and thus provided a worldwide audience that could understand the message the disciples were suddenly and miraculously speaking in their several languages (vv. 8-11; *see* TONGUES, GIFT OF). The story of the first Christian celebration of the festival contains a number of hints that the writer was aware of the association of the Festival of Weeks with the covenant-making at Mount Sinai—another event that had happened in the third month of the year (see Exod 19:1). The covenantal associations of the holiday in the Qumran literature seem to be an especially rich source of comparisons with the themes attributed to the celebration in Acts 2. An example is that new members were incorporated into the group on the date of the festival, just as the small band of Jesus' followers was augmented by "about three thousand persons" (Acts 2:41) who were baptized on the first Christian observance of Pentecost (*see* ACTS OF THE APOSTLES).

Josephus resorts to the word *Pentecost* as a name for the festival in both of his major histories. He refers to it in his paraphrase of the Law when he writes about the annual festivals. There he speaks about the passing of a period of time equaling a week of weeks (seven weeks) after which, on the fiftieth day, comes the holiday termed Pentecost (*Ant.* 3.10, 6). He makes another allusion to it in the course of his narrative about John Hyrcanus, the Hasmonean high priest and head of state, who ruled from 134 to 104 BCE. When Hyrcanus was campaigning with the Seleucid monarch Antiochus VII Sidetes against the Parthians, he and the Jews with him were allowed to stop traveling on Pentecost which, the historian says, fell on the day after the Sabbath (*Ant.* 13.8, 4).

It is especially interesting that Josephus mentions the festival as occurring on the day after the SABBATH (though he does not indicate this was always the case) because there was a dispute between Jewish groups about the day of the week when the holiday should take place. The community associated with the Dead Sea Scrolls believed that the Festival of Weeks had to fall on a Sunday in accord with their interpretation of Lev 23:16 ("on the day after the sabbath"; see also v. 11); the order of holidays in Lev 23 indicated to them that the Sunday in question was the one after completion of the Festival of Unleavened Bread (1/26 in their CALENDAR). In rabbinic literature it could theoretically be celebrated on any day of the week, since it was thought that the word *sabbath* in the scriptural expression "the day after the sabbath" referred to a holiday—in this case, the day following the first day of Unleavened Bread. In both *Jewish War* and *Antiquities*, Josephus relates an incident that occurred at the time of the troubles surrounding the reign of Archelaus (4 BCE–6 CE), Herod's son and successor as ruler in Judea. In particular, Josephus notes that a large crowd of Jews was present in Jerusalem for the feast following a seven-week period that Jews call Pentecost (*J.W.* 2.42–44; *Ant.* 17.254–55). That is, though it was a one-day festival, huge numbers of people made the journey to Jerusalem to celebrate it. Finally, Josephus claims that one of the signs portending the disaster that was to befall Jerusalem (in 70 CE), and that his contemporaries failed to appreciate, happened on Pentecost: the priests, preparing for the large crowds who would arrive during daytime, entered the inner court of the Temple complex the previous night and sensed a commotion, a din, and a voice announcing a departure from the place (*J.W.* 6.299–300). *See* FEASTS AND FASTS.

Bibliography: James C. VanderKam. "Sinai Revisited." *Biblical Interpretation at Qumran.* M. Henze, ed. (2005) 44–60.

JAMES C. VANDERKAM

PENUEL peh-ny*oo*-uhl [פְּנוּאֵל penuʾel]. 1. A city in Transjordan on the JABBOK River (Gen 32:22-32 [Heb. 32:23-33]). The exact location of the town, which the biblical text apparently places east of SUCCOTH and south of MAHANAIM, is debated. Several scholars identify Penuel and Mahanaim with a pair of ruins that lie on opposite sides of the Jabbok at a point where the river bends: Mahanaim is Tell edh-Dhahab el-Gharbi on the north side of the river, while Penuel is Tell edh-Dhahab esh-Sherqiyeh on the southern bank.

At Penuel, JACOB wrestled with a "man" (Gen 32:24 [Heb. 32:25]; Hos 12:4 calls him an "angel") prior to his reunion with Esau. Jacob named the site *Peniel* (peniʾel פְּנִיאֵל; Gen 32:30 [Heb. 32:31]), meaning "face of God," claiming to have seen God "face to face." However, in the following verse the form *Penuel* appears. The slight difference in spelling may indicate that there were variant forms of the name (compare the same confusion in the MT of 1 Chr 8:25 [Kethibh/Qere]). The name of the site is later echoed in Jacob's words to Esau—"to see your face is like seeing the face of God (pene ʾelohim פְּנֵי אֱלֹהִים)" (Gen 33:10)—showing that the encounter along the Jabbok is intimately connected to Jacob's encounter with Esau.

During the period of the judges, GIDEON destroyed a tower built at Penuel because its inhabitants, like the inhabitants of SUCCOTH, did not assist him in his pursuit of the Midianites (Judg 8:8-9, 17). After the division of Solomon's kingdom, the first king of the north, Jeroboam I, is said to have "built"—perhaps meaning "rebuilt"—Penuel (1 Kgs 12:25).

2. A descendant of Judah (1 Chr 4:4).

3. A descendant of Benjamin (1 Chr 8:25).

BRENT A. STRAWN

PEOPLE OF GOD [עַם אֱלֹהִים ʿam ʾelohim; λαὸς τοῦ θεοῦ laos tou theou]. The title with variations appears twice in the OT (Judg 20:2; 2 Sam 14:13) and once in the NT (Heb 11:25). Though the precise term does not occur frequently, the concept of the formation of a people, from the call of Abraham (Gen 12:1-3) to the vision of the new Jerusalem (Rev 21:9-27), is recurrent in the biblical text. The tribal god of a nomadic group was esteemed as its first ancestor, a kinsman who would come to its aid. "God," in "people of God," is an objective genitive of authorship and possession. Israel calls itself the people of God (more frequently, the people of Yahweh; NRSV, "people of the LORD") because it owed its national and religious existence to God's historical action. The title's accent is first on the priority and power of God's action.

The emergence of this people is a manifestation of God's purpose for creation. The end point of creation throughout the ANE, including Israel, was the emergence of a stable community in a benevolent, life-sustaining order. In Gen 12:2-3, God promised to make Abraham a great nation in whom all the families of the earth would be blessed. The choice of Israel is not a preference over others, but rather existence for others. To accomplish this purpose, Abraham and his descendants were charged to keep the way of the Lord by doing righteousness and justice (Gen 18:19). Sometimes the title was used to indict leadership (monarchy, priesthood) for abusive use of their authority at the expense of God's people (1 Sam 2:22-24; Isa 3:12-15). Through Israel, Yahweh would found a new social order. The religious identity of this people is represented in the qehal yhwh (קְהַל־יְהוָה), the assembly of the Lord, observant of torah (1 Chr 28:8). The torah's purpose is to produce a righteous society. The gathering of this people is an act of God, not only of biological generation. In the choice put before the people at the covenant renewal ceremony at Shechem, the families who followed Canaanite, Amorite, or other foreign gods freely chose Yahweh, Moses' God, as their God (Josh 24:14-16). God remains in the midst of his people who are called to transform the world by living torah, God's social order, so that the harmony in which God intends his creation to live will be clear to everyone.

The first Christians saw Jesus the Christ as the promised Messiah, their savior and king, and themselves as God's chosen people in him (Eph 1:13-14; Col 1:11-14; *see* SAINT). First Peter 2:9 preserves the primacy of God's action in this ELECTION: "You are ... God's own people, in order that you may proclaim the mighty acts of him who called you out of darkness into his marvelous light." By citing OT texts (Deut 7:6; 14:2), the author is indirectly asserting that the Christian community from its beginnings is grounded in the saving action of Abraham's God. But the people do not create this possibility. It is God's initiative in Christ in whom all creation coheres; in him all creation is reconciled to God (Col 1:17, 20). Through him God lives within them and walks among them (2 Cor 6:16).

Through Christ, God's people are gathered together as the assembly (ekklēsia ἐκκλησία) of the Lord. Possibly, the evangelist's use of the term *church* (ekklēsia) in Matt 16:18 is intended to call to mind the assembly of the Lord in the LXX translation of 1 Chr 28:8 (ekklēsia kyriou [ἐκκλησία κυρίου]; *see* CHURCH, IDEA OF THE). This community gathered in Christ, God's pilgrim people, will one day fully become the eschatological city described in Revelation. Acknowledging the primacy of God's activity, this city comes down from heaven and gathers humanity (Rev 21:2, 10). Its dimensions are such that it is of cosmic size (21:16). Its membership is international (21:24-26). It is neither a separate world nor a closed society. There will be no Temple because God dwells in its midst (21:22). It is a vision of God's desire of salvation for his creation promised to Abraham, father of a great nation, a blessing to all the families of the earth.

Bibliography: Gerhard Lohfink. *Does God Need the Church? Toward a Theology of the People of God* (1999); Norbert Lohfink. *Great Themes from the Old Testament* (1982); Paul S. Minear. *Images of the Church in the New Testament* (2004).

PAUL E. FITZPATRICK

PEOPLE OF THE EAST [בְּנֵי־קֶדֶם bene-qedhem]. An amorphous term referring to a number of different groups indicating they live to the east of the person assigning the epithet. Judges uses the phrase in reference to people associated with the Midianites and Amalekites (*see* AMALEK, AMALEKITES; MIDIAN, MIDIANITES) east of the Jordan River (6:3, 33; 7:12; 8:10). In 1 Kgs 4:30, the expression refers to those east of Israel, in contrast to Egypt in the west. Job is called the greatest of all the people of the east (Job 1:3), and his geographical location in the narrative suggests that here the phrase refers to people in Arabia.

KEVIN A. WILSON

PEOPLE OF THE LAND [עַם־הָאָרֶץ ʿam-haʾarets]. A term whose application changed from the premonarchic through the rabbinic periods. In the premonarchic era, "people of the land" appears to have been a general term for the free citizenry of any given place (e.g., the Canaanites in Num 13:28; NRSV, "people who live in the land"). The meaning of the expression during the monarchic period is debated and has been variously understood as the lower social classes, the elite, the free citizenry, or even a body of socially and politically important Judahites. During this period, the ʿam-haʾarets are involved in significant historical events (2 Kgs 11:12, 18-20; 21:24; 23:30, 35; Jer 1:18; 34:19; 37:2; 44:21; Ezek 7:27; 22:29).

In the postexilic era, the term began to be used negatively. In Ezra 4:4, those returning from exile were called "the people of Judah" (ʿam yehudhah עַם־יְהוּדָה), and the opposing local elites are called "people of the land." When Ezra is told that many of the returning exiles had intermarried with the local population, they are called the "peoples of the lands" (ʿamme haʾaratsoth עַמֵּי הָאֲרָצוֹת), pointing to the heterogeneity of the local population of Canaanites, Hittites, Perizzites, Jebusites, Ammonites, Moabites, Egyptians, and Amorites (e.g., Ezra 9:2). Later, the word ʿam alone is pluralized (Ezra 10:2, 11; Neh 10:30-31).

In post-biblical rabbinic texts, the term was used as a pejorative for those who were either ignorant of or did not observe the Torah. The people of the land reciprocated bitter antagonism toward scholars. Rabbi Akiva (*see* AKIVA, RABBI), who had been one of the ʿam-haʾarets until he was forty years old, recalled his own bitter antagonism toward the educated class (*Pesah.* 49b). In the NT, the scholarly elite epress negative sentiments in their application of the word *crowd* (ochlos ὄχλος) to the masses who are ignorant of the law (John 7:49). Jesus' encounters with the Pharisees possibly could reflect similar tension between the Pharisees and people who did not regularly observe certain laws (including Jesus and his disciples) (e.g., Mark 7:1-5; Luke 11:37-41). *See* ʿAM HAʾARETS.

RALPH K. HAWKINS

PEOR pee´or [פְּעוֹר peʿor]. Site of an infamous apostasy remembered by the Hebrew writers in recounting the story of Israelite wanderings prior to entering Canaan. The prophet BALAAM is identified as the instigator of the incident in which the Israelites participated in non-Yahwistic cultic festivities involving Moabite and/or Midianite women (Num 23:28; 25:3, 5, 18; 31:16; Deut 4:3; Josh 22:17; Ps 106:28). Peor may be equated with Reubenite BETH-PEOR in Moab (Deut 3:29; 4:46; 34:6; Josh 13:20). Tell al-Mashhad (Kh. 'Uyun Musa), a candidate for the ancient site near Mount Nebo, has been the subject of recent research determining that the tell reached its zenith in the late 8th to mid-6th cent. BCE. *See* BAAL-PEOR; MOAB, MOABITES.

Bibliography: Yohanan Aharoni. *The Land of the Bible.* Rev. ed. (1979); Francesco M. Benedettucci. "The Third Archaeological Investigation Campaign at the Site of Tell al-Mashhad (January–February 2003)." *LASBF* 52 (2002) 472–75; Moshe Weinfeld. *Deuteronomy 1–11.* AB (1991).

JASON R. TATLOCK

PERAZIM, MOUNT pi-ray´zim [הַר פְּרָצִים har peratsim]. Probably BAAL-PERAZIM, where Yahweh helped David to defeat the Philistines (2 Sam 5:19-20). In an oracle of judgment against the rulers of Jerusalem (Isa 28:7-22), Isaiah proclaims that Yahweh will fight against the people of Jerusalem as God once fought for Israel at Mount Perazim (Isa 28:21).

A. HEATH JONES III

PERCEIVE [בִּין bin, חָזָה khazah, רָאָה raʾah; θεωρέω theōreō, ὁράω horaō]. A number of verbs are alternately translated "see," "look," "understand," or "perceive." In the OT, one verb frequently translated "to perceive" is raʾah (e.g., Judg 6:22; 1 Kgs 3:28; Job 9:11; Isa 64:4). However, khazah is normally used when the situation is seeing God, and it essentially means "to see in a vision, envision" (Exod 24:11; Num 24:4; Ps 63:2 [Heb. 63:3]), and bin is used when the meaning is closer to "understanding" (2 Sam 12:9). In the NT, a variety of terms point toward the idea of perceiving, including theōreō (Matt 27:55; Mark 15:16; Luke 14:29; John 6:40; Acts 3:16; Rev 11:11) and horaō (Matt 28:7; Mark 16:7; Luke 16:23; John 1:18; 18:25), both of which convey the notion of conceptualization or understanding. Perceiving God and perceiving a plant, tree, or person are substantially different for biblical writers. One "sees" objects or material things and one "perceives" or conceptualizes God.

JAMES E. WEST

PERDITION puhr-di´shuhn [בְּלִיַּעַל beliyaʿal; ἀπώλεια apōleia; Lat. *perditus*]. Possibly derived from the Hebrew word "to swallow" (balaʿ בָּלַע) or the word "to become worn out" (balah בָּלָה), *perdition* (beliyaʿal) is synonymous with destruction and death in the OT. In the psalter, the author calls upon Yahweh for assistance from the "cords of death" and the "torrents of perdition" (Ps 18:4 [Heb. 18:5]). Second Samuel 22:5 reproduces the second phrase in its reworking of Ps 18 in order to highlight Yahweh's "steadfast love" for his "anointed," David.

Matthew holds that "destruction" is the end that awaits those who enter through the wide gate and take the easy road, while entering through the narrow gate and traveling the hard road culminates in "life" (Matt 7:13-14). That divergence between destruction or perdition (*perditus*) and life is articulated in Ezra's vision in 4 Esd 7:48. Ezra is told that most of the offspring of Mother Zion will go to perdition (4 Esd 10:10). The NT also speaks of the one "destined to be lost" or "destined for destruction" (KJV, "son of perdition"), alternatively associated with Judas, who was "lost," and the "lawless one," who will appear at the end of time to oppose God (John 17:12; 2 Thess 2:3). *See* ANTICHRIST; DESTROY, UTTERLY; DEVOTED; RUIN; WASTE.

DAVID M. REIS

PEREA puh-ree´uh [Περαία Peraia]. Name of a territory east of the Jordan River during the Roman period. This area was described by Josephus (*J.W.* 3.44) as extending from Machaerus in the south to Pella in the north, and from Philadelphia (ancient Rabbah, modern Amman) to the Jordan River, east to west, with its capital at Gadara (Umm Qais). Eusebius (*Onom.* 32.5–7; 33.5–7; and 136.7, 13; 18.3) further identified the northern border of Perea as being near Jabesh (either Tall al-Maqlub or Tall Abu al-Kharaz), with Madaba being outside of the territory, and Esbous (Heshbon) on its border. These data, along with the fact that the cities of Gadara, Pella, and Philadelphia were part of the Decapolis, would seem to indicate that the territory of Perea actually ran roughly from the river Arnon (Wadi Mujib) to the Wadi el-Yabis, and that it did not always extend beyond the plateau onto the Madaba Plain. Its capital may have been at Gadora (Tell 'Ain Jedur) near es-Salt.

The name *Perea* appears to have been derived from the phrase "beyond the Jordan" (peran tou Iordanou πέραν τοῦ Ἰορδάνου; e.g., Matt 4:25; Mark 3:8; John 3:26; Josephus, *J.W.* 2.57), a translation from the Hebrew (ʿever hayyarden עֵבֶר הַיַּרְדֵּן). While the term is used frequently by Josephus, it is not found in the NT except in variant readings of Luke 6:17 (*see* BEYOND THE JORDAN). Perea, along with Judea and Galilee, were Jewish districts (*m. B. Bat.* 3:2). During NT times Galilean Jews went through the territory of Perea to Jerusalem in order to avoid traveling through Samaria. Jesus and his disciples also used this route

(Luke 17:11; 18:31, 35; 19:1), spending time in Perea on occasion (Matt 19:1; John 10:40; 11:7). Jesus himself seems to have been baptized there (Matt 3:13; John 1:28). It was also in this region that John the Baptist was active during his ministry (John 1:28) and later died (Josephus, *Ant.* 18.116–19). *See* BETHANY.

During OT times much of this area of TRANSJORDAN was known as Gilead (Josh 12:2). With the emergence of Israel, the tribes of Reuben and Gad and half the tribe of Manasseh were given land there for an inheritance (Josh 12:6). All through the united monarchy, Gilead remained part of Israelite territory (1 Sam 11; 14:47; 2 Sam 10–12; 1 Kgs 4:13), but during the 9th cent. BCE the Syrians vied with Israel for its control, after which Jeroboam II was able to bring it once again solidly under Israelite hegemony. *See* GILEAD, GILEADITES.

Following the deportation of most of this region's Jewish population by the Assyrians in 732 BCE (2 Kgs 15:29), Gentiles began moving in, especially with the conquest of Alexander the Great. This community threatened the minority of postexilic Jews in ca. 152 BCE (1 Macc 5:9-13), resulting in a conquest of much of the area by Judas and Jonathan (1 Macc 5:24; 45–55). In an effort to Judaize the region, John Hyrcanus took the Madaba Plain from the Nabateans in 129 BCE (Josephus, *Ant.* 13.254). Later, in 88 BCE, Alexander Jannaeus added Amathus, Gadara, and possibly Pella to the north (Josephus, *J.W.* 1.86). This addition was short-lived, however, because in 63 BCE Pompey liberated the cities that the Jews had annexed, including Pella and Gadara (Josephus, *Ant.* 14.75). In ca. 57 BCE, Gabinius, the proconsul of Syria, made Perea an administrative district under Rome, with its capital, at least temporarily, at Ammathus (Tall Ammata) (Josephus, *Ant.* 14.89).

In 20 BCE, Perea became part of the kingdom of Herod the Great. After Herod's death, Augustus divided the kingdom among Herod's sons, with Perea going to Herod Antipas (4 BCE–39 CE) (Josephus, *J.W.* 2.93–95) and subsequently to Agrippa I (39–44 CE) (Josephus, *Ant.* 18.52; 18.237). Following a boundary dispute between Perea and Philadelphia and the death of Agrippa I, in 44 CE, Perea, along with Galilee and Judea, were given over to the Roman procurators until Nero bestowed Perea upon Agrippa II in 54 CE (Josephus, *J.W.* 2.52; 2.247). When Agrippa II died (ca. 100 CE), the territory became part of the Roman province of Syria. *See* PALESTINE, ADMINISTRATION OF.

PAUL J. RAY JR.

PERESH pee'rish [פֶּרֶשׁ peresh]. Peresh appears in a list of descendants of Manasseh as the son of MACHIR and of his wife MAACAH (1 Chr 7:16). *See* MANASSEH, MANASSITES.

PEREZ pee'riz [פֶּרֶץ perets; Φαρές Phares]. The son of Judah and TAMAR, Judah's daughter-in-law (Gen 38:29; 1 Chr 2:4; 4:1). Tamar was widowed and childless after the death of her husband ER, Judah's firstborn. Judah's second son ONAN refused to perform the duties of the LEVIRATE LAW and died as a result (Gen 38:8-10). Tamar tricked Judah into helping her conceive the twins, Perez and Zerah. Perez became the father of Hezron and Hamul (Gen 46:12; Num 26:21; 1 Chr 2:5) and ancestor of the Perezites (Num 26:20). Perez appears in the blessings of Boaz (Ruth 4:12) and in the genealogies of David (Ruth 4:18-22) and Jesus (Matt 1:3; Luke 3:33). *See* JUDAH, JUDAHITES; ZERAH, ZERAHITES.

CLAUDE MARIOTTINI

PEREZ-UZZAH pee'riz-uh'zuh [פֶּרֶץ עֻזָּה perets ʿuzzah]. At this place, UZZAH son of Abinadab died as he steadied the ark of God being brought to Jerusalem (2 Sam 6:3-8; 1 Chr 13:7-11). The narrator explains, "The LORD had burst forth with an outburst upon Uzzah" (parats yhwh perets beʿuzzah פָּרַץ יְהוָה פֶּרֶץ בְּעֻזָּה), taking perets be as "an outburst upon" (so Exod 19:22), the place name then meaning "Outburst on Uzzah." Alternately, perets could mean "an interruption (in a family line)" (Judg 21:15). The place name would then mean "Breach in Uzzah's Line." *See* ARK OF THE COVENANT.

DAVID L. THOMPSON

PERFECTION [תָּמִים tamim; τέλειος teleios, τελειότης teleiotēs, τελειόω teleioō, τελείωσις teleiōsis]. The biblical terms *perfection* and *perfect* commonly convey a sense of maturity, completion, or reaching a goal, often in terms of moral, ethical, cultic, or physical flawlessness.

In the OT, the adjective tamim is used forty-six times in cultic contexts (twice in Exodus, nineteen times in Leviticus, seventeen times in Numbers [mostly in chaps. 28–29], eight times in Ezek 43–46) in the sense of "without blemish" to describe the acceptability of a sacrificial offering. It is also used twenty-six times in the sense of "blameless" to describe the disposition and lifestyle of human beings and twice for the response of God toward such people (2 Sam 22:26; Ps 18:25 [Heb. 18:26]). Here the term approaches the concept of righteousness and justice in moral and ethical actions. A reasonable extension of this idea is seen in several references where the sense of integrity, honor, or truthfulness is evident (Josh 24:14; Judg 9:16, 19; Prov 28:18; Amos 5:10).

In the NT, teleiotēs and its cognates convey several senses. Matthew 5:48 uniquely in the NT refers to God as perfect—and, then, identifies God's perfection as the standard for Jesus' followers. This exhortation is not to some abstraction of perfection, but is rather tied concretely to the exercise of love (Matt 5:43-47). Similarly, Col 3:14 identifies love as the bond of perfection, and 1 John collocates love and perfection in contexts of obedience (2:5), love between believers (4:12), eschatological confidence (4:17), and vanquished fear (4:18). Related to this is the statement in Jas 3:2-12 that perfection is evidenced in those whose speech is without bitterness. Some theological traditions have summarized the biblical doctrine of perfection in the commands of Jesus to love God and neighbor completely (Mark 12:30-31).

Occasionally in the NT perfection language is used in a positional sense, indicating that believers, by virtue of their status as those redeemed by Christ, have reached a telic apex in human existence (1 Cor 2:6; Phil 3:15; Heb 5:14). In other texts, maturity is identified as the goal toward which believers are to strive (e.g., Eph 4:13; Col 1:28; 4:12; Heb 6:1; Jas 1:4).

Perfection has special significance in Hebrews, whose author observes that Jesus was holy, blameless, pure (7:26)—tempted, but without sin (4:15). This is central to the rhetoric of the letter, which identifies as an inadequacy of the old covenant that its prescribed means for dealing with sin, the priesthood and sacrifice, were incapable of leading persons on to the desired goal of perfection. This is overcome in Jesus in two ways. First, he is both the perfect priest and the perfect sacrifice, so that his self-offering can deal with human sinfulness once and for all. Second, he is the trailblazer or pioneer of human salvation, who opens up the path of perfect faithfulness. Perfection refers here to more than moral goodness. After all, Jesus, though "holy, blameless, undefiled, separated from sinners" (7:26), had still to become perfect (2:10; 5:7-9; 7:28). Thus, "perfect" has to do with Jesus' character and obedience, as well as with his becoming fully qualified for the task before him. Hebrews thus emphasizes that Jesus was like other humans in every respect, including the full experience of suffering and temptation, and yet walked faithfully the path of obedience to God, while at the same time presenting Jesus as the one who opened the road of maturation in holiness for others to follow. *See* SANCTIFY, SANCTIFICATION.

JEFFREY S. LAMP

PERFUME [בֹּשֶׂם bosem, רִקֻּחַ riqquah, שֶׁמֶן shemen; μύρον myron]. A perfume is a substance that releases a sweet fragrance, often derived from plants. There are a number of aromatic plants whose scents are classified as or serve as ingredients in perfumes or fragrances in the biblical text (*see* PLANTS OF THE BIBLE). Some fragrances were simply created from the petals of local flowers or scented wood that had been mixed with oil or fat and left in a pot until the oil absorbed the scent and could be spread on the body. The more exotic ingredients for true perfumes consisted of hard resins or spices (*see* SPICE), and many were mixed with olive oil to create ointments (*see* OINTMENT) or emulsions that could be applied to the skin as anointing oils (Exod 30:23-24) or placed as a soothing balm on the forehead. Egyptian tomb paintings show celebrants wearing perfumed cones on their head at social occasions, a pleasant addition to the scents of cooking and burning INCENSE and a display of wealth by the host. A few resins were used as aromatics for hair or beard, or burned as incense that would be fanned into bedding or garments. Some, like myrrh, were pulverized into a fine powder, placed in a sachet, and worn between a woman's breasts (Song 1:13).

Plant-based substances identified as perfume-making include ALOES, BALM, CALAMUS, CASSIA, CINNAMON, FRANKINCENSE, HENNA, MYRRH, NARD, and SAFFRON. Only one animal product is included in the lists of fragrances, ONYCHA, and it is extracted from the door membrane of a snail-like mollusk found in the Red Sea and used as a fixative agent when mixed with other fragrances (see the recipe for incense in Exod 30:34-35).

Since many of these plants had to be imported from Arabia and India, they were considered luxury items. Some—such as henna, nard, and saffron (the latter two of which enter Hebrew via Persian loanwords)—do not appear in the biblical text in preexilic context (only in the Song of Solomon). These exotic substances are not mentioned in the court narrative of Solomon or prior to the 8th cent. BCE in prophetic texts (Isa 43:24; Jer 6:20; Ezek 27:19). It seems likely that their widespread introduction to Israelite society came in the late monarchy or Persian period as a result of increased commercial activity between Judah and the Neo-Babylonian Empire and subsequently between Yehud and the far-flung mercantile interests of the Persian Empire.

One of the earliest examples of large-scale manufacture of perfumes during the Middle Bronze Age (2000–1850 BCE) is found on Cyprus at the site of Pyrgos and it may be presumed that these products, along with copper ingots and olive oil, were carried to ports throughout the Levant. A sign of just how much energy merchants were willing to expend to transport luxury items is found in the extensive pattern of overland and sea trade routes during the Roman period that extended along the coast of Africa down to Somaliland and Madagascar, across the Indian Ocean to Indonesia, and all along the Persian Gulf and the western coast of India bringing "cinnamon, spice, incense, myrrh, [and] frankincense" to the markets of every Roman city and province (Rev 18:13).

There was a variety of collection methods used to gather these materials, including stripping bark from trees (cinnamon), digging roots dug from the ground (MANDRAKE, nard), and gathering from flowers blossoms (saffron). In the case of frankincense and myrrh, trees were tapped and the "tears" of resin gathered once they dried. Since these items were precious and had to be transported over long distances, they were carefully packaged for transport in bags, alabaster jars (Matt 26:7), or perfume boxes (Isa 3:20). Undoubtedly, the packaging added to the high prices they commanded.

The profession of perfumer (roqqeah רֹקֵחַ) appears in the context of tabernacle/temple worship (Exod 30:25; 37:29; Neh 3:8), where perfumes were used in incense. Female palace servants (1 Sam 8:13) and craftsmen produced personal body products (Eccl 10:1). While some of the temple-based craft was restricted to members of the priestly community (Exod 30:37-38; 1 Chr 9:30), the majority would have been manufactured for the popular and luxury market. Since there was a lucrative market for perfumes among the elite classes throughout the ANE, the competition for creating specific perfumes, such as cyprinum, a fragrance based upon the scent of henna (*Lawsonia inermis*), may have been heated and the secret closely guarded.

It may be that these products are mentioned so rarely and in only a small number of contexts because of the expense involved. In the OT, they appear primarily in cultic situations in Exodus in recipes for anointing oil and sacred incense or in the erotic love poetry in the Song of Solomon where expense may take a back seat to seduction. The NT only speaks of expensive perfume in two very similar stories. The first, in Mark 14:3-5 (compare Luke 7:37-39), describes an unnamed woman who breaks an alabaster jar of nard and anoints Jesus' head with the fragrant ointment. In the other, Jesus' feet are anointed by Mary, the sister of Martha, with nard worth 300 denarii (= worker's pay for half a year; John 11:2; 12:3). In both cases, concern is expressed by the disciples, or by Judas alone in the John narrative, over the "frivolous" use of such an expensive item that could have been sold and the money distributed to the poor. The fact that the narratives are so careful to mention the container and the cost add to our understanding of its rarity among the common people. *See* BALSAM; BDELLIUM; CAMEL'S THORN; GALBANUM; GUM; STACTE.

Bibliography: Athalya Brenner. "Aromatics and Perfumes in the Song of Songs." *JSOT* 25 (1983) 75–81.

VICTOR H. MATTHEWS

PERGA puhr´guh [Πέργη Pergē]. A principal city in the ancient region of PAMPHYLIA in Asia Minor, twice visited by Paul during his first missionary venture. Perga is approximately 9 mi. (14 km) northeast of Antalya, 1 mi. (1.6 km) north of Aksu, and 3 mi. (4.8 km) west of the Cestrus River (now Aksu Çayï in modern Turkey). According to Strabo (*Geogr.* 14.4.2) the city could be approached by the Cestrus, navigable 60 stadia (7 mi., 11.5 km) up from the Mediterranean Sea, as implied also by the text of Acts (13:13-14).

The earliest settlement at Perga existed in the late Chalcolithic and Early Bronze ages on the plateau north of the later Hellenistic-Roman city. The name Perga itself proclaims a pre-Greek city, mentioned in a 13th-cent. BCE Hittite treaty as belonging within the southern kingdom of Tarhuntassa. Greek tradition claims the city was founded by the "miscellaneous throng" of Greek settlers who traversed Asia Minor after the Trojan War, led by Calchas, Mopsus, and Amphilochus (Herodotus, *Hist.* 7.91.1; Strabo, *Geogr.* 14.4.3). In a courtyard near the twin Hellenistic towers in Perga there remain four inscribed bases to statues (now lost) dedicated to the city's "founders," two being Calchas and Mopsus.

Greek influence predominated in Perga from the 7th cent. BCE onward, despite successive Lydian and Persian rule in the 5th cent. The city became a pan-Pamphylian cult center with its sanctuary of Vanassa Preiia (Artemis of Perga), located by Strabo (*Geogr.* 14.4.2) on a high place outside the city, but not yet discovered by modern archaeologists. Alexander the Great was welcomed to Perga in 333 BCE, and the city became the base for his military campaign into Pamphylia, with Pergaean guides leading the army from Phaselis. After Alexander's death, Perga was controlled successively by the Ptolemies and the Seleucids. With the battle of Magnesia (189 BCE), it became part of the Pergamene kingdom; but only four years later, when King Attalus III died, Perga, along with the whole Pergamene kingdom, was bequeathed to Rome. Periods of unrest in the 1st cent. BCE climaxed with the looting of the Temple of Artemis Pergaea by Verres in 78 BCE.

When Paul visited Perga in the 1st cent. CE, the city had not yet reached its zenith. The city flourished in the 2nd cent. under the patronage of Plancia Magna, a member of a wealthy and distinguished Roman family. She served as priestess of Artemis Pergaea and held the highest civic office of *demiurgus.* Several statues of her have been found in the city, as well as nearly a score of inscriptions mentioning her name, and her tomb (now almost totally destroyed) stood outside the later south gate. Her father, M. Plancius Varus, a Roman senator and once proconsul of Bithynia, and her brother, C. Plancius Varus, a Roman consul, had statues near the old Roman gate with inscriptions designating them as two of the four city "founders." During this period the city's theater, stadium, baths, and agora were built. In the 3rd cent. CE, Perga vied with Side for the title of metropolis, and was a bulwark of Roman resistance against Gothic and Persian invasions. Early Byzantine Christianity had a strong presence in Perga, as evidenced by delegates to the councils at Nicea (325 CE) and Ephesus (431 CE), and the remains of two basilicas in the city built in the 5th and 6th cent., respectively. Beginning in the 7th cent. the city suffered from Arab incursions, but resurged as a metropolitan bishopric in the 11th cent. when one of three basilicas on the acropolis was renovated. The Seljuk Turks conquered the region in the 11th cent., and the Ottoman Turks took control in the late 14th cent. CE, at which time (or sometime before) the city appears to have been almost entirely abandoned.

Paul and BARNABAS's initial visit to Perga on the first missionary venture occurred in 45 or 46 CE after a successful mission on the island of Cyprus. The text of

Acts tells us that Paul and his companions sailed from Paphos in Cyprus to Perga in Pamphylia, where John Mark (*see* MARK, JOHN) withdrew from the mission and returned to Jerusalem (Acts 13:13). There is no indication of Paul's preaching in Perga at this time, nor of John Mark's reasons for leaving, though later Paul characterized John Mark as a deserter (Acts 15:36-38). William Ramsay suggested that Paul had an attack of chronic malaria (compare Gal 4:13) and was forced to seek the recuperative highlands of Pisidian Antioch; but John Mark objected to this change of plans. Others have speculated that John Mark had qualms about Paul's intentional mission to Gentiles, fear of the rugged trek over the Taurus Mountains, or homesickness. Paul's second visit to Perga (ca. 47 CE) on the return trip of the first missionary venture included preaching, as well as departure from the port city of Attalia (Acts 14:25-26). Yet there is no solid evidence of an early Pauline church in Pisidia or Pamphylia. *See* PAUL, THE APOSTLE.

Bibliography: F. F. Bruce. *The Acts of the Apostles: The Greek Text with Introduction and Commentary.* 3rd ed. (1990); Clyde E. Fant and Mitchell G. Reddish. *A Guide to Biblical Sites in Greece and Turkey* (2003); William M. Ramsay. *St. Paul the Traveler and Roman Citizen* (2001).

KEVIN L. ANDERSON

PERGAMUM puhr´guh-muhm [Πέργαμος **Pergamos**, Πέργαμον **Pergamon**]. A city in western Asia Minor where one of the seven congregations addressed by Revelation was located (Rev 1:11; 2:12). The city's name means "citadel," since its central structures were built on top of an imposing hill that rose a thousand feet above the valley below. Located about 15 mi. from the Aegean Sea, Pergamum was a major political, cultural, and religious center.

Pergamum became prominent after the death of Alexander the Great in 323 BCE. During power struggles for control of the region, Pergamum's rulers established the city's independence and founded the Attalid Dynasty in the 3rd cent. BCE. The city's welfare was threatened by marauding Celtic tribes, which had come from Gaul, as well as by the neighboring Macedonian and Seleucid kingdoms, whose rulers sought to expand their own territories. By obtaining assistance from the Romans, Pergamum eventually brought much of western Asia Minor under its own control.

The city flourished during the 2nd cent. BCE. The acropolis was encircled with a wall and palaces were built. Revenue came from agriculture and manufactured goods, such as pottery and textiles. When Egyptian papyrus became difficult to obtain, the city began large-scale production of **membrana Pergamēna** (μέμβρανα Περγαμηνά), the writing material made from leather that became known as PARCHMENT. This made possible the development of a renowned library, second only to that of Alexandria in Egypt. Building projects included aqueducts, temples, gymnasiums, markets, and a theater that could accommodate 10,000 spectators. Pergamum's long-standing cooperation with Rome led the last of its rulers to bequeath the kingdom to the Romans in his will, thereby averting a power struggle after his death in 133 BCE. Under Roman rule the kingdom of Pergamum became the province of Asia. Burdensome tax policies led many to support the military campaigns that Mithridates VI of Pontus waged against Roman rule, and in 88 BCE the Roman residents of Pergamum were massacred. When the Romans regained control, Pergamum lost its status as a free city. Later, Roman administrators trying to prevent wealth from leaving the region confiscated funds that the Jewish community at Pergamum had planned to send to Jerusalem for the support of the Temple. The reign of Augustus brought increasing stability and prosperity to Asia, and in 29 BCE the province was given permission to build a temple honoring Rome and Augustus at Pergamum. Choosing Pergamum as the location recognized the city's historic importance as the center of Asia. In the 1st cent. CE other cities would seek similar honors, with Smyrna and Ephesus receiving permission to build provincial temples to Tiberius and the Flavian emperors, respectively. Under the Romans, Pergamum was one of the regional centers where court cases were heard. In the 1st cent. CE, increasing numbers of Pergamenes gained Roman citizenship. One of these, C. Aulus Julius Quadratus, was admitted to the Roman senate in the 70s CE, returning to serve as governor of Asia in the early 2nd cent.

Athena was Pergamum's patron goddess, revered as the bringer of victories. Her temple, featuring fine colonnades and statuary celebrating the defeat of the Celts, stood on the acropolis next to the library. Nearby was the great altar with its large marble staircase and side panels depicting the triumph of the Olympian gods over the giants, who represented the forces of chaos. Demeter, Hera, and Dionysus were among the other deities honored with sanctuaries.

Asclepius, the god of healing, was venerated at Pergamum from the 4th cent. BCE onward. Because of its renown, the Asclepian sanctuary attracted many visitors seeking help for various ailments through physical treatments and religious rites. In the late 1st cent. CE miraculous cures were reported, enhancing interest in the cult. During the 2nd cent. the sanctuary was renovated and expanded. The most famous member of the medical staff was Galen, who became court physician to the emperor Marcus Aurelius. The best-known patient was Aelius Aristides, a leading orator of the period (*see* MEDICINE AND HEALING, GODS OF).

The imperial cult centered on the temple built for Rome and Augustus. Many cities had local cults to the emperor, but the temple in Pergamum served the entire province. Coins picture the temple housing a statue of

Augustus in military garb with a spear in his right hand. Some also show the goddess Roma placing a victory crown on the emperor's head. Games were held in honor of the emperor, and the cities of Asia sent vocal groups to Pergamum to sing praises to the emperor and his household on imperial birthdays and other holidays.

A Christian congregation was established at Pergamum by the last third of the 1st cent. CE. In Rev 2:12-17 this church is commended for its faith, which remained unwavering even when a Christian named Antipas was killed in the city, either by the authorities or by mob action. The rest of the Christian community seems to have been left alone. Revelation evidently calls Pergamum "Satan's throne" (**ho thronos tou Satana** ὁ θρόνος τοῦ Σατανᾶ) because it was the only one of the seven cities where a Christian had been put to death (Rev 2:13). It is less likely that Satan's throne refers to a structure like the city's great altar or that it is a metaphor for the imperial cult, since the cult also flourished in other cities.

The principal issue facing the congregation was whether it was acceptable to eat what had been offered to idols (Rev 2:14-15; compare 1 Cor 8:1-13). Meat from sacrifices to Greco-Roman deities was often available at public festivals, at private meals in a temple or hall where religious rites were observed, and in the public market. Someone nicknamed Balaam, after a biblical figure associated with IDOLATRY (Num 31:16), taught that it was acceptable to eat such food. A group known as the Nicolaitans shared this view (Rev 2:14-15). Revelation, however, warns that this practice shows unfaithfulness to God. *See* REVELATION, BOOK OF.

Bibliography: Helmut Koester, ed. *Pergamon: Citadel of the Gods* (1998).

CRAIG R. KOESTER

PERICOPE puh-rik´uh-pee [περικοπή pericopē]. From **perikoptō** (περικόπτω, "to cut around"), *pericope* ("selection") is a rhetorical term for a portion of a text set apart for study or to be read in worship, e.g., a passage from the Psalms, a prophetic oracle, part of a narrative, a thought-unit from an epistle, or a parable. *See* EXEGESIS; LECTIONARY.

MARIANNE BLICKENSTAFF

PERIDA. *See* PERUDA.

PERIODS, HISTORICAL. Historical periods categorize eras, usually on the basis of the political and/or cultural situation. Relating to biblical times, periods are often named after the outside power controlling Israel. Because historical periods are interpretive, they can overlap. The SECOND TEMPLE PERIOD, for instance, comprises the Persian, Hellenistic, and Roman periods. Historical periods are distinct from archaeological periods, which are determined by developments in technology or settlement patterns. *See* ARCHAEOLOGY; HELLENISTIC PERIOD; PERSIAN PERIOD; ROMAN PERIOD.

KEVIN A. WILSON

PERISH [אָבַד ʾavadh; ἀπόλλυμι **apollymi**]. The English term *perish* refers to death or loss, often as the end of a process of deterioration, decay, or disease.

In the OT, the NRSV renders several Hebrew terms with *perish*, even though they may not convey the connotations of deterioration and loss. Examples include **karath** (כָּרַת) niph., "to be cut off" (Gen 41:36); **nafal** (נָפַל), "to fall" (Exod 19:21); **gawaʿ** (גָּוַע), "to expire" (Num 17:12-13 [Heb. 17:27-28]); **safah** (סָפָה) niph., "to be swept away" (1 Sam 26:10); **ʿavar** (עָבַר), "to pass [away]" (Job 36:12); **kalah** (כָּלָה), "to come to an end" (Isa 31:3); **damah** (דָּמָה) niph., "to cease" (Ps 49:12 [Heb. 49:13]); **damam** (דָּמַם), "to be silent" (Jer 8:14); and **shamem** (שָׁמֵם), "to be appalled" (Lam 4:5). The Hebrew word **ʾavadh**, on the other hand, coincides quite closely with its English counterpart. Comparative Semitic linguistics suggests that the basic meaning of the root is "to be lost, wander about, runaway" (compare Deut 26:5; 1 Sam 9:3, 20). More indicative of the theological dynamics of the term are the contexts in which it clusters: the consequences of doing evil (e.g., Pss 37:20; 68:2; Prov 11:10; 19:9) and of disloyalty to God or being an enemy of God (often involving a process of deterioration caused by natural phenomena or human enemies; e.g., Lev 26:38; Deut 8:19-20; Isa 31:3; Jer 8:14; Lam 4:5; Hos 10:7; Amos 1:8).

In the NT, circumstances closely parallel those in the OT. Apart from the relatively rare adjectives **phthartos** (φθαρτός, "perishable"; 1 Cor 9:25; 15:53-54; 1 Pet 1:18, 23, in reference to the decay of the body) and **aphtharsia** (ἀφθαρσία, "imperishable, not subject to decay"; 1 Cor 15:42, 50, 53-54; Eph 6:24), the NT regularly employs the term **apollymi** to denote "to lose" (participle "lost," e.g., sheep, son, life) and approximately forty times to denote incurring damage (e.g., wineskins, Mark 2:22; food, John 6:27; a weak person, 1 Cor 8:11) or being lost (e.g., hair of the head, Luke 21:18; Acts 27:34), or to emphasize the process of decay or loss (through a force of nature, Mark 4:38 par.; from hunger, Luke 15:17; by serpents, 1 Cor 10:9-10; through age, Heb 1:11). In several instances, NT usage of **apollymi** involves the concept of "life lost" or of "perishing" in reference to the eternal death that is the opposite of life in Christ (e.g., Luke 13:3-5; John 3:16; Rom 2:12). The metaphor of sheep lost from the good shepherd's fold illustrates this concept in John 17:12. *See* CORRUPTION; CUT OFF, TO; DAY OF THE LORD; DEATH, NT; DEATH, OT; FLESH IN THE NT; LOSE, LOST; RESURRECTION, NT; SIN, SINNERS.

Bibliography: J. Chinitz. "Death in the Bible." *JQR* 32 (2004) 98–103.

MARK E. BIDDLE

PERIZZITES per'i-z*ī*t [פְּרִזִּי perizzi]. A group of pre-Israelite people who lived in Canaan. They are always mentioned in conjunction with other groups. Perizzites are included in twenty-one of the twenty-seven lists of pre-Israelite people. In the common six-name lists, the Perizzites are usually found in the fourth position (Exod 3:8; 33:2; Deut 20:17; Josh 9:1; Judg 3:5). Since Perizzites are found in two-name lists with the Canaanites (Gen 13:7; 34:30), these two terms could refer to larger groupings of pre-Israelite peoples (see CANAAN, CANAANITES). The term *Perizzites* might be linked to **perazi** (פְּרָזִי, "resident of the open country") and **perazoth** (פְּרָזוֹת, "open country"). The term *Canaanites* might refer to people living in fortified cities, while the Perizzites live in unwalled towns. In the Amarna Letters (EA 27:89, 93; 28:12), a person named Pirizzi or Pirissi was sent as an emissary from Tushratta, king of Mitanni, to Amenhotep IV (Akhenaten). If this is a reference to the Perizzites, it might suggest a Hurrian connection for this group of people.

The Canaanites and the Perizzites were living in the land at the time of Abram (Gen 13:7) and Jacob (Gen 34:30). In Exod 3:8, the Lord promises Moses that he will bring the Israelites out of bondage in Egypt to the land belonging to the Canaanites, HITTITES, AMORITES, Perizzites, HIVITES, and Jebusites (*see* JEBUS, JEBUSITES). The Lord promises to blot out (Exod 23:23), drive out (Exod 33:2; Josh 3:10), or clear away (Deut 7:1) groups of people living in the land, including the Perizzites. The Israelites are not to worship the gods of the former inhabitants or follow their practices, but instead they are to destroy their religious artifacts. They are not to make covenants with these groups or intermarry with them (Exod 34:11-16). Sometimes the Israelites are told that they must defeat and destroy (Deut 7:1-2) or annihilate them (Deut 20:17).

Brief reports are made about pre-Israelite groups fighting with Joshua (Josh 9:1-2; 11:1-5). Such reports give little information about the nature of the specific groups. When the people of the tribe of Joseph complain that they do not have enough land, Joshua tells them to clear ground in the land of the Perizzites and the REPHAIM (Josh 17:15). There is a report of Judah defeating the Canaanites and Perizzites (Judg 1:4-5). Some texts suggest that the Perizzites lived in the hill country (e.g., Josh 11:3).

The Perizzites and other pre-Israelite groups were not exterminated. They continued to live in the midst of the Israelites, who intermarried with them and worshiped their gods (Judg 3:5). During monarchic times these groups were made slaves by Solomon (1 Kgs 9:20-21). In the postexilic period, Ezra learned that the Israelites had not separated from the people living in the land, including the Perizzites, but had intermarried with them (Ezra 9:1).

Peaceful coexistence with people of the land such as the Perizzites is indicated in the story of Abram (Gen 13:7), and Jacob desires keeping peace with them (Gen 34:30). However, other biblical writers view these groups as enemies (Josh 3:10; 9:1; 11:3; 12:8; 14:11; 17:15) and describe them negatively because they worship other gods (e.g., Exod 34:13-15). The assumption is that if the Israelites intermarry with them and make covenants with them, they will not remain faithful to the LORD (Exod 34:15-16; Ezra 9:1-15). *See* NATIONS.

Bibliography: Nadav Na'aman. "Canaanites and Perizzites." *BN* 45 (1988) 42–47.

STEPHEN A. REED

PERSECUTION. Persecution of God's people has occurred throughout history—as Jesus noted in speaking of "the blood of all the prophets" and "the blood of Abel to the blood of Zechariah" (Luke 11:50-51). The Israelites often faced adversaries (Isa 14:4-6; 29:20-21; Jer 11:19; 18:18; Pss 37:32; 38:20; 42:3, 10; 74:7-8) and appealed to God to judge and punish persecutors (Deut 30:7; Ps 119:84). Job accused his friends of acting as his persecutors (Job 19:22); even God, he thought, was persecuting him (Job 30:21). The psalmist appealed for divine intervention directed against enemies who "pursued the poor and needy" (Ps 109:16; compare Ps 119:157, 161).

Three major times of persecution occur in the OT: the exodus (Exod 1:9-10; 2:23-24), the days of the judges (Judg 2:11-16), and the events leading up to the exile, including the lives of prophets. Jeremiah, for instance, knew great suffering and persecution. He was put in the stocks (Jer 20:2), imprisoned (32:2-3; 37:15), and cast into a cistern (38:6). Israel's enemies were seen as combining forces against them, bringing "devastation and destruction" (Lam 3:46-48). Persecution was a hard fact of life to be faced bravely (Pss 94:5; 119:95, 110).

The book of Esther relates the story of two audacious Jews, Mordecai and Queen Esther, who upset the genocidal plans of Haman, "the enemy of the Jews" (Esth 3:1-15). The events described are placed during the reign of Ahasuerus (also called Xerxes, 486–465 BCE), king of the Persian Empire. The book is set against a hostile background and points to the inescapable nature of retributive justice (4:14), and the need for the persecuted to act boldly and astutely to ensure that justice prevails.

In the Maccabean era, intense Seleucid persecution erupted when ANTIOCHUS IV Ephiphanes (175–164 BCE) attempted to impose a program of enforced Hellenization. All the rites of the Jewish faith were ruthlessly attacked. Judas Maccabeus and his brothers put up a heroic resistance marked by terrible suffering. This persecution is reflected in the book of Daniel and culminated in the ABOMINATION OF DESOLATION—the sacrilegious offering of a pig on the altar of the Temple in Jerusalem (Dan 9:27; 11:31; 12:11). The history of the conflict is recorded in 1 Maccabees, and the

Maccabean martyrdoms are graphically portrayed in 2 Maccabees 6–7. *See* MACCABEES, MACCABEAN REVOLT.

The book of Judith, probably written during the Hasmonean period (164–63 BCE), is an apocryphal story of surprising reversals. Judith, a Jewish widow, beguiles and outwits Holofernes, the powerful leader of the Assyrian army, and routs his army by the little Israelite town of Bethulia. She praises God in a thanksgiving psalm that he "sets up his camp among his people; he delivered me from the hands of my pursuers" (Jdt 16:2). Judith raises some ethical questions as she delivers her people through lying, deception, and murder.

The harsh treatment experienced by God's people continued into NT times, both for Jesus and the early church. Jesus had warned his followers to expect persecution (Matt 23:34-37; Luke 11:49-51; John 16:2). He himself had suffered beating, mocking, and crucifixion, as all four Gospels show. His disciples were to expect similar treatment from their enemies (Matt 24:9-14; Mark 13:9-13; Luke 21:12-19). Still, hard times could be met confidently; Jesus promised the help of the Holy Spirit to empower them in dangerous situations (Mark 13:9-11; Luke 12:11-12; 21:15; Acts 1:8; 2:4; 4:8-13; 6:10; 7:55) and an advocate to comfort them (John 14:15-17; *see* PARACLETE).

The predicted persecution came upon the early church (Acts 5:17-42; 7:57-58; 8:1; 11:19; 14:19; 16:19-24). For a time, Saul of Tarsus was one of the most aggressive opponents of Christianity (Acts 8:3; 1 Cor 15:9; Gal 1:23). Then on the Damascus road he met the one he had so vigorously opposed (Acts 9:1-19*a*; 22:4-16; 26:9-18; 1 Cor 9:1; 15:8; Gal 1:16). Paul admitted that he had previously acted as a persecutor of the followers of the Way (Gal 1:13; Phil 3:6; compare 1 Tim 1:13).

Herod Agrippa I, grandson of Herod the Great (10 BCE–44 CE), imprisoned Peter and put James, John's brother, to death (Acts 12:1-4). Stephen, one of the serving seven (Acts 6:1-6), was martyred by stoning and prayed for his persecutors as he died (Acts 7:59-60; compare Luke 23:34). Persecution was a fact of life to be faced by the early Christians: "All who want to live a godly life in Christ Jesus will be persecuted" (2 Tim 3:12).

Jesus had prepared his followers for difficult times ahead when they might be required to present their faith in hostile circumstances and suffer persecution (Matt 10:17-23; Luke 21:12-15). After Pentecost, the apostles had openly announced their message as eyewitnesses of the life, death, and resurrection of their Lord (Acts 1:21-22; 3:15; 4:13, 33; 5:29-32; 10:36-43; 1 Pet 5:1; 1 John 1:1-3). Other Christian leaders, like Stephen and Philip, joined them and boldly declared the good news (Acts 6:8-10; 8:4-40; 9:27). Every Christian was called to share the faith and defend it, if the occasion arose, providing a rationale for Christian convictions (Col 4:6; 2 Tim 2:24-25; 1 Pet 3:15).

Paul's life-changing encounter entirely transformed his perspective (2 Cor 5:16-21). Now, as a convinced disciple of the Nazarene, he instructed believers to bless those who persecuted them (Rom 12:14; 1 Cor 4:12-13), following the teaching of his master (Matt 5:44; Luke 6:27-28, 35). He confidently affirmed, "I can do all things through him who strengthens me" (Phil 4:13). He insisted that the divine resources he claimed for himself were available to all sincere Christians, whatever the pressure or difficulty that might beset them (Rom 8:31-39). He often cited his personal experiences of persecution to encourage other believers facing comparable trials (2 Cor 1:5-7; 4:8-12; 12:10). The Thessalonians became examples of steadfastness under persecution (2 Thess 1:4); the author of 2 Thessalonians reminds them that God would use this persecution to show his justice and "to make you worthy of the kingdom of God, for which you are also suffering" (2 Thess 1:5). Paul viewed suffering as one of the ways God was working to accomplish his purpose.

First Peter notes Christ's own suffering, seeking to fortify Christians who were confronted with social pressure and subtle persecution (1 Pet 2:18-25; 3:13-18; 4:1-2, 12-19). In a similar way the letter to the Hebrews also offers encouragement to hard-pressed believers faced with opposition by recalling the supreme example of Jesus as well as other faithful servants of God in the past (Heb 11:4-40; 12:1-4).

The book of Revelation was directed to Christians who might be called upon to undergo suffering and even martyrdom for their faith (Rev 2:10; 6:9-11; 13:7; 17:6). If the book was written, as many scholars suggest, in the reign of Domitian (81–96 CE), there was apparently no general persecution underway. Nevertheless, the Roman Empire was becoming increasingly threatening to Christians. Antipas had already been martyred for his loyal Christian testimony (Rev 2:13). The seer of Patmos declared that Jesus was the supreme model, "the faithful and true witness" (Rev 1:5; 3:14), who had nobly suffered and died. Future suffering for his followers was a definite possibility, and they were summoned to be prepared. Believers shared in "the suffering" (**thlipsis** θλῖψις) and were called to "patient endurance" (**hypomonē** ὑπομονή; Rev 1:9; 2:2, 3, 19; 3:10; 13:10; 14:12). More suffering might be expected (Rev 2:9, 10), but God was on the "throne" (a key phrase in Revelation [3:21; 5:13; 7:10]), and his victory would ultimately ensure their final triumph (Rev 19:1-10; 21:1-8).

For roughly 200 years, from the time of Nero to the Decian persecutions of 250 CE, persecutions were mainly local and occasional, including those under the emperors Hadrian (117–38) and Marcus Aurelius (176–80). Christianity in the early 2nd cent. was technically illegal, but the laws against Christians were not strictly enforced—a point made clear in the correspondence between Pliny the Younger and the emperor Trajan (111–12). Later persecutions occurred under

Gallus (251–53), Valerian (257–60), and particularly Diocletian (303). Persecution stopped in 306, but after Constantine became the sole emperor in 323, Christians moved beyond tolerance into places of power and prominence in the Roman Empire.

Persecution is solemnly faced in the Bible, and the righteous may expect it (Job 12:4; Prov 29:10; Isa 51:12-13; Amos 5:10-12; Hab 1:13; Matt 5:10-12; John 15:20; Acts 14:22; 2 Tim 1:12; 1 Pet 4:12-14; Rev 16:5-7). It is seen as a vehicle whereby the kingdom of God is advanced (Acts 5:41; Rom 8:17-18; Phil 1:29; Rev 5:9-10). If the people of God act faithfully, there is nothing to fear, for God is sovereign, and his purpose will eventually triumph (Pss 27:1; 118:6; 2 Cor 2:14; Heb 13:6). Understood from the perspective of faith, persecution could be viewed as a source of blessing to those who accepted it in the right spirit, "knowing that suffering produces endurance, and endurance produces character, and character produces hope, and hope does not disappoint us" (Rom 5:3-5; compare 2 Cor 12:7-10). *See* ANTI-JUDAISM; ANTI-SEMITISM; CHRISTIAN-JEWISH RELATIONS; CHRISTIANS, PERSECUTION OF; HOLOCAUST AND BIBLICAL INTERPRETATION; JEWS, PERSECUTION OF; MARTYR; SUFFERING AND EVIL.

Bibliography: Daniel Boyarin. *Dying for God: Martyrdom and the Making of Christianity and Judaism* (1999); Elizabeth Castelli. *Martyrdom and Memory: Early Christian Culture Making* (2004); Craig A. Evans and Donald Hagner, eds. *Anti-Semitism and Early Christianity: Issues of Polemic and Faith* (1993); W. H. C. Frend. *Martyrdom and Persecution in the Early Church* (2004); Shmuel Shepkaru. *Jewish Martyrs in the Pagan and Christian Worlds* (2005); Geoffrey de Ste. Croix. *Christian Persecution, Martyrdom, and Orthodoxy* (2006); J. W. Van Henten. *The Maccabean Martyrs as Saviors of the Jewish People: A Study of 2 and 4 Maccabees* (1997).

ALLISON A. TRITES

PERSEPOLIS puhr-sep´uh-lis [Περσέπολις Persepolis]. One of the five royal capitals of the Persian Achaemenid Empire, alongside Babylon, Susa, Ecbatana (Hamadan), and Pasargadae. It is located in southwest Persia/Iran, in the province of Fars, near the river Pulwar, about 33 mi. (ca. 52 km) northeast of the modern city of Shiraz.

Persepolis derives from the Gk. Persepolis, which combines Persai (Πέρσαι, "Persians") and polis (πόλις, "city"). In fact, this is a Greek translation of the ancient Persian name *Parsa*, i.e., "The City of Persians." There are typological parallels of such names in biblical and ANE historical writings, e.g., pre-Davidic Jerusalem called (The City of) Jebus (yevus יְבוּס), after its ethnic inhabitances the Jebusites (1 Chr 11:5; *see* JEBUS, JEBUSITES); in the Babylonian Chronicles the city name al ia-a-hu-du and the name ʿir yehudhah (עִיר יְהוּדָה) in 2 Chr 25:28 both mean "The City of Judah." Today Persepolis is Takht-i Jamshid, i.e., "the Throne of Jamshid" (an Iranian mythological figure).

Persepolis was founded by Darius I, the Great (521–485 BCE), ca. 518 BCE, and gradually developed by his successors, particularly Xerxes I (biblical AHASUERUS; 485–465 BCE) and by ARTAXERXES I (Longimanus; 465–425/4 BCE). The site incorporates a large terrace, where Darius I erected the magnificent palace complex, Apadana, and the Throne Hall.

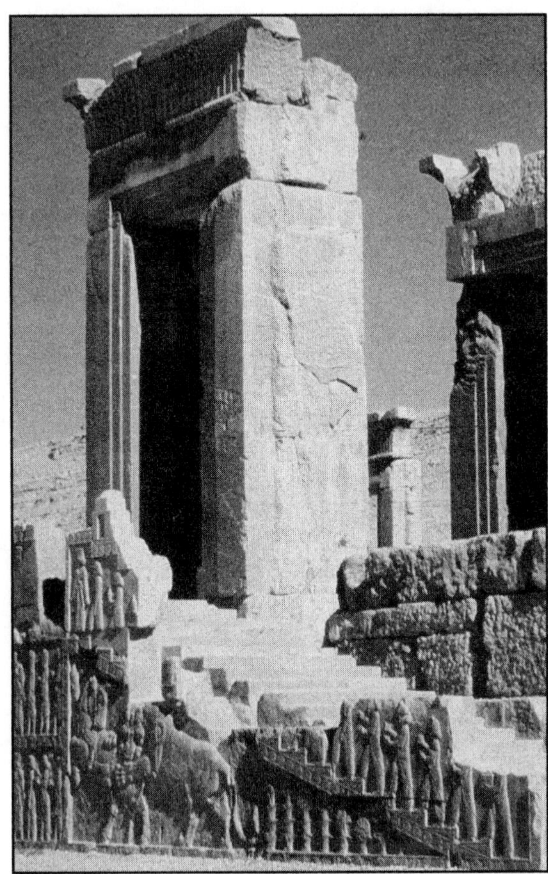

Alinari/Art Resource, NY

Figure 1: View of the entranceway staircase and the door of the Palace of Darius the Great in Persepolis. The reliefs from the staircase appear in the foreground, showing Persian dignitaries and a lion fighting with a bull. Persepolis, Iran.

Xerxes I completed his father's projects and built the Gate of All Nations and the Harem. The building area also includes the imperial treasury, military quarters, royal stables, and chariot places.

The core features of the city's architecture are numerous dark gray stone columns (topped with sculptures of lions, eagles, and double-headed bulls), the decorated walls (with plants, bulls, and lions), bas-reliefs (esp. on the stairways of the Apadana), and sculptures.

Its monumental ruins and artifacts testify to its being an extremely wealthy and glorious imperial center. According to Diodorus Siculus Persepolis was the richest city in existence (*Bibliotheke* 17.70.2). Persepolis has also a very large archive, one of the best documented in the Achaemenid Empire (over 2,100 texts already published). Since the political, economical, and administrative capitals of the empire were SUSA, Babylon, and ECBATANA, presumably Persepolis was a recreational site.

Persepolis was captured, looted, and partially ruined by Alexander the Great (330 BCE; Diodorus Siculus, *Bibliotheke* 17.70.1). Second Maccabees 9:2 recounts that ANTIOCHUS IV Epiphanes (175–164 BCE) attempted to control Persepolis and plunder its temples, but failed (ca. 164 BCE). However, 1 Maccabees claims Antiochus IV failed to plunder the rich city Elymais (biblical Elam) in Persia (1 Macc 6:1-4).

Bibliography: L. Allen. *The Persian Empire* (2005); P. Briant. *From Cyrus to Alexander: A History of the Persian Empire* (2002); J. Boardman, N. G. L. Hammond, D. M. Lewis, and M. Ostwald, eds. *The Cambridge Ancient History: Volume IV—Persia, Greece and Western Mediterranean* (1988); M. A. Dandamaev. *A Political History of the Achaemenid Empire* (1989); R. N. Frye. *The Heritage of Persia* (1962); I. Kalimi. *Reshaping of Ancient Israelite History in Chronicles* (2005); A. Sami. *Persepolis* (1958).

ISAAC KALIMI

PERSEUS puhr′see-uhs [Περσεύς Perseus]. A king of MACEDONIA and son of Philip V who ruled from 179 to 168 BCE. The author of 1 Maccabees mentions Perseus as one of the rulers "crushed in battle and conquered" by the Roman army during the Macedonian wars (1 Macc 8:5). Livy (*History of Rome* 44.40–42) and Plutarch (*Aem.* 19.4–6) both describe Perseus' defeat by the Romans at the battle of Pydna in 168 BCE, which effectively brought an end to the Macedonian kingdom and solidified Roman control of the region.

JESSICA TINKLENBERG DEVEGA

PERSEVERANCE. *See* ENDURANCE; STEADFASTNESS.

PERSIA, HISTORY AND RELIGION OF puhr′zhuh [פָּרַס paras; Περσίς Persis]. The Persians were Iranian tribes who developed into a major empire. Their religion is commonly referred to as Zoroastrianism, after Zoroaster, the Greek form of ZARATHUSTRA, or as Mazdaism (*see* AHURA MAZDA). This religion took shape among the Iranian tribes in Central Asia, and its oldest form is known from the Avesta sacred texts.

A. Historical Survey

Persia and *Persian* are names assigned by the Greek historians to certain ancient Iranian tribes. In modern usage, *Persia* refers to the political entity also called Iran, but, originally, the Persians were the Iranian inhabitants of the region of Parsa (later Pars), Greek Persis, modern Fars, in southwestern Iran near modern Shiraz, where the archaeological sites of PERSEPOLIS and Pasargadae are located. Other Iranian tribes known in antiquity are the Medes, Parthians, Sogdians, and SCYTHIANS (*see* MEDES, MEDIA; PARTHIA, PARTHIANS). Only the Persians are known from their own inscriptions (*see* PERSIAN, OLD).

The Iranians are defined by the languages they spoke, the Iranian subgroup of the Indo-Iranian group of languages, itself a branch of the Indo-European language family. The as-yet-undifferentiated proto-Indo-Iranians presumably inhabited the area of the modern Central Asian republics. From there, the Indians (or Indo-Aryans) may have started moving south into the subcontinent early in the 2nd millennium BCE, while the Iranian tribes may not have begun moving onto the Iranian Plateau until the end of the 2nd millennium BCE.

The AVESTA contains texts that were orally composed in Old Iranian, ca. 1500–500 BCE. They are hymns to deities and contain no narratives, mythical or otherwise. There are no historical references, but several lists of countries show that the texts originate in the area of Central Asia and Afghanistan. Deducing the historical-social context is a hopeless task, since it cannot be determined to what extent terminology denoting social-political structures reflects contemporary realities or is simply traditional.

We first hear of Persians (parsua) and Medes (matai) in the Assyrian annals from the 9th–7th cent. BCE as peoples encountered along the Zagros Mountains in western Iran. In Gen 10:2-3, MADAI (similar to matai) is listed as the son of Japheth and Ashkenaz as the son of Gomer son of Japheth. According to Herodotus, the first organized Iranian state was that of the Medes, founded by a legendary Deioces ca. 700 BCE, who passed it on to his son Phraortes (Herodotus, *Hist.* 1.96). The third Median king, Cyaxares, is known as the conqueror of Assur and Nineveh, while the last, Astyages, was overthrown by Cyrus (Kurush) II the Great in 550 BCE.

Before the arrival of the Persians in the 6th cent. BCE, Persia was part of the Elamite kingdom (*see* ELAM, ELAMITES), whose two capitals were Susa in the west and Anshan, near Persepolis, in the east. In his famous inscription on a clay cylinder (called the "Cyrus Cylinder") Cyrus assigned the Elamite title of king of Anshan to his ancestors, calling himself "king

Erich Lessing /Art Resource, NY

Figure 1: Cyrus Cylinder, British Museum, London, Great Britain

of Babylon, king of Sumer and Akkad, king of the four quarters, son of Cambyses the great king, king of Anshan, grandson of Cyrus the great king, king of Anshan, descendant of Teispes, the great king, king of Anshan" (*ANET,* 316). The origin of Cyrus and his three ancestors is quite obscure, however, since their names are both un-Iranian and un-Elamite.

Cyrus pursued an expansionist policy, adding numerous Iranian and non-Iranian territories in the west and northeast to his empire. In 539 BCE he took Babylon, and within four years a Babylonian-Transeuphratan satrapy had been established. About Cyrus' relationship with Judah and Jerusalem, our only source is the OT, where Cyrus is praised as a victorious conqueror, but the details of the conquest are unknown. According to Ezra, Cyrus was divinely inspired to rebuild the Temple and ordered all those in exile to come to Jerusalem and help in the building, notably those in Babylon (Ezra 1–2), and, under Darius, the original decree was allegedly found in Ecbatana (6:2-12). Further details about the government of Judah are also scarce, but Cyrus may have made it a province and appointed a Jew as governor, perhaps Sheshbazzar, who figures in this account.

The rebuilding of the Temple agrees with Cyrus' actions in Babylon according to the Akkadian inscription on the Cyrus Cylinder, a propaganda document composed by the priests of Marduk after Neo-Assyrian models, which provides no historically reliable details about the conquests after Babylon, nor does it portray Cyrus as a "human rights" champion (the paragraph adduced in evidence was added to the text of the Cylinder probably in the 1960s/70s as part of the Shah of Iran's propaganda). In this document, Cyrus relates how the people of Sumer and Akkad prayed to Marduk to deliver them from the evil king NABONIDUS, how Marduk chose Cyrus, a just ruler, king of Anshan, to help them, and how Cyrus entered Babylon peacefully. Thus Marduk saved the city, and Cyrus returned the divine statues that Nabonidus had removed and performed other pious actions (*ANET,* 315–16).

Cyrus' son CAMBYSES II (530–522 BCE) marched against Egypt in 525 BCE, where he added the regions to the west and south of Egypt to the empire and remained until he was apprised of a plot to dethrone him in Persia. On his way back to deal with the plot, however, he unexpectedly died. Cambyses' reign is known chiefly from Herodotus (*Hist.* 3.1–60), who depicts him as an increasingly demented person who committed crimes against temples and priests and even Persians. Our only other source is the local dignitary Udjahorresnet, who depicts Cambyses as having restored order in Egypt much in the same way Cyrus is depicted in the Cyrus Cylinder (Udjahorresnet inscription, lines 19–25; Tulli).

Cambyses' death provided the opportunity for the seven most important Persian families, who were clearly Iranian, to set one of their own on the throne. This was DARIUS, who killed an imposter king and proclaimed himself Ahura Mazda's chosen one. He claimed common descent with Cyrus from an ancestor Achaemenes, presenting himself as the true heir to the throne. In the course of two years, Darius brought all the rebellious provinces under control and added several new ones, and was stopped only in Greece. The Achaemenid Empire lasted for 200 years and was toppled only by Alexander in 330 BCE. Darius established his two capitals at Susa and Persepolis, the latter being the religious center of the empire and where the king celebrated the New Year, when his subjects came to his court bringing gifts.

Among the later Achaemenids were Darius' son Xerxes and Artaxerxes II, whose brother Cyrus the

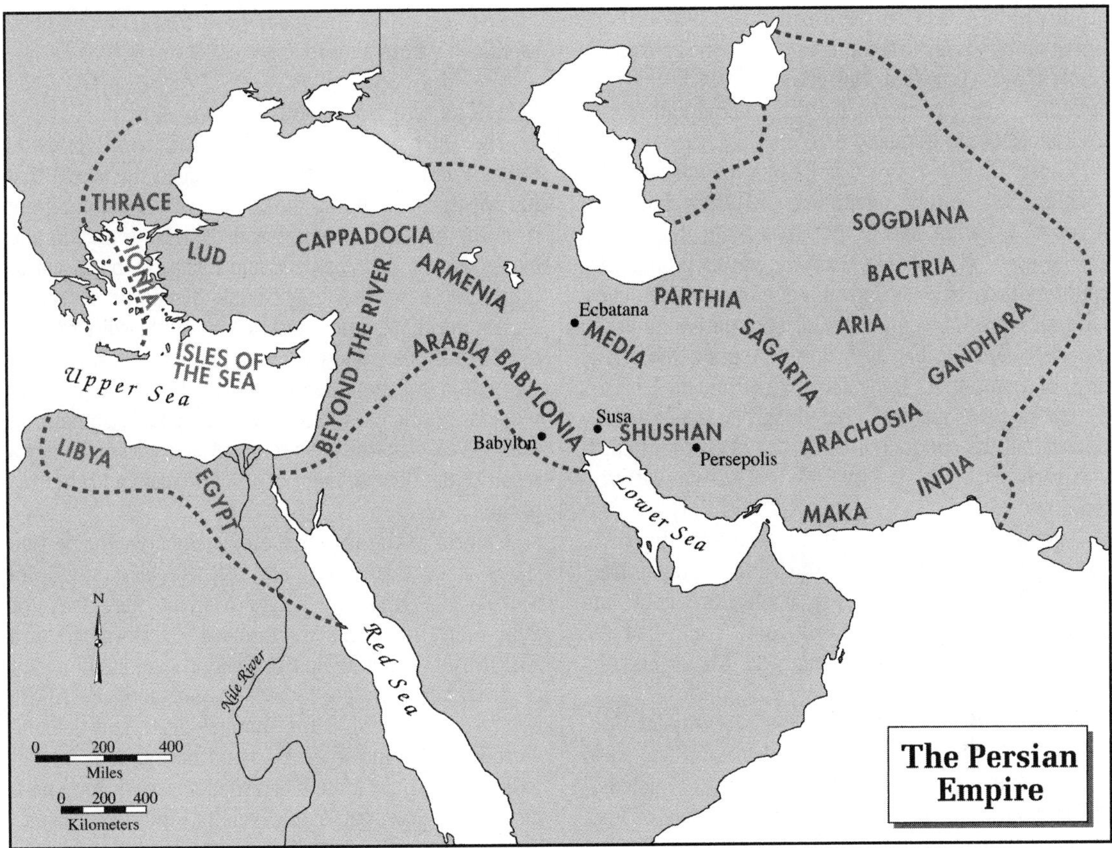

Figure 2: The Persian Empire

Younger rebelled and enlisted mercenaries from Greece, among them Xenophon. Which of the two names underlies the biblical AHASUERUS is not known (Ezra 4:6; Esth 1:1).

We have little information about the Achaemenid government of Judah other than what is in the OT. According to Ezra (7:25-26), who was sent by Artaxerxes I (465–424 BCE) on a mission to Jerusalem in 458 BCE, the indigenous laws (using the Persian word) were approved by the king. Nehemiah, who was sent in 445 as governor, tells us that the previous governors had levied tribute (5:4) and a personal tax (5:14-18). These had caused the people great distress, which Nehemiah was sent to alleviate.

After Alexander's death, Seleucus, one of his twelve generals, became king of Iran. His Hellenized dynasty was short-lived and was toppled by a Parthian named Arsaces (Arshak). The Parthian or Arsacid Dynasty, comprising names such as Mithridates (*see* MITHREDATH), Vologases, and Artabanus, was to last for half a millennium and was Rome's main competitor on its eastern frontier.

The last Parthian king, Artabanus IV, was overthrown in 224 CE by Ardashahr (Ardashir), the son of Pabag (Papak), a local king in Pars. Calling himself a descendant of Sasan and claiming descent from the by-then-legendary Darius, he founded the Sasanian (Sasanid) Dynasty, which came to an end in 650 CE with the Arab conquest and Islamization of Iran. Like their Achaemenid ancestors, the Sasanian kings extended their empire to the east and northeast, while fending off Roman attacks in the west. Ardashir's son Shahpur I defeated three Roman emperors in succession and annexed large territories of the eastern Roman Empire, including, after the battle with Valerian, Judea.

The Achaemenids, Parthians, and Sasanians referred to themselves as "king of Iranians," sometimes with the addition "of non-Iranians." The Sasanian expression **eran shahr** ("realm of the Iranians") gave rise to the modern name of Iran.

Under Ardashir and Shahpur I, MANI, calling himself the Apostle of Jesus Christ, founded his syncretistic gnostic religion, which quickly spread in and around Iran, but, under Shahpur's son and successor Varahran I and II, the high priest Kerdir rose to prominence, who is credited in the Manichean texts with having caused Mani's capture and execution. Kerdir accompanied Shahpur on his campaigns and, in his inscriptions, tells us how he placed Mazdaism on a firm basis throughout the empire, while "striking down" Jews, Shamans (Buddhists), Bramins (Hindus), Nazoreans, Christians, Maktags (Baptists?), and Zandigs (Manicheans).

Under Shahpur I's great-grandson, Shahpur II (309–79 CE), persecution of Christians intensified, as reported especially in Syriac sources, but only thirty years after his death, in 410 CE, under Yazdgerd I (399–420 CE), Christianity was legalized and a synod of the "Nestorian Church" was convened. Nestorianism was officially tolerated, and its leader bore the title of **eran katholikos**, Catholicos of the Iranians.

Khusro II (591–628 CE) is known for his extensive conquest of western territories, including Syria and Anatolia, Palestine, and Egypt. His sacking of Jerusalem and removal of the holy cross, however, prompted a counterattack by the Byzantine emperor Heraclius, who sacked a fire temple at Ganzak and extinguished the holy Adur-farnbag fire, one of the six most holy fires of Zoroastrian Iran. Thus, the Iranian Empire's last moment of grandeur lasted only a few years: by 630 CE, all the conquered lands had been returned. It was perhaps at this time that the oral Avesta was written down.

The last Sasanian king was Yazdgerd III (632–51 CE). In his second year, the Arabs entered Iraq, and, in 636 CE, defeated the Iranian armies at the battle of Qadisiyya. By 642 CE, they controlled the western provinces of Khuzistan and Media and, by 650 CE, also Fars.

Many Zoroastrians converted to Islam under pressure, and, in the 10th cent., a large group migrated to Gujarat, where they became the Parsees, "Persians," the largest community of Zoroastrians outside of Iran. In modern times, especially after the Islamic Revolution, large Zoroastrian groups are found in Britain, the United States, and in Canada.

Modern Zoroastrians face numerous challenges: dwindling numbers, not helped by strict censure of mixed marriages; lack of priestly training and local temples and schools; sectarian groups, some influenced by Western ideas; and, on the whole, uncertainty about their religious traditions.

B. Religion

Zoroastrianism as reflected in the Avesta is a development of the Indo-Iranian religion also reflected in the Old Indic Vedas. Like the Vedic religion, the Zoroastrian worldview is based on the contrast between an ordered cosmos characterized by light, health, and life, and chaos, characterized by darkness, disease, and death. The cosmic Order, Avestan **asha**, Vedic **rta**, is produced and guarded by the gods, in Iran specifically by Ahura Mazda, the All-knowing Lord. Among important similarities are the myths of the retention and liberation of the heavenly waters and the ritual importance of a magic plant that bestows visions and enormous strength on the one who consumes it, the Vedic **soma**, Avestan **haoma**. The most apparent differences between the two are, in the Avesta, the supreme status of one god, Ahura Mazda, around whom the other gods are organized, and two dualities of good and evil and the world of thought (of the gods) and that of living beings, which have no systematic counterparts in Vedic. The Vedas also have nothing to correspond to the mythical figure of Zarathustra, first and prototypical human poet-sacrificer, whom all humans must emulate.

1. The two worlds and the two states

The universe is divided into the two worlds of thought and of living beings, also called the world that has bones. The former is the domain of what man cannot reach by his normal senses and contains the good and evil gods and their helpers, and beings in both worlds must choose whether they belong to good or to evil.

Among those who chose to side with evil were the old Indo-Iranian **daewas**, who in Iran became what we would call demons or devils. This demonizing of what were originally benevolent sky gods is sometimes ascribed to "Zarathustra's reform," but was obviously a result of the development of strict dualism and the role of the choice.

Control of the universe oscillates between the two states of good and evil, the former ruled by Ahura Mazda, the latter by Angra Manyu, the Dark (or Evil) Spirit (in Pahlavi: Ohrmazd or Hormozd and AHRIMAN, also Foul Spirit). Every dawn, as the result of a successfully performed **yasna** sacrifice, Ahura Mazda is reinstated as the supreme ruler, and the universe is reborn in the ordered and harmonious form it took when Ahura Mazda banished darkness and chaos for the first time; but, every evening, Ahura Mazda and his creatures sicken and become weak, while his companion deities fight the powers of darkness and death throughout the night. The daily cycles are matched by the annual cycles and dawn by New Year.

The ordering principle of Ahura Mazda's cosmos is **asha**, which he also engendered, while that of chaos is the **druj**, the cosmic Deception or Lie, which deceives men and gods as to the true nature of **asha**, causing them to choose wrongly. Whoever chooses **asha** is **ashawan**, a sustainer of Order, while those who are deceived are **drugwant**, possessed by the Lie.

By his first sacrifice, Ahura Mazda, assisted by the **fravashis**, brought forth the heavenly lights. He and his helpers engendered or fashioned all good things (from unspecified materials) and set them in their proper places in the heavens and on earth and in the intermediate space.

2. The pantheon

The ordered cosmos is protected by numerous deities, who are as deserving of worship as Ahura Mazda, who also initiated and provided the model for their sacrifices.

Ardvi sura Anahita, the lofty, unattached one full of life-giving strength, is the heavenly river (the Milky Way), whom Ahura Mazda asked to come down from her lofty mountain to help him purify the wombs and semen of his living creatures to ensure good procreation. People with bodily imperfections are barred from sacrificing to her.

Mithra fights the forces of darkness throughout the night (presumably identified with the planet Venus), but specifically clears the path for the sun at dawn. From above, as the deified contract, he and his watchers oversee inter-human affairs, ensuring their regular functioning. Not entirely impartial, Mithra will aid the first to sacrifice to him. His steady companions are Rashnu, the god of what is straight and right, and Verthraghna, the incarnation of male strength, who bestowed his own strength and abilities on Zarathustra.

Vayu is the god of the space between earth and the sky, which surrounds it like a sphere and is thought to be a dual god, with one side that belongs to the Life-giving Spirit (above earth) and one that belongs to the Dark Spirit (below earth). Traveling into the beyond, the souls of the dead are therefore fearful of which Vayu they will encounter.

Tishtriya (Sirius, the Dog Star) ensures the seasonal rains, fighting the demoness of bad seasons and the demon of drought. Ashi is the goddess of the home and family, who also encourages Zarathustra before his fight with the Dark Spirit. Only the sexually mature and active may sacrifice to her.

Sraosha is the principal opponent of the forces of darkness, his main opponent being Aeshma, Wrath or rage, the embodiment of the dark sky. Sraosha's bird is the rooster, who wakes people at dawn, telling them to scorn the old gods and praise **asha** and not to let the demoness Sloth entice them to neglect their daily duties. Airyaman is the god of healing and harmony.

3. The life-giving immortals and the daena

The various elements of Ahura Mazda's primordial sacrifice became deities in their own right, the six called **amesha spenta** in the Young Avesta, "immortal" and "life-giving." The key term **spenta** implies swelling, that is, with the juices of fertility and life, and characterizes all things brought forth by Ahura Mazda through his Life-giving Spirit (**spenta manyu**). Entities endowed with this power are also said to be **sura** "endowed with life-giving strength" (e.g., Ardvi sura Anahita, the **fravashis**, Dawn, and the Renovation). The six are also correlated with elements in the world of the living. They are: **Vohu Manah**, Good Thought, Ahura Mazda's creative ability according to and with which he performed the sacrifice; **Asha Vahishta**, Best Order, what characterizes Ahura Mazda's creation, also the sun-lit sky and humans; **Khshathra Vairiya**, the Worthy Command, the royal command generated by the successful sacrifice, also metal; **Spenta Armaiti**, Life-giving Humility, Ahura Mazda's daughter and spouse and the embodiment of filial and spousal submission; **Haurwatat** and **Amertatat**, Wholeness and Undyingness, the absence of flaws and death that characterized Ahura Mazda's creation, also waters and plants, the result of and reward for the successful sacrifice. The Seven Life-giving Immortals include the six with Ahura Mazda at the head.

The term **daena** (Pahlavi **den**) originally denoted the faculty permitting humans to see into the world of thought. As such, she is personified as a female guide of the souls of the dead. She is also the totality of a person's thoughts, words, and deeds and looks beautiful or ugly accordingly. "The (good) **daena** of those who choose to sacrifice to Ahura Mazda" is the divine prototype of the **daena**.

4. Good and evil

According to the Young Avesta, Ahura Mazda's ordered cosmos was first threatened when the Dark Spirit tried to enter it with the intent to keep the heavenly waters from flowing, plants from growing, and the heavenly bodies from moving. His attempt was thwarted, however, by the **fravashis** and Ahura Mazda's heavenly Fire, and the Dark Spirit was confined within Ahura Mazda's world, where his damage could be controlled.

Good Zoroastrians are expected to counterbalance evil in this world by accumulating a surplus of good thoughts, words, and deeds, which are often said to be the foundation of the religion. When a person dies, after three days and nights, his or her soul travels into the beyond, where it is met by its **daena**, who leads it to a bridge and a judge holding a pair of scales. Its good and bad thoughts, etc., are weighed, and according to the balance, the bridge will widen and let the person across and up to heaven, or it will become so narrow that the person will fall into hell. In hell, it will suffer dire punishments until the end of time.

In the Avesta, good deeds include observing the purity rules and punishing those who transgress, as well as punishing (even killing) those who do the Dark Spirit's bidding, such as prostitutes and homosexuals. Even animals are in one or the other camp, and those belonging to evil can be killed for religious merit, a practice that is now being discontinued.

In the Old Persian inscriptions, we get a glimpse of the kings' values, foremost among which are truth, justice, and social rights. In the Pahlavi books, the principal virtues are moderation, patience, and hospitality; others are abstaining from vengeance, slander, lust, greed, and envy.

5. Pollution and purification

Pollution is basically the infection of living by dead matter, personified as a demoness. Not only corpses, but anything separated from the body, such as hair and nails and blood, count as dead matter, and must be disposed of properly. Corpses had to be left in a place where they could do the least damage to Ahura Mazda's creations, including earth, water, and fire. They were therefore exposed in barren places, and later in special enclosures on hilltops (towers of silence), where the bones would be picked clean by animals and birds. The Achaemenid kings were therefore entombed in rocks.

Blood from menstruation, which was caused when the Foul Spirit kissed his female companion, is one of the worst pollutants, and menstruating women were kept separated from living beings and had to be thoroughly purified.

6. Rituals

According to the Avesta, there were numerous major and minor rituals, some involving complex ritual activities, such as the yasna and the vedevdad sade; others were simply songs to deities and various geniuses.

The word yasna is derived from the verb yaza-, "to sacrifice" or "to sacrifice to," i.e., offer consecrated objects (concrete or not) as gifts to the deities

The yasna sacrifice is celebrated daily and so, at first sight, serves the purpose of renewing the daily existence, that is, bringing back dawn. It is modeled upon Zarathustra's first sacrifice, which, in turn, was the human replica of Ahura Mazda's primordial sacrifice. It is therefore also a New Year's (Iranian: New Day) sacrifice. As a reenactment of the cosmogony, its purpose is to remove the infection by the forces of darkness and evil and place Ahura Mazda back in command of the universe. During the yasna, the priests construct a microcosm in the image of the primordial creation by naming and ordering all its prototypical elements, beginning with the construction of finite time and adding the social and human elements.

The main ingredient of the sacrifice is the haoma, a mythical plant that was pressed for its juice and that conferred upon the presser various rewards. The fourth man to press it in the world of the living was Pourushaspa, whose reward was his son, Zarathustra. Similarly, in the later literature, Zarathustra is described as having been born after his parents had drunk a mixture of haoma and milk. In the yasna, the haoma is pressed about halfway through the ritual, just before the recitation of the Old Avesta, including "Zarathustra's five Gathas," and it would seem that its purpose is to regenerate Zarathustra in the person of the sacrificer to gain his power to overcome evil and to ensure a perfect sacrifice.

The videvdad sade is a long purification ritual, in which the yasna is recited from midnight till after sunrise, but with insertion of the chapters of videvdad before, within, and after the Old Avesta.

From Achaemenid and Sasanian times, we have copious evidence that sheep were regularly sacrificed. The bloody sacrifice was discontinued among the Parsees in India, but was practiced in Iran until recent times.

Among personal rituals, the coming of age (naujot, "new birth") is one of the most important. It was originally celebrated at the age of fifteen, but today at a much earlier age. On this occasion, the young person for the first time dons a white shirt (woven in one piece) and a girdle (an intricately woven belt of wool, with complex number symbolism). The shirt symbolizes Good Thought and the girdle the daena mazdayasni, and donning them makes the person a miniature cosmos, in which the girdle separates good from evil.

7. Eschatology

In the Pahlavi texts, the history of the world plays itself out in the limited time of four times 3,000 years set by Ohrmazd within which to overcome evil and achieve the return to the origins. It begins after Ohrmazd perceives the threat of an attack on the eternal and immaculate existence by the Foul Spirit. After having incapacitated the Evil One by reciting the Ahuna Vairiya, he makes the world of thought, which he populates with divine entities. He then fashions the world of living beings, but keeps it inside himself in the world of thought for a gestation period of 3,000 years. At the end of the second 3,000 years, it is then born into the world of the living, making Ohrmazd both its mother and father. At this point the Foul Spirit is awakened from his stupor and attacks the world of the living, setting it in motion. For another 3,000 years is the Mixture, the adherents of good fighting those of evil.

Zarathustra's birth marks the end of this period and the beginning of the last 3,000 years of the world of the living, setting in motion the events that will bring it to an end. He combats evil and sets the den in motion, but is opposed by those favoring the powers of evil and is assassinated. Before his death, his semen was intercepted by the divine messenger Neryosan and placed in a box at the bottom of a lake, and at the turn of the next three millennia, three times virgins will come and bathe in the lake. They will become pregnant and give birth to three sons. These three are the Revitalizers (saoshyant, "who shall make the world swell with life-giving juices"), the last being the Revitalizer par excellence (Pahlavi Soshans). The three will repeat Zarathustra's sacrifice, each bringing the world a step closer to perfection.

In the end, Soshans will perform the sacrifice to raise the dead, another son of Zarathustra, and Isadvastar will assemble those resurrected and pronounce final judgment, whereby the evil will be separated from the good, like white and black sheep, and go to hell to suffer their final punishments. The divine Erman and the Fire will melt the metal in the mountains, which will flow in a great river. All of humanity will pass through, the last remains of sin will be burned out, and all will be saved. Zarathustra will perform the last sacrifice in this world and Ohrmazd the last in the other world, whereby evil will be destroyed by the words of the *Gathas* and the world of the living will also become perfect, with no mountains or valleys.

Bibliography: J. Blenkinsopp. "The Mission of Udjahorresnet and Those of Ezra and Nehemiah." *JBL* 106 (1987) 409–21; M. Boyce. *A History of Zoroastrianism* (1991); P. Briant. *From Cyrus to Alexander: A History of the Persian Empire.* Peter Daniels, trans. (2002); L. S. Fried. *The Priest and the Great King: Temple-Palace Relations in the Persian Empire* (2004); J. R. Hinnells. *The Zoroastrian Diaspora: Religion and Migration* (2005); J. Kellens. *Essays on Zarathustra and Zoroastrianism.* P. O. Skjærvø, trans. and ed. (2000); M.

Stausberg, ed. *Zoroastrian Rituals in Context* (2004); A. Tulli. "Il Naoforo Vaticano." *Miscellanea Gregoriana* (1941) 211–80; J. Wiesehöfer. *Ancient Persia from 550 BC to 650 AD* (1996).

P. OKTOR SKJÆRVØ

PERSIAN PERIOD puhr´zhuhn. In the mid-6th cent. BCE, Media and Persia were united under the rule of CYRUS the Great, preparing the way for Cyrus' defeat of Babylon in 539 BCE, which marks the beginning of the Persian period. Persia's inheritance of areas controlled by Babylon made it the largest empire to date. The period lasts for roughly 200 years until Alexander the Great's defeat of the Persians under Darius III in 334–330 BCE. *See* PERSIA, HISTORY AND RELIGION OF.

KEVIN A. WILSON

PERSIAN, OLD puhr´zhuhn. An ancient Iranian language spoken in Achaemenid Persia (550–330 BCE), the modern province of Fārs, ancestor of Middle Persian (PAHLAVI) and modern Persian. It is written in a cuneiform script containing some forty signs.

The script was probably devised to record DARIUS I's (r. 522–486 BCE) account of the beginnings of his rule in a trilingual inscription at Bisotun (Behistun) in Old Persian, AKKADIAN, and Elamite. The decipherment of the Old Persian version in the early 19th cent. quickly led to that of the other two.

Other famous inscriptions are those on Darius' tomb near Persepolis, in which he describes his physical and intellectual abilities, and an inscription by XERXES I (r. 486–465 BCE), in which he describes how he destroyed the temples of the gods of a rebellious province and proscribed the sacrifices offered to them, enjoining upon them the worship of AHURA MAZDA.

The language was widely used in the Achaemenid Middle East, and many Old Persian words are found in the Aramaic parts of the OT. *See* PERSIA, HISTORY AND RELIGION OF.

Bibliography: Roland G. Kent. *Old Persian Grammar, Texts, Lexicon.* 2nd rev. ed. (1953).

P. OKTOR SKJÆRVØ

PERSIS puhr´sis [Περσίς Persis]. A Roman Christian whom Paul greets as "the beloved Persis." Paul commends him for having "worked hard in the Lord" (Rom 16:12). The name Persis means "Persian" and was a common name for a slave or freed slave. Persis is mentioned along with TRYPHAENA AND TRYPHOSA, other "workers in the Lord."

MARIANNE BLICKENSTAFF

PERSON [אָדָם ʾadham, אִישׁ ʾish, אֱנוֹשׁ ʾenosh, נֶפֶשׁ nefesh, פָּנִים panim; ἀδελφός adelphos, ἀνήρ anēr, ἄνθρωπος anthrōpos]. In both Hebrew and Greek, there is no one particular word for the English word *person.*

In the OT and NT the word *person* denotes either particular individuals or representative individuals. Study of the occurrences of the English word *person* does not allow for an investigation of the Bible's anthropology. For instance, the word *person* does not appear in the English of the creation stories. Consequently, there are various important aspects of the Bible's view of humankind, such as humanity's relatedness to the rest of creation, which may not be addressed here (*see* ANTHROPOLOGY, NT THEOLOGICAL; ANTHROPOLOGY, OT THEOLOGICAL).

Persons are distinct from inanimate objects (Gen 14:21), possessing breath and emotions and God-given life. Persons are either male or female (Num 5:6). The existence of persons is a bodily existence in which persons' bodies know a wide range of experience, from joy and singing (Job 33:26-27) to abject poverty (Job 31:19) and desolation.

Persons are made of flesh (Job 10:11) and can be identified as flesh (Ps 119:120). Consequently, since flesh is porous and vulnerable, persons are susceptible to physical afflictions and illness. Persons can be hungry and thirsty (Isa 29:8); they can suffer from disease (Lev 13:2), sometimes to such a degree that they are defined by a certain disease ("the leprous person"; Lev 14:2). At the same time, persons are disposed to healing and renewal (Num 19:18; 21:9). Persons can be restored to life after having died (2 Kgs 8:5), but inevitably every person's body dies (Eccl 3:2).

God created persons in God's own image (Gen 9:6). Consequently, the lives of persons are precious, and belong ultimately to God (Ezek 18:4). The prohibition against shedding the blood of an innocent person (Gen 9:6; Exod 21:12) is connected to the intrinsic sacredness of persons.

Connectedness to God is the most basic feature of being a person. The God-person connection may be manifest in persons being possessed by the Spirit of God (1 Sam 10:6), or being saved by God (Job 33:24). God may address a person and show God's glory to that person (Deut 5:24).

It is important for persons to know the will of God and so to know the statutes and instructions of God (Exod 18:16). Obedience to the laws of God is essential for persons, for this is the same as keeping faith with God (Num 5:6). It is of utmost importance that persons not sin against God (1 Sam 2:25). God's desire is for persons to be blameless (Job 8:20) and righteous (Ps 37:16). A person is meant to be orientated toward the one who created him or her. Consequently, a person may find it appropriate to consecrate a house to the Lord (Lev 27:14) or receive atonement mediated by a priest (Num 15:28). Disobedience of God's commands may result in being cut off from the presence of God (Lev 22:3).

The laws of God are for the purpose of keeping persons not only in right relationship with God but also in right relationship with one another. It is important to

God that persons relate to one another with compassion and justice: the blind person is not to be led astray on a road (Deut 27:18); economic justice should be expected for persons (Lev 25:26-28); poor and disadvantaged persons should be cared for (Job 31:16-19); social justice is due to persons (Isa 29:21). To treat other persons unjustly is at the same time to profane God (Ezek 13:19).

The two fundamental relationships of persons are to God and to one another. By virtue of being connected to God, the one who created all persons, persons are related to one another. There are some relationships (family, Gen 46:26; and tribe, 2 Sam 15:2) that are especially important.

The consequence of the intrinsic relatedness of persons is that persons affect one another's lives deeply, whether for ill or for good. Given the relatedness of persons, the consequence of a particular way of being a person affects other people. For instance, one person's envy oppresses others (Eccl 4:1-4). Persons are capable of taking away one another's lives through murder (Exod 21:12), or through accidental killing (Num 35:11). Persons are capable of taking away one another's freedom, through enslavement (Exod 21:2) or kidnapping (Exod 21:16) and, likewise, of being put in positions of various forms of slavery. Persons may exercise authority over other persons to the detriment of those others (Eccl 8:9). Persons are capable of greed, which stirs up strife (Prov 28:25).

On the other hand, persons are capable of love, even love between a slave and the master's household (Exod 21:5). Persons are capable of compassion and justice, for instance, in freeing slaves and sending them out with adequate provisions (Deut 15:13). Persons may be generous (Prov 11:25).

The word *person* may be qualified by reference to a particular trait. This use is found particularly in the wisdom literature and the Prophets. "This person" or "these persons" becomes representative of a group of people who share that trait, for instance stupidity (Job 11:12), deceitfulness (Job 13:9), laziness (Prov 26:13), haughtiness (Prov 21:24), quarrelsomeness (Prov 26:21), wickedness (Ezek 3:18), faithlessness (Zeph 3:4), wisdom (Prov 10:23), generosity (Prov 11:25), discernment (Prov 17:24), etc. The word *person* is also used to refer to an unnamed human who will do extraordinary things (Dan 11:21).

Person may also be used in legal contexts where it is a reference to what is normative for all (e.g., Deut 17:6), or for the particular group being addressed (e.g., a freed male slave; Deut 15:13).

In gender-sensitive translations, the majority of the appearances of the English word *person* render Greek words and constructions that are masculine-oriented: adelphos ("brother"), anēr ("man"), anthrōpos ("man"), or masculine pronouns.

The words psychē (ψυχή, "soul") and prosōpon (πρόσωπον, "face") may be translated as "person." For example, in the Greek psychē appears in Acts 2:41; 27:37; and Rom 13:1. Prosōpon appears in 1 Thess 2:17; Jude 16. Many other of the occurrences in English of the word *person* are the result of a particular usage for a Greek adjective, resulting in translations such as "blind person," or "spiritual person."

The appearance of the word *person* in the OT is related to a much smaller range of ideas than the questions involved in discussing the NT's view of personhood. Nevertheless, there are a number of important observations to be made on the basis of study of this word.

The NT, like the OT, regards persons (women and men) as living beings who are related to God and one another. While there are no passages using the word *person* that refer to the idea of persons being in the image of God, this is clearly assumed in the NT writings. Persons are bodily beings such that the word *person* can be used for physical presence as opposed to spiritual presence (1 Thess 2:17).

As a being connected to God, a person can be sent from God (2 Cor 2:17); be drawn to God (John 6:44); be taken up into heavenly paradise while still a mortal (2 Cor 12:2-3); be God's holy temple in which resides God's Spirit (1 Cor 3:16-17). This capacity for connection to the divine makes persons also vulnerable to negative spiritual forces, often described as "unclean spirits" (e.g., Matt 12:43-45). In both the OT and NT, a person can be saved by God (1 Pet 3:20).

The relatedness of persons to one another means that persons inevitably affect one another. This is why the characteristics of persons, such as wickedness (1 Cor 5:13) or righteousness (Matt 10:41), have significance not just for that particular person, but for others. The goodness or wickedness of persons produces good or evil around them (Luke 6:45). Paul and his coworkers' living for the sake of other persons is worthy of commendation (1 Thess 1:5). The NT particularly stresses the relationship that believers in Christ have to one another, and the importance of honoring such (1 Cor 14:30).

Societal structures, whether structures of government (Rom 13:1) or religious laws and traditions (Matt 15:5), are an indication of the relatedness of persons. A shared commitment to communal life is important for the health of persons. Followers of Christ may exemplify a particularly generous mode of communal life, where no needy person is found among them (Acts 4:34).

Some uses of the word *person* in the NT are representative, where *person* is used in reference to a mode of being human (Rom 10:5; 1 John 2:5, 10), or to a common human requirement (Matt 15:11, 20; Rom 13:1), or experience (Rom 7:1; Gal 3:15). English translations of the NT may use *person* also to refer to extraordinary human beings, such as Christ (Gal 3:16; compare 1 Pet 1:11).

The NT use of the word *person* shares much in common with the OT use and also connects the word to several distinctive ideas. Among the unique ideas related to *person* are that a person can be "in Christ" (2 Cor 2:17; 1 John 2:5), and relatedly, a person can be made righteous by faith apart from works of law (Rom 3:28; Gal 2:16). The demand on persons who are "in Christ" is that, because of the gift of righteousness they have received, they themselves must work righteousness (Jas 2:24). They must be pure and blameless, for, if they are not, they will not inherit the promise of the kingdom of God and of Christ (Eph 5:4). Persons who know Christ must obey his commandments (1 John 2:4). Moreover, persons can expect to be raised from the dead "on the last day" (John 6:44).

Bibliography: K. Berger. *Identity and Experience in the New Testament* (2003); Joel B. Green, ed. *What About the Soul? Neuroscience and Christian Anthropology* (2004); Aubrey R. Johnson. *The Vitality of the Individual in the Thought of Ancient Israel* (1964); Carol A. Newsom. *The Self as Symbolic Space: Constructing Identity and Community at Qumran* (2004); Han Walter Wolff. *Anthropology of the Old Testament* (1974).

ANN JERVIS

PERSON OF CHRIST. *See* CHRIST.

PERUDA pi-r*oo*'duh [פְּרוּדָא perudha'; Φαριδά Pharida]. A family head of temple servants whose descendants returned to Jerusalem with Zerubbabel after the exile (Ezra 2:55; 1 Esd 5:33; Peridai [peridha' פְּרִידָא], Neh 7:57).

PERVERSE, PERVERSITY [לוּז luz, עָוָה ʿawah, עִקֵּשׁ ʿiqqesh, תַּהְפֻּכָה tahpukhah; ἀποστρέφω apostrephō, διαστρέφω diastrephō, σκολιός skolios]. The idea of a perversion, a favorite topic in the book of Proverbs, is the negative form of the concept of the upright path or way. Things that are good—words, actions, groups—are all thought of as straight (yashar יָשָׁר), a standard by which one may measure how well the covenant with God is being fulfilled. The righteous are known for their straight talk, their civic virtue, and fidelity to responsibilities as family members (*see* RIGHTEOUSNESS IN THE NT; RIGHTEOUSNESS IN THE OT). This is not true of the unjust, the fool, and the sinner, in whom there is something that has bent away from the straight path, with predictable disastrous results (*see* SIN, SINNERS).

Perversity begins as a relational, spatial concept: one thing is more bent than another. One can imagine the meaning of such a concept in a world where the demands of carpentry and craftsmanship made a straight piece of wood far more useful than a warped, curved one. The Hebrew and Greek words often reflect simply bending or turning away from the straight edge (e.g., Deut 32:5, 20; 1 Sam 20:30; 1 Kgs 8:47; Prov 11:20; 12:8; 15:4; 17:20; 19:1; 22:5; 28:6, 18; Matt 17:17; Luke 9:41; Phil 2:15). In most cases, the text does not specify whether the crookedness resulting from such a turn was inherent (as in wood that is naturally bent: see Eccl 7:13, "Consider the work of God; who can make straight what he has made crooked?").

Elsewhere the concept clearly implies a human element of (wrong) choice, which would make perversity not a natural occurrence in nature, but a moral flaw. When paired with *faithless*, Jesus uses the term *perversity* to confront his skeptical audiences: a "faithless and perverse generation" greets Jesus' great miracles (Matt 17:17; Luke 9:41; compare the "perverse and crooked generation" in Deut 32:5, 20). In Prov 14:14 the words used imply backsliding of the mind (lit., heart in Hebrew; see Prov 11:20). The LXX of Prov 17:20 speaks of one who has a "perverse tongue," a changeable tongue, that is, one whose speech veers away from what is upright and expected. Isaiah 30:12 follows up on this theme: now the act of turning away includes despising God's word. Clearly, in these uses we have the basis for naming perverseness as a sin.

The nominal form of the word, *perversity* (Prov 2:14; 10:31; 16:28; 23:33), comes from the root hafakh (הָפַךְ) and means to overturn, turn away, or pervert, and so denotes all activities that involve a movement away from the cultural norms. Unlike the modern connotations of the word *perversity*, the biblical concept does not imply sexual deviance or sexual impurity, though these would certainly have been part of the behaviors condemned by the biblical authors.

CAROLE R. FONTAINE

PESACH. *See* PASSOVER AND FEAST OF UNLEAVENED BREAD.

PESAHIM. *See* MISHNAH; PASSOVER AND FEAST OF UNLEAVENED BREAD.

PESHARIM pesh'uh-rim [פְּשָׁרִים pesharim]. Pesharim are biblical interpretations based on a method of interpretation known as *pesher*. The pesharim assume that First Temple period prophets foretold and described events that took place in Second Temple times (in the lifetime of the authors). The authors of the pesharim believed that only the sectarian teacher could reveal the prophecies' real meaning. Such a reading of contemporary events and eschatological expectations into the words of the prophets is prominent in the DEAD SEA SCROLLS.

The Hebrew root pashar (פָּשַׁר) means "to explain" or "to expound." In Gen 40–41, when Joseph interprets Pharaoh's dreams, the OT uses the closely related word pathar (פָּתַר). All through the book of Daniel, peshar (פְּשַׁר) refers to the interpretation of dreams or visions. Daniel is asked to tell the meaning (peshar) of the mysterious writing on the wall at King Belshazzar's palace (Dan 5), and in Dan 7:16, he wonders about the true meaning (peshar) of his disturbing vision.

The pesher method often used wordplay, ALLEGORY, or references to other biblical passages to connect the biblical text to its interpretation. Such literary connections are often preceded by a formula giving the lemma, the biblical citation, followed by "Its pesher concerns," after which appears the contemporary significance bestowed upon the ancient text.

QUMRAN pesharim come in three varieties. First, sustained or continuous pesharim occur in verse-by-verse commentaries on the Prophets (Isaiah, Hosea, Micah, Nahum, Habakkuk, Zephaniah) and Psalms. Second, thematic pesharim are grouped around a specific topic rather than a particular biblical book. The most striking examples of this are 4Q174 and 11Q13 (*see* MELCHIZEDEK TEXT). A third type, isolated pesharim, are found occasionally embedded in other texts such as the DAMASCUS DOCUMENT.

Among the continuous pesharim is *Pesher Habakkuk* (1QpHab), the best-preserved manuscript, composed before the Roman conquest of Palestine in 63 BCE (*see* HABAKKUK COMMENTARY, PESHER). It deals with the early history of the sect, employing sobriquets to identify its main characters. The sectarian leader is the TEACHER OF RIGHTEOUSNESS. The pesher on Hab 1:5 (1QpHab I, 16) interprets those who disregarded the words of the Teacher of Righteousness from the mouth of God as "traitors" (bwgdym בוגדים). Later on, the Wicked Priest, the opponent of the Teacher of Righteousness, appears in an interpretation of Hab 2:5-6: "Its interpretation concerns the Wicked Priest" who at first ruled Israel justly, but then rebelled against the Torah for the sake of wealth (1QpHab VIII, 8–11). *Pesher Habakkuk* claims that God divulged "all the mysteries of the words of his servants, the prophets" to the Teacher of Righteousness (1QpHab VII, 4–5; *DSSSE*). The pesher implies that, before his time, no one knew what the prophets actually meant.

References in the pesharim can be used as direct sources for the history of Hasmonean times. The NAHUM PESHER mentions two rulers, ANTIOCHUS and DEMETRIUS (4Q169 3+4 I, 2–3), and uses various code words for other personages of the period, such as "Angry Lion" (4Q169 3+4 I, 4–6) for Alexander Jannaeus (104–76 BCE), "Ephraim" (4Q169 3+4 II, 2–8) for the Pharisees, and "Manasseh" (4Q169 3+4 III, 9; IV, 3–6) for the Sadducees. The PHARISEES were incensed about Alexander's practices in the Temple and questioned his legitimacy as a priest (*see* ALEXANDER JANNAEUS, JANNEUS). In their desperation, they invited Demetrius III Eukerus to invade Judea. When Alexander finally regained Jerusalem, he crucified 800 Pharisees. *Pesher Nahum* actually corroborates the sequence of events as narrated by Josephus (*Ant.* 13.372–83).

The Psalms pesher (1Q16, 4Q171, 4Q173) represents fragments of commentaries on isolated psalms dating from the Roman period. When a verse discusses the righteous and the wicked, the pesher interpolates the Teacher of Righteousness and the Wicked Priest or the Man of Lies, the sworn enemies of the Teacher (*see* PRIEST, WICKED). The sketchy biographical details about the Teacher of Righteousness, e.g., his confrontation with the Wicked Priest on the Day of Atonement, are mostly gleaned from the pesher texts. *Pesher Isaiah* A (4Q161) interprets the march of the Assyrians in Isaiah's day as the invasion of Judea by the Seleucids in 104–76 BCE. It prophesies the defeat of the Romans (known as the KITTIM) in the end of days and the rise to leadership of the Prince of the Congregation and the appearance of the Davidic Messiah (*see* MESSIAH, JEWISH).

Florilegium (4Q174) is a thematic pesher. Messianic in nature, it describes three temples: 1) the "temple of man," the sectarian group that serves as a replacement for the Temple of Jerusalem; 2) the contemporary defiled Temple in Jerusalem from which the sect distanced itself; and 3) the Temple to be built by God in the messianic age. It relies heavily on Psalms but freely quotes from other biblical books as well (*see* TEMPLE, JERUSALEM).

Isolated or embedded pesharim, such as those found in the *Damascus Document*, utilize proof texts to validate the beliefs of the Qumran sect or to show that events in its history have been prophesied in the Bible. Sobriquets often conceal from scholars the identities alluded to in the Dead Sea Scrolls, but to their contemporary readers the allusions must have been clearly understood.

The Gospels make use of a similar exegetical approach. Often a statement is followed by the formula "this was to fulfill what was spoken by the prophet," followed by a proof text from the Hebrew Scriptures (*see* FULFILL, FULFILLMENT). For example, Matt 2:15 explains that Jesus fled to Egypt until the death of the murderous King Herod by reference to Hos 11:1; and in Matt 2:17-18, the Gospel explains that Rachel weeping for her children in Jer 31:15 was fulfilled when Herod slew the infants. Isaiah's prophecy of "the voice of one crying in the wilderness" saying "prepare the way of the Lord" (Isa 40:3) refers to the ministry of John the Baptist who went out into the wilderness and preached repentance (Matt 3:3). This same verse appears as an embedded pesher in the RULE OF THE COMMUNITY (1QS VIII, 12–16) where it is taken as referring to sectarian interpretation of the Torah.

Rabbinic and medieval Jewish writings evidence some contemporizing biblical interpretation, but it never became a central technique in later Jewish exegesis (*see* JEWISH BIBLICAL INTERPRETATION).

Bibliography: George Brooke. *Exegesis at Qumran* (1985); Craig A. Evans. "Biblical Interpretation at Qumran." *Judaism in Late Antiquity.* Part 5. Vol. 2. *The Judaism of Qumran: A Systematic Reading of the Dead Sea Scrolls.* Alan J. Avery-Peck, Jacob Neusner, and Bruce D. Chilton, eds. (2001) 105–24; Maurya P.

Horgan. *Pesharim: Qumran Interpretations of Biblical Books* (1979); Lawrence H. Schiffman. *Reclaiming the Dead Sea Scrolls* (1994) 223–41.

LAWRENCE H. SCHIFFMAN

PESHER. *See* HABAKKUK COMMENTARY, PESHER; NAHUM PESHER; PESHARIM.

PESHITTA puh-shee´tuh. An important Syriac version of the Bible, parts of which originated in the earliest centuries CE. *See* ARAMAIC, ARAMAISM; VERSIONS, ANCIENT; VERSIONS, SYRIAC.

PESTILENCE [דֶּבֶר dever; θάνατος thanatos]. A pestilence is a virulent and devastating infectious DISEASE that becomes an epidemic and causes great suffering and loss of life (*see* PLAGUE). The term can also refer metaphorically to anything destructive. The LXX consistently renders **dever** with **thanatos**, meaning "death."

In the Bible, war, famine, and disease were interrelated phenomena that bring death and destruction. The triad of pestilence, hunger, and sword occurs several times as a form of divine retribution, especially in Jeremiah (14:12; 21:9; 27:8, 13) and Ezekiel (5:12; 6:11-12; 12:16). The book of Revelation borrows the same triad when pale Death kills by sword, famine, and pestilence (Rev 6:8). In Rev 18:8, the triad consists of pestilence, mourning, and famine.

The generic word *pestilence* (has several interpretations (Deut 28:21-25). First it is specified as consumption, fever, and inflammation (Deut 28:22). Pestilence affects the earth, animals, and plants, as well as humans, as the conditions of heat and drought (v. 22) could also metaphorically describe fever and dehydration. Finally, the last two types of pestilence, affecting crops, could also describe human experiences of fever and jaundice (mildew="yellowness"). These pestilences are active and punitive forces that pursue humans (Deut 28:45).

JOHN J. PILCH

PESTLE. *See* MORTAR AND PESTLE.

PETER AND ANDREW, ACTS OF. An older and longer version of the *Acts of Andrew and Matthias.* The narrative was composed between the 3rd and 5th cent. CE and is preserved in both Greek and Slavonic. It contains two scenes that dramatize the importance of conversion to Christianity. In the first, Peter, Andrew, and other apostles convert many to Christianity by a miraculous multiplication of grain; in the second, they win even more converts by passing a camel through an eye of a NEEDLE (compare Matt 19:24; Mark 10:25; Luke 18:25). Both episodes contain negative representations of women. *See* ANDREW AND MATTHIAS (MATTHEW), ACTS OF; APOCRYPHA, NT.

FRANCISCO LOZADA JR.

PETER AND PAUL, ACTS OF. A 6th- or 7th-cent. CE Gk. text that seeks to unite the apostles Peter and Paul in their missionary activity and their martyrdoms. It contains the story of Paul's journey from Gaudomelite to Rome; with Paul's arrival there, the text draws on the longer version of the *Passion of Peter and Paul* by Pseudo-Marcellus. It describes the same-day deaths of Paul by beheading and Peter by upside-down crucifixion, both earlier church traditions. The martyrdom of Perpetua is woven into the story of Paul's death. *See* APOCRYPHA, NT.

ROBERT E. VAN VOORST

PETER AND PAUL, MARTYRDOM OF. This narrative of the martyrdoms of the two apostles, also called *The Passion of Peter and Paul*, exists in a longer version in Greek, Latin, and Slavonic, and a much shorter Latin version. One of the latest works from the NT Apocrypha, it dates from the 6th or 7th cent. CE. Both versions relate mainly the death of Peter. They are drawn freely from the *Acts of Peter* and are supplemented from other NT apocryphal literature. Paul plays a minor, supporting role befitting his relative status to Peter in the church. In the longer version, Peter and Paul engage in a contest of miracles with Simon Magus, who claims to be the Christ (*see* MAGUS, SIMON). When Simon dies in this contest, Nero condemns Peter and Paul for causing his death. The *Quo vadis* legend ("Where are you going?" spoken by Christ to Peter as he flees Rome to escape martyrdom) is related, but at different points in the two versions. The locations of Peter's tomb on the Vatican hill and Paul's on the Ostian road, near the places of their executions, are stressed, promoting these tombs and (implicitly) the churches built over them as holy sites. *See* APOCRYPHA, NT; MARTYR; PAUL, ACTS OF; PETER, ACTS OF.

ROBERT E. VAN VOORST

PETER AND PAUL, PASSION OF. *See* PETER AND PAUL, MARTYRDOM OF.

PETER AND THE TWELVE APOSTLES, ACTS OF. This oddly named late 2nd-cent. CE tractate from Nag Hammadi presents a narrative with allegorical touches, possibly gnostic, about the encounter of the eleven disciples (including Peter) with a pearl merchant named Lithargoel, who turns out to be Jesus. Lithargoel attracts the poor but is rejected by the rich. He does not have with him the special pearl he is promoting; it is available only to those who journey to his celestial city. *See* APOCRYPHA, NT; NAG HAMMADI TEXTS.

ROBERT E. VAN VOORST

PETER TO PHILIP, LETTER OF. This tractate from the NAG HAMMADI TEXTS is a Coptic translation of a Greek original from the late 2nd or early 3rd cent. CE. It consists of a brief letter to the apostle Philip, attributed to the apostle Peter (132, 10-133, 7a), followed by a gnostic revelatory discourse from the risen Savior in response to a series of questions from the apostles (133, 17b-138, 7a) and a concluding section in which Peter affirms the gnostic conviction that "Jesus is stranger to this suffering" (138, 7b-140, 27). This pseudonymous writing invites Philip and his group, who are said to be "separate from us" (133, 2), to come together to receive instruction from the risen Christ. Peter was regarded as the preeminent authority of the authentic apostolic tradition in an emerging orthodox church. In this tractate, however, Peter is the central recipient of gnostic teaching that should be the content of apostolic teaching.

JAMES J. H. PRICE

PETER, ACTS OF. Written in Gk. ca. 170–190 CE, probably in Asia Minor or in Rome, the *Acts of Peter* is one of the earliest and most influential apocryphal acts. Most of the text has survived only in a Lat. version, which has encratite themes (e.g., permanent celibacy in marriage, preferring death by martyrdom to Christian marriage) not found in other versions. The final chapters also circulated separately as the *Martyrdom of Peter* (*see* PETER, MARTYRDOM OF), which survives in three Gk. manuscripts and several versions in the Eastern churches.

The *Acts* begins with Paul's departure from Rome for Spain (1–3), and continues with the arrival of Simon the magician in Rome and Peter's divinely guided journey to meet him there (4–6). After Peter authoritatively guides the Roman church, he has a lengthy miracle contest with Simon in the Roman Forum. Peter's many miracles include making a dog rebuke Simon and raising people from death (7–29). Despite his defeat of Simon, Peter is martyred by crucifixion, upside down at his humble request, the first appearance of this legend (30–41). The miracles and legends of the *Acts* show that this document draws on popular Christianity to present not an attack on Gnosticism (much less Simonian Gnosticism), which is very meagerly described here, but a defense of the truth and spiritual power of Christianity in the face of demonic power manifested in strong persecution. *See* APOCRYPHA, NT; JOHN, ACTS OF; PETER AND PAUL, ACTS OF.

Bibliography: Stevan Davies. *The Revolt of the Widows: The Social World of the Apocryphal Acts* (1980).

ROBERT E. VAN VOORST

PETER, APOCALYPSE OF. The *Apocalypse of Peter* is the earliest and most influential Christian exposition of the afterlife, describing in vivid detail the blessings of heaven and the torments of hell.

The *Apocalypse of Peter* was written in the second third of the 2nd cent. It uses imagery from *1 Enoch* extensively, and to a lesser extent *4 Esdras*, and it refers to 2 Peter's description of the transfiguration of Jesus. Theophilus of Antioch alludes to a verse of it around 180 CE. It was probably used by the author of the *Apocalypse of Paul*, and was included in the Muratorian Canon as one of the two official apocalypses. If its chap. 2 contains a reference to Simon bar Kokhba as a messianic pretender and persecutor of Christians, as seems likely, the work should be dated around 135–140 CE.

Originally written in Gk., the text survives in an Ethiopic version of the Pseudo-Clementine literature and in a Gk. fragment. A fragmentary Gk. text, less than half the size of the Ethiopic text, was discovered in the grave of a Christian monk at Akhmim, Egypt, during excavations in 1887. Despite being versions of the same Gk. original, the Ethiopic version and Gk. fragment have striking dissimilarities in wording, and most scholars hold that the fragmentary text is a later development than the Ethiopic version, which is probably closer to the original; but its exact wording is uncertain. Its provenance is Egyptian.

The *Apocalypse of Peter* is best known for its vivid, frightening descriptions of the physical and spiritual punishments of hell. In contrast to the canonical Revelation of John, its focus is not christological, but on the descriptions of different classes of sinners and their torturous punishment. Its main purpose is not, like most earlier apocalyptic, to keep believers faithful to God in the face of strong opposition (although this is not absent), but to reinforce moral standards in the church. Although its theology is doctrinally orthodox, and despite its popularity in the 2nd and 3rd cent., it gradually lost favor in the mainstream church. Its themes, however, continued to influence other Christian works from the *Apocalypse of Paul* to Dante's *Divine Comedy*. *See* APOCRYPHA, NT.

ROBERT E. VAN VOORST

PETER, FIRST LETTER OF pee´tuhr [Πέτρος Α Petros A]. The second of the seven CATHOLIC EPISTLES, 1 Peter presents itself as a communication from the apostle Peter. Written to churches located in the northern part of Asia Minor (modern Turkey) the letter urges readers, currently undergoing sporadic persecution for their faith, to endure persecution patiently, keeping in mind the suffering of Christ that has opened to them a new life and future. While avoiding irritating, unbelieving neighbors, Christians are to remain true to their faith in Christ, which will result in their redemption

- A. Structure and Outline of 1 Peter
  - 1. Structure
  - 2. Outline
- B. Analysis of the Letter
  - 1. Literary analysis
    - a. Author
    - b. Date
    - c. Literary unity
  - 2. Cultural surroundings and influences
    - a. Secular culture
    - b. Old Testament and Christian traditions

C. Theological Structure and Significance
   1. Theme and purpose
   2. Theological structure
      a. Theological logic
         i. Hope
         ii. Inheritance
         iii. Salvation
      b. Theological structure
      c. Controlling metaphor
   3. Significance
Bibliography

A. Structure and Outline of 1 Peter

1. Structure

As is the case with ancient Christian letters, 1 Peter has the usual epistolary opening (1:1-2). The passage that follows (1:3-12) serves more as an introduction (*Prooemium*) to the body of the letter (1:13–5:11), rather than the more usual form of prayer or blessing found in the Pauline Letters. The body is then followed with the usual epistolary closing (5:12-14).

The body itself, as also in the Pauline Letters, is divided into three parts, the body opening, body middle, and body closing. The dominance of the imperative form in 1:13–2:10, a form not used in 1:3-12, points to these verses as the beginning of that main body of the letter (body opening). The presence of the word *therefore* in 1:13 connects the body opening with the preceding section (1:3-12). The introductory use of the word *beloved* at 2:11 and 4:12, coupled with the benediction at 4:11 and 5:11, marks those sections as body middle (2:12–4:11) and body closing (4:12–5:11). The greetings, summary, and final benediction (5:12-14) are a formal epistolary conclusion.

2. Outline

I. 1:1-2 Epistolary opening
II. 1:3-12 Introduction (*Prooemium*)
   A. 1:3-5 A new life and its consequences
   B. 1:6-9 Present trials, future salvation
   C. 1:10-12 Salvation in Christ revealed to the Prophets
III. 1:13–2:10 Body Opening
   A. 1:13-25 Tasks (and Nature) of the Christian Community
      1. 1:13-21 Since lives of hope are holy, actions must conform
      2. 1:22-25 You have been begotten by God's word, and so must love one another
   B. 2:1-10 (Tasks) and nature of the Christian community
      1. 2:1-3 Desire appropriate things
      2. 2:4-10 You are a chosen people
IV. 2:11–4:11 Body Middle
V. A. 2:11-12 You are to thwart false accusations by good behavior
VI. B. 2:13–3:7 Call to appropriate subordination
      1. 2:13-17 All readers to civil authorities
      2. 2:18-25 Household slaves to their masters
      3. 3:1-6 Believing wives to their unbelieving husbands
      4. 3:7 Sub-unit. Believing husbands to show respect for their believing wives
   C. 3:8–4:11 Call to Right Conduct
      1. 3:8-12 Call to nonretaliation for evil
      2. 3:13-22 Call to right conduct facing suffering
      3. 4:1-6 Call to right conduct among unbelievers
      4. 4:7-11 Call to right conduct within the fellowship
VII. 4:12–5:11 Body Closing
   A. 4:12-19 Suffering of Christians in Present and Eschatological Context
   B. 5:1-5 Appropriate Conduct in Community
   C. 5:6-9 Appropriate Conduct in Eschatological Suffering
      1. 5:6-7 Toward God
      2. 5:8-9 Toward the devil
      3. 5:10-11 Conclusion
VIII. 5:12-14 Epistolary Closing

B. Analysis of the Letter

1. Literary analysis

Three literary problems associated with 1 Peter are the identity of its author, its date, and finally its literary unity: was it composed as a unified letter, or did it originate as an epistolary adaptation of an earlier baptismal homily? We shall investigate each of those questions in turn.

a. Author. The Gk. of this letter reflects an educated author who knew the theological situation in Asia Minor, a situation that fits the last years of the 1st cent. CE, some years after Peter's martyrdom in 64 CE. The author is familiar with the theological terminology of Paul's letters, and the names Silvanus (5:12) and Mark (5:13) are also associated with Paul (Mark: Acts 12:25; 13:5; 15:37-39; Col 4:10; 2 Tim 4:11; Phlm 24; Silvanus: 2 Cor 1:19; 1 Thess 1:1; 2 Thess 1:1). The only self-reference to the author, other than in the opening verse, is to *elder* (5:1), a term that is nowhere else attributed to Peter (*see* ELDER IN THE NT). The author's reference to himself as "a witness of the sufferings of Christ" cannot be a historical reference, since according to the Gospels, Peter was not present at the crucifixion. The author's reference to being a sharer in the glory to be revealed (5:10) fits the general eschatological tone of the letter and is not a covert reference to the transfiguration; 2 Pet 1:18 shows that such references associated with Peter are more direct. Again, the reference to Mark as "my son" does not refer to any physical relationship, just as the reference to Silvanus as "faithful brother" does not refer to a physical relationship. Finally, the reference to "She who is at Babylon, who is likewise chosen" (5:13; RSV) does not refer to Peter's wife, but to the church from which the letter is sent (NRSV, "Your sister church in Babylon, chosen together with you"). None of these references points to the historical Peter.

The language of the letter is closer to the defenders of Christianity in the 2nd cent. than to the letters of Paul. Further, the complex grammatical structures in this letter point to an educated author rather than to one who reproduced the ordinary Gk. spoken in the marketplace. When the author quotes the OT, the language bears a closer resemblance to the LXX (Gk. translation of the OT) than to the original Hebrew; the absence of obvious Semitisms (evidences of direct translation from Hebrew) shows that the author's native tongue was Gk.

Some have suggested that the author was Silvanus (the Lat. form of SILAS), who wrote down in Gk. the material that Peter, characterized in Acts 4:13 as "uneducated" and "ordinary," dictated to him. Yet the phrase "through Silvanus" to refer to the letter (1 Pet 5:12) is not used for the person who wrote a letter, but rather to the one who delivered it (e.g., Acts 15:23; see also Ign. *Rom.* 8:1; Ign. *Phld.* 11:2; Ign. *Smyrn.* 12:1; Ign. *Pol.* 14:1).

The emerging picture is therefore of a letter written in the name of Peter and delivered by Silvanus to a group of churches in Asia Minor who were experiencing difficulties related to their Christian faith. Following ancient custom, the unknown author, surely a follower of Peter, writes in the name of his teacher who is evidently revered in Asia Minor, applying to their situation insights into the Christian faith derived from Peter himself.

b. Date. If the author was not Peter himself, a date after Peter's death in 64 CE has much to commend it. The fact that the Christian faith was widespread enough in Asia Minor to provoke non-Christian reactions points to the late 1st cent. CE. The fact that the label *Christian* was sufficient to occasion a negative response (1 Pet 4:16) also points to that time, as does the reference to Rome as Babylon (5:13), a practice adopted by Christians and Jews after the Roman destruction of Jerusalem in 70 CE. References to PERSECUTION in the areas addressed (1:6; 2:20; 3:14; 4:1, 12; 5:9) have led some to attempt to locate such a persecution. Three examples are normally cited; those under Nero, Domitian, and Trajan.

We know of a persecution of Christians by Nero about the year 64, following the disastrous fire in Rome that Nero blamed on Christians. Yet there is no evidence for a general persecution of followers of Christ beyond the bounds of the city of Rome. There are references to persecutions during the reign of the emperor Domitian in the last years of the 1st cent. They were directed more against other Romans than against Christians, and resulted from Domitian's brutal and suspicious nature, and a desire to enrich his treasury by expropriating the estates of the condemned. Finally, we know about the persecution of some Christians during the reign of Trajan (ca. 110 CE) because of correspondence between Trajan and his legate Pliny the Younger. Trajan had dispatched Pliny to investigate the irregular finance and governance of provinces in northern Asia Minor. In the course of his duties, Pliny encountered groups of Christians and, after questioning some of them, had them put to death. Pliny's commission was not to persecute Christians. The fact that he had to ask Trajan about how to proceed shows that there was no official policy about Christians at that time. The upshot was that Christians were treated like other persons who, for whatever reasons, failed to show the proper respect for the emperor and hence of the Roman Empire (*see* CHRISTIANS, PERSECUTION OF).

The first systematic persecution of Christians as such does not occur until the middle of the 3rd cent. CE (249–51) under the emperor Decius. Hence, there is little evidence from the earlier persecution of Christians to fix a date for 1 Peter. One interesting bit of information in the Pliny-Trajan correspondence may lend a clue to the letter's date, however. Pliny reports (Pliny, *Ep. Tra.* 10.96) that some of the accused had recanted about twenty-five years earlier, perhaps during persecutions at the time Peter was written. In that case, 1 Peter was written in the 80s of the 1st cent.

c. Literary unity. The form and content of the letter led some scholars to posit that the letter originated as a baptismal homily later adapted to its present letter form. The evidence for that theory is as follows:

An examination of the content of the letter reveals an emphasis on the newness of the addressed Christians (1:3, 23: "born anew"; 2:2: "newborn infants"), along with a reference to baptism as the means to salvation (3:21). Again, it has been noted that the only places that identify the writing as a letter are 1:1-2 and 5:12-14. The rest is a general address to Christians suffering for their faith. Further, that emphasis on suffering seems to be presented in two forms: one indicates suffering as a future possibility (3:17); the other identifies it as a present reality (4:12). The latter reference is immediately preceded (4:11) by a benediction.

Such evidence led to the proposal that the body of the letter had had its origin as a baptismal homily that was addressed to converts at the time they were baptized as Christians (reference to baptism in 3:21; to NEW BIRTH in 1:3, 23; 2:2). That homily (1:3–4:11), which ended in a benediction, was then later adapted, with the addition of 1:1-2 and 4:12–5:14, into a letter that was sent to people who were undergoing actual persecution, encouraging them in the name of the martyred Peter.

Once widely held, that theory came under increasing scrutiny, and has now been largely discarded. Baptism (3:12) is hardly the central point of the letter. In fact, it has less prominence than Paul's discussion of baptism in Rom 6:1-4, but no one has proposed that that part of Romans had its origins as a baptismal homily. Such references were apparently part of the common early Christian tradition. The same can be said for the references to newness in relation to their former lives (compare 2 Cor 5:17; Gal 6:15; Heb 5:12-13). The benediction at 4:11 is not that uncommon (compare Rom 1:25; 11:36), and the references to suffering in 1:3–4:11 are not all future or hypothetical; 1 Pet 1:6 presumes suffering as a present reality and 3:17 points to the fact that some suffering is in accordance with God's will. Finally, there is evidence of a unity of theme throughout the letter: conflict brought about by faith in Christ (1:6-7; 2:4-8, 12, 18-20; 3:1-2, 9, 14, 15, 17; 4:1-2, 12-19; 5:8-10). Such a unity of theme indicates that the letter is not a composite creation, but was composed as a unified letter.

2. Cultural surroundings and influences

a. Secular culture. It is clear from the content that readers lived under the threat of persecution, simply for being Christians. While the suffering was widespread (4:17; 5:9), it was nevertheless sporadic (1:6; 5:10) and consisted primarily of verbal abuse (2:12; 3:9, 15). Apparently it had not yet become martyrdom for the faith, although the threat apparently existed (compare 4:12, although "fiery ordeal" may be meant metaphorically as in 1:7 rather than literally). In any case, the mere fact of being identified with the Christian faith was enough to elicit unfavorable attention.

Such persecution was due more to cultural expectations of Roman culture than to any official Roman policy against Christian faith. Indeed, it never was the policy of the Roman government to persecute or prohibit religions as such (the one exception was the Celtic religion, which included human sacrifice). The notion that Christianity was banned as an "illegal religion" has no basis in evidence from the 1st cent. The terms *legal* and *illegal* religion do not occur in any non-Christian Latin literature of this period; the use of "legal religion" (*religio licita*) occurs for the first time in the Christian apologist Tertullian (*Apol.* 21.1) and does not refer to Roman policy. Romans were suspicious of, but officially indifferent to, religious and cultural customs in the provinces, although they did not expect Roman citizens to participate in them. So long as taxes continued to flow from the provinces to Rome, Rome permitted foreign people their own religions and customs.

The basic problem for the Christians in 1 Peter was the fact that their faith prohibited them from acknowledging any Lord but Jesus. Yet such acknowledgment was a regular part of the religio-civic celebrations throughout the Roman Empire. In addition to festivals for local gods, in which all residents were to participate, there was a yearly empire-wide celebration on January 3, honoring the emperor (see Tacitus, *Ann.* 4.17). At such festivals everyone, young and old, was expected to participate. There were processions, feasts, games, and of course sacrifices to various deities. Those not participating in the processions might erect small altars in front of their houses, and offer sacrifices as the procession passed by. All such participation was impossible for the follower of Christ.

It is necessary to remember that in the Roman Empire religion and politics were inseparably connected, and both were intimately tied to the social fabric of the community. Therefore to be a religious nonconformist was at the same time to attack the social and political stability of the community. It was for social nonconformity that the Christians suffered. Once people became members of the Christian community, they could no longer participate in such normal community activities (compare 1 Pet 4:4) and that branded them as outsiders (compare 2:11).

In response to that situation, 1 Peter tells readers not to go out of their way to be condemnatory toward unbelievers, or offensive in the professions of their faith (see 3:15*b*-16*a*). Yet when Christian values conflicted with the core values of society they felt compelled by their faith to reject (e.g., 1:18; 4:3-4), Christians were to remain faithful to their core convictions even when that meant abuse and suffering.

Their example was Christ, who also had suffered unjustly. Yet as Christ did not abandon the world, neither are his followers to do that. Faithful Christians are to maintain exemplary conduct (e.g., 2:12, 15; 3:16; 4:15-16) and to be ready to explain to anyone who asks why they act as they do (3:15). Such exemplary conduct would make it clear that the goal of the Christian community was not the downfall of the social fabric of their community.

As long as social and political customs did not lead to a denial of their faith, Christians were expected to conduct themselves in every way as law-abiding citizens (compare 3:13-17). Such activity would produce a positive impression on pagan society (e.g., 2:15), and therefore Christians were to exercise love even toward those who persecuted them (ROME, EARLY CHRISTIAN ATTITUDES TOWARD).

b. Old Testament and Christian traditions. To address this situation, the author of 1 Peter drew on both OT and earlier Christian traditions. Justification for using such OT traditions is given in 1 Pet 1:10-12, where the author makes the specific point that the prophets in fact were addressing not their own generation, but the generation of the letter's Christian readers (1:12). The Spirit that motivated the prophets was the Spirit of Christ (1:11). Hence what they said was relevant to the current readers' own situation (1:10). An example of this use of the prophetic tradition occurs in 1 Pet 2:21-25, where the language of Isa 53 is applied to the events of Christ's passion, which, in turn, is exemplary for the way Christians are to conduct themselves (2:21).

In addition to these OT traditions, our author uses Christian traditions. In addition to the early traditions and vocabulary shared with the Pauline Epistles, our author employs what are called HOUSEHOLD CODES (see Eph 5:22–6:9; Col 3:18–4:1). Interestingly, he limits extended comments to the conduct of slaves and wives (1 Pet 2:18–3:6), probably because Christians, like those two groups, had few rights within Roman society. The indicated responses of those two groups to their limited rights are to be examples for the reactions of all Christians to their social predicament. The addition of advice to husbands (3:7) who were not similarly limited indicates the high regard with which women were held in the Christian communities. Although not compelled by society to extend gracious conduct to wives, Christian husbands are under such obligation, on peril of being ignored by God if they do not ("so that nothing may hinder your prayers," 3:7).

C. Theological Structure and Significance

1. Theme and purpose

There has been much discussion concerning the theme of 1 Peter. It has frequently been argued that suffering, both potential and actual, plays a central role in the discussions contained in the letter, seen either as the dominant theme, or serving as the basis for exhortation to those who suffer to remain faithful to Christ. Contained in that is also comfort to those suffering by assuring them such suffering does not mean they have been abandoned by God. That theme also provides insight into the author's concern to provide an understanding of Christian life that will enable the community to survive persecution with its faith intact.

A second theme often proposed as central to the letter is hope. Hope can be understood as related to, and providing the antidote for, the suffering the readers are currently undergoing. Such hope is seen as the counterpart to the theme of faith in Paul, giving the variegated discussion a central, underlying theme. Hope also points to a future when the present time of suffering will have been overcome, thus accounting for the eschatological strain in the letter.

Underlying both themes is the figure of Christ, whose unjust suffering and resurrection to final glory have also been seen as playing a central role in the letter. Christ's passion, death, and subsequent resurrection show how present suffering inflicted on the readers is related to their own future glory, thus providing the readers with a model for living faithful lives in the midst of a hostile society.

A final theme is the need for the nascent Christian community to maintain its integrity in the face of their hostile world. The emphasis on Christians as exiles and aliens in their cultural context reinforces the need for such inner coherence. Coupled with this, some have seen a corresponding emphasis on a call for social responsibility, including a witness to the faith when opportunity presents itself. Related to this emphasis, some have proposed that 1 Peter is in fact a call for assimilation of Christian values and practices to those of the surrounding society as a way to avoid social conflict, thus ensuring the survival of the Christian community. Others have countered that such a reading would undermine the thrust of the letter calling for faithfulness to Christ despite external hostility.

Finally, the need to reduce tension within the church has also been seen as thematic to the intention of the letter, specifically such tension as existed between the followers of Peter and of Paul, or between Paul and the Jerusalemite Christian traditions. Included in such an intent may be the desire to broaden the influence of the authority of Simon Peter, or of those who followed him.

Such a variety of proposals demonstrates its theological richness, but also shows the difficulty of identifying a single unifying theme. As a result, a more fruitful approach, rather than attempting to identify such a theme, will be to discern the interrelationships of the theological emphases contained within the letter. In that way we can identify the author's intentions without seeking to limit them to a unitary theme. The investigation of those interrelationships will proceed in terms of three rubrics, each of which will provide a perspective on the unified theological conception of our letter. Those rubrics are the letter's theological logic, its theological structure, and its ruling metaphor.

2. Theological structure

a. Theological logic. The events of the passion of Christ: his suffering, death, resurrection, and glorification constitute the grounds of the logic of 1 Peter. The logic thus grounded gives structure both to the new reality and consequently to the new behavior characteristic of those who follow Christ.

These basic events of the career of Jesus that free the Christians from their sinful past (1:19) conform to God's plan for sinful humanity, a plan that predates creation (1:20) and whose announcement by the prophets predates their occurrence (1:11). It is the proclamation of the new reality created by those events of Christ's passion, the "good news" (1:25*b*), that makes it possible for people to enter into that new reality. Such entry is described metaphorically as a "new birth" (1:3) with its consequent "newborn infants" (2:2); such begetting and birth occur through the proclaimed word of the gospel (1:23). The author uses three key concepts to describe the begetting and birth into the new reality; they are hope, inheritance, and salvation. These three concepts appear in the opening portion of the letter (1:3-12; the *Prooemium*) where each is introduced by a parallel structure: "into a living hope" (1:3), "into an inheritance" (1:4), and "for a salvation" (1:5*b*). The discussion of these three concepts, along with their consequences, provides the logical coherence of the rest of the letter.

i. Hope. This first of the elements of the new begetting and birth brought about by the generative power of the word of God (the "gospel") is characterized as "living hope" (1:3). The adjective "living" indicates its origin in the risen and living Christ, and also contrasts it to other hopes that cannot be characterized by their relationship to divine life. Such a new and unique HOPE is accompanied by a new set of loyalties that grow out of it. Such a new set of loyalties is at odds with those former loyalties attached to the old life (1:14; 4:4), and hence causes Christians who hold to these new loyalties to become exiled and alienated from the society that gave rise to those former loyalties (1:1, 17; 2:11). Such alienation brings with it rejection by those who hold to the former loyalties, and results in suffering brought upon those who hold the new loyalties (1:6; 2:18-20; 3:14, 17; 4:12). That such alienation and suffering belong to the new reality is shown by the fact that that was precisely the course of events visited upon Christ (2:21-24) upon whom the new reality is based (4:1-2).

ii. Inheritance. The second of the central realities brought about by the generative power of the word of God (the gospel) is expressed in the term *inheritance.* That the locus of this new inheritance is "in heaven" (1:4) shows that it stands in contrast to any former inheritance entered into as a result of physical birth. Because birth is always into a specific people, new birth means birth into a new people, a people that at one time did not exist (2:10) but that now exists through the deliberate decision of God (1:2; 2:9). First Peter describes this new people in terms of Israel as chosen people, and has taken over Israel's role as chosen people. The new people are grounded, as was Israel, in God's election (*see* INHERITANCE IN THE NT).

A new inheritance brings with it customs and practices appropriate to membership in this new people. For that reason ethical admonitions (2:11) follow directly on the description of the new people (2:9-10). Those new customs and practices (2:1-3, 4-5, 12, 13-16; 3:9; 4:8-11) are to be followed not only in relation to fellow Christians (1:22; 3:8-12) but also in relation to those outside the Christian fellowship where customs remain unchanged and still bound to the pagan societal structures (2:12-17; 4:3). Such activity not only maintains the integrity of existence as a new people (3:8; 4:8-11) but can also have the effect of winning over those who are offended by those new customs and practices (3:14-16).

iii. Salvation. The third reality brought about by the generative power of God's word in begetting a new people is described as *salvation* (1:5*b*), a term that refers primarily to deliverance at the time of the final judgment (1:9) to which all people will be subject (1:17*a*; 3:17; 4:5), both those living at the time and also the dead (4:6). Such judgment, although close at hand (compare 1:20), lies in the future. Since the fate of the Christians in that judgment will be glory (5:10), they face a future different from the future that awaits those who do not share in the new reality (4:17). That new and different future frees the Christian from present apprehension (5:7) and allows him or her to bear present suffering with joy, knowing such suffering is temporary and will soon end (1:6; 4:12). *See* SALVATION.

Therefore Christians can look forward to their future with hope (1:13), certain that, following the path Christ also followed (4:13), their present suffering will eventuate in future glory. It is just such hope, however, that was the first of the three realities that grow out of the new birth. In that way the third reality, salvation, leads again to the first, namely hope, thus demonstrating the complete reality described by these three consequences of the Christians' new birth through God's generative word in the gospel.

b. Theological structure. As with the theological logic of 1 Peter, its theological structure is also christocentric, growing out of the events of Christ's life. The theological structure is cast in the categories of past, present, and future, used in two sets of parallels. In the first set, Christ's past and the Christians' present are paralleled, as are Christ's present and the Christians' future. In the second set, which grows out of the first, the Christians' past is set in parallel contrast to their present, and the present is set in parallel contrast to their future. The result is that the pattern of events in Christ's passion becomes the temporal structure of the Christians' life.

The contrast between Christ's past and his present is paralleled to the contrast between the Christians' present and their future in passages throughout the letter. Typically they are centered on the contrast between Christ's suffering (past) and glorification (present). Although Christ was rejected by human beings (past), he is risen and glorified (present), showing that he had been chosen beforehand by God (2:4; compare 1:20) and thus the pattern is not accidental. Again, as a result of his exaltation (past), all supernatural powers are now subjected to him (present, 3:22).

Using that series of events, the author then contrasts what happened in the past to Christ with what is happening in the present to Christians. As Christ suffered (2:21; 4:1-2), was wounded (2:24), and died (3:18), so Christians in the present suffer at the hands of their contemporaries (3:14; 4:13, 14). Similarly, as Christ is now glorified (1:21; 3:22), Christians anticipate a future that will bring blessing (3:9, 14), salvation (1:5-6, 9), and glory (1:7; 5:1, 4).

In the second set of parallels, the author compares the Christians' past to their present, showing how great and beneficial that change has been. A physical birth (past) is contrasted to the new birth into the Christian community (present, 1:3). Their past life characterized by ignorance is contrasted to their present characterized by holiness (1:14). The have been rescued by Christ (present) from the formerly futile ways (past, 1:18), they have been moved from darkness (past) into light (present, 2:9); though formerly straying sheep (past) they have now been brought to their true shepherd (present, 2:25). Once, like the gentiles to whom they belonged, they were bereft of God but they now have been included into a new people of God and have been freed from the profligacy of their former life (2:10; 4:3-4).

Important as the contrast between past and present is, there is an equally important contrast between present and future. Like the contrast between past and present, it is pervasive throughout the letter. The Christians' present suffering will gain them honor, praise, and glory at Christ's (future) return (1:7; compare 1:13), just as their (present) good conduct in the face of false accusations will allow them to glorify God at the (future) final judgment (2:12; compare 4:11-12). Humbled at present under God's mighty hand, they will be exalted by that same God in the future (5:6). As newborn Christians, those who remain faithful in the midst of a difficult present (1:5-6; compare 1:9; 3:9, 10-11, 14; 4:12-13; 5:1, 2-4) will receive their new and imperishable inheritance (1:3-4; compare 2:2). The ignorance responsible for their present persecution will in the future come to an end (2:15) since "gentiles" will one day also have to give an account for their present behavior (4:4-5; compare 4:17).

Thus the formal parallelism between the past/present and present/future informs the content of the entire letter. The past/present contrast assures the readers that the present/future contrast will be as sure and complete as that former contrast has proved to be. Thus the emphasis on the contrast between once and now highlights the main intention of the letter, namely to strengthen the readers in the "now" of their persecution and suffering by assuring them that the glorious future will transform their present situation as surely as their present condition is transformed from the past. The key to the entire argument is the fate of Christ, whose past and present contrast assures the Christians of their glorious present/future contrast.

c. Controlling metaphor. As in other NT writings, 1 Peter draws heavily on the OT for language and concepts to describe the Christian community. From almost casual references to Sarah as model for the Christian wife (3:6) or the use of the word *flock* to designate the local congregation (5:2) to more substantial use of Isa 53 to describe Christ's passion (2:22, 24-25) or Ps 34 to characterize behavior within the community of faith (3:10-12), 1 Peter draws on the writings of the people of Israel for language used to describe the new people of God.

Unlike other NT writings, 1 Peter has taken over the language of Israel for the Christian community in such a way that Israel has become the controlling metaphor for the way the theology of this letter is expressed. The letter opens and closes with terms drawn from the life of Israel: it opens by addressing them as the CHOSEN people currently in EXILE in the Diaspora (1:1) and closes with the identification of Rome as Babylon (5:13), symbolizing the power that sent Israel into exile. In the same vein, the reason for the necessity of new conduct by Christians (1:15-16) is the quotation from Leviticus (e.g., 11:44-45; 19:2; 20:7, 26) that identifies the very nature of Israel, and, by derivation, of the Christian community as a holy people. Most evident of the constitutive nature of this language for the Christian community is the passage 1 Pet 2:9-10, where terms used to describe that Christian community are drawn from OT passages (Exod 19:6; 23:22; Isa 43:20-21; Hos 2:23) that describe the uniqueness of Israel as God's elect people.

In that way, the language, and thus the reality, of Israel as God's people passes into the language and hence the reality of the new people of God chosen in Christ. As a result, that language, and hence the reality to which it refers, is not simply illustrative. It is constitutive and foundational for the Christian community. God's chosen people, once Israel, has become the Christian community, composed of both Christians and Jews.

3. Significance

Writing in a time of hostility toward the Christian community and what it believed, 1 Peter is significant for any current situation in which general cultural norms are antithetical, if not hostile, to the church. In varying degrees, that is true of the contemporary world, from governments controlled by other religions persecuting followers of Christ, at one extreme, to a disdain for Christian values among culturally elite groups within a given culture at the other. By shaping the letter as he did, e.g., in terms of Israel as controlling metaphor and by employing the contrasts of past/present and present/future, all tied to the career of Christ, particularly his life, death, resurrection, and glorification, the author sought to enable his readers to withstand the abuse of a culture that found the very faithfulness of Christians to their community and its ideals offensive. The Greco-Roman culture posed a formidable threat to the existence of the Christian community. The continuing survival of the church in these early years within the Roman Empire points to the effectiveness of the witness of this letter, an effectiveness that continues to the present. *See* CHURCH, IDEA OF THE.

Bibliography: Paul J. Achtemeier. *1 Peter.* Hermeneia (1996); John H. Elliott. *1 Peter.* AB 37B (2000); Leonhard Goppelt. *A Commentary on 1 Peter.* J. E. Alsup, trans. (1993); J. Ramsey Michaels. *1 Peter* (1989); Pheme Perkins. *First and Second Peter, James, and Jude.* IBC (1995).

PAUL ACHTEMEIER

PETER, GOSPEL OF pee´tuhr, gos´puhl. A pseudonymous work from the early or mid-2nd cent. CE mentioned (but not quoted) by a few church fathers in the contest with Gnosticism and only partially preserved in manuscripts from modern archaeological excavations in Egypt. The text begins at the conclusion of a trial of Jesus before Pilate and Herod, then relates Jesus' death, burial, and resurrection, and breaks off at the beginning of his appearance to several followers in Galilee. It contains the first extant narrative in early Christian literature of the resurrection of Jesus itself, with two "men" (angels) who "sustain" Jesus in his departure from the tomb, and a speaking cross that emerges from the tomb after them, answering a heavenly voice that questions Jesus.

Recent scholarship no longer views the *Gospel of Peter* as gnostic or docetic, but as a mainstream document with occasional docetic touches. It was used by both the greater church (Mileto of Sardis and probably Justin) and Gnosticism; its acceptance by 2nd-cent. gnostics was a main factor in its rejection by the church at large. Helmut Koester and John D. Crossan have argued for a source of the *Gospel of Peter* that can be dated to the mid-1st cent. and was also a source for the Passion Narrative in the canonical Gospels. The majority conclusion has sharply denied this, maintaining that the *Gospel of Peter* is literarily dependent on the Synoptics, especially Matthew, and is supplemented with 2nd-cent. oral traditions from popular mainstream Christianity. *See* APOCRYPHA, NT.

Bibliography: Raymond E. Brown. "The Gospel of Peter—A Noncanonical Passion Narrative." *The Death of the Messiah* (1994) 2:1317–49; John D. Crossan. *The Cross That Spoke* (1988).

ROBERT E. VAN VOORST

PETER, MARTYRDOM OF pee´tuhr, mahr´turh-duhm. Written in Greek ca. 170–190 CE, probably in Asia Minor or in Rome, the *Martyrdom of Peter* is the final main division of the *Acts of Peter* (sections 30–41). It was separated from the *Acts of Peter* in the 3rd cent. CE and circulated independently. The *Martyrdom of Peter* survives in three Greek manuscripts and several versions in the Eastern churches: Coptic (fragmentary), Syriac, Ethiopic, Arabic, Armenian, and Slavonic.

Despite besting Simon the magician in a contest of miracles in the Roman Forum, Peter is condemned by the Roman prefect Agrippa to death by crucifixion. He asks to be crucified head down, because, as he says, he is not worthy to die in the same manner as Jesus. As he dies, he gives a lengthy, discursive sermon, complete with OT quotations and allusions, urging his followers to stay true to Christ. Because the several accounts of Peter's death in earlier Christian literature do not mention the way that he was crucified, it is likely (but not demonstrable) that this was a popular Christian legend arising in the 2nd cent. CE that sought to make Peter's martyrdom distinct among the many martyrologies of the time. To judge from the wide distribution of this document, and the influence it had on Christian life particularly in times of persecution, this legend contributed to its success. *See* APOCRYPHA, NT; PETER, ACTS OF.

ROBERT E. VAN VOORST

PETER, PREACHING OF. An early Christian work extant only in fragmentary quotations, primarily by Clement of Alexandria (*Strom.* 1.29.182; 2.15.68; 6.5.39–41; 6.5.43; 6.6.48; 6.7.58; 6.15.128; *Ecl.* 58). Clement attributes it to the apostle Peter, but Origen questions its authenticity (*Comm. Jo.* 13.17), and Eusebius considers it noncanonical (*Hist. eccl.* 3.3.2). Origen notes that the gnostic Heracleon quoted it.

The work is dated to the early 2nd cent. CE. Egypt is its most probable provenance. The original literary form is unknown. Its title, however, suggests the intent to present the content of the apostle Peter's preaching—i.e., basic Christian beliefs. Included with Peter's words is a speech of the risen Christ sending his twelve apostles into the world (frag. 3). The *Preaching* emphasizes the missionary role of the Twelve: they are to call all people to repentance and belief in the one God through Christ (frag. 3).

Scriptural proofs are central to the *Preaching*: "We say nothing apart from scripture" (frag. 4b). It claims that the main lines of the Christian kerygma concerning Jesus (his coming, death, resurrection, and assumption) are found in the "books of the prophets" (frag. 4a). It quotes Jer 31:31 (Christians have a "new covenant" with God; frag. 2d) and alludes to Isa 2:3 in calling Christ "Law and Word" (frag. 1). Both of these scriptural passages figure prominently in the proof text tradition common to Justin, Irenaeus, Tertullian, and other early catholic Christian authors.

Fragment 2 shows a self-consciousness of Christians as a "third race" that worships God in a manner distinct from "Greeks" (who worship idols and animals) and "Jews" (who, claiming to worship God, in fact worship "angels and archangels, the months and the moon").

Fragment 2a is a rhetorically polished philosophical description of God as "the incomprehensible," "the imperishable," and the "uncreated." With its stress on monotheistic belief and the errors of Greeks and Jews, the *Preaching* is an early example of Christian apologetic literature; it has a special affinity with the *Apology* of Aristides.

Bibliography: Wilhelm Schneemelcher. "The Kerygma Petri." *New Testament Apocrypha.* Vol. 2. Rev. ed. (1991) 34–41.

MARTIN C. ALBL

PETER, SECOND LETTER OF pee´tuhr [**Πέτρος Β Petros B**]. One of several early works ascribed to the apostle Peter by members of the early Jesus movement. Along with 1 Peter, it was admitted, with some difficulty and hesitation, into the NT canon (see Origen in Eusebius, *Hist. eccl.* 6.25.11 and Jerome, *Epist.* 120.11). This letter is one of the general or CATHOLIC EPISTLES and is an important pseudonymous work of the sub-apostolic period that has much to contribute to our understanding of early Christian theological and ecclesial evolution.

A. General Introduction

Second Peter has had, until recently, a precarious position in the Christian canon of holy books. At first its authenticity as a Petrine work was disputed, but it nonetheless found its way into the canonical list, only to be relegated to the lesser works of the NT list (*see* CANON OF THE NEW TESTAMENT). Though rarely read by past generations of believers and scholars, this work has received increased attention as modern readers have begun to appreciate its theological contribution to early Christian tradition and to understand its ecclesial setting, purpose, and strategy. The early faith communities and the existential clues they have left in their literature are of great interest and importance to later generations; such is the case for the ideological, religious, and theological significance of 2 Peter.

This three-chapter epistle treats a surprisingly large number of topics and issues for consideration. Between brief epistolary and body openings and an even more terse closing (1:1-2, 3-11; and 3:17-18), the author presents extended sections devoted to the issues of true prophecy, false prophets and teaching, and the Lord's day. The first of these sections (1:1-21), after dwelling at some length on the theme of "knowledge of our Lord Jesus Christ" (1:3-11), focuses on the issue of true prophecy by dwelling on Peter's reliability as eyewitness and bearer of authentic apostolic tradition (*see* PETER, THE APOSTLE). Thus, Simon Peter, the alleged writer, wishes to prepare for the period after his death by presenting a trustworthy record of his testimony (1:15). Appeal is made to two episodes in the Jesus tradition where the witness of Peter is crucial to establish a link between the alleged apostolic writer and the claims that will be made in regard to Jesus' coming; these allusions are, on the one hand, to John 21:18-19 where Jesus foretells Peter's death (1:13-15) and, on the other, to Mark 9:2-8 (and par.) where Peter and the apostles more generally are present at the manifestation of Jesus' glory (1:16-18). The Petrine author insists that the apostles have been witnesses to God's testimony concerning Jesus and are now guarantors of prophecy concerning his return or coming (see 3:4). It is not the appeal to Greek myths that supports Christian claims (1:16) but the Holy Spirit speaking through apostolic tradition (1:19, 21).

A second lengthy section (2:1-22) addresses the deception and punishment of the deviant teachers as false prophets. This long, colorful, and obscure section is a lengthy rewriting and expansion of Jude 4-16 and its stark alternating pattern of condemnation of earlier opponents and their heresy (*see* JUDE, LETTER OF). In place of Jude's sixfold depiction of unrelenting, impending judgment of troublesome opponents, one finds in 2 Peter a lengthy threefold treatment of false teachers, their teaching and activity, the certitude of divine punishment, and the harsh condemnation that awaits those who entice their fellow believers to apostasy and debauchery. Second Peter is both more hopeful for the godly and severe toward the ungodly than Jude. Also, the beliefs of the false teachers are presented with some specificity here (2:1*b*-2) and later in chap. 3 (3:3-7).

Thus, the third and final section (3:1-18) focuses more specifically on the problem at hand, namely, the false teachers' denial of the Parousia because of its delay (3:4-7). The author appeals first to cosmological arguments (the cosmological character of the beginning and the end of the world involving water and fire, respectively; 3:6-7), then to temporal and theological considerations (vv. 8-9) to explain the reason for the delay of Jesus' return. "The Lord's day," after God's benevolent patience has run its course, "will come like a thief" (3:10) and all manner of apocalyptic phenomena will take place, namely, the fiery, noisy passing of the heavens and the earth (vv. 10, 12; *see* DAY OF THE LORD). But in view of the holy conduct of the righteous and in accordance with God's promise, believers "wait for new heavens and a new earth, where righteousness is at home" (v. 13). In the meantime they are to "grow in the grace and knowledge of our Lord and Savior Jesus Christ" (v. 18).

How then do these three blocks of material relate first to one another and then to the author's purpose for writing? Clearly, these point to the climactic reproaches of 3:3-4 concerning Jesus' failure to return as judge as well as to his frequently mentioned role as lord and savior (e.g., 1:1, 8, 11, 14, 16). Equally, this block of material relates to the author's strategy and overall message.

B. Literary Analysis: Genre and Structure

1. Literary analysis

The style, language, and culture of 2 Peter are those of an educated Hellenist, not those of early Palestinian disciples. And though the author's style may at times be complex and even convoluted (e.g., 2:4-10*a*), there appears much mixing of Hellenistic and biblical vocabulary and traditions. Indeed the author's extensive rewriting of the biblical stories taken from Jude shows both a love for abstract language and knowledge of Stoic physics and the traditional pagan cosmological myths. Even allusions to the OT seem to be related to classical narratives. The allusion to the story of Noah (2 Pet 2:5) is like Deucalion and the flood story (Apollodorus, *Library* 1.7.2; Ovid, *Metam.* 1.313–90), and the story of the fallen angels "cast into hell" (tartaroō ταρταρόω; 2 Pet 2:4) is reminiscent of the casting of the Titans into Tartarus, the underworld (Hesiod, *Theog.* 721–819). The destruction and recreation of the cosmos (2 Pet 3:10-13) is comparable to Stoic cosmology (*see* STOICS, STOICISM). Thus, both the author's stress on Petrine tradition (Peter episodes) and characteristics (Semitic and Hellenistic names) and the appeals to the writings of Paul (2 Pet 3:15) and "other scriptures" (3:16) underscore the document's pseudonymous as well as Hellenistic character. Further, it is doubtful that the curious reference to "our beloved brother Paul" in 3:15*b*-16 points to the author as a Paulinist.

2. Genre

Second Peter, like Jude, has only the outward appearance of a letter, namely, a standard opening, a body, and a formulaic closing. These meager epistolary features, a phenomenon seen in other late NT writings, in this case serve to introduce the major portion of the document and invite the reader to entertain other literary genres.

The farewell discourse is the most instructive. This well-known biblical genre or sub-genre (see the speeches of Jacob [Gen 48–49], Moses [Deut 32–33], Joshua [Josh 22–24], David [1 Chr 28–29], Jesus [Mark 13 and par.; John 14–17], and Paul [Acts 20]) focuses or presupposes the forthcoming death of the hero; dwells on the themes of sorrow, reassurance, warnings, and advice; and perhaps gives lessons in history. The focus, as we have seen earlier, on the figure of Peter, either in self-defense or as eyewitness of Jesus' teaching and glory, points to the author's defense of Peter as trustworthy witness and as true prophet. Peter, before his death, is eager to leave the audience or reader a trustworthy source for recalling Jesus' teaching (1:15). Thus, the genre and structure of 2 Peter have much to tell us about the author's strategy and message. The discourse introduction (1:3-11) can be viewed as a tripartite structure that introduces the author's farewell discourse (see *4 Ezra* 14:28-36 for an instructive par.) as it presents the themes of God's benefactions (vv. 3-4), human effort expected in response (vv. 5-10), and finally the eschatological goal and reward of the believer's call and election (v. 11). These themes present the theological basis for the ensuing farewell discourse.

3. Structure

So it is in view of the above genre considerations that we propose the following discourse structure for understanding 2 Peter's purpose and overall message.

Epistolary Opening (1:1-2)
Discourse Structure (1:3–3:16)
  Discourse Introduction (1:3-11)
  Part 1: True and False Prophecy (1:12–2:22)
a. Peter and the Reliability of Apostolic Tradition (1:12-21)
b. False Teachers: Their Deception and Punishment (2:1-22)
  Part 2: Jesus' Return: Promise, Providence, and Salvation (3:1-16)
a. Delay of the Parousia, Repentance, End time (3:1-10)
b. Final Exhortation about Holy Conduct (3:11-16)
Epistolary Closing (3:17-18)

Thus, two principal parts of the work stand out, both introduced by the theme of "reminding or remembering" (1:12, 13, 15; 3:1, 2) and both insisting on the addressees' knowledge of apostolic tradition. The first section, 1:12–2:22, deals first with true prophecy as deriving from the original apostolic tradition, particularly with Peter as the inspired prophet or apostle, and second, with the false teachers who introduce heresies and fabrications (for this part 2 Peter borrows and rewrites much of Jude 4-16). The second section, 3:1-16, directs its attention to the defining issue of the polemics, i.e., the delay of the Parousia or Jesus' return (see 3:4-7). The primary issue, as we shall see, revolves around the exercise of Jesus' salvific role both as present lord and returning judge, the one the author repeatedly calls "our Lord and Savior Jesus Christ" (1:11, etc.).

C. Theological Analysis: Purpose and Strategy

Before addressing the issue of the author's purpose (and thus strategy), it is necessary to discuss two related issues, namely, 2 Peter's response(s) to the alleged statements of the false teachers and the nature of the heresy under scrutiny.

1. False teachers

It is frequently proposed that a number of passages in 2 Peter both preserve the teachers' objections and express the author's responses to their "cleverly devised myths" (1:16), the value or confirmation of prophecy (1:19), the idle or nonexistent character of divined judgment (2:3), or the delay or non-coming of the Lord (3:4). Second Peter then would be seen as a series of responses to such polemical statements by the false teachers or prophets. In structural and thematic terms, the crowning issue of the controversy concerns the last mentioned (the delay of the Lord's return) and that the other issues are related either to the author's strategy or to the polemics against the FALSE TEACHERS. Also important here are the christological titles employed in the work, especially "Lord and Savior."

2. Nature of the heresy

On the other hand, the nature of the HERESY has variously been viewed as 1) gnostic or spiritualist in character, 2) as Epicurean-like opposition to divine providence, or 3) as eschatological skepticism relating to the delay of Jesus' return. The first is less appealing since it anachronistically reads late gnostic developments into the sub-apostolic period. The other two provide interesting background for the study of 2 Peter and the early church more generally. The context for the second is Stoic debate against Epicurean pessimism concerning a noncaring divinity. The third option approaches more directly the christological concerns of 2 Pet 3:4-14, for whom the crowning issue of the debate seems to be the question of Jesus' return (*see* PAROUSIA).

3. Purpose

The above discussion brings us to a final statement of the author's purpose. While it is probably true that the most serious challenge to the Christian community and to the religious person generally, as it is expressed in 2 Peter, is that of denying divine providence ("all things continue as they were from the beginning of creation," 3:4*b*), it is nonetheless the first, interrogative statement of the false teachers that provides the author's and the Christian's point of reference for such an eschatological debate: "where is the promise of his coming?" The issue of 2 Peter is christological, for it is Jesus' lordship that is at stake; it is his return that motivates, at least in part, Christian behavior (see the addressees' question and its context in 3:11-13). As God's divine Son (2 Peter has a high CHRISTOLOGY) he is the promised one, who now provides assistance and protection, who will return to judge and to lead the righteous to his eternal kingdom—again, note that Jesus is here called "Lord and Savior" (1:11).

4. Strategy

We return to the author's strategy; since the promise can be traced through the eyewitnesses to the heavenly voice (1:16-18), the addressees can now believe and repeatedly hear Peter's final testimony (1:12-15) that the apostolic preaching about Jesus' "power and coming" (1:16), as well as about God's forbearance or benevolent patience (3:9), is a very reliable "prophetic message" (1:19) that dictates "what sort of people [believers]" ought to be in holy conduct and piety, while awaiting and hastening the coming of God's day (3:11-12). Additionally, 2 Peter warns, in graphic detail, about false teachers who propagate their destructive opinions and lead many, themselves included, on the path of destruction (2:1). The addressees are assured that the community's eschatological as well as soteriological teaching is reliable and inspired and is to serve as the foundation for a life of purity and commitment to God and to the Lord Jesus Christ. The latter, after all, has provided for their success and demands a firm effort on their part (1:5-10).

D. Brief Commentary

1. Epistolary opening (1:1-2)

Employing the traditional tripartite opening of the Hellenistic letter, the pseudonymous author begins by appealing to the apostle's Semitic as well as Greek names ("Simeon Peter") and by imitating the openings of the successful canonical letters of Jude and 1 Peter ("servant" and "apostle of Jesus Christ," respectively), to construct a believable testamentary Petrine work. Further, the addressees are designated in rather general terms as those "who have received [the] faith" and practice Jesus' righteousness (see 3:13). Finally, the traditional wish of "grace and peace" is related by the author to the crucial concepts of growth and knowledge (see 3:14, 18 and the further discussion below of the theme of knowledge).

2. Discourse introduction (1:3-11)

In place of the usual thanksgiving of ecclesial letters (see 1 Pet 1:3) 2 Peter formulates an interesting tripartite thematic prologue for the ensuing farewell discourse (see earlier discussion). The first part (1:3-4) addresses the theme of divine benefactions, i.e., God "gave us all things that pertain to life and godliness." Interestingly, these have come "through knowledge" of Jesus, that is, through his "great promises." The second part (vv. 5-10) discusses at length the effort required for supplementing one's faith. In the third part (v. 11) the author reiterates the goal and reward of this salvific process, whether participating in "divine nature" (v. 4), entering Jesus' "eternal kingdom" (v. 11), or experiencing heavenly righteousness (3:13).

3. Peter and the reliability of Apostolic tradition (1:12-21)

At this point the author introduces the first of two major, distinct parts of the document, each marked off by extended, complex recall formulas in 1:12-15 and 3:1-3. The first part is itself devoted to two opposing but complementary themes: true prophecy and its apostolic, particularly Petrine origin (1:12-21) and false prophecy as exemplified in the community's false teachers (2:1-22); the second major part deals more directly with the document's principal concerns, namely, the Lord's day, Jesus' return, and related issues of theodicy and moral practice (3:1-16).

In this long, foundational section (1:12-21) the author of 2 Peter sets out to accomplish a number of tasks, namely, the winning of the addressees' goodwill by insisting that they already know what is at stake (1:12), the setting up of the document's testamentary context by pointing to Peter's forthcoming death and the document's role as permanent, written record and reminder of Peter's teaching (1:13-15), the insistence that the writer and other apostolic figures witnessed both the glorious Lord Jesus and the heavenly voice as the source of the community's tradition (1:16-18), and finally a terse discussion of the reliability and origin of prophecy (1:19-21). It is at this point that the author employs two distinct Petrine episodes from the community's Gospels (see earlier) to establish, on the one hand, the document's testamentary character, namely, its claim to be Peter's final summation of the apostolic tradition before his death, as regards the subject at hand, and, on the other hand, to underscore the tradition's divine origin and christological character. In the first case the author appeals to Peter's forthcoming "putting off of the body," as foretold by the Lord, to justify the composition of 2 Peter as a perpetual means of recall of the community's tradition and as a firm link now and in the future between Jesus and the community of the faithful. In the second case the author employs apologetically the transfiguration story, not the venerable mythic traditions of the Hellenistic world, to characterize the apostolic tradition as heavenly in origin, as christological in character (about Jesus' salvific power and his coming as judge), and as communicated to the apostles on the holy mountain.

Thus the author can conclude this foundational section in vv. 19-21 by insisting that the community's tradition concerning the Lord Jesus' coming in power is a reliable prophetic message, one that comes from a heavenly source and that is embedded in the original apostolic preaching and indeed one that must serve now as a shining lamp for those who await the light bearer's return on the Lord's day. Peter and the other apostles have served and continue to serve as reliable witnesses to God's prophetic message concerning the community's soteriological and eschatological beliefs.

4. False teachers: Their deception and punishment (2:1-22)

To the extent that the apostolic witnesses, Peter in particular, are presented, in a first extended passage, as reliable mediums of God's prophetic message to the addressees, to an even greater extent the opponents, in a lengthy second panel, are condemned as false prophet-like teachers who deceive, teach false doctrine, and indulge in licentious practices. As noted earlier, the author has borrowed words, themes, and entire textual units from the Letter of Jude to construct a bitter threefold condemnation of the opponents' deceptive teaching and behavior and to insist on the divine punishment that awaits these ungodly people.

First, the author introduces the false teachers of the community by comparing them to the false prophets of the past and insists that their denial of the salvific Master will bring about their own swift destruction (1-3). To underscore their just punishment the author introduces a lengthy conditional sentence in vv. 4-10*a*, whose protasis (vv. 4-8 consisting of four clauses introduced by "if" [ei εἰ] and continued by successive "and" [kai καὶ] clauses) presents four OT examples and is balanced by a concluding apodosis in vv. 9-10*a*. In contrast to Jude, which underscores repeated examples of divine punishment, 2 Peter alternates evil and good models and concludes in v. 9 that God rescues the godly and "keep[s] the unrighteous under punishment until the day of judgment." Thus the examples of the sinful angels and the ungodly Dead Sea cities are counterbalanced by the righteousness of Noah and Lot and further underscore God's cosmic lordship or authority (see v. 10*a*).

There follow in quick succession two units condemning the teachers (10*b*-14 and 15-22), each of which presents a similar overall structure: an initial polemical characterization of the teachers ("bold and willful" people and "accursed children," v. 14*c*), a statement of accusation against them related to an OT story (the angels in v. 11 and Balaam and the beast of burden in vv. 15-16), a resumption (in 2:12 and 17) of the polemic by use of stark imagery borrowed from Jude 10 and 12 ("irrational animals" and "waterless springs," respectively), and an extension and conclusion of the theme of divine punishment by a series of loosely connected, complex statements. From beginning to end the entire chapter focuses on the reality and fate of the false teachers.

5. Jesus' return: Promise, providence, and salvation (3:1-16)

At this point 2 Peter introduces the second, and more crucial, part of the document, a part that, like the first (1:12-15), is also marked off by an extended, complex recall formula, featuring the terms *reminding, remember,* and *understand* (3:1-3). The beginning of the chapter (vv. 1-4) provides the reader with clues both for the author's purpose for writing and for understanding the thematic structure of the remainder of the document. It is generally agreed that v. 4 presents the core or flash points of the teachers' false teaching in the form of two stark statements denying both the Lord Jesus' return and the reality of divine providence. These two topics are subsequently treated in reverse order: vv. 5-7 and 8-10. Careful observation also suggests that v. 3 provides further clues for the author's focus, since 2 Peter accuses the teachers of making fun of or "scoffing" at the community's traditions and of living lives of debauchery or passion. It is no surprise that vv. 1-2 and 15*b*-16 are focused on the community's sources of authority and that vv. 11-15*a* are devoted to proper behavior or conduct. The author's discussion therefore focuses on four major issues, the first two introduced by v. 3 and the second two by v. 4.

a. Tradition. The false teachers scoff at or twist the Scriptures (see vv. 3 and 16). It is for this reason that the author speaks repeatedly of the community's tradition, true prophecy, knowledge of God and the Lord Jesus. This topic is the focal point of 3:1-2 where 2 Peter insists that the authority of Peter's memoirs, of the letter 1 Peter, of the OT prophets, and the apostolic message are crucial to the community's beliefs and practices. The teachers may scoff or twist these resources out of shape, whether Paul or the community's other authorities, but this only underscores their ignorance and unstable character (3:16).

b. Righteousness. Not only have the false teachers been accused of introducing "destructive opinions" (2:1) but of "indulging their own lusts" (3:3; see also 1:4; 2:10, 18). While they have followed the path of destruction, believers must live "lives of holiness and godliness" (3:11); they must be "without spot or blemish" (3:14). Thus, again, a question, this time from the community, concerning behavior (3:11-12), leads to a brief discussion of righteous living and its traditional foundation (vv. 13-15*a*).

c. Providence. From the teachers' own words we learn that divine providence is being called into question: "ever since our ancestors died, all things continue as they were from the beginning of creation" (3:4*b*). Thus, these would-be Christians reject the notion that everything is flux and opt instead for the immutability of the universe and thereby deny the possibility of divine intervention in cosmic and human affairs (see Philo, *Eternity* 7). Without skipping a beat, the author rejects such a notion of divinity and launches immediately instead into a cosmological argument concerning divine creation, purgation, and the eventual judgment of the world by the divine Word (vv. 5-7). The author insists that God is indeed active vis-à-vis the cosmos from its creation to its final dissolution and, the author adds, so is God's "judgment and destruction of the godless" (v. 7).

d. The Lord's return. We turn to the final and most central element of the document, the false teachers' denial, also expressed in their own words of mockery, that the Lord Jesus is to return: "where is the promise of his coming?" (3:4*a*). Thus, after having responded in 3:4*b*-7 to the statement that nothing changes, 2 Peter in 3:8-10 focuses on the theme of the Lord's return in terms of "delay," provides a reason for this divine respite (i.e., God's forbearance or mercy), and then reminds the addressees of the certitude of Jesus' return and of the stark nature of that day. Indeed, in divine terms, "the Lord is not slow about his promise ... but [in eschatological and christological terms] is patient ... not wanting any to perish" (3:9). Jesus will return as judge, despite the false teachers' mocking claims to the contrary, and lead the beloved "into the eternal kingdom" (1:11) but in the meantime he is the "Lord and Savior" (see the author's repeated use of these titles for Jesus—1:11; 2:20; 3:2, 18; see also 1:1), who has redeemed or bought them (2:2). So believers in the present are to "grow in the grace and knowledge of [the] Lord and Savior Jesus Christ" (3:18), while "waiting for and hastening the coming of the day of God" (3:12*a*).

6. Epistolary closing (3:17-18)

Second Peter here follows the traditional letter convention of direct address ("beloved"), brief negative and positive exhortations, and an even shorter, concluding doxology. This conclusion, like the overall document, exhibits a strong christological focus, whether "growth in grace and knowledge" is associated with the "Lord and Savior Jesus Christ" or whether the letter's doxology be a christological rather than a theological one. Thus the letter is particularly concerned about Jesus' salvific role in the life of believers and the exercise of his power as present lord and returning judge.

E. Theological and Religious Significance

Both the negative and positive aspects of 2 Peter's exhortation require a serious audience. Whether a stern rebuke of false teachers (threatened with divine judgment) or a promise of Jesus' forbearance (time for repentance), the letter is a plea to the addressees to consider the gift of faith as something "precious" (1:1) and as something that needs to grow as "grace and knowledge of [the] Lord and Savior Jesus Christ" (3:18), the one who "received honor and glory from God the Father" (1:17).

The letter of 2 Peter, like its predecessor Jude, reveals a fierce struggle against people judged to be false teachers and becomes a plea for eschatological and moral orthodoxy. The letter reveals some of the growth pains the early church experienced as it moved out into the Greek world and as its members dialogued with its contemporaries, striving all the while to protect the truth of its beliefs and the integrity of its morality. Nonetheless, the key issue for this author involves Jesus' salvific role, a role that calls for continued commitment to and knowledge of Jesus that recognizes his lordship and looks forward, through a time of holy conduct and piety, to his coming. Finally, it is the author's wish and strategy that the addressees may, at any time in the future, recall "Peter's" words (in this document) as prophecy about "the power and coming of [the] Lord Jesus Christ" (1:16).

Bibliography: R. J. Bauckham. *Jude, 2 Peter.* WBC 50 (1983); R. J. Bauckham. "2 Peter: An Account of Research." *ANRW* 2.25.2 (1988) 3713–52; J. Knight. *2 Peter and Jude.* NTG (1995); J. H. Neyrey. "The Apologetic Use of the Transfiguration in 2 Peter 1:16-21." *CBQ* 42 (1980) 504–19; J. H. Neyrey. "The Form and Background of the Polemic in 2 Peter." *JBL* 99 (1980) 407–31; J. H. Neyrey. *2 Peter, Jude.* AB 37C (1993); E. J. Richard. *Reading 1 Peter, Jude, and 2 Peter: A Literary and Theological Commentary* (2000); D. P. Senior and D. J. Harrington. *1 Peter,*

Jude, and 2 Peter (2003); D. F. Watson. *Invention, Arrangement, and Style: Rhetorical Criticism of Jude and 2 Peter* (1986).

EARL RICHARD

PETER, SLAVONIC ACTS OF. This late apocryphal romance ostensibly narrates Peter's experiences on the way to and in Rome, and his death. After a mysterious child urges him to sail to Rome, Peter buys the child from the ship's captain. The child works miracles in Rome, raising the dead whom Peter then returns to their graves. When the child appears after the crucifixion of Peter, the nails fall from Peter's body, and the child reveals himself to be Jesus. Its fantastical plot likely originated in popular Christian circles. Extant only in Slavonic, it probably has no literary connection to the *Acts of Peter*. *See* APOCRYPHA, NT; PETER, ACTS OF.

ROBERT E. VAN VOORST

PETER, THE APOSTLE pee'tuhr [Πέτρος Petros]. The most prominent disciple of Jesus, Peter is mentioned 155 times in the NT. His name was Simon (**Simōn** [Σίμων] in Matt 4:18) or Simeon (**Symeōn** [Συμεών] in Acts 15:14; 2 Pet 1:1) from Hebrew **shimeʿon** (שִׁמְעוֹן). He is also called **Bariōna** (Βαριωνᾶ, "bar Jonah" or "son of Jonah," Matt 16:17) or "son of John" (**huios Iōannou** [υἱὸς Ἰωάννου] in John 1:42). Jesus nicknamed him "Peter" (**Petros**, Mark 3:16), meaning "rock," which is "Cephas" (**Kēphas** [Κηφᾶς]), in Aram.); Paul ordinarily uses the Aram. "Cephas" (1 Cor 1:12; Gal 1:18).

A. Life and Character: A Synthetic Approach

A synthesis of NT stories provides the picture familiar in later Christian imagination. Peter and his brother Andrew were FISHERMEN on the Sea of Galilee, living in Capernaum where Jesus cured Peter's mother-in-law (Mark 1:29-31). The brothers left family and occupation to follow Jesus as part of the twelve disciples chosen to accompany Jesus on his ministry. Peter and the fishermen, James and John, sons of Zebedee, belonged to an inner circle of three disciples who witnessed some events that the others did not (Mark 5:37; 9:2-13; 14:32-41). As a literary device, the evangelists paint these privileged disciples failing to accept Jesus as suffering Messiah (Mark 8:31-38; 10:35-45; 14:32-42). After Jesus' resurrection, Peter became a premier APOSTLE and leader of the church known for powerful preaching and miraculous powers. The evangelists attribute this transformation to the prayer and intervention of Jesus (Luke 22:31-34; John 21:15-19) and the work of the Holy Spirit (Acts 2–3; 10). The disciple who had denied knowing Jesus in the high priest's courtyard (Mark 14:66-72) now spokes boldly before the Sanhedrin and was miraculously rescued from prison in Jerusalem (Acts 4:1-22; 5:17-22). Peter died as a martyr (John 21:18-19) in Rome under the emperor Nero (*1 Clem.* 5:4-5).

In the NT Peter is portrayed as the most outspoken of the twelve disciples, eager to raise questions and objections. He confesses Jesus to be the Messiah, but refuses to accept his prediction of suffering (Mark 8:27-33 and par.). Various stories show him to be impulsive, e.g., leaping into the sea, even trying to walk on water like Jesus (Matt 14:22-33) and lopping off a servant's ear in Gethsemane (John 18:10). He follows the arresting party to the high priest's courtyard (John 18:15-18), but becomes frightened when his identity as a disciple is suspected and denies his association with Jesus (Mark 14:66-72 and par.; John 18:25-27). The evangelists have Jesus predict that Peter will not manage to keep his bold promises to stand by him even if the other disciples fail (Mark 14:26-50 and par.). Thus the Gospels consistently depict Peter as a person flawed in character who is earnest in following Jesus. For the NT, then, he becomes a model disciple in whose life both God's grace and human dedication are evident.

B. Preeminent Disciple of Jesus: Four Gospels

In all three Synoptic Gospels, Peter is given primacy among the disciples of Jesus, named first in the lists of the Twelve (Matt 10:2-4; Mark 3:16-19; Luke 6:13-16; compare Acts 1:13; *see* TWELVE, THE). He is also named first in the inner circle of three (with JAMES and JOHN) who are close to Jesus and privy to special occasions such as raising a synagogue leader's daughter from the dead (Mark 5:37-43), witnessing Jesus' transfiguration on a mountain (Mark 9:2-13), hearing his prophecy concerning the end and the Temple (Mark 13:3-8), and seeing his agony in Gethsemane (Mark 14:33-42).

He takes the lead in recognizing Jesus as the Messiah (Mark 8:29; Luke 9:20) and the Son of the living God (Matt 16:16) in Caesarea Philippi. Even though in fear he denies Jesus three times, he repents in deep remorse (e.g., Matt 26:75) and is given special attention at Jesus' resurrection ("Go, tell his disciples and Peter that he is going ahead of you to Galilee," Mark 16:7; Luke 24:12). *See* DISCIPLE, DISCIPLESHIP.

1. Gospel of Mark

Each Synoptic Gospel highlights Peter's role as a model disciple in distinct ways. In the Gospel of Mark, Peter "immediately" leaves his fishing nets to follow Jesus, when Jesus calls him to "fish for people" (Mark 1:16-18). Though the first to confess Jesus as Messiah, he also rebukes Jesus for talking about suffering in Jerusalem. As a result, he is sternly rebuked by Jesus (8:33). He falls asleep at Gethsemane when Jesus directs him to pray (14:32-42), and he is afraid to acknowledge his association with Jesus in front of the high priest's servant (14:66-72). In Mark's narrative, therefore, Peter provides both positive and negative examples of discipleship. He may leave everything behind to follow Jesus, but he lacks faith and understanding at times. Some scholars speculate that the negative stories might indicate an anti-Petrine sentiment, but others see them as essential parts of the Gospel narrative intended to encourage the reader to be honest in faith and grow in understanding of the crucified Messiah who "came not to be served but to serve, and to give his life a ransom for many" (10:45), an idea contrary to the popular expectation of the time. Stories of Peter in Mark suggest that both faithfulness to one's calling and obedience to divine planning are hallmarks of true discipleship. They also demonstrate how challenging it is to follow the way of the Lord. The way to glory begins with humiliation, suffering, and even death on the cross (*see* MARK, GOSPEL OF).

2. Gospel of Matthew

In the Gospel of Matthew, Peter is featured as a representative of the disciples and is called the "rock" of faith authorized to build Jesus' church. Most notably, he is given continuous attention in chaps. 14–18 where he becomes the main character in conversation with Jesus on the way to Jerusalem. Peter's stature as leader of the church grows higher as the narrative unfolds.

In chap. 14, the disciples are weary in a boat battered by the waves and terrified by the unexpected arrival of Jesus, mistaking him for a ghost. Peter asks for permission to walk on the sea toward him. Even though he is frightened by the roaring water and begins to sink, he cries out "Lord, save me!" and is rescued (14:30). Peter is chided for "little faith," but his desire to reach Jesus and his cry for help become examples for believers facing crises and dangers.

In chap. 15, Jesus condemns the Pharisees and the scribes for their hypocrisy in dealing with purity laws and the obligation to care for parents, calling them "blind guides of the blind" who will be uprooted like a plant. Peter asks Jesus to explain his point, to which Jesus replies, "What comes out of the mouth proceeds from the heart, and this is what defiles" (15:18). The disciples are reprimanded for being "still without understanding," but Peter's inquiry prompts Jesus to define for them the true meaning of purity.

In chap. 16, Jesus asks his disciples an important question about his identity: "But who do you say that I am?" (16:15). Peter confesses him to be "the Messiah, the Son of the living God" (16:16). Jesus is pleased with his answer, saying that Peter is blessed with a privileged revelation from God his Father in heaven (16:17). In front of other disciples, then, Jesus says, "I tell you, you are Peter, and on this rock I will build my church, and the gates of Hades will not prevail against it" (16:18). This is a controversial text with a long history of interpretation and serious consequences. Depending on what they take "this rock" to be in Matthew's narrative context—the confessor (Peter the person), the confession (Peter's faith in Jesus as the Messiah and the Son of God), or the confessed (Jesus the rejected "stone" that has become the cornerstone; 21:42)—scholars have interpreted the foundation of the church in diverse ways. Their interpretations have led to passionate debates among Roman Catholic and Protestant theologians on the nature of Peter's authority—judicial or doctrinal. Peter is also given the keys of the kingdom of heaven (*see* POWER OF THE KEYS) and the authority to bind and loose on earth (*see* BINDING AND LOOSING), and his judgment, Jesus says, will be honored in heaven (16:19). Some interpreters take the symbol of the keys and the authority to bind or loose to mean that Peter was appointed the gatekeeper for the kingdom of heaven with a special power to admit and excommunicate people from the earthly church and the world to come. Others understand this verse to say that Peter was assigned to be the church's "chief rabbi" whose responsibility was to unlock the mystery of the kingdom of heaven and to explain the meaning of divine revelation to all people on earth. This second interpretation does not necessarily conflict with the juridical authority given to the whole community of the church to exercise its common decision to "bind and loose" unrepentant sinners after a due process (18:18). These two lines of interpretation have been used to uphold Peter's different roles and authorities in later churches.

In chap. 17, Peter witnesses Jesus' TRANSFIGURATION on a high mountain and overhears his conversation with Moses and Elijah. In excitement, he offers to build three tents, supposedly to give them shelter to carry on their conversation. Then, he hears a voice from heaven calling Jesus the beloved Son of God with whom God is pleased, and he is commanded to listen to Jesus. This story shows that Peter is blessed with direct revelation from God and given the privilege to see Jesus' glory, so he can understand Jesus' divine identity and teaching authority. His confession and commission in chap. 16 is thus validated by this epiphany. Peter's special relationship with Jesus is revealed in another story in 17:24-27. He is sent by Jesus to catch a fish in the sea to find a coin in the mouth to pay for their temple tax so that they might not give offense to the collectors. Some scholars consider this miracle story a composition by Matthew intended to address the question of Jewish Christians' obligation to the Temple in Jerusalem, even though it had been destroyed by Matthew's time. If this is true, this story may reflect the early church's view of Peter as an apostle to the circumcised.

In chap. 18, in which Jesus teaches community leadership and discipline, Peter asks how many times he should forgive an offender in the church. Jesus' answer of "seventy-seven times" (18:22) and the parable of the unforgiving servant (18:23-35) emphasizes the mandate for his followers to forgive one another because of God's immense generosity. For Matthew, Peter is undoubtedly the most prominent disciple of Jesus. His authority comes from Jesus, so his teaching binds the church in such areas as doctrinal belief, social relations, and community life (*see* MATTHEW, GOSPEL OF).

3. Gospel of Luke

In the Gospel of Luke, Peter first appears as a contrite sinner, confessing his sins to Jesus. This happens after Jesus teaches the crowds from his boat and tells him to cast nets in deep water. The catch of fish is so full that his nets begin to break and the boats almost sink. In awe of Jesus' extraordinary power, Peter kneels before him saying: "Go away from me, Lord, for I am a sinful man" (Luke 5:8). Jesus says: "Do not be afraid," and from then on Peter leaves everything to follow Jesus. Peter's response to Jesus' call thus exemplifies how encountering Jesus may bring change of heart and life. As the Gospel narrative continues, Peter becomes a spokesperson for the disciples trying to understand Jesus' teachings. For instance, hearing Jesus' parable about the slaves who were blessed for their readiness to welcome back their master at an unexpected hour, Peter asks Jesus whether it was told "for us or for everyone?" (12:41). Jesus replies with another parable saying that the "faithful and prudent manager" whom his master will put in charge of other slaves is the one who is found to be at work when his master arrives. In another instance, a ruler asks Jesus how to inherit eternal life, and Jesus instructs him to sell all that he owns to give to the poor and follow him. The ruler leaves without commitment, so Jesus says, "Indeed, it is easier for a camel to go through the eye of a needle than for someone who is rich to enter the kingdom of God" (18:25). Hearing this hard saying, Peter again asks Jesus on behalf of all disciples, "Look, we have left our homes and followed you" (18:28). Jesus promises them that, since they had left their homes and family for the sake of the kingdom of God, they would receive very much more in this age and in the age to come eternal life. Thus, Peter represented a model disciple eager to learn from Jesus about their duties and awards in serving the kingdom of God. It is also worth noting that Luke identifies Peter and John as the two disciples sent ahead to prepare the last supper for Jesus and his disciples (22:8). He also notes Peter's amazement at what happened in the empty tomb (24:12). Peter's role in preparing for the last supper and his presence at the tomb give him credence as witness and preacher of Jesus' death and resurrection, a main task he takes on in the Acts of the Apostles (*see* LUKE, GOSPEL OF).

4. Gospel of John

For the Gospel of John, the unnamed "beloved" disciple is the declared authority behind its traditions (John 21:24). Nevertheless, Peter is presented as a premier disciple with special rapport with Jesus. For instance, when Jesus declares himself the living bread from heaven saying, "Those who eat my flesh and drink my blood have eternal life, and I will raise them up on the last day" (John 6:54), "many of his disciples turned back" and left him (6:66). When Jesus asks the Twelve whether they also wished to depart, Peter says on their behalf, "Lord, to whom can we go? You have the words of eternal life. We have come to believe and know that you are the Holy One of God" (6:68-69). This statement sounds like the confession Peter makes in Caesarea Philippi in the synoptic tradition (Matt 16:16; Mark 8:29; Luke 9:20). His loyalty to Jesus stands in stark contrast to those who desert Jesus and the traitor among them, Judas (John 6:71). His exchange of words with Jesus regarding foot washing at the last supper reveals other characteristics of him, namely, humility and zeal, if also lack of understanding. Peter first refuses to be washed because Jesus is his Lord, but then earnestly asks for his hands and head also to be washed when he learns that the washing meant sharing life with Jesus and cleansing of sins (13:6-9). Peter's prominence is further evident in the fact that many disciples follow him to return, after Jesus' death, to their fishing job on the Sea of Galilee. When the risen Jesus appears on the shore telling them where to cast the nets, Peter immediately jumps into the sea to greet him ashore. It was there the risen Jesus asks Peter three times whether he loves him more than the fish they had just caught. Each time Peter answers, "Yes, Lord; you know that I love you," and three times Jesus commissions him to feed his lambs and tend his sheep (21:15-17). By asking Peter to publicly confess his love of Jesus three times, Jesus rehabilitates him from the three denials he committed at Jesus' trial. Also remarkable is the prophecy Jesus gives concerning Peter's martyrdom to glorify God: "But when you grow old, you will stretch out your hands, and someone else will fasten a belt around you and take you where you do not wish to go" (21:18). This prophecy indicates that

Peter's martyrdom is destined by God, just as Jesus' is. His death is not accidental or random, but in service of God's plan for the church (*see* JOHN, GOSPEL OF).

Among the twelve disciples, only Peter receives such personal attention in all four Gospels. His life, character, confession, courage, and enthusiasm, including flaws and failures, are recollected with affection and presented in candor. His relationship and interactions with Jesus serve as a model of genuine discipleship.

C. Leading Apostle in the Early Church

Just as the four Gospels present Peter as a preeminent disciple of Jesus from the beginning of his ministry in Galilee to his death and resurrection in Jerusalem, Paul's letters and the Acts of the Apostles preserve remarkable roles he played as a leading apostle of Jesus' movement after Easter, shaping the faith and mission of the early church.

1. Epistle to the Galatians

According to Paul, Peter was acknowledged as one of the pillars of the church in Jerusalem. Paul visited him the first time for fifteen days, probably to learn about the way of Jesus (Gal 1:18). Paul met him another time to discuss his mission to the Gentiles. Significant is the way in which Paul defined and legitimated his mission in relation to Peter's. Paul argued that he was entrusted with the gospel for the uncircumcised just as Peter was entrusted with it for the circumcised. And it was the same God who made Peter an apostle to the circumcised who sent him to the Gentiles (2:7-8). Paul also appealed to Peter's authority saying that Peter, James, and John accepted his commission by giving him and BARNABAS "the right hand of fellowship" and agreeing that they should preach the gospel among the Gentiles (2:9). While arguing for his own legitimacy, Paul evidently leaned on Peter's authority for support. Nonetheless, Paul confronted Peter for his hypocrisy when they met again in Antioch. Peter had come for a visit with the church in Antioch, which was ethnically mixed. He had no problem eating with Gentile Christians at the same table until some brothers arrived from James (2:11-14). For fear of offending the "circumcision faction" that insisted on observing purity laws even for Gentile converts, Peter separated himself from the Gentile Christians at the table. Even Barnabas followed him. Seeing them act unfairly against the Gentile Christians, Paul opposed Peter in public to defend the "truth of the gospel" that claims Christ's cross as necessary and sufficient for salvation for both the Jews and the Gentiles, who have received the same grace and equal standing from God in Christ. To burden the Gentile converts with Jewish laws would amount to denying the sufficiency of the cross for salvation. Jesus would have died in vain. Recalling his past encounters with Peter in Gal 2, Paul's intention was to refute the Jewish-Christian agitators, the so-called "Judaizers," who were preaching the absolute necessity of Jewish laws for salvation and thus limiting Christian freedom (*see* JUDAIZING). He vigorously argued that his gospel of grace for all, Jews and Gentiles alike, came as a direct revelation from the risen Lord Jesus he met on the way to Damascus. It is highly significant that even Peter, the apostle to the circumcised, endorsed his gospel of grace and his mission to the Gentiles. Meanwhile, believers ought to be vigilant, because even Peter the apostle could act wrongfully under pressure and would need to be corrected by the truth of the gospel (*see* GALATIANS, LETTER TO THE; PAUL, THE APOSTLE).

2. Acts of the Apostles

In the ACTS OF THE APOSTLES, Peter is the hero and focus of the first half of the narrative. His apostolic authority is firmly established at the beginning of the church in Jerusalem. His leadership qualities are characterized in a series of amazing stories.

a. Administrative skills. After Jesus' ascension, Peter urges the assembly of Jesus' followers in Jerusalem to choose another person in Judas' place to bear witness to Jesus' resurrection with them. The assembly agrees and by casting lots elects Matthias who had followed Jesus from the time of his baptism by John in Galilee until his death and resurrection in Jerusalem (Acts 1:21-22). So, there remains "twelve apostles" to lead the church, caring for its members in need and overseeing its missions in Judea and beyond.

b. Preaching prowess. Peter is also remembered as an eloquent preacher. On Pentecost, the crowds in Jerusalem are astonished by the extraordinary ability of the believers to speak in other languages used in Mesopotamia, Judea, Cappadocia, Pontus, Asia, Phrygia, Pamphylia, Egypt, Cyrene, and Rome. To this large gathering of Jewish pilgrims, Peter says with confidence that they were empowered by the Holy Spirit in fulfillment of Joel's prophecy concerning the last days (Joel 2:28-32). He then cites Ps 16:10 ("He was not abandoned to Hades, nor did his flesh experience corruption") and Ps 110:1 ("The Lord said to my Lord, 'Sit at my right hand, until I make your enemies your footstool'") to explain that Jesus must die and be raised from the dead in accordance with the Scriptures to demonstrate that he had been made the "Lord and Messiah" (Acts 2:36). The time of salvation had arrived, so they should repent and be baptized in the name of Jesus Christ in order to receive the gift of the Holy Spirit (2:38).

c. Miraculous power. Peter is portrayed as a wonder-worker like Jesus. With John beside him, he says to a crippled beggar at the Beautiful Gate of the Temple in Jerusalem: "I have no silver or gold, but what I have I give you; in the name of Jesus Christ of Nazareth, stand up and walk" (3:6). Then he takes the beggar by the right hand and raises him up. Immediately the beggar is cured, and enters the Temple with them, "walking and leaping and praising God" (3:8). In Jesus' name, Peter also heals Aeneas of Lydda who had been paralyzed and bedridden for eight years (9:33). Again, in Joppa, he raises Tabitha from the dead, a woman disciple respected for her charity works (9:40). These miracle stories show that Peter has become heir to Jesus' healing ministry.

d. Bold testimony. When Peter and John are arrested and interrogated by the rulers and elders of the council in Jerusalem over the healing of the crippled beggar, Peter uses this miracle to proclaim that Jesus the rejected stone had become the cornerstone of the church and that salvation had been given through no other name under heaven but Jesus (*see* TESTIMONY). Peter's boldness amazes the members of the council, and when ordered not to speak to anyone in the name of Jesus again, he says to their faces: "Whether it is right in God's sight to listen to you rather than to God, you must judge; for we cannot keep from speaking about what we have seen and heard" (4:19). When arrested again, Peter repeats: "We must obey God rather than any human authority" (5:29). Peter can make such a bold speech in the council, because he is now "filled with the Holy Spirit" (4:8). The stories of his arrest by King Herod, his miraculous release from the prison at night while under heavy guard, and Herod's horrific sudden death (12:1-23) provides encouragement to the disciples and proves Peter to be a genuine servant of the Lord. Peter's courage and boldness in making public testimony to Jesus make him an inspirational example for early Christians under similar harassment and persecution (4:29, 31; 28:31). *See* BOLDNESS, CONFIDENCE IN FAITH.

e. Judicial authority. There is a tragic story about Ananias and his wife Sapphira, who sell a piece of property but keep back a part of the proceeds before giving it to the church. Peter knows their secrets and confronts them about their lies to the Holy Spirit. Suddenly they die at his feet (5:9). This story serves as a serious warning regarding deceit before God. It also demonstrates Peter's authority to judge the members of the church.

f. Holy Spirit. Peter is filled with the HOLY SPIRIT not only to preach the gospel, heal the sick, and testify to Jesus Christ but also to lay hands on the believers in Samaria for them to receive the Holy Spirit (Acts 8:17). Simon the sorcerer is so attracted by Peter's power to dispense the Holy Spirit that he offers money to buy that power. Peter chastises him and warns him to repent from his greed and ask for God's forgiveness lest he should perish (8:18-23). The early church experiences the power of the Holy Spirit so much that it is hardly an overstatement to say that the Holy Spirit is the reason why it can survive and thrive in spite of afflictions and challenges. That Peter can lay hands on believers to receive the Holy Spirit is a clear sign of his authority and status as a leading apostle.

g. Heavenly vision. Peter is granted a special vision when he is visiting Simon the tanner in Joppa. While praying on a rooftop, he sees a large sheet lowered down from heaven with unclean animals, reptiles, and birds in it, and is ordered to kill and eat them. Peter is puzzled by this but it makes him realize later how his view of purity regarding food and Gentiles (10:28) needed to be changed, because God is impartial (10:34-35). All creation and all peoples are clean and pure in God's gracious will.

h. Gentile mission. Even though he is called "the apostle to the circumcised," Peter is one of the earliest apostles to work among the SAMARITANS (8:14) and the GENTILES (10:28; *see* NATIONS). After seeing the vision of unclean animals in Joppa, Peter is invited to visit Cornelius, an upright and God-fearing centurion in Caesarea. He is welcomed with great honor by Cornelius, who calls together his family and friends to hear Peter talk about Jesus. Realizing God's indiscriminate love for all peoples who fear God and do what is right, Peter tells him how God sent Jesus Christ to preach the gospel of peace to the people of Israel beginning with his ministry in Galilee and how he released those who were oppressed by the devil with the Holy Spirit and power because God was with him. Peter also testifies how he and other disciples followed Jesus to Jerusalem where he was crucified on the cross and died but was raised from the dead and appeared to them. And now they were chosen to preach to the world that the risen Jesus had been ordained by God as "judge of the living and the dead" (Acts 10:42) and it is through his name that sins will be forgiven. Thus, Peter gives the earliest apostolic **kērygma** (κήρυγμα, "proclamation") about Jesus. At that moment, the Holy Spirit falls upon CORNELIUS and those with him, and they begin to speak in tongues. Seeing what is happening, Peter does not hesitate to baptize them (10:44-48). Because of his contact with the centurion, Peter is criticized by the circumcised believers in Jerusalem. However, he asks his critics: "If then God gave them the same gifts that God gave us when we believed in the Lord Jesus Christ, who was I that I could hinder God?" (11:17). This experience in Caesarea persuades Peter to support Barnabas and Paul's plea, in the so-called first apostolic council of Jerusalem, to accept Gentile believers into the church without imposing Jewish laws on them (*see* JERUSALEM, COUNCIL OF). Peter evokes the incident in Caesarea to say that God had chosen him in earlier days to preach the message of the good news to the Gentiles so that they might become believers, and that God had shown impartiality by giving them the gift of the Holy Spirit. So, Peter concludes: "We believe that we will be saved through the grace of the Lord Jesus Christ, just as they will" (15:11). Peter thus lends his apostolic credibility to legitimating Paul's mission to the Gentiles and to bringing Jewish and Gentile believers closer to one another on the issue of the Jewish law.

Some scholars regard this pro-Gentile portrait of Peter to be in conflict with Paul's account in

Gal 2:11-14 of Peter withdrawing from table fellowship with Gentile believers, so they consider the Peter in Acts 15 to be Luke's literary attempt to reconcile Peter with Paul, the lead character in the second half of Acts. However, it is likely that Peter's behavior in Antioch was intended to maintain harmony and avoid public squabble between Paul and the brothers from James. Therefore his support of Paul and Barnabas in the apostolic council was also sincere as represented in Acts. The fact that Peter sat at the same table to eat with the Gentile believers in Antioch clearly showed that he was convinced of God's acceptance of Gentile believers just as he had witnessed in the case of Cornelius.

D. Impact and Legacy

Peter was called to follow Jesus as a disciple to fish for people and was believed to have ministered among the churches in Jerusalem, Antioch, and Rome, where he was martyred. His influence on the early church ran deep and his legacy long. Noteworthy is 1 Peter, which bears his name and may have been written by him—or, more precisely, by an associate who had been with Peter in Rome, such as Silvanus (Silas), identified as the bearer of the letter (1 Pet 5:12), or Mark. In reference to the historical circumstances implied in the letter, however, it was probably written by a disciple of Peter shortly after his martyrdom and the destruction of the Temple in Jerusalem. So, it serves as a witness to the importance of his teaching. In this letter, Peter's call for holy living stands out as a crucial message for believers suffering persecution (*see* PETER, FIRST LETTER OF).

Peter's influence in later centuries can also be attested by the pseudonymous 2 Peter (*see* PETER, SECOND LETTER OF), the apocryphal *Gospel of Peter, Apocalypse of Peter, Preaching of Peter, Acts of Peter, Slavonic Acts of Peter, Martyrdom of Peter, Acts of Peter and Paul, Martyrdom of Peter and Paul,* and *Acts of Peter and the Twelve Apostles,* circulated in some circles of the church, as well as his icons, paintings, and sculptures in Christian art and church architecture. *See* CHURCH, IDEA OF THE; CHURCH, LIFE AND ORGANIZATION OF; PETER AND PAUL, ACTS OF; PETER AND PAUL, MARTYRDOM OF; PETER AND THE TWELVE APOSTLES, ACTS OF; PETER, ACTS OF; PETER, APOCALYPSE OF; PETER, GOSPEL OF; PETER, MARTYRDOM OF; PETER, PREACHING OF; PETER, SLAVONIC ACTS OF.

Bibliography: R. E. Brown et al. *Peter in the New Testament: A Collaborative Assessment by Protestant and Roman Catholic Scholars* (1973); O. Cullmann. *Peter: Disciple, Apostle, Martyr.* 2nd ed. (1968); P. Perkins. *Peter: Apostle for the Whole Church* (1994); T. V. Smith. *Petrine Controversies in Early Christianity* (1985).

JOHN Y. H. YIEH

E. Quest for the Historical Peter

The Peter of Christian memory is embodied in the narratives of the Gospels and Acts, whose authors were dependent upon stories handed down from others. Since it is unlikely that Peter composed either of the letters attributed to him (*see* PETER, FIRST LETTER OF; PETER, SECOND LETTER OF), Paul's few comments are the only contemporary evidence. What plausible historical account emerges from critical analysis of these partial and conflicting remains?

1. Galilean fisherman (ca. 10?–29 CE)

Since most males in the 1st cent. died by the age of forty, it is unlikely that Peter was Jesus' age or older, because he would have been in his sixties or seventies when he died (ca. 60–64 CE). It is therefore more likely that Peter was about ten years younger than Jesus. Peter was married and lived in the same house with his mother-in-law (Mark 1:29//Luke 4:38). Jewish legal traditions considered males subject to the adult requirements of military service and the temple tax from age twenty (Exod 30:14; 38:26; Num 1:3; 26:2; *m. Sheq.* 1.1). The Essenes enrolled young men as adults at age twenty (1Q28a I, 6–11). Josephus reports becoming a Pharisee after exploring other Jewish sects and ascetic lifestyles at age nineteen. By age twenty-six (ca. 63–64 CE), Josephus was a member of a high-ranking delegation to Rome. Presumably he had married his first wife sometime earlier (*Life* 10–14). Males who did not belong to the educated elite may have married at a younger age.

Along with his brother Andrew, Peter engaged in fishing out of Capernaum (Matt 4:18; Mark 1:16; Luke 5:2-9). A reconstructed Galilean fishing boat discovered by archaeologists shows signs of repeated patching from other boats, a possible indication that such fishermen may have lived close to the economic margins. If so, a "no catch" night was a crisis (Luke 5:5). Small harbors, fish pools, and fish-preserving structures ringed the Sea of Galilee.

2. Disciple of Jesus (29–30/33 CE)

A variant tradition in John 1:44 locates Simon and Andrew in a different town, Bethsaida, along with another early follower, Philip. John also places Andrew among the disciples of John the Baptist (1:40). If so, the call stories found in the Synoptics (Mark 1:16-18; Luke 5:1-11) may have eclipsed an earlier interest awakened by the dramatic preaching of the Baptist. Stories of famous teachers often involved exchanges between the teacher and his youthful followers. Simon, assigned the nickname "Cephas" (Kēphas, the Aram. equivalent of Gk. Petros, "Peter," meaning "rock") by the teacher, clearly fills that narrative role in the Gospels. Was Peter actually a rough, outspoken person? Or is Peter's behavior, such as his ill-considered bravado and brash contradictions of his teacher (e.g., Matt 16:22//Mark 8:32), the narrative representation of youth? The historian cannot say. John identifies the anonymous sword-wielder in Gethsemane with Peter (John 18:10), creating further literary connections with the denial scenes.

3. Leader in Jerusalem (33–49? CE)

Peter was the first male disciple to encounter the risen Jesus (Mark 16:7; Luke 24:34; 1 Cor 15:5*a*). No details were preserved; even the locale was not specified. Though Luke 24 and John 20 situate appearances in Jerusalem, Mark, Matthew, and John 21 assume that the disciples had returned to Galilee. Luke–Acts has reshaped the story to keep the disciples in Jerusalem from Passover through Pentecost and beyond. A return to Galilee and perhaps even their earlier occupations (so John 21:1-14) is more plausible. Perhaps the next pilgrimage feast, Pentecost, was the occasion for a permanent return to Jerusalem. The Jesus movement, which Paul persecuted and then joined, was centered there. His private visit to Peter three years after his conversion (Gal 1:18; 34/36 CE) indicates that Cephas was the acknowledged leader of the group. However, an alternative leader with family ties to Jesus and his own resurrection vision, James, the brother of Jesus, is also on the scene (1 Cor 15:7; Gal 1:19). By the time Barnabas, Paul, and other representatives from the Antioch church meet with apostles in Jerusalem to discuss the status of non-Jewish converts in the community (ca. 49 CE), there are three dominant figures in Jerusalem: Cephas, James, the brother of the Lord, and John, the son of Zebedee (Gal 2:1-10; *see* JERUSALEM, COUNCIL OF). Despite his prominence among Jesus' disciples, Peter did not inherit the authority of his master as though he were the favored follower of a prophet or philosophic teacher. He could establish an authoritative teaching or determine how other apostles carried out their mission without the consensus of others in the movement.

4. Traveling missionary (50–60? CE)

Some time after the Jerusalem Council, Peter was in Antioch. Paul criticized him for leading Jewish Christians to withdraw from meal fellowship with non-Jewish believers to accommodate the objections of visitors from Jerusalem (Gal 2:11-14). The church appears to have agreed with Peter rather than Paul, who launched an independent mission. Paul presumed that the Corinthians knew that Peter (and his wife) were supported by local churches (1 Cor 9:5). Despite the "Cephas" faction among the Corinthians, Peter does not appear to have worked in that church.

5. Teaching and martyrdom in Rome (60?–64 CE)

It is not clear when Peter arrived in Rome, where he was martyred under NERO. Paul does not mention him in the greetings of Rom 16 (ca. 57/58 CE), so Peter may not have arrived there until shortly before his death. He was not a founder or bishop (episkopos ἐπίσκοπος) of the Roman church, a tradition related by the 2nd cent. CE (Irenaeus, *Haer.* 3.1, 5; Eusebius, *Hist. eccl.* 2.14.6; 2.25.5–8). The pseudonymous 1 Pet 5:1 employs the expression "fellow elder" (presbyteros πρεσβύτερος) of Peter. Early 2nd cent.-CE tradition claimed that Mark's Gospel was based on the reminiscences an aged Peter had shared with believers in Rome (Eusebius, *Hist. eccl.* 2.15.2). Paul's private visit with Peter in Jerusalem decades earlier had provided him with comparable information about Jesus.

The earliest references to Peter's martyrdom (John 21:18-19; *1 Clem.* 5.4–5; ca. 90–95 CE) have no traces of the later legends about his asking to be crucified upside down because he believed himself to be an unworthy disciple (*Acts Pet.* 37–41). Tacitus' report of crucified Christians set on fire as human torches (*Ann.* 15.44) and others condemned to deaths representing mythic figures (the charades of Danaids and Dirce referred to in *1 Clement*) on the Mons Vaticanus in Rome (the site of the Circus of Nero) indicates that the executions of 64 CE had been mythologized by the emperor himself. *First Clement* does not clearly include the deaths of Peter and Paul with these martyrs on the Vatican (*see* CHRISTIANS, PERSECUTION OF; MARTYR). The earliest memorial on the site (ca. 160 CE; Eusebius, *Hist. eccl.* 2.25.7; *see* ROME, CHRISTIAN MONUMENTS) fits the type of a small, uninscribed, limestone structure familiar among burials of persons too poor to afford marble facing or a carved mausoleum. No inscription or 1st-cent. burial remains were found in the traditional site. However, several early 2nd-cent. burials of poor persons around (but not intruding on) the location make it likely that Roman Christians had marked this plot as Peter's burial place in the 1st cent. CE. In death, Peter remained what he had been throughout his life, one of the urban masses quite beneath the notice of Rome's elite. The richly clad, solemn bishop and teacher of our stained glass windows is pure fiction.

Bibliography: Pheme Perkins. *Peter: Apostle for the Whole Church* (1994).

PHEME PERKINS

PETHAHIAH peth'uh-hī'uh [פְּתַחְיָה **pethakhyah;** Παθαιά **Pathaia**]. 1. A priest and descendant of Aaron associated with David (1 Chr 24:16).

2. A Levite (Neh 9:5) involved in the great communal confession and covenant sealing (Neh 9:38 [Heb. 10:1]) and probably the same Pethahiah who joined others in renouncing their foreign wives and children (Ezra 10:23; 1 Esd 9:23). *See* LEVI, LEVITES.

3. A Judahite son of MESHEZABEL serving in Jerusalem following the exile, who "was at the king's hand in all matters concerning the people" (Neh 11:24). Some interpreters understand this as an official Persian role, such as the one Ezra had held (Ezra 7:12). However, Pethahiah might simply have been a local administrator in Jerusalem, advising the king through official channels.

TERRY BRENSINGER

PETHOR pee´thor [פְּתוֹר pethor]. The home of BALAAM, the Mesopotamian diviner hired by BALAK, king of Moab, to curse the Israelites as they made their way from Egypt to Canaan (Num 22:4-6; Deut 23:4 [Heb. 23:5]). Pethor, according to Num 22:5, was located west of the Euphrates in the land of AMAW, a region mentioned occasionally in extrabiblical texts. Both the book of Numbers and the inscriptions of SHALMANESER III provide more specific information. First, Balaam himself states that he has come to the plains of Moab from Aram and the eastern mountains (Num 23:7). These vague geographical references point to the general area that stretched from central Syria all the way to the Euphrates. Greater specificity appears in Shalmaneser III's inscriptions. According to these texts, Pitru, the Hittite form of Pethor, was located along the Sajur River "on the other side of the Euphrates" (*ANET* 278). The Sajur connects with the Euphrates approximately 60 mi. (97 km) northeast of Aleppo, placing Pitru in Upper Mesopotamia in the area where these two rivers meet. Although no specific sites can be identified with certainty, Tell Ahmar, located 18 mi. (29 km) south of Carchemish, has been proposed. If the biblical Pethor and Pitru are in fact the same place, then Balaam traveled nearly 400 mi. (650 km) before encountering the Israelites.

TERRY BRENSINGER

PETHUEL pi´thy*oo*´uhl [פְּתוּאֵל pethuʾel]. The father of the prophet JOEL (Joel 1:1). Some LXX manuscripts have the name as **Bathouēl** (βαθουήλ), the same as the LXX rendering of BETHUEL.

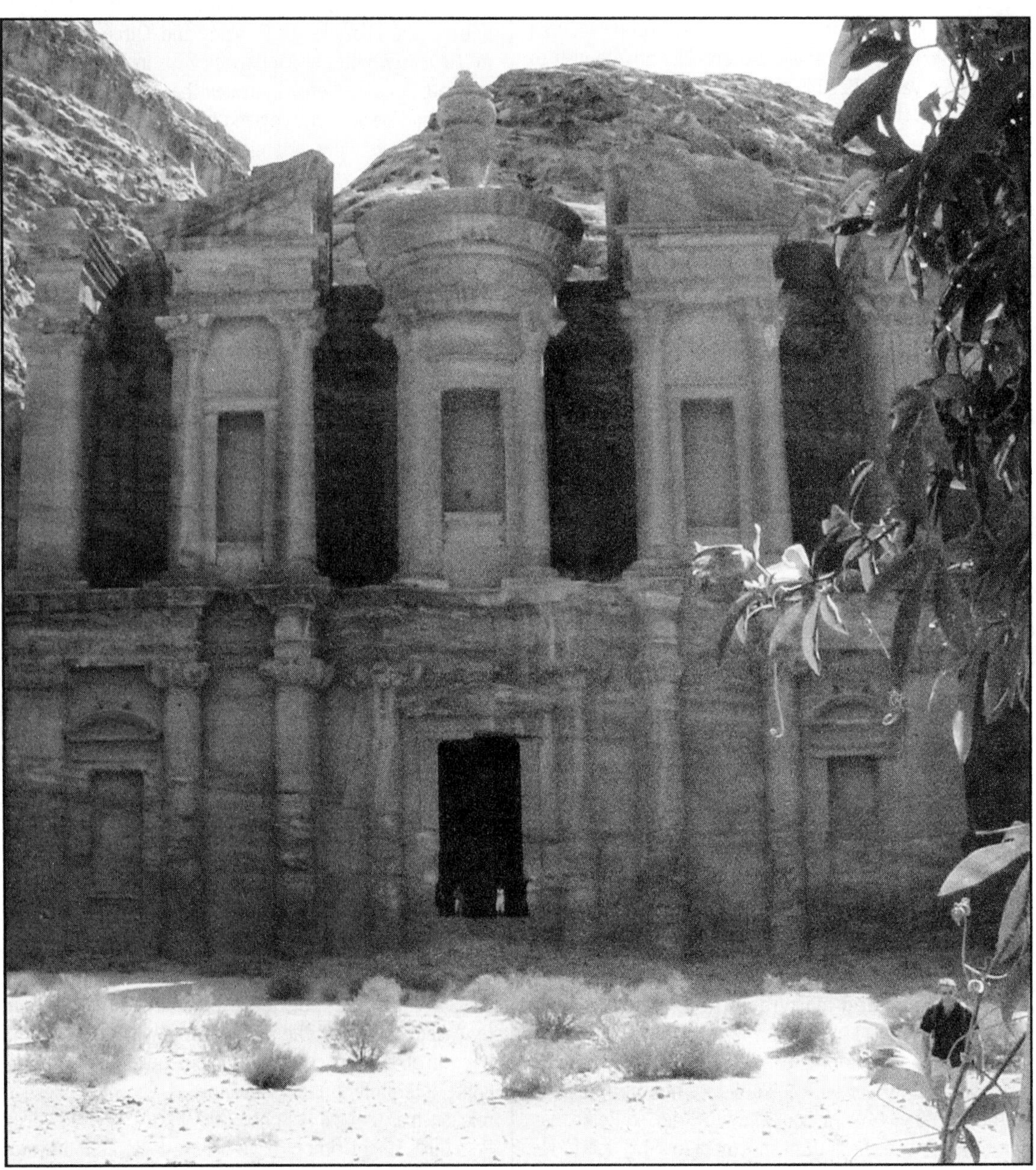

John Mark Wade

Figure 1: Ed-Deir (the Monastery)

PETRA pee´truh [Πέτρα Petra]. Located in the Wadi Musa Valley in southern Jordan, Petra is the capital of the Nabatean kingdom. The city stood on the flourishing overland trade route that linked Arabia and the Mediterranean Sea. The valley, surrounded by 300 m-high precipitous mountains of Nubian sandstone, is approximately 1.5 km long by 1 km wide. In the last quarter of the 1st cent. BCE, most of the city was constructed and remained independent until 106 CE when it was annexed by Rome. The principal rock-cut monuments of Petra are the Siq, the narrow gorge-entry into the city, the al-Khazna (the Treasury), theater, and the 800-plus tomb facades have been divided into four types, depending upon their decoration. The largest monument is the vast rock-cut Ed-Deir (the Monastery), 46.77 m in width by 48.30 m in height. Characteristic of both the Deir and the Khazna is that their facades have upper orders with a tholos framed by a broken pediment.

The most important of the freestanding structures are the Temple of the Winged Lions, the Great Temple, the Colonnaded Street, and the Qasr al-Bint Farʿun and its tripartite Monumental Gateway. The architecture of Petra has Egyptian, Assyrian, Persian, Parthian, and Greek Hellenistic elements, but it also displays an eclecticism that is Nabatean.

Numbers of churches were constructed in the Byzantine period, including the Petra and Ridge churches and the Blue Chapel. The site has Islamic and Crusader remains after which it eclipsed into obscurity.

MARTHA JOUKOWSKY

PETRONIUS, PUBLIUS. When 1st-cent. CE Roman emperor CALIGULA ordered a statue of his image be placed in the Jerusalem Temple and worshiped, he sent Publius Petronius, a Roman CONSUL, into Judea with an army to deal harshly with noncomplying Jews. But moved by their conviction, Petronius entreated Caligula to make peace.

KIMBERLY R. PEELER

PEULLETHAI pi-*oo*l´uh-th*i* [פְּעֻלְּתַי peʿullethay]. A Levite, a gatekeeper in the Temple in Jerusalem (1 Chr 26:5). His father, OBED-EDOM, also a "gatekeeper for the ark," worked closely with the temple musicians (1 Chr 15:21; 16:5). *See* LEVI, LEVITES.

PHANUEL fuh´ny*oo*´uhl [Φανουήλ Phanouēl]. The father of the prophetess ANNA, who prophesied the greatness of Jesus (Luke 2:36-38). The Hebrew name, PENUEL, means "face of God."

PHARAKIM fair´uh-kim [Φαρακείμ Pharakeim]. The ancestor of a family of temple servants who returned from Babylonian exile under ZERUBBABEL (1 Esd 5:31). This name is missing in the parallel lists (Ezra 2:51; Neh 7:53).

PHARAOH fair´oh [פַּרְעֹה parʿoh; Φαραώ Pharaō]. *Pharaoh* (Egyptian prʿ*3*), literally means "great house," i.e., the palace, a title for the king of ancient EGYPT. Although in common use the title is applied to any Egyptian king, its use for kings before the New Kingdom is anachronistic. Etiquette dictated that the Egyptian king be addressed indirectly, often as "your majesty" or "his majesty." During the late 2nd millennium BCE, prʿ*3* began to be used as a circumlocution for the king, much as "the White House" for the U.S. president or "10 Downing Street" for the British prime minister are used today. In the early 1st millennium BCE the term became one of the standard terms to designate the Egyptian king.

In biblical usage, *pharaoh* is a synonym for "king of Egypt" in conformity with 1st millennium BCE Egyptian convention. The Egyptian king is referred to alternately as king of Egypt, Pharaoh, or Pharaoh king of Egypt. Any of these formulations can be used with the king's name: Shishak king of Egypt (1 Kgs 11:40); Pharaoh Neco (2 Kgs 23:33); Pharaoh Hophra king of Egypt (Jer 44:30). The formal similarity between "Shishak king of Egypt" and "Pharaoh king of Egypt" lends the appearance that *Pharaoh* is the king's name. In fact, the term *pharaoh* is treated grammatically as if it were a proper name, never taking the definite article in biblical Hebrew.

A. Kingship and Divinity
B. Ideology of Kingship
C. Royal Titulary
D. Pharaoh in the Bible
Bibliography

A. Kingship and Divinity

In Egyptian cosmology, the king stood as intermediary between the earthly world and the worlds of the gods and the dead. Consequently, he was both human and divine. As a human being he was mortal and fallible. As he exercised the office of kingship, he was more than human, though not equal with the gods (*see* KING, KINGSHIP). His divinity was lesser and derivative. Whereas the gods were termed **nṯr** ʿ*3* "great gods," the king was **nṯr nfr** "good/perfect god," dependent on the gods for life, power, and success. Mythologically, his divinity was expressed in the epithets "Living Horus" and "Son of Re."

Horus the falcon was the patron god of kingship. Kingship was originally exercised by the gods. When Osiris was murdered and dismembered by his brother Seth, his wife, Isis, reassembled his body. Though he could not return to life on earth, Osiris was able to beget a son, Horus, who inherited the kingship. The Egyptian king exercised power as Horus on earth. The transition from one king to another was expressed as "the falcon/Horus has flown to heaven, (his successor) has risen in his place." The earliest element of the royal titulary was the Horus name, written in a **serekh**, a rectangular representation of the palace façade surmounted by a falcon.

The king was also the son of the solar god RE. This relationship could be expressed through divine conception: Re (or Amun-Re) visited the queen in the guise of the king in order to beget the future king. Thus the king was destined to rule from conception. The king's birth name was incorporated in his Son of Re name as part of his formal titulary.

The royal cult differed significantly from the cult of the gods. Worship of the living king was limited to a few sites outside Egypt proper, most notably the Abu Simbel temple of RAMESSES II in Nubia. Nonetheless, public images of the king with divine associations served propagandistic functions of exaltation and legitimation.

B. Ideology of Kingship

The king's primary responsibility was to maintain **maʿat** (order, truth, justice). The Egyptians believed that Re had placed the king in the land of the living to judge human beings, bring about **maʿat**, and rid the world of **isefet** (chaos and wrong). The king was to make offerings to the gods and funerary offerings to the dead (Assmann). In ancient cosmology creation involved the imposition of order on chaos. Yet chaos remained a constant threat against which kingship was the first and primary defense. The king fought back chaos through cultic ritual, wise administration, and military prowess.

The king maintained order in the cosmos by assuring that the temples were well maintained, the rituals of the cult were properly performed, and the offerings were made to the gods and the dead. Kings lavished endowments on the temples, constructing new chapels and donating the proceeds of their military exploits. Ideology dictated that the king, as the representative of the gods on earth and as intermediary between the earthly and heavenly worlds, perform all the sacred rites. In practice the priests served as the king's representative in offering the daily service in the temples. The king participated only in major festivals such as the New Year's Festival and the Opet Festival.

The earthly order for which the king was responsible was both physical and moral, encompassing security, stability, prosperity, and justice. A vast bureaucracy managed the fields and herds and administered justice. Although official corruption and abuse of power were denounced, **maʿat** was a conservative concept that tended to preserve the status quo, thus favoring the interests of the elite.

Other central themes of royal ideology included "uniting the Two Lands" of Upper and Lower Egypt and "smiting the enemies" of Egypt. Egypt's foundation myth attributed to its first king the act of uniting two disparate kingdoms into one. This political unity became symbolic of internal order and stability. Among the earliest images of kingship are images of the king grasping Egypt's enemies by the hair and preparing to smite them with a mace. As imperial aspirations arose, kings were expected also to "expand the borders" of Egypt, bringing order to the wider world and gaining access to the riches of neighboring lands. In times of peace, hunting expeditions served to demonstrate the king's prowess.

The king bore the protective image of an upraised cobra (or uraeus) on his brow, alone or paired with a vulture's head, representing the tutelary goddesses of Lower and Upper Egypt, respectively. The double crown combined the red (Upper Egyptian) and white (Lower Egyptian) crowns.

C. Royal Titulary

The royal titulary comprised five names. The first three are known by the epithets that preceded them: Horus, Two Ladies (Egyptian **nebty**, the tutelary goddesses of Upper and Lower Egypt), and Golden Horus. The final two names, known as the prenomen and nomen, were written inside protective rings called cartouches and served as the king's primary names. The prenomen or throne name was preceded by a standard title for king (**nsw-bit**, dual king or king of Upper and Lower Egypt). The nomen was preceded by the epithet Son of Re and included the king's birth name. Chosen upon accession to the throne, the titulary expressed the king's vision (theological, political, etc.) for his reign. Parallels have been drawn between the fivefold Egyptian royal titulary and the royal titles announced in Isa 9:6.

D. Pharaoh in the Bible

Pharaohs appear in three Torah narratives: SARAH pretends to be Abraham's sister and enters Pharaoh's harem (Gen 12:10-20); Joseph interprets Pharaoh's dreams and is appointed administrator of the kingdom (Gen 39–50); and the Israelites flee from Egypt after Moses brings a series of plagues on Pharaoh's people in the exodus story (Exod 1:11–18:10). Although the Egyptian king is a major character in these stories, he is never named. This practice, which conforms to the legendary character of the texts, frustrates attempts to make direct links between the biblical accounts and Egyptian history (*see* EXODUS, BOOK OF; MOSES).

Only four Egyptian kings are mentioned by name in the OT: SHISHAK (1 Kgs 11:40; 14:25; 2 Chr 12:2-9), NECO (2 Kgs 23:29-35; 2 Chr 35:20-22; 36:4; Jer 46:2), HOPHRA (Jer 44:30), and SO (2 Kgs 17:4). Unnamed pharaohs appear in two stories in 1 Kings prior to the first mention of Shishak: Solomon's marriage alliance with Pharaoh (1 Kgs 3:1) and Pharaoh's sheltering of Hadad (1 Kgs 11:17-22), which parallels the later narrative of Jeroboam and Shishak (1 Kgs 11:40). Usage in the prophetic literature varies. Jeremiah names both Neco and Hophra, whereas Isaiah and Ezekiel refer to the Egyptian king only by title.

Whereas the Torah narratives stress the power of the pharaoh, who holds the lives of Abraham, Sarah, Joseph, Moses, and the Israelites in his hands, the prophets seek to deconstruct this image of Pharaoh, declaring him to be a "broken reed of a staff" (Isa 36:6) and nothing but noise (Jer 46:17). The mighty arm of Pharaoh, which wielded the sword of power, God will break (Ezek 30:21-25).

In the NT, *pharaoh* appears only in reference to the OT narratives of Joseph and Moses (Acts 7:10-21; Rom 9:17; Heb 11:24-27). Similar references appear in Maccabees (1 Macc 4:9; 3 Macc 2:6-7; 6:4) and 4 Esd 1:10. First Esdras 1:25-38 recounts King Josiah's encounter with Pharaoh. Additionally, several Ptolemaic kings appear in Greek Esther (11:1) and in the books of Maccabees, but they are termed "king of Egypt" (**basileus Aigyptou** βασιλεὺς Αἰγύπτου), not *pharaoh. See* AKHENATEN; MERNEPTAH.

Bibliography: Jan Assmann. "State and Religion in the New Kingdom." *Religion and Philosophy in Ancient Egypt.* James P. Allen et al. (1989) 55–88; David O'Connor and David P. Silverman, eds. *Ancient Egyptian Kingship* (1995); Christiane Ziegler, ed. *The Pharaohs* (2002).

CAROLYN HIGGINBOTHAM

PHARAOH'S DAUGHTER [בַּת־פַּרְעֹה **bath-parʿoh;** θυγάτηρ Φαραώ **thygatēr Pharaō**]. 1. A royal daughter who acts as deliverer in Exod 2:5-10. She violates her father's order to throw all Hebrew male infants into the Nile by drawing one out and raising him as her own. She names him Moses, an Egyptian name meaning "born of" or "son of" (e.g., Thutmose, Rameses), but which she ties to the Hebrew verb **mashah** (מָשָׁה, "to draw out"). The NT includes two references to her (Acts 7:21; Heb 11:24). Her compassion contrasts with her father's cruelty. Moreover, her coming down to the water, seeing the basket, hearing the crying child, taking pity, and drawing him out of the water (Exod 2:5-6) parallel God hearing of the cries of the Israelites, seeing their misery, and coming down to deliver them (Exod 2:23-25; 3:7-8; Fretheim). In Jewish midrash this pharaoh's daughter is named BITHIAH, "daughter of Yah(weh)," highlighting her defiance of her father's command and Yahweh's adoption of her, which corresponds to her adoption of Moses. She is viewed as having rejected the gods of her land for devotion to Yahweh. She becomes connected to "Bithiah, daughter of Pharaoh, whom Mereb married" (1 Chr 4:17).

2. The first of Solomon's wives and part of a marriage alliance with Egypt (1 Kgs 3:1). The alliance underscores Solomon's commanding power in the region. Historically, Egyptian rulers often received foreign royal daughters but rarely sent their own. Pharaoh's daughter is listed first among Solomon's foreign wives (1 Kgs 11:1). The marriage alliance, however, does not survive into REHOBOAM's reign (1 Kgs 11:40; 14:25; 2 Chr 12:2).

As a dowry, Pharaoh's daughter received the city of Gezer, which Solomon rebuilt (1 Kgs 9:16-17). He built her a house in his palace complex (1 Kgs 7:8) and later a house outside Jerusalem (1 Kgs 9:24; 2 Chr 8:11). In the narrative of Solomon's reign, Pharaoh's daughter is mentioned from beginning to end in conjunction with those actions by which kings typically secure their legitimacy and establish their greatness: elimination of domestic rivals and dominance in international relations (1 Kgs 2:10–3:1), palace construction and royal administration (1 Kgs 7:7-8), fortification and building of cities (1 Kgs 3:1; 9:15-19), temple construction (1 Kgs 3:1), and worship (1 Kgs 11:7-8). In 2 Chr 8:11, however, Solomon moves her from being directly connected to Jerusalem and the house of David.

Bibliography: Terence E. Fretheim. *Exodus.* IBC (1991).

ELNA SOLVANG

PHARATHON fair´uh-thon [Φαραθών **Pharathōn**]. One of several Judean towns BACCHIDES fortified during the Maccabean war (1 Macc 9:50). Likely the same as PIRATHON. *See* JUDEA, JUDEANS; SELEUCID EMPIRE.

PHARISEES fair´uh-see [Φαρισαῖοι **Pharisaioi**]. The Greek term occurs for the first time in the NT (ninety-nine times) and is also used by Josephus (forty-four times). The term is not found in other early Jewish texts, or in the writings of Greco-Roman authors who refer to the Jews. Later references are found in noncanonical Christian texts (*Gospel of Thomas*, Oxyrhynchus Papyri) and in the writings of the church fathers of the 2nd cent. (Justin, Hippolytus, Hegesippus) and later (Origen, Eusebius). The Hebrew term (**perushim** פְּרוּשִׁים) is not attested before ca. 200 CE, when it is used in the Mishnah (*m. Hag.* 2:4–7; *m. Sotah* 3:4; *m. Toh.* 4.12; *m. Yad.* 4:6–8).

E. Pharisees in the New Testament
1. The Pharisees and Jesus
a. The conflicts regarding the Sabbath
b. Fasting and divorce
c. Tithing and ritual purity
d. The leaven of the Pharisees
e. The Pharisees' critique of Jesus
f. Jesus' critique of the Pharisees
2. The Pharisees and the early Christians
Bibliography

A. Terminology and Meaning

The Greek word **Pharisaioi** is the transcription of the Aramaic word **perishaya**ʾ (פְּרִישַׁיָּא, plural of the passive participle **perish** פְּרַשׁ that means "separated," or "distinguished"; see Dan 5:28). The Aramaic word is never used for a group that corresponds to the Pharisees, who occur in later Hebrew texts consistently as **perushim** and **perushin** (פְּרוּשִׁין). It appears that the Aramaic designation was replaced at the end of the 2nd or at the beginning of the 3rd cent. CE by the Hebrew term **perushim**. Origen still knew the Aramaic designation when he wrote of those set apart in his commentary on John 3:1 (*Comm. Jo.* 3.1).

It should be noted that the meaning of **perushim** and **perushin** in the rabbinic literature is not uniform; the terms refer to the Pharisees who were active before the destruction of the Temple in 70 CE (*m. Yad.* 4:6-8; *b. B. Bat.* 115b), and also to scrupulous religious eccentrics (*t. Sotah* 15:11-12; *b. B. Bat.* 60b).

The meaning of the Aramaic/Hebrew root **parash** (פָּרַשׁ) means 1) "to separate, to distinguish" (in the Qumran texts and in rabbinic literature), both in a positive sense (e.g., to separate from impure things, *m. Sotah* 9:15) and in a negative sense (e.g., to separate from the community, *m. Avot* 2:4), and 2) "to explain" (consistently in the OT, e.g., Lev 24:12; Num 15:34; Ezra 4:18; Neh 8:8; Esth 4:7; 10:2; Prov 23:32; Ezek 34:12). In the rabbinic literature, both meanings "to separate" and "to explain" are attested.

As a result of this dual meaning, two suggestions have been made for explaining the party term *Pharisee*: 1) the traditional explanation understands the Pharisees as "the separated ones" or "separatists"; 2) some interpret the term *Pharisees* as "the (precise) explainers (of the holy Scriptures)." With regard to the first explanation, which seems the more plausible one, the question arises whether this is a positive self-designation or a derogatory label used by others. Moreover, it is not immediately clear from what or from whom the people thus designated *separated.* The usage of the term in the various sources suggests that the designation *Pharisees* was used very early as a derogatory description, perhaps on account of this group's separation from the Maccabean resistance movement (1 Macc 7:12-13). By the 1st cent. CE the term seems to have had a positive meaning and was thus used as the designation of a major Jewish movement; both Paul and Josephus use the term in their self-description. It appears that the term was largely dropped after 70 CE when the traditional party affiliations had lost their significance and when scribal Pharisaism came to represent the entire Jewish people.

The term *Pharisee* is never defined in the sources. A Pharisee is a person who calls himself a Pharisee (as do Paul, Phil 3:5; Acts 23:6; and Josephus, *Life* 12), or who is called a Pharisee by others (see Luke 7:36-40 [Simon]; John 3:1 [Nicodemus]; Acts 5:34 [Gamaliel]; Josephus, *Ant.* 15.3 [Pollion]; *Ant.* 18.4 [Zadok, the cofounder of the Zealots]; *Life* 190 [Simon ben Gamaliel]). In in-group discussions such as those of the rabbis in the rabbinic literature, the characterization as a Pharisee would provide no relevant information about the individual and is thus usually omitted, with affiliations to a certain school (Hillel or Shammai) being more pertinent. The designation *Pharisee* appears to be only necessary when a person's standing within Judaism needed clarification in terms of one's close affinity to a strict mode of living as a pious and law-abiding Jewish person. Pharisees have a particular relationship with the Jewish law (Torah), which explains why the term *Pharisee* can be used as a synonym for the term *scribe.* The Pharisees are repeatedly described as people who transmit, preserve, and develop the tradition of the law in its written and oral form. Their understanding of tradition evidently was nonexclusive, which explains their interest in Jesus: they are prepared to listen to Jesus as long as he can demonstrate the continuity between his teaching and the Torah tradition.

B. Sources

The main sources for a description of the Pharisees are the writings of Josephus, the NT, several Qumran texts, other early Jewish writings, and later rabbinic texts.

1. Josephus

In three of his four writings, Josephus includes what is often characterized as idealized portrayals of the three "philosophies" of Judaism, i.e., the ESSENES, the SADDUCEES, and the Pharisees. In *J.W.* 2.162–66 he describes the Pharisees as affirming the significance of fate for human affairs and the immortality of the soul, while the Sadducees deny both positions. In *Ant.* 13.171–73 the Pharisees stand between the Sadducees who affirm free will and the Essenes who affirm fate, as they relate some matters to fate and others to free will. In *Ant.* 18.11–23, in addition to the disputes about fate and immortality, Josephus portrays the Pharisees as having their own traditions in addition to the holy Scriptures, while the Sadducees accept only the authority of the biblical laws. In *Life* 10–12 Josephus briefly describes again the three "philosophical schools" of Judaism, in each of which he received training (*see* JOSEPHUS, FLAVIUS).

In his historical narratives, the Pharisees are the only movement that plays an ongoing role. Josephus introduces them somewhat abruptly in the context of a brief sketch of the main Jewish groups during the time of the Maccabean Jonathan, who was high priest from 152–143 BCE (*Ant.* 13.171–72). They are the dominant party in Jewish society (*Ant.* 13.288, 298, 401–2; 17.41; 18.15–16; *J.W.* 2.162), but they are troublemakers from the time of the Hasmoneans (*J.W.* 1.110–14; *Ant.* 13.288–98, 399–400, 410–17) to Herod the Great (*Ant.* 17.41–45) and to Josephus' own time (*Life* 190–96).

Unfortunately, Josephus provides hardly any information about the piety of the Pharisees, about their activities in the synagogues and in the schools, or about their involvement in the priestly circles and in the Temple. He writes for a non-Jewish audience and describes the various Jewish groups in Palestine in the context of Greek-Roman parameters.

2. Qumran texts

Several Jewish texts, which were discovered in Qumran, are regarded as providing clues for the history and the teachings of the Pharisees. Several texts refer to a group whose members they describe as **drshy hkhlqwt** (דרשי החלקות, "Seekers After Smooth Things"), which are generally identified as Pharisees (CD I, 18–19; 4Q169 3–4 I 2, 7; III, 3, 6–7). This phrase represents a critique of the Pharisees' interpretation of the law, which is said to be "smooth," i.e., seductive: they teach a way of life that is agreeable to the masses. The author of the NAHUM PESHER (4Q169) distinguishes two major groups, Ephraim and Manasseh, corresponding to the Pharisees and the Sadducees, viewed from the "outside" by a third group, the Qumran people. A relevant text is the HALAKHIC LETTER, written between 159–152 BCE, a document purportedly sent by the leaders of the Qumran community to the leaders of the priestly circles in Jerusalem outlining some twenty laws. The priests who stayed in Jerusalem (and who accepted the new political order) are made responsible for allowing legal rulings to be practiced that contradict the teachings of the "sons of Zadok." Most scholars identify the "they"-group with the Pharisees or their forerunners who at that time exercised authority over the Temple and who have the support of the people. This early text already portrays the three major divisions within Judaism: the Qumran community (which may represent the Essenes), the priestly aristocracy in Jerusalem (Sadducees), and a non-priestly group that enjoys popularity among the people (the Pharisees or their forerunners).

3. Other early Jewish texts

Several writings that were written between 150 BCE and 70/100 CE have been linked with the Pharisees. The apocryphal book 1 Maccabees has been linked with Pharisaic circles, although attempts to identify a Pharisaic author have not be successful. The pseudepigraphical text Psalms of Solomon (*see* SOLOMON, PSALMS OF) is usually regarded as representing an authentic Pharisaic text: some psalms contrast the terms *we* and *they*; parts of the priesthood (1:7-8; 8:9-12) and the inhabitants of Jerusalem (2:3, 13) are criticized; the deeds of the righteous are contrasted with the deeds of sinners (3:6-12; 12–16); and resurrection is promised to those who fear God (3:16). The LIVES OF THE PROPHETS, a text that is concerned with the origins of the prophets and their graves (compare Matt 23.29; Luke 11:47), has been ascribed to an author who belonged to the Pharisaic-scribal milieu. The Scroll of Fasting (*Megillat Taanit*), which some date to the time before 70 CE, lists thirty-five days of joy during which fasting is prohibited; fourteen days remember events during the Maccabean revolt between 164–108 BCE, four days remember "victories" over the Sadducees during the early reign of Salome Alexandra (76–67 BCE), nine days remember successes in the resistance against Roman policies between 26–66/67 CE.

The *Liber antiquitarum biblicarum* (Pseudo-Philo) and the *Ezra Apocalypse* (*4 Ezra*) represent Pharisaism in its final phase as emerging rabbinic Judaism. The author of the Pseudo-Philo formulates the traditional Pharisaic program under the new conditions that pertain in Palestine after the destruction of the Temple (*L.A.B.* 27:14). The author of *4 Ezra* places his hopes for the Jewish nation in a more consistent adherence to the law.

4. New Testament

The term **Pharisaioi** occurs ninety-nine times in the NT: in all four Gospels (Matt 30; Mark 12; Luke 27; John 19 [also in the non-Johannine pericope John 8:3]), in Acts (9), and once in one of Paul's letters (Phil 3:5). The plural is used 86 times. The Pharisees are often mentioned in connection with another group.

The phrase "Pharisees and Sadducees" occurs in Matt 3:7; 16:1, 6, 11, 12 (the par. texts in Mark and Luke mentioned here only the Pharisees). Disputes between Pharisees and Sadducees are mentioned in Matt 22:34 and in Acts 23:6-8. A similar phrase is "the high priests and the Pharisees," as the high priestly aristocracy can be regarded as mostly Sadducean (compare Acts 4:1; 5:17); the phrase occurs at the beginning and at the end of Matthew's passion narrative (Matt 21:45; 27:62; see also John 7:32, 45; 11:47, 57; 18:3).

The Pharisees are more frequently grouped with the SCRIBES. We find the following phrases: "the scribes of the Pharisees" (Mark 2:16; Acts 23:9); "the Pharisees and their scribes" (Luke 5:30); "the Pharisees and the scribes" (Matt 15:1; Mark 7:1, 5; Luke 15:2); "the scribes and the Pharisees" (Matt 5:20; 12:38; 23:2, 13, 15, 23, 25, 27, 29; Luke 5:21; 6:7; 11:53; John 8:3); "the Pharisees and the teachers of the law" (Luke 5:17; compare Acts 5:34); "the Pharisees and the lawyers" (Luke 7:30; compare 14:3; also 11:43, 45-46, 52). The

Pharisees are also mentioned in connection with the Herodians (Matt 22:15-16; Mark 3:6; 12:13).

The Pharisees are described as having disciples (students) (Matt 22:15-16; Mark 2:18; Luke 5:33). They understand themselves to be disciples of Moses (Matt 23:2; John 9:28; see also 9:13, 15-16, 40: John regards the "Jews" in 9:18, 22, 28 as essentially identical with the Pharisees). The main context in which the writers of the Gospels mention the Pharisees is the conflict between Jesus and the Pharisees regarding the Sabbath commandment; other disputes concern fasting, tithing, and ritual purity (§E2).

The portrayal that is implicit in the Gospel accounts agrees with Josephus with regard to the assumption that the Pharisees were the most prominent and influential group in Palestinian Jewish life. For Josephus, the Pharisees are the most precise interpreters of the law, and in the Gospels they appear as scrupulous in their observance of the law, in particular concerning the Sabbath observance, tithing, and purity laws. At the same time, Jesus criticizes the Pharisees despite his high regard for them, charging them of hypocrisy (Matt 23:2-3); Josephus' critique of the Pharisees focuses on their political role, accusing them of deceit and subversion (e.g., *Life* 216, 245, 301–3).

5. Rabbinic texts

References to **perushim** and **perushin** in the Mishnah, the Tosefta, in the Babylonian and the Jerusalem Talmuds, and in the Tannaitic midrashim have traditionally been interpreted as references to the Pharisees, particularly in passages that recount legal debates with a group called **tsaddiqim** (צַדִּיקִים) or **tsaddiqin** (צַדִּיקִין). As the earliest of these rabbinic sources, the Mishnah, was compiled nearly 200 years after Jesus, scholars are much more hesitant today to use rabbinic debates as evidence for reconstructing the positions of the Pharisees in the 1st cent. Two problems need to be addressed if this material can be used with some confidence for a portrayal of the historical Pharisees. First, not all references to **perushim** and to **tsaddiqim** are automatically a reference to the Pharisees and the Sadducees: the former term is sometimes used for extreme ascetics or even heretics, while the latter term seems to have been substituted for the original word **minim** (מִינִים), which means "heretics." Second, the individual rabbinic traditions have to be carefully weighed in terms of their historical authenticity. References to "the sages" or "the scribes" can no longer be identified with the Pharisees. These problems notwithstanding, texts such as *m. Yad.* 4:6–8 are usually accepted as reflecting debates about ritual purity and impurity and the transmission of uncleanness between the Pharisees and the Sadducees.

C. History

As the sources for the Pharisees are scant, it is impossible to be certain about their origins and the various phases of their history. The following picture emerges from a cautious evaluation of the extant evidence.

1. Origins and identity

The hellenization program of Jewish aristocratic and priestly circles in Jerusalem in the 2nd cent. BCE threatened to undermine the existence of traditional Judaism. Two main parties led the resistance against the Jewish leadership who had secured the support of the Syrian king Antiochus IV Epiphanes: the priestly clan of the Hasmoneans, i.e., Matthathias and his son Judas Maccabeus and his brothers (1 Macc 2:1-28), and the party of the Hasideans (*see* HASIDIM) with their ties to the scribes (1 Macc 7:12-13). They were supported by Jews "who were seeking righteousness and justice" (1 Macc 2:29). The struggle, which eventually evolved into military confrontations, was driven primarily by religious motives: the Hasmonean resistance insisted on holding firm to the monotheistic worship of Yahweh, to the exclusive offering of sacrifices to Yahweh, to the food laws stipulated in the holy Scriptures, to circumcision, and the observance of the Sabbath and of the festivals.

After the initial successes, the anti-Hellenistic coalition dissolved quickly. As the victory over King Antiochus was attributed to God's favor on account of the pious Jews' faithfulness to keep the commandments and their willingness to suffer martyrdom, a debate ensued over how the Jewish people as a whole should comply with the law, not only in the cult in the Temple in Jerusalem but also in the private life of every individual. It is in this context that Josephus introduces the three Jewish "schools" of the Pharisees, the Sadducees, and the Essenes (*Ant.* 13.171–72) during the time of Jonathan Maccabeus (160–143 BCE). The *Halakhic Letter*, written ca. 159–152 BCE, confronts Jonathan, who is about to assume the high priesthood or has recently done so, with the alternative to either abandon the particular temple reform that had been introduced when the Temple was rededicated and thus side with the priestly elite of the sons of Zadok, or to accommodate to those who currently hold the authority over the Temple and who enjoy the support of the majority of the peoples. The verb for "separation" (**parash**) occurs in *Halakhic Letter* (4Q397 14–21 7–9). The name *Pharisee*, which seems to have been coined at this time, involved initially a dispute about who could legitimately call himself "a separated one." As it was HELLENISM, which had threatened the religious identity of Israel, the separation that the term alludes to should be understood as a separation from all pagan practices.

The Pharisees thus arose between 160–140 BCE from the scribes and the Hasideans as the proponents of the consistent necessity to study Scripture, to apply it to everyday matters, to follow the commandments as a nation (in the Temple) and as individuals (in one's private life), and to cultivate the tradition of the law and its interpretation and application. The Pharisaic movement thus continues the tradition of the Deuteronomistic view of history: obedience to God's will as revealed in the law brings salvation and blessing, whereas disobedience leads to exile. The Temple represented the ideal model of purity and holiness (*see* TEMPLE, JERUSALEM). If the legal observance was to be as comprehensive as possible, additional tradition besides the written Torah needed to be developed. If the nation could live in a state of purity analogous to the purity of the Temple, the latter would be effectively protected and thus God's salvation and blessing maintained. Many scholars detect in the goal to expand the holiness of the Temple to the entire life of all Jews in Israel a "democratization" of the piety of the Temple, which can be explained in terms of the influence of the individualism of Hellenistic culture, expressed in the Pharisaic movement as a personal decision for a particular form of piety. It is obvious, at any rate, that Pharisaism did not separate a Jew from the nation (as an exclusive "sect" would do); rather, it sought to help people become truly Jewish.

2. Historical developments

The Pharisees initially worked together with the HASMONEANS to address the many practical problems that had been introduced when the Hellenizers had outlawed the Torah as a whole, such as property rights of refugees, compensation for damages, amnesty, calendar adjustments, and other questions of TORAH observance. Conflict ensued when John Hyrcanus I (134–104 BCE) wanted to institutionalize the combination of the high priestly office with the political and military leadership of the nation (*see* Josephus, *Ant.* 13.288–98). The Pharisees evidently hoped that the normalization of the political and military affairs would allow the Hasmoneans to give up the high priestly office; in the rabbinic literature, this episode is linked with Alexander Jannaeus (103–76 BCE), perhaps because he is regarded by the rabbis as evildoer par excellence, while the initially pro-Pharisaic John Hyrcanus is not regarded that negatively (compare *b. Qidd.* 66a). Josephus relates that the Sadducees, now the more influential group, sought to reverse the legal practices that the Pharisees had introduced. The Pharisees, however, continued to enjoy the support of the large majority of the people, while the Sadducees' influence was limited to the wealthy (*Ant.* 13.296, 298).

This bifurcation of the nation caused several years of civil war (93–88 BCE) during the reign of Alexander Jannaeus during which thousands were killed (*J.W.* 1.88–92; *Ant.* 13.372–76). Many supporters of the Pharisaic opposition were forced to leave the country, and many were executed by the Jewish king. On his deathbed he advised his wife to make peace with the Pharisees and to grant them participation in the political affairs (*Ant.* 13.399–404), as they would be able to dispose the nation favorably toward her since the people trusted them (13.402). It is no coincidence that Josephus, in his older work, introduces the Pharisees in connection with Queen Salome Alexandra (76–67 BCE), King Alexander's widow (*J.W.* 1.110–14; see the par. account in *Ant.* 13.399–423). He describes the Pharisees as particularly diligent in observing the laws (*J.W.* 1.110), and he comments that while Queen Salome was in power that the Pharisees held authority (*Ant.* 13.409). The Pharisees proceeded to exact revenge on their adversaries, which eventually prompted the queen to provide safe havens for the supporters of her late husband. When Salome died, the Sadducees evidently favored her son Aristobulus II (69–63 BCE), while the Pharisees seem to have supported John Hyrcanus II (high priest 76–67 and 63–41 BCE, r. 47–41 BCE).

When Judea was incorporated into the sphere of influence of Rome by Pompey in 63 BCE (he imprisoned Aristobulus II and accepted John Hyrcanus II as high priest), the Pharisees continued to push for the legal/political enactment of their agenda of a holy people living according to the revealed will of God. Some see Josephus' remarks in *Ant.* 14.41 as evidence for the Pharisees' belief that Pompey's intervention in the affairs of Judea represented God's judgment over the Hasmonean leaders who were descended from priests but who had aspired to be kings as well, turning the Jews into a slaves. The Pharisees thus did not reject the foreign rule of the Romans, at least initially.

The only period for which Josephus provides more information is the reign of Herod I (40/37–4 BCE). When Herod had consolidated his rule over Judea and proceeded to punish his opponents, putting to death the members of the (Sadducean) Sanhedrin, Josephus singles out the Pharisee Pollion and his disciple Samaias who were spared for being honored by Herod for their previous support (*Ant.* 15.3–4). When they refused to swear the oath of allegiance with which Herod later hoped to secure the loyalty of the people, they were not punished, as were the others who refused (*Ant.* 15.370). In *Ant.* 17.41–45 Josephus relates that Herod punished 6,000 Pharisees with a fine when they refused to take the oath by which he made the people affirm their loyalty to the Roman emperor and to the king's government, and that he killed those of the Pharisees who (in his opinion) had corrupted some of the people at his court. The two sophistai (σοφισταὶ) of *J.W.* 1.648–55 (*Ant.* 17.149–67), Judas son of Sepphoraeus and Matthias son of Margalus, whom Josephus characterizes as being recognized for their knowledge of the law (*J.W.* 1.648), whose regular lectures in Jerusalem on the laws attracted a large following of students, are often regarded as Pharisees, even though Josephus describes them merely as Torah experts or scribes. If they were indeed Pharisees, a conclusion that is made plausible on account of their popular reputation, this episode is highly instructive for their combination of political goals and religious zeal: they think that they can take advantage of Herod's declining health and increasing despondency, they exhort their students and followers to avenge God's honor by tearing down the golden eagle over the temple gate that contradicted the ban on any iconographic representation of living beings, and they affirm that martyrdom and eternal bliss is preferable to ignorance and contravention of God's laws. The two rabbis and the forty young men who had begun to chop off the golden eagle were ordered by Herod to be burned alive.

According to the (later) rabbinic sources, the Pharisees were divided into the school of Hillel and the school of Shammai (*see* HILLEL THE ELDER, HOUSE OF HILLEL; SHAMAI THE ELDER). The legal opinions of Hillel and his followers were regularly more lenient than those of Shammai; they appeared to have taken into account the economic and social needs of the people and sought to find what they considered to be realistic expectations for ordinary Jews to observe the law.

Also according to the rabbinic sources, the Pharisees were organized in "fellowships" or cooperatives (**khevrah** חֶבְרָה; see *m. Demai* 2:3; 6:6, 9, 12; *m. Toh.* 7:4; *b. Bek.* 30b). The **khavarim** (חֲבֵרִים; e.g., *t. Demat* 2:2) are described as Jews who banded together to eat their food in conditions of ritual purity, which was required of the priests in the Temple when they consumed holy offerings. Some suggest that the **khavarim** should be identified with the Pharisees; others think they were a subgroup of the Pharisees, or a group that overlapped with Pharisaic concerns, or a different group of pious Jews altogether. As neither Josephus nor the NT refers to the **khavarim**, certainty is impossible. It seems to be clear, however, that there was no formal "membership" in the Pharisaic movement: it seems that a Jew regarded himself as a Pharisee, or was regarded as a Pharisee by others, if he followed the Pharisees' interpretation of the law in everyday life. The possibility cannot be excluded, however, that there existed circles and schools in the Pharisaic movement that had clearly identifiable organizational structures (as apparently existed in the Essene movement).

Josephus provides further information on the Pharisees in connection with their attempts to contain the effects of the rebellion against Roman rule after 66 CE (*J.W.* 2.411). The willingness to compromise and to have politically realistic dealings with the Romans and with their Herodian vassal rulers secured for the Pharisees their continued influence in the period after 70 CE when the Pharisaic movement became the intellectual, spiritual, and political establishment of rabbinic Judaism.

3. Influence in Jewish society

Some scholars reduce the role of the Pharisees in Jewish society in contrast to the witness of Josephus (Neusner), some increase the role of the Sadducees as the dominant group in both political and religious matters, also in contrast to the witness of Josephus (Sanders), and some maintain that Josephus' threefold division of Judaism (not including the later Zealots) is a misleading simplification that does not do justice to the numerous "Judaisms" in the Second Temple period (Boccaccini).

Some scholars have attempted to provide a sociological description of the Pharisees as being strongly represented in the "retainer class" of Judean society, i.e., the low-level government officials and educators on whom the aristocratic class depended (Saldarini). If correct, the Pharisees certainly would have had access to power, albeit somewhat indirectly.

Attempts to describe multiple Jewish "sects" based on the interpretation of individual literary texts do not appear to be fruitful. As both Josephus and *Halakhic Letter* provide evidence for the division of Judaism into three major religious movements, with the Pharisees described as the group with the most widespread support (*J.W.* 2.162: they hold the position of the leading school [**hairesis** αἵρεσις]), a picture that is at least indirectly confirmed by the NT texts (which do not mention the Essenes, however), there seems to be no good reason to substantially revise the traditional picture of Second Temple Judaism (Deines).

Paul's autobiographical statement in Phil 3:5 (compare Gal 1:14; Acts 22:3; 26:5) confirms the existence of the Pharisees in the second half of the 1st cent. Josephus' autobiographical comment in *Life* 12 also attests to the importance and popularity of the Pharisees in the 1st cent. Josephus does not claim that he "joined" the Pharisees but that he largely agreed with their tradition and their way of life. The fact that Josephus has practically nothing to relate about the Pharisees during the rule of the Roman prefects and procurators in the 1st cent. CE should not be taken as an indication that the Pharisees were left "out in the cold." Josephus has not written annals in which he records the events of each successive year.

The influence of the Pharisees among the Jewish population in Judea and in Galilee may explain the sudden appearance of numerous water pools for immersion for the removal of ritual impurity (*see* MIQVAH, MIQVEH), as well as the appearance of stone vessels and the reburial in ossuaries (presupposing belief in the resurrection of the body) since the middle of the 1st cent. BCE. There is no archaeological or literary evidence that links these practices with priestly (or Sadducean) circles.

The frequent connection that is made between the Pharisees and the scribes (twenty-one times in the NT) indicates that many (but certainly not all) scribes belonged to the Pharisaic movement. While only people with the proper genealogy could attain the priesthood, everyone could aspire to become a law expert. According to John 3:1 some members of the SANHEDRIN belonged to the circles of the Pharisees (Nicodemus).

There is thus no reason to doubt the presence of Pharisees in Galilee or their connection with the local synagogues reported in the Gospels. The controversies between Jesus and the Pharisees are a testimony to the eminent role that the Pharisees played in Jewish society: as both Jesus and the Pharisees focused on personal piety and on the proper interpretation and practice of the will of God, it was inevitable that they would clash if there was no agreement.

D. Theology and Piety

Since we have no primary sources written explicitly by Pharisees, we are dependent on the portrayals of non-Pharisees such as Josephus and the authors of the Gospels whose descriptions do not claim to be historically informative and objective but who write for their respective audiences.

1. Observance of the law

The emphasis on the observance of the law is not a characteristic of the Pharisaic movement alone: the Sadducees and the Essenes insisted on the need of following the law as well. However, the Pharisees are singled out by Josephus as a group that accurately interpreted the law (*J.W.* 2.162) and as the Jewish group who was proud of its observance of ancestral customs approved by God (*Ant.* 17.41). The term akribeia (ἀκρίβεια; "conformity, exactness, precision") describes the Pharisees' claim, acknowledged by Josephus, to accuracy, excellence, and precision in their interpretation and observance of the law.

The biographical sketches of Paul in Acts 22:3 and 26:5 confirm this portrayal: according to Luke, Paul is proud of the fact that he was "brought up in this city at the feet of Gamaliel, educated strictly [kata akribeian κατὰ ἀκρίβειαν] according to our ancestral law," and that he "belonged to the strictest party [kata tēn akribestatēn hairesin κατὰ τὴν ἀκριβεστάτην αἵρεσιν] of our religion and lived as a Pharisee."

The controversies between Jesus and the Pharisees over questions of the law (see §E2), regularly initiated by the Pharisees, confirm the centrality of the law and its correct interpretation for the Pharisees. The disputes between perushim and tsadduqim about intricate details of the observance of the law found in the rabbinical sources support this picture.

It is important to note that the Pharisees were interested not only in the correct interpretation of the law but also in correct behavior. The zeal of Saul/Paul, the Pharisee who persecuted the church asserting that "as to righteousness under the law" he was "blameless" (Phil 3:6), confirms that the zealous observance of the law and its commandments was a central element of the Pharisees' emphasis.

The Pharisees' precision in the interpretation of the law and their zeal for the punctilious observance of the commandments should not be confused with uncaring harshness. Josephus asserts categorically that the Pharisees were lenient in punishing people for breaking the law (*Ant.* 13.294) and cites as an example that when a certain Jonathan, a Sadducee, suggests that Eleazar should be executed for having spoken insultingly of doubts concerning John Hyrcanus' legitimacy, the Pharisees argue that he should merely be scourged and bound by chains. According to Acts 5:33-40, "a Pharisee in the council named Gamaliel, a teacher of the law, respected by all the people" recommends leniency when the leading priests and other council members want to put the apostles to death. The early rabbinic evidence again confirms this picture: in the disputes between perushim and tsadduqim about the details of the observance of the law, the Pharisees are more lenient.

2. The tradition of the elders

The laws that the Pharisees interpreted with precision and followed with zeal included not only the laws of the holy Scriptures but also the stipulations of the oral law, the tradition of the fathers (*see* ORAL LAW, ORAL TORAH; see Josephus, *Ant.* 13.297). The Sadducees rejected these traditions that were not written in the Law of Moses. During the reign of queen Salome, the Pharisees were permitted to reintroduce their regulations (*Ant.* 13.408). Paul asserts in Gal 1:14 that he was "far more zealous for the traditions of my ancestors." The term *tradition* (paradosis παράδοσις) describes instruction that has been handed down. Mark 7:3 describes the Pharisees as "observing the tradition of the elders" (compare Matt 15:2). In *m. Avot* 1:1 the tradition of the elders is traced from Moses via Joshua and the prophets to individuals in more recent times; the second-to-last and the last pair of teachers, all Pharisees (a fact that we know from other sources), are Hillel and Shammai and GAMALIEL I and his son Simeon I.

The sources of these traditions of the elders (or fathers) are according to Josephus the painstaking interpretation of the law (*J.W.* 2.162), rational considerations (*Ant.* 18.12), and the example of earlier teachers (*Ant.* 18.12). It would be wrong to assume that the Pharisees created all of the traditions, which they taught and observed: they preserve, transmit, and recontextualize ancient traditions that may have pre-Pharisaic origins. We should also note that the Pharisees were not the only group that preserved traditions not directly taught in the written law: any Jewish group that would insist on the normative relevance of the Torah for everyday life has to find practical solutions to new situations created by changing political and cultural circumstances.

These traditions of the fathers focused on at least the following areas: 1) purity rules concerning food and vessels containing food and liquids (Matt 23:25-26; Mark 7:1-23); *m. Or.* 2:12; *t. Abod. Zar.* 4:9); 2) purity rules concerning clean and unclean hands (Mark 7:1-5; *m. Yad.* 4:6); 3) purity rules concerning corpses and tombs (Matt 23:27-28; *m. Yad.* 4:7); 4) rules concerning the sanctity of the Temple and its cult (Matt 23:16-22; *t. Hag.* 3:35; *m. Sheq.* 6:1; Josephus, *Ant.* 18.15, 17); 5) tithing and the shares and dues of the priests (Matt 23:23; *m. Peah* 2:5-6; *t. Sanh.* 2:6); 6) observance of the SABBATH and of holy days, particularly as regards work and travel (Mark 2:23-28; 3:1-6; Luke 13:10-17; 14:1-6; John 5:1-18; 9:1-34; *m. Rosh Hash.* 2:5; *m. Eruv.* 6:2; *see* FEASTS AND FASTS); 7) marriage and divorce (Mark 10:1-12; Luke 16:18; *m. Yad.* 4:8; *m. Yebam.* 16:7; *m. Git.* 4:2-3).

The devotion to the written law and to the traditions of the fathers explains why the scribes played such an important role in the Pharisaic movement: Torah experts were needed both for the accurate interpretation of the law and for the legitimate application of the meaning of biblical law to specific and often novel situations in everyday life. Teaching the younger generation of law experts and also the population at large were logical extensions of the Pharisees' devotion to the law.

3. Belief in divine providence

Josephus ascribes to the Pharisees belief in the cooperation of providence and free will in human affairs: they attributed everything to Fate (heimarmenē εἱμαρμένη) and God (*J.W.* 2.162–63; compare *Ant.* 13.172; 18.13). According to *m. Avot* 3:16, Rabbi Akiva spoke of free will as well. According to Josephus, the Pharisees' position in this question stands between that of the Sadducees, who deny providence, and that of the Essenes, who trace all events to divine providence. The Pharisees rejected a deterministic worldview. They accepted both God's gracious sovereignty and obedience by free will. They thus propagated a view of morality and ethics in which human beings are responsible for their actions as their status before God is decisively impacted by their own will and by their actions. The Pharisees emphasized the study of the law because people can and should know what God expects them to do in their everyday lives. Paul's statement in Phil 2:12-13 implies a parallel understanding of this connection between divine providence and the free will of human beings: "work out your own salvation with fear and trembling; for it is God who is at work in you, enabling you both to will and to work for his good pleasure."

4. Belief in a future resurrection

The Pharisees believed that every good soul would pass into another body, while the bad souls would be punished forever (Josephus, *J.W.* 2.163). This belief distinguishes them from the Sadducees who believed that the soul perishes when people die (*J.W.* 2.165; compare Matt 22:23-33; Mark 12:18-27; Luke 20:27-40; Acts 23:8; compare 26:5-7), and from the Essenes who believed (according to Josephus) in the immortality of the soul but not in the resurrection of the body. The formulation in Mark 12:18 ("And there came to him the Sadducees, who say that there is no resurrection") seems to imply that the position of the Sadducees concerning resurrection differed from most, if not all, other Jews or Jewish groups (*see* RESURRECTION, EARLY JEWISH).

5. Messianic and apocalyptic expectations

The Pharisees seem to have championed various messianic and apocalyptic expectations, which cannot be reconstructed from the extant sources with any degree of precision. Josephus relates events at the court of Herod I that evidently involved messianic hopes that were stoked by Pharisees (*Ant.* 17.43–45). Some Pharisees responded to John the Baptist's prophetic preaching and wanted to be baptized (Matt 3:7). The Pharisees' question when the kingdom of God was coming (Luke 17:20) and the discussion about the identity of the Messiah as Son of David (and Son of God) between Jesus and the Pharisees (Matt 22:41-46; the par. texts Mark 12:35-37 and Luke 20:41-44 refer to scribes) confirm their interest in messianic beliefs (*see* MESSIAH, JEWISH). Josephus claims that the ZEALOTs followed the teachings of the Pharisees, with the exception of their love for freedom (*Ant.* 18.23), and that one of their founders was a Pharisee named Zaddok (*Ant.* 18.4, 9–10). If these claims are correct, the militant messianic ideas of the Zealot movement confirm the Pharisees' interest in messianic expectations. Moreover, when we take into consideration passages such as *Pss. Sol.* 17–18, granting that the *Psalms of Solomon* may reflect Pharisaic influence (if not authorship), the evidence seems to allow the conclusion that some Pharisaic circles expected the coming of the messiah in the near future. In view of their conviction that God's providence is linked with human action, some Pharisees were (eventually) willing to take specific action to make the messianic kingdom of God a reality. The zealous efforts to accomplish consistent holiness and ritual purity in everyday life may have played a role in this context as well (compare the words of Rabbi Phineas [*m. Sotah* 9.15], who links purity and holiness with the arrival of the resurrection of the dead).

6. Other beliefs

The Pharisees believed in the possibility of prophecy, which some of them practiced (*Ant.* 14.176 [according to *Ant.* 15.3, Samaias was the disciple of a Pharisee]; 15.4; 17.41–45; compare *J.W.* 3.352–54 for Josephus' prophetic dreams concerning the impending fate of the Jews and the destinies of the Roman generals). The Pharisees believe in the existence of angels and spirits, which the Sadducees deny (Acts 23:8). They believed in civil disobedience and they were willing to die for their basic convictions if they had come to the conclusion that the Jewish king or the Roman emperor acted in contravention of God's revealed will (*Ant.* 14.172–74; 15.3–4, 368–70; 17.42). They practiced a simple lifestyle; they despised luxury (*Ant.* 18.12;

compare Luke 16:14). It has often been assumed on the basis of Matt 23:15 that they engaged in missionary outreach, but this has been questioned (*see* MISSIONS; PROSELYTE).

E. Pharisees in the New Testament

Of the ninety-nine references to the Pharisees in the NT, eighty-nine are found in the four Gospels, while nine occur in the Acts of the Apostles; there is one reference in Paul's letters (Phil 3:5).

1. The Pharisees and Jesus

The conversations between Jesus and the Pharisees, which are without exception initiated by the latter, focus on questions of proper behavior: fasting, working on the Sabbath, tithing, and ritual purity. Jesus is presented as debating with and being talked about by the Pharisees in multiple sources and forms, so much so that scholars who are rather skeptical concerning the historical reliability of gospel material accept that Jesus' interaction with the Pharisees was a regular occurrence during his ministry. Some have questioned whether Mark's theological schema, which keeps Jesus in Galilee and away from Jerusalem (apart from the final week), and which forces him to place the interaction with the Pharisees in Galilee, corresponds to historical fact, arguing that the picture presented in the Gospel of John and in the Acts of the Apostles, where the Pharisees are placed in and around Jerusalem, might be closer to the truth. Some scholars regard the more frequent references to the Pharisees in Matthew and Luke as a multiplication of stage props, with Matthew presenting the Pharisees as Jesus' opponents par excellence, while Luke's characterization and utilization of the Pharisees is less hostile. Such interpretations are invariably linked with the reconstructed picture of the Pharisees that the individual interpreter finds most convincing. As there is no consensus concerning the political and legal influence or concerning the religious beliefs of the historical Pharisees, it is not surprising that some scholars find the portrayal of the Pharisees in the Gospels less problematic, if not more or less historically authentic and plausible.

a. The conflicts regarding the Sabbath. Repeated controversies between the Pharisees and Jesus concerning the observance of the SABBATH are reported by all four Gospels (Matt 12:1-8 / Mark 2:23-28 / Luke 6:1-5; Matt 12:9-14 / Mark 3:1-6 / Luke 6:6-11; Luke 14:1-6; John 9:1-41). The observance of the Sabbath was indeed a serious matter since it represented not only a confessional act that spoke of devotion to God but, together with circumcision, a fundamental characteristic of Jewish faith and life that distinguished Jews from pagans. Jesus' healing activity on the Sabbath was a deliberately provocative act (a person born blind can certainly wait one more day before being healed). All activities on the day of the Sabbath that could be construed as the "work" that the law prohibited were to be avoided, unless extenuating circumstances as defined by the experts of the law could be found to legitimate the activity. The Pharisees and (their) scribes found Jesus' behavior in violation of this principle. Jesus does not respond to the Pharisees' critique with a discussion about the correct interpretation of "work." He does not argue that, e.g., a healing does not constitute "work." Rather, he insists that doing good can never be wrong on the Sabbath (Mark 3:4), that compassion is a better guide to proper behavior than stipulations derived by scribes through exegetical-legal discussions (Matt 12:10-11), and that God's intentions for the Sabbath are distorted when his original purposes that were meant to benefit people are ignored (Mark 2:27). What is at stake in these debates is the question whether Jesus has the authority to interpret God's will in a manner that differs from the scribal exegesis of the Pharisees.

b. Fasting and divorce. According to Luke 18:12, the Pharisees fasted twice a week; the fact that Jesus is asked why neither he nor his disciples are fasting, while both the Pharisees and the disciples of John the Baptist practice fasting (Matt 9:14; Mark 2:18; Luke 5:33) confirms this practice (see also the Scroll of Fasting [*Megillat Taanit*], which lists thirty-five days of joy during which fasting is prohibited). According to *Pss. Sol.* 3.7–8, the fasting of the righteous atones for unknown sins. Jesus' critique of the Pharisees' fasting (Matt 9:15-17; Mark 2:19-22; Luke 5:34-39) is thus directed against an important element of Jewish piety. Jesus does not condemn the practice of fasting as such. Rather, he clarifies that the present time is a time for celebration, and people do not fast during festivals: as the "bridegroom" has arrived, the days of fasting have given way to seasons of joy and gladness and cheerful festivals (Zech 8:19). In Matt 6:16-18 Jesus criticizes the fasting practices of some people as external piety that is meant to impress onlookers rather than being a spiritual practiced directed toward God (note that this text does not identify the "hypocrites" with the Pharisees). *See* FAST, FASTING.

In the dispute concerning marriage and DIVORCE (Matt 19:1-9; Mark 10:1-12; Luke 16:18) Jesus sides neither with the more lenient school of Hillel nor with the stricter school of Shammai as regards legitimate grounds of divorce. Jesus grants that the law had allowed divorce on account of the hardness of heart of the people. Then he goes on to argue that people living in the last days for which the prophets had promised the exchange of hearts of stone for hearts of flesh (Ezek 11:19; 36:26), the time of God's new covenant when he would write his law on people's hearts (Jer 31:31-33) will live like the people in the first days after the creation of the world, fulfilling again God's intention of a permanent union between one man and one woman in marriage (*see* MARRIAGE, NT; MARRIAGE, OT).

c. Tithing and ritual purity. In the context of the Pharisees' program of the sanctification of everyday life, the TITHE was important because it safeguarded the concern to eat only food that was cultivated, harvested, sold, and bought in compliance with the law (Lev 27:30; Deut 14:22-29). Jesus does not criticize the Pharisees for tithing mint, dill, and cumin but for neglecting the weightier matters of justice, mercy, and faith (Matt 23:23; Luke 11:42; compare Luke 18:12). Similarly, the Pharisees concerned themselves with the ritual purity of the containers and cooking pots in a household (Lev 11:32-35; Num 19:14-15) and with the cleanness of one's hands, as this affected the purity of the food that is handled, stored, and consumed (*see* CLEAN AND UNCLEAN; DIETARY LAWS). As Jesus addresses these matters (Matt 15:1-20//Mark 7:1-23; Matt 23:25-26//Luke 11:37-44), his pronouncement that "there is nothing outside a person that by going in can defile, but the things that come out are what defile" (Mark 7:15) stands out. Jesus does not enter into a discussion about different types of ritual defilement or about the correct interpretation of the detailed regulations of Lev 11 specifying which animals could and could not be eaten by the people of God. Rather, Jesus establishes as a new principle, over against specific stipulations of the law that defilement comes from inside and not (or, rather, no longer) from the outside. Mark's editorial comment (Mark 7:19*b*) is the inevitable deduction both from the principle (v. 15) and from its elaboration (vv. 18*b*-19*a*): Jesus declares that food is no longer to be regarded as ritually unclean.

d. The leaven of the Pharisees. The only pronouncement of Jesus concerning the Pharisees that all three Synoptic Gospels relate is a warning to "beware of the yeast of the Pharisees and the yeast of Herod" (Mark 8:15; other manuscripts read "of the Herodians"). Matthew 16:6 has "the yeast of the Pharisees and Sadducees," while Luke 12:1 reads "the yeast of the Pharisees." Matthew relates this pronouncement to the teaching of the Pharisees and Sadducees (Matt 16:12), while Luke regards Jesus' warning as a reference to the hypocrisy of the Pharisees (Luke 12:1). Jesus' warning concerning the "yeast" (or leaven) of the Pharisees, a pronouncement that links them with the Herodians (Mark) and with the Sadducees (Matthew), can be understood in the context of the Pharisees' claim to be the sanctifying remnant (compare Rom 11:16) that takes the holiness and purity required by the law to the entire Jewish population. If correct, the pronouncement criticizes the Pharisees for their willingness to cooperate with Herod Antipas (or the Herodians more generally) and with the Sadducees whose influence over the people constitutes an increasingly dangerous situation for Jesus and his disciples, following the alliance of the Pharisees and the Herodians as early as Mark 3:6 who plot Jesus' removal (*see* HEROD, FAMILY).

e. The Pharisees' critique of Jesus. Mark, and even more so Matthew, intends his readers to understand that Jesus' approach to the observance of religious practices and to the interpretation of Scripture markedly differed from that of the Pharisees (Mark 2:24; Matt 9:11), that this difference became increasingly obvious in the course of Jesus' public ministry (Mark 7:1-5; 8:11; Matt 12:2; 15:1; 16:1), and that this was regarded as serious enough (Mark 12:13; Matt 12:24; 22:15; compare Luke 11:53-54) so that the Pharisees came to see it as a dangerous influence over the people that needed to be eliminated (Mark 3:6; Matt 12:14; 21:45-46; 27:62).

The Pharisees objected to Jesus' attitude and practice concerning the Sabbath, tithing, ritual purity, and the washing of hands (see §E1a–c), matters that had a fundamental religious role for the Pharisees: they believed that faithful observance of the law in these external matters indicates whether a person seeks to do God's will in areas that are hidden. The controversies between the Pharisees and Jesus occur precisely in areas of external piety, in questions of HALAKHAH, in matters of personal behavior.

From an early period onward, however, the Pharisees clashed with Jesus concerning the fundamental theological question of the origin of the power and authority that Jesus displayed in his healing and exorcism ministry. According to Matt 12:24, Pharisees declare Jesus' EXORCISMs to depend on his using the power of BEELZEBUL, the "ruler of the demons." In other words, they accuse him of being a sorcerer who invokes occult power. In Mark 3:22 it is a delegation of scribes from Jerusalem who make the same accusation (Mark 7:1 refers to a second delegation from Jerusalem, which consisted of Pharisees and some scribes). This discussion about Jesus' authority to heal is linked with the question whether he has the authority to pronounce sins to be forgiven: according to Luke 5:21, Pharisees and teachers of the law label Jesus' pronouncement of forgiveness to be blasphemy, which is an ominous charge that is repeated in Jesus' trial (Matt 26:65; Mark 14:64). According to Matt 27:62 and John 18:3 the Pharisees were involved (with the chief priests and the scribes) in having Jesus arrested and brought to trial before Pilate, where he is accused as a false teacher who was trying to lead Israel astray.

The Gospels also know of positive encounters between Jesus and the Pharisees. Luke speaks of repeated invitations of Jesus by Pharisees (Luke 7:36-50; 11:37-52; 14:1-6) and of well-meant advice that Pharisees give to Jesus (Luke 13:31). John 3:1-21 portrays NICODEMUS, a Pharisee and member of the Sanhedrin, as a sympathizer of Jesus (compare John 7:47-52).

f. Jesus' critique of the Pharisees. Jesus accepts the fundamental concerns of the Pharisees about matters of righteousness; note Matt 5:20: "For I tell you, unless your righteousness exceeds that of the scribes and Pharisees, you will never enter the kingdom of heaven" (compare Matt 23:1-3). His basic criticism focuses on the Pharisees' emphasis on external piety as an indication of, and pathway to, internal piety (Matt

15:17-20; Mark 7:15). Jesus emphasizes that the most scrupulous and correct observance of the laws does not indicate, nor lead to, a person's agreement with the will of God. Rather, it carries with it the tendency of arrogantly enjoying the applause of other people, of seeking to please oneself rather than God, and thus of losing God in and through such acts of external piety (Luke 16:15; 18:14). The NT term for this phenomenon is *hypocrisy* (*see* HYPOCRISY, HYPOCRITE). The Pharisees already knew of the dangers of a merely external piety, which is hypocrisy (*b. Sotah* 22b).

Jesus' woes against the hypocritical Pharisees (Matt 23:13-36; Luke 11:39-44) need to be understood in this context. 1) They represent an internal Jewish controversy rather than an arrogant and vicious dressing-down of Jews by Christians; unfortunately, later Christian tradition used these passages and made the term *Pharisee* in an unjustifiable pejorative fashion into a synonym for *hypocrite.* 2) Fiery denunciation was an established rhetorical tradition in internal Jewish debates since the days of Amos and Hosea, and examples in Jewish texts of the Second: Jews with beliefs or behavior that is regarded as aberrant are called *hypocrites* (*Pss. Sol.* 4:6-7; *As. Mos.* 7:5-10; 1QS IV, 14; Philo, *Embassy* 25, 162; Josephus, *Ag. Ap.* 2.142–44), blind (Wis 2:21; *1 En.* 90:7; Josephus, *Ag. Ap.* 2.142; *J.W.* 5.572), foolish or ignorant (Wis 13:1; Sir 50:26; *1 En.* 98:3, 9; 1QH IV, 8; Josephus, *Ag. Ap.* 2.37, 255; *J.W.* 3.381; 5.417, 566; *b. Yev.* 63b), guilty of economic sins (Wis 2:10; *Pss. Sol.* 4:9-13, 20, 22; *1 En.* 63:10; 94:6-8; *As. Mos.* 5:5; 7:5-7; 1QpHab VIII, 10–12), guilty of sexual sins (Wis 14:22-28; *Pss. Sol.* 2:11-13; 4:4-5; 8:9-10; CD IV, 19–21; V 6–12; Josephus, *J.W.* 5.402), unclean (1QpHab VIII, 13; *Pss. Sol.* 8:11-13, 22; *T. Levi* 16:1; *As. Mos.* 7:9-10; *m. Nid.* 4:1-2), snakes (Philo, *Embassy* 26, 166: *Pss. Sol.* 4:8), and destined for eschatological judgment (1QpHab X, 12–13; XI, 14–15; 1QS II, 7–9; *1 En.* 62:1-16; 94:9; 96:8; *Pss. Sol.* 14:9; *T. Levi* 15:2; *m. Sanh.* 10:1). Jesus' accusation that the Pharisees' interpretation of the law misses the point of God's will, as they pursue their own advantage (Matt 23:23, 16-22; Mark 7:8-13) agrees with the critique of the QUMRAN community, who accuse the Pharisees of exchanging the Torah with **khalaqoth** (חֲלָקוֹת, "smooth things"). 3) The denunciation of the Pharisees comes during the last week of Jesus' life and ministry, not at the beginning, the result of their rejection of Jesus as the messianic son of Man who preached and established the coming of the kingdom of God. This connection is evident in the first denunciation of the Pharisees as hypocrites in Matt 23:13: "You lock people out of the kingdom of heaven. For you do not go in yourselves, and when others are going in, you stop them." 4) The woes thus serve to delimit Jesus' position that focused on the coming of the kingdom of God and on the changes that this new reality is introducing both for the people and for the law, over against the dominant Jewish-Pharisaic position that focused on the law and its interpretation as a prerequisite for living according to the will of God.

2. The Pharisees and the early Christians

According to Acts 5:34 Gamaliel, a Pharisee and member of the Sanhedrin, was favorably disposed toward the Christians, preventing the execution of the apostles (see also Acts 23:6-9). Luke reports that Pharisees had become followers of Jesus and demanded that the new converts from paganism should be circumcised and ordered to keep the law of Moses (Acts 15:5).

Josephus recounts that the Sadducean high priest Ananus II convened the Sanhedrin to indict James, the brother of Jesus, for transgressing the law (*Ant.* 20.200). When James was executed (compare Acts 12:2), citizens "who were considered the most fair-minded and who were strict in observance of the law"—probably Pharisees—were offended, protested before King Agrippa II and before the Roman governor Albinus, with the result that Ananus was deposed (*Ant.* 20.201–3). It is unclear whether this incident attests to influential sympathizers with the Christians among the Pharisees, or to the standing of James in the society of Jerusalem, or simply to the unbending sense of justice of the Pharisees.

Paul was a former Pharisee (Phil 3:5); his continuous interpretation of Scripture and its application to new situations reflects Pharisaic practice, albeit in the completely different theological context of his conviction that Jesus was the promised Messiah whose death and resurrection fulfilled the law and the prophets and inaugurated the last days and the new covenant. His controversies with Jewish Christians who demanded that Gentile Christians should be circumcised and told to submit to the law were, evidently, controversies with Christian Pharisees. Thus, both Jesus and Paul engage the dominant religious movement of their nation, with which they shared many convictions and many practices. *See* JEWISH BIBLICAL INTERPRETATION; JUDAISM; RABBINIC LITERATURE.

Bibliography: Albert I. Baumgarten. *The Flourishing of Jewish Sects in the Maccabean Era* (1997); Gabriele Boccaccini. *Middle Judaism: Jewish Thought, 300 B.C.E. to 200 C.E.* (1991); Roland Deines. *Die Pharisäer* (1997); Roland Deines. "The Pharisees between 'Judaisms' and 'Common Judaism'." D. A. Carson, ed. *Justification and Variegated Nomism I* (2001) 443–504; Steve Mason. *Flavius Josephus on the Pharisees* (1991); Steve Mason. *Josephus and the New Testament* (1992, 2003); John P. Meier. *A Marginal Jew: Rethinking the Historical Jesus. Vol 3: Companions and Competitors* (2001); Jacob Neusner. *The Rabbinic Traditions about the Pharisees before 70* (1971); Anthony J. Saldarini. *Pharisees, Scribes and Sadducees in Palestinian Society* (1988;

2001); E. P. Sanders. *Judaism: Practice and Belief 63 BCE–66 CE* (1992); Günter Stemberger. *Jewish Contemporaries of Jesus: Pharisees, Sadducees, Essenes* (1995); Gerd Theissen and Annette Merz. *The Historical Jesus* (1998).

ECKHARD J. SCHNABEL

PHARPAR fahr´pahr [פַּרְפַּר parpar]. Pharpar was one of two rivers, along with the ABANA, named by NAAMAN as rivers of Damascus (2 Kgs 5:12). Naaman, the Syrian army commander, was stricken with LEPROSY and went to Israel to find Elisha for healing (2 Kgs 5:1-9). When told to wash in the Jordan River seven times, he angrily noted that these two rivers of Damascus were better than any water in Israel.

Whether these rivers were part of ancient Damascus proper or within the Damascus Plain about 10 mi. (16 km) south of Damascus is unclear. The modern Nahr al-Barada flows through Damascus and is thought to be the Abana by many scholars. The Pharpar is linked to the Nahr el-Awaj that forms from streams of Mount Hermon, eventually watering the oasis of Damascus in the plains. The Wadi Barbar, a small tributary of the Nahr el-Awaj, preserves the name. *See* RIVER; SYRIA.

MICHAEL G. VANZANT

PHASAEL fah´see-uhl. 1. Son of ANTIPATER and elder brother of Herod the Great (*see* HEROD, FAMILY). Antipater appointed his two sons governors over various territories. Phasael became the governor of Jerusalem, while Herod was appointed governor of Galilee (*Ant.* 14.158). Phasael appears to have ruled with greater moderation than Herod.

After Antipater's murder in 43 BCE, the Romans named Phasael and Herod tetrarchs, despite the protests of two Jewish delegations that demanded their ouster. In 40 BCE disgruntled elements of the Jewish aristocracy conspired with the Parthians to overthrow Roman rule; Phasael was betrayed into enemy hands and opted to commit suicide (*Ant.* 14.365–69). Herod memorialized Phasael by naming one of three monumental towers adjacent to his Jerusalem palace after his brother.

2. A son of Phasael (*J.W.* 1.275) who married Herod the Great's daughter Salampsio (*Ant.* 18.130).

3. Son of Herod the Great and Pallas (*J.W.* 1.562).

THOMAS V. BRISCO

PHASELIS fuh-see´lis [Φάσηλις Phasēlis]. A city on the southern coast of Asia Minor (modern Turkey) founded as a Greek colony by Rhodes in LYCIA in the 7th cent. BCE. Phaselis controlled three harbors and linked east and west trade. The ruins of the city are located near the modern village of Tekrova.

Phaselis is mentioned in a list of cities that received a letter from Roman consul Lucius (1 Macc 15:23). The letter instructed rulers and municipalities to treat the Jews in their region favorably. This request was prompted by a gift of a golden shield weighing 1,000 minas (about 1,250 pounds) given to the Roman ruler by Jewish ambassadors.

JOHN D. WINELAND

PHASIRON fas´uh-ron [Φασιρών Phasirōn]. The people of Phasiron, an otherwise unknown tribe attempting to join BACCHIDES's army besieging Bethbasi, were killed along with ODOMERA and his clansmen by Jonathan and the Hasmonean forces (1 Macc 9:66). *See* HASMONEANS.

PHI [φ ph, Φ Ph]. The twenty-second letter of the Greek alphabet. *See* ALPHABET.

PHICOL fi´kol [פִּיכֹל pikhol]. The commander of ABIMELECH's army. He is present on both occasions when Abimelech makes a covenant first with Abraham (Gen 21:22, 32) and later with Isaac (Gen 26:26). It is possible that the two stories represent a single incident reported in separate sources. *See* PHILISTINES.

PHILADELPHIA fil´uh-del´fee-uh [Φιλαδέλφεια **Philadelpheia**]. A Hellenistic name for two cities. 1. Initially named RABBAH of the Ammonites (modern Amman, Jordan), this city was known as Philadelphia in the Hellenistic era (but never in the Bible).

2. Philadelphia in Lydia (*see* LYDIA, LYDIANS) was located in the Roman province of Asia (modern Alasehir, Turkey). It is to this second Philadelphia that Rev 1:11 and 3:7-13 refer (*see* REVELATION, BOOK OF). The Philadelphia of Revelation was founded in the second half of the 2nd cent. BCE by either King Eumenes II of PERGAMUM, who ruled from 197 to 159 BCE, or his brother King Attalus II, whose reign lasted from 159 to 138 BCE. Attalus was known for his loyalty to his brother and was given the surname "Philadelphos" (**Philadelphos** Φιλάδελφος), which means "loyal to his brother."

The city is approximately 20 mi. east of SARDIS and 60 mi. east of SMYRNA, located on a 700 ft. plateau from the northern slopes of the Boz/Tmolus Mountains toward the River Hermus (modern Gediz). Prior to the founding of Philadelphia, a settlement called Callatebus existed there from ca. 900 BCE.

The region was fertile, and King Attalus brought in Macedonian veterans to settle the area. The area is prone to earthquakes, however, and a major earthquake destroyed the city in 17 CE. This tragedy had significant social effects. First of all, many residents lived outside the city for years because many buildings were unsafe, and they feared for their lives. Secondly, TIBERIUS CAESAR helped the city by remitting its tribute for five years to assist the rebuilding process (Strabo, *Geogr.* 12.8.18; 13.4.10). In response, the city added "Neocaesarea" ("new Caesar") to its name. Later, Philadelphia became "Philadelphia Flavia" under emperor VESPASIAN, in honor of his family name (Flavius). Revelation

3:12 refers to inscribing God's name and the name of God's city on the faithful victor, perhaps in deliberate contrast to the name of the emperor in the city's name "Philadelphia Flavia."

Philadelphia also received the "neokoros" (neōkoros νεωκόρος), the title of a temple custodian or the title of a city that had built a temple in honor of its patron god, making the city an official center for the imperial cult (see Acts 19:35, where neōkoros is translated "temple keeper"). The imperial cult was not initiated by the emperor but by the provincials. Traditionally, rulers in the eastern Mediterranean received divine honors. In many of these indigenous societies, locals believed their ruler to be either the son or the adopted son of the national deity (*see* EMPEROR WORSHIP). Alexander received such honors when he conquered the region. So did his Ptolemaic and Seleucid successors. The tradition was continued in a similar fashion when the Romans conquered the region. Cities competed vigorously to receive the neōkoros, because the title symbolized both civic pride and devotion to religious traditions. It also created a way of relating to the new imperial power in familiar religio-political ways. Finally, the neōkoros sought to establish and sustain strong, positive economic and political relations between the imperial court and a given municipality. Thus, a regional repression that was led by provincials against persons who did not participate in the imperial cult was possible.

In 92 CE, DOMITIAN decreed that at least half the vineyards in the provinces be destroyed and not be replaced (Suetonius, *Dom.* 7.2). This edict severely hurt Philadelphia because it had a strong wine industry. Ignatius visited the city and also wrote a letter to the church there en route to his martyrdom in Rome in the late 1st–early 2nd cent. CE (*see* IGNATIUS, EPISTLES OF). Ruins of the ancient city include an acropolis, a church, and a city wall from the Byzantine period. The museum in Manisa contains other archaeological finds from Philadelphia.

Bibliography: Colin J. Hemer. *The Letters to the Seven Churches of Asia in Their Local Setting* (1986); Simon R. F. Price. *Rituals and Power* (1984).

THOMAS B. SLATER

PHILADELPHIANS, LETTER TO THE. *See* IGNATIUS, EPISTLES OF.

PHILEMON, LETTER TO fi-lee´muhn [Πρὸς Φιλήμων **Pros Philēmōn**]. The shortest writing in the NT, this authentic letter by Paul bears the name of its recipient, a Pauline associate and slave owner who hosts a house church. The topic is Philemon's formerly pagan slave, ONESIMUS, who departed from home (v. 15), came to Paul in prison, and is being returned—with the letter—ahead of Paul's own anticipated arrival as a guest in Philemon's house (v. 22). The letter, probably written from Ephesus in the mid to late 50s CE, has a close connection to Colossians, because both exchange greetings by the same group of people and reference Onesimus (Col 4:9-14, 17; Phlm 2, 23). Ignatius of Antioch also mentions a certain Onesimus, a 2nd-cent. bishop of Ephesus (Ign. *Eph.* 1.3), but likely refers to another person, the name being a relatively common one in classical antiquity and not limited to slaves (see Livy, *Ab urbe condita* 44.16.4–5).

A. Epistolary Structure
B. Detailed Analysis
C. Religious Significance
Bibliography

A. Epistolary Structure

The LETTER contains four discrete sections. A salutation gives the senders, addressees, and formal greetings in a public hearing before the whole congregation (vv. 1-3). A thanksgiving offers prayers to the divine and sets the letter's tone with affective language and downright flattery (vv. 4-7). The body deals with the practical business at hand, deciding the future of Onesimus' labor (vv. 8-22). A closing sends conventional formulas of well-being, a peace wish, and further greetings by associates (vv. 23-25). This division is standard and familiar from ancient Greco-Roman letters found in the documentary papyri and in Paul's other correspondence.

B. Detailed Analysis

We know very little of the letter's context. The exegetical difficulties stem in part from Paul's diction, which is unusually deferential and circumspect. Because there is no context for this letter, interpreters routinely create one for it. One interpretation, found as early as John Chrysostom (4th cent.) and repeated ever since, is that Onesimus was a runaway slave who was subsequently captured and thrown in prison with Paul (*see* SLAVERY). The letter shows Paul returning Onesimus home to Philemon and appealing to Philemon as a mediator (see Pliny, *Ep.* 9.21 and 9.24). In another interpretation, Onesimus did not simply run away to freedom but ran specifically to Paul in prison to ask him to intercede with Philemon after some misdeed; thus, Onesimus could not have been a runaway slave according to the definitions of a *fugitivus* in Roman slave law (see *Dig.* 21.1.17.4–5 and 21.1.43.1). Among the problems with both hypotheses is imagining why any slave under any circumstances would run to a PRISON. And how could Paul, a prisoner, release Onesimus, another prisoner? Captured slaves often found themselves thrown into prison workhouses (*ergastula*) on the rural estates of wealthy landowners, never to be heard from again.

Onesimus must be, therefore, a visitor and not a fellow prisoner. Yet another approach takes this clue and claims that Philemon's congregation dispatched Onesimus to minister to Paul in prison, serving his meals and providing other financial assistance. The Roman Empire had, after all, no penal system. Incarceration was not a punishment but a detention before trial or execution. Guards generally threw the accused into any available strong room or secure hole and left issues like feeding, clothing, and other needs to the criminal's friends or family to supply, with bribery being common. A prisoner of rank could even request to keep a few household slaves in prison as domestic servants (Pliny, *Ep.* 3.16.8). Early Christian congregations would have known the dangers that an imprisoned Paul faced and at least on one occasion a congregation sent a representative (Epaphroditus) with money and other gifts to sustain Paul while in prison (Phil 2:25; 4:18). We have, then, a supporting precedent for this hypothesis.

Finally, it has been argued that Onesimus was the actual brother of Philemon (in blood relation). Onesimus was not a slave at all but a voluntary servant, a freeborn employee. This last, peculiar hypothesis, based on the KJV (which has the word *servant* instead of *slave*), was born of 19th-cent. American antislavery theology.

All these scenarios share a desire to supply a prehistory to the letter and a motivation for Onesimus. The goal is to solve the exegetical difficulties by the method of story creation, to tell Onesimus' story through narratology. But no matter which story of Onesimus they tell, even the most imaginative interpreters cannot restore to this Christian slave his voice or agency. Rather than explaining the letter by the method of story creation and inventing a prehistory for which there is little if any evidence, a more valuable approach is to focus on the letter's future and goals. The aim and function of the letter resemble that of a formal petition (recommendation, contract) among friends. Paul describes his relationship with Philemon as a "partnership" (**koinōnia κοινωνία**, vv. 6 and 17) and uses the technical language of an explicit "appeal" (vv. 9-10, 19). He asks for the "good deed" to be by consent and "not something forced" (v. 14). He uses affective language throughout—*fellow-workers, friend* (*beloved*), *brother*, your "old man" (vv. 1, 7, 9, 16, 20, 24)—and expresses joy over the love (v. 7) that grounds the whole proposition. The terminology reveals Paul's attention to the conventions of friendship and the assignment of friends to specific roles.

These roles include one for Onesimus. Important in the petition is Paul's advertisement of the slave's credentials: he has been able to serve Paul in Philemon's place (v. 13), has been adopted by Paul as "my child" (v. 10), has changed from "useless" (**achrēstos ἄχρηστος**) to "useful" (**euchrēstos** [**εὔχρηστος**]; v. 11, a pun on Onesimus [**onēsimos ὀνήσιμος**], which also means "useful"), and now has been made a "beloved brother" (v. 16). To underscore the slave's creditworthiness, Paul appends a personal voucher for any debts that might have accrued in the meantime (vv. 18-19) and emphasizes the language of receipts (v. 12): "so that you might have him back forever, no longer as a slave but more than a slave, a beloved brother—especially to me but how much more to you, both in the flesh and in the Lord" (vv. 15-16). The ritual of baptism, which Paul describes as an act of paternity (v. 10), transformed Onesimus into an extension of Paul's own self (v. 12), being sent in full confidence that Philemon will do "even more than I say" (vv. 12, 21-22). Paul anticipates a meeting soon to address the matter in person (v. 22). *See* BROTHER, BROTHERHOOD.

The discourse plays upon culturally charged moral values in Paul's fundamentally hierarchical ancient Mediterranean world. The anticipation of an open hearing and a public meeting raises the honor-shame stakes of Paul's petition to that of a face-to-face rhetorical encounter. Such encounters defined manhood by the honor (*dignitas*) and mastery (*auctoritas*) achieved in the successful domination of others. Importantly, Paul never calls Philemon a master (**kyrios κύριος**; NRSV, "Lord") but applies the title repeatedly to Jesus Christ alone (vv. 3, 5, 16, 20, 25), subordinating Philemon to another Lord. The affront is similar to the comment, "I say nothing about your owing me even your own self" (v. 19). Participating in his Greco-Roman conflict culture, Paul asserts his ritual authority as a "father" over Philemon's right as a master to determine the future of his own chattel slave.

The description of Onesimus also follows specific conventions in Greco-Roman culture. He is the "good slave," what the Romans called *servus frugi*, who does more than merely follow orders in mechanical fashion but completes and develops what the master had only suggested or even unconsciously desired. Onesimus is a living tool caught between two masters contesting each other over the rights to his labor. The principal device in the letter is, therefore, characterization—the rhetoric flattens Paul, Philemon, and Onesimus into stock types that ought to behave in certain ways under the given circumstances.

The technical language also points to a particular kind of document, the "journeyman apprentice" contract, such as those found among the OXYRHYNCHUS PAPYRI in Roman Egypt, especially associated with weavers and the textile industry. The aim of apprenticeship was the personal transformation of a slave or child from "useless" to "useful." These contracts use technical formulations of "doing service" under an agreement, of guaranteeing the slave's creditworthiness, of enumerating the slave's credentials for learning the trade, and of assuming any debts that might accrue (a final penalty clause). Journeyman apprentice contracts, therefore, provide a plausible context in which to read this letter's aim. It is a petition for Philemon to let Onesimus be apprenticed to Paul in the service of the gospel (compare v. 13).

C. Religious Significance

Odd as it might seem, the letter contains no general theology, doctrine, or gospel message about Jesus Christ. This absence becomes understandable, however, in light of the letter's particularity. The letter best exemplifies how Paul's writings are pieces of genuine correspondence, with particular occasions and destinations. In this letter, Paul's purpose is not evangelism to all Christians but business with a private owner about the services of a chattel slave. Although the letter's particularity caused some patristic authors as early as the 2nd cent. to doubt its value as Scripture and even its authenticity, the consensus of current scholarship finds the particularity of the letter good evidence of its authenticity. Modern attempts to find the religious or theological significance of the letter—Paul's so-called moral unease about slavery or that the letter really addresses proper employer-employee relationships and not slavery at all—have fallen short of persuasive power because they merely repeat hermeneutical games born of the 19th-cent. abolitionist era. Unfortunately, we cannot correct NT texts that support and participate in slavery, even when the interest to do so serves the noblest of aims.

For example, claims that the Letter to Philemon should guide morality and family values led to its use in the United States to support the Fugitive Slave Law of 1850 and the Supreme Court Dred Scott Decision of 1857, which quoted the letter in its majority opinion. Many of America's first biblical scholars, such as Moses Stuart (1780–1852), exhorted the nation to obey this "Pauline Mandate," as the Letter to Philemon was called, for the legality and morality of modern racial slavery. The use of the letter in the 19th-cent. American slave controversy is a warning today to move beyond simple appeals to "what the Bible says" as a foundation for Christian moral arguments. The Letter to Philemon reminds modern readers of the occasional nature of the Pauline correspondence and invites them to reflect on how their own daily activities and choices may participate in systems of oppression and dehumanization.

Bibliography: Peter Arzt-Grabner. *Philemon.* Papyrologische Kommentare zum Neuen Testament 1 (2003); Nils Alstrup Dahl. "The Particularity of the Pauline Epistles as a Problem in the Ancient Church." *Studies in Ephesians.* Nils Alstrup Dahl, ed. (2000) 165–79; Joseph A. Fitzmyer. *The Letter to Philemon: A New Translation with Introduction and Commentary.* AB 34C (2000); J. Albert Harrill. *Slaves in the New Testament: Literary, Social, and Moral Dimensions* (2006); Ronald F. Hock. "A Support for His Old Age: Paul's Plea on Behalf of Onesimus." *The Social World of the First Christians: Essays in Honor of Wayne A. Meeks.* L. Michael White and O. Larry Yarbrough, eds. (1995) 67–81; Eduard Lohse. *Colossians and Philemon: A Commentary on the Epistles to the Colossians and to Philemon.* Hermeneia (1971); Norman R. Petersen. *Rediscovering Paul: Philemon and the Sociology of Paul's Narrative World* (1985).

J. ALBERT HARRILL

PHILETUS fi-lee'tuhs [Φίλητος **Philētos**]. The author of 2 Timothy sounds a warning about the preachers Philetus and HYMENAEUS, who swerved from the truth by teaching that the resurrection had already taken place (2 Tim 2:17-18). Since Hymenaeus appears to have worked in Ephesus (1 Tim 1:3, 20), Philetus may have too. *See* PAUL, THE APOSTLE; TIMOTHY.

FLORENCE MORGAN GILLMAN

PHILIP fil'ip [Φίλιππος **Philippos**]. 1. Philip II, king of MACEDONIA (359–336 BCE), father of ALEXANDER THE GREAT (1 Macc 1:1). He unified Macedonia and overwhelmed the Greek city-states except Sparta to form the Hellenic League of Corinth in 337 BCE. He was assassinated before launching a military campaign against Persia (Josephus, *Ant.* 11.304–05), but his son Alexander accomplished his ambition to crush the Persian Empire and extend Greek rule "to the ends of the earth" (1 Macc 1:3).

2. Philip V, king of Macedonia (220–179 BCE; 1 Macc 8:5). His kingdom was invaded by the Roman armies. After being defeated at Cynoscephalae in 197 BCE, he signed a humiliating treaty relinquishing some territories but keeping his throne. The Romans used him as a bumper to thwart the aggression of ANTIOCHUS III, who reigned over Palestine and part of Asia Minor.

3. Philip the Phrygian (*see* PHRYGIA), governor of Jerusalem (2 Macc 5:22). He was appointed to this position in 169 BCE after Antiochus IV Epiphanes attacked the holy city and raided the Temple for its alleged revolt on the way back from his second campaign against Egypt. To enforce the policy of Hellenization, Philip burned the pious Jews who were hiding in caves to worship God on the Sabbath (2 Macc 6:11). As the Maccabean uprising gained ground, he wrote to PTOLEMY, governor of COELE-SYRIA and PHOENICIA (2 Macc 8:8), and maybe also to Lysias, who was in charge in Antioch (1 Macc 3:38), to request military reinforcement.

4. Philip the APOSTLE (Matt 10:3; Mark 3:18; Luke 6:14; Acts 1:13). He is mentioned in the Synoptic Gospels only in the lists of the twelve disciples, but several stories that reveal his character are preserved in the Gospel of John. Like Andrew and Peter, who were also from BETHSAIDA, he was one of the first disciples called to follow Jesus (John 1:43-44). He was enthusiastic in sharing the good news with others, so once he had recognized Jesus to be the Messiah prophesied in the Scriptures, he invited his friend Nathaniel to come to see Jesus (John 1:45-46). He was tested by Jesus on how to feed a crowd of 5,000 in the wilderness. He conceded

that even six months of wages could not buy enough bread to give a bit to every one (John 6:5-7), but he must have been amazed, more than anyone else, to witness Jesus feeding the multitude with five barley loaves and two fish from a boy. When Jesus visited Jerusalem for the Passover, some Greeks asked Philip to introduce them to Jesus. Jesus made an important declaration: "The hour has come for the Son of Man to be glorified" (John 12:23), referring to his imminent death that would give believers eternal life. The Greeks approached Philip probably because he had a Greek name, was from Bethsaida—a predominantly Greek city north of the Sea of Galilee—and presumably spoke Greek well. Philip was also inquisitive and eager to learn. When Jesus spoke about his departure for the Father at the Last Supper, Philip pleaded, "Lord, show us the Father, and we will be satisfied" (John 14:8). Hence, Jesus explained how the disciples had seen God when they saw him, because he was in God and God was in him. Philip remained faithful after Jesus' death and joined other disciples in the Upper Room to pray and wait for the Holy Spirit (Acts 1:13). Interest in Philip the apostle in later centuries can be seen in the Coptic *Gospel of Philip* (*see* PHILIP, GOSPEL OF), which shows a Valentinian Christian tendency, and in the Greek *Acts of Philip* (*see* PHILIP, ACTS OF), which recounts his miracles and martyrdom in Hierapolis and contains encratic and anti-marriage teachings.

5. Philip, son of Herod the Great and Mariamne II (Matt 14:3; Mark 6:17; Luke 3:19; *see* HEROD, FAMILY). He was half-brother of HEROD ANTIPAS and the first husband of HERODIAS. When Antipas became illicitly involved with Herodias, John the Baptist rebuked them and consequently was jailed and executed.

6. Philip the tetrarch, son of Herod the Great and Cleopatra of Jerusalem (Luke 3:1; *see* TETRARCH, TETRARCHY). He was half-brother of Herodias' first husband, Philip, and married Herodias' daughter SALOME, who asked for John the Baptist's head on a platter after dancing in a banquet to please Antipas (Mark 6:22). After the death of Herod the Great, he was granted by AUGUSTUS the tetrarchy of GAULANITIS, TRACHONITIS, Auranitis, Batanaea, and ITURAEA (Luke 3:1). He ruled with a good reputation over a mostly non-Jewish population for thirty-seven years (4 BCE–33/34 CE). He rebuilt Bethsaida as Julias (Josephus, *Ant.* 18.28; *J.W.* 2.168), and Panias as CAESAREA PHILIPPI (Matt 16:13; Mark 8:27) to honor the Roman emperor and his family. Though a Jewish prince, he imprinted the emperors' heads on his coins.

7. Philip the evangelist (Acts 8:5-13). Esteemed as reputable, Spirit-filled, and wise, he was one of the seven chosen by the church in Jerusalem, after the squabbling between Hellenistic Jewish Christians and Hebrew Christians, to care for the poor and the widows (Acts 6:5). After Stephen's martyrdom, he traveled to SAMARIA to preach the Messiah, cast out demons, and heal the paralyzed. Many Samaritans, including Simon the sorcerer, were converted. On the road to Gaza he preached the good news of Jesus to an Ethiopian eunuch, a court official of CANDACE, queen of the Ethiopians, by explaining the Servant Song of Isa 53:7-8 that the Ethiopian was reading. The eunuch believed and received baptism at once to become the first African Christian. Philip's evangelizing itinerary also took him to Azotos and other coastal cites. Finally he settled in Caesarea with four daughters who were prophetesses (*see* PHILIP, DAUGHTER'S OF). Paul visited them on his last journey to Jerusalem (Acts 21:8-9). Second-century CE sources, such as POLYCRATES and PAPIAS, seemed to have conflated Philip the apostle with Philip the evangelist as the same person (Eusebius, *Hist. eccl.* 3.31.3; 3.39.9; 5.24.2).

JOHN Y. H. YIEH

8. A companion of Antiochus IV EPIPHANES who attempted to take over the kingdom after his death. Hellenistic rulers often gave the title of *friend* (**philos** φίλος) to their high officials. According to 1 Macc 6:14-15, on his deathbed Antiochus IV Epiphanes turned the kingdom over to Philip and made him guardian of his son. This is a strange statement, because the young Antiochus was in the custody of LYSIAS, who immediately put him on the throne as ANTIOCHUS V Eupator when he heard of Antiochus Epiphanes' death. Philip returned to Antioch with the army and took over the city, apparently with the intention of taking the throne (1 Macc 6:55-63). Lysias, hearing of this, broke off his siege of JUDAS Maccabeus in Jerusalem and marched against Philip, defeating and killing him (ca. 163 BCE).

LESTER L. GRABBE

PHILIP, ACTS OF. A 4th–5th cent. CE miracle novel about Jesus' apostle PHILIP preserved in Greek, Syriac, and Latin fragments. It contains fifteen episodes ("acts") and an account of Philip's death. Philip raises the dead, calms a stormy sea, blinds and restores hordes of men, utters magical incantations, makes the earth swallow the high priest and 7,000 men, converses with a penitent leopard that becomes his follower, uses miracles to create faith, and causes bodily affliction to anyone who extends a hand against him. His death is romantic martyrology; hanged upside down by his pierced ankles, he smiles. Jesus appears after Philip's death in the form of Philip. Converted women begin to dress as men and converted couples cease sexual activity (which exemplifies the encratite theology of the work). *See* APOCRYPHA, NT; HIERAPOLIS; MARTYR.

Bibliography: James K. Elliott. *The Apocryphal New Testament.* Rev. ed. (1993).

RICHARD A. SPENCER

PHILIP, DAUGHTERS OF. In Acts 21:1-16, Paul's final journey to Jerusalem brings him to the home of PHILIP the evangelist in Caesarea. Philip's four unmarried daughters have the gift of prophecy (Acts 21:9) but never speak in the narrative. Ironically, while in Caesarea Paul's fate is prophesied by AGABUS of Jerusalem (Acts 21:10-14) and not by Philip's daughters. Luke seems to be more interested in the women's prophetic ability than their message (see also the widow prophet ANNA in Luke 2:36-38). There is no further information in the biblical text on the four sisters. *See* PROPHET, PROPHECY.

HEIDI S. GEIB

PHILIP, GOSPEL OF fil´ip, gos´puhl. The Coptic *Gospel of Philip* is one of the NAG HAMMADI TEXTS (Codex II, 3:51, 29–86, 19). It is not a "gospel" in the NT sense, but rather an anthology of loosely organized statements ("good news") used within the Valentinian gnostic tradition (*see* GNOSTICISM). Because the excerpts appear to derive from a variety of genres (e.g., sermons, treatises, and letters) and may reflect ideas from different Valentinian branches, they lack a recognizable order or progression of thought. Yet a number of overlapping themes appear throughout the text. Prominent among them are a discussion of the perfect realm of the Father; a distinction between the spiritual and material realms; the appearance of Jesus Christ as the revelation of truth; the nature of humanity and death; and the possibility of attaining a spiritual rebirth through gnosis.

Closely related to the attainment of Christian perfection is the text's discussion of five sacraments or "mysteries"—baptism, chrism, the eucharist, redemption, and the bridal chamber—that appear to have played a central role in Valentinian initiation rituals. It is possible that these rituals represent distinct stages of initiation leading to a spiritual transformation. Of the five, the bridal chamber has elicited the most attention for its description of the soul or "image" attaining a garment of "light" through its spiritual union with an angelic being. The text describes this moment of enlightenment as the return to the original androgynous condition that existed prior to the appearance of sexual differentiation, understood as the cause of death. As a result, the bridal chamber witnesses a rebirth in which the initiate becomes identified as a child of the Father, superior to both the material world and the natural processes of human generation and death. The *Gospel of Philip* thus emphasizes an ascetic spirituality that encourages the reader to transcend physical marriage and sexual relations, human activities associated with the unenlightened life.

While the ethical imperatives of the *Gospel of Philip* provide valuable evidence for the development of Valentinian theology, its interest in sacraments makes it equally important for understanding the history of catechetical instruction in early Christianity. Scholars generally date the gospel in the late 2nd to late 3rd cent., and its relation to Thomas Christianity and its interest in Syriac vocabulary have led some to speculate that its origins stem from a Syrian milieu.

DAVID M. REIS

PHILIPPI fi-lip´*i*, fil´i-p*i* [Φίλιπποι **Philippoi**]. Philippi is situated in eastern MACEDONIA (northern Greece) on the Via Egnatia overlooking an inland plain to the east of Mount Pangaeus/Pangaion. Philippi is named for PHILIP II (359–336 BCE), king of Macedonia and father of Alexander the Great. Philip named the city "Philippi" after himself when the citizens asked for his help against the Thracians. He built a wall around the city, some of which still remains.

The city was founded by immigrants from Thrace and known for its rich gold mines as well as for its many springs of water that rise in its hills (Strabo, *Geogr.* 7.34). Mountains surround this area on three sides with an open plain to the west. The current site was settled around 360 BCE when residents from Thasos annexed the territory and called it "Crenides" because of its springs (**krēnaios** [κρηναῖος], "spring, fountain"). It was also known for a brief period as "Datum" or "Daton" (Strabo, *Geogr.* 7.34).

Except for the wealth derived from the gold mines, Philippi was relatively unimportant until the Roman conquest of the region in 168–167 BCE. According to Diodorus Siculus (*Bib. Hist.* 16.3.7; 8.6), Philip II received 1,000 talents a year from the rich mines in the vicinity and treated Philippi as a "free city" within his kingdom. The wealth received here enabled him to enlarge his army and unify his kingdom. Pausanias, who traveled Greece during the reign of Hadrian (117–138 CE), called Philippi the "youngest city in Macedonia" (*Descr.* 6.10). The city is mentioned in a number of ancient authors (Dio Cassius, *Rom.* 47.35–49; Appian, *Bell. civ.* 4.102–38; Plutarch, *Brut.* 38–53).

After the famous Via Egnatia highway (begun ca. 145 BCE) was completed (ca. 130 BCE), it connected Byzantium (later Constantinople) with the Adriatic ports that led to Italy and it became Rome's primary route to the east. A result of that project is that Philippi became a major stopping place on the way to and from Rome. Besides making it possible to move troops more rapidly throughout the empire, this route also facilitated Paul on his missionary journey from Neapolis to Philippi, Amphipolis, Apollonia, and Thessalonica (Acts 16:12; 17:1). He left this road while journeying to Beroea (Acts 17:10).

With the emergence of the Second Triumvirate, made up of Octavian (later Emperor AUGUSTUS), MARK ANTONY (Marcus Antonius), and Marcus Aemilius Lepidus in 43 BCE, and following their proscriptions that led to the executions of some 300 senators and 2,000 knights in Rome, the only remaining threat to their control was the Republican army led by Cassius Longinus and Iunius Brutus, the murderers of

Julius Caesar. Leaving Lepidus to guard Rome, Octavian and Antony engaged the Republican forces just west of Philippi in two battles. Both Cassius and Brutus committed suicide after their defeat (Horace, *Carm.* 2.7.9–12). Following these battles, Antony settled many veterans from his army in Philippi and enlarged and fortified the city, making it a Roman colony that included Neapolis, Oisyme, and Apollonia. He also offered land to many of the triumviral soldiers from Rome who had earlier lost their land in Italy (Strabo, *Geogr.* 7.41; Pliny the Elder, *Nat.* 4.42; Diodorus, *Bib. Hist.* 51.4.6). Following his victory over Antony at Actium in 31 BCE, Octavian moved more settlers here from Italy (*see* ROMAN EMPIRE).

Philippi's colonial status brought with it the significant benefit of equal rights with Roman citizens and freedom from direct taxation. This was known as the *Ius Italicum* conferred normally on Italian cities (Acts 16:12)—the highest privilege possible for a Roman province. The new settlers, along with the previous residents, constituted the newly reformed colony that became known as *Colonia Augusta Julia Philippensis.* It was common in those days for the Romans to build or reconstitute communities as Roman colonies and then offer property to veteran soldiers and other citizens of Rome.

The official language of Philippi in the 1st cent. was Latin, the language of more than half of the inscriptions found there, but the marketplace language and that of the surrounding community continued to be Greek. The city was serviced by the nearby port of Neapolis, modern Kavala (Acts 16:11), some 10 mi. southeast of the city on the Via Egnatia. Remains from the Macedonian, Roman, and Byzantine periods, including remains of a sanctuary of the Egyptian gods Serapis and Isis, have been found on the acropolis at Philippi.

Around 49–50 CE, the apostle Paul started the first church in ancient Greece at Philippi (Acts 16:11-40) following his Macedonian vision at Troas (Acts 16:8-10). Although he was shamefully treated at Philippi (1 Thess 2:2), he nevertheless had a significant ministry in the city and spoke affectionately about the church and his ministry among them (Phil 4:10-20). His best-known converts at Philippi included Lydia, in whose house he began the church, the jailer and his family (Acts 16:14-15, 27-34), EPAPHRODITUS (Phil 2:25-30), Euodia and Syntyche, who were at odds with each other after Paul's departure (Phil 4:2), Clement, and others who served with Paul and Silas at Philippi (Phil 4:3). *See* LYDIA, LYDIANS; PAUL, THE APOSTLE.

The Philippian church contributed substantially to Paul's subsequent missionary activity (Phil 4:15-18) and became very dear to him. He visited here at least one more time (Acts 20:1-6; 1 Cor 16:5-6; 2 Cor 2:13; 7:5) and, on that visit, may have gone west to Illyricum (Rom 15:19). He may have written his letter(s) to the leaders of the church at Philippi (ca. 54–55 CE) from Ephesus or later while he was at Rome (ca. 60 CE). The letter itself originally may have been two or more separate letters (Phil 1:1–3:1 and 3:2–4:23) that were brought together into one document after the death of Paul. Scholars generally concede that the tone change in Phil 3:2–4:1 is so different from what is both before and following in the letter that now comprises Paul's letter to the Philippians that it may indicate the composition of two or more letters (*see* PHILIPPIANS, LETTER TO THE).

In the early 2nd cent. CE, Ignatius, bishop of Antioch of Syria, passed through Philippi on his way to Rome to face martyrdom (*see* IGNATIUS OF ANTIOCH). The Philippian church later sent a letter to Polycarp, bishop of Smyrna, requesting his assistance in collecting Ignatius' letters. Polycarp responded favorably to their request in his only letter that has survived (Pol. *Phil.* 13.2), though Irenaeus claims that he wrote several others (Irenaeus, *Haer.* 5.33.4). Polycarp's letter (ca. mid-2nd cent. CE) is helpful in understanding the continuing witness of the church in Philippi in the 2nd cent. and its concern for those in prison, but also for its hospitality. Like Paul, Polycarp addressed the presbyters (bishops) and deacons (Pol. *Phil.* 5.2–3; 6.1; compare Phil 1:1). In the post-Nicene era, the city became an important Christian center and had a metropolitan bishop (*see* POLYCARP, EPISTLE OF).

In the reigns of Trajan (97–117 CE) and Hadrian (117–38 CE), extensive repairs to the Via Egnatia were made, and later Marcus Aurelius (161–80 CE) made many building additions and improvements at Philippi. Several of the remains at Philippi date from the 2nd cent. CE, but most come from the 4th–6th cent. CE. These remains include a large forum (230 ft. × 485 ft.) and a rostrum for public speaking, with other buildings that can be dated to the time of Marcus Aurelius.

Philippi also has a large theater that dates from the time of Philip II, which was present during the ministry of Paul, and later was enlarged by the Romans in the 2nd cent. The location where Paul and Silas were imprisoned may possibly be identified with a Roman crypt found just west of Basilica A on the north side of the forum, but there is doubt about that. Portions of the Neapolis gate, through which they entered the city from the east, have also been discovered. Philippi has four large basilicas and a section of the ancient Via Egnatia, but nothing that remains at the ancient site sheds light on the church's organization, life, worship, and ministries in the 1st cent. Among the most significant discoveries at this site are some seven churches dating from the 4th to the 6th cent., the most prominent of which are commonly identified as Basilicas A and B. A number of other buildings were also found as well as tombs of both Christians and pagans dating from the 5th–6th cent. In the 4th cent. CE, the city was an important economic and cultural center and was praised for the purity of the Greek spoken there. The fate of Philippi after the 7th cent. is obscure, though the Slavs settled in much of the area in the 7th cent., and the Bulgarian invasions of ca. 812 forced the residents to flee the city and its fortress. The Ottomans finally captured the city in 1387.

Bibliography: Raymond E. Brown. *An Introduction to the New Testament* (1997); Werner G. Kümmel. *Introduction to the New Testament* (1975); John McRay. *Archaeology and the New Testament* (1991) 283–88; John E. Stambaugh and David L. Balch. *The New Testament in Its Social Environment* (1986).

LEE MARTIN MCDONALD

PHILIPPIANS, LETTER TO THE fi-lip´ee-uhnz [πρὸς Φιλιππήσιους pros Philippēsious]. Paul's letter to the Christians of Philippi is an exhortation to unity and steadfastness, presented as a letter of friendship that will nourish the familial relationship between people who already care deeply for one another. Philippians offers unique insight into the ways Jesus' death and resurrection have transformed Paul's own life and imagination (3:3-11), includes a hymn that is one of the most powerful and provocative expressions of early Christian convictions about Jesus (2:6-11), and makes an impassioned plea for Christian unity. Paul writes while a prisoner in Roman custody (1:7, 13-17; 4:22). Scholars have identified several locations where Paul might have been imprisoned as he wrote to the Philippians, each with implications for the dating of the letter, including Rome (61–63 CE), Ephesus (54–56 CE), Corinth (ca. 50 CE), and Caesarea (58–60 CE). None of these proposals, however, has generated consensus; the date and provenance of the letter thus remain open questions. The prescript names both Paul and Timothy as authors and, more specifically, as slaves of JESUS CHRIST, thereby signaling a central theme of the letter: the renunciation of self-interest, status, and power over others in favor of Christ-like servanthood, obedience, humiliation, and suffering, which strengthen the bonds of friendship between Paul and the Philippians and secure the unity of the church. As he awaits the resolution of his case, Paul encourages the Philippians to stand firm as they face their own adversity, and offers an array of examples—Paul himself, Christ, Timothy, and Epaphroditus—of those who have risked their lives in service for the gospel.

A. The Church in Philippi

Philippi is located in northeastern Greece, in the Roman province of Macedonia, near the seaport of Neapolis and astride the Via Egnatia, a major Roman trade route that crossed Macedonia. PHILIPPI was also important in Roman imperial imagination as the site where, in 42 BCE, Octavian and Mark Antony defeated Brutus and Cassius, the assassins of Julius Caesar, thereby laying the foundations for the rise of the Roman Empire. After claiming the title Caesar Augustus, Octavian granted Philippi the political status of a Roman city. The people of Philippi, who spoke both Greek and Latin, participated in devotion to the Greco-Roman pantheon, local deities, and foreign gods from Asia Minor and Egypt, alongside the cult of the emperors. Philippi would have featured extensive symbols of Roman imperial religion and order.

Acts 16:9-34 gives an account of the founding of the church at Philippi by Paul and SILAS (ca. 49–50 CE), whose proclamation leads to the conversion of LYDIA and her household, but also to beatings and imprisonment on the charge of disturbing the city and advocating traditions that threaten Roman custom (Acts 16:16-24). Philippians mentions none of the names or characters found in Luke's account, yet Paul and Luke concur on the key role women played in the leadership of the Philippian congregation (Acts 16:14-15; Phil 4:2-3), the identification of Paul and his missionary accomplices as "slaves" (Acts 16:17; Phil 1:1), conflicts around Roman custom, and Paul's imprisonment. Elsewhere, Paul confirms that he "suffered and was shamelessly mistreated at Philippi" (1 Thess 2:2) and that he received financial support from Christians in Macedonia while at Corinth (2 Cor 11:7-9). In 2 Cor 8:1-6 Paul lifts up the "churches of Macedonia" as models for their "abundant joy and extreme poverty," which overflowed in a wealth of generosity that surpassed their means (see Phil 1:5, 7; 4:10-20). It is noteworthy that Paul renounced his right of support from the Corinthian congregation (1 Cor 9:1-18), yet entered into a unique partnership with the Philippians (4:15)—all the more remarkable given their relative POVERTY.

Paul sustained regular correspondence with the congregation after he left Philippi. They supported him while he was in Thessalonica and perhaps elsewhere (4:15-16). When news of his imprisonment reached them, they sent a gift with one of their members, Epaphroditus (2:30; 4:18), who became ill and nearly died (2:26, 30). As Paul writes, Epaphroditus has regained his health and will return to Philippi (2:25-30), perhaps bearing the letter. Paul also plans to send Timothy (2:19-23) and hopes then himself to visit Philippi again (2:24).

B. Authenticity and Integrity of Philippians

While there is no dispute that Paul is the author of Philippians, repetition and abrupt transitions (e.g., 3:1-2) in the LETTER have given rise to claims that Philippians is a composite of two or three letters written over a brief period of time and later joined together. Some reconstructions identify 3:1*b*–4:20 (or 3:1*b*–4:1, 8-9) as an independent letter sent after Epaphroditus had arrived with the Philippians' gift, but before he had taken ill (2:25-30). Another letter, consisting of 1:1–3:1*a* and 4:21-23 (or 1:1–3:1*a*; 4:2-7; and 4:10-23), may have been sent after Epaphroditus' recovery and after Paul learned of dissension in the congregation. Some regard 4:10-20 as a "receipt" originally sent independently of the other portions. But none of these reconstructions has generated consensus and, even if composed from fragments of earlier correspondence, the canonical letter is a coherent rhetorical whole. Paul's note of thanks for the Philippians' gift (4:10-20), e.g., resumes the theme of partnership first introduced in the thanksgiving (1:3-11; see 1:5, 7). The prayer of thanksgiving, in fact, introduces several topics that recur throughout the supposed fragments: joy; contentment and confidence in the face of trials; unity; and partnership in the gospel and in suffering.

C. Christian Friendship and the Story of Jesus Christ

Philippians employs many of the topics and conventions associated with ancient discussions of friendship, including unity of spirit and mind (e.g., 1:27; 2:1-5; 4:2), partnership (or "fellowship"), and mutuality (e.g., 1:5-8; 2:1-4; 4:4-7, 15-19), even in the face of hardships (e.g., 1:12-18, 27-30; 2:25-30). Familial letters and letters of friendship often included reassurances about the writer's well-being (1:12-26) and expressions of concern for the recipients (1:27–2:18). Paul uses the conventions of friendship not only as a way to reaffirm the relationship he shares with the Philippians, but because his imprisonment and the adversity the congregation faces represent real threats to the Philippians' embodiment of the gospel.

Paul's central appeal in Philippians is not to ancient conventions of friendship, however, but to the story of Jesus Christ (2:6-11), which dramatically transforms the relationship between God and humankind, explains the origins of the community and its unity, and provides the defining model for the community's behavior. The examples Paul offers from his own life (1:12-26; 3:4-17) and the lives of TIMOTHY and EPAPHRODITUS (2:19-30) all conform to the central image of Christ's own self-emptying, slavery, humiliation, and obedience to God, even to the point of death on the cross (2:6-8). As God has vindicated Christ (2:9-11), so will God transform their "body of humiliation" into "the body of Christ's glory" (3:21). In this paradigm, Paul can even make of his imprisonment an occasion to affirm JOY and progress in the face of apparent obstacles (1:12-26), and he can call the Philippians to shine like stars in the world (2:15), despite the suffering and resistance they face.

D. Structure and Content

1. Address and thanksgiving (1:1-11)

Three features distinguish the salutation (1:1-2) and provide cues about matters Paul will pursue in the letter. First, the greeting identifies both Paul and Timothy as the senders. Timothy is also mentioned in the addresses of three other letters (2 Cor 1:1; 1 Thess 1:1; and Phlm 1), but in ways that suggest his subordination to Paul, while here he seems to be Paul's equal, as least insofar as both are identified as "slaves of Christ Jesus" (*see* SERVANT; SLAVERY). Timothy's status is in accord with his exemplary role in the life of the Philippian church: he is genuinely concerned for their welfare (2:20), will soon visit them (2:19, 23), and seeks the interests of Jesus Christ rather than his own (2:21). Second, the designation of Paul and Timothy as "slaves" (**douloi** δοῦλοι; compare 2:22) confirms their identification with Christ in his role as slave (**doulos** δοῦλος, 2:7) and lays the groundwork for the Philippians' own servanthood with Paul and Timothy in the gospel. Finally, Paul names the Philippians as "saints in Christ Jesus," and greets in particular "the bishops and deacons." The first identification locates the Philippians among those who have been set apart for service to God. The latter terms designate not fixed church offices, but those who serve by offering "oversight" and "help" for the sake of the congregation. Throughout the address, then, Paul's focus is on servanthood in Christ.

Paul's letters typically move from the address to thanksgiving and prayers for his addressees (1:3-11). Here Paul's prayer resonates with joy, mutual affection, and hope. Paul's inclusive words—"every time," "constantly," "in every prayer," "for all" (1:3-4)—weave a web of comprehensive mutuality between him and the Philippians. The Philippians share as partners in the gospel with Paul (1:5, 7), they are in his heart (1:7), and he yearns for them with the compassion of Christ (1:8). This is the language of deep friendship, emphasizing oneness, sharing, and a common focus (on Christ). Paul prays for their abundance in love, knowledge, insight, discernment, and "the harvest of righteousness" (1:9-11).

2. The progress of the gospel despite Paul's imprisonment (1:12-26)

As Paul prepares the Philippians to face their opponents (1:28), he first addresses his own circumstances.

Both his imprisonment (1:13-19) and the possibility of dying (1:20-26) become opportunities for Paul to demonstrate the renunciation of self-interest for the sake of others. He insists that his imprisonment, ordinarily a cause for shame, has actually helped to spread the gospel (*see* PRISON). The whole imperial guard now knows that he is imprisoned for the sake of Christ, and many other Christians have become even bolder in their proclamation (1:12-14). Still, Paul's imprisonment has provided an opportunity for others, who proclaim Christ out of selfish ambition, to increase his suffering (1:17). But as soon as Paul has named this reality, he diminishes its importance (1:18: "what of it?"). He cares only that "Christ is proclaimed in every way" (1:18). Paul then uses the question of his own life or death as yet another example of the renunciation of self-interest (1:20-26). He first affirms that "dying is gain" (1:20) and professes his desire "to depart and be with Christ" (1:23), then renounces his preference in favor of continuing in this life for their sake (1:24-26).

3. Paul's concern for the Philippians (1:27–2:18)

Now Paul's focus shifts decisively from his own circumstances to the adversity and disunity the Philippians face, first in an appeal to tenacity in the face of threats from outside the congregation (1:27-30), then in a call to unity and humility within the congregation (2:1-5), based on the story of Christ (2:6-11), and finally in a call to work out their salvation in such a way that they serve as beacons for the world (2:12-18). The heart of this section, if not the whole letter, is the story of the incarnation, self-emptying, obedience, humiliation, crucifixion, and exaltation of Jesus Christ (2:6-11).

a. Stand firm in adversity (1:27-30). Paul exhorts the Philippians to live worthily of their citizenship in the realm of Jesus Christ (1:27). Paul's language resonates with the political tones of ancient discussions of concord and unity in households and with appeals to the imagery of athletic contests. The Philippians are engaged in the same struggle Paul has been and still is fighting. The Philippians' opponents could be other Christians, like those who have been attacking Paul (see 1:15-17), or non-Christians among whom the Philippians live. But Paul is less interested in the opponents than in the Philippians' witness. They are to "stand firm in one spirit," "striving side by side with one mind." Their unity, in fact, is living evidence of their salvation, not least when they encounter the "privilege" of suffering for Christ (1:29).

b. Unity (2:1-5). Unity in the face of opposition from outside the church requires that the Philippians also address the causes of disunity within. The terms Paul uses to describe the internal sources of division—self-interest, selfish ambition, and conceit—echo what he had said about those who sought advantage in his own imprisonment (2:3-4; compare 1:17). Paul then speaks, in contrast, of love (2:2), humility, and putting others first (2:3-4), all of which express what it means to have "the same MIND that was in Christ Jesus" (2:5). The language of "being of the same mind" or "of one mind" (2:2) does not imply the kind of unity that might be achieved by authoritarian means or by imposing doctrinal or ethical straitjackets. Paul's goal is not "uniformity," but a common focus upon Christ that engenders the same love, faithful obedience, and HUMILITY that Christ himself embodied. At the heart of the church's unity is "the same mind that was in Christ Jesus."

c. The "Christ Hymn" (2:6-11). In order to remind the Philippians of what he means by "the mind of Christ," Paul cites a tradition his audience already knew well. The designation of this tradition as a hymn rests upon recognition of its rhythmic structure and evocative force (*see* HYMNS, NT). The first half of the hymn (2:6-8) tells the story of Christ's incarnation, his refusal to exploit his divine status or power, his becoming not merely human, but a slave, his life as one of the humiliated, and his obedience to God, culminating in his death on the cross (*see* KENOSIS). The second half of the hymn (2:9-11) asserts Christ's exaltation, his receipt of the name above all names, and the reality of his universal lordship. The hymn recounts the whole narrative of God's salvation of the world through Christ, thereby reminding the audience that they now reside under the lordship of Christ and in his story, which brings to an end the tyranny of death and sin since Adam's fall. At the same time, the hymn provides images of what it means to live in conformity to the way, or mind, of Christ. The hymn thus provides both the foundation and the paradigm for Paul's repeated calls to renunciation of self-interest, solidarity with the humiliated ones, and obedience, even to death. The unity of the congregation is rooted in the story of Christ and maintained in practices that conform to Christ's way.

d. Shine like stars in the world (2:12-18). The consequences Paul draws from the Christ Hymn focus first on the paradoxical assertion that while it is God who is at work among them, they are also to "work out their salvation in fear and trembling," that is, as an integral community that lives in humility and obedience before God (2:12-13). It is in their harmonious, unified, Christ-like conduct that the congregation bears mutual witness with Paul to the story of Christ. The image of shining like stars (2:15) suggests that the community lives not only in contrast to the darkness around them, but as a beacon by which others find illumination and orientation toward God.

4. Two other Christ-like models (2:19–3:1*a*).

Paul turns for a moment from his concerns for the congregation to travel plans for himself and two of his associates, Timothy (2:19-24) and Epaphroditus (2:25-30), who will represent Paul until he is able to visit Philippi again himself (2:24). As Paul commends these co-workers to the Philippians, he reiterates the dominant ethical concerns of the letter. Timothy will be "genuinely concerned" with their welfare, whereas others "seek their own interests" (2:20-21). Paul praises Epaphroditus especially because of his willingness to risk death for the sake of Christ and to provide services to Paul that the Philippians could not (2:30). Timothy and Epaphroditus thus provide two more examples of the Christ-like behavior to which Paul has been calling the congregation.

5. Conforming to Christ (3:1*b*-16)

The rejoicing of 3:1*a* gives way to harsh warnings against "the dogs," "evil workers," and "those who mutilate the flesh" (3:2). The altered tone of Paul's argument after 3:1 has led many to conclude that the material in this section originated under different circumstances than what precedes. Regardless of the origins of this material, the shift between positive and negative models continues a pattern Paul has already established in the letter. In this section, too, Paul alternates between negative (3:2, 18-19) and positive (3:3-17, 20–4:3) examples.

The heart of this section is yet another example of renunciation of self-interest and status, this time drawn from Paul's description of the consequences of his own transformation (3:3-14). Paul structures this description around two contrasting ways of engaging life, putting confidence in the flesh (3:3-6) versus knowing Jesus Christ (3:7-16). The initial focus on circumcision in 3:3 may suggest that the adversaries Paul has in mind are Jewish Christian missionaries who advocated circumcision. Paul quickly makes clear, however, that his real focus is not the practice of circumcision itself, but a larger field of practices that he designates "confidence in the flesh," of which circumcision is but one example. Paul lifts up, in contrast, "we" who are "the true circumcision," who "worship in the Spirit of God," and who "boast in Christ Jesus" (3:3). The contrasts do not demarcate competing religions, but describe radical epistemological alternatives (*see* CHRISTIAN-JEWISH RELATIONS).

Paul here uses the term "the flesh" elastically, first in reference to the physical body (3:2) and then to designate a world of values, ideals, practices, and identity markers by which humans know themselves and order their world, and upon which they claim legitimacy, power, and status (3:4-5; *see* FLESH IN THE NT). Lest he be accused of lacking the credentials to play the "confidence in the flesh" game, Paul lists a variety of qualifications that would have constituted a surpassing resumé (3:5-6). He then abruptly moves this list from the credit to the debit side of his personal ledger, asserting that all of it is as good as trash in comparison to the "surpassing value of knowing Christ Jesus" (3:7-8). Paul's hope now rests not on his own credentials or "righteousness," but in the righteousness of God that is his through the faithfulness of Christ (3:9). In 3:10-11 Paul further defines the focus and content of this knowledge by means of four chiastically arranged lines (a/b/b'/a') that describe Christian life as participation in both Christ's resurrection and his suffering and death. This is the goal toward which Paul is still running and toward which he urges the Philippians also to press (3:12-16).

6. The practice of heavenly citizenship (3:17–4:9)

Paul again urges the Philippians to imitate him and the others who live according to the example he has set (3:17). Another set of contrasting models then follows. Paul first describes the "enemies of the cross of Christ" as absorbed with their own needs, focused on "earthly things," and ultimately destructive (3:18-19). As he has throughout the letter, however, Paul turns quickly from this negative image to remind the Philippians of their heavenly citizenship (3:20; compare 1:27) and their hope of transformation from humiliation to exaltation. Paul then directs an exhortation (4:1-3) to unity and cooperation to particular members of the congregation, using language—"stand firm," "the same mind," and "struggling together in the work of the gospel"—that recalls Paul's initial exhortation to the Philippians in 1:27. A series of more general encouragements, emphasizing gentleness, prayer, God's nearness, and the promise of peace, brings the section to its conclusion.

7. Paul's thanks for the Philippians' partnership in the gospel (4:10-20)

At the beginning of the letter Paul affirmed the Philippians' "partnership" in the gospel (1:5, 7). Now, at the end, he returns to this theme, specifically to the "gift" (4:17) the Philippians had sent him via Epaphroditus (2:30; see 1:3). Paul's financial relationship with the Philippians is unique: no other church but theirs has shared with him in this way (4:15-16). Because Paul and the Philippians lived in an economy ordered around patronage, in which financial and social obligations shaped relationships, Paul is at pains to clarify what their gift signifies and its consequences for their friendship in Christ. The gift signifies, first, the revival of the Philippians' concern for Paul, following a time when they had lacked opportunity to show it (4:10; see 2:30), and second, their "partnership in Paul's distress" (4:14). Paul also perceives the gift as "profit that accumulates to your account" (4:17) and as "a fragrant offering, and a sacrifice acceptable and pleasing to God" (4:18). Paul mingles with these affirmations two disclaimers. First, he did not really need the gift but has learned to be content with whatever he has because he depends on God (4:11-13). Second, he did not seek the gift, but "profit" for their "account" (4:17). The most important help they had sent, in other words, was not the gift itself, but the Philippians' continuing commitment to Paul and the gospel that is demonstrated by it. Paul can therefore confirm not only that he has been "paid in full," but that their gifts represent a pleasing sacrifice to God (4:18).

Receipt of the gift thus becomes another opportunity for Paul to affirm the Philippians' friendship, partnership, and support of him, his own reliance on God in all circumstances, and the mutual enrichment that develops when friends in Christ put the interests of others first.

8. Final greetings and benediction (4:21-23)

Paul's final greeting is notable for his mention of members of "the emperor's household" among the saints who send their greetings to the Philippians (4:22). This could include those persons in the imperial administration who had responsibility for Paul or even the soldiers who guarded him, among whom the gospel had become known (1:13). Paul thus suggests one last time the power of gospel amid adversity.

E. Between Two Worlds

Philippians is typical of Paul's letters in its conviction that Christians live in a creation undergoing transformation, a divine work begun among the Philippians on the "first day" when they heard and responded to Paul's proclamation of the gospel, continuing as they pursue their partnership with Paul in the gospel, and anticipating the "day of Jesus Christ," when God will bring the work to conclusion (1:5-6; 2:13). The Christian community in Philippi thus lives between two rules and two worlds. One of these worlds is defined by self-interest, dissension, suffering, and death. In this world Caesar is Lord and savior (*see* EMPEROR WORSHIP), peace is the PAX ROMANA, and friendship involves navigating the asymmetrical relationships built around honor and shame and the obligations of patronage. The alternative world is focused on the lordship of Jesus Christ, the embrace of suffering for the sake of Jesus Christ (1:29; 3:10), and the hope of resurrection (3:10-11). Here friendship is rooted and manifested in mutual service and partnership in Christ. The story of Christ thus carries the seeds of affront to both the cultural values of the day and the social, political, and religious order of the human empires. Paul does not hesitate to name Jesus, not Caesar, as Lord (1:2; 3:20), nor to claim that the Philippians' real citizenship is not in the Roman order but in the heavenly realm of God (3:20).

Heavenly citizenship does not imply disconnection from this world, but steadfast witness—in prayer, joy, unity, and mutual servanthood—to the truth and power of the story of Jesus Christ (*see* KINGDOM OF GOD, KINGDOM OF HEAVEN). The letter to the Philippians focuses particularly on the communal character of this witness. While Paul offers various individuals, including himself, as examples of what it means to imitate Christ, his primary concern is the unity of the church, which together gives witness to God's oneness and to the reality of the peace attained in the crucifixion and resurrection of Jesus Christ (*see* CHURCH, IDEA OF THE). Salvation is worked out among the members of the community (2:12), which is God's good work (1:6; 2:13). There is little support in Philippians, even in the Christ Hymn, for traditional renderings of salvation as a drama of sacrificial atonement for the sins of individuals. Philippians links SALVATION to the recognition that the Lord of the whole creation is the one who renounced divine power and privilege, became a slave, suffered humiliation, and died on a Roman cross, thereby wrenching creation free of the power of enmity, self-interest, and death. *See* PAUL, THE APOSTLE.

Bibliography: Markus Bockmuehl. *The Epistle to the Philippians.* BNTC (1998); Charles B. Cousar. *Reading Galatians, Philippians, and 1 Thessalonians* (2001); Gordon D. Fee. *Paul's Letter to the Philippians.* NICNT (1995); Stephen E. Fowl. *Philippians.* The Two Horizons New Testament Commentary (2005); Peter T. O'Brien. *The Epistle to the Philippians.* NIGCT (1991); Carolyn Osiek. *Philippians, Philemon.* ANTC (2000); Stanley Stowers. "Friends and Enemies in the Politics of Heaven." *Pauline Theology.* Vol. 1: *Thessalonians, Philippians, Galatians, Philemon.* Jouette M. Bassler, ed. (1991) 105–21; Ben Witherington III. *Friendship and Finances in Philippi: The Letter of Paul to the Philippians* (1994).

STANLEY P. SAUNDERS

PHILISTINES

PHILISTINES fi-lis´teen [פְּלִשְׁתִּים pelishtim; Ἀλλόφυλοι Allophyloi, Φυλιστιείμ Phylistieim]. A people located on the southern coastal strip of ancient Canaan during the Iron Age. According to the OT, the Philistines were organized in a confederation of five city-states (or Pentapolis), consisting of ASHDOD, ASHKELON, EKRON, GATH, and Gaza (*see* GAZA, GAZITES), which were under the control of rulers referred to as tyrants (seranim סְרָנִים). The Philistines are presented as enemies of the Israelites, particularly during the period of the putative transition from a tribal to a monarchical society. Archaeological evidence suggests that they—at least initially—had a strong Aegean element in their material culture, which can be traced from the 12th cent. until ca. 600 BCE.

A. Textual Sources

1. Biblical texts

Although the Philistines are mentioned in scattered pentateuchal texts, these are generally viewed as anachronistic and of little value in historical reconstruction. Abraham dwelt in the land of the Philistines (Gen 21:32-34), and Abimelech, the Philistine king of Gerar, desired Isaac's wife, Rebecca (Gen 26). During the exodus, the Israelites decided not to go by way of the land of the Philistines (Exod 13:17). Of more consequence is the notice that the Philistines originated in CAPHTOR according to the Table of Nations (Gen 10:14). This echoes a tradition also found in Amos 9:7. Whether one identifies the biblical Caphtor with Cyprus or with Crete, they both point toward the Aegean world for the origin of the Philistines, a tradition in accord with the archaeological record.

Both Josh 13:2-3 and Judg 3:3 preserve a memory of the Philistine territory as outside that of Israel. The latter book also lists the Philistines among the enemies of nascent Israel (Judg 10:6-7). It is, however, only in the Samson cycle of stories (Judg 13–16) that the Philistines begin to play a central role in the biblical narrative. Although ostensibly a pan-Israelite hero, Samson is depicted as an individualist from the tribe of Dan, who oftentimes ran afoul of the Philistines owing to his taste for foreign women. Thus he engages in contests of wits with the Philistines (Judg 14:10-19), burns their fields (Judg 15:4-5), walks off with the city gate of Gaza (Judg 16:3), and kills thousands of them, particularly when he collapses the temple of Dagon on himself and the gathered Philistines (Judg 15:8, 15; 16:27-30).

The next narrative in which the Philistines play a leading role is the ark narrative (1 Sam 4:1*b*–7:1), in which the Philistines become an object of ridicule and satire in order to magnify the power of Yahweh and the ark. In this folktale the ark is captured in battle by the Philistines and placed in the temple of their god DAGON in Ashdod. There the ark wreaks such havoc, including toppling and breaking the statue of Dagon in addition to afflicting the Ashdodites with disease, that they send it on to Gath and from there to Ekron. Everywhere the result is the same. Therefore, the Philistines return it to Israel along with offerings of golden mice and tumors (or hemorrhoids).

Most of the biblical narratives dealing with the Philistines, however, center on the period of the rise of the monarchy, particularly in the David stories. The OT presents the introduction of the monarchy in Israel as a consequence of external pressures that needed a centralized bureaucracy to counter them. The expansion of the Israelites from the central hill country toward the west was opposed by an expansion of the Philistines from the coastal plain eastward. Much of the reign of Saul, Israel's first king, was spent countering the Philistine threat. After Saul's death in battle against the Philistines (1 Sam 31), it was left to David to decide the issue in Israel's favor.

The biblical picture of David's relations with the Philistines is somewhat ambivalent. On the one hand, David is presented as a Philistine foe. His first great deed is the defeat of the Philistine champion Goliath (1 Sam 17, although this deed is ascribed to one of David's heroes in 2 Sam 21:19). Once he became king over all Israel, the Philistines became cognizant of his threat to their hegemony and marched against him, only to be defeated and henceforth restricted to their southern coastal strip, without, however, being absorbed into the putative Davidic empire (2 Sam 5:17; 8:1; 21:15-22; 23:9-17; 1 Chr 11:12-19; 14:8-17; 18:1; 20:4-8). On the other hand, there are some texts that point to close relations between David and the Philistines. While on the run from Saul, David became a vassal of Achish, the king of Gath, and received the outlying town of Ziklag as his fiefdom (1 Sam 27). Although the text argues that David acted against the interests of his Philistine master (1 Sam 30), he seems to have given him no reason to suspect him of disloyalty, and it was only the suspicion of the other Philistine rulers that supposedly precluded David from participating in their final battle against Saul (1 Sam 29). In addition to these contacts with Gath, David won the loyalty of a number of Gittites, who served in his personal guard. These included Ittai the Gittite, who was one of the few who remained loyal to David at the time of Absalom's revolt, and possibly also his personal guard of CHERETHITES AND PELETHITES (2 Sam 15:18-22).

After the time of David, the Philistines were reduced to playing an incidental role in the biblical narrative. Although 1 Kgs 4:21 [Heb. 5:1] implies that Philistia was absorbed into Solomon's kingdom, in light of the flight of Shimei's slaves to Gath in search of sanctuary (1 Kgs 2:39-41) this appears unlikely. Minor border conflicts at Gibbethon are narrated in 1 Kgs 15:27 and 16:15-17. Nonetheless, a couple of stories indicate that the borders between Israel/Judah and Philistia were oftentimes porous. At a time of illness, King Ahaziah of Judah sent a delegation to consult an oracle of the god Baal-zebub at Ekron, for which he is roundly condemned in the text (2 Kgs 1:2-16). And at a time of famine, the Shunammite woman sojourned in Philistia (2 Kgs 8:2-3). Significantly, we are informed that the Aramean king Hazael campaigned against Gath (2 Kgs 12:17 [Heb. 12:18]) and the northern Philistine coast (in a LXX addition to 2 Kgs 13:22).

Although it would appear that Chronicles offers some additional information about the Philistine story, the Chronicler's use of this information within the context of the narrative casts doubts on its historical reliability. Thus the "good" kings Jehoshaphat and Uzziah/Azariah prosper against the Philistines (2 Chr 17:11; 26:6-7), while the "evil" kings Jehoram and Ahaz lose territory to them (2 Chr 21:16-17; 28:18).

The Philistines play a role among the traditional enemies of Israel in prophetic oracles against the nations (e.g., in Jer 47). A close reading of the text reveals that Gath had suffered a devastating fate and had been reduced in size and importance by the time of the literary prophets (e.g., Amos 1:6-8; 6:2). Finally, Isa 2:6 associates the Philistines with the forbidden activity of soothsaying.

2. Extra-biblical sources

While the biblical sources concerning the Philistines in many cases postdate the events narrated by a considerable amount of time, there are some contemporaneous sources from the ANE relating to Philistine history. For the period of their first appearance on the historical stage during the transition from the Late Bronze to Iron I ages these stem from Egypt, while as of the 8th cent. BCE onward they come from Mesopotamia (i.e., Assyria and Babylon) and are written in Akkadian. While there are some undeciphered inscriptions from the Iron Age I that have been attributed to the Philistines, the only inscriptions that can confidently be attributed to them are a handful written in a dialect of Canaanite dating to the latter part of Iron Age II.

a. Egyptian sources. At the time of the collapse of Bronze Age civilization throughout the eastern Mediterranean world, there were groups underway to which scholars since the 19th cent. have referred to as "Sea Peoples." Among them was a group mentioned in Egyptian sources as prst/plst, which is the equivalent of Philistine. They are first mentioned in the inscriptions of RAMESSES III (ca. 1184–1163 BCE), who connected them with the sea in his Deir el-Medineh Inscription. Most interest, however, is focused on the inscriptions and associated reliefs from his mortuary temple at Medinet Habu that are dated to his eighth year. The texts make the claim that he defeated them in large land and sea battles (*ANET*, 262–63), after which he settled them in fortresses according to Papyrus Harris I (*ANET*, 260–62).

Werner Forman/Art Resource, NY

Figure 1: Philistines in feathered headdresses being led away by Egyptians. Relief from the temple of Ramesses III at Medinet Habu, Thebes, Egypt.

The interpretation of these passages is debated, however. While some would claim that Ramesses withstood a massive two-pronged invasion of Egypt by the Sea Peoples and then settled at least the Philistines in what came to be known as Philistia in Canaan, others view the battle(s) as local uprisings by Egyptian mercenaries and point out that Papyrus Harris I doesn't mention where the fortresses were in which the Sea Peoples were settled, while yet others draw attention to the ideological layout of the mortuary temple and view the whole account as royal hyperbolic propaganda. At any rate, the reliefs convey much insight into the appearance, social structures, and technology of the Philistines and other Sea Peoples.

After Ramesses III, the Philistines are mentioned briefly in the Onomasticon of Amenope (ca. 1100 BCE) and in the Pedeeset Inscription of either an Egyptian official serving in Canaan or a Philistine serving in Egypt from the period of either the Twenty-Second or Twenty-Sixth Dynasty.

b. Assyrian and Babylonian sources. The first mention of the Philistines in an Assyrian text dates to 796 BCE, when Adad-nirari III (810–783 BCE) recorded their tribute among others on his campaign westward to the Mediterranean Sea (*ANET*, 281–82). It was only during the reign of TIGLATH-PILESER III (744–727 BCE) that the Philistines came into direct contact with Assyria. Tiglath-pileser inaugurated a new era for the Neo-Assyrian Empire, one marked by a vigorous program of conquest and expansion. In 734 BCE, Tiglath-pileser launched a lightning campaign to Gaza on the border with Egypt, thus gaining control over a major trade hub between Asia, Africa, and Arabia. Hanunu, the king of Gaza, fled to Egypt, but was allowed to resume his rule over his city as an Assyrian client (*COS* 2.117:284–92). In response to the Assyrian incursion, Mitinti of Ashkelon joined an anti-Assyrian coalition spearheaded by Damascus and Samaria. As a consequence, Tiglath-pileser spent the next two years dealing with the revolt, destroying Damascus and severely truncating the territory of Israel. Ashkelon was able to avoid destruction when Mitinti was deposed and replaced by the pro-Assyrian Rukibtu.

The Neo-Assyrian Empire reached its highpoint under the reigns of SARGON II (720–705 BCE) and his successors. After the death of his predecessor, however, revolts broke out in various parts of his kingdom. Among the rebels was Hanunu, who this time was not able to escape deposition and a presumably brutal punishment (*COS* 2.118:293–300).

In 713–711 BCE, it was Ashdod that rebelled against Assyrian rule with disastrous results. The city was captured together with its port Asdudimmu and Gath, which had become one of its satellites. Sargon took over the city and turned it and its holding into an Assyrian province.

After Sargon's death in 705 BCE, revolts broke out throughout his empire. In the Levant the leader of the anti-Assyrian forces was Hezekiah of Judah (2 Kgs 18–19; 2 Chr 32). The people of Ekron deposed their pro-Assyrian king Padi and replaced him with an anti-Assyrian one, after handing the former over to Hezekiah. After quelling the revolts in the east, the new Assyrian king SENNACHERIB (705–681 BCE) turned his attention to the Levant in 701 BCE. He crushed the revolt, truncated Judah, set Padi back on his throne, and distributed the bulk of Hezekiah's territory among the Philistine kings who had remained loyal to Assyria (*COS* 2.119B-D:302–05).

Following more than thirty years of frequent revolt against Assyrian rule, the Philistines finally accepted their vassalage and enjoyed the benefits of about half a century of peace and prosperity during the *pax assyriaca.* Indeed, the kings of Ashdod, Ashkelon, Gaza, and Ekron are listed among the Assyrian allies during Ashurbanipal's (669–627 BCE) campaign against Egypt in 667 BCE (*ANET,* 294; *see* ASHURBANIPAL, ASSURBANIPAL).

Following the death of Ashurbanipal, the Assyrian Empire declined rapidly until it was replaced by the Neo-Babylonian Empire, under whose sovereignty the Philistines now fell. Failure to negotiate shifting coalitions led to the conquest of Philistia by Nebuchadnezzar II (605–562 BCE) in 604 BCE (*see* NEBUCHADNEZZAR, NEBUCHADREZZAR). A glimpse into the desperate situation is given in the Aramaic Saqqara Letter sent by Adon, the king of one of the Philistine cities—presumably Ekron—to Egypt begging to no avail for help in the face of the Babylonian onslaught (*COS* 3.54:132–34). The last extra-biblical reference to the Philistines is in a Babylonian administrative text mentioning the deported kings of Gaza and Ashdod, but unfortunately not their names (*ANET,* 307–08). After this, the Philistines disappear from the historical record.

B. Archaeology

Owing to the geographical information contained in the OT, the continuous habitation of some of the Philistine cities, and the results of modern archaeological excavation, the area of Philistia can be delimited with some confidence. On the west it was bounded by the Mediterranean Sea and in the east by the SHEPHELAH, the low-lying Judean foothills. The northern border was defined by the YARKON RIVER in northern Tel Aviv, and the southern one by the Wadi of Egypt, the Wadi el-Arish. Philistine remains have also been found in the area of the Carmel range and in the Jordan Valley. However, whether this represents Philistine settlement or—more probably—trade relations is a subject for debate. Over the course of the years, most archaeological attention has been focused on answering the question of Philistine origins, which most scholars trace to Cyprus and the world of the Aegean. As work progresses, interest in the later phases of Philistine archaeology has moved closer to the center.

1. Pottery

Near the beginning of the 20th cent., a distinctive assemblage of light-colored pottery painted with black and red patterns was associated with the Philistines. This so-called bichrome pottery has since become the hallmark of Philistine material culture, although later studies have indicated that it represents but the middle stage of the development of Philistine pottery.

The first phase of Philistine settlement in Canaan in Iron Age IA (1200–1150 BCE) is represented by a pottery style derived from Late Bronze Age Mycenaean ware and is oftentimes referred to as Mycenaean IIIC:1 pottery. On account of its decoration with brownish-black patterns, it is also called Philistine monochrome ware.

The second and classic phase of Philistine settlement in Iron IB (1150–1000 BCE and into the 10th cent.) is represented by the aforementioned bichrome ware, which replaces the monochrome ware after about a generation. Lighter in color than its predecessor, this pottery consists of some eighteen distinct styles deriving from a number of cultural spheres, in which the Aegean element is most widespread. The bichrome decoration consists both of geometrical and animal patterns, in the latter of which birds and fish predominate.

A third phase in the development of Philistine pottery has also been identified in recent years. A marker of the 10th–9th cent., it is characterized by a style with dark reddish slip and by the so-called "Ashdod ware," which has decorations of concentric circles or stripes in the Phoenician style. In the 8th–7th cent., regional styles seem to predominate in the Philistine pottery assemblage.

2. Major excavations

The first excavations in Philistia took place at the end of the 19th cent. However, it was only with the excavation of Ashdod as of the 1960s that the archaeology of the Philistines entered the modern period. The locations of the Pentapolis sites of Ashdod, Ashkelon, and Gaza have remained common knowledge since antiquity. Ekron and Gath were located during the last two decades. All of these sites, with the exception of Gaza, which lies beneath the modern city, have been excavated using up-to-date methods. In addition to these central sites, many smaller and peripheral sites have been uncovered. Of these the major published ones include Tel Qasile, which lies on the Yarkon River in northern Tel Aviv and whose ancient name is unknown, and Timnah (at Tel Batash) on the border between Philistia and Judah (*see* QASILE, TEL; TIMNAH, TIMNITE).

The Iron Age city of Ashdod arose from the ruins of the Late Bronze Age city and grew steadily during the course of the next centuries. Many features of the material culture, particularly in the earlier stages of Philistine settlement here as elsewhere, evidence connections with the Aegean world.

This settlement process is more or less mirrored at Ashkelon, where the arrival of the Philistines was marked not only by a steady expansion of the city, which reached ca. 150 ha. in size, but also by a change in diet from one in which goats and lamb provided the major sources of meat to one in which pork and beef predominated. Contrary to previous assumptions that the Philistines' beverage of choice was beer, based on the presence of a pottery vessel originally labeled a "beer jug," it has been determined that wine was their preferred alcoholic beverage.

The site of Ekron at Khirbet el-Muqnna (Tel Miqne) in the Sorek Valley was definitively established with the find of an inscription mentioning the ancient name of the city, although the material cultural remains uncovered there as of the 1980s had made this a foregone conclusion. A major site of Philistine settlement as of Iron Age IA at which both monochrome and bichrome pottery was found and the change in diet mentioned above was evidenced, the city shrank in size in the 10th cent. BCE, which was probably occasioned by Ekron's position on the border with Israel/Judah. After two centuries of decline, Ekron revived and reached its zenith during the time of the *pax assyriaca* in the 7th cent., when it became the ANE's leading producer of olive oil and a major center of the textile industry. The presence of hearths, here as well as at other Philistine sites, during the Iron Age I indicates an initial Aegean element in their life and social structures.

Long disputed, it now appears generally accepted that Gath was located at a site named Tell es-Safi, which lies at the point at which the Elah Valley reaches the coastal plain, some 11 km south of Ekron. Although traces of Mycenaean IIIC:1 pottery have been found at Gath, it appears that the city only assumed major importance in Iron Age IB, when for the only time in their histories both Gath and Ekron were ascendant at the same time. Otherwise their fates appear to have been mirror images of each other. While Ekron shrank as of the 10th cent., Gath achieved its greatest extent. This period of prosperity was brought to an end at the end of the 9th cent., presumably by Hazael of Damascus, who appears to have conquered Gath, an event from which the city never recovered (2 Kgs 12:17 [Heb. 12:18]). Evidence for Hazael's siege of Gath may be seen in a unique siege trench that surrounded the city on three sides.

Unlike the other cities mentioned here, all of which were built on top of preexisting settlements, Tel Qasile seems to have been an original Philistine foundation and remained such throughout the Iron Age I. Afterward it passed into the cultural sphere of the Israelites. As a city founded by the Philistines, it provides valuable insight into Philistine architectural practices, some of which mirror Canaanite forms and some of which appear distinctive. Among the major finds were three superimposed temples of irregular shape, in which a variety of cultic objects were found.

As a border site, Timnah appears to have belonged to Philistia in Iron Age I and then passed to Judah in Iron Age II. The material culture is basically Canaanite with a Philistine overlay, which has led the excavators to propose that the Philistines represented no more than a ruling class imposed on a Canaanite population.

C. Religion and Cult

The OT provides a picture of the Philistine cult that makes it practically indistinguishable from the Canaanite one. According to 2 Kgs 1, the god Baal, who is known as the head of the Canaanite pantheon, was worshiped at Ekron. In addition, in 1 Sam 31:10 the Philistines deposit the armor of the slain Saul in the temple of ASTARTE. The only distinctive feature of the Philistine cult mentioned in the OT is their supposed chief god Dagon, the father of Baal and another Semitic deity, but one associated only with the Philistines in the OT (Judg 16:23*a*; 1 Sam 5:2-7; see also 1 Macc 10:83-84; 11:4).

In contrast to the OT's depiction of their cult, in which the masculine outweighs the feminine, the material remains from Philistine sites found thus far give pride of place to the feminine, which many see as a holdover of an Aegean mother-goddess cult. Among these many finds may be mentioned a type of figurine of a seated woman ("Ashdoda") found at Ashdod, a libation vessel in the form of a woman found at Tel Qasile, and the Ekron dedicatory inscription, which, besides mentioning a succession of rulers of the city, also mentions the name of the goddess in whose honor the temple in which it was found was dedicated, namely **ptgyh**, which is usually interpreted as an Aegean name. Interestingly enough, over the course of time the influence of the masculine element in the Philistine cult seems to grow more important, without, however, supplanting the feminine. Hence it would appear that the picture conveyed in the OT is more reflective of a late stage in the development of the Philistine cult than it is of an early one.

D. Conclusion

The Philistines appeared on the historical stage in Canaan in the early 12th cent. BCE. After a period of expansion during Iron Age I, they were limited to the southwestern coastal strip of Canaan. Although aspects of their material culture point to their origin in Cyprus and the Aegean world, they quickly became acculturated to their environment, although they retained some distinctive traits in their dietary habits and their emphasis on the worship of a goddess.

Bibliography: Neal Bierling. *Giving Goliath His Due: New Archaeological Light on the Philistines* (2002); John F. Brug. *A Literary and Archaeological Study of the Philistines* (1985); Barbara Cifola. "Ramses III and the Sea Peoples: A Structural Analysis of the Medinet Habu Inscriptions." *Or* 57 (1988) 275–306; Trude Dothan. *The Philistines and Their Material Culture* (1982); Trude Dothan and Moshe Dothan. *People of the Sea: The Search for the Philistines* (1992); Carl S. Ehrlich. *The Philistines in Transition: A History from ca. 1000–730 BCE* (1996); Israel Finkelstein. "The Philistines in the Bible: A Late-Monarchic Perspective." *JSOT* 27 (2002) 131–67; Seymour Gitin,

Amihai Mazar, and Ephraim Stern, eds. *Mediterranean Peoples in Transition: Thirteenth to Early Tenth Centuries* BCE (1998); Brian Hesse. "Animal Use at Tel Miqne-Ekron in the Bronze Age and Iron Age." *BASOR* 264 (1986) 17–27; George L. Kelm and Amihai Mazar, eds. *Timnah: A Biblical City in the Sorek Valley* (1995); Ann E. Killebrew. *Biblical Peoples and Ethnicity: An Archaeological Study of Egyptians, Canaanites, Philistines, and Early Israel 1300–1100 B.C.E.* (2005); Aren M. Maeir. "Notes and News: Tell es-Safi/Gath, 1996–2002." *IEJ* 53 (2003) 237–46; Amihai Mazar. *Excavations at Tell Qasile, Part One, The Philistine Sanctuary: Architecture and Cult Objects* (1980); Eliezer D. Oren, ed. *The Sea Peoples and Their World: A Reassessment* (2000); Nancy K. Sandars. *The Sea Peoples: Warriors of the Ancient Mediterranean 1250–1150* BC (1985); Christa Schäfer-Lichtenberger. "The Goddess of Ekron and the Religious-Cultural Background of the Philistines." *IEJ* 50 (2000) 82–91; Ilan Sharon. "Philistine Bichrome Painted Pottery: Scholarly Ideology and Ceramic Typology." *Studies in the Archaeology of Israel and Neighboring Lands.* Samuel R. Wolff, ed. (2001) 555–609; Bryan Jack Stone. "The Philistines and Acculturation: Culture Change and Ethnic Continuity in the Iron Age." *BASOR* 298 (1995) 7–35; Shelley Wachsmann. *Seagoing Ships and Seamanship in the Bronze Age Levant* (1998).

CARL S. EHRLICH

PHILO OF ALEXANDRIA *fi'*loh. First-century CE Jewish biblical exegete and thinker, also called Philo Judaeus, who brought together Jewish tradition and Greek philosophy.

In 39 or 40 CE Philo participated in a Jewish delegation to the Roman emperor Gaius CALIGULA. Because Philo refers to himself as among the elderly when he describes this experience, scholars assume his dates to have been ca. 20 BCE–50 CE. He was thus born soon after the transition in Egyptian governance (30 BCE) from the Ptolemies (Cleopatra) to the Romans (Augustus), and he would have been a contemporary of Jesus and Hillel (*see* HILLEL THE ELDER, HOUSE OF HILLEL). Although Philo provides few specifics about his life and virtually none about his family, we know from Josephus (*see* JOSEPHUS, FLAVIUS) that his brother was Alexander the alabarch (an official under Roman rule), who was extremely wealthy. One of Alexander's sons, Marcus, involved in trading, married Berenice, daughter of the Jewish king AGRIPPA I, and the other son, Tiberius Julius Alexander, turned away from Jewish practices and served in several high positions under the Romans.

Philo himself was profoundly loyal to the Jewish Scriptures, religion, and people. He was also thoroughly familiar with Greek philosophy, learning, and culture. His several references to the theater, sports, and banquets suggest that he enjoyed a comfortable, Hellenistic lifestyle. Philo may have come from a priestly family and was likely a teacher, perhaps in a private school or synagogue.

In 38 CE ALEXANDRIA witnessed a violent uprising against the Jews, which some scholars have called the first pogrom. Although Philo describes this event in two treatises (*Against Flaccus* and *On the Embassy to Gaius*), its exact causes continue to be debated. We do not know what happened to Philo himself during this uprising, but one consequence was his voyage to Rome and appearance before Caligula.

Most of Philo's works are commentaries on the Greek PENTATEUCH, whose authority he considered equal to the Hebrew original (*see* SEPTUAGINT). Philo himself probably knew little if any Hebrew. His commentaries can be classed in three series, with different forms, types of exegesis, aims, and audiences. For example, the Exposition of the Law is organized thematically, with treatises devoted to creation, lives of Israel's ancestors, the Decalogue, particular laws, virtues, and rewards and punishments. Occasionally interweaving non-biblical details and allegorical interpretations (*see* ALLEGORY) into his presentation, Philo retells biblical narratives, discusses laws, and assumes his readers have little or no knowledge of Jewish Scripture or practice. Though scholars disagree about his precise aims and audience(s) for this series, Philo may have been writing to instruct a mixed readership of Jews and non-Jews, whether friendly, curious, or hostile. He also composed two companion treatises, somewhat similar in style and presentation to the Exposition of the Law, on the life of Moses. Philo's Allegorical Commentary constitutes the greatest part of his writings; this is a verse-by-verse commentary on parts of Genesis, characterized by frequent references to secondary verses (mainly from the Pentateuch) and complex, sophisticated allegorical exegesis. It is generally assumed that Philo here expounded the deeper meaning of Scripture for like-minded Jews, similarly well-versed in Jewish tradition and Greek learning. Philo's third series, *Questions and Answers on Genesis and Exodus*, extant primarily in Armenian translation, presents separate questions and answers on individual biblical verses or parts of verses. Answers include both literal and allegorical interpretations, which reflect a wider range of positions than either of his other two commentaries. Debating the purpose of this work, scholars have suggested that it may have served as a basis for study in the synagogue or preliminary notes for the Allegorical Commentary. *See* JEWISH BIBLICAL INTERPRETATION.

Philo also composed philosophical treatises on such subjects as *That Every Good Person Is Free*, *On Providence*, and *Whether Animals Have Reason* (the last two treatises survive in full only in the Armenian translations). Some scholars question whether the treatise *On the Eternity of the World* is authentically Philonic. Besides his works related to the uprising in Alexandria,

Philo devoted a treatise (*On the Contemplative Life*) to a contemporary spiritual group of men and women known as the Therapeutae (men) and Therapeutrides (women), who lived by Lake Mareotis on the outskirts of Alexandria. These various writings may have been intended for both Jews and non-Jews. He also composed an apologetic work, the *Hypothetica*—perhaps addressed to one or more hostile critics—which, among other things, sympathetically presents Jewish laws and another Jewish group known as the ESSENES. Several of Philo's writings have been lost, including two treatises on covenants, a work on numbers, and two treatises that scholars are almost certain he wrote on Isaac and Jacob.

For a long time, scholars approached Philo as if he were virtually the sole representative of what is often called Hellenistic Judaism. It is now clear, however, that he belongs to a much wider intellectual tradition of Greek-speaking Jews that goes back at least as far as the translation of the LXX and includes such interpreters as ARISTOBULUS and the author of the *Letter of Aristeas* (*see* ARISTEAS, LETTER OF). Both of these sources evince the beginnings of allegorical interpretation, which is impressively developed in Philo's works. Philo, however, was influenced not only by such earlier Jewish exegetes but also by Greek scholars, who used etymological interpretations and allegorical exegesis to deepen the meaning of ostensibly frivolous stories, e.g., about the gods, in Homer and other writers. He was also strongly influenced by Greek philosophy, especially by what has come to be known as Middle Platonism, a blend of Platonist thought with Stoic and Pythagorean ideas (*see* GREEK PHILOSOPHY AND RELIGION; PLATO, PLATONISM).

The centerpiece of Philo's thought—and apparently his life—was belief in the one, true God. For Philo this God was both the personal God of Abraham, Isaac, and Jacob and the abstract philosophical notion of "the Existent" (to ōn [τὸ ὤν], lit. "being"). This dual concept of the divine is supported by Exod 3:14-15 (LXX), in which God reveals the divine name (ho ōn ὁ ὤν, "He who is") to Moses. Philo also believed that God interacted with creation through intermediary figures, which included, most prominently, the LOGOS, and God's creative and kingly powers. For Philo, the height of happiness was to "see God," an achievement that involved recognition of God's existence and perhaps an experiential component as well.

In several ways, Philo's thought displays a tension, or contrast, between the universal and the particular. According to him, the God of all creation was at the same time the particular God of the Jews, one who Philo claimed showed special watchfulness over the Jews. The basis of the particular, written Mosaic laws was the universal, unwritten law of nature, and to emphasize this universal basis, Moses began Scripture with an account of creation. Through allegorical interpretation, Philo universalized the particular, historical significance of biblical figures and events. Embracing the Platonic distinction between body and mind or soul, Philo viewed biblical details as symbolic of the quest of the soul. Israel's departure from Egypt, e.g., represented the soul's leaving behind the "land" of the body, sense, and passions. Similarly, Philo often saw biblical figures as symbolic of virtue, vice, or passion. The tortures Pharaoh suffered after bringing Sarah into his household (Gen 12:10-20), e.g., show what happens when virtue and vice come together in the same soul. Philo expressed openness toward and admiration for wise and virtuous people of all nations, who embodied the ideal of the citizen of the world, or kosmopolitēs (κοσμοπολίτης). Sometimes, however, he praised the Jewish nation above all others because only the Jews believed in and worshiped the one, true God.

Philo's writings were preserved by early church fathers (*see* APOSTOLIC FATHERS, CHURCH FATHERS), who found his concept of the logos and his allegorical approach to Scripture compatible with their own ideas. His influence was considerable, especially in CLEMENT OF ALEXANDRIA, ORIGEN, and EUSEBIUS. Some patristic writers even thought he was Christian. Among Jews, after Josephus, who describes Philo as "highly regarded in every respect" (*Ant.* 18.259), Philo was not again mentioned by name until 1573 CE, when Azariah de' Rossi (*Light of the Eyes*) discussed Philo's views. Though the rabbis may have willfully rejected Philo, it is more likely that they either were unaware of him or simply overlooked him. Whereas they composed their literature in Hebrew and Aramaic, Philo had written in Greek, and his interest in Greek philosophy and allegorical interpretation was quite different from the rabbinic focus on biblical laws and use of folkloric tales (*see* RABBINIC LITERATURE). Points of comparison exist between Philo and medieval Jewish philosophers like Saadya and Maimonides, but we cannot establish any direct influence. In modern scholarship on Jews and Judaism, Philo is increasingly claiming an important position. *See* HELLENISM; JUDAISM.

Bibliography: Ellen Birnbaum. "Two Millennia Later: General Resources and Particular Perspectives on Philo the Jew." *CurBS* 4 (2006) 241–76; F. C. Colson, G. H. Whitaker, and Ralph Marcus, trans. *Philo in Ten Volumes (and Two Supplementary Volumes)* (1929–62); David T. Runia. *Philo in Early Christian Literature: A Survey* (1993); David T. Runia. *Philo of Alexandria and the* Timaeus *of Plato* (1986); Thomas H. Tobin, S.J. *The Creation of Man: Philo and the History of Interpretation* (1983).

ELLEN BIRNBAUM

PHILO OF BYBLOS fī'loh, bib'los [Φίλων Βύβλιος Philōn Byblios]. Greek historian and grammarian, also known as Herennius Philo (ca. 64–141 CE). He is most celebrated for the *Phoenician History,* a Gk. work in nine books, extant only in fragments, that offers an account of the myths and religion of PHOENICIA. Philo claims to have derived and translated this information from the Phoenician writings of a certain Sanchuniathon, who was reputed to have lived before the time of the Trojan War. Sanchuniathon, in turn, credits the records of Taautos (identified by Philo with HERMES and the Egyptian god Thoth) as being his ultimate source. The work, therefore, presupposes a complicated and lengthy tradition history, the value and authenticity of which have been disputed by scholars. Because of its euhemerism and other Hellenistic features, some have dismissed the *Phoenician History* as a late and derivative pastiche of Hesiod's *Theogony.* Others, however, have pointed to similarities between it and the Ugaritic texts (*see* UGARIT, TEXTS AND LITERATURE) and Hittite Kumarbi myths (*see* HITTITE TEXTS) as evidence that some of the material is derived from genuine Phoenician traditions. The recent tendency has been to interpret the *Phoenician History* as a Hellenized rendering of older Phoenician materials. Biblical scholars note that the *Phoenician History* preserves elements of Phoenician mythology that aid in understanding the biblical world.

The extant passages of *Phoenician History* consist of six segments. The first is a cosmogony that begins with the primal elements of darkness and wind and resembles the creation story in Gen 1. With the emergence of desire, the darkness and wind intertwine, and the sun, moon, and stars appear, followed by insensate and then sensate beings. Storms develop, and the thunder jolts the sensate male and female creatures, the "Watchers of the Sky," into awareness and stirs in them a desire for each other. The second section addresses the history of culture, and particularly those culture heroes who made notable discoveries such as food-gathering, hunting and fishing, fire, shelter, clothing, boat-making, metallurgy, and medicine. This section is reminiscent of Gen 4:19-22, where inventors of certain human occupations and crafts are named. The third segment furnishes a history of Kronos, and is essentially a succession myth in three stages: Elioun and his consort Berouth give birth to Ouranos (Heaven) and Ge (Earth), who marry and succeed their parents. They have four children, Kronos, Baetylos, Dagon (Grain), and Atlas, but because Ouranos mistreats Ge, Kronos wages war on him, and then supplants and castrates him. Some scholars conjecture that Kronos' division of the world is similar to the apportioning of the nations by the Most High in Deut 32:8. Kronos takes numerous consorts and produces many children, among them Persephone, Athena, APOLLO, and ZEUS Belos. The next segment of the *Phoenician History* opens with the reign of Zeus and ASTARTE, who rule at Kronos' behest, and closes with Philo's own condemnation of the Greeks' distortions of these Phoenician myths. The penultimate segment furnishes a brief discussion of human sacrifice, including an account of how Kronos immolates his own son Ieoud, while the final segment discusses the sacred character of snakes.

The early church father EUSEBIUS (260–340 CE) relied heavily on Philo's *Phoenician History* in his attacks on pagan mystery cults, and because of this, many fragments of the *Phoenician History* are preserved in Eusebius' *Preparation for the Gospel* (*Praep. ev.* 1.9,10). Some brief passages survive in Porphyry (*Christ.* F.34 = *Praep. ev.* 1.9.20–21). According to the *Suda,* Philo was also the author of *On the Reign of Hadrian, On Cities and Their Famous Citizens,* and *On the Acquisition and Selection of Books.* He composed other works besides these, and brief excerpts of his *On the Jews* are extant in Eusebius (*Praep. ev.* 1.10.42–43) and Origen (*Cels.* 1.15).

Bibliography: Harold W. Attridge and Robert A. Oden. *Philo of Byblos: The Phoenician History: Introduction, Critical Text, Translation, Notes* (1981).

J. R. C. COUSLAND

PHILO, BIBLICAL ANTIQUITIES OF. *See* PSEUDO-PHILO.

PHILOLOGUS fil-ol´uh-guhs [Φιλόλογος **Philologos**]. A Roman Christian to whom Paul sent greetings (Rom 16:15). Philologus' name is paired with that of JULIA, who is possibly his wife or sister. With these two, Paul mentions NEREUS and his sister, OLYMPAS, and other "saints" who were perhaps part of a HOUSE CHURCH in Rome. *See* ROMANS, LETTER TO THE.

MARIANNE BLICKENSTAFF

PHILOMETOR fil´uh-mee´tor [Φιλομήτωρ **Philomētōr**]. The coronation of King PTOLEMY VI Philometor of EGYPT and his hostility to the Seleucid ANTIOCHUS IV are mentioned in 2 Macc 4:21 (see also 2 Macc 9:29; 10:13). *See* MACCABEES, SECOND BOOK OF.

PHILOSOPHY [φιλοσοφία **philosophia**]. Philosophy as it emerged in 6th-cent. BCE Greece is the effort to understand the cosmos based solely on human observation and reasoning.

For most OT writers, human reason cannot work independently. Rather, proper reasoning moves forward on the basis of God's revelation to Israel, delivered through dreams, prophecy, the priestly cult, or the law. Individual claims to revelation ought to be evaluated critically (Deut 18:22), but this evaluation takes place within the framework of Israel's broader revealed tradition. The sages of Proverbs presume that the mind can discern the ethical workings of the world simply by reflecting on experience, but they still recognize that the "fear of the Lord" is necessary for proper insight. Job and Ecclesiastes go further in their reasoned questioning of some traditional theological formulations. Still, both books recognize a limit to reasoned inquiry, at which point one must fall back on faith in the revealed God (Job 38:1–42:6; Eccl 2:12-26; 5:1-7). *See* WISDOM IN THE OT.

The word *philosophy* (**philosophia**) never appears in the LXX, and *philosopher* (**philosophos** φιλόσοφος) is used only in Dan 1:20 for Nebuchadnezzar's enchanters. In Judea, reactions against radical Hellenization sometimes involved suspicion of foreign knowledge or rationalistic speculation, and some sages identified wisdom increasingly with Israel's Torah (e.g., *Jub.* 12:16-18; Sir 1:26; 3:21-24). Others, often in the Diaspora, saw in Hellenistic philosophy useful parallels to Jewish distinctives like monotheism (Wis 13:1-10), sometimes reinterpreting themselves and their law as "philosophical" (4 Macc 7:1-23; *Let. Aris.* 130–300). Josephus (*J.W.* 2.119–66) models his Jewish "factions" on the Hellenistic philosophical schools: Stoicism (*see* STOICS, STOICISM), Epicureanism (*see* EPICURUS, EPICUREANISM), Platonism (*see* PLATO, PLATONISM), and Cynicism (*see* CYNICS, CYNICISM). PHILO OF ALEXANDRIA carried out a thorough Platonic and Stoic reinterpretation of Judaism, while still maintaining traditional Jewish practices.

In Col 2:8, philosophy (**philosophia**) is identified with "empty deceit," though it is unclear what kind of "philosophy" was influencing the Colossians. When Paul addresses Epicurean and Stoic "philosophers" (**philosophoi** φιλοσόφοι) in Acts, however, he capitalizes on points of contact with Stoic theology, even quoting EPIMENIDES and the Stoic ARATUS (Acts 17:18-31), and some of these philosophers respond enthusiastically (Acts 17:32-34).

Parallels between NT and philosophical theology or metaphysics are at most superficial. Jewish ideas like bodily resurrection remain foreign to the philosophical schools (see Acts 17:32). Despite Paul's ambiguous talk about "the flesh," the NT never accepts the Platonic view of the body as inherently corrupting. Any Platonic influence behind dualistic oppositions like light/darkness (John 1:5) or genuine/copy (Heb 9:24) likely comes via traditional Jewish thought (1QS III, 17–IV, 7; *1 En.* 9:1; 4Q201 IV, 7). The fiery dissolution of the elements in 2 Pet 3:10 is indebted more to the apocalyptic "Day of the Lord" than to the Stoic idea of periodic conflagrations. Even the Johannine "Word," being personal and incarnate, is probably only superficially related to the LOGOS theologies of Stoicism and Philo (John 1:1-18; compare Philo, *Heir* 205–206).

Unlike the philosophers, the NT writers again look to revelation as the basis for their reasoning (1 Cor 1:19-25). The natural theology in Rom 1:19-20 may parallel Stoic thought, but it describes for Paul a possibility that human beings universally reject. The NT also tends to assume, contrary to philosophical epistemologies, that nonrational attitudes determine one's intellectual response to the truth (Mark 4:9-13; John 5:31-47; 2 Cor 2:15-16).

New Testament writers do, though, employ philosophical styles of speech like the DIATRIBE, with its fictional dialogues and rhetorical questions (Rom 3:1-20; Gal 2:15-21; *see* RHETORIC AND ORATORY). Paul's depiction of debate as warfare in 2 Cor 10:3-5 also recalls Cynic and Stoic language. The emphasis in 1 Thess 2:2-12 on his lack of guile and purity of mind recalls the claims of some Cynics, as does the stress on Paul's "boldness" (**parrēsia** παρρησία) in 2 Cor 3:12 and Phil 1:20.

In NT ethics (*see* ETHICS IN THE NT) we find some affinities with Stoicism. Many parallel ethical injunctions reflect commonly shared values rather than philosophical influence on the NT, but the NT "household codes" may draw on philosophical teaching about households (e.g., Col 3:18–4:1; 1 Pet 2:13–3:7). Paul, like the Stoics, treats ethical wisdom as the fruit of the reasoning "mind" (**nous** νοῦς) (Rom 12:1-2), and this ethical reasoning sometimes appeals to "nature" (**physis** φύσις; Rom 1:26; 1 Cor 11:14). Paul too envisions an inner faculty of CONSCIENCE and a universal inner law (Rom 2:15), and claims to be self-sufficient (**autarkēs** αὐτάρκης) in any circumstances (Phil 4:11).

On the other hand, the NT praise of humility (Matt 11:29; Acts 20:19; Rom 12:16; Jas 1:9; 1 Pet 5:5) and promotion of "slavery" to God and to one another (Mark 10:42-45; Luke 2:29; Rom 6:16; 2 Tim 2:24; Rev 7:3) are foreign to philosophical ethics (compare Philo, *Heir* 1.7; *Names* 1.46). These differences arise in part from OT language about being "God's servant" and in part from the use of Christ's death as an ethical model. Where philosophy aimed at avoiding mental disturbance, the NT writers call believers to embrace the cross (Mark 8:34; Phil 2:3-8). Hardships are endured, not through Stoic detachment, but with hope in Christ's return (1 Cor 15:19). Hence, though love is encouraged by Hellenistic philosophers, **agapē** (ἀγάπη) is both qualitatively different and far more central in NT ethics (*see* LOVE IN THE NT). Finally, while philosophers generally view vice as the result of ignorance, Paul in particular insists that knowledge of the good is not enough without the Spirit's inner renewal (Rom 7:7–8:11).

Some have pointed out Cynic parallels with, e.g., the Q mission discourse (Luke 10:1-16), suggesting that the historical Jesus resembled a wandering Cynic. Yet such passages more likely reflect Jewish wisdom or prophetic traditions, particularly since Jesus seems to have focused his work in the conservatively Jewish countryside of Galilee.

Bibliography: Gerald F. Downing. *Cynics and Christian Origins* (1992); Paul Rhodes Eddy. "Jesus as Diogenes?" *JBL* 115 (1996) 449–69; Troels Engberg-Pedersen. *Paul and the Stoics* (2000); Troels Engberg-Pedersen, ed. *Paul Beyond the Judaism–Hellenism Divide* (2001); Everett Ferguson. *Backgrounds of Early Christianity.* 3rd ed. (2003); Abraham J. Malherbe. *Paul and the Popular Philosophers* (1989); Roland E.

Murphy. *The Tree of Life* (1990); J. Paul Sampley, ed. *Paul in the Greco-Roman World* (2003); Stanley K. Stowers. *The Diatribe and Paul's Letter to the Romans* (1981).

IAN W. SCOTT

PHILOSTRATUS, FLAVIUS. Flavius Philostratus (ca. 170–ca. 250 CE) studied rhetoric in Athens but wrote mainly in Rome as part of the imperial circle of Julia Domna, wife of Emperor Septimius Severus. His biographical interests are demonstrated by his *Lives of the Sophists*, but he is best known for his *Apollonius of Tyana*. Apollonius, a 1st-cent. philosopher and mystic from Tyana in Cappadocia, traveled all over the known world. Philostratus' long account charts his travels, teachings, and mighty deeds, concluding with a detailed account of his imprisonment, trial, and death at Rome, followed by later appearances to his doubting followers and his assumption into heaven. This BIOGRAPHY is often compared with the Gospels and other ancient biographies, but its length and sheer scale make it more like a novel or travelogue. Furthermore, the historicity of Apollonius and the central character, his disciple Damis, is disputed by classical scholars.

RICHARD BURRIDGE

PHINEAS. *See* PHINEHAS.

PHINEHAS fin'ee-huhs [פִּינְחָס pinekhas; Φινεές Phinees]. 1. The son of ELEAZAR and the grandson of Aaron, the first Israelite high priest (Exod 6:25; Judg 20:28; 1 Chr 6:4 [Heb. 5:30]; 6:50 [Heb. 6:35]; Ezra 7:5; also spelled "Phineas," 1 Esd 8:2, 29). When the Israelites began to have sexual relations with Moabite women and to sacrifice to their gods at PEOR in the Transjordan, Yahweh punished them with a plague (Num 25:1, 9). Phinehas pierced ZIMRI, an Israelite man, and COZBI, a Midianite woman, through the stomach with a single thrust of his spear, and Yahweh stopped the plague (Num 25:6-9; Ps 106:30; Sir 45:23). As a reward for his zealous act, Phinehas received a "covenant of perpetual priesthood" from Yahweh (Num 25:10-13). The zeal of Phinehas is celebrated in literature from the Hellenistic period (1 Macc 2:26, 54; 4 Macc 18:12) when Jews sought to preserve their practices and way of life from foreign influence. *See* HELLENISM.

Later, Phinehas returned to the Transjordan to investigate the report that the Transjordanian Israelites had erected an illicit altar (Josh 22:13-34). Accusing the Tranjordanians of "treachery" against God, Phinehas and his assistants reminded them that Israel had not yet cleansed itself from the indiscretions of Peor (Josh 22:17). Certainly it was no coincidence that the zealous priest headed the delegation.

2. The son of ELI and father of ICHABOD, who together with his brother Hophni ministered at the early cultic site of Shiloh. HOPHNI AND PHINEHAS abused the privileges of the priestly office (1 Sam 2:12-17, 22); as a consequence, Eli's family was deprived of the priesthood, and Phinehas and Hophni themselves were killed by the Philistines while accompanying the ark of the covenant on a failed military excursion (1 Sam 4:11).

3. The father of Eleazar, a priest living in Jerusalem during the time of Ezra (Ezra 8:33).

JASON R. TATLOCK

PHLEGON fleg'uhn [Φλέγων Phlegōn]. One of the Roman Christians whom Paul greets (Rom 16:14). Along with Asyncritus, Patrobas, Hermes, Hermas, and others, he was likely part of a HOUSE CHURCH in Rome. *See* ROMANS, LETTER TO THE.

PHOCYLIDES. *See* PSEUDO-PHOCYLIDES.

PHOEBE fee'bee [Φοίβη Phoibē]. A female resident of CENCHREAE (a seaport east of Corinth), Phoebe was the apparent deliverer of Paul's letter to the Romans. In commending her to that church (Rom 16:1-2), Paul urged them to receive her befittingly and help her in whatever she might need. This possibly involved assisting her in advance planning for Paul's intended visit to Rome and subsequent mission to Spain.

Paul refers to Phoebe using three key terms. The first is adelphē (ἀδελφή, "SISTER"), a common term for female Christians. The second, prostatis (προστάτις, "patroness"), presumably indicates that Phoebe was the legal BENEFACTOR of an ecclesial group that met in her home, where she likely had leadership responsibilities in the HOUSE CHURCH. Paul states that Phoebe had also been a patroness to himself personally, placing her in social standing above him and him below her as her client. The third term is diakonos (διάκονος, "DEACON"), meaning "minister" or "servant." Paul uses the term diakonos elsewhere (e.g., 1 Cor 3:5) to describe his own ministry and that of various other (male) servants of Christ. (The office of "deacon" likely had not been established at the time Paul wrote Romans; see 1 Tim 3:1-13). Because Paul refers to Phoebe as a diakonos (the same term he uses for male ministers), and because he apparently regards her as a leader who is well suited and worthy of doing important tasks at the church in Rome on his behalf, Phoebe has become a role model for women in ministry. *See* ROMANS, LETTER TO THE.

FLORENCE MORGAN GILLMAN

PHOENICIA fi-nish'uh [Φοινίκη phoinikē]. The word Phoinix (Φοῖνιξ) and the plural Phoinikēs (Φοίνικης) were used by the Greeks to refer to the people living in the territory of Phoinikē (Φοινίκη), the coastal fringe of the eastern Mediterranean. The root of phoinix is still unknown, and at present the etymological problem of its origin is unclear. The name *Phoenicians* may be derived from the Greek phoinos (φοινός), an Indo-European root meaning "red," a color closely related to the purple dye industry for which the Phoenicians were well known in the ancient world (see §B). It has also been suggested that the Phoenician coast was known as "the land of the purple" by the Hurrians (*see* HURRIANS). Phoenicia is part of the land of Canaan (*see* CANAAN, CANAANITES), and it is now a widely held view that the Phoenicians were the Iron Age descendants of the coastal Late Bronze Age Canaanites. The territory of Phoenicia lies between the mountains of Lebanon to the east and the Mediterranean Sea to the west with a surface area that varied from 7 to 30 mi. wide. The northern boundary was the isle of ARVAD, ancient Aradus, with the southern frontier in northern Palestine at Akko (Acre) and the promontory of Mount Carmel. The historical implications of this geographical situation are clear. With mountains practically dropping straight into the sea, overland passage is naturally difficult, thus promoting the growth of sea traffic on the Mediterranean conveniently endowed with natural harbors. Sea trade was therefore highly developed along the Canaanite-Phoenician coast from the 3rd millennium onward. The principal Phoenician cities, Byblos (*see* GEBAL, GEBALITES), Berytos (Beirut), Sarepta, SIDON, Akko (*see* ACCO, AKKO), and Akhziv were built on rocky promontories with naturally protected harbors. Two cities, TYRE and Arvad, were located on small islands close to the shore. The modern city of Tyre forms a peninsula joined to the mainland, due to the accumulation of sediments around the causeway built by Alexander the Great during his blockade of the city. The reefs at Arvad, Sidon, and Tyre provide outer supplementary anchorages for foreign ships, in addition to the harbors attached to the town itself. Phoenicia also had great agricultural resources with an exceedingly fertile agricultural hinterland with rivers and torrents that flowed through valleys. Most important, there were the vast forests in the mountains of Lebanon. The coastal cities also had access to a large variety of game in the neighboring mountains and fishing from the sea. An important phenomena in the strategic history of Phoenicia is the staunch independence of each city-state from its sister cities. Separated as they were by rivers, valleys, and mountains, the geographical terrain might account for why they never constituted a united nation even in the face of great danger from the Assyrian Empire, although at times one city-state had hegemony over the others.

A. History

1. The Early Iron Age

The transition from the Late Bronze to the Early Iron Age along the Phoenician coast was not characterized by abrupt or radical social disintegration. For reasons not yet understood, the major disruptions caused elsewhere in the Levant by the arrival of the SEA PEOPLES in the early 12th cent. BCE appear to have had a minimal effect upon the Phoenician coastal cities. Textual evidence about Phoenicia in this transition period is scarce, but it seems that Sidon was the major power in Phoenicia for part of the time. We learn from the report of Wenamun (*see* WENAMUN, JOURNEY OF), the envoy of the high priest of Amon at Thebes, that around 1080 BCE the Sidonian king boasted no less than fifty vessels, whereas trade between Egypt and Byblos was transported by no more than twenty ships. From the 10th cent. onward, this hegemony changes and it is Tyre that takes the lead in Phoenicia.

2. The 10th century BCE

The earliest documented relations between Phoenicia and the kingdom of Israel were good. HIRAM, king of Tyre, sent carpenters and masons to build a house for King David (2 Sam 5:11; 1 Chr 14:1; 2 Chr 2:3), although in 1 Chr 22:4 only the cedar wood is mentioned for the building of the house. In chronological terms, David's relation with Hiram has been the subject of some debate. When Solomon succeeded his father David, Hiram sent messengers to greet him with gifts mainly of CEDAR and timber of fir (1 Kgs 5:8-10) to which the new king replied with gifts of wheat and oil. The reigns of Hiram and Solomon (1 Kgs 5:12) were a period of prosperity with mutually beneficial economical relations, including exchanges of goods and techniques as well as joint commercial expeditions. The Bible mentions a maritime expedition to TARSHISH (1 Kgs 10:22), a city identified by some with historical Tartessos on the Iberian Peninsula, and another expedition to the shore of the Red Sea and to OPHIR (1 Kgs 9:26-28). The location of the latter is unclear, but East Africa, between Somalia to the south and Sudan to the north, remains a likely location. The development of Phoenico-Israelite naval expeditions to the Red Sea in the 1st millennium gave direct access to the gold-producing countries, thus breaking for the first time the Late Bronze Age traditional Egyptian monopoly over this commodity. Hiram and Solomon made considerable direct profits from their expeditions. Assyrian annals and the archaeological record bear witness to yet another commercial route for Tyre involving northern Syria and Cilicia from around the beginning of the 9th cent. BCE providing access to supplies of silver, iron, and tin.

In the Iron Age, Phoenicia was also a major supplier of craftsmen to the Israelite kingdom. Hiram's envoy is said to have been skilled "in gold, silver, bronze, iron, stone, and wood, and in purple, blue, and crimson fabrics and fine linen, and to do all sorts of engraving" (2 Chr 2:13-14). During this period, Phoenician deities were also worshiped in Israel (1 Kgs 11:5) and this endured for more than 300 years until the days of King Josiah (2 Kgs 23:13). Still a much-debated point is the territorial transfers between Solomon and Hiram (1 Kgs 9:10-14; 2 Chr 8:2). Hiram was given twenty cities in the Galilee by Solomon, but for some reason the cities did not please Hiram.

3. The second quarter of the 9th century BCE

In the second quarter of the 9th cent. BCE the worship of Phoenician gods continued in the kingdom of Israel. There was an agreement between OMRI (885/881–874 BCE), king of Israel, and ETHBAAL, king of the Sidonians (1 Kgs 16:31), whose capital was in Tyre. AHAB, the son of Omri, married JEZEBEL, Ethbaal's daughter (1 Kgs 18:18), who introduced the cult of BAAL (Melqart) into Samaria (1 Kgs 18:18). The Bible tells us that Ahab "erected an altar for Baal in the house of Baal, which he built in Samaria" (1 Kgs 16:32), pleasing his father-in-law, Ethbaal, king of the Tyrians and Sidonians (Josephus, *Ant.* 9.138). Jezebel brought priests from Phoenicia and the prophets of Baal ate at her table (1 Kgs 18:19). The marriage of JEHORAM, son of King Jehoshaphat, to the Samarian princess ATHALIA (the daughter of Jezebel) opened Jerusalem to the Tyrian gods. A later revolt against Queen Athalia (2 Kgs 11:4-16) resulted in the temple to Baal being torn down and its priest MATTAN killed before the altars. Later, (ca. 841 BCE) the usurper JEHU removed the worship of Baal from Israel (2 Kgs 10:28), demolishing the temple of Baal and turning it into a latrine (2 Kgs 10:27).

The most important event to take place in the 9th cent. BCE was the rise of the Assyrian Empire. King Ashurnasirpal II (883–859 BCE) arrived on the Mediterranean coast around 870 BCE, the first visit by an Assyrian monarch in 200 years. He received tribute from Phoenicia, including rare metals (gold, silver, copper, and tin), fine linen garments with multicolored trimmings, and precious materials (boxwood, ebony, and ivory from walrus tusks). He was succeeded by his son Shalmaneser III (858–824 BCE), who also received tribute from Tyre and Sidon of silver, gold, lead, bronze, and purple-dyed wool.

4. The 8th to 6th centuries BCE

The end of the 9th and first half of the 8th cent. BCE marked a period of greater political freedom for Phoenicia, as the Assyrians turned their attention north to the growing military presence of URARTU in southern Anatolia. The book of Kings provides less information on relations between Phoenicia and the kingdoms of Israel and Judah. Some scholars have suggested Phoenician influence in the biblical stories of the 8th-cent. BCE King AHAZ, who "made his son pass through fire" (2 Kgs 16:3) and Ahaz's grandson, King Manasseh, who also made his son pass through fire (2 Kgs 21:6). While there is minimal evidence that the Phoenicians performed child sacrifices in the time of the First Temple, a later source claims that a freeborn boy was offered to Saturn in the 4th cent. BCE, when Alexander the Great had Tyre under siege (Curtius, *History of Alexander* 4.3.23). According to Josephus (*Ant.* 9.243), child sacrifice might have been a Canaanite custom, which comports with the Phoenicians being coastal Canaanites. However, there is very little evidence to support these conjectures.

Peace treaties between Phoenicia and Israel and Judah were replaced by a new defensive arrangement against Assyrian incursions. Under TIGLATH-PILESER III (744–727 BCE) and SARGON II (721–705 BCE) Phoenicia was left unharmed on the provision that the cities pay taxes and offer tribute to the Assyrian monarch in order to safeguard their economic interests and freedom of trade. Assyrian tributary demands of metals (silver and iron) in particular exerted considerable financial pressure on the Phoenician cities. Later, SENNACHERIB (704–681 BCE) demanded regular annual tribute as a sign of fealty to the state. He invaded Phoenicia in 701 BCE, forcing King Luli of Tyre to flee to Cyprus. Sennacherib was followed by ESARHADDON (680–669 BCE), who advanced upon Sidon, seizing the city and its territory. In 668 BCE, the accession year of Ashurbanipal (668–631 BCE; *see* ASHURBANIPAL, ASSURBANIPAL), Tyre, Byblos, and Arvad offered tribute and naval assistance to the Assyrian monarch throughout his first campaign against Egypt. In 605 BCE the Babylonians under Nebuchadnezzar (*see* NEBUCHADNEZZAR, NEBUCHADREZZAR) succeeded in defeating the combined forces of Egypt and Assyria at Carchemish. Assyrian influence over the Levant began disintegrating. Around 585 BCE, Nebuchadnezzar began a thirteen-year siege of Tyre.

5. The Persian period

Under Persian rule, Phoenicia served as the primary naval arm of Persia's maritime operations in the Mediterranean. All four cities of Phoenicia—Tyre, Sidon, Byblos, and Arvad—were permitted to retain their dynastic autonomy. Sidon functioned as the regional headquarters and seat of a governor's residence throughout the Persian period. The Persians stationed a garrison in the city and created a pleasure garden (paradeisos παράδεισος) mentioned by Diodorus Siculus (*Bib. Hist.* 16.41.5). The end of the

5th cent. BCE was a period of growing internal unrest within the Achaemenid Empire. Several uprisings took place in Sidon in 362/1 BCE when the city was occupied by Persian military forces and placed under the authority of Mazaeus, satrap of Cilicia and Syria, in recognition of his assistance in suppressing the revolt. There was another rebellion resulting in the destruction of Sidon in 345 BCE, the fourteenth year of Artaxerxes Ochus' reign. In 333 BCE the arrival of Alexander marks the beginning of the Hellenistic period.

6. The Hellenistic and Roman periods

Alexander's conquest of Phoenicia in 333 BCE was followed by the Roman victory at the battle of Magnesia in 189 BCE, making the Romans virtual rulers of Phoenicia. It was only in 64 BCE, however, that the kingdom of the Seleucids was finally reduced to a Roman province (*see* SELEUCID EMPIRE).

The Acts of the Apostles attests that Christians, scattered by persecution, went as far as Phoenicia, Cyprus, and Antioch (Acts 11:19-20). Paul and Barnabas passed through Phoenicia and reported many Gentile converts to Christianity (15:3). Paul sailed into Tyre on his way to Jerusalem (21:2). *See* SYROPHOENICIAN WOMAN.

B. Material Culture

1. Ivory

Ivory carving was one of the skills for which the Phoenicians were known. Carved ivories were luxury objects (Ezek 27:6). Excavations in Tyre have yielded a series of ivory ornaments such as an Egyptianizing palm-capital. The palmette or "Paradise flower" is one of the most popular motifs of the Tyro-Sidonian repertoire. The "lady at the window," another popular motif, may be the sacred prostitute, the goddess ASTARTE, which could be related to Ishtar, the Mesopotamian goddess. Egyptian art was a cherished source of inspiration for artisans of various crafts commissioned by the state, reaching its apogee in the 8th cent. BCE. A popular Phoenician model depicts the head of a woman (sometimes Astarte) wearing a heavy wig of Egyptian type. Toward the middle of the 1st millennium BCE, popular art gradually exhibited less Egyptian influence.

2. Metal and glass

The reputation of the Phoenicians as skilled metalworkers (1 Kgs 7:14; 2 Chr 2:14) was also recorded in the 8th cent. BCE by Homer, who describes the Phoenician silver vessel awarded by Achilles as the first prize in Patroclus' funeral games. Bronze bowls thought to be of Phoenician origin and dating between the 9th and 7th cent. BCE have been found at Nimrud, where they are thought to have been brought as loot by the Assyrians. The Phoenicians also specialized in the production of jewelry using precious metals—gold in particular—and were actively involved in glass manufacture.

Erich Lessing/Art Resource, NY

Figure 1: The goddess Astarte, on her head the sun-disk and the Hathor-crown. Bronze and silver sheeted figure, Egyptian influence (8th cent. BCE). From Phoenicia. Louvre, Paris, France.

3. Purple dye

Phoenicia was renowned in antiquity for the production of fabrics dyed in PURPLE extracted from the *Murex* gastropods (*see* MUREX). Gastropods *Murex* (phylum Tronculus) and whelk were crushed together in an alkaline solution. This solution, when decanted and used for dyeing, stayed practically colorless in the container. However, when textiles (woolens, natural silk, or cotton) were taken out of the bath, they began to become purple in contact with oxygen in the air, reaching a shade dictated by the bath's concentration. This result cannot be obtained using *Murex* (phylum Brandaris) and *Thais* (*Purpura*) *haemastoma* alone. The fact that archaeologists have found piles of mixed shells of four species of gastropods on archaeological sites in Sidon, Sarepta, Tyre, and southern Italy leads one to suppose an evolution in the technique of purple dyeing after the 1st millennium BCE.

4. Shipbuilding

Shipbuilding was a leading industry supported by the proximity of the forests of LEBANON, where timber was always close at hand. *See* SHIPS AND SAILING IN THE NT; SHIPS AND SAILING IN THE OT.

C. Trade

Phoenician navigation and exploration were the result of geographical, historical, and political conditions that determined their expansion throughout the Mediterranean and the foundation of a series of landing stages and trading posts, many of which eventually became colonies. The Phoenicians' primary motivation was trade, especially for metals. Aegean imports were rare during the 12th and 11th cent. BCE as were any Phoenician imports to Greece from the East. This recession has been held to be one symptom of an Aegean "Dark Age" distinguished by illiteracy, poverty, and isolation from the outside world. These impressions of "darkness," however, have recently been dispelled to some extent by the excavations of graves at Lefkandi in Euboea that yielded eastern exotica dated ca. 950–900 BCE and in the Levant by finds of Euboean-type pottery imported to Tyre in the 10th cent. BCE. Phoenician presence in Crete has been documented by recent excavations at Kommos on Crete's southern coast where a Phoenician-type three-pillared shrine and imported Phoenician pottery were found. All this notwithstanding, the main impact of Phoenicia on Greek civilization was in the transmission of the ALPHABET to the Greeks and the Western world through trade. An important source of information about Phoenician trade is Homer, whose *Odyssey* described the Phoenicians as dominant at sea and in conflict with the Greeks and saw them as traders and pirates who frequented Greek waters.

CYPRUS was the first place the Phoenicians visited on their westward exploration. The establishment of the Phoenicians in Cyprus dates back to at least the mid-9th cent. BCE. The evidence for this comes from the site of Kition. Cyprus was used as a transit point for further commercial initiatives and many Phoenician-influenced sites on the island were important for the copper industry and international trade. Mass immigration of the Phoenicians took place during the 8th cent. BCE. Their presence is seen in Rhodes, the Dodecanese, North Africa, South Italy (Sicily and Sardinia), as well as the Mediterranean and Atlantic coasts of Spain.

Bibliography: Maria E. Aubet. *The Phoenicians and the West: Politics, Colonies and Trade.* 2nd ed. (2001); J. Doumet. "Ancient Purple Dyeing by Extraction of the Colour from *Murex* Phy. Tronculus, *Murex* Phy. Brandaris, *Thais Purpura Haemastoma* and Whelk Following the Natural History of Pliny the Elder." *Decade: A Decade of Archaeology and History in the Lebanon.* Claude Doumet-Serhal, ed. (2004) 38–49; Glenn E. Markoe. *Phoenicians* (2000).

CLAUDE DOUMET-SERHAL

PHOENIX fee′niks [Φοῖνιξ Phoinix]. A harbor on the southwest coast of CRETE, Phoenix was an intended but unattained destination on Paul's voyage to Rome (Acts 27:12-14). None of the ancient sources (Strabo, *Geogr.* 10.4.3; Ptolemy, *Geog.* 3.17.3; *Stadiasmus* 328–29; *Notitiae Graecae Episcopatum* 8.230; Hierocles, *Synecdemus* 651) give an exact location, but they point to the vicinity of Cape Muros. Whether it was on the east side (modern Loutro) or the west side (Phoinika Bay, which preserves the name) is disputed. Today the former has an adequate harbor but is exposed to the prevailing northeast winter wind, whereas the latter has no satisfactory harbor but faces southwest so as to provide protection from the northeast wind. One consideration is whether Acts 27:12*e* means "looking northeast and southeast" (RSV) or "facing southwest and northwest" (NRSV, most other translations, most commentaries). Another is whether western Cape Muros has been uplifted since the 1st cent., thus obliterating one harbor facing northwest and another facing southwest. Still another is why the FAIR HAVENS was unsatisfactory (vv. 8, 12*a*); perhaps it faced southeast and was therefore exposed to the winter wind. If so, Loutro was unsatisfactory for the same reason. Therefore the western side is more likely.

JAMES A. BROOKS

PHRYGIA frij′ee-uh [Φρυγία Phrygia]. Direct biblical references to Phrygia occur only in Acts. It is one of the territories listed in the Pentecost narrative in Acts 2:10 and one of the regions of Paul's travels mentioned along with Galatia in Acts 16:6 and 18:23. Phrygian cities mentioned in the NT include COLOSSAE, HIERAPOLIS, LAODICEA, Pisidian Antioch (*see* ANTIOCH, PISIDIAN), and arguably ICONIUM. In the LXX, 2 Macc 5:22 also refers to "PHILIP, by birth a Phrygian," appointed to govern Jerusalem by ANTIOCHUS IV. Old Testament references rely on the Assyrian identification of the Phrygians as the "Mushki" appearing as MESHECH (Gen 10:2; 1 Chr 1:5; Ezek 27:13).

Phrygia was a culturally defined territory with fluctuating boundaries on the west-central plateau of Asia Minor, an area of rock mesas, mountains, and broad river basins. At its greatest extent to the north, the territory included the valleys of the Tembris and the upper Sangarius rivers, including Pessinus and Gordion near Mount Dindymus. To the east, Phrygia extended as far as the Halys River, including Ancyra, and to the west to the area that included Midas City, Dorylaeum, and Aezani, known as Phrygia Epictetus ("acquired," a label from the Roman era). To the south, it extended to the fertile area known as Phrygia Paroreius ("along the mountains") and the lake area, including Philomelium, Pisidian Antioch, and Apameia. Central Phrygia was a mountainous area reaching elevations of 2,000 m. In antiquity, the forested Phrygian mountains produced pine, oak, and cedar timber, and its grazing lands provided for horses and sheep. Quarries, especially the one at Docimeium, supplied prized marble for export during the Roman era.

Phrygia takes its name from the ethnic group that entered Asia Minor, probably from Thrace, as part of the Indo-European incursions at the end of the Hittite Empire, ca. 1200 BCE (*see* HITTITES). The Phrygians built several of their most prominent sites over Hittite settlements at Gordion, Ancyra, and Boğazköy.

The Phrygian Empire arose during the 8th cent. BCE and flourished briefly. Excavations at the capital city at Gordion attest to the power and wealth of the kingdom, a high level of artisanship and architecture, and communication with Greek states in the west and the URARTU and Neo-Hittites in the east. The probable tomb of the most prominent of the Phrygian kings, King Midas, is the largest of nearly 100 tumulus graves, a mound 53 m high and 300 m wide. Excavation of the mound has revealed a burial chamber 5 by 6 m, complete with the remains of a large banquet.

The Phrygians worshiped a goddess named Matar, often with an epithet in Phrygian as *Matar Kubileya* (probably "Mother of the Mountain"). In the Greco-Roman era she was known as Cybele or "Mother of the Gods." Her temple-state at Pessinus was a major Phrygian city. Settlements in the highlands centered around fortified rock mesas called *kales* where the Phrygians' huge rock-cut monuments still stand. Most of these are large flat façades carved with square geometric designs surrounding a door-shaped niche for an image of the goddess, either as a space for placement of an image or as a rock-cut image. One such image in the monument at Arslankaya contains a massive rock-cut standing image of the goddess flanked by standing lions. Some of the monuments are inscribed in Paleo-Phrygian, an Indo-European language with an alphabet similar to Greek.

In the early 7th cent. BCE, the invasion of the CIMMERIANS ended the Phrygian Empire, probably destroying Gordion in a massive fire. The Cimmerians quickly receded, leaving the Lydians (*see* LYDIA, LYDIANS) to the west, with their capital at SARDIS, in ascendancy to rule most of the Phrygian territory. Phrygians never ruled Phrygia again, but their culture continued even though the territory was dominated by one external power after another.

In 546 BCE, the Persians overthrew the last Lydian king, Croesus, and dominated the region for nearly two centuries. Their cultural influence remained, including the worship of the deities Mên and Anaeitis, prominent in Phrgyia until the end of the Roman era.

With the arrival of the force of Alexander the Great in 334 BCE, Persian domination ended. At the former Phrygian capital, Alexander solved the puzzle of the Gordion knot, the legendary key to the control of Asia, by slicing through it with his sword. In the rivalries following Alexander's death, Phrygia came to be part of the Seleucid territory. The Jewish population that flourished in several Phrygian cities in later centuries immigrated under the Seleucids. SELEUCUS I granted Jewish settlers citizenship in cities he founded, and Antiochus III settled 2,000 Jewish families in Lydia and Phrygia at the end of the 3rd cent. BCE.

A massive incursion of three tribes of Celts (Galatians) crossed the Hellespont into Asia Minor in 278 BCE, allowed first as mercenaries for BITHYNIA in a time of complex rivalry for control of Asia. The Celts raided both the coastal areas and the interior of Asia Minor and were subdued in stages, driven first to northeastern Phrygia to the area around Ancyra, which became known as GALATIA. As they settled, they adopted religious and burial practices of the local population, including Phrygian devotion to the "Mother of the Gods." King Attalus I of Pergamum dealt the Galatians a decisive defeat in the late 3rd cent., but they held their own territory as a kingdom and remained a military force until their defeat by the Romans in 25 BCE. Galatia became a Roman PROVINCE incorporating the northeastern portion of Phrygia. The rest of Phrygia remained as part of the Roman province of Asia, acquired in 133 BCE when the last king of Pergamum bequeathed the territory to Rome.

Before Roman domination, the Hellenized portions of the territory were mostly cities established on the overland trade routes and installations to protect the holdings of Hellenistic rulers. Temple states dominated in some locations with populations of "sacred slaves." One prominent temple state was at Pessinus, the state of the "Mother of the Gods" ruled by the Attis, also the name of her subservient companion deity. Most of the population, however, lived in the villages that were the primary unit of social organization, and many country dwellers lived effectively as serfs. The Romans also established both imperial and privately owned estates in some of the more thinly settled areas of Phrygia. Phrygia was a patchwork of forms of social organization and land ownership.

In some locations the social and legal organization included guardian deities who functioned as enforcers in a form of "divine judicial system." Curses functioned as indictments, inscribed preemptively on tombs and buildings as protection or placed in the temple to request divine punishment for some offense already committed. The curses invoked divine retribution to cause the offender to suffer. Other inscriptions reveal belief in the effectiveness of the curses and the deities' enforcing power. These "confession inscriptions" acknowledged offenses as an appeal to the deities to terminate some form of suffering understood as a divine judgment and punishment for some offense. A number of the prominent deities in Phrygia reflect an ethos of divine judgment and vengeance: local forms of the "Mother of the Gods" and of Zeus functioning as overseers from the high places; the moon god Mên; the distinctively Phrygian deities the Holy and the Just; Dikaiosyne; Apollos Lairbenos; and others. The Roman imperial cult also took its place among the cults of Phrygia as it did elsewhere, and the Jewish population continued to thrive.

Abundant epigraphic evidence attests to the spread of Christianity in Phrygia during the 2nd and 3rd cent. CE in both the cities and the countryside. Christian symbols appear in reliefs on funerary monuments dated to the last half of the 2nd cent. Montanist (*see* MONTANUS, MONTANISM) inscriptions are also found widely in Phrygia. The Montanist movement, a version of Christianity known as the "Phrygian heresy," appeared around 170 CE and was centered at Pepuza in Phrygia, a location recently identified south of modern Usak. In the upper Tembris Valley, a collection known as the "Christians for Christians" inscriptions appear as early as 248 CE, and other inscriptions from the area indicate a Christian majority there before the end of the century. Christianity flourished well in most of Phrygia until the end of the Roman era, and its strength is also indicated in records of persecutions in Phrygian territory.

The Phrygian ethnicity and cultural identity also continued throughout the Roman era. This identity could be negative, such as the Greek equation of Phrygian ethnicity with slave status. Yet a form of Phrygian pride is also evident in neo-Phrygian inscriptions from the 2nd and 3rd cent. CE in the Greek alphabet, mostly appended as protective curses to tombstone dedications in Greek. These inscriptions indicate the preservation of the language in the Roman era. The references to Phrygia in Acts also indicate the recognition of the territory by ethnicity and language rather than by Roman provincial boundaries.

Bibliography: Ekrem Akurgal. *Ancient Civilizations and Ruins of Turkey: From Prehistoric Times until the End of the Roman Empire* (1978); Susan M. Elliott. *Cutting Too Close for Comfort: Paul's Letter to the Galatians in Its Anatolian Cultic Context* (2003); C. H. Emilie Haspels. *The Highlands of Phrygia* (1971); David Magie. *Roman Rule in Asia Minor to the End of the Third Century after Christ* (1950); Stephen Mitchell. *Anatolia: Land, Men, and Gods in Asia Minor* (1993); Lynn E. Roller. *In Search of God the Mother: The Cult of Anatolian Cybele* (1999).

SUSAN M. ELLIOTT

PHYGELUS fi'juh-luhs [Φύγελος **Phygelos**]. The Asian Phygelus, along with HERMOGENES, turned away from Paul during his imprisonment (2 Tim 1:15). It is unclear if Phygelus personally deserted Paul in Rome or if the "turning away" indicates a general withdrawal of support from the Asian church, of which Phygelus was a part. *See* ASIA.

KATHY R. MAXWELL

PHYLACTERIES fi'lak'tuh-ree [φυλακτήριον **phylaktērion**]. Phylacteries, from a Greek word meaning "amulet" (Hebrew **tefillin** תְּפִלִּין), are small boxes, made of the leather of a kosher animal, that contain scriptural passages and are fastened to the head and arm with leather thongs. As part of the remembrance of the exodus from Egypt, the Lord commanded that "these words" be as "a sign on your hand and as an emblem (**totafoth** [טוֹטָפֹת], "reminder") on your forehead" (Exod 13:9, 16; Deut 6:8; 11:18). The Greek term occurs only in the plural (**phylaktēria** φυλακτήρια) in Matt 23:5.

The meaning of the biblical Hebrew designation **totafoth** is unclear. The derivation of the term **tefillin** is most probably from its singular form, **tefillah** (תְּפִלָּה), meaning "PRAYER." Even though the Greek term **phylaktērion** means "amulet," there is no evidence in rabbinic literature that phylacteries were in any way connected with magical properties. Most scholars prefer to connect the term with **netifoth** (נְטִיפוֹת; Judg 8:26; Isa 3:19), meaning a "round jewel, pendant" worn by a woman on her forehead (*m. Shabb.* 6:1). In contrast, the mark of Cain (Gen 4:15) implies a physical sign of protection, perhaps a reference to tattooing the name of a god on the head or arm. (Another example of this protective sign is the mark on the foreheads of the righteous that spared them from punishment in Ezek 9:4).

Because the OT itself makes no mention of how phylacteries were to be constructed, it is possible that the passages regarding the **tefillin** were interpreted figuratively. While Deut 6:8 might imply a more concrete application of the "words," the exhortation to put them on the head, arm, doorposts, and gates in the context of the Passover celebration (Exod 13:9) could mean simply to keep the memory of God's deliverance and his commandments constantly in mind (*see* PASSOVER AND FEAST OF UNLEAVENED BREAD).

The *Letter of Aristeas* (159) in the 2nd cent. BCE already mentions phylacteries as physical objects worn on the body. Toward the end of the 1st cent. CE, they are mentioned by Josephus (*Ant.* 4.213), and the Gospel of Matthew critiques the scribes and Pharisees for wearing phylacteries to proclaim themselves pious when they are, in fact, hypocrites (Matt 23:5). Nevertheless, the actual form of pre-rabbinic phylacteries was not known until the discoveries at QUMRAN dated to the late Second Temple period and at Murabbaat (*see* MURABBAAT, WADI), occupied by refugees from the Bar Kokhba Revolt of 135 CE.

Phylacteries were secured to the head and forearm with leather thongs that passed through the box. Each box or capsule contained the four biblical passages concerning the commandment of phylacteries (Exod 13:1-10; 13:11-16; Deut 6:4-9; 11:13-21) written on leather slips. These slips were folded and tied with threads of animal tendon and hair and then placed in individual compartments. In the head phylactery, this leather capsule was stitched closed, and the strap passed below it. In the arm phylactery, there was but a single compartment with all the passages enclosed in it written on one slip, and the strap passed through this capsule.

Thirty fragments of phylacteries have been identified from the Judean Desert, made of vegetable-tanned, unbleached leather with the hair side facing out. One intact head phylactery (XQPhyl 1–4) from the Qumran region had a capsule measuring 13 × 20 mm and was paleographically dated to the Herodian period, the first half of the 1st cent. CE, thus pre-dating the MISHNAH. Overall, Qumran phylacteries are remarkably like those described in rabbinic texts as to their form, the writing material, and the manner of tying the parchments.

Rabbinic law required males over the age of thirteen to wear phylacteries; women were exempt (*m. Ber.* 3:3). The biblical passages found in the phylacteries from Qumran and those specified in rabbinic sources are to a large extent the same. However, some Qumran phylacteries include the TEN COMMANDMENTS and Deut 32. Further, in the Qumran phylacteries the passages appear in differing order and contain some orthographic variants and some variant biblical readings. The rabbinic tradition also testifies to disputes over the sequence of the passages (*b. Menah.* 34b). This debate even continued into the Middle Ages: Rashi held that the last two sections should contain Deut 6:4-9 and then Deut 11:13-21; Rabbenu Tam reversed this order. The Judean Desert yielded phylacteries similar to the view of Rashi but which evidence various sequences of passages. The complete phylactery from Murabbaat is of the Rabbenu Tam type, as seems to be the case for some other exemplars. It appears that these two traditions go back to Second Temple times and were in use concurrently.

The MISHNAH forbids any additional passages in the phylacteries except for the four prescribed ones (*m. Sanh.* 11:3). Some sectarian phylacteries do contain additional scriptural selections, such as the Ten Commandments. This passage was recited as part of the daily prayers (*m. Tamid* 5:1; *y. Ber.* 3c) and appears along with the Shema (*see* SHEMA, THE) in the Nash Papyrus (2nd cent. BCE). Phylacteries from Murabbaat conform more closely to Pharisaic-rabbinic halakhah and do not contain the Ten Commandments.

Scribal practice in the Judean Desert exemplars differs from that of the prescriptions of the TALMUD. For example, the Talmud does not allow corrections by means of writing between the lines. Words may not be broken at the ends of lines, nor may letters be crowded in at the end of the line if the word will not fit in the remaining space. All rabbinic phylacteries are written on one side of the parchment only and conform to a specific way of forming the letters. At Qumran, many of the tiny scrolls violate these rabbinic laws. It is possible that all of the later scribal regulations were not in force as yet, nor widely observed. Alternately, the sectarians simply may not have subscribed to Pharisaic regulations.

The phylacteries found in the Judean Desert, then, provide archaeological evidence from the Second Temple period to refine our knowledge about the history of these ritual objects. We can conclude that by the time of the manufacture of the Murabbaat phylacteries, in the early 2nd cent. CE, mishnaic prescriptions had become normative. Thus, the physical aspects of the phylacteries were standardized by the 1st cent., the contents of the scriptural passages were definitively established only by the 2nd cent., and the order of the passages was still not settled, but remained controversial, even into the Middle Ages.

The small number of phylacteries found at Qumran (where one might have expected to find many examples) might be explained by taking into consideration the minimal chances of their survival and the frequency of their use. Compared to later rabbinic phylacteries, the Qumran specimens are quite small. Due to their fragility, a number of them might have been lost. Their scarcity might also have to do with the extent of the practice of wearing phylacteries. According to rabbinic sources, phylacteries were not originally worn by all Jews, although this practice grew in popularity. The Qumran phylacteries might come from a time before this practice was universally observed. The Talmud indicates that phylacteries were worn by the especially devout rather than by the common people (*b. Shabb.* 130a; *b. Ber.* 47b; *b. Sotah* 22a), yet even the devout did not wear them all day, donning them for prayer and perhaps study. Possibly the requirement of ritual purity for wearing phylacteries led many not to wear them. Further, during the Hadrianic persecutions, donning phylacteries was forbidden on pain of death, resulting in a temporary abandonment of the practice even after the persecutions ceased (*b. Shabb.* 130b). *See* MEZUZAH.

Bibliography: Yehuda Cohn. *Tangled Up in Text: Tefillin in the Graeco-Roman World (4th Century BCE to 3rd Century CE)* (2006); David Rothstein. *From Bible to Murabba'at: Studies in the Literary, Textual and Scribal Features of Phylacteries and Mezuzot in Ancient Israel and Early Judaism* (1992); Emanuel Tov. "Phylacteries of Different Origin from Qumran?" *A Light for Jacob: Studies in the Bible and the Dead Sea Scrolls in Memory of Jacob Shalom Licht.* Yair Hoffman and Frank H. Polak, eds. (1997) 44–54; Geza Vermes. "Pre-Mishnaic Jewish Worship and the Phylacteries from the Dead Sea." *VT* 9 (1959) 65–72; Yigael Yadin. *Phylacteries from Qumran (X Q Phyl 1–4)* (1969).

LAWRENCE H. SCHIFFMAN

PHYSICIAN [רֹפֵא rofe᾽; ἰατρός iatros]. In the modern sense of a person certified to engage in diagnosis and therapy through naturalistic/scientific means, *physician* has no exact equivalent in the Bible. The Hebrew term rofe᾽ refers to a person who treats bodily injuries with medicinal substances (Jer 8:22; compare Exod 21:19), as well as embalmers (Gen 50:2). Yahweh is called a rofe᾽ in Exod 15:26 ("the LORD who heals you").

The Greek term iatros probably refers to a person who, for a fee, heals through naturalistic and/or religious therapies (Mark 5:26). Church fathers, such as Ignatius (Ign. *Eph.* 7.2), deemed Christ a fleshly and spiritual physician *par excellence* (compare Matt 9:12; Mark 2:17; Luke 5:31).

Physicians in the biblical world are part of a broader group best described as HEALTH CARE consultants, which includes midwives (Exod 1:15-16), prophets (2 Kgs 20:1-7), and priests (Lev 13), and perhaps a wide array of pagan sorcerers (Deut 18:10-11). Attitudes toward physicians range from positive (Luke in Col 4:14; Sir 38) to negative (2 Chr 16:12; Job 13:4; Luke 8:43).

Archaeologically, the activities of HEALING specialists are reflected in trephinated skulls from various periods and in the implantation of a bronze wire in a tooth at Horvat En Ziq, a Nabatean fortress in the northern Negev in the Hellenistic era. Attested medical instruments include bone spatulas at Tell Jemmeh (near Gaza, early 1st millennium BCE), and possible probes and medicinal vessels at Bethsaida in the Roman period.

Bibliography: Hector Avalos. *Health Care and the Rise of Christianity* (1999).

HECTOR AVALOS

PI [π p, Π P]. The seventeenth letter of the Greek alphabet, based on the Phoenician *pe. *See* ALPHABET.

PI-BESETH p*i*-bee'sith [פִּי־בֶסֶת pi-veseth; Βουβάστος Boubastos]. An Egyptian city in the eastern Nile Delta mentioned along with ON in Ezekiel's oracle against Egypt (Ezek 30:17). The archaeological site (Tell Basta) demonstrates that the city thrived from the Fourth Dynasty through the Roman period. The city was the chief cultic site of the cat-headed goddess Bastet and the home of Libyan pharaohs of the Twenty-second and Twenty-third Dynasties such as SHISHAK. Based on its Greek name, it is also known as Bubastis.

STEVE COOK

PICK [בָּחַר bakhar, חָרִיץ kharits; τρυγάω trygaō]. The NRSV translates kharits as an iron "pick" (2 Sam 12:31; 1 Chr 20:3), suggesting a tool with a sharp point attached to a handle. Semitic cognate words indicate a cutting instrument, although not necessarily a pick (*see* TOOLS). As a verb, *pick* means to pluck (Job 30:4; Jer 43:12; Luke 6:44) or select, especially in a military context (e.g., Exod 14:7; Judg 20:16; 2 Sam 10:9; 2 Chr 13:3; Dan 11:15).

KEVIN A. WILSON

PICTURE [דְּמוּת demuth]. An image or likeness of someone or something. The term appears in Ezek 23:15 describing Assyrian bas-reliefs depicting Babylonian officers. It is the same term used to denote the image of God in Gen 1:26. In 2 Esd 5:37, in a dialogue between Ezra and an angel, the angel indicates that Ezra can no more understand God's ways than he can produce a "picture of a voice."

DEREK E. WITTMAN

PIETY [יִרְאָה yir᾽ah; δικαιοσύνη dikaiosynē, εὐσέβεια eusebeia]. Piety is devout reverence for God portrayed through righteousness. The OT view of piety is "fear of the Lord," understood as active obedience to God (Gen 20:11; 2 Sam 23:3; Prov 1:7; 8:13; Isa 11:2-3; 33:6; compare Job 22:4). Piety in the NT includes appropriate, well-intentioned, outward religious activity. Jesus declared that overt "piety" for popularity will go unrewarded (Matt 6:1-18). Piety may have produced miracles, although this is denied by Peter (Acts 3:12). Piety is the result of a personal relationship with Jesus Christ, not self-imposed righteousness that is helpless for personal discipline (Col 2:23). *See* HOLY, HOLINESS, NT.

MICHAEL G. VANZANT

PIGEON [יוֹנָה yonah; περιστερά peristera]. Pigeons are members of the family Columbidae and are found in some 300 species worldwide. In the Bible, the terms DOVE and *pigeon* are often interchangeable and sometimes indistinguishable.

Pigeons are about 12 in. long and have plump bodies that were prized in Israel as food. The rich provided large cotes of pottery for their domesticated birds. People of moderate means had cotes of oven-baked clay, while the poor often cut holes over their house doors to allow pigeons to enter (Isa 60:8). Pigeons were used for sacrifice (Gen 15:9), especially by the poor in Israel without the means to offer larger animals (Lev 1:14). They were sold in the Second Temple (Mark 11:15 and par.). In Lev 5:7-10, the poor were to bring "two turtledoves or two pigeons" for a sin offering and a burnt offering. Pigeons or turtledoves were brought for purification of women after childbirth (Lev 12:6-8; Luke 2:24). *See* BIRDS OF THE BIBLE; TURTLEDOVE.

ROBERT E. VAN VOORST

PI-HAHIROTH p*i*'huh-h*i*'roth [פִּי הַחִירֹת pi hakhiroth]. A location in the eastern Nile delta between MIGDOL and the Sea of Reeds, east of Baal-zephon (Exod 14:2; Num 33:7). The Israelites reach Pi-hahiroth after turning back from Etham, a site probably located in the Wadi Tumilat (Exod 13:20). Pi-hahiroth was the last place the Israelites stayed before crossing the Sea of Reeds (Num 33:7). The meaning of the name Pi-hahiroth is unknown. Some have attempted to find an Egyptian derivation. One of the more plausible is Donald Redford's proposal of p3-ḥ3-rty, "the place of the widow," which might suggest a site near Lake Timsah. Others have put forth the Egyptian pr-ḥwt-ḥrt, a place near Pi-Ramesses. If pi is the Hebrew "mouth," the second element could correspond to a Semitic word for "canal." "Mouth [entrance] of the canal" would make sense as a toponym, as canals were built by the Egyptians in the eastern delta.

Bibliography: Donald B. Redford. "An Egyptian Perspective on the Exodus Narrative." *Egypt, Israel, and Sinai: Archaeological and Historical Relationships in the Biblical Period.* Anson Rainey, ed. (1987) 137–61.

KEVIN A. WILSON

PILATE, ACTS OF. The *Acts of Pilate*, also known as the *Gospel of Nicodemus*, is the combination of an account of the trial, death, and resurrection/ascension of Jesus (chaps. 1–16), with an account of Christ's descent into hell to release the righteous dead that had a major influence on medieval art and literature. The two accounts were originally independent apocrypha originating sometime in the 5th–6th cent. CE. Early fascination with an account of the crucifixion from Pilate's perspective is evident in references to such an apocryphon in Justin Martyr (*1 Apol.* 35.48), Epiphanius (*Pan.* 50.1.5–8), and Eusebius (*Hist. eccl.* 9.5.1), who knows it as an anti-Christian document. None of these can be securely identified with the known *Acts of Pilate* versions, which survive in various Latin text types as well as in Greek. Nothing supports the fictive claim to be the translation of a Hebrew original.

Acts of Pilate supplements the passion and resurrection material taken from the canonical Gospels with a variety of imaginative expansions and details. For example, when Jesus is brought into Pilate's presence, the legionary standards bow down. Pilate engages in an extensive judicial inquiry. NICODEMUS is the most prominent Jewish figure to testify on Jesus' behalf (5.1). Other Gospel figures appear as well: the paralytic (John 5:1-9); blind Bartimaeus (Mark 10:46-52); and the woman with the hemorrhage (here named Bernice or Veronica; Mark 5:25-34). Thus the leaders' charges that Jesus deserves death as a magician or devil-possessed exorcist are rejected. They introduce other charges: Jesus' claim to be king and Son of God. Other Jews report to Pilate the story of the magi's arrival in Herod's court (*Acts Pil.* 9.2). Pilate lashes out at the Jewish leaders for ingratitude toward their benefactors with the stubbornness of Israel in the wilderness as his prime example (*Acts Pil.* 9.2). *See* PILATE, PONTIUS.

Testimony to the resurrection occupies a section (*Acts Pil.* 12–16) that may have been added to an earlier passion account. Joseph of Arimathea, persecuted by Jewish leaders for burying Jesus, is rescued from jail by Jesus (*see* JOSEPH, JOSEPHITES). Jewish leaders receive detailed reports, first from the tomb guard who also questioned the women; then from a Galilean priest, teacher, and Levite who witness Jesus' encounter with his disciples there and his commissioning them to preach the gospel (including Mark 16:16-18). Nicodemus and Joseph again speak in defense of the truth about Jesus' resurrection (*Acts Pil.* 14–15). In addition, two sons of the aged Simeon (Luke 2:25), who had been raised from death by Jesus, also testify (*Acts Pil.* 16). The assembly concludes that if Jesus' movement endures fifty years, it will be eternal. A doxology praising God brings this section to an end.

The tradition about Jesus "harrowing hell" has been patched onto the passion and resurrection account by using Simeon's sons as witnesses. (The sons are named Karinos and Leucius, perhaps taken from the alleged author of *Acts of John.*) The righteous dead are baptized after Jesus frees them from Hades. *See* APOCRYPHA, NT; UNDERWORLD, DESCENT INTO THE.

PHEME PERKINS

PILATE, PONTIUS pon´shuhs pi´luht [Πόντιος Πιλᾶτος **Pontios Pilatos**]. The Roman prefect of Judea (26–37 CE) who crucified Jesus of Nazareth.

A. Background
B. Prefect of Judea
C. Jewish Sources
D. New Testament Sources
E. Last Years
Bibliography

A. Background

Little is known of Pilate prior to his arrival in the small yet turbulent province of Judea in 26 CE. He belonged to the equestrian class (a Roman knight) and probably attracted the Roman emperor Tiberius Caesar's attention through distinguished military service. He may have owed his appointment to L. Aelius Seianus, the prefect of the Praetorian Guard and Tiberius' confidant (whose alleged anti-Semitism is now disputed); though when Seianus fell in 31 CE, Pilate was not close enough to be affected.

B. Prefect of Judea

As the fifth Roman PREFECT of Judea, Pilate's main role was to maintain law and order in a territory subjugated only twenty years earlier (*see* JUDEA, JUDEANS). This is clear from his military title (*praefectus*), confirmed by a mutilated inscription found in CAESAREA MARITIMA in 1961. He commanded only auxiliary troops (five infantry cohorts and one cavalry regiment), but in difficult circumstances could call upon the legions under the neighboring and more powerful Syrian legate. Like earlier governors, Pilate made his capital in the predominantly Gentile coastal city of

Caesarea Maritima. Most troops were stationed here, while smaller garrisons were dispersed throughout the province, including a permanent cohort in Jerusalem. During festivals, Pilate arrived in the holy city with reinforcements (though the heightened military presence often created friction).

Rome had few officials in the provinces; routine administration was largely left to the Jewish priestly aristocracy in Jerusalem (*see* SANHEDRIN). The right to select high priests fell to the Roman governor (or perhaps now the Syrian Legate), but Pilate made no new appointments. Joseph CAIAPHAS was already in post when he arrived, and outlasted him by a couple of months. Presumably the two men worked reasonably well together.

Pilate possessed *imperium* or supreme magisterial power in the region. Whether, or to what extent, local courts had the right of capital punishment is disputed. Quite possibly they could execute for infringements against the Jewish Law while Pilate concerned himself with matters of national security. As governor, he also had financial duties: he oversaw the collection of taxes and, on three occasions, struck bronze coins (29/30, 30/31, 31/32 CE). Although these included symbols from the Roman cult (a wine bowl and an augur's wand), they do not seem to have been unduly offensive and were used well into the reign of Agrippa I (41–44 CE). *See* PALESTINE, ADMINISTRATION OF.

C. Jewish Sources

The fullest account of Pilate comes from Josephus, who describes his term of office in both the *Jewish War* (written ca. 75 CE) and *Antiquities of the Jews* (ca. 95 CE; *see* JOSEPHUS, FLAVIUS). A further event is described by Pilate's contemporary Philo of Alexandria in his *Embassy to Gaius* (written ca. 41 CE). Neither writer is flattering toward Pilate, and both use him to further their own rhetorical aims. When these are borne in mind, however, the broad sequence of events can be reconstructed.

One winter (perhaps his first in the province), Pilate replaced the garrison at Jerusalem with one whose standards contained (presumably honorific) images of the emperor (*J.W.* 2.169–74; *Ant.* 18.55–59). Regarding this as a contravention of the second commandment, the people protested before Pilate in Caesarea for five days. Finally, impressed by the strength of popular feeling, Pilate agreed to have the standards (i.e., the regiment) removed. The incident has the air of a new ruler testing public opinion; Pilate probably thought it ridiculous that standards that were perfectly acceptable in other parts of Judea were not tolerated in Jerusalem and absurd that provincials should dictate to him on military matters. He began his rule, then, with a firm, uncompromising attitude, though it is to his credit that he backed down in the face of overwhelming public outrage.

Some time later, Pilate extended a Jerusalem aqueduct. The project drew on Temple money and was perhaps planned as a cooperative venture between Roman and Jewish leaders. Things, however, soon soured: Josephus suggests that Pilate drained the money and notes that the people did not agree to the plan, leaving it unclear whether indignation concerned the aqueduct's route or the construction itself. When Pilate visited Jerusalem (presumably for a feast), he was met by rioting crowds. Anticipating trouble, however, he had dispersed plainclothesmen who, at an appointed signal, beat the rioters with clubs. According to Josephus, the fatalities were high (*J.W.* 2.175–77; *Ant.* 18.60–62).

The third incident is the execution of Jesus of Nazareth in a famous passage known as the *Testimonium Flavianum* (*Ant.* 18.63–64; also Tacitus, *Ann.* 15.44). This passage has undoubtedly been worked over by Christian editors, though the note that Pilate sent Jesus to the cross at the instigation of "the first men among us" may be Josephan and concurs with the Gospels (see §D). There is nothing improbable in Pilate's wishing to interrogate Jesus (however briefly): the case of John the Baptist was very similar (*Ant.* 18.118; Mark 6:17-29 par.) as was that of Jesus ben Ananias (*J.W.* 6.300–309). A messianic claimant with a following in the crowded Passover city was a clear threat to security, and Pilate would doubtless wish to eliminate him before he could cause an uprising (*see* MESSIAH, JEWISH).

About the same time, according to Philo (*Embassy* 299–305), Pilate set up aniconic gilded shields in honor of Tiberius inside the Roman *praetorium* (or headquarters) in Jerusalem (*see* TIBERIUS CAESAR). The reference to Tiberius' full name (including "son of the divine Augustus") within the holy city, however, caused offense, and resentment grew until four Herodian princes (presumably Antipas, Philip, and two others) were delegated to complain to Pilate (*see* HEROD, FAMILY). When the prefect refused to dismantle the shields, they took their grievances to Tiberius, who ordered them to be moved to the temple of Augustus at Caesarea. Philo's account is highly negative toward Pilate, describing him as a spiteful and angry person and referring to his venality, violence, thefts, assaults, abusive behavior, frequent executions of untried prisoners, and his endless savage ferocity. These insults, however, are stereotypical descriptions by Philo for people who act against the Jewish Law and need to be treated with some caution. This incident is often dated to Seianus' fall: Pilate's wish to honor the emperor and his reluctance to remove the shields would fit this turbulent time. The building of the Tiberieum at Caesarea—to which the above inscription was attached—may also date to this period.

Josephus' final incident recounts the end of Pilate's term of office (*Ant.* 18.85–105). A prophet claiming to be the Samaritan Messiah persuaded large numbers of people to accompany him up Mount Gerizim. When armed crowds gathered, Pilate, fearing insurrection, sent his cavalry against them, taking many prisoners and executing the ringleaders. Subsequently, the Samaritan leaders complained to Vitellius, the legate of Syria, explaining that they were refugees from Pilate's persecution rather than insurrectionists. Vitellius referred the matter to the emperor. Pilate hurried to Rome, arriving shortly after Tiberius' death (March 37) to find Gaius (Caligula) on the throne.

D. New Testament Sources

Most references to Pilate in the NT are brief and factual (e.g., Luke 3:1; Acts 3:13; 4:27; 13:28; 1 Tim 6:13). The fullest accounts are the descriptions of Jesus' Roman trial in the Gospels, though each has its own emphasis (*see* TRIAL OF JESUS).

Mark 15:1 introduces Pilate abruptly with no explanation (presumably readers were familiar with his name and role). The trial has two scenes. In the first (15:2-5), Pilate asks Jesus if he is the King of the Jews, to which Jesus remains silent, and Pilate is amazed (details that may have been inspired by Isa 52–53). In the second (15:6-15), the people ask Pilate to release one prisoner to them. When, stirred up by the chief priests, they demand Barabbas, Pilate asks them what he should do with "the King of the Jews," and they shout for crucifixion. Mark places most responsibility for Jesus' death on the Jewish leaders, but the parallels between the Roman and Jewish trials suggest that Pilate is not exonerated.

Matthew 27:1-2, 11-26 follows Mark closely, though a number of additions intensify Jewish involvement and lessen Pilate's responsibility: the dream by PILATE'S WIFE (27:19); Pilate's washing of his hands (27:14, a declaration of his own innocence based on Deut 21:1-9); and the cry of "the people as a whole" (27:25).

Luke briefly mentions the "Galileans whose blood Pilate had mingled with their sacrifices" (13:1). Nothing further is known of this, though it may be a reference to the incident with the aqueduct (see §C) and could explain the enmity between Pilate and Antipas (Luke 23:12—assuming the detail is historical). In Luke's trial narrative (23:1-25), the Jewish leaders bring Jesus to Pilate on three specific charges: perverting the nation, forbidding tribute to Caesar, and claiming to be Christ a king (23:2). The Gospel has already shown each of these to be false, underlining Jesus' innocence. Pilate in Luke is weak and vacillating; he learns that Jesus belongs to Galilee and so sends him to Antipas (who is in Jerusalem for the Passover, 23:6-12). When Jesus returns, Pilate says that he finds Jesus innocent, as too does Antipas (providing two witnesses to Jesus' innocence; Deut 17:6; 19:15). Yet Pilate does not have the strength of his convictions: his every verdict is overturned by the crowd, who finally have the murderer Barabbas released and Jesus crucified.

John's Pilate is the lengthiest and most complex figure (John 18:28–19:16). This Gospel presents seven scenes in which Pilate moves between the Jewish chief priests waiting outside and Jesus inside the *praetorium.* The reason for the movement is perhaps not so much to signal the indecision of Pilate as the convention in John (and biblical writing generally) to reduce powerful scenes to two main figures. As the narrative proceeds, it is clear that it is Pilate rather than Jesus who is on trial: he quickly shows that he is not on the side of Truth, a man more interested in his standing with the emperor than justice (19:12-13).

E. Last Years

Pilate's term of office was one of the longest of any governor of Judea (matched only by his predecessor Gratus' eleven years). To some extent this was because Tiberius disliked changing governors too frequently (*Ant.* 18.170–73; Tacitus, *Ann.* 4.6), but Pilate clearly could not have lasted so long if his governorship were as repressive as Philo's list of atrocities suggests. What comes across from the sources is a reasonably able governor, perhaps with little understanding of or sympathy for the people he governed and capable of acts of insensitivity, yet also able to compromise and back down in the interests of peace.

What became of Pilate is unknown. The fact that he did not return to Judea does not necessarily mean that Gaius upheld the charges against him; after more than a decade in the province, he may have simply thought that it was time for a new commission. Where history finished, Christian imagination began, and Pilate's life (and death) was a popular topic in both apocryphal literature and legend (e.g., *see* PILATE, ACTS OF). While the Eastern church, dwelling on his proclamation of Jesus' innocence, regarded him favorably (he was canonized in the Coptic Church; his feast date is June 25th), the Western church saw him as the enemy of Christ and delighted in devising ingenious and gruesome ends for him.

Bibliography: Helen K. Bond. *Pontius Pilate in History and Interpretation* (1998); John J. Rousseau and R. Arav. *Jesus and His World* (1995).

HELEN K. BOND

PILATE'S WIFE. An unnamed woman, referred to as "his wife" (hē gynē autou ἡ γυνὴ αὐτοῦ) in Matt 27:19, but clearly the wife of Pontius Pilate, the Roman procurator of Judea (26–36 CE), a position that made him judge in Jesus' trial and execution (*see* PILATE, PONTIUS). She sent word to Pilate to disassociate himself from Jesus because a DREAM about Jesus had troubled her sleep. Literarily, her dream forms a bracket with the dream of the MAGI (Matt 2:12), both of which are God's revelations to non-Jews that absolve them of culpability in actions against Jesus.

EMILY R. CHENEY

PILDASH pil'dash [פִּלְדָּשׁ pildash]. The sixth of eight sons born to NAHOR and his wife MILCAH, and thus Pildash was a nephew of Abraham (Gen 22:22). Rather than a person, the name may be eponymous, representing a tribe situated possibly in northern Arabia.

PILGRIMAGE [חַג khagh, מִקְרָא miqra']. The concept of pilgrimage—a journey to a foreign or holy place—holds that space is not homogeneous and provides many societies with liminality, a marginal experience of transition and potentiality. Pilgrimage to Zion, God's royal residence (Pss 46:4 [Heb. 46:5]; 76:2 [Heb. 76:3]), offers contact with the divine, mediated through sensory experience.

Exodus 23:14-17 lists three pilgrimage feasts—the Feast of Unleavened Bread, Feast of Harvest, and Feast of Ingathering—during which Israelite males must appear before the Lord, presumably at local sanctuaries (*see* PASSOVER AND FEAST OF UNLEAVENED BREAD). In Deut 16:1-17, Passover has replaced Unleavened Bread and is celebrated in the Temple; the Feast of Ingathering now receives its "booths" (possibly the tent camps of pilgrims to Jerusalem; *see* BOOTHS, FEAST OR FESTIVAL OF). This calendar shows marked centralization: the three festivals are observed in Jerusalem itself, and not only men but also women, children, servants, and sojourners must come (Deut 16:11, 14). Nevertheless, there is evidence the Northern Kingdom resisted this centralization (2 Chr 30:10-11).

Leviticus 23:4-44 suggests Passover and Weeks no longer required pilgrimage by the postexilic period but could be celebrated in every settlement, and Ezra allows Booths likewise to be celebrated in individual houses (Neh 8:13-18). SONGS OF ASCENT (esp. Pss 120, 123–131) are the postexilic hymns from such pilgrimages. Postexilic eschatology describes Jerusalem as the object of pilgrimage of all nations, who come to receive wisdom and bring wealth (Pss 76:11 [Heb. 76:12]; 87:4-5; 102; Isa 2:2-4; 60:1-7; Mic 4:1-4; Hag 2:6-9; Zech 14:16-19).

In the 1st cent., Josephus mentions large pilgrimage crowds in Jerusalem (*J.W.* 1.253; 2.280; 6.423–425; *Ant.* 14.337). Economic conditions had changed, and merchants could leave home for lengthy travel. Roads, cisterns, and ritual baths were repaired for each pilgrimage, Jerusalem homes opened for guests, tent cities arose (*m. Sheq.* 1.1), and no rent could be charged for pilgrims. Riots were common in such situations (Matt 26:5; Mark 14:1-2; *Ant.* 17.204–209). *See* WORSHIP, OT.

ROBERT D. MILLER II

PILHA pil'hah [פִּלְחָא pilkha']. One of the leaders of the people in postexilic Jerusalem who signed Ezra's pact to put away foreign wives (Neh 10:24).

PILLAR [עַמּוּד 'ammudh; מַצֵּבָה matsevah; στῦλος stylos]. The term *pillar* is used in two distinct ways in the OT, and this usage parallels almost perfectly two separate Hebrew words. The term 'ammudh refers to an architectural pillar, while matsevah designates a cultic object. In the NT, *pillar* (stylos) refers metaphorically to an architectural feature.

The Hebrew word 'ammudh is used almost exclusively for a pillar or a column as an architectural term, irrespective of the material of the pillar. In the biblical text, a pillar may be of wood (Exod 26:32; 1 Kgs 7:6), stone (Esth 1:6), or metal (1 Kgs 7:15).

That the pillar was a major structural element is shown in the Samson narrative. The blinded Samson is brought to a palace or temple of the Philistines and made to stand between the pillars (Judg 16:25-26). He pulled down the two pillars "on which the house rest[ed]," causing the roof (and possibly an upper story) to fall, killing himself and 3,000 Philistines (Judg 16:29-30). Such structural pillars are a typical feature of monumental structures in the ANE. Ceiling or roof beams were not long enough to span the entire width of a large structure, so pillars were set (often in pairs or rows) in a large room to hold the ends of the shorter horizontal ceiling or roof beams. Other biblical examples include the tabernacle (Exod 26:32; 27:9-17) and Solomon's palace (1 Kgs 7:2-6). The Solomonic Temple had two pillars 18 cubits tall in front of the vestibule (1 Kgs 7:15-22). There is debate whether the two bronze pillars of the Solomonic Temple, JACHIN AND BOAZ, were freestanding or structural.

Archaeological evidence of structural pillars has been found in numerous palaces and temples from the Early Bronze Age onward in Canaan. Typically, only the base for the pillar is present, but such bases clearly had a support pillar originally. Examples include the Early Bronze palace at AI and temples at MEGIDDO. Middle Bronze and Late Bronze examples include temples at HAZOR, Shechem (*see* SHECHEM, SHECHEMITES), and LACHISH, and palaces/dwellings at Megiddo, Tell Beit Mirsim, Tel Batash, and Tel Aphek. In these examples, the pillars were located in large rooms, and, as ceiling or roof supports, permitted larger open spaces without support walls. Such open spaces were perfect for ceremonial occasions involving larger groups of people.

In Iron Age Israel, pillared buildings were a common feature, in both domestic dwellings and in larger administrative complexes. A typical house of the Iron Age had two or three parallel long rooms or spaces and a broad room to the rear. Frequently, the structure would have a row of pillars defining one of the long room spaces. These pillars would support the beams for the ceiling or roof.

The larger pillared buildings, usually tripartite, are associated with administrative functions. Often located near the city gate and other administrative structures, these buildings have been variously described as stables, barracks, storehouses, and even shopping centers. While the function of the building may not be definite, the pillars definitely served a structural function of supporting beams for the roof or ceiling of the building, while giving maximum open space within the structure.

In a figurative usage, the OT speaks of a "pillar of cloud/smoke" and a "pillar of fire" that guided the Hebrews when they left Egypt and journeyed to Mount Sinai (Exod 13:21-22). The pillar of cloud/smoke also stood at the entrance to the tent of meeting when Yahweh met with Moses there (Exod 33:9-10; Num 12:5; Deut 31:15).

The second Hebrew word translated as pillar is **matsevah**, a term used exclusively for a pillar with covenantal, memorial, or cultic significance. The same word may be translated as "standing stone." These pillars may be unworked stones or shaped (often with a rounded top), but normally without inscriptions and designs that denote stelae (*see* STELE).

The uses of the term **matsevah** in the Jacob narrative demonstrate three meanings of the term: a marker of a theophany, a marker of a covenant, and as a memorial/grave marker. Jacob, fleeing from his brother, Esau, stops at the site that will become Bethel. His theophanic night dream led him to set up the stone that had served as his pillow as a cultic pillar (Gen 28:18). Jacob specifically states, "this stone, which I have set up for a pillar, shall be God's house" (Gen 28:22). Later in the narrative, as Jacob is returning to Canaan with his family, he and Laban, his father-in-law, make a covenant with each other. As part of that covenant they set up a pillar and a heap of stones as witness to the covenant (Gen 31:45-52). They both also call upon God as a witness (Gen 31:49, 53). After Jacob returns to Canaan, Rachel dies in childbirth. Jacob sets up a pillar as a memorial or burial marker (Gen 35:20).

In the passage from Gen 31, both the pillar and God are called to be a witness to the covenant between Laban and Jacob. That raises the question of the relationship of the pillar to God. Is the pillar there for God to see and remember the covenant or does the pillar represent God in some manner? That very question is the issue for most of the OT references to pillar.

A row of large pillars (up to 10 ft. in height) discovered by Macalister at Gezer (*see* GEZER, GEZERITES) has been interpreted as a Canaanite high place with the pillars having cultic significance or commemorating a covenant between participants represented by the pillars. The pillars could then represent the parties themselves or the deities of the parties who witnessed the covenant.

Jacob's setting up the pillar for Rachel's burial marker is the only biblical example that specifically mentions a burial marker. However, the pillar Absalom sets up for himself, since he has no son (2 Sam 18:18), seems to indicate a similar purpose of being a memorial. Likewise in the Ugaritic AQHAT epic, Danel is concerned because he has no son to set up a memorial pillar for him.

The primary usage of *pillar* in the OT is for a cultic object, and most frequently for pillars dedicated to pagan deities. The setting up and worship of such pillars is strictly prohibited. Among the regular injunctions from the Law and from the Prophets is that the Israelites are to pull down or destroy such pillars, and to avoid any worship of such. In Exod 23:24, the worship of pagan gods, especially their images, is prohibited; such idols are to be demolished and the pillars broken in pieces. Here the idols and pillars are in parallelism; the pillars represent the deities. Often pillars are mentioned along with altars and asherim as objects to be destroyed (Exod 34:13; Deut 7:5; 12:3; 2 Chr 14:3 [Heb. 14:2]).

Yet other passages allow pillars to be erected (as Jacob did to God in Gen 28:18-22 above). In Exod 24:4 Moses built an altar and set up twelve pillars according to the twelve tribes of Israel (these pillars represent the tribes). Isaiah 19:19 speaks of a future day when there will be an altar for Yahweh in the midst of the land of Egypt, and a pillar for Yahweh at its border (these pillars represent Yahweh).

Numerous pillars and groups of pillars have been found throughout sites in the Middle East. Many have been found associated with sanctuaries or cultic sites, such as those found at Hazor in the Middle Bronze shrine in Area C and temple area on the citadel, in the Middle Bronze temple at Shechem, in the Iron Age gate shrines at Dan (*see* DAN, TELL), and in the Israelite sanctuary at ARAD. At Arad, one pillar was discovered *in situ* in the Holy of Holies along with a second one that had merely fallen over from its original location. Since these two pillars were located in the Holy of Holies, they are interpreted as representing the deity or deities worshiped at Arad. Numerous groups of pillars have been discovered in the southern areas of Israel and Jordan. These pillars may represent deities or worshipers; the pillars in small groups of two or three may well represent deities, the larger groups of ten or so probably represent worshipers and may have had offerings placed at their base for the deities.

In the NT, *pillar* is used metaphorically as a symbol of strength. In 1 Tim 3:15, the household of God is called a "pillar and bulwark of truth," and in Rev 3:12, those who remain faithful to Christ will become pillars in the temple of God.

Bibliography: Uzi Avner. "Sacred Stones in the Desert." *BAR* 27 (May/June 2001) 30–41; Doron Ben-Ami. "Mysterious Standing Stones—What Do These Ubiquitous Things Mean?" *BAR* 32 (March/April 2006) 38–45; Carl F. Graesser. "Standing Stones in Ancient Palestine." *BA* 35 (1972) 34–63; Larry Herr. "Tripartite Pillared Buildings and the Market Place in Iron Age Palestine." *BASOR* 272 (1988) 47–67; Zeev Herzog. *Archaeology of the City* (1997); Zeev Herzog. "Israelite City Planning Seen in the Light of Beer-Sheba and Arad Excavations." *Expedition* 20 (1978) 38–43; Zeidan A. Kafafi and Hugo Gajus Scheltema. "Megalithic Structures in Jordan." *Mediterranean Archaeology* *and Archaeometry* 5 (December 2005) 5–22; Aharon Kempinski and Ronny Reich. *The Architecture of Ancient Israel* (1992); Elizabeth C. LaRocca-Pitts. *The Significance of Israelite Cultic Items in the Bible and Its Early Interpreters* (2001); Theodore J. Lewis. "Divine Images and Aniconism in Ancient Israel." *JAOS* 118 (1998) 36–53; Tryggve N. D. Mettinger. *No Graven Image? Israelite Aniconism in Its Ancient Near Eastern Context* (1995); Lawrence E. Stager. "The Shechem Temple." *BAR* 29 (July/August 2003) 26–35, 66–69; G. R. H. Wright. *Ancient Building in South Syria and Palestine* (1997).

JOEL F. DRINKARD JR.

PILLAR OF CLOUD AND FIRE [עַמּוּד עָנָן ʿammudh ʿanan, עַמּוּד אֵשׁ ʿammudh ʾesh]. The pillar of cloud (ʿammudh ʿanan) by day and of fire (ʾesh) by night first occurs in Exod 13:21-22, a theophany of Yahweh guiding Israel through the wilderness (the same pillar with two aspects, Exod 14:24). Exodus 14:19 equates the pillar with the accompanying ANGEL (see Exod 23:20). Yahweh communicates with Moses in the cloud, which descends at the entrance of the tent of meeting (e.g., Exod 33:9-11). This cloud, associated with the ark of the covenant, directs Israel's route through the wilderness (Num 10:33-36). These passages belong to the exilic version of the Pentateuch reflected in Deuteronomy (see Deut 31:14-15).

In the postexilic P edition, the cloud guiding Israel is related to the TABERNACLE (Num 9:15-22); it attests to, but veils, the presence of the glory of God (Exod 40:34-38). Aaron can approach only in the cloud of incense, kindled from the fire of the altar of burnt offering (Lev 16:12-13) provided by God (Lev 9:24). Thus, Isa 4:5 identifies the pillar of cloud and fire with the column of smoke and flame of the perpetual burnt offering in the Jerusalem Temple. The pillar of cloud is a warning in 1 Cor 10:1-2. *See* CLOUD, CLOUDS; DIVINE PRESENCE; FIRE; GLORY, GLORIFY; THEOPHANY IN THE OT.

WILLIAM JOHNSTONE

PILLAR OF SALT. *See* DEAD SEA; LOT'S WIFE.

PILLAR, OAK OF THE. *See* OAK OF THE PILLAR.

PILLARS, HALL OF. *See* HALL.

PILOT [חֹבֵל khovel; εὐθύνων euthynōn, κυβερνήτης kybernētēs]. A person skilled in directing a boat or a ship on its intended course and involved in maritime trade (Ezek 27:8, 27-29; Acts 27:11). It is metaphorically used to refer to the priest ELEAZAR's speaking with self-control in the midst of persecution (4 Macc 7:1) and as part of a different metaphor to illustrate the power of a person's tongue (Jas 3:4). *See* SHIPS AND SAILING IN THE NT; SHIPS AND SAILING IN THE OT.

EMILY R. CHENEY

PILTAI pil'tī [פִּלְטַי piltay]. Head of the priestly house of MOADIAH in the time of the postexilic high priest JOIAKIM (Neh 12:17).

PIN [יָתֵד yathedh, נָכָה nakhah]. A weaver uses a pin to fasten threads securely to the loom's beam. DELILAH attempted to use her loom as a trap, interweaving Samson's hair into the warp and tying it with a pin (Judg 16:14). Saul sought to kill David by pinning him to the wall with a spear (1 Sam 18:11; 19:10; compare 26:8). *See* NAIL; TOOLS.

VICTOR H. MATTHEWS

PINE, PINE TREE [בְּרוֹתִים berothim, תְּאַשּׁוּר teʾashur]. Pine trees have long needles and characteristic woody cones that remain complete, unlike the disintegrating CEDAR cone. The tall, slender trunks yield soft, whitish timber. In modern times pine timber is used commonly, but in biblical times it was favored for woodwork for grand houses, royal palaces (Song 1:17), and the holy sanctuary (Isa 60:13). Imported pine, like cedarwood, would have been expensive and was symbolic of wealth because it was not easily obtained. Pine trees were one of several resin-fragrant evergreen trees envisaged as usurping the dry, leafless desert species in Isa 41:19, an image of the bounty and richness to come.

There is confusion among botanists and translators as to the identity of several evergreen coniferous trees in Hebrew. In Isa 44:14 ʾoren (אֹרֶן) is rendered "cedar" (NRSV, NEB; KJV, "ash"), although elsewhere cedar is the translation of ʾerez (אֶרֶז). This once mentioned ʾoren may be the Aleppo Pine, *Pinus halepensis*, rather than the cedar. This pine tree is the only one native to Israel, and even that was not common in biblical times in spite of its abundance on the hills of modern Israel. The Calabrian Pine, *Pinus brutia*, is abundant in Lebanon and Cyprus from where it was imported into Jerusalem or used locally for shipbuilding (Ezek 27:6). Another species of pine, the Umbrella or Stone Pine, *Pinus pinea*, occurs in Lebanon, Cyprus, and westward where the well-known edible seeds are greatly esteemed; this is probably the fruitful evergreen tree mentioned in Hos 14:8 (NRSV, "CYPRESS"; KJV, "fir"). *See* PLANE TREE; PLANTS OF THE BIBLE.

F. NIGEL HEPPER

PINNACLE [שֶׁמֶשׁ shemesh; πτερύγιον pterygion]. The highest point or peak of a formation. In a message of comfort to Jerusalem, the LORD promises to adorn the city's pinnacles with rubies (Isa 54:12). In Matt 4:5 and Luke 4:9, the devil challenges Jesus to throw himself down from the pinnacle of the Jerusalem Temple to test the protection of God and God's angels. Here the Temple pinnacle is not only a high place but also a significant symbol of power. *See* DEVIL, DEVILS; TEMPLE, JERUSALEM.

KATHY R. MAXWELL

PINON pī´non [פִּינֹן pinon]. One of the clans of Edom descended from Esau (Gen 36:41; 1 Chr 1:52). The clan may be connected with PUNON, listed among the locations where the people of Israel camped in the wilderness (Num 33:42-43). Punon is often associated with Khirbet Fenan, south of the Dead Sea.

KEVIN A. WILSON

PIPE. *See* MUSICAL INSTRUMENTS.

PIRAM pī´ruhm [פִּרְאָם pirʾam]. King Piram of JARMUTH (Josh 10:3) is one of the five kings of the AMORITES who united to attack Gibeon for making a treaty with Joshua. The Israelites defeated the Amorites, eventually capturing and executing all five kings (Josh 10:1-27).

PIRATHON pihr´uh-thon [פִּרְעָתוֹן pirʿathon; Φαραθώμ Pharathōm, Φαραθών Pharathōn]. Variant PHARATHON. The significance of Pirathon for early Israel is demonstrated by its fame as the seat of government for nearly a decade during ABDON's tenure as judge in the premonarchical era (Judg 12:13-15) and as the hometown of BENAIAH, one of DAVID'S CHAMPIONS and key administrator in the days of the Davidic monarchy (2 Sam 23:30; 1 Chr 11:31; 27:14). Pirathon, situated by the biblical authors in the territory of Ephraim, is most likely preserved as modern Far'ata (southwest of Shechem), a site occupied in the Iron Age II.

Bibliography: David A. Dorsey. "Shechem and the Road Network of Central Samaria." *BASOR* 268 (1987) 57–70.

JASON R TATLOCK

PIRQE AVOTH. *See* SAYINGS OF THE FATHERS.

PISGAH, MOUNT piz´guh [פִּסְגָּה pisgah]. Mount Pisgah figures prominently in the narrative descriptions of the Israelite journey from Egypt to Canaan because it is from the "top of Pisgah" that Moses views the land of promise, albeit as one prohibited from crossing over (Deut 3:27; 34:1). The same vantage point is utilized by Balaam in seeking Yahweh's approval for cursing the Israelites, who are encamped within view of the peak (Num 23:14). The "slopes of Pisgah" (Deut 3:17; 4:49; Josh 12:3; 13:20) are sometimes interpreted as a proper name for a site in the Transjordanian tribal territory of Reuben (compare LXX, which also translates pisgah as a common noun referring to an area carved out of the mountainside). The matter is further complicated in light of Pisgah's relationship to Mount Nebo and to Mount Abarim (*see* ABARIM MOUNTAINS, NEBO, MOUNT). The latter is placed in apposition to Nebo in Deut 32:49; Pisgah and Nebo are likewise arranged in Deut 34:1. Abarim, however, is best understood as a mountain chain (Num 33:47-48), of which Nebo is a single peak. Pisgah, then, would constitute Nebo's summit.

Bibliography: Enzo Cortese and Alviero Niccacci. "Nebo in Biblical Tradition." *Mount Nebo: New Archaeological Excavations 1967–1997.* Michele Piccirillo and Eugenio Alliata, eds. (1998) 53–64.

JASON R. TATLOCK

PISHON pī´shon [פִּישׁוֹן pishon; Φισών Phisōn]. The first of four streams flowing from the river in Eden and around HAVILAH (Gen 2:11). Sirach compares the Torah, which overflows with wisdom, to the Pishon (Sir 24:23-25). *See* EDEN, GARDEN OF.

PISIDIA pi-sid´ee-uh [Πισιδία Pisidia]. A geographical region in the inland highland plateau in south-central Asia Minor mentioned in ancient texts, including two passages in the book of Acts (13:14; 14:24). Pisidia, located in the southern part of the Roman province of GALATIA, was encompassed by PHRYGIA on the north, LYCAONIA on the east, and PAMPHYLIA and LYCIA on the south and west. The latter two separated Pisidia from the Mediterranean Sea.

Pisidia was a land of challenges—topographically, culturally, and politically—for outsiders. The region, a part of the Taurus Mountains, had steep precipices that made travel through the area extremely dangerous. However, the rugged terrain was problematic in another way: it was occupied by those who rejected authority, outlaws and brigands who frequently attacked, robbed, beat, molested, or killed the outsider. Ancient records suggest that the native population had a spirit of independence with a history of turbulence, lawlessness, and violence; citizens who resisted occupation by other governments and rejected all outside authority. It is likely that Paul had Pisidia in mind, though names are not mentioned, as he spoke of his experiences in travel (2 Cor 11:26) where he faced "danger from rivers" and "danger from bandits." Though Pisidia was known for its mountainous surface, the province also had fertile valleys and freshwater lakes, a combination that encouraged the practice of agriculture and animal husbandry.

While the territory remained independent and free from occupation during the Persian and Hellenistic periods, it gained a new status in 25 BCE. AUGUSTUS declared Pisidia a part of the Roman province of Galatia and established the city of Antioch (*see* ANTIOCH, PISIDIAN) slightly outside the northeast border of Pisidia, which was at that time a military colony. Although approximately sixteen cities were named "Antioch" during the Seleucid period, Antioch of Pisidia and Antioch of Syria were the only two cities that continued to bear the name Antioch during the Roman period. Pisidia's notoriety in history derived from the fame of its capital, Antioch.

Antioch developed into an important urban center and military base during the Roman period due to its strategic location. Locally, Antioch functioned as a connecting link between other outlying military colonies established by Augustus and the international highway on which it was located. The highway was a part of a system of roads constructed by the Romans, which connected cities throughout the empire to Rome, the capital. Antioch was situated on an important section of that highway that traveled across Asia Minor from Antioch of Syria (*see* ANTIOCH, SYRIAN) on the east to EPHESUS on the west coast of Asia Minor. Antioch was Rome's leading military colony and administrative center in Pisidia, a position attained through favors it received from Rome, including the transfer of 3,000 retired veterans from Rome to Antioch. QUIRINIUS, the governor of Syria mentioned in Luke 2:2, was an honorary magistrate of Antioch and one who promoted the transfer of the veterans.

Pisidia played an important role in the spread of Christianity. Paul traveled through Pisidia two times on his first journey (Acts 13:14; 14:24). He announced a change in the direction of his ministry, a decision that established Antioch as a center of Christianity (Acts 13:46-47). We may assume that he traveled through Pisidia on his second (Acts 16:6-10) and third (Acts 18:22-23) journeys as well. During the early part of the 4th cent. CE, Antioch's status as a center of Christianity was enhanced with the conversion of Constantine to the Christian faith, which resulted in the legalizing of Christianity as a state religion.

Excavations at Antioch have provided important information concerning the impact of Rome and the Roman culture on Pisidia. While Pisidia and its people guarded against the influence of outside groups or governments, significant change came during the Roman era. The design of Antioch, the capital, was based on the Roman city plan, which included a new grid for streets, community facilities like public baths, colonnaded porticoes, civic buildings, and temples. The temple of Augustus demonstrated appreciation for the emperor, and evidence of the imperial cult. Though the new building activities began during the reign of Augustus, the majority of the construction took place during the latter part of the 1st cent. and continued on into the 2nd, 3rd, and 4th cent.

LAMOINE F. DEVRIES

PISPA pis´puh [פִּסְפָּה pispah]. One of JETHER's four sons and a descendant of Asher, head of one of Israel's tribes (1 Chr 7:38). *See* ASHER, ASHERITES.

PISTIS SOPHIA. The *Pistis Sophia*, a Coptic gnostic text found in the Askew Codex, is a manuscript that became known after the British Museum purchased it in the late 18th cent. The text, which scholars think comprises the first three of the codex's four books, records an extended post-resurrection dialogue in which Jesus, after eleven years of instruction, provides his disciples with a series of culminating discourses on various esoteric subjects. The first two books center on an explication of the nature of the mysteries of the heavenly realm, which unfolds through a discussion of Jesus' ascension into the divine world and his redemptive activity on behalf of the divine emanation, Pistis Sophia ("Faith-Wisdom"). During this ascent, Jesus meets Pistis Sophia, who had previously fallen from her home in the thirteenth aeon into the realm of chaos, where she experienced persecutions at the hands of a variety of evil powers. Passing through the lower aeons, Jesus meets Pistis Sophia below the thirteenth aeon and returns her to her original abode. Woven into this narrative are Jesus' teachings on the origin of sin and evil, the value of repentance, and the nature of postmortem existence. The disciples play an active role in these discussions and even receive illumination from Jesus that allows them to answer their own questions. Of particular interest in this text is Mary Magdalene who, along with John, surpasses all of the other disciples in knowledge (*Pistis Sophia* II.96). In addition, the text details its gnostic ideas through extensive discussions of a variety of biblical and extracanonical sources (e.g., Isa 19:3, 12; the Psalms; the Gospels; and *Pss. Sol.* 5). Scholars typically think the text derives from Egypt, where it was composed sometime during the second half of the 3rd cent. CE. *See* APOCRYPHA, NT; COPTIC LANGUAGE; GNOSTICISM.

DAVID M. REIS

PIT [בְּאֵר beʾer, בּוֹר bor, גּוּמָּץ gummats, פַּחַת pakhath, שׁוּחָה shukhah, שַׁחַת shakhath; ἄβυσσος abyssos, βόθυνος bothynos]. A hole in the ground, either naturally or humanly constructed, usually of sufficient depth that extraction is difficult or impossible. Often used literally (Gen 37:20; Matt 12:11), *pit* can also be a metaphor for destruction or disaster (Prov 26:27; Luke 6:39) or for the abode of the dead (Ps 30:3 [Heb. 30:4]; Sir 21:10). *See* ABYSS; BOTTOMLESS PIT; CISTERN; DEAD, ABODE OF THE; GEHENNA; HADES; SHEOL.

BYRON R. MCCANE

PITCH [זֶפֶת zefeth, כֹּפֶר kofer; πίσσα pissa]. A tarry substance. Pitch (**kofer**) is used to seal the inside and outside of the ARK OF NOAH (Gen 6:14). Likewise, Moses' mother plasters his BASKET with "BITUMEN and pitch" (**zefeth**) as a sealant against the river (Exod 2:3). Pitch is used metaphorically to refer to the unsightliness of God's judgment on Edom (Isa 34:9) and on Sodom and Gomorrah (2 Esd 2:9). Pitch (**pissa**) is used to stoke the fires that threaten Azariah and his companions (Sg Three 1:23); it is also used as an ingredient in Daniel's "cake" for the dragon idol, along with fat and hair (Bel 1:27).

JESSICA TINKLENBERG DEVEGA

PITCHER [גָּבִיעַ gaviʿa, כַּד kadh; κάλπη kalpē]. A pitcher is a form of pottery often associated with drawing, transporting, or storing water. Pitchers were bulbous-shaped clay jars, ranging in size from 18″–3′ in height to 12″–1½′ in diameter; size was appropriate to intended function. The word *pitcher* is only used three times in the NRSV to translate some form of pottery. In Eccl 12:6 a pitcher broken beside a fountain symbolizes the end of life. In Jer 35 God instructs Jeremiah to offer the Rechabites wine, which they had sworn by the command of their ancestor Jonadab never to consume. When Jeremiah offers the Rechabites wine in pitchers, they refuse, and God uses their obedience as an example to the wayward Judahites. In a reinterpretation of 1 Sam 23:13-17, the author of 4 Macc 3:12-18 emphasizes David's irrational desire in conflict with his reason when his men risk their lives to get David a pitcher of water he craves from a source inside the enemy's walls. David's reason wins out when he pours the water on the ground as an offering to God.

JOHN I. LAWLOR

PITFALL [פַּחַת pakhath, שִׁיחָה shikhah, שְׂבָכָה sevakhah; πρόσκομμα proskomma]. Figuratively, a pit or snare used by the arrogant to entrap the righteous (Ps 119:85; Lam 3:47), or by God for the wicked (Sir 39:24), or a lattice created by the wicked, who then step in it to their own detriment (Job 18:8). *See* PIT; TRAPS AND SNARES.

KATHY R. MAXWELL

PITHOM pi′thom [פִּתֹם pithom]. Pithom is one of two supply cities the Israelites built for the PHARAOH while they were slaves in Egypt (Exod 1:11), the other being RAAMSES, which is the Egyptian city pr-rʿ-ms-sw (Qatana-Qantir), the delta residence of the pharaohs of the Nineteenth and Twentieth Dynasties. The name *Pithom* is derived from the Egyptian pr-itm, "house of Atum," which could refer to any temple to the god Atum.

Pithom is often associated with TELL EL-MASKHUTA in the Wadi Tumilat. This identification is based on Papyrus Anastasi VI from the late 13th cent. BCE, which contains the report of a border official who notes that he has allowed a group of Shasu Bedouin from Edom to pass the fortress of Merneptah-Content-with-Truth, in ṯkw, in order that they might pasture their flocks at "the pools of pr-itm in ṯkw." Because ṯkw is the region of the Wadi Tumilat, Tell el-Maskhuta is often assumed to be Pithom. Indeed, the name Pithom is preserved in the Greek name of Maskhuta. Donald Redford has pointed out two problems with this identification, however. First, Maskhuta was not occupied prior to the 7th cent. BCE. If the biblical authors had this site in mind, therefore, its association with the exodus is anachronistic. Second, Papyrus Anastasi VI states that it is the pools of pr-itm that are in ṯkw. These could simply be pools in ṯkw belonging to a temple of Atum that was located elsewhere, since the Egyptians were unlikely to allow BEDOUIN to pasture their sheep in a temple. The most likely place for such a temple is at Pi-Rameses, as the text of Exod 1:11 explicitly connects Pithom with Pi-Rameses.

Bibliography: Donald B. Redford. "An Egyptian Perspective on the Exodus Narrative." *Egypt, Israel, and Sinai: Archaeological and Historical Relationships in the Biblical Period.* Anson Rainey, ed. (1987) 137–61.

KEVIN A. WILSON

PITHON pi′thon [פִּיתוֹן pithon]. One of Micah's four sons; a descendant of Benjamin (1 Chr 8:35; 9:41) and King Saul (1 Chr 8:33).

PITRU. *See* PETHOR.

PITY. *See* MERCY, MERCIFUL.

PLACE OF PRAYER [τόπος προσευχῆς topos proseuchēs, προσευχή proseuchē]. By the Second Temple period, Jews had begun to pray in groups at designated locations other than the Temple in Jerusalem, including Mizpah (1 Macc 3:46) and Ptolemais in Egypt (3 Macc 7:20). Paul visited a "place of prayer" near a river in PHILIPPI (Acts 16:13, 16). It is unclear whether a "place of prayer" was a SYNAGOGUE, associated with study as well as prayer.

BEATRICE J. W. LAWRENCE

PLACE OF THE SKULL. *See* GOLGOTHA.

PLAGUE [מַגֵּפָה maggefah, מַכָּה makkah, נֶגַע neghaʿ, נֶגֶף neghef; μάστιξ mastix, πληγή plēgē]. The Hebrew words generally translated *plague* are related to the verbs naghaf (נָגַף, "to strike, smite") or naghaʿ (נָגַע, "to touch") suggesting the term *affliction* might better render the culturally specific understanding of these words. In general the Hebrew words refer to epidemic events resulting in deaths, but efforts to identify each word with a specific disease are purely speculative. The unspecified plagues (neghaʿ) that God inflicted on Pharaoh and his household because of Sarai (Gen 12:17) specifically indicate skin conditions in Leviticus (13–14). However, translators render neghaʿ in Leviticus as "disease" rather than "plague." The widely known "ten plagues of Egypt" in Exodus are more often called SIGNS AND WONDERS, and only infrequently plagues. The biblical evidence indicates that the word *plague* covers a very comprehensive array of calamities such as natural disasters, sickness conditions, battle casualties, and the like (see 1 Kgs 8:37-40). Jesus is said to rid people of plagues (Luke 7:21), but the Gk. word mastigos (μάστιγος) may be better rendered "torment," "suffering," or perhaps even "wounds." The majority of NT instances of *plague* (plēgē) occur in Revelation and include fire, smoke, and sulfur (9:18, 20).

Throughout the Bible, it is clear that plagues are sent or withheld solely at the behest of God, often as punishment for Israel (Lev 26:21) or Israel's enemies (Zech 14:12; Jdt 5:12), or as a clear demonstration of God's power (e.g., the plagues in Egypt, Exod 9:14). Plagues are also often cited as signs of an end time (Luke 21:11; Rev 15:1). *See* APOCALYPTICISM; DISEASE; EXODUS, BOOK OF; PESTILENCE; PLAGUES IN EGYPT; REVELATION, BOOK OF.

JOHN J. PILCH

PLAGUES IN EGYPT. *Plagues* is the conventional term for the succession of ten disasters befalling the Egyptians in Exod 7–12. Interpreters have many ingenious suggestions in trying to explain what actually happened. The view taken below is that, while knowledge about conditions of life in Egypt has undoubtedly informed the narrative, these depictions are used to serve two main sets of theological affirmations. The combination of these two accounts explains complexities in the present narrative.

A. Naturalistic Explanations

The disasters described in Exod 7–12 seem to follow credibly the sequence of natural phenomena that could have happened in EGYPT over about a ten-month period (Hoffmeier, Humphreys). The turning of water into blood (plague 1) could be a figurative description of the river Nile laden with silt in its annual flood beginning in mid-June. The floodwaters overflowing its banks could have enabled frogs to spread over the land (plague 2). The receding waters and piles of dead frogs could have caused swarms of mosquitoes and flies (plagues 3 and 4) spreading disease among livestock (plague 5) and humans (plague 6). Hail (plague 7) in late winter could have flattened the early crops; later crops could have been wiped out by locusts (plague 8). The growing heat of spring could have triggered the hot south wind, which could have whipped up sand that could blot out the sun (plague 9). The whole sequence could then have coincided with the spring equinox, Passover time, when Israel commemorates deliverance from slavery finally forced on the Egyptians by the slaughter of all their firstborn (plague 10). However plausible, such naturalistic explanations are selective in the material in Exodus they choose (e.g., 7:19 states that not just the Nile, but all water in Egypt, even in storage vessels, was changed into blood). Above all, they shortchange the miraculous: the events are totally unprecedented (as explicitly stated in plagues 7, 8, and 10; Exod 9:18, 24; 10:6, 14; 11:6). Even Pharaoh's magicians are driven to confess, "This is the finger of God!" (plague 3; Exod 8:19 [Heb. 8:15]).

B. The Vocabulary for the Plagues in Exodus

The term *plagues* hardly does justice to the variety of terms used in the Heb. text. The headline term **nifla'oth** (נִפְלָאוֹת; "wonderful, unprecedented acts") occurs in Exod 3:20 (also, e.g., Ps 78:11), but not in the plague narrative itself. Traditionally, the plagues are referred to as ten "blows" (**makkoth** [מַכּוֹת]; *m. Avot* 5:6; see Deut 28:59-61). The term **makkoth** does not occur in the cycle (see 1 Sam 4:8), only its related verb "to strike" (**nakhah** [נָכָה]; Exod 7:25; 9:15, 25, 31–32; 12:12–13, 29; also Exod 7:17, 20; 8:16-17 [Heb. 8:12-13]).

Another verb, **naghaf** (נָגַף, "to strike"), is used as well (Exod 8:2 [Heb. 7:27]; 12:23, 27; see Josh 24:5), along with its associated nouns (**maggefah** [מַגֵּפָה], Exod 9:14; **neghef** [נֶגֶף], Exod 12:13). The term **negha'** (נֶגַע, "blow") occurs in Exod 11:1.

The general word for "plague" (**dever** דֶּבֶר) is used in Exod 9:3 in the context of plague 6, the cattle-pest. It is unlikely that **dever** is itself the technical term for cattle-pest. Rather, that plague is described as "the hand of the LORD," which is about to fall as "a devastating plague (**dever**)" (see also Exod 5:3; 9:15). The term "a mighty hand" (**yadh khazaqah** [יָד חֲזָקָה]; Exod 3:19; 13:9; 32:11; see Deut 6:21; 7:8; 9:26) may refer specifically to plague 10, the death of the Egyptian firstborn (see Exod 13:3, 9, 14, 16).

The plagues function as "signs" (**'othoth** [אֹתוֹת]; Exod 7:3; 8:23 [Heb. 8:19]; 10:1-2; see also 3:12; 4:8-9, 17, 28, 30) and "wonders" (**mofethim** [מֹפְתִים]; Exod 4:21; 7:3, 9; 11:9-10). The Exod 4 references suggest that **'othoth** connotes benefit for Israel and **mofethim** a threat to Egypt. *See* SIGNS AND WONDERS.

C. Two Accounts Combined, Two Theological Emphases

The above range of passages includes many from outside the narrower plague cycle in Exod 7–12. This suggests that the plague cycle should be considered not as a self-contained unit but as integral to a wider narrative. Like that wider narrative, the plague cycle in all probability combines two accounts, each with its distinctive theological emphasis (*see* EXODUS, BOOK OF).

The plague cycle is prefaced by two accounts of the commissioning of Moses and Aaron: Exod 3:1–6:1 (including some later additions) and 6:2–7:13. In the first account (the "non-Priestly version"), Moses is commissioned to go to Pharaoh to demand the release of Israel (Exod 3:18). As anticipated, that demand is met with a flat refusal (Exod 5). Pharaoh is forced to comply only when Yahweh unleashes all the unprecedented deeds of the plague cycle (Exod 6:1). *See* DOCUMENTARY HYPOTHESIS.

In the second account (the Priestly version), Aaron is brought into greater prominence. The plagues take on a cosmic dimension. Their purpose is not simply to force Israel's release but to work "mighty acts of judgment" (Exod 6:6; 7:4) on the gods of Egypt (Exod 12:12; Num 33:4) and to demonstrate Yahweh's universal power. As part of that demonstration this second account introduces Pharaoh's magicians (Exod 7:11), who are destined to be exposed as charlatans by Aaron.

Each of these commissioning accounts has corresponding material in the following plague narratives. The first, the non-Priestly version, is marked by a series of messages of accusation and threat delivered by Moses to Pharaoh that follow a broadly fixed pattern: "If you refuse [or equivalent] to let them go ... I will [unleash the following plague]" (plague 2, Exod 8:2 [Heb. 7:27]; plague 4, 8:21 [Heb. 17]; plague 5, 9:2; plague 7, 9:17; plague 8, 10:4). This pattern is partly present in plague 1 (7:17*b*); it is already exemplified in Exod 4:23, which, it will be argued below, is a fragment of plague 10 displaced to its present position by the P edition. Consistently throughout, these plagues are designed to compel Pharaoh to release Israel. They are conditional. Pharaoh is presented with a choice. He is a responsible moral agent. Consistently (except where the P-editor has intervened, esp. Exod 10:20), Pharaoh himself is responsible for the hardening of his heart (**kavedh** [כָּבֵד]; 8:15, 32 [Heb. 8:11, 28]; 9:7, 34), as stated at the outset (Exod 7:14). *See* HARDEN THE HEART.

Three plagues fall outside this pattern: 3, 6, and 9. It is striking that in 3 and 6, Pharaoh's magicians, introduced by P in Exod 7:11, make their reappearance; thus these plagues are likely to belong to the P-edition. A shared feature makes clear that all three do indeed belong to the P-edition: in none is a message delivered to Pharaoh. He is not warned; he has no choice. These plagues belong to the series of demonstrations of the power of Yahweh, who not only foreknows but preordains the hardening (**khazaq** חָזַק) of Pharaoh's heart as stated at the outset (Exod 7:3, 13). Pharaoh has to be obdurate, a plaything in Yahweh's hand (Exod 10:2), so that Yahweh can bring judgment on the gods of Egypt.

The P-editor has intervened at many points in the non-Priestly version of the plagues (with the possible exception of 5) to adapt them to his purpose, e.g., by the addition of Pharaoh's magicians in plague 1 (Exod 7:22), and especially radically in 10. As indicated above, Exod 4:22-23 belongs to the announcement of 10 (the past tense of the verbs in 4:23, "I said to you ... but you," in advance of any encounter between Moses and Pharaoh, does not fit its present context). Other anomalies confirm the intervention: Exod 10:28-29 appears to mark the end of the final dialogue between Moses and Pharaoh, and yet Exod 11:8 (and perhaps the whole of 11:4-8) continues that dialogue, thus including Exod 11:1-8 in plague 9. A concluding summary on the plague cycle is introduced in Exod 11:9-10, yet the continuation of plague 10 is to be found in 12:30-36. The P-editor has fragmented plague 10. In compensation, P has added Aaron's "wonder" at the beginning of the whole series in 7:8-13, thus creating a cycle of ten **mofethim** from Exod 7:8–11:10.

Two complex cycles thus stand in interaction with each other in Exod 7:8–12:36. The non-Priestly cycle of seven plagues (1, 2, 4, 5, 7, 8, 10), designed to force Pharaoh to release Israel, is dominated by the motif of death: from the death of the fish in the Nile in plague 1, to the death of the livestock in plague 5 (which once stood at the center of its cycle of 7 plagues), to the death of the firstborn in plague 10. The intervening pairs of plagues in the original non-Priestly cycle (2 and 4, human affliction; 7 and 8, destruction of vegetation) display a chiastic arrangement of intercession and apparent concession. The death of the firstborn represents an application of the law of retaliation (compare Exod 4:22-23; 21:23-25). Plundering the Egyptians, a motif that runs through the non-Priestly version (Exod 3:22; 11:2; 12:35-36), is designed to gain compensation for labor unjustly exacted from the Israelites in accordance with the law on the release of Hebrew slaves in Deut 15:12-18.

The addition by P of plagues 3, 6, and 9 might be regarded as substantiating the dominant traditional view that the ten plagues, as they stand, form the pattern 3+3+3+1. Rather, however, by adding the "wonder" in Exod 7:8-13 and concluding its series by the summary in Exod 11:9-10, and by its thorough editing of the intervening non-Priestly cycle, P has constructed a pattern in which the first and last of these "wonders" form an inclusio around the whole series by which the ordered life of the land of Egypt is undone and returned to primeval chaos. The first, Aaron's stick as all-devouring monster of the deep (**tannin** [תַּנִּין]; Exod 7:8-13; the agent of chaos threatening the ordered structure of creation, Isa 27:1; Ps 74:13; symbolic of Egypt itself, Isa 51:9-10; Ezek 29:3-5; 32:2), and the last, profound darkness (Exod 10:21–11:8), allude to the darkness over the face of the deep of Gen 1:2, the condition of the earth as "a formless void" before creation. By contrast, there is light as of the first act of creation throughout all Israel's dwelling-places (Exod 10:23; see Gen 1:3). The elevation of Aaron in the P-edition reflects his coming role as priest in the Tabernacle in which creation will be remade.

The whole P-cycle is interlinked by the theme of advancing recognition of Yahweh's power: it will be demonstrated to Pharaoh "that I am the LORD" (Exod 7:17); "that there is no one like the LORD our God" (Exod 8:10 [Heb. 8:6]); "that I the LORD am in this land [of Egypt]" (Exod 8:22 [Heb. 8:18]); "that there is no one like [Yahweh] in all the earth" (Exod 9:14); "that the earth is the LORD's" (Exod 9:29); "that the LORD makes a distinction between Egypt and Israel" (Exod 11:7).

P's radical intervention in plague 10 is connected with its radical revision of festivals in Exod 12–24. In the non-Priestly version, Passover is a seven-day festival culminating at Horeb with the making of the covenant (Exod 24:3-8; *see* PASSOVER AND FEAST OF UNLEAVENED BREAD). For the non-Priestly version, the final plague, the death of the Egyptian FIRSTBORN, provides the etiology for Israel's offering of their first-born males to God (Exod 13:1-2, 11-16; compare Deut 15:19-23). For P, the Levites become the substitutes for the firstborn of Israel (Num 3:11-13). Sinai is now detached from Passover and covenant and associated with the Festival of Weeks/Pentecost and lawgiving (Exod 19:1). Passover in Exod 12 is now a one-night festival. In contrast to the non-Priestly version, where there could be no threat to Israel now safe in Goshen, from an act against the Egyptians designed for Israel's liberation, Israel is now saved from the angel of death by the sign of the blood of the sacrificial victim, now a yearling (Exod 12:5) not a firstborn, daubed on their doorways. This is in line with P's lack of illusions about Israel: they too have to learn from the "signs and wonders" (the terms now used indiscriminately) to acknowledge the power of Yahweh (Exod 10:2). *See* EXODUS, BOOK OF.

Bibliography: James K. Hoffmeier. *Israel in Egypt* (1997); Colin J. Humphreys. *The Miracles of Exodus* (2003); John Van Seters. "The Plagues of Egypt: Ancient Tradition or Literary Invention?" *ZAW* 98 (1986) 31–39.

WILLIAM JOHNSTONE

PLAIN [בִּקְעָה biqʿah, כִּכָּר kikkar, מִישׁוֹר mishor, עֵמֶק ʿemeq, עֲרָבָה ʿaravah; πεδινός pedinos]. While each term is translated "plain" in various contexts, each has other, more specific geographical nuances as well. **Mishor** refers to an elevated plateau, such as the region directly east of the southern Jordan Valley and the Dead Sea. Specifically, the Madaba Plain extends south of Amman (Jordan) to the Wadi Dibon, the territory assigned to Reuben (Num 32:33-42). This region has long had the renown as the "breadbasket of Amman" because of its productive grain fields. The Moabite Plain, stretching between the Wadi Mujib and the Wadi Hesa, was the setting of Ruth's gleaning in a time of famine in Bethlehem (Ruth 1). **Biqʿah** refers to a valley plain such as the Megiddo/Jezreel Plain (the setting for the Gideon narrative, Judg 6:33) and the Harod Plain, north of the Carmel and Gilboa ridges, respectively. As an alluvial plain, this striking land formation was and is rich in grain production. **Kikkar** seems to refer to a circular/ovular region; in at least nine of its eleven OT uses the term refers specifically to the southwestern Jordan Valley, the region chosen by Lot (Gen 13:10-12; 19:17-29; 1 Kgs 7:46; 2 Chr 4:17). **ʿAravah** is a desert plain. The "**ʿarevoth** (עֲרְבוֹת) of Moab," prominent in the narrative of Israel's preparation for crossing into Canaan (e.g., Num 22:1; 26:3, 63), is to be distinguished from the Moabite Plain referenced above. The "**ʿarevoth** of Moab" refers to the region at the base of the eastern plateau, north of the Dead Sea, the eastern portion of the Jordan Valley. The long, slender region south of the Dead Sea, stretching all the way south to the Gulf of Aqabah, is known as the "ARABAH." Jesus' so-called SERMON ON THE PLAIN takes place on a **pedinos**, a "level place" (NRSV, Luke 6:17). *See* ISRAEL, GEOGRAPHY OF; SHEPHELAH; VALLEY.

JOHN I. LAWLOR

PLANE [מַקְצוּעָה maqtsuʿah]. A carpenter fashioning an idol uses a plane to smooth the surface and prepare it for carving and finishing (Isa 44:13). The prophet considers the skill associated with this task to be wasted on its product. *See* TOOLS.

PLANE TREE [עֶרְמוֹן ʿermon; πλάτανος platanos]. *Platanus orientalis,* frequently found in rocky stream beds (Sir 24:14) in the eastern Mediterranean region, is a large tree with flaking bark on its stout white trunk, large digitately lobed leaves, and flowers in several suspended balls. Plane is one of the choice trees envisaged in Isa 41:19 and 60:13. In spite of its size, Ezekiel (31:8) compared the plane unfavorably with the cedar of Lebanon (an image of proud Assyria). Plane, POPLAR, and ALMOND twigs seem to have been peeled by Jacob in order to encourage the birth of striped lambs and to deceive his uncle Laban (Gen 30:37). *See* PLANTS OF THE BIBLE.

F. NIGEL HEPPER

PLANK [שְׂדֵרָה sederah, לוּחַ luakh; σανίς sanis]. WOOD used in the structure of buildings (1 Kgs 6:9) or ships, e.g., planks of a ship representing Tyre (Ezek 27:5), and boards from Paul's wrecked ship, which transported survivors to Malta (Acts 27:44).

KATHY R. MAXWELL

PLANTS OF THE BIBLE. Plants served many purposes in the lives of biblical people. Cereals, herbs, spices, fruits, vegetables, and nuts supplied food; grapes were crushed to make wine and olives to make oil for consumption, anointing, and oil lamps; resinous plants and herbs were used as medicines, ointments, and cosmetics; trees provided various kinds of wood for building frames and panels, furniture, agricultural implements, and boats; water plants were employed to make writing materials and baskets; textile plants provided material for clothing, woven mats, rope, and other useful products.

The geography and climate of the Mediterranean area affected what sorts of plants would grow and the season for cultivation (*see* AGRICULTURE; ISRAEL, CLIMATE OF; ISRAEL, GEOGRAPHY OF). Many of the feasts and festivals were arranged around the agricultural year (e.g., offering first fruits Lev 23:9-22). A 10th-cent. BCE inscription, the Gezer calendar, divides the year into periods following the agricultural calendar beginning with the olive harvest in the fall, then planting grain once the land could be worked after the October–November rain, then a late planting, then hoeing flax, then barley harvest, then harvest and feasting, then vine tending, finally summer fruit. Familiar plants such as the various spices, the cedar, or the fig tree would became metaphors in biblical poetry, in oracles of the prophets in proverbs, and in the parables of Jesus.

This article surveys the types of plants mentioned in the Bible. More detailed information can be found in articles about specific topics noted in cross-references.

- A. Cereals
    1. Barley
    2. Wheat
- B. Flowers of the Field
    1. Broom
    2. Dove's dung
    3. Lily, lilies
    4. Mandrake
    5. Rose of Sharon
    6. Pleasant plants
- C. Herbs and Spices
    1. Aloes
    2. Calamus
    3. Camel's thorn
    4. Caper
    5. Cassia
    6. Cinnamon
    7. Coriander seed
    8. Cumin
    9. Dill
    10. Mint
    11. Mustard
    12. Nard
    13. Saffron
- D. Poisonous Plants
    1. Gall
    2. Weeds
    3. Wormwood
- E. Resinous Plants
    1. Frankincense
    2. Galbanum
    3. Mastic
    4. Myrrh
- F. Textile Plants
    1. Cotton
    2. Flax
    3. Silk
    4. Fibrous plants
- G. Thorns and Nettles
    1. Bramble
    2. Brier
    3. Crown of thorns
    4. Nettle
    5. Thistles and thorns
- H. Trees of the Forest
    1. Acacia
    2. Almug
    3. Cedar
    4. Cypress
    5. Ebony
    6. Holm
    7. Oak
    8. Pine
    9. Plane tree
    10. Poplar
    11. Scented wood
    12. Willow
- I. Trees of the Field
    1. Apple
    2. Date palm
    3. Fig
    4. Grapevine
    5. Mulberry
    6. Nut
        - a. Almond
        - b. Pine
        - c. Pistachio
        - d. Walnut
    7. Olive
    8. Pomegranate
    9. Sycamore
- J. Vegetables
    1. Beans
    2. Cucumber
    3. Garlic
    4. Gourds
    5. Lentil
    6. Melons
    7. Onion
- K. Water Plants
    1. Papyrus
    2. Rushes and reeds
- Bibliography

A. Cereals

In biblical times BREAD was the staple food of everybody except a few wealthy people. Bread is baked from flour made from milled cereal grains in the grass family, the principal ones being wheat and, especially among the poor, barley. These originated from wild grasses indigenous in the region. Their ears shatter on ripening making harvesting almost impossible; while the cultivated strains hold the grains together in the ears. This enables the farmer to cut and store the ears, which then must then be threshed to separate the grains from the husks or chaff. The hungry might eat the grains raw (as in Matt 12:1-8). Older translations of the Bible (such as KJV) use the word *corn* for both wheat and barley, which should not be confused with the New World maize or Indian corn (*Zea mays*). Other biblical cereals may have included the millet (*Panicum miliaceum*), a small annual grass with tiny grains (Ezek 4:9); also dura or sorghum (*Sorghum bicolor*) whose tall stems may have been used to hold the sponge lifted up to Jesus on the cross (Matt 27:48).

1. Barley

Barley (*Hordeum vulgare*) can tolerate drier conditions than wheat, so it was grown in the poorer, rockier soils cultivated by peasant farmers who used it for a coarse bread or "parched grain" (qali קָלִי), barley (or wheat) roasted without other preparation (Lev 23:14; Ruth 2:14; 1 Sam 17:17), as well as animal feed (1 Kgs 4:28). The stems are shorter than wheat and the fruiting heads (ears) with long whiskers (awns) nod over. *See* BARLEY.

2. Wheat

The wheat of Egypt and the eastern Mediterranean in biblical times was emmer (*Triticum dicoccum*). In the Mediterranean area, hard wheat (*T. durum*) came in about NT times. The so-called bread wheat (*T. aestivum*), which is dominant in the world today, rapidly replaced both of these in the major wheat-producing countries. In Pharaoh's dream the "seven ears of grain, full and good, growing on one stalk" (Gen 41:22) were probably a form of the hard wheat. Emmer stems grew to nearly the height of a man, with whiskery ears held almost upright. A fine flour for bread was made from the inner grains and considered suitable for the bread of Presence (Exod 25:30), as an offering (Lev 7:11-13), and the Passover (Matt 26:26; 1 Cor 11:23). However *wheat* also refers to a form of grits, the particles left after sifting, which may be the form employed for the raw cereal offering (Lev 2:1-6). *See* WHEAT.

B. Flowers of the Field

In most biblical lands the cool, moist springtime provides good conditions for the growth and flowering of the wild flora (krinon [κρίνον], "wildflower," Matt 6:28). As the summer produces high temperatures and dry conditions, many annuals seed and die; the leaves of perennials with bulbs or tubers wither; and shallow-rooted shrubs may lose their leaves. In a mainly rural and agricultural environment the biblical writers frequently referred to wild and cultivated plants (Isa 37:12; 40:6-7; Pss 37:2; 90:5-6). The prophet Isaiah employs many different terms for plants, though it is not always possible to identify his plant names with a particular species. Jesus refers to plants and seeds in several of his parables. The generic expression "flowers (NRSV, "lilies") of the field" (ta krina tou agrou [τὰ κρίνα τοῦ ἀγροῦ] in Matt 6:28; krina usually translates shoshannim [שׁוֹשַׁנִּים], "lilies") could include the purple anemone, the gladiolus, the crocus, the white Madonna lily, as well as some variety of poppy. Only the plants mentioned in the Bible are discussed here.

1. Broom

Broom, mentioned in 1 Kgs 19:4, is the white-flowered desert shrub *Retama raetam*. *See* BROOM.

2. Dove's dung

Dove's dung (mentioned in 2 Kgs 6:25) is the name of a white-flowered wild plant *Ornithogalum narbonense* (subspecies *brachystachys*), which makes the ground appear like bird droppings, hence its name. Its bulbs are edible (*see* DOVE'S DUNG).

3. Lily, lilies

The exact identity of the lilies mentioned in Song 2:2 (shoshannim) and Luke 12:27 (krina) is unknown. Suggestions include pretty spring wild flowers such as the windflower (*Anemone coronaria*), rather than true lilies in the genus *Lilium*, which are rare. Other candidates are hyacinth and crocus. The ornamental lily-work on the column capitals of Solomon's Temple (1 Kgs 7:22) was probably the lotus or water lily flower (*Nymphaea lotus*). *See* LILY.

4. Mandrake

Mandrake is a perennial herbaceous plant (*Mandragora officinarum*) with a forked taproot (that resembles a human torso) surmounted by a rosette of leaves ca. 30 cm long. In fall to early spring a congested head of purple flowers appears in the center of the rosette. By early summer the fruits develop, each like a small yellow tomato and sweetly fragrant. Typical habitat for this wild plant in the Mediterranean type of vegetation is the edge of cultivation and paths among old ruins. There is an ancient tradition that mandrake is an aphrodisiac (Gen 30:14-16). *See* MANDRAKE.

F. Nigel Hepper

Figure 1: Mandrake (*Mandragora officinarum*)

5. Rose of Sharon

Rose of Sharon (Song 2:1) is traditionally identified as the bulbous narcissus *N. tazetta* or the tulip *Tulipa montana*, both of which grow wild in the Sharon plain (*see* SHARON, SHARONITE).

6. Pleasant plants

Isaiah 17:10 cryptically refers to "pleasant plants," (nitʿe naʿamanim נִטְעֵי נַעֲמָנִים), which some scholars associate with Adonis and translate the Hebrew as "the shoots of Adonis"), perhaps a veiled reference to the gardens of Adonis or Naaman, a deity related to vegetation and worshiped in Syria and Phoenecia. In classical Greece "gardens of Adonis" referred to pots of quick blooming and withering plants that were set out in mid-summer to represent the deity (Plato, *Phaedr.* 276b). *See* PLANTS, PLEASANT.

C. Herbs and Spices

In a world without modern methods of preservation, fragrant herbs and spices were highly valued, yet only available to the wealthy, as they had to be imported. The common people would have to make do with gathered wild mints and other herbs. Herbs and spices were also valuable for seasoning food, medicine, ceremonies, feasts and fasts, and preparing bodies for burial. *See* BITTER HERBS; HYSSOP; OINTMENT; SPICE.

1. Aloes

Two distinct plants are mentioned as aloes in the Bible. The OT references (Num 24:6; Ps 45:8; Prov 7:17; Song 4:14) are to ligne-aloes or eaglewood (*Aquilaria agallocha*), a tree growing wild in Burma and northern Malaysia, which becomes infected with a fungus that makes the timber fragrant. The NT reference to the aloes used at Jesus' BURIAL (John 19:39) is to the bitter aloes (*Aloe vera*), a succulent plant growing wild in southwest Arabia and transported and cultivated in North Africa, Syria, and elsewhere. Its sword-like leaves provided the bitter flesh that was dried and sold as an embalming spice and purge. *See* ALOES.

2. Calamus

Calamus is the tuber of a water plant called sweet flag or "aromatic cane" (*Acorus calamus*) related to the wild arum but with iris-like tubers and leaves. The dried tuber was transported from its native Siberia for the sake of its fragrance (Exod 30:23; Song 4:14; Jer 6:20; Ezek 27:19). *See* CALAMUS; CANE.

3. Camel's thorn

A very prickly undershrub in the pea family, camel's thorn (*Alhagi camelorum*) occurs in salty semi-desert places. It is implied as a spice (perhaps CASSIA) in Exod 30:22-28 and mentioned in Sir 24:15. *See* CAMEL'S THORN.

4. Caper

Caper (ʾaviyonah אֲבִיּוֹנָה) refers to the fruit of the caper bush (*Capparis spinosa*) that the ancients believed to have medicinal properties. It was used as an aphrodisiac and stimulant to the appetite (Eccl 12:5; NRSV, "almond tree blossoms").

5. Cassia

Cassia is an aromatic bark from East Asia similar to cinnamon (Exod 30:24). It is used in anointing oil, along with aloes and myrrh (Ps 45:8). *See* CASSIA.

6. Cinnamon

The botanical identity of the biblical cinnamon (in perfumed oil for priests, Exod 30:23) is a matter of continuing discussion. It is usually considered to be the bark of cinnamon, a small tree (*Cinnamomum verum*) native to tropical forests in Sri Lanka and coastal India and hence an expensive imported item. The fragrant bark was part of the spice trade. *See* CINNAMON.

7. Coriander seed

The seeds of the common bitter herb coriander (*Coriandrum sativum*), though not actually white, were the MANNA provided by God to the wandering Israelites in the desert (Exod 16:31; Num 11:7; *b. Yoma* 75a). The leaves were used in soup and wine. *See* CORIANDER SEED.

8. Cumin

Cumin is a fragrant annual herb (*Cuminum cyminum*) that was beaten with a rod to prepare it for use (Isa 28:25, 27). Like coriander and dill, cumin belongs to the carrot family. It was part of a tithe, along with dill, based on a later interpretation of Deut 14:22-29 (*m. Maas.* 4:5). Cumin is included among the plants tithed in Matt 23:23. *See* CUMIN.

9. Dill

Dill is the well-known annual spicy herb *Anethum graveolens*, not anise, as in some translations. It has flat heads of yellow florets and comes from the carrot family. Along with cumin, it was a tithed seasoning (Matt 23:23). *See* DILL.

10. Mint

Mint was a popular herb in the genus *Mentha*, especially *M. longifolia* in the Mediterranean area. Mint is one of the herbs tithed by the Pharisees (Matt 23:23). Mint oil served as a seasoning. *See* MINT.

11. Mustard

Mustard is an annual plant, either the black mustard (*Sinapis nigra*) or perhaps the related white variety (*Sinapis alba*). Mustard is not mentioned in the OT. Although its seed is not the smallest known, it was a proverbial example of smallness (Matt 17:20; Luke 17:6; *m. Nid.* 5:2; *b. Ber.* 31a). Greco-Roman naturalists recognized this garden herb (Theophrastus, *Hist. Plant.* 7.1.1–3) for its rapid growth (Pliny, *Nat.* 19.170). The Mishnah prohibits planting mustard in gardens; it must be grown only in fields (*m. Kil.* 2:8-9; 3:2), a restriction observed in Matthew's version of Jesus' Mustard Seed parable (Matt 13:31-32). However, Luke depicts mustard planted in a garden (Luke 13:19). The bush can grow to a height of 10 ft., and while birds may eat the seeds or shelter among its leaves, they do not nest there.

12. Nard

Nard or spikenard (*Nardostachys grandiflora*) is a low herbaceous plant of the valerian family, with a strong, musky fragrance found in India. It is mentioned in the Bible (Song 1:12; 4:13; Mark 14:3; John 12:3) as an expensive perfume or ointment. *See* NARD; PERFUME.

13. Saffron

An expensive spice (Song 4:14) obtained from the orange-colored stigmas of the saffron crocus (*Crocus sativus*) that has pale purple flowers that are sterile. The plant is indigenous to the Himalayas, but the Bible probably refers to a local variety native to Asia Minor. It was used for medicine and as a dye, as well as for flavoring. *See* SAFFRON.

D. Poisonous Plants

Natural poisons occur in both animals and plants. Many kinds of snake (asp, viper) produce a fatal bite. Certain plants and fungi may have poisonous properties throughout or localized in parts such as root, leaves, or seeds. In the biblical times little was known about the properties of the active poisons except that in mild doses they appeared to act as healing stimulants. *See* POISON.

1. Gall

Gall is a type of gourd, the colocynth (*Citrullus colocynthis*), a desert vine creeping along the ground with yellow, ball-like fruits ca. 5 cm in diameter; the seeds contain a bitter dangerous purge. *Gall* becomes a metaphor for the bitterness of suffering (Lam 3:19; Acts 8:23), and in Matthew's version of the crucifixion it was mixed with the vinegar offered to Jesus on the cross (Matt 27:34; echoing the Gk. translation of Ps 69:22: "they gave me gall for my bread, and for my thirst they gave me vinegar" [69:21 in English translations]). Jesus' refusal to take it could be a reaction to the bitter taste or to the hastening of death implied by the offer of a poisonous substance. *See* GALL, HERB.

2. Weeds

Weeds may refer to a grass called darnel (*Lolium temulentum*), which has poisonous grains. Weeds are a metaphor for bad things: "Litigation springs up like poisonous weeds in the furrows of the field" (Hos 10:4). In Job, weeds are part of a curse: "If my land has cried out against me ... let thorns grow instead of wheat, and foul weeds instead of barley" (Job 31:38-40). In a parable, weeds (perhaps representing evildoers) are sown together with good grain by the farmer's "enemy"; when the harvest comes, the weeds will be separated from the wheat and burned (Matt 13:24-30). *See* WEEDS.

3. Wormwood

The whitish hairy leaves of wormwood (*Artemisia* species) yield a bitter infusion traditionally used in medicine against intestinal worms. In the Bible it is often linked with gall. It is symbolic of personal bitterness verging on poison (Prov 5:4; Lam 3:15, 19) or justice for idolatry (Deut 29:18) and Israel's disobedience (Jer 9:15). In Rev 8:10-11 when the star called Wormwood fell into the water, "a third of the waters became wormwood, and many died from the water, because it was made bitter." *See* WORMWOOD.

F. Nigel Hepper

Figure 2: Wormwood (*Artemisia herba-alba*)

E. Resinous Plants

In biblical times resin from certain trees and other plants was useful for medicines, cosmetics, incense, and perfumes. *See* BALM; BALSAM; BDELLIUM; COSMETICS; GUM; INCENSE; PERFUME; STACTE.

1. Frankincense

Frankincense is a fragrant resin obtained from incisions in the trunk and branches of desert trees *Boswellia sacra* and other species occurring in southern Arabia (Isa 60:6; Jer 6:20; Herodotus, *Hist.* 3.107) and eastern Africa and widely used in ritual contexts (an ingredient in incense, Exod 30:34-38) with bread and cereal offerings (Lev 2:1-2, 14-16; 24:7). *See* FRANKINCENSE.

2. Galbanum

Galbanum is a strong-smelling resin produced by a stout herbaceous giant fennel (*Ferula galbaniflua*), in the parsley family. It occurs wild on the dry mountainsides of northern Iran (Persia). The resin was burned as incense in the tabernacle rites (Exod 30:34-35). *See* GALBANUM.

3. Mastic

Mastic resin is produced from incisions in the trunk and branches of several species of pistachio relatives: the tree *Pistacia atlantica* and especially a variety of the lentisc bush *P. lentiscus* on the island of Cos. The mastic tree is mentioned in Sus 1:54. *See* MASTIC.

4. Myrrh

Resin produced by thorny bushes of *Commiphora*, especially *C. myrrha*, native in semi-desert areas of southeast Arabia and northeast Africa. Myrrh was highly valued in biblical times as a cosmetic and perfume. Myrrh was used in anointing oil (Exod 30:23) and as part of the cosmetic treatment given to Esther (Esth 2:12). Its fragrance perfumes the love poetry of Song of Songs (1:13; 3:6; 4:6, 14; 5:1, 5, 13). It was one of the gifts presented to the infant Jesus by the magi (Matt 2:11). In Mark 15:23, it is myrrh that is added to the drink offered to Jesus on the cross, perhaps as a numbing agent (*b. Sanh.* 43a has wine with frankincense given for that purpose). Myrrh was added to the aloes brought to prepare Jesus' body for burial (John 19:39). *See* MYRRH.

F. Textile Plants

In earliest times people dressed in animal skins (or even leaves according to Gen 3:7). Later, cloth was made of wool from sheep or goats or plant fibers (esp. flax; Hos 2:9) woven together. Plants were also used to weave baskets, mats, ropes, writing surfaces, and other items. *See* CLOTH, CLOTHES; TEXTILES.

1. Cotton

Cotton cloth first appears in India (ca. 3000 BCE), in Mesopotamia (ca. 1000 BCE), and the Aegean (6th–5th cent. BCE). Its existence in Persia is indicated in Esth 1:6, the only biblical example. *See* COTTON.

2. Flax

Probably the earliest such plant textile (fragments dating to the 7th cent. BCE have been found in the Judean desert) was LINEN, derived from the flax plant (*Linum usitatissimum*). The annual flax plant produced linen fibers from very ancient times (cultivated in Egypt as early as 4500 BCE), as well as linseed oil. It was grown in Egypt alongside barley (Exod 9:31). Flax plants have long bast fibers that separate from soaked green stems. After separation they are dried, crushed, and combed (Isa 19:9), and spun into threads for cloth (Hos 2:5, 9). The pure white clothes made from linen thread are frequently mentioned as garments of "fine linen" (Gen 41:42; Ezek 27:7). Linen was required for priestly garments (Exod 28:6; Lev 6:10). *See* FLAX.

3. Silk

Silk was produced by silk moth cocoons, the larvae of which fed on the white mulberry leaves in China. Another silk was independently provided by a different moth on the island of Cos, with a textile industry at Sidon. Silk is considered a luxury item along with jewels and "fine linen" in Rev 18:12. *See* SILK.

4. Fibrous plants

Several plants were widely used for their fibers to make baskets, mats, and ropes, e.g., fibers from the palm tree (*Phoenix dactylifera*); papyrus (*Cyperus papyrus*); reeds (*Phragmites australis*; *Typha domingensis*); and rushes (*Juncus* species). See §K below.

G. Thorns and Nettles

Biblical lands, having mainly dry, rocky, or sandy soil, abound in prickly, thorny, and stinging plants that protect them from browsing animals. They were the curse of Adam the gardener (Gen 3:18), and only too well known to farmers ever since. Hence it is no surprise that such plants were used in imagery throughout the Bible (e.g., negatively in Judg 8:7; Song 2:2; by comparison in Prov 15:19; 26:9; Isa 55:13; Matt 7:16; as worthless in 2 Sam 23:6; Ps 118:12; Nah 1:10; Heb 6:8; and in judgment in Isa 5:5-6; 7:23-25; Hos 9:6; Mark 4:18). The botanical identity of such plants is frequently dubious.

1. Bramble

The term *bramble* is strictly applicable to the blackberry *Rubus sanguineus*, but often used for various prickly plants. *See* BRAMBLE.

2. Brier

Brier is mainly used for the boxthorn shrub (*Lycium europaeum* and other species). This is probably the bramble mentioned by Jotham (Judg 9:14). *See* BRIER.

3. Crown of thorns

The Gk. stephanos (στέφανος, "crown") is a twisted wreath with which athletes would have been crowned. There are two shrubs that are main contenders for this crown; both are known as "Christ-thorn" (*Palirurus spina-christi*; *Ziziphus spina-christi*), in honor of the crown of thorns that Jesus was forced to wear before his crucifixion (Matt 27:29). *See* CROWN OF THORNS.

4. Nettle

The word *nettle* is usually reserved for certain herbaceous plants called stinging nettles (*Urtica* species) that have the ability to irritate anyone who touches them by secreting an irritating liquid on the skin, in contrast to thistles and thorns that simply prick (Job 30:7; Prov 24:31; Isa 34:13; Hos 9:6; Zeph 2:9). Nettles were also considered to be a type of weed that should be rooted out of one's field, a task that the lazy field owner fails (Prov 24:31). *See* NETTLE.

5. Thistles and thorns

Thistles and thorns are any variety of prickly weeds growing in fields and waysides. They are a hardship for humans forced to work the earth after exclusion from paradise (Gen 3:18). *See* THISTLE, THORN.

H. Trees of the Forest

Over fifteen tree species are mentioned in the Bible. There is usually a clear distinction in the Bible between wild and cultivated trees. The former are the natural trees of the forest (or wood) (1 Chr 16:33; Isa 7:2), while the latter are planted fruit trees of the field or orchard. In biblical times there was more forest or woodland than at the present day, but dense high forest was only to be found in the Lebanon mountains rather than in the land of Israel, where drier conditions supported lighter woodland and thickets; desert trees tended to be scattered or line streambeds. Timber was an essential requirement for buildings and fuel, the latter usually as charcoal (Lev 16:12), although fuel was also obtained from vine prunings (John 15:6), and even grass and chaff. Large timber, such as that required for Solomon's Temple in Jerusalem, had to be imported from Lebanon (1 Kgs 6). Although tree cutting was a humble task (Deut 29:11), woodworking was a skilled occupation. Jesus' legal father, Joseph, was a carpenter, a trade evidently followed by Jesus himself (Mark 6:3). *See* CARPENTER; WOOD.

1. Acacia

Acacia is a 3–5 m tall tree or shrub found in desert regions of Egypt, Arabia, Sinai, and Negev. Some specimens may grow as tall as 15 m. *Acacia raddiana* produces a durable wood that was used to build the ARK OF THE COVENANT, furnishings for the TABERNACLE, and the altar (Exod 25–27; 30; 35–38). Acacia wood was also used to build doors and coffins. *Acacia senegal* is a source for gum arabic. Acacias likely were plentiful in ABEL-SHITTIM, "meadow of the acacias" (Num 33:49; Josh 2:1; Mic 6:5). Acacia is one of the choice trees envisaged in Isa 41:19 as replacing the dry desert species (Isa 41:19). Some scholars think the burning bush Moses saw (Exod 3:2) was *Acacia nilotica. See* ACACIA; BUSH, BURNING.

2. Almug

Almug was one of the timbers imported for Solomon's Temple (1 Kgs 10:11-12), and was used to make musical instruments. There is no agreement among authorities as to the precise identity of this tree from Ophir brought by Hiram of Tyre: the Indian or Sri Lankan red sandalwood (*Pterocarpus santalinus*) or white sandalwood (*Santalum album*) are usually proposed. Josephus suggests a coniferous tree in Lebanon (*Ant.* 8.7). *See* ALMUG; MUSICAL INSTRUMENTS; TEMPLE OF SOLOMON.

3. Cedar

Cedar trees (*Cedrus libani*) are a long-lived evergreen that still grow on the mountains of Lebanon. Their forests were much reduced as the trees were exploited for their long, fragrant timbers to build Solomon's HOUSE OF THE FOREST OF LEBANON (2 Sam 7:2; 1 Kgs 7), as well as temples (1 Kgs 6:9; Ezra 3:7) and ships. Large Phoenician ships carried cedars to Egypt as early as the 4th millennium BCE. Cedars are large, stately coniferous trees (Ps 37:35) sometimes used in biblical imagery (Pss 29:5; 92:12; Amos 2:9). Cedarwood may have been used in oblations for purification in ritual cleansing for leprosy (Lev 14:4; Num 19:6), but this may have been other trees. *See* CEDAR.

4. Cypress

The cypress (*Cupressus sempervirens*) is a coniferous tree with small cones and evergreen overlapping scale leaves. The cypress occurs in the Levant and is now rare outside the mountains of Lebanon. Botanically, conifers are difficult to distinguish and collective words are used, and there may be confusion with the tall juniper (*Juniperus excelsa*). Cypress timber may have been used for the ARK OF NOAH (Gen 6:14) and for Solomon's Temple (1 Kgs 5:10). *See* CYPRESS.

5. Ebony

Ebony is a rare black wood traditionally identified as *Diospyros ebenum* from India and Sri Lanka, but more likely to have been the tropical African leguminous tree *Dalbergia melanoxylon.* It was imported into the Mediterranean area along with ivory (Ezek 27:15). *See* EBONY.

6. Holm

Found only in Isa 44:14 alongside the cedar and the oak, some scholars have identified the holm tree with the holm oak (*Quercus ilex*), a small evergreen. However, this connection is doubtful because the holm oak is rare in biblical lands. Isaiah says that the wood was being used to make idols, so the holm tree may refer to a type of hardwood tree. *See* HOLM TREE.

7. Oak

The kermes or calliprinos oak (*Q. coccifera* or *Q. calliprinos*) is usually identified as a nibbled bush or medium-sized tree of the mountains with evergreen, prickly leaves. One such tree is the traditional oak of MAMRE where Abraham camped (Gen 13:18). An alternative rendering is TEREBINTH, which is a large oak-like tree (*Pistacia atlantica*) of that region. The larger, deciduous Tabor oak (*Q. ithaborensis, Q. aegilops,* or *Q. macrolepis*), with lobed leaves, occurs on the lowland Plain of Sharon, as well as on Carmel and in the lower hill country. Solitary oak trees were often used as markers of graves (e.g., of Deborah, Rebecca's nurse [Gen 35:8]); however, in shady clumps immoral practices took place (Hos 4:13). *See* OAK.

8. Pine

There is confusion among botanists and translators as to the identity of evergreen coniferous trees mentioned in the Bible. For example, in some translations of Isa 44:14 the tree is called a "cedar" (NRSV, NEB; KJV, "ash"); however, it may be the Aleppo pine (*Pinus halepensis*) rather than the cedar. Pine is one of the choice trees envisaged in Isa 41:19 as usurping the dry desert species. A second species of pine, the umbrella or stone pine (*Pinus pinea*), occurs in Lebanon, Cyprus, and westward, where the edible seeds are esteemed; this is probably the fruitful evergreen tree mentioned in Hos 14:8. *See* PINE, PINE TREE.

9. Plane tree

The oriental plane tree (*Platanus orientalis*) frequently occurs in rocky streambeds in the eastern Mediterranean region. The plane tree is one of the choice trees envisaged in Isa 41:19 as replacing the dry desert species. In spite of its size Ezekiel (31:8) compared the plane unfavorably with the cedar of Lebanon (an image of proud Assyria). Jacob peeled plane twigs, together with poplar and almond (or left them smooth white after the bark has flaked), in order to encourage the birth of striped lambs and to deceive his uncle Laban (Gen 30:37), although there is no genetic basis for this folk procedure. *See* PLANE TREE.

10. Poplar

There is frequent confusion between poplars and willows, both being mainly trees growing on watersides. The famous passage in Ps 137:2-3, referring to willows, is certainly the Euphrates poplar (*Populus euphratica*), which grows by the Euphrates. Confusingly, its young leaves are long and very narrow, like some willows, while the leaves on older branches are almost round. It has one or more trunks several meters high and a rounded crown. The willow of Ezek 17:5 may also be the Euphrates poplar. The "willows of the brook" (Lev 23:40) may be oleander (which has poisonous properties) rather than willows or poplars. However, the white poplar (*P. alba*) occurs away from water and is more likely to have been one of the trees Jacob exposed in front of rams (Gen 30:37). The white poplar is likely the tree that provided the rustling leaves of 2 Sam 5:23, 24 and 1 Chr 14:14, 15 (not the balsam poplar or mulberry). *See* POPLAR.

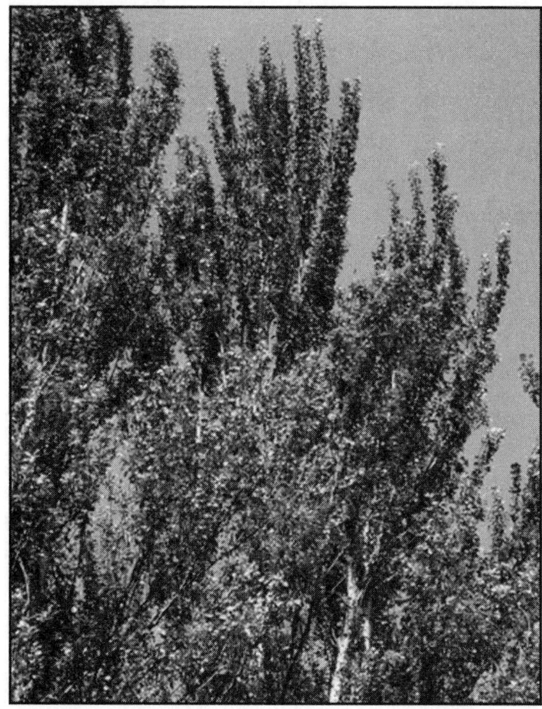

F. Nigel Hepper

Figure 3: White poplar (*Populus alba*)

11. Scented wood

This is the timber from the sanderac tree (*Tetraclinis articulata*), which is an evergreen conifer with small four-part cones. The only reference to it is in Rev 18:12, where it is being imported with many other exotic products that exemplify the decadent wealth of imperial Rome. The tree grows in northwest Africa, and its timber was esteemed by Greek and Roman woodworkers for fine cabinets and tables. *See* SCENTED WOOD.

12. Willow

In Israel there are two species of willow: *Salix acmophylla* and the white willow *S. alba*. Both grow in wet places that are not salty. Both species of willow are small trees with numerous stems and branches that easily root in moist soil. As discussed under poplar (§H10), there has been confusion between willows and poplars, due in part to their similar habitat and to the narrow willow-like young leaves of the Euphrates poplar (*Populus euphratica*). The "willows of the brook" collected for the Festival of Booths (or Tabernacles, Lev 23:40) may be either *S. acmophylla* or oleander *Nerium oleander*. It is apparent from Isa 44:3-4 that the writer was familiar with the stream habitat of willows. However, it is generally agreed that the willow of Ps 137:1-3 refers to the Euphrates poplar (*Populus euphratica*). *See* WILLOW.

I. Trees of the Field

Trees of the field are trees, shrubs, and vines cultivated in orchards or farm fields for the sake of their fruits. *See* AGRICULTURE; ORCHARD.

1. Apple

The "apples of gold" (Prov 25:11), "apple tree," and "apples" (Song 2:3, 5; 7:8; 8:5) are more likely to be apricots (*Prunus persica*) than the true apple (*Malus domestica*). *See* APPLE.

2. Date palm

The palm tree of the Bible is the date palm (*Phoenix dactylifera*) that has a tall, slender, unbranched trunk covered with old woody leaf-bases. The leaves, like huge feathers several m long, have a stout midrib making each leaf appear as a branch, hence the comment that people welcomed Jesus into Jerusalem by waving and spreading palm "branches" (John 12:13). The well-known sweet date is the fruit of this tree. The date palm flourishes in warm places such as Jericho ("the city of palm trees," Deut 34:3; 2 Chr 28:15), though it will grow in the hills (Judg 4:5) where its fruit is of poor quality. In addition to using the trunk for wood, the palm leaves are used in basket weavings and as roofing material. *See* DATES; PALM TREE.

3. Fig

Fig trees my have been planted beside houses (Mic 4:4) so that the large lobed leaves might provide shade (John 1:48). The large sweet fruits were eaten fresh or in dried cakes (1 Sam 25:18; 30:12). Biblical references to the fig tree abound (e.g., Judg 9:10, 11; 2 Kgs 20:7; Hos 9:10; Nah 3:12; Mark 11:13; Luke 13:6-7; John 1:48; Rev 6:13). *See* FIG TREE, FIGS.

4. Grapevine

A robust trailing or climbing shrub, the grapevine (*Vitis vinifera*) was one of the three most important crop plants of Bible lands. Its large palmate leaves, twisted tendrils, and hanging clusters of ripe GRAPES easily distinguish it. Grapevines were cultivated since at least the time of Noah (Gen 9:20), and vineyards are frequently mentioned in the OT (e.g., Isa 5:1-10) and NT (e.g., John 15:1-6). Grapes were eaten raw or dried (1 Sam 30:12), or they were made into WINE (Gen 9:21; Neh 13:15; Matt 26:27-29). *See* VINE, VINEYARD.

5. Mulberry

The mulberry tree is mentioned only in Luke 17:6 as a metaphor concerning believers' faith. The reference is to the black mulberry (*Morus nigra*), which was introduced into Palestine shortly before NT times from its native area in Iran (Persia). (The now common white mulberry [*Morus alba*], which yields silk, was introduced in the Middle Ages.) Black mulberry should not be confused with the sycamore fig-tree (*Ficus sycomorus*), which is sometimes called the sycamore fig, presumably owing to their superficial similarity. *See* MULBERRY, MULBERRY TREE.

6. Nut

Apart from almond, the nuts of the Bible grew wild.

a. Almond. Almond trees (*Amygdalus communis* or *Prunus dulcis*) bear decorative white flowers on the leafless trees very early in springtime, being one of the first to bloom. The fragrant almond nuts (seeds) were a favorite food (Gen 43:11). *See* ALMOND.

b. Pine. The seeds of the umbrella- or stone-pine (*Pinus pinea*) are popular nuts in some places where this tree grows. It is referred to in the Heb. of Hos 14:8 as the edible fruit of a coniferous tree (ra'anan [רַעֲנָן]; NRSV, "faithfulness").

c. Pistachio. Mentioned in Gen 43:11, these are likely to have been the little round seeds of the Atlantic terebinth or pistachio (*Pistacia atlantica* or *P. palaestina*), which are still sold in local markets, rather than the true pistachio (*P. vera*), which was cultivated later from Persia.

d. Walnut. In Song 6:11, the writer speaks of a "nut orchard," which suggests planted walnut trees (*Juglans regia*). *See* NUTS.

7. Olive

The olive tree (*Olea europaea*) is the most significant plant mentioned in the Bible. Olive trees so typify the lands of the Bible that the trees and their oil-rich fruits are frequently mentioned in their own right, as well as symbolically in verbal images (Deut 8:8; Hos 14:6; Rom 11:17-24). It was to the MOUNT OF OLIVES that Jesus led his disciples (Luke 22:39); and it is to this mountain that Zechariah (14:3-4) prophesied the coming day of the Lord. Olive oil was used for cooking food (1 Kgs 17:12) and for lighting (Matt 25:1-10). It was also used for healing (Luke 10:34), soothing the skin in a dry climate (Pss 23:5; 104:15; 133:2);,and for symbolic anointing (Exod 30:22-33; 40:9, 10; 1 Sam 10:1; 16:13; John 1:41). Both the fruit and its oil were dietary staples. Olives cannot be grown in warm climates like Egypt, which lack the winter chill needed to ripen the fruit; surplus oil was exported to Egypt (Hos 12:1). *See* OIL; OLIVE, OLIVE TREE.

F. Nigel Hepper

Figure 4: Olive (*Olea europaea*)

8. Pomegranate

The pomegranate (*Punica granatum*) is a large bush or small tree commonly planted in Israel, especially in warm situations. Its large fruits were brought back from the "promised land" by spies (Num 13:23). The form of the round fruits was later used to ornament part of Solomon's Temple (1 Kgs 7:20). Pomegranate fruits contain numerous seeds surrounded by tasty juice. *See* POMEGRANATE.

F. Nigel Hepper

Figure 5: Pomegranate fruit (*Punica granatum*)

9. Sycamore

This is the sycamore fig (*Ficus sycomorus*). Old trees have massive trunks with clusters of small fig fruits growing through the bark of trunk and branches. They are edible but not as delicious as the common fig. They are pollinated by a species of wasps, some of which die inside and pollute the fruit, so an ancient technique of cutting the young fruits was used to hasten their ripening and purity (Amos 7:14). Zacchaeus climbed up a sycamore to see Jesus (Luke 19:3-4). *See* SYCAMORE.

J. Vegetables

Gardens in biblical times (except those belonging to royalty cultivated for pleasure) were for the production of edible vegetables and herbs. *See* FOOD; GARDEN.

1. Beans

The vegetables given to Daniel and friends (Dan 1:12) evidently were beans. The broad bean (also called horse bean) is a stout leguminous annual with white flowers and large pods (*Vicia faba*, *Faba vulgaris*). Beans are mentioned in 2 Sam 17:28 and Ezek 4:9. *See* BEANS.

2. Cucumber

The cucumber of ancient Egypt that the Israelites longed for (Num 11:5) was the muskmelon (*Cucumis melo*), not our present-day Asian cucumber (*Cucumis sativa*). The muskmelon is an annual that trails extensively on the ground and bears separate male and female flowers among its large leaves. *See* CUCUMBER.

3. Garlic

Garlic (*Allium sativum*) is a familiar species of onion that was popular in ancient times (Num 11:5). Unlike typical onions, garlic bulbs are composed of separate cloves, each of which will grow a new plant, as the flowers do not produce fertile seeds. The cloves are strongly flavored and are used for culinary and medicinal purposes. *See* GARLIC.

4. Gourds

Gourd is a general term for plants yielding large fruits such as melons, squashes, cucumbers, and the poisonous wild vine the colocynth (*Citrullus colocynthis*) (1 Kgs 6:18; 2 Kgs 4:39). *See* GOURDS.

5. Lentil

An annual herb widely cultivated in dry biblical lands (2 Sam 23:11). It grows about 30 cm high, has slender compound leaves, tendrils, and small, mauve, pea-type flowers. The pods contain a few flattened round seeds usually reddish in color, which have for millenia been favored in stews and bread (Gen 25:34; Ezek 4:9). *See* LENTIL.

6. Melons

The well-known watermelon (*Citrullus lanatus* syn. *C.vulgaris*) with huge, round, juicy fruits was widely cultivated in ancient Egypt. It was one of the fruits and vegetables longed for by the wandering Israelites (Num 11:5). *See* MELONS.

7. Onion

A savory bulbous vegetable, related to leeks and garlic, all of which the wandering Israelites longed for in the desert (Num 1:5). *See* ONION.

K. Water Plants

1. Papyrus

The papyrus or paper-reed (*Cyperus papyrus*) grows in watery marshes (Job 8:11) mainly in Egypt. Its stalk easily bends over like a penitent (Isa 58:5). These triangular section pithy stalks were used for baskets (Gen 40:16); skiffs and boats (Isa 18:2); and paper (2 John 12). *See* PAPYRUS, PAPYRI.

2. Rushes and reeds

Rushes and reeds are general terms for water-loving marsh plants (Job 8:11; Isa 35:7), such as the rush (*Juncus* species in the strict sense), reeds (the tall grass *Phragmites australis*), cattail, or reedmace (*Typha angustifolia*), the sedges papyrus (*Cyperus papyrus*), and bulrush (*Scirpus lacustris*). In Pharaoh's dream, cows grazed in Nile reed grass (Gen 41:2). Isaiah compares the tall palm with the lowly reed, typifying senior leaders and lying prophets who will both be cut off from unfaithful Israel (Isa 9:14). Rushes and reeds were used to make rope and as fuel (Job 41:2, 20), and papyrus was used for Moses' basket (Exod 2:3). *See* BASKET; BULRUSH; REED; RUSHES.

Bibliography: F. Nigel Hepper. *Baker Encyclopedia of Biblical Plants* (1992); Philip J. King and Lawrence E. Stager. *Life in Biblical Israel* (2001); Michael Zohary. *Plants of the Bible* (1982).

F. NIGEL HEPPER

PLANTS, PLEASANT [נִטְעֵי נַעֲמָנִים nitʿe naʿamanim]. Most renderings of Isa 17:10 refer to "pleasant plants," but some authorities see this as a thinly veiled reference to the popular Greek mythology of Adonis because of the parallelism between "pleasant plants" and "slips of an alien god." Adonis was a nature deity associated with cult gardens, death, and rebirth. The Hebrew word ʾadhon (אָדוֹן) means "lord." *See* ADONAI, ADONAY; PLANTS OF THE BIBLE.

F. NIGEL HEPPER

PLASTER [טוּחַ tukh, עָפָר ʿafar, שִׂיד sidh; Aram. גִּיר gir]. The NRSV renders four OT terms as *plaster* (Lev 14:41-43, 45, 48; Deut 27:2, 4; Dan 5:5). In each of the contexts a coating of processed dust or limestone is to be removed from or applied to a wall or a monument. The slaking of limestone, a process known from very early times, involved heating limestone to very high temperatures, then mixing the powdery product with water to produce plaster; when dried and hardened, a water-resistant surface was produced. JERICHO and ʿAin Ghazal yielded plastered human skulls, and the excavation of Teleilât el-Ghassûl revealed painted plaster walls. *See* GHASSÛL, TELEILÂT EL; GHAZAL, ʿAIN.

JOHN I. LAWLOR

PLATE, PLATTER [קְעָרָה qeʿarah; παροψίς paropsis, πίναξ pinax]. Derived from the verbal root qʿr (קער, "to be deep"), qeʿarah refers to a service piece with an indentation (Exod 25:29; 37:16; Num 4:7; 7:13-85), also commonly rendered as "BOWL." Some commentators consider these "plates" cookware. There is no clear evidence whether their use was limited to the cult. In the NT, the platter (pinax) used in John the Baptist's beheading (Matt 14:8, 11; Mark 6:25, 28) was probably a flat serving piece made of wood. In Matt 23:25-26 Jesus describes hypocrisy as washing the outside of a plate (paropsis) or cup while the inside remains unclean (compare Matt 15:1-20; Mark 7:1-23; Luke 11:37-41).

STEVE COOK

PLATO, PLATONISM play'toh, play'tuh-niz'uhm. At his death, Plato (427–347 BCE) bequeathed a philosophical heritage that has not even yet spent its power. He was a student of Socrates (ca. 470–399 BCE), from whom—along with Orphic and Pythagorean traditions—he inherited a belief in the immorality of the soul, whose goodness in this life must be a person's chief concern, as well as a belief in an eternal, unchanging standard of virtue (not just what is good, but what is goodness itself) independent of changing circumstances. Plato appropriated the latter view in what is called his theory of Ideas or Forms. Whatever we see in this world of virtues such as love, truth, and beauty is but a shadow of the original, which exists in an unseen transcendent world of Forms. The ability to recognize that something in this world resembles its eternal archetype is due to an innate recollection of knowledge of the divine Forms acquired by the immortal soul before it "fell" from its celestial origin toward the world of sensible delights and became incarnated into a physical body. Plato's aim was to educate his students to contemplate these unseen realities rather than their earthly images perceived through their flawed natural senses, and to regulate their behavior in accord with them.

In his dialogue, the *Timaeus*, Plato applied these notions to a mythical account of the origin of the visible world that remained influential on Jewish and Christian thought from the beginning of the Common Era through the Renaissance. Even today there is considerable disagreement among scholars about its dating and how it is to be reconciled with his other works; indeed even his younger contemporaries (e.g., Speusippus, Xenocrates, ARISTOTLE) disagreed on its meaning.

According to this myth, the visible world is a living entity, whose divine and perfectly good maker—variously called "Demiurge," "God," and "Intellect"—brought it into being out of eternal formless matter (*Tim.* 30a) and organized it as a living being by supplying it with its own perfectly—indeed mathematically—regulated cosmic soul. Unlike the omnipotent God of the Bible, the Demiurge had not only to consult a predetermined pattern in the ideal realm of Forms eternally preexisting beyond him (*Tim.* 39e) but also to bend to his will a somewhat recalcitrant pre-cosmic material, in the process bringing into existence certain subordinate gods to assist him, especially in the creation of the bodies and mortal souls of humans and animating them with an immortal soul-substance similar to that of the cosmic soul. Although the result was a less than perfect world, it is obvious why later Jewish thinkers like PHILO OF ALEXANDRIA and the Christian Platonists saw in Plato's work a parallel to the biblical creation story and used it to bridge the gap between their beliefs and those of intellectual paganism.

Two developments of Plato's teaching are important for later Jewish and Christian thought: Middle Platonism, which became fully developed in the 1st cent. CE, and Neoplatonism, classically formulated by the philosopher PLOTINUS (205–70 CE). Both were marked by a deference to ancient authority, be it that of Plato or Pythagoras (*see* PYTHAGORAS, PYTHAGOREANISM), and contained a distinctly religious element; their watchword could aptly have been taken from Plato's dictum concerning the supreme goal of human effort: to assimilate oneself to God insofar as possible (*Theaet.* 176b).

The popular religious sentiment of these times was much more attracted to a philosophy like Plato's that explained—indeed revealed—the supreme cause of the world as a divine and paternal figure who could be touched upon by reflective thought, unlike the dreary calculations of the skeptical Academy, the dry moralism and mechanical cosmology of the Stoics (*see* STOICS, STOICISM), and the non-theistic atomism of the Epicureans. Middle Platonists (e.g., Philo of Alexandria, PLUTARCH, Moderatus, Alcinous, NUMENIUS) adopted Aristotle's logic and philosophy of mind, and maintained the tendency—characteristic of Plato, the "Old Academy" of his immediate successors, and contemporary Neopythagoreans—to make a sharp distinction between this world and the divine realm beyond it supplemented by an intermediate zone populated with spiritual powers (daimōn δαίμων), and to posit a dualistic view of soul and body that both Jews and Christians, even beyond the 4th cent., could embrace without denying either the bodily resurrection or the goodness of the physical creation. For Middle Platonists, the principal Platonic dialogue of reference was the *Timaeus*, interpreted to reveal three fundamental principles: 1) the supreme principle was God, identified with the supreme Form of the Good from the *Republic* and with the demiurge of the *Timaeus* (*Tim.* 39e) reconceived as a universal Intellect; 2) next was the archetypal Model of the *Timaeus*, conceived as the intelligible realm of Forms, perhaps identical with God's thoughts, existing either within the divine Intellect or—like Philo of Alexandria's LOGOS—occupying a distinct realm external and subjacent to it; 3) by contemplating these, God confers order upon the third and lowest principle, Matter, a preexisting stuff mysteriously agitated within its matrix, the receptacle of the *Timaeus* (*Tim.* 48e–49a).

The Neoplatonism of Plotinus and his successors (e.g., PORPHYRY, Iamblichus, Syrianus, Proclus, Damascius, Olympiodorus, Pseudo-Dionysius) represents a selective systematization of the works of Plato, plus elements from Aristotle and Stoicism, and is often described as the final form of Greek philosophy. Even though it became the dominant influence upon Christian theology from the 4th cent. until it was displaced by Aristotelianism in the Middle Ages, for some, such as the emperor Julian, it was a final attempt to revive classical philosophy as a viable alternative to the Christian faith. It resulted from linking the three principles outlined by Middle Platonists—supplemented by the cosmic soul of the *Timaeus* as a fourth principle—into a dynamic chain of emanation. From the supreme principle, now reconceived as an absolute "One" beyond all being and determination, originates the cosmic Intellect as the realm of the pure, unchanging being of the Platonic Forms. In turn, Intellect gives rise to the cosmic Soul as principle of life and becoming, which plays the demiurgic role of the Middle Platonic Intellect by imposing the forms it intuits in the cosmic Intelligence above it upon Matter, the final extremity of the emanational chain. Like Plotinus himself, Neoplatonists did not see themselves as coining a new philosophy, but believed that they had merely rediscovered the true meaning of Plato's teachings. *See* GREEK PHILOSOPHY AND RELIGION.

Bibliography: John Dillon. *The Middle Platonists: 80 B.C. to A.D. 220.* Rev. ed. (1996); John Dillon. *Neoplatonic Philosophy: Introductory Readings* (2004); W. K. C. Guthrie. *A History of Greek Philosophy* (1979–90); Plato. *Plato: Complete Works.* John M. Cooper and D. S. Hutchinson, eds. (1997); Richard T. Wallis. *Neoplatonism.* 2nd ed. (1995).

JOHN TURNER

PLEASED, TO BE [חָפֵץ khafets, רָצָה ratsah; εὐδοκέω eudokeō, χαίρω chairō]. In the OT, this verb denotes human reaction to other people, their words or actions, and circumstances (Gen 34:18; Judg 14:7; 2 Sam 3:36; 1 Chr 13:4). It also denotes the Lord's reaction to humans and their words or actions (Ps 41:11 [Heb. 41:12]), as well as the Lord's own actions (Ps 40:13 [Heb. 40:14]; 70:1 [Heb. 70:2]). The Lord's pleasure results in blessing (Num 14:8; 24:1; 1 Sam 12:22). Used negatively, the verb also communicates the Lord's displeasure with burnt offerings or polluted sacrifices (Ps 51:16 [Heb. 51:18]). In the NT, the verb conveys human reaction to others' words and action (Matt 14:6; Mark 14:11). When used of God it almost exclusively refers to the pleasure God takes in Jesus (Matt 3:17; 17:5; 2 Pet 1:17), the exception being when God is pleased with Enoch (Heb 11:5). Further, God is pleased with divine actions, especially with reference to Christ (Gal 1:15; Col 1:19-20).

KATHY R. MAXWELL

PLEDGE [אִסָּר ʾissar, עֲבוֹט ʿavot, עֵרָבוֹן ʿeravon, תְּשׂוּמֶת tesumeth; ἀρραβών arrabōn]. An object (Gen 38:17-20; Deut 24:12) or property (Neh 5:3) given as collateral in a loan transaction, limited by Israelite law (Lev 6:2-3 [Heb. 5:21-22]; Deut 24:17). In the NT, a pledge is a down payment (Eph 1:14; compare 2 Cor 5:5). *See* DEBT, DEBTOR; SURETY.

A. HEATH JONES III

PLEIADES plee'uh-deez [כִּימָה kimah]. A brilliant star cluster located in the constellation Taurus, its appearance in and disappearance from the night sky was employed throughout the ancient world to signal the beginning or end of the rainy seasons for both agriculture and navigation. The constellation is mentioned in the OT context of the divine construction of the cosmos (Job 9:9; 38:31; Amos 5:8). *See* ASTRONOMY, ASTROLOGY; COSMOGONY, COSMOLOGY; ORION.

Bibliography: G. R. Driver. "Two Astronomical Passages in the OT." *JTS* 7 (1956) 1–2; E. Robbins. "The Pleiades, the Flood, and the Jewish New Year." *Ki Baruch Hu.* R. Chazan et al., eds. (1999) 336–41.

ELLEN ROBBINS

PLEROMA pli-roh´muh [πλήρωμα plērōma]. *Pleroma* is that which fills or completes; fulfillment (of prophecy) or perfection. In theology *pleroma* acquires a technical referent, the full divine perfection, especially as present in Jesus (John 1:14) or salvation conveyed through him to believers (John 1:16). Second-century CE Valentinian Gnostic theologians (*see* GNOSTICISM) employed the word as a technical term for the reality of the divine cosmos in contrast to the deficiency of the fallen, material universe (Irenaeus, *Haer.* 1.1.3; 1.11.5; 1.12.4).

The noun appears infrequently in the LXX for **melo᾿ah** (מְלוֹאָהּ, "that which fills it"), especially in reference to earth (and heavens) in relationship to the Lord (e.g., Pss 24:1 [quoted in 1 Cor 10:26]; 50:12; 89:11 [Heb. 89:12]; 96:11). The expression also refers to the whole earth suffering destruction (Jer 8:16). A similar range of nontechnical meanings of *pleroma* occurs in Philo's writings. It can designate the full complement of a ship's crew (*Abraham* 116; *Moses* 2.62; *Spec. Laws* 4.186; *Good Person* 142) or the ballast carried (*Good Person* 41; 128). It can indicate perfection in a number or harmonic series in music (*Spec. Laws* 2.200; *Rewards* 109). With reference to the soul of the wise or of worshipers, *pleroma* designates the complete possession of the virtues in question (*Abraham* 268; *Spec. Laws* 1.272; *Rewards* 65). Hellenistic Greek does not use *pleroma* in the more technical theological senses that it acquires in later Christian authors.

In the NT, examples cover a similarly wide range of meanings. It designates the piece of cloth used to patch an old garment (Matt 9:16; Mark 2:21) as well as the full baskets of bread left over from the miraculous feedings (Mark 6:43; 8:20). Similarly, Paul speaks of Israel's hardening until the **plērōma** ("full number") of the Gentiles has come to believe (Rom 11:25) or alternatively of the riches to come when the "full inclusion" of Israel occurs (Rom 11:12). In these examples *pleroma* includes apocalyptic overtones of God's plan for the last days and the final salvation of humanity. Paul can use *pleroma* to refer to an earlier event in the unfolding of that plan when he speaks of the "sending" of God's son, "born of a woman, born under the Law," in the "fullness of time" (Gal 4:4). A similar temporal use of a point in which God's saving plan is accomplished occurs with reference to the exalted Christ in Eph 1:10. In a non-apocalyptic sense, Paul speaks of love as **plērōma** ("fulfillment") of the Law (Rom 13:10) and the "fullness of the blessing of Christ" with which he hopes to come to Rome (Rom 15:29; a reference to the spiritual blessings he anticipates sharing with the readers, Rom 1:11-12).

The word *pleroma* assumes a different range of theological overtones when it is used of attributes of divinity possessed by Christ or mediated through him to believers. The hymnic prologue to John's Gospel speaks of the unique Son as "full [plērēs πλήρης] of grace and truth" (John 1:14) and then of grace that believers have received from his **plērōma** (John 1:16). In these examples, "grace and truth" may be intended to reflect God's covenant attributes of "loving kindness and fidelity" (Exod 34:6), since v. 17 contrasts the Law through Moses with the "grace and truth" through Jesus. Thus the term still belongs to an understanding of how God's plan of salvation culminates in Jesus.

However, the possibility that *pleroma* refers to Jesus' participation in the divinity of God is suggested by the identification of the "only Son" with the incarnate Word in John 1:14 and the insistence that only the Son has seen and can reveal God (John 1:18). A distinctive christological use of *pleroma* emerges in Colossians and Ephesians. A hymnic passage in Col 1:15-20 celebrates the Son as the "image of the invisible God," an embodiment of God's creative wisdom, "firstborn of all creation" (Col 1:15), and as "head of the body, the church ... firstborn from the dead" (Col 1:18). An ambiguous phrase that speaks of "all the fullness" dwelling "in him" (Col 1:19) could refer either to a complete embodiment of God's creative activity or to the divine preeminence enjoyed by the risen Christ. Colossians later speaks of "the whole fullness of deity dwell[ing] bodily" (Col 2:9), followed by the affirmation that believers "have come to fullness in him" (Col 2:10), a sequence similar to that found in John 1:14-16. The association between Christ as divine fullness and his body, the church, reappears as the conclusion to an elaborate celebration of the lordship of the exalted Christ in Eph 1:23*b*. As in the other examples, their relationship to Christ ensures that believers are filled "with all the fullness of God" (Eph 3:19). Therefore any cosmological or metaphysical overtones that these passages employ in using *fullness* as a term for the way in which Christ participates in and mediates God can be grounded in the NT understanding of salvation.

Valentinian authors echo NT texts to provide a scriptural tie-in for a completely different speculative system (see echoes of Col 1:19 and Eph 3:19 in Irenaeus, *Haer.* 1.1.1; Clement of Alexandria, *Exc.* 21.1; *Gos. Truth* 16, 35). Primarily, the *pleroma* refers to the divine world that emanated from the unknown Father. Wisdom's disturbed passion either to create without a partner or to know God led to expulsion of her disturbed "light" from the "fullness" and the formation of the biblical god, his angelic realms, material creation, and humankind. As bearers of the "light," humanity will leave the "deficiency" of this world to return to the divine resulting in a restored "Pleroma" (*Treat. Res.* 49, 4–5; Irenaeus, *Haer.* 1.21.4; *Gos. Truth* 21, 8–21; 24, 20–25, 3; *Ep. Pet. Phil.* 134, 17–21). The *Gospel of Truth* (*see* TRUTH, GOSPEL OF) employs the whole range of the term *pleroma*: for the divine realm, for the knowledge of that realm brought by the Savior (Jesus), and for the spiritual state of the one who has received knowledge. Valentinian usage of *pleroma* is introduced as the true meaning of the NT (*Gos. Phil.* 68, 14 [Matt 6:6]; 84, 13 [John 8:32]). *See* FULFILL, FULFILLMENT.

PHEME PERKINS

PLINY plin´ee. Pliny the Younger was born in 61 or 62 CE. He was a successful lawyer and government official. While administering Pontus-Bithynia (in modern Turkey), Pliny wrote to the emperor TRAJAN to request guidance on what to do with Christians. Pliny reported that he executed Christians who refused to sacrifice to the Roman deities and the emperor's image but pardoned those who recanted. He asked Trajan what to do with those anonymously accused of being Christians (*Ep.* 10.96). Trajan approved of Pliny's policies, but forbade him from actively seeking out Christians or relying on anonymous accusations (*Ep.* 10.97). The correspondence does not describe why Christians were considered criminals. It does suggest that persecutions were localized and sporadic, since Trajan refused to lay down a general rule and ordered Pliny not to actively seek out the Christians. Pliny died in Pontus-Bithynia in 113 CE.

ADAM L. PORTER

PLOTINUS. According to the biography prepared by his student PORPHYRY, Plotinus was born around 205 CE. At the age of twenty-eight, he began studying philosophy in Alexandria. Ten years later, he joined Gordian III's invasion of Persia because he wished to study with Persian and Indian philosophers. Gordian was murdered, and Plotinus escaped to Rome. Here he became a favorite philosopher to leading families until his death in 270 CE. Porphyry published Plotinus' works in six books, each of which contains nine essays, hence the title *Enneads*. Although Plotinus claimed merely to articulate the truths that Platonism had already taught, he moved beyond Plato, especially by insisting on unity as his fundamental principle. This unity transcends even God and mind (or soul) (*Enn.* 6.9.6). His essays touch additionally on a variety of moral, ethical, and religious topics, including attacks on GNOSTICISM. Plotinus' connections to the highest levels of Rome's ruling class and the lasting influence of his doctrine make his work an important intellectual link between earlier classical and later Western thought, both philosophical and religious. *See* PLATO, PLATONISM.

Bibliography: Kevin Corrigan. *Reading Plotinus: A Practical Introduction to Neoplatonism* (2005); Lloyd P. Gerson. *Plotinus* (1994); Dominic J. O'Meara. *Plotinus: An Introduction to His Enneads* (1991).

HANS-FRIEDRICH MUELLER

PLOW [חָרַשׁ **kharash**; ἄροτρον **arotron**]. The metal blade or plowshare (**makhareshah** מַחֲרֵשָׁה; 1 Sam 13:20; Isa 2:4; Joel 3:10) affixed to the wooden plow, pulled by teams of oxen and guided by a human (1 Kgs 19:19; Sir 25:8), was used to create deep furrows in a cleared field that could then be sown with seed. Because this hot, dirty work was such a common sight (Luke 17:7), it served as a powerful metaphor in Micah's prophecy of the coming destruction of Jerusalem, when Zion would "be plowed as a field" (Mic 3:12). Plowing served as an element of several other metaphors and proverbs (Judg 14:18; Prov 20:4; Sir 38:25-26). *See* TOOLS.

VICTOR H. MATTHEWS

PLUMB LINE [אֲנָךְ **ʾanakh**]. A string with a stone or metal weight (plumb bob) attached, used by a builder to determine whether a stone or mud-brick wall is vertical. This instrument is also called a plummet (**ʾeven** אֶבֶן; Isa 34:11; Zech 4:10; **mishqoleth** מִשְׁקֹלֶת; 2 Kgs 21:13). As a tool used to measure straightness, the plumb line served as a metaphor for the moral assessment of Israel's kings (Ahab in 2 Kgs 21:13), of the nation's adherence to the covenant (Amos 7:7-8), and of the justice and righteousness expected of the people (Isa 28:17). *See* AMOS, BOOK OF; TOOLS.

VICTOR H. MATTHEWS

PLUMMET. *See* PLUMB LINE.

PLUTARCH pl*oo*´tahrk. This Greek biographer and essayist (ca. 45–125 CE) lived in the small city of Chaeronea but also traveled to Egypt and to Italy and served as a priest at Delphi. He is most famous for paired biographies of Greeks and Romans in his *Parallel Lives*. Seventy-eight miscellaneous essays, the *Moralia*, also survive and address diverse rhetorical, philosophical, moral, religious, educational, and antiquarian topics. A Platonist, deeply devout in traditional pagan religious practices, Plutarch conveys essential historical and religious information about the pre-Christian world as well as contemporary pagan parallels to the biographical narratives of the Gospels (*see* PLATO, PLATONISM). Plutarch's works also document the religious attitude of a highly educated and traditionally religious Roman citizen at the time of Christianity's early development.

Bibliography: Hans Dieter Betz, ed. *Plutarch's Ethical Writings and Early Christian Literature* (1978); Hans Dieter Betz, ed. *Plutarch's Theological Writings and Early Christian Literature* (1975); Frederick E. Brenk. *With Unperfumed Voice: Studies in Plutarch, in Greek*

Literature, Religion and Philosophy, and in the New Testament Background (2007); Donald A. Russell. *Plutarch.* 2nd ed. (2001).

HANS-FRIEDRICH MUELLER

POCHERETH-HAZZEBAIM pok´uh-rith-haz-uh-bay´im [פֹּכֶרֶת הַצְּבָיִים pokhereth hatsevayim]. Means "gazelle hunter" and is an example of a profession becoming a proper name. Pochereth-hazzebaim is among the cultic professionals returning from exile (Ezra 2:57; Neh 7:59; 1 Esd 5:34). He is one of ten heads of families called "Solomon's servant's" who are associated with and probably similar to the "temple servants" who assisted the Levites (Ezra 2:43; *see* NETHINIM).

MILTON ENG

POD [κεράτιον keration]. The seed pod of an evergreen in the Mediterranean called the carob tree. The pods, tasting similar to sweetened cocoa, are not usually a food source but can provide sustenance if needed. Pods are mentioned as the pig food that the desperate PRODIGAL SON considers eating (Luke 15:16).

KATHY R. MAXWELL

POEM OF ERRA. *See* ERRA EPIC.

POETRY IN THE NT. Poetry is less prominent in the NT than it is in the OT. As is the case with the OT, the boundaries between poetry and prose are blurry, which makes distinguishing between the two a difficult task. Strictly speaking, there is no Greek poetry in the NT following the meter, form, and rhythm that traditionally distinguished Greek poetry from prose. However, there appear to be a handful of brief quotations of Greek classical poets in the NT. In Acts 17:28, Paul supports his argument to the Athenians with the statement "as even some of your own poets have said," followed by the statement "For we too are his offspring." The latter appears to be a quotation from Aratus (*Phaen.* 5), although a similar line appears in Cleanthes' *Hymn to Zeus.* In addition, the phrase "In him we live and move and have our being," which precedes the reference to poets in this verse, has also been identified as a quotation from the 6th-cent. BCE poet Epimenides (*Cretica*), but this is less certain. In 1 Cor 15:33 Paul exhorts the Corinthians, saying, "Do not be deceived," followed by the phrase "Bad company ruins good morals." The latter was a widespread proverb derived from the comic poet Menander. And Titus 1:12 appears to be a quotation of a line from Callimachus (*Hymn to Zeus* 4).

Another way to approach the issue is to examine the relationship between NT poetry and the typical poetic forms of the OT. Among the abundant quotations of the OT in NT writings, there are a significant number of quotations of or allusions to poetic passages, some marked and some unmarked. These include Matt 4:6 (Ps 91:11-12); Matt 7:23 (Ps 6:8 [Heb. 6:9]); Matt 13:32 (Ps 104:12); Matt 13:35 (Ps 78:2); Matt 21:16 (Ps 8:2 [Heb. 8:3]); Mark 1:11 (Ps 2:7); Mark 11:9-10 (Ps 118:25-26); Rom 8:36 (Ps 44:22); and Rom 10:19-21 (Deut 32:21; Isa 65:1-2). There are also a number of passages that appear to be modeled on OT poetic parallelism. Luke 1–2 has several such passages, including the well-known praise of Mary, traditionally known as the MAGNIFICAT (Luke 1:46-55), and Zechariah's prophecy, traditionally called the BENEDICTUS (Luke 1:68-79). Scholars have pointed out the presence of hymn-like passages embedded in some of the letters in the NT and have suggested that they are remnants of the liturgy of early Christian groups (1 Cor 13:1-13; 15:3-5; Eph 1:3-13; Phil 2:6-11; Col 1:15-20; 1 Pet 1:3-5). Similarly, the throne-room ceremonies in the Apocalypse of John have over fifteen hymns (including Rev 4:8, 11; 5:9-10; 11:17-18). While scholars debate whether these hymns were adapted from preexisting liturgical materials or were composed by the author, they clearly have a poetic character. *See* HYMNS, NT.

Bibliography: Steve Moyise and Maarten J. J. Menken, eds. *The Psalms in the New Testament* (2004).

RUBÉN R. DUPERTUIS

POETRY, HEBREW. Roughly a third of the OT is verse (i.e., set in lines). This poetic corpus includes the three books of Job, Proverbs, and Psalms, and the several festival songs embedded in prose texts (Exod 15; Deut 32; Judg 5; 2 Sam 22) for which the Masoretes provided a distinct accentual system and/or special page layouts—the latter convention is now in evidence in (much earlier) manuscripts of most of these works from Qumran (Tov); Lamentations and Song of Songs; other poems or poetic fragments embedded within blocks of prose (e.g., Gen 4:23-24); and much of the Latter Prophets. Any reading of this material, however motivated (theologically, literarily, historically), will need to accommodate its poetic medium. The corpus as a whole remains centrally a part of the scriptural heritage of Judaism, Christianity, and Islam and has been a foundational source for poetry throughout history and throughout the world, and especially for all later (post-biblical) traditions of Hebrew verse (Carmi).

What follows is an account of biblical Hebrew poetry, its basic components, operative prosody, and leading characteristics. There is no atheoretical or neutral way of describing verse of any kind. The view on biblical verse presented here is itself laden with contestable theoretical assumptions at almost every step along the way and is but one way among many of accounting for this material. Its basic orientation is practical and pragmatic and chiefly descriptive. It is guided, on the one hand, by a strong conviction that biblical Hebrew verse is in most general respects just like any other verse tradition, especially regarding what we know of ancient poetic traditions, and thus biblical poems should be read and interpreted like other poems, with the same critical tools, with the same kinds of guiding assumptions in place, and, on the other hand, by an equally firm belief that what distinguishes the verse of the Bible is its historicity and cultural specificity, those peculiar encrustations and encumbrances that typify all human artifacts. The literary and the historical, then, are always in view here. Special attention is given to various dimensions and strategies of close reading (a most practical kind of criticism) through a reading of Ps 125.

A. What Is Hebrew Poetry?

1. Line structure

To define Hebrew poetry requires some awareness of what distinguishes poetry more generally, a topic that remains much debated and depends heavily on the particular theoretical disposition assumed. Yet beyond theoretical commitments (which are always germane) what counts as poetry is ever a configuration of specific historical, cultural, and ideological factors (Perloff). Almost all premodern (prior to ca. 1850 CE) poetry was set as verse, i.e., in lines—etymologically, the English term *verse* derives ultimately from Latin *versus*, lit., "turning," which, focusing on the turn at the end of the line, designated a line of writing, and especially a line of poetry. In fact, with the notable exception of a few modern genres (such as the "prose poem"), the line is the single differentia of poetry on which almost all critics and poets agree.

That biblical Hebrew poetry was arranged in lines (variously called cola, versets, half-lines, stichs, or hemistichs)—though a not incontestable proposition—is inferable from a wide variety of considerations. Several manuscript traditions exhibit a variety of special formatting that graphically displays line structure for a substantial portion of the biblical poetic corpus; the existence of single lines and triplets, alongside the more common couplet, shows that the line must be the basic unit of lineation. Parallelism presumes the individual line as its basic unit, being matched or repeated and set apart (see §A6). Parallelism in biblical poetry functions principally to mark line ends. The line also can be defined in terms of syntax and length. The acrostics in Pss 111 and 112 (as well as the ʾALEF [ʾ א] stanza [Ps 9:2-3] of the ACROSTIC poem in Pss 9–10) show the single line as a structural entity. Tropes, such as sound play (e.g., alliteration, see §F), appear frequently and precisely at the level of individual lines. In sum, there is a great deal of empirical warrant for positing the existence of the line in Hebrew verse, and thus, for referring to these lines as poetic, as verse.

Being nonmetrical, actual line lengths are never numerically consistent for long stretches. As a result, Hebrew poetic lines exhibit a general (though variable) symmetry in length that contrasts noticeably with the randomness of clause and sentence length in biblical Hebrew prose. Line boundaries normally converge with the end of discrete syntactic or phrasal units (even when sentences run on past line ends), and lines tend to be grouped chiefly in twos and threes (i.e., as couplets and triplets). Indeed, the characteristic closed and recursive shape of biblical Hebrew poetic rhythm is itself chiefly a product of end-stopping and parallelism. A clausal or sentential whole (frame) is articulated and then reiterated once or twice over, producing a pulsing series of progressions—one step forward, reiteration, and then another step forward, reiteration again, and sometimes twice over (in the case of triplets), and so on. The recursion of parallelism redoubles the syntactic frame, and in the process reinforces the projection of wholeness and the felt fullness of the stop at line end.

2. Beyond the line

The line, without which there can be no verse, is by itself insufficient to identify a specific instance of discourse as poetic, biblical or otherwise. In antiquity, e.g., lists of names, commodities, and the like, which are among the most mundane, nonpoetic forms of verbal communication, were commonly written out in lines (e.g., Josh 12:9-24; CAT 4.93, 99, 100; *TAD* C4.3, 4). What makes a poem includes something more than being set in lines, though deciding on what this something more is will vary depending on the specific poetic corpus in view. Aside from lineation, there are no intrinsic markers or clear-cut boundaries between poems and nonpoems, but only a cluster of intersecting and always local variables that signal the presence of poetry. Three variables (other than the line) are here offered for initial consideration.

3. Concision or compression

The first is concision or compression, which is commonly associated with poetry more generally. Concision may be measured in several ways. The typical poetic clause is shorter and less complex than its prose counterpart. This relative brevity is achieved principally through various forms of ellipses, e.g., verb gapping, double-duty prepositions, reduced usage of the so-called prose particles (definite article, relative particle, etc.), the net effect of which is to bring semantically important words closer together, adding layers of meaning and imagery and the impression of increased density. Further, the lines themselves, normally consisting of from two to six words, are fairly concise. Here, one might usefully compare some of the much longer written free-verse lines from modern Hebrew verse. The poems are also mostly shorter in terms of numbers of actual words used, and in relation to narrative poems from around the ANE (e.g., Gilgamesh, Atrahasis, Aqhat, Kirta).

4. Verbally inventive

"Verbally inventive" is a characterization borrowed from T. Eagleton. Poetry is often characterized as language that draws attention to itself through intensified language. The problem is that not all of what is routinely called poetry behaves in this manner. Hence, Eagleton's more modest phrasing and insistence that if poetry often uses language in "inventive" ways, it does not do so all the time. "Inventive" here is being used in a factual, not evaluative sense (Eagleton). Hebrew verse is often verbally inventive in this more modest sense. Its language routinely seems denser and more intense, with increased instances of wordplay and other tropes, ambiguity, allusion, etc. Sometimes a sense of verbal self-consciousness is detectable, as in the formal conceit of the alphabetic acrostic or in the insistence in Ps 19 that Day and Night and all the Heavens proclaim the glory of God but without literal speech (19:2-4). And in some poets, like Job, one is never in doubt of the verbal artistry on display, the inventiveness of the poetic idiom. Yet there, too, are other runs in Hebrew poems (e.g., as in many psalms) that appear much less linguistically self-conscious.

5. Difference from prose

There is a sense of difference between biblical poetry and biblical prose (the common language of, for instance, the historical books). Students of Hebrew literature to this day continue to find reading biblical poetry a more challenging exercise than reading prose. The act of reading poetry is more intense and laborious, typically requiring a slower pass through the text. It is not that this Hebrew is linguistically any different from the Hebrew of the prose texts—rare is the poetic tradition, however radical, that is not predicated on the linguistic conventions of the everyday language. Rather, the experiential difference follows because the poetic language so routinely involves higher concentrations of words and phrases with rare meanings or usages or simply rare words and phrases themselves, bold ellipses, sudden transitions in subject matter and grammar, and other stylistic difficulties.

In recent years much has been made of a putative poetry-prose continuum in biblical Hebrew literature (compare Petersen and Richards), with some even questioning whether such a notion as biblical Hebrew poetry has any real sensibility (Kugel). Biblical Hebrew is the self-same language, and there is nothing intrinsic to (most) rhetorical figures that proscribe their use as either poetry or prose. However, on the basis of the descriptions above (e.g., line, concision, verbal inventiveness, and a discernible poetic diction and texture), a sensible notion of Hebrew poetry is plainly achievable.

6. Parallelism

PARALLELISM is the repetition of patterns in adjacent phrases and has almost unexceptionally served as the defining formal feature of biblical Hebrew verse. But parallelism *qua* parallelism is unremarkable. In literature generally, written as well as oral, it is a common stylistic trope and has no significance as such for defining Hebrew verse. In fact, as many scholars have noted (esp. Kugel), as a trope parallelism is also to be found throughout Hebrew narrative prose. Moreover, a substantial portion (perhaps as much as a third) of the biblical poetic corpus comprises nonparallelistic lines. What is distinctive about parallelism in Hebrew verse is its prominent role in line fixing and in joining adjacent lines and the peculiar rhythm of recursion that it creates, neither of which applies to the use of parallelism in the prose portions of the Bible.

The articulation of line structure in biblical verse is varied. Such phenomena as line-end pause, sentence logic, line length, anaphora, semantic emphasis, and formal figures such as the alphabetic acrostic are routinely involved. Yet the main device used for fixing the line end in much of the biblical corpus is parallelism. Like the silence of a pause, parallelism marks the end of a line only belatedly, retrospectively. The unit most often iterated is the line, its shape emerging to match the adjacent lines that are set in equivalence. Isaiah 11:3 is a typical example:

and-not-according-to-the-vision-of-his-eyes will he judge
and-not-according-to-the-hearing-of-his-ears will he decide

welo᾽-lemar᾽eh ῾enaw yishpot
welo᾽-lemishma῾ ᾽ozenaw yokhiakh

וְלֹא־לְמַרְאֵה עֵינָיו יִשְׁפּוֹט
וְלֹא־לְמִשְׁמַע אָזְנָיו יוֹכִיחַ

Conjunction – Negative – Participle – Verb
Conjunction – Negative – Participle – Verb

The matching syntactic frames here are most exact. The onset of the frame established in the initial line is repeated in the second line and throws the ending of that first line into relief. Recognition of the reiterated frame as a whole enhances the closural force that accompanies the end of the second line, which itself mimes the line ending of the first line.

The full effectiveness of this kind of strategy for line marking depends to a large degree on familiarity with the techniques to be put into play. Appreciation of how parallelism signals line ends will not always be immediately perceptible from individual examples. But as the device is repeated over the course of a poem, perception increases. Consider Isa 11:3 together with vv. 4-5:

> And he shall not judge by what his eyes see,
> or decide by what his ears hear;
> but with righteousness he shall judge the poor,
> and decide with equity for the meek of the earth;
> and he shall strike the earth with the rod of his
> mouth,
> and with the breath of his lips he shall kill the
> wicked.
> And righteousness shall be the belt around his
> waist,
> and faithfulness the belt around his loins.
> (NRSV, slightly modified)

Here the listener is exposed four times in eight lines to the use of parallelism as a means for fixing local line ends.

Depending on the design of a given poem, other ad hoc features (e.g., logical or temporal connectors, thematic development, semantic emphasis), usually in combination with other considerations, may serve to underscore the beginnings and/or endings of lines. Notice in Isa 11:3-5 the use of the conjunctive WAW (w ו, meaning "and," "or," "but" in the NRSV) to head every line, serving as a kind of line-marking anaphora. But the conjunctive waws are especially important after the second lines of the four couplets, as they help to secure the integrity of those lines. Additionally, the symmetry of line length and the clausal nature of the lines themselves show that the line structure of Isa 11:3-5 is rather impressively indicated.

The parallel frame coerces auditors into considering two images together and giving rise to a new perception in the process. An example is provided by Gen 49:11 ("he washes his garments in wine and his robe in the blood of grapes"), where "washing in wine," an image of weal and superabundance (compare Deut 32:14), is perceived more violently in the parallel image of washing "in the blood of grapes."

B. Free Rhythms of Hebrew Verse

Until quite recently, the search for Hebrew meter has been a constant preoccupation of scholars. However, the simple fact is that Hebrew verse is not metrical (having a pattern in rhythm that can be observed and named). Biblical Hebrew is a stress-timed language, and stress figures prominently in the rhythmic drive of the language that naturally pulsates through its words and phrases. But the beat of the stresses in Hebrew poetry never finally exhibits a meter, a patterned rhythm. This is not because meter is unachievable in Hebrew. To the contrary, a plenitude of metrical verse exists in the various traditions that comprise the post-biblical Hebrew poetic corpus (Carmi). Rather, biblical verse is nonmetrical. Potentially, everything in the poem can contribute to the rhythm. The core of biblical poetry's "free rhythms" consists in configurations of its variable but constrained line, which is commonly grouped in twos and threes, and sometimes fours, with the language's strong word and word-group stress frequently reinforced through repetitions. Strict regularity of syllables is lacking. Nonetheless, stresses are made to fall within a limited range, with longer words having secondary stresses that may be separated by as many as two, three, and four syllables. These core constituencies, which give biblical verse its distinctive rhythmic signature, are enacted, often in combination with other aspects of the poem (e.g., lineation, syntactic patterns, tone, elements of meaning), in a myriad of ways to realize a specific poem's unique rhythm. That is, there is a certain "organic" structure to nonmetrical or free verse—no two such poems are ever really rhythmically alike.

Some sense of the kind of organic free rhythmic structures that typify biblical poems may be observed in Ps 19. The poem as a whole may be divided in two major sections, vv. 2-7 and vv. 8-15 (in the Heb.), each of which may be further halved (vv. 2-5*b*, 5*c*-7; vv. 8-11, 12-15)—each of these subsections is headed by a fronted topic word ("the heavens," "the sun," "the Torah of Yahweh," "your servant"). In the first half of the poem the lines are somewhat longer and relatively balanced within each couplet and triplet. Thematically, this part of Ps 19 focuses on creation and draws heavily on mythological imagery. The natural entities are personified throughout. The first section (vv. 2-5*b*) consists of four parallel couplets—though the parallelism is staged differently in each—and features the metaphorical language of speech, words, and voice. The repetition of the parallelism echoes the antiphonal praises of nature. The second section (vv. 5*c*-7) concentrates solely on the sun. It consists of two triplets with lines that run on, imitating something of the sun's daily trajectory of work. In the third section (vv. 8-11) an abrupt change in subject matter, tone, and feel is achieved. The relaxed ebb and flow of nature in the first sections gives way to the tightly controlled ritual of Torah study. The section consists of eight couplets, all parallel, and all roughly unbalanced—the first lines longer than the second ones. The exactness of the first six couplets is near perfect. Torah is mentioned in its various guises and the Tetragrammaton (YHWH) is used six times over in the same line position each time. Each of the first lines in these couplets comprises three major stresses, and each of the second lines contains two. The tight focus slackens a bit in v. 11 and even further in the poem's final section (vv. 12-15). Now the topic of focus is the servant, the speaker of the poem. The lines remain shorter than in the initial sections, but are not so strictly controlled as in section three. There are four couplets and a concluding triplet—the final triplet being an effective means of signaling closure (Smith). The final triplet replays various aspects of the poem, notably the language of speech (though here no longer metaphorical), and has one last reference to Yahweh.

The rhythmic profile realized in Ps 19 is typical of biblical poetry. Its backbone is the rhythmic movement of the syllables in biblical Hebrew (i.e., the loose alternation of stresses and slacks in words and phrases), materially no different from the spoken language or the language of Hebrew prose, except in its organization into tighter (e.g., Ps 19:8-10) and looser (e.g., Ps 19:2-5*b*) sequences. Hebrew verse is a kind of free verse, and its rhythms share strong family resemblance to other free-verse poems, such as Walt Whitman's *Leaves of Grass*. It is to free verse that students of biblical poetry should look first for models of reading, and not to the metrical traditions.

C. Poetry in the Ancient Near East

The portrait of biblical poetry so far painted—a nonmetrical form of discourse arranged as verse and characterized above all by terseness, verbal inventiveness, and a discernible poetic diction and texture—is one that in large and small ways resembles the other poetic traditions known from the ANE (e.g., Sumerian, Akkadian, Ugaritic). Though not at all surprising, neither is the fact of such broad similarities insignificant. Any construal of biblical verse must finally be squared with what we know about the various verse traditions from the surrounding ANE cultures. This is especially the case with respect to the Ugaritic poetic corpus, which provides biblical poetry with the semblance of a pre-history (Parker). Indeed, most of the genres of verse in the Bible are found in these contemporary poetic traditions (e.g., hymns, laments, love songs, proverbs). As a group, these verse traditions provide the earliest evidence for free verse (a poetic phenomenon otherwise mostly treated as a product of modernity). Though the historical rationale for privileging contemporary Near Eastern poetries for comparative purposes is incontrovertible, there is no reason not to read in light of all other poetry as well. One other such tradition, in particular, deserves highlighting: post-biblical Hebrew verse (Carmi). Often neglected by biblical scholars, this manifold and rich tradition of verse in Hebrew, through comparison and contrast, potentially can illuminate our understanding of biblical Hebrew verse on any number of topics (e.g., prosody, imagery, diction).

D. Nonnarrative Verse

As a practical matter, R. Alter notices that biblical verse is used for all manner of things except telling stories, which invariably in the OT are rendered in prose. Epic narrative verse is well known from the period and region (e.g., Gilgamesh, Kirta), so biblical writers could well have chosen to tell their stories in verse, had they so desired. To be sure, there are individual poems that incorporate narrative runs and sometimes even develop characters, but for the most part these forms are restricted in scale (e.g., Exod 15; Prov 7). Alter has also identified varieties of narrativity in certain Hebrew poems (e.g., 2 Sam 22). S. R. Driver, who much earlier also recognized the Bible's lack of epic verse, divided the nonnarrative poetry of the Bible into two broad types, lyric and gnomic. Though surely reductive, leaving many verse forms in the Bible unaccounted for, the two types are indeed pervasive.

1. Lyric

The term *lyric*, in its broadest sense, distinguishes the various nondramatic types of poetry. That is, one of its central identifying traits is the frequent absence of features and practices (plot, character, etc.) that are otherwise found in narrative. Since lyric poetry makes no recourse to plot or character, it must depend on language itself, e.g., the sound of words, rhyme, rhythm, imagery, and meter (Langer). The lyric also tends to be small in scale, features voice(s) instead of character(s), and is often highly fragmentary or nonsequential in structure. A core of lyric verse in the Bible (e.g., Psalms, Song of Songs) suggests rootedness in a tradition of song and music.

2. Gnomic

By "gnomic" Driver means didactic or wisdom poetry (e.g., Job, Proverbs, and Sirach). He defines this kind of verse broadly as consisting of observations on life and the conduct and character of human beings and societies. In many respects the basic medium of such verse is not unlike that of the lyric just described. Beyond thematic and performative differences (most wisdom literature would not have been sung), different life settings (e.g., teaching), and a preference for other kinds of genres (e.g., proverbs), the major modal difference is a higher incidence of discursive logic (*see* WISDOM IN THE OT).

3. Lament

Other subgroups of the biblical poetic corpus may also be isolated. For example, the LAMENT, in its various guises (individual and communal laments, funeral dirges, laments for destroyed cities), was an especially common ancient poetic genre. It shares much with lyric and didactic verse and may be distinguished, broadly, by its chief thematic concerns (suffering and loss), its typically dark and somber mood, and often (especially in funeral dirges) a fondness for unbalanced couplets. Like gnomic or didactic verse, laments were not necessarily sung.

4. Prophetic

Prophetic verse is broadly continuous with the other nonnarrative verse of the Bible. As in wisdom poetry, discursive logic is more freely on display, and the prophets tend to take up forms and genres from elsewhere, playing with and even warping them, and generally using them for their own ends. One might also highlight the oracular and visionary aspects that feature in many prophetic poems and that have had a strong influence on the Western literary poetic imagination (*see* ORACLE). Still other kinds of biblical poems abound (e.g., love songs, work songs, victory celebrations), and some even figure as insets for heightening and other purposes in prose narratives.

E. Poetic Structure

To ask about the principles, formal and thematic, by which a poem is generated is to emphasize the temporal and dynamic qualities of poetry (Smith). The formal structure is the repetition of certain physical features of the poem—sound, words, lines—or a relationship among such features. Thematic structure, on the other hand, results from the organization or deployment of those elements of a poem that arise from the symbolism contained in the words—semantics, tone, etc. The two—form and theme—can only be artificially disentangled for the purpose of analysis, and as often as not overlap and bleed into each other and work together. Form has generally been under-appreciated in biblical Hebrew poetry, despite Gunkel's highly influential brand of form criticism (*see* FORM CRITICISM, OT). The organic and nonsystematic realization of formal structure in most biblical poems is the likely cause, since the patterns of repetition never become very regular and often vary from one section of a poem to the next, as evidenced, e.g., in the varied manipulation of line and line groupings in Ps 19. The alphabetic acrostic (e.g., Pss 111; 112) is the best example of a given form in the Bible, and it is an explicitly graphic conceit, modeled after scribal school texts known as "abecedaries" and featuring the traditional sequence of (twenty-two) letter forms in the Hebrew ALPHABET. The psalmic "forms" isolated by form critics, on the other hand, exhibit mostly thematic structure. For example, the distinguishing features of the individual lament, such as address, complaint, petition, motivations, and expression of confidence, are all thematic in nature. They may be habitually associated with some formal feature (e.g., petitions are often rendered with imperative or jussive forms) and other formal features may figure in realizing an individual poem's larger structure—though these will vary from poem to poem; but in no way is there a constancy to the form as form that these psalms habitually take, i.e., they are nothing like the sonnet or sestina of the metrical tradition. The thematic elements in the individual lament, in fact, are a kind of discourse in which no sequential logic prevails and individual elements can be omitted, added, or exchanged without destroying the coherence or effect of the poem (Smith).

F. Sound

Sound in biblical poetry is also frequently under-appreciated, since the actual sounds of the spoken words and sung melodies are only imperfectly and belatedly known, if known at all, and, even when known with some confidence, are invariably lost in translation. Yet even in an age when poetry is written as much for the eye as for the ear (Hollander), poets still inevitably underscore the importance of sound to their craft. Sound patterns and repetitions abound in biblical Hebrew poetic art, mostly nonsystematically and often without strong or obvious semantic implications. Alliteration (e.g., the TSADE [ts צ] in Lam 3:52, **tsodh tsadhiwuni katsippor** [צוֹד צָדוּנִי כַּצִּפּוֹר]), the ʿAYINs [ʿ ע] and alefs in Isa 5:5 (**weʿattah qiweyithi laʿasoth ʿanavim** [וְעַתָּה קִוֵּיתִי לַעֲשׂוֹת עֲנָבִים]), as well as assonance and consonance (Ps 1:1) are all commonplace, routinely occurring locally, prominently as line-level tropes. Rhymes and chimes of various kinds can be heard, not infrequently, as well. The linguistic peculiarities of Hebrew phonology, morphology, and root structure are often exploited to good sonic effect. The same root may be repeated in syntactically warranted and sonically pleasing ways (e.g., the Hebrew lit. says, "on our watchtowers we watch," Lam 4:17) or different roots may be positioned so as to rhyme (e.g., lit., "moaning and groaning," Lam 2:5).

G. Poetic Collections

Poems, as singular acts of speech, always demand being read on their own, for their own sakes. Not insignificantly, however, ancient poems, and ancient biblical poems in particular, have been preserved mostly as parts of larger wholes. For biblical poems, this means they are typically either embedded in swaths of narrative prose (e.g., Exod 15; Judg 5; 2 Sam 1) or in collections of poems (e.g., Psalms, Song of Songs, Proverbs). Both contexts require the recognition of the embedded poems as the singular textual entities that they are (i.e., as poems) and call for reading strategies commensurate to the nature and sensibilities of the larger wholes of which they are a part. That is, these poems potentially may always "mean twice," once on their own and once in light of the fiction of the larger whole. Within narrative frameworks, the embedded poems are usually positioned to serve larger narrative functions, such as effecting closure (Exod 15; Judg 5) or realizing the didactic tradition of "last words" (Deut 32). But collections—lyric, prophetic, wisdom—often require different, nonnarrative strategies of reading, where fragmentation and the accommodation of fragmentation are often central aspects of the fiction enacted.

H. Orality and Literacy

Any reading of biblical poetry must hold together literacy and orality. On the one hand, communication in ancient Israel and Judah (and also Persian-period Yehud), like other traditional societies of the ANE, was overwhelmingly and fundamentally an oral affair (Niditch). And the roots of biblical verse as an art form were undoubtedly oral in nature as well—all written literature presently known was preceded by oral literature (Foley). In fact, biblical scholars have long assumed an originary phase of oral composition and transmission underlying most of the literature now found in the OT (e.g., Gunkel). However originally composed and transmitted, most (though not all) biblical Hebrew poetry was intended for oral performance, whether a more or less formal recitation or simply vocalized while reading to oneself. No doubt, also, there was a great deal of oral verse that was never recorded and thus lost. On the other hand, at least from the middle of the 4th millennium, when writing emerged in both Mesopotamia and Egypt, orality was always enacted within (and thus is shaped by) a context of literacy. And thus at no time in the history of the late-arriving Israelites and Judahites (ca. 1200 BCE) would writing not have been known and used in some capacity (e.g., among the royal and religious elites). These were not cultures with no knowledge of writing. In fact, however scant, extra-biblical Hebrew inscriptions do exist from as early as the 10th cent. (e.g., Gezer Calendar). And though specifics are not currently within our grasp, internal biblical representations and comparative evidence both support the likelihood that poetry was written down early on (maybe even early bookrolls, such as the "Book of Jashar" mentioned in Josh 10:13 and 2 Sam 1:18). How early is hard to say—the 8th and 7th cent. witness a considerable rise in the use of writing (to judge by the comparably large numbers of extent Hebrew epigraphs from these periods)—and only educated guesses may be made about its form and shape (e.g., written on papyrus, using word dividers but probably no visual indications of lineation; *see* WRITING AND WRITING MATERIALS). There are poems in the Bible, such as the several alphabetic acrostics (e.g., Pss 111; 112; 119; Prov 31:10-31; Lam 1–4; Nah 1:2-9), that clearly were intended for the eye (i.e., to be read), and many others that show an awareness of literacy, use literate tropes, or are effected in a literate mode (Niditch). All of the poetry in the OT, like all other poetry preserved from antiquity, has come down to us in written form.

I. How to Read a Biblical Poem

Poetry is an event, an act of reading or hearing (Attridge). It is an embodied event. A poem occurs when it is enacted (Smith), when it is spoken. Poetry, and here biblical poetry in particular, is ultimately all about reading. Readings (always in the plural) are the stuff out of which all construals of prosody and poetics are necessarily made and at the same time are what complete these construals (i.e., a prosody is only as good as the reading it helps to generate). Readings of poems are the ultimate justification of poetry, they are the gift of poetry. And readings of biblical poems (especially close, deep, lusciously savored, highly imaginative readings) are still rare and desperately needed.

There is no one right way of reading, no tidy, preset template or calculus guaranteed to generate meaningful, sure, and compelling readings. Reading is messy and full of risk. It is a practice, with many modes and an inestimable number of competing aims and outcomes. Proficiency (however measured) comes, much as it does in many other endeavors, through practice, as does the peculiar and pleasurable satisfactions that it brings.

A reading of the short Ps 125 is here offered, by way of conclusion, as but one example of what is possible. The psalm's title, "A Song of Ascents," explicitly announces the poet's lyric intent and embeds it within the larger sequence of "Songs of Ascents" (Pss 120–34)—whatever more the title may imply, it helps to build in a sense of coherence into this sequence of fifteen poems, and clearly sets this apart as an integrated sequence within the psalms. That is, in true lyric fashion, the poem will mean doubly, on its own and also as a part of a larger whole. As with many of the psalms in this sequence, it is short, does not abide closely by any of the well-known psalmic given forms, and shows a stylistic affection for repetition in various forms (Grossberg). The poem's larger identity emerges processually, and the meanings evolve. Emblematic is the poem's use of repetition. Excepting the fourfold repetition of the Tetragrammaton (Ps 125:1, 2, 4, 5), reiteration in this poem never spills over stanza boundaries. As a consequence, the specific sets of repetitions help articulate the contours of the individual stanzas, while the prominence of the trope itself adds a sense of stylistic unity to the whole. Such is the basic dynamic informing the poem. By contrast, repetition in many of the other poems in the Songs of Ascents is more global and serves as a unifying device (Grossberg).

The first stanza (vv. 1-2) is the most fragmented of the three. Meaning in the stanza is manufactured chiefly out of metaphor, explicitly, "like Mount Zion," and implicitly, "(just as) Jerusalem is surrounded by mountains/(so too) Yahweh surrounds his people." The whole is shaped as a statement about "those who trust in Yahweh." But as with all good lyric poetry the import lies as much in the saying as in the said. The imagery and diction of the stanza echo that of the old Zion tradition. But what has been mostly missed is the subtlety and creativity with which the poem does this. It is not simply a matter of revalorizing the Zion tradition. As Grossberg observes, the originality of the psalms emerges despite the mainly conservative compositional palette made up of familiar tropes and conventional imagery. The psalm likely dates from the postexilic period, by which time the Babylonian destruction of Jerusalem

(586 BCE) is a well-known fact. Thus, if the psalmist is to tap into the images associated with the Zion tradition, she will need to do so creatively in a way that does not depend on the inviolability of Jerusalem itself, and so she does. Instead of speaking about Jerusalem's beautiful walls and buildings, which at one time provided the visible token of Yahweh's beneficence, a visual testimony to the great king's invincibility, sovereignty, and reliability (compare Ps 48:6, 9, 13-14), and which are now demolished, the psalmist praises the mountainous nature of the site, which has persisted even amid violent destruction. The metaphors engaged here build on the substantiveness of mountains in general (i.e., they are normally perceived as unmovable, seeming to abide forever) and the fact that Jerusalem itself is surrounded by many hills. The shift in focus is subtle but all-important. In Ps 46:1-3, e.g., it is the assurance of Yahweh's ever-present help that bolsters the psalmist's confidence, even amid earthquakes and the toppling of mountains into the heart of the seas (compare Ps 46:6). In Ps 125 the mountains become "unshakeable" and they "endure" forever, not Yahweh enthroned on his temple mount (compare Exod 15:17; Num 23:21; Pss 46:5; 48:3; Isa 6:1), in Jerusalem, his chosen dwelling place (Pss 76:2; 78:68; 87:1-2; 132:13). Indeed, Yahweh in this psalm no longer functions as the main warrant motivating the psalmist's actions, but rather it is the psalmist's own agency (and those for whom he sings) upon which all is dependent, an agency that gets mediated liturgically (explicitly in vv. 4-5). Here, then, the mythic traditions of Zion provide the poet with his language and imagery, but they are herein refashioned so as to rehabilitate the core of the Zion tradition, its interest in Jerusalem (perhaps for pilgrims making their way to the holy city).

Furthermore, note that this reframing of the Zion tradition takes place out of the poet's choice of language and imagery. The stanza's main line of discourse is framed, semantically and syntactically, as a statement about those who trust in Yahweh. At this level note how the similes in the opening stanza are both predicated on verbless clauses. The lack of action inherent in verbless clause connote stability and surety, a fact that is nicely pointed up in the second line by the explicit negation of an active verb—"(which) does not totter" (NRSV, "which cannot be moved"). In other words, syntax underscores semantics. The only other verbless clause comes in the poem's closing line, "Peace (be) upon Israel!" The poem's opening and closing syntax mimes the stability and tranquility that the poem seeks to register.

The second stanza (v. 3) shifts gears formally and thematically. Formally, the stanza comprises two couplets of similar lengths. In both, the syntax continues on past line ends and the second is explicitly subordinated to the first. (Thus, the parataxis of the first stanza is tightened through syntax in the second—the whole (of v. 3) may be read as one complex sentence. As in the first stanza ("it is not shaken"), actions are framed negatively for a positive effect ("the scepter of wickedness shall not rest upon ... the righteous," "the righteous might not stretch out their hands to wrongdoing"). This contrasts with the third stanza in which there are no negatively framed statements.

The ultimate sense of the stanza is vague, perhaps intentionally so—note the highly figured use of terms such as "to rest," "scepter of wickedness," "lot," "to stretch out their hands to do wrong." Most would gloss the whole as either a veiled reference to the tyranny of foreign rule or as a rendition of the sapiential commonplace opposing the "just" and the "wicked." Both lines of interpretation are consistent with the larger poem. In the first type of reading "lot" refers to the "land" of Israel (Josh 15:1; Judg 1:3; Mic 2:5), which was originally assigned (Num 26:55; Josh 14:2) by the casting of actual "lots." The "scepter of wickedness" may be taken as a metaphor for wicked rulers (compare Ps 45:6; Isa 14:5). In the Ugaritic myths Mot is enthroned with a "staff of bereavement" in one hand and a "staff of widowhood" in the other (*CTU* 1.23.8–9); this is opposed to the more rightful "staff of rulership" (*CTU* 1.2.III.18; 1.6.VI.29). And the promise of "rest" in the land is a well-known political trope. Even "wrongdoing" frequently has political connotations in the OT (e.g., 2 Sam 7:10//1 Chr 17:9; Ps 89:23; Mic 3:10; Hab 2:12). The sapiential construal is activated mostly retrospectively as auditors move into the third stanza, and especially after the chiastic turn in v. 5 where "those inclined to their crookedness" are explicitly contrasted with "those upright in their hearts." On this reading "lot" refers more generally to "one's lot in life" (Ps 16:5; Wis 2:9), the "scepter of wickedness" points to general lawlessness (compare Ezek 7:11), and the sapiential associations of "wrongdoing" are elicited (e.g., Job 5:16; 6:29-30; 11:14; Ps 119:3; Prov 22:8). The twofold reference to "the righteous" draws on terminology that is encountered in psalms with a wisdom slant (e.g., Pss 1:5, 6; 33:1; 34:15; 37:12; 112:4, 6).

In the final stanza (vv. 4-5) attention shifts from "those who trust" and "the righteous" to the "the good." Another development that emerges from the poem's logic is the perception of a progressive stepping up of the poem's rhetoric, moving from declarative statement (vv. 1-2) to emphatic assertion (v. 3) to supplication (vv. 4-5), with the imperative ("do good") and jussive ("let them be made to walk") grammatically distinguishing the third stanza. The lines of the final stanza are also the most obviously figured of the poem, above all shaped chiastically:

A Do good, O Yahweh, to the good,
B   and to the upright of heart.
B´   But those inclined to crookedness,
A´ let Yahweh make them walk with the evil doers.
C Peace upon Israel! (author's trans.)

Here, too, the willing eye can find a patterned argument to the poem's line play, a movement from chaos (vv. 1-2) through syntax (v. 3) to the order and fine shaping of chiasm (vv. 4-5). And thus, there are a host of nonsemantic features that conspire to effect a sense of naturalness in the ending, as if the poem has achieved the very thing it set out to do. That is, there is no reason that the poem should close with entreaty to Yahweh. But it does, and it does so fittingly.

Ultimately, the several small and often subtle ripples of rituality that reverberate through the poem color our construal of the poem's semantics, how it means. The entreaty to Yahweh to do good to the good and to ensure that the not-good get their comeuppance becomes a most manifest realization of the "trust" that was a topic at the outset. And the concluding "benediction" ("Peace upon Israel!") rescues the poem from ending on a negative note while gesturing one last time to the larger sequence of poems where similarly benedictory exclamations abound: "Yahweh protects ... now and forever!" (Ps 121:8); "I will seek your good" (Ps 122:9); "Those who go out weeping ... shall come home with shouts of joy ..." (Ps 126:6); "Peace be upon Israel!" (Ps 128:8); "We bless you in the name of the LORD!" (Ps 129:8); "O Israel, hope in the LORD!" (Ps 131:3); and "May the LORD bless you!" (Ps 134:3). And yet for all the sense of satisfaction the poem does not end at a logical stopping place. Rather, the ending is another rendition of the poem's poetics of extravagance, a final apostrophe by which the poem both enacts and exposes its lyricism, its aspiration to make a happening out of words.

Bibliography: R. Alter. *The Art of Biblical Poetry* (1985); D. Attridge. *Poetic Rhythm: An Introduction* (1995); D. Attridge. *The Singularity of Literature.* (2004); A. Berlin. *The Dynamics of Biblical Parallelism* (1985); T. Carmi. *The Penguin Book of Hebrew Verse* (1981); F. W. Dobbs-Allsopp. "The Enjambing Line in Lamentations: A Taxonomy (Part 1)" and "The Effects of Enjambment in Lamentations (Part 2)." *ZAW* 113 (2001) 219–39, 370–85; F. W. Dobbs-Allsopp. *Lamentations.* Interpretation (2002); F. W. Dobbs-Allsopp. "Psalms and Lyric Verse." *The Evolution of Rationality: Interdisciplinary Essays in Honor of J. Wentzel van Huyssteen.* L. Shults, ed. (2006) 346–79; S. R. Driver. *An Introduction to the Literature of the Old Testament* (1897); ; T. Eagleton. *How to Read a Poem* (2006); J. M. Foley. *How to Read an Oral Poem* (2002); S. Geller. *Parallelism in Early Biblical Poetry* (1979); E. Gerstenberger. *Psalms, Part 2, and Lamentations.* FOTL (2001); E. Greenstein. "How Does Parallelism Mean?" *A Sense of the Text* (1982) 40–71; E. Greenstein. "Aspects of Biblical Poetry." *Jewish Book Annual* 44 (1986–87) 33–42; E. Greenstein. "On the Genesis of Biblical Prose Narrative." *Prooftexts* 8 (1988) 347–54; D. Grossberg. *Centripetal and Centrifugal Structures in Biblical Poetry* (1989); H. Gunkel. *The Legends of Genesis* (1966); J. Hollander. *Vision and Resonance: Two Senses of Poetic Form* (1975); J. Kugel. *Idea of Biblical Poetry* (1981); S. Langer. *Feeling and Form: A Theory of Art* (1953); R. Lowth. *Lectures on the Sacred Poetry of the Hebrews* (1787); S. Niditch. *Oral World and Written Word: Ancient Israelite Literature* (1996); M. O'Connor. *Hebrew Verse Structure* (1980); W. Ong. *Orality and Literacy: The Technology of the Word* (1982); D. Pardee. *Ugaritic and Hebrew Parallelism* (1988); S. Parker. *The Pre-Biblical Narrative Tradition* (1989); M. Perloff. "Lucent and Inescapable Rhythms: Metrical 'Choice' and Historical Formation." *The Line in Postmodern Poetry.* R. Frank and H. Sayre, eds. (1988) 13–40; D. Petersen and K. Richards. *Interpreting Hebrew Poetry* (1992); R. Pinsky. *The Sounds of Poetry: A Brief Guide* (1998); W. Schiedewind. *How the Bible Became a Book* (2004); B. Herrnstein Smith. *Poetic Closure: A Study of How Poems End* (1968); R. Thomas. *Literacy and Orality in Ancient Greece* (1992); E. Tov. "Special Layout of Poetical Units in the Texts from the Judean Desert." *Give Ear to My Words.* J. Dyk, ed. (1996) 115–28; W. G. E. Watson. *Classical Hebrew Poetry* (1984); S. Weitzman. *Song and Story in Biblical Narrative* (1997); Walt Whitman. *Leaves of Grass* (1895).

FRED W. DOBBS-ALLSOPP

POISON [חֵמָה khemah, רֹאשׁ roʾsh; κακός kakos]. A poison is a substance that injures or kills through chemical interaction within the body. Natural poisons occur in both animals and plants. Ingesting a poison is oftentimes fatal (2 Macc 10:13), except that in mild doses certain poisons may act as healing stimulants.

Many kinds of snakes produce a fatal venom that kills humans and animals that are bitten (Num 21:6; Deut 8:15; 32:33; Job 20:16; *see* ADDER; ASP; SERPENT; VIPER). While the Israelites were crossing the wilderness, the Lord sent poisonous serpents to punish them for speaking against God and Moses (*see* FIERY SERPENT OR POISONOUS SNAKE). God told Moses to make a serpent of bronze on a pole; when a person was bitten, he or she looked at the serpent on the pole and did not die (Num 21:6-9; *see* SERPENT, BRONZE).

Certain plants and fungi have poisonous properties. Sometimes the entire plant is poisonous while in other cases the poison is localized in parts such as root, leaves, or seeds. When one of Elisha's disciples collected gourds of the colocynth (*Citrullus colocynthis*) growing wild in the desert near Jericho during a famine, he expected them to be edible and cut them up into a stew. But the men eating the stew detected poison and said, "There is death in the pot" (2 Kgs 4:39-41). The man had gathered an extremely bitter purge that can be fatal. Less certain is the "poisonous weed" of Hos 10:4, which could be hemlock (*Conium maculatum*), a common weed of waste places. It grows

1–2 m high with mottled stems and parsley-like leaves and flat, white flower-heads. Extracts of this plant are said to have poisoned Socrates. *See* GALL, HERB; PLANTS OF THE BIBLE; WEEDS.

The OT uses *poison* metaphorically to illustrate harmful situations. Israel's encroaching enemies produce poisonous grapes, and their wine is like poison from serpents (Deut 32:32-33). Job compares his suffering to drinking poison (Job 6:4), and the psalmist laments that his enemies give him poison for food (Ps 69:21 [Heb. 69:22]). The Israelites experience God's wrath as drinking poisoned water (Jer 8:14; 9:15; 23:15). An oracle of the LORD says that the people have "turned justice into poison and the fruit of righteousness into WORMWOOD" (Amos 6:12*b*).

The term *poison* is used metaphorically in the NT to refer to harmful ideas or evil words. In Acts 14:2, unbelievers are accused of "poisoning" (from **kakoō** [κακόω], "to harm") the minds of Gentiles, so that they would not listen to Paul and Barnabas. In a treatise about "taming the tongue" (Jas 3:8), the author says that the tongue is "a restless evil, full of deadly poison (**kakos**)" because of the sometimes harmful consequences of speech.

F. NIGEL HEPPER

POISONOUS SERPENTS. *See* FIERY SERPENT OR POISONOUS SNAKE.

POISONOUS SNAKES. *See* FIERY SERPENT OR POISONOUS SNAKE.

POLICE [ῥαβδοῦχος **rhabdouchos**, στρατηγός **stratēgos**, ὑπηρέτης **hypēretēs**]. 1. Lictors or constables who carried bundles of rods as the means for beating and punishing offenders, and who received their orders from the Roman magistrates. In Acts 16:22-23, 35-39, under the orders of the Roman magistrates, these officials stripped Paul and Silas of their clothing, beat them, and placed them in prison because they had healed a slave girl and so had deprived her owners of the income from her divination activities.

2. Commanders responsible for the Temple in Jerusalem. Men of this rank accompanied the chief priests when the chief priests conferred with Judas (Luke 22:4), arrested Jesus (Luke 22:52), and demanded Jesus' crucifixion (John 19:6). In John 7:32, 45-46, these men were so impressed with Jesus' teaching that they failed to arrest him, but later accompanied Judas and the soldiers during Jesus' arrest (18:3, 12). They brought Peter and the apostles before the Sanhedrin for questioning (Acts 5:26).

EMILY R. CHENEY

POLITARCHS [πολιτάρχης **politarchēs**]. The title given to city officials encountered by Paul and Silas at Thessalonica (Acts 17:6, 8). Excavations in Northern Greece have produced approximately seventy inscriptions that mention politarchs. Politarch was a Greek title used in Macedonia from 2 BCE to 2 CE for the magistrates of free Greek cities, as opposed to Roman magistrates with Roman titles.

The office was held by the highest ranked magistrates in the leading cities, particularly of Macedonia. Appointments to the office were made annually. The number of politarchs appointed to the council varied from as few as one to as many as seven or more depending on the size of the **polis** (πόλις).

The magistrates were responsible for law enforcement in civic matters in the city. In Acts 17:6, 8 the politarchs restored peace in the city of Thessalonica following the disturbance at Jason's house. Their responsibility to Rome is clearly demonstrated in their concern with the charge that Paul and Silas were "acting against the decrees of Caesar, saying there is another king, Jesus" (Acts 17:7).

Bibliography: G. H. R. Horsley. "Appendix: The Politarchs." *The Book of Acts in Its Graeco-Roman Setting,* vol. 2. David W. J. Gill, ed. (1994) 419–31.

LAMOINE F. DEVRIES

POLLUTION. *See* CLEAN AND UNCLEAN; PROFANE.

POLYBIUS. A pro-Roman historian (200–118 BCE), born in Megalopolis in Arcadia. *The Histories*, Polybius' most famous work, extols the rise of Rome as a world power. Occasionally, *The Histories* references the plight of the Jewish people, including a description of the Ptolemaic general Scopas' attack on Jews and of Antiochus' conquest of Jerusalem (*Hist.* 16). Of the forty volumes written, only five are extant in complete form, though many more are fragmentary.

JESSICA TINKLENBERG DEVEGA

POLYCARP, EPISTLE OF. Polycarp, the bishop of SMYRNA for some decades, died a martyr's death at age eighty-six (ca. 155–160 CE) and was a major figure in early 2nd-cent. Christianity. His life and ministry spanned the era from late apostolic times to the emergence of catholic Christianity.

To the Philippians is Polycarp's sole surviving writing. Direct and unpretentious, this letter conveys exhortation and advice, often in the sermonic style of a word of exhortation. It draws heavily on the OT (in its LXX form) and early Christian writings, especially 1 Peter and *1 Clement*, but also Ephesians and 1 Corinthians. Responding to the Philippians' request for a discussion of righteousness, Polycarp wrote about an avaricious presbyter, Valens: for Polycarp, belief and behavior are two sides of one coin. Wrong behavior indicated wrong beliefs, and wrong beliefs inevitably produced wrong behavior—and both were characteristic of outsiders, i.e., nonbelievers. Thus Valens' financial irregularities were destabilizing in that they blurred the boundary between outsiders and insiders, and generated uncertainty about the meaning of *righteousness.* So Polycarp vigorously promoted both right belief and behavioral norms.

Though the letter's authenticity has been challenged by those questioning the Ignatian letters (to which Polycarp's letter, written about the time Ignatius was martyred, is the earliest witness), the challenges remain unpersuasive to the scholarly consensus. *See* IGNATIUS, EPISTLES OF; POLYCARP, MARTYRDOM OF.

Bibliography: Michael Holmes. "Polycarp of Smyrna, Epistle to the Philippians." *The Writings of the Apostolic Fathers.* Paul Foster, ed. (2007) 108–25.

MICHAEL W. HOLMES

POLYCARP, EPISTLE TO. *See* IGNATIUS, EPISTLES OF.

POLYCARP, MARTYRDOM OF pol'ee-kahrp, mahr'tuhr-duhm. A letter apparently written by an eyewitness less than a year after the event, the *Martyrdom of Polycarp* reports the arrest and execution (ca. 155–160 CE) of Polycarp, the eighty-six-year-old bishop of SMYRNA. It portrays Polycarp's death as "a martyrdom in accord with the gospel" (*Mart. Pol.* 1.1), i.e., one that seeks the salvation of others, displays endurance in suffering, and arises from a divine call rather than human initiative. The martyrdom expresses a response to threats posed by Rome and the surrounding pagan culture. *See* POLYCARP, EPISTLE OF.

Bibliography: Michael W. Holmes. *The Apostolic Fathers: Greek Texts and English Translations.* 3rd ed. (2007).

MICHAEL W. HOLMES

POLYCRATES. Late 2nd cent. Christian bishop of Ephesus. He was the leader of the Asian Quartodecimans, who thought that Easter should be celebrated annually on the fourteenth day of the Jewish month of Nisan. Polycrates presented this as an ancient tradition that stemmed from the apostles Philip and John and was followed by several prominent early bishops, including Polycarp and Melito. He also recorded traditions concerning the burial place of Philip and John (Eusebius, *Hist. eccl.* 3.31.3; 5.24.1–8).

MARK DELCOGLIANO

POLYGAMY. *See* MARRIAGE, OT.

POLYTHEISM. *See* GOD, OT VIEW OF; GODS, GODDESSES.

POMEGRANATE [רִמּוֹן rimmon; ῥοΐσκος rhoiskos]. A deciduous shrub or small tree (*Punica granatum*) thriving in a warm climate, with bright red flowers, ca. 3 cm diameter. The large round fruits, ca. 7 cm diameter, have a hard rind used for dyes and tanning leather. Inside, each of the numerous seeds is encased in delicious watery pulp. In ancient traditions the abundant seeds symbolized fertility. Spies sent by Moses brought back pomegranates from Canaan (Num 13:23). Gold likenesses of the fruit were used to ornament the hem of the priests' robes, and perhaps the "bells" were pomegranate flowers (Exod 28:33-34; 39:24-26). Later, latticework on the pillar capitals of the Temple was ornamented with 200 brass pomegranates (1 Kgs 7:20; 2 Kgs 25:17; 2 Chr 3:16; 4:13; Jer 52:22-23). The beauty and desirability of pomegranates are exemplified in the love poetry of Song 4:3, 13; 6:7. The Hebrew **rimmon** appears in place-names such as EN-RIMMON. *See* PLANTS OF THE BIBLE.

F. NIGEL HEPPER

POMPEY pom'pee. Gnaeus Pompeius (106–48 BCE) was an important Roman general during the civil wars at the end of the Republic. From the biblical perspective, his most important military campaign extended Roman control through Asia Minor, Syria, and Palestine (66–62 BCE). During this campaign, the HASMONEANS ARISTOBULUS II and HYRCANUS II asked Pompey to mediate their dispute. Aristobulus rejected Pompey's decision and fled to Jerusalem, prompting the Romans to capture the city. Pompey installed Hyrcanus as high priest and reorganized Palestine, removing Gentile areas conquered by the Hasmoneans from Jerusalem's control. Significantly, the Idumean ANTIPATER, Hyrcanus' advisor, established the positive relations with the Romans on which his son, King Herod, would later depend.

Returning to Rome, Pompey joined Crassus and Caesar to form the first triumvirate. After Crassus died fighting the Parthians, Pompey and Caesar fought several battles, which Caesar won. Pompey fled to Egypt, where he was assassinated.

ADAM L. PORTER

POND [אֲגַם ʾagham]. In Exod 7:19, ʾagham is among a series of terms for bodies of water in Egypt's delta.

PONTIUS PILATE. *See* PILATE, PONTIUS.

PONTUS pon'tuhs [Πόντος Pontos]. Pontus is a region in the northern part of modern Turkey. Its northern boundary is formed by the Black Sea (known in antiquity as the Pontus Euxinus), and to the south was the province of GALATIA. The westernmost city of the region was at Heraclea Pontica. A mountain range, the Pontic Alps, cut the coast from the interior of Anatolia. One of the few ancient routes from the Black Sea to the interior was from Amisus on the coast to Amaseia. There are two main rivers: the Halys, which crosses the central Anatolian plain, and the Iris. The coastal city of Trapezus provided access, via the mountain pass known as the Pontic Gates, to Persia.

The Black Sea coastline of Pontus was colonized by Greeks from the city of Miletos (Strabo, *Geogr.* 12.3.11) during the 7th cent. BCE. Among the cities were Sinope, Amastris, and Amisus. The kingdom of Pontus developed during the Hellenistic period. In 89 BCE, Mithridates VI Eupator annexed the Roman province of Asia, leading to the deaths of Italian merchants. This led to a series of campaigns against Mithridates by Rome, notably the one led by POMPEY the Great who was appointed to the command in 66 BCE. Pompey's victory and Mithridates' death allowed Pontus to become a Roman province in 65 BCE. It was joined with the older province of BITHYNIA to form a single administrative unit. Pompey reformed the administration of the new province, creating the *lex Pompeia*; this legal framework was still in use during the provincial governorship of the younger PLINY in the reign of Emperor TRAJAN. Pliny informs us about the way that Pompey set minimum ages for the holders of public office. The late 2nd-cent. CE Roman historian DIO CASSIUS (*Rom.* 37.20.2), who came from the joint province, also described aspects of the constitution.

Pompey created a series of new cities, and part of his legislation seems to have restricted the common Greek practice of multiple citizenships, perhaps to help establish these new foundations. The Augustan geographer STRABO (*Geogr.* 12.3.30, 31, 37–40), who was himself born at Amaseia around the time of the formation of the province, lists the seven cities: Pompeiopolis, Amaseia, Neapolis, Zela, Magnopolis, Megalopolis, and Diospolis. Although Amaseia had already been a city and royal center of administration, many of these cities appear to have been essentially new foundations; there is little suggestion of urban populations under Mithridates. These new cities were administered by a standard type of Greek civic magistrate known as archons. Nicopolis in the east of the province—Strabo (*Geogr.* 12.3.28) places it in Armenia—appears to have been settled by veterans from Pompey's army. The territory of the inland part of the former kingdom of Pontus was thus allocated to each of the new cities, while the old coastal Greek cities continued. Parts of the old Mithridatic kingdom of Pontus were allocated to client kings subject to Roman authority. Among them was the sanctuary city of Comana, which Pompey placed under the authority of Archelaos the priest (Strabo, *Geogr.* 12.3.33).

The province was linked by an east–west road that dated back to the Mithridatic kingdom. This cut through the mountains of Paphlagonia from Pompeiopolis to Nicopolis on the Armenian frontier. Essentially this road linked the Bosphorus (and thus Rome itself) with the east. A further road ran along the coast linking the former Greek colonies to Amisus and eventually Trapezus.

The province was reorganized by MARK ANTONY around 39 BCE. A client king, Darius, a grandson of Mithridates VI, was established. He was replaced by Polemo—perhaps on Darius' death—who had previously ruled in Cilicia; these events seem to have taken place by 36 BCE when Polemo, "king of Pontus," is recorded as campaigning with Antony against Artavasdes I in Parthia. However, it is clear that the new kingdom of Pontus was a reduced version of the province that had been established by Pompey.

Under AUGUSTUS, parts of the former kingdom remained under the control of client kings. Amaseia, probably under Galatian rulers, returned to Roman control in 3/2 BCE, giving focus to the newly formed region Pontus Galaticus, part of the province of Galatia. The control of Comana, which had been ruled by Dyteutus, was added to Pontus Galaticus in 34/35 CE. The former kingdom of rule by Polemo was added to the Roman Empire in 64 CE under NERO; this was known as Pontus Polemoniacus. Pontus had a senatorial status, though during the 2nd cent. it came under the control of the emperor in recognition of its strategic situation on the route to the east.

The region of Pontus is mentioned in the NT. Residents from Pontus were present in Jerusalem at Pentecost (Acts 2:9), suggesting a thriving Jewish community of a type known in detail from elsewhere in Anatolia. Some Jews may have been resident in the former Greek colonies such as Sinope, from where they may have settled in the Greek foundations along the northern coast of the Black Sea. Along with other regions of Asia Minor, Christians in Pontus were listed as one of the recipients of 1 Peter (1 Pet 1:1); it is perhaps significant that Pontus and Bithynia frame the list, suggesting a circular itinerary including CAPPADOCIA, Galatia, and Asia. Aquila, the Jewish tent-maker at CORINTH, was originally from Pontus, though he was resident in Rome (Acts 18:2; *see* AQUILA AND PRISCILLA).

Bibliography: David Magie. *Roman Rule in Asia Minor to the End of the Third Century after Christ* (1950); A. J. Marshall. "Pompey's Organization of Bithynia-Pontus: Two Neglected Texts." *JRS* 58 (1968) 103–9; Stephen Mitchell. *Anatolia: Land, Men, and Gods in Asia Minor. Volume 1: The Celts in Anatolia and the Impact of Roman Rule* (1993); Richard D. Sullivan. "Dynasts from Pontus." *ANRW* Vol. 2.7.2. Wolfgang Haase, ed. (1980) 913–30.

DAVID W. J. GILL

POOL [בְּרֵכָה berekhah; κολυμβήθρα kolymbēthra]. In the arid regions of the ANE, water collection and storage was a matter of great importance. Natural collections of water such as lakes or ponds were, and still are, extremely rare. Those areas with natural standing water were labeled usually ʾagham (אֲגַם), often translated "marsh." Exodus 7:19 and 8:5 describe "pools of water" in reference to offshoots of the Egyptian Nile.

The prophetic words of Isa 35:7 and 41:18 depict a day when the desert lands "shall become a pool." Psalms 107:35 and 114:8 also reflect on God who brings pools of water into the desert, and out of rocks. These references to standing water in natural environs are few. The majority of references to pools of water defines either reservoirs cut from rock, or blocked and dammed WADI or streambeds that provided a consistent supply of water once filled.

Pools served several purposes in the ancient world. The most common uses of these collected resources were for irrigation and for potable WATER. In times of warfare and siege, a city's ability to resist attackers often depended on the water supply. Often, the pools of cities were places of violence, or of important meetings. Second Samuel 2:13 describes a meeting between the armies of David and Abner at the pool of Gibeon that resulted in a bitter battle (*see* GIBEON, GIBEONITES). Later, the pool of Hebron was the site of David's brutal justice on the men who killed Saul's son, Ishbaal (2 Sam 4:12). The gruesome death of Ahab (1 Kgs 22:29-40) resulted in his chariot being washed of his blood at the pool of Samaria, the capital of the Northern Kingdom (22:38). On a lighter note, the pools of Heshbon "by the gate of Bath-rabbim" are used to describe the beauty of the beloved maiden in Song 7:4 [Heb. 7:5].

Similar to major CISTERNs such as those found in Megiddo, pools were placed in areas where the minimal rainfall run-off could be fed into the enclosure. Where numerous small cisterns were privately owned, most pools were civic projects constructed for public use. Elaborate channels carved into hillsides filled the pools with rainwater, or served as conduits from natural springs. The most famous of the latter variety is the pool of SILOAM on the southwestern edge of the original Old City of JERUSALEM known as the Ophel. This section of Jerusalem was the original city of David. The Gihon Spring on the eastern side of the city flows from the base of the high bluff that the city sits upon, and is actually in the lower Kidron Valley. The pool of Siloam was constructed inside the walls of the city. The Gihon Spring was protected by a Middle Bronze Age structure but was vulnerable to attack (*see* GIHON, SPRING). Hezekiah cut the meandering tunnel that now bears his name to allow the waters of the Gihon to flow beneath the city to the pool of Siloam (2 Kgs 20:20; 2 Chr 32:30). An inscription that contains the common word for pool (**brkh** ברכה) was inscribed inside the tunnel, relating the digging of the tunnel and the day of completion. The ever-increasing Assyrian threat motivated Hezekiah for this immense task. John 9:7 notes the Roman-period pool of Siloam. Recent excavations by Ronny Reich and Eli Shukron at the southern tip of the city of David ridge have revealed a massive step system leading down into the possible Roman pool of Siloam.

Numerous other pools of Jerusalem are noted in the text. Second Kings 18:17 describes a conversation between the Rabshakeh of Assyria and the representatives of Hezekiah at the "conduit of the upper pool" during the Assyrian siege of Jerusalem (compare Isa 7:3; 36:2). Isaiah 22:8-11 describes the actions of Hezekiah when he "collected the waters of the lower pool" (22:9). It also describes a RESERVOIR for the "water of the old pool" (22:11). These statements are in reference to military preparedness in a negative sense of not trusting God. Nehemiah's ride around the broken walls of Jerusalem included a stop at the King's Pool (Neh 2:14). Later, the rebuilding of the walls included "the wall of the Pool of Shelah of the king's garden" (Neh 3:15; *see* SHELAH, POOL OF). The vain attempts of the Teacher of Ecclesiastes to find pleasure included building "pools . . . to water the forest of growing trees" (Eccl 2:6).

BETH-ZATHA (Bethesda) was an important NT site. The story of Jesus' healing of the man who was lame displays the perceived healing capacity of this pool (John 5:1-9). Currently, the pool of Bethesda is identified with excavated ruins in the courtyard of St. Anne's Church in the Old City of Jerusalem, north of the Temple Mount.

A few miles south of Jerusalem are the "Pools of Solomon" that supplied Jerusalem with water through an aqueduct, at least during Roman times. The aqueduct flowed from three large pools near Bethlehem. One of the pools measures nearly 600 ft. in length with a depth of about 50 ft. These important pools supplied water to the temple precinct as well as to the city proper (see Josephus, *Ant.* 18.60–62). *See* WELLS.

South of the Pools of Solomon and Bethlehem stood the imposing fortress palace of Herod the Great (37–4 BCE) called the Herodion (*see* HERODIUM). One of Herod's monumental architectural undertakings, the Herodion's lower city included a massive pool with an island within it. This pool was used for swimming and boating. The water supply came from the Pools of Solomon to the north. The pools provided up to 400,000 cubic m of water per year for circulation and refreshment of Herod's recreational facility. Further, the desert fortress palace of Herod at Masada, overlooking the Dead Sea in the Jordan Valley, also enjoyed a massive swimming pool supplied by numerous cisterns cut into the mountainside.

These major city pools were manufactured reservoirs composed of broad and uncovered surface area, in contrast to cisterns. Examples of pools formed from damming wadi beds are found in Moab at Khirbat al-Mudaybiʿ, Madaba, and Dhiban in modern Jordan, in numerous small wadi systems in the Negeb, and in the steep valleys west of Qumran.

Smaller pools of water functioned in ritual purification rather than daily living. The **miqwah** (מִקְוָה) usually contained a two-way step system for cultic cleansing before entrance into the temple courts in Jerusalem (*see* MIQVAH, MIQVEH). Multiple examples are still visible along the southern walls of the Old City. One would walk into the pool down one side of the stairs and return up the other side after immersion. Qumran community members utilized several pools of water for ritual cleansing. Dead Sea Scroll notations on the "waters of washing" seem to imply that only members of the community could use the pools (compare 1QS V, 13–14). Both Herodium and Masada were later used by Jewish rebels during the first (70–74 CE) and the second (Bar Kochba, 132–35 CE) rebellions against Rome. The palaces received some remodeling to include synagogues and miqwoth (מִקְוֹת). *See* ISRAEL, CLIMATE OF; WATER WORKS.

Bibliography: Amihai Mazar. *Archaeology of the Land of the Bible: 10,000–586 B.C.E.* (1990); Hershel Shanks. "Where Jesus Cured the Blind Man." *BAR* 31 (2005) 16–23.

MICHAEL G. VANZANT

POOR [אֶבְיוֹן ʾevyon, דַּל dal, עָנִי ʿani; πένης penēs, πενιχρός penichros, πτωχός ptōchos]. The *poor* are people who have little or no money, land, or material possessions (*see* POVERTY). Because they do not have the power that comes with wealth, they enjoy no social standing or political influence (*see* MARGINAL, MARGINALIZATION).

The experience of the poor becomes a metaphor for the universal need for salvation. The poor have only one choice, and this is to depend upon God. While the Bible uses the language of being "poor" to speak about the universal experience of human poverty before God, it also condemns the injustice that helps create the actual deprivation of poverty and the inequalities between the wealthy and the poor. If one confines the study of how the Pentateuch deals with the poor by focusing only on the words for *poor* mentioned in its five books, the results will give an incomplete picture. While various Hebrew words for the *poor* occur only fifteen times in the Pentateuch, the poor are much more of a central concern in the Torah than that statistic indicates. The narratives of the Torah include stories of how people of means often use their status as an advantage in their dealings with those whose economic situation is precarious. The stories about Hagar illustrate the powerlessness of the poor. Sarah and Abraham use their Egyptian slave-girl HAGAR to acquire a son for themselves, and Sarah treats her so harshly that she attempts to run away (Gen 16:1-15). When Hagar's presence and service are no longer necessary, and when Sarah decides that Hagar and her child are troubling, Abraham agrees to send them away (Gen 21:9-14). But God saves Hagar and Ishmael from certain death and promises to make of him "a great nation" (Gen 21:15-20).

The legal traditions in the TORAH not only serve to delineate the rights of the poor (e.g., Exod 23:11) but also regulate how the more successful Israelites are to deal with those on the margins of the ancient Israelite economy (Exod 22:25; 23:6; Lev 19:10; 23:22; Deut 24:12, 14-15). For example, people who have completed service as bond slaves in repayment of a debt are to be given "gifts" that will enable them to make a fresh start (Deut 15:13-14). Without such help, the former slaves would eventually find that their newly acquired freedom brought them to the same kind of destitution that led them into bond slavery in the first place. The Deuteronomic law, then, sought to break the cycle of poverty that kept the poor in economic dependency. *See* SLAVERY.

The prophets saw the oppression of the poor as one symptom of Israel's failure to live according to traditional moral values. They accused the wealthy (Ezek 16:49; Amos 4:1) and the powerful (Isa 3:14-15; 10:2) of oppressing the poor. Since ancient Israel had an agricultural economy, ownership of LAND was essential to maintaining economic independence. Wealthy landowners were enlarging their estates by acquiring small family plots, concentrating the ownership of land in the hands of a few and creating a great number of landless farmers who were reduced to hiring themselves out as agricultural workers to survive (Isa 5:8; Ezek 22:29; Mic 2:1-3; Hab 2:5-6; *see* ISRAEL, SOCIAL AND ECONOMIC DEVELOPMENT OF). Amos announced that divine judgment was coming on Israel because of the oppression of the poor (Amos 5:11; 8:4, 6). Ancient Israel's prophets were not economic theorists or social critics. What they did was to make Israel appreciate the consequences of the injustice that infested the ancient Israelite social and economic system. The economically powerful and politically connected used their wealth and position to take advantage of the poor (Jer 5:27; Ezek 45:9; Hab 2:9; Mal 3:5). *See* PROPHET, PROPHECY.

While Wisdom literature does deal with the theme of the poor, its way of approaching this motif differs markedly from those of the Pentateuch and the Prophets because of the wisdom tradition's origins within the upper class. For example, one does not find the moral outrage at the oppression of the poor that one finds in prophetic literature. Ancient Israel's sages address the sons of society's upper class and warn them against laziness and inattention that will inevitably lead to poverty (Prov 10:4; 20:13). The sages assume that people "choose" poverty, albeit indirectly. A fundamental assumption of the wisdom tradition is that actions have consequences and that these consequences are quite predictable. According to Proverbs, those who live an undisciplined life will become poor (Prov 23:21). Success demands a disciplined life according to the sages. The book of Proverbs looks upon mistreatment of the poor as risk to the rich (Prov 22:16). Proverbs calls for the wealthy to defend the rights of the poor (Prov 31:9) and praises those who are generous to poor people (Prov 31:20). It warns against taking advantage of poor people's lack of status and power (Prov 22:22). Like the Torah, Proverbs advises people to be generous to the poor (Prov 14:21; 19:17; 21:13) because to do otherwise is an insult to God (Prov 14:31; 17:5).

The book of Psalms is replete with references to the "poor and needy." An important question of interpretation related to the psalms is the identification of the "poor and needy." Are the poor of the psalms the economically poor, or has the language of social and economic stratification and conflict become simply a convention in these prayers to speak about the community of Israel as a whole or about a group of the pious within the community? Have the poor become the pious in the psalms? The psalms consistently portray God as the protector and deliverer of the poor, the orphan, the humble, and the oppressed (e.g., Pss 9:18 [Heb. 9:19]; 10:14; 68:10 [Heb. 68:11]; 69:33 [Heb. 69:34]; 107:41; 109:31; 113:7; 140:12 [Heb. 140:13]; 147:6; 149:4). Those who experience exploitation ask for God's protection and strength in their conflict with the rich (Pss 12:1 [Heb. 12:2]; 69:33 [Heb. 69:34]) for the poor are those who depend upon God (Pss 10; 25; 34; 37; 82).

When the NT speaks of "the poor," it speaks both of the "working poor" and the genuinely destitute. Members of both groups had little social status and no political power in the Roman world. They existed on the margins of society and were vulnerable to exploitation at the hands of the wealthy. The NT does not idealize poverty and does not suggest that the poor have any special access to God, though the poor are specified as the beneficiaries of Jesus' mission (Matt 11:5; Luke 4:18; 7:22). Owning no significant possessions, being without political power, and having no social standing eliminates one type of temptation to dismiss Jesus' call to repentance—the temptation that comes with the self-sufficiency that wealth brings (Matt 19:24; Luke 12:16-21). Jesus implicitly condemns the oppression of the poor after he observes a poor woman donating all she has to the Temple (Mark 12:42-44; Luke 21:2-4). In parables, Jesus teaches that the poor and not the rich will be the ones welcomed at the table in the kingdom of God (Luke 14:13; 16:20-22). According to the Gospel of Matthew, the test of righteousness will be how people have treated those who live in poverty with hunger, thirst, and disease (Matt 25:31-46).

The NT does not suggest that poverty can be ignored or that its existence must be fatalistically accepted. Responding to Jesus' call to repentance enables the disciples to hear the call for justice that comes from Israel's prophetic tradition. It impels the disciples to sell what they have in order to give to the poor (Matt 19:21; Mark 10:21). Indeed, one way for the wealthy to give a tangible sign of their repentance is for them to distribute their goods to people in need (e.g., Luke 18:22; Acts 4:32-35). Paul gives no evidence of any spiritualization of poverty. For the apostle, the poor are simply those in need. He showed particular concern for the church of Jerusalem because so many of the faithful were in need there (Rom 15:26; 1 Cor 16:3; 2 Cor 9:1-15; Gal 2:10; *see* COLLECTION, THE). The apostle praises the churches of Macedonia for their generous contributions, even though they were living in poverty (2 Cor 8:9).

The book of James displays the passion of the Israelite prophets in condemning the wealthy who have exploited the poor (Jas 5:1-6). The author objects to economic stratification in the Christian community (Jas 2:2-6). Most often the NT reflects a type of solidarity that should characterize the community of faith—solidarity that makes social injustice unthinkable. The NT challenges the followers of Jesus to emulate his example of living on the margins with no home (Matt 8:20; Luke 9:58) and without the security that comes with political power, social status, or material possessions (e.g., Matt 19:21-30; Mark 10:17-31; Luke 18:22-30). The poor are blessed: the kingdom of God belongs to them (Luke 6:20). *See* LIBERATION THEOLOGY.

Bibliography: Leslie J. Hoppe, O.F.M. *There Shall Be No Poor among You: Poverty in the Bible* (2004); Norbert Lohfink. *Option for the Poor: The Basic Principle of Liberation Theology in Light of the Bible* (1987).

LESLIE J. HOPPE, O.F.M.

POPILIUS, GAIUS. The Roman Senate sent Gaius Popilius as an envoy to prevent the Seleucid king ANTIOCHUS IV Epiphanes from capturing Egypt in 168 BCE. As Antiochus approached Alexandria, Popilius met him and delivered tablets with the Senate's demand that he abandon Egypt. Antiochus requested time to consult with his advisors, but the arrogant Popilius responded by drawing a circle in the sand around Antiochus' feet and required a decision before he left the circle. The abashed Antiochus agreed to do as the Senate desired (Polybius, *Hist.* 29.27; Livy, *Hist.* 45.12). This humiliation angered Antiochus and undoubtedly contributed to his harsh punishment of Jerusalem, prompted by a report that Judea was in revolt (2 Macc 5:11-14).

ADAM L. PORTER

POPLAR [לִבְנֶה **livneh**, עֲרָבָה **ʿaravah**]. There is frequent confusion between poplar and willow trees, both found along watersides. In most instances **ʿaravah** refers to willows, but in Ps 137:2-3 it is certainly the Euphrates poplar (*Populus euphratica*), which grows by the Euphrates as well as the Jordan. The WILLOW of Ezek 17:5 may also be the Euphrates poplar.

The white poplar (*Populus alba*) occurs away from water (Hos 4:13). It is likely to have been one of the trees Jacob exposed in front of rams (Gen 30:37) and also the trees of 2 Sam 5:23-24; 1 Chr 14:14-15 (but not the balsam poplar tree or mulberry tree). *See* MULBERRY, MULBERRY TREE; PLANTS OF THE BIBLE.

F. NIGEL HEPPER

PORATHA por-ay'thuh [פּוֹרָתָא poratha']. One of Haman's ten sons killed by the Jews in Susa (Esth 9:8). *See* ESTHER, BOOK OF; HAMAN.

PORCH [אוּלָם 'ulam; πυλών pylōn]. An architectural space that joins the interior and exterior of a building, with or without a roof, as on Solomon's house (1 Kgs 7:6), the Temple (Ezek 8:16), and the house of the high priest (Matt 26:71). *See* ARCHITECTURE, NT; ARCHITECTURE, OT; TEMPLE, JERUSALEM.

PORCIUS FESTUS. *See* FESTUS, PORCIUS.

PORCUPINE. *See* HEDGEHOG.

PORPHYRY [בַּהַט bahat]. A purple or reddish-colored igneous stone with pieces of shiny stone throughout. It was used in the mosaic pavement of the palace of AHASUERUS (Esth 1:6), a lavish scene of wealth and ostentation. This is the only occurrence of this Hebrew word in the OT and its identification with porphyry is uncertain.

TRISHA GAMBAIANA WHEELOCK

PORTENT. *See* OMEN; SIGNS AND WONDERS; SIGNS IN THE NT; SIGNS IN THE OT.

PORTICO OF SOLOMON. *See* SOLOMON'S PORTICO.

PORTRAYALS OF BIBLICAL FIGURES IN ISLAMIC TRADITION. Three of the world's major monotheisms—Judaism, Christianity, and Islam—share a rich scriptural heritage. Many of the same stories with the same figures populate their holy texts. While some believers from all three faiths often will define one or both of the other monotheistic traditions as wholly alien or OTHER, such claims betray shared canonical textual origins as well as similar exegetical interests. Figures such as Noah, Abraham, Pharaoh, Moses, David, Solomon, Jesus, and Mary, to name just a few, are discussed in the Qur'an. They are found not only in the Qur'an but also in all types of literature of the Islamic tradition such as the Hadith (the sayings of the Prophet Muhammad), **tafsir** (Qur'anic commentary), and historical writings. In what follows, reference will be made to several Qur'anic passages and exegetical material, some of which I have translated from the Arabic. The Islamic exegetical tradition is enormous, but for the reader's benefit I have included reference in parenthesis to the most prominent English translations, as well as useful resources for studying specific traditions in greater depth.

A. Prophetic Figures

In Islamic tradition, several of the major characters of the OT and the NT are referred to as prophets and messengers. The most common term, **rasul**, used over 300 times in the Qur'an, generally means "messenger," "apostle," or "someone who was sent." It also has a more specific meaning of one who has been appointed by God to communicate a specific message. Biblical prophets who are explicitly referred to as messengers are Noah, Ishmael, Moses, Lot, and Jesus. Included in this list are also nonbiblical prophets: Hud, Salih, and Shuayb.

Another term used is **nabi** ("prophet"). Occurring less often in the Qur'an than **rasul**, yet inclusive of a greater number of biblical figures, the term is used in connection with many more biblical characters: Lot, Abraham, Isaac, Jacob, Joseph, Aaron, David, Solomon, Job, Idris (Enoch), Jonah, Zechariah, John the Baptist, Elisha, and Elijah. There are Qur'anic passages that refer to prophets but do not name them specifically. Later Muslim exegetes identify them by name, such as Ezekiel, Samuel, and Daniel (al-Tabari, *Jami' al-bayan*; *Lives of the Prophets*).

These messengers and prophets were sent to their people to spread the same belief that would be preached by Muhammad in the 7th cent. CE. As the Qur'an explicitly states in 6:87-90, it is to these men (Idris is not listed) that the Book, wisdom, and prophethood are given. They are entrusted to guide the people, to exhort them to follow the straight path. Other passages likewise express the notion that these biblical figures were recipients of revelation (Sura 3:84; 4:163).

The prophets preached monotheism. In this sense the message of the Qur'an is not a radically new message from that of the OT and NT, but rather it continues the message of the Bible. That said, according to Islam, the Bible as such is not God's revelation. **Tahrif** is the notion that the Jews and Christians who indeed received divine revelation over time corrupted God's word; therefore the OT and NT as they are preserved today are not the revealed word of God but rather the Qur'an is the true word of God, sent from above to the Prophet Muhammad, the seal of prophecy. Both Judaism and Christianity are given a special status as Ahl al-Kitab, "People of the Book," a term applied to pre-Islamic religions possessing sacred texts. Zoroastrians, Samaritans, and Mandeans are also included in this category, which, as Islam expanded east, also included Buddhists and Hindus who lived under Muslim rule.

Randomly referring to its characters in no sequential order, the Qur'an is a series of revelations given to Muhammad, ordered from the longest to shortest chapter, or sura. The one exception is the opening sura, the Fatihah. Whereas the Qur'an often mentions these figures in passing, events surrounding their lives are recounted in greater detail by exegetes and storytellers. Anyone somewhat acquainted with classical Jewish narrative interpretation of the Bible, MIDRASH, will find a striking similarity and overlap between Jewish and Islamic exegesis of the medieval period in terms of style and content.

These stories, which share details found in Jewish and Christian sources, fill in the gaps of the Qur'anic narrative and flesh out these characters with homiletical and historical flourishes. This is most evidenced in the *Qisas al-Anbiya*ʿ (lit., *Stories or Tales of the Prophets*). They are also known as the **Isra**ʿ**iliyyat**, a term applied to narratives about the "children of Israel" (**Banu Isra**ʾ**il**), although Jewish figures do not appear in many of the narratives. A precise definition of the term has eluded scholars; however, perhaps it is best defined as Muslim renditions of narratives found in the Jewish tradition.

*Qisas al-Anbiya*ʿ or **Isra**ʿ**iliyyat**, unlike the Qur'an, are ordered for the most part chronologically. In the early Islamic period, those gathering traditions looked favorably on these stories, which were considered early testimonies of the true religion, Islam. In fact, in the Qur'an God instructs Muhammad to consult those who have read the book if he doubts what God reveals to him (10:94). Keep in mind, however, that consulting these traditions for legal advice was prohibited, and despite its favorable acceptance early on, by the 14th cent., the term **Isra**ʿ**iliyyat** officially came to designate dubious traditions, the content of which was deemed objectionable. Be that as it may, the orthodox attitude toward the **Isra**ʿ**iliyyat** did not prevent their wide readership and preservation in various literary corpora throughout the centuries. In the introduction of al-Thaʿlabi's compilation of the *Tales of the Prophets* (*Qisas al-Anbiya*ʿ), he enumerates several reasons the Islamic sages transmitted stories about the prophets. Not only did they serve as a model for the Prophet Muhammad but also they offer moral instruction and guidance for all who are subject to transgressions. They are not dry and didactic, but rather colorful, fanciful stories that entertain, edify, and convey Muslim beliefs and mores in the same way that Jewish midrash not only fills in scriptural and theological lacunae but also transmits rabbinic teachings and religious, social, and cultural values.

In addition to collections of *Tales of the Prophets*, compilations of extra-Qur'anic traditions abound. Volumes of Qur'anic exegesis play an important role in the Islamic tradition and the production of different collections over the centuries reflects a heterogeneity often overlooked when discussing "the" Islamic tradition. Some of the major collections of **tafsir** are those of Muqatil Ibn Sulaman (d. 767 CE), al-Tabari (d. 923 CE), al-Thaʿkabi (d. 1035 CE), and Ibn Kathir (d. 1373 CE).

1. Noah

Generally speaking, the prophets are commissioned to warn the people of the consequences of their sinful behavior, but the people ignore the call. This is a recurring motif, exemplified in the case of Noah. In Sura 71, "Noah" (Nuh), God sends Noah to his people in order to warn them before a woeful scourge overtakes them. He tirelessly warns his people to turn from their sinful path, and to fear and obey God. He implores the people to seek forgiveness, but to no avail, for they willfully continue to follow those who will lead to their destruction. This story of divine retribution by the flood recurs more than once in the Qur'an. Whereas the biblical account of Noah and the flood devotes a great deal of attention to the building of the ark and its dimensions, and to the events surrounding Noah's family before and after the flood, the Qur'an devotes more attention to Noah's role as a messenger sent to warn his people to repent from their wicked ways. Unlike his voiceless biblical counterpart, the Noah of the Qur'an is vocal, yet his unrelenting, strident exhortations fall on deliberately deaf ears (7:7). Whereas, too, the immediate family members of Noah's family are saved in the biblical account, in the Qur'an one of Noah's sons is not saved. When Noah pleads with God to save his son, God responds that the son is guilty and thus not part of Noah's family (11:46). Instead, members of Noah's family are those who do not share his blood, but rather his righteousness.

2. Abraham

The prophets are evoked as exemplars of proper behavior and their strife is a harbinger of what Muhammad will confront when he brings his message to his people. One of the most prominent figures in the Qur'an is Abraham (Ibrahim). He is the quintessential **hanif**, pure monotheist, and "a friend of God" (4:125). In many respects, Abraham models the Prophet Muhammad. As has been noted by several scholars even as early as the 19th cent., Abraham is typologically connected to Muhammad, who is depicted as attempting to restore the religion of Abraham, which is neither Judaism nor Christianity. Parallels between their lives abound. Both completely reject the idolatry of their contemporaries and are forced to leave their homeland.

Both set up alternative religious beliefs and practices. Both suffer the verbal slings of their contemporaries.

The Qur'an (6:76-80) recounts Abraham's revelation of the one true God, who is not a celestial body (e.g., a star, the moon, or the sun). The **mufassirun**, Qur'anic exegetes, reiterate this story adding, as usual, details such as where the event took place, and in some instances a conversation with his mother or with both parents as to the nature of their god.

Although the Qur'an relates precious little about Abraham's early years, **tafsir** and *Qisas al-Anbiya*ʿ furnish more detail (Muqatil, *Tafsir Muqatil*; Ishaq ibn Bishr, *Qisas al-anbiya*ʿ *wa-mubtada*ʾ *al-dunya*; al-Masʿudi, *Muruj al-dhahab wa-maʿadin al-jawhar*; al-Tabari, *Taʾrikh al-rusul wa-al-Muluk*; al-Kisaʾi, *Vita Prophetarum auctore Muhammad ben Abdallah al-Kisaʾi*; Mujahid ibn Jabr, *Tafsir al-imam Mujahid ibn Jabr*; al-Thaʿlabi, *ʿAraʾis al-Majalis fi Qisas al-Anbiya*ʾ. For an English translation of narratives on the life of Abraham, see Brinner 2002. See also Firestone, Lowin, and Wheeler, who deal explicitly with traditions on Abraham.) The extra-scriptural sources share a basic motif. A tyrannical king, Nimrod (Namrud), sees a star, in some versions in a dream, a prophecy according to Nimrod's priest that a boy will be born who will overturn the idolatrous ways of the people and destroy his kingdom. Taking precautionary steps, Nimrod orders the slaughter of every boy born that year, and also decrees the segregation of men and women, except for when the women are ritually impure when sexual relations are prohibited. Nimrod's plans, however, are thwarted for Azar, Abraham's father, impregnates his wife and Abraham is born.

Of the several stories revolving around Abraham, the story of his battle against his father's idolatry is taken up in several Qur'anic passages (6:74, 79-83; 19:41-50; 21:51-71; 26:69-104; 29:16-25; 37:83-98; 43:26-28; 60:4). Abraham's pleas to his father to turn from Satan to the true God serve only to fuel Abraham's father's anger against his son. Abraham faces the same untoward reaction when he implores his father's people to abandon their gods (Sura 26:70-71).

Abraham smashes their idols except for the supreme God (21:51-71). When in horror they ask him who destroyed their idols, Abraham tells them that it was their chief who smote them. Riled up, they attempt to burn him at the stake, but God keeps him safe (21:69) by turning the fire cold. According to Muslim interpreters, Abraham was saved from the fire because he spoke the words: "God is sufficient for me. Most Excellent is He in whom I trust" (Brinner trans., 2002). Another tradition tells of God sending down an angel to keep Abraham company within the fire.

As in *Jub.* 12:1-8 and the *Apoc. Ab.* 1–8, in the *Stories of the Prophets* we read that Abraham's father was an idol maker. In one of the most respected collections of *Qisas al-Anbiya*ʿ, that of Thaʿlabi, his father gives Abraham the idols to obey. Abraham runs out with the idols and announces: "Who wants to buy that which does not cause harm or benefit?" No one buys. He takes them to the river and crushes their heads and says to them: "Drink" (author's trans.; see Brinner trans., 2002).

The other major episodes are Abraham and his son Ishmael building of the House of God, the Kaʿba in Mecca, the establishment of the pilgrimage to Mecca (the Hajj) and its environs during the month of **dhu al-hijja** (one of the Five Pillars of Islam), and Abraham's near-sacrifice of Ishmael. Sura 2:127 refers to Abraham and Ishmael in Mecca but does not provide a context for why and how they traveled there. The **mufassirun** narrate the story of the expulsion of Ishmael and Hagar from Abraham's household, which takes them to Mecca. In all versions, Abraham personally brings them to Mecca of his own volition, and then returns to Syria to be with Hagar. After some time, he goes to visit Ishmael. (For an in-depth analysis of Abraham's visits to Ishmael, see Firestone; Bakhos.) He asks Sarah for her permission to do so and she agrees to let him journey on the condition that he does not remain there, or dismount from his steed. When Abraham arrives in Mecca he is greeted by Ishmael's inhospitable wife who tells him that Ishmael is out hunting, or in some versions seeking food. Abraham asks her to convey a message to Ishmael: "Change the threshold of your door" (Bakhos). Upon Ishmael's return, Ishmael smells his father's scent, his wife gives him the message, and he knows that he must divorce his wife. After some time, Abraham visits again and Ishmael's second wife is everything the first was not. She offers him something to eat and washes his head. This time the message conveyed to Ishmael is that his threshold is sound. This story is also preserved in *Pirqe R. El.* 30, a 9th-cent. CE Jewish retelling of biblical stories.

In Mecca, Abraham and Ishmael build the Kaʿba, a cube-shaped structure, the spiritual and geographic focal point of Islam. Muslims circumambulate the Kaʿba seven times counterclockwise. Moreover, Muslims are required to face its direction when fulfilling the requirement for prayer five times daily (compare Sura 2:127-28).

Abraham's role in Islam cannot be underestimated. In fact, Abraham asks God to send a prophet to the Arabs, a prophet of their own race who could lead them to faith. Abraham, therefore, is not only the author of one of the fundamental rites of Islam, and the precursor to Muhammad who comes to call people to "the faith of Abraham," but also the one who presages Muhammad's mission in Arabia.

3. Moses

Moses is the biblical figure most often mentioned in the Qur'an, which provides ample details that are iterated in several suras. Sura 19 explicitly refers to Moses' status as a prophetic messenger as well as to his brother

Aaron, who is also named as a prophet (19:51-53). To a great extent, the story of Moses (Musa) is paradigmatic of the struggles the Prophet faces in spreading his message, and in many respects his mission prefigures that of Muhammad. Muhammad receives the Qur'an, like Moses receives the Torah (2:54).

Moses' life story is told from infancy when he was saved by his mother, who puts him in a basket and entrusts him to the waters of the Nile (Sura 28). Unlike the biblical story, in the Qur'an it is revealed to Moses' mother that she should suckle him and put him in the Nile. She is assured of his safety and is told that he would return to her and would be invested with a mission (Sura 28:7).

Moses' mission to free the Israelites from Egyptian bondage figures prominently in the Qur'an. Sura 14:5-6 is frequently cited. One of the oft-repeated stories is Moses' encounter with Pharaoh (Sura 7:103-41; 10:75-93; 17:101-04; 20:80-97; 26:10-66; 40:23-30). Other episodes in Sura 28 include the killing of the Egyptian and Moses' escape into the wilderness, his time in Midian, and his commissioning (28:33). The golden calf episode appears in Sura 7:142-60 and 20:81.

Despite the similarities, the Qur'anic account of Moses' commission is strikingly different from the biblical one. For in the Qur'anic account, Moses does not hesitate as in the Bible. For example, in Exod 3:6 Moses hides his face, and in 3:11 he questions, "Who am I that I should go to Pharaoh?" In Exod 3:13 Moses asks God what to do if the Israelites ask for God's name; in Exod 4:1, he asks God what to do if the Israelites do not believe Moses. He also notes his slow speech and even suggests to God that he send someone else (Exod 4:10, 13). This stands in contradistinction to the image of Moses in the Qur'an, where his reaction is one of steadfastness. As for his tongue, he requests that God untie it and give him assistance, as well as strengthen his weakness (Sura 20:25-26). The Moses of Exodus does not want to take on the responsibility, but the Qur'anic Moses responds as someone who is ready and will dutifully execute what is required of him. In fact, he asks for assistance in order to be more effective.

God indeed provides assistance. He not only sends Aaron along with him but also gives him a most unique rod. Moses' staff does more than turn into a snake (Sura 20:20; 26:32; 27:10). According to extra-Qur'anic sources, it slays dragons, quenches Moses' thirst with milk, and satisfies his hunger with honey (Brinner trans., 2002). Qur'an commentators disagree as to how Moses acquired the staff. Some say that his father-in-law, Shuʿayb, gave it to him, while others such as the early tafsirist Muqatil ibn Sulayman claim that the angel Gabriel gave it to him when he was heading for Midian by night (Brinner trans., 2002).

The Bible and Qur'an overlap a great deal in terms of the events in Moses' life, with the exception of his encounter with a mysterious person, al-Khidr. Sura 18:65-82 tells of Moses' encounter with an unnamed servant of God whom the Muslim exegetes identify as al-Khidr. He is endowed with esoteric knowledge that Moses seeks. The story shares resonances with popular late antique motifs, and the figure of al-Khidr is often associated with Elijah. The **mufassirun** have interpreted the story as a lesson from God to Moses about his pride (al-Tabari, *Taʾrikh al-rusul wa al-muluk*; al-Kisaʾi, *Qisas al-anbiyaʿ*).

4. Joseph

Joseph is another biblical figure who plays an important role in Islamic tradition. As in the case of prophets previously discussed, the trials of Joseph were precursors for the challenges the Prophet would face. Unlike other figures, the Joseph narrative is found complete in Sura 12 of the Qur'an, aptly titled "The Sura of Joseph." The special nature of the tale is clear from the beginning (Sura 12:3): the Qur'anic story emphasizes the protagonist's moral virtue. Joseph is an exemplar of one who is steadfast in times of tribulation, of one who withstands temptation and overcomes the "guile of women."

5. Jesus

In the *Stories of the Prophets*, we also learn that John, the son of Zechariah, was the first to believe in Jesus. When John's mother was pregnant with him she tells Mary that her child is bowing to Mary's in the womb (Brinner trans., 2002). We also learn that John was six months older than Jesus and was killed before Jesus was raised up to heaven.

After giving birth, Mary goes back to her people, who want to stone her for wanton behavior. When confronted with the accusation, she responds by pointing to the infant in the cradle. "How," they ask, "can we speak to a baby in a cradle?" At this the infant Jesus replies: "I am the servant of God. He has given me a Book and ordained me a prophet. His blessing is upon me wherever I go, and He has exhorted me to be steadfast in prayer and to give alms as long as I shall live.... Blessed was I on the day that I was born, and blessed I shall be on the day of my death and on the day I shall be raised to life" (Sura 19:29-31; author's trans.). Upon hearing this, they leave her alone. This is not the only time that the infant Jesus speaks. In the *Stories of the Prophets*, while Mary carries Jesus as they are making their way back to her people, he says to her that he is the Messiah of God (Brinner trans., 2002).

Jesus is frequently mentioned in the Qur'an, in ninety-three verses of fifteen suras, and although Muslims do not accept him as the second person of the Trinity—indeed this notion is vehemently opposed—he is a revered figure. The Qur'an refers to Jesus as God's messenger, prophet, messiah, and servant, but he is not divine; he is also God's word and a sign of grace (Sura 2:253). He is not greater than all the other prophets, and he was sent as a messenger to the Israelites. Special attention is drawn to his family, especially to Mary and Zechariah.

Denial of Jesus' divine status is succinctly stated in Sura 5:17. The notion of the incarnation is antithetical to the fundamental Islamic belief in the one, true, uncreated God. In fact, it is a prime example of the grave sin of associating anything or anyone with God. It is therefore no surprise that one finds several anti-Trinity references in the Qur'an (4:171; 19:35; 43:57-59, 63-65, 81) and explicit attacks against the notion that God had a son (5:72-75; 6:101; 9:30-31; 10:68; 21:26). Furthermore, the Qur'an repudiates the worship of both Jesus and Mary (5:116-18).

Jesus is not the second person of the triune Godhead; instead he is most often referred to as "Son of Mary." Jesus was a messenger of God who was given the **injil**, an Arabic term related to the Greek word for gospel, **euangelion** (εὐαγγέλιον; Sura 5:46). The **injil**, and the Torah before it, was corrupted according to Islamic tradition (see Sura 3:78 as a basis for this doctrine); thus it is not equivalent to what Christians deem the NT or Gospels.

Although the Qur'an does not relate stories about the life of Jesus in great detail, the extra-Qur'anic material narrates several incidents from Jesus' childhood. For example, prior to his prophetic mission when he was twelve years old, Jesus performed signs and wonders. According to one tradition, while his mother was staying in the house of an important Egyptian merchant, money was stolen from the generous merchant's house. Mary was distressed over this, and when Jesus saw his mother's grief, he instructed her to tell the merchant to assemble all the poor people who sought lodging in the merchant's house. Jesus then picked out two poor people, one blind, the other crippled, who turned out to have been the thieves. Soon after the event, the merchant hosted a lavish wedding dinner party for one of his sons. All the people of Egypt gathered at his house, but after feeding them for two months, a party from Syria visited him. On that day there was no drink. When Jesus saw how troubled the merchant was, he walked by two rows of large earthenware jars, placed his hand on their mouths, and they became full (Brinner trans., 2002).

Another incident is told of the time Mary and Jesus came to a small village and found a man who was hospitable to them. At the time, the tyrannical king forced the villagers on a rotating basis to provide food and drink for the king and his troops. Mary noticed that their host was aggrieved. She asked his wife what happened and she told Mary that it was her husband's turn to provide for the king and his troops, but they didn't have sufficient provisions. Mary then told Jesus about this and he turned water in jugs to wine. Jesus also resurrects the dead and, as in the *Gospel of Thomas* (2:1-5), he creates a bird from clay (Sura 5:110; compare Sura 3:49).

The Qur'an mentions Jesus' apostles (Sura 3:52). The disciples also ask for a sign from on high in a passage about a table from heaven (Sura 5:112-15). According to Kaʿb al-Ahbar, a 7th-cent. Jewish Yemenite convert who is a source of traditions about the prophets, a table descended from heaven upside down with all foods except meat. Others, such as Muqatil and al-Kalbi, as recorded in al-Thaʿlabi, report that God answered Jesus' prayer, admonishing, however, that whoever eats but does not believe will be cursed and made an example to future generations. Al-Thaʿlabi also includes mention of two small fish and six loaves of bread that were multiplied to feed 5,000 (Brinner trans., 2002).

With respect to Jesus' death, Islamic tradition holds that, despite the less than clear impression one gets from the Qur'an, Jesus was not killed; someone in his stead was crucified. Rather, he was taken by God and will witness against unbelievers at the end of time (4:157-59).

B. Other Figures

1. Mary

Other biblical figures, not deemed prophets, are mentioned in the Qur'an. Mary has a special status in Islamic tradition. She is given more attention in the Qur'an than any other woman. In fact, she is the only woman mentioned by name, and Sura 19 is named after her. She is not only the mother of Jesus but also is regarded as a righteous woman in her own right (Sura 3:42-43). In the Qur'an Mary's mother dedicates her unborn daughter to God (3:25-36). The end of Mary's mother's prayer is telling, for it calls attention to the birth of Jesus. In the very next scene, we discover that indeed God has protected Mary and entrusted her to Zechariah, another NT figure mentioned in the Qur'an (3:37; 6:85; 19:1; 21:89). In Luke 1:5, 36, we learn that Zechariah is the husband of Elizabeth, Mary's cousin. In the Qur'an, however, his role is that of her custodian.

Islamic tradition holds that Mary was a virgin and that the birth of Jesus was miraculous. In Sura 3, angels announce to Mary that she is chosen above all women and give the baby the name Messiah Jesus. When she inquires as to how this will come about, she is told that it will happen because of God's decree (Sura 3:45-47).

The Qur'anic annunciation in Sura 19 also differs from the Gospel version. In Sura 19, we read that Mary receives the news that she will give birth to a son from God's spirit, which comes to her in the guise of a full-grown man, who claims to be God's messenger (19:17). Here, too, she asks how this can be given that she is a virgin, and he replies that it is done (Sura 19:21). The responses to Mary's query echo the important message in the Qur'an of God's might. He is the all-knowing creator whose will comes to be.

2. Joseph

Joseph is never mentioned in the Qur'an, but in the interpretive tradition Zechariah charges him with taking care of Mary. We read in al-Thaʿlabi's *Qisas al-Anbiyaʾ* that Zechariah became too old to take care of Mary and asked for someone to take over the responsibility for Mary's care. Given that they were all facing hard times, no one volunteered, so they cast lots with pens and the lot fell to Joseph, an honest carpenter. In some traditions, he is her cousin. In Islamic tradition, Joseph is her guardian, not her husband (Muqatil, al-Tabari, al-Tha'labi). In the extra-Qur'anic traditions he is depicted as a constant companion who, like Mary, is pious and faithful to God. At one point, however, Joseph had the urge to kill Mary during their journey to Bethlehem, but the angel Gabriel interfered by telling Joseph that the baby was from the Holy Spirit (Brinner trans., 2002).

C. Conclusion

The above was a limited sampling of how Islamic tradition treats various biblical figures. Even a brief survey calls attention to the way in which the tradition shares common themes and concerns with Judaism and Christianity. The challenge of comparative studies is to detect the common treads while at the same time to appreciate the purpose and manner in which they are woven into each tradition.

Bibliography: Camilla Adang. *Muslim Writers on Judaism and the Hebrew Bible: From Ibn Rabban to Ibn Hazm* (1996); Carol Bakhos. *Ishmael on the Border: Rabbinic Portrayals of the First Arab* (2006); Marc Bernstein. *Stories of Joseph: Narrative Migrations between Judaism and Islam* (2006); William Brinner, trans. *ʿArai'ʾs al-Majalis fi Qisas al-Anbiyaʾ or "Lives of the Prophets"* (2002); William Brinner, trans. *Prophets and Patriarchs: The History of al-Tabari.* Vol. 2: *The Prophets and Patriarchs (Tarikh al-rusul wa-al-muluk)* (1987); Reuven Firestone. *Journeys in Holy Lands: The Evolution of the Abraham–Ishmael Legends in Islamic Exegesis* (1990); Shalom Goldman. *The Wiles of Women/The Wiles of Men: Joseph and Potiphar's Wife in Near Eastern, Jewish and Islamic Folklore* (1995); Brian M. Hauglid. "On the Early Life of Abraham: Biblical and Qur'anic Intertextuality and the Anticipation of Muhammad." *Bible and Qur'an: Essays in Scriptural Intertextuality.* John C. Reeves, ed. (2003) 87–105; G. R. Hawting and Abdul-Kader Shareef, eds. *Approaches to the Qur'an* (1993); John Kaltner. *Ishmael Instructs Isaac: An Introduction to the Qur'an for Bible Readers* (1999); Jacob Lassner. *Demonizing the Queen of Sheba: Boundaries of Gender and Culture in Postbiblical Judaism and Medieval Islam* (1993); Shari I. Lowin. *The Making of a Forefather: Abraham in Islamic and Jewish Exegetical Narratives* (2006); Walid Saleh. *The Formation of the Classical Tafsir Tradition: The Qur'an Commentary of al-Tha'labi (d. 427/1035)* (2004); Roberto Tottoli. *Biblical Prophets in the Qur'an and Muslim Literature* (2002); Brannon Wheeler. *Moses in the Quran and Islamic Exegesis* (2002); Brannon Wheeler. *Prophets of the Quran: An Introduction to the Quran and Muslim Exegesis* (2002).

CAROL BAKHOS

PORTRAYALS OF ISHMAEL IN ISLAMIC TRADITION. Ishmael, the son of Abraham and Hagar in the book of Genesis, is considered a messenger and a prophet in the Qur'an. According to the Islamic tradition, the prophets were biblical personalities who were directed by God on the straight path, and believers were exhorted to follow their guidance. A messenger is a representative of God among his people, with a specific mission, bringing a book or message to the people. There are instances, as in the case of Ishmael (Sura 19:54) and Muhammad, that both terms are used to describe an individual. Whereas all messengers are prophets, not all prophets are messengers. In the handful of verses that mention Ishmael, he is listed with Abraham, Isaac, and Jacob, and he is also listed among other prophets such as Jonah and Elisha, e.g., whose uprightness is deemed praiseworthy.

Other than reference to Ishmael and Abraham building and purifying the Kaba, the cube-shaped sanctuary in the Great Mosque in Mecca, specific events pertaining to his life are not mentioned in the Qur'an. Unlike Abraham and Moses, Ishmael does not figure prominently in the Qur'an. In fact, contrary to popular belief, the Qur'an does not explicitly refer to him as Abraham's intended sacrificial victim (compare Gen 22:1-19). Moreover, the Qur'an does not discuss the expulsion of Ishmael and his mother, Hagar, however, extra-qur'anic sources narrate the occurrences that take place upon their dismissal.

Although there is no mention in the Qur'an of Ishmael as the ancestor of the Arabs, genealogical systems of the 3rd–9th cent. attempted to legitimize Ishmael's Arab ancestry by preserving the tradition of his marriage into the Jurhum tribe, one of the legendary pre-Islamic Arab tribes affiliated with the holy city of Mecca. All Arab tribes, according to traditional genealogists, are derived from one of two great ancestors, Qahtan or ʿAdnan, the former associated with the true or original Arabs, the later with the Arabized northern tribes. The Jurhum tribe is of Qahtan. According to at least one genealogical system, that of Ibn al-Kalbi, whose form was finalized around 800 CE, the great ancestor, ʿAdnan, descends from Ishmael. Ishmael's marriage to a Jurhumite woman legitimizes him as an Arab, since the Jurhum are from Qahtan, the original Arabs. It furthermore establishes him as patriarch of the northern tribes, and thus progenitor of Muhammad, who is of the Quraysh, one of the northern tribes.

It is noteworthy that the complete Arabization of Ishmael was possible through marriage and not by birth, in comparison to Muhammad, whose is an Arab by birth. Furthermore, according to a tradition attributed to Ibn Abbas, the Jurhumites taught Ishmael Arabic, and according to the saying of the Prophet Muhammad, Ishmael was the first to speak in clear Arabic at the age of fourteen (Abu Ja'far al-Baqir).

Other traditions about Ishmael mention his twelve sons, the names of which correspond to the list of his descendants in Gen 25:13-16. When Ishmael was on his deathbed, he gave his inheritance to Isaac and his daughter Nesmah was given to Esau in marriage. According to Gen 28:8 her name was Mahalath, and in Gen 36:3, her name was Basemath. They also identify Ishmael as the first to ride a horse, and relate the story of Abraham's visits to him, a narrative also found in later rabbinic sources (e.g., *Pirqe R. El.* 30). *See* ABRAHAM, OT; HAGAR; ISHMAEL, ISHMAELITES; ISLAM; PORTRAYALS OF BIBLICAL FIGURES IN ISLAM.

CAROL BAKHOS

POSIDONIUS pos'i-doh'nee-uhs [Ποσιδώνιος **Posidōnios**]. A man sent by NICANOR along with THEODOTUS and MATTATHIAS to offer a treaty to JUDAS Maccabeus and his troops (2 Macc 14:19). In the parallel text (1 Macc 7:27-32), Nicanor either does not send envoys or their names are not mentioned.

POSSESSION, DEMONIC. *See* DEMONIAC.

POST, DOORPOST [מְזוּזָה **mezuzah**]. Doorposts are the vertical structural elements for a doorway, with the LINTEL as the upper horizontal member and the THRESHOLD as the lower horizontal member. Doorposts were usually of wood or stone. Mention is made of doorposts of individual houses (Exod 12:7; Deut 6:9), the temple at Shiloh (1 Sam 1:9), the inner sanctuary of the Solomonic Temple (1 Kgs 6:31), Solomon's palace (1 Kgs 7:5), and the restored Temple of Ezekiel's vision (Ezek 41:21). The same Hebrew word is used for posts of a city gate (Judg 16:3). Such a gatepost was excavated *in situ* at the site of Mudaybi, Jordan. Lamb's blood on the doorposts and lintel was a critical part of the Passover story (Exod 12:7, 22-24), and MEZUZAH became the place on the doorpost where the Shema was posted as a constant reminder of Israel's relationship with Yahweh (Deut 6:4-9). *See* ARCHITECTURE, OT; DOOR; FOUNDATION; HOUSE; SHEMA, THE.

JOEL F. DRINKARD JR.

POST-COLONIAL BIBLICAL INTERPRETATION. The task of post-colonial studies is twofold: 1) to analyze how European scholarship codified and studied cultures that European countries had colonized; and 2) to recover how the resistant writings of the colonized people have tried to redeem their cultures and restore their identity and dignity. The discourse, initiated in Edward Said's *Orientalism*, was associated with the study of sacred texts, historical documents, colonial records, and fictional accounts of societies that had been invaded and disrupted by European colonists. Post-colonialism began its career as a resistant and creative literature and only later was it turned into a theoretical category. It is seen no longer as a natural evolutionary progression following the departure of imperial powers, but as a series of critical and political protests that have taken place since the beginning of modern colonialism.

The central aim of post-colonial biblical criticism is to situate empire and imperial concerns at the center of the Bible and biblical studies. First, it has brought to attention the importance of empire—Assyrian, Egyptian, Persian, Greek, and Roman—as the context of many biblical narratives. While mainstream scholarship frequently restricts our understanding to theological, spiritual, and historical aspects of these narratives, post-colonialism adds the often neglected dimension of domination by an outside culture, specifically, the politics of imperialism. In doing so, it interrogates the text in various ways, asking, e.g., how the author portrays the empire: as benevolent or oppressive? Does the text support the imperial intentions of the empire or oppose these intentions? Where do the loyalties of the author lie—with the imperial power or with those subjugated by it? How does the author represent the occupied people—as victims or as grateful beneficiaries? Does the author speak about their resistance? Second, post-colonialism has exposed how both biblical figures and the colonized cultures have been distorted and defamed in colonial and theological literature. For example, post-colonial readings attempt to reconfigure the story of Mary Magdalene to show how (mostly) male ecclesiastical writers have relegated the "apostle to the apostles" to a minor role and defamed her as a repentant prostitute, a status that the NT does not support (*see* MARY). It has also exposed stereotypical images of the "OTHER" as lazy and unreliable.

Third, the retrieval hermeneutics embarked on by post-colonial criticism has unearthed the imaginative ways in which the colonized have appropriated the Bible.

The Indian convert K. M. Banerjea's claim that the Hindu Vedas contained superior notions of the sacrificial lamb is a notable case in point. These resistant discourses were a timely reminder that the colonized were capable of recovering and interpreting the gospel message in terms that were meaningful to their own experience, so that they did not have to rely on interpretations that had been distorted by the vested interests of Western denominationalism and cultural imperialism.

Fourth, post-colonialism has been able to intervene in the area of biblical translation and repair the cultural and theological damage sometimes done in that interpretive process. An illustration of this is the missionary version of the Shona Bible where the Supreme Being of the Shona people, who has no gender specificity, was transformed into a male god by translators. Finally, post-colonialism has been vigorous in addressing issues that have emerged in the wake of colonialism such as nationality, migrancy, DIASPORA, multiculturalism, and hybridity. *See* BIBLICAL INTERPRETATION, HISTORY OF; CULTURAL HERMENEUTICS; IDEOLOGICAL CRITICISM; MARGINAL, MARGINALIZATION.

Bibliography: K. M. Banerjea. *Dialogues on the Hindu Philosophy* (1903); Stephen D. Moore and Fernando Segovia, eds. *Post-colonial Biblical Criticism: Interdisciplinary Intersections* (2005); Edward W. Said. *Orientalism* (1979); R. S. Sugirtharajah. *Post-colonial Criticism and Biblical Interpretation* (2002).

R. S. SUGIRTHARAJAH

POSTMODERN BIBLICAL INTERPRETATION. Postmodern biblical interpretation includes an array of strategies that depart from the presuppositions of modern biblical criticism. Where modern biblical criticism strives for objectivity, postmodern critics value subjectivity. Where modern biblical criticism eschews political interests, most postmodern interpreters acknowledge a political component to their work (and through it promote social equality, cultural diversity, and resistance to heterosexual privilege). Where modern biblical interpreters emphasize rigorous methodological standards, postmodern interpreters emphasize the role of imagination. Modern biblical interpretation tends to treat biblical texts as if they contain a transparent meaning that the modern interpreter simply restates in contemporary terms. Such a model neglects the extent to which language creates varied interpretations (as the history of biblical interpretation amply illustrates). Linguistic expression is ambiguous, not because of shoddy composition, but as a necessary condition of linguistic communication. Jacques Derrida identified this ambiguity of language as "play"; the signs and symbols of language evoke a variety of possible meanings (*see* SEMIOTICS). Biblical interpreters have seized on the phenomenon of linguistic pliancy to argue for counterintuitive readings. The resulting startling readings are not based on outrageous whimsy; they articulate the many possibilities that linguistic expression permits.

The modern inclination to stress distinct, definite meaning at the cost of interpretive difference thus leads to the authorization of some sorts of criticism and the exclusion of others. According to postmodern interpreters, there is a willed refusal on the part of modernist interpreters to acknowledge alternatives to their standards of legitimacy. This "refusal" reveals a political impulse to this professedly apolitical and disinterested mode of discourse. Indeed, modern interpreters who simply identify their own approach with value-neutral, rational, scientific inquiry reinforce Jean-François Lyotard's accusation that enlightened modernity exercises an intellectual regime, the institution of will into reason. Postmodern interpreters typically challenge modern interpreters' claim that their conclusions derive from nonpartisan reason. Even though modernists claim to be objective interpreters, postmodernists argue that the modernists (typically male white European and North American scholars who have dominated the guild of biblical criticism) actually cannot escape interpreting from their own subjective social locations. Postmodern interpreters argue that there is no such thing as complete objectivity, and they often make their own social location the explicit criterion for their interpretive judgment. They show the ways that dominant-class interpreters use their institutional and social power to reinforce their own interests. Postmodernists may deliberately read the Bible against the grain of the dominant scholarship in order to articulate an alternative vision of biblical meaning that better coheres with the interests of women, the wider global community, and readers whose dissident understanding of Scripture has been suppressed in the name of cultural homogeneity.

These examples show some directions that a postmodern temper may take in biblical scholarship. Since postmodernity characterizes biblical interpretation not as a regulative method but as a sensibility, one cannot define or set boundaries for postmodern interpretations (though one can argue the justification of applying the characterization *postmodern* to particular readings). For just this reason, postmodern biblical criticism will probably not constitute itself as a distinct interpretive practice so much as it will influence the ways that particular interpreters approach their work. The resulting uncertainty over exactly what constitutes postmodern biblical interpretation thus befits a discourse that takes "uncertainty" as one of its hallmarks. *See* BIBLICAL INTERPRETATION, HISTORY OF; FEMINIST INTERPRETATION; IDEOLOGICAL CRITICISM; NARRATIVE CRITICISM; READER RESPONSE CRITICISM.

Bibliography: A. K. M. Adam. *Postmodern Interpretations of the Bible* (2001); A. K. M. Adam. *What Is Postmodern Biblical Criticism?* (1995); The Bible and Culture Collective. *The Postmodern Bible* (1997); Jacques Derrida. *Of Grammatology* (1967); Jean-François Lyotard. "Règles et Paradoxes et Appendice Svelte." *Babylone* 1 (1983) 67–80; Carol A. Newsom and Sharon H. Ringe, eds. *The Women's Bible Commentary* (1998); Daniel Patte et al., eds. *Global Bible Commentary* (2004); Fernando Segovia and Mary Ann Tolbert, eds. *Reading from This Place: Social Location and Biblical Interpretation.* 2 vols. (1995).

A. K. M. ADAM

POT [סִיר sir]. Pots were used for cooking and were included in lists of temple items (1 Kgs 7:40; 2 Kgs 4:38-41; 25:14; 2 Chr 35:13). Probably the ceramic vessel most commonly identified as a "pot" in archaeological remains is a cooking pot. *See* POTTERY.

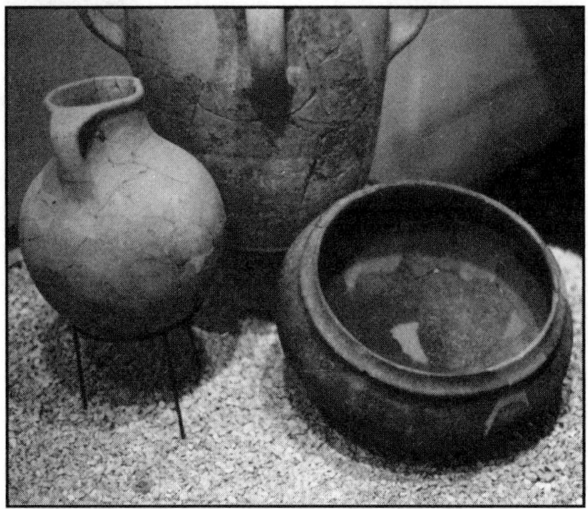

John C. H. Laughlin

Figure 1: Iron Age cooking pot

POTIPHAR pot'uh-fuhr [פּוֹטִיפַר potifar]. The Egyptian who purchases Joseph from the Midianites (Gen 37:36) or from the Ishmaelites (Gen 39:1). Traditional source criticism attributes this duplication to the redaction of Elohistic material in Gen 37 and Yahwistic material in Gen 39.

After he purchases Joseph, Potiphar notices Joseph's success and promotes him to a high-level position within the household: he "left all that he had in Joseph's charge" (Gen 39:6). Later, Potiphar imprisons Joseph after POTIPHAR'S WIFE (unnamed in the biblical text) accuses Joseph of rape. The interaction of Potiphar, Potiphar's wife, and Joseph shares similarities with the Egyptian *Tale of Two Brothers* in which the wife of Anubis accuses Bata, her brother-in-law, of assaulting her when she rejected his advances.

Potiphar may be a shortened form of POTIPHERA, an Egyptian theophoric name "he whom Re has given" (used for a priest of On; Gen 41:45, 50; 46:20), RE being the Egyptian sun god worshiped at ON (HELIOPOLIS). Potiphera is the name of Joseph's father-in-law, who was priest of On. Similar Egyptian names appear from the Twenty-Second Dynasty (945–745 BCE) onward.

Potiphar is a saris (סָרִיס), a term that is usually translated as "EUNUCH" (2 Kgs 20:18; 23:11; Esth 2:3; Isa 39:7; 56:3; Jer 34:19; 38:7). Yet, in reference to Potiphar, saris is often translated as "officer" or "official" (Gen 37:36; 39:1). Some scholars cite the lack of evidence of castration in Egypt and Potiphar's marital status as reasons for translating "officer," but the translation "eunuch" in Gen 37:36 and 39:1 is plausible as well. *See* JOSEPH, JOSEPHITES; OFFICER, OFFICIAL.

NYASHA JUNIOR

POTIPHAR'S WIFE pot'uh-fuhr. The wife of POTIPHAR, the Egyptian who purchased Joseph (Gen 37:36; 39:1). While she is unnamed in the biblical text, some later Jewish and Islamic sources refer to her as "Zulaikha" (with various spellings).

In Gen 39, she commands Joseph to have sex with her, but he refuses. Later, she repeats her command and grabs his garment. He leaves the garment in her hand and runs outside. She then calls to the men of the house, claiming that Joseph attempted to rape her but that she cried out (but see Deut 22:24). Finally, she accuses Joseph to Potiphar, and he imprisons Joseph.

In the history of interpretation of Gen 39, interpreters vary in their view of Potiphar's wife's actions toward Joseph. In many instances, interpreters regard Potiphar's wife as a *femme fatale* and treat Joseph as a righteous man (4 Macc 2:2-3; *T. Jos.* 9:2-3). Yet, some question Joseph's complicity (*b. Sotah* 36b; *Gen. Rab.* 87:7). Likewise, visual representations of Gen 39 provide a range of depictions of Joseph and Potiphar's wife's encounters.

Outside of the Bible, the "Potiphar's Wife" literary motif involves a woman who makes improper advances to a man and later accuses him of sexual assault or attempted sexual assault. This motif appears in the Egyptian "Tale of Two Brothers," the Qur'an's Sura 12, Book V of the *Iliad*, *Hippolytus* by Euripides, and many other texts. *See* JOSEPH, JOSEPHITES.

Bibliography: James L. Kugel. *In Potiphar's House: The Interpretive Life of Biblical Texts.* 2nd ed. (1994).

NYASHA JUNIOR

POTIPHERA puh-ti'fuh-ruh [פּוֹטִי פֶרַע poti feraʿ]. An Egyptian priest of On (Heliopolis) and father to ASENATH (Gen 41:45). The marriage of his daughter to the Hebrew patriarch Joseph gave Potiphera two grandsons, Manasseh and Ephraim (Gen 41:50). Potiphera is not to be confused with POTIPHAR, the official of Pharaoh's court to whom Joseph was sold in Gen 39, although some later commentaries on the story equated the two (e.g., *Jub.* 40:10). *See* JOSEPH, JOSEPHITES.

JESSICA TINKLENBERG DEVEGA

POTSHERD [חֶרֶשׂ kheres; ὄστρακον ostrakon]. Potsherds (usually called sherds) are the most common material remains found on archaeological sites from the Pottery Neolithic Period (ca. 5500 BCE) onward. When properly cleaned and analyzed, sherds, especially diagnostic ones such as rims, handles, and bases, can provide a reliable guide to the time periods the site was occupied (*see* POTTERY). Inscribed sherds are called OSTRACA. The image of Job scratching his sores with a discarded potsherd—garbage—illustrates his misery. Sirach illustrates the futility of teaching a fool with the image of someone attempting to glue potsherds together.

JOHN C. H. LAUGHLIN

John C. H. Laughlin

Figure 1: Photo of diagnostic potsherds

POTSHERD GATE [שַׁעַר הַחַרְסִית sha῾ar hakharsith]. City gate of preexilic Jerusalem exiting to the Hinnom Valley, perhaps near the southern end of the City of David. Possibly also identified as the "GATE BETWEEN THE TWO WALLS" and the "DUNG GATE," here Jeremiah prophesied the city's destruction by breaking an earthenware jug (Jer 19:1-13). *See* GATE; JERUSALEM.

JAMES RILEY STRANGE

POTTER'S FIELD. *See* AKELDAMA.

POTTER'S WHEEL [אָבְנָיִם ʾavnayim; τροχός trochos]. While the making of POTTERY goes back at least as early as the Pottery Neolithic era (6th millennium BCE), using a wheel to help shape or form the piece dates to the Chalcolithic Period (5th millennium BCE). What are believed to be wheel marks on certain vessels indicate that they were made on a slow wheel or *tournette.* A slow wheel utilized two stones: one had a conical base with a socket; the other was a stone disc with an oblong knob on one side that fitted into the socket of the other stone. The potter (or assistant) could then slowly turn the clay with one hand while shaping the vessel, or stop turning and use both hands. The potter, potter's wheel, and clay are used in Jer 18:1-11 to illustrate God's complete control over the people. Here ʾavnayim, translated "wheel," is literally the plural of "stone" (Jer 18:3).

The slow wheel was the only form of potter's wheel until the Middle Bronze Age (2000–1550 BCE), when a major revolution in ceramic technology took place. In order to make vessels with thin, uniform walls, centrifugal force was necessary, and potters began to use a "fast wheel" with a large stone as a flywheel or "kick wheel" attached with a wooden shaft to a smaller stone upon which the mat to hold the clay was attached. The potter created the necessary speed by "kicking" the flywheel with the foot, as the trochos in Sir 38:29-30. Until the Hellenistic-Roman periods, the finest pottery in Israel was made using this technique. For some reason, this valuable innovation was lost during the Late Bronze Age, but was reintroduced at some point during the Iron Age. The quality of pottery made with a fast wheel reached its highest point during the Roman Period from which comes the finest quality pottery ever made in the region.

JOHN C. H. LAUGHLIN

POTTERY. Pottery is among the most important discoveries on archaeological sites. Sir Flinders Petrie (d. 1942), a British Egyptologist who spent six weeks at Tell el-Hesi (*see* HESI, TELL EL) in 1890, was the first to recognize the value of pottery for establishing the chronology of a stratified tell. Properly collected, analyzed, and compared with the pottery from other sites, pottery remains, usually in the form of POTSHERDs, enable a pottery expert to date that part of a site from which the pottery was collected, provided the area of the site is not contaminated or disturbed in some way. Pottery analysis provides valuable information regarding trade relations, diet, manufacturing and firing tech-

John C. H. Laughlin

Figure 1: Iron I pottery vessels

niques, and the social and economic environments of the people who owned and used the vessels.

The image of a potter (yotser [יוֹצֵר]; from yatsar [יָצַר], "to form, fashion") is frequently used as an arresting metaphor for God, most often in late texts (Isa 45:9; 64:8; Jer 18:2-6, 11; 19:11; see also Isa 29:16; Lam 4:2; Rom 9:21; Sir 33:13). The author of Chronicles mentions families of royal potters who lived in Judah (1 Chr 4:23). *See* POT; POTTER'S WHEEL.

Bibliography: Ruth Amiran. *Ancient Pottery of the Holy Land* (1969); W. M. F. Petrie. *Tell el Hesy* (1891).

JOHN C. H. LAUGHLIN

POUND [λίτρα litra, μνᾶ mna, ταλαντιαῖος talantiaios]. A measure of weight (John 12:3; 19:39; Rev 16:21) or of weight equivalent for coins (Luke 19:13-25). Luke's version of the parable of the TALENTS (Luke 19:11-27) uses mna rather than the talanton (τάλαντον) of Matt 25:14-30. Although ancient measures were approximations at best, a Greco-Roman talent usually signified a huge debt. *See* MONEY, COINS; WEIGHTS AND MEASURES.

KIMBERLY R. PEELER

POVERTY [רֵאשׁ reʾsh, רֵישׁ rish, רֵישׁ resh; πτωχεία ptōcheia, ὑστέρημα hysterēma, ὑστέρησις hysterēsis]. In the Bible, *poverty* refers to a lack of material resources and economic power as well as to the political and social marginalization that results from this lack (Prov 10:15; 30:8; 31:7; Mark 12:44; Luke 21:4; 2 Cor 8:2, 9; Rev 2:9). Poverty is an important concern in the biblical tradition, though the individual components of that tradition differ in their analysis of the causes for and the responses to poverty. For example, the Deuteronomic tradition asserts that poverty would not exist in Israel if people observed the commandments (Deut 15:4-5); nevertheless, it recognizes that, for a variety of reasons, poverty will exist in the community (Deut 15:11). It calls for the people of Israel to be generous to the poor (Deut 15:7) and suggests strategies to ensure that poverty would never become a permanent feature of Israelite society.

On the other hand, the book of Proverbs generally sees poverty as the result of failures on the part of the POOR person (Prov 10:4; 13:18; 14:23; 20:13; 23:21; 24:33-34; 28:19). This book, whose intended audience was the sons of the upper classes, attempts to warn its readers about what happens when a person lacks diligence and leads a dissipated life. Still, Proverbs calls upon the wealthy to be generous toward the poor (Prov 19:17; 22:9) because it sees the existence of poverty as an affront to God (Prov 14:31).

Some of the prophets suggest that poverty is the result of decisions that the wealthy make to deprive others of what is rightfully theirs through economic exploitation and the corruption of the legal system (*see* WEALTH). Prophets who make this assertion announce divine judgment on a political, social, and economic system that allows poverty to exist (e.g., Isa 1:21-26; Amos 4:1-4).

The liturgical prayers of the OT use the vocabulary of poverty to emphasize the worshiper's total dependence on God. In these texts, poverty becomes a metaphor for the status of the worshiper before God (Pss 10:17-18; 72:2). Still, the psalms also recognize that poverty is the consequence of injustice that calls for divine judgment (Pss 10:2; 72:4).

The apocalyptic perspective that undergirds much of the NT affects a noticeable shift in the assessment of poverty. The poor are the fortunate ones, given the reversal of fortunes that will take place when the reign of God begins (Luke 6:20). Jesus advises his followers to make themselves poor for the sake of God's kingdom (Matt 19:21). Paul advises generosity toward the poor and he expends great efforts to collect funds to alleviate the poverty of the church in Jerusalem (Rom 15:25-28; *see* COLLECTION, THE).

The biblical tradition assumes that poverty does not just happen—it happens because people make it happen. In some instances, people are lazy and allow economic opportunities to slip through their hands. At other times, people use their political, social, and economic power to increase their wealth at the expense of others. In both instances, people create poverty. The Bible presents God as the protector of the poor, especially those unjustly deprived of their access to the bounty of the earth and the fruits of their labor (Jer 20:13). *See* ISRAEL, SOCIAL AND ECONOMIC DEVELOPMENT OF; SLAVERY.

LESLIE J. HOPPE, O.F.M.

POWER OF THE KEYS. In Matt 16:18-19, Jesus tells Peter that Peter is the rock (petra πέτρα; from which Simon's nickname *Peter* derives) upon which the church will be built, that he will be given the keys to the kingdom, and that "whatever you bind on earth will be bound in heaven, and whatever you loose on earth will be loosed in heaven." Luke, on the other hand, records Jesus accusing the lawyers of having taken away "the key of knowledge" so as to prevent all entry (Luke 11:52). The church fathers began early to read the Matthew passage as giving Peter—and hence the church authorities who traced their ordinations back to Peter—a great deal of authority over believers' salvation. The passage remains a sticking point between Protestant and Catholic theologians, since the former assert that Peter here represents all believers and not only the ordained clergy. It is a less significant passage for biblical scholars, and historians are likely to see it as Matthew's redaction (see Matt 18:18), rather than the words of the historical Jesus. The Evangelist thus raises Peter up from his shoddy appearance in Mark, where the nickname Peter may very well refer to Peter's hardheadedness. *See* BINDING AND LOOSING; PETER, THE APOSTLE.

NICOLE WILKINSON DURAN

POWER, POWERFUL [יָד yadh, כֹּחַ koakh, עוֹז ʿoz, תֹּקֶף toqef; δύναμις dynamis]. Power is the ability to influence or control entities and forces outside oneself, and the ability to withstand influence from other entities and forces. Biblical authors celebrate God's power as the ultimate power as manifested in creation, judgment, and redemption. Every aspect of the divine power is applied to humans in a secondary sense, since God's power is viewed as the source of humans' power and is the limit on any human claim to autonomous power. Paul ironically claims that God's power manifests itself in human weakness (2 Cor 12:9; see Isa 40:29).

God's power to influence others toward life is seen in the creation stories throughout the Bible. Whether in traditions that describe God speaking the world into existence *ex nihilo* (Gen 1; Jer 10:12; John 1:1-3; 2 Cor 4:6*a*; Heb 11:3) or in those that describe God mastering chaos (Job 38–41; Ps 74:12-17; Prov 8:22-31) or leading the people out of Egypt (Exod 15:6; Deut 4:37), the power of the divine, understood as potent influence to introduce and sustain life, is celebrated. When humans channel this life-giving potency to others, e.g., by raising the dead, they are also considered powerful (1 Kgs 17:17-24; 2 Kgs 4:32-37; Luke 7:11-17; John 11:28-44; Acts 9:36-43; Heb 11:35*a*). HEALING miracles also derive their aura of power in the Bible from direct connection to God's life-bringing, creative influence (2 Kgs 5:1-19; 20:1-11; Acts 14:8-18; *see* MIRACLE). Humans are considered the recipients of God's power when they procreate, especially in situations where procreation seems impossible (Gen 15:4-5; 21:1-7; 25:21; Judg 13:2-25; Luke 1:35; Rom 4:19-21; Heb 11:11-12). God gives humans power to do God's will, e.g., Moses' powers against Pharaoh (Exod 4:21; 9:16; Deut 34:12); Elisha's prophetic power (2 Kgs 3:13-20); or God's power for the king in battle (2 Chr 25:8).

In the NT, the themes of divine power exercised in life-bringing acts of creation (including healing), redemption, and judgment are focused on Christ as the divine agent of this power. Christ is not only the firstborn of creation (Col 1:15), he is also the agent of creation (John 1:1-3) and the firstborn from the dead (Col 1:18; Rev 1:5). In the Gospels, Christ's power to heal (Mark 1:30-31; John 9:1-17), to calm storms (Mark 4:35-41), and to walk on water (John 6:16-21) illustrates this creative power that has life-giving force and energy to control chaos. Luke can even use *power* (dynamis) synonymously with the Holy Spirit in describing Jesus' healing power (Luke 5:17; compare 4:36), and Jesus compared his act of healing to power going out from him (Luke 8:46). The Gospels call Jesus' actions "deeds of power" (Matt 11:20-23; 13:54-58), although strangely, he could do no deeds of power where the people did not believe in him (Mark 6:5).

God's power is also evident in JUDGMENT, particularly judgment of abuses of power. In the heavenly court, God is pictured as ruling among the other deities (Job 1:6-12; Ps 82:1-4). In Ps 82:1-4, God's power to judge among the other gods is correlated with the exercise of God's power in judgment on behalf of the powerless ("the weak and the needy," "the lowly and the destitute"). God grants power for judgment to the divinely chosen, human ruler for the purpose of executing justice on behalf of the powerless (1 Kgs 3:16-28; Ps 72:1-4; Luke 1:52). Whether from God in heaven (Ps 97:1-6; Jer 25:12-38; Ezek 32, 35, 38) or through a king in Zion (Pss 2:6-12; 89:19-26 [Heb. 89:20-27]), or through Jesus as Christ (Matt 26:64; Mark 14:62), divine power judges the nations. The Bible also speaks of human power or "powers" as forces of evil, over which God triumphs (1 Sam 4:3, 8; 2 Sam 18:19; Rom 8:38-39; Eph 6:12; Col 1:16; 1 Pet 3:22).

In the NT, God's power for judgment is through Christ. Christ and his followers are portrayed as eschatological judges of creation (Matt 25:31-46; Luke 22:28-30; Rom 2:16; Rev 20:4-15; 21:5-8). Since Christ's followers are destined to judge with him, they are not to place their trust in human courts (1 Cor 6:1-7).

God's power to judge among the nations implies that God is the source of redemptive power (Isa 1:24-28). The "mighty hand" (**yadh khazaqah** יָד חֲזָקָה) is a common description for God's power in redemption (Exod 3:19; Deut 6:21). God's power to redeem is combined in biblical descriptions of a renewed or NEW CREATION, whether understood as focused on Israel, the nations, and the earth as a whole (Isa 65:17-25; Amos 9:13-15; Rom 8:19-23; Rev 21–22). The power of Christ's redemption is also seen in the apocalyptic picture of Christ triumphing over evil forces in his death and resurrection (Col 2:13-15). *See* REDEEM, REDEEMER; SALVATION; STRENGTH.

MARK REASONER

PRAETORIAN GUARD pri-tor´ee-uhn. The title originally described the select group of legionnaires who guarded the praetor (commander) of a Roman army. Tradition held that P. Scipio Africanus inaugurated the first such guard. The praetor's location was the PRAETORIUM, a structure in the center of the camp; the term came to be applied to a governor's residence (Matt 27:27; Mark 15:16; John 18:28, 33; 19:9).

AUGUSTUS formed the praetorian guard in Rome to prevent his assassination—a lesson learned from Julius Caesar's death. It numbered nine (Suetonius, *Aug.* 49.1) or ten cohorts (Dio Cassius, *Rom.* 55.24.6), each consisting of 1,000 men. Augustus stationed only three cohorts in Rome. In 23 CE, however, Sejanus persuaded Tiberius to base all nine cohorts in Rome and erected a fortified camp for them on the eastern edge of the city (Dio Cassius, *Rom.* 57.19.6). The purpose of the guard now was to protect the imperial family, put down riots, and foil plots. CLAUDIUS was acclaimed emperor by the praetorian guard, a role they played more than once after that. Philippians 1:13 refers to the praetorium (NRSV, "imperial guard"), presumably meaning this camp, where some guardsmen have become devotees of Jesus.

EDGAR KRENTZ

PRAETORIUM pri-tor´ee-uhm [πραιτώριον **praitōrion**]. Headquarters of the *praefectus praetorii*, a Roman official serving as the GOVERNOR and judge of a region. In the NRSV, the word *praetorium* is replaced with "governor's headquarters" (Matt 27:27), "Pilate's headquarters" (John 18:28), "headquarters" (John 18:33), and "governor's headquarters" (Mark 15:16). In NT times the prefects and later the procurators of Judea resided in the praetorium of CAESAREA MARITIMA, built by Herod the Great (37–4 BCE; *see* PREFECT; PROCURATOR). Paul was imprisoned there from roughly 57–59 CE (Acts 23:35).

In 30 CE Jesus was tried and sentenced to death by Pilate (*see* PILATE, PONTIUS) in a praetorium in JERUSALEM (Matt 27:27; John 18:28, 33). This praetorium is also called a PALACE (**aulē** αὐλή), suggesting its identification with a former royal residence (Mark 15:16). Late in the 12th cent. CE, the Crusaders thought they had located the fortress Antonia (*see* ANTONIA, FORTRESS) on a rocky promontory in the northwest corner of the Temple Mount as the praetorium. This became the starting point of the *Via Dolorosa* (the traditional route that Jesus took from his sentencing to the cross). But the large pavement inside the monastery of the Sisters of Sion believed to be the "Stone PAVEMENT" of John 19:13 was built later (in the 2nd cent.) and situated outside the Antonia. Also, this fortress was never used as a royal palace.

Most scholars favor the Herodian Upper Palace as the praetorium of the Gospels. This luxurious palace, located in the Armenian Garden in the west of Jerusalem's Old City, was built around 23 BCE (Josephus, *J.W.* 5.166–83). At least one procurator, Gessius Florus, resided here in 66 CE (*J.W.* 2.301–8). But although impressive remains of the three fortified towers at the north end of the palace could always be seen in the area of today's Citadel, there was never a Christian tradition favoring this location.

The pre-Constantinian tradition identified the praetorium with ruins opposite the southwest corner of the Temple platform in the western part of the Upper City near the slope of the TYROPOEON VALLEY (Pilgrim of Bordeaux, *Itinerary* 16–17). The 5th-cent. Church of St. Sophia was built on this site. After the church's destruction in the 7th cent., however, the tradition was lost. The 11th cent. witnessed the erection of the Church of St. Mary of the Germans, partially preserved in the Jewish Quarter. Nearby, Naaman Avigad excavated the remains of a luxurious residence that he called a "Herodian Palatial Mansion." According to Josephus, the old Hasmonean royal palace where Herod the Great resided in former times (*Ant.* 15.292) was located in the same vicinity (*J.W.* 2.344). After the reign of AGRIPPA I (41–44 CE), the Hasmonean Palace remained in the possession of the Herodian family (*Ant.* 20.189–90). This would explain why Pilate resided there whereas the later procurators had their headquarters in the confiscated Upper Palace.

The praetorium mentioned in Phil 1:13 was located either at EPHESUS, Caesarea Maritima, or Rome, depending on one's reconstruction of the circumstances of Paul's imprisonment and resulting view of the provenance of the letter to the Philippians (*see* PHILIPPIANS, LETTER TO THE). *See* PALESTINE, ADMINISTRATION OF.

Bibliography: Naaman Avigad. *Discovering Jerusalem* (1983) 95–120; Raymond E. Brown. *The Death of the Messiah* (1994) 705–10; Max Küchler. *Jerusalem* (2007).

RAINER RIESNER

PRAISE [הָלַל halal, זִמֵּר zimmer, יָדָה yadhah, שָׁבַח shavakh, תְּהִלָּה tehillah; αἰνέω aineō, ἁλληλουϊά hallēlouia, ὑμνέω hymneō]. Praise is a human activity, oriented toward other(s) in a gesture of gratitude and exaltation for the person, accomplishments, and presence of the other. It may take the form of compliments or exuberant expressions that acknowledge the qualities of another. Frequent words, gestures, and expressions of praise are expressed without particular motivation or causal link with petition (as thanksgiving); the unsolicited and unmerited character of praise brings surprise, joy, and satisfaction and builds bonds between those praised and the ones who offer praise.

The most common Hebrew words for praise are halal (verb) and tehillah (noun). The most insistent call to praise appears in Ps 150, where a form of these words appears thirteen times in six verses. The commands to praise in this psalm specify its locations ("in his sanctuary ... in his mighty firmament," Ps 150:1), its motivations ("for his mighty deeds... his surpassing greatness!" Ps 150:2), and its forms (eight musical instruments mentioned, song, and dance). The psalm ends with a final call to praise God, "Hallelujah," from the Hebrew halelu-yah הַלְלוּ־יָהּ ("praise the LORD"; from hallu [הַלְלוּ] "shout, sing praise," plus yah, an abbreviation for Yahweh). Since this psalm forms the final crescendo of the Hebrew book of Psalms, the Hebrew title for the book, *Sepher Tehillim*, "The Book of Praises," seems most appropriate (*see* PSALMS, BOOK OF). The NT uses this psalter language by transliterating the Hebrew halelu-yah into Greek (hallēlouia), also rendered "Hallelujah" in English (Rev 19:1, 3, 4, 6). *See* HALLELUJAH.

In both the OT and NT, praise is most often oriented toward God. Of 437 occurrences of the English word *praise* (and its verbal forms *praises, praised, praising*) in the NRSV translation (representing different Hebrew and Greek words), the vast majority has God as direct object. Praise is motivated by gratitude for God's actions in the world (especially the more expansive ones), wonder and awe at God's qualities of creativeness, justice, and everlasting love, and joy over God's saving actions (e.g., Gen 29:35; Deut 32:43; 1 Chr 16:4; 2 Chr 5:13; Pss 113:1; 117:1; 135:1; 146:1-2; 147:1, 12; 148:1-14; 150:1-6; Isa 25:1; Dan 2:23; Joel 2:26; Luke 2:38; Rom 15:9; Eph 1:12-14; Phil 1:11; Rev 19:5). In this regard, praise differs radically from prayers (*see* LAMENT), which begin from an articulation of human need and crying out to God. Praise allows humans the opportunity to move beyond themselves, their needs, fears, and hopes, and to return something to their creator and redeemer. Praise offers ways for people to advance beyond themselves and to stretch their energies and activities toward the God who stands beyond them. Expressions of praise touch expansive chords in human experience.

Although words of praise are found throughout the OT, the Apocrypha, and the NT, most instances of a call to praise God occur in the book of Psalms, especially in the genre hymns of praise. This type of psalm generally consists of a call to praise/worship God, followed by a phrase or clause[s] that gives reasons to praise God; the psalm frequently concludes with a final call to praise/worship God. Psalm 117 provides an excellent example of a hymn of praise: "Praise the LORD, all you nations! Extol him, all you peoples! For great is his steadfast love toward us, and the faithfulness of the LORD endures forever. Praise the LORD!" (halelu-yah). The psalmist initiates the action with two commands (addressed to "all you nations, all you peoples") to praise and extol God. Usually considered a call to worship, this initial command is a second-person plural verb form ("all of you, praise God!"). In most cases the language of the psalm of praise (plural imperative) indicates a group of some kind (*see* WORSHIP, OT).

Reasons for praise of God in Ps 117 are clear: God's "steadfast love" and "the faithfulness of the LORD," which endures forever, ground the call to praise. These qualities encompass a web of relationships comprising the covenant relationship of God with Israel: "steadfast love" (*see* KHESED) indicates the bond by which God binds Godself to this people. The quality of "faithfulness" indicates the ongoing and utterly trustworthy character of that relationship that covenant partners can expect from God (*see* FAITH, FAITHFULNESS).

Motives for praise of God include and cover almost every aspect of human existence and also plant and animal life. Many hymns praise God's history of saving this people, so they mention God's saving activity in the past (e.g., Exod 15:21; Pss 111, 114, 135, 136). Other psalms sing with exuberance over the expanse of God's creative and sustaining activity in the world (e.g., Pss 8, 19, 29, 33, 103, 104). Some hymns praise God's goodness to people, especially for demonstrating loving-kindness and fidelity to covenant members who have suffered poverty and oppression (Pss 113, 145, 146). Motives to praise God come both from the past (God's actions in history) and from the present (God's continual loving activity). Although hymns of praise do not contain petitions, sometimes recalling God's past goodness and actions may serve as a subtle request for similar response in the future (*see* HYMNS, NT; HYMNS, OT).

Paying careful attention to the openings verses of hymns will show the who and the how of the worship of God that is envisioned in these hymns. For example, we learn much about the identity of worshipers from checking who is addressed in the imperative commands to praise God: you just, you heavenly beings, you peoples, all on earth, the earth, all you lands, people, or nations, or heavenly beings, or angels, or all creatures of the heavens or the earth, servants of the LORD, Jerusalem, sun and moon, shining stars, heavens, sea monsters and deep waters, lightning, hail, snow, clouds, animals, creatures that crawl and fly, kings of the earth, young men, women, old and young, Israel, people of Zion, everything that has breath. Human beings participate in praise of God that exceeds the capacities of men and women, suggesting a more cosmic view of reality in which human and nonhuman life participate together.

God's faithful people clearly are the prime actors in the praise of God, but all peoples are expected to join it. The list of those who offer praise shows how expansive is the notion of the praise of God, including even animals, heavenly bodies, and finally everything that breathes. Everything created by God is invited to join in jubilant praise of God. The range is far more cosmic than personal. Joining one's own praise with all others who praise already has an expansive quality to it. *See* MUSIC; WORSHIP, EARLY JEWISH; WORSHIP, NT CHRISTIAN.

Bibliography: Walter Brueggemann. *Israel's Praise: Doxology against Idolatry and Ideology* (1988); Patrick D. Miller. *They Cried to the Lord: The Form and Theology of Biblical Prayer* (1994); Claus Westermann. *Praise and Lament in the Psalms* (1981).

JOHN C. ENDRES, S.J.

PRAYER [תְּפִלָּה tefillah; προσευχή proseuchē]. The two terms normally translated by the word *prayer* in the OT and NT are neither identical nor even roughly exact equivalents. **Tefillah** is the general word for a prayer in Hebrew, especially for a prayer of supplication, but also apparently especially for a category of prayer known as the psalm of lament, occurring some twenty-one times in the book of Psalms. The Gk. term **proseuchē** is a technical term, a request for help made by speaking to a deity, usually in the form of a petition, vow, or wish prayer, but it is also used to designate the place of prayer, and in this sense **proseuchē** is often used in Jewish texts synonymously with the SYNAGOGUE.

Yet understanding the nature and role of prayer in its literary depiction in the Bible as well as in the cultural world of early Jewish and Christian antiquity requires exploration far beyond the narrow semantic constraints of a single word. Many words are used in connection with prayer and related behavior; in Hebrew: **palal** (פָּלַל, "pray"); **darash yhwh** (דָּרַשׁ יהוה, "seek the LORD"); **khanan** (חָנַן, "request"); **qara᾽ bashem** (קָרָא בַּשֵּׁם, "to call on the name"); **ʿathar** (עָתַר, "to entreat"); **yadhah** (יָדָה, "thank" or "confess"); **halal** (הָלַל, "to praise"); **barakh** (בָּרַךְ, "to bless"); and in Gk.: **proseuchomai** (προσεύχομαι, "to pray, petition"); **deēsis** (δέησις, "to petition, need"); **homologeō** (ὁμολογέω, "to confess, profess"); **ekzēteō** (ἐκζητέω, "to seek, inquire"); **aineō** (αἰνέω, "to praise"); **eucharisteō** (εὐχαριστέω, "to thank"); **eulogeō** (εὐλογέω, "to bless"); **dochazō** (δοχάζω, "to glorify"). Prayer can be understood broadly to comprehend human communication to God, which may include words and related ritual actions (*see* WORSHIP, EARLY JEWISH; WORSHIP, NT CHRISTIAN; WORSHIP, OT). This essay includes an overview of verbal prayer, that is, some of the many prayers, psalms, and hymns within scriptural and extra-biblical Jewish literature (*see* HYMNS, NT; HYMNS, OT; PSALMS, BOOK OF).

A. Prayer in the Old Testament

1. Prose prayers in narratives

The narrative descriptions of the OT may be very similar to actual prayer practices, but the narrative is also a construction and idealization of Israelite life and history. Thus our understanding of prayer in ancient Israel is necessarily limited by that prism. Three aspects of OT prayer warrant attention: 1) the prayers themselves—the contents and orientation of the many prayers that are found in the Bible; 2) the literary characterization of those offering prayers within the narrative context, whether prophets or priests, kings or everyday men and women; and 3) the development of formal public and corporate prayer in connection with the Temple and ultimately as liturgical practice in the absence of the Temple.

The presupposition underlying the depiction of praying in the Bible is that the God of Israel has personal characteristics and is intimately concerned with Israel, both as a people and as individuals in ongoing relationship. Israel's God is thus never considered wholly transcendent, but also immanent. This understanding of God is both universal and particular, based variously on the divine work of creation of the heavens and earth and all their inhabitants, angelic and human, and more particularly, on God as righteous covenant-maker with a particular people who has an ultimate plan for history and the world. Prayers in the OT presuppose a God who will hear and potentially respond through words, actions, or both. The narratives of the OT thus make manifest not only the role of prayer in the life of Israelites but also provide a glimpse of the divine character as well, although the divine character is never fully revealed and remains ultimately mysterious because it is seen through different prisms in the various books and narratives.

One way of conceiving of biblical prayer is to consider how human words to God negotiate different parts of that relationship—both between humans and God and among humans themselves—and what the prayers seek to do. Thus, there are prayers of petition for help, prayers of intercession that request help on behalf of others, prayers of confession that admit to wrongdoing, prayers of lament that mourn ill circumstances that have befallen, prayers of thanksgiving that acknowledge what God has done on behalf of the one praying, and prayers of praise that offer glory to God simply for God's own being (*see* CONFESSION; PRAISE; REPENTANCE IN THE NT; REPENTANCE IN THE OT; THANKSGIVING). This range of prayers is offered by individuals and by groups or the nation as a whole. There are many prayers contained in the narrative portions of the OT from Genesis to Kings, and Chronicles and Ezra–Nehemiah. We may distinguish between prayers that seem not to have been a part of the original text, but were inserted in a narrative, and more discursive prose prayers that seem always to have been part of the composition. Both kinds of prayers should be understood to play a role in the construction of character from a literary perspective, which may in turn suggest how prayer was considered to reflect and shape character in Israelite society and culture. The poetic prayers found in the prophetic books and the "prayer book" par excellence, the book of Psalms, also share similar patterns. In addition to second-person prayers that reflect direct engagement between God and human parties, there are also prayers uttered in the third-person voice, such as blessings or curses that call on divine power to affect people either in a positive or negative way (Gen 9:26-27; 14:19-20; 16:5; 27:27-29; Num 6:24-26; Deut 28:3-6; Ruth 2:20; *see* BLESSINGS AND CURSINGS).

Prayers serve both to characterize God and also to portray the role of those who pray. In the Pentateuch, Israelites and non-Israelites of no particular status sometimes offer prayers. From the fourth generation of human beings, that is, from the time of Enosh, human beings are said to "invoke the name of the LORD" (Gen 4:26). Although the phrase in the old J source of the Pentateuch anachronistically understands people to invoke the personal name of Israel's God, Yahweh, in prayer, the larger point is the recognition of prayer as a universal activity of all people. Abraham's nameless servant offers a petitional prayer to the "God of [his] master Abraham" (Gen 24:12-15) to provide a wife for Isaac. If we can understand the Egyptian slave Hagar's wish—"Do not let me look on the death of the child" (Gen 21:16)—as a prayer, this is even more poignant because she does not address God, although God hears and responds to the situation of this vulnerable woman's cry (Gen 21:17-19) with a promise for her descendants and physical provision for her thirst in the desert.

Some prayers are enjoined specifically for Israelites. All Israelite males are asked to present their offerings of first fruits in conjunction with a recitation addressed to God that acknowledges divine beneficence for the people in bringing them to the land (Deut 26:5-10). Deuteronomy also contains two passages that would become a standard part of the daily Jewish prayer requirement. The first is the Shema (*see* SHEMA, THE). Deuteronomy 6:4-9 begins "Hear, O Israel: The LORD (Yahweh) is our God, the LORD alone." Although not addressed to God directly, this passage affirms a commitment to the covenant and strict loyalty to God. The second is Deut 11:13-21. These two passages along with Num 15:37-41 would become a central feature of Jewish prayer life already by the time of the 2nd cent. BCE. The presence at Qumran of PHYLACTERIES (**tefillin** תְּפִילִין), prayer straps with tiny leather boxes attached in which were tiny pieces of leather scroll containing the Shema, indicates the importance of these passages from an early date. Another text that depicts the prayers of "all Israelites" is Lev 26:40-45. Written in the context of the Babylonian exile and from the perspective that grave sin had caused the destruction of Jerusalem and the expulsion of many of its inhabitants from the land, Lev 26:40 envisions that restoration might only occur through a confession of sin. The passage is written as an exhortation in the divine voice in first-person speech. If they confess their sin and the sin of their ancestors and humble their hearts, God will remember the divine covenant with Abraham, Isaac, and Jacob, and remember the land as well. In contrast to Lev 5:5-6 and Num 15:27, in which a sacrifice must accompany confession of sin, Lev 26 views the suffering borne of the exile as a sufficient expiation for human sin.

In addition to these depictions of universal prayer practices, more typically the narratives mention prayer or contain prayers in order to depict their role in Israel's history or their cultural position and status. Abraham, the ancestor of the Israelite nation, is depicted as a pious man, who builds an altar where he can "call on the name of the LORD" (Gen 12:8; 13:4). In the E strand of the Pentateuch, he is referred to as a prophet whose intercessory prayer can heal people (Gen 20:7, 17). Though more conversational and dialogic in nature than most prayers, Abraham's petitions to God to spare the city of Sodom if there are righteous people in it (Gen 18:23-33) might also be considered intercessory prayer, whose effectiveness is premised on his special status as the elect of God who must teach his descendants how to be righteous and just (Gen 18:18-19). Isaac, too, is considered to have special intercessory powers (Gen 25:21) to pray on behalf of his wife's barrenness, a petition to which God responds positively. Jacob, the wily trickster, also offers a prayer (Gen 32:9-12) that petitions God to spare him from his angry brother Esau, doing so on the basis of the very promised divine blessing that he had stolen from his brother!

Although some prophets are also called priests (Jeremiah, Ezekiel), the duties of priests are not connected directly with prayer in literature that describes the preexilic period, with the significant exception of Aaron on the annual DAY OF ATONEMENT. Aaron is expected to confess the accumulated sins of the people in a ritual transfer to the head of a goat (Lev 16:20-22). Priests of the house of Aaron and his descendants are also charged with offering a threefold priestly blessing over the people in connection with the powerful name of Israel's God: Yahweh (Num 6:24-26).

Prophets seem to have had a special responsibility for prayer as mediators between the divine and human realms, communicating between the heavenly and earthly spheres. Moses is depicted as the prophet par excellence from the day of his call to lead the people out of slavery in Egypt (Exod 3–4) and continuing with his mediatory role in delivering divine instruction to the people at Mount Sinai. Indeed, Moses' argument to Pharaoh to release Israel is premised on the notion that they will pray to God: "Let my people go, so that they may worship me in the wilderness" (Exod 7:16; compare Exod 4:23; 5:1; 8:1, 20; 9:1, 13; 10:3, 7, 11, 24). Such "worship" (ʿ**avodhah** עֲבֹדָה) is the same word for slavery or service in Hebrew and suggests that the rightful object for such exclusive worship is Yahweh, rather than an Egyptian pharaoh. Israel's proper worship is reflected in the paradigmatic hymn of praise after Israel's redemption from Egypt, the SONG OF THE SEA (Exod 15:1-18), and the song and dancing with timbrels by Miriam and the women (Exod 15:20-21). Miriam herself is referred to as a prophet in this instance (Exod 15:20), likely because of the close association of prophecy and song composition as divinely inspired activities in antiquity.

Moses, as a prophetic figure, remains in intimate communication with God. Moses is portrayed as an effective intercessor, first and foremost in the case of the golden calf when the establishment of the covenant, not to mention the fate of the people themselves, is in jeopardy. Moses' intercessory prayer for God to cease from his anger and to spare the people (Exod 32:11-13) appeals to God on the basis of maintaining international reputation and on the divine promise to the ancestors. The result of the prayer is a divine change of mind to desist from destroying the people, suggesting the reciprocity of the divine-human (prophetic) relationship. Moses' further petition to God to make manifest the divine glory (Exod 33:18) results in a unique theophany in which the divine name is proclaimed in connection with thirteen adjectival attributes relating to divine compassion and justice: Yahweh is "a God merciful and gracious, slow to anger, and abounding in steadfast love (**khesedh** חֶסֶד) and faithfulness, keeping steadfast love for the thousandth generation, forgiving iniquity and transgression and sin, yet by no means clearing the guilty, but visiting the iniquity of the parents upon the children and the children's children, to the third and the fourth generation" (Exod 34:6-7). The affirmation of these attributes became an integral part of the prayer tradition in postexilic prayers in the OT as well as in early Jewish and Christian prayers, especially confessions that draw upon the merciful attributes in anticipation of a continuation of that relationship (compare Neh 9:17; Ps 103:8; Joel 2:13; Jonah 4:2; Sir 2:11; *T. Zeb.* 9:7; 1QH[a] XII, 36–37; *T. Sim.* 4:4; *2 Bar.* 77:7; *Apoc. Ab.* 17:12; *Gk. Apoc. Ezra* 1:10-18). In the pentateuchal narrative, Moses calls upon these merciful attributes in order to forestall punishment of the Israelites' continuing apostasy (Num 14:13-19; compare also Deut 9:25-29). Moses' intercessory concern extends to his sister, Miriam, after she is smitten with leprosy, and he utters the shortest prayer of the Bible, in Hebrew only five words: "O God, please heal her" (Num 12:13). Moses also offers petitions that God might appoint a leader to succeed him (Num 27:16-17) and that he might cross the Jordan and enter the promised land (Deut 3:23-25).

Prophetic prayer also occurs in the Deuteronomistic History (Joshua–Kings), particularly in connection with the northern prophets Elijah and Elisha, who are patterned after the depiction of Moses in a number of ways including his prayerfulness. Elijah is shown to be an effective intercessor in reviving the life of a boy (1 Kgs 17:21-23; compare also Samuel, 1 Sam 7:5; 12:18-19, 23). He also petitions God for help in the contest with Baal (1 Kgs 18:36-37), and his prayers are answered quickly by God.

Among the prophetic books in the OT, Jeremiah stands out for its extensive use of the lament form of prayer. The five "confessions" of Jeremiah (Jer 11:18–12:6; 15:10-21; 17:14-18; 18:18-23; 20:7-18) depict a prophet who has intimate connection with God, who "consecrated" him from the womb for his prophetic task, and in that relationship gives voice to honest and deep anguish at his victimization: "But I was like a gentle lamb led to the slaughter.... But you, O LORD of hosts, who judge righteously, who try the heart and the mind, let me see your retribution upon them, for to you I have committed my cause" (Jer 11:19*a*, 20). "But you, O LORD, know me; You see me and test me—my heart is with you" (Jer 12:3*a*). The language of these prayers is similar to that found in the laments of the book of Psalms and at points becomes bluntly accusatory toward God: "O LORD, you have enticed me, and I was enticed; you have overpowered me, and you have prevailed. I have become a laughingstock all day long;

everyone mocks me. For whenever I speak, I must cry out, I must shout, 'Violence and destruction!' For the word of the LORD has become for me a reproach and derision all day long" (Jer 20:7-8). As prophet, Jeremiah also has the task of interceding on behalf of the people, and Israel's recalcitrance is the source of his frustration. The power of the prophet to intercede on behalf of the people is ultimately limited by God's sense of the people's unwillingness to repent of their sinfulness, which ruptures the covenant relationship and prevents God from accepting the prophetic plea anymore (Jer 7:16; 14:11-12; 15:1, 5-9) until divine judgment has run its course.

Amos offers another illustration of prophetic intercession. Twice, Amos pleads to God to forgive "Jacob" and twice God relents, but ultimately divine judgment is ordained (Amos 7:1-9). Samuel is also depicted as an intercessor (1 Sam 7:5; 12:18-19, 23). The postexilic book of Jonah provides an ironic twist on Mosaic intercession in which the divine attributes, which elsewhere provide a means of "reminding" God of the merciful aspect of the divine character, in Jonah's perverse mouth become an accusation toward God imbedded in his petition that he might die (Jonah 4:2-3) owing to the success of his prophetic mission. This too contrasts ironically with Moses' and other prophets' request to die out of a sense of failure (Num 11:10-15; 1 Kgs 19:2-4; Job 3; Jer 20:14-18).

Like prophetic prayer, the depiction of kings at prayer was also a significant part of positive character portrayal. Kings David, Solomon, and Hezekiah all offer significant prayers. David is the most prayerful figure in the DtrH, offering eight prayers. Solomon offers four. He petitions God for an "understanding mind" (1 Kgs 3:6-9) in order to judge and govern his people effectively, and God responds by giving him a "wise and discerning mind," which fits him for the task. The most important prayers of Solomon are the three spoken in connection with the dedication of the Temple. The longest of the three, 1 Kgs 8:23-53, contains seven petitions to God outlining seven cases in which divine forgiveness might be obtained, including situations of military defeat, sin against a neighbor, famine, drought, and plague. It also contains provision for the "foreigner's" prayer to be heard as well (1 Kgs 8:41-43). Solomon bases his petition on divine steadfast love (*see* KHESED) in connection with the divine election of the Davidic house. The prayer was revised during the exile in light of the experience of being without an operative Temple, signaling its symbolic unifying importance in the cultural memory of the exiles in Diaspora. The prayer depicts God hearing "in heaven your dwelling place" but it means clearly to emphasize the Temple in Jerusalem as the focal point for prayer. The prayer's importance for later Jewish practice is apparent in that subsequent prayers cite its wording (e.g., 2 Chr 20:5-12; 1 Macc 7:37-38; 3 Macc 2:2-20).

Hezekiah likewise offers momentous prayers, principally at the time of the Assyrian siege of Jerusalem. Accompanied by signs of lament and mourning, torn clothes and sackcloth, Hezekiah prays for deliverance from Sennacherib (2 Kgs 19:15-19//Isa 37:17-20). The immediate efficacy of the prayer is pronounced by Isaiah, and the ultimate preservation of Jerusalem from destruction enhanced its special divinely elect and inviolable status. The duplication of this account in the middle of the book of Isaiah thus places the efficacy of prayer as a central feature of the theology of that book, in which the fate of the divine covenant with David and Jerusalem (2 Sam 7) is contested but ultimately maintained in refigured form.

Women are rarely depicted as offering prayers in the OT. Children are essentially voiceless, inactive agents in regard to prayer though they are sometimes recipients of divine blessings. This is owing to the generally androcentric perspective of the narratives in which adult male characters and actions predominate and in a society in which most public leadership is held by men. Notable exceptions are Hannah's prayers in 1 Sam 1–2. Hannah petitions God in 1 Sam 1:11 for a son in exchange for her offering of him as a lifelong Nazirite. Hannah's subsequent pregnancy is attributed to God's "hearing" her and this serves also as the etiology for the name of the prophet, Samuel ("God hears"). In response to the divine provision for her pregnancy, Hannah offers a corporate prayer of praise and thanksgiving that extols God for bringing about surprising reversals in states of affairs. The poetic prayer of praise likely had a prior life outside the narrative. Even here, the prayers are not independent of the values of a patriarchal culture in which a woman's societal worth was chiefly determined by her ability to bear male offspring.

A second exception to the predominance of male prayers is the figurative depiction of the defeated city of Jerusalem as a widow and mother bereft of her children in the book of Lamentations. In Jewish practice, the book of Lamentations continues to be read on the Ninth of Av, a liturgy commemorating the destruction of the Temple, and in Christian tradition during Lent and Holy Week. The poetic language of the book of Lamentations describes Jerusalem in the third person and offers "the widow Zion's" first-person lament language in a distinctive poetic form (**qinah** קִינָה). The lament arises from the suffering and despair borne of the destruction of the Temple and Jerusalem and the experience of Babylonian exile, a situation of abandonment and desolation in which God refuses to hear and acknowledge the cry for help (Lam 3:8-9, 43-45; 3:49-50; 5:20). The book nonetheless holds out the hope that divine compassion will once again compel God to listen and respond (Lam 3:21-26, 32-33).

2. Postexilic trends

The book of Chronicles parallels the DtrH in many respects, but contains its own perspective on prayer and worship that is revealed in how it adapts its source material and the unique material it contains. Nowhere is the portrayal of a figure more changed than the adaptation of King David. His military exploits are downplayed and his sexual peccadillo with Bathsheba and murder of Uriah are not mentioned; rather, he is whitewashed and depicted as a founder of the Temple and its priestly Levitical order, a man of prayer who is chiefly concerned with the centrality of a well-run liturgical center. He appoints "Levites as ministers before the ark of the LORD, to invoke, to thank, and to praise the LORD, the God of Israel" (1 Chr 16:4; compare 1 Chr 6:31-32; 23:4-5, 30-31; 2 Chr 8:14). First Chronicles 29:10-19, a composition unique to the Chronicler, is David's final prayer before the end of his reign after he has made full provision and planning for the Temple. Containing elements of blessing, praise, and petition, David's prayer recognizes God as the source of all goodness and asks for divine guidance for Solomon and his subjects. The book of Chronicles has a different perspective on divine justice, judgment, and human repentance than the DtrH, which is reflected in the role of prayer in the book. The book vindicates King Manasseh, who is blamed for the fall of Jerusalem in the DtrH, by depicting Manasseh as a penitent sinner with humble heart who prays for forgiveness and is restored by God to Jerusalem (2 Chr 33:12-13). Manasseh can be understood as emblematic of the people as a whole in their experience of exile and their need for humility and repentant return to divine teaching. Manasseh's example apparently continued to inspire piety because at some point during the following centuries, the confessional Prayer of Manasseh was composed to "fill the gap" of the prayer mentioned in 2 Chr 33 (*see* MANASSEH, PRAYER OF). As a whole, the book of Chronicles reflects a stage in the postexilic period in which the Levites had assumed a unique liturgical role in Jerusalem as both prayer leaders and prophetic figures. Prayer was conceived as a two-way communicative conduit between God and people. This is especially apparent in the Chronicler's positive treatment of Jehoshaphat's reign, which depicts the king offering a prayer at the Temple on behalf of the nation (2 Chr 20:6-12), recognizing God's total sovereignty and their complete dependence on God. The Levite Jahaziel reveals the divine word to the king (2 Chr 20:15-17) and then leads prayers and songs as a prelude to God's victory over Israel's enemies (2 Chr 20:19-21).

Laments are voiced in the early literature and the psalms and continue to appear in the late literature, but confession of sin gains a more prominent profile in the postexilic period. Confession nonetheless has preexilic origins. The prophet in the 8th-cent. book of Hosea calls the northern kingdom of Israel to repentance and provides a brief prayer of petition: "Take away all guilt; accept that which is good, and we will offer the fruit (**parim** [פָּרִים], "bulls," i.e., "sacrifice") of our lips" (Hos 14:2 [Heb. 14:3]). The postexilic literature, by contrast, develops long, formalized, confessional prayers (Ezra 9:6-15; Neh 1:5-11; 9:6-37; Dan 9:4-19; compare Bar 1:15–3:8; LXX Dan 3; 4Q504; *Pss. Sol.* 9; 1QS I, 24–II, 1; CD XX, 28–30; LXX Prayer of Esther; 3 Macc 2:1-20). There are a number of variations in the confessional prayers, but they all share a theological perspective that emphasizes divine sovereignty and righteousness contrasting with human fallibility and weakness. They typically recall the history of divine mercy and redemption to the people Israel and on that basis petition for forgiveness and help. Confessional elements of these prayers include an admission of culpability, a declaration of solidarity with former generations, and the use of the hithpael of **yadhah** ("to confess"; compare Lev 26:40), thus reflecting the influence of both Deuteronomic and priestly theological traditions.

A pronounced feature of all postexilic prayers is their increasingly intricate uses of Scripture. Later prayers pattern themselves after earlier prayer forms, but also allude to, cite, and interpret texts and stories from earlier Scripture, even at a time when "Scripture" is still being written, and before all the texts that would eventually become the canonical Bible in subsequent centuries had been crystallized. Offering what was understood as **torah** (תּוֹרָה), divine teaching, back to God in prayer, in effect "praying Scripture," was a means of reaffirming the covenantal relationship with God by manifesting externally on the mouth that the Law, the TORAH, was written on the heart (Deut 30:14; Jer 31:33). The use of scripturalized language that appears in infinite and subtle variety in prayers required learning on the part of the pious. The fact that a famous figure gives voice to a prayer that is at once in line with the tradition but offers some subtle and unique twists may well signal a model for the transmission of the theological tradition through internalization of its language and forms. Individuals could make it their own by interiorizing its language and at the same time renewing it. The early Christian movement would understand this ability uniquely in connection with the gift of divine spirit (Acts 2). Judaism would continue with the composition of liturgical prayers that are interpretative reflections on Scripture.

3. The psalms as prayer and instruction in prayer

The book of Psalms is the largest collection of prayers in Scripture and it reflects a diverse range of theological perspectives. Some psalms extol God's work in the exodus, wilderness wandering, and deliverance into the land (Pss 78; 105; 106; 136); some psalms praise the city of Jerusalem and its Davidic king (Pss 72; 84; 87; 89; 132); some psalms give praise to God as creator or king (Pss 8; 19; 104; 145); and some psalms focus only on the concerns of an individual, whether in thanksgiving (Pss 30; 34) or in complaint (Pss 22; 69; 77). Metaphors used for God in the psalms include "rock," "king," "shepherd," "portion," "judge," and "light." The MT of the OT (*see* MT, MASORETIC

TEXT) contains 150 compositions (the LXX has 151) divided into five "books" thought to echo in some way the five books of the Pentateuch. The oldest Hebrew manuscripts do not have a title for the collection. The title "psalms" comes from the Gk. **psalmoi** (ψαλμοί), a translation of the Hebrew **mizmor** (מִזְמוֹר), meaning a song to be accompanied by a stringed instrument. In rabbinic and later literature, the book is called "Sefer Tehillim" or "Scroll of Praises" from the Hebrew verb **halal**, meaning "to praise." Indeed the associated word "hallelujah" (or "praise the LORD") occurs only in the book of Psalms. Yet another indication of its contents occurs at the end of book two of Psalms after Ps 72, which includes the sentence "The prayers (**tefilloth** תְּפִלּוֹת) of David son of Jesse are ended." *See* PSALMS, BOOK OF.

The psalms are almost entirely poetic prayers governed by the two-clause Hebrew verse structure with a wide range of poetic imagery. The two main types of prayers in the psalms are laments, which comprise roughly one-third of the psalms, and hymns of PRAISE. Laments are typically structured with an address to God, a LAMENT, a petition for help, and an expression of trust for God's help in the past or hope for divine response in the present. Laments articulate an important means of dealing with pain and suffering. Laments may also include elements of praise and thanksgiving as the prayer anticipates deliverance or response from God. Hymns are not typically connected with a singular occasion, but express the gratitude of individuals or the community to God (*see* HYMNS, OT).

Not all the psalms fall into neat categories of praise or lament, petition or thanksgiving. Some might better be classified as "homiletic reflections," such as the three verses of Ps 133, with its extended metaphor likening family-kin unity to the precious oil dripping on Aaron's beard and robe and to the sweet dew of northern Mount Hermon falling in southern Zion. Other psalms (such as Pss 1; 19; 36; 37) share wisdom vocabulary associated with the books of Job, Proverbs, and Ecclesiastes.

There is no explicit discussion about how the psalms were used and with rare exception (Ps 137 refers to the Babylonian exile, Ps 51 to the late exilic or postexilic period) they cannot be dated with certainty. Yet internal evidence from the content of some of the psalms as well as the appearance of poetic prayers outside the book of Psalms gives some evidence for their use in private devotion or public worship in the temples of the northern kingdom of Israel or in the southern capital of Jerusalem, whether before the exile during the period of the monarchy or after the exile during the Second Temple period. Psalms 120–134, e.g., contain the superscription "A Song of Ascent," which is thought to suggest the "ascent" to Jerusalem in the Judean hill country (*see* SONGS OF ASCENT). Israelites were supposed to make pilgrimage to Jerusalem three times a year for the Feasts of Weeks, Booths, and Passover (Deut 16:16), and these psalms were likely offered in song on the journey. Others seem to have accompanied sacrifice (Ps 118), while still others seem to have served as a substitute for sacrifice and perhaps were timed to correspond to the daily sacrifices: "Let my prayer be counted as incense before you, and the lifting up of my hands as an evening sacrifice" (Ps 141:2). The psalm-like composition in Jonah 2:2-9 was offered in a situation of grave peril.

In addition to understanding the psalms as discrete prayers of individuals and the people as a whole, whether in private or public at various points during the history of Israel and early Judaism in the postexilic period, we can also think of the psalms as a collection to be read and studied, that is, as part of Scripture. In this way, the words of humans to God become the reciprocal "word of God" again as teaching to humans. The first psalm is a wisdom psalm that contrasts the way of the righteous and the way of the wicked. The righteous, "their delight is in the law (**torah**, "teaching") of the LORD, and on his law they meditate day and night" (Ps 1:2). Standing as this psalm does at the beginning of the pentateuchal five books of the "**torah**" of Psalms, it invites those who read it to learn how to pray from its many examples. In this way, the book of Psalms is likened to a fountain of wisdom from which the righteous might drink, the diverse collection of prayers serving as paradigms, ready-made forms composed of words replete with the experience of the ages.

An additional feature of the psalms that is important in understanding the instructional character of the book is the use of superscriptions. Although many of the superscriptions refer to musical accompaniment, whether to which instruments would be used or which tune to employ in recitation, a number of the psalms include short narrative snippets indicating when they were (or might have been) recited. The traditional association of the psalms with David is clear from the seventy-three psalms ascribed to him in the OT (increasing to eighty-five in the LXX), of which nineteen are connected to a particular incident in his life. The confessional Ps 51 is perhaps the most famous with its superscription, "A Psalm of David, when the prophet Nathan came to him, after he had gone in to Bathsheba," thus associating the prayer with the adulterous and murderous affair of Uriah the Hittite and Bathsheba (2 Sam 11–12), a transgression of two of the Ten Commandments. While the historicity of such an association cannot be ascertained, the larger point would be that this prayer could well serve any man or woman who had likewise committed grievous sin. Praying such a psalm could help ripen their remorse, leading to confession, and ultimately, like David's story in 2 Sam 12 illustrates, forgiveness and restoration through a "clean heart" given by God.

Such a liturgical imagination might also be considered as part of a kind of "narratization" process in which the psalms, either in whole or part through singular verses, were woven into the narrative history of Israel. The thanksgiving hymn Ps 18 appears also in 2 Sam 22 after David's life had been spared by King Saul. First Chronicles 16:8-36, a composition that appears in connection with David's appointing of the Levites as ministers of the ark, is recognizable as Pss 96:1-13; 105:1-15; and 106:1, 47-48. In that way, the heightened rhetoric of the poetic prayers was understood to be as much a part of the prayer life of Israel as the less formal prose prayers. This phenomenon also goes along with a trend toward understanding the psalms as the prophetic prayers of King David.

The tradition of psalms composition and use continued well into the early Christian and rabbinic periods. Among the DEAD SEA SCROLLS are thirty-six manuscripts containing psalms. One is 11Q5, *Psalms Scroll*[a], a scroll dating from the 2nd cent. BCE that contains mostly psalms known to us from the Heb. (lying in main behind the NRSV translation). The first three "books" are in the same order, but the last two "books" show considerable variation and indeed include seven noncanonical psalms, one of which is the Hebrew version of Ps 151 known from the Greek psalter. Another collection is the nineteen prayers of the *Psalms of Solomon*, dating from the 1st cent. BCE at a time of Roman occupation of Palestine, that includes some of the earliest messianic expectation known to us in the pre-Christian era. The psalms call on divine help to overthrow wicked foreign powers as well as to cleanse the community of its internal corruption. The NT includes frequent psalms citations, some of which are not derived from the canonical book of psalms, thereby illustrating again the continued use and development of psalms compositions. The last words of Jesus from the cross according to two of the Gospels (Matt 27:46; Mark 15:34)—"My God, my God, why have you forsaken me?"—are the first words of Ps 22, an individual lament ascribed to David.

B. Prayer in the Septuagint

Although the Persian-era books of Chronicles and Ezra–Nehemiah already suggest the growing importance of prayer in their inclusion of long prayers placed in the mouths of the main characters, prayer as an essential part of Jewish life in the late Second Temple period is also evident from the LXX (*see* SEPTUAGINT). Not only is the activity of prayer mentioned with greater frequency but also an increasing number of prayers appear in the Greek literature. Several of the books that we know from the MT of the OT were augmented with prayers in their Gk. versions. The Greek book of Esther, which in its Hebrew version does not mention God, includes prayers of Mordecai (13:8-18) and Esther (14:1-19). Both prayers mention Haman and thus seem clearly to have been written for their narrative contexts, but they also use a great deal of conventional prayer language that in effect serves to "sacralize" the shorter version of Esther and to make the two main protagonists exemplars of piety rather than more secular heroes. The book of Daniel is augmented with the Prayer of Azariah and the Song of the Three Jews, both of which offer an example of Jewish faithfulness to God under the threat of apostasy (*see* AZARIAH, PRAYER OF; SONG OF THE THREE JEWS). Esther and Daniel offer perspectives from the Jewish Diaspora. These "additions" can be understood as a part of the pseudepigraphic trend in early Jewish literature, manifest also in the NT and in Greco-Roman culture generally, in which writings were attributed to an ancient or revered figure in order to enhance the authority and status of the writing. Likewise, these figures could serve as exemplars of righteous piety.

Like prayers in the OT, prayers embedded in the Greek compositions seem to be of two kinds: those that were written specifically for the narrative in which they are found because their content is closely linked to the narrative events, and those that are less closely tied to their context. To provide just one example for many as an illustration, the book of Judith includes two long prayers of rather different character. Judith 9:2-14 is a long petitional prayer that has close verbal links to its immediate narrative context as well as intertextual links to other scriptural traditions that provide a rationale for Judith's defensive act of violence in killing Holofernes. The second prayer, in Jdt 16:1-17, is actually designated a psalm. As a song of victory, it resembles the Song of the Sea (Exod 15) in form and function, yet tailored to new circumstances and understanding God's power to work victory through the hand of a woman. In a heightened rhetorical form, the psalm combines conventional phraseology found in other psalms and hymns with some descriptions in the third person of Judith's victory, which is ultimately attributed to God. In this way, the psalm of Jdt 16 is linked to the narrative but not tied to it inextricably. Both prayers are offered by the main character Judith within the narrative, though Jdt 9 makes a petition to God in the second person; Jdt 16 combines both third-person with first-person discourse. Whereas it is hard to imagine the book of Judith without the prayer of Jdt 9, because of its important role in the narrative plot, Jdt 16 could more easily be separated from the book. Just as the songs of Moses and Miriam in Exod 15 are widely thought to predate the prose account of the exodus, one can imagine that Jdt 16 may have circulated independently as a hymn of victory sung by the Hasmoneans to celebrate their triumph over the Seleucid encroachments in the 2nd cent.

Prayer holds a prominent place in other books of the LXX. Tobit contains four prayers (3:1-6, 11-15; 8:5-8; 13:1-17) that play an important means of expressing the author's theology and advancing the plot. The blessing in Tob 13:1-4 makes specific reference to the Diaspora conditions in which some Jews always lived after the exile. The Jewish witness to worshiping the one God was thus particularly important "among the nations" where they were scattered. The Hellenistic wisdom books of the LXX also evince an interest in prayer. The sage of Sirach urges: "But above all pray to the Most High that he may direct your way in truth" (37:15). Sirach contains twenty proverbs that relate to prayer as well as two prayers (Sir 36:22; 51:10-12). Especially worthy of note in Sirach is the emphasis on divine healing as a response to prayer (Sir 38:9, 14), which at the same time recognizes the God-given ability of physicians to heal (Sir 38:1-15). The 1st-cent. BCE Wisdom of Solomon contains a long prayer at its center, rooted in an expansive retelling in the first person of Solomon's dream in 1 Kgs 3. Whereas Solomon's speech to God in 1 Kgs 3:6-9 is not called a prayer, in the Wisdom of Solomon this element of the story is expanded and formalized. Solomon prays for the spirit of wisdom in a long prayer (Wis 9:1-18) with an invocation: "O God of my ancestors and Lord of mercy, who have made all things by your word, and by your wisdom have formed humankind to have dominion over the creatures you have made...." (Wis 9:1-2).

C. Prayer at Qumran and in Early Jewish Literature

The hundreds of prayers, hymns, and psalms found among the Dead Sea Scrolls also attest to the increasing importance of prayer to Jewish worship in the Greco-Roman period. The sheer quantity and variety of liturgical material found at QUMRAN came as something of a surprise, because little had been known about prayers and prayer practices in the 1st-cent. synagogue and elsewhere. The large cache is significant in part because it reflects the early period of development of Jewish prayer at the time of the emergence of Christianity. Daily fixed prayer would eventually become a mandated practice in rabbinic Judaism, but before this discovery, the earliest Jewish prayer book (*Siddur*) known was from the 9th cent. CE. Some of this liturgical material reflects sectarian ideas relating to a heightened eschatology with the expectation of messianic intervention, a strict dualism between good and evil spheres, and a reliance on the solar calendar, but the majority of the prayers shows no such signs of sectarian provenance and was likely part of the common inheritance of early Judaism generally. Given the continuing centrality of prayer as a religious practice, it is thus perhaps surprising that there are few direct links between the Qumran corpus and later rabbinic prayers, NT prayers, and early Christian worship. The material is quite diverse generically, including independent prayers, hymns, and psalms, prayers that are part of liturgies, and prayers that are part of narrative compositions. Among these, there are prayers for fixed times, whether daily or for specific festivals; and hymns, such as the sectarian *Hodayot*, poetic prayers of thanksgiving (1QH^{a}, 4Q427–432; *see* THANKSGIVING PSALMS). There are blessings (4Q286–290). There are Hebrew versions of prayers already known from their Gk. version (Sir 51:13-20; Tob 13; *1 En.* 84). A nonsectarian collection of daily prayers (4Q503–504), with a different prayer assigned for each day, is significant because it suggests that at least a subgroup of Jews during the Greco-Roman era was in the habit of offering prayer each day. There are many psalms, including not only psalms that also appear in the Bible but also many unique psalm compositions. There are prayers written in the name of Israel's kings, not only David but also Manasseh, as well as a prayer written in the name of Obadiah, whether the prophet or the steward of King Ahab. There is even a prayer written for the well-being of "King Jonathan" (4Q448), presumably Alexander Jannaeus, the high priest in Jerusalem (103–76 BCE). There are prayers, embedded in narratives, such as the sectarian *War Scroll* (1QM), that ascribe eschatological victory and praise to God and that bless God and the righteous and curse "Belial" the satanic force and his allies.

The priestly oriented, ascetic group that lived near the Dead Sea was only part of a larger community of Essenes that lived in Palestine. From what can be reconstructed from the community rules describing life in these communities, prayer was a central component. The *Rule of the Community* (1QS) describes a pattern in which one-third of each night is spent reading Scripture, one-third spent studying the community's laws, and one-third praying (lit., "blessing" together; 1QS VI, 7–8). Prayer at Qumran is also relevant to the study of Christianity because it provides a window into a community that was alienated from a large segment of Judaism, as was the early Jesus movement. Moreover, the community was estranged from the Temple, viewing the contemporary temple leadership as corrupt. There are two ways in which the Temple as a fulcrum for prayer (compare 1 Kgs 8) nonetheless shaped Qumran thinking. The first is that the purified community thought of itself in some way as a "sanctuary of men" (mqdsh ʾdm [מקדש אדם]; 4Q174 1 I, 6) as it offered its prayer and in other ways was obedient to the dictates of the law. In this way, the prayers and other worship they offered was in some ways an alternative to temple sacrifice, which they nonetheless seemed to view as essential and indeed wanted to reconstitute. Later rabbinic prayer would view the mandated daily liturgical prayer as a replacement for temple sacrifice (*b. Ber.* 26a-b). Some texts from Qumran (1QS IX, 5, 26; X, 6; CD XI, 21) liken prayer to sacrifice, and daily times of prayer are intentionally correlated with daily times of sacrifice.

While there is no contemporaneous evidence to support the idea that the statutory prayer of later rabbinic Judaism, the Shema and Amidah (lit., "standing" for the prayer posture), or Thirteen Blessings, was in place by the 1st cent. BCE or even CE, the Dead Sea Scrolls do suggest the possibility that sectors of the Jewish community offered prayer on a daily basis, perhaps some twice daily in the morning and the evening, while others offered prayer three times a day (Dan 6:10-13) to coordinate with the three sacrificial offerings.

D. Prayer in the New Testament

As a largely Hellenistic Jewish phenomenon in its origins and conceptual orientation, the early Jesus movement was heir to many Jewish practices and traditions, including the centrality and importance of prayer. In contrast to practitioners of Greco-Roman religions, Christians did not offer sacrifice in temples or possess devotional cult statues. Prayer was an accompaniment of sacrifice in Greco-Roman cultic practice as reflected in the common fixed expression "prayers and sacrifices" (**litai kai thysiai** [λιταὶ καὶ θυσίαι]; e.g., Pindar, *Ol.* 6.78). Prayers were said aloud by officiating priests. Underlying the practice of prayer in Greco-Roman culture was the notion of reciprocity—that for every gift offered or service rendered there was the expectation of a response in kind. Such social custom was thought to undergird relationships between the gods and human worshipers as well. The predominant form of early Christian worship by contrast was verbal prayer, unaccompanied by sacrifice. Moreover, Christian prayer, like Jewish prayer, did not carry with it the assumption of obligation on the part of God to respond, but rather called upon the divine relationship and beneficence of the past as the grounding of the relationship, with a hope for similar such intervention in the present and future. The doxological nature of Christian prayer also marks a distinctive difference from Greco-Roman prayer, which typically features supplication and petition. Thanksgiving and praise, two staple themes of Israelite and Jewish prayer, are also common in NT and early Christian prayers.

The NT speaks in a number of places of the expectation that prayer should be a frequent or even continuous activity. Thus Heb 13:15: "Through him, then, let us continually offer a sacrifice of praise to God, that is, the fruit of lips that confess his name" (compare Luke 18:1; Rom 1:9; 12:12; Eph 6:18; Col 1:9; 4:12; 1 Thess 1:2; 2 Thess 1:11; Phlm 4). Although there are fewer prayer texts in the NT than the OT and LXX, there are frequent mentions of prayer as an activity. The book of Acts offers a portrait of the early church as persevering in prayer as a unified company of believers (1:14; 2:46-47; 4:24-30). They are depicted as praying not only in customary Jewish locations, particularly the Temple (Acts 2:46-47; 3:1; 22:17-21), but also at times of leave-taking (Acts 20:36; 21:5-6) and at meals (Acts 27:35). A unique feature of Christian prayer as it developed was to pray in the name of Jesus. Although "Lord" (Gk. **kyrie** [κύριε], from **kyrios** [κύριος]) could be the name of God or Jesus, the salvific activity of Jesus came to be identified with his name. Thus the first Christians in Acts are those who "invoke the name" (Acts 9:14, 21), a phrase rooted ultimately in Joel 2:32 (compare Gen 4:26) quoted in Acts 2:21. Paintings in catacombs suggest that Jews prayed with arms outstretched while standing. Kneeling was another important posture for the first Christians (Acts 7:60; 9:40; 20:36; 21:5-6); such a posture of humility would have been anathema to Greeks and Romans. All prayer was said aloud, and speech generally was considered to have inherent power. Thus it was important to articulate the right words during prayer. Prayers in the NT include those of Jesus in the Gospels and those of Paul in his letters, as well as the prayers of early Christians in Acts and other writings.

1. Prayer in the Gospels

The Gospel of Luke's unique presentation among the Gospels of Jesus' infancy and childhood offers a portrait of pious Palestinian Jews during the 1st cent. CE. Prayer is a corporate activity associated with the courts of the Temple (Luke 1:10). Zechariah, the father of John the Baptist, is described as a priest (likely a Levite) whose incense is considered the equivalent of a petitional prayer (Luke 1:13). The mediatory role of angels (**mal'akhim** מַלְאָכִים; **angeloi** ἄγγελοι), as potential messengers transporting human prayer and communicating the divine will, already fully evident in the Qumran texts and other extrabiblical literature, is evident in the Lukan infancy narrative (*see* ANGEL). Aside from these characterizations of prayer, the prayers of Mary, Zechariah, and Simeon reflect traditional Jewish psalm-like prayers in continuity with the OT and extra-biblical liturgical compositions of the same era. Mary's prayer (Luke 1:46-55; the MAGNIFICAT) echoes the themes of Hannah's prayer after a miraculous birth (1 Sam 2:1-10), which praises God for the surprising reversals he has wrought: "He has brought down the powerful from their thrones, and lifted up the lowly; he has filled the hungry with good things, and sent the rich away empty" (Luke 1:52-53). Zechariah's prayer (Luke 1:68-79; the BENEDICTUS) begins with a blessing formula, a slight variant of a form that will become standard in rabbinic Judaism ("Blessed are you, O Lord our God, King of the Universe"). The hymn, which in form is much like a psalm of descriptive praise from the book of Psalms, is identified as a prophecy. Zechariah blesses God for the salvation that God has effected, promised through the prophets of old and through the ancestral covenant with Abraham, while at the same time looking toward the eschatological realization of salvation in the imminent future through a new prophet, the child John, whose vocation is to prepare the way for the Messiah. The third prayer, offered by Simeon (Luke 2:29-32; the NUNC DIMITTIS), is likewise a scripturalized composition that draws on language from various passages in Isaiah that describe the coming salvation of God in terms of glory and light that will be revealed to the nations (Isa 40:5; 42:6; 52:10). *See* HYMNS, NT.

All the Gospels model Jesus as an exemplar in his own prayer activity. Jesus offers laments at appropriate times in his life (Matt 27:46; Luke 23:46) as well as praise and thanksgiving (Matt 11:25-27; John 11:41-42). Jesus' desire to purge the Temple is rooted in the Isaianic vision that the Temple should be a house of prayer for all nations (Mark 11:17; compare Isa 56:7).

In the Gospel of Luke, Jesus prays at crucial points in his ministry, including at his baptism by John (Luke 3:21), before he chooses his disciples (Luke 6:12), at the time of the transfiguration (Luke 9:28-29), and on the Mount of Olives (Luke 22:41). At his death, Jesus signals the importance of intercession for others in his last words from the cross (Luke 23:34), an act that will be repeated by the first martyr, Stephen, at the moment of his own death (Acts 7:60).

The NT includes a number of texts that offer teaching about prayer (Matt 6:5-8; Mark 11:22-25; Luke 11:1-13; 18:1-14; Col 4:2-4; Jas 5:13-18; 1 Pet 3:12). It is in the context of such instruction about prayer that the LORD'S PRAYER appears. Jesus teaches his disciples how to pray. The slightly different versions that appear in two of the Gospels (Matt 6:9*b*-13; Luke 11:2*b*-4) presuppose a common source, perhaps the Q source, Q 11:2*b*-4 (*see* Q, QUELLE). Matthew's version is the longer and presumes the customary divine presence in heaven. Another 1st-cent. CE version is found in *Did.* 8:2. The seven petitions of this prayer contain nothing distinctively Christian. Although some have suggested that the Lord's Prayer may represent a short form of the Jewish daily prayer, the Eighteen Blessings, there is no firm evidence that these statutory prayers existed already in the 1st cent. CE. The intimacy of addressing God in prayer as "father" was already known in Judaism (Isa 63:16; 64:8; Sir 23:4-6; compare also Tob 13:4; Sir 51:10; 3; Wis 14:3; 4Q372 1 16; *Jos. Asen.* 12:8-15). The prayer includes a wish for the sanctification of the divine name (compare Lev 22:32). In Judaism, the divine name is understood to be the personal name of God, Yahweh, who stands in unique relationship to Israel (*see* GOD, NAMES OF). The first Christians understood Jesus to be another name of God (John 17:12; Phil 2:9-11). Sanctification of the name suggests the exclusive and unique worship of that Being, and the righteous behavior that results from such pure allegiance manifests the holiness of the God who has inspired it (Isa 29:23; Ezek 36:23-27). The opposite of sanctification would be the profanation or desecration of the Name, through idolatry, apostasy, or unrighteousness. Another element of the Lord's Prayer is hope for the eschatological reign of God as opposed to the oppressive rule of imperial powers. The prayer includes as well a petition for daily sustenance, which may also be an allusion to the daily bread or manna provided in the desert wilderness, which itself may be understood as a foretaste of the eschatological banquet, represented in Christian worship by the eucharistic bread or Lord's Supper (*see* EUCHARIST; MESSIANIC BANQUET). There is a petition for divine forgiveness of sins, which presumes a reciprocal forgiveness of the sins of one's fellows (compare Sir 28:2). There is also a petition for preservation from temptation or testing. The context of the prayer in Matthew emphasizes its simplicity by contrasting it with the pretense of hypocrites whose deeds do not match their words, and the wordiness of Gentile (Greco-Roman) prayers. Luke, on the other hand, portrays Jesus' teaching of the prayer as coming in response to the request of the disciples. Jesus' instruction also emphasizes the need for persistence in prayer (Luke 11:5-8).

The role of Jesus as either the object or mediator of worship does not appear prominently in the Synoptic Gospels, but as might be expected, the view of prayer in John is distinct from the Synoptics. Emblematic is Jesus' "high priestly prayer" in John 17:1-26. The prayer is consonant with the Platonizing, Hellenistic Jewish theology of John as a whole, beginning with the Johannine prologue (John 1:1-18) in which Jesus is identified as the Logos preexisting creation. The prayer is offered by Jesus at the end of his final meal with the disciples. Its tripartite structure concerns first, Jesus' prayer for himself (John 17:1-5), second, his prayer for his disciples (John 17:6-19), and finally, his prayer for future believers (John 17:20-26). Its rhetorical style is florid and repetitive, like the Fourth Gospel itself, using a small range of vocabulary in various nuanced ways. The prayer displays John's unique CHRISTOLOGY, that is, the unity of Jesus and God, and reflects the understanding that Jesus has already been given authority over all people to provide eternal life. Jesus also serves as intercessor for the disciples as well as future believers and as one who has special and esoteric knowledge of God. The prayer contains some of the same themes as the Lord's Prayer, such as the sanctification of the name, yet it moves beyond the Lord's Prayer in that Jesus prays for God as Father to glorify him and recognizes Jesus as a presence before creation. Unlike the Lord's Prayer, the "high priestly prayer" likely played no liturgical role outside the reading of the Gospel itself, yet its related teaching, specifically that disciples might pray and ask for things in Jesus' name (John 14:13), would have an influence on all subsequent Christian prayer that invokes the name of Jesus for efficacy. For John, answered prayer is likened to bearing fruit.

2. Paul and prayer

Many of the Pauline epistles follow a standard feature of Hellenistic letters, which is to begin with thanksgiving and to close with doxologies and benedictions. Philemon, e.g., begins with an address (Phlm 1-3), followed by a thanksgiving (Phlm 4-7) and the body of the letter itself (Phlm 8-20), and ends with a conclusion (Phlm 21-24) and final benediction in the name of Jesus Christ (Phlm 25). Many of the same features can be seen in Paul's longer letters. Compare, e.g., Rom 1:8-15 with the concluding blessing in Rom 16:25-27. The introductory prayer sets the theme and focus of the letter. So, e.g., the initial thanksgiving for the Corinthians of 1 Cor 1:4-9 introduces the themes of eloquent speech, transcendent knowledge, and spiritual gifts that will be discussed more thoroughly in the body of the letter. Thus, Paul is revealing the power of prayer to overcome the difficulties that are the cause of the letter and perhaps implicitly offering himself as a model of a righteous prayer.

The Pauline correspondence is larded with Scripture generally, including brief excerpts from the psalms. So, e.g., Rom 15:9-11 includes Ps 18:49, Deut 32:43, Ps 117:1, and Isa 11:10, all of which include mention of the "Gentiles." They are adduced to support Paul's larger argument that not only Israel but also the nations are called to glorify God. These serve to punctuate his work with prayer, which is another device that orients the letter as a whole to God as well as to the reader/hearer of the composition. The prayers to God in the second person refocus attention on God and—just as quotations from Scripture that appear in the letters (e.g., Rom 9:33)—provide the divine voice. Another notable feature of this shifting voice in the Pauline correspondence related to prayer is his exhortation to his audience to pray (Rom 12:12; Eph 5:20; 6:18; Phil 4:6; Col 4:2). Paul also requests prayer on behalf of himself (Rom 15:30-32; 2 Cor 1:11; Eph 6:19-20; 2 Thess 3:1-2; Phlm 22).

While much more could be said about prayer in the Bible and in early Judaism and Christianity, a central characteristic of Jewish and Christian prayers that distinguishes them from prayers in other religions in biblical times is that they reflect a close and intimate relationship with God, understood as both creator and redeemer. Whether the prayers occur as part of formal liturgical texts or they are independently offered in spontaneous contexts, Jewish and Christian prayers are permeated with scriptural language and metaphors as a means of expressing the continuity of that relationship. How prayers were used in Christianity in the first house churches and in early Judaism at the Temple and in relation to the developing institution of the synagogue is still not wholly known. What may be assumed is that the practice of prayer would of course continue in early Christian and early Jewish communities, which developed distinct regional differences. Such works as the *Didache*, *1 Clement*, and the later prayers in the *Martyrdom of Polycarp*, *Acts of Peter*, and the *Prayer of the Apostle Paul* are just a few Christian works from the 1st–3rd cent. CE containing prayers that shed light on continuing prayer practice. In Judaism, the statutory daily prayer would eventually be mandated for all adult male Jews. Aside from the gradual development of these fixed prayer forms, prayers would continue to be composed and included in the Targums, the Aramaic translations of the OT, as well as the Mishnah and Talmud as ongoing means of maintaining relationship with the Being whose ultimate will is the well-being and restoration of Israel and all the earth.

Bibliography: Samuel E. Balentine. *Prayer in the Hebrew Bible* (1993); Mark J. Boda. *Praying the Tradition: The Origin and Use of Tradition in Nehemiah 9* (1999); Esther Chazon. "Prayers from Qumran and Their Historical Implications." *DSD* 1 (1994) 758–72; John Endres. "The Spiritual Vision of Chronicles: Wholehearted, Joy-filled Worship of God." *CBQ* 69 (2007) 1–21; Daniel K. Falk. *Daily, Sabbath, and Festival Prayers in the Dead Sea Scrolls* (1998); Moshe Greenberg. *Biblical Prose Prayer as a Window to the Popular Religion of Ancient Israel* (1983); Tessel M. Jonquière. *Prayer in Josephus* (2007); Mark C. Kiley et al., eds. *Prayer from Alexander to Constantine* (1997); John Koenig. *Rediscovering New Testament Prayer: Boldness and Blessing in the Name of Jesus* (1992); Patrick D. Miller. *They Cried to the Lord: The Form and Theology of Biblical Prayer* (1994); Sigmund Mowinckel. *The Psalms in Israel's Worship* (1962); Judith H. Newman. *Praying by the Book: The Scripturalization of Prayer in Second Temple Judaism* (1999); Stefan C. Reif. *Judaism and Hebrew Prayer: New Perspectives on Jewish Liturgical History* (1993); Richard Sarason. "Communal Prayer at Qumran and among the Rabbis: Certainties and Uncertainties." *Liturgical Perspectives: Poetry and Prayer in Light of the Dead Sea Scrolls.* Esther G. Chazon, ed. (2003) 151–72; Eileen Schuller. "Prayer in the Dead Sea Scrolls." *Into God's Presence: Prayer in the New Testament.* Richard N. Longenecker, ed. (2001) 66–88; Elizabeth Theokritoff. "Praying the Scriptures in Orthodox Worship." *Orthodox and Wesleyan Scriptural Understanding and Practice.* S T Kimbrough, ed. (2005) 73–88; Bonnie Thurston. "Prayer in the New Testament." *Prayer from Alexander to Constantine.* Mark C. Kiley et al., eds. (1997) 207–10; Rodney Alan Werline. *Penitential Prayer in Second Temple Judaism: The Development of a Religious Institution* (1998).

JUDITH H. NEWMAN

PRAYER OF AZARIAH. *See* AZARIAH, PRAYER OF.

PRAYER OF JOSEPH. *See* JOSEPH, PRAYER OF.

PRAYER OF MANASSEH. *See* MANASSEH, PRAYER OF.

PRAYER OF NABONIDUS. *See* NABONIDUS, PRAYER OF.

PRAYER, LORD'S. *See* LORD'S PRAYER.

PREACHER, THE pree´chuhr [מַטִּיף mattif, קֹהֶלֶת qoheleth]. The preacher in the book of Micah refers to someone who spreads palatable teachings to the people, while they reject the warnings of Micah. Traditional translation of the word referring to the author of Ecclesiastes (1:1), alternately translated "Teacher" in the NRSV. *See* ECCLESIASTES, BOOK OF.

EMILY R. CHENEY

PREACHING [נָטַף nataf; εὐαγγελίζω euangelizō, κηρύσσω kēryssō, παρακαλέω parakaleō]. The telling of the ancient story of God's deliverance took varied forms in ancient Israel. Like other oral cultures, the message of redemption was often cast in story. Through narrative, values and commitments integral to the identity and well-being of the community were communicated to successive generations. Stories were lodged in the memories of those who told and heard them. As traditions developed and as the TORAH began to take on its written form, those who told the stories developed a homiletical intention. That is, creeds and affirmations became elaborated and contextualized to meet the needs and experiences of a contemporary group of hearers. In this process are the seeds of contemporary understandings of preaching.

One place where this development can be clearly witnessed is in the prophetic tradition. Beginning in the 8th cent. BCE, textual evidence appears for prophets who deliver not just brief oracles and statements from the Lord, but lengthy poems that reflected serious thought, rhetorical strategy, and flourish. Their impassioned cries for justice and their insistence that God cares for the poor and weak can be considered, in some measure, homilies. The prophets were addressing the community in a particular place and time, reflecting on the implications of their sacred traditions. Proclamation took other forms in the wisdom tradition and in liturgical poems and responses where, in poetic fashion, the stories of redemption were told and relived within the worshiping community (*see* WISDOM IN THE OT). There are at least two instances where there is an explicit, stated relationship between preaching and the work of the prophet. The first is in the book of Jonah where the prophet is called to "proclaim to [Nineveh] the message" (Jonah 3:2). Additionally, in Isa 61:1-2, the prophet is called to "bring good news to the oppressed" and to "proclaim liberty to the captives." *See* PROPHET, PROPHECY.

Following the destruction of the Temple and the dispersion of the community into captivity, the traditions of Israel were brought together into extended narratives; the Torah was given birth and the Jewish community became a community of "the book." The Torah, Prophets, and Writings became the focus of education, reflection, interpretation, and preaching. Serious study was ongoing, and the thoughts concerning Scripture carried the authority of Scripture itself. Faithful commentaries (*see* MIDRASH) of short sayings and later homilies and lectures were collected and exerted their own influence on synagogal preaching, which gave primacy to the reading and exposition of Scripture. These homilies entertained, persuaded, and inspired. Preaching became the center of communal religious life. The eventual translation of the Scriptures into Greek (the SEPTUAGINT) enabled a respectful hearing of the word in many parts of the empire. Hellenistic understandings of speech and rhetoric melded with tradition. The inherent understandings of Scripture and their explication informed the preaching of Jesus and, subsequently, the church.

Before the writing of the canonical Gospels, the memories and teachings of Jesus were preserved by the conversations of believers and by the preachers and teachers who presented Jesus as prophet, teacher, exemplar, and model for living (*see* TRADITION, ORAL). Each of the Gospels comprises, then, stories and sayings gathered from and within community. Each story was given a distinctive shape informed by the author's audience, interests, and theological perspectives. Much like the editors of the Pentateuch, who brought together strands of memory to tell a story about God and people, the Gospel writers fashioned a story about Jesus that proclaimed the good news. The Christian gospel (**euangelion** εὐαγγέλιον) announced SALVATION. Its KERYGMA or "proclamation" (**kērygma** κήρυγμα) was its announcement, its heralding, its publishing (Osborn). The Gospel writers are, in essence, preachers who tell a story. Subsequent generations of preachers, then, use their stories as foundational for their own witness to the ancient and continuing, living story of God's redemption among us (*see* GOSPELS).

In Luke 4, the Gospel writer uses words from Isa 61 to introduce the preaching and teaching ministry of Jesus. Jesus finds his place in the prophetic, preaching line of ancient Israel. The Gospels portray Jesus as a preacher who attracted eager audiences eager to hear him speak. He preaches and teaches in a variety of settings including the synagogues in Nazareth and Capernaum, on the mountainsides, in boats, marketplaces, and the temple courtyard. While it is not possible to determine with certainty the words actually spoken by Jesus, the Gospel writers are eager to bring to their own communities the essence of his proclamation (*see* JESUS CHRIST).

In the LXX, the verb **euangelizō** was used to evoke the image of someone racing to share good news that brings great joy. This verb appears in the Gospels, as does its near equivalent **kēryssō**. Both these verbs are translated as "preach." Usually the object of these verbs is "the word" (*see* WORD, THE). Jesus, then, takes his place in the line of prophets who were bringing to the community a word from God. While it is impossible to delineate in any satisfactory manner the major themes of Jesus' preaching, some generally agreed-upon options include the inauguration of God's reign (which means that life as it is known will be reversed or overturned), the Father's nearness, and God's care and concern for all peoples. In his preaching Jesus calls for radical change; he preaches the "gospel of God." The most notable mode of Jesus' preaching is the PARABLE, which paints a portrait of this realm or kingdom that has come, or is yet to come.

Jesus teaches and persuades in his teaching by using common language and local idiom. While his speech appears natural, his parables are not without careful construction and a definitive movement. Each intends to move the listening community to consider a question or observation important for their living. Interestingly, the preaching of Jesus is not always exegetical, as is the case in Luke 4:16-30. Nor is it expository. His proclamation often begins not in sacred text but in life experiences and situations that unfold around him, which he interprets against the landscape of the Scriptures. While this is not consistent with rabbinical models that are a part of his Jewish heritage, he does use literary forms—the parable, ALLEGORY, rhetorical questions, etc.—that are reflective of the rabbinic traditions. In his preaching, Jesus used graphic metaphor and image to bring a visual and often provocative power to his word. *See* RABBINIC INTERPRETATION; RABBINIC LITERATURE.

There is a unanimity in the Gospels that Jesus commissioned others to carry on his preaching, the spreading of the GOOD NEWS. Three of the Gospels conclude with stories that depict the risen Jesus commanding his followers to preach to all nations (Matt 28:19-20; Luke 24:47; John 20:21; compare the par. in Mark 16:15, though vv. 9-20 are probably a scribal addition to the original ending of Mark). *See* EVANGELISM; EVANGELIST; GREAT COMMISSION.

In Acts, Luke portrays the early disciples as preachers who carry out the final command and commissioning of Jesus. Peter's preaching in Jerusalem on the day of Pentecost ushers in a season of apostolic preaching. This preaching emphasizes the death and resurrection of Jesus and the HOLY SPIRIT as a sign of Jesus' continuing presence in the church and world. The preachers call for repentance and proclaim the assurance of God's forgiveness and the coming of the Holy Spirit. Their preaching is a call to belief and salvation. These themes, and others, are the seeds for the varied understandings and theologies of preaching found in contemporary church communities.

Bibliography: Yngve Brilioth. *A Brief History of Preaching* (1965); C. H. Dodd. *The Apostolic Preaching and Its Development* (1966); O. C. Edwards Jr. *A History of Preaching* (2004); Joachim Jeremias. *New Testament Theology: The Proclamation of Jesus* (1971); Ronald E. Osborn. *Folly of God: The Rise of Christian Preaching* (1999); Amos N. Wilder. *The Language of the Gospel: Early Christian Rhetoric* (1964); Paul Wilson et al., eds. *The New Interpreter's Handbook of Preaching* (2008).

MARY DONOVAN TURNER

PRECINCT [פַּרְבָּר parbar, פַּרְוָרִים parwarim]. This obscure Hebrew term of uncertain meaning is translated "colonnade" in the NRSV of 1 Chr 26:18 because of the suggestion that it refers to a partially open area. In the list of divisions of the gatekeepers, it refers to an area on the west side of the Temple. Parbar occurs only twice in the OT, in both instances referring to an area in the Temple structure. In 2 Kgs 23:11 (written parwarim; LXX pharoureim [φαρουρείμ]; NRSV, "precincts"), it is an area purged of horses dedicated to the sun during Josiah's reforms. *See* ARCHITECTURE, OT.

C. MARK MCCORMICK

PRECIOUS STONES. *See* JEWELS AND PRECIOUS STONES.

PREDESTINATION. God's preparation of the gifts of grace by which those whom God has elected will be brought to salvation and complete fulfillment (compare Rom 8:29-30). Election is explicitly mentioned in a number of NT passages (Rom 8:28-30; Eph 1:3-14; 2 Tim 1:9). It may also be the meaning of the imagery of the "book of life" in the OT (Exod 32:32; Ps 69:28 [Heb. 69:29]; Dan 12:1) and Revelation (3:5; 13:8; 17:8; 20:12; 21:27; *see* LIFE, BOOK OF).

While predestination is often discussed in relation to God's sovereignty over all things, the NT mentions it in relation to election "in Christ" (Rom 8:29; Eph 1:4; 2 Tim 1:9) and thus as part of a bilateral covenant (*see* COVENANT, NT AND OT). A number of questions have been debated through the centuries. Is predestination based on God's foreknowledge of faith and/or good works, as many have thought? Or, does God freely choose some for salvation, prior to any decision of their own (compare Rom 9:10-13)? If the latter, did God decide to elect some and reject others after human beings actually sinned (infralapsarianism) or prior to any human decision (supralapsarianism)?

Those who assert the priority of God's election are often accused of denying genuine human freedom. In response, they describe grace as liberating human freedom, not controlling or confining it. Those who object to strict predestination usually put forward one or more of these alternatives: 1) salvation is the result of the grace of God, while damnation is the result of human sin; 2) all persons are offered prevenient grace, but they are elected only if they respond with faith (Arminianism); or 3) the only appropriate response to the divine invitation is the "yes" of faith, though the offer of grace makes rejection impossible.

EUGENE TESELLE

PRE-EXISTENCE OF SOULS. In Homeric literature, the soul (psychē ψυχή) constitutes the life force, without which one is considered dead. One gives up one's soul at death, and there is no speculation on what happens to it afterward. Then, through the influence of the Orphic-Pythagorean myth of the transmigration of the soul or metempsychosis (metempsychōsis μετεμψύχωσις), Plato articulated a notion that souls exist both before and after their present habitation in bodies. Plato further developed an ontological dualism of body (sōma σῶμα) and soul and assigned reason, intelligence, and immortality (athanasia ἀθανασία) to the soul so that the cycles of regeneration of souls into different bodies will continue until a mature soul finally reaches the divine realm. Plato's theory of souls was only partially embraced by the Hellenistic philosophers. For example, Epicureans thought that the soul is dispersed at death, but the Stoics maintained that the soul outlives the body, while neither school dwelled on the pre-existence of souls. The dichotomy of body and soul was foreign to ancient Israelites, and therefore the notion of the pre-existence of souls is largely absent from the OT. Alexandrian Judaism during the Hellenistic period and later rabbinic Judaism entertained the idea that the Torah or the divine Wisdom personified had pre-existed and was the agent of the creation. It is against this background that the pre-existence of the Logos in John 1:1-18 should be interpreted. Otherwise, the NT contains no explicit mention of the pre-existence of human souls, as its primary language of hope is the resurrection of the body. *See* CHRIST; SOUL.

EUGENE EUNG-CHUN PARK

PREFECT pree'fekt [סְגַן seghan; ὕπατος hypatos]. One of the types of officials in, among others, the Persian governmental structure (Dan 2:48; 3:2-3, 27; 6:7; 1 Esd 3:14). *See* SATRAP, SATRAPY.

PRE-HISTORY IN THE ANCIENT NEAR EAST. The prehistoric period in the ANE refers to the Paleolithic Period through the Chalcolithic Period.

A. The Paleolithic Period ("Old Stone Age")
B. The Epipaleolithic ("End of the Paleolithic") Period
C. The Early Neolithic Period
D. The Late Neolithic Period
E. The Chalcolithic ("Copper-Stone") Period
Bibliography

A. The Paleolithic Period ("Old Stone Age")

Although the earliest evidence of prehistoric human culture dates to 2.5 million years in Africa, the oldest evidence for human presence in the LEVANT dates to ca. 1.5 million years at Ubeidiya, Israel, at the southern end of the Sea of Galilee. Hunters of the species *Homo erectus* sought game that was essentially African in nature, including elephant, giraffe, rhinoceros, and hippo. The characteristic stone tool of this part of the Stone Age (the Lower Paleolithic) is the "hand ax" or biface, generally associated with heavy-duty butchering of large game. There is no evidence for the use of fire in the Near East until about 700,000 years ago at Gesher Benot Yacob (Jisr Banat Yaaqov) in the JORDAN VALLEY, although it is unlikely that the ability to make fire at will does not appear until several hundred thousand years later.

The last part of the Lower Paleolithic period is the best represented, spread among hundreds of sites in Syria, Lebanon, Israel, and Jordan. Some sites are well preserved due to the protective characteristics of CAVEs, although the use of caves for dwellings is probably the exception in comparison to campsites located in the open air: caves were confined and dangerous, since other "hunters" also liked to frequent them. One of the longest records of occupation is at Tabun Cave just south of Haifa. Here the oldest artifact-bearing layers are probably 350,000 years old or more, with a persistent presence of human hunters until perhaps 50,000 years ago. Throughout this long period there is clear evidence of climate change from warm Mediterranean climate with a nearby beach to increasingly colder and drier conditions, witnessed by the retreat of the sea as more and more water became trapped in glaciers in the higher latitudes of the Northern Hemisphere.

Contemporary with the Lower Paleolithic cave sites of Israel and the Mediterranean coast of Syria and Lebanon, dense distributions of butchering tools are found throughout the southern and eastern deserts of Jordan as well as the steppe of central Syria. The desert oasis at Azraq in eastern Jordan has several sites at the edge of a former enormous Ice Age lake (or series of lakes). Although the area surrounding these points today includes some of the most desolate landscapes in the world, the contemporary landscape was similar to the grassland savannah of East Africa, testified by the presence of remains of elephant, rhinoceros, wild ass, and hartebeest. Another major area of butchery sites occurs in the al-Jafr Basin of southern Jordan, where the attraction of animals (and thus *H. erectus* hunters) was not so much the lakeshore, but wadis carrying strong spring discharges from the steep rim of the basin structure. Characteristic of all these desert localities is the dominating presence of bifaced tools called "cleavers" that have a cutting edge similar to the tool with the modern name.

By ca. 270,000 years ago, flakes, blades, and points (more efficient cutting tools made by using the Levallois techniques, preshaping tools on the stone core) replaced bifaces. This switch in tool preference and technological production is called the Middle Paleolithic. By this time *H. erectus* was evolving to "Archaic *H. sapiens*" and Neanderthals. Although caves remained important sources of evidence, open-air camps outnumbered cave and open sites of the Lower Paleolithic, almost ubiquitous across the terrain of lush Mediterranean vegetation, steppe grassland, and desert biomes. Climate fluctuated, ranging from cool and dry periods to warm and humid times, even warm and moist climatic episodes. But from ca. 60,000–40,000 years ago, climate became increasingly cooler and drier, and at the end of the Middle Paleolithic plant and animal resources that were necessary for hunter-gatherer populations became increasingly rare.

By 40,000 years ago, it is also clear that fully modern *H. sapiens sapiens* were the sole representatives of humans, although there is considerable controversy over the role of Neanderthals in this development. The 45,000-year timeline, initiating the Upper Paleolithic, marks a blurry change from an essentially homogeneous cultural phenomenon of the previous 1.5 million years to one that was characterized by two major contemporaneous cultural traditions separated by both geography and the means of producing stone tools. One tradition, the Levantine Aurignacian, is a probable evolution of the late Middle Paleolithic tradition in which irregularly shaped flakes were made into stone tools. The other tradition is the "Ahmarian," based on parallel-sided blades and also miniature pieces called "bladelets"; there is no clear antecedent for the Ahmarian. The Levantine Aurignacian is known principally from Lebanon and northern Israel; the Ahmarian is found mostly in southern Jordan and Israel, although there are territorial overlaps between the two traditions. The question arises: are these "ethnic" groups carrying on daily life in different cultural lifeways? Or are these patterns of tool manufacture and use related to the exploitation of different resources in different parts of the region?

The Upper Paleolithic endured climatic changes from cool and dry to warm and humid and finally cool and dry again. By 20,000 years ago, glacial conditions in Europe, northern Asia, and North America had reached the most severe states in paleoclimatological history. Average annual temperatures reached extreme lows, and precipitation was very sparse throughout the temperate zones. Large animals and seasonal plant resources that were so vital to Upper Paleolithic hunter-gatherer groups became rarer, and increasingly less preferred species of plants and animals necessarily were required to fulfill dietary requirements of human groups, and this shift to more intensive resource exploitation signifies a switch from the Upper Paleolithic to the Epipaleolithic, the "last gasp" of the Old Stone Age (22,000–12,000 BCE).

B. The Epipaleolithic ("End of the Paleolithic") Period

The Epipaleolithic period witnessed a continuation of the blade-bladelet focus of tool production, evidently an evolutionary process from the earlier Ahmarian tradition. Stone tools included many small bladelets that were shaped for use with other shaped microlithic (small stone) tools attached to the same shaft as arrows, harpoons, saws, or other implements. The Epipaleolithic period underwent a slow amelioration of the climate, with temperatures warming and precipitation increasing so that by 12,500 BCE conditions became even more pleasant than today. From the very beginning of the period the first evidence of the use of architecture in the form of temporary huts appeared.

The waterlogged deposits at Ohallo II, an early Epipaleolithic winter camp on the southwestern shore of the Sea of Galilee, provided a stunning array of preserved organic remains. Because environmental conditions normally are not conducive to preserving organic materials, prehistoric archaeology does not often benefit from such a find. Hundreds of bird bones, thousands of fish remains, and tens of thousands of seeds, including wild forms of wheat and barley, added unprecedented details to the menu these hunter-gatherers enjoyed, in addition to the meat from thousands of mammal bones (Nadel).

The last part of the Epipaleolithic shows a preference for shaping bladelets into geometric shapes, including triangles, rectangles, trapezes, and lunates, the last especially preferred after 12,500 BCE. Lunates characterized the Natufian period (12,000–9,600 BCE), a culture that experienced continued pleasant climatic conditions at the beginning, which afforded the possibility of establishing permanent or semi-permanent villages for the first time in human history. The first true cemeteries appeared at the villages, which signaled an identity of the society with a home territory. But a sudden and sharp deterioration of climate, which returned to the cold and dry late Upper Paleolithic conditions, curtailed the Natufian experiment with sedentary life, and for more than a thousand years the hunter-gatherers returned to a highly mobile way of life.

C. The Early Neolithic Period

By 10,000 BCE climate change to better conditions witnessed a return to sedentary life, with small villages appearing throughout the Levant, including such settlements at Jerf al-Ahmar in Syria and Jericho, Dhra and Zahrat al-Dhra near the shores of the Dead Sea. One aspect that contributed to stable residency was the emergence of agriculture; the farming of artificial species of wheat and barley began as only a supplement to food obtained from gathering wild plants and hunting, but the cereals were abundant and storable, which made it possible for people to maintain permanent dwellings near the fields (*see* AGRICULTURE). This change in the subsistence economy ushered in the Neolithic period, which ultimately led to major changes in the relationships of humans to the environment and among human societies. This early stage of the Neolithic, referred to as the Pre-Pottery Neolithic A (or PPNA), lasting until ca. 9,000 BCE, was characterized by round, semi-subterranean houses and the first true arrowheads (called Khiam points). The burial rituals of the Natufian period became elaborated in the PPNA, and public buildings evidently associated with ritual observances became common for the first time, especially in the northern Levant.

After 9,000 BCE population increased comparatively rapidly, with cereal and pulse farming providing the staples of a predictable diet, and the domestication of goats also provided up to half of the meat in the diet of the people. The period between 9,000–6,900 BCE is also marked by rectangular domestic dwellings with typical lime plaster floors that were built on ground level and a change in the production of standardized blade manufacture (called the "naviform" technique, especially used for making arrowheads, spear points, sickle blades, and knives). This remarkable florescence of cultural complexity is referred to as the Pre-Pottery Neolithic B (PPNB), which also witnessed a remarkable amplification of ritual activity. Small clay animal and human figurines became commonplace, but what was particularly remarkable was a growth in the ancestor cult, represented by the recreation of modeled plaster faces on human skulls found at several sites between modern Damascus and Amman. In addition to the "portrait skulls," the production of lime plaster human statues and busts at Jericho and Ain Ghazal indicates an extension of the ancestor cult to a mythical realm (Rollefson).

Severe dislocation of settlement patterns, including the abandonment of long-term farming villages in the Jordan Valley and Israel, marks the end of the Early and Middle PPNB by about 7,500 BCE, and the subsequent move of these farming populations into the Jordanian highlands ushers in the Late PPNB (7,500–6,900 BCE). The massive immigration into Jordan resulted in enormous growth of already existing settlements such as Ain Ghazal and Wadi Shueib (both of which mushroomed from ca. 5–7 ac. to more than 35 ac. in only a couple of generations) and to the founding of new towns almost as large at Basta and al-Sifaya. Architecture in the LPPNB also changed considerably as multi-story structures housing several (probably related) families were characteristic of the region. Statuary appears to have disappeared by the beginning of the LPPNB, although small family-oriented shrines may have maintained kinship-based ancestor veneration. Large cult buildings that were probably communal religious centers have been found at ʿAin Ghazal (*see* GHAZAL, ʿAIN), but their perceived absence at other LPPNB towns is probably a result of sampling problems (Rollefson).

D. The Late Neolithic Period

The translocation of people onto the Jordanian highlands solved the problems of the immigrants for a time, but the huge influx of people made unprecedented demands on the fragile ecosystem, and after about 500 years of megasite demands, local fields and pastures could no longer support large population concentrations. By 6,900 BCE towns throughout the highlands were either abandoned outright or, as was the case at Ain Ghazal and Wadi Shueib, experienced depopulation on the order of 75 percent. This was a turning point in Neolithic cultures of the Levant, when the steppe and desert became important new resource areas, where vegetation fed by the seasonal rains could be converted into meat, diary products, and hair or wool of the flocks of goats and sheep belonging to pastoral nomads who spent the greater part of the year away from farming territory in the wetter lands to the west and north.

Fired ceramics were still not part of the technological repertoire in the southern Levant, so this major change in lifestyles is termed the Pre-Pottery Neolithic C (PPNC), which lasted until about 5,500 BCE. Farmers reoccupied at least some parts of the Jordan Valley and Israel during the PPNC. Architecture reverted to smaller single-family dwellings, and the once-common use of solid lime plaster for floors was replaced with an ersatz flooring of crushed chalk and mud. Naviform blade production, the hallmark of the Early, Middle, and Late PPNB, virtually disappeared, as did the skull cult and ritual buildings.

Eventually, earlier experimentation with firing clay objects caught on as an essential component of the technological sphere, and this established the Pottery Neolithic period (5,500–4,500 BCE). A sudden cold snap with a severe decrease in precipitation that lasted about a century occurred at around 5,500 BCE, which exacerbated population decrease in the southern Levant but was less drastically felt in the north. Throughout the region domesticated pigs and cattle were added to the subsistence economy, although the relative importance of the different species (including sheep and goats) varied from one area to another.

During this time the Near East witnessed strong, clear-cut ethnic differences in material cultural terms with distinctive approaches to the production and decoration of pottery forms. In the earlier part of this era (6,350–5,800 BCE), e.g., Dark-Faced Burnished Ware of Syria, Yarmoukian pottery in most of Jordan and in large parts of Israel, and Jericho IX pottery in the rest of Israel are rarely found outside of their "stylistic boundaries." Throughout the region settlements remained small in population size, although some sites such as ʿAin Ghazal, Wadi Shueib, and Shaar Hagolan extended over areas that ranged from 20 to 50 ac. Architecture remained as single-family structures, although there was contemporaneous variability in round to rectangular structures, even within the same "pottery territory." Human burials are particularly rare in this section of the Pottery Neolithic period, and evidence of other ritual is similarly uncommon.

In the latter part of the Pottery Neolithic period ethnicity diverged even more, with several distinctive cultures in Syria (variously named *Byblos néolithique moyen*, Hassuna, Samarran, and Halafian), all overlapping to some degree in temporal terms. Although settlements were small and relatively short-lived in the three earlier cultures, irrigation on a limited scale allowed an extension of agriculture into the steppic borders of the Euphrates River and its major tributaries, and by the Halafian period, settlements became fewer but much larger.

By contrast, the Yarmoukian/Jericho IX dichotomy in the southern Levant appears to have been eliminated in the last half 500 to 600 years of the Pottery Neolithic period with the appearance of the Wadi Rabah culture, which is found widely, if sporadically, across Jordan and Israel. There are no indications of irrigation in the southern Levant at any time during the Pottery Neolithic, but there are clear indications that pastoral nomads were intensively utilizing the vegetation of the unfarmable steppe and desert as an independent subsistence strategy. Nevertheless, these groups were certainly in contact with farming settlements to exchange lambs and kids for cereals, legumes, and pasturage on fields after the harvest when the steppe and desert were barren and dry.

The close of the Pottery Neolithic period is poorly documented and dated, and there is considerable debate on how many distinct "cultures" were involved in the transition to the following archaeological period and what tempo was involved, particularly in the southern Levant. This is perhaps a result of the much more intensive investigation of this transition (particularly in Israel) and the consequences of estimating just how similar or different various aspects of a "culture" really are.

E. The Chalcolithic ("Copper-Stone") Period

The smelting of COPPER heralds a major technological innovation, although the distribution of this metal was limited to the southern Levant, principally restricted to the northern Negev settlements. Evidence of tool distribution in villages suggests that copper metallurgy was conducted on a household level (Levy and Shalev). Nevertheless, elegant metal objects made of copper alloyed with minor amounts of other metals (thus a low-grade bronze) have been identified as prestige items in several villages, including the magnificent hoard of ritual items from the cave of Nahal Mishmar, and these special objects suggest that ritual activities may have been alien to egalitarian social principles (Levy and Shalev).

Technically, the term *Chalcolithic* does not apply to northern Syria and Mesopotamia, for metallurgy in that region did not appear until the Bronze Age. In the northern Levant Neolithic developments continued on trajectories perhaps better described as setting the foundation for the Protohistoric Period just prior to the emergence of the well-known Mesopotamian city-states. The Halafian culture, e.g., appears to be a bridge for this protohistoric transition, involving increasing population growth and densities, mounting complexity of irrigation schemes, and the appearance of polychrome decoration on pottery.

In environmental terms, the period enjoyed an ameliorating climate that resulted in impressive population growth; there is an astounding increase in hamlets and villages in the 6th to 5th millennia. Most of the settlements reflect only 50–100 residents, although some, such as Teleilât el-Ghassûl at the northeastern edge of the Dead Sea, reached some 50 ac. in size and perhaps several thousand inhabitants. Part of the reason for this population expansion was probably due to continued experimentation with irrigation, including small-scale projects in the southern Levant that made it possible to expand fields into steppic landscapes. During this time the food menu became essentially "modern" with the addition of olives, grapes, dates, and other fruits. Added to the domesticated animals were donkeys, which greatly facilitated trade networks.

There is much argument over whether social and even political hierarchies had become established during this period. Impressive sanctuaries have been identified at Teleilât el-Ghassûl (see GHASSÛL, TELEILÂT EL) and EN-GEDI, suggesting that there was a priestly group that may have played an important role in social control. A distinctive distribution of large and small settlements in the northern Negev suggests there might be territorial cultural units indicating simple chiefdom political units, but this is not unanimously accepted. Differences in the quantities of grave goods in cemeteries (a new socio-religious concept that appears in the Chalcolithic) suggest to some that there are at least low-level differences in social rank, but this is not supported by distinctions in residential structures. *See* ARCHAEOLOGY.

Bibliography: Thomas Levy and Sariel Shalev. "Prehistoric Metalworking in the Southern Levant: Archaeometallurgical and Social Perspectives." *World Archaeology* 20 (1989) 352–72; Dani Nadel, ed. *Ohallo II, A 23,000-Year-Old Fisher-Hunter-Gatherers' Camp on the Sea of Galilee* (2002); Gary Rollefson. "Early Neolithic Ritual Centers in the Southern Levant." *Neo-Lithics* 2 (2005) 3–13.

GARY O. ROLLEFSON

PREPARATION DAY [παρασκευή paraskeuē]. The day when Jews made special arrangements to observe the SABBATH. Because the Sabbath was a day of complete rest, food had to be cooked, clothing prepared, and travel concluded before it began. To avoid profaning the Sabbath, work ceased before sunset on Friday and was prohibited until after sunset on Saturday.

According to the Gospels, Jesus was crucified on a preparation day. The Synoptic Gospels say people were preparing for the Sabbath (Matt 27:62; Mark 15:42; Luke 23:54), but John says they were preparing for the festival of Passover, a special Sabbath (John 19:14, 31, 42).

ADAM L. PORTER

PRESENCE OF GOD. *See* DIVINE PRESENCE.

PRESENCE, BREAD OF THE. *See* BREAD OF PRESENCE.

PRESIDENT [סָרַךְ sarakh]. One of the appointed officials in the governmental structure of Persia. Daniel was one of three presidents in charge of 120 satraps (Dan 6:2-7). *See* SATRAP, SATRAPY.

PRETTY. *See* BEAUTY.

PRIDE [גַּאֲוָה ga'awah, גָּאוֹן ga'on, גֹּבַהּ govah, גֵּוָה gewah, זָדוֹן zadhon, רוּם rum; ἀλαζονεία alazoneia, καύχημα kauchēma, καύχησις kauchēsis, ὑπερηφανία hyperēphania]. Pride usually refers to the arrogance, conceit, or vanity that individuals or nations hold about their accomplishments. In the OT, individuals are chastised for their pride (the opposite of HUMILITY), and pride is considered to be the path of evil (Prov 8:13). Proud persons believe that God is distant or absent, meting out no recompense (Ps 10:4). The character of the prideful is wanting. They lie and curse (Pss 31:18 [Heb. 31:19]; 59:12 [Heb. 59:13]), are violent (Ps 73:6), lack wisdom (Prov 11:2), are known as scoffers (Prov 21:24), and are greedy idolaters (Isa 2:11-17). In the extreme, prideful persons are murderers and oppressors of the poor (Ps 10:2-11). Such arrogance contains the seeds of its own destruction, for "[p]ride goes before destruction, and a haughty spirit before a fall" (Prov 16:18; see also Prov 29:23). Nevertheless, a prideful person may repent. King Hezekiah is praised for turning aside from his pride, thus delaying God's wrath (2 Chr 32:26).

Foreign nations are frequently chastised for displaying pride, believing that their accomplishments stem from their own abilities rather than from God's bequest. They use their wealth and power for their own purposes, overstepping their boundaries and ignoring the divine plan. However, God uses Assyria and Babylon as instruments to subdue Israel and Judah. Even so, Isaiah rebukes them when they prey upon the widow and the orphan, tyrannically wielding death and destruction to unimaginable levels (Isa 10:12; 13:11). Babylon, the city which is the "pride of the Chaldeans," will be destroyed and remain uninhabitable, as were "Sodom and Gomorrah when God overthrew them" (Isa 13:19; Jer 51:41). Similarly, Ashdod, "the pride of Philistia," soon will see its recompense (Zech 9:6). God also crushes the pride of Tyre (Isa 23:8-9), Edom (Jer 49:16), Moab (Isa 16:6; 25:11; Jer 48:29), and Egypt (Ezek 32:12). Ezekiel remembers Sodom's transgressions as the neglect of the poor and needy while it lived in prosperity (Ezek 16:49, 56); he uses Sodom as a symbol of Jerusalem and Judah who similarly have sinned.

In reference to Israel, pride is sometimes positive; usually, however, pride indicates arrogance or an affront to God that will soon be addressed, even if the source of pride—such as Zion or the Temple—is also held dear by God. Pride is found "in the name of the LORD," who answers the people's petitions and who supports them, even while other nations rely on chariots and horses—their military might (Ps 20:7 [Heb. 20:8], where **nazkir** [נַזְכִּיר], "we remember," is translated by "our pride is in"). The psalmist praises God, who "chose our heritage for us, the pride of Jacob whom he loves" (Ps 47:4 [Heb. 47:5]). Like the nations, Israel and Judah are judged for their misplaced pride, which is tantamount to evil, violence, and idolatry (Isa 9:9 [Heb. 9:8]; Ezek 7:10-20). God is even willing to profane the sanctuary—"the pride of [Judah's] power"—and sends destruction to Zion in order to bring justice (Jer 13:17; Lam 2:4; Ezek 24:21; compare Amos 6:8; 8:7). Isaiah expresses confidence, nonetheless, that God will bring deliverance to Israel, who once again will have (fitting) pride (Isa 4:2).

In the NT, pride is listed as one of many faults that cause people to stumble (Mark 7:22; 1 John 2:16). Yet pride can stem from hope and consolation, serving as encouragement for the community of faith (2 Cor 7:4; Gal 6:4; Heb 3:6).

SHARON PACE

PRIEST, WICKED. In the Qumran writings, "the Wicked Priest" is used five times (Habakkuk Commentary [1QpHab; Psalms Pesher[a] [4Q171]) to designate a high-priestly rival and enemy of the TEACHER OF RIGHTEOUSNESS, the leader of the Essene community. While the identity of the Wicked Priest is uncertain, it is often suggested that he was one of the non-Zadokite high priests Jonathan or Simon Maccabee. The Essenes viewed Jonathan and Simon as having claimed the high priesthood illegitimately (middle of the 2nd cent. BCE). *See* HABAKKUK COMMENTARY, PESHER.

SARIANNA METSO

PRIESTLY WRITERS. *See* DOCUMENTARY HYPOTHESIS; P, PRIESTLY WRITERS; PENTATEUCH; SOURCE CRITICISM.

PRIESTS AND LEVITES [כֹּהֵן **kohen**; בְּנֵי לֵוִי **bene lewi**, לְוִיִּם **lewiyim**; ἱερεύς **hiereus**, Λευίτης **Leuitēs**]. In Israelite religion and early Judaism to the fall of the Second Temple, priests and Levites were ritual specialists and mediators between God and people.

Telling the story of the priests and Levites in Israel and early Judaism from around the middle of the 2nd millennium BCE to the end of the Second Temple in the 1st cent. CE is notoriously difficult because of the nature of our sources. First, the texts that provide evidence for the preexilic era, the Deuteronomic and Priestly traditions, were only completed after the exile and their authors were far more concerned to legitimate their views on the proper roles of priests and Levites than to relate a factual record prior to their own day. Second, even though some other works addressing the priesthood in the Second Temple period were composed closer in time to the events that they narrate (e.g., Ezra–Nehemiah; Josephus), they too testify more convincingly to their authors' theological and institutional interests than to the raw events of the past. And third, because the sources are so conditioned by the interests of their authors and reflect such different moments in Israel and early Judaism's life, it is not possible to sidestep the first two problems by simply creating a composite portrait of the priesthood from the canonically unified sources.

Because of these evidentiary challenges, any history of the priests and Levites must be of two kinds. First, for the period prior to the composition of the religious texts that provide us with our evidence for the office's history, our history must be almost exclusively an account of events and of the changes that the office underwent in actual practice. Second, when we come to the period during which primary "histories" of the office, along with contemporary accounts of its development, begin to be written, our history must provide not only an account of contemporaneous actual practice of the office; it must also explicate the ideologies and theologies of the priesthood intended by those authors as they wrote their primary histories. As for the dominant characteristic of the history we write, the ideological and theological nature of our sources requires that it be perpetually tentative, in both kinds.

Before turning to the historical survey, the article discusses the relevant terminology for priests and Levites in the Bible, describes the general phenomenon of priesthood in the ANE and the Greco-Roman world, and rehearses briefly the history of scholarship on priests and Levites in the modern era.

A. Terminology

Hebrew terms deriving from the root **khn** (כהן) occur nearly 800 times in the OT (**kahen** [כִּהֵן], "to act as a priest"; **kohen**, "priest"; **kehunah** [כְּהֻנָּה], "priesthood"; an Aram. equivalent to **kohen**, **kahen** [כָּהֵן], occurs eight times in Ezra). The meaning of the root is disputed. It has been related to the Akkadian verb, **kanu**, which means "to bend down, to reverence," but this is uncertain. A more likely derivation is from the Semitic root **kwn**, "to stand upright." In any case, it is the only term used for priests of Yahweh in the OT. The term is also used for foreign priests (e.g., Egyptian, Gen 41:45; 47:22; Philistine, 1 Sam 5:5; 6:2; Moabite, Jer 48:7; Ammonite, Jer 49:3). Another word used for non-Israelite priests is **komer** (כֹּמֶר; always plural; NRSV, "idolatrous priests"; 2 Kgs 23:5; Hos 10:5; Zeph 1:4; see also possibly Hos 4:4).

The LXX usually renders **kohen** as **hiereus**, and variations of the same term are used throughout the NT over 150 times for priests, high priests, priesthood, acting as a priest, and priestly activities (e.g., Matt 2:4; 8:4; Mark 1:44; 15:1; Luke 1:9; John 1:19; Acts 9:1; Heb 7:11; 1 Pet 2:5; Rev 1:6; 5:10).

References to Levites number over 350 in the OT. The origin of the word **lewi** (לֵוִי) is uncertain. The root **lwh** (לוה) has been taken to mean "to turn, to whirl," suggesting that Levites were ecstatics. The root can also mean "to be attached, to accompany"; this makes sense of Leah's declamation at Levi's conception that "now this time my husband will be joined to me" (Gen 29:34), and resonates with the fact that the Levites were joined to Aaron (Num 18:2; *see* AARON, AARONITE; LEVI, LEVITES). Finally, the same root can have the meaning "to lend, to give as a pledge"; the pledge of Levites to God in place of the firstborn of Israel may echo this meaning (Num 18:6). Minean, an Arabic language, also used the root **lwh** to refer to consecrations to a god. The Greek **Leuitēs**, "Levite," appears for the Hebrew equivalents throughout the LXX, but only three times in the NT (Luke 10:32; John 1:19; Acts 4:36; see also **Leuitikos**, "levitical," in Heb 7:11).

B. Priesthood in the Ancient Near East and the Greco-Roman World

To fully appreciate the nature of the Israelite and early Jewish priesthood requires an understanding of the general phenomenon of priests. That priests were a cross-cultural phenomenon in the ancient world is clear already from the OT, which mentions Egyptian priests (Gen 41:45, 50; 46:20; 47:26), priests of Dagon (1 Sam 5:5), Philistine priests (1 Sam 6:2), priests of Baal (2 Kgs 10:19), priests of Chemosh (Jer 48:7), and priests of Baalim and Asherim (2 Chr 34:5).

At least in the ANE, the priest's fundamental identity is that of a mediator between the human and divine realms. Ancient Egypt's **hmw ntr**, "servant of the gods," Mesopotamian civilizations' **erib biti**, "temple enterer," Ugarit's **khnm**, "priests," and Israel's **hakkohanim wehalwiyim** (הַכֹּהֲנִים וְהַלְוִיִּם), "the priests and the Levites" all mediated between the human community and the gods through sacrifice or divination or teaching. (Exceptionally, ancient Greeks did not bestow the mediator's role on a particular "career" cultic functionary, leaving the approach to the deity instead to the individual worshiper [who received only modest assistance from sanctuary officials, the "priests," who were in turn appointed by the **polis** (πόλις, "city") for limited terms, and who had no special training for their mostly custodial duties]). The priests' mediation served to maintain a proper balance between the human community and the gods, and concomitantly within the human community that was structured in large part on the patterns decreed by the gods. From this broad perspective, priests and priesthood were not merely important for religion, but for the stability of human society altogether.

Priests performed this essential mediator role through their work as ritual specialists, performing circumscribed, routinized, and repeated actions in cultic contexts. In societies where the basic social unit was the extended family, elders (male and female) inherited the role of the ritual specialist from their seniors, and their actions were performed according to memory passed on to them as tradition by their predecessors. As civilizations became more complex and specialized, professional priesthoods developed. Under these conditions priests obtained their sanction not by tradition and inheritance, but by appointment, and they knew their proper functions and responsibilities not because they received and memorized a tradition, but through training and education.

The specific functions usually associated with the priestly office include sacrifice, divination, and teaching. While there are clearly various roles to play in a sacrificial cult—from preparing the ALTAR, to slaughtering animals and preparing grain offerings, to making the offering at the SANCTUARY altar—they all may be said to pertain to the act of sacrifice; thus, even ancillary and second-class officials (such as Levites in the Priestly Work, or the **kalu** priest of Mesopotamian civilizations) function as priests in this broadest sense of the word (*see* SACRIFICES AND OFFERINGS). In most ANE contexts the priest was an essential mediator between the layperson and the god. In virtually every ancient culture, to approach the purity and power of the divine was an act fraught with danger for anyone not possessing protection or permission to do so. Priests were specially set apart for this role, sanctioned for the task, and made holy for it by that sanction and by the observance of strict codes of purity. In this way, priests were the necessary go-betweens when laypersons sought contact with the deity through sacrifice.

The rationale for the priest's function as diviner and teacher was different. In these roles, priests and priestesses from Babylon to Delphi, Memphis to Antioch were necessary because of the special divinatory skills and mantic wisdom they possessed either through tradition and status (families, clans, or tribes) or training and education (more complex societies). While the quality that made priests essential mediators in the sacrificial act was ontological, a matter of their intrinsic nature, the skills and insight they acquired by formal or informal training and education were also necessary for the priestly roles of DIVINATION and accurate instruction.

Priests across the ancient world also functioned outside of cultic contexts, chiefly as scribes and judges. Like divination and teaching, these skills were acquired through training, and were not, like the capacity to approach the deity to make sacrifice, necessarily intrinsic to the being of the priest. Like sacrifice, divination, and teaching, however, they were functions that laity required from priests (or other professionals). Notably, scribal and judicial functions were explicitly about mediating among human beings, not between human and divine; thus, particularly in these roles, priests served as the glue that held human society together.

C. Modern Study of the Priests and Levites

The history of research on the priests and Levites of the OT roughly parallels the development of critical methods, which in turn progressed according to the dominant interest among scholars in writing Israel's history from the evidence of the OT. First came SOURCE CRITICISM and its emphasis on isolating the sources of the Pentateuch. When that effort did not provide access to the events narrated in the Bible, scholars pioneered form criticism with the hope of seeing human realities behind the sources (*see* FORM CRITICISM, OT).

Disappointed that form criticism did not provide the hoped-for window on the past "as it actually happened," scholars developed tradition criticism, hoping to read history behind the fundamental narratives that gave content to the forms and sources (*see* TRADITION HISTORY, OT). Most recently, scholars have employed social historical approaches to continue the pursuit of Israel's history. With respect to the history of Israel's priesthood, these developments have curiously brought us nearly full circle, more or less back to the perspective first achieved with the help of source criticism (*see* ISRAEL, SOCIOLOGY OF).

1. The precritical consensus

Prior to the rise of historical criticism, the traditional view of the priests and Levites more or less accepted the perspective that critical scholarship later assigned to the Priestly tradition. The Priestly work was able to dominate and overshadow other canonical portraits of the priesthood in precritical imagination for two reasons. First, it devotes by far the greatest amount of attention to the office, and second, it provides the narrative framework for the completed Pentateuch, effectively subsuming the perspectives of the other sources into its own (the Deuteronomic Tradition, the Yahwist Work, and the Holiness Code). Thus, the precritical portrait of the priests and Levites assigned their origin to Moses, a descendant of Levi (Exod 2:1; 7:16-20) who ordained his brother and fellow Levite Aaron to be the first preeminent priest, and Aaron's sons to be the priests who served with and under the Aaronites' direction (Exod 28; Lev 9). According to Num 3:8, the remaining Levites were dedicated to the cult's service in place of Israel's firstborn as an offering to God (see Exod 13:2). The Levites were designated according to their descent from the sons of Levi (Gershon, Kohath, and Merari) and were assigned second-rank duties in the sacrificial cult. The sequence of events in Num 16–18—a failed Levite rebellion against Aaron (Num 16), the selection by lot of Aaron and his descendants as chief priests (Num 17), and the subordination of the Levites to the Aaronites through the tithe system (Num 18)—confirmed Aaronite ascendancy and the Levites' second-class status. Additional Priestly episodes further underscored the first-rank status of Aaron's descendants (e.g., the "covenant of perpetual priesthood" granted Phinehas, grandson of Aaron in Num 25:13). The precritical consensus assumed that this three-tier priesthood—an Aaronite high priest assisted by other Aaronite priests who are assisted in turn by Levites—more or less endured through the preexilic, exilic, and postexilic periods to the fall of the Second Temple in 70 CE.

2. From Wellhausen to Albertz: Coming full circle

Julius Wellhausen formulated the basic elements of what is known as the DOCUMENTARY HYPOTHESIS, regarding the formation of the PENTATEUCH. Wellhausen intended this work to be the prolegomenon to a history of Israel, but at least with respect to the priesthood it led to the conclusion that there was little history to report before the late preexilic period. (Wellhausen did argue that the priesthood might have had Mushite (i.e., connected to the tradition of Moses) origins at Shiloh and Dan (*see* DAN, DANITE; SHILOH, SHILONITE). Wellhausen argued that only with Josiah's attempt to centralize the cult in Jerusalem did the priesthood first take on significance in Israel's life. At that time, the patronymic "Levite" was applied to priests, but only because they required the legitimacy of the affiliation to assume the privileges Josiah's reform accorded them (*see* JOSIAH). Deuteronomy invited all "Levites" to the central sanctuary where they could serve with their "fellow-Levites who stand to minister there before the LORD" (Deut 18:6-7). However, the reform was not entirely successful, as 2 Kgs 23:9 makes clear: priests of the high places did not all respond to the call to the central sanctuary, effectively negating the Deuteronomic effort to unify the cultic service of Yahweh under a single priesthood. To legitimate the subordination of the recalcitrant priests and their descendants to the priests who served faithfully in Jerusalem (according to Josiah's reform), Ezekiel introduced the distinction between Levites whose apostasy caused the exile, and the Zadokites who remained faithful (Ezek 44:10-15; *see* ZADOK, ZADOKITES). According to Wellhausen, the same two-tier priesthood was expressed later by the Priestly writers and later the Chronicler by the division of the priesthood between Aaronites and Levites.

Wellhausen's reticence regarding a history of the priesthood prior to Josiah's reform did not settle well even with his own disciples, W. R. Smith and A. Bertholet, who were among the first to study the Israelite priesthood in its wider ANE context as a means of going back in time. But attention to the literary sources remained a necessity, and it was left to K. Möhlenbrink to suggest that form criticism might be of assistance. Möhlenbrink identified a number of "Levitical" genres (lists, narrative, laws, and poems) and assigned them to various periods in Israelite history from around the conquest to the postexilic period. This schematization allowed Möhlenbrink to postulate about the Levites before the end of the monarchy. He argued that through Deut 33:8-11, a poem he says extols the virtue of Mushites, Levitical priests descended ostensibly from Moses, and we can see this as far back in time as the conquest. Möhlenbrink assigned the remaining genres to subsequent periods down to the Persian era, creating thereby at least a skeletal "history" of the priests and Levites prior to and beyond the Archimedean point of Josiah's reform.

A. H. J. Gunneweg took up a tradition historical approach to the question of the Levites' origin and the nature of their relationship to the priesthood. Focusing on Gen 49:5-7; Exod 32:25-29; and Deut 33:8-11, Gunneweg argued that the Levites were originally a "religious order" that belonged to the pre-monarchic AMPHICTYONY (a loose tribal association) but lacked specific tribal affiliation and land, and as such its members were dispersed among the tribes. On this reading, the Levites saw themselves as the guarantors of Israel's faithfulness to Yahweh. The affiliation of the Levites with the priesthood came with the Josianic reform—which their zeal prompted—and Deuteronomy was an attempt to grant them equal status with the existing priesthood (Deut 18:6-7). Gunneweg explained the affiliation of Aaronites and Zadokites with the Levites as innovations of the Priestly tradition and the Chronicler. Writing at nearly the same time, Aelred Cody also provided a history of the OT priesthood that balanced the source-critical approach of scholars like Gunneweg with the approach pioneered by Smith and Bertholet.

F. M. Cross made the next major contribution to research on the history of the priests and Levites, and thanks to the efforts of some of his students, his views have formed something of a post-Wellhausenian consensus. Like other successors to Wellhausen, Cross did not accept the idea that little could be known of the priesthood's history prior to Josiah's reform. Building on Wellhausen's speculation that there was in early times a Mushite priesthood affiliated with Shiloh and Dan, and depending on stories of conflict in the wilderness era (Exod 32; Num 12; 16–17; 25; etc.), Cross argued that well before the monarchy there was prolonged strife between a Mushite and Mushite-Kenite priesthood of Dan and Shiloh and the Aaronite priesthood of Bethel and Jerusalem. David's appointment of Abiathar, a Mushite-Levite, and Zadok, an Aaronite, reflected his attempt to resolve the old conflict with a unified priesthood serving the national cult (2 Sam 15:24-37). The Levites and Aaronites of the Deuteronomic and Priestly traditions were the later literary embodiments of these competing priesthoods.

While many efforts to write small segments of the history of Israel's priesthood continue to be produced well into the first decade of the 21st cent., none are as comprehensive as the efforts from Wellhausen to Cross. It is a mark of the former perspective's staying power, and especially of the abiding uncertainty regarding the priesthood's history prior to the late monarchy, that the last major effort of the 20th cent., that of Rainer Albertz in the context of his landmark study of Israelite religion, essentially returns to Wellhausen's hypothesis. Even with the help of social historical insights, Albertz is still compelled largely to put aside the advances into the pre-Josianic period made by the scholars who followed Wellhausen, and to resurrect Wellhausen's thesis for a new generation. However, Albertz makes important refinements on the Wellhausenian consensus that make his reconstruction quite attractive (see §D3).

D. Historical Survey of the Priests and Levites

As noted in the introduction to this article, the following survey of the history of the priests and Levites is heir to the historical skepticism of Wellhausen. It is also informed by a particular view of the literary history of the portions of the OT that provide us with much of the evidence we have for priests and Levites before and during the Second Temple period. It assumes that the Deuteronomic tradition dating to the exile provides the oldest substantial material in the OT addressing priests and Levites. The Deuteronomic Collection includes Deuteronomy (*see* DEUTERONOMY, BOOK OF), the DEUTERONOMISTIC HISTORY (Joshua–2 Kings, with the exception of Ruth), and a handful of the Latter Prophets. Dating to the early postexilic period, the Priestly Work provides the Bible's largest body of testimony regarding priests and Levites, writing their history from their ostensible origin in the time of Moses to the time when Israel entered the promised land (*see* P, PRIESTLY WRITERS). The Priestly Work includes major portions of Genesis, Exod 1–24, and Num 11–36, and virtually all of Exod 25–31 and 35–40, Lev 1–16, and Num 1–10. Created as a supplement and corrective to the worldview of the Priestly Work, the Holiness Code (Lev 17–26) is the latest material in the Pentateuch to address the priesthood. Outside of the Pentateuch sources for the priesthood's history include Haggai, Zech 1–8, Chronicles, and Ezra–Nehemiah, Third Isaiah, Malachi, 1 and 2 Maccabees, Sir 50, the *Aramaic Levi Document*, *Jub.* 30; 32, *1 En.* 12–16, Josephus, the Dead Sea Scrolls, and the NT. A handful of hints are also provided by rabbinic texts of a much later period.

1. Before the monarchy

Writing the history of the priesthood prior to the monarchy is very difficult: not only are the resources for researching and writing that history scarce, they are also late relative to the events they report, and they are very much shaped by the interests of their authors in legitimating realities in their own day. What follows, then, can offer little more than a sketch of the broad outlines of the office before the monarchy.

The biblical record reports no ordained priests among the ancestors, and for good reason; the authors of the pentateuchal sources are compelled by the shape of the story they want to tell to avoid introducing priests until the people have arrived at Sinai and Moses is receiving the law and instructions. However, the sources do indicate that other peoples the ancestors and the refugees from Egypt encountered had priests. Abram meets the mysterious MELCHIZEDEK (Gen 14); Joseph contends with POTIPHERA, priest of On and the father of Asenath (Gen 41), and with Pharaoh's priests (Gen 46); and JETHRO, Moses' father-in-law, is a priest of Midian (Exod 2; 3; 18). By contrast, the narratives assign sacerdotal functions among the ancestors exclusively to the elder males of the family. Abraham is called upon to sacrifice his son (Gen 22); Isaac offers a blessing to his son (Gen 27); and Jacob sacrifices on behalf of his household (Gen 31), makes a libation offering (Gen 35), and blesses his offspring and his grandchildren (Gen 48; 49). *See* PATRIARCHS.

These contradictory portraits of how the priesthood worked among the ancestors and their neighbors might lead one to reject the evidence for the kin-staffed, family-based priesthood as a historical fiction that somehow served the interests of the late preexilic, exilic, and postexilic authors responsible for the sources of the Pentateuch. However, Deut 33:8-11 and Judg 17–18, two texts with genuine claims to antiquity far greater than the source in which they appear (the Deuteronomic Collection), provide reason to accept the model as having had some basis in actual practice. These texts also provide a framework for understanding the earliest history of "Levites" and how they came to be associated with the family-based and professionalized priesthood.

Judges 17–18, widely regarded to be an ancient tradition incorporated by Deuteronomists into their history, first relates how a certain Micah of the hill country of Ephraim had constructed a family SHRINE, replete with ephod, teraphim, and an idol, and had designated his son as his priest by "filling the hand" (author's trans.; NRSV, "installed") of his son, an action clearly associated with the installation of priests (17:5; see Exod 28:41; 29:9). While this contradicts the preference for the elder male as priest in the ancestral traditions, it does provide evidence for the practice of assigning family or clan members the role of priest and of keeping shrines and other such devotional settings within the family. Archaeological evidence that families had their own shrines that exceeded the scope of the simple figurine nook is abundant (e.g., locus 2081 at Megiddo).

Judges 17 continues with the story of a "young man of Bethlehem in Judah, of the clan of Judah," "a Levite residing there" who set out from his homeland "to live wherever he could find a place" (17:7-8*a*). The Levite, "Jonathan son of Gershom, son of Moses" (18:30), seems to have been assigned the title because, although a resident of Bethlehem and a member of the tribe of Judah, he chose for himself an itinerant's life aimed at serving the God of Israel in some fashion or another.

Support for this understanding of the term *Levite* in this account comes from our second text, Deut 33:8-11. Also accorded an early date by critics, it reinforces the supposition that Levites were itinerants with its declaration that Levi and his descendants "said of his father and mother, 'I regard them not'; he ignored his kin, and did not acknowledge his children. For they observed your word, and kept your covenant" (33:9). Both texts indicate that Levites were not at first identified as such by tribal affiliation or priestly function, but by self-designation as itinerant "free agents" whose sole commitment was to the God of Israel.

The continuation of the story in Judg 17 offers a paradigm for how the transition from kin-staffed, family-based shrines to professionally staffed sanctuaries was made, and even an etiology for the association of Levites with the professional priesthood. The story in Judg 17 continues by observing that Jonathan "came to the house of Micah in the hill country of Ephraim to carry on his work" (17:8*b*). Seeing this, Micah invited Jonathan to stay and become his priest-for-pay, apparently because he saw in such an arrangement greater chances of obtaining God's favor than having his son continue as his priest (17:9, 13). Jonathan accepted the offer and Micah "installed the Levite" as he had done earlier with his son, by "filling his hand" (17:10-12).

The story in Judg 18 adds more to the paradigm by offering some evidence for why the shift toward a professional clergy came about. The text reports that the tribe of Dan, seeking to establish a home territory (or perhaps to expand on what they may already have had), sent scouts to Micah's household. During their visit there they asked Jonathan to inquire of the Lord whether they would have success in their mission (without revealing to him what it was). After what must have been an act of divination, his answer was that they would indeed succeed (18:1-6). When their mission brought them back to Micah's house, the Danites invited the Levite to become "priest and father" to them as a tribe, not merely to one man, an offer he did not refuse (18:14-20). From there he accompanied them on their expansionist quest, serving as their priest (much as Abiathar served as David's priest in his wanderings; 1 Sam 23:6-14), and when they finally conquered and settled a homeland and city he and his descendants served the tribe as priests (18:21-31). The story reveals the need more specialized, complex societies had for professional religious leadership. Unlike Micah, the Danites were not merely in the business of running a single household, but of expanding their territory and increasing their numbers by acts of conquest. Not only did this change force increasing specialization, it also demanded the presence of a professional priest who could be counted on to serve the whole tribe in his sacerdotal duties, not just one family.

It should probably be assumed that the shifting social dynamics just described produced many localized, group-affiliated priestly lines like the one established by the Danites, perhaps as many as there were locales that served as the cultic and political centers for distinct population groups (e.g., Dan, Shiloh, Shechem, Gibeon, Gibeah, Gilgal, Bethel, Jerusalem, etc.). That we do not hear about all of them in full detail, but only from hints left behind in much later texts, does not mean that they never existed; rather it indicates that by the time our sources came into existence this model of the priesthood had given way to later forms of the office.

What does this evidence suggest were the duties of the priest in the period before the monarchy and the establishment of the Temple? Although the evidence is negligible, already the three basic tasks priests performed across the ancient world are in evidence: the remains of altars in locus 2081 at Megiddo (and other sites from the same period and earlier) and the reference in Deut 33:10*b* indicate sacrifice. Deuteronomy 33:8, "Give to Levi your Thummim, and your Urim to your loyal one," and Judg 18:5-6 indicate that priests performed divination. And Deut 33:10*a* speaks in favor of teaching as yet another priestly duty. We may add that priests probably played central roles in what were likely the earliest, agriculture-based festivals celebrated by the people in the land of Cannan, the Feast of Unleavened Bread (Exod 23:15; 34:18-20), the Feast of Weeks (Exod 34:22), and the Feast of Booths (Deut 16:13).

As for when in the premonarchic period "Levites" came to be priests in the fashion just outlined, there is little certainty and even less consensus, and little more should be expected given the nature of the evidence. It is possible that these developments were quite early, in the centuries before the people emerged as definite tribal groups in Canaan, at least inasmuch as the employment of Levites as priests like the one in Judg 17–18 might have been one of the glues that began to bind disparate groups together to form "tribes" in the land. But this can only be speculation.

2. The monarchy

Sacral kingship came with monarchy in the ANE. Sacral kingship is the idea that kings were somehow divinely sanctioned, either by incarnating the deity, by being the son of the deity by birth or adoption, or by representing the divine on earth. Israel was no different in this regard, at least inasmuch as Davidic kings claimed divine election to dynastic succession (see 2 Sam 7). This special relationship made the Davidic king a de facto mediator between God and people: thus the king presided over sacrifices (2 Sam 6:12-13, 17; 1 Kgs 8:62-63), blessed the people (2 Sam 6:18; 1 Kgs 8:54-55), prayed before and for the people (1 Kgs 8), and even may have played the role of the religious ecstatic (2 Sam 6:14-15).

That kings possessed these powers would seem to have obviated priests for Israel, but the historical record indicates that it did not. To be sure, kingship was sacral in the ways just described, but the prior predilection for priests as mediators between God and people persisted and kings seem to have embraced priests as their partners in leadership of the community. Thus we learn that SAMUEL played the role of priest to Saul (e.g., 1 Sam 13), and David was accompanied in his exile from Saul's court by ABIATHAR, the only survivor of Saul's slaughter of the priests at Nob (1 Sam 22:20-23), who served him as a priest in his days as a rebel and later when he became king (1 Sam 23:6-14; 2 Sam 20:25). Both men were ritual specialists who mediated between their masters and God by making sacrifice and seeking oracles, and both conformed nicely to the paradigm for the "Levite-Priest" teased out from Deut 33:8-11 and Judg 17–18 (§D1) inasmuch as they were "free agents" (itinerants?) who joined themselves to their royal masters. Notably, any claim they might have to being "Levites" arises more readily from this fact than from their lineage. Indeed, the matter of their lineage as figures who acted as priests was only the subject of concern for later authors who wanted to secure for both some link to Levi (on the reasons for this, see §D4). According to 1 Sam 1, Samuel is an Ephraimite, but the Chronicler corrects that "mistake" in his genealogical record (1 Chr 6:33). Likewise, Abiathar is said to be an Elide (1 Sam 22:20-23; compare 1 Sam 14:3), and only with the help of 1 Chr 24:3, 6 is he given a certain Levitical lineage through the connection of Eli with Ithamar (and thus Aaron, and finally, Levi). As we shall see (§D4), there is plenty of reason to be suspicious of the "clarifying" genealogies of the Chronicler.

In any case, the affiliations of Samuel and Abiathar with Saul and David signal a significant turning point in the history of the priesthood. While they do point back to the early professionalized priesthoods that arose from the settled employment of itinerant Levites, and that surely sprang up widely among the tribes of Israel, Samuel and Abiathar also mark the beginning of the journey toward a single, "nationalized" priesthood that served by the permission and at the command of the king. Institutionalization of this special relationship between kings and their priests came when David appointed two men to serve him as priests, Abiathar and Zadok (2 Sam 20:25). It is important to note, however, that David's move did not necessarily bring to an end the activities of other priesthoods serving other tribes and groups. They surely persisted at least until Josiah's reform. Turning to David's priests and the question of why he appointed two men to the office, the lineage-based explanation offered by Cross (see §C2 above) seems unnecessary at least with respect to Abiathar, whose service to David was likely to have been the result of the hiring of the sort of "Levite" we encounter in Judg 17–18. He served David not because he came from a certain gene pool, but because his employer's needs for a priest and his social positioning as an itinerant "Levite" matched up so well.

Is there an equally non-lineage-based, functionalist explanation for David's selection of Zadok? The Jebusite hypothesis, thought to have been discredited by Cross' theory, offers just such an explanation. The hypothesis posited that Zadok had no lineage among the people of Israel because he was a priest of the existing cult in Jebus (the pre-Israelite name for Jerusalem) and that David's appointment of him alongside Abiathar was simply a means of integrating Jerusalem's existing population and cult into the people and religion that he and Abiathar brought to the city and the surrounding region. Thus, like Abiathar, Zadok was chosen not because of his bloodline, but because of his social position and the advantage he could bring to David. On this reading, then, the priesthood's partnership with the monarchy was not at all determined by lineage but by the actors' social functions and political needs.

However we explain David's double appointment of Abiathar and Zadok, Solomon undid the double appointment when he deposed Abiathar for siding with Adonijah in the struggle to succeed David and made Zadokites, regardless their origin, the sole providers of altar priests in Jerusalem (1 Kgs 2:26-27; 4:2). This turn of events is best explained if we accept the functional-political explanation for David's selection of Abiathar and Zadok in the first place. The former represented the pre-monarchic, tribal religion of the Yahweh believers, and the latter the urban, Canaanite religion of the Levant. Supporters for Adonijah and Solomon fell along the same lines, and Solomon's succession assured the victory of the urban, Canaanite traditions (as he was, after all, the son of a woman of Jerusalemite-Canaanite origins, Bathsheba; 2 Sam 11:3; 15:12; 23:34). Evidence for this view is the diminished interest in the liberation traditions of pre-monarchic Israelite religion on the part of the temple cult under Solomon and his successors, as well as the curious discovery of a serpent of Nehushtan in the Temple during Hezekiah's reform, cited as a relic of the Jebusite cult (2 Kgs 18:4).

The following history of the Zadokites as the line that supplied Israel's high priests is vastly underreported in 1 and 2 Kings, and the highly schematized genealogy in 1 Chr 6:3-15 (Heb. 5:29-41) of Zadok's twelve ancestors and twelve descendants down to Joshua, the first high priest after the exile (Hag 1:1), does not offer much help. To be sure, we read about Jeroboam's appointment of non-Levite priests to preside over his Northern Kingdom sanctuaries (1 Kgs 12–13), and about the role Jehoidada, priest in Jerusalem, played in the success achieved by King Jehoash (2 Kgs 12:2 [Heb. 12:3]), but the usefulness of both accounts to write history is suspect since they serve the aims of the Deuteronomic tradition so well. Likewise, we get little useful information on the activities of the priests staffing provincial sanctuaries until we learn of their deposition by Josiah in the late 7th cent.

We do have indirect reports of the activities of the Zadokites and the priests staffing the country sanctuaries in the critiques offered by the preexilic prophets, particularly those of the 8th cent. BCE. There is little good news to be had from them. While the overarching theme of the prophetic critique is that the cultic observances of Israel and Judah are meaningless in the light of the social injustices and religious infidelities committed by worshipers (e.g., Amos 5), the prophets save some of their most severe wrath for the failure of the priests to fulfill their teaching duties. The prophets assert that the ostensible guarantors of the purity and efficacy of Israel's worship bear much of the responsibility for Israel and Judah's infidelities because they have failed to offer sound cultic oversight. Hosea, condemning the Northern Kingdom's cult, blames its errant ways on the priests who, distracted by dalliances with cultic prostitutes, have neglected their duties as teachers of God's law and allowed Israel to stray into Baal worship and ignorance of God's requirements regarding proper sacrifice (Hos 4:4-6, 14). In Mic 3 the prophet attacks the "rulers," priests, and prophets, but like Hosea he singles the priests out for a failure of instruction and oversight (3:11), going so far as to charge them with accepting bribes for desired rulings (perhaps regarding the sufficiency of an impure sacrificial offering. Isaiah rails against the drunkenness of the priests and prophets, observing that their lack of sobriety has left the people bereft of sound teaching and access to God's word; as a consequence the word of God will turn on the priests (28:7-13).

Neither the 8th-cent. prophets' condemnation, nor the example of Israel's destruction by Assyria, nor Hezekiah's reforms had any impact on the actions of the temple priests if we give credence to the complaints laid against them by Jeremiah and Zephaniah. Both prophets were active at the dawn of Josiah's reform. Like his 8th-cent. predecessors, Jeremiah excoriates the priests for their failure to teach appropriately (2:8; 5:31; 14:18; see 18:18), and he may even have referred to them with his famous indictment of the scribes whose pen turns the law into a lie (8:8-9). Also like his forerunners, he condemns the prophets along with the priests for seeking unjust gain from their service (6:13; 8:10) and their general wickedness (23:33; 32:32). For all of this they shall be punished severely (2:26; 4:9; 8:1; 13:13; 23:34; 34:19). Although but a single verse, Zeph 3:4 puts an exclamation point on the preexilic prophets' central indictment of the priests: they "have profaned what is sacred, they have done violence to the law." The stage was thus well set for the next, and surely one of the most important eras in the history of the priesthood, the period of Josiah's reform and the Deuteronomic movement it birthed.

3. From Josiah's reform to the exile

Josiah's reform marked a turning point in the history of the priesthood (2 Kgs 22–23). By demanding the centralization of Judean worship in Jerusalem for the sake of his political reform and military ambitions, Josiah forced the closure of the country sanctuaries staffed by local priestly conclaves. These priestly groups were affiliated with the sanctuary sites since their genesis, surely in many cases through the hiring of itinerant Levites. Josiah's reform forced these country priests into sudden, uninvited retirement. At the same time, his reform made the Jerusalemite priesthood, the descendants of Zadok, the single priesthood permitted without prior qualification or claim to serve at the single altar of the single national sanctuary. The resulting sacerdotal labor surplus and the inevitable unrest among clergy groups that Josiah's action engendered surely constituted an enormous problem for Judah and thrust the office of the priesthood onto the political and religious center stage for the first time. How did Israelite religion manage this certain crisis?

As we saw above (§C2), the classic answer to this question is that the Deuteronomic tradition invited all priests to the Jerusalem Temple and legitimated them for equal service there by designating all priests as descendants of Levi (Deut 18:6-8). However, due to the refusal of the Jerusalem priests to grant the country priests equal rights to serve at the altar (in support of which 2 Kgs 23:9 is cited), the Deuteronomic proposal failed, and the resulting two-tier priesthood required legitimation by the appeals to archaic practice found in Ezek 44:10-15 and the Priestly Work, and later in the Chronicler.

There are difficulties with this hypothesis. First, it fails to contend with the fact that Deuteronomy itself refers to Levites in bipartite fashion. Deuteronomy 18:6 invites the single sojourner "Levite who dwells in your gate" (see Deut 12:12, 18; NRSV, "Levites who reside in your towns") to serve alongside the "fellow-Levites" who already "stand to minister there before the LORD" (18:7; see 17:8-13; 21:5). Second, 2 Kgs 23:9 does not imply that the Jerusalem priests reneged on the invitation to the country priests in Deut 18:7 to serve at the Jerusalem altar, let alone give evidence of hostility between the two groups; it only says that the latter did not come to Jerusalem, and instead remained in the country living off the generosity of their neighbors. Third, it overlooks the fact that the priests in Jerusalem were actually Zadokites, descendants of the Jebusite Zadok, and in no way Levites by lineage (or function, for that matter).

What are we to make of these facts? Rainer Albertz offers the foundations for a surprisingly simple explanation, one that has the advantage of acknowledging that the biblical testimony we depend on to reconstruct the history of the priesthood is to be treated first as theological and ideological literature, and only second as accurate historical reportage. Albertz argues that we should not read Deuteronomy's view of priests and Levites as reflecting any historical reality, but rather as the reform movement's attempt to override the dissension among priestly groups that centralization inevitably engendered: the Deuteronomic tradition's declaration that all priests descended from Levi is a historical fiction introduced to conjure the basis for a contemporary, unitary priesthood. Building on this insight, we add that the Deuteronomists perhaps meant the term *Levite* to refer to lineage and function. That is to say, it was intended to appeal to priestly groups who recalled their origins in the practice of employing itinerant Levites (see Judg 17–18) and to those who sought to legitimate themselves through appeals to ancestry. With the inclusion of Moses' blessing for Levi in Deut 33:8-11, the Deuteronomic tradition reinforced this double-barreled approach to leviticizing the priesthood inasmuch as the benediction defines the descendants of Levi by lineage and by function and social status.

Albertz argues further that the Deuteronomic reformers were not unaware of the labor surplus problem Josiah's reform would create. To respond to it they built into their idealized portrait of the unitary priesthood's origins a means of differentiating among descendants of Levi. The phrase "Levite in your gates" refers to the sacerdotalists left unemployed by the closure of the provincial sanctuaries, and the moniker "Levitical priests" (author's trans.; NRSV, "the priests, the sons of Levi"), as well as the simple, unqualified term "priests" (Deut 18:3; 19:17; see 21:5; 31:9) designates the Zadokites of Jerusalem. We add that on this reading, rather than signaling the failure of Josiah's reform, 2 Kgs 23:9 expresses the ideal the Deuteronomic tradition hoped to achieve, that the vast number of underemployed priests created by Josiah's centralization efforts would be cared for as **gerim** (גֵּרִים), figures not unlike the "functionally Levitical" Levites of the tribal period, and a class whose welfare was addressed by the Deuteronomic social legislation decreed by God through Moses (Deut 10:18; 24:17-21; 27:19).

One hardly needs evidence to suspect that this utopian vision of the Deuteronomic tradition achieved little success, for its too generously optimistic view of human nature surely doomed it from the beginning. It assumed the acquiescence of country priests to the premeditated destruction of their livelihood and to a substantial reduction in their quality of life; it depended equally on the Zadokites in Jerusalem willingly relinquishing substantial shares of their income to hordes of visiting country priests; it presumed that laypeople would generously meet the needs of the country priests left unmet by their only occasional service in Jerusalem; and it decreed that those very laity should also forego the sacerdotal services their priests had offered them for centuries at the local sanctuaries.

It should come as no surprise, then, that we already get hints of the plan's failure in literature composed within years of its inception. In the closing chapters of the DtrH we hear that Josiah's successors, Jehoahaz, Jehoiachim, and Jehoiachin each "did what was evil in the sight of the LORD" (2 Kgs 23:32, 37; 24:9), Deuteronomic shorthand for kings who promoted worship of Yahweh and other gods apart from Jerusalem (see 1 Kgs 11:1-8). Ezekiel 8 makes clear that after the first deportation, the sanctuary's keepers willingly relinquished control over it to worshipers of various foreign gods. Ezekiel 22:26 condemns the priests for failing to teach effectively. Jeremiah 28 suggests the complicity of priests with Hananiah in painting a false picture of Judah's prospects, and Lam 4:13, 16 poignantly testify to the impact of priestly malfeasance and the laity's failure to live up to any obligation of care they may have had for the priests.

Quite apart from the success or failure of the Deuteronomic vision for a unitary priesthood before the exile, its significance in setting the stage for the postexilic developments cannot be overlooked. As we see below (§D4), the nature of Persian rule in the postexilic period required of Judeans the single, unitary priesthood that eluded Josiah and the Deuteronomic movement; without it, Judea's autonomy within the Persian Empire would have been in jeopardy. Thus by establishing the notion that priestly legitimacy depended on Levitical lineage, and rooting that notion in the authoritative, original experience of Israel under Moses' leadership in the wilderness, the Deuteronomic writers predetermined one of the fundamental elements necessary for a group to compete for and win the coveted role of providing Judea's priestly class. For the first time, a claim to be of a certain bloodline was essential to a larger claim to priestly status and privilege.

The Deuteronomic reform movement, most active during the exilic period, also promoted other aspects of the priesthood that would be influential on postexilic ideologies and theologies of the priesthood. While Deuteronomy assigns to priests and Levites the traditional role of mediating between worshipers and God at significant cultic moments (see, e.g., Deut 26:1-11), this is a minor emphasis in the Deuteronomic tradition's view of the responsibilities of priests and Levites. The greatest emphasis is on their responsibility to teach and interpret Torah. Along with the judges of Israel they are to render decisions on questions of legal interpretation (Deut 17:9; 19:17; see 21:5); those who disobey their teachings and judgments are condemned to death (Deut 17:12); they are the guarantors of the authenticity of the "copy of [the] law" written for the king (Deut 17:18); and they instruct soldiers before undertaking holy war (Deut 20:2). A further signal of the connection the Deuteronomic tradition draws between priests and Levites and the Torah is their role in bearing the ark of the covenant (Deut 31:9; see Josh 4; 6).

The Deuteronomic focus on priests as teachers of Torah is unsurprising when seen in light of the tradition's understanding of virtually every other office it conceives of in the life of Israel. Deuteronomy 16:18–18:22, the "law of officials," provides rules regarding judges and the administration of justice, kings and their rule, the rights and responsibilities of Levites, and the provision and authenticity of prophets. The single unifying element in the legislation for each of these officials is that they are to observe and promote the laws that provide for God's rule over the people. This is clearest in the law of the king in Deut 17:14-20: rather than behave as a typical ANE monarch, occupying himself with building his military might and making beneficial alliances, Israel's king is to have a "copy of this law" (i.e., Deuteronomy) close at hand to read and keep so that he leads the nation in observing God's law. According to the Deuteronomic legislation, priests are different from judges, kings, or prophets in their role as teachers only inasmuch as their social status in traditional ANE cultures allowed and/or required of them different functions.

4. The Persian period

When we come to the Persian period our sources for the history of the priests and Levites present us with a striking contradiction: from no other era in the history of Israel and early Judaism do we have so much literature engaged with the priesthood, yet this literature is so little concerned to report the contemporary history of the office as to leave us as reliant on speculation about the priesthood's development under Persian rule as we are for other eras. Of course, the new dimension we add to the story at this point is that of the intensified ideological and theological debates embodied in the different proposals for imagining the priesthood. Thus, our story from this point on is often of the two kinds described in the introduction to this article, historical and ideological.

Beginning with the postexilic period, there is yet another new dimension to the priesthood's story that was not present before the exile: under Persian rule the office of the high priest becomes central to early Judaism's identity and development. This is in large part because Persian imperial policy made the high priest's office not only a locus of religious authority but also of political power. As a result, it eventually drew many claimants and engendered more than a few tussles for power among those claimants. Our story of the priesthood shall include these episodes, at least inasmuch as our sources permit us to report them. Notably, though, these conflicts did not commence immediately upon Judea coming under Persian control.

Of the Persian period sources, Haggai and Zechariah 1–8 are the earliest, dating to around 520 BCE. Haggai identifies Joshua as the returnees' high priest and as a son of Jehozadak (*see* JOZADAK; Hag 1:1). On the face of it, the significance of mentioning Joshua's parentage would seem, at most, to be to establish his Zadokite credentials. One must resist reading any more into this on the basis of 1 Chr 6:14-15 [Heb. 5:40-41], which makes Jehozadak the last high priest before the exile and a descendant of Aaron; establishing postexilic priests' Zadokite-Aaronite-Levite lineage is a typical concern of the Chronicler, and the fact that Ezra 7:1-5 inserts Ezra into Jehozadak's place in the same genealogy effectively eliminates any suggestions that the genealogy reflects actual history. The absence of concern for Joshua's lineage otherwise in Haggai indicates the relative lack of interest in the earliest days of the Persian period to legitimate priests by lineage. Confirmation and clarification of the unimportance of lineage claims early on may come from Zech 3:1-10, which does seek to clarify and defend Joshua's right to the office of high priest, but on the basis of his purity, not his genealogy. Moreover, the intensity of concern evidenced in Zech 3 and 6 to establish Joshua's suitability for the office does not come as a result of lineage-based challenges from counter-claimants, but rather from general doubt about the viability of the office altogether. Further proof that the priestly office was yet to attain the desirability that engendered later lineage-based competition for its possession comes from Hag 1:2-11, an oracle that makes clear that the laity had yet to see to the reconstruction of the Temple as the locus of priestly activity nearly two decades after their restoration to the land under Cyrus of Persia.

Regardless of the diminished quality of status accorded to the priests, Haggai and Zech 1–8 provide clear evidence that the roles priests played in early postexilic Judea were typical of earlier norms and of the conduct found among priests across the ANE world. Joshua and his peers were teachers of Torah (Hag 2:10-19); they provided oracles (Zech 7:3); and it seems certain that they also performed sacrifice for the people (see Hag 2:10-19).

As for the theological view of the priesthood that Haggai and Zechariah promoted, it seems to have been driven by the low status accorded priests, and particularly Joshua, and even more by the prophets' desire to invest the high priest with greater political authority than he had enjoyed before the exile. Indeed, Persian imperial policy would require an adjustment in Judean attitudes toward the balance of power between a potential king from the line of David and his erstwhile partner in leading the preexilic state, the high priest. Persia granted its subject peoples autonomy so long as they allowed the priests of their chief religion to govern them, and more important, to collect taxes from visitors to the sanctuary for the Persian authorities. That autonomy was quickly extinguished by Persian occupation of the homeland if indigenous peoples showed any signs of raising a king to power. That Judeans ran the risk of Persia's ire is apparent from their failure even to rebuild the sanctuary for nearly twenty years after their return (Hag 1:1-2), and politically dangerous sentiments in favor of restoring the Davidic monarchy are clearly indicated (and appeased) by Hag 2:20-23. That their foot-dragging included a lack of respect for priestly authority is obvious from Satan's doubt about Joshua and the cleansing he had to undergo in the heavenly council to qualify for his office (Zech 3). The passage is to be read as a visionary's way of recounting the public's low regard for the high priest. Also telling is the complex vision in Zech 6:9-15 that authorizes

Joshua's investment with authority normally accorded to royalty, while Zerubbabel, the true heir to Davidic kingship, appears largely as a bystander. The overall portrait, then, is one of Haggai and Zechariah helping to authorize a shift in power over the Judean community from heirs to the Davidic throne to high priests presiding over the temple cult. Again, that genealogy does not seem to be in play for the prophets suggests the absence of such concerns as yet, and concomitantly the lack of any serious competition among parties for the office. That calm in sacerdotal power politics was not to last long.

What changed to transform the priesthood from an office held in low regard by laity and potential priests alike, to one sought after and honored? The inevitability of the Persian policy's continued hold over Judean life was surely one factor; the power to control and define early Judaism under such circumstances would always be held by the priesthood. But without the economic resources to back up and reward the exercise of such power, the value of Persian authorization remained a chimera. Thus, improved material conditions in postexilic Judea were the second ingredient leading to the priesthood's ascendancy and to new competition for its possession. Although archaeological evidence for the standard of living in early postexilic Judea is poor, what little survives suggests that conditions were quite difficult. Judeans coming from Babylon with Persian authorization to repopulate the land had to contend with the adverse land claims and social, religious, and cultural norms of former refugees who had settled there during the exile, and they discovered that the infrastructure for a temple economy was in complete disrepair. As a result the returnees faced considerable hurdles on the way to fulfilling the Persian imperial mandate to repopulate Judea and make it the home of a profitable temple economy. Indeed, Hag 1:6; 2:16 confirm that inflation and poor crop yields, strong indicators of a weak agrarian economy, were the norm rather than the exception. Likewise, the economically and politically motivated delays in constructing a new Temple out of which to oversee such an economy made seizing power over the priesthood less than attractive (see, e.g., Ezra 4; Hag 1:1-6). Archaeological evidence for the later Persian period indicates, though, that these difficult conditions gradually improved, and the literary record indicates that Persia backed the economic restoration with its own resources and authority (Ezra 1:1-2, 7-8; 3:7; 5:13-17; 6:3, 14). With those changing circumstances, possession of priestly office and power changed from being a burden to a boon, and the gold rush was on. (For the archaeology of the Persian period, see Stern.)

The truth is, though, that we have only limited evidence for the specific dynamics of the competition that almost certainly ensued. This is unsurprising. In antiquity it was no one's practice, such as it is today, to record journalistically the events of political power struggles as they occurred. Moreover, the cases priestly groups made for their superior claim to office over others were not the sort of propositional arguments competitors for power make in our day. Instead, claims were based on appeals to antiquity and to the authority of founding figures and the influence of accepted traditions; as such they usually took the form of narratives of the archaic age ideologically shaped to confirm the victors' election to power in hoary antiquity. Finally, because in the ancient world winners in competitions for power controlled the media for shaping new traditions, they systematically extinguished narratives that conflicted with their accounts of how they came to power. There were no "objective" historians about to ensure that the stories of the defeated could also be told.

For this reason our chief evidence for reconstructing the competition for the PERSIAN PERIOD priesthood and its outcome is a winners' account of a time long before their own, the Priestly Work. We are left to read from the Priestly Work a portrait of the priesthood in the Persian period, answers to the classic questions about the identity and fate of priestly groups who competed for ascendancy, and P's theology of the priesthood.

As to the Priestly Work's portrait of the priesthood as evidence for actual postexilic practice, the first thing to note is the bipartite nature of the office: Aaronites were ordained to service at the altar and granted the lion's share of the perquisites attached to such service, while the rest of the Levites were given to the Aaronites as assistants and received considerably more modest provisions for their efforts. Exodus 28–29 and Lev 8–9 report God's command to Moses to ordain his brother Aaron and his brother's sons to the altar priesthood, as well as Moses' fulfillment of that command. According to these passages, by divine decree Aaron and his sons were to provide the high priests and altar priests for Israel. The Priestly Work also lays out the duties and perquisites of the Aaronites. They are to oversee the cultic activities associated with the Temple and the holy of holies (Exod 27–30), and they are the only priests permitted to approach the altar with sacrificial offerings, including the burnt, cereal, peace, sin, and guilt offerings (Lev 1–7; *see* TEMPLE, JERUSALEM). They control the URIM AND THUMMIM by which God's will is determined and the priests signal their judicial authority (Exod 28:29-30; Lev 8:5-9; Num 27:21; see Deut 33:8). They bestow the "Aaronic" blessing on the people (Num 6:22-27). They are garbed with special vestments, "a BREASTPIECE, an EPHOD, a ROBE, a checkered TUNIC, a TURBAN, and a SASH" (Exod 28:4), that distinguish them from other priests. They provide the priest who enters the holy of holies on the DAY OF ATONEMENT every year (Lev 16). They participate in priestly ordinations including their own (Lev 8). They are to distinguish for the people between the CLEAN AND UNCLEAN, the pure and the impure (Lev 11–14; see esp. 11:1; 13:1-2; 14:33-57). And according to Lev 10:8-11, they are to be clean and sober when approaching God in the Temple, distinguish between holy and profane, and teach the Lord's laws to the people (*see* HOLY, HOLINESS, OT).

The perquisites the Aaronites receive for their efforts were not inconsiderable. They received to eat within the sanctuary the sin, guilt, and food offerings, and the dozen weekly offerings of showbread (Num 18:9-11; Lev 2:3; 24:9; *see* BREAD OF PRESENCE). They received to eat at home with their families the loin and the breast of the OFFERING OF WELL-BEING brought by the laity (Lev 7:28-36). They kept the skin of any animal offering brought to the Temple (Lev 7:8). They received the best of the oil, wine, and grain, the firstfruits, every devoted thing, the meat of offerings of firstborn cows, sheep, and goats, and a redemption price of five shekels for human firstborn and blemished animals (Num 18:12-19). The generous number of sacrificial occasions legislated by the Priestly Work ensured that there were many opportunities for the laity to benefit the Aaronites according to the foregoing rules (see. Num 28). As a consequence of these generous perquisites the Aaronites required no share in the land of Israel (Num 18:20).

The remaining descendants of Levi, the Levites descended from Gershon, Kohath, and Merari, were set apart for service to the Aaronites (Num 3–4; 8; 18:1-3). The rationale for this designation of an entire class of people was that the Levites took the place of the firstborn of Israel due to God as sacrificial offerings (see Exod 22:29; 34:19-20). The Priestly Writers emphasize the all-embracing nature of their service to the Aaronites (Num 3:9; see Exod 38:21; Num 4:28, 33; 7:8), so much so that it is hard to describe in detail from their legislation what the Levites' precise duties were. Granted, the census of the Levites belonging to the lines of Gershon, Kohath, and Merari describes their particular responsibilities with respect to the transportation and care of the tent of meeting (*see* TABERNACLE), the ARK OF THE COVENANT, the other sacred VESSELS, and other cultic accoutrements (Num 4). In general, though, it was left to the Chronicler to articulate in greater detail the tasks of the Levites in the service of the Temple and the Aaronite priests. It seemed enough for the Priestly Work to dictate that Levites were at the beck and call of the Aaronites. Notably, the Priestly writers also emphasized with very serious measures the limitations on the Levites as temple servants vis-à-vis the Aaronites: they were not to approach the UTENSILS of the sanctuary or the ALTAR itself, and were they to do so, they and the Aaronites who had charge over them would die (Num 18:3).

The perquisites granted the Levites reinforced their second-tier status vis-à-vis the Aaronites. While they were to receive a tithe from all of Israel for their support, they were also to make a TITHE of that tithe to the Aaronites as their offering to the Lord (Num 18:21-32). The Levites also received a small portion of the booty the Israelites won through conquest (Num 31:30), and later legislation provided the Levites with cities of refuge and pasture land for the livestock they received (Num 35:1-5).

That this arrangement privileging Aaronites over Levites did not come about without conflict is also apparent from the Priestly Work. The well-known stories of tension among priestly groups betray this fact. The stories are concentrated in Num 16–18; 25. Numbers 16 reports a rebellion led by Korah and other Levites of Kohathite descent against Aaron (*see* KORAH, KORAHITES). Moses agreed to adjudicate the dispute through a contest of censers between Korah and his followers and Aaron. The result was poor for the rebels. They were destroyed along with their families, and the metal of their CENSERs was fashioned into covering plates for the altar to warn non-Aaronites not to approach the altar with INCENSE, lest they suffer the Kohathites' fate. Numbers 17 reports that God then ordered a staff from each tribe to be placed overnight in the tent of the covenant. In the morning, the blossoming staff would signal which tribe should have priestly leadership, settling the matter once and for all. Since Aaron lacked a staff of his own, although he was of the tribe of Levi, Moses gave to him alone the tribe's staff, and in the morning it had not only blossomed, it had even put forth ripe almonds (*see* AARON'S STAFF). This was taken to prove that God had elected Aaron and his descendants to lead Israel in its sacral life. God's instructions in Num 18 resoundingly affirmed the ascendant position secured by the Aaronites. As noted already, the Levites were assigned to assist the Aaronites in their priestly duties; Israelites were mandated to provide tithes to support the Aaronites and Levites; and Levites were required in turn to tithe their income to the Aaronites. Numbers 25 underscored the Aaronites' election to the altar priesthood. The people's rebellious affiliation with the women of Moab, to which the Levite Moses made only a halfhearted response, was finally stemmed by the zeal of PHINEHAS, grandson of Aaron, who slew an apostate Israelite and his Midianite bride in their wedding tent (25:1-9). For his trouble God rewarded him with a "covenant of peace," "a covenant of perpetual priesthood" (25:12-13). With this the descendants of Aaron were confirmed beyond all doubt in their ascendancy among Levites.

As noted above (§C2), the history of scholarship on the priesthood has read the foregoing evidence for the Priestly position on the roles of the Aaronites and Levites as an invitation to speculate on the genealogical origins of the preexilic and postexilic priesthood. Such speculation is predicated on the assumption that the terms *Aaronite* and *Levite* have to do with lineage. Given the lineage language in the Priestly Work, that assumption is not unreasonable. Yet our discussion of the origin of Levitical claims for the priesthood in the Deuteronomic Collection above (§D3) indicates that at its beginning such rhetoric was only rhetoric, and that, certainly before the exile, the priesthood in fact was a mix of the descendants of "functional Levites," who had settled into local sanctuaries, and Zadokites, who had no grounds (or reason) for making claims on Levitical lineage. It is doubtful that through the course of the exile circumstances changed so radically that by the Persian period all priests had to be authentically descendants of Levi, and that somehow the division of labor and privilege among Levites had become so finely tuned as the Priestly writers make it out to be. So the question becomes different from that of traditional scholarship. Rather than attempting to show that the Priestly Work's postexilic distinctions were somehow rooted in preexilic genealogies, it is necessary to explain why the Priestly writers felt compelled to embrace the Deuteronomic fiction of the priesthood's Levitical lineage and to make it more complex with the introduction of distinctions among kinds of Levites.

The answer lies in appreciating the power the Deuteronomic perspective had taken on over the course of the exile and its concomitant capacity to legitimate a victorious priestly group's claim to the high priest's office and the altar priesthood. The evidence for the influence of the Deuteronomic worldview on exilic and postexilic imagination and rhetoric is ubiquitous, a sure sign of its influence, if not its outright dominance. There is little doubt among commentators that the Deuteronomic perspective reshaped the prophecy of Jeremiah for exilic and postexilic audiences. It influenced the prophets Haggai and Zechariah and those who recorded their words. Accepting an exilic-era date for the Yahwist Work, the Deuteronomic worldview seems to have provoked it as a competing explanation for the exile that all the same had to mimic the rhetoric of the Deuteronomic writers to gain an audience (Van Seters). Many reckon that some form of the book of Job was shaped at least in part as a response to the Deuteronomic worldview. Still other later works of varying genres and from different eras reflect attempts to wrestle with real-life contradictions of the Deuteronomic notion of divine retributive justice (e.g., Ecclesiastes, Daniel).

Inasmuch as the Deuteronomic worldview exercised so much influence on exilic and postexilic religious imagination, it should not be surprising that attempts to legitimate proposals for the Second Temple priesthood would have readily taken Deuteronomy's terms for priestly identity to heart. As a result, the utopian vision of a unitary Levitical priesthood articulated by the Deuteronomic writers became a reality, but hardly in the manner they had hoped. The Deuteronomic writers extended a narrative invitation to priests of diverse origins to unite under the banner of a single Levitical identity; the Priestly writers used that literary summons to unity and equality to legitimate division and inequality. The reason the Deuteronomic writers' vision failed was the same reason the Priestly writers felt compelled to put it to such contrary use: there were surely more claimants to service in the Temple than its needs could bear, a historical reality to which the conflict stories testify.

The reason that the victorious party did not assume the identity of the Zadokites, the providers of the preexilic altar priesthood, seems obvious: Zadok did not appear in Israel's storyline until David's reign in Jerusalem and had no claim to be a Levite, and as such he was useless to establishing a claim to the office through an account of its origin in the Mosaic period. That Aaron filled that role instead also seems obvious: he was present in the Mosaic period and his Levitical ancestry was established in the Yahwist tradition's account of the call of Moses (Exod 4:14).

To sum up the Priestly Work's evidence for the priesthood as it was practiced in the Persian period: after competition among various claimant groups to the office and the victory of one group and the relegation of others to secondary status in the Temple's service, it was necessary to compose a narrative that legitimated this new state of affairs. Composed by the winners, this narrative assured recipients that from the days of Moses one branch of the Levitical line, the Aaronites, had been chosen to serve at the altar and supply Israel's high priests, and it confirmed that the remaining descendants of Levi were to serve as assistants to the Aaronites. It was the responsibility of both groups to maintain and operate the sanctuary where God and people could meet through cultic activity overseen by the priests. The Aaronites had the high privilege of approaching the altar with sacrifices, while the Levites were to perform the many tasks necessary to prepare for and clean up after the Aaronites' act of making sacrifice to God. The perquisites the laity provided to the priests for their maintenance were similarly unbalanced, with the Aaronites receiving the better and larger portion. Characterized in this way, the Priestly Work was likely intended to legitimate the end result of an extended struggle among claimants to the priestly office to determine its shape under Persian rule. It did so by assigning Aaronite identity to the competitor group that emerged victorious. It also granted members of the defeated priestly conclaves the opportunity to serve in the Temple as assistants to the newly minted Aaronites and it legitimated them in their role by assigning them Levite identity.

It is important to take note of the larger theology of the priesthood proposed by the Priestly Work as an antidote to dismissing it as nothing more than the self-justifying rhetoric of a winning faction. As indicated above (§C2), early Persian-period Judea was characterized by considerable political, economic, social, and cultural instability, and the infrastructure that supported improved conditions on all these fronts was lacking. Without strong leadership and a roadmap for constituting a new Judea—Judaism itself—the returnees could not count on a future for their community. The Priestly Work embodied a massive response to this looming crisis. In demonstrating the power of the God of Israel over cosmic chaos, it signaled God's capacity to bring order to the physical disorder of postexilic Judea (Gen 1:1–2:4*a*). It grounded in the era of Israel's idyllic wilderness dependence on God alone orderly patterns for the Temple and its practices that could replace the cultic chaos the returnees faced (Exod 25–31; 35–40; Lev 1–7). It addressed communal, social chaos with its symbolic proposal for ordered relations in the purity rules of Lev 11–15. It provided for the maintenance of Jewish identity apart from the Temple and its cult by requiring Jews to observe the SABBATH (Exod 31:14-16), CIRCUMCISION (Gen 17), and Passover (Exod 12; *see* PASSOVER AND FEAST OF UNLEAVENED BREAD) and by sending the high priest annually into the HOLY OF HOLIES to ensure the forgiveness of all believers' sins, regardless their access to the sacrificial cult in Jerusalem (Lev 16). With its legitimation of Levites and Aaronites as Israel's priests, it ensured that there would be leaders empowered to oversee and implement these provisions.

The Priestly writers' vision for postexilic Judea and its governance by the new Aaronites did not go uncontested. Objections came from several quarters, and some fragments of those dissenting perspectives survive in the OT. In what is perhaps a very late addition to the story of Israel's apostasy in the wilderness before the golden calf, Exod 32:25-29 provides a disturbingly violent account of the Levites' ordination-winning slaughter of the apostates and Aaron's role in leading the people astray. That the passage reflects the sentiments of dissenters from the Priestly formula for postexilic sacerdotal leadership seems obvious; less certain is that the dissent counseled by the episode should have included violence, but the implication is nonetheless apparent.

Accepting a late postexilic date for some portions of Ezek 40–48—a section of the book increasingly understood to have been composed over time by heirs to the historical prophet's vision—Ezek 44:10-16 is best understood as another of the faintly heard dissenting voices (and not the traditional consensus' first postexilic contribution to the debates about priestly identity; see above §C2). Presuming the terms set out by the Priestly Work, the passage explained the Levites' second-class status as punishment for cultic infidelities, but it turned the tables on the Priestly proposal by assigning the altar priesthood exclusively to the Zadokites who did remain faithful (Ezek 44:15). Clearly, this contradiction of Aaronite ascendancy was not without precedent; the DtrH told the story of David's and Solomon's validation of Zadok as the priest of the Jerusalem cult. Relying on that precedent, Ezek 44:10-16 clearly counted Aaronites among the Levites and argued for the ascendancy of its own priestly group.

Malachi and Isaiah dissent in broad terms from the Priestly exaltation of priests, decrying all priests' cultic and moral corruption (Isa 56:10-11; Mal 1:6-13), promising their rejection (Isa 56:9; Mal 2:1-3), and prophesying their replacement with new priestly orders. Demonstrating a certain respect for the Deuteronomic tradition, Malachi announces the corrupt priests' replacement with pure priests from Levi, the original priest and Torah teacher (Mal 2:4-7; 3:1-4; the rhetoric of Mal 3:1-4 echoes Num 25:6-13, showing that it knows the Priestly Work). Third Isaiah takes a more radical stance and promises that Judea's oppressed will become priests and even that Diaspora Jews will return to the land to be made priests and Levites by God (Isa 61:6; 66:21).

The most complete repudiation of the Priestly worldview appears in the Holiness Code, Lev 17–26 (*see* H, HOLINESS CODE). Although it is typically explained as a source cheerfully embraced by the Priestly writers, its outright contradiction of the Priestly limitation of holiness to the priests and to the innermost spaces of the Temple in its decree that sanctity extends even to the laity (Lev 19:1-2) suggests a contrary scenario. Even more suggestive of the Holiness Code's hostility to the Priestly worldview are the extraordinary limitations it implicitly places on priestly perquisites and the demands it makes on priestly purity. Leviticus 17:3-4 unequivocally converts all profane slaughter into sacrifice, decreeing that "anyone of the house of Israel [who] slaughters an ox or a lamb or a goat in the camp, or slaughters it outside the camp, and does not bring it to the entrance of the tent of meeting, to present it as an offering to the LORD before the tabernacle of the LORD, he shall be held guilty of bloodshed; he has shed blood, and he shall be cut off from the people." Somewhat disingenuously, Lev 17:5 says this statute is required to constrain Israelites from making sacrifices apart from the Temple. Its practical effect, however, would have been to encourage laity to declare most, if not all acts of sacrifice merely to be the necessary accompaniments to what would have otherwise been a profane slaughter; on that basis, the priests' perquisites would conceivably have been carried away by the laypersons who brought the sacrifices instead of remaining in the Temple to nourish the priests and their families. That this is not merely a fanciful reading of the legislation in Lev 17 is suggested by the powerful restrictions the code imposes on priests and the performance of their duties. Seen usually as little more than legislation intended to ensure the purity of priests, Lev 21:1–22:9 actually would have constrained priests from many of their duties; the most minor physical blemishes disqualify a man from priestly service, and priests in good standing who are defiled in the smallest way for any reason may not approach the altar or the sacred donations that are his sustenance. Altogether, the Holiness Code comes across like a utopian legislative parallel to the prophetic critique of the priestly corruption found in Third Isaiah and Malachi. Perhaps it is not surprising that lexical affiliation between the book of Ezekiel and the Holiness Code are particularly close.

The Priestly worldview was not without its supporters, too. Chronicles and Ezra–Nehemiah, to be read as a unified work, perpetuate and extend the Priestly tradition's division of the priesthood in "priests and Levites" and of assigning to the Aaronites the lead in serving at the Temple (1 Chr 6). As in the Priestly Work, the priests descend from Aaron (6:49), and Aaron is himself a Levite (6:3). Also, as in the Priestly Work, the Levites are temple servants, but one of the Chronicler's great innovations is to further define the roles of the Levites: they are given various and sundry assignments as singers, musicians, gatekeepers, treasurers, judges, and scribes, and "the descendants of Solomon's servants" (1 Chr 16; 24–27; Ezra 2:41-43, 55). Ezra 8:15 reports that Levites were reluctant at first to return from Babylon. While some take this as a signal that the division of labor in the Second Temple between Aaronites and Levites had already been determined before the return—arguing for a much earlier date for the Priestly Work than is assumed here—it is perhaps easier to understand this as an archaizing acknowledgment of the tensions between Levites and Aaronites. Perhaps by the time the Chronicler completed his work, the sort of angry dissent evident in Exod 32:25-29 had cooled to the diffidence communicated by the Levites in this episode.

The Chronicler's other important transformation of the Priestly Work's perspective on the priesthood was his firm leviticization of the Zadokites and other figures who perform priestly functions in Samuel–Kings. He provides Zadok with an unquestionably Levite lineage, but also in the line of Aaron (1 Chr 6:3-8 [Heb. 5:29-34]; 6:50-53 [Heb. 6:35-38]). Assuming that Ezek 44:10-16 has the meaning proposed above, the Chronicler might have been engaged here in an effort to muzzle any further dissent like that found there, proving that Zadokites were in fact Aaronides. He also gives Abiathar a place in the line of Leviticus (1 Chr 24:3, 6) and even extends the courtesy to Samuel (1 Chr 6:33).

As for the Chronicler's theological and ideological contribution to the history of the priesthood, while the Priestly Work legitimated the Mosaic, Torah-based origins of the postexilic office, the Chronicler's revision of the DtrH ensured its possession of a Davidic-royal imprimatur as well, even in the absence of kingship. The Chronicler devotes the lion's share of his writing to the reigns of David and Solomon, the two kingships that ruled over a united Israel. Much of the interest in the coverage of both kings is devoted to their efforts to arrange for and construct an independent Temple, set out its cultic practices, and establish its servants, the priests and Levites. According to the Chronicler, by the time the two kings finished their work, an independent priesthood commissioned by the Davidic line existed. (Moreover, the Chronicler tied up loose ends left by the DtrH, providing all of the priestly actors in the narrative Levitical credentials.) The consequence for the postexilic priesthood of this sort of revisionist history is obvious. The Chronicler's account responded to those who may still have doubted the efficacy of the temple cult and its leaders even after the Priestly Work provided it with Mosaic-era, Torah-based legitimation. Those objections probably depended specifically on the absence of the Temple and priests' preexilic partners and corollaries, court and king, as reason for their reservations (see Hag 2:20-23; Zech 3; 6:9-15). By locating a second foundation for the temple priesthood's legitimacy in the acts of the two kings of the United Monarchy, the Chronicler answered those doubts.

A look at the priesthood during the Persian period is not complete without acknowledging the intensified interest toward the end of the era in the high priesthood. It is not a surprising development. The cooling of factional disputes, the validation of a single priestly conclave as Israel's religious leaders, and the Persian policy of giving religious leaders secular authority encouraged the emergence of strong high priests. It also made high priests the focal point for kudos and complaints about early Judaism's religious and political direction under Persian rule. Evidence of this new concern with the high priesthood comes already in the much-debated list of only six high priests during the larger part of the Persian period in Neh 12:10-11. The number seems to many to be too formulaic to be trustworthy, but one recent commentator has made a strong argument that it is nonetheless plausible (VanderKam). Whatever its accuracy, the mere existence of the list in Nehemiah is a first sign of the intensified interest in the high priest's office and its holders.

Another indication that the politics of the high priestly office stirred passions is Nehemiah's report that he banished an unnamed priest (Neh 13:28). According to Josephus, this expelled priest was named Manasseh. Josephus offers a historically plausible explanation of Nehemiah's action and gives insight into the origin of the sanctuary at Gerizim in the bargain (*Ant.* 11.302–12; see Cross). Manasseh, the brother of Jaddua the high priest, had married Nikaso, daughter of Sanballat, the Persian-appointed governor of Samaria. Manasseh was pressured to forego his foreign marriage, presumably in part to void the possibility that he might follow Jaddua as high priest in the event of Jaddua's death. To preserve the marriage alliance, Sanballat offered Manasseh a sanctuary at Gerizim and his own high priesthood.

Before concluding our survey of the priesthood in the Hellenistic, Hasmonean, and early Roman periods, it is worth describing what priests actually did from the late Persian era to the end of the priesthood with the fall of the Second Temple. In addition to the duties the Priestly Work ascribed to priests and Levites, there were still other tasks for them to perform. If we are to believe the Chronicler, they served weekly rotations in twenty-four courses (1 Chr 24:4; *Ant.* 7.365). This suggests that, apart from the festivals, no more than thirty priests would have been sacrificing in the Temple daily. Of course, a large number of temple assistants, Levites, would have also been busy with their duties. Priests also offered rulings in matters of purity, offered prayers for worshipers, taught and interpreted Torah, and provided scribal and judicial services (Josephus, *Ag. Ap.* 2.187). Although it is not certain, some of these activities probably were undertaken to augment income received in the Temple. Of course, under virtually every imperial power the priests served as the tax collectors for their patrons and overlords.

5. The Hellenistic period

The sources reporting details of the priesthood from the period from Alexander the Great to the HASMONEANS are few, but they are vigorous in representing the history of the high priesthood from ONIAS I (ca. 320–290 BCE) to ALCIMUS (161–159 BCE). Some of these reports are of doubtful authenticity. For example, Hecateus of Abdera, quoted by Josephus, identifies a high priest in Alexander's day as "Hezekiah" but observes, probably accurately, that priests then exercised civic and ritual authority (*Ag. Ap.* 1.187–88). Josephus presents a legendary account of Alexander sparing Jerusalem because of an earlier vision (*Ant.* 11.325–36; see *b. Yoma* 69a). Yet some sources do offer plausible information. First Maccabees records a letter from Arius I of Sparta to Onias I expressing the Lacedemonians' affiliation with the Jews (1 Macc 12:7, 19-23; see *Ant.* 12.225–27). Josephus abbreviates Aristeas' account of the exchange between Ptolemy II Philadelphus and Eleazar (Simon I's successor) that led to the production of the LXX (*Ant.* 12.44–56). Although he likely oversimplifies Onias II's resistance to paying annual dues to Ptolemy III as a matter of greed—it was more likely a gesture of alliance with the Seleucids in the Third Syrian War—Josephus shows that Onias' tax-dodging facilitated the appointment of the Tobiad Joseph (Onias' nephew by marriage; *see* TOBIAS) as the Ptolemies' tax farmer and that he competed with the Oniads for control of the region (*Ant.* 12.157–85). Josephus identifies Onias' successor, SIMON the Just, and ascribes to him participation in the armed opposition to Hyrcanus (Joseph's son), which drove Hyrcanus to establish the Tobiads' desert retreat and consolidate Tobiad power (*Ant.* 12.228–29).

Sirach 50:1-21 adds to our knowledge of Simon and of the high priest's power, praising him not only for his priestly service (vv. 5-21) but also for his efforts to strengthen the Temple, build a reservoir, and fortify the city's walls (vv. 1-4). Second Maccabees 3:1 describes Simon's successor, Onias III, as a pious man and a worthy but unsuccessful opponent of the Hellenizers. Second Maccabees 3 reports that his first opponent, the extremist Hellenizer Simon, brother of MENELAUS and an ally of the Tobiads, sought twice to overthrow him. JASON, Onias' Hellenizing brother, succeeded in buying the office from Antiochus IV Epiphanes, and Menelaus (Simon's brother) outbid Jason in turn for the office. Onias publicly accused Menelaus of pilfering temple vessels for his own enrichment, so Menelaus had him assassinated (2 Macc 4). Both 1 and 2 Maccabees as well as Josephus report that the Seleucids assigned Alcimus to the high priesthood after Mene-laus (1 Macc 7:5, 14; 2 Macc 14:3; *Ant.* 12.387–413; 20.235–37). They also note that he held the office for two years through his alliances with Hellenizing forces, including the Seleucids. Onias II's son, Onias IV, fled to Egypt and is said by Josephus to have established a temple at Leontopolis (*Ant.* 13.62–73; see *J.W.* 1.33; 7.423).

Reaction to the priesthood's long-standing corruption, which intensified under Jason, Menelaus, and Alcimus, prompted responses in the ARAMAIC LEVI DOCUMENT; *Jub.* 30; 32; and *1 En.* 12–16. The *Aramaic Levi Document* imagines an ideal priesthood by reconstructing its origins through a sanitized expansion of the biblical portrait of Levi (Gen 34; 49:5-7). Dating to the 3rd cent. BCE, the *Aramaic Levi Document* retells Gen 34 to prove Levi's zeal for the purity of God's people. It narrates Levi's elevation to the priesthood in the heavens and on earth, Isaac's sacerdotal instructions to him, and his exemplary life. It also attributes to him a wisdom hymn celebrating his excellence as a teacher and judge. The *Aramaic Levi Document* may not have been intended as a polemical work, but its antiquarianism certainly argued that a "pure priesthood" could be found in Levi's story retold. The same may be said of *Jub.* 30 and 32, which closely resemble the *Aramaic Levi Document.* Written in the mid-2nd cent. BCE as a traditionalist counterbalance to the policies of the Hasmoneans, *Jubilees* also idealizes the origins of the priesthood by reworking Levi's story. Notably, both the *Aramaic Levi Document* and *Jubilees* signal how deeply ingrained the tradition of requiring Levitical lineage in Israel's priests had become. *First Enoch* 12–16, a 3rd-cent. BCE text that implicitly equates the sinful Watchers with errant priests, was surely written with a polemical aim (*1 En.* 15:3-4; see *Pss. Sol.* 8:13; CD V, 6–7; Nickelsburg).

6. The Hasmonean period

Many suppose that after Alcimus' death in 159 BCE there was a seven-year period without a high priest, but the evidence is not conclusive. Josephus reports that Judas Maccabee took the office at Alcimus' death (*Ant.* 12.414), and many speculate that the TEACHER OF RIGHTEOUSNESS at QUMRAN could have been the high priest in this period (VanderKam). At the same time, 1 Macc 10:15-21 seems to indicate that the office was vacant after Alcimus died and until Jonathan assumed it.

Whatever the truth about this seven-year period, the high priesthood resumed with Jonathan as its first undisputed Hasmonean possessor (152–142 BCE). He was able to secure his position thanks to the competition between Demetrius and Alexander, rival claimants to the Seleucid throne (1 Macc 10:15-21; *Ant.* 13.44–46). Simon followed his brother JONATHAN (142–135 BCE; 1 Macc 14:35–16:22; *Ant.* 13.213–29) and won Hasmonean autonomy from the Seleucids. He firmly combined royal, military, and sacerdotal powers in a single person. His son, John HYRCANUS, succeeded him (135–104 BCE; 1 Macc 16:23-24; *Ant.* 13.230–99), making both secular rule and the high priesthood hereditary and strengthening the Hasmonean double claim to royal and sacerdotal power (*Ant.* 13.230). Also noteworthy is Hyrcanus' encounter with the Pharisees. The Pharisee Eleazar suggested that Hyrcanus' pontificate was illegitimate because his mother had been a captive among the Seleucids and could have been defiled there, making Hyrcanus an offspring of a polluted woman (*Ant.* 13.288–92). Legendary or not, this episode reflects the natural tension between the Hasmoneans and pious Jews over the Hasmoneans' stewardship of the high priestly office, yet it is not a claim against the legitimacy of their priestly lineage (Schofield and VanderKam).

After Aristobulus (104–103 BCE; *Ant.* 13:301–18), Alexander Jannaeus strove to survive among the competing Seleucids and Romans (103–76 BCE; *Ant.* 13.320–407), badly undermining the purity of the priesthood and the nation along the way (e.g., *Ant.* 13.372, 380). On his deathbed he chose his wife, Alexandra, as his successor (76–67 BCE; *Ant.* 13.405–32); she in turn appointed as high priest her son Hyrcanus II over his brother ARISTOBULUS II (76–63 BCE; *Ant.* 13.408). The feud between the two drew Rome into Palestinian affairs and brought an end to independent Hasmonean rule (*Ant.* 14.95–96). After that, the office of the high priesthood was little more than a concession traded among parties at the whim of the Romans and their proxies.

The Dead Sea Scrolls join other sources in voicing dissatisfaction with the temple priesthood during this period. *Pesher Habakkuk* and *Psalms Pesher*[a] refer to a "Wicked Priest" widely believed to be one of the Hasmoneans (*see* PRIEST, WICKED). Not surprisingly, many texts idealize Levi and his descendants as the true priests Levi: 4Q225 2 II, 11–12; 4Q379 1 5; 5Q11 1 I, 2; 4Q175 14–20; *Aramaic Levi*; Levites: 11Q19 XXI, 1; XXII, 9–12; XLIV, 5, 14; LVII, 13; LX, 6–7, 12, 14; LXI, 8; 1QM XIII, 1; XVIII, 5–6; 4Q491 1–3 9; 4Q493 9–10; CD XIII, 3; 1QS I, 18–19; II, 11). The Dead Sea Scrolls group conceived itself as having the atoning function and holy status of priests (1QS V, 1–7; VIII, 5–6, 8–9; IX, 6; CD III, 18–IV, 4; 4Q174 I, 3–4) and as being subject to priestly purity and age rules (1QS V, 13; VI, 16–17; 1Q28a I, 8–17; II, 3–10; CD X, 6–8; XV, 15–17). Community members even identified themselves as Ezekiel's Zadokites and the Priestly Work's Aaronites (1QS V, 2, 9; IX, 14 [?]; 1Q28a I, 2, 24; II, 3). (In light of the Chronicler's merger of Zadokite and Aaronite lines under the lineage of Levi, the community's blurring of any distinction between Aaronites and Zadokites is unremarkable [see 1QS V, 2, 9; IX, 7].) Altogether, it seems fair to say that the community constructed its life as a polemic against an impure priesthood. That the polemic was directed at the priesthood in general more than it was at the high priest in particular is an interesting development in light of the importance attached to the office since the beginning of the Persian period. Perhaps we should not read too much into this, but it does suggest that with the corruption of the high priesthood in the hands of the "Hellenizers" and the Hasmoneans came also its decreasing relevance in the life of early Judaism.

7. The early Roman period to the fall of the Temple

From 63 BCE to 70 CE, the Temple priesthood was subject to the whims of Roman rule expressed by procurators and HERODIANS. The power the office enjoyed under the Persians, Greeks, and Hasmoneans was virtually absent. Indeed, a dizzying succession of no fewer than thirty high priests occupied the office during these years, and few of them received appointment for any other reason than their political value to the competing powers in the Levant.

Literary reflections on the priesthood are fewer for this period, perhaps in part because of the declining influence of the Temple and sacrifice at a time when alternative forms and forums for religious expression, such as the synagogue, blossomed in early Judaism. To be sure, some of the Dead Sea Scrolls referenced above were composed in this era, testifying at least to the Qumran group's enduring concern for the office as it was manifest in the Jerusalem Temple. But even this evidence should be considered in its proper context: the group had arrogated to itself and its patterns of worship in the desert any claims to embody a pure priesthood (Kugler), a move that reflected their view that the temple priesthood was corrupt beyond saving and could be replaced by worship apart from Jerusalem and devoid of animal sacrifice. With the Roman destruction of the Second Temple, any debate the Qumran proposal might have engendered was made moot: the temple priesthood was at an end.

Bibliography: R. Albertz. *A History of Israelite Religion in the Old Testament Period* (1992); J. Blenkinsopp. *Sage, Priest, Prophet: Religion and Intellectual Leadership in Ancient Israel* (1995); A. Cody. *A History of Old Testament Priesthood* (1969); F. M. Cross. "Aspects of Samaritan and Jewish History in Late Persian and Hellenistic Times." *HTR* 59 (1966) 201–11; F. M. Cross. "The Priestly Houses of Early Israel." *Canaanite Myth and Hebrew Epic* (1973) 195–215; A. H. J. Gunneweg. *Leviten und Priester* (1965); A. Hunt. *Missing Priests: The Zadokites in Tradition and History* (2006); R. A. Kugler. "Holiness, Purity, the Body, and Society: The Evidence for Theological Conflict in Leviticus." *JSOT* 76 (1997) 1–27; R. A. Kugler. "The

Priesthood at Qumran." *The Dead Sea Scrolls after Fifty Years: A Comprehensive Assessment*, vol. 2. P. W. Flint and J. VanderKam, eds. (2000) 93–116; R. A. Kugler. "The Priesthood at Qumran: The Evidence of References to Levi and the Levites." *The Provo International Conference on the Dead Sea Scrolls.* D. W. Parry and E. Ulrich, eds. (1999) 465–79; P. D. Miller. *The Religion of Ancient Israel* (2001); K. Möhlenbrink. "Die levitishcen Überlieferungen des Alten Testaments." *ZAW* 11 (1934) 184–231; R. D. Nelson. *Raising Up a Faithful Priest* (1993); G. W. E. Nickelsburg. *1 Enoch 1: A Commentary on the Book of 1 Enoch Chapters 1–36, 81–108* (2001); R. Nurmela. *The Levites: Their Emergence as a Second-Class Priesthood* (1998); D. W. Rook. *Zadok's Heirs: The Role and Development of the High Priesthood in Ancient Israel* (2000); L. Sabourin. *Priesthood: A Comparative Study* (1973); E. P. Sanders. *Judaism: Practice and Belief: 63 BCE–66 CE* (1992); A. Schofield and J. VanderKam. "Were the Hasmoneans Zadokites?" *JBL* 124 (2005) 73–87; W. R. Smith and A. Bertholet. "Levites." *Encyclopedia Biblica* 3. T. K. Cheyne and J. S. Black, eds. (1902) 2770–76; E. Stern. *Archaeology of the Land of the Bible, Vol. II: The Assyrian, Babylonian, and Persian Period (732–332 BCE)* (2001); J. C. VanderKam. *From Joshua to Caiaphas: High Priests after the Exile* (2004); John Van Seters. *Prologue to History: The Yahwist as Historian in Genesis* (1992); Roland de Vaux. *Ancient Israel: Its Life and Institutions* (1997); J. Wellhausen. *Prolegomena to the History of Israel* (1885).

ROBERT KUGLER

PRIESTS IN THE NT [ἱερεύς **hiereus**, ἀρχιερεύς **archiereus**]. Though priests of various religions were a common aspect of Greco-Roman religious life, NT understandings of priesthood are shaped primarily by their OT heritage.

The fundamental concept of priesthood throughout the Bible, as in the ancient world generally, is that of mediator (*see* MEDIATOR, MEDIATION). The priest functions to bridge the gap that separates the holy deity and sinful humanity (*pontifex*, the Latin term for *priest*, lit. means "bridge"). That the gap is bridged from both sides is illustrated in such texts as Deut 33:10, where priestly ministry mediates the word and will of God while facilitating the approach of sinful humanity to God by sacrifice and intercession. The priest represents God to people and people to God.

The NT assumes the view that human beings are not in direct relation to God, but are estranged from God and one other. While there are many variations in biblical understandings of priesthood, the fundamental image is the priest as God's provision of a mediator who facilitates reconciliation between God and people and among the people of God themselves. Priests thus exist for others. In the OT, priests existed for the sake of the nation, and Israel as a priestly community existed for the sake of the world (*see* PRIESTS AND LEVITES).

To be a priest is not a matter of personal achievement and dignity, but to be part of God's gracious provision to reconcile sinful humanity with the holy God and to facilitate life and community among human beings. As liminal beings, priests stood at the boundary (Lat. *limen*, "threshold") between holy and common, facilitating the presence of the holy God in the midst of a sinful people.

In the NT, the term *priest* (**hiereus**) occurs thirty-one times; its compound "high priest" (**archiereus**) occurs 122 times. Two abstract nouns usually translated *priesthood* occur twice each: **hierateia** (ἱερατεία; Luke 1:9; Heb 7:5) and **hierateuma** (ἱεράτευμα; 1 Pet 2:5, 9). The adjective *high-priestly* (**archieratikos** ἀρχιερατικός; Acts 4:6) occurs once. The related verbs **hierateuo** (ἱερατεύω, "to serve as priest"; Luke 1:8) and **hierourgeo** (ἱερουργέω, "to serve as priest"; Rom 15:16) each occur only once.

With the sole exceptions of Acts 14:13 (referring to a priest of Zeus) and Acts 19:14 (referring to a fictitious Jewish high priest), all NT references to priests as contemporary cultic officials are to Jewish priests. It is striking that even here, priests as ministers in the Temple receive little attention in the NT. They can be portrayed favorably and unpolemically, as valid representatives of the divine economy (e.g., Matt 8:4; Luke 1:8). They can also be portrayed negatively, but still without questioning their legitimacy (Luke 10:31). By far the majority of such references is to the high priest or the "chief priests," the collective term for the ruling priestly aristocracy in Jerusalem. Because they are among those who were accused of being involved in the death of Jesus, they are frequently depicted negatively in the NT.

The use of the term *priest* to designate a particular class of ordained Christian ministers distinct from the laity is not found in the NT. In the later NT period, priestly imagery was used metaphorically for cultic ministers (*Did.* 13.3; *1 Clem.* 40–44). It was not until the end of the 2nd cent. that ministers who presided at the EUCHARIST were called "priests" and not until the 3rd or 4th cent. that clergy as such were designated priests in contrast to the laity. The English word *priest*, when used to designate a member of the clergy, is not derived from the Greek **hiereus** (priest), but from **presbyteros** (πρεσβύτερος, "elder"), and is unrelated to the priestly vocabulary and imagery of the NT (*see* ELDER IN THE NT).

The NT uses priestly imagery for the person and work of Jesus as Christ. The Gospel of John portrays Jesus in cultic and sacerdotal terms as the one who offers himself as the sacrificial lamb (John 1:29, 36; 10:15-17) and whose great intercessory prayer is often called his "high priestly prayer" (John 17:1-26), though John does not speak explicitly of Jesus as priest. Paul refers to Jesus' atoning sacrifice and sin offering (Rom 3:21-25; 8:3) and speaks of him as the one who facilitates access to God (Rom 5:2) and who makes intercession for us before God (Rom 8:34), just as he can use priestly imagery for Christians who offer spiritual sacrifice (Rom 12:1) and for his own ministry to the Gentiles (Rom 15:15-16).

The only NT author to make explicit christological use of priestly vocabulary and imagery is the writer of Hebrews. For Hebrews, Jesus is the eternal high priest (Heb 3:1; 4:14; 5:6; 6:20; 7:3, 17, 21; 8:1), who stands on the divine side of reality and thus represents God (Heb 1:1-4, 8; 13:8), and is the truly human one taken from among human beings (Heb 2:5-18; 5:1-6), who shared human weakness and continues to intercede for sinful human beings (Heb 7:25). Hebrews handles this christological paradox chronologically: the preexistent divine Son became truly human and was then exalted as the divine and high priest intercessor. Priestly imagery facilitates the author's essential christological emphases. God's acceptance of humanity is not justified by the atoning act of a third party. By offering himself, Jesus represents God's own self-giving (*see* CHRISTOOGY).

Hebrews not only refers specifically to the high priesthood of Christ, but implicitly to the priestly role of believers in general by its repeated use of such cultic terminology and imagery as "approach" (Heb 4:16; 7:19, 25; 10:1, 22; 11:6) and "enter" (Heb 6:19-20; 9:12, 24-25; 10:19) in a cultic sense. These indirect and metaphorical uses of priestly imagery are important, but they do not represent a unified doctrine of priesthood; no NT author presents a systematic understanding of priesthood.

The only NT texts to use the specific terminology for priests for anyone except Jewish or pagan priests or for Christ as priest are 1 Pet 2:5, 9 and Rev 1:6; 5:10; and 20:6, all of which reflect Exod 19:6. This key text declaring Israel to be a **mamlekheth kohanim** (מַמְלֶכֶת כֹּהֲנִים, "priestly kingdom") was translated and understood in various ways in early Judaism, but generally referred to the priestly dignity conferred on Israel as a whole. The phrase did not mean that every Israelite was a priest, just as it did not mean every Israelite was a king. It did not abolish the distinction between king and people or between clergy and laity. Especially in the LXX translation of Exod 19:6 (**basileion hierateuma** βασίλειον ἱεράτευμα), the perspective of the original Hebrew is shifted from kingship to priesthood, from "priestly kingdom" to "royal priesthood." So translated, the text is now seen to affirm the dignity of the community of Israel as a whole as being royal in that it belonged to the king and as a body of priests in that it had a priestly function with regard to the nations of the world. The whole earth and all nations belong to God; Israel as a whole is called to the priestly service of mediating God's blessing to the world (compare also Isa 61:6). This Greek translation and understanding became the basis for the NT appropriation of the text.

Since Luther, the texts in 1 Peter and Revelation have often been interpreted to contrast the NT understanding of the "priesthood of all believers" with the presumed Jewish or Roman Catholic understanding of priesthood. Discussion has moved beyond the point where biblical texts are interpreted in this anachronistic fashion. So also, it is increasingly recognized that devaluation of "priestly," understood to represent ritual, tradition, and conservatism, in contrast to the "prophetic," understood positively as antiestablishment and progressive, was a grand oversimplification of the early Christian view. *See* CHURCH, IDEA OF THE; CHURCH, LIFE AND ORGANIZATION OF.

Bibliography: Raymond E. Brown. *The Critical Meaning of the Bible* (1981) 96–106; John H. Elliott. *The Elect and the Holy: An Exegetical Examination of 1 Peter 2:4-10 and the Phrase* βασίλειον ἱεράτευμα (1966); Richard D. Nelson. *Raising Up a Faithful Priest: Community and Priesthood in Biblical Theology* (1993); John M. Scholer. *Proleptic Priests: Priesthood in the Epistle to the Hebrews* (1991).

M. EUGENE BORING

PRINCE [אַדִּיר ʾaddir, נָגִיד naghidh, נָדִיב nadhiv, נָזִיר nazir, נָסִיךְ nasikh, נָשִׂיא nasiʾ, רָזוֹן razon, שַׂר sar; ἄρχων archōn, δυνάστης dynastēs, ἡγεμών hēgemōn, μεγιστάν megistan, τύραννος tyrannos]. Very occasionally in the OT, prince refers to the son of a king (e.g., 2 Kgs 10:13) or to a royal figure (e.g., David in Ezek 34:24; 37:25). Mostly, though, it signifies one who exercises influence (e.g., Gen 23:6; 1 Chr 7:40) or occupies a more formal leadership position (e.g., Isa 49:7; Lam 2:9). Sometimes the Hebrew word translated as "prince" refers to a preeminent leader (e.g., 1 Sam 25:30; 2 Sam 6:21; 7:8; 2 Chr 11:22). Ezekiel uses the phrase "princes of Israel" with reference to their responsibilities toward the Temple and the holy city (e.g., Ezek 45:7-8, 17; 48:21-22). The term prince may represent an earthly or non-earthly power. In Daniel, the archangel Michael is described as a "prince," whereas the "princes" of Persia and Greece may be earthly rulers or their heavenly counterparts (Dan 10:20). The phrase "Prince of Peace" may describe a messianic figure (Isa 9:6). Elsewhere, prince may carry messianic overtones and imply a link between messiah and Temple (Dan 9:25-26). In the poetic books, prince is often used to depict an uncomplimentary contrast between princes and the poor (e.g., 1 Sam 2:8; Ps 113:8) or the subjection of princes to God (e.g., Job 12:21; 29:10). In the Apocrypha, prince rarely refers to royalty (Bar 1:4 is an exception). Mostly it refers to identified leaders among the people (e.g., Jdt 5:2; 2 Macc 9:25; Sir 41:17), often occurring in parallel with "leaders," "judges," and "nobles" (Bar 1:9; Jdt 9:10; Sir 8:8). Judith 9:10 implies an ironic contrast between princes and ordinary people. See GOVERNOR; MESSIAH, JEWISH; NOBLES, NOBILITY.

TIM MEADOWCROFT

PRINCE HARDJEDEF, INSTRUCTION OF. *See* HARDJEDEF, INSTRUCTION OF PRINCE.

PRISCA, PRISCILLA pris'kuh, pri-sil'uh [Πρίσκα **Priska**, Πρίσκιλλα **Priskilla**]. A prominent woman in the early church, Prisca (Rom 16:3; 1 Cor 16:19; 2 Tim 4:19), or Priscilla (Acts 18:2, 18, 26), is always paired with her husband, Aquila. The couple traveled both independently and with Paul, spreading the gospel to Rome, Ephesus, and Corinth. Paul particularly honored their mutual sacrifice and assistance in establishing "all the churches of the Gentiles" (Rom 16:3-4; compare 1 Cor 16:19). Priscilla and Aquila supported themselves by the trade of tentmaking, or by "leather-working," which was easily transportable and suitable to evangelistic shoptalk with customers. Although a physically demanding occupation, there is no reason to doubt Priscilla's full participation with her husband (Acts 18:2-3; *see* TENTMAKER). During their sojourns in major cities, they hosted a HOUSE CHURCH in their residence (Rom 16:5; 1 Cor 16:19). In this domestic domain, Priscilla likely had authority, especially (but not only) among women and children, and prime opportunity for preaching, teaching, and caring for guests. As one who "explained the Way of God" to Apollos "more accurately," Priscilla is the only woman in Acts depicted as an authoritative teacher (Acts 18:24-26). *See* AQUILA AND PRISCILLA.

Bibliography: F. M. Gillman. *Women Who Knew Paul* (1992).

F. SCOTT SPENCER

PRISON [בֵּית הַסֹּהַר **beth hassohar**, בֵּית כֶּלֶא **beth kele'**; δεσμωτήριον **desmōtērion**]. Ancient legal systems allowed for incarceration of prisoners as they awaited trial, sentencing, transfer, execution, or other forms of punishment. Literature from the Roman period indicates substantive disagreements concerning the legitimacy of using imprisonment as a penal option. The lack of formal legal justifications, however, hardly meant that magistrates' actual practices did not include committing people to custody to shame them, quarantine them from public discourse, coerce a confession, or inflict punishment.

A consideration of prison in the ancient world cannot be limited to architecture or specific types of buildings; it encompasses custody in a general sense and different forms of detention. Terms for restraining and guarding (**'asar** אָסַר, **shamar** שָׁמַר; **deō** δέω, **tērēsis** τήρησις, **phylakē** φυλακή) can imply incarceration in various kinds of sites and conditions. While some cities included buildings reserved specifically for confining prisoners, imprisonment could occur in structures or enclosures such as quarries, military barracks, or buildings used for multiple governmental functions. For some, imprisonment meant living alone or in groups in such a fortified site. Others' imprisonment involved living under military guard in a camp or in their own homes. House arrest and better living conditions were often possible for prisoners of high social status.

Literary sources offer anecdotal glimpses into the conditions of imprisonment. Although practices varied widely across time, geography, and social strata, prisons were known for inflicting severe hardship, especially when prisoners were chained in place or to guards. Jailers were known as men of abject cruelty. Overcrowding, darkness, psychological distress, and malnutrition characterized the incarceration experience. Most prisoners required friends or relatives to supply their food and necessities. In addition to physical and emotional distress, prison settings also brought social shame upon their inhabitants and their associates. Nevertheless, some prisoners' conditions permitted modest freedoms, including reading, writing, and preparing defenses.

Biblical references to people in custody paint similar pictures. Diverse sites served the purposes: pits (Isa 24:22), cisterns (Jer 38:9, where Jeremiah is thrown to die), official structures meant to incarcerate many (Gen 39:20-23; Acts 16:23-28), military barracks (Acts 21:32–23:10), and house arrest (Acts 28:16, 30). Paul's imprisonments mentioned in Acts and the Pauline epistles usually describe him detained in military custody or house arrest.

Neglect and hardship characterize biblical portrayals of prisoners' experiences. Although Joseph enjoys special treatment in Pharaoh's prison, others there await execution (Gen 40:5-22), suffer isolation (Gen 40:23), and are unable to maintain hygiene (Gen 41:14). Imprisonment and chaining entailed suffering (1 Kgs 22:27; Ps 107:10; Isa 42:7; Jer 52:11; Acts 16:22-24), forced labor (Judg 16:21), and the imminence of death (Pss 79:11; 102:20 [Heb. 102:21]; Acts 12:1-4).

In the NT, imprisonment of various kinds, along with the attendant suffering, expresses opposition to the gospel (Luke 21:12; Acts 4:1-22; 5:17-42; 8:3; 12:1-11; 16:16-40; 2 Cor 11:23), and to visit prisoners is to serve Christ (Matt 25:36; Heb 10:34; 13:3). Although the potential for disgrace is acknowledged (2 Tim 1:8, 16), the imprisonment of believers confirms their fidelity to the gospel and functions ironically as a religious calling (Eph 3:1; 4:1; Phlm 1, 9). In some situations, incarcerated people find their settings providing new audiences and opportunities to make Christ known (Acts 21–28; Eph 6:19-20; Phil 1:12-14). *See* CHAINS, IMPRISONMENT; CRIMES AND PUNISHMENT, OT AND NT; DUNGEON.

MATTHEW L. SKINNER

PRISON GATE. *See* GUARD, GATE OF THE.

PRIZE [סָלַל **salal**, שָׁלָל **shalal**; ἄθλων **athlōn**, βραβεῖον **brabeion**, γέρας **geras**]. The Hebrew verb **salal** ("to prize") refers to valuing a person or object (Prov 4:8). Jeremiah says that those who have escaped destruction in war have received their life as a prize (Jer 21:9; 38:2; 39:18; 45:5). Most notably, however, the noun *prize* is used in wisdom literature and in Paul's writings as a metaphorical award given by God to victors in the game of living and dying righteously.

A geras is a gift of honor. In the Wisdom of Solomon, the gift or "prize (**geras**) for blameless souls" (Wis 2:22) is immortality (e.g., Wis 3:4; 5:15). Virtue itself is "victor in the contest for prizes (**athlōn**) that are undefiled" (Wis 4:2*b*). In 4 Maccabees, the martyrdom of seven brothers and their mother who refuse to forsake their religion in order to attain "the prize (**athlōn**) of virtue" (4 Macc 9:8-9; compare 15:29) is likened to a divine athletic contest for which the prize is immortality (4 Macc 17:11-12).

In 1 Cor 9:24-27, Paul presents himself as an example through an extended and mixed athletic metaphor. Like runners who compete to win "the prize" (**brabeion**), he practices self-discipline and strives for the ultimate goal. While Paul does not stress faithfulness to the law as do the Wisdom of Solomon and 4 Maccabees, the context of 1 Cor 8–10 displays a similar concern for righteous and faithful conduct with an eye toward immortality. Indeed, in Phil 3, Paul contrasts righteousness according to the law and the righteousness "that comes through faith in Christ" (Phil 3:9). Then follows a string of athletic allusions beginning with immortality as the goal, "the prize (**brabeion**) of the heavenly call of God in Christ Jesus" (Phil 3:14). Therefore, whether by faithfulness to the law or Christ, righteousness is proved and perfected in suffering for God and others.

MARK D. GIVEN

PROCHORUS prok´uh-ruhs [Πρόχορος **Prochoros**]. Prochorus is chosen, along with STEPHEN, among the seven named persons, "men of good standing," charged with the care of widows who were being neglected in the distribution of food (Acts 6:5; *see* SEVEN, THE). According to tradition, it is this Prochorus who compiled a version of the Apocryphal *Acts of John* from Leucius' gnostic version. Manuscripts of Prochorus' version still exist today. *See* JOHN, ACTS OF, BY PROCHORUS.

KIMBERLY R. PEELER

PROCHURUS, ACTS OF JOHN BY. *See* JOHN, ACTS OF, BY PROCHORUS.

PROCONSUL proh-kon´suhl [ἀνθύπατος **anthypatos**; Lat. *pro consule*]. A Roman official who governed a province. During the Hasmonean period, Aulus Gabinius, proconsul of Syria, divided Judea into districts, each locally governed by a SANHEDRIN. Paul and Barnabas encountered a proconsul named Sergius Paulus (*see* PAULUS, SERGIUS) who became a Christian believer (Acts 13:7-12). GALLIO, proconsul of Achaia, refused to try Paul when Jews who opposed Paul's teachings brought him before the tribunal (Acts 18:12-17). Paul escaped being brought before the proconsul in Ephesus after silversmiths of the shrines of Artemis fomented a riot in opposition to Paul's teaching that silver idols were not really gods (Acts 19:21-41). *See* PALESTINE, ADMINISTRATION OF.

MARIANNE BLICKENSTAFF

PROCURATOR prok´yuh-ray´tuhr. The Latin title for a regional governor in the Roman Empire. In the late 1st cent. CE, Tacitus used the term to designate the office held by Pontius Pilate (*Ann.* 15.44), as well as other regional officials who were appointed by the emperor to govern provinces for Rome. Pilate governed in the Roman province of Judea from 26–36 CE, and according to the NT he presided over the trial of Jesus. Based on an inscription dating to 31 CE, discovered in Caesarea Maritima in 1961, scholars have noted that Tacitus' use of *procurator* for Pilate was slightly anachronistic. The reconstructed inscription refers to Pilate as the "prefect" of the region, rather than the procurator. The emperor Claudius in 41 CE was most likely the first to apply the title *procurator* to his regional governors of equestrian rank. Fourteen prefects or procurators administered Judea during the period of Roman control between 4 BCE and the beginning of the Jewish revolt in 66 CE. In their official functions, there appears to be no significant difference between the office of prefect and that of procurator. In the NT, Pilate is called the "governor" (Matt 27:2; Luke 3:1).

MILTON MORELAND

PRODIGAL SON. This is the English title of the PARABLE of the SON who squanders his inheritance (while his brother remains dutiful), and is subsequently forgiven and welcomed back by his FATHER (Luke 15:11-32). Its occurrence only in Luke's Gospel may mean that it derives from sources known only to that author, or that the author crafted it to make one of his favorite points—that God rejoices at a sinner's repentance (e.g., Luke 15:1-10). *See* INHERITANCE IN THE NT.

NICOLE WILKINSON DURAN

PROFANE [חָלַל **khalal**; βέβηλος **bebēlos**, βεβηλόω **bebēloō**, κοινός **koinos**]. A technical category in the priestly purity system. Unlike "holy" or "impure" items, profane items compose an inert category, that is, they have no power. Rather, the forces of holiness (positive) and impurity (negative) act upon these neutral items. For example, a sacrificed animal undergoes a change in status from profane to holy; conversely, a contaminated pot of food has been altered from profane to impure status (compare Lev 11:34).

In later texts, "profane" often refers to the defilement of sancta, e.g., the sanctuary (Lev 21:12; 1 Macc 4:38), Israel (Ezek 22:26), God's name (Lev 19:12), the Sabbath (Neh 13:17; 1 Macc 1:45), or holy persons (Lev 21:9), a sin that incurs the death penalty (Lev 22:9).

In the NT, "to profane" continues to mean "to desecrate," e.g., the Sabbath (Matt 12:5) or the Temple (Acts 24:6), but more often the word *profane* refers to ungodliness (1 Tim 1:9; compare 6:20, "profane" conversation).

Bibliography: Jacob Milgrom. *Leviticus 1–16.* AB (1991).

HANNAH K. HARRINGTON

PROFANITY. *See* OATH.

PROMISE [ἐπαγγέλλομαι **epangellomai**]. Aside from the covenantal language between Yahweh and his people in the OT, other religions of the ANE did not speak of deities who made long-term promises, which might take generations to be fulfilled (*see* COVENANT, OT AND NT; FULFILL, FULFILLMENT). The repeated occurrences of such promises in Scripture thus make the concept of *promise* one of the distinctive features of the message of both testaments. God makes promises, their fulfillment is jeopardized in one way or another, partial fulfillments are recorded, and new promises are added to old ones. This places significant demands on believers. Trust is required—that God is able and willing to keep the promise—and patience, for fulfillment will come not now, but later. These are the elements that make up the theme of promise in Scripture.

No Hebrew word corresponds to the English word *promise.* Promises are usually introduced in the OT by the common verbs for speaking, although God will at times "take an OATH" in order to emphasize his commitment to keeping his word (e.g., Gen 22:16-18; Exod 13:5, 11; 32:13; 33:1). The idiom "to lift the hand" means essentially the same thing (e.g., Exod 6:8; Num 14:30; Neh 9:15). In the NT, **epangellomai** ("promise, profess, claim") and related terms are good equivalents to the English word *promise.*

A. Promise in the Old Testament

The promise to Abraham in Gen 12:1-3, 7 (compare Gen 15:18-21; 17:1-8) is a major theme that runs throughout the historical books of the OT. From Abraham was to come a great nation, to be blessed and a source of blessing, even to all the families (or nations) of the earth, and the land of Canaan was to be given to his descendants. The rest of Genesis is the story of the jeopardizing of that promise, by temporary exile (Gen 12:10-20), failure of Abraham and Sarah to have a child (e.g., Gen 15:1), and even by God's own command (Gen 22:1). The book ends with Abraham's descendants in exile in Egypt, and the great theme of Exodus is the beginning of fulfillment: being liberated from bondage to a great nation, being constituted as a nation at Sinai, and moving toward the promised LAND. In Exod 6:2-8, God spells out his intention to fulfill the promises made to Abraham, Isaac, and Jacob, and must add another, to be acted on immediately: "I will free you from the burdens of the Egyptians" (Exod 6:6). Shortly after the escape from Egypt, however, the sin of the golden calf (Exod 32–34) raised serious questions about whether the promise could ever be fulfilled. Moses succeeded in persuading God not to give up on the Hebrews, and part of his reasoning was an appeal to the promise: "Remember Abraham, Isaac, and Israel, your servants, how you swore to them by your own self" (Exod 32:13). The accounts of settlement in Canaan (Joshua–Judges), of the Philistine threat (1 Samuel), and the eventual success of David in giving them security (2 Sam 5), followed by their arrival at true nationhood under Solomon (1 Kgs 4–10), seemed to confirm almost all that God had promised Abraham. A new promise was offered to David, that he would never lack a descendant to sit upon the throne in Jerusalem (2 Sam 7).

God's major promises were associated with covenants. To Noah, God said, "I establish my covenant with you, that never again shall all flesh be cut off by the waters of a flood, and never again shall there be a flood to destroy the earth" (Gen 9:11). God's promise to Abraham is called a covenant in Gen 17:2, and Ps 132:11-12 refers to the promise to David as a covenant. These three were entirely covenants of promise, but the Sinai covenant added human responsibility: "If you obey my voice and keep my covenant, you shall be my treasured possession out of all the peoples. Indeed, the whole earth is mine, but you shall be for me a priestly kingdom and a holy nation" (Exod 19:5-6). A unique kind of nationhood was promised, but the new promise was conditional.

Leviticus and Deuteronomy elaborate the content of God's promises to a faithful people in the form of a series of blessings, but since the Sinai covenant was conditioned upon obedience, a series of curses follow the blessings (Lev 26; Deut 28). The possibility that the promises of the covenants made with Abraham and at Sinai might be rescinded was thus held before Israel in the starkest form, and even exile from the promised land was threatened. Leviticus, however, affirms the possibility of repentance (Lev 26:40-41) and appealed to the covenant with Abraham as a basis for HOPE, even after disaster.

Disaster did come. The story told in 1–2 Kings and elaborated in the prophetic books is one of perennial failure to be faithful to the commandments issued at Sinai, leading eventually to God's repudiation of the promise—at least for the time being (e.g., Amos 3:1-2; 8:2; compare Amos 7:17 with 2 Kgs 17:22; 25:21). The Northern Kingdom fell in the late 8th cent. BCE, and in 587 BCE Jerusalem with its Temple was destroyed. The Davidic dynasty came to an end. The upper classes were exiled to Babylonia, so nationhood, land, kingship, and blessing were no more. Psalm 77 raises the question of the failure of promise: "Will the Lord spurn forever, and never again be favorable? Has his steadfast love ceased forever? Are his promises (ʾomer [אֹמֶר], "word") at an end for all time? Has God forgotten to be gracious? Has he in anger shut up his compassion?" (Ps 77:7-9 [Heb. 77:8-10]). Similar questions appear elsewhere in the Psalms and in Lamentations. In Ps 77, a resolution is found in memory; in the past God has fulfilled his promises, and this provided a basis for hope: "I will call to mind the deeds of the LORD; I will remember your wonders of old" (Ps 77:11 [Heb. 77:12]). As to the promise to David, however, Ps 89 recounted at some length what God had said: "Once and for all I have sworn by my holiness; I will not lie to David. His line shall continue forever" (Ps 89:35-36*a* [Heb. 89:36-37*a*]). But kingship had come to an end: "now you have spurned and rejected him" (Ps 89:38*a* [Heb. 89:39*a*]), and the psalm offers no answer to that dilemma.

In spite of the loss of everything after 587 BCE, which prophets and the writer of Kings took to be fully deserved since Israel had proved unworthy to be called the people of God, some of the prophets insisted that God would be faithful to the promise, for his own sake (Ezek 36:22), although this would require radical transformations of human nature and society. Promise took on new forms in the eschatological passages in the prophetic books (*see* ESCHATOLOGY OF THE OT). God promised a new covenant to be written on the heart (Jer 31:31-34) and forgiveness of sin (Jer 33:8) to make it possible for people to live righteously. God's people would return to the promised land (Ezek 37:12-14 and many texts), and Jerusalem and the Temple would be rebuilt as the center of worship for all people (Isa 2:1-4). There would be no more war (Mic 4:3), no harm done to any living thing (Isa 11:9), no hunger (Ezek 36:30), and no human infirmity (Isa 35:5-6).

There were partial fulfillments of these hopes when some of the exiled Jews began to return to the promised land in 538 BCE, with eventual restoration of the Temple. The transformed nature of Judaism after the exile may be thought of as a fulfillment of the promise of a new covenant written on the heart, but the other promises have still not been fulfilled. Promise, which is a basis for hope, thus also puts demands on faith, trust, and patience. The glorious restoration promised in Isa 40–55, which never ensued, must have raised serious questions among the returnees about whether this was the expected fulfillment or not. So they questioned whether the time was right to rebuild the Temple (Hag 1:2-6).

B. Promise in the New Testament

The NT writers were convinced that God had fulfilled in Jesus Christ his promises made in the OT, and they could use the word in a quite sweeping way to refer to what God had accomplished in Christ without necessarily being specific about content. Sometimes promise means the gift of the Holy Spirit (Luke 24:49; Acts 1:4; 2:39; compare Gal 3:14). In Heb 4 it is rest, reinterpreting the word so as to refer no longer to rest in the land of Canaan, as in the OT (e.g., Josh 1:15), but participation in God's rest, as on the seventh day of creation. In 2 Tim 1:1 and Titus 1:2 it is life in Christ or eternal life. These are contents that do not directly correspond to specific OT promises. Possession of the land, glorification of Jerusalem, and reestablishment of kingship do not interest the NT writers, except to the extent that they can reinterpret them with reference to the work of Christ. Hebrews 11:8-16 speaks of the promise of land to Abraham, but spiritualizes it to represent heaven (Heb 11:19). Jesus' descent from David is important, but his kingship is also spiritualized and will be manifest on earth only in the last days (1 Cor 15:24-25; Eph 1:20-22; Rev 19:16). Jesus even denied that he had come to bring peace on earth (Matt 10:34).

Continuity appears in several of the NT's major emphases. Jesus' work as a healer was surely seen to be a fulfillment of texts such as Isa 35:5-6 and an indication that in him God had begun to fulfill his old promises (compare Matt 12:15-21; 15:29-31). He claimed to be able to forgive sins (Luke 5:17-26; 7:36-50) and at the Last Supper spoke of his impending death as the "new covenant" (Luke 22:20). A major part of the new covenant promise was the forgiveness of sins (Jer 31:34), which may account for Peter's association of the promise with both the gift of the Spirit and forgiveness (Acts 2:38-39).

The promise to Abraham was important to Paul, but he used it in a new way, showing no interest in the land or nationhood. Blessing and the reference to all the families (or nations) of the earth were valuable content, and the fact that the promise to Abraham was given long before the gift of the law at Mount Sinai and that "Abraham believed God, and it was reckoned to him as righteousness" (Rom 4:3; compare Gen 15:6) provide the scriptural basis for his claim that the promises had now been granted to all who believe, through the work of Christ (Rom 4:13-25; Gal 3:14-29). "Christ redeemed us from the curse of the law . . . in order that in Christ Jesus the blessing of Abraham might come to the Gentiles, so that we might receive the promise of the Spirit through faith" (Gal 3:13-14). In this verse, blessing, promise, and Gentiles are easily connected with the promise to Abraham, and in the next section of Galatians Paul used a typical rabbinic exegetical procedure to find Christ in Gen 22:18. The word *offspring* is singular, so Paul claimed it referred to only one of Abraham's descendants, namely Jesus. Then, using Gen 15:2-3 he concluded, "[S]o you see, those who believe are the descendants of Abraham" (Gal 3:7). "And if you belong to Christ, then you are Abraham's offspring, heirs according to the promise" (Gal 3:29). *Promise* was thus a key word for Paul's claim that the Gentiles were offered full and free access to God through Jesus

Christ. He developed the same argument in Rom 4, but having spoken of fulfilled promises, had to acknowledge the realities of the Christian life in Rom 6–7: God's best promises were coming true, but not all human imperfections had been overcome, and evil was far from having been eradicated on earth. Elsewhere he concluded: "But our citizenship is in heaven, and it is from there that we are expecting a Savior, the Lord Jesus Christ. He will transform the body of our humiliation that it may be conformed to the body of his glory, by the power that also enables him to make all things subject to himself" (Phil 3:20-21).

Having found a scriptural basis for this good news for Gentiles, Paul had to face a serious question concerning the promises of the OT, and he devoted three chapters of Romans to it. With the coming of Christ, were the promises no longer valid for Jews who did not believe in him? Romans 9–11 contain his struggle with that. "They are Israelites, and to them belong the adoption, the glory, the covenants, the giving of the law, the worship, and the promises" (Rom 9:4). He applied the OT theme of disobedience to the unbelieving Jews of his time (e.g., Rom 9:31-32; 10:3, 21), but could not believe God had completely given up on his promises: "I ask, then, has God rejected his people? By no means!" (Rom 11:1). As Paul neared his conclusion he asserted that "the gifts and the calling of God are irrevocable" (Rom 11:29), and "God has imprisoned all in disobedience so that he may be merciful to all" (Rom 11:32). But finally, he admitted that it is a mystery (Rom 11:33-36).

For the early Christians, experiences of having been forgiven, of entering into a new life that they attributed to the work of the Holy Spirit, and of entering into a new community, the church, were made possible because of faith in Jesus Christ as the Son of God who had died and risen for them. They explained these works as God's fulfillment of his promises to Israel. In order to do this, the early Christians selected and emphasized the parts of the OT that they found to be fulfilled by Jesus, while ignoring parts (such as the land) that did not interest them. They reaffirmed unfulfilled promises (such as peace on earth) as yet to come. A major form of that reaffirmation was the new promise that Christ would return at the time when God's victory over evil would become manifest and final (Matt 24; 25:31-46; 1 Thess 4:13–5:11; *see* ESCHATOLOGY OF THE NT; PAROUSIA). Revelation contains that promise: "Surely I am coming soon" (Rev 22:20). Jesus' return did not happen soon, as his followers expected, and so the later book of 2 Peter took up the subject of promise again, counseling patience (2 Pet 3:9). So, promises and partial fulfillments reappear throughout Scripture and provide the basis for hope, but the tensions created by still unfulfilled promises call for patience and may challenge believers' ability to trust. *See* FAITH, FAITHFULNESS.

Bibliography: Dennis C. Duling. "The Promises to David and Their Entry into Christianity." *NTS* 20 (1973/74) 55–77; Donald E. Gowan. *Eschatology in the Old Testament.* Rev. ed. (2000); Donald E. Gowan. *Theology in Exodus* (1994); Claus Westermann. *The Promises to the Patriarchs: Studies in the Patriarchal Narratives* (1980).

DONALD E. GOWAN

PROMISED LAND. *See* ABRAHAM, OT; DEUTERONOMY, BOOK OF; EXODUS, BOOK OF; ISRAEL, HISTORY OF; JOSHUA, BOOK OF; LAND.

PRONOUNCEMENT STORY. A term used mostly in form criticism to classify narrative units of material in the Gospels, such as a parable or a miracle story, whose conflict serves solely to emphasize the saying of Jesus that comes at the end of the narrative. *See* APOPHTHEGM; FORM CRITICISM, NT; JESUS, SAYINGS OF.

EMILY R. CHENEY

PROPERTY [אֲחֻזָּה **ʾakhuzzah,** יְרֻשָּׁה **yerushah,** נַחֲלָה **nakhalah,** קִנְיָן **qinyan;** κτῆμα **ktēma,** οὐσία **ousia**]. Property refers to LAND or goods over which persons, singly or as a group, claim ownership. Ownership, then, is the socially recognized entitlement to the exclusive possession, use, or disposal of some object. Property ownership rights are rooted in and shaped by social institutions. While in Western societies, we distinguish kinship, economics, religion, and politics as distinct social institutions, in antiquity only KINSHIP and politics (the household and the city) were of focal interest. For kin groups, there were indeed domestic economy and domestic religion, just as in the administrative **polis** (πόλις "city") there was political economy and political religion. In the area of the embedded economy of the ANE, property referred to human beings (*see* SLAVERY), domestic animals, things, and lands over which some person or group had the entitlements or rights of ownership. Laws outline responsibilities of property owners (e.g., Exod 21–22).

For Israel, of course, the Lord God of Israel ruled the sky and land ("Lord of heaven and earth") that was God's domain (Jdt 9:12; Matt 11:25; Luke 10:21). The basis for this dominion is that the Lord made the heavens and the earth (e.g., Gen 14:19; Exod 20:11; 2 Sam 18:9; 2 Kgs 19:15; Ezra 5:11; Pss 115:15; 121:2; 124:8; 134:3; 146:6; Isa 37:16; Luke 10:21; Acts 17:24; Rev 14:7). As such he was owner of that domain and could cede it to whomever he willed. All the repeated emphases in the Torah about God giving the land of Canaan as inheritance to Israel, even calling the people of Israel his inheritance, point to the vocabulary of property (e.g., Lev 27:22-24; Num 32–34; Deut 4:21; 24:4; 25:19; 26:1; Josh 13–21; compare Gal 3:6-29). The kings of Israel treated the people and lands in their domain as their property (see 1 Sam 8:11-18). Patriarchs did the same with their families (*see* HOUSEHOLD, HOUSEHOLDER).

The NT attests to the belief that with his resurrection, Jesus was made Lord (kyrios [κύριος]; Rom 1:3-4; Phil 2:6-11). The title *lord* was not a pious title, but had all the resonance of actual power wielding and ownership entitlements as it did in the practice of the Roman emperor. It is noteworthy that the reigning emperor, Claudius, likewise bore the title *lord.*

In both the OT and NT there is consideration for a property owner's responsibility to the POOR and landless, e.g., provisions for leaving grain at the edges of a field for the poor to glean (Lev 19:9-10; 23:22; compare Ruth 2:2-3), care of widows and orphans (Exod 22:21-24; Deut 10:18; 27:19; Pss 68:5 [Heb. 68:6], 146:9; Jer 49:11), and the establishment of a year of Jubilee (Exod 21:2-6; 23:10-11; Deut 15:1-18; Lev 25:1-55), which was a time for forgiveness of debts, freeing of slaves, and restoration of land (*see* DEBT, DEBTOR; JUBILEE, YEAR OF). Jesus taught his disciples and would-be disciples to forego property ownership in order to follow him (Matt 19:29; Mark 10:30; Luke 18:18-30), and the early church is depicted as a group in which property is shared communally (Acts 4:32-37; see 5:1-11). *See* COMMUNITY OF GOODS; INHERITANCE IN THE NT; INHERITANCE IN THE OT; OWNER; WEALTH.

BRUCE J. MALINA

PROPHECY OF AHIJAH THE SHILONITE. *See* BOOKS REFERRED TO IN THE BIBLE.

PROPHECY, FALSE [ψευδοπροφήτης pseudoprophētēs]. The notion of "false prophecy" is, in some measure, a category foreign to the OT, since no such phrase may be found in the Hebrew text (a prophet is designated only as a navi' [נָבִיא] or nevu'ah [נְבוּאָה], a "prophet"). Nonetheless, ancient Israelite literature attests that certain prophets behaved inappropriately, though the character of that malfeasance was diverse. For example, the Deuteronomic law code includes several prescriptions devoted to prophets. The first case (Deut 13:1-5 [Heb. 13:2-6]) involves prophets who offer omens or portents that come true, but who venerate deities other than Yahweh. Hence, such prophets receive a sentence of death. Though their words are "true," what they say leads to "treason" (Deut 13:5 [Heb. 13:6]). The second case (Deut 18:15-20) affirms a death sentence for the prophet who "speaks in the name of other gods." Deuteronomy 18:21-22 attests a third case, one in which a prophet speaks on behalf of Yahweh, but whose word does not take place. Here, though the words are false, the prophet has not led the people into idolatry and is not put to death. Such a prophet was thought to have spoken presumptuously, with the result that the people could simply ignore him (Deut 18:22). Negative judgments about prophets could stem either from the deity on whose behalf they spoke or from the content of their message (*see* PROPHET, PROPHECY).

At least two variables were at work when ancient Israelites assessed a prophet: whether or not they were prophets of Yahweh and whether or not what they spoke proved true. These variables worked themselves out in very different ways. If a prophet spoke on behalf of BAAL, e.g., 1 Kgs 18 (compare Jer 23:13), the audience would immediately be able to discriminate between that prophet and a prophet—in this case Elijah—who spoke on behalf of Yahweh. However, if two prophets began their speeches with the phrase, "Thus says the LORD," and then offered conflicting oracles, the people would have had a far more difficult time. Jeremiah 28 presents just such a case. Jeremiah and Hananiah both spoke on behalf of Yahweh, Hananiah predicting imminent restoration, Jeremiah pronouncing even greater destruction. After the two prophets had concluded their speeches, "the prophet Jeremiah went his way" (Jer 28:11). The people simply had to wait and see which prophet's words would be confirmed by later events.

Prophets could, of course, suffer critique for being immoral (e.g., committing adultery, lying, etc. [Jer 23:14]) or for offering oracles for monetary gain (Mic 3:11). An even more damning charge, however, was to suggest that a prophet was not communicating in a genuine way on behalf of the deity (see Jer 14:13-14). A "true" prophet was supposed to participate in the divine council (Isa 6:1-13; Jer 23:18, 22) or receive directly words from the deity (Jer 1:9; Ezek 2:8–3:3).

Some Yahwistic prophets clearly spoke oracles that did not come true. Ezekiel's pronouncement that Nebuchadnezzar would conquer Tyre is a classic example (Ezek 26:7-14). The book of Ezekiel attests that such a victory did not take place (Ezek 29:17-20) and instead promises that Nebuchadnezzar will conquer Egypt. Though he may have been inaccurate, the book of Ezekiel portrays him as a true prophet.

When the OT was translated into Greek, a new term, "false prophet," appeared. The creators of the Septuagint (LXX) used the phrase "false prophet" (pseudoprophētēs) on ten occasions to translate the Hebrew noun navi' ("prophet"; Jer 6:13; 33:7, 8, 11, 16; 34:9; 35:1; 36:1, 8; Zech 13:2; these references are to the LXX Jeremiah and may differ from the NRSV). In each instance, the presence of the Greek noun pseudoprophētēs reflects a translator's judgment that the prophet in question is in some sense false (pseudēs [ψευδής], "false" or "lying"). The character of that falsity varied, however. In LXX Jer 6:13, the prophet was "false" due to greed, whereas in LXX Jer 35:1, Hananiah was construed as a false prophet because he spoke words in opposition to Jeremiah.

This situation also obtains in the NT. The word pseudoprophētēs appears eleven times. Here, too, there is diversity of usage. Second Peter 2:1 and 1 John 4:1 refer to false prophets who have recently been active, though these texts do not describe their behavior. Elsewhere, Matt 24:11; 24:24//Mark 13:22 anticipate that false prophets will emerge and "lead astray" (compare *Did.* 16:3; *Acts Thom.* 79). The emphasis is more on the effect that they will have rather than on the particulars of what they do or say. The same may be said of Bar Jesus, "a certain magician, a Jewish false prophet" (Acts 13:6), who attempted to dissuade Sergius Paulus from becoming a Christian. The author of the Gospel of Matthew warns against "false prophets," admonishing his readers to test their words, i.e., to know them "by their fruits" (Matt 7:15; compare *Did.* 11:4–12). The Gospel of Luke pronounces a woe "when all speak well of you, for that is what their ancestors did to the false prophets" (6:26). Revelation characterizes the "second beast" (13:11-18), who is an agent of Satan, as "the false prophet" (pseudoprophētēs) on three different occasions (16:13; 19:20; 20:10).

DAVID L. PETERSEN

PROPHET IN THE NT AND EARLY CHURCH prof´it [προφήτης prophētēs]. The terms *prophet* and *prophecy* in the NT designate a variety of phenomena, including speech that names injustice or that builds up the community, revelatory visions and ecstatic utterances, altered states of consciousness, and symbolic actions that unmask and challenge the prevailing powers. Prophetic speech is not merely predictive, but combines aspects of memory, tradition, and hope to awaken vision and resistance. During the NT era, this resistance was focused on Roman imperial rule and its extension through the Herodian rulers and Jerusalem elites. Later generations of prophets directed their energies against the consolidation of power in the structures of the early church itself. Prophets arose especially in times of conflict and injustice. Women may have exercised significant leadership in the early church especially as prophets (Acts 21:9; 1 Cor 11:5; Rev 2:20).

The early Christians understood prophets to represent God's own voice, the continuing voice of the crucified and risen Jesus, or the movement of the Spirit. Christian prophets typically drew upon images, words, and themes of the biblical tradition, as well as the teachings of Jesus, even when speaking from direct revelation. Prophets were integral parts of Christian worshiping assemblies, which were themselves both endowed with the prophetic Spirit and called upon to exercise critical discernment of the prophetic voices among them (e.g., 1 Cor 14:26-33; 1 Thess 5:19-20).

The gospel traditions present John the Baptizer and Jesus as prophets. Both are called by God from birth and call others to repentance in anticipation of God's coming reign (Matt 3:1-12; 4:17; Mark 1:2-8, 14-15; Luke 3:1-17; John 1:19-28). John and Jesus both operate at the margins of their social settings and challenge the assumptions by which people around them have ordered their worlds. Jesus, especially, is presented as an eschatological figure whose ministry crosses the boundaries between the human and the divine. In their announcement of God's empire, their criticism and subversion of the dominant order, and their actions that point toward the reality of God's rule, John and Jesus combine the mode of the oracular prophets of the classical biblical tradition (e.g., Isaiah, Jeremiah, Ezekiel, Amos) with that of action prophets such as Moses, Joshua, Elijah, and Elisha. John's ministry of baptism in the wilderness, e.g., challenges the Jerusalem-based aristocracy and the efficacy of Temple sacrifices, while recalling Israel's encounters with God on the way from slavery to the promised land. Jesus' baptism by John signals Jesus' symbolic death to the powers of this world. Not only in his proclamation but also in his exorcisms and healings, parables, and practices of open table fellowship, Jesus functions as a prophet. Jesus' triumphal entry into Jerusalem and the cleansing of the Temple (Matt 21:1-17; Mark 11:1-19; Luke 19:28-48; John 2:13-22; 12:12-19) are prophetic sign-acts by which Jesus subverts Roman and Jewish social conventions, while asserting God's rule and drawing the ire of the ruling powers. Jesus' crucifixion is the definitive prophetic sign-act of his ministry.

The sayings source Q (*see* Q, QUELLE) is the work of early Christian prophets who transmitted the words of Jesus in oral performances; these traditions were later incorporated into Matthew and Luke. Each of the evangelists develops the image of Jesus as prophet, but Mark and Matthew also call for critical discernment in dealing with prophets in the church (e.g., Matt 7:15-20; Mark 13:22). John's Gospel and letters may have originated in communities in which prophets were still active, perhaps in ways that had given rise to conflict (see 1 John 4:1-3). For Luke, however, Jesus' prophetic identity is a major christological reference point that also provides the dominating plot device for both the Gospel and Acts. Luke's Jesus is the eschatological prophet promised by God in Isaiah (Luke 4:16-30), whose fate is that of all prophets at the hands of Israel's leaders (Luke 13:31-35). Peter, Paul, and Stephen are all depicted in Acts in ways that conform to the prophetic paradigm of proclamation, rejection and suffering, and even death. From Luke's perspective, the church itself is a prophetic, eschatological phenomenon, generated by the outpouring of the Spirit at PENTECOST (Acts 2:17-18; 4:31).

Paul names himself as an apostle, but also presents himself implicitly as a prophet. He describes his call in prophetic terms (Gal 1:15-16; see Isa 49:1; Jer 1:5) and claims that his gospel comes by divine revelation (Gal 1:12; see 2 Cor 12:1-7). Some of the traditions Paul incorporates in his letters may have been prophetic oracles (e.g., Rom 11:25-26; 1 Cor 15:51-52; 1 Thess 4:15-17). Most important, Paul repeatedly affirms the role of prophets in the churches he founded and to which he writes (Rom 12:6; 1 Cor 12–14; 1 Thess 5:19-20). Prophecy is the only item present in all of Paul's lists of charismatic gifts (Rom 12:6-8; 1 Cor 12:8-11, 28-30; 13:1-2) and the gift for which members of the community should strive (1 Cor 14:1-5), second in importance only to apostleship. Yet for Paul, prophecy is also imperfect—inferior to love—and will pass away (1 Cor 13:8-10). Prophecy must be tested (1 Thess 5:20-21). In 1 Corinthians, Paul is at pains to distinguish prophecy from tongues, a distinction that some members of the community may have rejected (*see* TONGUES, GIFT OF). Paul's concern is for speech that builds up the community rather than gifts that emphasize transcendent personal experiences.

Revelation is the most extensive and developed example of early Christian prophecy in the NT. While Revelation is often classified in the genre of apocalyptic literature, the seer identifies the book as "prophecy" (Rev 1:3; 22:7, 10, 18-19; compare 19:20) and suggests that he is a member of a community of prophets (Rev 22:9); moreover, the book has long been regarded by the church as prophecy. The entire book is a prophetic revelation, encompassing both letters and visions. Revelation draws upon the conventions and images of the prophetic traditions, especially Isaiah, Jeremiah, Daniel (also an apocalypse, but placed in the Christian canon as prophecy; *see* APOCALYPSE; APOCALYPTICISM), and Ezekiel, and employs a sophisticated blend of prophetic tools, including generic mixing, idiosyncratic speech patterns, oracles, hymns, and startling visions in order to affirm Christ's rule and to generate enduring resistance to Roman hegemony.

Already by the end of the NT era, the role of prophets was being circumscribed, due in part to the movement from charismatic to ordained and hierarchical patterns of leadership. Both the *Didache* (*Did.* 11) and the *Shepherd of Hermas* (Herm. *Mand.* 11) indicate that prophets were still active in the early part of the 2nd cent. CE, but were sometimes the cause of conflict or posed threats to the emerging institutional authority of the churches. During the mid-2nd cent., a renewal movement called the "New Prophecy" developed in PHRYGIA and spread through western and central Asia Minor, where political oppression, plagues, earthquakes, and economic pressures were generating widespread suffering. The New Prophecy clashed with the intellectual and ecclesial leaders of the emerging Roman-based church, especially over the growing authority of the bishops, accommodation to the Roman imperial order, and the leadership of women, as well as the nature of prophecy itself. As episcopal succession supplanted prophetic endowment, and as women were increasingly excluded from recognized leadership in the churches, the voice of prophets also diminished.

Bibliography: David Aune. *Prophecy in Early Christianity and the Ancient Mediterranean World* (1983); M. Eugene Boring. *The Continuing Voice of Jesus: Christian Prophecy and the Gospel Tradition* (1991); Richard Horsley and John S. Hanson. *Bandits, Prophets, and Messiahs: Popular Movements at the Time of Jesus* (1999); Richard Horsley with Jonathan A. Draper. *Whoever Hears You Hears Me: Prophets, Performance and Tradition in Q* (1999); Barbara Rossing. "Prophets, Prophetic Movements, and the Voices of Women." *A People's History of Christianity, Volume 1: Christian Origins.* Richard A. Horsley, ed. (2005) 261–86; Antoinette Clark Wire. *Corinthian Women Prophets: A Reconstruction through Paul's Rhetoric* (1990).

STANLEY P. SAUNDERS

PROPHET, PROPHECY prof'it [נָבִיא navi', נְבוּאָה nevu'ah; προφήτης prophētēs, προφητεία prophēteia]. There are no "prophets" per se in the OT. The English word *prophet* derives from the Greek word prophētēs, a noun that was used to translate the Hebrew noun navi' in early Greek versions of the OT. A related Greek verb, prophēteuō (προφητεύω), was used to translate the Hebrew verb nabba' (נָבָא, "to prophesy"). That usage continues, since most English translations of the OT use both the noun *prophet* and the verb *prophesy* to translate these same Hebrew words.

A. Introduction

The verb "to prophesy" in Greek (prophēteuō) means "to speak for or on behalf of someone." A "prophet" is a person who does such a thing. This sense comports well with the function of many Israelite prophets. They speak on behalf of the deity to the people, as the formula "Thus says the Lord" suggests, and, on occasion, they speak on behalf of an individual or the people as a whole to the deity. The term *prophet* does not, at least by dint of etymology, mean someone who forespeaks, i.e., someone who foretells the future, nor does it signify someone who "speaks forth," though prophets may, indeed, speak truth to various elements in Israelite society.

The etymology of the Hebrew noun **navi**ʾ is disputed. It may mean "someone who is called" or "someone who calls upon the gods." The former meaning is more likely. However, in attempting to define what prophets were in Israel and elsewhere in the ANE, one must move beyond etymology and seek a definition that comports with the behaviors of individuals known as prophets and with the literature associated with them.

Not all those individuals whom we think about as prophets were known simply as a **navi**ʾ. Persons in the OT who were characterized as a **navi**ʾ were sometimes known by other titles. For example, Gad, who is labeled as **navi**ʾ, is also described as a **khozeh** (חֹזֶה), a "seer" of David (2 Sam 24:11). (That same noun **khozeh** is used of Amos by his opponent Amaziah [Amos 7:12].) Or, Elijah, who is known as a prophet (1 Kgs 18:22) is also labeled **ish ha**ʾ**elohim**, "a man of God" (אִישׁ הָאֱלֹהִים; 2 Kgs 1:9). Moreover, some individuals who appear to belong to the roster of Israel's prophets (Isaiah, e.g.) are labeled as neither a prophet nor a seer. (Isaiah is known as a prophet in Isa 37–39, literature drawn from 2 Kgs 18–20.)

This terminological variety almost certainly reflects a long history during which *prophet* became the standard term by which intermediaries of originally distinct sorts were known. Several sorts of evidence point in this direction. First, references to intermediaries in the postexilic era are virtually always known as prophets (e.g., Hag 1:12; Zech 1:7; 13:4; Mal 4:5). Hanani's identity as **ro**ʾ**eh** (רֹאֶה "seer") is a noteworthy exception (2 Chr 16:7). Second, the author of 1 Sam 9:9 states that "the one who is now called a prophet (**navi**ʾ) was formerly called a seer (**ro**ʾ**eh**)." Ancient Israelite scribes attest that the prophetic terminology had a history, one in which the noun **navi**ʾ became the standard term for prophet.

If, prior to the exile, different sorts of prophets were known by various role labels, what do those distinctions signify? At a minimum, they appear to reflect the sorts of behaviors in which prophets were involved. The clearest example of a prophet known as a **ro**ʾ**eh**—that of Samuel in 1 Sam 9—suggests that he was known as a seer because he was an individual whom the people could consult for a fee in order to gain special knowledge. Samuel says to Saul and his servant, "I am the seer; go up before me to the shrine, for today you shall eat with me, and in the morning I will let you go and will tell you all that is on your mind. As for your donkeys that were lost three days ago, give no further thought to them, for they have been found. And on whom is all Israel's desire fixed, if not on you and on all your ancestral house?" (1 Sam 9:19-20). Then, in the morning, Samuel reported to Saul that he would make known to him "the word of God" (1 Sam 9:27).

This scene is not typical of the interactions of prophets with their audiences. Distinctive are Samuel's association with a shrine, his eating with his audience, and the presumed payment of a fee (1 Sam 9:8; compare Mic 3:11). Many readers of the OT expect prophets to offer unbidden words of woe. Here, Samuel is a fee-based consultant to the member of a significant family. Samuel's role is virtually that of a diviner. He can comfort Saul with the knowledge that the lost donkeys had been found. This report about the lost animals may or may not have stemmed from the deity. Some Israelite could have reported the location of the animals to someone in the city, where Samuel might have overheard it. More esoteric is the knowledge that Samuel offers about Saul and his ancestral house, namely, that Israel's desire is fixed on him and his lineage. But the most astonishing knowledge that Samuel possesses is the capacity, on the next day, to tell Saul "all that is on your mind" (1 Sam 9:19). This sort of omniscience can only refer to the sort of wisdom available to a representative of the deity. Samuel was remembered as a prophet, but he was originally titled a seer because of the specific form of behaviors and powers that he possessed. He was someone who had the ability to provide omniscient knowledge to humans.

Elijah was remembered as prophet, but he, like Samuel, was known by another title, in this case, "man of God." (Elisha, too, is known by this title, as are other individuals in the DtrH, e.g., 1 Kgs 13:1.) Again, there are certain actions that betray characteristic behavior of a "man of God." He personifies the power of the deity. Elisha, even more than Elijah, mediated the power of the deity through his deeds, and not just his words. Many of the stories about Elisha focus on his miraculous actions. Second Kings 4:1-7 offers a classic example. The widow of one of Elisha's followers (he had belonged to a group known as "the sons of the prophets") reports her financial plight to Elisha. Immediately after hearing that her children are to become slaves, Elisha tells her to start pouring oil from the one vessel in her house. It yields a fantastic amount of oil, which she is told to sell to pay off her debts and live on the remaining assets. In this case, the "man of God" (2 Kgs 4:7) simply acts on his own. There is no overt request to the deity for help. The same situation obtains when Elisha purifies some food that had been poisoned (2 Kgs 4:38-41). Holy men possessed the power of the deity and could use it at will.

Israel's long-term perceptions about prophets have made their way into these narratives about holy men. In another miracle story or legend, Elisha uses language that also appears on the lips of other prophets, "Thus says the LORD" (2 Kgs 2:21, compare Amos 2:1). Elijah, too, when confronting Ahab uses that same phrase twice (1 Kgs 21:19). And Elijah, when he was on Mount Carmel with the prophets of Baal, did not simply act, but instead prayed for God's help (1 Kgs 18:36-37). So, the portraits of these holy men have been somewhat obscured by the inclusion of language used about other prophets who were not necessarily prophets in the mold of an Elisha.

Other prophets were visionaries, or seers, though not diviner-seers in the mold of Samuel. They experienced visions. They engaged in what some contemporary scholars would call trances or possession behavior, and they reported those visions to other Israelites. Reports of visionary experience are widespread in the prophetic literature. In the Former Prophets, Micaiah ben Imlah, when summoned by two kings to offer a prophetic word about an upcoming battle, reports, "Therefore hear the word of the LORD: I saw the LORD sitting on his throne, with all the host of heaven standing beside him ..." (1 Kgs 22:19-23). Micaiah reports having observed the deliberations of the divine council. That vision is strikingly similar to one reported in the Latter Prophets. Isaiah reports that he, too, "saw the Lord sitting on a throne" (Isa 6:1). And in that vision, Isaiah also sees the divine council in action. Interestingly, the Hebrew noun **khozeh** ("seer" or "visionary") is never used of an Israelite prophet who provided vision reports.

The most frequent term for a prophet in the OT is **navi**ʾ. Over time it became the catchall term for prophet in ancient Israel. The one form of behavior that the other terms have not regularly attested is that of declaimer. And, though the noun **navi**ʾ does not literally mean "speaker," it is frequently used of prophets who make oral declarations, both oracles and prophetic sayings (see below for this distinction).

If one then draws back and considers the depictions of a diviner-seer such as Samuel, a man of God such as Elisha, a visionary such as Ezekiel, and a declaimer such as Amos, what might one identify as a common denominator? They were individuals who worked at the intersection of the world of the human and the divine. The same can be said for priests. Both were religious specialists. But priests and prophets worked in different arenas and possessed different qualifications. To be a priest, one had to be born into a priestly lineage (i.e., trace his parentage to a priest such as Levi or Aaron), had to learn the regulations in order to conduct the rituals at the Temple, and had to be ordained at the age of thirty. Though some prophets did belong to priestly lineages and did have some knowledge about rituals conducted at the Temple, there is no evidence that they were ordained into prophetic status. Instead, they report having been called or commissioned by the deity (so Isa 6; Jer 1; Ezek 1–3). And even those prophets for whom there is no commissioning report function as divinely authorized intermediaries (*see* CALL, CALLING, CALL STORIES).

Women in ancient Israel could not be priests; they could, however, be prophets, as was also the case in Mesopotamia (see below). Though no prophetic book bears a woman's name, five women in the OT are titled "prophet" or "prophetess": Miriam (Exod 15:20), Deborah (Judg 4:4), Isaiah's anonymous wife (Isa 8:3), Huldah (2 Kgs 22:14), and Noadiah (Neh 6:14). It would be difficult, indeed, to identify a core of prophetic activity based on the activities of these five women. When described as a prophet, Miriam was leading a group of women in musical praise of Yahweh's triumph at the Red Sea, including the first verse of a victory song attested in Exod 15. It may be that later authors thought of prophets as the creators of songs (see, e.g., Isa 5; Ezek 33:32) and labeled Miriam a prophet on that basis. Deborah receives three appellations: prophetess, wife of Lappidoth, and judge (Judg 4:4). In what follows in the narratives about her (Judg 4–5), it would be difficult to identify which activities are "prophetic." The most obvious might be Deborah's speaking on behalf of the deity to Barak (Judg 4:6-7). Isaiah 8:3 offers no evidence that would permit readers to know the reason that Isaiah named his wife as a "prophetess." Her sole role in that report is to give birth to a symbolically named child. Huldah is the individual most similar to male prophets. She is consulted by political leaders, as were both Jeremiah and Ezekiel. And she offers two oracles, each commencing with the phrase, "Thus says the LORD." The first of these oracles came true; the second did not. Finally, Noadiah is remembered, along with "the rest of the prophets," as having tried to make Nehemiah afraid. How she—or they—did this remains unclear. Their activity is, however, probably similar to that recounted in Neh 6:10-13, when Shemaiah "pronounced the prophecy against me." (Shemaiah had tried to frighten Nehemiah by telling him that his enemies were coming to kill him.) In sum, women were remembered as prophets, though their male counterparts radically outnumbered them. Interestingly, three of the five prophetesses are associated with males who were known as prophets: Miriam with Moses, Isaiah with his wife, and Noadiah with Shemaiah.

In the OT, there are several persons labeled as prophets who do not seem to otherwise belong with the aforementioned intermediaries. The author of Gen 20:7 characterizes Abraham as a prophet, since he will pray for Abimelech. Such a view is understandable, since some of Israel's prophets acted in an intercessory fashion. For example, Amos prayed successfully on behalf of Israel on more than one occasion (Amos 7:1-6). Clearly, for this biblical author the hallmark for being a prophet was his ability to intercede on someone's behalf. As noted, Deborah, a judge, is labeled a prophetess (Judg 4:4), probably because she spoke on behalf of the deity to Barak. Exodus 15:20 links Miriam to prophecy by dint of her work as a musician. Finally, Moses is likened to a prophet (Deut 34:10), apparently due to the immediate relationship he had with the deity. These texts attest that biblical authors labeled certain individuals as prophets based on one or another feature of their personae. Nonetheless, these individuals otherwise do not regularly function as intermediaries in the mold of an Elijah or an Isaiah.

Throughout much of the 20th cent., scholars offered diverse proposals to explain the source of or essential character of prophecy. Some claimed that divine inspiration or ecstatic behavior was a hallmark. Much of the discourse here was psychological. Others offered a more psycho-theological notion, suggesting that the prophets participated in the divine pathos of the deity. The notion that the prophets were poets represented yet a third tack, one that had difficulty accommodating the presence of so much prose in prophetic books. And then there were certain conceptual schemes, such as the claim that prophets developed a theological perspective known as ethical monotheism. And this notion suffered division, with some maintaining that the prophets were essentially concerned with ethical issues such as justice and righteousness and others claiming that the prophets developed the notion of monotheism. All such proposals suffer from one fatal flaw. They fail to take into account the radical diversity of those individuals known as prophets in ancient Israel. Just as it is difficult to speak of a quintessential prophetic message, so too it is difficult to identify one model of prophetic behavior. Instead, it is appropriate to recognize the fundamental diversity in prophetic performance, as is suggested by the various Hebrew words for prophets. Even in this diversity, however, it is appropriate to think about prophets as intermediaries, typically representing the deity to the world of humans and in ways related to but different from priests and technical diviners.

B. Prophecy in the Ancient Near East

Many interpreters of the OT have thought that prophecy and prophetic literature were distinctive features of Israelite culture (and this even though biblical texts themselves attest that prophets were associated with deities other than Yahweh—so the prophets of Baal in 1 Kgs 18). However, such a judgment needs to be put within the broader context of the many ways in which the literature of the OT is related to other literature from the ANE. Early on in the critical study of the OT, it became clear that the kinds of literature present in the OT were also attested in texts from the ANE. The legal collections in the Bible were placed in dialogue with such texts as the Hammurabi law code or laws from the Middle Assyrian period. Psalms were compared with hymns to deities in both Egypt and Mesopotamia. The book of Proverbs was, in at least in one case, understood to depend upon a collection of Egyptian maxims, the Instruction of Amenemope. And there are, of course, numerous other wisdom texts from the ANE that may be compared with biblical wisdom literature. Prescriptions for rituals at ancient Ugarit have been compared to descriptions of sacrifice in Leviticus. Put simply, most of the genres of literature present in the OT are attested in significant ways elsewhere in the ANE. Prophetic literature was, however, held to be an exception. This picture has now changed.

Scholars routinely refer to three texts as evidence that prophets were present in ancient Syria-Palestine, though outside the borders of Israel. The first is a narrative written in Egyptian, dating to the 11th cent. BCE. The story involves a journey of an Egyptian official, Wenamun, to the Phoenician coast in search of lumber for a pharaonic building project. While anchored in the harbor at Byblos, one of the sailors on his ship absconds with some gold and silver that Wenamun no doubt was going to use to purchase the aforementioned lumber. Wenamun remained at Byblos for roughly a month in unhappy dialogue with a local prince. At that point, "the god (Amon) seized a great seer from among his great seers, and he caused him to be in an ecstatic state, and he said to him:

> 'Bring up the god!
> Bring up the messenger who bears him!
> It is Amon who has sent him.
> He is the one who has caused that he come.'"
> (Nissinen, 220)

In this speech, the prophet is speaking "to him," the prince of Byblos. And Wenamun is the messenger to which the boy refers. The prophetic speech, therefore, offers an attempt to authenticate the credentials of Wenamun as a duly authorized servant of the Egyptian god Amon (*see* WENAMUN, JOURNEY OF).

Several features about this report are noteworthy. First, the text attests to possession behavior, which may be part of a prophetic performance (1 Sam 19:20; 1 Kgs 22:12 suggest that such behavior in Israel was associated with groups of prophets). Second, the person possessed speaks in his own voice, i.e., he utters a prophetic saying, not a divine oracle. Third, the deity who possesses the seer is apparently Amon, an Egyptian god, not a local Canaanite deity. This "ecumenical" form of prophecy may be compared to the biblical, though non-Israelite, Balaam, who becomes a visionary on behalf of Israel's God (Num 22–24). Fourth, the prophetic behavior and speech are associated in the narrative with the making of an offering, presumably a sacrifice. This connection between prophetic utterance and sacrifice is paralleled by the burnt offerings that precede two of Balaam's prophetic utterances (so Num 23:4-30). Clearly this brief episode in the Wenamun narrative attests to prophetic behavior that is in some consequential ways similar to prophetic behavior attested in the OT.

The second text from ancient Syria-Palestine, the Zakkur inscription, is briefer. Dating to the early 8th cent. BCE, it was erected by King Zakkur to celebrate his victory over a military alliance headed by the Aramean king BEN-HADAD. Zakkur reports that Ben-Hadad organized a coalition of sixteen kings who laid siege to

Hadrach. After Zakkur prayed to his god, Baalshamayn, that deity responded by speaking to him "through seers and through visionaries." Their response was conveyed in two separate speeches. In the first, they told Zakkur, "Fear not, for I have made [you] king, [and I who will st]and with [you], and I will deliver you from all [these kings who] have forced a siege against you ..." (Nissinen, 206). Then, in a second utterance, the prophets confirmed their earlier statement by proclaiming that Ben-Hadad and his coalition would be defeated.

One is immediately reminded of a Judahite king, Ahaz, who also confronted a military alliance (2 Kgs 16:1-20), and of Hezekiah, who suffered a military siege at the hand of the Neo-Assyrians (2 Kgs 18:9-37). In both cases, the prophet Isaiah offered words directly to the kings in question. And in both cases, Isaiah announced, as did the "seers and messengers," that God would surmount the military threat (see 2 Kgs 18:5-7). Even the diction used by those seers and messengers is similar to that of Isaiah. "Fear not" is on the lips of Isaiah on both occasions (Isa 7:4 and 37:6) as it was on those of the seers and the messengers. And the same basic word, *seer* (**khozeh**), is used in both the Zakkur inscription and in Isaiah ("the vision of Isaiah"; Isa 1:1).

The literature associated with the non-Israelite seer BALAAM son of Beor is of far greater significance than either of the aforementioned texts. In the OT, Balaam is depicted as one who receives "a word" from the Lord (Num 23:5), who has "the spirit of God" come upon him (Num 24:2), who speaks an ORACLE (Num 24:3), who sees "the vision of the Almighty" (Num 24:4), and who "hears the words of God" (Num 24:16). Though clearly not an Israelite, Balaam, whom the text locates near the juncture of northern Syria and northern Mesopotamia, shares many features with prophets of Yahweh.

Only recently has it become clear that this figure, Balaam son of Beor, was known outside Israel. In excavations that took place at Deir ʿAlla in 1967, an inscription, written in Aramaic and found in fragments, refers to "Balaam, son of Beor." In that inscription he is labeled "a seer of the gods" and associated with El. He, like the biblical Balaam, has a vision, though in the Deir ʿAlla texts it is probably a dream (*see* DEIR ʿALLA, TEXTS). He, like the biblical Balaam, envisions a future that has been enacted by the gods (Num 23:23, "See what God has done"; Deir ʿAlla, 1.5, "See the acts of the gods" [Nissinen, 210–11]). Both characters are privy to the world of divine decision making and communicate something of that world to their earthly compatriots. In both cases, the visions portend doom to certain individuals. There can be little question that one figure, a Balaam son of Beor, lies behind both of these texts, one biblical, one extra-biblical.

Further, what Balaam foresees in the Deir ʿAlla inscription is markedly similar to that which one finds elsewhere in biblical prophetic (and non-prophetic) texts. The non-biblical Balaam anticipates a time when normal social relationships will be disrupted: "The one who is esteemed esteems, and the one who esteems is esteemed ... and the deaf hear from afar ..." (Nissinen, 211). This pattern of reversal is also attested in biblical prophetic texts. Isaiah 3:5 offers a classic example: "the youth will be insolent to the elder, and the base to the honorable." Amos 8:9 exemplifies a comparable reversal, though in the heavens: "I will make the sun go down at noon, and darken the earth in broad daylight." The Aramean Balaam shares this rhetorical perspective about both social and cosmic disaster. In sum, Num 22–24 and the Deir ʿAlla inscription offer the clearest evidence that links the world of prophecy as known in the OT with prophets attested in literature from the ANE. Prophecy existed in various Levantine contexts. Moreover, visions seem to be a hallmark of prophecy in extra-biblical texts from Syria-Palestine.

Ancient Mesopotamia has yielded numerous texts that attest to the work of prophets. This literature dates to the Old Babylonian and Neo-Assyrian periods. Better known are the texts from ancient MARI, which date to the 18th cent. BCE. Mari, a city located on the Middle Euphrates River, was razed by the famous Hammurabi, king of Babylon. Prior to that destruction in 1765 BCE, it had been a prominent crossroads between Syria and Mesopotamia. Excavations have revealed a rich royal archive from the reign of King Zimri-Lim. This library included a number of texts preserving messages sent to the king from prophets. As is the case with prophets in the OT, the prophets in and around Mari were known by various titles. These include the **muhhum** and **apilum**. The former term derives from the verb meaning "to be ecstatic or possessed." Those individuals so labeled could convey messages from the deity to the king. The noun **apilum** derives from the verb "to answer." It has been a commonplace to suggest that the **apilum** was a prophet who responded to inquiries whereas the **muhhum** offered unsolicited oracles. However, in examining the texts in which these two names appear, individuals, whether titled **muhhum** or **apilum**, appear to perform in very similar fashion. Such a distinction is not attested among the biblical prophets (Ezekiel functioned in both ways). The **muhhum** appears to have ties to a particular temple, which was not always the case with the **apilum**.

Not all prophets wore such labels. Private individuals, i.e., those without any titles, could also present messages to the king. Further, the utterances of prophets were apparently conveyed to the king by people other than the prophets themselves. Shibtu, Zimri-Lim's wife, reported oracles and even solicited them when she deemed information necessary. These prophets spoke to the king on behalf of various deities (e.g., Adad, Dagan, Shamash). Unlike the world of biblical prophecy, women are prominent as prophets.

When one reads through the approximately fifty prophetic texts from Mari, the social context of what they address becomes evident (*see* MARI TEXTS, LETTERS). They addressed matters primarily involving the king, e.g., whether or not he will be victorious in battle, his personal well-being, or his support of particular temples. The king could be told that a battle in which he is about to engage will be won. The king can be admonished not to go out in public due to a possible revolt. Kings could be encouraged either to commence royal construction projects or to desist from them. The king can be admonished to provide "pure water" for a temple. Prophets also addressed issues related to the cities within the purview of the king, e.g., "Whoever commits an act of violence shall be expelled from the city" (Nissinen, 38). Such a topic is obviously related to the discourse of Israel's prophets. So, too, is the admonition that Abiya speaks to Nur-Sin, who in turn passes the utterance on to the king in written form: "If anyone cries out to you ... 'I have been wr[ong]ed,' be there to decide his case; an[swer him fai]rly. [Th]is is what I de[sire] from you" (Nissinen, 22). In both oracles, one is reminded of prophets depicted in the OT, especially Nathan and Gad, who have sometimes been characterized as court prophets. Both in Israel and in Mesopotamia, there was a close connection between the royal-political world and that of prophetic proclamation.

When one reads the Mari prophetic texts, one is struck by the presence of certain formulae, some of which may be readily compared with those in the OT. Typical is "Thus says Adad" (Nissinen, 21–22) or "Thus says Shamash" (Nissinen, 24–25). The respective prophets, Abiya and an unnamed individual, are clearly intermediaries who are conveying oracles, words spoken in the first person by the deity. Here, the similarity in rhetoric to that which occurs in the OT is clear, e.g., "Thus says Yahweh" (NRSV, "the LORD"; Amos 3:12). Less frequent at Mari is the phrase "in my dream" (Nissinen, 62–64; 67–69), which nonetheless attests to visionary behavior (the boundary between so-called waking and sleeping visions is notably permeable). That Akkadian phrase, "in my dream," functions similarly to introductions to vision reports in the OT, e.g., "And I looked up and saw" (Zech 1:18; 2:1; 5:1).

The issue of veracity was important. Prophets in ancient Mari addressed matters of state. And they sometimes did so publicly: "He did not utter his oracle in private, but he delivered his oracle in the assembly of the elders" (Nissinen, 38) or "This is what he kept proclaiming at the gate of the palace" (Nissinen, 73). Because of such public declarations, the kings insisted that the prophets be identified and held accountable. A number of texts conclude with statements such as "This is what this pr[ophet] said. I have now s[ent] the h[air and a fringe of the garment] of the prophet to my lord" (Nissinen, 54). These two objects—the hair and fringe—were preserved so that representatives of the royal court could identify the person if the prophecy proved errant or seditious. (First Kings 22 hints at a similar situation in Israel, involving the accountability of Micaiah ben Imlah for what he proclaimed.)

In the Neo-Assyrian period, prophetic activity is attested in a massive royal archive found at Nineveh. These 7th-cent. BCE texts, which date to the reigns of Esarhaddon and his son Assurbanipal, are more than 1,000 years younger than those from Mari. New elements have emerged, though these texts share many elements with their forebears. Terminological diversity remains, though one, new role label has achieved primacy, that of the **ragimmu** or proclaimer. This term emphasizes the character of these prophets as speakers. The term **mahhum** or ecstatic continues as does the phenomenon of people functioning as prophets even though they bore no comparable titles. An increasing number of prophets are female, a phenomenon that may be related to the deity to whom most of the Neo-Assyrian prophets are related. Many of the texts from Nineveh refer to prophets from another city located to the southeast of Nineveh: Arbela. A major temple devoted to Ishtar, a complex and primary deity associated with love and military activity, had been built there. And there were apparently a significant number of female devotees, some of whom functioned as prophets, communicating with rulers of the Neo-Assyrian Empire. Though the Neo-Assyrian prophets address the royal house, as they did in the Mari texts, the content of these texts is more homogeneous, often offering support to the king or those around him, e.g., the king or the king's mother. The following portion of an oracle to Esarhaddon is typical:

> "I am Ishtar of [Arbela]! Esarhaddon, king of A[ssyria]! In Assur, Ninev[eh], Calah and Arbe[la], I will give endle[ss] days and everlasti[ng] years to Esarhaddon, my king.... Fear not, king! I have spoken to you, I have not slandered yo[u]! I have inspi[red you] with confidence, I have not caused [you] to come to shame! I will lead [you] safely across the River."
> (Nissinen, 106–07)

One might imagine them being characterized as prophets of "peace," as does Jeremiah of his opponents.

Some of the texts on which the Neo-Assyrian prophecies were written differ from those discovered at Mari. At Mari, each prophecy or set of statements from one prophet was written on a single tablet. And this is true for some Neo-Assyrian texts as well. However, there are three texts in which multiple prophecies appear on the same tablet, now written in a horizontal format. In two instances, these longer tablets include oracles from multiple individuals. In one other case, a tablet is made up of five oracles, all from the same individual, La-dagil-ili, who is quoted in both of the other collections as well.

(Even though many of the prophets in Arbela were women, the most frequently cited person was a man.) The collection of La-dagil-ili's five oracles diverges from the others. In no other case did the compositor confront the issue of how to arrange the oracles from one person. In this case, the scribe confronted the task of integrating what were probably originally distinct oracles. At the outset, one finds an utterance describing a general state of peace, which is followed by one alluding to the defeat of the king's enemies. The central oracle alludes to a "covenant tablet" affirming the relationship between the king and Assur, the national god. The penultimate oracle calls upon the gods to join in this covenant in a ritual involving water whereas a final oracle admonishes Esarhaddon to provide appropriate food and drink for Ishtar. This tablet offers one an early extra-biblical example of the collection and editing of what might be termed prophetic literature.

One final feature of the Neo-Assyrian texts deserves comment. The prophets used figurative language to convey portions of their messages. In one text, in which the prophetess Mulissu-katbat offers assurances to Assurbanipal, she identifies herself using a simile, "Like a nurse I will carry you on my hip," and a metaphor "Fear not, you, my calf whom I rear" (Nissinen 127–28). La-dagil-ili speaks in even more specific imagery: "Like a winged bird over its fledgling, I will twitter above you, going around you, surrounding you. Like a faithful cub I will run around in your palace, sniffing out your enemies" (Nissinen 113). It is perhaps no accident that similes enrich biblical prophetic texts from the Neo-Assyrian period.

There is far less convincing evidence of prophetic activity and literature from ancient Egypt, even though some ancient Egyptian texts have been characterized as admonitory or prophetic. The Admonitions of Ipuwer has been likened to biblical prophetic literature primarily because it was perceived to offer challenges to Egyptian rulers comparable to those made by prophets to Israelite kings (*see* IPU-WER, ADMONITIONS OF). The Admonitions do address a king—"Authority, perception, and justice are with you" (*ANET*, 443)—and those topics concern biblical prophets as well. Moreover, this text describes a society in disarray, one in which there have been numerous "reversals," e.g., higher social classes are now serfs and the lower classes have achieved noble status, imagery shared by biblical prophetic literature. However, one of the essential features of prophetic literature is that it attests to the work of an intermediary who speaks on behalf of the deity. And there is no such discourse present in the Admonitions of Ipuwer. In fact, there are strong parallels between biblical and extra-biblical wisdom literature and the Admonitions of Ipuwer.

Some interpreters claim that the so-called Prophecies of Nefertiti are similar to biblical prophetic literature. This judgment is based in part on the presence of rhetoric about the future. A scribe, Nefer-rohu, speaks to the pharaoh about "what is going to happen" (*ANET*, 444). He anticipates a time of disaster, one in which "everything good is disappeared" (*ANET*, 445). The sun will have disappeared, rivers will dry up, and foreign enemies will overwhelm the land. This text attests the motif of reversals, which was also present in the Admonitions of Ipuwer. For example, "men salute respectfully him who formerly saluted" (*ANET*, 444). The social order will be "topsy-turvy" (*ANET*, 445). Only when a great king, who no doubt sponsored the creation of these "prophecies," is on the throne, will the society and land be at peace. Again, however, there is no evidence that such foresight is based on Nefer-rohu having communicated with the world of the divine. Instead, as was the case with Ipuwer, the literature seems to reflect the ethos and literary forms associated with the world of royal scribes in service to the court.

In sum, prophecy existed outside Israel. In Mesopotamia, as was the case in Israel, prophecy was not prominent in all times and places. In Israel, it was particularly important during times of crisis. And this appears to have been the case in Mesopotamia as well. Prophecy is particularly well attested in the Old Babylonian and Neo-Assyrian periods. In the former, Mari was under threat; in the latter, the royal succession—Assurbanipal to Esarhaddon—was particularly insecure. The Neo-Assyrian period was a time when prophecy flourished in Israel and Judah. In both Syria-Palestine and in Mesopotamia, prophets were known by different titles. Further, in both places prophets communicated with the deity in diverse ways, sometimes through visions, sometimes through auditions. The greatest difference between prophecy in Israel and in Mesopotamia involves the literature that the respective prophets and their tradents produced. For example, no texts from Mari or Nineveh are similar to the lengthy prophetic compositions in the OT, whether the prose essays of Ezekiel or the poetry of Jeremiah.

C. Prophecy in Israel

1. Prophecy and critical junctures

Some scholars have maintained that prophets often emerge in times of crisis or certain nodal moments in a society. Though all such generalizations remain open to challenge, the contexts in which many of Israel's prophets were active seems consistent with this claim. Though certain individuals, e.g., Abraham and Moses, were, at points, labeled as prophets, that understanding almost certainly depends upon models of prophecy based on the more "typical" prophets, e.g., an Amos or an Isaiah. Hence, to sketch a brief history of Israelite prophecy, one does well to begin with those individuals who seem to act in ways typical of others who are known as prophets.

The first "typical" prophets attested in the DtrH are Nathan and Gad. Both appeared when David reigned and addressed issues involving the new role of the king in Israel. This was a time of great social change in Israel. Israel had, until David became king, been a society in distress. They had been unable to thwart military challenges posed by the Philistines. The old pre-state order had failed. Hence something different was needed. Israel's own testimony affirms that Israel knew it was adopting a new form of governance, one used by other nations, and one that involved the potential for abuse—the king exercising power in inappropriate ways (so 1 Sam 8).

In this time of radical political change, kingship emerged, and so did a type of religious intermediary who could speak with authority to the king. One does well to consider the various issues that Gad and Nathan broached with David. 1) Soon after David had been anointed by Saul (1 Sam 16), an act that in effect made him king even before he had been designated as such by Judahites (see 2 Sam 2:4), David fled Israel to Moab. While there, the DtrH reports that Gad commanded David to return to Judah (1 Sam 22:5). This prophet was responsible for providing guidance to the nascent king about his responsibilities, namely, where he should reside. 2) David, the new king, wanted to build a temple. The creation of a temple in Jerusalem, a royal shrine, would be of great consequence. Though initially approving this project, Nathan received an oracle that forbade David from undertaking this project, allocating it to Solomon instead (2 Sam 7). This interaction involves the role of the king vis-à-vis ritual matters. 3) "In the spring of the year, the time when kings go out to battle" (2 Sam 11:1), David remained in Jerusalem. While there, he had sexual intercourse with Bathsheba and proceeded to have her husband killed on the battlefield. The prophet Nathan condemns David's behavior and pronounces judgment on him. Though David's deed is often viewed as a violation of Israel's moral ethos (adultery and murder), it should also be understood as misbehavior within the military ambit. David was serving as general and had misused the battlefield. Nathan, therefore, is addressing the new role of king in the context of military activity, a role that was quite different from the judge, the military leader prior to that time. 4) Second Samuel 24 presents a puzzling account, one in which Yahweh "incited" David against the people, such that David undertook a census to determine how many men would be available to fight, even after Joab, his general, had questioned the wisdom of such an act. Thereafter Gad appears to David and, as an intermediary for the deity, negotiates with David the punishment that the people will suffer. The report concludes with David acquiring the land on which, during Solomon's reign, the altar in Jerusalem will be built. Again, a prophet is involved in the world of war and ritual. 5) Finally, shortly before David's death, his son Adonijah attempted to secure the throne as David's successor. During that conflicted situation, David summoned Zadok, a priest, Benaiah, a military leader, and Nathan, the prophet, and commanded them to make Solomon king. In this case, the prophet was among three primary leaders who could assure a proper transition of royal authority. At the inception of the monarchy in Israel, the DtrH portrays prophets addressing the following issues: the role of the king in religious matters, the physical whereabouts of the king, the role of the king in war, and the issue of royal succession. Israelite historians portrayed prophets as having played prominent roles while the country charted the responsibilities of this new political actor, the king.

Within less than 100 years after the creation of the so-called united monarchy, various forces were at work that would lead to the reemergence of the two entities that had been held together under David and Solomon: Israel and Judah. Political, cultural, and economic factors all played into the dissolution of the united monarchy. From the perspective of Judahite historians, however, the role of the prophet was also critical at this formative moment. The prophet Ahijah announced to Jeroboam, a native of Ephraim, which was a part of the northern tribal confederation, that Yahweh would grant Jeroboam rule over ten tribes and leave Solomon (and the house of David) as rulers in Judah (1 Kgs 11:26-40).

Though the DtrH recounts a number of prophets active after Ahijah, the most prominent prophets are Elijah and Elisha. And both are related to crises and their resolution (and, of course, much more!). The narratives about Elijah commence with a reference to the third year, probably of a drought (1 Kgs 18:1). And this severe crisis sets the stage for what follows in the ensuing chapters. The narrator takes this problem as an occasion to report not only the return of the rains but also to address the theological issue of who is responsible for rains (Yahweh or Baal). Elisha is related not to a natural catastrophe but to the problem of dynastic instability in Israel as exemplified by the end of the house of Omri. Though many factors contributed to this revolt, the DtrH presents Elisha as pivotal. He calls for one of his band to anoint Jehu as king over Israel (2 Kgs 9:1-3). Again, the picture is clear: prophets are prominent during times of national crisis.

The history of prophecy in Israel changes somewhat in the 8th cent. For many years, it was customary to characterize this change as the shift from pre-classical to classical prophecy. This way of formulating the change is unfortunate, since it suggests that Gad and Isaiah are fundamentally different. Such may not be the case, since both Gad and Isaiah were linked in immediate ways to the kings during whose reigns they were active as prophets.

The transformations are more complicated. They involve both the prophet's audience, the character of the literature attesting to the prophet's work, and the political environment in the ANE. When one looks back on the activities associated with Gad and Nathan, and Elijah and Elisha, it is striking that they regularly involve kings or those associated closely with them (this is typically not the case with the "legends" about Elijah and Elisha). When one moves to Amos and Hosea, and a bit later, to Isaiah and Micah, the audience has broadened. Kings and matters of state are still present. However, priests, judges, and the ruling class (economically and politically) now become the subject of prophetic address. Moreover, though there are hints of this globalization in 2 Kgs 5, the prophets speak about other nations (Amos 1–2) and address specific foreign rulers (Isa 14:12-21). The reasons for this expansion in subject of address are probably multiple. As Israel became a state, it soon developed relations with other emerging nations. States such as Edom, Moab, and Ammon were also developing at about the same time monarchy emerged in Israel. Moreover, biblical authors claim that, under David and Solomon—at least for a time—Israel held sway over those states. It is therefore not surprising that an Amos or other later Judean prophets would address these nations on behalf of Judah's deity, who was understood to dwell in the nation's capital city. Out of that political milieu, certain theological postulates emerged. Israel's God was viewed as having cosmic authority. It is surely no accident that the psalms that attest to Yahweh's kingship refer to his universal sway, e.g., Ps 47:8: "God is king over the nations." If God is king over the nations, then God's prophets are empowered to speak to the nations on the deity's behalf. On theo-political grounds, the prophets began to address far broader issues than had been the case earlier.

The change that occurs in the 8th cent. also involves the sort of literature that Israel has preserved about the prophets. There is no prophetic book devoted to Nathan or Elijah. However, the OT preserves books attesting to prophets who were active in the 8th cent., and not before. Further, the sort of literature in these books is distinctive. Poetry predominates. Rather than comprising essentially reports about these prophets, even though such reports are present, the earliest of these books conserve that which prophets said.

The 8th cent. also saw the emergence of the Neo-Assyrian Empire. Though nascent Israel had confronted powerful enemies before (e.g., the Philistines and, later, the Arameans), the Neo-Assyrians presented a qualitatively different challenge, one that would spell doom for the Northern Kingdom. The superscriptions to the books of Hosea and Amos date the activities of these prophets to the reign of Jeroboam (786–746 BCE; Judean kings are mentioned as well). Just prior to his reign, the Neo-Assyrian emperor Adad-Nirari III had conducted military campaigns in Syria-Palestine. Israel, along with other states, was required to forfeit certain economic goods to him. And immediately after Jeroboam's death, Tiglath-pileser III began predatory invasions that affected both Israel and Judah. For prophets active during this century, the threat posed by the Neo-Assyrians would have been palpable. And it would remain so.

Amos and Hosea may be read as prophets commenting on life in the Northern Kingdom and anticipating disaster for that state at the hands of the Assyrian Empire. It is, therefore, no accident that the judgments foreseen by Amos and Hosea, as well as by later prophets, were often couched in military idioms. Amos identifies numerous ways in which the deity will punish Israel, e.g., "I will press you down in your place" (Amos 2:13); "I [will] punish Israel for its transgressions" (3:14). One reads such pronouncements and wonders how it is that the deity will undertake this action. Texts such as Amos 3:11 provide the answer: "An adversary shall surround the land, and strip you of your defense; and your strongholds shall be plundered" (so also Amos 6:14). References to exile (Amos 6:7) can only refer to the aftermath of military defeat. There can be little question but that Amos thought that Israel would suffer military assault.

The same may be said for Hosea. Though this prophet often speaks about the deity acting directly against Israel (e.g., 10:10, "I will come against the wayward people to punish them"), Hosea anticipates the destruction of the Northern Kingdom through military means. For example, 10:14 reads, "therefore the tumult of war shall rise against your people, and all your fortresses shall be destroyed, as Shalman destroyed Beth-arbel on the day of battle when mothers were dashed in pieces with their children." Both Hosea and Amos write with knowledge of Neo-Assyrian imperial might.

What had been from the perspective of Amos and Hosea a disaster on the horizon became for prophets active late in the 8th cent. and on into the 7th cent. an immediate and dire crisis, and now for both Israel and Judah. The threat to Israel posed by Tiglath-pileser III was severe. As a result, Israel joined forces with the Arameans in an attempt to create a military alliance strong enough to defend itself from the empire to the east. Not surprisingly, that alliance wanted Judah to become their ally. It is this occasion that elicits the first major burst of activity from Isaiah (though he reports that he had become a prophet several years earlier [ca. 738]). According to 2 Kgs 15–16, the so-called Syro-Ephraimitic coalition attacked Judah and immediately posed a threat to its capital, Jerusalem. Isaiah 7 reports the prophet's reaction to this situation. Ahaz, the king in Judah, felt that he had few options available to him. In order to preserve his nation, he had decided to seek help from the hand of the Neo-Assyrians themselves. Isaiah responded vigorously to this decision. His message to Ahaz was, essentially, twofold. First, the military coalition of which he was afraid would soon crumble. Second, Ahaz must trust that Yahweh will deliver Jerusalem. He should not seek help from the Neo-Assyrians. Were he not to follow these admonitions, he and Judah would be subject to later assault by the Neo-Assyrians.

Biblical texts attest that Ahaz failed to follow Isaiah's advice. He appealed for help to Tiglath-pileser III, who in turn attacked the coalition and defeated it ca. 732 BCE. Roughly ten years later, Israel, which had become a vassal to the Assyrians, violated that status, such that Tiglath-pileser III's successor, Shalmaneser V, came up against Israel and destroyed it, spelling the end of nationhood in the former Northern Kingdom. (It should be said that the book of Hosea appears to know and condemn the radical political instability in Israel just before its defeat [7:7], i.e., as a prophet he too is addressing this crisis.) Hence, during the first serious engagement between the states that venerated Yahweh and the Neo-Assyrian Empire, the prophet Isaiah had offered a proposal that had been ignored. Israel was defeated and Judah had become a vassal to the Neo-Assyrian Empire.

Near the end of the 8th cent., with new kings on the thrones of both Judah (Hezekiah) and Assyria (Sennacherib), the next major moment in the Neo-Assyrian crisis transpires. The episode is recounted in 2 Kgs 18–20, much of which also appears in slightly different form in Isa 36–39. Again, it involves coalitions, only this time Judah was part of the league attempting to defend itself from the Assyrians. The major players were Egypt and Babylon, but a number of Syro-Palestinian states, especially Tyre, were also involved. As was typical in the ANE, when a new king acceded to the throne, it often took several years for him to gain full control of the empire. Sennacherib took the Assyrian throne in 704, an accession that sparked rebellion to the south and west of the empire. Several years thereafter, the league was forming. Isaiah confronts this crisis at several points. In Isa 30:1-5, he indicts Judahites for making an alliance with Egypt (see also 31:1-3). Again, his voice is ignored. Judah joined the alliance and, soon thereafter, suffered attack by Sennacherib. At this point, Isaiah responds from the conviction that Yahweh will protect Zion from assault, the same position he held during the Syro-Ephraimitic crisis. He avers that the Assyrians will be defeated (e.g., 30:31; 31:8) and that Yahweh will deliver Zion (29:1-8). Isaiah's words regarding Sennacherib's attack are presented most explicitly in 2 Kgs 19:6-7: "Thus says the LORD: Do not be afraid because of the words that you have heard, with which the servants of the king of Assyria have reviled me. I myself will put a spirit in him, so that he shall hear a rumor and return to his own land; I will cause him to fall by the sword in his own land." The DtrH reports that, miraculously, Sennacherib and his army departed, having devastated many Judahite towns, but leaving Jerusalem intact. The crisis had been averted, as Isaiah had foreseen. Though the Neo-Assyrian Empire remained important well into the next century, there is little overt evidence from the book of Isaiah (or any other prophetic book dating early in the 7th cent.) that Judah existed in a crisis situation comparable to that posed by Sennacherib in 701 BCE.

Prophetic rhetoric of the 8th and early 7th cent. was forged on the anvil of the crises posed by the Neo-Assyrian Empire. It is difficult to discern oracles from prophets during much of the 7th cent. prior to the time just before the reforms associated with King Josiah. King Manasseh ruled on the Judahite throne from 686–642. He was apparently a loyal vassal to the Neo-Assyrians. As a result, Judah was not subject to military assault. Further, Judahite society during this time does not suffer the sort of socioeconomic critique that had been earlier leveled by Micah and, to a lesser extent, by Isaiah. Only in retrospect, as offered by the DtrH, is this time viewed as one of a religious crisis. In 2 Kgs 21, the historian indicts Manasseh for idolatrous religious practices. The text continues with a prose oracle, attributed to "the prophets," in which a national crisis is identified: the destruction of Judah and the exile of its citizens (21:10-15). Though the agent of Judah's destruction is not mentioned in this chapter, readers of 2 Kings learn several chapters later that the Neo-Babylonians will attack twice and then finally destroy Judah (chaps. 24–25). This crisis posed by the appearance of the Neo-Babylonians elicits a new burst of prophetic activity.

The period 630–620 BCE was a momentous one throughout the ANE. The last great emperor on the Neo-Assyrian throne, Assurbanipal, died in 627 BCE. Within one year, Babylonian troops had engaged those of Assyria and had been victorious. By that time it would have become clear to many throughout Mesopotamia and Syria-Palestine that the Assyrian Empire was crumbling and that the Babylonians would soon take their place. It was a time of geopolitical transition, one to which Judahite political and religious leaders responded. Josiah, according to the Chronicler's history, began his reforms in 627 BCE (the DtrH dates the beginning of his reforms to 621). The correlation between that date and Assurbanipal's death can hardly be coincidental.

Numerous prophets also address these changes—and in various ways. The book of Nahum is titled "an oracle concerning Nineveh" (1:1). Nineveh was the capital of the Neo-Assyrian Empire, renowned for its cultural significance and size (so, in hyperbolic fashion, Jonah 3:3). The book of Nahum puts what is happening to Nineveh within the purview of Israelite religion. Nahum anticipates the military destruction of Nineveh. Israel's God is at work in these events: "See, I am against you, says the LORD of hosts, and I will burn your chariots in smoke" (Nah 2:13). As with other prophets, he offers reasons for that eventuality: Nineveh is terribly violent. It is a "city of bloodshed, utterly deceitful, full of booty—no end to the plunder" (3:1). The final verse of the book concludes with the rhetorical question, "For who has ever escaped your endless cruelty?" The answer is, of course, no one. Since Nineveh has been cruel to everyone, it deserves extermination. Nahum, a Judahite prophet, is interpreting an international crisis—the destruction of Nineveh—from the perspective of Judahite religious traditions. The same may be said for Zephaniah, who also anticipates the destruction of Nineveh (Zeph 2:13-15).

The book of Habakkuk stems from a slightly later period. Unlike Nahum, Habakkuk names explicitly the Chaldeans (another way of depicting the Babylonians). Unlike Nahum and Zephaniah, Habakkuk does not refer to the Assyrians. It is as if they had already been defeated (Nineveh was destroyed in 612 BCE). Nahum and Zephaniah had proclaimed this as good news for Judah, which had suffered mightily at the hands of the Assyrians. But Judah now had to face the new rulers of the ANE. The book of Habakkuk construes the Babylonians as a people who are acting at the behest of Israel's deity: "For I am rousing the Chaldeans, that fierce and impetuous nation" (Hab 1:6). This Israelite prophet held, as did his forebears, that Judah's God was active in the international political crises that were affecting Judah. It was the task of the prophet to interpret these broader historical issues from the perspective of Israel's faith. In the case of Habakkuk, one may infer that Yahweh has roused the Chaldeans not to punish the Assyrians but rather to affect life in Judah itself. Habakkuk begins the book with a complaint about injustice, presumably in Judah (1:2-4). The deity responds by reporting that these Chaldeans "scoff at kings" (1:10). One might think he is referring to those on the throne in Judah. However, in the course of the dialogue between Habakkuk and God, the reader discovers that the Chaldeans will be more of a demonic force than one that will right the injustices about which Habakkuk is concerned. "Like Death they never have enough" (Hab 2:5).

These death-dealing Babylonians remain the subject of prophetic rhetoric as one moves into the 6th cent. They are no longer a distant threat but become an enemy at the door. The crisis that began in the late 7th cent. in the shift of power away from Assyria to Babylon has now worked its way insidiously into Syria-Palestine. At the turn of the century, Judah revolted from its status as vassal to Babylon (2 Kgs 24:1). The results were disastrous. Judah was attacked and subjugated in 598. Many of its leading citizens, including the king and Ezekiel, were taken into exile. Then, ten years later, after another mini-revolt, Judah was again attacked and Jerusalem was destroyed. If the Neo-Assyrian crisis involved a siege of Jerusalem, the Neo-Babylonian crisis spelled the very end of Judah as a monarchic state.

Both Jeremiah and Ezekiel attest to these cataclysmic events. Jeremiah is the first to allude to this challenge, but he does so in highly poetic fashion. At a number of places in the poetry that appears in the book's first ten chapters, Jeremiah alludes to "an enemy from the north," e.g., "for evil looms out of the north, and great destruction" (Jer 6:1). Such lines offer an almost mythic sense. Elsewhere, it seems clear that Jeremiah envisions the enemy from the north as a vast imperial army:

"See, a people is coming from the land of the
north,
a great nation is stirring from the farthest
parts of the earth.
They grasp the bow and the javelin,
they are cruel and have no mercy,
their sound is like the roaring of the sea;
they ride on horses,
equipped like a warrior for battle,
against you, O daughter Zion!"
(Jer 6:22-23)

Though in these poetic texts Jeremiah never offers the name of the enemy, it is difficult to imagine, particularly after the battle of Carchemish (605 BCE), when the Babylonians decisively defeated the Egyptians, that he could be referring to any army other than the troops of Nebuchadnezzar. This equation is made explicit in one of Jeremiah's prose sermons. "Therefore thus says the LORD of hosts: Because you have not obeyed my words, I am going to send for all the tribes of the north, says the LORD, even for King Nebuchadnezzar of Babylon ..." (Jer 25:8-9).

Much of the book of Jeremiah offers reasons why God is bringing an enemy agent against Israel and describes the days leading up to Jerusalem's destruction and its immediate aftermath. As such, one may read Jeremiah as yet another interpreter of the international crisis of which Judah was a part (see also his oracles against the nations [Jer 46–51]).

Ezekiel, too, attests to the assault on Judah by the Neo-Babylonian Empire. He does so in quite different fashion, however. And part of that difference may be a function of Ezekiel's physical location. Ezekiel offers a vision report regarding the destruction of the Temple and city (Ezek 9–11). That report is a highly impressionistic version of the destruction, one that focuses on the Temple and the departure of the deity from it. Jeremiah's account (Jer 39–40) oddly does not refer to the destruction of the Temple (that is mentioned only in the historical appendix, Jer 52, which was drawn from 2 Kgs 24–25). In sum, prophets, even though they might be viewing the same catastrophe, could focus on one and another aspect of its dimensions. The diverse ways in which Ezekiel and Jeremiah address the decimation of the Temple is a classic example. As prophets, they were interpreting the same momentous events, but for differing audiences.

Were Israel's prophets only exegetes of Israel's monarchic state, there would have been no more prophetic words after 587. The state had ceased to exist. Israel, however, was now living in a perpetual crisis situation. Some of its members were in diaspora, others lived in the land. Early on in the exilic period, Obadiah responds to this situation by calling for judgment upon Edom. According to that brief book, Edom was apparently involved in the victimization of Judah (Obad 13, "you should not have looted his goods"). In addition, Edomites handed over Judahite refugees to the conquering army (v. 14). Obadiah envisions "the day of the LORD" coming against Edom, but, unlike many of his prophetic predecessors, does not anticipate a particular nation that will attack Edom.

It was, however, more natural during this time of exilic duress for Judahites to focus on the empire that had destroyed their nation, the Babylonians. As a result, one is not surprised to discover invective directed against Babylon and its rulers. Isaiah 13:1-22 and 14:3-28, the initial chapters in that book's oracles against the nations, focus on the impending fall of Babylon. Though it will fall at the hand of another nation, the identity of that enemy remains vague (13:4-5). The same may be said for the brief oracle in Jer 50:1-3. Jeremiah uses again the allusive image of a nation from the north, but this time Babylon, rather than being the nation from the north, will instead be attacked by another northern enemy. (Surprisingly, Ezekiel does not include Babylon in his oracles against foreign nations.) Clearly, prophets active after Judah's defeat continue to observe the international scene and offer commentary when major changes are afoot.

That to which Isa 13–14 and Jer 50 attest in general terms, the defeat of Babylon, becomes explicit when the Persians appear on the scene. The Persians advanced into Mesopotamia during what Judahites were experiencing as the exilic period. A major portion of the book of Isaiah, chaps. 40–55, at a minimum, attests to this momentous change in the ANE. The figure of Cyrus was pivotal (Cyrus reigned ca. 550–530 BCE). Early on in his reign, Cyrus campaigned in northern Mesopotamia and Syria. Those alert to international affairs could surmise that Babylon would, in the not-too-distant future, suffer an assault from him. That expectation probably lies behind Isa 47, which foresees the demise of Babylon.

> "Come down and sit in the dust, virgin
> daughter Babylon!
>
> But evil shall come upon you,
> which you cannot charm away;
> disaster shall fall upon you,
> which you will not be able to ward off;
> and ruin shall come on you suddenly,
> of which you know nothing."
> (Isa 47:1, 11)

One must move to other portions of 2 Isaiah to discover how this disaster will occur. Isaiah 45:1 reads, "Thus says the LORD to his anointed, to Cyrus, whose right hand I have grasped to subdue nations before him and strip kings of their robes ...." The king of Babylon was one such king.

The time of exile was a period when a major shift in power occurred in the ANE—the demise of Babylon and the ascendance of the Persians. This seismic change was, yet again, the subject of prophetic address. In the eyes of the author of Isa 45, Cyrus is none other than a "messiah," someone anointed by Yahweh to do the Lord's will. For Judahites, Cyrus would be remembered as the one who permitted Judahites to return to the land and who authorized the rebuilding of the Second Temple, a process that would include the work of some of Israel's last named prophets, Haggai and Zechariah.

That the books of both Haggai and Zechariah date to the year 520 attests to the importance of that moment. In the broader ANE environment, Darius was now on the Persian throne. Conditions were ripe for the restoration of temple-based Yahwism in Syria-Palestine, but there were, apparently, impediments. However, both Haggai and Zechariah spurred the people and their leaders—both political and religious—to rebuild the Temple. Their efforts were successful; the Temple was rededicated in 515 BCE. This would be the last major historically defined moment during which Israelite prophets played an identifiable role.

In sum, prophets in Israel were associated with crucial moments in its existence: the emergence of monarchy, the dissolution of the united monarchy, problems in dynastic succession, the Neo-Assyrian crisis, the Neo-Babylonian crisis, and the period of exile and restoration of Judah. They were cognizant of the major changes in the international power structure, which they interpreted as initiatives of Yahweh. Prophets were heralds from that deity to the people during times of momentous change and crisis. During those periods when Israelite and/or Judahite life had a modicum of stability, prophets were far less prominent than they were during times of crisis.

2. Prophets in Israelite society

Prophets have often been viewed as individuals who stand on the edge of society, offering critical judgments about it, and existing at a remove from its important institutions. To be sure, the words of Micah appear consistent with that view. Within the compass of Mic 3:1-11, that prophet attacked: "heads of Jacob," "rulers of the house of Israel," "the prophets," "the seers," "the diviners," "chiefs of the house of Israel," and "priests." It is no wonder he, along with other prophets, were viewed as at odds with much of society in Judah. Nonetheless, close examination of the place of prophets in Israel suggests that many were integrally related to important social and religious institutions, particularly the royal court and the world of worship, especially that associated with temples.

Some scholars have maintained that prophecy in Israel roughly began and ended about the same time that monarchy existed. Though such a claim requires considerable nuance, it is striking that individuals whom most readers would think about as prophets—Nathan and Gad (and possibly Samuel)—begin to appear when David was on the scene. Moreover, named prophets cease to be prominent after the final members of the

Davidic line exercise power. Zerubbabel, a Davidic scion, was the subject of address by some of the last of Israel's named prophets (Haggai, Zechariah). It is as if prophecy was a mode of religious behavior that needed monarchy as its setting. Prophets spoke to and about kings, royal succession, wars, matters of state, and, generally, society ruled by a monarch.

Prophets could make kings. The DtrH includes several reports according to which a prophet was involved with the beginning of a king's reign. If Samuel is to be counted as a prophet, he anointed both Saul (1 Sam 10:1) and David (1 Sam 16:13). First Kings 11 recounts an encounter between Ahijah and Jeroboam. The latter had led an insurrection against Solomon. As Jeroboam was fleeing from Jerusalem, Ahijah met him and informed him that Yahweh was dividing the united monarchy into two parts, one of which, the Northern Kingdom, would be given to Jeroboam. He would reign over it as king. Here a prophet not only reports the creation of a state but announces who its first ruler will be. Later, in the history of that kingdom (2 Kgs 9:1-3), Elisha summoned one of his prophetic band and commanded him to anoint Jehu saying, "I anoint you king over Israel" (see 1 Kgs 1:34 and similar language about Nathan anointing Solomon). Then, in the 6th cent. BCE, Haggai offers an oracle on behalf of Zerubbabel as king (Hag 2:23). Prophets clearly functioned as emissaries of the deity when a king was to be chosen.

Once a king was on the throne, a prophet could interact with him in various ways, sometimes as royal adviser. Jeremiah's role vis-à-vis Zedekiah is instructive (Jer 38). Soon before the fall of Jerusalem, Jeremiah had been imprisoned on charges of deserting to the Babylonians. Zedekiah, whom the Babylonians had placed on the Judahite throne, summoned Jeremiah and met him at the Temple. Zedekiah reported to Jeremiah that he had a question for him. Though Zedekiah never actually asked the question, Jeremiah did give him advice, telling him that if he surrendered to the Babylonians, Judah and Jerusalem would be spared. If not, then the city would be razed and Zedekiah would die. After this interchange Zedekiah commanded Jeremiah not to report the substance of their conversation, a command with which, the narrator takes pains to demonstrate, Jeremiah complies.

Prophets could help heal kings (Isa 38:21), could admonish kings (Jer 21:12), and could critique kings (2 Sam 12 [Nathan's judgment of David]). There has been a tendency to describe some of these individuals as "court prophets." Such a label is understandable, particularly in the cases of Nathan and Gad, whose words addressed almost exclusively the royalty. However, it is more appropriate to think that many prophets could interact with the royal court. This was true for Isaiah and Jeremiah, among others. That activity did not, however, prevent them from speaking to others, e.g., priests, and about other topics.

A similar claim has been made about those prophets who are related in one way or another to the religious life associated with the Temple. They have been called "cultic prophets." Here, too, the notion that a prophet could be associated with the world of the priests does not necessarily mean that certain prophets worked only or primarily in that environment.

Prophets could be related to the world of worship in various ways. Some prophets belonged to priestly lineages. The superscription to the book of Jeremiah states that he was "of the priests who were in Anathoth" (Jer 1:1). This statement alludes to a priestly heritage that could trace its origins to Abiathar, a priest active during the time of David. Abiathar had sided with Adonijah in his desire to succeed David. When Solomon succeeded David, Solomon banished Abiathar to his "estate" in Anathoth, a small town ca. 3 mi. northeast of Jerusalem (1 Kgs 2:26-27). (Anathoth was one of the thirteen cities given to the Levitical priests [see Josh 21:13-19].) It is not clear what priestly prerogatives this priestly group would have possessed so many years after their removal from Jerusalem. One might argue that in this later period, Levites, though no longer involved in the service of sacrifice, could still be involved in the teaching of Israel's torah (Deut 33:10). Should that be the case, then one might suppose that reference to the word of the prophet and the instruction of the priest (Jer 18:18) might belong to the same world. In any case, an editor of the book of Jeremiah deemed that priestly relationship to be of sufficient importance to include it in the book's superscription.

Other prophets belonged to priestly lineages. Zechariah is listed as the grandson of an individual named Iddo (1:1). That name appears in Neh 12:16 within a list of priestly houses, which strongly suggests that Zechariah could be identified with Israel's priests. The case with Ezekiel is clearer. Ezekiel 1:3 reads, "The word of the LORD came to the priest Ezekiel son of Buzi." (The Hebrew phrase could be translated "The word of the LORD came to Ezekiel, the son of Buzi, the priest.") This statement seems utterly straightforward, namely, that Ezekiel was a priest. Yet the book elsewhere clearly indicates that he was viewed as a prophet (2:5). There is at least one problem with the notion that Ezekiel was a priest. In order to become a priest, one must not only belong to a priestly house, one must also be ordained at the Temple. The ordination ceremonies, described in Lev 8–9, must take place at the Temple, since they involved sacrifices. Further, one could be ordained only at the age of thirty (Num 4:3). These requirements—that ordination take place at the Temple and at the age of thirty—make it unlikely that Ezekiel was ever ordained. Ezekiel's call as a prophet took place in 593 BCE (the fifth year of the exile of King Jehoiachin, Ezek 1:2). Ezekiel was apparently thirty years old at that time (Ezek 1:1, "in the thirtieth year"). Moreover, he was already living in exile, far away from the Temple in Jerusalem. As a result, it is unlikely that he could have been ordained as a priest. He would have been eligible for that status, since he had lived according to the laws of purity (Ezek 4:14; compare Lev 21:18), but the vagaries of Israelite history probably prevented his ordination.

As noted, some prophets belonged to priestly lineages. Does that mean, however, when they acted as prophets they were undertaking behavior that might have been identified by an ancient Israelite as that belonging to the world of the priests? In at least one clear case, the answer appears to be positive. Zechariah 7 offers a report according to which representatives from Bethel travel to Jerusalem to seek information from "the priests of the house of the LORD of hosts and the prophets" (v. 3). Striking here is the implicit claim that such a question could be answered by either priests or prophets. Both could offer information from the divine world to humans. The text reports no answer from the priests. Instead, Zech 7:5-7 contains an interrogative response by Zechariah, challenging the motives of those who had posed the question. Then, in Zech 8:19, Zechariah receives a word from the deity, which constitutes the "real" response. The priests could, presumably, also have answered the people's question. But a prophet spoke instead.

The book of Joel offers comparable evidence. Israel confronted a crisis—either a military attack symbolized by a locust plague or a locust plague depicted as a military assault. Joel describes its impact on the ritual world: "the grain offering and the drink offering are cut off" (Joel 1:9). In order to address the problem, he challenges the priests to put on sackcloth and lament (1:13), to blow the trumpet in Zion (2:1), to sanctify a fast, and to call a solemn assembly (2:15). It is as if Joel were a high priest, admonishing others to undertake works of lamentation and admonition (e.g., the vocabulary of "return" [2:12-13]). The book of Joel recounts the activity of a prophet who works successfully within the world of priests and ritual behavior.

In other instances, Israel's prophets evidence knowledge about or experiences drawn from the world of ritual in less direct ways. Pride of place should go to the prominence of priestly vocabulary and ideas in the book of Ezekiel. The most obvious example is Ezekiel's use of priestly diction. Whereas other prophets might speak of sins, Ezekiel uses words such as "abomination" or "impurity," which are prominent in OT ritual texts (compare Lev 20:13; Ezek 18:12). Ezekiel deploys theological concepts important to the priests, e.g., the notion of the glory of Yahweh, which is of critical importance in the book's three major visions and in the priestly text of Exod 40:34-38 (e.g., Ezek 10). Scholars have drawn attention to similarities between Ezekiel and one particular priestly text, the so-called Holiness Code (Lev 17–26). Ezekiel and the Holiness Code share the conviction that both ritual and ethical behavior are of fundamental importance to the Israelite life as mandated by Yahweh. Further, both texts envision the possibility that Israel will suffer exile if Israel disobeys Yahweh's commandments. Both even use the vocabulary of Yahweh bringing a sword against some entity (Lev 26:33; Ezek 5). Finally, Ezekiel's vision of restoration is one that focuses on the Temple and its rituals (Ezek 40–48).

There are other important examples beyond Ezekiel. In Amos' final vision report (Amos 9:1-4), the prophet reports seeing Yahweh standing near (or on) the altar, probably the one at the Jerusalem Temple. The call narrative of Isaiah (Isa 6) is set at the Temple. The prophet envisions the deity as one enthroned above/in the Temple. There is overt reference to the Temple, the threshold, the altar, and tongs. The book of Haggai constitutes an apology on behalf of the construction of the Second Temple: "Go up to the hills and bring wood and build the house, so that I may take pleasure in it and be honored, says the LORD" (Hag 1:8). The book of Zechariah highlights the significance of the high priest (Zech 3) and envisions a time when the high priest and a descendant of David will jointly rule the community in Judah (Zech 4). Finally, Malachi is deeply concerned with the Levitical priesthood. The book associates that group with a special covenant (2:5), one that has subsequently been defamed. As well, the author of Isa 56–66 seems particularly concerned about inappropriate ritual behavior (e.g., Isa 58:13).

Therefore, it is unwise to erect an absolute boundary between the world of priests and prophets. Although the means by which an Israelite became a prophet—the sorts of experiences reported in the so-called "call narratives—differed from those by means of which priests were ordained, certain of their behaviors were very similar. Both uttered oracles and both could appear at temples.

Yet, even though prophets interacted with the worlds of the royal court and Temple, prophets could offer exceedingly critical judgments about those two institutions. As for the former, the "independent" stance of prophets was reported throughout the monarchy. Reports attesting to this role of the prophets appear in the DtrH. Nathan offers an early example. Even though Nathan worked at the court, he was able to confront David when he had committed adultery with Bathsheba and offer words of judgment that would affect not only David but also the son with whom Bathsheba was pregnant and the fate of David's lineage (2 Sam 12). In the 9th cent., Elijah serves as a parade example. The DtrH associates him with two kings: Ahab and Ahaziah. Just as was the case with Nathan, Elijah is depicted as having had personal encounters with both these kings. In both cases, he indicts and sentences them for specific behaviors. According to 1 Kgs 21, Ahab wanted a vineyard that had belonged to an individual named Naboth. The vineyard was part of his family's heritage. Ahab wanted the vineyard and, finally, let his wife Jezebel have Naboth falsely accused of cursing God and the king and have him killed. Elijah then meets Ahab and pronounces judgment upon both him and his wife. Then in 2 Kgs 1, Elijah confronts Ahaziah for having sought information about his health from a deity venerated in Ekron. Elijah's judgment could not have been harsher: "you shall surely die" (v. 16). These three prophetic encounters between prophet and king attest that the king is willing to hear the worst possible news from a prophet and still not kill him. Isaiah 7 and Jer 37 attest to this same ability of the prophet to interact directly with the king. That fact clearly suggests that the prophets had a powerful role vis-à-vis the monarch.

Not all prophets interacted with kings in the same and immediate fashion as did Nathan, Elijah, Isaiah, and Jeremiah. However, they regularly delivered oracles concerning kings and the states they governed. Hosea was highly critical of kings in the Northern Kingdom (5:1; 6:4) though recognizing that royal polity had been granted by Yahweh (13:10-11). And yet, kingship, along with the entire nation, could be destroyed. Amos was charged with having predicted that King "Jeroboam shall die by the sword" (Amos 7:11). Micah inveighs against the rulers of Judah (Mic 3:1, 9, though not explicitly against kings). Zephaniah foresees judgment against "the king's sons" (Zeph 1:8). The book of Jeremiah includes a collection of oracles directed against both the house of David and specific monarchs (Jer 21:11–23:8). It was not that prophets thought kingship was an inappropriate form of government. Rather, individual kings had not exercised their monarchic role properly. As a result, it should not come as a surprise that prophetic literature also includes the expectation that kings would once again rule after the demise of Judah (Jer 23:5-6; Ezek 34:23; Amos 9:11; Mic 5:2-5; Hag 2:23; Zech 6:9-13).

The prophets also offered dire judgments about priests, the future of the Temple, and the sacrificial system. For many years, such critiques were thought to mean that prophets rejected the worship life symbolized by the Temple. As should be clear by now, that is most unlikely, since many prophets belonged to priestly lineage and used priestly lore in their proclamations. They did, however, attack inappropriate behaviors within the ritual ambit, including those of both priests and laypeople. Amos indicted both a priest of Bethel and worshipers in the Northern Kingdom (2:8; 7:10-17). Hosea along with other prophets indicts those who worship gods other than Yahweh (Jer 2:23; Hos 2:13; Zeph 1:4-5). Isaiah challenges those who think that ritual behavior can cleanse them from their moral turpitude (Isa 1:10-17). Jeremiah critiques Judahites for false trust in the Temple (7:4). Isaiah 56–66 (65:1-7; 66:3, 17) and Malachi (1–2) discern diverse improprieties in ritual practice during the Second Temple period. As was with case with monarchy, the prophets, when addressing various infractions in the world of ancient worship, were not interested in damning the institution of the Temple so much as they were in identifying the various infractions that violated the norms attested in Israel's covenantal traditions regarding ritual activity (so esp. Lev 17–26).

D. Prophetic Literature

1. Defining prophetic literature

Prophetic literature is surprisingly difficult to define. It might seem natural to equate prophetic books with prophetic literature. But to do so would be to exclude the narratives about Elijah and Elisha, which would seem odd. Another possibility would be to suggest that prophetic literature is that literature spoken (or written) by prophets. To be sure, many poetic texts preserved in books attributed to prophets do appear to be sayings by these prophets. Micah 3:1 presents Micah himself speaking in his own voice: "And I said: Listen, you heads of Jacob and rulers of the house of Israel!" This is literature claiming to stem from the prophet himself. Micah 2:3 presents a different situation: "Now, I am devising against this family an evil from which you cannot remove your necks." The first-person pronoun appears again, but the "I" is no longer Micah; it refers instead to Yahweh. If the first instance may be described as a prophetic speech, then the second is an oracle, a saying from the deity, which the prophet is conveying to the people. Both are normally understood to belong to the world of prophetic literature, even though the "authors" of the speeches are different.

Micah 1:1 further muddies the water: "The word of the LORD that came to Micah of Moresheth in the days of Kings Jotham, Ahaz, and Hezekiah of Judah, which he saw concerning Samaria and Jerusalem." This superscription to the book of Micah is written in prose. Further, since it describes Micah in the third person, the verse seems unlikely to derive from the hand of Micah. It, as were many comparable texts in prophetic books, was probably written by someone who compiled the sayings of prophets and who composed the books that are now part of the OT. That is to say, considerable portions of prophetic books, which most people would want to count as prophetic literature, were written by someone other than the prophet whose name the book bears. One of the longest such texts may be found in Jer 36–45, a prose account of Jeremiah's prophetic activity beginning in 605 BCE and continuing until well after the destruction of Jerusalem, when Jeremiah was taken against his will to Egypt. In this case, the identity of the author is clear; he was Jeremiah's scribe, Baruch (Jer 45:1). There must have been other such individuals. For example, an unnamed author has written an account about Amos' encounter with Amaziah (7:10-17). The author of these verses is unknown. So the identity of those who wrote much of the literature found in prophetic books remains unknown, even though that literature is associated with prophets whose names have been preserved (there are, of course, unnamed prophets attested outside prophetic books, e.g., 1 Kgs 20:13, "a certain prophet";

1 Kgs 13:11, "an old prophet"). So the criterion of defining prophetic literature as that literature composed by prophets themselves does not work either.

This same situation obtains beyond the scope of prophetic books. There are substantial bodies of literature within the books of Kings that attest the activity of individuals normally construed as prophets. There is no book of Elijah, but there is certainly a collection of narratives about him, as there also is about Elisha. Some might claim that, since these narratives are part of Israel's historical literature, they should not count as prophetic literature. (Interestingly, the books of Kings have been included in the "Former Prophets," a label in part due to the presence of such prophets in those and other books that make up this section of the canon.) Such a judgment, however, would be unwise, since the literature devoted to these individuals, as well as other comparable texts, e.g., 1 Kgs 22, which recounts the activity of a prophet named Micaiah ben Imlah, reports primarily the activity of these prophets, and not only the affairs of state as is regularly the case elsewhere in the books of Kings.

Therefore, it seems appropriate to offer a fairly broad definition of prophetic literature, namely, as literature attesting to the activity of prophets, either stemming directly from them or reporting about them. It is not limited to that which named prophets themselves said or wrote.

This sort of definition does, however, raise an interesting issue, which can be exemplified by the following question: Does all literature in a prophetic book count as prophetic literature? The more scholars study the formation of biblical literature, the clearer it seems that much such literature has developed over a period of time. This is evident in a number of prophetic books, especially Isaiah and Jeremiah. It seems clear that Isa 40–66 were written considerably later than were many other chapters in the book. And though it has been a commonplace to attribute chaps. 40–66 to "individuals" known as Deutero- or Trito-Isaiah, it is likely that those twenty-seven chapters stem from various hands about whom precious little is known. Those anonymous persons composed literature of a sort that could be appended to earlier prophetic sayings, oracles, and narratives and not look radically different, i.e., a chapter such as Isa 59 has a similar rhetorical force as does Isa 1. These later compositions may have been originally spoken and then written down or originally written down without declamation.

If this is the case, there may be many more prophets attested in prophetic literature than the individuals for whom names have been preserved. So, e.g., the author of the discrete collection Isa 24–27 is unknown. And yet this composition is uniformly viewed as prophetic literature (though some might term it early apocalyptic literature). Nothing is known about the author of these four chapters. But since what that individual has written is included in a prophetic book and since it accords well with other late prophetic literature, that person might reasonably be called a prophet—an individual communicating on behalf of God to the world of humans.

2. Diversity of prophetic literature

Prophetic literature is, as are prophets themselves, diverse. Perhaps the most important distinction is that between prophetic prose and prophetic poetry. This is true for at least two reasons. First, some scholars have essentially identified prophecy with poetry. According to this way of thinking, prophets were inspired to speak by the deity. They were, then, quintessentially speakers. Such inspiration manifested itself in poetic utterance. Prose, by contrast, is more the product of the human mind, designed to be read as well as heard. Accordingly, one would accord higher status to poetry such as one finds in Ezek 19 than to the prose one finds in Ezek 20. Such a view, of course, necessarily devalues all the prose literature in prophetic books. Further, it fails to take into account the sometimes murky boundary between poetry and prose. For example, the RSV translated Ezek 17:3-10 as prose, whereas the NRSV printed those same verses as poetry. (The distinction between prose and poetry in biblical Hebrew literature is not absolute, though, in most cases, the distinction is reasonably clear, e.g., Exod 14 is clearly prose, and Exod 15:1-17 is poetry.) Since prophets in both the larger ANE context and Israel did far more than compose poetry, it seems inappropriate to limit prophetic literature to poetry.

Second, and more important, poetic prophetic literature is more difficult to comprehend. And, again, the reasons are multiple. Poetry by its very nature is more compact and rife with imagery than prose. Poetry, quite simply, offers more challenges to readers than do Hebrew prose narratives. So, when reading through the rich poetry in Joel, the reader is unsure whether the prophet is comparing a military destruction to a locust invasion or likening a locust invasion to a military destruction. Even a single verse can befuddle. Amos 2:13 conveys the punishment that God will work on Israel: "So, I will press you down in your place, just as a cart presses down when it is full of sheaves." The meaning of this statement is, however, difficult to grasp. Is Israel a road underneath the cart, the cart itself, or the sheaves? The picture is ambiguous, requiring the listener to think about the imagery in a way that readers often do not have to ponder prose (see Jer 38:23). Another feature of Hebrew poetry makes it difficult to modern readers—the presence of parallelism. Hebrew poetic texts are made up of relatively short lines. English translations print these out as distinct entities. For example, Amos 5:24 is made up of two poetic lines. Readers need to know that those two lines work together as a couplet. The first line, "But let justice roll down like waters," includes the verb that is implicit, but unstated, in the second line. And because there is no verb in the second line, the prophet could elaborate on the sorts of waters mentioned in the first line. There they were just "waters." In the second line, the reader learns that the waters will be "like an ever-flowing stream," i.e., not like the seasonal wadis that are so common in Syria-Palestine. Further, because there are two parallel lines, the prophet has the ability to develop the notion of what will be flowing: justice// righteousness. Those values are related and distinct. The very nature of Hebrew poetry permits the prophet to develop an idea even within the compass of two brief lines. Reading poetic prophetic literature requires attention to both imagery and parallelism, hallmarks of Hebrew poetry (*see* POETRY, HEBREW).

Scholars who have studied prophetic literature have observed that its authors used various genres of literature. This is true for both prose and poetic prophetic texts. As a result, readers of that literature are always well served to ask what sorts of prophetic literature they are reading. Though the list of such genres can be long, it is possible to highlight the most important forms of prophetic literature along with representative examples.

Prose prophetic literature has several basic types.

a. Commissioning report. Several prophetic books include reports of the way in which God commissioned an individual to work as a prophet. Amos, of course, reports that "the LORD took me from following the flock, and the LORD said to me, 'Go, prophesy to my people Israel'" (Amos 7:15). That one verse could be characterized as a report of Amos' commissioning. However, the phrase "commissioning report" is usually reserved for a set of longer texts in which there is an interaction between the prophet and the deity: Isa 6; Jer 1:4-10; Ezek 1:1–3:15. Each of these texts includes a dialogue in which the human encounters the deity, the deity gives the human a task, the human objects or demurs (this is implicit in Ezekiel's commissioning narrative), and the deity reaffirms the commission.

Although there is a more or less standard way in which these reports are written, they have been influenced significantly by the overall imagery and theology of the books in which they appear. Isaiah reports having experienced his commission at the Temple in Jerusalem. Jerusalem/Zion is of fundamental importance to this prophet, who lived in the capital of Judah. Jeremiah's commissioning narrative focuses on his reception of "the word of the LORD." This phrase permeates the entire book of Jeremiah. Finally, Ezekiel's report is concerned with the presence of "the glory of the LORD," a theological concern throughout Ezekiel's visions.

It is risky to assume that all of Israel's prophets had experiences of the sort attested in commissioning reports. Nonetheless, it remains the case that a number of prophets report that divine directives provide the impetus for their activities. This is true even for prophets for whom there is no commissioning report. For example, Hosea reports, within two symbolic action reports (see below), that Yahweh commanded him to undertake certain behaviors, e.g., "Go, take for yourself a wife of whoredom and have children of whoredom ... " (Hos 1:2). Hosea, like Jeremiah, was commanded to undertake a task by the deity. Isaiah 6:8, "Here am I; send me!" is the sole example in which a prophet volunteers.

b. Vision report. Biblical vision reports typically commence with a report about a visual experience, which is often then followed by comment about the meaning or significance of what the prophet has seen. (The alert reader will note that the commissioning reports of both Isaiah and Ezekiel also belong to the genre of the vision report: Isa 6:1, "I saw the Lord sitting on a throne"; Ezek 1:1, "I saw visions of God.") Important examples include: Micaiah ben Imlah (1 Kgs 22:19-22); Isa 6; Jer 1:11-13; Ezek 1:1–3:15; 8:1–11:25; 37:1-14; 40:1–48:35; Amos 7:1-9; 8:1-3; 9:1-4; Zech 1–6 (excepting the oracles in those chapters). Visionary discourse populates biblical books, e.g., Isa 1:1, "the vision of Isaiah son of Amoz, which he saw ..."; Isa 2:1, "the word that Isaiah son of Amoz saw ..."; Amos 1:1, "the words of Amos ... which he saw ..."; Nah 1:1, "the book of the vision of Nahum of Elkosh"; Hab 1:1, "the oracle that the prophet Habakkuk saw." Clearly, prophetic literature attests that Israelite prophets were "seers."

What do prophets see? On occasion, they report perceiving ordinary objects. Jeremiah reports seeing "a branch of an almond tree" (Jer 1:11). The interpretation of that vision, "for I am watching over my word to perform it," is built on a Hebrew pun, as the textual notes to the NRSV make clear. More typically, however, prophets see extraordinary things. Amos sees fire devouring the watery abyss (Amos 7:4); Ezekiel sees a phantasmagoric collection of half-animal, half-human figures (Ezek 1:4-14); Zechariah sees fantastic objects flying through the air (Zech 5). Perhaps most frequently, prophets see the deity, often enthroned (1 Kgs 22; Isa 6; Ezek 1:26).

Prior to the demise of Judah as a nation, prophets had visionary experiences that they were able to understand and to which they were able to respond. Amos 7:1-3 offers an excellent example. God allows Amos to see the deity forming locusts that are then devouring the grass of the land. Amos immediately perceives that the situation is dire and intercedes on Israel's behalf. Zechariah's visions provide a strong contrast. In his first vision (1:7-17), Zechariah sees some horses near myrtle trees but must ask an angelic interpreter what they mean. Here the prophet is a visionary but not someone who can explain the vision's significance. Clearly the role of the prophet in vision reports changes over time.

c. Symbolic action report. The OT contains a number of reports in which the deity commands prophets to undertake specific actions as a part of their prophetic vocation. These include Yahweh's command that Hosea marry a woman who is a prostitute (Hos 1), that Isaiah walk naked for three years (Isa 20), that Jeremiah buy, wear, and then bury a linen loincloth (Jer 13), and that Ezekiel build a miniature city with siege works portrayed against it (Ezek 4:1-3). Here the prophets are, literally, mimes, acting in strange ways and not necessarily speaking. The behaviors have meanings, but they are not necessarily self-evident. The meaning of Hosea's marriage is only revealed when the deity tells the prophet how to name his children and what the significance of their names truly is. In other cases, the behavior remains uninterpreted, i.e., Ezekiel's miniature city. One has the sense that this form of prophetic behavior was designed to encourage their audience—if the acts were performed publicly—to inquire about their meaning. Such dialogue may have encouraged a different form of communication than the simple delivery of a prophetic speech. This hypothesis surely explains the symbolic action reported in Ezek 24. When Ezekiel's wife dies, he is prohibited from mourning her in traditional fashion. As a result, the people ask, "Will you not tell us what these things mean for us, that you are acting this way?" (Ezek 24:19). One can imagine such a question being posed after prophets had performed symbolic actions.

d. Legend. The prophetic legend is a subset of the larger category, legend. Legends are literature that focuses on the sacred and its essential features. The OT contains legends about holy objects, e.g., the ark (2 Sam 6:6-7). There are, as well, legends about holy places, e.g., the holy ground reported in Exod 3:1-6. Even more frequent are narratives about holy people, people characterized in the OT by the label "man of god." Many of the stories told about Elijah and Elisha fall into this category. These stories focus on the extraordinary power possessed by the holy man. He embodies the power of the deity. Second Kings 6:1-7 offers a typical scene. One of Elisha's servants was using an ax, when the ax head fell into the Jordan River. Elisha responded by throwing a piece of wood into the water, whereupon the iron ax head floated to the surface. Such a story was surely told to emphasize the ability of this prophet to act in a miraculous way.

Legends depicted these holy men as powerful people, though not necessarily as "good" ones. The sacred is often dangerous, so dangerous in fact that it transcends the categories of good and bad. Second Kings 2:23-25 offers a case in point. Some young boys were remembered as having taunted Elisha. He responded by cursing them and summoning some bears, who mauled forty-two of the lads. One would misconstrue this narrative if one judged Elisha negatively for the violence done to the boys. As a legend, it was designed to highlight his power. More typical, however, the power of the holy man is used to help people, often those associated with the prophet. It is no accident that stories are told about both Elijah and Elisha (1 Kgs 17:8-24; 2 Kgs 4:1-7) in which the prophet assists a widow—in the case of Elisha, the widow of one of his retinue.

Second Kings 8:4 almost certainly attests to the kind of environment that produced these legends. This verse reports that the king had asked Gehazi, Elisha's servant, to tell him "all the great things that Elisha [had] done." Clearly, as a "man of God," Elisha was remembered for what he had done, not for what he had said. (The situation with Micah is palpably different, since he was remembered for what he had said; so Jer 26:18).

e. Prophetic historiography. It is no accident that "The Prophets," as a rubric for the second part of the Jewish canon, includes both so-called historical and prophetic books. "Kings" and "Prophets" belong together. This is true in at least two ways. Prophets were concerned with matters of state—both early and late in Judahite history. Nathan and Gad were associated with King David; Haggai and Zechariah both address the royal status of the Davidide Zerubbabel. And many prophets addressed kings during intervening times.

This strong correlation between kings and prophets is also attested in literary fashion. Portions of both Isaiah and Jeremiah appear in the books of Kings. Isaiah 36–39 is virtually identical to 2 Kgs 18:13–20:19. Similarly, the final chapter of the book of Jeremiah (52) is the same as 2 Kgs 24:18–25:30. The prophet Isaiah appears as a character in Isa 36–39 whereas Jeremiah is not present in Jer 52. Nonetheless, Jeremiah is there implicitly—and Jer 52 makes sense as the final chapter of that prophetic book, since it attests to the veracity of what Jeremiah had proclaimed, namely, that Judah would be destroyed and that many Judahites would go into exile.

Isaiah 36–39 comprises three episodes. In each, the prophet interacts with King Hezekiah. In the first (chaps. 36–37), Isaiah offers an oracle, assuring the king that the Neo-Assyrians will not conquer Jerusalem. In the second (chap. 38), Isaiah provides another oracle, again promising relief from the enemy armies and providing healing to the king, who had been mortally ill. In the final scene (chap. 39), Isaiah foresees the exile of Judah's royal house to Babylon. In all three moments, the prophet Isaiah is addressing the king concerning matters of historical consequence. The historical ramifications of the king's behavior are at stake. As a result, it is appropriate to characterize this literature as prophetic historiography, since in it the prophet plays a key role in both affecting and interpreting events concerning the royal house and the nation. Prophetic historiography attests to the conviction that prophets affect the course of history.

f. Biography. Biographic literature in the ancient world typically treated not only an individual but also a major theme or issue that was exemplified in that individual's life. Though few prophetic books focus on the life of the prophet, the book of Jeremiah offers a noteworthy exception. Jeremiah 37–44 follows the prophet from the year in which Zedekiah was placed on the Judahite throne by Nebuchadnezzar (587 BCE) to the time when Jeremiah was living in Egypt, after having been taken there against his will by Johanan son of Kareah. The author of these chapters portrays Jeremiah as an individual unable to control his own personal fate. He is imprisoned (chap. 37), thrown into a cistern (chap. 38), guarded by the Babylonians (chap. 39), and, finally, taken to Egypt, where he presumably died. Throughout these various events, the author makes clear that Jeremiah continued to receive and proclaim Yahweh's words and that the people routinely disregarded those words, just as they had in the past. The author is very explicit in announcing this theme: "neither he (Zedekiah) nor his servants nor the people of the land listened to the words of the LORD that he spoke through the prophet Jeremiah" (Jer 37:2)—and in the final chapter, "Yet I persistently sent to you all my servants the prophets ... but they did not listen or incline their ear" (Jer 44:4-5). This is the theme—a prophet who speaks Yahweh's words but who is not heeded—that turns this chronicle about a prophet's activities into a biography.

g. Divinatory chronicle. When reading literature about prophets, one often has the impression that they act in an unbidden fashion. They offer oracles that do not appear to have been requested. (The same may be said for prophetic oracles from ancient Mari.) Perhaps the classic poetic expression for this image occurs in Jer 20:9, where Jeremiah announces that though he tried to avoid speaking, the word of the Lord was like "a burning fire" inside him. There was a compulsion to speak.

Nonetheless, there are a number of texts, divinatory chronicles, that offer a different portrait, one in which prophets are solicited. First Samuel 9 portrays Samuel as a prophet or "seer" (v. 9), one who, for a fee (v. 8), will provide information otherwise unavailable to humans. In this instance, Saul and his compatriot hope to find out whether or not the journey on which they have embarked will be successful (v. 6). As one would expect, Samuel accedes to their request and provides the information that they had sought. Ezekiel 20 offers a comparable vignette. After the first deportation, but five years before Jerusalem was destroyed, "certain elders of Israel came to consult the Lord" (v. 1). The text does not report that which the elders wanted to know and it makes clear that, in this case, the deity will provide something other than that which the elders wanted. Nonetheless, this episode makes clear that Ezekiel as prophet was thought to be someone who could provide the desired information. Finally, Zech 7–8 attests to interaction between the prophet and a delegation from Bethel. They had been sent to ask: "Should I mourn and practice abstinence in the fifth month, as I have done for so many years?" (Zech 7:3). The book of Zechariah provides two prophetic responses to the people's question. The first occurs in Zech 7:5-7, an oracle in which the deity interrogates the delegation in judgmental fashion. The second follows in Zech 8:19. There, the prophet answers the question and adds the admonition "love truth and peace." This prophet's answer to the people's question involves more than the binary yes or no that might have been forthcoming from a priest. Instead, the first prophetic response explores the background of the question whereas the second one answers the question and follows it with religious counsel. Both the "consultations" involving Ezekiel and Zechariah demonstrate that prophets could function as diviners. However, those who sought knowledge from them might hear something more or different from that which they had expected.

h. Formulae and form. Poetic prophetic literature also includes a considerable variety. However, there is a feature common to all these genres. They all function as direct discourse. They appear to have functioned originally in an oral environment, portraying the declamatory role of Israel's prophets. Form criticism, as a discrete subdiscipline of biblical scholarship, has demonstrated that the prophets used identifiable forms of speaking. These forms or kinds of literature were well known in their society. The prophets adopted discourse from, especially, the law court, the Temple, and school to make their points. Needless to say, they could also compose poetry that did not depend upon such forms.

Scholars who have worked from a form critical perspective have attended to both formulae and form. As regards the former, they observed that a number of phrases recurred in prophetic literature. "Thus says the LORD" (Amos 1:3) or minimal variants thereof hold primary place in any such roster. Often characterized as "the messenger formula," this phrase reflects the role of the prophet as spokesman for the deity or the divine council. The prophet speaks on behalf of God when announcing an oracle. Prophetic books include many similar formulae, e.g., "Therefore says the Sovereign" (Isa 1:24); "Hear the word of the LORD" (Jer 2:4; Hos 4:1); "Hear this word that the LORD has spoken against you" (Amos 3:1); "Hear, you peoples, all of you" (Mic 1:2); "The LORD has commanded concerning you" (Nah 1:14). The prominence of verbs that involve oral discourse is striking. The prophets were speakers; their audience hearers. (In fact, Ezekiel apparently could simply announce the phrase, "Thus says the Lord GOD," whereupon the people would know that a prophet had been among them [Ezek 2:4-5].) These formulae are also important since they regularly appear at the beginning of oracles (whereas the phrase "says the LORD [e.g., Jer 21:3, 14]) often appears within or at the end of a speech. As a result, one may use these formulae as boundary markers between what were originally distinct speeches.

Important though formulae are for reading prophetic books, attention to the formal features of oracles and sayings is even more significant. Many such speeches appear to be structured in similar fashion.

For example, a number begin with an introductory formula, then move to an indictment of the party that is being addressed, offer a transitional phrase, and, finally, turn to a judgment based on the indictment. Amos 2:11-16 includes all these features, as do the rest of the oracles that make up Amos 1–2. Because of this consistent form, scholars have described it as a judgment oracle. Similar in juridical tone are texts labeled lawsuits, e.g., Isa 1:2-9; Mic 6:1-8 (a text that explicitly refers to a "case," v. 1); Jer 2:4-9 (note the language of "accusation," v. 9); Hos 4:1-4. A hallmark of these texts is the summoning of witnesses at the outset of the litigation, a summoning that is often followed by a series of charges presented to the jury and, sometimes, the outcome of the trial. In these two cases—judgment oracle and lawsuit—prophets appear to be using forms of speaking that derive from the ancient Israelite courts. They appropriated patterns of speaking known broadly in Israelite society and used them for their own purposes.

The same may be said for discourse at home in the world of ancient Israelite ritual and priestly practice. Prophetic books include hymns (e.g., Amos 4:13; 5:8-9; 9:5-6; Hab 3:2-15); liturgies (Isa 12); and laments (Jer 8:18–9:3). Such language would have been used at the Temple and perhaps elsewhere but was deployed in prophetic literature to serve the prophet's rhetorical purpose. For example, the hymnic language in Amos makes a theological point that, even in a time of judgment, Israel's God is praiseworthy. The book of Joel is particularly significant since it presents the prophet calling for rituals such as fasts in very much the way that a priest would have done (so Joel 1:13-20). He even tells the priests what words to use in their prayer to God (Joel 1:14). Amos also apparently uses priestly words, e.g., "Come to Bethel ... bring your sacrifices every morning ..." (Amos 4:4-5), but then turns such language on its head when he adds, "and transgress ... and multiply transgression." The call to worship becomes ironic. Prophets, it would seem, could function like priests and could also revise radically such priestly language. One of the most frequent forms of ritual discourse present in prophetic literature is the so-called oracle of salvation. That rubric does not so much refer to form as content, though the formula "fear not" is often present. Though particularly prominent in Isa 40–55 (e.g., Isa 41:14-16), such proclamations of weal occur in prior literature, e.g., Isa 7:7-9; Mic 5:10-15. Many oracles of salvation may originally have been priestly response to prayers, especially laments. Moreover, some such oracles, e.g., Amos 9:11-15, may well date to a period later than the prophet with whose book they are associated. Still, the inclusion of such ritual language would be consistent with the presence of other such discourse in prophetic books.

Language associated with ancient education and scribal practice constitutes a third discourse that prophets used. So-called wisdom forms appear in a number of prophetic books. They include the "graded numerical sequence" ("for three transgressions of Damascus, and for four" [Amos 1:3]); series of rhetorical questions (Amos 3:3-8); acrostic (Nah 1:2-8); and instruction (Isa 1:10-17). Such forms of speaking are well attested in OT wisdom literature. The presence of such wisdom discourse should not suggest that prophets were functioning as teachers. Rather, as was the case with language drawn from the court and the ritual sphere, prophets were adapting ways of speaking to suit their own ends. Here, the language of pedagogy could serve a message of judgment.

Other forms of speaking are not easily classified according to social institution. The woe oracle, which begins with the Hebrew word ʾoy (אוֹי) and then moves to a description of the lamented party and their fate, is often structured very much like a judgment oracle. However, since the initial word ʾoy was probably originally used in a funerary context, the prophets were suggesting that the party addressed was as good as dead. Prophets composed allegories (Ezek 17:2-10), a form of literature not limited to one social institution. The disputations or diatribes that populate the book of Malachi may reflect formalized arguments of a sort one might hear in any number of places. And prophets composed songs (Isa 5; Ezek 33:32), which are hardly the provenance of one sector of ancient society.

To conclude the analysis of prophetic poetry with a list of forms might give the impression that prophets were derivative artists. Such a judgment would be inappropriate, since much prophetic poetry is original both in form and in imagery. Many prophetic sayings are poems offering rich and original imagery. Jeremiah might have simply inveighed against Judah for worshiping Baal. Instead he used the imagery of flowing water and cisterns: "they have forsaken me, the fountain of flowing water, and dug out cisterns for themselves, cracked cisterns that can hold no water" (Jer 2:13).

3. The development and growth of prophetic literature

Divine oracles and prophetic sayings were relatively brief speeches. This is evident in both extra-biblical and biblical literature. Since Neo-Assyrian texts provide evidence of tablets on which several oracles have been transcribed, one may infer that the collection and arranging of oracles was an essential element for the production of prophetic literature in ancient Nineveh. The same may be said for biblical prophetic literature. Whether one looks at Isa 5, Amos 3, or Mic 1, one can see boundary markers between individual sayings. Someone, whether the originating prophet or a later scribe, collected these sayings. The same could be said for the legends associated with Elisha. Some individual or group compiled these stories into a document that could then be included in the DtrH. Such activity attests, at a minimum, to an archival mentality. These texts were to be preserved. Someone was convinced that these sayings—since many claimed to be of divine origin or about a person associated with the deity—bore special authority.

Jeremiah 36 attests to the process of inscription, the writing down of words that had been originally delivered orally. Jeremiah 51:59-62 reveals a different situation, one in which words that had been "written concerning Babylon" are rewritten and then read aloud in Babylon. It would seem that not all prophetic literature emerged out of an oral environment. There is significant evidence of prophetic literature that was written from the outset. There was flux in the oral/written environment. Words that were spoken could be written, and words that were written could be read.

Though oral performance may have been the dominant mode of prophetic activity, writing also appears prominently. Just as prophets could function as priests, they could as well work as scribes. Yahweh tells Isaiah to "take a large tablet and write on it ..." (Isa 8:1). Isaiah 30:8 includes a very similar admonition: "Go now, write it before them on a tablet, and inscribe it in a book [probably a scroll], so that it may be for the time to come as a witness forever." In Isa 8, Isaiah commands one of his disciples, "Bind up the testimony, seal the teaching among my disciples" (v. 16). The imagery is that of rolling up a scroll and sealing it with wax. Again, written records are part of prophetic activity. Another prophet, Habakkuk, is also involved in scribal work as a part of his prophetic activity. The deity mandates that he "write the vision, make it plain on tablets, so that a runner may read it" (Hab 2:2). And, of course, the imagery of writing is prominent in other prophetic literature (e.g., Ezek 2:9–3:3; 9:11; Zech 5:1-4; Mal 3:16).

Whereas some chapters in prophetic books appear to be "raw" assemblages—the oracles stand with no obvious relationship to one another—others appear to be more carefully collected or ordered. Jeremiah 21:11–23:8 constitutes a collection of prose and poetic material, all of which involves the royal house. In similar fashion, Jer 23:9-40 is an assemblage titled "concerning the prophets" (v. 9). In the latter entity, specific complaints in the poems give way to broader issues in the prose, i.e., the sayings appear to have been meaningfully organized.

Such arrangement can work on a larger scale. In the book of Hosea chaps. 4–14 are made up of two collections, 4–11 and 12–14. In each collection, the oracles move from the language of judgment to that of weal. And that same concern for a positive future appears at the end of the first section (chaps. 1–3) as well. All the literature that makes up the book of Hosea appears to have been integrated into this tripartite structure. As will become clear (see below), many other of the prophetic books have been carefully structured.

Over time, early prophetic collections were supplemented. Put another way, the originating literature elicited additions of one sort or another. Such supplementation reflected various impulses. One was an interest in commenting on or explaining the earlier material. Ancient manuscripts provide clear evidence of this process. For example, the Septuagintal book of Jeremiah, which almost certainly attests an earlier and shorter form when compared with the Heb., concludes Jer 28:15 with the clause, "Within this year you shall be dead." This statement occurs at the end of an oracle that Jeremiah has conveyed to his prophetic opponent Hananiah. The Heb. continues, "... because you have spoken rebellion against the Lord." That addition provides a rationale or explanation for why Hananiah must die. Such a rationale prevents Jeremiah from appearing as a vituperative prophet. Instead, he is simply conveying God's message to Hananiah. The addition is clearly designed to present Jeremiah in the best possible light.

Updating provided a second sort of supplementation. At numerous places, prophetic literature attests to earlier words that are now being cast in a new light. For example, the book of Isaiah includes oracles devoted to the nation of Moab. Those speeches begin in chap. 15 and continue to the end of chap. 16. The final oracle begins with the words, "This was the word that the LORD spoke concerning Moab in the past. But now the LORD says ...." What had been said earlier now needs to be put in a new light. In this case, there is good reason to think that Isaiah himself may have offered the new oracle.

There is a third sort of updating, one in which an earlier prophetic collection has been updated by someone other than the originating prophet. Isaiah 40–66 almost certainly stems from the hands of anonymous prophets writing during the 6th and, perhaps, 5th cent. This literature seems to have been inspired by Isaiah ben Amoz's literature, e.g., the concern for Zion, and how that concern might be articulated in a time after Zion/Jerusalem had been destroyed and, particularly in chaps. 56–66, rebuilt. Zechariah 9–14 and, perhaps, Malachi, Joel 3–4 (in the Heb.), and Isa 24–27 all comprise major updatings to earlier prophetic collections.

A final form of supplementation occurred after the prophetic books were more or less complete. Epilogues were added to some of them. Hosea 14:9 and Mal 4:4-6 offer the best examples. When the author of the former text wrote, "Those who are wise understand these things," that individual made an overt connection between the worlds of prophetic and wisdom literature. "These things" are the words uttered by Hosea. "Those who are wise" are the authors of literature such as the book of Proverbs. Such a connection serves the goal of integrating different portions of the canon. What might appear to be different kinds of literature (and theology)—prophetic saying and proverb—are, according to this mind-set, integrally related. Malachi 4:4-6 work in similar fashion, relating the words of Malachi to "the teaching of my servant, Moses," namely, the Pentateuch. Here, too, the epilogue serves the goal of canonical integration. Perhaps the best conclusion that can be offered to a discussion of the growth of prophetic literature appears in the book of Jeremiah: "and many similar words were added to them" (Jer 36:32).

4. Prophetic books

Prophetic books are themselves a distinctive form of prophetic literature. Many have been carefully structured, though in no clear case do two prophetic books share the same basic pattern. Some, e.g., Haggai, appear to present the oracles according to their order of original presentation. Many include discrete collections that have been included in the larger book, e.g., the oracles against the nations that may be found in many books, so Isa 13–23; Jer 46–51; and Ezek 25–32. Even more characteristic is the presence of a superscription. Every prophetic book includes at least a minimal introductory statement. Obadiah's is the briefest one: "the vision of Obadiah." More typical are those in Hosea, Amos, and Micah. Those superscriptions attest to the chronological setting of the prophet by referring to particular kings either in Israel or in Judah, though Haggai and Zechariah are dated to a Persian king. These superscriptions ground the book in specific historical moments. The prophets' words are not understood to be timeless. They need to stand the test of time (so esp. Deut 18; Isa 30:8*b*) and, hence, must be located in a specific time. Each prophetic book grew in a distinctive way. Isaiah was formed by the addition of major compositions, e.g., Isa 56–66. Jeremiah and Ezekiel grew by smaller accretions. Further, each prophetic book possesses a different textual history (see the entries on each biblical book).

Recent scholarly analysis of the so-called Minor Prophets has led a number of scholars to argue that those twelve books should be understood as a Book of the Twelve. Arguments on behalf of this case include the prominence of the theme of "the day of the LORD" throughout the twelve books and evidence for linking books by juxtaposition (e.g., the Lord roaring for Zion near the end of Joel [3:16] and near the beginning of Amos [1:2]). There are two different forms of the Book of the Twelve. The LXX, which may preserve an earlier form, contains the following order for the first six books: Hosea, Amos, Micah, Joel, Obadiah, and Jonah. Just as the differences between the ordering of the oracles between the LXX and Heb. forms of the book of Jeremiah have created two versions of that book, each with its distinct meaning, so too the different orders of the LXX and Heb. forms of the Book of the Twelve have yielded two distinct Books of the Twelve.

5. Prophetic literature and apocalyptic literature

A number of the prophetic books include literature that seems quite different from other portions of prophetic books. They focus on radical conflict, cosmic imagery, and avoid overt description of concrete historical affairs. Isaiah 24–27; portions of Isa 56–66; Ezek 38–39; Joel 2:30–3:21; and Zech 9–14 have regularly been included on this list. These chapters have been known by various titles: early apocalyptic, deutero-prophetic, late prophetic. And they have become part of a vexed debate, namely, whether or not that which one calls "apocalyptic literature" develops in some way out of prophetic literature. The book of Daniel contains the only undisputed example of apocalyptic literature in the OT, namely the visions in Dan 7–12. So, one way of posing this issue is to ask: What is the relationship of the visions in Daniel to the vision reports in prophetic literature?

There is, of course, a "canonical" relationship, at least in the LXX, and, subsequently, the Christian Bible, between Daniel and prophetic literature. Daniel has been placed immediately after Ezekiel and just before the Minor Prophets. Such a position suggests that at least some readers in the Greco-Roman period thought Daniel belonged among the prophets. The strongest warrant for that positioning would have been the prominent eschatological emphasis that Daniel shared with some prophetic literature, e.g., Isa 24; Ezek 38–39; Zech 14, and the presence of vision reports in Daniel and prior prophetic literature. It is surely no accident that Ezekiel, the book that immediately precedes Daniel, contains four powerful visions.

However, one must do more than simply observe the presence of visions. Rather, it is important to observe the trajectory of prophetic visions. Vision reports are one fundamental form of prophetic literature (see above). These reports do, however, evolve. As early as Amos and the extra-biblical Balaam, prophets reported visions of cosmic scale and fantastic imagery, e.g., a shower of fire destroying the great deep (Amos 7:4). These vision reports are relatively brief and the prophet understands what he has been shown. Isaiah 6, though functioning as the call narrative for Isaiah, is also a vision report. It is longer than those in Amos, yet its purport remains clear to the prophet. Things begin to change with Ezekiel. Three of the four visions are much longer than those of Amos and Isaiah. For example, the first vision runs for twenty-seven and one-half verses. It is filled with hybrid creatures—part human, part animal—whirring wheels, flashing light, and booming sound. Still, in that otherworldliness, Ezekiel is able to perceive the significance of what he sees: "This was the appearance of the likeness of the glory of the LORD" (Ezek 1:28*a*). Later in the 6th cent., ca. 520 BCE, Zechariah experienced multiple visions. They are not as long as the major visions in Ezekiel, but rather more similar in length to Ezekiel's vision of the valley of dry bones (Ezek 37:1-14). There is, however, a crucial difference between Ezekiel's and Zechariah's visions. Ezekiel understands what he sees; Zechariah does not. Hence, Zechariah's vision reports include a new element: a messenger who explains to the prophet that which he has seen (e.g., Zech 1:7-21). The prophet can still "see," but he does not "understand." The prophet becomes a seer without the capacity to interpret the vision. The messenger, this new type of intermediary, reappears in the book of Daniel (and in other apocalyptic literature such as 2 Esdras). Daniel experiences visions that he cannot understand and must depend upon an angelic interpreter to interpret them for him ("I approached one of the attendants to ask him the truth concerning all this," Dan 7:16).

Visionary revelation is one hallmark of apocalyptic literature. Though vision reports were present in prior prophetic literature, such focus on visionary revelation distinguishes apocalyptic literature from its prophetic precursors since prophets more frequently offered oracles and prophetic sayings rather than vision reports. In fact, some prophets appear to be suspicious of visionary rhetoric (Jer 23:16; Mic 3:6-8). Nonetheless, apocalyptic literature inherited the vision report, a standard form of prophetic literature, and developed it in significant ways. To this extent, there is a strong connection between prophetic and apocalyptic literature. Scholars have identified other features shared by late prophetic literature and apocalyptic literature, e.g., radical eschatology and cosmic symbolism (*see* APOCALYPTICISM).

"Messianic prophecy" is a concept associated with both prophetic and apocalyptic literature. It is important to understand what lies behind this phrase. In the OT, someone who is anointed can be called a "messiah." The act of anointing was used to inaugurate both the king and the high priest. Of these two offices, the noun *messiah* is normally used of a king (e.g., 2 Sam 23:1, "anointed"). Some prophetic texts announce an expectation of a new king on the throne. Any such text could be called a "messianic prophecy." The book of Isaiah contains two such texts. Isaiah 9:2-7 announces the imminent arrival of "a son given to us." This statement in the past tense almost certainly refers to the recent coronation of a Judahite king. As Ps 2:7 makes clear, a Davidic king was adopted by Yahweh as his son on the day of his coronation. Isaiah 9 refers to an adoption that has already taken place. Hence one may infer that the "endless peace" and other features of that king's rule will take place in the very near future. Isaiah 11:1-9 is similar in that it anticipates the marvelous reign of a member of the Davidic line. This text invests more time describing the features of that rule; it spells out in greater detail the "peace" attested in Isa 9. However, Isa 11 does not offer concrete evidence about when Isaiah thought this reign would take place. Much depends on to what period one dates the text. If Isaiah ben Amoz wrote these verses, then, like Isa 9, one would infer that this king's reign would take place during Isaiah's lifetime. If the prophetic saying dates to the period after Judah had been destroyed, then the arrival of such a king as messiah would have been anticipated in the 6th cent. BCE. (During that same century, Isa 45:1 attests that Cyrus, a Persian emperor, was also viewed as Yahweh's "messiah.")

In the late 6th cent., both Haggai and Zechariah anticipated the return of Davidic kingship. Haggai 2:23 anticipates the reinstitution of monarchy with Zerubbabel, a scion of the Davidic line. Zechariah anticipates two figures—a king and a high priest—ruling together (Zech 4). In this vision, Zechariah speaks overtly of two messiahs, "the two anointed ones," an expectation that follows standard Israelite tradition since both the high priest and the king were anointed when they entered office. There are echoes of such sentiment regarding the Davidic house in numerous late prophetic texts, e.g., Jeremiah's book of consolation (Jer 30:9), the epilogue to the book of Amos (9:11), and Deutero-Zechariah (9:9-10; 12:8). All such literature attests to the hope that Israel would reemerge as a nation and that a member of the Davidic line would sit on the throne. To the extent that apocalyptic literature anticipates the reinstitution of Davidic rule, it has inherited a significant tradition from prior prophetic literature. That expectation is fully attested in the NT. Early Christians believed that Jesus of Nazareth was the Messiah; the Greek work christos (χριστός), from which the title "Christ" derives, means "anointed one" (Luke 9:20). In order to warrant fully this claim, the Gospel of Matthew takes pains to trace Jesus' genealogy back to David (Matt 1:1-16), himself an anointed one (*see* MESSIAH, JEWISH).

E. Problems with Prophets

1. Prophets and conflict

One might expect that prophets, as religious specialists, would have held a place of honor in Israelite society. Some no doubt were. Both early, e.g., Nathan, and late, e.g., Haggai, biblical texts report that their audiences received and responded with utmost seriousness to their oracles and sayings. Not all prophets were treated in this fashion, however. Amos was accused of treason when he uttered oracles announcing that the shrines in Israel would be destroyed. This was not a case of a prophet without honor in his own country (compare Mark 6:4). Rather, Amos was perceived to be a foreign interloper, since he was a Judahite addressing those in the Northern Kingdom, Israel.

Prophets native to their own land were also perceived negatively. Early in the narratives about Elijah, Ahab characterizes him as "you troubler of Israel" (1 Kgs 18:17). In similar fashion, the DtrH portrays Micaiah through the words of "the king of Israel" as someone who "never prophesies anything favorable about me, but only disaster" (1 Kgs 22:8). These two cases imply that the words prophets spoke created perceptions of them as "troublers." They were not simply neutral mouthpieces of the deity.

Both the DtrH and prophetic books depict the audiences of the prophet often, though not always (Isaiah appears to be an exception), receiving their words with disdain or rejecting them outright. Hosea even quotes them: "The prophet is a fool, the man of the spirit is mad" (Hos 9:7). So, too, does Micah: "'Do not preach'—thus they preach—'one should not preach of such things; disgrace will not overtake us'" (Mic 2:6). The book of Jeremiah presents Jeremiah as someone threatened with death early in his time as a prophet. Here, again, the enemies of the prophet are quoted: "Let us cut him off from the land of the living" (Jer 11:19). This would not be the last time Jeremiah experienced a violent reaction to his words. Jeremiah was threatened with death again by "the officials" when he spoke an oracle announcing the destruction of Jerusalem (Jer 38:1-6). The book of Jeremiah even includes a report about a prophet, Uriah son of Shemaiah, being executed for speaking "words exactly like those of Jeremiah" (Jer 26:20-23). (Second Chronicles 24:20-22 presents a comparable case. Zechariah, who is the son of a priest, is possessed by "the spirit of God" and utters an oracle, commencing with the formula "Thus says God." The oracle angered the "the people," who then, with a royal mandate, stoned him to death.) Clearly, when prophets spoke words that challenged and angered their audiences, they were perceived negatively, even threatened with death and in certain cases killed. Such dire cases typically involve the proclamation of oracles concerning the nation and its national shrine.

The DtrH and prophetic books also depict a more particular kind of conflict, one between prophets. There is, of course, the famous scene between the prophets of Baal and Elijah (1 Kgs 18). But that was more of a contest—fatal to be sure—than a conflict. First Kings 22 and Jer 28 offer graphic stories of conflict between prophets. In the first case, Micaiah ben Imlah confronts about 400 anonymous prophets and another named Zedekiah ben Chenaanah. In the second, Jeremiah challenges Hananiah son of Azur. All of the aforementioned prophets are Yahwists. However, the words of Micaiah and Jeremiah prove, over a long period of time, to be true. This sort of conflict would obviously have been difficult for both prophets and people. In the case of Jeremiah, he had to "go his way" until he received a "word from the Lord" that would enable him to face down Hananiah publicly. And even when Hananiah was dead, the original conflict remained in place, since the downfall of Jerusalem, which would falsify Hananiah's original oracle, still lay several years ahead.

Prophetic conflict has often been examined using the language of "true versus false" prophecy (*see* PROPHECY, FALSE). Since these terms do not themselves appear in the biblical texts, it is difficult to use them to explain the aforementioned episodes. Biblical texts do offer binary categories that were designed to help the people distinguish between prophets: those who spoke on behalf of Yahweh versus those who spoke on behalf of other gods; those whose words proved to be true versus those whose words proved to be false. According to the book of Deuteronomy, there are clear instances in which a prophet may be ignored (Deut 18:22). Moreover, there are others in which the prophet is to be put to death (Deut 13:1-5; 18:20). The latter cases typically involve speaking on behalf of a deity other than Yahweh or speaking a word that Yahweh had not conveyed to the prophet (compare Deut 18:20 to 18:22).

It was, presumably, easy to distinguish between a prophet of Baal and a prophet of Yahweh. Far more difficult was the case in which Yahwistic prophets disagreed over predictions that lay well into the future. The only criterion that could be used was that attested in Jer 28:8-9, namely, comparing that which one prophet says now to what prophets have said over time. Jeremiah appeals to a consistent message of "war, famine, and pestilence against many countries and great kingdoms" (Jer 28:8), which had been spoken by his prophetic forebears. Ultimately, of course, many prophets, even portions of the book of Jeremiah (chaps. 30–31), offered a message of "peace," which is how Jeremiah characterizes the words of his opponent, Hananiah.

Much of the discussion of so-called true and false prophecy involves oracles that could be falsified, i.e., words that could be proved untrue by future events. Such is the case with Jeremiah and Hananiah, and Micaiah and Zedekiah. However, many prophetic oracles were not verifiable in that way. Rather, they offered admonitions, indictments, and explanations. When Amos says, "Ah, you that turn justice to wormwood, and bring righteousness to the ground" (Amos 5:7), he offers no comment about the future implications of that activity. Though his audience might disagree with him about the nature of their actions, there is nothing in the Deuteronomic prescriptions that might resolve a disagreement about "the facts."

Perhaps the most perplexing issue to contemporary readers is presented by those instances in which prophets appear to have said things that would not stand the test of Deut 18. Jonah is the clearest case. He pronounced a terse oracle: "Forty days more, and Nineveh shall be overthrown" (Jonah 3:4). Within the confines of that biblical book, Nineveh was not overthrown. In similar fashion, Ezekiel's judgment that Nebuchadnezzar would conquer Tyre did not come to pass (see above). Then, there are a number of prophetic texts written after the destruction of 587, literature that envisions a paradisal or utopian future, e.g., Isa 54:11-12; Ezek 40–48. These expectations, too, did not transpire. Nonetheless, this literature remained in the canon and expressed a powerful set of eschatological expectations that remained unfulfilled.

In the final analysis, prophecy, if by that phrase one may characterize the behavior of multiple prophets in a society, was not well equipped to handle disagreement between prophets. And it may be no accident that some of the most visceral prophetic conflicts, those reported in Jeremiah (chaps. 14:13-16; 23:9-40) and Ezekiel (chap. 13), occur close to the time when much prophetic literature had already been composed. Such public prophetic conflict may represent something of an Achilles' heel for this type of religious specialization.

2. The "end" of prophecy

There are no prophetic texts explicitly dated beyond the end of the 6th cent. BCE. That is not to say that portions of prophetic books, e.g., Isa 56–66, or even books like Malachi or Joel, were not written in the 5th cent., or perhaps later. It is, however, to affirm that those either writing or editing late prophetic literature were disinclined to identify it as deriving from the Second Temple period.

In addition, those texts that do stem from the Second Temple period refer to prophets either sparingly or in new ways. The book of Nehemiah attests the shadowy prophetess Noadiah and "the rest of the prophets" (Neh 6:14), but nothing is known about what they actually did to try and frighten Nehemiah. Moreover, the books of Chronicles, which also stem from the Persian period, view prophets differently than did the DtrH. Certain of the Levitical singers are known as prophets. First Chronicles 25:1 characterizes three Levites as those "who should prophesy with lyres, harps, and cymbals." Here clearly things prophetic have merged with the world of ritual music. Moreover, later in that same chapter, Heman, a Levite, is characterized as "the king's seer," in contrast to the Deuteronomistic picture in which David's prophets, Nathan and Gad, are not Levites. In similar fashion, 2 Chr 20 reports about the spirit of the Lord coming upon Jahaziel, who is a Levite. He then offers an oracle, introduced by the formula, "Thus says the LORD to you" (v. 15). This priest, though a Levitical singer, enacts a role more typical of preexilic prophets. Clearly, during the time of the Chronicler, Levites appear to have claimed prophetic status, one now associated with music and the world of psalmody (Asaph was a Levitical singer and there are psalms attributed to him [Pss 50; 73–83]. And some of these psalms appear to reflect prophetic rhetoric, e.g., Pss 50:16-21; 81:8-9).

During this same Persian period, prophetic literature was growing (see above). It is likely that some of that scribal activity would have occurred at the Temple. Since Levites were attested as prophets in Chronicles and since the book of Malachi proclaims overt concern for "the covenant of Levi" (Mal 2:4-9), there is prima facie reason to associate the Levites with the preservation of older prophetic literature and the creation of supplements to it. Put another way, two sorts of prophetic behavior—psalmody/the worship of song and the written composition of prophetic literature—belonged to the same world. Still, the world of the Temple was not homogeneous. Both Isa 56–66 and Malachi are regularly critical of many elements in the ritual world, particularly sacrificial practice. Moreover, both of these texts allude to sect-like groups (e.g., Isa 63:18; 66:5; Mal 3:16-17) that may have produced this type of literature, groups that may not have belonged to the priestly lineages who were enfranchised to participate in sacrificial ritual at the Jerusalem Temple. Simply put, Persian period prophetic literature was diverse, just as were its preexilic forebears.

Those who looked to the future during the Persian period included prophecy in that which they anticipated. In some postexilic prophetic literature, there are indications of a negative attitude toward things prophetic. Zechariah 13:2-6 creates an animus against anyone who would claim to be a prophet. Other prophetic texts expect the return of prophecy, either in collective form (Joel 2:28-29) or in a solitary prophet, Elijah, who will help loyal Yahwists survive the cataclysmic "great and terrible day of the LORD" (Mal 4:5). Since there is a clear expectation that prophecy will return in one form or another, one may infer that it was thought not to be part of the present time for those authors, perhaps because prophecy was now closely associated with the Temple and its personnel.

On religiohistorical grounds, one would expect prophets as non-technical intermediaries to exist in many times and places. However, certain social conditions were necessary for prophecy to flourish. One of those prerequisites in ancient Israel may have been a nation-state, which provided the object of prophetic address, its institutional support, and some measure of protection for prophets. With the end of Israelite statehood, some of those societal features vanished, which would have meant that intermediation, as exemplified in the activity of an Amos or Jeremiah, was no longer as necessary. Intermediation, then, occurred in new ways—through ritual life at the Temple, through inspired exposition of prior prophetic literature, and through the activity of apocalyptic seers. Later reports that the spirit of prophecy had vanished oversimplify complex transformations in the world of nontechnical intermediation during the Persian period.

F. Theology and Ethics

Prophets were individuals who spoke, wrote, and acted on behalf of the deity. As a result, it is appropriate to comment about their views of the deity as well as on their perceptions of religiously based values. Still, to do this is difficult and for a number of reasons. Prophets were active over both a long period of time and in a variety of contexts, both historical and social. To speak as if there were one prophetic theology or prophetic ethical stance is to risk homogenizing the literary and behavioral variety already examined in this article. Instead, it will be appropriate to highlight several features of Yahwistic theology that appear in prophetic literature.

The OT neither contains nor presents systematic theology. Instead there are narratives, reports, and poems that include various theological traditions, e.g., the notion that Yahweh is enthroned as king. This sort of tradition was stated as such in a number of biblical texts (e.g., Ps 99:1). Two of the most important theological traditions that Israelites themselves affirmed and that are present in Israelite texts are: Yahweh is king; Yahweh has made a covenant with Israel. Both of these traditions would have been at home, though with some differences, in the Northern and Southern Kingdoms. Two other traditions would have been prominent in Judah, namely, the convictions that Yahweh had chosen Zion as the deity's dwelling place and that God had designated the lineage of David as the divinely appointed form of polity.

Prophets not only inherited these traditions, they also explored their implications and, in some cases, turned them upside down. One prominent example of such prophetic working with traditions involves the covenant. According to its expressions in the Pentateuch, the covenant made at Sinai and reaffirmed on the plains of Moab comprised a contract between Yahweh and Israel. That covenant involved a number of stipulations, i.e., the covenant code (Exod 20:22–23:33) or the Deuteronomic law code, by means of which Israel was supposed to live. As a party to this treaty-like agreement, Israel agreed to follow those stipulations. Should Israel be obedient, the covenantal document outlined blessings that would ensue (see, e.g., Deut 28:1-14). If Israel disobeyed, then curses would follow (see, e.g., Deut 28:15-57). Prophets appear to have known such stipulations (e.g., Hos 4:2). Prophetic texts allude to both covenant curses (e.g., Isa 34:11-17) and covenant-like blessings (Jer 30:16, 19). Some prophetic texts, known as covenant lawsuits (e.g., Isa 1:2-9; Mic 6:1-8), reflect an imagined legal process by means of which the deity indicted Israel for having violated the stipulations of the covenant. Oracles of judgment reflect a comparable legal world in which an indictment has been made and a sentence has been passed (see above). In addition, living out of that covenantal world, prophets who lived in the 6th cent. and who had seen the covenant curses enacted could imagine the creation of a new covenant (Jer 31:31; compare Ezek 36:26). Prophets regularly used one or another feature of the Sinai covenant's "theo-logic" in formulating their oracles.

The same can be said about the conviction that Yahweh was king. A number of prophetic texts attest to Yahweh as enthroned in the divine council (1 Kgs 22; Isa 6; Jer 23:18, 22; Ezek 1). The prophets function as heralds of the divine council, speaking on behalf of the deity to the human world. As such, the prophets have the ability to address not only Israel but other nations as well. Though Jeremiah is the only prophet officially designated "as a prophet to the nations," each of the "major" prophetic books includes a sizable collection of sayings and oracles devoted to nations other than Israel (Isa 13:1–23:18; Jer 46:1–51:64; Ezek 25:1–32:32). Similar sections occur in the Book of the Twelve (e.g., Amos 1:3–2:3; Zeph 2:4-15). These prophets believed that Yahweh was a god whose decrees affected all nations. These oracles concerning other nations provide more than jingoistic rhetoric. They exemplify a conviction that God has a plan for all humanity: "this is the plan that is planned concerning the whole earth; and this is the hand that is stretched out over all the nations" (Isa 14:26).

To depict prophets as those who lived within Israel's theological world might give the impression that they were less than original. Such is hardly the case. They were able to take a tradition such as "the day of the Lord" and turn it upside down (Amos 5:18-20). Prior to the time of Amos, the day of the Lord had apparently been viewed positively—as a time when God would act on behalf of Israel. Amos affirms that God will act, but it will be a day of "darkness, not light" for Israel. In addition, texts such as Isa 43:19 affirm that some prophets thought Yahweh could act in new ways. Yet even here, that "new thing" is a rehearsal of an older tradition, a new exodus—from Babylon instead of from Egypt.

To speak of ethics in ancient Israel is to point to certain vocabulary and behaviors. It is not, however, to move outside the theological world of that culture. Israel's views of morality are innately linked to the aforementioned theological convictions. It is possible to maintain that the language of "righteousness and justice" summarizes well the moral norms embedded in the covenant (Amos 5:24). Moreover, just as Israel's law codes often focused on particular cases (e.g., Exod 22:1), so too Israel's prophets identified certain behaviors as violations of that social ethos. The prophets address very specific forms of moral infraction—they include real estate practices (Mic 2:2), sexual behavior (Hos 4:18; Amos 2:7), and the law court (Amos 5:10, 12).

Israelite prophets during the Neo-Assyrian period critiqued a style of life that stood in tension with concern for justice and righteousness. It became increasingly difficult to provide for economic justice when large estates were being created. People's land was being taken away, high interest rates became a financial burden, and debt slavery was rampant. When identifying these issues, the prophets were indicting social structures and not just the ethical behavior of individuals. At the same time, prophets draw attention to the plight of those individuals who were particularly disadvantaged. The widow and the orphan (e.g., Isa 1:17) symbolize those at risk in ancient Israelite society. Such prophetic rhetoric draws on concerns for these same people in Israel's covenantal literature (e.g., Deut 10:18).

Just as there was a close connection between prophets and priests, so too there were important similarities between a certain set of priestly prescriptions, the holiness code (Lev 17–26), and much of what may be found in prophetic literature, especially Ezekiel. An Amos (2:7*b*) as well as an Ezekiel would agree that true holiness involves behavior consistent with the norms of justice and righteousness. Israel could not act with moral impunity and expect that their sins would be forgiven through ritual action.

The affirmation of Yahweh's kingship laid the groundwork for certain moral principles. Foreign nations—and Israel—could be indicted for crimes against humanity, for violating universal moral norms. The oracles against the nations in Amos 1–2 indict those countries for heinous acts that virtually all humans would find repugnant, e.g., genocide (1:6, 9), violence against noncombatants (1:13), and acts of ritual degradation (2:1). Oracles against the nations also include indictments for prideful behavior that offended Israel's God (Isa 14). Finally, some foreign nations are condemned for having overstepped the roles assigned to them by Yahweh. For example, Assyria (so Isa 10:12-15) and Babylon (Jer 51:11-49) acted more violently toward Israel than God had intended. The prophets' moral universe was not limited to the boundaries of Israel as nation-state nor did it derive only from Israel's covenant with the deity.

Prophets were, therefore, both conservators and innovators. They worked on the basis of prior religious traditions and revamped them in new circumstances. If Micah spoke a resounding "No" to the continuation of the Temple in Jerusalem, Isaiah spoke a firm "Yes" to the importance of a Davidic ruler on the throne. If Amos (8:2) could proclaim that "the end has come upon my people Israel," Zechariah could speak of a time when "the remnant of this people" will possess all things (Zech 8:12).

Bibliography: Susan Ackerman. "Why Is Miriam Also among the Prophets? (And Is Zipporah among the Priests?)" *JBL* 121 (2002) 47–80; John Barton. *Oracles of God: Perceptions of Ancient Prophecy in Israel after the Exile* (1988); Ehud Ben Zvi and Michael Floyd, eds. *Writings and Speech in Israelite and Ancient Near Eastern Prophecy* (2000); Joseph Blenkinsopp. *A History of Prophecy in Israel* (1996); Stephen Cook. *Prophecy and Apocalypticism: The Postexilic Social Setting* (1995); Lester Grabbe. *Priests, Prophets, Diviners, Sages: A Socio-Historical Study of Religious Specialists in Ancient Israel* (1995); Norman Habel. "The Form and Significance of the Call Narratives." *ZAW* 77 (1965) 297–323; Martti Nissinen. *Prophets and Prophecy in the Ancient Near East* (2003); James Nogalski and Marvin Sweeney, eds. *Reading and Hearing the Book of the Twelve* (2000); Thomas Overholt. *Channels of Prophecy: The Social Dynamics of Prophetic Activity* (1989); David Petersen, ed. *Prophecy in Israel* (1987); David Petersen. *The Prophetic Literature: An Introduction* (2003); Gerhard von Rad. *The Message of the Prophets* (1967); Alexander Rofé. *The Prophetical Stories: The Narratives about the Prophets in the Hebrew Bible, Their Literary Types and History* (1988); Joachim Schaper. "Exilic and Post-Exilic Prophecy and the Orality-Literacy Problem." *VT* 55 (2005) 324–42; Marvin Sweeney. *The Prophetic Literature* (2005); Gene Tucker. "Prophecy and Prophetic Literature." *The Hebrew Bible and Its Modern Interpreters*. Douglas Knight and Gene Tucker, eds. (1985) 325–68; Claus Westermann. *Basic Forms of Prophetic Speech* (1967); Robert Wilson. *Prophecy and Society in Ancient Israel* (1980).

DAVID L. PETERSEN

PROPHETESS [נְבִיאָה nevi'ah; προφῆτις prophētis]. Female prophets appear in all three parts of the Jewish canon of Scripture (Torah, Prophets, and Writings) and throughout biblical history. The OT names five women as prophetesses: MIRIAM (Exod 15:20), DEBORAH (Judg 4:4), the woman who bears a child with Isaiah (Isa 8:3), HULDAH (2 Kgs 22:14; 2 Chr 34:22), and NOADIAH (Neh 6:14). Scholarship has not reached a consensus about the application of the title to each of these women. However, the presence of female prophets in the biblical text is evidence that women performed this role in ancient Israel. Additionally, the biblical text uses the verb "to prophesy" in connection with women on two occasions (Ezek 13:17; Joel 2:28 [Heb. 3:1]). While the OT does not identify any of the "writing" prophets as women, several scholars have suggested that the author of Second Isaiah was a woman. *See* ISAIAH, BOOK OF; PROPHET, PROPHECY.

STEVE COOK

PROPHETIC LAWSUIT. *See* LAWSUIT.

PROPHETS, SONS OF. *See* SONS OF PROPHETS.

PROPITIATION. *See* ATONEMENT.

PROSELYTE pros'uh-lit [προσήλυτος prosēlytos]. A Greek rendering of the Hebrew term ger (גֵּר; "sojourner, alien"). The word was not used by classical writers. It first appeared in the LXX (most frequently in the Pentateuch). In the OT the word denotes either a foreigner or sojourner, like Abraham among the Hittites (Gen 23:4) or Moses in Egypt (Exod 18:3), or a class of resident aliens (*see* FOREIGN, FOREIGNER; SOJOURNER; STRANGER). The latter resided in the land of Israel and, though lacking protection and privileges that were guaranteed to the natives by reason of their blood relationships, acquired a definite status similar to that of metics ("resident aliens") in Greek states. The resident aliens are often mentioned along with the poor, widows, and orphans (Lev 19:10; 23:22; Deut 24:19). The Israelites should treat them as equals with love (Lev 19:34). Such resident aliens were distinguished from other foreigners who were present in the country only temporarily, for instance, as travelers or merchants, and who had no protection or rights in Israel.

Due to the fact that the resident aliens had certain religious obligations (Exod 20:10; 23:12; Deut 5:14; 16:9-11, 14; 29:11) and gradually became integrated into the community of Israel, the concept acquired religious connotations, and both Greek and Hebrew words became technical terms for an incomer not to the Jewish land, but to Jewish religion, i.e., for a Gentile convert to Judaism. At first the term **prosēlytos** described those who were residents in the Jewish state, but later it referred also to all those who went over to Judaism, no matter where they lived. It is difficult to tell precisely when the final change took place, but it is clear that by the 1st cent. CE the term **prosēlytos** was religious in most cases. Since it was unfamiliar to the Gentile audience, both Josephus and Philo tended to avoid it: Josephus never used it, while Philo used it mostly in quotations from the LXX.

There is no scholarly consensus on whether Jews were actively seeking proselytes, i.e., whether Judaism of the Second Temple period was a missionary religion (in the bibliography below the positions of those who consider that it was—as well as those who deny it-are presented). The references to Jewish converts can be found both in Jewish and Greco-Roman sources (the latter are sometimes openly hostile). Josephus (*Ant.* 20.17–95) gave an extensive account of conversion of the most famous and influential among Jewish proselytes—a royal family of Adiabene. Tacitus (*Hist.* 5.5) referred to proselytes when he remarks that some were renouncing their ancestral religions and sending tribute to Jerusalem.

The epigraphic evidence for proselytes is very slim; only nineteen are referred to in inscriptions, mostly epitaphs. These texts represent no more than 1 percent of all known Jewish inscriptions and are spread over a period from the 1st cent. BCE to the 5th cent. CE. Half of epigraphic examples are women, which is a rather high percentage if compared with the total representation of women in inscriptions. However, the modest number of proselytes should not be pressed too far; our sources have many lacunae and it is not known whether it was obligatory to mention proselyte status in the epitaphs. Besides, the Roman laws from Hadrian onward treated the conversion of a Gentile as a capital crime, which evidently discouraged people from reporting such conversions on tombstones.

In the NT the term **prosēlytos** is attested four times: Matt 23:15; Acts 2:10; 6:5; 13:43. Each refers to converts. The reference in Matt 23:15 to the scribes and Pharisees who are eager to "cross sea and land" to make a single proselyte was often understood as a proof of Jewish missionary zeal, especially of the Pharisees. There is, however, no other evidence for Pharisaic missionary activity.

The attitude of rabbis toward proselytes varies from very favorable to quite hostile, though the favorable attitude prevails. The legal position of the proselyte was determined by the principle that the proselyte was like a newborn child, with the implication that the former pagan life had no legal existence.

Though the word **prosēlytos** was used as a technical term for a Jewish convert, it retains the basic literal meaning of the cognate verb "to come to." This served to widen the term's sphere of usage. Thus in the early Christian period, along with the traditional meaning there began to develop another one, namely a convert to Christianity.

Bibliography: Shaye J. D. Cohen. "Crossing the Boundary and Becoming a Jew." *HTR* 82 (1989) 13–33; Shaye J. D. Cohen. "Was Judaism in Antiquity a Missionary Religion?" *Jewish Assimilation, Acculturation, and Accommodation: Past Traditions, Current Issues, and Future Prospects.* Menahem Mor, ed. (1992) 14–23; Louis Feldman. *Jew and Gentile in the Ancient World: Attitudes and Interactions from Alexander to Justinian* (1993); Martin Goodman. *Mission and Conversion: Proselytizing in the Religious History of the Roman Empire* (1994); Kirsopp Lake. "Proselytes and God-fearers." *The Beginnings of Christianity, Vol. 5: Additional Notes to the Commentary.* Kirsopp Lake and Henry J. Cadbury, eds. (1933) 74–96; Irina Levinskaya. *The Book of Acts in Its Diaspora Setting* (1996); Scot McKnight. *A Light among the Gentiles: Jewish Missionary Activity in the Second Temple Period* (1991); James Carleton Paget. "Jewish Proselytism at the Time of Christian Origins: Chimera or Reality?" *JSNT* 62 (1996) 65–103; Lawrence H. Schiffman. *Who Was a Jew? Rabbinic and Halakhic Perspectives on the Jewish-Christian Schism* (1985).

IRINA LEVINSKAYA

PROSPERITY [טוֹב **tov**, צָלֵחַ **tsaleakh**, שַׂכַל **shakhal**, שַׁלְוָה **shalwah**, שָׁלוֹם **shalom**; πλουτέω **plouteō**]. Prosperity is a condition of productivity, prudence, or peace (well-being). There are several nuances to the meaning of this concept in the Bible, and thus the term should not be viewed as exclusively or primarily the acquisition of material goods. *Prosperity* and its related terms rarely indicate mere financial gain. Instead, they encompass sufficient growth, prudence, and goodness in every way and throughout life. *Prosperity*, or "to prosper," refers most often to success that comes as a gift of God and is normally dependent on the recipient's obedience to God's will (**tsaleakh**, e.g., God prospers Joseph's work in Gen 39:3, 23; see also Josh 1:8; 1 Chr 22:13; 29:23; 2 Chr 14:7; 24:20; 26:5; 31:21; 32:30; Ezra 5:8; 6:14; Pss 1:3; 37:7; Prov 28:13; Isa 48:15; 53:10; 54:17; Jer 2:37; 5:28; 12:1; Ezek 17:9). God provides people with prosperity (**tov**), literally "good" (e.g., Deut 28:11, 63; 30:5, 15; 1 Sam 2:32; 1 Kgs 10:7; Ezra 9:12; Job 20:21; 21:16; 36:11; Pss 25:13; 106:5; 128:5; Prov 13:21; 17:8, 20; 19:8; Eccl 7:14; Jer 44:17; Zech 1:17).

Prosperity also means well-being, peace, or good fortune (**shalom**, e.g., Job 15:21; Pss 37:11; 73:2, 3; Isa 48:18; 54:13; 66:12; Jer 33:6, 9; Dan 4:1; 6:25; Hag 2:9) or ease and careless calm (**shalwah**, e.g., Pss 30:6; 122:6; Lam 1:5; Jer 22:21; Ezek 16:49; Dan 4:27; Zech 7:7). To have insight that results in success or prosperity, one must be prudent (**shakhal**, e.g., 1 Kgs 2:3; 2 Kgs 18:7; Isa 52:13; Jer 10:21).

In the NT, the word *prospered* ("I have prospered," **peploutēka** [πεπλούτηκα], from **plouteō**, "to prosper or grow rich") only appears once, in a prophetic critique of the church in Laodicea (Rev 3:17). Apparently, that church measured its riches only in material ways. The succeeding verse (Rev 3:18) counsels, however, that the church may only become truly prosperous when it buys from God "gold refined by fire" (compare Zech 13:9; Mal 3:3; 1 Pet 1:7), a metaphor that renders God as the source of true wealth and righteousness. *See* PROVIDENCE; SHALOM; SUCCEED; WEALTH.

ABRAHAM SMITH

PROSTITUTION [זוֹנָה **zonah**; πόρνη **pornē**]. Female prostitution—a woman's participation in sexual intercourse outside marriage, typically in exchange for payment (but see Gen 34:31; Lev 21:14; Deut 22:21)—is well attested in the Bible and other ANE sources. Equally well attested is a profoundly ambivalent cultural attitude toward prostitution.

A. Social Ambivalence toward Prostitutes

1. Marginalized yet praiseworthy

There is no doubt that, at one level, the prostitute was stigmatized and even ostracized in the societies of the ANE. In Lev 19:29 and 21:9, e.g., prostitution is characterized as that which "profanes" or "defiles" (**khalal** חָלַל). Similarly, Prov 23:27 condemns the prostitute as a "deep pit." The prophet Amos curses his enemy Amaziah by decreeing, in the name of God, that Amaziah's wife will become a prostitute (Amos 7:17), and the apostle Paul castigates members of the house church in Corinth who would sleep with prostitutes (1 Cor 6:16). Prostitutes are at the same low level as tax collectors, who were hated and marginalized members of society (Matt 21:31-32).

Certain evidence even suggests that prostitutes lived on the outskirts of cities, their stigmatized status thus demarcated by their place within urban geography. In the Mesopotamian Epic of Gilgamesh (*see* GILGAMESH, EPIC OF), one of the many curses Gilgamesh's dying companion Enkidu heaps upon the prostitute Shamhat, whom he blames for bringing him into the world of humanity (and consequently into contact with the tragedies of death), is to implore that she have no home but the street and that she live in the shadow of the wall (*ANET*, 86). In the OT, the prostitute RAHAB actually lives within the city wall of Jericho, while her house proper stands on the wall's outer side (Josh 2:15). This detail is crucial to the plot of the Rahab story, for it is because her house abuts the city wall that she is able to facilitate the escape of the two Israelite spies who have taken refuge with her by lowering them through her window to land outside Jericho's perimeter. Rahab is subsequently lauded in biblical tradition for her role in securing the Israelite conquest of Jericho, to the extent that Heb 11:31 upholds her, alongside Abraham, Jacob, Joseph, and Moses, as a paradigm of faith. Rahab is also listed alongside Abraham as a paragon in Jas 2:25. Similarly, the Bible treats the widowed TAMAR's assumption of the role of prostitute as praiseworthy. Once he discovers that Tamar's reason for taking on a prostitute's guise was to fulfill her responsibility to bear a son for her deceased husband, her father-in-law, Judah, even declares, "She is more in the right than I" (Gen 38:26).

In the NT, Tamar and Rahab are two of only four women listed in Matthew's presentation of Jesus' genealogy (Matt 1:3, 5). Jesus praises prostitutes for their faith in the baptism of John and, eventually, in the message of Jesus' ministry (Matt 21:23-32), and Jesus likewise praises the faith of the sinful woman—often taken to be a prostitute—who washes and anoints his feet in Luke 7:36-50 (see §D). These passages clearly reflect a much more positive attitude toward prostitutes than those first quoted in this article. Still, there is ambivalence: even as the woman who washes and anoints Jesus' feet is praised, she is identified as sinful, because, presumably, she is a prostitute.

2. Liminal and independent

Phyllis A. Bird explains this ambivalence by suggesting that the institution of prostitution is something ANE societies (or at least the males) perceived as needed and even desired, and therefore the prostitute is accommodated. Still, because the prostitute threatens convention by functioning outside standard social order and acceptable roles for women, she is marginalized. Bird captures this ambiguity succinctly by describing the prostitute as a "legal outlaw"; she similarly describes prostitution in the biblical world as a tolerated liminal activity. Susan Niditch likewise uses the concept of liminality to characterize the prostitute, suggesting that as liminal entities generally are those who, to use Victor Turner's classic formulation, fall "betwixt and between" neatly defined categories, so does a prostitute fall between the two categories allowed women in the ANE, the positions of unmarried virgin and non-virgin wife.

The prostitute's role as a financial agent further places her in a "betwixt and between" position in her community. Bird has proposed, e.g., that at least part of the reason so much stigma is attached to the prostitute is that she controls the financial transactions in which she engages, which contravenes the normal ANE social order, where financial transactions were typically overseen by men. However, the ability of prostitutes to control their own financial destinies means they were among the few women within the ANE who were able to function independent of male authority.

The prostitute Rahab, for instance, is said to have had her own house in Jericho (Josh 2:1, 3, 18-19; 6:17, 22), and, since the point is made that she must gather her family there to protect them when the Israelites attack (Josh 2:18), the text seems to presume she otherwise lived in this house independent of the company—and of the authority—of her father and/or brothers. Her ability to function independently is also indicated in Josh 2:3, where the representatives of the king of Jericho who seek the Israelite spies are said to deal directly with Rahab rather than through a male intermediary. In addition, when she entered into an agreement—or what might even be called a treaty—with the two Israelites whom she sheltered, Rahab acted as an equal partner in the transaction, trading, as the men say, "Our life for yours" (Josh 2:14).

Judah likewise acknowledged Tamar, during the time she was disguised as a prostitute, to be his equal in their business dealings, thus agreeing to deposit with her a pledge—his signet, cord, and staff—until he could send the agreed-upon payment for her services, a kid from his flock (Gen 38:17-18). Yet after Tamar shed her prostitute's disguise, Judah exerted over her the authority an ancient Israelite man more typically held over women. Indeed, Judah (before he learned why she had assumed the prostitute's role) commanded that Tamar be killed for her alleged sexual misconduct (Gen 38:24).

B. Prostitution as Metaphor for Religious Apostasy

In addition to the texts just surveyed that concern actual prostitutes, we find passages in the OT that metaphorically employ the terms *prostitute*, *prostitution*, *whore*, and related lexemes (all derived from the Heb. root **znh** [זנה]) to suggest that the people of Israel, if they worship other gods instead of or in addition to the Israelite God Yahweh, play the prostitute by violating their covenant obligation to give Yahweh their exclusive fidelity. In legal materials, e.g., any Israelites who might devote themselves to other gods (e.g., Lev 17:7) or even to rituals or ritual agents deemed inappropriate within Yahwistic worship (e.g., Lev 20:5-6) are condemned as "prostituting themselves." Likewise, in the narrative complex that runs from Joshua–2 Kings (the so-called DEUTERONOMISTIC HISTORY), as well as in the related book of Deuteronomy, Israelite worship of other gods is condemned as prostitution (e.g., Deut 31:16; Judg 8:33). The Chronicles narratives, too, can deploy this language (1 Chr 5:25).

It is in the prophetic literature that the metaphorical identification of prostitution with religious apostasy is used most ubiquitously and also most problematically. In the OT, the problems stem from a second metaphorical move that is advanced by the prophets, which is to describe the covenant relationship of Yahweh and the Israelites—which in other sources is conceptualized using the language of a suzerain king (Yahweh) and that king's vassal subjects (Israel) or of a patriarchal authority (Yahweh) and that father's subject children (Israel)—as a relationship between a husband (Yahweh) and wife (Israel, or some representative subset of Israel: e.g., the capital city of Israel's northern kingdom, Samaria, or the capital of the southern kingdom of Judah, Jerusalem). To be sure, there are some profoundly appealing aspects of this prophetic reconceptualization, as the use of marriage language to describe the relationship of Yahweh and the Israelites allows for expressions of tenderness, of intimacy, and of deep, natural, and genuine affection between the people and God that are not as easily come by when the conceit of kingship or even of *paterfamilias* is employed. However, when the metaphor of Israel's covenant relationship with Yahweh as a marriage is combined with the metaphor of Israelite religious apostasy as prostitution, the unfortunate effect is that the language of, e.g., Leviticus and Judges, which saw all Israelite apostates as prostitutes, becomes gendered, so that apostasy becomes associated with the female. Under the terms of the metaphor of the Yahwistic covenant as a marriage, that is, it is a womanized Israel, or Judah, or Samaria, or Jerusalem/Zion that is forced to bear the guilt for all of the people's apostate behavior. Representative texts include Isa 1:21-23; 57:3, 6-13; Jer 3:1-3; 5:7-9; 13:20-27; 22:20-23; Lam 1:8-9; Ezek 16:1-63; 23:1-49; Hos 1–4; 9:1; Mic 1:6-7.

The ramifications of this gendering of apostasy can be unsettling. Some prophets, for example, make the metaphor of the female apostate concrete and thereby see not just the metaphorically female Israel, Judah, Samaria, Jerusalem/Zion, or Babylon as apostate but actual women as agents of apostasy. In Isa 3:16-24; 4:1; 32:9-14; Hos 4:13; Amos 4:1-3; Ezek 8:14; and Jer 7:18; 44:15-19, 25, e.g., women are singled out as particularly responsible for behaviors the prophets deem religiously unacceptable. In some texts, moreover, the identification between the metaphorically female and apostate Israel, Judah, Samaria, and/or Jerusalem/Zion and the alleged apostasies of actual women is made so facilely that a prophet can slip almost without notice from describing one to the other. Thus Isa 3:16–4:1 begins by castigating the "daughters of Zion" in vv. 16-24, then switches in vv. 25-26 to condemn "woman Zion," before returning its attention to Zion's women in Isa 4:1. Such easy identification further encouraged the prophets to blame women for the apostasies that rendered the entire population subject to Yahweh's wrath and judgment. The assigning of blame to women for the degeneration of Israel's metaphorical marriage to Yahweh in addition has the effect—when the prophet's metaphorical language becomes concretized—of setting wives up as the scapegoats in any actual marriages that are degenerating, while husbands are positioned as the aggrieved and wronged party. The metaphor can consequently empower these allegedly aggrieved and wronged husbands to respond, as does Yahweh, judgmentally, and with wrath. The implications for the justification of spousal abuse (both past and present) are chilling.

In the NT, this OT metaphor of "apostasy as prostitution" continues to be deployed, although in somewhat different ways. The book of Revelation in particular draws heavily on this image in its descriptions of the "WHORE OF BABYLON," who is said to represent the apostasies of the Roman Empire, as well as Rome's antagonism toward the peoples of the nascent Christian movement (Rev 17:1, 15, 16; 19:2). Revelation's metaphorical prostitute is, however, never portrayed as an unfaithful spouse to Yahweh, as in the OT prophets. Still, she shows disregard for Yahweh's authority over all the earth, she is the enemy of God's righteous ones, and she is depicted as a gaudy symbol of all sorts of abominations (Rev 17:3-6). All the nations of the earth have fornicated with her (Rev 17:2; 18:3). As in the OT, therefore, the brutal punishment of the Whore of Babylon (Rev 18:1-24) offers a religious justification for violence in relationships between men and women. Revelation 14:1-5, which depicts women as defilers of men, might also serve to condone such abuse.

C. The Question of "Sacred Prostitution"

An issue concerning prostitution in the OT requires discussion: the alleged existence in Israel of both male and female cult prostitutes, religious functionaries, that is, who participated in sexual acts within a ritualized context and for a religious purpose. Such behavior, it is alleged, although condemned by the biblical writers, was engaged in by some ancient Israelites in imitation of Mesopotamian ritual practices. Recent commentators, however, have argued that there is no clear evidence for any ANE or biblical ritual of cult prostitution.

The Hebrew terms commonly translated as "cult prostitute," or also "sacred prostitute" and "temple prostitute," are qadhesh (קָדֵשׁ; masc.; Deut 23:17 [Heb. 23:18]; 1 Kgs 14:24; 15:12; 22:46 [Heb. 22:47]; 2 Kgs 23:7; Job 36:14) and qedheshah (קְדֵשָׁה; fem.; Gen 38:21-22; Deut 23:17; Hos 4:14). Both stem from a root meaning "to be set apart, consecrated, holy," which, obviously, has no explicit sexual connotation. But because female qedheshoth (קְדֵשׁוֹת; pl.) show up in conjunction with prostitutes (zonoth זוֹנוֹת) in Hos 4:14, scholars have argued that the "holiness" of at least the female qedheshoth must involve ritual sex. The fact that the Mesopotamian equivalent to the Israelite qedheshoth, the qadishtu, has commonly been understood as a functionary of the goddess Ishtar, the Mesopotamian goddess of love and fertility, further suggests a connection between the role of the qedheshoth and ritualized sexual behaviors. Indeed, it is clear that the Mesopotamian qadishtu, who could bear children and serve as a wet-nurse, engaged in sexual activities of some sort.

Yet there is no evidence that the sexual activities of the Mesopotamian qadishtu were ritual in nature. Indeed, the assumption that the qadishtu was a particular functionary of the goddess Ishtar has been questioned. Students of Mesopotamian religion have also questioned whether other Mesopotamian ritual functionaries sometimes described as "sacred prostitutes" in fact performed such a role. Finally, regarding Hos 4:14, some scholars argue that the term zonoth ("prostitutes") is used metaphorically in this verse, as the prophet condemns those who commit apostasy in his eyes by accusing them of giving their devotions to other gods (see §B). All that is revealed in the juxtaposition of zonoth and qedheshoth, according to this interpretation, is that the ritual activities of the latter are viewed by Hosea as religiously inappropriate; that the nature of the inappropriateness is sexual misconduct is, however, not indicated.

D. Mary Magdalene's Mistaken Identity

Finally, we should consider the common assumption that the NT figure Mary Magdalene was a prostitute. This tradition stems from the interpretation noted above (see §A1) that takes the sinful woman who washes and anoints Jesus' feet in Luke 7:36-50 to be a prostitute (*see* WOMAN WHO ANOINTED JESUS) and the further interpretation that identifies this woman as Mary Magdalene (who first appears in Luke's Gospel as a follower of Jesus in the immediately succeeding passage, Luke 8:1-3, and whom early Christian exegetes associated with Jesus' anointing based on the story of Mary's anointing of Jesus in John 12:1-8). But the Mary who anoints Jesus' head (not feet) in John's Gospel is in fact Mary of Bethany, not Mary Magdalene (Mary of Magdala), and Luke 8:1-3 describes Mary Magdalene as being possessed by seven demons before becoming a follower of Jesus, not as one stigmatized by the sin of prostitution (*see* MARY). Indeed, nowhere in the NT text is Mary Magdalene labeled a prostitute; this identification is the product only of later Christian exegesis. *See* SEX, SEXUALITY; WOMEN IN THE ANCIENT NEAR EAST; WOMEN IN THE NT; WOMEN IN THE OT.

Bibliography: Phyllis A. Bird. "The Harlot as Heroine: Narrative Art and Social Presupposition in Three Old Testament Texts." *Semeia* 46 (1989) 119–39; Susan Niditch. "The Wronged Woman Righted: An Analysis of Genesis 38." *HTR* 72 (1979) 143–49; Robert A. Oden. "Religious Identity and the Sacred Prostitution Accusation." *The Bible without Theology: The Theological Tradition and Alternatives to It* (1987) 131–53; Jane Schaberg. "How Mary Magdalene Became a Whore." *BR* (1992) 37; Victor Turner. *The Ritual Process* (1969); Joan G. Westenholz. "Tamar, Qedeša, Qadištu, and Sacred Prostitution in Mesopotamia." *HTR* 82 (1989) 245–65.

SUSAN ACKERMAN

PROTESTS OF THE ELOQUENT PEASANT. *See* PEASANT, PROTESTS OF THE ELOQUENT.

PROTEVANGELIUM OF JAMES. *See* JAMES, PROTEVANGELIUM OF.

PROTO-LUKE. *See* LUKE, GOSPEL OF; SYNOPTIC PROBLEM.

PROVERB prov´uhrb [מָשָׁל mashal; παραβολή parabolē, παροιμία paroimia]. The word *proverb* describes various types of discourse in the Bible.

A. Uses in the Old Testament
B. Uses in the Ancient Near East
C. Uses in the Septuagint
D. Uses in the Deuterocanonical Literature
E. Uses in the New Testament
F. Conclusion
Bibliography

A. Uses in the Old Testament

The word most often translated as "proverb" in the OT is mashal, a word whose root meaning is "to be like." It occurs in verbal and noun forms some sixty times in the OT. The NRSV translates mashal in a number of ways, including "proverb," "oracle," "discourse," "allegory," "byword," and "taunt."

Readers of the biblical text most often associate the word *proverb* with short, usually two-line sayings in Hebrew poetic parallel structure that provide basic insights into human relationships. Proverbs 11:17, e.g., states, "Those who are kind reward themselves, but the cruel do themselves harm," and 11:25 says, "A generous person will be enriched, and one who gives water will get water." The word *proverb* is also associated with "comparison" sayings, such as, "Like a sparrow in its flitting, like a swallow in its flying, an undeserved curse goes nowhere" (Prov 26:2); with "better than" sayings, such as, "Better is open rebuke than hidden love" (Prov 27:5); and with numerical sayings, such as those found in Prov 30. Such sayings most likely originated in family settings in the ANE and were transmitted orally from one generation to the next. Eventually the collected sayings, the proverbial wisdom, of a people was set down in written form.

The DtrH states that Solomon composed 3,000 "proverbs" (1 Kgs 4:32). The book of Proverbs has the superscripted title "The proverbs of Solomon" (1:1), and two other divisions of the book, 10:1–22:16 and 25:1–29:27, are designated as "proverbs." Ezekiel references two-line proverbs in 18:2—"The parents have eaten sour grapes, and the children's teeth are set on edge"—and in 12:22: "The days are prolonged, and every vision comes to nothing." Job says to his three friends in 13:12 that their "maxims" (lit., "remembrances") are "proverbs of ashes." The epilogue to the book of Ecclesiastes states that the Teacher weighed, studied, and arranged many proverbs (12:9). The book of Proverbs warns of both the danger and the ineffectiveness of a proverb in the mouth of a fool (Prov 26:7, 9).

Brief sentence sayings are also designated "proverb" in the OT. The reaction of the people to Saul's ecstatic experience among a band of prophets in 1 Sam 10 becomes the "proverb": "Is Saul also among the prophets?" (1 Sam 10:12). David quotes a "proverb" in his words to Saul in 1 Sam 24:13: "Out of the wicked comes forth wickedness." In his condemnation of Judah's unfaithfulness to Yahweh, Ezekiel reminds his listeners of the "proverb": "Like mother, like daughter" (16:44).

Two of Job's speeches, in chaps. 27 and 29, are called "proverbs." In each instance, the text states that Job "continued the lifting up of his proverb" (NRSV, "again took up his discourse"), possibly indicating that the reader should approach all of the speeches in the book of Job as "proverb."

Mashal is used to designate certain prophetic speeches, such as Balaam's oracles in Num 23 and 24. In this narrative, mashal is used seven times to describe the words of Balaam (23:7, 18; 24:3, 15, 20, 21, 23; *see* ORACLE). Ezekiel's metaphorical stories of the eagles in 17:2-10 and of the boiling pot in 24:3-5 are called proverbs (NRSV, "allegory").

In Ezek 17:2, God commands Ezekiel to "riddle a riddle [khidhah חִידָה]" (NRSV, "propound a riddle") and "proverb a proverb [mashal]" (NRSV, "speak an allegory") to the house of Israel. Here, "riddle" and "proverb," or "allegory," are used together to describe a story whose meaning is much more than that derived from a literal reading. "Proverb" is also used in parallel construction with "riddle" in Ps 49:4 (compare 78:2) and in Prov 1:6.

The most common use of mashal in the OT is in reference to words of derision spoken by one people against another. In a beautifully constructed alliterative phrase in Deut 28:37, God says to the people that they will become "an object of horror [shammah שַׁמָּה]," "a proverb [mashal]," and a "byword [sheninah שְׁנִינָה] among all the peoples." In Jer 24:9, God tells the people that he will make them "a horror [zawaʿah זַוְעָה]," "an evil thing [raʿah רָעָה]," "a disgrace [kherpah חֶרְפָּה]," "a proverb [NRSV, "byword"; mashal]," "a byword [NRSV, "taunt"; sheninah]," and "a curse [qelalah קְלָלָה]" to "all the kingdoms of the earth." Other instances of the use of mashal in a negative sense include 2 Chr 7:20; Job 17:6; Pss 44:14; 69:11; Isa 14:4; Ezek 14:8; Mic 2:4; Hab 2:6. In Num 21:27, people who compose and sing taunt songs are called moshelim (מֹשְׁלִים).

B. Uses in the Ancient Near East

Numerous examples of the literary form called "proverb" in the OT are found in the ANE. The Egyptian Instruction of Amenemope (12th cent. BCE; *see* AMENEMOPE, INTRUCTION OF) is strikingly similar to Prov 22:17–24:22, suggesting some borrowing of common proverbial themes and sayings. The Instruction of Amenemope begins with the words,

"Give your ears, hear the sayings, Give your heart to understand them" (3.9–10; trans. *AEL*), while Prov 22:17 states, "Incline your ear and hear my words, and apply your mind to my teaching." Topics addressed by both documents include treatment of the poor (Prov 22:22; Instruction 4.4–5), relationships with angry people (Prov 22:24; Instruction 11.13–14), respect for tradition (Prov 23:10-11; Instruction 7.11–15), and how to behave in the presence of rulers (Prov 23:1-3; Instruction 13–18).

The Aramaic inscription "The Words of Ahiqar" (7th–5th cent. BCE), addressed to "my son," contains numerical sayings and gives advice about the discipline of children similar to Prov 23:13-14 ("Ahiqar" 81–82). Other ANE inscriptions that contain "proverbial" material include the Egyptian Instruction of Any (*AEL*, 135–46; *see* ANY, INSTRUCTION OF) and the Sumerian Instruction of Shuruppak (*ANET*, 594; *see* SHURUPPAK, INSTRUCTIONS OF).

C. Uses in the Septuagint

The LXX employs a number of words to translate mashal, the most common being parabolē. Parabolē is used to render the whole range of meanings and uses of the word mashal in the OT. The report of Solomon's compositions in 1 Kgs 4:32 (5:12 LXX) uses parabolē to name the works. The two-line sayings quoted in Ezek 18:2 and 12:22 are called parabolē, as are the brief sentence sayings found in Ezek 16:44 and the question about Saul in 1 Sam 10:12. Balaam's words in Num 23 and 24 and Ezekiel's metaphorical stories in chaps. 17 and 18 are referred to as parabolē.

Parabolē is also used in the LXX to translate mashal when the Hebrew word is being used to describe words of derision. In Deut 28:37, the LXX states that the people will become an ainigma (αἴνιγμα), a parabolē, and a diēgēma (διήγημα). In 2 Chr 7:20; Pss 44:14 (43:15 LXX); 69:11 (68:12 LXX); Mic 2:4; and Hab 2:6 parabolē is used in a negative sense.

While the LXX version of Prov 1:6 states that one of the purposes of the book is for the young learner "to understand a parabolē," the title of the book names the words of Solomon as paroimiai (παροιμίαι; see also Prov 26:7), while in 25:1, Solomon's works that Hezekiah's officials copied are called paideiai (παιδεῖαι). The references to Job's speeches in 27:1 and 29:1, called mashal in Hebrew, are called prooimion (προοιμίον) in the LXX. The derisive use of mashal in Job 17:6 is translated as thrylēma (θρύλημα), while in Isa 14:4, the negative use of the Hebrew word is rendered in Greek as thrēnon (θρῆνον). The composers of "taunt songs" in Num 21:27 are called ainigmatistai (αἰνιγματισταί) in the LXX.

D. Uses in the Deuterocanonical Literature

The word parabolē appears eleven times in the deuterocanonical books, nine times in Sirach and one time each in Tobit and the Wisdom of Solomon. It is used to describe learned words, as in Sir 3:29, "The mind of the intelligent appreciates proverbs, and an attentive ear is the desire of the wise," and Sir 47:15, "Your influence spread throughout the earth, and you filled it with proverbs having deep meaning." Paroimia occurs five times in Sirach in reference to wise words, and is used in 39:3 in a parallel construction with parabolē and in 47:17 in a list that includes parabolē and ōdē (ᾠδή, "song"). Nowhere in the deuterocanonical literature is parabolē used to describe words of derision spoken by one person to another.

E. Uses in the New Testament

Parabolē occurs forty-eight times in the NT in four books—sixteen times in Matthew, twelve times in Mark, eighteen times in Luke, and two times in the Letter to the Hebrews. The first use of the word parabolē is Matt 13:3-9. There Jesus tells the parable of the sower and the seed to people who gathered around him at the Sea of Galilee (see also Mark 4:1-9; Luke 8:4-8). Later the disciples come to him and ask him why he speaks in parables (Matt 13:10). Jesus responds in v. 13, "The reason I speak to them in parables is that 'seeing they do not perceive, and hearing they do not listen, nor do they understand,'" combining OT sapiential tradition with prophetic words from Isa 6:9-10 (see also Mark 4:10-20; Luke 8:9-15). In Matt 15:15-16, Peter asks Jesus to explain a parable to the disciples, and Jesus says, "Are you also still without understanding [asynetos ἀσυνέτος]?" The deuterocanonical book of Sirach states in 15:7 that "the one without understanding [asynetos; NRSV, "foolish"] will not obtain her [wisdom], and sinners will not see her" and Sir 27:12, in good two-line proverbial fashion, states, "Among stupid [asynetos] people limit your time, but among thoughtful people linger on."

The Gospel of Luke has the widest distribution of uses and nuances of meaning of the word parabolē in the NT. In Luke 4:23, Jesus quotes a brief sentence saying, calling it a parabolē: "Doctor, cure yourself!" (see 1 Sam 10:12; 24:13; Ezek 16:44). The parabolē Jesus tells in Luke 5:36 is more extended and contains two metaphorical images, a garment and a wineskin. In 6:39-42, Jesus uses a series of two-line poetic sayings reminiscent of the book of Proverbs: "Can a blind person guide a blind person? Will not both fall into a pit? A disciple is not above the teacher, but everyone who is fully qualified will be like the teacher. Why do you see the speck in your neighbor's eye, but do not notice the log in your own eye?"

Luke 8:4-15 contains the parable of the sower and the seed, an extended metaphorical story; Luke 12:13-21, the parable of the rich fool; Luke 12:41-48, the parable of the faithful and unfaithful servants; Luke 13:6, the parable of the fig tree; and in seven other places in the Gospel of Luke, stories told by Jesus are designated as parabolē (14:7; 15:3; 18:1, 9; 19:11; 20:9; 21:29). Thus, the use of parabolē in the NT includes many of the uses of mashal in the OT—to describe brief sentence sayings, two-line poetic wisdom words, and metaphorical stories. As in the deuterocanonical literature, parabolē is not used in the NT to designate words of derision spoken by one person to another.

The Greek word paroimia (see Proverbs and Sirach) occurs four times in the Gospel of John and one time in 2 Peter. The author of the Gospel of John states in 10:6 that Jesus used the image of the good shepherd to describe himself, but the disciples "did not understand" this "figure of speech [paroimia]." In John 16:25 Jesus explains to the disciples that up to this point he has spoken to them in "figures of speech" (paroimiai), but in the future he would speak to them "plainly" (parrēsia παρρησία) and then tells them that he is leaving the world and going to "the Father"; they reply in v. 29 that Jesus is now (finally?) speaking to them "plainly" (parrēsia) and not in "paroimia." In 2 Pet 2:22, the author refers to a true "proverb" (paroimia) in describing the fate of false prophets among the faithful: "'The dog turns back to its own vomit,' and 'The sow is washed only to wallow in the mud'" (see Prov 26:11).

F. Conclusion

In summary, *proverb*, mashal, in the OT is used to describe brief sentence sayings, two-line poetic parallel sayings, extended metaphorical stories, prophetic oracles, extended wisdom speeches, and words of derision spoken by one person against another. The LXX translators most often used parabolē to represent mashal in all of the variety of its meanings. The evidence from the deuterocanonical literature, however, attests only the use of parabolē to refer to brief sentence sayings and two-line poetic parallel sayings, with possible references to extended metaphorical stories. Nowhere in the deuterocanonical books is parabolē used to describe the words of prophets or words of derision spoken by one person against another.

The NT uses of parabolē parallel those of the deuterocanonical books, being limited to references to brief sentence sayings, two-line poetic parallel constructions, and extended (however brief) metaphorical stories. The narrative of the parable of the sower and the seed offers a limited connection between parabolē and OT prophetic speech. Thus we observe both a connect and disconnect between the OT mashal and the deuterocanonical and NT parabolē. The common ground—the connection—is found in the shared meaning of the words and stories of the collective wisdom of the people. But in the OT texts, the words of collective wisdom included words of derision spoken by others who hoped the worse for the Israelites. But such words are not called parabolē in the NT, perhaps suggesting an evolution in the meaning of the word from a broad idea of "wisdom" words, both positive and negative, to positive teaching words and metaphorical stories.

Bibliography: Joseph Blenkinsopp. *Sage, Priest, Prophet: Religious and Intellectual Leadership in Ancient Israel* (1995); Richard J. Clifford. "Your Attention Please! Heeding the Proverbs." *JSOT* 29 (2004) 155–63; James L. Crenshaw. *Old Testament Wisdom: An Introduction* (1998); John A. Emerton. "The Teaching of Amenemope and Proverbs xxii 17–xxiv 22: Further Reflections on a Long-standing Problem." *VT* 51 (2001) 431–65; Roland E. Murphy. *The Tree of Life: An Exploration of Biblical Wisdom.* 2nd ed. (1996); Timothy Polk. "Paradigms, Parables, and mesālîm: On Reading the māsāl in Scripture." *CBQ* 45 (1983) 564–83; Shamir Yona. "Shared Stylistic Patterns in the Aramaic Proverbs of Ahiqar and Hebrew Wisdom." *Ancient Near Eastern Studies* 44 (2007) 29–49.

NANCY DECLAISSÉ-WALFORD

PROVERBS, BOOK OF prov'uhrb [מִשְׁלֵי mishle; Παροιμίαι Paroimiai]. Proverbs is in the third section of the Jewish Scripture, "the Writings" (*see* KETHUBIM); in the OT, it is in the middle section, the wisdom literature, between the historical books and the Prophets. The book consists of instructions (chaps. 1–9; 22:17–24:22; 30:1-10; 31:1-9), two-line aphorisms (10:1–22:16; chaps. 25–29), lists (30:11-33), and a hymn (31:10-31). The material is of different dates, composed between the 10th cent. BCE to the Persian period (539–333 BCE).

A. Title

The full title of the book is mishle shlomoh ven-dawidh melekh yisraʾel (מִשְׁלֵי שְׁלֹמֹה בֶן־דָּוִד מֶלֶךְ יִשְׂרָאֵל), "The Proverbs of Solomon, son of David, king of Israel." The number value of all the Hebrew consonants in the phrase is 930, just short of the 934 lines of the book in Hebrew, suggesting that v. 1 is the title of the entire book (*see* NUMBERS, NUMBERING). The Hebrew word mashal (מָשָׁל), translated "proverb," the singular form of mishli, can refer to different kinds of literature: a two-line proverb, a parable (as in Ezek 17:2; 24:3), or a poem (as in Pss 49:4; 78:2). The noun may be related to the verb mashal (מָשַׁל), "to represent, be like," i.e., a comparison. The Vulgate refers to the proverbs as *parabolae*, meaning "parables."

B. Proverbs as a Collection

The book is a collection of previously existing collections: instructions, speeches, poems, and two-line sayings. The following division into an introduction followed by nine sections has broad scholarly support.

I. Introduction to the Book (1:1-7)
II. Instructions and Speeches (1:8–9:18)
III. The Proverbs of Solomon (10:1–22:16)
IV. The Words of the Wise (22:17–24:22)
V. Further Words of the Wise (24:23-34)
VI. The Proverbs of Solomon, Collected by King Hezekiah (25:1–29:27)
VII. The Words of Agur (30:1-14)
VIII. Numerical Sayings (30:15-33)
IX. The Words to King Lemuel of Massa (31:1-9)
X. Hymn to the Capable Wife (31:10-31)

Collecting and arranging traditional material was a recognized way of creating a new literary work in the ANE. Biblical examples are the Pentateuch, the Deuteronomistic History, and the Isaiah scroll. Old material was given fresh meaning through new juxtapositions. Proverbs' instructions in chaps. 1–9 are borrowed from Egyptian and Mesopotamian instructions to youths setting out on their careers. Juxtaposed with speeches of Woman Wisdom seeking disciples, they gain a metaphorical dimension (*see* SOPHIA). Exhortations to act prudently and to be faithful to home and profession (traditional aims of instructions) are broadened into exhortations to seek wisdom before everything else. Once the metaphorical level has been established in chaps. 1–9, the sayings and poems in the following chapters become means of gaining life-giving wisdom.

In chaps. 1–9, the editors made good use of contrasts, the most important being that between Woman Wisdom/Sophia (1:20-33; 8; 9:1-6, 11) and FOLLY, the deceptive woman (2:16-19; 5; 6:20-35; 7; 9:13-18). In the grand finale of chap. 9, the two appear in dramatic opposition: Woman Wisdom in 9:1-6, 11 and Folly in 9:13-18. But the deceptive woman is only one of two enemies in the youth's search for true wisdom. The other is deceptive men (always plural, 1:8-19; 2:12-15; 4:10-19). Woman Wisdom, Folly, and the deceptive men invite the youth to embark on a way of life. The contrasts seem to be developments of the familiar two ways: the way of the righteous and the way of the wicked (*see* WISDOM IN THE OT).

C. Date of Composition and the Historical Context

The mention of King Solomon (mid-10th cent. BCE) as the author (1:1; 10:1; 25:1) is more a description of genre than of date, for all wisdom literature was conventionally ascribed to Solomon, as psalms were to David and laws to Moses. The book is "by Solomon" in the sense that, as king, he would have collected, sponsored, or possibly even written various kinds of literature (1 Kgs 4:29-31). The best dating clue is Prov 25:1, "These are other proverbs of Solomon that the officials of King Hezekiah of Judah copied." Hezekiah, king of Judah (from 715–687 BCE), added proverbs (presumably chaps. 25–29) to an already existing collection under King Solomon's name, perhaps all or part of 10:1–22:16 (*see* SOLOMON).

It is difficult to date Proverbs by its language, editing devices, and themes. On the basis of comparative evidence, one can suggest that with the rise of the monarchy in the early 10th cent. BCE, palace scribes would have produced diplomatic and liturgical texts as well as the kind of *belles lettres* that included wisdom. By the late 8th cent., a collection attributed to Solomon must have been in circulation, when the servants of Hezekiah added a second collection to it (25:1). Because of its obvious indebtedness to the Egyptian Instruction of Amenemope, "The Words of the Wise" (22:17–24:22) had to have been written during the period of trade and cultural exchange with Egypt under the monarchy (*see* AMENEMOPE, INSTRUCTION OF). The proverb "My child, fear the LORD and the king, and do not disobey either of them" presumes a king was on the throne (Prov 24:21). It seems, then, that a substantial part of chaps. 10–29 was in circulation before the end of the monarchy in 586 BCE. When chaps. 1–9 were written and prefaced to the collection is difficult to say, though some scholars date it to the postexilic period. The entire book was probably edited at the same time as much of Israel's other literature, in the Persian period (539–333 BCE).

The question of who wrote Proverbs has been much debated over the last five decades. Before the 1960s it was generally assumed that the book was the work of sages, who were assumed to have been a distinct group in Israel on the basis of Job 15:18; Prov 1:5; 22:17; 24:23; and Jer 18:18. Beginning in the 1960s, two competing theories of authorship arose, one proposing that the material was composed in and for royally sponsored schools, and the other suggesting that at least some proverbs originated among common people.

Neither theory is adequate by itself. We know little about Israelite schools, and Proverbs could have been used in schools without originating there (*see* EDUCATION, OT). A folk origin is certainly possible for many proverbs, but the two-line sayings in their present form are polished, indebted to foreign literature, and consistent in their viewpoint, which strongly suggests they were written by scribes (*see* SCRIBE).

D. Proverbs' Sources: Ancient Near Eastern Wisdom Literature

Proverbs' authors revered ancient literature and drew freely from it. Father-son instructions are attested from the 3rd millennium both in Mesopotamia and in Egypt, as were proverbs. In Mesopotamia, more than twenty-eight collections of Sumerian proverbs are attested (3rd and 2nd millennia), and there are also Akkadian collections from a later period.

Proverbs shared three common assumptions of earlier wisdom literature: wisdom was practical, mediated through a hierarchy of agents, and "institutional." First, wisdom was practical rather than theoretical—knowing how to do something. A king was wise because he knew how to govern well; a jeweler was wise because he knew how to cut and set gems; and a woman was wise because she knew how to manage a household. Wisdom could refer to culture as well as to craft. The beliefs, social forms, and material traits of a particular group were considered part of the order of creation and thus informed by wisdom, for God made the world in wisdom (see especially Prov 3:19 and chap. 8).

Second, wisdom belonged preeminently to the gods and was mediated through a series of agents to human beings. Mediation is particularly clear in texts from Mesopotamia: all the gods were wise, but one in particular was preeminently so, Ea ("Enki" in Sumerian). It was on his advice that the gods created the human race and gave them the knowledge, crafts, and culture (e.g., writing, metallurgy, farming, rituals) needed for civilization and good service of the gods.

Third, heavenly wisdom came to the human race mediated by earthly institutions or authorities: the king, his scribes' literature, and heads of families. In Proverbs, the mediating institutions are the king (Solomon, 1:1; 10:1; 16:10; 20:8; 25:1; etc.), wisdom writings (e.g., 1:2, 6; 22:17, etc.), and the father (and sometimes the mother) in the instructions of chaps. 1–9.

Though Proverbs drew on the literature of its neighbors, it adapted freely. The instructions of Prov 1–9 are less specific than their Egyptian and Mesopotamian prototypes, for they urge readers to seek wisdom rather than to do particular actions. Proverbs emphasizes character rather than actions. Moreover, Proverbs' strong personification of Wisdom in Prov 1; 8; and 9 and its vivid descriptions of Wisdom's two enemies—the deceptive men (1:8-19; 2:12-15; 4:10-19) and the deceptive woman (2:16-19; 5; 6:20-35; 7; 9:13-18)—create a metaphorical level of discourse unknown in earlier wisdom literature. The Words of the Wise (Prov 22:17–24:22), e.g., recast sections of the Egyptian Instruction of Amenemope in the characteristic Hebrew two-line verse.

The other borrowed genre, the "saying," has also been reshaped. Akkadian and Syro-Palestinian sayings were extremely diverse, taking the form of witty sayings, observations on life, jokes, wordplays, humorous or ironic maxims, and proverbs, but Prov 10–31 focused on proverbs and made them all two-lined.

E. Significant Assumptions and Dramatizations of Proverbs

Proverbs operates with several assumptions: the world is "self-righting"; wisdom includes justice and piety and excludes folly and impiety; it includes "fear of the LORD"; and human beings are able to choose between two ways. Moreover, the book dramatizes moral possibilities by viewing human beings as types. These assumptions require comment.

1. The world is self-righting

Since God made the world in justice and wisdom, the world has the capacity to reward good deeds and punish wicked deeds (e.g., Prov 1:31: "therefore they shall eat the fruit of their way and be sated with their own devices"). The capacity is sometimes called the deed-consequence connection. Proverbs, however, sometimes speaks of the consequences of moral choice by attributing it explicitly to the Lord (over eighty times) or God; at other times it uses passive verbs, so that the reader assumes it is God's word.

2. Reverence for God

In Proverbs, "fear of the LORD" occurs fourteen times; twice it is said to be the beginning of wisdom (1:7; 9:10). "Fear of the LORD" is not a good translation of Hebrew yirʾath yhwh (יִרְאַת יְהוָה). For one thing, *Lord* is a title, and *Yahweh* is a proper name. For another, "fear of a god" does not mean the emotion of fear or even a reverent attitude. Rather, the phrase means revering a particular deity by performing the god's rituals and obeying the god's commands. Against the polytheistic context of the ANE, Israelites were to revere Yahweh to the exclusion of other gods. Since wisdom is a gift of the gods, the only way to acquire it is to seek it from the one deity that can grant it. In Proverbs, the deity could only be Yahweh.

3. Free will

Proverbs assumes that a human being is free and self-possessed. The book views life as action, and it frequently defines human beings through their organs of action: the organs of perception, decision, expression, and motion. Proverbs uses concrete images: eye, ear, mouth (tongue, lips), heart, hands, and feet (this style is especially clear in 4:20-27). The most important organ in Proverbs is the mouth, for words express the person better than anything else, and words are the medium through which discipline and knowledge are imparted. A major difference between Woman Wisdom and her enemies in chaps. 1–9 is the "truth" or reliability of their words. So strong is Proverbs' view of human freedom that the book virtually equates knowing the good with doing the good. The ignorance of the fool is not a simple lack of knowledge but an active aversion to it, an aversion arising from cowardice, pride, or laziness. Ignorance has an ethical dimension, and seeking wisdom is a moral obligation for human beings. The wise person is morally good; the fool is wicked. This blending of ethical and sapiential language seems to be an original contribution of Proverbs.

4. The two ways

Though Proverbs emphasizes personal freedom, it is acutely aware of the social consequences of individual acts and expresses these consequences by the metaphor of the "way." One's free choices place one on either of two paths, each with its own dynamic: "the way/path of the righteous" (e.g., 2:20; 4:18) or "the way/path of the wicked" (e.g., 4:14, 19; 12:26; 13:5, 6; 15:9; 25:26). The ways are not permanent states; one gets on and off by one's fundamental choices. One joins a community of people on the same path and shares their fate, as in the opening scene in 1:8-19. Thus Proverbs balances personal freedom and its social consequences.

5. Types

Proverbs uses types, usually antithetically paired, to describe behavior and its consequences. The contrasts add drama and liveliness to the saying. Each set of types is distinctive: pairings of the wise and the foolish show little interest in retribution from Yahweh, whereas divine retribution plays a major role in the righteous and wicked types; in the rich and poor types, riches are viewed positively as the result of diligence, but poverty is not blamed solely on laziness.

F. Personified Wisdom

Proverbs' personification of wisdom as a woman is exceptionally strong and persistent. Wisdom gives two powerful speeches to the youth (1:20-33; 8) and builds a palace and invites the youth to the dedicatory feast (9:1-6, 11). However, she has powerful enemies (2:12-19): deceptive men (1:8-19; 2:12-15; 4:10-19) and a deceitful woman (2:16-19; 5; 6:20-35; 7). Whence did this personification come?

Recent scholarship can be summarized under four headings: 1) Wisdom is a hypostasis of Yahweh; 2) she is derived from a Syro-Palestinian or Egyptian goddess; 3) she is derived from the Mesopotamian divine or semi-divine **ummanu** who was a sage and bringer of culture from heaven to earth; 4) she is a pure literary personification.

According to the first theory, an aspect of a deity, such as anger or wisdom or cultic presence, is reckoned an entity in itself (hypostasized) and personified. Such a theory is not an adequate explanation, however, for Prov 1:20-33 and 8:22-31 emphasize her distinction and subordination to Yahweh. For the second theory, solid evidence for such a goddess in Israel does not exist. The Egyptian goddess Maat is a pale and mute abstraction of "order," and there is no "order" in biblical religion comparable to that in Egyptian religion.

The third theory, that personified Wisdom is derived from culture-bringers in Mesopotamian mythology, explains the most features of Woman Wisdom and thus is the most likely; it is also compatible with the fourth theory that the personification is a literary creation. The Mesopotamian mythology was known in the Levant. The last in a series of culture-bringers is identified with Ahiqar, the hero of the 8th-cent. Aramaic tale Ahiqar (*see* AHIKAR, AHIQAR). Further, Philo of Byblos, a 1st- or 2nd-cent. CE savant, narrates a history of culture that alludes to the **ummanu** tradition. This interpretation finds support in the enigmatic Hebrew word in Prov 8:30*a*, ʾ**amon** (אָמוֹן). Though often translated into English as "nursling," it is best interpreted as a loanword from Akkadian **ummanu**, yielding the translation of Prov 8:30*a*: "then I was beside him, like a (heavenly) sage" (NRSV, "master worker"), i.e., as a heavenly figure mediating to the human race the knowledge they require to be good servants of God.

G. The Hebrew Text and Versions of Proverbs

The oldest Hebrew manuscripts of Proverbs are two fragments from Qumran: one ca. 30–31 BCE, and the other ca. 50 CE; both texts reflect the text type later selected by the rabbis as the standard. The Greek translators of the 2nd cent. BCE used a different Hebrew recension of Proverbs; over the years scribes added corrections to it to make it conform more literally to the Hebrew text. The result was many double translations of the SEPTUAGINT of Proverbs: entire verses (e.g., 1:7; 2:21; 3:15; 18:22; 29:25), and single lines (e.g., 1:14, 27; 6:25; 8:10; 29:7; 31:27, 29, 30). The translators were often baffled by the concise Hebrew sayings and devised many strategies to make sense of the text.

In the 2nd cent. CE, Proverbs was translated into Syriac (the Peshitta), for Syriac-speaking Christians. The Peshitta of Proverbs was probably translated by Jews, for the later Targum shows dependence on it. In 398 CE Jerome translated the Hebrew text of Proverbs into a polished Latin (*see* VULGATE). His work is valuable, for he had direct access to textual witnesses no longer extant and had the training and talent to use them properly; he also used ancient interpretive traditions, including some in which he received instruction from rabbis.

H. The Influence of Proverbs on Later Literature

Authors of the Second Temple period were aware of a corpus of sacred texts (including Proverbs) and "reread" these texts for new situations. A good example of rereading is Sir 24, which interprets Prov 8 with Torah and Temple in view. In Hellenistic Judaism, Proverbs influenced Wisdom of Solomon, written in the 1st cent BCE or 1st cent. CE. Wisdom of Solomon borrowed several Proverbs themes: personified Wisdom; Solomon the wise king; the righteous person as the point where divine action becomes visible in the world; God as a father who teaches his son (the righteous person or Israel) through a process of education; and the world protecting the righteous and punishing the wicked (*see* SOLOMON, WISDOM OF).

Wisdom literature is well represented in the library of the Qumran community: fragments of Proverbs (4Q102 and 4Q103), Job (4Q99–100) and *Targum of Job* (4Q157), Qoheleth (4Q109–110), and Sirach (2Q18 and 11Q5 XXI–XXII). Among nonbiblical wisdom texts are a description of the evils of Woman Folly (4Q184; compare Prov 5; 7; and 9), a poem on wisdom revealing the glory of God (11Q5 XVIII), and an instruction called Sapiential Work A (extant in fragments: 1Q26; 4Q415–418). Wisdom themes appear in sectarian documents such as the *Rule of the Community* (1QS), where the community head is the **maskil** (מַשְׂכִּיל), a wisdom term, "one who enlightens or instructs." Other texts stress knowledge and illumination (*see* DEAD SEA SCROLLS).

Early Christians regarded Jesus as a wisdom teacher and employed traditions about personified Wisdom to express his incarnation. Some sayings in the Q tradition (a presumed source of both Matthew and Luke) present Jesus as an emissary of Wisdom (Luke 7:35 and 11:49-50). In other Q sayings, Jesus himself seems to embody wisdom (see Luke 13:34//Matt 23:37; Luke 10:22// Matt 11:27). *See* WISDOM IN THE NT.

Proverbs influenced the Letter of James. Its instructions use exhortatory verbs and give reasons for the recommended behavior. Wisdom warnings appear: the danger of an unbridled tongue (Jas 3:5-10; compare Prov 10:18-21), presumptuous planning (Jas 4:13-17; compare Prov 16:1), and ill-gotten wealth (Jas 5:1-6; compare Prov 10:2-3). James exalts "wisdom from above" (Jas 3:13-18; compare Prov 2:6-11), which harks back to the view that wisdom is beyond human capacity but graciously given to human beings (Prov 8; Sir 24; *see* JAMES, LETTER OF).

The Fourth Gospel uses Proverbs' instructions to present Jesus as incarnate wisdom descended from on high to offer life and truth to human beings. As Woman Wisdom was with God from the beginning, even before the earth (Prov 8:22-23), so Jesus is the Word "in the beginning" who is with the Father before the world existed (John 1:1-2; 17:5). As Wisdom shows human beings how to walk in the right way (Prov 2:20-22; 3:13-26; 8:32-35), so Jesus functions as revealer in John (14:6). Jesus speaks in long discourses like Woman Wisdom (Prov 1:20-33; 8; compare John 14–17). Wisdom invites people to partake of her banquet, where the food and drink symbolize life and closeness to God (Prov 9:1-6, 11). Jesus does the same: "I am the bread of life. Whoever comes to me will never be hungry, and whoever believes in me will never be thirsty" (John 6:35). As Wisdom seeks friends (Prov 1:20-21; 8:1-4), so Jesus recruits disciples (John 1:36-38, 43), though the possibility exists of rejecting Wisdom (Prov 1:24-25; 7; 9) and Jesus (John 8:46; 10:25; *see* JOHN, GOSPEL OF).

Two NT hymns identify Jesus with God's creative word and heavenly wisdom: Col 1:15-20 and John 1:1-18. The Greek word **logos** (λογός, "word") in John 1 owes as much to wisdom traditions as to traditions of the word (*see* WORD, THE). Sirach 24:3 ("I came forth from the mouth of the Most High") and Wis 9:1-2 had already made "wisdom" and "word" parallel. Proverbs 8:22-23 ("The LORD created me at the beginning ... ages ago I was set up ...") and Sir 1:1 affirmed that wisdom comes from the Lord and remains with him forever. The Johannine prologue states that the Word was always with God (John 1:1-2).

I. Proverbs and Today's Seekers of Wisdom

Chapters 1–9 are more concerned with forming character than with urging specific actions; they teach respect for one's own freedom and dignity and inculcate obedience to God. The sayings, on the other hand, invite pondering. Their conciseness and euphony mark them immediately as different from ordinary speech, which is usually diffuse, repetitive, and meandering. The "differentness" makes a proverb appear given, revealed, always there, and so captures readers' attention. One becomes involved in its meaning. In the course of puzzling over the meaning, the saying becomes authoritative.

The entire book of Proverbs makes important contributions to contemporary seekers of wisdom. First, the quest for wisdom is depicted as a drama charged with conflict. Another voice, that of another woman or a group of men, also promises fellowship and life. In the end, however, their promises prove empty and even fatal. Any seeker of wisdom must therefore discern the authentic voice, and must reject as well as choose (compare John 10:3-5).

Second, acquiring wisdom is both a human achievement and a divine gift, a paradox stated most memorably in chap. 2. Though wisdom is a free gift, the way to it is through "discipline," i.e., willingness to learn from others, and the capacity to bear pain and contradiction in acquiring wisdom. One acquires wisdom by making oneself open to receive it as a gift.

Bibliography: Michael L. Barré. "'Fear of God' and the World View of Wisdom." *BTB* 11 (1981) 41–43; William P. Brown. *Character in Crisis: A Fresh Approach to the Wisdom Literature of the Old Testament* (1996); Richard J. Clifford. *Proverbs: A Commentary.* OTL (1999); Richard J. Clifford. "Your Attention Please! Heeding the Proverbs." *JSOT* 29 (2004) 155–63; Ellen F. Davis. *Proverbs, Ecclesiastes, and the Song of Songs.* Westminster Bible Companion (2000); Katherine J. Dell. *The Book of Proverbs in Social and Theological Context* (2006); Carol R. Fontaine. *Smooth Words: Women, Proverbs and Performance in Biblical Wisdom* (2002); Michael V. Fox. *Proverbs 1–9.* AB 18A (1999); Tremper Longman III. *Proverbs.* Baker Commentary on the Old Testament Wisdom and Psalms

(2006); Roland E. Murphy. *Proverbs.* WBC 22 (1999); Raymond C. Van Leeuwen. "The Book of Proverbs." *NIB* 5 (1997) 17–264; Bruce K. Waltke. *The Book of Proverbs.* NICOT (2005); R. N. Whybray. *Proverbs.* CBC (1994).

RICHARD J. CLIFFORD

PROVIDENCE [πρόνοια pronoia]. Providence is the action by which God sustains the creation and guides it toward God's intended purpose for it. Whereas creation is God's originating work for the cosmos, providence refers to God's ongoing relationship to the cosmos. While providence in Greek thought, from Plato to Plotinus and Seneca, was impersonal and related most often to Fate, the Jewish writer Philo related providence to a personal God, as did Christians. The Apocrypha places a heavy emphasis upon divine providence (compare Wis 14:3). In these contexts, *providence* is used similarly to Greek thought and is often a synonym for God (4 Macc 9:24; 13:19; 17:22) or as an attribute of God (3 Macc 4:21; 5:30).

Although the word *providence* is rare in the Bible, the concept of divine providence is common. Providence includes both foreknowledge and PREDESTINATION, as well as divine intervention. Job's three "friends" see providence as the cause of his ailments in response to Job's sins (Job 4:1-11). Daniel's three friends are preserved in the fiery furnace by providence (Dan 3:12-28). Jesus' suffering, death, and resurrection were providentially necessary (Luke 24:26). *See* ELECTION; GOD, NT VIEW OF; GOD, OT VIEW OF; VOCATION, NT.

KENNETH D. LITWAK

PROVINCE [מְדִינָה medhinah; ἐπαρχεία eparcheia]. An administrative term for a subdivision of an empire outside the imperial city or country. Ancient empires generally preferred to govern their territories through local client kings, transferring a territory to provincial status under direct imperial rule only when the region became inefficient, troublesome, or outright rebellious.

After losing their independence, the territories of Israel and Judah were at first administered by client kings. In northern Israel, the transition from quasi-independent kingdom to provinces of the Assyrian Empire is not entirely clear. Dor on the Mediterranean coast and MEGIDDO in the Jezreel Valley and Galilee seem to have been made into provinces in 732 BCE after Tiglath-pileser's victories there. Gilead in the region north and east of Galilee seems also to have been reorganized as a province at this time, but definitive documentation is lacking. In 722–720 BCE, the capital city of SAMARIA and its environs was also made into a province. Thus, by 720 BCE, all of Israel had become provinces of the Assyrian Empire. Then the territories of both Israel and Judah became provinces of the Babylonian (586 BCE), Persian (538 BCE), Ptolemaic (301 BCE), and Seleucid (200 BCE) empires. The repeated references in Ezra and Nehemiah to the province Beyond the River probably refer to the Persian provinces west of the Euphrates, though perhaps to Transjordan (e.g., Ezra 4:10-11; 5:6; 6:6; Neh 2:7, 9; 3:7).

Rome followed the general ANE pattern, but gradually practically all the territory under Roman control was given provincial status. From the time of AUGUSTUS, a distinction was made between senatorial provinces and those governed directly by the emperor. Senatorial provinces were governed by proconsuls appointed by the Senate. *Pro consule* means "in behalf of the consul" or chief magistrate of the senate (*see* PROCONSUL). Their term normally lasted one year. The NT refers to two such governors: GALLIO of ACHAIA (Acts 18:12-17) and Sergius Paulus (*see* PAULUS, SERGIUS) of CYPRUS (Acts 13:7). Order was maintained by small garrisons of auxiliary troops. The governors of imperial provinces were appointed by the emperor, reported directly to him, and could have legionary troops to enforce Roman directives and put down rebellion. Both types of provinces had governors of senatorial rank, a former consul or former praetor. SYRIA was the most important of such provinces. A third type of province also had governors appointed directly by the emperor. They were given the title *praefectus* or, from CLAUDIUS' time onward, *procurator* (*see* PROCURATOR). There were only a small number of such provinces, a category reserved for provinces regarded as potential hot spots or considered especially backward or resistant to Roman rule. Egypt was such a province, and in 6 CE Judea became such a province.

The following list of provinces relevant to NT study arranges them in order of their incorporation into the ROMAN EMPIRE. 1) Senatorial provinces: Macedonia (146 BCE); Achaea (146 BCE); Asia (133 BCE); Crete and Cyrenaica (74 BCE); Bithynia (74 BCE, with Pontus added in 64 CE); Illyricum (27–11 BCE); Cyprus (22 BCE, though already annexed without provincial status in 55 BCE). 2) Imperial provinces: Pamphylia (101 BCE, joined to Lycia in CE 43); Cilicia (67 BCE, joined to Syria in 22 BCE); Syria (64 BCE); Egypt (31 BCE); Galatia (25 BCE); Illyricum (made an imperial province in 11 BCE); Judea (6 CE); Cappadocia (17 CE); Lycia and Pamphylia (43 CE).

Roman provincial administration varied somewhat from province to province and during different periods of the same province, depending in part on who was emperor, the personalities and ambitions of the governors he appointed, and the local situations. Some areas of NT study where understanding provincial government bears on interpretation are: 1) the issue of whether the addresses of Paul's letter to the Galatians were inhabitants of ethnic GALATIA (the North Galatian hypothesis) or the Roman province of Galatia (the South Galatian hypothesis); 2) whether the SANHEDRIN had authority to execute the death penalty during Pilate's (*see* PILATE, PONTIUS) governorship (compare John 18:29-31); 3) the census of Luke 2:1-5; and 4) the jurisdiction to which Jesus (Luke 23:6-12) and Paul (Acts 23:34) belonged. *See* GOVERNOR.

Bibliography: David W. J. Gill and Conrad Gempf, eds. *The Book of Acts in Its Graeco-Roman Setting* (1994); E. Mary Smallwood. *The Jews under Roman Rule* (1976).

M. EUGENE BORING

PRUDENCE. *See* DISCRETION AND PRUDENCE.

PRUNING HOOK [מַזְמֵרָה mazmerah]. A tool used for pruning grapevines during dormant periods in order to maintain the vines, produce high-quality grapes, and speed the harvest. The curved and sharpened metal hook could easily cut away extra shoots and branches (Isa 18:5). At harvest, the hook was placed at the base of a clump of grapes and pulled toward the thumb in a motion like plucking the strings of a harp. Since warfare was so common, the prophets spoke of an idyllic time of peace when the metal blades of spears would be refashioned into pruning hooks (Isa 2:4; Mic 4:3). Joel reverses this image, calling for pruning hooks to be reshaped into spear points (Joel 3:10 [Heb. 4:10]). *See* TOOLS.

VICTOR H. MATTHEWS

PRUSA pr*oo'*suh [Προύσσα Proussa]. A Greek city located in the Roman province of BITHYNIA, identified with modern Bursa in northwestern Turkey. Founded in the late 3rd cent. BCE by King Prusias I (and/or Hannibal; Pliny the Elder, *Nat.* 5.148), Prusa boasted hot springs, fertile lands, and olive groves. Prusa was also the birthplace of the famous Greek orator, writer, philosopher, and historian Dio Chrysostom. There are no explicit references to Prusa in the Bible.

J. TED BLAKLEY

PSALM 151. Whereas the Heb. contains 150 psalms, the LXX features an additional Psalm 151. In certain Greek codices, this psalm is placed in an appendix with the superscription "This psalm is ascribed to David as his own composition, though it is outside the number." In Codex Sinaiticus, however, the psalm is presented as canonical within "The 151 Psalms of David" (*see* SINAITICUS, CODEX). The Hebrew version is attested in the Qumran PSALMS SCROLL (11Q5; dated ca. 30–50 CE) and is preserved as two separate psalms (151A and the fragmentary 151B), which the Greek version has conflated and shortened.

The LXX superscription situates Psalm 151 "after [David] fought in single combat with Goliath," while 11Q5 XXVIII, 3 has only "A Hallelujah of David the Son of Jesse" (*DSSSE*). Written in the first person and drawn from 1 Sam 16–17, the Greek psalm features David speaking of shepherding his father's flocks (Ps 151:1) and of his expertise with the lyre (Ps 151:2). David then recounts his selection by God and his anointing as king instead of his brothers (Ps 151:4-5). The final two verses briefly recount David's victory over Goliath.

Bibliography: Peter W. Flint. *The Dead Sea Psalms Scrolls and the Book of Psalms* (1997).

WILLIAM P. BROWN

PSALM HEADINGS, TITLES. *See* MUSIC; PSALMS, BOOK OF.

PSALMODY. *See* HYMNS, OT; MUSIC.

PSALMS OF SOLOMON. *See* SOLOMON, PSALMS OF.

PSALMS SCROLL. No book is represented by more copies in the DEAD SEA SCROLLS than the Psalms (thirty-nine manuscripts from the mid-2nd cent. BCE to the mid-1st cent. CE). The most prominent is the Psalms Scroll from Cave 11 (11Q5 ca. 50 CE), which preserves forty-nine compositions from Ps 101 to Ps 151, with at least one more (Ps 120) now missing. The Psalms Scroll challenges traditional ideas about the shaping of the book of Psalms (*see* PSALMS, BOOK OF). Many of its psalms follow a sequence different from traditional Bibles; three do not feature in the Hebrew psalter but are in other collections; and several others were previously unknown.

The Psalms Scroll has given rise to two views on the finalization of the book of Psalms. Some scholars explain the differences from the traditional Hebrew (or Masoretic) Psalter by classifying the Psalms Scroll as a liturgical compilation secondary to the traditional 150-psalm collection. In contrast, others maintain that the Psalms Scroll witnesses to a psalter stabilized in two stages (Pss 1–89 and 90 onward). Two or more psalters are represented among the Psalms scrolls, and the Psalms Scroll contains the second part of a true scriptural psalter.

Comparison with other Psalms scrolls tends to support the second position and indicates that at least two editions of the book of Psalms are represented in the scrolls. One of these is the traditional Masoretic collection of 150 psalms (e.g., Psalm scroll B from Masada). The other edition comprises the collection found in the Qumran Psalms Scroll preceded by Pss 1–89 (see *Psalms*[b] [11Q6], which preserves text from the earlier part of this Psalter; Pss 77:18-21; 78:1).

PETER FLINT

PSALMS, BOOK OF sahm [תְּהִלִּים tehillim; Ψαλμόι Psalmoi]. Psalms is not only the Bible's longest book; it is the Bible's most diverse, both literarily and theologically. Nowhere else in the Scriptures is found such a varied collection of religious poetry, with 150 psalms in the Hebrew text and 151 psalms in the LXX. As the product of several centuries of ancient Israel's religious life, the Psalter features an array of discursive forms including prayers, hymns, didactic poems, and even a wedding song. On the one hand, nearly every theological chord of the OT resounds throughout the Psalter. On the other hand, the Psalter consists primarily of human discourse, both joyous and anguished. In the psalms, the anthropological and the theological are inseparably wedded.

- A. Title(s)
- B. The Psalter as Collection
- C. Use and Function in Ancient Israel
- D. Language of the Psalms
- E. Genre
  - 1. Complaint or prayer psalms
  - 2. Hymn or praise psalms
  - 3. Thanksgiving psalms
  - 4. Other types
- F. Reading the Psalms as a "Book"
  - 1. Book I (Psalms 1–41)
    - a. Psalms 1–2
    - b. Psalms 3–14
    - c. Psalms 15–24
    - d. Psalms 25–34
    - e. Psalms 35–41
  - 2. Book II (Psalms 42–72)
    - a. Psalms 42–49
    - b. Psalm 50
    - c. Psalms 51–72
  - 3. Book III (Psalms 73–89)
    - a. Psalms 73–83
    - b. Psalms 84–89
  - 4. Book IV (Psalms 90–106)
    - a. Psalms 90–100
    - b. Psalms 101–106
  - 5. Book V (Psalms 107–150)
    - a. Psalms 107–110
    - b. Psalms 111–119
    - c. Psalms 120–134 (Psalms of Ascents)
    - d. Psalms 135–145
    - e. Psalms 146–150
- G. The Psalter's Coherence
  - 1. Anthropological
  - 2. Theological
- Bibliography

A. Title(s)

The title "Psalms" comes from the plural **psalmoi**, meaning "songs accompanied by stringed instrument," or simply "songs," and is preserved in the Latin title *Liber Psalmorum.* The Greek term for the singular, **psalmos** (ψαλμός), is a translation of the Hebrew **mizmor** (מִזְמוֹר) from the verb **zimmer** (זִמֵּר), "sing" or "accompany singing." The Hebrew term appears as a title for most individual psalms, usually translated "psalm," as in the title "A Psalm of David" (**mizmor ledhawidh** מִזְמוֹר לְדָוִד). In the Greek Codex Alexandrinus, the title for Psalms is **psaltērion** (ψαλτήριον), which refers to a stringed instrument. In English, the word *psalter* refers to a printed collection of hymns.

The title for the Psalter given in rabbinic tradition is **sefer tehillim** (סֵפֶר תְּהִילִּים; "Book of Hymns"), derived from the verb **halal** (הָלַל), meaning "praise," frequently used in the imperative form **halalu-yah** (הַלְלוּ־יָהּ), the Hebrew for "Hallelujah" ("Praise the Lord!"). The title, however, glosses over the variety of genres featured in the Psalter. Only Ps 145 is actually designated as "praise" (**tehillah** תְּהִלָּה) in its title. Moreover, the hymns in the Psalter are outnumbered by the complaint psalms or prayers by nearly two to one. Nevertheless, the Hebrew title appropriately discerns the overall aim of psalmic discourse, namely, to facilitate the move from complaint and petition to thanksgiving and praise.

One hundred nineteen psalms in the Psalter bear various titles, from the terse to the elaborate, such as those that identify a particular historical event in David's life (e.g., Pss 3; 51; 52; 142). (In the Heb. the superscriptions or titles are included in the psalm's first verse, whereas in English Bibles, the superscription directly precedes v. 1 and is therefore not enumerated.) The conclusion to Book II of the Psalter (Ps 72:20) reads, "The prayers [**tefilloth** תְּפִלּוֹת] of David son of Jesse are ended," thereby identifying most of Pss 1–72 as Davidic "prayers," with the exception of those psalms that bear different attribution in their titles (e.g., Pss 42–50; 72), as well as certain non-prayers (e.g., Pss 1; 2; 50). Conversely, the repeated attribution "of/for/concerning David"—the Hebrew preposition is ambiguous—is featured in many additional psalms beyond Ps 72, a total of seventy-three Davidic superscriptions throughout the Hebrew psalter. Other names and groups mentioned in the psalmic titles include Korahites or literally "sons of Korah" (Pss 42–49; 84–85; 87–88), Asaph (50; 73–83), Solomon (Pss 72; 127), Heman (Ps 88), Ethan (Ps 89), Moses (Ps 90), and Jeduthun (Pss 39; 62; 77).

Some of the titles bear generic orientation: "praise" (**tehillah**; Ps 145) and "prayer" (**tefillah** תְּפִלָּה; Pss 17; 86; 90; 102; 142). Other superscriptions are more technical and, consequently, more obscure to modern interpreters, such as **maskil** (מַשְׂכִּיל), attested thirteen times and possibly meaning "instructive poem" (e.g., Pss 32; 42; 44; 45; 52–55; 74; 78; 88; 89; 142 [compare Ps 47:7]).

Other terms are related to musical performance. Examples include the phrase "for the musical leader" or "choirmaster," which occurs fifty-five times (e.g., Pss 4; 6; 54; 55; 61; 67; 70). Other musical terms found in the titles remain enigmatic, such as "Deer of the Dawn" in Ps 22, **shiggayon** (שִׁגָּיוֹן, "lamentation"?) in Ps 7, **sheminith** (שְׁמִינִית, "eighth" as in eight-stringed instrument?) in Pss 6 and 12, "The Dove on Far-off Terebinths" in Ps 56, "Lily of the Covenant" in Ps 60, and "Lilies" in Pss 45; 69; and 80. Pending the discovery of a musical score from biblical times, we cannot reconstruct ancient Israel's sacred music (*see* MUSIC; MUSICAL INSTRUMENTS).

Finally, there are thirty-one "orphan" psalms, which bear no superscriptions, particularly in Books IV and V. Psalms 10 and 43 have no title because each was originally a continuation of the previous psalm.

B. The Psalter as Collection

Canonically, the book of Psalms is included in the third part of the Hebrew canon, the Writings (**kethuvim** כְּתוּבִים). This grouping covers the non-prophetic poetic books of the Bible (with the exception of Daniel, considered prophetic in the Christian canon), including the wisdom literature (Proverbs, Job, and Ecclesiastes), the Song of Songs, and Psalms, which assumes pride of place in the Hebrew canon. In the Christian canon Psalms comes second after the book of Job.

There are two systems of numbering the psalms in the Psalter, as evidenced in the Hebrew MT and in the Greek LXX. The latter counts Pss 9–10 and 114–115 as single psalms, as well as Pss 116 and 148 each as two psalms. The result is a discrepancy between the Greek and Hebrew textual traditions from Pss 8 to 147. The Latin Vulgate and the old Roman Catholic Bibles follow the LXX numbering, whereas all modern translations follow the Hebrew numbering of the psalms.

Internally, the 150 psalms that constitute the Psalter come from various collections and subcollections that derive from different geographical areas of the ancient Levant, as well as from different periods of ancient Israel's history. As evidenced from linguistic features and content, some psalms are evidently of northern origin (e.g., Pss 73–83), whereas most bear southern provenance, specifically Jerusalem. On a larger scale, the Psalter can be divided into five discrete units or "books," as suggested by the four doxologies that conclude each "book": 41:13 (Heb. 41:14); 72:18-20; 89:52 (Heb. 89:53); 106:48. The result is a structural division of the Psalter into five "books":

Book I: Psalms 1–41
Book II: Psalms 42–72
Book III: Psalms 73–89
Book IV: Psalms 90–106
Book V: Psalms 107–150

The Psalter's fivefold structure, according to rabbinic tradition, finds correspondence with the Torah or Pentateuch, as noted specifically in the *Midrash Tehellim* in the 1st cent. BCE. While the Hebrew psalter features David's name in seventy-three psalm titles, later versions, like the Greek and Syriac, cite his name even more frequently, leading to the assumption that David was author of the entire Psalter. The Greek translation (LXX), e.g., ascribes fourteen more psalms to David. The psalm scroll from Cave 11 at Qumran describes David as having composed a total of 4,050 psalms, which "he spoke through ... prophecy which had been given to him from before the Most High" (11Q5 XXVII, 11; DSSSE vol. 2). Also, the LXX version of Ps 151 refers to David having fashioned a "psaltery" (LXX Ps 151:2).

Within the Psalter's fivefold division are various smaller collections, some of which are delineated by particular superscriptions:

1. Davidic Collections	3–41; 51–72; 138–145
2. Korahite Collection	42(43)–49; 84–85; 87–88(89?)
3. Asaphite Collection	50; 73–83
4. Elohistic Collection	42–83
5. Enthronement Hymns Collection	93–100
6. Psalms of Praise Collection	103–107
7. Songs of Ascents Collection	120–134
8. Hallelujah Psalms	111–118; 135; 146–150

The first three collections connect their psalms to particular personages. In addition to Davidic collections, the other "personal" collections include that of the Korahites (a guild of temple singers; see 1 Chr 9:19, 31; 26:1, 19; 2 Chr 20:19; compare Num 16; 26:11) and Asaph (a temple singer appointed by David to oversee music performed in worship; see 1 Chr 6:39; 15:17; 16:7; 26:1; 2 Chr 5:12).

The so-called Elohistic collection includes a portion of the Korahite collection and all of the Asaphite collection. Its defining feature is a distinct though inconsistent preference for "God" (**'elohim** אֱלֹהִים) over "LORD" (**yhwh** יְהוָה) in reference to the deity (compare Pss 14 and 53). The enthronement hymns, lacking superscriptions, are united by content and style: they celebrate Yahweh's kingship over Israel and the nations. The SONGS OF ASCENT are distinguished by their unique superscription **shir hamma'aloth** (שִׁיר הַמַּעֲלוֹת, "song of ascents"), perhaps designating their use as songs of pilgrimage up the mountain to the Temple.

There are several psalms that lie outside the collections listed above. Psalms 1 and 2, e.g., bear no superscription, and hence are not part of the Davidic collection that follows but an introduction to the Psalter as a whole. Other "orphan" psalms include Pss 86; 89–92; 102; 108–110; 119; 136–137. Any reconstruction of the Psalter's growth involves speculation. The various superscriptions seem to function in part to place particular psalms into certain clusters. More broadly, Pss 2–89 form a corpus that presupposes a Davidic view of kingship. Some scholars, taking their cue from Ps 2, refer to this group (over half of the Psalter) as the "messianic psalms" collection (Books I–III), in contrast to Books IV–V, deemed the "theocratic collection," which develops the theme of divine kingship. In light of evidence gained from Qumran close to the turn of the Common Era, it appears that historically Books I–III were stabilized before Books IV and V. The thematic (and dramatic) shift from earthly to divine kingship is occasioned by Ps 89 (see §F3b). This movement is also paralleled with the decreasing number of psalms attributed to David in the ordering of psalms.

One can, moreover, note a rough movement from complaint psalms or laments to hymns throughout the psalter. In Book I, e.g., a string of lament psalms in Pss 3–13 is broken only by one hymn (Ps 8), whereas the last five psalms of the Psalter burst forth with universal praise. The Psalter begins with an indirect call to the study of God's TORAH (1:2) and concludes with a call to all-encompassing praise (150). This movement from earthly to divine kingship (see Pss 89–100) as well as from individual lament to communal praise forms a metanarrative thread, as it were, that ties this collection of discrete collections into a book.

C. Use and Function in Ancient Israel

The Psalter has been described as the "hymnbook of the Second Temple," which is true to a limited degree. Although notorious to date, some of the psalms were likely composed earlier than the Second Temple (520 BCE), namely, those that presuppose the existence of the Davidic monarchy and were later preserved as messianic psalms when the Davidic monarchy was no longer a historical reality. The traumatic experience of exile inspired the composition of some psalms (e.g., Pss 89; 137). But whether dated to the First or Second Temple, many psalms were clearly composed from the perspective of the Temple. According to psalmic tradition, the Temple was the destination of pilgrimage and the object of ultimate desire and religious fervor (see 23:6; 27:4; 42:2-4; 43:3-4; 69:9). In the Temple one could behold God's very presence (e.g., 17:15; 27:4; 42:2, 4; 63:2).

The psalms reflect something of the vibrant activity of ancient worship: references are made to festal events (Ps 81:3), temple visits (Pss 5:7; 65:4; 122:1-2), processions (24:7-10; 42:4; 118:26-27), sacrifices (4:5; 51:19; 107:22; 116:17), and benedictions (115:14-15; 121:3-8; 134:3; compare Num 6:24-26). Some psalms reflect antiphonal singing, as in Ps 118, as well as prescribe the accompaniment of various musical instruments in worship (Pss 149:3; 150:3-5). But whether in elaborate temple worship or in simple household rituals, the psalms were designed to be recited and sung, that is, performed. Even the term usually translated as "meditate" or "meditation" carries a distinctly discursive nuance (1:2; 19:14; 104:34). Private, silent reflection is not the aim of the psalms.

We find also in the psalms a certain fluidity of function. Psalm 30 is an obvious example: the psalm itself suggests that it was originally used as an expression of thanksgiving to God in response to an individual's recovery from illness (vv. 2-3, 11-12). The superscription, however, includes the following title: "A Song at the dedication of the temple," an occasion for its usage that simply cannot be inferred from the psalm's content and form. In short, the psalms held no copyright restrictions in their use and had various reuses in ancient Israel's life.

Some psalms seem to have little connection to corporate liturgy, at least as associated with the Temple. Many of the individual prayers for help, e.g., do not presuppose the background of worship. They are prayers to be heard by God, not by others. The presence of a priest is not assumed. Moreover, other psalms, instead of presupposing worship, indicate a distinctly didactic or instructional usage. Psalm 1, the introduction to the Psalter, commends the study of the "law" (**torah** תּוֹרָה). Psalms 32 and 34 refer to the importance of teaching (32:8-9; 34:11). Such psalms are sometimes referred to as "wisdom psalms," a debatable category. In any case, these psalms, together with those that commend God's torah (1:2; 19:7-10; 119), claim the Psalter as a book of instruction, in addition to being a hymnbook and prayer book.

D. Language of the Psalms

On the one hand, the language of the ancient psalms is by and large conventional. Both prayer and praise are expressed in stereotypical ways. On the other hand, such language is poetic, allowing for the imaginative use of metaphor and imagery. Poetry, by nature, is a much more compact and evocative style of discourse than prose. It is also elusive to define. Hebrew poetry, in particular, does not typically exhibit rhyme or fixed meter (*see* POETRY, HEBREW). Nevertheless, it does bear at least one distinctive feature, namely, the balancing of corresponding poetical lines, commonly called parallelism. A given line of Hebrew verse frequently consists of paired segments or couplets (bicola), although triplets (tricola) and more elaborate patterns are occasionally featured. In a poetic couplet, the second segment or colon can intensify, modify, or in some fashion complete the thought of the first segment. Furthermore, the relationship between the two cola may not be obvious or even parallel in any strict sense. Yet such pairing of clauses conveys a sense of lyrical elegance and symmetry. In addition, various poetic devices such as alliteration, assonance, wordplay, chiasmus, inclusio, and ellipsis abound in the poetry of the psalms. Take, e.g., the extended sentence in Ps 114:1-2.

> When Israel went out from Egypt /
>   the house of Jacob from a people of strange language //
> Judah became God's sanctuary /
>   Israel his dominion //

The circumstantial clause (v. 1) is composed of two parts or "cola" in which "Israel" and "house of

Jacob" serve as corresponding equivalents. In addition, "Egypt" and "a people of strange language" are set in parallel. The second colon expands the first. The main clause (v. 2), also cast in two parts, has its corresponding elements: "Judah" and "Israel," as well as "God's sanctuary" and "his dominion." Note, however, that the second colon of the main clause is elliptical: it lacks a verb.

Another example of such balanced parallelism, sometimes erroneously called "synonymous parallelism," can be seen in Ps 30:11:

> You have turned my mourning into dancing /
> you have taken off my sackcloth and clothed me with joy //

The second colon amplifies the first. The correspondence is clear: "mourning" finds its parallel partner in the image of "sackcloth"; "dancing" is associated with the apparel of "joy." Grammatically, the second colon deploys two complementary verbs to explicate and expand on the one verb featured in the first colon: "taken off" and "clothed" together illustrate in more graphic terms how God has "turned" the emotional disposition of the speaker.

Another common form of parallelism is contrastive or sometimes called "antithetical," as evinced in the following examples:

> For you deliver a humble people /
> *but* the haughty eyes you bring down //
> (Ps 18:27)

> Some take pride in chariots, and some in horses /
> *but* our pride is in the name of the LORD our God //
> (Ps 20:7)

The telltale sign is clearly evident in English, but not so in Hebrew: the connecting word in Hebrew is the same whether serving as a conjunctive or disjunctive (waw [w ו]). Frequently, it is entirely absent. Context is key on how to determine the grammatical relationship between the cola.

Some examples of Hebrew verse, however, do not fit neatly into parallel form, as in 113:3:

> From the rising of the sun to its setting /
> the name of the LORD is to be praised //

The first colon is merely prefatory for the second, whereby the second completes the thought of the first. Poetically, this is called enjambment.

E. Genre

Like snowflakes, no two psalms are identical. Nevertheless, many exhibit identifiable patterns. Analyzing psalms not unlike a field biologist would classify various species within the same genus, Hermann Gunkel identified different types of psalms. Each type, Gunkel argued, is characterized by common form, content, and setting in life, all constituting the psalm's genre. Genres, in short, establish "family resemblances." *See* FORM CRITICISM, OT.

Identifying the genre of a particular psalm, however, carries liabilities. It was once thought that the form of a particular psalm directly reflected its setting in life, that is, its institutional context of usage (e.g., temple worship, educational setting, family setting, etc.). Recent scholarship, however, has shown no rigid correspondence between the form and setting of individual psalms. Psalms of similar structure may reflect different settings of usage. Reception history has shown that a psalm can take on different settings, from public worship to individual devotion and vice versa. Still, genre analysis is quite useful in at least one respect. On the one hand, a genre conveys a set of expectations that enables the reader to identify a psalm's constituent parts and to sense how a psalm typically moves from beginning to end. On the other hand, serving as a sort of template, a genre can show how a particular psalm breaks the generic mold, thereby highlighting the psalm's distinctiveness within the family of psalms to which it belongs.

The three dominant genres exemplified in the Psalter are the complaint or prayer for help, the hymn or song of praise, and the thanksgiving psalm. Each type exhibits a shared literary pattern. Other psalms can be grouped together according to common theme, context, or style.

1. Complaint or prayer psalms

Sometimes called "LAMENTs," these psalms are most frequently cast in the first-person singular voice, "I." A simple example is Ps 13. Its constituent parts include invocation (v. 1), complaint (vv. 1-2), petition (vv. 3-4), and affirmation of trust and praise (v. 5). The complaint is cast as a question and contains an invocation to the Lord. The complaint describes the lamentable state of the speaker: he or she feels abandoned by God and bears "afflictions" and "sorrow," as well as social hostility (v. 2). The complaint itself, however, constitutes neither the center nor the aim of the psalm but rather serves as the preface to the petition that follows in vv. 3-4, in which God is called upon to restore the speaker's life. Completing its movement, the psalm concludes with an affirmation of trust and a vow to praise. The pattern of the complaint psalm, as with all forms in the Psalter, is typical but not uniformly applicable. Psalm 88, e.g., does not conclude in praise but remains in complaint.

Similar are the "communal complaints" or prayers whereby the corporate voice of the community is articulated. These psalms typically lament God's abandonment of the community and recall God's saving work in the past. A good example is Ps 79. Like the individual complaint, this communal psalm proceeds from complaint to God (vv. 1-5) to petition (vv. 6-12), and concludes with an expression of praise (v. 13). The initial complaint graphically describes Jerusalem's destruction, desecration, and international derision. The petition, which constitutes the bulk of the psalm, calls upon God to punish the nations and deliver Jacob (Israel). Reasons are given: the nations have violated Jacob (v. 7), Israel's desolation provides occasion for the nations to gloat over God's abandonment (v. 10*a*), God's reputation is at stake (vv. 9-10*a*), Israel has favored status before God (v. 13*a*). This last motivation serves as an effective transition to the concluding note of thanksgiving and praise sounded in the final two lines (v. 13*b*). As with the certain individual complaint psalms, several communal prayers do not conform to this pattern (e.g., 44; 89).

2. Hymn or praise psalms

There are at least twenty-eight hymns in the Psalter. The shortest psalm, Ps 117, features two common elements. The psalm opens with a command to give praise, a call to worship that includes not just Israel but all the nations. The second verse proclaims the reasons or bases for praise, drawn from God's character and activity. This mini-hymn concludes with the command: "Hallelujah" (NRSV, "Praise the LORD!").

In certain hymns, the call to praise dominates, such as in Ps 148, which calls upon various elements of creation to render praise to their creator. In other hymns, the proclamatory element is dominant (e.g., Pss 46; 48; 84; 87). The elucidated basis for praise in a given hymn focuses either on what God by nature is (or does) or on what God has done in the past. One scholar has designated the former as "descriptive praise" and the latter as "narrative" or "declarative praise," corresponding to the thanksgiving psalm described below (so Westermann). Some psalms, however, do not make such a hard distinction, such as Ps 136.

3. Thanksgiving psalms

Related to both the hymn of praise and the complaint or prayer psalm is the individual thanksgiving psalm. On the one hand, the thanksgiving psalm is an extension or complement of the lament. Recalling a past crisis of petition, thanksgiving psalms provide concrete testimony to answered prayer and display unwavering confidence in God's care and power to deliver. Central is the confession: "I sought the LORD, and he answered me, and delivered me from all my fears" (34:4). On the other hand, the language of thanksgiving is typically filled with expressions of praise, such as in the opening verse of Ps 111. Indeed, the hymn and the thanksgiving psalm are difficult to distinguish, owing to common vocabulary (see above). Nevertheless, the thanksgiving psalm revels in the rhetoric of proclamation, for the act of thanksgiving invariably involves a proclamation of what God has done for the individual or community in response to petition. Psalm 30 provides a paradigmatic example. Three times, no less, the speaker recounts his cry to God (vv. 2, 8), and testimony to God's salvific activity is recalled (vv. 2*b*-3, 7*a*, 11). Intermixed is the language of praise (vv. 4, 12*a*) and petition (v. 10).

4. Other types

Related to the thanksgiving psalms is the song of trust, whose most well-known example is Ps 23. The psalm conjoins two evocative metaphors for God, namely, shepherd and host. The speaker expresses the confident tone of trust in the God who protects and provides amid danger.

Other types of psalms can be categorized under thematic characteristics. These include the historical psalms, which recount the extensive history of the nation Israel, both in thanksgiving and in self-critique or confession (78, 105–106, 135–136).

Also attested are the royal psalms, which exhibit no fixed literary pattern but deal in some form or fashion with the earthly king. Psalm 2, e.g, celebrates the king as God's "son" and anointed one. Psalm 110 appears to be part of a coronation ceremony, while Ps 45 celebrates the marriage of the king. Psalm 72 outlines the solemn duties of the king, including giving due attention to the "poor" and "needy."

As a counterpart to the royal psalms are the enthronement psalms, which acclaim God's kingship as in the expression, "The LORD is king!" (93:1; 96:10; 97:1; 99:1). Related to them are the songs of Zion (46; 48; 76; 84; 87; 121–122). In these psalms, Zion is celebrated as the habitat for divinity, the place of God's holy abode, and the locus of protection from raging enemies. Psalm 48 gives the reader a virtual tour of Zion, God's habitation.

Two other categories of psalms are inseparably related, the torah and didactic psalms. These psalms refer specifically to God's torah or "instruction/law" (1; 19; 119). Psalm 119, the lengthiest psalm, is singularly devoted to the efficacy of divinely established instruction. Instruction is also what the didactic psalms provide: they function to instruct the reader about life before God. Diverse though they are, such psalms include at least 32; 34; 37; 49; 73; and (111) 112, if not others. All either adopt a tone of didactic prescription at some point in the psalm (e.g., 32:9; 34:12-15; 37:8; 49:16-17) or provide a profile of virtuous conduct or appropriated wisdom (e.g., 73; 112). Finally, there are those psalms that are not classifiable according to the common genres described above, such as the temple entrance liturgies of Pss 15 and 24 (see also 50; 82; 131; 133), or fit into more than one category, as in the so-called "mixed" psalms (e.g., 18; 36; 102; 119; 144).

F. Reading the Psalms as a "Book"

It is one thing to examine the Psalms as evocative poetry or as various literary forms functioning within certain, albeit hypothesized, settings. It is quite another to read the Psalms as a coherent collection, in effect a book. Connecting words and themes are evident between adjacent psalms and among clusters of psalms, as well as strategic positions of certain psalms with decisive themes, particularly at the "seams" of the five books (so Gerald Wilson). More broadly, one can discern the movement of certain themes and forms throughout the Psalter. For example, the complaint psalms are dominant in the first half of the Psalter, whereas praise psalms dominate the second half (particularly Books IV and V). In the last thirty psalms the Psalter's "center of gravity" shifts from petition to praise, as well as from individual to communal voice.

The Psalter begins with a commendation of obedience (Ps 1) and ends in a summons to praise (Pss 146–150). In between unfolds a dramatic movement that attains the heights of praise only first by descending into the depths of lament. In addition, the expressed aims of instruction and worship are tightly interwoven, suggesting that the Psalter in its final form bears a twofold purpose: instruction for life and worship before God. In this light, the Psalter can be considered both a book of liturgy and a book of instruction, a hymnbook and a catechism.

The following sections survey the various psalms in order, to provide, at the very least, an overview of the Psalter's content and variety and, at most, suggest how the various psalms connect with one other and function within discrete collections.

1. Book I (Psalms 1–41)

a. Psalms 1–2. Psalms 1 and 2 serve as a composite orientation to the Psalter by introducing two main themes that wend their respective ways throughout the book, namely, law (torah) and kingship. Psalm 1 opens with a beatitude ("Happy ...") that sharply distinguishes the righteous (a single individual in the Hebrew) from the wicked. Likened to a well-nourished tree (see 52:8-9 and 92:13), the righteous person flourishes, whereas the wicked are tantamount to chaff driven away by the wind (1:3-4). Both the righteous and the wicked have their respective paths to tread (v. 6). The righteous one delightfully "meditates" on torah (v. 2*b*); the wicked, by implication, do not. The term *meditate* (**haghah** הָגָה) in Hebrew is no private, silent affair; it designates discursive reflection, including poetic composing (compare 19:14; 104:34). To "meditate" is to recite, reflect on what is recited, and engage in poetic discourse in response. The Psalter is thus marked by its opening psalm as the poetic product of "meditation" on divine torah, human words in response to God's word.

On a very different order, Ps 2 plunges the reader into a scene of international conflict in which the foreign nations rally to attack Zion, the Lord's "holy hill" (2:1-6). The king proclaims by divine decree that he is God's designated "son" and is established on Zion as one anointed to hold sway over the foreign nations (vv. 7-9). The psalm ends with a dire warning: the kings are to "wise up" and serve the Lord with fear (vv. 10-11*a*); otherwise, they will "perish in the way" (v. 11), like the wicked in the previous psalm (1:4). As Ps 1 began, Ps 2 ends with a beatitude, one that commends taking refuge in God (v. 11*b*; compare 1:1). Together, Pss 1 and 2 conjoin various themes that pervade the Psalter: refuge and pathway, law and kingship, righteousness and royalty.

b. Psalms 3–14. These psalms form a subcollection populated mostly by petitions that call upon and affirm God's protection, all surrounding the central praise song of Ps 8. The royal voice of Ps 3, the first psalm in the Psalter that bears a title, mirrors the previous royal psalm: enemies surround the speaker (vv. 1, 6), whose cry for help leads to a pronouncement of trust and confidence (vv. 5-6, 8). The Lord responds from "his holy hill" (v. 4; compare 2:6). God is petitioned to strike the speaker's enemies and break "the teeth of the wicked" (3:7*b*; compare 2:9). Comparable to the image of refuge in Ps 2, God is a protective "shield" in Ps 3 (v. 3*a*).

Psalm 4, also a prayer for deliverance, features an admonition to trust in the Lord (vv. 4-5) and concludes with an affirmation of divine protection as the speaker sleeps in security (v. 8; compare 3:5). Psalm 5, a prayer for entrance into the Temple, develops the divine metaphors of refuge and protective shield (vv. 11-12) and adds a moral dimension: the Lord avoids "evil" and does not "delight in wickedness" (v. 4). Positively, God bears an "abundance" of **khesedh** (חֶסֶד, NRSV, "steadfast love"; v. 7*a*), on account of which the speaker is able to enter the Temple (*see* KHESED; LOVE IN THE OT). At the same time, the speaker indicts those who lie, setting their hearts on "destruction," and calls forth retribution (vv. 9-10)

Psalm 6, a prayer for physical healing, calls upon God to save the speaker's languishing life and to vindicate him before his enemies. As motivation, the prayer reminds God that his death will be of no benefit, for in the realm of the dead (Sheol) there is no praise or remembrance of God (v. 5; compare 30:9). The psalm concludes on a strong note of assurance (vv. 9-10). Psalm 7, a prayer for deliverance, declares the speaker's innocence or "righteousness/integrity" (vv. 3-4, 8) in the face of mounting persecution by unnamed "pursuers." God, in turn, is highlighted as "righteous judge," as well as "shield" (vv. 10-11). Retribution takes the form of both God's "deadly weapons" set against evildoers and the self-inflicted consequences of the wicked (vv. 12-16). The psalm ends with the speaker's resolve to sing praise.

Psalm 8 gives voice to such praise. Bracketed by acclamations of God's majestic name (vv. 1, 9), this psalm is unique within this collection of petitions. It affirms God's glory manifest in creation and divine strength against the unnamed enemy (vv. 1*b*-2). Following a question about God's care for mortals (v. 4;

compare 144:3), the psalm claims the exalted status of human beings vis-à-vis every living thing (vv. 3-8).

Psalms 9 and 10, originally one extended psalm cast in acrostic form, express both declarative praise or thanksgiving and an urgent appeal for justice. They mirror the seventh psalm's depiction of God as the enthroned king and judge of the world (9:7-8; 10:16). God's justice manifests itself, e.g., in the nations sinking in their own "pit" (compare 7:15) and the wicked getting "snared" by "their own hands" (9:15-16; 10:2). The second half, Ps 10, articulates both the flagrant discourse of the wicked, set against God (10:4, 6, 11, 13), and their violent machinations against the poor and helpless (10:8-10). The "poor" and the "needy" or "oppressed" are explicitly identified as rightful recipients of God's care (9:18; 10:9, 12, 14, 17-18).

A song of trust, Ps 11 declares God as the speaker's refuge amid the threat of violence perpetrated by the wicked. Flight from the wicked is tantamount to mistrust of God's power to protect. Indeed, nothing falls outside of God's scrutiny from on high even as God inhabits "his holy temple" (v. 4). Heaven and Temple, refuge and justice, find their convergence here. As the wicked prepare for violence in Ps 11, they promulgate lies and proliferate to near-universal scope in "this generation" in Ps 12 (vv. 1, 7-8). The wicked rely on the power of their speech to oppress the poor (vv. 2, 4-5). In response, God resolves to rise up and provide refuge.

Psalm 13, a short prayer for deliverance from personal enemies, likewise quotes the enemy (v. 4*a*). The speaker points out that God has a stake in preserving the speaker's well-being; otherwise, he will succumb to death's totalizing "sleep" (v. 3; compare 7:5) and his enemy will declare victory (v. 4). The psalm concludes with the speaker's resolve to give praise once deliverance occurs (v. 6).

Mirroring Ps 12, Ps 14 laments the prevalence of evildoers (vv. 3-4). God is portrayed peering down from heaven in search of anyone wise, but to no avail (14:2; compare 11:4). Fools deny God's efficacy (v. 1*a*; compare 10:4*b*), and so they act with impunity against the poor (v. 6). But the Lord is their "refuge" (v. 6*b*).

c. Psalms 15–24. This second subcollection runs in pairs with two (!) exceptions. It is bracketed on the "outside," as it were, by two temple entrance liturgies, and moving toward the center, represented by Ps 19, are two songs of trust (16, 23), two prayers for help (17, 22), and three royal psalms (18, 20–21), all arranged in chiastic fashion:

A	Psalm 15 (Entrance Liturgy)
B	Psalm 16 (Song of Trust)
C	Psalm 17 (Prayer for Help)
D	Psalm 18 (Royal Psalm)
E	Psalm 19 (Torah Psalm)
D′	Psalms 20–21 (Royal Psalms)
C′	Psalm 22 (Prayer for Help)
B′	Psalm 23 (Song of Trust)
A′	Psalm 24 (Entrance Liturgy)

Opening with a question, Ps 15 lists various qualifications for entrance into God's "holy hill," including speaking the truth, avoiding slander and bribes, refusaing to commit usury, and pursuing harmonious neighborly relations (vv. 2-5*a*). Like the Temple itself, the authentic worshiper "shall never be moved" (v. 5*b*).

A song of trust, Ps 16 begins by appealing for divine protection afforded by refuge (v. 1). The remainder of the psalm expresses trust and thanksgiving, including the confident proclamation, "I shall not be moved" (v. 8; compare 15:5*b*), and the resolve to worship only the Lord, "my chosen portion and my cup" (vv. 4-5). God makes known "the path of life" and imparts joy and security (vv. 9-11). Psalm 17 builds on the theme of refuge: the speaker prays to abide "in the shadow of [God's] wings" away from enemies (vv. 8-9). Confident in his righteousness, he also invites God to test his righteousness by confirming that he has "avoided the ways of the violent" (v. 4*b*) and, conversely, has walked unwaveringly upon God's "paths" (v. 5*a*).

Psalm 18, a royal thanksgiving, opens with a plethora of images of God's protective power: rock, fortress, shield, horn, stronghold, and fortress (v. 2). The speaker recalls an incident of distress that prompts a cry for help to God, who hears it "from his temple." A theophany ensues, convulsing creation (vv. 7-15) and setting the stage for God's deliverance (vv. 16-19). The speaker attributes God's salvific intervention to his own righteousness and purity (vv. 20, 24; compare 17:3-5) or loyalty (v. 25). God treats people accordingly: the loyal with loyalty and the crooked with perversity (vv. 25-27). God's "way is perfect," the speaker exclaims, a "shield for all who take refuge" (v. 30). A more prosaic account of the king's victory is cast in terms of the king's agency, demonstrating that God, "a rock," has enabled his success (vv. 31-42). In this royal psalm, deliverance and dominion are inseparably conjoined (vv. 37-48).

Positioned between Pss 18 and 20–21 is the distinctive hymn to God as creator and lawgiver, Ps 19, which moves from creation's silent testimony of God's glory to the specific image of the sun joyously making its trek across the heavens "like a warrior" (v. 5*b*; NRSV, "like a strong man"). In the context of the surrounding royal psalms, the sun takes on a distinctly militant, if not royal, persona. In the second half, the psalm shifts its focus to the efficacy of the law, which "enlightens the eyes" and "revives the soul" (vv. 7, 8). God's torah exhibits, as it were, its own radiance and power, consonant with the sun. The law also exposes the sins of the speaker, who petitions God to clear him from "hidden faults" and to protect him from the "insolent" for fear that they will have "dominion over" him (vv. 12-13). The speaker concludes with the petition that his "meditation" be accepted by the Lord (v. 14).

Psalms 20 and 21 are paired royal psalms, the first a benediction and prayer spoken on behalf of the community for success in battle, the second a thanksgiving for victory. Psalm 20 addresses the king, God's "anointed," with tidings of victory (v. 5). Divine help comes from the sanctuary in Zion (v. 2) as well as from "his holy heaven" (v. 6*b*). Success in battle is attributed not to technological superiority ("chariots" and "horses") but to the Lord (v. 7). The psalm concludes with a direct appeal to God for the king's victory. Psalm 21 is the response to God's fulfillment of Ps 20 (compare 21:2 and 20:4). Addressing God, the speaker enumerates what God has granted the king: crown, long life, glory and majesty, blessings, and joy (vv. 3-6). Unwavering trust on the part of the king, the speaker reports, is the motivating basis for God's **khesedh**, by which the king "shall not be moved" (v. 7). The psalm ends in praise (v. 13).

Lament follows royal thanksgiving with the appearance of Ps 22. The psalm moves deliberately, albeit in fits and starts, from utter despair to ecstatic praise. A complaint of abject abandonment by God opens the psalm, which then oscillates between expressions of self-debasement and suffering (vv. 6-8) and of God's majesty and legacy of care (vv. 3-5, 9-11). To highlight his suffering, the speaker enlists images of various wild animals attacking him (vv. 12, 13, 16, 21*a*), as well as images of physical debilitation (vv. 14-15, 17). The complaint climaxes with sharply pointed petitions (vv. 19-21*a*), but abruptly turns to thanksgiving, beginning with a mysteriously terse account of the speaker's deliverance (v. 21*b*). Praise is exhorted of the congregation as testimony to God's responsiveness to the "afflicted" (vv. 22-24). Like concentric ripples in a pond, the circle of praise expands to include the "ends of the earth" for breadth (v. 27), the dead in Sheol for depth (v. 29), and future generations for time (vv. 30-31), all to bear witness that "dominion belongs to the LORD" (v. 28*a*).

A song of trust, Ps 23 introduces new, albeit complementary, imagery for the saving God of the previous psalm, namely, that of a shepherd, who provides security in "green pastures," guidance along the "right paths," and abundant provision amid grave danger. As Ps 16 identifies God as the speaker's "cup" and "chosen portion" (16:5), so Ps 23 lifts up the image of an overflowing cup as a sign of God's gracious provision (23:5). Although no enemies are specifically mentioned in this idyllic psalm, the speaker uses the language of "pursuit" to anticipate the transformation of lurking danger into abundant blessing: "goodness" and "mercy" shall be his "pursuers" (v. 6*a*).

With the final affirmation of the speaker's desire to "dwell in the house of the LORD" in Ps 23, Ps 24 appropriately concludes the subcollection with another temple entrance liturgy. Prefaced by a statement of God's creation, Ps 24 enumerates, like Ps 15, the qualifications of purity and truthfulness (v. 4). The concluding scene depicts God, the divine king, entering through the temple gates, poetically personified by the command to "lift up your heads" (vv. 7-10).

d. Psalms 25–34. This grouping of psalms is characterized by the themes of "way" and "refuge," of integrity and Temple. A prayer for deliverance, the acrostic Ps 25 opens with a petition that the Lord "lift up" the speaker's "soul" (compare Ps 24:7, 9). Despite enemies and the threat of shame, the speaker declares his trust in God and his intention to "wait" (vv. 3, 5, 21*b*), as well as his need for forgiveness and mercy (vv. 7, 18). The speaker desires to be taught God's "ways," which are identified with "**khesedh** and faithfulness" (vv. 4, 10).

Picking up the theme of "way," the speaker in Ps 26 twice proclaims his innocence (vv. 1, 11) and confidently invites God to "test" him (vv. 1-2). As in Ps 1, the speaker does not associate with the "wicked" and the "worthless" (vv. 4, 5; compare 1:1). He proclaims his love for "the house in which [the LORD] dwells" (vv. 8, 12). It is there that the speaker sings a "song of thanksgiving" by proclaiming the Lord's "wondrous deeds" (v. 7). Psalm 27, likewise, expresses the desire to abide in the Temple to "behold the beauty of the LORD" (v. 4). As in Ps 25, the speaker expresses the desire to be taught the Lord's "way" (v. 11; compare 25:4). It is in the Temple that the speaker seeks the Lord's "face" and "goodness" (vv. 8, 13). As a "stronghold," the Lord provides "shelter in the day of trouble" (v. 5), as well as parental protection (v. 10).

In his cry for vindication, the speaker of Ps 28 makes petition before or within the "sanctuary" (v. 2). Seeking retribution against the wicked, the speaker declares the Lord as his "rock," "strength," and "shield"—that is, a "saving refuge"—as well as Israel's "shepherd" (vv. 1, 7-9). Psalm 29, a hymn, depicts a dramatic scene of worship in which the "God of glory" is manifest as a destructive thunderstorm over the "mighty waters" and the wilderness. Such demonstration of cosmic power confirms God's royal reign over creation (v. 10). As the psalm opens with a liturgical command to "ascribe to the LORD glory and strength," so it concludes with petition that the Lord give "strength to his people" (v. 11).

Psalm 30, a thanksgiving psalm, declares the speaker's deliverance from enemies and Sheol (death). The night of weeping has given way to joy in the morning, and "mourning" has turned to "dancing" (vv. 5, 11). The speaker recalls a time in which he felt firmly "established ... as a strong mountain" (vv. 6-7). But God's face became hidden. The speaker recalls the cry by which he reminded the Lord that his death would be of no use to God (v. 9; compare 6:5). But deliverance has occurred, with the result that praise and thanksgiving can again be conveyed by the now-restored speaker (v. 12).

In Ps 31, a prayer for deliverance, the speaker complains of being "beset as a city under siege" (v. 21). He implores God to "be a rock of refuge" and a "strong fortress" (v. 2) and defiantly declares his trust in God (v. 14). Trust leads to praise of God's power to deliver those who "fear" God (v. 19); they are delivered into "the shelter of [God's] presence" (v. 20). The psalm concludes with an exhortation for those "who wait for the LORD" to "be strong" and "take courage" (v. 24).

Like Ps 30, Ps 32 expresses thanksgiving for recovery from physical debilitation. The speaker regards his affliction as the just punishment of God, hence the appeal for forgiveness that opens the psalm (32:1). Confession of sin is articulated, and forgiveness is acknowledged (v. 5). Through mercy God becomes "a hiding place" for the speaker, who is surrounded by "glad cries of deliverance" (v. 7). The psalm abruptly moves to instruction concerning which "way" is to be chosen (v. 8; compare 25:8-9, 12; 27:11) and concludes with a call to praise (v. 11).

Psalm 33 answers the call to praise with a "new song" (vv. 1-3). The psalm lifts up God's role as creator. Creation by spoken word accounts for the heavens and the earth (vv. 6, 9). From God's vantage point in heaven, all nations are judged by their creator (vv. 13-14). Whereas Ps 32 opens with a beatitude concerning the forgiven individual, Ps 33 commends the nation "whose God is the LORD" (v. 12). The Lord's "counsel" brings the "counsel of the nations to nothing" (v. 10). The psalm concludes with the resolve to "wait for the LORD," Israel's "help and shield" (v. 20), and a petition for God's **khesedh** (v. 22).

The final psalm in this subcollection, the acrostic Ps 34, a thanksgiving song, commends taking refuge in God (v. 8) and cultivating "fear of the LORD" (vv. 9, 11). Reverence of God is grounded in personal testimony of deliverance from the speaker's "fears" (v. 4*b*). The ethical side to the "fear of the LORD," as explicated in vv. 13-14, is based on God's salvific work in behalf of the righteous (vv. 7-9, 17-22).

e. Psalms 35–41. This final subcollection of Book I consists of prayers for healings and thanksgiving psalms, as well as two psalms of instruction. Psalm 35, a petition, enlists God to fight in behalf of the speaker (vv. 1-3). The speaker appeals to God to reduce his enemies to "chaff before the wind" (v. 5; compare 1:4). The divine warrior delivers the "weak and needy" from the strong; such is God's incomparable character (v. 10). The speaker's enemies are "malicious witnesses" who repay evil for good (vv. 11-14). Seeking vindication, the speaker exhorts God to "wake up" and not neglect him (vv. 22-23).

Psalm 36 also dwells on the wickedness of the wicked, who exhibit "no fear of God" and, in turn, excel in the art of deception (vv. 2-4). In contrast, God's **khesedh**, as immeasurable as creation itself, works to "save humans and animals alike" (vv. 5-6, 10-12). God's "refuge," the "shadow of [God's] wings," extends to all peoples and provides an abundant feast, indeed the "fountain of life" (vv. 7-9). Psalm 37 is a didactic psalm cast acrostically. Anticipating retribution against the wicked, the speaker exhorts the reader to remain calm (v. 7), refrain from anger (v. 8), trust in God (v. 3), and "do good" (vv. 3, 27). As the wicked fade away, the meek (i.e., the righteous) shall inherit the land (vv. 11, 29, 34) because God is their refuge (v. 40).

Returning to prayer, Ps 38 seeks healing from sickness, and like Ps 32 connects sickness with sin. In addition, the speaker's companions distance themselves from him (v. 11), and his enemies "lay their snares" (v. 12). The speaker identifies God's angry "rebuke" and the speaker's "iniquities" as cause for his lamentable condition (vv. 1-2). The speaker confesses his sin (v. 18) and waits upon the Lord for response (v. 15), concluding with petition (vv. 21-22). Psalm 39 similarly petitions God for healing and attributes the speaker's condition to God's "stroke" (v. 10). The speaker first resolves to keep silent over his plight, but silence only exacerbates his condition (vv. 1-3). Breaking into petition, the speaker asks God for the "measure of [his] days" and reflects on his and humanity's fleeting existence (vv. 4-6, 11). The psalm concludes with the request that God turn away so that the speaker can find relief before he dies (v. 13).

Psalm 40, a song of thanksgiving, testifies to God's deliverance of the speaker from the "desolate pit," making his "steps secure" (v. 1-2). Hence, a "new song" is uttered, praise instead of lament. The speaker commends trust and right worship that is singularly devoted to the Lord and values obedience over sacrifice (vv. 4, 6-8). The latter half of the psalm returns to petition for deliverance from enemies and iniquities (vv. 11-15) and concludes in trust that God will deliver the "poor and needy" speaker again so that all can give praise (vv. 16-17).

The final psalm of Book I is also a prayer for healing from sickness. Psalm 41 begins with a beatitude regarding the poor and those who "consider" them because God responds favorably to them, granting healing (vv. 1-3). The speaker then petitions for healing caused by sin (v. 4) and deliverance from enemies and former friends who have betrayed the speaker (vv. 5-9). The psalm ends on a note of confidence that God has acted to uphold the speaker because of his "integrity" (vv. 11-12). Book I ends with a doxology (v. 13).

2. Book II (Psalms 42–72)

a. Psalms 42–49. Book II opens with a small collection of psalms designated as Korahite (lit., "sons of Korah"; see also Pss 84–85; 87–88). The collection is characterized by a prominent focus on Zion and on Sheol, the abode of the dead. The collection forms part of a larger grouping of psalms known as the Elohistic psalter (Pss 42–83).

Psalms 42 and 43, originally one lament psalm, open with the poignant imagery of a deer searching for flowing streams, representing the speaker's search for "the living God" (42:2). Water imagery for the speaker changes to tears of despair amid the taunts of others (v. 3). The speaker recalls two interlocking memories, one of praise-filled worship in "the house of God" (v. 4) and the other at the headwaters of the Jordan where "deep calls to deep" in liturgical mystery (vv. 6-7). Both experiences of God's awesome presence remain distant memories in light of the speaker's present condition. The speaker carries on a harsh dialogue between himself and his downcast "soul." The command to hope in God, cast in the form of a rebuke, is repeated three times (42:5, 11; 43:5) and confronts the speaker's state of depression (42:6*a*, 9-10; 43:2) but without complete resolution except for anticipation of praise (43:4).

Psalm 44, a communal complaint, opens with testimony of God's redemptive history with Israel, recalling both the exodus and settlement of the land (vv. 1-3). God is proclaimed as "my King and my God" through whom victory is achieved (vv. 4-5). Such was the past. Now, in the face of devastation, the community accuses God of rejection (vv. 9-16), resulting in defeat at the hands of their enemies, like "sheep for slaughter" (vv. 11, 22). Despite this, the people have remained true to God, even while God has not (vv. 17-21). The psalm ends in urgent appeal for God to awaken, "rise up," and "redeem" (vv. 23-26).

Much in contrast to the previous psalms, Ps 45 is an ode for a royal wedding. The king (compare 44:4), anointed by God, is declared blessed and is even addressed hyperbolically as God (v. 6). Self-identified as one "like" a "ready scribe" (v. 1), the psalmist also addresses the betrothed (vv. 10-12) and implores her to recognize the king as her "lord" (v. 11*b*). The psalm follows with the bride's wedding procession (vv. 13-15) and concludes with a divine promise of progeny and eternal praise (vv. 16-17). Psalm 46 broadens the horizons from royal palace to temple city, Zion, the object of God's help and strength. Zion, the psalm proclaims, is God's refuge even amid cosmic chaos and political upheaval (vv. 2-3, 6). The city "shall not be moved," for its help comes from God in the morning (v. 5). As victorious king, God destroys the weapons of war and commands the nations to desist from their warring ways (vv. 9-10).

Psalm 47, an enthronement psalm (see Pss 93–100), proclaims the Lord as the "great king over all the earth" who acts accordingly by achieving victory over the nations (v. 3), granting an inheritance of land to Jacob (v. 4), and assuming "his holy throne" (v. 8). As Israel gathers before God in worship, so the "princes of the peoples" gather in obedience to the exalted King (v. 9*a*). God owns the "shields of the earth" (v. 9*b*; compare 46:9*b*). Psalm 48 continues the note of praise with its focus on "the city of the great King," similar to Ps 46. On the outside, Zion inspires terror in the hearts of rebellious kings (vv. 4-7). From the inside, Zion upholds the Temple, the edifice of God, who is both refuge and guide (vv. 9, 12-14).

Psalm 49 begins its instruction on the transience of life by addressing the "inhabitants of the world" of every class and background (vv. 1-2). In contrast to the everlasting God, human life and wealth remain fleeting. Trust in wealth is vain, for all die, the wise and the foolish, the human and the animal (vv. 6-12). God abides in glory, but mortals cannot "in their pomp" (vv. 12, 20). Psalm 49 is the anthropological corollary and contrast to the Zion and enthronement psalms that precede it. So ends the Korahite group in this collection.

b. Psalm 50. An Asaphite psalm (see Pss 73–83), Ps 50 conveys God's lawsuit against Israel. As judge God "summons the earth" and gathers Israel for judgment (vv. 1-2, 4). God rejects Israel's sacrifices, which presume that God is hungry for animal flesh and blood (vv. 8-13). God accepts "no bull" (v. 9), for the whole earth belongs to God (vv. 10-11). Instead, what is acceptable is the sacrifice of thanksgiving (vv. 14, 23), which attests that God can be called upon "in the day of trouble" for deliverance (v. 15).

c. Psalms 51–72. Sometimes referred to as the "second Davidic Psalter," this general grouping features titles referencing certain events in David's life, in part drawn from 2 Samuel. The most well-known penitential psalm in the psalter, Ps 51, is attributed to David in light of the Bathsheba/Uriah affair. The speaker acknowledges his sin as an offense against God and, at the same time, appeals to God's mercy and **khesedh** for cleansing (vv. 1-5, 7, 9-10). As God's forgiveness is associated with joy, so the speaker anticipates praise and promises to teach others of God's "ways" (v. 13). As in the previous psalm and elsewhere, sacrificial offerings are deemed inadequate or offensive to God (v. 16; compare 50:7-13; 40:6-7). The speaker, instead, commends a "broken spirit" as the proper "sacrifice" (v. 17; compare 50:14, 23). The psalm concludes, contradictorily, with an appeal for Zion's restoration so that sacrifices can once again be offered properly (vv. 18-19).

As much as Ps 51 revels in self-judgment, Ps 52 casts judgment against another, an unnamed oppressor (v. 1). The title indicates "Doeg the Edomite" or "Saul." The psalm indicts the oppressor for his evil plotting (vv. 1*b*, 3), deceitful tongue (vv. 1*b*, 3*b*, 4), and taking "refuge" in wealth rather than in God (v. 7). The speaker concludes with a declaration of trust and thanksgiving while describing himself as a "green olive tree" planted in the Temple (vv. 8-9; compare 1:3; 92:13). Also attributed to David, Ps 53 repeats much of Ps 14, which condemns "fools" and "evildoers" for their lack of knowledge and oppressive ways. A more judgmental tone is evidenced in v. 5 than in Ps 14: God has rejected the oppressors.

A short prayer for deliverance, Ps 54 calls for vindication and retribution against unnamed enemies. The statement "God is my helper" and "upholder of my life" reflects the speaker's trust, and a freewill offering is promised in thanksgiving (v. 6). Also a prayer for deliverance, Ps 55 identifies not only anonymous enemies as the occasion of the speaker's petition but also the speaker's "equal" and "companion," one who "violated covenant" (vv. 13-14, 20-21). Betrayal is the occasion of the speaker's protest, who wishes that he were a "dove" and could fly away to "be at rest" (v. 6). The psalm ends on a confident note: whereas the righteous will not "be moved," the treacherous will be "cast down" (vv. 22-23).

Psalm 56, another complaint against enemies, vividly articulates trust in God's vindication of the speaker: God has "kept count" of the speaker's "tossings" and stored the speaker's "tears in" a "bottle," literally a flask (v. 8). Deliverance is anticipated, to be followed by the speaker's payment of vows and thank offerings (v. 12). Psalm 57, a composite psalm, beseeches God's mercy in response to the speaker's seeking "refuge" in the "shadow of [God's] wings" (v. 1*b*). Intermixed with urgent petition against enemies is the praise-filled petition that God "be exalted ... above the heavens" (vv. 5, 11). The second half of the psalm (vv. 7-11) is nearly identical with 108:1-5. The speaker proclaims his "steadfast" heart and his readiness to render musical praise (v. 8).

Psalm 58 appears to be a judgment against the gods who fail to judge the wicked, who act like serpents and lions (vv. 4-5, 6*b*) but are destined to be like the "snail that dissolves into slime" (v. 8). With such judgment carried out, the people will know that "there is a God who judges on earth" (v. 11). According to the superscription, Ps 59 is occasioned by Saul's death-warrant against David. The speaker proclaims his innocence and protests the unwarranted nature of his persecution (v. 3). He implores God to punish the treacherous, whom the speaker likens to roaming dogs, "bellowing with their mouths" (vv. 7, 15). And yet amid such threat, the speaker resolves to sing of God's **khesedh** in the morning and of God being a "refuge" and "fortress" (vv. 16-17).

Psalm 60 complains of God rejecting Israel (vv. 1-3) and petitions for victory (v. 5). As an answer, God lays claim to various regions of Israel as well as to surrounding countries (vv. 6-8). Nevertheless, the psalm concludes with another complaint and petition for help against the foe, culminating in trust that victory is won "with God" (v. 12). A prayer for protection of the king, Ps 61 declares God as "rock," "refuge," and "tower" (v. 3) and expresses the speaker's desire to abide in God's "tent" and find "refuge under the shelter of [God's] wings" (v. 4). Petition is given for the king's reign (vv. 6-7), followed by a resolve to render praise and pay vows (v. 8).

Psalm 62 articulates trust in God. God is acknowledged as the speaker's "rock" and "fortress" (vv. 1-2), followed by heated indictment made against an enemy (vv. 3-4). In vv. 5-8, the psalm returns to a serene disposition, culminating with a public admonition to trust (v. 8), followed by instructive reflection on the worthlessness of wealth (vv. 9-10). Power and **khesedh**, the speaker proclaims, belong to God (vv. 11-12). Also a psalm of trust, Ps 63 identifies God as the soul's object of desire, akin to thirst's craving (v. 1; compare 42:1). With thirst quenched, praise is the response to the speaker's encounter with God in the sanctuary (v. 4). The speaker's "soul" is sated with a "rich feast" (v. 5), and God remains the speaker's object of reflection day and night (vv. 6-8). By contrast, the speaker's enemies shall descend to Sheol while the king rejoices in God (vv. 9-11). Psalm 64, a prayer, urgently petitions God to hide the speaker from the "secret plots of the wicked" (vv. 1-2). Their mouths are like weapons targeting the "blameless" (vv. 3-4). The wicked act with impunity, convinced that no one can find them out (vv. 5-6*a*). In response, the speaker muses that the mind and heart are too deep to fathom (v. 6*b*). But God will find them out (v. 7). All will "fear" (v. 9), while the righteous will rejoice and take refuge in God (v. 10).

Psalm 65, a communal hymn, renders thanks to God for a good harvest. The speaker praises God for divine forbearance and for satisfying the community with "the goodness" of the Temple (vv. 3-4). God's "awesome deeds" include the deliverance of a people and the establishment of creation (vv. 5-7). God sustains the earth with a river; the furrows of the land are God's "wagon tracks," overflowing with fertility (vv. 9, 11-13). In similar fashion, Ps 66 opens with imperatives of praise for God's "awesome" deeds, including the exodus event (vv. 1-6). God tested and delivered Israel to "a spacious place" (vv. 8-12). Shifting from corporate praise to individual thanksgiving, the speaker resolves to offer various burnt offerings in thanksgiving (vv. 13-15) for God's protection, accompanied by words of proclamation (vv. 16-20). Continuing the theme of blessing from the two previous psalms, Ps 67 opens with a petition for divine favor for the sake of making known God's "way" and "saving power" (vv. 1-2). Praise is exhorted among the nations in thanksgiving for the earth's abundant produce (v. 6). Thus, "all the ends of the earth" are to revere God (v. 7).

Psalm 68, an elaborate victory hymn, exhorts the divine warrior to "rise up" and vanquish enemies (v. 1). As a "father of orphans and protector of widows" (v. 5), God provides a home for the desolate (v. 6*a*) and release to the prisoners (v. 6*b*). The speaker recounts the salvific work of the "God of Sinai" for Israel in the wilderness, convulsing the earth, bringing rain, and providing for a people (vv. 7-10). Victory over enemy kings is declared, and Zion, the mount of God's abode, is praised as the envy of the mountain of Bashan (vv. 11-16). God processes victoriously from Sinai to Zion, complete with an elaborate procession into the Temple (vv. 17-20, 24-27). Ascribing power to God, the psalm concludes with universal praise of the "rider in the heavens" (vv. 32-35; compare 29:1-2).

Of comparable length is the complaint of Ps 69, which opens with the familiar imagery of danger in "deep waters," followed by the dryness of sorrow (vv. 1-3, 14-15). The speaker complains of numerous enemies falsely accusing him of stealing (vv. 4-5) and beseeches God for protection of those who, like the speaker, have placed their hope in God (vv. 6-8). The speaker laments of social alienation (vv. 8, 20-21). He attributes his situation of conflict to his "zeal for [God's] house" (v. 9). The psalm concludes with praise to the God who "will save Zion" (vv. 30-35). Psalm 70, nearly identical with 40:13-17, is a desperate plea for deliverance from enemies who "desire to hurt" the speaker, who is identified as "poor and needy" (vv. 2, 5). Whereas the enemies speak only taunts ("Aha, Aha!"), those who seek God are called upon to proclaim in praise: "God is great!"

Invoking God as a "rock of refuge" and "fortress," Ps 71 articulates a prayer for deliverance from enemies in the context of old age. The speaker recalls his birth as an act of divine providence (v. 6) and lays claim to a life of continual praise (vv. 6*b*, 8). He beseeches God not to forsake him in his latter years (vv. 9, 18) and promises to give further praise by giving testimony of God's "deeds of salvation" (vv. 14-17). The psalm highlights God's incomparability and power (vv. 18-19). Psalm 72, attributed to Solomon (see also Ps 127), marks the conclusion to Book II and to the largest collection of Davidic psalms. Cast as a petition to God, the psalm prescribes the moral duties of the royal office. The king is to judge with righteousness (v. 2), deliver the poor and needy (vv. 4*a*, 12-14), and crush the oppressor (v. 4*b*). At the same time, the prayer makes petition that the king be God's agent of prosperity and peace (vv. 3, 6-7, 16), enjoy long life or reign as enduring as the sun and moon (vv. 5, 15; compare v. 17), and achieve dominion "to the ends of the earth" (vv. 8-11). The king's reign is to be a fertile rain that sustains a flourishing people (v. 6). So "the prayers of David son of Jesse are ended" (v. 20).

3. Book III (Psalms 73–89)

a. Psalms 73–83. This collection known as the Asaphite psalms (including Ps 50), likely of northern origin, reflects a strong interest in divine justice, Israel's history from exodus to exile, and Zion. Psalm 73, e.g, is a meditation on God's justice vis-à-vis the wicked. It opens with an affirmation of God's goodness to the upright (v. 1), but is followed by a self-confession of doubt (vv. 2-16). The speaker admits to being "envious" of the wicked for their prosperity (vv. 3-12) and consequently questions the worth of his own efforts at righteousness (vv. 13-14). Such dismay is diffused, however, as the speaker recounts entering into the sanctuary whereby the demise of the wicked is revealed (vv. 17-20) and affirms God's guidance in the hope of being received in glory to God, a vague reference to life after death (v. 24).

Psalm 74 corporately laments the destruction of the Temple. The psalm calls God to attend to the "perpetual ruins" of Zion, the divinely established abode of God (vv. 2-3). The sanctuary's destruction by God's foes (vv. 4-8) leads to pointed questioning of God's intentions for Israel (vv. 10-11). The psalm abruptly shifts from protest to trust and praise, affirming God's primordial sovereignty as illustrated in the vanquishing of Leviathan and the establishment of creation (vv. 12-17). The psalm returns to urgent petition for deliverance: God is exhorted to remember the covenant (vv. 18-23). Following the previous petition, Ps 75 gives thanks to God for divine victory. Bracketed by divine discourse (vv. 2-3, 10), the psalm affirms God's hand in establishing cosmic stability (v. 3) and in executing judgment against the wicked, who shall receive the cup of judgment (vv. 4-8). The speaker bursts forth with praise as God resolves to "cut off" the "horns of the wicked" and exalt "the horns of the righteous" (vv. 9-10). Psalm 76, a song of Zion, celebrates God's victory over the nations. As in Ps 46, Zion is deemed God's abode, where God breaks the weapons of war and defeats "both rider and horse" (vv. 2-6; compare 46:9). "Awesome" and "glorious," God renders judgment from heaven in behalf of the oppressed (vv. 7-9). By God's sovereignty even "human wrath" renders praise (v. 10). The psalm concludes with a call for tribute to the one who "inspires fear in the kings of the earth" (vv. 11-12).

Psalm 77 intermixes lament with memory. The speaker "refuses to be comforted" (v. 2*b*); meditating upon God inspires only moaning and exhaustion (v. 3). God's promises seem to have come to an end (vv. 5-10). But memory of God's "mighty deeds" of the past overtakes the lamenter's grief (vv. 11-20), including the redemption of a people and the subduing of the waters of chaos to clear the path for the exodus (vv. 15-20). The dramatic retelling concludes with Moses and Aaron's leadership of God's "flock" (v. 20). Psalm 78 continues the recounting of God's "glorious deeds" (v. 4). One of several "history" psalms (see also 105; 106; 135; 136), the psalm opens with a call to attention and the mandate to pass the historical legacy of God's redemption of a people onto the next generation (vv. 1-8). What follows vividly recounts God's great deeds and the people's recalcitrance and rebellion. The psalm narrates the exodus and the wilderness journey, recounting God's miraculous provisions and Israel's recalcitrance (vv. 9-12, 17-31). Judgment, repentance, then rebellion, and God's forgiving forbearance all follow in succession (vv. 32-42). As the Israelites remembered God as "their rock" (v. 35*a*), so God remembered them as "but flesh" and "wind" (v. 39). As the paradigm of divine power, the various plagues unleashed upon Egypt are retold (vv. 43-51; compare Exod 7–12). As in the ending of Ps 77, God led Israel "like sheep" to safety, to the "holy hill," and settled them in a divested land (vv. 42-55). Nevertheless, Israel continued to rebel, provoking God's wrath, but in a remarkable turnaround, God "awoke as from sleep" and defeated Israel's enemies (vv. 65-66). The psalm concludes with God's rejection of the Northern Kingdom and the election of Judah, Mount Zion, and God's servant David (vv. 67-72). Following upon the heels of Zion's election, Ps 79 laments the destruction of Jerusalem and God's "holy temple" (vv. 1-4). The community cries out for God's "anger" to be poured out upon the foreign nations (vv. 5-7) and appeals to God for forgiveness of past iniquities (vv. 8-9), as well as for deliverance and vengeance (vv. 9-10). Thanksgiving is anticipated by God's people, "the flock of [God's] pasture" (vv. 13).

Psalm 80, another corporate petition, reveals its northern origins in vv. 1-2. Appeal is made that the enthroned God "shine forth" (v. 1) to deliver Israel. The community prays that God's face "shine" for the sake of their salvation (see vv. 3, 7, 19). The psalm recalls the time when God took a "vine out of Egypt" and transplanted it in a new land. There it thrived until devastation struck with the Northern Kingdom's fall (vv. 8-16). The psalm concludes with the community's promise to "never turn back" (v. 18) and a petition for restoration (v. 19). As counterpart to the previous lament, Ps 81 opens with a call to praise with musical accompaniment "on a festal day" (vv. 1-5*a*). The remainder of the psalm is an admonition by God, who recounts Israel's deliverance from oppression, mandates right worship, and complains of Israel's disobedience (vv. 5*b*-12). The psalm concludes with a wish for Israel's obedience and divine provision of the "finest of the wheat" and "honey from the rock" (vv. 13-16).

Akin to Ps 58, Ps 82 conveys divine judgment against the heavenly council. Israel's God indicts the gods for not having implemented justice on earth, particularly for the "weak and the orphan," as well as the "destitute" and "needy" (vv. 2-4). The gods, moreover, act without understanding, and consequently the earth itself is shaken to its foundations (v. 5). God sentences the gods to a life of mortality (vv. 6-7). The psalm concludes with a petition for God to "rise up" against the nations of the earth (v. 8). As was done in heaven, so may it be on earth, the psalmist hopes. Psalm 83, the last of the Asaphite psalms (and of the Elohistic psalter), paints a picture of foreign nations, from Edom to Assyria, conspiring to wipe out Israel (vv. 2-8). The speaker implores God to defeat them, as was once done to Midian, to Sisera and Jabin (compare Judg 4–8). Only victory, the speaker proclaims, will demonstrate that the Lord alone is "the Most High over all the earth" (v. 18).

b. Psalms 84–89. This small grouping of psalms consists of four Korahite psalms (84–85; 87–88) surrounding a Davidic psalm (Ps 86), centralized for its fundamental theme of God's incomparability. Documenting the dissolution of the Davidic kingdom, Ps 89 concludes Book III and marks a dramatic transition into Book IV.

Psalm 84, a hymn composed for pilgrims, identifies the Temple as the object of ultimate desire. The speaker longs for God's "dwelling place" and declares his desire to remain there as a "doorkeeper" (vv. 2, 10). Similarly, the sparrow and the swallow find their home at God's altars (v. 3). Those who make pilgrimage to the Temple are deemed "happy" (vv. 4-7). A petition in the center of the psalm seeks blessing for God's "anointed" (vv. 8-9). The Lord is a "sun and shield," the source of blessing and protection (v. 11). Psalm 85 prefaces its prayer with affirmation of the Lord's past forgiveness and blessing of "Jacob" (vv. 1-3). Central is the corporate petition for God's restoration and **khesedh** (vv. 4-7). The psalm concludes with assurance that God will "speak peace to his people" and that "righteousness and peace will kiss each other" (vv. 8, 10). The central psalm in this collection, the Davidic Ps 86, identifies the speaker as "poor and needy"; he affirms his trust in God's **khesedh** and proclaims God's incomparability among the gods (vv. 1, 5, 8). The speaker seeks to be taught by God for the sake of his integrity (v. 11) and promises to render praise (vv. 12-13). The psalm concludes with petition for deliverance from the "insolent" (v. 14) and with an affirmation of God as "merciful and gracious, slow to anger and abounding in **khesedh**" (v. 15; compare Exod 34:6-7; Ps 103:8). Psalm 87, a short praise psalm, identifies Zion as the object of God's preferential love (v. 2) and Zion's citizens, though dispersed throughout various lands, as registered by God (vv. 4-6).

Psalm 88 is the darkest prayer of the Psalter: it never anticipates, let alone attains, the level of praise with which most individual laments conclude. The speaker complains of being near death, on the brink of the "Pit," where praise is impossible (vv. 3-7, 10-12), and of his estrangement from his companions (vv. 8, 18). God's "wrath" is singled out as the cause of the speaker's distress (vv. 7, 16). The psalm literally concludes with "darkness" (v. 18). For the first thirty-seven verses, Ps 89 is as different from the previous psalm as day from night. Attributed to "Ethan the Ezrahite," this psalm gives praise for God's enduring **khesedh** (vv. 1-2; compare 88:11). Such "steadfast love" is evidenced in God's covenant with David, which preserves "forever" the line of royal descendants (vv. 3-4, 28). God's incomparability (vv. 6-7; compare 86:8), lordship over creation (vv. 9-12), and justice (v. 14) are all lauded by the royal speaker. Specific focus is given to the terms of the covenant God established with David: victory over enemies, rule over an extensive kingdom, an enduring dynasty (vv. 19-37; compare 2 Sam 7). But all this is undone in the second half of the psalm: the speaker complains of God's rejection of the royal covenant, evidenced in the king's defeat by his enemies (vv. 38-45), and concludes with bitter questions about God's reliability, the inescapability of death (vv. 47-48; compare 88:4-6), and petition for God's **khesedh** (vv. 49-51). An abrupt doxology concludes Book III (v. 52). Psalm 89 paves the way for subsequent psalms that laud God's kingship over Israel, the nations, and the cosmos.

4. Book IV (Psalms 90–106)

a. Psalms 90–100. The shortest book of the Psalter is perhaps the most central theologically. Psalms 90–100 affirm God's sovereignty over Israel and the nations. Attributed to "Moses, the man of God," Ps 90 opens Book IV with a corporate lament. The Creator God is described as "our dwelling place" or refuge (v. 1). God is from "everlasting to everlasting," in contrast to mortals, who are mere dust, swept away like a dream or like withering grass (vv. 2-6). The psalm attributes the transience of human life, marked by "toil and trouble," to the "power of [God's] anger" (vv. 7-11). The psalmist asks for wisdom for how "to count our days" (v. 12) and concludes with an appeal to God for **khesedh** and prosperous work (vv. 13-14, 17). Psalm 91 similarly begins by declaring God as "shelter" and protective "shadow," "refuge," and "fortress" (vv. 1, 4). The psalm casts the theme of refuge as a matter of allegiance to God (v. 9) that ensures protection from all evil (v. 11). The psalm concludes with a divine promise of deliverance and prosperity (vv. 14-16). Psalm 92, a thanksgiving psalm designated for use on the Sabbath, proclaims God's **khesedh** and gives praise for God's great works (vv. 1-5). Divine majesty is contrasted with the wicked, who "sprout like grass" and are "doomed to destruction" (vv. 7-8). The speaker declares his thanks for God's victory over his enemies and counts himself among the righteous, who in contrast to the wicked "flourish like the palm tree" and are "planted in the house of the LORD" (vv. 10-14; compare 1:3; 52:8).

Psalm 93 is the first in a collection of hymns extolling God's kingship (93; 95–100; see also 47). In this psalm, as in subsequent psalms, the Lord is acclaimed "king" (v. 1; compare 96:10; 97:1; 99:1). God's lordship is evinced in the world's establishment (v. 2) and in God's power over the mighty floods (vv. 3-4). The psalm concludes in praise of God's sure decrees and holiness in the sanctuary (v. 5).

Psalm 94, a prayer for deliverance from the wicked, interrupts the series of enthronement psalms. It opens with a cry for God, the "judge of the earth," to execute vengeance upon the wicked, who presume that the Lord cannot detect their vicious crimes (vv. 6-7). The Lord, the creator of humanity, knows all people's thoughts (vv. 8-11). The speaker commends God's discipline, announces the return of justice (vv. 12-15), and proclaims the help he has received from God, his "rock" and "refuge," who will repay the wicked for their crimes (vv. 22-23).

Psalm 95 returns to the theme of divine kingship with praise to God in worship. The Lord is proclaimed as "King above all gods," whose hand holds all creation, from the mountains to the seas (vv. 3-4). The people are "the sheep of his hand" (vv. 6-7). The psalm concludes abruptly with a divine admonition for obedience in light of Israel's past rebellion in the wilderness (vv. 7*b*-11). Psalm 96 similarly commands praise and proclamation of God's "marvelous works" (v. 3). Above all the gods, mere idols (vv. 4-5; compare 95:3), the Lord is creator unequaled. Honor and majesty, glory and strength are due God (vv. 6-9). The Lord is proclaimed king (v. 10*a*; compare 93:1)—thus the world is "firmly established"—and judge (vv. 10*b*, 13; compare 94:2). In response, all of creation rejoices, including the sea (v. 11; compare 93:3-4). Psalm 97, like Pss 93 and 99, opens with an acclamation of divine kingship. In response, all the earth is to rejoice (v. 1). Vivid images of light and darkness describe God's theophany, before which the earth convulses and melts (vv. 2-5). The worshipers of idols, consequently, are "put to shame" as "all gods bow down" (v. 7), demonstrating the Lord's exaltation over creation and the divine assembly (v. 9).

Psalm 98 commands the singing of "a new song" in response to God's marvelous deeds, particularly victory over the nations (vv. 1-3). Even the sea and floods are commanded to roar in praise (v. 7; compare 96:11*b*) to herald the Lord's coming "to judge the earth" in righteousness (vv. 7-9). Psalm 99 opens with royal acclamation of the enthroned God. In response, both people and the earth tremble (v. 1). Unique to this enthronement psalm, God's holiness is repeatedly emphasized (vv. 3, 5, 9; compare 93:5). Moses, Aaron, and Samuel are identified as special priests who received God's decrees (vv. 6-8). The psalm concludes with a command to worship God "at his holy mountain" (v. 9). Psalm 100 serves as the concluding doxology for the enthronement psalms by its command for universal worship and its acknowledgment of God as the sole creator of Israel, "the sheep of his pasture" (v. 3; compare 95:7). Concluding the psalm is an affirmation of God's goodness and enduring **khesedh** (v. 5).

b. Psalms 101–106. Rounding out Book IV, the remaining psalms are a hodgepodge of forms and themes centered on creation (Ps 104) and history (Pss 105; 106). The last three psalms bear no superscription. Psalm 101, attributed to David, is a royal pledge to rule justly before God. The king resolves to "walk with integrity of heart," avoid evil, punish slanderers and the arrogant, purge the dishonest from his "house," and destroy the "wicked in the land" (vv. 2, 7-8). Psalm 102, in contrast, is a prayer for healing interspersed with declarative praise. The speaker complains of his body's deterioration, of social alienation, and of taunting enemies (vv. 3-11). Following is a hymn to the enthroned God who will rebuild Zion from its ruins and respond to the "prayer of the destitute" (vv. 12-17). Praise leads to proclamation: God has responded to the "groans of the prisoners" and set them free (vv. 18-22). The speaker prays that his life be preserved in midlife (vv. 23-24) and concludes with an affirmation of God's imperishability in contrast to the heavens, which will "wear out like a garment" and be changed "like clothing" (v. 26). The permanence of God's nature enables the children of God's servants to "live secure" (v. 28).

Complementing the previous psalm, Ps 103 articulates praise and thanksgiving. It begins with the speaker commanding his "soul" (**nefesh** נֶפֶשׁ) to "bless the LORD," the one who forgives and heals (compare

102:3-11), as well as redeems, provides, and renews one's strength (vv. 1-5). This God, whose "ways" are made known through Moses, works for justice for the oppressed, abounds "in **khesedh**" (compare Exod 34:6-7; Ps 86:15), and is compassionate "as a father" (vv. 6-13). In forgiveness, the Lord distances the sin from the sinner "as far as the east is from the west" (v. 12). God knows humans are "dust" (v. 14). The psalm concludes, as it began, with a command to bless the Lord, but is now directed to the heavenly hosts and creation (vv. 19-22). Continuing with creation, the hymn of Ps 104 vividly describes the "manifold" nature of God's "works" (v. 24). It begins, as does the previous psalm, with a command to the "soul" to bless the Lord (v. 1) and launches into praise of the Creator God, "wrapped in light as with a garment" (v. 2; compare 102:26), who created the heavens for God's abode (vv. 2*b*-3*a*) and the rest of creation as home for all of life, from birds to coneys, from lions to Leviathan (vv. 12-26). Each species has its habitation; each is abundantly sustained by God. Human beings are but one species among many that inhabit the world, all sharing space and the rhythm of time (vv. 19-23). Even Leviathan has its positive place and role as God's playmate (v. 26*b*; compare 74:13-14). As the psalmist rejoices in the Lord, the creator of all, so he enjoins God to "rejoice in his works" (vv. 31*b*, 34*b*). Acknowledging that the world portrayed in the psalm is not perfect, the psalm concludes with a call for the destruction of the wicked (v. 35).

As the previous psalm accounted for God's providence in creation, Pss 105 and 106 (like Ps 78) recount the history of God's works. Psalm 105 opens with a call to praise and to remember God's "wonderful works," "miracles," and "judgments" (v. 5), which are then recounted. Israel's history begins with God's covenant of land with Abraham, Isaac, and Jacob (vv. 9-11). The psalm recounts the story of Joseph (vv. 16-22) and of Israel's deliverance out of Egypt, including the plagues, through the agency of Moses and Aaron (vv. 23-38), followed by provision in the wilderness (vv. 39-42). Concluding the psalm, God's gracious deeds ground Israel's obedience to God's laws (vv. 43-45). Also recounting Israel's history, Ps 106 lays stress on Israel's recalcitrance in the face of God's deeds. Acknowledging Israel's sins, the psalm confesses negligence of God's "wonderful works," rebellion against God, disregard of the land, lack of faith in God's promise, assimilation with the nations, idolatry, and child sacrifice. God is repeatedly provoked to anger and executes punishment while also delivering the people for the sake of the covenant (v. 45). The psalm concludes with poignant appeal for salvation, and a doxology of blessing rounds out Book IV (vv. 47-48).

5. Book V (Psalms 107–150)

a. Psalms 107–110. Psalm 107 is the most extensive corporate psalm of thanksgiving in the Psalter. Opening with a command to render thanks to the Lord (vv. 1-3), the psalm presents four scenarios of distress: lost in the desert (vv. 4-9), imprisonment (vv. 10-16), illness (vv. 17-22), and danger at sea (vv. 23-32). In each case, "they cried to the LORD in their trouble," and the Lord responded with deliverance. Thanksgiving is then exhorted. The psalm concludes with praise to the God who "raises the needy out of distress" (v. 41) and exhorts the "wise" to consider the Lord's **khesedh** (v. 43). Psalm 108, a prayer for victory, opens with the speaker's resolve to render thanks to God (vv. 3-4). The psalm is identical with portions of two previous psalms: vv. 1-5 with 57:7-11 and vv. 6-13 with 60:5-12. The psalm features a petition for victory (v. 6), followed by divine pronouncement of God's victory over the surrounding nations, and concludes with complaint of God's rejection and petition for help from God (vv. 10-13).

Psalm 109, a prayer, describes a situation of false accusation against the speaker (vv. 2-5). What follows is a lengthy quotation of the imprecation uttered against him by his enemies. He is cursed with various calamities, from poverty to death (v. 16). The speaker counters with a petition that his "assailants be put to shame" by the God who "stands at the right hand of the needy" (vv. 26-31). Psalm 110, a coronation hymn by a court official, announces God's support of the king: he is to sit at the Lord's right hand (v. 1), rule over his enemies (v. 2), and be declared a "priest forever according to the order of Melchizedek" (v. 4; compare Gen 14:18). Victory in every battle is assured (vv. 6-7).

b. Psalms 111–119. Psalm 111 begins a series of praise psalms that extends to 118. Several open or conclude with the command "Hallelujah" (NRSV, "Praise the LORD!"). Psalms 111 and 112 are intentionally paired together and share acrostic structure. Psalm 111 renders praise for God's "wonderful deeds" and enduring righteousness (vv. 3*b*-4). God is "gracious and merciful," providing food to those who revere God and sending redemption to God's people (vv. 4*b*-5, 9). The psalm concludes on a sapiential note commending the "fear of the LORD" as the "beginning of wisdom" (v. 10; compare Job 28:28; Prov 1:7). Psalm 112 attributes comparable qualities to individuals (singular in the Hebrew) who "fear the LORD": their "righteousness endures forever" (vv. 3*b*, 9*b*); their progeny will be "mighty in the land" (v. 2*a*); they are "gracious, merciful, and righteous" (v. 4*b*), as well as generous to others (vv. 5, 9*a*).

Hymnic Pss 113 through 118 are known in Jewish tradition as the "Egyptian Hallel," all associated with the Passover meal. Psalm 113 gives praise to the Lord, "seated on high," who "raises the poor from the dust" and cares for the "barren woman" (vv. 4-9). Psalm 114 opens with Israel's exodus from Egypt and the choice of Judah as God's sanctuary (vv. 1-2), followed by an account of the sea's flight from God's rebuke and a command to the earth to "tremble" in worship before

God (vv. 3-8). Psalm 115 renders praise by contrasting God's power in the heavens with the impotence of idols, "the work of human hands" (vv. 1-8). Nevertheless, human beings are granted the earth by God for their charge (v. 16). God is identified as Israel's "help and shield," warranting Israel's trust (vv. 9-11). Because the dead cannot give praise, the praise by the living is urgent. Psalm 116 articulates praise to God in the form of thanksgiving for the speaker's deliverance from death and affliction (vv. 8-11). The remainder of the psalm details the speaker's response: lifting up the "cup of salvation," payment of vows (vv. 13, 18), and the offering of a "thanksgiving sacrifice" (v. 17). Psalm 117, the shortest psalm, exhorts the nations to give praise for the Lord's **khesedh**.

Psalm 118 renders thanksgiving to God for deliverance in battle. Opening and concluding with a command to give thanks for God's **khesedh** (compare 117:1-2), the psalm recounts a situation of distress on the battlefield that elicits urgent petition (vv. 5*a*, 10-13) and God's salvific response (vv. 5*b*, 14-18). On the heels of victory, the king seeks admittance to the Temple in order to render proper thanksgiving (vv. 19-20). Through the Lord's doing, the rejected stone "has become the chief cornerstone" (vv. 22-24).

Psalm 119, the longest psalm, consisting of 176 verses arranged acrostically and cast as a prayer for deliverance, is an extensive, repetitive meditation upon God's law or torah. It begins with a beatitude for those who "walk in the law of the LORD" (vv. 1-3). The speaker affirms his love for God's law and seeks to observe God's statutes wholeheartedly, imploring God for guidance and understanding, as well as for deliverance from the wicked, including princes (vv. 22-23, 61, 161). God's law is deemed life-giving and "firmly fixed in heaven" (vv. 89, 92-93). In the psalm refuge and word, salvation and law, are wedded together; both are objects of the speaker's longing (vv. 11, 40, 47, 174).

c. Psalms 120–134 (Psalms of Ascents). The following psalms constitute a series of pilgrimage songs that stress trust in God and regard the Temple as the locus of worship and blessing. Three times in the collection, God is proclaimed as the one "who made heaven and earth" (121:2; 124:8; 134:3). Psalm 120, a prayer for deliverance from one living afar, indicts the "deceitful tongue" (vv. 3-4) and laments having his residence in Meshech and Kedar, where war is favored (vv. 5-6). The speaker, in contrast, declares his allegiance to "peace" (v. 7). In Ps 121, a benediction, the Lord is Israel's "keeper," who untiringly provides protection from danger. Psalm 122 identifies the "house of the LORD" as the goal of pilgrimage (vv. 1-2). Jerusalem, the place of jurisdiction, is the destination for Israel's tribes (v. 4). The psalm concludes with a prayer for Jerusalem's peace (**shalom** שָׁלוֹם) and the speaker's resolve to seek Zion's good (vv. 6-9). Like Ps 121, Ps 123 begins with the speaker lifting his eyes to the Lord in heaven (vv. 1-2; compare 121:1). It is followed by a corporate prayer for mercy on account of the contempt the community faces from "the proud" (vv. 3-4). Psalm 124 conveys Israel's thanksgiving for deliverance by conjuring the hypothetical scenario of abandonment by God with the feared results of defeat at the hands of enemies (vv. 2-3) and inundation by flood (vv. 4-5). With God's help, however, Israel has "escaped like a bird from the snare" (v. 7). Help, the psalm concludes, is "in the name of the LORD, who made heaven and earth" (v. 8; compare 121:2).

Psalm 125 likens those who trust in the Lord to Mount Zion; they are immovable and steadfast (v. 1). God surrounds Israel as the mountains surround Jerusalem, protecting the land from the "scepter of wickedness" (vv. 2-3). The psalm concludes with petition for the Lord to do good to the righteous and grant peace to Israel (vv. 4-5). Psalm 126 recounts a time when the Lord restored Zion, eliciting joy from the community (vv. 1-3). The second half of the psalm petitions God for comparable restoration, turning the community's sowing of tears into a harvest of joy (vv. 4-6). Psalm 127 opens, like Ps 124, with a series of negative results: the people's diligence at work is done in vain unless the Lord is at work for them (vv. 1-2). The second half of the psalm commends the blessing of a large family (vv. 4-5). Psalm 128, similarly, commends reverence of God, whose reward is the prosperity of productive work and a large family (vv. 1-4). The psalm concludes with a benediction of blessing and peace from Zion (vv. 5-6).

Psalm 129, a corporate prayer for help, opens with a lament over enemy attackers who have "plowed" Israel's "back" (vv. 1-3). Petition is made that Zion's enemies "wither" away like "grass on the housetops" (v. 6). Psalm 130, a prayer for deliverance, gives voice to a cry "out of the depths" (v. 1). The speaker appeals to God's forgiveness and affirms his resolve to "wait for the LORD" (vv. 3-6). The psalm ends on a note of exhortation for Israel to "hope in the LORD" with confidence in God's "power to redeem" (vv. 7-8). Psalm 131 disavows the lofty or ecstatic aspirations of beholding God: the speaker admits that her "eyes are not raised too high" (v. 1; compare 121:1; 123:1-2). Instead, the speaker professes the serenity of a "calmed and quieted soul" like a "weaned child with its mother" (v. 2). The psalm ends with a call for Israel to "hope in the LORD" (v. 3).

Psalm 132 commemorates God's choice of Zion and the Davidic dynasty. The Lord is called to remember David's resolve to found a "dwelling place" for God (vv. 1-5). David's discovery of the ark and its transference to Zion are recounted as relived history (vv. 6-10). The Lord is implored to "rise up" and proceed to "your resting place" (v. 8). Recounted also is the Lord's "oath" to David, which holds successive kings responsible for keeping covenant for the sake of the dynasty's perpetuity (vv. 11-12). Psalm 133 celebrates the blessing of communal unity and harmony, likening it to the oil of holiness that consecrates the high priest Aaron and to the fertile dew that covers the mountains of Hermon and Zion, where "the LORD ordained his blessing" (vv. 1-3). Psalm 134 concludes the "Songs of Ascents" with a call to "bless the LORD" with lifted hands "to the holy place" (vv. 1-2) and a blessing from the Lord, "the maker of heaven and earth" from Zion (v. 3).

d. Psalms 135–145. This penultimate series features a particularly eclectic collection of psalms ranging from praise to complaint and includes instructional elements on Israel's history and the human condition. Psalms 135 and 136 give praise and thanksgiving for God's mighty deeds on behalf of Israel. Psalm 135 opens with a call to praise warranted by the Lord's goodness and in response to Israel's election (vv. 1-4). The Lord is exalted "above all gods" and is freely sovereign over all creation (vv. 5-7). The psalm recounts God's work in the exodus and in the conquest of Canaan (vv. 8-12), contrasts the impotence of the nations' idols with God's power (vv. 15-18; compare 115:3-8), and concludes with the command to "bless the LORD" (vv. 19-21). Psalm 136 provides greater detail of God's work with each statement accompanied by the refrain: "for his **khesedh** endures forever." The recitation of God's mighty works begins with creation (vv. 4-9) and seamlessly shifts to the exodus (vv. 10-15), the wilderness wanderings, and the conquest (vv. 16-22). With a summarizing account of God's deliverance of Israel and God's provision for "all flesh" (vv. 23-25), the psalm concludes as it began with a thanksgiving command (v. 26).

Psalm 137 is a wrenching lament over exile in Babylon. It opens with a scene of sorrow "by the rivers of Babylon," where the exiles are taunted with demands to sing a song of Zion from their captors (vv. 1-4). The psalm expresses a solemn pledge, cast in the form of a self-curse, to never forget Jerusalem (vv. 4-5) and concludes with a cry to God to execute vengeance against the Edomites and the Babylonians for Jerusalem's destruction (vv. 7-9). Psalm 138, by contrast, conveys thanksgiving within the "holy temple" for the Lord's **khesedh** and responsiveness to petition (vv. 1-3). The speaker envisions God receiving praise from "all the kings of the earth" because God "regards the lowly" (vv. 4-6) and concludes with an expression of confidence and petition that God protect the speaker from his enemies (vv. 7-8).

Formally, Ps 139 is a petition of deliverance from the wicked (vv. 19-24). Content-wise, the psalm affirms God's omniscience and omnipresence in relation to the speaker. God's presence is felt in even dark Sheol (vv. 7-12). The speaker boldly describes his own genesis as a mighty act of God and calls forth destruction of the wicked (vv. 13-22). The psalm concludes with petition for God to know the speaker's thoughts (compare v. 1) and to detect any "wicked" inclination on the speaker's part (vv. 23-24).

Psalm 140 is a prayer for deliverance from the wicked, whose slanderous tongue is "sharp as a snake's" (vv. 1-3). Amid petition, the speaker affirms his allegiance to God, his "strong deliverer" (vv. 6-7), and petitions that "burning coals fall" on the wicked (v. 10). The psalm concludes with affirmation that the Lord "executes justice for the poor" and that the "upright" will thrive in God's presence (vv. 12-13). Psalm 141, also a prayer for deliverance, petitions God for correction from the righteous (v. 5) and for a guarded mouth and heart to avoid evil (vv. 3-4). The speaker prays for singular devotion to God, his "refuge," and for protection from the traps of the wicked (vv. 8-10). Psalm 142, a prayer for deliverance, also speaks of "traps" laid by enemies (v. 3*b*) and like the previous psalm affirms God as the speaker's "refuge" (v. 5). The speaker prays for release from prison, so that he can "give thanks" to God's name (v. 7). Psalm 143 petitions God for release from judgment before whom no one is "righteous" (v. 2). The speaker complains of persecution by enemies and fondly recalls the past of God's deeds; his soul "thirsts ... like a parched land" (vv. 5-6; compare 63:1). The speaker desires to be taught God's way and will (vv. 8*b*, 10).

Psalm 144, a composite psalm of prayer, praise, and instruction, begins with a blessing of God, the "rock," "fortress," and "shield" of the king or warrior (vv. 1-2). Abruptly, the theme shifts to a teaching on the transience of human existence introduced with a question regarding God's care for mortals (v. 3; compare 8:4). The psalm then petitions God for the king's deliverance from "the hand of aliens" (vv. 5-8, 11), within which praise is given to the God "who gives victory" (vv. 9-10). The psalm concludes with a separate prayer for agricultural prosperity, ending with a beatitude (vv. 12-15). Psalm 145, a hymn of praise, extols God, the "King," for mercy, grace, forbearance, and **khesedh** (vv. 8-9; compare Exod 34:6; Ps 103:8). The speaker expresses thanksgiving for all of God's "wondrous works," including upholding the lowly and providing food for "every living thing" (vv. 5, 14-20).

e. Psalms 146–150. Psalm 146 begins the final series of psalms, each of which opens and ends with the command "Hallelujah!" (NRSV, "Praise the LORD!"). Together these psalms form the Psalter's doxological conclusion. Psalm 146 affirms God as creator of heaven, earth, and the sea (v. 6). This God, moreover, "executes justice for the oppressed," provides "food for the hungry," "sets the prisoners free," "opens the eyes of the blind," "lifts up" the lowly, and "upholds the orphan and the widow" (vv. 7-9). Psalm 147 also offers myriad reasons that warrant praise: the Lord "gathers the outcasts of Israel," "heals the brokenhearted," "binds up their wounds," "determines the number of the stars," "lifts up the downtrodden," provides for the land's fertility and animals with food, and delights in "those who fear him" (vv. 2-14). The psalm concludes by enumerating various accomplishments of God's command or "word": God's word enables frozen precipitation to fall and melt, the wind to blow, and Israel ("Jacob") to be instructed (vv. 15-20).

Psalm 148 is a roll call of praise issued to the various elements of creation, from the heavenly to the earthly. First the heavenly hosts and the celestial bodies are commanded, then all creatures, including "sea monsters and all deeps," and meteorological entities (fire, hail, snow, frost, and wind), mountains, trees, and animals (vv. 1-10). Next are the kings of the earth, men and women, both old and young, and last Israel (vv. 11-14). Psalm 149 begins where the previous psalm ends by narrowing the focus of praise to Israel. It enjoins Israel's worship to be performed with dancing and musical instruments (v. 3), as well as with weapons to "execute vengeance" on the nations (vv. 6*b*-9). Psalm 150 rounds out the Psalter with a simple and direct call to praise accompanied by various musical instruments (vv. 3-5). The final verse aptly commands "everything that breathes" to render praise (v. 6). Such is the aim of the **tehillim**.

G. The Psalter's Coherence

Within the rich variety of psalms described above, one can identify repeated themes that constitute the Psalter's coherence and relevance. Because the psalms are as personally introspective as they are theologically suggestive, their coherence can be addressed under two inseparably related angles, namely, the anthropological and the theological.

1. Anthropological

Because most of the psalms are cast as human speech embedded within a wide-ranging variety of settings, the question "What does it mean to be human?" is appropriate to pose to the Psalter. Indeed, the psalmist recasts it as an inherently theological question: "What are human beings that you are mindful of them, mortals that you care for them?" (8:4). The answer lies in God's creating humankind "a little lower than" the divine realm, "crowned with glory and honor." Cast in royal terminology, human beings are invested with inalienable, God-given dignity and power, with the earth as their charge (compare Ps 115:16; Gen 1:27-28). But that is not all. The question of human identity in Ps 8 is repeated in variant form in Ps 144, and the answer is entirely different: human beings "are like a breath; their days are like a passing shadow" (v. 4). Thus, the psalmic testimony of the human condition covers the extremes: human beings are both powerful and fragile, filled with dignity and fraught with affliction. They are at once endowed with nearly divine capacities and beset with physical and social debilitations. Pain and death, the psalms testify, constitute part of life, but also wholeness in right living and communion with God. Community is both a blessing when peace reigns (e.g., Ps 133) and a bane when alienation and persecution are the norm (e.g., Pss 22; 42; 55). The complaint psalms give vivid testimony of abuse committed by the "wicked" with impunity. Human beings exhibit the capacity to oppress others and wreak vengeance as well as to repent, show compassion, and work for reconciliation. The Psalter is like a "mirror" whereby the reader sees him- or herself as one is and as one ought to be.

The anthropological dissonance between humanity's elevation and its depravity invites, as James Mays notes, an eschatological orientation: human beings exist somewhere in between the now and the not yet of their readiness to live into God's image. In the meantime, they long for communion with others and with God. The psalms testify that God is the ultimate object of human yearning and that human beings are fully dependent upon God. Most broadly, human life is characterized in the psalms by the ultimacy of life and death. Walter Brueggemann discerns a comprehensive movement among the psalms: from orientation to disorientation and, finally, to new orientation. Psalm 22 is perhaps paradigmatic of all three milestones on the journey from life to death to new life. And what enables the passage from death to new life is a matter of God's **khesedh** or "steadfast love."

2. Theological

It is with good reason that Martin Luther called the Psalter "the little Bible" in his preface to the German Psalter (1531). Nearly every theological chord that resounds throughout the OT can be heard among the psalms, from covenant and history to creation and wisdom. In the psalms, the God who commands is also the God who sustains. The God of royal pedigree and the God of the "poor and needy," the God of judgment and the God of healing and forgiveness, God's hidden face and God's beaming countenance: all are profiled in the Psalter. The God of the Psalter is comparable to the profile of the human self, fraught with extremes.

Can one speak of a theological core for the Psalter? Identifying the "center" of the psalms reveals as much about how the interpreter treats the psalms in relation to his or her theological convictions as about how the Psalter is itself theologically shaped in its inexhaustible variety. Several recent proposals have been offered. James Mays identifies divine kingship as the Psalter's "root metaphor." Mays finds the center of the Psalter lodged in Book IV, specifically in the enthronement psalms. Taking into account both the divine and human sides of psalmic language, Jerome Creach identifies "refuge" as the Psalter's central metaphor. The sovereign God provides refuge; people seek refuge in situations of distress.

Proportionally lacking in both proposals are the instructional dimensions of the psalms, as reflected in the torah and didactic psalms. In these psalms and elsewhere the metaphor of "pathway" plays a significant role. Both *refuge* and *pathway* are intertwined in the first two psalms (1:1, 6; 2:12), and they make their way throughout the Psalter's variegated landscape. William Brown proposes, thus, a dual center to the Psalter, one that imbues the life of psalmic faith with both movement and destination, and discerns the God of the Psalms as both sovereign provider and divine pedagogue who provides the path of life. The psalms, in short, chart the movement of faith and paint the world of faith. *See* HYMNS, OT; MASKIL; MIKTAM; MIZMOR; WORSHIP, EARLY JEWISH; WORSHIP, OT.

Bibliography: William P. Brown. *Seeing the Psalms: A Theology of Metaphor* (2002); Walter Brueggemann. *The Message of the Psalms: A Theological Commentary* (1984); Jerome F. D. Creach. *Yahweh as Refuge and the Editing of the Hebrew Psalter* (1996); Hermann Gunkel. *Introduction to Psalms: The Genres of the Religious Lyric of Israel.* James D. Nogalski, trans. (1998); Martin Luther. *Luther's Works.* Vol. 35. Theodore Bachman, trans. (1956); James L. Mays. *The Lord Reigns: A Theological Handbook to the Psalms* (1994); James L. Mays. "The Self in the Psalms and the Image of God." *Teaching and Preaching the Psalms.* Patrick D. Miller and Gene M. Tucker, eds. (2006) 51–68; J. Clinton McCann. "The Psalms as Instruction." *Int* 46 (1992) 117–28; Sigmund Mowinckel. *The Psalms in Israel's Worship.* D. R. Ap-Thomas, trans. 2 vols. (2004); Harry P. Nasuti. *Defining the Sacred Songs: Genre, Tradition and the Post-Critical Interpretation of the Psalms* (1999); Claus Westermann. *Praise and Lament in the Psalms.* Keith R. Crim and Richard N. Soulen, trans. (1981); Gerald Henry Wilson. *The Editing of the Hebrew Psalter* (1985).

WILLIAM P. BROWN

PSALMS, NON-CANONICAL sahm. This article covers psalms that are found in certain editions of the book of Psalms (see PSALMS, Book of), but are not found in the Masoretic Text (*see* MT, MASORETIC TEXT). Prior to the discovery of the Dead Sea Scrolls, an article such as this would have focused on five noncanonical psalms, numbered 151–155, that are found in the Syriac Bible (*see* VERSIONS, SYRIAC). Three of these psalms (151, 154, and 155) were found in the Dead Sea Psalms Scroll (11Q5), which is generally conceded to be an edition of the book of Psalms and not merely a liturgical compilation. This scroll also contains three more (unnumbered) noncanonical psalms not previously known (often referred to as "Plea for Deliverance," "Hymn to the Creator," and "Apostrophe to Zion"), plus a prose catalog of David's compositions. (The scroll also includes Sir 51:13-19 and 2 Sam 23:1-7 among the psalms, but these will not be discussed here.) Other psalm-like texts have been found at Qumran as well, although whether they were considered part of some edition of the book of Psalms is unclear. All of the psalms found among the Dead Sea Scrolls are Jewish compositions written no later than the 1st cent. bce. Their presence in the scrolls confirms that the boundaries of the book of Psalms were not firmly fixed at this time.

The character of these noncanonical psalms varies. Some appear to be the product of devout readers of Psalms who selected images, phrases, and motifs that struck them as being particularly eloquent or true, and then wove those images into a coherent prayer that is nonetheless a new creation in its own right. Psalm 155 and the "Plea for Deliverance" are both examples of this kind of composition; they stand squarely in the tradition of personal prayer in Psalms. In the "Hymn to the Creator" we find a poem whose genre and theme is clearly represented among the earlier psalms, but which borrows much of its specific imagery from other texts, especially the book of Job (compare 11Q5 XXVI; Job 38). The "Apostrophe to Zion" seems to owe more to portions of the prophets and the final prayer of the book of Tobit (compare 11Q5 XXII; Tob 13:9-17). Three more "psalms" (from 11Q11) are incantations against evil powers.

These last might scarcely seem to be psalms at all (although compare Ps 91); however, one of them is specifically called "A Psalm of David" (11Q5 V) Indeed, the noncanonical psalms bear further witness to the trend of seeing King David as the author of the book of Psalms, a tendency already well under way in Jewish biblical interpretation in the Hellenistic period. Psalm 151 is presented as a verse narrative in which David relates his youth as a shepherd, his anointing by Samuel, and his defeat of "the Philistine." This psalm does not resemble other psalms as much as it resembles the superscriptions to the psalms connecting the poems with the life of David, which were increasingly added in various versions as time went on. A prose composition found toward the end of 11Q5 credits David with 3,600 psalms, plus 364 songs for daily offerings, 52 songs for Sabbath offerings, 30 songs for festivals, plus 4 for those stricken by demons, yielding a total of 4,050 songs (XXVII, 5–10).

This catalog also shows that many psalms were seen at this time as being part of temple worship and connected to the Jewish sacred calendar. A setting in the Temple is, of course, invoked by numerous canonical psalms. However, Ps 154 adapts the form and language used for temple hymns to a generalized sectarian setting. Like many such psalms, it begins with a summons to worship, but here the summons is specifically directed to the sectarian community, who are to announce God's power to the "simple ones." As with the temple hymns, the summons is followed by a reason for praise: "for to announce the glory of the Lord, wisdom has been given" (11Q5 XVIII, 1–3). After further adumbration of Wisdom's role, attention turns to those who glorify the Most High, an act tantamount to offering sacrifice. Their assembly is characterized by song, eating and drinking in "association," and "meditation on the Law of the Most High."

The provenance and date of Pss 152 and 153 are less certain; they are extant only in Syriac, and may not have been written in Hebrew. They are presented as prayers by David relating to the attack of a lion and wolf against his flock.

Bibliography: James H. Charlesworth and James A. Sanders. "More Psalms of David." *OTP* 2. James H. Charlesworth, ed. (1983) 609–24; Michael O. Wise, Martin G. Abegg Jr., and Edward M. Cook, eds. "Apocryphal Psalms of David." *The Dead Sea Scrolls: A New Translation* (2005) 571–77; Michael O. Wise, Martin G. Abegg Jr., and Edward M. Cook, eds. "Songs to Disperse Demons." *The Dead Sea Scrolls: A New Translation* (2005) 588–90.

WILL SOLL

PSALTER sawl'tuhr. Another name for the book of Psalms (*see* PSALMS, BOOK OF). *Psalter* can also refer to a particular version of the psalms (e.g., "Syriac Psalter"), or to a collection of psalms arranged for liturgical use.

PSEUDEPIGRAPHA *soo*'duh-pig'ruh-fuh. Traditionally, Jewish writings from the 3rd cent. BCE to the mid-2nd cent. CE that are not part of the OT or the OT Apocrypha. The designation means "falsely attributed writings," and reflects the prevalence of pseudonymous texts in the collection (*see* PSEUDONYMOUS WRITING). Texts that were first discovered among the Dead Sea Scrolls are not normally considered part of the Pseudepigrapha, although many fit the criteria for inclusion.

Defined principally in relation to existing canons, the category has always resisted the imposition of precise boundaries. Its early 20th-cent. formulation proceeded from a geologic conception of biblical literature, where, between the OT and the NT, the Pseudepigrapha occupied the "intertestamental" stratum alongside the Apocrypha, which it resembled in its number of texts, semblance of internal coherence, and general *Sitz im Leben.* The category has expanded radically over the last four decades, a result of the reevaluation of taxonomies and a resetting of chronological margins. At present, the standard collection of English translations (*OTP*) contains over five dozen highly heterogeneous compositions, ranging from the tale of *Ahiqar*, the Jewish version of which dates from the 5th cent. BCE, to the *Apocalypse of Daniel*, a Christian apocalyptic oracle from the 8th cent. CE. Yet despite their number and diversity, nearly all the Pseudepigrapha may be separated into two types, attributive and associative, which together accommodate a broad spectrum of literary genres, theological perspectives, and social functions.

Attributive Pseudepigrapha are pseudonymously ascribed to authoritative figures from the biblical past, and as such are normally related in the first person. These include apocalypses such as *1 Enoch*, *4 Ezra*, or *2 Baruch*, and testamentary and oracular literature such as the *Testaments of the Twelve Patriarchs* and the *Sibylline Oracles.* Prayers, psalms, hymns, and odes (e.g., the *Psalms of Solomon*) as well as prognostic-scientific treatises (e.g., the *Treatise of Shem*) are also accredited to figures from the biblical tradition. Attributive Pseudepigrapha are almost always new texts, i.e., they do not retell or rework a portion of the biblical record. Instead, they are linked to Scripture principally through their form and attribution, both of which express their function. Since many of these texts exhibit an apocalyptic worldview or otherwise reveal the existence of a transcendent reality, their functions generally correspond to those of apocalyptic literature.

Associative Pseudepigrapha are correlated to a biblical figure, story, or setting, and commonly take the form of third-person narratives. Some texts are a comparatively close retelling of Scripture (e.g., Pseudo-Philo's *Liber antiquitatum biblicarum*). Others substantially rewrite or recast a section of the biblical record, in effect fashioning a fresh account (e.g., *Jubilees*). Still others take their inspiration from Scripture to create an entirely new episode (e.g., *Joseph and Aseneth*). The motives for their composition vary as much as the quality of their exegetical relationship to Scripture. Some writings bridge gaps in an existing storyline, or extend it by means of supplemental biographic or descriptive information. Others attempt to resolve issues raised by a careful reading of the biblical text, or seek to disclose the text's deeper meaning. As with their scriptural antecedents, associative Pseudepigrapha can have didactic, explanatory, moralizing, hortative, or consolatory purposes. Stories about exemplary biblical figures, which can be quite entertaining, also served social functions by delineating appropriate patterns for personal or community behavior.

A few Pseudepigrapha resist ready classification. Certain texts are neither pseudonymous nor involve a biblical setting (e.g., the *Hellenistic Synagogal Prayers*), while excerpts from Judeo-Hellenistic authors preserved by the church fathers attest to lost historical and philosophical works.

For much of the 20th cent., scholars studied the Pseudepigrapha chiefly in order to illuminate the background to the NT. While this enterprise was (and remains) fruitful, it was eventually recognized that, as mainly Jewish texts, the Pseudepigrapha could exponentially do the same for early Judaism. There also was a growing appreciation of their intrinsic theological and literary qualities, and, collaterally, for their worth as objects of study in their own right. Despite their eventual exclusion from the OT and (with exceptions) the canons of Christianity, not all the Pseudepigrapha were marginal texts. In fact, the early *Enoch* books and *Jubilees* were among the most important postexilic Jewish writings. Both were valued highly by the Qumran community: portions of *Enoch* are preserved in twenty Dead Sea manuscript copies, while *Jubilees*, which is almost equally well represented, is cited authoritatively in the *Damascus Document* (CD XVI, 2–3). The NT letter of Jude quotes *Enoch* at vv. 14-15, and in other verses refers to stories preserved elsewhere in *1 Enoch* and in the *Assumption of Moses.* Similarly, the *Sibylline Oracles* and the *Testaments of the Twelve*

Patriarchs are products of a long-standing interest in these genres among Jews and Christians of antiquity. The question of the divine inspiration of some of the Pseudepigrapha persisted throughout early Christianity, which to a far greater degree than postbiblical Judaism transmitted and therefore preserved these texts. Indeed, many of the Pseudepigrapha were redacted or even composed in late antique Christian circles, or are now preserved only in manuscripts that do not antedate their Christian forms.

The Pseudepigrapha are products of an extraordinary time. The Hellenistic and Roman eras witnessed the multiform interaction of the biblical, classical, and Near Eastern traditions, the development of diverse streams of early Judaism and Christianity, and the advent of apocalypticism, mysticism, and religious sectarianism, all of which transpired within a pluralistic world infused by competing visions of the ecumene. Whether by creating new texts or by reworking and reinterpreting received writings, the Pseudepigrapha represent the literary responses of early Jewish and Christian communities to the complex tensions that arose between venerable traditions and present-day needs. *See* APOCRYPHA, DEUTEROCANONICAL; CANON OF THE NEW TESTAMENT; CANON OF THE OLD TESTAMENT.

Bibliography: L. DiTommaso. *Bibliography of Pseudepigrapha Research, 1850–1999* (2001); M. de Jonge. *Pseudepigrapha of the Old Testament as Part of Christian Literature* (2003).

LORENZO DITOMMASO

PSEUDO-CALLISTHENES. The Greek version of the Alexander Romance, a legendary sensationalized version of Alexander's life (*see* ALEXANDER THE GREAT). Callisthenes was a companion of Alexander who wrote an account of Alexander's military exploits. He died in 327 BCE, long before Alexander's conquests had ended, but his account circulated in antiquity. By about the 3rd cent. CE, a popular version of Alexander's life was circulating in Callisthenes' name, but it in sfact had nothing to do with Callisthenes; hence, it is now labeled "Pseudo-Callisthenes." Several variant versions of the story circulated in different languages, including Latin, French, and even Hebrew. The term *Pseudo-Callisthenes* tends to be reserved for the more original Greek version. Although some actual historical events might lie behind some parts of this version, it is mostly made up of imaginary and even miraculous or magical events. Other sources are preferred for Alexander's life and exploits.

LESTER L. GRABBE

PSEUDO-DANIEL. Three Aramaic texts found in Cave 4 at Qumran (4Q243–45) whose contents are not found in either the OT book of Daniel or in the Greek additions, but claim to be spoken by Daniel. The "Son of God" text (4Q246), sometimes called "Pseudo-Daniel," contains phrases that derive from the biblical book of Daniel. *See* DANIEL; DANIEL, BOOK OF; DEAD SEA SCROLLS.

EMILY R. CHENEY

PSEUDO-EUPOLEMUS s*oo*´doh-y*oo*-pol´uh-muhs. The name given to the author of two fragments preserved by Eusebius (*Praep. ev.* 9.17.1–9; 9.18.1–2). The first is attributed to Eupolemus and the second to an anonymous author. The author stresses Mount Gerizim and was probably a Samaritan, writing ca. 200 BCE. Pseudo-Eupolemus combined biblical narratives with Greek and Babylonian traditions. Enoch discovered astrology and Abraham taught astrology to the Egyptians. This treatment of astrology is intended to validate Judaism as an ancient and wise religion.

KENNETH D. LITWAK

PSEUDO-HECATAEUS. *See* HECATAEUS OF ABDERA.

PSEUDO-JONATHAN. *See* TARGUMS.

PSEUDO-JOSEPHUS. The name sometimes given to the unknown author of 4 Maccabees, which Eusebius (*Hist. eccl.* 3.10.6) attributed to Josephus. Many manuscripts of Josephus' works include the text of 4 Maccabees. However, several internal features of 4 Maccabees and the text's negative attitude toward Greek culture make it highly unlikely that Josephus is the author.

MARK DELCOGLIANO

PSEUDO-MATTHEW, GOSPEL OF s*oo*´doh-math´y*oo*. This Latin infancy gospel is primarily a reworking of the *Protevangelium of James* (*see* JAMES, PROTEVANGELIUM OF), composed sometime between 550 and 700 CE, probably during the early 7th cent. CE. It begins with a prologue containing a fictitious correspondence between Jerome and two bishops named Cromatius and Heliodorus. In his reply, Jerome explains that Matthew composed this gospel to a certain extent furtively, without intending that it would be published. By Jerome's time, the gospel had fallen into the hands of certain heretics, who published their own distorted version; thus the time had come to publish the gospel. Nevertheless, "Jerome" is careful to underscore that even though its author was an apostle and evangelist, its authority was not equal to the writings of the scriptural canon. The revised version of the *Protevangelium of James* follows immediately, accounting for around three-fourths of the *Gospel of Pseudo-Matthew*'s contents.

In rewriting the *Protevangelium of James*, this apocryphon smoothes out some inconsistencies with the canonical Gospels, although Christ's birth in a cave outside of Bethlehem remains. Influences from monasticism and Marian piety are also evident in the revision. The author adds a number of new traditions, including the presence of an ox and ass at Jesus' birth (in fulfillment of Isa 1:3). The most significant new material comes at the gospel's conclusion, which relates the flight of the Holy Family into Egypt, including their famous desert encounter with a miraculous date palm. In many manuscripts, a rewriting of the *Infancy Gospel of Thomas* follows (*see* INFANCY NARRATIVES; THOMAS, INFANCY GOSPEL OF), but this was not part of the original *Gospel of Pseudo-Matthew*. During the Middle Ages, this apocryphon was widely copied (surviving in over 130 manuscripts) and had great influence on medieval art and literature. In fact, the *Gospel of Pseudo-Matthew*'s popularity is probably the reason why no Latin version of the *Protevangelium of James* has survived. *See* APOCRYPHA, NT.

STEPHEN J. SHOEMAKER

PSEUDO-NARRATIVE OF MELITO. *See* MELITO, PSEUDO-NARRATIVE OF.

PSEUDONYMOUS WRITING s*oo*-don´uh-muhs. The phenomenon of pseudonymous writing, or pseudepigraphy, is attested in most literary cultures, including ancient Israel, early Judaism, and Christianity. Although the traditional perspective accepts the attribution of the biblical books at face value, the consensus among critical scholarship is that many are in fact pseudonymous. With texts such as Daniel, the evidence is clear. In other cases, such as Colossians, the issue remains unsettled. Several books in the Apocrypha are also pseudonymous, as are many (but not all) of the writings in the collection known as the PSEUDEPIGRAPHA. Postbiblical writings of early Christianity are regularly ascribed to biblical figures.

The production of pseudepigrapha is driven by diverse motivations, not all of which are relevant to the issue of pseudepigraphy in the Bible. There is no sense, e.g., that any of its pseudonymous texts derived from a malicious intent to deceive or the prospect of financial reward. It is important to recall as well that literary conventions, which by modern standards might appear deceptive or even fraudulent (e.g., the practice of dramatic composition, wherein invented speech is attributed to historical figures; *see* MIMESIS), were considered acceptable in antiquity. At the same time, we would be naïve to assume that ancient authors who wrote pseudonymous texts were unaware of the misleading nature of their action.

The principal impetus for pseudepigraphy in biblical and related literature was to support a text's authority. An attribution to a famous or respected figure validated the claims or doctrines of a text, and, if this figure was located in the distant past, accorded it the prestige of antiquity, which was another form of authority. The selection of pseudonym reflected the function of the text and expectations of the audience. Paul, the great letter-writer, was a natural choice for early Christian letters, while Daniel, who in several court tales forecast history on behalf of the Babylonian kings, was admirably suited as the visionary to whom the divine plan for human history was disclosed. It is possible that anonymous writings were at a later point credited to apposite figures from the past, or pseudonymously consigned to an already extant body of attributed work that they resembled in form or content. In cases such as Isaiah or the psalms, the ongoing desire to ascribe supplemental compositions of the same genre to the initial author might have been additionally motivated by love and honor or by a respectful sense of modesty, particularly if such compositions were produced by those who understood themselves as heirs to a special tradition or profession. Pseudonymous attribution in the historical apocalypses was essential to the device of *ex eventu* prophecy (a "prediction" written after an event but said to have been made by a person who lived before it), which in turn facilitated the underlying historiography. In writings whose messages might have been deemed seditious, pseudonymity could provide authority while simultaneously protecting their authors from official reprisal. *See* APOCRYPHA, DEUTEROCANONICAL; APOCRYPHA, NT.

Bibliography: E. G. Chazon and M. E. Stone, eds. *Pseudepigraphic Perspectives: The Apocrypha and Pseudepigrapha in Light of the Dead Sea Scrolls* (1999); B. M. Metzger. "Literary Forgeries and Canonical Pseudepigrapha." *JBL* 91 (1972) 3–24.

LORENZO DITOMMASO

PSEUDO-PHILO s*oo*´doh-f*i*´loh. Pseudo-Philo is the name given to the authors of the two groups of writings associated with the name of PHILO OF ALEXANDRIA or transmitted together with his writings: the *Liber antiquitatum biblicarum* and two Hellenistic-Jewish sermons on Jonah and Samson. The *Liber antiquitatum biblicarum* is the work most frequently associated with the name Pseudo-Philo.

Neither the author nor the original title of the book is known. The association with Philo results from the fact that the Latin translation has been transmitted with his writings. The title *Liber antiquitatum biblicarum* was not added to the text before Sichardus' first printed edition in 1527 on the basis of the analogy between the text and Josephus' *Jewish Antiquities*. Various versions of a Latin translation are preserved. Errors in the translation indicate a Greek basis for the Latin text, and its Hebraisms show that this Greek text in turn was translated from a Hebrew original, probably from Palestine. There are Hebrew sections of the *Liber antiquitatum biblicarum* in the medieval *Chronicles of Jerahmeel*, which are not ancient but retranslations from Latin. The original Hebrew text can be dated to the 1st cent. CE, although whether it was composed before or after 70 CE is disputed. Arguments for a date after 70 CE are the scarcity of references to temple worship, a possible reference to the destruction of the Temple in *L.A.B.* 19:7 (par. to 4 Ezra and 2 Baruch), and the lack of references to the messiah. Arguments for a date before 70 CE are the assumption that temple worship was continuing, use of a Hebrew text type suppressed around 100 CE, and the fact that *L.A.B.* 19:7 could also refer to the first destruction of the Temple in 587 BCE.

The text is a retelling of the biblical narrative from Adam to the death of Saul as a type of "rewritten Bible." It appears to end rather abruptly, which has led to conclusions about its being fragmentary although all extant versions end in the same way. Some parts of the biblical texts are summarized considerably (Leviticus, Deuteronomy) and others expanded on the basis of material not contained in the OT (e.g., the long account of the judge Kenaz in Judg 3:9, 11). Some events are not told in their temporal order but as a narrative insertion looking back on the event (e.g., Gen 22 in *L.A.B.* 18:5; 32:2-4; 40:2). The role of women is frequently expanded (e.g., Deborah and Jephthah's daughter Seila). *Liber antiquitatum biblicarum* is the earliest account of various haggadic motifs (e.g., Abraham's escape from Ur; *L.A.B.* 6). Some motifs are not found elsewhere (e.g., the Kenaz episode; *L.A.B.* 25–28). The book cannot be attributed to any specific Jewish group or sect but appears to reflect the Palestinian milieu of the 1st cent. The fundamental message of the book is God's covenant with Israel, the Torah and the importance of Israel's obedience to it, the avoidance of idolatry, and the avoidance of intercourse with Gentiles. It is imperative that the leaders obey God, as otherwise they will lead the people astray. There is a strong interest in the fate of people after death and the world to come (*L.A.B.* 33:2-5; 44:10), in judgment, and in the salvation of the just (*L.A.B.* 16:3; 23:6, 13; 28:10; 51:5). In spite of Israel's frequent desertion, God is regarded as eternally faithful to his people.

The sermons were not written by either Philo or the author of *Liber antiquitatum biblicarum* (assuming the work was originally composed in Hebrew). They reflect a different philosophy, although they also use Stoic concepts to interpret the OT. They have only been preserved in an Armenian translation of the original Greek. They may be the only preserved Greek synagogal sermons. *De Jona* is on the goodness of God, and *De Sampsone* on the just Jew.

Bibliography: Bruce N. Fisk. *Do You Not Remember? Scripture, Story, and Exegesis in the Rewritten Bible of Pseudo-Philo* (2001); Daniel J. Harrington. "Pseudo-Philo." *OTP* 2 (1985) 297–377; Pieter W. van der Horst. "Pseudo-Philo." *TRE* 27 (1997) 670–72; Frederick J. Murphy. *Pseudo-Philo: Rewriting the Bible* (1993).

JUTTA LEONHARDT-BALZER

PSEUDO-PHOCYLIDES *soo*'doh-foh-sil'uh-deez. A Hellenistic Jewish poet (ca. late 1st cent. BCE–1st cent. CE) who wrote under the name of Phocylides of Miletus, a 6th-cent. BCE moral poet. Pseudo-Phocylides' *Sentences*, a poem in Greek classical style, includes moral precepts based on the Pentateuch and wisdom literature that offer advice for everyday living, particularly in the areas of sexual ethics and social relations. The work seems to be intended for Gentiles. Similar Hellenistic Jewish moral teachings are found in Josephus (*Ag. Ap.* 2.190–219) and Philo (*Hypothetica* 7.1–20). The HOUSEHOLD CODES in the NT (Eph 5:21-33; Col 3:18–4:1) resemble *Sentences* 175–227, and parts of *Sentences* 5–79 are found in the ORACLES (*Sib. Or.* 2:56–148). *See* ETHICS IN THE NONCANONICAL JEWISH WRITINGS.

Bibliography: John J. Collins. *Jewish Wisdom in the Hellenistic Age* (1998).

MARIANNE BLICKENSTAFF

PSI [ψ ps, Ψ Ps]. The twenty-fourth letter of the Greek alphabet. *See* ALPHABET.

PSYCHOLOGY AND BIBLICAL STUDIES. Although the Bible knows nothing of modern psychological theory, it is a richly psychological text. Psychology is the study of human behavior, and the Bible not only describes human behaviors, attitudes, motivations, interactions, and relationships, it is also the product of human behaviors—memory, personality, thinking processes, perception, and interpersonal interactions. Psychological factors continue to be at work in the ongoing reading, exegesis, and interpretation of the Bible.

The roots of psychology originally lay in theology and the biblical descriptions of the nature, habits, and transformations of the psyche (soul). Following the emergence of scientific psychology in the late 19th and early 20th cent., many efforts were made to apply psychological theory to the Bible with mixed results. As biblical studies expanded beyond historical-critical methods in the late 20th cent., scholars rediscovered psychology as a vital tool for understanding the Bible.

Psychological biblical criticism is not a method. It is a way of reading the biblical text that is sensitive to psychological factors that may be at play. Psychological criticism draws on a wide array of psychological theories, including behaviorism, depth psychology, object relations, cognitive and learning theory, family relations theory, and many more. It also examines different dimensions of the biblical text: the writers and historical situations that lie behind the text; the personalities, descriptions, myths and symbols, and psychological dynamics expressed in the text; and interaction between the text and readers or communities of interpretation.

Recovering the extensive history of biblical psychology developed prior to the modern period is one fruitful area for engaging psychological perspectives. Recognizing the importance of symbol and psychodynamic processes in the text can potentially enrich exegesis. The "hermeneutics of suspicion" prominent in contemporary hermeneutics recognizes that unconscious factors can be at work in the production and interpretation of the text. Psychological perspectives can shed light on biblical experiences of healing, dreams, or speaking in tongues. Above all, psychological approaches can illuminate how contemporary individuals and communities read and interpret the Bible and amplify it in preaching, liturgy, culture, and art.

Psychological criticism at its best seeks an appropriate fit between the biblical phenomena under consideration and the theoretical framework used. It recognizes potential cultural and historical distances between contemporary theories and the ancient world. It remembers always that the text is a text, that literary genres and transmission have shaped it, and that it may give us limited data for interpretation. Used carefully, psychological criticism yields insights into the biblical text that are not otherwise available, and it remains an essential tool for scholars of the Bible.

Bibliography: J. Harold Ellens and Wayne G. Rollins, eds. *Psychology and the Bible: A New Way to Read the Scriptures* (2004); D. Andrew Kille. *Psychological Biblical Criticism* (2001); Wayne G. Rollins. *Soul and Psyche: The Bible in Psychological Perspective* (1999); Wayne G. Rollins and D. Andrew Kille, eds. *Psychological Insight into the Bible: Texts and Readings* (2007).

D. ANDREW KILLE

PTAH-HOTEP, INSTRUCTION OF. This Egyptian Middle Kingdom wisdom text contains proverbial advice, admonitions, and worldly observations that Vizier Ptah-hotep wished to pass on to his young successor. In form and content, it parallels the parent's advice to youth in Prov 1–9, and echoes concerns of the royal sages of Prov 15–24. Ptah-hotep's description of old age is a forerunner to Ecclesiastes' parable about aging (12:1-7). Shrewd yet ethical, Ptah-hotep discusses workplace disputes, successful marriage, public behavior, ethical duties, ill-considered romances, and the virtues of silence and wise speech, which even a slavewoman at the grindstone may display. *See* PROVERBS, BOOK OF.

CAROLE R. FONTAINE

PTOLEMAIS tol'uh-may'uhs [Πτολεμαΐς **Ptolemais**]. 1. The name of Acco during Hellenistic and Roman times (1–2 Maccabees; Acts 21:7). *See* ACCO, AKKO.

2. A seaport in Egypt (3 Macc 7:17).

PTOLEMY tol'uh-mee [Πτολεμαῖος **Ptolemaios**]. The Ptolemaic Dynasty ruled Egypt from the death of ALEXANDER THE GREAT (323 BCE) until the final defeat and death of CLEOPATRA VII in 30 BCE at the hands of the Romans. Over this period of almost three centuries, all fifteen of the kings were called "Ptolemy," which sometimes creates problems of precise identity in inscriptions and even literary sources. With all its ups and downs, this was a remarkable achievement for a single dynasty in ruling so long. Many other individuals outside this Egyptian dynasty shared this name.

1. Ptolemy I Soter was Alexander the Great's childhood companion. Although the question of whether Alexander's empire would remain intact was not immediately put to the test, Ptolemy was made satrap of Egypt and seems to have recognized the strategic position of this domain from the beginning. It was almost twenty years before the Diadochi (the "successors" of Alexander) began to take the title of king, but Egypt was essentially Ptolemy's realm from the beginning and he worked tirelessly to maintain control of it. Ptolemy I (323/305–282 BCE) was a worthy founder of the Ptolemaic Dynasty (his father was Lagus, which is why the dynasty is sometimes called the Lagids). He was a true polymath, not only being a general and strategist of considerable ability but also a statesman and a man of learning and culture. His history of Alexander's conquests served as the basis of the most reliable account extant, and he perhaps began the famous library of Alexandria, the Museon, though possibly this was done by his son. Most of his life was taken up with fighting, first under Alexander and then during the period of the Diadochi. He aided SELEUCUS I in returning to Babylon in 312 BCE after the latter was driven out by ANTIGONUS. This is why when Ptolemy seized southern Syria and Palestine after the battle of Ipsus in 301 BCE, Seleucus did not press his legitimate claim to the territory. Even the last fifteen years of Ptolemy's life were taken up with expansion: into Cyprus and the Aegean islands (at the expense of Demetrius Poliorcetes). But he was one of the few of Alexander's companions to die peacefully.

2. Ptolemy II Philadelphos was chosen in preference to his elder half-brother Ptolemy Keraunos. Ptolemy I's son was already associated with him on the throne before his father's death. Ptolemy II (282–246 BCE) had a long reign in which he pursued cultural as well as political matters, such as building the famous lighthouse Pharos and bringing the library of Alexandria to completion, if he did not begin it. Yet his rule had its share of war as he tried to maintain the Ptolemaic Empire in the Aegean and Asia Minor. We know little of the First Syrian War (274–271 BCE) with ANTIOCHUS I, except that the Seleucids withdrew, giving unexpected victory to the Egyptians. Ptolemy II's attempts to influence events in the Aegean area were thwarted by the Macedonian king Antigonus Gonatas in the Chremonidean War (267–261 BCE) and some Egyptian holdings in Asia were lost in the Second Syrian War (ca. 260–253 BCE) with Antiochus II. He made peace with Antiochus by giving him his daughter Berenice Syra in marriage, which led to disastrous consequences for Antiochus' son Seleucus II. Ptolemy divorced his first wife to marry his sister Arsinoe, a strong and independent woman, though her influence on her brother has often been exaggerated. He also established diplomatic relations with Rome, which was engaged in the First

Punic War with Carthage (264–241 BCE). Ptolemy's reign has regularly been interpreted in idyllic terms as one of economic prosperity as well as cultural achievement, but recent studies have suggested that his fiscal policies were in fact disastrous, spending more than the economy could sustain, which led to the financial crisis in his son's reign. For scholars of Judaica, Ptolemy II is known most widely as the Ptolemy of the *Letter of Aristeas*, but much of that letter is a literary invention and probably tells us little about Jewish history (*see* ARISTEAS, LETTER OF).

3. Ptolemy III Euergetes I (246–221 BCE) was still a crown prince, Ptolemy III, when he had to put down a revolt in Cyrenaica. He then received an urgent message for help from his sister Berenice, shortly after taking the throne. She had married Antiochus II, but after his death she was under siege from Antiochus' first wife. Ptolemy took an army to her aid but found she had already been killed. He thus initiated the Third Syrian War (246–241 BCE) by first taking Antioch, then moving on eastward to occupy Babylon and Seleucia-on-the-Tigris and perhaps even other areas; however, he was forced to make peace with Seleucus II and returned home because of a revolt of the Egyptians (the first of many in Ptolemaic history), partly because a number of low Nile floods produced a famine. In the *Canopus Decree*, Ptolemy III claims to have bought grain from abroad at great expense.

4. Ptolemy IV Philopator followed Ptolemy III as king. After a period of positive growth in the first part of Ptolemaic rule, a decline marked by dynastic crises began with the reign of Ptolemy IV (221–204 BCE). A negative evaluation of his reign was already found in the Greek historian POLYBIUS (*Hist.* 5.34). His main achievement—the defeat of Antiochus III at the battle of Raphia in the Fourth Syrian War (219–217 BCE)—was vital, but it in fact produced only a defensive outcome. This was sufficient to allow him to reign at ease (he had a particular interest in literature), but he had achieved his success in part by using native Egyptian troops, which is thought by many to have laid the ground for future civil disorders since the Egyptians naturally expected some civic rights in return. During the rest of Ptolemy IV's reign Antiochus III continued to strengthen his own position. The battle of Raphia and a possibly authentic visit to Jerusalem by Ptolemy IV are mentioned in 3 Macc 1:1-7.

5. Ptolemy V Theos Epiphanes (204–180 BCE) was only six years old when he took the throne. Ptolemy V was in no position to defend his realm, and Egypt suffered considerably. This included loss of most territories in the Aegean and Asia Minor. The main event was the forfeiture of Palestine and southern Syria to Antiochus III in 200 BCE, during the Fifth Syrian War (202–194 BCE). An agreement was finally sealed with Ptolemy's marriage to Cleopatra I, a daughter of Antiochus. The coronation of Ptolemy and his wife is the event described on the famous ROSETTA STONE. It has recently been argued that the assertion that Coele-Syria's revenues were given as a dowry to Cleopatra (Josephus, *Ant.* 12.154) is not totally wrong (though perhaps only a portion). In any case, Ptolemy apparently planned to try to recapture the Syro-Palestinian possessions but was assassinated first by his generals.

6. Ptolemy VI Philometor (180–145 BCE) came to the throne as a six-year-old boy. His regents planned an invasion of Antiochus IV's realm, and proclaimed a joint rule of Ptolemy VI, his wife Cleopatra II, and his younger brother Ptolemy VIII (Physcon). Antiochus seems to have anticipated the Ptolemaic intent to attack his territory, so he attacked first (170 BCE); Antiochus was victorious and made Ptolemy VI his ward, but the regents reinstituted the joint rule of Ptolemy VI, Ptolemy VIII, and Cleopatra II. This cooperation led to another invasion by Antiochus in 168 BCE, but this time the Romans warned the Seleucid king off. The joint rulers of Egypt quarreled, eventually ending with Ptolemy VI ruling alone for the next twenty years. After 150 BCE, Philometor became involved in the struggle over the Seleucid throne, with hopes of regaining Coele-Syria, but was killed in fighting against Alexander Balas. Ptotemy VI through VII were in some sense rivals to each other.

7. Ptolemy VII Neos Philopator, who ruled briefly (145 BCE), is generally thought to have been the son of Philometor and Cleopatra II. However, some think Ptolemy VII was actually a son of Euergetes and Cleopatra II (called Ptolemy Memphites) who was killed by Euergetes in 131 BCE.

8. Ptolemy VIII Euergetes II (145–116 BCE) initially ruled along with his brother Ptolemy VI and sister Cleopatra II (170–145 BCE). Ptolemy VIII was given Cyrenaica in 163 BCE, but he continued to try to enlist Roman support in taking the Egyptian throne. With the death of Ptolemy VI, Ptolemy VIII had his chance to take the Egyptian throne and marry his rival's widow Cleopatra II. Euergetes later married Cleopatra II's daughter, Cleopatra III; the two wives (mother and daughter) became rivals. Cleopatra II drove Euergetes out of Egypt for a time (131–130 BCE), but when he succeeded in returning, she in turn fled to Syria. By 124 BCE, however, the co-rulership of Ptolemy VIII and Cleopatra II and III had been restored.

9. Ptolemy IX Soter II was the elder son of Euergetes and Cleopatra III who became governor of Cyprus until his father's death. As Ptolemy IX (Lathyrus) he ruled alongside his mother (116–107 BCE). Cleopatra III favored his younger brother Ptolemy X, whom she set out to add as a co-ruler; Cleopatra II, however, frustrated her efforts. The three ruled together until the death of Cleopatra II within the year. Soter then ruled as the junior partner to his mother until she managed to put Alexander on the throne in 107 BCE. Soter fled to Syria but returned to take Cyprus. He also ruled in Cyrenaica. Ptolemy IX became involved in the struggle between the rival Seleucid dynasts as a means

of returning to the Egyptian throne, but his mother and brother prevented him. Ptolemy IX ruled again from 88–80 BCE, when his brother Ptolemy X was expelled from Egypt.

10. Ptolemy X Alexander I controlled Cyprus until his mother, Cleopatra III, helped make him co-ruler of Egypt from 107–88 BCE. Cleopatra III died in 101 BCE, and Ptolemy X took his wife Cleopatra Berenice III as his co-ruler. In the meantime, an illegitimate son of Ptolemy VIII named Ptolemy Apion took up rule in Cyrenaica. At Ptolemy Apion's death in 96 BCE, his will left Cyrenaica to Rome. Ptolemy X also decided to leave Egypt to Rome in his will; he was driven from Egypt by a revolt in 88 BCE, however, and Ptolemy IX returned to take up his second period of rulership. Alexander was killed shortly afterward in trying to retake the throne.

11. Ptolemy XI Alexander II was a son of Ptolemy X and stepson of Cleopatra Berenice III. When Ptolemy IX died in 80 BCE, his daughter Cleopatra Berenice III took the throne. This sole rulership did not last, though, probably because of Roman intervention. Ptolemy XI was associated with her on the throne soon after her assuming it. Yet within a few days of marrying his stepmother, he ordered her murder. The people of Alexandria were incensed at this violent bid for power against a popular queen and killed Ptolemy XI in a riot.

12. Ptolemy XII Neos Dionysus (80–58, 55–51 BCE) was a son of Ptolemy IX. After killing Ptolemy XI, the Alexandrians had to fill the vacant kingly office; if they did not, Rome would soon move to do so. Ptolemy XII (Auletes) was invited to take the throne, apparently without Roman intervention. Ptolemy XII married his sister Cleopatra VI (though she was apparently deposed from her position for a time after 69 BCE). Egypt became a bone of contention among various Roman factions, with some arguing for annexation of the country as a Roman province. Ptolemy XII's response was to spend great sums bribing various influential Romans. He also established relations with POMPEY, who was dealing with various matters in the east and had headquarters in Damascus. Later, after Pompey's mission was complete, Ptolemy XII offered an enormous sum to both Caesar and Pompey in 60 BCE (during the First Triumvirate) to be granted kingship by the Romans. Cyprus was not part of the package, however, and the Romans annexed it. For the people of Alexandria this annexation of Cyprus and the high taxes needed to pay Ptolemy XII's bribes were too much, and they drove the king out of Egypt and appointed his wife Cleopatra VI and daughter Cleopatra Berenice IV as co-rulers. Back in Rome, Ptolemy XII continued to cultivate leading Romans, with special attention paid to Pompey. Finally in 55 BCE, Gabinius, the pro-consul of Syria, took an army to Egypt with Pompey's support. The Hasmonean (former) king and high priest HYRCANUS II (*see* HASMONEANS) and ANTIPATER (the father of Herod the Great; *see* HEROD, FAMILY) provided him with grain for the campaign and also persuaded the Jews near PELUSIUM, who were guards over the entrance to Egypt, to join the Romans as allies. Ptolemy XII had his daughter Berenice IV executed (Cleopatra VI had died in the meantime). Ptolemy XII's daughter Cleopatra VII (51–30 BCE) was associated with him on his throne in his last year.

13. After Ptolemy XII's death, his ten-year-old son Ptolemy XIII (51–47 BCE) reigned jointly as the husband of his nineteen-year-old sister Cleopatra VII. Cleopatra soon managed to dislodge him from the throne, but this was only temporary. In 49 BCE Cleopatra was herself evicted from the joint rule by Ptolemy XIII's supporters at court and fled to Syria. At this point, Egypt became caught up in the Roman civil war. Pompey, after his defeat at Pharsalia, came to Egypt and sought support from Ptolemy XIII; instead, the king's guardians arranged to have Pompey assassinated. Julius Caesar (*see* CAESAR, JULIUS) arrived on the scene soon afterward and stayed for a period of time. He intervened to reconcile Ptolemy XIII and Cleopatra (having become Cleopatra's lover) and arranged to have Cyprus returned to Ptolemaic rule. For the most part the Egyptians were hostile to the Romans, however, and Ptolemy XIII's guardians brought in an army against Alexandria ("the Alexandrian War"). Caesar was in some difficulties, militarily, but managed to hold out until reinforcements arrived (including Jewish soldiers under Antipater). Ptolemy XIII died in the fighting.

14. Ptolemy XIV (47–44 BCE) was the younger brother of Cleoptra VII. Caesar placed Cleopatra back on the throne as joint ruler with Ptolemy XIV after the death of Ptolemy XIII. Caesar left Egypt in 47 BCE; shortly afterward, Cleopatra had a child (Caesarion), who was almost certainly fathered by Caesar. In 46 BCE, Cleopatra and Ptolemy XIV traveled to Rome and remained there until after Caesar's assassination. Back in Egypt in 44 BCE Cleopatra had her brother Ptolemy XIV assassinated.

15. Cleopatra had her son Caesarion recognized as Ptolemy XV (ca. 44–30 BCE), associating him with her on the throne. The next fifteen years were the story of Cleopatra and MARK ANTONY. She would have abdicated in favor of her son, if it would have secured him the throne. In the end, though, Caesarion was executed on Octavian's orders after the deaths of Mark Antony and Cleopatra.

Bibliography: Norman Davis and Colin M. Kraay. *The Hellenistic Kingdoms: Portrait Coins and History* (1973); Günther Hölbl. *A History of the Ptolemaic Empire* (2001).

LESTER L. GRABBE

16. Alternately known as Ptolemaios, he was governor/satrap (201–163 BCE) and then king (163–130 BCE) of COMMAGENE, a Hellenistic kingdom in southern Anatolia near Antioch, after he led a revolt

and declared its independence. These events form part of the context for 1 Macc 7.

EMILY R. CHENEY

PUAH pyoo'uh [פּוּאָה pu'ah, פּוּעָה pu'ah]. 1. In Exod 1:15-21, Puah is a MIDWIFE (whether Hebrew or Egyptian is unspecified) who attends Hebrew women during childbirth. When commanded by Pharaoh to kill all the male newborns, Puah and her colleague SHIPHRAH defy the ruler through trickery by saying that the Hebrew women are literally "beasts" (NRSV, "vigorous") who can give birth on their own. It is striking that the name of the Pharaoh is never recorded, yet Puah, the humble woman who saves Israel by her courage, is mentioned by name. For their valor, God rewards the midwives with "houses" (NRSV, "families"), a possible reference to having children, being heads of midwife guilds, or receiving divine protection.

2. Puah is a descendant of Issachar. He is listed as the son of Dodo and the father of Tola (Judg 10:1) or as Issachar's son and Tola's brother (1 Chr 7:1). *See* ISSACHAR, ISSACHARITES; PUNITE; PUVAH.

SHARON PACE

PUBLIC SQUARE. *See* SQUARE, PUBLIC.

PUBLIUS puhb'lee-uhs [Πόπλιος Poplios]. From the Latin, "of the people," Publius was a common praenomen (first name) in the Roman Empire. When Paul is shipwrecked on Malta, he comes under the care and hospitality of Publius, the "leading man of the island," which is likely an official designation of Publius' governorship of Malta (Acts 28:7-8). In response to Publius' hospitality, Paul cures his father of a fever and dysentery.

JESSICA TINKLENBERG DEVEGA

PUBLIUS PETRONIUS. *See* PETRONIUS, PUBLIUS.

PUDENS pyoo'dinz [Πούδης Poudēs]. Mentioned with the Christians in Rome who send greetings to Timothy (2 Tim 4:21), listed after Eubulus, and followed by Linus, Claudia, and all other Christians in Rome. According to later tradition (the *Acts of Saints Pudentiana and Praxedis*), a wealthy Roman widower named Pudens hosted Peter during his visit to Rome. Pudens later dedicated his house as a Christian church, which was said to have been frequented by Pope Pius I. Pudens' daughters, Praxedis and Pudentiana, were also recognized as saints. Some sources identify the Pudens of the *Acts* with the Pudens mentioned in 2 Timothy.

KATHY R. MAXWELL

PUL puhl [פּוּל pul]. The name "Pul" referred to TIGLATH-PILESER III (1 Chr 5:26), the Assyrian king (745–727 BCE) who established the Neo-Assyrian Empire over Babylonia under the name of Pulu (Babylonian King List A iv 8, *ANET*, 272). Pul received tribute from Menahem of Israel (2 Kgs 15:19-20). Whether it is the throne-name or the original monarchic name, the name is likely a wordplay on the Akkadian word **pulu**, "limestone block."

Bibliography: J. A. Brinkman. *A Political History of Post-Kassite Babylonia, 1158–722 B.C.* (1968) 240–41.

DAEGYU J. JANG

PUNIC TEXTS. The term *Punic* designates primarily Canaanite populations from the Syro-Lebanese coast who settled near the Mediterranean coast in North Africa, Iberia, and in the islands of the western Mediterranean. Punic texts were composed ca. 500–146 BCE. Fewer than 6,000 Punic texts exist, most excavated at Carthage (Tunisia). Nearly all are brief votive texts inscribed on stone steles dedicated to one or more deities. The votive inscriptions are formulaic: "For (the Lady Tinnit Face-of-Baal and for) the Lord Baal Khamon [is] this vow that (name) son/daughter of (name) vowed. She/he/they heard the sound of his/her/their voice."

The Phoenician-Punic language group is closely related to biblical Hebrew. Numerous Punic words are cognate with biblical Hebrew terms (e.g., Pun. **sadhe**, "field"; **tsava'**, "army"), especially religious and sacrificial words (e.g., Pun. **kuhin**, "priest"; **nadr**, "vow"; **zibkh**, "sacrifice"; **minkhah**, "offering"; **'ula**, "holocaust"). A few Punic texts invoke curses and blessings, similar to biblical law. A Punic inscription found at Marseilles concerns temple sacrifice, specifying payments to priests, procedures for sacrifices in which a portion of the victim is retained by the sacrificer (Pun. **shlmm**), and similar details. Similarities between this inscription and the sacrificial laws of Leviticus invite close study. A 3rd-cent. BCE epitaph refers to the spirit of the deceased "rejoicing with the holy ones" (Pun. **qudshim**). An enigmatic text on lead appears to be a legal document involving quittance of a debt.

Bibliography: Jacob Hoftijzer and Karel Jongeling. *Dictionary of the North-west Semitic Inscriptions* (1995); Karel Jongeling and Robert M. Kerr. *Late Punic Epigraphy* (2005); Charles R. Krahmalkov. *Phoenician-Punic Dictionary* (2000); Charles R. Krahmalkov. *A Phoenician-Punic Grammar* (2001); J. Brian Peckham. *The Development of the Late Phoenician Scripts* (1968).

PHILIP C. SCHMITZ

PUNISHMENT. *See* CHAINS, IMPRISONMENT; CRIMES AND PUNISHMENT, OT AND NT.

PUNITE pyoo'nit [פּוּנִי puni]. PUVAH is named as eponymous ancestor of the Punite clan, in the tribe of Issachar (Num 26:23), despite the dissimilarity in name (compare PUAH in 1 Chr 7:1).

PUNON pyoo´non [פּוּנֹן punon]. Punon was a stopping place for the Israelites between Zalmonah and Oboth on their journey from Egypt to the Plains of Moab (Num 33:42-43).

The location for ancient Punon is likely modern-day Feinan, a large copper production site on the eastern edge of the ARABAH in ancient Edom (modern Jordan). An Edomite chief, PINON (Gen 36:41), may be named after the site. Located at the juncture of Wadi el-Gheweir and Wadi esh-Sheger, Punon received the ample water required for large-scale smelting of copper. Along with two other nearby major smelting centers, Punon played an important role in Egyptian copper trade during the Early Bronze Age. When the Israelites arrived, the site had either already been abandoned (ca. 1400 BCE) or was in the early stages of revival (ca. 1200 BCE). After a long period of abandonment, Punon renewed intensive smelting activities during the Iron Age (ca. 1200–700 BCE). Later activity is seen during the Nabatean through early Arabic/Islamic periods.

The story of Moses and the bronze serpent (Num 21:4-9) may have occurred near Punon, with Oboth mentioned as the encampment site. The availability of copper to make the bronze serpent supports traditions placing the story in the area. *See* SERPENT, BRONZE.

MICHAEL G. VANZANT

PUR pyoor [פּוּר pur]. The term means "lot" (Esth 3:7; *see* LOTS). In the book of Esther (9:24-26), **pur** is mentioned as a (rather strained) way of connecting the story with the festival of PURIM. Haman "had cast Pur—that is 'the lot'" to destroy the Jews, hence the name of the festival.

NICOLE WILKINSON DURAN

PURAH pyoo´ruh [פֻּרָה purah]. To assuage GIDEON's fears, Yahweh instructed him to take his servant Purah and spy on the Midianite camp (Judg 7:10-11).

PURE. *See* CLEAN AND UNCLEAN.

PURIFICATION [טָהֳרָה tohorah, חַטָּאת khatta᾿th, נִדָּה niddah; ἁγνίζω hagnizō, ἁγνισμός hagnismos, καθαρισμός katharismos]. In the OT, *purification* refers to the process whereby a person removes impurity that interferes with communal and religious life (*see* CLEAN AND UNCLEAN). Impurity can be caused by numerous events and objects, and purification is achieved through a variety of means, depending on the cause of the impurity. The practice of BAPTISM developed from this concept and similarly emphasizes the theological concept that a person must be purified and prepared to encounter the divine.

BEATRICE J. W. LAWRENCE

PURIM pyoo´rim [פּוּרִים purim]. A festival in the Jewish liturgical calendar falling on the fourteenth day of the month of ADAR, which commemorates the Jews' deliverance from HAMAN's genocidal plot through the actions of Esther and Mordecai. The book of Esther reports how the holiday derives its name from the "lots" (a Hebraicized form, in the plural, of the Babylonian term **pûru**, "lot" or "fate") cast to determine the date of attack (Esth 3:7; 9:24). As this connection may well be a secondary addition to the story, a question remains as to whether the book or the holiday existed first.

Purim, a festival not prescribed in the Torah, has obscure origins that may well be non-Jewish. Its name has led some to suggest that Babylonian festivals and myths underlie Purim and the Esther story. As the story is set in the Persian Empire, it is instead possible that either the Persian Farvardigan festival or the new year's festival served as its antecedents. Alternatively, Purim may have originated in Palestine itself, taking over the Jewish holiday "the day of Nicanor" (the thirteenth day of Adar), which commemorated a Maccabean victory reported in 1 Macc 7:26-49 and 2 Macc 14:12–15:36. In the latter text the reference to the following day as "Mordecai's day" links the two holidays.

Celebration of Purim includes the reading of the Megillah (the scroll of Esther) in the synagogue, gifts of charity to the poor, exchanges of food, and an abundant meal. It is a joyous and playful occasion with a carnival-like ambience. Celebrants dress in costume, engage in role-playing, and sound noisemakers at the mention of Haman's name. Reflecting the well-lubricated atmosphere of the Esther story itself, the Talmud even instructs persons to imbibe so much wine that they can no longer distinguish between the phrases "cursed be Haman" and "blessed be Mordecai." See ESTHER, BOOK OF; FEASTS AND FASTS.

LINDA DAY

PURITY, RITUAL. *See* CLEAN AND UNCLEAN.

PURPLE [אַרְגָּמָן ᾿argaman; πορφύρα porphyra]. In the ancient world, purple goods were typically made with a dye extracted from the MUREX family of sea snails. Because of the difficult and lengthy production process, purple dye was very expensive, making purple cloth a luxury item. In the OT, the manufacture of purple textiles is often associated with PHOENICIA in general and the city of TYRE in particular (2 Chr 2:14; Ezek 27:16). As a status symbol, purple cloth was often connected with royalty (Judg 8:26; Esth 1:6; Song 3:10) and honor (Esth 8:15; Dan 5:16, 29). It is high praise to say that the wife in Prov 31:21-22 can provide such goods to her family.

Purple cloth was also used in the tabernacle, the royal residence of God. The curtains for the walls were woven of blue, purple, and crimson yarns (Exod 26:1; 36:8). The interior curtain that divided the holy place from the most holy place was a similar cloth embroidered with cherubim (Exod 26:31; 36:35), as were the screens at the entrance of the tabernacle and the court

(Exod 26:36; 27:16; 36:36-37). Some of the priestly garments—including the ephod and the breastpiece—were also made from blue, purple, and crimson yarns (Exod 28:6-8, 15). Even the ashes of the altar were holy enough to be draped with a purple covering whenever the tabernacle was dismantled (Num 4:13). This imagery carried over into Solomon's Temple, where the curtain dividing the holy place from the most holy place was made of blue, purple, and crimson cloth (2 Chr 3:14).

Purple is also associated with luxury and royalty in the NT. When the Roman soldiers mock Jesus as a king, they place a purple robe on him (Mark 15:17, 20; John 19:2, 5). In the parable of the rich man and Lazarus, the wealth of the rich man is illustrated by his purple robes (Luke 16:19). In Revelation, the woman representing Rome is dressed in purple and scarlet (Rev 17:4; 18:16), but after her destruction the merchants mourn because Rome is no longer able to buy imported goods, such as purple cloth (Rev 18:12). Paul's first convert in Europe is Lydia, "a dealer in purple cloth" (Acts 16:14). This suggests that she was a person of some wealth, which is consistent with the fact that she may have hosted a church in her house (Acts 16:40; *see* LYDIA, LYDIANS). *See* COLORS.

KEVIN A. WILSON

PURPOSE, PURPOSE OF GOD. The divine will, intentions, or plans may be conveniently labeled as God's purpose. Human beings often have purposes that are opposed to the divine and need to be realigned with those of God.

The purposes of both human beings and God spring from the heart (**lev** לֵב). God declares that actions are right when they are carried out "in accordance with all that was in my heart" (2 Kgs 10:30; compare 2 Sam 7:21; 1 Kgs 9:3). Those who act according to the divine purpose are said to be "after [God's] own heart" (1 Sam 13:14; Jer 3:15). God's faithfulness is undertaken "with all my heart and all my soul" (Jer 32:41). God does not "willingly [lit., "from his heart"] afflict or grieve anyone" (Lam 3:33); that is, suffering is not the ultimate purpose of God for Israel.

The words **zamam** (זָמַם, "to intend") and **mezimmah** (מְזִמָּה, "purpose, intent") are used almost exclusively of people's evil thoughts or harmful intentions (e.g., Gen 11:6; Deut 19:19; Job 21:27; Pss 10:2, 4; 17:3; 37:7, 12; 139:20; Prov 12:2; Jer 11:15). Proverbs contains five instances when the noun signifies "prudence" or "discretion" (Prov 1:4; 2:11; 3:21; 5:2; 8:12) and one when the verb denotes simple deliberation (Prov 31:16). These terms are used most often by the prophet Jeremiah of God's purpose to chastise Israel (Jer 4:28; 23:20; 30:24; compare Lam 2:17) and execute judgment against Babylon (Jer 51:11-12). Zechariah, too, ponders God's intention to judge Judah for disobedience (Zech 1:6; 8:14), but also to do good (8:15). According to Job 42:2 God's purposes are unassailable: "I know that you can do all things, and that no purpose of yours can be thwarted."

The terms **khashav** (חָשַׁב, "to plan") and **makhashavah** (מַחֲשָׁבָה, "thought, plan, purpose") are common in wisdom literature with reference to humans. People can devise evil plans (Ps 140:2, 4; Prov 6:18; 16:30; 24:8), but are no match for the LORD's plans, which endure for generations (Ps 33:10-11). "The human mind may devise many plans, but it is the purpose (**ʿetsah** עֵצָה) of the LORD that will be established" (Prov 19:21). Human plans formulated with counsel (Prov 15:22; 20:18) and diligence (Prov 21:5) are successful; but "[c]ommit your work to the LORD, and your plans will be established" (Prov 16:3). The contrast between human and divine plans finds classic expression in Joseph's words: "Even though you intended to do harm to me, God intended it for good" (Gen 50:20). On the superiority of God's thoughts to human ones, see Isa 55:8-9. According to Jeremiah, the divine purpose can be conditional. God will turn back judgment if the people repent (Jer 26:3; 36:3) and not stubbornly pursue their own plans (Jer 18:11-12). In the end, God "determined" to destroy Jerusalem (Lam 2:8). The divine plan to destroy Babylon stood firm (Jer 50:45), but God declared further "plans" for Israel, "plans for your welfare and not for harm, to give you a future with hope" (Jer 29:11).

Other words expressing purpose are yaʿats (יָעַץ, "to counsel") and ʿetsah ("counsel, plan"). The expression "plan of the LORD" (or "plan of the Holy One of Israel," Isa 5:19) occurs five times (Ps 33:11 [NRSV, "counsel"]; Prov 19:21 [NRSV, "purpose"]; Isa 19:17; Jer 49:20; 50:45). God's "plan" occurs prominently in prophetic oracles against the nations, emphasizing its universality (Isa 14:24-27; 19:12, 17; 23:8-9; Jer 49:20; 50:45) and prevailing efficacy (Isa 14:24, 27; 44:26): "[D]eclaring the end from the beginning and from ancient times things not yet done, saying, 'My purpose shall stand, and I will fulfill my intention' " (Isa 46:10; compare 25:1, "plans formed of old, faithful and sure").

The verb yatsar (יָצַר, "to frame, devise, purpose") is used by both Jeremiah and Isaiah in wordplay, since the same God who "shaped" or "made" (i.e., "created") the world also "shapes" historical events (Isa 37:26; 45:7; 46:11; Jer 18:11).

Accomplishment of the divine will is what pleases God. "Whatever the LORD pleases he does, in heaven and on earth, in the seas and all deeps" (Ps 135:6; compare 115:3; Jonah 1:14). This vocabulary is significant for ethics, since human performance of the divine will also pleases God (Pss 143:10; 147:10-11; Prov 12:2, 22; 15:8; Isa 58:2; Hos 6:6).

In the NT, the verb boulomai (βούλομαι, "to will, want") and noun **boulē** (βουλή, "will, resolve, purpose") are predominant in Luke–Acts (**boulomai**, sixteen out of thirty-seven times; **boulē**, nine out of twelve times). Only in Luke–Acts do we find the expression **he boulē tou theou** (ἡ βουλὴ τοῦ θεοῦ, "purpose/will of God," four times). God's will, proclaimed by John the Baptist, could be rejected (Luke 7:30); the plan of God is linked with divine foreknowledge and predestination concerning Jesus' death (Acts 2:23; compare 4:28); David's death completes his service to God's purpose in saving history (Acts 13:36); and "the whole purpose of God" is a cipher for Paul's preaching the gospel (Acts 20:27). **Boulē** is used of God's design or purpose also in Eph 1:11 and Heb 6:17. **Boulomai** has a divine subject only seven times. In Matt 11:27 and Luke 10:22, the Son has the prerogative to reveal the Father to people. In Luke 22:42, Jesus pleads, "Father, if you are willing, remove this cup from me." The allotment of spiritual gifts is in accordance with what the Spirit "chooses" (1 Cor 12:11). God's will to bring humanity to salvation (Jas 1:18) was confirmed with an oath because God "desired" (**boulomai**) to reveal "the unchangeable character of his purpose (**boulē**)" (Heb 6:17). God's saving purpose is potentially universal, with God "not wanting any to perish" (2 Pet 3:9).

The terms **thelō** (θέλω, "to will, be willing, want") and **thelēma** (θέλημα, "will") are more common than **boulomai/boulē** in the NT. The verb **thelō** is most often used of human will or desire, but 39 of 208 times it is used of God or Christ. The noun **thelēma** has a divine reference 50 out of 62 times. Matthew distinctively refers to "the will of my/your Father in heaven" (7:21; 12:50; 18:14), and John to "the will of him who sent me" (4:34; 5:30; 6:38-39). Paul routinely declares that his apostleship is "by the will of God" (e.g., 1 Cor 1:1; 2 Cor 1:1). The will of God initiates the salvation of human beings (Gal 1:4; Eph 1:5, 9, 11; Col 1:27; Heb 10:10), desired by God for everyone (1 Tim 2:4). Believers are to seek (Matt 6:10), discern (Rom 12:2; Eph 5:17), be filled with (Col 1:9; 4:12), and do the will of God (Heb 10:36; 13:21; 1 Pet 4:2), as the incarnate Son did (Matt 26:42; Heb 10:7, 9). God's will for believers in the NT includes sexual purity (1 Thess 4:3); arrangement of roles in the church (1 Cor 12:18); consistent rejoicing, prayer, and thanksgiving (1 Thess 5:16-18); and even the outcome of travel plans (Acts 18:21; 1 Cor 4:19; 16:7; Jas 4:15).

The term **prothesis** (πρόθεσις, "intention, resolve, purpose") is used of God's purpose five times in Pauline literature. The election of Jacob was determined by God's purpose (Rom 9:11), as was the manifestation of divine grace through Christ (Eph 3:11). The calling and salvation of believers is also in accord with the divine purpose (Rom 8:28; Eph 1:11; 2 Tim 1:9). *See* ELECTION; PREDESTINATION.

KEVIN L. ANDERSON

PURSE [כִּיס kis; βαλλάντιον **ballantion**, γλωσσόκομον **glōssokomon**, μαρσίππιον **marsippion**]. A purse is a form of bag (*see* BAG, BAGGAGE) with the specific function of holding weights or money, especially for merchants. Gold is kept in a purse, which is used in parallel with scales (Isa 46:6). *Purse* may describe a group's source of income (Prov 1:14).

The NT uses *purse* to refer to a pouch or money bag. Jesus told his disciples to go out preaching the gospel without a purse (**ballantion**; Luke 10:4; 22:35-36) and to make for themselves purses that do not wear out, namely a treasure in heaven (Luke 12:33). Judas Iscariot objected to the use of expensive ointment to anoint Jesus because he wanted it sold and the money put into the common purse (**glōssokomon**), from which he stole (John 12:6; compare John 13:29). Sirach 18:33 also refers to a small sack or purse (**marsippion**) that holds money.

KENNETH D. LITWAK

PURSUE [רָדַף radhaf; διώκω diōkō]. Frequently used in a military context, *pursue* carries a connotation of not only chasing but capturing and destroying one's enemies (Deut 28:22; Josh 10:19; 2 Sam 17:1-2; Lam 3:66; Jdt 14:4). This tenacity to carry the chase to the end is greatly magnified if it is God doing the pursuing (Job 13:25; 19:22; Ps 83:13-15 [Heb. 83:14-16]; Jer 29:18-19; Nah 1:7-8). This sense of relentlessness is then implicit when applied to the pursuit of such states of affairs as justice (Deut 16:20; Sir 27:8), righteousness (Isa 51:1), love (1 Cor 14:1), and peace (Ps 34:14 [Heb. 34:15]; Heb 12:14; 1 Pet 3:11).

A. HEATH JONES III

PUT poot [פּוּט **put**; Φούδ **Phoud**]. The Hebrew term **put** designates both a person and a nation in the Bible.

1. The person, Put, is the third son of Noah's second son Ham (Gen 10:6). Unlike his brothers Cush, Egypt, and Canaan, who are the eponymous ancestors of an extensive list of "nations," there is no patronymic of progenitors associated with Put. In such an ethnographic list, the absence of a record of Put's descendants implies that the author was less familiar with this nation and its sociopolitical alliances than with the other members of this North African political-military league.

2. Uncertainty persists about the specific national referent to biblical Put (Jer 46:9; Ezek 27:10; 30:5; 38:5). Though translated in some English versions as "Libya" following the LXX, which translates the term when it represents a nation as **Libyes** (Λίβυες), *Put* most likely refers to phonetically similar ancient Punt. Punt was a nation to the southeast of Egypt roughly consistent with the contemporary region of Somaliland near the Horn of Africa. Put was geographically distant from Judah and its people were known to the Judean audience of the OT primarily because of their participation in the larger Egyptian-Cushite league. Because of Put's distance from and infrequent contact with Judah, the vague biblical references to this nation far across the Red Sea from Judah's southernmost port at Elath (*see* ELATH, ELOTH) are understandable.

When Libyans were the intended ethnic entity, distinctive gentilics were employed (*see* LIBYA, LIBYANS). Three times the plural gentilic term **luvim** (לוּבִים), "Lubim," is used describing the people from "Lub" or "Libya." In each of these instances the term is used to refer to people from Libya participating in Egyptian expeditionary legions (2 Chr 12:3; 16:8; Nah 3:9). In the former two instances, this term is used to refer to Libyans precisely at the time that they would have been most instrumental in the politics of this region, during the reign of Pharaoh SHISHAK of the Twenty-second (Libyan) Dynasty. In the latter instance, Nah 3:9 presents the term **luvim** with the term **put**, suggesting that they were distinct entities both participating in Egypt's armies.

A subsequent reference to Libyans can be found in Dan 11:43. In this instance, the defective plural gentilic **luvim** is used to refer to members of an Egyptian triumvirate designated because of their wealth. Again, when the referent is clearly intended to be citizens from Libya, these terms, not a form of the term Put, are used.

Determining that Put is not Libya poses a problem particularly for the interpretation of the Table of Nations (Gen 10). It is implausible that a nation that figures as prominently in the history of the region would be omitted from this extensive list of nations, particularly from the list that includes Egypt, its known ally (e.g., Gen 10:6). Against this, however, it should be noted that the patronymic of national origins in the Table of Nations is not universal. Further, Gen 10:13 describes a group called the **lehavim** (לְהָבִים), "Lehabim," and deems them descendants from Egypt. This is the most likely eponymous ancestor for the Libyans inasmuch as such subordination of Libya to Egypt is precisely what the reader would expect in this relationship between sovereign and vassal. Such a power imbalance was common except during the reign of the Twenty-second Dynasty in Egypt. Hence, the presence of the Lehabim and not Put includes the Libyan populace in the scope of the Table of Nations.

RODNEY S. SADLER JR.

PUTEOLI py*oo*-tee´oh-lee [Ποτίολοι **Potioloi**]. A seaport on the north shore of the bay of Naples, also known as Dicaearchia (**Dikaiarcheia** Δικαιάρχεια). A Roman colony from 194 BCE, Puteoli became the major trading port serving Rome. Connected by the *Via Campania* to the *Via Appia* and benefiting from a natural harbor enhanced by a breakwater, Puteoli prospered at least until the 2nd cent. CE, but declined after the development of Ostia. Egyptian grain supplies, on which Rome depended, were landed at Puteoli, as were goods from all parts of the eastern Mediterranean, including Palestine. With goods came people, banking and business links, and cults. Serapis was established at an early date, and other oriental cults, including a Nabatean temple, coexisted with the Greek and Roman. A Jewish population is attested from toward the end of the 1st cent. BCE.

Puteoli was the transit port for several journeys recorded by Josephus and the location of some noteworthy episodes. An impersonator of Alexander, one of the executed sons of King Herod, was feted by the Jewish community and adherents of the dynasty before being exposed by Augustus on reaching Rome (ca. 4 BCE; *J.W.* 2.104; *Ant.* 17.328–30).

The Alexandrian Jewish delegation, including Philo, seeking redress on matters of civic rights, awaited audience with Caius (Caligula) at Puteoli, and there learned of the scheme to install his statue in the Temple in Jerusalem (ca. 39–40 CE; Philo, *Embassy* 185–89). The emperor was preoccupied with building projects at Baiae and also built a pontoon bridge linking Puteoli with Misenum (Dio Cassius, *Rom.* 59.17.1–3; Suetonius, *Cal.* 19).

Paul landed at Puteoli on his journey to Rome for trial and was able to meet with a Christian community there (ca. 62 CE; Acts 28:13-14). The origins of this church are unrecorded, but its existence in a major trading port at an early date is unremarkable.

NICHOLAS H. TAYLOR

PUTHITE py*oo*´th*it* [פּוּתִי **puthi**]. One of four Calebite families listed as coming from KIRIATH-JEARIM (both a personal and place name) (1 Chr 2:53). *See* CALEB, CALEBITES.

PUTIEL py*oo*´tee-uhl [פּוּטִיאֵל **puti'el**]. Putiel's unnamed daughter was married to ELEAZAR, and they were the parents of PHINEHAS (Exod 6:25). Eleazar was a son of Aaron, making Phinehas Aaron's grandson. The name Putiel may be Egyptian in origin.

PUVAH py*oo*´vuh [פֻּוָּה **puwwah**]. The second-named son of Issachar (Gen 46:13), listed as PUAH in 1 Chr 7:1. Puvah is also cited as the eponymous ancestor of the PUNITE clan (Num 26:23), where there is some confusion and lack of correspondence of the name with "Punites." *See* ISSACHAR, ISSACHARITES.

PYRAMID TEXTS. A term used by Egyptologists to refer to the oldest Egyptian funerary literature inscribed on the antechambers and burial chambers of royal pyramids in the late Old Kingdom and First Intermediate Period (2375–2055 BCE). The spells functioned to awaken, protect, and transform the dead king so that he could ascend to the heavens—either to the circumpolar stars in the northern sky, to the constellation Orion in the southern sky, or to the sun god in the east. No pyramid contains all 800 known spells. King Unas' pyramid was the first to contain pyramid texts, but these archaic spells may find their origins in the early 3rd millennium BCE. Some spells may represent proto-Canaanite language, not Egyptian, perhaps the first instance of written Semitic. Pyramid texts form the basis of later Egyptian netherworld literature, and many spells survive into the New Kingdom BOOK OF THE DEAD.

Bibliography: R. O. Faulkner. *The Ancient Egyptian Pyramid Texts* (1969).

KATHLYN MARY COONEY

PYRE [מְדוּרָה **medhurah**]. A pyre is a circular pile of combustible material, usually wood, used for burning a dead body (Isa 30:33). *See* GEHENNA; MOLECH, MOLOCH.

PYRRHUS pihr´uhs [Πύρρος **Pyrros**]. Father of Sopater, one of Paul's companions (Acts 20:4), and from Beroea, where Paul had preached previously (Acts 17:10-15).

PYTHAGORAS, PYTHAGOREANISM. Pythagoras was a philosopher and mathematician born in Samos (Italy) ca. 570 BCE. He is best known for the geometric theorem that bears his name. Among his other contributions to intellectual knowledge is his discovery of musical ratios. He founded a sect whose doctrines included the immortality and transmigration of souls. Membership required certain initiation rites and ascetical practices.

For the biblical world, Pythagoreanism is important for its symbolic numerology, a sort of mystical speculation based on numbers and their perceived qualities. This numerology was especially popular in the late Hellenistic and imperial periods of Greco-Roman history. The ancients, especially the Pythagoreans and those influenced by them, believed that numbers represented fundamental elements in the universe, that is, numbers had various objective qualities, like odd and even. Some biblical numerology probably had its roots in Pythagorean numerological traditions. Extrabiblical works and archaeology indicate that a kind of Pythagoreanism flourished in NT times. For example, the number seven was thought to represent the cosmos, and certain numbers could be conceived of as plane numbers (square, triangular, etc.); the triangles 666 (Rev 13:18) and 153 (John 21:11) are primary instances. The Essenes' calendar may have been Pythagorean.

SUSAN F. MATHEWS

PYTHON. In Greek myth, the serpent or dragon that guarded the oracle at Delphi and was slain by Apollo. By the early Roman period, the term was used of ventriloquists, whose ability was often attributed to a divining spirit that possessed them. In Acts 16:16, Paul and his companions encountered a slave girl who had "a spirit of divination" (**pneuma pythōna** πνεῦμα πύθωνα). But the phrase can also be translated as "a python spirit," "a python as spirit," or, following an alternate reading in some manuscripts, "a spirit of a python." This is an unusual use of the term, but Paul's command that the spirit leave the girl (Acts 16:18) appears to imply that her divinatory powers are viewed in Acts as the result of possession.

RUBÉN R. DUPERTUIS

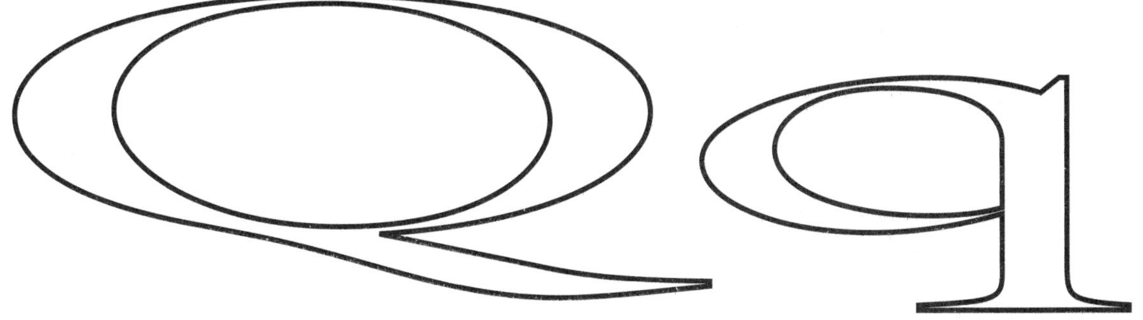
Qq

Q, QUELLE kvel´eh [Ger. *Quelle*, "source"]. In research on the SYNOPTIC GOSPELS, this letter represents the hypothesis that a source stands behind the portions of text common to the Gospels of Matthew and Luke (also known as the "double tradition") but unaccounted for in the Gospel of Mark. Most of these shared verses depict the words of Jesus (e.g., the temptation, Luke 4:1-13//Matt 4:1-11; large segments of the "Sermon on the Mount/Plain," including Luke 6:20-23// Matt 5:3-12). The Q source follows the versification of the Gospel of Luke; hence, Q 7:34 is the same as Luke 7:34.

There is no direct, historical evidence of a Q-source in early Christianity; there are examples, however, of collections of Jesus' sayings (e.g., the *Gospel of Thomas*). Nonetheless, proponents, assuming the independence of Matthew and Luke a priori, support this theory based on three literary arguments surrounding the common material: 1) the common tradition occurs in different narrative locations in their respective accounts; 2) Luke regularly contains the earlier version of these verses; and 3) Luke shows no awareness of special Matthean material (so-called "M"). For proponents, Q-material places scholars a generation closer to the historical Jesus than other Gospel stories.

A majority of biblical scholars holds to this theory. But the opposition to this hypothesis, while a minority, remains influential (e.g., Mark Goodacre). Generally, they advocate for Luke's literary dependence on the Gospel of Matthew in order to account for this material. *See* REDACTION CRITICISM, NT; SOURCE CRITICISM; SYNOPTIC PROBLEM.

Bibliography: Mark Goodacre. *The Case against Q: Studies in Markan Priority and the Synoptic Problem* (2001).

EMERSON B. POWERY

QAʿAQIR, JEBEL. Jebel Qaʿaqir, a large cemetery of the Early Bronze Age IV (ca. 2200–2000 BCE) in the Judean foothills 12 mi. west of Hebron, was discovered by William G. Dever and excavated by him in 1967–71. The expedition investigated hundreds of typical Early Bronze Age IV shaft tombs that had been robbed, and systematically excavated some forty tombs with disarticulated secondary burials. The pottery and copper artifacts belong to Dever's southern "Family S," very similar to the material from nearby LACHISH and Tell Beit Mirsim (*see* MIRSIM, TELL BEIT).

The only dwellings at the site were several enlarged natural caves, one of which (G23) yielded fragments of some 1,800 Early Bronze Age IV vessels. Also on the ridge above the cemeteries were a few rambling "boundary walls," a potter's kiln, several large cairns, an enigmatic dolmen-like structure, and a possible cult installation with large standing stones.

Bibliography: William G. Dever. "A Middle Bronze I Site on the West Bank of the Jordan." *Arch* 25 (1972) 231–33; William G. Dever. "New Vistas on the EB IV ("MB I") Horizons in Syria-Palestine." *BASOR* 237 (1980) 35–64; Seymour Gitin. "Middle Bronze I 'Domestic' Pottery of Jebel Qaʿaqir: A Ceramic Inventory of Cave G23." *ErIsr* 12 (1975) 46*–62*; Patricia Smith. "The Physical Characteristics and Biological Affinities of the MB I Skeletal Remains from Jebel Qaʿaqir." *BASOR* 245 (1982) 65–73.

WILLIAM G. DEVER

QADES, TELL. A Canaanite city in Galilee, 10 km (6 mi.) northwest of Hazor. At around 25 ac., it is the largest tell in Upper Galilee. It is identified with biblical KEDESH, a fortified town allotted to Naphtali (Josh 19:37) that served as a city of refuge (Josh 20:7) and a levitical city apportioned to the Gershonites (Josh 21:32; 1 Chr 6:76). Though Tell Qades is often identified with Kedesh-Naphtali (Judg 4:6), the geographical description (Judg 4:11) suggests a location for the latter site in the Lower Galilee, possibly Khirbet Qadish. During the reign of King Pekah of Israel, Tiglath-pileser of Assyria captured "all the land of Naphtali," including Kedesh, and carried its inhabitants into captivity (2 Kgs 15:29). In the Hellenistic period, Demetrius II went "to Kadesh in Galilee" with an army to remove Jonathan the Hasmonean from leadership (1 Macc 11:63, 73).

Tell Qades was first identified with biblical Kedesh by Edward Robinson (1794–1863). William F. Albright visited the site in 1925 and was the first to identify its different historical periods. There have been a series of subsequent surveys, soundings, and excavations conducted at the site. A step-trench cut into the northern mound in 1953 revealed deposits from the Early Bronze Age through the Hellenistic and Arabic eras. About 500 yds. north of the site, a 3rd-millennium BCE cultic-cave was excavated, the contents of which suggest rituals connected with funerary and mortuary cults. A Roman temple on the hill east of the site was in use during the 2nd and 3rd cent. CE and was apparently dedicated to the Syro-Phoenician god Baal Shamin. Renewed excavations have uncovered a Byzantine mortuary chapel in the center of the southern mound, and farther south substantial Hellenistic remains have been uncovered just below the surface. This part of the settlement was apparently abandoned in the mid-2nd cent. BCE.

Bibliography: William F. Albright. "Bronze Age Mounds of Northern Palestine and the Hauran: The Spring Trip of the School in Jerusalem." *BASOR* 19 (1925) 5–19; Edward Robinson. *Biblical Researches in Palestine and the Adjacent Countries, in the Years 1838 and 1852* (1856).

RALPH K. HAWKINS

QASHISH, TEL. Tel Qashish is located on the northern bank of the KISHON River, in the northwestern end of the Jezreel Valley, on the route leading to the Acco Valley. The small village is identified with DABBESHETH, mentioned in relation to the border of the tribe of Zebulun (Josh 19:11).

Tel Qashish was excavated by Amnon Ben-Tor of the Hebrew University of Jerusalem as part of the Yoqneʿam Regional Project (*see* JOKNEAM; QIRI, TELL). There were fifteen strata of habitation on the tel, spanning the Early Bronze Age I until the Persian period. The Early and Middle Bronze Age strata were characterized by domestic buildings and fortifications.

Bibliography: Amnon Ben-Tor, Ruhama Bonfil, and Sharon Zuckerman. *Tel Qashish: A Village in the Jezreel Valley: Final Report of the Archaeological Excavations (1978–1987)* (2003).

SHARON ZUCKERMAN

QASILE, TEL. A site situated on the northern bank of the YARKON RIVER, about 1 mi. from the Mediterranean coast. Its ancient name is unknown. Excavations in 1949–51, in 1956, in 1971–74, and in 1982–84 revealed a 4-ac. town that existed between the 12th and 10th/9th cent. BCE. The founders were probably Philistines who extended their core settlement territory in the late 12th cent. The local economy was based on seafaring, trade, and agriculture; the Yarkon River was used as a natural harbor. Strata XII–X, dated to ca. 1130–980 BCE, demonstrate gradual development and growth, culminating in the well-planned town of Str. X, which was violently destroyed by heavy fire. Architectural features include a large hall from the earliest occupation level (XII) with freestanding hearth, recalling Aegean and Cypriot traditions. Three successive temples from Str. XII–X were revealed with a spacious courtyard at their front and a small attached shrine to their west. The temples' plans differ from one another and, though based on Canaanite ideas, they exhibit great originality and variability and have some parallels in the Aegean world. A rich collection of cult objects and various other gifts exhibit an artistically rich variety based on Canaanite traditions, yet also indicate originality, freedom from conventions, and some connections to Cypriot and Aegean traditions. A well-planned dwelling quarter of Str. X in the southern part of the site is one of the best examples of such urban quarters in the Iron Age I. Intersecting streets create insulae; the houses are of the so-called "four room" type. Rich finds from these houses illustrate wealth and trade connections with Phoenicia, Cyprus, and Egypt. The heavy destruction by fire of Str. X was attributed to a conquest of the region by David, though other causes like a natural disaster must also be taken into account.

During the 10th/9th cent. BCE, the town was partially rebuilt (Strata IX–VIII), though not as densely as in the previous period; at that time it could have been serving the Israelite united monarchy as a port town. After an occupation gap, a small settlement existed on the site in the late 8th and 7th cent. Two Hebrew ostraca found on the surface of the mound belong to this period. One mentions "gold of Ophir belonging to Beth Horon, 30 shekels"; the other reads "(belonging) to the king, one thousand and one hundred [units] of oil . . . Hiyahu." It is assumed that the "king" is one of the kings of Judah.

During the Persian period, a large building at the top of the mound perhaps served as an administration building or a farmstead. Water supply was from a rock-cut square well. During the Hellenistic and Roman periods, there was a small settlement on the site. Isolated structures from the Byzantine period include a public bathhouse on the mound and a synagogue with Samaritan inscription at the foot of the mound. An Early Islamic caravanserai was found on the top of the mound.

Bibliography: B. Maisler. *Two Hebrew Ostraca from Tell Qasile. JNES* 10 (1951) 265–87; Amihai Mazar. *Excavations at Tell Qasile, Part One* (1981); Amihai Mazar. *Excavations at Tell Qasile, Part Two* (1985).

AMIHAI MAZAR

QATABAN. An ancient Southwest Arabian kingdom located in modern Yemen between the Wadi Bayhan and the Wadi Harib. Its capital was Timna. Qataban flourished during the 1st millennium BCE. Its origins are obscure. It first appears during the 7th cent. BCE as an ally and dependency of the kingdom of Saba. Later, between the 5th and 1st cent. BCE, it seems to have risen to the first rank, extending its dominion westward over the high plateaus of Yemen. Although the names of more than twenty rulers of Qataban are known, it is difficult to arrange them in chronological sequence. Qataban must have come into frequent conflict with the neighboring kingdoms of Saba and Hadramawt, but the historical record is silent. At the beginning of the Common Era, the power of

Qataban declined, undermined by desert nomads who took control of Timna. The kingdom survived on the upper part of the Wadi Bayhan before it was conquered at the end of the 2nd cent. CE, first by Hadramawt and then by Saba. Like the other South Arabian kingdoms, Qataban had its own dialect and its own pantheon with a national god, Amm. Its architecture and sculpture show a high level of civilization, marked toward the end by a strong Hellenistic influence. *See* ARAB, ARABIAN, ARABIA.

FRANÇOIS BRON

QATABANIA. *See* ALPHABET; QATABAN.

QEDAH, TEL EL. *See* HAZOR.

QEDEIS, ʿAIN. *See* HEZRON.

QEDISH, KHIRBET. *See* KEDESH.

QEIYAFA, KHIRBET. The site of Khirbet Qeiyafa is some 5 ac., located on the hills that border the Elah Valley. Its location is of strategic significance, as the site is on a main road that runs from the region of Philistia to cities in the hill country such as Jerusalem, Bethlehem, and Hebron. The Iron Age and the Hellenistic period are both represented at the site. Some have suggested that the Iron Age component of the site is Philistine, while others have suggested that it is Judean (even Davidic). Further excavation will be necessary to clarify this issue.

Excavations began at Qeiyafa in 2007; of particular import are Qeiyafa's fortifications, with casemate walls some 4 m wide and preserved to a height of 2.5 m. Moreover, portions of the city gate have been excavated and some of its megaliths weigh ca. 5 tons. Some residential architecture has been found at this fortified site.

During the 2008 expedition season, a small inscription was found, incised on the interior of a body-sherd. Carbon 14 tests were performed (on associated carbonized remains) and suggest a date sometime between the middle of the 11th cent. and the early 10th cent. BCE, thus providing a basic chronological time frame for the inscription. Of significance is the fact that the script itself is not the Old Hebrew script, but rather a precursor from which the Old Hebrew script derived (*see* HEBREW LANGUAGE). Although this is an important inscription, it would be tenuous to base arguments about the nature and extent of literacy during this time on this inscription.

CHRISTOPHER A. ROLLSTON

QERE-KETHIBH kuh-rayʹkuh-theevʹ [קְרֵא כְּתִיב **qereʾ-kethiv**]. A combination of two Aramaic terms meaning "(what is) read (aloud) or pronounced" (*Qere*) and "(what is) written" (*Kethibh*). The combination describes a phenomenon in the Hebrew text of the OT where two different words are indicated by one written form. Since the consonantal alphabet and the vowel pointing are separate systems for Hebrew, the consonants may indicate one word and the vowels another. For some people, the order in which these terms occur designates which form has primary authority: "Qere/Kethibh" gives authority to the pronounced form, while "Kethibh/Qere" gives authority to the written form.

Such forms may involve a difference in grammar only. For instance, in Ruth 3:4 the form **weshakhovti** (וְשָׁכָבְתִּי) occurs, where the Kethibh indicates a first-person common singular verb ("I will lie down"), but the Qere reads as a second-person feminine singular verb (**weshakhavte** וְשָׁכַבְתְּ, "you will lie down"). Nonetheless, some Qere-Kethibh forms do express a semantic difference.

How these forms arose has been the subject of much debate. Scribes may have used the forms to correct what they considered a faulty text. In the example above, the Kethibh form ("I will lie down") is grammatically inconsistent with its context, since Naomi is giving Ruth instructions ("go and ... lie down"). Since there is a long tradition of considering the consonantal text as holy and not subject to change, a SCRIBE may have used the vowel pointing system to indicate a more grammatically consistent form without changing the consonantal text itself. Alternatively, these forms may simply be preserving two separate traditions. Perhaps a scribe was using two different manuscripts when copying the Ruth text above and encountered a discrepancy. The scribe could have used the Qere/Kethibh as a strategy to preserve both readings.

Forms described as "Perpetual Qere" (*qere perpetuum*) are consistently pronounced differently from their written forms. One of these is the divine name (the TETRAGRAMMATON). It is written with the consonants **yhwh** (יהוה), but with the vowels for the word **ʾadhonay** (אֲדֹנָי, "my Lord"). *See* ARAMAIC, ARAMAISM; HEBREW LANGUAGE; TEXT, HEBREW, HISTORY OF.

ANNA BRAWLEY

QERE-KETHIV. *See* QERE-KETHIBH.

QERE-KETIV. *See* QERE-KETHIBH.

QESITAH [קְשִׂיטָה **qesitah**]. A coin or unit of money of unknown value, consistently translated in the NRSV as "piece(s) of money" (Gen 33:19; Josh 24:32; Job 42:11). *See* WEIGHTS AND MEASURES.

QIDDUSHIN [קִדּוּשִׁין **qiddushin**]. Qiddushin is the seventh tractate of the third order of the MISHNAH, *Nashim* (*Women*). Qiddushin (which translates to "sanctification[s]") focuses primarily on the betrothal of a woman by a man: the betrothal gift, process, and legal stipulations. The tractate also contains discussions concerning the differences between men and women in the obligation to perform commandments, the status of offspring produced from a man and woman of unequal social status, appropriate relations between men and women, appropriate and inappropriate jobs for unmarried men, and the kinds of crafts men should teach their sons.

BEATRICE J. W. LAWRENCE

QIMHI, DAVID. *See* KIMCHI.

QIRI, TELL. A site on the eastern slopes of the Mount Carmel range, 2 km south of Yoqneʿam. Tell Qiri was excavated as part of the Yoqneam Regional Project (see JOKNEAM; QASHISH, TEL). Occupation of the site spanned from the 5th millennium BCE until the Roman-Byzantine period. The site's Iron Age remains, represented by successive strata of domestic buildings and rich ceramic assemblages, included several cultic vessels and evidence for animal sacrifice in an Early Iron Age dwelling.

Bibliography: Amnon Ben-Tor et al. *Tel Qiri: A Village in the Jezreel Valley: Report of the Archaeological Excavations (1975–1977)* (1987).

SHARON ZUCKERMAN

QOF kohf [ק q]. The nineteenth letter of the Hebrew alphabet. *See* ALPHABET.

QOHELETH. *See* ECCLESIASTES, BOOK OF.

QOM, KHIRBET EL. Khirbet El-Qom, probably biblical MAKKEDAH, is a small site 12 mi. west of Hebron at the juncture of the Judean foothills and the inner mouth of the Lachish Valley. It was excavated in 1968–71 by William G. Dever in a salvage project designed to stop robbing of a vast Iron Age cemetery.

Tomb I, a typical Iron Age Judean bench tomb, produced two mid-8th cent. BCE inscriptions. Number 1 reads, "Belonging to Ophai, son of Nethanyahu; this is his tomb-chamber." Number 2 reads, "Belonging to Ophah, daughter of Nethanyahu." The most important Hebrew inscription (no. 3) was recovered from Tomb II, reading something like, "For Uriyahu, the governor, his inscription. Blessed be Uriyahu by Yahweh. From his enemies he has been saved by his Asherah. (Written by Oniyahu)." Yahweh's ASHERAH—whether the latter is taken as the name of the Canaanite-Israelite goddess (Asherah), or merely her tree-like symbol (asherah)—occurs again in the roughly contemporary Hebrew inscriptions at KUNTILLET ʿAJRUD in the eastern Sinai desert. These inscriptions have revolutionized our understanding of ancient Israelite religion, underscoring the persistence of polytheism until the end of the monarchy.

In 1971, J. S. Holladay investigated a 10th–7th cent. BCE two-way gate and a stretch of city wall on the hill above the cemetery (Field I). In Field II, L. T. Geraty recovered several 4th–3rd cent. BCE Aramaic and Greek ostraca, one (no. 3) mentioning an Edomite shopkeeper named Qos-yada and a Greek named Nikeratos, dated to 277 BCE by a probable reference to Ptolemy II Philadelphus.

Bibliography: William G. Dever. "Iron Age Epigraphic Material from the Area of the Kh. El-Kôm, West of Hebron." *HUCA* 40–41 (1969–70) 139–204; David A. Dorsey. "The Location of Biblical Makkedah." *TA* 7 (1980) 185–93; Lawrence T. Geraty. "The Khirbet el-Kôm Bilingual Ostracon." *BASOR* 220 (1975) 55–61; J. S. Holladay. "Khirbet el-Qôm." *IEJ* 21 (1971) 175–77; Ziony Zevit. "The Khirbet el-Qôm Inscription Mentioning a Goddess." *BASOR* 255 (1984) 39–47.

WILLIAM G. DEVER

QOPH. *See* QOF.

QOSEIMEH, ʿAIN. *See* KARKA.

QUADRATUS kwahd´ruh-tuhs. The earliest known Christian apologist, Quadratus addressed an apology to the emperor Hadrian ca. 124–25 CE. Eusebius (*Eccl. hist.* 4.3.1–2) preserves the only surviving information about him, including a fragment of his apology. *See* APOLOGETICS; APOSTOLIC FATHERS, CHURCH FATHERS.

Bibliography: Paul Foster. "The *Apology of Quadratus.*" *ExpTim* 117 (2006) 353–59.

MICHAEL W. HOLMES

QUAIL [שְׂלָו selaw; ὀρτυγομήτρα ortygomētra]. According to the account of Israel's journey through the desert, the people craved meat. Thus, God provided them not only with manna, but with great numbers of quails as well (Exod 16:13; Num 11:31-32; recalled in Ps 105:40; Wis 16:2; 19:12). The established translation of selaw as "quail" need not be disputed. The texts clearly refer to some kind of bird (compare Ps 78:27), and the quail (*Coturnix communis*) meets the requirements of the story. The meat of this conspicuously fat bird is regarded as delicious. Further, quails are migratory, appearing in impressive flocks, carried by the wind (Num 11:31). In the month of March, they return in large numbers seemingly overnight. During their exhausting journey from Africa, they are easily caught whenever they alight to rest. *See* BIRDS OF THE BIBLE.

GÖRAN EIDEVALL

QUARRY [מַסָּע massaʿ, מַקֶּבֶת maqqeveth]. Rock quarries are mentioned infrequently in the Bible, though judging by archaeological evidence the practice of quarrying stone for building monumental structures was known in Syria-Palestine from as early as the Early Bronze Age (*see* ARCHITECTURE, OT). Large, rectangular quarried stones (also called ashlars) were desirable both for their beauty and for the increased stability and load-bearing strength they offered relative to fieldstone and mortar. The use of ashlars in construction also served as a demonstration of central power and authority, as their quarrying on a large scale required the mustering of significant amounts of skilled and unskilled labor, funds, and logistical support. Thus, an ashlar building testified to the power of the king who built it, and, in the case of a temple, to the greatness of the deity who inhabited it. Most biblical references to quarries and quarrying have to do with the construction of Solomon's Temple in Jerusalem.

The books of Kings take considerable care to point out that the Temple was constructed using stone that was quarried, as opposed to fieldstone. First Kings 5:17 describes how Solomon's workers, with Tyrian assistance, quarried the stones. First Kings 6:7 stresses the fact that the stones for the Temple's initial construction were dressed and finished entirely at the quarry (**massa'**), so that no chiseling or other such noise was heard at the temple site. This is probably an echo of the earlier tradition that an ALTAR to Yahweh must always be built of fieldstone (Exod 20:24-25), because the use of a chisel would profane the structure. It would be impractical to build a structure of the Temple's scale using exclusively fieldstone, but by restricting the actual process of dressing the stones to the off-site quarry, the temple site itself was kept free of pollution, and the tradition was still honored. In any event, the practice of fully dressing ashlars for temple construction in the field, rather than on-site, is archaeologically attested at other sites, including Tell Tayinat in Syria (*see* TAYINAT, TELL).

A cluster of references to "quarried stone" (**'avne makhtsev** אַבְנֵי מַחְצֵב) relates to the repairs to the Temple undertaken during the reigns of Joash (2 Kgs 12:12) and Josiah (2 Kgs 22:6; 2 Chr 34:11). The LXX reading of **lithos tetrapedos** (λίθος τετραπέδος) in 2 Chr 34:11 is of particular interest, as it emphasizes the fully dressed, rectangular cut of the ashlar masonry, as opposed to a less costly—but also less beautiful—partial dressing in which only some faces of the stones were finished.

The language of quarries and quarrying appears only twice in the Bible outside of the context of the Temple. Ecclesiastes 10:9 includes a proverbial saying of "whoever quarries stones will be hurt by them" among examples of the "evil" that the speaker has seen in observing the world. Here the inherent danger of working in a quarry is used to illustrate the dangerous, unpredictable nature of life. Isaiah 51:1 includes a command from God to those who "pursue righteousness" to "look to the rock from which you were hewn, and to the quarry (**maqqeveth**) from which you were dug." The figure refers to Abraham and Sarah, implying that the covenant made by Yahweh with those ancestors is the source of the righteousness that Isaiah's audience should seek.

D. MATTHEW STITH

QUART [χοῖνιξ **choinix**]. Word used for the Greek dry measure that is about the same weight as a modern quart (Rev 6:6). *See* WEIGHTS AND MEASURES.

QUARTER, SECOND. *See* SECOND QUARTER.

QUARTERMASTER [שַׂר מְנוּחָה **sar menukhah**]. Jeremiah 51:59 identifies SERAIAH as a "quartermaster" (NRSV). The Hebrew phrase means literally "officer of the resting place," one who prepares overnight resting quarters for soldiers on a journey. It is preferable to read "officer (or chief) of tribute" (**sar minkhah** שַׂר מִנְחָה). Seraiah as such was most likely the brother of Jeremiah's scribe Baruch (compare Jer 32:12), who was sent to Nebuchadnezzar to bring tribute.

MILTON ENG

QUARTUS kwor'tuhs [Κούαρτος **Kouartos**]. A Christian listed with seven others in the concluding greetings in Paul's letter to the Romans (16:23). Because Paul calls him "our brother," it is likely that Quartus was a Christian brother rather than brother by birth to someone else in the list.

QUEEN [מַלְכָּה **malkah**, מְלֶכֶת **melekheth**; βασίλισσα **basilissa**]. In the OT, the title *queen* is used in reference to royal women of foreign countries: Sheba (1 Kgs 10:1-13; 2 Chr 9:1-12), Vashti (Esth 1:1-20), Esther (Esth 2:17), and an unnamed king's wife (Dan 5:10). The term also occurs in Jeremiah's polemic against the "QUEEN OF HEAVEN" (Jer 7:18; 44:17-19, 25) and for unspecified admirers of the woman in Song of Songs (6:8-9). The LXX, with the exception of Jer 7:18, uses **basilissa**. The NT uses of **basilissa** are also references to foreign women: the queen of the South (i.e., Sheba; Matt 12:42; Luke 11:31; *see* SHEBA, QUEEN OF); the CANDACE, queen of the Ethiopians (Acts 8:27); and Babylon, who rules as queen (Rev 18:7). Since *queen* is applied to both admired and reviled women, the limited use of the title does not suggest a negative view of royal women.

In contemporary Western monarchies the term *queen* refers to a female monarch or the wife of a king. The biblical uses of *queen* appear to follow this pattern. Sheba/the queen of the South, the Queen of Heaven, the Candace, and Babylon are presented as female monarchs, while the references in the books of Esther, Song of Songs, and Daniel are to the highest-ranking royal women of the palace.

The majority of biblical queens, however, are not called *queen*. Athaliah, e.g., is the wife of a king, mother of a king, and for six years sole monarch of Judah (2 Kgs 11:3), but she is never titled *queen*. Collective reference to the wives of the king (e.g., 1 Kgs 4:11; 2 Chr 11:21; 21:17) and specific mention of prominent wives (e.g., Bathsheba, Jezebel) occur throughout the narratives of Israel's monarchy, and Herodias is mentioned in the NT (Matt 14:1-11; Mark 6:17-28); yet, again, the term *queen* is never applied.

In Isa 49:23 the term **sarah** (שָׂרָה), which typically means "princess," is set parallel to *kings* to refer to queens of foreign nations who will submit to a restored Jerusalem. In Neh 2:6 the term sheghal (שֵׁגָל) identifies the queen next to Artaxerxes. In Ps 45:9 [Heb. 45:10; LXX 44:10] sheghal identifies the king's new wife or the mother of the king who welcomes her. The LXX identifies her as basilissa. The LXX also uses basilissa to refer to the female royal monarch at the head of the list of exiles (Jer 29:2 [LXX Jer 36:2]).

While the LXX uses basilissa, the Hebrew version of Jer 29:2 introduces yet another term to refer to the queen: gevirah (גְּבִירָה), which is related to a verb meaning "to be strong, mighty." In Jer 29:2 and in Jer 13:18, where Jeremiah announces the future toppling of the royal house, the "mighty" or "great" woman is likely the mother of the king. The LXX of 2 Kgs 10:13 uses a term meaning "mighty" to translate the Hebrew gevirah. The kin of King Ahaziah of Judah explain they are in the Northern Kingdom to seek out "the sons of the king and the sons of the dynasteuousē (δυναστευούσῃ)." The likely gevirah or dynasteuousē would be the mighty queen Jezebel. Rather than translating gevirah as "great" or "mighty lady," however, most English Bibles have "queen" or "queen mother."

While the Jeremiah and 2 Kgs 10:13 passages may refer to mothers of kings, pharaoh's wife is called gevirah in 1 Kgs 11:19. It appears to be an honorary title; the LXX has tēn meizō (τήν μείζω), "the great." In 1 Kgs 15:13, however, something more is at stake. King Asa removes MAACAH, identified as his mother, from being gevirah for making something for the goddess Asherah. The LXX describes Maacah as removed from being "leader" (hēgoumenēn ἑγουμένην). The parallel report in 2 Chr 15:16 in the LXX has Maacah removed from serving (leitourgousan λειτουργοῦσαν) Astarte.

Some scholars have suggested Hittite parallels to the dismissal of Maacah. There are two examples of Hittite queens in the New Kingdom period being deposed from the position of tawananna: 1) the widow of King Shuppiluliuma, whose husband's heir Murshili II charged her with witchcraft, theft, and the introduction of foreign practices; 2) Danuhepa, who was tried and killed for unknown reasons. Neither widowed queen was mother of the king who deposed her; the title tawananna was not equivalent to "king's wife" or "mother of the king." The Hittite tawananna exercised religious leadership as high priestess of the sun-goddess of Arinna. Images on Hittite seals suggest that the office of the tawananna and the title *queen* were linked, and most often it was not the wife of the current king bearing these titles. Maacah's dismissal for religious activity and the dismissal of the two Hittite priestesses have led some scholars to suggest the gevirah was a position of religious leadership. There have been various proposals regarding the focus of the gevirah's religious devotion and whether, for some period, Maacah's attention to Asherah had a legitimate place within the religion of Israel and Judah.

The tawananna title was also used during the earlier Hittite Old Kingdom Period. In this period, the tawananna played a role in royal succession, in addition to exercising authority as priestess; however, she was the king's aunt, sister, or daughter, and she was not called *queen*. Some have suggested that the gevirah played a role in succession in Judah and point to Bathsheba's advancement of her son Solomon to succeed David (1 Kgs 1). However, Bathsheba is David's wife and she is never called gevirah. Though Jezebel (2 Kgs 10:13) or Hamutal or Nehushta (Jer 13:18; 29:2) might have been gevirahs, Maacah is the only royal woman in Israel or Judah identified by name. The position of gevirah has visibility and authority, and extends from early in the divided monarchy (i.e., Maacah) to the exile (Jer 29:2), but the specific form, content, and length of service remain under discussion.

The scarcity, inconsistency, and indefiniteness of titles for biblical royal women are not that different from the pattern in other ANE kingdoms. The presence and significance of female monarchs, wives, and mothers of kings, however, are visible in the texts and material remains.

There is a nearly complete list of the mothers of the kings of Judah in the regnal notices in 1–2 Kings. These notices announce and assess the reign of each Judean king and synchronize it with the reign of his Israelite counterpart (e.g., 1 Kgs 14:21-22; 22:41-43; 2 Kgs 14:1-4). The notice identifies the father and the name of the king's mother for each king except Jehoram (2 Kgs 8:16-18) and Ahaz (2 Kgs 16:2-3). The inclusion of the mother distinguishes the Judean regnal notices from those of Israel (e.g., 2 Kgs 13:1-2, 10-11) and from other ANE king lists. The addition presents the monarchy as a royal house within which a key woman also functioned. Some scholars suggest that the inclusion of the mother of the king indicates that she held an official position in the Judean monarchy; many draw a connection to the gevirah position from which Maacah was removed (1 Kgs 15:13).

Throughout 1–2 Kings, the regnal notices underscore the continuity and assess the faithfulness of the Judean monarchy. The inclusion of the queen mothers signifies that they are a part of that continuity and that assessment. While Judah adopted dynastic succession, David's appointment of Solomon (1 Kgs 1) suggests the eldest son did not always inherit the throne and royal mothers might get involved in matters of succession. Haggith is not depicted in the events of 1 Kgs 1, but in the narrative leading up to Solomon's anointing, Adonijah is identified as "son of Haggith" and Solomon as Bathsheba's son. David swears to Bathsheba, "Your son Solomon shall succeed me as king" (1 Kgs 1:30).

Various biblical passages highlight the involvement of queens in the counsel of kings and in royal administration. Proverbs 31:1-9, attributed to a King Lemuel's mother, counsels restraint and directs the king to care for the poor and needy. In Dan 5:10-12, the Babylonian queen encourages the king not to fear the writing on the wall and identifies someone who can interpret it. In 1 Kgs 14:1-20, the Israelite king Jeroboam sends his wife to the prophet Ahijah to inquire covertly about their ill son. She returns not only with the announcement of her son's imminent death but also with an oracle concerning the nation. In 1 Kgs 2:13-24, Bathsheba agrees to present to Solomon Adonijah's request to marry Abishag. Whether Bathsheba saw this as an opportunity to remove her son's archrival or was genuinely surprised by Solomon's violent refusal is not clear, but Solomon's hospitality to his mother and initial assurances that her request would be granted suggest that the offering of counsel was neither strange nor forbidden. Such counsel—like the actions of the king—was subject to review. The regnal notices of Jehoram (2 Kgs 8:16-18) and Ahaziah (2 Kgs 8:25-27) blame their inappropriate leadership of Judah on Israelite influence through wife and mother. Psalm 45 reminds the new queen that international delegations and the wealthy will seek her favor (Ps 45:12 [Heb. 45:13]) and warns her to turn her loyalty from her "father's house" (Ps 45:10 [Heb. 45:11]) to her new husband. Michal assists her husband, David, to escape the murderous intentions of King Saul, her own father (1 Sam 19:11-17).

While the terminology related to queens and the historical details of their lives remain sketchy, the general portrait of queens that emerges depicts them as symbols of a nation. They are an integral part of the Davidic monarchy and part of the process of ruling.

Bibliography: Susan Ackerman. *Warrior, Dancer, Seductress, Queen: Women in Judges and Biblical Israel* (1998); Nancy R. Bowen. "The Quest for the Historical Gĕbîrâ." *CBQ* 64 (2001) 597–618.

ELNA SOLVANG

QUEEN OF HEAVEN [מְלֶכֶת הַשָּׁמַיִם **melekheth hashamayim**]. According to Jer 7:16-20 and 44:15-25, some ancient Israelites—both in Judah, before its fall to Babylon in 586 BCE, and in Egypt, where they took refuge after the Babylonian onslaught—burned incense, poured out libations, and baked cakes to honor a goddess known only as the Queen of Heaven. In exchange, according to the Queen's adherents, she made available plenty of food and kept them safe from enemy attack. It is particularly women, moreover, who seem devoted to the Queen of Heaven; thus they become, in Jer 44:25, the object of Jeremiah's special scorn.

Together, these data suggest that the Queen of Heaven is a syncretistic deity who combines in her character aspects of the west Semitic goddess ASTARTE and Mesopotamian ISHTAR. Both Astarte and Ishtar can be called "Queen of Heaven" or related titles in extrabiblical sources; both, like the Queen of Heaven, have associations with fertility and with war; and the making of offering cakes seems a particularly important ritual in both of their cults. Indeed, the Hebrew name of these offering cakes, **kawwanim** (כַּוָּנִים), is derived from the Akkadian term **kamanu**, used in Mesopotamia to describe cakes baked for Ishtar. Also in Mesopotamia, women were particularly associated with Ishtar worship, especially through their ritual imitation of the mourning in which Ishtar engaged after the untimely death of her young husband, Tammuz. According to Ezek 8:14, Israelite women likewise wept over Tammuz at the time of Babylon's incursions into Judah.

The appeal of Ishtar's cult to some Judeans in the early 6th cent. BCE is explained in part by their experience of Babylon's military might and their conviction that this might was effected by Babylon's gods: such powerful gods, so this logic goes, are more worthy of worship than Yahweh, the God of Israel, whose ability to protect Israel's people seemed to have waned. But the special appeal this cult had for women may also result from the religious reforms promulgated by King Josiah a few decades previous, which had arguably compromised women's ability to participate in the cult of Yahweh: by centralizing Yahwistic worship in Jerusalem, e.g., and so making it more difficult for women—especially women with childcare responsibilities (compare 1 Sam 1:22)—to be present for important ritual occasions.

SUSAN ACKERMAN

QUEEN OF SHEBA. *See* SHEBA, QUEEN OF.

QUEEN OF THE SOUTH [βασίλισσα νότου **basilissa notou**]. The Queen of the South to which Jesus refers (Matt 12:42; Luke 11:31) is most likely the Gentile queen of Sheba (1 Kgs 10:1-13; 2 Chr 9:1-12). She asked Solomon hard questions and marveled at his answers and wealth. Jesus says that the queen will rise up at the judgment and condemn Jesus' audience because she came from the ends of the earth to hear Solomon's wisdom. Jesus condemns his audience for asking for signs instead of seeking wisdom from him. His audience is hearing someone greater than Solomon but rejecting Jesus' wisdom (compare Luke 7:35; 11:49; and par.). *See* SHEBA, QUEEN OF.

KENNETH D. LITWAK

QUEER THEORY. *See* GAY INTERPRETATION; HOMOSEXUALITY; LESBIAN INTERPRETATION.

QUELLE, Q. *See* Q, QUELLE.

QUFIN, KHIRBET. *See* MAARATH.

QUINTILIAN. Born in Calagurris (now Calahorra) in Spain, Marcus Fabius Quintilianus (ca. 35–100 CE) was a rhetorician and teacher in Rome, where he established a successful school. His only surviving work, the lengthy *Institutio oratoria* (*The Education of the Orator*), was written in the early 90s CE and is the fullest extant account of classical rhetoric, detailing a student's training from infancy to full maturity. Roughly contemporary with NT writings, *Institutio oratoria* is an invaluable resource for understanding rhetorical theory and training as practiced in the early Roman period and, consequently, for situating early Christian literature in its broader literary and cultural context.

RUBÉN R. DUPERTUIS

QUINTUS MEMMIUS. *See* MEMMIUS, QUINTUS.

QUIRINIUS kwi-rin′ee-uhs [Κυρήνιος Kyrēnios]. Not unlike Pontius Pilate (*see* PILATE, PONTIUS), who escaped the silence of history through his role in the passion of Jesus Christ, Publius Sulpicius Quirinius, also a Roman governor, became a figure of lasting significance in connection with the birth of Jesus. According to Luke, "In those days [of King Herod of Judea; Luke 1:5] a decree went out from Emperor AUGUSTUS that all the world should be registered. This was the first registration (apographē ἀπογραφή) and was taken while Quirinius was governor of SYRIA" (Luke 2:1-2).

According to Josephus (*Ant.* 17.354; 18.1–10, 26, 29; 20.102; *J.W.* 2.433; 7.253), Quirinius was installed as "governor" of Syria in 6 CE, whereas Herod the Great died in 4 BCE (*Ant.* 17.190–91). Was Luke aware of this ten-year discrepancy and, if so, would not the appearance of inaccuracy detract considerably from the "clear certainty" (hē asphaleia ἡ ἀσφάλεια; Luke 1:4, authors' trans.; NRSV, "truth") that he sought to instill through his own account?

Attempts to explain this chronological conundrum take three tracks: 1) there was an earlier census, otherwise unknown, that Luke records, or Quirinius also served as ruler over Judea in a prior period that overlapped with Herod the Great; 2) Luke was either unaware of the discrepancy or did not concern himself with such imprecision since he simply intended his audience to link Jesus' birth with a well-known event during the momentous rule of Augustus; 3) King Herod refers to ARCHELAUS, Herod's son, (*Ant.* 17.194–95, 202; *J.W.* 1.668), who was deposed in 6 CE when Augustus annexed Judea to Syria and ensconced Quirinius as governor. We offer a new solution.

First, the contours of Quirinius' public career are clear enough from Josephus' *Jewish Antiquities* and Tacitus' *Annales.* Not surprisingly, Josephus singles out Quirinius' census of 6 CE (in the thirty-seventh year after Octavian's defeat of Antony at Actium; *Ant.* 18.26) that sparked such violent reaction among Jews and functioned as a prime catalyst for Judas the Galilean and the zealot resistance that would foment the Jewish war against Rome (66–73 CE; *Ant.* 17.354; 18.1–10; 20.102; *J.W.* 2.433; 7.253). At first blush, Luke might seem to have the same interest (Luke 2:1-5), since he has the revered Gamaliel compare the stirrings of the Jesus-messianist "party" quite favorably over against "Judas the Galilean" whose following "at the time of the census (apographē) ... were scattered" (Acts 5:33-39)—i.e., the days when the Jesus movement was born. For Luke there appears to be something qualitatively different about the followers of Messiah Jesus and these other popular uprisings against Rome's authority (compare Luke 21:8-9).

Josephus emphasizes how Quirinius was sent by the emperor Augustus, and in Judea, personally oversaw the assessment of Jewish property, the liquidation of Archelaus' estate, and the replacement of the high priest Joazar with the well-known An(a)nus of the Gospels (*Ant.* 18.1–29). Although Tacitus does not mention Quirinius' consular appointment over Syria, his account (*Ann.* 3.22–23, 48; compare 2.30) is fully consistent with Josephus', portraying Quirinius as a *novus homo* ("new man") who enjoyed considerable influence under Augustus and Tiberius. Born (ca. 51 BCE) into a plebian family from Lanuvium, Quirinius quickly demonstrated military prowess, and probably as proconsul of Crete and Cyrene (ca. 15 BCE) defeated the rebellious Marmarides (Florus, *Epit.* 2.31). By 12 BCE Quirinius had earned a consulship, most likely over Pamphylia/Galatia (*Inscrip. Lat. Sel.* 9502, 9503; Dio, *Rom.* 54.28.2), and sometime before 2 CE had squelched the fierce "Cilician" brigands, the Homanadenses, near Lake Trogitis (Strabo, *Geogr.* 12.6.2), which was rewarded with Augustus' "insignia of triumph." In the following years, Quirinius became an adviser to the exiled Tiberius on the island of Rhodes and then to Gaius Julius Caesar in the east. He married Aemilia Lepida, whose patrician pedigree included Sulla and Pompey. Under Tiberius, Quirinius' stature had increased (*Ann.* 2.30) but then waned considerably toward the end of his life. Although Quirinius was divorced and childless (Suetonius, *Tib.* 49) and embarrassed Lepida in his latter years (*Ann.* 3.22–23), at his death in 21 CE Tiberius granted him a state funeral, himself delivering a panegyric on Quirinius' loyal service (*Ann.* 3.48).

Second, primary texts for Roman census-taking and taxation are sparse; but epigraphic evidence has revealed complex, non-uniform systems that reflect Rome's practice of adapting local customs: 1) Under Augustus, previous city taxation (*tributum*) comes under imperial power; provincial censuses are subsumed to the will of the emperor; 2) Augustus ordered the first provincial censuses, including registration of property as well as of persons, one year after completing a census of Roman citizens; assuming the role of "censor" in 29 BCE (Augustus' *Res gest. divi Aug.* 6.1), he administered the census at least three times (27, 11, and 4 CE; Suetonius, *Aug.* 27; compare Dio, *Rom.* 52.42.1; 53.22.5; 54.35.1; 55.13.4; 59.22.3); 3) There is no evidence that a single census of all the provinces was conducted simultaneously. Yet Augustus' decree to register a single province as in his edicts regarding Cyrene (7/6 and 4 BCE) could logically be construed as his "will" to canvas the whole Roman world; 4) Neither is it known whether provincial censuses occurred in regular intervals, though inscriptions point to a fourteen-year cycle for Egypt; 5) One inscription (*Inscrip. Lat. Sel.* 2683) lists Quirinius as "governor" (*legatus*) conducting a census in Apamea, Syria (no date); 6) Josephus details the tumultuous last years of Herod the Great and Augustus' uncontested interventions against this "client" king (*Ant.* 16–17). That Archelaus is the "king" of Luke 1:5 and 2:1-40 finds no support whatever in the evidence and destroys Luke's intricate interlacing of the births of Jesus from Nazareth and John from Judea (Luke 1:5-80) when both Galilee and Judea were under the same control of Herod "king of Judea" (37–4 BCE).

Third, in telescoping the later census with the birth of Jesus, Luke follows a convention of Hellenistic rhetorical-historiography that he repeats at the end of his first volume when he foregrounds Jesus' ascension to the same day as his resurrection (Luke 24:36-51 corresponds to Acts 1:3*b*-11; compare, e.g., Diodorus Siculus' linking passages). Such "end" telescoping constrains Luke's audience to hear the assumption of Jesus' universal lordship in resonance with "all that Jesus did and taught from the beginning," culminating in a Roman cross and resurrection (Acts 1:1-3*a*). Moreover, Luke's synchronism of the beginnings of the zealot movement with the birth of Jesus exhibits another ploy of historiographical-narrative performance developed by Polybius (ca. 200–118 BCE). By aligning the main action with an auxiliary event (insurrection) that will emerge again later in the narrative (Luke 23:18-19, Barabbas; Acts 5:33-39, Theudas/Judas the Galilean; Acts 21:37-40, the "Egyptian"), Luke leads his audience to comprehend the overarching "plan of God" by which the powerful players of Rome and Judea would coalesce again to shame and depose another "king" of the Jews through yet another governor's "assessment": "The King of the Jews—this one!" (Luke 23:38, author's trans.; NRSV, "This is the King of the Jews"). Herod (Luke 1:5), Quirinius (Luke 2:2), Herod Antipas (Luke 23:6-12), and Pilate (23:1-25) combine unwittingly to facilitate a very different lordship and kind of "decree" that issues in the "good news" of the release of sins to all the nations (Luke 24:44-49; see Acts 4:23-31).

Therefore Luke's superlative "first" (Luke 2:2) may refer to more than one Roman taxation that "laid the mines" for the violent detonation at the infamous intrusion of 6 CE. Possibly Luke erred in his correlation of Jesus' birth with Quirinius' census (Tertullian claims Saturninus as governor; *Marc.* 4.19; compare *Ant.* 17.89). But in light of the data, it is more likely that Luke intended to alert his audience at the beginning to the absolute authority claimed by Rome and the inevitable clashes of lordship that would mount and build to a climax when Paul reached the center of empire at the "end" of the narrative (Acts 28:15-31; see Luke 20:20-26). Jesus, not Caesar Augustus, is the Lord, the Savior, the true herald and giver of the "good news of peace" to all the world (see Priene Inscription, *OGIS* 458).

Bibliography: Hermann Dessau. *Inscriptiones Latinae Selectae* (1997); David P. Moessner. "'Listening Posts' Along the Way: 'Synchronisms' as Metaleptic Prompts to the 'Continuity of the Narrative' in Polybius' *Histories* and in Luke's Gospel–Acts." *The New Testament and Early Christian Literature in Greco-Roman Context.* John Fotopoulos, ed. (2006) 129–50.

DAVID P. MOESSNER AND JOHN GAY

QUIVER [אַשְׁפָּה ʾashpah, תְּלִי teli]. A case used to carry and store arrows. The bow and arrow were used for both hunting and warfare from as early as 3000 BCE. Since the bow was delicate, strung with animal tendons and sinews, it was kept in a quiver (Gen 27:3). Quivers are depicted on the Lachish reliefs from Nineveh.

The quiver provided a ready metaphor for biblical writers. Isaiah states that God hid him in a quiver, reserving him for special use (Isa 49:2). Jeremiah 5:16 compares the quiver of the unnamed enemy of Israel and Judah to an "open tomb" to illustrate the extent of their rapaciousness. The psalmist uses a full quiver as an analogy for a man who has many sons (Ps 127:5).

RALPH K. HAWKINS

QUMRAN koom´rahn. Khirbet Qumran is the modern Arabic name of a site located on the northwest shore of the DEAD SEA. Although some scholars have identified Qumran with the CITY OF SALT mentioned in Josh 15:61-62, the COPPER SCROLL (3Q15) indicates that Qumran should be identified with SECACAH, another desert town mentioned in this passage.

A. Identification and History of Exploration

Qumran was visited by early explorers but attracted little attention before the discovery of the first DEAD SEA SCROLLS in 1946–47. In February–March 1949, Roland de Vaux of the École Biblique et Archéologique Française de Jerusalem and G. Lankester Harding, the chief inspector of antiquities in Jordan, conducted excavations in Cave 1 and confirmed that this was the

Figure 1: Site Plan

cave from which the first scrolls had been removed. Two years later (1951) they conducted a first season of excavations at Qumran, followed by large-scale excavations in 1953–56.

More recently, other expeditions have explored different parts of the site, including the settlement and cemetery (Yitzhak Magen and Yuval Peleg), residential caves to the north (Magen Broshi and Hanan Eshel), and the cemetery (Broshi, Eshe, and Freund; see Galor). *See* ARCHAEOLOGY.

B. Description of the Settlement and Occupation Phases

De Vaux divided the sectarian settlement at Qumran into three phases, which he termed "Period Ia," "Period Ib," and "Period II." De Vaux dated Period Ia to the third quarter of the 2nd cent. BCE (ca. 130–100 BCE), Period Ib from ca. 100–31 BCE, and Period II from ca. 4 BCE–68 CE. A late Iron Age settlement preceded Period Ia, and Period II was followed by a brief phase of Roman occupation (Period III).

1. Iron Age

Qumran was first inhabited during the late Iron Age (8th–7th cent. BCE). The Iron Age settlement consisted of a rectangular building with a row of rooms along the east side of an open courtyard. An enclosure attached to the west side of the building contained a large round cistern (L110; L refers to *locus*, an archaeological division of space). This occupation phase ended with the fall of the kingdom of Judah ca. 586 BCE.

2. Period Ia

Qumran had been abandoned for several hundred years when the sectarian settlement was established. This settlement was modest in size and brief in duration. Parts of the ruined Iron Age building were rebuilt and reoccupied. A new channel was built to supply the Iron Age cistern and two new pools (L117 and L118) nearby. Since coins of Alexander Jannaeus (103–76 BCE; *see* ALEXANDER JANNAEUS, JANNEUS; MONEY, COINS) were plentiful in the next phase (Period Ib), de Vaux assigned Period Ia to the reign of John HYRCANUS I (135–104 BCE).

3. Period Ib

According to de Vaux, the sectarian settlement at Qumran acquired its definitive form during the reign of Alexander Jannaeus, when it expanded greatly in size. The main entrance to the settlement was through a gate by a two-story high watchtower (L9–L11). The tower guarded the main point of entry into the settlement, giving access to a passage that divided the site into two main parts: an eastern sector dominated by the tower (de Vaux called this the "main building"), and a western sector centered on the round Iron Age cistern (described by de Vaux as the "secondary building"). The main building incorporated remains of the Iron Age building and consisted of rooms grouped around a central, open-air courtyard.

The largest room in the settlement (L77) is located on the south side of the main building. It functioned as an assembly hall and communal dining room, as indicated by the adjacent pantry (L86 in Period Ib), which contained over 1,000 dishes. A potters' workshop (L64 and L84) was located in the southeast part of the main building.

The rooms in the secondary building included storerooms, industrial installations, and workshops. An open-air courtyard to the west of the round cistern (L111) gave access to two rooms (L120 and L121) that apparently were used for storage. A large stone mortar found in association with the Period Ib floor in L105 suggests that some of the rooms in this area were used for food preparation, as in Period II.

The hydraulic system was greatly expanded in Period Ib and remained in use with modifications until the destruction of the sectarian settlement at the end of Period II. The water was brought by aqueduct from Wadi Qumran, which flows into the Dead Sea to the south of the marl terrace on which the settlement sits. Branches of the aqueduct wound through the settlement and supplied all of the pools. Decantation basins in front of each pool or group of pools served as settling tanks, catching the silt carried by the flood waters.

According to de Vaux, the end of Period Ib was marked by an earthquake and a fire. Evidence for earthquake destruction was found throughout the settlement but is perhaps clearest in the case of one of the pools (L49), where the steps (L48) and floor had split and the eastern half had dropped about 50 cm. This crack continues to the north and south. The wooden shelves with stacks of dishes in the pantry (L86) collapsed onto the floor. Earthquake damage is also evident in the tower, where the lintel and ceiling of one of the rooms at the ground level collapsed.

The testimony of Josephus (*see* JOSEPHUS, FLAVIUS) enabled de Vaux to date the earthquake to 31 BCE (*J.W.* 1.370–80). In addition to the earthquake damage, a layer of ash that had blown across the site when the wood and reed roofs burned indicates there had been a fire. De Vaux concluded that the earthquake and fire were simultaneous but admitted that there was no evidence to confirm this.

4. Period II

De Vaux relied on the numismatic evidence to date the beginning of Period II to the time of Herod's son and successor, Herod ARCHELAUS (4 BCE–6 CE). According to de Vaux, the buildings damaged by the earthquake and fire were not repaired immediately. Because the water system ceased to be maintained, the site was flooded and silt accumulated to a depth of 75 cm. The silt overlay the layer of ash from the fire, indicating that the period of abandonment was subsequent to the fire.

Following the abandonment the site was cleared and reoccupied. Some of the damaged structures in the settlement were strengthened while others were abandoned. The tower was reinforced by the addition of a sloping stone rampart or glacis. The dishes in the pantry (L86), which had fallen and broken in the earthquake, were left lying on the floor at the back of the room. A row of wooden posts on plastered mud brick bases was erected to support the ceiling at the eastern end of L77, and the dining room was now moved to the second-story level of this room.

After the earthquake the pool that had been split (L48–L50) and a toilet in the adjacent room (L51) went out of use. In the secondary building, the eastern wall of open-air courtyard L111 was doubled in thickness and the courtyard was now roofed over. A staircase installed in L113 led to a dining room on the west side of the secondary building (above L111, L120–L123). Workshops, ovens, and silos were installed in many of the rooms in the secondary building in Period II.

De Vaux identified a large room in the center of the main building (L30) as a "scriptorium." The debris of the second-story level yielded long, narrow, mud brick tables and a bench covered with plaster, as well as a plastered platform and inkwells.

A cemetery containing about 1,100 graves is located 50 m to the east of the site. The graves, which are marked by heaps of stones, are arranged in rows along the top of the marl plateau and on hills to the north and east. The bodies were placed in a loculus or niche at the bottom of a rectangular trench. In all but one of the burials the feet of the deceased are oriented to the north and the head faces south. Other graves located on hills to the south do not have the same regular alignment. Of the forty-three graves that de Vaux excavated on the plateau and on hills to the north and east, all but three contained adult male burials (the three exceptions are adult females). Graves on hills to the south that included large numbers of women and children have been identified as Bedouin burials.

The sectarian settlement at Qumran came to an end with a violent destruction by fire, apparently at the hands of the Roman army at the time of the First Jewish Revolt (68 CE).

5. Period III

Following the destruction in 68 CE, the main building was occupied by a small garrison of Roman soldiers, apparently until the fall of MASADA in 73 or 74 CE.

C. A Revised Chronology for Qumran

The fact that Period Ia yielded no coins and only a few potsherds that are indistinguishable from those of Period Ib suggests that de Vaux's Period Ia might not exist. Instead, most of the architectural remains attributed to Period Ia could belong to Period Ib. If de Vaux's Period Ia does exist, the currently available evidence suggests that it should be dated to the early 1st cent. BCE instead of ca. 130–100 BCE.

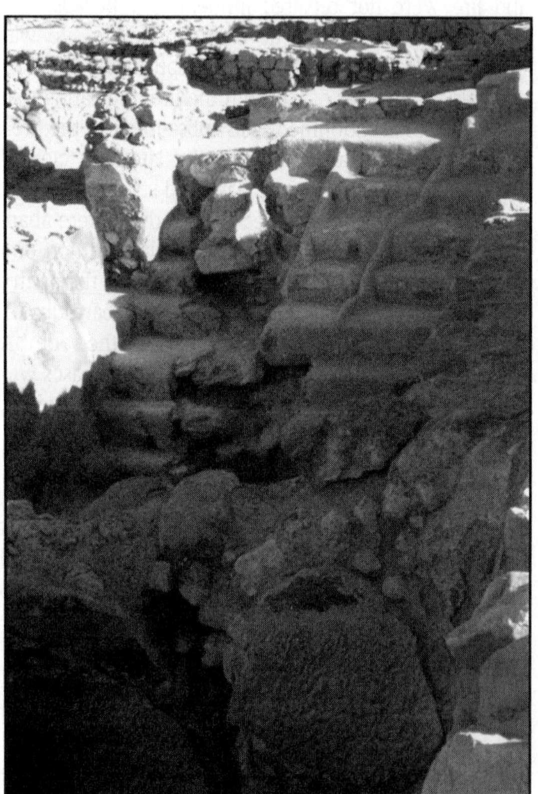

Jodi Magness

Figure 2: Qumran miqveh

According to de Vaux, Qumran lay in ruins and was unoccupied for about thirty years after the earthquake of 31 BCE. This period of abandonment ended when the site was reoccupied ca. 4–1 BCE. However, attributing the burial of a hoard of silver Tyrian tetradrachmas found in L120 to the end of Period Ib instead of the beginning of Period II (as de Vaux suggested) means that the site was not abandoned after the earthquake of 31 BCE. The inhabitants immediately repaired or strengthened many of the damaged buildings but did not bother to clear those beyond repair.

The settlement of Period Ib continued without interruption until 9/8 BCE or some time thereafter, when Qumran suffered a deliberate, violent destruction by fire, as indicated by the layer of ash that de Vaux associated with the earthquake. The site was reoccupied early in the reign of Herod Archelaus in 4 BCE or shortly afterward. Perhaps the destruction is connected with the turmoil that erupted in Judea after the death of Herod the Great in 4 BCE.

D. The Nature of the Qumran Community

The Qumran community probably consisted of about 150–200 members, although the number could have fluctuated. Most of the members of the community apparently lived outside the settlement, in tents, huts, and some of the caves. The rooms inside the settlement seem to have been used for communal purposes: dining rooms, assembly rooms, kitchens, workshops, and industrial installations.

Archaeological and literary evidence indicates that Qumran was inhabited by the same Jewish sect that deposited the scrolls in the nearby caves. Many scholars identify this community with the ESSENES mentioned in ancient historical sources (Flavius Josephus, PHILO OF ALEXANDRIA, and PLINY the Elder).

The sectarian lifestyle finds physical expression in the archaeological remains at Qumran. The large number (ten) and large sizes of the ritual baths (**miqwah** מִקְוָה; **miqweh** מִקְוֶה; *see* MIQVAH, MIQVEH) were necessary for the maintenance of the high level of ritual purity required of members. The communal meals of the sect took place in two dining rooms.

Bones deposited under potsherds outside the dining rooms apparently represent the remains of animals consumed at the communal meals, and perhaps reflect the sectarian belief that these meals were a substitute for participation in the temple sacrifices. The large number of dishes found in pantries adjacent to the two dining rooms should be understood in light of the sectarian belief that impurity could be transmitted through food and drink (*see* CLEAN AND UNCLEAN). For this reason the sectarians were served individual portions instead of dining from common dishes, as was customary in the Greco-Roman world. The sectarian concern with the transmission of impurity also explains the presence of a potters' workshop at Qumran, which enabled the community to ensure the purity of the pottery by manufacturing it themselves.

Recently proposed theories that interpret Qumran not as a sectarian settlement but as something else (e.g., villa, manor house, commercial entrepot, fort, pottery manufacturing center) divorce the scrolls from the site of Qumran; in other words, advocates of these theories argue that the inhabitants of Qumran did not use and deposit the scrolls in the nearby caves. This argument is disproved by archaeology, as the same types of pottery, some of which are distinctive to Qumran, are found in both the scroll caves and in the settlement. Furthermore, all of the alternative theories create more problems than they solve in terms of understanding the archaeological evidence. For example, if Qumran was not a sectarian settlement, how do we account for the large number of ritual baths (and their large sizes), the animal bone deposits, and the large adjacent cemetery? These features and others are best understood in light of the sectarian community's lifestyle, halakhah, and purity concerns. De Vaux's description of Qumran as a sectarian community center is still the most convincing. *See* ESCHATOLOGY IN EARLY JUDAISM; ETHICS IN THE NONCANONICAL JEWISH WRITINGS; MANUSCRIPTS FROM THE JUDEAN DESERT; RIGHTEOUSNESS IN EARLY JEWISH LITERATURE; SECTS, SECTARIANS.

Bibliography: Katharina Galor, Jean-Baptiste Humbert, and Jürgen Zangenberg, eds. *Qumran, the Site of the Dead Sea Scrolls: Archaeological Interpretations and Debates, Proceedings of a Conference Held at Brown University, November 17–19, 2002* (2006); Jean-Baptiste Humbert and Alain Chambon. *Fouilles de Khirbet Qumrân et de Aïn Feshkha I* (1994); Jean-Baptiste Humbert and Jan Gunneweg, eds. *Khirbet Qumrân et `Aïn Feskha II* (2003); Jodi Magness. *The Archaeology of Qumran and the Dead Sea Scrolls* (2002); Jodi Magness. *Debating Qumran: Collected Essays on Its Archaeology* (2004); Jodi Magness. "Qumran: The Site of the Dead Sea Scrolls: A Review Article." *RevQ* 88 (2007) 641–64; Roland de Vaux. *Archaeology and the Dead Sea Scrolls* (1973); Roland de Vaux. "Archéologie." *Les 'Petites Grottes' de Qumrân* (1962) 1–36; Roland de Vaux. "Fouille au Khirbet Qumrân, Rapport préliminaire." *RB* 60 (1953) 83–106; Roland de Vaux. "Fouilles au Khirbet Qumrân, Rapport préliminaire sur la deuxième campagne." *RB* 61 (1954) 206–36; Roland de Vaux. "Fouilles de Feshkha." *RB* 66 (1959) 225–55; Roland de Vaux. "Fouilles de Khirbet Qumrân, Rapport préliminaire sur les 3e, 4e, et 5e campagnes." *RB* 63 (1956) 533–77.

JODI MAGNESS

QUMRAN SCROLLS. *See* DEAD SEA SCROLLS.

QUMRAN, KHIRBET. *See* QUMRAN.

QUOTATIONS. There are numerous links between the various books of the Bible. These links can be described in a variety of ways, but one form is the quotation. A quotation is when the reader is particularly directed to the source by either a specific formula ("It is written"; "It is said") or by other syntactical clues such as "so that" or "therefore." In the OT, there are references to a *Book of Jashar* (Josh 10:13; *see* JASHAR, BOOK OF) and a *Book of the Wars of the Lord* (Num 21:14; *see* WARS OF THE LORD, BOOK OF), but it is the NT's use of the OT (which its authors would have regarded simply as "Scripture") where quotations occur in abundance. There are over 300 quotations in the NT, an average of more than one per chapter. They are particularly frequent in Romans (sixty), Matthew (fifty-four), Acts (forty), and Hebrews (thirty-seven), and taking into account their smaller size, also in 1 Peter (twelve in five chapters) and Galatians (ten in six chapters). There are some books where there are no explicit quotations (1–2 Thessalonians; 1–2–3 John; Revelation), though they are not devoid of allusions and echoes (e.g., the reference to Cain in 1 John 3:12). Revelation is particularly interesting in that there are no explicit quotations but over 200 allusions where the reference is unmistakable (e.g., Rev 2:26-27, alluding to Ps 2:8-9).

The books most frequently quoted in the NT (Psalms, Isaiah, Deuteronomy) are also the books most frequently quoted in the DEAD SEA SCROLLS, including some of the same verses (Gen 1:27; Deut 18:15; 2 Sam 7:14; Isa 61:1; Amos 9:11). This shows that the NT authors did not operate in a vacuum but were part of an interpretive tradition. For example, it was common practice to interpret one text in the light of another by means of a common word. We see this in the NT when both Paul and 1 Peter bring together a number of "stone" texts from the OT (Rom 9:33; 1 Pet 2:6-8) and when Paul relates Gen 15:6 ("it was reckoned to him as righteousness"; Rom 4:3) to Ps 32:1-2 ("Blessed is the one against whom the Lord will not reckon sin"; Rom 4:7-8). Indeed, it may be that some texts are quoted precisely because they were being used by rival groups (e.g., Lev 18:5). Though the 300 or more NT quotations are drawn from twenty-four of the OT books, over half of them come from certain well-known sections (Gen 12–22; Exod 3; 20; Lev 19; Deut 5–9; 29–32; Pss 2; 8; 16; 22; 69; 110; 118; Isa 6–8; 40–66; Jer 31; Zech 8–13).

When NT quotations are compared with the OT texts, we often notice discrepancies between them. There are several reasons for this. The first is that the OT section of an English Bible is based on the Hebrew text, whereas the NT writers generally quoted from its Greek translation (known as the SEPTUAGINT, abbreviated LXX). Since the two languages have very different structures, it is quite rare for them to result in identical English translations. Second, it was often necessary to adjust the precise wording of the quotation to fit the new context. This was often stylistic (just as a modern Bible uses modern language) but was sometimes deliberate (Acts 7:43 says "I will remove you beyond Babylon," but Amos 5:27 was referring to the northern exile: "I will take you into exile beyond Damascus"). Third, there was no single text called the LXX that was the same in every city or library. Individual books circulated independently and had their own character (e.g., the chapters in Jeremiah are in a different order in the Hebrew than in the Greek text). This could be because they were based on different Hebrew texts (we know that different texts existed from the Dead Sea Scrolls) or that they were faulty translations (the Hebrew text consisted only of consonants and was sometimes ambiguous). As a result, there were attempts to revise some of the LXX books and it may be that the NT authors used some of these texts. A fourth explanation is that, in many cases, texts were probably quoted from memory (Paul hardly took dozens of scrolls on his journeys), leaving open the possibility of differences between the written source texts and the remembered texts.

Finally, quotations are used in a variety of ways in the NT. Matthew's use is often called "christological" or "messianic," since he seeks to show how the ancient prophecies have been fulfilled in Jesus (e.g., Matt 1:23; 2:6, 15, 18). This is not his only use, however. Scripture can be quoted as instruction (Ten Commandments), illustration (Jonah), and prediction (Daniel). Paul applies Scripture to a range of issues facing the early church (in a manner sometimes called "ecclesiological"), notably the inclusion of Gentiles (Rom 9–11) and the importance of faith (Rom 4; Gal 3). Stephen's speech in Acts 7 recounts Israel's history (of rebellion), while Heb 11 recounts Israel's heroes of faith. A major debate in scholarship is whether the first hearers and readers of the NT documents would have understood the quotations in the light of their original contexts or more atomistically (as the author of Hebrews says on one occasion, "But someone has testified somewhere" [Heb 2:6]). Studies of literacy in the 1st cent. CE would suggest not, but other scholars argue that new converts would have undergone rigorous catechetical instruction. *See* NEW TESTAMENT, OT QUOTATIONS IN THE.

Bibliography: Richard B. Hays. *Echoes of Scripture in the Letters of Paul* (1989); Steve Moyise. *The Old Testament in the New* (2001); Stanley E. Porter. *Hearing the Old Testament in the New Testament* (2006); Christopher D. Stanley. *Arguing with Scripture* (2004).

STEVE MOYISE

QURAN. The Qur'an (sometimes spelled Koran) is the sacred text of Islam, which is believed by Muslims to be the perfectly preserved word of God. According to the Islamic sources, sometime around the age of forty the Prophet Muhammad (570–632 CE) received the first of a series of revelations through the angel Gabriel that continued intermittently throughout the remaining twenty-two years of his life. The Qur'an, which means "recitation" in Arabic, is the record of those revelations. It takes its name from the opening word of chap. 96 (iqraʾ, "Recite!"), which is generally held to be the first part of the text to be revealed.

Erich Lessing / Art Resource, NY

Figure 1: Qur'an manuscript, 13th cent. Sura 176. Ben Yussuf Library, Marrakesh, Morocco.

The 114 suras (chapters) of the Qur'an vary in length and total just over 6,000 verses. Each has a title that is derived from a word or name found within it. In some cases this is an important figure or central theme present in the sura, and in others it is an obscure term appearing only once. Examples of these titles include "The Cow," "Women," "The Table," "Abraham," "Mary," "The Spider," "Divorce," and "The Disaster." Muslims refer to the suras by these titles, while it is more common for non-Muslims to use a numbering system as a way of identifying the suras. According to that system, the suras listed above by their names are known as suras 2, 4, 5, 14, 19, 29, 65, and 101. Every sura but 9 ("Repentance") begins with the words "In the name of God, the merciful and compassionate." This superscription is missing from sura 9, probably because it was originally part of sura 8 before being split off from it.

The organizing principle of the Qur'an is length, not chronology. This is seen in the fact, noted above, that the oldest material in the text is believed to be found in sura 96. While no hard and fast rule is strictly followed, the relative length of the suras appears to be a factor in their order and arrangement. After a brief introductory chapter (al-fatiha, "The Opening"), the lengthiest chapters follow, and they get progressively shorter until the end of the book. The longest chapter is 2 ("The Cow"), which contains 282 verses, while the shortest is sura 108 ("The Abundance"), with only three verses.

In most editions of the Qur'an each sura is designated as either "Meccan" or "Medinan." This is a distinction based upon the hijrah ("migration") of Muhammad. In order to escape the persecution they were experiencing in Mecca because of their beliefs, Muhammad and a small group of his followers moved to Medina, a city some 250 mi. to the north. This relocation, which occurred in 622 CE, ensured the survival of the nascent Muslim community, and its importance is seen in that it was chosen as the starting point of the Islamic calendar, which operates on a lunar system and is now in the first half of its 15th cent. Those suras revealed prior to the migration are referred to as Meccan, while those received after it are Medinan. There are ninety suras from the Meccan period and twenty-four from the Medinan period. These designations, which are not found in the oldest copies of the Qur'an, have been the subject of debate among scholars, with some calling for subcategories under the two main headings like Early Meccan and Late Medinan. The two groups of suras are easily distinguishable by length and content. Generally speaking, the Meccan suras tend to be briefer sections that contain warnings about the dangers of polytheism and that urge the listener to embrace worship of the one true God. The Medinan suras are lengthier and focus more on issues concerning communal life and how to coexist with non-Muslims. Given the length-based organizing principle mentioned above, this means most of the earlier Meccan suras are found later in the Qur'an. Therefore, if one wishes to get a sense of the likely original chronology of the material the suras should be read in reverse order.

Muslims consider only the Arabic text to be the authentic Qur'an, with translations into other languages being interpretations of the original. The Arabic is distinguished by its poetry, the most characteristic feature of which is rhyme. This underscores the fact that, as its name suggests, the Qur'an is a text that is meant to be recited out loud rather than read quietly. The history of the use of the text, including the high status enjoyed by those who are professionally trained to recite it and the presence of radio stations that broadcast it throughout the day, testifies to this.

Those familiar with the Bible often find reading the Qur'an to be a strange or confusing experience. Unlike many portions of the biblical text, the Islamic one does not have an overarching story or follow a clear chronological order. It is a blend of narratives, teachings, warnings, and guidelines that can strike the uninitiated reader as being random or haphazard. In fact, many scholars have argued that the text possesses an internal logic and coherence based on principles and elements different from those commonly associated with the biblical literature. A further aspect that complicates things for the Bible reader is the presence of biblical characters and stories in the Qur'an. In these parallels, biblical traditions and figures are presented in ways that support and reflect the Islamic literary context in which they are situated.

The Qur'an originally circulated orally, although portions of it were written down while Muhammad was still alive. After his death it was committed to writing, and the traditional Muslim view holds that its present canonical form dates from the time of Muhammad's third successor, the Caliph Uthman (r. 644–56 CE). As the first Arabic literary text, the Qur'an has been studied intensely since the earliest decades of Islam, with particular attention paid to matters of lexicography, grammar, and meaning. *See* ISLAM; PORTRAYALS OF BIBLICAL FIGURES IN ISLAMIC TRADITION; PORTRAYALS OF ISHMAEL IN ISLAMIC TRADITION.

Bibliography: John Kaltner. *Ishmael Instructs Isaac: An Introduction to the Qur'an for Bible Readers* (1999).

JOHN KALTNER

Rr

RA. *See* RE.

RAAMAH ray'uh-mah [רַעְמָא raʿemaʾ, רַעְמָה raʿemah; Ῥαγμά Rhagma, Ῥεγμά Rhegma]. 1. Raamah has traditionally been identified as one of the descendants of Cush and the father of SHEBA and DEDAN (Gen 10:7; 1 Chr 1:9; *see* CUSH, CUSHITE).

2. The town Raamah has become loosely identified with the southern Arabian peninsula. In Ezek 27:22 traders from Sheba and Raamah are said to have traded with TYRE in precious stones and gold. If the LXX reading of Rhagma for Raamah (Ezek 27:22) is correct, then the oasis of Nagran could possibly be identified with Raamah. In Hebrew, raʿemaʾ means "thunder," and in ancient sources it is noted that Nagran was known as the city of thunder.

JOSEPH R. CATHEY

RAAMIAH. *See* REELAIAH.

RAAMSES ray-am'seez [רַעַמְסֵס raʿamses]. The name of a city in the eastern delta of Egypt on the Pelusiac branch of the Nile. The name is taken from the Egyptian pr-rʿ-ms-sw, which means "The House of (Pharaoh) RAMESSES." The town name is often transcribed as Pi-Raamses to avoid confusion with the name of the PHARAOH. In the book of Genesis, Raamses is listed as the region where the descendants of Jacob settled in the land of EGYPT during the famine in Canaan (Gen 47:11; NRSV, "Rameses"). Although no region called "Raamses" is known from Egyptian records, this text probably is to be understood as referring to the region around the city of Raamses. According to Exod 1:11, the Egyptians later enslaved the Hebrews and made them build Raamses and Pithom as storage cities. It is subsequently mentioned as the starting point for the exodus (Exod 12:37; Num 33:3, 5).

Raamses is identified with Qantir, the delta residence of the pharaohs of the Nineteenth and Twentieth Dynasties. The site is 2 km northeast of Tell el-Dabʾa, the capital of the HYKSOS during the preceding Second Intermediate Period. Building of Pi-Raamses was begun under Seti I, although most of the construction at the site was done under his son Raamses II, from whom the city takes its name. PITHOM (Exod 1:11), which the Bible associates with Raamses, may not have been a city at all. Its name means "The House of Atum," which some scholars theorize may have been a temple in Pi-Raamses. Although one of the most impressive cities in Egypt during the Nineteenth and Twentieth Dynasties, Pi-Raamses was abandoned after the New Kingdom, possibly due to a change in the course of the Pelusiac branch of the Nile River.

Identification of Pi-Raamses was made difficult by the fact that the city had been dismantled by the pharaohs of the Twenty-First and Twenty-Second Dynasties and reused as building material for other cities, particularly Bubastis and Tanis. Because the reused blocks of stone, as well as the stelae and statues, still bore inscriptions of Raamses II, these sites were early on identified as candidates for the site of Pi-Raamses. Excavations at Qantir that began in 1929 led to its identification as Pi-Raamses, an identification that is widely accepted today.

Papyrus Leiden 348 states that ʿApiru were used in the building of the temple in Pi-Raamses. The ʿApiru were a class of people well known from Late Bronze Age documents in both Canaan and Egypt. Due to the similarity of the words *ʿApiru* and *Hebrew*, this text has often been taken as secondary confirmation of the biblical account of the exodus. More recent studies have pointed out difficulties in the identification of *ʿApiru* with *Hebrew*, and scholars are now much less inclined to accept this theory (*see* HABIRU, HAPIRU). But the fact that the previous capital of the Hyksos was located to the southwest makes it likely that Semites were still living in the area during the Nineteenth and Twentieth Dynasties.

Bibliography: Manfred Bietak. *Avaris and Piramesse: Archaeological Exploration in the Eastern Nile Delta* (1979); Donald B. Redford. "An Egyptian Perspective on the Exodus Narrative." *Egypt, Israel, and Sinai* (1987) 137–61.

KEVIN A. WILSON

RABAH, WADI. In 1952, archaeological excavations led by Jacob Kaplan in the Wadi Rabah, a tributary of the YARKON RIVER, about a kilometer east of biblical APHEK, exposed a Chalcolithic structure that overlay an earlier building associated with distinctive pottery and stone tools. Kaplan originally placed this new phase at the beginning of the Chalcolithic period, but it is now widely accepted that it more properly occupies a later part of the Pottery Neolithic period, the earlier half of the 6th millennium BCE. Typical for the pottery of this phase is "Dark Faced Burnished Ware," exemplified in small, thin bowls, well-fired and with shiny red or black burnishing, although there is a broad range of decorative techniques and a wide array of forms. Sickle blades are characteristic of the stone tool inventory (blade sections backed and truncated on both ends). Arrowheads were extremely rare.

Bibliography: Avi Gopher and Ram Gophna. "Cultures of the Eighth and Seventh Millennia BP in the Southern Levant: A Review for the 1990s." *Journal of World Prehistory* 7(3) (1993) 297–353; Jacob Kaplan. "Excavations at Wadi Rabah." *IEJ* 8 (1958) 149–60.

GARY O. ROLLEFSON

RABBAH rab´uh [רַבָּה rabbah, רַבַּת בְּנֵי עַמּוֹן **rabbath bene ʿammon**]. 1. "Rabbah of the Ammonites" (Deut 3:11; 2 Sam 12:26; 17:27; Jer 49:2; Ezek 21:20) is to be distinguished from the Rabbah of Josh 15:60, a border town in the tenth district of Judah. Rabbah of the Ammonites is identified with the ancient citadel (Jebel al-Qalʿah) in the heart of the modern city of Amman, the capital of the Hashemite Kingdom of Jordan. Josephus refers to **Arabatha** (᾿Αραβαθά) and **Rabathas** (῾Ραβαθᾶς) in his *Ant.* (7.129, 160). Under the influence of Hellenization the city's name was changed to Philadelphia.

Sitting at 2,700 ft. above sea level, Rabbah—Amman—is located approximately 40 mi. east-northeast of Jerusalem, about 24 mi. east of the Jordan River and 23 mi. northeast of the Dead Sea. Damascus is situated north-northeast approximately 110 mi. The western edge of the 600-mi.-wide desert separating Amman and Bagdad lies only 10–15 mi. east of Amman.

The biblical history of the site begins with its association with Og, king of Bashan, the last of the Rephaim, whose iron "bed" was noted for its size (Deut 3:11). It is next mentioned in the context of the summary of the tribal territory of the Gadites who settled on the east side of the Jordan (Josh 13:24-28). The NRSV reads, "Aroer which is east of Rabbah" (Josh 13:25) but more accurately should read "Aroer, which is before the face of Rabbah" (**ʿal-pene rabbah** עַל־פְּנֵי רַבָּה); Aroer is well south of Amman. Rabbah is perhaps best known in the OT as the geographical setting for the Ammonite War Narrative (2 Sam 10–12)—the larger narrative event by which the David/Bathsheba/Uriah incident (2 Sam 11:1–12:25) is framed. The narrator reports that Joab "captured the royal city" (2 Sam 12:26); Joab's report to David was that he had "captured the city of water" (2 Sam 12:27). Joab's apparent reference seems to have derived from Rabbah's control of a fortified water source in the headwaters of the Wadi Amman, a tributary of the Wadi Jabbok. It appears that the subduing of Rabbah by David (compare 2 Sam 12:29-31; see also 1 Chr 20:2-3) brought the city and the entire Ammonite domain under Israelite control. In spite of the Davidic domination of the Ammonites, in the run-up to the conclusion to Absalom's rebellion against David, it was an Ammonite of Rabbah—Shobi, son of Nahash—along with two other companions who provided David and his entourage with needed supplies (2 Sam 17:27-29).

Subsequent to the division of the Israelite monarchy, Rabbah regained independence and achieved relative prominence. The remaining biblical texts in which Rabbah is referenced are prophetic texts in which judgment is anticipated for the city. The mid-8th cent. Amos oracle (1:13-15) anticipates destruction of the city and exile of its king because of an Ammonite attempt to enlarge its territory at the expense of the pregnant women of Gilead. Likewise, Jeremiah's late 7th-cent. oracle against the Ammonites (Jer 49) anticipates the desolation of Rabbah (Jer 49:2) and the exile of the Ammonite deity Milcom, his priests, and his attendants (Jer 49:3). Interestingly, the late 7th–early 6th cent. Rabbah is anticipated as factoring into an option laid before the king of Babylon; he would come to a "fork in the road," at which point he would have to decide, through divination, whether to take the road to Rabbah of Ammon or to Judah and Jerusalem (Ezek 21:18-27). It seems he opted in the direction of Jerusalem. Ezekiel's oracles against nations, like those of Amos and Jeremiah, include an oracle against the Ammonites, in which Rabbah is anticipated as being turned into a "pasture for camels" (Ezek 25:5).

While the biblical data seem to attest to the continual occupation of Rabbah from at least the time of Og through the OT period and beyond, archaeological work at the citadel points toward occupation dating to the Neolithic Era (8000 BCE); the excavations at ʿAin Ghazal point to substantial settlement reaching back as far as the prehistoric era. Various 20th-cent. archaeological surveys of the area reported the presence of dolmens, which have subsequently disappeared or been destroyed. These same surveys yielded surface (unstratified) pottery of Early Bronze (2900–2200 BCE) vintage.

Bronze Age (2200–1550 BCE) tombs that yielded a small collection of cylinder seals were discovered in excavations on the citadel; also the remnants of a glacis dating to this period have been encountered in examination of Jebel al-Qalʿah.

The Amman Airport structure offers one of the very tangible evidences of Late Bronze Age (1550–1200 BCE) culture at Rabbah. Nearly 15 m square, this structure featured exterior walls 2 m thick. The initial interpretation of the structure as a temple has been more recently questioned. In addition to the impressive wall system, two other features of the structure are noteworthy. Among the ceramic remains associated with the building were found generous amounts of imported Cypriot and Mycenaean forms and wares; this was a major influencing factor in dating the building to 1300–1200 BCE. Furthermore, a significant amount of burnt human bones was discovered in the excavation; it is this feature that has led to the suggestion that the building served some sort of funerary function.

Subsequent to the Ammonite War (2 Sam 10–12) Rabbah came under Israelite suzerainty—a status that seems to have continued until the division of the Israelite monarchy at the end of the Solomonic era. The Ammonite kingdom and capital seems to have flourished under Assyrian suzerainty (mid-9th–mid-7th cent. BCE) and the ensuing Babylonian control. Iron Age occupation is particularly well attested. Two specific inscriptional artifacts give witness to Ammonite history and culture in and around Rabbah during this era. The first, the Amman Citadel Inscription, discovered on Jebel al-Qalʿah in 1961, is a generally rectangular-shaped piece of white limestone on which eight lines of text were found. The beginning and end of each line were lost and some letters were chipped out, but enough text remains to clarify the genre of the text as that associated with the construction—perhaps dedication—of a structure of some sort. On the basis of paleographic evidence, the text has been dated to the mid-9th cent. BCE. The second, the Siran Bottle Inscription, was discovered at Tal Siran, now part of the campus of the University of Jordan, in 1972. The bottle was made of bronze; the inscription is eight lines in length and is completely readable. Among the many contributions of this textual artifact is the particular value that this text makes in identifying three Ammonite kings of the 7th cent. BCE. A third item of interest is the 9th-cent. BCE Yarah-Azar figure rendered in limestone—a small statuette (.45 m in height) of an Ammonite official. The figure's base bears a badly worn inscription, which seems to identify the figure as one "Yarah-Azar" (*ANEP*, fig. 64). Tombs, rich with a variety of artifacts, have been dated to around 800 BCE; finds included ceramic assemblages, small jewelry items, and a few figurines.

Relatively little Persian material associated with the citadel has come to light, although the nearby Tobiad caves, northwest of Amman, should not go unmentioned.

Rabbah came under the influence of Hellenization and its name was changed to "Philadelphia" under the rule of Ptolemy II Philadelphus in the 3rd cent. BCE; he both rebuilt the city and incorporated it into the province of Syria. In 218 BCE the Seleucid king Antiochus took the city, but did not achieve real control of the city until early in the 2nd cent. BCE.

In 63 BCE Philadelphia was made a part of the Decapolis as the southernmost of the cities; this resulted in the city being made the focus of extensive building efforts. Remains of this concentrated construction initiative are still very evident in the form of the amphitheater at the foot of the citadel, along with other structures such as the nymphaeum, the odium, and the Temple of Hercules, which cuts an impressive profile on the citadel. Other Roman remnants include portions of a colonnaded street and several tombs. Its status as a city of the Decapolis was enhanced by its location on a major trade route established under the rule of Trajan—a route that extended from the Gulf of Aqabah in the south to Damascus in the north. Under Trajan Philadelphia was also made a part of the province of Arabia. A series of tower-like structures that were found to surround Amman were initially identified as Iron Age defense towers ringing the city. Several of these towers have been dated, by excavation, to the Roman era and seem to have served as farmsteads rather than watchtowers.

Philadelphia was made the seat of a bishopric toward the end of the 4th cent. CE, subsequent to Constantine's declaration of Christianity as the religion of the empire. Records indicate that the bishop of Philadelphia attended the Council of Nicea (325 CE), the Synod of Antioch (341 CE), and the Council of Chalcedon (451 CE). During the 4th–7th cent. numerous early Christian churches were constructed in the vicinity, including one on the citadel. Evidence suggests that the city declined somewhat toward the end of the 7th cent.

The city came under Arab control in 635 CE in conjunction with the transition to Arab domination during the second half of the 7th cent., at which time the city was renamed "Amman," its current name. An Umayyad mosque and palace have come to light on Jebel al-Qalʿah, attesting to the Arab control of the city. Under Arab rule the region from the Arnon to the Jabbok became known as the "Belqa" region, of which Amman was the most prominent city. During the extended period from the late 6th cent. to the 19th cent. the city gradually slipped into decline, a situation that was contributed to by shifting trade patterns, a series of earthquakes, and general neglect.

Under the control of the Turkish Ottomans the fortunes of Amman began to change and eventually it became the capital of the Emirate of Transjordan under the British Mandate. From about 1975 to the present the population of the city has grown from 250,000 to nearly 3 million. The Amman Museum is presently and appropriately located on the citadel.

Bibliography: William W. Hallo and K. Lawson Younger Jr. *The Context of Scripture Volume Two: Monumental Inscriptions from the Biblical World* (2001); Larry Herr, ed. *The Amman Airport Excavations, AASOR 47–48* (1983); James B. Pritchard. *The Ancient Near East in Pictures Relating to the Old Testament.* 2nd ed. (1969).

JOHN I. LAWLOR

2. A town in the hill country of Judah named in a list of towns allotted to the tribe of Judah (Josh 15:60). It is listed after KIRIATH-JEARIM, indicating that the towns were in close proximity to each another. The exact location of Rabbah is not known, although some suggest that it is the town of Rubutu mentioned in the AMARNA LETTERS.

DEREK E. WITTMAN

RABBI, RABBONI rab'*i*, ra-boh'*ni* [ῥαββί **rhabbi**, ῥαββουνί **rhabbouni**]. Throughout RABBINIC LITERATURE, *rabbi* means "master" and "teacher of disciples." As such, a rabbi serves as a metaphoric "father." These meanings are still in use in the modern era. *Rabbi* derives from the Hebrew term **rav** (רַב), meaning "mighty," "great," or "numerous." In its construct form, **rav** serves as a title to designate the chief of a group of officers. In the OT, it occurs most frequently as **rav-thabbakhim** (רַב־תַבָּחִים), "captain of the guard" (2 Kgs 25:8, 10, 11, 20; Jer 39:9; 40:2, 5; 52:14, 19). Occurring less frequently is the construct **rav-saris** (רַב־סָרִיס), meaning "chief eunuch," "chief of officers," or "palace master" (Dan 1:3; rendered Rabsaris in 2 Kgs 18:17) in the NRSV. In Esth 1:8, **rav-beyitho** (רַב־בֵּיתוֹ) is rendered "palace official" and in Jonah 1:6, **rav hakhovel** (רַב הַחֹבֵל) is the ship's captain.

In the NT **rav** is transliterated into Greek as **rhabbi** or **rhabbouni** (Mark 10:51; John 20:16). The term **rhabbi** is glossed as "teacher" (**didaskalos** διδάσκαλος) in Matt 23:8 and John 1:38, and becomes "**rhabbouni**" in John 20:16. The term *rabbi* is transliterated frequently in Mark, Matthew, and John but is absent in Luke. In almost every NT citation, the term *rabbi* refers to Jesus. Even assuming a late 1st-cent. CE date for the Gospels, these passages are among the earliest uses of *rabbi* to mean "teacher" or "master of disciples." It is likely that the term is used anachronistically in the NT (that is, it was applied as a title for Jesus retrospectively) and only came into vogue after 70 CE.

In the earliest layers of rabbinic literature (*see* MEKILTA; MISHNAH; SAYINGS OF THE FATHERS; SIFRA, SIFRE), the term *rabbi* most often means "teacher" (although it can refer to the master of a slave; *m. Pesah.* 8:1–2) and also is used anachronistically to refer to biblical characters such as Moses and Elijah (*t. Sotah* 4:7). Most proto-rabbinic characters who lived before 70 CE are referred to in rabbinic literature with other titles, such as "elder" or "father." The title "elder" (**zaqen** זָקֵן) was given to Hillel the Elder (*m. Shev.* 10.3), Shammai (*m. Or.* 2:8), and GAMALIEL (*m. Or.* 2:12; *see* HILLEL THE ELDER, HOUSE OF HILLEL; SHAMMAI THE ELDER). The title "father" (**'av** אָב) was given to Abba Saul (*m. Avot* 2:8; compare Matt 23:8-9, which uses three terms: *rabbi* [**rhabbi**], *teacher* [**didaskalos**], and *father* [**patēr** πατήρ]).

In the 2nd and 3rd cent. CE, archaeological evidence shows the term used as an honorific title for a teacher or communal leader. The burial inscriptions in the catacombs of Beth-Shearim refer to rabbis and perhaps their disciples. The term *rabbi* regularly appears there, as does the term **berebbi** (בֵּירְבִּי), which may mean a disciple of or a son of a rabbi (from **beth rabbi** [בֵּית רַבִּי], "of the rabbi's house or school"). A lintel discovered in Galilee refers to the "academy of" (**beth midhrasho** בֵּית מִדְרָשׁוֹ) Rabbi Eliezer Hakappar (ca. the end of the 2nd cent. CE). It is possible that this academy was named for the rabbi after his death.

Other forms of the term *rabbi* were also used. In addition to *rabboni* (**rhabbouni**) in John 20:16, the term *rabban* (**rabban** רַבָּן), "our master," in early rabbinic literature (again anachronistically) refers to the Jewish patriarch or "prince" (**nasi'** נָשִׂיא). Descendants of Gamaliel the Elder through his descendant Judah the Prince (editor of the Mishnah, ca. 200 CE) are afforded the title "Rabban" (*see* JUDAH THE PRINCE, RABBI). In many rabbinic texts YOHANAN BEN ZAKKAI is also called "Rabban."

By the 3rd cent. CE, rabbinic Judaism had spread among Babylonian Jews. There the term was shortened to its biblical Hebrew origin, and rabbis from Iraq were called Rav (**rav**). The political head of that Jewish community was given the honorific title "Rabbana" (**rabban'a** רַבָּנָא), "our master." In a still later era, the heads of the Gaonic academies (ca. 500–1000 CE) in Palestine, Babylonia, and North Africa were honored with the title "Rebbenu" (**rabbenu** רַבֵּינוּ), "our master." A brief history of the various uses of the title *rabbi* is recounted in the *Epistle of Rab Sherira Gaon of Pumbedita* (ca. 906–1006 CE). *See* TEACHER.

Bibliography: Lee Levine. *The Rabbinic Class of Roman Palestine in Late Antiquity* (1989).

BURTON L. VISOTZKY

RABBINIC INTERPRETATION ruh-bin'ik. Rabbinic interpretation of Scripture is the preeminent form of Jewish biblical exegesis (*see* BIBLICAL INTERPRETATION, HISTORY OF; JEWISH BIBLICAL INTERPRETATION). The earliest rabbinic readings of the Bible often mimicked modes of interpretation found within the biblical text. These exegeses sought to understand difficult words, expand the purview of the law where it was not explicit, and to fill in gaps in the biblical narrative. Early rabbinic interpretation of Scripture also explicated verses of the Bible by means of other verses.

Following the destruction of the Second Temple in 70 CE, the first generations of rabbis, the Tannaim (*see* TANNA, TANNAIM), divided into two distinctive "schools" of thought on the interpretation of the Bible. The school of Rabbi Ishmael (*see* ISHMAEL, RABBI) tended to read more literally, attempting to understand the plain meaning of the text. Rabbi Ishmael's hermeneutic principle was that Torah is expressed in normative human discourse. The opposing school of Rabbi Akiva (*see* AKIVA, RABBI) tended to read the Bible more as a code that needed to be solved. This inclined Akivan-style exegesis more to allegory and hyper-interpretation, reading the superfluities of Scripture as indicative of new meanings, often unrelated to the biblical context. The Akivan school in particular ignored the broader context of a passage as a means of determining its meaning (despite the penchant for contextual proofs attributed to his student, Rabbi Simeon ben Yohai). Throughout the 1st millennium of rabbinic interpretation, it was standard practice to atomize verses of the

Bible into constituent phrases, individual words, and sometimes even single letters. This tendency to ignore context allowed the rabbis to read a rabbinic agenda in the words of the Bible (*see* MIDRASH).

The interpretive norms of the Akivan School are sometimes anachronistically attributed to the 1st-cent. CE sage Hillel (*see* HILLEL THE ELDER, HOUSE OF HILLEL) and enumerated as seven rules. These listings are historically insecure, and certainly not as early as Hillel. In any case, the Akivan mode of biblical interpretation may be characterized as a broad attitude of allegorical reading, not unlike that of the Alexandrian school of the church fathers. For its part, Rabbi Ishmael's school produced a list of thirteen exegetical rules. Some of these Ishmaelean norms can be inferred from Scripture, while others have distinct parallels in Hellenistic interpretations of Homeric epics and of dreams.

In general, the rabbis distinguish between two distinct realms of interpretation, each presaged in scriptural literature. The first is of the behavioral norms and laws found in the Bible: HALAKHAH. The second, more indeterminate in character, is of the nonlegal passages and narratives of the Bible: HAGGADAH. These two realms of discourse, legal and nonlegal, persist through rabbinic literature up to the present time (*see* RABBINIC LITERATURE). Because of the "indeterminacy of belief" that permeates the haggadah, it is the biblical interpretation of the rabbis for halakhah that determines the differences within their schools. Although the Akivan and Ishmaelean schools have many notable differences regarding the biblical derivations of the halakhah, they share a common corpus of haggadic narratives and interpretations.

The very close readings of the Bible, which began in the earliest eras of rabbinic interpretation, persisted and expanded in the later periods. The rabbis of the era of the TALMUD, the Amoraim (*see* AMORA, AMORAIM), often took Akivan allegorical methods to an extreme, sometimes even obliterating the straightforward contextual meaning of a given biblical passage. By the end of the amoraic period, in the late 5th or early 6th cent., a reaction against this form of reading caused the rabbis to distinguish between **peshat** (פְּשָׁט; more literal, contextual readings) and **derash** (דְּרָשׁ; atomistic, freely interpretive readings). The Babylonian rabbi Mar bar Rav Huna proclaimed that scripture could not lose its literal sense (*b. Shabb.* 63*a*). This insistence on maintaining the contextual reading is similar to that of the Antiochene church fathers' notions of **theōria** (θεωρία) and **historia** (ἱστορία). It is also the harbinger of what would later become a movement toward **peshat** in medieval rabbinic interpretation of the Bible.

In the post-Talmudic period, the heads of the rabbinic academies or Gaonim collected many of the extant norms for biblical interpretation. One collection is pseudonymously attributed to the Tanna Rabbi Eliezer son of Rabbi Yose Hagalili. This medieval listing contains thirty-two or thirty-three norms (depending on the version). Similarly, the Gaon Samuel ben Hofni (d. 1013 CE) listed forty-nine modes of rabbinic exegesis. In truth, these listings are not comprehensive, as exactitude of method was always a handmaid to ideology in rabbinic interpretation of the Bible.

During this post-Talmudic period, especially following the advent of Islam, the influence of Arabic grammarians and Karaite Jewish literalists moved rabbinic interpretation more and more toward contextual readings. This is especially evident in the Arabic translation and **tafsir** commentary of the Egyptian-born Rav Saadia Gaon of the Babylonian rabbinic academies (882–942 CE). This penchant for **peshat**, which grew throughout the gaonic period (ca. 500–1000 CE), reached an apogee during the period of medieval commentators (ca. 1000–1500 CE).

Along with Saadia's translation of the Torah into Arabic, the rabbinic community long had made use of Aramaic Bible translations or TARGUMS. The earliest extant Targums are known to us from among the DEAD SEA SCROLLS. Within the rabbinic community, Targums range from the somewhat literal translation attributed to Aquila/Onkelos, a contemporary and reputed disciple of Rabbi Akiva, to the loose retellings of the Torah, replete with midrashic additions, most dating from the gaonic era. These Targums appear in many forms and fragments; the earliest among them is likely *Targum Neofiti*, a complete Targum to the Pentateuch. The latest among these texts is *Targum Pseudo-Jonathan*, which has elements that date after the advent of Islam. Manuscript research has yielded many fragmentary Targum traditions. Almost by definition, these Targums contain a strong element of rabbinic interpretation, apparently prepared for synagogue audiences.

The rabbinic interpreter of Scripture par excellence was Rabbi Solomon ben Isaac (Troyes, France, 1040–1105), known to latter generations by the acronym Rashi (*see* RASHI). Rashi combined traditional, atomistic, midrashic readings of Scripture with occasional reference to **peshat** exegesis in his attempt to produce a commentary on the Bible that preserved the older rabbinic traditions while also explicating the meaning of the biblical text. Rashi's grandson, Samuel ben Meir, or Rashbam (northern France, ca. 1085–1174) vigorously disputed Rashi's inclusive methods and instead produced a commentary almost entirely devoted to **peshat** exegesis. This move to contextual reading is one of the hallmarks that distinguish the medieval commentators, particularly of northern France, from the earlier, more atomistic midrash. In the next generation of rabbinic interpreters, Rabbi Moses ben Nachman or NACHMANIDES (Gerona, Catalonia, 1194–1270) offered more philosophical exegeses of Scripture. In keeping with his time and place, Nachmanides was a controversialist, engaging in a famous Catholic–Jewish disputation in Barcelona in 1263 under the aegis of King James I. Nachmanides' tendency to philosophical exegesis may also be seen in the "philosophic-scientific" commentaries of Rabbi Levi ben Gershom or Ralbag (Provence, 1288–1344).

In the later Middle Ages, rabbinic interpretation continued to develop in parallel with the interpretive trends of the outside (primarily Christian) world. Yet rabbinic interpretation always focused on the halakhah and haggadah within the biblical text. Even as philosophical interpretation continued in the rabbinic community, homiletical discourse also occupied rabbinic exegetes. These rabbinic sermons, keyed to the weekly Torah readings in the traditional synagogue, explored themes that occupied the Jewish communities of Europe, even as they linked these concerns to the biblical text. As was the case from the very beginnings of rabbinic interpretation and up to the modern era, rabbinic interpretation of the Bible tended to read the community of contemporary listeners into the fabric of the biblical text being interpreted.

In the early modern era, again in keeping with non-Jewish trends of interpretation, rabbinic interpreters first offered apologetic for and then reluctantly accepted modern theories of biblical origins, composition, and exegesis (*see* BIBLICAL CRITICISM). More recently, literary theories and even postmodern strategies of reading have entered the repertoire of rabbinic interpretation. It remains the goal of rabbinic interpreters to hear and understand the word of God in Scripture speaking afresh to every generation.

Bibliography: Michael Fishbane. *Biblical Interpretation in Ancient Israel* (1985); Daniel Frank. *Search Scripture Well: Karaite Exegetes and the Origins of the Jewish Bible Commentary in the Islamic East* (2004); James Kugel and Rowan Greer. *Early Biblical Interpretation* (1986); Saul Lieberman. "Rabbinic Interpretation of Scripture." *Hellenism in Jewish Palestine* (1950) 47–82; Martin Jan Mulder and Harry Sysling, eds. *Mikra: Text, Translation, Reading and Interpretation of the Hebrew Bible in Ancient Judaism and Early Christianity* (1988); Magne Saebø, ed. *Hebrew Bible/Old Testament: The History of Its Interpretation. I/1: Antiquity, I/2: The Middle Ages* (1996; 2000); Burton L. Visotzky. "Jots and Tittles: On Scriptural Interpretation in Rabbinic and Patristic Literatures." *Fathers of the World: Essays in Rabbinic and Patristic Literatures* (1995) 28–40; Azzan Yadin. *Scripture as Logos: Rabbi Ishmael and the Origins of Midrash* (2004).

BURTON L. VISOTZKY

RABBINIC LITERATURE. Rabbinic literature traces its antecedents back into the Bible and claims rabbinic forebears from the late biblical era up to the early 1st cent. CE. Despite this etiological mythos, the rabbinic movement only began with the destruction of the Jerusalem Temple by the Romans in 70 CE and the concomitant demise of the priestly cult. In this post-Temple era, rabbis (*see* RABBI, RABBONI) came to the fore as authorities within the Jewish community and began the process of creating what would become rabbinic literature. Part of this process was the collation of traditional laws and customs transmitted within the Jewish community during Second Temple times. This apodictic style of asserting laws and customs by virtue of traditional authority was buttressed by and in turn gave authority to the rabbis (*see* MISHNAH). Once the canon of Scripture was determined, the process of interpreting those documents formally continued as biblical commentary. This appeal to Scripture as authority gave rise to a literature of exegesis of both the laws and the narratives of the Bible, which also buttressed rabbinic authority within the community (*see* HAGGADAH; HALAKHAH). Each of these two "genres" of rabbinic literature, the "mishnaic" and the "midrashic," persists throughout its history (*see* MIDRASH).

The literature may be periodized by its major works or historic events. The era from the destruction of the Jerusalem Temple until the publication of the Mishnah is called Tannaitic, after the title of the rabbis of that period. The era of Mishnaic interpretation that followed and produced the two Talmuds (*see* TALMUD; TALMUD, JERUSALEM) is called Amoraic, after the title of those rabbis (*see* AMORA, AMORAIM). The next period is named the Gaonic era, after the heads of the rabbinic academies, the last of which died in 1040 CE. For the purposes of this article we divide the most recent millennium into two eras: the first we call "medieval," which arbitrarily comes to a close with either the expulsion of the Jews from Spain in 1492 or with the publication of the great compendium of Jewish law, the *Shulkhan ʿArukh,* in 1565. The latter period is dubbed "modern" and continues from the 16th cent. to the present.

A. Tannaitic Literature (ca. 70–200 CE)

1. Midrash Halakhah

The earliest rabbis, called Tannaim (*see* TANNA, TANNAIM) studied the TORAH, and collected the traditional laws and customs that had been handed down through generations (*see* ORAL LAW, ORAL TORAH). Most often the same rabbis engaged in both activities; and their conclusions are presented in two differing ways, with and absent biblical support. In the former cases, these rabbis interpreted Scripture to determine its meaning in legal and narrative contexts. These readings were complemented with interpretations that sought to tie traditional laws and customs to biblical authority. These biblical exegeses continued the work of biblical interpretation that began within Scripture itself and continued in every Jewish community both before and following the destruction of the Jerusalem Temple (*see* RABBINIC INTERPRETATION). By the end of the 2nd or in the early 3rd cent. CE, these rabbinic interpretations were arranged according to the pentateuchal texts they considered. There was no extensive tannaitic commentary attached to Genesis due to its paucity of legal materials. Tannaitic commentaries, called Midrash Halakhah or Tannaitic Midrash, are extant for Exodus (*see* MEKILTA), Leviticus, Numbers, and Deuteronomy (*see* SIFRA, SIFRE). The works were produced by two separate "schools" of rabbis, that of Akiva (*see* AKIVA, RABBI) and Ishmael (*see* ISHMAEL, RABBI), each with their own biblical hermeneutic.

2. Mishnah/Tosefta, Baraitot

Simultaneously, the rabbis collected and reorganized the corpus of Tannaitic teaching into broad topical categories or orders. By the end of the 2nd or beginning of the 3rd cent. CE these teachings, usually presented apodictically in the name of a rabbinic (rather than biblical) authority, were organized as Mishnah. The Mishnah is arranged into six major orders (Agriculture, Calendar, Women, Torts, Sacred Things, and Purities). Each order is subsequently divided into tractates, which are divided into chapters and then into subsections. Shortly after the Mishnah was published, a companion work called the Tosefta also was produced following the same organizing principles (*see* TOSEPHTA, TOSEPTA, TOSEFTA). It remains debated whether the Mishnah was orally published or propagated in written format. The exact relationship between the Mishnah and the Tosefta is also currently subject to debate. Certain statements of tannaitic rabbis that are not found in the Mishnah but which are preserved in the Tosefta, the Midrash Halakhah, or in the later Talmudic corpora are called "baraitot" (sing. BARAITA; lit. "outside," meaning not part of the Mishnah).

These rabbinic texts constitute the Tannaitic literature: on the one hand midrash organized around the authority and rabbinic exegesis of the Torah, and on the other hand the collections of statements of rabbinic authority, ordered with the Mishnah (*see* SAYINGS OF THE FATHERS). This earliest rabbinic literature was not edited before the late 2nd or early 3rd cent. CE.

B. Amoraic Literature (ca. 200–500 CE)

1. Talmud

a. Jerusalem. As the existence of the Tosefta indicates, almost immediately following the publication of the Mishnah it became an object for further commentary, study, expansion, and interpretation. Many of the apodictic laws quoted in the Mishnah were given the support of biblical proof texts (*see* APODICTIC, APODEICTIC). Passages of the Mishnah that had become obscure were clarified. When Tannaitic texts appeared to be in contradiction, these traditions were harmonized to make the Tannaitic corpus appear monolithic. Where tannaitic rabbis were quoted as disagreeing, later rabbis attempted to determine which opinion was preferable. Dialectical discussion examining almost every facet of the Mishnaic text was the rule of the day. In Roman Palestine in the 3rd and 4th cent. these opinions and discussions were recited and commented upon in turn. Legends about the Tannaitic rabbis and even many of the Amoraic rabbis were added to the record. By the early 5th cent. these unruly discussions, harmonizations, and stories were edited into a Gemara (*see* GEMARA) or commentary on the Mishnah. The Mishnah and Gemara combined to yield a body of literature known as the *Talmud Yerushalmi* (Jerusalem Talmud).

b. Babylonian. A similar process took place in the rabbinic community of Sassanian, Zoroastrian Babylonia from ca. 220 CE to the end of the 5th cent. This included a more extensive process of dialectic that took place over five generations and more. The legends of the rabbis of the land of Israel were supplemented by stories of the Babylonian rabbis. The final product was edited in the early 6th cent. by the rabbis of the local academies and gave rise to a second Talmud, the Babylonian. This work came to dominate rabbinic discourse in subsequent centuries.

2. Midrash

In addition to their Talmud, the rabbis of the land of Israel were also intensively engaged in biblical exegesis. Having inherited a corpus of halakhic exegesis, noted above, the Amoraic rabbis turned to a variety of modes of interpretation to produce miscellanies of commentary on Genesis, Leviticus, Song of Songs, and Lamentations. *Genesis Rabbah* examines virtually every verse of the book of Genesis, offering exegeses of difficult words and phrases, filling in narrative gaps in the biblical account, polemicizing against nonrabbinic "heresies" (Gnosticism and Christianity among them), and occasionally offering what seem to be full-blown homilies. By contrast, *Leviticus Rabbah* considers fewer than 20 percent of the verses of Leviticus, ignoring the details of ritual purity and leprosy in favor of moral homilies and folklore. A significant portion of this material is paralleled in *Pesiqta of Rab Kahana*, which organizes its largely homiletic midrashic material around the lectionary cycle for special Sabbaths and holidays. *Song of Songs Rabbah* offers allegorical readings of Song of Songs and presumes that the beloved and lover represent God and Israel. Finally, *Lamentations Rabbah* uses the biblical laments over the destruction of the First Temple to offer consolation and theodicy for the destruction of the Second Temple and the Roman oppressions that followed in subsequent centuries. Just after the redaction of the Babylonian Talmud, *Ecclesiastes Rabbah* served as an encyclopedic collection of rabbinic haggadic traditions, using the verses of that biblical book as organizing rubrics. Other works of midrash followed in subsequent eras.

C. Gaonic Literature (ca. 500–1040 CE)

1. Talmud commentaries

Following the publications of their respective Talmuds, whether in writing or orally, the academies of Palestine and Babylonia devoted their curriculum to the study and elucidation of these documents. Under the supervision of the heads of the academies of Sura and Pumbeditha in Babylonia, systematic commentaries were offered on the Babylonian Talmud.

2. Responsa, codes, and liturgy

The Gaons of Babylonia and the land of Israel also received a constant stream of letters asking for legal decisions; and their responses set halakhic standards for the communities within and outside their immediate orbit of influence. Ultimately, the responsa of the Babylonian Gaonate proved to have greater reach and were instrumental in establishing rabbinic law throughout the Jewish communities of the Mediterranean basin and beyond. These responsa were collected and became the first independent compendia of Jewish law. A responsum of Amram Gaon (d. 875 CE, Sura, Babylonia) addressed the subject of Jewish liturgy and, having circulated in writing, began the process of fixing and essentially canonizing rabbinic liturgy from its earlier, more fluid, oral forms. In this period, liturgical poetry flourished and served as a link between the Sabbath liturgy and the lectionary readings of the Torah. The custom of creating liturgical poetry persisted well into the medieval era.

3. Midrash and Targum

The process of writing midrash continued during this period as well. Following the Islamic conquest in the 7th cent., travel from Jewish Babylonia to the Jewish communities of the Mediterranean was much simpler. As a result, the customs and literature of the two formerly distinct communities were shared. This often precludes accurate modern scholarly identification of provenance of these midrashic texts. *Midrash Mishle* offers a commentary cum Midrash to the book of Proverbs. *Seder Eliahu Rabbah* and *Zuta* purport to be the teachings of the prophet Elijah to an anonymous rabbi. This work is unusual in that it is not organized around a biblical book, but is a first-person narrative of morals, ethics, stories, and maxims, along with anti-Karaite polemics that date it to ca. 9th cent. From the same era, *Pirqe Rabbi Eliezer* retells the Torah from Genesis through Numbers (and ends abruptly, leading to the conclusion it is fragmentary). This midrash has asides and fanciful diversions (such as chap. 10, on Jonah's tour of the underseaworld while in the belly of the fish), including references to Islam. Much of the "retold" text is in archaized Hebrew; but were it in Aramaic, it would resemble Targum Pseudo-Jonathan with which it shares many midrashic traditions. Although Aramaic was waning at this time in favor of Arabic usage, the late versions of the TARGUMS were certainly favorites of the rabbis for inculcating synagogue attendees with rabbinic values through their interpretive and loose translations of the scriptural lectionary.

In keeping with the responsa that the Gaons wrote, Rav Aha of Shabha (680–752 CE), Gaon of the Babylonian school of Pumbedita, pioneered a format of asking a question related to Jewish law in the synagogue or academy, which he then answered by teaching a text from the Mishnah. These public questions, or **sheʾeltoth** (שְׁאֵלְתוֹת), served as a popular homiletic form, since following the teaching of the halakhah, the rabbi ended with a peroration of haggadah. While the sheʾeltot literature is in Aramaic, the opening query formula, rendered in Hebrew: **yelamdenu rabbenu** (יְלַמְּדֵנוּ רַבֵּנוּ), "teach us, our master," gave rise to a broader midrashic genre in Hebrew called "Yelamdenu" or "Tanhuma" midrash. A variety of these works is extant on all five books of the Pentateuch.

4. Mystical literature

One other phenomenon must be noted for rabbinic literature of the Gaonic era; rabbinic mystical and apocalyptic literature begins to abound. Descriptions of God's throne-room, chariot, and body vie with angelology, prayers to angelic beings, accounts of ascents to heaven and descents to hell. Speculation on the mysteries of the works of creation and about the eschaton also takes a place in the rabbinic library. While these works were unquestionably esoteric, mainstream rabbinic literature refers to them and alludes to their content (e.g., *Midrash Mishle* 10).

D. Medieval Literature (ca. 1000–1500 CE)

By the close of the Gaonic era (1040 CE), rabbinic influence had spread throughout the Jewish communities of the Islamic Mediterranean world and the Christian European world as well. Under the cloud of conflict between Christianity and Islam, rabbis continued to produce literature along lines similar to those of Gaonic times. One of the greatest commentators on the Talmud was Rabbi Solomon ben Isaac of Troyes, France (ca. 1040–1105). Rashi, as he is known by the acronym of his name, offered apparently simple explanations that opened the text to generations of students of the Talmud, explicating the laws, difficult words, and passages. Also in the 11th cent., Rabbi Isaac ben Jacob of Fez, or al-Fasi, as he is called, epitomized the Talmud text by publishing an extract of the legal materials and omitting the haggadah. Another great Talmudic commentator from that era was Rabbenu Hananel ben Hushiel of Kairawan, now in modern Tunisia.

Rabbi Moses ben Maimon, called Rambam or MAIMONIDES (1135–1204 CE), wrote a commentary on the Mishnah and a legal extract of the *Talmud Yerushalmi.* A leader in the Sefardic community, Maimonides also wrote many responsa. Following the format of Islamic law, Maimonides also compiled a compendium of rabbinic law, virtually eliminating the Talmudic sources and, instead, presented only the dictates of halakhah in simple Hebrew. His work, the *Mishneh Torah,* became a monument of Jewish law for subsequent generations. Maimonides also wrote a great work of philosophy and theology titled *The Guide for the Perplexed.* As with most of his work, it was written in Arabic.

In the 13th cent., Rabbi Asher ben Yehiel wrote an influential legal commentary on the Talmud. Like most Jews enduring the Crusades, Rabbi Asher lived a peripatetic life, moving from Germany to France and ultimately to Spain. His son, Rabbi Jacob ben Asher, built on his father's work and reorganized his halakhic compendium into a four-part structure called the Four Pillars, abbreviated as Tur (**tur** טוּר, "Pillar"). This work, in turn, was the subject of an extensive commentary in the 16th cent. by Rabbi Joseph Karo. Karo then converted his commentary into his own compendium of Jewish Law, the *Shulkhan ʿArukh,* published in 1565 CE. This legal code remains the central work of Jewish law today. Yet even a rabbi as devoted to halakhah as Karo had a mystical bent, which he recorded in his work *Maggid Mesharim.*

In addition to these works centering upon Talmud, the medieval rabbis did not neglect scriptural commentary. RASHI wrote what continues to be the most influential rabbinic commentary on the Bible. His grandson, Rabbi Samuel ben Meir (1085–1174 CE), rejected Rashi's midrashic approach for more literal and contextual exegesis. Yet even after rabbinic interpretation shifted from the midrashic, atomistic style to the genre of commentary, the earlier midrash was not neglected. In the 13th cent., Rabbi Shimon HaDarshan collected an anthology, which he called the *Yalkut Shimoni,* from over fifty works of midrash. Another mode of Jewish expression in this era, perhaps in response to the Crusades, was an outpouring of liturgical poetry. These works, composed in archaic Hebrew, were singularly allusive and intertextual with the Bible and earlier midrash.

Finally, posing as a biblical commentary and written in an Aramaic approaching jargon, in the late 13th cent. Rabbi Moses de Leon composed his magisterial *Zohar,* which he attributed to the Tanna, Rabbi Shimeon ben Yohai. The *Zohar* was a great change from earlier rabbinic literature in that it reimagined God's relationship to the universe in a new way, positing a system of divine emanations (**sefiroth** סְפִירוֹת). The mythopoetic commentary in fact took the form of narrative, offering moral and theological insights in a manner unseen since the startling marriage of Aristotelian philosophy and rabbinic literature achieved by Maimonides in his *Guide.*

E. Modern Literature (1500–present)

Since the advent of printing, modern rabbinic literature has been published at a dizzying pace. Of course, calling the last half-millennium "modern" requires ignoring the historic divide in Jewish history wrought by the political emancipation of the Jews and the enlightenment of the late 18th cent. Throughout the broader period, however, Talmudic study and commentary continued apace, as did the publication of rabbinic legal codes for each Jewish community. Rabbis continued to be asked legal queries and issued formal responsa, while within each community liturgical innovation and liturgical poetry continued to be produced. New Bible commentaries and midrashic collections were regularly published.

In the 19th and 20th cent., a significant shift took place as rabbinic literature found a place in the Western academic curriculum. Critical scholarship on the previous two millennia of rabbinic literature became the norm, often under the influence of Christian and secular academic discourse. Modern methods of study, from the historical-critical to the literary, were and continue to be used to advance the study of rabbinic literature and even Jewish mysticism. In Jewish centers such as Israel, New York, and at universities throughout the world, the study of rabbinic literature continues unabated. A recent signal advance is Bar Ilan University's "Judaic Responsa," a global Jewish database containing almost the entirety of the rabbinic literature surveyed here.

Bibliography: Hermann L. Strack and Günter Stemberger. *Introduction to the Talmud and Midrash* (1992); Burton L. Visotzky. "The Literature of the Rabbis." *From Mesopotamia to Modernity: Ten Introductions to Jewish History and Literature.* Burton L. Visotzky and David Fishman, eds. (1999) 71–102.

BURTON L. VISOTZKY

RABBITH rab'ith [רַבִּית **rabbith**]. One of thirteen cities listed as being included in the territory allotted to the tribe of Issachar (Josh 19:17-23). Three additional cities are listed as border cities, with a total tally of sixteen cities. *See* DABERATH; ISSACHAR, ISSACHARITES.

RABBONI. *See* RABBI, RABBONI.

RABMAG rab´mag [רַב־מָג rav-magh]. The title of NERGAL-SHAREZER, an official of King Nebuchadnezzar of Babylon who was present when the Babylonians besieged, conquered, and destroyed Jerusalem (Jer 39:3; *see* BABYLON, OT; NEBUCHADNEZZAR, NEBUCHADREZZAR). The title is mentioned again when Nergal-sarezer is listed among the officials who had Jeremiah brought out from prison and handed over to GEDALIAH (Jer 39:13). *Rabmag* is probably Akkadian in origin, as it is similar to some Assyrian terms.

DEREK E. WITTMAN

RAB-SARIS rab´suh-ris [רַב־סָרִיס rav-saris]. The reference is to a high official whose title literally means "chief of the eunuchs." In Assyria, two officials with this title—one serving the king and the other the crown prince—led divisions of the central standing army. In 2 Kgs 18:17, the rav-saris' forces are supplemented by the contingents of the TARTAN and the RABSHAKEH. In Jer 39:3, 13, the Babylonian king's rab-saris appears alongside his subordinate, the RABMAG (commander of 500 horse troops).

JOANN SCURLOCK

RABSHAKEH rab´shuh-kuh [רַב־שָׁקֵה rav-shaqeh]. The title of a high-ranking Assyrian official that literally means "chief cupbearer." The Bible treats *Rabshakeh* as a personal name. As SENNACHERIB's emissary, the Rabshakeh delivered a threatening speech to HEZEKIAH in Hebrew (not in Aramaic, the language of international diplomacy), so that all Jerusalem would understand (2 Kgs 18:13–19:13; Isa 36:1–37:13).

LJUBICA JOVANOVIC

RACAL ray´kuhl [רָכָל rakhal]. A city, otherwise unknown, to which David sent spoils from his retaliatory campaign against the Amalekites who attacked Ziklag (1 Sam 30:29). Many interpreters follow the LXX in reading the word *Carmel* for *Racal*, since Carmel is near Hebron and is a location where "David and his men had roamed" (compare 1 Sam 30:31).

NATHAN D. MAXWELL

RACE. *See* ANTHROPOLOGY, NT CULTURAL; ANTHROPOLOGY, OT CULTURAL; ETHNICITY; RACE, SPORT; RACISM.

RACE, SPORT [מֵרוֹץ merots; τρέχω trechō]. Racing in the ANE and in the Greco-Roman world developed out of a need for swift messengers to carry news of wars and disasters from one village to another. (See 2 Sam 18:19; 1 Kgs 1:5; Prov 1:16; Isa 59:7; Hab 2:2; 1 Cor 9:24, 26; Heb 12:1.) Later, of course, competition arose merely for the sake of praise. *See* COURAGE; GAMES, NT.

JAMES E. WEST

RACHEL ray´chuhl [רָחֵל rakhel; Ῥαχήλ Rhachēl]. Means "ewe." Rachel is the youngest daughter of LABAN and the sister of LEAH. As JACOB's wife, she was the biological mother of Joseph (*see* JOSEPH, JOSEPHITES) and Benjamin (*see* BENJAMIN, BENJAMINITES), and the grandmother of Ephraim (*see* EPHRAIM, EPHRAIMITES) and Manasseh (*see* MANASSEH, MANASSITES), clan heads of what became the northern kingdom of Israel.

Best known, perhaps, as the object of her cousin Jacob's great love (Jacob is smitten from the moment he sees her and immediately kisses her; Gen 29:10-11), Rachel is depicted as a complex figure. Genesis introduces her as "graceful and beautiful" (29:17) and also as a shepherd (29:9), the only woman in the Bible who explicitly holds this position. She is portrayed on the one hand as a resourceful figure (who dares, e.g., to steal her father's household gods; *see* TERAPHIM) and also a paradigmatic barren woman who desperately longs for children (Gen 30:1). She eventually gets her wish, but also tragically dies young in childbirth. Jacob, who seeks refuge in her father's house, falls in love with Rachel and offers to work seven years for her father in order to marry her (Gen 29:20). At the end of those years, however, her father switches brides, and Jacob discovers in the morning that he had married her sister LEAH instead (Gen 29:23-25). Beloved Rachel becomes Jacob's bride a week later, but Jacob works for her an additional seven years.

The narrator does not disclose Rachel's feelings for Jacob. In contrast to Leah, whose naming of the children repeatedly show how desperately she longs for Jacob's affection, Rachel repeatedly longs for a son/child and sees herself in competition with her sister. Her anguished plea to Jacob illustrates this desperation ("When Rachel saw that she bore Jacob no children, she envied her sister; and she said to Jacob, 'Give me children, or I shall die!'" [Gen 30:1]). When Jacob's angry response does not help, Rachel resorts to a surrogate, her servant BILHAH, who then conceives and bears two sons on Rachel's behalf. The names she bestows on the sons disclose her feelings and hopes as she competes with her sister for fertility: she names the first son Dan (meaning "judge"; *see* DAN, DANITES), saying "God has judged me, and has also heard my voice and given me a son" (Gen 30:6); she names the second Naphtali (meaning "to wrestle"; *see* NAPHTALI, NAPHTALITES), saying, "With mighty wrestlings I have wrestled with my sister, and have prevailed" (Gen 30:8; note the parallel with Jacob's wrestling with God in Gen 32). When Rachel finally conceives and bears Joseph, his birth does not completely satisfy her longings, as is evident when she names him Joseph (meaning to "to add"), saying, "May the LORD add to me another son!" (30:24). On the road back to Canaan, Rachel gives birth to that hoped-for other son but dies in childbirth. The ambiguous name she gives the child as she dies, BEN-ONI (meaning either "son of my sorrow" or "son of my strength") is changed by Jacob to Benjamin ("son of my right hand").

The relationship between Rachel and Leah is one of only three somewhat developed stories about sisters in the OT (the others are Lot's daughters in Gen 19 and Zelophehad's daughters in Num 27; 36; and Josh 17). Their story begins with competition but changes to collaboration when Rachel negotiates with Leah for the mandrakes (presumed fertility plant) that Leah's son found and relinquishes time with Jacob in return. Whereas sibling rivalry among brothers in Genesis leads to murder (*see* CAIN and ABEL in Gen 4) or attempted murder (see Joseph and his brothers in Gen 37), the sisters' rivalry leads to the birth of children. When the sisters eventually move from competition to collaboration, their subsequent unity is indicated as they speak in unison in response to Jacob's decision to return to Canaan with Jacob (Gen 31:14-16). Jointly they report that their father has swindled them out of their inheritance.

In a baffling account, Rachel steals her father's teraphim (**terafim** תְּרָפִים), usually translated as "household gods" (Gen 31:19). She hides them in her camel's saddlebags, then sits upon them. When her father comes looking for them, she audaciously, and ironically, excuses herself for not rising before him by saying she is menstruating, thereby playing on the anxiety generated by women's menstruation. Not knowing who is responsible, Jacob utters a curse upon the one who stole the **terafim** (which some scholars interpret as a cause of her early death). Scholars debate the meaning of Rachel's theft: is it an attempt to secure for herself the family authority (possibly in lieu of her sister, as Jacob did), an expression of pious attachment to her family's traditions, or revenge against a father who had cheated her?

Rachel dies young in childbirth on the road back to Canaan (Gen 35:19-20) and is the only matriarch not buried at the family cave of MACHPELAH. Jacob places a **matsevah** (מַצֵּבָה), a stone pillar (*see* PILLAR), on her grave, the location of which is unnamed in Gen 35:16-20, but appears later to be associated with RAMAH. Jacob also invokes poignantly Rachel's memory and premature death in his exchanges with his sons and with Pharaoh (see Gen 48:7), and his love for her binds him uniquely to her two sons, especially Joseph.

Rachel is also the only matriarch who is repeatedly remembered in the OT outside of Genesis (SARAH appears only once after Genesis in Isa 51:2; and Leah in Ruth 4:11). First Samuel 10:2 refers to the tomb of Rachel as a landmark. Jeremiah specifically mentions Rachel in his message of hope, illustrating that her longing for her children moves God to act on Israel's behalf. Depicting Rachel as an inconsolable mother, weeping for her children, Jeremiah reports that her voice and tears elicit God's promise of restoration (31:15-18; see also Matt 2:18, which quotes from this passage). The prophet Hosea alludes to Rachel when referring to Jacob who "served for a wife, and for a wife he guarded sheep" (Hos 12:12). The community in the book of Ruth blesses Ruth and Boaz by reference to Rachel and Leah (in this order) who "together built up the house of Israel" (4:11). Tradition locates RACHEL'S TOMB in Ramah, slightly north of Jerusalem, and the site has become a pilgrimage site especially for women wishing to become mothers.

TAMARA COHN ESKENAZI

RACHEL'S TOMB [קְבֻרַת רָחֵל **qevurath rakhel**]. Rachel is buried in Ramah, north of Jerusalem and south of Bethel in the territory of Benjamin. Several passages allude to the site.

Genesis 35:16-21; 48:7 record that Rachel died giving birth to Benjamin south of Bethel but north of the border of the Judahite clan Ephrath(ah) (*see* EPHRATHAH, EPHRATHITES). At this period the boundaries of Ephrath(ah) were from Tekoa in southern Judah to just north of Jerusalem. In later times Ephrath(ah) was reduced to the area surrounding Bethlehem. Hence the anachronistic glosses identifying Ephrath(ah) with Bethlehem (Gen 35:19; 48:7) and the subsequent misplaced modern "tomb of Rachel."

In 1 Sam 9–10 Saul leaves his home in Benjaminite Gibeah south of Ramah and travels north into adjacent Ephraim. There Samuel tells him to go back home to Gibeah, but that on the way he will "meet two men by Rachel's tomb in the territory of Benjamin" (1 Sam 10:2). This is consistent with the location of the tomb at Ramah.

Just a bit farther and before reaching Gibeah, Saul passes the "oak of Tabor" (1 Sam 10:3). Judges 4:5 calls this tree near Ramah the "palm of Deborah," heroine of the battle at Mount Tabor (Judg 4–5), an identification facilitated by the phonetic similarity between "Deborah" and "Tabor." In an alternate etiology for the tree of Deborah/Tabor tree, Gen 35:8 relates that Rachel's nurse "Deborah" is said to be buried just south of Bethel under "the oak" (Gen 35:8; NRSV, "an oak") that is called "the Oak of Weeping" (NRSV, "Allon-bacuth"). Surely "the oak" about which any reader would have known is not named after Rachel's nurse but is the well-known Deborah/Tabor tree near Rachel's tomb referred to in Jer 31:15: "A voice is heard in Ramah, lamentation and bitter weeping. Rachel is weeping for her children."

LAMONTTE M. LUKER

RACISM. Racism is grounded in the 19th-cent. belief that a particular group of people is superior to another based on assumptions about social and moral traits predetermined by innate biological characteristics. This biological understanding of racism assumes that race is immutable, typically determined by skin color, and consists of a core inherited "essence." In the early 20th cent., scholars theorized race as an anthropological construct rather than a biological reality, and since then definitions of racism abound depending on the social, cultural, geopolitical, and ideological commitments of the interpreters. Regardless of how one chooses to define racism, one fact remains: it is systemic and survives because of the intentional or unintentional use of power to isolate, separate, and exploit. Racism is enforced and maintained by the legal, cultural, religious, educational, economic, political, and military institutions of societies. Thus, racism is more than a personal attitude; it is institutionalized, indeed, woven throughout the very fabric of societies that have a history of oppression based on prejudice, stereotypes, or other types of "difference" among its people. The ideological thread that holds this system of oppression in place is manifested through both active and passive forms, and it is the passive (or covert) forms of racism that have seeped into the guild of biblical scholarship and influenced interpretations of race in antiquity.

Racism is a thorny issue for biblical interpreters mainly because of the elusive and emotionally laden nature of this phenomenon, which leads to what may be considered "interpretive quicksand"—best avoided rather than engaged. Avoidance, however, is no longer a viable option given the variety of interpretive perspectives that offer solid ground for those committed to reconciling the perplexing contradictions that exist in contemporary church and society with the teachings contained in biblical texts. Although scholars across a wide range of disciplines might agree that racism is a modern construct and thus beyond the purview of ancient studies, biblical scholarship is now understood as having deeply embedded "racializing" tendencies inherited from the intellectually dishonest historiography of the 19th-cent. philosophical movements in Germany that effectively erased Africa and Africans from the map of antiquity. The covert racism embedded in this interpretive tradition was inherited by biblical scholars in the United States and invariably led to racialized studies about the historical Jesus, the missionary activities of Paul, and many other aspects of the Bible, including the "myth of Ham" (Gen 9:18-25). This racism has been exposed and new hermeneutical frameworks for dismantling the "racializing" readings of biblical texts are now available.

Even before the scholarship dealing with the racialized origins of contemporary U.S. biblical interpretation, African American biblical interpreters have been on the forefront of addressing questions related to race in the Bible, initially during the 1970s and 80s, through investigations of the "presence" of Blacks in the Bible, and since the 1990s, through a variety of reconstructive cultural and historical interpretations and "ideological" readings of biblical and extra-biblical writings. In addition, African American biblical scholars have offered corrective responses to "white supremacist" interpretations of the Bible, most notably through the work of OT scholar Charles B. Copher and NT scholar Cain Hope Felder. Copher's critical survey of "racialist interpretations" of the so-called curse of Ham and Felder's conceptual framework for analyzing the "racial motifs in biblical narratives" introduced a fresh wave of scholarship dealing with racism in the Bible and contemporary biblical scholarship at the close of the 20th cent.

African American biblical interpreters are not alone in their quest for more race-critical readings of the Bible. Latino/a and Asian American scholars are also providing many useful studies that deal with race and the Bible. Indeed, the collaborative projects generated by "underrepresented" racial and ethnic interpreters of the Bible identify convergences and differences in reading strategies among different groups of interpreters and also highlight the challenging intersectionalities of race, gender, sex, and class. Several European Americans are also challenging the guild to consider the political, theological, ethical, and ideological stakes implicit in reading for race and ethnicity in the Bible.

Classicist Frank M. Snowden Jr. (1911–2007) provided one of the most persuasive studies about racism or color prejudice in the classical world. In *Blacks in Antiquity*, Snowden amassed a wealth of information about Ethiopians in the Greco-Roman experience and concluded that there was no racism or color prejudice in antiquity. Appealing to a wide range of positive depictions of Ethiopians, Snowden provided a critical guide for addressing the race question in the ancient world. Moreover, Snowden's research was conducted over a fifteen-year period and published in 1970 on the heels of the tumultuous civil rights movement, thus offering a timely, soothing balm for the race question in his own contemporary setting.

Although several scholars have noted limitations in Snowden's basic hypothesis regarding racism and racial prejudice in antiquity, generally his claims are regarded as the unrelenting benchmark upon which biblical scholars, church historians, and others exploring matters related to race in the ancient world begin and summarily end their research. His work, therefore, functions as a convenient justification for focusing on race as solely a product of modernity. Such a focus invariably lets the classical writers and the classical world off the hook when it comes to exploring questions related to race in antiquity. Furthermore, some scholars appeal to Snowden's work as a way of absolving themselves of the responsibility of taking seriously the racialized attitudes that may have existed in the ancient world as well as their own subconscious racializing interpretive tendencies that continue to shape the hermeneutical assumptions and methods they employ.

Fortunately, during the first decade of the 21st cent., a new wave of scholarship is demonstrating how racism was indeed "invented" in antiquity and to some degree holds "symbolic" significance for the authors of ancient texts. The categories of "race" and "ethnicity" are also being analyzed more critically as interchangeable social constructs, which enable interpreters to assess the identity-making strategies of the ancients. Moreover, scholars are now acknowledging how attitudes about race and racism in the present affect how one interprets race and ethnicity in the past.

Racism influences the interpretation of biblical texts—not only from the standpoint of the racialized assumptions embedded in the very methods that are used for biblical interpretation but also in the uninterrogated norms or assumptions that frame the interpreters themselves. Beyond this, racism also impacts the interpretation of biblical texts in that the ancient world itself may not be as untainted by racialized assumptions as we would want it to be (*pace* Snowden). Given these complex exegetical challenges, responsible biblical interpreters must now raise questions about the insidious connection between "reading race" and "reading the Bible." *See* AFRICAN INTERPRETATION; ASIAN INTERPRETATION; ETHNICITY; IDEOLOGICAL CRITICISM; POSTMODERN BIBLICAL INTERPRETATION.

Bibliography: Randall C. Bailey. "Academic Biblical Interpretation among African Americans in the United States." *African Americans and the Bible.* Vincent L. Wimbush, ed. (2000) 696–711; Denise K. Buell. *Why This New Race? Ethnic Reasoning in Early Christianity* (2005); Denise K. Buell and Caroline J. Hodge. "The Politics of Interpretation: The Rhetoric of Race and Ethnicity in Paul." *JBL* 123 (2004) 235–52; Gay L. Byron. *Symbolic Blackness and Ethnic Difference in Early Christian Literature* (2002); Charles B. Copher. *Black Biblical Studies* (1993); Richard Delgado and Jean Stefancic. *Critical Race Theory: An Introduction* (2001); Cain Hope Felder. *Troubling Biblical Waters: Race, Class, Family* (1989); David M. Goldenberg. *The Curse of Ham: Race and Slavery in Early Judaism, Christianity, and Islam* (2003); Ivan Hannaford. *Race: The History of an Idea in the West* (1996); Benjamin Isaac. *The Invention of Racism In Classical Antiquity* (2004); Sylvester Johnson. *The Myth of Ham in Nineteenth-Century American Christianity: Race, Heathens, and the People of God* (2004); Shawn Kelley. *Racializing Jesus: Race, Ideology and the Formation of Modern Biblical Scholarship* (2002); Tat-siong Benny Liew, ed. *The Bible in Asian America* (2002); Peter T. Nash. *Reading Race, Reading the Bible* (2003); Daniel Patte. *Ethics of Biblical Interpretation* (1995); Frank M. Snowden Jr. *Blacks in Antiquity: Ethiopians in the Greco-Roman Experience* (1970); Frank M. Snowden Jr. *Before Color Prejudice: The Ancient View of Blacks* (1983).

GAY L. BYRON

RADDAI rad'*i* [רַדַּי radday]. Raddai is listed as the fifth of seven sons of JESSE (1 Chr 2:14) and the older brother of David.

RADDANA, KHIRBET. A ruin near the modern village of Bireh to the east ancient AI (et-Tell). Salvage excavations were carried out there between 1969 and 1972. Four phases of occupation were evident at the site. Early Bronze pottery was found in the first phase, but no buildings were uncovered from this period. The second and third phases were dated to Iron Age I, with occupation in this period coming to an end after the site was destroyed. A final layer shows slight evidence of use during the Byzantine period. The excavators cautiously identified the site with biblical BEEROTH (Josh 9:17; 2 Sam 4:2-3).

KEVIN A. WILSON

RAFT [דֹּבְרָה dovrah, רַפְסֹודָה rafsodhah; σχεδία schedia]. An object used to transport people and goods over water. Rafts conveyed lumber from Lebanon for the construction of both Temples in Jerusalem. Hiram of Tyre sent precious wood to Solomon by raft (1 Kgs 5:9 [Heb. 5:23]); according to the Chronicler, Hiram delivered the timber specifically to Joppa (2 Chr 2:16 [Heb. 2:15]). When the Temple was rebuilt after the exile, wood came from Lebanon by the same means (1 Esd 5:55 [Gr. 5:53]; compare Ezra 3:7). Such shipping rafts would have been towed by other crafts. The book of Wisdom celebrates divine providence and wisdom by noting how sailors are able to travel safely through the sea on a fragile raft, even calling Noah's massive ark a raft on which the hope of the world took refuge (Wis 14:5-6).

STEVE COOK

RAGAU. *See* RAGES; REU.

RAGES rah'guhs [Ῥάγοι Rhagoi]. Tobit frequently traveled in Media, and he left ten talents of silver in trust in Rages (Tob 4:1, 20), which he sent his son Tobias to recover (5:6; 6:13; 9:2, 5). The book of Tobit places the town of Rages in Media "in the mountains" (author's trans.; NRSV, "in a mountainous area") two days' east of Ecbatana (5:6). This is presumably the "Raga in Media" of Darius I's Bisotun inscription and the Rhaga or Rhages (Rhagae) of the classical authors, located one day from the Caspian Gates (Arrian, *Anab.* 3.20), or about 500 stadia to the south of them (Strabo, *Geogr.* 11.9.1; 11.13.6, citing Apollodorus of Artemita). Citing Arrian, George Rawlinson suggested that the ruins of Median Rhagae might be Qal'e-ye Erij, near Varamin, southeast of Tehran, but the site has not been excavated. The city's exact location remains unknown. The name survives in the town of Ray just south of Tehran.

The book of Judith describes Ragau (Rhagau Ῥαγαύ) as "the great plain that is in the territories (en tois horiois [ἐν τοῖς ὁρίοις], author's trans.; NRSV, "on the borders") of Ragau" (Jdt 1:5) and states that Arphaxad was captured "in the mountains of Ragau" (1:15). While some associate Ragau with Rages, Ragau here may be identical with Rhagiana, a fertile area between the Alborz Mountains and the Great Salt Desert (Isidore Charax, *Parthian Stations* §7), and one of the districts of Media (Ptolemy, *Geography* 6.2; Diodorus Siculus, *Bib. Hist.* 19.44.2).

The *Avesta* includes Ragha in a list of place names from eastern Iran (*Videvdad* 1.15) and, perhaps, in *Yasna* 19.18, where it is called "Zarathustrid" (**zarathushtri**), but this is probably not Median Raga. Some Pahlavi texts state that Zarathustra was from Ragh, and in the 19th cent. CE, it was thought that Zarathustra had made it a Zoroastrian center, a view that is now outdated.

Rhagae was refounded by Seleucus Nicator and named Europus (Strabo, *Geogr.* 11.13.6). The medieval city was described by Muslim geographers, by which time it was already falling into ruin.

Bibliography: Gherardo Gnoli. *Zoroaster's Time and Homeland* (1980) 23–26, 64–66; Guy Le Strange. *The Lands of the Eastern Caliphate: Mesopotamia, Persia, and Central Asia, from the Moslem Conquest to the Time of Timur* (1905) 214–18; George Rawlinson. *The Five Great Monarchies of the Ancient Eastern World.* 3 vols. (1881) 2:272–73.

P. OKTOR SKJAERVØ

RAGUEL ruh-gy*oo*´uhl [ʽΡαγουήλ **Rhagouēl**]. Father of Sarah with his wife Edna, and relative to Tobit (Tob 3:7), Raguel, bound by the Law of Moses to allow TOBIAS to marry Sarah as he is her kinsman (Tob 7:10), gives the couple half of all he owns in celebration of their marriage (Tob 8:21). *See* TOBIT, BOOK OF.

JESSICA TINKLENBERG DEVEGA

RAHAB ray´hab [רָחָב **rakhav**, רַהַב **rahav**; ʽΡαχάβ **Rhachab**, ʽΡαάβ **Rhaab**]. 1. The woman who helps Joshua's spies in Jericho (Josh 2), Rahab (**rakhav**) has been the subject of countless studies. The first thing revealed about Rahab, even before her name, is that she is a prostitute. Since **zonah** (זוֹנָה), the Hebrew word for "prostitute," has been translated in various ways ("harlot, adulteress, cultic prostitute"), there has been much speculation about Rahab's occupation and character. Phyllis Bird argues that the meaning of **zonah** here does not indicate a cultic prostitute and that nothing in the story suggests that Rahab is a hierodule. Neither, argues Bird, does anything in the story suggest that Rahab is an adulteress, one who engages in extramarital, illicit sexual relations. There is a critical distinction between being an adulteress and a prostitute: the first offends a theoretical proprietary ownership of the woman's body. Because Rahab seems to be autonomous (Josh 2:1, 15), or at least as autonomous as a woman could be in that time and place, there is no reason to suspect the word has connotations of adultery. Rahab, it seems, is a woman who sells her body in exchange for money or goods. She owns her own house, perhaps a kind of bordello, which may have led Greek interpreters to call her an "innkeeper," which is consistent with Josephus' reference to her (*Ant.* 5.7–8).

There are three verses that mention Rahab in the NT. First, Matthew puts her in the genealogy that links Jesus to Abraham (Matt 1:5). According to Matthew, she is the mother of BOAZ (the husband of RUTH). The significance of her mention (if it is indeed Joshua's Rahab) in Matthew's genealogy has been the subject of much consideration. One view is that evoking the name of Rahab along with Ruth, TAMAR (Matt 1:3), and "the wife of URIAH the Hittite" (Matt 1:6) suggests that Matthew is taking special notice of the inclusion of Gentiles in Jesus' birth narrative. Another explanation is that this genealogy contains women considered to be sexually suspect and reflects Matthew's theology of a "higher righteousness." The remaining two occurrences of Rahab in the NT are found in the Catholic Epistles. The author of Hebrews praises Rahab for her faith (Heb 11:31) while the author of James lauds her for her works (Jas 2:25).

Bibliography: Phyllis Bird. *Missing Persons and Mistaken Identities* (1997).

TERESA J. HORNSBY

2. The ANE knew a large number of CHAOS monsters (e.g., LEVIATHAN, Tannin, Tehom, TIAMAT, and Yam) that were involved in various cosmogonies. The name *Rahab* (**rahav**) is often translated "DRAGON" or "surger," alluding to the restlessness and surging of the ocean. Ancient Near Eastern cognates for Rahab are sketchy at best, a possible exception being the Akkadian **raʾabu** ("tremble with rage"). Best known among the cosmogonies is the battle between MARDUK and Tiamat. In this account, Marduk kills Tiamat and splits her corpse into halves. The upper half is made into the heavens and the lower half comprises the land and waters.

The OT knows of Rahab, Tannin, Tehom, and Yam within its textual history. Various poetic texts of the OT preserve the original chaotic battle between Yahweh and Rahab. The surviving texts portray Yahweh and Rahab engaging in battle before the creation of the heavens and earth (e.g., Job 26:12; Ps 89:7-13 [Heb. 89:8-14]). A number of the texts hearken back to the ANE motifs of total defeat. For instance, Job 9:13 notes that both Rahab and her helpers are destroyed in this tumultuous battle with Yahweh (see also *Enuma Elish* I, 125-27). In wisdom literature such as Ps 87:4 and in the prophets such as Isa 30:7 and 51:9-10, Rahab is synonymous with Egypt. Just as Rahab was powerless to save herself against Yahweh, so also was Egypt powerless to save Israel. *See* COSMOGONY, COSMOLOGY.

JOSEPH R. CATHEY

RAHAM ray´huhm [רַחַם **rakham**]. Son of SHEMA and father of JORKEAM, descendants of Hebron, one of Caleb's sons (1 Chr 2:44).

RAHEL, RAMAT ray´hel [רָמַת רָחֵל **ramath rakhel**]. An ancient tell (Khirbet Salih) located on a hilltop about midway between the Old City of Jerusalem and Bethlehem, strategically situated to control the roads leading to Jerusalem from the south and the west. The location is most likely biblical BETH-HACCHEREM (LXX Josh 15:59*a*; Neh 3:14). The site was first excavated by Y. Aharoni in 1954 and later between 1959 and 1962. Excavations resumed in 2004 under the direction of O. Lipschits, M. Oeming, and Y. Gadot.

The generally accepted view is that there were seven periods of occupation. The site was first settled in the late 8th–early 7th cent. BCE (Stratum VB), yielding scanty architectural remains but a large number of storage jar handles, stamped with royal seal impressions (*see* LMLK SEALS). An imposing palace stood on top of the mound in the next stratum (VA; 7th cent. BCE). The palace was built of ashlar blocks and decorated with proto-Aeolic capitals and window balustrades (compare Jer 22:14). The western part of the palace was surrounded by a garden, with pools, drains, and channels of water.

During the late 4th–3rd cent. BCE, the garden went out of use and other buildings were erected on top of it. From this period numerous small finds have been discovered, among them about 200 stamped jar handles with the name of the province Yehud. In the 2nd cent. BCE the palace and garden were destroyed, and a Jewish village was built on top. From this period eleven Jewish baths were discovered, two columbaria, and many Yehud and Jerusalem stamped jar handles, all dated to the Hasmonean occupation.

The next occupation level is a small, unfortified village from the Early Roman period (Stratum IVA; 1st cent. BCE–1st cent. CE). After its destruction ca. 70 CE, the site remained abandoned until the 3rd cent. when a Roman-style house with a bathhouse was erected (Stratum III). Between the middle of the 5th and the 6th cent., a Christian church was built on the tell with an attached monastery complex and a large village around it (Stratum II). This church should be connected to the other, bigger church excavated down the hill, the church of the Kathisma ("the Seat"), which was mentioned in Byzantine sources as the place where Mary, mother of Jesus, rested during her journey to Bethlehem. Scanty remains found upon the ruined Byzantine stratum dating from the Umayyad and the early Abbasid periods (7th–8th cent. CE) continued probably until the 11th cent. This was the last occupation of the tell.

Bibliography: Y. Aharoni et al. *Excavations at Ramat Rahel 1: Seasons 1959 and 1960* (1962); Y. Aharoni et al. *Excavations at Ramat Rahel 2: Seasons 1961 and 1962* (1964); O. Lipschits, M. Oeming, Y. Gadot, B. Arubas. "Ramat Rahel 2005." *IEJ* 56 (2006) 227–35; O. Lipschits, M. Oeming, Y. Gadot, D. Vanderhooft. "Seventeen Newly Excavated YEHUD Stamp Impressions from Ramat-Rahel." *TA* 34 (2007) 74–89.

ODED LIPSCHITS

RAIN [גֶּשֶׁם geshem, זֶרֶם zerem, מָטָר matar, שֶׁטֶף shetef; βροχή brochē, ὄμβρος ombros, ὑετός hyetos]. In the Mediterranean climate of ancient Israel, the Israelites hoped that God would provide rain "in its season" (i.e., autumn and spring; Deut 11:14; Job 29:23; compare Ezra 10:13; 2 Esd 8:43). In metaphorical terms, rain served as both a reward for the righteous (Ps 68:7-10 [Heb. 68:8-11]) and a punishment for the wicked (i.e., a rain of fire and sulfur; Ps 11:6). In Wisdom literature, rain is a sign of God's wise plan for creation (Sir 1:2) and the basis for proverbial admonitions against quarreling or boasting (Prov 19:13; 25:14). *See* DROUGHT; EARLY AND LATE RAINS; ISRAEL, CLIMATE OF; SEASONS.

VICTOR H. MATTHEWS

RAINBOW [קֶשֶׁת qesheth; ἶρις iris, τόξον toxon]. The OT uses the Hebrew word *bow*, meaning the weapon, to refer to the bow-shaped object seen in the sky after rain: it is the "bow in the clouds" (Gen 9:13). A similar image is found in the Wisdom of Solomon (Wis 5:17-23), which imagines God combating enemies with shafts of lightning that "will leap from the clouds to the target, as from a well-drawn bow."

After the flood (Gen 9:12-17), God hangs the bow in the sky where it will serve as a reminder of God's promise to never again destroy all flesh with a flood because of human wickedness. This action may function as a triple entendre, whereby the hanging up of the bow as a sign of the cessation of God's battle with creation refers to a literal rainbow, as well as to the reestablishment after the flood of the bow-shaped dome or FIRMAMENT that holds up the heavenly waters.

According to Sirach, the rainbow encircling the vaulted sky testifies to God's work as creator (Sir 43:11). Sirach also compares the high priest Simon to a rainbow (Sir 50:7). In Revelation, a rainbow surrounds the throne on which the divine presence is seated (Rev 4:3; compare 10:1), recalling the glory of the divine presence as Ezekiel saw it (Ezek 1:28).

Bibliography: Paul J. Kissling. "The Rainbow in Genesis 9:12-17: A Triple Entendre?" *Stone-Campbell Journal* 4 (2001) 249–61.

PAUL J. KISSLING

RAISIN CAKES [אֲשִׁישָׁה ʾashishah, צִמּוּק tsimmuk]. Raisin cakes, perhaps made by compressing a clump of crushed, DRIED GRAPES into a solid mound, were a delicacy of wine-growing regions (Song 2:5). Because of their relative imperishability, they were often used as food during travel and as military rations (1 Sam 25:18; 30:12; 2 Sam 6:19; 16:1; 1 Chr 12:40 [Heb. 12:41]). Another word that may refer to raisin cakes is **tsimmuk**, which the NRSV renders as "clusters of raisins."

Raisin cakes were also featured in cultic observances involving BAAL. In Hos 3:1, the people of Israel are said to "turn to other gods and love raisin cakes" (NRSV) or, alternately, "turn to other gods who love raisin cakes" (author's trans.). These cakes are probably comparable to the dough cakes (**kawwanim** כַּוָּנִים) made for the QUEEN OF HEAVEN (Jer 7:18). *See* FERTILITY CULT; HOSEA, BOOK OF.

RALPH K. HAWKINS

RAKKATH rak´uhth [רַקַּת **raqqath**]. Rakkath appears in Josh 19:35 in a list of the fortified cities within the borders of Naphtali (*see* NAPHTALI, NAPHTALITES). Various identifications have been made for Rakkath beginning with rabbinic tradition. In the Jerusalem Talmud it is written that Rakkath was the precursor to the city of TIBERIAS.

JOSEPH R. CATHEY

RAKKON rak´on [רַקּוֹן **raqqon**]. Meaning "narrow place," "strait," or "marshy bank," Rakkon appears in Josh 19:46 as one of the cities in the territory of Dan (*see* DAN, DANITES). It is generally identified as a city in the vicinity of JOPPA. Scholars such as Noth have identified Rakkon with Tel er-Reddet while others have suggested a reference to Nahr el-Barideh. Since the LXX does not preserve a reading at this point some have suggested dittography of the preceding river name ME-JARKON (**me hayyarqon** מֵי הַיַּרְקוֹן).

JOSEPH R. CATHEY

RAM ram [אַיִל **ʾayil**]. 1. The ram (a male sheep) is a valuable animal within flocks (Gen 31:38; Deut 32:14; 2 Kgs 3:4; 2 Chr 17:11; Ezek 27:21; 34:17) and figures as an offering in inaugural and festal sacrifices (Gen 15; Exod 29; Lev 8–9; 16:3; 23:18; Num 6–7; 15:6-7; 23; 28–29; 1 Chr 15:26; 2 Chr 29; Ezek 43; 45–46) as well as in offerings that accomplish forgiveness (Lev 5:14–6:7 [Heb. 5:14-26]; 16:3, 5; 19:20-22; Num 5:5-10). The ram's skin, typically dyed red (Exod 25:5; 26:14; 35:7, 23; 36:19; 39:34), features in arrangements for the cult. To this extent, the ram stands as a metonym for the act of sacrifice. The ram also has symbolic significance in the visions of Daniel (Dan 8).

In Gen 22, the ram is sacrificed instead of Isaac. The story rejects human offerings, not because Abraham disobeys God but because Yahweh desires nomadic sacrifice rather than the urban sacrifice instanced in other ancient mythologies. Melito of Sardis later compared the ram of Gen 22 to Christ's redemption (fragment 10), and the rabbis taught that the sound of the ram's horn with prayer and fasting would cause God to answer the community as Yahweh had once answered Abraham on Moriah (*m. Taan.* 2:5).

Within the sacrificial system of Israel, this makes the ram the precedent of human redemption. Every male firstborn among man and beast belongs to God and, in the case of clean animals, should be offered in sacrifice (Exod 13:2; Deut 15:19-23). Impure animals and humans are to be redeemed, that is, bought out of their sacrificial status (Exod 13:11-16). Offering a lamb redeems an ass (Exod 13:13; 34:20), while five shekels as measured in the sanctuary redeems a person (Num 18:15-18; compare Lev 5:15, where the shekel of the sanctuary is used to value the ram). The link between the offering of the firstborn male and redemption with a ram underlies the later usage of monetary redemption (Mic 6:7). *See* ANIMALS OF THE BIBLE; SACRIFICES AND OFFERINGS.

Bibliography: Bruce Chilton. "The Hungry Knife: Towards a Sense of Sacrifice." *The Bible in Human Society: Essays in Honour of John Rogerson.* M. D. Carroll et al, eds. (1995) 122–38.

BRUCE CHILTON

2. Ram (**ram** רָם) was the great-grandson of Judah and ancestor of King David (1 Chr 2:9-10). Ram was the grandson of Perez, who was born to Judah by his daughter-in-law Tamar. He is listed in the genealogy of Boaz in Ruth 4:19. The genealogy of Jesus in Matthew gives his name as Aram (Matt 1:3-4).

3. The firstborn son of Jerahmeel (1 Chr 2:25-27).

4. The name of the clan to which Elihu belonged (Job 32:2).

KEVIN A. WILSON

RAM OF ORDINATION [אֵיל מִלֻּאִים **ʾel milluʾim**]. A sacrifice used for the priestly consecration of Aaron and his sons, issued as a divine command in Exod 29:15-34 and fulfilled in Lev 8:22, 29. In type, it stands between the holy and most holy offerings. It is mentioned in the *Temple Scroll* (11QT[a] XV, 3). *See* PRIESTS AND LEVITES; SACRIFICES AND OFFERINGS.

LJUBICA JOVANOVIC

RAM, BATTERING. *See* BATTERING RAM; WAR, METHODS, TACTICS, WEAPONS OF (BRONZE AGE THROUGH PERSIAN PERIOD); WAR, METHODS, TACTICS, WEAPONS OF (HELLENISTIC THROUGH ROMAN PERIODS).

RAMAH ray´muh [רָמָה **ramah,** רָאמַת **raʾmath;** Ῥαμά **Rhama**]. This name designates four places in the Bible. It is sometimes alternated with the related forms RAMOTH and Ramathaim. The toponym means "high place, hill, eminence," or the like. In 2 Kgs 8:29 and 2 Chr 22:6, Ramah is a shortened form for RAMOTH-GILEAD. 1. A town in Benjamin (*see* BENJAMIN, BENJAMINITES) located north of Jerusalem. This site is probably to be identified with modern er-Ram, though some prefer identification with Ramallah a bit farther north. This Ramah first appears in the topographic list in Josh 18:25, where it is located among the towns of Benjamin. It is also mentioned, in passing, as a site in Benjamin in the stories of DEBORAH (Judg 4:5) and the Levite's concubine (Judg 19:13). In the former case, the site is noted for its nearness to Bethel, in the latter, to GIBEAH.

The biblical figure who is most prominently associated with Ramah of Benjamin is SAMUEL. Ramah is the home of Samuel's parents Elkanah and Hannah (1 Sam 1:19; 2:11), from which they journey to Bethel for Hannah's fateful encounter with Eli. The form Ramathaim, found in 1 Sam 1:1, should be taken as an alternate name for the same location, rather than a different place. Later, once Samuel has taken up his office as judge and prophet, he establishes his own home and seat at Ramah, itinerating from there on a circuit including Bethel, GILGAL, and Mizpah (1 Sam 7:15-17; *see* MIZPAH, MIZPEH). It was at Ramah that the elders of Israel sought Samuel to ask that he give them a king (1 Sam 8:4), to Ramah that Samuel returned after his final conflict with Saul (1 Sam 15:34) and his anointing of DAVID (1 Sam 16:13), and at Ramah that Samuel was buried after his death (1 Sam 25:1; 28:3).

In 1 Sam 19, David's flight from the jealous King Saul leads him to Ramah. David apparently seeks to shelter himself under the authority of Samuel. The prophet and the fugitive take refuge at a place called NAIOTH in Ramah. There, Saul's messengers, sent to retrieve David, are distracted from their mission when they fall into a prophetic frenzy, a fate that also befalls Saul himself when he comes (1 Sam 19:18-24). The meaning and significance of *Naioth* is uncertain, but the most satisfactory suggestion is that the term designates a particular precinct or compound within Ramah, possibly the dwelling place of a band of charismatic prophets affiliated with Samuel. Such an understanding would account for the prophetic episodes experienced by Saul and his henchmen, bearing in mind that the other occurrence of such an episode on the part of Saul (1 Sam 10:10) also takes place in the presence of a prophetic band.

In the period of the divided monarchy, Ramah of Benjamin was located within the territory of Judah, but very near to the border with Israel. Because it sat on the main road connecting Jerusalem to the north, the site had considerable strategic importance. BAASHA of Israel, in the early 9th cent. BCE, attempted to subdue Judah by seizing and fortifying Ramah, effecting a blockade on commercial traffic to Jerusalem and the Judahite heartland (1 Kgs 15:17). ASA of Judah sought to break the blockade by the expedient of bribing BEN-HADAD of Aram-Damascus to attack Israel from the north. This tactic was successful, as the Aramean invasion drove into Israelite territory as far as the shores of Lake Kinneret, and compelled Baasha to withdraw from Judah (1 Kgs 15:18-21). Asa razed the new fortifications at Ramah and used the materials to fortify his nearby outposts of GEBA and Mizpah.

Ramah is mentioned in two prophetic oracles from the 8th cent. BCE, both making reference to the invasion of Judah by the combined forces of Israel and Aram known as the Syro-Ephraimitic Crisis. Hosea 5:8 calls for warning trumpets to be sounded in Gibeah, Ramah, and Beth-aven, all Benjaminite sites on the likely route of an invader marching from SAMARIA or the Jezreel Valley to Jerusalem. In Isa 10:29, a similar route is traced for advancing enemies, which probably reflects the same scenario. The Isaiah text is somewhat ambiguous in context, however, and could conceivably point to a different episode. In any case, the mention of Ramah in these oracles suggests that it remained among the key strategic outposts of Judah during this period.

After the fall of Jerusalem to the Babylonians in 586 BCE, Ramah was no longer a border town. It appears, however, that its location on a major trade route lent it new significance as the staging point for the caravans of exiles and Babylonian troops who were departing for Mesopotamia. The site is explicitly mentioned in this connection in Jer 40:1, where Jeremiah is released by the Babylonian commander NEBUZARADAN after he has been brought to Ramah in chains with other Judahite exiles-to-be. It appears that Ramah was the "point of no return," and so it was at Ramah that Jeremiah had to decide whether to accompany the exiles to Babylon or to remain in Judah. Presumably, his record of advocating cooperation with Babylon instead of resistance earned Jeremiah exemption from forcible deportation. The cryptic reference to Ramah in the poetic description of Rachel weeping for her lost children in Jer 31:15 may well reflect the laments of the departing exiles that Jeremiah heard there. In the postexilic period, Ramah appears in several geographic lists that probably reflect census lists from the Persian period (Ezra 2:26; Neh 7:30; 11:33). These lists consistently place Ramah in Benjamin, and near Geba, as one would expect.

In the NT, Ramah is mentioned once. Matthew 2:18 quotes Jer 31:15 as a prophecy that has been fulfilled by Herod's slaughter of innocent children in and around BETHLEHEM, as he sought to eliminate the infant Jesus. The reference to Ramah is somewhat puzzling, since the Ramah to which Jeremiah refers is clearly located in Benjamin, north of Jerusalem, far from Bethlehem. The connection is explained by the conflicting traditions about the location of the tomb of RACHEL, wife of Jacob. Some traditions of Rachel's burial locate her tomb at ZELZAH, a Benjaminite site near Ramah (1 Sam 10:2). Jeremiah's reference to Rachel in his poetic description of the departing exiles seems to presume such a tradition. Other traditions, however, locate Rachel's burial place at Ramat Rahel (*see* RAHEL, RAMAT) on the way south from Jerusalem to Bethlehem. Thus, Matt 2:18 appropriates the oracle based on the mention of Rachel.

2. A town in Simeon (*see* SIMEON, SIMEONITES) located in the Negeb (*see* NEGEB, NEGEV), probably to be identified with Tel Ira, in the Beersheba Valley. This Ramah appears in a toponym list (Josh 19:8) and, as "Ramoth of the Negeb," as one of the towns to which David gave his booty (1 Sam 30:27). The site is also mentioned on one of the ARAD OSTRACA,

where it appears to be a fortress of Judah on or near the Edomite border.

3. A town on the boundary of Asher (*see* ASHER, ASHERITES) somewhere in the vicinity of TYRE (Josh 19:29). No modern identification can be made with certainty.

4. A town in Naphtali, possibly at modern er-Rameh, in the vicinity of HAZOR (Josh 19:36). *See* NAPHTALI, NAPHTALITES.

Bibliography: Yohanan Aharoni. *The Land of the Bible: A Historical Geography* (1979).

D. MATTHEW STITH

RAMAT EL-KHALIL. *See* KHALIL, RAMAT EL.

RAMAT MATRED. *See* MATRED, RAMAT.

RAMATHAIM-ZOPHIM. *See* RAMAH.

RAMATHITE ray′muh-th*i*t [רָמָתִי **ramathi**]. SHIMEI the Ramathite was in charge of David's vineyards (1 Chr 27:27). *Ramathite* likely indicates that Shimei was from one of the cities named RAMAH.

RAMATH-LEHI ray′muhth-lee′h*i* [רָמַת לְחִי **ramath lekhi**]. The place where SAMSON, spirit-filled, slew 1,000 Philistines with a donkey's jawbone (Judg 15:14-17). The name means "raised jawbone." *See* LEHI.

RAMATH-MIZPEH ray′muhth-miz′puh [רָמַת הַמִּצְפֶּה **ramath hammitspeh**]. A town serving as a boundary marker in the Gadites' allotment (Josh 13:26).

RAMBAN. Acronym of Rabbi Moses ben Nachman (1194–1270), also known as Nachmanides. An important figure for the Jewish community in medieval Catalonia, the Ramban was competent in medicine, talmudic scholarship, philology, and mysticism. He wrote commentaries on the Song of Songs, the book of Job, and the Pentateuch. His exegetical approach drew heavily on the Spanish tradition of interpretation, which focused on linguistic analysis and the plain meaning of the text, but he also engaged in dialogue with predecessors like Ibn Ezra (*see* IBN EZRA, RABBI ABRAHAM) and RASHI. In both his person and his work, the Ramban represents the culmination of over 1,000 years of Jewish interpretive practice. *See* RABBINIC INTERPRETATION.

PHILLIP MICHAEL SHERMAN

RAMESES. *See* RAAMSES.

RAMESSES ram′uh-seez [רַעְמְסֵס **ra**ʿ**meses**; רַעַמְסֵס **ra**ʿ**amses**]. Ramesses was the name of eleven Egyptian kings in the late 2nd millennium BCE. The historical era comprising the Nineteenth and Twentieth dynasties, from the reign of Ramesses I through that of Ramesses XI, is often termed the Ramesside period (*see* EGYPT).

1. Ramesses I was the first in the line of kings Egypt named Ramesses ("born of [the sun-god] Re") who came to power against the backdrop of the AMARNA period, the reigns of AKHENATEN (Amenhotep IV) and his immediate successors in the late 14th cent. BCE. Akhenaten revolutionized the social, political, and religious landscape of Egypt.

Akhenaten's successors embarked on a program of restoration, erasing the reforms and reviving the old customs and institutions. The dynastic line ended with the boy-king Tutankhamun, who died childless. The throne passed to civilian and military leaders, first Vizier Ay and then General Horemhab. Lacking a son to succeed him, Horemhab appointed as his successor the vizier and general Ramesses who already had a son and grandson.

Although he reigned little more than a year, Ramesses I founded a dynasty that ruled Egypt for over a century. He and his successors sought to recapture the power and prestige Egypt enjoyed at the height of the Eighteenth Dynasty, a program carried to its fullest under his grandson, Ramesses II. Ramesses I modeled his throne names after those of Ahmose, founder of the Eighteenth Dynasty. His son, Seti I, combined elements of the throne names of the great Eighteenth Dynasty kings Thuthmose III (*see* THUTMOSE) and Amenhotep III.

2. Ramesses II was the most famous Ramesses, known in modern times as "Ramesses the Great" and frequently identified as the PHARAOH of the exodus (*see* EXODUS, BOOK OF). Ramesses II was a young boy when his father, Seti I, ascended the throne. By his mid-teens he was accompanying his father into battle and learning the tasks of administration. He was crowned prince-regent in Seti I's seventh year, solidifying his position as heir and pharaoh-in-training. Nine years later Seti I died, and Ramesses, a young man in his mid-twenties, became king in his own right.

The Hittite Empire (*see* HITTITES) constituted Ramesses II's greatest challenge. At its zenith the Egyptian Empire incorporated almost the entire Levant, but during the 14th cent. BCE, Hittite expansion encroached on Egypt's Syrian territories. Like his father before him, Ramesses II mounted military campaigns to reestablish Egyptian sovereignty over the region. The key battle occurred at Kadesh on the Orontes River in Ramesses II's fifth year. According to Egyptian accounts, the king's heroism saved the day. The Egyptians, misled by local spies into believing that the Hittites were still far to the north, allowed their troops to become strung out as they approached Kadesh. The Hittites were actually hiding behind the city and ambushed the Egyptians while they were crossing the river. The Egyptians were thrown into a panic, until Ramesses II charged into the fray on his chariot and rallied his troops. With the aid of a late arriving unit of elite soldiers, the Egyptians were able to regroup and prevent a rout, but were forced to withdraw without regaining control over the region.

Periodic skirmishes over the next fifteen years accomplished little, and in Ramesses II's twenty-first year he concluded a peace treaty with the Hittites, copies of which are extant in both Egyptian and AKKADIAN.

In Asia, as in NUBIA, imperial administration was under an overseer of foreign lands whose permanent residence was in Egypt. A small number of Egyptian soldiers and administrators was permanently posted in the Levant with vassal princes managing day-to-day administration of individual city-states.

Egypt enjoyed stability and prosperity during the sixty-six year reign of Ramesses II (1279–1213 or 1304–1237 BCE). Royal donations enriched temple complexes throughout the Nile Valley. Ramesses II commissioned more monuments than any other Egyptian king. At THEBES he completed the Great Hypostyle Hall, begun by his grandfather, in the Karnak temple and constructed a forecourt in the Luxor temple. Across the river on the west bank, he built the Ramesseum (his mortuary temple) and a complex of tombs for himself and his family in the Valley of the Kings and the Valley of the Queens. At Abydos he built his own cenotaph temple (secondary mortuary temple) and completed his father's. Prince Khaemwaset oversaw major construction projects at MEMPHIS on his father's behalf, including the Serapeum (underground burial complex for the Apis Bull) and the great temple of Ptah, where he served as high priest. Ramesses II also built several temples in Nubia, including two at Abu Simbel. These impressive structures, dedicated to Ramesses II and his chief wife Nefertari, were cut into the cliffs and flanked by colossal statues. The great temple was oriented so that twice each year the rising sun would penetrate to the innermost sanctuary and illuminate the four colossal statues representing Ptah, Amun-Re, Re-Horakhty, and Ramesses II.

The quantity of monuments bearing the names of Ramesses II is due in part to policies that sped up production. While the king commissioned countless life-size and colossal statues, he also usurped the statues of earlier kings, which were recarved in his likeness and with his names. Sunken relief replaced raised relief on most monuments, reducing the total surface area that had to be cut back.

Ramesses II sired nearly 100 children, many of whom he outlived, including his twelve oldest sons. His thirteenth son MERNEPTAH succeeded him. From Merneptah's reign comes the first reference to Israel—on a stela celebrating victory over the Libyans.

The identification of Ramesses II as the pharaoh of the exodus is tempting, but strictly circumstantial. The "Israel Stela" seems to place some entity called Israel in Canaan by the fifth year of Merneptah, but provides no details regarding their settlement history. The exodus narrative itself contains details drawn from the Rameside period, including the construction of Pi-Ramesses, which establishes the earliest possible date for the final editing of the text. Such details could not have been written before the reign of Ramesses II, but could be anachronisms introduced for the sake of verisimilitude by a later author who knew of Pithom and Pi-Ramesses as cities from an earlier era and assumed they were contemporaneous with the exodus.

The decline that began in the latter years of Ramesses II accelerated after the death of his heir, Merneptah. The ensuing struggles resulted in the emergence of a new dynastic line, which modeled itself after the reign of Ramesses II. With the exception of the founder Sethnakhte, the kings of the Twentieth Dynasty all bore the name Ramesses.

3. Ramesses III was the son and successor of Sethnakhte. Inscribed bowls from sites in the Negev indicate continued Egyptian dominance over that region during his reign. The settlement of the PHILISTINES along the southern coastal plain dates from his reign. Ramesses III repulsed a land and sea attack on the Nile Valley by the SEA PEOPLES, a coalition of tribes that included the Peleset or Philistines, but ceded them the Mediterranean coastal plain north of Sinai. The latter years of his reign reveal a rapidly declining central authority, including labor strikes by the necropolis workmen and a conspiracy by members of the harem to assassinate the king and place one of his sons on the throne.

4. During the later Twentieth Dynasty other kings named Ramesses witnessed the collapse of Egypt's empire as the kings were forced to concentrate on internal struggles. Although the kings continued to mount expeditions to the copper mines of Timna, north of modern Elath (*see* ELATH, ELOTH) in southern Israel, at least through the reign of Ramesses V, few Egyptian artifacts of any significance appear at Canaanite or Proto-Israelite sites after the reign of Ramesses III.

Bibliography: Manfred Bietak. *Avaris and Piramesse: Archaeological Exploration in the Eastern Nile Delta.* Rev. ed. (1986); Rita E. Freed. *Ramsses II: The Great Pharaoh and His Time* (1987); Kenneth A. Kitchen. *Pharaoh Triumphant: The Life and Times of Ramesses II* (1982); Joyce A. Tyldesley. *Ramesses: Egypt's Greatest Pharaoh* (2000).

CAROLYN R. HIGGINBOTHAM

RAMIAH ruh-m*i*´uh [רַמְיָה ramyah; Ἰερμάς Iermas]. The first of seven sons of PAROSH who dismissed their foreign wives and children as God's covenant required (Ezra 10:25). In the parallel, 1 Esd 9:26, the name is Iermas, which some translations render "Hiermas," but the NRSV corrects to Ramiah.

RAMOTH ray´moth [רָאמוֹת raʾmoth, רָמוֹת ramoth]. 1. *See* RAMOTH-GILEAD.

2. A Levitical city in the territory of Issachar given to the sons of Gershom (1 Chr 6:73 [Heb. 6:58]). A parallel Hebrew text in Josh 21:29 lists the city as JARMUTH, although the LXX version of this text reads

"Ramoth," which is most likely the original form. Ramoth is probably the city of Issachar's territory listed in Josh 19:21 as REMETH. Ramoth's location is uncertain but some scholars associate Ramoth with Kokab el-Hawa, a towering site (ca. 1,000 ft. above sea level) on which stands the crusader castle Belvoir, overlooking the Jordan Valley. They make this assessment by connecting the site's lofty position with the meaning of Ramoth, "heights."

3. A Judahite city in the Negev whose elders received spoils from David after he routed the Amalekites (1 Sam 30:27). The location of the site is unknown.

TERRY W. EDDINGER

RAMOTH-GILEAD ray'muhth-gil'ee-uhd [רָמֹת גִּלְעָד **ramoth gil`adh**]. Located on the plateau east of the Jordan River in the tribal territory of Gad (Deut 4:43; Josh 20:8; 21:38; *see* GAD, GADITES) near the border between ancient Israel and Syria. Various suggestions regarding the identification of Ramoth-gilead with an archaeological site in the region have been offered. Archaeological work in the second half of the 20th cent. at Tell er-Rumeit, located about 7 km south of Ramtha on the Syrian border and approximately 60 km north of modern Amman (Roman Philadelphia), provides strong evidence for its identification with Ramoth-gilead of the OT.

Deuteronomy and Joshua give Ramoth-gilead a prominent place in the early stages of Israel's history in the land. Deuteronomy 4:43 records the Mosaic identification of Ramoth-gilead as the central-most of the three cities of refuge on the east side of the Jordan River; Josh 20:8 has Joshua implementing the assignment of the cities. In addition, Joshua designated Ramoth-gilead as one of the forty-eight Levitical cities, according to Josh 21:38. The continued importance of the city in the period of the united monarchy is indicated by its identification as the location of BEN-GEBER, one of twelve Solomonic officials assigned to organizing and providing the monthly royal cuisine (1 Kgs 4:13).

Subsequent to the late-10th cent. BCE division of the monarchy, Ramoth-gilead became part of the Northern Kingdom; its strategic location near the Syrian border made it something of a buffer between Israel and Syria, and, consequently, control of the city was a continuing high priority for both the Israelites and the Arameans. The first of two theologically charged narratives attesting to this is the incident that portrays Israelite kingship confronted by the conflict between true and false prophets recorded in 1 Kgs 22 (compare 2 Chr 18). The Israelite king AHAB invited the king of Judah, JEHOSHAPHAT, to join him in his attempt to regain possession of Ramoth-gilead, which had come under the control of the Arameans. Jehoshaphat agreed to join Ahab in his endeavor only after prophetic word regarding the outcome was sought. Conflicting word from the prophets of Ahab and the prophet MICAIAH ben-Imlah resulted in a disguised Ahab and his royally clad southern counterpart engaging the Arameans. The word of Micaiah ben-Imlah proved to be true when the disguised Ahab was slain and the Israelite army routed.

The second incident similarly depicts the Israelite king JORAM being joined by AHAZIAH, the king of Judah, in waging war against the Syrians at Ramoth-gilead, where Joram was wounded, although not mortally (2 Kgs 8:25-29). While Joram returned to Jezreel to recover from his wound Elisha sent a prophet to Ramoth-gilead to anoint JEHU, one of the Israelite commanders maintaining a garrison there, as king in place of Joram. Jehu subsequently assassinated both Ahaziah and Joram, thus bringing the Omride Dynasty to its end.

JOHN I. LAWLOR

RAMP, SIEGE [סֹלְלָה **solelah**; χάραξ **charax**]. A siege ramp was a structure "cast-up" around or against the walls of cities or fortresses to prevent the escape of inhabitants, thereby laying siege. It was a platform for siege engines or towers, allowing the invading forces the capacity to attack the inhabitants and walls with arrows, stones, battering rams, and even fire.

This type of warfare was common in the ancient world. Joab used siege ramps against the walls of the town of Abel of Beth-maacah where the rebellious Sheba son of Bichri was hiding (2 Sam 20:15). Sennacherib intended to build a siege ramp against Jerusalem but was divinely foiled (2 Kgs 19:32; Isa 37:33). The prophets predicted Babylonian siege ramps against Jerusalem (Jer 6:6; Ezek 4:2; 17:17; 21:22; 26:8), and Jesus foretold Roman siege ramps (NRSV, "ramparts") against Jerusalem (Luke 19:43). *See* BATTLEMENT; WAR, METHODS, TACTICS, WEAPONS OF (BRONZE AGE THROUGH PERSIAN PERIOD); WAR, METHODS, TACTICS, WEAPONS OF (HELLENISTIC THROUGH ROMAN PERIODS).

MICHAEL G. VANZANT

RAMPART [חֵיל **khel**, חֵל **khel**, מָצוֹר **matsor**; χάραξ **charax**]. A raised earthen mound or embankment or a fortification wall (Hab 2:1). The term can be used for the outer defenses of a city, as at Abel of Beth-maacah (2 Sam 20:15). *Rampart* is used in reference to JERUSALEM in Lam 2:8; however, Jerusalem's extensive use of ramparts was limited to the north side of the city, since deep natural valleys protected the other sides. Nahum uses the term metaphorically when he speaks of the sea as the "rampart" of THEBES (Nah 3:8). Jesus prophesied that soon the enemies of Jerusalem would set up ramparts against the city and besiege it (Luke 19:43). *See* FORTIFICATION.

TERRY W. EDDINGER

RAM'S HORN, SHOPHAR. *See* MUSICAL INSTRUMENTS.

RAMSES. *See* RAMESSES.

RANSOM [כֹּפֶר kofer; λύτρον lytron]. The price paid to redeem someone or something, to cancel a debt or obligation, or to secure an exemption for punishment. In the OT, ransom is usually found in conjunction with the price of a penalty for an offense (of individuals, e.g., Exod 21:30; Num 35:31; of groups, Isa 43:3; 4 Macc 17:21). The term can refer to the redemption of a slave (Lev 19:20) or an animal (Lev 27:27). In the 1st-cent. CE Greek world, the term was commonly used for the release of captives or prisoners. In the NT, the term is used of Jesus' sacrifice for humanity (Matt 20:28; Mark 10:45; compare 1 Pet 1:18; Rev 5:9). *See* ATONEMENT; REDEEM, REDEEMER; SALVATION.

TERRY W. EDDINGER

RAPE. An act in which one person uses force to commit sexual violence against another. In the OT and ANE the rape of a woman is usually treated as an offense against another male. Thus, the biblical perception of rape is different from the modern understanding, which places emphasis on the lack of consent of the victim and the violation of an individual's body. Although in the biblical material a woman's consent (or lack thereof) does play a role in determining whether a rape has occurred, the offense is understood legally as a crime against another man, such as her father or husband.

In the OT, the subject of rape appears in both legal and narrative contexts. The legal texts concerning rape are found within a larger collection of laws that deal with sexual relations between men and women (Deut 22:13-30 [Heb. 22:13–23:1]). Two texts within this section, 22:25-27 and 22:28-29, are usually classified as rape laws. The first addresses the case of a woman who is engaged to be married. The second deals with a virgin who is not engaged. These texts reflect patterns and themes that are similar to law codes found elsewhere in the ANE. In biblical and ANE law, there are three issues in dealing with rape: 1) the marital status of the female victim; 2) the woman's consent or lack of consent; and 3) the identity of the offended party.

Deuteronomy 22 contains laws that deal with adultery and other sexual crimes. The marital status of the woman is a key factor in determining the nature of the offense and the extent of punishment for both adultery and rape. The woman is characterized as married, engaged, or not engaged. The male offender is charged with adultery in cases where he has sexual relations with a woman who is married or engaged. The offender's punishment is death (v. 22 and vv. 23-24). The woman is also put to death if the sexual encounter was consensual. In cases that involve rape—when the woman does not consent—she is not punished. In biblical law, like in ANE law, a woman's consent is tied to the context in which the act occurred. If the crime occurs in the city, the woman's consent is assumed since presumably someone would hear her if she cried out. (For a deuterocanonical example of a woman who does cry out in the context of a town, see Sus 24–26.) If, however, a man meets the woman in the open country and seizes her, the act is considered nonconsensual and only the male offender is put to death (vv. 25-27). In such a circumstance, the woman might have tried to cry out, but no one would have heard her. In the last law (vv. 28-29), the rape of a virgin who is not engaged, the perpetrator is required to pay the bride price to her father. The male offender must marry the woman without the possibility of divorce. The crime is viewed as a financial loss to the father since his daughter is no longer marriageable. The no-divorce clause, however, suggests that this law intends to provide for the financial security of the female victim.

There are three narrative incidents of rape in the OT. They occur in Gen 34; Judg 19; and 2 Sam 13. All three stories follow a similar progression. The initial rape is followed by excessively violent male responses, resulting in some kind of social fragmentation. In Gen 34, Shechem rapes Dinah, daughter of Jacob, as she is going out to visit the women of the region. After the encounter, Shechem and his father, Hamor, negotiate with Jacob and his sons for Dinah's hand in marriage. The sons, however, deceive the Shechemites, the latter agreeing to have the town's men circumcised as part of the marriage agreement. Simeon and Levi, both blood brothers of Dinah, retaliate by killing all of the men of Shechem with the sword. The brothers' violent act of retribution enrages Jacob. The story ends with the family bitterly divided over the incident.

Judges 19 recounts the horrible gang rape of a Levite's concubine in Gibeah. The scene contains significant literary allusions to the story of Sodom and Gomorrah (Gen 19). In fact, most scholars assume that the Judges narrative is dependent on the Genesis material. Both the Gen 19 and Judg 19 stories are more properly understood not as a condemnation against homoeroticism (both mobs seek to "know" the visiting males) but instead as a failure of hospitality. In the ancient world, male on male sexual violence or rape constituted a social shaming or humiliation on one's opponent or enemy. In Judg 19, similar to Gen 19, the violent mob demands that an old Ephraimite man send out his Levite guest so that they might sexually humiliate the visitor. The host offers his daughter and the Levite's concubine instead. When the mob refuses, the Levite takes his concubine and throws her out to the crowd. After they brutally rape her all night, she is left for dead. The Levite returns home and proceeds to cut his concubine's body into pieces, which he sends to the tribes of Israel as a summons to battle. A bloody civil war follows in which the tribe of Benjamin is almost completely destroyed. This intertribal conflict is part of the larger social and moral decline that characterizes the end of the book of Judges. In the third rape text, 2 Sam 13, David's son Amnon rapes his half-sister Tamar. After the sexual violation, Amnon humiliates Tamar by sending her away. David, however, does not do anything to address this situation.

Tamar's brother, Absalom, secretly plots his revenge and eventually kills Amnon. David's post-rape silence creates tension between the king and his son, Absalom. These dynamics lead inevitably to Absalom's rebellion against his father. The events in 2 Sam 13 begin to fulfill the prophet Nathan's oracle that internal strife will violently divide David's house.

Beyond similar progression and themes among the rape narratives, these texts share common vocabulary. The Hebrew verb used for rape (ʿ**anah** עָנָה) appears in all three texts and is accompanied by verbs of force in all three texts to describe the sexual violation. The term **nevalah** (נְבָלָה, "disgraceful thing") also occurs within all three stories, primarily in the idiom "to do a disgraceful thing in Israel." This phrase serves as an evaluative response to the rapes (Gen 34:7; Judg 20:6; 2 Sam 13:12). *See* DINAH and TAMAR.

Bibliography: Cheryl B. Anderson. *Women, Ideology, and Violence: Critical Theory and the Construction of Gender in the Book of the Covenant and the Deuteronomic Law* (2004); Alice A. Keefe. "Rapes of Women/ Wars of Men." *Semeia* 61 (1993) 79–97; Carolyn Pressler. *The View of Women Found in the Deuteronomic Family Laws* (1993).

FRANK M. YAMADA

RAPHAEL raf′ay-uhl [רְפָאֵל refaʾel; ʿΡαφαήλ **Rhaphaēl**]. Meaning "God heals." 1. An ancestor of Tobit (Tob 1:1; *see* TOBIT, BOOK OF). The name is lacking in some Greek manuscripts.

2. In the books of Tobit and *1 Enoch* (*see* ENOCH, FIRST BOOK OF), Raphael is one of seven angels who stand in God's presence (Tob 12:15; *1 En.* 20:1-7; *see* ANGEL). In Tobit, Raphael hears the prayers of Tobit and Sarah and comes to their assistance (Tob 3:16-17). Disguised as a human, Raphael accompanies Tobit's son Tobias on his journey to Media and arranges the marriage between Tobias and Sarah. He protects Tobias from the demon Asmodeus, who has killed Sarah's first seven husbands on their wedding nights. In keeping with the meaning of his name, Raphael later provides a way for Tobias to cure Tobit's blindness. In *1 Enoch*, Raphael is the one who binds the demon AZAZEL (*1 En.* 10:5-7).

KEVIN A. WILSON

RAPHAH ray′fuh [רָפָה **rafah**]. Raphah (REPHAIAH in 1 Chr 9:43) is listed among the descendants of Benjamin as the son of Binea and father of Eleasah (1 Chr 8:37), although he is not included in other Benjaminite lists (e.g., 1 Chr 7:6-12).

RAPHAIN raf′ay-in [ʿΡαφαίν **Rhaphain**]. An ancestor of Judith (Jdt 8:1).

RAPHIA ruh-fi′uh [ʿΡαφία **Rhaphia**]. A city located 20 mi. southwest of Gaza on the coast of Palestine, identified with modern Tel Rafah. Raphia is the last fortress on the "way of Horus" in Papyrus Anastasi I (pAn I.27.7–8), a 13th-cent. BCE text that describes itineraries through Canaan. The "way of Horus" was the Egyptian name for the road that ran from the Nile delta across the Sinai Peninsula into Palestine. The OT refers to this road as "by way of the land of the Philistines" (Exod 13:17), a road purposefully avoided by the Israelites during the exodus. The Egyptians established a string of fortresses along this road to guard it. Raphia's position at the eastern end marked it as the first town in Palestine. Although Raphia is not mentioned in the OT, it occurs in a number of Egyptian and Mesopotamian sources, such as the triumphal relief of Shoshenq I (King Shishak of Egypt), who campaigned against Jerusalem in the late 10th cent. BCE (1 Kgs 14:25-28; 2 Chr 12:1-12).

Raphia was the site of the battle between Ptolemy IV Philopater and Antiochus III in 217 BCE in the struggle between the Ptolemies and the Seleucids over control of Palestine (3 Macc 1:1). It was destroyed by the Hasmoneans in 97 BCE, but was rebuilt by the Romans in 55 BCE.

KEVIN A. WILSON

RAPHON ray′fon [ʿΡαφών **Rhaphōn**]. A town in Gilead usually associated with Er-Rafeh. According to 1 Macc 5:37-44, Gentiles under the leadership of a man named Timothy had begun to attack the Jews living in Transjordan following the rededication of the Temple in Jerusalem. Judas Maccabeus and his army conducted a campaign through Transjordan to liberate Jews who were under attack. The decisive battle between the Maccabeans and the army of Timothy came at Raphon, where the Gentiles were defeated.

KEVIN A. WILSON

RAPHU ray′fyoo [רָפוּא **rafu**ʾ]. The father of PALTI, the Benjaminite among the twelve men (one from each tribe) whom Moses charged with the task of scouting the land of Canaan to determine its fruitfulness and the strength of its inhabitants (Num 13:9).

RAQQA, KHIRBET ER. *See* JOKDEAM.

RAS ABU TABAT. *See* TABBATH.

RAS ET-TAHUNA. *See* ZEMARAIM.

RAS SHAMRA rahs-shahm′ruh. Ras Shamra lies on the coast of modern Syria and is the location of the ancient city of Ugarit. *See* UGARIT, HISTORY AND ARCHAEOLOGY.

RAS SHAMRA TABLETS. *See* UGARIT, HISTORY AND ARCHAEOLOGY; UGARIT, TEXTS AND LITERATURE.

RAS, BEIT. The modern village of Beit Ras is 5 km north of Irbid in Jordan. Late in the 1st cent. CE, the Romans founded a city, CAPITOLIAS, on the site. Coins issued by the city show that it was founded in 97/98 CE. The coins depict the main temple of the city, which was dedicated to Jupiter Capitolinus. The site has been continuously occupied since then. The ancient city reached its peak prosperity in the 2nd and 3rd cent. CE, with a mixed population of Nabateans, Romans, and Greeks. After the Islamic conquest in the 7th cent., the city's name was changed from Capitolias to Beit Ras and has remained so ever since.

Excavations have uncovered two levels of a marketplace in the center of town. A structure across from the marketplace has been identified as the city's main church. Capitolias was important enough to have a bishop, who represented the city at the councils of Nicea (325 CE) and Chalcedon (451 CE). In 2002, the Jordanian Department of Antiquities announced the discovery of a Roman amphitheater.

ADAM L. PORTER

RASHI. Solomon ben Isaac (1040–1105), commonly known as Rashi, the most popular Jewish biblical exegete of all time, was born in Troyes, in northern France, where he spent most of his life, except for time spent studying in the talmudic academies of Mainz and Worms. He was a leading rabbinic figure of his day, a spiritual and communal leader renowned for his wisdom, scholarship, modesty, and devotion to the truth.

Rashi wrote commentaries on almost the entire corpus of the Hebrew Bible, as well as an indispensable and arguably more important commentary on the Talmud. His commentaries, which are steeped in the rabbinic tradition, feature a newly discovered sensitivity to context, which leads to selectivity in the choice of midrashic material for inclusion. In many cases, Rashi modifies midrashic comments in keeping with his exegetical goals. While Rashi's commentaries usually focus on the text, he occasionally refers to contemporary social or economic conditions. The impact of the Crusades is especially felt in his commentary on Psalms, written after 1096, which applies numerous references to the nation Edom to the Christian Crusaders. His commentary on the Song of Songs shows the influence of contemporary Christian exegesis. Rashi was a brilliant stylist, and his blend of contextual exegesis and ethical homiletics characterized by clarity, concision, and felicity of expression have helped assign his commentary pride of place in the canon of classic Jewish texts that are still studied widely today. *See* RABBINIC LITERATURE.

BARRY DOV WALFISH

RASSIS ras'is [Ῥασσεις Rhasseis]. A city whose inhabitants were attacked by the Assyrian army under HOLOFERNES (Jdt 2:23; NRSV, "Rassisites"). It is only mentioned in the Judith passage, and the location is uncertain, although it has been identified by some as Mount Rossos or as a corruption of Tarsus.

JESSICA TINKLENBERG DEVEGA

RATHAMIN rath'uh-min [Ῥαθαμείν Rhathamein]. One of the three administrative districts in southern Samaria transferred by DEMETRIUS II Nicator of Syria to Maccabean control around 148 BCE. The other two districts were Aphairema and Lydda, east and west of Rathamin, respectively (1 Macc 11:34).

Starting in the 150s BCE, various claimants to the throne of the Seleucid kingdom sought Maccabean support by offering them concessions (1 Macc 10:6, 18-20, 25-44). Demetrius II confirmed these concessions (1 Macc 11:30-37). The transfer of Rathamin, Aphairema, and Lydda to Jerusalem probably indicates that the bulk of the population in these territories was Jewish. Modein, the home of the Maccabees (1 Macc 2:1), was just south of Rathamin. The territories remained under Jerusalem's control until the Romans assumed direct control of Judea and Samaria in 6 CE.

Rathamin is probably a corruption of "Ramathaim" (1 Sam 1:1), the home of the prophet Samuel. The district was also known as "ARIMATHEA," the home of one of Jesus' followers (Matt 27:57; John 19:38).

ADAM L. PORTER

RATTLE-SISTRUM. *See* MUSICAL INSTRUMENTS.

RAVEN [עֹרֵב ʿorev; κόραξ korax]. It is evident from Lev 11:15 and Deut 14:14 ("every raven of any kind") that ʿorev could be used in a broad, generic sense, covering all birds belonging to the *Corvidae* family, including ravens, crows, jackdaws, and rooks. Still, this apparently onomatopoeic term is usually, and probably correctly, translated "raven." Although some characteristics attributed to the ʿorev by biblical authors, such as this bird's propensity to feed on corpses and carcasses (Prov 30:17), are equally applicable to the raven and the CROW, the reference to its intensely black color (Song 5:11) would seem to favor the raven (*Corvus corax*). As a bird of prey that feeds on corpses, the raven is classified among the "detestable" and certainly unclean birds (Lev 11:13-19; Deut 14:12-18).

In the story of the flood, both the biblical version (Gen 8:7) and the Babylonian version (*see* GILGAMESH, EPIC OF), the captain sends out a raven to search for land. Another narrative reflecting a rather close relationship between ravens and human beings is found in 1 Kgs 17, where Elijah, sent into the wilderness, is fed by ravens. The seemingly trivial fact that the raven is able to obtain food for itself and its young is cited as evidence for God's providential care (Job 38:41; Ps 147:9; Luke 12:24). *See* BIRDS OF THE BIBLE; CLEAN AND UNCLEAN.

GÖRAN EIDEVALL

RAZIS ray'zis [Ῥαζίς Rhazis]. One of the Jerusalem elders. When NICANOR sent troops to arrest him in an effort to frighten the Jews, Razis took his own life rather than suffer the indignity of arrest by the enemy. His story (2 Macc 14:37-46) attests an early belief in resurrection.

RAZOR [מוֹרָה morah, תַּעַר taʿar]. Except for symbolic occasions (Ezekiel's sword in Ezek 5:1), the principal barbering tool was the razor. Forged of bronze and later of iron, with a rounded end to accommodate the curves of the face and head, this instrument was kept sharp to prevent irritation and to do an efficient job (see Ps 52:2 [Heb. 52:4] for comparison with a sharp tongue). The metaphorical mention of Assyria as a hired razor in Isa 7:20 suggests that barbering may have been a paid service. Individuals who could not afford a barber probably used their personal, multi-purpose knife. The razor was usually used on the face or head, but Levites shaved their bodies before being consecrated (Num 8:7). Since hair grows back, shaving is a temporary means of changing one's appearance when in mourning (Isa 15:2; Jer 16:6), entering a new community (Deut 21:12-13), or fulfilling a nazirite vow (Num 6:5, 9-17). Samson (Judg 13:5; 16:17) and Samuel (1 Sam 1:11), by contrast, were prohibited from ever using razors. *See* NAZIR, NAZIRITE; PENKNIFE; SHAVING; TOOLS.

VICTOR H. MATTHEWS

RE ray. The Egyptian sun-god Re was associated with creation, kingship, and the afterlife. Worshiped in many places, his chief cultic centers were at HELIOPOLIS and THEBES. At Heliopolis, he was joined with the creator Atum to form Atum-Re, the self-creative source of all existence. At Thebes, he was joined with Amun ("hiddenness") to form Amun-Re, the hidden one made visible.

The Egyptian king ruled as the "son of Re." One version of the afterlife casts the deceased as Re, dying in the west only to be revived at dawn after a perilous journey through the underworld. *See* EGYPT.

CAROLYN HIGGINBOTHAM

READER RESPONSE CRITICISM. Reading is a partnership between author/compiler and audience. The author creates a text, and the reader derives meaning. Both author and audience are governed by the sociocultural contexts in which they live and the assumptions that they bring to the text. This approach to literary works, including the Bible, differs from the emphasis on attempting to determine authorial intention.

Reader response methods begin by identifying a unique, theoretical audience and by postulating this audience's most likely interpretation of a text, given the audience's social context and history. Consequently, reader response criticism represents not only a literary but also a sociological approach to a text.

A historical reader response approach identifies the characteristics of ancient audiences to elucidate probable interpretations of the biblical materials shortly after they were written. A contemporary reader response approach addresses the interests and norms of a specific congregation to facilitate the homiletical interpretation of the same biblical materials. To bridge the gap between ancient and contemporary interpretations of Scripture, one may use these methods together on the same text.

Two brief examples illustrate the utility of reader response methods for the interpretation of biblical materials. The study of characteristics of a postexilic audience's social and behavioral interests might facilitate the exploration of reasons for the compilation of diverse materials from three prophets into their current form in the book of Isaiah. A comparison of the socioeconomic and theological concerns mirroring those found in Paul's letters and the very different economic and theological concerns reflected in the letter of James might illuminate why early audiences preserved and eventually canonized both Paul's letters and the non-Pauline perspectives of James. In these examples, the key to interpretation is as much on the audience's response as on the author's intent.

Reader response perspectives carry both advantages and drawbacks for scriptural interpretation. These models are useful because: 1) authorial intention and reader response are not always congruent; and 2) most biblical materials are either anonymous or attributed to authors about whom we have limited biographical information. Reader response criticism provides a useful approximation of the early reception of the biblical materials, especially when limited or contradictory data preclude an informed theory of authorial intention. However, a caveat about the limitations imposed by circular reasoning is required. The text under examination normally contributes some of the data used for the description of the hypothetical audience. This theoretical construct, in turn, guides the interpretation of the text. Consequently, some degree of selectivity and subjectivity is inherent in the process. The astute practitioner can mitigate these pitfalls by including extra-textual data and models from social theory among the data to be considered in the formulation of the hypothetical audience. *See* BIBLICAL CRITICISM; LITERARY INTERPRETATION, NT; LITERARY INTERPRETATION, OT; SOCIAL SCIENTIFIC CRITICISM, NT; SOCIAL SCIENTIFIC CRITICISM, OT.

Bibliography: Donald J. Hirsch Jr. *Validity in Interpretation* (1967); Wolfgang Iser. *The Act of Reading: A Theory of Aesthetic Response* (1978); Randall C. Webber. *Reader Response Analysis of the Epistle of James* (1996).

RANDALL C. WEBBER

REAIAH ree-ay'yuh [רְאָיָה reʾayah]. Three different men named Reaiah are mentioned in the OT.

1. A grandson of Judah and son of Shobal (1 Chr 4:2; named HAROEH in 1 Chr 2:52).

2. A Reubenite of the family of Joel, whose father is Micah and whose son is Baal (1 Chr 5:5).

3. The ancestor of temple servants who returned from the Babylonian exile with ZERUBBABEL (Ezra 2:47; Neh 7:50).

JOAN E. COOK

REALM OF THE DEAD. *See* DEAD, ABODE OF THE.

REAP [קָצַר qatsar; θερίζω therizō]. Reaping (harvesting, gathering) was vital in agriculturally based economies (Lev 23:22; Ruth 2:9; Matt 6:26; Luke 12:24) and often served as a metaphor for divine judgment (Isa 17:5; Jer 12:13; Rev 14:15-16) and the rewards and consequences of human effort (John 4:37-38; 1 Cor 9:11; Gal 6:7-9). *See* AGRICULTURE.

JAMES E. WEST

REASON [מַנְדַּע manda'; ἔννοια ennoia, λογός logos, νοῦς nous, φρόνημα phronēma]. The Bible ranges in its opinion about reason (also translated variously, e.g., as "knowledge" or "mind"), the capacity of human beings to seek truth or knowledge through rational thought. An illustration of perhaps the most negative view of reason appears at 2 Cor 10:1-6. There reason is actually described as an enemy; it needs to be subdued so that obedience to Christ may follow. Proverbs 3:5-8 and 1 Cor 13:8-13 regard reason slightly less dimly, although it is still seen as deficient. Proverbs labels reason unreliable, at least in contrast with Yahweh. Human wisdom does not necessarily shun evil, while fear of Yahweh does. In 1 Corinthians reason is associated with speech and thought. The limited capacity of children to reason is contrasted with adult rationality as an analogy for the shortfall of human reason now when compared with some fulfilled future realization of knowledge.

According to Wis 13:1-9 and Rom 1:18-23 reason is not all bad; however, humans do not make ideal use of it. People should be able to learn about God from the universe, declares Wisdom; yet many fail to do so and hence are blameworthy. They are misled to think that the universe itself is divine. Romans similarly indicates that reason ought to be able to learn about God through the cosmos. However, the wicked fail to exercise this faculty properly and instead worship false deities.

Sirach 17:5-14 considers reason good while, nonetheless, limited. On the one hand, the Lord gave reason or the ability of critical thinking to human beings. On the other hand, they were not supposed to think too much but rather to take the Lord's word on things.

Some of the better ratings of reason surface in Isa 29:13-14; Dan 4:34-37; Wis 17:12-13; and 4 Macc 1:1-6. All of these verses hold reason up as a valuable thing. A punishment for insincerity and halfheartedness is that the community's wise and discerning persons will lose their wisdom and discernment, which Isaiah compares with an equally unhappy consequence of prophets and seers being blinded (29:10). After Nebuchadnezzar's humiliation as an unbathed grass-eating outcast from society, Daniel shows him regaining his sanity or reason. This made the king fit for office once again and caused him to recognize God as the true sovereign. Both Wisdom and 4 Maccabees figure that reason controls passions. The former says reason can ward off fear, while fear when victorious establishes ignorance. The latter claims that reason as rational judgment is the chief virtue. It rules over the emotions that hinder self-control (namely, gluttony and lust), justice (e.g., malice), and courage (namely, anger, fear, and pain).

Because reason urges a person toward Christlikeness, Phil 2:1-8 and 1 Pet 4:1-6 offer it the highest praise. Philippians suggests that reason leads us to be loving, humble, and solicitous in service to each other just as Christ Jesus himself was. Reason leads us, like Christ, to accept suffering, reports 1 Peter, but also to reject desires such as licentiousness, passions, drunkenness, revelry, carousing, and lawless idolatry.

EDWIN C. HOSTETTER

REBA ree'buh [רֶבַע reva']. One of the five kings of Midian killed by Moses' army (Num 31:8; Josh 13:21). The kings, along with all the men of Midian, were slain on the Lord's order as revenge for their deception in a previous encounter at PEOR (Num 25:16-18). Numbers connects their deaths to that of BALAAM (Num 31:8). Joshua held that their demise occurred at the same time as the killing of the Amorite king SIHON (Josh 13:21). *See* MIDIAN, MIDIANITES.

JESSICA TINKLENBERG DEVEGA

REBECCA. *See* REBEKAH.

REBEKAH ri-bek'uh [רִבְקָה rivqah; Ῥεβέκκα Rhebekka]. Rebekah (Gen 22:23; 24:15–28:5; 29:12; 35:8; 49:31; or "Rebecca," Rom 9:10-12) is the second matriarch in the Hebrew family line after SARAH. She is the wife of ISAAC, the mother of JACOB and Esau (*see* ESAU, ESAUITES), and the daughter of BETHUEL, son of NAHOR and MILCAH. The main narrative involving Rebekah (Gen 24–28) begins when Abraham sends a servant to his hometown in Mesopotamia to find a wife for his son Isaac (*see* ABRAHAM, OT). The servant is concerned about whether a woman will be willing to go with him, but Abraham assures him that an angel of God will go before him. The servant leaves with ten camels and many valuable gifts. Upon arriving at the well by the outskirts of Nahor, he prays to God that the woman to whom he will ask help in watering the camels will respond affirmatively and will be God's choice for Isaac. No sooner is the prayer uttered than Rebekah, described as a virgin who is very fair to look at (24:16), appears with a water jar on her shoulder. She gives the servant water to drink and then proceeds to water his numerous camels. He gives her a heavy gold ring and gold bracelets, asks about her parentage, and whether there is room for him to lodge at her father's house. She describes her family and indicates that there is sufficient food and room for him to stay. He thanks God for his success. This classic type-scene of the woman at the well (compare Gen 29:1-30; Exod 2:11-22) depicts Rebekah as beautiful and gracious.

Rebekah's brother LABAN runs out to meet Abraham's servant and takes care of his camels and his men. Then Abraham's servant explains his mission and Bethuel and Nahor respond positively. The servant spends the night and gives more jewelry to Rebekah and gifts to her family. Abraham's servant is now eager to be on his way, but Rebekah's family wishes her to stay for ten days. She is queried and agrees to go immediately. She and her maids ride back to Canaan where Isaac and Rebekah see each other from a distance. Isaac takes Rebekah into his mother's tent and consummates their marriage.

At first Rebekah is barren, as is true of Sarah before her and RACHEL after her, but Isaac prays for her and she conceives the twins Esau and Jacob. The pregnancy is turbulent and when Rebekah inquires of the Lord, the Lord reveals that two nations are in her womb, that one is stronger than the other, and that the elder will serve the younger. After the twins are born, a famine drives the family to the land of Gerar, where Isaac passes Rebekah off as his sister out of fear that the Gerarites will kill him if he tells the truth about their relationship. Unlike the similar stories about Sarah and Abraham (Gen 12; 20), Rebekah is not actually taken into the foreign ruler's household.

When Isaac is old and blind and ready to give his blessing to his elder son Esau, Rebekah overhears Isaac's instructions to Esau and tells Jacob to get two kids so that she can prepare food for Isaac before Esau does and can trick Isaac into blessing Jacob rather than Esau. Although Isaac is suspicious, he is finally persuaded to bless Jacob. Many commentators have denounced Rebekah's manipulation of Isaac. However, some have pointed out that she is carrying out the mandate given to her when she inquires of God during her pregnancy. In any case, Rebekah is the protagonist in this episode. Overall she plays a more significant role than Isaac in this part of the ancestral narrative.

Esau is naturally angry and Rebekah instructs Jacob to go back to her relatives in Mesopotamia. She gets Isaac's agreement on this plan. When Jacob arrives he meets Rachel, Laban's daughter, and tells her that they are related and that he is Rebekah's son. The only other information the reader learns about Rebekah is about the death of her nurse Deborah (Gen 35:8) and of Rebekah's own death and burial alongside Abraham and Sarah and Isaac (Gen 49:31), in the field at MACHPELAH, east of Mamre, in Canaan. Rebekah is an independent, assertive, clever character who overshadows her husband, Isaac, about whom we learn much less than his wife.

In the NT, Paul contends that Abraham's only true heirs are those born to him as a result of a promise (Gen 18:10). He further illustrates this concept with Sarah and HAGAR, two mothers, and with Rebekah, one mother with two sons, of whom God promises that the elder will serve the younger (Rom 9:10-12).

Bibliography: Alice Ogden Bellis. *Helpmates, Harlots, and Heroes: Women's Stories in the Hebrew Bible* (1994) 80–84.

ALICE OGDEN BELLIS

REBEL, REBELLION [מָרַד maradh, מָרָה marah, פָּשַׁע pashaʿ, סָרַר sarar; στασιαστής stasiastēs]. The OT attests to the conviction that the government was given by God. There are accounts of rebellions, but they are only seen as God's will if they are successful, e.g., David's succession to Saul (1 Sam 16). Similarly, during Absalom's rebellion and his flight from Jerusalem David mentions that he will come back if it is the will of God (2 Sam 15:25-26). The OT also describes people rebelling against God by breaking his commandments (Isa 1:2; 63:10; Ezek 5:6), and the theme of the people's rebellion against God in the wilderness is carried out through different biblical books (Num 27:14; Josh 22; Ps 78).

When in Hellenistic times the government was influenced by Greek values, rebellion against it was seen as acceptable, even necessary, in order to uphold the divine laws. The Maccabees based their revolt on obedience to the Torah (1 Macc 2:24-27); they saw themselves in the tradition of Phinehas (1 Macc 2:26) and his fight against intermarriage of Israelites and the nations (Num 25:1-15). The ultimate success of the Maccabean revolt gave it justification as God's will and set a precedent of rebellion as zeal for God and his Torah.

This zeal also played a role in the Jewish war against the Romans. The causes of that rebellion were manifold: the Roman lack of understanding for the specific Jewish situation increased the atmosphere of tension and unrest, while poverty and the social problems of large land holdings also caused discontent among the poor. Thus religious zeal for the Torah, social tension, and cultural factors combined to lead to the Jewish revolt against Rome.

At first the aristocracy joined the war to maintain control and fortify the country (Josephus, *J.W.* 2.562–68). After Vespasian conquered Galilee and Idumea (*J.W.* 3.309–4.120, 550–56), different rebel factions were driven into Jerusalem where they fought at first against the aristocratic government and then among themselves. The sicarii (*J.W.* 2.272–77; *Ant.* 20.182–215) were adherents of a family who, like the Maccabees, dedicated themselves to the fight against Roman rule (Judas the Galilee, 6 CE; *J.W.* 2.118,

433; 7.253–57; Acts 5:37; James and Simon, 46–48 CE; *Ant.* 18.102; Menahem ben Jehuda, 66 CE; *J.W.* 2.408, 433–48; Eleazar ben Jair, 66–70 CE; *J.W.* 2.447; 7.163–209; 7.304–406).

The zealots (*J.W.* 18.23; *Ant.* 18.9; *see* ZEALOT) appeared as a distinct group in the winter 67–68 CE in a civil war with the provisional government (*J.W.* 4.162–207). With John of Gischala and the Idumeans (*J.W.* 4.208–35), they established a reign of terror in Jerusalem (*J.W.* 4.283–344; 355–65; 7.262–70). From November 67 CE, John of Gischala, an impoverished Galilean nobleman, took over the city and the Temple Mount (*J.W.* 4.389–97), until in 69 CE he was driven out of the city onto the Temple Mount by Simon bar Giora (*J.W.* 5.20, 98–103), until Jerusalem was conquered by the Romans and the Temple destroyed.

However, the different groups produced common coins. Thus they agreed on certain common goals: independence from Rome and the importance of the Torah. Unlike the Maccabees, their fight was unsuccessful and thus lacked the traditional justification of previous rebellions. After the Bar Kochba revolt in the 2nd cent. CE the thought of rebellion as expression of zeal for Torah was abandoned.

JUTTA LEONHARDT-BALZER

REBIRTH, RENEWAL [חָדַשׁ **khadhash,** חָלַף **khalaf;** ἀναγεννάω **anagennaō,** παλιγγενεσία **palingenesia**]. Rebirth and renewal refer to the life-giving activity of God in effecting a transforming new birth and/or renewal for persons and the created order. In the OT, God renews strength and life (Pss 103:5; 104:30; Lam 5:21 [**khadhash**]; and Isa 40:31; 41:1 [**khalaf**]). Philo apparently reads the OT with the Stoic understanding of rebirth following the cyclical conflagration (Philo, *Eternity* 89–93) and individual senses, e.g., the soul's rebirth at death (Philo, *Cherubim* 114). Philo and Josephus employ **palingenesia** in reference to the renewed post-flood world (Philo, *Moses* 2.65; compare *1 Clem.* 9:4) and Israel's postexilic restoration (Josephus, *Ant.* 11.66). The NT includes the concepts "renewal of all things" (Matt 19:28) and "rebirth" (**palingenesia**; Titus 3:5), as well as "new birth" (1 Pet 1:3) and "born anew" (**anagennaō**; 1 Pet 1:23; compare John 3:3).

A. The Old Testament

1. God's acts of renewal

God renews strength and life (Pss 103:5; 104:30; Lam 5:21 [**khadhash**]; Isa 40:31; 41:1 [**khalaf**]). God's initial creative activity gives birth to the cosmos and infuses it with life. God gives birth to humanity with the "breath of life" (Gen 2:7). God renews life after sending the flood (Gen 7–9), then gives birth to a people through whom God intends to carry out a life-giving mission to all of humanity (Gen 12:3; 18:18) and creation. When God's people find themselves in Egypt as slaves, God rebirths them through the exodus by making a way through the waters (birth imagery(?); Exod 14:21-22; compare Gen 1:9-10).

In exile, their plight is analogous to their former Egyptian bondage, requiring a new exodus, depicted as national and cosmic rebirth (Isa 35; 40–55), with Jerusalem as the center of the renewed cosmos (Isa 2:1-4; 65:17-25). Ezekiel's vision of the valley of dry bones depicts exile as death, a plight requiring the resurrecting power of God's Spirit to regenerate and renew the nation (Ezek 37:1-14). Israel's rebirth includes God's making a new covenant with them (Jer 31:31-34; 32:36-41) in which he gives them a new heart (Jer 24:7; Ezek 11:19-20; 36:25-27), cleanses them from sinful practices with "clean water" (Ezek 36:25), and places the divine Spirit in/among them, thereby transforming them from a disobedient, idolatrous people into those enabled to obey God's statutes and ordinances (Ezek 36:27).

2. Relational renewal

At the beginning of the monarchy, Saul is proclaimed Yahweh's choice for king, but some of the people do not accept his authority (1 Sam 10:24-27). After he succeeds in routing the Ammonites, the people "renew" his kingship to indicate their solidarity behind him (1 Sam 11:14). Jonathan, the Hasmonean high priest, solidifies crucial political relationships when he renews friendship between Israel and Rome and the Spartans (1 Macc 12:1-17; 14:18, 22; 15:17).

B. The New Testament

1. Cosmic rebirth

Jesus' resurrection is the primary reference point for conceptions of rebirth and renewal in the NT (*see* RESURRECTION, NT). References to cosmic renewal (Matt 19:28; Rev 21:5) are best understood with Jesus' death and resurrection in mind.

Matthew 19:28 speaks of Jesus' enthronement along with the Twelve, who judge the twelve tribes of Israel "at the renewal of all things (**palingenesia**)." The "judging" or "ruling" by the Twelve implies an extended period, an age that would clearly include something like Israel's renewal as envisioned by the prophets (see §A1) and most probably a resurrection of the dead. Some argue that Matthew understands this new age to be initiated by a Stoic-like replacement of the cosmos following its destruction. However, since the language from Isaiah and Ezekiel discussed above (§A1) suggests transforming renewal (not replacement) of the present cosmos—analogous with the transforming renewal (not replacement) of Jesus' body in his rebirth from death to life—**palingenesia** here is better understood as the new age initiated by a transforming eschatological renewal of Israel and the present cosmos. The God who created all things is about to renew them (Rev 21:5; compare Acts 3:21). This context of cosmic renewal is presupposed in NT references to corporate and personal renewal/regeneration.

2. Corporate and personal rebirth

a. John 3 and 1 John. In John 3:3 Jesus tells Nicodemus, "No one can see the kingdom of God without being born from above/again" (**anōthen** ἄνωθεν). The word **anōthen** can be translated as either "from above" (indicating source) or "again" (indicating sequence). Typical of John, both meanings seem intended to explicate God's activity through the Spirit in effecting rebirth whereby children are born into God's family (John 1:12-13) in order to see/enter the kingdom of God (John 3:3, 5, 7). To have this "eternal life" (John 3:15), one must be born "of water and Spirit" (or, perhaps, "water, that is, Spirit"; John 3:5). The Spirit is the active agent/source of rebirth, which is dependent upon the Son of Man being "lifted up/exalted" on the cross (John 3:14; 8:28; 12:32-34). By this act of grace the crucified Christ will "draw all people to [himself]" (John 12:32; compare 6:44) with those who exhibit ongoing faith in him thereby having eternal life (John 3:15). However, the Spirit is unavailable to effect rebirth until after Jesus is "glorified" (John 7:39) in his crucifixion, resurrection, and return to God. Evoking their belief/trust in him with his resurrection appearance (implicit in John 20:21; compare Thomas' explicit unbelieving stance in 20:25), the disciples themselves are reborn when the Son breathes (**enephysēsen** [ἐνεφύσησεν]; as in Gen 2:7) upon them and they receive (or are baptized with) the Spirit (John 20:21-22; compare 1:33). Hence, "You must be born from above" in John 3:7 is not a command to Nicodemus, but rather states what is necessary for Israel and individual Israelites to enter the kingdom of God. "Out of water" in John 3:5 could refer to baptism, the Spirit (with the **kai** [καὶ] between *water* and *Spirit* meaning "that is" rather than "and"), or the fluids of normal human birth. Since there is no baptism with water when rebirth is portrayed in 20:21-22 and no explicit reference to Christian baptism anywhere in John, *baptism* seems an unlikely reference. With no definite articles in the phrase "water and Spirit," the grammar suggests a close relationship between water and Spirit. In fact, 7:38-39 explicitly identifies "living water" with the Spirit and affirms that Jesus, the Spirit-endowed Son (1:33), is the Spirit's source. But the third alternative, the water accompanying birth, is more persuasive because it has parallel structure in its favor, both in the immediate context (3:5-6) and in the similar thematic announcement in the Gospel's prologue (1:12-13). Those born "of [birth] water" (3:5) equals "what is born of the flesh" (3:6) and those born "of blood or of the will of the flesh or of the will of man" (1:13). Those "born of Spirit" (3:5) equals "what is born of the Spirit" (3:6) and "children of God ... born of God" (1:12-13). The contrast here is between persons reborn from above by means of the Spirit and those who are not.

As in Ezek 36:25-27, "rebirth from above" includes God's placing his Spirit in/among his people, effecting both cleansing from sinful practices and transforming of hearts, thus enabling obedience to God. Birth from above enables participation in the character of the God whose Spirit regenerates (John 3:6*b*). That natural human birth is not sufficient for entering God's kingdom, therefore, is something a teacher of Israel familiar with Ezek 36–37 should know (3:7, 10). God's Spirit must regenerate even Israel (pl. "you"; **hymas** ὑμᾶς in v. 7) and individuals within Israel (sing. "no one," 3:3, 5) if they are to enter God's kingdom (compare Ezek 37:1-14). Hence rebirth from above is life-transforming and results from the Father's sending the Spirit-endowed Son to mediate the regenerating Spirit to those who follow him (3:34; 7:39; 14:17, 26; 15:26; 16:13; esp. 20:21-22), thereby making them corporately and individually a part of God's family and life (1:12-13). In John, then, rebirth is based on Jesus' death, resurrection, and return to God and entails a reception of the Spirit or baptism with the Spirit. In his death, the Son "draws all people" to himself (12:32), and thus the Father draws all to the crucified Christ (6:44). Hence, the Father, Son, and Spirit engage together in a life-giving (i.e., regenerating) pattern of activity toward the whole world (3:16) enabling ongoing faith in the crucified one. However, John's narrative does not describe the internal dynamics of the initial moment of new birth (i.e., whether it chronologically precedes the exercise of saving faith or occurs when humans respond with saving faith to the prior regenerating activity of God).

First John develops the pattern of life characterizing those in God's family by using perfect-tense verbs to describe the continuing results of being "born of God." They include doing righteousness as a reflection of the character of the righteous one (2:29), not habitually engaging in sin (3:9; 5:18), loving one another (4:7), believing that Jesus is the Messiah (5:1), and conquering the world through faith/faithfulness (5:4).

b. Acts. Pentecost depicts a theological pattern similar to John 20:19-23 as the Son receives the Spirit from the Father and pours out the regenerating Spirit on his followers (Acts 2:33). Blowing in like the wind (Acts 2:2; compare Ezek 37:1-14), the Spirit restores representative Israel (the 120 Jews from all the nations [2:5]). Israel is in essence "born again from above" (compare John 3:7), recreated into an expanding ecclesial community of faith, worship, and fellowship where persons are restored to fellowship with God and one another in order to participate in God's mission in the world.

c. Paul and the Pauline tradition. Apart from Titus 3:5 (treated separately below), explicit rebirth terminology does not appear in the Pauline corpus. However, related language does appear, including the phrase "new creation" (kainē ktisis καινὴ κτίσις), Paul's shorthand for the new age that God has inaugurated by graciously invading the cosmos through Jesus' death and resurrection in order to reclaim and establish sovereignty over a world enslaved by the powers of sin and death (2 Cor 5:17; Gal 6:15). Although this "new creation" has truly begun in the realm of the crucified and risen Christ, it is not consummated until God's reign comes in fullness (1 Cor 15:20-28). Persons "born according to the Spirit" (Gal 4:29) are adopted into this realm, i.e., into God's family for the purpose of being conformed to the image of God's Son, their elder brother (Rom 8:12-16, 29; Gal 4:1-7). Here the life-giving presence of the Holy Spirit is most focused (2 Cor 3:6), and persons are liberated from sin's reign and "made alive" (Rom 6:4, 13; compare Eph 2:1-5; Col 2:12-13). They are transformed into "new creatures" that continue to be renewed (Rom 12:2; 2 Cor 4:16; Col 3:10) until they are fully formed into the image of their elder brother, the firstborn from the dead (1 Cor 15:20-28, 35-49; Col 1:18), and the cosmos itself is fully redeemed (Rom 8:18-25).

As in John, the internal dynamics of the initial moment of birth/adoption engendered by the Spirit are not entirely clear. Nor is its relationship to baptism. Although some NT passages might suggest a connection between baptism and Spirit-reception (Acts 2:38), in Paul's understanding reception of the Spirit does not necessarily occur at baptism but is connected with hearing the faith-eliciting proclamation about the crucified Christ (Gal 3:1-5; 1 Thess 1:5; compare Eph 1:13). Even so, one seems to be definitively incorporated into Christ only when that hearing issues in faith that is embodied in the co-crucifixion and co-resurrection of baptism (Rom 6:1-11), which Paul describes in language similar to the experience of faith (compare Gal 2:15-21). Baptism, then, is the definitive sign of being incorporated into Christ's body where the life-giving presence of the Holy Spirit is most focused. Therefore, at baptism, one is "immersed" in the same Spirit (1 Cor 6:11*b*; 12:13) whose regenerating work occurs before, during, and after that baptism.

d. Titus 3:1-7. Titus 2:11-14 depicts God's transforming salvific activity aimed at forming a people whose practices bear public witness to it. On the basis of the change from what they once were (3:3), Titus is counseled to remind his people to engage in such public practices toward all (Titus 3:1-2). Enlarging on Titus 2:11-14, vv. 3:4-7 attribute this change to the salvific in-breaking of God. God saved us, v. 5 declares, "through washing (loutrou λουτροῦ) of rebirth (palingenesias παλιγγενεσίας) and renewal (anakainōseōs ἀνακαινώσεως) by the Holy Spirit." This prepositional phrase gives rise to a number of interrelated ambiguities including: 1) whether loutron (λουτρόν, "washing") is being used metonymically to refer to baptism or metaphorically in reference to cleansing from sins; 2) whether the kai ("and") indicates that two separate experiences are in view (regeneration effected by washing; renewal effected by the Spirit) or connects regeneration with renewal as a single experience (a washing effected by the Holy Spirit).

Since nowhere else in the Pauline corpus does Spirit reception explicitly occur at baptism, and since the writer clearly had the word *baptism* at his disposal, it is better to understand "washing" here metaphorically as a cleansing from the sorts of sins referred to in v. 3. Given the clear emphasis on the Spirit in Titus 3:5-6, the Spirit is its active agent. This conclusion makes it more likely that the kai ("and") is better understood as joining rebirth (palingenesia) and renewal (anakainōsis), with both phrases describing the cleansing. Hence, God's means of salvation is through the Holy Spirit's cleansing, which is characterized by rebirth and renewal.

One might still argue that rebirth and renewal refer to two aspects of the single event of the Spirit's cleansing and then explicate those as new birth followed by sanctification and/or Spirit baptism. But this places too much emphasis on the internal dynamics of the word loutron ("washing") when the passage focuses on the Spirit and his salvific work as a whole. Hence, rebirth and renewal are best taken as practically synonymous, each referring to the life-generating and renewing effects of the Spirit's cleansing of former sins (Titus 3:3), thus enabling God's newly created people to live transformed lives.

The ultimate purpose of this rich outpouring of the Spirit "through Jesus Christ our savior" (compare John 20:19-23; Acts 2:33) is described in Titus 3:7 as "in order that, having been justified/rectified by that one's grace, we might become heirs according to the hope of eternal life." Given the sentence structure of vv. 4-7, the regenerating and renewing cleansing could be understood as prior to, following, or constitutive of "having been rectified." Because of this ambiguity, this text sheds little definitive light on an order of salvation. Rather, it focuses on the transforming effects of God's saving activity seen as a whole, i.e., on the life-generating and renewing effects of the Spirit's work whereby the audience makes a significant break with their past (Titus 2:12*a*; 3:3) and is enabled to live transformed lives (Titus 2:12*b*; 3:1-2, 8). As Paul formulates the conceptuality elsewhere (Rom 6:4), they have died with Christ to their old existence and been raised with him to walk in "newness of life."

e. First Peter. In 1 Pet 1:3 the Father "rebirths" (**anagennaō** ἀναγεννάω) the audience through the definitive past act of raising Jesus from the dead. Their transformation is evident in that they no longer engage in their former pattern of behavior (1 Pet 4:3-4) and now exhibit "obedience to the truth" and "genuine mutual love" (1 Pet 1:22). Because they have been reborn (1 Pet 1:23; **anagegennēmenoi** [ἀναγεγεννημένοι], a causal perfect participle of **anagennaō**), with its ongoing transformative effects, they can be exhorted to "love one another deeply from the heart" (1 Pet 1:22-23). Here their rebirth is "through the living and enduring word of God ... the good news that was announced to you" (1 Pet 1:23, 25; compare Jas 1:18). In 1 Peter then, the Father's vehicle for the audience's rebirth is the Spirit-empowered (1 Pet 1:12) proclamation of the good news about Jesus' resurrection. While their reborn life together is clearly characterized by faith/fidelity (1 Pet 1:5, 7, 9, 21), the precise timing of their initial exercise of faith in relation to their rebirth is not specifically addressed. And although Jesus' resurrection is the basis for both their rebirth and the water baptism that "now saves" the audience (1 Pet 3:21), precisely how the two are related is not clear. *See* BAPTISM; FAITH, FAITHFULNESS; IMAGE OF GOD; JUSTIFICATION, JUSTIFY; NEW BIRTH; NEW HUMANITY; RESTORATION; SANCTIFY, SANCTIFICATION.

Bibliography: Helmut Burkhardt. *The Biblical Doctrine of Regeneration* (1978); Gordon Fee. *God's Empowering Presence: The Holy Spirit in the Letters of Paul* (1994); David C. Sim. "The Meaning of παλιγγενεσία in Matthew 19.28." *JSNT* 50 (1993) 3–12; Peter Toon. *Born Again: A Biblical and Theological Study of Regeneration* (1987).

ANDY JOHNSON

RECAH ree´kuh [רֵכָה **rekhah**]. A town associated with a brief genealogy of Recahites in 1 Chr 4:11-12, part of the genealogy of David in 1 Chr 2–4.

RECHAB, RECHABITES ree´kab, rek´uh-b*i*t [רֵכָב **rekhav**, בֵּית הָרֵכָבִים **beth harekhavim**]. *Rechab* is the name of two men in the OT, while *Rechabites* refers to the house of Rechab (**beth harekhavim**, the descendants of Rechab), a group that follows a distinctive way of living. The name *Rechab* relates to the words for riding a horse (**rakhav** רָכַב) and riding in a chariot (**rekhev** [רֶכֶב] or **merkav** [מֶרְכָּב]), and is similar to the term for chariot (**rekhuv** [רְכוּב] or **merkavah** [מֶרְכָּבָה]). 1. Son of RIMMON of Beeroth, a Benjaminite city. Together with his brother, BAANAH, Rechab was a military leader in the forces of Saul's son, ISHBOSHETH, who had succeeded his father as king of the northern tribes. The brothers assassinated Ishbosheth and presented his head to David. David, who was presumably negotiating to become king of all Israel, prudently had the two brothers killed for assassinating Ishbosheth, who was described as a "righteous man" (2 Sam 4:1-12).

2. The ancestor of JONADAB, founder of the house of the Rechabites (**beth harekhavim**), who first appears in the account of the bloody coup waged by the future king JEHU of Israel. Jonadab, son of Rechab, consents to ride in Jehu's chariot and supports Jehu's slaughter of all the worshipers of BAAL gathered in the temple of Baal in Samaria (2 Kgs 10:15-28).

3. Over two and a half centuries after Jonadab and Jehu, the Rechabites appear in Jer 35. JAAZANIAH gathers the house of the Rechabites in an upper room in the Temple complex. (This implies a small membership, though there may have been other Rechabites elsewhere.) The Rechabites are offered wine, but they decline, citing the rule of their founding father, Jonadab: "You shall never drink wine, neither you nor your children, nor shall you ever build a house, or sow seed; nor shall you plant a vineyard, or even own one; but you shall live in tents all your days, that you may live many days in the land where you reside (Jer 35:6*b*-7). Indeed, the Rechabites affirm that they and their wives, their sons, and their daughters abstain from wine, do not build houses or occupy them, and do not have vineyards or fields or engage in raising crops. They live in tents as sojourners (Jer 35:8-10). They have come to Jerusalem only to seek refuge from the invasion of King Nebuchadnezzar. Their presence in Jerusalem during a time of invasion does not mean they have shifted from living in tents to living in houses, because refugees within a walled city may well live in tents or even in the streets. Jeremiah contrasts the fidelity of the Rechabites to the infidelity of the people of Judah (Jer 35:19). For Jeremiah, the Rechabites represent a unique example of enduring loyalty to human rule within the larger Yahwistic community. Their loyalty to the rule of their founder offers a marked contrast with the disloyalty of the people of Judah to divine rule.

Though the Rechabites share some features with the Nazirites (*see* NAZIR, NAZIRITES), they do not make specific vows to God or live by specific rules of purity (other than their abstinence from drinking wine). Their distinctive way of life is also similar to the later ESSENES (as described by Philo), who have renounced wealth and land in order to live by the laws of their fathers (*Good Person* 77–80).

Scholars generally concur in viewing the Rechabites as a minor, somewhat sectarian movement, or more specifically as a kinship group committed to a particular lifestyle. The Rechabites rigorously disengage from the basic features of settled life—wine, houses, vineyards, fields, and seeding—and as such, they have often been identified as ascetic, nomadic stock keepers. Many scholars compare them with Diodorus Siculus' description of the NABATEANS in the 4th cent. BCE, a people who did not live in houses, plant grain or raise fruit trees, or drink wine. The Nabateans supported themselves by stock raising and serving as traders (Diodorus Siculus, *Bib. Hist.* 19.94.2–3).

The Rechabites also resemble the KENITES, and a connection between the two groups is supported by a reference to families of scribes dwelling at JABEZ: "These are the Kenites who came from HAMMATH, father of the house of Rechab (1 Chr 2:55). Traditionally, the Kenites are the descendants of TUBAL-CAIN, father of tent-dwellers, herders, and metal-workers (Gen 4:17-22). If there truly is an association between the Kenites and Rechabites, there is a possibility that the Rechabites were, like the Kenites, nomadic metal-workers. Such a trade could have included making and repairing chariots, which could explain Jonadab's presence in Jehu's chariot (2 Kgs 10:15-28). However, it is not necessary to identify everyone associated with the Kenites as a metal-worker; moreover, Jonadab's presence in Jehu's chariot primarily represents his endorsement of the religious motivation for Jehu's assassinations.

Jeremiah 35:19 claims that at least one Rechabite always stands before God. Others who "stand before God" include Moses and Samuel (Jer 15:1) and Jeremiah himself (Jer 15:19; 18:20). This suggests a priestly or cultic role for the Rechabites (e.g., Deut 10:8; 18:7). Mazar has suggested that inscriptions at KUNTILLET ʿAJRUD may describe the religious activity of the Rechabites. But the language about always standing before God could just as easily refer to non-priestly activities, though it could have contributed to shaping later tradition about the Rechabites (compare 1 Kgs 10:8; 12:6, 8; 2 Chr 9:7; 10:6, 8).

The Rechabites' lifestyle resembles a kind of primitivism, probably an attempt to reenact a notion of life patterned on the wilderness period, or a kind of counter-cultural reaction to the excesses of the prosperous, indulgent life in the Omride period in Israel, the time for which the founder, Jonadab, is cited as a zealous Yahwist. The wilderness period was a time without the comforts of established cities or fields and without sacrifices or oblations (Jer 7:21-23; Amos 5:25), and it was a time of special faithfulness (Jer 2:2; Hos 2:14-15 [Heb. 2:16-17]). Indeed, Hos 12:9 (Heb. 12:10) envisions that God will show Israel favor by letting them dwell in tents again as in the days of old.

The distinctive lifestyle of the Rechabites was quite possibly intended to display their disconnection with what they saw as the disastrous features of life under the monarchy, especially in the north, and served as a form of protest and resistance (van der Toorn). In this interpretation, they were symbolically acting out the consequences of offending God: "You have built houses of hewn stone, but you shall not live in them; you have planted pleasant vineyards, but you shall not drink their wine (Amos 5:11 warns: see also the curses in Deut 28:30 and Zeph 1:13, and the blessings in Isa 65:21-22 and Amos 9:14). By renouncing a settled lifestyle, the Rechabites resemble the prophets—and they perhaps serve even as an intercessory group standing before God (Knights). Levenson suggests that the prophet Jeremiah believed that the obedience of one generation could secure the gift of life for future generations. The Rechabites may have shared Jeremiah's belief.

Other references to the Rechabites include the title for Ps 71 in Greek (Ps 70 in the LXX): "For David; of the sons of Jonadab and the first ones taken captive. Eusebius mentions that one of the priests of the sons of Rechab sought to stop the stoning of James the Just (*Hist. eccl.* 2.23.17). An apocryphon titled *The History of the Rechabites* portrays the Rechabites as an idealistic community and seems to be a Christian reworking of Jewish traditions.

Bibliography: H. L. Bosman. "The Rechabites and 'Sippenethos' in Jeremiah 35." *Theologia Evangelica* 16 (1983) 83–86; Robert R. Carroll. *Jeremiah.* OTL (1986); Frank Frick. "The Rechabites Reconsidered." *JBL* 90 (1971) 279–87; Gerald L. Keown, Pamela J. Scalise, and Thomas G. Smothers. *Jeremiah 26–52.* WBC 27 (1995); C. H. Knights. "Kenites = Rechabites?: 1 Chronicles II 55 Reconsidered." *VT* 43 (1993) 10–18; C. H. Knights. "The Nabataeans and the Rechabites." *JSS* 38 (1993) 227–33; C. H. Knights. "'Standing before Me for Ever'—Jeremiah 35:19." *ExpTim* 108 (1996) 40–42; Jon D. Levenson. "On the Promise to the Rechabites." *CBQ* 38 (1976) 508–14; Amihai Mazar. *Archaeology of the Land of the Bible: 10,000–586 B.C.E.* (1990); S. Talmon. "1 Chron. ii, 55." *IEJ* 10 (1960) 174–80; Karel van der Toorn. "Ritual Resistance and Self-Assertion: The Rechabites in Early Israelite Religion." *Pluralism and Identity: Studies in Ritual Behaviour.* Jan Platvoet and Karel van der Toorn, eds. (1995) 239–59.

HERBERT B. HUFFMON

RECONCILE, RECONCILIATION. [גָּאַל gaʾal, כִּפֶּר kipper, רָצָה ratsah; ἀποκαταλλάσσω apokatallassō, διαλλάσσω diallassō, καταλλάσσω katallassō]. The word *reconciliation* indicates a change in social relationship in which two parties previously at enmity with each other exchange friendship and peace (e.g., diallassō and related terms: Xenophon, *Oec.* 11.23; *Hell.* 1.6.7; Plato, *Phaed.* 60c; *Symp.* 213d; Josephus, *J.W.* 1.320; 5.415; *Ant.* 7.295; 7.153; katallassō and related terms: Herodotus, *Hist.* 5.95; 7.145; Josephus, *Ant.* 3.295; 6.144; 7.184; 7.196). Greco-Roman authors, including the Jewish historian Josephus, employ the language of reconciliation in contexts of conflict between warring parties, whether military conflict (Aristophanes, *Av.* 1588; Plato, *Resp.* 566e), marital conflict (Josephus, *Ant.* 7.185; 7.196; 11.195; P. Oxy. 1.104.26), or conflict between citizens (Thucydides, *Hist.* 4.59.4; 4.61.2; Josephus, *Ant.* 6.353; Dio Chrysostom, *Nicom.* 21; *Conc. Apam.* 16).

A. Old Testament and Apocrypha

1. Hebrew

While there is no single Hebrew word corresponding to the Gk. terms for *reconciliation*, there are several concepts that convey the healing of relationships connoted by reconciliation: "to become acceptable" (**ratsah**), e.g., in 1 Sam 29:4; "to cover over" (**kipper**), e.g., in Jer 18:23, where **kipper** is related to FORGIVENESS; and "to redeem" (**ga'al**), e.g., in Isa 43:1; 44:22-23; 48:20; 52:9, where God's redemption indicates that God has already turned toward the people and no longer wishes to punish them (*see* COVENANT, OT AND NT; MERCY, MERCIFUL; REDEEM, REDEEMER).

2. Greek

The LXX employs reconciliation language on occasion for the resolution of conflict between individuals (**katalassō**: Jer 31:39 [MT 48:39]; **diallassō**: 1 Sam 29:4; 1 Esd 4:31).

Second Maccabees 1:5 narrates a prayer that asks God to respond to the pleas of the Jewish people by overlooking their sins and being reconciled to them. In 2 Macc 5:20, after a period of divine anger, reconciliation may ensue (compare 8:29). In 2 Macc 7:32-33, after God vents disciplinary anger, the suffering of the seven brothers moves God to forgive and to be reconciled to the Jewish people. Second Maccabees' reconciliation language therefore functions within a pattern: the people's sin leads to God's anger and punishment, God is satisfied, God responds to the people's prayers for mercy, and reconciliation is achieved between God and the people.

B. New Testament

1. Matthew 5:24

In Matt 5:24 the Gk. verb **diallassō** indicates the reconciliation that must take place between community members before bringing an offering to God. The passive form of the verb expresses the same notion as the active form: an individual must take the necessary action to persuade a community member to be restored to friendly relations.

2. 2 Corinthians 5:18-21

The apostle Paul uses the verb **katallassō** six times (Rom 5:10; 1 Cor 7:11; 2 Cor 5:18, 19, 20) and the noun **katallagē** (καταλλαγή, "reconciliation") four times (Rom 5:11; 11:15; 2 Cor 5:18, 19). The verb **apokatallassō** (another term for the word *reconcile*), an otherwise rare term, occurs three times in the disputed Pauline corpus (Eph 2:16; Col 1:20, 22). The lack of later Christian reconciliation language and the paucity of other Jewish and NT instances suggests Paul himself as the source of early Christian reconciliation language as he drew from the Greco-Roman milieu to express his understanding of the effects of Christ's saving work.

In 2 Cor 5:18-21 Paul employs the verb *reconcile* (**katallassō**) three times and the noun *reconciliation* (**katallagē**) twice. Whether or not he incorporated traditional material, the Pauline stamp on 2 Cor 5:18-21 is clear (e.g., v. 19*b*: "not counting their trespasses against them; v. 20*c*: "we entreat you on behalf of Christ, be reconciled to God"). Second Corinthians 5:19 is grammatically difficult. The apostle asserts that "God was reconciling the world to himself through Christ" (author's trans.). God is not only the agent of reconciliation but also the one toward whom reconciliation is directed. Paul appears to be the first Greek author to speak of the offended party (God) initiating reconciliation. In all other instances of the word group, the offending party, whether the sole offender or a party within a situation of mutual offense, persuades the offended to cease hostility and anger. In the case of Paul, God is never the object of the verb **katallassō** or **apokatallassō** in either the active or passive voice. God rather initiates and unilaterally completes reconciliation. God accomplished what humanity could not for itself (contra 2 Maccabees). The divine reconciliation of humanity entails the reconciliation of the entire world to God (2 Cor 5:19), even though that world remains full of human trespass and sin (2 Cor 5:19, 21). The world is reconciled, not God. The term *world* in 2 Cor 5:19 parallels *all* in 2 Cor 5:14. Christ died "for all; therefore all have died." As a result of Christ's work, Paul envisions a "new creation" in which "everything old has passed away; see, everything has become new!" (2 Cor 5:17). Reconciliation is therefore an objective state.

Paul's understanding is that God accomplishes reconciliation exclusively by means of Christ's work. Paul emphasizes reconciliation "by" (**en** ἐν) or "through" (**dia** διά) Christ's vicarious death (2 Cor 5:14-15; compare Rom 5:10). Second Corinthians 5:19 explains v. 18. God's reconciling of the world in Christ may be defined as not counting their trespasses. God's nonreckoning of sin has ample precedent in the OT (Ps 31:2 [LXX]; Jer 31:34). As the apostle says with respect to Abraham in Rom 4:7-8: "Blessed are those whose iniquities are forgiven, and whose sins are covered; blessed is the one against whom the Lord will not reckon sin." Paul explains that a sort of interchange has taken place (2 Cor 5:20-21). Prior to Christ's death, human beings lived for themselves (2 Cor 5:14-15).

Thanks to the benefits of Christ's death, no longer is that the case. Trespasses are no longer counted against humanity (2 Cor 5:19). Christ became "sin" in order that "we" might become the "righteousness of God" (compare Rom 8:3-4; Gal 3:13). What does it mean for Paul to write that Christ became sin? Some have thought that the apostle is referring to the Levitical sin offering, but the immediately preceding words about the one who "knew no sin" rule out a reference to the sin offering. Nothing in the context signals a change from "sin" (in the phrase "knew no sin") to "sin offering" (where Christ became sin). The interchange is between "sin" and the "righteousness of God," not between "sin offering" and the "righteousness of God." (Paul may have been aware of the martyr tradition in 2 and 4 Maccabees and interpreted this tradition in terms of Christ's sacrificial death.) Christ stands in humanity's place in order that humanity may stand in Christ's place before God. Christ absorbs God's wrath against sin. As a result, God views humanity as if it were righteous. God imputes Christ's righteousness, but God's work in Christ goes further. Christ fully identifies with sin and its effects even as those in Christ enjoy Christ's righteousness and sinlessness. This bestowal of righteousness is God's means of bringing about a "new creation" (5:17). Those who receive the imputed righteousness of God really are a NEW CREATION, even though the transformation will not be complete until the end of time when the justified are saved (*see* JUSTIFICATION, JUSTIFY; RIGHTEOUSNESS IN THE NT).

In the chapters preceding 2 Cor 5:18-21 Paul elaborates on the ministry of the new covenant and Spirit (3:6, 8) and the ministry of righteousness that endures (3:9, 11). The ministry of reconciliation in 2 Cor 5 defines this new covenant ministry in terms of Christ's reconciling death "for all." The completed results of reconciliation are then proclaimed to humanity through God's ambassadors. Even though the reconciliation of the world has been fully accomplished by God through Christ, paradoxically, that objective state of affairs must be appropriated personally by individuals. The God who reconciled the world to himself has therefore given to Paul and others "the ministry of reconciliation." Through these messengers comes the divine summons to "be reconciled." Note that the apostle does not say "reconcile yourselves to God." The sense is passive: "Be reconciled." God is the implied agent. Although most commentators view this sentence as requiring the audience's response, Paul does not explicitly address the audience until 6:1. The pronoun *you* is absent in the preceding verses. Paul is not suggesting a second experience of reconciliation to God, but rather a divinely enabled appropriation of the objective state of reconciliation. This subjective appropriation takes place by means of proclamation (compare Rom 10:16-17). Because reconciliation expresses an objective state between God and humanity, Paul does not use the language in the context of other relationships. He does not employ the language for relationships between believers. Reconciliation remains an evangelistic emphasis. At the same time, while God's reconciliation with humanity is complete in Christ and is appropriated by means of a proclamation with miraculous, life-giving power, people may still deny for themselves this new reality. The Corinthians' reception of Paul as God's ambassador serves as evidence that God's reconciliation of the world has been subjectively appropriated. Following the audience's anticipated appropriation of reconciliation comes Paul's request in 6:1. With the Corinthians' restoration comes the responsibility to work together with God. *See* CORINTHIANS, SECOND LETTER TO THE.

3. Romans 5:8-11; 11:15

In Rom 1:18–3:20 Paul charges all humanity with sin. God's wrath has been provoked "against all ungodliness and wickedness" (1:18). Paul labels "us" "sinners" in Rom 5:8. In parallel language in 5:6 "we" are "weak" and "ungodly." He further describes the state of the weak and ungodly "sinner" in 5:10 as enmity against God. Romans 8:7 defines such enmity as involving an active hostility of the mind of the flesh that consciously refuses to submit to God's law. The relationship between God and sinner, when considered apart from Christ, stands broken (*see* SIN, SINNERS).

In spite of humanity's active opposition, Rom 5:5, 8 stresses the aggrieved party's response. God demonstrates an utterly counterintuitive love in the face of human sinfulness. God unilaterally initiates reconciliation and rapprochement with fallen humanity. Humanity does not attempt rapprochement with God (compare Rom 3:11). God overcomes the shame of sin by a divine love that accepts the individual without qualification. The reconciliation of Rom 5:10 parallels justification and peace in Rom 5:1. Whereas justification stresses a right relationship with God, reconciliation stresses the change from a prior state of enmity to friendship.

As in 2 Cor 5:18-21, God effects reconciliation by means of Christ's sacrificial death (Rom 5:8-11; see Rom 5:1). "By his blood" echoes God's means of atonement "now" available in 3:26. Paul's repetition of formulaic language throughout 5:6-11 stresses Christ's instrumental role. The language parallels Rom 14:15; 1 Cor 8:11; 15:3; 2 Cor 5:14; and Thess 5:9-10. As a result of Christ's death, "we" enjoy the sure hope of salvation from God's eschatological wrath at the final judgment (5:9-10). In place of enmity, "we" enjoy peaceful and harmonious relations with God (5:1). Reconciliation on the basis of Christ's work is, as in 2 Cor 5, an objective state of affairs that prompts joy and praise on the part of the believer. This objective state forms the basis for Paul's contrast of two contrasting corporate realities in Adam and in Christ. Participation in Christ brings about certain deliverance from eschatological wrath

(5:12-21). Indeed, God's act of reconciliation provides the basis for that hope (5:4-5).

In Rom 11:15, Paul argues that God's seeming rejection of Israel benefits the entirety of the Gentile world with reconciliation. As is the case with other Pauline reconciliation texts, "reconciliation" is worldwide. As for the Jewish people, God's future acceptance of them will trigger the resurrection of the dead. *See* ROMANS, LETTER TO THE.

4. Colossians 1:20-22

The arguments in favor of a pre-Pauline hymn in Col 1:15-20 are hardly decisive. The cosmic dimension of these verses is consonant with the cosmic emphases elsewhere in Colossians. Reconciliation language moves beyond sinful humanity or the world, as in the undisputed letters, to a more universal scope including all things in heaven and on earth. The entire universe is reconciled to God by the peace obtained through the blood of Christ's cross (1:20). Such universal reconciliation is a fitting result for the "firstborn of all creation" through whom "all things in heaven and on earth were created, things visible and invisible, whether thrones or dominions or rulers or powers" (1:16). The Creator is acting to bring about a restoration of the fallen creation.

Consistent with the undisputed Pauline corpus, God is the unstated subject of the verb *reconcile* (apokatallaxai [ἀποκαταλλάξαι], aorist active infinitive of apokatallassō) in Col 1:20. Christ may very well be the subject of the verb in 1:22. A virtual equation of God and Christ would not be surprising, since the fullness of God was pleased to dwell in Christ (1:19). Christ remains the subject of the main clauses in 1:15, 17, 18 and is central to the act of reconciliation in 1:19-20. Christ sacrificially reconciles "in his fleshly body through death" (1:22). Peace is possible only "through the blood of his cross" (1:20). The emphasis therefore remains on Christ throughout these verses. Whereas God reconciles the world in 2 Cor 5 and Rom 5, in Col 1:20-22 the focus is on Christ as reconciler, even as other attributes of God are predicated of Christ in Colossians.

The objects of Christ's reconciling activity are those "once estranged and hostile in mind, doing evil deeds" (1:21). The benefits of this activity are applied to "us." Although humanity was once characterized by a hostility of mind and evil deeds, Colossians emphasizes the moral change that results from Christ's reconciling work. The reconciled will be presented "holy and blameless and irreproachable" (1:22). Christ's reconciling work creates a genuine renewal in moral character. *See* COLOSSIANS, LETTER TO THE.

5. Ephesians 2:12-17

Reconciliation between Jew and Gentile is the subject of Eph 2:12-17. In this passage, the author claims that Christ's reconciling work dissolves the hostility between Jew and non-Jew, as the barrier between them is broken (2:14) and the hostility slain (2:16). A new society dawns in which Christ now dwells. The barrier wall is a metaphor that likely refers to the law, which separated Jew and Gentile. In Pauline theology, the Mosaic law is rendered inoperative by Christ's death (see Rom 6:15; 7:1-6; Gal 2:19; 3:24-25). Consequently, the law need no longer divide humanity. If the law's division of the world into Jew and Gentile has been superseded by a new humanity in Christ, the grounds for hostility are now abolished as well. By means of Christ's work on the cross, hostility is "put to death" (2:16). Jews must abandon disdain for Gentile sinners (see Gal 2:15-16). In agreement with other Pauline reconciliation passages, the message of peace must be proclaimed (2:17). *See* EPHESIANS, LETTER TO THE.

Bibliography: Murray J. Harris. *The Second Epistle to the Corinthians: A Commentary on the Greek Text.* NIGTC (2005); Harold W. Hoehner. *Ephesians: An Exegetical Commentary* (2002); Robert Jewett. *Romans: A Commentary.* Hermeneia (2007); I. Howard Marshall. "The Meaning of 'Reconciliation.'" *Unity and Diversity in New Testament Theology: Essays in Honor of George E. Ladd.* Robert A. Guelich, ed. (1978) 117–32; Ralph Martin. "Reconciliation and Forgiveness in the Letter to the Colossians." *Reconciliation and Hope: New Testament Essays on Atonement and Eschatology.* R. Banks, ed. (1974) 104–24; Ralph P. Martin. *2 Corinthians.* WBC 40 (1986); Frank J. Matera. *II Corinthians: A Commentary.* NTL (2003); Thomas R. Schreiner. *Romans.* BECNT 6 (1998).

A. ANDREW DAS

RECORDER, OFFICER [מַזְכִּיר mazkir]. A high-ranking officer in Israel's royal court. Since the term literally means "one who causes to remember," some scholars suggest this person functioned as an archivist of national events. Others suggest that the officer was a royal herald. JEHOSHAPHAT served as recorder during the reigns of David and Solomon (2 Sam 8:16; 1 Kgs 4:3). JOAH son of Asaph was a recorder who, along with two other royal officials, served as Hezekiah's representatives to the Assyrian RABSHAKEH (2 Kgs 18:18, 37). Joah son of Joahaz was Josiah's recorder, and he and two other officials delivered money for repair of the Temple (2 Chr 34:8).

Bibliography: Arnold A. Anderson. *2 Samuel.* WBC 11 (1989).

TERRY W. EDDINGER

RECORDS OF THE CHRONICLES OF KING DAVID. *See* BOOKS REFERRED TO IN THE BIBLE.

RED [אָדֹם ʾadhom; πυρρός pyrros]. *Red* is a color term that describes hues ranging from brown to wine-red. In Scripture, *red* can refer to a person's complexion (Gen 25:25; Job 16:16), a dish of lentils (Gen 25:30), a heifer (Num 19:2), water (2 Kgs 3:22), wine (Prov 23:31), sins (Isa 1:18), robes (Isa 63:2, stained with blood or wine), shields (Nah 2:3), horses (Zech 1:8; 6:2; Rev 6:4), the sky (Matt 16:2-3), or a dragon (Rev 12:3).

The Hebrew term ʾ**adhom** is related etymologically to both Adam and the earth, which is seen as reddish, as well as Edom (based on the red lentils for which Esau sold his birthright; Gen 25:30; *see* EDOM, EDOMITES). Horses and cows are a ruddy brown, cooked lentils a yellowish brown, and wine and blood are more what English calls *red.* (Note that "Red Sea" does not use ʾ**adhom**; see the NRSV footnote "Sea of Reeds" [e.g., Exod 10:19]; *see* RED SEA, REED SEA.) In Isa 1:18 (compare Isa 63:2), *red* is used metaphorically in stark contrast to white to show the extent of divine forgiveness.

The color red encompasses both SCARLET and CRIMSON, which refer primarily to textiles: yarn, fabric, or garments. The female shield louse (*Kermococcus vermilio*), which is found on the kermes oak, is the source for the dye. The insects are gathered, dried, and then dissolved in water to produce a colorfast red dye. It takes the bodies of 70,000 insects to produce 1 lb. of dye. *See* COLORS.

Bibliography: Athalya Brenner. *Colour Terms in the Old Testament* (1982).

MARY P. BOYD

RED HEIFER [פָּרָה אֲדֻמָּה **parah** ʾ**adhummah**]. According to the book of Numbers, the ashes of a special red cow were used to purify those defiled by death, the strongest contaminant in the Israelite system of impurities (*see* DEATH, POLLUTION OF). A corpse was irrevocably impure and those who had been in contact with it were required to purify themselves under penalty of death by divine agency. If one was not properly purified, corpse impurity became a danger to the sanctuary, even if no direct contact with it was made (Num 19:13, 20).

The ashes of a physically perfect red cow, which had never been worked, were necessary for the purification ritual from corpse impurity (Num 19:2). This cow must have been specially consecrated and burned in a pure place outside of the community, its blood sprinkled seven times toward the sanctuary, and its ashes preserved for later use by the priests in a special mixture called **me niddah** (מֵי נִדָּה; "water for cleansing"; Num 19:9; *see* WATER FOR IMPURITY). According to the Mishnah, the burning of the cow took place on the Mount of Olives in Second Temple times (*m. Parah* 3:6).

The red cow ritual was probably considered sacred since, although it was not burned at the holy altar, the unblemished cow was designated as a **khatta**ʾ**th** (חַטָּאת; "sin offering"), and a consecrated priest sprinkled some of the cow's blood in the direction of the sanctuary, thus linking the burning of the animal with the altar. Cedarwood, hyssop, and scarlet wool were thrown into the conflagration. The redness of the cow, cedar, and wool draws attention to the cow's red blood, which is the sacred agent of purgation.

Curiously, all persons involved in making the purification ash became impure. The priest who prepared the purgation mixture and the persons who burned the cow and collected the ash were required to bathe and launder their clothes; they remained impure until evening (Num 19:7-10). This paradox is found similarly with other **khatta**ʾ**th** sacrifices, which absorb impurity from various sancta although they function as purgation agents (compare Lev 6:27-28 [Heb. 6:20-21]).

Individuals needing purification from corpse impurity were required to come to the priest, who mixed spring water with ashes from the red cow creating **me niddah** and sprinkled this mixture on them using a sprig of hyssop. This procedure was performed on the impure person or object on their third and seventh days of impurity (Num 19:18-19). Washing and laundering were also required; metal objects were purified by fire (Num 19:19; 31:19-24; *see* CLEAN AND UNCLEAN).

References to the red cow rite are found in other biblical texts. For example, the psalmist mourns his sin and begs for purification with symbolic reference to the hyssop of the red cow rite: "Purge me with hyssop, and I shall be clean; wash me, and I shall be whiter than snow" (Ps 51:7 [Heb. 51:9]). Hebrews mentions this ritual along with other sacrificial rites of the OT in an effort to contrast their limitations with the blood of Christ's sacrifice (Heb 9:13-14). While the author concedes that under the old covenant the blood of the red cow was a powerful agent against defilement, for him, only Christ's blood is truly effective in purging sin.

The Pharisees and Sadducees of the MISHNAH argued over the correct standard of purity for those who participated in the red cow rite. The Sadducees, who did not regard a purifying person pure until sunset, would not let any such person participate. The Pharisees, who subscribed to the water purification rite for those who made the ash, would intentionally make the participants impure so that they would have to immerse and, to the dismay of the Sadducees, be in this intermediate status when they performed the rituals. In this case, the Qumran sectarians would have sided with the Sadducees (4Q277 1 1–13; 4Q395 8–10; 11Q19 LI, 2–5).

The sanctity of the rite was upheld by the Qumran and rabbinic authors (compare *m. Parah* 2:3). The author of 4Q277 allows only priests to perform the rite, including collection of ash and disposal of the blood, and 4QMMT refers to the red cow as a sacrifice (**khatta**ʾ**th**; 4Q277 1 6–7; 4Q395 8). Another text requires the vessel that contains the cow's blood to be first sanctified at the temple altar and all participants in the rite to be pure (4Q276 1 3–4; compare *b. Zevah.* 20*b*). Curiously, the priestly garments are not allowed for use in this rite. This may be simply due to the fact that the rite is not conducted at the Temple or it may be that the author did not want the holy vestments to become defiled.

Other post-biblical texts seem to authenticate the red cow ritual for the period of the Second Temple and even beyond it (compare *Barn.* 8:1). The Mishnah claims that only a few red cows were burned in Jewish history, but, since only a minimal amount of ash was required to make the purgation water, the ashes of an entire cow could last a long time (*m. Parah* 3:5). The Jerusalem Talmud records instances of rabbis using the red cow ash for corpse purification (*y. Ber.* 6:10*a*). The SAMARITANS are reported to have used it until the 14th cent. CE. They continued to sprinkle the purgation water in the direction of their sanctuary even after its demise.

Bibliography: Joseph Baumgarten. "The Red Cow Purification Rites in Qumran Texts." *JJS* 46 (1995) 112–19; Mary Douglas. *In the Wilderness: The Doctrine of Defilement in the Book of Numbers* (1993); Hannah K. Harrington. *The Purity Texts* (2004) 71–85; Baruch A. Levine. *Numbers 1–20.* AB 4 (1993) 457–79; Jacob Milgrom. "The Paradox of the Red Cow (Num, xix)." *VT* 30 (1981) 62–72; David P. Wright. "Purification from Corpse-Contamination in Numbers XXXI 19–24." *VT* 35 (1985) 213–23.

HANNAH K. HARRINGTON

RED SEA, REED SEA red'see' [יַם־סוּף yam-suf; ἐρυθρὰ θάλασσα erythra thalassa]. The phrase "Red Sea" can be a troublesome one for interpreters of the OT. Its accuracy as a translation of the Hebrew yam-suf is highly dubious, its meaning and etymology debated, and its geographic referent variable and sometimes uncertain. However, the frequent occurrence of the image of the Red Sea, especially as associated with the exodus, testifies to its importance in the conceptual world of ancient Israel.

The English phrase "Red Sea" commonly used as a translation for yam-suf derives from the LXX erythra thalassa, which means "red sea." This translation was followed by Jerome in the Vulgate. There is no apparent support for reading suf as "red" in biblical Hebrew. It is clear, however, that at least some occurrences of yam-suf do refer to the Gulf of Aqaba, a finger of the Red Sea, which lends at least some credibility to this translation.

Among scholars, the most broadly supported option for translating yam-suf is "Reed Sea," or something similar. The OT uses suf as a term for weeds, reeds, or other such water plants (Exod 2:3, 5; Isa 19:6; Jonah 2:5 [Heb. 2:6]; *see* REED), and there is a possible Egyptian cognate that means "papyrus reeds" or the like. Hence, yam-suf would be an appropriate designation for a body of water known to contain or be bordered by reeds.

A third possible understanding of yam-suf supposes that the word suf should in fact be vocalized as sof (סוֹף) and that it derives from a Hebrew verb suf, meaning "to come to an end." Accordingly, the (putative) yam-sof would mean "Uttermost Sea" and refer to the boundless, chaotic ocean that marked the end of the created world in the ANE worldview. Such an understanding of the Hebrew text is suggested once in the LXX, which, in 1 Kgs 9:26, reads eschatē thalassa (ἐσχάτη θαλάσσα, "last sea").

Determining which translation is to be preferred (or if more than one might be appropriate in different contexts) requires a survey of the biblical occurrences of the phrase. This survey will also point out some of the issues and difficulties that face the interpreter in seeking to understand the use of yam-suf in the OT.

As noted above, some OT uses of yam-suf almost surely refer to the Gulf of Aqaba. The account of Solomon's maritime trade with OPHIR in 1 Kgs 9:26-28 centers on the port of EZION-GEBER, which the text locates "near Eloth on the shore of the yam-suf." While the precise location of ancient Ezion-geber is not certain (the island port of Jezirat Faraun seems the most compelling candidate), the reference to Eloth, which is certainly to be sought at or near the site of modern Eilat and Aqaba, along with the likelihood that Ophir was located somewhere on the southwest coast of Arabia or the Red Sea coast of Africa, makes it virtually certain that the text here refers to the Gulf of Aqaba. Other texts whose use of yam-suf almost certainly has the Gulf of Aqaba in mind include the summary statement of the (idealized) borders of the promised land in Exod 23:31 and the oracle against Edom in Jer 49:21.

Within the narrative of the Israelites' wandering in the wilderness, there is a cluster of occurrences of the phrase derekh yam-suf (דֶּרֶךְ יַם־סוּף), "The Way of the yam-suf" (see Num 14:25; 21:4; Deut 1:40; 2:1). The formulation here suggests an established road or route that would probably have one end or the other at the designated location. The geographic context of these references (near Edom) suggests that they might well refer to the Gulf of Aqaba also, though they could conceivably be understood to refer to one of the other possible options. A similar line of reasoning suggests that the reference to yam-suf in Jephthah's recitation of the Israelites' wilderness travels in Jdg 11:16 also has the Gulf of Aqaba in mind.

It has been proposed that a small number of yam-suf occurrences (Exod 10:19; 13:18; Num 33:10-11) refer to the Gulf of Suez, the arm of the Red Sea separating EGYPT from the Sinai Peninsula. Such an identification is by no means certain, however, and these references could also be taken to refer either to the Gulf of Aqaba or to the "Sea of the Exodus."

The majority of OT occurrences of yam-suf are in the context of either the description of Yahweh's victory over Pharaoh's army and deliverance of the Israelites (e.g., Exod 15:4) or later references to that event (e.g., Ps 106:7, 9). The NT and Apocrypha occurrences of **erythra thalassa** also refer to this event (Acts 7:36; Heb 11:29; Jdt 5:13; 1 Macc 4:9; Wis 19:7). However, the precise identification of the body of water in view remains a matter of much debate and disagreement. Thus, the phrase "Sea of the Exodus" serves to refer to this body of water, wherever it may have been.

The account of the miraculous deliverance of Israel at the sea in Exod 14 does not mention the **yam-suf** as the location of this event. Instead, the text refers generically to "the sea," and locates the Israelites "in front of Pi-hahiroth, between Migdol and the sea, in front of Baal-zephon" (Exod 14:2). None of these locations can be identified with confidence, though many candidates have been suggested. The impossibility of definitively fixing the location described in Exod 14 leaves open a range of possibilities for understanding the **yam-suf** references that have the Sea of the Exodus in view.

Those who favor the "Reed Sea" translation of **yam-suf** tend to propose locations for the Sea of the Exodus among the various lakes and marshes that lay between the head of the Gulf of Suez and the mouths of the Nile. Depending upon the particular reconstruction of the hypothetical route of the Israelites' journey, different bodies of water, including the Ballah Lakes and the Bitter Lakes, have been proposed (*see* EXODUS, ROUTE OF THE). All of these lakes and marshes would have been surrounded by reeds, explaining the designation **yam-suf**. By contrast, the saltwater gulfs of Aqaba and Suez do not support significant growths of reeds or other plant life. While this perspective offers a sensible understanding of the Hebrew term, and also allows for coherent reconstruction of a proposed exodus route, it does not explain the unquestioned application of **yam-suf** to the Gulf of Aqaba in the OT period.

There are also substantial difficulties inherent in insisting that all references to **yam-suf** must refer to the Gulf of Aqaba, on the grounds that some of them certainly do. Most important is the impossibility of constructing a coherent hypothetical exodus route in which the Sea of the exodus and the Gulf of Aqaba could be the same. Inflexibly understanding **yam-suf** to refer to the gulf requires the assumption that all the subsequent texts that connect the **yam-suf** to the Sea of the Exodus stand in sharp, almost defiant tension with the exodus narrative itself, which is implausible, given the supreme importance of that narrative to Israel's sense of history and identity.

While the precise location of the Sea of the Exodus is a crucial point in the arguments for and against the understandings of **yam-suf** described above, it is a matter of virtual indifference to the camp that favors the "Uttermost Sea" translation. In this understanding, the final victory of Yahweh over Pharaoh's troops, coming at least on the fringes of the primeval, chaotic ocean, takes on decidedly mythic overtones. The precise location of the event is far less important than its theological and mythological content. Yahweh's manipulation of primal forces on behalf of Israel and in opposition to Pharaoh echoes the victory over CHAOS in the CREATION and attests Yahweh's supreme power and his unique solicitude toward Israel. In practical terms, thinking of the Sea of the Exodus in these more mythic terms also serves to at least reduce the tension surrounding the use of **yam-suf** both for this sea and for the Gulf of Aqaba. Both could be considered, in a sense, to be parts of the Uttermost Sea.

An additional datum that might accord with this more inclusive understanding of **yam-suf** lies in the somewhat murky origins of the LXX translation **erythra thalassa**. This Greek term was applied not only to the Red Sea as modern geography designates it, but, in at least some contexts, to the entire Indian Ocean, including even the Persian Gulf. If this larger body of water is in view, then it certainly might have seemed to be the Uttermost Sea, and the waters of the Nile Delta and the gulfs of Aqaba and Suez could all be understood to be parts of it.

As is evident from even the brief survey above, the critical issues surrounding the translation and geographic referent of **yam-suf** are unlikely ever to find definitive resolution. The interpreter is faced with a term of considerable importance in the literature of the OT, but also of considerable ambiguity. It may be, however, that the meaning and significance of **yam-suf** for readers of the OT are not finally dependent upon the resolution of the technical, critical issues.

The **yam-suf**, in the context of the exodus narrative, represents a barrier, a hazard insurmountable by the Israelites. Whether the narrative has in mind a reedy marsh in the delta, an arm of the Red Sea, or the indeterminate cosmic ocean, the import of the events at the **yam-suf** was clearly understood by Israel: there Yahweh definitively demonstrated power over the forces of nature, the forces of chaos, and the forces of Pharaoh; there also Yahweh showed his unequivocal favor and intent to care for Israel. It matters little, under such a conception, precisely where this sea was located, or how its name was vocalized. For Israel, every insurmountable obstacle or terrifying threat was, in effect, the **yam-suf** and Pharaoh's onrushing army once again. The memory of Yahweh's mighty actions at that original **yam-suf**, somewhere on the border between history and myth, was a source of confidence and hope for Israel, regardless of location or translation.

D. MATTHEW STITH

REDACTION CRITICISM, NT ri-dak´shuhn. Redaction criticism is the study of the way in which the Gospel writers (in this context "redactors") molded their source material. It attempts to discover their literary and theological agendas and to learn more about the communities from which they came.

Redaction criticism (German *Redaktionsgeschichte*) was pioneered by German NT scholars in the 1950s, especially Willi Marxsen on Mark, Günther Bornkamm on Matthew, and Hans Conzelmann on Luke. They built on the earlier work of source critics and form critics and attempted to show how the evangelists knitted together traditional materials, analyzing subtle differences between the SYNOPTIC GOSPELS and looking for repeated motifs for evidence of the evangelists' theological agendas. Conzelmann, e.g., used redaction criticism to argue that Luke replaced the cross-focused eschatological proclamation of his predecessors with a salvation-historical viewpoint where there is no theology of the cross and the end is no longer imminent.

The dominance of redaction criticism has been challenged by the development of newer methods like NARRATIVE CRITICISM, in which there is less interest in the historical, source-related questions that are presupposed by the redaction critic. Nevertheless, redaction criticism remains a popular method in the literary-historical study of the Gospels and provides a promising means of distinguishing an evangelist's views from those of his source material. The beginning student can learn how to practice redaction criticism in four steps: 1) acquire a synopsis of the Gospels and begin looking at parallel passages; 2) choose a passage, preferably from the "triple tradition" (occurring in all three Synoptics) and begin to find the similarities and differences between Matthew, Mark, and Luke, marking the differences with (ideally colored) pencils; 3) focus on the differences between the Gospels and attempt to find places where the evangelists do the same thing elsewhere in their Gospels; 4) find an explanation for the kinds of change that have been isolated, ideally an explanation that draws on characteristics of the Gospel in question.

Given the consensus view that Mark's Gospel was the first to be written, redaction criticism is naturally easier to practice with Matthew and Luke than it is with Mark, whose sources we do not possess. The method has other limitations. The excessive emphasis on what is distinctive in each Gospel can be misleading. Matthew, e.g., might like something in Mark so much that he reproduces it verbatim—he might think that a given section of Mark expresses his own view better than anything he can add himself. Similarly, redaction criticism does not allow sufficiently for the effect that a source Gospel might have had on a given evangelist. It is possible, e.g., that Mark's Gospel fundamentally altered Matthew's views. Further, redaction critics sometimes make too speedy a correlation between the fine details of the text and the postulated background in the evangelists and their communities. When these limitations are borne in mind, redaction criticism still has a great deal to offer those interested in the historical-critical study of the NT.

Bibliography: G. Bornkamm, G. Barth, and H. J. Held. *Tradition and Interpretation in Matthew* (1963); H. Conzelmann. *The Theology of St. Luke* (1960); W. Marxsen. *Mark the Evangelist: Studies on the Redaction History of the Gospel* (1969); Steven L. McKenzie and Stephen R. Haynes. *To Each Its Own Meaning: An Introduction to Biblical Criticisms and Their Application* (1999); Norman Perrin. *What Is Redaction Criticism?* (2002).

MARK S. GOODACRE

REDACTION CRITICISM, OT ri-dak´shuhn. The terms *redaction* and *redactor* reflect the German terms for *editing* and *editor*, respectively. "Redaction criticism" could simply be defined as the study of how the OT documents were edited. However, ancient editing and authorship differ from modern practice. In literary source criticism, the word *redaction* referred to the ways in which the hypothetical sources of the OT books were combined. According to Julius Wellhausen, J and E were thoroughly conflated by a redactor (the Jehovist). Next, Deuteronomy was juxtaposed with JE as an appendix. Finally, the major sections of P were inserted into the JED book as a structural framework for the whole, producing the present Pentateuch.

However contested Wellhausen's scheme might be, scholars early on recognized that literature in the ANE typically arose from a writer combining, coordinating, and supplementing preexisting literary sources. The biblical writers' own use of materials found elsewhere in the Bible itself also illustrates this common ancient mode of composition. Most interestingly, the textual evidence for Jeremiah in both the MT and LXX allows interpreters access to the text of a biblical book in two distinct editions, allowing a direct view into the formation of a biblical book. Thus empirical evidence validates a literary combinatory model of composition and warrants a critical method that analyzes this process of composition.

Early form critics saw the redactor as merely a transcriber and anthologist, attributing hermeneutical significance to the process. Still, some form critics like Gerhard von Rad argued that the transformation both of the media of the tradition and its context entailed a powerful hermeneutical dynamic. Likewise, Martin Noth's analysis of the DtrH envisioned a writer forging a literary whole from disparate literary traditions. Though he eschewed the term *redactor*, Noth's work engendered subsequent redaction-critical studies of the Former Prophets and beyond. Interestingly, while NT redaction criticism moved toward developing sophisticated models of the composition of the Gospels, OT redaction criticism stayed focused mainly on reconstructing increasingly over-refined models of literary growth, often failing to make coherent sense of the text in its final form. In the meantime, purely synchronic literary criticism, often appealing to the concept of canon, increasingly dominated exegetical approaches to the material's final form.

Redaction criticism could be conceived as an integrative method describing the kinds, levels, and mechanisms of conceptual unity operating in documents thought to possess compositional diversity. Redaction criticism begins by discerning, through analytical methods like source- and form-criticism, the source materials behind a text. The redaction critic then explores how the material was reshaped and organized, assessing both the possible intentionality at work as well as the literary effect of the final text. The redaction critic also inquires into the historical, cultural, and social contexts for such compositional processes. Redaction criticism thus potentially integrates synchronic and diachronic concerns in a single method.

Bibliography: Martin Noth. *The Deuteronomistic History* (1981); Gerhard von Rad. *The Problem of the Hexateuch and Other Essays* (1966); Jeffrey Tigay, ed. *Empirical Models for Biblical Criticism* (1985); John Van Seters. *The Edited Bible: The Curious History of the "Editor" in Biblical Criticism* (2006); Julius Wellhausen. *Prolegomena to the History of Ancient Israel* (2003).

LAWSON G. STONE

REDEEM, REDEEMER [גָּאַל gaʾal, פָּדָה padhah; ἀγοράζω agorazō, ἐξαγοράζω exagorazō, λυτρόω lytroō]. The simplest meaning of the word *redeem* is "to buy back." *Redeem* can also mean to ransom, rescue, or liberate. A redeemer is someone who buys back or rescues. The Hebrew padhah (redeem or ransom) is used frequently in the laws concerning sales (*see* LAW IN THE OT). Land, houses, and crops given to the Temple can be "redeemed" (gaʾal), i.e., bought back, for the price plus a fifth (Lev 27:15, 19, 31). Leviticus 25 designates the obligation of a close male relative to buy land or a person belonging to the clan. Jeremiah 32:6-12 describes an instance of land redemption in operation and indicates that Jeremiah became the owner—neither Hanamel nor other clan members retained claim.

The short story of Ruth speaks of redemption twenty-three times (e.g., 4:1-6). Boaz becomes a redeemer in two ways: he is purchaser of the land, and he becomes husband to the wife of a deceased relative, in order to produce heirs for him (*see* LEVIRATE LAW).

Redemption also referred to slavery. In Exod 21:8 a slavewoman purchased as a wife must be redeemed (set free) if the purchaser decides that she is not fit for a wife. Leviticus 25 imposes the obligation to redeem (buy the freedom) of an enslaved family member (Lev 25:35-54); if a family cannot afford to redeem a family member, the indenture will last until the year of jubilee, at which time the slave is redeemed (*see* JUBILEE, YEAR OF; SLAVERY).

Redemption is related to the act of avenging a murder (*see* BLOODGUILT). The Heb. root gaʾal becomes goʾel (גֹּאֵל, "avenger") in the phrase goʾel haddam (גֹּאֵל הַדָּם), which describes someone acting in the interests of the family to pursue and execute the killer of a family member (Num 35:19, 21, 24, 27; Deut 19:6, 12; Josh 20:3, 5, 9; 2 Sam 14:11; *see* AVENGER OF BLOOD).

The root padhah also is used in the cultic context of sacrifice, where the sacrifice stands in the place of the one who needs redemption. Numbers 18:15-16 requires sacrificing firstborn males; however, humans and "unclean animals" (e.g., donkeys) were replaced by substitute animals (Exod 13:13; 34:20; compare Gen 22:13) or money (Num 18:16). First Samuel 14:45 uses padhah in a distinctive way. Saul made a vow (1 Sam 14:24) and his son Jonathan unknowingly violated the vow. Rather than execute Jonathan, the army "redeemed" him. What they did is not stated.

The term *redeem* (padhah) can we used with regard to God's rescuing action. *Redeem* is used rather frequently with "life" as object (e.g., 2 Sam 4:9; Lam 3:58). Psalms of lament beseech God to draw near, set free, and redeem the psalmist from his enemies (e.g., Ps 69:18 [Heb. 69:19]). God redeems the people from oppression and violence (Ps 72:14).

Many references to national redemption are to the exodus from Egypt (e.g., Deut 24:18), sometimes emphasizing God's power, sometimes Israel's liberation (*see* PASSOVER AND FEAST OF UNLEAVENED BREAD). Twice Hosea has the LORD reject redemption (Hos 7:13; 13:14). Other prophets promise redemption from exile (Isa 35:9-10; Mic 4:10).

The language of redemption comes into its own in Isa 40–55. Isaiah 43:1; 44:22-23; 48:20; and 52:9 all proclaim the redemption (gaʾal) of Judean exiles. Padhah appears in Isa 50:2 and 51:10. In Isaiah's use of redemption, the LORD has already turned toward his people, judgment is over, and redemption is beginning. Redemption will only finish when exiles have returned to their homeland. Even the nations will share in the event.

The participle goʾel ("redeemer") is one of the chief titles for God in these chapters (Isa 41:14; 43:14; 44:6; 47:4; 48:17; 49:7, 26; 54:5, 8). Aside from these occurrences, the title is rare. Using this title probably preserves the traditional connotation of a relative who intervenes in a family member's distress (compare Exod 4:22, "Israel is my firstborn son").

Only in Ps 130:7-8 do we find the expression "redeem from iniquities." The theological perception that the power of sin is the greatest threat to the well-being of the people of God probably entered Israelite consciousness with the prophets. Jeremiah, e.g., promised a new covenant written on their hearts (Jer 31:31-34).

The emerging strain of inward piety can be connected to the prophets who composed the oracles in Isa 56–66. Three times God is given the title "redeemer" (Isa 59:20; 60:16; 63:16). One of these (Isa 63:16) expresses the contradiction between the title and Israel's erring ways; Isa 64:5-8 confesses corporate sin and requests divine intervention to remold Israel.

The strain of piety that is deeply conscious of sin and places its hope in God's redeeming power over sin links the OT and the NT. The title "redeemer" is not used in the NT, but many passages describe Jesus as one who liberates, saves, or redeems.

The Gospel of Luke is the only Gospel to use the term *redemption.* Luke speaks of redemption as the urgent hope of Jews living at the time of Jesus (Luke 1:68; 2:38; 24:21), a hope for national restoration and renewal (compare Acts 1:6). In Luke 21:28, Jesus mentions a future redemption as the last event of history. Mark and Matthew include the saying: "the Son of Man came ... to give his life a ransom for many" (Matt 20:28; Mark 10:45), an expression of sacrificial atonement.

Paul and his disciples called significantly upon the language of redemption. The fullest Pauline statement is found in Rom 3:23-25*a*: "[S]ince all have sinned and fall short of the glory of God; they are now justified by his grace as a gift, through the redemption that is in Christ Jesus, whom God put forward as a sacrifice of atonement by his blood, effective through faith." Paul claims that humans are set free from powers that alienate them from God—sin (Rom 1:18–3:20), such as the "curse" of the law (Gal 3:13; 4:1-7), elemental spirits (Gal 4:8-9), the power of darkness (Col 1:13), and, ultimately, death (Rom 8:21-25). Redemption is a transaction between God, the Son, and the believing community, entailing forgiveness for sin and power to liberate humans from the propensity to sin. *See* ATONEMENT; MESSIAH, JEWISH; SACRIFICES AND OFFERINGS; SALVATION.

DALE PATRICK

REED [אֵבֶה ʾeveh, אַגְמוֹן ʾaghmon, אָחוּ ʾakhu, גֹּמֶא gomeʾ, סוּף suf, קָנֶה qaneh; κάλαμος kalamos]. Although it is impossible to identify plants of the Bible with complete accuracy, the reeds and rushes represented by various translations of Hebrew and Greek were probably the common reed (*Phragmites communis*), the cattail (*Typha angustifolia*), or one of a variety of plants that grow primarily in marshy areas along rivers, lakes, and other bodies of water in the Near East (*see* PLANTS OF THE BIBLE). The yam-suf (יַם־סוּף, "Sea of Reeds") refers to the body of water associated with the exodus (e.g., Exod 13:18; *see* RED SEA, REED SEA).

The reed had many practical uses. The Iron Age (1200–586 BCE) archaeological record suggests the existence of instruments that employed single or double reeds (*see* MUSICAL INSTRUMENTS). The "measuring reed" for determining the dimensions of the Temple (Ezek 40:3-8; 42:16-19) reoccurs in Revelation, where it measures the dimensions of the heavenly Temple and the new Jerusalem (Rev 11:1; 21:15, 16). Reeds were used to make papyrus, a writing surface widely used in the biblical world. In 3 John 13 the reed is a "pen" used by the author (*see* PAPYRUS, PAPYRI; WRITING AND WRITING MATERIALS).

The reed served as a metaphor for human frailty and unreliability. The reed is a symbol for wicked people (Job 8:11) and weak leaders (Isa 9:14), or it is related to God's judgment on nations (Isa 19:15); the growth of reeds and rushes can also stand for the land's restoration (Isa 35:7). The prophet Ahijah declared, "The LORD will strike Israel, as a reed is shaken in the water" (1 Kgs 14:15), and the Assyrian Rabshakeh warned Jerusalem not to rely on Egypt, "that broken reed of a staff" (2 Kgs 18:21). Third Maccaabees speaks of human frailty under God's judgment—"as a reed is shaken by the wind" (2:22).

Jesus asks his audience whether they consider John the Baptist "a reed shaken by the wind" (Matt 11:7; Luke 7:24). Matthew characterizes Jesus' ministry of compassionate healing as a fulfillment of the Isaianic servant who "will not break a bruised reed" (Matt 12:20//Isa 42:3). Roman soldiers give Jesus a reed as a mock scepter, only to strike him with it (Matt 27:29-30; Mark 15:19).

Bibliography: Joachim Braun. *Music in Ancient Israel/Palestine* (2002); Irene Jacob. *Plants of the Bible* (2003); Hyun Kim. "An Intertextual Reading of 'a Crushed Reed' and 'a Dim Wick' in Isaiah 42.3." *JSOT* 83 (1999) 113–24.

JAMES K. MEAD

REED SEA. *See* RED SEA, REED SEA.

REELAIAH ree'uh-lay'yuh [רְעֵלָיָה reʿelayah]. Reelaiah was among those returning from the Babylonian exile with Zerubbabel in the Persian period (Ezra 2:2). The name occurs as Raamiah (raʿamyah רַעַמְיָה) in a parallel passage (Neh 7:7). Other words based on the root from which Reelaiah is derived (raʿal רַעַל) convey the notion of reeling under divine judgment (Isa 51:17, 22), fitting for an exilic name apparently connoting the idea of staggering from Yahweh's condemnation.

JASON R. TATLOCK

REFINING [זָקַק zaqaq, צָרַף tsaraf; πυρόω pyroō]. The process of removing impurities from metal, ORE, WATER, or WINE (*see* METALLURGY).

GOLD and SILVER are both described as being refined to make a high-quality metal for the Temple. The altar of incense (*see* INCENSE ALTARS) is constructed of refined gold and the wall paneling of refined silver (1 Chr 28:18; 29:4). The isolating and bleak process of MINING and refining is described in Job 28:1-11. The rigors of the endeavor become the springboard for a discussion of wisdom, which the farthest recesses of the earth cannot divulge, for it is found only through the LORD's own pathway (Job 28:12-28).

Not only metal and ore but also wine and water may be refined. The feast God prepares on Mount Zion, signifying the reward for the righteous in the days to come, includes rich food and wines "strained clear (refined)" (Isa 25:6). Elihu, of the book of Job, speaks of the unfathomable aspects of nature, as when God refines or distills mist from rain (Job 36:27). The top-quality wine and metals that come from refining allow for this statement about the integrity of God's word: "Your promise is well tried (refined), and your servant loves it" (Ps 119:140). Similarly, "This God—his way is perfect; the promise of the LORD proves true (is refined); he is a shield for all who take refuge in him" (Ps 18:30 [Heb. 18:31]).

The most commonly used context for the metaphor of refining is God's testing of human beings and chastisement for sin. Normally, God does the testing, but a prophet may also serve as God's representative. Jeremiah is told he is "a tester and a refiner" of God's people (Jer 6:27). This occasion brings forth divine pathos, as God laments that the refining of the people has been in vain (Jer 6:28-30). In the same way, God declares to the prophet Ezekiel that the people's trials have only resulted in their becoming dross (Ezek 22:18). Besides the people, the priests are singled out for refining; the prophet Malachi speaks of a time when the Levites will be refined and purified so that their offerings will be marked by righteousness (Mal 3:3).

Various postexilic references use the symbol of refining to indicate that God indeed takes the people back. In Second Isaiah, refining, or testing, allows the people again to be God's chosen (Isa 48:10). In Zechariah, refining prompts the people to call on God's name—a cry to which God responds. Echoing the covenant made at Sinai, God declares, "They are my people," who, in turn, accept their obligations with these words: "The LORD is our God" (Zech 13:9).

The image of refining is also used in eschatological and apocalyptic imagery. The DAY OF THE LORD, a time of future divine judgment, is described as "a refiner's fire" (Mal 3:2). Refining is not only a process the wicked undergo, for sometimes the just are tested. In the book of Daniel, e.g., it is the wise who are refined, even though they bring many to righteousness (Dan 11:35). The refining is sometimes characteristic, therefore, of God's inscrutable plan. Indeed the "many" as opposed to the "wicked" described at the end times will be purified and refined, even as evil continues (Dan 12:10).

In the NT, the awesome nature of the one like a Son of Man who comes in judgment is indicated by his arresting appearance, including this description: "his feet were like burnished bronze, refined as in a furnace" (Rev 1:15). The author of the book of Revelation calls upon the complacent Christians of Laodicea to adopt an impassioned faith; he pleads with them to buy his "gold refined by fire" so that they openly attest to their commitment even when threatened (Rev 3:18).

SHARON PACE

REFORM. *See* ISRAEL, HISTORY OF.

REFUGE [חָסָה **khasah,** מַחְסֶה **makhseh,** מָעוֹז **maʿoz;** καταφεύγω **katapheugō**]. A shelter or protection from danger or distress, *refuge* is a common metaphor for God in the OT (Deut 32:37). The word appears most frequently in the Psalms (Ps 142:5 [Heb. 142:6]), where the profession of Yahweh as refuge distinguishes the righteous from the wicked (Pss 2:12; 34:8 [Heb. 34:9]; 37:39-40; 52:7 [Heb. 52:9]; 64:10 [Heb. 64:11]; compare Prov 14:32).

The figurative use of the language draws on experiences of seeking protection from enemies during warfare (2 Sam 22:3, 31; Pss 18:2, 30 [Heb. 18:3, 31]; 61:3-4 [Heb. 61:4-5]), taking shelter from the elements (Judg 9:15; Isa 4:6), or observing animals hiding from predators (Ps 104:18). Important related expressions include "STRONGHOLD" (Joel 3:16), "secure height," "strong tower" (Ps 61:3 [Heb. 61:4]), "rock" (Isa 17:10), and "shade" (Isa 4:6). In some texts, God's refuge is associated closely with the security of the Temple (Ps 73:28; compare Isa 14:32). References to God's "wings" sometimes appear in such texts (Pss 36:7 [Heb. 36:8]; 57:1 [Heb. 57:2]; 61:4 [Heb. 61:5]), but this language is not necessarily inspired by the outstretched wings of the cherubim as sometimes thought (see Ruth 2:12).

Verbal expressions such as "I seek refuge" often appear alongside declarations of trust and hope. In the NT, those who have taken refuge in God's unchangeable promises seize the hope set before them (Heb 6:18). Taking refuge in God implies a choice of Yahweh over human resources as the basis of life and faith (Ps 44:6-7 [Heb. 44:7-8]). *See* CITY OF REFUGE.

Bibliography: Jerome F. D. Creach. *Yahweh as Refuge and the Editing of the Hebrew Psalter* (1996).

JEROME F. D. CREACH

REFUGE, CITY OF. *See* CITY OF REFUGE.

REFUGEE [פְּלֵתִים **palthim**]. A person or people who seeks protection from national or political atrocities, or must travel to find safety from such atrocities. In Jer 50:28, the people are called "fugitives and refugees" following the destruction of the Solomonic Temple and exile to Babylon.

REGEM ree'guhm [רֶגֶם **reghem**]. One of six sons of JAHDAI listed in 1 Chr 2:42-55, in the second genealogy of Calebites (see 1 Chr 2:18-24).

REGEM-MELECH ree'guhm-mee'lik [רֶגֶם מֶלֶךְ **reghem melekh**]. The name of a person accompanying SHAREZER, sent to inquire of the temple priests and prophets concerning the continuation of fasting in commemoration of the Temple's destruction (Zech 7:2). This visit occurred as the rebuilding of the Temple neared completion in the fourth year of DARIUS, the

Persian king (518 BCE). The meaning of the Hebrew term **reghem** is uncertain; **melekh** means "king."

TERRY W. EDDINGER

REGISTRY, REGISTRATION [כְּתָב **ketav**, פָּקַד **paqadh**; ἀπογραφή **apographē**]. Counting or numbering of a population according to tribe or lineage was conducted to determine troop strength (Num 1:3; 26:2), provide a tax base (Exod 30:12-16; Luke 2:1-5), or to assign Levitical cultic roles (Num 3:14-15). The OT refers to many registrations, most famously that by David, which the Deuteronomist attributes to Yahweh but the Chronicler to Satan (2 Sam 24:1; 1 Chr 21:1). In the NT, Joseph registers as a descendant of David (Luke 2:1-5). *See* CENSUS; ENROLLMENT; GENEALOGY; TAXES, TAXATION.

JAMES E. WEST

REGNAL NOTICE. A literary formula used to present the reigns of the kings of Israel and Judah in 1–2 Kings. It included an introduction (e.g., 1 Kgs 15:1-2), an evaluative history of the reign of the king (e.g., 1 Kgs 15:3-7), and a conclusion (e.g., 1 Kgs 15:8). Regnal notices are primarily theological, noting a king's faithfulness to the covenant and his emulation of David, the ideal king, or of Jeroboam I of Israel, the paradigmatic bad king (e.g., 1 Kgs 15:33-34; 16:25-26).

RALPH K. HAWKINS

REHABIAH ree'huh-bi'uh [רְחַבְיָה **rekhavyah**, רְחַבְיָהוּ **rekhavyahu**]. The only son of ELIEZER, Rehabiah is said to have had numerous sons (1 Chr 23:17; 26:25), including ISSHIAH, one of the chiefs of the Levites (1 Chr 24:21).

REHOB ree'hob [רְחוֹב **rekhov**]. A word meaning "broad, open place" or "plaza." 1. The father of Hadadezer, king of ZOBAH (2 Sam 8:3, 12), a people of Syrian descent (2 Sam 10:8).

2. One of the Levites who signed a covenant with Nehemiah (Neh 10:11).

3. A city at the extremity of the spies' travels within Canaan (Num 13:21). It fell within the land allotted to the tribe of Asher in northern Israel (Josh 19:28, 30) but was given to the Levites (Josh 21:31; 1 Chr 6:75). However, Canaanites maintained possession of the city (Judg 1:31). The site is identified with Tell el-Gharbi, located 10 km east-southeast of Acco. *See* BETH-REHOB.

TERRY W. EDDINGER

REHOBOAM ree'huh-boh'uhm [רְחַבְעָם **rekhavʿam**; Ῥοβοάμ **Rhoboam**]. Son of SOLOMON and the Ammonite woman NAAMAH (1 Kgs 14:21, 31), and grandson of DAVID. Rehoboam is noted for precipitating the division of the kingdom of Israel. He retained the southern tribal areas of Benjamin and Judah under his control. These tribes survived as the kingdom of Judah until the Babylonian invasion and conquest in 586 BCE. Rehoboam lost the northern tribes, who formed their own union, Israel, which lasted until 722 BCE.

A. Dates
B. Literary Sources
C. The Division of the Kingdom
D. Historical Problems
  1. Coincidence with Shishak
  2. Building projects described in Chronicles
E. Theological Judgments
Bibliography

A. Dates

For many interpreters the reference to the invasion of Judah by Pharaoh SHISHAK I (Sheshonq) in the fifth year of Rehoboam's reign (1 Kgs 14:25; 2 Chr 12:9) provides an anchor for dating this king. Shishak (931–910 BCE) is reckoned to have invaded Judah in 925 BCE, placing Rehoboam's accession ca. 930 BCE. His seventeen-year reign (1 Kgs 14:21) would place his death at ca. 913 BCE. According to some historians this chronology is problematic. Some scholars have shortened the reign to 922–915 BCE, whereas others have inserted almost the full seventeen years into 926–910 BCE. Recent archaeological work at Tel Rehov (*see* REHOV, TEL) in the eastern Beth-shan Valley, where there are clear destruction levels that can be linked to Shishak's invasion, has raised even more questions regarding Iron Age chronology (*see* CHRONOLOGY OF THE OT).

B. Literary Sources

The literary accounts for the reign of Rehoboam are 1 Kgs 11:43–14:31 and 2 Chr 9:31–12:16. There are some striking similarities between the two accounts, but also some equally noticeable ideological differences. Unlike the Kings account, the Chronicler makes much of the activities of the Levitical priests who fled south after the accession of JEROBOAM in the north (2 Chr 11:13-17). Their initial influence upon Rehoboam was positive (2 Chr 11:17).

The so-called Deuteronomist, on the other hand, complements this brief story of the division with his description of the activities of Jeroboam after he had become king in the north (1 Kgs 12:25-33). Jeroboam established Dan and Bethel as border towns and sanctuaries, staffing them with non-Levitical priests. He compounded his apostasy by installing there golden calves as objects of worship.

In the Chronicler's account brief mention is made of Rehoboam's family and the bestowing of power on his sons in the regional centers he established (2 Chr 11:18-23). Also in the Chronicler's account is the enigmatic reference to the "fortified cities" established by Rehoboam throughout Judah. While many scholars and chronographers see the strengthening of these centers as prelude to the invasion of Shishak, this is far from certain.

Of particular interest is the space devoted to the activities and prophecies of SHEMAIAH, not so much in the Kings account, where he is mentioned only in passing (1 Kgs 12:22) as he advises against an invasion of the north, but in the Chronicler's account (2 Chr 12:5-8). In the latter version he pronounces judgment on Judah and Jerusalem at the agency of Shishak. This is followed by an act of repentance on the part of Rehoboam and his entourage, and the deliverance of the city. The Chronicler also claims as a source the records of this prophet and IDDO the seer that had been preserved (2 Chr 12:15).

C. The Division of the Kingdom

According to both major literary traditions, the Deuteronomist in 1 Kings and the Chronicler, Rehoboam was responsible for the division of the kingdom of Israel, which had been united during the reigns of David and Solomon. The two descriptions of the division are almost identical, save for a few minor linguistic variations. Both agree that the primary cause of the division was the imposition by Rehoboam of harsher conditions of labor on the majority northern tribes. The original domestic policy over all Israel, which involved a pattern of labor and supply, had been established by Solomon (1 Kgs 4:1-6). The purpose of this system was the maintenance of a central court and administration, the supply of a standing army, and other court trappings (1 Kgs 4:7-28).

Both literary traditions recall the court discussions with the elders and the young men who were part of the system of advisors for the newly appointed king. Both also mention that the young men were those with whom Rehoboam had grown up (1 Kgs 12:8; 2 Chr 10:8). The advice from the two groups could not have been more different. The older men suggested a conciliatory move toward the northern tribes and an easing of the burden of taxation and supply of resources. The younger men advised against conciliation and adopted a hard-line approach that involved submission or the threat of violence.

The nature of this advice suggests a deep division within the court between the old regime and the new. We also know from the story of David that divisions had long existed between the northern tribes and the southern tribes and that it took David a period of negotiation to satisfy the demands of the north in the establishment of the united kingdom (2 Sam 5:1-5). Solomon had already introduced the system of regular regional taxation, and, as the young men surrounding Rehoboam admit, it was a burden likened to "whips" (1 Kgs 12:11; 2 Chr 10:11). This suggests a system of forced labor and a reluctant workforce, and probably exploited divisions already felt in David's negotiations with the northern tribes following his seven-year reign in Hebron. Solomon's system differed from that proposed by the young only in degree. Perhaps the elders' advice signified a change in domestic policy for the Jerusalem court. The sending of HADORAM, the court official responsible for forced labor, to the northern tribes, and his subsequent fate (1 Kgs 12:18; 2 Chr 10:18) highlights the explosive nature of this issue among the tribes.

While the story of Rehoboam's failure to listen to and to concede anything to the north is dominant in these accounts, both sources place blame for the subsequent history of both the northern tribes (Israel) and the southern (Judah) on the activities of Jeroboam ben Nebat in the north. It was he who, according to the Deuteronomist, deliberately established an alternative form of cult in the north, contrary to the Deuteronomistic ideal (1 Kgs 12:25-33), and it was he, according to the Chronicler, who inaugurated a different form of priesthood than the hereditary Levitical one (2 Chr 11:14).

Some scholars have sought parallels with the state organization reflected in the story of the division of the kingdoms and that of surrounding nations. This can be a valuable exercise, but needs to be balanced by the observation that any centralized state organization needs certain structures in place to be effective. Given the common environment and political climate of the contemporary ANE, there will be inevitable similarities.

D. Historical Problems

Within the broader context of contemporary scholarship on the OT, there must be an acknowledgment of the doubt cast upon the very existence of a formerly united, now divided kingdom. No attempt can be made here to solve the matter (*see* ISRAEL, HISTORY OF), but there is a growing body of historians who regard these stories as fiction with a strong element of ideological and religious propaganda. If, as many argue, these stories were finally composed, or compiled in the late postexilic period, and possibly in the Hellenistic period, they stand as cautionary tales relevant to their period of production, and are not accounts of "pure" history.

1. Coincidence with Shishak

As indicated above, the reference to Shishak in both sources and the scant references to an Asian campaign by Shishak I (Sheshonq) in Egyptian sources have prompted numerous scholars to use the apparent coincidence as a dating point. A triumphal relief in Karnak lists several cities throughout the Levant that Shishak claimed to have destroyed. The Chronicler certainly uses the impending invasion, the attack, then the Egyptians' supposed leniency toward Jerusalem as a cautionary tale of apostasy and repentance (2 Chr 12:1-8), which appears to be contradicted in 2 Chr 12:9-10. The Deuteronomist refers to it only in passing (1 Kgs 14:25-28//2 Chr 12:9-11), but omits reference to Rehoboam's repentance and stay of total destruction on Jerusalem (compare 2 Chr 12:12).

In spite of the attractiveness of the apparent coincidence of Shishak's campaign, and the happenings during the reign of Rehoboam in Jerusalem, several scholars now doubt the precise link. Donald Redford is not alone among Egyptologists who have raised the difficulty of the extremely poor quality of the records of Shishak's reign in Karnak. The records offer no single campaign account, but simply a list of several towns and cities that were claimed to have been destroyed. These cities and the routes on which they are located would have been very familiar in Egyptian sources from the 3rd millennium BCE.

In any event both accounts (1 Kgs 14:25-28; 2 Chr 12:2-12) make much of the fate of the one major city that does not appear on the list, namely Jerusalem, and although they both involve Shishak in its siege and deliverance, no comparable record exists in Egyptian sources.

2. Building projects described in Chronicles

Not only has the direct link between Rehoboam's reign and Shishak's Asiatic campaign now been placed under suspicion, the list of apparent building activities of Rehoboam, recorded in 2 Chr 11:5-12, can probably be divorced from any discussion of Shishak. Several scholars and historians have assumed that the list of building projects refers to a defensive strategy on the part of Rehoboam in anticipation of the Egyptian invasion. Not only would this have presupposed a remarkably sophisticated intelligence system to provide such information to the Judean court but there are other problems with this interpretation. They are: 1) a careful reading of the Chronicler's account shows that the building project is quite distinct from the invasion of Shishak, and no indication is given as to whether it preceded the invasion or was a reaction to it; 2) the list of the projects does not coincide with the Shishak list at Karnak; the list of cities in 2 Chr 11 is of regional centers coinciding with the districts established early in the monarchy; 3) the archaeological evidence from these sites, such as it is, does not show extensive building projects in the mid-10th cent. BCE; 4) some of the language used of the project is unusual; instead of the usual word for "fortress" (mivtsar מִבְצָר), the more subtle "cities for defense" (ʿarim lematsor עָרִים לְמָצוֹר) is used; 5) the project must be linked up with the establishment of the sites as centers of government, staffed by Rehoboam's sons and family members (2 Chr 11:22-23); 6) through this project Rehoboam "held Judah and Benjamin" (2 Chr 11:12).

All of this suggests a strategy directed toward the control of the two tribes left to Rehoboam, Judah and Benjamin, precipitated by the secession of the northern tribes. The project is a matter of internal security with his own family members in charge. Such a move would have been typical of young dynasties.

E. Theological Judgments

After this account of his reign, Rehoboam disappears from the pages of the OT. His contribution to the history of Israel was decisive, namely the division of the kingdoms because of his threat of tyrannical actions toward the northern tribes. Each literary tradition adds its own commentary to the basic outline of his reign. The Chronicler, possibly as an explanation of his relatively long survival (twelve years) following Shishak's invasion, inserts the activity of Shemaiah the prophet, and his words provide an explanation for not only Rehoboam's reign but for the length of years Jerusalem survived.

Although Rehoboam was a decisive factor in the histories of the kingdoms of Judah and Israel, it was his contemporary and rival in Israel, Jeroboam ben Nebat, who receives the dubious honor of being not only remembered continually by the subsequent history but being held up as an exemplar of evil and apostasy.

Sirach recalls Rehoboam's foolishness in contradistinction to Jeroboam ben Nebat, who led the people to sin. In the NT, Rehoboam is listed among Jesus' ancestors in Matthew's genealogy (1:7).

Bibliography: Nicolas Coldstream and Amihai Mazar. "Greek Pottery from Tel Rehov and Iron Age Chronology." *IEJ* 53 (2003) 29–48; D. Geoffrey Evans. "Rehoboam's Advisers at Shechem and Political Institutions in Israel and Sumer." *JNES* 25 (1966) 273–79; T. R. Hobbs. "The 'Fortresses of Rehoboam': Another Look." *Uncovering Ancient Stones.* Lewis M. Hopfe, ed. (1994) 41–64; Gary N. Knoppers. "The Disappearing Solomon: The Disappearance of the United Monarchy from Recent Histories of Israel." *JBL* 116 (1997) 19–44; Abraham Malamat. "Kingship and Council in Israel and Sumer: A Parallel." *JNES* 22 (1963) 247–53; Amihai Mazar. "Pharaoh Shishak's Campaign to the Land of Israel." *The Early Biblical Period: Historical Studies.* Shmuel Ahituv and Baruch A. Levine, eds. (1988) 139–50; Donald B. Redford. *Egypt, Canaan and Israel in Ancient Times* (1992).

T. R. HOBBS

REHOBOTH ri-hoh'both [רְחֹבוֹת rekhovoth]. Meaning "wide, broad places" or "plaza," the place name Rehoboth refers to two locations in the OT.

1. The name of a well built by Isaac, etymologically defined as "The LORD has made room for us" (Gen 26:22). Many scholars assume that this location is Wadi Ruhayeb, southwest of Beersheba.

2. Genesis 36:37 and 1 Chroncles 1:48 identify a Rehoboth as the place from which the Edomite king SHAUL originated. Depending on one's dating of the Edomite king list of Gen 36, this site is either Ras er-Rihab or Wadi al-Ghuwayr.

JAMES E. WEST

REHOBOTH-IR ri-hoh'both-ihr' [רְחֹבֹת עִיר rekhovoth ʿir]. The place name Rehoboth-Ir occurs in Gen 10:11. It means "plazas of the city" or "city squares," perhaps denoting a suburb of NINEVEH or the city of Nineveh itself. If Rehoboth-Ir is indeed a description of Nineveh, there may be an intentional wordplay on the name of RAHAB, the mythical sea monster defeated at creation, which hints at Nineveh's ultimate defeat by Yahweh. *See* REHOBOTH.

Bibliography: Jack Sasson. "Rehovoth 'îr." *RB* 90 (1983) 94–96.

JAMES E. WEST

REHOV, TEL. Tel Rehov (often spelled Rehob; Arab. Tell es-Sarem), located between the Jordan River and the Gilboa ridge, in the Beth Shan Valley, is one of the largest mounds in the land of Israel (10.4 ha.). The place is identified with Rehov mentioned in several Egyptian and Akkadian texts of the Late Bronze Age as well as in Shoshenq I's (biblical SHISHAK) list of conquered cities (ca. 925 BCE), where it is mentioned aside Beth-Shan. Rehov in the Beth-Shan Valley is not mentioned in the OT.

Excavations at the site were conducted between 1997–2005, directed by Amihai Mazar on behalf of the Institute of Archaeology of the Hebrew University and sponsored by John Camp. The mound is composed of two parts, an upper mound and a lower mound. The upper mound was surrounded during the Early Bronze Age II–III by a massive fortification system, including a 9.5 m wide mud brick and earth rampart. No remains from the Middle Bronze Age have been found so far. Evidence for continuous development of the Canaanite city from the Late Bronze Age until the beginning of the 10th cent. BCE was revealed in the lower city, where six occupation levels from this period were identified. This evidence fits Judg 1:28, which recalls Canaanite continuity in this region until the eve of the monarchy.

The main period explored at Tel Rehov is the Iron Age IIA (11th–10th cent. BCE). Three strata from this period were defined: VI, V, and IV. The city was densely built according to a well-ordered town plan, with parallel blocks of buildings, though no fortifications were found. The architecture is unusual for Iron Age Israel: the walls were built of mud bricks without stone foundations; wood was a common building material and served as foundations for both walls and floors, and there were none of the "pillared buildings" that were so common in Israelite towns. An open-air sanctuary uncovered next to a dwelling quarter perhaps served the local neighborhood. In another area, beehives were found, the first of their kind to be uncovered in the Levant. A partial destruction of Stratum V may have occurred during Shishak's invasion; Stratum IV came to an end in violent destruction by fire probably caused during the wars against HAZAEL, king of Damascus (ca. 830 BCE).

Rich finds from these three strata represent a specific regional aspect of the Iron Age IIA material culture in northern Israel. The finds are evidence of international trade with Phoenicia, Cyprus, and Greece. A rich collection of cult objects includes decorated ceramic horned altars, a ceramic model shrine decorated with unique molding, clay figurines, dozens of seals and seal impressions, a unique ivory object showing an enthroned human figure, and three alphabetic inscriptions incised on pottery jars, one of them mentioning the biblical name **nmsh** (נמש; NIMSHI) known as JEHU's father or grandfather. Thus Rehov must have been one of the most important cities in the northern kingdom of Israel.

Following the Aramean conquest the city was reduced to the upper mound, thus to one-half of its former size. During the 8th cent. BCE (Str. III), the city was surrounded by a 9.5 m wide city wall, probably intended to stand against the Assyrian threat. This new city ended with dramatic destruction, most probably during the Assyrian conquest in the year 732 BCE. Following this destruction, the city was not revived, except for a few squatters and evidence of an Assyrian presence in the form of graves with Assyrian pottery (Str II). The site was abandoned soon afterward.

After a gap of about 1,000 years, a small village was founded on the summit of the mound in the 8th cent. CE. It survived until the 12th cent. CE.

Bibliography: H. Bruins, J. van der Plicht, and A. Mazar. "^{14}C Dates from Tel Rehov: Iron Age Chronology, Pharaohs, and Hebrew Kings." *Science* 300, no. 5617 (2003) 315–18; N. Coldstream and A. Mazar. "Greek Pottery from Tel Rehov and Iron Age Chronology." *IEJ* 53 (2003) 29–48; A. Mazar. "The 1997–1998 Excavations at Tel Rehov: Preliminary Report." *IEJ* 49 (1999) 1–42; A. Mazar. "Three Tenth–Ninth Century B.C.E. Inscriptions from Tel Rehov." *Saxa loquentur: Studien zur Archäologie Palästinas/Israels.* C. G. den Hertog, U. Hübner, and S. Münger, eds. (2003) 171–84; A. Mazar. "Greek and Levantine Iron Age Chronology: A Rejoinder." *IEJ* 54 (2004) 24–36; A. Mazar, H. Bruins, N. Panitz-Cohen, and J. van der Plicht. "Ladder of Time at Tel Rehov: Stratigraphy, Archaeological Context, Pottery and Radiocarbon Dates." *The Bible and Radiocarbon Dating: Archaeology, Text, and Science.* T. Levy and T. Higham, eds. (2005) 193–255.

AMIHAI MAZAR

REHUM ree'huhm [רְחוּם **rekhum**; Ῥαούμ **Rhaoum**, Ῥεούμ **Rheoum**]. 1. One of eleven leaders of those returning from exile in Babylon (Ezra 2:2). It appears that one name has fallen out of this list since Neh 7:7 and 1 Esd 5:8 record twelve names, perhaps symbolic of all Israel. Nehemiah 7:7 lists Rehum as NEHUM.

2. A Persian official (NRSV, "royal deputy") who wrote to Artaxerxes concerning the rebuilding of the walls in Jerusalem (Ezra 4:8-24; 1 Esd 2:16-30). In response, Artaxerxes enjoined the work to stop, an order that Rehum and the officials carried out with force. This event is difficult to date; it is often assumed to precede the time of Nehemiah.

3. A Levite, son of Bani, who helped repair the wall under Nehemiah (Neh 3:17). The list of workers is only partial and likely comes from an independent source that was later incorporated into Nehemiah's memoirs.

4. A family leader who signed the covenant of Nehemiah (Neh 10:25 [Heb. 10:26]). This list and covenant may not belong originally in this context.

5. A priest or priestly clan associated with Zerubbabel and Jeshua. Many interpret it as an error for, or alternate form of, HARIM (Neh 12:3; compare 12:15).

MARK RONCACE

REI ree´*i* [רֵעִי reʿi]. One of David's warriors who did not support ADONIJAH in his efforts to succeed his father David as king (1 Kgs 1:8). Some manuscripts suggest that the Hebrew word is not a proper name but means "a friend" (**reʿeh** רֵעֶה) of SHIMEI or describes Shimei as David's friend.

EMILY R. CHENEY

REINS. *See* BIT.

REJECT [מָאַס maʾas; ἀθετέω atheteō, ἀποδοκιμάζω apodokimazō]. To do away with completely, to discard, or to cut oneself off from another. The OT weaves the ongoing pattern of God's choosing a people with their rejection and refusal to follow God's statutes. Whether their rejection of God is active (e.g., making idols) or passive (e.g., Adam accepting the forbidden fruit from Eve), both result in a breach between God and humanity. The Scriptures do not allow a middle ground regarding whom humanity chooses to serve. Either they accept the decrees of God, or they reject and despise God completely. Leviticus 26:14-39 details how God will abhor and reject Israel if they turn away from keeping all of the Law (compare 2 Kgs 17:16-20; 23:27). Similarly, Saul is rejected as king for failing to follow the commands of God (1 Sam 15:23, 26). Though making good on the promise to cut off those who reject God, God also offers a way out. In Lev 26:40-45, God makes provision for those who repent and turn from their wicked ways. God will not "spurn them, or abhor them so as to destroy them utterly" (Lev 26:44).

The theme of rejection and repentance carries over into the NT. Listeners to Jesus either accept or reject his teaching, and his followers should expect similar treatment (Luke 6:22; 10:16). Religious teachers reject Jesus as the Messiah (Luke 7:30; 9:22; 17:25; compare Isa 53:3) and challenge Jesus' authority to teach and do miracles (Mark 11–12). In response, Jesus quotes Ps 118:22 to show that they have rejected the CORNERSTONE of the kingdom of God (Mark 12:10; compare Matt 21:42; Luke 20:17; Acts 4:11; 1 Pet 2:7).

Lest the believer despair of being able to fully accept God as king and so fear being forever cut off, the Scriptures make clear that despite the fact that the chosen have rejected God, God cannot completely reject them (Lam 3:31; Zech 10:6; Rom 11:1-2). For the sake of God's own name (1 Sam 12:22) and the covenantal promises, God provides a way of salvation and full acceptance into the kingdom.

PHILIP G. MONROE

REJOICE. *See* JOY.

REKEM ree´kuhm [רֶקֶם reqem]. 1. One of the five kings of Midian killed by the Israelites on their journey to Canaan (Num 31:8; Josh 13:21); it is possible, however, that this is a place name, not a person.

2. Son of Hebron in the line of Caleb (1 Chr 2:43).

3. Son of Peresh, a descendant of Manasseh, and member of one of the Machir clans in Gilead; brother of Ulam (1 Chr 7:16).

4. A town in the territory of Benjamin (Josh 18:27). Its exact location is unknown, but it appears in a list of places located in the western part of the region. Rekem is also the ancient designation for PETRA.

MARK RONCACE

RELEASE, YEAR OF. *See* YEAR OF RELEASE.

RELIGION [δεισιδαιμονία deisidaimonia, εὐσέβεια eusebeia, θρησκεία thrēskeia]. Respect and awe for the sacred and divine, strict observance of religious ritual, or conscientiousness in morality and ethics. *Religion* occurs in the NRSV in 1–4 Maccabees and the NT, but most frequently in 4 Maccabees. For example, Antiochus IV Epiphanes refers to the priest Eleazar's religion as **thrēskeia** when compelling him to eat pork (4 Macc 5:7, 13), while Eleazar and the narrator use **eusebeia** (4 Macc 5:18; NRSV, "piety"), perhaps emphasizing that true religion is a matter not only of outward observances but of inward devotion and integrity.

In the NT of the NRSV, **eusebeia** is rendered as *religion* only in 1 Tim 3:16 (compare other translations at 1 Tim 6:5-6; 2 Tim 3:5; Titus 1:1). In other uses of **thrēskeia**, Paul speaks of belonging to "the strictest sect of our religion" (Acts 26:5). According to Jas 1:26-27, the religion of one who does not control the tongue and deceives the heart is empty. Pure and undefiled religion is an active concern for others and keeping one's self unstained by the world (see Col 2:18; 3:23).

Finally, **deisidaimonia** refers to religiosity or a system of cultic belief or practice. While other words for religion can have negative connotations, **deisidaimonia** was used the most often to refer to superstition, such as by Festus in reference to Judaism (Acts 25:19; compare Acts 17:22). *See* DEVOUT; GODLY; HOLY, HOLINESS, NT.

MARK D. GIVEN

REMAIN [יָשַׁב yashav; μένω menō]. The concept of remaining, abiding, or continuing steadfast is found in both the OT and the NT. The OT also contains a concept of God's rescue of a "REMNANT" and their restoration in the land. (See Isa 10:21-22; Jer 44:14;

and Ezekiel's "vision of the dry bones," Ezek 34.) The verb also means "place," "set," or "cause to dwell," depending on its context (Gen 47:6, 11; Lev 23:43; 1 Sam 12:8). In the NT, "remaining" concerns holding one's ground against opposition or maintaining constant adherence or devotion, as when Jesus says "remain in me" (John 15:11, 16; also Phil 1:25). *See* ABIDE; STEADFASTNESS.

JAMES E. WEST

REMALIAH rem´uh-li´uh [רְמַלְיָהוּ **remalyahu**]. Remaliah, the second-last king of the Northern Kingdom and father of PEKAH, ruled from 736–731 BCE (2 Kgs 15:25-37; 16:1-5; 2 Chr 28:6; Isa 7:1-9; 8:6).

REMEMBER, TO [זָכַר **zakhar**; μιμνῄσκω **mimnēskō**]. Remembering is related to covenant (*see* COVENANT, OT AND NT). The first reference to remembering is in the Noah story. As the ark floats on the floodwaters, God remembers Noah and makes the waters subside (Gen 8:1). God hangs a bow in the sky as a sign of the covenant that God will never again destroy all flesh by flood (Gen 9:12-17). God remembers humankind (Gen 19:29; 30:22; 1 Sam 1:19), and God remembers the covenants with humankind (Exod 2:24; 6:5; Lev 26:42, 45; compare Ps 105:8). The people are called to remember God and what God requires of them, especially to remember the day they were brought out of slavery (Exod 13:3; *see* PASSOVER AND FEAST OF UNLEAVENED BREAD); the SABBATH (Exod 20:8); and their long wandering in the wilderness (Deut 8:2).

Remember is used in texts of judgment against the people when they have not remembered God (Isa 17:10), or when God remembers iniquity and wickedness (Jer 14:10; Hos 7:2; 9:9; Rev 18:5). *Remember* also is used in words of hope that God will not remember the people's sins (Isa 43:18-19, 25), and Jerusalem will not remember her disgrace (Isa 54:4); God will remember the people as a father remembers a son (Jer 31:20). God remembers Rachel and Hannah, who conceive and bear sons who will become patriarch and prophet for Israel (Gen 30:22-23; 1 Sam 1:11, 19-20).

The word occurs some forty-five times in the book of Psalms alone, often in laments crying out to God to remember (Pss 25:7; 74:2, 18, 22; 89:47), and also in gratitude that God has remembered (Pss 78:39; 136:23; compare 8:4; 111:5). Thus, remembering is an action of both God and people. God remembers; the people remember. The people call upon God to remember; and God, through the prophets, admonishes the people to remember. Memory, the account of the actions of God on behalf of the people, is the fundamental shaping element of the faith of ancient Israel (*see* MEMORIAL, MEMORY). Remembering is a communal activity through which identity and right living are realized and maintained.

The Greek verb **mimnēsko** corresponds closely in meaning to the Hebrew **zakhar**. The Lukan infancy narratives, with their strong OT overtones, provide good examples of the correspondence. In Luke 1:54, Mary sings to God "in remembrance of his mercy," and Zechariah states that God "has remembered his holy covenant" (Luke 1:72). The followers of Jesus remember his words (Luke 24:6-8; Acts 20:35) and the things prophesied about him (John 12:16); remembering becomes the basis of the tradition "handed down" (1 Cor 11:2; compare 1 Cor 4:17).

The uses of the word *remember* in both the OT and NT suggest that remembering is about more than the mind; remembering is about covenant and requires response. In the OT, the instructions for observing the Passover state: "Remember this day on which you came out of Egypt" (Exod 13:3); "this day shall be a day of remembrance for you" (12:14). Luke 22:19 and 1 Cor 11:24-25 describe the purpose of the LORD'S SUPPER as a remembrance of Jesus and his new covenant: "Do this in remembrance of me." Remembering is depicted not simply as a "bringing to mind," but as an active, participatory event, in which God and people somehow mysteriously interact.

Bibliography: Ronald S. Hendel. *Remembering Abraham: Culture, Memory, and History in the Hebrew Bible* (2005); Michael A. Signer, ed. *Memory and History in Christianity and Judaism* (2000).

NANCY DECLAISSÉ-WALFORD

REMEMBRANCE. *See* MEMORIAL, MEMORY.

REMEMBRANCE, BOOK OF. *See* BOOKS REFERRED TO IN THE BIBLE.

REMETH ree´mith [רֶמֶת **remeth**]. Remeth is one of sixteen towns allotted to the tribe of Issachar in Josh 19:21. The names of the Levitical cities of JARMUTH (Josh 21:29) and RAMOTH (1 Chr 6:73 [Heb. 6:58]) may be variant spellings of the same place.

REMNANT [יֶתֶר **yether**, פְּלֵיטָה **peletah**, שָׂרִיד **saridh**, שְׁאָר **she'ar**, שְׁאֵרִית **she'erith**; λεῖμμα **leimma**, ὑπόλειμμα **hypoleimma**]. While remnant may be used for anyone or anything left behind following a disaster, it occurs most frequently in the Latter Prophets where it is used to depict a people reduced to a vestige of its former grandeur. "Remnant" is the English translation of four Hebrew words used to convey this motif. Two indicate those who remain or are left behind (**she'ar, she'erith**) and two suggest those who survived or escaped (**peletah, saridh**). These Hebrew words are used interchangeably, and sometimes two or three appear in the same phrase or sentence. A fifth word (**yether**), also translated "remnant," occurs less frequently.

The political turbulence and insecurity that frame the background of prophetic books are understood to be orchestrated by Yahweh. In a number of instances, Yahweh's anger is described as reducing the surrounding nations to a remnant of their past greatness. For example, after Yahweh unleashes his fury against the king of Assyria, "the remnant of the trees of his forest will be so few that a child can write them down" (Isa 10:19). Yahweh "will cut off from Babylon name and remnant, offspring and posterity" (Isa 14:22; see also Jer 25:20; 47:4-5).

Primarily, however, Yahweh's anger is unleashed against his own people so that only a remnant will escape the devastating consequences. The negative impact of God's actions, however, is only part of the full picture envisioned by the prophets, for they also speak of the restoration of what has been lost. This twofold notion of desolation and promise is encapsulated in the name of Isaiah's son, SHEAR-JASHUB ("a remnant shall return"), who accompanies Isaiah when he goes to meet King Ahaz (Isa 7:3). The son's name is ominous, in that it presages the coming catastrophe for Judah and Jerusalem brought by Assyria (Isa 7:18-25), the rod of God's anger (Isa 10:5). Although the "people Israel were like the sand of the sea, only a remnant of them will return. Destruction is decreed" for them (Isa 10:22). However, the son's name is also hopeful in that it portends restoration from Assyrian invasion. The returning remnant will now lean on "the Holy One of Israel" (Isa 10:20) and return to "the mighty God" (Isa 10:22). Yahweh will provide a highway from Assyria and the surrounding nations "to recover the remnant that is left of his people" (Isa 11:11). Indeed, when King Hezekiah beseeches Isaiah to offer a "prayer for the remnant that is left" (Isa 37:1-4; see 2 Kgs 19:1-4), Yahweh's response is that "the surviving remnant of the house of Judah shall again take root downward, and bear fruit upward; for from Jerusalem a remnant shall go out, and from Mount Zion a band of survivors" (Isa 37:31-32; see 2 Kgs 19:30-31). While the first part of Isaiah concerns the remnant surviving Assyrian invasion, the latter part of the book also addresses "the remnant of the house of Israel" that has experienced Babylonian deportation. Yahweh has sustained them from birth and rescued them (Isa 46:3-4). The notion of Yahweh preserving a remnant of his people echoes the words of Joseph to his brothers when he reveals his identity to them: "God sent me before you to preserve for you a remnant on earth, and to keep alive for you many survivors" (Gen 45:7).

Isaiah's largely positive portrayal of restoring the remnant that survives is also found in Micah and Zephaniah. In Micah, the remnant is portrayed as those who are lame and cast off (Mic 4:7). Although surrounded by many nations, they will again become strong like a lion in the forest (Mic 5:5-8 [Heb. 5:4-7]). Yahweh's anger will not last forever; he will forgive the iniquity of the remnant of his people (Mic 7:18). Zephaniah also refers to the restoration of the remnant that will again take possession of the seacoast and have houses in Ashkelon (Zeph 2:7). The remnant will plunder Moab making it like Sodom and Gomorrah (Zeph 2:9). Zephaniah also emphasizes that the remnant will consist of those who are humble and lowly and will exclude the proud who exult in their power. The restored remnant will do no wrong and utter no lies (Zeph 3:11-13). These passages in Isaiah, Micah, and Zephaniah picture the remnant restored to power as an ideal community purged of those whose transgressions turned Yahweh's anger against them.

While there are also places in Jeremiah that speak of a remnant that will experience restoration and be fruitful and multiply (Jer 23:3; 31:7), Jeremiah's message is more notably directed toward judgment on the remnant that survived Babylonian invasion and remains in Jerusalem. Yahweh summons Babylon to glean the remnant of Israel like a grape-gatherer moving his hand over the branches (Jer 6:9). "Death shall be preferred to life by all the remnant that remains" (Jer 8:3). In a vision of good and bad figs, Jeremiah says that those who go into exile are like the good figs, while the remnant that remain in the land will be like figs that are so bad they cannot be eaten (Jer 24:1-10). When Babylon's occupation of Jerusalem is complete and Gedaliah is installed as governor, Jeremiah's message changes. The remnant in Judah who are now scheming to flee to Egypt (Jer 42:15-17) are warned not to go there (Jer 42:19). If they do such a thing, everyone will perish in Egypt by famine and by sword (Jer 44:7, 12), "so that none of the remnant of Judah who have come to settle in the land of Egypt shall escape or survive or return to the land of Judah" (Jer 44:14). Restoration and return will only be for those who are in Babylonian exile.

Haggai refers to those who have come back from Babylonian exile and whom he encourages to rebuild the Temple as "the remnant of the people" (Hag 1:12-14; 2:2). Likewise Zechariah refers to those who have returned as "the remnant of this people" (Zech 8:6, 11, 12). Ezra also addresses the community who has returned from exile as "a remnant" (Ezra 9:8, 13-15).

In the NT, *remnant* is found only in Paul's letter to the Romans. He quotes Isaiah who "cries out concerning Israel, 'Though the number of the children of Israel were like the sand of the sea, only a remnant of them will be saved'" (Rom 9:27; see Isa 10:22). While Isaiah is referring to the remnant that will return after Assyrian invasion, Paul is citing this text in his argument in Rom 9–11 that the remnant are the Jews who are "chosen by grace" (Rom 11:5).

EDGAR W. CONRAD

REPENTANCE IN THE NT [μετάνοια metanoia; μετανοέω metanoeō]. In the NT repentance is conveyed primarily by the noun **metanoia** and related verb **metanoeō** and denotes the complete reorientation of one's whole being to God. It entails acknowledging sin and turning away from all that hinders wholehearted devotion to God's will, along with resolute turning to God with renewed trust and obedience. In Greco-Roman literature the word conveys, literally, a "change of mind," but the NT use of the word is deeply influenced by the OT's notion of "turning" to God (shuv [שׁוּב]; *see* REPENTANCE IN THE OT) as an "about face," a change in direction and return to covenant fidelity. Thus, repentance involves far more than intellectual change or remorse; it entails a new or renewed relationship with God that transforms all the dimensions of one's life, including conduct, and is akin to conversion. Repentance is completed by faith and inseparably linked to it (see Mark 1:15). The words strephō (στρέφω) and epistrephō (ἐπιστρέφω, "to turn") can function as synonyms of repentance (see Acts 3:19; 26:20). The verb metamelomai (μεταμέλομαι), occasionally translated as "repentance," refers more narrowly to a change of mind or feeling that is not necessarily accompanied by true turning to God (see Judas in Matt 27:3). *See* CONVERSION; FAITH, FAITHFULNESS; SIN, SINNERS.

The vocabulary of repentance plays a prominent role in the Synoptic Gospels and in Acts, appearing less frequently in the NT epistles. The NT places a distinctive stamp upon it by linking it with the kingdom of God and faith in God's saving work in Jesus Christ.

In the Gospels of Mark and Matthew, repentance is central to the proclamation of both John the Baptist and Jesus. John the Baptist highlights the urgent necessity of it in view of the in-breaking kingdom or rule of God, the imminent arrival of one stronger than he (the Messiah), and the inevitable judgment that will accompany this time of fulfillment (Matt 3:1-12; Mark 1:1-8). In Mark, John urges fellow Jews to submit to "a baptism of repentance for the forgiveness of sins" (Mark 1:4) as a pledge of authentic reorientation of life. His water baptism does not itself mediate forgiveness of sins, but rather prepares people for the key saving events associated with the coming of the "one who is more powerful" who will baptize with the Holy Spirit. In Matthew, John also warns them not to rely on their Abrahamic ancestry at the coming judgment, but rather to bear behavioral "fruit worthy of repentance" (Matt 3:7-10).

In Mark and Matthew, repentance is also the keynote of Jesus' inaugural preaching. Like John the Baptist, Jesus believes that radical transformation is required for life in the kingdom of God and issues a call to repentance in view of its nearness. He also explicitly links repentance with faith in the gospel (Mark 1:15). Since God's kingdom or rule is present with power in Jesus' own ministry, repentance and belief in the gospel is associated with response to him and takes the form of discipleship. When he sends his twelve disciples out in mission, they, too, proclaim repentance (Mark 6:12).

Repentance is featured most prominently in the NT throughout Luke–Acts. The Gospel of Luke, like Mark and Matthew, summarizes John the Baptist's message as a call to repentance (Luke 3:3). But when John urges the crowds who come to him to bear "fruits" (plural) that are "worthy of repentance," he goes a step further, fleshing out what they entail (Luke 3:7-14). Repentance is not among the first words on Jesus' lips in Luke, as in Matthew and Mark, but he clearly defines his mission in terms of it: "I have come to call not the righteous but sinners to repentance" (Luke 5:32). Parables of Jesus found only in Luke (e.g., the prodigal son in Luke 15 and the Pharisee and the tax collector in Luke 18) provide some of the NT's most memorable images of repentance, as do unique stories of Jesus' encounters with individuals such as ZACCHAEUS (Luke 19) and the penitent thief on the cross (Luke 23). In Luke, Jesus highlights the divine joy occasioned by repentance (Luke 15:7). And at the end of Luke's Gospel, the risen Lord commissions his disciples with words that summarize the import of his life, ministry, death, and resurrection: "repentance and forgiveness of sins is to be proclaimed in his [the Messiah's] name to all nations, beginning from Jerusalem" (Luke 24:47).

In Luke's second volume, the Acts of the Apostles, the church proves faithful to this task, for repentance is the heart of the message it proclaims, repeatedly forming the conclusion to the missionary sermons of its central figures, Peter and Paul (Acts 2:38; 3:19; 5:31; 8:22; 13:24; 17:30; 19:4; 20:21; 26:20). The call to repentance is extended to both Jews and Gentiles (Acts 11:18). Jews are presented with a second opportunity to repent of their rejection of God's Messiah and to turn to him in faith; Gentiles are to turn from idols to the living God who will give them life. For both, repentance leads to baptism in Jesus' name, incorporation into the renewed people of God, forgiveness of sins, and the gift of the Spirit.

While the language of repentance is an important aspect of the apostle Paul's missionary preaching in Acts, it is rarely found in his own letters. Paul's understanding of the newness of life occasioned by the revelation of God in Christ is embraced by his concept of "faith" and conveyed with specialized vocabulary (e.g., in terms of baptism into Christ's death or new creation). The same is true for the Gospel of John, which focuses on "believing" and speaks in its own specialized terms of new birth and movement from death to life or from darkness to light (e.g., John 3). The most unsettling references to repentance in the NT appear in Hebrews' discussion of apostates, to whom a "second repentance" is denied (Heb 6:4-6; 12:17; *see* UNFORGIVABLE SIN). The vocabulary of repentance also appears in the book of Revelation, notably in the opening letters to seven churches who stand under the threat of judgment (Rev 2:5, 16, 21-22; 3:3, 19; see also 9:20-21; 16:9, 11). Here, as elsewhere in the NT, repentance is associated with judgment; however, it is also associated with joy (Luke 15:7) and with the goodness and patience of God (Rom 2:4; 2 Tim 2:25; 2 Pet 3:9). Indeed, it is God's saving work in Jesus Christ that makes forgiveness and new life possible. Repentance, in concert with faith, is a response that appropriates this divine gift.

FRANCES TAYLOR GENCH

REPENTANCE IN THE OT [שׁוּב shuv]. The OT describes repentance more with reference to action than to feelings (such as contrition). The most common verb is **shuv** ("to turn, return"). One turned away from unrighteousness (Jer 18:11; Ezek 18:21; Zech 1:4) and turned to (2 Chr 15:4) or returned to (Isa 55:7) God, so a radical change in one's way of life was involved. This verb is also translated "repent" (1 Kgs 8:47-48; Jer 34:15), especially when it is not followed by a preposition. Related verbs include **yadhah** (יָדָה, "to confess"; Lev 5:5) and **sur** (סוּר, "to turn aside," i.e., from evil; Ps 34:14 [Heb. 34:15]). The NRSV has appropriately translated the niphal of **nhm** (נחם) as "to change one's mind, relent" (e.g., Exod 32:14; 1 Sam 15:29; Joel 2:13-14; Jonah 3:9-10), rather than the "repent" of older translations, since "repent" in English suggests turning away from sin—a notion that would be inappropriate when God is the subject.

Repentance is seldom referred to explicitly in the Torah and Former Prophets (see Deut 30:10; 1 Kgs 8:35, 47-48), but it appears in positive and negative ways in the Latter Prophets. Although it has regularly been claimed that the preexilic prophets called Israel to repentance, careful study of their books has shown that they mostly spoke of Israel's having turned away (Hos 7:16; 11:7) from Yahweh and of their failure to return (Isa 9:13 [Heb. 9:12]; Jer 5:3; 8:6; 15:7; 44:5; Hos 5:4; 7:10; 11:5; Amos 4:6-11) to him as the basis for the day of judgment, which was now at hand. A few times they appealed for repentance (Isa 1:27; 30:15; Jer 18:11; Hos 12:6 [Heb. 12:7]; 14:1-2 [Heb. 14:2-3]). Most of their message, however, was announcement of impending judgment because repentance had failed. Jeremiah 3:12–4:1 is addressed to the remnant of the Northern Kingdom, which had already experienced judgment.

Once the judgment had come with the fall of Jerusalem in 587 BCE, appeals for repentance began to play a more significant role in the messages of the exilic and postexilic prophets (Isa 44:22; 55:7; Ezek 14:6; 18:21-32; Joel 2:12-13; Zech 1:3-4; Mal 3:7). An important part of their message, however, was the claim that restoration as the people of Yahweh would come true only because of Yahweh's faithfulness, which would make it possible for them to repent. Jeremiah spoke of God's promise to restore the exiles to their land and to "give them a heart to know that I am the LORD," and then they would return to him (Jer 24:6-7). Ezekiel said it would be restoration that would finally make it possible for the people to remember their evil ways and loathe themselves for their iniquities (Ezek 36:31; compare 16:59-63). Second Isaiah spoke of redemption before return (Isa 44:22). These are some of the texts that seem to say forgiveness makes repentance possible, rather than the reverse, as might seem logical and as other texts put it (e.g., Deut 30:10; Ezek 18:30-32; Zech 1:3; Mal 3:7).

Although the prophets spoke of the failure of the nation to repent, repentance did first involve individual decisions that could eventually transform society. Jeremiah reminds us of this both when he speaks of God giving "a heart to know that I am the LORD" (Jer 24:7), which will lead to repentance, and also when he promises a new covenant written on the heart (Jer 31:31-34). Ezekiel also looked forward to repentance at the individual level in promising God's gift of a new heart and a new spirit, again making repentance possible (Ezek 36:25-32). Psalm 51 provides an excellent example of what true repentance meant to the individual Israelite. After the appeal to God for cleansing from sin (Ps 51:1-2 [Heb. 51:3-4]), the awareness of guilt having produced a feeling of being defiled, the psalmist confesses his sin, acknowledging that this is a personal issue between him and God (since only God can fix what is wrong), and expressing the intensity of his feelings of guilt (Ps 51:3-5 [Heb. 51:5-7]). This is followed by a renewed appeal for cleansing (Ps 51:6-12 [Heb. 51:8-14]) and for reestablishment of a right relationship with God (Ps 51:9, 11 [Heb. 51:11, 13]). A promise of what the forgiven sinner intends to do follows (Ps 51:13-15 [Heb. 51:15-17]), but he knows this is no bargain with God, for there is nothing he can do to earn forgiveness (Ps 51:16 [Heb. 51:18]). The best he can do is to humble himself before the compassionate God (Ps 51:17 [Heb. 51:19]).

What made repentance possible for the Israelite was thus the prior assurance that God desired to forgive. When Joel called for a national time of repentance (Joel 2:13), he quoted Exod 34:6-7, God's revelation of the divine nature: "gracious and merciful, slow to anger, and abounding in steadfast love," a classic OT passage concerning divine forgiveness. After the sin of the golden calf, Moses had interceded on behalf of sinful people without mentioning the need for repentance on their part (Exod 32:7-14, 30-32; 34:9), and the resolution of the crisis seems to have come about solely via God's self-revelation in Exod 34:6-7. A similarly striking point of view appears in Daniel's prayer, in which he confesses his sin and the sins of his people, showing that he was repentant, but he depended solely on God's righteousness in his appeals for forgiveness for them all (Dan 9:15-19).

The OT thus reveals divine forgiveness to be a more complex matter than the simple pattern of human initiative, repentance, followed by a divine response, forgiveness.

Bibliography: William L. Holladay. *The Root Shubh in the Old Testament* (1958); Jacob Milgrom. *Cult and Conscience: The ASHAM and the Priestly Doctrine of*

Repentance (1976); Norman Snaith. *The Seven Psalms* (1964).

DONALD E. GOWAN

REPHAEL ref′ay-uhl [רְפָאֵל refa᾿el]. A son of SHEMAIAH and one of the Korahite gatekeepers at the Temple in Jerusalem (1 Chr 26:7). *See* KORAH, KORAHITES.

REPHAH ree′fuh [רֶפַח refakh]. In the genealogy of Joseph's sons, Rephah is listed as an Ephraimite (1 Chr 7:25). His father's name is not given, perhaps because the text of vv. 23-25 was revised. Rephah is not listed in the only other Ephraimite genealogy (Num 26:35-36).

REPHAIAH ri-fay′yuh [רְפָיָה refayah]. Means "God healed." 1. One of the descendants of David: grandson of Hananiah, son of Jeshaiah, and father of Arnan (1 Chr 3:21).

2. One of the four leaders of 500 Simeonites who destroyed a remnant of Amalekites at Mount Seir and lived there "to this day" (1 Chr 4:42-43).

3. A mighty warrior of the tribe of Issachar and a son of Tola (1 Chr 7:2).

4. One of the descendants of Saul: son of Binea and father of Eleasah (1 Chr 9:43). He is listed as RAPHAH in 1 Chr 8:37.

5. Son of Hur and ruler of half the district in Jerusalem who led efforts in repairing the city wall (Neh 3:9).

BRUCE W. GENTRY

REPHAIM ref′ay-im [רְפָאִים refa᾿im]. 1. The term **refa᾿im** occurs eight times in the Hebrew text with reference to the underworld's inhabitants (*see* DEAD, ABODE OF THE; SHEOL). The texts are all poetic, generally dated as exilic or postexilic. The dead **refa᾿im** are lifeless and flaccid. They tremble before Yahweh (Job 26:5) but cannot praise him (Ps 88:10; compare 6:5). They are roused by a newcomer, only to note his new weakness (Isa 14:9-11; compare Ezek 32:21). The **refa᾿im** are deceased vassal kings in Isa 14, but in Proverbs they include all foolish people, forming an assembly at rest (Prov 2:18; 9:18; 21:16). One apocalyptic passage envisages their resurrection in reference to Yahweh's people, but precludes it for Israel's enemies (Isa 26:14, 19).

There are two notable features of the biblical portrayal of rephaim. First, there are very few Hebrew references altogether to the underworld's inhabitants. The only other term, **᾿elohim** (אֱלֹהִים), occurs in this sense even more rarely (1 Sam 28:13; Isa 8:19-21). Second, the biblical **refa᾿im** remain shadowy and effete. Unlike the Ugaritic **rpum** with whom they are often compared, they are never individually named or linked with a founder/patron, and they have no reported contact with the living through necromantic consultation or commemorative feast. Whether these features of the canonical text are due to relative disinterest by ancient Israelites, casual disregard by the texts' compilers, or censoring disapproval by biblical redactors remains an open question.

Older scholarship generally interpreted **refa᾿im** as "weak ones" (compare Isa 14:9-11), from **rafah** (רָפָה, "to be weak"), despite the different final consonant. Now, given the Ugaritic evidence, most scholars derive it from **rafa᾿** (רָפָא, "to heal"), giving "healers/providers (of fertility and life)."

The equivalent Ugaritic term **rpum** also occurs in several texts with arguably different meanings. Most scholars see references to the deceased in the BAAL Cycle's concluding hymn to Shaphash and in a so-called funerary ritual (KTU 1.6:VI.45–48; 1.161), and references to the living in the fragmentary Rephaim texts (KTU 1.20–22). Brian Schmidt argues that interest in the dead did not emerge until much later and that Ugaritic **rpum** always indicates the living. However, neither his overall thesis nor his specific arguments has been generally accepted. The stem **rp᾿m** occurs further in a few other extant Semitic texts, always indicating the dead. Two royal Phoenician inscriptions wish tomb robbers "no resting place with the **rp᾿m**," while a Neo-Punic inscription mentions "divine **rp᾿m**." The parallels between Hebrew, Ugaritic, and other Semitic texts are intriguing, but the relationship between the various meanings of the stem remains unclear.

Bibliography: Philip S. Johnston. *Shades of Sheol* (2002); Brian B. Schmidt. *Israel's Beneficent Dead* (1994).

PHILIP S. JOHNSTON

2. The Rephaim is an ethnic term designating a people who once occupied portions of the Levant, especially the TRANSJORDAN. The translation of Rephaim as "GIANTS" is probably derived from two differing traditions. One was their association with the Anakim (*see* ANAK, ANAKIM, ANAKITES), a people described as exceedingly tall (Deut 1:28; 9:2). The second was the identification of OG, king of Bashan, as one of the Rephaim (Josh 12:4; 13:12), whose bed was reported to have been over 13 ft. × 6 ft. (Deut 3:11), and whose land was called Rephaim country (Deut 3:13).

According to the Deuteronomic tradition, the Rephaim were known by a number of different names. Deuteronomy 2:10-11 notes that a people called the Emim were considered part of the Rephaim, though the Moabites called them Emim (*see* EMIM, THE). The Rephaim also inhabited Ammon, though the Ammonites called them ZAMZUMMIM (Deut 2:20-21). The Deuteronomic tradition of identifying these groups with the Rephaim contrasts with the tradition reflected in Gen 14:5, where Chedorlaomer is reported to have defeated the Rephaim at Ashteroth-karnaim, the ZUZIM (who may be the same as the Zamzummim) at Ham, and the Emim at Shaveh-kiriathaim. Those traditions that refer to a Valley of the Rephaim near Jerusalem (Josh 15:8; 18:16;

2 Sam 5:18, 22; 23:13; *see* REPHAIM, VALLEY OF) also contrast with the Deuteronomic location of the Rephaim in the Transjordan.

E. THEODORE MULLEN JR.

REPHAIM, VALLEY OF ref′ay-im [עֵמֶק רְפָאִים ʿemeq refaʾim]. Recognized as a fertile farming valley from the Late Bronze Age onward, this agricultural center, known in modern times as Wadi el-Ward, is located southwest of Jerusalem. The valley is named in Joshua as part of a natural geographical boundary between the tribes of Judah and Benjamin (Josh 15:8; 18:16).

After David ascended to the throne, the Philistines assembled in the valley of Rephaim in order to subdue the growing power of this king. On both occasions, David received an oracle from Yahweh that encouraged him to move against the Philistines (1 Sam 5:18-25; 1 Chr 14:9-17). Another story relates how three of David's champion warriors broke through a Philistine encampment in the valley of Rephaim in order to fetch him a drink of water from the well of Bethlehem. The story illustrates the humble nature of King David, because he refused to drink the water that his men had secured at the risk of their lives (2 Sam 23:13-17; 1 Chr 11:15-19).

Isaiah used the image of the valley in order to describe the aftermath of the destruction of the Syro-Ephraimite alliance. Fugitives from Damascus and Israel ("Ephraim") would resemble the ears of grain that remained in a harvested field (Isa 17:5-6).

BRUCE W. GENTRY

REPHAN ref′uhn [Ῥαιφάν Rhaiphan]. A god mentioned in Stephen's speech in Acts 7:43. Stephen is quoting from the LXX version of Amos 5:26, which refers to Moloch and Rephan. The Hebrew of Amos 5:26 instead reads SAKKUTH AND KAIWAN (sikkuth סִכּוּת, kiyun כִּיּוּן), which are possibly references to the planet Saturn. No deity named Rephan is known from ancient sources. The variant reading may have arisen from a confusion of the Hebrew letters kaf (kh כ) and resh (r ר).

KEVIN A. WILSON

REPHIDIM ref′i-dim [רְפִידִים refidhim]. A site on the exodus route between the Wilderness of Sin and the Wilderness of Sinai (Exod 17:1; 19:2). Numbers 33:12-15 establishes the order of places visited as the Wilderness of Sin, Dophkah, Alush, Rephidim, and the Wilderness of Sinai. Dophkah and Alush are mentioned only in this passage and their location is uncertain. The location of Rephidim, as well as the other toponyms, is dependent on the reconstruction of the exodus route. Since Rephidim is the last camping place before the Israelites arrive at Mount Sinai, Rephidim's location is heavily dependent on the site of Mount Sinai. Three general areas have been proposed for Sinai: a southern location near Jebel Musa, a location in the northern part of the Sinai Peninsula, and the Hejaz southeast of the Gulf of Aqaba. Scholars who identify Sinai with Jebel Musa have often proposed Wadi Feiran as the site of Rephidim.

Exodus 17:1-7 presents the story of the sojourn at Rephidim. The people complain to Moses because they find no water to drink. Moses presents their claim to God, who commands Moses to strike the rock at Horeb (an odd reference, since they have not yet arrived at Sinai). Moses does so, and the rock produces water. The name of Rephidim is then changed to MASSAH, which means "testing," and MERIBAH, which means "quarreling." The same story is repeated in Num 20:1-13, but the story is set at Kadesh. The events at Rephidim are reflected in Ps 95:8. The Amalekites attacked Israel at Rephidim, but were defeated (Exod 17:8-13).

KEVIN A. WILSON

REPROACH [חֶרְפָּה kherpah, כָּלַם kalam; ἀνεπίλημπτος anepilēmptos, ὀνειδίζω oneidizō, ὀνειδισμός oneidismos]. *Reproach* fundamentally connotes an experience of dishonor or humiliation (Ps 69:7 [Heb. 69:8]; Prov 19:26), particularly in a public context, be it at the individual (Gen 30:23; Tob 3:10) or national level (Ezek 21:28 [Heb. 21:33]; Tob 3:4). It is appropriate, therefore, that the removal of such reproach results in adulation for the one who reestablishes the lost honor (1 Sam 17:25-27). Also, despite the possibility of unjustifiable criticism (Job 19:3), reproach can be a legitimate form of rebuke for inappropriate behavior (Wis 2:12). An unwillingness to respond appropriately in the face of a clearly manifested divine proclamation of repentance is especially worthy of a vehement rebuke, like that expressed by Jesus in Matt 11:20-24. As with other paradoxical Beatitudes, Jesus turns a negative into a positive by making reproach a blessing when one is falsely criticized on account of the Christian faith (Matt 5:11-12; author's trans.; NRSV, "when people revile you"). Isaiah 51:7 serves as an OT precedent for the underlying principle that the righteous should not greatly concern themselves with the misguided reprimands of the unfaithful. Justifiable reproach, conversely, is an important matter and the NT utilizes the idea of being "above reproach" as the ideal standard for Christian living (1 Tim 3:2; 5:7). *See* SCOFFER; TAUNT.

JASON R. TATLOCK

REPTILE [רֶמֶשׂ remes; ἑρπετόν herpeton]. Solomon's vast wisdom extends to reptiles (1 Kgs 4:33). Peter's vision of animals in the sheet includes reptiles (Acts 10:12; 11:6). Fools make idols in the image of reptiles (Rom 1:23). James notes that while humans can tame animals, including reptiles, they cannot tame their own tongues (3:7). *See* CREEPING THINGS; SERPENT.

A. HEATH JONES III

RESAIAH ri-say′yuh [Ῥησαίας Rhēsaias]. Judean leader who returned to Jerusalem after the exile (1 Esd 5:8), the same as REELAIAH in Ezra 2:2.

RESCUE [יָשַׁע yasha', נָצַל natsal; ἐξαιρέω exaireō]. To rescue means to save or deliver. Biblical use of the verb *rescue* denotes a removal from danger to a place of safety and security. Both God and individuals rescue the people. God is remembered for rescuing the Israelites from the Egyptians and the people surrounding Israel (1 Sam 10:18; 12:11). Reuben plans to rescue Joseph but fails (Gen 37:22). David rescues the people of Keilah (1 Sam 23:5). The people pray to God for rescue from hardships and danger (Pss 22:8; 35:17; 71:2; 82:4; 144:7; Matt 6:13). *See* SALVATION.

JAMES E. WEST

RESERVOIR [מִקְוָה miqwah; ἀποδοχεῖον apodocheion, λάκκος lakkos]. Storage of water was critical for urban centers like Jerusalem (Sir 50:3). In preparation for the siege of 701 BCE, Hezekiah created a reservoir that was fed by the Siloam tunnel (2 Kgs 20:20; Isa 22:11). Such man-made reservoirs or "pools," some tied to canals, were also used to water groves of trees (Eccl 2:6) and fields (Exod 7:19). Sirach 39:17 refers to reservoirs in which God commanded the cosmic waters to stand at creation (compare Gen 1:9-10). *See* CISTERN; POOL; WATER WORKS.

VICTOR H. MATTHEWS

RESH raysh [ר r]. The twentieth letter of the Hebrew alphabet, derived from the Semitic word *ri'sh, "head." *See* ALPHABET; HEBREW LANGUAGE.

RESHEPH ree'shif [רֶשֶׁף reshef]. 1. A descendant of Ephraim, son of Rephah and father of Telah (1 Chr 7:25).

2. A West Semitic deity known to both harm and heal, also regarded as a god of battle and plague, which he spread by his bow and arrows. Resheph appears in bronze sculpture and glyptic scenes on seals and amulets from Egypt, Syria, and Palestine as a bellicose deity, often holding a weapon and shield. This imagery, as reflected in the "flashes [rishpe רִשְׁפֵּי] of fire" in Song 8:6, is symbolic of plague, an association that colors the understanding of reshef in modern English translations.

In the OT, reshef appears in poetic contexts as a supernatural agent of destruction in the service of Yahweh (although the NRSV does not translate reshef as a proper name in these instances). In this connection, Resheph is mentioned alongside hunger and pestilence (Deut 32:24; NRSV, "burning"; Hab 3:5; NRSV, "plague"), hail (Ps 78:48; NRSV, "thunderbolts"), and weapons of war (Ps 76:3 [Heb. 76:4]; NRSV, "flashing"). The "sons of Resheph" is a class of supernatural agents of mortal affliction (Job 5:7; see NRSV footnote).

Bibliography: William J. Fulco. *The Canaanite God Rešep* (1976).

JOEL S. BURNETT

RESIDENT ALIEN [גֵּר ger; πάροικος paroikos, προσήλυτος prosēlytos]. The resident alien, SOJOURNER, or STRANGER was a foreign-born permanent resident. Resident aliens could not depend on social and legal protection afforded to Israelite family members, but Pentateuchal laws explicitly afforded them basic social services, religious inclusion, and freedom from oppression, often because the Israelites themselves had been resident aliens in Egypt.

JOAN COOK

RESPECT [הָדַר hadhar, יָרֵא yare', מוֹרָא mora'; ἐντρέπω entrepō, φοβέω phobeō]. Respect is an attitude of deference and obedience owed to superiors who have assigned (parent, husband, slave owner) or acquired (scribes, teachers, bishops) power (e.g., Eph 5:33; Titus 2:9; Add Esth 1:22). Superiors may also gain HONOR by showing respect for their underlings (compare Luke 18:2-4). One respects elders, parents, and leaders (Lam 5:12; Rom 13:7; Tob 14:13; Sir 3:3-11; Bar 4:15), as well as God (Mal 1:6) and God's commandments (Prov 13:13). God (the absent landlord) expects the "tenants" to respect the son, but they do not (Matt 21:37; Mark 12:6; Luke 20:13). The scribes and Pharisees expect signs of respect as a form of self-importance (Mark 12:38-39; Luke 11:43; 20:46). Valuable things, whether actions (service or counsel) or items, are shown respect or honor (Luke 15:43; Acts 5:34; 1 Cor 12:23; 1 Tim 3:4). *See* AUTHORITY; FEAR.

CAROLE R. FONTAINE

REST [מָנוֹחַ manoakh, מְנוּחָה menukhah, נוֹחַ noakh, שַׁבָּת shabbath, שָׁבַת shavath, שַׁבָּתוֹן shabbathon, שָׁקַט shaqat; ἀνάπαυσις anapausis, ἀναπαύω anapauō, κατάπαυσις katapausis, καταπαύω katapauō]. Forms of the English term *rest* occur 274 times in the OT, seventy-three times in the Apocrypha, and fifty-two times in the NT. More than twenty Hebrew words are translated in this way in the OT, while the Greek terms anapausis and katapausis, along with their cognates, as well as the term loipos (λοιπός, "remainder"), lie behind the Apocrypha and NT renderings. Discounting those occurrences that convey the sense of rest as "remainder" (*see* REMNANT), the uses of the word *rest* may be grouped in several distinct thematic categories, most of which could be expressed by more than one of the many terms for rest in the original languages.

One meaning of *rest* in the Bible is "to rest on" (in some cases represented in Hebrew or Greek by an implicit or explicit form of the verb "to be" plus a preposition "upon"). The idea of one thing or person resting on another can connote a physical relationship, as in Exod 26:32, where in a description of the tabernacle's construction four pillars of acacia are to rest on four bases of silver (compare Judg 16:29). Yet the phrase can also communicate a spiritual dynamic, as when in Isaiah the spirit of the Lord is said to rest on the shoot from Jesse (Isa 11:2; compare Num 11:25-26; Isa 25:10; Ezek 44:30; Luke 2:25; 10:6; 1 Pet 4:14; Sir 5:6; 44:22-23;). Further, Paul notes that faith does not rest on (i.e., find its basis in) human wisdom (1 Cor 2:5), nor does the law rest on faith (Gal 3:12).

An emotional state of peace is another connotation of *rest.* The unsettled state of a person's emotions can be described as lacking rest (e.g., Job 3:26; Ps 22:2 [Heb. 22:3]; Eccl 2:23), and, conversely, those who are blessed are at rest (i.e., peace; e.g., Deut 33:12). In 2 Cor 2:13, Paul says his mind could not rest (i.e., was troubled) because he did not find Titus (compare 2 Cor 7:13).

Physical rest is the basic human need for physical renewal by ceasing work or travel. Verbal forms and nouns (i.e., a place of rest) are used to express physical rest. For example, Prov 24:33-34 rebukes the lazy person, noting that "a little folding of the hands to rest" can lead to poverty. In Mark 6:31, Jesus recognized that his disciples had become exhausted and were in need of physical renewal (compare Ruth 2:7; Matt 26:45; Mark 14:41; Jdt 1:16; 10:21). The concept of physical rest finds an extension as a word picture describing death as rest, as in Job 3:17, where the weary are said to be at rest, and Rev 6:11, where the dead in Christ are exhorted to "rest a little longer" (compare 2 Esd 7:75). *Rest* can also carry the connotation of stopping an activity. Genesis 2:3 records that on the seventh day of creation "God rested from all the work that he had done," meaning that God had completed the process (compare Ruth 3:18).

The idea of physical rest finds a specific connotation in the SABBATH day as a day to stop physical work and be refreshed. The rhythm of Sabbath observance is grounded both in creation (Exod 20:8-11) and in the exodus (Deut 5:12-15), and served as a sign of the covenant (Exod 31:16-17). The day, moreover, had the very practical purpose of refreshing people and animals relieved from a day of work (Exod 23:12). Special days of festival or solemn observance extended the concept of the Sabbath, since they were considered set apart for special purposes beyond the normal rhythm of weekly existence (e.g., Exod 16:23; 31:15; Lev 16:31; 23:3, 24), and the principle of Sabbath extended to periods of agricultural rest in which the land was not worked (Exod 23:10-11; Lev 25:4). Finally, the concept of rest also applies to the year of relief found in the Jubilee (Lev 25:8-55; *see* JUBILEE, YEAR OF).

Rest can be rest from war. Portions of the OT narrative literature use the statement "the land had rest" (**haʾarets shaqetah** [הָאָרֶץ שָׁקְטָה]; i.e., "was at peace") to speak of a time free from war, and the assertion plays a special role in the sin–judgment–deliverance cycle of Judges (Josh 11:23; 14:15; Judg 3:11, 30; 5:31; 8:28; 2 Chr 14:1, 5; 1 Macc 14:4). Also, David, Solomon, and other kings are said to have experienced rest from having to engage their enemies (e.g., 2 Sam 7:1, 11; 1 Kgs 5:4 [Heb. 5:18]; 8:56; 2 Chr 15:15).

As God led the Israelites from an existence of wandering to their settlement in Canaan, the inheritance of the land is referred to as rest (e.g., Deut 3:20; 12:9-11; Josh 1:13, 15; Ps 95:11; Isa 63:14). Some scholars understand the promise given to the patriarchs concerning the land to be presented as fulfilled in the OT history from Joshua to 2 Kings. Thus, Josh 1:13 reads, "Remember the word that Moses the servant of the LORD commanded you, saying, 'The LORD your God is providing you a place of rest, and will give you this land.'" The concept finds extension in Zion as God's resting place (Ps 132:14), and particularly the holy of holies in the Temple as the place where God was understood to dwell (2 Chr 6:41; contrast Isa 66:1; Acts 7:49).

Rest can refer to eschatological rest. In Isaiah especially, the rest idea points to a future hope for the nation (e.g., Isa 14:3; 32:18; 57:2; 63:14), and eschatological rest stands as an important theme in the second main movement of 2 Esdras (7:32, 36, 38, 75, 91; 8:52; 10:24), not surprising given the eschatological orientation of this section of the book. In Matt 11:28-29, Jesus' invitation—"Come to me, all you that are weary and are carrying heavy burdens, and I will give you rest"—probably alludes to Sir 51:23-27 and Exod 33:14. In saying, "Come to me . . . I will give you rest," Jesus thus stands in the place both of Wisdom and Yahweh as providing rest for people. Scholars have debated vigorously about the nature of God's promised rest in Heb 4:1-11. Some suggest it refers to a state of existence that can be experienced in this life. Others have pointed to a spatial interpretation of the rest as entrance into the heavenly holy of holies upon death or at the end of the age. Given Hebrews' orientation to the high-priestly ministry of Christ, perhaps preferred is an interpretation that understands Hebrews' rest as participation in the Sabbath of the DAY OF ATONEMENT provided for those who benefit from the great high priest's sacrifice (compare Lev 16:29-31; 23:26-32). Both in the decisive forgiveness of their sins (Heb 10:14-23) and through entrance into the very presence of God at death (Heb 12:23), Christ's followers experience the ultimate blessings of true rest both in the "now" of this life and "not yet" of the life to come.

Bibliography: Niels-Erik Andreasen. *The Old Testament Sabbath: A Tradition-Historical Investigation* (1972); Harold W. Attridge. "'Let Us Strive to Enter That Rest': The Logic of Hebrews 4:1-11." *HTR* 73 (1980) 279–88; Samuele Bacchiocchi. "Sabbatical Typologies of Messianic Redemption." *JSJ* 17 (1986) 153–76; D. A. Carson. *From Sabbath to Lord's Day: A Biblical, Historical, and Theological Investigation* (1982); Donald A. Hagner. *Matthew 1–13.* WBC 33A (1993); Jon Laansma. *'I Will Give You Rest': The Rest Motif in the New Testament with Special Reference to Mt 11 and Heb 3–4* (1997); Gnana Robinson. "The

Idea of Rest in the Old Testament and the Search for the Basic Character of Sabbath." *ZAW* 92 (1980) 32–42; Herold Weiss. "The Sabbath in the Synoptic Gospels." *JSNT* 38 (1990) 13–27.

GEORGE GUTHRIE

RESTITUTION. *See* CRIMES AND PUNISHMENT, OT AND NT.

RESTORATION [שׁוּב shuv; ἀποκαθίστημι apokathistēmi]. The basic sense of the English word *restoration* implies return to a state that had once existed but had been lost. The main word in the OT is shuv ("to turn, return"). In the Greek NT it is apokathistēmi ("to re-establish, restore, reinstate"). There are many examples of restoration in the Bible, but some passages have particularly theological or religious connotations. Three primary theological restorations can be found in the biblical texts: 1) restoring the captive Jews to their land after the exile; 2) restoring the kingdom to Israel; and 3) restoring cosmic conditions to their primal state before the sin of Adam and Eve. The last two are naturally related, but the first two fit better the OT context, while the last is better suited to the NT worldview.

The threat of deportation from the land because of the sins of the people was one that is frequently mentioned in the OT. Key passages are Lev 26 and Deut 28, both of which assign rewards for obedience but concentrate on the punishments that will follow disobedience. The culmination of the punishments in each case is being "scattered among the nations" (Lev 26:33) and the land left desolate. Many of the prophets prophesied conquest, destruction, and deportation because of sins against God (e.g., Jer 20:1-6; 24:1-10; 27:1-22; 29:1-32; Amos 5:26-27; 7:16-17). In the end, this took place first with regard to the Northern Kingdom about 722 BCE, which was taken captive by the Assyrians (2 Kgs 17), and then almost a century and a half later the Southern Kingdom fell to the Babylonians (2 Kgs 24–25). Those who survived this destruction were often referred to as a REMNANT.

The first restoration related to the physical captivity of Israel and Judah. There was no restoration of the Northern Kingdom—they became the "ten lost tribes" who did not return to the land but continued to live across the Euphrates. As for the Southern Kingdom, after a period of about half a century (described as "seventy years") the Persian conquest of Babylon opened up the way for some of those in captivity to return to Judah and rebuild the Temple, as described in Ezra 1–6, Haggai, and Zech 1–8. This return was much heralded in biblical literature. The pattern of sin–captivity–return is found in many passages (such and Lev 26 and Deut 28 cited above). The people had returned from exile and were restored to their land, as they saw it (compare Ezra 2:1; Neh 7:6).

Yet in spite of this physical restoration, Judah remained a subject nation under a succession of empires: Persian, Greek, and Roman. Only briefly, for less than a century, they were an independent nation under the rule of the HASMONEANS. Thus, a succession of literature looked forward not just to being in the land and able to worship at the Temple but toward a restoration, an idealized rule. Some prophetic passages picture a nation in which people lived an idyllic existence under a restored "house of David" (compare Jer 16:14-15; 23:5-8; 30:8-9; Amos 9:8-15). A key NT passage is found in Acts 1:6, which refers to the restoration of the kingdom to Israel. In some Jewish literature, the language of restoration is used in the context of some sort of a messiah (messianic expectations varied considerably among the Jews), such as the *Pss. Sol.* 17–18.

The ultimate goal was the restoration of the earth to its pristine state, perhaps regarded as the state before the sin of Adam (or the fall of the angels in such writings as *1 Enoch*). This seems to entail a number of ideas or images. For example, we have Mal 4:5-6 [Heb. 3:23-24] where Elijah comes before the "day of the LORD" to turn the hearts of the parents to the children and vice versa. The more graphic image, however, is to refer to "new heavens and a new earth" (Isa 65:17-25; Rev 21:1–22:5). In some cases, this takes place gradually rather than suddenly. For example, in *2 Baruch* the messiah "begins to be revealed" at a particular time, implying that he is only gradually revealed (*2 Bar.* 29–30). It is only when he is fully revealed that the resurrection of the dead and final judgment take place. Similarly, *4 Ezra* has a temporary messianic reign of 400 years, after which the messiah dies (*4 Ezra* 7:26-44). Only then does resurrection and judgment take place. A heavenly Jerusalem seems to be the ultimate goal (*4 Ezra* 10:25-27).

LESTER L. GRABBE

RESURRECTION OF CHRIST, BOOK OF, BY BARTHOLOMEW THE APOSTLE. *See* BARTHOLOMEW THE APOSTLE, BOOK OF THE RESURRECTION OF CHRIST BY.

RESURRECTION, EARLY JEWISH [ἀνάστασις anastasis, ἐξανάστασις exanastasis]. Resurrection was an innovation in Hebrew thought. The First Temple period survived quite nicely without it. Exactly what was believed in this long period of time is a puzzle, because the early texts in the Bible have so little to say about AFTERLIFE in general (*see* RESURRECTION, OT). This is in distinct contrast to the mythological texts of Israel's neighbors, which are replete with references to the realm of the dead. Apparently—and this is an educated guess—the redactors of the Bible were appalled by the afterlife beliefs that many Israelites were tempted to share with the Canaanites and did nothing to spread the beliefs further. Archaeological remains, which include grave goods, suggest that there were popular notions of afterlife among the Israelites that differed very little from Canaanite customs. Where the text gives us details, it appears as though the dominant understanding of the afterlife in First Temple times was that the dead went to SHEOL (she'ol שְׁאוֹל). This was a place of darkness where all the dead went, regardless of their moral or immoral life on earth (compare Deut 32:22; Amos 9:2). It was not a reward or punishment for anything. In the famous recall of Samuel from the dead, he complains that the medium has interrupted his slumber (1 Sam 28:15).

A. The Old Testament Concept of Resurrection
B. Resurrection in Philo and Josephus
C. Resurrection in Rabbinic Judaism

A. The Old Testament Concept of Resurrection

The imagery of resurrection (Isa 26:19; Ezek 37:1-14) appears in the Bible before the actuality of the promise. The first sure reference to resurrection occurs in Dan 12:2. This is a prophecy of the end of time, which states that some of those who sleep in the dust of the earth, will arise (qits קִיץ), some to shame and everlasting contempt (see Isa 66) and some to everlasting life. This prophecy, dated by scholars not to the Babylonian and Persian period in which the book of Daniel is set but to the Maccabean Wars of 168–165 BCE, is basic to all other Jewish, Christian, and Muslim views of resurrection. Before unpacking its significance, this article will look at the intervening passages of the Second Temple period that lead up to this prophecy.

Although both the book of Ecclesiastes (3:16-22; 9:3-10) and the book of Job (14:10-12) question any beatific afterlife, there are some passages in the later prophets that develop tropes and images that end in the literal prophecy of resurrection in Dan 12. A number of these passages discuss the issue pointedly enough that they must have been written in polemical distinction to ideas of the afterlife known to the writers, whether from Canaanite, Persian, or Greek cultures, or from developing parallel doctrines within the Israelite tradition. The most famous of these preparatory passages is Ezek 37:1-14, where the prophet envisions corpses being reassembled from their bones to become fully realized human beings on earth. This vivid description of the dead being reassembled in their flesh seems like it is the parade example of resurrection, but careful reading reveals that it is merely a metaphor for the prophecy, a vision that does not prophesy the future but signifies that the prophet's own preaching of the spirit will reanimate the people who are depressed and demoralized by exile. Rather than personal immortality, it is the more relevant consolation that, although punished, God has not left them and continues to guide Israel's existence.

Isaiah 24–27 is the most ambiguous case. Is it a literal reference or another prophetic vision whose meaning is symbolic? The crux is Isa 26:19: "Your dead shall live, their corpses shall rise. O dwellers in the dust, awake and sing for joy!" It certainly seems to prophesy resurrection, with a description of corpses rising from the dust. But when viewed in context, it too appears to be a discussion of Israel's present time, this time an exhortation to live in the spirit of the Lord. The imagery of sleeping and waking and dew on dry ground does not describe a literal resurrection but encourages the renewal of the kingdom. There is the further difficulty of dating these three chapters. Are they from Isaiah of Jerusalem, as chaps. 1–39 are, or do they come from later periods, from unnamed prophets conventionally grouped together and called Second Isaiah (Isa 40–55) or Third Isaiah (Isa 56–66), or perhaps from even later? If one presumes that this passage describes an actual resurrection, there is the further problem of dating the passage. In this scholar's opinion, the text is early and does not discuss literal resurrection.

Whether or not these earlier passages reflect an actual belief in resurrection, the imagery in the passages in Isaiah and Ezekiel is crucial for the development of the actual belief as expressed in Daniel. It is of course quite possible that the idea came from Zoroastrianism, where resurrection is standard (*see* ZOROASTER, ZOROASTRIANISM). But the imagery of resurrection in the OT is demonstration that resurrection has become acculturated into a native Jewish doctrine as well. In Zoroastrianism, resurrection is the common lot, but it is not so in the earliest Israelite thought. The resurrection promised in Daniel is not for all, only for some. Some of those resurrected will be specially punished. These must be the oppressors of the Jews in the Maccabean Revolt, even though the description of the punishment of oppressors in 2 Macc 7 is that they will get no resurrection, which suggests that the notion of resurrection was generalized to all the righteous fairly quickly. But only some of those who sleep in the dust were prophesied to receive resurrection in 2 Maccabees; the oppressors die with no hope of resurrection. In each case, besides vengeance on the oppressors, one might even detect some social criticism of the upper-class SADDUCEES, who did not believe in resurrection, in the vision of the apocalypticists. In general, many different ways of envisioning the resurrection can be seen in the early material. Second Maccabees 7 relates a very literal, physical resurrection in which the bodies of the martyrs are returned to earth to live out their lives, which were cut short. Daniel suggests an astral reward for some. No doubt this fulfills God's promise in Deut 1:1–3:22; Prov 7, and elsewhere that those who follow the law will have long life.

Other interpretations of Dan 12 would include *1 En.* 102, where the souls of the righteous are resurrected from Sheol where they have been dwelling. In *2 Bar.* 49–51, all the dead are raised in their previous bodies for judgment, then transformed into their heavenly form or judged to perdition. In *4 Ezra* 7:76–99, the intermediate state is further detailed. All of these are interpretations and reinterpretations of the Dan

12 passage. Every interpretation from literal resurrection to resurrection of the soul can be read out of that passage.

But there is a further aspect of the prophecy in Daniel. Among those receiving resurrection in Daniel were "those who are wise" (NRSV) or more literally "those who make others wise." They will shine "like the brightness of the sky, and those who lead many to righteousness, like the stars forever and ever" (Dan 12:2-3). This appears to signify some kind of "angelic" status for those who lead many to righteousness. This is a tradition of astral immortality, even astral exaltation, in that the recipients are transformed into an angelic or immortal astral form. Like resurrection, all of this is saved for the very end of time. Some other social locations in which resurrection and ascension are discussed include conversion, as in *Joseph and Aseneth* (e.g., *Jos. Asen.* 15:3-4), where immortality and incorruptibility are part of the rewards of conversion to Judaism.

B. Resurrection in Philo and Josephus

Philo and Josephus represent special cases in 1st-cent. Judaism (*see* JOSEPHUS, FLAVIUS; PHILO OF ALEXANDRIA). They both speak of immortality of the soul, but they are writing for Greco-Roman audiences who understand the significance of these terms in Platonic philosophy (*see* PLATO, PLATONISM). Philo promulgates Platonism, though he translates biblical notions allegorically into Platonic philosophy with great facility. Josephus may only be adopting the language of the Greco-Roman world to explain Jewish culture, but it is more likely that people lucky enough to be educated in both cultures saw the Greek notion of IMMORTALITY as the functional equivalent of the native Hebrew notion of resurrection. In any event, both Philo and Josephus describe persons, such as the ESSENES (if, as seems likely, they are the Dead Sea Scroll sectarians), who are known to believe in resurrection. It thus appears that their use of the concept of the immortality of the soul, a Platonic doctrine, is a hermeneutical attempt to explain resurrection to Greco-Roman intellectuals familiar with the Platonic form of immortality. Josephus describes earthly bodies perishing while souls become divine (*J.W.* 3.362–72). Josephus depicts the PHARISEES as believing that the soul goes from one body to another (*J.W.* 2.163), which is consonant with Platonism but may well describe a resurrection doctrine that also includes an intermediate state as a soulless body in heaven. This seems to be roughly consonant with the rabbinic notion in later texts. In any event, the rabbis did not interpret resurrection as strictly as Christians, because they did not have to explain the resurrection of Jesus as the prime example of what was going to happen to the faithful dead.

Philo, a prominent Jewish philosopher, offers an explicit argument for the immortality of the soul. The body is matter, which deteriorates, but the soul is by nature immortal (*Creation* 135; *Spec. Laws* 1:345). At the moment of death, the virtuous soul is released to beatific closeness with God (*Contempl. Life* 13; *Creation* 77; *Giants* 14). God, however, may choose to destroy the souls of the sinners (*Alleg. Interp.* 1.107; *Prelim. Studies* 57; *Rewards* 60). Philo also uses some of the language of astral immortality in describing the soul as the stuff of the stars (*Sacrifices* 5; *Giants* 61) and in speaking of Moses and other Hebrew prophets as attaining to God's divinity. In a most striking interpretation of creation, Philo suggests that the creation in Gen 1 is the soul or form of humanity, while that of Gen 2 is the material creation of Adam and Eve, thus illustrating the action of form or ideas upon matter in the Platonic system (*Alleg. Interp.* 1.92).

No one is sure that the Essenes produced the DEAD SEA SCROLLS. Yet there are hints of resurrection in Josephus' and Philo's description of the Essenes, and we now have good texts showing that the Dead Sea Scroll sectarians believed in resurrection. According to Josephus, the Essenes immortalize the soul (*Ant.* 18.18). He also says that the Essenes believed the soul to be imprisoned in the body but, once released, it is borne aloft (*J.W.* 2.155). Good souls receive a reward in an abode beyond the ocean, an idea that seems to rely on the Greek notion of the Isles of the Blessed. Definitive proof that the Dead Sea Scroll sectarians believed in resurrection can now be found in 4Q521 2 II, 11–12: "And the Lord will perform marvelous acts such as have not existed, just as he sa[id], [for] he will heal the badly wounded and will make the dead live, he will proclaim good news to the poor" (*DSSSE*). In this passage, Ps 146 is reinterpreted in order to bring in a reference to resurrection, just as the rabbis did (below). Change of form of the virtuous resurrected (angelomorphism) can be found in at least one very important place, 1Q28b IV, 24–28, where the priestly leader seems to be identified with the angel of the presence. Hodayot[a] (4Q427) 7 I + 9 6–12 and 4Q431 1 1–9 preserve a thanksgiving psalm with a passage that shows that the reciter of the hymn can be raised from normal human existence to the heavenly heights, seemingly to live as an angel, which is directly parallel to the eschatological prophecy in Dan 12. Since this hymn has a liturgical dimension, it looks as though the rewards of the end time could be anticipated in the Sabbath liturgy of the group, just as it is in the rabbinic community.

C. Resurrection in Rabbinic Judaism

In Judaism God has not yet begun this task of resurrection, which awaits the last days. The rabbis were less interested than Christians in explaining exactly how God was planning to accomplish his promise to the righteous. The rabbis are clear that it happens on the DAY OF JUDGMENT, which has not yet occurred but which shall occur on a perfected earth. The centrality of resurrection in rabbinic thought can be seen in the main rabbinic discussion of the conception in *b. Sanh.*

10:1. The rabbis take the Dan 12 passage quite literally, though they hardly mention it explicitly in their texts. They divide humanity at the end of days into three groups: those who are resurrected for reward, those who are resurrected for punishment, and those in between, about whom the prophecy in Dan 12 says nothing. *Roshosh HaShanah* 16b–17a discusses the fates of these middling people, using terminology very similar to Zoroastrian thought on the subject. The Hillelites and Shammaites disagree about the ultimate fate of these people. The Shammaites hold that they will be sent to GEHENNA but will be freed if they repent by crying out to the Lord. The Hillelites, to the contrary, argue that God immediately grants them eternal life. In general, the rabbis thought that a good God would not withhold this great reward without justification. Other places in rabbinic literature also make clear that the judgment of sin is not purely an arithmetic process of discovering whether a person was predominantly good or bad. With characteristic hyperbole, they stress that sincere repentance and contrition can outweigh even a whole life of sinning. But since one never knows one's date of death, one should lead each day as though it presaged the end. Consequently, rabbinic liturgy contains a fervent prayer blessing God for the gift of resurrection, contained in the *Amidah*, the famous prayer of eighteen paragraphs, which is said at every service. *See* RABBINIC INTERPRETATION; RESURRECTION, NT.

ALAN F. SEGAL

RESURRECTION, NT [ἀνάστασις anastasis, ἐξανάστασις exanastasis]. The doctrine of resurrection is first securely manifested in biblical writing in Dan 12, which can be dated a bit more than a century and a half before Jesus was born (approximately 168 BCE is a well-established date for the composition of the visions at the end of Daniel). Resurrection may be generally defined as the doctrine that after death the body will be reconstituted and revivified by God as a reward for the righteous and/or faithful. But resurrection is central to Christianity in a way that it is not to any of the other 1st cent. sects of Judaism. Because the resurrection of Christ was experienced as an event for the early Jesus movement, Christianity needed to define what resurrection was in a way that was not necessary to other Jews in the 1st cent. It is one thing to know that God has promised resurrection to the righteous faithful in Daniel, presumably in his own way and at the appropriate time, and another to express what exactly happened to Jesus on the first Easter and how those who heard his message might gain the same reward.

A. Paul
B. Gospels and Acts of the Apostles
C. Revelation
D. Other Early Christians
   1. Barnabas
   2. Docetism and Gnosticism
   3. The letters of Clement
   4. Ignatius
   5. Tertullian
   6. Origen
   7. Athenagoras
   8. Augustine
Bibliography

A. Paul

Paul is the first Christian writer to express what resurrection was, apparently from descriptions of the risen Christ, which came to him in visionary experience ("a revelation of Jesus Christ," Gal 1:11-12). Paul argues that though he never knew the man Jesus, he can claim to be an apostle because Christ appeared to him (1 Cor 15:3-9; compare 9:1). From his experience of the risen Christ, Paul writes a short treatise on the resurrection (1 Cor 15:12-58). Paul claims that our flesh will be transformed into another kind of body (1 Cor 15:42-44). He calls the physical, fleshly body, in which we live our earthly lives, a sōma psychikon (σῶμα ψυχικόν)—that is, a psychic body, or a natural body, that is left behind (*see* BODY; FLESH IN THE NT). The resurrected body is an immortal and incorruptible body (sōma pneumatikon σῶμα πνευματικόν), or SPIRITUAL BODY.

The sōma pneumatikon (spiritual body) is a complete contradiction in any Platonic or Aristotelian system (*see* PLATO, PLATONISM). Paul, in fact, seems to be contrasting the Platonic view of humanity (the unredeemed body composed of soul and flesh) with a more natively Jewish view of the redeemed body, one that has been infused or transformed by the Spirit. For Paul, both psychic, fleshly life and pneumatic, spiritual life are bodily. But the bodies—heavenly and earthly—are quite different. As Paul shows, the pneumatic body is what Christ gained in his resurrection and has affinities not with the stuff of the earth but with the heavenly, immortal bodies of the sun, the stars, and constellations (1 Cor 15:40-42), likely an interpretation of the prophecy in Dan 12 that "those who are wise shall shine like the brightness of the sky…like the stars forever" under the influence of a Hellenistic cosmology.

Paul calls this process a "transformation" in several related ways (Rom 12:2; 1 Cor 15:51-52; 2 Cor 3:18; Phil 3:21). Paul understands this process to have begun with the resurrection of Christ and to continue until the final consummation of history. Believers are transformed into the "image (eikōn εἰκών) of his son" (Rom 8:29; compare Phil 3:21; 1 Cor 15:49). His terminology for transformation is often based on the Grk. word morphē (μορφή), "form." His verbs imply that believers will be changed, even "morphed" into "the image of his son" or "his Christ," using terms like symmorphizomai (συμμορφίζομαι, "being transformed together with"). In Phil 3:10, Paul uses the term metaschēmatizō (μετασχηματίζω, "change the structure of") to describe how our lowly body will become his glorious body. Thus, faith in Christ begins a process of transformation that will end in the resurrection of believers, and this explains Paul's terminology of being "in Christ."

In 1 Cor 15:51-57, Paul discloses the aim and purpose of this transformation. We shall not all fall asleep (i.e., die). At the last trumpet, presumably the trumpet of Gabriel or Michael, the archangel of God, the dead will all be raised immortal and changed. The perishable body will put on imperishability, just as the baptisand puts on new clothing after the ceremony. In 1 Thess 4:16 Paul gives an alternative description of the consummation that has sometimes been called "the rapture" even though the term *rapture* is not biblical. The verb harpazō (ἁρπάζω, "seized" or "caught up") from 4:16 is the basis of this terminology. In 1 Thess 4:16 Paul describes the final consummation, not the beginning of a tribulation.

B. Gospels and Acts of the Apostles

The Gospels' interpretation of resurrection does not in every way correspond to Paul's description. One may wonder whether they do not explicitly shade Paul's description to avoid some religious difficulties in Paul's conception. Mark, the earliest Gospel, contains no description of Jesus' resurrection, instead presenting us with an empty tomb, which signifies the mystery of Easter (Mark 16:1-8). The later Gospels expand the story of the empty tomb but do not describe the actual resurrection. It is worth noting that Paul has nothing to say about the empty tomb at all, though he certainly mentions that Jesus was buried and rose and describes it as a transformation, though he was not an eyewitness to it. Some of the differences can be explained by noting that Paul's knowledge of Christ came from Paul's own personal spiritual visions of him, so his description of Christ's current status stressed the spiritual side of the resurrection. The Gospels, on the other hand, stress Jesus' humanity and messiahship. So he is fully human and appears in human form, arguably even in fleshly form, after his resurrection, as he eats, walks, talks, and in these ways is indistinguishable from ordinary humans (Matt 28:9-10, 17-20; Luke 24:13-48; John 20:14-29; 21:1-24).

Matthew, Luke, and John all add important post-resurrection appearances of Jesus. But they concentrate on the ordinariness of Jesus' bodily presence. In Matthew, the women see Jesus himself as they leave the tomb (28:9-10). He personally commissions his followers to make disciples of all nations and to baptize in the name of the Trinity, clearly a later addition from the liturgical life of the community (28:19-20). Even more important, the women actually take hold of his feet, showing that he is a physical presence, having the same body that was lying in the tomb, now resurrected (28:9). This is a statement, like being shown the exact place where the body had lain (28:6), that emphasizes the physicality of the resurrection. All these details are easily understandable as elaborations to answer potential antagonistic interpretations of the Markan version. The last statement is one of comfort—he will be them always, to the end of time—another ancient liturgical fragment (Matt 28:18-20). The passage also has important links to the apocalyptic vision in Dan 7:14: "His dominion is an everlasting dominion that shall not pass away, and his kingship is one that shall never be destroyed." It is this passage, rightfully understood as a prophecy, that Jesus' death and resurrection is taken to fulfill. Jesus, then, sits enthroned in heaven next to God, as the "son of man" (manlike figure) who will bring judgment to the evil dominions on earth.

Even more important is the attention given to the physical resurrection of Jesus in the Gospel of John. Even in the "spiritual Gospel," Jesus has been resurrected bodily and physically (John 20:14-29). The two exceptions to the physicality of the resurrection come at the beginning of the passage. When Mary is told not to embrace the risen Jesus, as he has not yet returned to the Father (20:17-18), one hardly knows what this implies about the body of the risen Christ. And then (20:24-26) Jesus appears to the disciples in a locked room. While it seems clear that the story is constructed for the purposes of showing the miraculous power of the appearance, it does not necessarily dispute the physicality of the resurrection body. On the contrary, what comes next shows that physicality is just what is implied. But the miracle of Jesus' materialization in the locked room shows precisely that the church wanted to emphasize the miraculous character of the appearance and, at the same time, emphasize that it is not merely a ghost or spirit. Jesus had to rise in his body, not merely as a spirit.

What of Luke's account? The story of the appearance on the road to Emmaus (Luke 24:13-35) provides a precedent for a number of issues, including the Lord's Supper (24:30). From this clue, it seems obvious that the story is also intended to demonstrate that the empty tomb tradition, at first thought to be an idle story worthy only of women within the community (24:11), describes exactly what happened. And no less an authority than Jesus himself demonstrates it (24:25-26). Luke's inclusion of an affirmation of the empty tomb suggests quite strongly that the tradition of the empty tomb did not take hold within the early church right away. In Luke we have the final defense of the reality of the empty tomb that suggests that Jesus' resurrection must be more than the appearance of a spirit or a ghost. Jesus' resurrection is a physical resurrection.

In fact, Luke's presentation of the resurrected Jesus demonstrates his corporeality without allowing his physicality to determine unambiguously the form of his existence. On one side of the ledger we find evidence that Jesus' post-resurrection existence was out of the ordinary. He disappears and appears suddenly (24:31,

36), in the same way that an angel appears to Cornelius (Acts 10:30) and that is reminiscent of angels in Israel's Scriptures (e.g., Gen 18:2; Dan 8:15; 12:5). His appearance is elusive, both to the two disciples on the Emmaus road (24:15-16) and to his followers gathered in Jerusalem (24:36-37); the latter regard him as a "spirit," a "ghostly apparition," the disembodied residue of a dead person. This analysis of things is flatly contradicted by Jesus, however, who goes to great lengths to establish his physicality. Jesus grounds the continuity of his identity ("It is really me!"), first, in his physicality—in the constitution of flesh and the density of bones (24:39), and then by eating broiled fish in the presence of his disciples (24:41-43; compare Tob 12:15, 19). In Luke's report of Jesus' post-resurrection existence, we find no witness to resurrection as escape from bodily existence (as one would expect if a Platonic dualism were presumed here); his, rather, is a transformed materiality, a bodily resurrection.

Luke thus navigates between two popular views for imaging the afterlife. First, he shows that Jesus' disciples did not mistake him for a cadaver brought back to life, a reanimated corpse. Luke distinguishes Jesus' resurrected body from the resuscitated bodies of the widow's son in Nain (7:11-17), Jairus' daughter (8:40-42, 49-56), Tabitha (Acts 9:36-43), and Eutychus (Acts 20:7-12). Second, he certifies that neither is Jesus an "immortal soul" free from bodily existence. Jesus is present to his disciples, beyond the grave, as a fully embodied person.

In Luke, the ASCENSION is a separate process, not included within the resurrection itself but placed temporally at the end of the post-resurrection appearances. The story is narrated twice by Luke—once at the end of the Gospel (24:51) and again at the beginning of the Acts of the Apostles (1:9-11), also written by Luke. What makes this interesting is that Luke is aware of the primitive KERYGMA, which he repeats in two key places: "God exalted him at his right hand as Leader and Savior that he might give repentance to Israel and forgiveness of sins. Being therefore exalted at the right hand of God, and having received from the Father the promise of the Holy Spirit, he has poured out this that you both see and hear" (Acts 5:31; 2:33-34; also Luke 20:42-43). The proof of this is Ps 110:1. Indeed, Ps 110, a psalm of David, mentions that a second "Lord" is enthroned in heaven, which can be reinterpreted by means of Dan 7:13.

Throughout the Gospels, several other aspects of resurrection become clear. The term *resurrection*, for example, appears frequently in Paul but infrequently in the Gospels. There, it is explicitly part of Jesus' polemic with the PHARISEES. Against the SADDUCEES (who are characterized as not believing in resurrection, neither as a spirit nor as an angel [Acts 23:8]), the Pharisees do believe in resurrection, as do the Essenes (if the Dead Sea Scrolls represent their beliefs). And we have seen that Paul himself believes that resurrection is going to entail transformation into a new kind of body. Apostolic, proto-orthodox Christianity would agree that resurrection could not be merely spiritual, as proto-gnostic groups believed. So a great deal depends on the outcome of this controversy. According to the Gospels, the Sadducees are anxious to trip Jesus up in his description of the event (Matt 22:23-33; Mark 12:18-27; Luke 20:27-40). Luke also uses resurrection as the main difference of opinion in the trial of Paul in Acts 23. Indeed, it is one of several places in which the Paul of Acts says that resurrection is the center of his Christian faith.

Conflicts with Pharisees and Sadducees are an opportunity for the evangelists to specify what they mean by resurrection. Matthew relates this example of a question posed by the Sadducees: If a woman is married to seven brothers in order, with whom would she live in the resurrection? The Matthean Jesus replies that marriage and divorce are not issues in the resurrection; the faithful are like angels in the resurrection. They do not marry, perhaps meaning they have no sex or gender. The resurrected faithful exist as the angels do, as immortal beings in the heavens (Matt 22:23-30). Jesus further argues that the Scriptures (e.g., Exod 3:15) say, "I am the God of Abraham, the God of Isaac, and the God of Jacob." God is God of the living, not of the dead (Matt 22:32). That means logically that Abraham, Isaac, and Jacob are still alive. Since we know that they died, we must conclude that they were resurrected. The point of the passage, for the evangelists, is that one can demonstrate the truth of resurrection apart from the events of Jesus' life.

The significance of the resurrection in the Gospel of Luke is, if anything, heightened in Luke's second volume, the Acts of the Apostles, where it becomes the focus of controversy in varied settings—whether, e.g., in Jerusalem at the Temple (4:1-2) or the Sanhedrin (23:6-10), or in Athens in the marketplace (17:16-18) or the Areopagus (17:19-34). The resurrection of Jesus is the focus of the message of salvation in Luke and Acts. Theologically, it is part of God's purpose for Israel and the world. Christologically, it confirms Jesus' status as the agent of God's covenant blessings of salvation (e.g., 2:22-36). Jesus, not only as Israel's Messiah, but as universal Lord, grants repentance and forgiveness of sins to Israel and the nations in view of the day of judgment when he will act as the appointed judge (e.g., 5:31; 11:18; 17:30-31). And eschatologically, the resurrection of Jesus anticipates and certifies the culmination of God's salvation of his people and the full realization of God's rule among humankind.

C. Revelation

Revelation, written by a prophet named John imprisoned on Patmos (Rev 1:9-11), comes at least a generation after the Gospels and records the vicissitudes of Christians being martyred in Asia (that is, Anatolia, the western part of Turkey). It begins with a message of hope and patient endurance, long a Jewish martyrological theme, to each of seven churches in danger (*see* MARTYR). It explicitly mentions that the seven stars are the angels of the seven churches, based on the long tradition that stars and angels are comparable (1:20). The message he brings is that resurrection is the reward for suffering: "Do not be afraid; I am the first and the last, and the living one. I was dead, and see, I am alive forever and ever; and I have the keys of Death and of Hades. Now write what you have seen, what is, and what is to take place after this" (1:17-19).

The understanding of the transformation to a resurrection body depends on Dan 12, as we have seen. But it also depends on the enthronement of Jesus as the "son of man" in Dan 7:13. The early Christians identified the "SON OF MAN," the human or angelic representation of God, with the risen Christ. Christians took the second "Lord" of Ps 110:1 to refer to Jesus. Thereafter, the risen Christ was understood as an aspect of the divinity. For the Gospel of John, the Christ also became logos (**logos** λόγος), God's intermediary form and light (John 1:1-5), which was Philo's term for God's principal hypostasis as well (e.g., *Spec. Laws* 1.45–50). Christ as "son" is said to be above the angels, just as Moses is enthroned and worshiped by the stars in Ezekiel the Tragedian's work (Ezek. Trag. 68–69). This is made explicit in Heb 1:8, where the "son" is identified with the Elohim in Ps 45:7. Of course, there were other conceptions of Jesus—as prophet or son, for example—but they were all summed up in the earliest Christian designation of Jesus as LORD, the name of God (*see* JESUS, METAPHORS FOR). And it was this identification of Christ as the human figure of God enthroned in heaven, the same vision that Ezekiel the Tragedian saw, which was vouchsafed to Paul and to John of Patmos.

D. Other Early Christians

1. Barnabas

If we look at the *Letter of Barnabas*, an early apostolic writing probably dating from the end of the 1st cent. or beginning of the 2nd cent., we see that Barnabas prominently displays the promises of Dan 12, which he understood as resurrection of the flesh, in his picture of the coming end (e.g., 4:1-14). The evidence from Barnabas suggests that the missionaries have to distinguish their message from that of the Jews, who were better known though not as emphatic proselytizers. Not many of the Jews living in Diaspora were enthusiastic believers in resurrection. That is more characteristic of revolutionaries and millenarians living in the land of Israel and also of the Pharisees, who had not yet made major inroads in Diaspora Judaism, and who believed in resurrection but with so much flexibility that it could have easily accommodated IMMORTALITY of the soul as well. Most Jews who spoke and thought in Greek were involved in a significant hermeneutical process, a translation process that allowed them to understand AFTERLIFE as continuous with immortality of the soul, thus combining native Jewish ideas with Greek philosophical ones (*see* GREEK RELIGION AND PHILOSOPHY; HELLENISM). The reason for the continuous growth in interest in resurrection, despite the wider view of immortality of the soul, is due principally to the centrality of the notion of resurrection in the preaching of the Christian faith. Tertullian said that the resurrection of the dead is the hallmark of Christian faith (*Res.* 1). Christians acknowledge that their faith depends upon the resurrection event in Jesus' life.

For their part, the church fathers take aim at immortality of the soul as the doctrine to defeat. They learn their task from the Stoics, Epicureans, and Cynics. Although the earliest fathers do not concentrate on the intellectual cogency of the resurrection, they do preach it steadfastly, fixing on immortality of the soul as a hostile doctrine because immortality of the soul vitiated the special salvation the cross brought to the faithful alone. If immortality were a natural property of the soul, no one would need a savior. If immortality were a natural property of the soul, one would only need an operational manual for the soul as an ethical guide, the right moral instructions to train the body to care properly for the soul.

2. Docetism and Gnosticism

Apostolic Christianity shows a distinct tendency towards an explicit description of bodily resurrection. The history of the philosophical speculation on resurrection begins with an intellectual challenge: the struggle against docetic Christology. DOCETISM, from the Greek word **dokeō** (δοκέω, "to appear to be"—in the sense of "to seem to be," with the connotation of [mistakenly] seeming to be human), promulgated the notion that Jesus, being divine, only seemed to suffer and die. In reality Christ's divine nature was never compromised. This is an obvious way out of a deep ambiguity about Jesus' nature. Docetism is an obvious way to preserve Jesus' divinity at the moments when he seems most tragically human and lacking in divinity.

The claim that Jesus only appeared to be human is characteristic of the gnostic writers (*see* GNOSTICISM). The gnostics and others suggested that Jesus only seemed to die, although the body was putrid and infected. Therefore, Jesus subsequently only seemed to be resurrected. His resurrection was merely the revelation of his true divinity, the re-manifestation of his true divinity.

Interest in Gnosticism has increased considerably since the discovery in 1947 of the Nag Hammadi collection of thirteen mostly Coptic codices, evidently from a monastic library dating back to the first centuries of the Christian era in Egypt. Some gnostic texts, especially those having to do with Seth, seem to delight in revaluing the stories of the Bible, most particularly the primeval history, into mythological stories in which the God of the OT figures as a demon, while the gnostics themselves were those whom the OT treats as enemies, like the Cainites. These Sethian gnostic documents focus on how the gnostics retain their secret truths in order to reascend to the savior. Talk of resurrection is only metaphoric.

3. The letters of Clement

Clement of Rome served as bishop at the end of the 1st cent., according to church tradition. *First Clement,* a letter from Rome to Corinth and weakly attributed to Clement, is usually listed with the writings of the apostolic fathers. It tries to settle the issue of the nature of resurrection by means of an ambiguous phrase, "immortal knowledge": Jesus has willed that Christians would have immortal knowledge through him (*1 Clem.* 36:1-2). This terminology is a clever attempt to bridge the growing gap between religious experience and ecclesiastical authority. At the same time, *1 Clement* emphasizes the resurrection of believers. But it begins by describing the resurrection of Christ metaphorically as a tree. The tree sheds, which refers both to the death of Christ and the death of believers. From there the cycle of rebirth begins. Clement thus analogizes the resurrection with the phoenix, a mythological bird supposed to die in a self-conflagration and rise again from its own ashes, the point being that resurrection is part of the natural order (*1 Clem.* 24–26).

Second Clement states that we must be raised in the flesh, because Jesus became flesh and called us while we were in the flesh, and so we must receive reward in the flesh (*2 Clem.* 9).

4. Ignatius

Ignatius demonstrates in his writing that physical resurrection, martyrdom, angelic status, and heavenly exaltation continue to be seen together in early Christianity. Ignatius desires martyrdom so that he can become a true disciple of Christ (Ign. *Rom.* 4).

Although Ignatius follows the martyr tradition begun for Christian piety by the narrative of Stephen's martyrdom (Acts 7), he does not yet use the term *martyr* (martys [μάρτυς] "witness"), which had not yet become the standard title for voluntary death as an act of faith. The specifically Christian interpretation of the tradition—using the term "witness" as a metaphor of a legal trial—evolves slowly out of Christian experience. Even without the specific vocabulary of Christian martyrdom, Ignatius' description is deeply dependent on bodily resurrection. It is no surprise that when he outlines his creed to the Smyrneans, he outlines a very physical resurrection. After having outlined his creed, which emphasizes the physical pain of the crucifixion, Ignatius talks about the coming resurrection as fully physical bodies (Ign. *Smyrn.* 1–3). To the Ephesians, he even writes that he hopes to be resurrected in his bonds so that he can be in the same lot with the Ephesians (Ign. *Eph.* 11:2), who are suffering persecution. There is no doubt that the physicality of the resurrection continues to cohere with issues of martyrdom.

5. Tertullian

By the end of the 2nd cent., the resurrection of the body had become a major topic of controversy among Christians, as well as for the pagan critics of Christianity. The body was what guaranteed to the Christians that they personally would be resurrected in the end time. The opposition claimed that resurrection was not something to be desired because it was impure and not logically the continuation of the thinking mind. In some way, then, the battle was not just about resurrection but about what kind of persons we essentially are.

Although Justin and Irenaeus founded the patristic apologetic tradition, it was Tertullian who wrote a treatise directly discussing the resurrection of the flesh, developing the new Latin vocabulary to a technical one. Like Tatian, Tertullian writes out of the Stoic philosophical tradition. Like Tatian, Tertullian's conception of the resurrection is a recreation of body and soul with a reassembling of the physical parts, instead of a spiritual process of spiritual, dynamic development, as in Paul. Following the Stoics, Tertullian thinks that even the soul has a material reality, being made up of very fine matter. In this, he is following the Greek tradition, which sometimes called even spiritual substances exquisitely fine bodies.

Tertullian wrote *The Resurrection of the Flesh* at the beginning of the 3rd cent. His opponents were gnostics and probably Valentinians. He criticizes his opponents' notion that one receives gnosis at baptism and hence can consider oneself resurrected and saved as well. Those who deny that the flesh is raised are also refusing to recognize that Christ lived in the flesh and that he was raised in the flesh (*Res.* 2). Following Dan 7:13, many fathers suggest that Christ has been taken bodily into heaven. Tertullian is cognizant of the conflict that this raises in Scripture. Paul's statement that "flesh and blood cannot inherit the kingdom of God" means for Tertullian not only that the spirit is necessary for humans to enter the kingdom (1 Cor 15:50) but also that death will end because corruption cannot enter heaven (1 Cor 15:51).

Tertullian compensates by describing the process of the self's perception through faith. He even envisions a flesh infused with spirit that is free of every malady, thus re-importing Paul's pneumatology. Tertullian is evidently aware of rabbinic midrash on this point and uses it effectively to make his point. He thus argues that when the children of Israel wandered for forty years in the desert, neither their shoes nor their clothes wore out, neither their hair nor their fingernails grew (*Res.* 58). Through this midrash, Tertullian demonstrates that if God could sustain the children of Israel in the desert miraculously, he can certainly preserve the body of the faithful for its future resurrection. So the saved rise with every infirmity, malady, and bodily handicap removed (*Res.* 57). The resurrection body will contain all the same organs that we have but they may not all be used (*Res.* 59–62). We will have no need for organs of digestion or sex. For flesh and spirit are as a bridegroom and a bride.

At the end of his life when Tertullian becomes a Montanist (an apocalyptic movement that expected the end of the world immediately; *see* MONTANUS, MONTANISM), he can combine his notions of fleshly resurrection with apocalypticism. Tertullian decides that the resurrection body will be like the angels (*Res.* 62). The importance of this statement is not in the identity between the two but in the immortalizing of the perfected believer. The emphasis on the fleshly nature of the resurrection is a mark of the importance of this early battle between gnosticism and orthodoxy over the nature of the body. We have seen that this is just as certainly an argument over human identity, gender, and transcendent significance. Behind it, the nature of the believer's responsibility toward martyrdom was being expressed as well.

6. Origen

Origen claims that he is merely restating the Pauline concept of spiritual bodies. But he has traveled, in reality, a great distance from the apocalyptic mysticism of Paul. Origen's notion of a "spiritual body" has taken its lead from Paul but, like Valentinianism, the concept is the immortal soul of Platonism in disguise (*Fr. Ps.* 1.5). He sees souls as the stuff of the stars and the perfected souls as the heavenly bodies. Origen allows everything but the natural immortality of the soul. For him, it is the saving work of God that immortalizes the soul, just as it was for Philo (*Princ.* 2.10.8).

Evidently one problem with his perception is that it threatened the personal identity of the believer. Origen reassures the believer that the visible form (eidos εἶδος) of the body will not be lost, but will be gloriously changed (*Fr. Ps.* 1.5). For this Origen returns yet again to the Pauline term "spiritual body" (sōma pneumatikon), but he loads it this time with different ammunition. This time, he fills the term with the implications of the spermatic logos of Stoicism (*see* STOICS, STOICISM), an emanation of the primeval fire that animated all things in the universe. Thus, Origen forges yet one more link between Christianity and Greek philosophy. His notion of personal identity is the Platonic notion of the soul.

Having disputed the natural immortality of the soul, Origen believes that God, being merciful, would not condemn any soul to permanent perdition. The sinners and even the demons will be eventually restored to their permanent position (*Princ.* 2.10.8). In so doing, Origen steals UNIVERSALISM from the pagan philosophers and claims it for Christianity, though it is hard to understand how it can be reconciled with many apocalyptic passages in Christian Scriptures. But for Origen, as for the rabbis, God could not for eternity refuse a soul SALVATION. For Origen, following Plato, evil souls must go back to earth for a new trial. For others, bliss will be immediate, because they have comported themselves in such a way as to warrant their reward. Thus, Origen embraces the Platonic notion of reincarnation. Once having given up flesh, there is no reason for the soul ever to want to be reincarnated in it, except to be given another chance to prove itself. Like the rest of the Platonists, Origen feels that the incarnation of the soul is just but it is a remedy for previous infractions.

7. Athenagoras

For Athenagoras, bodily resurrection is the guarantee that we are human beings. To be perfected as humanity, we have to retain our bodily humanity; resurrection for him is the guarantee of that bodily perfection as humans. Death is but a temporary state for the faithful, a state in which their identity is temporarily dispersed. To survive forever merely as a disembodied soul would be to survive at the expense of the essence of our humanity. The human being cannot be said to survive if the body has decomposed. It is not human survival unless the same body, newly perfected, is restored to the same soul (*Res.* 25).

8. Augustine

For Augustine, the vocabulary has to agree with Paul: resurrection refers to a spiritual body at the end of history, when the earthly things will be perfected (*Serm.* 362.18.21). Augustine describes the intermediary realm in which the faithful dead live. At the Second Coming, nature itself will change and be perfected. To have the form of a body, without the flesh of corruption, means for Augustine that none of the acts of the flesh (eating, drinking, begetting, etc.) will continue in heaven. Human beings will finally achieve the status of angels (stars) in the afterlife and this will become the model for a perfected earth in the end times (*Serm.* 362.18.21).

Augustine must explain why, when souls can contemplate God in heaven, it should be necessary for them to have a body at all. For Augustine, the answer is more scriptural than philosophical. He does adduce reasons, if not an actual proof. The purpose of having a spiritual body in heaven has to do with the identity of the believer and also with its purpose in heaven, to meditate upon God. The spiritual body is both infinitely superior to the soul and, at the same time, only complete when it has become a spiritual body. Augustine analogizes with the incarnation. If God can be incarnate, then the perfected soul can be embodied as a spiritual body. But the highest pleasures are reserved for a spiritual body (*Serm.* 12.35). He then says that even after we have reached the felicity of bodiless existence there is the further felicity of returning to a perfected body, so that the wise and ascetic in this world live as if they are already in the perfected world to come.

In his most extensive treatment of our final disposition, *The City of God*, Augustine locates the ultimate good in being reincorporated without the evils of corporeal life. But he also uses that peculiar future state to demonstrate that hellfire and punishment for the damned will be real. How else could the soul be punished except in a body (*Civ.* 19.1–17)? The saved have precisely the converse issue. They will be souls together in salvation, a community of those saved, just as the church creates a community on earth. They will need an incorruptible body for their reward: so, in order to be happy, souls need not flee from every kind of body, but must receive an incorruptible body. And in what incorruptible body will they more fittingly rejoice than in the one in which they groaned while it was corruptible (*Civ.* 12.26).

Augustine is driven to the conclusion from which Paul started: the body that the faithful will enjoy eternally is like a fleshly body but it is not a fleshly body. It is not even a material body. It is perfected flesh, with eyes that can see the invisible things of God (*Civ.* 22.29).

Either, therefore, God will be seen by means of those eyes because they in their excellence will have something similar to mind by which even an incorporeal nature is discerned—but that is difficult or impossible to illustrate by an example or testimony of the divine writings—or else, which is easier to understand, God will be so known by us and so present to our eyes that by means of the spirit he will be seen by each of us in each of us, seen by each in his neighbor and in himself, seen in the new heaven and the new earth and in every creature that will then exist (*Civ.* 22.29). For Augustine this means being subsumed into the body of Christ, who is the only member of the Trinity to take on human form. Indeed for him, meditating on the Trinity is a way to anticipate the last and final consummation, which in *The City of God* Augustine compares with the Sabbath (*Civ.* 22).

In short, Augustine believes that the saved Christians will enjoy eternity as a community of perfected beings, like angels. As opposed to Origen, Augustine sees the final disposition of the soul only at the PAROUSIA, the Second Coming, when all the faithful are resurrected. The living will be transformed but the dead will find their souls reclothed. The soul, rather than hating the body (as in Platonism), yearns for the body in order to complete its repentance (as in late Neo-Platonism). The difference, for Augustine, is that repentance must be done in a single lifetime and may only be accomplished by those who believe in the Christ. Augustine himself certainly had plenty of experience with repentance, having been a religious quester himself. Indeed, the interior life of the convert dominates his writings. One might say that his psychology was far advanced beyond his eschatology because it contains implications that take him far beyond the purview of Christian beliefs about the end.

The Nicene Creed affirmed that Christians must firmly await the life of the aeon to come. For the Cappadocians, this meant affirming both the immortality of the soul and the resurrection of the dead, a formula which was by now the standard way of dealing with the opposing concepts of afterlife in Christian thought. There was certainly a difficulty in affirming both of them simultaneously. But for Augustine, both could be affirmed sequentially. Upon death, the correctly believing and acting soul could attain the immortality of the soul that had originally been the Greek notion, while at the end of time, the soul would be returned to a body for the fulfillment that was contemplated by Daniel and the Jewish apocalypticists (of which Christianity was certainly the primary example). Immortality of the soul now; resurrection of the body at the last trumpet.

The return, one might object, is not really resurrection of the flesh but only a resurrection into a spiritual body resembling in some respects the fleshly body it inhabited on earth. From another perspective, however, the soul can already be said to be a spiritual body. In any event, this formulation satisfied Augustine.

With his doctrine of the embodied fulfillment of time, he avoids the Greek philosophical notion that the soul merely discorporates and finds its final fulfillment. There is an immortal soul but it will be punished at death. Augustine never sees a return to the body as a return to bodily pleasures in the apocalyptic end. All of earthly pleasure is purged away. It is the body of an angel to which the faithful return, to contemplate God the more completely. The result is an interesting synthesis: the soul is immortal but only in the intermediate state. At the last JUDGMENT, it shall be judged again. Only the elect shall return to the perfected body at the end of time. There, it is most fully itself for the soul is not fully an individual. The synthesis is, in a way, a systematic description of the pictures of the last judgment in the Christian apocrypha, combining a notion of a soul that survives death with a final judgment.

This synthesis may not be as satisfactory intellectually to us as is the synthesis of Gregory (that is, if the soul is not fully individual, then it is not fully the same as the original person on earth). But we live in a different world than Augustine. Augustine represents the forceful partnership of the civil authority with the church and provided the synthesis most in line with the desired, new unification of the Christian Roman Empire. That is part of the importance of Augustine; the church seized upon his thought because it so thoroughly supported the orthodox position. The state seized upon his thought because it gave it the justification to demand higher allegiances from its inhabitants. But minority groups not part of the Christian synthesis, like the Jews, were forced into very subservient roles. Many were forced out or murdered or converted or eventually left the territory controlled by Roman Christendom. Those who remained were constantly stripped of their rights as individuals and communities.

Augustinianism was, understandably, not immediately attractive to the intellectual community. After Augustine, the first generation of Greek Byzantine thinkers begin, in fact, to reappropriate the solution of Origen. In some ways, then, the intermediate stage of philosophically sophisticated theology becomes the more predominant pattern at first. On the other hand, Christianity eventually found a powerful ally in the notion of immortality of the soul, even though it flatly contradicts the claims of the NT.

Like an irritation, this contradiction produced a pearl of a solution, after intense intellectual activity. Not even Socrates cared as much about the immortality of the soul. He died confident of the concept but he did not expound as much on the subject as the typical church father did because the church had to explain the saving message of Jesus' martyrdom and at the same time had to argue that this reward was greater than the reward of immortality of the soul.

It took centuries for the church to undo the damage that natural philosophy seemed to do to the Christian message. The conceptualization of the resurrection and the many different discussions of its properties carried the hopes, desires, and polemical furies of the early Christians. And yet, at the beginning it was based on one of the greatest mysteries of all times, resurrection of the body. In the end, faith demands taking on the burden of that mystery and struggling with its difficulties. It is that struggle that makes resurrection not only the center of the Christian faith but representative of the struggle that all people of faith have with the modern world and its differing scientific assumptions. *See* DEATH OF CHRIST; ESCHATOLOGY OF THE NT; RESURRECTION, EARLY JEWISH; RESURRECTION, OT.

Bibliography: David Aune. *The Cultic Setting of Realized Eschatology in Early Christianity* (1972); Peter Brown. *The Body and Society: Men, Women and Sexual Renunciation in Early Christianity* (1988); Raymond E. Brown. *The Virginal Conception and Bodily Resurrection of Jesus* (1973); Caroline Walker Bynum. *The Resurrection of the Body in Western Christianity* (1993); Adela Collins. *Cosmology and Eschatology in Jewish and Christian Apocalypticism* (1996); John J. Collins. "Apocalyptic Eschatology and the Transcendence of Death." *CBQ* 36 (1974) 21–43; John J. Collins. *The Apocalyptic Vision of the Book of Daniel* (1977); John Dominic Crossan. "Empty Tomb and Absent Lord (Mark 16:1-8)." *The Passion in Mark.* W. Kelber, ed. (1976) 134–52; Joanne E. McWilliam Dewart. *Death and Resurrection.* Message of the Fathers of the Church 22 (1986); W. H. C. Frend. *Martyrdom and Persecution in the Early Church: A Study of a Conflict from the Maccabees to Donatus* (1967); Robert Kraft. *The Didache and Barnabas* (1965); G. W. E. Nickelsburg. *Resurrection, Immortality, and Eternal Life in Intertestamental Judaism* (1972); Elaine Pagels. "The Mystery of the Resurrection." *JBL* 93 (1974) 276–88; Elaine Pagels. *The Gnostic Paul: Gnostic Exegesis of the Pauline Letters* (1975); Pheme Perkins. *Resurrection: New Testament Witness and Contemporary Reflection* (1984); Alan Scott. *Origen and the Life of the Stars: A History of an Idea* (1991); Alan F. Segal. *Life After Death: A History of the Afterlife in Western Religion* (2004); Alan F. Segal. *Heavenly Ascent in Hellenistic Judaism, Early Christianity, and Their Environments* (1980); Alan F. Segal. *Paul the Convert: The Apostolate and Apostasy of Saul of Tarsus* (1988); N. T. Wright. *The Resurrection of the Son of God* (2003).

ALAN F. SEGAL

RESURRECTION, OT. The concept of resurrection of the dead did not develop until the Second Temple period (after 587 BCE). The First Temple period (ca. 950–587 BCE) gives us no proof of a conception of resurrection nor of any other AFTERLIFE that can be called beatific, like paradise—i.e., a reward for good behavior on earth. It could be that there was no idea of the afterlife at all, but that would make the Hebrews unique among world cultures and especially out of place in the ANE, where elaborate ideas about postmortem existence and even more elaborate funeral rituals were everywhere part of literature, myth, and social life.

Two personages in the OT—Enoch (Gen 5) and Elijah (2 Kgs 2)—can be said to have achieved a beatific afterlife, in that they are assumed bodily into heaven without dying. Nothing suggests that this was viewed as a common fate of humanity. Indeed, from the text alone, it is hard to understand why Enoch might have received this reward. One has to look at the mythical stories told about Enoch in later Hebrew tradition and like characters in other cultures to gain some understanding of the story. Moses, legendarily, was later added to the number of those assumed into heaven, on account of the report that no one knows of his grave. But these are later traditions.

Most biblical terms for the dead can be found in the book of Isaiah—predominantly positive terms like "souls," "divine ones," "healers," "holy ones," "knowing ones," and "those who pass over." A large number of scholars have concluded from this usage that the dead had a powerful role in the lives of the living in the oldest period of Israelite thought; they might even heal the sick and revive the dead, as sometimes seems possible in Canaanite religion. But so far we have no direct evidence that the dead themselves were resurrected.

There are some passages that hint at a more complicated relationship between the Israelites and their Canaanite environment. For instance, Saul, when he feared God's disfavor, sought the services of a necromancer, following a practice that he himself had specifically forbidden, according to the narrative (1 Sam 28:6-14; *see* NECROMANCY). In this incident, he recalls the ghost of Samuel, who is even described as a god in 1 Sam 28:13 (ʾ**elohim** אֱלֹהִים). He comes up from the ground. The name for the underground home of the dead is SHEOL (**sheʾol** שְׁאוֹל or שְׁאֹל), which could be related to Saul's name in Hebrew, **shaʾul** (שָׁאוּל), since it comes from the same root.

Psalm 115:16-18 gives a short and very articulate view of the cosmos of the Hebrews: "The heavens are the LORD's heavens, but the earth he has given to human beings. The dead do not praise the LORD, nor do any that go down into silence." Moreover, the dead are cut off both from the living and the presence of God: "For Sheol cannot thank you, death cannot praise you; those who go down to the Pit cannot hope for your faithfulness" (Isa 38:18).

But such a clear statement that Yahweh's dominion stops before the gates of Sheol is perhaps too hasty, or perhaps it is but the oldest notion in the Bible, to be replaced by newer ones. Certainly other passages suggest other relationships between Yahweh and the afterlife. Especially Pss 16:10-11; 49:15; and 73:24, as well as Deut 32:39 and 1 Sam 2:6 should be consulted. But these passages seem to describe rescue from death rather than return from death. They underline that Yahweh is God of the living. Psalm 1:5, which says that the wicked will not stand in judgment, seems to mean only that the wicked will not be able to stand the severe trials awaiting them when they are brought to justice.

When Sheol is mentioned, untimely death is quite frequently present too. Jacob, distraught over the presumed death of Joseph, says: "I shall go down to Sheol to my son, mourning" (Gen 37:35). When the brothers tell him they must bring Benjamin back to Egypt he says: "You would bring down my gray hairs with sorrow to Sheol" (Gen 42:38). The brothers say the same things about their father (Gen 44:31). Yet in the end, Jacob has a peaceful death: "When Jacob ended his charge to his sons, he drew up his feet into the bed, breathed his last, and was gathered to his people" (Gen 49:33). David instructs Solomon not to allow Shimei ben Gera or Joab to live but to bring his gray head down to Sheol in blood (1 Kgs 2:9), not peace (1 Kgs 2:6). Afterward, David rests with his people and is buried in the city of David. The deaths of Shimei ben Gera and Joab contrast with David's.

The phrase "being gathered to one's ancestors" (lit., fathers, i.e., forefathers, kin) appears to indicate proper burial and, if so, the term *fathers* is used as a common plural, including both genders, as both men and women were buried in the same way and in the same places. It is possible that the phrase originally indicated the practice of mixing the bones of the family in common for final disposition, which is an Iron Age innovation, evidenced throughout the biblical period.

The phrases "being gathered to one's ancestors" and "resting with one's ancestors" are not exactly equivalent with being buried, as Jacob is "gathered" several weeks before his body is buried in the land of Israel (Gen 50:1-13). But it is possible that they merely anticipated the successful conclusion of the funeral process in the foreshortened narrative. If so, the expression outgrows its original context in immediate burial. It may even suggest that there was a ritual process of merging one's individuality with the collective ancestry of the people in the year or so that it took the flesh to decay, leaving the bones only.

Israelite burial locations and styles, as everywhere, depended on the deceased's station in life. There is also a great deal of variation in burial, including jar burials, individual burials in coffins (wood or ceramic) or without, cist tombs, pit burials, bench or niche burials, and communal or family tombs. Grave goods were very common. In the Late Bronze Age for Israel, during the settlement period (1200–1000 BCE), there is a distinct difference between lowland and highland patterns of burial, suggesting that the Israelite and Judahite patterns are more often seen in the hills, which were the strongholds of early Israelite tribal life. The lowland patterns are considerably more sophisticated, as one would expect, since that is where the civilized Canaanite cities were.

The word for dead spirits in ancient Hebrew is **refaʾim** (רְפָאִים), which essentially means ghosts or spirits (*see* REPHAIM). Yet there are not many grounds for optimism about what lies beyond the grave, though **nefesh** (נֶפֶשׁ; "breath") and **neshama** (נְשָׁמָה; "breath") both offer a basis for later Second Temple notions of immortal souls in a beatific afterlife. In the First Temple period, the Bible does not describe an afterlife with the intensity of the Mesopotamians or Canaanites. If it existed in popular religion (as seems obvious), there is no reason to suspect that it would be any more beatific than the Canaanite notions. Neither the Canaanite nor Babylonian conceptions of the afterlife contained much about reward or punishment or represented the reward for the righteous.

True, the **refaʾim** logically represent the survival of the identity of persons. But to call **nefesh** or **rpʾ** (רפא) an "intermediate state" is to assume that the ancient Israelites expected an amelioration in the afterlife, for which there is little evidence. In the Second Temple period, resurrection becomes possible, though there is no sure evidence for it until Dan 12:2-3, usually dated to the 2nd cent. BCE. How the dead were to participate in "the day of the LORD," which the prophets sometimes predict, is not evident. Likely, it was to be enjoyed only by the living, at first.

The real issue is not whether someone survives death but whether that someone is punished or enjoys a beatific afterlife. We must be careful of this distinction throughout: When **rpʾ** or **nefesh** means nothing more than "shade" or "ghost" or "spirit" in describing the afterlife, then it is no different from a host of other words for "ghost" throughout world religions.

There are a few ambiguous places where Sheol is depicted as being under the power of God (Job 8:3-7; 26:6; Ps 139:8; Amos 9:2). These passages underline the constant biblical refrain that God is the only God. They contradict the notion that Sheol contains no presence of God. It is hard to know whether this represents an evolutionary step in the development of monotheism or merely an alternative poetic trope that the psalmists and prophets could use. In these passages Yahweh is God of the living and the dead, of this world and the next. The statements are most probably part of the biblical polemic against other gods, in this case, against the notion that there is another god who is "lord of the underworld," as there was in every other culture surrounding Israel. Psalms 49:15 and 73:26 seem to suggest that the good will remain with God forever, and this may imply the beginning of a new notion of life after death, even as early as the First Temple period, but it is only a hint, and Psalms and Job are particularly difficult to date. It would be incautious to conclude that this demonstrates resurrection or any specific notion of afterlife.

In this category we might well put the intriguing passage in 1 Sam 2:6: "The LORD kills and brings to life; he brings down to Sheol and raises up." The phrase occurs in the "Song of Hannah" after the birth of Samuel. Normally the passage has been interpreted by means of a parallel passage in another psalm, Deut 32:39, "The Song of Moses," which states, "I kill and I make alive; I wound and I heal; and no one can deliver from my hand." In the latter case, most scholars have been convinced that the reference is to two separate persons, one whom God preserves and the other whom he kills. The text describes reversals in this life. In 1 Sam 2:6 as well, this phrase seems to be a stock attribute of God's power, as in the cycle of stories concerning Elisha and the evil kings of Israel: "When the king of Israel read the letter, he tore his clothes and said, 'Am I God, to give death or life, that this man sends word to me to cure a man of his leprosy?'"

It is possible that the phrase in 1 Samuel was originally meant to claim that it was Yahweh, the God of Israel, who brings up spirits (so that the medium of Endor was operating under the aegis of the God of Israel after all). In this case, one would posit that Israel's God was propounded as the God of the underworld too, at least in some part of Israelite territory, and that the later stories are attempts to extinguish necromantic practices. No doubt there are voices in the Israelite past who could have assented to this proposition.

If there is no beatific afterlife and no judgment, then it does not much matter whether the "soul" is a "wraith" or a "spirit" or a "ghost" or a "shade." There is nothing after death to be desired. Resurrection and a beatific life, significant parts of Second Temple beliefs, do not develop until the Hellenistic period, and then in the specific context of martyrdom. *See* RESURRECTION, EARLY JEWISH; RESURRECTION, NT.

Bibliography: James Barr. *The Garden of Eden and the Hope of Immortality* (1993); Elizabeth Bloch-Smith. *Judahite Burial Practices and Beliefs about the Dead* (1992); Jon D. Levenson. *Resurrection and the Restoration of Israel: The Ultimate Victory of the God of Life* (2006); Alan F. Segal. *Life After Death: A History of the Afterlife in Western Religion* (2004).

ALAN F. SEGAL

RETRIBUTION [נָקָם naqam, שׁוּב shuv, שִׁלֵּם shillam; ἀνταπόδομα antapodoma]. Retribution means that God gives to individuals and communities a degree of suffering that somehow corresponds to their sin or offense. The idea of retribution serves as a corner-stone for the central theological claim that God governs the world with justice.

The OT speaks frequently regarding God's activity in dealing with sin. **Naqam** usually carries the notion of *divine* vengeance, that God will terribly punish errant nations and individuals (e.g., Jer 15:15). God maintains a balance in the universe that induces harmony and well-being. The word **shalom** (שָׁלוֹם) expresses that balance. Often, SHALOM is translated "well being," "health," or "a debt paid," as well as "peace." The Israelites inhabited a world in precarious balance, where every action (human or divine) affected the equilibrium toward either greater harmony or to chaos and destruction. When someone violated communal or individual norms, that person tipped the balance away from **shalom**, threatening the community's prosperity and well-being. By acting against the perpetrator (by execution, banishment, loss, or disease) God restored the harmony. The related word **shillam** describes how God restores the balance (e.g., Isa 59:18; 66:6).

The Hebrew root **shuv** speaks of return, and sometimes means "repentance." **Shuv** also expresses a different kind of return, a "re-tribution." For the ancient Israelite, negative influences had to be balanced by a corresponding action. God takes what an individual does and "returns" it with a proportionate punishment: "... and God also made all the wickedness of the people of Shechem fall back (**shuv**) on their heads" (Judg 9:57).

The Israelites derived great comfort from the knowledge that God reliably punished iniquity, particularly the sins of their enemies (Isa 59:18). When faced with an imbalanced and unfair universe, some writings insisted that divine retribution was only delayed and that the faithful must be patient (Hab 2:3). Unfortunately, things often turned out badly for the beleaguered people, and their enemies remained unpunished. Therefore, there arose a series of alternative ways to understand divine justice.

For example, the Wisdom tradition raised strong objections to the doctrine of retribution (*see* WISDOM IN THE OT). People suffered for no apparent reason while harmful, predatory people lived long and carefree lives (*see* THEODICY). Their evil did not return to them. Some Israelites explained this lack of retribution by accusing the sufferers of being guilty of sin they had not admitted. In the prologue of the book of Job, a perfectly righteous man received affliction appropriate for the worst sinner. Job says that God is under no obligation to reward good behavior or punish the bad (1:20). However, his friends argue that even though Job seems innocent, God has punished him because he must have done something heinous. In the long debate between Job and his friends, his position changes, though the subject never does. Now Job claims that God treats him unfairly. He deserves reward and not retribution for his good behavior. However, Job concludes that there is no discernible way to determine God's actions (42:1-6).

Belief in retribution assumes that the universe makes sense. Qoheleth, the author of the book of Ecclesiastes, questions whether there is any evidence of that. He considers the finality of death and wonders if there is any balancing or corresponding justice in the world (e.g., Eccl 8:11). But even he, the great skeptic, hopes that things will one day work out. The bad people will finally end up with what they deserve, while the good enjoy satisfaction (Eccl 8:12-13).

Among the later works of the OT (6th–2nd cent. BCE), sages and prophets developed a new idea that justified their belief in divine retribution. God's vengeance, they said, takes place after an individual dies. Divine judgment happens to people in the afterlife. One finds some bare hints of this idea in the books of Daniel and 2 Maccabees: "Many of those who sleep in the dust of the earth shall awake, some to everlasting life, and some to shame and everlasting contempt. Those who are wise shall shine like the brightness of the sky, and those who lead many to righteousness, like the stars forever and ever" (Dan 12:2-3; compare 2 Macc 7:9, 14, 23).

Sages asked, how is it fair that the righteous suffer. The author of the Wisdom of Solomon (180–130 BCE) assures them not to worry. After they die, the righteous will receive their reward and recompense in heaven (Wis 2:4*b*, 9*b*), and the wicked will receive God's retribution (Wis 4:18).

All the various OT positions on retribution are represented in some form in the NT. Using agricultural imagery, Paul succinctly expresses the traditional understanding of the doctrine of retribution: "Do not be deceived; God is not mocked, for you reap whatever you sow. If you sow to your own flesh, you will reap corruption from the flesh; but if you sow to the Spirit, you will reap eternal life from the Spirit" (Gal 6:7-8).

Retribution in the afterlife, offered tentatively in the latest OT writings, becomes a central pillar of Christian hope. But there still remain strong objections to the teaching of retribution. The Gospel of John portrays Jesus denying a causal relationship between suffering and sin and thus denying the relevance of retribution. His disciples point to a man born blind and ask, "Rabbi, who sinned, this man or his parents?" His answer is both ambiguous and profound: "Neither this man nor his parents sinned" (John 9:3). In this paradigmatic example, Jesus rejects retribution as the cause of suffering. People suffer, but not because of their sins and not from the retributive activity of God. Similarly, in Luke, Jesus refers to a natural disaster attributed to God's judgment. He rejects the notion that their suffering results from their sin: "Or those eighteen who were killed when the tower of Siloam fell on them—do you think that they were worse offenders than all the others living in Jerusalem? No, I tell you; but unless you repent, you will all perish just as they did" (Luke 13:4-5). While Jesus denied the connection between sin and suffering in the examples above, he also threatened sure punishment against the wicked and eternal life in heaven for followers (Matt 25:31-46).

The martyred Christians under the altar of God complain of the absence of retribution: "how long will it be before you judge and avenge our blood on the inhabitants of the earth?" (Rev 6:10). In 2 Thessalonians the notion of retribution is both brutal and certain: "inflicting vengeance on those who do not know God" (2 Thess 1:8).

The early Christians believed that retribution would come upon their enemies and persecutors in eschatological time, the end of history, when God will judge and remake the world (*see* ESCHATOLOGY IN THE NT). Jesus divides the human community into wheat and weeds, gathered for destruction or storage (Matt 13:30). Revelation speaks of repaying the community's enemies double for their deeds (18:6). Elsewhere in Revelation retribution appears as a bureaucratic process: "And the dead were judged according to their works, as recorded in the books" (20:12).

In both the OT and NT, divine retribution offered a way to make sense of the world. It presumed that God maintained the moral order of the universe. Suffering came as divine punishment. However, human experience did not always fit this paradigm. Divine retribution never completely dominated or eliminated alternative explanations for human suffering in the Bible. Ultimately, the attempt to defer the entire moral balancing of the universe to some future time provided for some an explanation of what plainly remained an unfair world. *See* AFTERLIFE; JUDGMENT; PAROUSIA; SIN, SINNERS.

Bibliography: James Crenshaw. *Defending God: Biblical Responses to the Problem of Evil* (2005); Klaus Koch. "Is There a Doctrine of Retribution in the Old Testament?" *Theodicy in the Hebrew Bible.* James Crenshaw, ed. (1983) 57–87; David Penchansky. *What Rough Beast? Images of God in the Hebrew Bible* (1999); Stephen Travis. *Christ and the Judgment of God: The Limits of Divine Retribution in the New Testament* (2009).

DAVID PENCHANSKY

RETURN [שׁוּב shuv; ἐπιστρέφω epistrephō]. Beyond the basic meaning of "to go/come back," in the OT *return* often denotes a major theological theme of repentance (i.e., Deut 30:2; Job 22:23; Ps 51:13 [Heb. 51:15]; Isa 44:22; 2 Chr 30:6-9). In prophetic writings, the term expresses the heartfelt plea for Yahweh's people to repent (Jer 3:1-14; 4:1-2; 31:21; Hos 12:6 [Heb. 12:7]; 14:1-2 [Heb. 14:2-3]). Even severe judgment did not always induce the people to return to Yahweh (Amos 4:6-11). Return can be reciprocal: in Zech 1:3-4, Yahweh promises to return to Israel if Israel returns to Yahweh. Sirach 17:24-29 also equates repentance and return. The same theme appears in the NT at 1 Pet 2:25 in an allusion to Isa 53:6: the sheep who went astray have now returned to the shepherd. Another theologically charged use of *return*, associated with rejoicing, is its reference to Israelites returning from exile (Isa 10:21-22; 35:10; 51:11; Jer 31:1-9, 21).

BRUCE W. GENTRY

REU ree'*yoo* [רְעוּ re῾u; Ῥαγαύ Rhagau]. Reu's life as an independent figure does not receive much attention in the biblical texts; instead, the writers of both the OT and NT essentially mention Reu in terms of his role as the ancestor of Abraham (Gen 11:18-21; 1 Chr 1:25) and Jesus (Luke 3:35). Reu, therefore, is merely one link in the chain of individuals going back to Adam through the line of Shem.

JASON R. TATLOCK

REUBEN, REUBENITES r*oo*'bin, r*oo*'bi-n*i*t [רְאוּבֵן re᾽uven, בְּנֵי רְאוּבֵן bene re᾽uven, רְאוּבֵנִי re᾽uveni; Ῥουβήν Rhoubēn]. 1. Reuben was the first of Jacob and Leah's sons, the firstborn of all Jacob's children (Gen 29:31-32), and the eponymous patriarch of the Reubenites. While the name Reuben literally means "Behold, a son," Genesis has Leah provide a different account: "It means 'God has seen my distress' and 'Now my husband will love me'" (Gen 29:32). Her dual pronouncement seems to suggest composite sources (likely J and E), each with its own explication of Reuben's name, later combined by a redactor.

Reuben plays a pivotal role at several points in the narrative line of Genesis. He collects the mandrakes that Rachel then demands as an aphrodisiac; in exchange for them, Leah requests an additional night with Jacob, resulting in the birth of Issachar (Gen 30:14-16). Reuben later has sexual relations with his father's concubine Bilhah, leading to the loss of his birthright to his brothers Judah and Joseph (1 Chr 5:1). He speaks on behalf of Joseph when his brothers seek to kill him (Gen 37:21-22), and seems surprised and distressed to find Joseph sold to the Ishmaelite traders (Gen 37:29). Later, Reuben chastises the other brothers for their violence against Joseph, and is finally instrumental in reuniting the family in Egypt (Gen 42:37).

As a consequence of his relationship with Bilhah, however, Jacob's final speech to his sons calls Reuben "unstable as water," and posits his family's decline from prominence (Gen 49:4).

2. A tribe whose eponymous ancestor was Reuben the son of Jacob. According to Numbers, the Reubenites and Gadites had chosen lands east of the Jordan for their inheritance, the better to graze their cattle (Num 32:1-48). However, Moses assumed they lacked the will to take the western land, and called down the wrath of the Lord upon them (Num 32:10). By agreeing to cross the Jordan to do battle, the Reubenites later inherited lands in the southeastern portion of Canaan (Num 32:33). The Reubenite territories were bordered by the Jordan River and Dead Sea to the west and extended to the east to include "all the towns of the tableland" listed in Josh 13:16-20. These tableland cities are elsewhere attributed to other tribes, however; e.g., Gad receives both Heshbon (Josh 21:39) and Dibon (Num 32:34), cities that are counted for Reuben in Josh 13. Curtis suggests that this confusion about Reubenite cities indicates that the tribe of Reuben never fully migrated Transjordan at all. Some members continued to live in the West, where they were absorbed by Judah; the small contingent that migrated east was subsumed into Gad, eventually leading to the demise of the Reubenites as a separate entity (Curtis 1965).

In later OT texts, the Reubenites are mentioned only sporadically. The tribe is among those who set up an altar in their region of the Jordan against the wishes of the western tribes (Josh 22:9-12). They fail to come to the aid of the judges in order to care for their sheep in the Song of Deborah (Judg 5:16-17). The tribe wages war on Hagrites in the time of Saul (1 Chr 5:10, 20), and some are among those who acclaim David at Hebron (1 Chr 11:42). While many texts list Judah's family first in genealogical tables (as in 1 Chr 2), the Reubenites maintained the first position in several other later sources. For example, the tribe remains preeminent in the listings of descendants and inhabitants of the land in Exod 6:14; Num 1:20; 26:5.

Around 740 BCE, they are conquered and carried into exile by the king of Assyria (2 Kgs 15:19-29; 1 Chr 5:26). Ezekiel later offers a vision of a restored Israel in which the Reubenites receive their "portion" and gate (Ezek 48:6, 31).

The lone NT mention of the Reubenites is at the sealing of the tribes, which occurs in Rev 7:5-8. As with the other tribes, 12,000 of the tribe of Reuben are sealed for salvation. Interestingly, here Reuben is listed second to the tribe Judah, as in much of the OT.

Reuben also appears in extra-biblical literature of the Hellenistic period, most notably in the *Testament of Reuben.* In this Second Temple Jewish writing (with Christian interpolations), the author relates in first person the affair between Bilhah and Reuben, but emphasizes Reuben's innocence, stating, "For if I had not seen Bilhah bathing in a sheltered place, I would not have fallen into this great lawless act. For so absorbed were my senses by her naked femininity that I was not able to sleep

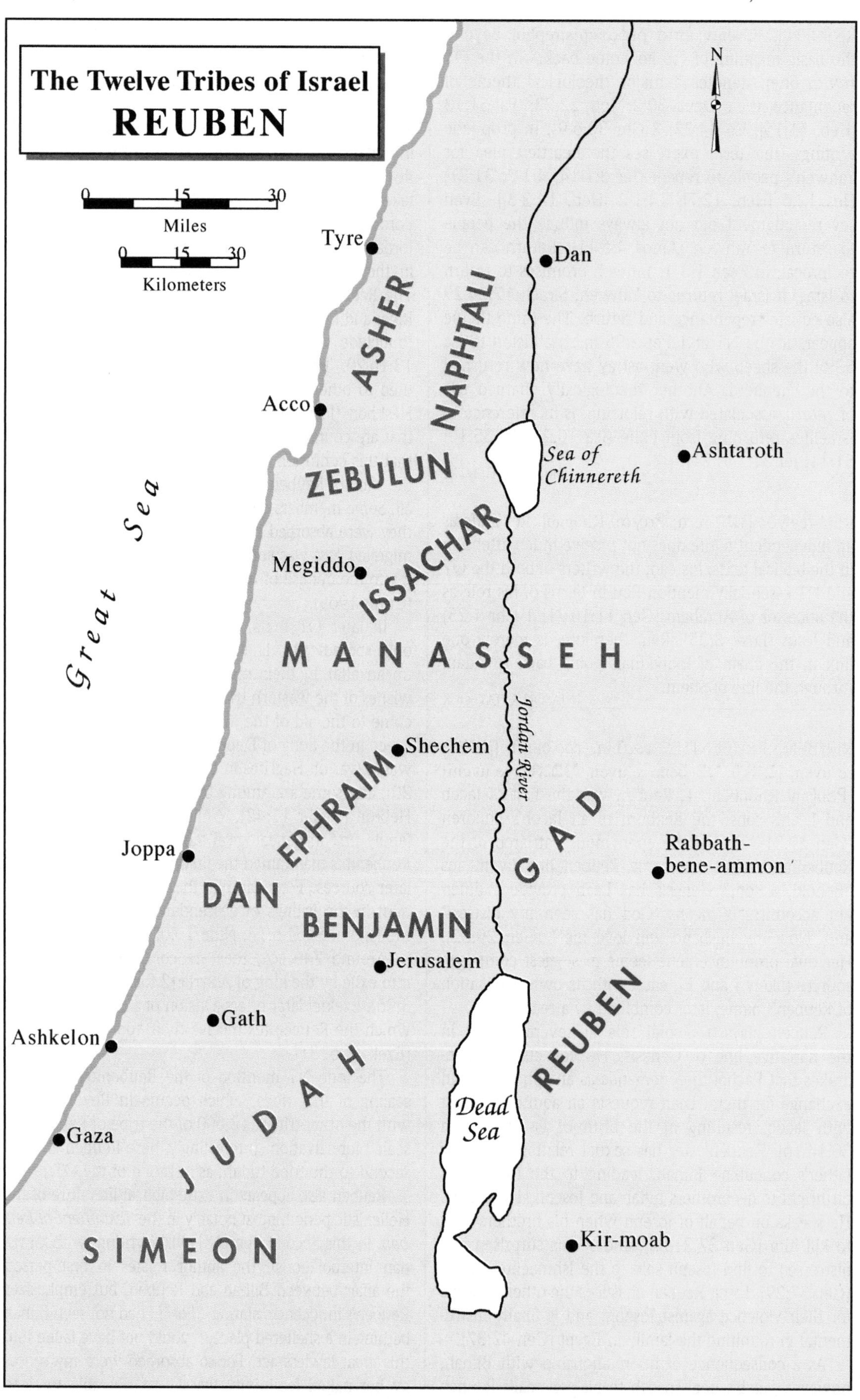
The Twelve Tribes of Israel
REUBEN
N
0 15 30
Miles
0 15 30
Kilometers
Tyre
Dan
ASHER
NAPHTALI
Acco
Sea of Chinnereth
Ashtaroth
ZEBULUN
Great Sea
ISSACHAR
Megiddo
MANASSEH
Jordan River
Shechem
EPHRAIM
GAD
Joppa
Rabbath-bene-ammon
DAN
BENJAMIN
Jerusalem
Gath
Ashkelon
REUBEN
JUDAH
Dead Sea
Gaza
Kir-moab
SIMEON

until I had performed this revolting act" (*T. Reu.* 3:11-12; *OTP* 1). He also suggests that Bilhah's drunkenness was instrumental in the affair (3:13). He thus places the responsibility squarely on her; the author is left to exhort his sons that "women are evil ... and whomever they cannot enchant by their appearance they conquer by a stratagem" (*T. Reu.* 5:1-2; *OTP* 1). Jubilees, however, places the blame for the affair exclusively on Reuben, indicating he stole into Bilhah's tent after glimpsing her and caused her great shame, with no mention of her complicity or bewitching (*Jub.* 33:2-4). There is, overall, a great diversity in estimations of Reuben and the Reubenites in both biblical and extra-biblical literature, indicating the complex interpretive history of the patriarch in Israelite and Jewish traditions.

Bibliography: John Briggs Curtis. "Some Suggestions Concerning the History of the Tribe of Reuben." *JBR* 33 (1965) 247–49; Gerhard von Rad. *Genesis: A Commentary.* OTL (1973); Ishay Rosen-Zvi. "Bilhah the Temptress: The Testament of Reuben and 'The Birth of Sexuality.'" *JQR* 96 (2006) 65–94.

JESSICA TINKLENBERG DEVEGA

REUEL r*oo*′uhl [רְעוּאֵל reʿuʾel]. Means "friend of God" or "God is a friend." 1. One of the sons of Esau by his wife Basemath (Gen 36:4), Reuel was father of Nahath, Zerah, Shammah, and Mizzah (Gen 36:17).

2. One of the names given to Moses' father-in-law (Exod 2:18), also called Jethro (Exod 3:1) and Hobab (Judg 1:16). Other passages refer to Reuel as the father of Hobab (Num 10:29). Moses' father-in-law, a Midianite priest, was a worshiper of Yahweh (Exod 18:10-12), and it has been suggested that the Israelites learned Yahweh worship from the Midianites. Because the Midianites and the Edomites lived in the same general area, a connection between the clan of Reuel, son of Esau, and Moses' father-in-law is possible.

3. The father of Eliasaph, one of the Gadites' leaders (Num 2:14).

4. A grandfather of the Benjaminite Meshullam (1 Chr 9:8) who lived in postexilic Jerusalem.

KEVIN A. WILSON

REUMAH r*oo*′muh [רְאוּמָה reʾumah]. A CONCUBINE of NAHOR, Abraham's brother, who bore four children: Tebah, Gaham, Tahash, and Maacah (Gen 22:24). Reumah's name means "exalted."

REVELATION. *See* APOCALYPSE; APOCALYPTICISM; AUTHORITY; DIVINATION; HIDE, TO; INSPIRATION AND REVELATION; PROPHET, PROPHECY; REVELATION, BOOK OF; VISION.

REVELATION, BOOK OF rev′uh-lay′shuhn ['Αποκάλυψις 'Ιωάννου Apokalypsis Iōannou]. This book is also called the Apocalypse of John (Apokalypsis Iōannou). As a collection of visions addressed to seven churches in Asia Minor, it depicts the conflict between the allies of God and the forces of evil. The visions move in cycles through series of threats that culminate in scenes of worship in the heavenly throne room. The book climaxes with the defeat of evil, a new heaven and earth, and the descent of the new Jerusalem, where the redeemed worship God and Christ the Lamb.

A. Social and Historical Context

Revelation was written by a Christian prophet named John in the latter part of the 1st cent. CE. The congregations addressed by it faced challenges ranging from persecution to assimilation and complacency.

1. Authorship

a. Identity. The author identifies himself as JOHN, which seems to be his true name (Rev 1:1, 4, 9; 22:8). He received visions on the island of Patmos, but does not say more about his identity (1:9-11). His familiarity with local issues suggests that he had prior contact with the Christians to whom he writes. John was probably of Jewish background. He knows the OT well, assumes that Christians are true Jews (2:9; 3:9), and writes a peculiar form of Greek, which might mean that his first language was Hebrew or Aramaic.

Traditionally, the author was identified as John the son of Zebedee, one of the twelve apostles of Jesus. This was the view of Justin Martyr, who wrote in the mid-2nd cent. CE (*Dial.* 81.4). Later in the century Irenaeus ascribed Revelation and the Fourth Gospel to the apostle John (*Haer.* 3.11.1; 4.20.11). The idea that the apostle wrote Revelation was accepted by other writers of the period and continues to be affirmed by some interpreters. Many others, however, find this unlikely since the author never claims to have seen the earthly Jesus and does not call himself an apostle. For him the apostles are founding figures from the past, and he does not include himself among them (Rev 18:20; 21:14).

Some early Christians thought that if the Gospel was written by the apostle then Revelation might come from a church elder named John (Eusebius, *Hist. eccl.* 3.39.4–6; 7.25.16). Many modern interpreters agree that Revelation and the Fourth Gospel have different authors, but also say that neither book was written by the son of Zebedee (see §F2). Revelation never suggests that its author was an elder. John the author of Revelation cannot be identified with any other known figure from the early church.

b. Social location. John calls himself a "servant" of Jesus Christ, which means he belongs to Christ and is obedient to him (Rev 1:1*b*). Since this title is used for all Christians, it places John among other believers (1:1*a*). Using kinship language, he calls himself the "brother" of those to whom he writes (1:9). All who profess the same faith belong to the same family and are to support and encourage one another (19:10). He is a priest in the sense that all Christians are priests, worshiping the one true God (1:6*b*).

John's distinctive role is that of a prophet. He tells of receiving an inspired message from God and Jesus, which he was to send to congregations in Asia Minor (1:9-11). Although he does not call himself a prophet, he says that he was divinely commanded to prophesy (10:11) and refers to his book as prophecy (1:3; 22:7, 10, 18, 19). His familiarity with congregations throughout the province of Asia suggests that he traveled from place to place. He refers to other legitimate Christian prophets as "your brothers the prophets," but he does not suggest that these prophets belonged to the same group or that he was their leader (22:9). John's rivals included a prophetess nicknamed Jezebel and some traveling teachers or apostles, whose message he opposed (2:2, 20). He responds to their influence with his own prophetic word.

2. Date

Revelation was probably written between 80 and 100 CE. A more precise date is difficult to determine. Since Revelation is mentioned by Justin Martyr, it must have been composed before the middle of the 2nd cent. CE. Several factors suggest that it was put in final form in the closing decades of the 1st cent. CE.

The beast from the sea personifies a tyrant, who is said to have died and come back to life (13:3, 12, 14). This beast resembles the emperor NERO, who persecuted Christians in Rome, committed suicide in 68 CE, and yet was rumored to be alive and preparing to return to power (*Sib. Or.* 4:119–24, 138–39; Dio Chrysostom, *Pulchr.* 21.10). Some have argued that Revelation was written in the late 60s in response to Nero's persecution, but since Revelation alludes to stories about Nero's return, the book was probably written after the end of Nero's reign.

The name Babylon is used for Rome, the city on seven hills that rules the world (Rev 17:5, 9, 18). Apocalyptic Jewish writings of the late 1st and 2nd cent. refer to Rome as Babylon (*Sib. Or.* 5:143; *4 Ezra* 3:1-2, 29-31; *2 Bar.* 67:7). Just as Babylon destroyed the First Temple in 587 BCE, Rome destroyed the Second Temple in 70 CE. Therefore, it seems likely that Revelation was composed sometime after 70 (*see* BABYLON, NT; ROMAN EMPIRE).

John pictures the Temple under siege in Rev 11:1-2. Some take this to mean that the actual Temple was still standing and therefore date Revelation to 68–70 CE, shortly before the Romans destroyed the sanctuary. The vision does not, however, refer to the earthly Temple but uses siege imagery to depict threats against the Christian community. The Temple was a common metaphor for the Church and the vision fits well in the period after 70 CE (compare 1 Cor 3:16; 2 Cor 6:16; Eph 2:20-22; Rev 3:12).

The heads of the beast represent seven kings. Five have fallen, one is reigning, and one is yet to come (Rev 17:9-10). This cryptic passage is sometimes mined for clues as to which emperor was reigning when John wrote, but there is no consensus about how best to do this. Some begin counting the kings with Julius Caesar, others with Augustus, Gaius, or Nero. Some include the three emperors who ruled briefly in 68–69 and others exclude them. Alternatively, some count only the emperors who were deified or died violently. Finally, it may be that the seven kings simply represent an era of oppressive power. The vision yields no reliable information about Revelation's date.

Those who place Revelation in the late 1st cent. CE often date it to 95–96 CE. This follows Irenaeus, who said that John saw his visions toward the end of the reign of DOMITIAN, who died in 96 CE (*Haer.* 5.30.3). The final years of Domitian's reign have been pictured as a time of heightened pressure to worship the emperor, with threats of persecution against those who resisted. Such a scenario has been seen as the context in which John wrote his visions of the beastly tyrant (Rev 13:1-18; 17:1-6).

Nevertheless, there are good reasons to consider dates ranging from 80–100 CE, rather than choosing a specific date like 95. Irenaeus assumed that Revelation was penned by John the apostle, but this is probably not correct. Therefore, one might also question whether his view of the date is accurate. There is little evidence that Domitian's reign was marked by intensified pressure for people in Asia Minor to participate in the imperial cult or that he singled out Christians for persecution. Rather than responding to a specific crisis, John's book addresses issues that were common in the final decades of the 1st cent. CE.

3. Setting

John says that he received his visions on the island of PATMOS, which is in the Aegean Sea off the coast of Asia Minor or modern Turkey. He was there "because of the word of God," which probably means he was banished because of his preaching (1:9). Those deemed guilty of promoting superstition were sent to islands—and Christianity was regarded as a superstition by its opponents. Those relegated to islands had to support themselves but were not subjected to forced labor.

The SEVEN CHURCHES he addresses were located in the Roman province of Asia and faced several issues (1:4, 11). First, some were persecuted because of their faith. The process began with verbal denunciation by persons in synagogues. Since there were Jewish communities in nearly all the cities mentioned in Revelation, the conflict between Christians and Jews seems to have been limited to two locations (2:8-11; 3:7-13). When denunciations portrayed Christians as a threat to the social order, the civic authorities could imprison them. If Christians refused to compromise, they could be put to death (*see* CHRISTIAN-JEWISH RELATIONS; JEWISH CHRISTIANITY).

Persecutions in the 1st cent. CE were local and sporadic. Roman authorities did not carry out sustained campaigns against Christians (Pliny the Younger, *Ep.* 10.96). Nero's persecution of Christians in the mid-60s was confined to Rome. In the churches addressed by Revelation, a Christian named Antipas had been killed at Pergamum, but others there seem to have been left alone (Rev 2:13). The potential for persecution was evident in SMYRNA and PHILADELPHIA, but John's visions of widespread violence go beyond the experience of his readers (13:8, 15).

Second, some faced issues of assimilation to Greco-Roman culture. A specific problem concerned eating meat that had been offered to pagan deities. Civic festivals included meals and distributions of sacrificial meat, while gatherings of friends and businesspeople were held in temples. Christians seeking to maintain social and commercial contacts would have felt pressure to participate. Some at PERGAMUM and THYATIRA thought it acceptable to eat sacrificial meat, following the teaching of Balaam and a prophetess nicknamed Jezebel (2:14, 20). This latitudinarian approach might also have been shared by the NICOLAITANS (2:6, 15). In contrast, John argues that readers should resist idolatry and the social and economic pressures that lead to compromise—although zeal for truth should not lead to a loss of love (2:2-4).

Third, some congregations were complacent. SARDIS had a reputation for being alive, yet was spiritually dead (3:1-2). Christians at LAODICEA were rich, yet tepid in faith (3:14-17). Here the problem was not persecution but prosperity. Economic well-being had diminished faith commitments, so that a congregation became an innocuous part of its cultural context. The vision of the harlot later showed how the preoccupation with wealth bred an easy tolerance of violence, arrogance, and religious infidelity (17:1-6; 18:1-24).

Those addressed by Revelation faced a spectrum of issues relating to life in the Roman world. Later these issues reappear in the visions of the beast, false prophet, and harlot, who personify violence, idolatry, and the preoccupation with wealth. The beast has traits of Rome and its rulers (see §E3). The visions of its brutality relate the local threats of violence to the wider claims of the empire. The false prophet induces people to worship the beast (13:11-18; 19:20). This fits practices in the imperial cult, which received broad local support in Asia Minor throughout the 1st cent. CE. The vision relates local questions of accommodating idolatry to the practice of deifying human beings, which is shown to be tyrannical. Finally, the harlot's obsession with wealth calls into question the complacency of those who are prosperous. Amassing riches is linked to selling out to a debauched commercial network (18:1-20).

B. Genre

Readers approach different literary genres in different ways. Interpretation is affected by what kind of material they think they are reading. Revelation has features of several literary types.

1. Apocalypse

Revelation identifies itself as an APOCALYPSE (**apokalypsis**, 1:1*a*). The term refers to the disclosure of what has been hidden. A revelation is not designed to conceal meaning but to convey it. The term *apocalypse* has come to be used for a specific kind of literature.

It designates a work with a narrative framework in which a revelation of transcendent reality is given by an otherworldly being to a human recipient. Typically it discloses a supernatural world and points to salvation at the end of time. Other examples of apocalypses are *1 Enoch*, *4 Ezra*, and *2 Baruch* (*see* APOCALYPTICISM; ESCHATOLOGY IN EARLY JUDAISM; ESCHATOLOGY OF THE NT).

Most apocalypses are pseudonymous. The author assumes the name of a person from the past, like Enoch or Ezra, while writing for an audience in a later period. John, however, departs from this practice by writing in his own name. He says that God gave the revelation to Jesus, who sent it through an angel to John, who now discloses it to the readers (1:1). The work has a vertical dimension in that John is shown God's heavenly throne room where angels and other heavenly beings reside (4:1–5:14; 7:9-17; 15:1-8). Its horizontal or temporal aspect looks forward to the final defeat of evil and appearance of a new creation (19:11–22:5).

John uses this established literary form to give the readers a transcendent perspective. His apocalypse takes them into a heavenly world so they can see this world from a heavenly point of view. He discloses the nature of God's conflict with evil and assures readers of God's final victory. This enables them to see the present in light of God's future, giving them incentive to remain faithful. An apocalypse can also serve as protest literature. The visionary world shows that the present order is not absolute or final. Readers need not conform to the patterns of idolatry, violence, and avarice that dominate the world. The present order will pass away, but God's purposes will endure.

2. Prophecy

Revelation is also called a prophecy (1:3). Its opening lines resemble those of prophetic books in the OT (Jer 1:1-2; Ezek 1:1-3; Amos 1:1). Many parts of Revelation recount visionary experiences like those attributed to biblical prophets. The heavenly throne room (Isa 6:1-4; Ezek 1:4-28; Rev 4:1-11) and new Jerusalem (Ezek 40:1–48:35; Rev 21:1–22:5) are good examples. Other sections include what John purports to have heard, such as words from God's throne (Rev 1:8), the risen Christ (22:12-13), or the Spirit (14:13).

Some assume that prophecy mainly predicts future events. Revelation looks to the future, since its visions extend to the new heaven and new earth (21:1). But it is clear that the whole book is prophecy, which means it includes more than prediction (1:3; 22:7, 10, 18, 19). There are condemnations of sin, calls for repentance, and words of encouragement. Warnings are sometimes given in conditional form, so that the threat will be carried out only if repentance does not occur (2:5, 16; 3:3). The promises and blessings are not so much predictions of events as expressions of God's commitment to the faithful (2:7, 10-11; 14:13; 19:9). The Hebrew prophets include a comparable range of material.

The main function of prophecy, in the context of Revelation, is to promote faithfulness to God and Jesus. Prophetic witnesses wear sackcloth as a visible call to repentance and faith (11:3). They have authority to bring plagues, but nothing is said about their ability to predict the future. True prophecy is known by its witness to Jesus (19:10). Similarly, false prophets like Jezebel and the beast from the land are denounced for leading people into idolatry, not for wrongly foretelling the future (2:20; 13:11-18; 16:13-14; 19:20). People are to respond to prophecy by "keeping" it, which has to do with fundamental commitments (1:3). To "keep" Revelation's prophetic message is to worship God (22:9). *See* PROPHET IN THE NT AND EARLY CHURCH.

3. Letter

Revelation begins and ends like a LETTER. The standard opening of an ancient letter had three elements: the name of the sender, the intended recipients, and a greeting. This pattern is used in early Christian letters, which were usually addressed to congregations and read aloud (1 Thess 5:27). Instead of the usual Greek greeting (**chairein** [χαίρειν], "greetings"), Christian letters began "Grace to you and peace" (e.g., 1 Thess 1:1; 1 Pet 1:1-2). The grace and peace were often said to come from God and Jesus (Rom 1:1-7; 1 Cor 1:1-3; Phil 1:1-2), and sometimes praise to God was included in the greeting (Gal 1:1-5). The letters typically ended with an expression like "The grace of our Lord Jesus Christ be with you" (1 Cor 16:23; Gal 6:18; 1 Thess 5:28).

Revelation includes the standard introduction for a letter: "John to the seven churches that are in Asia. Grace to you and peace" (Rev 1:4). Like other Christian letters, Revelation addresses several congregations and its message is to be read aloud (1:3). The greeting of grace and peace comes from God, the seven spirits before his throne, and Jesus Christ, and it includes words of praise (1:4-6). Like other NT letters Revelation concludes "The grace of the Lord Jesus be with all the saints. Amen" (22:21).

The letter format shows that Revelation is to be read contextually. Its visionary contents speak to the congregations identified in its opening salutation. Some interpreters limit Revelation's epistolary aspect to the first three chapters, which deal specifically with the churches in Asia Minor, but this can lead to a noncontextual reading of the rest of the book. Epistolary elements frame Revelation, so that the entire work can be read as a message to the seven churches. This means that interpreters should take the context of Revelation seriously, as they do when interpreting other NT letters.

C. Literary Features

Revelation says that it recounts visions that John received. Interpreters can grant that genuine visionary experiences lie behind the book, while recognizing that John has written of them in an established literary format using his own distinctive style.

1. Language and style

a. Idiosyncratic Greek. Revelation is written in Greek, the dominant language of the eastern Roman Empire, yet its syntax is idiosyncratic. Sometimes the genders and cases of nouns, adjectives, and participles do not agree. Participles are used in place of finite verbs and vice versa. Sentence after sentence begins with kai (καί, "and"). New constructions can depart markedly from accepted Greek practice. For example, references to God might begin with the correct participial construction ho ōn (ὁ ὤν) or "the one who is," then shift to the odd combination of a definite article with a finite verb: ho ēn (ὁ ἦν), literally, "the was" (1:4).

Assessments of John's Greek vary. Many suggest that Greek was his second language. While writing in Greek, he may have thought in Hebrew, since some of his unusual constructions have counterparts in Hebrew or Aramaic. It is not clear whether John's own knowledge of Greek was imperfect or whether he reflects speech patterns shared by others in his social context. Some propose that he deliberately flouted the standards of Greek that were used by the elite. If so, his peculiar style accents the countercultural quality of his message (*see* GREEK LANGUAGE).

b. Repetition. Revelation often lists many similar items to give a sense of magnitude, e.g., "every tribe and language and people and nation." Moreover, such lists are repeated in varying forms in different contexts, creating cross references. For example, the Lamb redeems people of every tribe and nation, whereas the beast oppresses people of every tribe and nation (5:10; 13:7). Listing phenomena like lightning, thunder, and rumbling conveys divine majesty. Repeating the list connects visions in which God is worshiped as the Creator with those in which he confronts his opponents (4:5; 8:5; 11:19; 16:18).

c. Hymnic elements. Hymns of praise occur throughout Revelation. Initially, the heavenly company ascribes glory, honor, and power to God (4:11), then repeats the list along with wealth, wisdom, might, and blessing when praising the Lamb (5:12). Again, listing many items magnifies the praise, while using similar lists for God and the Lamb shows that they are to be worshiped together. Repeating the praises in a later vision helps establish worship as a goal of divine action (7:10-12).

The hymns seem to have been composed to fit the present literary context. The announcement of God's kingdom foreshadows the conflict with evil to come (11:15-18). The psalm-like praise of God's justice leads to enacting justice against the beast's followers (15:3-4; 16:4-7). The victorious Hallelujah chorus celebrates the defeat of the harlot (19:1-8). The style and content of the hymns might reflect worship patterns in the churches known to John. But since he never quotes the OT verbatim, it is unlikely that he includes exact citations of hymns (*see* HYMNS, NT).

2. Structure

The literary shape of Revelation has a number of important features. First, many sections are structured in groups of seven: seven churches, seven seals, seven trumpets, and seven plagues (*see* SEVEN, SEVENTH, SEVENTY). Each constitutes a large unit within the book. Second, there are groups of unnumbered visions, including those of the woman and the dragon, the beast, Babylon the harlot, and the great battle and millennial kingdom. It is not clear that these occur in groups of seven. Third, the book is punctuated by scenes of worship in heaven, as creatures, elders, and the redeemed praise God and the Lamb. Typically these scenes include hymn-like passages. Fourth, some vision sequences are interrupted by scenes that introduce new elements. For example, six seals are opened, bringing visions of threats (6:1-17), but angels halt the action so readers can see a vision of the redeemed (7:1-17) before the final seal is opened (8:1). Fifth, major sequences may overlap, a technique known as intercalation; e.g., seven angels with plagues appear in 15:1, but the focus shifts to the redeemed by the glassy sea in 15:2-4 and only returns to the angels in 15:5. Sixth, there are repetitive elements: e.g., the world is darkened in 6:12-14; 8:12; and 16:10, and the sea is turned into blood in 8:9 and 16:3.

Given this complexity, there are various ways to consider the book's structure. Some suggest that the incongruities and repetitions show that Revelation is a compilation of sources or an edited version of an older apocalypse. Most, however, treat Revelation as a unified composition because of its consistent style and language. Working with the present form of the book, some assume that Revelation outlines events in chronological order, ending with the defeat of evil and appearance of a new world. The repetitions and interruptions in the action, however, pose a challenge for linear reading.

An alternative is that the book recapitulates the message of God's victory several times, so that major sections culminate in the scenes of heavenly celebration. This is a promising approach, but it needs to be nuanced to take the book's forward movement into account. The visions are arranged in cycles but also move forward: plagues affect a fourth of the earth, then a third of it, and finally the whole world (6:8; 8:7-12; 16:3-11). Satan is cast down from heaven, later thrown into the abyss, and finally destroyed (12:7-12; 20:1-3, 7-10).

Structurally, Revelation's visions spiral forward. Readers are taken through a circle of threats and into the presence of God several times as the story moves toward final salvation. Scenes of heavenly worship signal transition points. The pattern is established in the first half of the book, chaps. 1–11. This section has three groups of seven visions: the churches, the seals, and the trumpets. Immediately before or after the seventh vision in a series, readers are taken to the heavenly throne room. The second half of the book, chaps. 12–22, also has three series of visions. Only one series—the bowl plagues—has numbered visions, but each continues leading readers through a circle of threats and into the heavenly throne room. The book as a whole can be outlined as follows:

Introduction in 1:1-8
1) Seven Churches 1:9–3:22
2) Seven Seals 4:1–8:1
3) Seven Trumpets 8:2–11:18
4) Dragon, Beast, and the Reign of God 11:19–15:4
5) Seven Bowls and the Fall of Babylon 15:1–19:10
6) Great Battle to the New Jerusalem 19:11–22:5
Conclusion 22:6-21

3. Overview of contents

The introduction identifies the book as a revelation and prophecy, then uses a letter format to greet seven churches (1:1-8). The first series of visions (1:9–3:22) begins when John is told to write what he sees in a book and send it to the churches (*see* VISION). Christ appears to him as a majestic figure, who addresses each congregation in turn. The messages follow the same pattern: an initial statement from Christ, words of reproof and encouragement, then promises to the one who conquers and an appeal to listen. The congregations face issues ranging from persecution to assimilation to complacency (see §A3).

The second series (4:1–8:1) begins in the heavenly throne room, where creatures and elders worship God as Creator of all things. John sees CHRIST the slaughtered and yet living Lamb, who takes a scroll from God's hand. As he opens each of its seals, a threat appears. Four horsemen bring conquest, violence, food shortages, and death. Then the martyrs under the heavenly altar ask how long God will let evil continue, and when judgment looms over the earth, people ask who can stand in the face of such wrath. As if in response, the threat is interrupted so that John can see the redeemed. Initially he hears about 144,000 from the twelve tribes of Israel, who are sealed as a sign of divine protection. But when he turns to look at them, he sees a countless multitude from all nations praising God and the Lamb. When the seventh seal is opened, a graceful silence follows.

The third series (8:2–11:18) begins as prayers of the saints rise before God and an angel hurls fire from the heavenly altar onto the earth. Seven angels blow trumpets bringing plagues. Fire burns plant life, the sea turns to blood, rivers become bitter, and a third of the heavenly bodies are darkened. Demonic creatures from the underworld torment the ungodly, and demonic cavalry kill a third of humanity, but people do not repent. Then threats are interrupted again, and John is told to eat a scroll and prophesy. During this interlude he pictures the community of faith as a temple under siege and tells of two witnesses prophesying in sackcloth. The witnesses are killed and raised. But only when many have come to glorify God does the seventh trumpet announce God's kingdom.

The fourth series (11:19–15:4) introduces the second half of the book. Satan the dragon threatens a woman who gives birth to the Messiah. She flees to the wilderness, and the dragon is cast down from heaven by the angelic warrior Michael and his allies. When the evil dragon comes to earth, a seven-headed beast rises from the sea to do his bidding. The beast dominates the earth and threatens the saints. Another beast rises from the land to deceive and coerce people into worshiping the sea beast. This figure is later called the false prophet, and he forces all who buy and sell to bear the name or number of the beast, which is 666. Nevertheless, a new song is heard from heaven, and angels call the world to worship God and warn of the judgment that will fall on those who worship the beast. The sequence culminates with the redeemed beside heaven's glassy sea, praising God (*see* SEA OF GLASS, GLASSY SEA).

The fifth series (15:1–19:10) begins when angels from the heavenly sanctuary pour bowls of wrath onto the earth. These afflict the followers of the beast with sores, water that turns to blood, heat, and darkness; yet they do not repent. Kings gather for battle at Armageddon, then judgment falls on Babylon the great (*see* ARMAGEDDON, OT AND NT). Babylon is pictured as a bejeweled harlot who rides the seven-headed beast and is drunk on the blood of the saints. Yet the beast turns against the harlot city and burns it with fire, so that one agent of evil destroys another. The kings, merchants, and seafarers who obtained great wealth from Babylon mourn the city's demise—and their own loss of income—but angels declare that the city deserved to fall because of its arrogance, greed, and brutality. In the end, voices from heaven celebrate God's saving action.

The sixth and final series (19:11–22:5) begins with the battle that was anticipated by the kings gathering at Armageddon. Christ is a rider on a white horse, who defeats the beast and false prophet with the sword from his mouth. Satan, the power behind the beast, is confined to the abyss for a thousand years, while the saints reign with Christ. Then Satan is loosed and defeated, the dead are raised, and the last judgment takes place. A new heaven and earth appear and the NEW JERUSALEM descends (*see* NEW HEAVEN, NEW EARTH). The river of the water of life flows through the city and the tree of life is there. The nations bring their glory into the city and the redeemed worship

God and the Lamb. The conclusion of the book, like its introduction, identifies its prophetic character and uses the form of a letter to extend a final word of grace.

4. Narrative aspects

a. Narrator. John narrates his story in the first person. His perspective extends from the chambers of heaven to the door of the abyss (9:1-2), but he is not omniscient. Others must explain what stars and lampstands signify, who can open God's scroll, who belongs in the great multitude, and who the harlot and beast are (1:20; 5:4-5; 7:13-14; 17:6-7). John follows directives from heaven and is open to correction (19:10; 22:8-9). His responsiveness makes him an example for readers.

b. Characterization. Major characters appear in pairs. God is the Creator, who is enthroned in heaven and surrounded by beings who honor him for bringing all things into being (4:1-11; 10:6; 14:7). His adversary is Satan the dragon, who wears diadems as a sign of his aspiration to power (12:3, 9). If God is the Creator, Satan is a destroyer (11:18). God's throne means life and salvation for his people, while Satan's throne brings them death (2:13; 7:10). God is faithful and true, while Satan works through deception (6:10; 12:9).

Christ the Lamb shares the throne of God. The Lamb was slain and yet is alive. Through his self-sacrifice he conquers, redeeming people of every tribe and nation for God's kingdom (5:5-10). The seven-headed beast shares Satan's throne and, like the Lamb, has been slain and returned to life (13:1-3). But where the Lamb conquers by dying for others, the beast conquers by inflicting death on others (11:7; 13:7*a*). The Lamb delivers people of every tribe and nation but the beast oppresses people of every tribe and nation (13:7*b*). In the Lamb and the beast readers see the difference between the power of God and the working of evil.

Those who belong to the Lamb have a seal on their foreheads, consisting of his name and the name of his Father (7:3; 14:1). Being sealed does not exempt people from suffering but provides assurance of a future in God's kingdom. In contrast, those who belong to the beast bear a mark on their foreheads or right hands. The mark is the beast's name or number, which is SIX HUNDRED AND SIXTY-SIX (13:16-18). Receiving the mark allows people to buy and sell freely and it spares them from condemnation by the beast, but it subjects them to the future judgment of God (14:9-11; 16:2). In Revelation everyone belongs to someone. The question is whether one's identity is defined by the Lamb, who redeems or literally "purchases" people for God through his blood (5:9; 14:3-4), or by the beast, whose mark lets people purchase in the marketplace (13:17).

Cities are sometimes personified. The new Jerusalem holds the future for God's people and is pictured as the bride of the Lamb (19:7; 21:2). She wears fine linen, gold, gems, and pearls (*see* BRIDE OF CHRIST). As a bride, her relationship with the Lamb is characterized by faithfulness and purity. In contrast, Babylon is the harlot city, which rides on the beast. The harlot also wears gold and jewels, but her appearance is debauched and garish. Her relationships with her clients are defiling and reduce intimacy to a commercial transaction (17:1-6). Babylon drinks in violence and death, but in New Jerusalem death and grief are taken away, as people drink the water of life (18:24; 21:4; 22:1). The contrasting visions are to repel readers from Babylon's obsession with wealth and violence while attracting them to Jerusalem's vision of healing and redemption.

c. Imagery. Major images have multiple layers. Evil figures like the beast and harlot blend elements from various OT powers with allusions to the Roman Empire (see §§E3, 4). Images of the people of God, like the two witnesses and the woman clothed with the sun, fuse aspects of biblical Israel and the church (see §D6). The layers enable readers to see themselves and their world as part of a larger reality.

Images are evocative, with a center of meaning and wider circle of associations. Most details contribute to the sense of the whole. John conveys the majesty of the SON OF MAN by describing his robe, hair, eyes, feet, and voice. The stars in his hand and lampstands around him are explicitly said to signify angels and churches (*see* LAMP, NT), but the other details do not have independent significance (1:12-20). Similarly, the beast's heads are said to symbolize mountains and kings, but its leopard- and bear-like qualities simply emphasize its savagery (13:1-2; 17:9).

Many have treated Revelation's imagery as a code, which John used in order to slip his message past Roman censors to Christians on the mainland, who held the key to interpretation. This idea is colorful but implausible. When John says that the beast's heads are seven hills, even non-Christian readers would link the beast to Rome, the city on seven hills. John uses picture language to shape the way readers see things. He portrays Jesus as a Lamb to convey the sacrificial significance of his death, not to conceal his identity. Similarly, depicting the ruling power as a beast emphasizes its threatening qualities.

d. Plot. Revelation's plots and subplots revolve around God's battle with evil. Major movements in the first part of the book relate to John's desire to know the contents of the sealed scroll in God's hand (5:1-4). The seals are opened by the slaughtered Lamb, and ominous visions appear, but the contents of the scroll are not yet revealed. Only when readers have seen that threats alone do not bring repentance does an angel appear with the open scroll (9:20-21; 10:1-2). He gives the scroll to John, who consumes it and is told to prophesy (10:11). What then appears is a vision of the faithful bearing witness in sackcloth, a visible call for repentance (11:3). They suffer—as did the Lamb—and yet their witness expresses God's will for the world.

Threats against the church intensify in the second half of the book. The plot unfolds in a stylized way as Satan, the beast, the false prophet, and the harlot are successively introduced into the story and then defeated in reverse order:

Satan thrown from heaven to earth (Rev 12)
 Beast and false prophet conquer (Rev 13)
  Harlot rides on the beast (Rev 17)
  Harlot destroyed by the beast (Rev 17)
 Beast and false prophet are conquered (Rev 19)
Satan thrown from earth into the abyss (Rev 20)

The turning point in the action comes when the beast turns against his former ally, the harlot, and destroys her with fire (17:16). Afterward, Christ defeats the beast and false prophet by his word (19:11-21). Finally, Satan is incarcerated for a thousand years before suffering a final defeat (20:1-3, 7-10). The overthrow of evil and the blessings given to the faithful show that God's justice will be done.

e. Spatial and temporal aspects. Spaces in the visionary world extend from heaven to earth and the abyss below the earth. Action moves easily from one realm to another. Angels hurl coals from the celestial altar onto the earth (8:5) and pour bowls of plagues from heaven on the sun, sea, and air (16:3, 8, 17). Locations can be so fluid that it is not always clear where the action takes place. For example, the woman clothed with the sun seems to give birth to the messianic child in heaven before she flees to a desert. Yet the child is then snatched up to God's heavenly throne, which suggests that the birth actually takes place on earth (12:1-6).

Places can be personified (see §C4b) and a single place can encompass the world. John tells of two witnesses being slain in the street of the great city. In Revelation the great city is usually Babylon, a place of opulence and violence. Yet it is also Sodom the city of sin, Egypt the place of bondage, and Jerusalem where Jesus was crucified. In this one place are found the inhabitants of the whole earth (11:7-10). Locations in the visionary world often cannot be identified with sites in the ordinary world. For example, when the angel opens the abyss, unleashing hordes of demonic beings, one would be hard-pressed to locate the abyss' entrance on a map (9:1-2).

Time in the visionary world has a fluid and surreal quality. Satan is cast down from heaven immediately after the Messiah's birth and exaltation to heaven (12:5-9), and Satan rages about the earth knowing that his time is short (12:12). This so-called "short" time extends until the end of the book, when the Messiah returns and Satan is banished from the earth to the abyss (20:1-3). In the visionary world Satan's raging lasts for three and a half years, which is 1,260 days or forty-two months (12:6, 14; 13:5). Yet this brief time encompasses the whole period between Christ's exaltation and return.

D. Theological Perspectives

1. God

The God of Revelation is already known from Israel's Scriptures. John takes up the tradition that God is "the one who is," then looks to the past and future by adding that God also "was and is to come" (1:4). God is called the ALPHA AND OMEGA, the first and last letters of the Greek alphabet (1:8; 21:6). This continual existence in the past, present, and future sets God apart from other beings. The language echoes Isa 44:6: "I am the first and I am the last; besides me there is no god." God is before all things as their Creator and he will bring all things to their fulfillment.

God is the world's rightful ruler. His reign is recognized by the hosts of heaven and the creatures of earth and sea, but other powers seek to dominate and ruin the world God made (Rev 5:13; 11:18). Therefore, actions against these hostile forces come from God's throne. Paradoxically, God's power is revealed in the slaughtered Lamb, who builds God's kingdom through his blood (5:9-10). God's authority challenges human attempts to make their own power absolute. Revelation critiques human efforts to deify their rulers. When people put themselves in the place of God, the result is tyranny (13:4-8).

God is just, yet questions persist. How long will God allow evil to operate, so that justice is denied to suffering people (6:9-10)? The visions affirm that God is merciful as well as just. The plagues press the ungodly to repent, and when this fails to occur God sends witnesses to continue calling for repentance (9:20-21; 10:11; 11:3). God's justice will bring evil to an end (15:3; 19:2), but God also continues to call for change, for repentance, before God's justice is complete (*see* GOD, NT VIEW OF; JUSTICE, NT).

2. Jesus

John hears that Jesus is the Lion of Judah and Root of David, the ruler who will build God's kingdom (5:5; compare Gen 49:9-10; Isa 11:1). He also sees that the power of the Lion is conveyed in the slaughtered Lamb (Rev 5:6). The blood of the crucified Messiah establishes the kingdom by ransoming people to worship God as true priests (Rev 5:9-10). The imagery recalls the sacrifice of the Passover lamb, which led to Israel's deliverance from slavery and redemption to be God's priestly people (Exod 12:3, 27; 19:6). The Lamb's blood also connotes atonement for sin and reconciliation with God (Lev 17:11; Isa 53:4-7; Rev 1:5). The LAMB is the central image for Jesus in Revelation.

Jesus is the King of kings, who confronts the forces of evil (19:16). The Lamb has a militant and confrontational side. If people are oppressed by tyrannical forces, then saving means liberating them from bondage. Christ comes as a warrior—not against the earth but against those who destroy the earth (11:18). His main opponents are the beast and false prophet, whose dominion is marked by deception and coercion. His weapon is his word, which ends their oppressive rule (19:15, 20-21).

Revelation has a high CHRISTOLOGY. The Lamb shares God's throne (3:21; 7:17). They exhibit the same wrath against evil (6:16; *see* WRATH OF GOD) and together provide SALVATION (7:10). God is called the Alpha and Omega, the beginning and the end (1:8; 21:6), and these same expressions are used for Jesus (1:17; 22:13). Jesus is not a second god but shares the existence of the one true God. Revelation clearly distinguishes angels, who cannot be worshiped (19:10; 22:8-9), from Jesus, who is rightly worshiped as one worships God (4:10-11; 5:8-10, 13-14). In and through Christ, God reigns (11:15).

3. Spirit

The Spirit of God inspires prophetic oracles in Revelation. When John sees and hears things "in the spirit," he does so in a spiritual state brought about by God's Spirit (1:10; 4:2; 17:3; 21:10). When the exalted Christ addresses the seven churches with words of admonition and encouragement, each message concludes with an appeal to "listen to what the Spirit is saying to the churches" (2:7, 11, 17, 29; 3:6, 13, 22). Here the words of the Spirit are those of the risen Christ. Elsewhere the Spirit speaks along with other heavenly beings, affirming that those who die in the Lord find rest, and inviting all to receive the book's message (14:13; 22:17). The significance of the seven spirits before God's throne is disputed (1:4; 3:1; 4:5; 5:6). They may be seven angelic beings, although some propose that they represent the sevenfold fullness of God's Spirit. In any case, the focus of the Spirit's prophetic work is to promote the worship of God by bearing faithful witness to Jesus (19:10). *See* HOLY SPIRIT.

4. Creation

God is the Maker of all things and the world is his CREATION. The four creatures around his throne have the faces of a lion, ox, eagle, and human being. As the heavenly representatives of the created order they praise God for bringing all things into existence (4:6-11). Their praise extends in waves throughout the universe, so that every creature in heaven and on earth and under the earth and in the sea joins in acclaiming God and the Lamb (5:13). This vision of creation's harmony is central to John's apocalyptic worldview. God's adversaries seek to ruin the earth (11:18). The beast and harlot corrupt earth's peoples and reduce its wealth to mere commodities, which are exploited for their own ends (18:3, 11-14). Because God created heaven, earth, and sea, he refuses to let these powers dominate the world (10:6; 14:7; 19:2).

Visions of plagues falling on earth and sea stand in tension with this central affirmation of the world as God's creation (8:6–9:21; 16:1-11). It is clear that the plagues are not directed against the created order but against those who reject God and ally themselves with evil. As fire falls from heaven and waters turn to blood, God's adversaries experience threats on every side. The plagues confront the ungodly while leaving them alive so that they have opportunity to turn away from evil. If the creation suffers, it does so as God pressures his adversaries to repent (9:20-21; 16:9, 11). Just as the faithful who suffer are promised new life through resurrection, the creation has a future in being made new by God (21:1-5).

5. Evil

SATAN the dragon is the personification of EVIL. He is identified as the serpent who has deceived people into sin since the beginning (12:9; Gen 3:1). The devil has also had the role of denouncing people as sinners before God (Rev 12:10; Zech 3:1). But after the birth and exaltation of Jesus, Satan was expelled from heaven by Michael and his angels (Rev 12:5, 7-9). Knowing this reframes the way people perceive evil. The devil rages furiously about the earth and seems invincible. Yet this vision shows the opposite: he acts so ferociously because he is now wounded, banished from heaven, and has only a limited time left (12:12). Those who think evil is supreme will give in to it, but those who know it is losing have incentive to resist.

Satan's power infiltrates the political structures personified by the beast (see §E3). The political order is not inherently evil but becomes a tool of evil in John's visions. Its principal manifestation is idolatry, the deification of human power that leads to tyranny. Similarly, evil infiltrates economic life. Goods ranging from gold and jewels to fine cloth can play a positive role in the new Jerusalem, but in Babylon's world order they become fuel for an arrogant and brutal power (see §E5). God acts in part by turning evil against itself, so that the violent beast destroys its own ally the harlot (17:16). Finally, God confronts the satanic power itself, bringing evil to an end (20:7-10).

6. People of God

The people of God include biblical Israel and the followers of Jesus. The vision of the woman clothed with the sun brings together traits of God's people from many times and places (12:1-17). Like biblical Zion she is in labor, giving birth to the Messiah (compare Ps 2:8-9; Isa 66:7-8). Like Israel of old she is carried on eagles' wings to the desert where God preserves her (Exod 19:4). Yet her children include those who hold the testimony of Jesus (Rev 12:17). All belong to the same people. Finally, the new Jerusalem has the names of the twelve tribes on its gates and the names of the twelve apostles on its foundations (21:12-14). The story of Israel continues within the church.

God's people are called from all nations and are to bear witness to all nations. The two witnesses in 11:3-12 represent the whole church. They wear sackcloth as a visible call for repentance. Like Moses, Elijah, and Jeremiah they have power to bring plagues (Exod

7:19; 1 Kgs 17:1) and preach with fire (Jer 5:14). Like Zerubbabel and Joshua the priest, they are called lampstands and olive trees (Zech 4:3, 14). Like Jesus they are killed and resurrected. These witnesses are afflicted and yet testify to the truth before the nations. They portray the vocation of the Christian community.

7. Salvation and judgment

Revelation recognizes that sin is present in the church and the world. Christ calls the churches to repent of idolatry, complacency, and lovelessness (2:5, 16; 3:3, 19). The call includes warnings about sin's consequences as well as promises of blessing for the faithful (3:16, 20). Sin is also part of the wider world, and God's desire is that the world repents. PLAGUE visions reveal God's judgment against the wicked (9:20-21). When these plagues do not bring change, however, the judgments are interrupted so that God's witnesses can prophesy in sackcloth as a visible call for repentance (11:3). Angels call the world to turn to God, warning of judgment against the ungodly and promising blessing to the faithful (14:6-13). When more plagues occur, the ungodly are left alive so that they still have opportunity to repent, even if they do not do so (16:9, 11).

Revelation also understands that evil forces influence people. Satan and his allies personify oppressive powers that go beyond any one person's sin. They enmesh people in a web of falsehood and wrongdoing. Insofar as people are sinful they are accountable and are to repent. Insofar as they are held captive by these powers they must be liberated. By enacting judgment against Satan and his agents, God brings deliverance for those in bondage (19:1-2).

After Satan's demise, the dead are raised for final JUDGMENT. Two sets of books are opened. First, the books of deeds point to human accountability. People are responsible for their actions (20:12-13). Second, the book of life signifies divine grace (*see* LIFE, BOOK OF). People are placed in this book by the mercy of God from the foundation of the world (13:8; 17:8). Both human accountability and divine grace come into play. But in the end, people are saved by grace, by having a place in the book of life of the Lamb, who died to redeem people from every tribe and nation (5:9-10; 20:15; 21:27).

Revelation depicts horrific judgments on the opponents of God, who are warned of torment in the lake of fire (14:10). At the same time, its vision of the new Jerusalem depicts a salvation that is vast. The city's gates stand open. The kings and nations, who were often allied with evil, are given hope that they too might have a place there (21:24-25). The message works through the interplay of warning and promise. People are warned of the need to repent because sin and judgment are real. They are also encouraged to trust God because the promise of salvation is real.

E. Special Topics

1. Four horsemen

As the Lamb opens the seals on God's scroll, four horsemen appear (6:1-8). The first has a bow and conquers. The second holds a sword and takes peace from the earth. The third holds the scales used in commerce and announces food shortages. The fourth is death, followed by Hades, who personifies the realm of the dead. Futuristic interpreters assume that they signal specific moments of conquest or death at the end of the age, but historical interpreters note that the horsemen would have been meaningful to 1st-cent. CE readers. Issues of conquest, violence, food shortages, and death were real for John's audience. These figures call into question the claims of the Roman Empire to provide security, peace, and prosperity. The images of the horsemen identify points of vulnerability, stripping away the pretensions of readers who think they are secure (3:17).

2. 144,000

This number is TWELVE times 12,000, which has a sense of completeness. Initially John hears that this represents the number of those who are sealed for God (7:4). The seal is placed on the forehead and consists of the name of God and the Lamb (see §C4b). John then hears that 12,000 are called from each of the twelve tribes of Israel, yielding the requisite 144,000. Note that John has not yet seen this group. When he turns to look, he sees a countless multitude from every nation—all who are cleansed by Jesus the Lamb (7:9). Earlier, the promise of the messianic Lion was fulfilled in the slaughtered Lamb (5:5-6). Here the promise to redeem many from the twelve tribes is fulfilled in the countless multitude from every tribe, who belong to the Lamb.

Some limit the group to martyrs, who follow the Lamb to death (14:4*a*). This is unlikely, however, since the 144,000 are the "redeemed" (agorazō [ἀγοράζω], "buy, purchase"), a term used for all Christians (5:9; 14:3-4). Futuristic interpreters often assume that the 144,000 are Jews who will convert to Christianity at the end of the age. In 7:1-17, however, the 144,000 and great multitude offer two perspectives on the people of God. The imagery shows the church's continuity with biblical Israel.

3. Beast

The BEAST is Satan's agent and shares his throne. Like Satan the dragon, it has seven heads and ten horns (12:3; 13:1-2). In the beast, evil takes political form. It has traits of the Roman Empire and its individual emperors. Its heads represent the seven hills on which Rome is built and seven kings (17:9). The beast rules the nations and has its own ruler cult (13:4). Its blasphemous names recall how emperors were acclaimed "god" and "son of god." The beast is said to have died and returned to life (13:3, 12, 14). This may allude to the story that Nero had survived death and would someday return to power (Tacitus, *Hist.* 2.8–9; *Sib. Or.* 5:361–65). Like the beast, Nero was known for persecuting Christians (Rev 13:7). John does not expect Nero himself to return, but alludes to the story to show that in Nero the beastlike qualities of the empire show their true face.

The beast is also a power that goes beyond Rome. It has the features of a lion, bear, leopard, and ten-horned monster, which represent the successive empires of the Babylonians, Medes, Persians, and Greeks (Dan 7:1-8; Rev 13:1-2). Combining these features, Revelation shows that the tyrannical aspects of many empires are part of the same reality. Later writers combined the visions of the beast with other evil figures to create a composite picture of the ANTICHRIST.

4. 666

This is the number of the beast, which corresponds to its name (13:17-18). John tells readers to "calculate" (psēphizō ψηφίζω) the number, which means adding up the numerical values of letters in a word. This practice is called gematria. Each letter in the Greek and Hebrew alphabets corresponded to a number: a = 1, b = 2, etc. Combining the values of letters yielded a total for a word. The problem is that the letters of many names can add up to 666. Writers using gematria usually provided clues so that readers could guess the name before doing the calculations. The beast has traits of Nero (see §E3), and it seems likely that 666 fits the name Nero Caesar if the name is written in Hebrew (*see* NUMBERS, NUMBERING).

A problem is that John wrote in Greek and his readers might not have known Hebrew. The names of other emperors have been suggested, but these require even more complex calculations. Some suggest that sixes refer to imperfection, but six did not commonly have such connotations. Others think the number is a general reference to humankind. Again, this is unlikely since "calculate" indicates the use of gematria. Interpretation must begin with the context not with the number. Given the beast's Nero-like traits, some form of Nero's name is likely.

5. Babylon the harlot

The harlot exemplifies arrogance, opulence, and brutality. Wearing purple and scarlet clothing and jewels, she is drunk with the blood of the saints (17:1-6). The harlot, like the beast, fuses traits of many oppressive powers. She is called Babylon, a brutal and domineering power, who subjugates nations (compare Jer 50–51). The city is also like Nineveh, who was cruel to the nations she conquered even as she lured them into debauchery like a prostitute (Nah 3:4). The city has a commercial empire like that of Tyre, a place derided as a prostitute for its ability to lure clients into a glittering network of sea trade (Isa 23:17; Ezek 27:3).

Early readers would have identified the harlot with Rome, the city on seven hills, who ruled the nations of the world and solidified her control by vast networks of trade (17:9, 18; *see* ROME, CITY OF). The prosperity brought by Roman rule was intoxicating to the nations, who became numb to her violence against the innocent (18:3, 24). The imagery shows people compromising their integrity for the sake of gain and a society enamored with wealth that masks corruption. The vision calls for readers to disengage from the debased economic practices that ultimately lead to the city's own demise.

6. Armageddon

This is the place where kings gather for war against God (16:16). The battle leads to the defeat of the beast and false prophet (19:11-21). "Armageddon" is probably based on words meaning "mountain of Megiddo." MEGIDDO was a place of defeat for God's adversaries (Judg 5:19; 2 Chr 35:20-22). The place suggested the grief that would occur at God's final victory over the nations (Zech 12:11). The name does not give the geographical location of the conflict but underscores that it means triumph for God. Christ comes as a mounted warrior, but does not use conventional military tactics (Rev 19:11). His one weapon is his word, pictured as a sword from his mouth (19:15). Those who accompany Christ are not said to fight. Armageddon is the victory that Christ wins through the power of his word (19:21). *See* ARMAGEDDON, OT AND NT.

7. Millennium

Satan is confined to the abyss for a MILLENNIUM or thousand years. During this time the saints rule with Christ (20:1-6). The martyrs are resurrected for life in this kingdom. Other faithful people also seem to be included, although the Greek is less clear about this. Revelation does not say where this kingdom is located. Some think it is on earth. Since the 2nd cent. CE, many have argued that this fulfills OT promises about an earthly paradise where the wolf and lamb will live peaceably (Isa 65:25). But this is not mentioned in Revelation. Others suggest that those enthroned in the millennial kingdom are in heaven since previous throne scenes were in heaven (e.g., Rev 4:4; 11:16). The problem is that the only reference to location is personal: the saints are "with Christ" and reign "with him" (20:4, 6). The assurance of a future with Christ is central to the vision.

Futuristic interpreters understand the millennial kingdom to be a period of time that will begin at a definite point in the future. But others do not think this vision fits easily into ordinary categories of time and space. If the door to the abyss cannot be located on a map (20:3), it is unlikely that the beginning of the millennium can be placed on a calendar (20:4). John's account of redemption is highly stylized. Satan, the beast, and the harlot are successively introduced and then defeated in reverse order (see §C4d). The story of redemption is also stylized, as the saints reign for a thousand years (20:4-6) and then forever in the new Jerusalem (22:5). The emphasis is theological rather than chronological. The future of the faithful centers on life with God and the Lamb (*see* SAINT).

F. Revelation's Place in the Scriptures

1. Use of the Old Testament

The OT is used throughout Revelation. John's commission to write his book is reminiscent of Daniel's encounter with a heavenly being (Rev 1:9-20; see Dan 10:2-14) and Ezekiel's call story (Rev 10:8-11; see Ezek 2:8–3:3). This tacitly places John in the company of Israel's prophets. His reports of visions also draw on the prophets: e.g., the heavenly throne room in Rev 4 recalls Ezek 1 and Isa 6, the beast in Rev 13 has the features of the monsters in Dan 7, and the new Jerusalem in Rev 21–22 resembles the city of Ezek 40–45. John's words sometimes blend multiple OT passages as in Rev 1:7, which combines the Son of Man's coming on the clouds from Dan 7:13 with the grief of the tribes from Zech 12:10.

John does not cite the OT using a formula like "it is written." He never quotes it exactly according to any known Hebrew or Greek version. Some think John worked directly with a Hebrew text of the OT, while others think he might have known a Greek translation. The most frequent allusions are to Daniel, Isaiah, Ezekiel, and Psalms, although there are also connections to many other books. Sometimes the older biblical language helps disclose the nature of sin and evil, as in the critique of Babylon's greed and brutality (Rev 18; compare Isa 13; 21; 47; Jer 50–51; Ezek 26–28). Imagery from the plagues in Egypt (Rev 16:1-21; compare Exod 7:14–12:32) and the coming day of the Lord convey the character of divine judgment (Rev 6:12-17; compare Isa 13:10; Joel 2:30-31; Zeph 1:15), while the prophetic oracles of salvation help to show Christian hope (Rev 21:1-6; compare Isa 25:7-8; 65:17-18).

Theologically, Revelation's constant reliance on the OT assumes that God will be faithful to the promises of salvation and the warnings of judgment against evil that were spoken by Israel's prophets. At the same time, Revelation does not have a mechanistic notion of promise and fulfillment. The absence of verbatim quotations and the preference for paraphrase and allusion recognize that God has freedom in the way he will keep his word. The OT promises concerning the messianic Lion are kept—but in the unexpected form of a crucified Lamb (Rev 5:5-6; compare Gen 49:9-10).

2. Relationship to other New Testament writings

Revelation and John's Gospel and epistles have traditionally been ascribed to the apostle John (see §A1). There are some similarities in content. The Gospel and Revelation depict Jesus as the Word (John 1:1; Rev 19:13), the lamb (John 1:29; Rev 5:6), and a shepherd (John 10:11; Rev 7:17). Images of light and living water are used (John 4:10; 8:12; Rev 21:23; 22:1). Jesus and his followers are said to "conquer" by faithfulness (John 16:33; 1 John 5:4; Rev 5:5; 12:11).

Nevertheless, the differences in style and content make it almost certain that these writings were composed by different people. The Gospel does not name its author but traces its origin to the anonymous Beloved Disciple, who was with Jesus at the Last Supper (John 21:20-24). In contrast, Revelation names its author as John, yet never claims that he was one of Jesus' early disciples (Rev 1:1). The Gospel is written in clear and accurate Greek, whereas the Greek of Revelation is idiosyncratic. Similarities in imagery can best be ascribed to a common reliance on the OT. For example, the Gospel relates seeing the one who is pierced to the crucifixion, while Revelation applies it to the second coming (John 19:37; Rev 1:7; compare Zech 12:10).

Revelation has some elements in common with other NT writings. These include the image of the community of faith as a temple (Rev 3:12; compare 1 Cor 3:16; Eph 2:19-21), the warning that Jesus will come like a thief (Rev 3:3; 16:15; compare Matt 24:42-44; Luke 12:39-40; 1 Thess 5:2), and the call for the one with ears to listen (Rev 2:7, 11; compare Matt 11:15; Mark 4:23). The woes that appear when the seven seals are opened bear some resemblance to the tribulations depicted in the Synoptic Gospels (Rev 6:1-17; compare Matt 24:3-44; Mark 13:3-31). It is not clear that John had read any of the Gospels or Paul's letters, but he seems to have been familiar with some of the same traditions.

3. History of canonization

Revelation's inclusion in the Christian canon is related to its history of interpretation. The book was widely accepted by Christians in the mid- to late 2nd cent. CE. It was used by Justin Martyr, who lived in Ephesus and later in Rome (*Dial.* 81.4). In western Syria it was attested by Theophilus of Antioch and in Asia Minor by Melito of Sardis (Eusebius, *Hist. eccl.* 4.24, 26). In Egypt it was used by Clement of Alexandria (*Strom.* 6.106). In the West, it was often cited by Irenaeus, a bishop in Gaul, who understood that its teaching about the millennium affirmed a future for creation and justice for the faithful who suffered (*Haer.* 5.28–33). Tertullian of Carthage in North Africa valued its moral exhortations against sin (*Pud.* 19). The apostle John was understood to be its author. A challenge to Revelation came from Marcion, who disliked its Jewish character. Another came from opponents of the Montanists, a group that emphasized the prophetic spirit and had a sensuous view of the millennium. Critics tried to discredit Revelation by ascribing it to the heretic Cerinthus.

John's Apocalypse remained popular in the early 3rd cent. CE. Hippolytus of Rome drew heavily on it in his writing of his treatise *On Antichrist.* Revelation was also cited by Cyprian of Carthage (*Eleem.* 8.14), Origen of Alexandria (*Comm. Jo.* 2.42–63), and others, who valued its emphasis on faith and moral life. Some in Egypt thought that Revelation envisioned a millennial kingdom devoted to physical enjoyment. Responding to the theological issue, Dionysius of Alexandria distanced Revelation from the Gospel of John. On stylistic and theological grounds Dionysius insisted that Revelation must have been written by a different author (Eusebius, *Hist. eccl.* 7.52.1–27). Since he assumed that the Gospel was penned by the apostle, this meant that Revelation did not have apostolic authorship, and this diminished its status in the East.

In the 4th and 5th cent., Revelation continued to be widely accepted in the West. Victorinus of Pettau in central Europe wrote *On the Apocalypse*, the earliest extant commentary on it, noting that its visions repeated similar threats of plagues as it looked for God's final victory over evil. Tyconius, a Donatist writer, composed a commentary on the Apocalypse that is no longer extant but held that Revelation rightly pictured the present time of the church, which exists in a conflicted and imperfect world (Gennadius, *Of Famous Men* 18). His approach was adopted by Augustine, who used Revelation for his work *The City of God.* Jerome noted doubts about the book (*Epist.* 129.3), but he reissued Victorinus' commentary in edited form, emphasizing the book's moral aspects.

Eastern churches in this period were divided in their attitudes toward Revelation. After Dionysius' critique of apostolic authorship, many expressed doubts about the book's authority. Eusebius was not sure whether it was to be placed among the accepted or the rejected books (*Hist. eccl.* 3.25.2–4). Revelation was not included in the list of the Council of Laodicea (ca. 360) or cited by John Chrysostom, Theodore of Mopsuestia, or Theodoret. The early Syriac Peshitta translation of the NT did not include it. Nevertheless, it was used by Methodius in *The Symposium* and was listed as authoritative by Athanasius of Alexandria in his Easter letter of 367. Beginning with Oecumenius who wrote *Commentary on the Apocalypse* in the 6th cent. CE, Greek commentaries were written on the Apocalypse, usually focusing on its theological and moral dimensions. By the 12th cent. CE it was accepted in the Armenian Church (*see* CANON OF THE NEW TESTAMENT).

G. Hermeneutical Approaches

A basic interpretive question concerns the relationship of the visionary world to the ordinary world of time and space. Everyone recognizes that Revelation uses at least some symbolic language. The question is how the imagery relates to the world in which people live.

1. Futuristic interpretation

Popular futuristic interpretation assumes that prophecy is history written in advance. First, this means that Revelation's visions are to be taken literally. When John tells of fire falling from heaven, he is predicting that someday actual fire will fall from the sky. In practice, the literalism is selective. Futuristic interpreters regularly note that the four horsemen are not actual horsemen but symbols of coming conflicts (6:1-8). The beast is to be an actual evil figure but will not have seven physical heads (13:1). Second, the visions are said to predict specific events in a chronological sequence. For example, the four horsemen signify successive disasters, the sixth seal brings an earthquake, then 144,000 Jewish Christians are sealed, etc. (6:1–7:8). In practice this also is done selectively. Scenes that fit awkwardly at one point are thought to anticipate events that occur at some other time.

The futuristic approach often assumes that modern interpreters can understand Revelation better than its early readers, since they live closer to the end of the age. Some approaches also insert episodes from other books into Revelation in order to create a complete scenario of the end. For example, Paul's comment about the saints being caught up to meet the Lord in the air (1 Thess 4:17)—something often called the rapture—is inserted at Rev 4:1. This means that subsequent threats affect only those who were not previously Christians. The result is that Revelation's call for perseverance seems less relevant for those who do not expect to face the kinds of conflicts depicted in the book.

2. Historical and social interpretation

Historical interpretation, in contrast, presupposes that Revelation addressed the context for which it was written. The assumption is that the book was designed to shape the viewpoints of readers in the seven churches. Modern readers must ask how its earliest audience would have understood it, which disciplines interpretation. Some kinds of historical interpretation try to link Revelation to specific events, like the fall of Jerusalem. Other forms explore connections with broader social patterns. Revelation is understood in light of the worship practices, commercial networks, and leadership structures that were typical in Asia Minor in the late 1st cent. CE. This approach envisions the context in terms of a period rather than a specific date.

Some forms of historical inquiry make rather direct connections between Revelation's imagery and 1st-cent. CE life. Accordingly, the beast represents Rome and its emperor, and the worship of the beast is the imperial cult. Problems can arise, however, when interpreters assume that the visions directly mirror the context in which John wrote. For example, it is not clear that receiving the mark of the beast corresponded to any specific practice that was known to the readers (13:16-17). Interpreters must recognize that some elements correspond to 1st-cent. CE realities while others shape the readers' perspectives by using images of a different order.

Historical interpreters make connections with modern concerns by analogy. Readers in Western Europe and North America may not face issues of eating food sacrificed to idols (2:14, 20), but they may be pressured to compromise their convictions in other ways. The imperial cult is not practiced now as it was in antiquity, but modern readers may face other forms of political and economic imperialism. Discerning analogies between ancient and modern contexts allows the book to continue shaping the perspectives of its readers.

3. Theological interpretation

Modern theological interpretation is often informed by a historical reading of the text. Theological questions, however, give special emphasis to aspects of the book that transcend the immediate historical context. The assumption is that there is continuity in God, Christ, and human beings. Historical interpreters look for analogies between the problems people faced in antiquity and those faced by people today. Theological interpreters ask what the visions reveal about the abiding reality of sin. From a historical perspective, one sees the imperial cult in the worship of the beast. From a theological perspective one sees the human propensity to absolutize their own power.

Literary aspects of the visions help disclose broader theological perspectives. The beast and harlot exhibit the traits of empires that existed long before John's time (see §§E3, 5). The problem he addresses is not only Rome but the powers of evil that lie beneath it. Difficulties arise, however, when Revelation's visions too quickly become timeless truths. General statements about God and the world lack the polemical edge that characterizes John's book. He saw the forces of evil that had been at work long before his time taking particular forms in his context. His message was not limited to informing readers about broad issues. It called for resistance and faithfulness in the world in which they lived. Contextually informed theological reading does the same.

Bibliography: David E. Aune. *Revelation.* WBC 52A (1997); David E. Aune. *Revelation.* WBC 52B (1998); David Barr. *Tales of the End* (1998); Richard Bauckham. *The Climax of Prophecy* (1993); Richard Bauckham. *The Theology of the Book of Revelation* (1993); G. K. Beale. *The Book of Revelation.* NIGCT (1999); M. Eugene Boring. *Revelation.* IBC (1989); Adela Yarbro Collins. *Crisis and Catharsis* (1984); John J. Collins. *Apocalyptic Imagination* (1998); Steven Friesen. *Imperial Cults and the Apocalypse of John* (2001); Craig R. Koester. *Revelation and the End of All Things* (2001); J. Nelson Kraybill. *Imperial Cult and Commerce in John's Apocalypse* (1996); Harry O. Maier. *Apocalypse Recalled* (2002); Frederick J. Murphy. *Fallen Is Babylon* (1998); Grant R. Osborne. *Revelation.* Baker Exegetical Commentary on the New Testament (2002); Mitchell G. Reddish. *Revelation.* Smyth and Helwys Bible Commentary (2001); Barbara R. Rossing. *The Choice between Two Cities* (1999); Elisabeth Schüssler Fiorenza. *The Book of Revelation: Justice and Judgement* (1985); Thomas B. Slater. *Christ and Community* (1999); Stephen S. Smalley. *The Revelation to John: A Commentary on the Greek Text of the Apocalypse* (2005); Leonard L. Thompson. *The Book of Revelation: Apocalypse and Empire* (1990); Arthur W. Wainwright. *Mysterious Apocalypse* (1993).

CRAIG R. KOESTER

REVENGE. *See* AVENGE; AVENGER OF BLOOD; VENGEANCE.

REVERENCE [יָרֵא yare'; εὐλάβεια eulabeia, φόβος phobos]. A deep, abiding, and profound sense of respect, awe, and humility in the presence of the one reverenced. The OT uses the word group yare' (323 times), which is generally translated "revere." Yare' means "to fear, be afraid of," but came to refer to the cause of fear or awe and then to the proper attitude or disposition of the one holding the other in reverence. When one holds another in reverence, one is respectful and obedient to that other, so that in the OT reverence does not refer so much to an emotion as it does an action or a behavior. In the NT, eulabeia, often translated "reverence," means "good service" and hence a reverential attitude or disposition. In its verbal form, the Greek word group means "to be afraid, concerned," while the noun forms mean "reverence, respect." In Greek, the word properly equivalent to the English "FEAR" is phobos: "There is no fear [phobos] in love, but perfect love casts out fear; for fear has to do with punishment, and whoever fears has not reached perfection in love" (1 John 4:18). Phobos is sometimes translated "reverence" (e.g., Eph 5:21; 1 Pet 3:2, 16). See 2 Kgs 4:1; Job 28:28; Prov 24:21; Jer 2:19; 26:19; Heb 5:7; 12:28; Rev 15:4.

JAMES E. WEST

REVILE. *See* SCOFFER.

REVOLT. *See* BAR KOCHBA, SIMON; JERUSALEM; JEWISH WARS; MACCABEES, MACCABEAN REVOLT; REBEL, REBELLION; ZEALOT.

REWARD [גְּמוּלָה gemulah, גָּמַל gamal, עֵקֶב ʿeqev, פְּעֻלָּה peʿullah, שָׂכָר sakhar, שָׁלֵם shalam; μισθός misthos]. That actions have consequences is axiomatic in modern thought. The further conviction of the biblical materials is that the God of the covenant is integrally involved—actively or passively, directly or indirectly—in bringing about such consequences. Thus, a schema in which actions are "rewarded" with befitting outcomes serves as a presupposition of nearly all biblical narrative and discourse. God sees, knows, and requites with justice: the righteous with blessing and the wicked with just recompense. Yet not all of the biblical corpora bear witness to this premise in the same way or without qualification, or, indeed, without some disquiet in the face of human experience that appears to contradict the thesis. It will be necessary then, following a survey of the vocabulary of reward, to observe the diversity of the biblical witness to this central motif.

A. Vocabulary of Reward

The notion of reward is presupposed or appealed to throughout the whole of biblical literature and is by no means limited to use of the English word itself. Although the NRSV has forty-three occurrences of *reward* (in all its forms) in the OT and twenty-six in the NT (with another twenty-five in the deuterocanonical books), this hardly begins to hint at the ubiquity of the idea in the biblical canon, however variously articulated. Nonetheless, it will be useful to offer a preliminary sketch of the relevant vocabulary. The NRSV translates nearly a dozen different Hebrew (and Aramaic) words or expressions as "reward," among which the following are the most common: 1) **sakhar**, "wages, payment, reward" (Gen 15:1; 2 Chr 15:7; Ps 127:3; Prov 11:18; Eccl 4:9; 9:5; Isa 40:10; 62:11; Jer 31:16); 2) **shalam**, "to repay, reward, requite" (1 Sam 24:19 [Heb. 24:20]; Prov 13:13, 21; 25:22); 3) **gamal**, "to deal with (bountifully)" (Ps 18:20 [Heb. 18:21]; 2 Sam 22:21); 4) **gemulah**, "reprise, reward" (2 Sam 19:36 [Heb. 19:37]; Ps 28:4; compare Jer 51:56); 5) **peʿullah**, "recompense, reward" (Ps 109:20; Isa 49:4; compare Isa 40:10); 6) **ʿeqev**, "end, result, wages" (Ps 19:11 [Heb. 19:12]; Prov 22:4). It is important to note that in none of these cases is "reward" the only, nor necessarily even the most common, meaning of the term; rather, context suggests or requires the translation "reward." The notion of reward is not semantically tied to a limited and specialized vocabulary in the OT.

The situation is somewhat different with the NT, where "reward" is characteristically a translation of **misthos**, "wages, reward" (compare cognates **misthapodosia** [μισθαποδοσία], Heb 10:35; 11:26; and **misthapodotēs** [μισθαποδότης], Heb 11:6) when the context is ethical or religious (e.g., Matt 5:12; 6:1; Mark 9:41; Luke 6:35; 1 Cor 3:14; Rev 22:12) rather than commercial, where the translation "wage" is more fitting (e.g., Matt 20:8; Rom 4:4; 1 Cor 3:8; 1 Tim 5:18; Jas 5:4). Thus, with just a few exceptions (**apodidōmi** [ἀποδίδωμι], "repay," Matt 6:4, 6, 18; **antapodosis** [ἀνταπόδοσις], "recompense," Col 3:24; compare **brabeion** [βραβεῖον], "prize," 1 Cor 9:24; Phil 3:14; **stephanos** [στέφανος], **stephanoō** [στεφανόω], "crown, prize," 1 Cor 9:25; 2 Tim 4:8; Rev 2:10; etc.), the NT vocabulary of "reward" is largely the translation of words with **misth-** roots. But here again, the concept is not exhausted in a bounded set of terminology.

With regard to both the OT and NT, it should be noted that whereas the English word *reward* connotes consequences that are positive and even gratuitous, the biblical vocabulary is more characteristically neutral in itself. Once again, the context determines the particular nuance, and most of the terms surveyed above might just as well refer to a negative recompense in another context (e.g., 2 Macc 8:33; Rev 22:12). It is necessary, then, to expand the inquiry from a narrow semantic focus to consider the function of the notion of reward or requital in the theologies of the biblical writings.

B. Reward in the Old Testament

The default picture in which good and evil, obedience and disobedience, are requited by God is especially characteristic of the primary OT narrative spanning Joshua to 2 Kings and introduced by Deuteronomy (the so-called DEUTERONOMISTIC HISTORY). Here God rewards Israel for covenantal faithfulness and punishes disobedience, so that blessing and bounty, political and military success, are the promised outcomes for God's people among the nations should Israel keep covenant; but hardship, exile, and destruction are the consequence of unfaithfulness, not least for turning to other gods. Moses expounds this thesis at considerable length in the programmatic statements of Deuteronomy (e.g., 11:8-32; 28:1–32:52) and it becomes the undergirding thesis controlling the narration of Israel's story. In this way the Deuteronomistic narrative functions both to explain Israel's plight and to enjoin faithfulness to the covenant.

As such, the primary OT narrative only rarely hints at the more complex picture found elsewhere in the OT, and one could be (mis)led by these texts, if read in isolation from the rest, toward a mechanistic conception of temporal recompense. It is also important to note that the promises are characteristically corporate or national in scope and covenantal in context. It is particularly the obedience and fortunes of the people as a people, rather than as individuals, that is at issue, even if at times an individual stands as a representative of the whole. These narratives do not then have as a first interest the destiny of individuals nor a concern regarding their just treatment as individuals (contrast Ezek 18) but rather the need to interpret the history of God's people as a hortatory narrative.

If the DtrH offers the thesis of action and fitting consequence, a similar outlook is reinforced from different perspectives in other OT literatures. The prophets' frequent calls to repentance are predicated on the premise that the current or impending misfortune is the result of covenant unfaithfulness and that a turn from disobedience will lead to an outpouring of blessing and reversal of fortune (Isa 1:18-20; Jer 4:1-2; 31:16; 32:16-25; Zech 6:15). Whether viewed prospectively or retrospectively, the exile in particular is viewed as the direct consequence of such unfaithfulness, but the reward of restoration and vindication awaits the faithful when the God of Israel intervenes on behalf of the people. The Chronicler shares this general vision of reward and punishment, though it has been argued that here JUDGMENT is more immediate and individual than with the parallels of 1 Samuel–2 Kings.

With wisdom literature and the psalter, however, more diverse and pensive voices emerge, reflecting especially upon the fate and responsibilities of the individual. If the Deuteronomist requires and assumes divine intervention as a means of reward or judgment, proverbial wisdom characteristically presumes a more integral relation between deed and consequence, as much a matter of natural consequence as specific divine intervention. Proverbs frequently appeals to this "deed–consequence nexus" in which reward or calamity follows, respectively, as a matter of course from prudent or foolish actions. Actions bear consequences, but of a predictable sort; God's recompense takes the form of a reaping commensurate with the sowing (e.g., Prov 11:18; 12:24; 16:22; 20:4; 22:8).

While presupposing the basic picture of divine provident justice (e.g., Ps 1:6), the remonstrations of certain psalms (e.g., Pss 10, 13, 44, 73), of Job, and of Ecclesiastes imply that a formulaic schema is too simplistic and human experience too anomalous to be accounted for in mechanistic terms. For, according to human observation, it seems that blessing and calamity fall upon the good and the evil with apparent indiscrimination. Though no single answer is proffered in these texts, they share in common a claim that what can be observed is not the totality of reality (e.g., Job 38:1–39:30; Pss 49:1-20 [Heb. 49:2-21]; 73:17-28), so God's faithful are not to judge hastily by appearances only. Thus, an appeal to eschatological hope becomes an increasingly viable reconciliation of the dilemma, whether in the form of salvation-historical resolution or even postmortem recompense.

C. Reward in Early Judaism

A thoroughgoing eschatological solution to the dilemma of temporal injustice comes to the fore with the deuterocanonical and pseudepigraphical literature, especially with the rise of the martyrological tradition and apocalypticism within the distressed Judaism of the Second Temple era. The injustices of this life, especially the suffering of the righteous at the hands of the unrighteous, will be fully requited in a life or world to come. With this appeal to the eschatological horizon, the whole notion of reward and requital takes a decisive turn that is reflected in the Second Temple and later Tannaitic literatures (*see* TANNA, TANNAIM). This is not at all to say that temporal judgment is set aside altogether, only that individual (not to say individualistic) eschatology becomes a primary domain of reflection and quite frequently the explicit basis of motivation for the righteous and faithful life (e.g., 2 Esd 2:34-37; 7:33-36; 2 Macc 12:41-45; 4 Macc 10:13–11:6; 18:1-24; Sir 11:26; ; 36:1-22; Wis 5:15-16; *1 En.* 104:1-13; *Pss. Sol.* 3:11-12; 9:5; compare 1QS IV, 7–13).

The degree to which a "reward theology" defines the soteriology of early Judaism remains a matter of ongoing dispute. E. P. Sanders has set the terms of the debate with his massive and influential argument that the role of **torah** [תּוֹרָה] obedience was by no means that of meriting salvation but, rather, that Judaism gave priority to the divine initiative of election in making covenant with God's people. It is this, rather than human effort or an amassing of good deeds, by which the faithful Jew found standing in the covenant. Thus, as Sanders would put it, early Judaism could be characterized as "covenantal nomism": Jewish allegiance to the law (i.e., "nomism" from **nomos** [νόμος]; "law") is not a mechanical striving to be ethical but a relationally motivated faithfulness to the electing God of the covenant. An important corrective to distorted construals of ancient Judaism, Sanders' construct of covenantal nomism has won widespread assent within NT scholarship. Still, not a few have queried whether, in defining Judaism in terms of covenantal nomism, Sanders has been fair to all of the evidence or allowed for enough variety in the *de facto* soteriologies of various Judaisms. While there can be no question that a theology of reward is amply attested in early Judaism, the question of how that theology functioned in the larger worldview and to what extent the various NT writings are continuous or discontinuous with their Jewish counterparts continues to occupy scholars of early Judaism and the NT.

D. Reward in the New Testament

It would be a mistake to assume that reward theology is to be found only within early Judaism, as if nascent Christianity moved in a completely different direction. The notion of eschatological reward is found throughout the NT writings. To be sure, the centrality of the crucifixion and resurrection of Jesus as saving events along with the emphasis on justification by faith (at least in Paul, though compare the Johannine tradition) naturally mutes a thoroughgoing emphasis on reward for obedience, but by no means is it absent from the NT.

The language and concept of reward figures prominently in the teaching of Jesus as it is presented in the canonical Gospels, and in this respect, he stands broadly in the tradition of contemporary Judaism. On the other hand, Jesus' use of the motif is directed rhetorically toward reconfiguring and subverting prevailing assumptions, so that the reward motif is subordinated to a proclamation of a kingdom characteristically defined in terms of its eschatological reversal of fortune. Those well rewarded and highly esteemed in the present age are not necessarily so in the kingdom of God, and those who are poor, marginalized, and persecuted in this life enjoy consolation, vindication, and reward in the kingdom (e.g., Matt 5:3-12; Mark 10:28-31; Luke

6:20-35; 12:13-21; 14:16-24; 16:19-31). Moreover, Jesus likewise asserts that those who are presumed, or who presume themselves, to be righteous are in peril, while the repentant unrighteous have found favor with God. Particularly in the parables, Jesus provocatively reconfigures reward as a matter of grace toward the undeserving and unexpected rather than an obligation owed to the righteous (e.g., Matt 20:1-16; 21:28-32; Luke 8:9-15; 15:11-32). The reward motif also well serves Jesus' insistence that religious piety must only be the expression of sincere motives. That which is calculated to win human acclamation goes unrewarded by "your Father in heaven"; for such people, fleeting human approval exhausts all the reward there will be (Matt 6:1-18). Although a theology of reward is found in some measure in all of the Gospels, Matthew especially emphasizes the theme and grants it the strongest soteriological emphasis (Matt 5:12, 46; 6:1-2, 4-6, 16, 18; 7:24-27; 10:41-42; 25:31-46).

In general terms, Paul too reflects the Jewish tradition in which eschatological reward is related to human deeds (e.g., Rom 2:6-16; 1 Cor 3:8, 14; 9:17-18, 24-25; 2 Cor 5:10; Eph 6:8; Phil 3:14). Here, however, one finds a difficult to resolve tension between his insistence that justification is a matter of faith apart from works or "works of the law" (e.g., Rom 4:1-12; 9:11, 32; Gal 2:16; compare Eph 2:8-9; 2 Tim 1:9; Titus 3:5) and the claim that humans are judged according to their works (e.g., Rom 2:6-11; 1 Cor 3:5-17; 2 Cor 5:10; 11:15; Col 3:23-25). Various syntheses have been offered, yet none is without its difficulties, nor has any commanded the assent of a majority of Pauline scholars. It must be held at least possible that Paul's thought on the matter is not systematic enough to be satisfactorily synthesized. The diversity of outlook can be attributed to the variety of Paul's rhetorical situations so that the two strands of thought are not ultimately reconcilable. While this might rightly be judged a council of despair, the unsystematic character of Paul's extant writings at least cautions against a too-facile solution.

It has often been suggested or assumed that reward is essentially a different category than salvation and has to do not with inclusion into the sphere of eschatological redemption but with varying degrees of blessing within it. The fact that certain of the key texts (esp. Rom 2:6-16; 2 Cor 5:10; and perhaps 1 Cor 9:24-27) seem to speak of eternal destiny rather than mere enjoyment of reward or a differentiation among the redeemed is problematic for this proposal. Others propose that while there is truly a judgment according to deeds, its outcome can only be negative. Accordingly, those outside of Christ are judged and invariably found wanting, while those in Christ are likewise judged according to works, but now according to the surrogate obedience of Christ with whom they are united in baptism. In this case, one must infer that Rom 2:6-16 can only be speaking hypothetically (or of Gentile Christians) when it promises eternal life according to works for those seeking glory, honor, and immortality. Finally, it could be argued that while those in Christ are truly judged according to works, human actions are essentially evidential in character, revealing a genuineness of faith by means of concrete acts of obedience. Although Paul will disavow "works" as grounds for justification, especially works regarded as meritorious (e.g., Rom 4:1-5), he is equally insistent that obedience to God follows invariably from faith for those in union with Christ. This suggestion gains greater plausibility when it is noted that precisely in those letters where Paul makes his most strenuous arguments for justification by faith apart from works—Galatians and Romans—we find equal insistence that obedience and transformation follow justification as a matter of course (e.g., "obedience of faith," Rom 1:5; 16:26; compare Rom 6:21-23; 8:4, 12-13; 15:18; "the fruit of the Spirit," Gal 5:22-23; compare Eph 2:8-10; Titus 2:11-14).

In both the Pauline corpus and the remaining texts of the NT, the promise of eschatological judgment and reward plays an important hortatory role as motivation for steadfastness in the face of trial or hostility (1 Thess 2:14-16; 2 Thess 1:6-12; Heb 10:32-36; 11:26; Jas 5:7-11; 1 Pet 3:9-12; 2 John 8; Rev 11:18; 22:12). God's recompense toward those hostile to the Christian movement and the corresponding vindication of the faithful become not only the incentive for perseverance but also ground a stance of nonretaliation that cedes the prerogative of judgment to the justice of God.

It is sometimes objected that the NT's overall theology of reward raises a conundrum with respect to ethics: Does not the promise of reward when used as a motivation for moral actions subvert nobler motives, essentially removing the conditions of altruism? This would perhaps be true if eschatological reward were the only motive to which the authors appealed, but, as it is, an appeal to reward is but one of many ways in which the NT texts commend a just and moral life. When, however, the notion of reward is placed within the context of correlative motivations—the love for God and neighbor, the self-giving example of Jesus as crucified Messiah, gratitude for the mercy of God, and the expression of the fruit of the indwelling Spirit—the reward motif is more properly understood as a metaphorical network with a compelling rhetorical function. That which God rewards is that which is of ultimate, rather than merely transitory, value. The language of reward, drawing upon its Jewish precedent, is thus a means of valuation, of reconfiguring the world according to a vision of the reign of God. As such, reward language is not only sometimes apocalyptic in form but also always so in function, that is, revelatory (**apokalypsis** ἀποκάλυψις) of the divine will that seeks to reorder human affections, aspirations, and actions according to the mission of God.

Bibliography: D. A. Carson et al., eds. *Justification and Variegated Nomism.* Vol. 1: *The Complexities of Second Temple Judaism* (2001); Simon J. Gathercole.

Where Is Boasting? Early Jewish Soteriology and Paul's Response in Romans 1–5 (2002); Jože Krašovec. *Reward, Punishment, and Forgiveness: The Thinking and Beliefs of Ancient Israel in the Light of Greek and Modern Views* (1999); Patrick D. Miller Jr. *Sin and Judgment in the Prophets: A Stylistic and Theological Analysis* (1982); E. P. Sanders. *Paul and Palestinian Judaism: A Comparison of Patterns of Religion* (1977); Kent T. Yinger. *Paul, Judaism, and Judgment according to Deeds* (1999).

GARWOOD P. ANDERSON

REZEPH ree´zif [רֶצֶף retsef]. A Mesopotamian city located between Palmyra and the Euphrates. The city was probably conquered and absorbed into the Assyrian empire in the 9th cent. BCE; it is listed as a provincial capital in Assyrian records. When the Assyrian official RABSHAKEH stood outside the walls of Jerusalem and tried to intimidate King Hezekiah into surrendering, he cited Rezeph as one of eight cities that had been unable to withstand the might of the Assyrian army (2 Kgs 19:12-13; par. Isa 37:11-12). Rabshakeh implied that the gods of those cities had been unable, or unwilling, to rescue them. Rabshakeh also claimed that Yahweh sent the Assyrian army to punish the Israelites (2 Kgs 18:22, 25; par. Isa 36:7, 10). Rabshakeh's speech is an example of the propagandistic techniques that Assyria used to maintain control of its empire.

Bibliography: A. Kirk Grayson. "Assyrian Militarism." *CANE* 2:959–68.

BRUCE W. GENTRY

REZIN ree´zin [רְצִין retsin]. 1. The Aramean leader of the anti-Assyrian coalition consisting of Damascus, Tyre, Philistia, Israel, and perhaps Edom. Rezin may have usurped the throne, since he was not from Damascus according to Assyrian records; the year in which he took the throne is unknown. Rezin paid tribute to the Assyrian king TIGLATH-PILESER III in 738 BCE, but by 735 he had rebelled and organized the coalition. When King Ahaz of Judah refused to join, Rezin and his ally PEKAH of Israel attacked Jerusalem in an effort to depose AHAZ and install a "son of Tabeel" (Isa 7:6) who would support the coalition. This conflict is often called the Syro-Ephraimite War (2 Kgs 16:5-9; compare Isa 7–8). Rezin's attempt to take Jerusalem and depose Ahaz failed (Isa 7:1-10). According to 2 Kgs 16:7-8, Ahaz asked for Tiglath-pileser's assistance during the siege of Jerusalem. Many scholars, however, think the Assyrian king had already planned on quashing Rezin's coalition. Indeed, after subduing Phoenicia and Philistia in 734, Tiglath-pileser crushed the Syro-Ephraimite alliance in 733–732. The attack on Aram and its allies is mentioned briefly in the annals of Tiglath-pileser. The OT reports simply that the king of Assyria defeated Damascus, exiled its people to KIR, and killed Rezin (2 Kgs 16:9). Aram ceased to be an independent state; thus, Rezin was its last king before it was incorporated into the Assyrian Empire. (The statement in 2 Kgs 16:6 that Rezin conquered Elath is typically understood as a scribal error in which the name Edom has been mistakenly changed to Aram—the two words are extremely similar in Hebrew.) *See* ARAM, ARAMEAN.

2. The name of one of the families of temple servants who returned from Babylonian exile (Ezra 2:48; Neh 7:50).

MARK RONCACE

REZON ree´zuhn [רְזוֹן rezon]. An Aramean king. Rezon son of Eliada served under HADADEZER, king of Zobah, but abandoned his master, probably when Hadadezer was defeated by David (2 Sam 8:3-8). Rezon became the leader of a group of outlaws, with whose aid he became king of Damascus. Some scholars identify Rezon with Hezion, the grandfather of Ben-Hadad I (1 Kgs 15:18) and the founder of a dynasty of powerful Aramean kings. According to the DtrH's theological reading of Israelite history, God used Rezon to punish SOLOMON for his unfaithfulness (1 Kgs 11:23-25).

CLAUDE MARIOTTINI

RHEGIUM ree´jee-uhm [Ῥήγιον Rhēgion]. The city is mentioned in Acts 28:13 as a stopping point on Paul's journey to Rome. Located on the tip of the Italian peninsula in Calabria, the modern city is known as Reggio di Calabria. The city sits at the southern base of the Aspromonte ("sour mountains") in an area known as Magna Graecia, across the Strait of Messina opposite Sicily.

According to Strabo (*Geogr.* 6.258), the area was originally settled in the 8th cent. BCE as a Greek colony of Chalcis (Khalkis on the island of Euboea, Greece). With its strategic location on an important sea route, Rhegium became a significant commercial and cultural port for much of its early history. The high point was in the 5th cent. BCE when Pythagoras of Rhegium became famous for his innovative sculpture. Its location also attracted many foreign and regional invaders, as well as natural disasters. The city was destroyed by Dionysius I, tyrant of Syracuse, in 387 BCE. Diodorus Siculus, the 1st-cent. BCE Greek historian, reports that the inhabi-tants of Rhegium were sold into slavery (*Bib. Hist.* 14.106–8, 111–12). During the Punic Wars, the city was an ally of Rome. Roman army veterans settled in the city in the 1st cent. CE, at which time it was named Rhegium Julium.

In the narrative of Acts, Paul is in the custody of a Roman cohort of Augustus on his way to Rome. Having departed from Caesarea (Acts 27:1), his ship traveled to Sidon, Cyprus, then Myra in Lycia, where the travelers boarded an Alexandrian ship to Italy by way of Crete. The ship ran aground at Malta after a storm, and the group of prisoners and guards eventually boarded another Alexandrian ship "with the Twin Brothers as its figurehead" (Castor and Pollux, gods of the sea; Acts 28:11), and sailed to Syracuse, Rhegium, Puteoli, and finally Rome.

MILTON MORELAND

RHESA ree´suh [Ῥησά Rhēsa]. In Luke's genealogy (3:27) Rhesa is the son of ZERUBBABEL, postexilic governor of Judah (Ezra 3:2; Hag 1:1), but ABIUD appears instead in Matthew's genealogy (Matt 1:13).

RHETORIC AND ORATORY. Rhetoric is the art of creating spoken and written discourse that informs and persuades an audience to think and take action as deemed appropriate by a speaker. Oratory is the art of effective public speaking.

The books of the OT exhibit a variety of literary genres, rhetorical techniques, and figures of speech and thought. These were shaped by the needs of an oral culture and were devised to help the hearers remember what was spoken. Thus figures of repetition, like PARALLELISM and CHIASM, are prominent. Also found in abundance are figures that aid memory like antithesis and contrast, metaphors and similes. Larger units of texts are structured by *inclusio*, catchwords, repeated topics, and climax. These techniques are obvious in the poetic literature, where the writer is conscious of artistry; wisdom literature, where the needs of learning and memorizing are central; and in prophetic literature, which needs to persuade an audience to conform to the stipulations of covenant. Although mainly predating the Hellenistic era in which rhetoric became highly conceptualized, the rhetoric of the OT has many similarities to Greco-Roman rhetoric due to the shared needs and parameters of human communication and oral and written culture.

According to tradition, Corax of Sicily initially conceptualized rhetorical theory (476 BCE) and his student, Tisias, introduced rhetoric to Greece. An ambassador from Sicily, Gorgias, introduced rhetoric to Athens (427 BCE) and founded a school of rhetoric there. The judicial and political needs of democratic society in Greece prompted the further systematization of rhetoric and its secure place in public life in the Greek city-state. The Sophists added rhetoric to the school curriculum. Isocrates, a student of Gorgias, founded a school (ca. 390 BCE) that combined the Sophists' rhetorical techniques with public oratory, and created a rhetorical approach to literature. His school became a model for secondary education in the Greco-Roman world.

The pragmatic approach to rhetoric as taught by the Sophists that emphasized winning a legal case versus moral truth was rejected by the philosophers. Socrates (469–399 BCE) and Plato (ca. 427–347 BCE) made a sharp distinction between dialectic, seeking the truth through question and answer, and rhetoric, seeking to persuade but not necessarily to obtain truth. Aristotle (384–322 BCE) tried to bridge the chasm between rhetors and philosophers, arguing that both dialectic and rhetoric concern knowledge—the former philosophical knowledge and the latter political knowledge.

The works of the first Roman rhetorician, Cato the Elder, indicate that the Romans borrowed Greek rhetoric in the late 3rd cent. BCE. As it did in Greece, rhetoric had judicial and political application, was the mainstay of secondary education, and strongly pervaded literary composition. In his writings, Cicero, the greatest Roman orator (1st cent. BCE), provided the most complete understanding of the theory of rhetoric and the practice of oratory in the Roman Republic. With the advent of the empire, Rome usurped Greece as the center of rhetorical study. However, the influence of rhetoric in politics declined with the accompanying dearth of debate in an imperial government. Rhetoric could still be found in public rhetorical exercises on various topics called declamations.

Ancient rhetoric classified rhetoric in three species: judicial, deliberative, and epideictic. The judicial species concerns accusation and defense and was used primarily in the law court. The deliberative species involves persuading and dissuading an audience of the expediency of a course of action, particularly in political contexts. The epideictic species concerns praise and blame and was used in speeches in public ceremony like festivals and funerals.

The practice of rhetoric was discussed under the five categories of invention, arrangement, style, memory, and delivery. Invention concerns creating arguments from ethos (moral character), pathos (emotion), and logos (inductive and deductive reasoning) to support or refute propositions. Arrangement involves ordering the parts of a speech and its proofs in a persuasive manner. Arrangement is more precisely defined for judicial rhetoric than for deliberative or epideictic and comprises six key elements: 1) an *exordium* or introduction that works to obtain the attention and good will of the audience; 2) a *narratio* that presents the background of the case at hand; 3) a *propositio* listing the propositions to be developed; 4) a *probatio* or the main body where the propositions of the rhetor's case receive supporting argumentation; 5) a *refutatio* that refutes the propositions of the opposing side; and 6) a *peroratio* or conclusion that summarizes the argumentation and appeals to the emotions of the audience so it will take the desired action. Style is the careful selection of words and figures of speech and thought to further support the argumentation of invention. Memory and delivery involve the practical steps for delivering a speech.

The NT was composed in the context of Hellenism. The texts of the NT were written to differing extents using the conventions of Greco-Roman rhetoric that permeated the Mediterranean basin in the 1st cent. CE. These conventions are found in schoolbook exercises (progymnasmata προγυμνάσματα), rhetorical handbooks by Aristotle (*Rhetorica*), Cicero (*De Oratore*,

De Inventione), and Quintilian (*Institutio Oratoria*) among others, and in extant rhetorical speeches and other works.

From apostolic times biblical interpreters have acknowledged the role of Greco-Roman rhetoric in the NT, but rhetoric's role in interpretation was uneven in subsequent interpretation. During the Reformation with its renewed academic study of Greek, the role of rhetoric in the NT was reaffirmed. German scholarship in the 19th cent. produced the first systematic works on biblical rhetoric, particularly analysis of genre and style. However, this work was truncated by the waning of rhetoric in education in the 20th cent., so much so that rhetoric's role in interpretation was conscripted to style only.

The rhetoric of the NT has been a renewed focus of interpretation since the mid-1970s. All of the books of the NT have been studied in light of Greco-Roman conventions of invention, arrangement, and style. It is a matter of debate if any NT authors received a formal education at the secondary level that included rhetoric and if any consciously used this skill in composing their works (*see* EDUCATON, NT). However, a wide range of rhetorical conventions appears in part or the whole of NT books. These can be attributed to anything from skill gained from daily public interchange all the way to formal rhetorical training.

In the NT, invention or creation of proofs relies heavily upon quotation of the OT, citation of authorities like eyewitness testimony, early Christian teaching, and traditional examples. These are often used as reasons supporting a proposition in the form: "This is true, because ...." The full or partial form of arrangement from *exordium* to *peroratio* characterizes many of the NT letters. Important figures of speech and thought support the argumentation. Antithesis, hyperbole, irony, metaphor, personification, and repetition are prominent.

Regarding the Gospels, the sayings of Jesus were orally transmitted and written down according to patterns found in the progymnasmata for the elaboration of a CHREIA. A chreia is a saying, account of an action, or both, attributed to an individual or group that is useful for daily living. Chreiai were commonly used in philosophy and biography and could be elaborated using rationales, contraries, analogies, examples, citation of authorities, exhortations, and conclusions. The basic units of the Synoptic Gospels are simple and elaborated chreiai of the words and deeds of Jesus and the Apostles. Mark 1:14-15 is a simple chreia: "Now after John was arrested, Jesus came to Galilee, proclaiming the good news of God, and saying, 'The time is fulfilled, and the kingdom of God has come near; repent, and believe in the good news.'" Mark 9:38-40 is an elaborated chreia.

Regarding the NT letters, all those of Paul exhibit rhetorical conventions of invention, arrangement, and style to some degree. The study of Galatians by Hanz Dieter Betz is classic study in this regard. He outlined Galatians as epistolary prescript (1:1-5), *exordium* (1:6-11), *narratio* (1:12–2:14), *propositio* (2:15-21), *probatio* (3:1–4:31), *exhortatio* (5:1–6:10), and epistolary postscript (6:11-18). While Betz identified the genre of the letter as judicial rhetoric in which Paul defends himself against accusations of opponents, it is currently understood as deliberative rhetoric in which Paul persuades the Galatians to adhere more firmly to his gospel and dissuade them from embracing an opposing one. Arguably, the most telling use of Greco-Roman rhetoric in the Pauline Epistles is found in 2 Cor 10–13, where Paul demonstrates a unique blend of irony and boasting that exhibits the finest principles of Greco-Roman oratory, especially those found in Plutarch's *On Praising Oneself Inoffensively.*

Bibliography: R. Dean Andersen Jr. *Ancient Rhetorical Theory and Paul.* Rev. ed. (1999); Hans Dieter Betz. *Galatians.* Hermeneia (1979); George Kennedy. *A New History of Classical Rhetoric* (1994); George Kennedy. *New Testament Interpretation through Rhetorical Criticism* (1984); Burton L. Mack. *Rhetoric and the New Testament* (1989); Burton L. Mack and Vernon K. Robbins. *Patterns of Persuasion in the Gospels* (1989); James J. Murphy and Richard A. Katula. *A Synoptic History of Classical Rhetoric.* 2nd ed. (1994); Duane F. Watson. "Paul and Boasting." *Paul in the Greco-Roman World: A Handbook.* J. Paul Sampley, ed. (2003) 77–100; Duane F. Watson. *Rhetorical Criticism of the New Testament: A Bibliographic Survey* (2006); Duane F. Watson and Alan J. Hauser. *Rhetorical Criticism of the Bible* (1994).

DUANE F. WATSON

RHETORICAL CRITICISM, NT. Rhetoric as the art of communication was central to education in the Greco-Roman world and probably exerted an influence on the formation of NT texts. It also shaped early and medieval NT biblical commentary, though it was eclipsed by the historical-critical method. Renewed attention to rhetoric began in the mid-20th cent. with the work of Amos Wilder and James Muilenburg and took two forms: as form-critical study and, paradoxically, as a literary alternative to historical-critical study. George Kennedy, Hans Dieter Betz, and others showed how classical rhetorical forms could be discerned in early Christian texts, while others highlighted rhetoric as a synchronic precursor to narrative analysis. Recently, socio-rhetorical interpretation has provided a programmatic approach to the literary, sociocultural, and ideological textures of NT texts by drawing additionally on 1) rhetoric as hermeneutics (Burke); 2) ideological and feminist criticism (Schüssler Fiorenza); 3) cultural anthropology; and most recently, 4) analysis of human cognition.

Bibliography: Hans Dieter Betz. *Galatians: A Commentary on Paul's Letter to the Churches in Galatia.* Hermeneia (1979); Kenneth Burke. *Counter-Statement*

(1931); James D. Hester and J. David Hester, eds. *Rhetorics and Hermeneutics: Wilhelm Wuellner and His Influence* (2004); George A. Kennedy. *New Testament Interpretation through Rhetorical Criticism* (1984); James Muilenburg. "Form Criticism and Beyond." *JBL* 88 (1969) 1–18; Vernon K. Robbins. *Exploring the Texture of Texts: A Guide to Socio-Rhetorical Interpretation* (1996); Elisabeth Schüssler Fiorenza. *Rhetoric and Ethic: The Politics of Biblical Studies* (1999); Amos N. Wilder. *Early Christian Rhetoric: The Language of the Gospel* (1971).

L. GREGORY BLOOMQUIST

RHETORICAL CRITICISM, OT. An approach to biblical texts that focuses on the way language is employed in the composition of a text for the purpose of persuading its audience. Grammatical particles, figures of speech (e.g. chiasmus, choice of metaphors and imagery, wordplay), and other stylistic features such as strings of rhetorical questions (notably in Job) and parallelism have a rhetorical impact on the hearer and reader. This also applies to the arrangement (not always chronological: 2 Sam 4:4), inner structure, and boundaries of literary units in the text. Key terms (e.g., "brother" in Gen 4) and key phrases are repeated through a text (e.g., refrains in poetry; prophetic formulas) selectively to influence and create an impression on the audience. Inverted quotations (e.g., Gen 27:29 and Num 24:9; Hag 1:10 and Zech 8:12) are a form of intended INTERTEXTUALITY. The full identity of a major character may be withheld so as to build up suspense: though he is introduced in 1 Sam 16:11, David's name is only mentioned in v. 13. Suspense is also achieved by means of the "three-and-four structure": three times Delilah tries Samson in vain; the fourth time she succeeds (Judg 16:4-21).

It is the combination of such features that makes a text unique, and not just a specimen of one literary form (from which it may have evolved). The rhetorical features of a text may give us some idea of the writer's (or the final redactor's) thought and intention.

Bibliography: Yairah Amit. *Reading Biblical Narratives: Literary Criticism and the Hebrew Bible* (2001); James Muilenburg. "Form Criticism and Beyond." *JBL* 88 (1969) 1–18; L. J. de Regt, Jan de Waard, and J. P. Fokkelman, eds. *Literary Structure and Rhetorical Strategies in the Hebrew Bible* (1996); Meir Sternberg. *The Poetics of Biblical Narrative: Ideological Literature and the Drama of Reading* (1985).

L. J. DE REGT

RHETORICAL QUESTION. A rhetorical question does not expect an answer but issues a command, offers a tentative statement, or evaluates a situation. Most famously, God's question to Adam in the garden, "Adam, where are you?" (Gen 3:9), is not asked to elicit information; it is a summons for Adam to appear. (See also Gen 4:6; Exod 5:22; Jer 8:14; Ezek 18:31; Matt 27:46; Acts 9:4.)

JAMES E. WEST

RHO [ρ Ρ r R]. The eighteenth letter of the Greek alphabet, based on the Phoenician *roʾsh. *See* ALPHABET.

RHODA roh'duh [Ῥόδη **Rhodē**]. Meaning "rosebush." A young woman in the home of MARY (mother of John Mark) who announces the arrival of Peter following his miraculous escape from prison (Acts 12:13). Rhoda's announcement that Peter was "at the gate" is treated with skepticism by those gathered (Acts 12:15). In this, her story parallels Luke's account of the resurrection appearance, at which the disciples dismissed the pronouncement of Mary and the other women (Luke 24:11).

JESSICA TINKLENBERG DEVEGA

RHODES rohdz [Ῥόδος **Rhodos**]. Rhodes is mentioned in Ezek 27:15; Acts 21:1; and 1 Macc 15:23. In Ezek 27:15, Rhodes is listed as one of many economic powers trading with Tyre in some versions. The NRSV reading of "Rhodians" is taken from the LXX, although the Hebrew has "Dedanites." In 1 Macc 15:23, Rhodes is one of the recipients of a message from the Roman consul Lucius declaring an alliance between Rome and the Jewish people. In Acts 21:1, Rhodes is one of the cities Paul passes through en route to Jerusalem. The island of Rhodes is approximately 45 mi. long and 22 mi. wide. It is located in the southeastern portion of the Aegean Sea between Asia Minor and Crete. It began as a Minoan colony ca. 1600 BCE. Rhodes was also the name of its capital, a port city that had a significant role in economic and political affairs in antiquity. It is probably to Rhodes the city that Acts 21 refers.

Rhodes' Mount Atabyrion (approximately 4,000 ft. high) served as a point of reference for ancient sailors. Zeus was worshiped on its summit. According to legend (e.g., Diodorus Siculus, *Bib. Hist.* 5.55–59; Pindar, *Ol.* 7.54–76), the island arose from the sea and was physically a part of Apollo/Helios, the sun god. A cult to Apollo continued in Rhodes for an extensive period in antiquity.

Rhodes' influence was due to its strategic location. Its eastern harbors could facilitate or hinder entry into the Aegean. It was also a major port for shipping from Greece, Cyprus, Palestine, and also Asia Minor. Thus, its appearance in Acts 21 as a major port of call between Cos and Patara was quite plausible.

By the 6th cent. BCE, Rhodes had become the premier economic power in the eastern Mediterranean region and it established its colonies in Sicily, the Balearic Islands, and the eastern coast of Italy. During the Hellenistic period, Rhodes' economic, cultural, and political influence grew substantially. The city funded political and economic enterprises among its neighbors. The poet Apollonius resided there, a sculptural school was there, and the Stoics Panaetius and Poseidonius taught there. Julius Caesar, Cicero, and Cato also studied in Rhodes. During this period, the city had a temple to Aphrodite, a shrine to Dionysus, a stadium, and a gymnasium. Ruins have also been found of a temple to Zeus and Athena.

Rome's victory at Pydna in 167 BCE severely undermined Rhodes' influence in the region when Rome declared Delos a free harbor. Crassus made Rhodes more subservient in 43 BCE. Rhodes remained very popular throughout the Roman period due to its renowned beauty and as the home of the Colossus of Rhodes, one of the seven wonders of the ancient world. The statue depicted Apollo. Built between 304 and 292 BCE, it stood 90 ft. high and was made of bronze. It commemorates a victory over Demetrius ca. 304 BCE (Diodorus Siculus, *Bib. Hist.* 20). The statue was destroyed partially by an earthquake in ca. 227 BCE and completely by Arabs in 653 CE. Rhodes was also the home of the statue of the winged Nike of Samothrace that celebrated a victory over Antiochus III in 190 BCE. The statue is now in the Louvre.

THOMAS B. SLATER

RHODOCUS rod´uh-kuhs [Ῥόδοκος Rhodokos]. A soldier in JUDAS Maccabeus' army, who betrayed him by providing information to Antiochus EUPATOR and who was subsequently imprisoned for this deception (2 Macc 13:21).

RIBAI ri´bi [רִיבַי rivay]. Ribai, a Benjaminite from GIBEAH, is listed as the father of Ittai (2 Sam 23:29) or Ithai (1 Chr 11:31), one of the Thirty, David's inner band of warriors.

RIBLAH rib´luh [רִבְלָה rivlah]. Two different locations are named Riblah in the OT. The disparate locations are reflected in the multiple spellings among textual witnesses. 1. Riblah was one of the cities bordering Canaan on the northeast in the Transjordan (e.g., Num 34:11). Although its identification is tentative, some have suggested that Riblah be identified with modern Irbid, 25 km northeast of PELLA.

2. In 2 Kings (e.g., 2 Kgs 23:33), Riblah is in the land of Hamath on the eastern bank of the Orontes, 32 km south of Homs, situated at a very strategic crossroad in Syria. Two major events happened at Riblah after the decline of the Assyrian Empire. In 609 BCE Pharaoh NECO II deposed King JEHOAHAZ of Judah (2 Kgs 23:33-34). Likewise, after the conquest of Jerusalem in 586 BCE, the Babylonian king Nebuchadnezzar deposed King ZEDEKIAH of Judah (2 Kgs 25:6; compare Jer 39:5-6; 52:9-10, 26-27). *See* NEBUCHADNEZZAR, NEBUCHADREZZAR.

Bibliography: Yoel Elitzur. *Ancient Place Names in the Holy Land* (2004).

JOSEPH R. CATHEY

RICHES. *See* WEALTH.

RIDDLE [חִידָה khidhah]. The noun **khidhah** occurs just seventeen times in the OT. Such limited use provides the interpreter with little context for determining its full range of meanings. Compounding the difficulty is that eight of its seventeen occurrences are in a single narrative, that of the marriage of Samson in Judg 14 (vv. 12, 13, 14, 15, 16, 17, 18, and 19), and four times the noun appears with a denominative verb as part of cognate accusative construction (**khud khidhah** [חוּד חִידָה], "riddle a riddle"; Judg 14:12, 13, 16; Ezek 17:2).

The word appears outside of biblical Hebrew with certainty only in Aramaic in Dan 5:12, *Ahiqar* (line 99), the Targumim, and in Syriac. Scholars surmise that the Semitic root of **khidhah** is **ʾkhd** (אחד), which most likely means "grasp, seize." Thus the basic idea of **khidhah** may be "something which is grasped or seized."

The first occurrence of the word **khidhah** in the OT is Num 12:8, a passage in which God chastises Aaron and Miriam for questioning Moses' special relationship with God. God says to them, "With him I speak face to face—clearly, not in riddles; and he beholds the form of the LORD." *Riddles* is paralleled in this passage with "visions (**marʾah** מַרְאָה) and dreams (**khalom** חֲלוֹם)" (v. 7 [Heb. v. 6]), both of which were means of communication from God that required interpretation by those with special insights (e.g., Joseph and Daniel).

Judges 14 recounts a **khidhah** posed by Samson to his wedding companions: "Out of the eater came something to eat. Out of the strong came something sweet" (v. 14). The riddle is posed as a wager; whoever of the companions could answer the riddle would receive "thirty linen garments and thirty festal garments" (vv. 12-13). The wedding companions were unable to find an answer to the riddle, so they coerced Samson's wife to pry the answer from him.

In 1 Kgs 10:1 (see also 2 Chr 9:1), the Queen of Sheba visits Solomon to test him with **khidhoth** (חִידוֹת, translated by the NRSV as "hard questions"). The narrative states that Solomon "answered all her questions (lit., "words," **devarim** [דְּבָרִים]) and "there was nothing hidden from the king that he could not explain to her" (1 Kgs 10:3).

Psalms 49:4; 78:2; Prov 1:6; Ezek 17:2; and Hab 2:6 use *riddle* in parallel poetic construction with *proverb* (**mashal** מָשָׁל). The basic verbal meaning of *proverb* is "to be like," suggesting that a proverb, like a metaphor, suggests to the hearer a likeness between two objects or ideas that the hearer may not have concluded without the benefit of the suggestion. Thus we may surmise that the word *riddle* in the OT falls into the same semantic range of meaning as the word *proverb*.

In Dan 8:23, one of the vision narratives, Gabriel interprets a vision for Daniel and tells him that a king will arise "bold of countenance" and "skilled in khidhoth." In the Aramaic portion of the book of Daniel, Daniel is described as having "an excellent spirit, knowledge, and understanding to interpret dreams, explain riddles (ʾakhidhan אֲחִידָן) and solve problems" (Dan 5:12).

The LXX translates khidhah in a number of ways. In Num 12:8; 1 Kgs 1:10; 2 Chr 9:1; Prov 1:6; and Dan 8:23, khidhah is translated as ainigma (αἴνιγμα). The translation of khidhah in Ezek 17:2 is diēgēma (διήγημα); and in Judg 14; Pss 49:5; 78:2; and Hab 2:6, the Hebrew word is translated as problēma (πρόβλημα).

The word problēma is not found in the deuterocanonical literature. Ainigma occurs in Sir 39:3, which points out to the reader the obscurity of the meaning of parables (ainigmasi parabolōn αἰνίγμασι παραβολῶν), and in Sir 47:15 Solomon is said to have filled the earth with "proverbs having deep meaning" (parabolais ainigmatōn παραβολαῖς αἰνιγμάτων).

The word diēgēma is found in 2 Macc 2:24 in a description of the abundance of historical records available to the writer of the story of Judas Maccabeus—"the flood of statistics involved and the difficulty there is for those who wish to enter upon the narratives of history" (historias diēgēmasin ἱστορίας διηγήμασιν). In Sir 8:8 the hearer is urged to give heed to "the discourse (diēgēma) of the sages."

The only NT occurrence of any of the three Greek words used to translate the Hebrew word khidhah is found in 1 Cor 13:12. The NRSV, following in the tradition of the translation history of the 1611 Authorized Version, renders the verse as "For now we see in a mirror dimly, but then we will see face to face." The Greek words translated "through a mirror dimly" are di esoptrou en ainigmati (δι᾽ ἐσόπτρου ἐν αἰνίγματι), meaning literally, "through a glass in a riddle."

A *riddle*, according to the early 20th-cent. scholarship, is a question that assumes an answer. The OT text presents the concept of riddle, khidhah, in a number of ways: 1) that which posits a connection between concepts and ideas that seemingly have no connection; 2) that which gives insight into the relationship between God and humanity; and 3) that which guides humanity in its quest to find a place in the created world.

Bibliography: Eleanor Cook. *Enigmas and Riddles in Literature* (2006); Carl McDaniel. "Samson's Riddle." *Did* 12 (2001) 47–57.

NANCY DECLAISSÉ-WALFORD

RIDGE OF JUDEA *joo*-dee'uh [πρίων τῆς Ιουδαίας priōn tēs Ioudaias]. The ridge of Judea is mentioned (Jdt 3:9) in connection with the western campaign of Nebuchadnezzar's general HOLOFERNES, who camped south of the Plain of Esdraelon near Dothan. It has been argued that the ridge of Judea is a misreading of mishor (מִישׁוֹר, "plain") for massor (מַשּׂוֹר, "a saw") in which case the Greek translator would have read "saw" (priōn) metaphorically.

JOSEPH R. CATHEY

RIGHT HAND [יָמִין yamin; δεξιός dexios]. In Hebrew, the word "right hand" can simply mean to the right (as opposed to left) side literally (Gen 13:9; 24:49; Num 20:17) or metaphorically as departing from the commandments to the right hand or left (Josh 1:7). It also represents the literal right hand (Gen 48:13; 2 Sam 20:9). The right hand was apparently the main hand for giving a blessing (Gen 48:14, 17-18), and Jacob deliberately overrode Joseph's wishes to have Manasseh as his firstborn receive Jacob's primary blessing. God swears oaths by "his right hand" (Isa 62:8). The right hand also seems to stand for the person, as when the right ear lobe, thumb of the right hand, and right big toe had blood put on them, making the priest or Israelite clean (Lev 8:23; 14:14, 17).

The right hand represents the power of God, as seen in the Song of Moses: "Your right hand, O LORD, glorious in power" (Exod 15:6; compare Job 40:14; Ps 20:6 [Heb. 20:7]). It also represents the power of people to do good, as in the case of Jael (Judg 5:26), or evil (Matt 5:30). The right hand gives good things, such as God giving David pleasures forevermore (Ps 16:11) or refuge from enemies (Ps 17:7), or wisdom giving long life (Prov 3:16). The right hand holds symbols of authority (Rev 1:16). Being at someone's right hand is to occupy a place of honor (Ps 45:9 [Heb. 45:10]; 110:1). In the NT, being at the right hand—dexios, with (Luke 6:6) or without (Matt 20:21) cheir (χείρ, "hand")—often refers to Ps 110:1 and is used especially of Jesus at God's right hand (Matt 26:64; Acts 2:33; Heb 12:2). Barnabas and Paul received the "right hand of fellowship," acceptance of or partnership with their mission, from the pillars in the Jerusalem church (Gal 2:9).

KENNETH D. LITWAK

RIGHTEOUSNESS IN EARLY JEWISH LITERATURE [צֶדֶק tsedheq, צְדָקָה tsedhaqah; δικαιοσύνη dikaiosynē]. The concept of righteousness has a broad range of meanings in the early Jewish texts. The Apocrypha, Pseudepigrapha, Philo, Josephus, and the Qumran writings all have their own idea of the term. Common to all is the idea that righteousness governs relationships and fundamental to all is the biblical conviction that righteousness is found in God (2 Chr 12:6; Neh 9:8; Pss 103:17; 111:3; 116:5; Jer 9:24; Dan 9:14; Zeph 3:5; Zech 8:8). Human beings mirror God by being righteous themselves in their observance of God's will and their behavior towards each other. The fundamental difference between the sources consists in the details of their idea of righteousness, of the time of the judgment, and in their attitude towards human failure.

A. Terminology

1. English

The English term *righteousness* refers to the quality of being righteous, right, or just, as well as to rightfulness as such and that which conforms to God's standards and which is acceptable to God. Thus the term with its ethical and religious connotations is broader than the related term *justice*, which is limited to the judicial context.

2. Hebrew

There is no difference between the two Hebrew nouns except that **tsedheq** is male and **tsedaqah** is female. The fundamental meaning is "righteousness" or "justice," deriving from the fundamental meaning of "straightness"; however, there are instances where they can mean "integrity" (Job 31:6), "vindication" (Ps 103:6; Jer 51:10), "deliverance" (Mic 7:9; NRSV, "vindication"), or "equity" (2 Sam 8:15). Fundamentally the meaning involves not only justice at a court of law but correct behavior in social frameworks. The term is focused on one's function within the demands of specific relationships, and its meaning depends on whether the emphasis is on interaction among human beings or with God. Thus forensic, ethical, as well as religious elements are involved.

3. Greek

In the LXX the most frequently used term to translate the Hebrew nouns is **dikaiosynē** (δικαιοσύνη), "righteousness," "justice," less frequently with terms for "purity," "blamelessness," "judgment," "mercy," or "compassion." The term **dikaiosynē** in classical Gk. has the meaning of conformity with the traditions or customs, the fulfillment of one's duty (e.g., Plato, *Resp.* 433a). Therefore it is an important virtue (compare Plutarch, *Fort.* 97e). In legal context the idea is to give each their due (Aristotle, *Rhet.* 1.9). The LXX, however, links this concept to God's rules and his judgment. This broadens the context and opens the term not only to forensic and ethical but also to religious connotations. The judicial connotations are always near (compare Isa 43:9, 26), but mercy, truth, and salvation are also involved (Deut 32:4; Mic 7:9; Ps 102:11, 17). There is the conscious combination of righteousness with salvation (Pss 64:5; 70:15; Isa 46:12; 51:5; 59:17; 61:10), with mercy (Gen 19:19; 20:13; 24:27; Exod 15:13; 34:7; Prov 20:22), or with God's faithfulness to his covenant (Isa 38:19; 39:8; Dan 8:12). Consequently human righteousness consists in the observance of God's will (Isa 5:7; Tob 14:7; Wis 5:6). But in spite of this broadening of the Gk. term the forensic sense of "justice" is more prominent than in the Hebrew.

B. God's Righteousness

1. Righteousness as justice

The righteousness of God is related to the power with which he rules creation. His deeds constitute his righteousness, and due to his supreme power he alone can be called righteous (Sir 18:2). Like the Hebrew Scriptures, the LXX links God's righteousness with his holiness in Deut 32:4; Ps 144:17. God's judgment is always just (*Jub.* 21:4; *Pss. Sol.* 5:1; 8:24; 9:3-4). As he rules history, his judgment of Israel's failings occurs through historic events. Thus his punishment of Israel through the hands of its enemies (*L.A.B.* 35:4) or Pompey's entry into the Temple are interpreted as signs of God's just judgment over Israel (*Pss. Sol.* 8:17, 26).

The idea of God as lord of history led to the importance of God as judge in apocalyptic thought. Thus in *1 En.* 62:3 the kings and rulers of the earth will recognize God as the ultimate judge. The strictness of God's judgment brings to light all the good and evil deeds of humankind (*4 Ezra* 7:33-35; 9:13). God's righteousness, which must be revealed in the end, is the basis of the apocalyptic expectation of a final judgment.

The apocalyptic worldview is also important in Qumran, where the righteousness of God's judgment is also emphasized. It is based on his creative activity (1QH[a] IX, 26–31). The justice of God and of his judgment is acknowledged even in the confession of one's sin (1QS X, 11–12). Forgiveness only derives from God's goodness (1QH[a] XII, 36–37; XIX, 8–10). Only God is righteous (1QS XI, 20–22) and from him all human righteousness derives; only he can enable his elect to repent and improve their lives (1QH[a] VIII, 17–20; XII, 31–32).

The Hellenistic authors regard God's righteousness more along the Gk. meaning of the term. Philo also emphasizes that only God is righteous (*Dreams* 2.194), particularly as judge (*Moses* 2.279; *Flight* 82), but for him it is a virtue of God, who combines all the virtues (*Unchangeable* 79). Here the importance of the proper distribution—of one's faculties as well as of judgment—is more important than any relational implications. Josephus does not often use righteousness in connection with God, but where he does, it is not in the context of virtues but with greater emphasis on God's judgment and his truth (*Ant.* 2.108; 11.55; *J.W.* 7.323). A similar forensic interpretation can be found in 4 Macc 4:21 where Antiochus' persecutions are seen as God's just punishment for the disobedient Israel.

In rabbinic thought the idea of God's righteousness continues to be important: God as cause of order and as lord of judgment is associated with the name Elohim and God's mercy with that of Yahweh (*Exod. Rab.* on Exod 3:14). God judges all humankind, righteous and unrighteous (*Abot* 4:29). Here the emphasis moves away from immediate eschatological expectation or direct historical application and focuses on an ethical interpretation of righteousness.

2. Righteousness as faithfulness

Already the LXX emphasizes God's righteousness in his being faithful to his promises (Isa 40–66; the psalms; compare also 1 Kgdms 2:2; 2 Esd 9:15; Tob 3:2). God's lasting covenant with Abraham and his descendants is seen as an expression of this righteousness (*Jub.* 22:15), and the promise to Abraham is seen as prophecy of a righteous Israel dwelling in the land given by God (*Jub.* 1:15-18; 36:6). God cares for Israel (Bar 5:9; *Pss. Sol.* 8:32). He will bring Israel back from among the nations (*T. Naph.* 8:3). God as the righteous and just, who has created all order and rules over the world, is expected to be true to his chosen people (2 Macc 1:24-29). Here again God's righteousness manifests itself in his activity within history and particularly within his history with Israel. The relationship with Israel defines God's righteousness as faithfulness to his promise.

Also in Qumran the idea of God's faithfulness to the covenant is important. However, the interpretation of the addressees of the covenant is different. Israel is no longer the nation as a whole but the community of the righteous. Thus during the Covenant Liturgy the priests recount God's righteousness in his actions on behalf of Israel (1QS I, 21–22). The Levites immediately afterwards list Israel's transgressions (1QS I, 22–24), which show that Israel as a whole has broken the covenant. Then all the members of the congregation confess their sins (1QS I, 24–II, 1). Thus the idea of God's covenant is limited to the community, as outside it there is no awareness of transgression and thus no repentance. God's covenant with Israel only continues in the community as righteousness can only be found among them.

3. Righteousness as mercy

Already the LXX links God's righteousness with his mercy, e.g., in Ps 114:5. The same link is established in *Jub.* 31:25. God can be seen as righteous in that he does not punish human sin but remains true to his goodness (Tob 3:2). But although mercy is an important aspect of God's righteousness, it is only rarely identified with it; in *4 Ezra* 8:32-38, God shows his righteousness and goodness in taking pity on those without good works. Thus they do not have any claim to God's mercy. This identification should, however, not be overemphasized for the punishment of the wicked is stressed in 7:33-35 and 9:13. Thus the expectation of mercy only extends to God's people, and not to everyone.

Similarly in Qumran the conviction is that God's righteousness consists in his saving activity on behalf of those who serve him, particularly in that he redeems them when they stumble (CD XX, 20; 1QS I, 21; X, 23; XI, 3, 5, 6, 12, 14). When they see the error of their ways and join the community, the members have a chance at attaining righteousness.

C. Human Righteousness

1. Righteousness as justice

In wisdom texts the idea of human justice occurs mainly in the context of government. Following God, particularly the rulers are expected to show righteousness in just judgment (Wis 1:1; 9:3). Even the wicked deserve a fair trial (Sir 42:2).

In Hellenistic Jewish writings the above-mentioned link between virtue and righteousness led to a more democratic interpretation of human righteousness. Philo and Josephus frequently maintain the Gk. meaning of the term with its emphasis on justice (*Ant.* 11.268) and virtue (*Ant.* 6.160; 9.182; *Life* 7). For Philo it is the just distribution to all (*Creation* 51), related to equality (*Spec. Laws* 2.204; 4.231). Thus it is required in a judge (*Spec. Laws* 4.56), but any wise person should aim for it. The *Letter of Aristeas* applies justice to everyone. On the one hand just rulers are expected to be fair and moderate (209). Righteousness in employers consists in not exploiting the people who work for them (258–259) and in officers in not risking the lives of their men unnecessarily (281). But this attitude is not limited to the powerful. Thus the laws about unclean animals are interpreted as calling all the people who observe these rules to righteous behavior towards those who are weaker than they are (147). Similarly in *Sib. Or.* 3.630 there is a warning not to oppress anyone. The general idea of justice as virtue in one's dealings with other people reflects the Greek idea of one's duty within a civic context, even though one's ethical behavior is based on the Jewish Torah.

2. Righteousness as observance of the social and divine rules

Fundamentally, righteousness is the appropriate behavior required by God (*1 En.* 94:1; 1QS VIII, 20–IX, 6). The righteous are in God's hand (Wis 3:1), and he preserves them (*1 En.* 48:7). Therefore the Jews can be called a righteous people, particularly when they receive the benefits of God's covenant (Wis 10:15, 20; 16:23; 18:7; *1 En.* 93:2; *Jub.* 16:26; 20:9; 25:3; 36:6; *Sib. Or.* 3:218, 234, 580). In this context it is noteworthy that this identification occurs frequently in the context of the covenant with Abraham, which is an indication of the importance of Gen 15:6 for the early Jewish interpretation of righteousness.

In wisdom texts the contrast between the righteous wise and the wicked is presented as a conflict, in which the righteous are persecuted by the wicked (Wis 2:12-20; 5:1-7). Righteousness is related to truth (Wis 5:6), not only in a wisdom context but also in *1 En.* 10:16; *4 Ezra* 7:114; *Let. Aris.* 306. The fundamental conviction is that, just as God himself is just, so are his commandments (*Pss. Sol.* 14:1-5; 4 Macc 13:26; *Let. Aris.* 131). Therefore their observance leads to righteousness. Some texts affirm that the righteous are guided by God (*Pss. Sol.* 18:8), which means that they receive his help in doing what is right.

In apocalyptic writings the contrast between the righteous and the wicked appears as that of the Jews versus the other nations. The Jews are depicted as interested in righteousness and virtue and not in the erroneous ways of other nations. This attitude expresses itself in the protection of the weak and the respect for other people's property and rights (*Sib. Or.* 3:218-47). Righteousness consists in observing the rules of God (*Jub.* 20:2-4), particularly the commandments about honoring one's parents, respecting one's neighbors, and refraining from pollution (*Jub.* 7:20, 26). Positively the idea of righteousness is closely related to the Jewish social structure as outlined by the Torah. Negatively righteousness means turning from the nations' ways to God (*Jub.* 1:15). But the privileges of access to the rules for a life pleasing to God do not lead to an attitude of superiority: the righteous are humble (*4 Ezra* 8:49). The prayer of the righteous has a special power (*1 En.* 47:2; *4 Ezra* 7:45-47). Occasionally the term can describe a particular group as opposed to the people as a whole (*1 En.* 93:6; 103:9). This shows that some authors found it difficult to associate the Israel of their present with the righteous people of the promise. Therefore righteousness is linked with the messianic age (*1 En.* 38:2; 53:6). It is the messiah (*Pss. Sol.* 17:26-35; 18:8; *1 En.* 38:2), the elect one (*1 En.* 39:6; 51:2-3; 53:6), or the Son of Man (*1 En.* 46:3; 48:4; 71:14) who is associated with the introduction of a rule of righteousness.

Examples of the righteous in the Jewish literature of the time are particularly the patriarchs (Enoch: *T. Benj.* 9:1; Isaac: *Jub.* 31:23; 36:6; Jacob: Wis 10:10; Simeon and Levi: *Jub.* 30:23; Joseph: Wis 10:13; Moses: *L.A.B.* 24:6; David: *L.A.B.* 62:9; Solomon: *Pss. Sol.* 1:2), but above all Abraham is associated with righteousness on account of his behavior throughout his life (*Jub.* 14:6; 23:10; compare 17:15-18; 19:8; also in 1 Macc 2:52; Philo, *Alleg. Interp.* 3.228; *Heir* 94–95; *Virtues* 216). The faith that was counted as righteousness in Gen 15:6 is mainly seen as referring to Abraham's firmness in trials (1 Macc 2:52; Sir 44:19-21; *Jub.* 18:14-16; 19:8-9; *Abot* 5:3-4; *Avot R. Nat.* 33; *Gen. Rab.* 55.1), and only in Sir 44:19-21 as referring to his circumcision. There is a strong link between Abraham's covenant and his righteousness in Neh 9:8 (LXX); Sir 44:19-21; *Jub.* 18:14-16; *b. Ned.* 32a; *Exod. Rab.* 23.5; *Mek.* 40b.

For the people in Qumran righteousness consisted in following God's statutes in the way they were interpreted by the community (CD XX, 27–33; 1QS I, 13; III, 1; IV, 4). They acknowledge that perfect righteousness is unattainable (1QH[a] XII, 29–30). Therefore to be able to do that is a sign of God's grace (1QH[a] XV, 14, 17). The true commandments of God are revealed to the community through their founder, the Teacher of Righteousness (1QpHab I, 12–13), and in the *Hodayot* he is presented as praying in the tradition of the suffering righteous as known from the biblical psalms (1QH[a] X–XVII). The Teacher alone has received the true interpretation of the words of the prophets (1QpHab VII, 4–5) and only those who are faithful to him and suffer in consequence are seen as righteous (1QpHab VIII, 1–3). Consequently the members of the community dedicate themselves to performing righteousness (1QS I, 5–6) and regard themselves as "children of righteousness," while those who do not follow their ways show themselves to be ungodly, "children of deceit" (1QS III, 20–25). The members of the community follow the Teacher of Righteousness into the desert to prepare for God's coming (1QS VIII, 13; IX, 19–26) by studying the Torah in the interpretation revealed to them (1QS VIII, 15). This means that they truly observe the Torah (1QpHab VIII, 1–2), which all the other Jews do not. As in the OT the terminology of righteousness defines the relationship between God and chosen people, but the relationship does not extend to a nation but to a group of elect. There is a mixture between an awareness of God's grace in their election and an emphasis on the observance of the rules of the community as the only way to righteousness.

In spite of the non-sectarian context, in rabbinic thought the fundamental contrast between the righteous who observe the commandments and thus remain in the covenant and the ungodly is also important (*b. Abod. Zar.* 4a; *Midr. Cant.* 2.1 [62a]). Some traditions distinguish between the wholly righteous, the average, the penitent, and the wholly ungodly (*bar. b. Rosh. Hash.* 16b; *Sifre Deut.* 307; *t. Qidd.* 1.14; *Avot R. Nat.* 40; *y. Rosh. Hash.* 57a, 49; *bar. b. Sukkah* 53a). However, the aim of this distinction is not to be able to place people in categories and thus to judge them. The people are called to observe the commandments without thought of reward (*Abot* 1:3). Here as well, Abraham is regarded as the ideal righteous person, for whom the world was created (*Sifre Deut.* 38; 47; *Gen. Rab.* 35 on 9:12). But there are also rabbis who are regarded as righteous, e.g., Onias the rainmaker (ca. 80 BCE; *m. Taan.* 38) and Hanina ben Dosa (ca. 10–80 CE, *b. Sotah* 49a). The prayer of the righteous is regarded as particularly powerful: they are thought to effect healing (*Deut. Rab.* 10.3) and to live beyond death (*b. Ber.* 18b; *b. Taan.* 7b), and their death was expected to expiate sin (*b. Moed Qat.* 28a).

As seen above, Hellenistic Jewish authors also interpret righteousness in terms of individual ethics. Philo lists righteousness as one of the main virtues (*Alleg. Interp.* 2.18; *Sobriety* 38; *Migration* 219); the righteous person is perfect in his soul and in his deeds (*Prelim. Studies* 90), and achieves harmony in all the parts of the soul (*Alleg. Interp.* 1.72). Such a person is the true representative of humanity (*Migration* 121), who in spite of their own perfection remain with the unrighteous in order to cure them (*Migration* 61; 124; *Worse* 123). Following the Greek use of the term, righteousness for Philo is more a human virtue (*Abraham* 27; 56; *Prelim. Studies* 31; *Sacrifices* 84). Thus the patriarchs are particular examples of righteousness (*Alleg. Interp.* 3.77, 228; *Worse* 121). Similarly in Josephus the heroes of the OT are called righteous (*Ant.* 9.33; 10.38; 14.172), but in Josephus the tendency is to see the one who is righteous as the person who obeys God's commands (*Ag. Ap.* 2.293; *Ant.* 6.165; 8.208), which is closer to the general Jewish interpretation of the term.

3. Righteousness as mercy

Human righteousness can also express itself in mercy and benevolence, particularly towards those who are disadvantaged; therefore, almsgiving is one of the most important expressions of righteousness (Prov 10:2 (LXX); Tob 14:11; Dan 4:27 (LXX); *b. B. Bat.* 8b).

D. Effects of God's Righteousness

1. Salvation of the godly

On a mundane level the righteousness of the wise and just has its effects in this world: it is going to be remembered and their descendants will benefit from their good fortune (Sir 44:10). Similar, but more closely related to the Greek idea of righteousness as virtue, is the thought that righteousness contains its own reward, as expressed in *Let. Aris.* 267.

On the other hand, the book of Job shows that the idea of the suffering of the righteous was a problem for Jewish thought. Some texts solve this by assuming that there is no righteousness at all among humankind (*Jub.* 21:21), not even among all the generations of Israel (*Jub.* 23:21). Even in those texts that refer to human righteousness there is an awareness that this derives from God's grace (*Jub.* 16:26). God is the origin of all righteousness (Wis 12:16) and his wisdom guides the holy ones (Wis 10:17). In this approach there is an awareness that even the righteous ones sometimes lose their way (Wis 5:6), and at times the whole people of God suffers (Wis 10:15; 17:2; *4 Ezra* 10:22). This approach, however, is usually combined with the expectation that the righteous can expect God to help them on their way (*Pss. Sol.* 10:3; 15:7). Thus in *Pss. Sol.* 9 God's just judgment comes over Israel, which deserted him; human good and evil actions lead to salvation or punishment, but honest repentance and trust in God's covenant leaves hope for God's mercy over Israel. Even the righteous can stumble, and even their salvation depends on God (*Pss. Sol.* 9:7). God will gather a righteous people for himself (*Pss. Sol.* 17:26-27, 29, 32). The righteous are redeemed while the sinners cannot expect pardon (*Pss. Sol.* 3:5-12). The punishment of the righteous is like the chastisement of a child, so that the sinners cannot gloat at their fate (*Pss. Sol.* 13:6-7).

The problem of the difference between the expectation of a righteous people and the experience of actual iniquity is also taken up in apocalyptic literature. There is a very positive picture of the righteous: God's wisdom is revealed to them (*1 En.* 48:7; 93:10; 104:12-13); the righteous are also the wise (*1 En.* 91:10). As in wisdom literature, the expectation is that the righteous will be rewarded (*4 Ezra* 7:17), not only in the future (*1 En.* 62:8; 99:10), but also in prosperity in this life (*1 En.* 1:8; 10:18; 94:4). The righteous are supported by God, not only in the material sense but also spiritually (*1 En.* 41:8). God strengthens the faith of the righteous (*1 En.* 108:13); he even appoints angels to watch over them (*1 En.* 100:5), and they can expect to rise from the grave (*1 En.* 62:15). The Son of Man strengthens the righteous (*1 En.* 48:4). At the end of time they can expect to be illuminated by the light of God (*1 En.* 38:4; 58:2-3) and be taken from the earth (*1 En.* 60:23; 62:15). A person who dies righteous is truly blessed (*1 En.* 81:4). Those who instruct people in righteousness can expect a special reward (Dan 12:3). Instruction about righteousness is always regarded as important; such instruction is mentioned about Enoch (*1 En.* 13:10; 14:1; 91:3-4, 18-19; 94:1, 3-4), Noah (*Jub.* 7:20, 26), Abraham (*Jub.* 20:2), Levi (*Jub.* 31:15; *T. Levi* 13:5), and Solomon (Wis 1:1).

But there is also an awareness of a bleaker reality. Israel's sin led to the loss of the land (*4 Ezra* 14:32). Israel's falling away is sometimes seen as a sign of the end (*4 Ezra* 5:11). Consequently, apocalyptic texts emphasize that, as humankind cannot last before God, they have to appeal to God's mercy instead of their human righteousness (Dan 9:18), for the world is too full of iniquity (*4 Ezra* 4:27). This iniquity delays the coming judgment (*4 Ezra* 4:39). When God restores Israel, this is due not to Israel's merits but to his righteousness and mercy (Bar 5:9). Particularly the good deeds of the righteous will save Israel as God looks at them and not at the unrighteous (*4 Ezra* 8:26-36; *2 Bar.* 14:7). The prayer of the righteous praises and supplicates on the day of judgment (*1 En.* 47:1-2), and the angels pray for the people (*1 En.* 39:5). This knowledge of the failings of the people does not, however, lead to the expectation of hope for the wicked. Even after Ezra has emphasized the failings of his generation (*4 Ezra* 8:26-36), he is called to focus on the salvation of the righteous and not on that of the wicked (*4 Ezra* 9:13). Thus there is a strong awareness of the mistakes of the righteous but no interest in the fate of the ungodly. Very rare are the instances when God's salvation extends even to every person under the influence of Belial and to the nations (*T. Zeb.* 9:8).

By contrast, in Qumran God's righteousness is particularly seen in his saving actions towards the community alone (CD XX, 20; 1QS I, 21; X, 23; XI, 3, 5, 6, 12, 14). The terms occur mainly in 1QH[a] (fifteen times) and 1QS (twelve times), mostly in contexts of individual and communal confessions of sin. As only God is righteous (1QH[a] XII, 29–31; XX, 30–31; 1QS I, 21–II, 4), human beings can only hope that God's righteousness shows itself in his cleansing them from their impurity (1QH[a] XII, 37; XIX, 30–31). In God's righteous judgment the members of the community put their hope (1QS XI, 12–16), for they expect him to cleanse his elect through his spirit (1QS IV, 18–23). The community becomes the chosen people of God, which is saved from the assaults of evil at the end (1QM XIII). Thus the great war at the end of time will mark the final purification of the elect.

2. Punishment of the wicked

In wisdom literature the conviction that knowledge of God is righteousness (Wis 15:3) divides humankind into those who know God and those who do not and leads to the expectation that God's judgment will come upon the unjust (Wis 1:8; 17:2). Again, the fundamental conviction is that God's judgment is just (Wis 12:13), although at times the righteous suffer (Wis 2:10, 18-19; 3:1-2). Based on their knowledge of God, ultimately the righteous will judge the nations (Wis 3:8). This shows once again the expectation that righteousness will have its reward, even if in the present this may not be visible. The opposing view is that the wicked do not have to expect punishment and the righteous do not receive reward for their behavior, so that it does not pay to be too righteous (Eccl 2:14-16; 7:15-16; 8:14; 9:2). Against such ideas there is only the hope for a balance in the future. Therefore a large number of texts emphasize the salvation of the righteous from the persecution of the sinners and the sinners' punishment (*Pss. Sol.* 2:34-35). The sinners as well as the foreign nations can only expect retribution (*Pss. Sol.* 17:22), and the righteous will praise God when they see that those who bent the law will be punished (*Pss. Sol.* 4:8). The fate of the unrighteous is death (*Pss. Sol.* 9:5; 13:11). Sometimes human evil is attributed to the actions of an evil personification, e.g., Beliar (*Jub.* 1:20), but this does not detract from the responsibility of the individual. The same writings that refer to the doings of Beliar/Mastema/the devil advocate the punishment of the sinner as righteous action—not only punishment by God (*Jub.* 21:4), but also the burning of the harlot (*Jub.* 20:4) or Levi's and Simeon's killing of the Shechemites (*Jub.* 30:18, 23). The punishment corresponds to the sin (*1 En.* 100:7), thus Cain killed Abel with a stone and was killed by his house falling on top of him (*Jub.* 4:31), and whether there was any influence on the perpetrator is irrelevant for the justice of the judgment.

Particularly in apocalyptic contexts the importance of God's judgment on the ungodly cannot be underestimated (*1 En.* 27:3; 38:1; 60:6). The expectation for the future is that God will restore his elect and they will overcome their enemies; they will be redeemed and see their curses on their adversaries having effect (*Jub.* 23:30). The prayer of the righteous can invoke God's judgment on the wicked (*1 En.* 47:1-2; 97:1, 3, 5), but not even the intercession of the righteous can preserve them from their fate (*1 En.* 12–16). The righteous will be rewarded and the sinners will be destroyed (*1 En.* 38:1-2). The ungodly will be informed about their failings (*1 En.* 13:10; 14:1). Against the idea that there is no reward for the righteous after death (*1 En.* 102), the righteous can be assured of a judgment after death. This judgment rewards them and punishes the sinners (*1 En.* 103) without regard to wealth or status (*1 En.* 63:9; 96:4). The righteous will see not only the unjust rulers be judged (*1 En.* 62:12), but also all sinners (*1 En.* 91:12; 97:1). The wicked will have no place to escape to (*1 En.* 97:3). God will hand over the sinners to the righteous to do with them as they please (*1 En.* 95:3; 96:1), the expectation being that they will mercilessly kill them (*1 En.* 98:12; 99:3, 6). Their death is final (*1 En.* 98:13-14); unlike the righteous they have no hope of an afterlife. Even in *4 Ezra* with its struggle for hope for the people the angel does not allow the supplication of the righteous for the undeserving on the day of judgment; everyone will be judged on their own merits (7:102-115). Thus there is the awareness of a present unjust age and the expectation of the coming of righteousness with the destruction of iniquity in the age to come (*1 En.* 10:16, 21; 39:6; 81:8; 107:1; *Jub.* 23:26). The final vision is that the present evil age will end, all unrighteousness will be destroyed, and only the righteousness of God and his people will remain.

This is also the expectation of the community of the Qumran writings, with the difference that they only expect themselves to survive the purification of judgment. Even members of the community who swear the oath of entry but do not enter the community with the honest intention to observe their rules will not be cleansed by the spirit of God but remain with the forces of evil (1QS II, 25–III, 12) and share the fate of the non-community members. The ultimate battle between the forces of light and of darkness leads to the destruction of all iniquity, of every unrighteous person and particularly their leader, Belial/Mastema (1QM XVII) as well as to the purge of the elect from those among the community who are tainted by iniquity (1QM XVI, 11–XVII, 15). Those members of the community who fall in battle are shown to have never truly been a part of the elect.

A similar idea of unrighteous being found among God's people can be found in Hellenistic Jewish historiography: God's judgment on the unjust is a given also in the Hellenistic context (3 Macc 2:3). The Maccabean wars demonstrate that the problem of who could be counted among the righteous was virulent: Judas Maccabeus calls on God's righteousness when he punishes Joppa (2 Macc 12:6), and thus claims the righteous cause for himself. God's support of his cause shows itself not only in his victories themselves but also in the fact that the Jews who fell in the battle against Gorgias turn out to have secretly owned idols, so that their death proves to be the just judgment of God for their sins (2 Macc 12:39-42). The conclusion is that in a righteous war only the wicked need to fear death. Here the same thought of divine judgment through death in battle occurs as in 1QM, but Hellenistic Jewish writings find God's punishment of the wicked strictly within history. Such a complex claim to righteousness is, however, unusual. More frequently the punishment is of foreigners or open transgressors. Thus foreigners who interfere with Jewish customs face divine punishment (Ptolemy Philopator in 3 Macc 2:21-22; Apollonius in 4 Macc 4:13). Similarly Philo regards God's judgment of the Egyptians as righteous (*QE* 1.10), and he also approves of righteous anger, particularly of the Levites in the service of God (*Flight* 90; *Dreams* 1.91; 2.7). In *Let. Aris.* 131 the law is seen as belonging necessarily together with the punishment for transgressions. Thus in Hellenistic writings the expectation of punishment is in history, not in a future judgment.

E. Conclusion

In early Judaism the concept of righteousness links humankind with God. Righteousness is the attitude of God in which he addresses humanity and in righteousness human beings can face God the creator and judge. God is righteous as just judge of his creation, as faithful partner in the covenant with Israel, and as merciful savior of his elect. The Jews have the rules and wisdom according to which they can live their lives righteously. The difference between the traditions is in the interpretation of these aspects.

In Judaism in general the observance of the divine commandments makes people righteous. Wisdom traditions regard righteousness more precisely in terms of insight into God's plans and a life according to his order. Rewards and punishment should occur within this world. Philo's interpretation of righteousness as virtue and the Hellenistic Jewish historians' reading of God's punishment as occurring through historical events follow similar lines.

As the number of righteous in the present was found to have been small and they felt themselves oppressed, the expectation of a future judgment grew. At the same time the need arose to face the failings of the people of God. Some traditions answer this by hoping for God's mercy to his remaining faithful in his promise to Israel and letting the just deeds of a part count as righteousness for all (*4 Ezra*); others reinterpret Israel in terms of a smaller, clearly defined community of elect (Qumran) and abandon the idea of the nation as God's righteous people. For both the hope for salvation and righteousness lies in God's mercy, and neither expects this mercy to extend to the unrighteous, those who do not ask for God.

In conclusion, early Jewish literature finds in righteousness the outline of a social order among human beings and a relationship with God; it struggles with human failure to live accordingly and lives in the hope of the strength of God's promise.

Bibliography: B. Bryne. "Living Out the Righteousness of God." *CBQ* 43 (1981) 557–81; G. L. Cockerill. "Melchizedek or 'King of Righteousness.'" *EvQ* 63 (1991) 305–12; L. Gaston. "Abraham and the Righteousness of God." *HBT* 2 (1980) 39–68; W. Grundmann. "The Teacher of Righteousness of Qumran and the Question of Justification by Faith in the Theology of the Apostle Paul." *Paul and Qumran.* J. Murphy O'Connor, ed. (1968) 85–114; D. Hill. "DIKAIOI as a Quasi-Technical Term." *NTS* 11 (1965) 296–302; D. Hill. *Greek Words and Hebrew Meanings: Studies in the Semantics of Soteriological Terms* (1967); J. Kampen. "'Righteousness' in Matthew and the Legal Texts from Qumran." *Legal Texts and Legal Issues: Proceedings of the Second Meeting of the International Organization for Qumran Studies Cambridge 1995* (1997) 461–87; J. W. Olley. *"Righteousness" in the Septuagint of Isaiah* (1979); Benno Przybylski. "*Tsedeq, Tsedaqah* and *Tsaddiq* in the Dead Sea Scrolls." *Righteousness in Matthew and His World of Thought* (1980) 13–38; J. Reumann. *"Righteousness" in the New Testament: "Justification" in the United States Lutheran-Roman Catholic Dialogue.* Responses by J. Fitzmyer and J. Quinn (1982); H. Ringgren. "God's Righteousness." *The Faith of Qumran: Theology of the Dead Sea Scrolls.* E. T. Sander, trans., J. H. Charlesworth, ed. (1995) 63–67; P. Sacchi. "From Righteousness to Justification in the Period of Hellenistic Judaism." *Hen* 23 (2001) 11–26; E. P. Sanders. *Paul and Palestinian Judaism* (1977); P. Stuhlmacher. *Reconciliation, Law, and Righteousness* (1986); H. Ulfgard. "The Teacher of Righteousness, the History of the Qumran Community, and Our Understanding of the Jesus Movement: Texts, Theories and Trajectories." *Qumran Between the Old and New Testaments.* F. J. Cryer and T. L. Thompson, eds. (1998) 310–46; N. W. Watson. "Some Observations on the Use of DIKAIOO in the Septuagint." *JBL* 79 (1960) 255–66.

JUTTA LEONHARDT-BALZER

RIGHTEOUSNESS IN THE NT [δικαιοσύνη **dikaiosynē**]. In the NT the word *righteousness* is the translation of the Gk. word **dikaiosynē**. The majority of occurrences of **dikaiosynē** are translated "righteousness," although **dikaiosynē** is also rendered with words such as *justice, justification, piety, right,* and "what is right." The related adjective **dikaios** (δίκαιος) means "righteous," "good," "just," "right," "proper," "in a right relationship with God," "honest," and "innocent." The opposite of the term *righteousness* is *unrighteousness* (adikia ἀδικία), with the related adjective *unrighteous* (adikos ἄδικος).

A. Righteousness in Hebrew and Greek Cultural Contexts

Righteousness has rich cultural and conceptual backgrounds in both Hebrew and Greek origins. In Hebrew, tsedhaqah (צְדָקָה) may come from an Arabic root connoting "straightness," so that one infers a thing conforming to a norm or standard. Yet in biblical usage *righteousness* indicates a richness of meaning that is difficult to capture with simple English terms. Righteousness in the biblical view presupposes a covenantal relationship between two parties in which both participants are actively engaged in the relationship. Covenants may be between God and humans (or humanity) or between humans (as individuals or groups). Acts that honor and preserve a covenant are deemed righteous—so that such activity is righteousness—whereas acts that corrupt and violate a covenant are regarded as unrighteous and constitute unrighteousness. Covenantal righteousness (or unrighteousness) is not merely ethical in nature; rather, the issue is whether or not an act conforms to and preserves the covenantal relationship (*see* COVENANT, OT AND NT).

In Greek thought, a righteous person was dikē (δίκη). This term was applied to persons who observed or conformed to tradition or custom. The word dikē denoted one who fulfilled social and religious obligations. A person was regarded as being righteous who observed legal norms and civic duties. Moreover, in Greek culture Dikē was a mythological personification, the virgin daughter of Zeus who effected just judgment and right punishment. The language of righteousness touched on the significance of all of life, since in Greek culture there was extensive emphasis on virtue.

One sees the Hebrew and Greek cultural currents converging in the LXX. There is a decisive change in the nuances of the dikaiosynē word group through the influence of OT thought. In the LXX, the Greek emphasis on righteousness as virtue is modified, even replaced, by the fundamental question of how humanity is to stand before the judgment of God. The law is the standard of righteousness in the covenant between God and humanity (*see* LAW IN THE OT). The basic Greek notion of righteousness (as the fulfillment of secular legal standards and civic duties) becomes in the LXX the idea of God's people fulfilling obligations to God and to God's theocratic social order. Thus, the Gk. term *righteousness* takes on a consistently and explicitly religious sense through its usage in the LXX. In the NT, *righteousness* has much the same sense as in the LXX. However, in the NT the distinction is even greater. Here, the Greek idea of righteousness as virtue and civic duty (which emphasizes individual achievement) is virtually replaced by the OT notion of righteousness (which emphasizes relationship to God and God-created social order).

B. Righteousness in the New Testament Writings

In the NT there are various ways in which one may think about righteousness. There is righteousness as a relationship between God and humanity and righteousness as a relationship between human beings. There is also the notion of God's righteousness (that is, God is righteous or God demands righteousness) and human righteousness (that is, humanity acts in accordance with God's will). At times interpreters debate which of the basic senses of the term *righteousness* is to be understood in various NT texts.

In all, *righteousness* and its related terms occur approximately 300 times in the NT. The pattern of usage is remarkable, because the majority of them occur in Paul, and in Acts, a book about Paul's work. There are 64 occurrences in the Gospels (28 in Matthew; 2 in Mark; twenty-eight in Luke; and six in John); twenty-five occurrences in Acts; 138 occurrences in the thirteen canonical Pauline epistles (72 of which are in Romans); 13 in Hebrews; 9 in James; 8 in 1 Peter; 12 in 2 Peter; 11 in 1 John; 1 in Jude; and 21 in Revelation.

1. The Gospels and Acts

Given the importance of the concept of covenant and the attendant notion of righteousness in the OT, it is striking that there is a seeming lack of stress on the concept of righteousness in the teaching of Jesus. As J. H. P. Reumann states the matter, Jesus material associates righteousness with judgment and rarely with saving righteousness. Even the idea that God is righteous is rarely stated (see John 17:25). In short, a NT theological treatment of righteousness necessarily looks to and beyond the Gospels for a complete picture of righteousness in the NT. Nevertheless, the material on righteousness in the Gospels demands careful scrutiny in its own right.

a. Matthew. The author of Matthew shows a pronounced concern with righteousness. First, it is God's will that humans are to fulfill righteousness (3:15; 5:6, 10; 6:33). Second, righteousness is human life lived in accordance with God's will (Matt 5:20; 6:1). The Matthean Jesus tells his disciples that their righteousness must exceed that of the scribes and Pharisees (Matt 5:20). In the Sermon on the Mount, he demonstrates a high standard of righteousness through his teachings on the law (Matt 5:17-48) and exhorts his listeners to "be perfect" (Matt 5:48).

b. Mark. The author of Mark uses the adjective *righteous* (**dikaios**) twice. In 2:17, in a somewhat sarcastic statement ("I have come to call not the righteous but sinners"), Jesus defends his call of the tax collector Levi. Jesus' reference to "the righteous" at face value indicates those who were self-righteous. Yet, in turn, in Mark 6:20 Herod Antipas regards John the Baptist as "righteous and holy." This correlation of "righteous" and "holy" seems to indicate an understanding of life lived in accordance with God's will.

c. Luke and Acts. The author of Luke's sole use of **dikaiosynē** in the Gospel is coupled with "holiness"; righteousness and holiness are held together in an equation similar to that found in Mark 6:20, where righteousness is life in obedient relation to God. In turn, Luke's several uses of the adjective *righteous* are defined by the first use of that word in Luke 1:6, where he describes the "righteous" parents of John the Baptist, Zechariah and Elizabeth, as "living blamelessly according to all the commandments and regulations of the Lord." In this instance, the notion of being "righteous" is clearly related to law observance. However, in Luke, *righteous* does not always explicitly mean law observance. At the time of Jesus' death (Luke 23:47), a centurion says of Jesus, "Certainly this man was **dikaios**" (which is most often translated "innocent"). Then, in Luke 23:50, Luke states that Joseph of Arimathea was "a good and righteous man."

In the second volume of his two-volume work, Acts of the Apostles, Luke makes clear that righteousness is doing God's will; in Acts 13:10 Luke holds together "righteousness" and "the straight paths of the Lord." Similarly, in Acts 3:14, Jesus is "the Holy and Righteous One." These uses of *righteousness* show that righteousness is doing God's will in life.

d. John. In John, there is little "righteousness" language; however, the notion of the concept is evident. The author uses *righteousness* twice (John 16:8, 10) in reference to the vindication of Jesus before those who opposed him in his ministry. In John, the "Advocate" will come and will show or prove "righteousness": that Jesus has indeed gone to God who sent him (14:26; 15:26). In turn, three uses of the adjective **dikaios** show that it means "right" or "godly" (John 5:30; 7:24; 17:25).

2. The Pauline epistles

Paul's authorship of the thirteen epistles attributed to him in the NT is a matter of debate. Thus, the treatment of "righteousness" in what follows will work first in relation to the seven undisputed epistles, especially Romans, and only secondarily in relation to the disputed letters (*see* PAUL, AUTHORSHIP).

a. The undisputed Pauline epistles. Romans, Galatians, and Philippians are the three letters that present the fullest or clearest evidence of Paul's thinking on righteousness.

In Romans many interpreters say that Paul's writing about "righteousness" and "the righteousness of God" is the heart of the epistle. The cluster of words related to the term *righteousness* is rich in Romans, with the noun *righteousness* heading up the list (thirty-four times) and the verb "to justify" (or, "to rightwise" or "to make right") standing in second place with fifteen occurrences. 1) Paul states that righteousness in humans is the result of God's declaring or pronouncing them to be righteous. Thus, righteousness is said to have been "reckoned" to Abraham; indeed, Paul insists that it was Abraham's faith that was reckoned to him as righteousness (Rom 4:9-10). The righteousness reckoned to Abraham (and by implication, to others) is his standing with God. 2) Paul uses the enigmatic phrase "the righteousness of faith." Here, Paul means to name something that is different from righteousness through observance of the law. While some writings, like the Gospel of Matthew, continue to assert that law observance is of primary importance for followers of Jesus (Matt 5:17-20), Paul claims that God mediates righteousness to humanity through faith, not law (Rom 4:11-13). 3) Paul uses the phrase "the righteousness of God" explicitly in Romans (1:17; 3:5, 21-26; 10:3). The phrase is ambiguous in Gk., as in English, and may be understood to mean "God is righteous" or "God gives righteousness." Interpreters who contend that "the righteousness of God" means "God gives righteousness" typically see salvation as a human possibility, wherein "the righteousness of God" is the righteousness that God requires of humanity and that God actually gives as a gift to the person of faith (*see* FAITH, FAITHFULNESS). Here, faith is the condition for the reception of the gift of righteousness from God. The righteousness of God is understood to mean that God acts in Christ and, in turn, humans react by having faith, so that God then gives the believing human "righteousness." By contrast, other interpreters understand "the righteousness of God" to mean "God is righteous," and they contend that salvation is purely the work of God, despite the failures of humanity. Here, God acts in Christ, and part of that action is the creation of faith on the part of human beings who otherwise would have no faith. Thus, in this second understanding, "the righteousness of God" is the power of God at work to save humanity through the creation of faith in humans. 4) At times Paul explicitly says that righteousness is a gift from God (Rom 5:17). In this regard Paul makes clear that this righteousness is itself the source of the vitality of the Spirit at work in the believer (Rom 8:10-11). 5) Interpreters recognize that Paul uses the language of righteousness in terms of ethics. Particularly in Rom 6 Paul admonishes his readers to present their members to God as instruments of righteousness (Rom 6:13). In this context Paul insists that righteousness is the lordly figure to which believers are bound in order that they may experience the ongoing process of sanctification (Rom 6:15-23).

In Gal 2:15-21, Paul makes some of his strongest statements about "righteousness" (dikaiosynē) and dikaioō (δικαιόω, "to justify"). This passage reflects a heated difference, discussion, and debate that went on in the 1st cent. over the role of the law in the life of believers, particularly Gentile believers. Paul builds a contrast between faith and law, arguing that the believer is "justified" through faith, not by law. Paul argues that the one who is justified has a right standing with God, so that by implication righteousness is to be understood as a right relationship with God.

In Philippians—particularly Phil 3—Paul contrasts "a righteousness of my own that comes from the law" with "one that comes through the faith of Christ, the righteousness of God based on faith" (3:9, author's trans.; NRSV, "one that comes through faith in Christ, the righteousness from God based on faith"). Here, two forms of righteousness stand over against each other. On the one hand, there is a humanly achieved righteousness that results from law observance; on the other hand, there is righteousness that is a gift from God to those who believe. Righteousness in both instances refers to the human being's standing before God. Yet in this contrast it is clear which version of righteousness Paul was adopting. Formerly as a zealous Pharisee, Paul had observed the law (Phil 3:7) in order to stand "blameless" (Phil3:6). Nevertheless, as a follower of Jesus, Paul had foregone his former prerogatives from law observance in order to be found "in Christ" with a new righteousness that came as a gift from God through Paul's faith in Christ (Phil 3:9). The outcome of Paul's embrace—or being embraced—by this new righteousness was that he knew Christ and his resurrection, and he held the hope of resurrection from the dead for himself (and others who shared the new righteousness).

In 1 Cor 1:30, Paul speaks of "our righteousness" in conjunction with wisdom, sanctification, and redemption. His point is clear: God is the source of all these things. Paul's mention of wisdom, sanctification, and redemption in the same context indicates that righteousness is an integral part of Christian life.

In 2 Corinthians there is more extensive use of the notion of righteousness (3:9; 5:21; 6:7, 14; 9:9, 10; 11:15). Paul speaks of himself and others as ministers of a new covenant, a covenant by Spirit not letter (of the law; 3:7-11). In this context he contrasts "the ministry of condemnation" (the work of the covenant of the letter) with "the ministry of justification" (the work of the covenant of Spirit). Paul sometimes uses the terms *righteousness* and *justification* synonymously (*see* JUSTIFICATION, JUSTIFY). Justification (or righteousness), here, is the substance of the work of the new covenant. Second Corinthians 5:21 presents a similar understanding of righteousness (or justification). Then, 2 Cor 6:7 speaks of righteousness as a weapon of God's power, whereas 2 Cor 6:14 contrasts righteousness with "lawlessness." Second Corinthians 9:9-10 speaks of God's righteousness and, then, Christians' righteousness; in turn, 2 Cor 11:15 speaks again of "ministers of righteousness." Thus, one sees that Paul uses the language of righteousness in various ways in 2 Corinthians, so that there is no developed reflection on righteousness in this epistle—though the various references do make clear that righteousness is God's work in relation to humanity.

First Thessalonians and Philemon have too little of the language of righteousness to draw conclusions as to Paul's understanding and presentation of this idea.

b. The disputed Pauline epistles. Ephesians 4:24 couples the mention of righteousness with holiness, another way of saying that righteousness has to do with one's standing before God. Then, Eph 5:9 mentions righteousness in conjunction with that which is good and that which is true, saying that the good, the right, and the true are the sources of appropriate Christian living. Referring to "the whole armor of God," Eph 6:14 mentions "the breastplate of righteousness," again, a desirable characteristic of Christian life. (Colossians presents too little information to draw conclusions about righteousness.) Second Thessalonians speaks of righteousness in terms of God's eschatological judgment, an indication that God's judgment is just or right (1:5). The Pastoral Epistles (1 and 2 Timothy, Titus) consistently present righteousness as a fundamental and necessary characteristic of the Christian's life (e.g., 2 Tim 2:22; Titus 2:12; 3:7). *See* PAUL, THE APOSTLE.

3. Hebrews

The "righteousness" language in Hebrews, for the most part, relates to materials from the OT and is striking in the context of the other NT treatments of righteousness. Hebrews 1:9 cites Ps 45:7; Heb 8:12 cites Jer 31:34 (with possible awareness of Isa 43:25); Heb 10:30 cites Deut 32:35; and Heb 10:37-38 cites a combination of Hab 2:3-4 and Isa 26:20.

Moreover, there is a strong connection between "righteousness" and "faith." In Heb 11 several statements make this connection explicit: "By faith" Abel offered an acceptable sacrifice and "received approval as righteous" (Heb 11:4). "By faith" Noah took heed and "became an heir to the righteousness that is in accordance with faith" (Heb 11:7). And "through faith" Gideon, Barak, Samson, Jephthah, David, Samuel, and the prophets "administered justice (dikaiosynē)" (Heb 11:32-33). Both terms (*faith* and *righteousness*) are difficult to define in these connections, though while faith seems to be the disposition of those named, righteousness seems sometimes to be both a human characteristic and a divine bestowal. In combination, however, faith seems to be the indisputable basis for righteousness, which itself either puts one into a right relationship to God or refers to the right relationship itself.

4. James

James' reflection on righteousness is controversial because of an ostensible conflict with Paul. Careful attention to and comparison between James and Paul finds that these two NT authors use the same Greek words in very different ways. What James means by "works" that justify the person is what Paul means by "the obedience of faith" that reveals the person's justification. These two authors are not necessarily in conflict but are speaking at odd angles to each other.

James uses the verb "to justify" three times (Jas 2:21, 24, 25) in the famous passage that discusses "works" and "faith alone." Abraham is the key character that James uses to register his point: that doing something is necessary to experience justification. James does not specify what it is that persons must do—other than "works" as evidence of faith—but he does clearly present the activity of justification as the work of God.

In turn, James' three uses of dikaiosynē (*righteousness*) present James' flexibility in using this term. James writes, "Your anger does not produce God's righteousness," a statement that seems to indicate that righteousness is that which is in accordance with God's will and acceptable to God (Jas 1:20). It is, in other words, human activity in keeping with God's purposes. In Jas 2:23, as James cites Gen 15:6 ("Abraham believed God, and it was reckoned to him as righteousness"), he seems to assume that the righteousness of Abraham was his willingness to sacrifice Isaac at God's command. Thus, Abraham did not merely believe, but he believed and began to take action upon that belief; and so, he was justified. In Jas 3:18, he says simply, "And a harvest of righteousness is sown in peace for/by those who make peace." Self-evidently, righteousness is the result of faithful action done in accordance with God's will.

James uses the adjective *righteous* as if it were a noun in 5:6, 16. The verses refer to "the righteous one" and "the righteous," indicating a person who is spiritually sound ("The prayer of the righteous is powerful and effective," Jas 5:16).

In sum, James writes to motivate a vigorous style of Christian life, to dissuade persons away from a kind of inert piety. In writing of righteousness, James advances his cause by encouraging and exhorting his readers to active Christian living that honors and does God's will.

5. First Peter

Predominantly, 1 Peter's understanding of righteousness is seen in two uses of the noun *righteousness* (dikaiosynē) and three uses of the adjective *righteous* (dikaios). First Peter 3:10-12 cites Ps 34:12-16 to indicate that the Lord's eyes are upon "the righteous," who are described as those who "desire life and desire to see good days, [who] keep their tongues from evil and their lips from speaking deceit; [who] turn away from evil and do good; [who] seek peace and pursue it" (1 Pet 3:10-11). Here, righteousness is understood as actions in relation to other humans, but also probably toward God as well. In turn, in 3:18, Christ is described as "the righteous [one]" who suffered for sins in behalf of "the unrighteous." This reference to the righteous one is clearly an allusion to his behavior in behalf of and in relation to other humans, but almost certainly (given the soteriological value of the suffering of the righteous one) it is to be seen as living in relation to God's will. Finally, the epistle once again cites an OT text (Prov 11:31) in the Septuagintal version (1 Pet 4:18). Here, "the righteous [one]" is contrasted with "the ungodly and the sinners." Here, righteousness is standing before God, as is indicated by the reference to judgment in the preceding verse (1 Pet 4:17).

The noun *righteousness* (dikaiosynē) occurs in 2:24 in a passage that interpreters typically regard as liturgical material. The pertinent phrase states that Christ did what he did in order that we might die to sin and live to righteousness. Thus, there is a sharp contrast between sin and righteousness: righteousness is a way of life lived in keeping with God's will and purposes. Furthermore, another use of the term *righteousness* mentions suffering "for righteousness' sake" (NRSV, "doing what is right") so that again righteousness is a standard of God's will for humanity (1 Pet 3:14).

6. Second Peter and Jude

Most interpreters think that there is some literary relationship between 2 Peter and Jude, with the majority of scholars understanding that the author of 2 Peter knew and used Jude in composing his epistle. Whatever the relationship may be, there is a sharp contrast between the two documents in terms of their use of the language of righteousness. Second Peter uses various forms of "righteousness" several times, in contrast to Jude's single occurrence.

Three uses of *righteous* cluster in 2 Pet 2:7-8 in references to the OT character Lot (compare Gen 19). He is called a "righteous man," in contrast to "the licentiousness of the lawless" and "lawless deeds that he saw and heard." Moreover, we read of Lot's "righteous soul," which was vexed by what he saw and heard. Here, *righteous* describes a way of living that is in keeping with God's will.

Second Peter also speaks of "the righteousness of God." This phrase might be interpreted to be either God's activity or God's standard, but the phrase itself is part of a seemingly high christological declaration, "the righteousness of our God and Savior Jesus Christ"

(1:1). Without attempting to settle the theological and christological questions that arise from this striking formulation, we can see that 2 Peter is likely referring to "the righteousness of. . .Christ," which is most likely an allusion to Christ's own suffering in behalf of humanity. Second Peter next mentions "Noah, a herald of righteousness"(2:5)—apparently indicating Noah's pre-flood preaching of God's will for human life. The third use of *righteousness* (in 2:21) speaks of "the way of righteousness" in conjunction with "the holy commandment that was passed on to them," a clear reference to a manner of life in keeping with the ordinances of God. Second Peter 3:13 uses the language of Isa 65:17 and 66:22 ("new heavens and a new earth") in saying, "But, in accordance with his promise, we wait for new heavens and a new earth, where righteousness is at home." This statement indicates God's standard or God's creatures doing God's will. Together these statements show a fluid use of "righteousness" language.

7. First John

First John has eleven occurrences of "righteousness" language: three uses of the noun *righteousness* (**dikaiosynē**), six uses of the adjective *righteous* (**dikaios**), and two uses of the noun *unrighteousness* (**adikia ἀδικία**). The usages of these terms fall into clear patterns: 1) God is "just" or "righteous" (1 John 1:9; 3:7). 2) Jesus Christ is "righteous" (1 John 2:1, 29). 3) "Righteousness" is human activity that is consistent with God's will, which humans may or may not do (1 John 2:29; 3:7, 10). 4) Believers are "righteous" if they do righteousness (1 John 2:29; 3:12). 5) Unrighteousness is sin or failure to do God's will (1 John 1:9; 5:17).

8. Revelation

The Revelation to John has twenty-one occurrences of *righteousness* language: *righteous* (five times), *righteousness* (two times), *judgment* or "righteous deed" (two times), "to harm" or "do damage" (eleven times), and *iniquity* (one time). The use of this language is striking and falls into observable patterns. Indeed, Revelation shares many of the patterns of usage that were observed in 1 John.

God (Rev 15:3; 16:5), God's judgments (Rev 16:7; 19:2), and believers, who are called holy and who do righteousness (Rev 22:11), are all referred to as being "righteous" or "just." In turn, "righteousness" is associated with a rider on a white horse, a figure of judgment (Rev 19:11). God's activity is called "judgment" (Rev 15:4), and the bride of the Lamb is clothed in "righteous deeds" (Rev 19:8). Then, negatively speaking, Revelation refers repeatedly to "doing harm" or "doing damage" (Rev 2:11; 6:6; 7:2, 3; 9:4, 10, 19; 11:5; 22:11), which is primarily the result of the activity of the forces of evil. Finally, Revelation refers to iniquities (Rev 18:5), a term that is effectively equivalent to sins (*see* SIN, SINNERS).

C. Conclusion

Righteousness (and its cognates) is a prominent, if not dominant, theme in portions of the NT. The range of senses in the NT in which righteousness is meant includes God's own righteousness, human righteousness in relationship to God, and human righteousness in human relationships. Different NT authors use "righteousness" language in different (though not widely different) ways. Careful attention to the NT language of righteousness in various contexts is necessary to discern exactly what the NT authors are attempting to communicate through their uses of this language.

Bibliography: M. Barth. *Justification: Pauline Texts Interpreted in the Light of the Old and New Testament* (1971); M. T. Brauch. "Perspectives on 'God's Righteousness' in Recent German Discussion." E. P. Sanders, ed. *Paul and Palestinian Judaism* (1977) 523–42; R. Bultmann. "ΔΙΚΑΙΟΣΥΝΗ ΘΕΟΥ." *JBL* 83 (1964) 12–16; J. D. G. Dunn. "'Righteousness from the Law' and 'Righteousness from Faith': Paul's Interpretation of Scripture in Rom 10:1-10." *Tradition and Interpretation in the New Testament.* G. F. Hawthorne and O. Betz, eds. (1987) 216–28; E. Käsemann. "'The Righteousness of God' in Paul." *New Testament Questions of Today* (1969) 168–82; L. E. Keck. "'Justification of the Ungodly' and Ethics." *Rechtfertigung.* J. Friedrich et al., eds. (1976) 199–209; B. Przybylski. *Righteousness in Matthew and His World of Thought* (1980); J. H. P. Reumann. *"Righteousness" in the New Testament* (1982); M. L. Soards. "The Righteousness of God in the Writings of the Apostle Paul." *BTB* 15 (1985) 104–109; M. L. Soards. "Käsemann's 'Righteousness' Reexamined." *CBQ* 49 (1987) 264–67; S. K. Williams. "The 'Righteousness of God' in Romans." *JBL* 99 (1980) 241–90.

MARION L. SOARDS

RIGHTEOUSNESS IN THE OT [צֶדֶק **tsedheq**, צְדָקָה **tsedhaqah**, צַדִּיק **tsaddiq**]. Words derived from the verbal root **tsdq** (צדק) occur in the OT no less than 525 times. The basic meaning of the root is "to do the right." The word and its derivations appear to be West Semitic in origin. The only East Semitic attestation of it is in the Akkadian text of a 14th-cent. Amarna letter from one Abdu-hepa of Jerusalem to the king of Egypt in which he says, "See, my Lord, I am right (**tsa-du-uq**) about the people . . ." (*CAD* 16:59).

In West Semitic language **tsadaq** occurs in Amorite, Old South Arabic, Ugaritic, Phoenician, Aramaic, Arabic, and Syriac.

West Semitic languages and dialects display a range of meanings for **tsdq** that include right or proper conduct, order, legitimacy of succession, loyalty, truth, and responsibility.

The occurrences of the root **tsdq** in the OT attest to and confirm the meaning of the root found in other West Semitic languages. In most of its occurrences in the biblical text, the word carries a nuance of meaning that goes beyond simply "not doing the wrong." It involves obedience to the covenant relationship between the people of Israel and Yahweh, an obedience incumbent upon both the people and their God.

Thus, righteousness in the OT is a relational concept rather than a matter of strict obedience to a set of rules and regulations. It is God's share in human history (Heschel) and the most important idea in the OT with regard to all human affairs (von Rad). An example of the relational nature of righteousness is found in Deut 24:10, 12-13: "When you make your neighbor a loan of any kind, you shall not go into the house to take the pledge. . . . If the person is poor, you shall not sleep in the garment given you as the pledge. You shall give the pledge back by sunset, so that your neighbor may sleep in the cloak and bless you; and it will be to your righteousness (NRSV, "credit") before the LORD your God." The prophet Amos condemns unrighteous practices in Israel: "They lay themselves down beside every altar on garments taken in pledge; and in the house of their God they drink wine bought with fines they imposed" (Amos 2:8).

Various derivations of the root **tsdq** are found in thirty of the thirty-nine books in the OT, most often in the prophets, psalms, and wisdom literature. Their occurrences in the Pentateuch and the historical books are fewer but nonetheless significant for understanding the meaning and interpretation of the word. The most commonly occurring form of the word is **tsaddiq** and is used to describe God, individual humans, and groups of humans; the form is not often used to describe things or actions, where the preferred form is **tsedhaqah** or **tsedheq**.

A. The Pentateuch and Former Prophets

1. References to individuals and groups of people

The word *righteous* occurs for the first time in the biblical text in the story of Noah. The genealogy of Gen 6:9 states that Noah was a righteous man, and in 7:1 God declares to Noah, "I have seen that you alone are righteous before me in this generation." The next appearance of the word is in the narrative in Gen 15 in which Abram believed the words of the Lord, and the Lord "reckoned it to him as righteousness" (v. 6).

In Gen 18:19, God declares that Sarah and Abraham would have a child in their old age because God chose Abraham "that he may charge his children and his household after him to keep the way of the LORD by doing righteousness and justice" (**mishpat** מִשְׁפָּט). Later in the same chapter, Abraham challenges God not to destroy Sodom and Gomorrah if as few as ten righteous people are found in their midst (18:23-33).

In the Gen 20 story of Abraham and King Abimelech of Gerar, after God reveals to Abimelech the true identity of Sarah, the king inquires whether God would destroy a righteous (NRSV, "innocent") people (v. 4). Jacob claims that he is righteous (NRSV, "honest") in his dealings with Laban in Gen 30:33; and Judah declares Tamar "more in the right" than he in Gen 38:26.

In the book of Genesis, therefore, various derivations of the root **tsdq** are used by God to refer to individuals, by individuals to refer to others (those inside and outside the community of ancient Israel), and by individuals to refer to themselves. The pattern continues in the remainder of the Pentateuch and the DtrH.

In the law code of Exod 23:7-8, the people are commanded to be careful to preserve the integrity of those who are "in the right," and in Deut 6:25 God reminds the Israelites that the reason they are to observe the commandments of God is so that they will be "in the right." In Deut 9:4-6, however, God reminds the people that when they enter the land of promise and possess it, it will not be because of their righteousness, but because of God's promise to the ancestors.

Righteousness was particularly incumbent upon the monarchy in ancient Israel, since the ruler was the guarantor of the stability of society. In one of the narratives of the conflict between Saul and David, David states that the Lord rewards each person's individual righteousness and faithfulness (**ʾemunah** אֱמוּנָה) (1 Sam 26:23). In another, Saul declares that David is "more righteous" than he (1 Sam 24:17). And in 2 Sam 22:21, 25, David sings that the Lord has rewarded him according to his righteousness. Solomon celebrates his father's righteousness in 1 Kgs 3:6.

When the queen of Sheba visits Solomon at his palace in Jerusalem, she states that all that she had heard about the king was true—all his accomplishments and his wisdom. And she declares that God had placed Solomon on the throne of Israel to execute justice and righteousness (1 Kgs 10:1-9).

2. References to the interactions among people

A number of passages that include a derivation of the root **tsdq** have to do with right relationships among people, particularly among the people of Israel. Leviticus 19:15; Deut 1:16; and 16:18-20 deal with the issue of due process in legal disputes. Deuteronomy 1:16 says, "I charged your judges at that time: 'Give the members of your community a fair hearing, and judge rightly between one person and another, whether citizen or resident alien.' "

In Lev 19:36 and Deut 25:15, God admonishes the Israelites to have only right weights and measures because, according to Lev 19:36, "I am the LORD your God, who brought you out of the land of Egypt," and "so that your days may be long in the land that the LORD your God is giving to you" (Deut 25:15).

3. Descriptions of God and the works of God

The first human declaration of the righteousness of God is that of Pharaoh in Exod 9:27. Moses sings of God's justice and righteousness in Deut 32:4 and praises Zebulun for carrying out the righteousness (NRSV, "justice") of the Lord in Deut 33:21; David echoes Moses' words concerning God's righteousness in 2 Sam 23:3. In Judg 5, Deborah and Barak sing of the righteousness (**tsidhqoth** צִדְקוֹת) of the Lord, and Samuel speaks of the righteousness (**tsidqoth**) of the Lord in his farewell address to the Israelites in 1 Sam 12:7.

Deuteronomy 4:8 declares that the Torah of the Lord is righteous (NRSV, "just"), and in Deut 33:19, Moses sings of right sacrifices.

B. The Latter Prophets

Eleven of the fifteen books of the Latter Prophets contain words derived from the root **tsdq**. Some form of the word occurs no less than eighty times in the book of Isaiah alone, with an additional twenty times in Jeremiah, forty times in Ezekiel, and twenty-three times in the Book of the Twelve.

The prophets attribute righteousness to God and speak of righteousness as a gift from God, given to the people at Sinai. As spokespersons of the covenant, they admonish the people to seek to do righteousness as part of their covenant loyalty to God. As in the Pentateuch and Former Prophets, righteousness is not simply "not doing the wrong," not even "strict adherence to the Torah," but actively seeking to do the right in all aspects of human and divine relationships. Amos 5:21-24 reminds the people that unless their festivals, solemn assemblies, offerings and sacrifices, and songs of worship were offered in the right spirit, they would not be accepted. Rather, God desires justice and righteousness.

1. God's righteousness

The prophets speak of God's righteousness as they call the people to righteousness, but most often in terms of God's actions rather than God's character. Isaiah certainly declares that the Lord is exalted by justice and shows himself holy by righteousness (5:16); but he proclaims that God "filled Zion with justice and righteousness" (33:5) and that the Lord "put on righteousness like a breastplate, and a helmet of salvation on his head" (59:17). In Jer 9:24, God says, "I act with steadfast love, justice, and righteousness in the earth."

God is righteous and that righteousness affects God's actions in history and the character of the created order. In Isa 45:8, the Lord commands, "Shower, O heavens, from above, and let the skies rain down righteousness; let the earth open, that salvation may spring up, and let it cause righteousness to sprout up also"; in 61:11 God promises, "as the earth brings forth its shoots, and as a garden causes what is sown in it to spring up, so the Lord GOD will cause righteousness and praise to spring up before the nations." The prophet Joel calls the people to "rejoice in the LORD your God; for he has given the early rain in righteousness" (2:23; NRSV, "for your vindication").

Of greater concern to the prophets, however, is the behavior of the people, particularly those who are in authority over the people. Isaiah and Jeremiah, especially, look forward to a time when a righteous king would sit on the throne of Israel, bringing peace and prosperity to the people. Isaiah speaks of one who will come and establish and uphold the throne of David "with justice and with righteousness from this time onward and forevermore" (9:7), and of a shoot from the stump of Jesse (11:1) who will judge the poor with righteousness "and decide with equity for the meek of the earth" (11:4). Jeremiah looks forward to a day when God will "raise up for David a righteous Branch" who will "execute justice and righteousness in the land" (23:5).

2. Justice and righteousness

The various words derived from the root **tsdq** are used in parallel construction (in both narrative and poetic texts) with *justice* some eighty times. An examination of the two words in their tandem usage provides additional insight into the meaning of *righteousness.*

Abraham Heschel suggests that the word *justice* implies the ability to discern between good and evil and the act of discerning between good and evil, while *righteousness* is the innate quality that drives one to act on that ability to discern. Thus, according to Heschel, righteousness goes beyond justice, in that justice connotes adherence to a code of conduct (the Torah), while righteousness embodies a burning compassion for others.

The two words occur together eighteen times in the book of Isaiah. The opening words of the book bemoan the current state of affairs in Jerusalem: "How the faithful city has become a whore! She that was full of justice, righteousness lodged in her—but now murderers!" (Isa 1:21).

In Isa 5:7, the prophet emphasizes the significance of the parallel concepts of justice and righteousness in a carefully crafted play on words: "For the vineyard of the LORD of hosts is the house of Israel, and the people of Judah are his pleasant planting; he expected justice (**mishpat**), but saw bloodshed (**mispakh** מִשְׂפָּח); righteousness (**tsedhaqah**), but heard a cry (**tseʿaqah** צְעָקָה)." The lack of adherence to the covenant stipulations resulted in physical harm to the people; the lack of an innate sense of covenant loyalty resulted in the crying out of the people.

Isaiah 32:16 states that when God reigns over the world, "justice will dwell in the wilderness, and righteousness . . . in the fruitful field." But v. 17 gives pride of place to righteousness, stating that "the doing" of righteousness will be **shalom** (שָׁלוֹם; NRSV, "peace") and "the working out" (NRSV, "result") of righteousness will be quietness and trust forever.

Ezekiel admonishes the rulers of the people in 45:9, "Thus says the Lord GOD: Enough, O princes of Israel! Put away violence and oppression, and do what is just and right." In Amos 5:7 and 6:12, the prophet uses what appears to be a proverbial saying to describe the sins of the people: "You have turned justice into poison and the fruit of righteousness into wormwood" (see also Jer 9:15 and 23:15).

3. Covenant love, faithfulness, and righteousness

Righteousness in its various iterations is also paralleled in OT texts with KHESED (**khesedh** חֶסֶד), the word used to describe the covenant relationship between God and the Israelites, and with forms of the root **ʾmn** (אמן; esp. **ʾemeth** [אֱמֶת]), whose basic meaning has to do with constancy and reliability.

The prophet Hosea says to the people: "Sow for yourselves righteousness; reap steadfast love (**khesedh**); break up your fallow ground; for it is time to seek the LORD, that he may come and rain righteousness upon you" (10:12).

Isaiah describes a future ruler of the line of Jesse in 11:5 with the words "Righteousness shall be the belt around his waist, and faithfulness the belt around his loins." And in 16:5, "Then a throne shall be established in steadfast love in the tent of David, and on it shall sit in faithfulness a ruler who seeks justice and is swift to do what is right."

God's heartfelt speech to Israel in Hos 2 includes the words, "And I will take you for my wife forever; I will take you for my wife in righteousness and in justice, in steadfast love, and in mercy (**rakhamim** רַחֲמִים)" (2:19).

Jeremiah admonishes his hearers not to boast in their own abilities, but to boast that they understand and know their God who says to them, "I am the LORD; I act with steadfast love, justice, and righteousness in the earth" (Jer 9:24).

Interestingly, though, the words *righteousness* and *justice* do not occur in God's self-description in Exod 34:6, although *merciful*, *steadfast love*, and *faithfulness* do.

C. The Psalter

Words derived from the root **tsdq** occur in the psalter 141 times, in every type of psalm. As in the prophetic works, the word is paired with justice, steadfast love, and faithfulness in a number of psalms.

1. God's righteousness

Righteousness is attributed to the Lord in the psalter and is often tied to the deity's saving actions and deliverance of the people. Psalm 7:10-11 declares that God saves the upright in heart and that God is a righteous judge. The singer of Ps 36 says, "Your steadfast love, O LORD, extends to the heavens, your faithfulness to the clouds. Your righteousness is like the mighty mountains, your judgments are like the great deep; you save humans and animals alike, O LORD" (vv. 5-6). In Ps 51:14, the psalmist implores God, "Deliver me from bloodshed, O God, O God of my salvation, and my tongue will sing aloud of your righteousness" (NRSV, "deliverance").

In Ps 48:10, God's right hand is described as righteous (NRSV, "filled with victory"); in Ps 50:6 the heavens declare God's righteousness; Ps 97, an enthronement psalm, states that righteousness and justice are the foundations of God's throne (v. 2; see also 89:14); and the singer of Ps 85 declares that righteousness will go before God and will make a path for his steps (v. 13).

2. God's righteous works

The works of God are described as righteous in numerous places in the psalter. Psalm 19:9 states that the ordinances of the Lord are "true and righteous altogether." Psalm 99:4 praises God the king who has carried out justice and righteousness in Jacob. The great Ps 119 contains fifteen words from the root **tsdq**, most often in descriptions of the Torah. Verses 7, 62, 106, 160, and 164 celebrate God's righteous ordinances. Verse 142 states that God's righteousness is an everlasting righteousness, and God's Torah is truth. The singer of Ps 145 declares that the Lord is "righteous (NRSV, "just") in all his ways, and kind in all his doings" (v. 17).

3. The righteous person in Psalms

In Ps 143:2, the psalmist declares that "no one living is righteous" before God, and, while the psalm singers rarely declare their own righteousness, they speak often of "the righteous." A few instances of declarations of self-righteousness are found in the psalter. In Ps 7:9, the singer asks God to judge the psalmist according to his/her own righteousness.

The psalter opens in Ps 1:6 with a promise that God "watches over the way of the righteous," and numerous other psalms address God's care for the righteous. Psalm 5 declares that God blesses the righteous and covers them with a shield (v. 12); the singer of Ps 34 states, "The eyes of the LORD are on the righteous" (tsaddiq; v. 15); in Ps 55:22, the righteous are assured that God will never permit them to be moved; and Ps 92:12 maintains, "The righteous flourish like the palm tree, and grow like a cedar in Lebanon."

In the royal Ps 72, the singer requests that God give to the king justice and righteousness; and in Ps 82:3, the psalmist asks that there be justice and righteousness for the weak, the orphan, the lowly, and destitute.

The singers of Pss 33 and 64 command the righteous to rejoice in the Lord (33:1; 64:10); in Ps 68:3, they are admonished to be joyful, to exult, and to be jubilant before God; and in Ps 97:12 they are to rejoice in the Lord and give thanks to his holy name.

Psalm 112 states that the one who fears the Lord will have righteousness that endures forever and that that person will never be afraid (vv. 3, 8, 9).

4. The righteous and the wicked

The contrast between the righteous and the wicked (rashaʿ רָשָׁע) is pervasive in the psalter, and first encountered in the wisdom of Ps 1, in which the psalm singer proclaims that "the LORD watches over the way of the righteous, but the way of the wicked will perish" (v. 6). More than thirty psalms throughout the book deal with the subject, even the closing doxological Ps 146, which states, "the LORD loves the righteous. . . but the way of the wicked he brings to ruin" (vv. 8-9).

In Ps 37, another wisdom psalm, the words *righteous* and *wicked* occur twenty-three times in forty verses as the psalm singer encourages the righteous ones not to be envious or fearful of the wicked ones.

D. The Wisdom Books (Job, Proverbs, Ecclesiastes)

As in the book of Psalms, the contrast between the righteous and the wicked is a major theme of the wisdom books of the OT. In the book of Proverbs, the righteous and wicked appear in dichotomy in a total of fifty-seven verses, in almost every chapter of the book. (Interestingly, the two words occur together in only two verses in 22:17–24:22, the portion of Proverbs that has many similarities with the 12th-cent. BCE Egyptian Instruction of Amenemope.) In 3:33, we read, "The LORD's curse is on the house of the wicked, but he blesses the abode of the righteous"; in 12:21, "No harm happens to the righteous, but the wicked are filled with trouble"; and 29:2 states, "When the righteous are in authority, the people rejoice; but when the wicked rule, the people groan."

Words derived from the root tsdq occur in the book of Job thirty-five times. In 4:17, Job asks, "Can mortals be righteous before God?" and in 25:4, "How then can a mortal be righteous?" (see also 9:2 and 15:14). And yet Job declares his righteousness: "I, who called upon God and he answered me, a righteous (NRSV, "just") and blameless man" (12:4); "I hold fast my righteousness, and will not let it go" (27:6); "I put on righteousness, and it clothed me; my justice was like a robe and a turban" (29:14). And Job speaks with confidence that he will be found righteous in the end: "I have indeed prepared my case; I know that I shall be righteous" (13:18; NRSV, "vindicated"); "let me be weighed in a righteous (NRSV, "just") balance, and let God know my integrity!" (31:6). God has the last word in the debate over righteousness in the book of Job. In the midst of God's reply to Job "out of the whirlwind," God says to Job, "Will you even put me in the wrong? Will you condemn me that you may be righteous?" (40:8; NRSV, "justified").

Forms of the root tsdq occur in the book of Ecclesiastes eleven times. The teacher laments in 3:16 that "I saw under the sun that in the place. . .of righteousness, wickedness"; in 7:15, "In my vain life I have seen everything; there are righteous people who perish in their righteousness, and there are wicked people who prolong their life in their evildoing"; and in 8:14, "There are righteous people who are treated according to the conduct of the wicked, and there are wicked people who are treated according to the conduct of the righteous." The teacher does not provide a solution to the question of the fates of the righteous and the wicked, but concludes in 12:13-14, "Fear God, and keep his commandments; for that is the whole duty of everyone. For God will bring every deed into judgment," suggesting that, in the end, God's righteousness (doing the right) will prevail over the earth and over humanity.

E. Conclusion

The concept of righteousness is pervasive in the books of the OT. Righteousness, as described in the OT, is about right relationships on both the cosmic and human level, relationships based on the covenant promises made between God and the people of Israel at Sinai; it has less to do with attitude than with action, less to do with inner mind-set than with outward manifestation.

The acts of God in creation, the acts of God in relation to humanity, the acts of humanity in relation to God, and the acts of humanity in relation to humanity are described and critiqued within the parameters of righteousness. The God of Israel who claims to be righteous calls those who would worship him to be righteous. Nowhere in the OT is the righteousness of God cited as a reason for the condemnation of humankind; it is, rather, depicted as a characteristic of God that is kindly shared with humanity in its quest to emulate the God of the covenant. The OT, particularly the psalms and wisdom literature, draws a sharp distinction between the righteous and wicked, between those who seek to carry out the covenant promises and those who seek their own self-interest.

Righteousness is thus about placing the interest of all—all people and all of creation—above one's own desires and indulgences. It is, in the end, about "doing the right" in all realms of human existence. Meanings of the root tsdq in other West Semitic languages include the ideas of right conduct, legitimacy, loyalty, and truth, but only in the biblical text are these ideas combined with and connected to the covenant relationship between God and people.

Bibliography: Abraham J. Heschel. *The Prophets: An Introduction.* Vol. 1 (1962); Gert Kwakkel. *According to My Righteousness: Upright Behavior as Grounds for Deliverance in Psalms 7, 17, 18, 26, and 44* (2002); J. Clinton McCann Jr. *A Theological Introduction to the Book of Psalms* (1993); R. W. L. Moberly. "Whose Justice? Which Righteousness? The Interpretation of Isaiah v 16." *VT* 51 (2001) 55–68; Gerhard von Rad. *Old Testament Theology.* Vol. 1. D. M. Stalker, trans. (1962); Peter Stuhlmacher. *Reconciliation, Law and Righteousness: Essays in Biblical Theology* (1986); Moshe Weinfeld. *Justice and Righteousness in Israel and the Nations* (1985).

NANCY DECLAISSÉ-WALFORD

RIMMON rim´uhn [רִמּוֹן rimmon]. Means "pomegranate." *Rimmon* is the name of at least three different locations of the OT. It is also the name of a Benjaminite and a designation for the god HADAD. 1. A site in Lower Galilee on the northern border of the tribal territory of Zebulun. Joshua 19:13 names the site in outlining the boundaries of Zebulun's territorial inheritance. First Chronicles 6:77 identifies Rimmon (RIMMONO) and its pasture lands as territory given by Zebulun to the Levitical Merarites. The present-day, Rummana, located about 9 km north of Nazareth, on the southern edge of the Beit Netofa Valley, is generally regarded as this Rimmon.

2. Judah's southernmost district, outlined in Josh 15:21-32, includes "Ain and Rimmon" (Josh 15:32 NRSV), but perhaps should be read as "En-Rimmon." Likewise, Josh 19:1-9 outlines Simeon's territory and lists "Ain, Rimmon" (19:7 NRSV), which conceivably is also best read as "En-Rimmon." EN-RIMMON was a site in Judah and Simeon. Given the nondistinct nature of the Judah-Simeon border, it is probable that the same town is referenced in both descriptions. First Chronicles 4:32 likewise lists Rimmon as a Simeonite city. Nehemiah 11:29 cites En-Rimmon among the cities in which some Judahites took up residence in the reestablished postexilic province of Judea. Consensus seems to locate the site approximately 14 km northeast of Beer-sheba and 3 km west-southwest of Tell Halif.

3. The rock of Rimmon was located in the southern reaches of Ephraimite territory, a few kilometers north of the Benjaminite border. It was to this location that 600 Benjaminite warriors fled for refuge when the amassed Israelite army nearly extinguished the tribe of Benjamin as a consequence of the Gibeah incident. Upon realizing the desperate plight of the remaining Benjaminites, the nation sent an overture of peace, whereupon they returned and a means was devised for salvaging the tribe (Judg 19–21; see esp. 20:45, 47; 21:13).

4. A Benjaminite, apparently a descendant of the salvaged tribe, from the town of Beeroth approximately 3 km south of Gibeon; the father of Rechab and Baanah, the two assassins of Ishbosheth, the son of Saul (2 Sam 4:2, 5, 9). Perhaps there is intended irony in naming the father of Ishbosheth's murderers, an event that brought to an end the potential for any Saulide dynasty, in light of the place to which the 600 Benjaminites fled, the protection of which factored into the events that led to Saul's kingship.

5. A designation for Hadad, the Aramean storm deity referenced in the context of Elisha's cleansing of the Syrian military commander, Naaman. Naaman, who had just been healed of his leprosy, proclaimed allegiance to Yahweh, but immediately and somewhat apologetically, sought Elisha's understanding about continued worship in the house of Rimmon (2 Kgs 5:18; compare also 1 Kgs 15:18, "TABRIMMON" ["Rimmon is good"] the father of the Aramean king, Benhadad).

JOHN I. LAWLOR

RIMMON, HORVAT rim´uhn. Horvat Rimmon (Khirbet Umm er-Ramamin) is in the southern SHEPHELAH, 1.2 km south of Tel Halif. Eusebius (*Onom.* 88.17–18), commenting on Rimmon in the inheritance of Simeon (Josh 19:7), refers to Eremmon as a Jewish village 16 mi. from Eleutheropolis. That, indeed, corresponds to the distance between Beth Guvrin (Eleutheropolis) and RIMMON. The nearby mound of Tel Halif (*see* HALIF, TEL) is generally identified with the biblical Rimmon or Hormah. However, in the Hellenistic Period a settlement was founded here, and the biblical name "Rimmon" became identified with this site from that time onward.

Three seasons of excavations (1978–80) and some later soundings were carried out at the site. The first settlement at Rimmon was built at the end of the 2nd and beginning of the 1st cent. BCE and continued until the Bar Kochba War (*see* BAR KOCHBA, SIMON). The site was not abandoned, and it continued to be occupied from the mid-2nd until the mid-3rd cent. CE, although only a few remains were found, including coins.

Significantly, four synagogues were built in the central compound, each above the earlier one. In the mid-3rd cent. CE the first "broad house" SYNAGOGUE was built, with the long northern wall containing a square niche facing Jerusalem. The second, a rectangular building with a narrow "narthex" on the south, was constructed at the end of the 4th cent. CE; the short northern wall facing Jerusalem contained a bema. In the 5th cent. CE, two rows of columns were added to the central prayer hall to reinforce the roof, converting the structure into a "basilica-type" synagogue. The fourth synagogue, paved with square flagstones, was constructed at the beginning of the 7th cent. CE. It was dated by coins found below the pavement, some of them intentionally placed, and was in use for slightly less than a century. The pavement contains a carpet-like central area decorated with five incised rosettes; a seven-branched MENORAH was added later to the north. The synagogues were incorporated into a closed compound used by the local community for their social needs, including a long magazine west of the synagogue containing the community's treasury. *See* IDUMEA.

Bibliography: Amos Kloner. "The Synagogues of Horvat Rimmon." *Ancient Synagogues in Israel: Third–Seventh Century C.E.* Rachel Hachlili, ed. (1989) 43–48, pl. XXV–XXVII; Amos Kloner and Tessa Mindel. "Two Byzantine Hoards from the Ancient Synagogue of Horvat Rimmon." *Israel Numismatic Journal* 5 (1981) 60–68, pls. 14–15; Joseph Naveh and Shaul Shaked. *Amulets and Magic Bowls* (1985).

AMOS KLONER

RIMMONO ri-moh´nuh [רִמּוֹנוֹ rimmono]. Town allotted to the Merrarites (1 Chr 6:77 [Heb. 6:62]). Variant of RIMMON.

RIMMON-PEREZ rim´uhn-pee´riz [רִמֹּן פֶּרֶץ rimmon parets]. Meaning "pomegranate rift." Rimmon-Perez occurs in the list of campsites traversed by Israel during the exodus in Num 33:19-20. It is listed as a stop between Rithmah and Libnah. Some equate Rimmon-Perez with Wadi er Rummun in the Negev, but that identification is not certain.

RING. *See* JEWELRY.

RINNAH rin´uh [רִנָּה rinnah]. The second of four sons of Shimon and a descendant of Judah (1 Chr 4:20).

RIPHATH rī´fath [רִיפַת rifath]. Son of GOMER, grandson of JAPHETH, and great-grandson of Noah (Gen 10:3; 1 Chr 1:6, where NRSV follows the Hebrew, which reads "Diphath" here). The genealogies in which the name appears link nations by geographic, cultural, and political association. Israel understood Riphath to be most closely related to the Greeks and Medes. In Ezekiel's apocalyptic vision of the future, God brings the descendants of Japheth (GOG, Gomer) to righteous judgment when Israel is redeemed (Ezek 38; similarly Rev 20:8).

SHARON PACE

RISSAH ris´uh [רִסָּה rissah]. An Israelite camping site in the wilderness between Sinai and Ezion-Geber (Num 33:21-22) in an itinerary attributed to P. Its location is unknown. According to Jewish Midrash, the list illustrates the miraculous nature of the wilderness journey, made possible only with divine assistance.

RITHMAH rith´muh [רִתְמָה rithmah]. One of the Israelites' early stopping points on their wilderness journey (Num 33:18-19). Its location is unknown.

RITUAL. Ritual is the means by which a group of people defines certain life events and their beliefs about the meaning of those events through proscribed actions. By studying actual groups of people whose way of life resembles ancient biblical culture, anthropologists have contributed new insight to ritual theory, and hence to the meaning of biblical rituals including sacrifice, meals, purification, marriage, initiation, gender roles, consecration of leaders, and death. For example, Rene Girard, in the 1970s, applied his theory of the violent origins of culture to the Bible. Girard theorized that the ritual of sacrifice was built on a scapegoating mechanism; one person or animal would die, having been vested with all the crimes and sins of the society (*see* ATONEMENT; SACRIFICES AND OFFERINGS). Though the gospel accounts neatly fit this scheme, Girard sees them as exposing the innocence of the sacrificial victim, while other religions cover up the victim's arbitrary and innocent nature. Other scholars who have contributed to modern ritual theory include Victor Turner, Arnold van Gennep, Clifford Geertz, Catherine Bell, and Ronald Grimes.

Anthropologist Mary Douglas and biblical scholars Jon Levenson, Howard Eilberg-Schwartz, Frank Gorman, Hyam Maccoby, Ithamar Gruenwald, Jay Sklar, and others have fruitfully examined the presence of ritual and its contribution to meaning in OT texts, for instance, in rituals of purity (*see* CLEAN AND UNCLEAN), formation of FAMILY through marriages, the symbolic meaning of MEALS, ways of dealing with DEATH, initiation rites such as CIRCUMCISION, the ritual purpose behind certain laws, and the practice of sacrifice. With the exception of Nancy Jay's analysis of biblical and Christian sacrifice, there has been minimal interest among NT scholars in examining ritual elements in the NT. *See* ANOINT; ANTHROPOLOGY, NT CULTURAL; ANTHROPOLOGY, OT CULTURAL; BAPTISM; FEASTS AND FASTS; MARRIAGE, NT; MARRIAGE, OT; MEN AND MASCULINITY IN THE BIBLE; WOMEN IN THE ANCIENT NEAR EAST; WOMEN IN THE NT; WOMEN IN THE OT.

Bibliography: Catherine Bell. *Ritual Theory, Ritual Practice* (1992); Mary Douglas. *Purity and Danger* (1966); Nicole Wilkinson Duran. *Power of Disorder: Ritual Elements in Marks' Passion Narrative* (2009); Howard Eilberg-Schwartz. *The Savage in Judaism* (1990); Clifford Geertz. *Interpretation of Cultures* (1973); Arnold van Gennep. *Rites of Passage* (1960); Rene Girard. *Violence and the Sacred* (1977); Frank H. Gorman Jr. *The Ideology of Ritual: Space, Time, and Status in Priestly Theology* (1990); Ronald L. Grimes. *Beginnings in Ritual Studies* (1994); Ithamar Gruenwald. *Rituals and Ritual Theory in Ancient Israel* (2003); Nancy Jay. *Throughout Your Generations Forever* (1992); Jon D. Levenson. *Death and Resurrection of the Beloved Son* (1993); Hyam Maccoby. *Ritual and Morality: The Ritual Purity System and Its Place in Judaism* (1999); Jay

Sklar. *Sin, Impurity, Sacrifice, and Atonement* (2005); Victor Turner. *Ritual Process* (1969).

NICOLE WILKINSON DURAN

RIVER [נָהָר nahar; ποταμός potamos]. The Hebrew and Greek words for *river* are used principally of watercourses that have water year-round, especially the JORDAN RIVER and the EUPHRATES RIVER, and a dozen others less frequently. Another word, *brook* (nakhal נַחַל), usually refers to streambeds or valleys that have water from runoff only during the rainy season, although nahar and nakhal often overlap in meaning. The word for *river* may also refer to irrigation canals in Mesopotamia (Ps 137:1; Ezek 1:1) and perhaps also in Egypt (Exod 7:19). The NILE RIVER is generally called simply the Nile, although occasionally also a "river" (Isa 19:5; Wis 19:10). The Euphrates is often called simply "the River" (Ps 72:8; Isa 8:7), although the NRSV often substitutes or adds "the Euphrates" (e.g., Josh 24:2). In the Persian period, the region west of the Euphrates was a district called "Beyond the River" (Ezra 4:10).

Like the word *sea* (yam יָם), with which it is often used as a parallel term in biblical poetry, *river* also has a mythological meaning: in the plural it is used as one of the titles of the storm god's watery adversary (Hab 3:8; see NRSV footnote), called in Ugaritic by the parallel titles "Prince Sea" and "Judge River" (*see* Pss 24:2; 89:25 [Heb. 89:26]; Rev 12:15). The *river* is also a parallel term for the Sea of Reeds (miyam-suf מִיַּם־סוּף), which the Israelites crossed during the exodus. In biblical narrative, the crossing of the Reed Sea and the crossing of the Jordan River bracket the period of the exodus, with the connection between these crossings affirmed in Josh 4:23. In poetry the chronology is collapsed, as in Pss 66:6; 114:3.

In ANE mythology, the home of the high god was a cosmic mountain from whose base the principal rivers of the world flowed. In the Bible, from Eden, the garden of God (Ezek 28:13), there flows a river that divides into four branches to water the world (Gen 2:10-14). Likewise, from the house of God, the Temple on Mount Zion in Jerusalem, flows a river (Ps 46:4 [Heb. 46:5]). The principal source of water for ancient Jerusalem was the spring Gihon ("the gusher"), one of the four rivers of Eden (*see* GIHON, SPRING). From the restored Temple will flow a river of living waters providing supernatural fertility (Ezek 47:1-12; Joel 3:18 [Heb. 4:18]; Zech 14:8; see also Isa 33:21; 66:12). This language is alluded to in the NT, where Jesus, who himself is a replacement for the Temple (John 2:21), is also called a source of "living water" (John 4:10; 7:37-38). In the end time the "river of the water of life" will flow from the throne of God and the Lamb (Rev 22:1).

A possible mythological dimension of another Hebrew word occasionally translated "river" (shelakh שֶׁלַח) is as a boundary that had to be crossed by those who died as they entered the underworld (Job 33:18), like the river Hubur in Mesopotamian mythology and the river Styx in Greek mythology. *See* ABANA; AHAVA; BROOK; CHEBAR; FLOOD; GOZAN; ISRAEL, GEOGRAPHY OF; JABBOK; KISHON; PHARPAR; PISHON; SEA; ULAI; VALLEY.

MICHAEL D. COOGAN

RIVER OF EGYPT. *See* EGYPT, RIVER OF; EGYPT, WADI OF.

RIVER ORDEAL. *See* LAW IN THE OT; TRIAL BY ORDEAL.

RIVER, EUPHRATES. *See* EUPHRATES RIVER.

RIVER, JORDAN. *See* JORDAN RIVER.

RIVER, NILE. *See* NILE RIVER.

RIVER, TIBER. *See* TIBER RIVER.

RIVER, TIGRIS. *See* TIGRIS RIVER.

RIZIA ri-zi´uh [רִצְיָא ritsya᾿]. Arah, Hanniel, and Rizia are the three sons of ULLA listed among the descendants of Asher (1 Chr 7:39).

RIZPAH riz´puh [רִצְפָּה ritspah]. Rizpah was the daughter of Aiah and concubine of Saul who produced two sons (2 Sam 21:1-9). Following Saul's death, his son ISHBAAL's Transjordanian-based kingdom had minimal authority. Ishbaal's general, ABNER, went "in to" Rizpah and made her his own (2 Sam 3:7). This act was a claim to the throne or at best an act of treason (see 1 Kgs 17–25). When Ishbaal questioned Abner's loyalty to Saul's house, Abner responded by defecting to David (2 Sam 3:7-21).

After David became king, a famine in the land was seen as punishment for Saul's slaying of Gibeonites (see Josh 9). David atoned for the offense by hanging seven sons of Saul, including Rizpah's two sons (2 Sam 21:1-9). Rizpah protected their bodies from birds and beasts for some months until the rains came, ending the famine (2 Sam 21:10-14). Rizpah literally means "hot coals" and proved to be so for Ishbaal.

MICHAEL G. VANZANT

ROAD [דֶּרֶךְ derekh; ὁδός hodos]. The first roads used by humans were animal paths that followed the easiest lay of the terrain. Over time, humans developed methods for constructing and maintaining roads. The use of vehicles beginning ca. 3000 BCE increased the need for well-constructed roads. The primary purpose of roads was to facilitate military transportation, but they were also used for communication by governments, trade, and personal business (*see* TRADE AND COMMERCE). Because of their essential role in human culture, roads are referred to throughout the Bible.

The OT contains numerous references to roads (*see* TRAVEL AND COMMUNICATION IN THE OT). **Derekh** is the most common word used for "road" in the OT. **Derekh** is often used with the name of the city to which it led. Some translators (such as the NRSV) think that in this construction **derekh** means "in the direction of" or "by way of," but other translators think it is used as a noun that preserves actual names of roads.

Evidence for roads in the ANE exists from the time of the Sumerians onward. The OT indicates that roads were constructed by removing boulders, brush, and other obstacles and then filling in the holes and leveling the surface (Prov 15:19; 22:5; Isa 40:3; 57:14; 62:10; Hos 2:6). Ancient roads typically were wide enough to accommodate two lanes of traffic. The Minoans (ca. 2000–1400 BCE) and Mycenaeans (ca. 1400–1200 BCE) engaged in extensive road construction. The Assyrians (911–612 BCE) built numerous roads to facilitate administration of their empire. Their roads were made of packed dirt, and various intervals were marked by road signs, guard posts, and wells. The Persians (539–331 BCE) expanded and developed the Assyrian system of roads. Classical Greece (ca. 500–323 BCE) lacked a unified road system, but crudely constructed roads were built and maintained by local city-states with special care given to routes to sacred places.

The Romans built thousands of miles of roads throughout their empire. They learned the craft from the Etruscans, but Romans were the first to use paving extensively on open roads. They adapted the construction process to local conditions, but it generally involved the following steps: surveying a straight route and marking it with furrows; clearing boulders, trees, and other obstacles; digging a trench down about three feet to firm ground; packing a bed of sand and large stones; pounding or rolling a hard layer of pebbles and gravel; fitting together paving blocks cut from basalt, granite, or porphyry to form a crown that would aid drainage; and installing a curb of vertical stones, drainage ditches, and footpaths along the sides. Sometimes ruts were carved into the surface to prevent skidding. Lesser-used roads were paved with gravel or packed dirt.

Two major international highways traversed the land of Canaan and Transjordan from north to south (*see* HIGHWAY). The VIA MARIS—also called the Great Trunk Road or Coastal Highway—began at Aleppo and passed through Damascus, Hazor, Megiddo, the Sharon plain, Gaza, and ended at Memphis in Egypt. The KING'S HIGHWAY (Num 20:17; 21:22) began at the Via Maris in Damascus and passed south through Rabbath-ammon, Heshbon, Dibon, Kir-hareseth, Bozrah, and Elath. A third highway, the National Highway, passed through the highlands of Israel, connecting Jezreel, Dothan, Samaria, Shechem, Bethel, Jerusalem, Hebron, and Beersheba. Approximately 245 roads from the OT period have been identified.

The Roman road system in Palestine consisted of four north–south roads intersected by numerous east–west roads (*see* TRAVEL AND COMMUNICATION IN THE NT). However, most of the Roman roads were not built until the time of Hadrian. Various roads are mentioned in the Gospels, such as the one that Jesus took during his final entry to Jerusalem (Matt 21:8) and the road to EMMAUS on which he walked with two disciples after his resurrection (Luke 24:13-35).

Many of Paul's travels recorded in Acts took place on Roman roads. During his second missionary journey, Paul would have traveled a Roman road that led from Antioch to Tarsus, Derbe, Iconium, Lystra, and Pisidian Antioch (Acts 15:41–16:6). During his third journey, he would have continued on this road to Apamea, Laodicea, and Ephesus (Acts 19:1). During his second journey, he would have traveled the Via Egnatia from Neapolis to Philippi, Amphipolis, Apollonia, and Thessalonica (Acts 16:11–17:1). Built in 148 BCE, this was the first major road constructed outside Italy. After Paul disembarked at Puteoli during his journey to Rome, he would have traveled northeast to Capua where he would have been able to travel the APPIAN WAY to Rome (Acts 28:13-16).

Bibliography: Yohanan Aharoni. *The Land of the Bible: A Historical Geography.* 2nd ed. Anson F. Rainey, trans. and ed. (1979); Lionel Casson. *Travel in the Ancient World* (1994); Raymond Chevallier. *Roman Roads.* N. H. Field, trans. (1976); David A. Dorsey. *The Roads and Highways of Ancient Israel* (1991).

GREGORY L. LINTON

ROAD MARKER [צִיּוּן **tsiyun**]. A sign, most likely a cairn or heap of stones, erected to mark a road or pathway (*see* GUIDEPOST). Such markers are still used in some places in the Near East. Addressing the northern tribes who are being led into exile by the Assyrians, Jeremiah instructs them to "set up road markers for yourself" and "make yourself guideposts" so that they will be able to retrace their steps (Jer 31:21). Thus, Jeremiah uses the metaphor of marking a path to reassure the northern exiles that they will return to Israel.

JOHN I. LAWLOR

ROBBER, ROBBERY. *See* CRIMES AND PUNISHMENT, OT AND NT.

ROBE [כְּתֹנֶת **kethoneth**, מְעִיל **meʿil**; ἔνδυμα **endyma**, ἐσθής **esthēs**, ἱμάτιον **himation**, ποδήρης **podērēs**, στολή **stolē**, χλαμύς **chlamys**]. The robe is an outer garment that is worn over a tunic or inner garment. It may be as simple as a rectangular piece of fabric or it may be cut and sewn. The quality of a robe could serve as a marker of status. Jacob gave his son Joseph a special robe that helped to arouse his brothers' envy (Gen 37:3-4). Jonathan gave David the robes of a prince (1 Sam 18:4). The soldiers dressed Jesus in a rich robe when they mocked him as one who claimed to be a king (Matt 27:28, 31; Luke 23:11; John 19:2, 5). An example of an especially ornate robe is the blue priestly garment described in Exod 28 and 39. It had a bound opening and its lower hem was trimmed with pomegranates embroidered in blue, purple, and crimson. The pomegranates alternated with golden bells. This robe was worn over a linen tunic.

Because it was conventional to wear a robe, the removal of a robe could signal extraordinary behavior. As a sign of humility, Jesus removed his robe before washing the disciples' feet (John 13:4, 12). Those who are grieving remove their robes and put on sackcloth (Isa 3:24; Jonah 3:6) or tear their robes (2 Sam 13:19; Job 1:20). *See* CLOTH, CLOTHES; MANTLE.

Bibliography: P. Horn. "Textiles in Biblical Times." *CIBA Review* 4 (1968) 3–37.

MARY P. BOYD

ROCK. *See* GOD, METAPHORS FOR; GOD, NAMES OF; ISRAEL, GEOLOGY OF; PETER, THE APOSTLE.

ROCK BADGER [שָׁפָן **shafan**]. A small mammal that belongs to the hydrax family and resembles the rabbit in its appearance and size but has shorter ears. Among the Israelites it was considered unclean because it was classified as an animal that chewed its cud (Lev 11:5; Deut 14:7). Actually, it has no cud; that it constantly moves its jaws leaves the impression of chewing cud. *See* ANIMALS OF THE BIBLE.

EMILY R. CHENEY

ROCK OF ESCAPE [סֶלַע הַמַּחְלְקוֹת **selaʿ hammakhleqoth**]. A site in the MAON wilderness where David narrowly escaped from Saul (1 Sam 23:28). Saul and his forces were closing in on David, who had taken refuge on the side of a mountain. But when a messenger arrived with news that the Philistines were raiding part of Saul's territory, he gave up his pursuit of David. Consequently, the mountain was called the "Rock of Escape" (NRSV). The literal meaning of **hammakhleqoth** seems to be "divisions," which may be a reference to the well-timed withdrawal of Saul's troops from their pursuit of David.

RALPH K. HAWKINS

ROD [מַקֵּל **maqqel**, שֵׁבֶט **shevet**; κάλαμος **kalamos**, ῥάβδος **rhabdos**]. A variety of words, with a variety of functions, is reflected in the NRSV *rod.* Least frequently, the rod (**maqqel**) reflects a live stick or branch, as in Gen 30:37-41, where Jacob uses rods of particular types so that the flocks would conceive young who were striped, speckled, and spotted. Elsewhere, the NRSV translates **maqqel** as "stick" (e.g., 1 Sam 17:43). More frequently, the rod (**shevet**) is used for discipline. Thus, especially in wisdom literature, parents discipline their children with a rod (Prov 13:24), and boys and fools are similarly corrected (Prov 22:15; 26:3). Such corporal punishment was deeply imbedded in Israelite culture: it was as natural as bridling a horse or whipping a donkey (Prov 26:3) and was felt to be so beneficial that it could save the lives of those reproved from Sheol, namely premature death (Prov 23:14). Servants were also beaten with rods (Exod 21:20).

This image could also be used of God, who used a rod to reprove the Davidic kings (2 Sam 7:14), foreign rulers (Ps 2:9), individuals (Job 9:34; 21:9), or all Israel (Lam 3:1—the singular represents the nation); such uses may be metaphorical. God could even use foreign nations as his rod (Isa 10:5), namely as his vehicle of punishment. Psalm 23:4 very cleverly reverses the image of God's rod as punishment, insisting that "your rod and your staff" comfort, rather than punish, the individual who accepts God as the divine shepherd. According to Isa 11:4, the messianic king will "strike the earth with the rod of his mouth"—in other words will be so powerful that he will discipline effectively through words alone. Rods had a variety of other purposes; they were used for grinding seeds (Isa 28:27), for divining (Hos 4:12), and for measuring (Ezek 40:3, translated in the NRSV as "measuring reed").

The NT uses of *rod* are similar to the OT. Revelation 2:27; 12:5; and 19:15 use the image of "a rod of iron" from Ps 2:9. Revelation 11:1 and 21:15-16 mention a measuring rod. Acts 16:22 and 2 Cor 11:25 describe rods used to beat people. The depiction of "Aaron's rod that budded" in Heb 9:4 reflects Num 17 (translated in the NRSV as "staff"). In addition, there are several overlapping words used in the Bible to reflect more specialized types of rods, including the stick, STAFF, and SCEPTER.

MARC ZVI BRETTLER

RODANIM roh'duh-nim [רוֹדָנִים **rodhanim**; Ῥόδιοι **Rhodioi**]. The Israelite perspective on the origins of their neighbors is conceptualized in the so-called Table of Nations found in Gen 10. Rodanim, the ancestor of the nation of RHODES, is identified in this passage as the son of Javan, the son of Japheth, the son of Noah. The Hebrew of Gen 10:4 and 1 Chr 1:7 provides two divergent spellings of the name (**dodhanim** [דֹּדָנִים] and **rodhanim**, respectively), the Gk. renders it **Rhodioi** in both verses. Not only does the NRSV follow the Gk. in this regard, but it does so as well by referencing the RHODIANS in Ezek 27:15 where the Hebrew lists DEDAN, a descendant of Ham. *See* DODANIM.

JASON R. TATLOCK

ROEBUCK [יַחְמוּר **yakhmur**]. The English term *roebuck,* the male of the roe deer, is used by the NRSV in Deut 14:5 and 1 Kgs 4:23 [Heb. 5:3]. *See* ANIMALS OF THE BIBLE.

ROGELIM roh'guh-lim [רֹגְלִים **roghelim**]. David fled Jerusalem across the Jordan River to Mahanaim in Gilead following the revolt of Absalom. BARZILLAI, from the town of Rogelim in Gilead, supplied David and his men with provisions (2 Sam 17:27-29; 19:31 [Heb. 19:32]). Although near the JABBOK River, the exact location of Rogelim is unknown, with two sites being possibilities. Tell Bersinya has been proposed on toponymic similarities with Barzillai, but Nelson Glueck's survey of the region revealed no Iron Age pottery at the site. The alternate is the Iron Age tell of Dhaharat Soqʿa, 2 km from Tell Bersinya. Both locations are west-southwest of Irbid, Jordan.

Bibliography: Nelson Glueck. *Explorations in Eastern Palestine IV.* AASOR 25–28 (1951).

MICHAEL G. VANZANT

ROHGAH roh'guh [רָהְגָּה rohgah]. A descendant of Asher, listed among the sons of SHEMER (1 Chr 7:34).

ROLL [פָּקַד paqadh, גָּלַל galal; ἀποκυλίω apokyliō]. The noun *roll* means a military roster or muster (Judg 21:9; 1 Sam 14:17). According to Amos 5:21-24, Yahweh spurns festivals and music, preferring that justice "roll down" like water (Amos 5:24). A large stone rolled in front of a tomb served as a door (Mark 16:3).

A. HEATH JONES III

ROMAMTI-EZER roh-mam'ti-ee'zuhr [רֹמַמְתִּי עֶזֶר romamti ʿezer]. Son of HEMAN and one of the musicians appointed by David to serve in the Temple (1 Chr 25:4, 31). These musicians were trained singers who could also play several musical instruments. Their duties were assigned by lot. *See* MUSIC.

ROMAN EMPIRE roh'muhn. Legend has it that Rome began as a small village in 753 BCE. Over subsequent centuries the republic grew, and the city extended its influence throughout Italy and beyond. After civil war, Augustus reunited the empire in 30 BCE and subsequently became its first emperor. By the 1st cent. CE, Rome's empire extended from Britain in the northwest, through (present-day) France and Spain to the west, across Europe to Turkey and Syria in the east, and to the south along North Africa. Rome ruled an estimated 60–65 million people of diverse ethnicities and cultures. The empire was hierarchical with vast disparities of power and wealth. For the small number of ruling elite, both in Rome and the provinces, life was quite comfortable. For the majority of non-elite, it was at best livable and at worst very miserable. There was no middle class, little opportunity to improve one's lot, and few safety nets in adversity.

A. The Roman Empire

1. Structures of power

The Roman Empire was an aristocratic empire. A small elite of about 2 to 3 percent of the population, headed by the emperor, controlled political power, ruling largely for their own advantage. They exercised power, controlled wealth, enjoyed high status, and determined the social experience and "quality" of life of the rest of the empire's inhabitants. As an agrarian empire, wealth and power were based in elite control of land, its production, and cheap labor including slaves. Rents, tributes, and taxes on production, distribution, and consumption of goods transferred wealth to the elite. Not to pay taxes was regarded as rebellion because it refused recognition of Rome's sovereignty over land, sea, human labor, and production.

The Roman Empire was also a legionary empire. The much-vaunted Roman army, comprising approximately twenty-five legions of about 6,000 men each, intimidated and forcibly coerced submission (*see* LEGION). Legions also spread Roman presence and control by building roads and bridges and improved productivity by increasing available land through clearing forests and draining swamps. Special taxes and levies on food, housing, clothing, and equipment for war in areas where legions were based ensured adequate supplies at the expense of local populations (*see* PAX ROMANA).

In addition, the elite controlled various forms of communication or "media" such as designs on coins, monuments, and various buildings, as well as civic festivals and entertainments. Civic rhetoric and a legal system biased in favor of elites maintained order and removed threats. Networks of patronage and displays of elite civic good deeds called euergetism (such as funding a festival or food distribution) extended control, maintained the *status quo*, and enforced the elite's interests. Rome also ruled by forming often tensive alliances with elites in the provinces such as the puppet king Herod and the Jerusalem high priestly families.

Emperors mentioned in the biblical text include AUGUSTUS and TIBERIUS CAESAR (Luke 2:1; 3:1). Relationships between the EMPEROR and the elite were complex. Since the rewards of power were great, these relationships usually combined deference to the emperor, interdependence, competition for immense

Roman Emperors 49 BCE–138 CE	
Julius Caesar	49–44 BCE
Augustus (Octavian)	31 BCE–14 CE
Tiberius	14–37 CE
Gaius (Caligula)	37–41
Claudius	41–54
Nero	54–68
Galba	68–69
Otho	69
Vitellius	69
Vespasian	69–79
Titus	79–81
Domitian	81–96
Nerva	96–98
Trajan	98–117
Hadrian	117–138

Figure 1: Roman Emperors 49 BCE–138 CE

wealth and power, tension, and mutual suspicion. Amidst various power struggles, several emperors were murdered including CALIGULA (37–41 CE), CLAUDIUS (41–54 CE), Galba (68–69 CE), Vitellius (69 CE), and DOMITIAN (81–96 CE). Others such as NERO (54–68 CE) and Otho (69 CE) committed suicide. Civil war in 68–69 CE saw four emperors (Galba, Otho, Vitellius, and VESPASIAN), backed by various legions, claim supreme power for short periods of time. The victor, Vespasian (69–79 CE), provided some stability with two sons who succeeded him, TITUS (79–81 CE) and Domitian (81–96 CE).

2. Divine sanction

In addition to ownership of resources, military force, and working relationships with the elite, emperors secured power by claiming the favor of the gods. Imperial theology proclaimed that Rome was chosen by the gods, notably Jupiter, to rule an "empire without end" (Virgil, *Aen.* 1.278–79). Rome was chosen to manifest the gods' rule, presence, and favor throughout the world. The hierarchical and exploitative structure of the empire was thus presented as being divinely sanctioned. Religious observances at civic occasions were an integral part of Rome's civic, economic, and political life (*see* ROMAN RELIGIONS).

Individual emperors needed to demonstrate that they were recipients of divine favor. Various accounts narrate amazing signs, dreams, and experiences understood to show the gods' election of particular emperors. For example, in the civil war after Nero's suicide in 68 CE, three figures (Galba, Otho, and Vitellius) claimed power for short periods of time before Vespasian emerged as the victor. In legitimating Vespasian's rule as the divine will, Suetonius describes a dream in which Nero sees Jupiter's chariot travel to Vespasian's house (*Vesp.* 5.6). The dream presents Vespasian as Nero's divinely legitimated successor. Similarly, Tacitus describes the gods deserting one emperor, Vitellius, to join Vespasian, thereby signifying their election of Vespasian (*Hist.* 1.86).

The gods' continuing sanction for emperors was both recognized and sought in the imperial cult, a vast range of practices for honoring the emperor. Temples dedicated to specific emperors and images of emperors located in other temples were focal points for offering thanksgiving and prayers to the gods for the safekeeping and blessing of emperors and members of the imperial household. Incense, sacrifices, and annual vows expressed and renewed loyalty. Street processions and feasting, often funded by elites, expressed honor and gratitude, as well as commemorating significant events such as an emperor's birthday, accession to power, or military victories. Acts of imperial worship were also incorporated into the gatherings of artisan or religious groups (*see* EMPEROR WORSHIP). Elites played a prominent role in these activities, sponsoring celebrations, maintaining buildings, and supplying leadership. These diverse celebrations presented the empire—presided over by the emperor—as divinely ordained. They displayed and reinforced the elite's control. They invited and expressed, encouraged and ensured the non-elite's submission.

Participation in the imperial cult was not compulsory. Its celebration was neither uniform across the empire nor consistent throughout the 1st cent. Whereas in many cities sacrifices and incense were offered to the emperor's image, in the Jerusalem Temple, for example, daily sacrifices and prayers were offered for the emperor but not to his image. While participation was not required, it was actively encouraged, often by local elites who funded activities and buildings, and who served as priests or leaders of imperial celebrations. Elite men and women served as priests for the imperial cult (and for numerous other religious groups also) because they could fund celebrations and gain societal prestige. Such elite priestly activity, eligible for both men and women, was not a lifetime vocation requiring seminary training and/or vows of celibacy. Rather good birth, wealth, social standing, and interest in enhancing one's civic reputation were needed.

3. Elite values

With the emperor, members of the elite created, maintained, and exercised power, wealth, and prestige through crucial roles: warrior, tax-collector, administrator, patron, judge, priest. These roles express key elite values. First among these were domination and power. The elaborate celebration called a "Triumph" took place in Rome when a victorious general entered the city, displaying booty and captives taken in battle, parading captured enemy leaders, executing them, and offering thanks to Jupiter for Rome's victory. The

Triumph, such as that celebrating Rome's destruction of Jerusalem in 70 CE, paraded Rome's military might, conquering power, hierarchical social order, legionary economy, and divine blessing.

Second, elites valued civic display through civic and military offices, patronage, and civic good deeds (euergetism) that enhanced their honor, wealth, and power. Third, elites exhibited contempt for manual labor. They depended on and benefited from the work of others such as peasant farmers, artisans, and slaves. Slaves provided physical strength as well as highly valued skills in education, business, and medicine. They performed all sorts of roles, including working the land, serving domestically, meeting the sexual needs of their owners, educating elite children, and being business and financial managers of a master's estates and commercial affairs (*see* SLAVERY).

Fourth, elites valued conspicuous consumption. They displayed wealth in housing, clothing, jewelry, food, and ownership of land and slaves. They also displayed it in various civic good deeds: funding feasts, games, and food handouts, presiding at civic religious observances, building civic facilities, erecting statues, and benefiting clients. They could afford such displays not on the basis of investments but because taxes and rents provided a constant (coerced) source of wealth (*see* TAXES, TAXATION).

And fifth, elites valued superiority, sustained by and expressed through the ability to subject, coerce, exploit, and extract wealth. Rome was superior to provincials, the wealthy and powerful elite to the non-elite, and males to females.

4. Non-elites

Most of the population, however, about 97 percent, comprised non-elites, almost all of whom lived in varying levels of poverty. It is not surprising that most early Christians belonged to this group. Without a middle class, an enormous gap separated the non-elite from the elite's power, wealth, and status. For most, life was a struggle for survival. Some made an adequate living from trade. Most scraped by either from trade, artisan skills, or farming. Most knew periods of surplus and of deprivation so that regularly many non-elites lived at or below subsistence levels. If crops failed, taxes increased, or elites withheld food supply and forced up prices, there was little safety net. Food shortages and poor health were commonplace. Perhaps up to 50 percent did not reach age ten while most non-elite adults seem to have died by age thirty or forty. Elite life spans were longer. Urban life for non-elites was crowded, dirty, smelly, and subject to numerous dangers: floods, fires, food shortages, contaminated water, infectious diseases, human and animal waste, ethnic tensions, and irregular work. Rural life also knew most of these dangers. Poor crop returns meant immediate food shortages, limited seed for next year, few options with which to trade for what a peasant could not produce, the likely breakup of extended families if some were forced into cities to find work, and the inability to pay taxes or repay loans thus risking seizure of land. Anxiety and stress about daily survival were rife.

5. Resistance

Faced with material domination and deprivation, as well as personal humiliation and the loss of dignity, how did non-elites negotiate this world? Much effort was needed for survival. Cooperation through deferential and submissive behavior enhanced this goal. Studies have shown, though, that whenever dominating power is asserted, there is resistance. Sometimes this resistance was open and violent such as the revolt in Judea against Rome in 66–70 CE (*see* JEWISH WARS). Usually, though, such revolts were quickly and harshly crushed. More often, protests were hidden or "offstage," disguised, calculated, self-protective, anonymous, and intended not to change the system but to assert dignity and facilitate survival.

Such actions might comprise a work slowdown or telling stories with an alternative or counter ideology. The subjugated might imagine fantasies of violent revenge and judgment on elites and/or a reversal of roles in favor of non-elites. They may employ coded talk with secret messages of freedom ("the reign of God" or "kingdom of God") or "double-talk" that seems to submit to elites ("Give to the emperor the things that are the emperor's") but contains, for those with ears to hear, a subversive message ("and to God the things that are God's," Matt 22:21). They may reframe an elite action intended to humiliate (such as paying taxes) by attributing to it a different significance that dignifies the dominated (the coin in the fish's mouth supplied by God attests God's sovereignty, not Rome's; Matt 17:24-27). They may create communities that affirm practices and social interactions that somewhat imitate but also differ from domination patterns: "You know that the rulers of the Gentiles lord it over them, and their great ones are tyrants over them. It will not be so among you; but whoever wishes to be great among you must be your servant" (Matt 20:25-26; compare 1 Cor 12:13; Gal 3:28).

Such webs of protest have been called a "hidden transcript." It envisions human dignity and interaction that is an alternative to the elite's "public transcript" or official version of how society is to be run. The NT writings can, in part, be thought of as "hidden transcripts." They are not public writings targeted to the elite or addressed to any person who wants to read them. They are written by and for followers of Jesus, who was crucified by the empire, to assist these followers in negotiating Rome's world (*see* ROME, EARLY CHRISTIAN ATTITUDES TOWARD).

B. Rome's Empire: Visible and Invisible in the New Testament

The most obvious sign of the empire's presence in the NT involves four groups of imperial personnel: emperors (Mark 12:13-17; Luke 2:1-3; 3:1; John

19:12-15; Acts 25:8-12, 21; 26:32; 1 Pet 2:13-17; 1 Tim 2:1-2), client kings appointed by Rome (Herod, Matt 2; ARCHELAUS, Matt 2:22; HEROD ANTIPAS, Mark 6:14-29; AGRIPPA I, Acts 12:1-23; Agrippa II, Acts 25:13–26:32), governors (Pilate, Matt 27:11-26; John 18:28–19:22; Sergius Paulus, Acts 13:4-12; GALLIO, Acts 18:12-17; FELIX and Festus, Acts 24–25), and soldiers of various ranks such as tribunes (about six per legion commanding 1,000 men; Mark 6:21; Acts 21:31-37; 22:24-29; 23:10, 15-23), centurions (about sixty per legion commanding eighty to one hundred men; Matt 27:54; Luke 7:1-10; Acts 10–11), and

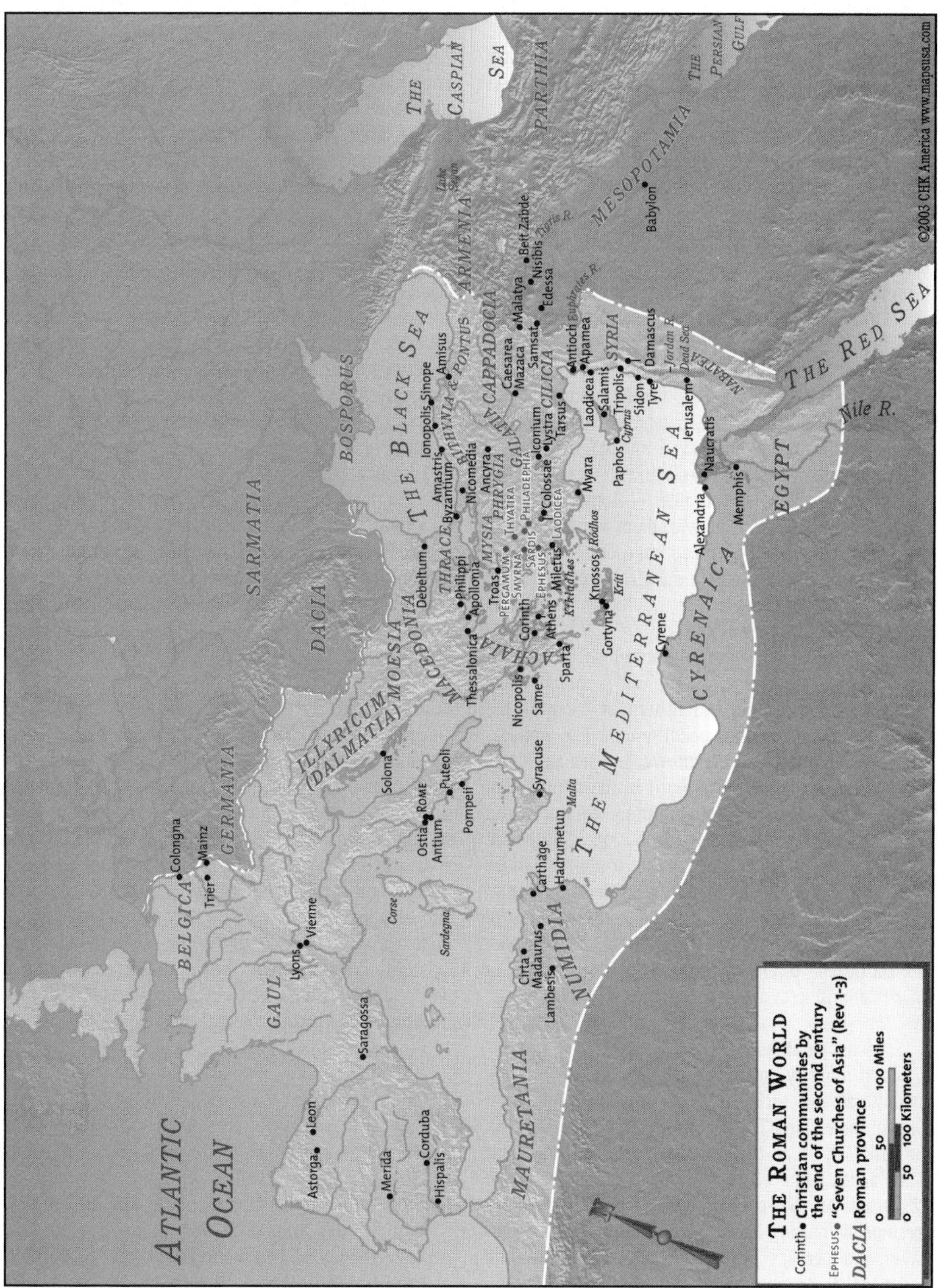

Figure 2: The Roman World

unranked soldiers (Mark 15:16-20; John 19:2, 23, 25, 32) of various functions (cavalry and spearmen, Acts 23:23), and of various military units (PRAETORIAN GUARD, Acts 28:16; Phil 1:13; a detachment [up to 600 soldiers], John 18:3). *See* FESTUS, PORCIUS; HEROD, FAMILY; PAULUS, SERGIUS; PILATE, PONTIUS; PRAETORIUM.

Recognizing these faces of empire is relatively easy. Much more difficult, though, is the recognition that even when explicit references to imperial personnel are absent, the NT texts assume and continue to engage Rome's world. The empire provides the ever-present political, economic, societal, and religious framework and context for the NT's claims, language, structures, personnel, and scenes.

In addition to our lack of knowledge of the Roman imperial world, another issue can prevent 21st -cent. readers from recognizing these imperial realities, namely the relationship between religion and politics. Modern people often think of religion and politics as separate and distinct with religion being personal, individual, and private, and politics being societal, communal, and public. In the 1st cent. Roman world, however, no one pretended religion and politics were separate. Rome claimed its empire was ordained by the gods. Some religious leaders in Jerusalem such as chief priests and scribes were the political leaders of Judea and allies of Rome (Josephus, *Ant.* 20.251). Jesus conflicts with them not just as religious figures but as religious-political-economic leaders. The NT texts do not spell out such connections. They assume that readers know how the Roman world was structured and what it was like.

When Jesus calls Galilean fishermen to follow him (Mark 1:16-20), for example, the call is more than a personal matter. Fishing and fishermen were deeply embedded in the Roman imperial system. The emperor was considered to be sovereign over the sea and land, and his sovereignty was expressed in the structure of the imperial economy through fishing contracts and taxes on the catch and its distribution. The scene assumes these realities. Jesus' call to James, John, Andrew, and Simon Peter manifests his declaration that the kingdom or empire of God is at hand in the midst of Rome's empire (Mark 1:15). Two different sets of loyalties clash. The disciples' response to Jesus redefines their relationship to and involvement in Rome's world.

1. Jesus' parables

Jesus' ministry, including his parables, reflects the agricultural and socio-economic practices and structures of the empire. The parables are full of allusions to the reality of life in the empire. People squabble over inheritances (Luke 12:13-14) and indebtedness (Luke 12:58-59). An elite person increases his landholdings, presumably outside the city and through agents or slaves and perhaps through default and foreclosure (Luke 14:18). Another has purchased five yoke of oxen, enough animal power for perhaps 100 acres. If this is half of his arable land, his (minimally approximate) 200 acres is very much larger than small peasant holdings of up to about 6 acres (Luke 14:19). Absentee landowners employ administratively skillful slaves to manage and increase their master's wealth (Matt 24:45-51; Luke 12:36-48; 19:11-27). Some elite landowners keep their land and wealth in the family through inheritances (Luke 15:11-32). Some build bigger barns for their crops (Luke 12:16-21). They own hardworking slaves from whom even more is expected (Luke 17:7-10). They hire day laborers from a city or village marketplace to work in a vineyard (Matt 20:1-16) or they rely on the labor of their sons (Matt 21:28-32). Through their agents, they take violent and fatal action against tenants who themselves use violence to refuse handing over their rent payment in the form of a percentage of the yield (Matt 21:33-46). Jesus' acts of supplying abundant food occur in a world of frequent food shortages (Matt 14:13-21; 15:32-39). The Gospels are peopled with sick folks, a reflection of imperial society where poor food supply, living conditions, and hard work frequently made people sick.

Parables also reflect political structures. The parable of the king and the unforgiving servant employs imperial realities of tax and tribute collection, as well as patronage (Matt 18:23-35). The king who invites elites to the wedding feast of his son is insulted when they refuse the invitation and murder the messengers (Matt 22:1-14). He burns their city, a common form of punishment for the incompliant (compare Rome's burning of Jerusalem in 70 CE). The Lukan form of this parable, the great banquet, reflects common urban geography and socio-political structures (Luke 14:15-24). Having been rejected by three elite invitees, the host orders his slave into "the streets (or squares) and lanes of the town" to invite "the poor, the crippled, the blind, and the lame" (Luke 14:21). When the city's poor do not fill his banquet hall, he sends the slave out again. He goes to those who are even more socially and geographically marginal, outside the city walls on the highways and under the hedges. These are not peasants in rural villages but the dispossessed and beggars, perhaps because they defaulted on a loan or taxes, who are seeking to eke out a living. Their existence is so far removed from the host's elite urban world, and they have been so damaged by it, that they need to be coerced into entering it.

2. Paul

Paul's language commonly echoes imperial language. In Rom 1:16-17, for example, he defines the gospel as "the power of God for salvation to everyone who has faith, to the Jew first and also to the Greek. For in it the righteousness of God is revealed through faith for faith." Paul's initial concern with power echoes the pervasive reality of the empire. The term "good news" or "gospel" often denoted the empire's benefits, such as an emperor's birth, military conquest, or accession to power (Josephus, *J.W.* 4.618). In Isaiah (especially Isa 40:1-31; 52:7), though, it speaks of God's saving activity and the establishment of God's reign or empire. Salvation named the blessings of Rome's world, especially its security and order achieved through (military) deliverance from any "foreign" threat. Righteousness or justice formed a constituent part of Rome's mission to "to crown peace with law" (Virgil, *Aen.* 6.851–53; *Res gest. divi Aug.* 34). There was a temple to *Iustitia* in Rome, the goddess Justice, understood to be at work through Rome's rule. The language of faith and fullness was also central to imperial claims. The goddess *Fides* (loyalty or faithfulness) was understood to be active through the empire's rulers. The emperor represented Rome's loyalty or faithfulness to treaties and alliances (*Res gest. divi Aug.* 31–34). But such loyalty required a reciprocal loyalty comprising submission to Rome's will and cooperation with Rome's self-benefiting rule. The important question, once these links have been recognized, concerns the effect of using such language. Paul is clearly not endorsing Rome's claims. Is he redefining the language, and if so, what relationships exist between his claims concerning God's activity in the world and Rome's?

These examples provide a small glimpse into the importance of the empire for the NT writings even when the empire does not seem to us to be present. This pervasive presence raises a question. How do the NT texts negotiate Rome's empire? How do they guide followers of Jesus, crucified by the empire, in living their daily lives and discipleship in the midst of the empire?

C. Diverse Christian Negotiation of the Empire

It is often thought that the empire persecuted Christians continually during the 1st cent. when the NT was being written, but this view is not sustainable. There is no evidence for empire-wide persecution of Christians until the mid-3rd cent. The emperor Nero does attack some Christians living in Rome after the fire of 64 CE. Tradition has it that Paul and Peter were killed in this outburst. Nero's actions, though, were not directed at all Christians throughout the empire, were not sustained, and may have been motivated more by the need to find a scapegoat than by particular objections to Christian practice or doctrine. The NT writings do refer to persecutions (Mark 10:30), perhaps referring to local harassment (sometimes involving civic officials) brought by local residents if Christians refused to take oaths to local or imperial gods, or to imprisonment of apostles like Paul (Phil 1:12-13; 1 Thess 1:6).

If Christians did not have to fear being thrown to the lions or being imprisoned on a daily basis, how did they negotiate Roman power? As with many issues, the NT writings do not address this issue with one voice.

1. Submission

At one end of the spectrum of views are exhortations to submit to the empire. There are instructions to pray for the emperor (1 Tim 2:1-2; Titus 3:1-2) and to honor him (1 Pet 2:17). As surprising as it may sound, the latter instruction probably authorizes Christians to participate in imperial cult activities, including sacrifices, while they honor Christ in their hearts (1 Pet 3:15). In Rom 13:1-7, Paul instructs the Christians in the empire's capital city to be "subject to the governing authorities" since they have been "instituted by God." This is a difficult passage, partly because of contradictions within the passage (if these authorities are always seeking the good as "servants of God," why would anyone resist them or fear them?) and partly because of contradictions with Paul's teachings about the present evil age (Rom 1:18; 3:11-14) and the fact that Jesus was crucified by Rome. The passage in Rom 13:1-7 certainly does not tell the full story. At best its instruction seems to address some situation in Rome (refusal to pay taxes perhaps mentioned in Rom 13:6?) for which this flattering presentation is appropriate. It is difficult to generalize the passage for all interactions or to take it as Paul's final word on the matter.

2. The evil empire under judgment

At the opposite end of the spectrum are rhetorical attacks on the empire that name or reveal its structures as evil and demonic and anticipate its demise, condemned by God. Jesus names the realities of self-benefiting elite rule that depletes the poor when he says, "to those who have, more will be given; and from those who do not have, even what they seem to have will be taken away" (Luke 8:18; compare Amos 4:1-3; 5:10-13; 6:3-7; 8:4-6; Mic 2:1-9; 6:9-16). A parable names elite greed when a slave (boldly) comments to a very wealthy landowner, "You take what you did not deposit, and reap what you did not sow" (Luke 19:21; compare John 4:37; 1 Cor 3:9). The "rich man" who plans to build larger barns for his grain and goods is identified as a fool because in ignoring God's just and life-giving purposes for all creation, he is not "rich toward God" (Luke 12:16-21). Jesus challenges a very rich ruler to sell what he owns and redistribute his money to the poor (Luke 18:18-27). Jesus warns against the scribes (Luke 20:45-47) who interpret the traditions and make alliances with other elite groups such as chief priests (Luke 20:19) to enrich themselves, devouring "widows' houses" for which "they will receive the greater condemnation" (Luke 20:47).

The scenes involving Jesus and Pilate expose the powerful and manipulative ways of a Roman governor. While these scenes are commonly understood as depicting the weak Pilate forced to crucify Jesus against Pilate's will, such a view takes no account of the realities of Roman rule in which the governor has life-and-death power, is allied with the Jerusalem elite, yet must maintain the upper hand in exercising power. Pilate variously taunts the Jerusalem leaders, gains wonderful declarations of loyalty to Caesar from them, polls the crowds to assess levels of support for Jesus, manipulates the crowds to support the elite agenda, and disguises the elite's commitment to kill Jesus as the people's will. Pilate emerges as astute, skillful, and very powerful (Luke 23:1-25).

The empire is, accordingly, revealed to be under judgment and its destruction by God is imminent according to Paul (1 Cor 15:24). Luke is adamant that God will reverse the *status quo* whereby the powerful are brought down and the lowly lifted up (Luke 1:52; 4:18-19) and the way of life of the rich and full is condemned (Luke 6:24-25). Mark's Jesus confronts a demon named "Legion," a key military unit in the Roman army and instrument of the empire's power, destroying it by casting it into the sea (Mark 5:1-20). Matthew and Luke also see the empire as in the devil's control (Matt 4:8-9; Luke 4:5-7). Matthew probably imagines Rome's demise when he says that "all the tribes of the earth will mourn" at the return of Jesus in power (Matt 24:27-31). The book of Revelation imagines Rome's downfall (Rev 18:1-24; 19:17-21). Already the empire is under judgment; destructive imperial practices bring about its own destruction (Rev 6:1-8). It has failed to heed God's merciful warnings (Rev 8–9). It is in the devil's control in promoting imperial worship (Rev 13). The empire will bow to God's sovereignty when "all nations" worship (Rev 15:4) and participate in the "healing of the nations" (Rev 22:2).

Significantly, these rhetorical attacks and scenarios of imagined violence depicting Rome's demise allow no role for violence by followers of Jesus in resisting Rome. John's Jesus specifically contrasts his kingdom/empire with Rome's in that Jesus' followers do not resort to violence (John 18:36; compare Matt 26:51-53).

3. Imitation, ambivalence, and alternative communities

While NT texts reveal the evil and demonic qualities of the empire, and anticipate and imagine its imminent downfall, the question of how believers are to live in its midst remains. Revelation 18 calls believers to "come out of her" (Rev 18:4). John's Gospel exerts much energy depicting a dualistic world—life or death, light or darkness, truth or falseness, God or Caesar—suggesting, ideally, little room for compromise or even societal participation for Jesus-believers. The fact that the text seeks to create such a division suggests considerable societal compromise and participation.

In most NT writings, what emerges, even within the same book, is an ambivalent mixture of pragmatic cooperation to ensure survival, non-violent but active resistance expressive of faithfulness to God's purposes, and the shaping of alternative communities with practices and commitments that differ from imperial ways. At times the writings also imitate imperial ways even while they require believers not to be conformed to this world (Rom 12:2).

Imitation can take a number of forms. Identifying God as "Father"—as John's Gospel does some 120 times—evokes, among other things, the imperial title of *pater patriae*, "Father of the Fatherland" or "Father of the Country" (e.g., Suetonius, *Vesp.* 12), which identified the emperor as Jupiter's agent and embodiment of Jupiter's rule. Numerous titles used for Jesus—shepherd, Lord, savior—were used of emperors. Imperial claims to manifest the gods' sovereignty, presence, blessings, and will are matched by similar presentations of Jesus' roles but in relation to God's "empire/kingdom" and purposes (e.g., Matt 1:23; 4:17; 5:1–7:29; 1 Cor 8:6).

At times, the Gospels imitate and employ imperial realities without any critique in order to instruct followers about God's ways. Just as slaves, for example, must be ready for an absent master to appear at any time, so followers must be ready for Jesus' return (Matt 24:45-51). Just as an angry master punishes a slave who had experienced a tax break but denied mercy to another, so God will punish one who has experienced God's forgiveness but does not forgive another (Matt 18:23-35). Just as slaves wash another's feet, so must Jesus-believers (John 13:12-17). Paul frequently uses military images to describe aspects of Christian existence (2 Cor 10:3-6; Phil 2:25; 4:7; compare Eph 6:10-17). Imitation is also evident in the examples above in which NT writers imagine Rome's destruction and the forcible imposition of God's purposes. They attribute to God the ways and methods of Caesar. Imitating imperial ways indicates how deeply ingrained the NT texts are in the imperial world.

Ambivalence of societal interaction—cooperation yet disguised critique—is evident in Jesus' difficult instruction about taxes: "Give to the emperor the things that are the emperor's, and to God the things that are God's" (Matt 22:17-22; Mark 12:13-17; Luke 20:21-26). Paying taxes expressed submission to Rome's and the elite's sovereignty while non-payment was regarded as rebellion. Jesus' instruction cleverly combines loyalty and deference with his own subversive agenda. He employs ambiguous, coded, and self-protective speech to uphold payment of a coin bearing the emperor's image (contrary to the Ten Commandments), while also asserting overriding loyalty to God. He balances apparent compliance with hidden resistance. "The things that are God's" embraces everything since God is creator: "The earth is the LORD's and all that is in it" (Ps 24:1). The "hidden transcript" says that the earth does not belong to Caesar, despite Rome's claims of ownership (the "public transcript") that the tax represented. But instead of saying, "Pay Caesar nothing," Jesus orders giving to Caesar Caesar's things. The verb translated "give" or "render" (**dounai** [δοῦναι], from **didōmi** [δίδωμι]) literally means "to give back." Following Jesus' instruction, disciples "give back" to Caesar a blasphemous coin that, contrary to God's will, bears an image. Paying the tax is a subversive way of removing this illicit coin from Judea. As far as Rome is concerned, the act of paying looks like compliance. But Jesus' instruction reframes the act for his followers. "Giving back" to Caesar becomes a disguised, dignity-restoring act of resistance that recognizes God's all-encompassing claim.

Similar actions are described in Matt 5:39-41 where Jesus offers in the place of violence ("Do not resist an evildoer," i.e., violently) the alternative strategy of active, non-violent resistance. In situations of social inequalities, the inferior turns the other cheek to show that he or she has not been humiliated or beaten into submission. To the superior, the gesture is ambiguous: has submission been achieved or not? In situations of economic inequality, the poor person gives up even his undergarment to expose his or her humanity and the heartlessness of the powerful. In contexts of military power, the coerced employs a strategy that seizes the initiative and puts the soldier off-guard. In the context of desperate needs, actions of justice are the appropriate responses.

Evident throughout is the strategy of forming communities of disciples of Jesus marked by social interactions that differ from imperial values. Unity and new household bonds are to be nurtured (Phil 1:27-28; 2:1-4; 4:1-3). The poor, not the rich, receive preferential treatment (Jas 2:1-7). Prayer is a form of imperial dissent as disciples pray for the fullness of God's reign/ empire and will to be established (Matt 6:9-13). The Lord's Supper is to display God's justice in ensuring all have adequate food (1 Cor 11:17-34; compare Matt 14:13-21; the eschatological vision of Isa 25:6-10*a*). Acts of mercy and justice sustain one another (Matt 6:1-18). Paul collects money from Gentile churches for Jewish believers (Rom 15:25-33). Practical love—expressed in a wide range of relational commitments (1 Thess 5:11-14) and practices—is to be the hallmark (Matt 22:34-39; Rom 12:9-21; 13:8-10; 1 John 3:16). The sick are to be healed (Matt 11:2-6; compare the eschatological vision of wholeness in Isa 35:5-6). The dead are to be raised, lepers cleansed, and demoniacs exorcized (Matt 10:8). The hungry are to be fed, the thirsty supplied, the homeless housed, the imprisoned visited, the sick healed, and the naked clothed (Matt 25:31-46). Given the deplorable living conditions for non-elites in cities throughout the empire, such communities and practices begin to repair imperial damage at local levels, continue Jesus' ministry of Jubilee (Luke 4:18-19; compare Lev 25:10-17), and anticipate the eschatological completion of God's purposes. *See* JUBILEE, YEAR OF.

Bibliography: Warren Carter. *Matthew and the Margins: A Sociopolitical and Religious Reading* (2000); Warren Carter. *Matthew and Empire: Initial Explorations* (2001); Warren Carter. "Are There Imperial Texts in This Class? Intertextual Eagles and Matthean Eschatology as 'Lights Out' Time for Imperial Rome (Matthew 24:27-31)." *JBL* 122 (2003) 467–87; Warren Carter. *Pontius Pilate: Portraits of a Roman Governor* (2003); Warren Carter. "Going All the Way? Honoring the Emperor and Sacrificing Wives and Slaves in 1 Peter 2:13–3:6." *A Feminist Companion to the Catholic Epistles and Hebrews.* Amy-Jill Levine and Maria Mayo Robbins, eds. (2004) 14–33; Warren Carter. *The Roman Empire and the New Testament: An Essential Guide* (2006); Warren Carter. *John and Empire: Initial Explorations* (2007); John Dominic Crossan and Jonathan L. Reed. *In Search of Paul: How Jesus' Apostle Opposed Rome's Empire with God's Kingdom* (2004); Dennis Duling. "Empire: Theories, Methods, Models." *The Gospel of Matthew in Its Roman Imperial Context.* John Riches and David C. Sim, eds. (2005) 49–74; Steven Friesen. *Imperial Cults and the Apocalypse of John: Reading Revelation in the Ruins* (2001); Peter Garnsey. *Food and Society in Classical Antiquity* (1999); Peter Garnsey and Richard Saller. *The Roman Empire: Economy, Society, and Culture* (1987); Edward Gibbon. *History of the Decline and Fall of the Roman Empire.* Vol. 1 (2001); William Herzog. *Prophet and Teacher: An Introduction to the Historical Jesus* (2005); Richard Horsley. *Hearing the Whole Gospel: The Politics of Plot in Mark's Gospel* (2001); Richard Horsley. *Jesus and Empire: The Kingdom of God and the New World Disorder* (2003); Richard Horsley, ed. *Paul and Politics* (2000); Richard Horsley. *Paul and the Roman Imperial Order* (2004); Wes Howard-Brooks and Anthony Gwyther. *Unveiling Empire: Reading Revelation Then and Now* (2001); Janet Huskinson, ed. *Experiencing Rome: Culture, Identity, and Power in the Roman Empire* (2000); Gerhard Lenski. *Power and Privilege: A Theory of Social Stratification* (1984); Tat-Siong Benny Liew. *Politics of Parousia: Reading Mark Inter(con)textually* (1999); Stephen Moore. *Empire and Apocalypse: Postcolonialism and the New Testament* (2006); Ched Myers. *Binding the Strong Man: A Political Reading of Mark's Story of Jesus* (1988); Simon Price. *Rituals and Power: The Roman Imperial Cult in Asia Minor* (1984); James C. Scott. *Weapons of the Weak: Everyday Forms of Peasant Resistance* (1985); James C. Scott. *Domination and the Arts of Resistance* (1990); Collin Wells. *The Roman Empire* (1995); Klaus Wengst. *Pax Romana and the Peace of Jesus Christ* (1987); Charles R. Whittaker. "The Poor." *The Romans.* Andrea Giardina, ed. (1993) 272–99.

WARREN CARTER

ROMAN PERIOD. For the biblical world, the Roman period began when the Romans took control of the region in 63 BCE. During this period, Roman technology was put to use in extensive building projects including highways, amphitheaters, and aqueducts. Trade networks grew as imports arrived via ship from Italy and were transported along the new road system. The Jews revolted against Rome in 66–73 CE, resulting in the destruction of the Second Temple, and again in 132–35 CE, but were unable to drive the Romans out.

The end of the Roman period is often dated to 330 CE, when Constantine moved the capital from Rome to Byzantium/Constantinople. *See* JEWISH WARS; ROMAN EMPIRE.

KEVIN A. WILSON

ROMAN RELIGIONS. In order to understand the place of Roman religions in the 1st-cent. world, it is necessary to forget much of what is normally associated with the term *religion* in the modern West. Any notion of religion as a monotheistic, exclusivistic, faith-based entity focused on afterlife and entirely separate from governmental institutions must be dropped. This may seem like a harsh prescription, but not to do so is to risk viewing Roman religions through the lens of modern expectations for what constitutes religious activity. While this may yield a more comfortable engagement with the ancient world, it will not lead to a realistic and ultimately helpful view.

Because the history of the church has had such a remarkable impact on most aspects of Western society, it is difficult to imagine a world in which there was no such thing as Christianity. Yet that is the task presented. The earliest strains of Christianity developed in an environment where modern ideas about religion did not exist. Instead of focusing on a single, more or less personal deity, revealed through prophetic word and sacred Scripture, the Romans saw cosmic power reflected through a wide spectrum of gods, demigods, spirits, and heroes. Instead of emphasis on personal belief in a deity and the living of an ethical life based on that belief, the Romans recognized their duty to either individual or corporate ritual actions as the key to pleasing the divine forces that controlled their lives. Instead of thinking about how proper belief and piety in this life would provide assurance of an eternal life after death, the Romans viewed their religious activities as crucial to a successful experience in the present life. Instead of seeing religion, at least in theory, as completely separate from political and civic concerns, the Romans thought that the success of their government—whether local or imperial—was contingent on the favor of the gods and therefore on the appropriate honoring of those deities by military and governmental officials. In order to envision such a world, each of these alternative views will be examined in detail.

A. Differences between Roman Religion and Modern Concepts

1. Not one God but many

Prior to the rise of Christianity, Jews comprised virtually the only monotheists in the Roman Empire. Outside the province of Syria-Palestine, Jews made up a sizable minority in some Roman cities, including Rome and Alexandria. They were not, however, nor did they want to be, part of the mainstream of Roman religious understanding and practice. Going back to Etruscan roots and heavily influenced by Greek tradition, Roman religions were dominated by a multiplicity of divine forces that served as a web of power controlling the lives and fortunes of people at all levels of society. The gods emerge as key players in the earliest mythical stories about the founding of Rome, and each successive ruling body or ruler incorporated the stories of the gods into their propaganda. The family of Julius Caesar was said to be descended from Venus, and Caesar Augustus used a close connection with Apollo to establish and sustain his rise to power (*see* AUGUSTUS; CAESAR, JULIUS).

These multiple deities echoed the realities of human rule on earth. JUPITER served as king of the gods with the close assistance of Juno and Minerva. These three deities made up the Capitoline Triad, a grouping that went back to Etruscan traditions. Roman polytheism reflected a very diverse and widespread development. As with Greek traditions, individual deities could have different stories of origins and be credited with different attributes depending on the source and context. A goddess like Juno was associated with the Greek goddess Hera and in that guise served as wife of Jupiter and queen of the gods. She also had a deep and varied independent heritage including associations with fertility, military success, and economy. Even Jupiter took on different roles and appearances as he was honored throughout the Roman world, e.g., Jupiter Optimus Maximus in Rome, Jupiter Amicalis (the friend) in Pergamum, and Jupiter Dolichenus in the east. Much of this variety was due to association with local deities. Roman polytheistic perspectives meant that it was not necessary—although it was sometimes possible—for one deity to supersede another. Instead, the gods of the Roman conquerors could usually be associated with long-established local deities, and thereby Roman power could be fused with existing local authority.

In a similar way, gods from the provinces could be adopted and become popular in Rome. In the late 3rd cent. BCE, the Senate of Rome ordered that the cult of the Great Mother (Magna Mater or Cybele) should be brought from Asia Minor to Rome. Other deities came to the capital in more subtle ways. Egyptian deities like Isis and Serapis became very popular and were even favored by some emperors in the 1st cent. Scholars continue to debate the origins of the god Mithras, but by the 2nd cent. CE, worship of this divinity was spread widely across the Roman world. Acceptance of any divinity was no doubt based on its legacy and perceived fields of influence. If the story behind a god appeared to be of ancient origin and if enough people were convinced that their lives were improved based on the favor of that god, the popularity of that deity would grow.

Added to this mix of public deities to whom one owed devotion was an equally diverse selection of household deities that would be worshiped within the home. Among these the *Lares* and *Di Penates* appear frequently and seem to receive the most attention. In the case of the *Lares*, one possible explanation is that these spirits were representative of deceased family members who remained close to the household and needed to be appeased. For wealthy Romans, casts made from wax death masks of the deceased were displayed as a constant reminder of that presence. The Roman understanding of the spirit world required attention to both the cosmic and the very intimate. Divine forces could also be experienced in both the private and public spheres. Vesta was goddess of the hearth and was expected to sustain the existence of each home. At the same time, at Vesta's shrine in the forum, virgin priestesses guaranteed the continued success of the city of Rome by maintaining the flame of the civic hearth.

2. Not belief but practice

The Roman system of religions required not affirmation of a particular belief or creed, but rather the regular performance of rituals in honor of the gods relevant to one's life. The basic form of this ritual was sacrifice, but offerings could be made in a wide variety of ways. Wealthy people in a community were expected to provide the funds necessary to purchase animals for sacrifice at the main temples of the city. People of lesser means were supposed to attend these rituals—which also served as important social functions—but they also made their own modest offerings of birds, incense, or even grain on small altars. The basic idea was that gods who lived above would smell the burning offering and be pleased with the sacrifice. Of course this is an idea that goes back much further into history and is even described in the biblical tradition (Gen 8:21).

The grand civic sacrifices took the form of festivals that began with a huge parade through the town, or sometimes between the city and a sacred site. This was a way of promoting the cult and also commemorating important aspects of the history of the city. Along the way, people could see the sacred objects and symbols being carried by participants in colorful procession. They also saw the animals being led to the sanctuary for slaughter. These processions were a popular subject for relief carvings, many of which have survived from the Roman world. The enclosure wall for the Altar of Peace (*Ara Pacis*) in Rome features two views of a procession including religious authorities and the family of the emperor Augustus. Not only does this composition announce the succession of the Julio-Claudian dynasty, it also recalls the famous frieze depicting the Panathenaic Procession from the Parthenon in Athens. Thus the monument connects Augustus and his descendants to the glorious traditions and cultures of the past.

Foto Marburg/Art Resource, NY

Figure 1: Sacrificial Procession (detail), relief from the *Ara Pacis*. Louvre, Paris, France.

Once they arrived at the sanctuary, participants heard music and saw ritual reenactments of stories related to the deity being honored. After the animal had been killed, its internal organs were examined for indications of sickness or other unworthiness. The Romans developed a whole system of reading the entrails of sacrificial victims to indicate the success or failure of upcoming battles or other undertakings. Unless the offering was a holocaust or whole burnt offering, only a portion of the animal was burned on the altar. Some ancient commentators wondered why the gods were offered fat and bones while the meat of the animal was divided up among the participants and onlookers. Celebrating the festival of a god must have been a great opportunity for socializing and getting some protein in one's diet. It's not surprising that such attendance and the practice of "eating meat sacrificed to idols" became an issue for Paul and his early churches (1 Cor 8).

All of these activities took place in the courtyard surrounding the temple, not in the sacred building itself. The temple was where the statue of the divinity was located, and thus was seen as literally the house of the god. When the doors of the temple were opened, the god could look out into the courtyard and see the proceedings unfold. It might have been possible to gain access to the temple when rituals were not in progress. In addition to housing the cult statue, many temples also featured beautiful objects of art that had been accumulated as offerings. Out in the courtyard, there would be numerous smaller altars, statues, and other dedications that were set up by individuals and cities who wanted to make a public display of their devotion.

Because religious practice was a part of every aspect of Roman society, it is important to recognize that formal ceremonies at large temple complexes were only one facet of ritual observance. Honoring the gods involved many other activities as well. Going back to Greek traditions, theatrical performances and dance were associated with the god Dionysus (sometimes, but not always referred to as "Bacchus" by the Romans). Games and other athletic activities were also done in honor of certain deities. The games at Olympia—dedicated to Zeus—were probably the most venerable example, and they continued through the Roman period. Other regions held games to show regard for their local deities. The Panathenaic games honored Athena, while the Pythian games at Delphi were dedicated to Apollo. Even a new god such as the deified emperor Augustus was honored with games in cities throughout the empire. Victory in any of these games meant great fame for the winner and honor for the home city. At the same time, being caught cheating in the games was understood to be an insult to the gods and a disgrace for the athlete and his or her hometown.

In the context of modern medicine, it may seem unusual that even medical practice was intimately tied with religious ritual. Although some physicians practiced independently, the worship of healing gods such as Asclepius/Aesculeipius was very common throughout the Greek and Roman worlds. In response to a plague in the 3rd cent. BCE, the Roman Senate ordered that the snake of Asclepius be brought from Epidaurus in Greece to Rome. Healing sanctuaries are often found in association with Roman army installations as well. Sites dedicated to healing deities can sometimes be identified by terra-cotta representations of different body parts, which were no doubt intended as offerings to show gratitude for the healing or anticipated healing of particular afflictions.

In teaching about Roman religions, the question of belief inevitably arises: "Did they really believe all this stuff?" The idea of belief as it is commonly discussed in modern Christian contexts is not really a widespread issue for the Romans. While some philosophers raise questions about the "reality" of the gods and the futility of trying to honor them, it was largely accepted that the key to happiness in life was to make sure that the right gods were appeased by the right means, according to the correct calendar. Generations of people had come to understand that this type of ritual observance was the key to maintaining the balance of all the different forces that ultimately controlled the universe, and thereby human life within it. If one's parents, grandparents, great-grandparents, and beyond had found meaning and success in this system, on what basis might this be questioned? This deep commitment to the traditional polytheistic perspective made Christian claims for a new way of believing even the more difficult to accept. In this light it is even more remarkable that these radical Christian claims were able to succeed.

3. Not an afterlife but this life

Roman religious thinking tended to focus on the maintenance and improvement of life in this world rather than prospects for some kind of positive treatment in the afterlife. For the vast majority of people, death was seen as a transition to the underworld—ruled by the god Hades, sometimes known also as Pluto. The underworld was a shadowy existence without the color and vividness of earthly life. People in the "place of shades" were merely shadows of their previous selves. Although a descent into a deeper region of Tartarus could be seen as a condemnation to punishment, the usual fate of the dead was this drab existence of Hades. For this reason, the Christian understanding of hell as a place of punishment could not be equated directly with the Roman Hades.

Nor was there a direct parallel for later Christian understandings of heaven. For the Romans, only a few privileged people could expect to avoid Hades and experience a more meaningful or positive existence after death. Throughout the imperial period, increasing numbers of people seem to have hoped for transfer to the Elysian Fields, a place of fertility and peace where they could live out eternity. Even more unusual was the heroic figure who, because of great accomplishments, was elevated to the heavens to live among the gods. This also becomes the fate of emperors and some of their family members who are officially deified by vote of the Roman Senate, and receive divine honors thereafter. For the vast majority, however, there was very little to look forward to after death.

For the survivors, however, there were very important ways in which deceased family members were to be entombed and remembered. Death was both a loss and a source of shame, but if the family responded with proper ritual activity, they could correct the imbalance of forces and return to normal life. As is often the case, our knowledge about funerary practice is limited to evidence from those in society who had sufficient means to leave behind traces of their life and death. There must have been a great majority of people who could not afford elaborate preparation for burial or a funerary monument.

After mourning, the deceased was taken to a tomb outside the walls of the city. The cemetery or "necropolis" was literally the city of the dead and was placed near the city gates. Here, deceased persons remained close to, yet separate from, the living community. They were considered to be part of a collective sense of spiritual existence or divinity known as *di manes*. Latin tombstone inscriptions often are dedicated *dis manibus* ("to the divine spirits"). The "afterlife" for these people was therefore directly tied to proper burial and maintenance of their tombs. This allowed descendants to provide honor and remembrance during regular celebrations of ancestors such as the *dies parentales* (February 13–21). For families of means, the burial monuments also became a way of advertising their wealth along with devotion to their ancestors. Of course modern study of the Roman world is greatly aided by their burial customs. Decoration and design of tombs along with excavation of grave goods has provided much information about how the Romans lived and died.

Although the Roman religious calendar called for regular remembrance of departed family and community members, that remembrance served to make death part of the ongoing life of Roman society. As mentioned above, the purpose of Roman religions was to balance the various external forces that had the potential to control one's life and to make sure that the divinities and spirits who controlled those forces were properly honored. This ritual process was laid out in detailed form as part of the religious calendar of the Romans. As such, it was possible to keep track of the various observances and participate where necessary. The idea was that proper attention to these rituals would ensure a happy and successful life in this world. Since any kind of special status in the afterlife was well beyond the reach of most people, religious devotion was not intended to provide assurances of life after death.

While it was essential to follow the proper rituals in order to ensure that you had a good life, it was also possible to use similar ritual practice to bring negative fortune to others. This practice is still followed today when people pray for success in battle or seek retribution against enemies, but in antiquity it was a very developed practice. One way to wish evil on another was to use curse tablets (usually sheets of lead) on which evil wishes were made to various deities. These notes were then rolled up and hidden in a temple precinct, or thrown into a sacred spring, such as the one in the courtyard of the temple to Sulis Minerva in Bath, England.

The evil wishes tended to be very specific in terms of the punishment that was sought. Wishing gastrointestinal problems or other illness on one's enemy was one common practice. Given the lack of medical knowledge at the time, sudden illnesses were often seen as punishment from one of the gods. Curse tablets were used in response to a wide variety of wrongs. Some were as simple as cursing the person who stole money or an article of clothing. Retribution over affairs of the heart was also very common. Many inscriptions cursed the one who had "stolen" a lover. Those who offered curse tablets vowed to make special offerings to the deities in question once the curse had taken effect.

It was also possible to try and manipulate one's own fortunes or those of another through various magical practices. Since much in the natural world was not understood, the Romans thought that different kinds of spells and incantations could alter the course of nature and bring about changes in health, weather, or fortune. These practices were largely done in secret, and involved mystical or unintelligible wording. In some cases, a string of divine names was inscribed to give protection to a home or sanctuary. The clandestine nature of the magical arts made them suspect in broader Roman society. They were usually not controlled by official priesthoods, and therefore could be used in inappropriate ways. The Roman concept of *superstitio* was used to describe these actions that did not conform to accepted public standards of religious ritual. This, of course, did not stop the practices but largely drove them underground. It is not surprising then that once the Romans became aware of the inexplicable and—to them—bizarre practices and teachings of the early Christians, they also labeled them as superstitions.

4. No separation of religion and state

Perhaps the most dramatic difference in how the Romans viewed religion from most modern, Western views is that there was no attempt to separate the affairs of state from religious practice. Since religion served as the glue that held together the many forces that controlled human lives and society, it was only natural that all facets of government included regular interaction with religious institutions and rituals.

In many ways, military success was at the foundation of the amazing power and influence of the Roman Empire, and that success was understood to be due to the favor of the gods. As god of war, Mars served as focal point for prayers and sacrifices, but many other deities could be invoked as well. Reliefs showing a military leader offering sacrifice before a battle or giving thanks after a military campaign are very familiar. The tradition of official triumphs honoring the conquering generals and emperors also included many religious components. One relief panel from the Arch of Titus near the forum in Rome shows images of soldiers carrying religious objects from the Jerusalem Temple into the city. The opposite panel shows the emperor in his chariot being led by a divine figure (probably the goddess Roma), and being crowned by a winged victory. Of course, the story of Constantine's dream, in which he is told that he will conquer under the sign of the cross, builds on this tradition of divine blessings for military endeavors, but substitutes the Christian god for the various Roman divinities. Individual soldiers also found religious meaning in their service. The importance of sanctuaries to healing gods has already been mentioned, but it is also common to find other sanctuaries proximate to Roman army camps. Based on archaeological evidence, it appears that the mystery deity Mithras was especially popular among the troops.

Religious concerns are common from the very foundation of cities and colonies. Coins commemorate the ritual act of plowing the first furrow of a newly founded city, and discussion of city planning included the proper location for temples and shrines. As mentioned above, the civic calendar revolved around a strict cycle of festivals and sacrifices honoring the deities of the city and their help in the great accomplishments of the past. Even the treaties between cities and other political powers were understood to be the result of religious concepts of harmony made possible by the gods. The *Ara Pacis* in Rome was erected to honor the end of the civil war with Marc Antony and the establishment of peace by Augustus. The fact that he had used superior—and sometimes ruthless—military power to establish this peace was not considered to be a problem.

Priesthoods of the various temples in a city were important sources of power and influence. Some were held on a hereditary basis so that certain families controlled the worship of particular deities. A letter from the emperor Claudius to the city of Alexandria stipulates that priests of the divine Augustus should be selected by lot, apparently in an effort to prevent one group from dominating the office. Priests and other wealthy citizens were also responsible to provide the funds necessary to hold celebrations and sacrifices at the temples. This could include paying for victims, wine, and incense for use during the ceremonies, as well as the cost of construction, decoration, and repair of temple complexes. These forms of benefaction served as a kind of charitable service to the community and a limited kind of redistribution of wealth.

The fusing of religious and political power was most obvious in the person of the Roman emperor. Prayers and offerings were made on a regular basis for the good health (*salus*) of the emperor, who served as *pontifex maximus*, chief priest of Roman religion. Since priesthoods were a source of great power in the society, it was natural that the emperor would hold a position where he was able to control other priests and religious practices. The role of emperor emerged out of the chaos that brought about the end of the republic. The military successes of Octavian, who became the first emperor, brought about unparalleled personal success and honor. At least publicly, however, he was careful to refuse honors that might be construed as divine worship. He took on the venerable name Augustus, which recalled the glorious past of Rome. Augustus showed great piety in reestablishing the worship of the gods, building or rebuilding temples, and collecting the sacred oracles of Roman tradition. His supporters also used literary forms steeped in religious tradition to promote the Augustan regime. The *Aeneid* by Virgil built on the Greek model of Homer's epics to relate the history of Rome. Of course the divine narrative foreshadowed Augustus and culminated in his coming to power.

Modern scholars commonly refer to religious honors for the emperor as the "imperial cult." Unfortunately, this terminology of "cult" implies an organized system of religious observance, whereas the evidence for honors offered to the emperors comes in a wide variety of forms. Some scholars argue that offering divine honors to the emperor only took place in the eastern provinces, but in Rome and the West heroes who had done extraordinary things had long been honored with celebrations and even sacrifices normally reserved for the gods. A title like *savior* had been used regularly to honor generals and rulers. In order to explain the military success and supreme power of the emperor, it was quite natural to see him as a representative of the gods on earth. At the very least, the spirit or *genius* of the emperor and his family was honored as deriving from the divine.

According to the example of Augustus, excessive or divine honors were supposed to be prohibited during the lifetime of the emperor. If he ruled wisely and well, an emperor could be honored with divinization by the Roman Senate after death. In contrast, emperors who demanded divine honors during their lifetime could suffer a *damnatio memoriae* where the Senate decreed that all mention of their reign (including inscriptions and statuary) be stricken from the public record. The presence of erasures on inscriptions and even figures chiseled out of relief carvings is evidence for this practice. Even under Augustus, however, there were ways to honor the emperor that emphasized his connections to the gods. All around the empire, he allowed temples to be built to his divine spirit (*genius*), as long as they were also dedicated to the goddess Roma. In Rome itself, Augustus built a new forum featuring a temple dedicated to Mars the Avenger in honor of his victory over the assassins of Caesar. In one corner of the complex stood a small chapel featuring a colossal statue, probably depicting the *genius* of Augustus. The statue appears to have measured almost 11 m in height.

Augustus stressed his descent from the divinized Julius Caesar by using the title "son of god" (*divi filius*) in all of his propaganda. In addition, monuments to his great deeds always referred to the divine figures that were responsible for his success. The monument to his victory over Antony and Cleopatra at Actium featured a huge altar to Mars as well as a display of the bronze rams taken from the sunken ships of the enemy. Since success in battle was a sign of piety and the favor of the gods, Roman emperors after Augustus continued to reinforce and explain their amazing power by highlighting their connection to the divine. Thus the language used to describe Jesus as "son of God" and the close identification of humans and the divine was very well known to the people of the time.

B. Conclusion

All of the aforementioned elements make up only a portion of the ritual activity and social significance involved in Roman religions. From a modern perspective, this diverse collection of practices may seem hopelessly complicated and chaotic. For the Romans, however, their religious practice made sense and met their needs for centuries. Order and meaning were provided by long-standing family traditions and by an official civic calendar that laid out the schedule for festivals and special observances throughout the year. Fragmentary remains of these calendars have been found in a number of sites, and they serve to underline how everyone in the city or region would have been aware of the religious and social obligations that needed to be fulfilled. Feast days, anniversaries of important events, games and festivals, and public sacrifices are all listed on the schedule. In addition, the calendar noted how these religious events affected the schedule for conducting business. Romans would have learned from very early on how to plan their lives according to this calendar. Based on their social position and occupation, they would have understood the obligations and opportunities that the calendar described. While the practice of Roman religions might have been hectic, noisy, and bloody at times, it was not chaotic, and to the contrary religious activities provided a vital infrastructure for Roman society.

This fundamental importance of religion in Roman society helps to explain how difficult it would have been for someone who opted not to participate in these religious practices. For centuries, Jews had remained apart from these rituals and structured their society around a different religious understanding and a different calendar. In the 1st cent. CE, followers of Jesus were suddenly faced with a religious choice that threatened the very fabric of their social world. The Jesus follower who decided not to participate in the traditional Roman cults was choosing to ignore a huge portion of what it meant to live in that society. It was a religious decision that had huge ramifications for all aspects of life.

These very real consequences for choosing to follow Jesus highlight several important lessons. First, they underline the power of the early Christian message and the commitment that was needed to accept and adopt it. Second, they put into high relief the amazing success of the churches in providing alternative forms of social structure and meaning for those who chose to join. Finally, they lead to an understanding of how quickly a system of religious ritual, calendar, social hierarchy, and governmental activities came to dominate the Byzantine Empire and other Christian forms of government after the 4th cent. Religious practice, belief, and authority were given a properly Christian context, but they continued to control all aspects of society in a way that seems very foreign to modern Western understandings.

Bibliography: Mary Beard, John North, and Simon Price. *Religions of Rome*. Vol. 1: *A History* (1998); Ittai Gradel. *Emperor Worship and Roman Religion* (2004).

DANIEL M. SCHOWALTER

ROMANS, LETTER TO THE [Πρός Ῥωμαίους Pros Rhōmaious]. Romans is the longest and most theologically dense letter written by Paul the apostle. The theological importance of Romans in the history of Christianity has fostered a tendency to use the rubrics of systematic theology to describe the argument of the letter. Some of the Reformers, for instance, divided the first half of Romans into two sections, one dealing with justification (chaps. 1–5) and the other with sanctification (chaps. 6–8). Paul certainly deals with significant theological issues in Romans. But he is writing a letter and not a systematic theology. Ancient LETTERs tended to fall into a formal (and somewhat natural) pattern, and the letters of the NT are no exception. The three basic parts of the letter (opening, body, and closing) are clearly seen in Romans, although each of them is elaborated at much greater length than usual. The opening, with identification of the sender, an address to the readers, and a greeting, is found in 1:1-7. It is followed by a thanksgiving (1:8-15), typical especially of Paul's letters, and an announcement of the letter's theme (1:16-17). Then follows the body of the letter (1:18–15:13). The conclusion of the letter (15:14–16:27) also follows the ancient letter pattern, with modifications and elaborations typical of the NT and arising from the particular situation addressed in Romans.

Since Paul is writing a letter, it is important not to impose an elaborate theological structure on the letter that is foreign to its nature. Still, Romans is a particular kind of letter, a "tractate letter," in which a careful and coherent argument can be discerned. The language of "gospel," prominent in both the letter opening and closing (1:1, 9, 15, 16; 15:16, 19, 20; 16:25), and standing in pride of place in the statement of the letter's theme (1:16), suggests that Romans is Paul's rehearsal of "his gospel" (see 2:16), applied to the particular situation of the Roman Christians and defended from its detractors. Unlike other letters of Paul that are explicitly organized according to the issues of the recipients (e.g., 1–2 Corinthians), Romans is organized by the logic of the argument that Paul presents. The major stages in this argument are relatively clear. Most can be readily identified by the use of certain formal features—e.g., "I appeal to you therefore, brothers and sisters" (12:1)—or by shifts in vocabulary and argument. The only serious uncertainty about the major divisions of the letter occurs with respect to chap. 5. Connections with chaps. 1–4, particularly in the use of "righteousness" language, might suggest that this chapter is the conclusion of the first major section of the letter. But the linguistic and conceptual parallels between 5:1-11 and 8:18-39 suggest rather that the chapter belongs with what follows—a conclusion reinforced by the transitional tone of 5:1: "Therefore, since we are justified by faith ...."

A. Structure of Romans

1. The Letter Opening (1:1-17)
   a. Prescript (1:1-7)
   b. Thanksgiving and Occasion: Paul and the Romans (1:8-15)
   c. The Theme of the Letter (1:16-17)
2. The Gospel Message of Justification by Faith (1:18–4:25)
   a. The Universal Reign of Sin (1:18–3:20)
      i. The Plight of the Gentiles (1:18-32)
      ii. The Plight of the Jews (2:1-29)
      iii. The Guilt of All Humanity (3:9-20)
   b. Justification by Faith (3:21–4:25)
      i. Justification and the Righteousness of God (3:21-26)
      ii. "By Faith Alone" (3:27–4:25)
3. The Gospel Promise: The Hope of Salvation (5:1–8:39)
   a. The Hope of Glory (5:1-21)
      i. From Justification to Salvation (5:1-11)
      ii. The Reign of Grace and Life (5:12-21)
   b. Freedom from Bondage to Sin (6:1-23)
      i. "Dead to Sin" through Union with Christ (6:1-14)
      ii. Freed from Sin's Power to Serve Righteousness (6:15-23)
   c. Freedom from Bondage to the Law (7:1-25)
      i. Released from the Law, Joined to Christ (7:1-6)
      ii. The History and Experience of Jews under the Law (7:7-25)
   d. Assurance of Eternal life in the Spirit (8:1-30)
      i. The Spirit of Life (8:1-13)
      ii. The Spirit of Adoption (8:14-17)
      iii. The Spirit of Glory (8:18-30)
   e. The Believer's Security Celebrated (8:31-39)
4. The Gospel Defended: God's Faithfulness and Israel (9:1–11:36)
   a. Introduction: The Tension between God's Promises and Israel's Plight (9:1-5)
   b. Defining the Promise, Part 1: God's Sovereign Election (9:6-29)
   c. Understanding Israel's Plight: Christ as the Climax of Salvation History (9:30–10:21)
      i. Israel, the Gentiles, and the Righteousness of God (9:30–10:13)
      ii. Israel's Accountability (10:14-21)
   d. Summary: Israel, the Elect and the Hardened (11:1-10)
   e. Defining the Promise, Part 2: The Future of Israel (11:11-32)
   f. Conclusion: Praise to God in Light of God's Awesome Plan (11:33-36)
5. The Transforming Power of the Gospel: Christian Conduct (12:1–15:13)
   a. The Heart of the Matter: Total Transformation (12:1-2)
   b. Humility and Mutual Service (12:3-8)
   c. Love and Its Manifestations (12:9-21)
   d. Submission to Authorities (13:1-7)
   e. Love and the Law (13:8-10)
   f. Living in Light of the Day (13:11-14)
   g. A Plea for Unity (14:1–15:13)
      i. Do Not Condemn One Another (14:1-12)
      ii. Do Not Cause Fellow Believers to Stumble (14:13-23)
      iii. Put Others First (15:1-6)
      iv. Receive One Another (15:7-13)
6. The Letter Closing (15:14–16:27)
   a. Paul's Ministry and Travel Plans (15:14-33)
   b. Greetings (16:1-23)
   c. Doxology (16:25-27)

B. Detailed Analysis

1. Historical situation

a. Paul. The claim in the letter's opening that it was written by the apostle Paul has never been seriously challenged. To be sure, the letter also claims that Tertius is the "writer" of the letter (16:22). But this is simply the identification of the AMANUENSIS, or scribe. Ancient letters were often dictated by the writer and written down by an amanuensis. These amanuenses were sometimes given considerable responsibility for the wording and sometimes the content of the letter. But the similarities in vocabulary and argument between Romans and other letters (esp. Galatians and 1 Corinthians) suggest that Tertius has probably followed Paul's oral dictation quite closely.

Paul indicates in 15:14-29 that his apostolic ministry was at a pivotal point as he wrote Romans. In a strongly worded statement, he claims that "from Jerusalem and as far around as Illyricum I have fully proclaimed the good news of Christ" (15:19). Illyricum was the name of the Roman province occupying what is now most of Bosnia and Croatia. "As far around as" creates the picture of an arc; and an arc drawn from Jerusalem to Illyricum covers most of the territory that Paul evangelized on his three great "missionary journeys" recorded in the book of Acts. What Paul is saying here, then, is that he has "filled" these regions with the good news. He has planted vibrant Christian churches in significant cities, and these churches are now able to carry the good news to their surrounding areas.

Paul is looking for virgin gospel territory, and his gaze is drawn to Spain, at the opposite end of the Mediterranean Sea (15:24*a*). But before heading for Spain, he must make two important visits, to Jerusalem (v. 25) and then Rome (v. 24*b*). Paul must go to Jerusalem to deliver the money he has collected from the Gentile churches to relieve the poverty of Christians in Judea. This collection was an important project of Paul's on his third missionary journey (see also 1 Cor 16:1-4; 2 Cor 8–9). But the collection was more than a relief effort (*see* COLLECTION, THE). Paul also saw it as a practical means of bringing together two groups in the early church that were beginning to draw apart from each another: (mainly) Jewish Christians in the Diaspora, and Gentile Christians in Judea. This was why Paul was concerned about the way the collection would be received in Jerusalem (15:30-33). Paul does not explicitly say why he plans to stop in Rome after his visit to Jerusalem. But the verb that he uses in 15:24*b* ("to be sent on by you") implies that he hopes to secure logistical and perhaps financial support for his ministry in Spain. Paul's home base of Syrian Antioch was a long way from Spain, and he evidently felt the need to find support closer to his new missionary territory.

From these details it is clear that Paul must be writing the Letter to the Romans sometime on the third missionary journey (Acts 18:23–21:16). Other indications in Romans point more precisely to his three-month stay in CORINTH, recorded in Acts 20:2-3 (that it was Corinth where Paul stayed in "Greece" is evident from 2 Cor 13:1, 10). Phoebe, a prominent Christian woman whom Paul commends to the Romans in 16:1-2, is from Cenchreae, the port city near Corinth. The Gaius with whom Paul seems to be staying (16:23) is probably the same man whom Paul mentions having baptized at Corinth (1 Cor 1:14). And there is some reason to think that the city official Erastus (16:24) is the same Erastus who is mentioned in an inscription from Corinth. Paul, then, wrote Romans from Corinth toward the end of his third missionary journey. Establishing an absolute date depends on the overall chronology of Paul's missionary work. But 57 CE is a reasonable estimate.

b. The Roman Christians. The NT provides no direct information about the origin or history of the Christian churches in Rome. The book of Acts (*see* ACTS OF THE APOSTLES) records that Jews (and converts to Judaism) from Rome were among those who were gathered on the day of Pentecost in Jerusalem (Acts 2:10-11). It is natural to think that these Jewish Christians would have been responsible for initiating the Christian movement in Rome. This supposition fits the claim of a later church father (Ambrosiaster) that Christianity in Rome had its origins in the synagogues and that no apostles were involved. To be sure, this denial contradicts another tradition to the effect that Roman Christianity had its origins in the preaching of Peter (or, in some forms, Peter and Paul together). But there is good reason to be skeptical about this latter tradition. It is in this very letter of Romans that Paul enunciates his ministry principle of not building "on someone else's foundation" (15:20). It is unlikely that he would write a letter of the nature of Romans or plan a visit of the sort he describes in 1:8-15 to a Christian community founded by Peter (*see* ROME, CHURCH OF).

The Jewish community in Rome out of which the Christian movement emerged was of considerable size in the 1st cent. CE. Jews met in a number of SYNAGOGUEs that were not apparently bound together in any kind of larger organizational structure. The Roman historian Suetonius records an event in the life of the Jews in Rome of potentially considerable importance for the interpretation of Romans in the Life of Claudius. He says that the emperor Claudius expelled Jews living in Rome because of rioting due to Chrestus (*Claud.* 25.2). It is generally agreed that *Chrestus* is a corruption of the Gk. **Christos** (Χριστός) and that the rioting among the Jews was the result of conflicts over the claim of Jesus to be the **Christos**, or Messiah. The expulsion order would certainly have included both Jews and Jewish Christians. Less certain is the date when this expulsion occurred. A later writer, the 5th-cent. Orosius, dated the expulsion to 49 CE, and most scholars are inclined to accept this date. The date would fit well into the probable chronology of the book of Acts, which claims that Priscilla and Aquila were in Corinth during Paul's second missionary journey "because Claudius had ordered all Jews to leave Rome" (Acts 18:2). That "all" the Jews would have been expelled by Claudius is also a matter of some debate. But our sources provide sufficient grounds for concluding that a significant number of Jews were forced to leave Rome about eight years before Paul wrote to the Christian community there. The fact that Priscilla and Aquila are back in Rome as Paul writes Romans (16:3) reveals that the expulsion order had been allowed to lapse, perhaps after the death of Claudius in 54 CE.

By this time, judging from the evidence of Romans itself and from what we know of the growth of the Christian movement elsewhere, the Christian community in Rome included GENTILES as well as Jews. And the tensions between the two groups that we can document elsewhere in the early church probably affected the Roman Christians also. The forced absence of all (or at least most) Jewish Christians from Rome probably exacerbated these tensions. For during those years, the Christian movement in Rome, which had originated among the Jews, would have become an exclusively Gentile phenomenon. When Jewish Christians began to filter back into Rome, they would have found themselves in the minority. It would have been natural for them to resent the dominance of the Gentiles and to feel disenfranchised from the movement that they had initiated. The Gentiles, in their turn, may well have felt that it was time for the Christian movement to move away from its Jewish roots. This scenario is admittedly hypothetical, but it fits an overall pattern of social tension and matches the situation that did exist in many segments of the early Christian movement. At the same time, it offers a plausible social setting for the situation that Paul addresses in Rom 14:1–15:13, which probably reflects tensions between Jewish Christians and Gentile Christians in the Roman community (*see* CHRISTIAN-JEWISH RELATIONS; JEWISH CHRISTIANITY; JUDAISM).

2. Text and literary history

As is the case for the other letters of Paul, the text of Romans as we have it in the Greek NT and on which our English versions are based has solid early attestation. Of course, as in every NT book, there are passages where the particular wording of the original text is in some doubt. But, for most of the letter, there are few serious textual problems. This changes a bit in the last two chapters of the letter. The manuscript tradition offers some interesting options to the form of the sixteen-chapter text printed in our Bibles, options that have been the starting point for theories about the literary history of the letter (*see* TEXT, NT; TEXT CRITICISM, NT). The manuscripts witness to six different forms of these last chapters.

1. 1:1–14:23, 15:1–16:23, 16:25-27
2. 1:1–14:23, 16:25-27, 15:1–16:23, 16:25-27
3. 1:1–14:23, 16:25-27, 15:1–16:24
4. 1:1–14:23, 15:1–16:24
5. 1:1–14:23, 16:24-27
6. 1:1–15:33, 16:25-27, 16:1-23

The basic variable in these options is the status of the doxology (16:25-27). As a glance at the evidence reveals, it is omitted entirely in a few manuscripts and occurs in three different places in others: at the end of the letter, after chap. 14, and after chap. 15 (and in one set of manuscripts, it occurs both after chap. 14 and at the end of the letter). These differing placements of the doxology suggest some uncertainty about the doxology itself but also raise larger questions about the original form of Romans. For instance, it is suggested that the placement of the doxology after chap. 15 in the important early papyrus manuscript P^{46} might point to an earlier form of Romans that lacked chap. 16. This chapter, along with chap. 15, is also lacking in three manuscripts of the Vulgate, while three early church fathers, Tertullian, Irenaeus, and Cyprian, make no reference to chaps. 15–16. It is possible, then, that the bulk of what we now call the Letter to the Romans existed in an earlier form, which Paul expanded when he sent it to Rome. Even more intriguing is the possibility that the original letter to Rome did not include chap. 16. After all, this chapter includes greetings to twenty-five individuals, two families, one "house church," and an unspecified number of "fellow believers." Yet Paul has never visited Rome. Is it not more likely, then, that this chapter was originally addressed to another church? Ephesus surfaces as a likely candidate, since this is where Priscilla and Aquila are located when last mentioned in Acts (18:19) and because Paul greets "the first convert in Asia" (Rom 16:5; Ephesus was an important city in the Roman province of Asia). It is thought that chap. 16 might have been a letter in its own right, whose purpose was to commend Phoebe. Or, after sending the fifteen-chapter form of the letter to Rome, Paul might have added the sixteenth chapter and sent the whole to Ephesus.

But none of these scenarios is very likely. As the evidence above indicates, there is no manuscript evidence for a fifteen-chapter form of Romans. The placement of the doxology between chaps. 15 and 16 does not necessarily indicate any uncertainty in the tradition about chap. 16. Nor does the number of people Paul greets in Rom 16 necessarily constitute a problem for a Roman destination. As has been noted, Jewish Christians had been forced to leave Rome, and Paul may have met many of them, who had now returned to Rome, during his travels in the eastern Mediterranean. Priscilla and Aquila are a case in point. Some manuscript evidence for a fourteen-chapter form of the letter does exist, but almost certainly as a later development in the history of the text of Romans.

Finally, the status of the doxology (16:25-27) requires comment. While few manuscripts actually omit the doxology, its varied placement among the manuscripts does give rise to suspicion that it was added later to the text. Internal evidence is thought to point in the same direction. Some of the language in the doxology is more typical of Ephesians and Colossians than of Romans. Those who think that Ephesians and/or Colossians were written by a disciple of Paul attribute the doxology to the same individual or school of thought. On the other hand, almost all the manuscripts do include the doxology, and a good number of the very best ones place it at the end of the letter. Moreover, several of its features make it an eminently fit ending for the letter. For these reasons, scholars in the last several years have been a bit more inclined to accept the doxology as authentic, and this seems to be on the whole the best option.

3. Audience

Something of the composition of the Roman Christian community can be learned by an analysis of the names of people whom Paul greets in Rom 16. Unlike our custom, names in the ancient Roman world usually indicated something about people's ethnic origin, and often also about their social standing or even profession. The names in Rom 16 suggest a diverse community that included people from a wide range of social classes and economic standing. They also point to the ethnic diversity in the Roman Christian community. And it is this matter of the ethnic makeup of Paul's audience in Romans that is especially important for the interpretation of the letter. For Romans gives significant attention to the relationship between Jew and Gentile in the saving plan of God. Identifying Paul's audience in the letter would help to explain his intentions in writing what he does on this theme. Of course, determining the ethnic composition of the Roman Christian community in general does not necessarily settle the matter of the audience of the letter. For Paul might have directed his letter to a particular group within the larger community. Only the evidence of the letter itself can enable us to pinpoint the makeup of Paul's audience.

The letter, however, appears to send out mixed signals on this issue. Several features of Romans suggest that Paul was writing for a mainly Jewish-Christian audience. 1) He sends greetings to Priscilla and Aquila, as well as to his "relatives" Andronicus, Junia, and Herodion (16:3, 7, 11). 2) He addresses the argument in 2:17-29 to a "Jew" (2:17). 3) Paul says that he writes to "those who know the law" (7:1), and he speaks of them having lived "under the law" (6:14, 15; see 7:4). *Law* throughout Romans, with only rare exceptions, refers to the TORAH, the law of Moses that God gave to the people of Israel. 4) He calls Abraham "our ancestor according to the flesh" (4:1). 5) Romans is filled with quotations of and allusions to the OT (almost one-third of all Paul's OT quotations are found in Romans), and with argument about the status of Jews and their place in salvation history (e.g., 2:17–3:8; 3:27–4:25; 9–11).

Indications of a Gentile-Christian audience, on the other hand, while fewer, are perhaps even clearer. 1) Paul identifies his readers as Gentiles in the letter opening and closing. In 1:5-6, he claims to be an apostle given the commission to work "among all the Gentiles" and then includes his readers among those Gentiles. Similarly, in 1:13, Paul expresses the desire to "reap some harvest among you as I have among the rest of the Gentiles." And in 15:15-16, Paul explains that he has felt it appropriate to write to his audience quite boldly "because of the grace given me by God to be a minister of Christ Jesus to the Gentiles." 2) Paul claims explicitly to be directing his discussion of the place of Israel in salvation history to "you Gentiles" (11:13; and he continues to address this same group with second-person plural verbs throughout vv. 14-24).

Romans, then, appears to have a double character, pointing in two different directions in terms of the audience. A minority of scholars resolves this tension in favor of a Jewish-Christian audience. They acknowledge that there may have been a few Gentiles in Paul's intended audience (11:13) but deny that any of the evidence for a Gentile-Christian readership from elsewhere in the letter is convincing. But this view is hard to sustain in the face of 1:5-6 and 15:15-16. These texts, coming in the letter's opening and closing, constitute strong evidence for a Gentile audience. It is for this reason that several scholars have recently concluded that Romans is addressed exclusively to Gentile Christians, perhaps GODFEARERs, Gentiles who had adopted Jewish customs and studied Torah. Such Gentile Christians would "know the law" and be able to follow arguments from the OT because of their involvement in the synagogue. Paul's address of a "Jew" (2:17) gives no indication of the makeup of his audience because it is a literary device. Direct address of a fictional discussion partner is a regular feature of the diatribe, a literary style that Paul uses extensively in Romans. Similarly, Paul's greetings in chap. 16 provide no evidence for the letter's audience, since they are all indirect greetings: he calls on his readership to extend his greeting to these people. Most of these points are well taken. It is particularly important to recognize, as 11:13-24 makes clear, that arguments about the Torah, the ultimate significance of the OT, or the status of the people of Israel in the plan of God would have been as relevant to Gentiles as to Jews. As Galatians also makes clear, Gentile Christians needed to figure out "who they were"; they needed to understand what their commitment to a Jewish Messiah meant, at both a theological and practical level (*see* MESSIAH, JEWISH).

However, while clearly more compelling than an identification of the audience as exclusively (or mainly) Jewish, the exclusively Gentile view is probably also too extreme. Paul claims to be addressing "all God's beloved in Rome" (1:7), and there were indisputably Jews among "God's beloved" in Rome. The main argument of the letter would indeed be important for Gentile Christians to hear; but aspects of that argument (esp. chaps. 4 and 9–10) would seem to have even greater relevance to Jewish Christians. One of the key threads that runs through Paul's argument is the concept of "the Jew first and also the Greek" (1:16; 2:9, 10; see 15:8-9). This motif makes best sense if Paul addresses both groups. The tension between the "strong" and the "weak in faith" that Paul addresses in Rom 14:1–15:13 also favors a mixed audience. To be sure, it has been claimed that the section simply rehearses general Pauline parenesis (compare 1 Cor 8–10) and thus indicates nothing about the situation in Rome. But the specifics that Paul includes in the section make this unlikely. It is also the case that the identification of the two "parties" Paul rebukes is not entirely clear. They may have been people of uncertain ethnic identity who were quarreling about dietary rules and observances of special days that were popular in the Greco-Roman world. Or, less likely, the "weak" may have been Jews and not Jewish-Christians at all. But the widely held view that that the two groups were divided over the status of certain Jewish traditions within the church makes very good sense. The tensions reflected here probably reflect the historical/social situation that resulted from Claudius' expulsion of the Jews from Rome. The natural fit between the situation that seems to be presupposed in these chapters and the historical background of the community also constitutes good evidence for this way of viewing the chapters.

Paul, then, directs Romans to a mixed audience of Jewish and Gentile Christians. The fact that he can single out Gentiles in his address (1:5-6, 13) and conclusion (15:15-16) may suggest that Gentiles were in the majority. But it also—and more importantly—indicates that Paul viewed the community in Rome as falling within the scope of his calling to minister to Gentiles.

4. Nature and genre

Romans is a letter, as its opening and closing sections reveal. These passages reveal formal characteristics that were typical of ancient letters. But classifying Romans as a letter is only a first, and not very helpful, step in understanding its nature and the way it should be read. For ancient letters are of many different types. Some were very brief notes about specific matters addressed to a narrow audience—e.g., letters written by a businessperson to a colleague about a financial transaction. At the other extreme were fairly long letters on topics of general importance addressed to a wide and undefined audience—e.g., Cicero's letters about Roman public policy. The letters of Paul fall between these extremes. The Letter to Philemon, the most personal of all Paul's letters, is nevertheless concerned with larger church issues. And the most general of Paul's letters contain personal remarks that would be of interest only to the immediate addressees. This is manifestly the case in Romans. Paul writes to a specific Christian community in a specific set of circumstances (see above). He addresses a problem in the Roman Christian community (14:1–15:13), goes into considerable detail about his own travel plans, and sends greetings to a long list of individuals in the community. Romans is manifestly an occasional letter.

But the most striking feature of Romans is the long sustained argument that makes up the body of the letter. In strong contrast to most of his other letters, this argument proceeds with no direct reference to the situation of the Roman Christians. To be sure, Paul interjects questions along the way. But these questions are not questions the Roman Christians are asking but questions brought up by Paul himself to clarify his teaching and to move his argument along from topic to topic. Even Paul's exhortations about authentic Christian living in 12:1–13:14 have no ostensible reference to the circumstances of the Roman Christians. This practice changes in 14:1–15:13, where Paul directs his teaching to specific groups in the Roman community. Even here, however, there is some reason to think that the tension between these two groups in Rome reflects a fundamental tension within the Christian movement in Paul's day, and that by tackling the specific problem in Rome he tackles the larger issue as well. All this suggests that Romans should be put into the category of a "treatise" or "tractate" letter. Such a letter develops a self-contained argument of wide-ranging importance. Of course, the circumstances of the Roman community have undoubtedly influenced the selection of topics and the way that Paul develops them. Without dismissing the significant and broadly applicable theology that Paul develops in this letter, then, it is important to see that theology as genuinely contextualized. Paul is not writing a systematic theology in a vacuum. He is bringing to bear on the situation of the Roman Christian community broad theological teaching that they need to hear. It is the nature of the problem in Rome—divisions between Jewish and Gentile believers—that leads Paul to develop the theological argument as he does.

Various attempts to identify more specifically the genre of Romans have been proposed. It has been put into the category of "diatribe," a dialogical argumentative genre associated with Cynic-Stoic philosophers (the best example is the *Discourses* of Epictetus, 1st–2nd cent. CE). Romans certainly shares features of the DIATRIBE: the use of a fictional "debating partner," a question-and-answer format, and the emphatic negative mē genoito (μὴ γένοιτο, "By no means!"). But the diatribe is not so much a literary genre as a style of writing that might occur within almost any genre. Romans has also been classified as a "memorandum," an "epideictic" letter, an ambassadorial letter, a "letter essay," and a "protreptic letter"—to name just a few. Some of these classifications reflect categories of ancient rhetoric, and these have undoubtedly influenced the method of Paul's argument at various points. But Romans does not fit cleanly into any of these generic categories. Paul seems to have borrowed from various styles and rhetorical methods to put together his argument in the Letter to the Romans (*see* RHETORICAL CRITICISM, NT).

5. Purpose

Several of the issues treated in this article come together in a question that is central to an accurate reading of Romans: Why has Paul written such a long and theologically dense letter to a Christian community that he had never visited before? Answering this question accurately would provide great help in interpreting the letter. The particular theological and practical issues that Paul treats in Romans can be understood on their own. But putting them into their appropriate context as means to a larger argumentative purpose would help to assess their significance. Unfortunately, the letter itself gives no explicit answer to this question. The closest it comes to a purpose statement is in 15:15, where Paul claims that he has written quite boldly "by way of a reminder." Clearly, this provides little help in determining the purpose of Romans. Therefore a decision about purpose depends on the nature and direction of the argument of the letter itself, seen in the context of the historical and literary factors that have been examined above. The subjectivity inherent in this enterprise has resulted in considerable debate over this matter. Answers to the question of purpose fall into two broad categories: those that explain the purpose of the letter in terms of Paul's own circumstances; and those that focus on the Roman Christians' circumstances as the key to the answer.

a. Paul. The section above on the historical situation outlined Paul's circumstances as he writes. Having completed a significant stage in his ministry, he has stopped for three months in Corinth. He is preparing for a momentous visit to Jerusalem and plans then to initiate a new ministry in Spain, passing through Rome on his way. Attention is drawn to three of these localities as backdrop to Paul's purpose in writing Romans.

Paul's next major destination as he writes Romans is Jerusalem. He not only mentions this destination in Romans but talks about the purpose of the visit and asks the Romans to pray for it (15:25-33). The main reason for this visit, he says, is to deliver the "collection," the money he had been soliciting from Gentile Christians in his missionary churches to aid the Jewish Christians in Judea. Paul hopes by means of this collection to signify in a tangible way the need for unity between these two groups in the early church, as Gentile Christians recognize their indebtedness to Jews and Jewish Christians and Jewish Christians, in turn, recognize the validity of the Gentiles' standing as members of God's people. Paul's request for prayer indicates his deep concern about the success of this ministry. So it is possible that the body of Romans reflects Paul's wide-ranging thinking on the theological issues that lie behind his visit to Jerusalem. This would explain the dominance of the Jewish/Gentile issues in Romans. But it has considerable difficulty explaining the inclusion of many other topics. And one has to wonder why Paul would send a draft of his thinking on this matter to a church with which he had not had previous relations.

Corinth may stand for another way of thinking about the purpose of Romans. It is here that Paul is "catching his breath" after about ten years of intense ministry. Those years involved extensive travel, particularly in the Greek-oriented cities of the eastern Mediterranean. As "apostle to the Gentiles," Paul has been especially involved in extending God's saving grace to Gentiles and in crafting a theology that would both embrace Gentiles as full members of God's people and tie the early Christian movement firmly to its OT roots. This theological task involved Paul in endless controversy. So it might be that Romans is Paul's attempt to set down the theology that he has hammered out through the controversies of those past years. The letter might contain, as it were, Paul's "doctrinal statement." One element of Romans that could be cited in favor of this view is the careful balance it maintains on key issues such as the significance and role of the Law—in contrast, for instance, to the clearly polemical stance he adopts on this issue in Galatians. Such balance suggests that Paul may be writing in a context where he does not have to argue a particular position. There is something to be said for this proposal. But it leaves two large questions unanswered. 1) Why the particular selection of topics that we find in Romans? A lot of attention is given to the Law and to the place of Israel in God's plan; but issues that are significant in other letters of Paul, such as christology, eschatology, and ecclesiology, are hardly mentioned. 2) Why send this "doctrinal statement" to Rome?

The latter question might be answered by focusing on Paul's next missionary destination: Spain. One of the reasons he is traveling through Rome on his way to Spain is to solicit logistical and perhaps financial assistance. In order to garner such support, however, Paul will have to convince the Romans that his theological views deserve their support. Romans, then, may, indeed, be Paul's "doctrinal statement," sent to pave the way for his visit and request for support. The selection and manner of treatment of topics could in large measure be determined by the need to reassure the Romans about Paul's views on especially contentious issues. Paul's pioneering Gentile evangelism made him a controversial figure in the early church. Rumors (often inaccurate) about Paul's views were circulating widely, something to which Paul draws attention to in Romans itself (3:8). This understanding of Paul's purpose goes a long way toward explaining the content of the letter, and is almost certainly part of Paul's purpose in writing. But there are reasons to wonder if it is finally adequate as a comprehensive explanation, especially in light of Rom 14:1–15:13.

b. The Roman Christians. The various hypotheses that locate the purpose of Romans in Paul's own circumstances suffer from a similar objection: other NT letters, and, indeed, letters in general, are usually directed to the concerns of the recipients. To be sure, this objection must not be given the status of an absolute: letters, both ancient and modern, will sometimes be addressed to a particular audience for the convenience of the writer. And the concerns of the readers may also be interpreted very generally. For instance, Paul may have judged that the Roman Christians would benefit from a general overview of his gospel teaching. But, granted the occasional nature of most of the NT letters, it is quite appropriate to ask whether the letter suggests a purpose that might have had the Roman Christians particularly in view. The 19th-cent. scholar F. C. Baur broke with the tradition that saw Romans as a timeless theological treatise and stressed its occasional nature. Typical of his overall approach to the NT, he attributed to Romans a polemical purpose: to challenge Jewish Christians about their views on the Law and ELECTION. Some passages in Romans could fit with such a purpose; but many do not. A better starting point for this approach is the passage where Paul clearly addresses himself to the situation of the Romans: 14:1–15:13.

Accepting the majority view that this text reflects a division in the Roman community between Gentile and Jewish Christians, and that the division was over the continuing relevance of certain requirements related to the law of Moses, it is natural to think that Paul's main purpose in writing was to heal this division. This proposal would explain why Paul focuses so much of the letter on the relation of Jews and Gentiles, the role of the Law, and the status of Israel. These were the theological issues that lay at the root of the division in Rome; and Paul hopes that by changing their convictions about these theological matters he can achieve his goal of getting the two factions to "receive" each other (15:7). Such a purpose would also explain why Paul takes such a balanced approach to so many of these issues: he needs to change the convictions of both groups. Further, it fits with Paul's expressed intention in at least one key passage: Rom 11:11-32, where Paul explicitly claims that his argument at this point is designed to stifle Gentile "boasting" over Jews and Jewish Christians (11:18; see vv. 20, 25).

These considerations make it very probable that one of Paul's reasons for writing Romans is to foster a new spirit of unity among the squabbling Roman Christians. But it is doubtful if we can elevate this concern into the sole purpose of the letter. Some of the material in Paul's theological exposition (most of Rom 5–8, for instance) would seem to have little bearing on this issue. And if this had been Paul's dominant purpose, it is likely that he would have signaled this intention early in the letter and made reference to it regularly. Instead, nothing is said about this division until chap. 14. As has been noted above, the Letter to the Romans is unlike every other letter of Paul (except, perhaps Ephesians) in developing a sustained theological argument without reference to the readers.

This survey of options reveals that several specific suggestions have merit but that no one proposal is capable of explaining the letter as a whole. It can only be concluded that Paul writes with more than one purpose. A multifaceted purpose makes especially good sense in this case because the specific proposals all have a common denominator: the challenge of crafting a theology that would maintain continuity with the OT at the same time as it provided for the inclusion of Gentiles as full members of God's people. This was the central issue in Paul's missionary career to this point. It was the motivating force in the collection for the saints in Jerusalem. It would have been one of the most important issues for Paul to address if he hoped to gain support from the Roman Christians. And it is the theological problem that generates the disputes in the Roman church. These reasons converge to explain why Paul writes this particular letter to the Roman Christians. The dispute among them mirrors the larger problem of the church in Paul's day, a problem that has resulted especially from Paul's missionary successes in the Gentile world. By writing about the gospel as he understands it and by focusing on the implications of that gospel for both Jews and Gentiles, Paul is able to prepare for his own visit to Rome at the same time as he addresses a pressing issue among them. These varied circumstances required Paul to write a letter that dealt extensively with wide-ranging theological issues. It is for this reason that Romans justly has the reputation as one of the most important contributions to Christian theology ever written.

C. Theological and Religious Significance

1. Angle of view

The particular matters that are given pride of place in a summary of the theological significance of Romans will depend considerably on the angle at which we approach the letter. Especially since the time of the Reformation, Romans has been viewed as a book whose key concern is the individual human being. Romans is a letter about each person's sinfulness (1:18–3:20), their justification by faith rather than by works (3:21–5:21), their victory over sin, the Law, and death (chaps. 6–8), and their transformed life (12:1–15:13). Of course, notable for its absence in this quick survey are chaps. 9–11. Advocates of this traditional reading of Romans struggled to explain the presence of these chapters, sometimes seeing them as an elaboration of salvation in terms of election, sometimes dismissing the section as an excursus motivated by Paul's personal interest. It is just this failure to incorporate chaps. 9–11 successfully in the argument of the letter that stimulated scholars in recent decades to reconsider the nature of Romans. Perhaps, it was argued, concerns about people groups play a more prominent role in the letter than had been seen in the past.

Coupled with this new emphasis on Rom 9–11 came questions about whether Paul would have shared the modern preoccupation with the individual (*see* COLLECTIVIST PERSONALITY; INDIVIDUAL, INDIVIDUALISM). Added impetus for this approach to Romans came from the implications of a new way of understanding the basics of Jewish soteriology. Careful analysis of Jewish writings from Paul's day revealed that Jews held to a corporate view of salvation. Jews were saved because they belonged to the people with whom God had entered into covenant. Adherence to Torah was the way that Jews maintained their covenant status. When Paul contrasts faith and works, therefore, the focus is not on general anthropology (human believing versus human doing) but with salvation history (law as a marker of old covenant status versus faith in

Christ as the marker of new covenant status). And he criticized adherence to the Law not so much because people could never do enough "works" to be saved but because the Law, being the Torah that God gave as an exclusive possession to Israel, excluded Gentiles from the people of God. The burning question for Paul was not Martin Luther's "How can a sinful human being get right with a holy God?" but "How can Gentiles be given full covenant status alongside Jews?" (author's paraphrase; *see* COVENANT, OT AND NT).

This way of reading Romans is recent enough that it is still undergoing considerable scholarly assessment and critique, and opinions about its validity range widely across the spectrum from full acceptance to full rejection. It is probably best, then, to see in this newer reading not a replacement of the older reading but a correction to it. There is no doubt that the perspective on Romans inherited from the Reformers tends both to foster a misunderstanding of the true nature of the Jewish religion and to overlook the important emphasis on "people" concerns. The obvious focus on this issue in chaps. 9–11 is matched by similar concerns throughout the book (e.g., 3:28-29; 4:16-18; 15:8-13; the motif of "Jew first and also the Greek"). But the new perspective goes too far in dismissing the degree to which the good news that Paul proclaims in Romans is, in fact, directed to fundamental human concerns. The gospel that Paul explains and defends in Romans is, first of all, the "good news" that every person has the opportunity by faith in Christ to find acceptance with God. At the same time, reflecting the Israel-centric nature of salvation history, Paul divides human beings between Jew and Gentile and directs special attention to the way the gospel overcomes the differences between them.

2. Salvation history

As in all of his letters, Paul in Romans works out of a basic sense of the development of God's plan of salvation over time. Scripture for Paul told a story, in which creation, the fall into sin, the establishment of Israel and the giving of the Law, Israel's failure, marked by the exile, and the prophetic hope for national (and universal) renewal were the defining moments. Paul's theological task is to attach the new and climactic event in salvation history, the coming of the Messiah, to that history. And so in Romans Paul strikes a careful balance between continuity and discontinuity in this history of SALVATION. God's new work in Christ is tied very firmly to OT promise (1:2; 3:21; 9–11; 15:9-12) at the same time as it is presented as a new work that takes place outside the realm of the Law and the covenant it represents (3:21; 7; 9:30–10:4). Two verses, in particular, enunciate this perspective very clearly. Romans 3:21 claims that God's righteousness has been manifested "apart from law," but, at the same time, is "attested by the law and the prophets." And in Rom 10:4, Paul asserts that Christ is the "end" of the Law, the word *end* probably having the sense of culmination or climax: Christ ends the Law by bringing what it has been pointing toward all along. Paul's argument in Romans also draws from the familiar Jewish apocalyptic contrast of the "old age" and the "new age." The old age is determined by ADAM, who introduced sin and death into the world, while the new age is determined by Christ, who, through his obedience, offers life to the world (5:12-21). The Law, with its impossible demand, rules the old age, while grace rules the new (6:14, 15; see 7:7-25; 8:3). The old age is dominated by the "flesh," symbolizing human frailty, while the new is dominated by God's Spirit (8:4-11). Believers are to avoid the pattern of living characteristic of "this age" (12:2; NRSV, "this world") as they allow their minds to be transformed by Christ. Paul clearly finds this two-age framework a useful means of highlighting the benefits that believers in Christ enjoy. It should be emphasized that these two ages do not neatly equate with OT and NT. Abraham, e.g., because he was justified by faith, partakes to some degree of the blessings of the "new age." *See* APOCALYPTICISM.

3. The righteousness of God and justification

A cluster of words derived from the same Greek root has a significant role in the teaching of Romans: *righteousness*, *righteous*, *justify*, *just*. That these words are closely related is evident from passages such as 1:17 ("righteousness of God," "the one who is righteous") and 2:13 ("righteous," "justified"). In the Greek OT (the LXX), this word group often refers to behavior that is expected of those who are in covenant relationship with God. Romans sometimes uses righteousness language in this same way (e.g., 6:16) but more characteristic is the use of the language in its basic legal sense to refer to the "right standing" of Christians before God (e.g., 3:24, 28; 5:1, 9). *Justification*, the word applied to this concept, is accomplished through Christ's death (3:24; 5:9) and is appropriated by people through their faith (3:28; 5:1; and see chap. 4). Justification is to be understood as the creative declaration of God that a person is "innocent" before him (see 2:13). This "forensic" sense of justification is now widely acknowledged by both Protestant and Roman Catholic scholars (*see* JUSTIFICATION, JUSTIFY). A point of greater disagreement currently is the place of justification in Paul's theological argument. Is the doctrine basically about how a person is saved, with a focus on the invitation offered in the gospel to each person to respond by faith? Or is the doctrine basically about how one can tell who is in the people of God, with a focus on the inclusion of Gentiles? Certainly Paul emphasizes in Romans that the latter is a key implication of justification. But the doctrine itself appears to be more about how a person finds acceptance with God. Also controversial is the meaning of a key phrase in Romans, the "righteousness of God." It occurs eight times in Romans (1:17; 3:5, 21, 22, 25, 26; 10:3 [twice]) and outside of Romans only in 2 Cor

5:21. It is usual to claim that the phrase reflects the language of the OT covenant: God's righteousness is faithfulness in doing what God has promised to God's people. But there is also evidence that God's righteousness reflects a more basic concept: God's commitment to uphold God's own character and purposes. Paul may be using the phrase in this sense in 3:25 and 26. Particularly significant for Paul's announcement that "the righteousness of God" is revealed in Christ and the gospel (1:17; 3:21) are Isaiah's prophecies about God establishing "his righteousness" (NRSV, "deliverance") in the last day (Isa 46:13; 51:5-6). In these texts, God's righteousness is parallel to his "salvation" and suggests that the phrase refers to God's intervention to vindicate his people. Particularly distinctive to Paul's teaching on righteousness in general is his insistence that this "righteousness" of God would not be confined to Israel or based on the Law but is available to anyone who believes (*see* RIGHTEOUSNESS IN THE NT).

4. The human plight

In order to show why God must act in Christ to make his righteousness available, Paul devotes considerable space in Romans to the human plight. This plight, Paul insists, is universal. All human beings have sinned (3:23) and are therefore justly deserving of God's wrath (1:18). Using typical Jewish polemic, Paul accuses the Gentiles of the root sin of IDOLATRY, which has manifested itself in sexual sin and in all manner of other departures from God's will (1:18-32). But he is even more concerned to show why Jews, the recipients of God's covenant, need to respond to the righteousness that God offers in Christ. He accuses them of presuming on their covenant status when, in fact, their disobedience of God has, in effect, nullified that covenant standing (2:1-29). Both Jew and Gentile, Paul concludes, are "under the power of sin" (3:9). Paul's way of putting this matter gets to the heart of his analysis of the human condition. The problem is not just that people sin; it is that they are helpless slaves under the power of sin (*see* SIN, SINNERS). Humans therefore do not need a teacher to explain to them what sin is and how to avoid it; they need a liberator who can set them free from sin's power. It is just this notion of liberation that Paul picks up in the language of "redemption" in 3:24 where he explains how God has acted for us in Christ (*see* REDEEM, REDEEMER). In 5:12-21 Paul traces the universal reach of sin back to the first sin of Adam. Using the OT concept of corporate solidarity, he suggests that all human beings were somehow involved in Adam's sin and have therefore inherited the condition of death that he introduced into the world. While Paul's understanding of "death" in this context, and elsewhere in Romans, has some allusion to physical death, the more important aspect of death is the notion of condemnation (compare 5:12 and 5:19 with 5:18).

5. The Law (Torah)

Paul uses the word *law* far more often in Romans than in any other of his letters (74 occurrences out of 121 total in Paul). As the Jewish context and explicit claims make clear (e.g., 2:12; 5:13), *law* in Romans refers basically to TORAH, understood as the body of commandments given to the people of Israel through Moses. To be sure, Paul can extend this basic sense of the word at times, either to refer to the OT as a whole (3:19, where *law* refers to a series of quotations drawn from Psalms and the Prophets), or to basic moral requirements that God has revealed to all people (2:14). But it is the Law as a critical factor in salvation history that receives most of Paul's attention. The Jews' possession of the Torah solidified their pride in being the only people whom God had chosen for himself (see 2:17-22). During the two centuries immediately preceding Paul's Letter to the Romans, the Jewish people had experienced both persecution and dispersion. Both situations led to a renewed emphasis on adherence to Torah as a means of preserving Jewish identity. It is this confidence based on possession of the Torah that Paul attacks in chap. 2. Having the Law without doing it, he insists, will be of no ultimate benefit to the Jews. And Paul's pessimistic view of human beings in general (3:9-18) means that the Torah can never be obeyed deeply enough to secure salvation for the Jewish people (3:20, 28).

Paul also analyzes the place and purpose of Torah in the history of salvation. The typically balanced approach of Romans to theological issues emerges again in Paul's treatment of the Law. He strongly affirms its divine origin (7:12) and even claims that his preaching of justification by faith "upholds the law" (3:31; see 8:4). But he also makes clear that the Torah, because it was given to a people already locked up under sin, could never deliver them from their plight (7:7-25; see 8:3). In fact, the coming of Torah exacerbated the sin problem, since it imposed a series of very clear demands that could not be met (3:20; 4:15; 5:20; 7:7-12). It is for this reason that Paul can identify the Torah as one of those powers of the old age from whose bondage people must be delivered in order to experience the blessings of the new covenant (7:1-6). Christ has brought the era of the Law to an end (10:4). Some interpreters think that Paul in these contexts is addressing a Gentile audience, and that it is only Gentiles who must not come under the domain of Torah. But there is no good reason to restrict his focus to Gentiles in these contexts. Indeed, Paul's focus is on the Jewish people and their experience of Torah, from which he extrapolates to refer to the experience of human beings with "law" of any kind (see 2:14-15; 3:20 ["no human being"]). The teaching on Torah and its works therefore functions in Romans ultimately as a way of analyzing the human condition as such. Finally, however, it is important also to note that Paul gives Jews who look to Christ for their spiritual standing liberty to continue to follow Torah if they so choose (this is the implication of his warning to the "strong" in 14:1–15:13 not to judge the "weak").

6. Israel

Paul's dismissal of Torah as a defining possession of the people of God is also an indirect attack on Israel's claim to be God's people. Much of Paul's polemic in Romans, indeed, would seem to be directed against the notion that the Jewish people can claim any kind of exclusive or even preferable standing with God. Paul "levels the playing field" between Jew and Gentile, claiming that there is now "no distinction" between them (3:22; 10:12) and that God's grace is now open equally to "everyone" (e.g., 3:22; 10:4, 11-13). At the same time, Paul also enunciates the principle "to the Jew first." These two perspectives emerge right next to each other in the letter's theme statement, setting the agenda for much that follows: the gospel is "the power of God for salvation to everyone who has faith, to the Jew first and also to the Greek" (1:16). The principle "to the Jew first" cannot be confined to the historical sequence of gospel preaching; as 3:1-8 and chaps. 9–11 reveal, it has continuing theological importance for Paul. It is in chaps. 9–11 that Paul turns to the question of Israel. His purpose is to show that the word of God has not "failed" (9:6). As so often is the case in Romans, Paul's previous argument has created the need for this denial. For he has portrayed Christians, Jew and Gentile together, as those who have inherited the covenant blessings once given to Israel. Those who are "led by the Spirit" are the children of God (8:14); they are the ones who are "called" (elect; 8:28) and who are destined for glory (8:18, 30). Abraham's spiritual descendants are not (or at least not only) Jews, but all who believe as Abraham did (4:11-12, 16). All this seems to fly in the face of the promises and privileges that God had granted to Israel in the OT. The claim of Paul that his gospel is rooted in the OT and, therefore, the validity of the gospel itself, seem to be in doubt. In chaps. 9–11, then, Paul must, in order to guard the continuity of salvation history, explain how the present situation—many Gentiles streaming into the kingdom, most Jews rejecting the gospel—can be squared with God's word of promise to Israel. He makes two points particularly relevant to this discussion (*see* ABRAHAM, NT AND EARLY JUDAISM).

First, the situation in Paul's day is not fundamentally different than it has always been. From the beginning of Israel's history God has selected only some from within national Israel to be his true people (9:9-29). This remnant of faithful Israelites continues to exist in Paul's day in the form of Jews—like himself—who, in response to God's elective grace, have accepted Jesus as their Messiah (11:1-10). Second, the situation in Paul's day is being used by God to bring "all Israel" to salvation (11:11-32; see v. 26). What exactly is Paul affirming here? Some have suggested that he is affirming the continuing election of Israel through her own covenant. As Gentiles are saved through their Christ covenant, so Jews are saved through their Torah covenant. But in Romans, Paul has too closely tied salvation to Christ—for both Jew and Gentile (10:11-13)—for this to be a viable option. Others think that "all Israel" is a way of describing all the elect people of God—both Jews and Gentiles. But, again, Paul has too consistently used "Israel" throughout this context for national Israel to make this a likely option. Probably, then, Paul is affirming that the present rather small remnant of Jewish believers will enjoy a significant increase—perhaps in a single great mass conversion at the time of Christ's return (11:26*c*?). "All Israel," as OT usage makes clear, does not necessarily mean "every single Israelite"; it more often means, as it probably does here, "a significant or representative number of Israelites." Paul therefore affirms the continuing significance of Israel, as national body, in God's plan and purpose. His election of that nation, despite the turn to include the Gentiles as equal partners in the new covenant, continues to have spiritual consequences (11:2, 28-30).

7. Life as worship of God

The people who experience the "mercies of God" abundantly poured out in the gospel are expected to respond in lives given over to God and his service. This is their "spiritual worship" (12:1; see 6:12-13). Standing at the head of Paul's exhortations about Christian living, this demand sums up and sets the agenda for all that follows. Paul thus "Christianizes" all of life, suggesting that, for the believer, there can be no such thing as a "secular" life separate from the spiritual life. Such consistent service of God requires a fundamental transformation in the way God's people think. The "debased mind" that characterizes people apart from Christ (1:28) must be renewed so that it can recognize and carry out God's purposes (12:2).

In chaps. 12–13, Paul touches on some of the ways in which transformed Christians will live out their lives of worship and service. With a glance ahead, perhaps, at the conflict between the "weak" and the "strong" in 14:1–15:13, Paul urges that the Roman Christians learn to appreciate the unity of Christ's body, the church, and take their proper place within it (12:3-8). The following section features a series of brief exhortations, remarkable for the degree to which Paul borrows from the teaching of Jesus (e.g., compare v. 14*a* with Luke 6:28; v. 17 with Matt 5:39). The overarching theme, stated almost as a title in v. 9, is "genuine love" (NRSV, "let love be genuine"; there is, however, no verb in the Gk.). Paul emphasizes the fundamental role that love plays in Christian worship by heralding it as the "fulfilling of the law" (13:8-10). Between these texts Paul calls on all people to "be subject to the governing authorities" (13:1-7). Serious grumbling about the burdensome Roman taxation (mentioned by Roman historians) may have been the occasion for this exhortation (see

vv. 6-7). But the call for submission to authorities may also be directed against a distinctly Christian problem: the tendency among early Christians to become so focused on their new spiritual status that they neglected or even treated with disdain the structures of this world. Paul draws on standard OT and Jewish teaching to remind the Roman Christians that governing authorities are chosen by God and serve God's purposes. While Paul mentions here no exception to the command of submission, it would be wrong to read this passage as an unqualified endorsement of the authority of government. "Submission" requires Christians to recognize their place "under" the authorities; but the far more fundamental call to worship and serve God by carrying out his will (12:2) means that Christians will at times have to disobey the authorities.

It would be easy to view Paul's exhortations in chaps. 12–13 as generalized moral admonition. But this would ignore the very important eschatological framework within which Paul has set these exhortations. Paul only hints at this underlying framework in 12:2, where he urges believers not to be conformed to this "age" (NRSV, "world"). Nevertheless, this passage reflects the informing perspective of salvation history, with its fundamental division between the "old age" and the "new age." The old age of sin, death, and rebellion against God continues, but Christians no longer belong to it; and they should not live as if they do. *See* ESCHATOLOGY OF THE NT; FAITH, FAITHFULNESS; PAUL, THE APOSTLE.

Bibliography: Paul Achtemeier. *Romans.* IBC (1985); Karl Barth. *The Epistle to the Romans* (1933); F. C. Baur. "Über Zweck und Veranlassung des Römerbriefs und die damit zusammenhängenden Verhältnisse der römischen Gemeinde." *Tübinger Zeitschrift für Theologie* 3 (1836) 59–178; John Calvin. *Commentaries on the Epistle of Paul the Apostle to the Romans* (1947); C. E. B. Cranfield. *A Critical and Exegetical Commentary on the Epistle to the Romans.* ICC. 2 vols. (1975, 1979); Karl P. Donfried, ed. *The Romans Debate.* 2nd ed. (1991); J. D. G. Dunn. *Romans 1–8.* WBC 38A (1988); J. D. G. Dunn. *Romans 9–16.* WBC 38B (1988); Joseph A. Fitzmyer. *Romans: A New Translation with Introduction and Commentary.* AB33 (1993); Harry Gamble Jr. *The Textual History of the Letter to the Romans: A Study in Textual and Literary Criticism.* SD 42 (1977); Klaus Haacker. *The Theology of Paul's Letter to the Romans.* New Testament Theology (2003); Ernst Käsemann. *Commentary on Romans* (1980); Martin Luther. *Luther's Works. Vol. 4. Lectures on Genesis: Chapters 21–25.* Jaroslav Pelikan, ed. (1964); Douglas J. Moo. *The Epistle to the Romans.* NICNT (1996); Mark D. Nanos. *The Mystery of Romans: The Jewish Context of Paul's Letter* (1996); Thomas R. Schreiner. *Romans.* Baker Exegetical Commentary on the New Testament (1998); Stanley K. Stowers. *A Rereading of Romans: Justice, Jews, and Gentiles* (1994); Peter Stuhlmacher. *Paul's Letter to the Romans: A Commentary* (1994); A. J. M. Wedderburn. *The Reasons for Romans* (1991); N. T. Wright. "The Letter to the Romans." *NIB* 10 (2002) 395–770.

DOUGLAS MOO

ROME, CHRISTIAN MONUMENTS. The earliest extant Christian monuments in Rome were places of burial. The Roman catacombs, dating from the 1st cent. CE, are approximately 60 mi. long and contain about half a million remains. Christians were buried in narrow shelves with some type of Christian symbol at the burial site along with a brief inscription on a plate of some type. Some remains were placed in a somewhat larger space called a *cubiculum.* By 200 CE, Christian cemeteries had become more visible and recognizable. Examples include the cemetery of Domitilla and also the Memoria Apostolorum, both built in the second half of the 2nd cent. By the end of the 3rd cent. CE, burial places for the popes became identifiable Christian landmarks.

The Red Wall in the Vatican necropolis was built ca. 160 CE and an aedicule was added ca. 200, according to Eusebius (*Hist. eccl.* 2.25.6–7). Approximately fifty years later, supporting walls were added to the aedicule. St. Sebastiano on Via Appia replaced a pagan place of worship on that site around 200 CE. The basilica of St. John and St. Paul may have an ancient 1st-cent. Christian shop in its foundation. This edifice grew in the first centuries from a single room to its present basilica. St. Crisogono was built ca. 300 in the Trastevere. The Pudentiana was built in the 2nd cent. and remodeled in the 4th. Paintings at the St. Martini ai Monti are dated ca. 200. The Capella Greca in St. Priscilla (ca. 200 CE) is the oldest extant Christian fresco art. Many of the pre-Constantine places of worship were close to the wall of Servius Tullius in poorer neighborhoods of Rome where Christians converted residential structures into churches.

Constantine was clearly the great builder of the first Christian centuries in and around the city of Rome. He built covered, circular cemeteries that also included mausoleums. These cemeteries had a clerestory at one end supported by an interior column. Examples include St. Lorenzo, St. Sebastiano, and St. Peter. Constantine also built great houses of worship. St. Peter's Basilica was built over a non-Christian cemetery near Nero's circus. Constantine initially built several basilicas on imperial property with imperial monies on the fringe of the city. They include the Constantiniana, the Sessoriana of the Holy Cross in Jerusalem, St. Peter, the Apostolorum, St. Lawrence, and Via Labicana. The latter contained a mausoleum for Constantine himself. In 313 CE he also built St. Giovanni in Laterno, one of the first basilicas within the city proper. After Constantine, Christian art became more illustrative than symbolic.

THOMAS B. SLATER

ROME, CHURCH OF. The rapid emergence of groups of followers of Jesus in the capital of the ROMAN EMPIRE had a profound effect on the long-term development of Christianity. In the NT period, Rome was also the place of writing or reception of a number of the most influential texts (*see* ROME, CITY OF).

A. Early Evidence
B. Jews and Gentiles
C. Location and Organization
D. Peter, Paul, and Persecution
Bibliography

A. Early Evidence

The earliest evidence that followers of Jesus were meeting in Rome is Paul's Letter to the Romans (Rom 1:7, 15). He writes in 55–58 CE and has long known about them (Rom 1:8, 13; 15:22). This probably puts the inauguration of house churches comprising people arriving from the eastern Mediterranean back into the 40s CE. In Rom 16, Paul greets a large number of individuals and five groups: 1) the ekklēsia (ἐκκλησία, "assembly, church") in the house of Prisca and Aquila (Rom 16:3-5); 2) "those . . . who belong to the family of Aristobulus" (Rom 16:10); 3) "those in the Lord who belong to the family of Narcissus" (Rom 16:11); 4) "the brothers and sisters who are with" Asyncritus and others (Rom 16:14); and 5) "all the saints who are with" Philologus and others (Rom 16:15). The impression, strengthened by reading Paul's discussion in Rom 14–15 of difficulties about eating together, is that a number of groups meet in houses or apartments around the city. One of Paul's aims appears to be to draw these groups into a more unified network (see esp. Rom 15:7).

The earliest text that alludes to the Christians at Rome as a single body is 1 Pet 5:13, with greetings from "she who is in Babylon" (i.e., Rome; see, e.g., Eusebius, *Hist. eccl.* 2.15.2). More explicitly, *1 Clement*, at the end of the 1st cent. CE, is written on behalf of "the church (ekklēsia) of God that sojourns at Rome" to a similarly described church at Corinth (superscription). Each of these texts represents an early instance of the church at Rome seeking to exert influence elsewhere. The first external text to address the church at Rome as a single body is the letter from Ignatius (*To the Romans*, early 2nd cent.). However, the actual diversity of Christian groups continued well into the 2nd cent. CE. There were differences in approach to the Christian life, seen in the contrast between the formalism of *1 Clement* and the more charismatic ethos of the *Shepherd of Hermas* (early 2nd cent.). There were also conflicts between groups. Justin Martyr, writing in the middle of the 2nd cent., mentioned several groups that he saw as heretical, including followers of Marcion and Valentinians (Justin, *Dial.* 35.6). However, the early texts produced in or sent to Rome probably signal enough linkage among most of the Christians to say that they shared an identity as being part of "the church of Rome," even though it operated as a number of house churches that differed somewhat in culture.

A number of NT texts originated in Rome. The very early church tradition represented by Papias (writing 110–30 CE) links Mark with Peter (Eusebius, *Hist. eccl.* 3.39.14–15), who is placed at Rome by 1 Peter (which also mentions a Mark in 1 Pet 5:13), *1 Clem.* 5, and many other traditions. Rome continues to be a widely supported option for the origin of Mark's Gospel. In that case, stress on persecution and suffering (Mark 8:34-38; 13:9-13 and the prominence of the passion) suggests a Gospel written in the aftermath of Nero's action against the Christians. (Other scholars noting the prominence of Galilee prefer an origin nearer there during the sufferings of the revolt against Rome.) In fact, persecution and suffering is a theme common to all the NT texts for which an origin at Rome has been frequently suggested: 1–2 Peter, Hebrews, and some or all of the Prison Epistles attributed to Paul—Ephesians, Philippians, Colossians, 2 Timothy, and Philemon. The question of the origin of these writings is complicated by discussion of possible pseudonymity. In addition, some scholars argue for an Ephesian origin for Philippians and Philemon. None of these texts provides much information about early Christianity at Rome. Philippians does include Paul's disquiet about some other Christians in his vicinity (Phil 1:15-18; 2:20-21) and his joy at success for the gospel among some connected with the Roman authorities (Phil 1:12-14; 4:22). Acts 28 is disappointingly slight in its reference to Christians at Rome. They come out to meet Paul (Acts 28:15) but then disappear. The Jews whom Paul then meets seem largely unaware of them (Acts 28:22).

Christians first appear clearly in the archaeological record in catacombs at the beginning of the 3rd cent. (*see* ROME, CHRISTIAN MONUMENTS). In that period, Christian imagery begins to appear in these underground burial complexes in several parts of the city. The monument to Peter that forms the focus of Constantine's Vatican church dates from the middle of the 2nd cent., although as with other monuments of similar style it had no inscription to give us more certainty of identification. Peter Lampe argues that surrounding 2nd-cent. burials, which were too simple to have distinguishing features, would also have been Christian. The earliest non-Christian writers to refer to Christianity at Rome are from the early 2nd cent.: Tacitus and Suetonius describe Nero's persecution of Christians and explain who they are (Tacitus, *Ann.* 15.38–45; Suetonius, *Nero* 38.16). Suetonius also describes an event under Claudius that many scholars see as the key to understanding the early history of Christians at Rome (see §B).

B. Jews and Gentiles

The Jesus movement and its early leaders were Jewish. Yet by 55–58 CE, Paul writes to the followers of Jesus at Rome as though they were predominantly Gentile (Rom 1:5-6, 14-15; 11:13-32; 15:15-16). Peter Lampe and many other scholars see a clue to understanding this in Suetonius, *Claud.* 25.4. In a list of Claudius' actions toward various groups, Suetonius writes that Claudius expelled the Jews from Rome because of the commotion they were making "with Chrestus as instigator." If "Chrestus" should be read as "Christus," then the text is a garbled account of an expulsion of Jewish Christians (in 49 CE if one accepts Orosius, *Hist.* 7.6.15; compare Acts 18:2), which left a Gentile majority among the Christian groups at Rome.

If Chrestus is not Christ, Suetonius must be referring to a Chrestus (a fairly common, predominantly slave or freedman name) who needs no introduction to his readers, in which case it is just a coincidence that 1st-cent. Jewish history included both a Chrestus and a Christus. On the other hand, if Chrestus is Christ, Suetonius or his source misspelled Christus and misunderstood the relationship between Christ and events at Rome. Acts 18:2 and 28:22 must describe matters in ways that do not quite fit the facts. Frequent misspelling of *christianus* as *chrestianus* is mentioned in 2nd-cent. Christian writers (Tertullian, *Apol.* 3; Justin, *1 Apol.* 4.5). However, Suetonius gets *christianus* right (*Nero* 16.2, unless a Christian copyist has corrected it). Moreover, since Suetonius sees no need to explain who Christ is, the misspelling and misunderstanding become less probable. As for the Acts evidence, many scholars have questioned the historical reliability of Acts. However, disagreement with Acts is a factor that must be considered in weighing the relative probabilities of the options for the identity of Chrestus.

In terms of the early history of Christians at Rome, one consideration is probably more important than all the above: Paul writes all his letters as if to predominantly Gentile recipients. Paul may be selectively addressing only certain people. However, it also seems clear that the churches in most of the empire rapidly became predominantly Gentile. The Christian groups at Rome fall within that pattern and need no special explanation.

If Suetonius is not testimony to a catastrophic falling-out in the late 40s CE, the question of the degree of continuing relationship between Christians and the Roman synagogues becomes an issue. Mark Nanos argues that the Christians are within the synagogues when Paul writes Romans. Nanos sees him as seeking to make the Gentiles' behavior appropriate to synagogue life. The "weak in faith" of Rom 14:1 are seen as non-Christian Jews. Conversely, Andrew Das sees the "weak" as "God-fearing" Gentiles, formerly attached to synagogues and following much of Jewish practice, but now facing contempt from other Gentile Christians who were never linked to synagogues. Other scholars see the "strong" and "weak" as Gentile and Jewish Christians or as more-Pauline and less-Pauline Christians, all usually outside the synagogues.

A factor to bear in mind in evaluating this is that there were numerous synagogues in Rome, differentiated by factors such as allegiances or origins of members (e.g., those of the Agrippans [*CIJ* 1:365] and of the Tripolitans [*CIJ* 1:390]). Many early synagogues were based in houses, as were the Christian meetings. A group of Christian Jews who arrived in Rome from Antioch, for instance, might set up their own house-meeting, which they could see as a synagogue. Differentiation between house churches and synagogues is less clear than one might imagine.

C. Location and Organization

House-meetings were necessarily fairly small, especially among the nonelite, for whom accommodation in Rome typically meant a small, badly lit apartment. Lampe seeks to locate the Christians by noting where Jewish groups and Christian catacombs were found, supplementing this with evidence from locations of early *titulus* churches and literary and legendary references. He concludes that the main locations were Transtiberim and the area outside the Porta Capena. These were low-lying, fairly poor areas at the western and southern peripheries of the city. Transtiberim in particular was an area with a large immigrant population (Philo, *Embassy* 155; 157) and a heavy concentration of apartment blocks.

The prevalence of Greek names in Rom 16 indicates that most were either immigrants or slaves (or freed slaves or their descendants). Several of those with Latin names fall into one of those categories too (e.g., Aquila). Romans 16 is not directly representative of the churches in Rome; Paul, who had never been to Rome, had met many of those greeted. However, most Christians at Rome were probably rather like them. There was certainly one immigrant-led house church (Rom 16:5) and each of the slave groups mentioned, those of the families of Aristobulus and Narcissus (16:10, 11), might themselves have constituted a house church (interestingly, the one type of setting in which Christians were likely to meet in houses rather than apartments).

The only possible indications by Paul of authority figures in the Roman house churches are if the householders are implied as having such a position. First Peter 5:1-2 talks of presbyters who are overseeing (**episkopountes** ἐπισκοποῦντες) their flock. *First Clement* writes synonymously of bishops (**episkopoi** ἐπίσκοποι) and presbyters in a single city (*1 Clem.* 42:4–5; 44; 47:6; 54:2; 57:1). Clement's twofold church order consists of these and deacons (*1 Clem.* 42:4–5). The place of the (single) bishop in a church is one of Ignatius' main interests in every letter except *To the Romans*, in which a bishop is not named and episcopacy is not discussed. The *Shepherd of Hermas* gives positive evidence about the structure at Rome. There are presbyters "who preside over the church" (*Herm. Vis.* 2.4.2–3). (He does use the term *bishops* but in a less clear way; *Herm. Sim.* 9.27.2.) It is hard to avoid the conclusion that, although an individual sometimes held a special role among the Roman Christians (*Herm. Vis.* 2.4.3), there was a plurality of leadership until about the middle of the 2nd cent. when we reach the time of Hegesippus' visit to Rome (Eusebius, *Hist. eccl.* 4.22.1–3).

D. Peter, Paul, and Persecution

First Clement 5 is convincing testimony that Peter and Paul died in Rome, as many later traditions also asserted. First Peter also attests Peter's presence (whether or not the letter is pseudonymous). His absence from Paul's letter to Rome probably means Peter was not there by 55 CE. Given Luke's interest in presenting a united front between Peter and Paul, Peter's absence from Acts 28 suggests he was not in Rome at the beginning of the 60s. Ignatius describes the church at Rome as having been instructed by Peter and Paul while they were free (*Rom.* 4.3), although this could refer to letters. The early 2nd cent. *Apocalypse of Peter* refers to his death at Rome under Nero (*Apoc. Pet.* 14). The tradition of Peter's inverted crucifixion is first attested in *Acts Pet.* 37 (late 2nd cent.). Paul presumably did arrive in Rome as a prisoner, around 61 CE, as described in Acts 28. The complexities of assessing his possible further movements are beyond the scope of this article. Eusebius cites Origen for Paul's death under Nero (*Hist. eccl.* 3.1.3) and cites Dionysius of Corinth for Paul teaching with Peter and dying at the same time as him (*Hist. eccl.* 2.25.8), although by beheading (*Hist. eccl.* 2.25.5), as would befit a Roman citizen.

Tacitus sees the violent punishment of Christians by Nero following the fire of Rome in 64 CE as unjust and excessive, but as reflecting their unpopularity. They were "a class hated for their abominations," characterized by "hatred of the human race" (Tacitus, *Ann.* 15.44), "a class of men given to a new and mischievous superstition" (Suetonius, *Nero* 16.2). In 64 CE, the Christians were an identifiable group, sufficiently widespread in Rome to have a general reputation. The Roman writers do not link the Christians with the synagogues, although Tacitus does link Christian origins to Judea. The extent of persecution is unclear. To make Nero's point, significant numbers must have been involved, although Tacitus' "immense multitude" sounds excessive. In any case, the trajectory of development of the churches at Rome seems to continue fairly steadily, as far as we can tell from the occasional documents that bear witness.

For Eusebius, the next persecutor is Domitian. The focus is not particularly on Rome. However, Eusebius does identify Flavia Domitilla as a Christian (*Hist. eccl.* 3.18). She was exiled when her husband, T. Flavius Clemens, was executed, despite both being from the imperial family. Suetonius (*Dom.* 15–17) and Cassius Dio (*Hist.* 67.14.2) link this to "atheism," while Dio also mentions "Jewish ways." These accusations could relate to Christianity but they could be about Judaism. Similarly, the evidence from *1 Clement* of "sudden and repeated misfortunes" (1.1) is also ambiguous as to whether it relates to persecution.

Bibliography: Raymond E. Brown and John P. Meier. *Antioch and Rome: New Testament Cradles of Catholic Christianity* (1983); A. Andrew Das. *Solving the Romans Debate* (2007); Karl P. Donfried, ed. *The Romans Debate.* Rev. ed. (1991); Karl P. Donfried and Peter Richardson, eds. *Judaism and Christianity in First-Century Rome* (1998); Erich S. Gruen. *Diaspora: Jews amidst Greeks and Romans* (2002); Peter Lampe. *From Paul to Valentinus: Christians at Rome in the First Two Centuries.* Marshall D. Johnson, ed. (2003); Mark D. Nanos. *The Mystery of Romans: The Jewish Context of Paul's Letter* (1996); H. Dixon Slingerland. *Claudian Policymaking and the Early Imperial Repression of Judaism at Rome* (1997).

PETER OAKES

ROME, CITY OF rohm [Ῥώμη Rhōmē]. Rome was the capital and biggest metropolis of the Roman Empire. Parts of the Roman hills have been settled since the 14th cent. BCE. The city, however, was founded by the Etruscans, probably around 650 BCE; the traditional date of 753 BCE is based on legend. Etruscan kings ruled the city until 510/509 BCE.

A. Stages in the Development of the City

Etruscans founded the Temple of Jupiter on Capitol Hill, the Via Sacra on the Forum, and the sewer canal Cloaca Maxima, which served as drainage for the Forum area and emptied into the Tiber River south of Tiber Island; in imperial times it was entirely underground. The Etruscans built large stone houses, an extensive city wall, the Temple of Vesta and the royal residence Regia, which in Republican times became the office of the Pontifex Maximus. At the foot of the Palatine Hill, a circus was established. The Etruscan kings started the tradition of games and triumphal processions. With boundary stones they marked the city limits as a sacred line, called the *pomerium*, which remained basically unchanged until the time of the emperor Claudius (41–54 CE). It does not always coincide with later city walls and with the later urbanized areas. Military missions and certain foreign cults such as the Jewish or Egyptian religions were banned from the *pomerium.*

In Republican times, from the 5th cent. until 31 BCE, the Senate, patrician magistrates (under two consuls), and tribunes managed the city's life. Narrow alleys

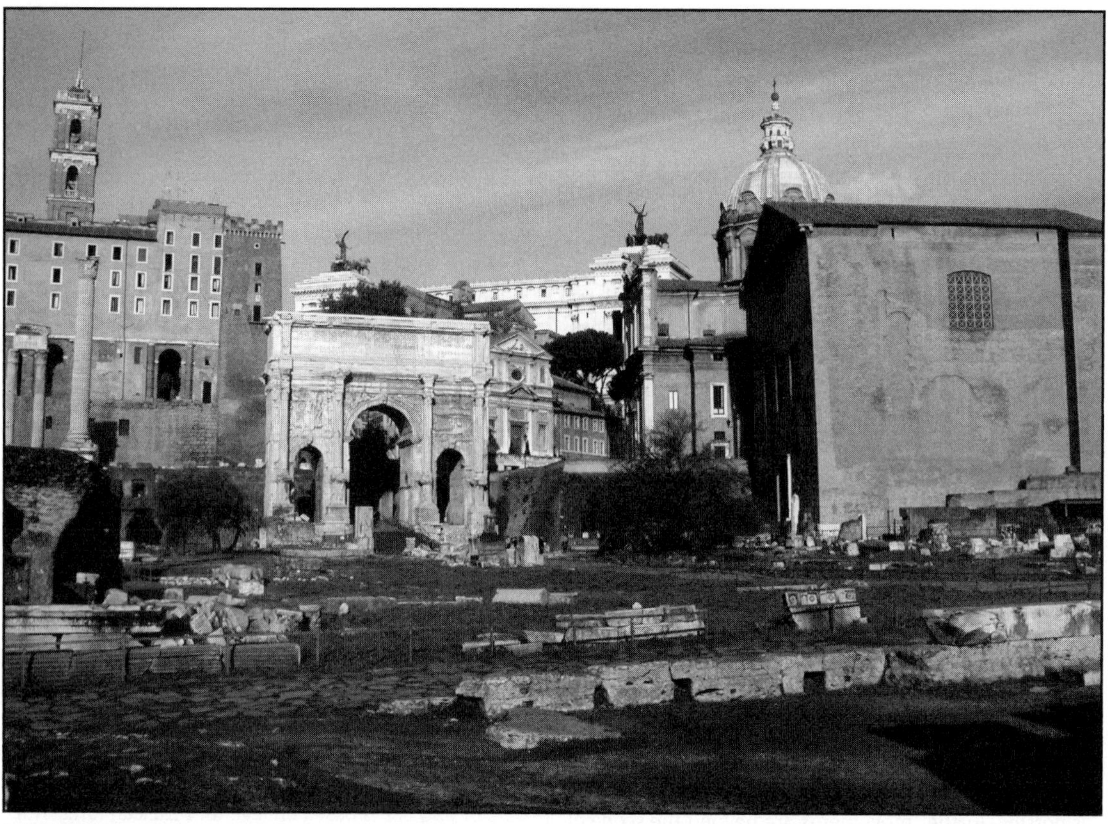

Todd Bolen/BiblePlaces.com

Figure 1: Arch of Septimus Severus and Julia Curia.

wound through the quarters. After the Gallian invasion in 387 BCE, the Republican, so-called Servian city wall was built in 378–350 BCE; it included the Aventine hill, which, nonetheless, stayed outside the *pomerium.* During the first two centuries of the republic, at least eight new temples were built, e.g., the Aesculapian sanctuary on Tiber Island (291 BCE). Busy building activities within the city paralleled the external political expansion. Already in 312 BCE, a first aqueduct fed running water into the city; others followed, until in late imperial times eleven aqueducts provided water for more than 1,000 fountains, public baths, and private homes. In 221 BCE, the Circus Flaminius was created on Mars Field. From 179 BCE, formerly wooden bridges were built with stone piers; in late imperial times nine bridges crossed the Tiber River. In the 2nd cent. BCE, streets were paved for the first time. Southwest of the Aventine Hill, large storage buildings received goods from trade ships moored to wharves. A triumphal arch marking the victory in the Second Punic War, porticos, basilicas, and marble statues lent a monumental façade to the city of the 2nd cent. BCE. Basilicas at the Forum served as market halls. Foreign cults entered the city, e.g., for Hercules and the Muses, already in 205/4 BCE for the Anatolian Mother Goddess Cybele (Magna Mater), to whom in 191 BCE a temple on the Palatine hill was dedicated. In the 1st cent. BCE, several urban quarters were developed outside the *pomerium*, and more temples were erected. On Mars Field, Pompeius in 55 BCE built the first theater made of stone, the model for all Roman theaters. Under Julius Caesar, many stores at the Forum had to give way to the new Basilica Julia.

Across from it, the Forum Iulium was constructed. Caesar built anew the Circus Maximus, which had existed at the foot of the Palatine Hill since pre-Republican times; under Augustus 55,000–60,000 spectators cheered the cart races—or made eyes at the opposite sex (Ovid, *Ars* 1.135–66). To counterbalance the numerous high tenement houses and narrow streets, Caesar and other sponsors (Lucullus, Sallust, Maecenas) established parks in and near the city; in imperial times there were almost thirty. A first public library opened in 39 BCE.

In imperial times, Augustus divided the city into fourteen regions. According to his own words, he restored eighty-two temples, which had deteriorated during the civil wars, and also founded new ones (*R. gest. divi Aug.* 20). Marble and travertine now were the building materials for sanctuaries, not tuff anymore; the architecture followed Greek models. At the Forum Romanum, Augustus completed the Basilica Julia begun by Caesar, erected the Basilica Aemilia and, following Caesar's example, named a new forum after himself, the Augustus Forum. Later emperors continued this tradition of constructing a forum named after themselves near the Forum Romanum (Vespasian, Domitian, Trajan). Augustus opened public libraries on Mars Field and near the Apollo Temple on the Palatine Hill; in the 4th cent. CE, Rome boasted twenty-eight public libraries. On Mars Field, Augustus had the monumental Ara Pacis and his own mausoleum erected as well as an obelisk from Egypt, which served as the needle of a huge sundial. Also on Mars Field, in 25 BCE, his friend Agrippa completed the antecedent of the Pantheon. In the same year, workers started the construction of the nearby Agrippa thermal baths, the oldest of the monumental public baths in Rome, with which emperors such as Nero (54–68 CE), Titus (79–81 CE), or Trajan (98–117 CE) decorated the city. The thermal baths were centers of social life, where not only bathing and massages but also conversation, ball games, and other sports were cultivated. Libraries were connected with them; in their proximity restaurants and bordellos flourished. The largest ruins of thermal baths preserved are those of Caracalla (211–17 CE) and Diocletian (284–305 CE). In addition, hundreds of private thermal baths existed. In the 2nd cent. CE, the Christian theologian and philosopher Justin lived in an apartment above the "bath of Myrtinus."

Tiberius (14–37 CE) built the Praetorian Camp in the northeast, Caligula (37–41 CE) a third stadium (*circus*) in the Vatican gardens. Under Caligula and then Claudius (41–54 CE), two new aqueducts were built to supply water to the growing city. Claudius included the Aventine Hill and parts of Mars Field in its *pomerium.* Nero (54–68 CE) completed Caligula's stadium, dedicated a new temple to his deified predecessor Claudius, and opened another large food market in the east of the city, the *Marcellum Magnum.* His new palace, the "Golden House," stretched from the Palatine Hill to the slopes of the Esquiline Hill. In 64 CE, a fire destroyed ten of the fourteen city regions. Nero accused the Christians of arson and crucified and burned many of them in the Vatican gardens. In the valley between the Palatine and Esquiline hills, where

David Bivin/LifeintheHolyLand.com

Figure 2: Colosseum interior.

a pond of Nero's destroyed "Golden House" had been located, Vespasian (69–79 CE) built the Coliseum. This amphitheater gave room to up to 50,000 spectators, who watched the gladiators fight.

At the beginning of his reign, Domitian (81–96 CE) erected the Arch of Titus, which commemorated the fall of Jerusalem (70 CE) and the triumph over the Jews that Titus and Vespasian celebrated at Rome in June 71 CE. On the Palatine Hill, Domitian enjoyed new luxurious palace buildings. The location of his stadium on Mars Field is still recognizable (Piazza Navona). Nerva (96–98 CE) completed Domitian's Forum Transitorium. Trajan's (98–117 CE) large forum with reliefs of the Dacian wars on the famous Trajan column connected the Forum Romanum with Mars Field. Hadrian (117–38 CE) constructed the Pantheon in the form it still has today. There are remains of his mausoleum near the Vatican (today's St. Angel's Castle) and of his temple for Roma and Venus on the Forum Romanum. Seven years after his death, Antoninus Pius (138–61 CE) dedicated a temple on Mars Field to him, the *Hadrianeum*. Antoninus Pius, in 141 CE, also devoted a temple to his deceased wife, Faustina, on the Forum Romanum. The impressive Aurelian city wall did not originate until much later (270–75 CE).

B. Population of Ancient Rome

In imperial times, presumably one million people from all over the empire lived in Rome, with various languages, customs, and religions. The waters of the Syrian river Orontes, Juvenal joked, emptied into the Tiber River. They imported eastern rhythms, music, and ways of life so that Rome, according to him, was Greek (*Sat.* 3.60–83).

Richer people lived in luxurious apartments or in villas (*domus*) with floor heat, running water, and sewer pipes. The majority of the population, however, crowded in tenement houses built of bricks and wood (*insulae*). Five or six floors high, they often became deadly fire traps. Most of them had no water supply of their own and no latrines. The ground floors were used as stores, workshops, or storage rooms. The higher one climbed in them, the smaller and darker the dwelling units became. Loud noises, odors, and crowdedness were normal. At night sleep was disturbed by carts that clattered under the windows, since Caesar had banned any cart traffic from the jammed streets of the city during daytime. In the 4th cent. CE, more than 44,000 entrances to *insulae* were counted in Rome, beside 1,791 entrances to *villae*.

C. Jews and Christians in Rome

In 63 CE, Pompeius conquered Judea and deported hundreds of Jews to Rome as slaves. Later many of them were freed by masters, who mostly were Roman citizens. These freedmen then received Roman citizenship, as it was the rule in Rome up until about 19 CE. When, in 19 CE, Tiberius expelled Jews from Rome, Jewish freed persons and their descendants, because of their Roman citizenship, could not be banned from the city without individual trials. In order to get rid of them, Tiberius circumvented this legal difficulty by drafting Jewish freedmen of Rome, allegedly 4,000, to fight against the bandits of Sardinia. In the 1st cent. CE, at least three Roman synagogues of Jewish freed persons existed: the synagogue of the *Augustesioi*, where freed persons of the emperor met, as well as the synagogues of the *Agrippesioi* and the *Volumnenses*. These names suggest that after Pompeius Jewish slaves continued to stream into Rome through large households, i.e., through the households of Volumnius, Agrippa, and the emperor. Volumnius in 8 BCE served as Augustus' legate in Syria and was, like Agrippa, a friend of Herod the Great. Other synagogues of the 1st cent. CE were at least those of the "Vernaculi" and the "Hebrews," as well as a Jewish worship place near the Republican wall. Through travel, the Jews of Rome stayed in touch with Jerusalem and its temple (Acts 2:10). On the whole, the inscriptions show about fourteen synagogues in imperial Rome. They existed independently from one another and were only loosely connected. In a similar way, in the first two centuries, Roman Christianity was divided into many distinctive groups (see below).

Jews of the 1st cent. CE lived in three city quarters. Many crowded in Trastevere, a densely populated area west of the river. Other rather poor Jews settled in the unhealthy valley of the Via Appia outside the Porta Capena. And other Jewish groups lived in the city's northeast in the neighborhood of the Porta Viminalis, where they founded a synagogue already in the 1st cent. CE; they probably also started the first Jewish catacomb (Villa Torlonia) on the Via Nomentana as early as the 1st or 2nd cent. CE, as radiocarbon dating suggests. All three areas were located outside the Republican wall and the *pomerium* (see for Philippi Acts 16:13).

Christianity seems to have entered the city in the 40s CE through Jewish Christians, who attended one or several synagogues in Rome. Their Christian proclamation stirred up unrest in the synagogues, which evoked the attention of Roman officials. At least the key figures of this inner-Jewish quarrel were expelled in 49 CE by Claudius' administration, among them the Jewish Christians Aquila and Prisca (Acts 18:2). After this, the Roman Christians seemed to have gathered in house congregations on their own, aside from the synagogues, although the separation from Judaism and its ideas was a slow process; many personal connections and cultural exchanges (e.g., in the fields of theology or catacomb architecture, which the Christians copied from the Jews) still existed even in the 2nd cent. However, when Paul wrote Romans in the second half of the 50s, the Roman Christians' congregational life was organized apart from the synagogues. Most Roman Christians, in addition, were of non-Jewish descent. Nonetheless, many of these "Gentile Christians" may have adhered to a synagogue as sympathizers of Jewish monotheism before their baptism. In 64 CE, even Nero knew to distinguish Christians from Jews in Rome.

Like the Jews, the early Christians lived at the periphery outside the *pomerium*: in Trastevere and the Appian Valley outside the Porta Capena. Both quarters were populated by lower-class immigrants from the provinces, who spilled into town on the Via Appia and the Tiber River.

Other Christians dwelled in between these two quarters on the Aventine Hill, others on Mars Field. Although persons from socially low strata predominated in Roman Christianity, all strata were represented, even senatorial nobility. In 96 CE a relative of the emperor Domitian, Flavia Domitilla, was banned to an island because of her Christian faith, which hindered her from acknowledging Domitian as a god (Eusebius, *Hist. eccl.* 3.18.4; Cassius Dio, *Rom.* 67.14.1).

D. Organization of the Early Christian Communities in Rome

Roman Christianity consisted of a variety of house congregations (Rom 16) that gathered in private homes. There was no local center for the Christians in town. This multiplicity fostered theological pluralism. In 2nd-cent. Rome, various Christian groups not only adhered to (what was only later called) "orthodoxy" but also to Marcionite, Valentinian, Carpocratian, modalistic, Montanist, quartodecimanian teachings or to those of Cerdo or Theodotus. A Jewish-Christian circle still observed the Torah. Others favored a logos theology, which was too complicated for less educated Christians. Some groups believed in a thousand-year-long eschatological reign of Christ; others did not.

The house congregations, spread around the city, were only loosely connected. Some sent leftovers of their eucharist to other Christian groups in order to document their ecclesiastical unity. The groups also exchanged written material. Often they coordinated communication with churches outside of Rome, so that outsiders might perceive the various Roman house churches as "the Roman church." A monarchic bishop, however, who at least directed the "orthodox" house congregations did not come onto the Roman stage before the second half of the 2nd cent. Earlier, the various house churches were led solely by their own presbyters; only sometimes did the city's presbyters gather at a central convention.

On the whole, the various Christian groups tolerated one another, i.e., no group labeled another as heretical, with a very few exceptions. It was not until the last decade of the 2nd cent. that the bishop Victor, the representative of the "orthodox" house churches, began to excommunicate other Christian groups in town. Victor was the first full-blown monarchic bishop in Rome.

At the latest in the middle of the 2nd cent., Christians identified a simple grave in the Vatican necropolis as St. Peter's tomb. Around 160 CE, they decorated it with a modest monument, an *aedicula*. At the latest, at the end of the 2nd cent., a tomb of St. Paul was also shown at the Via Ostiensis. Already in the 90s CE, *1 Clement* (5:4-7; see also Ignatius, *Rom.* 4:3) claimed that both apostles suffered martyrdom in Rome—possibly in connection with Nero's massacre in 64 CE. The narrative of Acts stops short before a martyrdom of Paul. Acts rather emphasizes that Paul, although guarded by a soldier, could teach relatively freely in Rome (28:16-31). Luke kept negative sides of the Roman reign, such as Paul's martyrdom, from his readers where he could. Revelation displays an entirely different tendency. In the Roman Empire, it was a rare document of political-economical protest against Rome, this "Babylon," a "whore," who seduces the nations (13:7; 17:2, 4, 15; 18:3, 7, 11, 15-17, 19, 22-24).

Bibliography: R. R. Holloway. *Constantine and Rome* (2004); P. Lampe. *From Paul to Valentinus: Christians at Rome in the First Two Centuries* (2003); P. Lampe. "Early Christians in the City of Rome: Topographical and Social Historical Aspects of the First Three Centuries." *Christians as a Religious Minority in a Multicultural City.* M. Labahn and J. Zangenberg, eds. (2004) 20–32; L. V. Rutgers. *The Jews in Late Ancient Rome* (1995).

PETER LAMPE

ROME, EARLY CHRISTIAN ATTITUDES TOWARD. Twenty years ago, study of the relationship between early Christian texts and the ROMAN EMPIRE was a fairly minor field within scholarship. It focused mainly on study of specific texts such as the "render to Caesar" passages (e.g., Matt 22:21), the book of Acts, Rom 13:1-7, Revelation, and a wide range of postbiblical narrative texts that center on the martyrdom of a person or group (such as *Martyrdom of Peter*). Today, the field is a major area in NT scholarship and studies cover the whole NT and a range of other early Christian texts.

The conventional view that, except for Revelation, NT texts are broadly supportive of or neutral toward the Roman Empire has come under sustained attack from scholars such as Richard Horsley, Neil Elliott, and Warren Carter. They see in many of the NT texts a fairly sustained rhetoric of resistance to the Roman Empire, which these scholars interpret as resistance to empire in general—an interpretive move that can have profound implications for the use of the NT in the present-day political theology.

All NT texts were written in territory ruled by Rome. The question is to what extent the texts were shaped by attitudes that the writers and their audiences held toward the empire. In Revelation, the shaping is stark. Especially in chap. 17, the author clearly has a very negative view of Rome, which is linked with the death of some Christians (Rev 17:6). The author looks forward to Rome's destruction (Rev 18:1–19:3). Luke–Acts is also very consciously set in the Roman Empire, most obviously in Luke's notices of historical settings (Luke 2:1-2; 3:1-2) and in the geographical structure of Acts, moving from Jerusalem to Rome. However, the ambiguity of attitudes to Rome is indicated in the portrayal of the many Roman officials. They range from models of excellence

(CORNELIUS in Acts 10) to dubious figures, addicted to bribes (FELIX in Acts 24:26). Attitudes to Rome are directly dealt with in the question to Jesus about taxes (Matt 22:15-22; Mark 12:13-17; Luke 20:20-26) and in Rom 13:1-7. Scholars are divided on the extent to which the compliant instruction, in these passages, to pay taxes to Rome is couched in language that qualifies Rome's authority so much as to represent a form of resistance to Rome. The case is hard to maintain for Rom 13, but a number of scholars have argued that tactical reasons, such as the need to preserve the Christian community under a dangerous regime, account for Paul's apparently compliant language there.

Beyond these passages, there is now debate about every major book in the NT. Early Christian eschatology has been described as a challenge both to the empire's authority in general and to the imperial "Golden Age" idea in particular (*see* ESCHATOLOGY OF THE NT). Christology has been seen by some scholars as a challenge to the lordship of Caesar. Early Christian ethics and community structures have been treated as a challenge to basic social structures of the empire (such as patronage). Many specific texts and terms (such as *Legion* in Mark 5:9 and *coming* in 1 Thess 4:15) have been studied for their political significance. Methods used in this field range from conventional historical study to postcolonial approaches and, particularly, James C. Scott's work on "hidden transcripts."

In assessing these issues, there are a number of contexts to bear in mind: 1) OT and other early Jewish texts about the relationship of the people of God to empires; 2) general attitudes to Rome and its empire in the eastern provinces; 3) the social and political situation of the ministry of Jesus; 4) the situation and experiences of the early Christian groups among whom the NT texts were written; 5) the nature of Roman imperial ideology and of its dissemination around the empire. The wide range of these factors makes it inevitable that the relationship between the NT and its political environment is a complex one.

Many Jewish writings developed specifically in relation to experience under imperial powers: Assyria, Babylon, Persia, the Seleucids (such as ANTIOCHUS Epiphanes in Daniel and the Maccabean literature), and Rome (esp. in the *Psalms of Solomon* and the DEAD SEA SCROLLS). This led to complex reflection both on theological topics such as the relationship between imperial rulers and God's plans, and on practical topics about living well under, or resisting, imperial control. New Testament writers inherited this complexity, along with the ambiguity of 1st-cent. attitudes to Rome, the awe-inspiring protector and the oppressive collector of taxes. Jesus comes into this situation as a preacher among poor peasants, announcing a change of authority in the world. He is then crucified. His followers form groups, often unpopular outsiders (Tacitus, *Ann.* 15.44), in towns and cities around the Roman Empire. They thrive on the communication networks that the empire underpins but they face various kinds of conflict with other groups and, eventually, from the Roman government. As Christian theology and practice develops, it interacts with Roman ideology, in ways ranging from borrowing of language to direct conflict of views. This builds to a peak in the 2nd cent., when refusal to acknowledge the imperial cult becomes—for both sides—a key identifying mark of Christians (Pliny the Younger, *Ep.* 10.96; *Mart. Pol.* 10:1).

The NT writings sit at various places in a complex matrix. Reflection on how a text that one is studying should be located is valuable both for proper contextual interpretation of the text and for any consequent use to which some readers will put the text in reflecting on the social and political context of their own community.

Bibliography: Warren Carter. *The Roman Empire and the New Testament: An Essential Guide* (2006); John Dominic Crossan and Jonathan L. Reed. *In Search of Paul: How Jesus' Apostle Opposed Rome's Empire with God's Kingdom* (2004); Neil Elliott. *Liberating Paul* (1995); Richard A. Horsley, ed. *Paul and Politics* (2000); Richard A. Horsley, ed. *Paul and the Roman Imperial Order* (2004); Peter Oakes, ed. *Rome in the Bible and the Early Church* (2002); John Riches and David Sim, eds. *The Gospel of Matthew in Its Roman Imperial Context* (2005); James C. Scott. *Domination and the Arts of Resistance* (1990).

PETER OAKES

ROOF [גַּג gagh, קוֹרָה qorah; δῶμα dōma, στέγη stegē]. The roof of an ancient house was often flat and made of mud, clay, and/or straw. The roof of a temporary shelter roof might be made of reeds or rushes. Permanent, open, flat rooftops provided cool places of rest. Peter was waiting for his meal on the roof of a house when he experienced the vision of the unclean animals (Acts 10:9-16).

KATHY R. MAXWELL

ROOF CHAMBER. *See* CHAMBER.

ROOM. *See* CHAMBER; THRONE; UPPER ROOM.

ROOT [שֹׁרֶשׁ shoresh; ῥίζα rhiza]. The part of a plant that extends into the ground to provide support and nourishment. Metaphorically, people are "rooted up" from a location like roots pulled from the ground (Deut 2:15; 1 Kgs 14:15), but Israel will one day take root again in the land (Isa 27:6; Hos 14:5). Roots are a symbol of morality, both good and bad. An unbelieving heart is like a root that produces poison (Deut 29:18 [Heb. 29:17]). Fools take root (Job 5:3), and the roots of the unrighteous wrap around rocks (Job 8:17) and dry out (Job 18:16; compare Hos 9:16). Yet the root of the righteous, which will never be moved, bears fruit (Prov 12:3, 12; compare Jer 17:8).

John the Baptist preaches that the ax is laid at the root of the tree, namely those who do not repent (Matt 3:10). The one who receives Jesus' words with joy but abandons faith quickly is seed sown on rocky soil, without root (Matt 13:6, 21). Isaiah refers to a stump or root of JESSE (Isa 11:1, 10), which Paul cites in reference to Jesus (Rom 15:12; compare Rev 5:5). Believers are to be rooted in love and in Christ (Eph 3:17) and let neither money (1 Tim 6:10) nor bitterness (Heb 12:15) take root.

KENNETH D. LITWAK

ROPE [אַגְמוֹן ʾaghmon, חֶבֶל khevel, עֲבֹת ʿavoth; ζευκτηρία zeuktēria, σχοινίον schoinion]. Ancient ropes were twisted and braided from long plant fibers or animal hair. The distinction between ropes and smaller cords is not always clear (e.g., Isa 5:18; *see* CORD, ROPE). Rope (ʿ**avoth**) was used to guide a plow animal (Job 39:10) or attach a cart (Isa 5:18). It could bind Samson but not withstand his strength (Judg 15:13-14; 16:11-12). Another type of rope (**khevel**) was used for rescue, to lower the Hebrew spies from Rahab's window (Josh 2:15) or to maneuver Jeremiah into and out of a pit (Jer 38:6, 11-13). When replacing a belt (Isa 3:24) or wrapping around the head while one was dressed in sackcloth (1 Kgs 20:31-32), a rope was a sign of poverty or humility. The same word describes ropes laid as a snare (Job 18:10), employed to pull down city walls (2 Sam 17:13), or tied to tent stakes (Isa 33:20). The word ʾ**aghmon**, which commonly describes bulrushes, suggests a rope in Job 41:2 that is used to snag Leviathan (in the previous verse, **khevel** depicts a fishing line used for the same purpose). Ropes appear in the NT only with reference to their use on ships (Acts 27:32, 40).

TONY W. CARTLEDGE

ROSETTA STONE roh-zet´uh. A stone found by Napoleon's expedition in el-Rashid (Rosetta), Egypt, in July 1799. The face of the stone contains the same inscription in two languages (Egyptian and Greek) and three alphabets (hieroglyphics, demotic, and Greek). The stone is 3.75 ft. high, 2.38 ft. wide, and .9 ft. thick.

The stone dates from March 27, 196 BCE, and contains a copy of decrees passed to celebrate the

Todd Bolen/BiblePlaces.com

Figure 1: The Rosetta Stone, British Museum, London, Great Britain.

first anniversary of the reign of Pharaoh Ptolemy V Epiphanes. Because the same text was repeated three times, the Rosetta Stone was a primary key to deciphering hieroglyphics. The stone is now housed at the British Museum.

KEVIN A. WILSON

ROSH rosh [רֹאשׁ ro'sh]. According to the Heb., Rosh was one of the ten sons of Benjamin who migrated with him to Egypt (Gen 46:21). The LXX lists him as Benjamin's grandson. Rosh's name does not appear in the corresponding lists in Num 26:38-40 or 1 Chr 8:1-2.

ROSH HA-SHANAH rosh'huh-shah'nuh [רֹאשׁ הַשָּׁנָה ro'sh hashanah]. The term literally means "head of the year" and refers to the Jewish NEW YEAR festival, celebrated on the first day of the seventh month. Leviticus 23:24 prescribes the blowing of the shofar (ram's horn) on Rosh Hashanah, a custom preserved by modern Judaism.

RUBY [כַּדְכֹּד kadhkodh; ἄνθραξ anthrax]. Ruby is the red variety of corundum and a prized luxury trade good (Isa 54:12; Ezek 27:16). Rubies are second only to diamonds in hardness. Tobit imagines that the streets of the restored Jerusalem will be paved with rubies (Tob 13:16). *See* JEWELRY; JEWELS AND PRECIOUS STONES.

RUDDER [οἴαξ oiax, πηδάλιον pēdalion]. An underwater blade attached at the stern of a boat or ship that is used to steer the vessel. A ship's rudder is small, but a slight change in its position alters the course of the much larger ship. James compares the human tongue to a rudder: although the tongue is a small organ, its affect on human behavior can be great (Jas 3:4). The author of 4 Maccabees, who argues that reason should govern the emotions, praises the aged martyr Eleazar for using the "rudder of religion" to steer the "ship of religion over the sea of the emotions" (4 Macc 7:1-3). That is, Eleazar refused to save his life by eating pork, because he reasoned that he would be setting a bad example for younger Jews.

KENNETH D. LITWAK

RUDDY [אַדְמֹנִי 'adhmoni]. *Ruddy* is used to translate 'adhmoni ("red") in the context of male beauty, perhaps referring to the complexion or hair. It is used with reference to David (1 Sam 16:12; 17:42), a male consort (Song 5:10), and a people (Lam 4:7).

RUE r*oo* [πήγανον pēganon]. The list of tithed spices in Luke 11:42 is based on the requirement to tithe "all the yield of your seed" (Deut 14:22; 26:12). Jesus notes the meticulous attention of the Pharisees to comply with this law but condemns them for failing to act on injustice. Rue (*Ruta chalepensis*) grows wild, and its leaves produce scented oil and flavoring. Since it is not a cultivated plant, rue is not subject to the tithe, but its mention in Luke may be based on confusion over the sound of the word *rue* in Aram. (shivra' שְׁבְרָא) and the word for dill (shivtha' שִׁיבְתָא; compare Matt 23:23). *See* DILL; SPICE.

VICTOR H. MATTHEWS

RUFUS r*oo*'fuhs [Ῥοῦφος Rhouphos]. Meaning "red."
1. According to Mark, Simon of Cyrene was the father of Rufus and Alexander (Mark 15:21). The synoptic parallels do not refer to Simon's children (Matt 27:32; Luke 23:26).

2. An associate of Paul's, to whom he sends greeting (Rom 16:13). Paul considers Rufus' mother to be "a mother to me also." There is no evidence that this is the same Rufus as mentioned in Mark's Gospel.

JESSICA TINKLENBERG DEVEGA

RUG [צָפִית tsafith, שְׂמִיכָה semikhah]. The covering JAEL, the wife of Heber, uses to enfold SISERA after he agrees to turn aside into her tent for rest while fleeing from Barak (Judg 4:18). While he is wrapped in this heavy garment and "fast asleep from weariness," Jael is able to slay him with a tent peg (Judg 4:21). The expression "spread the rugs" for feasting appears in an oracle about the enemies of Israel becoming comfortable (Isa 21:6).

JESSICA TINKLENBERG DEVEGA

RUHAMAH. *See* LO-RUHAMAH.

RUIN [עַוָּה 'awwah, תֵּל tel; ὄλεθρος olethros, ῥῆγμα rhēgma]. A variety of biblical vocabulary expresses the idea of destruction or DESOLATION. The Hebrew word tel has made its way into the English language and describes the many large mounds in the Middle East. Large mound ruins were known at least from the exilic period (e.g., Ezra 2:59; Neh 7:61; Ezek 3:15) and were used by the biblical writers as symbols of destruction and judgment. The final act of holy war for the Israelites was to offer up the town of their enemy as a tel 'olam (תֵּל עוֹלָם, "perpetual ruin"), a place never to be built upon again (Deut 13:16 [Heb. 13:17]; Josh 8:28; compare Josh 11:13; Jer 49:2 [NRSV, "mound(s)"]). The dramatic repetition of the term 'awwah is used by Ezekiel to express the unprecedented destruction of Jerusalem (Ezek 21:27 [Heb. 21:32]). An alternative vision of hope is proclaimed in Jer 30:18, where the fortune of Joseph includes the rebuilding of their city upon the ruins (NRSV, "mound"). *Ruin* also refers metaphorically to spiritual destruction of the unwise or disobedient (Prov 10:14; 19:3; Rom 14:15; 1 Tim 6:9; 2 Tim 2:14; compare Luke 6:49).

BRUCE W. GENTRY

RUJM EL-HIRI. *See* HIRI, RUJM EL.

RULE OF THE COMMUNITY. The *Serekh ha-Yakhad* ("*Rule of the Community*") is a composite document that records the religious beliefs and practices and the organizational rules of the Yachad, commonly identified with the community of ESSENES living at Khirbet QUMRAN near the Dead Sea from ca. 150 BCE to 68 CE.

An almost completely preserved form of the *Rule of the Community* (1QS), comprising eleven columns on five leather sheets stitched together, was among the initial discoveries in Cave 1 at Qumran in 1947. Ten further fragmentary manuscripts were discovered in Cave 4 (4QS[a-j]) and another in Cave 5 (5QS or 5Q11). Recently, a tiny fragment from Cave 11 (11Q29) was identified as yet another possible copy of the *Serekh.* These additional twelve (eleven?) copies show both wide agreement with 1QS as well as major differences that illuminate the textual development of the work.

The contents of 1QS may be summarized as follows. 1QS I, 1–15: The most fully preserved manuscript has an introduction that emphasizes the Torah of Moses as foundational and paints the community as "the sons of light" in contrast with "the sons of darkness," i.e., those outside. The community members are the true keepers of the covenant, striving for perfection in their ritual conduct. The cultic festivals are celebrated according to the solar calendar (not the lunar calendar used in the Jerusalem Temple), and community members hold their property in common.

1QS I, 16–III, 12: A liturgical section includes the ceremony for entry of novices into the community, the annual renewal of the covenant for all members, which presumably took place in the same ceremony, and a condemnation of those who refuse to enter into the covenant or do so with an impure heart.

1QS III, 13–IV, 26: A theological section on the two spirits states that while God has predetermined everything, there are two opposing cosmic powers struggling to influence the life and destiny of every human being: the spirit of truth (or light) and the spirit of wickedness (or darkness). On the one hand, each person is allotted to the power of one or the other of the spirits. On the other hand, each person is simultaneously influenced by both spirits: they fight in the heart of the person who does either good or evil according to which of the spirits dominates more. Only in the predetermined end will God eliminate evil and the spirit of truth reign.

1QS V, 1–VI, 23: The rule section begins with the principles of community life. Each member takes an oath "to return to the Torah of Moses" as it has been revealed to the priests called "sons of Zadok" and to the members of the community. Various rules for community life follow, such as for separation from outsiders, for the meeting of the full members of the community (**hrbym** הרבים, "the many"), and for accepting new members into the community. The manuscripts 4QS[b] and 4QS[d] provide a shorter and perhaps more original form of the text for these columns.

1QS VI, 24–VII, 25: A casuistic penal code completes the corpus of rules regulating the life of the community (cols. 5–7). The penal code is quite heterogeneous, the units apparently collected haphazardly and possibly compiled as the result of the court proceedings in the meetings of "the many." The penalties vary from short-term punishment to permanent expulsion.

1QS VIII, 1–IX, 26*a*: This section has been seen by some scholars as a "manifesto" or the program of the community, possibly originating in the period when the founding of the community still lay ahead. The interpretation of this section is difficult, however, and further complicated by the absence of any parallel of 1QS VIII, 15–IX, 11 in 4QS[e]. The section begins with an introduction comparable to the one in col. 5, and is followed by a penal code exhibiting some differences from the one in col. 6. The latter part of col. 9 includes two sections addressed to a community official called "the Instructor" or "wise leader" (**hmskyl** המשכיל).

1QS IX, 26*b*–XI, 22: A lengthy hymn concludes 1QS. The hymn contains a calendrical section that lists the community's times of prayer. In 4QS[e], the hymn is replaced by a calendrical text.

The importance of the *Rule of the Community* for the Essenes is attested by the large number of texts it has influenced. Sections of the *Rule of the Community* are quoted in Cave 4 manuscripts of the *Damascus Document* (4Q266 frag. 10 and 4Q270 7), the *Miscellaneous Rules* (4Q265; formerly *Serek Damascus*), a manuscript titled simply the *Rule* (5Q13), and possibly the *Ritual of Marriage* (4Q502 16). Other manuscripts related to the *Rule of the Community* are *Rebukes Reported by the Overseer* (4Q477; formerly *Decrees*), *Communal Ceremony* (4Q275), and *Four Lots* (4Q279). To the scroll of 1QS two other texts, the RULE OF THE CONGREGATION (1Q28a) and the *Words of Blessing* (1Q28b) were attached and may be seen either as two independent works or as appendixes to 1QS.

Bibliography: Philip S. Alexander and Gaza Vermes. *Qumran Cave 4, XIX: Serekh ha-Yahad and Two Related Texts* (1998); Michael A. Knibb. *The Qumran Community* (1987) 77–144; Sarianna Metso. *The Textual Development of the Qumran Community Rule* (1997); Sarianna Metso. *The Serekh Texts* (2007).

SARIANNA METSO

RULE OF THE CONGREGATION. One of the two appendices to the *Rule of the Community* (1QS) manuscript from Cave 1 at Qumran (*see* DEAD SEA SCROLLS), the *Rule of the Congregation* (1Q28a) is attested also in eight or nine very fragmentary manuscripts in cryptic script from Cave 4. The best-preserved copy of this Hebrew composition dates from the early 2nd cent. BCE. The title derives from the work's opening line, "This is the rule for all of the congregation of Israel in the last days" (1Q28a I, 1), as well as from repeated references to the congregation in the remainder of the work. Both the very beginning of the composition as well as the final part clearly speak of the end time, which gave rise to the alternative title "Messianic Rule." The final part of the document (1Q28a II, 11a–22) appears to describe a meal in the presence of two messiahs: a priestly and a lay messiah. The description of the meal closely resembles the communal meal outlined in the *Rule of the Community* (1QS VI) and concludes with an admonition to proceed in this manner at every meal.

The bulk of the composition (1Q28a I, 6–II, 11a) comprises regulations for the organization of the congregation that resemble the constitutional rules found in the *Damascus Document*. One of the most striking features of this overtly messianic text is the close relationship that it bears to other communal rules. This has been variously explained as a feature of Qumran messianism, which perceives the present community as mirroring the end time; or as an indication that the text is not messianic at all; or that the text has a messianic framework within which we find constitutional rules whose origin is independent of the framework.

The *Rule of the Congregation* portrays a community in which women and children played a prominent part. The question of its relationship to the *Rule of the Community* has recently been reopened. Two recent suggestions are that the whole scroll should be taken as a collection of smaller compositions or, conversely, to take both appendixes as an integral part of the *Rule of the Community* from Cave 1.

Bibliography: Charlotte Hempel. "The Earthly Essene Nucleus of 1QSa." *DSD* 3 (1996) 253–67; Lawrence H. Schiffman. *The Eschatological Community of the Dead Sea Scrolls* (1989).

CHARLOTTE HEMPEL

RULER OF SYNAGOGUE [ἀρχισυνάγωγος archisynagōgos]. Although data are sparse concerning the specific functions of the leader (or official) of the synagogue, the role was apparently local and primarily administrative and liturgical, making provisions for and presiding over Sabbath worship. Given that private homes were the more common setting for synagogue assemblies during the NT era, the office may often have been held by the homeowner and meeting host, and the archisynagōgos was typically of sufficient means to have a reputation as a benefactor. The archisynagōgos was assisted by one or more liturgical "servants." Together these offices may have provided the general pattern for the elder and deacon of the early Christian house churches. In the NT, archisynagōgos is used in reference to three named figures (Jairus: Mark 5:22, 35, 36, 38; Luke 8:49; compare Matt 9:18; Crispus: Acts 18:8; Sosthenes: Acts 18:17) and two unnamed (Luke 13:14; Acts 13:15). *See* SYNAGOGUE.

GARWOOD P. ANDERSON

RULERS OF THE CITY. *See* AUTHORITIES, CITY.

RUMAH r*oo*'muh [רוּמָה rumah]. The home of Josiah's wife ZEBIDAH (2 Kgs 23:36). The location of Rumah is uncertain. Josephus mentions a Ruma in Galilee (*J.W.* 3.233), which is identified with the modern town of Khirbet Rumeh. Most ancient witnesses to Josh 15:52 list Rumah as a site near Hebron in Judah, but the MT (and NRSV) read "Dumah." If the site was in Galilee, then the statement about the origin of Josiah's wife could imply that Josiah's kingdom extended far north into the old kingdom of Israel (compare 2 Chr 34:6-7). If the site was near Hebron, Josiah's kingdom may have been much smaller.

Bibliography: Yoel Elitzur. "Rumah in Judah." *IEJ* 44 (1994) 123–28.

ADAM L. PORTER

RUNNER. *See* RACE, SPORT.

F. Nigel Hepper

Figure 1: Rush (*Juncus effusus*)

RUSHES [גֹּמֶא gome', סוּף suf]. A general term for water-loving marsh plants (Isa 19:6; 35:7; Hos 13:15), such as the rush (*Juncus* species in the strict sense), but also reeds (the tall grass *Phragmites australis*), cattail or reedmace (*Typha angustata*), and even the sedges papyrus (*Cyperus papyrus*) and bulrush in the strict sense (*Scirpus lacustris*). Rushes, reeds, and other grasses of the field were used for fuel to heat cooking pots (Job

41:20). *See* BULRUSH; PAPYRUS, PAPYRI; PLANTS OF THE BIBLE; REED.

F. NIGEL HEPPER

RUST [חֶלְאָה khel'ah; βρῶσις brōsis, ἰός ios]. Usually, rust means the corrosion of metal, but the various terms translated "rust" in the Bible are most often used metaphorically to suggest destruction or calamity upon a city or person. Ezekiel describes the lewdness of Jerusalem as a rusting copper pot (Ezek 24:6-12), the corrosion of which cannot be removed even with searing heat. Jesus relates that the treasures of the kingdom of heaven are impervious to rust (**brōsis**, "corrosion") and destruction (Matt 6:19-20). The letter of James depicts the rusting wealth of the rich testifying on behalf of the poor (Jas 5:3); the term used in this instance (**ios**) is also employed earlier in the letter to describe the corrosive effects of untamed speech and is there translated as "poison" (Jas 3:8).

JESSICA TINKLENBERG DEVEGA

RUTH r*oo*th [רוּת **ruth**; Ῥούθ **Rhouth**]. Meaning "friend." Ruth is introduced as the Moabite daughter-in-law of ELIMELECH and NAOMI, natives of Judah who search for sustenance in Moab (*see* MOAB, MOABITES). When Elimelech and his sons die, Ruth's sister-in-law Orpah stays with her people at Naomi's bidding, whereas Ruth swears loyalty to Naomi, her people, and her God, and she returns with Naomi to Judah. Although BOAZ, a wealthy relative of Naomi, lives nearby, he does not immediately redeem the impoverished Ruth, who gleans in his fields. The reason for Boaz's hesitancy becomes clear: he is not the closest relative or "next-of-kin"—the one who must marry the widow and raise up children in the deceased's name (*see* LEVIRATE LAW). When the next-of-kin is found and refuses his duty, Boaz is free to marry Ruth. Their child OBED is the progenitor of Jesse, the father of King David. In contrast to other biblical accounts in which the foreign woman is feared as a source of idolatry, the portrayal of Ruth provides another stance where even a Moabite can be a model of fidelity to the commandments and become an ancestress of kings. In Matt 1:5, Ruth is one of four women from the OT identified in the genealogy of Jesus. *See* RUTH, BOOK OF.

SHARON PACE

RUTH, BOOK OF [רוּת **ruth**; Ῥούθ **Rhouth**]. In the time of the judges of Israel, a family from Bethlehem of Judah migrates to Moab to escape famine. There they are overwhelmed by tragedy; within ten years, all the menfolk die, leaving the woman, Naomi, and her two Moabite daughters-in-law bereaved and childless. Hearing that God has provided food for the people of Judah, Naomi returns to her homeland, accompanied by a resolute Ruth who vows to stand with her to the end. In Bethlehem, the widows must support themselves, and Ruth finds a way by gleaning. Her efforts are rewarded beyond expectation when she happens upon the field of Boaz, a relative of Naomi's deceased husband. His generous patronage sustains the women throughout the harvest. But they must eventually take extreme measures to secure for themselves a more permanent livelihood. Ruth approaches Boaz at the threshing floor in the middle of the night and proposes marriage. All's well that ends well when Boaz accepts responsibility and promptly arranges to redeem Naomi's land and take Ruth as his wife. God blesses the union with a son who proves to be the father of Jesse, the father of David. The book thus recounts the grievous loss of Naomi's family and their eventual restoration through the faithfulness (**khesedh** חֶסֶד) of a Moabite daughter-in-law and an Israelite kinsman. Their loyal acts are all the more remarkable because they transcend not only self-interests but also cultural boundaries. God too is at work in this story of survival, quietly but faithfully providing for those in need.

A. Structure of the Book

I. Journey to Moab and back
  Prologue: family history of displacement, depletion, death (1:1-5)
  Homeward journey and negotiation of kinship ties (1:6-18)
  Naomi's bitter lament to the women of Bethlehem (1:19-22)
II. Gleaning for survival
  Naomi agrees to Ruth's plan to glean (2:1-3)
  Boaz publicly shows favor to Ruth (2:4-17)
  Ruth reports to Naomi (2:18-23)
III. Ruth's visit in the night
  Ruth agrees to Naomi's plan to "find security" (3:1-6)
  Boaz privately promises to secure redemption for the women (3:7-15)
  Ruth reports to Naomi (3:16-18)
IV. Resolution at the gate and Naomi's restoration
  Boaz formally "settles the matter" before town elders (4:1-12)
  Ruth and Boaz marry and women celebrate the birth of a son (4:13-17)
  Epilogue: family history culminating in David (4:18-22)

B. Analysis and Interpretation

1. Literary analysis

There is general agreement that the form of the book is a short story, that is, a narrative that has been carefully crafted to move through various scenes before reaching a climax and denouement. The book opens with a crisis—famine, displacement, barrenness, and death—that will be resolved by the story's end. It is structured symmetrically in four chapters that highlight the themes of loss and restoration. The first chapter, consisting of three scenes (family history of loss, 1:1-5; negotiation of kinship ties among women, 1:6-18; Naomi's lament before the women, 1:19-22), is balanced by the three scenes of the final chapter (negotiation of kinship ties among men, 4:1-12; celebration of women over Naomi's restoration, 4:13-17; family history of fecundity, 4:18-22). Likewise, the middle two chapters, each consisting of three scenes, parallel one another (deliberation between Ruth and Naomi about means of survival, 2:1-3 and 3:1-5; encounter between Ruth and Boaz, 2:4-17 and 3:6-15; Ruth's report to Naomi, 2:18-23 and 3:16-18). At the end of each chapter, a narrative transition reviews past events and subtly points to what is to come (1:22; 2:23; 3:18; 4:17*b*).

The steady movement from emptiness to fullness is further underscored by the purposeful repetition of words and images. Often a strategic doubling forms a literary bracket that rounds out the story's themes. Upon her arrival in Bethlehem, Naomi laments that "the LORD has brought me back empty" (1:21, **heshivani** [הֱשִׁיבַנִי]; Hiphil of the root **shwb** [שׁוּב]). Although the verb *return* recurs throughout (esp. in chap. 1) to reinforce the journey motif, this particular form occurs only one other time at the end, when the women bless Yahweh for providing Naomi's "restorer of life" (4:15, **meshiv** [מֵשִׁיב]; Hiphil ptc. of **shwb**). Similarly, Naomi's use of the word *empty* (**reqam** רֵיקָם) is overturned when Ruth returns from the threshing floor loaded with barley rather than "empty-handed" (3:17). Naomi is left without "her sons" (**yeladheha** [יְלָדֶיהָ], 1:5), an unusual designation for married men. With Obed's birth, she holds a "child" (**yeledh** [יֶלֶד], 4:16) in her arms again. Other instances of doubling include the words translated *security* (**menukhah** [מְנוּחָה], 1:9; **manoakh** [מָנוֹחַ], 3:1); *wings/ cloak* (**kanaf** [כָּנָף], 2:12; 3:9); *substance/ worth* (**khayil** [חַיִל], 2:1; 3:11; compare 4:11); *cling* /"stay close" (**davaq** [דָּבַק], 1:14; 2:8, 21, 23); and not least of all, *faithfulness* (**khesedh**, 1:8; 2:20; 3:10).

Naomi is arguably the central figure of the drama. It is her loss that is foregrounded at the start. In poetic language that recalls Job's indictment against God (esp. Job 27:2), she laments that Yahweh has testified against her, that "Almighty has dealt bitterly" with her and "brought calamity" upon her (1:20-21). Her use of the epithet "Shaddai" (traditional translation "Almighty" is prompted by LXX **pantokratōr** [παντοκράτωρ] and Vg. *omnipotens*) is poignant in its irony, because outside of Job, this divine name occurs predominantly in the ancestral narratives in Genesis and is associated with the God of blessing and fecundity. The charge that God is responsible for her calamities amounts to a widow's cry for redress, and the rest of the narrative is occupied with its steady resolution.

Ruth, however, is deservedly the heroine. She is the vehicle for Naomi's restoration. With extraordinary devotion, she forfeits the security of her homeland and joins her fate to a woman with no prospects (1:11-13). The narrative affords her no time or space to mourn her own losses. She is intent on survival and constantly on the move, *going* (**halakh** [הָלַךְ], eleven times), *coming* (**boʾ** [בּוֹא] thirteen times), *gleaning* (**laqat** [לָקַט], twelve times), *working/ acting* (**ʿasah** [עָשָׂה], eight times). She treks back and forth between Naomi and Boaz, the two of whom never meet. Her solidarity with Naomi, industry and diligence, willingness to take risks, and eventual union with Boaz enable Naomi to be reintegrated into the life of the community.

In this ancient story, however, women need men to survive. And Boaz—Naomi's relative and upstanding citizen—readily does his part. He welcomes the foreign woman (2:10) and grants her special privileges in his field. He invites her to his "table" and breaks bread with her. His generous provision of grain sustains the women and renews Naomi's hope (2:20). When prompted by Ruth, he moves expeditiously to make formal arrangements for the women's permanent livelihood. It is fitting that all the townspeople celebrate his marriage to Ruth (4:11-12), which not only unites two deserving people but also ensures the perpetuation of Naomi's family.

So, when Ruth gives birth to Naomi's redeemer (4:13-14), the story comes full circle. But the happy ending belies its subtle complexity. Significant gaps and ambiguities resist easy interpretation. Why does Naomi respond to Ruth's pledge of loyalty with silence (1:18)? Why do Naomi's male relatives initially do nothing? Why does Boaz fail to identify his family connections to Ruth in chap. 2 and why does he wait for her to suggest marriage? Whence the sudden emergence of Elimelech's land (4:3)? How are the practices of levirate marriage and land redemption related to each other? Why do the townswomen declare that "a son has been born to Naomi" (4:17)? Sometimes the puzzlement has to do with the complexity of human motivations, and sometimes with the modern reader's lack of information about ancient customs. But the uncertainties are also a function of the storyteller's art. The element of surprise adds to the delight of reading. Ambiguities create multiple interpretive possibilities and invite engagement.

Moreover, the story is not so idyllic in its depiction of the challenges and risks that women must overcome just to survive. One must not gloss over the trauma of widowhood, especially in the absence of male offspring. Indeed, the special protection afforded them in biblical law indicates their extreme vulnerability. Ruth must resort to gleaning as a pauper, even when that exposes her to potential harassment (2:9, 15, 22). In approaching Boaz at the threshing floor, she makes herself sexually vulnerable. Perhaps her willingness to take the risk is a function of her loyalty to her mother-in-law. But it also highlights the desperate plight of women who have few or no other options. In the end, they are dependent on the town elders to determine their welfare. Attention to such cultural biases makes this story of women all the more remarkable, especially when the women of Bethlehem, who have the last spoken words, declare that Ruth is "more ... than seven sons" (4:15).

2. Date and purpose

The debate concerning the dating of the book remains lively, with proposals ranging from the time of David and Solomon to the postexilic era. Arguments revolve around issues of the language of the text, the customs assumed in the story, literary parallels and their provenance, and the book's ideological or theological orientation. All of these criteria are subject to underlying assumptions and biases, and have not led to any sure consensus. An examination of the Hebrew text indicates a combination of standard and late biblical Hebrew features, suggesting a transitional period in the language. The date of the book lies somewhere between the late preexilic to the early postexilic era.

Discussions concerning the book's purpose have often been tied to its dating. A proposal that has appealed to many is that the book emerged in the postexilic period as a polemic against the exclusionary policies of Ezra and Nehemiah and the forced dissolution of foreign marriages (Ezra 9–10; Neh 13). According to this view, Ruth was written to subvert the establishment's narrow interpretation of marriage laws. Others who date the book earlier have argued that it functioned as an apologia for David's dynasty. The depiction of David's ancestors as models of piety and good conduct was meant to defend his right to the throne against his detractors. But the story does not have an overtly polemical or propagandistic tone, and to tie the book narrowly to a specific political agenda during a specific historical context is misguided. It runs the risk of obscuring the story's multiple layers of meaning—social, political, religious, and aesthetic. Indeed, Ruth is a masterfully crafted story, meant both to delight the reader and to provide a model of faithfulness. It witnesses to God at work in the life of a family, and by extension (4:18-22), the life of the nation. It elevates the virtue of loyalty. It commends an inclusive attitude toward outsiders, a perennial social concern.

C. Theological and Religious Significance

1. Models of faithfulness

In Jewish tradition, the book belongs among the five festal scrolls (Megilloth) and is read during the Feast of Weeks, a celebration of the harvest season. The festival also commemorates the gift of Torah, and this association too is appropriate for Ruth, who, according to the rabbis, modeled obedience to Torah by her extraordinary kindness. Indeed, the scroll was written "to teach how great is the reward of those who do deeds of kindness" (*Ruth Rab.* 2:14). Early Christian interpreters also emphasized how Ruth's loyalty to Naomi went beyond the requirements of the law and thus earned her a place in the genealogy of Jesus Christ (e.g., Ambrose, *Exp. Luc.* 3).

Modern interpreters also expound on the portrayal of exemplary religious life. The principal characters of the book—Ruth and Boaz especially—embody the meaning of **khesedh**, that is, loyalty, faithfulness, and kindness that surpass the requirements of the law. Ruth models **khesedh** in her resolute commitment to Naomi, in her free decision to care for her mother-in-law's needs (1:8; 3:10). Boaz also goes beyond what is required or expected when he provides grain for the widows (2:20) and sees to Ruth's marriage and the redemption of Naomi's land.

2. Divine providence and human agency

Related to this motif is the kindness of God (1:8; 2:20). Human kindness and divine kindness work together to transform Naomi's sorrow to joy. Considering where and how God appears in the book illuminates the interplay. The narrator reports divine activity twice, once at the beginning and once at the end. God's gift of food (1:6) and gift of conception (4:13) thus frames the book, forming a broad theological horizon. Elsewhere, God's name proliferates on the lips of people who invoke blessing on one another, indeed, even in routine greetings (2:4). These exchanges reinforce the notion of God who provides: God is said to provide security, refuge, reward for good deeds, redemption, and offspring. These good wishes are fulfilled as the story progresses, but often by the very people who utter and receive the prayers. In the opening dialogue, Naomi invokes Yahweh as the one to grant her daughters-in-law "security" (**menukhah**) (1:9); she later takes it upon herself to find that "security" (**manoakh**) for Ruth (3:1). Boaz asks that Ruth find refuge under God's "wings" (**kanaf**, 2:12), but Ruth calls upon him to make good on that prayer by spreading his "cloak" (**kanaf**, 3:9) over her in espousal.

The interplay is also evident in the rhetoric of blessing. When Naomi hears of Ruth's "accidental" encounter with Boaz (2:3-4) and his remarkable generosity, she declares: "Blessed be he by the LORD, whose kindness has not forsaken the living or the dead!" (2:20). There is an ambiguity in the Hebrew syntax, so that the "kindness" may be attributed to either the Lord or Boaz (compare Gen 24:27; 2 Sam 2:5). Indeed, Naomi's eyes are opened to the kindness of God still at work in her life precisely because of Boaz's concrete acts of kindness. Elsewhere, there is a weaving together of divine agency and human agency in the structure of the blessing, so that Yahweh's making/giving (**nathan** נָתַן) is parallel with women's building and bearing (4:11-12).

In this backdrop of blessing, a discordant note is sounded by Naomi's complaint concerning Yahweh's harsh treatment of her (1:13, 20-21). This lament is steadily resolved in the story, but is not to be muted. For Naomi, divine sovereignty is a given. God is creator of famine and harvest, plenty and want, good and bad. She recognizes that sometimes Providence is very bitter. Yet, because of the fundamental belief in God's sovereignty, her complaint bespeaks a profound faith. Indeed, couched in the language of biblical laments, this speech about God, too, plays a critical part in the reversal of her plight.

Thus, in the deft construction of the story, God acts in and through human agents, in the way they speak and behave toward one another. There is no miraculous deliverance or mighty act of God. Instead, providence is experienced in mundane human acts—gleaning, caring for needy relatives, getting married, being accountable for one's prayers—for God is present in the glory of the ordinary. Ordinary people living ordinary but faithful lives act as God's agents of redemption.

3. Kinship and otherness

A Moabite heroine in the OT is striking, given the scandalous associations with Moab in Israel's genealogical imagination (Gen 19:30-38; Num 25:1-5) and the general animosity depicted in biblical texts (Num 22; Deut 23:3-5; Jer 48). Ruth offers a counter-vision. Moab provides for a hungry Israelite family (contra Deut 23:4). Moabite women are elevated as paragons of **khesedh** (Ruth 1:8). Ruth's marriage with a prominent man of Bethlehem is celebrated, not excoriated. The story's remarkable vision of kinship reaching across boundaries invites a more expansive construction of community. But the story also registers an anxiety about that vision. The ambivalence is signaled by a recurring emphasis on Ruth's Moabite ethnicity (1:22; 2:2, 6, 21; 4:5, 10), as well as a repeated interrogation of her identity (2:5; 3:9, 16; compare 1:19). These point to an underlying tension between kinship and otherness. Through the widespread use of dialogue, however, the story negotiates that tension toward a reconstruction of identity. Those who question Ruth undergo profound changes in their self-understanding.

When Boaz inquires about the connections of the stranger gleaning in his field (2:5), he is met with this query from Ruth: "Why have I found favor in your sight, that you should take notice of me (**lehakkireni** [לְהַכִּירֵנִי], Hiphil of the root **nkr** [נכר]), when I am a foreigner (**nokhriyah** [נָכְרִיָּה]; 2:10)?" The wordplay exploits the root **nkr**, which may mean either "to treat/act as a stranger" (Piel/Hithpael) or "to recognize" (Hiphil), to confront Boaz with a moral choice: will he regard Ruth as a stranger or acknowledge her? The man responds admirably to the implicit challenge and displays remarkable hospitality. He does so in a public setting, where he, as the landowner, exercises considerable authority. His behavior thus functions as an important moral witness. At the end of the day, however, he refrains from identifying himself to Ruth as Naomi's relative, a point that the narrator belabored (2:1, 3). It takes another interrogation of identity at the threshing floor (3:9) before Boaz more fully recognizes her as his kindred (**ʾesheth khayil** [אֵשֶׁת חַיִל], 3:11; compare **ʾish gibbor khayil** [אִישׁ גִּבּוֹר חַיִל], 2:1) and embraces his own identity as "next-of-kin" (3:12-13). Ruth's presence in Bethlehem thus generates a self-interrogation on the part of Israel.

That self-interrogation becomes all the more pressing because of Ruth's implied pride of place in David's genealogy. Indeed, in early Jewish interpretation, David's dubious origins posed a scandal that had to be addressed. Again and again, *Ruth Rabbah* cites a revision of the law prohibiting Ammonites and Moabites from entering the assembly of Israel that allowed both Ammonite and Moabite women to enter the assembly (Deut 23:3) (e.g., *Ruth Rab.* 1:4; 2:5). The urgency with which the issue is repeatedly taken up indicates that this gendered reading should not be dismissed lightly. It registers a profound anxiety about Israel's very identity. The Moabite within Israel represents a destabilizing force that subverts rigid constructions of identity and necessitates an ongoing openness to the other. Such implications were not lost on the rabbis. In an intriguing midrash on Ruth 2:5, Doeg the Edomite argues that David's Moabite ancestry makes him unfit, and challenges the revised law by suggesting that if Moabite women are acceptable, then the principle may be applied more broadly to Edomites and Egyptians (*Ruth Rab.* 2:5; compare Deut 23:7-8). Indeed, this precedent may apply to anyone desiring to enter Israel's assembly.

For Christian readers, Ruth's place in David's line is valorized by her inclusion in the Matthean genealogy (Matt 1:5), where she is joined by Tamar, Rahab, and "the wife of Uriah." These women of questionable repute and non-Israelite descent prepare the way for the scandal of Jesus' origins (Mary's extraordinary conception), and, more generally, for the gospel's inclusion of all nations.

Bibliography: Athalya Brenner, ed. *A Feminist Companion to Ruth* (1993); Athalya Brenner, ed. *Ruth and Esther: A Feminist Companion to the Bible* (1999); F. W. Bush. *Ruth, Esther.* WBC (1996); Edward F. Campbell Jr. *Ruth.* AB 7 (1975); D. N. Fewell and D. M. Gunn. *Compromising Redemption: Relating Characters in the Book of Ruth* (1990); J. A. Kates and G. Twersky Reimer, eds. *Reading Ruth: Contemporary Women Reclaim a Sacred Story* (1994); André LaCocque. *Ruth.* K. C. Hanson, trans. CC (2004); Kirsten Nielsen. *Ruth: A Commentary.* E. Broadbridge, trans. OTL (1997); L. Rabinowitz, trans. *Midrash Rabbah*, vol. 8 (1983); Saint Ambrose of Milan. *Exposition of the Holy Gospel According to Luke.* Theodosia Tompkinson, trans. (1998); Katharine Doob Sakenfeld. *Ruth.* IBC (1999).

EUNNY LEE

Abbreviations

General Abbreviations

*	reconstructed prototype of hypothetical letter or word form
Akkad.	Akkadian
AM	Anno Mundi (creation of the world)
ANE	Ancient Near East
Aram.	Aramaic
b.	born
BCE	Before the Common Era (replaces B.C.)
C	centigrade
c.	common
ca.	circa
CE	Common Era (replaces A.D.)
cent.	century
chap(s).	chapter(s)
Chr	Chronicler
cm	centimeter(s)
col/s.	column/s
d.	died
D	Deuteronomist source (of the Pentateuch)
Dtr	Deuteronomistic
DtrH	Deuteronomistic History/Historian
E	Elohist source (of the Pentateuch)
ed(s).	editor(s), edited by
e.g.	*exempli gratia,* for example
esp.	especially
et al.	*et alii,* and others
etc.	*et cetera,* and the rest
f. or fem.	feminine
fig.	figure
frag.	fragment
ft.	feet (measurement)
FS	Festschrift
g	grams
Gk.	Greek
ha.	Hectare(s)
Heb.	Hebrew manuscripts
i.e.	*id est,* that is
in.	inch(es)
J	Jahwist or Yahwist source (of the Pentateuch)
km	kilometers
L	liters
LB	Late Bronze

lb(s)	pound(s)
lit.	literally
LXX	Septuagint (the Greek Old Testament)
m	meters
m. or masc.	masculine
MB	Middle Bronze
mi.	miles
mm	millimeters
MS(S)	manuscript(s)
MT	Masoretic Text (of the Hebrew Bible)
n(n).	note(s)
n.d.	no date
no(s).	number(s)
n.p.	no place; no publisher; no page
NHC	Nag Hammadi Codex
NS	new series
NT	New Testament
OT	Old Testament
P	Priestly source (of the Pentateuch)
P. Oxy.	Oxyrhyncus Papyri
p(p).	page(s)
par. or //	parallel
Q	Qumran (or Quelle)
r.	ruled
repr.	reprinted
rev.	revised (by)
ser.	series
sq. mi.	square mile(s)
suppl.	supplement
T	Tomb (Nag Hammadi)
Tg(s).	Targum(s); Targumic
trans.	translator, translated by
v(v).	verse(s)
vol(s).	volume(s)
yd(s).	yard(s)

Bible Translations

ASV	American Standard Version
CEV	Contemporary English Version
CSB	Catholic Study Bible
GNB	Good News Bible
JB	Jerusalem Bible
KJV	King James Version
LB	The Living Bible
NAB	New American Bible
NCB	New Century Bible
NEB	New English Bible
NIV	New International Version
NJB	New Jerusalem Bible
NJPS	New Jewish Publication Society Tanakh
NKJV	New King James Version
NLB	New Living Bible
NOAB	New Oxford Annotated Bible

NRSV	New Revised Standard Version
REB	Revised English Bible
RSV	Revised Standard Version
TEV	Today's English Version
TNK	Tanakh

Old Testament

Gen	Genesis
Exod	Exodus
Lev	Leviticus
Num	Numbers
Deut	Deuteronomy
Josh	Joshua
Judg	Judges
Ruth	Ruth
1–2 Sam	1–2 Samuel
1–2 Kgs	1–2 Kings
1–2–3–4 Kgdms	1–2–3–4 Kingdoms (LXX)
1–2 Chr	1–2 Chronicles
Ezra	Ezra
Neh	Nehemiah
Esth	Esther
Job	Job
Ps(s)	Psalm(s)
Prov	Proverbs
Eccl	Ecclesiastes
Song	Song of Songs (Song of Solomon, or Canticles)
Isa	Isaiah
Jer	Jeremiah
Lam	Lamentations
Ezek	Ezekiel
Dan	Daniel
Hos	Hosea
Joel	Joel
Amos	Amos
Obad	Obadiah
Jonah	Jonah
Mic	Micah
Nah	Nahum
Hab	Habakkuk
Zeph	Zephaniah
Hag	Haggai
Zech	Zechariah
Mal	Malachi

New Testament

Matt	Matthew
Mark	Mark
Luke	Luke
John	John
Acts	Acts

Rom	Romans
1–2 Cor	1–2 Corinthians
Gal	Galatians
Eph	Ephesians
Phil	Philippians
Col	Colossians
1–2 Thess	1–2 Thessalonians
1–2 Tim	1–2 Timothy
Titus	Titus
Phlm	Philemon
Heb	Hebrews
Jas	James
1–2 Pet	1–2 Peter
1–2–3 John	1–2–3 John
Jude	Jude
Rev	Revelation

Apocrypha and Septuagint

Bar	Baruch
Add Dan	Additions to Daniel
Pr Azar	Prayer of Azariah
Bel	Bel and the Dragon
Sg Three	Song of the Three Jews
Sus	Susanna
1–2 Esd	1–2 Esdras
Add Esth	Additions to Esther
Ep Jer	Epistle of Jeremiah
Jdt	Judith
1–2–3–4 Macc	1–2–3–4 Maccabees
Pr Man	Prayer of Manasseh
Ps 151	Psalm 151
Sir	Sirach (Ecclesiasticus)
Tob	Tobit
Wis	Wisdom of Solomon

Pseudepigraphical and Early Patristic Books

Ahiqar	*Ahiqar*
Apoc. Ab.	*Apocalypse of Abraham*
Apoc. Adam	*Apocalypse of Adam*
Apoc. Dan.	*Apocalypse of Daniel*
Apoc. El. (C)	Coptic *Apocalypse of Elijah*
Apoc. El. (H)	Hebrew *Apocalypse of Elijah*
Apoc. Mos.	*Apocalypse of Moses*
Apoc. Sedr.	*Apocalypse of Sedrach*
Apoc. Zeph.	*Apocalypse of Zephaniah*
Apocr. Ezek.	*Apocrypon of Ezekiel*
Aris. Ex.	Aristeas the Exegete
Aristob.	Aristobulus
Artap.	Artapanus
Ascen. Isa.	*Mart. Ascen. Isa.* 6–11
As. Mos.	*Assumption of Moses*

2 Bar.	*2 Baruch (Syriac Apocalypse)*
3 Bar.	*3 Baruch (Greek Apocalypse)*
4 Bar.	*4 Baruch (Paraleipomena Jeremiou)*
Bk. Noah	*Book of Noah*
Cav. Tr.	*Cave of Treasures*
Cl. Mal.	Cleodemus Malchus
Dem.	Demetrius (the Chronographer)
El. Mod.	*Eldad and Modad*
1 En.	*1 Enoch (Ethiopic Apocalypse)*
2 En.	*2 Enoch (Slavonic Apocalypse)*
3 En.	*3 Enoch (Hebrew Apocalypse)*
Eup.	Eupolemus
Ezek. Trag.	Ezekiel the Tragedian
4 Ezra	*4 Ezra*
5 Apoc. Syr. Pss.	*Five Apocryphal Syriac Psalms*
Gk. Apoc. Ezra	*Greek Apocalypse of Ezra*
Hec. Ab.	Hecataeus of Abdera
Hel. Syn. Pr.	*Hellenistic Synagogal Prayers*
Hist. Jos.	*History of Joseph*
Hist. Rech.	*History of the Rechabites*
Jan. Jam.	*Jannes and Jambres*
Jos. Asen.	*Joseph and Aseneth*
Jub.	*Jubilees*
L.A.B.	*Liber antiquitatum biblicarum* (Pseudo-Philo)
L.A.E.	*Life of Adam and Eve*
Lad. Jac.	*Ladder of Jacob*
Let. Aris.	*Letter of Aristeas*
Liv. Pro.	*Lives of the Prophets*
Lost Tr.	*The Lost Tribes*
3 Macc.	*3 Maccabees*
4 Macc.	*4 Maccabees*
5 Macc.	*5 Maccabees* (Arabic)
Mart. Ascen. Isa.	*Martyrdom and Ascension of Isaiah*
Mart. Isa.	*Mart. Ascen. Isa.* 1–5
Odes Sol.	*Odes of Solomon*
Ph. E. Poet	Philo the Epic Poet
Pr. Jac.	*Prayer of Jacob*
Pr. Jos.	*Prayer of Joseph*
Pr. Man.	*Prayer of Manasseh*
Pr. Mos.	*Prayer of Moses*
Ps.-Eup.	Pseudo-Eupolemus
Ps.-Hec.	Pseudo-Hecataeus
Ps.-Orph.	Pseudo-Orpheus
Ps.-Phoc.	Pseudo-Phocylides
Pss. Sol.	*Psalms of Solomon*
Ques. Ezra	*Questions of Ezra*
Rev. Ezra	*Revelation of Ezra*
Sib. Or.	*Sibylline Oracles*
Syr. Men.	*Sentences of the Syriac Menander*
T. 12 Patr.	*Testaments of the Twelve Patriarchs*
T. Ash.	*Testament of Asher*
T. Benj.	*Testament of Benjamin*
T. Dan	*Testament of Dan*
T. Gad	*Testament of Gad*

T. Iss.	*Testament of Issachar*
T. Jos.	*Testament of Joseph*
T. Jud.	*Testament of Judah*
T. Levi	*Testament of Levi*
T. Naph.	*Testament of Naphtali*
T. Reu.	*Testament of Reuben*
T. Sim.	*Testament of Simeon*
T. Zeb.	*Testament of Zebulun*
T. 3 Patr.	*Testaments of the Three Patriarchs*
T. Ab.	*Testament of Abraham*
T. Isaac	*Testament of Isaac*
T. Jac.	*Testament of Jacob*
T. Adam	*Testament of Adam*
T. Hez.	*Testament of Hezekiah (Mart. Ascen. Isa.* 3:13–4:22*)*
T. Job	*Testament of Job*
T. Mos.	*Testament of Moses*
T. Sol.	*Testament of Solomon*
Theod.	Theodotus, *On the Jews*
Treat. Shem	*Treatise of Shem*
Vis. Ezra	*Vision of Ezra*

Philo of Alexandria

Latin		**English**	
Abr.	*De Abrahamo*	*Abraham*	*On the Life of Abraham*
Aet.	*De aeternitate mundi*	*Eternity*	*On the Eternity of the World*
Agr.	*De agricultura*	*Agriculture*	*On Agriculture*
Anim.	*De animalibus*	*Animals*	*Whether Animals Have Reason (= Alexander)*
Cher.	*De cherubim*	*Cherubim*	*On the Cherubim*
Conf.	*De confusione linguarum*	*Confusion*	*On the Confusion of Tongues*
Congr.	*De congressueru ditionis gratia*	*Prelim. Studies*	*On the Preliminary Studies*
Contempl.	*De vita contemplativa*	*Contempl. Life*	*On the Contemplative Life*
Decal.	*De decalogo*	*Decalogue*	*On the Decalogue*
Deo	*De Deo*	*God*	*On God*
Det.	*Quod deterius potiori insidari soleat*	*Worse*	*That the Worse Attacks the Better*
Deus	*Quod Deus sit immutabilis*	*Unchangeable*	*That God Is Unchangeable*
Ebr.	*De ebrietate*	*Drunkenness*	*On Drunkenness*
Exsecr.	*De exsecrationibus*	*Curses*	*On Curses (= Rewards 127–72)*
Flacc.	*In Flaccum*	*Flaccus*	*Against Flaccus*
Fug.	*De fuga et inventione*	*Flight*	*On Flight and Finding*
Gig.	*De gigantibus*	*Giants*	*On Giants*
Her.	*Quis rerum divinarum heres sit*	*Heir*	*Who Is the Heir?*
Hypoth.	*Hypothetica*	*Hypothetica*	*Hypothetica*
Ios.	*De Iosepho*	*Joseph*	*On the Life of Joseph*
Leg. 1, 2, 3	*Legum allegoriae* I, II, III	*Alleg. Interp.* 1, 2, 3	*Allegorical Interpretation* 1, 2, 3
Legat.	*Legatio ad Gaium*	*Embassy*	*On the Embassy to Gaius*
Migr.	*De migratione Abrahami*	*Migration*	*On the Migration of Abraham*
Mos. 1, 2	*De vita Mosis* I, II	*Moses* 1, 2	*On the Life of Moses* 1, 2
Mut.	*De mutatione nominum*	*Names*	*On the Change of Names*
Opif.	*De opificio mundi*	*Creation*	*On the Creation of the World*
Plant.	*De plantatione*	*Planting*	*On Planting*
Post.	*De posteritate Caini*	*Posterity*	*On the Posterity of Cain*
Praem.	*De praemiis et poenis*	*Rewards*	*On Rewards and Punishments*
Prob.	*Quod omnis probus liber sit*	*Good Person*	*That Every Good Person Is Free*

Prov. 1, 2	*De providentia* I, II	*Providence* 1, 2	*On Providence* 1, 2
QE 1, 2	*Quaestiones et solutiones in Exodum* I, II	*QE* 1, 2	*Questions and Answers on Exodus* 1, 2
QG 1, 2, 3, 4	*Quaestiones et solutiones in Genesin* I, II, III, IV	*QG* 1, 2, 3, 4	*Questions and Answers on Genesis* 1, 2, 3, 4
Sacr.	*De sacrificiis Abelis et Caini*	*Sacrifices*	*On the Sacrifices of Cain and Abel*
Sobr.	*De sobrietate*	*Sobriety*	*On Sobriety*
Somn. 1, 2,	*De somniis* I, II	*Dreams* 1, 2	*On Dreams* 1, 2
Spec. 1, 2, 3, 4	*De specialibus legibus* I, II, III, IV	*Spec. Laws*	*On the Special Laws* 1, 2, 3, 4
Virt.	*De virtutibus*	*Virtues*	*On the Virtues*

Josephus

Latin		**English**	
A.J.	*Antiquitates judaicae*	*Ant.*	*Jewish Antiquities*
B.J.	*Bellum judaicum*	*J. W.*	*Jewish War*
C. Ap.	*Contra Apionem*	*Ag. Ap.*	*Against Apion*
Vita	*Vita*	*Life*	*The Life*

Dead Sea Scrolls and Related Texts

Number	**Abbreviation**	**Name**
	CD	Cairo Genizah copy of the *Damascus Document*
	1Qap Gen ar	*Genesis Apocryphon*
	1QH[a]	*Hodayot*[a] *or Thanksgiving Hymns*[a]
	1QpHab	*Pesher Habakkuk*
	1QM	*Milhamah or War Scroll*
	1QS	*Serek Hayahad or Rule of the Community*
	1QIsa[a]	Isaiah[a]
	1QIsa[b]	Isaiah[b]
1Q20	1Qap Gen ar	*Genesis Apocryphon*
1Q21	1QTLevi ar	*Testament of Levi*
1Q26	1QInstruction	*1QInstruction, formerly Wisdom Apocryphon*
1Q28a	1QSa	*Rule of the Congregation* (Appendix a to 1QS)
1Q28b	1QSb	*Rule of the Blessings* (Appendix b to 1QS)
3Q15		*Copper Scroll*
4Q17	4QExod-Lev[f]	
4Q22	4QpaleoExod[m]	
4Q58	4QIsa[d]	*4QIsaiah*[d]
4Q82	4QXII[g]	
4Q120	4QpapLXXLev[b]	
4Q127	4QpapParaExod gr	*ParaExodus*
4Q163	4Qpap pIsac	*Isaiah Pesher*[c]
4Q171	4QpPsa	*Psalms Pesher*[a]
4Q174	4QFlor (MidrEschat[a])	*Florilegium,* also *Midrash on Eschatology*[a]
4Q175	4QTest	*Testimonia*
4Q177	4QCatena[a] (MidrEschat[b])	*Catena*[a], also *Midrash on Eschatology*[b]
4Q180	4QAgesCreat	*Ages of Creation*
4Q182	4QCatena[b] (MidrEschat[c])	*Catena*[b], also *Midrash on Eschatology*[c]
4Q213-14	4QLevi ar	*Aramaic Levi*
4Q242	4QPrNab ar	*Prayer of Nabonidus*
4Q246	4QapocrDan ar	*Apocryphon of Daniel*
4Q252	4QCommGen A	*Commentary on Genesis A,* formerly *Patriarchal Blessings* or *Pesher Genesis*
4Q265	4QSD	*Miscellaneous*

4Q266	4QD[a]	*Damascus Document[a]*
4Q271	D[f]	*Damascus Document[f]*, formerly Damascus *Document[c]*
4Q274	4QTohorot A	*Tohorot A*
4Q285		*Sefer Hamilhamah*
4Q299	4QMyst[a]	*Mysteries[a]*
4Q319-330	4QCalDoc A-I	*Calendrical Document A-I,* also *Mishmarot*
4Q320	4QCalDoc A	*Calendrical Document A,* formerly *Mishmarot A*
4Q325	4QCalDoc D	*Calendrical Document,* formerly *Mishmarot E[b]*
4Q334	4Qord	*Order of Divine Office*
4Q337	4QCalDoc F	*Fragment of Calendar*
4Q365	4QRP[c]	*Reworked Pentateuch[c]*
4Q378	4QapocrJosh[a]	*Apocryphon of Joshua[a]* formerly *Psalms of Joshua[a]*
4Q383	4QapocrJer A	*Apocryphon of Jeremiah A*
4Q384	4QpapApocrjer B?	*Apocryphon of Jeremiah B?*
4Q385a	4QapocrJer C[a]	*Apocryphon of Jeremiah C,* formerly *Pseudo-Moses[a]*
4Q387	4QJer C[b]	*Apocryphon of Jeremiah C,* formerly *Pseudo-Moses[b]*
4Q387b	4QapocrJer D	*Apocryphon of Jeremiah D*
4Q388a	4QJer C[c]	*Apocryphon of Jeremiah C,* formerly *Pseudo-Moses[c]*
4Q389	4QJer C[d]	*Apocryphon of Jeremiah D,* formerly *Pseudo-Moses[d]*
4Q390	4QapocrJerE (psMos[e])	*Apocryphon of Jeremiah E*
4Q394	4QMMT[a]	*Miqsat Maase ha-Torah[a]*
4Q395	4QMMT[b]	*Halakhic Letter[b]*
4Q396	4QMMT[c]	*Halakhic Letter[c]*
4Q397	4QMMT[d]	*Halakhic Letter[d]*
4Q398	4QMMT[e]	*Halakhic Letter[e]*
4Q399	4QMMT[f]	*Halakhic Letter[f]*
4Q400	4QShirShabb[a]	*Songs of the Sabbath Sacrifice[a]*
4Q414	4QRitPur A	*Ritual Purity A,* formerly *Baptismal Liturgy*
4Q415	4QInstruction[a]	*Instruction[a]*, formerly *Sapiental Work A[d]*
4Q416	4QInstruction[b]	*Instruction[b]*, formerly *Sapiental Work A[b]*
4Q417	4QInstruction[c]	*Instruction[c]*, formerly *Sapiental Work A[c]*
4Q418	4QInstruction[d]	*Instruction[d]*, formerly *Sapiental Work A[a]*
4Q418a	4QInstruction[e]	*Instruction[e]*
4Q418c	4QInstruction[e]	*Instruction[f]*
4Q423	4QInstruction[g]	*Instruction[g]*, formerly *Sapiental Work A[e]* also *Tree of Knowledge*
4Q434	4QBarki Nafshi[a]	*BarkhiNafshi[a]*
4Q502	4QpapRitMar	*Ritual of Marriage*
4Q503	4QpapPrQuot	*Prières quotidiennes* or *Daily Prayers*
4Q504	4QDibHam[a]	*Dibre Hame 'orota* or *Words of the Luminaries[a]*
4Q507	4QPrFêtes[a]	*Prières pour les fêtesa* or *Festival Prayersa*
4Q510	4QShir[a]	*Shirot[a]* or *Songs of the Sage[a]*
4Q512	4QpapRitPur B	*Ritual Purity B*
4Q521	4QMessAp	*Messianic Apocalypse*
4Q524	4QT[b]	*4QTemple Scroll,* formerly *Halakhic Text*
4Q525	4QBeat	*Beatitudes*
7Q2		*Epistle of Jeremiah*
11Q5	11QPsa	*Psalms Scroll[a]*
11Q10	11QtgJob	*Targum of Job*
11Q11	11QApPs	*Apocryphal Psalms*
11Q13	11QMelch	*Melchizedek*
11Q18	11QNJ ar	*New Jerusalem*
11Q19	11QT[a]	*Temple Scroll[a]*

MISHNAH, TALMUD, AND RELATED LITERATURE

Abbreviations distinguish the versions of the Talmudic tractates: *y.* for Jerusalem and *b.* for Babylonian. A prefixed *t.* denotes the tractates of the Tosefta and an *m.* those of the Mishnah. A prefixed *bar.* denotes a baraita (an authoritative Tannaitic rule external to the Mishnah).

Avod. Zar.	*Avodah Zarah*
Avot	*Avot*
Arak.	*Arakhin*
B. Bat.	*Bava Batra*
B. Metz.	*Bava Metzia*
B. Qam.	*Bava Qamma*
Bek.	*Bekhorot*
Ber.	*Berakhot*
Betzah	*Betzah (= Yom Tov)*
Bik.	*Bikkurim*
Demai	*Demai*
Eruv.	*Eruvin*
Ed.	*Eduyyot*
Git.	*Gittin*
Hag.	*Hagigah*
Hal.	*Hallah*
Hor.	*Horayot*
Hul.	*Hullin*
Kelim	*Kelim*
Ker.	*Keritot*
Ketub.	*Ketubbot*
Kil.	*Kilayim*
Maas. S.	*Maaser Sheni*
Maas.	*Maaserot*
Mak.	*Makkot*
Makh.	*Makhshirin*
Meg.	*Megillah*
Meil.	*Meilah*
Menah.	*Menahot*
Mid.	*Middot*
Mikw.	*Mikwaot*
Moed	*Moed*
Moed Qat.	*Moed Qatan*
Nash.	*Nashim*
Naz.	*Nazir*
Ned.	*Nedarim*
Neg.	*Negaim*
Nez.	*Neziqin*
Nid.	*Niddah*
Ohal.	*Ohalot*
Or.	*Orlah*
Parah	*Parah*
Peah	*Peah*
Pesah.	*Pesahim*
Qinnim	*Qinnim*
Qidd.	*Qiddushin*
Qod.	*Qodashim*
Rosh. Hash.	*Rosh HaShanah*

Sanh.	*Sanhedrin*
Shabb.	*Shabbat*
Shev.	*Sheviit*
Shevu.	*Shevuot*
Seder	*Seder*
Sheq.	*Sheqalim*
Sotah	*Sotah*
Sukkah	*Sukkah*
Taan.	*Taanit*
Tamid	*Tamid*
Tehar.	*Teharot*
Tem.	*Temurah*
Ter.	*Terumot*
T. Yom	*Tevul Yom*
Uq.	*Uqtzin*
Yad.	*Yadayin*
Yev.	*Yevamot*
Yoma	*Yoma (= Kippurim)*
Zabim	*Zabim*
Zevah.	*Zevahim*
Zera.	*Zeraim*

Targumic Texts

Tg. Onq.	*Targum Onqelos*
Tg. Neb.	*Targum of the Prophets*
Tg. Ket.	*Targum of the Writings*
Frg. Tg.	*Fragmentary Targum*
Sam. Tg.	*Samaritan Targum*
Tg. Isa.	*Targum Isaiah*
Tg. Neof.	*Targum Neofiti*
Tg. Ps.-J.	*Targum Pseudo-Jonathan*
Tg. Yer. I, II	*Targum Yerushalmi I, II*
Yem. Tg.	*Yemenite Targum*
Tg. Esth. I, II	*First or Second Targum of Esther*

Other Rabbinic Works

Avad.	*Avadim*
Avot. R. Nat.	*Avot of Rabbi Nathan*
Ag. Ber.	*Aggadat Bereshit*
Bab.	*Babylonian*
Der. Er. Rab.	*Derekh Eretz Rabbah*
Der. Er. Zut.	*Derekh Eretz Zuta*
Gem.	*Gemara*
Gerim	*Gerim*
Kallah	*Kallah*
Kallah Rab.	*Kallah Rabbati*
Kutim	*Kutim*
Mas. Qet.	*Massekhtot Qetannot*
Mek.	*Mekilta*
Mez.	*Mezuzah*
Midr.	*Midrash*

Midr. Tann.	*Midrash Tannaim*
Pal.	*Palestinian*
Pesiq. Rab.	*Pesiqta Rabbati*
Pesiq. Rab Kah.	*Pesiqta of Rab Kahana*
Pirqe R. El.	*Pirqe Rabbi Eliezer*
Rab.	*Rabbah*
S. Eli. Rab.	*Seder Eliyahu Rabbah*
S. Eli. Zut.	*Seder Eliyahu Zuta*
Sem.	*Semahot*
Sef. Torah	*Sefer Torah*
Sifra	*Sifra*
Sifre	*Sifre*
Tzitz.	*Tzitzit*
Sof.	*Soferim*
S. Olam. Rab	*Seder Olam Rabbah*
Tanh.	*Tanhuma*
Tef.	*Tefillin*
Yal.	*Yalqut*

Apostolic Fathers

Barn.	*Barnabas*
1–2 Clem.	*1–2 Clement*
Did.	*Didache*
Diogn.	*Diognetus*
Herm. *Mand.*	Shepherd of Hermas, *Mandate*
Herm. *Sim.*	Shepherd of Hermas, *Similitude*
Herm. *Vis.*	Shepherd Hermas, *Vision*
Ign. *Eph.*	Ignatius, *To the Ephesians*
Ign. *Magn.*	Ignatius, *To the Magnesians*
Ign. *Phld.*	Ignatius, *To the Philadelphians*
Ign. *Pol.*	Ignatius, *To Polycarp*
Ign. *Rom.*	Ignatius, *To the Romans*
Ign. *Smyrn.*	Ignatius, *To the Smyrnaeans*
Ign. *Trall.*	Ignatius, *To the Trallians*
Mart. Pol.	*Martyrdom of Polycarp*
Pol. *Phil*	Polycarp, *To the Philippians*

Nag Hammadi Codices

Act Pet.	*Act of Peter*
Acts Pet. 12 Apos.	*Acts of Peter and the Twelve Apostles*
Allogenes	*Allogenes*
Ap. Jas.	*Apocryphon of James*
Ap. John	*Apocryphon of John*
Apoc. Adam	*Apocalypse of Adam*
1 Apoc. Jas.	*(First) Apocalypse of James*
2 Apoc. Jas.	*(Second) Apocalypse of James*
Apoc. Paul	*Apocalypse of Paul*
Apoc. Pet.	*Apocalypse of Peter*
Asclepius	*Asclepius 21–29*
Auth. Teach.	*Authoritative Teaching*
Dial. Sav.	*Dialogue of the Savior*

Disc. 8–9	*Discourse on the Eighth and Ninth*
Eugnostos	*Eugnostos the Blessed* (III, 3), (V, 1)
Exeg. Soul	*Exegesis of the Soul*
Frm.	*Fragments*
Gos. Eg.	*Gospel of the Egyptians*
Gos. Mary	*Gospel of Mary*
Gos. Phil.	*Gospel of Philip*
Gos. Thom.	*Gospel of Thomas*
Gos. Truth	*Gospel of Truth*
Great Pow.	*Concept of our Great Power*
Hyp. Arch.	*Hypostasis of the Archons*
Hypsiph.	*Hypsiphrone*
Interp. Know.	*Interpretation of Knowledge*
Marsanes	*Marsanes*
Melch.	*Melchizedek*
Norea	*Thought of Norea*
On Anointing	*On the Anointing*
On Bap. A	*On Baptism A*
On Bap. B	*On Baptism B*
On Euch. A	*On the Eucharist A*
On Euch. B	*On the Eucharist B*
Orig. World	*On the Origin of the World*
Paraph. Shem	*Paraphrase of Shem*
Plato Rep.	Plato, *Republic 588b-589b*
Pr. Paul	*Prayer of the Apostle Paul*
Pr. Thanks.	*Prayer of Thanksgiving*
Sent. Sextus	*Sentences of Sextus*
Soph. Jes. Chr.	*Sophia of Jesus Christ*
Steles Seth	*Three Steles of Seth*
Teach. Silv.	*Teachings of Silvanus*
Testim. Truth	*Testimony of Truth*
Thom. Cont.	*Book of Thomas the Contender*
Thund.	*Thunder: Perfect Mind*
Treat. Res.	*Treatise on the Resurrection*
Treat. Seth	*Second Treatise of the Great Seth*
Tri. Trac.	*Tripartite Tractate*
Trim. Prot.	*Trimorphic Protennoia*
Val. Exp.	*Valentinian Exposition*
Zost.	*Zostrianos*

New Testament Apocrypha and Pseudepigrapha

Acts Andr.	*Acts of Andrew*
Acts Andr. Mth.	*Acts of Andrew and Matthias*
Acts Andr. Paul	*Acts of Andrew and Paul*
Acts Barn.	*Acts of Barnabas*
Acts Jas.	*Acts of James the Great*
Acts John	*Acts of John*
Acts John Pro.	*Acts of John (by Prochorus)*
Acts Paul	*Acts of Paul (or Acts of Paul and Thecla)*
Acts Pet.	*Acts of Peter*
Acts Pet. (Slav.)	*Acts of Peter (Slavonic)*
Acts Pet. Andr.	*Acts of Peter and Andrew*
Acts Pet. Paul	*Acts of Peter and Paul*

Acts Phil.	*Acts of Philip*
Acts Phil. (Syr.)	*Acts of Philip (Syriac)*
Acts Pil.	*Acts of Pilate*
Acts Thad.	*Acts of Thaddaeus*
Acts Thom.	*Acts of Thomas*
Apoc. Pet.	*Apocalypse of Peter*
Ap. John	*Apocryphon of John*
Apoc. Dosith.	*Apocalypse of Dositheus*
Apoc. Messos	*Apocalypse of Messos*
Apoc. Thom.	*Apocalypse of Thomas*
Apoc. Vir.	*Apocalypse of the Virgin*
(Apocr.) Ep. Tit.	*Apocryphal Epistle of Titus*
(Apocr.) Gos. John	*Apocryphal Gospel of John*
Apos. Con.	*Apostolic Constitutions and Canons*
Ps.-Abd.	*Apostolic History of Pseudo-Abdias*
(Arab.) Gos. Inf.	*Arabic Gospel of the Infancy*
(Arm.) Gos. Inf.	*Armenian Gospel of the Infancy*
Asc. Jas.	*Ascents of James*
Assum. Vir.	*Assumption of the Virgin*
Bk. Barn.	*Book of the Resurrection of Christ by Barnabas the Apostle*
Bk. Elch.	*Book Elchasai*
Cerinthus	*Cerinthus*
3 Cor.	*3 Corinthians*
Ep. Alex.	*Epistle to the Alexandrians*
Ep. Apos.	*Epistle to the Apostles*
Ep. Chr. Abg.	*Epistle of Christ and Abgar*
Ep. Chr. Heav.	*Epistle of Christ from Heaven*
Ep. Lao.	*Epistle to the Laodiceans*
Ep. Lent.	*Epistle of Lentulus*
Ep. Paul Sen.	*Epistles of Paul and Seneca*
Gos. Barn.	*Gospel of Barnabas*
Gos. Bart.	*Gospel of Bartholomew*
Gos. Bas.	*Gospel of Basilides*
Gos. Bir. Mary	*Gospel of the Birth of Mary*
Gos. Eb.	*Gospel of the Ebionites*
Gos. Eg.	*Gospel of the Egyptians*
Gos. Eve	*Gospel of Eve*
Gos. Gam.	*Gospel of Gamaliel*
Gos. Heb.	*Gospel of the Hebrews*
Gos. Marcion	*Gospel of Marcion*
Gos. Mary	*Gospel of Mary*
Gos. Naass.	*Gospel of the Naassenes*
Gos. Naz.	*Gospel of the Nazarenes (Nazoreans)*
Gos. Nic.	*Gospel of Nicodemus*
Gos. Pet.	*Gospel of Peter*
Ps.-Mt.	*Gospel of Pseudo-Matthew*
Gos. Thom.	*Gospel of Thomas*
Gos. Trad. Mth.	*Gospel and Traditions of Matthias*
Hist. Jos. Carp.	*History of Joseph the Carpenter*
Hymn Dance	*Hymn of the Dance*
Hymn Pearl	*Hymn of the Pearl*
Inf. Gos. Thom.	*Infancy Gospel of Thomas*
Inf. Gos.	*Infancy Gospels*
Mart. Bart.	*Martyrdom of Bartholomew*
Mart. Mt.	*Martyrdom of Matthew*
Mart. On.	*Martyrdom of Onesimus*
Mart. Paul	*Martyrdom of Paul*

Mart. Pet.	*Martyrdom of Peter*
Mart. Pet. Paul	*Paul Martyrdom of Peter and Paul*
Mart. Phil.	*Martyrdom of Philip*
Melkon	*Melkon*
Mem. Apos.	*Memoria of Apostles*
Pre. Pet.	*Preaching of Peter*
Prot. Jas.	*Protevangelium of James*
Ps.-Clem.	*Pseudo-Clementines*
Rev. Steph.	*Revelation of Stephen*
Sec. Gos. Mk.	*Secret Gospel of Mark*
Vis. Paul	*Vision of Paul*

Works in Greek and Latin, Some with English Translations

Achilles Tatius

Leuc. Clit.	*Leucippe et Clitophon*	*The Adventures of Leucippe and Clitophon*

Aelian

Nat. an.	*De natura animalium*	*Nature of Animals*
Var. hist.	*Varia historia*	

Aeschines

Ctes.	*In Ctesiphonem*	*Against Ctesiphon*
Fals. leg.	*De falsa legatione*	*False Embassy*
Tim.	*In Timarchum*	*Against Timarchus*

Aeschylus

Ag.	*Agamemnon*	*Agamemnon*
Cho.	*Choephori*	*Libation-Bearers*
Eum.	*Eumenides*	*Eumenides*
Pers.	*Persae*	*Persians*
Prom.	*Prometheus vinctus*	*Prometheus Bound*
Sept.	*Septem contra Thebas*	*Seven against Thebes*
Suppl.	*Supplices*	*Suppliant Women*

Aesop

Fab.	*Fabulae*	*Fables*

Albinus

Epit.	*Epitome doctrinae platonicae*	*Handbook of Platonism*
Intr.	*Introductio in Platonem*	*Introduction to Plato*

Alexander of Aphrodisias

De an.	*De anima*
Comm. An. post.	*In Analytica posteriora commentariorum fragmenta*
Comm. An. pr.	*In Aristotelis Analyticorum priorum librum i commentarium*
Comm. Metaph.	*In Aristotelis Metaphysica commentaria*

Comm. Mete.	*In Aristotelis Meteorologicorum libros commentaria*	
Comm. Sens.	*In librum De sensu commentarium*	
Comm. Top.	*In Aristotelis Topicorum libros octo commentaria*	
Fat.	*De fato*	
Mixt.	*De mixtione*	
Probl.	*Problemata*	

Ambrose

Abr.	*De Abraham*	
Apol. Dav.	*Apologia prophetae David*	
Aux.	*Sermo contra Auxentium de basilicis tradendis*	
Bon. mort.	*De bono mortis*	*Death as a Good*
Cain	*De Cain et Abel*	
Enarrat. Ps.	*Enarrationes in XII Psalmos davidicos*	
Exc.	*De excessufratris sui Satyri*	
Exh. virginit.	*Exhortatio virginitatis*	
Fid.	*De fide*	
Exp. Isa.	*Expositio Isaiae prophetae*	
Exp. Luc.	*Expositio Evangelii secundum Lucam*	
Exp. Ps. 118	*Expositio Psalmi CXVIII*	
Expl. symb.	*Explanatio symboli ad initiandos*	
Fid. Grat.	*De fide ad Gratianum*	
Fug.	*De fuga saeculi*	*Flight from the World*
Hel.	*De Helia et Jejunio*	
Hex.	*Hexaemeron libri sex*	*Six Days of Creation*
Hymn.	*Hymni*	
Incarn.	*De incarnationis dominicae sacramento*	*Sacrament of the Incarnation of the Lord*
Instit.	*De institutione virginis*	
Isaac	*De Isaac vel anima*	*Isaac, or the Soul*
Jac.	*De Jacob et vita beata*	*Jacob and the Happy Life*
Job	*De interpellatione Job et David*	*Prayer of Job and David*
Jos.	*De Joseph patriarcha*	
Myst.	*De mysteriis*	*The Mysteries*
Nab.	*De Nabuthae historia*	
Noe	*De Noe et arca*	
Ob. Theo.	*De obitu Theodosii*	
Ob. Val.	*De obitu Valentianiani consolatio*	
Off.	*De officiis ministrorum*	
Paen.	*De paenitentia*	
Parad.	*De paradiso*	*Paradise*
Patr.	*De benedictionibus patriarcharum*	*The Patriarchs*
Sacr.	*De sacramentis*	*The Sacraments*
Sacr. regen.	*De sacramento regenerationis sive de philosophia*	
Spir.	*De Spiritu Sancto*	*The Holy Spirit*
Symb.	*Explanatio symboli*	
Tob.	*De Tobia*	
Vid.	*De viduis*	
Virg.	*De virginibus*	
Virginit.	*De virginitate*	

ANAXIMENES OF LAMPSACUS

Rhet. Alex.	*Rhetorica ad Alexandrum (Ars rhetorica)*	

ANDRONICUS

[Pass.]	*De passionibus*	*The Passions*

ANTH. PAL.	*Anthologia palatina*	*Palatine Anthology*
ANTH. PLAN.	*Anthologia planudea*	*Planudean Anthology*

ANTONINUS LIBERALIS

Metam.	*Metamorphōseōn synagōgē*	

APOLLODORUS

Library	*The Library*	

APOLLONIUS OF RHODES

Argon.	*Argonautica*	*Argonautica*

APOLLONIUS SOPHISTA

Lex. hom.	*Lexicon homericum*	*Homeric Lexicon*

APPIAN

Bell. civ.	*Bella civilia*	*Civil Wars*
Hist. rom.	*Historia romana*	*Roman History*

APULEIUS

Apol.	*Apologia (Pro se de magia)*	*Apology*
De deo Socr.	*De deo Socratico*	
Dogm. Plat.	*De dogma Platonis*	
Flor.	*Florida*	
Metam.	*Metamorphoses*	*The Golden Ass*

AQUINAS, THOMAS

ST	*Summa Theologiae*	

ARATUS

Phaen.	*Phaenomena*	

ARCHIMEDES

Aequil.	*De planorum aequilibriis*	*Equilibriums of Planes*
Aren.	*Arenarius*	*The Sand-reckoner*
Assumpt.	*Liber assumptorum*	
Bov.	*Problema bovinum*	
Circ.	*Dimensio circuli*	*Measurement of a Circle*
Con. sph.	*De conoidibus et sphaeroidibus*	*On Conoids and Spheroids*
Eratosth.	*Ad Eratosthenem methodus*	*To Eratosthenes on the Mechanical Method Theorems*
Fluit.	*De corporibus fluitantibus*	*On Floating Bodies*
Quadr.	*Quadratura parabolae*	*Quadrature of the Parabola*
Sph. cyl.	*De sphaera et cylindro*	*On the Sphere and Cylinder*
Spir.	*De lineis spiralibus*	*On Spirals*
Stom.	*Stomachion*	

ARETAEUS

Cur. acut.	*De curatione acutorum morborum*
Cur. diut.	*De curatione diuturnorum morborum*
Sign. acut.	*De causis et signis acutorum morborum*
Sign. diut.	*De causis et signis diuturnorum morborum*

ARISTOPHANES

Ach.	*Acharnenses*	*Acharnians*
Av.	*Aves*	*Birds*
Eccl.	*Ecclesiazusae*	*Women of the Assembly*
Eq.	*Equites*	*Knights*
Lys.	*Lysistrata*	*Lysistrata*
Nub.	*Nubes*	*Clouds*
Pax	*Pax*	*Peace*
Plut.	*Plutus*	*The Rich Man*
Ran.	*Ranae*	*Frogs*
Thesm.	*Thesmophoriazusae*	
Vesp.	*Vespae*	*Wasps*

ARISTOTLE

De an.	*De anima*	*Soul*
An. post.	*Analytica posteriora*	*Posterior Analytics*
An. pr.	*Analytica priora*	*Prior Analytics*
Ath. pol.	*Athēnaīn politeia*	*Constitution of Athens*
[Aud.]	*De audibilibus*	*Sounds*
Cael.	*De caelo*	*Heavens*
Cat.	*Categoriae*	*Categories*
Col.	*De coloribus*	*Colors*
Div. somn.	*De divinatio per somnum*	*Prophesying by Dreams*
Ep.	*Epistulae*	*Letters*
Eth. eud.	*Ethica eudemia*	*Eudemian Ethics*
Eth. nic.	*Ethica nichomachea*	*Nichomachean Ethics*
Gen. an.	*De generatione anamalium*	*Generation of Animals*
Gen. corr.	*De generatione et corruptione*	*Generaion of Corruption*
Hist. an.	*Historia animalium*	*History of Animals*
Inc. an.	*De incessu animalium*	*Gait of Animals*

Insomn.	*De insomniis*	
Int.	*De interpretatione*	*Interpretation*
Juv. sen.	*De juventute et senectute*	*Youth and Old Age*
[Lin. ins.]	*De lineis insecabilibus*	*Indivisible Lines*
Long. brev.	*De longitudine et brevitate vitae*	*Longevity and Shortness of Life*
[Mag. mor.]	*Magna moralia*	
[Mech.]	*Mechanica*	*Mechanics*
Mem. rem.	*De memoria et reminiscentia*	*Memory and Reminiscence*
Metaph.	*Metaphysica*	*Metaphysics*
Mete.	*Meteorologica*	*Meteorology*
[Mir. ausc.]	*De mirabilibus auscultationibus*	*On Marvelous Things Heard*
Mot. an.	*De motu animalium*	*Movement of Animals*
[Mund.]	*De mundo*	*World*
[Oec.]	*Oeconomica*	*Economics*
Part. an.	*De partibus animalium*	*Parts of Animals*
Phys.	*Physica*	*Physics*
[Physiogn.]	*Physiognomonica*	*Physiognomonics*
[Plant.]	*De plantis*	*Plants*
Poet.	*Poetica*	*Poetics*
Pol.	*Politica*	*Politics*
[Probl.]	*Problemata*	*Problems*
Protr.	*Protrepticus*	
Resp.	*De respiratione*	*Respiration*
Rhet.	*Rhetorica*	*Rhetoric*
[Rhet. Alex.]	*Rhetorica ad Alexandrum*	*Rhetoric to Alexander*
Sens.	*De sensuet sensibilibus*	*Sense and Sensibilia*
Somn.	*De somniis*	*Dreams*
Somn. vig.	*De somno et vigilia*	*Sleep and Waking*
Soph. elench.	*Sophistici elenchi*	*Sophistical Refutations*
[Spir.]	*De spiritu*	*Spirit*
Top.	*Topica*	*Topics*
[Vent.]	*De ventorum situ et nominibus*	*Situations and Names of Winds*
[Virt. vit.]	*De virtutibus et vitiis*	*Virtues and Vices*
Vit. mort.	*De vita et morte*	*Life and Death*
[Gorg.]	*De Gorgia*	
[Xen.]	*De Xenophane*	
[Zen.]	*De Zenone*	

Arrian

Anab.	*Anabasis*
Epict. diss.	*Epicteti dissertationes*
Peripl. M. Eux.	*Periplus Maris Euxini*
Tact.	*Tactica*

Artemidorus Daldianus

Onir.	*Onirocritica*

Athanasius

Apol. Const.	*Apologia ad Constantium*	*Defense before Constantius*
Apol. sec.	*Apologia secunda (= Apologia contra Arianos)*	*Defense against the Arians*
[Apoll.]	*De incarnatione contra Apollinarium*	*On the Incarnation against Apollinarius*
C. Ar.	*Orationes contra Arianos*	*Orations against the Arians*

C. Gent.	*Contra gentes*	*Against Pagans*
Decr.	*De decretis*	*Defense of the Nicene Definition*
Dion.	*De sententia Dionysii*	*On the Opinion of Dionysius*
Ep. Adelph.	*Epistula ad Adelphium*	*Letter to Adelphius*
Ep. Aeg. Lib.	*Epistula ad episcopos Aegypti et Libyae*	*Letter to the Bishops of Egypt and Libya*
Ep. Afr.	*Epistula ad Afros episcopos*	*Letter to the Bishops of Africa*
Ep. Amun	*Epistula ad Amun*	*Letter to Ammoun*
Ep. cler. Alex.	*Epistula ad clerum Alexandriae*	*Letter to the Clergy of Alexandria*
Ep. cler. Mareot.	*Epistula ad clerum Mareotae*	*Letter to the Clergy of Mareotis*
Ep. Drac.	*Epistula ad Dracontium*	*Letter to Dracontius*
Ep. encycl.	*Epistula encyclica*	*Circular Letter*
Ep. Epict.	*Epistula ad Epictetum*	*Letter to Epictetus*
Ep. fest.	*Epistulae festales*	*Festal Letters*
Ep. Jo. Ant.	*Epistula ad Joannem et Antiochum presbyteros*	*Letter to John and Antiochus*
Ep. Jov.	*Epistula ad Jovianum*	*Letter to Jovian*
Ep. Marcell.	*Epistula ad Marcellinum de interpretatione Psalmorum*	*Letter to Marcellinus on the Interpretation of the Psalms*
Ep. Max.	*Epistula ad Maximum*	*Letter to Maximus*
Ep. mon. 1	*Epistula ad monachos i*	*First Letter to Monks*
Ep. mon. 2	*Epistula ad monachos ii*	*Second Letter to Monks*
Ep. mort. Ar.	*Epistula ad Serapionem de more Arii*	*Letter to Seapion Concerning Death of Arius*
Ep. Ors. 1	*Epistula ad Orsisium i*	*First Letter to Orsisius*
Ep. Ors. 2	*Epistula ad Orsisium ii*	*Second Letter to Orsisius*
Ep. Pall.	*Epistula ad Palladium*	*Letter to Palladius*
Ep. Rufin.	*Epistula ad Rufinianum*	*Letter to Rufinianus*
Ep. Serap.	*Epistulae ad Serapionem*	*Letters to serapion concerning the Holy Spirit*
Ep. virg. (Copt.)	*Epistula ad virgines (Coptice)*	*First (Coptic) Letter to Virgins*
Ep. virg. (Syr.)	*Epistula ad virgines (Syriace)*	*Second (Syriac) Letter to Virgins*
Ep. virg. (Syr./Arm.)	*Epistula ad virgines (Syriace et Armeniace)*	*Letter to Virgins*
Ep. virg. (Theod.)	*Epistula exhortatora ad virgines apud Theodoretum*	*Letter to Virgins*
Fug.	*Apologia de fuga sua*	*Defense of His Flight*
H. Ar.	*Historia Arianorum*	*History of the Arians*
Hen. sōm.	*Henos sōmatos*	*Encyclical Letter of Alexander concerning the Deposition of Arius*
Hom. Jo. 12:27	*In illud Nunc anima mea turbata est*	*Homily on John 12:27*
Hom. Luc. 12:10	*In illud Qui dixerit verbum in filium*	*Homily on Luke 12:10*
Hom. Matt. 11:27	*In illud Omnia mihi tradita sunt*	*Homily on Matt 11:27*
Inc.	*De incarnatione*	*On the Incarnation*
Mor. et val.	*De morbo et valitudine*	*On Sickness and Health*
Narr. fug.	*Narratio ad Ammonium episcopum de fuga sua*	*Report of Athanasius concerning Theodorus*
Syn.	*De synodis*	*On the Councils of Arimimum and Seleucia*
Tom.	*Tomus ad Antiochenos*	*Tome to the People of Antioch*
Vit. Ant.	*Vita Antonii*	*Life of Antony*

ATHENAEUS

Deipn.	*Deipnosophistae*

ATHENAGORAS

Leg.	*Legatio pro Christianis*
Res.	*De resurrectione*

Augustine

Acad.	*Contra Academicos*	*Against the Academics*
Adim.	*Contra Adimantum*	*Agaiinst Adimantus*
Adnot. Job	*Adnotationum in Job liber I*	*Annotations on Job*
Adv. Jud.	*Tractatus adversus Judaeos*	*In Answer to the Jews*
Agon.	*De agone christiano*	*Christian Combat*
An. orig.	*De anima et eius origine*	*The Soul and Its Origin*
Arian.	*Contra sermonem Arianorum*	
Bapt.	*De baptismo contra Donatistas*	
Beat.	*De vita beata*	*Baptism*
Bon. conj.	*De bono conjugali*	*The Good Marriage*
Brev. coll.	*Breviculus collationis cum Donatistas*	
C. du. ep. Pelag.	*Contra duas epistulas Pelagianorum ad Bonifatium*	*Against the Two Letters of the Pelagians*
C. Jul.	*Contra Julianum*	*Against Julian*
C. Jul. op. imp.	*Contra secundam Juliani responsionem imperfectum opus*	*Against Julian: Opus Imperfectum*
C. litt. Petil.	*Contra litteras Petiliani*	
C. mend.	*Contra mendacium*	*Against Lying (to Consentius)*
Catech.	*De catechizandis rudibus*	*Catechizing the Uninstructed*
Civ.	*De civitate Dei*	*The City of God*
Coll. Max.	*Collatio cum Maximino Arianorum episcopo*	
Conf.	*Confessionum libri XIII*	*Confessions*
Cons.	*De consensu evangelistarum*	*Harmony of the Gospels*
Contin.	*De continentia*	*Continence*
Corrept.	*De correptione et gratia*	*Admonition and Grace*
Cresc.	*Contra Cresconium Donatistam*	
Cur.	*De cura pro mortuis gerenda*	*The Care to Be Taken for the Dead*
Dial.	*Principia dialecticae*	
Disc.	*De disciplina christiana*	
Div.	*De divinitate daemonum*	*The Divination of Demons*
Div. quaest. LXXXIII	*De diversis quaestionibus LXXXIII*	*Eighty-three Different Questions*
Div. quaest. Simpl.	*De diversis quaestionibus ad Simplicianum*	
Doctr. chr.	*De doctrina christiana*	*Christian Instruction*
Don.	*Post collationem adversus Donatistas*	
Duab.	*De duabus animabus*	*Two Souls*
Dulc.	*De octo Dulcitii quaestionibus*	*The Eight Questions of Dulcitius*
Emer.	*De gestis cum Emerino*	
Enarrat. Ps.	*Enarrationes in Psalmos*	*Enarrations on the Psalms*
Enchir.	*Enchiridion de fide, spe, et caritate*	*Enchiridion on Faith, Hope, and Love*
Exp. Gal.	*Expositio in epistulam ad Galatas*	
Exp. quaest. Rom.	*Expositio quarumdam quaestionum in epistula ad Romanos*	
Faust.	*Contra Faustum Manichaeum*	*Against Faustus the Manichaean*
Fel.	*Contra Felicem*	*Against Felix*
Fid.	*De fide rerum quae non videntur*	*Faith in Thiings Unseen*
Fid. op.	*De fide et operibus*	*Faith and Works*
Fid. symb.	*De fide et symbolo*	*Faith and the Creed*
Fort.	*Contra Fortunatum*	*Against Fortunatus*
Fund.	*Contra epistulam Manichaei quam vocant Fundamenti*	*Against the Letter of the Manichaeans That They Call "The Basics"*

Gaud.	*Contra Gaudentium Donatistarum episcopum*	*Against Gaudentius the Donatist Bishop*
Gen. imp.	*De Genesi ad litteram imperfectus liber*	*On the Literal Interpretation of Genesis: An Unfinished Book*
Gen. litt.	*De Genesi ad litteram*	*On Genesis Litarally Interpreted*
Gen. Man.	*De Genesi contra Manichaeos*	*On Genesis Against the Manicheans*
Gest. Pelag.	*De gestis Pelagii*	*Proceedings of Pelagius*
Gramm.	*De grammatica*	
Grat.	*De gratia et libero arbitrio*	*Grace and Free Will*
Grat. Chr.	*De gratia Christi, et de peccato originali*	*The Grace of Christ and Original Sin*
Haer.	*De haeresibus*	*Heresies*
Immort. an.	*De immortalitate animae*	*The Immortality of the Soul*
Incomp. nupt.	*De incompetentibus nuptiis*	*Adulterous Marriages*
Leg.	*Contra adversarium legis et prophetarum*	
Lib.	*De libero arbitrio*	*Free Will*
Locut. Hept.	*Locutionum in Heptateuchum libri septem*	
Mag.	*De magistro*	
Man.	*De moribus Manichaeorum*	*The Morals of the Manichaeans*
Maxim.	*Contra Maximinum Arianum*	*Against Maximimus the Arian*
De mend.	*De mendacio*	*On Lying*
Mor. eccl.	*De moribus ecclesiae catholicae*	*The Way of Life of the Catholic Church*
Mor. Manich.	*De moribus Manichaeorum*	*The Way of the Life of the Manichaeans*
Mus.	*De musica*	*Music*
Nat. bon.	*De natura boni contra Manichaeos*	*The Nature of the Good*
Nat. grat.	*De natura et gratia*	*Nature and Grace*
Nat. orig.	*De natura et origine animae*	*The Nature and Origin of the Soul*
Nupt.	*De nuptiis et concupiscentia ad Valerium comitem*	*Marriage and Concupiscence*
Oct. quaest. Vet. Test.	*De octo quaestionibus ex Veteri Testamento*	*Eight Questions from the Old Testament*
Op. mon.	*De opere monachorum*	*The Work of Monks*
Ord.	*De ordine*	
Parm.	*Contra epistulam Parmeniani*	
Pat.	*De patientia*	*Patience*
Pecc. merit.	*De peccatorum meritis et remissione*	*Guilt and Remission of Sins*
Pecc. orig.	*De peccato originali*	*Original sin*
Perf.	*De perfectione justitiae hominis*	*Perfection in Human Righteousness*
Persev.	*De dono perseverantiae*	*The Gift of Perseverance*
Praed.	*De praedestinatione sanctorum*	*The Predestination of the Saints*
Priscill.	*Ad Orosium contra Priscillianistas et Origenistas*	*To Orosius against the Priscillianists and the Origenists*
Psal. Don.	*Psalmus contra partem Donati*	
Quaest. ev.	*Quaestionum evangelicarum libri II*	
Quaest. Hept.	*Quaestiones in Heptateuchum*	
Quaest. Matt.	*Quaestiones in evangelium Matthaei*	
Quant. an.	*De quantitate animae*	*The Magnitude of the Soul*
Reg.	*Regula ad servos Dei*	
Retract.	*Retractationum libri II*	*Retractions*
Rhet.	*De rhetorica, Rhetores Latini*	
Secund.	*Contra Secundinum Manichaeum*	
Serm.	*Sermones*	
Serm. Dom.	*De sermone Domini in monte*	*Sermon on the Mount*

Solil.	*Soliloquiorum libri II*	*Soliloquies*
Spec.	*De scriptura sancta speculum*	
Spir. et litt.	*De spiritu et littera*	*The Spirit and the Letter*
Symb.	*De symbolo ad catechumenos*	*The Creed: For Catechumens*
Tract. ep. Jo.	*In epistulam Johannis ad Parthos tractatus*	*Tractates on the First Epistle of John*
Tract. Ev. Jo.	*In Evangelium Johannis tractatus*	*Tractates on the Gospel of John*
Trin.	*De Trinitate*	*The Trinity*
Unic. bapt.	*De unico baptismo*	
Unit. eccl.	*De unitate ecclesiae*	*The Unity of the Church*
Util. cred.	*De utilitate credendi*	*The Usefulness of Believing*
Util. jej.	*De utilitate jejunii*	*The Usefulness of Fasting*
Ver. rel.	*De vera religione*	*True Religion*
Vid.	*De bono viduitatis*	*The Excellence of Widowhood*
Virginit.	*De sancta virginitate*	*Holy virginity*
Vit. Christ.	*De vita christiana*	*The Christian Life*

Aulus Gellius

Bell. afr.	*Bellum africum*	*African War*
Bell. alex.	*Bellum alexandrinum*	*Alexandrian War*
Noct. att.	*Noctes atticae*	*Attic Nights*

Bede

Eccl. Hist.	*Ecclesiastical History of the English People*

Berossus

Hist.	*History of Babylon*

Bion

Epitaph. Adon.	*Epitaphius Adonis*	*Lament for Adonis*
[Epith. Achil.]	*Epithalamium Achillis et Deidameiae*	*To Achilles and Deidamea*

Caesar

Bell. civ.	*Bellum civile*	*Civil War*
Bell. gall.	*Bellum gallicum*	*Gallic War*

Callimachus

Aet.	*Aetia (in P.Oxy. 2079)*	*Causes*
Epigr.	*Epigrammata*	*Epigrams*
Hec.	*Hecala*	*Hecale*
Hymn.	*Hymni*	*Hymns*
Hymn. Apoll.	*Hymnus in Apollinem*	*Hymn to Apollo*
Hymn. Cer.	*Hymnus in Cererem*	*Hymn to Ceres or Demeter*
Hymn. Del.	*Hymnus in Delum*	*Hymn to Delos*
Hymn. Dian.	*Hymnus in Dianam*	*Hymn to Diana or Artemis*
Hymn. Jov.	*Hymnus in Jovem*	*Hymn to Jove or Zeus*
Hymn. lav. Pall.	*Hymnus in lavacrum Palladis*	*Hymn to the Baths of Pallas*

CAN. AP.	*Canones apostolicae*	*Apostolic Canons*

CATO

Agr.	*De agricultura (De re rustica)*	*Agriculture*
Orig.	*Origines*	*Origins*

CEB. TAB.	*Cebetis Tabula*	

CHARITON

Chaer.	*De Chaerea et Callirhoe*	*Chaereas and Callirhoe*

CHRYSOSTOM (See John Chrysostom)

CICERO

Acad.	*Academicae quaestiones*
Acad. post.	*Academica posteriora (Lucullus)*
Acad. pr.	*Academica priora*
Agr.	*De Lege agraria*
Amic.	*De amicitia*
Arch.	*Pro Archia*
Att.	*Epistulae ad Atticum*
Aug.	*De auguriis*
Balb.	*Pro Balbo*
Brut.	*Brutus or De claris oratoribus*
Caecin.	*Pro Caecina*
Cael.	*Pro Caelio*
Cat.	*In Catalinam*
Clu.	*Pro Cluentio*
Corn.	*Pro Cornelio de maiestate*
Deiot.	*Pro rege Deiotaro*
Div.	*De divinatione*
Div. Caec.	*Divinatio in Caecilium*
Dom.	*De domo suo*
Ep. Brut.	*Epistulae ad Brutum*
Epigr.	*Epigrammata*
Fam.	*Epistulae ad familiares*
Fat.	*De fato*
Fin.	*De finibus*
Flac.	*Pro Flacco*
Font.	*Pro Fonteio*
Har. resp.	*De haruspicum responso*
Inv.	*De inventione rhetorica*
Leg.	*De legibus*
Leg. man.	*Pro Lege manilia (De imperio Cn. Pompeii)*
Lig.	*Pro Ligario*
Lim.	*Limon*
Mar.	*Marius*
Marcell.	*Pro Marcello*
Mil.	*Pro Milone*
Mur.	*Pro Murena*

Nat. d.	*De natura deorum*	
Off.	*De officiis*	
Opt. gen.	*De optimo genere oratorum*	
De or.	*De oratore*	
Or. Brut.	*Orator ad M. Brutum*	
Parad.	*Paradoxa Stoicorum*	
Part. or.	*Partitiones oratoriae*	
Phil.	*Orationes philippicae*	
Pis.	*In Pisonem*	
Planc.	*Pro Plancio*	
Prov. cons.	*De provinciis consularibus*	
Quinct.	*Pro Quinctio*	
Quint. fratr.	*Epistulae ad Quintum fratrem*	
Rab. Perd.	*Pro Rabirio Perduellionis Reo*	
Rab. Post.	*Pro Rabirio Postumo*	
Red. pop.	*Post reditum ad populum*	
Red. sen.	*Post reditum in senatu*	
Rep.	*De republica*	
Rosc. Amer.	*Pro Sexto Roscio Amerino*	
Rosc. com.	*Pro Roscio comoedo*	
Scaur.	*Pro Scauro*	
Sen.	*De senectute*	
Sest.	*Pro Sestio*	
Sull.	*Pro Sulla*	
Tim.	*Timaeus*	
Tog. cand.	*Oratio in senatu in toga candida*	
Top.	*Topica*	
Tull.	*Pro Tullio*	
Tusc.	*Tusculanae disputationes*	
Vat.	*In Vatinium*	
Verr.	*In Verrem*	

CLEMENT OF ALEXANDRIA

Ecl.	*Eclogae propheticae*	*Extracts from the Prophets*
Exc.	*Excerpta ex Theodoto*	*Excerpts from Theodotus*
Paed.	*Paedagogus*	*Christ the Educator*
Protr.	*Protrepticus*	*Exhortation to the Greeks*
Quis div.	*Quis dives salvetur*	*Salvation of the Rich*
Strom.	*Stromata*	*Miscellanies*

COD. JUSTIN. *Codex justinianus*

COD. THEOD. *Codex theodosianus*

COLUMELLA

Arb.	*De arboribus*
Rust.	*De re rustica*

CONST. AP. *Constitutiones apostolicae* *Apostolic Constitutions*

Cornutus

Nat. d.	*De natura deorum (Epidrōme tō n kata tēn Hellēniken theologian paradedomenōn)*	*Summary of the Traditions concerning Greek Mythology*

Corp. herm. *Corpus hermeticum*

Cosmas Indicopleustes

Top.	*Topographia christiana*	*Christian Topography*

Cyprian

Demetr.	*Ad Demetrianum*	*To Demetrian*
Dom. or.	*De dominica oratione*	*The Lord's Supper*
Don.	*Ad Donatum*	*To Donatus*
Eleem.	*De opere et eleemosynis*	*Works and Almsgiving*
Fort.	*Ad Fortunatum*	*To Fortunatus: Exhortation to Martyrdom*
Hab. virg.	*De habitu virginum*	*The Dress of Virgins*
[Idol.]	*Quod idola dii non sint*	*That Idols Are Not Gods*
Laps.	*De lapsis*	*The Lapsed*
Mort.	*De mortalitate*	*Mortality*
Pat.	*De bono patientiae*	*The Advantage of Patience*
Sent.	*Sententiae episcoporum de haereticis baptizandis*	
Test.	*Ad Quirinum testimonia adversus Judaeos*	*To Quirinius: Testimonies against the Jews*
Unit. eccl.	*De catholicae ecclesiae unitate*	*The Unity of the Catholic Church*
Zel. liv.	*De zelo et livore*	*Jealousy and Envy*

Demetrius

Eloc.	*De elocutione (Peri hermeneias)*	*Style*

Demosthenes

Andr.	*Adversus Androtionem*	*Against Androtion*
[Apat.]	*Contra Apatourium*	*Against Apaturius*
1–3 Aphob.	*In Aphobum*	*1–3 Against Aphobus*
Aristocr.	*In Aristocratem*	*Against Aristocrates*
1–2 Aristog.	*In Aristogitonem*	*1–2 Against Aristogeiton*
1 [2] Boeot.	*Contra Boeotum i–ii*	*1–2 Against Boeotos*
C. Phorm.	*Contra Phormionem*	*Against Phormio*
Call.	*Contra Calliclem*	*Against Callicles*
[Callip.]	*Contra Callipum*	*Against Callipus*
Chers.	*De Chersoneso*	*On the Chersonese*
Con.	*In Cononem*	*Against Canon*
Cor.	*De corona*	*On the Crown*
Cor. trier.	*De corona trierarchiae*	*On the Trierarchic Crown*
[Dionys.]	*Contra Dionysodorum*	*Against Dionysodorus*

Epitaph.	*Epitaphius*	*Funeral Oration*
[Erot.]	*Eroticus*	*Eroticus*
Eub.	*Contra Eubulidem*	*Against Eubulides*
[Everg.]	*In Evergum et Mnesibulum*	*Against Evergus and Mnesibulus*
Exord.	*Exordia (Prooemia)*	
Fals. leg.	*De falsa legatione*	*False Embassy*
Halon.	*De Halonneso*	*On the Halonnesus*
[Lacr.]	*Contra Lacritum*	*Against Lacritus*
[Leoch.]	*Contra Leocharem*	*Against Leochares*
Lept.	*Adversus Leptinem*	*Against Leptines*
[Macart.]	*Contra Macartatum*	*Against Macartatus*
Meg.	*Pro Megalopolitanis*	*For the Megalopolitans*
Mid.	*In Midiam*	*Against Meidias*
Naus.	*Contra Nausimachum et Xenopeithea*	*Against Nausimachus*
[Neaer.]	*In Neaeram*	*Against Neaera*
Nicostr.	*Contra Nicostratum*	*Against Nicostratus*
[Olymp.]	*In Olympiodorum*	*Agaiinst Olympiodorus*
1–3 Olynth.	*Olynthiaca i–iii*	*1–3 Olynthiac*
1–2 Onet.	*Contra Onetorem*	*1–2 Against Onetor*
De pace	*De pace*	*On the Peace*
Pant.	*Contra Pantaenetum*	*Against Pantaenetus*
1–3 [4] Philip.	*Philippica i–iv*	*1–4 Philippic*
Pro Phorm.	*Pro Phormione*	*For Phormio*
[Poly.]	*Contra Polyclem*	*Against Polycles*
Rhod. lib.	*De Rhodiorum libertate*	*On the Liberty of the Rhodians*
Spud.	*Contra Spudiam*	*Against Spudia*
1 [2] Steph.	*In Stephanum i–ii*	*1–2 Against Stephanus*
Symm.	*De symmoriis*	*On the Symmories*
[Syntax.]	*Peri syntaxeōs*	*On Organization*
[Theocr.]	*In Theocrinem*	*Against Theocrines*
[Tim.]	*Contra Timotheum*	*Against Timotheus*
Timocr.	*In Timocratem*	*Against Timocrates*
Zenoth.	*Contra Zenothemin*	*Against Zenothemis*

Didymus

Comm. Eccl.	*Commentarii in Ecclesiasten*
Comm. Job	*Commentarii in Job*
Comm. Oct. Reg.	*Commentarii in Octateuchum et Reges*
Comm. Ps.	*Commentarii in Psalmos*
Comm. Zach.	*Commentarii in Zachariam*
Dial. haer.	*Dialogus Didymi Caeci cum haeretico*
Enarrat. Ep. Cath.	*In Epistulas Catholicas brevis enarratio*
Fr. Cant.	*Fragmentum in Canticum canticorum*
Fr. 1 Cor.	*Fragmenta in Epistulam i ad Corinthios*
Fr. 2 Cor.	*Fragmenta in Epistulam ii ad Corinthios*
Fr. Heb.	*Fragmentum in Epistulam ad Hebraeos*
Fr. Jer.	*Fragmenta in Jeremiam*
Fr. Jo.	*Fragmenta in Joannem*
Fr. Prov.	*Fragmenta in Proverbia*
Fr. Ps.	*Fragmenta in Psalmos*
Fr. Rom.	*Fragmenta in Epistulam ad Romanos*
In Gen.	*In Genesim*
Incorp.	*De incorporeo*

Man.	*Contra Manichaeos*	
Philos.	*Ad philosophum*	
Trin.	*De Trinitate*	

Dig.

Digesta

Dinarchus

Aristog.	*In Aristogitonem*	*Against Aristogiton*
Demosth.	*In Demosthenem*	*Against Demosthenes*
Phil.	*In Philoclem*	*Against Philocles*

Dio (Cassius Dio)

Rom.	*Romaika*	

Dio Chrysostom

Achill.	*Achilles (Or. 58)*	*Achilles and Cheiron*
Admin.	*De administratione (Or. 50)*	*His Past Record*
Aegr.	*De aegritudine (Or. 16)*	*Pain and Distress of Spirit*
Alex.	*Ad Alexandrinos (Or. 32)*	*To the People of Alexandria*
Apam.	*Ad Apamenses (Or. 41)*	*To the Apameians*
Aud. aff.	*De audiendi affectione (Or. 19)*	*Fondness for Listening*
Avar.	*De avaritia (Or. 17)*	*Covetousness*
Borysth.	*Borysthenitica (Or. 36)*	*Borysthenic Discourse*
Cel. Phryg.	*Celaenis Phrygiae (Or. 35)*	*At Celaenae in Phrygia*
Charid.	*Charidemus (Or. 30)*	
Chrys.	*Chryseis (Or. 61)*	
Compot.	*De compotatione (Or. 27)*	*Symposia*
Conc. Apam.	*De concordia cum Apamensibus (Or. 40)*	*On Concord with Apamea*
Consuet.	*De consuetudine (Or. 76)*	*Custom*
Consult.	*De consultatione (Or. 26)*	*Deliberation*
Cont.	*Contio (Or. 47)*	*In the Public Assembly at Prusa*
In cont.	*In contione (Or. 48)*	*Political Address in the Assembly*
[Cor.]	*Corinthiaca (Or. 37)*	*Corinthian Discourse*
Def.	*Defensio (Or. 45)*	*Defense*
Dei cogn.	*De dei cognitione (Or. 12)*	*Olympic Discourse*
Dial.	*Dialexis (Or. 42)*	*In His Native City*
Dic. exercit.	*De dicendi exercitatione (Or. 18)*	*Training for Public Speaking*
Diffid.	*De diffidentia (Or. 74)*	*Distrust*
Diod.	*Ad Diodorum (Or. 51)*	*To Diodorus*
Divit.	*De divitiis (Or. 79)*	*Wealth*
Exil.	*De exilio (Or. 13)*	*Banishment*
Fel.	*De felicitate (Or. 24)*	*Happiness*
Fel. sap.	*De quod felix sit sapiens (Or. 23)*	*The Wise Man is Happy*
Fid.	*De fide (Or. 73)*	*Trust*
1 Fort.	*De fortuna i (Or. 63)*	*Fortune 1*
2 Fort.	*De fortuna ii (Or. 64)*	*Fortune 2*
3 Fort.	*De fortuna iii (Or. 65)*	*Fortune 3*

Gen.	*De genio (Or. 25)*	*The Guiding Spirit*
1 Glor.	*De gloria i (Or. 66)*	*Reputation*
2 Glor.	*De gloria ii (Or. 67)*	*Popular Opinion*
3 Glor.	*De gloria iii (Or. 68)*	*Opinion*
Grat.	*Gratitudo (Or. 44)*	*Friendship for Native Land*
Hab.	*De habitu (Or. 72)*	*Personal Appearance*
Hom.	*De Homero (Or. 53)*	*Homer*
Hom. Socr.	*De Homero et Socrate (Or. 55)*	*Homer and Socrates*
Invid.	*De invidia (Or. 77/78)*	*Envy*
Isthm.	*Isthmiaca (Or. 9)*	*Isthmian Discourse*
De lege	*De lege (Or. 75)*	*Law*
Lib.	*De libertate (Or. 80)*	*Freedom*
Lib. myth.	*Libycus mythos (Or. 5)*	*A Libyan Myth*
1 Melanc.	*Melancomas i (Or. 29)*	*Melancomas 1*
2 Melanc.	*Melancomas ii (Or. 28)*	*Melancomas 2*
Ness.	*Nessus (Or. 60)*	*Nessus, or Deianeira*
Nest.	*Nestor (Or. 57)*	*Homer's Portrayal of Nestor*
Nicaeen.	*Ad Nicaeenses (Or. 39)*	*To the Nicaeans*
Nicom.	*Ad Nicomedienses (Or. 38)*	*To the Nicomedians*
De pace	*De pace et bello (Or. 22)*	*Peace and War*
Philoct. arc.	*De Philoctetae arcu (Or. 52)*	*Appraisal of the Tragic Triad*
Philoct.	*Philoctetes (Or. 59)*	
De philosophia	*De philosophia (Or. 70)*	*Philosophy*
De philosopho	*De philosopho (Or. 71)*	*The Philosopher*
Pol.	*Politica (Or. 43)*	*Political Address*
Pulchr.	*De pulchritudine (Or. 21)*	*Beauty*
Rec. mag.	*Recusatio magistratus (Or. 49)*	*Refusal of the Office of Archon*
Regn.	*De regno (Or. 56)*	*Kingship*
1 Regn.	*De regno i (Or. 1)*	*Kingship 1*
2 Regn.	*De regno ii (Or. 2)*	*Kingship 2*
3 Regn.	*De regno iii (Or. 3)*	*Kingship 3*
4 Regn.	*De regno iv (Or. 4)*	*Kingship 4*
Regn. tyr.	*De regno et tyrannide (Or. 62)*	*Kingship and Tyranny*
Rhod.	*Rhodiaca (Or. 31)*	*To the People of Rhodes*
Sec.	*De secessu (Or. 20)*	*Retirement*
Serv.	*De servis (Or. 10)*	*Servants*
1 Serv. lib.	*De servitute et libertate i (Or. 14)*	*Slavery and Freedom 1*
2 Serv. lib.	*De servitute et libertate ii (Or. 15)*	*Slavery and Freedom 2*
Socr.	*De Socrate (Or. 54)*	*Socrates*
1 Tars.	*Tarsica prior (Or. 33)*	*First Tarsic Discourse*
2 Tars.	*Tarsica altera (Or. 34)*	*Second Tarsic Discourse*
Troj.	*Trojana (Or. 11)*	*Trojan Discourse*
Tumult.	*De tumultu (Or. 46)*	*Protest against Mistreatment*
Tyr.	*De tyrannide (Or. 6)*	*On Tyranny, or Diogenes*
Ven.	*Venator (Or. 7)*	*The Hunter*
Virt. (Or. 8)	*De virtute (Or. 8)*	*Virtue*
Virt. (Or. 69)	*De virtute (Or. 69)*	*Virtue*

Dio of Prusa

Dis.	*Discourse*

Diodorus Siculus

Bib. Hist.	*Biblioteca Historica*

Diogenes Laertius

Vit. Phil.	*Vitae philosophorum*	*Lives of the Philosophers*

Dionysius of Halicarnassus

1–2 Amm.	*Epistula ad Ammaeum i–ii*	
Ant. or.	*De antiquis oratoribus*	
Ant. rom.	*Antiquitates romanae*	
Comp.	*De compositione verborum*	
Dem.	*De Demosthene*	
Din.	*De Dinarcho*	
Is.	*De Isaeo*	
Isocr.	*De Isocrate*	
Lys.	*De Lysia*	
Pomp.	*Epistula ad Pompeium Geminum*	
[Rhet.]	*Ars rhetorica*	
Thuc.	*De Thucydide*	
Thuc. id.	*De Thucydidis idiomatibus*	

Dioscorides Pedanius

[Alex.]	*Alexipharmaca*	
Mat. med.	*De materia medica*	

Epictetus

Diatr.	*Diatribai (Dissertationes)*	
Ench.	*Enchiridion*	
Gnom.	*Gnomologium*	

Epiphanius

Pan.	*Panarion (Adversus haereses)*	*Refutation of All Heresies*

Euripides

Alc.	*Alcestis*	
Andr.	*Andromache*	
Bacch.	*Bacchae*	*Bacchanals*
Cycl.	*Cyclops*	
Dict.	*Dictys*	
El.	*Electra*	
Hec.	*Hecuba*	
Hel.	*Helena*	*Helen*
Heracl.	*Heraclidae*	*Children of Hercules*
Herc. fur.	*Hercules furens*	*Madness of Hercules*
Hipp.	*Hippolytus*	
Hyps.	*Hypsipyle*	
Iph. aul.	*Iphigenia aulidensis*	*Iphigenia at Aulis*
Iph. taur.	*Iphigenia taurica*	*Iphigenia at Tauris*
Med.	*Medea*	*Medea*

Orest.	*Orestes*	*Phoenician Maidens*
Phoen.	*Phoenissae*	
Rhes.	*Rhesus*	
Suppl.	*Supplices*	
Tro.	*Troades*	*Daughters of Troy*

EUSEBIUS

Chron.	*Chronicon*	*Chronicle*
Coet. sanct.	*Ad coetum sanctorum*	*To the Assembly of Saints*
Comm. Isa.	*Commentarius in Isaiam*	*Commentary on Isaiah*
Comm. Ps.	*Commentarius in Psalmos*	*Commentary on Psalms*
Dem. ev.	*Demonstratio evangelica*	*Demonstration of the Gospel*
Eccl. theol.	*De ecclesiastica theologia*	*Ecclesiastical Theology*
Ecl. proph.	*Eclogae propheticae*	*Extracts from the Prophets*
Hier.	*Contra Hieroclem*	*Against Hierocles*
Hist. eccl.	*Historia ecclesiastica*	*Church History*
Laud. Const.	*De laudibus Constantini*	*Praise of Constantine*
Marc.	*Contra Marcellum*	*Against Marcellus*
Mart. Pal.	*De martyribus Palaestinae*	*The Martyrs of Palestine*
Onom.	*Onomasticon*	*List of Names*
Praep. ev.	*Praeparatio evangelica*	*Preparations for the Gospel*
Theoph.	*Theophania*	*Divine Manifestation*
Vit. Const.	*Vita Constantini*	*Life of Constantine*

FIRMICUS MATERNUS

Err. prof. rel.	*De errore profanarum religionum*
Math.	*Mathesis*

FLORUS

Epit.	*Epitome of Roman History*

GAIUS

Inst.	*Institutiones*

GALEN

Simp. Med.	*De simplicium medicamentorum temperamentis ac facultatibus*

GORGIAS

Hel.	*Helena*
Pal.	*Palamedes*

GREGORY OF NAZIANZUS

Ep.	*Epistulae*
Or. Bas.	*Oratio in laudem Basilii*

GREGORY OF NYSSA

Deit.	*De deitate Filii et Spiritus Sancti*

Gregory the Great

Moral.	*Expositio in Librum Job, sive Moralium libri xxv*	*Moralia*

Heliodorus

Aeth.	*Aethiopica*	

Heraclitus

All.	*Allegoriae (Quaestiones homericae)*	

Herodotus

Hist.	*Historiae*	*Histories*

Hesiod

Op.	*Opera et dies*	*Works and Days*
[Scut.]	*Scutum*	*Shield*
Theog.	*Theogonia*	*Theogony*

Hieronymus (See Jerome)

Hippocrates

Acut.	*De ratione victus in morbis acutis*	*Regimen in Acute Diseases*
Aff.	*De affectionibus*	*Affections*
Alim.	*De alimento*	*Nutriment*
Aph.	*Aphorismata*	*Aphorisms*
Arte	*De arte*	*The Art*
Artic.	*De articulis reponendis*	*Joints*
Carn.	*De carne*	*Fleshes*
Coac.	*Praenotiones coacae*	
Decent.	*De habitu decenti*	*Decorum*
Dent.	*De dentitione*	*Dentition*
Epid.	*Epidemiae*	*Epidemics*
Fist.	*Fistulae*	*Fistulas*
Fract.	*De fracturis*	*Fractures*
Genit.	*Genitalia*	*Genitals*
Int.	*De affectionibus internis*	*Internal Affections*
Jusj.	*Jus jurandum*	*The Oath*
Lex	*Lex*	*Law*
Liq.	*De liquidorum usu*	*Use of Liquids*
Loc. hom.	*De locis in homine*	*Places in Man*
Med.	*De medico*	*The Physician*
Mochl.	*Mochlichon*	*Instruments of Reduction*
Morb.	*De morbis*	*Diseases*
Morb. sacr.	*De morbo sacro*	*The Sacred Disease*
Mul.	*De morbis mulierum*	*Female Diseases*
Nat. hom.	*De natura hominis*	*Nature of Man*
Nat. mul.	*De natura muliebri*	*Nature of Woman*

Nat. puer.	*De natura pueri*	*Nature of the Chile*
Oct.	*De octimestri partu*	
Off.	*De officina medici*	*In the Surgery*
Praec.	*Praeceptiones*	*Precepts*
Progn.	*Prognostica*	*Prognostic*
Prorrh.	*Prorrhetica*	*Prorrhetic*
Septim.	*De septimestri partu*	
Steril.	*De sterilitate*	*Sterility*
Vet. med.	*De vetere medicina*	*Ancient Medicine*
Vict.	*De victu*	*Regimen*
Vict. salubr.	*De ratione victus salubris*	*Regimen in Health*

HIPPOLYTUS

Antichr.	*De antichristo*	
Ben. Is. Jac.	*De benedictionibus Isaaci et Jacobi*	
Can. pasch.	*Canon paschalis*	
In Cant.	*In Canticum canticorum*	
Cant. Mos.	*In canticum Mosis*	
Chron.	*Chronicon*	
Comm. Dan.	*Commentarium in Danielem*	
Fr. Prov.	*Fragmenta in Proverbia*	
Fr. Ps.	*Fragmenta in Psalmos*	
Haer.	*Refutatio omnium haeresium (Philosophoumena)*	*Refutation of All Heresies*
Helc. Ann.	*In Helcanam et Annam*	
Noet.	*Contra haeresin Noeti*	
Trad. ap.	*Traditio apostolica*	*The Apostolic Tradition*
Univ.	*De universo*	

HOMER

Il.	*Ilias*	*Iliad*
Od.	*Odyssea*	*Odyssey*

HORACE

Ars	*Ars poetica*	
Carm.	*Carmina*	*Odes*
Ep.	*Epistulae*	*Epistles*
Epod.	*Epodi*	*Epodes*
Saec.	*Carmen saeculare*	
Sat.	*Satirae*	*Satires*

IAMBLICHUS

Vit. Pyth.	*Vita Pythagorae*

INSCRIP. LAT. SEL.

Inscriptiones Latinae Selectae (H. Dessau, ed.)

IRENAEUS

Epid.	*Epideixis tou apostolikou kerygmatos*	*Demonstration of the Apostolic Preaching*
Haer.	*Adversus haereses*	*Against Heresies*

Isocrates

Aeginet.	*Aegineticus (Or. 19)*	
Antid.	*Antidosis (Or. 15)*	
Archid.	*Archidamus (Or. 6)*	
Areop.	*Areopagiticus (Or. 7)*	
Big.	*De bigis (Or. 16)*	*On the Team of Horses*
Bus.	*Busiris (Or. 11)*	
Callim.	*In Callimachum (Or. 18)*	*Agaiinst Callimachus*
De pace	*De pace (Or. 8)*	
Demon.	*Ad Demonicum (Or. 1)*	
Ep.	*Epistulae*	
Euth.	*In Euthynum (Or. 21)*	
Evag.	*Evagoras (Or. 9)*	
Hel. enc.	*Helenae encomium (Or. 10)*	
Loch.	*In Lochitum (Or. 20)*	
Nic.	*Nicocles (Or. 3)*	
Ad Nic.	*Ad Nicoclem (Or. 2)*	
Panath.	*Panathenaicus (Or. 12)*	
Paneg.	*Panegyricus (Or. 4)*	
Phil.	*Philippus (Or. 5)*	
Plat.	*Plataicus (Or. 14)*	
Soph.	*In sophistas (Or. 13)*	
Trapez.	*Trapeziticus (Or. 17)*	*On the Banker*

Jerome

Chron.	*Chronicon Eusebii a Graeco Latine redditum et continuatum*
Comm. Abd.	*Commentariorum in Abdiam liber*
Comm. Agg.	*Commentariorum in Aggaeum liber*
Comm. Am.	*Commentariorum in Amos libri III*
Comm. Eccl.	*Commentarii in Ecclesiasten*
Comm. Eph.	*Commentariorum in Epistulam ad Ephesios libri III*
Comm. Ezech.	*Commentariorum in Ezechielem libri XVI*
Comm. Gal.	*Commentariorum in Epistulam ad Galatas libri III*
Comm. Habac.	*Commentariorum in Habacuc libri II*
Comm. Isa.	*Commentariorum in Isaiam libri XVIII*
Comm. Jer.	*Commentariorum in Jeremiam libri VI*
Comm. Joel.	*Commentariorum in Joelem liber*
Comm. Jon.	*Commentariorum in Jonam liber*
Comm. Mal.	*Commentariorum in Malachiam liber*
Comm. Matt.	*Commentariorum in Matthaeum libri IV*
Comm. Mich.	*Commentariorum in Michaeum libri II*
Comm. Nah.	*Commentariorum in Nahum liber*
Comm. Os.	*Commentariorum in Osee libri III*
Comm. Phlm.	*Commentariorum in Epistulam ad Philemonem liber*
Comm. Ps.	*Commentarioli in Psalmos*
Comm. Soph.	*Commentariorum in Sophoniam libri III*
Comm. Tit.	*Commentariorum in Epistulam ad Titum liber*
Comm. Zach.	*Commentariorum in Zachariam libri III*
Did. Spir.	*Liber Didymi de Spiritu Sancto*
Epist.	*Epistulae*
Expl. Dan.	*Explanatio in Danielem*
Helv.	*Adversus Helvidium de Mariae virginitate perpetua*

Hom. Matth.	*Homilia in Evangelium secundum Matthaeum*
Interp. Job	*Libri Job versio, textus hexaplorum*
Jo. Hier.	*Adversus Joannem Hierosolymitanum liber*
Jov.	*Adversus Jovinianum libri II*
Lucif.	*Altercatio Luciferiani et orthodoxi seu dialogus contra Luciferianos*
Mon. Pachom.	*Monitorum Pachomii versio latina*
Monogr.	*Tractatus de monogrammate*
Nom. hebr.	*De nominibus hebraicis (Liber nominum)*
Orig. Hom. Cant.	*Homiliae II Origenis in Canticum canticorum Latine redditae*
Orig. Hom. Luc.	*In Lucam homiliae XXXIX ex Graeco Origenis Latine conversae*
Orig. Jer. Ezech.	*Homiliae XXVIII in Jeremiam et Ezechielem Graeco Origenis Latine redditae*
Orig. Princ.	*De principiis*
Pelag.	*Adversus Pelagianos dialogi III*
Psalt. Hebr.	*Psalterium secundum Hebraeos*
Qu. hebr. Gen.	*Quaestionum hebraicarum liber in Genesim*
Reg. Pachom.	*Regula S. Pachomii, e Graeco*
Ruf.	*Adversus Rufinum libri III*
Sit.	*De situ et nominibus locorum Hebraicorum (Liber locorum)*
Tract. Isa.	*Tractatus in Isaiam*
Tract. Marc.	*Tractatus in Evangelium Marci*
Tract. Ps.	*Tractatus in Psalmos*
Tract. var.	*Tractatus varii*
Vigil.	*Adversus Vigilantium*
Vir. ill.	*De viris illustribus*
Vit. Hil.	*Vita S. Hilarionis eremitae*
Vit. Malch.	*Vita Malchi monachi*
Vit. Paul.	*Vita S. Pauli, primi eremitae*

John Chrysostom

Adfu.	*Adversus eos qui non adfuerant*	
Aeg.	*In martyres Aegyptios*	
Anna	*De Anna*	
Anom.	*Contra Anomoeos*	
Ant. exsil.	*Sermo antequam iret in exsilium*	
Ascens.	*In ascensionem domini nostri Jesu Christi*	
Bab.	*De sancto hieromartyre*	*Babyla Babylas the Martyr*
Bab. Jul.	*De Babyla contra Julianum et gentiles*	
Bapt.	*De baptismo Christi*	
Barl.	*In sanctum Barlaam martyrem*	
Bern.	*De sanctis Bernice et Prosdoce*	
Catech. illum.	*Catecheses ad illuminandos*	
Catech. jur.	*Catechesis de juramento*	
Catech. ult.	*Catechesis ultima ad baptizandos*	
Cath.	*Adversus Catharos*	
Coemet.	*De coemeterio et de cruce*	
Comm. Isa.	*Commentarius in Isaiam*	
Comm. Job	*Commentarius in Job*	
Comp. reg. mon.	*Comparatio regis et monachi*	
Compunct. Dem.	*Ad Demetrium de compunctione*	
Compunct. Stel.	*Ad Stelechium de compunctione*	
Cruc.	*De cruce et latrone homiliae II*	
Cum exsil.	*Sermo cum iret in exsilium*	

Dav.	*De Davide et Saule*
Delic.	*De futurae vitae deliciis*
Diab.	*De diabolo tentatore*
Diod.	*Laus Diodori episcopi*
Dros.	*De sancta Droside martyre*
Educ. lib.	*De educandis liberis*
El. vid.	*In Eliam et viduam*
Eleaz. puer.	*De Eleazaro et septem pueris*
Eleem.	*De eleemosyna*
Ep. carc.	*Epistula ad episcopos, presbyteros et diaconos in carcere*
Ep. Cyr.	*Epistula ad Cyriacum*
1 Ep. Innoc.	*Ad Innocentium papam epistula I*
2 Ep. Innoc.	*Ad Innocentium papam epistula II*
Ep. Olymp.	*Epistulae ad Olympiadem*
Ep. Theod.	*Letter to Theodore*
Eust.	*In sanctum Eustathium Antiochenum*
Eutrop.	*In Eutropium*
Exp. Ps.	*Expositiones in Psalmos*
Fat. prov.	*De fato et providentia*
Fem. reg.	*Quod regulares feminae viris cohabitare non debeant*
Fr. Ep. Cath.	*Fragmenta in Epistulas Catholicas*
Freq. conv.	*Quod frequenter conveniendum sit*
Goth. concin.	*Homilia habita postquam presbyter Gothus concionatus fuerat*
Grat.	*Non esse ad gratiam concionandum*
Hom. Act.	*Homiliae in Acta apostolorum*
Hom. Act. 9:1	*De mutatione nominum*
Hom. Col.	*Homiliae in epistulam ad Colossenses*
Hom. 1 Cor.	*Homiliae in epistulam i ad Corinthios*
Hom. 1 Cor. 7:2	*In illud: Propter fornicationes autem unusquisque suam uxorem habeat*
Hom. 1 Cor. 10:1	*In dictum Pauli: Nolo vos ignorare*
Hom. 1 Cor. 11:19	*In dictum Pauli: Oportet haereses esse*
Hom. 2 Cor.	*Homiliae in epistulam ii ad Corinthios*
Hom. 2 Cor. 4:13	*In illud: Habentes eundem spiritum*
Hom. 2 Cor. 11:1	*In illud: Utinam sustineretis modicum*
Hom. Eph.	*Homiliae in epistulam ad Ephesios*
Hom. Gal.	*Homiliae in epistulam ad Galatas commentarius*
Hom. Gal. 2:11	*In illud: In faciem ei restiti*
Hom. Gen.	*Homiliae in Genesim*
Hom. Heb.	*Homiliae in epistulam ad Hebraeos*
Hom. Isa. 6:1	*In illud: Vidi Dominum*
Hom. Isa. 45:7	*In illud Isaiae: Ego Dominus Deus feci lumen*
Hom. Jer. 10:23	*In illud: Domine, non est in homine*
Hom. Jo.	*Homiliae in Joannem*
Hom. Jo. 5:17	*In illud: Pater meus usque modo operatur*
Hom. Jo. 5:19	*In illud: Filius ex se nihil facit*
Hom. Matt.	*Homiliae in Matthaeum*
Hom. Matt. 9:37	*In illud: Messis quidem multa*
Hom. Matt. 18:23	*De decem millium talentorum debitore*
Hom. Matt. 26:39	*In illud: Pater, si possibile est, transeat*
Hom. Phil.	*Homiliae in epistulam ad Philippenses*
Hom. Phlm.	*Homiliae in epistulam ad Philemonem*
Hom. princ. Act.	*In principium Actorum*
Hom. Ps. 48:17	*In illud: Ne timueris cum dives factus fuerit homo*
Hom. Rom.	*Homiliae in epistulam ad Romanos*

Hom. Rom. 5:3	*De gloria in tribulationibus*	
Hom. Rom. 8:28	*In illud: Diligentibus deum omnia cooperantur in bonum*	
Hom. Rom. 12:20	*In illud: Si esurierit inimicus*	
Hom. Rom. 16:3	*In illud: Salutate Priscillam et Aquilam*	
Hom 1 Thess.	*Homiliae in epistulam i ad Thessalonicenses*	
Hom. 2 Thess.	*Homiliae in epistulam ii ad Thessalonicenses*	
Hom. 1 Tim.	*Homiliae in epistulam i ad Timotheum*	
Hom. 1 Tim. 5:9	*In illud: Vidua eligatur*	
Hom. 2 Tim.	*Homiliae in epistulam ii ad Timotheum*	
Hom. 2 Tim. 3:1	*In illud: Hoc scitote quod in novissimis diebus*	
Hom. Tit.	*Homiliae in epistulam ad Titum*	
Hom. Tit. 2:11	*In illud: Apparuit gratia dei omnibus hominibus*	
Ign.	*In sanctum Ignatium martyrem*	
Inan. glor.	*De inani gloria*	
Iter. conj.	*De non iterando conjugio*	
Adv. Jud.	*Adversus Judaeos*	*Discourses against Judaizing Christians*
Jud. gent.	*Contra Judaeos et gentiles quod Christus sit deus*	
Jul.	*In sanctum Julianum martyrem*	
Juv.	*In Juventinum et Maximum martyres*	
Kal.	*In Kalendas*	
Laed.	*Quod nemo laeditur nisi a se ipso*	*No One Can Harm the Man Who Does Not Injure Himself*
Laud. Max.	*Quales ducendae sint uxores (=De laude Maximi)*	
Laud. Paul.	*De laudibus sancti Pauli apostoli*	
Laz.	*De Lazaro*	
Lib. repud.	*De libello repudii*	
Liturg.	*Liturgia*	
Lucian.	*In sanctum Lucianum martyrem*	
Macc.	*De Maccabeis*	
Mart.	*De sanctis martyribus; Homilia in martyres*	
Melet.	*De sancto Meletio Antiocheno*	
Natal.	*In diem natalem Christi*	
Non desp.	*Non esse desperandum*	
Oppugn.	*Adversus oppugnatores vitae monasticae*	
Ordin.	*Sermo cum presbyter fuit ordinatus*	
Paenit.	*De paenitentia*	
Paralyt.	*In paralyticum demissum per tectum*	
Pasch.	*In sanctum pascha*	
Pecc.	*Peccata fratrum non evulganda*	*Against Publicly Exposing the Sins of the Brethren*
Pelag.	*De sancta Pelagia virgine et martyre*	
Pent.	*De sancta pentecoste*	
Phoc.	*De sancto hieromartyre Phoca*	
Praes. imp.	*Homilia dicta praesente imperatore*	
Prod. Jud.	*De proditione Judae*	
Prof. evang.	*De profectu evangelii*	*Lowliness of Mind*
Proph. obscurit.	*De prophetarum obscuritate*	
Quatr. Laz.	*In quatriduanum Lazarum*	
1 Redit.	*Post reditum a priore exsilio sermo I*	
2 Redit.	*Post reditum a priore exsilio sermo II*	
Regr.	*De regressu*	

Reliq. mart.	*Homilia dicta postquam reliquiae martyrum*	
Res. Chr.	*Adversus ebriosos et de resurrectione domini nostri JesuChristi*	
Res. mort.	*De resurrectione mortuorum*	
Rom. mart.	*In sanctum Romanum martyrem*	
Sac.	*De sacerdotio*	*Priesthood*
Sanct. Anast.	*Homilia dicta in templo sanctae Anastasiae*	
Saturn.	*Cum Saturninus et Aurelianus acti essent in exsilium*	
Scand.	*Ad eos qui scandalizati sunt*	
Serm. Gen.	*Sermones in Genesim*	
Stag.	*Ad Stagirium a daemone vexatum*	
Stat.	*Ad populum Antiochenum de statuis*	
Stud. praes.	*De studio praesentium*	
Subintr.	*Contra eos qui subintroductas habent virgines*	
Terr. mot.	*De terrae motu*	
Theatr.	*Contra ludos et theatra*	
Theod. laps.	*Ad Theodorum lapsum*	*Exhortation to Theodore after His Fall*
Vid.	*Ad viduam juniorem*	*To the Young Widow*
Virginit.	*De virginitate*	

John Malalas

Chron.	*Chronographia*	

John Philoponus

Comm. De an.	*In Aristotelis De anima libros commentaria*	

Josephus (See p. 875)

Justin

1 Apol.	*Apologia i*	*First Apology*
2 Apol.	*Apologia ii*	*Second Apology*
Dial.	*Dialogus cum Tryphone*	*Dialogue with Trypho*

Justinian

Edict.	*Edicta*	
Nov.	*Novellae*	

Juvenal

Sat.	*Satirae*	*Satires*

Lactantius

Epit.	*Epitome divinarum institutionum*	*Epitome of the Divine Institutes*
Inst.	*Divinarum institutionum libri VII*	*The Divine Institutes*

Ir.	*De ira Dei*	*The Wrath of God*
Mort.	*De morte persecutorum*	*The Deaths of the Persecutors*
Opif.	*De opificio Dei*	*The Workmanship of God*

LIVY

Hist.	*The History of Rome*	

LONGINUS

[Subl.]	*De sublimitate*	*On the Sublime*

LONGUS

Daphn.	*Daphnis et Chloe*	*Daphnis and Chloe*

LUCIAN

Abdic.	*Abdicatus Disowned*	*Disowned*
Alex.	*Alexander (Pseudomantis)*	*Alexander the False Prophet*
[Am.]	*Amores*	*Affairs of the Heart*
Anach.	*Anacharsis*	
[Asin.]	*Asinus (Lucius)*	*Lucius, or The Ass*
Astr.	*Astrologia*	*Astrology*
Bis acc.	*Bis accusatus*	*The Double Indictment*
Cal.	*Calumniae non temere credendum*	*Slander*
Cat.	*Cataplus*	*The Downward Journey, or The Tyrant*
Char.	*Charon*	
Demon.	*Demonax*	
Deor. conc.	*Deorm concilium*	*Parliament of the Gods*
Dial. d.	*Dialogi deorum*	*Dialogues of the Gods*
Dial. meretr.	*Dialogi meretricii*	*Dialogues of the Courtesans*
Dial. mort.	*Diologi mortuorum*	*Dialogues of the Dead*
Dom.	*De domo*	*The Hall*
Electr.	*De electro*	*Amber, or The Swans*
[Encom. Demosth.]	*Demosthenous encomium*	*Praise of Demosthenes*
Eunuch.	*Eunuchus*	*The Eunuch*
Fug.	*Fugitivi*	*The Runaways*
Gall.	*Gallus*	*The Dream, or The Cock*
Hermot.	*Hermotimus (De sectis)*	*Hermotimus, or Sects*
Icar.	*Icaromenippus*	
Imag.	*Imagines*	*Essays in Portraiture*
Pro imag.	*Pro imaginibus*	*Essays in Portraiture Defended*
Ind.	*Adversus indoctum*	*The Ignorant Book-Collector*
Jud. voc.	*Judicium vocalium*	*The Consonants at Law*
Jupp. conf.	*Juppiter confutatus*	*Zeus Catechized*
Jupp. trag.	*Juppiter tragoedus*	*Zeus Rants*
Laps.	*Pro lapsu inter salutandum*	*A Slip of the Tongue in Greeting*
Lex.	*Lexiphanes*	
Luct.	*De luctu*	*Funerals*
Men.	*Menippus (Necyomantia)*	*Menippus, or Descent into Hades*
Merc. cond.	*De mercede conductis*	*Salaried Posts in Great Houses*

Musc. laud.	*Muscae laudatio*	*The Fly*
Nav.	*Navigium*	*The Ship, or The Wishes*
Nigr.	*Nigrinus*	
Par.	*De parasito*	*The Parasite*
Peregr.	*De morte Peregrini*	*The Passing of Peregrinus*
Phal.	*Phalaris*	
[Philopatr.]	*Philopatris*	*The Patriot*
Philops.	*Philopseudes*	*The Lover of Lies*
Pisc.	*Piscator*	*The Dead Come to Life, or The Fisherman*
Pseudol.	*Pseudologista*	*The Mistaken Critic*
Rhet. praec.	*Rhetorum praeceptor*	*A Professor of Public Speaking*
Sacr.	*De sacrificiis*	*Sacrifices*
Salt.	*De saltatione*	*The Dance*
Sat.		*Saturnalia Conversation with Cronius*
Scyth.	*Scytha*	*The Scythian, or The Consul*
Somn.	*Somnium (Vita Luciani)*	*The Dream, or Lucians Career*
Symp.	*Symposium*	*The Carousal*
Lapiths		
Syr. d.	*De syria dea*	*The Goddess of Syria*
Tim.	*Timon*	
Tox.	*Toxaris*	
Tyr.	*Tyrannicida*	*The Tyrannicide*
Ver. hist.	*Vera historia*	*A True Story*
Vit. auct.	*Vitarum auctio*	*Philosophies for Sale*

Martial

Epi.	*Epigramma*

Menander

Dysk.	*Dyskolos*
Epitr.	*Epitrepontes*
Georg.	*Georgos*
Mis.	*Misoumenos*
Mon.	*Monostichoi*
Perik.	*Perikeiromenē*
Phasm.	*Phasma*
Sam.	*Samia*
Sik.	*Sikyonios*
Thras.	*Thrasonidis*

Methodius of Olympus

Lib. arb.	*De libero arbitrio*
Res.	*De resurrectione*
Symp.	*Symposium (Convivium decem virginum)*

Minucius Felix

Oct.	*Octavius*

Nepos

Ag.	*Agesilaus*
Alc.	*Alciabiades*
Arist.	*Aristides*
Att.	*Atticus*
Cat.	*Cato*
Chabr.	*Chabrias*
Cim.	*Cimon*
Con.	*Conon*
Dat.	*Datames*
Di.	*Dion*
Epam.	*Epaminondas*
Eum.	*Eumenes*
Ham.	*Hamilcar*
Han.	*Hannibal*
Iph.	*Iphicrates*
Lys.	*Lysander*
Milt.	*Miltiades*
Paus.	*Pausanias*
Pel.	*Pelopidas*
Phoc.	*Phocion*
Reg.	*De regibus*
Them.	*Themistocles*
Thras.	*Thrasybulus*
Timol.	*Timoleon*
Timoth.	*Timotheus*

Nicander

Alex.	*Alexipharmaca*
Ther.	*Theriaca*

Nicolaus of Damascus

Hist. univ.	*Historia universalis*	*Universal History (in Athanaeus)*
Vit. Caes.	*Vita Caesaris*	

Nonnus

Dion.	*Dionysiaca*
Paraphr. Jo.	*Paraphrasis sancti evangelii Joannei*

Orac. chald.	*De oraculis chaldaicis*	*Chaldean Oracles*

Origen

Adnot. Deut.	*Adnotationes in Deuteronomium*
Adnot. Exod.	*Adnotationes in Exodum*
Adnot. Gen.	*Adnotationes in Genesim*
Adnot. Jes. Nav.	*Adnotationes in Jesum filium Nave*

Adnot. Judic.	*Adnotationes in Judices*	
Adnot. Lev.	*Adnotationes in Leviticum*	
Adnot. Num.	*Adnotationes in Numeros*	
Cant. (Adulesc.)	*In Canticum canticorum (libri duo quos scripsit in adulescentia)*	
Cels.	*Contra Celsum*	*Against Celsus*
Comm. Cant.	*Commentarius in Canticum*	
Comm. Gen.	*Commentarii in Genesim*	
Comm. Jo.	*Commentarii in evangelium Joannis*	
Comm. Matt.	*Commentarium in evangelium Matthaei*	
Comm. Rom.	*Commentarii in Romanos*	
Comm. ser. Matt.	*Commentarium series in evangelium Matthaei*	
Dial.	*Diologus cum Heraclide*	*Dialogue with Heraclides*
Enarrat. Job	*Enarrationes in Job*	
Engastr.	*De engastrimytho*	*Witch of Endor*
Ep. Afr.	*Epistula ad Africanum*	
Ep. Greg.	*Epistula ad Gregorium Thaumaturgum*	
Ep. ign.	*Epistula ad ignotum (Fabianum Romanum)*	
Exc. Ps.	*Excerpta in Psalmos*	
Exp. Prov.	*Expositio in Proverbia*	
Fr. Act.	*Fragmentum ex homiliis in Acta apostolorum*	
Fr. Cant.	*Libri x in Canticum canticorum*	
Fr. 1 Cor.	*Fragmenta ex commentariis in epistulam i ad Corinthios*	
Fr. Eph.	*Fragmenta ex commentariis in epistulam ad Ephesios*	
Fr. Exod.	*Fragmenta ex commentariis in Exodum*	
Fr. Ezech.	*Fragmenta ex commentariis in Ezechielem*	
Fr. Heb.	*Fragmenta ex homiliis in epistulam ad Hebraeos*	
Fr. Jer.	*Fragmenta in Jeremiam*	
Fr. Jo.	*Fragmenta in evangelium Joannis*	
Fr. Lam.	*Fragmenta in Lamentationes*	
Fr. Luc.	*Fragmenta in Lucam*	
Fr. Matt.	*Fragmenta ex commentariis in evangelium Matthaei*	
Fr. Os.	*Fragmentum ex commentariis in Osee*	
Fr. Prin.	*Fragmenta de principiis*	
Fr. Prov.	*Fragmenta ex commentariis in Proverbia*	
Fr. Ps.	*Fragmenta in Psalmos 1–150*	
Fr. 1 Reg.	*Fragmenta in librum primum Regnorum*	
Fr. Ruth	*Fragmentum in Ruth*	
Hex.	*Hexapla*	
Hom. Cant.	*Homiliae in Canticum*	
Hom. Exod.	*Homiliae in Exodum*	
Hom. Ezech.	*Homiliae in Ezechielem*	
Hom. Gen.	*Homiliae in Genesim*	
Hom. Isa.	*Homiliae in Isaiam*	
Hom. Jer.	*Homiliae in Jeremiam*	
Hom. Jes. Nav.	*In Jesu Nave homiliae xxvi*	
Hom. Job	*Homiliae in Job*	
Hom. Judic.	*Homiliae in Judices*	
Hom. Lev.	*Homiliae in Leviticum*	
Hom. Luc.	*Homiliae in Lucam*	
Hom. Num.	*Homiliae in Numeros*	
Hom. Ps.	*Homiliae in Psalmos*	
Hom. 1 Reg.	*Homiliae in I Reges*	

Mart.	*Exhortatio ad martyrium*	*Exhortation to Martyrdom*
Or.	*De oratione (Peri proseuchēs)*	*Prayer*
Pasch.	*De pascha*	*The Pascha*
Philoc.	*Philocalia*	
Princ.	*De principiis (Peri archōn)*	*First Principles*
Res.	*De resurrectione libri ii*	
Schol. Apoc.	*Scholia in Apocalypsem*	
Schol. Cant.	*Scholia in Canticum canticorum*	
Schol. Luc.	*Scholia in Lucam*	
Schol. Matt.	*Scholia in Matthaeum*	
Sel. Deut.	*Selecta in Deuteronomium*	
Sel. Exod.	*Selecta in Exodum*	
Sel. Ezech.	*Selecta in Ezechielem*	
Sel. Gen.	*Selecta in Genesim*	
Sel. Jes. Nav.	*Selecta in Jesum Nave*	
Sel. Job	*Selecta in Job*	
Sel. Judic.	*Selecta in Judices*	
Sel. Lev.	*Selecta in Leviticum*	
Sel. Num.	*Selecta in Numeros*	
Sel. Ps.	*Selecta in Psalmos*	

OROSIUS

Hist.	*Historiarum Adversum Paganos Libri VII* ("Seven Books of History Against the Pagans")

OVID

Am.	*Amores*
Ars	*Ars amatoria*
Fast.	*Fasti*
Hal.	*Halieutica*
Her.	*Heroides*
Ib.	*Ibis*
Med.	*Medicamina faciei femineae*
Metam.	*Metamorphoses*

PAUSANIAS

Descr.	*Graeciae description*	*Description of Greece*

PERIPL. M. RUBR.

Periplus Maris Rubri — The Periplus of the Erythraean Sea

PERSIUS

Sat.	*Satirae*

PHILO OF ALEXANDRIA (See pp. 874–75)

PHILODEMUS OF GADARA

Adv. Soph.	*Adversus sophistas*
D.	*De Diis*
Hom.	*De bono rege secundum Homerum*
Ir.	*De ira*

Lib.	*De libertate dicendi*	
Mort.	*De morte*	
Mus.	*De musica*	
Piet.	*De pietate*	
Rhet.	*Volumina rhetorica*	
Sign.	*De signis*	
Vit.	*De vitiis X*	

PHILOSTRATUS

Ep.	*Epistulae*	
Gymn.	*De gymnastica*	
Imag.	*Imagines*	
Vit. Apoll.	*Vita Apollonii*	
Vit. soph.	*Vitae sophistarum*	

PHOTIUS

Lex.	*Lexicon*	

PINDAR

Isthm.	*Isthmionikai*	*Isthmian Odes*
Nem.	*Nemeonikai*	*Nemean Odes*
Ol.	*Olympionikai*	*Olympian Odes*
Paean.	*Paeanes*	*Hymns*
Pyth.	*Pythionikai*	*Pythian Odes*
Thren.	*Threnoi*	*Dirges*

PLATO

[Alc. maj.]	*Alcibiades major*	*Greater Alcibiades*
Apol.	*Apologia*	*Apology of Socrates*
[Ax.]	*Axiochus*	
Charm.	*Charmides*	
Crat.	*Cratylus*	
[Def.]	*Definitiones*	*Definitions*
Ep.	*Epistulae*	*Letters*
[Epin.]	*Epinomis*	
Euthyd.	*Euthydemus*	
Euthyphr.	*Euthyphro*	
Gorg.	*Gorgias*	
Hipparch.	*Hipparchus*	
Hipp. maj.	*Hippias major*	*Greater Hippias*
Hipp. min.	*Hippias minor*	*Lesser Hippias*
Lach.	*Laches*	
Leg.	*Leges*	*Laws*
Menex.	*Menexenus*	
[Min.]	*Minos*	
Parm.	*Parmenides*	
Phaed.	*Phaedo*	
Phaedr.	*Phaedrus*	
Phileb.	*Philebus*	
Pol.	*Politicus*	*Statesman*
Prot.	*Protagoras*	

Resp.	*Respublica*	*Republic*
Soph.	*Sophista*	*Sophist*
Symp.	*Symposium*	
Theaet.	*Theaetetus*	
Tim.	*Timaeus*	

Plautus

Amph.	*Amphitruo*
Asin.	*Asinaria*
Aul.	*Aulularia*
Bacch.	*Bacchides*
Capt.	*Captivi*
Cas.	*Casina*
Cist.	*Cistellaria*
Curc.	*Curculio*
Epid.	*Epidicus*
Men.	*Menaechmi*
Mil. glor.	*Miles gloriosus*
Most.	*Mostellaria*
Pers.	*Persae*
Poen.	*Poenulus*
Pseud.	*Pseudolus*
Rud.	*Rudens*
Stic.	*Sticus*
Trin.	*Trinummus*
Truc.	*Truculentus*
Vid.	*Vidularia*

Pliny the Elder

Nat.	*Naturalis historia*	*Natural History*

Pliny the Younger

Ep.	*Epistulae*
Ep. Tra.	*Epistulae ad Trajanum*
Pan.	*Panegyricus*

Plotinus

Enn.	*Enneades*

Plutarch

Adol. poet. aud.	*Quomodo adolescens poetas audire debeat*
Adul. am.	*De adulatore et amico*
Adul. amic.	*Quomodo adulator ab amico internoscatur*
Aem.	*Aemilius Paullus*
Ag. Cleom.	*Agis et Cleomenes*
Ages.	*Agesilaus*
Alc.	*Alcibiades*

Alex.	*Alexander*	
Alex. fort.	*De Alexandri magni fortuna aut virtute*	
Am. prol.	*De amore prolis*	
Amat.	*Amatorius*	
[Amat. narr.]	*Amatoriae narrationes*	
Amic. mult.	*De amicorum multitudine*	
An. corp.	*Animine an corporis affectiones sint peiores*	
[An ignis]	*Aquane an ignis utilior*	
An. procr.	*De animae procreatione in Timaeo*	
An. procr. epit.	*Epitome libri de procreatione in Timaeo*	
An seni	*An seni respublica gerenda sit*	
An virt. doc.	*An virtus doceri possit*	
An vit.	*An vitiositas ad infelicitatem sufficiat*	
Ant.	*Antonius*	
[Apoph. lac.]	*Apophthegmata laconica*	
Arat.	*Aratus*	
Arist.	*Aristides*	
Art.	*Artaxerxes*	
Brut.	*Brutus*	
Brut. an.	*Bruta animalia ratione uti*	
Caes.	*Caesar*	
Cam.	*Camillus*	
Cat. Maj.	*Cato Major*	*Cato the Elder*
Cat. Min.	*Cato Minor*	*Cato the Younger*
Cic.	*Cicero*	
Cim.	*Cimon*	
Cleom.	*Cleomenes*	
Cohib. ira	*De cohibenda ira*	
Adv. Col.	*Adversus Colotem*	
Comm. not.	*De communibus notitiis contra stoicos*	
Comp. Aem. Tim.	*Comparatio Aemilii Paulli et Timoleontis*	
Comp. Ag. Cleom. cum Ti. Gracch.	*Comparatio Agidis et Cleomenis cum Tiberio et Gaio Graccho*	
Comp. Ages. Pomp.	*Comparatio Agesilai et Pompeii*	
Comp. Alc. Cor.	*Comparatio Alcibiadis et Marcii Coriolani*	
Comp. Arist. Cat.	*Comparatio Aristidis et Catonis*	
Comp. Arist. Men. compend.	*Comparationis Aristophanis et Menandri compendium*	
Comp. Cim. Luc.	*Comparatio Cimonis et Luculli*	
Comp. Dem. Cic.	*Comparatio Demosthenis et Ciceronis*	
Comp. Demetr. Ant.	*Comparatio Demetrii et Antonii*	
Comp. Dion. Brut.	*Comparatio Dionis et Bruti*	
Comp. Eum. Sert.	*Comparatio Eumenis et Sertorii*	
Comp. Lyc. Num.	*Comparatio Lycurgi et Numae*	
Comp. Lys. Sull.	*Comparatio Lysandri et Sullae*	
Comp. Nic. Crass.	*Comparatio Nicae et Crassi*	
Comp. Pel. Marc.	*Comparatio Pelopidae et Marcelli*	
Comp. Per. Fab.	*Comparatio Periclis et Fabii Maximi*	
Comp. Phil. Flam.	*Comparatio Philopoemenis et Titi Flaminini*	
Comp. Sol. Publ.	*Comparatio Solonis et Publicolae*	
Comp. Thes. Rom.	*Comparatio Thesei et Romuli*	
Conj. praec.	*Conjugalia Praecepta*	
[Cons. Apoll.]	*Consolatio ad Apollonium*	
Cons. ux.	*Consolatio ad uxorem*	

Cor.	*Marcius Coriolanus*
Crass.	*Crassus*
Cupid. divit.	*De cupiditate divitiarum*
Curios.	*De curiositate*
De esu	*De esu carnium*
De laude	*De laude ipsius*
Def. orac.	*De defectu oraculorum*
Dem.	*Demosthenes*
Demetr.	*Demetrius*
Dion	*Dion*
E Delph.	*De E apud Delphos*
Eum.	*Eumenes*
Exil.	*De exilio*
Fab.	*Fabius Maximus*
Fac.	*De facie in orbe lunae*
Flam.	*Titus Flamininus*
Fort.	*De fortuna*
Fort. Rom.	*De fortuna Romanorum*
Frat. amor.	*De fraterno amore*
Galb.	*Galba*
Garr.	*De garrulitate*
Gen. Socr.	*De genio Socratis*
Glor. Ath.	*De gloria Atheniensium*
Her. mal.	*De Herodoti malignitate*
Inim. util.	*De capienda ex inimicis utilitate*
Inv. od.	*De invidia et odio*
Is. Os.	*De Iside et Osiride*
Lat. viv.	*De latenter vivendo*
Lib. aegr.	*De libidine et aegritudine*
[Lib. ed.]	*De liberis educandis*
Luc.	*Lucullus*
Lyc.	*Lycurgus*
Lys.	*Lysander*
Mar.	*Marius*
Marc.	*Marcellus*
Max. princ.	*Maxime cum principibus philosophiam esse disserendum*
Mor.	*Moralia*
Mulier. virt.	*Mulierum virtutes*
[Mus.]	*De musica*
Nic.	*Nicias*
Num.	*Numa*
Oth.	*Otho*
Parsne an fac.	*Parsne an facultas animi sit vita passiva*
Pel.	*Pelopidas*
Per.	*Pericles*
Phil.	*Philopoemen*
Phoc.	*Phocion*
[Plac. philos.]	*De placita philosophorum*
Pomp.	*Pompeius*
Praec. ger. rei publ.	*Praecepta gerendae rei publicae*
Prim. frig.	*De primo frigido*
Princ. iner.	*Ad principem ineruditum*
Publ.	*Publicola*
Pyrrh.	*Pyrrhus*

Pyth. orac.	*De Pythiae oraculis*
Quaest. conv.	*Quaestionum convivialum libri IX*
Quaest. nat.	*Quaestiones naturales (Aetia physica)*
Quaest. plat.	*Quaestiones platonicae*
Quaest. rom.	*Quaestiones romanae et graecae (Aetia romana et graeca)*
Rect. rat. aud.	*De recta ratione audiendi*
[Reg. imp. apophth.]	*Regum et imperatorum apophthegmata*
Rom.	*Romulus*
Sept. sap. conv.	*Septem sapientium convivium*
Sera	*De sera numinis vindicta*
Sert.	*Sertorius*
Sol.	*Solon*
Soll. an.	*De sollertia animalium*
Stoic. abs.	*Stoicos absurdiora poetis dicere*
Stoic. rep.	*De Stoicorum repugnantiis*
Suav. viv.	*Non posse suaviter vivi secundum Epicurum*
Sull.	*Sulla*
Superst.	*De superstitione*
Them.	*Themistocles*
Thes.	*Theseus*
Ti. C. Gracch.	*Tiberius et Caius Gracchus*
Tim.	*Timoleon*
Tranq. an.	*De tranquillitate animi*
Trib. r. p. gen.	*De tribus rei publicae generibus*
Tu. san.	*De tuenda sanitate praecepta*
Un. rep. dom.	*De unius in republica dominatione*
Virt. mor.	*De virtute morali*
Virt. prof.	*Quomodo quis suos in virtute sentiat profectus*
Virt. vit.	*De virtute et vitio*
Vit. aere al.	*De vitando aere alieno*
[Vit. poes. Hom.]	*De vita et poesi Homeri*
Vit. pud.	*De vitioso pudore*
[Vit. X orat.]	*Vitae decem oratorum*

Pollux

Onom.	*Onomasticon*

Polybius

Hist.	*Historical*

Pomponius Mela

De Chorog.	*De Chorographia*

Porphyry

Abst.	*De abstinentia*
Agalm.	*Peri agalmatōn*
Aneb.	*Epistula ad Anebonem*
Antr. nymph.	*De antro nympharum*

Christ.	*Contra Christianos*	
Chron.	*Chronica*	
Comm. harm.	*Eis ta harmonika Ptolemaiou hypomnēma*	
Comm. Tim.	*In Platonis Timaeum commentaria*	
Exp. Cat.	*In Aristotelis Categorias expositio per interrogationem et responsionem*	
Isag.	*Isagoge sive quinque voces*	
Marc.	*Ad Marcellam*	
Philos. orac.	*De philosophia ex oraculis*	
Quaest. hom.	*Quaestiones homericae*	
Quaest. hom. Odd.	*Quaestionum homericarum ad Odysseam pertinentium reliquiae*	
Sent.	*Sententiae ad intelligibilia ducentes*	
Vit. Plot.	*Vita Plotini*	
Vit. Pyth.	*Vita Pythagorae*	

PTOLEMY

Geog.	*Geography*	

PTOLEMY (THE GNOSTIC)

Flor.	*Epistula ad Floram*	*Letter to Flora*

QUINTILIAN

Decl.	*Declamationes*	
Inst.	*Institutio oratoria*	

RES GEST. DIVI AUG.	*Res gestae divi Augusti*	
RHET. HER.	*Rhetorica ad Herennium*	

RUFINUS

Adam. Haer.	*Adamantii libri Contra haereticos*	
Anast.	*Apologia ad Anastasium papam*	
Apol. Hier.	*Apologia adversus Hieronymum*	
Apol. Orig.	*Eusebii et Pamphyli Apologia Origenis*	
Basil. hom.	*Homiliae S. Basilii*	
Ben. patr.	*De benedictionibus patriarcharum*	
Clem. Recogn.	*Clementis quae feruntur Recognitiones*	
Greg. Orat.	*Gregorii Orationes*	
Hist.	*Eusebii Historia ecclesiastica a Rufino translata et continuata*	
Hist. mon.	*Historia monachorum in Aegypto*	
Orig. Comm. Cant.	*Origenis Commentarius in Canticum*	
Orig. Comm. Rom.	*Origenis Commentarius in epistulam ad Romanos*	
Orig. Hom. Exod.	*Origenis in Exodum homiliae*	
Orig. Hom. Gen.	*Origenis in Genesism homiliae*	
Orig. Hom. Jos.	*Origenis Homiliae in librum Josua*	

Orig. Hom. Judic.	*Origenis in librum Judicum homiliae*	
Orig. Hom. Lev.	*Origenis Homiliae in Leviticum*	
Orig. Hom. Num.	*Origenis in Numeros homiliae*	
Orig. Hom. Ps.	*Origenis Homiliae in Psalmos*	
Orig. Princ.	*Origenis Libri Peri archōn seu De principiis libri IV*	
Sent. Sext.	*Sexti philosophi Sententiae a Rufino translatae*	
Symb.	*Commentarius in symbolum apostolorum*	

Sallust

Bell. Cat.	*Bellum catalinae*	
Bell. Jug.	*Bellum jugurthinum*	
Hist.	*Historiae*	
Rep.	*Epistulae ad Caesarem senem de re publica*	

Seneca

Ag.	*Agamemnon*	
Apol.	*Apolocyntosis*	
Ben.	*De beneficiis*	
Clem.	*De clementia*	
Dial.	*Dialogi*	
Ep.	*Epistulae morales*	
Helv.	*Ad Helviam*	
Herc. fur.	*Hercules furens*	
Herc. Ot.	*Hercules Otaeus*	
Ira	*De ira*	
Lucil.	*Ad Lucilium*	
Marc.	*Ad Marciam de consolatione*	
Med.	*Medea*	
Nat.	*Naturales quaestiones*	
Phaed.	*Phaedra*	
Phoen.	*Phoenissae*	
Polyb.	*Ad Polybium de consolatione*	
Thy.	*Thyestes*	
Tranq.	*De tranquillitate animi*	
Tro.	*Troades*	
Vit. beat.	*De vita beata*	

Sextus Empiricus

Math.	*Adversus mathematicos*	*Against the Mathematicians*
Pyr.	*Pyrrhoniae hypotyposes*	*Outlines of Pyrrhonism*

Sophocles

Aj.	*Ajax*	
Ant.	*Antigone*	
El.	*Elektra*	
Ichn.	*Ichneutae*	

Oed. col.	*Oedipus coloneus*	
Oed. tyr.	*Oedipus tyrannus*	
Phil.	*Philoctetes*	
Trach.	*Trachiniae*	

STOBAEUS

Ecl.	*Eclogae*	
Flor.	*Florilegium*	

STRABO

Geogr.	*Geographica*	

SUETONIUS

Aug.	*Divus Augustus*	
Cal.	*Gaius Caligula*	
Claud.	*Divus Claudius*	
Dom.	*Domitianus*	
Galb.	*Galba*	
Gramm.	*De grammaticis*	
Jul.	*Divus Julius*	
Nero	*Nero*	
Otho	*Otho*	
Poet.	*De poetis*	
Rhet.	*De rhetoribus*	
Tib.	*Tiberius*	
Tit.	*Divus Titus*	
Vesp.	*Vespasianus*	
Vit.	*Vitellius*	

TACITUS

Agr.	*Agricola*	
Ann.	*Annales*	
Dial.	*Dialogus de oratoribus*	
Germ.	*Germania*	
Hist.	*Historiae*	

TERENCE

Ad.	*Adelphi*	
Andr.	*Andria*	
Eun.	*Eunuchus*	
Haut.	*Hauton timorumenos*	
Hec.	*Hecyra*	
Phorm.	*Phormio*	

TERTULLIAN

An.	*De anima*	*The Soul*
Apol.	*Apologeticus*	*Apology*
Bapt.	*De baptismo*	*Baptism*

Carn. Chr.	*De carne Christi*	*The Flesh of Christ*
Cor.	*De corona militis*	*The Crown*
Cult. fem.	*De cultu feminarum*	*The Apparel of Women*
Exh. cast.	*De exhortatione castitatis*	*Exhortation to Chastity*
Fug.	*De fuga in persecutione*	*Flight in Persecution*
Herm.	*Adversus Hermogenem*	*Against Hermogenes*
Idol.	*De idololatria*	*Idolatry*
Jejun.	*De jejunio adversus psychicos*	*On Fasting, against the Psychics*
Adv. Jud.	*Adversus Judaeos*	*Against the Jews*
Marc.	*Adversus Marcionem*	*Against Marcion*
Mart.	*Ad martyras*	*To the Martyrs*
Mon.	*De monogamia*	*Monogamy*
Nat.	*Ad nationes*	*To the Heathen*
Or.	*De oratione*	*Prayer*
Paen.	*De paenitentia*	*Repentance*
Pall.	*De pallio*	*The Pallium*
Pat.	*De patientia*	*Patience*
Praescr.	*De praescriptione haereticorum*	*Prescription against Heretics*
Prax.	*Adversus Praxean*	*Against Praxeas*
Pud.	*De pudicitia*	*Modesty*
Res.	*De resurrectione carnis*	*The Resurrection of the Flesh*
Scap.	*Ad Scapulam*	*To Scapula*
Scorp.	*Scorpiace*	*Antidote for Scorpian's Sting*
Spect.	*De spectaculis*	*The Shows*
Test.	*De testimonio animae*	*The Soul's Testimony*
Ux.	*Ad uxorem*	*To His Wife*
Val.	*Adversus Valentinianos*	*Against the Valentinians*
Virg.	*De virginibus velandis*	*The Veiling of Virgins*

THEOCRITUS

Id.	*Idylls*	

THEOD. — THEODOTIAN

Vg.	*Vulgate*	

THEODORET

Car.	*De caritate*	
Hist. eccl.	*Historia ecclesiastica*	*Ecclesiastical History*
Phil. hist.	*Philotheos historia*	*History of Monks of Syria*

THEON OF ALEXANDRIA

Comm. Alm.	*Commentarium in Almagestum*	*Commentary on the Almagest*

THEOPHILUS

Autol.	*Ad Autolycum*	*To Autolycus*

THEOPHRASTUS

Caus. plant.	*De causis plantarum*	
Char.	*Characteres*	
Hist. plant.	*Historia plantarum*	
Sens.	*De sensu*	

Tyconius

Reg.	*Liber regularum*

Varro

Rust.	*De re rustica*

Virgil

Aen.	*Aeneid*
Ecl.	*Eclogae*
Georg.	*Georgica*

Xenophon

Ages.	*Agesilaus*
Anab.	*Anabasis*
Apol.	*Apologia Socratis*
[Ath.]	*Respublica atheniensium*
Cyn.	*Cynegeticus*
Cyr.	*Cyropaedia*
Eq.	*De equitande ratione*
Eq. mag.	*De equitum magistro*
Hell.	*Hellenica*
Hier.	*Hiero*
Lac.	*Respublica Lacedaemoniorum*
Mem.	*Memorabilia*
Oec.	*Oeconomicus*
Symp.	*Symposium*

Periodicals, Reference Works, and Serials

AA	*Archäologischer Anzeiger*
AAA	Annals of Archaeology and Anthropology
AAeg	*Analecta aegyptiaca*
AAHG	*Anzeiger für die Altertumswissenschaft*
AARDS	American Academy of Religion Dissertation Series
AAS	*Acta apostolicae sedis*
AASF	Annales Academiae scientiarum fennicae
AASOR	Annual of the American Schools of Oriental Research
AASS	*Acta sanctorum quotquot toto orbe coluntur.* Antwerp, 1643–
AB	Anchor Bible
AB	*Assyriologische Bibliothek*
ABAT2	*Altorientalische Bilder zum Alten Testament.* Edited by H. Gressmann. 2d ed. Berlin, 1927
ABAW	Abhandlungen der Bayrischen Akademie der Wissenschaften
AbB	*Altbabylonische Briefe in Umschrift und Übersetzung.* Edited by F. R. Kraus. Leiden, 1964–
ABC	*Assyrian and Babylonian Chronicles.* A. K. Grayson. TCS 5. Locust Valley, New York, 1975
ABD	*Anchor Bible Dictionary.* Edited by D. N. Freedman. 6 vols. New York, 1992
ABL	*Assyrian and Babylonian Letters Belonging to the Kouyunjik Collections of the British Museum.* Edited by R. F. Harper. 14 vols. Chicago, 1892–1914
ABQ	*American Baptist Quarterly*

ABR	*Australian Biblical Review*
ABRL	Anchor Bible Reference Library
AbrN	*Abr-Nahrain*
AbrNSup	Abr-Nahrain: Supplement Series
ABW	*Archaeology in the Biblical World*
ABZ	*Assyrisch-babylonische Zeichenliste.* Rykle Borger. 3d ed. AOAT 33/33A. Neukirchen-Vluyn, 1986
ACCS	Ancient Christian Commentary on Scripture
ACEBT	*Amsterdamse Cahiers voor Exegese en bijbelse Theologie*
ACNT	Augsburg Commentaries on the New Testament
ACO	*Acta conciliorum oecumenicorum.* Edited by E. Schwartz. Berlin, 1914–
AcOr	*Acta orientalia*
ACR	*Australasian Catholic Record*
AcT	*Acta theologica*
ACW	Ancient Christian Writers. 1946–
ADAJ	*Annual of the Department of Antiquities of Jordan*
ADD	*Assyrian Deeds and Documents.* C. H. W. Johns. 4 vols. Cambridge, 1898–1923
ADOG	Abhandlungen der deutschen Orientgesellschaft
AE	*Année épigraphique*
AEB	*Annual Egyptological Bibliography*
Aeg	*Aegyptus*
AEL	*Ancient Egyptian Literature.* M. Lichtheim. 3 vols. Berkeley, 1971–1980
AEO	*Ancient Egyptian Onomastica.* A. H. Gardiner. 3 vols. London, 1947
AER	*American Ecclesiastical Review*
Aev	*Aevum: Rassegna de scienze, storiche, linguistiche, e filologiche*
ÄF	Ägyptologische Forschungen
AfK	*Archiv für Keilschriftforschung*
AfO	*Archiv für Orientforschung*
AfOB	Archiv für Orientforschung: Beiheft
ÄgAbh	Ägyptologische Abhandlungen
AGLB	*Aus der Geschichte der lateinischen Bibel (= Vetus Latina: Die Reste der altlateinischen Bibel: Aus der Geschichte der lateinischen Bibel).* Freiburg: Herder, 1957–
AGJU	Arbeiten zur Geschichte des antiken Judentums und des Urchristentums
AGSU	Arbeiten zur Geschichte des Spätjudentums und Urchristentums
AHAW	Abhandlungen der Heidelberger Akademie der Wissenschaften
AHR	*American Historical Review*
AHw	*Akkadisches Handwörterbuch.* W. von Soden. 3 vols. Wiesbaden, 1965–1981
AION	*Annali dell'Istituto Orientale di Napoli*
AIPHOS	*Annuaire de l'Institut de philologie et d'histoire orientales et slaves*
AJA	*American Journal of Archaeology*
AJAS	*American Journal of Arabic Studies*
AJBA	*Australian Journal of Biblical Archaeology*
AJBI	*Annual of the Japanese Biblical Institute*
AJBS	*African Journal of Biblical Studies*
AJP	*American Journal of Philology*
AJSL	*American Journal of Semitic Languages and Literature*
AJSR	*Association for Jewish Studies Review*
AJSUFS	Arbeiten aus dem Juristischen Seminar der Universität Freiburg, Schweiz
AJT	*American Journal of Theology*
AJT	*Asia Journal of Theology*
ALASP	Abhandlungen zur Literatur Alt-Syren-Palästinas und Mesopotamiens
ALBO	Analecta lovaniensia biblica et orientalia
ALGHJ	Arbeiten zur Literatur und Geschichte des hellenistischen Judentums
Altaner	Altaner, B. *Patrologie.* 8th ed. Freiburg, 1978

ALUOS	*Annual of Leeds University Oriental Society*
AMS	*Acta martyrum et sanctorum Syriace.* Edited by P. Bedjan. 7 vols. Paris, 1890–1897
AMWNE	*Apocalypticism in the Mediterranean World and the Near East. Proceedings of the International Colloquium on Apocalypticism.* Edited by D.Hellholm. Uppsala, 1979
Anám	*Anámnesis*
AnBib	Analecta biblica
AnBoll	Analecta Bollandiana
ANEP	*The Ancient Near East in Pictures Relating to the Old Testament.* Edited by J. B. Pritchard. Princeton, 1954
ANESTP	*The Ancient Near East: Supplementary Texts and Pictures Relating to the Old Testament.* Edited by J. B. Pritchard. Princeton, 1969.
ANET	*Ancient Near Eastern Texts Relating to the Old Testament.* Edited by J. B. Pritchard. 3d ed. Princeton, 1969
ANF	*Ante-Nicene Fathers*
Ang	*Angelicum*
AnL	*Anthropological Linguistics*
AnOr	Analecta orientalia
AnPhil	*L'année philologique*
ANQ	*Andover Newton Quarterly*
ANRW	*Aufstieg und Niedergang der römischen Welt: Geschichte und Kultur Roms im Spiegel der neueren Forschung.* Edited by H. Temporini and W. Haase. Berlin, 1972–
AnSt	*Anatolian Studies*
ANTC	Abingdon New Testament Commentaries
ANTF	Arbeiten zur neutestamentlichen Textforschung
AnthLyrGraec	*Anthologia lyrica graeca.* Edited by E. Diehl. Leipzig, 1954–
ANTJ	Arbeiten zum Neuen Testament und Judentum
Anton	*Antonianum*
Anuari	*Anuari de filología*
ANZSTR	Australian and New Zealand Studies in Theology and Religion
AO	*Der Alte Orient*
AOAT	Alter Orient und Altes Testament
AÖAW	Anzeiger der Österreichischen Akademie der Wissenschaften
AOBib	Altorientalische Bibliothek
AoF	Altorientalische Forschungen
AOS	American Oriental Series
AOSTS	American Oriental Society Translation Series
AOT	*The Apocryphal Old Testament.* Edited by H. F. D. Sparks. Oxford, 1984
AOTAT	*Altorientalische Texte zum Alten Testament.* Edited by H. Gressmann. 2d ed. Berlin, 1926
AOTC	Abingdon Old Testament Commentaries
APAT	*Die Apokryphen und Pseudepigraphen des Alten Testaments.* Translated and edited by E. Kautzsch. 2 vols. Tübingen, 1900
APF	*Archiv für Papyrusforschung*
APHM	Grohmann, A. *Arabic Papyri from Hirbet el-Mird.* Bibliothèque du Muséon 52. Louvain: Publications Universitaires, 1963.
APOT	*The Apocrypha and Pseudepigrapha of the Old Testament.* Edited by R. H. Charles. 2 vols. Oxford, 1913
APSP	*American Philosophical Society Proceedings*
AR	*Archiv für Religionswissenschaft*
ARAB	*Ancient Records of Assyria and Babylonia.* Daniel David Luckenbill. 2 vols. Chicago, 1926–1927
ArBib	The Aramaic Bible
Arch	*Archaeology*
ARE	*Ancient Records of Egypt.* Edited by J. H. Breasted. 5 vols. Chicago, 1905–1907. Reprint, New York, 1962

ARG	*Archiv für Reformationsgeschichte*
ARI	*Assyrian Royal Inscriptions.* A. K. Grayson. 2 vols. RANE. Wiesbaden, 1972–1976
ARM	Archives royales de Mari
ARMT	Archives royales de Mari, transcrite et traduite
ArOr	*Archiv Orientální*
ArSt	Arabian Studies
AS	Assyriological Studies
ASAE	*Annales duservice des antiquités de l'Egypte*
ASAW	Abhandlungen der Sächsischen Akademie der Wissenschaften
ASNU	Acta seminarii neotestamentici upsaliensis
ASOR	American Schools of Oriental Research
ASP	*American Studies in Papyrology*
Asp	*Asprenas: Rivista di scienze teologiche*
ASS	*Acta sanctae sedis*
AsSeign	*Assemblées du Seigneur*
ASSR	*Archives de sciences sociales des religions*
ASTI	*Annual of the Swedish Theological Institute*
AsTJ	*Asbury Theological Journal*
AT	*Annales theologici*
ATA	Alttestamentliche Abhandlungen
ATANT	Abhandlungen zur Theologie des Alten und Neuen Testaments
ATD	Das Alte Testament Deutsch
ATDan	Acta theologica danica
ATG	*Archivo teológico granadino*
AThR	*Anglican Theological Review*
Atiqot	*ʿAtiqot*
ATJ	*Ashland Theological Journal*
ATLA	American Theological Library Association
ATR	*Australasian Theological Review*
Aug	*Augustinianum*
AugStud	*Augustinian Studies*
AuOr	*Aula orientalis*
AUSS	*Andrews University Seminary Studies*
AVTRW	Aufsätze und Vorträge zur Theologie und Religionswissenschaft
AzTh	Arbeiten zur Theologie
B&R	*Books and Religion*
BA	*Biblical Archaeologist*
Bab	*Babyloniaca*
BAC	Biblioteca de autores cristianos
BAG	Bauer, W., W. F. Arndt, and F. W. Gingrich. *Greek-English Lexicon of the New Testament and Other Early Christian Literature.* Chicago, 1957
BAGB	*Bulletin de l'Association G. Budé*
BAGD	Bauer, W., W. F. Arndt, F. W. Gingrich, and F. W. Danker. *Greek-English Lexicon of the New Testament and Other Early Christian Literature.* 2d ed. Chicago, 1979
BaghM	*Baghdader Mitteilungen*
BAIAS	*Bulletin of the Anglo-Israel Archeological Society*
BAP	*Beiträge zum altbabylonischen Privatrecht.* Bruno Meissner. Leipzig, 1893
BAR	*Biblical Archaeology Review*
BARead	*Biblical Archaeologist Reader*
Bar-Ilan	*Annual of Bar-Ilan University*
BASOR	*Bulletin of the American Schools of Oriental Research*
BASORSup	Bulletin of the American Schools of Oriental Research: Supplement Series
BASP	*Bulletin of the American Society of Papyrologists*
BASPSup	Bulletin of the American Society of Papyrologists: Supplement

BAT	Die Botschaft des Alten Testaments
BBB	Bonner biblische Beiträge
BBB	*Bulletin de bibliographie biblique*
BBET	Beiträge zur biblischen Exegese und Theologie
BBMS	Baker Biblical Monograph Series
BBR	*Bulletin for Biblical Research*
BBS	*Bulletin of Biblical Studies*
BCH	*Bulletin de correspondance hellénique*
BCPE	*Bulletin du Centre protestant d'études*
BCR	Biblioteca di cultura religiosa
BCSR	*Bulletin of the Council on the Study of Religion*
BDAG	Bauer, W., F. W. Danker, W. F. Arndt, and F. W. Gingrich. *Greek-English Lexicon of the New Testament and Other Early Christian Literature.* 3d ed. Chicago, 1999
BDB	Brown, F., S. R. Driver, and C. A. Briggs. *A Hebrew and English Lexicon of the Old Testament.* Oxford, 1907
BDF	Blass, F., A. Debrunner, and R. W. Funk. *A Greek Grammar of the New Testament and Other Early Christian Literature.* Chicago, 1961
BE	Milik, J. T. *The Books of Enoch.* Oxford: Clarendon, 1976.
BEATAJ	Beiträge zur Erforschung des Alten Testaments und des antiken Judentum
BEB	*Baker Encyclopedia of the Bible.* Edited by W. A. Elwell. 2 vols. Grand Rapids, 1988
BeO	*Bibbia e oriente*
Ber	*Berytus*
BerMatÖAI	Berichte und Materialien des Österreichischen archäologischen Instituts
BETL	Bibliotheca ephemeridum theologicarum lovaniensium
BEvT	Beiträge zur evangelischen Theologie
BFCT	Beiträge zur Förderung christlicher Theologie
BFT	Biblical Foundations in Theology
BGBE	Beiträge zur Geschichte der biblischen Exegese
BGU	*Aegyptische Urkunden aus den Königlichen Staatlichen Museen zu Berlin, Griechische Urkunden.* 15 vols. Berlin, 1895–1983.
BHEAT	*Bulletin d'histoire et d'exégèse de l'Ancien Testament*
BHG	*Bibliotheca hagiographica Graece.* Brussels, 1977
BHH	*Biblisch-historisches Handwörterbuch: Landeskunde, Geschichte, Religion, Kultur.* Edited by B. Reicke and L. Rost. 4 vols. Göttingen, 1962–1966
BHK	*Biblia Hebraica.* Edited by R. Kittel. Stuttgart, 1905–1906, 1925^{2}, 1937^{3}, 1951^{4}, 1973^{16}
BHL	*Bibliotheca hagiographica latina antiquae et mediae aetatis.* 2 vols. Brussels, 1898–1901
BHLen	*Biblia Hebraica Leninradensia.* Edited by A. Dotan. Peabody, Mass., 2001.
BHO	*Bibliotheca hagiographica orientalis.* Brussels, 1910
BHS	*Biblia Hebraica Stuttgartensia.* Edited by K. Elliger and W. Rudolph. Stuttgart, 1983
BHT	Beiträge zur historischen Theologie
BI	*Biblical Illustrator*
Bib	*Biblica*
BibB	Biblische Beiträge
BiBh	*Bible Bhashyam*
BibInt	*Biblical Interpretation*
BibLeb	*Bibel und Leben*
BibOr	Biblica et orientalia
BibS(F)	Biblische Studien (Freiburg, 1895–)
BibS(N)	Biblische Studien (Neukirchen, 1951–)
BIES	*Bulletin of the Israel Exploration Society* (= *Yediot*)
BIFAO	*Bulletin de l'Institut français d'archéologie orientale*
Bijdr	*Bijdragen: Tijdschrift voor filosofie en theologie*
BIN	*Babylonian Inscriptions in the Collection of James B. Nies*

BIOSCS	*Bulletin of the International Organization for Septuagint and Cognate Studies*
BiPa	Biblia Patristica: Index des citations et allusions bibliques dans la littérature. Paris, 1975–
BJ	*Bonner Jahrbücher*
BJPES	*Bulletin of the Jewish Palestine Exploration Society*
BJRL	*Bulletin of the John Rylands University Library of Manchester*
BJS	Brown Judaic Studies
BJVF	*Berliner Jahrbuch für Vor- und Frühgeschichte*
BK	*Bibel und Kirche*
BKAT	Biblischer Kommentar, Altes Testament. Edited by M. Noth and H. W. Wolff
BL	*Bibel und Liturgie*
BLE	*Bulletin de littérature ecclésiastique*
BLit	*Bibliothèque liturgique*
BMes	Bibliotheca mesopotamica
BN	*Biblische Notizen*
BNTC	Black's New Testament Commentaries
BO	*Bibliotheca orientalis*
Böhl	Böhl, F. M. Th. de Liagre. *Opera minora: Studies en bijdragen op Assyriologisch en Oudtestamentisch terrein.* Groningen, 1953
BOR	*Babylonian and Oriental Record*
Bousset-Gressmann	Bousset, W., and H. Gressmann, *Die Religion des Judentums im späthellenistischen Zeitalter.* 3d ed. Tübingen, 1926
BR	*Biblical Research*
BRev	*Bible Review*
BRL2	*Biblisches Reallexikon.* 2d ed. Edited by K. Galling. HAT 1/1. Tübingen, 1977
BSAA	*Bulletin de la Société archéologique d'Alexandrie*
BSac	*Bibliotheca sacra*
BSAC	*Bulletin de la Société d'archéologie copte*
BSC	Bible Student's Commentary
BSGW	Berichte der Sächsischen Gesellschaft der Wissenschaften
BSOAS	*Bulletin of the School of Oriental and African Studies*
BT	*The Bible Translator*
BTB	*Biblical Theology Bulletin*
BThAM	*Bulletin de théologie ancienne et médiévale*
BTS	*Bible et terre sainte*
BTZ	*Berliner Theologische Zeitschrift*
Budé	Collection des universités de France, publiée sous le patronage de l'Association Guillaume Budé
Burg	*Burgense*
BurH	*Buried History*
BV	*Biblical Viewpoint*
BVC	*Bible et vie chrétienne*
BW	*The Biblical World: A Dictionary of Biblical Archaeology.* Edited by C. F. Pfeiffer. Grand Rapids, 1966
BWA(N)T	Beiträge zur Wissenschaft vom Alten (und Neuen) Testament
BWL	*Babylonian Wisdom Literature.* W. G. Lambert. Oxford, 1960
ByF	*Biblia y fe*
Byzantion	*Byzantion*
ByzF	*Byzantinische Forschungen*
ByzZ	*Byzantinische Zeitschrift*
BZ	*Biblische Zeitschrift*
BzA	Beiträge zur Assyriologie
BZAW	Beihefte zur Zeitschrift für die alttestamentliche Wissenschaft
BZNW	Beihefte zur Zeitschrift für die neutestamentliche Wissenschaft

BZRGG Beihefte zur Zeitschrift für Religions und Geistesgeschichte
CA *Convivium assisiense*
CAD *The Assyrian Dictionary of the Oriental Institute of the University of Chicago.* Chicago, 1956–
CaE *Cahiers évangile*
CAGN *Collected Ancient Greek Novels.* Edited by B. P. Reardon. Berkeley, 1989
CAH Cambridge Ancient History
CahRB Cahiers de la Revue biblique
CahT Cahiers Théologiques
CANE *Civilizations of the Ancient Near East.* Edited by J. Sasson. 4 vols. New York, 1995
CAP Cowley, A. E. *Aramaic Papyri of the Fifth Century B.C.* Oxford, 1923
Car *Carthagiensia*
CAT Commentaire de l'Ancien Testament
CB *Cultura bíblica*
CBC Cambridge Bible Commentary
CBET Contributions to Biblical Exegesis and Theology
CBM Chester Beatty Monographs
CBQ *Catholic Biblical Quarterly*
CBQMS Catholic Biblical Quarterly Monograph Series
CBTJ *Calvary Baptist Theological Journal*
CC Continental Commentaries
CCath Corpus Catholicorum
CCCM Corpus Christianorum: Continuatio mediaevalis. Turnhout, 1969–
CClCr *Civilità classica e cristiana*
CCSG Corpus Christianorum: Series graeca. Turnhout, 1977–
CCSL Corpus Christianorum: Series latina. Turnhout, 1953–
CCT *Cuneiform Texts from Cappadocian Tablets in the British Museum*
CDME *A Concise Dictionary of Middle Egyptian.* Edited by R. O. Faulkner. Oxford, 1962
CF *Classical Folia*
CGTC Cambridge Greek Testament Commentary
CGTSC Cambridge Greek Testament for Schools and Colleges
CH *Church History*
CHJ *Cambridge History of Judaism.* Ed. W. D. Davies and Louis Finkelstein. Cambridge, 1984–
Chm *Churchman*
CHR *Catholic Historical Review*
ChrCent *Christian Century*
ChrEg *Chronique d'Egypte*
ChrLit *Christianity and Literature*
CIC *Corpus inscriptionum chaldicarum*
CIG *Corpus inscriptionum graecarum.* Edited by A. Boeckh. 4 vols. Berlin, 1828–1877
CII *Corpus inscriptionum iudaicarum.* Edited by J. B. Frey. 2 vols. Rome, 1936–1952
CIJ *Corpus inscriptionum judaicarum*
CIL *Corpus inscriptionum latinarum*
CIS *Corpus inscriptionum semiticarum*
CJ *Classical Journal*
CJT *Canadian Journal of Theology*
Cmio *Communio: Commentarii internationales de ecclesia et theología*
CML *Canaanite Myths and Legends.* Edited by G. R. Driver. Edinburgh, 1956. Edited by J. C. L. Gibson, 1978[2]
CNS *Cristianesimo nella storia*
CNT Commentaire du Nouveau Testament
Coll *Collationes*
Colloq *Colloquium*
ColT *Collectanea theologica*

Comm	*Communio*
Comp	*Compostellanum*
ConBNT	Coniectanea neotestamentica or Coniectanea biblica: New Testament Series
ConBOT	Coniectanea biblica: Old Testament Series
Cont	*Continuum*
COS	William W. Hallo, ed., *The Context of Scripture.* (3 vols.; Leiden: E. J. Brill, 1997–)
COut	Commentaar op het Oude Testament
CP	*Classical Philology*
CPG	*Clavis patrum graecorum.* Edited by M. Geerard. 5 vols. Turnhout, 1974–1987
CPJ	*Corpus papyrorum judaicorum.* Edited by V. Tcherikover. 3 vols. Cambridge, 1957–1964.
CPL	*Clavis patrum latinorum.* Edited by E. Dekkers. 2d ed. Steenbrugis, 1961
CQ	*Church Quarterly*
CQ	*Classical Quarterly*
CQR	*Church Quarterly Review*
CRAI	Comptes rendus de l'Académie des inscriptions et belleslettres
CRBR	*Critical Review of Books in Religion*
CRINT	Compendia rerum iudaicarum ad Novum Testamentum
CRTL	Cahiers de la Revue théologique de Louvain
Crux	*Crux*
CSCO	Corpus scriptorum christianorum orientalium. Edited by I. B. Chabot et al. Paris, 1903–
CSEL	Corpus scriptorum ecclesiasticorum latinorum
CSHB	Corpus scriptorum historiae byzantinae
CSJH	Chicago Studies in the History of Judaism
CSR	*Christian Scholar's Review*
CSRB	*Council on the Study of Religion: Bulletin*
CT	*Cuneiform Texts from Babylonian Tablets in the British Museum*
CTA	*Corpus des tablettes en cunéiformes alphabétiques découvertes à Ras Shamra-Ugarit de 1929 à 1939.* Edited by A. Herdner. Mission de Ras Shamra 10. Paris, 1963
CTAED	*Canaanite Toponyms in Ancient Egyptian Documents.* S. Ahituv. Jerusalem, 1984
CTJ	*Calvin Theological Journal*
CTM	*Concordia Theological Monthly*
CTQ	*Concordia Theological Quarterly*
CTR	*Criswell Theological Review*
CTU	*The Cuneiform Alphabetic Texts from Ugarit, Ras Ibn Hani, and Other Places.* Edited by M. Dietrich, O. Loretz, and J. Sanmartín. Münster, 1995.
CUL	*A Concordance of the Ugaritic Literature.* R. E. Whitaker. Cambridge, Mass., 1972
CurBS	*Currents in Research: Biblical Studies*
CurTM	*Currents in Theology and Mission*
CV	*Communio viatorum*
CW	*Classical World*
CWS	Classics of Western Spirituality. New York, 1978–
DACL	*Dictionnaire d'archéologie chrétienne et de liturgie.* Edited by F. Cabrol. 15 vols. Paris, 1907–1953
DB	*Dictionnaire de la Bible.* Edited by F. Vigouroux. 5 vols. 1895–1912
DBAT	*Dielheimer Blätter zum Alten Testament und seiner Rezeption in der Alten Kirche*
DBSup	*Dictionnaire de la Bible: Supplément.* Edited by L. Pirot and A. Robert. Paris, 1928–
DBT	*Dictionary of Biblical Theology.* Edited by X. Léon-Dufour. 2d ed. 1972
DCB	*Dictionary of Christian Biography.* Edited by W. Smith and H. Wace. 4 vols. London, 1877–1887
DCG	*Dictionary of Christ and the Gospels.* Edited by J. Hastings. 2 vols. Edinburgh, 1908
DCH	*Dictionary of Classical Hebrew.* Edited by D. J. A. Clines. Sheffield, 1993–
DDD	*Dictionary of Deities and Demons in the Bible.* Edited by K. van der Toorn, B. Becking, and P. W. van der Horst. Leiden, 1995

DHA	*Dialogues d'histoire ancienne*
Di	*Dialog*
Did	*Didaskalia*
DISO	*Dictionnaire des inscriptions sémitiques de l'ouest.* Edited by Ch. F. Jean and J. Hoftijzer. Leiden, 1965
DissAb	Dissertation Abstracts
DivThom	*Divus Thomas*
DJD	Discoveries in the Judaean Desert (of Jordan)
DJG	*Dictionary of Jesus and the Gospels.* Edited by J. B. Green and S. McKnight. Downers Grove, 1992
DLE	*Dictionary of Late Egyptian.* Edited by L. H. Lesko and B. S. Lesko. 4 vols. Berkeley, 1982–1989
DLNT	*Dictionary of the Later New Testament and Its Developments.* Edited by R. P. Martin and P. H. Davids. Downers Grove, 1997
DNP	*Der neue Pauly: Enzyklopädie der Antike.* Edited by H. Cancik and H. Schneider. Stuttgart, 1996–
DNWSI	*Dictionary of the North-West Semitic Inscriptions.* J. Hoftijzer and K. Jongeling. 2 vols. Leiden, 1995
DOP	*Dumbarton Oaks Papers*
DOTT	*Documents from Old Testament Times.* Edited by D. W. Thomas, London, 1958
DPAC	*Dizionario patristico e di antichità cristiane.* Edited by A. di Berardino. 3 vols. Casale Monferrato, 1983–1988
DPL	*Dictionary of Paul and His Letters.* Edited by G. F. Hawthorne and R. P. Martin. Downers Grove, 1993
DRev	*Downside Review*
DrewG	*Drew Gateway*
DSD	*Dead Sea Discoveries*
DSSSE	*Dead Sea Scrolls: Study Edition.* Edited by F. H. Martínez and E. J. C. Tigchelaar. New York, 1997–1998.
DTC	*Dictionnaire de théologie catholique.* Edited by A. Vacant et al. 15 vols. Paris, 1903–1950
DTT	*Dansk teologisk tidsskrift*
Duchesne	Duchesne, L., ed. *Le Liber pontificalis.* 2 vols. Paris, 1886, 1892. Reprinted with 3d vol. by C. Vogel. Paris, 1955–1957
DunRev	*Dunwoodie Review*
EA	El-Amarna tablets. According to the edition of J. A. Knudtzon. *Die el-Amarna-Tafeln.* Leipzig, 1908–1915. Reprint, Aalen, 1964. Continued in A. F. Rainey, *El-Amarna Tablets, 359–379.* 2d revised ed. Kevelaer, 1978
EAEHL	*Encyclopedia of Archaeological Excavations in the Holy Land.* Edited by M. Avi-Yonah. 4 vols. Jerusalem, 1975
EB	Echter Bibel
EBib	*Etudes bibliques*
ECR	*Eastern Churches Review*
ECT	*Egyptian Coffin Texts.* Edited by A. de Buck and A. H. Gardiner. Chicago, 1935–1947
EdF	Erträge der Forschung
EDNT	*Exegetical Dictionary of the New Testament.* Edited by H. Balz, G. Schneider. ET. Grand Rapids, 1990–1993
EEA	*L'epigrafia ebraica antica.* S. Moscati. Rome, 1951
EEC	*Encyclopedia of Early Christianity.* Edited by E. Ferguson. 2d ed. New York, 1990
EECh	*Encyclopedia of the Early Church.* Edited by A. di Berardino. Translated by A. Walford. New York, 1992
EfMex	*Efemerides mexicana*
EFN	Estudios de filología neotestamentaria. Cordova, Spain, 1988–
EgT	*Eglise et théologie*
EHAT	Exegetisches Handbuch zum Alten Testament
EKKNT	Evangelisch-katholischer Kommentar zum Neuen Testament

EKL	*Evangelisches Kirchenlexikon.* Edited by Erwin Fahlbusch et al. 4 vols. 3d ed. Göttingen, 1985–1996
Elenchus	*Elenchus bibliographicus biblicus* of *Biblica,* Rome, 1985–
ELKZ	*Evangelisch-Lutherische Kirchenzeitung*
EMC	*Echos dumonde classique/Classical Views*
Enc	*Encounter*
EnchBib	*Enchiridion biblicum*
EncJud	*Encyclopaedia Judaica.* 16 vols. Jerusalem, 1972
EPap	*Etudes de papyrologie*
Epiph	*Epiphany*
EPRO	Etudes préliminaires auxreligions orientales dans l'empire romain
ER	*The Encyclopedia of Religion.* Edited by M. Eliade. 16 vols. New York, 1987
ERAS	*Epithètes royales akkadiennes et sumériennes.* M.-J. Seux. Paris, 1967
ERE	*Encyclopedia of Religion and Ethics.* Edited by J. Hastings. 13 vols. New York, 1908–1927. Reprint, 7 vols., 1951
ErIsr	*Eretz-Israel*
ErJb	*Eranos-Jahrbuch*
EstAg	*Estudio Agustiniano*
EstBib	*Estudios bíblicos*
EstEcl	*Estudios eclesiásticos*
EstMin	*Estudios mindonienses*
EstTeo	*Estudios teológicos*
ETL	*Ephemerides theologicae lovanienses*
ETR	*Etudes théologiques et religieuses*
ETS	Erfurter theologische Studien
EuroJTh	*European Journal of Theology*
Even-Shoshan	Even-Shoshan, A., ed. *A New Concordance of the Bible.* Jerusalem, 1977, 1983
EvJ	*Evangelical Journal*
EvK	Evangelische Kommentare
EvQ	*Evangelical Quarterly*
EvT	*Evangelische Theologie*
ExAud	*Ex auditu*
Exeg	*Exegetica* [Japanese]
ExpTim	*Expository Times*
FAT	Forschungen zum Alten Testament
FB	Forschung zur Bibel
FBBS	Facet Books, Biblical Series
FBE	Forum for Bibelsk Eksegese
FC	Fathers of the Church. Washington, D.C., 1947–
FCB	Feminist Companion to the Bible
FF	*Forschungen und Fortschritte*
FF	Foundations and Facets
FGH	*Die Fragmente der griechischen Historiker.* Edited by F. Jacoby. Leiden, 1954–1964
FHG	Fragmenta historicorum graecorum. Paris, 1841–1870
FiE	*Forschungen in Ephesos*
FMSt	Frühmittelalterliche Studien
FO	*Folia orientalia*
FoiVie	*Foi et vie*
ForFasc	*Forum Fascicles*
Foster, *Muses*	Foster, Benjamin R. *Before the Muses: An Anthology of Akkadian Literature.* 2 vols. Bethesda, 1993
FOTL	Forms of the Old Testament Literature
Fran	*Franciscanum*
FRLANT	Forschungen zur Religion und Literatur des Alten und Neuen Testaments

FT	*Folia theologica*
Fund	*Fundamentum*
FZPhTh	*Freiburger Zeitschrift für Philosophie und Theologie*
GAG	*Grundriss der akkadischen Grammatik.* W. von Soden. 2d ed. Rome, 1969
GAT	Grundrisse zum Alten Testament
GBS	Guides to Biblical Scholarship
GCDS	*Graphic Concordance to the Dead Sea Scrolls.* Edited by J. H. Charlesworth et al. Tübingen, 1991
GCS	Die griechische christliche Schriftsteller der ersten [drei] Jahrhunderte Gesenius
Gesenius, *Thesaurus*	Gesenius, W. *Thesaurus philologicus criticus linquae hebraeae et chaldaeae Veteris Testamentia* Vols. 1-3. Leipzig, 1829–1842.
GKC	*Gesenius' Hebrew Grammar.* Edited by E. Kautzsch. Translated by A. E. Cowley. 2d. ed. Oxford, 1910
Gn	*Gnomon*
GNS	*Good News Studies*
GNT	Grundrisse zum Neuen Testament
GOTR	*Greek Orthodox Theological Review*
GP	*Géographie de la Palestine.* F. M. Abel. 2 vols. Paris, 1933
GR	*Greece and Rome*
GRBS	*Greek, Roman, and Byzantine Studies*
Greg	*Gregorianum*
GS	*Gesammelte Studien*
GTA	Göttinger theologischer Arbeiten
GTT	*Gereformeerd theologisch tijdschrift*
GTTOT	*The Geographical and Topographical Texts of the Old Testament.* Edited by J. J.Simons. Studia Francisci Scholten memoriae dicata 2. Leiden, 1959
GVG	*Grundriss der vergleichenden Grammatik der semitischen Sprachen.* C. Brockelmann, 2 vols. Berlin, 1908–1913. Reprint, Hildesheim, 1961
HAL	Koehler, L., W. Baumgartner, and J. J. Stamm. *Hebräisches und aramäisches Lexikon zum Alten Testament.* Fascicles 1–5, 1967–1995 (KBL3). ET: *HALOT*
HALOT	Koehler, L., W. Baumgartner, and J. J. Stamm, *The Hebrew and Aramaic Lexicon of the Old Testament.* Translated and edited under the supervision of M. E. J. Richardson. 4 vols. Leiden, 1994–1999
HAR	*Hebrew Annual Review*
Harris	Harris, Z. S. *A Grammar of the Phoenician Language.* AOS 8. New Haven, 1936. Reprint, 1990
HAT	Handbuch zum Alten Testament
HBC	*Harper's Bible Commentary.* Edited by J. L. Mays et al. San Francisco, 1988.
HBD	*HarperCollins Bible Dictionary.* Edited by P. J. Achtemeier et al. 2d ed. San Francisco, 1996
HBT	*Horizons in Biblical Theology*
HDR	Harvard Dissertations in Religion
Hell	*Hellenica: Recueil d'épigraphie, de numismatique et d'antiquités grecques*
Hen	*Henoch*
Herm	*Hermanthena*
Hesperia	*Hesperia: Journal of the American School of Classical Studies at Athens*
HeyJ	*Heythrop Journal*
HibJ	*Hibbert Journal*
HKAT	Handkommentar zum Alten Testament
HKL	*Handbuch der Keilschriftliteratur.* R. Borger. 3 vols. Berlin, 1967–1975
HKNT	Handkommentar zum Neuen Testament
HNT	Handbuch zum Neuen Testament
HNTC	Harper's New Testament Commentaries
HO	Handbuch der Orientalistik
Hok	*Hokhma*

HolBD	*Holman Bible Dictionary.* Edited by T. C. Butler. Nashville, 1991
Hor	*Horizons*
HR	*History of Religions*
HRCS	Hatch, E. and H. A. Redpath. *Concordance to the Septuagint and Other Greek Versions of the Old Testament.* 2 vols. Oxford, 1897. Suppl., 1906. Reprint, 3 vols. in 2, Grand Rapids, 1983
HS	*Hebrew Studies*
HSAT	*Die Heilige Schrift des Alten Testaments.* Edited by E. Kautzsch and A. Bertholet. 4th ed. Tübingen, 1922–1923
HSCP	*Harvard Studies in Classical Philology*
HSem	Horae semiticae. 9 vols. London, 1908–1912
HSM	Harvard Semitic Monographs
HSS	Harvard Semitic Studies
HT	*History Today*
HTB	Histoire du texte biblique. Lausanne, 1996–
HTh	*Ho Theológos*
HTKNT	Herders theologischer Kommentar zum Neuen Testament
HTR	*Harvard Theological Review*
HTS	Harvard Theological Studies
HUCA	*Hebrew Union College Annual*
HUCM	Monographs of the Hebrew Union College
HumTeo	Biblioteca humanística e teológica
HUT	Hermeneutische Untersuchungen zur Theologie
HvTSt	*Hervormde teologiese studies*
IAR	Iraq Archaeological Reports
IATG[2]	Schwertner, Siegfried M. *Internationales Abkürzungsverzeichnis für Theologie und Grenzgebeite.* 2d ed. Berlin, 1992
IB	*Interpreter's Bible.* Edited by G. A. Buttrick et al. 12 vols. New York, 1951–1957
IBC	Interpretation: A Bible Commentary for Teaching and Preaching.
IBHS	*An Introduction to Biblical Hebrew Syntax.* B. K. Waltke and M. O'Connor. Winona Lake, Indiana, 1990
IBS	*Irish Biblical Studies*
ICC	International Critical Commentary
ICUR	*Inscriptiones christianae urbis Romae.* Edited by J. B. de Rossi. Rome, 1857–1888
IDB	*The Interpreter's Dictionary of the Bible.* Edited by G. A. Buttrick. 4 vols. Nashville, 1962
IDBSup	*Interpreter's Dictionary of the Bible: Supplementary Volume.* Edited by K. Crim. Nashville, 1976
IDS	*In die Skriflig*
IEJ	*Israel Exploration Journal*
IESS	*International Encyclopedia of the Social Sciences.* Edited by D. L. Sills. New York, 1968–
IG	*Inscriptiones graecae.* Editio minor. Berlin, 1924–
IJT	*Indian Journal of Theology*
IKaZ	*Internationale katholische Zeitschrift*
IKZ	*Internationale kirchliche Zeitschrift*
ILCV	*Inscriptiones latinae christianae veteres.* Edited by E. Diehl. 2d ed. Berlin, 1961
Imm	*Immanuel*
Int	*Interpretation*
IOS	*Israel Oriental Society*
IPN	*Die israelitischen Personennamen.* M. Noth. BWANT 3/10. Stuttgart, 1928. Reprint, Hildesheim, 1980
Iran	*Iran*
Iraq	*Iraq*
Irén	*Irénikon*

IRT	Issues in Religion and Theology
ISBE	*International Standard Bible Encyclopedia.* Edited by G. W. Bromiley. 4 vols. Grand Rapids, 1979–1988
Isd	*Isidorianum*
Istina	*Istina*
IstMitt	*Istanbuler Mitteilungen*
Itala	*Itala: Das Neue Testament in altlateinischer Überlieferung.* 4 vols. Berlin, 1938–1963
ITC	International Theological Commentary
Iter	*Iter*
Itin (Italy)	*Itinerarium* (Italy)
Itin (Portugal)	*Itinerarium* (Portugal)
ITP	Hayim Tadmor, *The Inscriptions of Tiglath-Pileser III, King of Assyria.* Jerusalem, 1994
ITQ	*Irish Theological Quarterly*
IZBG	*Internationale Zeitschriftenschaufür Bibelwissenschaft und Grenzgebiete*
JA	*Journal asiatique*
JAAL	*Journal of Afroasiatic Languages*
JAAR	*Journal of the American Academy of Religion*
JAARSup	Journal of the American Academy of Religious Supplement Series
JAC	Jahrbuch für Antike und Christentum
JACiv	*Journal of Ancient Civilizations*
Jahnow	Jahnow, J. *Das hebräische Leichenlied im Rahmen der Völkerdichtung.* Giessen, 1923
JAL	Jewish Apocryphal Literature Series
JANESCU	*Journal of the Ancient Near Eastern Society of Columbia University*
JAOS	*Journal of the American Oriental Society*
JAS	*Journal of Asian Studies*
Jastrow	Jastrow, M. *A Dictionary of the Targumim, the Talmud Babli and Yerushalmi, and the Midrashic Literature.* 2d ed. New York, 1903
JB	Jerusalem Bible
JBC	*Jerome Biblical Commentary.* Edited by R. E. Brown et al. Englewood Cliffs, 1968
JBL	*Journal of Biblical Literature*
JBQ	*Jewish Bible Quarterly*
JBR	*Journal of Bible and Religion*
JCS	*Journal of Cuneiform Studies*
JdI	*Jahrbuch des deutschen archäologischen Instituts*
JDS	Jewish Desert Studies
JDS	Judean Desert Studies
JDT	*Jahrbuch für deutsche Theologie*
JE	*The Jewish Encyclopedia.* Edited by I. Singer. 12 vols. New York, 1925
JEA	*Journal of Egyptian Archaeology*
JECS	*Journal of Early Christian Studies*
Jeev	*Jeevadhara*
JEH	*Journal of Ecclesiastical History*
JEOL	*Jaarbericht van het Vooraziatisch-Egyptisch Gezelschap (Genootschap) Ex oriente lux*
JES	*Journal of Ecumenical Studies*
JESHO	*Journal of the Economic and Social History of the Orient*
JET	*Jahrbuch für Evangelische Theologie*
JETS	*Journal of the Evangelical Theological Society*
JFSR	*Journal of Feminist Studies in Religion*
JHI	*Journal of the History of Ideas*
JHNES	Johns Hopkins Near Eastern Studies
JHS	*Journal of Hellenic Studies*
Jian Dao	*Jian Dao*
JJA	*Journal of Jewish Art*
JJP	*Journal of Juristic Papyrology*

JJS — *Journal of Jewish Studies*
JJT — *Josephinum Journal of Theology*
JLA — *Jewish Law Annual*
JLCRS — Jordan Lectures in Comparative Religion Series
JMedHist — *Journal of Medieval History*
JMES — *Journal of Middle Eastern Studies*
JMS — *Journal of Mithraic Studies*
JNES — *Journal of Near Eastern Studies*
JNSL — *Journal of Northwest Semitic Languages*
JÖAI — *Jahreshefte des Österreichischen archäologischen Instituts*
JOTT — *Journal of Translation and Textlinguistics*
Joüon — Joüon, P. *A Grammar of Biblical Hebrew.* Translated and revised by T. Muraoka. 2 vols. Subsidia biblica 14/1–2. Rome, 1991
JPJ — *Journal of Progressive Judaism*
JPOS — *Journal of the Palestine Oriental Society*
JPS — Jewish Publication Society
JQR — *Jewish Quarterly Review*
JQRMS — Jewish Quarterly Review Monograph Series
JR — *Journal of Religion*
JRAS — *Journal of the Royal Asiatic Society*
JRE — *Journal of Religious Ethics*
JRelS — *Journal of Religious Studies*
JRH — *Journal of Religious History*
JRitSt — *Journal of Ritual Studies*
JRS — *Journal of Roman Studies*
JRT — *Journal of Religious Thought*
JSem — *Journal of Semitics*
JSHRZ — *Jüdische Schriften aus hellenistisch-römischer Zeit*
JSJ — *Journal for the Study of Judaism in the Persian, Hellenistic, and Roman Periods*
JSNT — *Journal for the Study of the New Testament*
JSNTSup — Journal for the Study of the New Testament: Supplement Series
JSOR — *Journal of the Society of Oriental Research*
JSOT — *Journal for the Study of the Old Testament*
JSOTSup — Journal for the Study of the Old Testament: Supplement Series
JSP — *Journal for the Study of the Pseudepigrapha*
JSPSup — Journal for the Study of the Pseudepigrapha: Supplement Series
JSQ — *Jewish Studies Quarterly*
JSS — *Journal of Semitic Studies*
JSSEA — *Journal of the Society for the Study of Egyptian Antiquities*
JSSR — *Journal for the Scientific Study of Religion*
JTC — *Journal for Theology and the Church*
JTS — *Journal of Theological Studies*
JTSA — *Journal of Theology for Southern Africa*
Jud — *Judaica*
Judaica — *Judaica: Beiträge zum Verständnis des jüdischen Schicksals in Vergangenheit und Gegenwart*
Judaism — *Judaism*
JWSTP — *Jewish Writings of the Second Temple Period: Apocrypha, Pseudepigrapha, Qumran Sectarian Writings, Philo, Josephus.* Edited by M. E. Stone. CRINT 2.2. Assen/Philadelphia, 1984
K&D — Keil, C. F., and F. Delitzsch, *Biblical Commentary on the Old Testament.* Translated by J. Martin et al. 25 vols. Edinburgh, 1857–1878. Reprint, 10 vols., Peabody, Mass., 1996
KAH 1 — *Keilschrifttexte aus Assur historischen Inhalts.* L. Messerschmidt. Vol. 1. WVDOG 16. Leipzig, 1911

KAH 2	*Keilschrifttexte aus Assur historischen Inhalts.* O. Schroeder. Vol. 2. WVDOG 37. Leipzig, 1922
KAI	*Kanaanäische und aramäische Inschriften.* H. Donner and W. Röllig. 2d ed. Wiesbaden, 1966–1969
Kairós	*Kairós*
KAR	*Keilschrifttexte aus Assur religiösen Inhalts.* Edited by E. Ebeling. Leipzig, 1919–1923
KAT	Kommentar zum Alten Testament
KB	*Keilinschriftliche Bibliothek.* Edited by E. Schrader. 6 vols. Berlin, 1889–1915
KBANT	Kommentare und Beiträge zum Alten und Neuen Testament
KBL	Koehler, L., and W. Baumgartner, *Lexicon in Veteris Testamenti libros.* 2d ed. Leiden, 1958
KBo	*Keilschrifttexte aus Boghazköi.* WVDOG 30, 36, 68–70, 72–73, 77–80, 82–86, 89–90. Leipzig, 1916–
KD	*Kerygma und Dogma*
KEK	Kritisch-exegetischer Kommentar über das Neue Testament (Meyer-Kommentar)
Kerux	*Kerux*
KHC	Kurzer Hand-Commentar zum Alten Testament
KI	*Kanaanäische Inschriften (Moabitisch, Althebraisch, Phonizisch, Punisch).* Edited by M. Lidzbarski. Giessen, 1907
KK	*Katorikku Kenkyu*
KlPauly	*Der kleine Pauly*
KlT	Kleine Texte
KS	*Kirjath-Sepher*
KTU	*Die keilalphabetischen Texte aus Ugarit.* Edited by M. Dietrich, O. Loretz, and J. Sanmartín. AOAT 24/1. Neukirchen-Vluyn, 1976. 2d enlarged ed. of *KTU: The Cuneiform Alphabetic Texts from Ugarit, Ras Ibn Hani, and Other Places.* Edited by M. Dietrich, O. Loretz, and J. Sanmartín. Münster, 1995 (= *CTU*)
KUB	*Keilschrifturkunden aus Boghazköi*
Kuhn	Kuhn, K. G. *Konkordanz zuden Qumrantexten.* Göttingen, 1960
KVRG	Kölner Veroffentlichungen zur Religionsgeschichte
L&N	Louw and Nida. *Greek-English Lexicon of the New Testament: Based on Semantic Domains.* Edited by J. P. Louw and E. A. Nida. 2d ed. New York, 1989
LAE	*Literature of Ancient Egypt.* W. K. Simpson. New Haven, 1972
LAE[3]	*Literature of Ancient Egypt.* W. K. Simpson. 3d rev. ed. New Haven, 2003
Lane	Lane, E. W. *An Arabic-English Lexicon.* 8 vols. London. Reprint, 1968
LAPO	Littératures anciennes du Proche-Orient
LASBF	*Liber annuus Studii biblici franciscani*
Laur	*Laurentianum*
LÄ	*Lexikon der Ägyptologie.* Edited by W. Helck, E. Otto, and W. Westendorf. Wiesbaden, 1972
LB	*Linguistica Biblica*
LCC	Library of Christian Classics. Philadelphia, 1953–
LCL	Loeb Classical Library
LD	Lectio divina
LEC	Library of Early Christianity
Leš	*Lešonénu*
Levant	*Levant*
LexSyr	*Lexicon syriacum.* C. Brockelmann. 2d ed. Halle, 1928
LIMC	*Lexicon iconographicum mythologiae classicae.* Edited by H. C. Ackerman and J.-R. Gisler. 8 vols. Zurich, 1981–1997
List	*Listening: Journal of Religion and Culture*
LJPSTT	Literature of the Jewish People in the Period of the Second Temple and the Talmud
LQ	*Lutheran Quarterly*
LR	*Lutherische Rundschau*
LS	*Louvain Studies*
LSJ	Liddell, H. G., R. Scott, H. S. Jones, *A Greek-English Lexicon.* 9th ed. with revised

	supplement. Oxford, 1996
LSS	*Leipziger semitische Studien*
LTK	*Lexicon für Theologie und Kirche*
LTP	*Laval théologique et philosophique*
LTQ	*Lexington Theological Quarterly*
LUÅ	Lunds universitets årsskrift
Lum	*Lumen*
LumVie	*Lumière et vie*
LW	*Living Word*
MAAR	Memoirs of the American Academy in Rome
Maarav	*Maarav*
MAMA	*Monumenta Asiae Minoris Antiqua.* Manchester and London, 1928–1993
Mandl	Mandelkern, S. *Veteris Testamenti concordantiae hebraicae atque chaldaicae, etc.* Reprint, 1925. 2d ed. Jerusalem, 1967
MAOG	Mitteilungen der Altorientalischen Gesellschaft
MARI	*Mari: Annales de recherches interdisciplinaires*
MBPF	Münchener Beiträge zur Papyrusforschung und antiken Rechtsgeschichte
MBS	Message of Biblical Spirituality
McCQ	*McCormick Quarterly*
MCom	*Miscelánea Comillas*
MCuS	*Manchester Cuneiform Studies*
MDAI	*Mitteilungen des Deutschen archäologischen Instituts*
MDB	*Mercer Dictionary of the Bible.* Edited by W. E. Mills. Macon, 1990
MdB	*Le Monde de la Bible*
MDOG	Mitteilungen der Deutschen Orient-Gesellschaft
MEAH	*Miscelánea de estudios arabes y hebraicos*
Med	*Medellin*
MEFR	*Mélanges d'archéologie et d'histoire de l'école français de Rome*
MelT	*Melita theologica*
MGWJ	*Monatschrift für Geschichte und Wissenschaft des Judentums*
MH	*Museum helveticum*
Mid-Stream	*Mid-Stream*
Mils	*Milltown Studies*
MIO	*Mitteilungen des Instituts für Orientforschung*
MM	Moulton, J. H., and G. Milligan. *The Vocabulary of the Greek Testament.* London, 1930. Reprint, Peabody, Mass., 1997
MNTC	Moffatt New Testament Commentary
MPAIBL	Mémoires présentés à l'Academie des inscriptions et belleslettres
MS	*Mediaeval Studies*
MScRel	*Mélanges de science religieuse*
MSJ	*The Master's Seminary Journal*
MSL	*Materialien zum sumerischen Lexikon.* Benno Landsberger, ed.
MSU	Mitteilungen des Septuaginta-Unternehmens
MTSR	*Method and Theory in the Study of Religion*
MTZ	*Münchener theologische Zeitschrift*
Mursurillo	Mursurillo, H., ed. and trans. *The Acts of the Christian Martyrs.* Oxford, 1972
Mus	*Muséon: Revue d'études orientales*
MUSJ	*Mélanges de l'Université Saint-Joseph*
MVAG	Mitteilungen der Vorderasiatisch-ägyptischen Gesellschaft. Vols. 1–44. 1896–1939
NABU	*Nouvelles assyriologiques breves et utilitaires*
NAC	New American Commentary
NAWG	*Nachrichten (von) der Akademie der Wissenschaften in Göttingen*
NBD[2]	*New Bible Dictionary.* Edited by J. D. Douglas and N. Hillyer. 2d ed. Downers Grove, 1982

NBf	*New Blackfrairs*
NCB	New Century Bible
NCE	*New Catholic Encyclopedia.* Edited by W. J. McDonald et al. 15 vols. New York, 1967
NE	*Handbuch der nordsemitischen Epigraphik.* Edited by M. Lidzbarski. Weimar, 1898. Reprint, Hildesheim, 1962
NEA	*Near Eastern Archaeology*
NEAEHL	*The New Encyclopedia of Archaeological Excavations in the Holy Land.* Edited by E. Stern. 4 vols. Jerusalem, 1993
NEchtB	Neue Echter Bibel
NedTT	*Nederlands theologisch tijdschrift*
Nem	*Nemalah*
Neot	*Neotestamentica*
NETR	*Near East School of Theology Theological Review*
NewDocs	*New Documents Illustrating Early Christianity.* Edited by G. H. R. Horsley and S. Llewelyn. North Ryde, N.S.W., 1981–
NFT	New Frontiers in Theology
NGTT	*Nederduitse gereformeerde teologiese tydskrif*
NHC	Nag Hammadi Codices
NHL	*Nag Hammadi Library in English.* Edited by J. M. Robinson. 4th rev. ed. Leiden, 1996
NHS	Nag Hammadi Studies
NIB	*The New Interpreter's Bible*
NIBCNT	New International Biblical Commentary on the New Testament
NIBCOT	New International Biblical Commentary on the Old Testament
NICNT	New International Commentary on the New Testament
NICOT	New International Commentary on the Old Testament
NIDB	*New International Dictionary of the Bible.* Edited by J. D. Douglas and M. C. Tenney. Grand Rapids, 1987
NIDBA	*New International Dictionary of Biblical Archaeology.* Edited by E. M. Blaiklock and R. K. Harrison. Grand Rapids, 1983
NIDNTT	*New International Dictionary of New Testament Theology.* Edited by C. Brown. 4 vols. Grand Rapids, 1975–1985
NIDOTTE	*New International Dictionary of Old Testament Theology and Exegesis.* Edited by W. A. VanGemeren. 5 vols. Grand Rapids, 1997
NIGTC	New International Greek Testament Commentary
NJahrb	*Neue Jahrbücher für das klassiche Altertum (1898–1925); Neue Jahrbücher für Wissenschaft und Jugendbildung (1925–1936)*
NJBC	*The New Jerome Biblical Commentary.* Edited by R. E. Brown et al. Englewood Cliffs, 1990
NKZ	*Neue kirchliche Zeitschrift*
Notes	*Notes on Translation*
NovT	*Novum Testamentum*
NovTSup	Supplements to Novum Testamentum
NPEPP	*New Princeton Encyclopedia of Poetry and Poetics*
NPNF[1]	*Nicene and Post-Nicene Fathers,* Series 1
NPNF[2]	*Nicene and Post-Nicene Fathers,* Series 2
NRTh	*La nouvelle revue théologique*
NTA	*New Testament Abstracts*
NTAbh	Neutestamentliche Abhandlungen
NTD	Das Neue Testament Deutsch
NTF	Neutestamentliche Forschungen
NTG	New Testament Guides
NTGF	New Testament in the Greek Fathers
NTL	New Testament Library
NTOA	Novum Testamentum et Orbis Antiquus
NTS	*New Testament Studies*

NTT	*Norsk Teologisk Tidsskrift*
NTTS	New Testament Tools and Studies
NumC	*Numismatic Chronicle*
Numen	*Numen: International Review for the History of Religions*
NuMu	*Nuevo mundo*
NV	*Nova et vetera*
OBO	Orbis biblicus et orientalis
ÖBS	Österreichische biblische Studien
OBT	Overtures to Biblical Theology
OCD	*Oxford Classical Dictionary.* Edited by S. Hornblower and A. Spawforth. 3d ed. Oxford, 1996
OCP	*Orientalia christiana periodica*
OCT	Oxford Classical Texts/Scriptorum classicorum bibliotheca oxoniensis
OCuT	Oxford Editions of Cuneiform Texts
ODCC	*The Oxford Dictionary of the Christian Church.* Edited by F. L. Cross and E. A. Livingstone. 2d ed. Oxford, 1983
OEANE	*The Oxford Encyclopedia of Archaeology in the Near East.* Edited by E. M. Meyers. New York, 1997
OECT	Oxford Early Christian Texts. Edited by H. Chadwick. Oxford, 1970–
OGIS	*Orientis graeci inscriptiones selectae.* Edited by W. Dittenberger. 2 vols. Leipzig, 1903–1905
OiC	*One in Christ*
OIC	*Oriental Institute Communications*
OIP	Oriental Institute Publications
OLA	Orientalia lovaniensia analecta
OLP	Orientalia lovaniensia periodica
OLZ	*Orientalistische Literaturzeitung*
Or	*Orientalia* (NS)
OrAnt	*Oriens antiquus*
OrChr	*Oriens christianus*
OrChrAn	Orientalia christiana analecta
Orita	*Orita*
OrSyr	*L'orient syrien*
OTA	*Old Testament Abstracts*
OTE	*Old Testament Essays*
OTG	Old Testament Guides
ÖTK	Ökumenischer Taschenbuch-Kommentar
OTL	Old Testament Library
OTM	Old Testament Message
OTP	*Old Testament Pseudepigrapha.* Edited by J. H. Charlesworth. 2 vols. New York, 1983
OTS	Old Testament Studies
OtSt	Oudtestamentische Studiën
PAAJR	*Proceedings of the American Academy of Jewish Research*
Pacifica	*Pacifica*
PapyCast	Papyrologica Castroctaviana, Studia et textus. Barcelona, 1967–
Parab	*Parabola*
ParOr	*Parole de l'orient*
PaVi	*Parole di vita*
Payne Smith	*Thesaurus syriacus.* Edited by R. Payne Smith. Oxford, 1879–1901
PDM	*Papyri demoticae magicae.* Demotic texts in *PGM* corpus as collated in H. D. Betz, ed. *The Greek Magical Papyri in Translation, including the Demotic Spells.* Chicago, 1996
PEFQS	Palestine Exploration Fund Quarterly Statement
PEQ	*Palestine Exploration Quarterly*
Per	*Perspectives*

PerTeol	*Perspectiva teológica*
PG	Patrologia graeca [= Patrologiae cursus completus: Series graeca]. Edited by J.-P. Migne. 162 vols. Paris, 1857–1886
PGL	*Patristic Greek Lexicon.* Edited by G. W. H. Lampe. Oxford, 1968
PGM	*Papyri graecae magicae: Die griechischen Zauberpapyri.* Edited by K. Preisendanz. Berlin, 1928
Phil	*Philologus*
Phon	*Phonetica*
PIASH	Proceedings of the Israel Academy of Sciences and Humanities
PIBA	Proceedings of the Irish Biblical Association
PJ	*Palästina-Jahrbuch*
PL	Patrologia latina [= Patrologiae cursus completus: Series latina]. Edited by J.-P. Migne. 217 vols. Paris, 1844–1864
Pneuma	*Pneuma: Journal for the Society of Pentecostal Studies*
PNTC	Pelican New Testament Commentaries
PO	Patrologia orientalis
POut	De Prediking van het Oude Testament
Presb	*Presbyterion*
ProEccl	*Pro ecclesia*
Proof	*Prooftexts: A Journal of Jewish Literary History*
Protest	*Protestantesimo*
Proy	*Proyección*
PRSt	*Perspectives in Religious Studies*
PRU	*Le palais royal d'Ugarit*
PS	Patrologia syriaca. Rev. ed. I. Ortiz de Urbina. Rome, 1965
PSB	*Princeton Seminary Bulletin*
PSTJ	*Perkins (School of Theology) Journal*
PTMS	Pittsburgh Theological Monograph Series
PTS	Patristische Texte und Studien
PVTG	Pseudepigrapha Veteris Testamenti Graece
PW	Pauly, A. F. *Paulys Realencyclopädie der classischen Altertumswissenschaft.* New edition G. Wissowa. 49 vols. Munich, 1980
PWSup	Supplement to PW
PzB	*Protokolle zur Bibel*
Qad	*Qadmoniot*
QC	*Qumran Chronicle*
QD	Quaestiones disputatae
QDAP	*Quarterly of the Department of Antiquities in Palestine*
QR	*Quarterly Review*
Quasten	Quasten, J. *Patrology.* 4 vols. Westminster, 1953–1986
R&T	*Religion and Theology*
RA	*Revue d'assyriologie et d'archéologie orientale*
RAC	*Reallexikon für Antike und Christentum.* Edited by T. Kluser et al. Stuttgart, 1950–
RANE	Records of the Ancient Near East
RAr	*Revue archéologique*
RÄR	*Reallexikon der ägyptischen Religionsgeschichte.* H. Bonnet. Berlin, 1952
RawlCu	*The Cuneiform Inscriptions of Western Asia.* Edited by H. C. Rawlinson. London, 1891
RB	*Revue biblique*
RBB	*Revista biblica brasileira*
RBén	*Revue bénédictine*
RBL	*Ruch biblijny i liturgiczny*
RBPH	*Revue belge de philologie et d'histoire*
RCB	*Revista de cultura bíblica*
RCT	*Revista catalana de teología*

RdT	*Rassegna di teologia*
RE	*Realencyklopädie für protestantische Theologie und Kirche*
REA	*Revue des études anciennes*
REAug	*Revue des études augustiniennes*
REB	*Revista eclesiástica brasileira*
RechBib	Recherches bibliques
RechPap	*Recherches de papyrologie*
RefLitM	*Reformed Liturgy and Music*
RefR	*Reformed Review*
REg	*Revue d'égyptologie*
REG	*Revue des études grecques*
REJ	*Revue des études juives*
RelArts	Religion and the Arts
RelEd	*Religious Education*
RelS	*Religious Studies*
RelSoc	*Religion and Society*
RelSRev	*Religious Studies Review*
RelStTh	*Religious Studies and Theology*
RES	*Répertoire d'épigraphie sémitique*
RES	*Revue des études sémitiques*
ResQ	*Restoration Quarterly*
RET	*Revista española de teología*
RevExp	*Review and Expositor*
RevistB	*Revista bíblica*
RevPhil	*Revue de philologie*
RevQ	*Revue de Qumran*
RevScRel	*Revue des sciences religieuses*
RGG	*Religion in Geschichte und Gegenwart.* Edited by K. Galling. 7 vols. 3d ed. Tübingen, 1957–1965
RHA	*Revue hittite et asianique*
RHE	*Revue d'histoire ecclésiastique*
RHPR	*Revue d'histoire et de philosophie religieuses*
RHR	*Revue de l'histoire des religions*
RIBLA	*Revista de interpretación bíblica latino-americana*
RIDA	*Revue internationale des droits de l'antiquité*
RIM	The Royal Inscriptions of Mesopotamia Project. Toronto
RIMA	The Royal Inscriptions of Mesopotamia, Assyrian Periods
RIMB	The Royal Inscriptions of Mesopotamia, Babylonian Periods
RIME	The Royal Inscriptions of Mesopotamia, Early Periods
RIMS	The Royal Inscriptions of Mesopotamia, Supplements
RISA	*Royal Inscriptions of Sumer and Akkad.* Edited by G. A. Barton. New Haven, 1929
RivB	*Rivista biblica italiana*
RivSR	*Rivista di scienze religiose*
RlA	*Reallexikon der Assyriologie.* Edited by Erich Ebeling et al. Berlin, 1928–
RLV	*Reallexikon der Vorgeschichte.* Edited by M. Ebert. Berlin, 1924–1932
RNT	Regensburger Neues Testament
RocT	*Roczniki teologiczne*
RomBarb	*Romanobarbarica*
RoMo	Rowohlts Monographien
RQ	*Römische Quartalschrift für christliche Altertumskunde und Kirchengeschichte*
RR	*Review of Religion*
RRef	*La revue réformée*
RRelRes	*Review of Religious Research*
RS	Ras Shamra

RSC	*Rivista di studi classici*
RSém	*Revue de sémitique*
RSF	*Rivista di studi fenici*
RSO	*Rivista degli studi orientali*
RSP	*Ras Shamra Parallels*
RSPT	*Revue des sciences philosophiques et théologiques*
RSR	*Recherches de science religieuse*
RST	Regensburger Studien zur Theologie
RStB	*Ricerche storico bibliche*
RTAM	*Recherches de théologie ancienne et médiévale*
RThom	*Revue thomiste*
RTL	*Revue théologique de Louvain*
RTP	*Revue de théologie et de philosophie*
RTR	*Reformed Theological Review*
RuBL	*Ruch biblijnu i liturgiczny*
RUO	*Revue de l'université d'Ottawa*
SA	Studia anselmiana
SAA	State Archives of Assyria
SAAB	*State Archives of Assyria Bulletin*
SAAS	State Archives of Assyria Studies
SAC	Studies in Antiquity and Christianity
SacEr	*Sacris erudiri: Jaarboek voor Godsdienstwetenschappen*
Salm	*Salmanticensis*
SANT	Studien zum Alten und Neuen Testaments
SAOC	Studies in Ancient Oriental Civilizations
Sap	*Sapienza*
SAQ	Sammlung ausgewählter Kirchen- und dogmengeschichtlicher Quellenschriften
SB	*Sammelbuch griechischer Urkunden aus Aegypten.* Edited by F. Preisigke et al. Vols. 1– , 1915–
SB	Sources bibliques
SBA	Studies in Biblical Archaeology
SBAB	Stuttgarter biblische Aufsatzbände
SBAW	Sitzungsberichte der bayerischen Akademie der Wissenschaften
SBB	Stuttgarter biblische Beiträge
SBFLA	*Studii biblici Franciscani liber annus*
SBL	Society of Biblical Literature
SBLABib	Society of Biblical Literature Academia Biblica
SBLABS	Society of Biblical Literature Archaeology and Biblical Studies
SBLBAC	Society of Biblical Literature The Bible and American Culture
SBLBMI	Society of Biblical Literature The Bible and Its Modern Interpreters
SBLBSNA	Society of Biblical Literature Biblical Scholarship in North America
SBLCP	Society of Biblical Literature Centennial Publications
SBLDS	Society of Biblical Literature Dissertation Series
SBLEJL	Society of Biblical Literature Early Judaism and Its Literature
SBLGPBS	Society of Biblical Literature Global Perspectives on Biblical Scholarship
SBLHS	*The SBL Handbook of Style*, Edited by P. Alexander et al. Peabody, Mass., 1999
SBLMasS	Society of Biblical Literature Masoretic Studies
SBLMS	Society of Biblical Literature Monograph Series
SBLNTGF	Society of Biblical Literature The New Testament in the Greek Fathers
SBLRBS	Society of Biblical Literature Resources for Biblical Study
SBLSBS	Society of Biblical Literature Sources for Biblical Study
SBLSC	Society of Biblical Literature Septuagint and Cognate Studies
SBLSP	Society of Biblical Literature Seminar Papers
SBLStBL	Society of Biblical Literature Studies in Biblical Literature

SBLSymS Society of Biblical Literature Symposium Series
SBLTCS Society of Biblical Literature Text-Critical Studies
SBLTT Society of Biblical Literature Texts and Translations
SBLWAW Society of Biblical Literature Writings from the Ancient World
SBLWGRW Society of Biblical Literature Writings from the Greco-Roman World
SBM Stuttgarter biblische Monographien
SBS Stuttgarter Bibelstudien
SBT Studies in Biblical Theology
SC Sources chrétiennes. Paris: Cerf, 1943–
ScC *La scuola cattolica*
ScEccl *Sciences ecclésiastiques*
ScEs *Science et esprit*
SCH Studies in Church History
SCHNT Studia ad corpus hellenisticum Novi Testamenti
Schol *Scholastik*
Scr *Scripture*
SCR *Studies in Comparative Religion*
ScrB *Scripture Bulletin*
ScrC *Scripture in Church*
ScrHier Scripta hierosolymitana
ScrTh *Scripta theologica*
ScrVict *Scriptorium victoriense*
SD Studies and Documents
SDAW Sitzungen der deutschen Akademie der Wissenschaften zu Berlin
SE *Studia evangelica I, II, III* (= TU 73 [1959], 87 [1964], 88 [1964]. etc.)
SEÅ *Svensk exegetisk årsbok*
SEAug Studia ephemeridis Augustinianum
SecCent *Second Century*
Sef *Sefarad*
SEG Supplementum epigraphicum graecum
SEL *Studi epigrafici e linguistici*
Sem *Semitica*
Semeia *Semeia*
SemeiaSt Semeia Studies
SFulg *Scripta fulgentina*
SHANE Studies in the History of the Ancient Near East
SHAW Sitzungen der heidelberger Akademie der Wissenschaften
Shofar *Shofar*
SHR Studies in the History of Religions (supplement to *Numen*)
SHT Studies in Historical Theology
SIDIC *SIDIC* (Journal of the Service internationale de documentation judeo-chrétienne)
SIG *Sylloge inscriptionum graecarum.* Edited by W. Dittenberger. 4 vols. 3d ed. Leipzig, 1915–1924
SJ Studia judaica
SJLA Studies in Judaism in Late Antiquity
SJOT *Scandinavian Journal of the Old Testament*
SJT *Scottish Journal of Theology*
SK *Skrif en kerk*
SKKNT Stuttgarter kleiner Kommentar, Neues Testament
SL *Sumerisches Lexikon.* Edited by A. Deimel. 8 vols. Rome, 1928–1950
SLJT *St. Luke's Journal of Theology*
SMBen Série monographique de Benedictina: Section paulinienne *SMSR Studi e materiali di storia delle religioni*
SMSR *Studi e materiali di storia delle religioni*

SMT	*Studii Montis Regii*
SNT	Studien zum Neuen Testament
SNTA	Studiorum Novi Testamenti Auxilia
SNTSMS	Society for New Testament Studies Monograph Series
SNTSU	Studien zum Neuen Testament und seiner Umwelt
SO	*Symbolae osloenses*
SÖAW	*Sitzungen der österreichischen Akademie der Wissenschaften in Wien*
Sobornost	*Sobornost*
SOTSMS	Society for Old Testament Studies Monograph Series
Sound	*Soundings*
SP	Sacra pagina
SPap	*Studia papyrologica*
SPAW	Sitzungsberichte der preussischen Akademie der Wissenschaften
Spec	*Speculum*
SPhilo	*Studia philonica*
SQAW	Schriften und Quellen der alten Welt
SR	*Studies in Religion*
SSEJC	Studies in Early Judaism and Christianity
SSN	Studia semitica neerlandica
SSS	Semitic Study Series
ST	*Studia theologica*
St	*Studium*
StABH	Studies in American Biblical Hermeneutics
StC	Studia catholica
STDJ	Studies on the Texts of the Desert of Judah
SThU	*Schweizerische theologische Umschau*
SThZ	*Schweizerische theologische Zeitschrift*
STJ	*Stulos Theological Journal*
STK	*Svensk teologisk kvartalskrift*
StOR	Studies in Oriental Religions
StPat	*Studia patavina*
StPatr	Studia patristica
StPB	Studia post-biblica
Str	*Stromata*
Str-B	Strack, H. L., and P. Billerbeck. *Kommentar zum Neuen Testament aus Talmud und Midrasch.* 6 vols. Munich, 1922–1961
STRev	*Sewanee Theological Review*
StSin	Studia Sinaitica
StudBib	Studia Biblica
StudMon	Studia monastica
StudNeot	Studia neotestamentica
StudOr	Studia orientalia
StZ	Stimmen der Zeit
Su	*Studia theological varsaviensia*
SubBi	*Subsidia biblica*
Sumer	*Sumer: A Journal of Archaeology and History in Iraq*
SUNT	Studien zur Umwelt des Neuen Testaments
SVF	*Stoicorum veterum fragmenta.* H. von Arnim. 4 vols. Leipzig, 1903–1924
SVTP	Studia in Veteris Testamenti pseudepigraphica
SVTQ	*St. Vladimir's Theological Quarterly*
SWBA	Social World of Biblical Antiquity
SwJT	*Southwestern Journal of Theology*
SymBU	Symbolae biblicae upsalienses
T&K	*Texte & Kontexte*

TA	*Tel Aviv*
TAD	*Textbook of Aramaic Documents from Ancient Egypt. Newly Copied, Edited and Translated into Hebrew and English.* Edited by Bazalel Porten and Ada Yardeni. Winona Lake, IN *(1986–1993)*
TAPA	*Transactions of the American Philological Association*
Tarbiz	*Tarbiz*
TB	Theologische Bücherei: Neudrucke und Berichte aus dem 20. Jahrhundert
TBC	Torch Bible Commentaries
TBei	*Theologische Beiträge*
TBl	*Theologische Blätter*
TBT	*The Bible Today*
TCL	Textes cunéiformes. Musée du Louvre
TCS	Texts from Cuneiform Sources
TCW	*Tydskrif vir Christelike Wetenskap*
TD	*Theology Digest*
TDNT	*Theological Dictionary of the New Testament.* Edited by G. Kittel and G. Friedrich. Translated by G. W. Bromiley. 10 vols. Grand Rapids, 1964–1976
TDOT	*Theological Dictionary of the Old Testament.* Edited by G. J. Botterweck and H. Ringgren. Translated by J. T. Willis, G. W. Bromiley, and D. E. Green. 8 vols. Grand Rapids, 1974–
TdT	Themen der Theologie
Teol	*Teología*
Teubner	Bibliotheca scriptorum graecorum et romanorum teubneriana
Text	*Textus*
TF	*Theologische Forschung*
TGI	*Textbuch zur Geschichte Israels.* Edited by K. Galling. 2d ed. Tübingen, 1968
TGl	*Theologie und Glaube*
TGUOS	Transactions of the Glasgow University Oriental Society
THAT	*Theologisches Handwörterbuch zum Alten Testament.* Edited by E. Jenni, with assistance from C. Westermann. 2 vols., Stuttgart, 1971–1976
Them	*Themelios*
Theo	*Theologika*
Theof	*Theoforum*
Theol	*Theologica*
ThH	Théologie historique
THKNT	Theologischer Handkommentar zum Neuen Testament
ThPQ	*Theologisch-praktische Quartalschrift*
ThSt	Theologische Studiën
ThT	*Theologisch tijdschrift*
ThTo	*Theology Today*
ThViat	*Theologia viatorum*
ThWAT	*Theologisches Wörterbuch zum Alten Testament.* Edited by G. J. Botterweck and H. Ringgren. Stuttgart, 1970–
TI	*Teologia iusi*
TimesLitSupp	*Times Literary Supplement*
TJ	*Trinity Journal*
TJT	*Toronto Journal of Theology*
TLG	*Thesaurus linguae graecae: Canon of Greek Authors and Works.* Edited by L. Berkowitz and K. A. Squitier. 3d ed. Oxford, 1990
TLL	*Thesaurus linguae latinae*
TLNT	*Theological Lexicon of the New Testament.* C. Spicq. Translated and edited by J. D. Ernest. 3 vols. Peabody, Mass., 1994
TLOT	*Theological Lexicon of the Old Testament.* Edited by E. Jenni, with assistance from C. Westermann. Translated by M. E. Biddle. 3 vols. Peabody, Mass., 1997

TLZ	*Theologische Literaturzeitung*
TNTC	Tyndale New Testament Commentaries
TOTC	Tyndale Old Testament Commentaries
TP	*Theologie und Philosophie*
TPINTC	TPI New Testament Commentaries
TPQ	*Theologisch-praktische Quartalschrift*
TQ	*Theologische Quartalschrift*
Transeu	*Transeuphratène*
TRE	*Theologische Realenzyklopädie.* Edited by G. Krause and G. Müller. Berlin, 1977–
TRev	*Theologische Revue*
TRSR	Testi e ricerche di scienze religiose
TRu	*Theologische Rundschau*
Trumah	*Trumah*
TS	Texts and Studies
TS	*Theological Studies*
TSAJ	Texte und Studien zum antiken Judentum
TSK	*Theologische Studien und Kritiken*
TTE	*The Theological Educator*
TThSt	Trierer theologische Studien
TTJ	*Trinity Theological Journal*
TTKi	*Tidsskrift for Teologi og Kirke*
TTZ	*Trierer theologische Zeitschrift*
TU	Texte und Untersuchungen
TUAT	*Texte aus der Umwelt des Alten Testaments.* Edited by Otto Kaiser. Gütersloh, 1984–
TUGAL	Texte und Untersuchungen zur Geschichte der altchristlichen Literatur
TUMSR	Trinity University Monograph Series in Religion
TV	*Teología y vida*
TVM	Theologische Verlagsgemeinschaft: Monographien
TvT	*Tijdschrift voor theologie*
TWNT	*Theologische Wörterbuch zum Neuen Testament.* Edited by G. Kittel and G. Friedrich. Stuttgart, 1932–1979
TWOT	*Theological Wordbook of the Old Testament.* Edited by R. L. Harris, G. L. Archer Jr. 2 vols. Chicago, 1980
TynBul	*Tyndale Bulletin*
TZ	*Theologische Zeitschrift*
UBL	Ugaritisch-biblische Literatur
UF	*Ugarit-Forschungen*
UHP	*Ugaritic-Hebrew Philology.* M. Dahood. 2d ed. Rome, 1989
UJEnc	*The Universal Jewish Encylopedia.* Edited by I. Landman. 10 vols. New York, 1939–1943
UNP	*Ugaritic Narrative Poetry.* Edited by Simon B. Parker. SBLWAW 9. Atlanta, 1997
UNT	Untersuchungen zum Neuen Testament
UrE	Ur Excavations
UrET	Ur Excavations: Texts
USQR	*Union Seminary Quarterly Review*
UT	*Ugaritic Textbook.* C. H. Gordon. AnOr 38. Rome, 1965
UUA	Uppsala Universitets arskrift
VAB	Vorderasiatische Bibliothek
VAT	Vorderasiatische Abteilung Tontafel. Vorderasiatisches Museum, Berlin
VC	*Vigiliae christianae*
VCaro	*Verbum caro*
VD	*Verbum domini*
VE	*Vox evangelica*
VF	*Verkündigung und Forschung*
VH	*Vivens homo*

Vid	*Vidyajyoti*
VL	*Vetus Latina: Die Reste der altlateinischen Bibel.* Edited by E. Beuron, 1949–
VR	*Vox reformata*
VS	*Verbum Salutie*
VS	*Vox scripturae*
VSpir	*Vie spirituelle*
VT	*Vetus Testamentum*
VTSup	Supplements to Vetus Testamentum
WÄS	*Wörterbuch der ägyptischen Sprache.* A. Erman and H. Grapow. 5 vols. Berlin, 1926–1931. Reprint, 1963
WBC	Word Biblical Commentary
WC	Westminster Commentaries
WD	*Wort und Dienst*
WDB	*Westminster Dictionary of the Bible*
Wehr	Wehr, H. *A Dictionary of Modern Written Arabic.* Edited by J. M. Cowan. Ithaca, 1961, 1976[3]
WHAB	*Westminster Historical Atlas of the Bible*
WHJP	World History of the Jewish People
WKAS	*Das Wörterbuch der klassischen arabischen Sprache.* Edited by M. Ullmann. 1957– .
WMANT	Wissenschaftliche Monographien zum Alten und Neuen Testament
WO	*Die Welt des Orients*
WTJ	*Westminster Theological Journal*
WTM	*Das Wörterbuch über die Talmudim und Midraschim.* J. Levy. 2d ed. 1924
WUANT	Wissenschaftliche Untersuchungen zum Alten und Neuen Testament
WUNT	Wissenschaftliche Untersuchungen zum Neuen Testament
WUS	*Das Wörterbuch der ugaritischen Sprache.* J. Aistleitner. Edited by O. Eissfeldt. 3d ed. Berlin, 1967
WVDOG	Wissenschaftliche Veröffentlichungen der deutschen Orientgesellschaft
WW	*Word and World*
WZ	*Wissenschaftliche Zeitschrift*
WZKM	*Wiener Zeitschrift für die Kunde des Morgenlandes*
WZKSO	*Wiener Zeitschrift für die Kunde Süd- und Ostasiens*
YCS	Yale Classical Studies
YOS	Yale Oriental Series, Texts
YOSR	Yale Oriental Series, Researches
ZA	*Zeitschrift für Assyriologie*
ZABeih	Zeitschrift für Assyriologie: Beihefte
ZABR	*Zeitschrift für altorientalische und biblische Rechtgeschichte*
ZAC	*Zeitschrift für Antikes Christentum/Journal of Ancient Christianity*
ZAH	*Zeitschrift für Althebräistik*
ZÄS	*Zeitschrift für ägyptische Sprache und Altertumskunde*
ZAW	*Zeitschrift für die alttestamentliche Wissenschaft*
ZB	Zürcher Bibel
ZBK	Zürcher Bibelkommentare
ZDMG	*Zeitschrift der deutschen morgenländischen Gesellschaft*
ZDMGSup	Zeitschrift der deutschen morgenländischen Gesellschaft: Supplementbände
ZDPV	*Zeitschrift des deutschen Palästina-Vereins*
ZEE	*Zeitschrift für evangelische Ethik*
ZHT	*Zeitschrift für historische Theologie*
Zion	*Zion*
ZKG	*Zeitschrift für Kirchengeschichte*
ZKT	*Zeitschrift für katholische Theologie*
ZKunstG	*Zeitschrift für Kunstgeschichte*

ZNW	*Zeitschrift für die neutestamentliche Wissenschaft und die Kunde der älteren Kirche*
Zorell	Zorell, F. *Lexicon hebraicum et aramaicum Veteris Testamenti.* Rome, 1968
ZPE	*Zeitschrift für Papyrologie und Epigraphik*
ZPEB	*Zondervan Pictorial Encyclopedia of the Bible.* Edited by M. C. Tenney. 5 vols. Grand Rapids, 1975
ZRGG	*Zeitschrift für Religions- und Geistesgeschichte*
ZS	*Zeitschrift für Semitistik und verwandte Gebiete*
ZST	*Zeitschrift für systematische Theologie*
ZTK	*Zeitschrift für Theologie und Kirche*
ZWKL	*Zeitschrift für Wissenschaft und kirchliches Leben*
ZWT	*Zeitschrift für wissenschaftliche Theologie*

Charts, Illustrations, and Maps